SUMMARY CONTENTS

TABLE OF CONTENTS

The Oxford History of the Laws of England

THE OXFORD HISTORY OF THE LAWS OF ENGLAND

General Editor: Sir John Baker, Q.C., LL.D., F.B.A., Downing Professor of the Laws of England, and Fellow of St Catharine's College, Cambridge

The Oxford History of the Laws of England will provide a detailed survey of the development of English law and its institutions from the earliest times until the twentieth century, drawing heavily upon recent research using unpublished materials.

The Oxford History of the Laws of England

VOLUME XI
1820–1914

English Legal System

OXFORD

UNIVERSITY PRESS

OXFORD

UNIVERSITY PRESS

Great Clarendon Street, Oxford OX2 6DP

Oxford University Press is a department of the University of Oxford.
It furthers the University's objective of excellence in research, scholarship,
and education by publishing worldwide in

Oxford New York

Auckland Cape Town Dar es Salaam Hong Kong Karachi
Kuala Lumpur Madrid Melbourne Mexico City Nairobi
New Delhi Shanghai Taipei Toronto

With offices in

Argentina Austria Brazil Chile Czech Republic France Greece
Guatemala Hungary Italy Japan Poland Portugal Singapore
South Korea Switzerland Thailand Turkey Ukraine Vietnam

Oxford is a registered trade mark of Oxford University Press
in the UK and in certain other countries

Published in the United States
by Oxford University Press Inc., New York

British Library Cataloguing in Publication Data

Data available

Library of Congress Cataloging in Publication Data

Data available

Typeset by Newgen Imaging Systems Pvt Ltd., Chennai, India
Printed in Great Britain
on acid-free paper by
Antony Rowe, Chippenham, Wiltshire

ISBN 978-0-19-9258819

1 3 5 7 9 10 8 6 4 2

PART TWO: PUBLIC LAW   *Stuart Anderson*

ABBREVIATIONS

Statutes of UK Parliament: the regnal year is included in a first citation of a statute until 1853. Then the modern series published by HM Stationery Office begins, the annual volumes having reliable indices.

Law Reports: Abbreviations of series of Law Reports are not listed here. The names of nominate series follow standard practice for the nineteenth and twentieth centuries as listed in Halsbury's *Laws of England* (4th aand 5th eds, 2009), Consolidated Tables, Cases A–L pp. xi–xlvi. Further assistance may be found in C. W. Ringrose (ed.), *Where to Look for your Law* (14th edn, 1962) and also within D. Raistrick's very thorough *Index of Legal Citations and Abbreviations* (3rd edn, 2008).

AJLH	American Journal of Legal History
Am. J. Comp. Law	American Journal of Comparative Law
Am. J. Int. Law	American Journal of International Law
Am. Soc. Of Int. Law	American Society of International Law
Anglo-Am. Law Rev.	Anglo-American Law Review
App.	Appendix
Att.-Gen.	Attorney-General
B.	Baron of the Exchequer
Bt	Baronet
BIHR	Bulletin of the Institute of Historical Research
Bl. Comm.	Blackstone's Commentaries on the Laws of England
BYIL	British Yearbook of International Law
CB	Chief Baron
CCC	County Courts Chronicle
CFLQ	Child and Family Law Quarterly
Ch. Chs	Chapter, Chapters
CJCP	Chief Justice of Common Pleas
CJK(Q)B	Chief Justice of King's (Queen's) Bench
CLE	Council for Legal Education
CLJ	Cambridge Law Journal
CLP	Current Legal Problems
Con. and Ch.	Continuity and Change
Cornhill Mag.	Cornhill Magazine
Crim. Law Rev.	Criminal Law Review
DC	Departmental Committee

DNB	Dictionary of National Biography
East P. C.	East, Pleas of the Crown
Econ. Hist. Rev.	Economic History Review
Edinburgh Rev.	Edinburgh Review
Eng. Hist. Rev.	English Historical Review
Hale H.P.C	Hale, History of the Please of the Crown
Hawk P. C.	Hawkins, Pleas of the Crown
Hist. J.	Historical Journal
Hist. St. Ind. Rels	Historical Studies in Industrial Relations
Holdsworth, HEL	Sir W.S. Holdsworth, History of English Law
ICLQ	International and Comparative Law Review
ILS	Incorporated Law Society
Int. Rev. Soc. Hist.	International Review of Social History
J., JJ.	Justice, Justices
JBS	Journal of British Studies
JCPC	Judicial Committee of the Privy Council
JEH	Journal of Economic History
J. Hist. Geography	Journal of Historical Geography
J. Hist. Ideas	Journal of the History of Ideas
J. Hist. Int. L.	Journal of the History of International Law
JLTRTE	Journal of Law and Economics
JLE	Journal of Law and Economics
JLH	Journal of Legal History
JLS	Journal of Legal Studies
JPOS	Journal of the Patent Office Society
JPTOS	Journal of the Patent and Trade Mark Office Society
JP	Justice of the Peace
JR	Juridical Review
J. Soc. Hist.	Journal of Social History
JSPTL	Journal of the Society of Public Teachers of Law
KC	King's Counsel
LAS	Law Amendment Society
LC	Lord Chancellor
LCO	Lord Chancellor's Office
Leg. Ob.	Legal Observer
LG	Law Gazette
LJ, LJJ	Lord Justice, Lord Justices
LHR	Law and History Review
LJ	Law Journal

LM	Law Magazine
LN	Legal Notes
LQR	Law Quarterly Review
LR	Law Reporter
LS	Legal Studies
LT	Law Times (journal)
MLR	Modern Law Review
MPLA	Metropolitan and Provincial Law Association
MR	Master of the Rolls
NA	The National Archives
NAPSS	National Association for the Promotion of Social Science
NILQ	Northern Ireland Legal Quarterly
19C Fict.	Nineteenth-century Fiction
ODNB	Oxford Dictionary of National Biography
OED	Oxford English Dictionary
OJLS	Oxford Journal of Legal Studies
P &P	Past and Present
para., paras	Paragraph, paragraphs
PDA	Probate, Divorce and Admiralty Division (High Court)
PRO	Public Record Office
QC	Queen's Counsel
Quart. Rev.	Quarterly Review
RC	Royal Commission
SC	Select Committee
Sjt	Serjeant
Sol.-Gen.	Solicitor-General
SJ	Solicitors Journal
SLT	Scots Law Times
State Tr.	State Trials
TLR	Times Law Reports
TNAPSS	Transactions of the National Association for the Promotion of Social Science
TRHS	Transactions of the Royal Historical Society
VC	Vice-Chancellor
VCH	Victoria County History
Vict. St.	Victorian Studies
West. Rev.	Westminster Review
YLJ	Yale Law Journal

TABLE OF CASES

Note: Criminal prosecutions all indexed under the defendent's name.

TABLE OF LEGISLATION

MANIFEST[1]

The *Oxford History of the Laws of England* rounds off its long cavalcade with three Volumes devoted to that period of relative peace across Europe running from the defeat of Napoleon to the terrible war against the two Kaisers. As the story in these Volumes opens in 1820, a precocious Britain was set to become an industrial and largely urban society. The population in England was beginning a relentless expansion, much of it being drawn into towns, or bred in them, for work in factories, mines, transport, building, education, finance, government, and professional life. Agriculture and rural production, which had for so long sustained the bulk of her people, would become secondary as types of labour became more specialized—that crucial key in economic expansion already identified by Adam Smith and his followers. Villages and small towns that were intensely local and knew only their inward hierarchies were being replaced by large agglomerations of people who allied themselves to their equals in their regions, and even across the nation. Thus was rank giving way to class.

By the last decades of Queen Victoria's long reign, despite intermittent depressions and despite the drudge-like lives of much of its working population, the country was to enjoy unexampled prosperity as the commercially dominant force in the world. Optimists could see no end to this expansion of power and riches, and they robed their country in a noble imperialism. Freedom and equality of its people, guaranteed under the rule of its law, constituted a precious inheritance. British governors saw their cause as moral rather than economic, and they became intent on teaching it to all their subject races. These fine sentiments were easily compounded:

Thine equal laws by Freedom gained,
Have ruled thee well and long:
By Freedom gained, by Truth maintained,
Thine Empire shall be strong.[2]

---

[1] For the Customs, a cargo is listed in a manifest. Here, it is the readers who undertake the inspection of the hold.

[2] Thus AC Benson, Master of Magdalene College, Cambridge, versifying Edward Elgar's *Pomp and Circumstance March No. 1* for the coronation of Edward VII—an event made famous to contract lawyers for its initial frustration by appendectomy. Christianity being the other crucial element in the imperial mix, the chorus contained the much-bellowed lines:
Wider still and wider, shall thy bounds be set,
God who made thee mighty, make thee mightier yet.

Pessimists, however, were becoming alarmed at the bellicose rivalries of the European Powers. At home they were dismayed by the rise of a working class urgent for democratic rights and improved chances in life. The tensions would lead the country soon enough into serious domestic confrontations—over votes for women and conditions of work in the mines, the docks and the railways, as well as the smouldering grudges of a subjugate Ireland. Then came the maelstrom of war. For Britain thereafter, decades of dessication would follow, as the debts of this and a second World War withered the economy and Empire was bleached into Commonwealth.

LEGAL REFORM IN A PERIOD OF RAPID CHANGE

The implacable changes of the period—economic, social, cultural, political—demanded reforms and new growths in the English system of common law, using that term in an embracing sense to include not only equity and the civilian jurisdictions but also a growing use of statute to effect legal change. These shifts would occur with a speed not previously known, and in various ways they would seem profound. From them, indeed, would emerge modified versions of an 'English common law', whose influence spread, both in the former colonies in North America, where it had long been established, and in the new 'second British empire' which grew after the decline of the first.[3] That diaspora gives the common law today a place in the pantheon of major legal systems, particularly when characterizing the legal inheritance on both sides of the Atlantic. But in the shifting course of reform there was almost always a powerful drag effect—a fear of the unpredictable results of altered systems, a concern that existing balances of power and prestige would be undermined. An atmosphere of concession and accommodation, of experiment and qualification, pervaded the diffuse business of keeping this 'common law' functioning in the face of such unexampled challenges.

Volumes XI–XIII do not attempt to trace the history of the common law as it fanned out across the Empire, any more than they deal with the position of the law of Scotland or Ireland. These are separate tasks. We must content ourselves with intermittent observations on the relationship between the English core and the imperial penumbra as it was until 1914. Most colonies fleshed out their law around a common law kernel through developments that they sought from Britain or introduced for themselves. Only rarely did the English take up these alterations for examination and possible adoption at home. Indeed, the

---

[3] Below, Ch.VII.

tendency to ignore such comparisons becomes more noticeable as the nineteenth century moves on.[4]

The amount of material to be covered in any reasonably complete history of nineteenth-century English law is very considerable, for law wove its strands into so much of the social fabric. How it did so became increasingly apparent as written records proliferated, as they so evidently did. Nonetheless, these volumes do not seek to provide a social history of the law, or examine closely the impact of law on society. Rather, they seek to offer primarily a history of the law itself, focusing on its institutions and doctrines, and considering how these changed in response to changes in the wider world. We have sought to cover the major aspects of legal development in England during the ninety-four years from 1820. We have not, however, treated every aspect in equal detail. These volumes bring to a close a long history of ideas and institutions that have made the common law a distinctive and important inheritance, comparable with the civilian tradition by which Continental countries derived their own laws in varied ways from Roman law foundations. The organization and content of contributions to the Series have shaped our own approach. We follow their broad pattern set by the division into Institutions, Public Law, and Private Law. In the common law this can be treated only as a convenient outline, since, as the whole becomes more elaborate, the overlaps increase. The distinction between the public and the private in law has applications which shift with the development of governmental administration and the desire to decrease or increase the degree of regulation affecting the economic and social activities of individuals, classes, and other divisions within a society, arising from differences of gender, ethnic origin, nationality, religion, or education.[5]

English common lawyers have long resisted the erection of a complete structure of legal classifications deriving from an explicit constitutional foundation. In the nineteenth century, civil law, criminal law, administrative law and so on, displayed an open-ended quality that was fundamentally at odds with engineered pyramids of obligation and entitlement such as was introduced into continental systems by codification. It was not just that English law got by with what was enough for present needs. The whole system had developed out of practical experience that allowed for additions by analogy, or re-definition, or pretence (as with legal fictions). Most of those who in some sense ran it—Parliamentarians, civil servants, those engaged in local government, as well as judges, magistrates, and lawyers—found the result preferable to pre-conditioned categorization. So much of what did not happen, as well as what did, can be explained through

[4] Below, pp. 251–4.
[5] M. Horwitz, 'The History of the Public/Private Distinction' (1982) 139 *U Pennsylvania LR* 1423–8.

the preferences of those with the power and prestige to get their way. But there were other driving forces, not least those which expressed a growing political consciousness in the lower social orders. One part of that novelty was a realization that the tools of law could, with persistence, be turned to their advantage.

We hope that these volumes will be of interest not just to legal historians but to judges, legal scholars, and practising lawyers, whose main concerns are not in history for its own sake, and to historians to whom legal matters and patterns of thought are one part of their conspectus. General histories of the period still neglect to offer much account of law as a distinctive factor in managing government or in contributing to the wider culture.[6] In part, this may reflect the fact that the legal terrain is often regarded by historians as unfamiliar and sometimes forbidding. We hope that these volumes will help explain to a wider historical audience, both how law worked, and how it reacted to social change. The Volumes, let it be added, do not pretend to be a general history of their period or country; nor do they set their own subject against the state of the law today or the criticisms that are made of it in theory or practice.

We have aimed to capture a sense of the nature and meanings of law in the late Georgian, Victorian, and Edwardian periods, and to show the possibilities offered by law for people to advance their own interests, and the limitations and frustrations it posed for them. The insight of those with legal training naturally carries with it the insiders' tendency to admire the constructions of their specialism, using the language which is the mortar of the craft and has about it an attractive adhesiveness.[7] Legal historians today are well aware of the need to distance themselves from their material. On the whole, they strive to avoid the many dangers of treating it with the reverence conjured by Sir Frederick Pollock's obeisances to 'Our Lady, the Common Law'. In its own way, legal language is as forbidding for the untrained as that of natural sciences, and sometimes as obscure as that of sociology and theology can be. When the historian's period is relatively remote, the language recorded in documents may well issue its own warnings against the dangers of misinterpretation. By the nineteenth century, there is a greater proximity to our own understandings, and differences of meaning may be subtle. Those who tackle this period have constantly to remind themselves not to transplant a twenty-first century assumption back into the conditions of what was still a very different age; nor must they seize on some interpretation of past usage

---

[6] Regretted, for instance, by M. Lobban, 'Law and Politics in the Nineteenth Century' (paper given at the British Legal History Conference in July, 2007).

[7] For the difficulties of drawing any line between 'internal' and 'external' histories of the law, when approaching so complex a period, see, e.g., S. Hedley, 'Words, Words, Words: Making Sense of Legal Judgments, 1875–1940' in C. Stebbings (ed.), *Law Reporting in Britain* (1995), 169–96; M. Lobban, 'The Tools and Tasks of the Legal Historian' in A. Lewis and M. Lobban (eds), *Law and History* (Current Legal Issues, vi; 2004), 1–32.

which fosters a case that they are championing for their own time. Indeed, legal language exposes itself as a particular case for the post-modern divination that statements stand to be understood as those who receive them wish to treat them, rather than as those who made them intended. How else could legal fictions have had such moments in the development of the common law?

HISTORIES OF MODERN ENGLISH LAW

Systematic historical study of English law as a whole received its first extensive treatment by Sir William Holdsworth, whose forty-year, sixteen-volume Odyssey ended with six volumes devoted to the eighteenth and nineteenth centuries up to the Judicature Acts 1873–75.[8] All that he so assiduously recorded remains one starting point for today's historian. But Holdsworth was born a Victorian and his appreciation of modern historical developments glows with a sense of their fulfilment in the cause of his nation. As his work approached its close, an escapee to Britain, Sir Leon Radzinowicz, showed, in his *History of English Criminal Law*, what wealth of original material was available to the historian who took a branch of law and set it in its larger context.[9] A certain admiration for what he found in England understandably informed his judgement and later writers of Foucaultesque mien have treated him with considerable, but undeserved, harshness.

In the comfortable conditions of modern academic life, historical treatment of many fields in which law played a significant role became the subject of ideological confrontation. A British movement to study law in a broader context was well under way by the time that evidence of Critical Legal Studies began to cross the Atlantic eastwards.[10] Revisionist histories of government structures, civil liberties, the legal professions, the judiciary and legal process, of corporate, labour,

---

[8] *A History of English Law* (1903–66). Even Holdsworth faltered at the end, Vols XIII–XVI being completed by A.L. Goodhart and H.G. Hanbury. Before him, A.V. Dicey's *Law and Opinion in England in the Nineteenth Century* (1905, 1914) was an influential compound of intellectual influences, legal developments and minatory soothsaying: for which, see below, Vol VIII, Pt 2, Ch. VII. There were also valuable contributions to *Select Essays in Anglo-American Legal History* (1907), esp. Vol. I, Parts 4 and 5. For the flow of works that established historical jurisprudence as a nineteenth-century art form, see below, pp. 102–11; K.J.M. Smith and J.P.S. McLaren, 'History's Living Legacy: An Outline of "Modern" Historiography of the Common Law' (2001) 21 *Leg. St.* 251, 253–64, and *cf.* 317–22.

[9] This *History* appeared in five volumes, 1948–86, the last with Roger Hood. For reactions, see Smith and McLaren 'Living Legacy' 281–9.

[10] There had been important British catalysts before and after the Second War, notably in the public law field, in the extensive investigations of Sidney and Beatrice Webb and their followers, and then such writers as Sir Ivor Jennings and W.A. Robson, Hermann Levy, and Wolfgang Friedmann. In the 1960s, the appearance of B. Abel-Smith and R.B. Stevens' *Lawyers and the Courts* (1967) raised the flag considerably higher, joined as it was by A. Harding's *Social History of English Law* (1966).

social welfare, criminal, family, and accident law built up unsettling pictures of legal operations in the past.[11] Here were portrayals that no longer simply marked the point from which to measure enlightened progress. Among them came unremitting claims that everything was determined at root by the selfish interests of the powerful, whether consciously adopted or merely assumed as the natural order of things. These in their turn have attracted counter-criticism. The greatest scholars of the history of the common law as a whole have, after all, stressed the Adam-Smith-like contributions of the mass of people engaged in resolving legal difficulties, intent on their immediate needs and desires, who have little or no interest in fulfilling some larger scheme of understanding.[12]

Other ways of tackling the records blossomed, with insights not just from a range of historians—political, administrative, economic, social, technological— but from sociologists, anthropologists, political scientists, and philosophers. Broad surveys stood alongside detailed investigations of legal areas and were expanded by critical biographies and case-history elaborations.[13] Legal history became not only about the establishment and development of legal rules essentially as sources of law, but extended to the psychological and social impact of all 'legal relationships' in von Savigny's embracing sense.[14] On the home front, far more importance attached to collective action such as that of political parties, professional and trade associations, amateur and professional lobbyists, rioters, strikers, the stimulators of purpose-driven rowdiness; and equally to dealings between individuals that displayed anything from greed, perversity, and the will to dominate, to generosity, decency, altruism, and good, solid judgment.[15] As contemporary Britain has adjusted to its middle-ranking, post-Imperial condition in

---

[11] The series of Penguin titles, which included H. Street, *Freedom, the Individual and the Law* (1963), G. Borrie and A.L. Diamond, *The Consumer, Society and the Law* (196.) and K.W. Wedderburn, *The Worker and the Law* (1965), all emphasized the historical contingencies of their subjects and set in motion a 'law and society' movement that would in some respects prove to have parallels to realist and later critical writing in the United States. For the historical significance of the intensive, organic realism of Willard Hurst and his school, see Smith and McLaren, 'Living Legacy', 273–81, 289–303.

[12] This forms the *Leitmotif* of S.F.C. Milsom, *Historical Foundations of the Common Law* (2nd edn, 1981).

[13] Two general texts were A.H. Manchester, *Modern Legal History of England and Wales, 1750– 1950* (1980), and W.R. Cornish and G.de N. Clark, *Law and Society in England, 1750–1950* (1989). The latter, it will be appreciated, has certain umbilical ties to the present volumes. The master of the case history is A.W.B. Simpson. His essays are now collected in *Leading Cases in the Common Law* (Oxford, 1995), together with *Cannibalism and the Common Law* (Chicago, 1984). They and others have a distinctive place at various points in these Volumes.

[14] A conception introduced to British readers in translation by William Guthrie. See his Introduction to F.C. von Savigny, *Conflict of Laws* (1869).

[15] G.R. Rubin and D. Sugarman's edited collection, *Law, Economy and Society, 1750–1914* (1984), epitomized the first stage of development, with its mixture of achievement and incitement to the research community.

a collaborating Europe that is fighting for its stake in global trade and world order, the need to compare constitutional forms and legal systems has greatly increased the flow of historical writing. There is a cornucopia brimming with reactions against modernistic certainties, including those that in their time used history to classify stages of human development towards more advanced and rational understandings. These Volumes contain the results of research into primary sources by each author. They also contain a critical survey of research and speculation undertaken by scholars from Britain and other countries. The history of English law in the modern period is now a flourishing discipline. Equally, it is a necessary one. Law is mostly deployed to resolve social problems of the moment and to organize how policies and desires can be carried out. All too easily the immediate purpose for relying on a legal principle becomes the only thing that counts; and then, all too easily, 'text without context becomes pretext'.

Retrieving historical context remains crucial to a fuller understanding of the phenomenon of law. In the latter twentieth century, as those in industrialized parts of the world came to live without directly confronting elemental violence, scepticism took the place of ideological commitments and the many-faceted notion of post-modernism provided an alluring philosophical premise. Among its targets, history came to be treated as a purposeless exercise and one therefore that was wholly misleading. The provider of knowledge about the past was confronted with the impossibility of establishing the truth of events, since each recipient of the information would interpret what they were told by reference to their own personality and experience. That nihilistic attack deserved and, so far as we are concerned, secured its answer from such authors as Richard Evans.[16] A warrior from the litigious battlefield of Holocaust denial, his *In Defence of History* (1998) recognizes that historians must use surviving evidence to explore reactions to events from varied individual and social perspectives. At the same time he welcomes that endeavour as a vital tradition in securing collective understanding about the present, and indeed the future, of the human condition. Exploring history in this ever-critical way provides the real chance of putting scepticism to worthwhile ends. Historiography began stretching out for such new perspectives, and at the same time for more detailed exploration of what is to be found in its sources, from a time well before the elevation of the art of deconstruction into a fundamental philosophical premise, as in the linguistic theory of Jacques Derrida.[17]

The authors have, sometimes individually and sometimes as part of their joint deliberations, had such a welter of advice and criticism from colleagues

---

[16] See also, e.g., J. Tosh, *The Pursuit of History: Aims, Methods and New Directions in the Study of Modern History* (3rd edn, Harlow, 2000).

[17] See in more detail, Lobban, 'Tools and Tasks' 8–14.

and friends that it would take too much space to name them all and would be an embarrassment to draw up a partial list. We trust that they will take it in good part if we offer them our gratitude only in a collective form. The one exception must be Sir John Baker who, as General Editor of the *Oxford History of the Laws of England*, invited us to join his parade of authors and has been at hand as mentor and guide from the time when we first sketched our plans and divided up tasks. That, it has to be said, was several years ago. We thank him, as we do our publishers, for the forbearance that they have had to show while we worked towards completion of the three final Volumes in the *Oxford History of the Laws of England*.

We would all wish to thank the law faculties in our respective universities— Cambridge, Otago, Keele, Queen Mary, London, Brunel, and Cardiff—for their institutional support, just as we thank their library staff for much practical assistance. Michael Lobban would like to add his particular thanks to the British Academy for electing him to a Research Readership in 2003–2005, to work on his contributions to Vol. XII. William Cornish likewise is specially grateful to the Leverhulme Trust for the award of an Emeritus Fellowship for 2004–2006.

We end this display of wares with some remarks on the organization of the writing:

(i)   The three Volumes are each divided into Parts, within which come sets of Chapters. Volume XI is devoted mainly to the sources of English law, the intellectual frameworks and institutions within which they were understood, the constitutional arrangements for the legislature, central and local executives, and the judicial system, this last providing the crucial core from which professional lawyers operated. Volume XII treats the major categories of private rights and responsibilities: property, contract, commercial law and torts. Volume XIII considers five 'topics' which changed in major ways between 1820 and 1914: criminal law, law as an instrument in social protection and control, family law, labour law, and rights relating to personality and intellectual property.

(ii)   Detailed footnoting to historical sources and literature occurs in the course of the narrative; but to provide exhaustive bibliographies of primary and secondary works would have taken a great many pages. Thanks partly to the publication of many specialized works and partly to digitization, the growth of bibliographies for many of our subjects has already been exponential. That is also true of access to primary records that previously were at best available only after very considerable perseverance.

(iii) In the tradition of common law legal scholarship, each Volume has Tables of Cases and of Statutes covering the materials in that Volume. In Volumes

XI and XII, there is a Names Index and a Subject Index for the volume. In Volume XIII, these Indices cover all three Volumes. The Names Index allows the reader to know where an individual is mentioned in the text or footnotes. The entries are not intended as biographical surveys in disguise. The Subject Index identifies where in the narrative a topic is discussed. There are numerous points at which a subject is dealt with in more than one Part or Chapter. An important function of the Indices is to show where this is so.

WRC

JSA

RCJC

MJWL

PP

KJMS

Part One

ENGLISH LAW IN AN INDUSTRIALIZING SOCIETY

I

Introduction*

ANY legal history worth salting must deal not only with what the law was but how and why it became so: the pressures that led to shifts in the law itself and the rationalizations offered for them. So far as evidence can be winkled out, it should also look at outcomes, for most legal change produces unintended effects. There may be large consequences from supposedly minor adjustments; there may be rejections of new law through non-activation or reversal. Between these poles any number of variants arise, which have to do with those who sought to rely on their rights and those who were obliged to meet their responsibilities, those who used the channels marked out by law to achieve their ends, and all those who were affected at some remove by the rights and duties of others. This is territory where legal history merges into the social, economic, political, and administrative.

Volumes XI–XIII, which end this *Oxford History of the Laws of England* in a period of unprecedented economic and social change, are much concerned with new legal developments. The present Chapter and those which follow in this Part aim to set the general scene for subjects that will be described later in more detail. The remainder of Volume XI concentrates on the structure of the English legal system, including the constitutional framework within which government operated and the intellectual stimuli to its functioning. Volume XII deals with the major elements of its inherited Private Law and the manner in which they were re-fitted for a more complex age, giving larger understandings of property, contract, commercial law, and tort. Volume XIII takes up five subject areas—some primarily public in orientation, some private, some increasingly mixed—where, between 1820 and 1914, any original clay was substantially remoulded. The volume covers the criminal law and its techniques of detection, prosecution, and punishment; provisions for social aid in accordance with the earnest moral endeavour of Victorian thought and action; family law as it came to apply both to the interests of the propertied classes and the great body of people supported by manual labour; labour law as it faced class conflict through the demands and actions of employers and trade unions; and the development of conceptions that would

* In this Part, Chapters II, III, VII, VIII and IX are by William Cornish, Chapters IV is by Michael Lobban, and Chapters V and VI are by Keith Smith.

protect individuals against external intrusions upon their personal lives and allow them exclusive control over the results of their intellectual endeavours.

The first task of this initial Part is to outline the nineteenth-century frame of government and law. At the very heart of the common law system lay a triangle of continuity.[1] Along one side, a set of courts had built up which, despite some considerable re-shaping, would keep to certain basic divisions—between superior and inferior courts, between civil and criminal process. Along a second side, there was an ever-clearer division of professional lawyers into barristers, with their rights of audience in the superior courts, and attorneys-cum-solicitors, with their own monopolies in such matters as conveyancing. Along the third side, as for centuries before, was the convention that the superior judges were drawn from the practising bar. Here was the institutional foundation of the common law system bred in England, a base-plate which shaped so much of the relations between legal institutions and the other branches of government.[2] Filling the space thus enclosed were the established procedures of these superior courts and the substantive legal rules generated in large measure from their decisions—a definitive process for so much of this *Oxford History*. On the stamping ground thus measured out, there were arenas flagged as *'common law'* in the strict sense: the law of the three royal courts of common law; then there was *equity*, being the law mainly applied in the courts of Chancery; and thirdly, *civilian law*—an inheritance of both ecclesiastical and Admiralty rules. By 1876, these arenas would together become common jurisdictional territory for all the courts of the new Supreme Court of Judicature; but not so as to alter the content and meaning of the substantive rules or remedies that were previously available only in one of the arenas.[3]

On a separate plane rose those buttresses which sustained, first, the Parliament, consisting of Monarch, Lords and Commons, as the sovereign legislature of the country; and secondly, the executive, which—at least formally—retained the Monarch at its centre until the franchise reforms of 1832; and thereafter was in the charge of Prime Minister and Cabinet, themselves all members of one or other House of Parliament. The 'Glorious Revolution' of 1689 had established new perceptions of a legislature, a central executive and a judiciary—each of them distinct, and in varying degrees separate. Between them, the three entities provided legally defined channels for governmental and private energies which were with time to become the hallmark of 'progressive' societies—as they liked to distinguish themselves from 'backward' communities.[4] In *L'Esprit des Loix*, the Baron

---

[1] The development of the legal system is treated in detail in Pts 3 and 4 of this volume.

[2] See A. W. B. Simpson, 'The Survival of the Common Law' in his *Legal Theory and Legal History* (1987), Ch. 16.

[3] See below, Pt 3, Ch. VI.

[4] This distinction, like the related concepts of 'society', 'state', and 'sovereignty', was premised upon a variety of ill-defined assumptions. See, for instance, its restrictive effect upon the very idea of international law: see below, pp. 264–5.

de Montesquieu had held the example of Britain up to the world and the upper ranks of its peoples were well satisfied in being such a model.

Secondly, this Part turns to issues of what could be identified as law. Starting from inherited beliefs about the sources of English law, Chapter III on that subject and Chapter IV on theories of law and government deal with the drive to distinguish law clearly from other moral structures. That discussion touches on the related hope, espoused by some engaged in public discussion, but certainly not by all, that its principles and rules would be expressed in codified legislation, with a written constitution as its top storey. In England codification was to prove a movement with only very partial success; but it instituted a debate about the theory of law that would intensify over the latter part of Victoria's reign, as the subject became an academic discipline as well as a craft practice.[5]

To a degree this would prove to be an internal debate among those attracted by distinctively legal philosophy. But that intellectual activity cannot be isolated from other schemes of thought about conditions of society. Accordingly, the next element in this Part addresses two external frames of reference—religious belief and political economy, together with ideological beliefs and sociological understandings which provided the warp to their weft (Chapters V and VI). The effect of strands of intellectual history upon the functioning law is always complex and often diffuse. A legal history has most to say when the law's means become significant in their own right in contributing to social ends. That perception lies behind the content of every volume in this *Oxford History* but it needs to be borne in mind, particularly in the modern period. Reading historical materials through the minds of those who wrote them and those for whom they were written has become a pre-emptive basis of historical scholarship. Where the gap in time is relatively brief the differences of understanding may be the less easy to appreciate and the scope for misinterpretation by unthinking reliance on today's assumptions all the greater.

Finally, in Chapters VII–IX we turn outward to the place of Britain and its vaunted Empire in relation to other nation states. It was in this context that notions of legislative sovereignty, and indeed the very nature of law, gained much of their modern character. In the nineteenth century ideas of a law of nations and of private international law were obliged to break their European frame, given the competition to trade with and colonize the inhabitable globe. The prospects for an international legal order would appear to be slender in the decades of hostility that would make the first half of the twentieth century so terrible. Nonetheless the preceding attempts to build that order had an impact that cannot be ignored, even in respect of English common law.

[5] See Ch. II(5).

II
Government and People

1. GUARANTEE OF A RULE OF LAW

By 1820, educated Englishmen considered themselves the bearers of a distinctive degree of personal liberty. They were ready to think that they enjoyed freedoms unknown in Continental Europe—above all freedom from unregulated interference in their lives by those with political power over them. None of these liberties and protective guarantees were unconditional; but the security that bolstered their individual liberties was commonly thought to stem from that 'rule' or 'reign' of law which had grown with the fashioning of the non-absolutist state. The root idea of responsibility under law as a curb on the excesses of arbitrary power had classical expression in Plato and Aristotle and had surfaced as a political ideal under many social conditions thereafter. But as it blossomed in eighteenth-century Britain, it had taken particular forms. Since the securing of the Protestant succession in 1689, parliamentary government had involved constraints on monarchs which somehow fitted their limited capabilities. Autocracies might flourish in France, Austria, Saxony, Prussia, and Russia. But the balance of powers struck with William of Orange and Mary Stuart would provide a solid buttress for the English aristocracy and gentry; and the Georges from Hanover lacked the mettle to mount any fundamental assault upon it. An individual's legal right to protection of life and bodily security, personal freedoms, and private property had become governed by what was regarded as 'ordinary law', without any distinct form of justice being administered in special prerogative courts such as those that had been deployed by Tudor and Stuart monarchs.[1] It was a secular law that stood to resist not only royal pretensions to hold the reins of governmental power, but also those of the Established Church.[2]

That 'ordinary law' was the statute law and the rules recognized and applied in the royal courts, particularly the courts of common law and equity. So far as concerned the judges of the three royal courts of common law—King's Bench,

---

[1] The civilian jurisdictions in admiralty and prize, and over the probate of wills and matrimonial causes tended to be seen also as part of this 'ordinary law': see below, Pt 3, Ch. V.

[2] As to the Church of England's constitutional position and its courts, see below, Pt 2, Ch. III.1.

Common Pleas, and Exchequer—they could be removed from office only by vote of both houses of parliament.[3] The harsh experiences of early modern England had inculcated an unswerving faith in English law as the bedrock of a liberal constitution. Life and limb were regulated by a criminal law of offences against the person and by civil liability for injuries to the person. These were the rules that established the extent to which one individual was responsible towards others and could at the same time prevent others from harming him or her. The writ of habeas corpus required any imprisoner, public or private, to show legal grounds for the restraint.[4] The penal offences and civil liability for libels and slanders protected the reputation of individuals against defamatory attacks on their 'personalities'.[5]

As for private property, so much was it the outward sign of an individual's very consequence that it sat surrounded by a deep moat of legal protection. The true English freeman held property or had real prospects of doing so. When denouncing general search warrants in *Entick* v. *Carrington*, Lord Camden had echoed a common sentiment, deriving from John Locke, by insisting that:

[t]he great end, for which men entered into society, was to secure their property. That right is preserved sacred and incommunicable in all instances, where it has not been taken away or abridged by some public law for the good of the whole.[6]

So Sir William Blackstone taught succeeding generations through his *Commentaries on the Laws of England*,[7] doing much to sustain a faith in the common law of the land as the guarantor of this crucial security of property. His insistence on its sanctity made it subject to even fewer qualifications than applied to the rights to life and to liberty.[8] In the ill-temper of the seventeenth century, many would have weighed those basic rights rather differently. English society

---

[3] See below, pp. 32, 989–91, 1002–3.

[4] For its use in family issues, however, see XIII, pp. 731–2, 810–11.

[5] Below, pp. 852–7.

[6] (1765) 19 St. Tr. 1029 at 1066.

[7] In four Books, 1765–9; on this theme, see esp. Bk. 1 Ch. I, 'Of the Absolute Rights of Persons'. Our interest in Blackstone must be confined to the continuing influence of his major work long into the nineteenth century (for which, see esp. J. W. Cairns 'Blackstone: An English Institutist' (1984) 4 *OJLS* 318; S. F. C. Milsom 'The Nature of Blackstone's Achievement' in *Selden Society Lectures 1952–2001* (2005), 499; W. Prest, *William Blackstone* (2008), esp. Ch. 14). The quality of argument in the *Commentaries* has provoked scepticism, if not derision, from various modern scholars—led with verve by Daniel Boorstein in *The Mysterious Science of the Law* (Chicago, 1941). Such criticism only adds to the fascination of his appeal for many generations of laymen as well as initiates in the law.

[8] His presentation, as elsewhere, propounded an unexceptionable truth, only to admit qualifications upon it expressed in uncertain but strictly limited terms: as with, in this context, the right of parliament to expropriate property on condition that compensation be provided: see e.g. A. W. B. Simpson, 'Victorian Law and the Industrial Spirit' in *Selden Society Lectures, 1952–2001* (2005), 615.

had become stable enough for the right of a people to overthrow a tyrant to be a matter for philosophic speculation, rather than an urgent practicality.[9] By the early nineteenth century, the English had lost the 13 colonies of the American seaboard to their own landed gentlemen, who had set about establishing a novel form of democratic rule with separations and balances of power more strongly delineated than in the mother country that they had renounced. Far more unsettling had been the spectacle of the French revolution, with its Republic and then First Empire, its expropriations of aristocratic property and its replacement of the old *police* by an aggressive bureaucracy of Napoleonic snoopers. Drawn into protracted wars to settle the balance of power in Europe, the English landed class came to fear that the rule of law under parliamentary governance could not after all be taken simply as a given. Despite the final victory over Napoleon in 1815, the upper ranks of the country would remain anxious that the sharing of authority among themselves could not be sustained, despite their support for programmes of moral cleansing and their insistence that redress against those who might attack others, break promises or abuse property must be through the regular courses of law and the legal system.

The first condition for government under law was characterized by Jeremy Bentham and his disciple John Austin as a 'habit of obedience'—a shared determination among the people to live in a degree of harmony.[10] Theorists of the Enlightenment, from Locke to Rousseau and Burke, had sought to express this fundamental understanding as a social contract. In consequence, emerging governments, led by the United States, were adopting written constitutions that set forth the powers of legislature, executive, and judiciary so as to define the legal character of the state. But the deeper reality was always the need for some measure of shared trust, and the English—or at least those Englishmen and their families who had some share in property and power—had moved a century earlier to an assumption that government could be under law—an assumption that, by and large, the law then operated to sustain.[11]

The Parliament, which the Bill of Rights had affirmed as supreme, was nominally a triumvirate, but one in which the Crown played only a formal part. Royal assent to bills passed by the two Houses was never withheld—a Hanoverian 'convention of the constitution' no longer open to reversal. Eighteenth-century monarchs, however, had kept charge over executive government in the Kingdom as a whole. Still in 1820, their powers to act under the royal prerogative were

---

[9] Cf. *Comms*, i, Ch. 2, III with Locke's *First Treatise on Government*, ii, paras 149, 227.

[10] See below, Ch. IV.1, IV.2.

[11] The Union for which that Parliament legislated, had begun with the engrafting of Wales onto England in the fourteenth century. For the incorporation of Scotland in 1707, then Ireland in 1800, see below at p. 236.

considerable, since that prerogative justified any action of the central executive that Parliament had not chosen to limit. Nonetheless Parliament had intervened and continued to do so increasingly, the first great constraints lying in its control of the power to tax and to maintain a standing army—those issues that had been of such moment in the contests between Parliament and the Stuarts. After 1689 both matters had become the subject of annual Acts which renewed, and, where necessary, altered or extended the Crown's powers. On the political balance thus struck, Georgian kings and their advisers had been able to conduct a long series of wars in Europe and across the world in pursuit of the great issue that remained within the royal prerogative—the conduct of relations with other nations.[12]

In this perception the rule of law could be treated as a corollary of parliamentary sovereignty. Eighteenth-century politicians and writers who admired the consti-tutional foundation of 1689 had shown little enough concern that Parliament had thereby acquired the power to turn the law on sections of its peoples, so as to make a mockery of its 'reign' or 'rule'. To have acknowledged a higher set of legal values to which even Parliament must adhere was not a direction favoured by the survivors of the seventeenth-century struggles. Their concern was to elim-inate the taint of Stuart appeals to the ultimate authority of kings, posited as a divine right. As it was, the Bill of Rights categorically denounced James II's practice of deploying the royal prerogative to invalidate legislation or suspend it in relation to particular cases.[13] Sufficient control over Parliament was taken to exist in its own edict that elections to the Commons must take place at least every seven years.[14] The legislature itself remained capable of extending the life of parliaments as it chose, thanks to its untrammelled sovereignty.[15] In this order of things there was no place for the judiciary (or indeed any other form of ulti-mate council) to nullify parliamentary legislation by finding it incompatible with a basic Constitution or any catalogue of the 'true, ancient and indubitable rights and liberties of the people'.[16] In our period political pressures would lead to constitutional changes, sometimes expressed in positive legislation, but more

[12] See below, p. 265–6.

[13] Even James had not attempted to legislate by promulgating his own decrees.

[14] The Septennial Act 1715, 1 Geo. I, st. 2, c. 3, had extended from three years to seven the period before which the Crown was obliged to call a new Commons election (eventually to be reduced to five years by the Parliament Act 1911, s 7). The requirement that Parliament at least meet once in three years (see 6 & 7 Wm & Mary c. 2, 1694) would in time be bolstered by a convention that it should meet at least once a year.

[15] Blackstone, who thought little of apologies for the Septennial Act, asked how a Parliament could have prolonged even its own life: *Comms*, i, 2.VII.3.

[16] In the Bill of Rights of 1689 this fine phrase acknowledged the new monarchs' acceptance of the common and statute law and custom of their realm; but the content of that law, for the most part, was left without further definition in the document.

typically evolving as 'conventions', which could not be the subject of adjudication in courts, but which in practice could not be reversed or altered without risking a political crisis.

Albert Venn Dicey, the late Victorian theorist of the British Constitution, treated these conventions as sophisticated mechanisms for adjusting the relationship between the strictly legal and the purely political.[17] A parliamentary enactment was certainly necessary for any increase in the range and independence of the electorate for the lower House. However, the conduct of business in the two Houses was organized through Standing Orders; and while this procedural web appeared to be enshrined in rules, the Orders were nonetheless set and amended solely by each House for itself. Then again, the relation between the Upper and Lower Houses throughout Victoria's reign depended on more evidently 'conventional' understandings that were also political, it being accepted, for example, that over the vital question of raising public revenue, a Commons bill must initiate the process. Only at the end of our period had political tension between the two Chambers become so grave and persistent that the Liberal government would insist on a legal framework which curbed the powers of the Lords to reject bills from the Commons. The Parliament Act 1911 placed strict constraints on the ability of the Lords to refuse a 'money bill' from the Commons: and a more measured limitation on their entitlement to reject other public bills.[18] In consequence a statute could exceptionally be a text passed by the Commons and signed by the Crown, it having been a convention for some 200 years that royal assent would always be given.

Mixed into the politics of securing this change was an affirmation of the convention that major legislation needed to be grounded upon a pre-election promise that it would be introduced. The immediate cause had been the Lords' rejection of the Finance Bill of 1909, embodying the 'People's Budget'. This high Tory insistence on rectitude was justified by asserting that the government had no 'mandate' for its policy that had been spelled out in the Liberal manifesto on which they won the 1906 election. The Asquith Cabinet responded by securing a new election in 1910 that was to be fought as a way of taking the political temperature on the Budget proposals. Yet another election was then needed only months later to gain support for 'clipping the wings' of the Lords by the Parliament Act.[19]

---

[17] *Introduction to the Study of the Law of the Constitution* (1885), Part III.

[18] The Lords' refusal of a money bill could be maintained only to the end of the Session, a money bill being one concerned only with the raising of revenue. The power to decide on particular instances was conferred on the Speaker of the Commons. Other bills were to become law, despite the Lords having rejected the bill from the Commons in three successive sessions of Parliament. The latter period would be further reduced by the Parliament Act 1949.

[19] The 'Constitutional Convention' which sought to mediate between Liberal proponents and Conservative antagonists at one stage proposed that 'constitutional bills' needed to be passed either

The requiring of an election pledge, however, was at the 'political' pole of what could constitute a convention. How central and how wide-ranging did the manifesto have to be in order to satisfy the requirement? The very idea left a good deal of scope for political posturing.

2. SOCIAL RELATIONS AND THE PARLIAMENTARY FRANCHISE

Adopting a rule of law can be accounted 'itself an unqualified good', as E. P. Thompson unexpectedly wrote.[20] Nonetheless, for many who have speculated about its constituent qualities, it was and has remained no more than a necessary first step towards a better society. It insists that legality is an essential presupposition for political liberty. It posits a society which places all subjects under its law, making them in-laws, rather than outlaws. Beyond that the characteristics that theorists—juristic and political—consider to be its requisites vary over time with types of society and national structures for conducting government. Blackstone's rule of law supported the constitutional arrangements that in 1689 had laid novel foundations for a limited monarchy. But his first purpose, three-quarters of a century later, was to justify what had become that status quo. It was certainly not a doctrine that addressed the great goals of equality and fraternity, so powerful in the rhetoric of the Enlightenment in continental Europe.

In 1820 the much-vaunted freedom of the individual under law gave the bulk of the English people only a highly conditional share in it. The dependent members of families were under the dominion of their paterfamilias—not just the children below majority,[21] but even more the wife, who by common law rule was treated as a subjugate unity with her husband.[22] This was so down the many ranks of society. At the lowest socio-economic levels, it was true that formal notions of slavery—legal ownership by a master of his workforce—had disappeared in the UK and its place in British colonies, in the United States and elsewhere was already vigorously contested by the anti-slavery movement led by William Wilberforce, Thomas Clarkson, and other Evangelicals. Nonetheless the prospects open to unskilled workers to earn or produce enough to live on were often enough precarious. Labourers in agriculture and building trades, handweavers, factory and

---

by both Houses, or that there be a specific referendum on the issue. But since the Conservative opinion was that a Home Rule Bill for Irish governance was 'constitutional', while the Liberal view was the opposite, the compromise made no progress.

[20] *Whigs and Hunters* (1975), 273.

[21] The 1841 census was the first to record numbers of population under 21: it was 36%—a proportion that would fall to 30% by 1911.

[22] See XIII, pp. 729–32.

mine hands, domestic servants, clerks, the trampers after work, the feckless, the luckless—all were subject to the iron realities of survival. Their subordinate social condition was set within notions of property and contract that derived practical force from both civil and criminal law.[23] This, for the Tory apologist, Richard Oastler, placed them in 'a state of slavery, more horrid than are the victims of that hellish system, "colonial slavery"'.[24] Telling political badinage, undoubtedly; but not an issue that the law itself contained the means to rectify.

Who then could depend upon the beneficence that flowed from protection under law? The population of England and Wales as a whole was measured by the first Census of 1801 at nearly 9 million and by 1821 it has already bounded to 12 million, just over half being women.[25] If the right to elect members of the Commons is taken as a first indicator, we must start from the constitution of the unreformed Commons, with its two members for each county and its gradual accretion of borough seats, given particular form in an original charter and then shaped by all manner of subsequent history. Of the latter, Westminster and Yorkshire accorded the vote to a fairly wide range of its male populace, while at the other extreme, the ancient, rotten boroughs, such as Old Sarum and Grampound, had decayed into curious oddities. The Commons of 1820 therefore embodied much of what is implied in the notion of paternal government by the landed upper class—that interplay of wealth, social position, and patronage down the social scale that survived the long wars with France and from some perspectives looked set to continue for any foreseeable future.

Even remembering that a considerable proportion of the populace as a whole were under age, the proportion of those who enjoyed the inherited franchise was small. In the unreformed Parliament, some 300,000 adult men had the right to vote for the Commons, being in one way or another persons of substance. They were part of those upper cohorts of society marked out by their property. But these people maintained many links with those of lower status who were (in the usage of the time) their 'friends'. And this engendered a sense that the conditions and concerns of lesser folk would not go entirely ignored in the central councils of the Kingdom. While many parliamentary seats remained in the apparent gift of large landowners, the expensive rigmarole of an election contest was often avoided by quite generous condescension on their part towards their social

---

[23] For the theories of political economy and the legal consequences upon relations between master and servant, see below, pp. 192–205 and XIII, pp. 629–32, 667–83, 692–708.

[24] *Leeds Mercury*, 29 September 1830.

[25] In 1821 Scotland had just over 2 million people; this number would more than double by 1911. Ireland held nearly 7 million in 1821, and would add more than another million by 1841, before falling away, for the rest of the century, thanks to the potato famine, emigration, and other causes.

inferiors. As Frank O'Gorman has shown, loyalty and sympathy came only at a well-understood price.[26]

The concessions and rationalizations made in the First Reform Act of 1832, gave all men owning or occupying substantial landholdings the vote.[27] This increased the electorate to some 650,000; but by then the population was touching 14 million. The beneficiaries were a widening middle class, associated with manufacturing and distributing the new industrial products, the financing of economic developments, the fomenting of colonial and foreign trade, and the spread of professional services and government regulation. The great mass of ordinary labour remained outside. A growing indignation against this exclusion produced the Chartist movement, with its demands for democratic rights for all adult males, secret ballots, annual parliaments, frequent elections, and other demotic guarantees. Particularly through the economic downturn of 1837–42, Chartism posed a real threat of insurrectionary activity. It involved militaristic forces training by night. Occasionally they were put to use, as notably in the attack on Newport in 1839, when a crowd of some 8000 men sought to secure the release of a number of local Chartists who were under arrest.[28]

The proportion of workers in factories, mines, workshops, shipping, railways, and other transport continued its rise. The population, just short of 16 million in 1841, would grow by well over 10 per cent in each decade to 1911, when the total figure reached 36 million. The actual numbers engaged in agriculture and fisheries would stay more or less constant through that period, but their proportion would decline from 22 per cent to 9 per cent.[29] That is one stark measure of the shift of population from country into city and town, there to struggle in the grim conditions detailed in investigative reports and emotive novels on slums, overcrowding, dangerous diseases, drink, crime, and work that broke backs and spirits.

Trailing these primary demographic shifts, periodic extensions in the franchise for the Commons would eventually be enacted—and likewise changes in various electorates for local government bodies.[30] The Second Reform Act of 1867

[26] F. O'Gorman, *Voters, Patrons and Parties: The Unreformed Electorate of Hanoverian England 1734–1832* (Oxford, 1989); also his *The Emergence of the British Two-Party System* (1982); and see R. Stewart, *Party and Politics, 1830–1852* (Basingstoke, 1989).

[27] In the English counties, freeholders of land rated at 40s, copyholders, and long leaseholders paying £10 per annum rent, and shorter leaseholders rated at £50; in the boroughs, the main franchise went to householders, as 40s freeholders or £10 tenants, with freeholders also having some rights to vote for the county seats.

[28] The confrontation was put down by the authorities calling in soldiers and the leaders were condemned to death—a sentence then commuted to long terms of transportation: see D. V. A. Jones, *The Last Rising* (Oxford, 1985).

[29] Those recorded were mostly male; so the figures exclude the many contributions of women and children to agricultural production.

[30] For these latter, see below Pt 2, Ch. V; XIII, Pt 2, Ch. II.

was driven forward by a clamour that spoke as much to Tories as to Whigs (or Conservatives and Liberals, as they were coming to be called). The association between land ownership or occupation and the right to vote would long remain but it would be extended to embrace more sectors of the populace. All male freeholders in the towns, together with lessees who occupied dwellings with an annual value for rates of £12, were added, thus doubling the electorate to around 2 million.

Nonetheless it was a 'leap in the dark' empowering new 'masters' who were badly in need of education—thus did the gentry and the middle classes express their fears. From this juncture the movement towards full democracy seemed inevitable to many, but there were other elements in the equation. Despite the urgings of the early feminists and their allies, led by John Stuart Mill, women did not in 1867 secure the parliamentary franchise on the same basis as men;[31] but two years later they did obtain it for municipal councils.[32] In addition, the introduction of a secret ballot in 1872 had great impact.[33] No longer could landlords watch that their tenants voted to order—a change that lifted fetters from the Irish in particular. Political parties turned to importuning voters with 'programmes' setting out their proposals for legislation. That in turn called for much greater discipline from party whips in both Houses and so ushered in the modern relationship between ministers and their own back-benchers.[34]

In 1884–5, a further extension of the parliamentary suffrage gave the vote to two male adults in three, by bringing in small-scale agricultural tenants and lodgers. Great complications ensued over who exactly was still excluded. The most evident category remained women. After the respectable campaigning of suffragists, the dramatic confrontations aroused by the civil disobedience of the

---

[31] *Chorlton* v. *Lings* (1868) LR 4 CP 374—this despite Brougham's Acts of Parliament Abbreviation Act 1850 (13 & 14 Vict. c. 21, s 4) which prescribed that words of masculine gender in a statute were to be understood to include those of feminine gender unless expressly provided to the contrary. Resolutely, the Court of Common Pleas insisted that, because there was no evidence of women having voting rights for the Commons over the previous 300 years, past practice settled the matter 'expressly'. By the time of the case, 5346 women in Manchester were seeking to have their names placed on the voters register: see N. St.John-Stevas, 'Women in Public Law', in R. Graveson and F. R. Crane, *A Century of Family Law* (1957), 256, 263–6.

[32] Municipal Franchise etc Act 1869, s 9. Since only borough ratepayers qualified, there remained an indirect discrimination against women. Jacob Bright's amendment which secured the concession was a response to the considerable agitation against the *Chorlton* decision (above, n.31). In 1870, Bright promoted a bill to secure women the parliamentary suffrage on the same basis as men, but it was defeated in Committee by a considerable majority. In any case, women as well as men had from 1834 been entitled to vote on membership of Boards of Guardians of the Poor Law if they satisfied the property qualification.

[33] Ballot (Parliamentary and Municipal Elections) Act 1872, ss 4, 20.

[34] See below, pp. 308–11.

suffragettes, and in the end the crucial contribution of women to war work, their admission to the parliamentary franchise became inevitable. It was granted in 1918; but still women voters had to be aged 30, while all men, irrespective of where and how they lived, were enfranchised at 21.[35]

Britain did not progress through its great economic and imperial transformation by some effortless conviction that all things and all creatures were indeed bright and beautiful, wise and wonderful, thanks to divine providence. Christian hymns might proclaim so,[36] but the reality was otherwise.[37] What England did have was a distribution of power, wealth, and political temper that allowed it to deal with social change by concession before confrontations could build up that might not be capable of containment by the state. With the Reform Act of 1832 those who argued that Parliament itself must broaden political franchises in stages that reflected the rising position of lower social groups, had a first precedent for their arguments.

Real threats of social unrest continued in Britain until the final stand-off with the Chartists in 1848, organized for the government with military precision by the aged Duke of Wellington.[38] The spirit of revolution that had ignited so defiant an upsurge in the France of 1789 had soon enough sparked restive crowds in London and other British towns, stirred by the democratic visions of radical orators. During the quarter-century of wars against the French the beacons of a new world had never been extinguished. After the final defeat of Napoleon, disturbances at home flared and were tackled by attempts at repression, such as the ill-judged 'Peterloo' Massacre in St Peters Fields, Manchester in 1819 and the Six Acts, then pushed through by the Home Secretary, Viscount Sidmouth (Addington). Their intent was to repress militaristic formations, to make large political gatherings subject to permission from magistrates and to impose stamp duties and other curbs on the radical press, thereby eroding freedom of speech and the right to bear arms.[39] Individual liberty was not a cause that could be allowed to override any threat to the security of the state from within. The rule

[35] Most of the other public disabilities cast upon women would be removed in the following year: Sex Disqualification (Removal) Act 1919. The age limit for women voters would be reduced to 21 in 1928, disparagers referring to this enfranchisement as the 'flappers' vote'.

[36] Mrs Cecil Alexander's Children's Hymn of 1848 radiated reassurance, in a verse no longer much found in hymnals:

> The rich man in his castle,
> The poor man at his gate,
> He made them, high and lowly,
> And ordered their estate.

[37] See below, pp. 153–7.

[38] For the movement, see e.g. J. T. Ward, *Chartism* (1974).

[39] 60 Geo. IV cs. 1, 2, 4, 6, 8, 9. See M. Lobban, 'From Seditious Libel to Unlawful Assembly: Peterloo and the Changing Face of Political Crime, *c.* 1770–1820' (1990) 10 *OxJLS* 307–52.

of law was judged by the ruling classes not to be infringed precisely because the Acts had been passed by the sovereign Parliament.

In 1830, the southern counties saw fitful challenges to the prevailing order through threats made in the name of 'Captain Swing', and the Reform Bill riots succeeded them soon afterwards. From this time, the movement towards modern policing could be instituted bit by bit. But, save in London, it was to be organized at a local level in order to cauterize the ambitions of central government. The army could still be brought in as a last resort to deal with truly serious threats to civil peace; but it did not prove necessary or desirable to arm the police, at least in England. Central government would confine its role in policing mainly to financial support out of taxation, though for this it would extract the right to inspect the borough and county police forces in the name of value for money.[40] It was an outcome that tells a great deal about the ways in which central power was contained in the early decades of Victoria's reign.

3. EXECUTIVE POWER SUBJECT TO LAW

A country with a modern written constitution will set forth in that foundation document the structure around which central, regional, and perhaps smaller units of administration may legally be formed, and may state what their main powers will be. It is then to be expected that more detailed legislation will elaborate on the exercise of those powers through a whole complex of instruments from legislative enactments, formal regulations and procedural rules, down to documents notifying normal practices and administrative guidelines that today are characterized as 'soft law'. It is one of the curiosities of the evolution of modern government in Britain, however, that at the apex of executive government, the organization of business came to be distributed as a matter of political practice, rather than under law laid down according to a documented plan.

Certainly at subordinate levels beneath the central authority, the benches of magistrates, the corporate bodies of the boroughs and many other institutions had to accept that their powers were limited by law. The judges used both common law remedies and the prerogative writs to keep these bodies and individual office-holders in legal line. At these levels, as we shall see, judicial review of governmental activities was indeed part of the rule of law and its impact would grow steadily through the nineteenth century.[41] But there was nothing essentially novel about what would occur. The operation of controls over local life had for centuries been primarily in the hands of those who held sway over their manors, their justices' bench, their parishes, their counties. It was a characteristic of continuing

---

[40] See XIII, pp. 41–44.   [41] See below, Pt 2, Ch. VI.

significance in both rural and urban life as industrialization penetrated different parts of the country. The lively use of Parliament to sanction specific schemes of development had been an eighteenth-century phenomenon, whether the subject was an enclosure of village land, or the establishment of a turnpike road or a canal, or a corporation with, for instance, a power of compulsory purchase, or the securing of a full divorce.[42] In all this the precondition of legality was constantly being reinforced, however tough the outcomes might be for those who lost out from the process.

As the nineteenth century unfolded, local and private legislation tended to give place to public statutes which granted powers in more or less standard form across the UK as a whole, or for England and Wales, Scotland or Ireland. Local inwardness, local initiative, local pride would remain a signal focus of Victorian life. At the same time the consciousness of a national identity would grow, which those in the southern Kingdom tended to call 'English'—or 'British' when it suited them to touch on the wider political embrace. So far as legal systems were concerned, the divisions of jurisdiction meant that it was English common law that was exported (albeit in some modified form) to most of the colonies of the Empire.[43] Legal conceptions of the structure of government played their own part in solidifying the idea of the nation, rather than a local community, as the core of social existence under complex industrial conditions.

In 1820, the power of executive government remained formally with the king in person. Both George IV and his brother, William IV, expected deferential consultation by their Crown servants, who included not only their political advisers but also their permanent administrators, who were becoming civil servants rather than placemen. In practice, the Ministers in charge of the growing number of central departments would treat royal criticism as calling up their capacities for discreet and politic tact. Over the previous century the Hanoverians had evolved a practice of appointing a first minister and around him a group of close advisers, who formed what would be called the Cabinet. These ministers stayed in office only so long as they retained the royal favour, a practice that had coloured much of high politics in the reign of George III. Even he learned that he could express displeasure by dismissing one or more of them only if he could find other advisers better fitted to his purpose. Achieving the reform of the franchise in 1832 was a stormy experience, partly because William IV was opposed to it; but the terms finally hammered out left the propertied classes able to treat the consequences for the legislature as less than a root reform.[44] In its immediate aftermath came

---

[42] The growth in the nineteenth century of general legislation is well instanced in the discussion of social reforms in XIII, Pt 2.

[43] See below, pp. 238–41.   [44] See below, pp. 301–2.

the episode in which William replaced the Whig leadership with the Tory Peel, and learned in a matter of months that he no longer had the practical ability to maintain a government that could not keep the confidence of a newly elected Commons.[45]

From this it followed that the ministers in the Cabinet and lesser government positions were to be chosen and retained by the Prime Minister and he would pick them from members of the lower or upper House whose loyalty and ability he trusted. Ministers would therefore be responsible collectively for the conduct of government, primarily to the House of Commons and ultimately therefore to the electorate.[46] They would be responsible individually to Parliament for the department or other executive body over which they presided. This required them to answer for accusations of malpractice or neglect by those under them, though it never became clear to what extent convention obliged them to resign from office once they admitted the fault.[47] Why theoretically they should shoulder such blame stemmed from the legal principle that suits for maladministration lay against the department or office for which officers acted, not against them personally. In the nineteenth century, French law was building towards the opposite approach, under which individual servants of the state were placed under personal responsibility for their acts. This was hailed as an incentive to act properly within the scope of powers prescribed in law. Dicey would engage in protracted discussion of which approach more faithfully realized the idea of a Rule of Law, the object of which was to demonstrate the virtues of the common law's position.[48] Gratifying though Britain's political and judicial leaders would find his theoretical conclusion, the argument was inherently difficult to substantiate.

Overall the framework set a balance, rather than a separation, between legislative and executive power.[49] It was a structure for modern government which could give effect to the rule of law ideal and its acceptance grew out of political practice that had been building since the decades when the younger Pitt assumed

[45] Over the formation and continuance of governments, two prerogatives did remain. The monarch was not obliged to accept a Prime Minister's request to dissolve Parliament for an election; and he or she also decided who among leading figures in a victorious party should be called to become Prime Minister.

[46] Disraeli sought dissolution after losing the 1868 election without first going to the Commons for a vote of no confidence and so marked a distinct change: he acknowledged the electorate, and not the Commons, as holder of the decisive power.

[47] For the importance of having a minister answerable for the conduct of otherwise autonomous bodies within central government would be plainly demonstrated by the acrimonious history of the Poor Law Commission, set up in 1834 to supervise the New Poor Law: see XIII, Pt 2, Ch. II.

[48] Dicey, Law of the Constitution, Ch.12; cf. esp. W. I. Jennings, The Law and the Constitution (1933), Ch. 6.2.

[49] This was the image sustained for later Victorian generations by Walter Bagehot in his The English Constitution (1867), Ch. 6.

the premiership. But as with any design that left ultimate issues to be settled by active politicians, rather than a constitutional court, it had its built-in risks. In these Volumes there is much about the growth of government administration at both the central and the local levels. The party winning an election gained the opportunity for up to seven years to put through legislation, provided that it found itself able to withstand whatever criticism might be levelled against its bills by 'His or Her Majesty's Opposition' or by individual members of either House. Parliament could therefore be induced by the governing party, thanks to its majority in the Commons, to confer executive authority in terms that gave very considerable discretion to ministries, central boards, and commissions, or to general and special bodies at county, borough, parish, or district levels, and so forth. It would often give them powers to draft their own regulations. It could even confer on a Department's subordinate legislation the same 'sovereign' status as that accorded by the Bill of Rights to parliamentary enactments; but that would soon enough provoke criticism from those who adhered to theories of minimal government and detected conspiracies in corners of Whitehall.[50]

Measures which directly threatened the rule of law as a curb on executive action were most likely to appear when the country came under threat of invasion or major internal disturbance. Victorian England became a country too economically powerful for attacks from outside to be directed against home territory, and, at least once militant Chartism died away, insurrectionary activities could, for the most part, be handled under the criminal law and the imposition of constraints on the freedom to engage in political demonstration and discussion that were relatively marginal in practice, if ultimately threatening in general character.[51] It would not be until the outbreak of hostilities in 1914 that Parliament would—at a day's notice—succumb to the government's demand that it be given the wholly extraordinary powers to restrain individuals in person and to take over their property that were sketched in its first Defence of the Realm Act.[52] Then in the aftermath, an Emergency Powers Act of 1920 would confer on governments the ability, even in times of peace, to bring similar measures into operation without having to secure new legislation first.[53]

In all these shifts, conservatives who still believed that the role of government should be restricted to the maintenance of peace and of justice under law, turned to Dicey's version of the rule of law as their weapon against a rise of 'Whitehall' that necessarily undermined the liberty of the individual, for the protection

[50] See n. 54, below.

[51] Ireland, however, would induce a different story, Westminster using a long series of Coercion Acts in attempts to control protest.

[52] From this the government would spin out a spider's web of Defence of the Realm Regulations.

[53] For the effects during World War I, see A. W. B. Simpson, *In the Highest Degree Odious: Detention without Trial in Wartime Britain* (Oxford, 1992), Chs 1–3.

of which Parliament had been accorded supremacy more than two centuries before.[54] As the country had moved towards a full democracy, government pro-grammes of social support expanded and the judiciary found itself increasingly pressed to settle the scope of powers conferred on public bodies. English law was slowly developing its own criteria by which judges could review the actions of public administrators, as distinct from those of legislators. The types of issue were uncomfortably diverse. It was one thing to decide whether a claimant was entitled to an old age pension, or national insurance benefit because of unem-ployment or loss of earnings through sickness: these rules, having been laid down by legislation, needed interpretation in order to settle their scope. It was quite another matter to determine where a garden suburb should be built and what facilities it should have, when these were policy choices that legislation left to be made by governments and their advisers. It is a crucial, but challenging, subject, and is reserved for later discussion.[55]

The British constitution, never having been spelled out in an overarching doc-ument, had the appearance of considerable flexibility. It had acquired a backbone from successive records of political settlements among the powerful, commenc-ing with Magna Carta in 1215. But while the doctrine of parliamentary suprem-acy had been set out in forthright terms in the Bill of Rights, that document had simply assumed the existence of Parliament in its threefold manifestation. If Parliament had to be found defined in legal terms, then it was a bundle of customary practices recognized as a matter of common law. As just noted, the modern constitution had acquired flesh through the practice of Cabinet govern-ment—flesh that changed from adherence to the royal will to retention of the confidence of the Commons.

To Blackstone the role of ministers of the Crown had no part in an exposition of constitutional law. Those who set out to explain the activities of the legislature and the central executive in the nineteenth century for the most part wrote as historians of the evolution of governmental practice or as analysts who strove to pinpoint what it was that kept that practice conjoined.[56] Not only were they to a considerable extent in agreement, but they in the main admired the result. Here was a robust form of government capable of managing an ever-growing Empire. T. B. Macaulay made this emergence of 'The Ministry' a crowning glory of his resplendently Whiggish *History of England*;[57] and Walter Bagehot treated it as a vital element in what he termed the 'efficient', as distinct from the 'dignified',

[54] The charge would be led by Lord Hewart CJ, in *The New Despotism* (1929).

[55] See below, pp. 512–21.

[56] See esp. O. Hood Phillips, 'Constitutional Conventions: Dicey's Predecessors' (1966) 29 *MLR* 137–48.

[57] (1855), iv: 434–5.

aspects of the constitution.[58] J. S. Mill likewise gave prominence to the many unwritten maxims constituting the 'positive political morality of the country' in his influential *Considerations on Representative Government*.[59] Others who wrote on British constitutional evolution sought to capture the foundational quality of customary practices, whether they expressed themselves as historians identifying customary practices in government *simpliciter* or as lawyers regarding those practices as imbued with 'normativity', albeit that they were not justiciable in courts. This was true of the legal theorists, John Austin and his London rival, John James Park,[60] at the catharsis of 1832, just as it was of barrister-historians such as Henry Hallam and—a generation later—Sir Erskine May and Homersham Cox.[61]

As we shall see, the idea that a British colony might shed its chrysalis and emerge as a self-governing dominion gave new impetus to defining in statutory terms the power and practices of many institutions which were simply presumed to have effect in the practice of Westminster, Whitehall, and the English courts of common law.[62] Alpheus Todd, emigrant to Canada, would publish *On the Parliamentary Government in England* just as that Dominion was created.[63] The talented W. E. Hearn, professing a succession of subjects in Melbourne University, published *The Government of England: Its Structure and Development*,[64] in which he emphasized the difficulty of expressing in legal terms the roles of Prime Minister and cabinet in abiding by the conventions of responsible government, while pointing up how crucial it was that the duties as well as the powers ascribed to these offices be respected. The tendency in his reflections was, if anything, to play down the importance of stating them as a matter of law. This was also to be found in the writer from whom Dicey would claim to have learned most, E. A. Freeman. Yet in his *Growth of the English Constitution: From Earliest Times*, Freeman would in effect take law only to define the established institutions and recognized doctrines that were acknowledged by Blackstone in the 1760s—a strategy which in his view was used by lawyers to justify the considerable scope that remained for the royal prerogative. This made acknowledgment of customary practices in the course of government the more essential in that they differed in kind. As he concluded:

---

[58] *The English Constitution* (1867), Ch. 1.

[59] (1861), Ch. 5.

[60] J. Austin, *The Province of Jurisprudence Determined* (1832), Lecture 5; J. J. Park, *The Dogmas of the Constitution: Four Lectures* (1832).

[61] H. Hallam, *The Constitutional History of England: From the Accession of Henry VII to the Death of George III* (1827); followed by Sir E. May, *The Constitutional History of England since the Reign of George III* (1861); H. Cox, *Institutions of the English Government* (1863).

[62] Below, pp. 242–4.

[63] In two vols, 1867, 1869.

[64] 1867.

by the side of our written Law, there has grown up an unwritten or conventional constitution. When an Englishman speaks of the conduct of a public man being constitutional or unconstitutional, he means something wholly different from what he means by his conduct being legal or illegal.[65]

Dicey therefore saw it as his task in his *Introduction to the Study of the Law of the Constitution* (1885) to explain how, within a structure dominated by the legal doctrine of parliamentary supremacy as a means of grounding a rule of law, these constitutional practices could be accepted as having force in terms recognized as in some sense compulsive. He found this not by suggesting that constitutional conventions were law in the straightforward sense that courts would see to their enforcement, any more than that ministers might theoretically be subjected to the ancient process of impeachment.[66] Rather he claimed it to lie in the fact that failure to respect a convention would lead to a breakdown in legal powers. Of this his illustration was that if Parliament was not summoned to a yearly sitting (as convention prescribed), the annual enactments of powers to maintain the army and to apply government revenue to legitimate purposes would cease. Those who acted without this authority would commit criminal offences. The recognition of conventions acted as bridge between what he labelled legal sovereignty and political sovereignty:

[I]f Parliament be in the eye of the law a supreme legislature, the essence of representative government is that the legislature should represent or give effect to the will of political sovereign, *i.e.*, of the electoral body or the nation.[67]

This was an explanation that turned on its in-built capacity to sustain itself and many later theorists have doubted its coherence. Yet it identified a constraining set of values which large tranches of the British people considered essential to the functioning politics of the homeland and empire. Accordingly the conception has remained central to constitutional debate in common law systems.

4. LAW REFORM AND ITS POLITICAL BACKGROUND

Political Kernels

A survey of legal developments through the stages of the nineteenth century is likely to emphasize the course of national politics, because parliamentary

---

[65] 1st edn, 1872, 109.

[66] Sir William Anson, also a law don at Oxford, whose *Law and Custom of the Constitution* (Oxford, 1886) appeared a year after Dicey's book, was not so circumspect. He would at one point claim that both the privileges of each House of Parliament and the prerogative of the Crown were rights conferred by law 'and as such their limits are ascertainable and determinable, like the limits of other rights, by the courts of law' (5th edn, 192–3).

[67] 7th edn, 1908, 429–30.

legislation would become the major engine for removing old constraints and eventually for introducing schemes of social welfare for the benefit of the wider populace. The present Volumes do not trace in any detail the political history of the period; nor do they survey the social allegiances and antagonisms so closely bound into that history. Likewise, the Volumes do not record the measures of production and distribution, or finance and profit, which marked the economic transformation of the century under review. All are subjects that now have a very considerable literature.

Of the changing political stage an introductory sketch must suffice. In the eighteenth century, country people typically saw themselves in local heirarchies presided over by aristocrats and landed gentry, in which manual work in the fields was given out by a middling level of tenant farmers. Where a village had such a structure, the manorial family was likely to adopt a paternal stance towards those beneath—condescension, severity, and compassion mingling according to taste. With townspeople, social gradations were somewhat more varied, but they tended also to be seen as ladder-like. In the nineteenth century, as urbanization took its hold, a whole set of perceptions grew around notions of class, marked by differences of geography, language, accents, religion, education, housing, property, earning, and social mobility.[68] And so the older sense of vertical rank began to be overlaid with horizontal perceptions, as associative bonds formed according to socio-economic position, seen as much in regional and national terms as in purely local alliances.

In the nineteenth century, earlier laws that had applied to social groups in order to discriminate against them tended to disappear, although attitudinal change by no means followed as a matter of course. That was true of religious tests that had marked out the privileges of the Church of England, just as it was of the law on married women's property.[69] The game laws provided an instance. Not only had the poaching of birds and animals from the estates of landowners long been a pursuit fiercely prosecuted by the very class that it protected: those who did not rank as gentry were, by seventeenth-century edicts, forbidden to hunt.[70] But with game becoming such a symbol of gentility there developed an undercover trade to pass it from poachers up to middling-rankers whose dinner tables needed the mark of social pretension. Eighteenth-century legislation had sought to stop this commercialization, but the position could not be sustained. The game laws were

---

[68] For leading insights, see A. Briggs, *The Age of Improvement, 1780–1867* (1959), 8–20; H. Perkin, *The Origins of Modern English Society* (1969), Ch. 2; E. P. Thompson, *The Making of the English Working Class* (rev. edn, 1980).

[69] See below, pp. 385–8; XIII, pp. 760–66.

[70] See P. B. Munsche, *Gentlemen and Poachers 1671–1831* (Cambridge, 1981).

even then being denounced—Blackstone calling the criminal sanctions 'questionable'. By 1831 they had to be stripped of their social differentiation.[71]

When the period covered by these Volumes begins, Tories had formed the King's government, with only a single interruption, from the years preceding the French revolution. Under the younger Pitt, those politically engaged had taken to the idea that there must be some measure of 'economical reform' if England was to avoid another schism such as had convulsed it in the mid-seventeenth century. The wars with France, which drew to a close only in 1815, induced fears that left the owners of landed wealth clinging to old ways even when, with peace, critics of the existing political structure became increasingly vociferous. In the end, the parliamentary reform of 1832 was pushed through and the Whig government of 1830, which pulled it off, would govern for another decade. The single interruption to this—Peel's short term as Tory prime minister in 1834–5—finally settled that the responsibility of the government in power was to the Commons rather than the Crown.

The economic conditions of the 1830s and 1840s brought to a head a 'class struggle' over the key issue of free trade across British frontiers, and more specifically over the protection of British agriculture by Corn Laws which impacted on foreign imports when grain and flour prices fell because of a glut from good harvests.[72] The argument was central to writings on political economy and that context is considered in Chapter VI of this Part. Its political repercussions at the national level were considerable, for all the convolutions that it engendered. Even in 1828, the Tory government had conceded that the barriers to importation laid down in the Corn Laws should be lowered quite considerably by introducing a sliding scale of import duties.[73] It took several years after the electoral reform of 1832 for the question to revive; under Melbourne the Whigs could continue in office without altering the sliding scale. But then antagonism to the protection of agriculture was led by manufacturing interests who proclaimed the case for cheap food, thus allying their own interests with that of their workers. The Tories, with Peel as Prime Minister when they took over by a great margin in 1841, contained leaders and a following who were willing enough to stand against the

---

[71] Notably by the Game Act 1831, 1 & 2 Wm. IV, c. 32, which repealed 27 enactments dating from 1390 onwards. See C. Kirby 'English Game Law Reform', in *Essays in Modern English History in Honor of Wilbur Cortez Abbott* (Cambridge, MA, 1941), Ch. 11.

[72] See below, pp. 168–9.

[73] The governing legislation was enacted in 1815 (55 Geo. III c. 26), with the country fearful of its ability to provide enough food for itself, particularly if a foreign power were able to prevent imports from abroad, as Napoleon, striking at Britain's mastery of the seas, had sought to do. The great agricultural interests had no wish to see their high returns of the war years reduced in the peace. The 1828 Act (9 Geo. IV, c. 60) replaced a single bar on imports of corn until the price for British corn reached £4.

Anti-Corn Law League and maintain the existing duties. But suddenly in 1845 Lord John Russell, now the Whig leader, was converted to the cause of repeal; and Peel showed that personally he had become convinced of the abolitionist case. The contretemps that then overran each of the two parties, ended with Peel getting his repeal through Parliament,[74] but immediately losing the reins of government, thanks to challengers in his own party, led by Disraeli. It proved to be a debilitating division of loyalties that took more than a decade to begin to heal. Russell's difficulties were less fundamental. He was obliged to form a government despite the mutual grudges between the younger Earl Grey and Lord Palmerston, which had prevented him from doing so 18 months previously.

Although, therefore, it was not the Whigs who carried the reform, the triumph of the entrepreneurial class, for which Corn Law repeal was emblematic, meant, so it was said, that 'by the middle of the nineteenth century government policy in Britain came as near laisser-faire as has ever been practicable in a modern state'.[75] It was also a measure of the growing belief that industrialization, and with it colonial expansion, was indeed bringing England remarkable economic success. The mid-century 'age of equipoise', as W. L. Burn epitomized it, would remain in balance for a quarter-century. Ordinary people could hope for a degree of improvement in their life chances; the prosperity of the country, as many were coming to believe, would put paid to the grinding conditions of existence observed in industrial districts by Engels, Mrs Gaskell, and reformers appalled by the horrors of factories and mines and the squalor of filthy cities.

Central government in the 1850s saw rather more flux. Five ministries took office: two for the Tories were led by the earl of Derby and lasted only for ephemeral terms (1852; 1858–9); two for the Whigs were led by Palmerston (1855–8, 1859–65); and one was a coalition of a sort, formed under the earl of Aberdeen (1852–5). Amid this shifting, it was apparent that national politics continued to be run largely by the aristocracy, backed in the Commons by a membership that remained more gentrified than professional or commercial;[76] and more generally that members of both Houses remained their own men, not yet in the grip of strict party discipline. So it was that W.E. Gladstone became Peel's President of the Board of Trade in 1843 until he resigned over the increased grant to the Irish College at Maynooth. In Aberdeen's mixed ministry he gained the Chancellorship of the Exchequer and but did not then have a place in Palmerston's succeeding cabinet of 1855. He did, however, come back under the latter in 1859, again as

---

[74] 9 & 10 Vict. c. 22.

[75] E. J. Hobsbaum, *Industry and Empire* (1968), 197; and for a review of the historical debate, see A. J. Taylor, *Laissez-Faire and State Intervention in Nineteenth Century Britain* (1972).

[76] With a good parade, however, of barristers.

Chancellor, and so positioned himself to lead the Whigs-turned-Liberals after the Second Reform Act.

Politics and the Lower Orders

The politicization of parts of the working class, which had become manifest in the wars with France, would continue in the unsettled conditions of peace after 1815. Tom Paine's attack on the monarchical pretensions of George III in *The Rights of Man* (1791–2) continued to be widely read by the working populace as they became more literate. In the years after 1815 the concept of economic organization not on the basis of unrelenting competition between investors in business but on an ideal of cooperation, was stimulated by the writings and the example of the factory owner, Robert Owen. It led to a brief spell of experiment with a system of production in which the workers were the collaborators, but they scarcely flourished. The signal achievement of the cooperative movement in England would come from the 1840s onwards in the distribution of household goods.

Disaffected by the failure of the 1832 reforms to concede anything to the claims of skilled manual workers, the Chartist movement had flourished fitfully for a decade and more from 1838. The consequent protests had to be dealt with, but the upper classes could disdain the cause itself as well-nigh inconceivable. Enthusiasts for overturning the existing order continued to argue for the redistribution of land. Some looked to socialized solutions involving land nationalization or periodic redistribution by government. Others agitated for highly radical re-division of landholdings among individuals, which was intended to lead to a great increase in the private ownership of smallholdings.[77] With varying degrees of enthusiasm these root-and-branch critics sought a world in which government and law would be replaced by harmonious cooperation.

From the Chartist period onwards, advocacy of 'collectivist' alternatives to a liberal democracy would grow in Britain, as in other advanced societies. The Irish journalist, Bronterre O'Brien, made the case for such fundamentally socialistic measures as nationalization of mines and other basic industries, government purchase of land on a major scale and the reduction of private property to a condition lasting only until death.[78] The barrister, Ernest Jones, argued for a 'Parliament of Labour'—the vesting of political power in institutions centred in the workplace, rather than in separate representational bodies of the kind that had grown in strength both in limited monarchies such as Britain and in republics set up in

---

[77] The boisterous Irish Chartist, Feargus O'Connor, set up a Chartist Land Company as basis for cottage farming; but it failed: A. M. Hadfield, *The Chartist Land Company* (1970).

[78] See e.g. Ward, *Chartism*, 221–6.

the wake of revolutions.[79] The idea of syndicalist governance thus joined the splay of theories for social transformation. Of these, Karl Marx's use in *Das Kapital* of the analytic tools of Adam Smith, David Ricardo, and fellow economists in order to savage their portrayal of the virtues of competitive, minimally regulated, markets would in the twentieth century have an extraordinary influence on European and world history.

For our concerns with the Victorian legal system, such uncompromising assaults on liberal capitalism remained a marginal factor. Only tiny cliques in Britain became committed to extreme methods of assuring the political and economic future of the proletarian masses. The Social Democratic Foundation was set up in 1881 by Henry Hyndman after reading Marx; and then run by him autocratically in the manner of a would-be charismatic.[80] Wider circles absorbed such literature in the process of working out more moderate political philosophies for evolutionary change. Trade unionists and other working-class activists, middle-class sympathizers from politics and industry, idealistic university men, gained from their comparisons some measure of what could and should be achieved in terms of social reform through legislation, public administration, and collective action.

1867: The Crucial Shift

Already by the 1860s, among leaders of opinion there were reformers enough, particularly within a radical wing of the Whig party, who sought a second reform of the parliamentary franchise. So long as Palmerston led the party he deflected any real spirit of change but after his death in 1865 there was no holding the suffrage question back. It was Derby's Conservatives, pushed by Disraeli, who hammered out the final terms of the 1867 Reform Act. For their pains they would lose the 1868 election to Gladstone's Liberals, for the new electorate had an instinct that the latter were more likely to foster the spirit of change. Education, above all else, began to be required for children of all levels. The systems of social support acquired greater moral specificity—sorting the deserving poor from the undeserving, taking action against root causes of miserable existence, such as the employment of women and children in grossly debilitating work, imposing regulations to insanitary and unsafe conditions in towns and so on.[81]

---

[79] See XIII, p. 633.

[80] His refusal to countenance other views was one instance of the schismatic tendency in Victorian socialism. Hyndman's last organization was a National Socialist Party.

[81] See the instances explored in XIII, Pt 2.

When Disraeli returned as Prime Minister in 1874 his government cast a watchful eye towards the new electors of 1867, just as had the Liberals before him; but even more the Conservatives were engaging with powerful sectors of production, business, and finance; and in succeeding decades they would become the natural party of both landed and capitalist interests—and yet attractive enough to be backed also by a working-class following.[82] When Disraeli retired in 1880, the Party reverted to aristocratic roots, soon enough taking as leader, Robert Gascoigne-Cecil, Third Marquess of Salisbury, who formed governments in 1885, 1886–92 and 1895–1902.[83]

The subterranean shift in the loyalties of voters posed many difficulties for the Liberals, who in office under Gladstone in 1880–5 and then 1892–4, were turning towards radical policies that they would not have countenanced under Palmerston. They played with various schemes of land nationalization and other re-distribution of property. Gladstone's commitment to some form of Irish Home Rule led to the split away of Whigs loyal to earlier ideas (under the Marquess of Hartington—later Duke of Devonshire). For the same reason Gladstone lost his powerful ally, Joseph Chamberlain, who would join Salisbury in a Conservative and Unionist Party in 1890. The Liberals were left as a coalition of interests, led increasingly by professionals, among them lawyers who included Asquith, Loreburn, Haldane, and Lloyd George.

Labour and the Established Parties

The skilled trade unions drew together in the Trades Union Congress from 1868 onwards, and saw two miners' representatives elected to Parliament in 1874. Then in the later 1880s mass unions of the semi-skilled and unskilled began to pursue large-scale strikes that delivered serious economic blows to dock work, mining, and later among the engineers. At the same time, the case for a gradualist turn towards socialism was being fostered by the Fabian Society and similar groups, with some sympathy from those who counted as radical liberals. Led by Keir Hardy, the first prospects would emerge for an Independent Labour Party (formed in 1893), drawing its strength from a close association with the growing trade unions. The Labour Representation Committee, also formed by Hardie and his associates to secure seats in the Commons, had a small success in the 1902 election. As we shall see in Chapter IV, the Victorian *fin de siècle* saw an alteration

[82] R. T. McKenzie and A. Silver, *Angels in Marble: Working Class Conservatives in Urban England* (1968).

[83] A. J. Balfour, his nephew and successor to the premiership in 1902, formed a Cabinet quite as well-stocked with grandees.

in the ways in which the advocates of individual freedom as a prime virtue were coming to regard its role for the future. This 'new liberalism', drawing inspiration from German transcendental idealism, sought to encourage the idea of the state as the guarantor of basic support for all its citizens, so that each might have the prospect of fulfilling whatever personal capacities they held within themselves.[84]

Such was the resonance of these growing ideas, that when in the last days of 1905 the Liberals were returned in a landslide victory against the Conservatives, the number of 'leftist' Members increased significantly, and the Labour Party was officially formed. The Liberal government set out on a determined course of social protection through legislation under the leadership of Campbell-Bannerman and then Asquith. Increased opportunities for education, old age pensions, action against loss of jobs, and national insurance against unemployment and ill-health in work, led the action.[85] Differential taxation of income was introduced as a new element in paying for the novel schemes.[86] And Lloyd George, as Chancellor of the Exchequer, raised the thorny issue of land ownership.[87] The Liberals sensed well enough that they were losing the support of the propertied who had been their rank-and-file in the mid-Victorian generations but who now were rounding out their shift to the Conservatives. The Liberals' future depended on sustaining the loyalty of ordinary people who looked to central and local governments to manage crucial elements of their well-being through life. Only in this way would it be possible to circumscribe the growing independence of the labour movement as a political and industrial force. As the government would learn from the disturbing series of strikes by railwaymen, dockers, miners, and others in 1910–12, in matters economic as well as social, there were alliances among working men that could lead to politics being conducted in the workplace, drawing upon French ideas of syndicalism; or else that in Parliament Labour would succeed so far as to form a government.

By 1923, there would for a short term be a Labour government, dependent though it was on Liberal support. In between, war broke out on a scale that changed social and political ideas and practices in unforeseeable measure, marked first and foremost by the admission of women to the parliamentary franchise. At a single stretch, the electorate would grow from a pre-War figure of 7 million to a post-demobilization figure of 20 million.[88] The prospect of a Triple Alliance between miners, dockers, and railwaymen stood as a threat that might

[84] See below, pp. 117–23.

[85] See below, pp. 205–18; XIII, pp. 499–506, 552–4, 591–7.

[86] See below, pp. 218–26.

[87] His land campaign was at the core of his highly controversial 'People's Budget' of 1909, much of which was directed at increasing the flow of revenue from landed property.

[88] The restriction of the franchise to women over 30 (removed only in 1928) was the main restriction keeping the proportion of men higher. In 1919 the electorate was 65% male: A. J. P. Taylor, *English History, 1914–1945* (1965), 115–16.

bring the functioning economy quickly to its knees. Its test would come in the General Strike of 1926. In the immediate aftermath of the peace with Germany, the British government had to give way in Ireland and negotiate the ominous partition between a virtually independent Catholic Free State in the south and the six counties of the north that stayed in the union with England, Wales, and Scotland in order to protect their Protestant majorities.

'Party' and Parliamentarians

The idea of 'party' as a driving force in politics had woven a changing course through the eighteenth century. From what has just been outlined can be sensed how much this continued into Victorian and Edwardian Britain. Party brought the alignment of numbers to the battles for the power to govern. It could strengthen that power if there were only two major groups in contention. Operation of the system was likely to weaken where three or more parties had seats enough to require coalitions and liaisons before a government could be formed and maintained. From the Reform Act of 1832 onwards, a two-party system gradually became the norm, the electorate having reasonably clear choices over what the vote was about. Even so, for the mid-third of the century, party implied only conditional loyalty from individual members of Lords and Commons. Independence of political judgment formed part of their self-perception, supported as it largely was by their upper-class background and the financial security that sustained it. It remained therefore for Cabinets to persuade, rather than to insist upon, their people supporting their legislative measures as well as their executive policies; likewise with oppositions.

Allied to this, came freedoms of attitude which meant that both the Tory and the Whig party developed considerable variations of opinion among their supporters. There would be major issues on which the divisions were more marked within parties than between them. This was as apparent within the Tories after Lord Liverpool's retirement in 1827, as it would be over free trade and the Corn Laws in the 1840s. Modern party discipline became suddenly more apparent after the reforms of 1867. The greater spread of interests, not just across the new electorate but equally among those elected to the Commons, taken together with the impact of the secret ballot upon the process of electing (which was introduced in the 1872), meant that parties had to offer clearer statements of their proposed programmes, and had to insist that their Members were 'whipped' into line, and that more parliamentary time was devoted to bills promoted by government departments. As we shall see, it was at this juncture that much of the old quasi-independence dissolved away.[89]

---

[89] See below, pp. 301–15.

Politicians, Proponents from Without, and Law Reform

These few paragraphs sketching the root shifts in the high politics of Britain deal with an ever-present element in the modern history of English law. The great political leaders—the Prime Ministers, the members of Cabinet in such crucial positions as Lord Chancellor, Chancellor of the Exchequer, President of the Board of Trade, and Home Secretary—could become decisive voices in settling whether, and if so how, new or extended legislation was to be deployed in reaction to social and economic change in Britain. In 1906, for instance, the Prime Minister, Campbell-Bannerman, became the decisive backer of trade union leaders in their demand for legislation exempting unions, as quasi-corporate institutions, from any liability in tort—notably that arising from their organization of strikes and other collective pressure on employers. The Trade Disputes Act of that year was accordingly passed despite outraged cries in the legal press and elsewhere that this was an utter denial of the rule of law in the face of sectional interest.[90] His decision must be understood against the shifts of allegiance among voters, which by the 1920s would leave the House of Commons to be contested by three parties—Conservative, Liberals, and Labour. In this the Liberal party lost its old position. Given the 'first-past-the-post' system for electing Members to constituencies, its role would become that of a makeweight. Its support might be needed to enable one of the other parties to form a government, but it would thereafter desert its senior partner at its peril, since causing a new election was likely to reduce its own popularity with the electorate.[91]

Political leaders were likely to become involved in legislative change only after more diffuse discussion had built up into campaigns that could no longer be ignored. The sudden exposure of a scandal might prove a catalyst for legislation, as might the airing of issues in the press or discussion at a national level. So far as legal measures were concerned, much happened through such non-official bodies as the Law Amendment Society and its cousin, the National Association for the Promotion of Social Science. Lobbying groups sprang up regularly, many of them fighting single-issue campaigns. Even with the changes after 1867, it is important to avoid reading events from a perspective of today's form of centralized government, dominated by statements from the ruling party, devised by their civil servants, and then attacked by their opposition. Victorian England continued to be a great age of local political initiative. The ways in which old forms of local government were replaced with new or revised authorities, and how they then arrived at new accommodations with the central ministries who in one or other sense

---

[90] The Act also conferred very considerable exemption from liability on trade union officers and members: see XIII, pp. 704–6.

[91] See Jennings, *Law and the Constitution*, Ch. 4.

supervised them, is a complex story which is explored more fully in Part Two of this Volume and in much else that has to do with domestic policy.[92]

5. AN INDEPENDENT JUDICIARY

Lacking any arrangement that placed Parliament apart from executive government, the structure of the modern British system avoided direct confrontations over the use of legislative powers that could follow when each institution was in the control of different parties. The ideal of an independent judiciary, however, had been sustained since the Protestant succession, the great step to that end having been secured by the Act of Settlement 1701,[93] which abrogated the monarch's power to remove a serving judge from office.[94] Those barristers who wanted to cap out a successful career in the law by appointment to a judgeship would be likely to seek a seat in the Commons as a way of getting noticed. Equally, kings and their confidants had an eye for promising youngsters who might later be appointed as law officers and chief justices. These patterns would remain familiar in Victorian England. As we shall see, there would be allegations of party preference; and, since the Lord Chancellor played a leading role in making or recommending judicial and similar appointments, it was he who would stand accused.[95]

There were also institutional connections at the highest levels between the judiciary and the other branches of government. The Lord Chancellor both presided in the House of Lords as a political chamber and sat in the Cabinet.[96] At the same time, he ran the Court of Chancery with little enough assistance, and he played a leading role in deciding cases on appeal before the House of Lords—a role continuing for the House that was by no means as distinct from the legislative as it became after 1875.[97] Unlike the royal judges, his term of office would last only as long as his government's. His presence as a 'universal joint' at the fulcrum of the system of government was not just an inconsequential oddity. Since the office was given to an established judge or very senior barrister (notably the Attorney-General or Solicitor-General to the Crown), it reassured lawyers

---

[92] See esp. below, Pt 2, Ch V; XIII, Pt 1, Chs II, III, V.2; XIII. Pt 2, Chs II, III.3, IV, V.

[93] 1 Anne c. 22.

[94] George III also gave up the royal disposition to re-appoint the judges on accession to the throne. Other practices—paying salaries only after a delay, refusing any pension, granting sinecures—would disappear before 1820. S. Shetreet, *Judges on Trial* (Amsterdam, 1976), Ch. 1.

[95] See below, Pt 4, pp. 962–4.

[96] In the brief Cabinet of All the Talents (1806–7) both the Lord Chancellor, Erskine, and the Lord Chief Justice, Ellenborough, had been members, though the latter appointment aroused criticism and it did not occur again. The Master of the Rolls continued as an MP until the appointment of Lord Romilly in 1851, who did not seek re-election as an MP in 1852.

[97] See below, Pt 3, Ch. II.1; L. Blom-Cooper and G. Drewry, *Final Appeal* (Oxford, 1972), Ch.1.

that the right men would be appointed judges.[98] Not just the Lord Chancellor, but other ennobled judges, were able to take part in legislative debates, notably when questions of constitutional significance were at stake or law reform in a technical sense was the issue.

While a sturdy independence characterized much of the attitudes of those chosen to be judges, still they were drawn from a profession and social class which believed that the senior judiciary had a strategic role in managing and maintaining the governance of Britain, but at a distance. The judges who became truly revered among lawyers, were those who combined quick, energetic perception of what the cases before them were really about with an encyclopaedic knowledge of legal sources—men such as Willes, a judge of Common Pleas, and Blackburn, a judge of Queen's Bench and after 1876, a Lord of Appeal in Ordinary. With the Second Reform Act, and then the Judicature Act of 1873, the idea of judges as technocrats, working within their own sphere, began to grow. They more readily foreswore commenting on political issues and expected in return not to be the subject of criticism by politicians or the press.[99] It was a complex shift that reflected the need in a democracy for the judiciary to be seen as above and apart from the running of legislative and executive government.[100]

Numerous factors, some with long historical roots, continued to contribute to this idea of separation and with it the understanding that justice in England could not be secured by bribery, corruption, or the more evident forms of bias (including an interest in the outcome of the case being tried). The use of juries and justices of the peace brought elements of lay judgment into the processes of the courts of common law, and the quarter and petty sessions of JPs; and whatever the failings of these citizen-adjudicators, on many matters they reduced the role of professional judge to that of umpire and instructor on matters of law.[101] The number of those judges could therefore be kept small and accorded an elevated social status.

[98] So proposals to hive off some of the Lord Chancellor's triple duties to a Minister of Justice would come to nought. The evident danger to legal interests was that the Minister would not necessarily be a lawyer of any kind: see R. B. Stevens, *Law and Politics: The House of Lords as a Judicial Body, 1800–1976* (Chapel Hill, 1979) Ch. 2.

[99] R. B. Stevens, *Law and Politics: The House of Lords as a Judicial Body, 1800–1976* (Chapel Hill, 1979) traces these shifts in great detail among those who served as judges in the House of Lords in the period 1800–1976. A late example of a judge who could not forbear political partisanship was Grantham J. He even got away with attending a Conservative Party meeting while in office.

[100] For the place of these political considerations in settling the manner and style of judgments, see below, pp. 64–7.

[101] At the local level, the powers given to justices of the peace made little distinction between establishing rules, carrying them out, and adjudicating disputes upon them. Only in the course of the nineteenth century did a greater separation of tasks gradually take hold, partly through the establishment of new authorities for counties and boroughs and for particular functions, such as policing and poor relief. See esp. below Pt 2, Ch. V; XIII, Pt 1, Ch. III.

No corps of judges, under instructions to investigate the allegations being made to their courts, developed within central government as it did in the civilian systems of mainland Europe. English judges were therefore much less dependent on government for progression through the ranks. Their protection from dismissal, should they refuse to do what the government was advocating before them, was a major factor in establishing the modern belief that English courts were not corruptible. Judges might become insane or singular in their views; but the 'system' (meaning in particular the Lord Chancellor) found ways of dealing with such embarrassments when occasionally they occurred, just as it dealt with antagonisms between individual judges and difficulties in their private lives.[102]

The very structure of English courts thus underpinned their reputation for fairness. This of course is not to say that the moral assumptions and the sociopolitical beliefs of judges had no effect on their judgment at the points where ideological issues came into play, for no adjudicative system can provide perfect objectivity. It was, however, true that, at least among those who had a political presence, there had grown a sense that the very structure of government placed adjudication apart from the enactment of legislation and, even more, the activities of executive government. Rectitude in providing justice had become a virtue well before other assertions of Victorian moral earnestness. Nonetheless, it was a value purchased at a price. To a large extent litigants in both civil courts and defendants charged with crime had themselves to finance their preparation and representation in court, or rely upon their own connections for help—a highly questionable factor for a large part of the population.[103]

Even while party allegiance remained an important factor in deciding who should be appointed to the superior court benches, politics provided no simple key indicating how judges would then decide the cases that came before them or the reasoning that they would use in directing juries or reaching their own judgments. Their prime responsibility was to dispose of the particular disputes before them and that might turn on myriad circumstances—reactions, for instance, for or against particular witnesses, views on where it was proper for appellate bodies to intervene and a great host of other factors—which for the most part were well-removed from the rough and tumble of political allegiance and antagonism. As we shall see in relation to civil liability, much of their time was given over to deciding which of the contesting parties was a rogue and which a saint, if indeed either characterization could be held applicable. In that process, moral feeling was one decisive factor.[104]

---

[102] For the position regarding superior court judges, see below, Pt 4, pp. 978–84. Compare that for County Court judges, pp. 1002–4; and for stipendiary magistrates, pp. 1001–10.

[103] See, e.g., below pp.625–30.

[104] For evidence of this in the context of contract law see XII, Pt 2, Ch. IV.

If a case raised a question about the scope of the applicable legal rule, the choice
open to the judge would be constrained to an extent by general principles for determining the source of law, which are discussed in the next Chapter. As we shall
see, those general principles left considerable room for manoeuvre at their margins, making them means towards a conclusion, rather than ends in themselves. As
Parliament gained in democratic strength, and the judiciary came to be appointed
primarily for their legal talent, rather than partly as a political reward, it may appear
that judgments were more regularly crafted to disguise whatever moral, political,
or economic preference the judge might really have. Perhaps some greater respect
for Parliament's choice of language in expressing its will is to be found at the end of
Victoria's reign than at its beginning. But even that is dependent on many factors
that are not simple to balance. For one thing, both the frequency of legislation on
some topics increased, and the art of drafting both public and private documents
became more sophisticated.[105] Lord Esher MR, would claim:

The law of England is not a science. It is a practical application of the rule of right and
wrong to the particular case before the Court, and the canon of law is, that the rule should
be adopted and applied to the case, which people of honour, candour and fairness in the
position of the two parties would apply in respect of the matter in hand.[106]

Criticisms could be offered of every phrase in that summation. Rules established by
statute or precedent had a central place in determining what the 'rule of right and
wrong' was and how it should apply to given sets of facts. What Esher expressed
was the satisfaction felt by many Victorian judges and lawyers that the system they
operated had its ways of tempering rules of law and procedure in order to comply
with their deep sense of moral propriety. As men of honour and determination,
and thanks both to their social position and their professional experience, they had
a self-confident understanding of what amounted to justice between those before
them in court. Deciding how to balance the public interests that gave every branch
of law its own objectives against the particular circumstances of a case could be difficult, but they believed themselves better fitted to the task than any others.

6. REFORM OF THE COURT SYSTEM: A GROWING HIERARCHY OF GOVERNMENT

The core of the English legal system—the royal courts of common law and
Chancery, together with the legal professions that sustained them—had to
change in order to meet the challenges of industrialization and its accompanying

---

[105] To the reasoning deployed in judgments we return below, pp. 64–70.

[106] Quoted in (1898–9) 24 *LM*. 403; see M. Lobban, 'The Politics of English Law in the Nineteenth
Century', paper to the British Legal History Conference, Oxford, July 2007.

urbanisation. The judges and the legal professions accepted proposals provided that they went step by cautious step and did not trespass too far upon basic understandings. Their response to the denunciations of critics in and out of Parliament was generally to do what seemed necessary at the time, but no more.

In all measures of court reform, the umbilical relation between legal practitioners and the judiciary remained a first consideration. It was equally so with other essential elements in professional relationships, such as the basic division of practitioners into barristers and solicitors. The bar alone practised advocacy in the superior courts (though of course they could appear elsewhere). Solicitors prepared such litigation, presented cases in lesser courts and also undertook conveyancing, the administration of estates, and a great range of other practical affairs that called for their legal skills or worldly experience. In these professions there would be many interstitial developments, but they would mostly serve to simplify and strengthen the one great divide.[107]

So far as concerned the schema of superior civil courts, a Supreme Court of Judicature for England and Wales would eventually be set up, to be housed principally in the Gothick splendours of G. E. Street's Law Courts in the Strand.[108] The new hierarchy seemed a bold design, but much about it harked back to inherited glories, real or imagined.[109] Much also stemmed from the long series of reforms beginning in the earlier nineteenth century, which had already drawn the powers and procedures of the different non-criminal courts rather closer together.[110] The new Supreme Court accordingly rationalized the trial and first appellate level of civil litigation, but it did so largely for superior cases alone.[111] There came into existence a High Court composed of three Divisions: Queen's Bench, Chancery and—for the civilian inheritance—Probate, Divorce, and Admiralty.[112] In all these courts the whole diverse body of English law—common law, equity, and civilian—was to be applicable, but the various rules were not to be subverted by wiping out their historical basis. Above the High Court was placed a unitary

---

[107] The development of the legal professions is analysed in depth, below Pt 4, esp. Chs II–IV.

[108] The new Court was established by the Judicature Acts 1873, 187; see below, Pt 3, Ch. VII. For Street's grand design, see D. B. Brownlee, *The Law Courts: The Architecture of George Edmund Street* (New York, 1984); and for court architecture in England generally, see C. Graham, *Ordering Law* (Aldershot, 2003).

[109] A more ambitious plan to bring superior criminal trials within the same framework lapsed. Once criminal appeals became more regular, they were heard in courtrooms in the Law Courts: see generally below, Pt 3, Ch. VI.

[110] See in general, XIII, Pt 1, Ch. IV.

[111] For the replacement of a medley of local civil courts by the County Court structure in 1846—a highly significant step, see Pt 3, Chs XI, XII.

[112] In this the Queen's Bench Division represented a coalescence of the three common law courts: below, pp. 763–4.

Court of Appeal;[113] and, thanks to a reprieve, the House of Lords was retained as a second level of appeal.[114] In almost all respects, the Appellate Committee of the Lords continued to function as a court of final appeal that was separate from the legislative body. Some of its members were henceforth appointed specifically for the role as Lords of Appeal in Ordinary, the rest comprising the current Lord Chancellor, his predecessors, and other ennobled lawyers of high distinction. Until the opening of the twenty-first century, so it would continue, its form a reminder of its origins in ways that were scarcely any prejudice to its modern independence in the structures of government.

It was by means of judicial precedents set forth in the judgment of these superior courts that rules having the force of law would continue to evolve.[115] The great bulk of contentious legal business was nonetheless conducted in inferior courts. On the criminal law side, much fell to the justices of peace, sitting either in their Quarter Sessions or, for more minor issues, in Petty Sessions. In the largest cities they were to some extent replaced by Stipendiary (or Police) Magistrates. Trials of serious offences on indictment were decided by a jury under instruction from an Assize judge or Chairman of Quarter Sessions. On the civil law side, various institutions which had agglomerated from earlier stages of legal history, were replaced by the modern County Courts in 1846, institutions operating under legislative authority and run by central government—a successful rationalization shown by the fact that these courts regularly had extensions of subject-matter given to them.[116] Wherever a salaried judge took office under these schemes, the appointment was on the principle that there should be no removal from office save for bad behaviour.[117] Justices of the peace, though they served in an honorific capacity, no longer held office only for the duration of the monarch's reign. So in their turn they had a measure of security that allowed them independence of judgment.

Our picture of the court structure that after 1832 began to be revised by a stream of enactments to provide a more coherent hierarchy, is drawn in detail in Part Three of this Volume. But one aspect deserves emphasis in the present context. There was much about the re-forming of the whole that was pragmatic and experimental, particularly in the lower strata of courts. That was no novelty. In the pre-industrial world there had always been opportunities to develop courts

[113] Likewise with appeals from inferior civil jurisdictions when they went to Divisional Courts and the Court of Appeal.
[114] See below, pp. 535–7.
[115] See below, pp. 444–8.
[116] But for the politics see below, pp. 876–84.
[117] cf above, p. 32.

by local initiative to meet local needs.[118] Thus in the eighteenth century, courts of requests had spread as debt-collecting agencies and adjudicators over other minor contractual disputes mainly because local traders pressed Parliament to establish one for their city or town. They thus became one precursor of the later county courts.[119]

As manufacturing and commerce became more complex, that tradition evolved in notable ways. New procedures were needed, which in some cases would involve reference to more or less permanent arbitral bodies for settling internal confrontations without resort to courts. Harry Arthurs has demonstrated how this provided machinery for competitors in commodity exchanges, manufacturers, and dealers in many trades, and for members of friendly, building and other such societies, including trade unions. When eventually government instigated schemes for social welfare operating throughout the country, these also tended to breed their own tribunals for dispute settlement.[120] Arthurs roundly attacked the representation of the late Victorian hierarchy of royal courts as a closed system, alone administering the 'common law of England'.[121] With many of these arbitral bodies the bench might have no general legal training; and would have no guarantee of continuation in office that was accorded to judges and stipendiary magistrates. What they could bring to the task was an experience and understanding of the world in which the tribunal operated; and, as with justices of the peace, this meant a concatenation of local knowledge and attitudes that could vary from the sympathetic to the censorious.

How far, then, did the central courts use their power of intervention to ensure fair process and even fair decision-making on the substantive questions at stake? A form of administrative law grew haltingly as the common law courts ruled on the scope of the ancient prerogative writs, and also interpreted statutes which conferred judicial and executive powers on government departments, local authorities, minor courts, and other 'public' institutions. It was a development

---

[118] Likewise, it had been natural to turn to leading figures of a community—lords of the manor, justices, clergy, freemen of a borough, land agents, attornies—to adjudicate or mediate informally in disputes between ordinary people.

[119] Below, pp. 851–7.

[120] H. W. Arthurs, 'Without the Law': Administrative Justice and Legal Pluralism in Nineteenth-Century England (Toronto, 1985), esp. 52–4. S. Kyd, Law of Awards (1794) was an early treatise on the subject.

[121] His concern was to rectify the narrowness of Holdsworth's account of the legal system in his History of English Law. See also Lord Parker of Waddington, The History and Development of Arbitration (1959); P. L. Sayre, 'Development of Commercial Arbitration Law' (1928) 37 Yale LJ 595–617.

that Dicey insisted was of high significance to the modern functioning of a rule of law.[122] It is treated in detail in Part Two of this Volume.[123]

It has its parallel in the private sphere. The deployment of arbitration as an alternative mechanism for settling disputes without resort to litigation in court was no novelty.[124] The practice depended on all the parties involved agreeing to the submission to arbitration and it could well contribute to securing a settlement which all could live with, however reluctantly. Arbitration had a natural appeal in a period so attracted by the virtues of non-interference by governments. Apart from anything else, it aided the continuance of the central court structure with its small, cohesive group of superior judges, drawn from a limited pool of barristers who had their own competitive *esprit de corps*. In the seventeenth century, common law courts, eager to expand business, had allowed a party engaged in an arbitration to remove it into their jurisdiction at any stage before the arbitrator had given his award.[125]

With time, the advantages of agreements to arbitrate became more apparent: the procedures were private, they could take place in an atmosphere that encouraged mutual accommodation between the disputants, they might well be cheaper, quicker, not open to appeal, or more convenient for other reasons. As the case-loads of courts changed, they had come to regard arbitral process beyond their jurisdiction less jealously. A statute of 1698 had required the courts to order a party to keep an undertaking to participate in an arbitration and also to enforce the arbitrator's award.[126] In the eighteenth century, the courts remained hostile to agreements that directly ousted their jurisdiction in favour of an arbitral settlement.[127] But what of an agreement to submit an issue to arbitration and obtain an award before a court could have jurisdiction to consider the matter itself? When that issue was tested, the House of Lords held that the pursuit of the arbitration must take place first. However, their decision left it open for a court to decide that it would alter the assessment when 'public policy' dictated.[128] What these circumstances could be was left to the judges' discretion. There could after all be issues about the rudiments of due process (the right to be heard, the right to insist that

---

[122] In *Law of the Constitution*, Ch. 12, Dicey drew what he saw as stark contrasts concerning the responsibility of government officers for unlawful acts in the course of duty under English common law and French *droit administratif*.

[123] Below, Pt 2, Ch. IV.

[124] For early evidence, see e.g. Sir J. Baker, *Oxford History of the Laws of England*, vi: 333–4.

[125] The leading decision had been *Vynior's Case* (1610) 8 Co. Rep. 796.

[126] Arbitration Act 1698, 9 Will. III c. 15.

[127] Lord Kenyon CJ's decision in *Thompson* v. *Charnock* (1799) 8 T.R. 139 put the matter beyond peradventure.

[128] *Scott* v. *Avery* (1856) 5 H.L.C. 81. The judges were summoned to give opinions on the question, but proved to be sharply divided.

arbitrators be without personal interest or evident preference for one side over the other, and so on). Equally, issues about the true state of English law could arise and, in 1889, each party was accorded the right to require the arbitrator to state a case to the High Court in order to obtain a ruling on it.[129] English judges felt no compunction to define the types of issue that would give grounds for intervention.[130] To this extent only, arbitration became a process under the supervision of the 'ordinary law'. Nonetheless, a much greater readiness to respect the terms of the agreement to arbitrate prevailed than in earlier times.

[129] Arbitration Act 1889, s 19. By the Common Law Procedure Act 1854, arbitrators had been given power to state such a case, but could not be compelled to do so: see E. J. Cohn 'Commercial Arbitration and the Rules of Law: a Comparative Study' (1941) 4 *U Toronto LJ* 1–32 at 19.

[130] Scrutton LJ would make this particularly plain in the leading case of *Czarkinow* v. *Roth, Schmidt* [1922] 1 KB 478 at 487–8.

III

Sources of Law

THIS Chapter concentrates on the sources of English law that were treated within the system as rules of recognition—as authority, in other words, for what the law was, rather than as mere descriptions of propositions that courts would apply as law. In formal terms, legislation and judicial precedent were the two sources that predominated, as they had for centuries. Some legal writings, together with established customs and similar practices, might also rate on occasion; but if they were admitted at all as sources, they tended to be treated as secondary.

These understandings were already part of the structure of the English legal system and they have not in essence varied very much since. However, by the period of the first franchise reforms, books were beginning to appear that treated the very rules for finding and using the law in resolving disputes with a new sophistication. In particular, Sir Fortunatus Dwarris' *Treatise on Statutes* appeared in 1830–1[1] and James Ram's *Science of Legal Judgment* in 1834[2]—both to enjoy evident success, not least in the United States. Their publication suggests a shifting emphasis in court advocacy, since their focus was on permissible ways of arguing how the rules of English law were to be identified and applied. The readership must have been largely professional.[3] In their turn these identification techniques linked to even more primal questions. What made legal rules and principles distinct from ethical ideas of other kinds? What forms should judicial reasoning take? To these issues we return later in this Part.[4] What has first

---

[1] Dwarris was an English barrister, born in Jamaica and knighted for a Report on the island, favouring abolition of slavery. The *Treatise on Statutes* had a 2nd edition in 1848 and later US editions with transatlantic references. Vol. 1 is an exhaustive historical study of Parliament and its legislative process; Vol. 2 is mainly devoted to statutory interpretation by the courts. For later literature, see n. 66.

[2] As a young barrister, Ram published a number of treatises of which this was one. After practising as a barrister in East Anglia, Ram wrote a colourful volume, *Treatise on Facts as Subjects of Inquiry by a Jury* (1861) which concerned inferences that are to be drawn from facts proven in court in numerous situations. So it was a sourcebook on advocacy and reactions to it. Many of the instances were drawn from classical and modern literature.

[3] See below, pp. 60–61.

[4] See below, pp. 64–72.

to be considered is the hierarchy of norms in which parliamentary sovereignty accords primacy to legislation; but places it nonetheless in the complex inheritance of principles and rules contained in judicial precedent, one aspect of which included the interpretation of statutory texts by courts.

1. STATUTES AND SECONDARY LEGISLATION

General, Local, and Private Legislation

Statute had primacy as a legal source—as had secondary legislation, provided that it was made under statutory authority. So the doctrine of parliamentary supremacy dictated.[5] The British perception of sovereignty held Parliament responsible to no higher legal authority, either as part of the state constitution or because of any law of nature or of nations. Legislation had an increasing impact on the people in general as well as on a local basis or as an intervention in private affairs. While it is only in the nineteenth century that the flow of enactments covering the government's revenue, the organization, and powers of executives at central and local level, the range of the criminal law and the regulation of both the economy and the condition of the people assumed truly major importance, in all these fields there had been legislation in earlier centuries, some of it of very considerable importance, as preceding Volumes of this *Oxford History* make clear.

A characteristic of eighteenth-century parliaments, however, had been the prominence of 'local' and 'private' legislation.[6] Those with the resources and perseverance could acquire the powers they needed for local initiatives of many kinds, such as the building of turnpike roads and canals, and the enclosure of landholdings. So too with the resolution of essentially individual disputes or uncertainties—over, for instance, the title to specific land, the terms of family trusts, or the granting of a full 'parliamentary' divorce. The root character of this process had been that an issue between individuals was resolved by the investigation of parliamentary committees, not on the basis of existing legal rules but as a matter of particular policy. It had perhaps the character of a variation of common law by the courts of equity. Above all, it suggested how the notion of what was legislative and what was judicial shifted with time. Certainly it had

---

[5] By the nineteenth century, the authentic text of legislation was secured by its parliamentary enrolment. The courts refused to countenance any investigation into whether the proper procedure for enacting private bills had been followed: *Edinburgh and Dalkeith Rly* v. *Wauchope* (1842) 8 Cl. & F. 710, HL.

[6] The usage of these terms, as indeed to some extent of the contrasting category of 'public and general' Acts, shifted somewhat over time: for details, see e.g. S. Lambert, *Bills and Acts* (Cambridge, 1971).

affected the self-conception of the House of Lords as a chamber with overlapping roles, in which 'lay' peers still had a role in the disposal of appeals from inferior courts. A complex change would take place from the late eighteenth century, by which the regular resort by the propertied to strictly private legislation would wane, but local legislation would wax. General law-making likewise grew apace. It would become a crucial part of government intervention in social organization. In our period, general acts would provide machinery both for local improvements and for altering private relationships that took the decision-making away from Parliament and gave it to courts or commissions, as with, for example, the approval of local enclosures of land. There were also general Acts which introduced standard clauses into private legal acts, either on a mandatory or a presumptive basis, as with reforms of conveyancing and the terms authorizing the establishment of railways. On these fronts we shall come across plenty of examples.[7]

As with statute, it was the procedure by which precedents were brought into existence—the fact that they were pronouncements made in the higher courts while giving reasons for judgment—which gave them their stamp of authority. Law reports were no mere historical record; they were normative in that they foretold what the rules were to be applied in future. In this the common law acquired much of its distinctiveness from civilian systems. The latter found the law to be applied in the statutes, decrees, and ordinances of the sovereign, particularly once the major parts of the law became codified. Given the long tradition of scholarly study of law in their universities, they also attached significance to juridical writings and opinions. Partly in consequence, they tended not to accord the same directive force to what the courts stated in reaching particular decisions.

There was an inherent tension in the trains of thought for applying the different sources of law to particular instances. In general, statutes were drafted to encompass all the cases to which they were to apply. There were many difficulties in doing so with precision and much was left at the edges for the courts to settle by interpretation of the enactment. Whatever the situation in a particular instance, their reasoning was in essence deductive. When it came to case law, there would often be previous statements by judges of sufficient generality that a court's task would also be to deduce whether or not a case fell within the principle stated. But rationalizing their decisions by propounding general principles was a goal towards which courts were in many circumstances still proceeding. Starting from the question, what rule should be applied to particular circumstances, much reasoning was inductive rather than deductive: what rule appeared to have

---

[7] In the 1840s, the practice spread. Thus 1844 saw enactment of standard clauses, in various forms, relating to conveyancing, railways, and joint stock companies: see 7 & 8 Vict. c.s. 76, 85, and 100.

been applied in earlier relevant judgments? Could it be generalized sufficiently to apply also to the different circumstances of the subsequent case? Should the rule be subject to new limitations or exceptions?

This scope for constant reassessment allowed a flexibility which English lawyers were apt to admire as a necessary refinement in pursuit of justice. But inevitably it rendered the law only conditional. Moreover, in the traditional techniques of the three courts of common law for disposing of civil actions, the starting point was still, in 1820, whether a form of action was available for the type of claim made by a plaintiff. The learning necessary to understand and argue issues of the scope of legal redress in this way was not for those without legal training. From the seventeenth century, these formulaic mysteries encasing the common law began to dispel. Until this period, the acceptability of a writ had been a matter that could be raised only on demurrer, as an alternative to putting the case to a jury. Gradually opportunities to challenge the outcome of a case after a jury's verdict were introduced. So by our period justifications for decisions were becoming direct statements about legal outcomes rather than statements about forms of pleading that were permitted under a given writ.

Another factor had been the appearance of a literature that did more than list the operative effects of the law. Instead it sought to classify rights and duties under large, serviceable categories in a manner that often involved very considerable steps of induction. Blackstone had written his *Commentaries* as an 'institute' to enable gentlemen students to view English law as a comprehensible whole. The work proved to be a major signpost along this changing path for a century and more. Thanks to frequent revisions, it remained a first recourse in studying and understanding English law.

2. LAW EVIDENCED AND LAW MADE BY JUDGES

In formal terms secondary to legislation, the precedents established by judicial decisions were nonetheless sources of authority that were the judges' own. So they attracted a special loyalty from lawyers of every rank, much as they had from the time when printing had allowed their regular promulgation and preservation.[8] Precedents were to be found in the decisions of the superior court judges and the reasons they vouchsafed for their judgments. The reporting of cases had begun to expand and improve from the mid-eighteenth century; but for many decades it would remain a private business which depended to some degree on the capacities of individual editors and publishers. Only in 1865 would an 'official series'

---

[8] See Sir J. Baker, *Oxford History of the Laws of England*, vi: 486–9; N. Duxbury, *The Nature and Authority of Precedent* (Cambridge, 2008), Chs 1, 2 (esp. pp. 17–18).

of Reports be instituted, run by an Incorporated Council for Law Reporting. On this body legal practitioners and judges took care to secure representation. The supply of this starting material for so much legal enterprise was not to be given over simply to a government publisher.[9]

In the common law, where the rule to be applied in litigation was at stake—and equally when the issue concerned how a statute was to be interpreted—judges and lawyers constantly sought out precedents. But if no prior rule appeared to be in point and the case was thus one of first impression, it would have to be decided by reference to 'principle', or 'reason', or some governing view of social objective or ethical principle. Much that was crucial to the adaptation of the law would be settled through pronouncements justifying what judges thought was just in the circumstances—rationalizations that in the eighteenth century might well have drawn on explicit moral precepts.[10] These derived sometimes from the preachings of the Established Church; but increasingly from a view of expediency—a weighing of competing utilities, in the form of a rough estimate of what, across the social and economic range, would produce greater happiness.

The courts of common law, Chancery, and the civilian jurisdictions, together with the appellate bodies above them, considered that they held the essential rules of their part of the legal system as a whole in their body of precedent. This basic understanding allowed common law judges to continue in the tradition of Coke and Blackstone that their decisions did not lay down new law. Rather their pronouncements expressed what was already *common* throughout their jurisdiction—albeit dormant perhaps and awaiting the reviving embrace of a judicial declaration. It was a convenient theory, which with time would allow the emergence of a more structured set of rules associated with the concept of *stare decisis*; which is discussed in the next section. Allowing the common law to fold into its rules the practices of lawyers, financiers, traders, and masters—even on occasion the behaviour of families—allowed an understated adaptation of principles and rules so as to fit them within prevailing social mores.

The common law's standard form of trial—by jury—allowed plenty of scope for finessing distinctions between custom and legal rule. Lord Mansfield had made bravura use of the possibilities by developing commercial principles within the common law in league with a regular special jury of City merchants.[11] In the mid-nineteenth century, according to the roseate recollection of Lord Halsbury, London special juries included 'the first merchants of the City' and 'better

---

[9] See below, Pt 4, Ch. V.4.

[10] For the influences of moral intuition and associated ideas in the nineteenth century, see below, Ch. IV.3.

[11] J. Oldham, *The Mansfield Manuscripts and the Growth of English Law in the Eighteenth Century* (Chapel Hill, 1992), i: 82–99.

tribunals...for the administration of the commercial law, it was impossible to obtain'; but their replacements (probably because of the wider qualification rules of the Juries Act 1870) had drained them of their abilities and commercial litigants soon began to prefer trial by judge alone.[12]

The principles of equity, generated mainly in the court of Chancery,[13] were—at least in origin—expressions of exceptional need. Before the Court came cases where the common law called for qualification or alteration or better enforcement in response to the dictates of some higher justice. The whole procedure stemmed from medieval notions of the monarch as the ultimate fount of justice, with a power therefore to correct injustices when they occurred from applying the common law without sufficient discrimination.[14] This opposite character continued to colour the jurisdiction, and detractors of equity, appearing as they did in each generation, had long deplored it as ungoverned discretion.[15] Against attacks that equity was thus the most formidable instrument of arbitrary power that could be devised—a denial within the legal system itself of any rule of law— the decisions of Lord Chancellors had increasingly hardened into established rule. In private law, since the Restoration of Charles II, that process had become of vital importance.[16] Precedent thus became increasingly significant,[17] even with

---

[12] Quoted by R. B. Ferguson, 'The Adjudication of Commercial Disputes and the Legal System in Modern England' (1980) 7 *British J. L. & Soc.*141–57 at 144.

[13] The Court of Exchequer's jurisdiction in equity came to an end in 1841: see below pp. 656–8.

[14] One device for spelling out the moral virtues in equity's variations of common law came to rest in the dozen or so Maxims of Equity: equity will not suffer a right to go without remedy; only those with clean hands can ask for equity's assistance, the person who comes to equity must do equity; and so forth. (They were displayed systematically in the eighteenth century, starting with R. Francis, *Maxims of Equity* (1728), building on earlier understandings: see D. E. C. Yale (ed.), *Lord Nottingham's Chancery Cases* (vol. I) 73 Selden Soc. (1954), pp. lviii–lxii). Even the precautionary proposition that equity follows the law (when in practice it existed to introduce variations and exceptions) helped to ensure that fundamental rules of common law—those for instance that defined the types of estate in freehold land—were not altered in ways that would re-write their characteristics or would waive their application out of some sense of favour towards a particular party.

[15] Selden's squib, which held equity to be measured by the length of the Chancellor's foot, had been echoed by later detractors such as Lord Kames and Jeremy Bentham. Civilians might share the same suspicion of this open courting of moral feeling.

[16] Dwarris, *Statutes*, ii: 709, offered a typical apology: 'New discoveries and inventions in commerce have given birth to new species of contracts, and these have been followed by new contrivances to break and exclude them, for which the ancient simplicity of the common law had adopted no remedies; and from this cause, courts of equity, which admit a greater latitude, have...been obliged to accommodate the wants of mankind.'

[17] Lord Eldon, High Tory LC for 26 years between 1801 and 1827, can be found preferring to follow a case that was precisely in point, even though a great deal might be urged against it: *Townley* v. *Bedwell* (1808) 14 Ves. Jun. 591 at 596. On other occasions he refused to follow a decision that he judged to be against 'principle': see *Aldrich* v. *Cooper*, below, n. 52. Many opinions in the superior courts are referred to in Ram, *Science of Judgments*, Ch. 14, which indicate that, where he thought it necessary, a judge would depart from an earlier decision, rather than find a basis for distinguishing it.

equity's interventions, for all their appeal to an ultimate morality.[18] As equity had become more evidently rule-based, it had provided a number of qualifications upon common law principles that were of high importance to the emergence of a money-based economy; complex management structures proved necessary for both landed and industrial wealth. It was a small boost from equity that had prevented the common law structure of the strict settlement of land from collapsing at the behest of the current tenant for life.[19] It was an instruction from equity which had allowed a debtor to be sued in a common law court by an assignee of the debt without having to face the accusation that he was maintaining another's suit.[20] It was a prohibition from equity that gave the mortgagor the ability to repay his debt even after the date on which it was due.[21] Above all, equity imposed its own liability on trustees who held property for other beneficiaries—a device with protean applications.[22] A court which could supply such needs within the legal system could not be feared in the way that destroyed the prerogative tribunals of early modern England.

As for those courts with quite separate legal functions—notably the civilian courts administering ecclesiastical, probate, and admiralty law—precedent there had also acquired a significant role; but in the eighteenth century the records of their decisions had remained largely private, handed on by the judges and advocates of Doctors' Commons as part of their own mystery.[23] It continued to have about it the air of secret doctrine known only to initiates.[24]

---

[18] See Ram's account of how Chancery could be defended: *Science of Judgments*, Ch. 3. In the eighteenth century, there had been pronouncements from common law judges that Chancery decisions applying common law rules were not to be taken as high, or even as any, authority of what the common law was. But Lord Eldon objected to the Vice-Chancellor asking the King's Bench for advice on a rule that was clear beyond question: *Goodenough* v. *Powell* (1826) 2 Russ. 229. Equity deserved its own respect. Thus the rule in *Clayton's Case* (1816) 1 Mer. 572—a decision of Sir William Grant MR—was applied by King's Bench in *Bodenham* v. *Purchas* (1818) 2 B. & Ald. 39 at 46–8) as 'an authority of great weight,' decided on 'the soundest principles.'

[19] For the strict settlement of land in the nineteenth century, see XII, Pt 1, pp. 79–94.

[20] For the earlier history, see Holdsworth, *HEL*, vii, 534–7.

[21] *Ibid*, v, 330–2, vi, 663–5.

[22] See esp. XII, Pt 1, Ch. 6; XIII, Pt 2, Ch. III.1.

[23] For the ecclesiastical jurisdiction, see R. H. Helmholz, 'Records and Reports: The English Ecclesiastical Courts', in A. Wijffels (ed.), *Case Law in the Making* (Berlin, 1997), i: 83. In *Sir William Scott, Lord Stowell, Judge of the High Court of Admiralty* (Cambridge, 1987), H. J. Bourguignon has shown how that great figure (brother of Lord Eldon) derived his knowledge of a range of shipping matters and of the *ius gentium* regarding vessels in time of war for the purposes of prize law. He made a long study of civilian writings and precedents at common law as well as the decisions of his own court. He did not start from a clean sheet, as earlier writers had supposed, e.g. E. S. Roscoe, *Lord Stowell* (1916), 243–4.

[24] In *Velley* v. *Burder* (1837) 1 Curt. 372, 389–90, Dr Lushington, Judge of the London Consistory Court, expatiated upon the binding effect of the appellate court above him, the Court of Arches. He took a position very much of his time: that he could depart from its decisions only if there were 'very

3. JUDICIAL PRECEDENT AND *STARE DECISIS*

The doctrine of judicial precedent in its modern form was essentially a Victorian rationalization:

The common law did not develop a system of case-law by adopting explicit premises as to the authority of cases. It passed imperceptibly from a time when what was said in the course of cases was evidence of the law—of the legal custom applying in common to all parts of the realm—to a time when the law pronounced in the cases was itself the material of a substantial part of the system of law.[25]

So long as the House of Lords acted as an ultimate authority in the settlement of disputes by voting rather than by articulating reasons for judgment, it was difficult to treat its decisions as settling legal rules in a general sense.[26] Equally, while there remained three distinct courts of common law, the extent to which each would follow the precedents set by the others when sitting in banc had to be limited by their apparent independence and the reasons for conserving it. Since all the judges of these courts also conducted trials in the assize courts on circuit, this provided a lower level of decision-making that added to the case law for subsequent citation in argument and judgment. Moreover, the intermediate jurisdictions in error were a strange labyrinth with paths that were only somewhat straightened in 1830.[27] The competition for jurisdiction between these courts, if it retained any real justification, lay in fears that judges might exhibit naked bias or more subtle forms of inclination towards one party or against another. To dispel these mistrusts, plaintiffs (but not defendants) had come to have some measure of protection, thanks to their choice of forum.[28]

Probably the triumvirate of common law courts survived as much by the simple anchor of tradition. However that may be, it was accepted as a convention based on 'comity' that each bench would respect decisions of the others. As James Ram showed in 1834, the matter was not put in terms of any binding rule.[29] A consistent

---

peculiar circumstances', stressing how exceptional this would be. See J. Evans, 'Precedent in the Nineteenth Century', in L. Goldstein (ed.), *Precedent in Law* (Oxford, 1987), 35–72 at 46–52;

[25] Evans, 'Changes in Precedent', at 35–6. The expressions, *stare decisis* and *ratio decidendi*, had their place in Roman law and its derivatives and in earlier common law. These occurred as part of discussions of the need for certainty and finality in law derived from precedents; but their meaning was, to say the least, somewhat variable.

[26] For the evolution of Lords' jurisdiction in this context, see esp. R. B. Stevens, *Law and Politics*, Ch. 1; J. B. Landau, 'Precedents in the House of Lords' (1951) 63 *Juridical Rev.* 222–33.

[27] See below, Pt 3, pp. 601–2.

[28] This was a rather remote justification since it only affected references of legal issues to the court in banc.

[29] *Science of Judgment*, 6–7. So the issue continued to be regarded: see e.g. Brett MR, *The Vera Cruz (No. 2)* (1884) 9 PD 96 at 98. As Brown J. of the US Supreme Court would put it, 'Comity is not

line of authority would command very great respect; but a single precedent would not be followed if to do so was 'plainly unreasonable and inconvenient'.[30] Each court in banc might therefore refuse to accept a precedent set by that very court, as well as a decision of one of the other courts; and judgments given at *nisi prius* would not necessarily be followed in later courts of the same level. Only the precedents of the House of Lords and the Court of Exchequer Chamber were taken to be binding on the three courts below and on the Chancellor in equity.[31] Even so decisions might be found to have been misreported, or decided without any sufficient argument, or distinguished on their facts—perhaps after investigation of the details of the case that were on record.[32]

What then of the question whether appellate courts were bound by their own previous decisions—an issue that has stood in modern times as the ultimate mark of *stare decisis*? Restructuring the superior civil courts by the Judicature Acts would give the question new force; but earlier in the century, the House of Lords had begun to treat its own decisions as binding. By the end of his long occupancy of the Woolsack, Lord Eldon was prepared to commit himself to the view that the House was bound to apply its own earlier decision, even where subsequent judges doubted its correctness, unless special circumstances allowed it to be distinguished.[33] In 1844 it ruled that, for there to be a valid celebration of a marriage, a member of the Established clergy must be present;[34] and in 1861, the House, led by Campbell CJ, insisted that it must accept that decision as the law, even though it went against the better judgment of most of those hearing the appeal.[35] Robert

a rule of law, but one of practice, convenience and expediency': *Mast, Foos* v. *Stover Mfg* 177 US 485, 488 (1900).

[30] So it was expressed by Parke B., *Mirehouse* v. *Rennell* (1833) 1 Cl. & F. 527, 546; and Campbell CJ in *Bright* v. *Hutton* (below, n. 36 at 391; but these two judges were leaders of the movement for stricter ideas of the force of precedent.

[31] Various judges considered that the Lords' decision in *Kettle* v. *Townsend* (temp. Will III) 1 Salk. 187 to be incorrect, but felt that only the Lords themselves could overrule it: cf. Lord Eldon, *Hills* v. *Downton* (1800) 5 Ves. Jr. 557, 565, disapproving of the decision as having been decided with no lawyer sitting in judgment, but finding reason to distinguish it. For a similar view of a decision of Exchequer Chamber, see Parke B., *Garland* v. *Carlisle* (1834) 2 Car. & M. 31 at 64–5; Ram, *Science of Judgment*, Ch. 18, section 1.

[32] Ram, *Science of Judgment*, Ch. 18, listed 13 types of argument for treating a precedent as having enhanced authority (section 2). He then found 21 arguments for disregarding a decision (section 3).

[33] *Fletcher* v. *Sondes* (1827) 1 Bli. (N.S.) 144, 247–8.

[34] *R* v. *Millis* (1844) 10 Cl. & F. 88. This precedent, though set after consulting the judges, was a decision of six judicial Lords who divided equally, and the decision appealed from had therefore to stand. In a later view of the position in an appeal court, such an equal division of opinion showed no concordance and so 'judicial comity' did not require it to be followed: *The Vera Cruz* (above, n. 29)).

[35] *Beamish* v. *Beamish* (1861) 9 H.L.C. 274. VII. Only a decade before, Lord St Leonards had stuck to the general formula that decisions of the Lords were to be followed unless it would be unreasonable or inconvenient: *Bright* v. *Hutton* (1851) 3 H.L.C. 341, 387, 388. But there the House was faced with an

Stevens has argued that this step must be seen in its own context.[36] It was taken by a court of final resolution that still had no permanent judges of its own and remained in some sense part of the upper legislative House.[37] This was moreover a time when courts did not always distinguish clearly between deciding the same case again and applying the rule derived from one case to another raising similar issues.[38]

Even so, an understanding seemed to be emerging that the final instance in the great common law structure could only give sufficient stability and certainty if it regarded what it had concluded once as a settlement of argument for all time. After the Appellate Committee of the Lords took distinct form, with Lords of Appeal in Ordinary as part of its membership,[39] it continued to insist that its own precedents were not open to reversal. Blackburn, one of the first appointees, was firmly of this view.[40] In *London Tramways* v. *London County Council*, the bluff Lord Chancellor, Halsbury, pronounced that the rule had been 'established now for some centuries' and was 'universally assumed by the profession' in the interests of legal certainty.[41] As Pugsley has shown, this undoubted exaggeration

earlier precedent, *Hutton* v. *Upfill* (1850) 2 H.L.C. 674, which was decided by Lord Brougham, effectively sitting alone in the Lords, and upholding a decision of his own brother, Master Brougham! The two cases, moreover, arose out of the winding up of a single company and so had about them elements of what today might be regarded as an issue estoppel. Brougham threatened to seek legislation that would in effect restore his own decision, incurring the animosity in particular of Lord Campbell—an advocate of strict precedent, who nonetheless in the second case, found reason for distinguishing it.

[36] Stevens, *Law and Politics*, 79–98. Issues of first moment could involve re-argument and the seeking of opinions from the common law judges: as for instance in *Fletcher* v. *Sondes* (above, n. 34) or in the 15-year saga, *Birtwhistle* v. *Vardill* (1835) 2 Cl. & F. 571, (1840) 7 Cl. & Fin. 895. In the latter, the Lords eventually held that a child legitimated under Scots law by the subsequent marriage of his parents could not be the heir to an English landed estate. In that case Lord Brougham urged his fellow judges, 'in an open and manly way [to retrace] their steps, rather than persist in their error' (at 922); but his vociferous campaign to persuade the House to recognize the heirship came to naught.

[37] Lay peers were still being used to make up a quorum—on a daily rota. For legal membership, see below, pp. 532–35.

[38] The expression, *res judicata*, had not yet acquired its limited modern meaning of an embargo on retrying the very issue that had been decided in previous litigation: see D. Pugsley, 'London Tramways (1898)' [1996] *JLH* 172, 183, n. 32

[39] For its rescue and re-formation by the Judicature Act 1875, see below, pp. 535–42.

[40] See Evans, 'Precedent', 58, n.95.

[41] [1898] A.C. 375. This report wrongly gave the plaintiff's name as London Street Tramways, a smaller outfit separate from London Tramways. The latter had already litigated to the Lords and lost an argument with the LCC over whether the Council had power under the Tramways Act 1870, s 43, to acquire the tramway without compensating LST for losses over and above the value of the physical track. This was why the 1898 case was an attempt to persuade the Lords that they should admit the possibility of not following an earlier decision of their own, thus opening the door to a reconsideration of the decision in the earlier case. Pugsley (*London Tramways*) suggests that the audacious running of this argument followed from the critical remarks made by Sir Frederick Pollock in his

nonetheless represented a well-endorsed view stretching back some 70 years.[42] The decision was taken to put the rule beyond question, finding some echo with the keystone courts of the dominions.[43] Scrutton LJ would sneer: 'All judges make mistakes. Only the House of Lords do not make mistakes because there is no-one to tell them that they do.'[44] Indeed, it was only after his retirement that the Court of Appeal would finally adopt the principle that it too was bound by its earlier decisions, save where they were reached in ignorance of a statute or a binding decision, or had created a conflict between one another.[45] The resilience with which the Lords defined their once-for-all role expresses a confidence in their own capacities that seems particularly of its period. Certainly there was pressing need to give settled answers to legal questions. With the small number of superior judges, the demand for rules fit for an immense Empire was hard to meet.[46] Better a rule that, short of statutory overturning, had to be taken as settled than a conditional rule always open to revision in later litigation. So plainly the most senior judges felt.

In his apologia for the doctrine of precedent, Holdsworth claimed for it an ideal flexibility, amounting to a formula which allowed for cautious extension and revision of legal rules, but nothing that in essence disturbed the declaratory rationale—that judges were only uncovering a principle or rule.[47] Even after the House of Lords' self-denying ordinance in *London Tramways*, the scope for limiting a prior decision certainly remained considerable. The art of distinguishing a rule set by precedent, particularly by finding that the facts were not on all fours, had been deployed by judges great and small since at least the eighteenth century.[48] It might well be used where the earlier decision had been the subject of

---

First Book of Jurisprudence (1896). Duxbury, however, finds no evidence that this in turn was stirred by a running antagonism between Pollock and Halsbury: *Frederick Pollock and the English Juristic Tradition* (Oxford, 2004), 318–19.

[42] Pugsley, *London Tramways*, 179–81 (App.).

[43] In the same period, the Privy Council held itself not to be strictly bound by its own decisions: *Ridsdale* v. *Clifton* (1877) 2 PD 276 (Cairns LC); *Tooth* v. *Power* [1891] AC 284 (Lord Watson)—a difference, according to Evans, that can be explained only by the accidents of history: 'Precedent', 58, 61–2. Highest appellate courts in the dominions also refused to go quite as far as the House of Lords: J. D. Murphy and R. Rueter, *Stare Decisis in Commonwealth Appellate Courts* (Toronto, 1981), Chs 3, 4. Thus the Supreme Court of Canada, which had to hear appeals from the civilian jurisdiction of Quebec as well as from common law provinces, held itself bound by its own precedents save for 'exceptional circumstances': *Stuart* v. *Bank of Montreal* (1909) 41 SCR 516.

[44] S. Uglow, A. W. B. Simpson (eds), *Biographical Dictionary of the Common Law* (1984), 469; see e.g. T. E. Scrutton, *Law of Copyright* (4th edn, 1904), 119.

[45] *Young* v. *Bristol Aeroplane* [1944] KB 718. The Court assumed that it had indeed long been bound by its earlier decisions, produced some specific authority in point, and dismissed the occasional dictum to the contrary.

[46] Hence e.g. the building of a general law of contract by judicial precedent, as analysed by P. S. Atiyah , *The Rise and Fall of Freedom of Contract* (1979).

[47] *History of English Law*, xii: 146–62.

[48] See generally, Ram, *Science of Judgments*, 12, 48–52.

criticism among judges and practitioners, or even where a particular judge found it wholly unreasonable. In turn there could then be aspersions against unwarranted distinctions that were, as Lord Hardwicke had once put it, 'slight and cobweb'.[49] Here too were assumptions that would gain in legal sinew with time. Where one court was bound by the earlier decision of another, it was obliged to apply the *ratio decidendi* of that case, but not *obiter dicta* that were no more than judicial adumbrations on other matters. In the 1930s the dichotomy between the two would lead to much scholarly disputation in the pages of the *Law Quarterly Review*.[50] How far, in particular, must the later court treat the earlier judge's formulation of the applicable rule as binding *ratio*, rather than passing *dictum*? What scope was left for the later judge to engage in 'restrictive distinguishing' that reformulated the earlier rule, as distinct from pointing to a factual difference in the cases which justified following a different rule?

In the early nineteenth century, it remained not unknown for judges to express hesitations about how to decide a case over considerable periods. They might reserve their decision until the body of their brothers could be consulted; they might hear re-argument after a search for further precedent or a better report; they might discount cases as wrongly reported or for not having been reported; they might note that a case dealing with a new issue was decided only for its particular facts; and so on.[51] It may also be noted that the House of Lords, hearing an appeal in error, continued their occasional practice of seeking the opinions of the common law judges on issues of law raised in a case. However, they would not necessarily accept the advice they were offered by all or a majority of the judges who responded.

4. INTERPRETATION OF STATUTES BY COURTS

Despite his obeisences to parliamentary sovereignty, Blackstone had treated much on the statute book as unsatisfactory, as became evident in his treatment of the approach of courts to statutory interpretation.[52] The complaint would continue to

---

[49] *Tomlinson* v. *Gill* (1756) Amb. 330. Best CJ, reporting the view of Lord Mansfield, was firmly against 'subtilties and refinements being introduced into our law…our jurisprudence should be bottomed on plain broad principles …': cited in Ram, *Science of Judgment*, 252–5.

[50] See A. L. Goodhart, 'Precedent in English and Continental Law' (1935) 50 *LQR* 40, 196; W. E. S. Holdsworth (1934) 50 *LQR* 180; C. K. Allen, 'Case Law: An Unwarrantable Intervention' (1935) 51 *LQR* 333.

[51] Witness the lengths to which Lord Eldon went in *Aldrich* v. *Cooper* (1803) 8 Ves. Jun. 382, 388 *et seq.* to consider a forgotten decision of Lord Hardwicke's, *Robinson* v. *Tonge*, resurrected by Cox in his 5th edn of Peere Williams' Reports in 1793. It had come down through a private note in the hands of the great equity authority, Lord Redesdale. Eldon consulted him but ended by finding the case contrary to the thrust of other authority.

[52] *Comms*, i, Introduction, para. 3.

surface often enough, for there had been no system established even for drawing up legislation promoted by the government. Instead each ministry had its own tactics which were part of their ever-growing need for legal advice. In 1867, the office of Parliamentary Counsel was established as a resource to which a Department could turn if it chose. Henry Thring as its first head did much to establish what was needed to produce an effective draft for legislation, the first requirement being adequate instructions and behind them, adequate discussion of the policies being aimed at. Equally assiduous was his successor, Courtenay Ilbert.[53] Since departments could choose to rely instead on the skills of their own civil servants, or of legal practitioners consulted on an *ad hoc* basis or seconded to their service for a limited period, the quality of legislation would continue to be variable.[54] By the late nineteenth century judges tended to voice their criticisms of particular legislation more in sorrow and less in anger; but still they were regularly faced with obscurities and inadequacies of drafting for which they did not care.

A considerable section of Dwarris' book presented judicial pronouncements on the proper approach to the interpretation of enactments.[55] Concluding that statutes—for the most part like wills, deeds, contracts, and royal grants [56]—must be read so as to understand and give effect to their intent, he starts with attention to the long-lived 'Mischief Rule' and is even able to call in aid that high legalist, Baron Parke, who on one occasion remarked: 'We must always construe an act so as to suppress the mischief and advance the remedy.'[57] But Parke soon qualified any prospect of a free-ranging search for what Plowden had once called the 'soul' of the law—its 'internal sense' and 'reason'[58]—by insisting, as modern judges do, that it is the words used that determine the legislature's intent; and that accordingly it is often difficult to discern what that motive or purpose was.[59]

---

[53] Thring's general instructions were eventually published as *Practical Legislation, the Composition and Language of Acts of Parliament and Business Documents* (1903). The experience which they embodied was acknowledged in Ilbert's Charpentier Lectures, *The Mechanics of Law Making* (New York, 1914).

[54] For numerous examples, see XIII, Pt 2; and on the general problem, *ibid.*, pp. 610–19.

[55] Note similarities of approach to John Chipman Gray's discussion of the subject in *The Nature and Sources of the Law* (1909), Ch. 8.

[56] Courts would reformulate the terms of private documents, at least by implying terms into them where the document remained silent on the question, or even by writing terms into a formal document, such as a will or a trust. A certain growth in the tendency to take documents at their face value occurred, as individuals more regularly consulted professional lawyers and legal treatises offered detailed models as precedents.

[57] *Lyde* v. *Bernard* (1836) 1 M. & W. 113, 114. The mischief in question was the defect in the common law that the statute sought to correct, as the Barons of the Exchequer had formulated the rule in *Heydon's Case* (1584) 3 Co. Rep. 7a.

[58] *Eyston* v. *Studd* (1574) 2 Plowd. 459.

[59] Dwarris, *Statutes*, ended his account of the judge's role with observations on the line between interpretation and judicial legislation (see ii: Ch. 9). He accepted that the judges have sometimes

The judges had long claimed to adhere where possible to a principle—the so-called 'literal rule'—by which the words of a statute were to be interpreted by 'their ordinary and familiar signification and import, regard being had to their general and popular use nothing adding thereto, nothing diminishing'.[60] That did something to enhance their claim to be deciding objectively and without resort to personal opinions, feelings or ethical strictures. But they continued to qualify that stance, sometimes by reliance on Baron Parke's 'golden rule',[61] and sometimes by resort to a whole splay of presumptions expressed in maxims such as *ut res magis valeat quam pereat* and *expressio eorum quae tacite insunt*.

Later, general Interpretation Acts and the incorporation of definition clauses into particular statutes would reduce the need to delve around in order to discover the 'mischief' that the statute was intended to eradicate.[62] In any case the judges stood out against hearing arguments as to what ministers, promoters, and others said about meaning during the progress of a bill and rarely would they consider the reports of preceding Royal Commissions or Parliamentary or Ministerial Committees. The Assize circuits could scarcely carry their own copies of Parliamentary Debates or Blue Books.[63] More fundamentally, the judges insisted upon interpreting statutes as they saw fit after hearing argument before them. Thus it was, in their view, that the balance of power between legislature and bench had to be set, even as true democracy approached. Further English texts would tackle statutory interpretation afresh in the 1870s. To an ill-defined degree, it continued to be said that judges would not allow 'a fraud on the law or an insult to an Act of Parliament'. [64] What was more evident was the tendency to resort to presumptions as starting points, such as the restrictive interpretation of penal statutes, the presumption against retrospective effect, the requirement that for an act to affect the position of the Crown it must say so, the avoidance of collision with other principles, the choice of the solution most agreeable to justice or reason, the choice of meaning that was consonant with international obligations.

---

overstepped the mark, for instance, in stretching the language of the Statute of Frauds 1677; but he placed the blame elsewhere, under the rubric, 'Legislature, supineness of' (2nd edn at 629–30, 708).

[60] Tindal CJ, *Everett* v. *Mills*, cited in Dwarris, *Statutes*, ii.

[61] *Becke* v. *Smith* (1836) 2 M. & W. 191, 195; repeated in *Grey* v. *Pearson* (1857) 6 H.L.C. 61 at 106. An earlier version had been adopted by Parker LCJ, *Mitchell* v. *Torup* (1766) Parker 227, 233. This was probably much what Bentham meant when he criticized Blackstone by describing the latter's view of the Mischief Rule as replacing interpretation by alteration: *Comment on the Commentaries* (ed. J. H. Burns and H. L. A. Hart, Oxford, 1977), 137–61.

[62] Brougham's Acts of Parliament Abbreviation Act 1850 made a start (see above, p. 15, n. 31). The Interpretation Act 1889 provided a more sophisticated version.

[63] On the difficulties of getting judges to refer to anything for which they could not all have copies in front of them, see Lord Rodger, of Earlsferry, 'Thinking about Scots Law' (1996) 1 *Edinburgh Law Rev.* 3–24 at 17–18.

[64] See *Fox* v. *Bishop of Chester* (1829) 1 Dow. & Cl. (HL) 416, 429.

A large portion of P. B. Maxwell's *On the Interpretation of Statutes*[65] was cast in this mould; likewise H. Hardcastle's *The Construction and Effect of Statutory Law.*[66] The guidelines on how to construe statutes formed a web of rationalization which judges used to justify their acceptance of one argument over another. Referring to such propositions could lend weight to what was no more than off-the-cuff preference.

5. CODIFICATION OF BASIC LEGAL PRINCIPLES

In the early nineteenth century, the balance between what was set forth in statute and what was left as part of common law had little about it that was pre-ordained; and so matters would largely remain in the development of the modern law. The issue was, however, long the subject of argument between the supporters of tradition and the advocates of rationalizing reform. As the polities of the European continent loosened the trappings of feudal government, the states that emerged were often larger than before and were searching for their own legitimacy. The changes set in train a determination to state their general laws of civil and criminal responsibility, of trade and of court procedures, in the form of codes. It was a reshaping that could help to replace overlordly power with government under a rule of law—a *Rechtsstaat*. It could well lead to an intellectual shift in which legal sources were taken to consist solely in the Codes and other legislative acts or decrees. In face of this urge to legislate, there was likely to be some withering of the sense that there existed a body of rules known to those who exercised judicial power and expressed in their reasons for judgment. Precedent (*jurisprudence* in French terminology) accordingly tended to lose its status as a source of law.[67] Instead, scholars in universities gained increasing respect and admiration for their exposition, commentary and exegesis upon the codes themselves, providing *doctrine* (again in the French sense) that held its own authority for those seeking to settle what the law was.

These European legal codes, which derived, at least in part, through various historical channels from Roman Law or interpretations of it, had their own models in the immense Prussian Code of 1794 and in the French *Code civil* of 1806, so enthusiastically engendered by Napoleon. Yet it was an Englishman, Jeremy Bentham, who made the case for codification with particular spirit, urging the need to replace custom and judicial practice with a coherent and complete panoply

---

[65] 1875 (12 edns to 1969).

[66] 1879, which after four editions was converted into W. F. Craies' *Treatise on Statute Law* (1907, 8 edns to date).

[67] For the interplay from comparative perspectives, see e.g. W. H. Bryson and S. Danchy (eds), *Ratio Decidendi: Guiding Principles of Judicial Decisions* (Berlin, 2006).

of publicly stated rules. Certainly his writings on the subject attracted numerous countries to the cause as the nineteenth century progressed. Bentham's long voyage as a moral philosopher had as its engine his self-proclaimed 'genius for legislation' and it was still running at speed in 1820, when he had another 12 years to live. It would carry him into massive plans for legal 'codification' (the word is his own); into writings on many elements in social life, pursuing ideas of economic liberalism but backing them by state provision against communal disaster; into attempts at practising his novel ideas—as with his Panopticon scheme for prisons, poor law workhouses, asylums for the insane and the like; into advocacy of complete democracy (for adult males); and into plans for executive government that would cast the citizenry in the role of constant watchdog and critic of official acts and omissions.

Bentham left no completed version of his Code of Codes, the *Pannomion*— which was to comprise a constitutional code and under it four codes of private law, civil procedure, penal law, and criminal procedure; but his writings explored basic issues about the structure and the content of each part of the whole. We shall return below to fundamental aspects of his analysis of the nature of law and the need to justify its policies by the principle of utility, rather than by some ineffable moral sense.[68] Despite what was put about by his disparagers, he by no means believed that the Codes could be so complete and unchanging that the role of the judges would be simply to apply them to cases before their courts. He foresaw a regular process for revising the texts to meet new circumstances, which would often start from an 'ameliorative-suggestive function' assigned to the judges (the term being a typical piece of his conflated word-smithery). This would draw them into the business of necessary law reform, without leaving them with their distinct power of decision by reference to earlier precedents. In that process, he believed that they should act, as did Lord Mansfield, by reference to principle, rather than to authority.

The influence of these ideas was felt both in foreign countries and also within the British Empire, notably in India. After the 1857 Mutiny, Britain assumed the direct reins of government and saw codification as the instrument that, so far as possible, would make English common law part of the great Imperial mission to civilize the teeming peoples of the sub-continent.[69] Not so at home. Against attempts to codify the common law there was a tide of resistance that flowed throughout the century, as often enough since. It was a rebuttal of the Benthamic programme, powered above all by the judges and the practising professions working in the interstices of the legal system.

---

[68] See below, Ch. IV.1.   [69] See below, pp. 240–1.

There were determined efforts from the period of the First Reform Act onwards to get down to the business of English codification. Because of its patchwork effects it is worth summarizing even at this early stage. It was led by lawyers who had some measure of sympathy with radical arguments for legal reform. Henry Brougham exhausted the House of Commons in 1828 with a six-hour speech on the subject of the defects of English common law and its machinery,[70] and it caught a mood of impatience for change that had strong links to the cause of parliamentary reform.

Soon enough Commissioners were investigating the tangled interstices of the land law and conveyancing and others were looking to the prospects of codifying, or at least re-stating, criminal law and procedure, and of re-working the very texture of civil procedure.[71] The land law would over time be patched by a succession of statutes that, at least until the major re-designing of the subject and its coordinates in 1925, would fall well short of any code.[72] Civil procedure was gradually re-set. Particularly in the 1850s, Commissions recommended that old limitations on the structure of judicial bodies, on remedies in the different courts and the application of particular rules and changes were introduced by statute.[73] Two decades later, it became possible to create a single hierarchy of superior civil courts to hear disputes based on rules drawn from common law, equity, and the civilian jurisdictions; but in large measure the changes were in jurisdiction and practice, not in the substantive content of the rules themselves.[74] Between 1833 and 1850, two sets of Commissioners wrestled long to produce Criminal Law and Procedure Codes, but at the end of their efforts the judges and law officers returned what was in effect a vote of no confidence in their drafting and, at base, in the very project itself.[75] Of all branches of law to which laymen should be entitled to access through clear statement, criminal law was the obvious case. But it was said in riposte that potential criminals knew well enough already what they

---

[70] See *Speeches of Lord Brougham with Historical Introductions* (1838), ii, 319–486; Holdsworth *HEL*, xiii, 296–308.

[71] At the same period, the reforms of legislature, municipal government, and poor law administration gave major areas of public law a statutory basis which approached the idea of statutory codification.

[72] In 1826, the Benthamite, James Humphreys, had published his own Land Law Code; but the Land Law Commission went about its reforms at an interstitial level: see XII, Pt 1, pp 47–58.

[73] For the intermediate stages in reforming and coalescing the jurisdictions of the common law and chancery courts, see below, esp.Pt 3, Chs III.1, IV.1–3.

[74] The Judicature Act 1873, s 25 listed instances of conflict between rules deriving from common law, equity, or civilian jurisdictions, and indicated which was to be preferred. It also stated a general preference for equity over common law, which reflected the refining quality of the former. But the clashes were a minor aspect of the grand rebuilding of the system of courts: see below, Pt 3, pp. 770–3.

[75] XIII, Pt 1, pp. 191–203.

should not do.[76] A code would only rigidify the ability of the courts to mould common law principles to fit the cases before them, and that would be a constriction of far greater moment. Instead, after further work, the mass of statutes on parts of the criminal law were consolidated—with amendments that rationalized the possible sentences for different crimes and made occasional adjustments to definitions of the crimes themselves.[77]

In the 1870s, FitzJames Stephen returned from a term as Law Member of the Viceroy's Council in India, enthused with the cause of codification to which he had been contributing there, as had Sir Henry Maine before him. But his own Criminal Code for England failed to secure enactment. Fellow members of a Royal Commission to consider his draft accepted that it should go forward. But then the commanding Lord Chief Justice, Cockburn, raised a plethora of objections to its General Part and promised more for the rest. In England it was shelved, though it would be the basis of enactments in Queensland, Western Australia and other colonies.[78] Opposition from senior judges was undoubtedly a main source of resistance, but other difficulties were to be anticipated as well. No Justice Ministry had emerged, criminal law being the charge of the Home Office. Its day-to-day preoccupations were with policing and detection, the carrying out of punishments, particularly in custodial institutions, and managing criminal courts at the superior and summary levels.[79] Systematic statement of the definitions of criminal liability was far removed from its main objectives. On the other hand, the business of applying the principles to particular cases was one part of the law where, as justices of the peace, English gentlemen were engaged in running the system. How could a code of criminal law and procedure ever be expected to pass the scrutiny of a Parliament made up of such men?[80]

In the late nineteenth century, codes would be enacted on a number of relatively specific aspects of commercial law, largely because of pressure from groups with financial or business interests. They wanted legal advice grounded on the plain speaking that they thought legislative language provided; they abhorred opinions from their barristers built out of the nuanced weighing of judicial pronouncements into a seat on the fence. The codes covered bills of exchange,

---

[76] Coleridge J. was of the opinion that the public already knew enough about the criminal law and needed no code to guide it: *PP* 1854 (303), liii, p. 401.

[77] XIII Pt 1, pp. 203–5.

[78] See XIII, Pt 1, pp. 205–16.

[79] The absence of a Justice Ministry can also be seen as an impediment in the way of reforms of the land law, both in its substantive rules and its conveyancing practices.

[80] See A. H. Manchester, 'Simplifying the Sources of the Law: An Essay in Law Reform' (1973) 2 *AALR* 395–415.

partnership, sale of goods, and marine insurance. But even these fell short of the codes of commercial law that were finding a place in many Continental countries.[81] The only serious movement for uniformity between different parts of the UK (of the kind that would later bring about the Uniform Commercial Code in the United States) was abandoned amid the mutual hostilities of English and Scots lawyers.[82]

Full Benthamic codification was inspired by an embracing modernism which strove to reduce the role of tradition and accumulated experience as far as possible. The draftsman would take from the existing sources of legal rules, domestic and foreign, and from commentaries and proposals relating to them, in order to find the examples which best fitted expedient outcomes for the whole community. Whatever was deemed fit for the complex and diverse conditions of India,[83] most of those charged with maintaining the English legal system in its homeland exhibited no desire to institute a regime that would upset the balances set by the long evolution of their own 'common law' system.[84]

6. THE SUBORDINATE AUTHORITY OF LEGAL LITERATURE

The sense that English law consisted in the principles that the courts would apply to litigation before them was heavily underscored by the reluctance of judges to accord to writings about law any regular status in themselves as a *source* of that law. The universities of the European continent had for centuries built great schools of law, where professors pronounced *ex cathedra* upon doctrines and principles, and their profound dogmatics gave instruction to judges on the rightful course of the law. Some of that tradition surrounded the education and practice of the civilian lawyers of Doctors' Commons.[85] But, as is recorded in earlier volumes of this *History*, the English common lawyers for the most part held to an obverse tradition. In it the formation and custody of the essential law was kept to the judges, who were themselves drawn from the practising bar. William Blackstone—a man of civilian training, and no great success in the common law courts as barrister or judge—had begun to repair the absence of systematic

---

[81] See XII, Pt 3, pp. 771–81, 859–61, 711–19. In interpreting these codes, case law from before and after the enactments would continue to be treated as legal sources within the rules that accommodated both the concept of parliamentary sovereignty and of judicial interpretation.

[82] See Lord Rodger of Earlsferry, 'The Codification of Commercial Law in Victorian Britain' (1991) 80 *Proceedings of the British Academy* 149–70.

[83] See below. pp. 240–1, 250–1.

[84] For late nineteenth-century 'jurisprudential' writings that stressed the essential value of judge-made concepts and principles, see below, pp. 123–31.

[85] See below, pp. 696 *et seq*.

exposition; and lacuna it was, as the long-lasting success of his *Commentaries* would come to demonstrate.[86] That great work did, indeed, acquire a special status as one authority upon which judges would directly rely.[87]

As the ensuing trickle of books on legal subjects became a well-stocked stream, they took the form of legal treatises, many of them surveying the history of their subject in telling or tedious detail. By the 1820s, in England, as in the United States, they were pouring forth and a certain number would gain recognition from the bench. These tended to be the works of practising barristers or judges no longer living.[88] The indefatigable James Ram listed works which judges had called authoritative and others which were regarded 'with much respect'.[89] They were not just the line of great classics stemming from Glanvile and Bracton onwards, but extended, to take two instances out of a great many, to *Callis on Sewers* and *Nolan on the Poor Laws*.[90] On the *lex mercatoria* and the *ius gentium* they encompassed the great civilian authors of Europe. Nonetheless the general run of books expounding the law lacked the standing of law reports.[91] Their citation by counsel and in judgments tended to be supportive rather than primary. There was some tradition that the works of living authors were not to be cited, though it was not always followed.[92] Academic authors would later bemoan this;[93] but barrister authors could well benefit, since in court their opponents could not quote their books against them.

To say that this body of literature was only tangentially a source of law is not to deny influence, but only to clarify the form that the influence took. Treatises on a field of law, whether wide or narrow, gave an organized account of a subject where otherwise there might only be personal recollection, or a record in a file, such as those kept by judges for their own use, or some published collation

---

[86] For the continuing role of the *Commentaries* in the formation of young lawyers, see M. Lobban, 'The English Legal Treatise and English Law in the Eighteenth Century', in S. Danchy et al. (1997) 13 *Juris Scripta Historica* 69–88. For Blackstone's links to earlier inspirers of an institutional account of the common law as a whole, notably Sir Matthew Hale, see A. W. B. Simpson, 'The Rise and Fall of the Legal Treatise' (1981) 48 *U Chi. Law Rev.* 632, 652–8.

[87] Not, however, until he was dead and Lord Mansfield no longer Chief Justice: J. Oldham, 'Lord Mansfield, *Stare Decisis* and the *Ratio Decidendi*' in Bryson and Danchy, *Ratio Decidendi*, 137, 149.

[88] Hence also the common style of practitioners' texts which set out statutes, garnered precedents, and left the public to consult the authors for more specific advice.

[89] Ram, *Science of* Judgment, Ch. 12. The list shows how very considerable, by 1834, the range of texts aimed at legal practitioners had become.

[90] In Ram's treasury, base metal also displayed: an example is Heath J.'s view of Lord Coke: 'In every part of his conduct, his passions influenced his judgment. *Vir acer et vehemens*': *Jefferson* v. *Bishop of Durham* (1801) 1 Bos. & Pul. 106 at 131; see Ram, *Science of Judgment*, 85.

[91] For the development of law reporting in our period, see below, Pt 4, Ch. V.4.

[92] There were occasions when a judge took this to heart, as in the mysterious instance of Kekewich J.: for which see Pugsley, '*London Tramways* (1898)' [1996] *JLH* 172.

[93] See e.g. the correspondence in 1932 between Prof. H. C. Gutteridge and Lord Atkin: G. Lewis, *Lord Atkin* (1983), App. 1.

of material—perhaps by date, perhaps by alphabetical listing. Some of the most saleable practitioners' handbooks of the nineteenth century continued older 'magpie' traditions. But, particularly once teachers from the new law schools became engaged in legal publishing, treatments of major subjects tended to offer a theoretical framework of some kind. In that way the law could be claimed as a 'scientific' discipline, worthy of serious study as such, rather than a jumble of information about how things had been done, and should therefore be done again. Those who were not yet masters of a field would naturally turn to these interrelated descriptions in search of memorable templates on which to develop arguments, submissions, judgments. The first book on a subject to undertake the task would be of particular significance. Once done, others would appear, but the subject-matter generally left little room to introduce major shifts in the structure of accounting for it. Later books would add detail and take up points of controversy. They were needed whenever statutes entered the domain and had to be incorporated. As will become apparent from much of what follows in these Volumes, it was often in the earlier nineteenth century that treatises of the modern type first appeared. As a phenomenon, they accordingly play a vital part in expanding the legal system for the industrial and imperial era.

7. CUSTOM AS A SOURCE OF LAW

To round out our discussion of the sources of law, we return to that sense of law as a gradual compounding of moral understanding and social practices through which custom came to have a legal effect. The very evolution of a common law of the realm amounted to a recognition of the force of custom in a fundamental sense.[94] This body of law had long been treated as 'reasonable usage throughout the whole realm, approved time out of mind in the king's courts of record'. Sir Edward Coke had found it to consist in the particular wisdom and experience of the common lawyers themselves; it was therefore not open to plead and prove a custom before a court as a basis for demonstrating a common law rule. As a basic proposition this had about it the same mysterious ambivalence as Blackstone's treatment of the common law as always having existed, the judges serving only to reveal it when previously it had not been appreciated. To those within the system, Coke's sophistry would have a reassuring resonance even in the ever-shifting world of the nineteenth century.[95]

[94] For the various senses of custom, see M. Lobban, 'Custom, Common Law Reasoning and the Law of Nations in the Nineteenth Century', in A. Perreau-Saussine and J. B. Murphy (eds), *The Nature of Customary Law* (Cambridge, 2007).

[95] For the historical trajectory of such ideas, see Lobban, 'Custom, Nature and Authority: The Roots of English Positivism', in D. Lemmings (ed.), *The British and their Laws in the Eighteenth Century* (Woodbridge, 2005), 27–58.

The common law, however, recognized that certain customs, when supported by specific proof, could be pleaded in order to establish that a general rule of common law should be varied or displaced. First, there were communal practices, followed for instance by the inhabitants of a village or town, under which copyhold land was held.[96] The formal test of longevity required the custom to have been in existence from the accession of Richard I in 1189, but that might be presumed unless there was evidence or a reason to the contrary. It had to be continuously practised thereafter, it had to be certain, and it had to be reasonable. These severe criteria gave juries and judges plentiful opportunities to reject assertions of a binding local custom when they were so minded.

Secondly, there were individual usages by which a person with title to one piece of land could establish rights over another's land. These had to fall within set categories of easement or *profit à prendre*, but they did not have to satisfy any further criterion of reasonableness. Traditionally, particular instances had to be shown to have existed from time immemorial, but by our period a tendency to presume that, after enjoyment within living memory, there must have been a 'lost modern grant' of the right.[97] The reference to the notion of grant gave a clue to what this form of custom achieved. The right was of a type that could be expressly granted by conveyance. Its recognition out of long-held practice was a supplement where evidence of an actual grant failed. That was a natural circumstance in a world when rights in land had been freed of feudal obligation but the world was still one of slow social change and patchy literacy. By the nineteenth century, dealings in land would be embedded in conveyancing practice and the need to rely on customary relationships was receding.

Thirdly, there were commercial practices that could be taken to be established customs of the trade in question and could therefore affect both proprietary and contractual rights and duties. This mixed the attributes of the first two categories, since it took a practice of a communal group and applied it to the settlement of a particular dispute. Lord Mansfield was remembered in succeeding generations not least for his effective use of a regular jury of City of London merchants to determine whether a particular form of dealing had become so much a standard that he should adopt it into the common law. There had been examples before, as there would be afterwards, where judges expressed a conviction that they knew better, by insisting that they alone truly appreciated the 'artificial reason' of the law. For example, *Atwood* v. *Sellar*[98] tested whether in marine insurance the cost of damage to the ship should be borne by the shipowner alone (particular

---

[96]   For the assimilation of copyhold during the nineteenth century, see XIII, Pt 1, pp. 53–9.
[97]   For nineteenth-century developments of such rights, see XII, Pt 1, p. 61.
[98]   *Attwood* v. *Sellar* (1879) 4 QBD 342 and see (1880) 5 QBD(CA). See XII Pt 2, p. 715.

average—which was the law in many other states), or should be shared with cargo owners (general average). Although there was strong evidence that, for some 80 years, particular average had been the practice followed by average adjusters in England, the Queen's Bench, led by Cockburn CJ, held that the common law rule was and remained general average—an established principle that the practice of loss adjusters could not be taken to displace. Manisty J., however, dissented, treating the customary approach as so well established that nothing short of new legislation could justify changing it.[99]

As the Victorian world filled with economic adventure, the role that proven custom could play in determining mutual rights and obligations tended to give place to a looser invocation of reasonable expectations, for instance, in the interpretation of contracts whose express terms were incomplete. As we shall see, the basic rule became that terms would only be implied into contracts where they were necessary to give the agreement business efficacy. Nonetheless the scope for intervening was considerable. Likewise, the interpretation of written terms was a 'question of law' for the judge rather than the jury.[100] This was part of that shift from status to contract which Henry Maine identified as the characteristic of progressive societies. But at the same time it was a complex process in which the increasing use of standard terms, presumptions laid down by statute and the imposition of regulatory laws could make 'contract' something other than simply the enforcement of terms reached by adults who had been fully aware of consequences of their explicit agreement. Therein lay the continuing significance of Coke's characterization of the common law as an appreciation lodged in the collective understanding of its practitioners. This became the more so as litigation about transactions came to be the province of judges, sitting without a jury or requiring their juries to act within the compass of their direction, given in relatively precise terms.[101]

8. THE LANGUAGE OF JUDGMENT

In the three ensuing Chapters, attention shifts to aspects of the intellectual climate in the nineteenth century which had important impacts on the English legal system. First, come jurisprudential reflections on the idea of law itself, as different traditions of natural law came to be displaced in favour of positivistic conceptions of law as a phenomenon separate from general morality. Then, the

---

[99] Manisty, 352–3.

[100] A rule that had evolved when jurors were not necessarily literate.

[101] M. Lobban, 'The Strange Life of the English Civil Jury, 1837–1914', in J. Cairns and G. McLeod (eds), The Dearest Birthright of the People of England (Oxford, 2002), 173.

temporal moralities derived from religious doctrine are discussed for their ener-
gizing of behavioural control through the criminal law and other legal mechanisms. Thirdly, the emergence of political economy is explored, as a technique
for analysing the efficiency of government in a society increasingly dominated by
liberal capitalism. Here were three modes of thinking about legal issues, which
might be deployed in parallel towards a particular conclusion, or might set up
oppositional forces in the minds of individuals, quite as much as they did between
social groups with conflicting interests.

By way of transition to these subjects, it is useful to consider how far judges
used 'external' modes of thought in forming and justifying their own views.
Beyond the courtroom, certainly, Victorian judges and lawyers were willing
enough to express themselves generally on public affairs. They sat, for example,
in the House of Lords; they gave evidence to Royal Commissions; they participated in the programmes of the Law Amendment Society and the Social Science
Association; they wrote up their 'reminiscences'; and, in their judicial office at
Assizes, they addressed grand juries on the virtues and difficulties of the criminal law system and other issues of legal or national policy. Equally, there were
lower court judges and stipendiaries who took up political cudgels over social
difficulties which recurred before them: the activities of rapacious moneylenders
and implacable debt collectors, for example; the plight of deserted wives whom
their husbands would not support; the lot of children, abandoned or maltreated.
In these settings their opinions would draw on much the same streams of thought
as were shared among their social equals and were likely to reflect one of the
viewpoints current within the 'establishment' of their day. In each generation
there would be judges preternaturally fearful of change and others who tended
to welcome it—whether the arguments were over differences of class, economic
activity, gender, age, nationality, education, or any another matter.

However, something more complex and indirect occurred in court when as
advocates they were putting arguments for their clients, or as judges they were
stating conclusions upon the dispute before them, either in summing up to a jury
or as a judge sitting as decider. Decision-making in the superior courts in England,
as already said, held a central place in formal legal reasoning. The French concept that codes and other ordinances alone could constitute 'la loi' was as foreign
to English assumptions as was the American acceptance of a Constitution with
which all law, legislative or judicial, must comply.[102] Compared with the tersely
formulaic nature of reasons for judgment that became the tradition in France

---

[102] J-L. Goutal, 'Characteristics of Judicial Style in France, Britain and the USA' (1976) 24 *Am.
J. Comp. L.* 43–71, and the comment by F. H. Lawson, 'Comparative Judicial Style' (1977) 25 *Am. J.
Comp. L.* 364–71.

and other civilian countries, English decisions were discursive in style and carried the imprimatur of the particular judge. If he was speaking for his fellows,
it was mostly because they agreed with his view and his expression of it, not
because the court was expressing its 'composite' opinion, which hid measures of
disagreement among the members.[103] On any joint bench there was scope for dissenting judgment. These were practices that heightened the judiciary's sense of its
independence from other arms of government. Legal practitioners accordingly
sought to divine the political leanings, moral sensibilities, and attitudes to legal
doctrine which brought the judges to life as personalities, quirkish or eccentric
though they might be.[104]

A judicial decision in England typically provided a summary of the issues at
stake and of the facts, which were either being adjudicated upon (at trial), or
which were being taken from the record made at trial (on appeal). If counsel
had raised substantial arguments about the applicable law, which was the case
in most appeals, the judge or judges would be taken up with reviewing previous
case law, or with choosing between rival interpretations of statutory provisions
proposed by counsel; and it was in doing this that the judge might refer to policy
considerations or make policy assumptions that ranged outside the identification
and analysis of legal sources. But any such discussions were likely to be incidental
to the main object of the procedure, which was to apply the current law (to the
extent that it could be ascertained from statute or earlier case law) to the circumstances at issue between the two sides.

The English judicial system did not separate off 'questions of law' (including questions of statutory interpretation), so as to introduce a type of cassation
in which an appellate court ruled on a legal issue that was in some measure
detached from the particular litigation, and then returned its answer to another
court for application in the case. If an English appeal court found that the judge
below had misdirected the jury or had itself reached an unsustainable view of
the law or its application to the facts, it would either direct a new trial or would

---

[103] Lawson ('Judicial style'), emphasized the distinctiveness of oral statement in the practice of
English judges, and, related to that, the lack of any judicial conference as a regular mechanism in
the process of reaching decisions. Both were factors that in different ways derived from jury trial at
common law.

[104] Hedley considers that in the pre-Judicature Act period, the bar felt that they had a role in keeping judges in order; whereas subsequently they became more distanced in attitude: S. W. Hedley,
'Words, Words, Words: Making Sense of Legal Judgments, 1875–1940', in C. Stebbings (ed.), *Law
Reporting in England* (1995) 169–86. The shift may well have to do not only with the creation of a
novel appeal structure but also with the reduced centrality of circuit life and the fact that fewer
judges were coming to have had experience in politics as well as pursuing their career at the bar.

impose its own view of what should have been ordered in the first place.[105] It was through these mechanisms, related closely to the very cause to be determined, that the English conception of appellate process strove to satisfy the need for legal certainty. Within its own limits the judgments often commented on this crucial objective. Clarity about legal rules allows individuals to plan major aspects of their property, business, employment, and family affairs as well as their dealings with government. It reduces the prospect of disputes remaining unresolved until adjudicated by judgment from the bench or a jury's verdict. It is as important an attribute of a legal system as is the ability to trust the independence and the incorruptibility of its judges.

As a force precedent depended on the flow of litigation and that inevitably posed its own hazards. The lack of sympathy for wholescale codification of legal principle only added to the sense that common law was too much at the risk of hazard.[106] From such decisions as there were, the need to generalize gained a new urgency in the shifting sands of economic and social change. Thus arose the pressure to treat even single judgments of appellate courts as binding on the very same court.[107] Equally this attitude encouraged a categorical form of judicial pronouncement in preference to one that directly expressed a moral or political justification from the bench. For one thing, to seek to formulate judgments from basic principles courted counter-argument; individuals, enterprises, and governments might be encouraged to protest or to seek legislative amendment. Better to stand forth as lofty figures who could interpret the practices of the past so that any advances in the law appeared to accrete through a process of gradual evolution. There would be instances, of course, where judges felt impelled to speak out against economic and social results that would follow from deciding cases before them one way rather than another. We shall refer both to the evident reluctance of some early nineteenth-century courts to offer their remedies to those who invested in early forms of commercial corporations, just as, increasingly through the century, they would insist that the law should provide weapons against trade unionists who resorted to strikes and other attempts to coerce employers.[108] These, however, were a very small proportion of all the business of the courts.

---

[105] Once appeals by defendants convicted of criminal offences were regularized in 1907, an acquittal or variation of sentence was the normal order of the Court of Criminal Appeal.

[106] For the fate of codification projects in Britain, see above, pp. 55–59 and the reference there to further discussions elsewhere in the volumes.

[107] Above pp. 48–53. For the associated idea that 'the court is governed by the principle of law, and not by the hardship of the case', Ram (*Science of Judgment*, 227) offers a number of dicta; see also P. S. Atiyah, *From Principles to Pragmatism* (Oxford, 1978).

[108] See XII, Pt 3, pp. 617–18; XIII, Pt 3, Chs II, III.

Even by 1914, the number of superior court judges remained a small coterie, and their views were likely to have an influence on the choice of new appointees, which was for the most part made by the Lord Chancellor of the day.[109] There were political and personal differences between individual appointees, but because of their long experience in the competitive school of the bar, they had good cause to know what the proprieties were when giving judgment from the bench. Decisions by appeal courts were often expressed at greater length once the new system of judicature for civil litigation opened in 1876—a trend which would become more marked after 1918. The same did not occur in either France or the United States.[110] The English appellate jurisdictions were now composed of judges whose sole function was to consider legal issues arising in civil litigation.[111] Older ideas also carried forward: complex cases required greater expatiation, as did cases that called for a review of a whole train of case law or statute. With time the spread of professional advice led to more substantial preparation of litigation among the propertied, and this might well turn on the drafting of original documents, such as contracts, wills or company prospectuses, memoranda, and articles of association in which the advisers involved had set out detailed provisions which nonetheless did not resolve the difficulty that had later arisen.

There have been attempts at characterizing how nineteenth-century judges, taken as a group, used moral and economic propositions in judgment. A. V. Dicey, who engaged in intellectual history in order to express his horror of the 'collectivist' world gathering strength around him, believed that judge-made law tended to be out of step with the governing strain of socio-political attitudes of the period in which a precedent was adopted. The moral and political influences upon the higher judiciary, by his argument, constituted a cross-current to the dominant 'public opinion' of their day. In one passage he chose to 'lay it down as a rule that judge-made law has, owing to the training and age of our judges, tended at any given moment to represent the convictions of an earlier era than the ideas represented by parliamentary legislation'. Indeed he went so far as to claim that 'if a statute...is apt to reproduce the public opinion not so much of to-day as of yesterday, judge-made law occasionally represents the opinion of the day before yesterday'.[112]

---

[109] Below, Pt 4, pp. 962–4.

[110] Goutal, 'Judicial Style', 56–71, esp. 61–5; Hedley notes that the language used was simply more, not more convoluted: 'Words', at 169.

[111] For this new court, see below, Pt 3, paras. 798–804. The House of Lords acquired its first two Lords of Appeal in Ordinary, able to sit with Lord Chancellors and other peers who had attained high judicial office at this juncture.

[112] *Law and Public Opinion in England in the Nineteenth Century* (2nd edn, 1914), 367–70, esp. 369.

He proceeded by example, but the few instances on which he relied lack conviction because he was so casual in identifying what was the prevailing 'public opinion' at a given time, and what was the counter-opinion that the judges continued to pursue. To find a first instance, he had to resort to the eighteenth century, remarking on the judges' insistence that the cornering of markets for food remained a criminal offence at common law even when Parliament had repealed a line of old statutes covering much the same ground. Since this instance arose before our period, it will not be pursued here. Given, however, that the judges' reaction came under wartime conditions when there was sudden popular indignation about this type of trading conduct, can it really be said that the judges were out of touch with contemporary opinion? What they refused to accept was a contention supported by conclusions that political economists had impressed on Parliament in calmer times.[113] Dicey apparently thought the economists were right, the anxious poor wrong.

A second example taken up by Dicey is even more curious. It concerned the insistence of equity judges that an agent must account to his employer for any profit that he made out of the relationship which went undisclosed. The rules imposing this duty he described as

admitted by every conscientious man to be morally sound, but which are violated every day by tradesmen, merchants, and professional men, who make no scruple at giving or accepting secret commissions; and these rules Parliament hesitates or refuses to enforce by statute.

Was it that these judges learned their sense of propriety from an old respect for honesty that had passed away? The classic instance of the equitable duty arose in 1726.[114] As will be emphasized later, it was a major aim of the law of contracts, torts, and equitable responsibilities to oppose fraud, and by no means only in respect of this type of conduct.[115] Unscrupulous commercial conduct of many kinds was already a major reason for clarifying and strengthening legal principle, rather than leaving the outcome of litigation to the moral instincts of juries. The clashes of attitude were scarcely a matter of 'very old fogeydom' set against a 'watch-your-own-back' cynicism of youth.

---

[113] The higher courts would react to a similar upsurge against monopolists during the First World War: see W. R. Cornish, 'Legal Control over Cartels and Monopolization, 1870–1914. A Comparison', in N. Horn and J. Kocka (Göttingen, 1979), *Law and the Formation of the Big Enterprises in the 19th and early 20th Centuries*, 280–303, esp. 283–7, 297–9.

[114] *Keech* v. *Sandford* (1726) Sel. Cas. t. King 6; it was then extended to others who entered fiduciary relationships. For the historical evolution of this language, see L. S. Sealy, 'Fiduciary Relationships' [1962] *CLJ* 69–81; [1963] *CLJ* 119–40.

[115] See XII, Pt 2, Ch. IV.

A more intriguing investigation into the moral and social attitudes of judges has examined the style in which judgments are expressed. Some scholars of the judicial process, notably in the United States, have argued that, for a period during early industrialization, the judges as a cohort abandoned their formalistic reliance on precedent and statute as legal sources. Their judgments went instead to the economic and social justifications for their conclusions, their objective being to shift legal principles in favour of the efficient operation of free, and therefore competitive, markets of a flourishing capitalism.[116] Once, however, this legal goal had been achieved, they would revert to hierarchical forms of expression that disguised their 'real' motivation, which continued to be the shaping of the law to fit those same demands upon it.

Even assuming that this argument is sustainable for the United States,[117] could it equally hold true for the English? Researchers who looked for a similar tidal shift in the early and middle periods of industrialization could find little evidence for it.[118] The issue was tested by R. B. Ferguson who analysed four groups of cases reported on sale of goods law, for the periods 1801–5, 1881–90, 1897–1905, and 1971–5. In these decisions he could find no 'instrumentalist' shift towards judgments expressed in moral or economic terms, only to be later changed back. Certainly there was some tendency to dismiss arguments as 'absurd' or 'contrary to common sense', as distinct from having no basis in law. Since the cases concerned sales, judges might pronounce that business people would not countenance what was being proposed by one of the parties before the court. But ratiocinations of this rather rudimentary kind occurred in all the periods studied, just as they continue to be frequent in modern times.[119] The judges were making no contribution to the philosophy of mind as an analysis of how sensory

---

[116] Karl Llewellyn (*The Common Law Tradition* (Chicago, 1960); *Jurisprudence* (Chicago, 1962), 178–92) called the novel frankness a 'grand tradition' and others labelled it an 'instrumentalist approach': see esp. W. J. Chambliss and R. B. Seidman, *Law, Order and Power* (1971), 125–31; M. Horwitz, *The Transformation of American Law, 1780–1860* (1977), Chs 1, 8. Contributors to the debate then questioned each facet of this theory: see e.g. A. W. B. Simpson, 'The Horwitz Thesis and the History of Contracts' (1979) 46 *U Chicago Law Rev.* 632–79.

[117] For evidence that something of the phenomenon occurred in early colonial developments, see below, p. 248.

[118] Notably P. S. Atiyah, who concentrated instead on their extra-judicial statements: *The Rise and Fall of Freedom of Contract* (Oxford, 1979), 388–90, 660–1.

[119] R. B. Ferguson, 'The Horwitz Thesis and Common Law Discourse in England' (1983) 3 *OxJLSt* 34–58. See also his 'Legal Ideology and Commercial Interests' (1977) 4 *British J. L. & Soc.* 18, 35–8; and 'The Adjudication of Commercial Disputes and the Legal System in Modern England' (1980) 7 *British J. L. & Soc.* 141–57. For a demonstration that in 1979 the judicial House of Lords regularly justified their opinions by invoking this sort of loose pronouncement: W. T. Murphy and R. W. Rawlings, 'After the Ancien Regime: The Writing of Judgments in the House of Lords, 1979/80' (1981) 44 *MLR* 617–57, (1982) 45 *MLR* 36–61.

perceptions become knowledge through an accumulation of experience.[120] Rather their judgments have an interest because they illustrate such mental processes at work in deciding socially important disputes. Sir Paul Vinogradoff, great scholar of medieval law, would entitle his introduction to the historical jurisprudence of his day, *Common-Sense in Law*. The nub of his characterization was this:

> Although the details of legal rules are complicated and technical, the operations of the mind in the domain of law are based on common sense, and may be followed without difficulty and by persons of ordinary intelligence and education. Jurisprudence may be likened in this respect to political economy, which also is developed from simple general principles and yet requires a great deal of special knowledge when it comes to particulars.[121]

The relation between the simplicity of root perceptions and the complexity of the rules that they engendered encapsulates an ever-present tension—one which helps to explain what is referred to as the autonomous nature of legal reasoning. The law, as a skilled profession, built up its esoteric knowledge through language pregnant with implications. Judges, practitioners and jurists had to understand a whole network of interrelated ideas each with its own clusters of subordinate concepts. By the Edwardian years, those clusters often had multiple layers of rules, practices, and expectations that were both much altered and often more dense than had been the case a century before. Much of the judges' task in formulating governing rules consisted in arriving at expressions which delimited rights and responsibilities to an acceptable degree, taking account of definitions and analogies already there and at the same time measuring up to their rational or emotive notions of what was just. As will become apparent from the many instances of this process at work in the remaining parts of these three Volumes, it is very largely what individual judges said and did that matters. The difficulty with generalizations about the way in which 'the judiciary' thought is that quite frequently the author cites an individual instance or two without showing how far these were representative. As Steve Hedley has argued, even with the judgments of individual judges, to disentangle what is

---

[120] Cf. e.g. the impact of the Scottish school of 'common-sense' philosophers, from Thomas Reid to Sir William Hamilton, who would influence jurists such as James Lorimer: see below, pp. 123–4, 129, 262.

[121] P. Vinogradoff, *Common-Sense in Law* (New York, 1914): Russian émigré and Oxford Professor, he used the book to attack Austin's view of laws as orders from the sovereign: 'the common law, with which [jurists] have principally to deal, stands or falls with the admission of legal principles obtained not by command but by retrospective estimates of right and justice' (p. 15).

a personal reaction from discussion of the arguments presented in court by
either side about both the proven facts and the applicable law may soon enough
become an intractable task.[122]

[122] '"Superior Knowledge or Revelation": An Approach to Modern Legal History' (1989)
Anglo-Am. Law Rev. 179–200. His illustration is *Fearon* v. *Earl of Aylesford* (1884) 12 QBD 539; (1884)
14 QBD 792—the opening shot in the wrangles over the Countess's long-term adultery which led to
the *Aylesford Peerage* case (for which see XIII, p. 805).

IV

Theories of Law and Government

WRITING in 1905, A. V. Dicey famously defined the era from about 1825 to 1870 as a period in which legal and political thought was dominated by the ideas of Jeremy Bentham and his followers. Dicey was right to note the importance of Bentham, even if his characterization of Benthamism was open to debate.[1] Bentham's intellectual energy and range was enormous. He was a legal theorist, who challenged the woolly thinking of an earlier generation of common lawyers, and who sought to put jurisprudence on a new scientific foundation. By the 1820s, he was already recognized as the great philosopher of law reform, whose writings were to inspire repeated attempts to codify the English criminal law, and reform procedure. At the same time, he was a major political theorist, who developed a radical democratic theory, which found its fullest expression in his *Constitutional Code*. This work also embodied a third strand in Bentham's thought, his ideas on how to create modern, accountable bureaucratic structures of government.

The three strands of Bentham's thought formed part of an integrated whole. The *Constitutional Code* was the radical culmination of a lifetime's work. But if Bentham's own thinking was joined-up, his legacy turned out to be a highly fragmented one. For the different strands of his work were taken up by different people, and they took them in different and often unBenthamic directions. The first strand, that of jurisprudence, fell into the hands of John Austin, who gave the world—reluctantly and posthumously—a version of Bentham's analysis of sovereignty and other legal concepts, which filleted out both the politics and the criticism of the common law. By defining the 'province of jurisprudence' as excluding legislation, Austin's jurisprudence laid the foundations for formalist works, which sought to draw principles and doctrines only from the material of

---

[1] In equating Benthamism with 'individualism', and in claiming that it 'exactly answered to the immediate wants of the day' by working out plans 'which corresponded to the best ideas of the English middle class', Dicey was attributing to Bentham the dominant political ideology of his own youth, whose passing he so sorely regretted in 1905: but it said very little about Bentham himself. A. V. Dicey, *Lectures on the Relation between Law and Public Opinion in England during the Nineteenth Century* (1905), 170, 172.

the common law. Such an approach perhaps reached its apogee at Harvard, in the works of C. C. Langdell, but its assumptions (and its vocabulary of concepts) also inspired generations of treatise writers in England from the 1860s onwards. Common lawyers found further ammunition for the intellectual defence of their system against the encroachments of a potentially interventionist sovereign legislature in the work of Henry Maine, who questioned Austin's theory of sovereignty, and rooted legal ideas in evolutionary developments found in different kinds of community. By the end of the century, common law theorists such as Frederick Pollock—who came of age in 1866, before the passing of the second Reform Act, and who died in 1936, in an era of universal suffrage—felt content to write works which largely ignored legislation, and saw the common law develop as the reflection of the community's values as interpreted by judges. They used Benthamic analytical tools for a highly unBenthamic purpose.

The science of legislation—what law ought to be—was generally regarded by jurists as a separate science to be cultivated by others. But since a purely formal science of legal concepts did little to indicate how the law should be developed, debates in moral and political philosophy were inevitably relevant not only for legislators, but also for judges. In this area, the legacy of Bentham was rather more mixed. To begin with, his successors did not share Bentham's political radicalism. Universal suffrage would not be won thanks to the unanswerable power of genius, but thanks to political and social pressure on the part of the unenfranchised over the long term; and the Chartists and Suffragettes carried no banners bearing Bentham's name. Bentham's most important intellectual heirs, such as J. S. Mill, were rather more elitist, feeling that good government needed those with particular talents. Nor did utilitarian thought dominate. In the decades following Bentham's death, judges and politicians, who had a range of political and moral outlooks, were able to draw on a range of moral theories, both intuitionist and utilitarian. For our purposes, a significant outcome of the debates on moral philosophy was the development of a consensus that there existed axioms of morality shared by the community, which were largely the result of common sense. Philosophers disagreed profoundly on the foundations of these axioms, and how to resolve disputes between them: but they did not ask judges, or citizens, to decide every moral issue on the basis of a direct utilitarian calculation, or seek the voice of inner intuition.

The question of the influence of Bentham's ideas on the administrative state has been chewed over for decades by historians debating the nineteenth-century 'revolution in government'.[2] Clearly, some of Bentham's followers played

---

[2] Dicey's thesis was importantly debated in O. R. McDonagh's 'The Nineteenth-Century Revolution in Government: A Reappraisal' (1958) 1 *Hist. J.* 52–67; H. Parris, 'The Nineteenth-Century

central roles in developing areas of regulation, as Edwin Chadwick did in the area of poor law, sanitary, and police reform. At the same time, in many areas, key developments in regulation were driven by pragmatic responses by the state to emerging social problems, without any kind of administrative blueprint for guidance. Moreover, by the 1860s, if there was one intellectual colossus who most dominated the public sphere, it was Mill, whose most famous work, *On Liberty*, defended a view which held not only that the state should act in a *laissez-faire* way, but that public opinion should do so as well. Both as a moralist, and as a political economist, Mill defended the free-trade, non-interventionist state which Dicey celebrated so much. Indeed, Mill came close to defending 'negative' liberty as in itself being a value, something which was itself very unBenthamic.

As Dicey perceived, this mid-Victorian view of liberty was increasingly challenged after 1880. It was not just that the pressure of a new electorate was forcing governments to pass more interventionist legislation than they had before. At the same time, new schools of thinkers, influenced by idealist philosophy, theories of evolution, and new ideas on social utility, began to develop theories which saw the state much more in communitarian terms and which justified more state intervention.

1. THE THOUGHT OF JEREMY BENTHAM

In 1820, Jeremy Bentham was 72 years old. It was more than 40 years since he had written *An Introduction to the Principles of Morals and Legislation*. This work had a limited impact when it was published in 1789, but by the time of its second edition, in 1823, Bentham's name was far better known, and he had acquired a core of dedicated followers keen to propagate his views. Bentham's interest in codification dated from the 1770s and early 1780s,[3] when he had drafted not only the *Introduction*, but also a series of manuscripts on the nature of law and its classification.[4] Asking himself, as a young man, whether he had a genius for anything, he had 'fearfully and tremblingly' answered that his genius was for legislation.[5]

Revolution in Government: A Reappraisal Reappraised' (1960) 3 *Hist. J.* 17–37; and L. J. Hume, 'Jeremy Bentham and the Nineteenth-Century Revolution in Government' (1967) 10 *Hist. J.* 361–75.

[3] On codification, see Ch. III, pp. 55–61.

[4] Those on the nature of a law, seeking to develop the concluding chapter of the *Introduction*, were published in the twentieth century, under the title *Of Laws in General* (ed. H. L. A. Hart, 1970). A revised edition of this work, edited by Philip Schofield under the title *Of the Limits of the Penal Branch of Jurisprudence*, is forthcoming. A volume of other materials, entitled *The Elements of Critical Jurisprudence* is to be published (edited by Douglas Long) in the Collected Works of Jeremy Bentham.

[5] 'Memoirs of Bentham', in J. Bowring (ed.), *The Works of Jeremy Bentham*, 11 vols (Edinburgh, 1838–43), x, 27.

After the turn of the nineteenth century, some of his jurisprudential writings became known, thanks to Etienne Dumont's French editions of his writings, *Traités de législation civile et pénale*. In Bentham's view, these editions 'paved the way for acceptance more or less favourable' to codification.[6] He began to offer to draw up a code of laws for any state which would accept his offer; though he was unwilling to commence the task of drawing up any code until his offer had been accepted. Finally, in April 1822, Bentham received notification that his offer had been accepted by the Cortes of Portugal, and he was finally ready to begin the task.[7]

Bentham's commitment to the project of codification derived from his theories of law, originally developed in the 1770s, when he reacted to the vision of law found in Sir William Blackstone's *Commentaries on the Laws of England*.[8] In this work, Blackstone had sought to put English law into an institutional structure borrowed from continental civilian jurists. Like them, he opened the work with a theoretical discussion, which set out the natural law principles which were to be the key to the work. Blackstone's work was not only hugely influential in the late eighteenth century, but continued to be republished well into the nineteenth century.[9] Its prime use was in providing an elegant and comprehensive introduction to the rules of English law. But its popularity and influence—and the fact that it seemed to be the definitive statement of the common lawyer's theory of his law— also made it an ideal target for Bentham, who had himself attended the lectures on which the work was based.

Bentham felt that Blackstone had used meaningless language when describing the law. His definitions of law produced nothing but a 'labyrinth of confusion'.[10] From an early period, Bentham was concerned to use language precisely. He was particularly worried about the use of fictions by common lawyers to explain and justify their system. Two fictions which stood at the heart of

---

[6] Quoted in P. Schofield, *Utility and Democracy: The Political Thought of Jeremy Bentham* (Oxford, 2006), 240.

[7] His various offers are traced in Schofield, *Utility and Democracy*, 244–9.

[8] See esp. G. J. Postema, *Bentham and the Common Law Tradition* (Oxford, 1986); D. Lieberman, *The Province of Legislation Determined: Legal Theory in Eighteenth Century Britain* (Cambridge, 1989); M. Lobban, *The Common Law and English Jurisprudence, 1760–1850* (Oxford, 1991).

[9] For instance, J. F. Hargrave edited a 21st edition in 1844. Robert Maugham, secretary of the Incorporated Law Society also produced a series of texts on various areas of law, using readings from Blackstone and other writers. In 1841, H. J. Stephen produced his own *New Commentaries on the Laws of England*, partly based on Blackstone, which would be regularly reprinted into the twentieth century, and remain examination fodder for articled clerks.

[10] J. Bentham, *A Comment on the Commentaries and a Fragment on Government* (ed. J. H. Burns and H. L. A. Hart, 1977), 16. *A Fragment on Government* was first published anonymously in 1776. The broader material from which it was drawn, *Comment of the Commentaries*, was first published in 1928.

Blackstone's vision of the common law were the social contract—which was used to explain the grounds and extent of political obligation—and natural law, which was presented as the highest form of law, by which the validity of positive law was to be tested. At an early stage in his thinking,[11] Bentham distinguished between real and fictitious entities. Real entities were those which could be perceived by the senses (such as pleasure and pain, or an apple). Fictitious entities, by contrast, could not be perceived by the senses (such as 'power' or 'obligation', or 'ripeness'). They were the creation of language, or words which did not correspond to things. They could not be defined (as real ones could) *per genus et differentiam*.[12] They could only be defined by being related to real entities, though a process Bentham called paraphrasis.[13] This entailed taking a sentence containing a fictitious entity and expounding it in another sentence, using real entities. In this way, a fictitious entity could be expounded by showing its relationship with the real entities of which it was ultimately composed. A phrase including the 'fictitious' entity of 'duty' could thus be expounded by being transmuted into a sentence using the 'real' entity of having pain inflicted. If it was not possible to do this with a fictitious entity, Bentham argued, then it was a 'non-entity', utterly devoid of meaning.

In Bentham's view, when jurists such as Blackstone invoked concepts such as the law of nature, and when American and French revolutionaries used the language of natural rights, they were invoking 'non-entities' and talking nonsense. For Bentham, 'nothing that is at once intelligible and true can be collected from anything said by our Author [Blackstone] or by anyone else of the phantom of the Law of Nature'. It was nothing but a 'formidable non-entity'.[14] Instead of invoking reason or rights, the jurist could only make sense of the concept of law by relating it to the real entities of commands and punishments, which ended in pleasure or pain. A law, in Bentham's definition, was

an assemblage of signs declarative of a volition conceived or adopted by the *sovereign* in a state, concerning the conduct to be observed in a certain *case* by a certain person or class of persons, who in the case in question are or are supposed to be subject to his power: such volition trusting for its accomplishment to the expectation of certain events which it is intended such declaration should upon occasion be a means of bringing to pass, and the

[11] The following draws on Schofield, *Utility and Democracy*, Ch. 1. See also D. G. Long, *Bentham on Liberty: Jeremy Bentham's Idea of Liberty in relation to his Utilitarianism* (Toronto, 1977), Ch. 1.

[12] Words such as 'duty' and 'right' had no superior genus of which they were a species, but were 'each of them a head itself under which substances may be classed according as they have that property'. Quoted in Schofield, *Utility and Democracy*, 8.

[13] 'By the word paraphrasis may be designated that sort of exposition which may be afforded by transmuting into a proposition having for its subject some real entity, a proposition which has not for its subject any other than a fictitious entity'. Quoted in Schofield, *Utility and Democracy*, 25.

[14] Bentham, *Comment*, 17, 20.

prospect of which it is intended should act as a motive upon those whose conduct is in question.[15]

All legal concepts which had any function in a legal system—such as duty, obligation, power, or right—had to be similarly capable of being related to these real entities.[16]

Bentham's definition of law posed a challenge for the common lawyers. First, he undermined their claim that English law was rooted in the law of nature, or reason. By definition, he argued, the law of nature could not be a genuine law, since 'a real Law is a command, [...] an expression of the will of some person, and there is no person of whose will the Law of Nature can be said to be the expression'.[17] Natural law could not be seen as God's command: since no person had ever perceived God, Bentham argued that anyone claiming to have knowledge of God could only be speaking nonsense.[18] When people invoked natural law as a standard by which to judge conduct, they were therefore doing no more than expressing their own 'sentiments about what is right and what is wrong'.[19] Instead of appealing to positive standards, they appealed only to their own subjective sentiments. What other theorists referred to as the moral sense or common sense, Bentham called 'the principle of sympathy and antipathy'; and he argued that it was the negation of all principle, since it offered no 'external consideration, as a means of warranting and guiding the internal sentiments of approbation and disapprobation'.[20]

Secondly, Bentham argued that English law could not be seen as a body of customary law. Those customs which existed in the community—what he called customs *in pays*—could not themselves be regarded as laws, since they lacked the obligatory force which came from command and threatened punishment. They became obligatory only when 'legalized' by judges, announcing that punishment would be inflicted on the party who failed to conform to the custom.[21]

---

[15] Bentham, *Of Laws in General*, 1.

[16] See *ibid.*, 252. For a recent invaluable discussion of the relationship between Bentham's jurisprudence, his philosophy of language, and the principle of utility, see P. Schofield, 'Jeremy Bentham, the Principle of Utility, and Legal Positivism' (2003) 56 *Current Legal Problems* 1–40.

[17] Quoted in Lieberman, *Province*, 225.

[18] Schofield, *Utility and Democracy*, 21. See further, J. E. Crimmins, *Secular Utilitarianism: Social Science and the Critique of Religion in the Thought of Jeremy Bentham* (Oxford, 1990), 175.

[19] J. Bentham, *An Introduction to the Principles of Morals and Legislation* (ed. J. H. Burns and H. L. A. Hart, 1970), 27.

[20] Bentham, *Morals and Legislation*, 25.

[21] If people were compelled to follow the customary mode, 'it is by something further than that of which custom is made up [...] it is by the acts of others [...] as are Laws or out of which Law is made'. Bentham, *Comment*, 308. See also *Comment*, 183. See also Lieberman, *Province*, 223; M. Lobban, *A History of the Philosophy of Law in the Common Law World, 1600–1900*; vol. 8 of *A Treatise of Legal Philosophy and General Jurisprudence* (ed. E. Pattaro, Dordrecht, 2007), 163–5.

Instead of being a body of customs deriving their authority from the community, the common law was composed of a large series of individual judgments by different courts. It operated *ex post facto* and without the proper commands needed to guide conduct. It was a non-entity, something which did not exist.[22] 'As a system of general rules, the Common Law is a thing merely imaginary', Bentham wrote, 'and the particular commands, which are all that (in the way of command) there ever was of it that was real, can not every where, indeed can seldom, be produced.'[23] The real commands found in the common law system were only those given by the judges to the officials—such as the executioner—who were to carry out the sentence.[24] This was like the law a man made for his dog: he waited until the dog misbehaved, and then beat him for it. Like the dog, the public had to guess the rule which was to guide their conduct and to make their own predictions about how the judiciary might behave in future. Bentham admitted that people could infer rules from the common law, but these rules could never be authoritative, and were hence always unstable as guides.

It was Bentham's critique of the common law which led him, early in his career as a jurist, to turn his mind to codification. In his view, only written law enacted by a legislator could be properly regarded as law. Nor was it enough merely to recast common law in statutory form. Instead, a complete body of law—a *pannomion*—had to be created. Bentham wished to see a code enacted which would be comprehensive and complete. Nothing would be law which was not contained in the code. The new code would leave no *terrae incognitae*. Under the system he had in view, 'a man need but open the book in order to inform himself what the aspect borne by the law bears to every imaginable act that can come within the possible sphere of human agency'.[25] Bentham realized that in order to construct such a code, he had first to create a perfect plan of legislation. The groundwork for this was an analytical exercise, by which Bentham clarified the meaning of legal terms and concepts, showing on the way how the common lawyers had confused them.[26] In this process, he sought to uncover and explain the universal terms by which the particular jurisprudence of any country could be explained. In particular, he sought to explain the notion of 'a law'. In his view, any 'complete' law comprised both civil and penal aspects, the former giving an exposition of the rights and titles protected by the sanction enforced by the latter. Every complete law ended in an offence. In Bentham's system, the civil law would stand at the

---

[22] J. Bentham, *Legislator of the World: Writings on Codification, Law and Education* (ed. P. Schofield and J. Harris, Oxford, 1998), 123–4.

[23] Bentham, *Comment*, 119–20.

[24] Lieberman, *Province*, 233–4.

[25] Bentham, *Of Laws in General*, 346.

[26] See Lobban, *Common Law*, Ch. 6.

heart of the code, and would be designed to maximize the four sub-sets of utility: subsistence, abundance, security, and equality.[27] The penal law would give effect to the civil law. A complete code would set out all the rules of substantive law, removing any need for the judges to create law by judicial legislation.[28] But it would be backed by a new form of 'natural' procedure, which would allow judges to hear all relevant evidence, hearing cases in the same natural way in which a father heard disputes between family members. In the early part of his career, Bentham believed that his complete code of penal and civil law could be enacted by any ruler under any form of government: it was for this reason that he was prepared to offer his services to any ruler, including Catherine the Great of Russia.[29]

Bentham also set out the principles on which the code should be constructed. The key to both morals and legislation was the principle of utility. Bentham grounded his moral theory in his materialist philosophy: 'Nature has placed mankind under the governance of two sovereign masters, *pain* and *pleasure*. It is for them alone to point out what we ought to do, as well as to determine what we shall do.'[30] The only way in which one could make sense of morals was by using the standard of the real sensations of pleasure and pain: it was in the end a matter of fact. It was this morality which was to guide the legislator:

[T]he happiness of the individuals, of whom a community is composed, that is their pleasures and their security, is the end and the sole end which the legislator ought to have in view; the sole standard, in conformity to which each individual ought, as far as depends on the legislator, to be *made* to fashion his behaviour.[31]

In the second edition of the *Principles of Morals and Legislation*, Bentham restated the principle of utility as the 'greatest happiness principle', seeking the greatest happiness of the greatest number. Morality was therefore a matter of calculation, with the legislator having to take into account the numbers affected, and all the

[27] See P. J. Kelly, *Utilitarianism and Distributive Justice: Jeremy Bentham and the Civil Law* (Oxford, 1990).

[28] There has been some debate about whether Bentham wished to allow his judges room for direct-utilitarian adjudications (within a code of general principles), or whether they were to act mechanically. Bentham's view, developed in his early writings and put into institutional form in the *Constitutional Code*, was to allow judges to suggest changes to the code (while making provisional judgments) which the legislator could then adopt. See Lobban, *History*, 170. For the debate, see Postema, *Bentham and the Common Law Tradition*, 406 and J. R. Dinwiddy, 'Adjudication under Bentham's Pannomion' (1989) 1 *Utilitas* 283–9.

[29] Bentham's brother Samuel worked in Russia between 1780 and 1791, and was employed by Catherine the Great to establish a shipyard, where Samuel had the idea of a central inspection house, which was later developed by his brother in the *Panopticon*.

[30] Bentham, *Morals and Legislation*, 11.

[31] *Ibid.*, 34.

pleasures and pains which would be experienced by all parties if certain legislation were enacted. This could, in theory, entail sacrificing the interests of a minority for those of the majority.[32] This result might be rare, given the legislator's duty
to take into account factors such as the intensity, duration, and remoteness of
pleasures and pains, which might result in the minority's pains outweighing the
majority's pleasures. However, the result would always occur in the case of the
delinquent who was to be punished: it was not that his happiness (in offending)
counted for less, but 'that it is necessary to the greatest happiness of the greatest
number, that a portion of the happiness of that one be sacrificed'.[33]

   As Bentham developed his theory of law, he also developed a theory of
punishment,[34] in writings published in French by Dumont in 1811 as *La Théorie
des Peines*. In this work, Bentham developed a utilitarian theory of punishment,
premised on the notion that punishment was designed to reform the criminal
and to deter crime. Like Beccaria, Bentham favoured reforming criminal punishments and was an opponent of the death penalty. But unlike Beccaria, he did
not base his views on humanitarian concerns for the prisoner, but rather on
whether severe punishments were necessary. Dumont's edition was widely read,
and welcomed by criminal law reformers in England as a major contribution to
the debate.[35] To Bentham's chagrin, this contribution turned out to be more theoretical than practical. For by the time of Dumont's publication, Bentham had
spent many years failing to persuade the government to adopt his scheme to build
and run a Panopticon prison, and had become embittered by this failure.

   In the circular prison which was Bentham's Panopticon, the inspector would
be able to see everything which was happening in the prison, while the prisoners
themselves would be unable to see him. The Panopticon—that machine to 'grind
men good'—seemed to represent a strong, centralized supervisory state, where
liberty had no value, but the state was to force people to conform to the dictates
of utility:[36]

If it were possible to find a method of becoming master of everything which might happen to a certain number of men, to dispose of everything around them so as to produce on

---

   [32] J. R. Dinwiddy, *Bentham* (Oxford, 1989), 26–7.

   [33] Bentham, *Legislator of the World*, 250.

   [34] This was an indispensable corollary to his wider work: 'No punishment, no government; no
government, no political society.' Bentham, 'Principles of Penal Law', in Bowring (ed.), *Works of
Jeremy Bentham*, i, 528.

   [35] J. Semple, *Bentham's Prison: A Study of the Panopticon Penitentiary* (Oxford, 1993), 39–40. See
further, XIII, Pt 1, Ch. V.

   [36] See M. Foucault, *Discipline and Punish: The Birth of the Prison* (Harmondsworth, 1985);
M. Ignatieff, *A Just Measure of Pain: The Penitentiary in the Industrial Revolution, 1750–1850*
(Harmondsworth, 1989); R. Evans, *The Fabrication of Virtue: English Prison Architecture, 1750–1840*
(Cambridge, 1982).

them the desired impression, to make certain of their actions, of their connections, and of all the circumstances of their lives, so that nothing could escape, nor could oppose the desired effect, it cannot be doubted that a method of this kind would be a very powerful and a very useful instrument which governments might apply to various objects of the utmost importance.[37]

Bentham's writings on the Panopticon, as well as his writings on the Poor Laws, have been taken as central to his developing ideas on how to organize the administrative state.[38] A number of historians have seen Bentham's writings as providing a theoretical blueprint for the institutions of social control—prisons, workhouses, and asylums—which were built in early Victorian England.[39]

Bentham's failure to get his project off the ground helped radicalize him. He had long felt that the legislator was justified in setting rules of conduct, which would best promote utility, rather than leaving each individual to judge how to act for himself, since the legislator (as Philip Schofield has put it) was 'capable of taking a more correct view of the future consequences of actions'.[40] However, the failure of the Panopticon project helped to persuade him that the legislator could not simply be trusted to advance the greatest happiness of the greatest number, since he might have his own particular, sinister interest. The more Bentham reflected on this, the more he sought to develop a theory to resolve it. His turn to radicalism made him rethink his notion of sovereignty and the state. This also made him rethink his approach to codification, for he now saw codification of constitutional law as the key to the enterprise.

When Bentham had first outlined his ideas about law, he had rejected the fictions on which much English constitutional thought was based, but without making democratic accountability a central part of his theory. Following Hume, he ridiculed the notion that there had been an original contract of government. The Lockean idea that men entered into a contract to secure pre-existing rights was nonsense, for no rights could exist before governments were created. It was natural for men to seek the security offered by political society, since this best promoted their happiness; but there was no one moment when this had occurred. Rather, a habit of obedience to government had developed, echoing that found in the patriarchal family.[41] A state existed when 'a habit of submission to the punishments and

[37] J. Bentham, 'Panopticon, or Inspection House', in Bowring (ed.), *Works of Jeremy Bentham*, iv: 37–172, quoted in E. Halévy, *The Growth of Philosophic Radicalism*, trans. M. Morris (1972), 82–3. See also G. Himmelfarb, 'The Haunted House of Jeremy Bentham', in her *Victorian Minds* (1968), 32–81 at 75–7.

[38] On this, see L. J. Hume, *Bentham and Bureaucracy* (Cambridge, 1981).

[39] The most balanced and nuanced discussion is in Semple, *Bentham's Prison*, esp. Ch 6.

[40] Schofield, *Utility and Democracy*, 49.

[41] Lobban, *History*, 156–7.

obedience to the commands of persons of a certain description among them' had developed in a community.[42] Bentham dismissed the Lockean notion that the people had a right to resist when the ruler broke the contract: instead, he pointed out, people would disobey the ruler when they were persuaded of the utility of doing so; and if a sufficient number reached this 'juncture for resistance', then the ruler would be overthrown.[43] Bentham recognized, in his early writings, that there was a distinction between the commands of a legislator and the 'investitive' powers by which persons were appointed to offices,[44] but he did not in these early writings talk much about how rulers were constituted, save by the 'habit' of their subjects. But he did speak of constitutional laws *in principem*, whereby rulers imposed obligations on themselves. Such 'laws' could not be enforced by legal or political sanctions—since there was no one who could judge or coerce the sovereign—but they could be enforced by the moral sanction, the force of public opinion. If that sanction were ignored, then the ruler risked being overthrown.

By the time he drafted his *Constitutional Code* in the 1820s, Bentham had revised his theory of sovereignty, thanks to his discovery of the power of sinister interests. A sinister interest was one which was in opposition to the interest of the whole community. Various powerful groups were prone to advance their own sinister interests at the expense of the community. Prime among them— indeed the first to be identified as such by Bentham—were the lawyers, whose sinister interest was to promote expense and delay in the law. By 1810, Bentham came to realize that rulers were also prone to follow their sinister interests, rather than the general interest, and began to argue for radical parliamentary reform. In his *Constitutional Code*, Bentham therefore sought to devise a structure which would prevent the development of sinister interests, to ensure that the interest of the rulers—and all officials in the system of government—coincided with the general interest, which they would feel it was their own interest to advance.

Where previously he had spoken of the 'sovereign' as the ruler whose commands were obeyed, he now stated that '[t]he sovereignty is in *the people*'. That sovereignty was exercised 'by the exercise of the Constitutive authority',[45] by which the people invested the officials in the state with their powers. His reformulation reflected his later concern to create a system which promoted the security of the people, and thereby the greatest happiness. This could only be done if the 'possessors of efficient power'—the rulers—were dependent on 'the originative

[42] Quoted in Schofield, *Utility and Democracy*, 225.

[43] J. Bentham, *Fragment*, 483–4.

[44] Schofield, *Utility and Democracy*, 227

[45] J. Bentham, *Constitutional Code*, vol. 1 (ed. F. Rosen and J. H. Burns, Oxford, 1983), 25.

power of the body of the people'.[46] Nonetheless, the legislature so elected was to be omnicompetent and unlimited in its powers to make laws. It was not to be judged by any other power in the state. Bentham's reformulation was in effect a refinement of his earlier ideas on the relationship between the sovereign and subject, rather than representing a different theory of law from that espoused in his earlier writings.[47] However, the theory of the *Constitutional Code* was a radical one: it required a representative democracy, and one in which the entire machinery of government would be transparent, and under the ever watchful eye of the Public Opinion Tribunal. Bentham's constitution would not be policed by a judiciary, with any power of judicial review. Rather, it was to be policed by the people, who invested the officials with their power and who would be able to see much more clearly under the new system of accountability how and when officials went wrong.

Bentham's codification project had moved from being a theory of law and law reform to become a wider theory of government and how to control it. 'In place of limits', Bentham noted, the legislature 'has checks [...], securities, provided for good conduct on the part of the several members, individually operated upon.'[48] Much of Bentham's writings in the 1820s entailed developing a set of securities against misrule, an architecture of the state which would prevent sinister interests emerging in its fabric. The aim of constitutional law was to make the interests of the rulers and the ruled coincide. This entailed maximizing the aptitude of officials, and minimizing the expense of government. Officials would be accountable for their actions, both through lines of accountability to those who appointed them, and through publicity. For Bentham, only a fully democratic system could reconcile the tension between the job of the legislator in promoting the greatest happiness of the greatest number, and his belief that every individual was the best judge of his own pleasures and pains.

After his death in 1832, Bentham was dissected in the Webb Street school of anatomy, after an address had been given to all his fellow-disciples by the surgeon Thomas Southwood Smith. Bentham had wanted his body dissected for the sake of utility—to further medical knowledge—and his body, or Auto-Icon, was subsequently housed in University College London. But Bentham and his memory were not universally venerated, as Thomas Carlyle's famous attacks demonstrated. Nor did his project for radical political reform find a receptive audience. Although a group of Philosophic Radicals continued to spread the message in

---

[46] J. Bentham, *Rights, Representation and Reform: Nonsense upon Stilts and other Writings on the French Revolution* (ed. P. Schofield, C. Pease-Watkin, and C. Blamires, Oxford, 2002), 409.

[47] H. L. A. Hart, *Essays on Bentham: Jurisprudence and Political Theory* (Oxford, 1982), 228; Lobban, *History*, 160.

[48] Bentham, *Constitutional Code*, i, 42.

the 1830s, their importance and influence should not be exaggerated.[49] Moreover, these followers were in practice far less radical than the master. The voices calling for the most radical reform remained an extra-parliamentary movement, who would in the decade after Bentham's death call for universal adult male suffrage and the secret ballot in the Chartist movement. But their vision of political reform owed nothing to Bentham, having its roots in the political radicalism of Thomas Paine and the London Corresponding Society of the 1790s, and in the early socialism of the Owenites.[50]

If Bentham's influence on the pace of political reform was small in the decades after his death, it was much greater when it came to administrative reform and law reform. Men who had come under Bentham's influence, such as Chadwick and Southwood Smith, would play important parts in numerous areas of government growth in the 1830s and 1840s.[51] Bentham's work, which came to a wider audience when John Bowring produced an 11-volume edition of his writings (between 1838 and 1843), also exerted great influence in spurring law reform.[52] Although Blackstone's *Commentaries* continued to be republished, few by the 1830s shared his apparent complacency that all was well with the common law. Bentham's attacks on Blackstone's natural law theory had hit their target. Nonetheless, Bentham's projects remained far too radical for most English stomachs, and his influence was indirect. In law reform, it would be the reformist Henry Brougham and his Law Amendment Society who would have most influence. In legal theory, it was John Austin who would present a more acceptable, politically neutered, form of the jurisprudence developed by Bentham.

2. JOHN AUSTIN'S REFORMULATION OF THE PROVINCE OF JURISPRUDENCE

In 1819, John Austin wrote to Bentham that he had 'no violent desire for any other object than that of disseminating your doctrines'.[53] The doctrines he had in mind were not Bentham's ideas on political reform, or democratic accountability.

---

[49] On the movement, see W. Thomas, *The Philosophic Radicals: Nine Studies in Theory and Practice, 1817–1841* (Oxford, 1979) and J. Hamburger, *Intellectuals in Politics: John Stuart Mill and the Philosophic Radicals* (New Haven, 1965).

[50] On the ideology of Chartism, see esp. G. Stedman Jones, 'Rethinking Chartism', in his *Languages of Class: Studies in English Working Class History, 1832–1982* (Cambridge, 1983). On Owenite socialism, see G. Claeys, *Citizens and Saints: Politics and Anti-Politics in Early British Socialism* (Cambridge, 1989).

[51] This is explored further below, Pt 1, Ch. VI.

[52] See also S. E. Finer, 'The Transmission of Benthamite Ideas, 1820–59', in G. Sutherland (ed.), *Studies in the Growth of Nineteenth-Century Government* (1972), 11–32.

[53] Quoted in W. E. Rumble, *The Thought of John Austin: Jurisprudence, Colonial Reform and the British Constitution* (1985), 18. On Austin, see also W. E. Rumble, *Doing Austin Justice: The Reception*

They were rather his ideas about the nature of law and legal reasoning. Dumont's rescensions aside, Bentham's own jurisprudential works were not published in the nineteenth century, and it was Austin who acquired a reputation as the most important English writer on jurisprudence in the nineteenth century. Austin's politics were significantly different from Bentham's. Whereas Bentham died in 1832 a democrat, whose dream was radically to recast the constitution, Austin died in 1859 a conservative, whose last work—A Plea for the Constitution—opposed any kind of political reform, and praised the 'political aristocracy' which had the time and talent to rule. Although Austin's conservatism grew over the long and unproductive years before his death, his disagreement with Bentham's radicalism dated from the late 1820s.[54]

Austin popularized a version of the jurisprudence Bentham had developed in the 1770s and 1780s—before his mind turned to constitutional law—and used it to explain the uncodified common law. In contrast to the hyper-productive Bentham, who never stopped writing all his life, Austin's oeuvre consisted of an incomplete set of Lectures on Jurisprudence, delivered at the University of London. Some of these lectures were published as The Province of Jurisprudence Determined in 1832, and the rest appeared posthumously in 1863 in an edition produced by his vivacious wife. Bentham was not the only influence on this work. While preparing his lectures, Austin spent six months in Bonn, in 1827–8, where he came to admire the Roman law scholarship of the German Pandectists, though without finding the Kantian philosophy on which it was based congenial. The lectures were delivered between 1829 and 1833, to audiences which were very small, but select, for they included John Stuart Mill, Edwin Chadwick, and John Romilly.

The Province laid out the bases of Austin's positivist theory of law. According to his definition, every law 'properly so called' was a command issued by a determinate rational being, which was backed by the threat of a sanction which that being had the power to exert.[55] The subject matter of jurisprudence was the positive laws 'set by a sovereign person, or a sovereign body of persons, to a member or members of the independent political society wherein that person or body is sovereign or supreme'.[56] Just as Bentham had sought to distinguish between the task of the expositor and the censor, whereby the former expounded what the law was, and the latter evaluated and criticized it, so Austin distinguished the sphere of law and morals. The task of jurisprudence was to consider the positive laws

---

of Austin's Philosophy of Law in Nineteenth-Century England (2005); W. L. Morison, John Austin (1982).

[54] Rumble, The Thought of John Austin, 25.

[55] Austin, Lectures on Jurisprudence, or the Philosophy of Positive Law, 2 vols (4th edn, ed. R. Campbell, 1873), 91–4.

[56] Ibid., 181.

'without regard to their goodness or badness'.[57] The task of exploring the relation of positive law and morals was to be left to the science of legislation. The jurist was not to confuse the law as it was, with the law as it ought to be.

Unlike Bentham, the Unitarian Austin felt that the laws of God were properly called laws, since they derived from a superior being with power to punish in the afterlife.[58] However, he agreed that the laws which the jurist was to study were the positive laws enacted and enforced by the rulers in a political society. Such positive law did not include rules found in custom or international law: since they were enforced by indeterminate sanctions imposed by indeterminate bodies, they were defined as 'positive morality'.[59] Austin's theory of the state and sovereignty echoed that of the early Bentham. The sovereign, who issued commands, was legally illimitable in any state, since he was the source of law. His sovereign nature was constituted by the fact that the bulk of any given society gave him habitual obedience, while he obeyed no superior himself.[60] Although Austin did not spend much time developing the notion, he agreed with the early Bentham that the sovereign could be limited by the moral sanction, if the ruler feared arousing the resistance of subjects whose expectations had been thwarted.[61] But unlike Bentham, he had little interest in developing a constitutional structure by which rulers could be held to account. For Austin's theory, it made no difference whether the sovereign was an absolute monarch, a democracy, or a mixed constitution, even though there might be difficulties in exactly locating the sovereign in the latter case.

Instead of being an active legislator, Austin's sovereign was the formal source of all positive law. He did not share Bentham's abhorrence of judicial lawmaking, regarding it as 'highly beneficial and even absolutely necessary'.[62] Although he wanted to see English law codified—and played an important (if brief) role on the Criminal Law Commission of the 1830s—he did not share Bentham's ambition to create a *pannomion* in which the role of the judge would be severely curtailed. Instead, his lectures offered a theory and justification of judicial law-making, which was congenial to a generation of jurists faced with the problem of developing principles of private law untouched by Parliament. In Austin's view, the

---

[57] *Ibid.*, 176–7.

[58] According to L. and J. Hamburger, *Troubled Lives: John and Sarah Austin* (Toronto, 1985), 15, Austin 'for a time became an unbeliever', under Bentham's influence. The reasoning of the *Province* suggests he had recovered his faith.

[59] On international law, see below, Pt 1, Ch. VIII.

[60] Austin, *Lectures*, 226.

[61] Lobban, *History*, 177–8.

[62] Austin, *Lectures*, 224n.

judges were not 'oracles of the law', finding the law in reason or in the customs of the community, as Blackstone had seen them. Rather,

[t]he portion of the sovereign power which lies at [the judge's] disposition is merely delegated. The rules which he makes derive their legal force from authority given by the state: an authority which the state may confer expressly, but which it commonly imparts in the way of acquiescence.[63]

The common law was a body of judge-made law. A judge developing the law could draw from sources which did not have the force of law within the system (such as custom or divine law), or simply use 'his own views of what law ought to be (be the standard which he assumes, general utility or any other)'.[64] But the usual way judges operated, he argued, was to extend existing rules by 'consequence and analogy'. These rules were capable of being found in a line of precedents, teased out of their *rationes decidendi*. While Austin had some difficulties in explaining how sovereign commands could be extracted from a developing case law composed of individual judgments, his was the most penetrating analysis of the common law method of judicial law-making yet attempted.[65]

Although Austin claimed not to be dealing with the science of legislation, three of the six lectures published as the *Province* were devoted to discussing the principle of utility. Austin's concern in these lectures was particularly to reject the notion that a moral sense existed, by which right and wrong could be known. His denial of the existence of a moral sense was therefore part of his argument demonstrating the separation of law and morals. In these lectures, Austin offered a significantly different version of utilitarianism from Bentham's. Following William Paley, he treated utility as an index to the divine will, rather than being itself the source of any moral obligation. The law of God was to be inferred from observing the tendency of general actions. This generated a form of rule-utilitarianism, which entailed making conduct 'conform to *rules* inferred from the tendencies of actions' rather than determining how to act 'by a direct resort to the principle of general utility'.[66] In Austin's view, the only occasion for a direct resort to utility was in cases of disobedience to a government: for while it was a general rule dictated by utility that governments be obeyed, on occasion, the mischief of obedience might be outweighed by the utility of rebellion.

Austin's rule-utilitarianism was premised on the view that it was far too difficult for the mass of people to infer the divine will from the tendency of an infinite variety

---

[63] *Ibid.*, 104.

[64] *Ibid.*, 660.

[65] Rumble, *Thought of John Austin*, 110; Lobban, *History*, 180–1; W.L. Morison, 'Some Myth about Positivism' (1958) 8 *Yale LJ* 212–33.

[66] Austin, *Lectures*, 116.

of acts. Discovering the best moral solution was a product of experience and expertise. Such correct and good moral rules as existed had been formed not by the reasoning of individual people, but from the observation and experience of generations
of people. Insofar as current rules stood in need of correction and reformation, this
was to be the task of experts in a position to study the principle of utility and observe
the tendencies of action. Once the experts had obtained this knowledge, the leading
principles could be taught to the poor and uneducated, who would no more be able
to master the details than they could master the complexities of political economy.
Austin's rule-utilitarianism thus served to justify existing moral positions, while
giving a role to experts to develop the moral rules to be followed by society. No
doubt, for Austin, the judges would have been among that cadre.

However congenial this brand of utilitarianism might have been for the judiciary, many later commentators felt that Austin had violated his own strict separation of law and morality by even talking of utility. Instead, his fame was to rest
primarily on his analysis of legal concepts. Austin defined general jurisprudence
as the study of principles, notions, and distinctions which were common to every
system of law. These principles, 'abstracted from positive systems', were 'necessary' notions, insofar as 'we cannot imagine coherently a system of law (or a system evolved in a refined community), without considering them as constituent
parts of it'.[67] They included the notions of duty and right, person and thing, act,
forbearance, and omission. Austin spent much time drawing distinctions—such
as that between will, motive, intention, and negligence—which would prove of
great use to lawyers seeking to develop legal rules in an age when the jury's role
was being diminished.

By getting the structure of concepts right, Austin intended to provide the conceptual materials for a systematic treatment of the content of the common law as
a whole. This required him to relate his concepts to his fundamental positivist
definition of what a law was. Like Bentham, Austin rejected the Lockean language of natural or absolute rights which Blackstone had used. 'I *have* no right',
Austin noted, 'independently of the injunction or prohibition which declares that
some given act, forbearance or omission, would be a violation of my right.'[68] This
meant that Austin took a very Hobbesian view of liberty:[69]

Political or civil liberty is properly the mere liberty from legal obligation left by a
Government to its own subjects, which liberty the Government may or may not couple
with a legal right to it … If not, then the right to liberty is any right to do or forbear,
which is not comprehended by any other specified right whatever.[70]

[67] *Ibid.*, 1108.
[68] *Ibid.*, 794.
[69] See Q. Skinner, *Hobbes and Republican Liberty* (Cambridge, 2008).
[70] Austin, *Lectures*, 816–17.

It also meant that all the rights protected by the law of obligations—rights to property, person, and reputation—derived from duties imposed on others by the sovereign.

In Austin's view, rights were generated indirectly, through duties imposed by the sovereign on others. But this did not mean that one could not *describe* rights without reference to commands or sanctions. Austin distinguished between 'primary' rights—'which exist *in* and *per se*: which are, as it were, the ends for which the law exists'—and secondary rights, which gave remedies, and which arose out of injuries or wrongs. Strictly speaking, the only laws which were *necessary* in any legal system were those which gave remedies, or imposed punishments,[71] for they were the 'means or instruments for making the primary available'.[72] Often, indeed, the 'primary' right was not defined or described at all, but was implied in the 'secondary' right which gave redress. But sometimes, these primary rights were more complex, and needed to be set out separately. For instance, if it were true theoretically that any person's property rights were merely the product of an infinity of duties of non-interference imposed on others, the law was rendered more comprehensible if it set out the titles to property by which rights were conferred and extinguished, and duties imposed. In Austin's view, the broad content of a right could be described and set out, as well as the means of acquiring it.

This analysis had echoes of Bentham's division between the civil and penal parts of a law. However, unlike Bentham, his aim was not to create a complete code of laws enacted by legislation, but to explain the content of the common law. The more he focused on the rights and remedies of the common law, the more the notion of command slipped out of view. Instead of the commands of the sovereign, the rights of the subject came to take the prime place. Even the remedies identified by Austin were related more to the rights they protected than to the commands of the sovereign. Thus, the 'secondary' rights relating to civil injuries were classified by reference to the rights which were infringed.[73] Austin divided the law of civil injuries into two parts. The first dealt with infringements of rights against the whole world (dealing with torts); the second with infringements of rights against particular people (dealing with contracts). Torts were further divided into rights of vindication, rights of satisfaction, and rights of prevention.[74] The first of these concerned actions such as those to recover possession of a house, or to abate a nuisance. The second considered when the right

---

[71] 'For the remedy or punishment implies a foregone injury, and a foregone injury implies that a primary right or duty has been violated. And, further, the primary right or duty owes its existence as such to the injunction or prohibition of certain acts, and to the remedy or punishment to be applied in the event of disobedience': Austin, *Lectures*, 794.

[72] *Ibid.*, 789.

[73] *Ibid.*, 63.

[74] *Ibid.*, 64–5.

was 'virtually annihilated' and pecuniary compensation was required. The third dealt with injunctive relief. This was hardly a taxonomy of duties. It was merely an analytical relation of breaches back to the rights they protected. There was even some circularity here. Primary rights were largely defined by the secondary rights; but these secondary rights themselves only made sense if one knew what primary rights they protected. Later jurists continued to worry about Austin's structure, and questioned whether it was correct to begin with rights, rather than duties. But the common lawyers who queried his structure did not seek to relate the 'duties' they had in mind to sovereign commands.[75]

Austin's analytical jurisprudence was therefore helpful for the common lawyers—for it gave them new definitions and distinctions—and it did not challenge the common law way of thinking about the substance of law in the way Bentham did. Published in the year of the Great Reform Act, Austin's jurisprudence neatly provided its readers with what they wanted to hear. On the one hand, his Hobbesian stress on the power of the state, locating sovereignty in the Crown-in-Parliament, offered a perfect constitutional theory for a new age of legislative activism. It is not insignificant that that great champion of parliamentary sovereignty, A. V. Dicey, was an admirer of Austin. In Dicey's constitution, judges would be duly deferential to their sovereign masters. On the other hand, Austin had also drawn the political sting of Bentham's attack on the common law, defending the standing of the judiciary, and portraying their task as a technical one. The common law was to be seen as a system of authoritative rules derived from case law which provided remedies for wrongs not given prior definition by the sovereign.

3. INTUITIONISTS AND UTILITARIANS, 1820–75

Although Dicey felt confident in characterizing the period after 1825 as the era of 'Benthamism', contemporaries were less convinced of the influence of the Philosophic Radicals.[76] In his *Autobiography*, J. S. Mill noted that 'they had little

---

[75] Austin's classifications were influenced by his focus on civil law, and he was therefore criticized for being able to find no adequate place for duties (as in criminal law) which 'do not correspond to any rights'. Mill therefore criticized Austin's structure: J. S. Mill, 'Austin on Jurisprudence', in *Essays on Equality, Law and Education* in J. M. Robson and S. Collini (eds), *Collected Works of John Stuart Mill* (Toronto, 1984), 167–205, at 200. Others echoed Mill's criticism of Austin's arrangement. See Pollock's typically unsophisticated bluff approach (taking the view that it was better to commence with duties) in *First Book of Jurisprudence* (1896), 70 *et seq.*

[76] This group which included William Molesworth (the editor of Hobbes's collected works), J. R. Roebuck and George Grote, as well as those who had attended Austin's lectures, Chadwick and Romilly.

enterprise, little activity' in Parliament in the 1830s.[77] As late as 1861, he told a French correspondent that the principle of utility remained 'very unpopular' in England, where 'the school of Bentham has always been regarded (I say it with regret) as an insignificant minority'.[78] While Mill may have exaggerated this—for the influence of men like Chadwick on administrative reform was not inconsiderable—it is clear that the utilitarians did not have all of the argument in the 1830s. Indeed, Bentham's mechanical utilitarianism was famously derided by Carlyle, who poked fun at 'Bentham with his *Mills* grinding thee out morality'.[79]

Bentham's moral theory was attacked by a school of conservative thinkers, whose intellectual inspiration was Samuel Taylor Coleridge. Coleridge was appalled that the 'guess-work of general consequences' should be 'substituted for moral and political philosophy'.[80] For him, true morality had to be rooted in religion. He rejected the empiricism of the utilitarians, and was strongly influenced by German idealist philosophy, much of which he had read in his youth. Like Kant, he felt that not all knowledge was derived from experience. Instead, knowledge was in part *a priori*, with the mind putting order into the data perceived by the senses, through ideas which were not derived from experience. He therefore distinguished between the 'understanding', which perceived and organized sensory data, and 'reason', which perceived the intuitional and abstract categories that allowed thinkers to perceive the underlying reality.

For Coleridge, moral knowledge derived from intuition, rather than from experience. Unlike beasts, humans were not driven by mere appetites, but had a will, which was the source of their moral sense, or the knowledge of right and wrong. Intuitive ideas of good and evil could be discovered by reason guided by the will. Such ideas were above understanding, since they were not to be empirically proved, and they took the form of conscience.[81] Coleridge's moral intuitions had a transcendental independence, beyond the conception of subjects. This 'knowledge, or sense, may very well exist, aye, and powerfully influence a man's thoughts and actions, without his being distinctly conscious of the same, much more without his being competent to express it in definite words'.[82] Coleridge's

---

[77] Mill, *Autobiography*, 202.

[78] Quoted in J. B. Schneewind, *Sidgwick's Ethics and Victorian Moral Philosophy* (Oxford, 1977), 174. As Schneewind shows, Mill's *Utilitarianism* turned this school into what the Idealist F. H. Bradley would in 1876 call 'our most fashionable philosophy'.

[79] T. Carlyle, *Sartor Resartus* (ed. R. Tarr, Berkeley and Los Angeles, 2000), 293, quoted in F. Rosen, *Classical Utilitarianism from Hume to Mill* (2003), 169.

[80] S. T. Coleridge, *On the Constitution of Church and State* (3rd edn, ed. H. N. Coleridge, 1839), 70.

[81] S. T. Coleridge, *Aids to Reflection* (4th edn, ed. H. N. Coleridge, 1839), 99–100. On the relationship between law and religion, see below, Pt 1, Ch. V.

[82] Coleridge, *Constitution of Church and State*, 12.

moral theory was also teleological. Man was 'the creature destined to move progressively towards that divine idea which we have learnt to contemplate as the final cause of all creation, and the centre in which all its lines converge'.[83]

For Coleridge, the institutions of a state were living forms, also guided by the teleological idea of its 'ultimate aim'.[84] A constitution, he argued, is 'an idea arising out of the idea of State'. Our whole history demonstrated the continued influence of such an idea, and 'the result has been a progressive, though not always a direct or equable, advance in the realization of the idea'. The science of history, he noted, 'studied in the light of philosophy, as the great drama of an ever unfolding Providence, [...] infuses hope and reverential thoughts of man and his destination'.[85] In contrast to Bentham, he sought to develop a constitutional theory which could define and preserve the existing institutions. Coleridge's idealistic interpretation of English history saw the development of the state as a balance of the permanent and the progressive.[86] The former element was represented by landed property, the latter by the commercial classes: 'in the first estate the permanency of the nation was provided for; and in the second estate its progressiveness and personal freedom'. But the moral health of the nation required the existence of a third estate, the clerisy or national church, whose task was 'to secure and improve that civilization, without which the nation could be neither permanent nor progressive'.[87]

Coleridge's moral philosophy was anything but democratic, for he argued that 'it is the privilege of the few to possess an idea'.[88] The poor, brutalized by their poverty, lacked the capacity for it, and so had to be guided by the elite. In his later work, he therefore advocated the establishment of a cultural elite, or 'clerisy', which would guide the community. They would be 'at the fountain heads of the humanities, in cultivating and enlarging the knowledge already possessed and in watching over the interests of the physical and moral science'. They would provide a source of ethical guidance for the community. The clerisy 'comprehended the learned of all denominations, [...] all the so-called liberal arts and sciences, the possession and application of which constitute the civilization of a country, as well as the theological'. All these, who directed their studies to the 'nobler

---

[83] Quoted in C. Parker, *The English Idea of History from Coleridge to Collingwood* (Aldershot, 2000), 25.

[84] See P. Edwards, *The Statesman's Science: History, Nature and Law in the Political Thought of Samuel Taylor Coleridge* (New York, 2004), 38.

[85] Coleridge, *Constitution of Church and State*, 18–19, 34.

[86] 'The line of evolution, however sinuous, has still tended to this point, sometimes with, sometimes without, not seldom, perhaps, against the intention of individual actors, but always as if a power, greater and better than the men themselves, had intended it for them': Coleridge, *Constitution of Church and State*, 33.

[87] *Ibid.*, 46–7. See also Edwards, *The Statesman's Science*, 184–5.

[88] Coleridge, *Constitution of Church and State*, 12.

character of our nature', would be 'led by the supernatural in themselves to the contemplation of a power which is likewise superhuman'.[89]

Coleridge was the great Romantic philosopher of conservatism in the decades around Bentham's death. He also provided intellectual inspiration for a group of theologians and moralists in Cambridge in the 1830s, who adopted a similar idealist position, openly critical of empiricism and utilitarianism. These thinkers stressed the development of moral knowledge over time, as human insights into the workings of divine providence developed. Much of the debate turned on the issue of whether scientific research had to be premised on the theological insights. In these debates, the Coleridgean F. D. Maurice (later one of the protagonists of Christian Socialism), argued that science demanded God as its foundation, since knowledge of God was essential for all other knowledge. Just as God was essential for any understanding of the physical world, so conscience, which transmitted to humans the law of God, was the rule of morality.[90]

The most important intuitionist philosophy developed at this time was William Whewell's.[91] Whewell agreed with the Coleridgean view that our knowledge developed historically on the basis of intuitions. Two elements were involved in every act of knowledge: ideas and perceptions. In each branch of scientific inquiry, fundamental ideas were supplied by the mind itself, independently of experience. These ideas formed the structure which made sense of the data obtained by experience and observation. While the ideas, or intuitions, were timeless, the human capacity to grasp them developed over time with scientific knowledge. Ideas provided the categories with which to make sense of the data obtained by induction; but in turn, the concepts were refined and clarified in the light of data obtained by induction. Whewell also developed an intuitionist theory of morals. He held that moral knowledge was acquired through the conscience, and that moral rules were self-evident necessary truths. Moral knowledge was progressive, in the same manner as scientific knowledge. Just as there were fundamental ideas in the sciences—such as space—which were refined over time, so there were fundamental ideas in morals—benevolence, justice, truth—which became better understood over time. These innate ideas helped us to make sense of the world, and structure our knowledge. The intuitionists' attack on utilitarianism is significant, for it articulated a powerful counter-view as to the basis of moral obligation, which appealed to many conservatives.[92]

[89] *Ibid.*, 46–9.

[90] See Schneewind, *Sidgwick's Ethics*, 99–101. On Maurice and Christian Socialism, see below, Pt 1, Ch. VI, pp. 189–90.

[91] On Whewell, see R. Yeo, *Defining Science: William Whewell, Natural Knowledge and Public Debate in early Victorian Britain* (Cambridge, 1993).

[92] Whewell's vision of the development of moral knowledge was one likely to be congenial to Peel, who appointed him to the mastership of Trinity College, Cambridge.

This view of moral knowledge was likely to be congenial to many Tory judges, not least John Taylor Coleridge, the nephew of the poet. It was also significant for eliciting a response from John Stuart Mill, the dominant intellectual figure of the mid-nineteenth century. The son of the radical utilitarian James Mill, he had spent much of his youth in the company of Bentham, whose writings—much more than those of his father—opened his eyes to the principle of utility.[93] He had also been taught Roman law and jurisprudence by Austin, both privately and in the classes at University College. Mill's legal training was profound, his intellectual apprenticeship completed by his editing Bentham's massive *Rationale of Judicial Evidence* between 1824 and 1826. By then, however, Mill had already given up the idea of a career in law, and he was only ever to turn his pen to the philosophy of law when reviewing the works of others, notably Austin. Instead, his name was made by the theoretical tomes, *A System of Logic* (1843) and *The Principles of Political Economy* (1848), and by the more popular works elaborating his political thought, *On Liberty* (1859), *Considerations on Representative Government* (1859), *Utilitarianism* (1861) and *The Subjection of Women* (1869). In these works, he sketched out his view of the grounds of morality, and the proper sphere of government. These were questions which Austin's jurisprudence had not explored in any detail, but which had been central to Bentham's theories. In politics, Mill stood on the radical wing of the Liberal party, sitting in Parliament from 1865–8. Less radical than Bentham, or his father, had been in the 1820s, his work also offered important modifications to the theory of Bentham.

By 1830, Mill had already suffered the most famous nervous breakdown in intellectual history, and had rebelled against the dry, soulless, calculating system drilled into him by his father.[94] His realization that pleasure was not all a matter of calculation would make him rethink his brand of utilitarianism. In the decade which followed, he was in some degree influenced by Carlyle and Maurice. Mill acknowledged that the great seminal minds of the age were Bentham and Coleridge: 'every Englishman [...] is by implication either a Benthamite or a Coleridgean'.[95] He rejected the idealist epistemology of Coleridge and his followers, setting out his views most fully in his *System of Logic*, a work widely regarded to have bettered Whewell's approach. However, having engaged in the debate

---

[93] J. S. Mill, *Autobiography*, in *The Collected Works of John Stuart Mill*, vol. 1 (ed. J. M. Robson and J. Stillinger, Toronto, 1981), 66.

[94] For Mill's life, see N. Capaldi, *John Stuart Mill: A Biography* (Cambridge, 2004). The general literature on Mill is huge, but see esp. A. Ryan, *The Philosophy of John Stuart Mill* (2nd edn, Basingstoke, 1987); J. Skorupski, *John Stuart Mill* (1989); D. Lyons, *Rights, Welfare and Mill's Moral Theory* (Oxford, 1994); and J. Skorupski (ed.), *The Cambridge Companion to Mill* (Cambridge, 1998).

[95] Mill, 'Bentham', in *Essays on Ethics, Religion, and Society* (vol. 10 of *Collected Works of John Stuart Mill*, ed. J. M. Robson, F. E. L. Priestley and D. P. Dryer), 77; 'Coleridge,' *ibid.*, 121.

with the rival school, Mill presented a highly modified version of the utilitarianism he had learned on the knees of his father and Bentham.

Mill felt that while Bentham was a great reformer, who had for the first time brought precision into moral philosophy, his system of thought had left much out. Bentham's mechanical view of man was flawed. Dismissing Bentham's view that the game of push-pin was equal in value to poetry, since both produced happiness,[96] Mill pointed to the existence of higher pleasures and sentiments, which should be cultivated by education. 'Next to selfishness', he noted, 'the principal cause which makes life unsatisfactory, is want of mental cultivation.'[97] Bentham had not seen that man was 'capable of pursuing spiritual perfection as an end'. Most strikingly, he had failed to recognize the existence of conscience.[98] Mill did not share Coleridge's views about the conscience, accepting the utilitarian view that the moral sense could not be a test of right and wrong. However, he noted—as Bentham had not— the existence of the conscience as a fact in human nature.[99] It was (he noted in *Utilitarianism*) 'a feeling in our own mind; a pain, more or less intense, attendant on violation of duty, which in properly-cultivated moral natures rises, in the more serious cases, into shrinking from it as an impossibility'.[100] For Mill, this feeling did not come from an innate moral sense, but was developed by social experience.

Just as Bentham failed to notice the nature of conscience, so he failed to see the factors which held a society together. If Bentham's system may have taught how to best organize the material or business aspects of any social arrangement, the 'Germano-Coleridgean' school had been right to draw attention to the need to consider history. It was an error to fail to 'acknowledge the historical value of much which had ceased to be useful' and to fail to recognize 'that institutions and creeds, now effete, had rendered essential services to civilization, and still filled a place in the human mind, and in the arrangements of society, which could not without great peril, be left vacant'.[101] Coleridge and his antecedents had corrected this by seeking a philosophy of society and a philosophy of history. They had shown that societies were held together by systems of education which developed discipline, as well as feelings of allegiance and loyalty among the members of a community. Mill drew the conclusion that '[a] philosophy of laws and institutions, not founded on a philosophy of national character, is an absurdity'.[102]

[96] J. Bentham, *The Rationale of Reward*, in Bowring, (ed.), *Works of Jeremy Bentham*, ii: 253.

[97] Mill, 'Utilitarianism', in *Essays on Ethics, Religion, and Society* (vol. 10 of *Collected Works of John Stuart Mill*, ed. J. M. Robson, F. E. L. Priestley and D. P. Dryer), 215.

[98] Mill, 'Bentham', 95.

[99] *Ibid.*, 97.

[100] Mill, 'Utilitarianism', 228.

[101] Mill, 'Coleridge', 138.

[102] Mill, 'Bentham', 99.

Mill's interest in history was also sparked by his reading of the Saint-Simonians and Auguste Comte, whose anti-theological view was perhaps more to Mill's personal tastes than Coleridge's mysticism.[103] Comte's work in particular made him explore the question of whether it was possible to develop a social science. In the *System of Logic*, he explored the question of whether a science of society could be developed, by seeking uniformities in the different states of society. For Mill, the 'state of society' included the degree of knowledge, and moral and intellectual culture existing in the community, the state of industry, the common beliefs, and the state of its government and laws.[104] Mill did not accept Comte's view that social science would show that all societies developed in the same way, but he did feel that there were empirical laws of society, which could be traced, some of which were 'uniformities of coexistence, some of succession'.[105]

These views about human nature and the nature of society made Mill rework the principle of utility. This principle was to be treated as the ultimate criterion of morality, but did not have to be directly invoked in every moral decision. In Mill's view, utility was 'much too complex and indefinite an end to be sought except through the medium of various secondary ends'.[106] In practice, the community was guided by 'secondary principles' or ordinary rules of moral action. Mill noted that both utilitarians and intuitionists agreed that such principles were needed since 'morality of an individual action is not a question of direct perception, but of the application of a law to an individual case'. They also agreed on the content of these rules. Their disagreement lay in the foundations of these rules, or 'the source from which they derive their authority'.[107] If it was easy enough to agree on the nature of the 'secondary principles', things became more complicated when these principles came into conflict, when there had to be a direct appeal to a higher principle, the most effective of which was the principle of utility.[108] For Mill, theories of the moral sense could offer only generalities, which failed to descend into detail. Morality required a means of ascertaining what was right and wrong: as soon as this was sought, all moralists (Mill claimed), even Kant himself, in effect reverted to utilitarian forms of argument.

The secondary or intermediate principles were taught by experience. Coleridge had taught Mill that the fact people had held a belief for a long time showed that it could not be a fallacy, but had to be accounted for. In *Utilitarianism*, he reiterated the point that mankind had learned the tendencies of actions from experience

---

[103] Comte's views are discussed further below.
[104] J. S. Mill, *A System of Logic, Collected Works*, 8, 911–12.
[105] *Ibid.*, 8, 917. This was to evoke the Comtean notion of Social Statics and Social Dynamics.
[106] Mill, 'Bentham', 110–11.
[107] Mill, 'Utilitarianism', 206.
[108] Mill, 'Bentham', 110–11.

over time. Current established rules were to be presumed good, though they were open to being tested by the philosopher applying higher principles.[109] Nor were these higher utilitarian principles simply ones of individual psychological hedonism. Like all moral principles, they looked to the public interest, considering the consequences of everyone being allowed to perform the act in question, and not merely the consequences for oneself.

This was to suggest that the rules of morality were to be found in the community's practice, but that they could be tested and challenged by those more expert. Like many of his generation, Mill was attracted by the elitism of Coleridge's clerisy. In his view, the conservative poet had vindicated against Bentham 'the principle of an endowed class, for the cultivation of learning, and for diffusing its results among the community'.[110] Mill doubted that it was good for mankind, in all places and at all times, to be 'under the absolute authority of a majority of themselves' or 'under the despotism of Public Opinion'. The power of the majority was salutary as long as it was used defensively, and not offensively: as long as its 'exertion is tempered by respect for the personality of the individual, and deference to superiority of cultivated intelligence'.[111] Mill's elitism was also seen in his *Considerations on Representative Government*, where he argued for a system whereby the task of governing and drafting legislation would be left to men of character and learning. It was also to be seen in his view that liberal, democratic forms of government were unsuitable for 'barbarians' or 'those backward states of society', whose members needed to be coerced rather than 'guided to their own improvement by conviction or persuasion'.[112] For Mill, the cultured and educated elite could help develop the higher moral feelings necessary for the greater happiness of society, acting as 'public moralists'.[113]

While Mill did not develop a theory of law, he did famously discuss the nature of justice and the limits of coercion. In *On Liberty*, Mill argued that '[t]he only purpose for which power can be rightfully exercised over any member of a civilized community, against his will, is to prevent harm to others'.[114] In his view, harm occurred when one person injured another's interests, 'which, either by express legal provision or by tacit understanding, ought to be considered as

---

[109] Mill, 'Utilitarianism', 224.

[110] Mill, 'Coleridge', 150.

[111] Mill, 'Bentham', 106–7, 109. Mill's concern with the danger of the tyranny of the majority was a major theme of *On Liberty*.

[112] J. S. Mill, *On Liberty*, in *Essays on Politics and Society* (vol. 18 of *Collected Works of John Stuart Mill*, ed. J. M. Robson and A. Brady, Toronto, 1977), 224.

[113] For such a view of the mid-Victorian intellectual elite, including Mill, see S. Collini, *Public Moralists: Political Thought and Intellectual Life in Britain, 1850–1930* (Oxford, 1991).

[114] Mill, *On Liberty*, 223.

rights'.[115] For Mill, where the interests of others were not affected, an individual should be left to make his own choices, though those choices might be influenced by that person's education or by the advice of others. But 'if he has infringed the rules necessary for the protection of his fellow-creatures, individually or collectively', then, 'society, as the protector of all its members, must retaliate on him: must inflict pain on him for the express purpose of punishment, and must take care that it be sufficiently severe'. [116]

Scholars have long debated whether this view was consistent with his utilitarianism, given that it seemed to place the right to liberty above the good of utility. Mill himself insisted that he did not derive his argument from an abstract right, independent of utility.[117] That the two notions were compatible can be seen from his discussion in *Utilitarianism* of justice and utility. In Mill's view, the original notion of justice derived from the idea of conformity to law, that there were acts which were worthy of being punished, because they violated another's rights. The notion of justice was social: it developed when 'the animal desire to repel or retaliate a hurt or damage to oneself, or to those with whom one sympathizes, widened so as to include all persons, by the human capacity of enlarged sympathy, and the human conception of intelligent self-interest'. The right protected, according to this definition, was a claim which was considered sufficiently important by people to be guaranteed by society. The idea that rights existed which needed such protection derived from utility, having its root in the fundamental human need for security. It was people's very awareness of their social nature which made them recognize rights:

Our notion, therefore, of the claim we have on our fellow creatures to join in making safe for us the very groundwork of our existence, gathers feelings round it so much more intense than those concerned in any of the more common cases of utility, that the difference in degree (as is often the case in psychology) becomes a real difference in kind. The claim assumes that character of absoluteness, that apparent infinity, and incommensurability with all other considerations, which constitute the distinction between the feeling of right and wrong and that of ordinary expediency and inexpediency.[118]

If, in Mill's view (as outlined in *On Liberty*), purely self-regarding conduct should remain unregulated by rules imposed by legislators or moralists, it was not because there was an innate right to non-interference, but because utility demanded it. This was an altogether more subtle interpretation of the nature and derivation of rights from that to be found in Austin; and it was one which left the Austinian sovereign wholly out of the discussion.

---

[115] *Ibid.*, 276.   [116] *Ibid.*, 280.
[117] *Ibid.*, 224.   [118] Mill, *Utilitarianism*, 245–51.

Mill did not outline exactly what the rights were which needed protection by law. To begin with, his argument was addressed not merely to legislators, but also to moralists, for he recognized the coercive force of both kinds of rules. Moreover, he noted that not all activities which could count as harms should be subject to legal control. In many cases, those who engaged in legitimate activity caused pain or loss to others. For example, society admitted no right not to suffer from trade competition, though it did provide a right to be protected from fraud or force.[119] Equally, the state could, if it chose, interfere more to regulate trade: its choice not to do so, Mill asserted, was the result of a utilitarian view of what best promoted the efficient working of the economy.

At first glance, Mill's *On Liberty*, which aimed to protect the individual from the tyranny of the majority, looked like a manifesto for the mid-century era of *laissez-faire* and individualism. Mill argued against using government action for the people's benefit, feeling it was better to leave people to help themselves by their own voluntary or collective action. He seemed to be hostile to collectivism. One of his strategies to persuade his readers that the public had no jurisdiction over private concerns was to invoke the example of the 'bad workmen' in many industries, who employed 'a moral police, which occasionally, becomes a physical one, to deter skilful workmen from receiving, and employers from giving, a larger remuneration for a more useful service'.[120] Readers who were unsympathetic to workmen who wanted the bad to be paid as well as the good would see that the state had no business to interfere in other private matters. Moreover, Mill's liberty seemed to be a commodity only for the independent, financially secure classes, for he took a tight view of the poor who were unable to maintain themselves or their children. In his view, laws which forbade marriage unless the couple could show that they were able to support a family were not an infringement of liberty, but were legitimate examples of the state forbidding mischievous acts which were injurious to others.[121]

At the same time, however, Mill's works were replete with the language of altruism, of the need to cultivate fellow feeling and the development of social ties: indeed, the very notion of social feelings underpinned his version of utilitarianism.[122] Mill's utilitarianism was not the dry, calculating kind associated with Bentham. If the ultimate basis of his moral theory was utilitarian, he

---

[119] Mill, *On Liberty*, 292–3.
[120] *Ibid.*, 287.
[121] *Ibid.*, 304.
[122] Mill, *Utilitarianism*, 231; Collini, *Public Moralists*, 68. Contemporaries argued that he had failed to reconcile the individualism of *On Liberty* with the altruism of *Utilitarianism*: F. Harrison, 'John Stuart Mill' (1896) 40 *Nineteenth Century* 487–508 at 499–500.

acknowledged the role of moral rules recognized by the common sense of the community:

The moral rules which forbid mankind to hurt one another (in which we must never forget to include wrongful interference with each other's freedom) are more vital to human well-being than any maxims, however important, which only point out the best mode of managing some department of human affairs. They have also the peculiarity, that they are the main element in determining the whole of the social feelings of mankind.[123]

This was a view which accorded significant weight to moral feeling and to altruism. It also opened the way for a more collectivist approach to politics. Writing before 1867, Mill had been anxious about the growth of democracy, and sought to qualify it with 'fancy franchises'. Nonetheless, in his later life, he did begin to argue in favour of greater state intervention, noting that the abiding sins of the modern state were indolence and indifference. Now a passionate campaigner for women's rights, he argued that female participation would 'infuse into the legislature a greater determination to grapple with the great physical and moral evils of society'.[124]

Mill's work elicited a conservative response from one prominent lawyer, James Fitzjames Stephen. He wanted to defend the notion of a state with a limited but efficient government, which would allow the flourishing of free individuals; while an elite set of men of character would improve the general tone of life in the community. In many ways, this was not a vision Mill would have found alien. However, after the passing of the Second Reform Act in 1867, lawyers like Stephen—and Henry Maine—felt that the forces of stability and order needed a stronger defence than Mill could offer. Coming from the Whiggish side of liberalism, they preferred forms of government which were guided by an experienced elite. They had both served as Law Member in India, and had sympathy for firm, bureaucratic government. Although they were both devotees of freedom of contract and individualism, they reacted strongly to Mill's brand of liberalism, which by the 1870s appeared to them to open a dangerous door towards popular government.[125]

Stephen set out his views most fully in *Liberty, Equality, Freedom*. In it, he took Mill's work as its target. He argued that in *On Liberty, Utilitarianism*, and *The Subjection of Women*, Mill had abandoned Benthamite utilitarianism in favour

---

[123] Mill, *Utilitarianism*, 255.

[124] Mill, Speech on Women's Suffrage, 26 March 1870, in J. S. Mill, *Public and Parliamentary Speeches* in *The Collected Works of John Stuart Mill*, vol. 29 (ed. J. M. Robson and B. L. Kinzer, Toronto, 1988), 387.

[125] For Stephen, see esp. K. J. M. Smith, *James Fitzjames Stephen: Portrait of a Victorian Rationalist* (Cambridge, 1988), 44–54. Maine's views are discussed below.

of a version of Comtean positivism. Stephen claimed that the motto, 'Liberty, Equality, Freedom' was the creed of a religion, the Religion of Humanity. This religion (Stephen argued) held that 'the human race collectively has before it splendid destinies of various kinds, and that the road to them is to be found in the removal of all restraints on human conduct, in the recognition of a substantial equality between all human creatures, and in fraternity or general love'.[126] While considering himself to be Mill's disciple in many respects, he regarded *Utilitarianism* and *The Subjection of Women* as embracing the forms of equality and fraternity to which he objected. Stephen disliked the stress on social feelings found in *Utilitarianism*, detecting in it a tinge of Comte. Against Mill's belief that if all men were put on an equal footing, they would treat each other as brothers, Stephen argued that many men were bad, and most indifferent, and would often find themselves 'compelled to treat each other as enemies'.[127] Stephen dismissed Mill's version of utilitarianism, though still claiming to be a utilitarian himself, in the sense that an external standard had to be appealed to, which might be best referred to as happiness, or expediency:

To say [...] that moral speculation or legislation presupposes on the part of the moralist or legislator a desire to promote equally the happiness of every person affected by his system or his law is, I think, incorrect [...] the happiness which the lawgiver regards as the test of his laws is that which he, after attaching to their wishes whatever weight he thinks proper, wishes his subjects to have, not that which his subjects wish to have.[128]

For Stephen, liberty was not in itself a value, as Mill had appeared to assume in his work. Like Hobbes and Bentham, he argued that it was nothing more than absence of restraint. All societies were held together by systems of coercion; the question for utility to determine was how far it was to be exerted. Mill's attempt to draw the line by invoking the harm principle failed to convince Stephen. For Stephen, governments had to act 'upon such principles, religious, political and moral, as they may from time to time regard as most likely to be true'.[129] These needed enforcement by coercion. In his view, it was social morality which held

---

[126] *Liberty, Equality, Freedom* (2nd edn, 1874), 2. Although Mill admired the methodology of Comte's early work, the *Cours de Philosophie Positive* (1830–42), he did not admire his later *Système de Politique Positive* (1851–4), where he developed his notion of altruism and the religion of humanity. For Mill's reaction, see 'The Positive Philosophy of Auguste Comte' (1865) 83 *Westminster Review* 339–405, and 'Later Speculations of Auguste Comte' (1865) 84 *Westminster Review* 1–42 (and *Collected Works*, x: 261–368). Stephen may have associated Mill's altruistic later works with Comte, since it was the latter who introduced the term 'altruism' into public discourse. For a discussion of the issues, see T. Dixon, *The Invention of Altruism: Making Moral Meanings in Victorian Britain* (Oxford, 2008), Ch. 2.

[127] *Ibid.*, 281.

[128] *Ibid.*, 283–4.

[129] Quoted in Smith, *James Fitzjames Stephen*, 168.

society together, and which had to be articulated and enforced by the state. In effect, it was for the government to articulate and enforce the prevailing morals which held the community together; something which entailed taking a position even on questions of religion.[130] If, in practice, Stephen did not wish for a more interventionist government than Mill, he did argue that intervention in matters Mill had sought to define as private was justifiable to reinforce cohesive social values. Moreover, while Stephen's view was that the moral majority should be able to impose its view on the minority, that view was in practice to be articulated by an intellectual elite, which included himself.

Besides attacking Mill on liberty, Stephen also criticized his views on equality, considering that Mill regarded this (as he did liberty) as a higher value than utility. For Stephen, inequality was inevitable in society, and any attempts to legislate against it were futile. If there was a natural inequality in society, then the law should reflect it, rather than trying to work against the grain. Stephen was particularly worried by the notion that there might be class-based legislation. *Liberty, Equality, Freedom* was well received, and was later described by Ernest Barker as 'the finest exposition of conservative thought in the latter half of the nineteenth century'.[131] However, the work did not achieve the canonical status of Mill's work, and it ran to no more than two nineteenth-century editions. Stephen landed some effective blows against Mill—notably on the harm principle—but the parameters of debate were moving elsewhere by the mid-1870s.

If Stephen's work did not set the tone of a wider debate on politics, it does give a vivid insight into the mind of a prominent judge. Fear of democracy, resistance to the development of social rights, and a commitment to the role of an elite set of judges in developing the moral voice of the community were surely characteristic of the late nineteenth-century judiciary, many of whom liked the notion that judges were to articulate the values to guide the community, without being keen on a democratic conception of the community whose values they purported to apply.

4. THEORIES OF EVOLUTION

In the middle of the nineteenth century, scholars in all fields increasingly turned their attention to empirical studies of human development. There was a growing interest in social science and in theories of evolution. The work of Auguste Comte was particularly influential. His *Cours de Philosophie Positive* described 'sociology'

---

[130] See esp. Stephen's views on the criminal law, which needed to reflect popular beliefs while at the same time being developed and controlled by the judiciary: Smith, *James Fitzjames Stephen*, Ch. 3.

[131] E. Barker, *Political Thought in England, 1848–1914* (2nd edn, 1928), 150, quoted in J. A. Colaiaco, *James Fitzjames Stephen and the Crisis of Victorian Thought* (1983), 165.

as the highest of the sciences. He also set out a 'positivist' methodology, which held that only empirically verifiable facts could be possible objects of knowledge, and that science produced empirical laws connecting them. 'Positivism' became a key word in Victorian science and philosophy, and one whose meaning was wholly distinct from the legal positivism associated with Austin's theory of law as the posited commands of a sovereign. Comte's work also contained a theory of evolutionary progress. He argued that the development of the various sciences, and the human mind, always progressed through three stages: the theological, metaphysical, and 'positive', or scientific. The third stage—in which empirical laws would replace all theoretical or metaphysical speculation—was the goal towards which the philosopher and scientist aspired. This empirical theory was wholly secular, though in later work Comte sought to introduce a spiritual element through his notion of the Religion of Humanity.[132] Comte's work influenced Mill, when writing his *System of Logic*, and it was popularized in the 1840s and 1850s by G. H. Lewes.[133] Indeed, the very term 'social science', which came into increasing use in the 1830s, and which obtained an organized expression in the name of the Social Science Association founded in 1857, may have been adopted by the English from its use by Comte.[134]

By the 1850s, a number of English writers were seeking to explore the science of society. In 1857, H. T. Buckle published a *History of Civilization in England*, which sought to do for history what had been done for the natural sciences: to discover whether 'the actions of men, and therefore of societies, [are] governed by fixed laws, or are … the result either of chance or of superfluous influence'.[135] He felt that the regularities of human conduct meant that a scientific history was possible. In the same year, Herbert Spencer began to look to evolution as the key to his system of philosophy.[136] His life's project was to create a Synthetic Philosophy, which would systematize the truths of each specific science. By 1857, he had come to see that the key to this was a general law of evolution. Spencer's view of evolution owed more to physics than to biology: he 'aimed at nothing less than a mechanical interpretation of the universe in which every event could be

---

[132] See M. Pickering, *Auguste Comte: An Intellectual Biography*, vol. 1 (Cambridge, 2006); T. R. Wright, *The Religion of Humanity: The Impact of Comtean Positivism on Victorian Britain* (Cambridge, 1986); C. D. Cashdollar, *The Transformation of Theology, 1830–1890: Positivism and Positivist Thought in Britain and America* (Princeton, 1989).

[133] G. H. Lewes, *Comte's Philosophy of the Sciences: Being an Exposition of the Principles of the Cours de Philosophie of Auguste Comte* (1853).

[134] L. Goldman, *Science, Reform and Politics in Victorian Britain: The Social Science Association, 1857–1886* (Cambridge, 2002), 307. See further, below, Pt 1, Ch. VI.

[135] H. T. Buckle, *History of Civilization in England*, 2 vols (1851–61), i, 8.

[136] H. Spencer, 'Progress: Its Law and Cause' (1857) 11 *West. Review* (N.S.) 445–85. See, in general, J. W. Burrow, *Evolution and Society: A Study in Victorian Social Theory* (Cambridge, 1966).

explained in terms of the relations of cause and effect between incident forces'.[137] Arguing that the first cause of the universe was unknowable, he derived a law of evolution from the physical laws of matter and motion. Evolution entailed growing complexity and concentration. Societies displayed tendencies to aggregate (as in the growth of towns and population) and then to become ever more heterogeneous (with the division of labour). Spencer continued to work on this great project for the rest of his life. His work was often aimed at a popular audience, rather than at the academy. Thanks to this, he acquired a very great influence in the later nineteenth century, even if, by the time of his death in 1903, his work was 'already being exiled to the lumber-room of redundant Victoriana'.[138]

Throughout his career, Spencer was concerned with finding a scientific basis for ethics. In developing his view, he drew on a wide range of influences, including utilitarianism, Comtean positivism, and even moral intuitionism.[139] In his early work, *Social Statics* (1851), he argued that instead of seeking happiness directly, the theorist should develop rules of action scientifically, by establishing the conditions leading to happiness.[140] In his view, there were certain moral rights which were 'necessary' for the attainment of human happiness. Happiness came from the exercise of one's faculties; and since this required the freedom to exercise them, each person had a right to exercise them freely, a right limited only by a similar right in all other people.[141] Much of the rest of the book was devoted to an elucidation of these rights, which were of the purest *laissez-faire* type. After 1857, he began to rework his theories in light of his turn to evolution. In 1879, he published the *Data of Ethics*, which 'became the definitive statement of the evolutionary approach to ethics'.[142] In this work, he sought to explain the evolution of the moral consciousness. His approach was influenced by the theories of Jean-Baptiste Lamarck, who had argued that species mutated in response

[137] M. W. Taylor, *Men versus the State: Herbert Spencer and Late Victorian Individualism* (Oxford, 1992), 77.

[138] K. T. Hoppen, *The Mid-Victorian Generation, 1846–1886* (Oxford, 1998), 474. By contrast, in 1896, Frederic Harrison wrote that Mill had not been as original or as systematic as Bentham or Spencer: 'John Stuart Mill', 508.

[139] Although a utilitarian, insofar as he took happiness to be the ultimate end, he also contended that there were moral instincts, which gave moral axioms for reason to develop: H. Spencer, *Social Statics, or the Conditions Essential to Human Happiness Specified, and the First of them Developed* (1851), 23–31 ('even the disciples of Bentham have no alternative but to fall back upon an intuition of this much derided moral sense, for the foundation of their own system').

[140] His method led Mill to doubt whether Spencer was really a utilitarian. For their exchange of views, see Mill, *Utilitarianism*, 258n and Spencer, *The Data of Ethics* (1894; 1st edn, 1862), 57. Spencer continued to insist that he was a utilitarian, though he called his version 'rational', as opposed to 'empirical'.

[141] Spencer, *Social Statics*, 76–8.

[142] Dixon, *Altruism*, 184.

to environmental change, and were able to pass on the higher characteristic they had acquired in their lives to their descendants. Spencer's view of moral intuitions had little in common with either the Coleridgeans on the earlier schools of Shaftesbury or the Scottish school of common sense philosophy, led by Thomas Reid. He argued that

moral intuitions are the results of accumulated experiences of Utility, gradually organized and inherited ... I believe that the experiences of utility organized and consolidated through all past generations of the human race, have been producing corresponding nervous modifications, which, by continued transmission and accumulation, have become in us certain faculties of moral intuition—certain emotions corresponding to right and wrong conduct, which have no apparent basis in the individual experiences of utility.[143]

For Spencer, each individual inherited the characteristics which had been acquired by the experience of his predecessors: the new-born baby was not a blank sheet who needed to learn moral lessons from his own experience of pleasure and pain. His vision of the development of moral ideas was thus distinct both from the version of the intuitionists and the utilitarians.

In his moral theory, Spencer used the Comtean terminology of altruism and egoism. He argued that altruistic feelings would come increasingly to the fore, as society developed from the simple military predatory to more complex industrial societies. However, this did not translate into a demand for the state to intervene to promote social cooperation and foster altruism. Although he spoke of society as an organism, seeing its development in terms akin to those of biology, he insisted that society had no common consciousness. It had no moral personality which could justify claims against the interests of individual members. Unlike individual organisms, the complex, modern industrial society had evolved as the product of spontaneous voluntary co-operation between individuals. If moral evolution was leading to an increasingly altruistic society, this was not something which could be accelerated or coerced by the state.

Spencer's vision of evolution translated into a conservative form of individualism. Where other practically minded devotees of social science—such as the members of the Social Science Association—sought to use empirical methods as a tool for social policy, Spencer's organic view of society and theory of evolution warned against any assumption that the state had the power or knowledge to engage in social engineering. For him, there was an individualistic social order which was not the product of human design, and which might be damaged by foolish intervention. Society was so complex that the effect of legislation could not be predicted. Progress was a slow, natural development, which could not be accelerated by the

---

[143] Spencer, *The Data of Ethics*, 123.

state. By the 1880s, Spencer was therefore arguing for minimalist state intervention. The essential function of the state was to protect individual rights, secure the fulfilment of contracts, and defend against external aggression.[144] Spencer had expressed a version of this view in *Social Statics*, when he spoke of the Law of Equal Freedom, under which every man could claim the fullest freedom to exercise his faculties compatible with the like freedom for others. By 1884, in *The Man versus the State*, he was increasingly strident in opposing interventionist legislation.

At the same time that Buckle and Spencer were turning to evolution to explain the development of human society, Henry Maine was also turning to history to explain legal evolution. In 1861, he published what would be one of the most popular and influential works on law in the second half of the nineteenth century—*Ancient Law*. This was a work which influenced both legal audiences—for whom Austin's jurisprudence would have to be read alongside Maine's—and also wider political ones. Maine shared the mid-century enthusiasm for studying his subject empirically and historically, eschewing both *a priori* and theological forms of reasoning. However, although the Positivist Frederick Harrison thought that Maine was more a social philosopher than a jurist in the strict sense,[145] his methodology seemed to owe little, if anything, to Comte or Spencer. Unlike Positivist social scientists, Maine did not seek to develop a social scientific explanation of the progress of societies and made no normative claims about the path of evolution, for his prime interest lay in qualifying and correcting the dominant Austinian form of jurisprudence, by describing and analysing the development of legal concepts over time.[146] His work owed more to German historiography, notably that of Niebuhr,[147] as well as the developing sciences of geology and philology.[148] But if Maine's methodology offered little to the growing band of social scientists, his conclusions about the trends of legal development were enthusiastically embraced as if they were scientific truths.[149]

Maine wished to reach a larger audience than merely law students. He felt that law was regarded too much as a professional matter, and that jurisprudence should

[144] Taylor, *Men versus the State*, 144. See further, below, Pt 1, Ch. VI, p. 205.

[145] G. Feaver, *From Status to Contract: A Biography of Sir Henry Maine 1822–1888* (1969), 26. Harrison himself was a devotee of Comte, translating the *Système de Politique Positive* in 1875–7 and writing his own Positivist *Order and Progress* in 1875.

[146] J. F. Stephen sensed a hint of the flaws of Comtean Positivism in Maine's work, Stephen, 'English Jurisprudence' (1861) 114 *Edinburgh Rev.* 456–86 at 484.

[147] See N. O'Brien, '"Something Older than Law Itself": Sir Henry Maine, Niebuhr and '"the Path not Chosen"' (2005) 26 *JLH* 229–51.

[148] Maine's work in *Ancient Law* does not seem to have owed anything to Charles Darwin's 1859 *Origin of Species*.

[149] His methodology was debated more among anthropologists and historians. See the essays in A. Diamond (ed.), *The Victorian Achievement of Sir Henry Maine: A Centennial Reappraisal* (Cambridge, 1991).

be cultivated more widely.[150] An indefatigable journalist, he also held numerous posts as a teacher of jurisprudence (first at the inns of court and later at Oxford and Cambridge), and as a civil servant, notably in India. A number of lucrative, but not unduly time-consuming jobs left him the leisure to write extensively. In his road-map of legal evolution, *Ancient Law*, Maine set out six stages of legal development. In the earliest stages of society, he argued, law consisted of the pronouncements of heroic kings, acting on the basis of what was believed to be divine inspiration. This era gave way to one in which law was made by oligarchs acting as the repositories of law, which was in turn followed by the era of codes, when primitive law was set into writing. For Maine, those societies (such as Rome) which put their laws into a code early in their history became progressive, while those (such as India) which did so late became 'stationary'. In progressive societies, law always lagged behind social necessity and opinion, and a gap grew which had to be filled. It was filled first by fictions, next by equity, and finally by legislation.[151] The last of the 'amelio-rating instrumentalities' was legislation by 'the assumed organ of the entire soci-ety', whether that was in the form of a Parliament or an autocratic prince. The age of legislation was in effect that of the Austinian sovereign:

Its obligatory force is independent of its principles. The legislature, whatever be the actual restraints imposed on it by public opinion, is in theory empowered to impose what obli-gations it pleases on members of the community.[152]

Although Maine did not challenge the analytical vocabulary of Bentham and Austin, insofar as it applied to contemporary society, he felt that it left much unsaid. Resolving law into a command of a sovereign may have solved some problems of definition, but it left open the 'whole question [...] as to the motives of societies in imposing these commands on themselves, as to the connection of these commands with each other, and the nature of their dependence on those which preceded them, and which they have superseded'. Bentham's view that societies modified law according to their views of general expediency was true, but 'unfruitful', and said nothing substantive about the impulse prompting the modification.[153] But if it was flawed, Maine felt that Bentham's approach was at least better than that of the natural lawyers, notably Rousseau, who abandoned the careful observation of existing institutions in favour of 'the unassisted con-sideration of the natural state, a social order wholly irrespective of the actual

---

[150] Collini, *Public Moralists*, 252–3.

[151] For a summary of Maine's views, see Lobban, *History*, 192–3, and more fully R. C. J. Cocks, *Sir Henry Maine: A Study in Victorian Jurisprudence* (Cambridge, 1988).

[152] H. S. Maine, *Ancient Law: Its Connection with the Early History of Society and its Relation to Modern Ideas* (with introduction by F. Pollock, 1930), 35.

[153] Maine, *Ancient Law*, 135.

condition of the world and wholly unlike it'.[154] He was even less impressed with
the critical philosophy of Kant, for whom the ontological grounds of the rules of
morality were more important than the rules themselves.[155] As Maine saw it, one
needed to look for the development of law in the community, and this had to be
done by using an empirical methodology.

Maine was no philosopher, and was not concerned with exploring the higher
foundations of moral obligation. Instead, he was interested in tracing the development of the middle axioms, the rules which were accepted and acted on by
communities which regarded them simply as matters of common sense.[156] These
needed to be traced empirically through history. Like the geologist, the jurist
should begin by analysing the simplest particles of which the world was made up,
and tracing their development over time.[157] Maine's history traced the evolution
of an ancient patriarchal society into a modern individualistic one. Over time,
there was a gradual dissolution of family dependency, and a growth of individual obligation, arriving at a society where all the relations of persons arose from
the free agreement of individuals. In the modern age, only those who did not
possess the faculty of forming a judgment on their own interests—children and
lunatics—were still regulated by a law of status. Maine summed up this development in his famous aphorism that 'the movement of the progressive societies has
hitherto been a movement *from Status to Contract*'.[158]

Maine's work sought to trace this evolution in different areas of law, showing
how various modern legal concepts had developed out of older forms rooted in sta-
tus-based patriarchal societies. Maine's discussion of the evolution of contract was
particularly significant. The very notion of contract, he pointed out, was a modern
one. Thinkers who rooted political obligation in legal notions of an ancient social
contract missed a central point: in primitive societies, the individual created few
or no rights or duties for himself. Rather, '[t]he rules which he obeys are derived

---

[154] *Ibid.*, 99. Maine argued that Natural Law had its roots in the positive system of Roman law,
which eighteenth-century French thinkers abandoned in their search for rights in the wholly
abstract State of Nature.

[155] Maine, *Ancient Law*, 369.

[156] Indeed, in his brief discussion of utility, in *The Early History of Institutions*, Maine spoke of
Bentham as articulating the principle as 'a working rule of legislation', which assumed the existence of a modern sovereign and legislature: 'No doubt his language seems sometimes to imply that
he is explaining moral phenomena; in reality he wishes to alter or re-arrange them according to a
working rule gathered from his reflections on legislation. This transfer of the working rule from
legislation to morality seems to me the true ground of the criticisms to which Bentham is justly
open as an analyst of moral facts': *The Early History of Institutions*, 7th edn, 400. Maine also argued
that Austin's jurisprudence was consistent with any ethical theory, and not merely utilitarianism,
ibid., 368–9.

[157] Maine, *Ancient Law*, 136.

[158] *Ibid.*, 182.

first from the station into which he is born, and next from the imperative commands addressed to him by the chief of the household of which he forms part.
Such a system leaves the very smallest room for contract.'[159] The very idea of contract developed over the long term. Maine sketched its evolution in Roman law,
from the *nexum* to the consensual contracts ('from which all modern conceptions
of contract took their start'), and speculated whether this history 'exemplifies the
necessary progress of human thought on the subject of Contract'.[160]

Maine's theory of a society based on contract has often been seen as an ideal
social theory for the era of free trade liberalism and political economy.[161] Indeed,
Maine himself asserted that political economy was 'the only department of moral
inquiry which has made any considerable progress in our day'. Yet his vision of
the contracting economy was at the same time a very moral one. Having accepted
that the modern legislature was Austinian in nature, Maine commented that its
role was small. Political economy taught that the province of imperative law was
to be curtailed, while that of contract was to be expanded, increasingly to take
its place.[162] The growth of contract law was accompanied by the development of
morality. The very character of modern frauds—and Maine clearly had in mind
recent financial frauds, such as the Royal British Bank scandal of 1856—showed
'clearly that, before they became possible, the moral obligations of which they
are the breach must have been more than proportionately developed'.[163] It was
the very confidence reposed by the many which afforded the opportunity for
the fraudulent few, and which made it so shocking. The conclusion to be drawn
was that morality had not declined since Roman times, but rather that it 'has
advanced from a very rude to a highly refined conception—from viewing the
rights of property as exclusively sacred, to looking upon the rights growing out
of the mere unilateral repose of confidence as entitled to the protection of the
penal law'.[164]

In Maine's later work, written on his return from India, he developed his criticisms of the Austinian concept of sovereignty. He noted that the word 'law' was
associated both with the idea of 'order' and that of 'force'. While the notion of
force had been accorded primacy by Bentham and Austin, it was also true that
'the contemplation of order in the external world has strongly influenced the

---

[159] *Ibid.*, 337–8.

[160] *Ibid.*, 358.

[161] E.g., Lobban, *History*, 198.

[162] Maine, *Ancient Law*, 332: 'the law even of the least advanced communities tends more and
more to become a mere surface-stratum, having under it an ever-changing assemblage of contractual rules with which it rarely interferes except to compel compliance with a few fundamental principles, or unless it be called in to punish the violation of good faith'.

[163] *Ibid.*, 333.

[164] *Ibid.*, 334.

view taken of laws proper by much of the civilised part of mankind'.[165] Maine
again accepted that Austin's analysis was the one which the modern student of
jurisprudence had to use in identifying law. But he felt that his theory, developed
in the context of modern England, was of limited value, particularly when applied
to different kinds of societies. In particular, it was unable to explain the working
of customary law, which was so central to primitive societies. Customary law was
not obeyed in the same way as enacted law was: '[w]hen it obtains over small areas
and in small natural groups, the penal sanctions on which it depends are partly
opinion, partly superstition, but to a far greater extent an instinct almost as blind
and unconscious as that which produces some of the movements of our bodies'.[166]
It was only as societies expanded, and a sovereign began to legislate more actively
on his own principles, that force became central.

At the core of the Austinian explanation of positive law was the notion that
whatever the sovereign permitted, he had to be taken to have commanded. Maine
accepted that this was true as a formal definition, but he found it had no practical application in societies with bodies of customary law. In Runjeet Singh's
Punjab, that most despotic of rulers never felt he had the power to change customary law. What was true of the Punjab was also true of the old common law.[167]
The customary law of all countries—including the common law—generally had
an origin claimed for it which was independent of the sovereign.[168] The theory
that what the sovereign permitted he commanded was a mere artifice of speech,
which assumed that courts acted 'in a way and from motives of which they are
unconscious'.[169] A theory which saw the sovereign's power in his ability to alter
the common law said nothing practical about its working. Maine therefore
argued that Austin should have gone further than his formal definitions, to
'examine that great mass of rules, which men in fact obey, and which have some
of the characteristics of laws, but which are not (as such) imposed by Sovereigns
on subjects, and which are not (as such) enforced by the sanction supplied by
Sovereign power'.[170] For Maine, a comprehensive jurisprudence required a closer
study of ethics.

The customary foundations of law were also seen in the fact that law had emerged
in an adjudicatory, rather than in a legislative context. 'Nobody should know

---

[165] H. S. Maine, *The Early History of Institutions* (7th edn, 1905), 373–4.

[166] Maine, *Early History*, 392.

[167] '[M]y Oriental example shows that the difficulty felt by the old lawyers about the Common
law may have once deserved more respect than it obtained from Hobbes and his successors', Maine,
Early History, 381–2.

[168] *Ibid.*, 368.

[169] *Ibid.*, 368, 364.

[170] *Ibid.*, 367.

better than an Englishman', he noted, that the Roman institutional method was not an arrangement which spontaneously suggested itself: 'So great is the ascendancy of the Law of Actions in the infancy of Courts of Justice, that substantive law has at first the look of being gradually secreted in the interstices of procedure.'[171] In the earlier stages of society, law courts and the remedies they offered assumed a prominent place, since they were the means of settling disputes which had hitherto been left to private vengeance. Abstract legal concepts only developed later. For instance, Maine noted that the very idea of abstract legal rights was not one which was clear to Roman lawyers. Rather, they considered the parties to a suit as bound together by a 'chain of law'. This *vinculum juris* or obligation signified both rights and duties: '[b]ut it was the Courts of Justice which had welded this chain'.[172] Over time, the centrality of the courts faded from view, and people could perceive the rights in the abstract, reaching a stage when 'law has so formed our conscious habits and ideas that Courts of Justice are rarely needed to compel obedience'.[173]

The development of law-abiding habits meant that the coercive power of the state was less and less visible and intrusive. In developing this argument, Maine clearly did not have in mind a society which got into the habit of obeying the regular commands of a sovereign busybody. He noted that:

The great difficulty of the modern Analytical Jurists, Bentham and Austin, has been to recover from its hiding-place the force which gives its sanction to law. They had to show that it had not disappeared and could not disappear; but that it was only latent because it had been transformed into a law-abiding habit. Even now their assertion, that it is everywhere present where there are Courts of Justice administering law, has to many the idea of a paradox—which it loses, I think, when their analysis is aided by history.[174]

The habit of obedience which underpinned the Benthamic and Austinian sovereign had therefore to be explained in terms of a customary disposition cultivated over time, to obey the rules which would be enforced by a court. With Maine's work, Austin's commanding sovereign was effectively neutered, and common lawyers were left free to study and celebrate their ancient, developing customary system of law. Maine's qualifications of Austin proved highly influential among lawyers, who read the older man's jurisprudence with the younger man's qualifications. Lawyers took from Maine the comfort that the common law could still be regarded as a customary system, under the control of lawyers.

Paradoxically, however, Maine's longer-term influence was limited. The arguments in *Ancient Law*, that legal developments were tied to social developments,

[171] H. S. Maine, *Dissertations on Early Law and Custom* (1883), 389.
[172] *Ibid.*, 391.
[173] *Ibid.*, 385–6.
[174] *Ibid.*, 389.

and that law had to adapt to keep up with changes in society, might have been expected to encourage jurists to look more at the purposes of law, and to the relationship between law and society. After all, this work had presented a significant challenge to scholars who thought that the ideas found in Roman law were timeless, and that legal problems could be resolved by the abstract analysis of legal concepts. Yet his brand of historical jurisprudence did not take root. Analytical jurisprudence continued to flourish, and rather than being succeeded by a school of historical or sociological jurists, Maine's work was subjected to increasing criticism from specialists who pointed to the errors in his detailed discussions. Nevertheless, in the wider public debate, Maine's motto about the path of legal evolution was to remain a political mantra.

5. INDIVIDUALISM VERSUS SOCIALISM, 1880–1914

In A. V. Dicey's view, the passing of the Second Reform Act ended the era of 'Benthamism or individualism' and inaugurated the age of collectivism. Twenty years of liberal government between 1846 and 1868 had seen very small government, with liberal activists (like Richard Cobden, John Bright, and Robert Lowe) seeking to legislate to remove government intervention which hindered the freedom of the individual. Prime among the legislative targets were the ending of the protectionism of the Corn Laws and the securing of 'freedom of contract' in industry. It was this world that Dicey looked nostalgically back to when writing *Law and Opinion* in 1905.

In fact, the impact of the change wrought in 1867 was not felt until the 1880s, when Gladstone returned to power, bringing with him a more interventionist form of liberalism than had existed before. Gladstone's new ministry seemed to many liberals of the old school to be abandoning the main tenets of liberal policy. Legislation such as the Employers' Liability Act, the Ground Game Act, and the Irish Land Act appeared to many to be a direct attack on freedom of contract. G. J. Goschen, a member of the liberal government of the mid-1860s, bemoaned the fact in 1885 that '[w]e seem almost to have arrived at this formula—little freedom in making contracts, much freedom in breaking them'.[175] Dicey complained that the Land Act made the rights of landlord and tenant depend on status, rather than contract, and was therefore retrogressive.[176]

As Goschen realized, much of public opinion was moving in a different direction. There had been 'an awakening of the public conscience as to the moral

---

[175] Quoted in Taylor, *Men versus the State*, 10.
[176] A. V. Dicey, *Lectures on the Relation between Law and Public Opinion in England during the Nineteenth Century* (1905), 263.

aspects of many sides of our industrial arrangements'.[177] The public conscience was awakened to the appalling conditions in which many of their fellows lived by works such as Andrew Mearns's *The Bitter Cry of Outcast London*, publicized in the pages of W. T. Stead's campaigning *Pall Mall Gazette*. In an age of economic depression, it became apparent to many that the old economic shibboleths— which required the poor to be severely self-reliant—could no longer be invoked. In an age of more assertive trade unionism, and at a time when the working-class vote was becoming increasingly important and finding new organizational outlets, many new questions were raised about the role of the state in alleviating social conditions.

It was in this context that polemicists began to oppose 'individualism' and 'socialism' or 'collectivism'. The word 'socialist' now gained a far wider currency than it had ever enjoyed before, a fact reflected in William Harcourt's much-discussed comment of 1887, 'We are all socialists now'. The word had been used before 1880, to refer to the utopian radicalism associated with foreign writers, such as Fourier and Saint-Simon. By the 1880s, the word was used much more broadly, and might refer to any kind of collectivist or interventionist social policy.[178] The range of those supporting 'socialist' policies was broad. It included new radical political organizations such as H. M. Hyndman's Social Democratic Federation (founded in 1883) and the Fabian Society (formed in 1884), which aimed to give a political voice to the working classes mobilized by the New Unionism of the late 1880s. It also included liberals (such as L. T. Hobhouse or D. G. Ritchie), who rejected the 'vulgar' or 'bureaucratic' socialism associated with these bod ies, but who favoured growing state intervention and had an organic view of the community. It even included some individualists, like Henry Sidgwick, who was prepared to support some 'socialist' measures. Sidgwick's definition of socialism was far from that which would appeal to Marxists like Hyndman: it was 'the requirement that one sane adult, apart from contract or claim for reparation, shall contribute positively by money or services to the support of others'.[179]

The counter-point to socialism was individualism. This was encapsulated in the motto of the Liberty and Property Defence League, founded in 1882: 'Individualism *versus* Socialism'. Where the notion of individualism had been associated before 1880 with selfishness, it was now championed as a virtue. Prime among its champions was Herbert Spencer, whose manifesto, *The Man versus*

---

[177] G. J. Goschen, *Essays and Addresses on Economic Questions* (1905), quoted in Dixon, *Altruism*, 230.

[178] See M. Freeden, *The New Liberalism: An Ideology of Social Reform* (Oxford, 1986), 25–39; S. Collini, *Liberalism and Sociology: L. T. Hobhouse and Political Argument in England, 1880–1914* (Cambridge, 1979), 32–43.

[179] Quoted in Taylor, *Men versus the State*, 224.

the State (1884) was described by Ritchie as 'the most conspicuous work of recent years in defence of Individualism and in opposition to the growing tendency of state intervention'.[180] Individualism was more a social or political theory than an economic one. By the 1880s, developments in economic thought made it less plausible for individualists to argue that economic science dictated the necessity of a policy of *laissez-faire*.[181] However, men like Spencer and his followers argued that evolutionary science proved that any retreat from individualism would be damaging. In their view, a move to interventionism seemed to fly in the face of the individualistic trend of evolution. Maine himself had appeared to endorse such a view when he wrote, in *Village Communities*, that 'no-one is at liberty to attack several property and to say at the same time that he values civilization. The history of the two cannot be disentangled.'[182]

By the 1880s, many individualists had also been seduced by what came to be known as Social Darwinism. Darwin's *Origin of Species*, published in 1859, had made a huge impact on Victorian society. While it had come too late to influence either Spencer or Maine in the development of their own ideas, both men drew on the theory of natural selection in their later thoughts. It was Spencer, rather than Darwin, who (in 1864) first coined the phrase 'survival of the fittest'. In *The Man versus the State*, he noted the irony that just at the moment when 'the beneficent working of the survival of the fittest' had been impressed on all cultivated people, they had turned to 'doing all they can to further the survival of the unfittest!' Elsewhere, he wrote,

If left to operate in all its sternness, the principle of the survival of the fittest, which, ethically considered, we have seen to imply that each individual shall be left to experience the effects of his own nature and consequent conduct, would quickly clear away the degraded.[183]

This crude brand of Social Darwinism had clear limits as a theory. Darwin himself was not crudely Darwinian. While the *Origin of Species*—which did not discuss humanity—had seen evolution in terms of the ruthless competition of individuals, in his later *Descent of Man* he did discuss the evolution of the moral sense and of social instincts, showing that nature could be a moral teacher.[184] Nor was Spencer usually as crude; for, as has been seen, he spoke of altruistic sentiments being essential in the development of humanity, even if the altruistic impulse was an individual, voluntary one. Moreover, as Spencer's critics pointed out, in order to

---

[180] D. G. Ritchie, *The Principles of State Interference* (London, 1891), 3.
[181] On economic thought, see below, Pt 1, Ch. VI.
[182] Quoted in Collini, *Liberalism and Sociology*, 27.
[183] Quoted in Taylor, *Men versus the State*, 87–8.
[184] See Dixon, *Altruism*, Ch. 4.

create the proper conditions for a Social Darwinian selection to occur, one would have to remove all law and property, so that proper competition could commence.

Nevertheless, the Social Darwinian challenge remained important. On a theoretical level, the idea that natural selection was the motor of progress posed a challenge to those who wished to develop a broader communitarian vision. On a practical level, it justified Spencer and his supporters in opposing legislation such as the Factory Acts and Poor Law, and in supporting organizations such as the Charity Organisation Society, which aimed to channel voluntary contributions to the deserving poor. It was, moreover, a vision which appealed to the likes of Maine. Like Spencer, Maine was appalled at the prospect of democratic collectivism. In his *Popular Government*, published in the conservative *Quarterly Review* and issued as a book in 1885, he praised Spencer's 'admirable volume', *The Man versus the State*. For Maine, the principle of the 'survival of the fittest' had echoes of pre-Darwinian theories of political economy, and was rooted in Malthusian pessimism about the pressure of population allowing only the disciplined and restrained to prosper and survive. The central principle of political economy, the population principle, he said, had—through Darwin—'become the central truth of all biological science', though it was 'evidently disliked by the multitude', and had been 'thrust into the background by those whom the multitude permits to lead it'. Like Spencer, he was particularly worried by the prospect of the socialism of the mob. '[I]f the mass of mankind were to make an attempt at redividing the common stock of good things', he wrote, 'they would resemble, not a number of claimants insisting on the fair division of a fund, but a mutinous crew, feasting on a ship's provisions, gorging themselves on the meat and intoxicating themselves with the liquors, but refusing to navigate the vessel to port'.[185]

Spencer's was not the only brand of individualism available. A more moderate version, which rested on a refined utilitarianism rather than a theory of evolution, was put forward by Henry Sidgwick.[186] He was another Liberal in politics, though by the mid-1880s his political sympathies were with those Liberals who left the party over Home Rule for Ireland (who included Dicey). A friend of Maine, Sidgwick was also unsympathetic to the development of socialist ideas, holding to essentially mid-Victorian views of individualism and economics.[187] He remained committed to utilitarianism, for he was unconvinced by intuitionist approaches to moral philosophy, considering them unable either to provide

---

[185] H. S. Maine, *Popular Government* (1885), 37, 45–6.

[186] On Sidgwick, see esp. Schneewind, *Sidgwick's Ethics* and B. Schultz, *Henry Sidgwick: Eye of the Universe* (Cambridge, 2004).

[187] A supporter of the Charity Organisation Society, he opposed giving votes to paupers, fearing that it might undermine attempts to make them self reliant. See C. Harvie, *The Lights of Liberalism: University Liberals and the Challenge of Democracy, 1860–86* (1976), 196.

principles from which specific judgments could be derived or to provide answers when different principles came into conflict. In such cases, he thought that even those who claimed to argue from intuition or common sense had to resort to utilitarian reasoning. Nonetheless, Sidgwick had at the same time to admit that the ultimate foundations of the moral system were based on an intuition, that rational beings had to aim at the good; and that the good of one person was of no greater value than the good of the other. Sidgwick was also sceptical about the possibility of creating an ideal code of utilitarian ethics, given the great complexity of calculating the potential felicific consequences of any action. However, he argued (like Mill) that the morality of common sense could provide a defensible guide to action, providing middle axioms, which had to be tested and guided by the principle of utility.

Like Spencer, Sidgwick was an individualist. The individualist position was supported by two generalizations: 'the psychological generalization that individuals are likely to provide for their own welfare better than Government can provide for them, and the sociological generalization that the common welfare is likely to be best promoted by individuals promoting their private interest intelligently'.[188] Freedom of contract remained an essential component in his vision. The role of the legislature was

(1) to secure to every sane adult freedom to provide for his own happiness, by adapting the material world to the satisfaction of his own needs and desires, and establishing such relations with other human beings as may in his opinion conduce to the same end; (2) to secure him from pain or loss, caused directly or indirectly by the actions of other human beings—including in this loss any damage due to the non-performance of engagements made without coercion or deception.[189]

He spoke of an 'Individualistic Minimum' of government intervention, which entailed the 'middle axiom' of utilitarianism, 'that individuals are to be protected from deception, breach of engagement, annoyance, coercion, or other conduct tending to impede them in the pursuit of their ends, so far as such protection is conducive to the general happiness'.[190] Since this was only a 'middle axiom', it was open to modification, for the generalizations given above might not always hold true. Unlike Spencer, Sidgwick therefore did not rule out greater state intervention, though in the current state of society he felt there were limits as to how far this should go. Sidgwick accordingly supported the Poor Law, though not redistributive taxation.

[188] H. Sidgwick, *The Elements of Politics* (1891), 139.
[189] *Ibid.*, 53, quoted in Collini, *Liberalism and Sociology*, 18.
[190] Sidgwick, *Elements of Politics*, 55.

In the years after 1880, utilitarianism—both in Sidgwick's classical and Spencer's bastardized versions—became increasingly associated with individualism. The anti-individualist position came at this time to be associated with an idealist school of philosophy which exerted considerable influence in academic circles down to the First World War. The key founder of this movement is generally acknowledged to be Sidgwick's contemporary at Rugby school, T. H. Green. Professor of moral philosophy in Oxford, Green died in 1882 at the age of 45, having inspired a new school of idealists who would develop his ideas over the next four decades. Although Green's own politics were those of a mid-century liberal, his philosophy inspired a set of followers who were far more collectivist in outlook. Green and his students (notably D. G. Ritchie) developed a version of liberal theory which was more communitarian, and which stressed the role of the state in helping the citizen to be able to live a worthwhile life. It was a philosophy which well fitted the intellectual demands of the time.[191]

Green and his followers did not seek to build on the intuitionist theories of Coleridge and Whewell—regarding the foundations of their thought as having been discredited by Mill's assault—but took their inspiration from Kant and Hegel, whose works were regularly translated with commentaries in the last three decades of the century.[192] They also returned to the classics, drawing on Platonic and Aristotelian ideas. Green rejected the empiricist epistemology found in the tradition of Locke, Hume, and Mill. Following Kant, he held that the basic categories of thought were not derived from experience, but were themselves the preconditions of experience. It was through a unifying principle supplied by consciousness that objects of experience were related to each other and understood.[193] Green referred to the 'single self-conscious principle' which related all phenomena to each other as the 'eternal consciousness'. It represented the unity of knowledge. It was an insight into the mind of the divine for an era of a crisis in faith. In Green's view, men were ever tending towards this eternal consciousness,

---

[191] As Gertrude Himmelfarb pointed out, the posthumous *Principles of Political Obligation* and *Prolegomena to Ethics* were published in 1883, the same year as *The Bitter Cry of Outcast London*: Himmelfarb, *Poverty and Compassion: The Moral Imagination of the Late Victorians* (New York, 1991), 247.

[192] On Green and his idealist followers, see S. M. den Otter, *British Idealism and Social Explanation: A Study in Late Victorian Thought* (Oxford, 1996); A. Vincent and R. Plant, *Philosophy, Politics and Citizenship: The Life and Thought of the British Idealists* (Oxford, 1984); A. Vincent (ed.), *The Philosophy of T. H. Green* (Aldershot, 1986); P. P. Nicholson, *The Political Philosophy of the British Idealists: Selected Studies* (Cambridge, 1990). For broader studies of the intellectual foundations of 'New Liberalism', see Freeden, *New Liberalism* and P. F. Clarke, *Liberals and Social Democrats* (Cambridge, 1978).

[193] T. H. Green, *Prolegomena to Ethics* (3rd edn, ed. A.C. Bradley, Oxford, 1890), para. 32, p. 35.

as 'the one divine mind gradually reproduces itself in the human soul'. Although it was never fully realized 'in any life that can be observed',

Yet, because the essence of man's spiritual endowment is the consciousness of having it, the idea of his having such capabilities, and of a possible better state of himself consisting in their future realisation, is a moving influence in him. It has been the parent of the institutions and usages, of the social judgments and aspirations, through which human life has been so far bettered.[194]

This eternal consciousness was the telos of every individual, but it could only be attained with the collective development of humanity. As institutions and social arrangements developed, so the understanding of the good developed. Green insisted that the growth of moral ideas was not merely the progressive discovery of means of pleasure, but rather consisted of an 'increasing enlightenment as to what should be done', according to the ideal of the eternal consciousness. It implied 'a progressive determination of the idea of the end itself'. This end was not simply the good of each individual, but the development of a common good; for it was in the development of the community that the interest in moral qualities developed.[195]

Green's thinking built on a notion of the free moral will derived from Kant and Hegel. His notion of reason and will followed Kantian lines. Reason was 'the self-objectifying consciousness', which constituted the capability in man of seeking an absolute good, and 'which alone renders him a possible author and a self-submitting subject of law'.[196] For him, the free will was by definition the *good* will.[197] Hegelian influences could be found in his view that the 'self-seeking consciousness of man' gave rise to a set of social relations, which gave content to the ideal, 'working through generations of men'. The social state supplied interests 'of a more concrete kind than the interest in fulfilment of a universally binding law, but which yet are the product of reason, and in satisfying which he is conscious of attaining a true good—a good contributory to the perfection of himself and his kind'.[198] However, he was somewhat sceptical of Hegel's statist view. To begin with, he felt that one could only speak of freedom (in the sense of 'determination

---

[194] *Ibid.*, para. 180, p. 189.
[195] *Ibid.*, paras 241, 243–4, pp. 259, 261–2.
[196] *Ibid.*, paras 202–3, pp. 213–14.
[197] *Ibid.*, para. 154, p. 161.
[198] T. H. Green, 'On the Different Senses of "Freedom" as applied to Will and to the Moral Progress of Man', in P. Harris and J. Morrow (eds), *Lectures on the Principles of Political Obligation and Other Writings* (Cambridge, 1986), 232. In contrast to Kant, who rooted morality in a categorical imperative based on pure reason, Hegel had sought to locate it in actual communities. For him, freedom found its expression in the state and society, with the community being the expression of the rational will of its members.

by reason, autonomy of the will') in relation to individuals. Furthermore, he noted that the realization of such freedom in any society had been imperfect. As he put it, one could hardly speak of the state as the realization of freedom for 'the untaught and under-fed denizen of a London yard with gin-shops on the right and on the left'.[199]

Green's philosophy led him to emphasize the importance of rights. In his view, since individuals had to be free to will the ideal objects identified by reason, their freedom had to be protected by rights. His view of rights was not a Lockean one, which saw them inhering in man in a notional pre-social state. Nor did he think that existing positive law was ever all that it ought to be, so that rights would simply be what was protected by law. Instead, he argued that there was a system of rights and obligations which should be maintained by law. He called these rights 'natural' because they were 'necessary to the end which it is the vocation of human society to realise'.[200] Green's *jus naturae* (or *Naturrecht*) was more than morality, since it concerned outward acts capable of enforcement by law: it was a test of what the law should be. It was not deduced from original rights, but was 'relative to the moral end to which perfect law is relative'. It presupposed man's moral end. The nature of rights was discovered by considering what powers had to be secured to people to attain their end:

[T]he claim of right of the individual to have certain powers secured to him by society, and the counter-claim of society to exercise certain powers over the individual, alike rest on the fact that these powers are necessary to the fulfilment of his vocation as a moral being, to an effectual self-devotion to the work of developing the perfect character in himself and others.[201]

Moreover, all rights were social. There was no natural right to act as one liked irrespective of society. Rather, '[i]t is on the relation to a society—to other men recognizing a common good—that the individual's rights depend, as much as the gravity of a body depends on its relations to other bodies'.[202]

This perspective entailed a fundamental rethinking of liberal thought. In contrast to the branch of liberalism which derived its ideas from the Hobbesian notion that liberty was absence of constraint, and that government and law was a matter of coercion which restricted liberty, Green argued that the theorist had to look at the development of society, and the development of man through society.

---

[199] Green, 'On the Different Senses of "Freedom"', 233.

[200] T. H. Green, *Lectures on the Principles of Political Obligation*, para. 9, p. 17.

[201] *Ibid.*, paras 20–1, pp. 22–3.

[202] *Ibid.*, para. 99, p. 79. At para. 103 (p. 82), he noted that a 'right is a power of which the exercise by the individual or some body of men is recognised by a society either as itself directly essential to a common good or conferred by an authority of which the maintenance is recognised as so essential'.

To do so would show that freedom was to be thought of in terms of moral ends, and that government was to be seen in terms of a will to those ends, rather than as force. The philosopher needed to look at the processes by which men were clothed with rights and duties, independent of the existence of any sovereign power. The sovereign state did not create rights, but gave a fuller reality to rights already existing. It secured and extended 'the exercise of powers, which men, influenced in dealing with each other by an idea of common good, had recognised in each other as being capable of direction to that common good, and had already in a certain measure secured to each other in consequence of that recognition'.[203] A state therefore presupposed other forms of community, and the rights arising from them. These rights were then developed and articulated in the state. It was therefore an idea, rather than force, which gave birth to the state, and to rights.[204]

Like Maine, Green conceded that Austin's formal definition of sovereignty might be suitable for thoroughly developed states, where no legal control could be exerted over institutions with the power to make and enforce laws. But it only told half the story. Unlike Maine, who made no efforts to develop his own theory of the state, Green spelled out that '[t]he essential thing in political society is a power which guarantees men rights, i.e. a certain freedom of action and acquisition conditionally upon their allowing a like freedom in others'.[205] A political society was more complete, the more complete and extensive its guarantees of this freedom. What held political societies together was not the force exerted by the ruler, or the simple habit of people to obey:

That which determines this habitual obedience is a power residing in the common will and reason of men, i.e. in the will and reason of men as determined by social relations, as interested in each other as acting together for common ends. It is a power which this 'universal' rational will exercises over the inclinations of the individual, and which only needs exceptionally to be backed by coercive force.[206]

Whereas Maine derided Rousseau, Green felt that his notion of a general will was to be taken seriously. Whereas Austin's habit of obedience seemed a matter of fact, Green tied it to his idealist philosophy.

Green's rethinking of the notion of the state, freedom, and rights made him also rethink the scope of state action. He disagreed with Mill's notion that the business of law was only to prevent interference with the liberty of individuals.

---

[203] *Ibid.*, para. 132, p. 103.
[204] *Ibid.*, para. 136, p. 106: 'There is no right but thinking makes it so—none that is not derived from some idea that men have about each other.'
[205] *Ibid.*, para. 91, p. 73.
[206] *Ibid.*, para. 92, p. 74.

In his view, the real function of government was to maintain the conditions of life in which morality would be possible, morality being in Green's Kantian definition 'the disinterested performance of self-imposed duties'.[207] The state could intervene wherever obstacles existed impeding the human capacity for self-determination. Green explained his ideas to a wider public in a lecture published in 1881, on 'Liberal Legislation and Freedom of Contract'. In it, he noted that legislation passed since the 1867 Reform Act—such as the Employer's Liability Act—had been criticized for interfering with freedom of contract, the sacred principle of the mid-century. In the lecture, Green tried to get his liberal audience to think again about freedom, presenting a popular version of his ideas. He wanted his hearers to think of freedom in the positive sense: 'the liberation of the powers of all men equally for contributions to a common good'. When people spoke of freedom as something worth having, 'we mean a positive power or capacity of doing or enjoying something worth doing or enjoying'. The notion of freedom as absence of constraint was hollow, he noted, for the freedom of the savage could not be compared with the freedom of the humblest citizen of a law-abiding state At the same time, he reminded his auditors of the centrality of society in securing freedom. Every one had an interest in securing the free use and enjoyment of property, such as was compatible with an equal right in others, 'because such freedom contributes to that development of the faculties of all which is the highest good for all'.[208] This meant that some laws which appeared to restrict freedom of contract—those regulating labour conditions, sanitation, or education—were in fact necessary to enhance freedom:

Every injury to the health of the individual is, so far as it goes, a public injury. It is an impediment to the general freedom; so much deduction from our power, as members of society, to make the best of ourselves. Society is, therefore, plainly within its right when it limits freedom of contract for the sale of labour.[209]

Nevertheless, although Green was on the most advanced wing of the Liberal party, his own ideas of the range of state intervention were not especially radical: many of them were perfectly compatible with the views of other liberals of his day.[210]

---

[207] *Ibid.*, para. 18, p. 22.

[208] T. H. Green, 'Liberal Legislation and Freedom of Contract', in P. Harris and J. Morrow (eds), *Lectures on the Principles of Political Obligation and Other Writings* (Cambridge, 1986), 200.

[209] 'Liberal Legislation and Freedom of Contract', 201.

[210] He supported education reform, temperance reform, and land reform, notably to prevent land being tied up in settlements. Freeden has challenged the traditonal view that Green's brand of Idealism was responsible for the transformation of liberal ideas. In his view, Idealism was only one element in a general progressive movement in politics and ideology which drove liberalism towards

Green's thinking did, however, inspire a school of followers, whose ideas in turn would be influential on the debates on collectivism at the turn of the twentieth century. For instance, his student D. G. Ritchie (who died at the age of 50 in 1903) argued for much greater state intervention in his *Principles of State Interference*, developing Green's notion that the state should provide the environment in which people could achieve their self-realization. Richie was instrumental in fusing Green's notion of the moral state to the agenda of political reconstructions adopted by the New Liberals.[211] In his work, Ritchie particularly sought to counter Herbert Spencer arguments, arguing that society was the prime object of evolution, rather than the individual.

The influence of philosophy on the debates over policy should not be exaggerated. As Stefan Collini has written, 'Idealism was only ever a minority taste, though an ingredient in many of the intellectual cocktails of this period.'[212] Less philosophical ideas—those derived from evangelicalism and humanitarianism, which stressed the moral values of virtue and character—were likely to have as great a purchase on public debate as anything which went on in the universities. Nor was Idealism a united philosophical school. For instance, the idealist theory of the state developed by Green's pupil Bernard Bosanquet was a much more Hegelian version, which other liberals who were inspired by Green, such as L. T. Hobhouse, found sinister and potentially authoritarian. Nor did Bosanquet's enthusiasm for a notion of the general will prevent him from opposing old age pensions or being a strong supporter of the Charity Organisation Society, which opposed state intervention to alleviate poverty, preferring to stamp out 'pauperism' by improving the moral character of the poor.

Idealist philosophy was at most one among many ingredients in the political debates after the turn of the century. Moreover, it was often only one influence among many, even on the philosophically minded participants in the debate. For instance, L. T. Hobhouse, who was perhaps the most authoritative theorist of 'New Liberalism',[213] brought quite a load of idealist baggage to his theory. But he was also critical of aspects of the theory, and sought to develop a theory of moral evolution which had no counterpart in Green's thought. In particular, he felt that Green's Idealism failed to take empirical science seriously, and argued that 'a philosophy that was to possess more than a speculative interest must rest

collectivism. In retrospect, he argues, it came to seem more important than it was: *New Liberalism*, 16–19, 55–60.

[211] Freeden notes that 'among the Idealists it was Ritchie, not Green, who assisted most in formulating a new liberal theory of the state': *New Liberalism*, 58. See also den Otter, *British Idealism*, 170.

[212] Collini, *Liberalism and Sociology*, 45.

[213] Especially in his work *Liberalism* ([1911]).

on a synthesis of experience as interpreted by science'.[214] In his view, the key to this project was to be found in a theory of evolution which did not depend on individualism.

Finally, it should be noted that much of the reorientation of thinking about policy at the turn of the twentieth century reflected new ideas about economics, as much as it reflected new philosophical ideas about the relationship between the state and the individual. Just as Mill was able to rethink some of the fundamental problems of political economy towards the end of his life, so many other liberal utilitarians could modify their view of what liberty entailed and what utility dictated, when they saw economics in a new light.[215]

6. LATE NINETEENTH-CENTURY JURISPRUDENCE

Much of this turn in social and political thought passed over the heads of judges and jurists. J. F. Stephen and H. S. Maine were exceptional, as jurists, in making a mark with works on wider issues of political and social theory. By the 1870s, legal scholarship was becoming an increasingly professional matter, as the law curriculum was reinvigorated in the ancient universities, and as scholarly lawyers turned their minds to writing systematic treatises on distinct areas of law. Those who now wrote works of jurisprudence, such as T. E. Holland, Frederick Pollock, and John Salmond, also published works aimed at students of particular areas of law. They did not seek to write works on moral or political philosophy for a learned audience. The approach of the 'English school' can be seen in Pollock's views on the subject. Pollock was not uninterested in philosophical and ethical questions. Indeed, in 1880 he published a book on the life and philosophy of Spinoza, though it made no noticeable impact on his juristic writings.[216] In this same year, Pollock encountered the second, expanded, edition of the Scottish jurist James Lorimer's *The Institutes of the Law*. Lorimer was very familiar with continental philosophy, both legal and moral, and had read his Hegel. By contrast, he noted that '[u]tilitarianism [...] scarcely crossed the Border, and never crossed the Channel at all'.[217] His view of *Naturrecht* echoed the kind of philosophy developed by Green for his Oxford audiences. Pollock's reaction is telling, particularly since it came

---

[214] Quoted in Collini, *Liberalism and Sociology*, 150.

[215] For the economists, see Ch. VI, 'Law and Political Economy'.

[216] F. Pollock, *Spinoza: His Life and Philosophy* (1880). See further, N. Duxbury, *Frederick Pollock and the English Juristic Tradition* (Oxford, 2004), 89–96. Pollock argued that Spinoza's views on law and government 'distinctly belongs to the general doctrine characteristic of the English school of jurisprudence', whose genealogy was to be traced from Hobbes, via Bentham and Austin, to Maine (*Spinoza*, 310–11).

[217] J. Lorimer, *The Institutes of the Law: A Treatise on the Principles of Jurisprudence as Determined by Nature* (2nd edn, Edinburgh, 1880), ix.

from a man whose admiration for Savigny was considerable.[218] Reviewing the work, he admitted to having known of *Naturrecht* 'as a thing existing in German books', but he had never come across it to any serious extent. 'As I came to the last page I said to myself with a mental gasp and shiver, "Ugh! Ugh! now I know what *Naturrecht* is". Lorimer's work was the only one in English which adequately set out 'a view of the nature of jurisprudence diametrically opposed to that of the English analytical school'. For Pollock, it fell into the trap which the English avoided of failing to see the distinction between the realm of morality and that of law, by discussing the law as it should be. All that the jurist needed to know of morals was that a settled society existed with a settled common opinion of right and wrong, and a view that some rules of conduct had to be enforced by compulsion. Questions about the nature of moral obligation had no place in a text on jurisprudence. 'We may take the morality of men living together in settled societies as an existing and sufficiently ascertained fact', Pollock said. 'It is for the moralist and the metaphysician to analyse it if they can; enough for us that it is there.' Indeed, 'we may safely contend, without prejudging the issue between transcendental and empirical theories of duty, that profitable discussion of the origin and nature of laws in general must follow, and not precede, the scientific study of laws as they exist'. Having trawled his way through Lorimer, he was unimpressed, finding that the Scot had by a high-flying and circuitous route arrived 'at obvious general conclusions, or [...] at more precise ones by a slenderly disguised appeal to the principle of "what is vulgarly called expediency"'.[219]

Late nineteenth-century jurists had an ambivalent reaction to John Austin. Pollock referred to him as 'that clever but very narrow and grossly overrated dialectitian' whose work continued to be fed to students because 'a cocksure dogmatic theory, however bad, is good stuff to examine, and cram for examination'. F. W. Maitland was blunter still: 'J.A. = 0'.[220] At the same time, they accepted his definition that the 'province' of their study was only to study the positive law enforced in the courts. Austin himself was frequently criticized for including his

---

[218] Pollock had been influenced by Savigny's analytical jurisprudence, in his *System des heutigen Römischen Rechts* while writing his treatise on the law of contract, first published in 1876. It was only after 1880 that his enthusiasm for Savigny began to wane. See XII, pp. 309–12.

[219] The quotations above are taken from F. Pollock, 'The Nature of Jurisprudence', in his *Essays in Jurisprudence and Ethics* (1882), 18–28. Compare his view in *An Introduction to the History of the Science of Politics* (1890), 109–14, where he argued that both schools of political theory were equally dogmatic, but that the key point for the jurist to note was that the pure science of positive law was 'altogether independent of ethical theories'.

[220] C. H. S. Fifoot (ed.), *The Letters of Frederic William Maitland* (1965), 253; M. D. Howe (ed.), *The Pollock-Holmes Letters: Correspondence of Sir Frederick Pollock and Mr Justice Holmes 1874–1932*, 2 vols (Cambridge, 1942), ii: 263.

chapters on utility.[221] Moreover, they also agreed that students needed to learn the basic legal concepts provided by Austin's brand of analytical jurisprudence. Austin's jurisprudence remained dominant, primarily for its analytical value.[222] In the 1870s and 1880s, a new generation of jurists produced textbooks which analysed basic legal concepts for students, in a more accessible and digestible way than was found in the incomplete *Lectures*.[223] T. E. Holland, professor of international law in Oxford, presented readers with a view of the scope of his project which would have pleased Austin. It was to explain the few simple ideas which underlay the infinite variety of legal rules. The tools he aimed to provide were vital, for 'an uncodified system of law can be mastered only by the student whose scientific equipment enables him to cut a path through the tangled growth of enactment and precedent, so as to codify for his own purposes'.[224] Works such as these took care not to stray into the province of legislation, or to discuss the nature and purpose of law in a more philosophical way. John Salmond, the author of another influential work on jurisprudence, acknowledged that jurisprudence in its widest sense embraced the study of all species of obligatory rules in human action, and would include the study of natural law and international law, as well as the study of civil law, or the law of a state. However, he limited his own discussion to exploring 'the science of the first principles of the civil law', by which he meant 'those more fundamental conceptions and principles which serve as the basis of the concrete details of the law'. This subject dealt with material to be found in the various 'practical' fields of civil law; and provided tools not only for the systematic study of law (or legal exposition), but also for the historical study of civil law, and the critical study, or science of legislation.[225] Pollock, who also

---

[221] Frederic Harrison said that his discussion of utility 'is perfectly beside his own avowed method, and I think in itself almost worthless': 'The English School of Jurisprudence: Part I—Austin and Maine on Sovereignty' (1878) 24 *Fortnightly Review* (N.S.) 475–92 at 479. Another critic, Pollock, therefore regarded Holland's book as the 'first work of pure scientific jurisprudence' in England: Pollock, *Introduction to the History of the Science of Politics*, 63.

[222] For discussion of the jurisprudence of this era, see R. Cosgrove, *Scholars of the Law* (New York, 1996); D. Sugarman, 'Legal Theory, the Common Law Mind and the Making of the Textbook Tradition: Some Aspects of the Intellectual History of Modern Legal Thought and Education', in W. Twining (ed.), *Legal Theory and the Common Law* (Oxford, 1986), 25–61; P. Schofield, 'Jeremy Bentham and Nineteenth-Century English Jurisprudence' (1991) 12 *JLH* 58–88; M. Lobban, 'Was there a Nineteenth Century "English School of Jurisprudence"?' (1995) 16 *JLH* 34–62; N. Duxbury, 'English Jurisprudence between Austin and Hart' (2005) 91 *Virginia Law Review* 1–91.

[223] Such works included W. Markby, *Elements of Law, Considered with Reference to Principles of General Jurisprudence* (2nd edn, Oxford, 1874); T. E. Holland, *The Elements of Jurisprudence* (2nd edn, Oxford, 1882); J. Salmond, *Jurisprudence, or the Theory of the Law* (2nd edn, 1907); W. Jethro Brown, *The Austinian Theory of Law* (1906).

[224] Holland, *Jurisprudence* (2nd edn), 1.

[225] Salmond, *Jurisprudence* (2nd ed), 4–7.

wrote a *First Book of Jurisprudence*, setting out basic concepts for the law student, had an ambivalent view of the value of such works. In his view, works which were in effect abstract grammars of law were best regarded as preparing the ground for the real task of the jurist, which was to provide a scientific exposition of English law.[226]

At the same time, jurists followed Maine in qualifying Austin's command theory. Instead of seeing all law in modern societies as the commands of a sovereign, Holland defined law as 'a general rule of external human action *enforced* by a sovereign political authority'.[227] In common with all jurists who had read Maine, he accepted that customary rules existed prior to their legal enforcement, but insisted that it was state recognition—albeit retrospective—which gave them the force of law.[228] Holland himself rejected the view of the German historical school that law was begotten in the people by any kind of *Volksgeist*. But other jurists appeared willing to edge in that direction. In an essay on 'Law and Command' written in 1872, Pollock stated that Austin's focus on command 'seriously obscures the organic relation of law to the community'.[229] Drawing the theoretical conclusions implicit in Maine's history, Pollock said that

[i]f we once admit that the sovereign has nothing to do with making the custom into law beyond a general silent assent, then it is surely the better way to refer the validity of the custom at once to the assent of those who made it, for after all the existence and power of the sovereign depend directly or indirectly [...] on the assent of the nation, and when the nation, or some part of it, makes a rule to itself by a gradual and indefinite consent, it seems hardly needful to suppose that such consent becomes operative by a feigned transmission through a sovereign.[230]

This definition, Pollock pointed out, would allow for the acknowledgement that international law was more than the positive morality Austin had characterized it to be.[231] Moreover, rethinking law in this way meant that law could be seen as

---

[226] F. Pollock, 'The Nature of Jurisprudence', in his *Essays in Jurisprudence and Ethics* (1882), 8.

[227] Holland, *Jurisprudence* (2nd edn), 34 (emphasis added).

[228] *Ibid.*, 49: 'It does not *proprio motu* then [at the time of a judgment] for the first time make that custom a law; it merely decides as a fact, that there exists a legal custom, about which there might up to that moment have been some question, as there might about the interpretation of an Act of Parliament'.

[229] F. Pollock, 'Law and Command' (1872) 1 *LM* 189–205 at 191.

[230] *Ibid.*, 198.

[231] Other writers on international law were equally keen to stress that the jurist seeking to understand law should focus his attention on the question of order, rather than force. See J. Westlake, *Chapters on the Principles of International Law* (Cambridge, 1894), 2–3; T. J. Lawrence, 'Is there a true International law?' in his *Essays on Some Disputed Questions in Modern International Law* (Cambridge and London, 1885), 16, discussed in Lobban, 'English Approaches to International Law in the Nineteenth Century', in M. Craven, M. Fitzmaurice, and M. Vogiatzi (eds), *Time, History and International Law* (Leiden, 2007), 65–90 at 83–6.

part of the normal development of society, rather than as an abnormal restraint imposed by a legislator. It would allow the recognition of 'the systematic unity which is the real informing body of law'.[232]

Similarly, John Salmond argued that law emanated from the community, finding its expression through the judges. In his view, while the formal source of customary law was the state's power of enforcement, its material source was 'popular conscience embodie[d] [...] in popular usage'.[233] Custom was 'the embodiment of those principles which have commended themselves to the national conscience as principles of truth, justice, and public utility'. While accepting that the law was distinct from private morality, Salmond nonetheless saw it as a moral system. For him, the primary function of the state was 'to maintain right, to uphold justice, to protect rights, to redress wrongs'. Justice was the end, law the instrument, 'and the instrument must be defined by reference to its end'. The aggregate of rules which made up the legal system was 'not a condition precedent of the administration of justice, but a product of it'. The development of law occurred through the progressive substitution of fixed principles for individual judgments about justice, largely developing 'spontaneously within the legal tribunals themselves'.[234]

Jurists such as Pollock or Salmond, who conceived of law as developing along with community morality, had no interest in philosophizing on *Naturrecht*, for they were not attracted by the idealist view that such a law was an ideal type to which positive law should ever be tending.[235] Rather, they saw morality as a matter of fact, or a matter of social practice which the jurist had to accept, but not analyse or explain. Pollock took a common-sense view of morality. Theories of ethics only sought to make explicit what was already implicit in practical morality. 'The scientific basis of working morals is not in any formulated rules or propositions', he noted, 'but in the mass of continuous experience half-consciously or

---

[232] F. Pollock, 'Law and Command', 203.

[233] Salmond, *Jurisprudence* (2nd edn, 1907), 49–50, 121.

[234] *Ibid.*, 144, 13–14.

[235] Compare the practical view of Frederic Harrison: having anticipated some of H. L. A. Hart's criticisms of Austin's command theory (notably the fact that many rules of law could not meaningfully be analysed as commands backed by sanctions), and criticized Austin's scheme of classification, he argued that '[Jurisprudence] can be placed no higher than a systematic arrangement of rules established by practical convenience; and the attempt to base it on psychological principles, or theories of abstract logic, seems arbitrary and quite illusory. Practical convenience is the source of law; and technical convenience is the aim of all classification of law.' Harrison's view tended towards pragmatism: 'even in law, *right* never means more than that the courts will enforce a given claim to an individual advantage, provided the doing so does not work some countervailing disadvantage to others of overwhelming and specific kinds': 'The English School of Jurisprudence. Part II: Bentham and Austin's Analysis of Law' (1878) 24 *Fortnightly Review* (NS) 682–703 at 698–9, 702.

unconsciously accumulated and embodied in the morality of common sense'.[236] In his view, it did not require moral philosophy to ascertain the kind of conduct which promoted the welfare of society: for this was 'just what the common experience of mankind has been doing for all the time that men have lived together'.[237] The fact that one might not have an absolute standard of right and wrong was beside the point: '[a]ll that we need is a standard sufficiently adapted to the conditions of life in which we act and judge for the time being'. He therefore rejected the intuitionist approach for the 'historical'—or empirical—one. Pollock found Spencer's utilitarian evolutionary theory particularly attractive, arguing that moral feeling was the result of 'certain social feelings and tendencies of man, guided by ancestry and individual experiences of utility'.[238]

This left unanswered the question of how judges were to deal with novel questions, or how the practitioner should advise clients. Pollock addressed these issues in an essay on 'The Science of Case Law', where he sought to apply the inductive method to legal reasoning. Pollock began with the premise that like cases would be treated alike, and that precedents would be followed. In advising a client on a novel case, the lawyer would need to select the right kind of cases with which to compare the set of facts before him. Out of these materials, he would infer a conclusion which would indicate how the new case would be decided. Although Pollock claimed that the method was a kind of scientific induction which might generate predictions, his description of how lawyers found their answers hardly promised scientific precision. He described the task as a job for experts, who 'acquire an unconscious habit of looking at the matters of their own art in the right way, which may almost be called an instinct'.[239] What guided the lawyer and the highest court to the right decision was 'an ideal standard of scientific fitness and harmony'. Pollock's ideal standard was not a Kantian notion, but the common sense of the common lawyer:

This is rather a matter of fact than a matter of theory or even of convention, and is the natural result of the judges having been long trained in legal habits of mind. The ideal standard is, in fact, nothing else than the objective side of the legal habit of mind itself, when considered as independent of the particular individuals in whom the habit is formed. It cannot be found in any one book or in any one lawyer, but only in the collective opinion of legal experts.[240]

---

[236] F. Pollock, 'Mr Spencer's Data of Ethics', in his *Essays in Jurisprudence and Ethics* (1882), 352–77 at 353.

[237] *Ibid.*, 359.

[238] *Ibid.*, 370.

[239] F. Pollock, 'The Science of Case Law', in *Essays in Jurisprudence and Ethics* (1882), 237–60 at 249.

[240] Pollock, 'The Science of Case Law', 251.

This ideal standard modified over time, but so slowly that at any given moment it could be regarded as fixed. Moreover, he conceded that judges constantly decided what the law should be, when case law was silent or ambiguous, despite jurists' protestations that the lawyer dealt only with law as it was, and not as it should be.[241] In effect, they decided according to what the collective opinion of experts decided the ideal to be. In another article, 'The Casuistry of Common Sense', Pollock suggested that a similar method could be used to predict how ethical questions might be determined in future. Practical moral judgments, he suggested, were made in a similar way to legal ones, following settled precedents—the 'existing standard of positive morality'—while also regarding an ideal standard.[242] Pollock's common sense had nothing to do with the philosophy of Thomas Reid. It was the bluff common sense of the 'right-thinking' Victorian Englishman,[243] and the right-thinking judge. Although Pollock later abandoned his claims regarding prediction, he continued to conceive of law as developed by men of learned character such as himself.[244]

In 1883, Pollock succeeded Maine in the chair of jurisprudence at Oxford University. His chair required him to give a historical and comparative treatment to jurisprudence, and Pollock fully realized his duty to work in the spirit of that 'illustrious leader', Maine.[245] If historical and comparative jurisprudence was more to his taste than the analytical brand,[246] however, Pollock did not carry Maine's torch. Although his successor in the chair, Paul Vinogradoff, sought to reinvigorate the tradition of Maine, the version of historical jurisprudence which began with *Ancient Law* largely ran into the sand.[247] Pollock himself had no clear ideas on what specifically jurisprudential insights the historical or comparative method could give. As Duxbury has put it, he treated the historical and comparative methods 'as an exercise in rummaging through the past or through other

---

[241] F. Pollock, 'The Casuistry of Common Sense', in *Essays in Jurisprudence and Ethics* (1882), 261–86 at 283.

[242] *Ibid.* at 276.

[243] 'When we appeal to the moral sense of mankind—meaning thereby the civilized part of mankind whose character and circumstances are like enough to our own to make their opinions worth considering—or more specially, as we sometimes do, to the moral sense of Englishmen, we mean that there is a certain way of thinking on questions of morality which we expect to find in a reasonable civilized man': 'The Casuistry of Common Sense', 270.

[244] On Pollock's ideas on prediction, and how they compared with Holmes, see Duxbury, *Pollock*, 116–24.

[245] Duxbury, *Pollock*, 49.

[246] N. Duxbury, 'Why English Jurisprudence is Analytical' (2004) 57 *Current Legal Problems* 1–51 at 7.

[247] S. Collini, D. Winch, and J. Burrow, *That Noble Science of Politics: A Study in Nineteenth-Century Intellectual History* (Cambridge, 1983), 209. On Vinogradoff, see N. O'Brien, '"In Vino Veritas": Truth and Method in Vinogradoff's Historical Jurisprudence' (2008) 29 *JLS* 39–61.

legal systems to find new ways of exhibiting the genius of the common law'.[248] The study of legal history in late nineteenth century England took two forms.[249] The first was its study by those, such as Maitland, who did not look to history for lessons for the lawyer, but rather sought to uncover the past. Maitland told Dicey in 1896, 'I have not for many years past believed in what calls itself historical jurisprudence.'[250] For Maitland, a legal training was a vital prerequisite for the legal historian; but a knowledge of 'the remoter parts of history' was not a pre-requisite for the lawyer.[251] Pollock famously dabbled in this kind of history, getting top billing on Maitland's masterpiece, the *History of English Law*.[252] Equally well known is the fact that Maitland hurried to finish his writing, to ensure that Pollock's rather more inexpert contribution would be kept to a minimum. The second form of study of legal history was that engaged in by doctrinalists seeking to make sense of and explain areas of law. Perhaps the most notable early exponent of this was O. W. Holmes, much of whose *Common Law* was devoted to attempting to understand the shape of particular legal doctrines through tracing their evolution in the common law. Holmes's larger project of drawing out general doctrinal principles from a study of the development of the common law was not echoed by English scholars.[253] Nonetheless, scholars on both sides of the Atlantic did engage in legal-historical research, to explore the history of complex doctrines, such as consideration in contract law. If Mainite social theory withered, doctrinal legal history flourished on both sides of the Atlantic, at a time when private law scholarship was especially fruitful, as lawyers sought to uncover and systematize the principles of tort law and contract.[254]

It has been generally agreed by scholars that English jurisprudence in the late nineteenth and early twentieth centuries was in a pretty sorry state.[255] It took H. L. A. Hart's engagement with Austin to breathe new life into it in the 1950s.

[248] Duxbury, *Pollock*, 115.

[249] For a detailed treatment, see K. J. M. Smith and J. P. S. McLaren, 'History's Living Legacy: an Outline of "Modern" Historiography of the Common Law' (2001) 21 *Legal Studies* 251–324.

[250] P. N. R. Zutschi (ed.), *The Letters of Frederic William Maitland* (1995), ii: 105.

[251] F. W. Maitland, 'Why the History of English law is Not Written', in H. A. L. Fisher (ed.), *The Collected Papers of Frederick William Maitland* 3 vols (Cambridge, 1911), i: 493.

[252] F. Pollock and F. W. Maitland, *The History of English Law before the time of Edward I* (Cambridge, 1895).

[253] His friend Pollock was perhaps the one scholar who might have done so: but rather than write a book on the theory behind common law doctrines (as *The Common Law* was), he wrote treatises on contract and tort, often drawing on Holmes's ideas.

[254] Prominent American scholars in this field included J. B. Ames, J. B. Thayer, and J. H. Wigmore. In England, this approach was taken in the interwar years by tort scholars such as P. H. Winfield. Moreover, those private lawyers who did not themselves undertake legal-historical research nevertheless handled their doctrine with one eye on their historical development.

[255] Duxbury, 'English Jurisprudence', 4.

Theory was weak because lawyers were more interested in the practical issue of the 'analysis and consolidation of the actual doctrines of law under systematic titles' and with 'preparing the way for the ultimate consolidation of our system into a form which shall be worthy of its past history'. To do this, as Frederic Harrison argued in 1879, a combination of the analytic, the historical, and the comparative was needed:

The substance of our jurisprudence now must be the systematic analysis of all the leading titles and doctrines which are found in a working code; the reduction of these to a series of digests arranged on a general principle; and the collation of these rules with the bodies of law now governing the lives of people in a state of advanced civilisation for their ultimate end.[256]

At the end of our period, jurisprudence therefore remained the servant of the practical lawyer, who was primarily interested in understanding and arranging doctrine. It was not a means through which he would gain access to the broader insights of philosophers, sociologists, or policy-makers.

---

[256] F. Harrison, 'The English School of Jurisprudence. Part III: The Historical Method' (1879) 25 *Fortnightly Review* (N.S.) 114–30 at 126, 130.

V
Law and Religion

1. REINFORCING TWO FACES OF SOCIAL MORALITY: REPRESSION AND COMPASSION

Well before the 1820s, beside their important constitutional and institutional roles,[1] Christianity and Christian ethics had assumed a manifest core significance in the nation's evolving social and political values and objectives. Consequently, providing any sort of account of the role of religion in Victorian law necessarily requires some initial acquaintance with the religio-legal scene to be found at the end of the eighteenth century and the early decades of the nineteenth. However, while significant religious belief or dogma would endure and influence opinion and attitudes throughout the Victorian era, it was an influence that markedly fell away or changed in its nature well before the century's end.

In terms of its political position or function, the Established Anglican clergy largely inhabited mainstream Toryism and, less typically, Whig circles, as in the case of the celebrated wit and commentator, the Reverend Sydney Smith.[2] At a local level, the clergy might play a key secular role as councillor in the business of their parish vestry, or even as a Justice of the Peace.[3] Religious pastoral care and instruction tended to be characterized by understatement, if not outright neglect.[4] While in a more diffused sense contributing to the ambient moral climate, it was implicitly accepted that Christian religion and its precepts were, by

---

[1] Below, Pt 2.

[2] See J. C. Clark, *English Society 1660–1832, Religion, ideology and politics during the ancien regime* (Cambridge, 1985, revised 2000) for the argument that the 1832 Reform Act was, to a substantial degree, the consequence of growth in religious dissent and decline in the position of the Established church.

[3] From the 1830s, the number of clergymen appointed to sit as magistrates steadily declined. The Church authorities indicated concern over the possible incompatibility of pastoral and penal roles. The Whig government of this period also expressed discomfort at the possible problems of combining these duties: W. Jacob, *The Clerical Profession in the Long Eighteenth Century 1680–1840* (Oxford, 2007), 233–4. Also for the decline from the 1820s in Essex, see P. King, *Crime, Justice and Discretion in England 1740–1820* (Oxford, 2000), 123.

[4] P. Virgin, *The Church in an Age of Negligence: Ecclesiastical Structure and Problems of Church Reform 1700–1840* (Cambridge, 1989).

and large, not to be strenuously inserted into the everyday affairs of parishioners. Until Wesley's appearance in the mid-eighteenth century and the eventual sever-ance of Methodists from the Established church, Christian ethics were rarely the banner under which social and political ambitions were advanced. Even then, no serious social and political programme was presented; spiritual regeneration through revelation was at that time the primary Wesleyan ambition. Broader objectives and political activism, however, arrived with the late eighteenth cen-tury Anglican Evangelical revival. For Evangelicals, the means and goal were blindingly clear: direct and fervent engagement with people's lives rather than traditional church rituals saved souls; spiritual re-birth and eventual salvation through atonement were to be gained by combining personal rectitude with per-forming God's good works in all areas of social existence.[5]

Wesleyans and other Dissenters who broke away from the Established church shared much of Evangelicalism's dissatisfaction with mainstream Anglicanism's tepid, milk and water Christian faith. For these religious groups, divine revela-tion through the primacy of Biblical scripture and commitment to Christ guided all conduct; bringing this understanding of their faith directly to the population at large was the supreme mission. However, despite being a considerably larger body than the Anglican Evangelicals, the early nineteenth-century potential influence of Methodists was less significant than that of Evangelicals because of the former's relative weakness and latter's strength of support amongst the professional and governing classes.[6] Absorption of revivified Christian gospel by this social and political strata crucially translated into the establishment of a wide range of campaigning societies intent on influencing and improving many features of the population's manners, morals, and institutions. Naturally, as part of their mission, the content and enforcement of the nation's laws were of con-siderable interest to the Evangelicals. Over the course of the subsequent century, Christian moralizing, initially in its Evangelical form and later of a more diffuse character, played a frequently visible role in influencing the law's scope, content, and process of enforcement. And while not exclusively at work within the orbit of the criminal law,[7] it was within that particular context where Christian moralism most conspicuously operated as a motivating force.

Especially over the first half of the nineteenth century, in many respects Utilitarianism and Evangelicalism were the two competing and complementary

---

[5] For the varieties of Evangelicalism, see D. Bebbington, *The Nonconformist Conscience* (1982) and B. Hilton, *The Age of Atonement* (Oxford, 1988), Ch. 1.

[6] e.g. (1825) 15 *Blackwood's Mag.* 395.

[7] Religious ethics and practice in relation to commercial law and cognate areas are examined as part of 'Law and Political Economy', below, Ch. VI.

social, political, and economic working ideologies;[8] in one sense, they constituted a blend of manners, morals, and outlook that became the essence of Victorianism. Carlyle's inimitable late 1820s lament, 'Sign of the Times', captured the impact of this powerful ideological coalition on the period's social and religious climate: a ' "superior morality" of which we hear so much . . . produced [by] that far subtler and stronger Police, called Public Opinion'.[9]

At first blush, Utilitarianism's and Evangelicalism's respective core beliefs and social philosophies suggested inherent antipathy: divine revelation set against secular rationalism; self-denial versus the pursuit of self-interest. Yet by curious alchemy, they frequently combined to produce the middle and governing class response to large-scale problems of the times, including education, health, factory regulation, and penal laws. Consequently, it became a truism that weekday professionals and businessmen were Sunday Evangelicals. Personal responsibility, self-improvement, together with social progress and national prosperity were common objectives of Evangelicals and Utilitarians; these were the shared goals which spawned collective allegiance to dominant notions of political economy and practical offshoots, including the Society for the Suppression of Mendicity.[10] For both persuasions, moral failure through indulging in immediate gratifications and neglecting essential future aims was the certain route to individual and national impoverishment. Spiritual needs were met by taking deep draughts from the book of Exodus and the Gospels; intellectual or practical nourishment might be offered by self-improving Utilitarian bodies such as Brougham's Society for the Diffusion of Useful Knowledge—waggishly dubbed the 'Steam Intellect Society'.[11] For secular Utilitarianism, temporal achievements were initial and final aims; for Evangelicals a pure soul and salvation were ultimate goals. Yet, commonality of earthly objectives greatly exceeded philosophical differences, famously making possible support and collaboration between the avowed atheist Bentham and the saintly Wilberforce in respect of the proposed building of the former's

[8] On the balance of influence between these two forces, see e.g. E. Paul, *Moral Revolution and Economic Science* (Westport, 1979) and Hilton, *Age of Atonement*.

[9] (1829) 49 *Edin. Rev.* 439–59, 452.

[10] Established in 1818, it enjoyed royal patronage, with organized support from Evangelicals, the Quaker (and close friend of Wilberforce) William Allen, and Utilitarians such as David Ricardo. The Mendicity Society's broad twin aim was assisting beggars and vagrants who were victims of misfortune to regain moral self-respect and employment, and to facilitate prosecution of those judged incorrigibly work-shy. For officially assembled evidence of the extent of and concern over London vagrancy, see the *House of Commons Select Committee on the State of Mendicity and Vagrancy in the Metropolis, PP* 1814–15 (473), iii, 1 and *PP* 1816 (396), v, 1.

[11] By Thomas Love Peacock in *Crotchet Castle* (1831). To ensure consumption of only wholesome reading material the Evangelicals set up various bodies including the 'Society for the Diffusion of Pure Literature'. Thomas Bowdler's *Family Shakespeare* (1818) offered a work stripped of real and imagined 'profaneness and obscenity'.

Panopticon penitentiary,[12] later broadly realized in Millbank's construction. And it was much the same joint belief in equating the deemed immorality of unproductive behaviour and homelessness with vagrancy and criminality, which led to successful joint efforts to give sharper summary teeth to the vagrancy laws in the 1820s.[13]

But there was considerable complexity in this relationship. As well as many shared aims, between these ideologies ran an infinite range of cross-currents in beliefs and objectives. For instance, while undiluted Benthamic Utilitarianism had no truck with religion, many adhering to a progressive rationalist approach to politics and law were by no means divorced from Christian faith. Yet, at the same time, the religious underpinnings of the *ancien regime's* penal philosophy was Paley's gospel of utility and expediency, one directly inspired by his own construction of God's will. Moreover, amongst Paley's fiercest critics were not only the broad coalition of humanitarian/rationalist figures (such notables as Romilly, Mackintosh, Lushington, and Brougham) but also the leading group of Evangelical penal reformers. For them, morality was a matter of direct divine revelation; what might promote greatest human happiness was not a question of calculation and expediency.[14] Buxton was a prime example of one driven by a powerful brew of Evangelical inspiration while also hugely adept in marshalling Utilitarian/rationalist arguments favouring penal law revisions. Only in the crudest sense might the clichéd contrast be drawn between Evangelical emotionalism and dispassionate Utilitarian calculation. Overall, though each started from a distinct point of reference, they broadly shared the objectives of a more humane and effective system, with Evangelicals never losing sight of the ultimate determinant of success: redemption.

2. CRIME AND EARTHLY PUNISHMENT

Evangelical activism had engaged itself on a broad and fundamental social and political front from the 1780s. The directly politically active membership of the Evangelicals, the Clapham Sect, or 'the Saints', as their parliamentary brigade was styled, enjoyed a high profile, including amongst their members the Macaulays, Stephens, and Venns, together with William Wilberforce and Henry Thornton, rector of Holy Trinity, Clapham. Tenacious parliamentary and national campaigning led principally by William Wilberforce and later Thomas Fowell Buxton constituted the most fervent and determined representation of a

---

[12] *Collected Works of Jeremy Bentham, Correspondence 1797–1800* (ed.) J. R. Dinwiddy (Oxford, 1984), vi.

[13] See XIII, Pt 1.

[14] Especially, T. Gisborne, *Principles of Moral Philosophy* (1789).

much broader coalition of religious or plain humanitarian inspired supporters.[15] The involvement of the leading lights of late eighteenth and early nineteenth-century Evangelicalism, along with others of differing moral complexions in the abolition of the slave trade and eventually the use of slaves in the British Empire, is well documented.[16] Of similar breadth of persuasion were campaigners seeking the decapitalizing of all or most criminal offences with the substitution of imprisonment or transportation.

Religious inspiration figured prominently in developments associated with capital punishment well into the 1830s. Along with Quakers, Wilberforce and Buxton,[17] as Evangelicals, were typical in opposing the Paleyite regime of widespread capital threats, with the discretionary carrying out of executions. Romilly's largely unsuccessful attempts to reduce the span of capital statutes consistently gained the active support of parliamentary Evangelicals and Quakers who had set up the 'Society for Diffusion of Knowledge upon the Punishment of Death and the Improvement of Prison Discipline' in 1808, known as the 'Capital Punishment Society'.[18] Together with campaigners motivated by utilitarian calculation rather than divine inspiration, Evangelicals also argued the rationalist case against capital punishment. Buxton in particular more than once in the Commons demonstrated a formidable command of the full spread of anti-capital punishment arguments.[19] Indeed, both Buxton and Wilberforce in Parliament, supported by organized Evangelicals and Quakers outside, played a pivotal role in ensuring the establishment of the 1819 Select

[15] On the development of the Evangelical strain within the Anglican Church, see D. Bebbington, *Evangelicalism in Modern Britain: A History from the 1730s to the 1980s* (1989). On the schisms amongst Evangelicals in the first half of the nineteenth century, see G. Carter, *Anglican Evangelicals: Protestant Secessions from the Via Media c. 1800–1850* (Oxford, 2001).

[16] For the early campaign to ban the slave trading, see J. Oldfield, *Popular Politics and British Anti-Slavery: The Mobilisation of Public Opinion against the Slave Trade 1787–1807* (Manchester, 1995). On the later campaign to prohibit the use of slaves in British colonies, see F. Kingsberg, *The Anti-Slavery Movement in England: A Study in English Humanitarianism* (1968).

[17] Generally, XIII, Pt 1, and Wilberforce, *Practical View* (1797); Buxton *An Inquiry* (1818). Also, B. Montague, *A Brief Statement of the Proceedings in Both Houses of Parliament ... with a View to the Amendment of the Criminal Law* (1811). The principal Evangelical-inspired philosophical refutation of Paley was T. Gisborne, *Principles of Moral Philosophy* (1789). Not all Evangelicals took this view, Spencer Perceval when Prime Minister was a defender of the status quo on punishment: *PD* 1811 (s1) 19: 655. See also the extreme views of the severe Evangelical Robert Seeley, *The Perils of the Nation: An Appeal to the Legislature ...* (1843 edn).

[18] By the Evangelically inclined Montague and the Quaker anti-slaver, William Allen. See Montague's *An Account of the Origin and Object of the Society for the Diffusion of Knowledge upon the Punishment of Death* (1812). Montague was the author of a substantial clutch of anti-capital punishments tracts. For example, *Some Inquiries respecting the Punishment of Death for Crimes without Violence* (1818); *On the Effects of Capital Punishment as applied to Forgery and Theft* (1818); and *Thoughts on the Punishment of Death for Forgery* (1830).

[19] For example, *PD* 1819 (s1) 39: 806–14.

Committee on Criminal Laws. Moreover, a substantial proportion of the pro-reform petitions which rained on Parliament in the period running up to 1819 was the handiwork of Quakers and Evangelical groups. This was emphatically true of the petition delivered by the Corporation of the City of London, which marshalled a forceful combination of practical and Christian moralist reform arguments.[20]

As a consequence of adroit political manoeuvring led by Mackintosh and Buxton, against Government wishes,[21] two separate Select Committees were appointed in 1819: one to examine the state and function of prisons; the other to consider the criminal law. Both Committees included several leading Evangelicals such as Buxton, Wilberforce, and Holford. As shown elsewhere,[22] this Evangelical faction along with other staunch penal reformers like Mackintosh and Lushington, persisted in their mission for rather greater reform innovation in the criminal justice system than Peel, as Home Secretary, was prepared to concede.[23] Arguably, more than any other reformist factions, it was Evangelicals and Quakers who provided the enduring core of determined, informed, and organized campaigning both in and outside Parliament, that ensured the capital question never retreated long from public or parliamentary prominence. While the true nature of Peel's personal inclinations towards capital punishment reform are disputable, religiously inspired activism was at least a principal force in ensuring that by the 1820s neglect of the subject was not a political option.

Aside from capital punishment, the particular involvement of Evangelical individuals and societies, in alliance with Utilitarians, was especially extensive in respect of prison reform. Prison and transportation were inevitably linked to the capital question: a strategy for replacing the capital threat was a pre-condition of scaling down the vast range of capital offences.[24] For John Howard and George Holford, both Evangelicals, religious instruction and salvation were

---

[20] The Quaker banker, Samuel Hoare, was chief organizer of the 'Petition of the Corporation of London, Complaining of the Criminal Law', *PD* 1819 (s1) 39: 81. Amongst the petition's 'general principles' for incorporation in the criminal law, was the 'diffusion of Christianity, by which we are daily taught to love each other as brethren, and to desire not the death of a sinner, but rather that he should turn from his wickedness and live' (84).

[21] By appointing a single committee to consider both prisons and the criminal law, the government appeared to hope that the review process might be more easily controlled and slowed to a politically less threatening pace. See the detailed account in XIII, Pt 1 and R. Follett, *Evangelicalism, Penal Theory and the Politics of Criminal Law Reform 1808–1830* (2001), Ch. 9.

[22] For the 1824 Select Committee on Criminal Laws and the range of Peel's consolidation and procedural measures, see XIII, Pt 1.

[23] For Buxton's prominent role in the close fought attempts during the late 1820s and early 1830s to de-capitalize all forms of forgery, see Follett, *Evangelicalism*, 178–81.

[24] XIII, Pt 1.

explicit central components of their national prison schemes.[25] Along with Quakers[26] and fellow travellers, Evangelicals were the backbone of the Society for the Improvement of Prison Discipline and Reformation of Juveniles, established in 1818.[27] Success in achieving improvements in the physical conditions of prisoners was at the cost of the eventual dominance of the 'separate system' of cellular isolation. Widespread employment of this technique was inspired by the virulent strain of Evangelicalism which possessed Millbank's Chaplain, Whitworth Russell.[28] The results of this practice were pitiful:

This unwise project for spiritually drilling the felons into repentance was...a failure; the incidental circumstance that the discipline was over-tinctured with the views of one particular school did not increase the chance of success. The terrors of the law were abundantly preached in the chapel, tracts were diligently circulated in the wards, and the turnkeys transformed into Scripture readers, and sent on pastoral visits from cell to cell. Of course, all the readiest rogues played the inevitable game, donned a sanctimonious demeanour, and curried favour by hypocrisy; while a few of the weaker sort went mad under the combined influences of solitude, malaria and Calvinism.[29]

It was an extreme technique of the 1820s and 1830s that contrasted with earlier Evangelicals, such as Howard and Holford, whose regime of gospel instruction to convert criminals also allowed for a modest level of daytime socializing amongst prisoners.[30] And as Buxton maintained, the alternative to capital punishment was religious education, 'hard labour and occasional solitary confinement'.[31]

As indicated, Evangelicalism's engagement in the general cause of punishment reform was a shared venture with individuals and groups less directly motivated by powerful Christian belief.[32] Those such as Romilly, Mackintosh,

---

[25] John Howard, *The State of the Prisons in England and Wales* (1777). *Select Committee* (Holford) *Reports*, PP 1810–11 (199), iii, 567 and (217), iii, 691; 1812 (306), ii, 313.

[26] Especially banking families such as the Frys, Gurneys, and Hoares. Also James Nield, disciple of Howard and author of *State of the Prisons in England, Scotland and Wales* (1812) and J. J. Gurney (brother of Elizabeth Fry) *Notes on a Visit Made to Some of the Prisons in Scotland and the North of England* (1819).

[27] Most particularly Samuel Hoare, its chairman, and Thomas Fowell Buxton, author of *An Inquiry [into] Prison Discipline* (1818). Buxton became a Quaker on marriage in 1807 but expressed an Evangelical allegiance in 1811. By the time of its winding up in 1832, the Society had issued several extensive critical reports on the state and management of prisons which were instrumental in the enactment of prison legislation in 1823 and 1824.

[28] Brother of Lord John Russell working along with William Crawford. See XIII, Pt 1.

[29] W. L. Clay, *The Prison Chaplain: A Memoir of the Rev. John Clay* (1861), 77.

[30] See Wilberforce's parliamentary comments on the use of 'solitude' in PD 1819 (s1) 39: 830.

[31] PD 1821 (s2) 5: 900.

[32] See XIII, Pt 1; and for the dispute on Peel's role and motivation, see V. Gatrell, *The Hanging Tree* (Oxford, 1994), Ch. 21 (Tory reactive pragmatism interpretation), and B. Hilton, 'The Gallows and Mr Peel', in T. Blanning and D. Cannadine (eds), *History and Biography Essays in Honour of Derek Beales* (Cambridge, 1996), 88, (principled liberal-Tory progressive interpretation).

and Lushington, though occasionally invoking Christian morality, were as much charged with a more secular form of humanitarian mission. Added to this in varying strengths was the force of non-divine utilitarian calculation seeking a more effective and efficient criminal justice system.[33] At the same time, penal reformers of all persuasions subscribed to the notion that the characteristics of the criminal justice system should be in broad harmony with public opinion.[34] Furthermore, there was also a large measure of agreement on the alleged corrupting effects of severe penal laws on the manners and sensibilities of the population.[35] But while Evangelicals in this way shared common ground or objectives and reinforced a broad reformist coalition, they were a considerable distance apart from such allies in other areas of the law: this was most distinctly true in respect of so-called 'offences against morality'.

3. ENFORCING THE LAW OF CHRISTIAN MORALITY

Societies bent on the reforming of social manners and morals, of saving individuals and the nation from decadence, depravity and decline, were no rarity in Victorian England. Often Wesleyan in origin, such societies sought to save souls by biblical education and personal persuasion. Getting underway in the late eighteenth and early nineteenth century, Evangelicalism adopted a rather firmer line in dealing with sin. If people lacked the moral fibre to practise self-denial, the pleasures of immorality would be denied them by invoking terrestrial law to ensure they followed God's law. And where English law was found wanting, Evangelicals felt duty bound to seek enactment of supplementary measures. Evangelicals did, indeed, believe in the 'possibility of indicting men into piety or calling in the Quarter Sessions to the aid of religion …'.[36]

Located at the core of God's self-appointed law enforcement agency in Victorian England were the Evangelicals. Their key moment in history had been Wilberforce's crusade to reform the nation's manners and morals, boosted by the inestimable benefit of royal patronage and the Privy Council's 1787 'Proclamation for the Encouragement of Piety and Virtue; and for preventing and punishing of Vice, Profaneness, and Immorality'. More than merely enjoining the nation to mend its moral ways, the Proclamation was addressed to the civil authorities:

our judges, mayors, sheriffs, justices of the peace…to be very vigilant and strict in the discovery, and effectual prosecution and punishment of all persons who shall be guilty of

---

[33] See XIII, Pt 1.

[34] e.g. Mackintosh, PD 1823 (s2) 9: 413; and Buxton, PD 1819 (s1) 39: 812 and 1821 (s2) 5: 906.

[35] e.g. On the Effects of Capital Punishment as Applied to Forgery and Theft (1818) written by Montague for the Capital Punishment Society. Similarly, Romilly, Observations (1786).

[36] Sydney Smith (1819) 32 Edin. Rev. 28–48; and XIII, Pt 1.

excessive drinking, blasphemy, profane swearing and cursing, lewdness, profanation of the Lord's day....[37]

The notion that national as well as personal salvation was at stake inhabited religious, moralistic, and economic discourse throughout the nineteenth century: continued toleration of 'impiety and licentiousness, and that deluge of profaneness, immorality and every kind of vice...' corrupted not merely individuals but threatened to 'provoke God's wrath and indignation' against the state.

Set up a few months later by Wilberforce, Evangelical brethren and other Anglican sympathizers, the 'Society for giving Effect to His Majesty's Proclamation Against Vice and Immorality'[38] was the principal engine of enforcement of moral rectitude, and the prototype for a host of subsequent similar Victorian bodies aimed at galvanizing local officials who lacked the necessary backbone and zeal. Its original and later membership was dominated by the aristocracy and upper echelons of the Established church, with a relative sprinkling of politicians such as Wilberforce. Moreover, in the pursuit of law enforcement, as well as establishing a system of informants, Evangelicals were also encouraged (when of appropriate standing) to seek membership of local magistrates' benches. Without doubt, there was a more benign, philanthropic dimension to this powerful concern with immorality. This manifested itself in the establishment of an abundance of charitable bodies, such as the wonderfully specific, graphically entitled 'Friendly Female Society for the Relief of Poor, Infirm, Aged Widows, and Single Women, of Good Character, Who Have Seen Better Days' (1802). However, especially in the early decades of the nineteenth century, it was Evangelicalism's censorious interventionism through resort to legal proceedings which established its followers' reputation as zealous moral crusaders.

Victorian England's marked Sabbatarianism, and the formidable 'Lord's Day Observance Society', owed much to the Proclamation Society's 1801 reincarnation: the 'Society for the Suppression of Vice and the Encouragement of Religion and Virtue'.[39] As identified in the Royal Proclamation, the list of target offences was extensive, spanning gambling, obscenity, drunkenness, prostitution, and Sabbath

---

[37] Copies of the Proclamation were distributed by the Home Office to all High Sheriffs with instructions to activate their Magistracy. The Proclamation is reproduced in Radzinowicz, *History*, iii, App. 3. There had been a failed attempt in the Commons a few weeks earlier to establish machinery for examining the 'state of the penal laws'. The initiative (provoked by dissatisfaction with the lack of proportionality between offences and punishments) was squashed by Pitt who argued that such an inquiry would tend to undermine the standing of existing penal laws: *Parl. Hist.* (1786–88), xxvi, 1058.

[38] Its foundation membership boasted, amongst others, five Dukes, the Archbishops of Canterbury and York, and 18 Bishops. The Society took care to detail the 'prudential methods' to be followed by those providing information leading to possible prosecution. *Ibid.*, pp. 496–7.

[39] On the Society's composition, see M. Roberts, 'The Society for the Suppression of Vice and its Early Critics' (1983) 26 *His. J.* 159 and *Making English Morals: Voluntary Association and Moral*

breaking. An express overarching philosophy was that the 'most efficient way to prevent the greater crimes is by punishing the smaller, and by endeavouring to repress that general spirit of licentiousness which is the parent of every species of vice'.[40] And although the Society successfully prosecuted the full range of offences, it was profanation of the Sabbath which generally outnumbered all other charges. Regarded by Evangelicals as 'intended for strengthening our impression of invisible and eternal things',[41] protection of Sundays from the incursion of ungodly activities—including work—was a key feature for improving the population's morals and manners. Prior to the Proclamation, Sabbatarianism had been notionally reinforced by legislation in 1781.[42] Armed with these provisions, in its first year of existence, the Vice Society had shown its determination to maintain the sanctity of the Lord's day by achieving over 600 convictions for Sabbath breaking in London.[43]

Such was the importance attached to keeping Sunday holy, that a by-product of the Vice Society, the 'Society for Promoting the Observance of the Sabbath', was established in 1809 to focus specifically on this cause. Further bodies, especially the long enduring Lord's Day Observance Society, maintained an anxious watch over the nation's Sunday activities for the remainder of Victoria's reign. Coupled with this vigilance was a continuing determination to enact new legislation to meet fresh challenges to the integrity of the Sabbath. Indicative of the period's mores and concerns were the views of the 1832 Select Committee, whose membership sported Buxton, Baring, Ashley (Shaftesbury), and Peel. A tightening of the laws enforcing Sabbatarianism was proposed to counter

...systematic and widespread violation of the Lord's Day, which in their judgment, cannot fail to be highly injurious to the best interests of the People and which is calculated to bring down upon the Country the Divine displeasure.

Conversely, there were 'abundant grounds, both in the Word of God and in the history of past ages, to expect that His Blessing and Favour would accompany such an endeavour to promote the Honour due to His Holy Name and Commandment'.[44]

Reform in England 1787–1886 (Cambridge, 2004), 74–5. Its new recruits included the prominent and fervent penal reformer Patrick Colquhoun, then appointed a committee member.

[40] *Life of William Wilberforce* (1838), i: 131.

[41] R. and S. Wilberforce (eds), *Correspondence of William Wilberforce* (1840), i, 373.

[42] 21 Geo. 3 c. 49. Abortive attempts were made in the 1790s to add to such legislation measures aimed at increasing the rewards for informing on Sabbath breaking and to prevent the sale of newspapers. *Parl. Hist.* (1794–5), xxxi, 1428–34; *Parl. Hist.* (1798–1800), xxxiv, 1006–14.

[43] In part attributed to the successful crusade of prosecutions, by the mid-1820s the Vice Society's annual tally of prosecutions for the offence had fallen to 14: *Report of the Society for the Suppression of Vice* (1825).

[44] *Report*, PP 1831–2 (697), vii, pp. 4 and 13. But by the late 1840s, fear of God's displeasure and an inclination to reward keeping the Sabbath holy were eclipsed by welfare concerns for workers.

During the 1830s the Lord's Day Observance Society strenuously promoted a clutch of almost successful parliamentary initiatives to prohibit all Sunday games, public transport, and work. However, a measure of success was achieved in the 1840s and 1850s, preventing Sunday collections and delivery of mail, as well as greatly restricting the number of public music performances.[45] Trollope's inspired mid-century creation, the chilling Evangelical, the Reverend Obadiah Slope, provided a deadly satirization of this disposition.

Most active clergymen have their hobby, and Sunday observances are his. Sunday, however, is a word which never pollutes his mouth—it is always 'the Sabbath'. The 'desecration of the Sabbath,' as he delights to call it, is to him meat and drink:—he thrives upon that as policemen do on the general evil habits of the community. It is the loved subject of all his evening discourses, the source of all his eloquence, the secret of all his power over the female heart.[46]

These concerns at the apparent strength of Sabbatarianism led those of lesser conviction to set up opposition bodies, such as the 'Anti-Sabbatarian National Sunday League' in 1855. Dickens, a celebrated supporter, famously evoked the joylessness of a worker's London Sunday:

...nothing to see but streets, streets, streets. Nothing to breathe but streets, streets, streets...Nothing for the spent toiler to do but to compare the monotony of his six days with the monotony of his seventh.[47]

And while a trickle of Parliamentary Reports on Sabbath observance from the 1850s indicates a decline in sensitivities towards Sabbatarianism, the relative relaxation of laws over the remainder of the century was never less than cautious and always carried out in the face of a substantial body of sustained opposition.[48]

Beyond Sabbatarianism, active concern of religious bodies, and especially Evangelicals, for the nation's public and private morality, extended over the widest span of social behaviour, embracing entertainment, sports, gambling, what was published, blasphemy, and fornication. As well as the innate sinfulness, such failings were viewed as signalling a likely progression into even deeper forms of criminality. Evangelicalism's distaste for entertainments including the theatre was well captured in the puritanical observation that 'if Vice were to come

[45] For parliamentary petitions enjoining legislative measures, see e.g. PD 1833 (s3) 16: 723 and 1231. For bills, 16: 898 and 1232; 17: 1326; 1836 33: 5 and 1067.

[46] Barchester Towers (1855), Ch. 4.

[47] Little Dorrit (1855–7), Ch 3. Quoted in I. Bradley, The Call to Seriousness: The Evangelical Impact on Victorians (1976), 105–6.

[48] Undoubtedly much opposition to the freeing up of restrictions on the sales of intoxicants and the permitting of Sunday entertainments was motivated as much by public order and social concerns, especially in relation to gambling. See below.

in person to take up her residence in London, she would naturally visit the play-house'.[49] In all of these areas religiously inspired organizations both sought to enforce and often to strengthen existing laws. At the opening of the nineteenth century, the Vice Society's recorded tally of prosecutions over one year in London reveals convictions for the sale of obscene books and prints, brothel keeping, running disorderly public houses, and gaming.[50] The formation and evolution of public and political attitudes along with legislative activity in each of these fields almost invariably involved the activities of religious bodies, a practice which continued throughout the whole of the Victorian age.

Licentiousness was a target of Christian and particularly Evangelical attention in two particular forms: sexual relations outside marriage; and unseemly or immodest representation of, or allusion to, sexuality in a fashion which might be labelled 'obscene'. In some respects, the most extreme examples of attempts to curb what Evangelicals regarded as licentiousness were their efforts in 1800 to make adultery a criminal offence, punishable by fine or imprisonment.[51] Less contentious moves to deal with prostitution were focused principally on seeking to curb the offence caused by the outward manifestations of the trade. Later in the century, Non-conformist and Evangelical led groups (especially the National Vigilance Association) were particularly active in attacking sexual exploitation and championing the more general cause of moral purification through legal proscription.[52] The hyper-sensitivity towards sexual impropriety and obscenity of Evangelicals and Non-conformists infiltrated all stratas of Victorian society, notably colouring notions of indecency and heavily boosting prurient tendencies.

On a more practical front, it propelled the Vice Society into the vigorous pursuit of sellers of obscene books and materials. As indicated in the Proclamation, 'dispersing poison to the minds of the young and unwary' was a particular concern.[53] Not only did the Vice Society bring or promote prosecutions, it also developed the practice of making representations on matters of concern directly to the Home Office.[54] Dissatisfied with existing measures, in the 1820s, 1830s, and

[49] Attributed to the Rev. John Venn, in J. Pratt, *Eclectic Notes* (1800), 164 quoted in Bradley, *The Call*, 102. See also, 'Public Morality and Social Control', XIII, Pt 1, Ch. X.

[50] Table of Convictions 1804, reproduced in Radzinowicz, *History*, iii, App. 4, 504.

[51] William Eden (later Lord Auckland), the author of the greatly esteemed reformist *Penal Law* (1771), introduced a bill for the 'Punishment and more effectual Prevention of the Crime of Adultery' *Parl. Hist.* (1800–1), xxxv, 225–301. Supporters included the Archbishop of Canterbury (301), Pitt, and Wilberforce (301–26).

[52] See XIII, Pt 1, Ch. X, also Bebbington, *The Nonconformist Conscience* and E. Bristow, *Vice and Vigilance* (1977). The National Vigilance Association was established in 1885.

[53] The Vice Society successfully sought the insertion of provisions in the 1824 Vagrancy Act under which obscene displays became a summary offence.

[54] e.g. cited by Bristow, *Vice and Vigilance*, 53 and 240–1. The National Vigilance Association initiated the obscene publications prosecution of Vizetelly in 1888 and drafted the bill which became

1850s Evangelicals successfully sought a strengthening of the law regulating the public display of obscene works, importation of obscene articles, together with the seizure and destruction of obscene publications.[55] Even public reading habits were strongly mediated if not censored by the Evangelical or Non-conformist conscience, powerfully influencing the business practices of book sellers and private lending libraries.[56] While Evangelicals and Non-conformists were notable for their public activism, the broader, inter-denominational character of religious influence and involvement is apparent from the composition of many campaigning bodies. For example, in later Victorian times, the National Vigilance Association's first chairman was the Bishop of Southwell, with its council members including many other bishops and also Cardinal Manning. Established in 1880, the rather less aggressive Church of England Purity Society, with the Archbishop of Canterbury as President (reinvented as the White Cross Society in 1890) adopted more of a missionary role amongst the fallen to save both bodies and souls from sexual exploitation.

Gambling and excessive consumption of alcohol had figured in the Proclamation and remained in the calculations of government and employers throughout the nineteenth century. For the religiously inspired, gambling and intoxication seriously threatened to distract individuals from responsible and moral lives; for those more concerned with terrestrial consequences, these vices subverted both the national and individual economic progress, while adding to the social burden of supporting the self-impoverished. Of course, members of the governing and employing classes were often also doubly concerned at the contagion of immorality by virtue of its impact on their own religious sensibilities. As well as prosecuting unlawful gaming, state-sponsored gambling in the form of lotteries was toppled by the Evangelicals in the 1820s.[57] Legislative action later in the century, aiming to regulate gambling was almost inevitably promoted, or at the very least strenuously endorsed by both Anglican and Non-conformist campaigning groups, including the formidable National Anti-Gambling League, established in 1890.[58]

Compared with gambling, alcohol consumption generated a more equivocal and evolving nineteenth-century religious response across practically every

the Indecent Advertisements Act 1889. See XIII, Pt 1, Ch. X.

[55] In the Vagrancy Act 1824; Customs Consolidation Act 1853; Campbell LCJ's Obscene Publications Act 1857. See XIII, Pt 1, Ch. X.

[56] See XIII, Pt. 1, Ch. X.

[57] Including Wilberforce, Colquhoun, and others, including Romilly. In the Commons, Wilberforce, *PD* 1816 (s1) 34: 1086, 36: 686. Also, D. Miers, *Regulating Commercial Gambling* (Oxford, 2004), Ch. 5.

[58] See XIII, Pt 1, Ch. X. Also, Bebbington, *The Nonconformist Conscience* and B. Harrison, 'State Interference' in P. Hollis (ed.), *Pressure from Without* (1974), 289.

denomination. Until the 1850s, Anglicans, including Evangelicals, took no principled stand against the consumption of alcohol. Indeed, brewing figured amongst the commercial backgrounds of a number of leading Evangelicals and Quakers, including Buxton and Hanbury. Moreover, the Beer Act 1830 was engineered to free up the 'benign' drinking of beer in the hope of lowering working-class consumption of pernicious and disabling quantities of cheap spirits. Formed in 1831, the National British and Foreign Temperance Society claimed its leading members from both Evangelicals and Non-conformists, especially Methodists and Baptists. In line with the informing philosophy of the Beer Act, the Society's principal target was excessive spirit drinking. Yet by the end of the decade, as the relaxation of regulation on beer sales became discredited, the Society took on a total abstinence stance.

More broadly, a gradual adjustment of focus of Anglican, Non-conformist, and Catholic churches to include not only individual salvation but also broader social welfare increased internal pressure to confront alcohol abuse and its dire consequences more forcefully. Campaigning groups including the Church of England Temperance Society, established in the early 1860s, now sought the population's social and moral elevation as a route to religious enlightenment—practically reversing the original Evangelical objective of purified morality through religion.[59] Out-and-out prohibition was the cause of a few societies including the Non-conformist United Kingdom Alliance set up in 1853. For the rest of the century this and other less extreme groups were notable in their sustained agitation to either increase the restrictions on the sale or consumption of alcohol, or, at the very least, to ensure the rigorous enforcement of existing legislation.[60]

4. CHRISTIANITY AND THE POLITICAL AND ECONOMIC STATUS QUO

While the people's (principally the working class's) morals, sensibilities, and salvation were being protected by these forms of religiously inspired activism, an additional uncompromisingly political dimension intruded into the enforcement of blasphemy laws. Irreligion was seen as socially and politically corrupting the suggestible young: the 'blasting influence of an unchristian education on the

[59] Originally the Church of England Total Abstinence Society. Its Establishment credentials were complete when the Queen became its patron in 1875. Harrison, *Drink and the Victorians*, 183–8. On the long, but less prominent role, of Quakers in the abstinence movement, see L. Shiman, *Crusade Against Drink in Victorian England* (1988), 57–9.

[60] e.g. Harrison, *Drink and the Victorians*, Ch. 9; and A. Shadwell, *Drink, Temperance and Legislation* (1902). And see XIII, Pt 1, Ch. X. On the political influence of religious nonconformists, see Bebbington, *The Nonconformist Conscience*, Ch. 3.

minds of youth'.[61] For Wilberforce, radical assaults on the 'inequality of property' were dangerous enough. However, even more threatening was 'sapping the foundations of the social edifice...by attacking Christianity', for the 'high and noble may be restrained by honour; but religion only is the law of the multitude'.[62] The sometimes overlapping nature of blasphemy, obscenity, and sedition charges often exposed the broader political and class credentials of Anglicans and especially Evangelicals. Together with parliamentary performances, their enthusiasm for blasphemy and sedition prosecutions confirmed a powerful attachment to existing institutional structures and consequent distribution of political power: essentially, while often socially progressive, most Evangelicals, like the Established church generally, were politically conservative.

An early indicative illustration of the severe Evangelical stance on blasphemy was provided by *Williams*, a prosecution successfully brought by the Proclamation Society in 1797 for the defendant's publishing of Paine's *Age of Reason*. Paine's uninhibited attack on the Christian religion provoked several prosecutions as being 'a libel on the religion of the state'. As Ashhurst J. reminded Williams, 'all offences of this kind are not only offences against God, but crimes against the law of the land, and punishable as such, inasmuch as they tend to destroy those obligations whereby civil society is bound together; and it is upon this ground that the Christian religion constitutes part of the law of England'.[63] Wilberforce and his fellow society members demonstrated considerably less than Christian charity by declining to follow the advice of Erskine, as prosecution counsel, insisting that the hapless and impoverished Williams be brought before the King's Bench for final judgment: one year's hard labour coupled with a recognisance of £1000.[64] Such behaviour doubtless contributed to their unpopularity even amongst those such as the rarely less than illiberal Eldon who confessed that the 'more I see of the "modern Saint[s]" character the less I like it'.[65]

This reputation for inflexible over-zealousness was compounded by several other successful prosecutions including one of blasphemous libel against the radical Richard Carlile for republishing Paine's *Age of Reason*. In the following year

[61] William Howley, Bishop of London, *A Charge Delivered to the Clergy of the Diocese of London* (1814) and R. Hole, *Pulpits, Politics and Public Order in England 1760–1832* (Cambridge, 1989), 202.

[62] R. and S. Wilberforce, *The Life of William Wilberforce* (1838), 5, 40.

[63] (1797) 26 St. Tr. 654, 716–17. On the frequently declared link between blasphemy and sedition from the 1780s to the 1830s, see Hole, *Pulpits, Politics and Public Order*, 200–13. Bentham's work contained much implicit and some explicitly anti-Christian sentiment. See, *ibid.*, 202–5 and J. Steintrager, 'Morality and Belief: The Origin and Purpose of Bentham's Writings on Religion' (1971) 6 *The Mill Newsletter* 3.

[64] After this episode Erskine declined to act for the Vice Society. J. L. High (ed.), *Speeches of Lord Erskine*, i: 592–3 (Chicago, 1876).

[65] August 1808, quoted in R. Melikan, *John Scott, Lord Eldon* (Cambridge, 1999), 18.

the Vice Society was reinforced by the newly established, more openly politically motivated, Constitutional Association in bringing a series of actions against blasphemers and avowed republicans,[66] including Richard Carlile's sister Mary Ann, and William Benbow. Both convictions generated hostile parliamentary attention. In presenting a petition for Carlile's release, Joseph Hume characterized the Vice Society and Constitutional Association as 'little better than conspiracies against the liberty of the subject'. Defending the prosecutions, Wilberforce argued that all that was 'most valuable depended upon the preservation of the sacred institutions of the country'.[67] Benbow's conviction for obscene libel provoked a shower of Commons' criticism. According to the philanthropist Samuel Whitbread, the Constitutional Association was as 'odious in principles as it had proved itself malignant in practice'. For Stephen Lushington—closely allied with Evangelicals in anti-slavery and capital punishment campaigns—the Vice Society was a 'set of cowardly pusillanimous hypocrites, who prosecuted the poor and helpless, but left the great and noble unmolested'.[68] Battered but unbowed, Wilberforce remained unshakable in his belief that 'enforcing the laws…would best promote the morals of the people, upon which the happiness of the nation mainly rested'.[69] If nothing else, such prosecutions are likely to have speeded the two societies' decline, which set in from the mid-1820s.

At a more general and explicit level, especially in the early first half of the nineteenth century, the Anglican church, including Evangelicals, staunchly defended its special political status:

The very loss of our church establishment, though, as in all human institutions, some defects may be found in it, would in itself be attended with the most fatal consequences. No prudent man dares hastily pronounce how far its destruction might not greatly endanger our civil institutions. It would not be difficult to prove, that the want of it would also be in the highest degree injurious to the cause of Christianity; and still more, that it would take away what appears from experience to be one of the most probable means of its revival.

Additionally, the poor and working classes were regarded as duty-bound to accept that 'their lowly path has been allotted to them by the hand of God…'.[70] This

---

[66] Prosecution for blasphemous libel of Mary Ann Carlile in 1821 for selling a pamphlet entitled 'An Appendix to the Theological Works of Thomas Paine'. On conviction she was sentenced to a year's imprisonment and fined £500: (1821) 1 St. Tr. (NS), 1033. The atheist William Godwin's less inflammatory *An Enquiry concerning Political Justice, and its Influence on General Virtue and Happiness* (1793) attracted rather less attention from the authorities.

[67] *PD* 1823 (s2) 8: 709 and 732.

[68] *PD* 1821 (s2) 5: 1486 and 1491.

[69] *Ibid.*, 1493.

[70] Wilberforce, *A Practical View* (1797), 405 and 411. Similarly, T. Gisborne, *An Enquiry into the Duties of Men in the Higher and Middle Classes* (1794).

orthodoxy was well captured in the Christian response to Paine's subversive *Rights of Man*. Here Christian duty was set out by Wilberforce's close and long-time associate Hannah More, in her staggeringly popular *Cheap Repository Tracts* between 1795 and 1798. In fictionalized form and selling for a penny or less, these homilies served up easily digested social and political propaganda opposing the period's radical, often anti-Christian, politics.[71] It was a gospel of the disadvantaged being obliged to accept what Providence had allocated them in life, coupled with the social and religious responsibility of the well off to look after the poor; these were perfectly meshing, complementary duties and expectations. Within Parliament, Evangelical backing for measures such as the Combination Acts 1799–1800 was consistent with this philosophy, as were other political responses, especially during the unsettled post-Napoleonic war years. At this time, Wilberforce gave wholehearted support for the repressive 'Six Acts', limiting public meetings and press reporting, and suppressing *habeas corpus*. His endorsement of the last measure was for the 'sake of the patient poor, [and] for the sake even of the turbulent themselves'.[72] Wilberforce's subsequent opposition to a parliamentary enquiry into the Peterloo Massacre of 1819 appeared to rest principally on the claim that the process would entail Parliament taking evidence from many who 'professed the new system and morality, and who defied the laws of God and Man'[73]—a process which itself would ascribe to them an unmerited degree of credence or respectability. In part this earned Wilberforce a low key but stinging portrait by Hazlitt a few years later, hinting at, though frequently denying charges of rank hypocrisy, and concluding Wilberforce to be a 'fine specimen of moral equivocation'.[74]

More broadly, practically all denominations and factions of the organized Christian church confirmed this conservative political outlook most vividly in

---

[71] Bought also by the well-to-do for distribution amongst the poor, over 2 million copies were sold in the first year of publication. A new series of these tracts was published from 1817. A. Stott, *Hannah More: The First Victorian* (Oxford, 2003).

[72] *PD* 1817 (s1) 36: 1122. Wilberforce was a member of the Commons' Secret Committee whose report led to the legislation. See XIII, Pt 1, Ch. IX.

[73] *PD* 1819 (s1) 12: 135.

[74] e.g. 'Mr Wilberforce is a less perfect character in his way. He acts from mixed motives. He would willingly serve two masters, God and Mammon. He is a person of many excellent and admirable qualifications; but he has made a mistake in wishing to reconcile those that are incompatible.... He goes hand and heart along with Government in all their notions of legitimacy and political aggrandizement, in the hope that they will leave him a sort of *no-man's ground* of humanity in the Great Desert, where his reputation for benevolence and public spirit may spring up and flourish.... He is coy in his approaches to power; his public spirit is, in a manner, *under the rose*. He thus reaps the credit of independence without the obloquy, and secures the advantages of servility without incurring any obligations. He has two strings to his bow: he by no means neglects his worldly interests, while he expects a bright reversion in the skies. Mr Wilberforce is far from being a hypocrite; but he is, we think, as fine a specimen of *moral equivocation* as can be well conceived: *The Spirit of the Age* (1825), 'Lord Eldon—Mr Wilberforce'.

the 1830s and 1840s in their negative responses to Chartism. But while Chartism was by no means anti-Christian, 'the Christian Chartist Churches' movement emphatically rejected the anti-democratic credentials of both the conformist and Non-conformist religious establishment. In turn, the mainstream bodies were hostile to Chartism's strongly politically subversive stance, with its extreme parliamentary franchise demands. To a large degree, Christian Socialism was an oppositional reaction to Chartism's radical political programme. As will be seen, although Christian Socialism's targets were a combination of the social and the economic, it fundamentally diverged from Chartism in its outright rejection of extensive parliamentary reform and universal suffrage.[75]

5. LEGISLATING FOR SOCIAL COMPASSION AND PROGRESS

Running broadly in the opposite direction, throughout the whole of the nineteenth century, most Christian denominations (excluding Catholicism on matters such as divorce) could also be seen pursuing socially progressive and non-repressive ambitions. While long associated with enforced Christian morality and firm government, whether Tory or Whig in complexion, an extensive catalogue of religiously inspired social reforms can be attributed particularly to Anglican and Non-conformist activism. For instance, general animal welfare and the proscribing of their use in cruel sports were early causes. In 1824 Buxton became first chairman of the Royal Society for the Protection of Cruelty to Animals, which succeeded in bringing about the criminalizing of many cruel animal sports in 1835, and in subsequent years prosecuting offenders.[76] Lord Ashley, later seventh Earl of Shaftesbury, indefatigable philanthropist, high Tory, and devout Evangelical, was a central and enduring driving force for regulating and inspecting the conditions of factories and mines. To a large degree, it was Shaftesbury who shocked the middle classes into legislative action by publicizing the horrors of child employment in mines, factories, and as chimney sweeps. Eventual legislation in the 1840s was strengthened in the 1860s in no small measure as a

---

[75] H. Faulkner, *Chartism and the Churches* (New York, 1916), *passim*, and E. Norman, *Church and Society in England 1770–1970* (Oxford, 1976), 168–70.

[76] Cruelty to Animals Act, 1835, 5 & 6 Will. 4 c. 59. Prior to this the Evangelical influenced attempts at such legislation, for example bills against bull-baiting introduced in 1800 and 1802 *Parl. Hist.*, xxxv, 202, xxxvi, 829. They were opposed as being legislation unfairly aimed at the working class. The Cruelty to Animals Bill, *PP* 1809 (208) i, 651; *PD* 1809 (s1) 14: 553; amended version 1810 (s1) 16: 726, 845–6. Although not specifically aimed at cruel sports, these bills failed largely over the alleged giving to magistrates of excessively wide powers. The stock justifications for proposed animal cruelty legislation were humanitarian, the inherent evil of cruelty and its morally debasing effects on those guilty of it.

consequence of Shaftesbury's persistent campaigning and lobbying; a campaign which produced the paradoxical spectacle of the Tory philanthropist Shaftesbury opposed by the Radical, doctrinaire free-trader John Bright.[77]

Of equal fame is Shaftesbury's role during this period in the provision of basic education in 'ragged schools', where along with literacy and numeracy, poor and vagrant children might absorb the fundamentals of Christian morality and religion. Shaftesbury's role in education was well within the strong Evangelical and broader Christian tradition inspired by the likes of Robert Raikes, who already in the 1780s had begun his Sunday School Movement. Early nineteenth-century educational developments became largely driven by the various Christian denominations: in 1811 Anglicans set up the National Society for Promoting the Education of the Poor in the Principles of the Established Church, with Non-conformists following in 1812 with the British and Foreign School Society. By the 1830s, these activities were attracting low-level Government grants. This was despite many in Parliament, like Cobbett, who would 'not consent to take from the people a single farthing in the way of taxes' to bring literacy to the working classes by increasing the number of 'schoolmasters and schoolmistresses—that new race of idlers'.[78] However, serious state engagement in education only began with the establishment of the Privy Council's Education Committee in 1839, principally in response to steady cross-denominational pressure. This, along with the influence of individual philanthropists and progressive radicals, set central Government on course for increasing acceptance of enlarged funding of church schools together with the training of teachers and the full embrace of compulsory elementary education in the 1870s. Well before then, there had emerged at least a broad inter-denominational consensus on the central worth of education: the moral value of the 'intellectual improvement of every human being', whatever their class, and emphatically seen by some as a 'duty no less sacred than [God's] spiritual welfare ...'.[79]

Of course, there was a very distinct grain of truth in Engels' (and others) assertion that different denominational schools operated in a competitive environment,

---

[77] Mines and Collieries Act 1842 5 & 6 Vict. c. 99; Factories Act 1847 10 & 11 Vict. c. 29. Shaftesbury originally took up the campaign in 1831. See also Shaftesbury's *Children's Employment Committee*, *PP* 1840 (203–504), x and *Children's Employment Commission Report*, *PP* 1842 (381–2) xvi, and 1843 (431–2) xiv; N. Thomas, *The Early Factory Legislation* (1951). For the split of Evangelical opinion on the 10 hours movement, see Hilton, *Age of Atonement*, 212–13. Shaftesbury was substantially responsible for the appointment of a Royal Commission initiated to investigate the industrial employment of children in 1862, following which child protection was extended by the Factory and Workshops Act of 1864 and 1867 (27 & 28 Vict. c. 48; 30 & 31 Vict. c. 103). Resistance to observing regulations on the use of child chimney sweeps was only really overcome after legislation in 1875. See also Bright and the 'Manchester School' in 'Law and Political Economy', Ch. VI, below.

[78] *PD* 1833 (s3), 20: 735.

[79] F. Kingsley, *Charles Kingsley: his letters and memories of his life* (1877), ii: 417.

being founded 'simply and solely in order to bring up children...in their particular faiths; and, if possible, now and again to filch the soul of some poor little child from a rival ...'.[80] Ironically, while arguably the predominant force behind the establishment of widely available elementary education, it could also be suggested that the ameliorative effects of church schools and frequent fierce Christian inter-denominational squabbling delayed the eventual full introduction of compulsory elementary state education.[81] In good measure, the initial appeal of central financial support for church schools was that they might be trusted to inculcate non-seditious education which might safely confirm rather than challenge providential social ranking. Just such concerns prompted the Established church to lead the opposition to early attempts to provide more widely available secular parish based education. Efforts in the 1840s to ensure better and more extensive elementary education for child factory workers were substantially undermined by inter-denominational in-fighting. Moreover, the Established church long proved singularly resistant to a dominant secular, state appointed schools' inspectorate.

Conflict and determination amongst Established and Non-conformist groups to influence the administration and content of elementary education was in great evidence during the uneasy passage of the Education Act 1870. Indeed, in readiness for the anticipated battle for the power to influence the religious education of young minds, the two main opposing forces had grouped into the National Education Union (advocating continuation of denominational divisions) and the National Education League (supporting non-sectarianism), whose leadership included the politically emerging Joseph Chamberlain. Months of parliamentary wrangling finally produced the 'Cowper-Temple clause', a compromise which, while explicitly banning 'catechism or religious formulary', failed seriously to inhibit their continued teaching. Consequently, the Established church, while suffering some diminution in its direct control of elementary schooling, continued as a significant force in the field.[82] Far from expiring, the running

---

[80] F. Engels, *The Condition of the Working Class in England* (1844), ed., trans. W. Henderson and W. Chaloner (1958), 125.

[81] Beside raising the nation's awareness of the educational and moral needs of such children, acting as chairman of the Ragged School Union, Shaftesbury was closely associated with the enactment of the Industrial Schools Act 1857, set up for the educating, moralizing, and training of deprived and criminally vulnerable children. See C. Seymour, *Ragged Schools Ragged Children* (1995). Evidence from these activities fed into the 1861 Commission on Education and the 1870 Education Act. Evangelicalism was well represented in the case of deprived and orphan children, most famously by Thomas Barnardo's Homes whose value was effectively recognized in the Custody of Children Act 1891. Shaftesbury's involvement in child protection also manifested itself in the establishment of the (eventually) NSPCC in the 1880s which was substantially instrumental in the passing of the Prevention of Cruelty to, and Better Protection of, Children Act 1889. See more generally on child welfare, XIII, Pt 4.

[82] Provisions in the 1870 Act aimed at inhibiting the over-representation of denominational groups on the new School Boards were initially far from completely successful. Yet, by the opening

conflict between Established Anglicans and Non-conformists over educational influence purposefully re-ignited with the setting up of the Bryce Commission (1895) and during the subsequent 1902 Education Bill debates. Setting the stage for many decades, the eventual 1902 Act facilitated perpetuation of largely Anglican church schools by financially beneficial provisions under which existing school 'Board' grants could be supplemented by local rates.

Beyond education, one further significant, religiously driven area of nineteenth-century social and legal reform related to the treatment of lunatics. Here, both Quakers and especially Evangelicals including Wilberforce and Shaftesbury, were prominent in efforts to ensure what was regarded as appropriate care of lunatics, which eventually resulted in the Lunatics Act 1845 and later provisions. Eighteenth-century legislation[83] had sanctioned a dual system of care for lunatics: licensed private 'mad houses' for those with means, and parish responsibility for pauper lunatics. Both forms of care became notorious for failings and abuses.[84] Early well-regarded alternatives were established by the Quakers, under the Society of Friends' York Retreat set up in 1792 by William Tuke. Here a diet of religion together with the fostering of self-control and suitable 'normalizing' occupations were in strong contrast to regimes of restraint and punishment common elsewhere.[85] However, as in other areas of social reform, it was Evangelicalism which propelled individuals and societies into national activism. The 1807 Select Committee into the 'state of criminal and pauper lunatics in England' included Romilly (then Solicitor General), the Christian philanthropist Samuel Whitbread, and Wilberforce. Its Report resulted in the first serious legislative attempt to facilitate a national scheme for the building of county asylums for criminal and pauper lunatics. Local reluctance to incur the necessary cost ensured a severely limited adoption of this permissive legislation.[86]

While the 1808 Act was relatively modest in its achievement, the Committee's Report was unsparing in documenting the grim state of affairs which fuelled a succession of more innovative bills between 1816 and 1819.[87] All failed in the

---

of the twentieth century, the new (state) local non-denominational Board Schools were providing education for more than half of eligible children: J. Hurt, *Elementary Schooling and the Working Classes 1860–1918* (1979) and G. Machin, *Politics and the Churches in Great Britain 1869 to 1921* (Oxford, 1987).

[83] Principally 17 Geo. II, c. 5 (1744) and 14 Geo. III, c. 9 (1774).

[84] e.g. K. Jones, *Lunacy, Law and Conscience 1744–1845* (1955), Chs 2–4, revised in *Asylum and After* (1993). See also XIII, Pt 4.

[85] The Tuke family (Samuel Tuke and Daniel Tuke) remained engaged in the welfare of lunatics throughout a substantial part of the nineteenth century. See Samuel Tuke, *Description of the Retreat* (York, 1813).

[86] County Asylums Act 1808, 48 Geo. III c. 96.

[87] The 1815 Select Committee included two Claphamites: Lord Robert Seymour and William Smith. It produced six Reports between 1815 and 1816 cataloguing the system's extensive abuses and failings. Analysed in Jones, *Lunacy.*

Lords largely on inchoate concerns over the propriety of state intrusion into parish or private matters. For Lord Eldon the prospect of extending state involvement into private asylums was fundamentally odious for there 'could not be a more false humanity than an over humanity with regard to persons afflicted with insanity'.[88] Such anti-statist or anti-centralizing arguments were soon to inhabit the seismic changes governing poor relief brought in by the 1834 Act. In respect of lunacy reforms, renewed interest in the treatment of lunatics generated by the Evangelical Lord Robert Seymour in 1827 led to the appointment of a Commons' Select Committee which included the recently elected member for Woodstock, the then Lord Ashley. Consequential legislation in the following year enabled the appointment of a body of inspecting and reporting commissioners, one of whom was Ashley, a position he held for more than 50 years.[89]

6. LOSS OF PLACE; LOSS OF FAITH

Looking back across the nineteenth century, it is apparent that Christianity functioned as a powerful inspirational force individually for broad-gauged figures such as Wilberforce, Buxton, and Shaftesbury, and collectively for religious groupings, including the Evangelicals. Beyond the effects of their direct agitation and campaigning for law revision and enforcement, lay the more diffuse influences of religiously inspired social and political activities. Evolving manners and morality fed into social and political expectations and assumptions. Christian beliefs were constitutionally embedded in the state, which recognized the privileged position of the Established Church of England[90] in a range of ways, both financial and jurisdictional. Christian religion was viewed by the propertied classes as a key force for social stability, acting as vital ballast in turbulent times. At the same time, the role of religion in moral regeneration was taken to be of overriding importance, it being universally accepted that moral regeneration benefited both individuals and the nation. To this end, the Stipendiary Curates Act 1813 and Church Building Acts 1818 and 1824 were targeted at boosting (by £1½ million) the building and running of hundreds of new churches in urban areas.[91]

But while acceptance of Christianity's role remained largely unchanged over the course of the nineteenth century, political expediency caused the steady

---

[88] *PD* 1819 (s1) 40: 1345.

[89] County Asylums Act 1828 9 Geo. IV c. 40 and the Madhouse Act 1828 9 Geo. IV c. 41.

[90] On the Established Church's constitutional position, Pt 2, below.

[91] (1813) 53 Geo. III c. 149, (1818) 58 Geo. III c. 45, (1824) 5 Geo. IV c. 90 and c. 103. The 1818 Church Building Act was the handiwork of Vansittart, the Evangelical Chancellor of the Exchequer. Between 1810 and 1870 close to 4000 new or rebuilt churches were consecrated. O. Chadwick, *The Victorian Church* (1966–70), ii, 227. The Anglican Church Building Society was established in 1818.

dismantling of the Established church's privileges, a process emphatically beginning with the Repeal of the Test Acts (1673 and 1678) in 1828 and 1829. Effectively, this lifted the previous bar on all except Anglicans from public civil and military office, including membership of the House of Commons. Even more distressing for many Protestant constitutionalists was the Catholic Emancipation Act 1829, removing the disqualification of Catholics from Parliament and, in practical terms, enfranchising them. It was a reform which generated much political and constitutional alarm for some, believing that an inevitable corollary of spiritual allegiance to Rome was a foreign political affiliation; in effect, that Catholics represented an ever-present potential fifth column in the British body politic. For constitutionalists, such as Eldon, the Established Church of England was 'inseparably part of the state' and therefore removal of its privileges weakened both Church and state.[92]

Some areas of social reform aroused considerable resistance from mainstream religious opinion. For example, changes of divorce law in 1857 attracted strenuous, religiously based opposition from some prominent politicians, including Gladstone, to sanctioning the re-marriage of divorced adulterers.[93] On matters of church ritual and questions of doctrine, the Judicial Committee of the Privy Council generated considerable disquiet amongst high churchmen with its 1864 overruling of the Ecclesiastical Court of Arches' decision in the 1860 heresy case, involving *Essays and Reviews* (below). Lord Chancellor Westbury's judgment for the Privy Council provoked a 'virulent' personal attack from Dr Pusey, the leading Oxford high churchman, after Newman's defection to Rome. In place of the Privy Council's jurisdiction, Puseyites called for establishment of an exclusively Ecclesiastical Court of Appeal, made up of bishops, to adjudicate on all religious disputes. Defending Westbury and the Privy Council, Fitzjames Stephen returned Pusey's invective, with interest, characterizing Pusey's performance as 'positively indecent and hardly gentleman-like; showing an almost grotesque' incapacity to understand basic legal principles, and giving the 'English Church judicial and legislative powers akin to the Catholic Church..., an arena for jugglers' tricks'.[94]

---

[92] *PD* 1828 (s2) 59: 1492, 1499–1500.

[93] J. Parry, *Democracy and Religion, Gladstone and the Liberal Party 1867–1875* (Cambridge, 1986), 37.

[94] 'Dr Pusey and the Court of Appeal' (1864) 70 *Fraser's Mag.* 644, 646. Pusey had accused Westbury of having 'poisoned the springs of English justice for all ages in all matters of faith'. See also Stephen, 'The Privy Council and the Church of England' (1864) 69 *Fraser's Mag.* 521. And, for instance, Gladstone's extensive criticism of the Privy Council's judgment in the *Gorham* case (1850), overthrowing the Court of Arches' decision. Parry, *Democracy and Religion*, 35 and 158; also the upset caused by the Privy Council's *ultra vires* finding in the Colenso affair (1862–4) where the Bishop of Cape Town attempted to deprive Bishop Colenso of his see on heresy grounds: P. Hinchcliff, *J. W. Colenso: Bishop of Natal* (1964).

Not only did the Established church continue to suffer removal of privileges,[95] but all Christian denominations and beliefs came under the most fundamental of all attacks from the scientific challenge of evolutionism. Rather than a sudden, intellectually shattering event, the 1859 publication of Darwin's *The Origin of the Species* represented the culmination of three decades of accumulating scientific evidence, chipping away at the bedrock of Christian creationism. While not a direct assault on Christian beliefs, Darwin's observations demonstrated the non-immutability of species was manifestly a substitution of accident and chance for Divine intelligent design. Extensive unease over social morality's vulnerability[96] without the reinforcement of Christian belief—Carlyle's society 'at once destitute of faith and terrified at scepticism'—proved largely unfounded. More broadly, Darwinism was met by a diversity of emotional and intellectual accommodations across the span of Christian denominations, with the humanist philosophy and agnosticism of Auguste Comte claiming a fair portion of the intelligentsia.[97]

Of the majority who did not shed Christianity, some responded by choosing the route of pure unshakable belief leading to Rome via Newmanism; that 'desperate leap into a blind fanaticism' as a hostile Thomas Arnold characterized such conversions. Others, most spectacularly in the trial of the alleged heterodoxy of *Essays and Reviews* (1860),[98] sought to meet scientism with a restated, historically untainted account of core Christian belief. But overwhelmingly, Christian denominations, including the Established Anglican church, met science and secularism with a measure of passing anxiety, eventually subsiding into relative indifference. In one form or another, faith was sustained by adhering to the great Coleridgean contrast between 'Reason and Understanding', with spiritual imagination acting as an inseparable element of 'Reason'.[99] By the 1860s,

---

[95] See Pts 2 and 3 below; and XIII, Pt 4, for the modification and removal of Ecclesiastical jurisdiction on divorce and abolition of church rates in 1868. For the University 'Tests Agitation', see C. Harvie, *The Lights of Liberalism* (1976), Ch. 4.

[96] The move from Evangelicalism to agnosticism in one generation was famously witnessed in Fitzjames Stephen's family. And also for worries over the morality of the masses, see K. Smith, *James Fitzjames Stephen* (Cambridge, 1988), Ch. 8 'Rationalism's Burden'.

[97] Non-Christian rationalists produced a variety of responses to which the spiritually needy might turn, including J. S. Mill's supremely vapid 'Religion of Humanity', 'Utility of Religion' (1850–8) and also 'Theism' (1868–70) published posthumously in *Three Essays on Religion*. Also, Comte's much earlier *Cours de philosophie positive* (1830–42) (outlined by G. H. Lewes in *Comte's Philosophy of the Sciences* (1853) and *Système de politique positive* (1851–4).

[98] I. Ellis, *Seven Against Christ: A Study of 'Essays and Reviews'* (1980); J. F. Stephen, *Defence of the Rev. Rowland Williams* (1862); and, generally, J. Moore, *The Post-Darwinian Controversies* (Cambridge, 1979).

[99] Most especially, B. Wiley, *Nineteenth Century Studies* (1955), Ch. 1, 'Samuel Taylor Coleridge'; and O. Chadwick, *The Secularization of the European Mind in the Nineteenth Century* (Cambridge, 1975).

intellectual disputes over the nature and relationship of science and religion might be openly aired by interested parties at forums such as the Metaphysical Society.[100]

And while some way from disappearing, the rhetoric of atonement and damnation greatly moderated.[101] Yet the twin notions of a Christian's personal and social responsibility continued largely undiminished. For most, Christianity could still be invoked to underwrite individual and social morality. And, as the late nineteenth-century campaigns against prostitution, gambling, and alcohol demonstrate, Christian religion remained a significant factor in several areas of law-making and enforcement. However, at the same time Anglican and Nonconformist churches were increasingly expressing concerns over the ideology and consequences of liberal market capitalism.[102] Against this background, establishment of Christian Socialism in the late 1840s and an Evangelical revival of the late 1850s—apparently undeflected by later Darwinian revelations—developed into the formidable social missions of the Methodists, along with those of Catholics, and, by the 1870s, the Salvation Army. In the last case, 'General' William Booth's army engaged in a long-enduring battle against the evils of extreme poverty, ignorance, and vice in the most basic and practical fashion to save bodies as well as souls.

Beyond broad Non-conformist forces enjoying a measure of direct political influence through their association with Gladstonian Liberalism,[103] the second half of the nineteenth century witnessed Christian denominations distinctly leaning away from Wilberforcian political sentiments. By now, more representative of many was Charles Kingsley's reproof that too often Churches had 'used the Bible as if it was a mere special constable's handbook—an opium dose for keeping beasts of burden patient while they were being overloaded—a mere book to keep the poor in order ...'.[104] Yet despite the reincarnation of Christian Socialism in the 1870s, none of its varied manifestations remotely approached Marxist, (effectively) committed statist, leanings. In the 1880s, Thomas Hughes rejected the 'paternal state, the owner of all property finding easy employment

---

[100] A. W. Brown, *The Metaphysical Society: Victorian Minds in Crises 1869–1880* (New York, 1947) and A. V. Benn, *The History of English Rationalism in the Nineteenth Century* (1906), ii, Ch. 15.

[101] Most conspicuously from the efforts of the Rev. F. D. Maurice and his Christian Socialist acolytes such as Charles Kingsley and Thomas Hughes; and later by the likes of Stewart Headlam and Brooke Foss Westcott. For the Christian Socialist assault on capitalism, see 'Law and Political Economy', Ch. VI, below.

[102] For this gradual transformation, see E. Norman, *Church and Society in England 1770–1970* (Oxford, 1976), Ch. 4 and see 'Law and Political Economy', Ch. VI, below.

[103] Particularly, Parry, *Democracy and Religion, passim.*

[104] From 'Tracts for the times', *Politics for the People* (1848). Kingsley's best-known sympathetic treatments of the working classes are *Alton Locke* (1850) and *Yeast* (1848).

and liberal maintenance for all citizens, reserving all profits for the community, and paying no dividends to individuals'.[105] Even Christian Socialism's most radical exponent, Stewart Headlam, notwithstanding his long embrace of Fabianism, showed no coherent adherence to any truly collectivist, socialist manifesto. His only serious dalliance with the creed was his sustained advocacy of radical 'Land Reform' through a redistributive tax regime.[106] More significantly, it was in the nineteenth century's final decades that a disparate range of church figures such as Manning, Booth, and Mearns, along with diverse Christian Socialist organizations,[107] were especially prominent in campaigns to raise the chronically grim, unhealthy habitation standards of large swathes of the working classes. In turn these pressures were partly instrumental in the enactment of a cluster of ameliorative social measures, including the Housing Act 1890 and subsequent broader welfare legislation.[108]

---

[105] *Rugby, Tennessee* (1881); Norman, *The Victorian Christian Socialists*, 92.

[106] Headlam's relatively small and radical 'Guild of St Matthew' formed in London's East End in 1877, survived for over 30 years as a strong presence and voice within the broad Christian Socialist Movement. He was a member of the Fabian Society in 1886, two years after its establishment. By contrast, the socialism of Brooke Foss Westcott's Christian Social Union supported the progressive reform of social institutions eventually seen after the Liberal victory of 1906. Westcott's Establishment credentials were confirmed by his appointment as Bishop of Durham in 1890: Norman, *The Victorian Christian Socialists, passim*, esp. Ch. 6

[107] Especially Brooke Foss Westcott's Christian Social Union (1889), the Christian Social League (1894), and Christian Socialist League (1906). And see 'Law and Political Economy', Ch. VI, below.

[108] The Rev. Andrew Mearns published an exposé of appalling south London slum conditions in *The Bitter Cry of Outcast London* in 1883. Mearns, Secretary of the London Congregational Union, gave extensive and pungent evidence to the *Royal Commission on the Housing of the Working Classes. First Report and Evidence 1884–5, PP* 1884–5 (c.4402) xxx, 1174–82. The Royal Commissioners included Cardinal Manning and the Bishop of Bedford. In 1890 William Booth published his sensational account of working-class housing overcrowding, *In Darkest England and the Way Out*. The Quaker B. S. Rowntree's *Poverty: A Study of Town Life* (1901) pioneered innovatory techniques of social investigation. The aged Lord Shaftesbury latterly expressed concerns that state subsidised rents of housing risked destroying the moral vigour of the working classes ('The Mischief of State Aid' (1883) 14 *Nineteenth Century* 934). Decades earlier in 1851 he had been a prime mover of the Lodging Houses Act which provided local authorities with powers to build low-rent working-class accommodation. The distinction between 'regulated' rents at less than the fully realizable market rate and 'subsidised' rents was ideologically subtle. For the influential role of religious groups in the enactment of the Artizans and Labourers Dwellings Improvement Act 1875 (the 'Cross Act'), see 'Law and Political Economy', Ch. VI below.

VI
Law and Political Economy

THOUGH patently a fundamental political question, the state's role in the creation and distribution of wealth almost inevitably involves law-making and
enforcement. Most basically, the state may choose between non-intervention
or some degree of engagement in wealth-generating activities or the processes
of its distribution. The latter course can entail anything from the provision of
broad, facilitative legal structures, to detailed, mandatory requirements. The
law's involvement raises an additional tier of issues relating to why and how the
law was employed as a conduit of economic and social government policy. This
essentially functionalist analysis relates principally to centrally inspired legislative activity, where usually particular express or implicit policy ends are being
pursued. The further considerable question, of whether courts operated as an
autonomous institution, generating their own policies on political economy,
involves examination of approaches to statutory interpretation and the deployment of common law or equity notions. In broad terms, this chapter seeks to provide an overview of the relevant leading features of Victorian political economy
which actively informed attitudes, assumptions, and policies manifested in law-
making: both through legislation and by courts in their creative and interpretive
roles. By 'political economy' is meant that sizeable element of political ideology
and policies which concerns itself with the principles of the effective creation of
a nation's wealth and its appropriate distribution. More detailed reflections on
the relationship of specific economic considerations to particular areas of legal
development will be found in the treatment of those individual topics.

Collectively, these matters may be conveniently separated into two periods,
very roughly reflecting discernible stages of political economic development:
1815–50 and 1850–1914. Within these periods two distinct but obviously related
fields of policy and law-making require separating: first, those most directly
affecting the economy and wealth generation; and secondly, those concerning
the state's social philosophy on intervention in the distribution and spending
of profits and wealth. The legal system's involvement in the economy of wealth
generation draws in consideration of the law governing the many dimensions of
commercial and industrial activity, including labour relations. Distribution of

wealth through applied social policy reaches across areas of law affecting working conditions, taxation, housing, health, education and, most prominently, welfare support of the poor and destitute.

1. FACILITATING A LIBERAL ECONOMY: 1815–1850

An Emerging 'Science' of Political Economy

As an appropriate starting point for an overview of England's political economy, 1815 recommends itself for two principal reasons: first, the end of the Napoleonic Wars caused the shedding onto the labour market of nearly a third of a million demobbed servicemen, creating immediate and serious practical strains on the country's economic and, consequently, social and political system; secondly, price controls and protectionism, one key feature of the entrenched economic landscape, came under political scrutiny in the course of the 1815 renewal of the Corn Laws, in some respects the *raison d'être* of a regulated market. Social and political tensions, sometimes leading to open conflict, generated during this period of shifting the country's economy from a war to a peace time footing forced reviews and fresh justifications for often long-established economic attitudes and assumptions. It was a period when so-called 'classical' political economy gained a secure place in, at least, the nation's intellectual, political, and parliamentary discourse; so much so, that some, like the *Edinburgh Review's* Francis Jeffrey, were prepared to assert that it was the 'surest guarantee for justice, order and freedom, and the only safe basis for every species of moral and intellectual improvement'.[1]

By a system of import duties and export credits, the Corn Laws were originally established to protect and nurture English grain production and national self-sufficiency. From the early nineteenth century, a production shortfall led to the necessity of grain imports, with tariffs seen as artificially inflating food prices by restricting cheaper imports. As Adam Smith's celebrated economic critique *The Wealth of Nations* (1776) had maintained, a protectionist trading system permitted self-interested producers to sell at inflated prices to consumers' manifest disadvantage. In essence, Smithian theory argued that only a free trade market could reconcile naturally conflicting interests of producers and consumers. Market manipulation cheated consumers and bred inefficiency amongst producers. A free-market pursuit of self-interest by both producer and consumer

---

[1] (1825) 43 *Edin. Rev.* 2 and F. Fetter 'The Influence of Economists in Parliament on British Legislation from Ricardo to John Stuart Mill' (1975) 83 *Journal of Political Economy* 1051.

benefited both parties and conduced to the highest level of the nation's general welfare.[2] These core beliefs, refined by David Ricardo,[3] fuelled the public wrangle over the Corn Laws (Importation Act) of 1815. While in the government's reasonable belief not lacking some strategic benefit in addressing concern over the rapidly rising population,[4] the 1815 Act was commonly viewed as a capitulation to English landed interests. Indeed, Ricardo's rent theory claimed to demonstrate that the interests of landlords were 'always opposed to the interest of every other class in the community'. Organized working-class agitation followed, stoked up by fears of rising food prices; and commercial and industrial forces vociferously opposed the Act because of the believed inflationary effects that rising food prices would have on the cost of labour, thereby eroding competitiveness in foreign markets.

Moves toward the practical adoption of a free-market economic theory had indeed been seen earlier in the century. Termination of the East India Company's monopoly on Indian trade came in 1813. On the domestic front, repeal of the Statute of Artificers in 1814 and the London Assize of Bread in 1815 were of symbolic rather than great practical consequence. The former legislation required magistrates to set the wages and conditions of apprentices and journeymen in

---

[2] *Inquiry into the Nature and Causes of the Wealth of Nations* (1776). The basic tenets of Smithian political economy rested on claimed immutable natural laws of social order, deducible by moral reasoning. Most fundamentally, individuals shared a natural preference for enlightened self-interest which, in the long-term, benefited society: a natural harmony of interests that should be reflected in the Nation's law.

[3] *Principles of Political Economy and Taxation* (1817) and *On Protection to Agriculture* (1822). Two features of Ricardo's *Principles* of particular relevance related to land. Reinforcing Malthus's attack on the Speenhamland system of poor relief for those in employment (below), Ricardo argued that such payments distorted the free market level of agricultural wages: supplementing labourers' wages through the poor rate levy encouraged farmers to lower them. His theory of rent propounded in opposition to renewal of the Corn Laws in 1815, linked population growth to rising land values and rents as a consequence of the arable use of what was formerly only marginally viable land. In turn, lower yields from such land would force up grain prices.

[4] B. Hilton, *Corn, Cash, Commerce: The Economic Policies of the Tory Governments 1815–1830* (Oxford, 1977). The state's willingness to intervene in agriculture was powerfully illustrated by its authorization of enclosure of common land, particularly over the course of the eighteenth century in the cause of commercial efficiency. This was supplemented by a Board of Agriculture (1793–1822) aimed at encouraging improved farming techniques. The net outcome of seventeenth and eighteenth-century parliamentary enclosure was probably a small degree of improved agricultural efficiency. 'Its most important outcome was to increase the share of income taken by the landed elite; it was part of the creation of a more hierarchical rural society of large landed estates and tenant farmers facing a mass of landless labourers. The rise of the great estates, enclosure, and clearances produced a major change in rural society, but were not crucial to the improvement of yields and output': M. Daunton, *Progress and Poverty, An Economic and Social History of Britain 1700–1850* (Oxford, 1995), 117; and *passim* Chs 2–4 'Agriculture and Rural Society'. Concerns over the nation's ability to feed its markedly increasing population figured in the political economic analyses of Smith, Ricardo, and most centrally in Malthus. See 'Political Economy, Evangelicalism and Social Policy', below.

certain trades. To a degree, such freeing of state restrictions downgraded the economic power of skilled labour, whilst permitting employers an unrestricted choice of whom to employ and under what conditions. The Assize of Bread had empowered magistrates to fix the price of bread based on the price of flour and reasonable profit margins for bakers. In an attempt to thwart the artificial cost inflation induced by some millers of flour, the market for bread was thrown open to competition in the hope of lowering bread prices. Although in part intended to act as a counterforce to the Corn Laws, it further aggravated rather than mollified working-class Corn Law agitation.

But while freeing the labour economy from some forms of wage control, legal restraints on the economic power of labour had been increased at the end of the eighteenth century. An important component of Smith's *Wealth of Nations* was a free market in labour to ensure its most efficient employment. However, insofar as the ability to organize collective bargaining could be regarded as an element of a free market, the common law (reinforced by the Combination Acts of 1799/1800), acted against it by criminalizing such practices.[5]

Political Economy, Evangelicalism, and Social Policy

Basic endorsement of a *laissez-faire* or free-market economic philosophy by no means carried an inevitable set of social policy implications: *laissez-fairism* in wealth generation might be coupled with state interventionist social policies of welfare support and wealth distribution.[6] However, the dominant political and cultural mind-set of early nineteenth-century England regarded these theoretically separable outlooks as tightly interconnected. This relationship was no more apparent than in respect of the state's response to pauperism.[7] Under late eighteenth-century legislation,[8] Elizabethan Poor Law was supplemented to permit the subsidizing of low wages in rural areas by monetary payments, and for magistrates to authorize payment of 'outdoor relief' to the needy for short periods of illness or 'distress'. Additional local initiatives could be even more innovatory. In free-market economic terms, the most threatening were those, such as the 'Speenhamland' system of 1795, under which parishes could subsidize labourers' wages based on a cost of bread index and number of dependants.

---

[5] See 'Economic Policy, Capitalism and Labour' below.

[6] The absence of whole-hearted, universal adherence to *laissez-faire* economics across the political parties is well illustrated by the running divide between high Tories and liberal Tories over the question of Corn Laws repeal—something which was to split the party in 1846. See the treatment of this by B. Hilton, *A Mad, Bad, and Dangerous People, England 1783–1846* (Oxford, 2006), 264–8, 314–28; and Hilton, *Corn, Cash, Commerce, passim*.

[7] Generally, XIII, Pt 2.

[8] Gilbert's Act 1782 (22 Geo. III c. 83) and Poor Relief Act 1796 (36 Geo. III c. 23).

While offering short-term alleviation, this edifice of poor relief came under reasoned attack from emerging professional economists as undermining the nation's economic well-being. Most vividly, the Reverend Thomas Malthus's *Essay on Population* (1798)[9] offered a geometric–arithmetic equation and analysis of the grim consequences threatened by an imbalance between population growth and food production. Malthusian principles claimed to demonstrate that poor relief tended to remove natural, rational restraints on improvident early marriage and large families; and that poverty's powerful incentive to gain work and achieve self-sufficiency would only be dulled by the existence of wage subsidies and poor relief. As a contemporary observed, both Malthus and his *Essay* 'attained a scientific reputation in questions of moral and political philosophy'.[10] David Ricardo's *Principles of Political Economy and Taxation* offered searching analytical support for Malthus's 'iron law of wages', arguing that the more of the nation's 'wages fund' was paid out in poor relief, the less would be available for workers' pay.

The clear and direct tendency of the poor law, is in direct opposition to these obvious principles: it is not, as the legislature benevolently intended, to amend the condition of the poor, but to deteriorate the condition of both poor and rich; instead of making the poor rich, they are calculated to make the rich poor; and whilst the present laws are in force, it is quite in the natural order of things that the fund for the maintenance of the poor should progressively increase, till it has absorbed all the net revenue of the country, or at least so much of it as the state shall leave to us, after satisfying its own never failing demands for the public expenditure.[11]

In simplistic terms, the 'iron law of wages' maintained that the labouring classes' standard of living could never rise above subsistence level because of the natural cycle of working population increase leading to an over-abundance of labour, which in turn depressed wages and the birth rate. Whether or not soundly based,[12] the essence of such 'scientific' arguments powerfully reinforced concerns over the rising cost of alleviating poverty and the growing political and social culture which sought individual self-control and responsibility, heralded in Smith's *Wealth of Nations*. Indeed the Utilitarian-inspired[13] reformed Poor Law mantra

---

[9] The emphasis of Malthus's analysis shifted during subsequent editions of the *Essay* (Hilton, *The Age of Atonement* (Oxford, 1988) Chs 2 and 3) but the central economic arguments on the damaging effects of Poor Relief remained.

[10] William Hazlitt, *The Spirit of the Age* (1906 edn, orig. pub. 1825), 'Mr Malthus', 183.

[11] *Principles of Political Economy and Taxation*, 126. For J. S. Mill's eventual abandonment of the wage fund theory, see below. For philosophical differences between Smith, Ricardo, and Malthus, see Hilton, *A Mad, Bad and Dangerous People*, 342–6.

[12] Cf. Daunton, *Progress and Poverty*, Ch. 17, and XIII, Pt 3.

[13] Bentham alluded to this notion, discussed by J. R. Poynter, *Society and Pauperism* (1969), 122–44.

of less eligibility[14] was the pithy articulation of this deterrent-based economic attack on the old system of support which allegedly encouraged idleness and discouraged individual productive industry.

But such reasoning also served an arguably even more important function during this period: Malthus provided late eighteenth-century Anglican orthodoxy with an economic rationalization for its broad political adherence to the view that Providence had decreed society's division between the ruling rich elite and the poor working classes.[15] Indeed, Malthus's *Essay on Population* was in large measure an attempted express rebuttal of William Godwin's *Inquiry Concerning Political Justice*,[16] which both undermined Christian ethics and preached that only a socially dynamic society could induce a reining back of sexual passions and promote population stability. Through the science of political economy Malthus sought to show that only the compelling need of labour to provide the basics of subsistence would divert the masses from unproductive indolence and sexual gratification; poverty and social inequality were the inescapable consequence of finite resources, whose allocation was subject to the open competitive forces of a market economy. In essence, earthly existence was a providentially sanctioned discipline and trial for the afterlife. With this sequence of assertions, Malthus had produced an 'ideological alliance of political economy and Christian theology'.[17] Such a rationale provided the broad philosophical underpinnings of the developing discipline of political economy over the first three decades of the nineteenth century, lingering on in increasingly enfeebled form until the 1850s.

Malthus's fundamental thesis, linking Providence's natural social and economic order, as most spectacularly taken up by the Scot, Thomas Chalmers,

---

[14] See the 1817 *Report of the Select Committee on the Poor Laws PP* 1817 (462) vi and the *Report of the Royal Commission on the Poor Laws PP* 1834 (44) xxviii; also XIII, Pt 2.

[15] See Bishop Butler, Wilberforce etc in 'Law and Religion', Ch. V, above.

[16] *An Enquiry concerning Political Justice and its Influence on General Virtue and Happiness* (1793). D. C. Somervell, observed, that as Godwin's seditious but 'ponderous and pretentious' book cost three guineas, 'Pitt did not interfere with Godwin; he thought the price of the book sufficient for the security of the Government', *English Thought in the Nineteenth Century* (2nd edn, 1929), 32. Concern over population growth outstripping a nation's resources had in different ways been raised by many before Malthus, including Hume, *Of the Populousness of Ancient Nations* (1752) and Robert Wallace, *Various Prospects of Mankind, Nature and Providence* (1761). Godwin maintained that the general growth in happiness of the masses through social equality would lead to a diminution in sexual appetite and, consequently, a stabilized population.

[17] A. Waterman, *Revolution, Economics and Religion: Christian Political Economy 1798–1833* (Cambridge, 1991). Rather than a necessary linkage between political economy and Christian theology, describing it as an *alliance* is probably more appropriate. Both Ricardo and James Mill were inclined towards religious scepticism. However, for claims of the broad significance of religious institutions and philosophy for the political and economic developments of the 1820s–1830s, see also Clark, *English Society 1660–1832*, and Hole, *Pulpits, Politics and Political Order in England*, passim.

became the age's religio-economic gospel competing with morally distinct Utilitarian political economy (below). Such was the Chalmers' phenomenon that his apparent devotees included Canning, Peel, Huskisson, Vansittart, Mackintosh, and Romilly. Most particularly, Chalmers' tracts on *laissez-faire* and a market economy, adopted by sympathizers such as Bishop John Sumner,[18] became the economic voice of mainstream Evangelical opinion.[19] In common with Malthus, while strongly supporting private charities (where discretionary material relief could be dispensed with lessons on self-help and even more generous helpings of spiritual nourishment) he was an entrenched opponent of state intervention to alleviate poverty under the Poor Laws. Chalmers also attacked the over-abundance of capital supplied by un-godly, avaricious speculators, which allegedly led to the economically destabilizing over-supply of goods. But significant differences separated Malthus and Chalmers: most especially, where Chalmers was a free trader, who supported removal of the Corn Laws, Malthus favoured many protectionist devices. Yet while the age's celebrated expounder of religio-economic philosophy, Chalmers' views on the Poor Laws received a resounding rebuff by the social and economic intervention represented by the 1834 Act. Although punitive in a fashion which he could endorse, the whole meddling administrative edifice of state welfare provision was utterly contrary to the voluntarism and self-responsibility espoused by Chalmers. Indeed, this coupled with the many divisions within the broad Evangelical creed, might caution that claims of its impact on political economy of the period should be restricted to one of broad ethical endorsement or legitimisation of *laissez fairism*. And even this could hardly be ascribed to Evangelical high Tories such as Drummond and Shaftesbury, or even the liberal Tory *Times* when expressing marked reservations over the 'parrot gabble about political economy, which is now so common in and out of Parliament [after] a few lectures of some pedant [giving] by rote a few abstract rules'.[20]

---

[18] *A Treatise on the Records of Creation* (1816). Sumner was Bishop of Chester from 1828, and appointed Archbishop of Canterbury in 1848.

[19] Especially, *Discourses on the Christian Revelation* (1817), *Christian and Civic Economy of Large Towns* (1821–6), and the *Bridgewater Treatises* (1833). For a detailed analysis of the involvement of Evangelicals in the discourse of political economy in the first half of the nineteenth century, see Hilton, *Age of Atonement*. As Hilton amply demonstrates, deep theological, political, and economic views divided Evangelical factions. This was most marked between the 'moderate' Claphamites led by Wilberforce (supporting a liberal-Tory social and economic stance) and the high paternalistic, Evangelical Tories, typified by Henry Drummond, Thomas Sadler, Richard Oastler, and Shaftesbury. Many of the latter resisted the Reform Act 1832 and harboured long-standing suspicions over the benefits of industrialization and economic *laissez-fairism*. But even within factions, attitudes to social and economic policies frequently lacked consistency (Chs 1–3).

[20] 19 March 1831, p. 5.

Chalmers' celebrity and authority as the representative voice of religio-economic philosophy waned from the mid-1830s.[21] This was a consequence of two primary forces: Whig and liberal Tory administrations began to recognize the irresistible need for social interventionism; and a slowly growing belief amongst politicians and economists in the optimistic Smithian claim that population growth could be accommodated by an expanding, free-trade economy, which yielded lower prices and higher wages.[22] It was a claim increasingly accepted by influential economists, such as Nassau Senior, and which staunch free-trade propagandists, such as Richard Cobden, would relentlessly promote in the 1840s.

Beyond poor relief measures, prior to 1815 the state largely absented itself from matters of social welfare. This rested principally on the basis of fundamental political assumptions and beliefs as to the state's role, reinforced by the steady absorption of notions of free-market economic liberalism. However, an exceptional legislative intervention and check on industrial freedom was Robert Peel senior's Health and Morals of Apprentices Act 1802.[23] This early instance of factory regulation was largely regarded by fellow mill owners as an unthreatening curb on manufacturers which would neither severely compromise their economic efficiency nor foreign competitiveness. As was long to remain the case, protecting health and moral welfare chimed well with both humanitarian and Evangelical notions of beneficial capitalism and also with what was regarded as the legitimate function of poor relief: support for the immature and vulnerable. Moreover, as early nineteenth-century Owenite cooperative industrial philosophy and practice (initially, at least) appeared to demonstrate, even extensive welfare provisions in conditions of employment were by no means incompatible with the return of handsome profits.[24]

As for the physical infrastructure of an increasingly industrial urbanized nation, until well into the nineteenth century, matters relating to housing,

---

[21] For the diverse range of oppositional 'Christian economy' developing in universities at this time, see Hilton, Age of Atonement, 36–49.

[22] In respect of the relevance of population growth, Ricardo's Utilitarian (secular) economic treatise of 1817, On the Principles of Political Economy and Taxation, took more or less the same view as Malthus on the static nature of the economy and the need to hold wages at subsistence level. M. Milgate and S. Stimson, Ricardian Politics (Princeton, 1991).

[23] 42 Geo. III c. 73. The Act limited the working day of apprentices in textile mills to 12 hours and required both the provision of clothing, some literacy instruction, along with separate sleeping arrangements for boys and girls. Enforcement measures proved inadequate in the hands of Quarter Sessions. See J. Innes, 'Origins of the Factory Acts: The Health and Morals of Apprentices Act 1802', in N. Landau (ed.), Law, Crime and English Society 1660–1830 (Cambridge, 2002), 230.

[24] Robert Owen's paternalistic industrial philosophy (originally supported by Bentham and Wilberforce) was set out in his A New View of Society (1813–16) and Report to the County of Lanark (1821). Though the movement eventually foundered in the 1840s, Owen's notions of political economy, particularly that labour was the basis of value were taken up in the 1830s by radicals and socialists. J. Harrison, Robert Owen and the Owenites in Britain and America (1969).

sanitation, and roads, rested almost exclusively on local initiatives facilitated by locally relevant legislation. Creation of Improvement Commissioners had grown from the 1720s, yet the financing and execution of municipal schemes was haphazard, random in effect, and almost completely unregulated when it came as to quality, density, or any other general environmental or health requirement.[25] Furthermore, active civic interventionism was by no means seen by all as desirable. Many, including Hazlitt in the early 1820s, viewed the steady accumulation of local, especially urban, corporate powers with considerable suspicion:

Corporate bodies are more corrupt and profligate than individuals, because they have more powers to do mischief and are less amenable to disgrace or punishment. They feel neither shame, remorse, gratitude, nor good-will...Public bodies are so far worse than the individuals comprising them, because the *official* takes place of the *moral sense*.[26]

Finally, at this early nineteenth-century stage, to what extent did the common law and equity facilitate or thwart an emerging capitalist *laissez-faire* economy? At a generalized level, it is highly debatable just how sympathetic the courts were towards the developing late eighteenth and early nineteenth-century economy.[27] For instance the historical evidence on the specific and key position of contract law has been subject to conflicting interpretations. In particular, suggestions[28] of the common law's late eighteenth-century calculated accommodation with the emerging, and eventually dominant, economic philosophy of *laissez-faire* are open to refutation.[29] First,

---

[25] E. Jones and M. Falkus, 'Urban Improvement and English Economy in the 17th and 18th Centuries' (1979) 4 *Research in Economic History* 212. On the mixed public and private system of turnpike trusts, see T. Barker and D. Gerhold, *The Rise and Rise of Road Transport 1700–1990* (1993). The function and relationship of both national and local taxes to the production and distribution of wealth is considered below.

[26] William Hazlitt, *Table Talk* (1908 edn, orig. pub. 1821) 'On Corporate Bodies', 264–5. A theme also taken up by Herbert Spencer in 'Railway Murders and Railway Policy' (1854) in *Essays* (1891), iii: 60.

[27] e.g. cf. P. O'Brien, *Power without Profit: The State and the Economy 1688–1815* (1991) and 'Central Government and the Economy 1688–1815', in R. Floud and D. McCloskey (eds), *The Economic History of Britain since 1700* (Cambridge, 1994), i: 205, with Daunton, *Progress and Poverty*, Ch. 18. O'Brien suggests that in 'particular areas' of law, economic growth was constrained by the state's failure to provide 'proper legal conditions conducive to (a) the operation of efficient markets for the exchange of commodities; (b) for raising long-term capital; and (c) for the regulation of credit supplies' (*Economic History*, (1994) 230). In contrast, Daunton concludes, 'A strong case may be made that the legal system was able to respond to the changing needs of the economy, and that the British State in the eighteenth century was remarkably effective and strong' (502).

[28] Most powerfully in P. Atiyah, *The Rise and Fall of Freedom of Contract* (Oxford, 1979). Also in a principally American context by M. Horwitz, *The Transformation of American Law* (1977).

[29] A. W. Simpson (1975) 91 *LQR* 247 and (1979) 46 *U. Chicago LR* 533; J. Barton, (1987) 103 *LQR* 118; and J. Baker (1980) 43 *MLR* 467. And see Vol XII, Pt 2 and D. Hay, 'The State and the Market in 1800: Lord Kenyon and Mr Waddington' (1999) 162 *Past and Present* 101–62.

as a matter of chronology, by the time Mansfield's influence had established itself, while the judiciary by no means always presented a united and uniform front in all contractual contexts across a range of early nineteenth-century case law, the predominant doctrinal view favoured the enforcement of hard bargains, with the award of damages for breach. Furthermore, there is little to support the thesis that the Victorian judiciary as a whole fashioned the common law (or equity), or approached statutory construction with the objective of facilitating economic development consistent with the period's political economic ideology.[30] Within and beyond contract law, as the century advanced it will be seen that common law and equity steered a somewhat erratic, unpredictable course, depending on the particular aspect or area of economic activity. Broadly, whether the court was developing the common law or interpreting a statute, the judiciary could be observed both reinforcing *laissez-faire* attitudes in some instances, and obstructing capitalistic endeavour in others.

Economic Policy, Capitalism, and Labour: Dependence and Conflict

Through a blend of time, circumstances, and political pragmatism, reinforced by the growing orthodoxy of a refined Smithian *laissez-fairism*, the 30 years leading up to the death of the Corn Laws in 1846 witnessed the piecemeal dismantling of a collection of legal inhibitions on the full-blooded pursuit of free trade.[31] Additionally, two particular conditioning factors were highly germane to free-trade ambitions: monetary and fiscal policies. In 1819 new legislation facilitated the resumption of the gold standard (effected in 1821) and of cash payments, thereby placing a premium on liberalizing and increasing the volume of foreign trade. To this end in 1822 the Navigation Laws of 1651 protecting the trading rights of British shipping were revised, though not abolished. The further liberalizing-related prospect of removing or reducing duties on imports was dependent on securing alternative revenue sources or budget surpluses. In the highly sensitive case of corn, duties were cut in 1827. Five years later the East India Company's monopoly on British trade with China was terminated.[32] Although Chartist agitation ran well into the 1840s, to a degree it was absorbed by Cobden and Bright's essentially middle-class Anti-Corn Law League, with its hyperbole lacerating the

---

[30] On the tort liability of manufacturers and consumer protection, see XII, Pt 4.

[31] For the complex cross-currents of government, political and economic policies during the 1820s, see B. Gordon, *Economic Doctrine and Tory Liberalism 1824–1830* (1979) and Hilton, *A Mad, Bad and Dangerous People*, 286–308. For the fiscal constraints and opportunities, see M. Daunton, *Trusting Leviathan, The Politics of Taxation in Britain, 1799–1914* (Cambridge, 2001), Ch. 2.

[32] See A. Howe, 'Restoring Free Trade: The British Experience 1776–1873', in D. Winch and P. O'Brien (eds), *The Political Economy of British Historical Experience 1688–1914* (Oxford, 2002), 193–213.

ruling class and its promises of lower food prices through the sweeping away of trade protection.[33]

While some great distance from endorsing the League's depiction of the landed classes as 'power proud plunderers [or] blood sucking vampires',[34] Peel further modified the Corn Laws in 1842 and completely removed them in 1846.[35] Rather than as a direct response to the campaigning pressure of the League and 'Manchester School' of economic liberals, Peel (though splitting the Tories) regarded his policy as both a way of reconciling class antagonisms, quelling residual social unrest, and delivering long-term national economic stability. Set doggedly against this strategy were high Tory social and economic paternalists who continued to view this free-trading economic liberalism as 'in its very essence a mercenary, unsocial, democratising system, opposed to all generous actions, all kindly feelings. Based on selfishness—the most pervading as well as the most powerful of our vicious propensities—it directs that impulse into the lowest of all channels, the mere sordid pursuit of wealth.'[36]

These evolving features and philosophies of capitalistic economic liberalism over the first half of the nineteenth century developed alongside—or in opposition to—the collective ambitions of the country's labour force. Trade specific legislation enacted at various stages of the eighteenth century, coupled with the general relevance of criminal conspiracy, outlawed workmen's combinations.[37] At the century's conclusion, dominant political opinion had come to endorse Wilberforce's characterization of the pressure and agitation from workmen's combinations as a 'general disease in our society'[38] requiring comprehensive legal intervention. The subsequent Combination Acts of 1799 and 1800 punished with summary and 'exemplary justice' all collective agreements and actions to improve wages or working conditions, or interfere with the operation of an employer's business. However, in a limited gesture at showing even-handedness, provisions were inserted into the 1800 Act declaring illegal employers' associations formed to depress wages or in some way worsen employees' working conditions.[39]

---

[33] e.g. M. Taylor, *The Decline of British Radicalism 1847–1860* (Oxford, 1995).

[34] Quoted by H. Perkin, *The Origins of Modern English Society 1780–1880* (1969), 277.

[35] Partly on the back of reintroducing income tax. Daunton, *Trusting Leviathan*, Ch. 4.

[36] G. F. Young, 'Free Trade' (1849) 86 *Quart. Rev.*, 148–83; Daunton, *Poverty and Progress*, 554.

[37] J. Orth, *A Legal History of Trade Unionism 1721–1906* (Oxford, 1991), Ch. 2.

[38] *Parliamentary Register*, 8 (1799) Ch. 2.

[39] But, while convicted employees faced immediate imprisonment of up to three months, employers were initially only subject to a fine. Some argued that such an employers' strategy would be economically self-defeating. R. Torrens, *On Wages and Combinations* (1834).

Beyond this tailor-made form of summary liability, also lay the severe threat of common law criminal conspiracy, recognized both before and after 1800:

[I]t was true that every man had a right to demand what wages he thought his services deserved; this was the law of the land, and the law of [economic] reason; but still the manner of making such demand was everything—it could not legally be thus made in a body.[40]

Use, or the threat, of general conspiracy charges carried real coercive power in that not only could conviction render defendants liable to substantial periods of imprisonment, but even the sheer cost of successfully defending such indictable charges could constitute a severe financial penalty.[41]

However, significant legal change arrived with the Combination Act 1824,[42] which recognized the legality of combinations. Boosting the political expediency of conceding the right to unionize (just five years after the highly liberty restricting 'Six Acts') was the belief of some political economists in the reform's largely neutral effect: the free play of market forces would rapidly teach organized labour the so-called iron laws of economics and most especially the realities of a limited 'wage fund'. Giving evidence to Hume's Commons Select Committee, both economists McCulloch and Malthus argued that regulating combinations by legislation was superfluous: attempts to extract better wages or conditions beyond the natural market level, determined by supply and demand, would ultimately be self-defeating. Even though restraint of trade was arguably a central component of union economic power,[43] to the government, such liberation of organized labour was fully consistent with the general pursuit of a free-market economy and the repeal of specific eighteenth-century wage-fixing provisions.[44]

---

[40] Sir John Sylvester, at the Old Bailey, *The Times*, 9 November 1810, quoted by Orth, *History* 36. See also e.g. *Hammond and Webb* (1799) 2 Esp. 719 and *Ferguson and Edge* (1819) 2 Stark. 489.

[41] Individual worker liability for breach of a contract of employment under the Master and Servant Act 1823 (and earlier legislation) also constituted a powerful brake on strike action. On the effects of the 1823 and 1867 Acts (until removed in 1875), and thousands of annual prosecutions, see R. Steinfeld, *Coercion, Contract and Free Labor in the Nineteenth Century* (Cambridge, 2001) and C. Frank, 'The Defeat of the 1844 Master and Servants Bill', in D. Hay and P. Craven (eds), *Masters, Servants and Magistrates in Britain and the Empire 1562–1955* (Chapel Hill, 2004), 402.

[42] On the background and substance of the 1824 and 1825 Acts, XIII, Pt 3.

[43] As courts would eventually conclude (below).

[44] Utilitarian J. McCulloch 'Combinations Laws' (1824) 39 *Edin. Rev.* 315, 318, also *Principles of Political Economy*. The 1824 *Select Committee Report*, PP 1824, (51), v, and Joseph Hume, the Select Committee's promoter, *PD* 1824 (s2) 10: 143. Hume invoked the authority of the recently deceased Ricardo. Others, including Thomas Chalmers (*Christian and Civic Economy*, vol. 3, Ch. 20), adopted much the same line as McCulloch. The actual degree of influence exercised by (largely Utilitarian) political economic theory on the liberalizing of the Combination laws is debatable: cf. W. Grampp, 'The Economists and the Combination Laws' (1979) 93 *Quarterly Jnl. of Econ.* 501 and Gordon, *Economic Doctrine and Tory Liberalism 1824–1830* . However, at government request, the Utilitarian

But faith in the natural self-adjusting mechanisms of the market was rapidly undermined through an upsurge in labour activism, fuelled by a favourable economic climate and driven by demands for higher wages, shorter hours, or for the protection of established working practices against cost-cutting technical innovation. An unnerved Parliament sought to modify recent reforms with enactment of the Combination Act 1825. As a principal proponent of the Liverpool Government's *laissez-faire* ideology, Huskisson reaffirmed the immutable economic reality, that although 'labour was the poor man's capital', employers must enjoy that 'perfect freedom … to give employment to that labour'.[45] So, while leaving untouched the new legality enjoyed by voluntary combinations, the 1825 legislation deployed summary criminal liability to curtail the potential economic leverage of unions by circumscribing their ability to coerce fellow workers into joining a union and striking against an employer.

As well as conceding to organized labour the legal, political, and economic power to bargain, the Act created a largely ignored arbitration system controlled by magistrates for settlement of disputes between employers and workers. Crucially, however, the 1825 Act left ambiguous the forms of collective action which might still be subject to indictment as common law conspiracy. Over the subsequent half century, with varying degrees of accommodation by the courts,[46] employers successfully exploited this absence of legal clarity, thereby limiting the industrial power of unions. Increasingly common in judicial pronouncements, when construing the effect of the 1825 legislation, was the individualistic assertion of the likely dire national consequences of the law not recognizing political economy's imperative: that everyone 'may make what bargain he pleases for his own employment…; and men may associate together; but they must not by their association violate the law…; they must not do what would prejudice another

economist Nassau Senior was active in the 1830s and 1840s in investigating the believed economic consequences of the actions of combinations. To realize his concept of free labour (not subject to the pressure of organized labour), Senior proposed greater use of specifically formulated criminal offences in substitution for criminal conspiracy as an anti-combination weapon. M. Curthoys, *Governments, Labour and the Law in Mid-Victorian Britain* (Oxford, 2004), 21–4.

[45] *PD* 1825 (s2) 12: 1292, as President of the Board of Trade, seeking appointment of a further Commons' Select Committee to examine the operation of the 1824 Act. The socialist-labour response to this was Thomas Hodgskin, *Labour Defended against the Claims of Capital* (1825). Identifying Huskisson as the mouthpiece of capitalism, Hodgskin sought to reinterpret the political economy of Smith, James Mill, Ricardo, and McCulloch to support the claims of workers to the full product of their labour. More generally, D. Stack, *Nature and Artifice: The Life and Thought of Thomas Hodgskin* (1998).

[46] XIII, Pt 3. The 1834 case of the 'Tolpuddle Martyrs' involved convictions under the Unlawful Oaths Act 1797. The political embarrassment caused by the opportunistic misuse of this provision resulted in the granting of pardons and return from transportation after four years.

man. [Permitting this] would lead to the most melancholy consequences to the working classes' as well as for manufacturers.[47]

The broadly unsympathetic judicial stance[48] towards organized labour's quest for collectivist industrial and economic power clearly needs to be read against several contextual features, most especially the social unrest of the Luddite, Swing, and Chartist periods. These largely working-class manifestations of social, economic, and political discontent well demonstrated abilities to organize social disorder by collective action aimed at damaging property or creating extensive disorder. While far from being simple fellow travellers of such agitators, the sometimes sympathetic developing union movement, for the most part confined to skilled manual workers, was no doubt seen in that unfavourable light from the Bench.[49] Aside from these potentially distorted judicial perceptions, there was the political and economic reality of the growth in unionized labour. Beyond the establishment of regional or national unions representing particular trades, creation of more politically and economically ominous generalized unions covering several trades was from time to time attempted. Yet it would be the 1850s before general unions would achieve any degree of solidity and permanence.[50]

Social Consequences of Economic Policies—Interventionism

Open and widespread political espousal of a Smithian, liberal competitive market in the 1820s and 1830s was reinforced by a cluster of professional (Utilitarian) economists, principally Ricardo, James Mill,[51] James McCulloch,[52] and Nassau Senior.[53] The problematic nature of the relationship between Smith's *laissez-fairism*

---

[47] Lord Campbell CJ, *Hewitt* (1851) 5 Cox 162, 163. The central importance of the legality of picketing was recognized by legislative intervention in 1859 (Molestation of Workmen Act, 22 Vict. c. 34). However, the broad rights to picket apparently given under the Act were over the years scaled down by the courts. For example, *Druitt* (1867) 10 Cox 592, where 'black' or 'threatening looks' were held capable of constituting illegal intimidation.

[48] For the strategic use of economic power by employers as an alternative to legal proceedings to thwart union action, see M. Lobban, 'Strikers and the Law, 1825–51', in P. Birks (ed.), *The Life of the Law* (1993) 211, *passim*.

[49] The inconclusive case of *O'Connor* (1842) 4, St. Tri. (N.S.) 1200 was one high profile conjunction of Chartist agitation, union strikes, and conspiracy charges.

[50] XIII, Pt 3.

[51] *Elements of Political Economy* (1821). James Mill was effectively Ricardo's mentor in encouraging both the publication of *Principles* and his seeking election to the Commons in 1819.

[52] The widely popular public lectures followed by *Discourse on the Rise, Progress, Peculiar Objects, and Importance of Political Economy* (1825); *The Principles of Political Economy* (1825).

[53] *Outline of the Science of Political Economy* (1836). First holder of Oxford's Drummond Chair of Political Economy.

and the diverse gamut of Utilitarian economic theories is well recognized.[54] However, the shared central prominence that both ideologies ascribed to the power of natural, individualistic, self-preference meant that Utilitarianism and classical political economy were commonly regarded as much of a muchness:

['Rationalist']: But the Political Economists, in directing the attention to 'the greatest happiness of the greatest number' wish to provide for the solid comforts and amelioration of home life... ['Sentimentalist']: Yes, in a very notable way, after their fashion... They would starve the poor outright, reduce their wages to what is barely necessary to keep them alive.[55]

Essentially, Bentham's greatest happiness principle could be credibly translated into any system which promoted the nation's greatest economic success; utility could lend itself to both severe forms of *laissez-fairism* as well as considerable extensions of state intervention.[56] The economically and socially moderate *Times* well captured the limits of *laissez-fairism*: 'The general axiom of economists' laissez faire, is a purely economical lesson, of the highest importance to Governments. But then it should be recollected that it is purely economical; that it disclaims all collateral moral considerations.'[57] The core question was, of course, one of degree: how far should *laissez-fairism* be permitted to operate and when was state intervention necessary to effect the most generally beneficial outcome? As later asserted by J. S. Mill, the pragmatic rule of thumb was that *laissez-fairism* '... should be the general practice; every departure from it, unless required by some great good, is a certain evil'.[58] The Poor Law Act 1834 was the most obvious and prominent progeny of a marriage between the body of *laissez-fairism* and the Utilitarian mindset. Much in the early examples of factory and health legislation initiatives (below) further illustrates the conceptual convergence between dyed-in-the-wool economic liberalism and Utilitarian felicific calculation.

Both rested on a belief in man's rational calculating, self-interested, and trainable nature. In consequence, the appropriate institutional structures and laws could bring about generally desirable individual and social outcomes. This held

---

[54] Conveniently summarized by R. D. Collinson Black, 'Bentham and the Political Economists of the Nineteenth Century' (1988) *The Bentham Newsletter* 24, reprinted in *Jeremy Bentham*, ed. B. Parekh (1993), iv, 3.

[55] W. Hazlitt, *The Plain Speaker* (1925 edn, orig. pub. 1825) 'The New School of Reform—A Dialogue between a Rationalist and a Sentimentalist', 193. And the lampooning of James Mill and McCulloch in Peacock's *Crotchet Castle* (1831). Cf. the more serious, sympathetic treatment of F. Jeffrey (1825) 43 *Edin. Rev.* 2.

[56] H. Parris, 'The Nineteenth Century Revolution in Government: A Reappraisal Reappraised' (1960) *Hist. J.* 35.

[57] 13 June 1848, p. 4.

[58] *Principles of Political Economy*, Collected Works, iii, 945. Even Smith's *Wealth of Nations* allowed for exceptional cases where *laissez-fairism* would not serve the nation's interest, such as external defence, internal law and order, state education, and even a major network of roads.

good whether the question was of criminal vagrants or work-shy paupers. In the case of poor relief, the right system of economic incentives and disincentives promised to convert 'the able bodied idle into productive, autonomous individuals, gaining the inestimable benefits of moral self-respect and economic self-sufficiency; freeing the state of the burden of poor relief'. The favoured Benthamite procedure of structured administrative investigation, assembly of findings, and consequential reform proposals was outwardly satisfied by the 1832 Royal Commission on the Poor Laws. However, the not-so-rare practice of manipulating evidence to support prior conclusions characterized the Commission's proceedings and 1834 Report, directed and composed by Nassau Senior, a doctrinaire *laissez-faire* economist, and Edwin Chadwick, Bentham's instinctively interventionist former secretary. As the basis of the Poor Law Amendment Act 1834, the Report explicitly embraced a social mechanism linking self-interest and a liberal market economy. Most centrally, in common with other *laissez-faire* economists, Senior regarded the widely deployed outdoor relief system as undermining the natural market setting of wage levels. Removal of such relief with the insistence of workhouse residence, and substituting the key principle of less-eligibility (greater misery) would liberate the labour market and achieve the most generally beneficial economic outcome of higher productivity coupled with higher wages. Among many fiercely attacking the substance and operation of the 1834 Act, and particularly attempts to extinguish outdoor relief, *The Times* declared on more than one occasion that the country would not tolerate such centralized hegemony: 'The national palate nauseates it. You cannot, by pushing or screwing, send it down the nation's throat. The people will not have it ...'.[59] But against this sentiment, believed damaging local departures from the national scheme were the target of a centralized, supervisory administration, a Poor Law Commission, replaced in 1847 by a Poor Law Board, presided over by a minister accountable to Parliament.[60]

In the case of the often appalling physical and social consequences of a substantially unfettered industrial economy, there was a largely common response from cross-party free-market liberals and Utilitarian economists. The factory reform movement and the anti-reformists comprised a complex and peculiar cluster of groupings and ideologies: reformist high-Tory philanthropists and Evangelicals were pitted against many Whig and liberal parliamentarians supported by Utilitarian economists in alliance with industrialists. Reform agitation over limitation of working hours and increased safety, led initially in Parliament

---

[59] 6 July 1844, p. 5.
[60] For the detailed implementation and evolution of the Poor Law reforms, see also XIII, Pt 2.

by Michael Sadler and then Lord Shaftesbury,[61] was met by a Royal Commission on Factories which, like the Poor Law Commission, had solid Benthamite ambitions. In its first Report,[62] Chadwick and his colleagues broadly endorsed the basic *laissez-faire* arguments put up by the anti-reformists defending the commercial imperative of an unregulated labour market for responsible free-acting adults. The underpinning rationale of free adult agency (still making regular appearances in the late nineteenth century)[63] completely discounted the stark realities of economic pressures exerted by limited employment opportunities for many of the semi-skilled or unskilled working population. After 1834, it was often the case of them facing the economic and socially engineered choice of taking work for grindingly low wages and conditions or entry to the workhouse.

Such a political economic stance coincided with and mutually reinforced the well-articulated common law doctrinal preference for freedom of contract. In the *Edinburgh Review*, Benthamite political economist James McCulloch advanced the socio-economic justification for even unregulated factories:

abuses were rare instances; speaking generally, factory work people, including non-adults, are as healthy and contented as any class of the community obliged to earn their bread in [*sic*] the sweat of their brow... Whatever may be the state of society in [great towns] we hesitate not to say, that it would have been ten times worse but for the factories. They have been the best and most important academies. Besides taking children out of harm's way, they have imbued them with regular, orderly, and industrious habits.[64]

Thus, the compelling economic virtues of *laissez-fairism* could be rendered compatible with the absence of state regulation. For its part, *The Times* was in no doubt about what the 'shallow reasonings [of] the school of your half-taught pretenders to political economy [represented]: warfare between humanity and greediness'.[65] But a compromise was struck: as Whig free-trader Thomas Macaulay observed at the time, the 'general rule—a rule not more beneficial to the capitalist than to the labourer—is that contract [of employment] shall be free and that the State shall not interfere between master and... workman. [However]

---

[61] See 'Law and Religion', Ch. V, above.

[62] *PP* 1833 (45), xx.

[63] e.g. Cross, the Tory Home Secretary in 1874. P. Smith, *Disraelian Conservatism* (1967), 214.

[64] (1835) 61 *Edin. Rev.* 463. Economic consequences clearly attended the care, including education, of children. Under the Factory Act 1833, child workers were required to attend elementary schooling outside the factory premises. However, time spent at school could mean the loss or reduction of a child's wage contribution to an impoverished family. After 1834, schooling could not be provided by Poor Law Boards. For the gradual involvement of the state in supporting elementary schooling run by voluntary religious bodies, see Ch. V, above, 'Law and Religion' and XIII, Pt 2.

[65] 22 January 1841, p. 4. Similarly, 27 January 1847, p. 4.

children cannot protect themselves and are therefore entitled to the prohibition of the public.'[66] Women also achieved this status of economically 'unfree' agents, thereby enjoying (some) protection from exploitation under the Mines Act 1842. Despite the limited scope of the Factories Act 1833 and severe problems of enforcement,[67] it constituted a foot in the door against principled, blanket opposition to state interference with trade and industry. Nevertheless, subsequent more restrictive legislative regulation continued to attract staunch opposition from a broad coalition of free-traders, including the anti-Corn Law League and its leader John Bright. Rather than resort to the familiar uncompetitiveness argument against regulation, Bright opposed regulation on the grounds that completely free trade would itself be the 'best and surest protection' for all workers.[68] As in other areas of creeping state intervention, the key to effectiveness was almost always to be the establishment of an adequate, centrally controlled inspectorate. At the same time, early limited judicial constructing of factory legislation suggested no great appetite to offer a protective approach to workers.[69]

Legislation protecting factory workers was the health issue most immediately connected with the state's role in dealing with the consequences of an expanding industrial economy. England's relatively rapid industry-driven urbanization spawned its own particular social problems, most especially those of housing and sanitation, problems which were only incidentally addressed by laws covering poor relief and working conditions. Certainly some employers well understood the economic benefits to be derived from healthy, well-housed workers—most famously Robert Owen's factory villages. However, the driving forces of *limited* state intervention in matters of poor relief and factory workers' protection (secular and Evangelical humanitarianism, philanthropy, Utilitarian, and *laissez-faire* beliefs) had far less relevance to matters of health and housing. Urban living conditions had only in the most limited sense been central government's business by the early decades of the nineteenth century. The paternalistic provision of housing, albeit often of a poor state, in an agrarian economy was far less frequently replicated in urban industrial areas; and when it was, economic rents would often be expected from employees. In broad terms, housing and health would

---

[66] Similarly, by a member of the Children's Employment Commission in 1842, *First Report*, PP 1842 (381–2) xvi, App. 195. Quoted from the *Leeds Mercury*, June 1832 by D. Fraser, *The Evolution of the Welfare State* (2003) 22.

[67] The central concern (expressed largely through a succession of Royal Commissions and Select Committees) beyond the next half century was the protection and education of children and women, in the work place, especially textile factories and mines. See generally, R. Gray, *The Factory Question and Industrial England 1830–1860* (Cambridge, 1996). And see 'Law and Religion', Ch. V, above, and XIII, Pt 2.

[68] *Leicestershire Mercury*, April 1844, and Fraser, *Evolution*, 27.

[69] e.g. *Ryder v. Mills* (1850) 3 Exch. 853.

only become the state's business when poor social conditions became sufficiently acute and widespread to make central government inaction politically impossible.[70] Coupled with the ever-present suspicion of unwanted state intrusion, was the ever-present economic brake: a general resistance at a national or local level to fund social intervention. It was a reality at the core of disputes over poor relief, the loss of cheap child labour, the establishing of professional policing, and the setting up of a prison-building programme.[71]

While long suspected, the link between disease, poor health, housing, and sanitation only became credibly authenticated by the 1840s. One Select Committee even expressly made out a moral and economic case for state protection from ill-health of workers 'by whose hands the great riches derived from...trade are chiefly formed ...'.[72] Though such evidence had been emerging from the new Poor Law Commissioners,[73] it was Chadwick's massive 1842 Report on the sanitary condition of the Labouring Classes which first established the irresistible truth of the debilitating effect of poor environment on health. A sizeable motive for Chadwick's pursuit of the link between poverty and public health was the potential savings in the cost of poor relief. The burden of disabling diseases 'would render it good economy on the part of the administrators of the Poor Laws to incur the changes for preventing the evils when they are ascribable to physical causes, which there are no other means of removing'.[74] Chadwick's evidence and conclusions[75] were soon confirmed by Southwood Smith's influential Health of Towns' Commission, set up by Peel, and reporting in 1844 and 1845.[76] As in other areas of intervention, localism rather than Chadwick's centralizing ambitions was the preferred point of state entry. Local initiatives under the Municipal Corporation Act 1835, reinforced by the growth of local Acts, had produced a measure of alleviation of some urban conditions in certain areas. But beyond the paving and lighting of streets, the heavier capital investment required for water and sewage projects proved singularly resistible to reformed corporations, where

[70] Early examples include the Cholera Act 1832 and the Vaccination Act 1840. It might not be completely cynical to suggest that the cross-class reach of these diseases may have spurred parliamentary concern and action.

[71] See XIII, Pt 1.

[72] Slaney's 1840 Select Committee on the 'Health of the Inhabitants of Large Towns' had already concluded that in default of local improvements central direction was required.

[73] For the Poor Law Commissioners and the medical relief of the poor, see XIII, Pt 2.

[74] Appendix A, 1, Fourth Annual Report of Poor Law Commissioners 1838, and S. Finer, *The Life and Times of Sir Edwin Chadwick* (1952), Ch. 3. For the central Poor Law Commissioners, Local Poor Law Guardians and medical treatment of the poor, XIII, Pt 2.

[75] Finer, *Sir Edwin Chadwick*, Ch. 3.

[76] (1850) 38 *Quart. Rev.* 436. He regarded the Public Health Act 1848 as an 'imperishable monument of that great statesman's [Peel] far-reaching sagacity', embodying the principles of Peel's Health of Towns' Commission.

the potential increased rates burden acted as a powerful brake on undertaking municipal improvements.

The eventual outcome of Chadwick's (and others) investigations was the General Board of Health, created by the much fought-over[77] Public Health Act 1848. With Chadwick as Secretary[78] (and Shaftesbury as a Board Member) the General Board recognized central government's role in public health, largely as a facilitator or adviser to local health boards. However, arming the Board with a reserved right of intervention marked an innovation in central government's social philosophy as to its appropriate sphere of responsibility. By the early 1850s, Peelites were persuaded of the necessity for exceptional central intervention. The Tory *Quarterly Review* was able to accept that 'centralisation is, in fact…legitimate, provided its actions be based on ascertained public requirement, national or provincial. It is only when these limitations are disregarded, when the exception becomes the rule…that centralisation becomes excessive and obnoxious.'[79]

But for the reasons and forces which made enactment of the 1848 Act highly contentious, the General Board of Health enjoyed only a short life, ending in 1858.[80] Resistance to the Board's creation rested on the reality and reputation of the Poor Law Commission's style and substance of central administration, including an intrusive inspectorate. More of the same in the broad area of public health was an unappetizing prospect for many local public bodies, with overlapping, sometimes rival administrative powers, which might include local authorities, water commissioners, poor law guardians, street commissioners, and improvement commissioners. Secondly, apart from a virtually perpetual local disinclination to surrender local autonomy on any subject to unwelcome central meddling, there were powerful local financial interests at stake. Private water companies naturally resisted regulatory intrusion which threatened profits that, as was generally asserted, only the free market ought to determine. Similarly, factory and industrial plant owners mobilized opposition to regulatory regimes which would operate to their perceived economic disadvantage. Adding legislation governing factory and individual employment practices, and working conditions, there was now threatened a further basis for centralized interference with the untrammelled pursuit of profits. Despite the collective resistance of these local political

---

[77] XIII, Pt 2.

[78] See also the *Royal Commission on the Health of Towns, First Report*, PP. 1844 (s72) xvii and Nuisance Removal Act 1846 (9 & 10 Vict. c. 96). Also, C. Hamlin, *Public Health and Social Justice in the Age of Chadwick 1800–1854* (Cambridge, 1998), Chs 7 and 8.

[79] 'Sanitary Consolidation—Centralization—Local Self-government' (1850) 38 *Quart. Rev.* 436. Similarly, 'The Sanitary Question' (1847) 36 *Fraser's Magazine* 371.

[80] Chadwick was sacked in 1854 through a combination of personal animosity and his association with the then unpopular cause of centralization—similar to the reasons behind his dismissal in 1847 from the Poor Law Commission. Chadwick's replacement was the more emollient Dr John Simon.

administrative and commercial interests, by the end of the 1850s the principle of local authority responsibility and funding of sanitation and ancillary matters had gained broad assent.

If anything, the state's intervention in the distinct but related public health problem of poor housing was even more contentious than sanitation. While drainage, sewage disposal, and the availability of water were key elements of wholesome living accommodation, the nature and quality of building construction could also have a considerable impact on the health of occupants. Above all, house building was viewed as purely a matter of speculative enterprise. It combined two powerful ideologies: the sanctity of private property and the freedom of the market economy. Making headway against these would inevitably be a formidable challenge for even the most ardent social interventionist. Rising urban land prices coupled with expanding demand from ever-increasing numbers of industrial workers were compelling incentives for speculative builders to maximize the use of space at the lowest cost. At the same time, landlords would expect market rate rents. Dense occupancy levels and overcrowding were predictable, natural outcomes of demand generally outstripping supply. And, of course, wage levels determined what rents could be afforded and what landlords were prepared to make available for rents manageable by workers. The frequent outcome of these economic driving forces was graphically described in Dr James Kay-Shuttleworth's, *The Moral and Physical Condition of the Working Classes* (1832). In the specific example of cotton mill workers, grim living conditions of the many entailed: 'dilapidated, badly drained, damp … [housing. In turn, demonstrating] an intimate connexion subsists among the poor, between the cleanliness of the street and that of house and person. Uneconomical habit, and dissipation are almost inseparably allied …'.[81]

The miserable effects of leaving the building of dwellings largely unregulated and subject to market forces were increasingly manifest with the decades of growth of urban slums prior to initial and tentative intervention. Depending on location, building controls, whether under local Acts or by-laws (or, in London's case, the Building Act 1774 and Metropolitan Building Act 1844),[82] were subject to enormous variation as to the rigour of controls and level of enforcement. This remained the case until the centralized demands and controls of the Local Government Act 1858. Shaftesbury's Lodging Houses Act 1851[83] was, essentially, an aberration, owing much to the great man's tenacity and the provision's apparently unthreatening nature which enabled local authorities to finance the building of wholesome worker accommodation through rates or by borrowing; but

[81] Kay-Shuttleworth (1970 edn), 28.
[82] J. Burnett, *A Social History of Housing 1815–1985* (2nd edn, 1986), Ch. 3.
[83] 14 & 15 Vict. c. 34.

the scheme remained largely unadopted. Crucially, even these innovatory powers were expressly subject to the economic and Poor Law imperatives that the rents charged for such local authority accommodation should not be of a level that amounted to a hidden wages subsidy.

Law and Refining a Capitalist Economy

While the industrial free market was curbed by a modest degree of social legislation in the early part of the nineteenth century, the law's/state's intervention in business and commerce proceeded on a rather different footing. As already noted, much intervention was in the form of deregulation (the dismantling of 'mercantilism'), driven by a brew of pragmatism and *laissez-faire* ideology. Beyond this, legal intervention in business and the economy took a variety of approaches, many of which involved setting up facilitative or enabling structures. Other measures sought to curb or constrain anticipated anti-competitive practices. However, the steady motivation of successive Whig and Tory governments and their legislative interventions was, by and large, the effective operation of a liberal economy. And, while the foundation of *laissez-faire* ideology in contracts was furnished by the common law, most of commercial law's superstructure was constructed by legislation. As will be seen, in some areas the courts performed a significant role in creative legislative interpretation.

The immediate commercial adjuncts to freedom of contract included bills of exchange, credit facilities, together with legal procedures supporting recovery of debt. A business need for credit and paper money or negotiable instruments was the motor powering development of the banking system, many elements of which remained untouched by legislation until the Bank Charter Act 1844. Wartime suspension of the convertibility of bank notes into gold bullion had granted private banks substantial freedom in the issuing of bank notes. But reintroduction of the gold standard in 1821 brought a degree of automatic control over the supply of money and credit.[84] In essence, the belief was that such a money supply control mechanism would only inhibit unrealistic, improvident, and undesirable commercial speculation. Moreover, it promised to bring future confidence in the security of money and market stability, avoiding economic lurches between booms and depressions. Enactment of the Bank Charter Act 1844[85] was final

---

[84] See Hilton, *Corn, Cash and Commerce.*

[85] The Act set up the basic framework of British banking which operated until the 1930s. Regulations under the Act meant the phased extinction of bank notes except those of the Bank of England, the supply of which was largely governed by its holdings of gold bullion. This represented a victory for the 'currency' school over the 'banking' school which maintained that the money supply should be determined by the demands of trade. See A. Gambles, *Protection and Politics:*

affirmation of the desire of central government to both centralize note issue and regulate the money market and bank rate by the automatic gold standard mechanism, while reserving to itself the facility to intervene when thought necessary. In effect, it was a policy of regulated non-intervention and legal compromise of the free money markets advocated by the Act's opponents.

Whether a case of large-scale, unsuccessful capitalist speculation launched on credit or no more than the imprudent personal borrowing of an individual, the relevance to the broader economy of creditors' ability to recover debts is plain. The availability of imprisonment for debt[86] at a creditor's instigation was a coercive device increasingly restricted as the nineteenth century progressed. Yet, even by the 1840s, over 13,000 languished in the main London debtors' prisons, such as the Fleet and the Marshalsea. Central to reforms were the eventual introduction of the county court system in 1846 and the potential mediating role of these courts in determining the appropriateness of imprisonment as a sanction for debt. Most especially, the main determinant of eligibility for imprisonment was the refusal of a debtor to meet a judgment even when able to pay. Pursuit of multiple debts by multiple creditors of defaulting business concerns or individuals always raised the possibility of bankruptcy. The ability of large-scale creditors to recover at least part of their losses had obvious implications for the lending and credit policies of bankers, financial credit houses, and the functioning of the credit economy generally.

The Select Committee on Bankruptcy Laws 1818[87] chronicled the inconsistencies and abuses of the existing bankruptcy laws. Confinement of bankruptcy proceedings to 'traders' was justified by Blackstone on the basis that, unlike others, they could legitimately as a necessary part of business 'encumber [themselves] with debts of any considerable value'.[88] In other words, wholesale traders or manufacturers properly supported their entrepreneurial ventures with credit. This rationale conditioned the consequences of bankruptcy provisions under which on the surrendering of the debtor's estate to his creditors for an agreed dividend, not only would debts be discharged at less than full value, but the debtor would receive a percentage rebate from the cash value of his estate on which to launch a fresh

---

Conservative Economic Discourse 1815–1852 (1999), *passim*. Consistent with a free market ideology was the modification of the usury laws by the Usury Act 1837 (7 Will. IV & 1 Vict. c. 80) and complete abandonment in 1854 which removed the 5% interest rate limit on loans. Repeal had been proposed by a Commons Select Committee in 1818 (*PP* 1818 (376), vi). See Bentham's early well-known attack on this fetter on the free market of credit, *Defence of Usury* (1787).

[86] J. Cohen, 'The History of Imprisonment for Debt and its Relation to the Development of Discharging Bankruptcy' (1982) 3 *JLH* 153.

[87] *Report PP* 1818 (376), vi. See J. Hoppit, *Risk and Failure in English Business* (Cambridge, 1987), and XII, Pt 3.

[88] *Comms*, ii, Ch. 31, 'Bankruptcy', 473.

business start. The administrative and judicial shambles was given legislative attention in the early 1830s.[89] But the arcane distinction between 'traders' and the rest,
which had generated an impressive number of imaginative court constructions
endured until 1861.[90] Even then, the search for a solution to identifying and punishing collusive or fraudulent bankruptcies eluded legislators and courts until enactment of the Bankruptcy Act 1883, which owed more to the effective lobbying of
particular interest groups than pursuit of economic ideology,[91] and by which time
the use of limited liability corporations was growing.

In some part, the coming of the joint stock company was a consequence of
the desire of commercial and industrial enterprises to limit their exposure to the
possible financial catastrophe of insolvency and bankruptcy or imprisonment
for debt. The speculative fiasco of the early eighteenth century which burnt not
only the fingers of a host of large-scale investors but those of government too,
had resulted in the Bubble Act 1720 which placed highly restrictive and punitive
limits on joint stock organizations. Long, lingering suspicions of corporate bodies
as potential vehicles for fraud or other nefarious business practices ensured that
the protective benefits of legal incorporation (either by private bill or royal charter) was relatively rarely granted and generally confined to transportation or utility ventures with large capital demands and likely consequential public benefit.
However, lawyers' ingenuity provided capitalist enterprise with unincorporated
societies or joint stock companies resting on a hybrid partnership—trust device,
which, crucially, meant that a company's assets could not be subjected to legal
action by a partner-trustee's creditors. In this fashion, the financial risks of investment could be limited.[92]

An extensive period of judicial acquiescence in the widespread use of the trust
technique ended with a bout of early nineteenth-century speculative fever when
the punitive Bubble Act provisions were deployed against what the courts sensed
to be shady enterprises.[93] Uncertainty over the legal effect of trust devices was
compounded by a further outbreak of judicial antagonism led by Lord Eldon in

---

[89] (1831) 1 & 2 Will. IV c. 56.

[90] 24 & 25 Vict. c. 134. For the use of summary justice for small debts and the distinct class element in available debt enforcement procedures, see M. Finn, *The Character of Credit: Personal Debt in
English Culture, 1740–1914* (Cambridge, 2003).

[91] As well as the objective of some reformers to punish the immoral behaviour of bankrupts,
regardless of economic efficiency, there was also a steady tension between officialism and just leaving the initiative in the hands of creditors. See the *Royal Commission on the Court of Bankruptcy,
Report PP* 1854 (1770), xxiii, the *Committee on the Bankruptcy Act 1869, Report PP* 1877 (152), lxix, and
V. Markham Lester, *Victorian Insolvency* (Oxford, 1995).

[92] J. Getzler and M. Macnair, 'The Firm as an Entity before the Companies Acts', in P. Brand,
K. Costello, and W. Osborough (eds), *Adventures of the Law* (Dublin, 2005), 267.

[93] e.g. *Dodd* (1808) 9 East 516 and *Stratton* (1809) 1 Camp. 549.

response to a fresh speculative frenzy in the mid-1820s,[94] culminating in the 1825 bubble crash and demise of over 40 provincial banks. In simplistic terms, the 1825 repeal of the Bubble Act arguably represented Parliament's re-affirmation of the centrality to the economy of *laissez-fairism* in England:

Where extensive commercial interests were constantly at work, a great degree of specu-lation was unavoidable, and if kept within certain limits, this spirit of speculation was attended with much advantage to the country. [Parliament should not] prevent men from spending their own money as they pleased.[95]

Yet, effectively side-stepping the intended purpose of the 1825 Act, some judicial support for Eldon's hostile approach to unincorporated companies survived.[96] However, within a few years, Brougham, as Lord Chancellor, provided the judicial lead towards a more sympathetic treatment of unincorporated bodies, endorsing their worth as a valuable business facility.[97] It reflected a broad Whig, liberal Tory, and City strain of opinion on the overall economic benefits of such legal facilitation of established commercial practices.[98]

This political and judicial realignment occurred in a business environment about to experience the first great investment surge in railways, which, like the earlier canal network, demanded a combination of extensive capital backed up by special powers enabling compulsory land acquisition. Such steady pressure ensured that the broad question of the state's appropriate response to economic and business requirements remained very much a live issue. An ultimately abortive review of the potential for partnership law being developed as a more certain and flexible business instrument left the possibility unrealized until the end of the century.[99] As an element of early 1840s broadly liberal economic strategy, Peel and Gladstone's Companies Act 1844 regularized trust-based corporations by a system of registra-tion. Incorporation no longer depended on any centralized official determina-tion[100] of the appropriateness of such legal status; compliance with the detailed

---

[94] Lord Eldon in the vanguard with his *obiter* in *Ellison* v. *Bignold* (1821) 2 J. & W. 503, and Abbott CJ in *Josephs* v. *Pebrer* (1825) 3 B. & C. 639. For a detailed analysis of the division of judicial attitudes, see R. Harris, *Industrializing English Law: Entrepreneurship and Business Organisation 1720–1844* (Cambridge, 2000), Ch. 9.

[95] Lord Liverpool, *PD* 1825 (s2) 12: 1195 and Harris, *Industrializing English Law*, Ch. 10.

[96] Best CJ in *Duvergier* v. *Fellows* (1828) 5 Bing. 248.

[97] *Walburn* v. *Ingilby* (1833) 1 My. & K. 61.

[98] On the complex amalgam of formative forces, including litigant demands and strong pressures from commercial interest groups, see Harris, *Industrializing English Law*; T. Alborn *Conceiving Companies* (1998); and esp. XII, Pt 3.

[99] 1837 Report of Bellenden Ker on partnerships, *PP* 1837 (530), lxiv. The 1851 Select Committee on the Law of Partnership proposed a change in the law to provide partnerships with limited liability, *Report PP* 1851 (509), xviii, enacted by the Limited Partnership Act 1909.

[100] In formulating the appropriate reforms, Gladstone took over the Select Committee set up in 1841 by Melbourne's previous administration, *PP* 1844 (119), vii.

registration requirements was the sole qualifying basis for incorporation. In theory at least, detailed disclosure requirements of the 1844 Act sought to free up and simplify commercial speculation while offering investors a fair measure of intelligence on the nature of ventures and the risk of losing their shirts on sham or shakey enterprises. Yet this legislative intervention did nothing to inhibit the speculative mania for railway shares; a particular bubble that burst in 1845. Furthermore, the sensitive question of the financial exposure of investors and the ability to limit their liability for a company's debts was left to one side for future resolution.

Gladstone's legislative brief on government intervention in business matters was substantial, going beyond the generality of the Companies Act 1844. Both banks and railways merited specific attention. Special circumstances and the economic impact of banks and the Bank of England became the subject of the particular requirements of the Joint Stock Banks and Charter Act 1844.[101] Expansion of the railways, as well as having national economic consequences, also presented central government with an instance *par excellence* of the singular problem of whether, and how, effective monopolies should be regulated in a liberal economy.

Gladstone's Railway Act of 1844 constituted further legislative interventionism in an area of the economy increasingly subject to a potent brew of both statutory and common law regulation. The principal driving force of such intervention was the manifestly obvious commercial reality that, as Peel observed, 'railways were a practical monopoly [and consequently it was parliament's] duty to see the public's rights were not interfered with by those in possession of the monopoly'.[102] Just what protective, anti-monopolistic actions Peel had in mind became apparent with the 1842[103] and 1844 Railway Acts which regulated the level of railway profits through Board of Trade powers to control carriage rates, coupled with reserve powers to take railway lines into state ownership. Additionally, railway companies were compelled to offer a basic level of service over all tracks, subject to a designated maximum fare. While not the only area of actual or potential monopolistic power, railways, along with water supply (below) presented the clearest challenge to the functioning of a liberal economy, with free-market competition as a foundation expectation. From their creation in the 1820s, railway companies were required to seek private Acts for incorporation along with powers for necessary compulsory land acquisition.[104] The detailed scrutiny of all aspects of railway schemes could and did constitute a parliamentary regulatory

[101] 7 & 8 Vict. c. 113 and 7 & 8 c. 32.

[102] *PD* 1840 (s3) 65: 909.

[103] The 1842 Act set up a Railway Department at the Board of Trade for the promotion of safety through an inspectorate and, where necessary, criminal prosecutions.

[104] The Land Clauses Consolidation Act 1845 (8 & 9 Vict. c. 18) and the Railway Clauses Consolidation Act 1845 (8 & 9 Vict. c. 20) sought to generalize the procedures for the compulsory acquisition of land and the settling of levels of compensation.

system based on the feasibility and desirability of capital ventures. However, no manifest economic (or social) overall strategy was apparent over the key decades when railway company incorporation was being granted.[105]

The mid-nineteenth century not only witnessed the early stages of legislative intervention in the way and conditions under which railway companies were permitted to operate, but also judicial engagement with monopolistic practices taking hold of the railways' freight trade. Beside their greater speed and technological superiority over canals and road freight carriers, railway companies often faced no competition from rival railway companies. Consequently, ownership of tracks usually constituted a rail monopoly power over freight transport in that area or region. Legislative recognition of the potential for exploitation of *de facto* monopolies came in the form of broad prohibitions against unreasonable or prejudicial freight charging, or failure to offer competitors reasonable access to railway services. Under legislation in 1854, the Court of Common Pleas adjudicated on complaints of anti-competitive behaviour by railway companies. It was a role with which, according to Lord Campbell CJ, the courts were unhappy: 'Parliament attempting to make his judges railway directors.'[106] Over a period of 30 years until the 1870s[107] when this regulatory role was reassigned to Special Railway Commissioners, in their attitude to railway monopolies the courts were 'remarkably consistent: independent carrier–plaintiffs always won. This striking pattern was a consequence less of written law than of the tacit conviction of... Victorian judges and juries that corporate monopolism was against the public interest and, therefore, law'.[108] In short, the courts resisted moves by railway companies to gain a monopoly in freight carriage by seeking to eliminate the competition of their rival 'middle-men' freight carriers.

Up to a point this was an unsurprising response. The common law's antipathy towards clear monopolies had been long established, as Bayley J. starkly reaffirmed in 1830: 'Monopolies are against the law.'[109] Monopolies, whether local, regional or national, were manifestly the antithesis of competitive free trade. Their acceptance and statutory creation was premised on the belief that

---

[105] R. Kostal, *Law and English Railway Capitalism 1825–1875* (Oxford, 1994).

[106] Quoted by R. Jackson, *The Machinery of Justice* (7th edn, Cambridge, 1977), 112n.

[107] The Railway and Canal Traffic Act 1854 (17 & 18 Vict. c. 31) as substantially revised by the Regulation of Railways Act 1873, sought to maintain a competitive freight and mail carrying market between rival road, canal, and railway companies. The 1873 Act furnished 'Railway Commissioners' with wide investigatory and price controlling powers. Board of Trade supervision of railway safety under the Rail Regulation Act 1842 was strengthened by a second Railway Regulation Act 1873 and subsequent legislation.

[108] Kostal, *Railway Capitalism*, 218 and the analysis of case law, 185–214.

[109] Tenterden CJ, in *Duvergier* v. *Fellows* (1830) 10 B. & C. 826, 827.

an overall widespread benefit would be derived from such protection from market forces, as for example, in the case of the granting of patents (below). Beyond such exceptions, monopolies were, as an extreme form of restraint of trade, unlawful at common law. Yet, over the years, the judicial approach to restraint of trade was far from consistent or obviously principled. In the area of master and servant, the courts showed a ready willingness to use the common law both to declare unlawful agreements by groups of employers to hold down wages and to deny the legality of workers' combinations to force wages up. However, the judiciary showed themselves ready to enforce anti-competitive market rigging contracts or other restrictive practices amongst businessmen and traders.[110] Indeed, while having no truck with attempts by railway companies to monopolize the freight business, courts distinguished, and permitted, anti-competitive arrangements amongst companies to maintain passenger fares and freight charges.[111] In essence, at mid-century the judiciary were discriminatory in their stance towards restraint of trade as to what was against public policy and interest; and as later judgments were to emphasize, the courts would not readily undermine the powerful doctrinal adherence to the enforceability of contracts.

Pre-dating the creation of the railway network, both canal and water companies raised similar though less acute questions relating to Parliament's and the common law's approach to the potential economic abuses of complete or near monopolies. In respect of water suppliers, before the Companies Act 1844 some efforts were made as a condition of the necessary granting of incorporation to establish a degree of competition in the area of operation. However, in some cases early in the nineteenth century the benefits of lower prices came at the expense of a deteriorating service. The strong linkage of sound water to public health, especially in expanding urban areas, forced Parliament into conceding the sanctioning of regulated water monopolies[112] whereby private water companies operated under a regime governing matters of quality, supply, and service. In a very broad sense, canals could be regarded as a transport precursor of railway tracks in that both required substantial capital investment for their construction and special land acquisition powers; although the scale of compulsory land acquisition for canals and the concerns generated by such an assault on sacrosanct property rights was far exceeded in the railway age. But railways and canals differed in crucial respects. Most especially, safety and efficiency arguments which

---

[110] e.g. *Hearn* v. *Griffin* (1815) 2 Chitty 407 and *Wickens* v. *Evans* (1829) 3 Y. & T. 318.

[111] *Shrewsbury and Birmingham Railway* v. *L.N.W.R.* (1851) 21 L.J. Q.B. 89.

[112] On the several Royal Commissions and Select Committees, see J. Foreman-Peck and R. Millward *Public and Private Ownership of British Industry, 1820–1990* (Oxford, 1994) and B. Rudden, *The New River: A Legal History* (Oxford, 1985).

railway companies used to maintain monopoly powers over the running of trains on their own tracks had little relevance to canals. Additionally, major roads and turnpikes could offer a reasonable degree of competition for some forms of canal freight. On top of this, the sheer economic scale and presence of the larger railway companies in the country's economy in itself came to represent a malign threat of market dominance. As a consequence of these distinctions, the anti-competitive practices and problems which arose in relation to railways never materialized in the same way with canals.

Finally, an overview of law and political economy during the first half of the nineteenth century needs to turn to taxation's key function: fiscal measures straddle and link the political economy of generating wealth and the political and social policy entailed in matters of wealth distribution. Broadly, fiscal objectives look to facilitating state activities including waging wars, encouraging or supporting sectors of economic activity, and allocating revenue in the pursuit of particular social ends, such as poor relief, education, and public health initiatives.[113] In short, the potential range of state activities is intimately related to its ability and willingness to raise revenue, or at least borrow against future anticipated revenues.

As a scene-setting summary of the nature and reach of taxes levied by the 1820s, Sydney Smith's satirical evocation is hard to match:

Taxes upon every article which enters into the mouth or covers the back or is placed under the foot. Taxes upon everything which it is pleasant to see, hear, feel, smell or taste. Taxes upon warmth, light and locomotion. Taxes on everything on earth or under the earth, on everything that comes from abroad or is grown at home. Taxes on the raw material, taxes on every fresh value that is added to it by the industry of man. Taxes on the sauce which pampers man's appetite, and the drug which restores him to health; on the ermine which decorates the judge, and the rope which hangs the criminal; on the poor man's salt and the rich man's spice; on the brass nails of the coffin, and the ribbons of the bride; at the bed or board, couchant or levant, we must pay. The schoolboy whips his taxed top; the beardless youth manages his taxed horse, with a taxed bridle, on a taxed road; and the dying Englishman, pouring his medicine, which has paid 7 per cent., into a spoon that has paid 15 per cent., and expires in the arms of an apothecary who has paid a licence of a hundred pounds for the privilege of putting him to death. His whole prosperity is then immediately taxed from 2 to 10 per cent. Besides the probate, large fees are demanded for burying him in the chancel. His virtues are handed down to posterity on taxed marble, and he will then be gathered to his father to be taxed no more.[114]

---

[113] On the fundamental consequences of fiscal policy for the state's activities, see Daunton, *Trusting Leviathan, passim* and below.

[114] (1820) 33 *Edin. Rev.* 'Poor Law' 91–108.

Over the previous 20 years, the fiscal conventions and practical politics governing taxation had been subject to both innovation and retrenchment. Pitt's 1799 bending of the convention that taxation of income was only permissible in war time marked the period's most singular fiscal innovation. However, as became clear at the termination of the Napoleonic wars, Parliament's willingness to truck with a combined backward looking and pre-emptive 'war' tax at the re-opening of hostilities in 1799 did not later translate into acceptance of a peace time income tax.[115] Though due to terminate at the cessation of the conflict, a combination of national debt and a government appetite for progressive (modest) social relief measures, encouraged Liverpool's administration to seek a short-term extension of the tax in 1816 and again in 1819.[116] Fuelled by a vociferous alliance of interests, including merchants, bankers, and traders, Parliament resisted the invitation. Even though administrative measures had been taken in 1803[117] to meet widespread complaints of the intrusive quality of income tax assessment, as a major and recurrent objection, this claim continued to figure prominently in debates well into the 1840s: that '... inquisitorial visiting which laid open to the world, with most ruinous effect, the exact situation of every man's affairs'.[118] Not until the 1840s would such objections be outweighed by

---

[115] Accumulated war debts from the War of the First Coalition (1793–7) and other loans to the Exchequer had generated a budgetary crisis in 1797. Land tax, the self-imposed tax of a predominantly landed Parliament, no longer carried the potential to rescue substantial budgetary deficits. W. R. Ward, *The English Land Tax in the Eighteenth Century* (Oxford, 1954), *passim*. Before his open introduction of income tax in 1799, in anticipation of further war debts, during the previous year Pitt had sought to avoid the ideological objections of direct income taxation by enacting new forms of graduated assessed taxes, on the manifestations of wealth—arguably an indirect tax on income. Indeed, as an alternative to liability for such assessed taxes, tax payers could opt for graduated scale payments on the basis of declared income. However, a lower than anticipated revenue yield on assessed taxes led Pitt to impose income tax as the (temporary) saviour of the 'fiscal-military state': imposition of income tax in 1799 thus sought to deal with both existing and expected budgetary problems. J. Brewer, *The Sinews of Power: War, Money and the English State, 1688–1783* (1989), xvii.

[116] Its attractions were clear: by 1815, income tax was contributing marginally under a fifth of tax revenue. B. Mitchell and P. Deane, *Abstract of British Historical Statistics* (Cambridge, 1962), 386–94. And see the Chancellor of the Exchequer, Vansittart, giving the first of many government speeches justifying the need for income tax, *PD* 1815 (s1) 29: 853.

[117] Principally, a move from a scheme where taxpayers were required to submit a return of aggregated income, to one where different streams of income were assigned to distinct schedules of liability, some of which specified tax to be deducted at source. Under the Income Tax Act 1806 these included rent paid on estates and houses (A), profits from government stock and dividends (C), and salaries and pensions from 'office' (E). Incorporated bodies were not directly taxable on income or profits until after the First World War. Their shareholders paid tax on dividends. For the complexities of the tax liability of charities in the nineteenth century, see C. Stebbings, 'Charity Land: A Mortmain Confusion' (1991) 12 *JLH* 7, and Daunton, *Trusting Leviathan*, 211–18.

[118] *PD* 1816 (s1) 33: 435. On earlier objections to the tax's inquisitorial nature, see C. Stebbings, 'The Budget of 1798: Legislative Provision for Secrecy in Income Taxation' (1998) *British Tax Rev.* 651.

more pressing concerns, permitting significant changes to be effected in the country's tax regime.

2. CAPITALISM, COMPROMISE, AND COLLECTIVISM: 1850–1914

The apparent success of Peel and Gladstone's broad version of liberal economics largely, though not entirely,[119] left politically undisputed the supremacy of a free-market economy. Yet there were consistently prominent voices, such as *The Times*, seeking to ensure that orthodox political economy theory was tempered by humane realities:

Its philosophy is cold, selfish, arrogant. It disclaims all protections for all classes; it repudiates all State interference on behalf of the oppressed; it comforts the poor and the aged with 'laissez faire' and union houses. It has but one nostrum; and that nostrum it is ever prescribing in the frigid language of political economy.[120]

Aside from philosophical reservations of this nature and the openly political, socialistic ambitions of some trade unionists and their middle-class promoters,[121] one of the most persistent critiques of the liberal economy and its consequences came from certain Christian denominations. More generally, in contrast with its stance in the first half of the nineteenth century, organized religion in the second part increasingly manifested a fundamental discomfort with capitalistic ethics and their social consequences. Occasional religious or quasi-religious attacks on capitalism had certainly been delivered in the early nineteenth century, including Carlyle's stinging *Past and Present* creation of the 'Mammon-Gospel; of Supply-and-Demand, Competition, Laissez-faire, and Devil take the hindmost... one of the shabbiest Gospels ever preached'.[122] But Christian, and especially

---

[119] From the late 1840s to the early 1870s, J. S. Mill's *Principles of Political Economy* (1848) rapidly became the orthodox exposition of political economy. While less dogmatically hostile to limited state intervention in the operation of market forces, he remained firmly attached to belief in the fundamental necessity of (educated) self-interest as the driving force of social and economic advancement (below). Opposition to Mill's limited dilution of out and out *laissez-fairism*, along with the admission of occasional state social interventionism, came most prominently from Herbert Spencer. For Spencer, strict allegiance to the classical creed of Malthusian *laissez-faire* meant that not only was the state's organization of poor relief misguided and ultimately socially damaging, even its engagement in the provision of education and matters of public health was to be condemned: *Social Statics* (1850). It is not entirely coincidental that *The Economist*, for which Spencer had worked as assistant editor in the late 1840s and early 1850s, strongly espoused untainted principles of classical political economy.

[120] Addressed particularly to Cobdenite economic policies, 21 June 1844, p. 4. Similarly e.g. 30 January 1846, p. 5 and 18 May 1847, p. 6.

[121] G. R. Searle, *Morality and the Market in Victorian Britain* (Oxford, 1998).

[122] *Past and Present* (1843) (Oxford, 1909), intro. G. K. Chesterton, pp. 189–90.

Evangelical, ethical rationalization and firm embrace of *laissez-fairism* along with a competitive market economy, was subjected to its first emphatic clerical rejection in the late 1840s. It provoked the *Quarterly Review* into a spluttering rebuke:

Incredible as it may appear, there is, it seems a clique of educated and clever but wayward-minded men—the most prominent among them two *clergymen of the Church of England*—who from a morbid craving for notoriety or a crazy straining after paradox, have taken up the unnatural and unhallowed task of preaching...not indeed such open and undisguised *Jacobinism and Jacquerie* as we have just been quoting, but under the name of *Christian Socialism*—the same doctrines in a form not less dangerous for being less honest[123] [original emphasis].

Formed in 1848, led by Frederick Denison Maurice and Charles Kingsley, the Christian Socialist group's[124] collectivist economic mantra of industrial organization was co-operation rather than competition. Opposing the organized antagonism between employer and worker, through their weekly 'Politics for the People' they promoted co-operative production schemes, where managers were elected and profits distributed, wholly or partly, amongst employees. The prevailing ideology of a free-market industrial economy was ringingly denounced as dehumanizing exploitation:

The whole system of modern manufacture, with its factory slavery; its gaunt and sallow faces; its half-clad hunger; its female degradation; its abortions and ricketty children; its dens of pestilence and abomination; its ignorance, brutality and drunkenness; its vice in all its hideous forms of infidelity, helpless poverty, and mad despair—these, and if it were possible, worse than these are the sure fruits of making man the workman of mammon, instead of making wealth the servant of humanity for the relief of man's estate...That system of political economy which makes *wealth* and not *man*, the ultimatum, is based on a monstrous fallacy that in taking the *rents of the landlords, and the profits of the capitalists*, as the measures of good and evil, instead of taking the *condition of the cultivators, and the condition of the labourers* (the many) as the sure index of the character of a system... *Man* is the stable element. *His* condition is the standard; *his* improvement is a good; *his* deterioration is an evil.... Man is not useful as he produces wealth, but wealth useful as it sustains man, ameliorates his condition...gives opportunities for his further cultivation, and aids in the great scheme of human regeneration.[125][original emphasis]

---

[123] J. W. Croker, 'Revolutionary Literature' (1851) 89 *Quart. Rev.* 491–543, 524. The published works of Maurice and Kingsley were the *Quarterly's* chief targets.

[124] See later revivals, including Henry Holland's Christian Social Union, 1889. More generally, see E. Norman, *The Victorian Christian Socialists* (Cambridge, 1987). One of the movement's staunchest supporters was Thomas Hughes, and also 'Law and Religion', Ch. V above, (author of *Tom Brown's Schooldays*, 1857 MP and vociferous advocate of Trade Union rights.

[125] *Christian Socialist* 18 January 1851, 'The Aims of Political Economy' reproduced in E. Evans (ed.), *Social Policy 1830–1914* (1978), 42.

Yet, while succeeding in their campaign for the legal facilitation[126] of certain forms of co-operative industrial and commercial ventures, the movement's initial manifestation fizzled out after six years.

Despite this, the concept of co-operative schemes enjoyed a certain vogue in wider circles, especially in the 1860s.[127] Prominent amongst the promoters of such ventures was the Social Science Association, whose *Trades' Societies and Strikes* (1860) identified a variety of possible forms of industrial 'partnerships'. Significantly, the Society's membership included many Christian Socialists or sympathizers.[128] In essence, the Association saw co-operative schemes as mutually beneficial structures capable of resolving the fundamentally competing claims of capital and labour. And while faltering in its first incarnation, Christian Socialism gave long-lasting prominence to the question of the appropriate response of the Christian church to increasingly evident social squalor and injustice following in the wake of a booming capitalist economy. Indeed, a slightly less combative version of anti-*laissez-faire* Christian Socialism re-emerged in the 1880s. At this stage the ideology was broadly represented in a cluster of bodies, including Brooke Westcott's Christian Social Union (1889), the Non-conformist Christian Socialist League (1894), and Anglican Christian Socialist League (1906).[129]

Though not rivalling the active collectivist scepticism of Christian Socialism towards the competitive liberal economy, the mid and late Victorian eras saw an articulated spiritual discomfort amongst mainstream Christian clergy with capitalist economics, coupled with a determination by some to infuse 'true' Christian morality into business ethics.[130] As a supplement to, and refinement of, a commercial law framework, a solid body of Christian business ethical literature

---

[126] The Industrial and Provident Societies Act 1852, contained a 'Frugal Investment' clause providing limited liability co-operatives for workmen and farmers. Parliamentary representations of Christian Socialists were a force in the more general campaign for limited liability of stock companies to enable small investors to boost the value of their savings. See e.g. Viscount Gooderich, *PD* 1854 (s3) 134: 763. Six out of 17 witnesses before the 1850 Select Committee on limited liability were Christian Socialists. J. Saville, 'Sleeping Partnerships and Limited Liability 1850–56' (1956) *EHR* 418.

[127] The earliest co-operative store was set up in 1844 in Rochdale. By the 1860s, over 400 had been established and were, initially at least, targeted at customers from the lower classes. P. Gurney, *Co-operative Culture and the Politics of Consumption in England 1870–1930* (Manchester, 1996).

[128] Including Maurice, Hughes, and Ludlow. Although both the Majority and Minority Reports comprising *Trades' Societies and Strikes* supported co-operatives, the Minority (Ludlow and Hughes) favoured a far higher level of co-operative integration between employers and workers. See L. Goldman, *Science, Reform and Politics in Victorian Britain: The Social Science Association, 1857–1886* (Cambridge, 2002), Ch. 7.

[129] See generally, Norman, *The Victorian Christian Socialists*, and Ch V above.

[130] See the large range of examples cited by J. Garnett, 'Commercial Ethics: A Victorian Perspective on the Practice of Theory', in C. Cowton and R. Crisp, *Business Ethics* (Oxford, 1998), 117. For the considerable influence of later Christian Socialist thinking on the Church of England's leadership in the early twentieth century, see E. Norman, *Church and Society* (Oxford, 1976), Ch. 6.

appeared, seeking to guide practices that were happily both morally defensible and profitable. While most were unconcealed didactic exercises, occasionally ethical propaganda was delivered in fictional guise, such as the enormously popular *The Successful Merchant* (1852).[131] Some examples even flew clearly in the face of fundamental *laissez-fairism*, by advocating avoidance of practices that might seriously damage competing traders.[132] Such economic altruism even resonated with a few later professional economists, and most especially the pivotal figure of Alfred Marshall,[133] who denied that self-interest was the only effective economic driving force, advocating instead 'economic chivalry' as an element of collectivist moral progress. Moreover, Marshall's own socio-economic creed openly conceded that 'some temporary material loss [might be] submitted to for the sake of a higher and ultimate greater gain... Thus gradually we may attain to an order of social life, in which the common good overrules individual caprice, even more than it did in the days before the sway of individualism had begun.'[134]

Aside from the sharpening of religious scruples over the harsh moral imperatives and social consequences of capitalism, during the second half of the nineteenth century three broad, competing aspects of political economy generated extensive continuing political dispute and legal engagement: first, just how 'free' a market was desirable, and how the nation's wealth should be shared, and what was the necessary extent to which industrial processes and commercial practices should be regulated? Secondly, what were the appropriate rights and limitations under which the state should permit organized labour to function? Finally, what was the state's social responsibility for the welfare of its citizens? As already seen, all of these fundamental questions had been inconclusively encountered earlier in the century. With the emergence of 'New Liberalism' and socialist movements in the final decades of the century, distinct shifts in political and economic thinking would propose and promote new solutions to old problems, with considerable implications for the role of the state and the law.

As will later become apparent, an element in such shifts in political and economic thinking was the significant conceptual modification of the nature and substance of political economic theory. Taking place from the 1870s, these changes in part sprang from an earlier strengthening in the broad acceptance of the necessity and benefits of a more rigorous approach to social scientific investigation and

---

[131] Written by the Methodist William Arthur about the life of grocer Samuel Budgett. And the popular Christian practices business primer, T. Binney's calculating cryptic, *Is it possible to Make the Best of Both Worlds?* (1853) Garnett, 124–5, 133.

[132] J. W. Gilbirt, *A Practical Treatise on Banking* (1849), Garnett, 126.

[133] *Principles of Economics* (1890). From 1885, Professor of Political Economy at Cambridge. For Marshall's key place in the evolving social science of 'neo-classical' economics, see S. Collini, D. Winch, and J. Burrow, *That Noble Science of Politics* (Cambridge, 1983), Ch. X. See below for Marshall's very important informing role in the social and collective economics of New Liberalism.

[134] *Principles of Economics* (8th edn, 1920), 752.

speculation. In its various guises, from Smith, Malthus, Ricardo, up to Mill, as an early social science, Classical political economy rested on assertions of immutable, self-regulating laws of human behaviour. Sharing much of Utilitarianism's crude characterization of human nature and psychology, the 'science' of political economy largely excluded the functioning of non-economic aspects of individual and collective behaviour. Rather than a genuine social science, Carlyle's monochromatic 'dismal science' of political economy increasingly became regarded as more closely resembling an *a priori* based ideology.[135]

This erosion of the social scientific credentials of Classical political economy accompanied the steady advance in the sophistication of Victorian social scientific theory and its ambitions: the belief that society's reconstruction might proceed on a truly social scientific basis by mimicking the scientific methodology applied to natural sciences; essentially, by employing extensive historical investigation and empirical social observation to falsify or confirm hypotheses. It was an intellectual change principally fuelled by the social scientific philosophy of Auguste Comte,[136] partially mediated through Mill's *Logic* (1843), and later promoted by the membership of the Social Science Association.[137] Yet, despite Mill's own articulation of, and allegiance to, 'scientific' or inductively constructed social scientific theory, his *Political Economy* (from 1848 onwards) exhibited few signs of actually being influenced by empirical or historical evidence. And while in the 1870s the likes of W. S. Jevons and Henry Sidgwick made clear inroads into the orthodoxy of Mill's *Political Economy*, it took Alfred Marshall to establish that political economy was 'not a body of concrete truth, but an engine for the discovery of concrete truth'.[138]

Regulating the Economy: Employment Conditions and Commercial Structures

EMPLOYMENT CONDITIONS

Legislative restrictions on the freedom of individuals to choose hours worked were extended beyond the textile industry in the 1860s and 1870s.[139] But such

[135] 'The Nigger Question', Thomas Carlyle, *Critical Essays*, v 7 (1869), 79–110 at 84. Originally published in *Fraser's Mag.* (1849).

[136] G. H. Lewes, *Comte's Philosophy of the Sciences* (1853) was the major popularizing work. On Comte and Theories of Government, 'Theories of Law and Government', Ch. IV, above; also citations of Comte's works in 'Law and Religion', Ch. V, above.

[137] Goldman, *Science, Reform and Politics*, 293–320.

[138] Collini, Winch, and Burrow, *That Noble Science of Politics*, 311–37; N. Annan, *Leslie Stephen, The Godless Victorian* (1984), 297. Some of the elements of the methodological approach developed in Marshall's *Principles of Economics* (1890) appeared a decade earlier in *The Economics of Industry* (1879).

[139] Including the Factory and Workshop Acts 1864, 1867, and 1878.

protective limitations and fetters on economic freedom were still confined to women and children. Men of full age retained the largely unshackled privilege of working to the limits of their endurance. Even after the increasing safety requirements and levels of inspection demanded by the Factories and Workshop Act 1878,[140] the position of men remained unaffected. Again, the restriction of working hours in the retail trade, effected by the Shops Act 1886, related only to women and young people. In the specific case of railways, high injury rates to both public and employees eventually resulted in the Railway Servants (Hours of Labour) Act 1893, followed by the Railway Employment (Prevention of Accidents) Act 1900.[141] And as a consequence of substantial parliamentary representation, state intervention in the working day of miners arrived with the Coal Mines Act 1908, limiting underground shifts to eight hours.[142] Opposing colliery owners unsuccessfully fielded the orthodox economic counter-claims that increased production costs led to international uncompetitiveness and infringement of freedom of employment contracts. Just such arguments had sunk Joseph Chamberlain's progressive Eight-hour Bill back in 1892, when he had expressly cited W. S. Jevons' justification that the state was entitled 'in passing any law...which in its ulterior consequences, adds to the sum total of happiness'.[143] Arguably, an even greater ideological inroad was the Liberal government's legislative intervention in settling minimum wage levels in certain industries. Following proposals from the House of Lords Select Committee on the Sweating System in 1890,[144] local and central government began to deploy economic pressure on certain commercial suppliers to ensure basic minimum levels of wages and working conditions of suppliers' employees.

Direct legislation to set minimum wages in these exploitative trades was inhibited by a combination of doctrinaire objections to interference with a free labour market, coupled with fears of rendering uneconomic the employment of certain unskilled workers, thereby producing unemployment. In the early 1890s a national minimum wage was a manifesto ambition of the emerging Labour Party. Additionally, the Royal Commission on Labour (1894) had received

---

[140] The 1878 Act followed campaigning by organized labour and the proposals of the *Royal Commission on the Working of the Factories and Workshop Acts Report 1876*.

[141] G. Alderman *The Railway Interest* (Leicester, 1973) and H. Parris *Government and the Railways in the Nineteenth Century* (1965). Such was the concern at the level of railway accidents that a Royal Commission on Railway Accidents was established in 1884, followed by a series of safety enactments.

[142] And later the Shops Act 1911, ensuring weekly half-day closing.

[143] Quoted with approval by *The Times*, 24 March 1892, p. 7.

[144] *Fifth Report, PP* 1890 (169), xvii. Limited improvement in conditions were required by the Factory and Workshop Act 1891. The 'sweating system' was created principally around London's East End migrant population. See J. Schmiechen, *Sweated Industries and Sweated Labour* (1984).

evidence from those of socialist persuasion, including the Webbs' promoting the same objective. Though resisting such an economically extremely radical move, as an element of its broader strategy to facilitate the effective operation of the labour market, the new Liberal administration brought in the Trade Boards Act 1909. Alongside the national system of labour exchanges, Churchill's 1909 legislation set up a collection of independent trade boards comprising representatives of workers, employers, and (government-nominated) independent members, charged with formulating appropriate wage levels for specific trades.[145] While in good measure the 1909 Act was enacted to head off extreme examples of worker exploitation, the driving force of minimum wage legislation in the mining industry was the sheer economic power of organized labour. Strikes from 1910 to 1912, generating both extensive civil conflict and threats to the nation's key power supply, resulted in the Coal Miners (Minimum Wage) Act 1912, which established 26 District Boards for settling local minimum wages.

Beyond regulation of wages and working hours was the growing problem of industrial injury. With mechanization had come an increased vulnerability of workers to accidental harm and the question of the extent of an employer's legal responsibility for such harm. Over the course of half a century the common law's *laissez-fairest* inspired treatment of injured employees came under scrutiny and eventual legislative modification, despite opposition from strenuously deployed economic arguments. As with any other financial costs, employers were ever concerned with competitiveness and profitability. Alongside the state intervention of factory legislation, regulating the safety of industrial premises and processes, was the matter of the legal consequences of workplace injury, whether or not sustained as a consequence of breach of safety regulations. By the 1830s the courts had displayed a marked unwillingness to recognize an employer's responsibility for injury to one employee by another.[146] Resistance to vicarious liability by invoking the doctrine of 'common employment' was to characterize the common law's response for much of the nineteenth century. And while recognizing an employer's direct responsibility to provide an employee with a reasonably safe system of work, the common law showed itself more than ready to debar an employee from compensation for harm eventuating from a risk voluntarily assumed by them.[147]

Underpinning this employment of the *volenti* principle was the almost omnipresent economic rationale of voluntary contractual agency: an employee had a free-market choice of accepting or declining risky work; he had the option of

---

[145] Initially the trades included shirt-making, tailoring, lace, and confectionery.

[146] *Priestly* v. *Fowler* (1837) 3 M. & W. 1, and generally XII, Pt 4.

[147] *Dymen* v. *Leach* (1857) 26 L.J. Ex. 221.

ensuring that the wages reflected the nature of any consequent risk.[148] Indeed, with the exception of Edwin Chadwick, and possibly McCulloch, who favoured factory-owner liability, earlier political economists offered no wisdom on the subject.[149] Early legislation covering an injured employee's death, the highly restricted Fatal Accidents Act 1846, offered severely limited opportunities for successful compensation actions by personal representatives on behalf of dependants. Not until the 1890s[150] did the common law begin to reflect the political and social shift in attitudes and expectations of increasingly organized labour by exhibiting a greater scepticism towards the legal and economic fiction of the *volenti* principle.

In the face of the common law's doctrinaire attachment to personal fault and broad resistance to recognizing employers' accident liability, from the 1860s a variety of attempts were undertaken to legislate for liability.[151] But headway only followed the formation of the TUC and the trickle of 'workers' MPs' whose abortive bills and campaigning eventually led to a Select Committee review, chaired by Robert Lowe. To the stock economic arguments against liability of potential unemployment and lower wages, was added claims that the growth of injury support funds, organized by unions, friendly societies or employers, rendered legislative intervention unnecessary.[152] Though persuaded of the essential correctness of the doctrine of common employment, the Committee favoured a limited change, introducing employer liability for harm caused by delegated duties negligently executed by a manager. The subsequent Employers' Liability Act 1880 embodied a combination of an expanded delegation principle and specific provisions introducing wide-ranging liability for railway companies.[153] Yet while limited in ambit, not only did the Act constitute a foot in the door of employer negligence liability, equally important was the economic ramifications and change in practices: the widespread taking out of employer liability insurance[154] which, in effect,

---

[148] House of Lords in *Bartonshill Coal Co* v. *Reid* (1858) 3 Macqu. 265.

[149] See particularly, A. W. B. Simpson's analysis of *Priestly v Fowler* and Chadwick's 1833 proposals, 'A Case of First Impression, Priestly v Fowler (1837)', in Simpson, *Leading Cases in the Common Law* (Oxford, 1995), 100–34, 129–32.

[150] *Smith* v. *Baker* [1891] AC 325. And in respect of the doctrine of common employment, *Johnson* v. *Lindsay* [1891] AC 371.

[151] See P. Bartrip and S. Burman, *The Wounded Soldiers of Industry* (1983) and H. Smith, 'Judges and the Lagging Law of Compensation for Personal Injuries in the Nineteenth Century' (1981) 2 *JLH* 258.

[152] *PP* 1877 (285), x.

[153] In essence, Lowe's Select Committee proposal. Joseph Chamberlain, as Gladstone's President of the Board of Trade, was a staunch supporter of the bill. A Royal Commission on the position of railways, *PP* 1877 [Cd. 1637], xlviii, was established principally because of the special dependent working structures of railway employees in relation to each other, and the high rate of injuries sustained in that industry through fellow employee negligence.

[154] The special Employers' Liability Assurance Corporation was established for just such a purpose.

increasingly spread the costs of accidents across industrial and manufacturing processes.

This economic consequence became more marked following Chamberlain's Workmen's Compensation Act 1897, which, in the case of specific dangerous industries, discarded the requirement of negligence in imposing responsibility for injuries upon employers. Indeed, the limited success of the 1880 Act followed from the frequent difficulty in establishing negligence and the required degree of delegation, both of which were the subject of extensive judicial logic-chopping and hair-splitting.[155] Further legislation in 1906 not only widened the coverage to most industries, but extended compensation provisions to death or disablement caused by particular industrially induced diseases.[156] But for no type of enterprise did the law require that an employer insure against potential compensation claims. Consequently, in the case of small-scale concerns compensation awards might threaten their future economic viability or even precipitate their collapse. On the courts' side, the appellate interpretive culture of the Workmen's Compensation Acts manifested a split between the doctrinaire judiciary (predominantly in the Court of Appeal) construing relief narrowly, and the more innovative strain of judiciary, found largely among members of the House of Lords.[157]

COMMERCIAL STRUCTURES

No compelling political or economic case was made out for the granting of limited liability to corporate stockholders during the enactment debates of the Companies Act 1844. However, increasingly in the late 1840s and early 1850s, complex legal devices of varying effect[158] were resorted to for shareholders' protection from unlimited financial risk. And while the mutual economic benefits to relatively small middle-class investors and new enterprises of investment capital were officially recognized,[159] no immediate legislative endorsement of a general

---

[155] Bartrip and Burman, *Wounded Soldiers*. Additionally, in some areas the practice of employers imposing on employees express contracting-out provisions became established, with some employers contributing to a mutual aid scheme as a substitute. Government attempts to outlaw contracting-out and abolish common employment doctrine failed in 1893 in the face of powerful opposition. See *PD* 1893 (s4) 20: 2–62, esp. Asquith (Home Secretary), 2–14 and Chamberlain, 14–27. Contracting-out of the effects of legislation was restricted by the 1897 Act to cases where the alternative compensation terms were 'not less favourable'.

[156] The Workmen's Compensation Act 1906 followed the favourable assessment and recommendation of the Digby Committee on the operation of the 1897 Act, *PP* 1904 [Cd. 2208], lxxxviii.

[157] e.g. *Raine* v. *R. Robson and Co* [1901] AC 404. See R. Stevens, *Law and Politics, The House of Lords as a Judicial Body 1800–1976* (Chapel Hill 1979), 164–70.

[158] e.g. see the limited legal effect expressed in *Greenwood's Case* (1854) 3 De G.M. & G. 459 and. XII, Pt 3.

[159] Particularly the *Select Committee on Investments for the Savings of the Middle and Working Classes Report*, *PP* 1850 (508); *Select Committee on Partnership Report*, *PP* 1851 (509), xviii; and the *Royal Commission on Mercantile Laws Report*, 1854 [1791], xxvii.

right of limited liability was offered. Yet apparent City encouragement convinced the Aberdeen administration that permitting limited liability was fully consonant with a liberal market and freedom of contract. Furthermore, supporters of limited liability attacked its absence as being against the 'first principles of political economy... anti-free trade... and contrary to the high authority on political economy, Mr John Stewart [sic] Mill ...'.[160] Cobden argued that the effect of unlimited liability was 'one of the social blots in this country that capital had a tendency to accumulate in great masses and in few hands'. Removal of unlimited liability would 'tend to bridge over the gulf which now divided different classes, and diminish that spirit of alienation between employers and employed ...'.[161] Vice-President of the Board of Trade, resolute doctrinaire liberal marketeer, Robert Lowe reflected that the law of joint stock companies had 'always been legislated for by persons in a state of excitement from the Bubble Act onwards'. Individuals should be permitted to arrange business investment on whatever conditions were mutually agreeable; the law should not interfere with the laws of human nature: protection in the market 'lull[ed] their vigilance to sleep [helping] fraudulent men mislead and delude them'.[162] Or, in *The Times* direct, less sympathetic epigram:

complete 'laissez faire' in commerce: an insular maxim that every man has a right to make his fortune if he can, and to ruin himself if he thinks fit.[163]

By 1856 Palmerston's government had carried legislation liberating companies to determine their own arrangements for the debt liability of their shareholders.[164] The moderate, gradual rise of resort to limited liability incorporation (accelerating from the 1870s) suggests that the absence of such a legal facility placed no obvious restraint on capitalistic enterprise in the first half of the nineteenth century.[165] Even the creative use of limited liability to engage in sharp, not to say fraudulent, practice was regarded by both the House of Lords in its judicial

[160] *PD* 1854 (s3) 134: 178–9.
[161] *PD* 1854 (s3) 134: 785.
[162] *PD* 1856 (s3) 140: 112 and 138.
[163] 23 September 1857, p. 6.
[164] Initially, subject to some restrictions under the Limited Liability Act 1855 (18 and 19 Vict. c. 133) removed by the Joint Stock Companies Act 1856 (19 & 20 Vict. c. 47). Banks were placed in largely the same position in 1858 (21 & 22 Vict. c. 62) and insurance companies in 1862 (25 & 26 Vict. c. 89). Gladstone resigned from his post as Chancellor of the Exchequer early in 1855 and voted against the Act.
[165] The sensational and catastrophic failure in 1866 of Overend, Gurney and Co, the second largest bank and discount house (after the Bank of England) not only shook the country's financial foundations but also showed up the restricted protection in limited liability companies for shareholders with less than fully paid up shares. See G. Elliott, *The Mystery of Overend and Gurney* (2006). As a consequence, there remained lingering concerns over the nature and availability of limited liability for the rest of the century: *Select Committees on the Limited Liability Acts Reports, PP* 1867 (329), x, and *PP* 1877 (365), viii; and *Committee on Company Law Report, PP* 1895 [Cd. 7779], lxviii.

capacity,[166] and Parliament generally, not to be a sufficient justification for removing or seriously modifying the consequences of limited incorporation on creditor rights: extending credit to limited companies was regarded as a freely assumed risk of the market.[167]

Growth in the size of companies facilitated by limited liability also increased opportunities for industrial market sector dominance for both sales and in relation to supply sources. While large corporations might choke off or severely limit competition, except with clear monopolies such as railways,[168] successive governments showed no inclination to interfere in the name of free trade. It was a reluctance bred from belief in frequent, well-represented, corporate claims of the need for general efficiencies or economies of large-scale production, and the competitive demands of overseas trade. Furthermore, even though espousing a broad commitment to a free-market economy, settling the nature of remedial legislative intervention was in itself a sufficiently daunting prospect as to inhibit possible action. Similarly, the courts showed little appetite to deploy the common law against anti-competitive practices of cartels, trade associations, and the like, and to regard them as against the public interest.[169]

Trade Unions: Enfranchisement and Political Realities

The state's legislative and common law response to the emerging economic power of organized labour in the second half of the nineteenth century provided a marked contrast to its treatment of capitalist enterprise. By the 1850s the virtues of economic liberalism were largely undisputed amongst the two main political parties. However, while the moral and political underpinnings of the system for generation of wealth and profits were philosophically uncontentious, this could

---

[166] *Salomon* v. *A. Salomon & Co* [1897] AC 22. However, the earlier House of Lords decision in *Derry* v. *Peek* (1889) 14 AC 337 exempting from liability company directors and promoters for prospectus misstatements (unless fraudulent) was rapidly extinguished by the Directors' Liability Act 1890 (53 & 54 Vict. c. 64).

[167] Echoing reservations expressed earlier in the century, both Mill and Marshall had their doubts about the desirability and economic benefits of the corporate separating of ownership and control. Especially in the case of the limited liability of shareholders, both saw dangers of economic inefficiency, wasteful speculation, and moral irresponsibility. Marshall, *Principles*, 279–85; Mill, *Principles*, Ch. XI, book IV. More generally, on the balance struck between the legal rights of shareholders and company directors, XII, Pt 3.

[168] Established in 1873, the Railway Commission had powers to validate price fixing agreements. The Railway and Canal Traffic Act 1894 gave the Commission power to regulate freight prices.

[169] In a series of House of Lords decisions, esp. *Mogul SS* v. *McGregor Gow* [1892] AC 25; *Nordenfeldt* v. *Maxim Nordenfeldt* [1894] AC 535; and *North Western Salt* v. *Electrolytic Alkali* [1914] AC 461. See XII, Pt 3. For the disagreement amongst political economists on the response to anti-competitive practices, see G. Searle, *Morality and the Market in Victorian Britain* (Oxford, 1998).

hardly be said of the share of this wealth to which worker-producers ought to be entitled. As trade unions established solid institutional qualities, developed regional and national characteristics, so the economic consequences of their ambitions and actions grew to a level which governments found increasingly unable to ignore. Over the second half of the nineteenth and into the twentieth century, successive governments were forced to seek resolution of a group of connected questions relating to the state's recognition of the economic, political, and legal powers it was willing to cede to organized labour: most specifically, the legal nature of union identity; the extent of their immunity for losses caused by strike action; the limits of legal picketing; and the ability to impose the labour monopoly of a closed shop or a demarcation of skills.

These fundamental questions were not set in a purely political context, but were also framed by particularly germane beliefs of political economy, standing almost unchallenged until the 1860s: first, the concept of a delimited 'wage fund' which 'naturally' determined wage levels; and secondly, the 'natural' effect on wages of the labour supply. Interference with these market mechanisms, it was predicted, would generate the usual trio of mutually damaging consequences: uncompetitiveness, loss of trade, and increased unemployment.[170] In broad terms, from the 1820s until the late 1860s, successive governments saw the state's role in relation to labour disputes as essentially 'neutral', confined to maintaining the peace between protagonists. Occasional urgings from both labour and employers for a government to break dead-locked strikes by conciliatory intervention were in most cases firmly resisted. Taking this prevailing view of its role in political economy, governments were content to permit the labour market and wages to find their own 'natural' balance.[171]

For their part, the courts and the common law were proving highly resistant to even recognition of unions' legitimate legal standing. The mid-1860s decision of *Hornby* v. *Close*[172] confirmed that most unions were bodies whose object was the illegal restraint of trade—an easy conclusion in an era of robustly espoused *laissez-faire*.[173] Though not 'illegal' in a criminal sense, the taint of restraint of trade excluded unions from even limited protection of their assets against dishonest

---

[170] J. R. McCulloch, *A Treatise on the Circumstances which determine the Rate of Wages* (1851) and W. S. Jevons, *Trade Societies, Their Objects and Policy* (1868). Latterly also the Social Science Association which mounted a series of 'Lectures on Economic Science' aimed at enlightening workers on the immutable and irresistible law of political economy. Goldman, *Science, Reform and Politics*, 226–32.

[171] See official correspondence cited by Curthoys, *Governments, Labour and the Law*, 25–9.

[172] (1867) LR 2 QB 153. Similar much earlier judgments including *Turner* (1811) 13 East 231. Generally, XIII, Pt 3.

[173] e.g. Robert Lowe (1867) 123 *Quart. Rev.* 365. But divisions in judicial ranks appear two years later in *Farrer* v. *Close* (1869) 4 LR QB, where two members of the bench questioned the conclusion that strikes were necessarily in restraint of trade.

employees, and also rendered their contracts unenforceable. More generally, *Hornby* v. *Close* reinforced the broadly held philosophy that unions were inherently, politically, and economically, undesirable associations. And, in the context of labour relations, the courts accepted that *laissez-faire* was, in Carlyle's antipathetic terms, 'mutual hostility named fair competition'.[174]

However a counter-current that would soon constitute a powerful ally in the advance of trade union legal rights was the contemporary revision of the wage fund theory—a key element of orthodox political economy: essentially, that within the price of any article a fixed sum was available for labour after the deduction of all other production costs; and consequently, the maximum economic wage payable to each worker was dependent upon the size of the labour force employed for production. Therefore, organized strikes for higher wages would necessarily be self-defeating. But following William Thornton's *On Labour* (1869) discrediting the theory, his illustrious friend, J. S. Mill also publicly, in the columns of the *Fortnightly Review*, radically revised his own position. As Mill's biographer St John Packe remarked: with his *Fortnightly* articles,

Mill was widely thought to have signed the capitulation of classical Political Economy. He had given up his own remaining speculative objection to the labour movement, and by reason of his tremendous reputation gave great impetus to Trade Unionism all over Europe.[175]

Prior to this, fresh assessments of the nature of unions from other quarters[176] had fed into the 1867 Royal Commission on Trades Unions, which in 1869 produced

---

[174] *Past and Present* (1843), Book 3, Ch 2, 'Gospel of Mammonism'.

[175] M. St. John Packe, *The Life of John Stuart Mill* (1954), preface F. A. Hayek, 488. In fact, since 1862 Mill's *Principles of Political Economy* had supported the legal existence of trade unions in that 'far from being a hindrance to a free market of labour, [they] are the necessary instrumentality of that free market; the indispensable means of enabling the sellers of labour to take due care of their own interests under a system of competition'. *The Collected Work of John Stuart Mill* (Toronto, 1965), iii: 932. Similarly, H. Fawcett, *Manual of Political Economy* (1863). However, this denial of the inherent 'restraint of trade' nature of trade unions cut no ice with the court in *Hornby* v. *Close*. Unions and their promoters made extensive propagandist use of Mill's and Fawcett's theoretical support. See E. Biagini, 'British Trade Unions and Popular Political Economy, 1860–1880' (1987) 30 *Hist. J.* 811.

[176] On the influence of the 1867 'Memorandum on Combinations' drawn up by Henry Thring, Home Office counsel, and of F. D. Longe's earlier, *A Refutation of the Wage-Fund Theory of Modern Political Economy as Enunciated by Mr Mill, MP and Mr Fawcett, MP* (1866), see Curthoys, *History of Trade Unionism*, 74–80. Thring maintained that the courts had been over-restrictive in their construction of unlawful union coercion and that the criminal law was probably an inappropriate means of delimiting union actions. On the contested ability of unions to increase wage rates, Thring adopted Longe's *Refutation* of the (then) dominant wage-fund theory. Broadly in line with other prominent commentators, including Lowe (*ibid.*), Godfrey Lushington (author of 'Workmen and Trade Unions', published in *Questions for a Reformed Parliament* (1867)), and Bagehot (*Economist*, 27 April 1867), Thring argued that the full recognition of unions would be the

an equivocal, split Report on the nature and value of organized labour.[177] The Majority of Commissioners regarded the general common law governing unions and sound political economy as substantially coincidental. However, Mill's subsequent endorsement of unionism and, more generally, the effective realignment of economic orthodoxy undermined the economic reservations deployed in the Commission's Majority Report, creating a significant force for more favourable (for unions) legislative reform.[178] Thereafter, attempts to use political economy theory as a fundamental objection to recognition of the positive value and legality of unions lost much of their credibility.[179]

Leaning marginally in the direction of the Minority Report, Gladstone's Trade Union Act and Criminal Law Amendment Act, both of 1871,[180] eliminated the risk of restraint of trade proceedings and confirmed the ability of unions to register as friendly societies, thereby protecting their assets from employees' fraud

most efficacious method of curbing the undesirable aspects of union rules and practices. Lushington succeeded Thring at the Home Office in 1869.

[177] Particularly as a consequence of Fawcett's and Frederic Harrison's efforts. Biagini, 'British Trade Unions and Popular Political Economy 1860–1880'. See XIII, Pt 3 for the Commission's composition and contrasts between the Majority and Minority Reports.

[178] Though half-hearted attempts were made to shore up the theory, notably by Millist, J. E. Cairnes (*Essays in Political Economy* (1873); *Some Leading Principles of Political Economy* (1874)) its doctrinaire force irresistibly declined through the 1870s.

More broadly, W. S. Jevons, Cairnes' successor to the Chair of Political Economy at University College London, led the attack on the classical theory of value, espoused from Ricardo to Mill: *The Theory of Political Economy* (1871). (See also Henry Sidgwick's overview in 'The Wages Fund Theory' (1879) 25 *Fortnightly Review* 401–13 and T. Cliffe Leslie, *Essays in Political and Moral Philosophy* (1879)). Jevons laid the foundations of marginalism (below), taken up and developed by Alfred Marshall, the dominant voice of Neo-classical political economy from the mid-1880s. Marshall shifted much of the basis of political economy from Classical economics foundational abstract, self-seeking individualism, to an empirically leaning acceptance of co-operative, altruistic economic endeavour: that even wealth might be beneficially exchanged for improving 'the quality of life'.

Such notions would clearly be of significant relevance in supporting greater state welfare interventionism (below). Marshall provided the main evidence for the Royal Commission on the Aged Poor (1893) and Local Taxation (1899). He was also a member of the Royal Commission on Labour (1891–4). On the distinction between Jevons and Marshall, and Marshall's theories of consumer demand, supply of agents of production (land, labour, capital), the relationship of supply and demand, the creation of 'value' and its share amongst the agents of production, see below and 'A Separate Science: Polity and Society in Marshall's Economics', in Collini, Winch, and Burrow *That Noble Science of Politics*, 311–37.

[179] However, as most economists continued to suggest, there were distinct economic limits to just what proportion of a producer's net profits might realistically be diverted to wages.

[180] *Final Report, PP* 1868–9 [Cd. 4123], xxxi. More radical pro-union proposals came in the Minority Report with the philosophical radical, Frederic Harrison, the Christian socialist, Thomas Hughes, and the Earl of Litchfield, manifesting a general distaste for *laissez-faire* economics, and advocating greater equality of economic bargaining power between employers and workers, with power to enforce a closed shop.

or theft.[181] On the highly charged question of the limits of coercive powers that unions should have at their disposal, the Molestation of Workmen Act 1859 had been very narrowly construed by the courts against the unions.[182] However, partly because of a contemporary climate of industrial strife, the Criminal Law Amendment Act made an inadequate effort to clarify or explicitly enhance picketing powers, leaving the delimiting of this key component of economic leverage in judicial hands. Suspicions of a largely unsympathetic, if not outright hostile judiciary, were broadly confirmed in the immediately succeeding years. Illegal coercive industrial action by unions was given a wide construction, rendering unlawful almost all forms of attempts to persuade.[183] In adopting this interpretation of the common law, the judiciary, according to one of its most consistently vociferous exponents, Bramwell B., were protecting the fundamental rights of individual enterprise and responsibility: 'for the total aggregate happiness of mankind is increased by every man being left to the unbiased, unfettered determination of his own free will and judgment as to how he will employ his industry and other means of getting on in the world'.[184]

In substantial measure, Gladstone's 1874 election defeat was a consequence of organized working-class displeasure with Liberal reluctance to give legislative recognition to increased union political and economic power. Acting well beyond the extremely limited reform proposals of a new Royal Commission,[185] with cross-party support, Disraeli's administration went some way to redeeming Tory pre-election pledges on union powers[186] in the form of the Employers and

---

[181] As well as recognition of the voting power of the newly enfranchised section of the working classes, public unease at union intimidation and direct violence (particularly in Sheffield in 1866) was a major political reason behind the setting up of the Royal Commission. The remedy for legal protection of trade union property came in two forms: first, (the so-called) Russell Gurney's Act 1868 (31 & 32 Vict. c. 116) directly adapted the general larceny law to make such dishonesty subject to prosecution; and secondly, protection was provided by the temporary provisions of the Trade Union (Protection of Funds) Act 1869, (32 & 33 Vict. c. 61) giving the right of special summary proceedings against dishonest employees.

[182] Especially resort to the language of conspiracy by Bramwell B. in *Druitt* (1867) 10 Cox 592 and cf. *Shepherd* (1869) 11 Cox 325. For the inconsistent judicial approach to picketing and the longstanding Tory support for the protection provided by the 1859 Act, see Orth, *A Legal History of Trade Unionism*, Ch. 8.

[183] Particularly in *Bunn* (1872) 12 Cox 316 and *Hibbert* (1875) 13 Cox 82. For the 1871 legislation and judicial response, XIII, Pt 3.

[184] The pre-1871 Acts case of *Druitt* (1867) 10 Cox 592, 600; *The Times*, 24 August 1867; Curthoys, *History*, 83.

[185] *PP* 1875 [Cd. 1157], xxx, chaired by Lord Cockburn CJ. Crucially, the majority was opposed to giving immunity from prosecution for conspiracy to break individual employment contracts. This was effected by repeal in 1875 of the Master and Servant Act 1867.

[186] Particularly to the Parliamentary Committee of the Trade Union Congress set up in 1868. On the claimed extensive role of senior Home Office officials, see Curthoys, *History, passim*.

Workmen Act 1875 and Conspiracy and Protection of Property Act 1875. Their combined effect appeared to guard trade unionists against the consequences of collective industrial action, provided that such actions were in furtherance of an immediate, specific dispute,[187] and not damaging to public interest. Most basically, the new law embodied the political recognition of the right of individual workers to combine to match or balance the economic power of capital. By these measures, as Mill and other political economists had contended, something closer to a truly liberal, free market could be achieved. Yet, at the same time, such legislation was undeniably also an implicit acceptance of the inherently anticompetitive objectives and practices promoted by trade unions.

Against this legislative background, over the subsequent two decades the perception, substance, and ambitions of trade unions underwent developments of considerable economic and political consequence. First, the evolving political presence of the TUC seeking election of parliamentary representation of unionism (reinforced by the further franchise reforms of 1884–5) was followed in 1893 by the formation of the Independent Labour Party, espousing a highly interventionist economic programme which included a legal minimum wage, an eight-hour day and nationalization of land and major industries. Dyed-in-the-wool socialist demands of this nature were also the core of the Minority Report of the Royal Commission on Labour published the following year.[188]

As trade unionism moved towards establishing what was to become its parliamentary wing—the Labour Party—employers sought to staunch the flow of economic power in the unions' direction by resort to imaginative legal action. In the main, their endeavours were eventually well rewarded by a largely accommodating judiciary. Most especially, the question whether unionists were liable for damages for third party economic harm was resolved by the Court of Appeal in employers' favour in 1893.[189] By the opening of the twentieth century, the Lords was prepared to hold that 'malicious' economic pressure on employers' third party suppliers was capable of constituting the tort of conspiracy.[190] And despite

---

[187] For the detailed provisions and effects see XIII, Pt 3.

[188] *Final Report of the Royal Commission on Labour*, PP 1894 [Cd. 7421], xxxv. Considered in detail in XIII, Pt 3. The Majority (including some non-socialist trade unionists) underscored the importance of well-organized representation of labour and capital engaged in a legislative structure of conciliation and arbitration. This non-confrontational system was overseen by the Labour Department of the Board of Trade established by the (relatively neglected) Conciliation Act 1896.

[189] *Temperton* v. *Russell* [1893] 1 QB held secondary industrial action against a supplier constituted the tort of inducing breach of contract. And see XIII, Pt 3.

[190] Apparent inconsistency with the line taken by the House of Lords in respect of employers trade cartels in the *Mogul Case* (1892) AC 25 and *Allen* v. *Flood*, was dismissed in *Quinn* v. *Leathem* [1901] AC 495.

a strong Divisional Court ruling in 1891 (led by Lord Coleridge CJ,[191] who professed himself mindful of the 'changing temper of the times') that coercion under the Conspiracy and Protection of Property Act 1875 was restricted to physical violence to person or property, within five years the Court of Appeal had largely trumped this with its casuistic distinction between lawfully informing others of the substance of a dispute and illegal picketing to persuade others to support industrial action.[192] Emasculation of serious union economic power was all but completed in 1901 by the Lords with the *Taff Vale Railway Case*, holding unions themselves subject to tortious legal action for damage caused with their authority in pursuit of an industrial dispute.[193] The consequential vulnerability of often very extensive union assets to legal appropriation by aggrieved employers greatly compromised union economic leverage.

Predictably, once again the whole question of the appropriate role of trade unions in the country's political economy was put before a Royal Commission in 1903. The Majority Report favoured giving unions full corporate status, while offering immunity of some but not all union funds from legal action for damages.[194] However, the new Liberal government's distinct inclination to accept this compromise was thwarted by persuasive pressure from a combination of the TUC and the proto-Labour Party's 29 MPs, miner MPs, along with a clutch of sympathetic Liberals. Capitulation to such pressure produced the Trade Disputes Act 1906,[195] broadly assigning to unions the economic privilege of immunity against tort actions for damages caused in contemplation of an industrial dispute. These special rights were underwritten by reaffirming and extending the legality of peaceful picketing to cover attempts to persuade individuals to support industrial action. Though leaving unresolved murky risks of actions for conspiracy against the public interest, the reality and legality of extensive trade union political and economic power had been conceded by the state. Not only was this viewed as an inevitable consequence of determined political representation both within and outside Parliament, but voluntarism in industrial relations had widely come to be regarded as most likely to eliminate

---

[191]   *Gibson* v. *Lawson* [1891] 2 QB 545 at 559. Lord Coleridge praised (the long-standing supporter of unions) 'Mr Justice Wright's excellent work on the Law of Criminal Conspiracies and Agreements' and 'reasonings' on the subject (560).

[192]   Lyndley, A.L. Smith, and Kay LJJ in *J. Lyons and Sons* v. *Wilkins* [1896] 1 Ch 811.

[193]   [1901] AC 426. In 1905 the House of Lords confirmed that encouragement to break contracts of employment was a tort for which an employer could recover damages: *South Wales Miners' Fed.* v. *Glamorgan Coal Co* [1905] AC 239. Analysed in detail in XIII, Pt 3.

[194]   *Report of the Royal Commission on Trade Disputes and Trade Combinations*, PP 1906 [C. 2825], lvi. The economic benefits of a stable, union organized, labour market was taken to be a powerful ground in favour of the full legal recognition of unions. See XIII, Pt 3.

[195]   *Ibid.*

the damaging excesses of organized class adversarialism, promote harmony, and national economic advancement.

Thus, within the course of 80 years, this dimension of political economy was refashioned and rebalanced: common and statute law had radically shifted from seeking to suppress trade unions through criminal sanctions, to granting them the status of privileged organizations, able to exercise local and national economic power untrammelled by the general criminal or civil law. Furthermore, as a significant coda to the 1906 legislation, the Trade Union Act 1913 legalized the use of union funds in the direct pursuit of political objectives, thereby permitting organized labour to reinforce its future economic standing and impact through political and parliamentary measures, most especially through a Labour Party that might form future governments.[196]

The State and Citizens' Welfare: Shifting Political and Economic Ideologies

In broad terms, Tory and Liberal party social and economic ideologies between the 1860s and early 1900s were hardly distinguishable: support for a liberal free market; a forced concessionary approach to the power of organised labour; a largely reluctant ameliorative addressing of chronic social problems; a strong desire to encourage enterprise and individual self-reliance; and an ever-watchful eye for signs of serious social instability.[197] Alongside this basic political consensus was a growing realization that a free-market economy incorporated no automatic, self-adjusting mechanism for distributing a more generous share of wealth and profits to workers, thereby helping to resolve the manifest adverse social consequences of booming capitalism. And while The Times was ready to certify that 'laissez faire doctrine is as dead as the worship of Osiris',[198] the nature and extent of the state's appropriate response, if any, generated no broad agreement.

Representing the most resolute form of anti-state interventionism, Herbert Spencer's The Man Versus the State (1884) and broad claims for 'Social Darwinism' made little political or intellectual headway. In the opposite direction, fermentation of 'New Liberalism', beginning in the 1880s,[199] produced an integrated brew

---

[196] Such use of union funds was subject to membership ballot and regulation by the Registrar of Friendly Societies. The 1913 Act overturned the House of Lords' ruling in Amalgamated Society of Railway Servants v. Osborne [1910] AC 89. See D. Tanner, Political Change and the Labour Party 1900–1918 (1990).

[197] W. Greenleaf, The British Political Tradition, vol. 2; The Ideological Heritage (1983), 196–231.

[198] 8 March, 1883, p. 9; similarly 27 October, 1883, p. 9.

[199] By theorists such as T. H. Green, J. A. Hobson, D. G. Richie, and later L. T. Hobhouse. For concerns that expanded welfare provisions would act as a disincentive and jeopardize economic progress, see e.g. H. Sidgwick, The Method of Ethics (1874).

of social and economic policies. This agenda recognized the reality of political change by advocating greater state intervention, incorporating a redistributive tax regime feeding into an expanded social welfare programme.[200] J. A. Hobson's 'underconsumption' thesis even promised to combine increased economic efficiency alongside greater social equity.[201] Most basically, 'New Liberalism' rejected the powerful, long-standing social and economic assumption that impoverishment was either the inevitable and unchangeable feature of the natural order of society or that poverty was generally a culpable condition, deserving no more than the barest, subsistence level relief. Consequences of economic forces that were beyond the control of the working classes were now being seen as the appropriate target of state interventionism. Within the sphere of national practical politics, the Radical liberal Joseph Chamberlain became the most notable early advocate of many such policies, first serving Gladstone and then, following the Home Rule schism, joining Salisbury.[202] Not long after enactment of the third franchise reform, Chamberlain roused an audience in Warrington by declaring

We have to account for and grapple with the mass of misery and destitution in our midst, co-existent as it is with the evidence of abundant wealth and teeming prosperity. It is a problem which some men would put aside by reference to the eternal laws of supply and demand, to the necessity for freedom of contract and the sanctity of every private right in property. Ah, gentlemen, these phrases are the convenient cant of selfish wealth. ... I shall be told tomorrow 'this is Socialism...'. Of course, it is Socialism. The Poor-Law is Socialism, the Education Act is Socialism, the great part of our municipal work is Socialism; every kindly act of legislation by which the community recognises its responsibility and obligations to its poorer members is socialistic, and it is none the worse for

[200] Later underpinned by Alfred Marshall's authoritative economic analysis, *Principles of Economics* (1890). M. Freeden, *The New Liberalism: An Ideology of Social Reform* (Oxford, 1978); and B. Murray, *The People's Budget 1909/1910 Lloyd George and Liberal Politics* (Oxford, 1980).

[201] As later modified, Hobson (with co-author A. F. Mummery) argued that because the well-to-do could not spend the whole of their income, which could have boosted consumption, they invested too much which in turn increased production of too many unsold goods—leading to periodic crises and unemployment. Economic advance and stability might be secured by greater levels of production being balanced by increased consumption, through a combination of higher public and government spending. This would be a consequence of a greater spread of wealth effected through redistributive taxation and broader welfare schemes. Particularly, *The Physiology of Industry* (1889).

[202] Though not an element of 'New Liberalism' in the sense of being associated with the 1906 Liberal Government, Chamberlain's early social radicalism had much in common with the Liberal Government's welfare philosophy. On Chamberlain's social radicalism, see R. Jay, *Joseph Chamberlain: A Political Study* (Oxford, 1981). Compare Chamberlain's 1885 attack on the 'excessive inequality in the distribution of riches' with Lloyd George's 1908 Commons' pensions' rejoinder that: 'The wealth of the country is enormous [and] growing at a gigantic pace. I do not think it is too much to expect the more favoured part of the community who have got riches so great that they have really to spend a good part of their time in thinking how to spend them, to make a substantial contribution to improve the lot of the poorer members of the same community...', *PD* 1908 (s4) 189: 875.

that. Our object is the elevation of the poor, of the masses of the people—a levelling up which shall do something to remove the excessive inequalities in the social condition of the people, and which is now one of the greatest dangers as well as the greatest injury to the State.[203]

A combination of factors are identifiable as driving these ideological revisions, including anxieties over 'national efficiency'—whether the working population's physical capacities and educational standard were adequate to take on the economic (and military) challenges of Germany and the United States.[204] But dominant amongst these background factors was the twin advance of working-class enfranchisement and trade union power. After the Reform Act 1884, working-class voters were in the majority. Initially under Liberal colours, union-sponsored working-class MPs appeared in parliament from 1874. Formation of a cluster of socialist groups and the Independent Labour Party in 1893, all promoting prominent welfare and collectivist policies, threatened to steal many vital working-class votes from both Liberals and Tories. Though socialist parties were far from attracting an automatic or natural working-class allegiance, the electoral appeal for a substantial proportion of workers of greater state welfare intervention in areas such as housing, health, education, and unemployment, was beyond doubt.[205]

These looming political realities were reflected in Tory and Liberal responses from the 1870s to early 1900s in a range of legislation—some Tory, more Liberal—covering both central and local government social reforms, in many respects, more innovatory in their nature than in practical impact. However, the increasing municipalization by some local authorities of transport, utilities, housing, and medical services was on a sufficient scale to prompt the establishment of Select Committees on Municipal Trading by 1900.[206] Directly reflecting *Real-politik* of the period, the greatest legislative interventions relate to the powers of organized labour and, latterly, workmen's compensation, followed by the Unemployed Workmen Act 1905. The Liberal electoral victory of December 1905 followed Tory fragmentation over trade protectionism, a Liberal party campaign offering vague

---

[203] 8 September 1885. Reported in the *Manchester Guardian* 9 September 1885. Reproduced in Evans (ed.), *Social Policy*, 130. Compare Gladstone four years later, below. For parallels between Chamberlain's social philosophy and that of late nineteenth-century Anglicanism, see P. d' A. Jones, *The Christian Socialist Revised 1877–1914* (Princeton, 1968), and Law and Religion, Ch. V above.

[204] The 1904 Inter-Departmental Committee on Physical Deterioration confirmed the extreme problems of poor physique and general health of would-be working class recruits for the Boer War.

[205] P. Thane, 'The Working Class and State "Welfare" in Britain 1880–1914', (1984) 27 *Hist. J.* 877–900. For developments in the provision of free state elementary and secondary education, see Ch. V, above, 'Law and Religion' and Vol XIII, Pt 2.

[206] *Report of Select Committee Municipal Trading*, PP 1903 (270) vii, 1 and *Return*, PP 1909 (171), xc, 1.

assurances of social reform harnessed to free trade[207] and, crucially, the pledge to reverse the series of judgments greatly constricting trade union political and economic leverage. While rapidly honouring the latter, Campbell-Bannerman's administration, containing a substantial proportion of Gladstonian Liberals, showed no immediate inclination to launch into an extensive social reform programme. For much of Gladstonian economic and welfare individualism still had considerable currency in substantial sections of the parliamentary party, and was typified by the great man's reaffirmation of the late 1880s:

If the Government takes into its hands that which the man ought to do for himself, it will inflict upon him greater mischiefs than all the benefits he will have received or all the advantages that will accrue from them. The essence of the whole thing is that the spirit of self-reliance, the spirit of true and genuine manly independence, should be preserved in the minds of the people, in the minds of the masses of the people, in the minds of every member of that class. If he loses his self-reliance, if he learns to live in a craven dependence upon wealthier people rather than upon himself, you may depend upon it he incurs mischiefs for which no compensation can be made.[208]

Measures, such as the Education (Provision of Meals) Act 1906, [209] and the Old Age Pensions Act 1908 were initiated by a group of more radical Liberal and Labour backbenchers, supported by extra-parliamentary pressure. The Liberal Government's more enthusiastic unequivocal promotion of welfare legislation resembling that advocated by 'New Liberalism's' ideologues did not get under way until 1909. At this stage, under Asquith's premiership, the cabinet's most forceful social radicals, Lloyd George and Winston Churchill, were being copiously briefed by the Webbs' protégé, the young William Beveridge and other like-minded civil servants. But Fabian collectivism found no advocates amongst such prominent Liberal progressives; rather, the forthcoming welfare legislation

---

[207] On Chamberlain's 1903, Tory splitting, protectionist trade tariff policy, see A. Sykes, *Tariff Reform in British Politics 1903–1913* (Oxford, 1979). Also, A. Marrison, *British Business and Protection 1903–1932* (Oxford, 1996), and A. Howe, *Free Trade and Liberal England 1846–1946* (Oxford, 1997).

[208] Speech in Cheshire, 26 October 1889; A. W. Hutton and H. J. Cohen (eds), *The Speeches of W.E. Gladstone* (1892), x: 132. Distinct elements of the political economy promoted by Mill and Fawcett in the 1860s and 1870s assert themselves in late Gladstonian social policy. For example, while a long-standing supporter of unions, Fawcett saw it as imperative that the state should not remove the incentive for economic self-responsibility: for 'any scheme, however well intentioned...will indefinitely increase every evil it seeks to alleviate if it lessens individual responsibility by encouraging the people to rely less upon themselves and more upon the state'. *Manual of Political Economy* (1863), 130, quoted by S. Collini, *Public Moralists Political Thought and Intellectual Hope in Britain, 1850–1930* (Oxford 1991), 185.

[209] Inspired by a combination of humanitarian and economic concerns (above, Inter-Departmental Committee on Physical Deterioration) along with the Education (Administrative Provisions) Act 1907, and the Children Act 1908, the Liberal government sought to improve the physical and moral welfare of children.

was of the Hobhouse variety, seeking to facilitate individuals achieving their full social and economic potential through a cluster of more limited interventions and adjustments to the operation of existing institutions and the labour market.[210]

Against such an ideological background, two related clusters of welfare interventions were particularly significant: public health and housing; and the Poor Law, along with pensions. Their review is complemented by consideration of the developing features of taxation, the main mechanism for funding welfare initiatives.

PUBLIC HEALTH AND HOUSING

On the death of the General Board of Health in 1858, its powers and responsibilities under the Public Health Act 1848 were inherited by the Privy Council and Home Office. Contrary to long-standing economic assertions, the combination of increasing industrialization and urbanization with subsequent public health consequences was not being adequately met by self-ordering, free-market mechanisms. Moreover, while increasingly apparent that local authorities were often unwilling or unable to tackle pervasive public health problems, the few central government initiatives only attacked particular problems, including air pollution and aspects of sanitation.[211] Accumulating evidence of the nature and extent of public health problems from a substantial cluster of official investigations[212] of the late 1860s and early 1870s, initially resulted in the combining of public health and poor law ministerial responsibility under the 1871 Local Government Board Act, followed by Disraeli's Public Health Act 1875. The two Acts made substantial administrative inroads in bringing together responsibility for a range of health areas formerly dispersed across many *ad hoc* bodies. The 1875 legislation compelled the establishment of local health authorities with the appointment

---

[210] In *The Labour Movement* (1893), L. T. Hobhouse (a leader writer for the *Manchester Guardian*) argued that trade unions, co-operatives, and socialism all rested on the notion of mutual dependence. Like the Fabians, he favoured a minimum national wage. Adopting Marshall's view expressed in *Principles of Economics,* Hobhouse maintained that manufacturers' profits (net of labour cost, rent, and capital interest) should be shared by 'real creditors': the community at large: *Democracy and Reaction* (1904). Hobhouse and Hobson shared a broad welfarist stance, influencing much of post-1906 'New Liberalism'. Hobhouse was appointed the first Professor of Sociology at the LSE in 1907. S. Collini, *Liberalism and Sociology: L. T. Hobhouse and Political Argument in 1880–1914* (1979).

[211] The Alkali Act 1863 (26 & 27 Vict. c. 124) established a central government inspectorate. See the *Select Committee on Noxious Vapours Report,* PP 1862 (486), xiv. The Sanitary Act 1866 (29 & 30 Vict. 90) included local authority duties to take action to deal with public nuisances. Under the Public Works Loans Act 1853, local authorities could fund health measures by capital borrowings from central government. Generally on the administrative and legal control of individual and civic pollution, see XIII, Pt 2.

[212] Especially those on river pollution, *PP* 1867 [Cd. 3835], xix; 1870 [Cd. 737, 181], xl; the Sanitary Commission Reports of 1869 and 1871 [Cd. 281], xxxv.

of medical officers of health for all districts, half funded by the central Local Government Board.[213] A host of other responsibilities also lay on local authorities: to ensure that the streets were configured healthily, adequately paved and lit; that no new houses were built without water supply; and that domestic drainage was connected to a sewage system. These obligations were underwritten by unlimited rating powers.

Significantly, the 1875 Act also permitted (subject to the Local Government Board consent) the municipal assumption of control over utilities, including water and gas supplies. Such schemes were indirectly encouraged in that all profits could be set against the local rates burden. Beyond these vital public health measures,[214] the 1875 Act permitted local authorities to build and acquire land for conversion into municipal parks. By-laws might also be deployed to prevent the dangerous or unhealthy use of public places. Before the 1875 legislation, additional specific powers were often taken by corporations under private Acts. One of the most celebrated examples of extensive municipal enterprise of this nature was Birmingham Corporation under Joseph Chamberlain's leadership, which in the 1870s directed profits from the construction of shops and offices into city slum clearance, house building, and sanitation works.[215] Though establishing mandatory requirements and a facilitatory framework, the ideological objections to central government's intervention was in part met by preserving a large measure of local agency and wide discretion for municipal innovation. But crucially, the 1875 Act, as consolidated by subsequent legislation, solidly established the principle of central government's political obligation to ensure that errant local authorities were led in the appropriate direction. All in all, the enactments of the Disraeli government substantially dented the application of Gladstonian minimal state ideology.

In the particular case of housing, Shaftesbury's largely neglected Lodging Houses Act 1851 was supplemented by the Artizans and Labourers Dwellings Improvement Act 1868, which, on certification of the local medical officer, permitted the compulsory demolition of unsanitary houses. However, the committed attack on urban slums and often appalling working-class living conditions came with the Artizans and Labourers Dwelling Improvement Act 1875 (the 'Cross' Act) empowering local authorities to carry out large-scale slum clearance through compulsory house purchase. Yet despite a keen, detailed understanding of the depth of the problems

---

[213] By this time central government was also contributing to the cost of education and policing.

[214] Earlier significant legislative measures in this direction included the Metropolitan Poor Act 1867, permitting the establishing of distinct infirmaries for treatment of the poor.

[215] Particularly, 'Birmingham: The Making of a Civic Gospel', in A. Briggs, *Victorian Cities* (1968 edn), 184.

highlighted both by Select Committees and Royal Commissions,[216] followed by further enabling legislation,[217] the overall effects on the extensive stock of poor housing were modest. As Chamberlain had demonstrated, fundamental to success was the presence of municipal initiative and civic ambition. Central government's facilitation, combined with enterprising localism, was the limit of the state's readiness to involve itself in the provision of wholesome housing for the working classes until beyond the First World War. As both central and local government understood, the sticking point was ideological and economic: who would or should finance clearance and rebuilding schemes? Full economic rents for houses were largely beyond the means of the industrial-worker occupants; who would or should subsidize rents—ratepayers or taxpayers? A free private enterprise market in housing simply had not, and possibly could not with existing wage levels, provide adequate housing for the working classes.[218] By 1913 Lloyd George could assure the voters of Swindon of his readiness to deal with poor housing conditions and shortages directly: because of local authority indolence, he had 'come to the conclusion that the central government have got to do it...to build houses ourselves'.[219] The decisive anti-market move towards the state sanctioning of subsidies would initially come through rent restriction legislation as a special wartime provision, followed within a few years by building subsidies.

POVERTY AND PENSIONS

By 1914, to a considerable degree, the provision of state welfare support through the Poor Law had been ideologically and practically outflanked by distinct and focused developments in the fields of unemployment relief, medical health insurance, workers' pension provisions, and public health legislation, including increasing central and local attempts to improve the stock of working-class housing. In the evolving political environment of a collective shift towards state welfare, the 1909 Report of the Royal Commission on the Poor Law took stock of just what function the Poor Law ought to perform in the early twentieth century.[220]

---

[216] *House of Commons Select Committee Reports, 1881 and 1882, PP* 1881 (358), vii and 1882 (235), vii; *Royal Commission on the Housing of the Working Classes, PP* 1884–5 [Cd. 4402], xxx.

[217] Including the Artisans' Dwellings Act 1882 (45 & 46 Vict. c. 54); Housing of the Working Classes Act 1885 (48 & 49 Vict. c. 72); Housing of the Working Classes Act 1890 (53 & 54 Vict. c. 16); and Housing of the Working Classes Confirmation Order (1 Ed. VII.) 1901. The high level of compensation payments payable to owners was an important factor in suppressing local authority slum clearance.

[218] Though a significant advocate of welfare reforms in the post-1905 era of the Liberal government, in the mid-1880s, the economist Aldred Marshall proposed, as a means of alleviating housing problems, the imposition of migration controls to keep the surplus poor out of cities: 'The Housing of the London Poor' (1884) 45 *Contemporary Review* 224.

[219] Speech reported in *The Times*, 23 October 1913.

[220] For a detailed analysis, see XIII, Pt 2.

Not unnaturally, the Majority and Minority reports reflected differing ideologies among the Commission's membership. Common ground existed on a number of matters, including the desirability of integrating Poor Laws into local government administrative responsibilities, the state provision of medical and employment services, together with pensions. But a fundamental division of opinion revolved around the core Poor Law notion of less eligibility. Adhering to the 1834 Act's philosophy, the Majority favoured its modified retention since less eligibility captured the essential distinction between the undeserving and deserving poor—those who could be held morally responsible for their condition and those who could not. Loss of this distinction in the allocation of relief jeopardized the essential incentive needed to motivate the bulk of the population to work. Indeed, for the Majority the nation's economic wellbeing was jeopardized by a disturbing growth in the number of 'useless and costly inefficients': 'no country, however rich, can presently hold its own in the race of international competition if hampered by an increasing load of their dead weight'.[221] The Majority's proposed new administrative solution of Public Assistance Committees, run by local authorities, embraced both charitable bodies and state agencies, covering the dispensing of relief for destitution, unemployment, and sickness.

Rather than seeking to identify moral inadequacy and less eligibility, for the Fabian-led Minority,[222] pauperism was the outcome of a diverse range of causes, each of which needed specifically identifying and treating by the appropriate specialist-based local authority committee. Placing enormous faith in the diagnostic and therapeutic abilities of medical and social services, the Minority recommended that 'Maintenance should be freely provided...on condition that [paupers] submit themselves to physical and mental training that they may prove to require'.[223] Use of labour exchanges to employ and dismiss workers would be obligatory. Additionally, the Minority proposed an ideologically radical scheme

---

[221] *Royal Commission on the Poor Law, Report PP* 1909 [Cd. 4499] xxxvii, 644.

[222] A Fabian and Labour quartet headed by Beatrice Webb, whose report was drafted by Sidney Webb. Research by the Fabians on Poor Law policy since 1834 printed as part of the Report was later published as *English Poor Law Policy* (1910). Founded in the mid-1880s, and powered by the likes of the Webbs, George Bernard Shaw, and Graham Wallas, the Fabian Society championed the cause of gradualist socialism—socialism by instalments. Its solidly middle-class professional, intellectual membership aimed to convert the nation to socialism largely through the provision of empirical studies of contemporary social problems and appropriate reform programmes. As well as land nationalization (to secure for the general good increased land values), Fabianism sought e.g. large-scale expansion of municipal activity and extensive central government intervention in welfare, work, and industry. Despite Beatrice Webb having regarded Bentham as the spiritual forebear of Fabianism—with J.S. Mill acting as the evolutionary link—*laissez-faire* capitalism was regarded as a failing, wasteful, and socially unfair means of production. R. Harrison, *The Life and Times of Sidney and Beatrice Webb 1858–1905* (2000) and B. Webb, *Our Partnership* (1948 edn), 210.

[223] Part II of the *Minority Report*, 328.

of state intervention in the functioning of the economy during depressions: the Ministry of Labour would organize both the retraining of surplus labour and launch public works programmes: 'that the duty of so organising the National Labour Market as to prevent or to minimise unemployment should be placed upon a minister responsible to Parliament ...'.[224]

Far in advance of the social philosophy of even New Liberalism, these social-ist proposals were ignored, as were both reports generally. Rather, the political necessity for such action was not pressing, with other forms of welfare relief and post-war economic boom absorbing or masking Poor Law problems until the 1920s. Crucially, the Liberal Government's own national programme for con-tributory schemes (inconsistent with the Majority Report)[225] of unemployment and sickness benefit was being formulated principally by Churchill and Lloyd George.[226] Neither the moralistic discrimination of the Commission's Majority revamped Poor Law nor the Minority's Fabian socialism attracted them. Rejecting the explicit centralist collectivism of the latter, in Churchill's terms, rather than impair the 'vigour of competition', Liberal social policy aimed 'to mitigate the consequences of failure;...to draw a line below which we will not allow persons to live and labour, yet above which they may compete...Nothing in our plans will relieve people from the need of making every exertion to help themselves ...'.[227] Moreover, neither Lloyd George nor Churchill had the slightest intention of surrendering to others any part of the great political credit for their own considerable social innovations.

Returning to the administration of the new Poor Law, from its earliest days the uneasy partnership between the central administration (Poor Law Board after 1847) and local guardians had created enormous variations, both in respect of the rate of local building of workhouses and in the rigour with which the law's spirit and rules were enforced. Most especially, the central hostility to the undermining effects of outdoor relief payments had a limited and patchy impact on its wide-spread practice. Central efforts to reduce radically the practice by the Outdoor Relief Prohibitory Order 1844 (modified in 1852) failed, as did the objective of a uniform system embodied in the Act. Among consistent opponents of this car-dinal feature of the 1834 legislation, *The Times* declared the Act to be a 'dead

---

[224] *Minority Report*, p. 1215 'Summary of Proposals'.

[225] Indeed, a single flat rate national insurance contribution payable by all, regardless of income level, amounted to a regressive tax.

[226] The appeal of contributory schemes was economic in two respects (i) reduced costs for the national exchequer; and (ii) the ideological appeal of economic individual responsibility of people enjoying contracted-for benefits as of right: neither state largesse nor a full capitulation to collectivism.

[227] *Liberalism and the Social Problem* (1909), 82 and 396; quoted by M. Daunton, *Wealth and Welfare An Economic and Social History of Britain 1851–1951* (Oxford, 2007), 546.

artificial statute [that] has not been able to connect itself with the life around it'.[228] Throughout the Victorian period, the overwhelming majority of paupers still lived outside workhouses, receiving outdoor relief. As well as a consequence of local humanitarian sentiments, and in spite of contrary Malthusian arguments, this approach was regarded as more economically attractive: it eliminated the need to build costly, large capacity workhouses, and it held down the number of relatively expensive 'in-house' paupers.[229]

Despite further measures aimed at reinvigorating the economic and punitive moral philosophy underpinning the 1834 Act, decade by decade saw a diminution in the once widespread credibility of these foundational beliefs. Coupled with this was a greater willingness to accept that for the able-bodied unemployment and poverty were not principally a consequence of idleness and moral inadequacy. One small instance indicating this evolving view was the Public Works Act 1863 which provided local authorities with power to borrow in order to generate public works projects for absorption of locally unemployed.[230] Moreover, growing understanding of the relationship between poor health and poverty incidentally often raised the level of medical services available to sick paupers above that accessible to the employed poor. However, from 1852 the Poor Law Board authorized medical care for poor family 'bread-winners', even while employed. Again, the prime motivation for Poor Law guardians was the sound local economic sense of keeping such impoverished people and their families in work and out of the workhouse.[231] From the mid-1860s this process resulted in workhouse medical wards being described as 'state hospitals'. Indeed, this practice was embodied in legislation restructuring the provision of Poor Law medical services in London in the late 1860s, a trend gradually followed throughout the country.[232]

As was expressly acknowledged in promoting this legislation, the foundational philosophy embodied in the 1834 Act now had no relevance to the 'sick, who are

[228] 6 July 1844, p. 5 and 8 July 1844, p. 4. Bowing to widespread local pressure, the 1852 Relief Regulations Order introduced a limited formal degree of flexibility for unions to give outdoor relief to 'able bodied' men.

[229] The proportion of 'in house' and 'outdoor' relief shifted towards 'in house' in the final decades of the nineteenth century. In 1858 the national figures were c. 12% indoor relief, c. 88% outdoor relief; by 1900, c. 34% indoor, c. 66% outdoor: Local Government Board Report 1899–1900.

[230] Public Works Act 1863, 26 & 27 Vict. c. 70. The Act was a response to the cotton 'famine' in the Lancashire cotton mills.

[231] And see the medical profession's attitudes evinced in the Reports of the Select Committee on Medical Poor Relief, XIII, Pt 2.

[232] Metropolitan Poor Act 1867 (30 & 31 Vict. c. 6). Two years earlier the government had set up a Metropolitan Common Poor Fund to spread some Poor Law costs. It was a significant shift away from locally funded relief. But the steady, incremental improvement in 'medical relief' for the poor was far from unopposed. For example even in the mid-1880s, in relation to the Medical Relief Disqualification Removal Bill, speech of Lord Bramwell, PD 1885 (s3) 300: 232–3.

not proper objects of such a system'.[233] But, of course, however much a theoretical distinction might be drawn between the state's care of sick paupers and the more innovative notion of direct care of the poor, the running of one into the other was predictable, and recognised as a desirable objective by the 1881 Royal Commission on Local Government. Moreover, the process had been boosted by linking responsibility and administration of poor law and public health matters under the 1871 Local Government Board Act,[234] where prior sympathy for this approach had existed. Additionally, in the following year the principle of localism in the provision of health care was compromised by the introduction of (half) centrally funded Medical Officers of Health for each local health authority set up by the Public Health Act 1872.

Such administrative coalescing of the separate elements of individual and collective social welfare reflected the growing perception at local and central levels of their physically interconnected nature; that alleviation of these increasingly apparent large-scale health problems revealed in the statistics of social investigations, including those of Mayhew, Booth, Rowntree, and others, could only occur through a broad revision of social philosophy. At its most basic level, a liberal market economy might legitimately be combined with greater collective social responsibility and interventionism. It was to be a process of re-evaluation driven by a combination of political revelation, necessity, and opportunism on the part of Tories and Liberals in accommodating the rising political fortunes of trade unions and the emerging Labour Party. Those most acquainted with the harsh, demeaning, often crippling social consequences of the nation's economic triumph were now well on the way to significant participation in the democratic process—most notably after the 1867 and 1884 franchise reforms.[235] The 'respectable' working classes might, where able, follow Smiles' injunction and strive for social elevation and economic independence, even join the millions by then in friendly societies and co-operatives. But, contrary to Smiles' prediction,[236] this was not to make them the most staunch defenders of the social and political status quo.

[233] PD 1867 (s3) 185: 163; and Fraser, Evolution of the British Welfare State, 101.

[234] Local Government Act 1871 (34 & 35 Vict. c. 70). George Goschen, the Local Government Board's first President, made early efforts to coordinate the actions of London local Poor Law Boards with the Charity Organisation Society established in 1869. Goschen's aim, partly achieved, was to shift responsibility for the 'deserving' poor to charities, while reserving 'less eligibility' workhouse rigours for 'non-deserving' cases and an improved care regime for true dependants: children, the elderly, and sick. See A. Brundage, The English Poor Laws 1700–1930 (Basingstoke, 2002), Ch. 6.

[235] It is accepted that Gladstone's 1874 defeat turned more on the unfavourable view taken by workers of the Trade Union Act 1871.

[236] Samuel Smiles, Self-Help (1859), 1–4. Aside from friendly societies and their like, in 1861 Gladstone set up the Post Office Savings Bank to encourage thrift and self-dependence.

In the closing decade of the nineteenth century, the twin strains of welfare relief for the aged and for the unemployed increasingly influenced attitudes towards the more amorphous notion of Poor Law support. The Report of the Royal Commission on the Aged Poor showed the influence of economists who were now challenging the crude deterrent philosophy embodied in the Poor Law and its claimed relationship to an efficient market economy.[237] Though shying away from proposing state supported pensions, the Commission condemned the low levels of relief and harshness of workhouse regimes.[238] Previously, the Commons 1899 Select Committee (whose membership included Lloyd George) was troubled by the potential effects of a state supported pension on working-class financial prudence and savings habits. Most centrally, the debate was over whether pensions should be contributory.[239] Yet by 1908, despite Asquith's reservations, and in the face of opposition from the Charity Organisation Society, friendly societies and even some unions,[240] Lloyd George powered by the necessary budget surplus and 'New Liberalism', had given the nation a means-tested, non-contributory old age pension. By any measure the Pensions Act constituted a radical social welfare innovation. Unlike Poor Law relief, pensions came from the central state as of right, without the need for destitution and, not least, without stigma. Moreover, not only did the measure rescue a large section of Poor Law dependants, it also threw into unflattering relief the continuing nature and administration of the Poor Law.

As well as from the provision of state pensions, the Poor Law client base was also to suffer invasion by developments relating to the relief of unemployment. In the mid-1880s, rioting by London unemployed workers had help persuade the

[237] Particularly A. Marshall, *Principles of Economics* (1890). Also H. Sidgwick, *The Methods of Ethics* (1874) and J. Thorold Rogers, *Manual of Political Economy* (2nd edn, Oxford, 1869).

[238] *Royal Commission on the Aged Poor Report* 1895 (Cd. 7684).

[239] *Report of Commons Select Committee on Aged Deserving Poor*, PP 1899 (296) v, ix. From the 1850s, non-contributory pension schemes were enjoyed by civil servants and Post Office employees. Contributory pension schemes followed in the private sector for all grades of employees in a range of organizations, from banks to railway companies. Generally, L. Hannah, *Inventing Retirement: The Development of Occupational Pensions in Britain* (1986).

[240] Some union and friendly society opposition was to a degree assuaged by the relief that pension payments might offer from meeting sick benefit claims in old age. Formed in 1869, the Charity Organisation Society aimed to eliminate the enormous poverty in East London through better coordination and professionalism of the diverse bodies then carrying out charitable work. Pauperism was seen by the Society as the consequence of personal moral failings rather than an endemic social problem. The Society took a militant approach to separating the deserving poor who might receive aid from the undeserving poor who were directed to the even more severe Poor Law authorities. Charles Booth's extensive social investigations, 'Life and Labour of the People in London', beginning in the mid-1880s, seriously challenged the Society's claims of the low incidence and causes of poverty. G. Steadman Jones, *Outcast London: A Study in the Relationship between Classes in Victorian Society* (Oxford, 1971).

government of the benefit of authorizing local public works projects to absorb surplus labour.[241] While far from making extensive inroads into unemployment levels, the scheme, promoted until the 1900s, did establish the principle of a degree of state responsibility for the poor (though not destitute) unemployed. Manifest recognition of this intervention in the operation of a liberal market economy came with the Unemployed Workmen Act 1905. Enacted by the expiring Tory government as a response to a period of large-scale unemployment, the legislation sought to set up a national network of committees whose principal purpose was to establish labour exchanges to link those seeking work with employers seeking workers.[242] The implications of this (initially) three-year scheme for the provision of Poor Law relief were plain enough. So much so, that the future of labour exchanges was made contingent upon the findings of the Royal Commission on the Poor Law set up in 1905 by the outgoing Balfour administration.

Under the succeeding Liberal government's broad, though vague, social policy agenda, the number and use of labour exchanges expanded rapidly. Their severance from the Poor Law (effected by the Labour Exchanges Act 1909)[243] and the removal of control of existing exchanges from local authorities placed them in the hands of the Board of Trade, financed by central funds. The innovation was presented as not so much an interference with the free-market economy, but as a facilitative measure designed to enhance market efficiency. The second major element of Churchill's and William Beveridge's assault on unemployment, the National Insurance Act, was eventually enacted in 1911.[244] The pernicious link between 'uncertain' employment and feckless working-class attitudes had been argued over decades by many social commentators. In the 1860s, Henry Mayhew had sought to dislodge the common belief of 'men in smooth circumstances' that workers' failure to apportion irregular earnings across periods of unemployment was undeniable evidence of moral fault.[245] Funded by employer and employee contributions, supplemented by central payments, the objective was to enable workers in industries prone to market-driven fluctuations to survive periods of

---

[241] Instituted by Joseph Chamberlain as President of the Local Government Board in Gladstone's government 1886: 'Pauperism and Distress: Circular Letter to Boards of Guardians'. Chamberlain's circular offered 'to deal promptly' with loan applications for the setting up of such projects. See also the Fabian tract of John Burns, *The Unemployed* (1893), who argued for labour exchanges as part of a new period when 'laisser [sic] faire has been abandoned' (18).

[242] The 1905 Act required committees to be made up of representatives from local authorities, Poor Law guardians, and charity organizations.

[243] The Minority Report of the Royal Commission on the Poor Law (1909) strongly supported labour exchanges.

[244] For the Bismarckian influence on the scheme, see E. Hennock, *British Social Reform and German Precedents: The Case of Social Insurance 1880–1914* (Oxford, 1987).

[245] *London, Labour and the London Poor* (1861), ii, 367.

forced unemployment. Again, as with the labour exchanges, it was a measure characterizable as complementary to a liberal economy rather than an interference with it. Of course, as was readily apparent to some, the two measures could also be read as strengthening a worker's overall economic leverage: they made more remote the need to have resort to demeaning Poor Law support; and to a degree, they enhanced worker mobility, thus inhibiting local (wage lowering) over-supply of labour. Beveridge described unemployment insurance as providing for the 'maintenance of the reserves while standing idle and of the displaced man while waiting re-absorption'. In the case of labour exchanges, Beveridge had observed that some 'measure of protection for those within a trade or district against the competition of those outside is an essential... consequence of the system... The aim... is not simply the fluidity, but the organised and intelligent fluidity of labour—the enabling of men to go where they are wanted, but at the same time the discouraging of movement to places where men are not wanted.'[246] All in all, the state's former uninvolved role in one cardinal feature of a capitalist system—the labour supply—had been extensively compromised. Yet, in the event, the measure attracted practically no parliamentary opposition.

The National Insurance Act not only introduced unemployed benefit insurance, but also health insurance. As with unemployed benefit, health insurance spread the financial burden between worker, employer, and the state. Both schemes also removed from those workers covered the social and economic decision on whether to plan for the contingencies of unemployment or illness. To that degree, individual social and economic self-responsibility was no longer demanded by the state. Whilst a financial partner in both schemes, administration of the 1911 Act was placed principally in the non-state hands of the medical profession, trade unions, friendly societies, and insurance companies.[247] In some measure, this involvement was a *quid pro quo* for their reluctant acceptance of the schemes. Not only was this seen to limit public costs, but the use of private organizations helped to retain the substance and appearance of the continuing importance of voluntaryism in the provision of such services.

Taxation and Redistributing Wealth

Until the reintroduction of income tax in 1842, relatively little in the way of political or theoretical discourse sought to link fiscal and broad economic and

---

[246] *Unemployment: A Problem of Industry* (1909), 229; and Fraser, *The Evolution of the British Welfare State*, 'Documentary Appendix' 7C and 7D.

[247] For later outspoken criticism of the trend for legislating to exclude the role of courts in welfare disputes, see, most notably, Lord Hewart CJ's *The New Despotism* (1929), where he expressed open contempt for the 'pretensions and encroachments of bureaucracy' (v).

social policy. Indirect taxes (customs and excise duties) paid by all consumers, accounting for over 70 per cent of tax revenue until late Victorian times, were arguably both regressive in being a proportionately unequal burden on society's poorest, and a hindrance on free trade and business. Yet free traders could be found rejecting income tax and arguing for the retention of higher indirect tax; while at the same time, some dyed-in-the-wool protectionists supported income tax and reduced indirect taxation.[248] Moreover, beyond generalizations, earlier political economists offered no clear coherent philosophy of taxation to be prayed in aid; and even these generalizations were sometimes open to a range of conflicting constructions.[249] And when the language of political economy was resorted to by ministers while discussing fiscal matters, it was more likely to be a justificatory prop rather than a motivation in the formulation of policy.[250]

Partly to cope with budget deficits and to hold down government borrowing, through to the 1840s several unsuccessful attempts were mounted by Tory administrations to tax incomes and profits, in addition to the vast range of established direct and indirect taxes. On these occasions Whig opposition rested primarily on its alleged inequitable spread amongst the classes. However, periodic economic depressions severely diminished the revenue produced by indirect taxation, in turn causing governments to increase tax rates, with socially painful and divisive consequences. But if new sources of revenue were politically inaccessible, then increased budget funding could only flow from a generally more successful economy.

Open political articulation of the relationship between the growth of national wealth, government spending and fiscal policy became more pronounced in the 1830s on the back of a potent combination of contemporary factors: most particularly, periodic free-trade agitation (especially over the Corn laws, a target not only of entrepreneurs but also of Chartism[251]), the rising need for a measure of government social intervention, set against deepening budgetary deficits. While divisions within both Whig and Tory parties ensured that no significant fiscal

---

[248] Hilton, *Corn, Cash and Commerce*, 260.

[249] On the contrast between direct and indirect tax, Adam Smith's general principles of taxation, distinguished tax on luxuries and that on necessities, supporting its repeal on social grounds for basics such as salt, soap, and candles. Tax on wages was not favoured on the grounds of inefficiency in collection costs and possible inequities. *Inquiry*, Book V, Ch. 2. Bentham seems to have taken a similar line on indirect tax, but supported a profits tax on commerce and industry as a means of relieving what he regarded as the excessive tax burdens on land. For example, *Proposal for a Mode of Taxation* (1794) and T. Dome, 'Bentham and J. S. Mill on Tax Reform' (1999) 11 *Utilitas* 310. For Ricardo's equivocal stance, see C. Shoup, *Ricardo and the Tax System* (New York, 1960), 218–24 and *passim*.

[250] Hilton, *A Mad, Bad and Dangerous People*, 275.

[251] The tax system was one target of Chartism which maintained that it both helped generate poverty and worked to the benefit of the wealthy. Daunton, *Trusting Leviathan*, 56.

reforms occurred, conflicting views on the links between political economy and taxation were often aired. Peel's brief minority administration made no headway in the mid-1830s with his proposed reintroduction of income tax aimed at reconciling competing class interests, relieving the poor's tax burden, and facilitating generally beneficial lower trade tariffs. With momentous matters of franchise and then Poor Law reform pressing in, along with the certainty of staunch opposition to such a change from cross-party vested interests, the Whigs under Melbourne showed no appetite for the fiscal shift required to adopt Peelite policy. Seeking to satisfy free-traders (campaigning for abolition of tariffs but opposing income tax as hostile to capital investment) and to balance the nation's accounts, the 1841 Whig budget lowered many indirect taxes, hoping to increase overall revenue by a boost in domestic consumption. Failure of this strategy, and a Whig defeat in the summer general election, presented the incoming Peel government with a large budgetary deficit, the result of government expenditure amidst a trade depression.[252]

Peel's innovatory reintroduction of income tax in 1842 was expressly justified as essential for boosting trade and industry, quelling continuing social unrest, raising consumption and meeting poverty by lowering the prices of basic necessities.[253] For the liberal Tory *Times*, the policy put Peel in the 'first rank of financial statesmen'. It was a 'great measure in comparison with which all other financial propositions of recent years sink into insignificance'.[254] Along with parliamentary critics, the Whig inclining *Morning Chronicle* censured Peel's illicit use of a 'war tax [as] proof of [his] complete financial exhaustion'.[255] As before, income tax was opposed on several fronts by a coalition of forces: claiming that it was likely to facilitate excessive government spending at home and on foreign adventures; also that it was hostile to commercial and industrial investment;[256] and that it was unacceptably inquisitorial. In the last respect, even the otherwise sympathetic *Times* felt obliged to concede that the tax's intrusiveness was a necessary but 'most grievous evil'.[257]

However, not only did Peel's 1842 fiscal strategy succeed, but three years later, with the expiration of this short-term measure, Peel was back in parliament[258] seeking (and getting) an extension of income taxing powers, principally on

---

[252] Daunton, *Progress and Poverty*, 552–3.

[253] 12 March 1842, p. 13.

[254] *PD* 1842 (s3) 61: 916–17.

[255] 15 March 1842, p. 2.

[256] The theoretical backup for this contention was provided by McCulloch's *A Treatise on the Principles and Practical Influence of Taxation and the Funding System* (1845).

[257] 15 March 1842, p. 4.

[258] A hint from Goulborn, Peel's Chancellor of the Exchequer in 1842, that income tax would be a long-lasting measure, was picked up by *The Times*, 27 April 1842, p. 6.

social grounds: to meet Chartism's challenge by keeping down indirect taxes, thereby suppressing the cost of basic consumables. Thus, he was able to achieve the formidable task of balancing the competing, powerful political and economic interests of commerce, manufacturers and landowners, free-traders and protectionists; those wishing to see an expansion of interventionism by the state and those seeking its shrinkage. But, topped with the complete abolition of the Corn Laws in 1846,[259] it was a manoeuvre which ultimately split the Tories.

Returning to power that year, the Whig government under Russell retained the Tory peacetime income tax, as did all subsequent administrations of whatever stripe throughout the rest of Victoria's reign, and beyond. Certainly, initially for both Whig and Tory, and later Liberal governments, the fiscal orthodoxy was that income tax remained a temporary measure, contingent upon transient, extraordinary revenue needs. It was a philosophy freely espoused by both Gladstone and Disraeli in their early careers as Chancellors of the Exchequer. However, by the late 1850s, in the aftermath of the Crimean War and growing government expenditure on domestic concerns, such talk of income tax as a temporary expedient increasingly became little more than an empty and declining ritual. From this point, the principal contentious questions became whether for taxation purposes, all *types* of income should be treated alike—or subject to 'differentiation', and whether all taxpayers regardless of circumstances, should be subject to the same rate of tax.

Until the second half of the nineteenth century, the broad question of *who* should pay and *what* revenue sources might be taxed had tended to concentrate on the distinction between direct and indirect taxation. The latter's great virtues were the relative low cost and efficiency of its collection, along with limited risks of evasion and non-intrusiveness into payers' private professional circumstances. By contrast, direct taxation was administratively inquisitorial, expensive and, to a degree, open to evasion—especially in respect of commercial and professional profits.[260] However, as already noted, indirect taxation was seen by many as essentially regressive: it was a disproportionate and unfair burden on the nation's poor, taxing even the basic necessities of their lowly existence. Conscious of this rumbling political charge, Peel, and later Gladstone, also

---

[259] Daunton, *Progress and Poverty*, 553–7.

[260] Characteristics identified by many including Adam Smith and Mill. The latter was far less worried about the inquisitorial nature of income tax assessment than the unfairness caused by the evasion of full liability by many: '[T]he variable gains of professions, and still more the profits of business...can still less be estimated with any approach to fairness by a tax collector...The unscrupulous succeed in evading a great proportion of what they should pay; even persons of integrity in their ordinary transaction are tempted to palter with their consciences...' *Principles*, Book V, Ch. 3, section 5.

appreciated that more than simply an additional revenue source for rescuing the nation from budgetary disasters, the reintroduction of income tax could also serve as a demonstration of the desire for an equitable spreading of the general fiscal burden. This is implicit in Gladstone's imaginative characterization of 'direct and indirect taxation [as] two attractive sisters who have been introduced into the gay world of London, each with an ample fortune, both having the same parentage [of] Necessity and Invention—differing only as sisters may differ …'.[261]

But while recognizing the political imperative for a fair and equitable spread of fiscal burdens across all classes, both Peel[262] and Gladstone resisted any logical extension of this philosophy in relation to the types of income and taxpayers' personal circumstances. Differentiation for tax rate purposes between 'spontaneous' income (such as rents), and 'precarious' income (like wages or profits), had been found at least feasible by a Commons' Select Committee on Income and Property tax in the early 1850s.[263] Yet politically, most, including Gladstone, regarded movement away from flat tax rates as wholly divisive; a change likely to upset the relative broad toleration of the fiscal regime reached by this time. Differentiation was viewed as likely to detonate a chain reaction across a range of opposing interest groups each seeking special tax concessions,[264] upsetting the comparative taxation equilibrium which had evolved by mid-century. Not that differentiation between earned and unearned income completely lacked advocates. In essence, both Mill and McCulloch saw earned income as meriting more generous fiscal treatment than unearned income, because the former was a consequence of capital enterprise and investment.[265] But powerful reaffirmation of most politicians' resistance to such logic continued to be displayed from time to time. For example, in 1869 Gladstone's Chancellor of the Exchequer, the formidable Robert Lowe, bamboozled and teased his parliamentary audience with speculation on the fundamental conceptual challenge of even pinning down the nature of income, let alone its differentiation:

It is like 'now'. In a moment it flies from you while you stop. It is the notion of a man's annual revenue, abstracted altogether from the sources whence it comes and the purposes for which it goes. That is the idea of an income: and the moment you begin to say you ought to pay more on this schedule and less on that, or abolish, as the Hon. Gentleman says a Schedule altogether, you are not amending the income tax but destroying it and making, instead of it, an unfair and bungling property tax. Unless you look at income

---

[261] PD 1861 (s3) 162: 584; quoted by Daunton, *Trusting Leviathan*, 172.
[262] PD 1842 (s3) 61: 914–15.
[263] *Report*, PP 1852 (510) ix.
[264] PD 1853 (s3) 125: 1383–4. And B. Sabine, *Short History of Taxation* (1980), 64–7.
[265] Mill, *Principles*, Book V, Ch. II, section 4. McCulloch *Treatise on Taxation* (1845).

without reference to the sources whence it comes, or whither it goes, it is impossible to maintain an income tax by any argument.[266]

Throughout this same period proposals for the graduation of tax rate also fared politically much the same as differentiation on broadly similar grounds. Yet the notion of proportioning tax liability to a person's wealth or ability to pay was by no means an alien concept to the fiscal system. From 1799, income tax had only been levied on those enjoying an income in excess of £60; and up to £200 the rate was graduated. Moreover, in calculating liability child allowance was incorporated until 1806. Peel's 1842 reintroduction of income tax while not conceding child allowance, set the bar at incomes of £150 and above, thereby excluding from liability the great majority of the population—a policy which continued for the remainder of the century. Until the 1880s, the almost universal political orthodoxy was that extracting higher rates of income tax from the well-to-do was destructive of the 'whole principle of property, to the principle of accumulation, and through that principle, to industry itself, and therefore to the interests of both poor and rich …'.[267] Mill, while supporting differentiation, opposed graduation, regarding it as a tax on enterprise, penalizing those who worked harder and saved to invest.[268] However, such arguments were not seen as directly applicable to death or inheritance taxes. Consequently, Gladstone felt free to apply a graduated rate to the new succession duty on property introduced in 1853, paid by those who inherited.[269]

By the 1880s both the political and theoretical credibility of a more overt redistributive fiscal regime were gaining significant advocates. Central Exchequer subventions of increasing local government responsibilities and civic initiatives, prompted broader reviews of taxation practice generally.[270] Liberal radicals, including Joseph Chamberlain,[271] openly supported the principle of graduated tax

---

[266] *PD* 1869 (s3) 194: 1533, and invoking the alleged authority of Adam Smith.

[267] Gladstone, *PD* 1863 (s3) 170: 622.

[268] *Principles*, Book V, Ch. II, section 3.

[269] Succession Duty Act 1853, 16 & 17 Vict. c. 50. On land tax and succession duty, see also XII, Pt 1. Mill also favoured a graduated tax on inherited wealth: *Principles*, Book V, Ch. II, section 3.

[270] Inadequacies in the machinery of assessment and collection of rates led to deepening shortfalls between rising local expenditure and relatively static local revenues. It was a difference which central government felt increasingly obliged to make up, with either formalized annual payments (e.g. as with policing and education) or *ad hoc* grants in aid. On subvention processes, see the Local Government Act 1888. *The Royal Commission on Local Taxation, Final Report PP* 1901 (Cd. 638) xxiv produced no clear-cut solution to the funding gap between what local rates could raise and the necessary expenditure of local authorities. See also J. Wilson, 'The Finance of Municipal Capital Expenditure in England and Wales 1870–1914' (1997) *Financial History Review* 4; and Daunton, *Trusting Leviathan*, 256–301.

[271] During his election campaign of 1885, Chamberlain argued for increased spending on social reform funded by 'equality of sacrifice' through both differentiated and graduated tax structures. Sabine, *Short History of Taxation*, 132–3.

rates, as did a new generation of political economists, like Alfred Marshall, as one ramification of marginal cost-benefit analysis.[272] Indeed, strengthening a socially redistributive fiscal policy could be seen with increased central government domestic spending being partly underpinned by a shift from indirect to direct taxes from the early 1890s.[273] And while not going as far as actually incorporating graduated income taxation in his 1894 budget, as Gladstone's Chancellor of the Exchequer, Sir William Harcourt voiced support for the notion 'as a sound principle of finance'.[274] Moreover, in 1894, Harcourt introduced a graduated scale of death duties, thereby significantly boosting revenue from this source as well as demonstrating the Liberals' sense of social equity by spreading the nation's fiscal burden in a more progressive fashion across all classes, including the landed wealthy.[275] Indeed, such was its apparent impact on the psyche of estate owners, that Wilde's creation Lady Bracknell, in *The Importance of Being Ernest* (1895), reflects that

What between the duties expected of one during one's lifetime, and the duties exacted from one after one's death, land has ceased to be either a profit or a pleasure (Act 1, Pt 2).

Prior to Asquith's Liberal budget of 1907, a Select Committee had confirmed the 'practicability' of 'differentiating' and 'graduating' income tax.[276] Reinforced by this endorsement, the government's budgetary provisions differentiated types of income, with a lower rate payable on earned than unearned income. At the same time, graduated estate duty rates were significantly increased on larger estates. Asquith pinned the government's fiscal colours to the parliamentary mast in justifying increasing and redistributing the tax burden in unequivocal terms:

[I]f we are to have social reform we must be ready to pay for it, and when I say 'we' I mean the whole nation—the working and consuming classes as well as the wealthier class of direct tax payers… [S]trengthening of our national credit and the provision for social reform, are to be the governing aims of our policy.… [277]

---

[272] *Principles of Economics* (1890). Similarly later, A. Pigou, *Wealth and Welfare* (1912). And see Daunton, *Trusting Leviathan*, 142–7. As a proportion of government revenue, income tax rose from approximately 10% in the mid-1870s to around 17% by the mid-1890s.

[273] Beside rising social welfare demands, higher government revenues were required for propping up local authority finances, along with the great cost of rearming the national defence forces, and paying for the Boer War at the end of the decade.

[274] e.g. *PD* 1890 (s3) 343: 1093.

[275] See M. Daunton, 'The Political Economy of Death Duties: Harcourt's Budget of 1894', in N. Harte and R. Quinault (eds), *Land and Society in Britain 1700–1914* (Manchester, 1996), 137. Inheritance or succession duty was introduced by Gladstone in 1853. For Mill's support for this form of taxation, see *Principles*, Book V Ch. 2.

[276] *Report of the Select Committee on Income Tax*, PP 1906, (Cd. 365), ix.

[277] *PD* 1907 (s4) 172: 1192. Elsewhere, Asquith also readily acknowledged the sizeable revenue demands of armaments. On tax liability being proportionate to means, see Lloyd George, e.g. *PD* 1911 (s5 HC) 32: 1939–40.

Outstripping Asquith's fiscal innovations of 1907, Lloyd George's inflammatory 1909 budget not only introduced graduation of income tax[278] and again raised death duties, but more provocatively, it proposed various new forms of land taxation.[279] In terms of tax innovation, Lloyd George's three-pronged fiscal attack on rising land values constituted the most economically radical element of the 'People's Budget' proposals of 1909. However, such land tax provisions were far from original: the 1870s had seen economists, including Mill and Fawcett, along with bodies like the Land Tenure Reform Association, advocate similar measures.[280] By the early 1900s, principally as the consequence of urbanization, many estate owners had enjoyed decades of substantially increased land values. These rises followed urban improvement 'effected by the labour and at the cost of other people [including] the municipality...and ratepayers'. In addition to justifying taxation on the grounds of economic equity, and very much echoing Joseph Chamberlain's early 1880s rhetoric, Winston Churchill also threw in a charge of monopoly exploitation: 'the land monopolist...renders no service to the community, [he] has only to sit still and watch complacently his property multiplying in value'.[281] Of course, this form of land value tax was most directly a tax on landed wealth, interests that were exceedingly well represented in the House of Lords. Yet, as demonstrated by the Parliament Act 1911, even a resolute obstructionist Lords could not ultimately resist the new political climate and determined power of the Commons.

With the increased tax burden falling largely on the landed and those with high or unearned incomes, Asquith's Liberal administration sought to maintain its core middle-class appeal, as well as win over a greater proportion of the strengthening Labour Party's natural constituency. Moreover, holding down or lowering indirect taxes on food and consumables, meant no obvious compromise of a free-trade philosophy was necessary, thereby heading off Chamberlain's protectionist momentum.[282] The Tory Lords' induced constitutional confrontation and subsequent 1910 Liberal election victory was not unreasonably construed as

---

[278] As well as graduated income tax, incomes over £5000 incurred a supplemental 'super tax'. The budget eventually became law in April 1910.

[279] By 1914, direct taxes had for the first time exceeded indirect taxes, with increased income tax accounting for 27%, the largest single source of tax revenue.

[280] See below.

[281] Chamberlain, quoted by J. Garvin, *Life of Joseph Chamberlain* (1932), i, 392. Churchill, *The People's Rights* (1909), 119 and Fraser, *Evolution of the British Welfare State*, 171. The proposed duties were a levy on the increase in land value as realized on sale; a capital tax on unused land, and tax on the reversionary interest value on the expiration of leases. Controls on land development were introduced by the Housing and Town Planning Act 1909. The 1909 budget offered economic innovation in the form of a development fund of £1 million for improvement of the rural economy.

[282] Of contemporary political economists, see esp. J. A. Hobson's theory of 'under-consumption', e.g. *The Industrial System* (1909) and *The Economics of Distribution* (1900); discussed in Daunton, *Trusting Leviathan*, 341–52.

a national endorsement of this form of fiscal innovation, helping to power the opening of an era of welfarism. And with the Parliament Act of 1911, the House of Lords' ability to vote down financial bills was removed. At least for some Liberal theorists, the virtuous fiscal circle was now complete: social reform, increased taxation levels of those who could afford to contribute more, and free trade were complementary strategies: putting more money in the pockets of low earners would help correct 'under consumption' thereby effecting both economic efficiency and greater social equity.[283]

Turning away from legislation to the role of courts in fiscal matters, though all forms of taxation were, and are, very much the creatures of legislation, enforcement was, both before and after Victorian times, almost exclusively in the hands of central and local government administration. Even when formal adjudicatory roles in tax matters were assigned to the courts, until post-1914 resort to them was extremely limited. Prior to Pitt's income tax of 1799, the collection of land and assessed taxes was carried out by groups of local lay commissioners, appointed by and under the ultimate control of the Treasury.[284] With the introduction of income tax they were augmented by lay 'General Commissioners' and 'Special Commissioners' of income tax.[285] Taxation disputes between the authorities and individuals were usually dealt with internally by the General Commissioners, or, less often, by Special Commissioners. The judicial interpretation of fiscal legislation only began in earnest in the late 1860s.[286] Appeals on points of law from decisions of tax Commissioners were authorized from 1874, under section 9 of the Customs and Inland Revenue Act.[287] But, up to 1915, business was exceedingly thin, with fewer than a total of 30 cases appealed from the Special Commissioners to the High Court. However, unsurprisingly, Lloyd George's introduction of 'super tax' greatly expanded the appeal rate thereafter.[288]

---

[283] Daunton, *Trusting Leviathan*, 360–71.

[284] The Treasury also appointed the many tiers of the extensive bureaucratic army of central and local customs and excise officials responsible for effectively collecting the largest proportion of government revenues until the beginning of the twentieth century.

[285] Special Commissioners were central, paid officials first appointed under the Income Tax Act 1805 (45 Geo. 3, c. 49) to deal with more complex or sensitive questions of income tax, including granting charitable exemptions. From 1842 their role was to ensure confidential handling of business or commercial information collected for tax assessment purposes. See Peel, *PD* 1842 (s3) 61: 912. On the functioning of the whole range of tax tribunals, see C. Stebbings, *Legal Foundations of Tribunals in Nineteenth Century England* (Cambridge, 2000), *passim*.

[286] *Partington* v. *Attorney-General* (1869) LR 4 HL 100 at 122. Here Lord Cairns insisted that tax liability was subject to strict statutory construction: it must come within the 'letter' of the law.

[287] Appeals to Quarter Sessions were permissible by aggrieved ratepayers on the grounds of inaccurate assessment or other forms of maladministration.

[288] H. Munroe, *Reflections on the Law of Tax* (1981), 81–82. For an analysis of the political division amongst Law Lords on taxation appeals, see Stevens, *Law and Politics*, 170–6.

3. OVERVIEW: POLITICAL ECONOMY, THE STATE'S ROLE, AND THE LAW

Dicey's description of the nineteenth century as comprising three periods: 'Legislative Quiescence' (1800–30), 'Benthamism or Individualism' (1825–70), and 'Collectivism' (1865–1900), has attracted considerable critical fire as well as a high degree of endorsement.[289] Indeed, in 1869 a leader in *The Times* expressed sentiments bearing a distinct resemblance to some elements in Dicey's analysis:

Forty or fifty years ago…Politicians then fancied that Government was responsible for a great deal…The age of economists succeeded; the Corn Laws were abolished…and the opinion became widely prevalent that Government had very little to do with the state of the people, except to let well alone. That age too has already passed away, and we are beginning to perceive that neither Protection nor Free trade is a principle capable of Governing the whole science of domestic legislation….[290]

Most contentious has been the accuracy of Dicey's characterization of the 1830s–1870s as a period marked by its 'individualism' and the influence of Benthamite ideas. Clearly, running against Dicey's thesis is the accelerating legislative trend from the late 1830s involving state intervention in both spheres of political economy: the imposition of controls on the operation of private industrial and commercial concerns; and the increasing engagement of central and local government in a range of social welfare areas such as education, public health, and the Poor Law.[291] Equally apparent were the principal forces driving the state's intervention: initially the growing social consequences of industrialization coupled with urbanization; the manifest 'social deficit' of capitalism, underscored by the allied forces of Tory paternalism, Evangelical fervour, cross-party humanitarianism, and Utilitarian ideology. Moreover, a dominant economic philosophy embracing *laissez-fairism* and a liberal market was not inherently hostile to legislative intervention: not only was legislation necessary to undo earlier 'mercantilism' or anti-competitive laws, but, especially from the 1840s, new laws were increasingly

---

[289] *The Relation between Law and Public Opinion in England* (1905). Dicey's best known critics include O. MacDonagh, 'The Nineteenth Century Revolution in Government: A Reappraisal' (1958) 1 *Hist. J.* 52; D. Roberts, *Victorian Origins of the British Welfare State* (New Haven, 1968); and W. Lubenow, *The Politics of Government Growth* (1971). Qualified support for Dicey's thesis is found in H. Parris, 'The Nineteenth Century Revolution in Government: A Reappraisal' (1960) 3 *Hist. J.* 17 and *Constitutional Bureaucracy* (1969); J. Hart, 'Nineteenth Century Social Reform: A Tory Interpretation' (1965) 31 *Past and Present* 39. And see the detailed analysis in XIII, Pt 2.

[290] 28 June 1869, p. 8.

[291] Taking 'social welfare' in its broadest sense, parallel engagements had occurred within the criminal justice system, where central government had become increasingly involved in regulating the substance and structures of punishment. See XIII, Pt 1.

deployed to facilitate a liberal market economy or regulate its undesirable anti-competitive manifestations.[292]

In its own time, the emerging 'science' of political economy was commonly identified with Utilitarianism. At root, Utilitarianism enabled the economy, social welfare, and the state to be viewed in pragmatic terms. While fielding a cluster of political economists (Ricardo, McCulloch, Senior, and the Mills) theoretically attached to *laissez-faire* and a liberal market, the countervailing collectivistic aim of greater social benefit (happiness) flexibly applied could trump a non-interventionist, individualistic ideology.[293] In the context of political economy, seeking to identify Utilitarianism as either collectivistic or individualistic, interventionist or non-interventionist, is an analytically doubtful, if not futile exercise.[294] This is nowhere more apparent than in Utilitarianism's prominent role in the substance and enactment of the Poor Law reforms, a measure combining severe individualistic notions of self-responsibility with emphatically centralist regulation and superintendence. Furthermore, Utilitarianism was in competition with other potent forces making identification of individual influence singularly problematic. Added to this, Utilitarian 'expediency', Tory paternalism, and Evangelical humanitarianism, often led to the same economic and social policy conclusions, albeit from elementally different premises.[295]

Claims of a significant role for Benthamism in economic and social legislation carry most credibility in respect of the creation of the machinery or apparatus for the growth in state intervention. While initially often feeble in enforcement and outcome, the regulatory model procedure much favoured by Utilitarians— central enquiry, review of expert evidence, then regulation enforced by an inspectorate—rapidly became the orthodoxy of the Victorian age.[296] Administrative

---

[292] e.g. respectively, the companies legislation, and railway and canal regulation.

[293] Significantly, the five principal Utilitarian (inclined) journals were all advocates of increased government intervention. See F. Roberts, *The Social Conscience of the Early Victorians* (Stanford, 2002), 442–3.

[294] H. Perkin, 'Individualism versus Collectivism in Nineteenth Century Britain: A False Antithesis' (1977) 17 *JBS* 105. Moreover, the meaning of the terms 'individualism' and 'collectivism' are far from undisputed. Most basically, in the case of Utilitarianism, the pursuit of self-interest (the pain and pleasure calculus) suggests fundamental individualism. But political concern for the greatest social happiness/welfare and consequential state intervention are the hallmarks of collectivism.

[295] See Ch. V, above, 'Law and Religion'.

[296] On the age's prominent practitioner, Edwin Chadwick, see A. Brundage, *England's 'Prussian' Minister Edwin Chadwick and the Politics of Government Growth 1832–1854* (1988). However, Utilitarians were far from content with the system of parliamentary scrutiny of bills and legislative proposals. See e.g. J. S. Mill, *Thoughts on Parliamentary Reform* (1859) and *Considerations of Representative Government* (1861); and Edwin Chadwick's *A Paper on the Chief Methods of Preparation for Legislation Especially Applicable to the Reform of Parliament* (1859).

development and growth were practically inevitable corollaries of such central government ambitions and intervention. Moreover, beside the necessity of central (and later local)[297] administrative expansion to support and facilitate the broadening range and degree of intervention, it is also arguable that bureaucratic growth was a consequence of sheer administrative momentum and rising professional expertise.[298] It was a development feared by some as speeding the nation towards political acceptance of an enfeebled, intellectually dependent society. By rigging the evidence, 'Government Commissioners' foisted on the public 'misleading self-serving reports: The tendency of the whole system is to depress individual thought and effort;... to cramp the development of individual ideas and check the individual search after truth [instead of individuals] battling the questions until the truth has been won by self-exertion.'[299]

Such views aside, the weight of evidence does not suggest that a developed and skilled civil service became the dominant initiating force in matters of economic and social intervention. Rather, although in a position to influence the nature of possible 'solutions' to the political pressures and broader influences confronting their masters, a skilled bureaucracy[300] made state intervention an immediately more viable, attractive, and likely response. Additionally, although rightly long regarded as a bulwark against central government intrusion, exploitation of the tradition of local government could also be viewed as a statist Trojan horse: the first stage of centrally imposed regulation often began with relatively uncontroversial permissive local authority powers, later followed up by the politically less dramatic step to mandatory provisions. And, of course, an inestimable political benefit of intervention through municipal agency was that at least a substantial element of any necessary expenditure could be placed on the backs of ratepayers.[301]

Increasingly, allegiance to *laissez-fairism* meant a continued belief in the virtues of competition, but not necessarily an unregulated market: state intervention could facilitate or enhance desirable competitiveness. As the mid-Victorian

---

[297] Depending on particular circumstances and the extent of private enterprise, huge variations existed in the level of 'public' works carried out through local initiatives. Until the facilitatory powers granted by the Municipal Corporations Act 1836 were increasingly taken up in the 1840s, local government administrative structures (beyond those for Poor Relief) in most areas remained rudimentary.

[298] MacDonagh and Roberts, above.

[299] J. Toulmin Smith, *Government by Commissions Illegal and Pernicious* (1849), 174.

[300] Including prominent central departmental administrators such as James Kay-Shuttleworth, John Simon, Godfrey Lushington, Henry Taylor, Thomas Southwood Smith, and Henry Cole. More generally, on the professional and administrative influences on mid and late Victorian governments, see R. MacLeod (ed.), *Government and Expertise. Specialists, Administrators and Professionals 1860–1919*, (Cambridge, 1988) 1–24.

[301] Central government expenditure stabilized during the 1860s and 1870s.

period was reached, resort to the language of commercial *laissez-faire*, private enterprise, and individual self-help, more than ever assumed a ritualistic quality; the continuum of economic and social intervention was consolidated when 'expediency' so demanded; it became a practical reality reflecting an unself-conscious progression from dogma to disposition. This response was particularly apparent following the fundamental political shifts manifested in the franchise reforms of the 1860s and 1880s, with allied pressures from organized labour and growing anxieties over the nation's ability to cope with the foreign competition when other advanced economies were opting for national protection over free trade.

Finally, beyond such political and institutional forces, and in some respects running alongside them, were the judiciary and courts. The evidence of their impact on Victorian political economy is mixed: common law and equity courts over the century running up to the 1850s showed a pragmatic willingness to recognize doctrinal adaptation and innovation in many areas of commercial and property law which facilitated economic activity, including trusts, mortgages, and contract law. This is consistent with suggestions that the judiciary, while adhering to a formalistic, precedent-based application of law, could also embrace the contemporary philosophy of a liberal market economy. Yet insofar as it is possible to speak of a collective nineteenth-century political ideology, there were distinct limits on how far the courts were prepared to venture in accommodating the demands of a capitalist economy. Exceptionally, some members of the judiciary could even be witnessed openly deploying the common law in a patently obstructionist fashion. This was most notably true of the formidable Lord Eldon in his stand against unincorporated joint stock companies. In contrast, Lord Bramwell in the 1880s and 1890s openly espoused *laissez-fairism* across a range of matters.[302] On a broader front, the judicial revival of common law conspiracy along with interpretive attitudes were transparently deployed to thwart legislation designed to protect trade unions from criminal proceedings; an hostility capped at the turn of the century with the House of Lords' recognition of trade union civil liability in the *Taff Vale* judgment and other landmark decisions.

But more typically, the courts manifested a general resistance to drawing on non-legal concepts and factors in the production of judgments, and most especially a disinclination to act creatively in the cause of market efficiency.[303] This was

[302] e.g. Bramwell's doctrinal antipathy to strict and vicarious liability (*G.W.R.* v. *Bunch* (1888) 13 AC 48); undermining the objectives of the Employers' Liability Act 1880 by deployment of the *volenti* principle (*Membury* v. *G.W.R* (1889) 14 AC 179) and minority judgment in *Smith* v. *Baker and Sons* [1891] AC 325; explicit endorsement of the strong 'free trade' view (with Lords Halsbury and Watson) in *Mogul Steamship Co* v. *McGregor* [1892] AC 25; Bramwell's consistently *laissez-faire* approach to the construction and enforcement of contracts (e.g. *G.W.R.* v. *McCarthy* (1887) 12 AC 218).

[303] Generally, there is only very limited historical support for claims that nineteenth-century judicial decisions were focused on ensuring efficiency in the use of economic and social resources. Cf. e.g. R. Posner, *Economic Analysis of Law* (1st edn, 1972).

markedly true in the case of some property rights. Most basically, a free market economy requires clearly defined, easily enforced, and simply transferable property rights.[304] While arguably satisfied in respect of personal and some intangible property, large areas of other property rights failed to meet these criteria, especially the disposal of interests in land during the nineteenth century. At a theoretical level, this was a serious deficiency, in that classical political economists identified land and its system of ownership (along with capital and labour) as a key component of a commercial economy.[305] Devised to prevent the dissipation or fragmentation of landed wealth, strict settlements also constituted one of the primary legal mechanisms inhibiting the fullest or most effective economic exploitation of land. Yet in the early decades of the nineteenth century, the general view of the economic effects of land settlements was typified by Brougham's claim that the law 'hit…very happily the just medium between too great strictness and too great latitude, in the disposition of landed property'.[306] Neither was much judicial inclination shown to upset this claimed felicitous legal equilibrium. However, as one feature of the broader free trade campaign, from the 1840s claims that strict settlements inhibited the development and sale of land became the focus of broadening political agitation for land reform leading up to the liberalizing Settled Land Act 1882.[307] Even more radically, in the early 1870s, some, including Mill[308] and the Land Tenure Reform Association, scandalized mainstream contemporary opinion[309] by advocating special taxes on increased land

[304] On the particular question of the economic agency of women, see B. Griffin, 'Class, Gender and Liberalism in Parliament 1868–1882': The Case of the Married Women's Property Act' (2003) 48 *Hist. J.* 62.

[305] Including Malthus, Ricardo, McCulloch, and J. S. Mill. Reviewed by F. M. Thompson, 'Changing Perceptions of Land Tenures in Britain 1750–1914', in D. Winch and P. O'Brien (eds), *The Political Economy of British Historical Experience 1688–1914* (Oxford, 2002), 120. On improving the system of transferring interests in land, see XII, Pt 1.

[306] *PD* 1828 (s2) 18:181. A view given broad support a year later by the Real Property Commissioners. *First Report, PP* 1829 (263), x.

[307] A. Offer, *Property and Politics 1870–1914* (1981) and B. English, *Strict Settlement* (1983). Generally, on the nature of Victorian and early Edwardian developments of the strict settlement, see XII, Pt 1. Many economists, including Adam Smith, maintained that because of their lack of long-term personal interest, tenants for life under strict settlements were likely to neglect sound economic development of land: *Wealth of Nations*, Book 3. Prominent amongst other socially and economically driven land reforms of the period were the Settled Land Acts 1856–1864, allowing landowners to charge for improvements of land subject to settlements, and the Agricultural Holdings (England) Acts 1875 and 1883. The 'Farmers' Alliance' campaigning group succeeded with enactment of the 1883 legislation which awarded agricultural tenants the entitlement to compensation for certain forms of land improvements carried out during their tenancies.

[308] *Principles* (1871 edn), Book V, Ch. II, section 5.

[309] The Liberty and Property Defence League, set up in 1882 to counter the Association, and more extreme organizations (such as the English Restoration League, the Land Nationalisation Society and Land Reform Union) numbered Lord Bramwell as its inaugural president and one of

values. Partly this was sought in the cause of social and economic equity, but also in order to encourage a greater spread of land ownership and improved economic efficiency in its use. Within less than 40 years, as part of a socially redistributive fiscal policy, such proposals had gained legislative force.[310]

Aside from land, property rights relating to patented inventions and water were subject to less than benign neglect by the common law. In an age when technical innovation was forming a base for home-grown enterprise, some economists urged that those who developed novel machines and processes should have an exclusive right to exploit their idea for a limited period. Protection from imitation was needed to encourage investment in necessary research and development. While an old patent system existed under which the Crown granted such rights, the procedures for application long remained painfully cumbrous and remarkably expensive.[311] Even after the grant, a patentee could still face the challenge that his specification failed to reveal any sufficient invention; thus even the truly inventive would strive to disguise what they had discovered.[312] Before reform in 1852, a short-term system for protecting industrial designs against copying, even where the shape in question was technical, began to enjoy more frequent use than did invention patents. In the middle decades of the century, a group of severe free-marketeers tried to secure abolition of the patent system, such as it was. Though unsuccessful, divisions of opinion among economists, as well as manufacturers, meant that major businesses continued to develop without much reliance on the imperfect types of industrial property that Parliament, supported by the courts, had made available.[313]

A similar story of judicially unsupported enterprise can be seen in relation to water's exploitation. Though the social and economic importance of water

its most vociferous supporters. Generally, N. Soldon, 'Laissez Faire as Dogma: The Liberty and Property Defence League 1882–1914', in K. Brown (ed.), *Essays in Anti-Labour History* (1974), 24 and A. Ramasatry, 'The Parameters, Progressions and Paradoxes of Baron Bramwell' (1994) 38 *AJLH* 322. Also, *Laissez Faire* (1884) and *Economics versus Socialism* (1888) where Bramwell affirmed express allegiance to Smith, Ricardo, and McCulloch, and latterly Herbert Spencer. For his opposition to J. S. Mill's land and property views, see *The Times*, 16 February 1885. On Tort and Contract, see XII, Pts 2 and 4. For the distinct Christian Socialist involvement in land reform movements, see Norman, *The Victorian Christian Socialists*, Ch. 6.

[310] Thompson, *ibid*. Implemented by Asquith's administration under the Finance Act 1909; and see Churchill's view, above. Rather than for economic reasons, compulsory purchase powers to enhance public health were awarded to local authorities in 1875. For the ideological conflicts between Mill's differing views on social and economic intervention expressed in *Political Economy* and *On Liberty*, see G. Himmelfarb, *On Liberty and Liberalism* (New York, 1974), esp. Chs IV and V.

[311] Heavily satirized by Dickens' creation the 'Circumlocution Office' in *Little Dorrit*, first published in serial form (after the 1852 changes), between 1855 and 1857.

[312] See XIII, Pt 5. Cf. H. Dutton, *The Patent System and Inventive Activity during the Industrial Revolution* (Manchester, 1984) and C. MacLeod, *Inventing the Industrial Revolution* (Cambridge, 1988).

[313] See XIII, Pt 5.

rights hardly needed underscoring, as a consequence of conceptual rigidity, the common law courts displayed a singular reluctance to be seduced by extra-legal commercial or economic reasoning, and consequently the source of most legal developments was private or general legislation.[314] Finally, beyond particular examples of judicial responses to the apparent needs of developing various forms of property law, the treatment of railway capitalism—that exemplar of Victorian economic enterprise—offers one further significant illustration of the extent of the common law's doctrinal and conceptual insulation from the economic ambitions and activities of the period. Here, more than simply failing to facilitate expansion of the railway network, historical evidence compels the conclusion that the common law had a largely 'negative' effect on the development of railway capitalism.[315]

---

[314] J. Getzler, *A History of Water Rights* (Oxford, 2004), *passim*.

[315] Kostal, *Railway Capitalism, passim*. However, the arguably greater good of free market competition was served by the judicial insistence of breaking railway companies' rail freight monopolies.

VII

Empire's Law

1. COLONIES INTO EMPIRE

In considerable measure the spectacular wealth and power that would accrue to the British was built out of territorial acquisition and adventurous trading across the globe. British producers and merchants rode high in the colonies, and equally in foreign states in Europe, the Near East, and then further afield in Asia and Africa. We turn in this Chapter therefore to two countervailing forces: from one direction there was a diffusion of common law ideas as the British Empire grew in size and range; from the other, constraints upon common law systems from principles of international law became more perceptible. Both forces affected home-grown law in the nineteenth century as never before.

At the same time, these Volumes are part of a Series that traces the growth of English law in its homeland. Accordingly, no extended treatment is offered either of law within other parts of the UK, or the colonies to which 'English common law' was in one way or another transplanted. This Chapter aims to note how both the essential constitutional doctrines and the major rules of private law could fare in the process of adapting the common law to its novel environments; for, among other things, that suggests the extent to which *English* common law was dependent upon its own circumstances of time and socio-political development. Chapter VIII treats public international law with a focus upon the extent to which it was allowed to leech into municipal English law, as well as conditioning British conduct of foreign affairs. Chapter IX outlines the emergence of the conflict of laws, or private international law, as a distinct discipline within English municipal law—but one that cannot be severed from either the spread of common law in the Empire or the growth of public international law.

2. COLONIES AND EMPIRE

In its nineteenth-century apotheosis, the British Empire was hailed as a glory on which the sun would never set, bringing enlightened liberties and untold opportunities to its subject races.[1] Such claims were no novelty—empires turn

---

[1] Older histories used 'Empire' for the whole span, describing the period to American Independence as the 'first', or the 'old' Empire. In the post-colonial world, with its greater sensitivities about what

to such comfortable rhetoric once they are established.[2] Only the scale of the British domains set them apart. As was proudly (if impressionistically) trumpeted, Victoria's Empire extended perhaps to a quarter of the earth's territory and a quarter of its population.[3] True it was that throughout Victoria's reign, the places that by then had become leading British colonies were full of movements for local legislatures, as also for virtually complete separation. By 1867 the provinces of Canada would merge into a federation that was given dominion status; to be followed by Australia in 1901, New Zealand in 1907, and the Union of South Africa in 1909. In 1902, J. A. Hobson used the title, *Imperialism*, for a denunciation of late nineteenth-century colonialism as a ploy of capitalistic oligarchs—a deconstruction that would become the handbook of all those who strove to end European domination over their country.[4] In the case of Britain that would be the upshot in the course of little more than a half-century. In the wake of two world wars, a string of colonies and dependencies were breaking free, some after long-standing relationships (as above all in the case of India), many under much shorter tutelage of one form or another. Anti-colonial historians writing in the latter twentieth century would reveal the greed, harsh discipline, and oppression behind the beneficent show of British paternalism and aid towards self-realization that had expressed the faith of the imperialists.

Today we are left only with the shadowy British Commonwealth. As an entity the Commonwealth has no legal foundation.[5] Yet one of the continuing legacies of the whole Imperial adventure has been the transplantation of a legal and constitutional system to a whole range of states that continue to acknowledge this juridical birthright: a democratic legislature, an executive responsible to that legislature, a judiciary administering laws that apply to government as well as to natural persons and legal personalities. Inevitably these ideals of a rule of law have not survived where a powerful autocracy denies basic rights to its peoples. But even in the most malign cases, the common law inheritance remains

the British did and why they did it, 'Empire' tends to refer to the age of high governance by the Imperial state, the first signal being the Great Exhibition of 1851 in London, which Prince Albert generated for his adoring wife, Queen Victoria. Its full monstrance displayed the share-holding in the Suez Canal, purchased for the nation in 1874 by Benjamin Disraeli, who proceeded to secure for his widowed, captivated, Queen, the title 'Empress of India'. See e.g. E. Hobsbawm, *The Age of Empire, 1875–1914* (1987). The old usage still survives in recent general surveys, such as those referred to in n. 68 below.

[2] For comparisons of law in the Roman and other empires, James, Lord Bryce, historian of the Holy Roman Empire and for 30 years Regius Professor of Civil Law in Oxford, wrote with a perception that still deserves attention: *Essays on Jurisprudence and History* (1901) i: Lects 1, 2.

[3] For the spread of English Common Law, see B. H. McPherson, *The Reception of British Law Abroad* (Brisbane, 2007); and for the literature, see J. Dupont, *The Common Law Abroad* (Littleton CL, 2001).

[4] It led Lenin, for instance, to publish *Imperialism, the Highest Stage of Capitalism* (1916).

[5] R. R. Wilson, *International Law and Contemporary Commonwealth Issues* (1971), Ch. 1.

a standard for which the oppressed may at least yearn; and when political conditions become less intolerant, they may invoke it. One part of its continuing appeal is that it provides a cultural tie across countries that are to be found on or around every habitable continent.

British colonies became an Empire almost by osmosis. In the early modern period, England had been a somewhat delayed entrant into the business of colonization that grew with the Renaissance, notably across the Atlantic and around the Cape of Good Hope to alien lands with prospects of extraordinary riches. Her interests had been concentrated closer to home. Long conflicts had cut away her possessions in France; and she would see in the coalescence with Scotland and the subjection of Ireland—the latter a frustrating experience that would result in a *United* Kingdom for the British Isles only in 1800—a unity in constitutional terms, but a volatile confrontation in political reality.[6] Nonetheless from the reign of Elizabeth onwards, English mercantile adventures took off, swashbuckling voyagers were sent forth by London investors to the Levant, to Russia, to India; so also to North America, where trade mingled with wider communitarian ideals—and new settlements began to thrive.

These adventurers had looked to the British monarchs for protection, just as those monarchs watched for gains to their realms. Competition with the Spanish, Dutch, and French led in the eighteenth and early nineteenth centuries to the acquisition of more and more British colonies and dependencies, thanks in part to that naval dominance by which Britannia ruled the waves. But that period had also delivered the first immense lesson in the government of colonial societies. Thanks to their narrow, mercantilistic view of English interests, George III and his advisers had lost the American colonies, which thenceforth would evolve their own common law genome. Gradually thereafter, Canada, Australia, New Zealand, the Cape Colony, and other provinces of southern Africa would gain importance for a variety of reasons; and above all India would become the Koh-I-Noor in the Crown, dazzling from every facet in its richly varied cut.

In the reverses triggered by the American Declaration of Independence, liberals in Britain, following both Adam Smith and Edmund Burke, became notably sceptical about colonization, pointing to the high cost of colonial adventures and the grave uncertainties of any adequate return from them. But as the country became more deeply embroiled in the acquisition of Asian and African territories, the ideology of Empire evolved. British determination and high moral tone

---

[6] So far as concerned legal systems, also a unity for Ireland, as for Wales; but not for Scotland, which was brought into a joint Kingdom by the accession of James VI of Scotland to the English throne in 1603 (as James I), and was governed by a single Parliament at Westminster under the Treaty of Union 1707. For a comparison of developments in the three legal systems, see R. S. Tompson, *Islands of Law: A Legal History of the British Isles* (New York, 2000).

could alone provide the will and the means to convert decrepit, selfish, corrupt old societies into pillars of righteous government, where economic progress could flourish not just for British investors but for the colonial population in some wider sense. Many politicians and electors, judges and lawyers, churches and their flocks, generals and their armies, took up this national cry of support for the immense business of gaining and maintaining a hugely polygenic Empire. In this evolution of attitudes, many advanced liberals surrendered the scepticism of their intellectual forebears, succumbing to visions of the social improvement that might be wrought.[7]

The growing ideology of virtuous Imperial progress had roots in that alliance of religious sense of mission and economic calculation which we have already investigated. One element undoubtedly was the Evangelicalism within the established Church and other missionary bodies, which taught the need of conversion on earth to Godly beliefs and service as the key to salvation in the afterlife. The movement took as its first great social creed the abolition of slavery, not least in British shipping and colonies, but then also in the Americas, Africa, and elsewhere. Indeed, as the impact of the Christian religions began to wane, the incitement to rectitude transposed itself into secularized form, the moral force of Empire replacing that of the deity.[8] It found expression, inevitably, in the precepts, principles, and structures that made up its legal and administrative systems; but those institutions took consequential form, building upon the fact of a colonization rather than questioning its justification.

3. CONSTITUTIONAL STRUCTURES AND ADMINISTRATIONS

The Place of the Crown

It was only in the half-century from the 1860s that, across much of its Imperial territories, Britain directed government in a full, modern sense. In the eighteenth century, overseas affairs remained part of the personal prerogative of the monarch. The actual machinery for exerting legal control over British colonies

---

[7] For this shift of ideological beliefs in both British and French political thought, see J. Pitts, *A Turn to Empire: The Rise of Imperial Liberalism in Britain and France* (Princeton, 2005); D. S. A. Bell, 'Empire and International Relations in Victorian Political Thought' (2006) 49 *Hist J.* 281–98; and, in his edited volume, *Victorian Visions of Global Order* (Cambridge, 2007), the essays by C. Sylvest, 'The Foundations of Victorian International Law', Ch. 3 and K. Mantena, 'The Crisis of Liberal Imperialism' (Ch. 6); M. Craven, *The Decolonization of International Law* (Oxford, 2007).

[8] See e.g. E. Stokes, *The English Utilitarians and India* (1959), Ch. 4, tracing the attempts to structure government of the Indian territories by Bentham's principle of utility.

was small and limited. The Hanoverian kings had directed colonial affairs very largely through their Privy Council, a body with formal recognition within the structure of the British state.[9] Over time the Council would prove capable of expanding the central executive, for it might set up committees and offices for particular purposes in home affairs, such as public health and education. But, as already noted, by and large the necessities of an industrial economy at home and large territories abroad could not be managed within its confines. With the Prime Minister and his Cabinet conducting executive government at the growing centre, each Minister came to have his own department of officials, who were civil servants (as distinct from the military). And so there developed a Ministry which covered the Colonies, and separately a Board of Control for the East India Company.[10] After the Mutiny of 1857 the latter was superseded by a separate government department under a Secretary for India.

Throughout Victoria's reign, as Britain was evolving her own political institutions, with their curious, but reasonably stable linkages between legislature, executive, and judiciary, Parliament was beginning to grant equivalent institutions for her varied colonies. Those that were peaceable, and had a reasonably numerous population of Europeans, could expect government in their own community to move from a simple command structure under the Crown's governor to an appointed legislature, then a representative legislature and, finally, virtual independence as a dominion. By contrast, those with large local populations, or with dissidents ready to resort to violence or mass protest, could be governed only by direct authority with prominent military backing.

Source of Legal Authority in Colonies: The Conquered and the Settled[11]

The legal dogma justifying British authority in its colonies had become established by the early eighteenth century, fortified by concepts shared through the

---

[9] For Blackstone, the Privy Council was the principal institution of consultation at the disposal of the King; he did not see the Cabinet as even an informal body having any separate standing: *Comms* i, Ch. 5.

[10] The great civil servant of the Colonial Office was Sir James Stephen, father of Leslie Stephen, man of letters, and FitzJames Stephen, controversialist, codifier, and judge. Sir James held a prominent place in the relentlessly Evangelical Clapham Sect. Important officers of the India Board were James Mill, Bentham's acolyte and publicist, and his remarkable son, John Stuart Mill. The interconnections between Evangelicalism, Benthamite utility and colonial policy form an intricate web in the intellectual and functional history of Empire: Pitts, *Turn to Empire*, Ch. 5.

[11] Roberts-Wray, *Commonwealth and Colonial Law* (1966), 157–8; A. Berridale Keith, *The British Commonwealth of Nations: Its Territories and Constitutions* (1940); for the position in the various territories, see the 14 volumes in the Series (ed. G. W. Keeton and D. Lloyd, 1952–67), *The British Commonwealth: Development of its Laws and Constitutions*; A. C. Castles, *Introduction to Australian Legal History* (Melbourne, 1971); and 'The Reception and Status of English Law in Australia' (1962) 3

ius gentium of the European states. It started with a simple division. A colony would be treated as *conquered* where there was a native tribe, race, or prince, or a prior European occupant, which had been overcome by force or displaced by treaty.[12] These initiatory steps were essential activities of the British monarch acting under the royal prerogative.[13] If, on the other hand, any native tribes or peoples of the territory were 'primitive'—if, in particular, they had little by way of established agriculture—they could then, as a polity, be disregarded. The territory would be *settled*, rather than conquered. In that case, the post-1689 ascendancy of Parliament required a legislative enactment to be the kernel of legal authority.[14] These principles of acquisition applied, whether the essential impetus was a public concern (as with the penal settlement in New South Wales), or was a mercantile or other essentially private venture, backed by a Crown charter to form a British colony in trust.[15] Whichever the mode of acquisition, legal formalities rarely impeded the imperious drive to acquire new territories ahead of other European powers, or in displacement of them.

In settled lands, the English civilian population would arrive carrying with them their common law, with its much-vaunted liberties, together with such statute law of England as was suited to the circumstances of the colony. Here was the key to considerable adaptability. Blackstone had said that there would be 'very many and very great restrictions' on the rules and statutes that would apply in a colony; and he cited as unsuitable for transplantation 'the artificial

Adelaide LR 1; B. Kercher, *An Unruly Child: A History of Law in Australia* (Sydney, 1995), Part II; B. H. McPherson, *The Reception of English Law Abroad* (Brisbane, 2007).

[12] The notion of 'conquest' was initially wide, including all accessions other than those coming to the Crown by descent (as when James VI of Scotland became James I of England in 1603). It was after 1689, that the case of 'plantations by settlement' were distinguished, notably by Holt CJ in *Dutton v. Howell* (1693) Shower PC 24; and then in Privy Council Memorandum of 1722, *Case No. 15 Anon*, 2 Peere Wms 75.

[13] *Lyons v. East India Co* (1836) 1 Mod. PC 175; *Phillips v. Eyre* (1870) LR 6 QB 1. The elegant explanation espoused by the Privy Council in 1722 retained a feudal ring: 'the conqueror, by saving the lives of the people conquered, gains a right and property in such people': *Case No. 15 Anon.* (above, n. 12).

[14] Lands claimed by right of occupancy only by finding them 'desart and uncultivated'. From this stemmed a continuing determination to disregard claims of many kinds by the native peoples. For the most part it is only recently that legislatures and courts have come to regard the results as abrogating fundamental rights. This new theme is by no means confined only to settled colonies and plays an important part in any account of the adaptation of English laws to colonial conditions: see P. Karsten, *Between Law and Custom* (2002), esp. 49–118.

[15] When disputes arose over their application, there could be a major political battle in the offing: as when, in the reconciliatory steps in the aftermath of the Boer War, the Liberal Prime Minister, Campbell-Bannerman, restored local independence to the Transvaal. He was able to do so by Letters Patent without needing a statute. The Conservatives in the House of Lords would have obstructed the latter. It was this concession that laid the ground for the four South African territories to bring their country into its Union in 1909—altogether a fortuitous bit of legal footwork.

refinements and distinctions incident to property of a great and commercial people' and 'the laws of police and revenue', as well as other more specific matters.[16] It was relatively rare, however, for the issue to be forced to the point of litigation. Matters were more complicated in conquered territories where there was already a people with legal rights from a former regime. It was then vital to define the extent to which that system of law would continue in place for the existing locals and Europeans, as well as for newcomers. The matter had to be left to prerogative decision-making in the name of the English Crown. The British Empire was a thing of rapid formation, change, and decay. A single legal system arching over the whole dominion—after the manner of Rome—was never in prospect.[17]

At the next level down, there would be questions about which later English laws, notably those enacted by the Westminster Parliament, would apply in a colony. In the case of a settled colony, if Parliament dealt with the matter expressly, then well and good. Where, however, the issue was left as a matter of implication, then ultimately a court would have to determine whether Parliament must have intended its statute to apply in the colonies as part of the inherited English law. The essential question in either case was whether the rules were necessary for the 'peace, order and good government of the colony'. In relation to 'conquered lands', it was for the Crown to decide what law applied and to which groups.[18] In the Cape Colony and Ceylon (Sri Lanka) the inheritance of Roman-Dutch law was allowed to remain, gradually to be influenced by English notions and procedures.

In India all sorts of variations were permitted to the different parts of the country, one-third of which was governed through treaties with local rulers, who thereby accepted British protection and at the same time a measure of subjugation.[19] Until the East India Company gave its last executive roles to the British government itself, its commercial operations did much to shape the growth of courts that had a considerable degree of independence from interference and worked under a rule of law.[20] The three main areas for commerce involving the British

---

[16] *Comms*, i, 106–7. From the common law, it was likely that a colony would take its basic constitutional structure, legal status of constables, riot and other public order offences, homicide, rape, and theft; together with a very considerable range of civil law principles.

[17] See above, n. 2.

[18] The results could seem authoritarian and arbitrary to those who had to live with them. This prerogative would not be curbed until the Crown set up a local legislature and then only to the extent prescribed for it.

[19] See below, pp. 264–5.

[20] See generally, A. Gledhill, *India* in the Series, *The British Commonwealth: The Development of its Laws and Constitutions* (2nd edn, 1964), vol. v, Chs 1–4, 10; M. Rama Jois, *Legal and Constitutional History of India*, vol. ii (Bombay, 1984).

and other expatriates (Bombay, Calcutta, and Madras) acquired Presidential courts and applied the commercial and criminal laws of England to the extent that they were applicable to the country's conditions. To this the main exception was that Hindus and Muslims retained their personal laws (of inheritance, marriage, caste, religious usage, and institution). With typical pragmatism, in these territories the British set up *muffassal* courts to which Indians could resort, in part in order to allow them to retain their personal law. In these courts it was not English law in any form, but 'justice, equity and good conscience' that was to apply.[21] They proved to be popular because they were mostly quick and fair in comparison with surviving local institutions. As for the rest of the country, justice was first administered by Revenue Officers, but they tended to acquire a judicial officer and later, in important instances, a Chief Court. One British ideal for colonization was that native peoples should be persuaded by moral influence to adopt fairer forms of government and rights established by law, but not that they should be forced into an obedience that ran counter to their own religious and cultural morality. One lasting institution of British legal influence was therefore the extensive resort to codification, Benthamic in inspiration and eclectic in its borrowings.[22] Independence would finally come by virtue of Westminster's Indian Independence Act 1947, and with it the division into India and Pakistan, in the hope of diffusing religious tension. In the two countries, much of the inherited English Law and its codified variants would remain, being accepted for the degree of justice and certainty that it was thought capable of maintaining in countries with ever-growing populations that were capable of being fired by mutual grievances on a grand scale.

It remained a matter of prerogative that the Crown should determine whether a territory was settled or conquered.[23] The difference could be important in the earliest stages of setting up British rule—for instance over the establishment of courts and other legal institutions.[24] The enactment setting up a settled colony would in effect make the Crown's governor the local autocrat, fortified by the troops that he commanded. What alternative could there be, where, for instance, the object was to found a penal colony such as New South Wales at an immense

---

[21] See above, pp. 55–61.

[22] See, e.g. A. Gledhill, *The Republic of India: The Development of its Laws and Constitution* (1951), 154–6, 175–80, 192–6, 237–45.

[23] *Nabob of the Carnatic* v. *East India Co* (1792) 2 Ves. Jun. 56. Nice applications of the theory led to the North Island of New Zealand being classed as conquered (thanks to acknowledgment of the Treaty of Waitangi 1842, made with some of the northern Maori tribes), while the South Island was settled (though there were also Maori tribes there).

[24] It would lead into curious mazes: British statutes which formed part of the initial inheritance in a settled colony were operative under the general theory of the common law, and could therefore be amended by a colony's legislature. But statutes which, by statement or 'necessary intendment', were to apply to the colony concerned, were effective 'by paramount force' and could not be altered locally: per Willes J., *Phillips* v. *Eyre* (1870) LR 6 QB 1; Castles, *Introduction* (above), 115.

distance and in a pre-telegraphic age?[25] More pressing questions about the application of British legislation would present themselves. As already mentioned, it might be left for 'discovery' by a court whether British legislation was meant to apply to a colony. Once a local legislature was set up how far could that body repeal or amend an imperial statute that did apply there? Local legislation was not valid if it was repugnant to the applicable British law, and had not been specifically approved by submission to the Colonial Office for parliamentary approval.

These issues came to a head in the colony of South Australia, soon after it was granted a representative legislature. From 1859, Benjamin Boothby, an eccentric judge of the colony's Supreme Court, launched wholesale attacks on the legitimacy of important legislation being enacted by the colony's newly responsible Parliament. Insisting on the innate superiority of the English tradition, he struck down enactments creating local courts and a new type of land titles registration—the original version of the 'Torrens system'.[26] His conflicts with other judges on the court, whose very appointments he challenged, and with the local legislature, on a range of other matters, became so complicated that the very legal system was in substantial jeopardy.[27] The Colonial Office, when told what was going on, at first stonewalled. But soon enough it had to recognize that, once basic constitutional assumptions were challenged, anarchy threatened. It agreed with the South Australian government's proposal for an Imperial enactment and this became the Colonial Laws Validity Act 1865. It legitimated all colonial legislation, save that which was repugnant to Imperial statutes intended to have paramount force in the colony concerned.[28] In so doing it affirmed the ultimate supremacy of Westminster enactments; but at the same time it sapped Boothby's claims that local legislative, administrative, and judicial acts were subject to the tightest of Imperial constraints.[29]

In terms of basic constitutional structure, the pattern of thought permeated by the doctrine of parliamentary sovereignty was decisive. The granting of measures

[25] In that colony, after 30 years from its founding in 1788, the scope of the governor's power to legislate by proclamation began to be strenuously questioned. The prime issue, not surprisingly, concerned the levying of taxes. A local appointed legislature was then created in 1823 and the applicability of earlier British law was settled by the Australian Courts Act 1828 (9 Geo. IV c. 83), s 24: see Castles, *Introduction*, 118–26.

[26] For the disdain of this conveyancing system exhibited by most British commentators, see XII, pp. 215–16.

[27] For details of the imbroglio, see D. Pike 'Introduction of the Real Property Act in South Australia' (1961) 1 *Adelaide LR* 169; Castles, *Introduction*, 155–6; A. C. Castles and M. Harris, *Lawmakers and Wayward Wigs* (Adelaide, 1987); Kercher, *Unruly Child*, 97–102.

[28] Dicey gave a bland account of the Act's provisions, fitting it neatly into his structural view of the Imperial constitution: *Introduction to the Study of the Law of the Constitution* (1908 edn), 105–15.

[29] For his misbehaviour, Boothby would in the end be moved from office by the governor in council (under Burke's Act of 1782, 22 Geo. III c. 75, s 3).

of self-government to colonies led the Westminster Parliament into the writing of constitutions for legislative bodies, appointed or elected or both; for the setting up of executive institutions led by ministers who were also members of the legislature; and for an independent judiciary secured through rules on appointment, duration of office, and possible removal for sufficient cause. Even with the coming of federal dominion status—for Canada first, in 1867—the power structure would for decades remain pyramidal. The UK granted a subordinate governmental structure, rather than complete independence.[30] And on the judicial front, ultimate appeal in most cases lay to the Privy Council.[31]

At the next level of constitution-making, there would prove to be varied outcomes: were parliaments to be bicameral or unicameral? What were to be the procedures for election or appointment to them? If there was to be an Upper House, what function was it to perform? What mechanism would untie deadlocks between chambers? How were Prime Ministers and their cabinets, collectively and individually, to be made responsible to the legislature? What matters were the exclusive province of the courts? How were different jurisdictions to be defined? Who were to be judges and how could their independence be guaranteed? Experiments in constructing the details of democratic government went on partly at the stage when a written constitution was drawn up, but partly, as in the home country, in response to particular pressures. In 1893, New Zealand would concede the vote for its unicameral legislature to women—an influential precedent for other parts of the common law world.[32]

In large measure, the political conditions of the particular colony would determine the various upshots. For example, when Canada attained dominion status in 1867, the federal legislature took a bicameral form designed to accommodate a large European minority—the French in Quebec. Nonetheless, there would be grave disputes over the respective spheres of federal and provincial competence in matters of legislation. As we shall see, the Judicial Committee of the Privy Council, once established in 1833, would become the ultimate jurisdiction to which appeal could be made in such matters.[33] But that technique meant that the Australian High Court had to assume the burden instead—a form of political

---

[30] Typically, the movement towards cutting the bond of legal sovereignty took several decades, the Statute of Westminster 1931 drawing the line for the final severance.

[31] But this meant that the Judicial Committee entered the lists of controversy in any Federation where legislative power was divided between the centre and the provinces or states. Hence the exclusion of appeals on the fields of competence *inter se* provided in the Australian Constitution of 1900, s 74.

[32] Electoral Act 1893, passed by a large majority after considering bills on the subject for seven years: N. Atkinson, *Adventures in Democracy: A History of the Vote in New Zealand* (2003).

[33] The basis for Judicial Committee jurisdiction varied from one constitutional document to the next, with curious variations. In New South Wales at one stage (1828–50), the power to appeal was

exposure, but one that judges drawn from within the national community were probably better equipped to appreciate and therefore solve.

4. THE IMPERIAL INHERITANCE OF LAW

Judges and Other Adjudicators

However rough the idea of command from the Valhalla of Westminster might appear, it cemented in place the legal structure of common law inheritance. There it was at the outset in small communities of British immigrants, threatened by hostile native peoples, or by lack of food and shelter, but filling with adventurers hungry for land rights and the opportunity to build a life for themselves, or to make money out of having others do the hard labour. Historians recalling this process have been obliged, whatever their reluctance, to recognize the degree of loyalty, even reverence, which English law and legal process attracted in these new societies. If there were precedents in the English sources, and if no special circumstances rendered them otiose, they were applied with relief, and often with a sycophantic admiration.[34] The forming of these new societies, or the re-forming of government as the British took over from earlier colonial masters, was partly enlightened, but often also benighted. The Hobbesian strain in the human psyche had to be reckoned with, the true source of power loudly asserted and given effect—by force if necessary, but where possible by that more commodious surrogate, the law. Little wonder then that judges and magistrates were ready to rely on previous decisions, rather than branching out into uncharted territory of laws that they would construct to answer the cases before them.

The fraternities of colonial judges and lawyers disputed over this law and its application. Much therefore turned on their own background. At the outset, they came from England, or, to a lesser extent, from Ireland or Scotland. Most judges would have been admitted as barristers to one of the Inns of Court in London and would have practised before the courts of common law, equity, or (after 1857) the divorce and probate courts. The legal practitioners of a colony—barristers or solicitors in separate or fused professions—expected the exclusive rights of audience in court and in the conveyancing of land which had come to sustain

---

left out altogether, and had to be substituted by the Committee itself granting leave to appeal when it considered there was justification enough: Kercher, *Unruly Child*, 74.

[34] To an extent, reference was made in colonial courts to decisions from other common law jurisdictions and in the United States (the latter particularly in Canada, for obvious reasons). The sources were far from easy to obtain, so there appears to have been some informal network of information in place. As ever, it seems that those able to finance expensive litigation got best access. See Karsten, *Law and Custom*, 498–503.

their status and incomes at home.[35] Soon enough the colonies themselves began to provide their own practitioners (often the sons of the previous generation of lawyers). If they aspired to success and rank, it remained common enough through the nineteenth century to send them to London to read for the bar. That formed an important cement in the common law pyramid, but in time it would tend to crumble. Locals inculcated in London might react against the condescension and narrowness of British attitudes to colonies and their peoples. In cases such as Janakinath Bose and Mahatma Gandhi it would help to hone rhetorical skills and moral attitudes that would sharpen the cause of independence from the Empire.[36]

Colonial Legislation and Subordinate Hierarchies

Command theory exerted its greatest constraints as colonies in the Empire were given local legislatures by Imperial legislation. They would acquire representative government on the Westminster model. But there would be limitations on the subject-matter which they might cover or certain enactments would have first been approved by the Queen-in-(her Imperial)-Parliament. This meant, as a first control, that the Colonial Office in London would monitor what could be done; but ultimately, the matter could become an issue on which the courts could rule. In a system that had come to respect the independence of the judiciary, the separate structure of colonial courts had its own apex. In the case of the colonies, this had long been the Privy Council, but it was only in 1833 that a distinct Judicial Committee of the Council was set up to mark this division of basic function. Within English common law many factors militated against systematic structures for appeal to higher courts, and this is no more than a peripheral instance. The assumption was that there could be cohesion and certainty in the legal system of the Empire only if appeals could be referred up to a judicial body in London. As with appellate proceedings in England itself, procedural constraints and very significant costs discouraged much use of this ultimate resort to the keystone court. As a result the Judicial Committee of the Privy Council could function on an occasional basis.[37] Dealing with an increasing case-load was indeed something of

---

[35] See D. Duman, *The English and Colonial Bars in the Nineteenth Century* (1983), 122–5. He treats the change for the bar as occurring from the 1870s onwards.

[36] After the Mutiny in India, the 'Bengali Babu' of middle-class Indian lawyers became increasingly prominent politically, though their veneer of Englishness was derided by Europeans: Stokes, *Utilitarians and India*, 282–97, 304–5, 318–19.

[37] For those who constituted the Judicial Committee, see below, pp 558–62.

a conjuror's trick and its performance became more controversial as legal professions blossomed in the colonies.[38]

In particular, it became entangled in the politics of those parts of the Empire that were becoming federations. Federation occurred when there was the political will to press for it in the colonies themselves. But before and after the event, there was generally as much scepticism internally as there was enthusiasm—the French of Lower Canada continued to fear the English of Upper Canada; or in the Australian colonies, the preference for free trade in dominant New South Wales against the protectionism of weaker Victoria reflected differences in economic opportunity. A concern over foreign ambitions—the intentions of the United States as to the Western Canadian seaboard, or those of Germany towards New Guinea—might tip the colonies into demanding federation, but the consequent balance of powers between the linked units was likely to remain unsettled and from time to time to require litigation to resolve it. In Canada there were some indications in the British North America Act 1867 of an agreement to favour Federal power, but in the 1870s and 1880s the Judicial Committee, led by the Scots Lord of Appeal, Lord Watson, tended to favour the Provinces.[39] There would be later shifts of emphasis, largely depending on a single personality among the members of the Judicial Committee.[40] As the Committee became the arbiter between hostile groupings in the dominions and colonies, their judgments inescapably appeared to take political sides. The Canadian experience in the late nineteenth century was indeed so controversial that the Australian Constitution of 1900 forbade appeals to the Privy Council on issues relating to the distribution of legislative powers between Commonwealth and States.[41]

The details of the Judicial Committee's record into modern times we will deal with later.[42] In terms of lasting influence, two characteristics deserve to be picked out here: the first was the attachment of Imperial optimists to the Privy Council as a symbol of ultimate jurisdiction. The lawyers among them fostered a plan that the Committee should evolve into a truly Imperial Court of Appeal, which might

[38] Sometimes it became all too plain that the Committee took little interest in the issue before them, making mistakes over the facts, and dealing with the case in a brief space of time despite the immense business involved in bringing it to London.

[39] For the line of cases and the intensive debates about them, see D. B. Swinfen, *Imperial Appeal*, 45–9.

[40] Loreburn, Liberal Lord Chancellor, 1906–12, more evidently favoured the Federation, but Haldane LC, a successor, proved to be a disciple of Watson.

[41] The exclusion of *inter se* questions would generate controversial differences of view between Judicial Committee and High Court: for the history, see e.g. Kercher, *Unruly Child*, 171–4.

[42] Below, pp. 550–3; and see P. A. Howell, *The Judicial Committee of the Privy Council, 1833–1876* (1979); Swinfen, *Imperial Appeal* (1987).

have representatives of the Dominions sitting upon it regularly.[43] There was even a prospect that it might become a roving court for the Empire—as was, for instance, the High Court of Australia for its continent. The idea lost whatever attraction it had, as Empire faded into Commonwealth. The second, altogether more elegiac in tone, clung to the existing idea of a judicial hierarchy of norms, with the Committee as the Imperial keystone, its decisions binding, under the concept of *stare decisis*, on all jurisdictions from which an appeal lay to it, while remaining of only persuasive authority for courts in the separate UK pyramid. Empire and Commonwealth countries might therefore feel both old loyalties and political conveniences in having a remote tribunal in London to settle difficult issues from afar.[44] They might well preserve this last vestige of the commands of the Imperial centre long after the legislative and executive cords had been severed. [45]

5. THE COMMON LAW IN RESOLVING DISPUTES

Law in Colonial Courts

The second point at which English law is refracted by the legal history of the varied parts of Empire concerns the adaptation, first of substantive and procedural rules themselves, and secondly of the way in which they were applied in practice. Here major strides have been made by historians working on court records and sources such as legal texts in the settled colonies where the community (or at least its upper stratum) was British by descent. A leading part in the work has occurred in the United States, where the sources were at first ransacked for evidence of capitalist promotion, in the form of the 'instrumentalist' theory used in denunciatory fashion by Morton Horwitz and other critical legal scholars; or for evidence that the law, sometimes despite its internal rationalisations, fulfilled goals of economic efficiency—an approach dear to writers of the Coase-cum-Posner school.[46]

---

[43] For Lord Brougham, instigator of the Judicial Committee, this carried the prospect that appeals from various jurisdictions in Britain itself would also lie to this court, rather than the House of Lords: see below, pp. 547–8.

[44] There were, however, many tensions about this. Canada early obtained an exemption from appeals in criminal cases, whereas some countries of the 'new' Commonwealth would much later hold on to Privy Council appeals precisely to deal with imposition of the death penalty.

[45] New Zealand, for instance, would give up appeals to the Privy Council only in 2004, even though, as a self-governing dominion, she had power to effect the abolition under the Statute of Westminster 1931 (as to which see *Moore* v. *Irish Free State* [1935] AC 484; Swinfen, *Imperial Appeal*, Ch. 5).

[46] For a sceptical view of both opposed schools, stemming from their use of nineteenth-century case-law, see A.W.B. Simpson 'The Horwitz Thesis and the History of Contracts' (1979) 46 *U. Chicago LR* 533–601; and '*Coase* v. *Pigon* Re-examined' (1996) 25 *JLS* 53–97, with Addendum 99–101.

The materials were then worked more carefully and fully to justify less committed conclusions than those of either of the confrontational schools. This has been replicated in similar investigations across jurisdictions in Canada, Australia, and New Zealand. Peter Karsten has offered an impressive summation of the case law evidence, in which he argues, first from a mainly US perspective, and then from British colonial materials, for an anti-instrumentalist interpretation.[47] From his own detailed investigations and those of others, he claims that within many of these territories, across the nineteenth century, those who dispensed justice—judges, jurymen, justices, arbitrators—did not force outcomes of rigid, cost-cutting efficiency on the disputants before them, but were prone to sympathetic attitudes towards the less fortunate or the less dominant—to tenants who sought compensation for their improvements or title to cut timber, to debtors who could not meet the strict terms of their obligations, to the victims of accidents over which they had no control, to workers whose contracts of employment for some reason ended before due time.

At various junctures in our Volumes the riches on display in such work and the colonial history on which they are built is touched upon. They concentrate attention particularly on questions of land rights, arising from geographical differences and from the need to reduce virgin lands to pasture and arable field and to handle relations between absentee landowners and local farmers and builders. Equally they concern the extent to which the British arrivals imposed their selfish regimes of land ownership, overriding the cultural understandings of native peoples.[48] When it came to transactions in general, there were many signs of severity in the contract law which evolved progressively in England to meet the needs of 'the workshop of the world', and by extension its splay of colonies. This sanctity of contract was at its height in the great age of Imperialism, when the superior courts of England and Wales were drawn together into a single judicial hierarchy and the common law judges could constrain the moral relativism of equity and its advocates.[49]

Land Rights in Colonies

In the home country since Tudor times, advocacy of 'improvement' in place of 'waste' had sustained the movement towards enclosure and re-allocation of interests in land. Sophisticated legal institutions (freehold interests, copyhold, leases,

---

[47] P. Karsten, *Heart versus Head: Judge-made Law in Nineteenth-Century America* (1997); and *Between Law and Custom* (2002).

[48] P. McHugh, *Aboriginal Societies and the Common Law* (Oxford, 2004) provides a fine-grained set of comparisons.

[49] W. R. Cornish and G. de N Clark, *Law and Society in England, 1750–1950* (1989), 200–26.

mortgages, and other charges) sustained beliefs about the crucial importance of private property, so essential to John Locke's concept of a labour theory of value and later to Adam Smith's vision of economic growth stemming from the individual's willingness to increase his economic activity if he could be assured that the results of his activities would be treated as private goods. In colonies only colonizing powers could bring about the division of labour and its exercise on a sufficient scale to achieve economic and social progress. Hence native populations were increasingly treated as incapable of deserving land rights, and the doctrine of *res nullius*, so infuriating to modern critics, was put in place in order to deprive them of more than passing interests.[50] By the 1830s and 1840s much notice was being taken of the optimistic calculations of Edward Gibbon Wakefield, tireless proselytizer of free enterprise colonization, in which the terms for the initial sale of land set the social balance between capitalists and labourers in new agricultural economies.[51]

It was part of this process in England that unchanging traditional rules and practices in agricultural production were being replaced by specific contractual terms set as negotiated obligations between the parties involved. From that shift in understanding flowed many consequences, but none more crucial than the question of what disciplines for due and complete performance could be built into the terms of leases, production contracts, sales of commodities, and so into the law touching their enforcement. They had a considerable history: from the practice of imprisoning debtors, both *in terrorem* and after judgment; through the use of the conditional bond to ensure the promised performance; to equity's willingness to upset penalty clauses.[52] In the nineteenth century, as contracting became more diverse and sometimes more informal, rules which distinguished 'entire' from 'apportionable' contracts became more prominent. There was certainly some tendency in English judgments to attach minatory consequences to contracts that were entire: if, for instance, a builder, a supplier of goods, or a worker, did not complete the whole performance but only part of it, he could claim no portion of the agreed sum for the work, the goods or the service. In its strictest applications this rule was applied even when the claimant could not be blamed (as where he died or was

---

[50] P. G. McHugh, *Aboriginal Societies and the Common Law: A History of Sovereignty, Status and Self-Determination* (Oxford, 2004), Chs 3, 4; J. McLaren, A. R. Buck and N. F. Wright (eds), *Land and Freedom: Law, Property Rights and the British Diaspora* (Dartmouth, 2001); and their edited vol., *Despotic Dominion: Property Rights in British Settler Societies* (Vancouver, 2004), esp. their initial essay, 'Property Rights in the Colonial Imagination and Experience', 1–22.

[51] P. Karsten, ' "They seem to Argue that Custom has made a Higher Law": Formal and Informal Law on the Frontier' in Buck *et al., Land and Freedom*, 63–82.

[52] There is here a complex pattern of laws which form the background of judgments about just how exhortatory the modern law of contract was becoming. It also involves an appreciation of the developing law of insolvency, bankruptcy of traders, and limitation of liability.

injured[53]) or where he had performed the great bulk of what he had undertaken. And it applied not only where the claimant was clearly at fault in breaking off the contract, but also where there had been an argument over which of the two sides could be blamed (so that, in respect of service, the real issue might be about whether a dismissal was wrongful; or it might be about whether strike action by workers was lawful, and so did not attract sanctions under Master and Servant laws and their later replacements).[54]

In Karsten's material, there is evidence, both in the United States and the settled British colonies, that judges were averse to applying entire contract rules mechanically. From streams of cases dealing, for example, with nautical work, agricultural labour, building work and supplies and so on, he shows that these courts did not side with the master, the purchaser, or the commissioner as a matter of course, in order to buttress contract discipline. Rather, they sought to use the basic rules so that, after taking account of the facts and their background, the result would favour the side that weighed more in the moral balance.[55] Included within this 'equitable' approach were cases where in effect employers lost because they sought the full rigour of the law for quite minor defiance or default. Karsten's case is that in relatively remote communities, where the demands of industrial production as yet had nothing like the same impact as in England, a good measure of communal understanding prevailed which caused some relaxing of severely individualistic legal doctrines in this sphere.[56]

This material related to the situation in settled colonies. Where conquest led to common law/civilian divergences, notably in Quebec and in Ceylon and South Africa, the situation was necessarily more complex. Towering above all there is the case of India. There the first question must be what is to be made, given its geographical, economic, and cultural divergences, of the great movement to codify—to provide not just constitutional statutes from Westminster but also to empower the making of codes of civil and criminal law and of civil and criminal procedure. Much

[53] A classic formulation of the entire contract doctrine was built around understandings of *Cutter* v. *Powell* (1795) 6 T.R. 320. The case itself concerned a seaman who was held to have contracted for the full journey from Jamaica to London for a sum much above the going rate. When he died en route, his estate was unable to claim a *quantum meruit* for the work completed. But the bargain was easily characterized as 'entire' from its special nature and could have been treated as out of the ordinary. Instead, such was its psychological appeal that it was generalized and taken as the norm: see below, XIII, Pt 2, pp. 645–6.

[54] For questions over what strikes could be regarded as justifiable from 1871 onwards, see XIII, pp. 673–9.

[55] Within common law systems, use of the jury to decide cases at trial provided considerable outlet for communal sympathies, wherever the trial took place. It is striking in Karsten's material how far appellate courts were ready to intervene in setting to rights what they thought were unjustifiably harsh verdicts of juries.

[56] Likewise, for issues over compensation for personal injuries negligently caused, notably at work: see below, XII, Pt 4, 1002–12.

of this was achieved between 1859 and 1872, when the Indian Contracts Act was passed.[57] Leading theorists and rhetoricians took part in drafting the Indian Codes, many of them claiming some adherence to Utilitarianism. Some therefore were modernizers of Bentham's own kind, ready enough to impose British solutions on the whole populace, country as well as city, in all but deeply personal matters such as family and inheritance where Muslim and Hindu law had to persist. Others, notably those with long experience of Indian conditions, were alive to the grip of custom, to the remoteness of village life from that of cold, darkly industrialized Britain and to the growing resentment of greedy British planters and merchants.[58]

In formulating the Contracts Act, for instance, there were sharp differences of opinion over legal discipline in connection with the sanctions that peasant farmers would face if they failed to honour contracts for producing indigo for European 'factory' planters. The terms were often in practice ruinous and the whole business close to slavery, backed as it had been with criminal penalties for breach.[59] These were to go, but what should replace them? Should there be orders of specific performance? Or an entire contract rule, subject only to very limited variation? Or enforcement of penal bonds if they had been given? On the other hand, should the fact of a hard bargain avoid the contract on the assumption that it must have been obtained by threats or undue influence? These were issues of great immediacy to farming and trade in British India. They were resolved in the end much in line with common law principles, but not before confrontations and stand-offs between the grand old Commissioners drafting the Contracts Bill in London and the Governor-General's Council (with Maine, and then Stephen, as its Law Member) in Calcutta. It was an episode that seriously strained the bonds of Imperial supremacy.[60]

6. ENGLISH PERCEPTIONS OF COLONIAL DEVELOPMENTS

What did the extension of English ideas of a legal system to a range of countries mean for the development of English law itself? Only to a very limited extent were reformist ideas tested in a colony and then used as a model in arguments

[57] The Codes included the Penal Code and the Criminal and Civil Procedure Codes (1859–61); the Succession Act (1865); and the Indian Contract and Evidence Acts (1872).

[58] For an exploration of the understandings by which the British managed the relations between English law and local customary law, see M. B. Hooker, *Legal Pluralism* (1975); L. Benton, *Law and Colonial Cultures: Legal Regimes in World History, 1400–1900* (Cambridge, 2002). For comparisons within England itself, see H. W. Arthurs, '*"Without the Law": Administrative Justice and Legal Pluralism in Nineteenth-Century England*' (Toronto, 1985).

[59] See A. and B. Rao, *The Blue Devil: Indigo and Colonial Bengal* (Delhi, 1992).

[60] Whitley Stokes, *Anglo-Indian Codes* (1887), i, 534; Atul Chandra Patra, 'Historical Background of the Indian Contract Act 1872' (1962) 4 *J. Indian L. Inst.* 373, 393–9.

in Parliament or the courts in the heart of Empire: electoral rights for women, protection of relatives from the worst aspects of complete freedom to leave one's property on death as one chooses, systems of compulsory arbitration in labour disputes.[61] But just as often, novel policies introduced into colonies were rejected or ignored at home. Much of the Antipodes and North America gained Torrens systems for registering land titles, dedicated to indefeasible title and built around a register open to the public. But to the landowners of England publicity of the extent of landed domains would reveal an utterly private knowledge, which alone, so owners felt, kept a greedy or an increasingly egalitarian state from increasing taxation or taking up the popular cry for land nationalization.[62] At the same time many lawyers had their own interest in continuing their private conveyancing practices. Conveniently they could denounce indefeasibility of title, a central precept of the Torrens approach, as an abnegation of the authority of the judges.

At a fundamental level also, the introduction of federal structures, with their divisions of power between the national legislature and those of the provinces, could appear to undermine the unitary structure of the UK. In Canada or Australia, federal constitutions could be conferred which still preserved the notion of Imperial sovereignty since the divisions of power were at a secondary level. But what were the implications for the place of Ireland within the UK itself? To Dicey, parliamentary supremacy required that Westminster should not devolve part of its powers to an Irish Parliament so as to divide sovereignty between two bodies. Liberal radicals pressed the case for Irish Home Rule on just this basis, and split their Party on the question. But a wall of conservative opinion stood against it and for this Dicey provided a constitutional theory which he put with increasing shrillness.[63] In the late Victorian age, the positivist inculcation of law as command became fired with political immediacy. It smouldered with other increasing discontents facing the British electorate, such as those between the House of Commons and House of Lords, and those stemming from labour and Irish representation in the Commons. These were arguments that rang through the age of high Empire for the British, where parliamentary sovereignty was widely viewed at home as a towering perfection.

<hr />

[61] J. Finn, '"Should We not Profit from such Experiments when We Could?" Australasian Legislative Precedents in British Parliamentary History' (2007) 28 *JLH* 31–56.

[62] Hence the fear that a titles register would provide a source of public information about landholding: cf. above, n. 26.

[63] Observable at once in the titles of his tracts, *England's Case against Home Rule* (2nd edn, 1886); *A Leap in the Dark* (1893); *A Fool's Paradise* (1913). Each denounced a new Home Rule Bill and found plentiful targets in the detailed proposals, which tended to embody contorted compromises: see R. A. Cosgrove, *The Rule of Law: Albert Venn Dicey, Victorian Jurist* (Chapel Hill, 1980), Chs 6, 7, 10; T. H. Ford, *Albert Venn Dicey: The Man and his Times* (1986), Chs 8–10, 12.

To those who held real power in Britain the outworks of the Empire remained secondary, even subjugate. Colonies might prove themselves worthy of increasing degrees of political independence but they were scarcely societies from which the British should learn. This was as true of English judges as it was of Cabinet ministers and Governor-Generals.[64] A tone of ineffable patronage filled the speeches of Lord Chancellors and Law Lords as they received colonial judges in London or steamed forth themselves on Imperial tours.[65] It was an echoing, in talk among lawyers, of the general rhetoric used by enthusiasts of Empire and it took on the inspirational glow that is so characteristic of the Edwardian moment. The urge to promote moral improvement had grown with the spread and strength of British domains and a Blackstonian admiration of the common law was a strongly shared belief.

Upper and middle-class Britons considered it not just their privilege but their duty to provide their own institutions and opportunities to the peoples under their tutelage. But there were many opinions about the true path to that high end. At one pole—that of radical liberals—was a stream of opinion showing genuine sympathy for the democratic cause. The colonial peoples should be raised to a level of education and moral decency that would allow for self-governance and an end to any dependent relationship with the Mother Country. At the other pole—that of unbending conservatives—lay a belief in an innate superiority of the British character that could not be transmitted to lesser stock. To attempt to do so would be fundamentally unsettling. Relations with the educated locals should therefore remain strictly at arms length as part of necessary discipline and legal constraints. This was the version of Imperialism that roused such fervour in Britain as the country celebrated Victoria's Diamond Jubilee in 1897 and two years later found itself locked in a South African War against Boer intransigence. Likewise it infected government in India, reaching its zenith under the Viceroyship of Lord Curzon (1898–1906).[66]

The legal structures of English public and private law were embedded to a depth that could support either of these political forces. Soon enough the liberal vision would come to dominate: independence would be granted by the Westminster Parliament, entrusting the populations of the different states with their own political futures, either alone or in federations. Their ability to live up

---

[64] So far as legislative proposals were concerned, see Finn, 'Precedents'.

[65] For what they tended to say, cf. Lord Rodger of Earlsferry, 'Thinking about Scots Law' (1996) 1 *Edinburgh Law Rev.* 3–24 at 19–23.

[66] Neatly pinned down in the squib:
'My name is George Nathaniel Curzon;
I'm a most superior person,
My cheek is pink, my hair is sleek,
I dine at Blenheim once a week.'

to the basic standards of functioning democracies has proved regrettably vari-able and in some the types of legislative institutions with which they started have been abolished or hideously transfigured. Yet all those parts of the Empire that acquired a common law system retain the language and conceptual relationships of that system and with this the ideals from which resistance to tyranny and the suppression of the fundamental rights of individuals can with time be re-bred. That has to be counted as one of the lasting values of that global encirclement of power which the world had not previously experienced and will probably not again, at least in that form.[67]

Recent historians of the British Empire have not lingered long over the details of legal structure which the British transferred.[68] Yet the great American histo-rian of industrialization, David Landes, lists the *desiderata* for a developing state to bring about lasting economic growth: secure rights of private property; secure rights of personal liberty; enforcement of contracts, explicit or implicit; stable government under known rules; responsive government that hears complaint and makes redress; honest government in which economic actors are not motivated to secure advantage or privilege inside or outside the marketplace; moderate, effi-cient, ungreedy government, holding taxes down, reducing government's claim upon social surplus, while avoiding privilege.[69] These were conditions which eighteenth-century Britain had in greater measure than elsewhere in Europe and which enabled it to build towards its remarkable technological changes and com-mercial and financial success of the mid-nineteenth century. In this course the expansion of colonies became a crucial element. The management of these heter-ogenous societies fell well short of perfection, for the self-interest of the colonists was a driving force that was often enough less than benign. Nonetheless a striv-ing for these fundamental elements of civil society, embodied in the legal system, was passed to these peoples as they became independent states. The history of the English common law in the British Empire remains a factor that has yet to be sufficiently acknowledged by those who look at the adventure as a phenomenon in the round.

[67] Thereby, perhaps, the British came to satisfy Adam Smith's support for the American colonies in 1776: 'To found a great empire for the sole purpose of raising up a people of customers, may at first sight appear a project fit only for a nation of shopkeepers. It is, however, a project altogether unfit for a nation of shopkeepers; but extremely fit for a nation whose government is influenced by shopkeepers. Such statesmen, and such statesmen only, are capable of fancying that they will find some advantage in employing the blood and treasure of their fellow-citizens to found and maintain such an empire' (*Wealth of Nations*, ii, iv 7 iii).

[68] See e.g. L. James, *The Rise and fall of the British Empire* (1991); T. O. Lloyd, *Empire: The History of the British Empire* (2001); N. Ferguson, *Empire: How Britain Made the Modern World* (2003).

[69] D. S. Landes, *The Wealth and Poverty of Nations: Why Some are so Rich and Some so Poor* (1998), 217–23.

VIII

International Law

1. A 'POSITIVE' INTERNATIONAL LAW AND ITS OPPONENTS[1]

For centuries before 1820, those for whom social existence must needs be something other than the ruthless pursuit of power and fortune, had searched for a legal order above that of the selfish interests of rulers or communities. Their dream was of a system of obligation that would condition foreign relations by principles rather than by mere political expedience coupled with armed aggression. As modern states evolved from tribes, kingdoms and cities, this aspiration had found expression in the natural law tradition of Western Christendom, bred in part from Roman law example but more from medieval notions of governance by God's anointed on earth. The Church's scholars taught that resort to war required

---

[1] See, in general, A. Nussbaum, *Concise History of the Law of Nations* (1954); J. H. W. Verzijl, *International Law in Historical Perspective*, 11 vols (1968); W. Grewe, *Epochs of International Law* (Baden, 1983, trans. M. Byers, Berlin, 2000); H.-U. Scupin, 'History of the Law of Nations, 1815–World War I' (1984) *Encyclopedia of Public Int. Law*, ii, 767; A. Cassese, *International Law* (Oxford, 2001); S. C. Neff, 'A Short History of International Law', in M. D. Evans (ed.), *International Law* (2nd edn, Oxford, 2006), Ch. 2.

For English perspectives, see H. Lauterpacht and R. Y. Jennings, 'International Law and Colonial Questions, 1870–1914', in E. A. Benians et al. (eds), *Cambridge History of the British Empire* (1959), iii: 667–710; D. H. N. Johnson, 'The English Tradition in International Law' (1962) 11 *ICLQ* 416–45; C. Sylvest, 'International Law in Nineteenth-Century Britain' (2004) 75 *BYIL* 1–69; J. R. Crawford, 'Public International Law in Twentieth-century England', in R. Zimmermann and J. Beatson, *Jurists Uprooted* (Oxford, 2004), 681–707 (with list of nineteenth-century English Treatises); M. Lobban, 'English Approaches to International Law', in M. Craven et al. (eds), *Time, History and International Law* (Leiden, 2007), 65–90.

For reflections, see R. Higgins, 'Time and the Law: International Perspectives on an Old Problem' (1997) 46 *ICLQ* 501–20; P. Allott 'International Law and the Idea of History' (1999) *J. Hist. Int. Law* 1–22; I. J. Hueck 'The Discipline of the History of International Law' (2001) 3 *J. Hist. Int. Law* 194–217; M. Craven, 'International Law and its Histories' and R. Lesaffer 'International Law and its History: The Story of an Unrequited Love', both in M. Craven et al. (eds), *Time, History*, 1–26, 27–42; also Craven's *The Decolonisation of International Law* (Oxford, 2007).

And see P. Macalister-Smith and J. Schwietzke, 'Bibliography of the Textbooks and Comprehensive Treatises on Positive International Law of the 19th Century' (1999) 1 *J. Hist. Int. Law* 136–212.

divine sanction and princes might look for Papal approval of their intentions. That was unlikely to be withheld when it came to crusades against infidels.

The ultimate hope for international law has long been that it can help to avert war and other belligerence between nations.[2] But the idealistic view of St Augustine and St Thomas Aquinas that wars were legal only if justifiable in the eyes of the deity began to lose place in favour of more complex rationalizations which could take account of situations where each side proclaimed the justice of its cause and the outcome of battles was taken as the test of who was ultimately right. To achieve this Hugo Grotius had distinguished from natural law (*ius naturale*) a secondary law of nations (*ius gentium*). And so, as this law of nations drew increasingly into line with the political objectives of nation states, war was held to be instituted when one sovereign declared it against another, legal doctrine providing no supervailing measure of its rightness or wrongness. The most that international law could aim for was to regulate relations between the belligerents themselves and in relation to neutral states. Its principles would, for instance, cover declarations of war by sovereigns, bombardments and sieges of towns, blockades of ports, seizure of ships and their cargo, reprisals, impressments of soldiers and sailors, forced deployment of captured enemy and even the treatment of prisoners.

As Stephen Neff suggests, eighteenth-century assertions about the basis of international law drew inspiration from obverse intellectual traditions. Hobbesian theorists justified the need for sovereign power within a state as a protection against the destructive belligerence of humans so long as they were left in a raw state of nature. From this it followed that each sovereign power must decide for itself when and how war had to be waged. Social contractarians, in contrast, saw war as an honorific duel between competing states in which each agreed in advance to accept victory in battle as deciding the contention between them. During the course of hostilities there was taken to be agreement to observe the *ius gentium*.[3] In the nineteenth century, as war or the threat of hostilities became a recurrent condition in international relations, expositions of international law would treat war and peace as primary distinctions. Much of the conduct of war operates at the most evidently political pole of what can be treated as 'law'. Thus it has something of the character that constitutional conventions assume in the internal operations of a nation state. But whereas in a democracy these conventions operate under the ultimate power of the enfranchised voters to bring governments to heel through the electoral process, international relations in the

---

[2] W. O. Manning's early contribution to the English literature, *Commentaries on the Law of Nations* (1839) is largely concerned with the laws of war from a Christian perspective: see Sylvest, 'Nineteenth Century', 24–5.

[3] *War and the Law of Nations* (Cambridge, 2005), Part 2.

nineteenth century lacked any supervailing authority of an equivalent kind, save where common principles, such as those of the Europe-wide *lex mercatoria*, were accepted in national courts as the governing law of a state.[4]

For most, the answers drew upon positivistic tendencies already apparent in Continental treatises in the eighteenth century. In them the *ius gentium* had begun to shed its 'naturalistic' inheritance, since sovereign states by their very definition owed no pre-existing obligations over their conduct. Nevertheless those states could be expected to adhere to the requirements of international law by their consent, either expressed in their treaties, or implied from their membership of the European family of 'gentlemanly states'. The Swiss, Emerich de Vattel, writing in the age of Blackstone, had placed novel emphasis both on the defining principle of liberty and on the actual practice of states as the source of obligation.[5] The empiricist implications of his writing would be picked over by scholars across Europe.[6] Mansfield and Blackstone were pointing in the same direction when they called for evidence that a rule of the *ius gentium* had entered English law—through Act of Parliament, judicial precedent, or some undeniable acceptance in British practice.[7] If taken seriously, this was an approach with a double entrenchment of the declaratory theory of precedent. For how could there be initial recognition of any unprecedented rule of international law, save by explicit treaty? As we shall see, a century later the severest among the common law judges began to treat principles of international law in this vein.[8]

'Positivism' characterized the movement in political philosophy away from religious and other moral preconception in favour of proof by scientific observation of natural phenomena, including human behaviour. The term would gain currency in the nineteenth century from the writings of Auguste Comte, social philosopher of France in its post-Revolutionary phase. Comte developed a theory of human societies as evolving from an initial condition of blind subservience to theocratic dictates, through a 'metaphysical' stage when leading thinkers questioned the inherited assumptions of their people by reference to such ideals as the Rights of Man, to a third, ultimate condition in which government occurred through application of purely scientific method, a stage which he labelled

---

[4] Thus in England, the Court of Admiralty found much of its law in these shared customs of mercantile sea trade, recognized within the *ius gentium*: see below, p. 262.

[5] *Droit des gens, ou principes du droit naturel* (1758, first English edn, 1760).

[6] De Vattel's successors included rational systematizers such as G. F. von Martens and Klüber: for whom see Koskenniemi, *The Gentle Civiliser of Nations: The Rise and Fall of International Law, 1870–1960* (Cambridge, 2001), 19–24.

[7] *Triquet v. Bath* (1764) 3 Burr. 1478, following Talbot LC in *Barbuit's Case* (1737) Cas. T. Talb. 281. Mansfield was counsel in the earlier case, as was Blackstone in *Triquet*; hence its appearance in the *Comms*, iv, Ch. 5.

[8] See below, pp. 272–6.

'positivist'. The quest for evidence of what should count as international law that had begun with de Vattel could claim to be an important step towards such positivist policy-making and became the matrix of much theorizing of the subject. It explained, and so justified, the government of an established state, together with its dependencies, by insisting that the foundation of its law lay in the existence of institutions conferring constitutional sovereignty. Equally, it could epitomize those elements in the relationships between independent states which by their mutual consent amounted to 'law'.

Eighteenth-century England had contributed very little to the European search for a rationalization of the law of nations. As the country grew towards its industrial and commercial dominance during Victoria's reign, however, it would impress upon conceptions of the law of nations, or the law between nations, a set of standards that were ever more determined by positivistic tenets.[9] The first of these confined international law strictly to relations between sovereign states.[10] The British were drawn to treat the growing pyramid of Empire as a structure to which international legal obligations could attach only at its summit.[11] So, while British contributions to international law thinking would become more significant, they would be primarily at a pragmatic level, finding sources in the results of diplomatic practice, the treaties that flowed from that activity, and to some extent the precedents set by litigation in national courts and arbitrations organized by the voluntary submission of states.[12] The work provided additions to the corpus of inherited doctrine in a century when ideas for legislative, executive, or judicial institutions operating at an international level were still largely a prospect for the future. Compared with today, there was much about this Victorian international law that gave it an air of sanguine experiment.

In his unending search for utilitarian solutions that improved social organization through legislation, Jeremy Bentham had proposed the re-titling of the *ius gentium* so as to characterize it as a foundation for relations between nations— *ius* inter *gentes*.[13] It was largely left to his disciple, John Austin, to spell out the

---

[9] Grewe, *Epochs*, sought to credit England as the dominant force in the subject for the period 1815–1914. But the typology is inherently over-simple and in this case unlikely, given the depth of discussion from around the 'civilized' world: see Koskenniemi, *Gentle Civiliser*, 6–7.

[10] See below, p. 264 *et seq.*

[11] Koskenniemi, *Gentle Civilizer*, esp. Ch. 2; A. Anghie, *Imperialism, Sovereignty and the Making of International Law* (Cambridge, 2004), Ch. 2; and note the works cited in Ch. VII n. 7 above.

[12] The Congress of Vienna led to a Quintuple Alliance between the victors over Napoleon and France itself which was novel in seeking to guarantee peace across Europe, rather than in individual states: see Neff, 'Short History', 44–6. See generally W. Grewe, 'The Role of International Law in Diplomatic Practice' (1999) 1 *J. Hist. Int. Law* 22–37.

[13] With his usual honesty he noted an earlier use of the term (*Introduction to the Study of Morals and Legislation* (1781), 6). He wrote about aspects in four papers published only in his *Collected Works* (ed. Bowring, 1843), ii. In the course of these, he considered the possibility of a universal

consequences within a 'command theory' of the nature of law.[14] With his analytic scruple, Austin distinguished the positive law of a sovereign state from, on the one hand, divine law, answerable at the seat of eternal judgment; and, on the other, the 'positive morality' that characterized the law between nations. That morality was *positive* in the sense that the states which acknowledged it regarded it as laid down (posited) in order to condition their dealings with each other.[15] The absence of sanctions in a sense equivalent to those that gave legal backbone to the 'municipal' legal systems of states was nonetheless a stark reality. As Austin insisted, the will of states to become bound was not disciplined by any higher authority with power to compel adherence to its commands by calculable sanctions; and so, for the most part, it was a will that was not law 'properly so called' in the sense of rules by which courts or other tribunals would adjudicate contentions. It was not a body of doctrine that could be studied independently of its moral quality. At most, a state which failed to comply with its treaty obligations or to observe established customs might meet belligerence, or, short of that, some loss of economic advantage or of face. These sanctions, however, would be imposed by the state, or concert of states, when claiming that an international norm had been violated. Only after the debacle of the First World War, would that structural lacuna begin to be filled. It would come with the setting up of the League of Nations, the Permanent Court of Justice at The Hague and other supra-national bodies with authority to foster international law-making, to secure adherence to that law by executive action or to adjudicate upon its application.

Austin's first expression of his views on international law, in *The Province of Jurisprudence Determined* (1832), appears to have attracted little interest for some 30 years.[16] It was probably the re-publication of that volume in his posthumous *Lectures on Jurisprudence* (1861) that had real impact. By then there were sufficient audiences, in the universities and public life, for this application of legal positivism to be taken seriously. Even so, the concept of international law had too insistent a potential—in the business of diplomacy, in the striking of accords

international code, the causes of war, and a plan for universal and perpetual peace. See further, M. Janis, *The American Tradition in International Law* (Oxford, 2004), 11–21.

[14] For the subtlety of his views, see Lobban, 'English Approaches', 78–80. Not least was Austin's acknowledgment that some positive morality might be law strictly so called, i.e. when it is 'an imperative law set by a sovereign to a sovereign'. J. F. Stephen, unsurprisingly, provided one instance of a '"vulgar Austinian" view of international law, hostile to it and uncomprehending of it' (*ibid.*, 77–8).

[15] It could therefore be analysed in similar fashion to internal systems, in a way that distinguished it from moral obligations that did not carry the same expectation that they would be observed.

[16] Richard Wildman would publish *Institutes of International Law* (1849–50), which strongly denied that the subject had divine origins as part of natural law, but the book made no mention of Austin: Sylvest, 'Nineteenth Century' 29–37.

between states and in the settlement of running disputes between states—for it simply to be discounted as something other than law. The *ius gentium* had been recognized in English courts by the statements of Mansfield, Blackstone, and others that it could form part of the common law;[17] and it had long been treated as a direct source of law in the civilian courts of Admiralty and Prize at Doctors' Commons, where the small band of advocates and judges held doctorates in civil law from the Universities of Oxford or Cambridge.[18]

The Victorian authors who took up the cause found their own parries to Austin's argument. As English treatises and other scholarly writings on the subject emerged in the great age of Empire, most accepted at least some of the basic tenets of Bentham and Austin, whilst advocating ways of meeting Austin's doubts over to the very idea of international *law*. Those who sought to dispel this scepticism about the root character of their subject relied upon the evidence of the consent of sovereign states to its principles as a sufficient basis for binding obligation. They accordingly denied claims, stemming in particular from Grotius and his successors, for a *ius gentium* compounded of the assertions of scholars, expressing universal truths deduced by human reason. The new empiricism—a search for actual precedents in international practice—could be accepted as part of the demystifying thrust of the positivist approach. In this sense it was early stamped on the major American treatise, that by the diplomat and Harvard professor, Henry Wheaton.[19] Equally, it characterized the writings in England of the urbane Edward Hall, the acute but pedantic Erskine Holland, the practical and learned John Westlake, the formidable Lassa Oppenheim and even the Rev. Dr T. J. Lawrence.[20] Likewise, it was reflected in works by English men-of-affairs

---

[17] Blackstone had taken from the civilian authors of his time the notion that the law of nations was a component part of the law of nature and distinct from municipal law; but he made no attempt to settle a hierarchy of these norms in relation to English law, with its sovereign Parliament: *Comms*, i, 38–44; Janis, *American Tradition* (Oxford, 2004), 2–11. For a century, common law and equity courts would continue to follow Blackstone's apparently generous line. In our period, see e.g. *Novello* v. *Toogood* (1823) 1 B. & C. 554, 562 (Abbott CJ); *De Wutz* v. *Hendricks* (1824) 2 Bing. 314, 315–16 (Best CJ); *Emperor of Austria* v. *Day* (1861) 3 De G. F. & J. 217, 244 (Campbell CJ); but then sterner views would gain ground: see below, p. 274.

[18] See below, pp. 696–7 At the Reformation, Henry VIII had established Regius Chairs of Civil Law in each university in order to instil its precepts in the would-be doctors. As the subject grew in the nineteenth century, Oxford acquired the Chichele professorship of international law (1855) and Cambridge the Whewell chair in the subject (1867). For the civilians and the teaching of international law in the various law schools from 1850 onwards, see Lobban, 'English Approaches', 66–72. For the role of Whewell among his contemporarties, Sylvest, 'Nineteenth Century', 22–8.

[19] *Elements of International Law* (1836, 6 edns to 1866); *History of the Law of Nations in Europe and America* (1845); see Janis, *American Tradition*, Ch. 2.

[20] W. E. Hall, *Treatise on International Law* (1880, 8 edns to 1924); Sir Erskine Holland, *Elements of Jurisprudence* (1880, 13 edns to 1924), 79 ('law only by analogy') and his *Lectures on International Law* (ed. Walker, 1933); J. Westlake, *International Law*, 2 vols (1904–7, 2nd edn, 1910–13); L. Oppenheim,

who found it natural to underpin the foreign and colonial politics of their mighty country with accommodating notions of international legal obligation.[21] Among these were the Crown's advisers in international law matters—on the common law side, the Attorney-General and Solicitor-General; on the civilian, the Advocate-General. Some of these men, including Lord Chief Justice Cockburn, Lord Russell of Killowen and Lord Finlay, had considerable knowledge of the subject, and corresponding influence.[22] To this tally should be added a number of judges—notably Lord Hannen and Sir Edward Fry.[23]

If the measure of a rule was its acceptance by states, then, at least in all circumstances short of express treaty, the rule would exist only to the extent that it was followed. International law was in danger of losing any normative quality, becoming instead a set of descriptive hypotheses that would be valid only so far as states continued to accept them. Indeed, there were discussions of how close this brought international law to the less exact natural sciences such as botany, with its classificatory descriptions.[24] For those who found it crucial to preserve the distinctive quality of 'oughtness' in this sphere, arguments tended to revolve around the theoretical place of the sanction-like consequences of failing to abide by an accepted international rule, which could include gunboat diplomacy, trade barriers, seizures of ships and goods, armed forays to teach lessons or impose a measure of self-defence, and ultimately war.[25] This strand of theory would culminate in the work of Hans Kelsen. He insisted that the quality of law

International Law (1905–6, 8 edns to date); T. J. Lawrence, *Principles of International Law* (1895, 7 edns to 1929). In general, Crawford, 'Twentieth-century England', 680–701, esp. at 685–92.

[21] The first Whewell professor of the subject in Cambridge was Vernon Harcourt (later Liberal Home Secretary and Chancellor of the Exchequer), who wrote stern letters on international affairs to *The Times* as 'Historicus'—they were later collected and had undoubted influence. As an aspirant at the Bar, F. E. Smith (the future Lord Birkenhead) published a spirited *International Law* (1899, 6 edns to 1927). In the first generation of teachers and authors, Phillimore, Twiss, Mountague Bernard (the first Chichele professor) and Westlake (Harcourt's successor in Cambridge) all played important roles in international law practice of one form or another. Bernard, for instance, supplied the British defence to US allegations that the country had given neutralist aid to the South: see his much-praised *Historical Account of the Neutrality of Great Britain during the American Civil War* (1870). Long before, in 1799, Sir James Macintosh had delivered lectures on international law at Lincoln's Inn, which were published in 1835: see Johnson, 'English Tradition', 418.

[22] For Cockburn, see below , pp. 271, 273–6; for Russell's views, see 'International Law' (1896) 12 *LQR* 311.

[23] Hannen for his conduct of the Behring Sea Arbitration (below, p. 271); Fry not least for his outstanding library of the subject, left to the British Library of Political and Economic Science.

[24] Thus Westlake: 'As is fitting in a science dealing with living subjects, in which there is always so much shading off, we have not made the classification of law depend on a verbal definition like those of geometry, but have followed the practice approved in natural history, in which classifications are founded on likeness to types' (*International Law*, i, 7).

[25] For a simple version of the distinction between identifying legal sources and commenting on them from a moral perspective, see Lawrence (2nd edn, 1897), 23.

was in essence normative (a prescription of what ought to happen) rather than descriptive (an explanation of what does happen). As a correlative, propositions of law are to be found in legal sources, recognized within their own heirarchy of norms. Appreciation and criticism of his profound work, however, did not make headway in England until the inter-war years.[26]

In any case, counter-currents played a very distinct part in the first writings in Britain on the subject, and this was largely thanks to the role of the English civilians. During the crucial battles for maritime control during the Napoleonic wars, the Prize Court had regular and wide-ranging recourse to the principles of the *ius gentium*.[27] The Admiralty judge, Sir William Scott (Lord Stowell), demonstrated an exceptional mastery of international law, representing it much as it had stood before the innovative thinking of de Vattel and his followers.[28] In mid-nineteenth century, Sir Robert Phillimore published a three-volume set of *Commentaries on International Law* (1849–54) which retained the old, and in his case heavily Christian, universalism;[29] as did another learned civilian, Sir Travers Twiss.[30] The latter, for instance, argued that a war had to be just in order to be legal—an idea that had been central to the foundational writings of Vitoria and Grotius, but had lost a good deal of its centrality by the nineteenth century.[31] Later still the Edinburgh professor, James Lorimer, also maintained the natural law basis of the subject. His writing bore the stamp of Hegel's ennoblement of the nation state as the means of fulfilling the capacities of individual subjects, and had affinities to the work of the fervent Italian scholar, Mancini. Between them, they brought a strain of historical romanticism to international law scholarship, which nonetheless could conjure dark ideas of racial superiority.[32] In England, however, this

---

[26] His pupil and critical admirer, Hersch Lauterpacht, would do much to make Kelsen's international law known in Britain: Koskenniemi, *Gentle Civilizer*, Ch. 5.

[27] Prize law would indeed continue to be treated as a body of rules distinct from English law: see, notably, *The Zamora* [1916] 2 AC 77, where the Judicial Committee accepted that a British statute could override that law; but that if it did so, the British court applying the enactment 'would be deprived of its proper function as a Prize Court': see G. Lushington, *Manual of Prize Law* (1866).

[28] See above, p. 257.

[29] Further editions came in 1871 and 1879. For the fourth volume, on conflicts in private law, see below, Ch. IX, text at n. 23. Phillimore's premises bear striking resemblance to those of the first great writer in the American tradition, Chancellor Kent—see his *Commentaries on American Law*, i: 1–200 (1826; note the English edns by J. T. Abdy in 1866 and 1878); Janis, *American Tradition*, Ch. 2.

[30] *The Law of Nations considered as Independent Political Communities: On the Rights and Duties of Nations in Time of War* (1861–3, 2nd edn, 1875, revised 1884).

[31] Mountague Bernard, sometimes considered drily positivist, wrote an essay pleading for a humane exercise of the rights of war, 'Growth of Laws and Usages of War', *Oxford Essays* (1856). In the same year, C. M. Kennedy published *The Influence of Christianity on International Law* (Cambridge, 1856): Sylvest 'Nineteenth Century', 31–8.

[32] *The Institutes of the Law of Nations: A Treatise of the Jural Relations of Separate Political Communities* (1883–4); see Johnson, 'English Tradition', at 434. Lorimer was given to aspersions on the

'naturalistic' tradition faded in the years when the courts of the civilians were being eclipsed by those of common law and equity. Institutional and theoretical shifts worked cautiously but unremittingly in tandem.[33]

Those jurists who refused to accept sovereign command as the prime characteristic of law were readier to find analogies between the internal law of communities and the principles binding states. In England, Sir Henry Maine adhered to a utilitarian view of the function of law in any society; but historical relativism led him to treat as law the communal traditions and accepted relationships in primitive societies that had no written edicts and very little by way of overt sanction for non-conformity.[34] For James, Lord Bryce, international law was one illustration of the undue narrowness of the whole Austinian characterization of law.[35] Sir Frederick Pollock, normally the ally of Maine and Bryce against undue positivism, was more hesitant.[36] It was no surprise, all in all, that the Marquess of Salisbury, as Prime Minister, could dismiss international law as depending 'generally on the prejudices of the writers of text-books'.[37]

It is fair to say that the nuances that British writers brought to the precise characterization of international law were of less moment than their arguments over the 'positive' rules and principles to which states committed themselves through treaty and practice. Soon enough, the attitudes that were common to their writings were being disparaged by Continental idealists as an *école historico-pratique*.[38] A disdain for the pragmatism and urbane expediency of the common law in general was shown often enough by lofty civilian scholars from many branches of legal expertise. In relation to international law, it could be compounded because the British rarely lost sight of the commanding ambitions of their Empire, which seemed particularly to condition their attitudes to any international juristic order.[39]

proclivities of the English. His *Treatise* had only one edition: see Crawford, 'Twentieth Century', 689.

[33] See Lobban, 'English Approaches', 66–70.

[34] Maine (for whom, see above, Ch. IV) first explained his position in *Ancient Law* (1861), which coincided with the re-publication of Austin's ideas (above, p. 259); see also Maine's lectures as Whewell Professor, *International Law* (1888); C. Lindauer 'From Status to Treaty' (2002) 15 *Canadian J. L. & Jurisprudence*, 219.

[35] J. Bryce, 'The Nature of Sovereignty', in *Essays in Legal History and Jurisprudence* (1901), Lecture X.

[36] Pollock, *Essays in Jurisprudence and Ethics* (1882), 35; 'The Sources of International Law' (1902) 18 *LQR* 418–29 at 420. Pollock was prepared to admit that international law rules were still 'on the way to become law' but he took them seriously: N. Duxbury, *Frederick Pollock and the English Juristic Tradition* (2004), 106–7; Johnson, 'English Tradition', 421–2.

[37] *The Times*, 26 July 1897. Of course he would rely upon it when it suited: see below, p. 265.

[38] See Neff, 'Short History', 38–46.

[39] In his *International Law*, I. Peace (Cambridge, 1904), Westlake devoted four Chapters (3–6) to problems of state creation and succession. In his *Chapters on the Principles of International Law*

2. INTERNATIONAL LAW AND SOVEREIGN STATES

The ideas embedded in a positive international law were built upon four core doctrines, to which the leading powers—especially those with strong colonial ambitions—were prepared to countenance. Its obligations arose only between sovereign states, they had effect whatever the strength or weakness of such states, different theories determined what evidence was necessary to be regarded as a sovereign state, and it was not for one sovereign state to interfere in the internal governance of another.

Responsibility in International Law

The law of nations, or between nations, as already mentioned, applied to sovereign states conceived not just as territorially independent but as civilized enough to be admitted to the European family of Christian countries. After American independence, the circle certainly included the United States; but it excluded not just remote and unfathomable countries of Asia (such as China and, for some time, Japan) and Africa (such as its 'Mahometan States').[40] Given the bitter legacy of invasion, for many in Europe it shut out the Ottoman Turks. Dealings with the rulers of barbarian peoples had therefore to be purely *ad hoc*.[41] While some loosening of this incomprehension and hostility occurred as the nineteenth century proceeded, it left the European powers free to annex territories as colonies without legal question, whether by conquest or by settlement. If tribal rulers or elders were cajoled or pressured into signing over their lands that was not something that they or their successors could later challenge on grounds of unconscionability.[42] Anghie cites, as an extreme instance of conceptual manipulation, the treatment of these leaders as sovereigns purely for the purpose of making the cession that would subordinate their state beneath the horizon of international law.[43] The only

(Cambridge, 1894), he devoted three of the 11 essays to the treatment of colonies and natives: see Anghie, *Imperialism, Sovereignty*, 39.

[40] As referred to by Lord Stowell in *The Helena* (1801) 4 C. Rob. Adm. R. 3 at 7; C. H. Alexandrowicz, 'Doctrinal Aspects of the Universality of the Law of Nations' (1961) 37 *BYIL* 506–15; and his *Introduction to the History of the Law of Nations in the East Indies* (1967).

[41] The inclusion of Turkey within the Treaty of Paris in 1856 was a step towards greater integration that appealed more to those with internationalist instincts than to those intent on colonization. As to the attitudes of the Court of Admiralty on such questions, essentially the same view would be applied; but truly basic rules, which must have been 'familiar to the knowledge or observation' of such countries, might be treated as governing the situation: see Lord Stowell, *The Hurtige Hane* (1801) 3 Chr. Rob. Adm. R. 324, 327–8; see further, Lobban, 'English Approaches', 68–9.

[42] See n. 49 below.

[43] Anghie, *Imperialism, Sovereignty*, Ch. 2 providing a wholesale critique of the manipulations which big powers brought to this question in their own interests; Jianming Shen, 'The Relativity and Historical Perspective of the Golden Age of International Law' (1999) 6 *Int. Legal*

constraints upon the acquisition of such territories were those accepted by the international law family. When in 1887 Britain saw Portugal proclaiming a purely 'paper' annexation of territory between its colonies of Angola and Mozambique, not accompanied by any significant settlement, Salisbury, as Foreign Secretary, was quick to inform the country that its declaration had no legal effect on the conduct of rival states.[44]

The most notorious competition of its kind—the late nineteenth century 'grab for Africa'—was therefore an issue between the European players. When Bismarck called the Africa Conference in Berlin in 1884, they alone were its participants.[45] Even the professed determination to make Leopold II of the Belgians reduce the level of slavery and inhumane treatment of the native population in his personal fiefdom of the Congo was a morally clouded objective. In reality the Conference was as much directed to breaking his monopoly on foreign trade in the Congo Basin in favour of 'free trade', divided up among the participating nations.[46]

Equality of Responsibility

Within the European family of international law adherents, the size or prosperity of a state was irrelevant once it was accepted to be a sovereign member. The proposition had suited a Europe of overlapping kingdoms and principates, for which the *ius gentium* had been a regular source of reference.[47] The concept cast a gloss of objectivity over the immense differences in power and wealth that existed between different states.[48] As Britain (or nominally the East India Company) acquired territories across the Indian sub-continent it proceeded partly by treaty with princes. For decades Britain was ready enough to treat them as sovereigns, even though British protection had to be bought by regular tribute. When, however, the

Theory 15; D. Kennedy 'International Law and the Nineteenth Century' (1997) 17 *Quinnipiac LR* 99; O. Korhonen 'The Role of Outlaws in the History in International Law' (2000) 94 *American Soc. of Int. Law Proceedings,* 45; Simpson, *Outlaw States,* Chs 2–5, 8. Cf. M. F. Lindley, *The Acquisition and Government of Backward Territory in International Law* (1926).

[44] See Lauterpacht and Jennings, 'International Law, 1870–1914', 680.

[45] The Final Act of the Berlin Conference would in some measure constrain new colonizations; but its effect was to foster the practices of imposing 'colonial protectorates', acquiring 'political leases' or entering 'condominia', in place of outright annexations: see Lauterpacht and Jennings, 679–87; S. E. Crowe, *The Berlin West Africa Conference* (1942).

[46] The British did, however, lead continuing attempts to improve native conditions in the Congo, which eventually forced King Leopold to cede the territory to the Belgian state in 1908. The British then refused to recognize the Belgian Congo as a state until satisfied with its progress.

[47] Anghie, *Imperialism, Sovereignty,* Chs 1, 2; A. Riles, 'Aspiration and Control: International Legal Rhetoric and the Essentialization of Culture' (1993) 106 *Harvard LR* 723–40.

[48] For the tendency to regard the leading states of the world, in economic and military terms, as having special authority over world affairs—a hegemony which may even have legal acknowledgment—see Simpson, *Outlaw States,* esp. as regards 1815–1914, Chs 4 and 5.

uprisings of 1857 led to the institution of direct British rule, legislation quickly degraded the status of these 'sovereigns' to that of subjects. As for the Muslim King of Delhi: when charged with complicity in the insurrection, he found himself unable to plead sovereign immunity; and that at a time when that plea was treated as having no exceptions.[49] The British called the whole outbreak a Mutiny, confident that they were the real rulers even before the insurgence broke out.

Identification of States

Recognition of states, as of governments over states, had scarcely been an issue under the European universalism of the *ius gentium*. In the nineteenth century, however, the jurists—many of them proclaimed positivists—were debating the conditions that justified admission to the circle of sovereign nations mutually bound by their individual willingness to observe the rules of international law. Two main schools of thought contested whether a state, before admission, must satisfy legal standards set by those states already within the circle—thus making recognition the very act that constituted the new state for purposes of international law; or whether, on the other hand, the existence of the state came about by its assumption of governmental power over a given territory and recognition by other states was a purely political act amounting to a declaration evidencing that pre-existing fact. The first, constitutive, theory turned on judgments about the methods by which a regime came to hold sway over its territory—whether by orderly succession or by insurgency or revolution. The second, declaratory, theory, opted for a straightforward pragmatism which allowed international law standards to be applied between states despite the continuing political divisions between them. The necessities of the twentieth century would lead to the latter becoming the predominant approach.[50]

Internal Independence

The concept of sovereignty required that the international community accept the independence of each state over its own population and territory. That meant that

---

[49] See Westlake, *International Law, Peace*, 82, cited in Lauterpacht and Jennings, 'International Law, 1870–1914', 684–5.

[50] See generally, J. R. Crawford, *The Creation of States in International Law* (2nd edn, 2009), Ch. 1. As to the recognition of governments, the British adhered to the policy that there must either be popular acceptance in advance of the assumption of power, or some evidence of sufficient ratification. This principle it applied, for instance, to the *coup d'état* of Louis Napoleon in 1852 and his overthrow by the Third Republic in 1870; and also to the Spanish revolutions of 1869 and 1874 and that in Portugal in 1910. But the rapid changes of the post-1918 period led to recognition on a purely factual basis.

other states had no right to intervene in its internal government; nor within the country was there to be any interference with the use and enjoyment of property, national resources or commerce; nor any exercise of jurisdiction. Internal affairs, even where a government conducted or permitted the most flagrant abuses of its own peoples, were not a matter for international law. The law of war governed conflicts between national armed forces, not between different sectors within a state, whether in outright civil war, sporadic attacks from terrorists, or violent protest arising out of hunger, political opposition, or conditions of labour.[51] The prime humanitarian cause of the modern world—the elimination of slavery—fell first to be addressed at the stage of trans-shipment from one part of the world to another. Only by treaty could the issue become an obligation affecting sovereigns within their own territory.[52] Likewise with other extreme examples of degradation: savage punishments, unremitting labour, persecution of minorities, subjugation of women, killing of unwanted babies, and so on through the dreadful catalogue of inhumanities that only increased with advancing technologies.

3. ADVANCES IN INTERNATIONAL LAW: ENGLISH PERSPECTIVES

Writing in 1959, Hersch Lauterpacht and Robert Jennings presented the period 1870–1914 as filled with promise for the future of international law, thanks at root to the relatively pacific relations of the great powers.[53] In their view, the ideal of an international society, subject across continents to legal constraints, was seeping gradually into the perceptions of political leaders and their advisers. They counted the contributions of Imperial Britain, however pragmatic and self-interested they might be, as among the more significant. Certainly Victorian international lawyers showed a self-confidence that contrasts starkly with the dread-filled lamentations over the neglect of the subject in Britain that would fill the inter-war period.[54] By then, the debacle of the First World War had shown how paper-thin were the attempts to set standards of decent and cooperative behaviour between potential belligerents;[55] and indeed the hopes for an ordered international society

---

[51] See e.g. Neff, *War and the Law of Nations*, Ch. 7.

[52] By this technique the British did lead continuing attempts to improve native conditions in the Congo, which eventually forced King Leopold to cede the territory to the Belgian state in 1908. Britain then refused to recognize the new state until satisfied with its progress on this score.

[53] Their essay ('International Law, 1870–1914') appeared in a volume devoted to Imperial history.

[54] See e.g. A. Pearce Higgins, 'The Present Position of the Study of International Law in England' (1923) 39 *LQR* 507–16.

[55] The Treaty of Paris brought the Crimean War to a close in 1856. When in 1870 Russia unilaterally denounced its obligations under the Treaty, Britain led the protests against an act which implied that even conventions had nothing other than conditional effect. A London Conference of

seemed in ashes. Who in the 1920s could tell whether the twin phoenixes of the
League of Nations and the Permanent Court of Justice at The Hague would prove
capable of long-distance flight?

In the later nineteenth century, there were advances in substantive doctrines of
international law, wrought partly through the mechanisms of treaties and partly
through acknowledgment of established practices in the course of settling disputes between states. By their side, procedures evolved that would open prospects
for international institutions to make and maintain international norms or settle
disputes between states as to their international obligations.

Humanitarian Law

Consider the movement for an international consensus which would denounce
and eradicate inhuman conditions of labour. The British had built a rich portion
of their early colonial wealth on West Indian sugar production and export. It was
grown and harvested by the sweat of African slaves shipped over by buccaneering
merchantmen who did extravagantly well out of their triangular voyages around
the Atlantic. In 1771 Lord Mansfield had overcome his political scruples to the
extent of ruling that a Jamaican slave, allowed to go free in England, could not
be reclaimed there by his purchaser.[56] A seed of decency was germinating in the
fields of respectable opinion and, after long campaigns, slavery came to be seen
as the abnegation of the very idea of humanity. One of the first enactments of
the Reformed Parliament abolished (subject to compensation) the institution of
slavery throughout its colonies.[57] Britain could afford to take the high ground,
since her sprouting economy was fertilized by cheap manual labour at home and
across the Empire without needing a workforce founded formally on ownership
of human beings.[58]

Already in 1807 the British Parliament had outlawed British trans-shipment of
Africans across the Atlantic into slavery in the Americas. Eight years later, the
Congress of Vienna cast its own aura of enlightenment by its general denunciation of slavery. But without rights to board slave-ships and remove their shackled
cargo, the international policing of such a brutal business had little meaning.

1871 patched over the dispute with a Protocol that gave in to certain Russian demands concerning
the neutralization of the Black Sea. Its point was nonetheless that *pacta sunt servanda* was the foundation of the law of treaties. It was not a principle subservient to some exaggerated respect for the
autonomy of sovereign states.

   [56] *Sommersett's Case* (1771) 20 St. Tr. 1, following earlier dicta of Holt CJ.

   [57] 3 & 4 Will. IV c. 85.

   [58] A comparison between labour conditions in industrial Britain and those on slave plantations
was never far from the imagery of radical critics: see e.g. Robert Oastler, above, p. 12.

It would not be until the 1860s, when the American civil war freed black slaves there, and Alexander II ordered the emancipation of Russian serfs, that the great nations could contemplate pressing lesser states to give up slave regimes. As already mentioned, this became one of the major demands of Bismarck's Africa Conference of 1884 and the subsequent pressure on Leopold II of Belgium to eradicate forced labour of the native peoples of the Congo.[59] Within the same decades—a period when socialist and syndicalist groups became much more prominent in Europe and elsewhere—discussions were under way towards eliminating compulsory, low-paid labour, particularly in colonies.[60] Britain was at first reluctant to accept that any international obligation could be placed over its own governance of the economy of its territories; plainly its business and financial communities had much to lose.[61] Its view shifted with the parliamentary victory of the Liberals in 1906 and it became a prominent supporter of a Convention on the issue, which would be under the supervision of an international institution. Such a body would indeed come into existence in 1919 as the International Labour Organisation.[62]

One striking achievement was the initiation at Geneva in 1863 of what became the Red Cross.[63] Concerned initially with the plight of soldiers in the wake of battle, which its first champion, the Swiss, Henry Dunant, had witnessed at Solferino, the idea blossomed rapidly in favour of an independent authority, acknowledged and supported by governments through a Convention for the Amelioration of the Condition of the Wounded in Armies in the Field.[64] The International Committee strove to create practical instruments for the neutrality and protection of wounded soldiers, and volunteer forces for relief assistance on battlefields. The nature of the enterprise meant that it had to have international status and to this end a considerable band of states were prepared to act together.[65] The result was a major impetus to international humanitarian law.

---

[59] See above, p. 265.

[60] Partly this would be inter-governmental, but partly also private (see next note).

[61] The inaugural meeting of the International Association for Labour Legislation in Paris, 1900 was composed primarily of scholars. The British were not present.

[62] The Swiss government fostered the process with a technical and then a diplomatic Conference in Berne in 1905 and 1906. The Treaty of Versailles, founded upon its Covenant of the League of Nations, included the setting up of the ILO within its terms.

[63] The International Committee of the Red Cross took the name in 1876, the symbol being that used to distinguish medical officers in the field. The Red Crescent, first used by the Ottoman armies in the Russo-Turkish War of 1876–8, gained reciprocal recognition at that time, and led to the affiliation of the two International Committees.

[64] It would be extended to naval forces in 1907 in the wake of the Second Hague Peace Treaty.

[65] It would soon lead to affiliate Red Cross societies at the national level.

Commercial Prospects and Advancing Technologies

Treaty-making among the Christian states of Europe had medieval antecedents,[66] not just for settling confrontational disputes but also in order to secure mutual advantages, many of them in commercial and financial matters. The rapid growth of trade across continents in the nineteenth century, evolving out of novel technologies of steam, gas, and electric power, construction using iron and other minerals, road, rail, sea, and eventually air transport, telegraphy and radio transmission, gave rise to many pressures for collaborations between states. The volume of treaty-making involving Britain and like countries began inexorably to grow.[67] In the latter nineteenth century the older practice of bi-lateral arrangements began to expand into the negotiation of multi-lateral conventions, many of them open to adherence by all countries of the world or by those of a region. A few of these set up unions of the participant countries, which signalled the establishment of supra-national bodies charged to administer the agreement, and perhaps taking a role in fostering revisions of its actual text.[68] There might even be provision for the arbitral settlement of disputes between member countries. Here were further international institutions acting under authority conferred by the assent of those states to the initial agreement—adding to an international legal order that was not simply dependent on the continuing goodwill of individual countries.

Inter-State Arbitration

The development of arbitration as a means of settling legal disputes between states was much fostered by practice between the United States and the UK. Within little more than a decade of American Independence the continuing familial, economic, linguistic, and other cultural ties between the two countries—not least that of the common legal inheritance—had brought processes for formal dispute settlement into existence. The Jay Treaty of 1794 had provided for mixed commissions adjudicating on the basis of law. These in the end had dealt with a number of issues over boundaries and wartime neutrality which established a sufficient measure of mutual trust for further arbitrations between the two to occur every decade or so thereafter. They included such settlements at

---

[66] Johnson, 'English Tradition' at 430–1 points to the Treaties of Lambeth and Paris (1217, 1259) concerning the Minquiers and Echehot islets in the Channel.

[67] The UK Treaty Series was first published in 1892: see Johnson, 'English Tradition', at 416–17.

[68] For instance, the International Postal Union (1875), the Paris Union for Industrial Property (1883), the Berne Union for Authors' Rights (1886), various treaties on railways and, after the *Titanic* disaster, an international ice patrol (1914).

the political nerve-centre as the Geneva arbitration, established by a Treaty of Washington in 1871. It dealt with Britain's failure to prevent the surreptitious fitting out of vessels in Liverpool, thanks to which the forces of the South were able to attack shipping supplies to the North during the American Civil War. The ship which the South re-named *The Alabama* gave its name to the whole controversy.[69] In 1893 the high-powered Behring Sea Tribunal ruled in favour of freedom of the seas against the US claim to property in fur seals on islands in that Sea. This was soon followed by the arbitration over Venezuela's threats to invade British Guiana—which were in reality fostered by President Cleveland's government in pursuit of the Monroe Doctrine; so also with the arbitration over the United States-Canada boundary of Alaska.[70]

In the two decades before 1914, the great powers became increasingly boisterous in their confrontations and their alliances. The edgy diplomacy that this bred looked to the developments in treaty-making and arbitration practice for some way of restraining the outbreak of war until the avenues for peaceful resolution of disputes had been given every chance. These efforts would culminate in the two Hague Peace Conferences, that of 1899 being called by the Russian Tsar, Nikolai II, and that of 1907 by the United States. From the 1899 Conference came Declarations and Conventions on both land and sea warfare and a Convention for the Pacific Settlement of Disputes, which established the Permanent Court of Arbitration (from 1903), the most significant supra-national body to that date. In form it did no more than create a tribunal in waiting, with a slate of potential arbitrators and a staff of officers, to which countries could turn. But bilateral treaties that dealt with the settlement of future disputes began to provide that there would, if necessary, be reference to the Permanent Court.

The 1907 Conference resulted in the conclusion of no less than 13 conventions, partly covering the ground of the previous Conference. For all the worthiness of the achievement, the great powers, Britain not least among them, saw to it that neither proceeding touched current disputes or colonial questions. They made plain that their sovereign freedom to protect their 'vital interests' remained an exception to dispute settlement agreements and they resisted any attempt to define and so constrict what those interests might be. Britain attempted at one stage to promote a compromise on the subject which would have required compulsory arbitration, while leaving it to each party to decide whether the exception applied. When the Germans pointed out the contradiction, they were accused of having no will for peace.

[69] For Cockburn CJ's role on the tribunal, see below, p. 273; Lobban, 'English Approaches', 72–8.

[70] Settled by arbitration in 1903 under the Hay-Herbert treaty to a moderate degree in the US's favour, thanks to the position taken by the British member, Lord Alverstone.

4. INTERNATIONAL LAW AND ENGLISH LAW:
THE CAUTION OF COMMON LAWYERS

What then was the relation of the general range of international law to the municipal law of England? How far could its recognized rules be treated as a source of law before English courts? International law had come to consist of the mutual agreements between nations, together with customary practices between them that could be said to command general acceptance; and these differences of source determined their impact in the English sphere. But in relation to both, the British conception of parliamentary sovereignty provided a premise on which the courts built their own ideas.

Many treaties only affected the conduct of states; but there were those—particularly regarding trade, finance, and government liability—which had direct impact on individuals, who accordingly would wish to assert their entitlements in domestic proceedings. The unqualified faith in parliamentary sovereignty led to the dualist position that Britain's obligations to its partner states were norms of a separate, and limited, order. Treaty-making remained a matter for the government of the day, under the royal prerogative. But even where the treaty was plainly meant to govern legal relations between individual persons, this could have no consequence in English law until statute had given it effect. Transformation was required; the courts had no power to find that the treaty had been incorporated into municipal law through case law or practice.[71] Accordingly, it was the language of the British enactment which settled the scope of the obligation. Only 'in cases admitting of doubt, the presumption would be that Parliament intended to legislate without violating any rule of international law, and the construction has been accordingly'.[72]

As for customary international law, the issue became part of an extraordinary set-piece, R v. Keyn,[73] which was decided precisely as the Supreme Court of Judicature was being set up to embody the whole business of superior court reform. Ferdinand Keyn, the Prussian Kapitan of a German vessel, *The Franconia*, was responsible for ramming a Britisher, *The Strathclyde*, some two miles from Dover Beach, thereby causing deaths among its passengers and crew.[74] The collision had

---

[71] Affirmed in *The Parlement Belge* (1880) 5 PD 197; *Walker* v. *Baird* [1892] AC 491. For the less categorical position that came to prevail in the United States, see Janis, *American Tradition*, 61–8. And transformation could fail: in the course of the great parliamentary contests of 1911, the House of Lords rejected the Naval Prize Bill which would have accepted the setting up of an International Prize Court.

[72] Dr Lushington, *The Annapolis* (1839) Lush. Adm. 295; and see *Ellerman Lines* v. *Murray* [1931] AC 126 at 147—a case where, clearly enough, the statute was not meant to adopt the Convention in question in full (it related to the employment of seamen after wrecking).

[73] (1876) 2 Ex D 63.

[74] There were oddities about this eventual conclusion by the courts: see esp. A. W. B. Simpson, 'The Ideal of the Rule of Law: *R. v. Keyn*' in his *Leading Cases in the Common Law* (1995) 227 at 232–3.

occurred within British territorial waters, since international law had by then accepted a conventional limit of three miles from the shore (or one cannon-shot to it).[75] Shipping disasters in the Channel played hard on the sensibilities of the English in the 1870s and this accident caused a public furore against Keyn.[76] He was convicted at the Old Bailey of manslaughter of an 18-year-old woman passenger either through his negligence in causing the accident or else through failing to help survivors—both matters, however, on which there had been significant arguments in his defence.[77]

A full Court of Crown Cases Reserved convened to decide the question whether an English court had jurisdiction over a foreigner for a crime committed on a foreign ship in peaceful transit across British waters.[78] Lord Cockburn CJ, with considerable learning and a decided hauteur, led a bare majority (seven judges to six) to the conclusion that there was no such jurisdiction.[79] In consequence any prosecution would have to be brought in Germany.[80] Merchant ships fell to be treated as territory of the country of their flag; and while there were several exceptions to that assumption,[81] none displaced it here. In Cockburn's view of the English sources, the courts of common law had no criminal jurisdiction over territorial waters beyond the shore; and Admiralty's jurisdiction did not extend to criminal charges. That position could have been reversed by a statute of the British Parliament. But, in the majority's view, the numerous statutes which did touch the subject of territorial waters failed to introduce criminal jurisdiction over foreigners on foreign vessels. This was the question which most clearly divided the majority of the judges from the minority.[82]

---

[75] See further below, n. 83.

[76] Among the dread incidents in the same seaway in 1875 were the collision of *The Northfleet* and *The Murillo*, and the wrecks of *The Schiller* and *The Deutschland*—the last springing Gerard Manley Hopkins to high emotion over the loss of five Franciscan nuns from Salzköller.

[77] For the maritime background and the details, see Simpson, 'Rule of Law' at 231–42.

[78] An initial Court of six was divided and, following the practice at the time, Lord Cairns LC decreed that the process should start afresh before 14 of the 28 superior judges. He was minded to sit himself, but Cockburn objected: G. Marston, 'The Centenary of the Franconia Case' (1976) 92 LQR 93, 103–5.

[79] *Ibid.*, 106–7. Cockburn's penchant for a hard-nosed, authority-based, version of international legal obligations is also very apparent in the Treaty of Washington Arbitration (see *PP* 1872 (61), lxix, 1, 23; 1873 (145), lxxiv, 419, p. 23) and on the Royal Commission on Fugitive Slaves (*PP* 1876 [C. 1516–I] xxviii, 285, p. xxxi); see also above, n. 22

[80] It was taken for granted that a sovereign state enforced its own penal laws, and never those of another state. See below, pp. 279–80.

[81] It was arguable that the crime was committed on *The Strathclyde*, so that jurisdiction followed from the fact of its being a British ship; but only two of the minority judges were prepared to consider this approach.

[82] There was plentiful scope for interpretation of the implications of these statutes and the minority duly held to the opposite construction. There was an argument, which counsel for the

In the end, for most of the judges, the outcome turned upon issues of English legal history and the interpretation of relevant British statutes.[83] Counsel made reference to a raft of learned tracts, most of them in the *ius gentium* tradition, on the rights of littoral states each to govern their own territorial waters. As might be expected, they showed variations which stretched back to Roman disputes over whether the basis of the *ius gentium* was the political *imperium* of the state or its proprietary *dominium* over the territory.[84] Sir Robert Phillimore, as the last of the English civilians, treated these sources familiarly, but even he found that they did not *require* a littoral state to take criminal jurisdiction over events in its territorial waters. The common law judges who made up the rest of the majority did not dismiss these sources on any strict Austinian view, but they examined them critically. Cockburn certainly proved to have little time for learned 'publicists' (as they were then labelled).[85] To Lord Mansfield's incorporation of international custom into common law, the majority emphasized his proviso that there must be a precedent for doing so. Taken strictly this would mean that there could be no reliance on an international law rule to meet an issue of first impression, so far as English law was concerned. The minority, by contrast, adhered to the Blackstonian view of the law of nations as forming part of the common law.[86]

The decision, infused with deep respect for parliamentary sovereignty, buttressed common law ramparts not only against any idea that international legal obligations might override the commands of the British legislature,[87] but also against

Crown refused to pursue, that customs legislation had extended the Port of Dover to the three-mile limit—as to which, see Marston, *The Marginal Seabed* (Oxford, 1981), 281–5. Since no further appeal lay from the *Keyn* decision, representatives of some of the victims brought civil actions; but these were disqualified as *res judicata*: *ibid.*, 139–40; Simpson, *Rule of Law*, 254–7.

[83] The case became a pointillistic exercise from which it became hard to make out any general *ratio decidendi*. In the view of Cecil Hurst, Foreign Office Legal Adviser in the 1920s, the case settled that the territorial waters formed no part of national territory: 'Whose Bed is the Sea?' (1923–4) 4 *BYIL* 34. Ever since, as the economic potential of these waters and their seabed has multiplied, the significance of the case has been a matter of high debate. There has been considerable criticism of the court for its incomplete appreciation of historical sources, and the common law slant that it placed upon them: see e.g. Marston, *Marginal Seabed*; and in the context of federal Dominions, D. P. O'Connell, 'Problems of Australian Coastal Jurisdiction' (1958) 34 *BYIL* 199—but note his later obverse stance, 'The Juridical Nature of the Territorial Sea' (1971) 45 *BYIL* 303.

[84] The writers included the great names of Italy, France, the German states, Switzerland, the Low countries, and the United States.

[85] See esp. his exhaustive review of doctrinal pronouncements (pp. 174–93); cf. Grove J. 110–11; Amphlett JA, 122–3 (both in dissent).

[86] See above, 260. Blackstone had regarded this general principle as necessary with the comforting pronouncement that Britain, unlike an absolutist monarchy, could not otherwise adapt its law to take account of the *ius gentium*. Why Parliament could not take on this role, as it did with treaty implementation, was left obscure: see *Comms*, iv, 66–7.

[87] As to which, see the Scottish decision, *Mortensen v. Peters* 1906 8 F (JC) 93.

the notion that the existence of an international law rule might make an English judge readier to fill any gap left by absence of legislation than it would in deciding a purely domestic issue. From a different angle, Brian Simpson has argued that the majority of the court was expressing a strongly positivist disapproval of adjusting the law's established standards elastically in response to popular outrage. As he shows, many who offered the government advice about pursuing the prosecution stressed the political unwisdom of trespassing so far upon German sensibilities in a high season for moral outrage. Parliament of course had an unlimited power to change the law; and soon enough, by the Territorial Waters Jurisdiction Act 1878, it created a criminal jurisdiction which covered foreigners in passage over British waters on foreign vessels.[88] The immanence of the rule of law might therefore be a value to which judges would subscribe, just as they would when they refused to depart from their own precedents. But it provided no fundamental criterion against which to measure the acts of an implacably sovereign legislature, of which the Westminster Parliament was the great exemplar.

For some commentators, the *Keyn* decision established that, as with treaty obligations, the courts lacked any general power to incorporate customary international law into English law.[89] If there was no relevant statute, then for a rule to become part of municipal law there would need to be evidence at least that the British government accepted the rule or an earlier precedent established by an English court. In the politically sensitive decision, *West Rand Central Gold Mining Co v. R*,[90] Lord Alverstone CJ appeared to come even closer to adopting such a rule explicitly; and that perhaps represents the closest that the common law came to erecting a sanitary cordon against the would-be world of international law publicists.[91] The case arose out of the British government's re-annexation of the Transvaal from the Kruger regime after the first stage of the Boer War. The Divisional Court held that the government was not bound by the regime's mining concessions; nor was it liable to meet obligations arising from the terms on which that the regime had commandeered gold for its war chest. In the upshot the court disposed of the case by refusing to find sufficient evidence of any international law obligation to the contrary.[92] It imbued an attitude which Westlake had already

---

[88] Simpson, 'Rule of Law', Ch. 9.

[89] See e.g. W.S. Holdsworth, 'The Relation of English Law to International Law', in his *Essays in Law and History* (1945), 260–72 at 263–6. Pollock called Cockburn's judgment 'a brilliant and frank exposition of [a] perverse insularity' (1932) 48 *LQR* 40–1.

[90] [1905] 2 KB 391.

[91] There were signs of its survival in the inter-war period, see e.g. the views of Lord Atkin in *Commercial and Estates Co of Egypt v. Board of Trade* [1925] I KB 271, 295, CA, and *Chung Chi Cheung v. R* [1939] AC 160, 167–8, JC. It has not, however, survived into modern law.

[92] A conclusion which in itself was later doubted: see Lauterpacht and Jennings, 'International Law, 1870–1914', 684–5.

condemned as demonstrating 'the baneful effects of Austin's narrow definition of law'.[93]

The centre of gravity for English ideas about international law during the country's great Imperial period lay in an adherence to positivism that to some extent was refined by larger perceptions of historical experience. When from mid-century it did start to acquire its own substantial literature, much of it appeared to adopt attitudes that then marked English common law more generally. The arguments over Austin's view of international law as positive morality bore a family likeness to arguments over judicial decision-making as a source of law and its relation to that habitual obedience underlying a command theory as a qualification needed to give the theory some attachment to reality. It was not in the interests of the common law's guardians to resolve arguments over the declaratory or the innovative nature of the judicial function. Instead the current of case law was left to swell and its practical importance would remain high even in an age which made far greater use of statute than ever before. The guarded relationship between Parliament and the judiciary meant that the clash of arms was better left untried, the more so as democracy evolved.

With international law, little English learning had come down from the eighteenth century that could stand beside the masterworks of the *ius gentium*. But those Englishmen who led opinion on international law—the statesmen, judges, legal practitioners, government legal advisers, and others who had to wrestle with practical dealings between states, together with those in their midst who became the leading British writers—were intent on finding its rules primarily in those sources which had a parallel in their own legal system. Inter-state treaties after all established texts resembling statutes; and the decisions of courts and international arbitrators provided judicial precedents of at least persuasive authority.

As with the common law itself, scholarship of the subject, while by no means totally discountenanced, was left as an authority of secondary significance, to be called in aid when there was no better evidence from more standard sources. In civilian Europe, the *ius gentium* tradition had undergone tremors related to the seismic shifts produced by national codifications. A highly schematic conception of international law, in its own way a form of rationalistic positivism, was adopted by the followers of de Vattel. However, in the later nineteenth century there was once more a shift to an idealistic invocation of higher principle—a set of beliefs that the future of mankind must be secured by observing fundamental decencies that were far removed from the selfish interests of the most powerful

---

[93] Commenting on the Report of a preceding Commission (*PP* [1901] [Cd. 623] which had reached the same conclusion: Westlake, 'The Nature and Extent of title by Conquest' (1901) 17 *LQR* 392, 394–5.

states. Leading scholars in the universities were the harbingers of this courageous resurrection and the *Institut de Droit International*, formed in 1873 at Ghent, gave it a significant voice.[94] Within a few weeks, a more open meeting in Brussels was held to consider the prospects for immediate and large-scale action such as the codification of international law itself.[95] It had before it David Dudley Field's draft outline of such a code, which covered both the public and private sides of the subject. It had first been debated at the Social Science Association's Meeting in Manchester in 1866.[96] Its ideals would prove to be utopian—no more achievable then than it would prove subsequently.

Despite the interest that Bernard, Westlake, Twiss, Holland, and Lorimer took in it, the *Institut* was dominated by an internationalist philosophy that found only limited response in the pragmatic world of English lawyers. Perhaps it would have achieved more if the British had had the will to offer real support. That would have been so only if the true powers in its international affairs—the government, the political parties, the judges, and leaders of legal practice—had shown some greater sense of commitment. As it was, the British behaved with much the same reluctance that infected dominant powers before and after them. On subsidiary issues the adoption of rules that could be labelled law, if carefully expressed, would bring benefits to dealings between nations. To that they would lend the authority of the British state. But on the great issues of international relations, they had no intention of making prior, general commitments in the form of principles which they would feel obliged to treat as binding upon themselves. It was with that mindset that the British and their Empire were soon enough drawn into devastating war across the European continent.

---

[94] For the formation and leading ideas of the *Institut*, see esp. Koskenniemi, *Gentle Civilizer*, Ch. 1. Its membership was confined to 50, most of them leading jurists.

[95] This Association for the Reform and Codification of International Law (which would become the International Law Association) at first worked in tandem with the more exclusive *Institut*, its meetings following on from the latter's: see Manning, *Law of Nations* (2nd edn, 1875), Ch. 1.

[96] Indicative of the rush of interest in the subject, the Association made much of it at its meetings for 1873–5—the very years when the two Belgian developments were set on foot.

IX

Private International Law

1. RESOLVING CONFLICTS OF LAW

By the time that international law was taking its nineteenth-century form, the judicial function had become a core attribute of the sovereign states that were its subject. How each state divided the jurisdiction of courts within its own territory (including its dependent colonies) was a vital aspect of its supremacy. The practice in each would turn on the course of its individual history, the distinctions that it might draw between civil, criminal, and other causes and its conception of judges and other adjudicators.[1] At least within the extended European family of civilized nations, each state came to hold territory that was looked upon as exclusive. The courts would mostly hear proceedings arising out of events occurring within their own bounds. Those subject to claims or accusations would be present for the proceedings or would at least have notice of them. But 'cross-border' disputes had become endemic between the cities of medieval Italy, the provinces of pre-Revolutionary France, the principates of the Holy Roman Empire and the Netherlands provinces freed from Spanish domination after 1648. By the nineteenth century the number of such disputes was growing rapidly. New technologies of transport, growth of international trade, movements of people to and from colonies, increased possibilities of emigration both by volunteers and by the persecuted—all these things greatly increased the prospect of litigation involving a foreign element of some sort.

While the questions were at root conceived as part of international law,[2] they could equally arise within the sub-divided territory of a nation, rather than across its borders with another independent state. Long and intense debates in the earlier *ius gentium* had arisen before overarching ideas of sovereign states

---

[1] Thus in England, in the early modern period, foreign trading and shipping agreements had been the subject of an internecine struggle for jurisdiction between King's Bench and Admiralty, in which the former's blatant incursion resulted in English law being applied to foreign transactions by fictitious pleading about the place of contracting: see e.g. Sir J. Baker, *Introduction to the History of English Law* (4th edn, 2002), 123–4.

[2] See J. Westlake, 'On the Relation between Public and Private International Law', (1856) *Juridical Society Paper* 173.

had become a political reality and a plethora of small jurisdictions led to conflicts of laws among peoples who had only informal ties of race, language, and
other understandings forged in a common culture. The immense impulses on
the Continent towards national unifications, sparked by the French Revolution,
came to be underpinned by unitary legal systems grounded on codified laws.[3] In
such countries private international law lost its role from the perspective of the
internal state. By contrast the UK continued its three separate jurisdictions, in
one of which, Scotland, the law had a basis quite distinct from that in England
and Wales or in Ireland; and to its growing Empire Britain applied the same
constitutional assumption. The American Federation likewise retained separate
laws and courts in the various states. This was to be a difference with considerable impact as the conflict of laws began to assume modern forms in advanced
states. It contributed to the idea that private international law was essentially a
branch of municipal law in each state, rather than one branch of international
law in general.

2. COMMON LAW CONCEPTIONS[4]

In the *ius gentium* various schools had disputed over the questions in classificatory terms that would form a bridge between public and private international
law. English judges might rely upon the pronouncements on the subject to be
found in learned treatises, perhaps describing them simply as 'international'.[5]
So far as concerned the public law of a state, including its criminal and revenue
law, the principle of territoriality was by and large taken to confine legal enforcement to proceedings before its own courts.[6] There was no prospect of having the
punishments or penalties imposed by those courts carried out with the aid of
courts and institutions in other countries—where, for instance, the miscreant
or his property might be.[7] The most that would develop, and that only slowly,

---

[3] See above, p. 236.

[4] See generally, A. Sack, 'Conflict of Laws in the History of English Law', in M. Culp (ed.), *Selected Readings on Conflict of Laws* (1956); for the progress of this separation and the prospects for its reversal, see A. Mills, 'The Private History of International Law' (2006) 55 *ICLQ* 1–50.

[5] See below pp. 281–2.

[6] Each state would enforce its own criminal and other public law in its tribunals, sometimes even
in respect of activities that occurred outside their territories—such as the plotting of insurrection
from abroad. But nowhere was there any tendency for them to enforce the criminal law of another
state, even where a defendant belonged to that state: *Huntington* v. *Attrill* [1893] AC 150, JC; cf. e.g.,
R. v. *Keyn*, above, Ch. VIII, text at n. 82.

[7] Differences between legal systems threw up nice questions about what was 'penal'. When a
reckless American lady on horseback mowed down a French officer in the Bois de Boulogne, she
was prosecuted for criminal negligence in France. As well as convicting her the court awarded the
victim damages; the latter part of the judgment, being for personal compensation, was severed

were international treaties for the extradition of alleged criminals to the country where they committed a crime in order that they might stand trial there.[8] Without such a mutual arrangement the British view was that no obligation to extradite arose. Detention of the criminal in order to do so was wrongful.[9] Such was the allegiance to the concept of state sovereignty.

When, however, it came to civil litigation the same scruples were less compelling. If X in State A and Y in State B concluded a contract for performance in State C and Y allegedly broke its terms, could X choose to sue Y in A, B or C?[10] If so, the law of which state would determine whether the contract had been validly made? Which law would settle the questions of its interpretation, breach and remedies? And if X won in A or C, could he have the judgement recognized and enforced in Y's State, B, where Y's assets were likely to be? These are root issues of private international law, as it emerged in the industrializing and colonizing sectors of the world. To conclude that none of the laws or the courts of any of the countries could hear the dispute would be an evident denial of justice—something that could be regarded as 'contrary to nature'. But when it came to more specific rules and limitations for dealing with the various issues, the solutions propounded by older civilian writers fell somewhere between two poles. The one, imbued with strong ideas of feudal or communal loyalty, strove to treat the law of the place where the issue arose as governing; the other sought, where possible, to give priority to the personal law of individuals which they were deemed to carry with them wherever they went. These magnetic tensions would seem to align with intellectual divisions between positivists and natural lawyers, but in ways that could be obscure.[11]

and enforced by English process: *Raulin* v. *Fischer* [1911] 2 KB 93; and see also the leading case, *Huntington* v. *Attrill*, above, n. 6.

[8] Particular arrangements between states concerning political refugees dated back to the fourteenth century. But it was only with the Jay Treaty of 1796 and the Webster Ashburton Treaty of 1842, both between the United States and the UK, that reciprocal rules began to take the general form given place in the Extradition Act 1870. See e.g. E. Clarke, *Law of Extradition* (1867); B. H. Giles 'Extradition and International Law' (1967) 1 *Auckland Law Rev.* 111.

[9] In 1836 Campbell A-G and Rolfe S-G advised that the Lieutenant-Governor of the Bahamas could not seize Spaniards who had already been convicted and were being transported, when they were shipwrecked on his coasts: see W. Forsyth, *Cases and Opinions on Constitutional Law* (1869) 341.

[10] It is useful to start with a contract example, for it was in that context that Lord Mansfield had initially recognized that the laws of England might, where appropriate, refer to another law. So when dealing with a contract legally made abroad, an English court might apply the law of the country where the cause of action arose: *Holman* v. *Johnson* (1775) 1 Cowp. 341, 344.

[11] Since the discussions had, until this period, been organized around an institutional classification of issues under 'statutes' relating to persons, things or both (so-called mixed statutes), the darkness only deepened. Where, for instance, did one place a question of succession to property on a person's death? The civilian classification informs an intermediate English work of 1823, Jabez

The common law perspective was positivistic in the same sense as that which underpinned its public international law. It was the great American judge, Joseph Story, who produced the first foundational treatise on the subject for common lawyers. His *Commentaries on the Conflict of Laws* reviewed the existing case law from both sides of the Atlantic and brought into account much of the inherited civilian learning on the matter—a tradition stretching back to Roman law sources.[12] By way of pedigree, Story gave particular prominence to Ulrich Huber's pithy and practical discussion of conflicts of law, written for the Dutch Provinces in 1689.[13] From Huber he was able to reconcile the admission of foreign law into jurisdictions maintained by all-powerful states: nations could not countenance any penal law other than their own being of effect in their courts, but in civil matters they could admit foreign law by virtue of their own private international law rules. This was a condescension that they could decently offer in a spirit of comity. Story's *Commentaries* were at once also published in Edinburgh. Shortly thereafter, from the British side, came William Burge's learned *Commentaries on Colonial and Foreign Law*.[14] While Burge's work earned the respect of Story, Savigny, and others, it lacked the power of synthesis to be found in Story, whose work was widely (but not uncritically) welcomed in France, Germany and elsewhere, as well as in England.[15]

The British gained further treatises in mid-century when Robert Phillimore devoted a fourth volume of his *Commentaries upon International Law* to the

---

Henry, *Treatise on the Difference between Personal and Real* [i.e. 'thing-ly'] *Statutes*. As to the meaning of 'statutes', cf. Sir F. Dwarris, *General Treatise on Statutes: Their Rules of Construction, and the Proper Boundaries of Legislation and Judicial Interpretation* (1830), which used the term in the modern English sense, but also had a short section on its usage in the traditional law of nations (ii: 647–51). Both authors, together with Burge (see below, n. 14), had strong West Indian connections— where the English governing class built great fortunes out of trade that was international.

[12] 1st and 2nd US editions, 1834 and 1841, English editions, 1835 and 1842. For immediate recognition in English courts, see Tindal CJ, *Huber v. Steiner* (1835) 2 Bing. N.C. 202. For its contents and impact, see E. G. Lorenzen, 'Story's Commentaries on the Conflict of Laws—One Hundred Years After' (1934) 48 *Harvard LR* 15–38; K. H. Nadelmann, 'Joseph Story's Contribution to American Conflicts Law' (1961) 5 *AJLH* 230–53 and 'Bicentennial Observations on the Second Edition' (1980) 28 *Am. J. Comp. Law* 67–77.

[13] *Praelectiones Juris Romani et Hodierni* (1689), Tit. 3, Pt 2, Bk 1: 'De Conflictu Legum Diversarum in Diversis Imperiis'; D. J. Davies, 'The Influence of Huber's De Conflictu Legum on English Private International Law' (1937) 18 *BYIL* 49–63. Huber by no means attracted the same adherence among Continental scholars. Other civilians to whom Story gave particular attention included the Voets, father and son, Froland, Boullenois, and Bouhier.

[14] Published in London in 1838 in four volumes, Burge having risen to be Attorney-General in Jamaica. For contemporaneous publications in Continental countries, see Nadelmann, 'Story's Contribution', 68.

[15] The school of 'statutory' classification (above, n. 11) disappeared in response to his aminadversions on its obscurities.

subject;[16] and John Westlake produced a shorter, but long-lasting, *Treatise on Private International Law*.[17] In 1896, A. V. Dicey would publish his long-awaited *Conflict of Laws*.[18] The work, that most iconic of English treatises, followed a form that had a special appeal in the decades of high Empire. The common law on the subject, developed very largely out of precedent,[19] was dubbed by Dicey in his best Austinian manner, 'judicial legislation'.[20] He set forth his summation of it in a series of Rules, each of which was then elaborated, illustrated and commented upon in an exhaustive review of decisions, dicta and writings.[21] That result could well be labelled 'private codification' and was in its way the precursor of the American Restatement of the subject. As such it accommodated the judges' preference for their own shaping of the law in a form that a statutory code would have inhibited. Under a line of distinguished editors, *Dicey* has kept its particular authority, for there remain basic issues on which even today English courts have never reached a final conclusion and the views of authors have therefore commanded special respect.[22]

Expressing heavy debts to both Story and Westlake, Dicey introduced his Rules with First Principles I–VI—precepts or maxims of strongly utilitarian character. Even at the very end of the century, he confined the whole subject to conflicts of private rights between 'civilized countries'—that characteristic limitation upon international law as a whole in the Imperial period.[23] In relation to these countries

---

[16] (1854–61), iv: *Private International Law or Comity*.

[17] Subtitled: *Or the conflict of laws, with principal reference to its practice in the English and other cognate systems of jurisprudence* (1858, 7 edns to 1925). In 1878 J. A. Foote would produce his rather similar *Foreign and Domestic Law* (with 4 edns to 1914). The special subject of *Foreign Judgments* was dealt with by F. T. Piggott (2nd edn, 1884).

[18] *Digest of the Law of England with reference to the Conflict of Laws*. Dicey built upon his earlier monograph, *Law of Domicil as a Branch of English Law* (1879). For the fatigues of writing the larger work, see R. A. Cosgrove, *The Rule of Law* (1980) 163–9.

[19] The Rules governing service out of the jurisdiction were an exception, as were the Judgments Extension Act 1865 and the Foreign Marriages Act 1892.

[20] He objected to the term 'private international law' partly in obeisance to Austin's characterization of international law as only positive morality (*Conflict*, 12–15).

[21] Both the Harvard professor, Beale, and Westlake questioned the desirability of this form in otherwise favourable reviews: (1896) 10 *Harvard LR* 168, 12 *LQR* 397.

[22] See P. M. North, 'Private International Law in the Twentieth Century', in J. Beatson and R. Zimmermann, *Jurists Uprooted* (2004), 483–515.

[23] i.e. the states of Europe, North America, and Europeanized colonies, as distinct from more heterogenous states in Africa, Asia, and Latin America, with particular mention of Turkey and China. Rights arising under the latter were to be given effect only where the English court considered it appropriate—no rule of law for them: see Dicey, *Conflict*, App. Phillimore had earlier insisted that the higher level of mutual obligation between Christian states stemmed from their prevailing religion: *Commentaries on International Law*, (1861), iv, Ch. 1. No court could be obliged to take account of the law or judgments of another country which contravened 'immutable law of Right written by the finger of God on the heart of man', such as opposition to slavery and familial ill-treatment (pp. 13–15).

there was a positive legal obligation on English courts to recognize and enforce any right duly acquired under their laws (Principle I).[24] This principle applied in respect of any matter for which the foreign court could give effective judgment (III).[25] However, there were qualifications—first concerning the legitimacy of foreign judgments;[26] and then more generally, where there would be inconsistency with a British statute intended to have extra-territorial effect, with 'the policy of English law', with 'the maintenance of English political institutions', or where 'the Principle of such right involves interference with the authority of a foreign sovereign' in his own territory (II).[27] Apart from this, an English court could take jurisdiction in any case where the parties voluntarily submitted to it (IV); and parties to a transaction were entitled to have their choice of law respected, where they made a nomination (VI).[28] These six Principles, said Dicey, placed a reader 'in the right position for appreciating the meaning and effect of the body of rules which regulate the extra-territorial recognition of rights'. They are shot through with respect for the sovereign authority of independent states over their territories that was so much part of positivist international law in general.

If the substantive laws governing issues were the same in different states and were applied with equal assiduity and fairness in each of them, there would be only a residual role for private international law in any legal system. But often enough there were implacable conflicts between substantive laws or there were procedural, remedial, or costs disadvantages in one place compared with another. A positivist view of private international law countenanced an emphasis on expediency. After all, any rule that one country might adopt—permitting a court to order, for instance, that a defendant do or refrain from doing something in another country—might well be taken reciprocally into the law of other countries; and that on balance might well be disadvantageous. The common law literature before Dicey had laid considerable stress on the 'comity' between sovereigns by which they admitted foreign law into the proceedings of their courts. Even Phillimore, that late repository of the *ius gentium* tradition in England, considered that *private* international law issues arose through such comity and not by any divine precept or rational dictate.[29]

---

[24] pp. 22–31. It must therefore be acquired under that law (Principle V).

[25] pp. 39–41. A judgment concerning title to foreign land could not be regarded as 'effective': see XIII, text at n. 69 *et seq*. For 'comparative efficacy' in jurisdiction over divorce, see below, pp. 293, 840–2.

[26] See below, pp. 289–90.

[27] pp. 32–8. The absence of any reference to moral or religious values is of course a key: cf. Phillimore, above, n. 23.

[28] pp. 42–61.

[29] Phillimore opens his volume with a chapter on Comity which he characterizes as a matter of concession between sovereigns, rather than any force of obligation. For him, a breach of comity could never justify retaliation by act of war: *Commentaries*, iv, 13–15.

So there was scope to consider the particular conflict that arose, the relative advantages of procedure and cost and even suspicions that the courts of a country were open to bribery or showed a distinct bias in favour of their own citizens. Some of the worst aspects of forum shopping by claimants might thus be alleviated.[30]

Dicey's analysis of actual rules to be found in case law and elsewhere is positivistic in other respects. He claimed the book to be a statement of what the law is, divorced from considerations of what it should be. The history of the subject, including its civilian roots, so prominent in Story, Burge, Phillimore, and Westlake, lost ground in the new work. Here was an account confined more rigorously to English and American authorities as they ranked in their time.[31] This did not prevent Dicey from offering copious advice to judges on the best solution where none was clear from the authorities. He also asserted that the English law thus described had much common ground with the private international law of other civilized states, as witnessed in writings of jurists of the stature of Story and Savigny; and he made references to their writings. Yet those giants at base represented the opposed schools of positivism and naturalism—philosophic premises that could trigger intransigent argument. This would become all too apparent during the first attempts to reach international accord by conventions on private international law principles.[32]

F. C. von Savigny's great theoretical treatise on the resolution of conflicts of law[33] appeared six years after Story's. In contrast to the latter, Savigny's portrayal of an ideal private international law was imbued with the civilian faith that higher principles directed its course. As they had long done, jurists would uncover these principles, which were immanent. To this they would bring their historical learning, which in civilian Europe meant above all the study of Roman law doctrine and its later assimilation into the *ius gentium*. He accordingly rejected the view that this branch of international law was based upon convenience and political calculation between sovereigns. It was a position antagonistic to the very idea that states each held dominion over their geographical territories and were obliged to other states only by voluntary acts of their own will, which they might change over time.[34]

---

[30] See further below, pp. 288–9.

[31] Dicey's first edition contained notes on US cases by the distinguished J. B. Moore; but these disappeared subsequently.

[32] See below, XIII, pp. 841–2.

[33] *System des heutigen Römischen Rechts*, viii (1840); (translated in an edition by W. Guthrie as *A Treatise on the Conflict of Laws and the Limits of their Operation in Respect of Place and Time* (Edinburgh, 1869)).

[34] See Lorenzen, 'Story's Commentaries', 31–2.

The doctrine could moreover be given nationalistic colour, as it was by the Italian jurist and statesman, P. S. Mancini.[35] Mancini started with the individual, who was conceived as carrying his personal law wherever he went and should therefore be entitled to rely upon it in the courts of other countries. This personal law, moreover, was now to be the law of his nationality, rather than any more local domicil.[36] In Mancini's rationalization this personal law was to govern all matters save those that depended on the *ordre public* of the forum state, or on the choice of a particular law by the persons involved. In Continental Europe this rousing idea would have great attraction as part of the movement towards the self-determination of its peoples.

Just as with public international law, the private side was close to constitutional politics and particularly to nineteenth-century ideas of the nation state. But naturalists and positivists made very different assumptions about how to express that proximity. In the following paragraphs we explore a little further the relation between basic conceptions and leading doctrines of the subject as they evolved through this gestatory period.

3. DOMICIL AND NATIONALITY— A CONCEPTUAL DIVIDE

The connection of a person to the country with which he was most closely associated already had a long history in the *ius gentium*, stretching back to Roman law precepts. It was the law of this domicil which, according to most writers, determined the capacity to marry, to enter contracts and other arrangements, and the disposition of assets on death.[37] Nineteenth-century contenders for personal law, as against territorial law, were arguing that it should be the presumptive approach in other legal situations. The definition of domicil, however, was a troubling conception, both as a matter of formulation and as a matter of proof. In the common law view, domicil was the place where a person had his or her permanent home—the place which was fixed at birth by family connection:[38] legitimate children acquired their father's domicil, bastard children, their mother's.[39]

---

[35] *Della Nazionalità come Fondamento del Diritti delli Genti* (Lecture, Turin 1851).

[36] See below, p. 286.

[37] For an introduction to the private international law affecting marriage, divorce, matrimonial property, and rights over children and similar matters, see XIII, Pt 4, Ch. VII.

[38] Its first use appears to have been in the civilian jurisdiction by Sir Leoline Jenkins: see Phillimore, *Commentaries*, iv, 39–40. The suit concerned succession to the personal estate of Queen Henrietta Maria.

[39] One of the many sources of difficulty in comparisons with civilian legal systems was that 'domicil' could be used with varying meaning according to context. Thus at mid-century, French law was said to use the term in at least five ways—electoral, jurisdictional, notarial, indigential, and

It would come to be accepted that individuals could have only one domicil and could never be without one. They would retain it until they were legally able and willing to change it.[40] A wife, however, was obliged to take her husband's domicil for the duration of the marriage. A domicil of choice could be achieved by taking up residence in a new jurisdiction with an *animus manendi*—a fixed and settled intention to remain there for good. Accordingly, individuals (other than minors or married women) retained the power to change their domicil of their own volition. The concept had a strong appeal to liberals, being unassociated with any idea of state grant.

Rules based on a relatively flexible concept of personal attachment had suited the political arrangements between kingdoms, principalities, and republics of the European continent before the post-feudal conditions sparked by the French Revolution. But once the state became the focus of exclusive power and loyalty, the political relationship between it and its citizens intensified and nationality tended to acquire an overarching importance. Accordingly, even rules of private international law came to turn on that allegiance to the state which nationality crystallized. The voluntarist notion of domicil was progressively displaced by nationality as a crucial connecting factor in codes of private law, starting with Napoleon's *Code civil*. From mid-century, when Mancini gave such patriotic force to the concept of a personal law of national origin, one civilian country after another took nationality, rather than domicil, as the key factor in much private international law.[41]

In the UK, a binding obligation of loyalty to the Monarch unquestionably gained an immense Imperial significance, but nationality had its legal effects in matters of public obligation. In English law, nationality arose out of the simple geographical fact of birth in any British domain, no matter who the parents were. It was also taken to be irreversible, save where statute altered the situation. This would have a distinct impact, when it came to wartime searches of belligerent vessels. During the War with the United States in 1812, the British had taken British-born seamen off American ships, including even those who had obtained American nationality in order to avoid impressments into the British navy. Only in the wake of the American civil war would the Naturalisation Act 1870 allow a Briton to surrender his nationality voluntarily.[42]

---

successionary: see (1861) 11 *LM & LR* 339, 346–7 (a disparaging review of O. S. Round, *English Law of Domicil* (!861)). Even the third edition of Phillimore's *Commentaries* (1879) Ch. 5, spent energy in arguing that a person could not have two domicils in English law .

[40] At mid-century, however, this was still not clear beyond argument.

[41] See Lorenzen, 'Story's Commentaries', 32–4.

[42] 33 & 34 Vict. c. 14. It also permitted the children of foreigners born in Britain to elect to take their parents' nationality.

Both the UK and the United States had kept the jurisdiction of most of their courts confined to limited areas within their union. Hence the private international law of each was taken to relate to their purely regional divisions as well as to inter-state issues.[43] The personal law of individuals thus needed to be associated with part-territories and the overarching concept of nationality was thus inappropriate. In the constitutions of civil law countries, however, the legal system was often conceived as a national structure, with jurisdictional regions only for administrative reasons. This was the assumption that allowed nationality to be the touchstone of personal obligations in codes of civil law; and if the country was pursuing a policy of registering its nationals in order to track their identity, as many were, this at least provided a straightforward means of proof for all legal issues, private as well as public.[44]

English antagonisms against governmental authority acquiring any unnecessary knowledge of private affairs—important when it came to wealth and welfare, as much as whereabouts—stood against such outgrowths of the idea of nationality. So in private law, and indeed in certain public fields, such as revenue and bankruptcy, the concept of domicil survived. It would prove to have a useful adaptability as the Empire stretched to ever more exotic climes and the British who worked in the outreaches divided into those who were there strictly for their term of service and those who, for whatever reason, would stay on for good. Men among the latter (if not their wives and children) could acquire a domicil of choice in the new country, provided at least that it was 'civilized'. Where an Englishwoman died in China in circumstances that would have earned her a domicil of choice had she been in a 'civilized' country, she was held not to gain a domicil there. So her estate was liable to pay British legacy duty.[45]

Domicil was a puzzling notion, but English and American law adhered to it. Because of the distinction from nationality, it could lead into the logical circumlocutions of a *renvoi*. If (say) a woman died a national of State A but with a domicil in State B, and the private international law of each state referred the distribution of her assets to the other, only an arbitrary axe-blow could cut the Gordian

---

[43] In the UK, this large truth was not taken to be upset by the existence of the House of Lords as a final instance for appeals from its three jurisdictions. So equally in federations of states with a senior court for the whole country.

[44] In mid-century, Lord Kingsdown appeared to suggest that in Britain the common law might shift in the same direction: *Moorhouse* v. *Lord* (1860) 10 H.L.C. 272. The editor of Story's *Conflict of Laws* took this up; but the House of Lords soon stamped on it: *Udny* v. *Udny* (1869) 1 ScD&A 441, esp. at 459–60 (Lord Westbury).

[45] *Re Tootal's Trusts* (1886) 23 Ch D 532; an approach later mollified by the House of Lords, *Casdalgi* v. *Casdalgi* [1919] AC 145.

knot.[46] But it was scrupulous, indeed zealous, lawyers who set about resolving the dilemma—without definitive results.[47] The issue continued to rankle. A Hague Conference Convention of 1905 which aimed to eliminate the conflicts of law over the distribution of deceased estates was signed by only seven states and Britain played no part in its drafting.[48]

4. JURISDICTION OF ENGLISH COURTS

Behind any conflict of substantive laws lay issues about the choice of courts between countries: what, for example, was an English court to do if it suspected that foreign judges were likely to be biased in favour of their own citizens or particular litigants, or that they might be bribed? Should it take account of the fact that more of the parties or witnesses would be in one country or another, or that an order by a foreign court would be more readily carried out in its own territory than an order of an English court, or that conflict of laws principles of a foreign court were open to criticism? What was to happen if more or less the same suit had already been launched in a place where doubts about probity or capability were being aired? Comity between sovereigns had as its concomitant that there might be reasons of public policy for refusing to decide an English case by reference to a foreign law. Equally an English court might refuse to take jurisdiction over a case with a foreign element, or might refuse to recognize a foreign judgment because of its own public policy. If such issues were left to the court's discretion, as in Anglo-American law, Savignians saw a pragmatism that undermined proper respect for the rule of law.

As a general principle, English courts would take jurisdiction over a case only when the defendant to a civil action was present in its territory or had voluntarily submitted to the jurisdiction of the court.[49] There was then some hope that, if liable, defendants might be compelled to satisfy judgments—through the appropriation of their assets, or by proceeding against them personally for the contempt of court inherent in failure to abide by or satisfy a judgment.[50] The common law took a decidedly casual view of what might be a sufficient presence in England.

---

[46] The subject even gained a monograph by the learned J. Pawley Bate, *Notes on the Doctrine of Renvoi* (1904).

[47] In 1900, *l'Institut de Droit International* rejected a complex resolution in favour of renvoi, by 21 to 6, Westlake being one of the majority: Westlake, *Private International Law*, 7th edn, 34–5.

[48] See Westlake, *Private International Law* (5th edn, 1912), 33–4.

[49] *Voinet* v. *Barrett* (1855) 55 L.J. Q.B. 39; *Carrick* v. *Hancock* (1895) 12 *TLR* 59; *Schibsby* v. *Westenholz* (1870) LR 6 QB 155; *Copin* v. *Adamson* [1875] 1 ExD 17. The Admiralty rule was that a ship subject to *in rem* proceedings must be in an English port or within three miles of the coast: *The Clara Killam* (1870) LR 3 A & E 161.

[50] Dicey, *Conflict*, Rule 46, replete with extensive illustration and comment.

If the defendant was passing through the country, it was enough to serve the writ on him or her in that fleet moment. Foreign commentators were severe in their judgment against such presumption, for all its simplicity.[51] Circumstances were then added, category by category, in what became Order 11 of the Rules of the Supreme Court 1883. The courts came thereby to have a discretion to order service of the writ out of the jurisdiction on a defendant who was not domiciled or ordinarily resident in England—as for instance where the action concerned a contract made in England or was intended to be governed by English law; or where the action was over title to English land or over deeds, wills, or personal obligations affecting it.[52] In these instances it was the discretionary element that was likely to offend the advocates of a strict legalism.

5. RECOGNITION AND ENFORCEMENT OF FOREIGN JUDGMENTS

When it came to recognition and, if need be, enforcement of a foreign court's judgment in England, an opposite attitude prevailed, which might provoke further foreign censure. The common law had long subjected these supplementary steps to the requirement that intermediate proceedings be launched before an English court. An innate suspicion of things foreign was part of the reason, as was the view that there should be reciprocal arrangements between countries by treaty before there could be any mere registration of the foreign judgment. An English court would order recognition and enforcement only if the defendant had been domiciled or resident in the foreign country concerned or had submitted voluntarily to the proceedings there—a stricter rule than that for an English court's own jurisdiction.[53] Countries, such as France, where the courts took jurisdiction on the nationality or residence of the *claimant*, were considered to be going too far in protecting their own.[54] The foreign judgment had to be for

---

[51] *Phillips* v. *Eyre* (1871) LR 6 QB 1, 28; cf. *Western Bank* v. *Perez* [1891] 1 QB 304 at 309–11, 316–17.

[52] The Order reflected earlier practice particularly in the Court of Chancery. First introduced as part of the 1883 Rules for the Supreme Court of Judicature, it was gradually broadened with time.

[53] Westlake, *Private International Law*, Ch. 12; Dicey, *Conflict*, Ch. 16. An early statute in the field, the Judgments Extension Act 1868, did introduce mutual registration of judgments between the different jurisdictions of the UK. But it was a special exception: not even the Empire was accorded like treatment: see e.g. *Emanuel* v. *Simon* [1908] 1 KB 302 (judgment of a Western Australian court, terminating a partnership and ordering payments, was not enforceable in England against a defendant who was neither domiciled nor resident in Western Australia, and who, on being served with the initial writ in England, had taken no part in the Australian proceedings).

[54] In the leading case, *Schibsby* v. *Westenholz* (1870) LR 6 QB 155, the foreign judgment in question was by the Tribunal de Commerce de Caen, and had been given without even serving notice of the proceedings on the non-French defendants; see also *Rousillon* v. *Rousillon* (1880) 14 Ch D 351. Even

a specified sum and it had to be final, rather than interlocutory; but it did not matter that it was still subject to an appeal.[55]

When these various conditions were satisfied, the English court would rarely permit the substance of the successful foreign proceedings to be reopened—a shift away from earlier, less defined, practice. Only in extreme cases—of fraud, public policy, and (possibly) absence of due process—would it be possible to secure a re-examination. Mistakes of fact or law were generally not enough, even if they concerned English law.[56] In describing the run of cases that settled and illustrated these rules before 1914, North notes their geographical confines.[57] It was only judgments from states in the European family or from Empire courts that even became the subject of reported English proceedings. Private international law was still a set of mutual rules between 'civilized' states. Their courts alone warranted a sufficient degree of trust.[58]

6. CHOICE OF LAW

Where English courts took jurisdiction, they might well have to work out the circumstances in which the law of another country would be applied in resolving the case before them. While the flow of case law would long remain too slender for all the tasks in hand, it had built up into a certain corpus by the time that the treatise writers were seeking to mould its larger shape. Any court is likely to be uneasy about its ability fully to understand and apply foreign law, but the more so in a tradition of accusatorial process such as that at common law, where there was no practice of referring such issues to independent experts. Instead, in England the foreign law had to be established by expert witnesses called and cross-examined by the parties. The issues could then become very difficult to resolve. The judges took comfort from the proposition that a decision by them on the content of foreign law was deemed to be a question of 'fact', not of 'law', and so formed

---

the French had doubts: they would not recognize judgments given on an equivalent basis in other countries which had followed their own lead.

[55] *Nouvion* v. *Freeman* (1889) 15 App Cas 1, HL.

[56] *Henderson* v. *Henderson* (1844) 6 Q.B. 288; *Godard* v. *Gray* (1870) LR 6 QB 139; *Ochsenbein* v. *Papelier* (1873) LR 8 Ch App 695; *Rousillon* v *Rousillon* (above, n. 54); *Huntingdon* v. *Attrill* [1893] AC 150. A claim of fraud could allow the substance of the claim to be reopened: *Abouloff* v. *Oppenheimer* (1882) 10 QBD 295, CA—concerning a judgment of the District Court of Tiflis, Russia; *Vadala* v. *Lawes* (1980) 25 QBD 310.

[57] North, 'Twentieth Century', 514–15.

[58] A borderline illustration is *Sirdar Gurdyal Singh* v. *Rajah of Faridkote* [1894] AC 570: the native Court of Faridkote had ordered Singh, a defaulting treasurer of that state, to repay moneys, even though he was domiciled and resident in Jhind and had not appeared in the proceedings. The Judicial Committee held that the judgment should not be enforced by a Jhind court: the Faridkote decrees were 'a nullity by international law'.

no precedent for proceedings between other parties.[59] The *ius gentium* had long held to the principle that only issues of substance could be referred to another law, procedure being a matter for law of the forum. The common law accepted this limitation without quibble, holding that 'procedure' included all questions of remedial relief, including such issues as the availability of specific performance, injunctions, and the assessment of damages—differences about which could well be a prime reason for forum shopping.[60]

As to choice of law rules for the main branches of civil liability, there were many developments in the 62 years between the first editions of Story and Dicey. These we illustrate here in relation to general obligations, leaving issues of family law until we reach that subject.[61]

Contracts

One point at which advocates of the personal locked horns with proponents of the territorial concerned the capacity to contract: questions of infancy, weakness of mind, and so forth. Story refused to accept the civilian view that this must be a matter of the personal law.[62] Instead he treated the law of the place of contracting as governing. So likewise with most other general issues of contracting—validity, nature, obligation, and interpretation. However, where the contract was to be performed in another country, its law would be used instead to settle such questions, if, as Lord Mansfield had said, the parties 'had a view' to the application of that law.[63] As an interesting instance of will theory in determining the existence, scope and effect of contracts, the rule would in time move beyond actual expressions of which law was to apply to a transaction, to more difficult cases where the court would have to presume that intention.[64]

By the later nineteenth century, it was common for courts to find that the parties must have intended to contract according to the law of the place where they

---

[59] Story, *Commentaries*, para. 637; Westlake, *Private International Law*, paras 413–14. It would be for the jury to decide whether proof of the difference from English law had been made out sufficiently for the latter to be replaced.

[60] Story, *Commentaries*, paras 620 *et seq.*; Dicey, *Conflict*, Rule 188. Inevitably there were differences of view over such borderlands as the effect of the Statute of Frauds on proof of a contract (*Leroux* v. *Brown* 1852 12 CB 801—*lex fori* determined its relevance); statutes of limitation (likewise treated as procedural); availability of damages for a shipping collision (*The Halley* (1868) LR 2 PC 193, JC, reversing Phillimore's valiant application of the *lex loci delicti* to the issue: (1867) LR 2 A & E 12).

[61] See below, XIII, Pt 4, Ch. VII.

[62] In the civilian view only the issue of formalities was referred to the place of the contract.

[63] *Robinson* v. *Bland* (1760) 2 Burr. 1077.

[64] For the importance of party choice, H. Yntema, 'Contract and Conflict of Laws: "Autonomy" in Choice of Law in the United States' (1955) 1 *New York Law Forum* 46.

made the contract, rather than where it was to be performed. Thus a shipping company, responsible for transporting baggage from London to Mauritius under a contract signed in London, could rely on an exemption clause against loss of one parcel because English law held the clause valid, while Mauritian law did not.[65] As the Judicial Committee pointed out, while final delivery was to be in Mauritius, the baggage was to pass through other countries en route—a good practical reason for choosing the law of the place of contracting. Yet Mansfield's case itself had shown that doing so was only a presumption: Robinson had lent Bland a sum to meet a gaming debt in Paris and Bland had drawn a bill of exchange there to discharge the loan in a fortnight. Since the bill was to be met in London, that was taken to show an intention that English law should apply.

Inevitably, cases would also arise where the parties in different countries concluded the contract by correspondence, and it seemed artificial to make (say) a question of interpretation turn on where the contract was finally concluded (an issue in itself on which contract laws could conflict). Westlake saw that the courts were deciding which law to apply by themselves bringing into account the various terms and circumstances in which contracts were made—a process which he characterized as determining the 'proper law of the contract', in the sense of being the law with which in all the circumstances the contract had most connection.[66] His phrase would only become standard after Lord Simonds adopted it in 1951.[67] This was a shift away from the language of 'presumed intent'—a recognition of what was already happening in response to the inescapable complexities of modern transactions. The question of the applicable law would be a dominant issue when there was a clear difference of rule or public policy between the two legal systems. But there were cases enough where the opposed parties were fighting over the meaning of a contractual word or phrase as it applied to facts which themselves were in contention. The alleged conflict of laws would then go to supposed differences about the correct approach to interpretation and to such often

---

[65] *P & O Steamship* v. *Shand* (1865) 3 Moo. PC (N.S.) 272. Mauritius applied the *Code civil* of Napoleon. Fortunately a decision of the Cour de Cassation reached the same result as the JC (case of the ship *Alma*). For other leading decisions in the period to 1914, *Jacobs* v. *Crédit Lyonnais* (1883) 12 QBD 589 (contract between English parties for shipment of a cargo to London for payment there binding despite effect of *force majeure* rule at place of shipment); *Re Missouri Steamship* (1888) 42 Ch D 321, (public policy objection to contractual exemption clause according to the *lex loci contractu*; contract nonetheless upheld because of indications that law of place of performance (England) was to apply); and see *Royal Exchange Assurance* v. *Vega* [1902] 2 KB 384; *British South Africa Co* v. *De Beers* [1910] 2 Ch 502.

[66] Westlake, *Private International Law*, 236–7. He treated the reference to the parties' intention in *Shand's* case as nominal, rather than substantial, suggesting that it would not have been referred to if the public policy objection had arisen under English law, rather than the Mauritian French law; cf. *Re Missouri* (above, n. 65). Dicey was more circumspect: see *Conflict*, Rule 146.

[67] *Bonython* v. *Commonwealth of Australia* [1951] AC 201 at 219.

associated questions as how terms would be understood in a particular market or trade and what understandings must be treated as assumptions underlying the transaction. Once a court had worked through these possibilities it might well be that no sufficient difference existed between the two systems to need the application of any private international law.

Property

The subjects of succession to property on death and of the ownership and other rights in property during a marriage had long been issues to which the *ius gentium* gave attention. We shall refer to them in relation to family property, but plainly they are matters in which personal law is likely to play a role.[68] Aside from that, there were many questions affecting property which arose from dealings *inter vivos* and from injuries and deprivations outside the scope of contracts. With moveable property there could be questions concerning title, the lesser interests of bailees and so on, which could be characterized as distinct from purely contractual considerations. Civilian doctrine had traditionally referred these matters also to the personal law of the owner of the property and there had been some indications that English law would adopt the same rule.[69] However, given the rapid growth of international trade, the individual transfer of corporeal objects and the granting of rights in them, for instance by way of pledge, were generally referred to the *lex situs* of the goods.[70]

What was coming to matter was the commodity, not a person's relationship to it. Indeed in the 1840s the same general approach was accepted by leading civilian authorities—in Germany, Savigny, in France, Foelix.[71] Commodity dealers needed plainer rules than an inquiry into the domiciliary laws of particular owners. (So indeed did private consumers, but their concerns scarcely determined the shift in approach.) There were major differences, for instance in laws of sale, over whether delivery of the object was a necessary step in transferring its ownership or whether a contractual agreement making the transfer would suffice; so equally with rules concerning whether defective title to a chattel could or could not be cured in a sale to an innocent purchaser or in open market—and if so in what

---

[68] Below, XIII, Pt 4, Ch. VII, pp. 836–8.

[69] *Sill* v. *Worswick* (1791) 1 H. Bl. 690; *Philips* v. *Hunter* (1795) 2 H. Bl. 406. Lord Chelmsford's later assertion of the same approach (*Liverpool Marine Credit* v. *Hunter* (1868) LR 3 Ch App 479) was confined in the textbooks to the special rules concerning ships.

[70] Leading cases included *Freeman* v. *East India Co* (1822) 5 B. & Ald. 617; *Cammell* v. *Sewell* (1860) 1 H. & N. 746; *Liverpool Marine Credit* (above, n. 69); *City Bank* v. *Barrow* (1880) 5 App Cas 664.

[71] As Westlake made plain: *Private International Law*, 199–202.

circumstances. It was inevitable across commercially vibrant countries that such a shift would take place.

Even less was it possible to resolve issues relating to intangibles by reference to simple guiding principles. The characterization of debt in common law systems as a value capable of transfer to another by assignment led to the rule that its effectiveness was governed by the law of the place where it was properly recoverable. But where it was a secured debt, the law of the place where the security was would be preferred to either that of the contract or the domicile of the debtor. Financial instruments, such as bills of exchange and promissory notes, drew a variety of solutions from civilian and common law authors.[72] Most complex of all was the distribution of assets, whether of traders or non-traders, upon an insolvency or an assignment to creditors in general, which might involve the distribution of property under concurrent bankruptcy proceedings in different countries.[73]

As to land, civilian doctrine went some way in referring issues to the law of its location, but not with the unrelenting commitment to territoriality that would characterize some of the decisions and writings of common lawyers. For them sanctity of property rights and the territoriality of the state drew together in an insistence that issues concerning rights in land were governed by the *lex situs*. Direct questions of title to non-English land, stemming from an assertion of the tort of trespass, could not even be litigated in England.[74] Despite this, less direct issues might be accommodated within the jurisdiction. These could include cases in equity, which were held to turn on the personal nature of Chancery's jurisdiction over defendants. Hence specific performance might be granted to carry out a contract to settle the boundaries of foreign land;[75] or to require a trustee to give effect to a trust interest over foreign land.[76] Respect for territoriality might lead the court to take into account the law of the *situs* in actually deciding the case.[77] But in the nineteenth century this was not necessarily so. Particularly when it scented fraud, Chancery might turn to its own law as justification for intervening in a dispute over rights in foreign land. It used the personal nature of the

---

[72] The complexities could be considerable, since the drawer, acceptor and indorser of a bill might all be in different countries, and the place for payment might be different again: see Westlake, *Private International Law*, 315–27.

[73] Westlake, *Private International Law*, Ch. 6; Dicey, *Conflict*, Rule 177.

[74] A line of cases from *Carteret* v. *Petty* (1676) 2 Sw. 323 led to *British South Africa Co* v. *Companhia de Moçambique* [1893] AC 632. See Westlake, *Private International Law*, Ch. 8; Dicey, *Conflict*, Ch. 22.

[75] *Penn* v. *Lord Baltimore* (1750) 1 Ves. Sen. 444.

[76] *Arglasse* v. *Muchamp* (1682) 1 Vern. 75 provides an early example from Lord Nottingham.

[77] As in *Bank of Africa* v. *Cohen* [1909] 2 Ch 129.

injunction to order defendants not to continue equivalent proceedings before foreign courts and might require undertakings from them to deal with the land in certain ways if the plaintiff won in the English proceedings.[78] This might well achieve justice, however much it offended the self-respect of the country where the land was situate. Lord Chancellors had an instinct for where their duty lay.

Torts

With issues of tort or delict, the private international law of all countries had to face the prospect of differences of principle and nuance: liability might be premised on different concepts, including the questions whether liability was strict or required proof of negligence or intention; how issues of causation would be approached; and whether there was any complete defence or a limitation of liability. If, as at common law, the availability of injunctive, monetary, or other remedies was for the *lex fori*, this avoided intractable problems, but it could encourage forum shopping.[79] As we have seen, contests over trespass to land in another jurisdiction were considered too intricate to be a subject that an English court could take into its own hands.[80] Apart from that, the courts were inclined to open their doors. But the cautious solution at which they arrived, notably in the high politics of *Phillips* v. *Eyre*,[81] was to require that the conduct be wrongful both by English law and the law of the place where it occurred. Edward Eyre—once an explorer of Australia, but later the Governor of Jamaica—had suppressed an uprising on that island by military intervention that was claimed to be wholly excessive. However that might be, the Jamaican legislature had passed an act of indemnity protecting him from suits claiming damages for the consequences. An English civil suit against him therefore failed because his actions had become unchallengeable in Jamaica, albeit after the event.[82] Where, by contrast, the strict

---

[78] See Westlake, *Private International Law*, paras 130–1. Thus Lord Eldon in *Harrison* v. *Gurney* (1821) 2 Jac. & W. 563 appointed a receiver over the foreign lands in order to provide effective relief; and also ordered the trustees not to proceed on the matter in the courts of the *situs*.

[79] Savigny argued for reference to the *lex fori*, characterizing delictual wrongs as expressing moral principles of special meaning to the country concerned: *Conflict of Laws* (trans. W. Guthrie, 1869), 176. Westlake found it difficult to see the difference from contractual liability: *Private International Law* (1st edn, 1858), 230–4.

[80] Above, n. 74. The same approach would be applied to patents and similar immaterial property because they involved state grants applicable only in their own territory. But despite a decision from the Supreme Court of Victoria to that effect (*Potter* v. *Broken Hill* (1905) VLR 612, affirmed (1906) 3 CLR 479), the English textbooks would ignore the question for successive editions.

[81] [1870] 6 QB 1 (preceded by *The Halley*, above, n. 60).

[82] The indemnity raised fundamental issues about the doctrine of parliamentary supremacy. For the great English controversy over Eyre's conduct in Jamaica, see Pitts, *Turn to Empire*, 150–60;

test was satisfied, an English court would have the comfort of applying its own law, on liability as much as on remedies.[83]

7. ENGLISH SOLUTIONS SET IN ENGLISH COURTS

In 1820 the very idea of private international law as part of English Law was only beginning to form in common law minds. By 1914 its main problems and their detailed consequences had been discussed in some detail, with answers hazarded or proffered in case law and occasional statutes, underpinned by substantial texts. In its early years, the writers who shaped it drew more heavily on comparative learning than would be the pattern for much of the twentieth century.[84] It emerged in the environment of scholarly exchange between the nations accorded status in international law, and the private side separated from the public only gradually. Its growing insularity is marked by the failure of Britain to play much part in the movement to settle solutions to conflicts of private law by international convention. Content to spread English solutions across its Empire, Britain adhered to none of the six conventions reached by the four Hague Conferences on Private International Law of 1893–1904.[85]

In its way this seems part of the British response to the increasing jealousy against it in international politics. More immediately, it is the consequence of the growth of precedents in a system that accorded them such significance as a source of law. As judges went about the short-term business of resolving particular conflicts, their reasons for decision were seized upon in the great repositories of the subject and in the textbooks through which the growing ranks of lawyers were instructed. The flow of decisions was still limited, but that only encouraged the belief that 'judicial legislation' was its appropriate vehicle. The common lawyers appropriated the field as their own in a world where statutory direction was invading so much else and the prospect of international solutions even to private law problems was beginning. As case law accumulated it buttressed a juristic

---

R. W. Kostal, *The Jurisprudence of Power: Victorian Empire and the Rule of Law* (Oxford, 2006).

[83] Later the Court of Appeal considered it enough to sustain English jurisdiction that the activity was unjustifiable because criminal in the place of wrongdoing, even if it was not delictual there, but only in England: *Machado* v. *Fontes* [1897] 2 QB 231 (publishing a libel in Brazil). This served to emphasize that the Court would apply English law in actually deciding the case. Dicey had disapproved of this outcome before the decision was reached: *Conflict*, Rule 176.

[84] Even the arrival of Jewish and other jurists of great distinction, driven west by the horrors of 1930s' persecutions, would begin to reverse the trend only gradually: see North, 'Twentieth Century' 514–15.

[85] Apart from the Convention on Civil Procedure, these were concerned with aspects of family law and will be referred to below, XIII, pp. 841–2. See generally, K. Lipstein 'One Hundred Years of the Hague Conferences on Private International Law' (1993) 42 *ICLQ* 553–653, esp. Pt III.

concentration on past answers, rather than ideal solutions. Comparisons by the learned, which had little enough appeal to practising common lawyers, could mostly be left for the speculations of the reflective in their separate sphere.

In this the perception of sources was distinctively British. Starting with the limited provisions of the French civil code, a movement to embody private international law in the codified sources began in civilian systems. By 1898 a much more elaborate coverage was included in the German Civil Code, showing that it was perfectly possible to produce such a design by legislation. Later the United States would engage in its typical process for harmonization by generating a Restatement of the subject which could give influential guidance to courts at both the State and the Federal levels. So eventually it would be that basic codes on matters of jurisdiction and the recognition and enforcement of judgments would be worked out within the auspices of the European Union; and within the law of obligations steps would be taken by treaties designed to set down the substantive principles for resolving conflicts concerning contractual and non-contractual issues. More broadly, the Hague Conferences on Private International Law would generate international agreements having potentially world effect—the kind of step which brings back links between public and private international law. The scene has, in the century since 1914, undergone a sea-change of considerable enrichment—certainly so far as the UK is concerned.[86]

---

[86] For the impacts of legal change from the perspective the inter-war period onwards, see North, 'Twentieth Century', 498–515.

Part Two

PUBLIC LAW

I

Parliament

THIS chapter describes Parliament as a law maker—what had to be done to turn a proposal into a law. It begins with the Commons, and particularly with the relation between the Commons and the government. It was trite law throughout our period that Parliament's sovereignty gave its laws a finality no other rule-making possessed, and trite politics that the Commons was the primary initiating chamber. Well before 1914 the government came to possess a near monopoly of access to this legislative machinery, which was different from the near veto power it possessed in 1820. This section accordingly traces the decline of the private member and the decline of the Lords. It describes how far the important category of local and private legislation also fell under executive control, which was partly a function of increased control over the Commons, partly of increased control over local government authorities, who were the prime sponsors of this form of legislation.

Judges merit scarcely a footnote. Uniformly they considered statutes only the object of interpretation. Questions of validity of public general legislation simply did not arise; there is nothing to record. Very occasionally they arose for local and private legislation, but when they did judges likewise confined their role to interpretation. Early in our period some judges thought their interpretive role different for local and private legislation, as will be seen, but the mood did not last. Looking back in 1893 Bowen LJ ridiculed his predecessors for that pretension; statutes were statutes, even if some were better written than others.[1]

Broadly speaking, there were two long-term transitions, the first beginning long before our period starts and the second ending after it finishes. In the first the government, once the king's, though living in dialogue with the Commons, became instead wholly dependent upon the Commons for its continued existence. From the late eighteenth century onwards royal patronage, which had sustained governments by providing reliable supporters in the Commons, was removed by a series of financial and administrative reforms designed to reduce the costs of government, hence to meet public criticism and remove pressure for

---

[1] *R v. Great Western Railway* (1893) 62 LJ KB 572.

franchise reform. George IV, as regent and as king, sought less control over the personnel of government and its measures than his father had done. Bullied by Wellington, his political impotence was demonstrated by his failure to prevent Catholic emancipation in 1829. The king's influence over his government further diminished with the return of the Whigs in 1830, and with the manner of the passing of the Reform Act 1832, when William IV was manoeuvred into promising a far larger creation of peers to swamp the Lords than he wished. The king's dismissal of his government in 1834 rebounded upon him when he failed to find an alternative. Such a demonstration of plenary prerogative power was never attempted again. His choice of pretext—that he thought the Whigs too weak in the Commons to merit their office—only emphasized where real power lay.

Party made this independence from the monarch possible, and it is conceivable that with the weakening of party identification in the mid-century stronger royal control might have returned.[2] But the two most likely actors, Peel and Prince Albert, died young, and by the time Victoria emerged from her seclusion her influence was limited to the occasional veto of reprobates or radicals as ministers, an imperious barrage of correspondence to her advisors, and (that power beloved of Conservatives and constitutional lawyers) the ability sometimes to select a prime minister from among the leadership of the majority party when the party itself had not clearly identified its man. So the period between the two Reform Acts 1832 and 1867 has been labelled a period of 'parliamentary government', recognizing that governments were usually made, ended, and replaced by the Commons.[3] Defeat in the Lords could only weaken, not destroy, and even the results of elections were not clear until a motion of confidence made in the Commons interpreted the verdict.

In the second transition liberalism transformed into democracy. Where once a government had been chosen and sustained by the Commons it became instead the current embodiment of the people's will, the winner of a plebiscitary general election, sustained by that vote until, usually, the electorate voted the rival party into office in its place. Parties acquired an existence extraneous to Westminster. The Commons became more sharply divided, the majority representing the electoral mandate of a party to govern. The second Reform Act marked the beginning, the third in 1884 the decisive turn, when traditional parliamentary seats were converted from dual- into single-member constituencies containing a roughly equal number of voters, a move justified by democracy but devised by Lord Salisbury to save the countryside and perhaps the suburbs for

---

[2] A. Hawkins, '"Parliamentary Government" and Victorian Political Parties c. 1830–c. 1880' (1989) 104 *EHR* 638–69.

[3] See the works cited in Hawkins '"Parliamentary Government"'.

the Conservatives. Control of small constituencies by individual landowners, which had been reduced but by no means abolished by the 1832 Act, disappeared with the second Reform Act. Open voting was replaced by the secret ballot in 1872, not least in an attempt to stop employers from seizing the directing interest that landowners had vacated.

After 1884 about two-thirds of men in England and Wales could vote, fewer in Scotland or Ireland, which they could exercise only on a 'first past the post, winner takes all' basis that perpetuated and reinforced a two-party system. It was an incomplete parliamentary democracy for men, not even the beginnings of one for women. Moreover, its nature was contested between the parties, because the Conservatives had permanent control of the Lords. When the Conservatives held office the Lords was somnolent, virtually otiose save for providing comfortable berths for senior ministers. The country then experienced a form of party government. But the Liberals in office were allowed no such latitude, for then the Conservatives insisted that the Lords had a referendal function, justifying rejection of Liberal measures they deemed not to have been fairly put to and endorsed by the electorate. From this collision there could have emerged a reconstituted Lords or a regular use of the referendum, either of which would have required something like a Constitution Act to spell out the ramifications. Instead the crisis produced the Parliament Act 1911, which reduced the Lords' powers and produced party government in its modern form.

1. THE COMMONS AS A LEGISLATIVE ASSEMBLY

In a history of nineteenth-century law, legislation naturally takes centre stage, and with it the perception that Parliament's importance was as sovereign legislator. Equally, the focus is mostly on the Commons, for by the mid-century the Lords was willing to acknowledge what had been true for a long time, that it was a reviewing rather than an initiating chamber.[4] But the Commons had not evolved to give legislation primacy. Bagehot ranked the Commons' legislative function in the 1860s as only third in importance behind its elective function in giving its confidence to Her Majesty's Government and its educative function in shaping the nation's political consciousness.[5] As Peter Fraser has written, through into the mid-century the Commons was 'still thought of as the "grand inquest of the nation", where independently of parties or of ministers all aspects of the

---

[4] SC of House of Lords on Despatch of Public Business, Report, PP 1861 (321), xi, 417; W. Bagehot, 'English Constitution', in N. St. John-Stevas (ed.), The Collected Works of Walter Bagehot (1966–86), v, 268.

[5] 'English Constitution' in St. John-Stevas, Collected Works, v, 288; see also vi, 41, 45.

nation's life were represented and all its needs that admitted of a political remedy were resolved'.[6] It was a debating chamber premised upon the value of informed opinion, its procedures egalitarian to the point that until 1835 ministers had no formal priority in arranging its business. Its character as a chamber oppositional to the king, manifested in the slogan 'grievances before supply', gave it internal procedures that encouraged spontaneity at the expense of the orderly processing of official business.

Further, each parliamentary session was self-contained, consisting usually of some 125 working days or thereabouts, between February and mid-summer each year.[7] Business not concluded when Parliament was prorogued had to be reintroduced afresh in the next session; it could not simply be resumed where it had been left off. This annual rhythm reflected and suited the Commons' ancient role of annually voting supply to the government, reinforced by the need for annual renewal of the Mutiny Acts, but it distorted legislative possibilities. Each year bills lapsed for lack of time, others were rushed through only partly digested. Yet public general legislation became the vehicle through which politicians reacted to social and economic change, and sought to mould it. Indeed Bagehot's careful ranking of the Commons' functions was written explicitly to counter the common popular view that the only appropriate measure of scrutiny of the Commons' performance each year was its legislative output for the session. In practice that meant scrutiny of the government's performance, since legislation had become primarily government business, not wholly to the exclusion of private members' legislation, but predominantly so. Gladstone, for example, could pillory Palmerston in 1856 for his inept legislative record by reminding his readers that as long ago as 1841 Peel had used just that yardstick when moving the downfall of Lord Melbourne's administration: 'those, he contended, who are unable to legislate, are disentitled to govern'.[8]

Even in the unreformed Commons governments accepted some responsibility for most legislation, for when ministers were not actually the proposers they were often active in lending support to what was notionally a private member's bill.[9] Sometimes that was a form of co-option. Thomas Estcourt's Licensing Act 1828, for example, was co-sponsored by Peel and Dawson, the Financial Secretary, and had quite a different orientation from what Estcourt had first

---

[6] P. Fraser, 'The Growth of Ministerial Control in the Nineteenth-century House of Commons' (1960) 75 *EHR* 444, 455.

[7] I. Jennings, *Parliament* (2nd edn, Cambridge, 1970), 95; *Return of Number of Days on which House of Commons Sat [etc]*, PP 1881 (445), lxxiv, 109; P. Jupp, *British Politics on the Eve of Reform* (Basingstoke, 1998), 198.

[8] W. E. Gladstone, 'The Declining Efficiency of Parliament' (1856) 99 *Quart. Rev.* 521.

[9] Jupp, *British Politics*, 168.

proposed.[10] Professor Jupp shows that individual enthusiasts could succeed in sponsoring significant legislation in the 1820s, through persistence in the House, building opinion there through floating bills and instituting select committees, usually in conjunction with pressure from without, taking care also to consult government and receive its advice. 'Robert Slaney on the poor laws, Thomas Potter Macqueen on the laws of settlement, Robert Gordon on lunatic asylums and Robert Wilmot Horton on emigration are exemplars in this respect', though not all their activity resulted in new law.[11] With ministries few and small, political and legislative initiative often rested with such individual members, but, even so, government advice, neutrality, and support, be it in votes or in the provision of Commons time, were often critical.[12]

In the 1820s competition for parliamentary time seems to have been manageable. A rule change in 1811 that had earmarked two days a week for 'orders'— the progressing of business previously introduced into the House—and which should have brought greater regularity to the legislative process, seems not to have been strictly enforced, so it was common for government business to be deflected by matters of the moment.[13] There was no crisis however; governments did not have to struggle for supply, and their ministers habitually secured some 60 or 70 Acts annually from the 70 or 80 bills they introduced, as against private members' 15 to 20 Acts a year.[14] There was time enough for everyone, even if it was disorganized.

Commentators then and now agree that the 1832 election changed the Commons. Its sessions, though longer than before, were too short to accommodate increased ministerial and private members' ambition to legislate. Ministers' responsibility for preparing and carrying legislation grew by degrees, wrote Earl Grey, and chiefly since the passing of the Reform Act 1832.[15] But ministers could not dictate to the Commons. They had no extensive spoils system to bribe members into support, nor were there many places in government to use as rewards for faithful service. Old corruption had been dismantled. Parties were formed in Parliament, not extraneously, so party discipline could not be enforced as it would be a century later. Thus persuasion was needed for each government

[10] Jupp, *British Politics*, 170; S. Anderson 'Discretion and the Rule of Law: The Licensing of Drink in England, c.1817–40' (2002) 23 *JLH* 45–59.

[11] Jupp, *British Politics* 175. Sturges Bourne is perhaps a better example, for his poor law legislation in 1818 and 1819: D. Eastwood, 'Men, Morals and the Machinery of Social Legislation, 1790–1840' (1994) 13 *Parl. Hist.* 190–205.

[12] Jupp, *British Politics*, 174–8.

[13] Jupp, *British Politics*, 442.

[14] Figures from Fraser, 'Growth of Ministerial Control', 455n and Jupp, *British Politics*, 181.

[15] Henry, Earl Grey, *Parliamentary Government Considered with Reference to Reform* (2nd edn, 1864), 21–2.

measure, which very largely meant persuasion in the chamber. At the same time the chamber was the arena in which responsibility of the government to the Commons for their policies and acts of executive authority was daily manifested. So Commons' procedures had to accommodate conflicting objectives. There was a shift of initiative towards government—associated with the increased importance of legislation—and within that a further shift to make debate more efficient so that measures could be thoroughly and fairly assessed. But it was also inherent in parliamentary government that all government's actions and neglects were open to scrutiny, as they had always been, hence a need for considerable leeway for individuals to raise these matters. The government was responsible to the Commons in the Commons.

The basic settlement introduced in 1835 lasted until at least the 1860s, though always with encroachments from both sides, always with refinement and modification. It was that the government should have just two order days a week secured for its business, private members one order day for the progression of their bills, and the remaining two days should be notice of motion days for topical debate and the introduction of bills. The formula acknowledged the government's duty to lead the House, while accepting that government and private members could have different agendas. It showed something of a preference for legislative proposals, though, importantly, government order days had also to be used for voting supply. The aim, however, was only that there be reasonable and predictable provision for debate. As a select committee later put it, ministers should have preference 'not only in the introduction of their Bills but in opportunities for pressing them upon the consideration of the House'.[16] Petitions, which flooded the House in an ever-rising tide, were still to be received, but after 1836 they were not to be open to impromptu debate.[17]

Though from 1848 there was polite interest in the French notion of *clôture*, nobody sought to regulate the course or duration of debate, not least because ministers did not necessarily expect all their bills to pass. But the division of time was becoming precarious. Adjournments from order days cut into notice days and, especially, it was difficult to structure notice days to cater for both the impromptu debates of important issues and the long-term, consciousness-raising motions which often bored the House inquorate. So some members used procedural opportunities on order days to divert the agenda their way, and the House

---

[16] *SC on Business of the House*, Report, PP 1861 (173), xi, 431, para. 26.

[17] The new practice was formalized into a Standing Order in 1842: C. Leys, 'Petitioning in the Nineteenth and Twentieth Centuries' (1955) 3 *Political Studies* 45–64; T. E. May, *A Treatise on the Law, Proceedings, and Usage of Parliament* (6th edn, 1868), 515–18. May calculated that in the five years to the end of 1842 the Commons received 70,072 petitions, compared to 28,283 in the five years to the end of 1832: 515n.

responded by removing numerous formal stages in the legislative process (for example, that a clause proposed to be added to a bill be now read), since it was on such occasions that members could raise colourable amendments designed to raise their own issues or merely to delay.[18] The result, sometimes referred to as the 'rule of progress', aimed to confine debate on the principle of a bill to its second and third readings, detailed examination of its clauses to the committee stage, and new amendments to the report stage.

By 1861 the House usually conceded government a third order day in mid-session, giving it theoretical control of about half the Commons' time.[19] Importantly, however, order days used for seeking supply were apt to be diverted into a miscellany of member-initiated debates, because the House could not bring itself to abandon the ancient maxim of 'grievances before supply'. The symbolism was heavy, but the political point simple: notice days were often of strictly minority interest, so members' issues were much better raised when ministers had to listen. So in the early part of the session, when it was imperative to pass military estimates to enable the renewal of the Mutiny Acts, a great part of what was nominally government time was effectively ceded to members. Little legislation could get under way until after Easter, which often left too little time for it to pass through both Houses before the session ended. Within the logic of mid-century parliamentary government, solutions were necessarily compromises: in 1861 the government's third order day became permanent, but was always to be a supply day so as to leave members their opportunities. The government was also allowed a reversionary interest in the Tuesday motion day, should motions not exhaust the time, a base from which there was much future expansion. By 1861, then, government may have acquired more of the Commons' time, but the ethos was still one of sharing with members, whose claims were not strenuously denied.

More radical procedural changes were rejected because they would upset the constitutional balance. The first, raised in 1848 and revived in 1861 and 1869, was to allow bills that had passed their Commons stages to carry over in the Lords next session.[20] This drew arcane objections that such an incursion into the effect of prorogation would impinge upon Crown prerogatives, and there were some practical difficulties with extending the time it took to pass a bill. But the House rejected it principally because it might strengthen the power of the Lords, who,

---

[18] *SC on the Business of the House*, Report, *PP* 1854 (213), vii, 11, 61–2; cf. M. Rush, *The Role of the Member of Parliament Since 1868* (Oxford, 2001), 65.

[19] *SC on Despatch of Public Business of the House*, Report, *PP* 1861 (173), xi, 431, para. 25.

[20] All reprinted in *SC on Business of the House (abridged procedure on partly considered Bills)*, *PP* 1890 (298), xi, 1; it was considered by Gladstone as part of the 1882 reforms too: see E. Hughes, 'The Changes in Parliamentary Procedure, 1880–1882', in R. Pares and A. J. P. Taylor (eds), *Essays Presented to Sir Lewis Namier* (1956), 289–319.

rather than feeling obliged to pass an unpalatable bill under pressure of time, might now shelve it for a session.[21] The second radical proposal was to shift part of a bill's progress out of the chamber to morning sittings before committees, several of which could sit contemporaneously. The thoroughgoing version of this proposal, from Erskine May in 1854, was that a bill's early stages should henceforward be taken in one of six grand committees, bills being grouped by subject area so as to attract specialist members.[22] Milder versions of the idea were developed too, but fear of government manipulation, compounded by the severe difficulty of finding an appropriate way of selecting committee members, saw even those rejected in 1854, 1861, and 1871.[23] To allow government to by-pass the chamber would diminish the influence of minorities unacceptably.

After the second Reform Act the tone of debate began to change. Disraeli's convention-breaking resignation on defeat in the 1868 election without waiting for an adverse vote in the Commons, coupled with the emergence of both Conservative and Liberal parties as centralized and autonomous bodies, not dependent on the shifting allegiance of parliamentary adherents, signalled an impending transfer of authority. Responsibility to the electorate gradually replaced responsibility to the Commons as the central facet of a government's existence. The two-party system strengthened. As both parties came to seek election on the basis of their legislative proposals, and as the franchise expanded again, it became plausible to assert that the Commons' duty was primarily to pass government legislation, not just to consider it. Government should not only have the lion's share of parliamentary time for its business, but should also be able to curtail debate to bring questions to the vote. The transition was not complete until after the third Reform Act, and its logic was still being worked out at the end of our period, but even in 1872 one iconoclastic Liberal minister could reject values such as 'grievances before supply' as 'obsolete words and fine phrases', and another could twice propose that the Commons should adopt the *clôture* to reduce time-wasting discussion.[24]

Likewise, short-term party advantage began to colour debate on procedural change. Both parties in the 1870s sought to make the motion that the House move

---

[21] *SC on Despatch of Public Business* 1861, Report, questions 142–3, 153.

[22] 'The Machinery of Parliamentary Legislation' (1854) 99 *Edin. Rev.* 243; *SC on Business of the House* 1854, Report, 69–70.

[23] *SC on Business of the House* 1854, Report, 69, 87–8; *PD* 1861 (s3) 162: 1522–8; *SC on Business of the House*, Report, *PP* 1871 (137), ix, 1, 47–8. 'Supplementary chapter by Sir Courtney Ilbert KCSI' in J. Redlich, *The Procedure of the House of Commons* (1908), iii, 202–24 at 208–11.

[24] *PD* 1872 (s3) 209: 1093–4 (Lowe); Knatchbull-Hugessen: *SC on Public Business* 1871, Report, 6; *SC on Public Business*, Report, *PP* 1878 (268), xviii, 1, 17. '*Clôture*' was the common usage until anglicized by Speaker Brand in a suggestion to Gladstone in 1881: Hughes, 'Changes in Parliamentary Procedure', 310.

into a committee to discuss supply purely formal, to prevent members seizing the moment to raise their own issues, but each denounced the other's proposal, similar though they were.[25] And though both parties were enormously relieved when Speaker Brand unilaterally took a closure power to end Irish members' obstruction in 1881, Gladstone's consequent new general rules, which needed 19 days of debate to pass, were treated as a party measure, not the basis for a lasting settlement.[26] In turn the Conservatives' remodelling of Brand's closure rule to reduce safeguards for minorities and vest its control more completely in the majority of the House took 14 days to pass, and their invention of the 'guillotine', an enhanced closure rule forcing a vote on all outstanding questions and amendments, drew vehement predictions of the day when such tools would rebound against them.[27] 'You think yourselves safe in the protection of the House of Lords', one Irish member warned the Conservatives presciently as they introduced the guillotine, 'but it is just possible that at a future time you may not have a House of Lords to protect you.'[28] Such was the pattern, with innovations introduced to curb Irish obstruction later turned to more ordinary party purposes and tightened to make majority control more effective.[29]

These changes did not yet eclipse the public role of the private member. Though the number of private members' bills passing into law fluctuated considerably from year to year depending on political circumstance, the five-year running average was very steady at about 21 from the 1868/9 session through to 1894.[30] Professor Jupp's exemplars of the 1820s had their counterparts in the 1870s: A. J. Mundella, for example, sometime Chartist, later an 'advanced' employer and factory owner.[31] He co-sponsored the Wages Attachment Abolition Act in 1870, and saw the bill he unsuccessfully introduced in 1869 be partially (and unsatisfactorily) taken up by the Liberal government as the Trade Union Act and the Criminal Law Amendment Act in 1871. In 1872 and 1873 he introduced bills to render the latter judge-proof, leading to the Conservatives' Conspiracy and Protection of Property Act and Employers and Workmen Act of 1875. In 1876 he successfully sponsored a bill to amend the Trade Union Act. In all this he was acting for the Trades Union Congress. It in turn supported his own campaign for

[25] *SC on the Business of the House 1871*, Report; *PD* 1872 (s3) 209: 1039–98; *SC on Public Business 1878*, Report, 66; *PD* 1879 (s3) 243: 1318–84.

[26] Redlich, *Procedure of the House*, i, 165–75.

[27] *PD* 1887 (s3) 313: 784; 315: 1594, 1630–31.

[28] *PD* 1887 (s3) 315: 1660 (Healy).

[29] Jennings, *Parliament*, 127–30, 242–3.

[30] *PP, Return of Public Bills*, annual. Successful non-ministerial bills first introduced in the Lords dwindled over the same period from about six per year to two or three.

[31] This account of his legislative endeavours is taken from W. H. G. Armytage, *A.J. Mundella, 1825–1897* (1951).

extension of the Factory Acts, the main vehicle for which was the Factory Acts Reform Association. This campaign saw one of Mundella's bills incorporated into the Liberals' Factory and Workshop Act 1871, and another into the Conservatives' Factory Act 1874. In addition, in 1872 he successfully sponsored an arbitration bill for the TUC, which it had got from the county court judge and pioneer of industrial arbitration, Rupert Kettle. At the urging of his constituency's borough council he co-sponsored the Borough Fund Act 1872, which, catching just the right moment to win government support, enabled local authorities to charge the costs of applying for local Acts on to the rates, greatly expanding their ability to acquire and run public utilities. From 1877 to 1879 he introduced bills to abolish the property qualification for membership of school boards and town councils, unsuccessful each time, but enacted in very much the same form by the Conservatives in 1880. Much later, spurred again by constituency interests, he introduced a merchandise marks bill, which became part of the government's 1887 Act. And finally he piloted into legislation the Prevention of Cruelty to, and Better Protection of, Children Act 1889, which combined enforcement powers useful for the swiftly rising NSPCC and regulation of the employment of street children and child theatrical performers.

These are all examples of successful pressure from without, where a member intimately connected with pressure groups acted as bridgehead to Parliament and as liaison with government. He lobbied and led delegations, and when he was not introducing his own bills he worked for government bills which subsumed his own, and pressed in committee for the amendment of other members' bills.

Similarly, Russell Gurney, a Conservative and a lawyer, worked for years with, for, and through the Married Women's Property Committee and the Social Science Association to achieve the Married Women's Property Act 1870 and the Medical (Qualifications) Act 1876. The latter, blessed by the government, prised open the door to the medical profession for women, the former, without government support and mangled by the Lords, was merely an unsatisfactory step on the way to the Liberals' settlement of the issue in 1882, itself a consequence of prolonged pressure from without.[32] But in addition to these well-known measures Gurney in 1870 also successfully sponsored a Shipping Dues Exemption Act, a fitting subject for a Member of Parliament for Southampton, and co-sponsored the Life Assurance Companies Act. Then in 1871 he successfully promoted an Act facilitating loans to poor law boards, co-sponsored the Workshop Regulation Act, and became the latest, but not the last, private member to fail to persuade government to allow a public prosecutors bill to pass.[33] Even in 1872, when he

[32] L. Holcombe, *Wives and Property* (Oxford, 1983); C. Blake, *The Charge of the Parasols* (1990).
[33] P. Kurland and D. Waters, 'Public Prosecutions in England 1854–79' [1959] *Duke LJ* 493.

was heavily concerned with work outside Parliament, his name can be found as a co-sponsor of the successful Grand Juries (Middlesex) Act.

The differences between these men's experience and that of Slaney, Macqueen, Gordon, and Horton in the 1820s are perhaps twofold, but are differences of degree only. First, for Mundella particularly, government's own willingness to legislate on these social issues gave him greater opportunities for seeing his proposals carried into law through incorporation into government measures, to some extent counteracting the much greater competition for Commons' time. Secondly, both men were sometimes more obviously spokesmen in a way that their predecessors were not.[34] The Married Women's Property Committee and Trades Union Congress would have found other MPs if need be, though perhaps less prestigious in the TUC's case. Nonetheless Mundella and Gurney represent a generation of members for whom legislation was still a personal activity, even if it was very clearly as a junior partner to the government.[35]

Such activity was possible so long as members and pressure groups could rely upon parliamentary time being available year on year to maintain momentum. But on the one hand it was being reduced by the needs of the government, and on the other competition among members was increasing. In the 1820s about 50 private members' bills were introduced each year, increasing to the mid-60s by the early 1850s, where the rate remained until after the 1868 election.[36] Then the rise was dramatic: 100 bills in 1872, 130s and 140s through to the 1884–5 session, higher still later.[37] Even in 1854 private members' bills talked out on the days specially set aside for them were waiting a month for rescheduling.[38] Some extra time for private members' bills was available late at night, but from 1872 no opposed business could be taken after a specified hour, opposition to be signalled by a mere entry on the order paper.[39] In 1872 Mundella's factory bill had to wait three months for its second reading, the crucial stage for any bill; in 1888, when a very high placing in the lottery for priority had become critical, his first child cruelty

---

[34] Eastwood, 'Men, Morals'.

[35] J. Parry, *The Rise and Fall of Liberal Government in Victorian Britain* (New Haven, 1993), 229–30.

[36] Fraser, 'Growth of Ministerial Control', 455n; Jupp, *British Politics*, 168; PP, *Return of Public Bills*, annual; Parry, *Rise and Fall*, 230.

[37] PP, *Return of Public Bills*, annual. The figures rose to the 240s and 250s at the end of the 1880s, topping 300 in the 1893–4 session before falling back. Given that opportunities for progressing bills were reducing some explanation for these further increases is needed. Members may sometimes have been hunting in packs: Mundella when President of the Board of Trade faced additional pressure to get rail freight charges reduced from the fact that 'no fewer than seven private members were printed for presentation to the house of commons', Armytage, *Mundella*, 291.

[38] SC on the Business of the House 1854, Report, 100 (Pakington) and see 78 (May).

[39] May, *Treatise* (6th edn, 1873), 282.

bill was one of the vast majority that did not get even that far.[40] It was clear by
then that private members had merely a token role in initiating legislation. The
Social Science Association, which had used both routes to success, arming private members and lobbying ministries, wound itself up in 1886, since by then the
only reliable route to influence was direct communication between an interest
group and a ministry.[41] Ministries offered expertise, legitimacy, and continuity.

In 1887 and 1888 James Bryce MP sought to persuade the Commons to restore
to private members some of their former ability to introduce useful legislation
independently of government, and have it passed.[42] The demand clearly existed,
as Bryce noted, but getting a private member's bill to the starting line turned
on winning a high ranking by lottery, so there was no correlation between a
bill's importance and its even being discussed. Procedural rules made private
members' bills particularly easy to block, since once stalled they were difficult
to reschedule. There was pathos in Bryce's pleading, for he set his sights low.
Members, he said, might be surprised to know of 'the great many small amendments to the law and small administrative questions affecting the social welfare
of the people' once effected by private members' legislation, and even if a bill
failed it was surely in the public interest for there to be an extended debate of
some of these issues. But his only practicable suggestion was that the lottery be
replaced by a popularity poll among members, the bills with greatest initial support proceeding to second reading stage. His critics quickly pointed out that that
would inevitably be worked by the whips and thus effectively reduce private initiative. In 1891 the government refused to countenance even the most modest procedural change to aid private members' bills.[43] Subsequent attention fell almost
entirely on ways to expedite government business, and in 1914 a select committee
comprising entirely private members failed to agree a solution, lapsing without
reporting.[44] All this left private members' bills at the margin of politics to be sunk
or supported as ministers chose.[45] A government unable to agree upon a measure
might shunt it off into the private members' process, as prime minister Asquith
famously did with women's suffrage—hopeful that he could stifle it, or, if not,
that that momentous constitutional change would not taint him personally—but
such cynical or desperate uses were rare.[46]

---

[40] Armytage, *Mundella*, 125, 276.

[41] L. Goldman, 'The Social Science Association, 1857–1886' (1986) 101 *EHR* 95–134.

[42] *PD* 1887 (s3) 311: 380; 1888 (s3) 322: 1408, 1774.

[43] *PD* 1891 (s3) 351: 1068.

[44] *SC on House of Commons (Procedure)*, Reports, *PP* 1913 (246), vii, 15; 1914 (378) vii, 593.

[45] P. Rowland, *The Last Liberal Governments* (1968), i, 79n; ii, 154n.

[46] Rowland, *Last Liberal Governments*, ii, 36–8. Compare Disraeli's co-option of Gladstone's private member's bill in 1868 to end the vexed question of church rates: J. P. Ellens, *Religious Routes to
Gladstonian Liberalism* (University Park, Pennsylvania, 1994), 254.

The reason for this decline was that government control of Commons time and process tightened further in the late 1880s. During his 1868–74 ministry Gladstone had adhered still to the notion that fullness of debate was sacrosanct, compelling the Commons to sit until any hour of the morning to reach a division.[47] That value soon weakened. As W. H. Smith explained it in 1888, ministers had work to do in the mornings, as did the growing number of members who earned their living in commerce, finance, and the professions, though no doubt the increasing influence of oppositional party politics played its part too.[48] So a fixed closing time was instituted, which could be coupled with a closure motion to bring debate to a conclusion and not just an end. Government was to have freedom to stipulate the order of business in the House on days when it had priority, which in practice meant some four days out of five, since it habitually appropriated private members' days early in the session. In addition, on all but four occasions for moving the House into committee on questions of supply there was to be no opportunity for general debate.

That left just one general area of Commons activity to be brought under government control. Members could still propose amendments in committees of supply, which they used to introduce debate on the conduct and policies of departments listed in the estimates. Consequently the civil service estimates, which had taken 16 days in 1869, and a mere 13 in 1875, took 31 in 1887 as other opportunities for members had been removed.[49] A select committee, however, was inclined to agree that 'review of the administration of the country...is extremely valuable. It may be indulged in to an inordinate degree in respect of certain parts of that administration, but it is one of the prime functions of Parliament.'[50] It would be neither feasible nor desirable to shift that type of discussion out of the chamber and into a sub-committee, as had been proposed. Supply days had thus taken on their essential modern character as Opposition days for criticizing government policy. From 1896, however, they were limited to 20 days per session, to prevent their undue encroachment on government time. Government now had virtually complete control of the timetable. Balfour's well-known 'parliamentary railway time-table' in 1902, which sought to micro-manage the chamber in the government's interest, merely confirmed that fact.[51]

Yet still, it seemed, there was insufficient time. 'Every year the machine breaks down, and its failure is confessed', wrote Sir Courtney Ilbert, parliamentary

[47] Rush, *Role*, 66, quoting Lord George Hamilton.

[48] *PD* 1888 (s3) 321: 1400; and see Rush, *Role*, 94–103.

[49] *SC on Estimates Procedure (Grants of Supply)*, Report, *PP* 1888 (281), xii, 27.

[50] *SC on Estimates Procedure* 88 (Courtney). 'Inordinate' referred to Irish members' criticism of the Irish Constabulary.

[51] Redlich, *Procedure*, i, 193–203.

draftsman and clerk of the House of Commons.[52] One casualty was departmental and other uncontentious legislative business, which was often squeezed out. Any legislation, controversial or mundane, was liable to be passed in a state its sponsors knew to be imperfect, time necessary for tabling and discussing amendments being unavailable.[53] In 1888, Ilbert recounted later, the leaders of both parties agreed to suppress the question whether the Local Government Bill permitted women to become county councillors, because the obscurity of the drafting was spotted so late that to table a clarification would have cost three days in a very hot July, risking the bill.[54] Thirty-eight days out from the end of the session there were 33 government bills pending.[55] The Conservatives responded by reviving the proposal for breaking the annual cycle for legislation, allowing partially progressed measures to be resumed in the following session.[56] Liberal fear of the Lords was too strong, however, and too well founded for that to be acceptable.

Instead stages of some public legislative business were moved out of the chamber.[57] Gladstone had made a stuttering start in 1882, without great enthusiasm from anyone else. In 1888, however, that significant step was made permanent, with bills deemed uncontroversial being sent upstairs to a committee after their second reading, instead of taking the committee stage in the House. Selection of suitable bills was cautious to start with, but by the early 1900s, when party solidarity in the chamber had become overwhelming, there was less compunction about sending even substantial party measures to such a standing committee. After its landslide victory in the 1906 election the Liberal government decided to make that the normal course for all but the most controversial bills, forcing its reconstitution of standing committees through by guillotine in 1907, and arming their chairmen with powers of closure. Money bills were excluded from this new streamlining, but when, in 1909, Conservative opposition threatened to submerge the finance bill in an ocean of amendments, the logic of party government produced yet a further means of closure: the 'kangaroo', which enabled the majority to empower the Chairman of Ways and Means to choose which amendments should proceed. There was Conservative outrage, of course, but

[52] Ilbert, 'Supplementary chapter' in Redlich, *Procedure*, iii, 207.

[53] *Select Committee on House of Commons (Procedure)*, 2nd Report, *PP* 1906 (181), viii, 463, 504 (evidence of Sir C. Ilbert).

[54] *SC on House of Commons (Procedure)*, 2nd Report, *PP* 1906 (181), viii, 463, 500.

[55] *PD* 1888 (s3) 345: 1679.

[56] *SC on Business of the House (abridged procedure on partly considered bills)*, Report, *PP* 1890 (298), xi, 1.

[57] Ilbert, 'Supplementary chapter' in Redlich, *Procedure*, iii; *SC on House of Commons (Procedure)* 1906, 2nd Report, 463; Rush, *Role*, 48–50; Hughes 'Changes in Parliamentary Procedure'; Jennings, *Parliament*, 269.

it was followed in 1919 by Conservative refinement of the device.[58] Democracy, even incomplete democracy, meant election of a party government. Law had to be processed through the chamber, with greater or lesser difficulty, but it was not made there.

2. THE HOUSE OF LORDS

Throughout our period the Lords operated in two distinct modes. There was an excited mode, when the peers and their ladies would flock to town for some controversial matter, and a normal mode with low attendances and lower participation. Suitably, the historian of Wellington's ministry adopts a half-measure for assessing the Lords: it sat for about half the time the Commons did, the proportion of participant members was about half that of the Commons, and what he counts as an active debater or active committee member requires only half in the Lords what it does in the Commons.[59] Anecdotes about the desultory conduct of Lords' business were commonplace from at least the mid-century onwards. The normal daily attendance in the 1850s was about 75, from a House of some 400, representing a pool of some 100 fairly frequent attenders and about the same number of casuals, and it was much the same in the quiet years of Balfour's government in the early twentieth century, when the House numbered some 600.[60] Fewer spoke in the chamber, in quiet years about a fifth of total membership or less, but nearly a third when controversial business such as Catholic relief in 1829 or the Liberals' legislative programme in 1906 stirred their lordships' imagination.[61] Then the numbers voting would also increase dramatically. Three-quarters cast a vote on the Catholic Relief bill in 1829, three times the usual figure, and 425 voted in 1909 in the division that rejected Lloyd George's budget.[62]

In 1909 all those 425 would have attended too, but until 1868 it was possible for peers to vote by proxy in some divisions. Wellington, as prime minister from 1828 to 1830, mustered between 51 and 72 proxies, depending upon the issue, and there were occasions in the 1830s and 1840s when over 100 peers voted by proxy.[63] The practice was dying, however; though there were 104 occasions on which proxy votes were used between 1815 and 1868, only two fell in the last decade and nine between 1849 and 1859.[64] Normally, leaving aside the great occasions and the big

[58] Jennings, *Parliament*, 240–1.

[59] Jupp, *British Politics*, 195–239.

[60] A. Adonis, *Making Aristocracy Work* (Oxford, 1993), 52–3.

[61] Jupp, *British Politics*, 201; Adonis, *Making Aristocracy Work*, 53.

[62] Jupp, *British Politics*, 257; R. Jenkins, *Mr. Balfour's Poodle* (1954), 67.

[63] Jupp, *British Politics*, 255.

[64] E. A. Smith, *The House of Lords in British Politics and Society 1815–1911* (1992), 43.

divisions, the Lords' business was conducted by a core of perhaps 40 peers, many of them ministers or former ministers, some very senior, few enough for it to be managed *ad hoc*, without need for the detailed Standing Orders that increasingly ruled the Commons.[65]

As Bagehot put it, in the mid-century liberal constitution the position of the Lords as a legislating house was somewhat peculiar.[66] It could not originate money bills, widely defined to include any provision that imposed a pecuniary burden directly or indirectly, because the Commons would simply decline to consider them.[67] In theory that stretched as far as bills authorizing fees to be charged or salaries paid to an official. But in practice the Commons would tolerate a financial element in a Lords' bill, but only if the Lords printed it in red ink to signify that it did not actually *pass* that House, but was included to indicate to the peers a clause that would later be added in the Commons. Nor could the Lords amend a money bill or a money clause in a general bill sent up from the Commons, though this prohibition was merely conventional, resting on long acquiescence. It too was subject to tolerance by the Commons if it thought the Lords' amendment was merely trying to help—which the Commons would acknowledge by solemnly making a special entry in its Journal. Beyond that it was all a matter of practice and political expediency, for the Lords' powers were otherwise the same as the Commons'.

A government's major legislation would nearly always be started in the Commons, but 'law reform [and] minor social questions' might as well start in the Lords, and in the mid-century many did.[68] The 1857 Divorce and Matrimonial Causes bill began in the Lords, for example, as did its precursor a year earlier. Over the course of the four sessions from 1852–3 to 1856 the Lords sent down 104 bills to the Commons, resulting in 74 such useful, but undoubtedly minor, measures as the Common Law Procedure Act and the Bills of Sale Registration Act of 1854, the Purchasers' Protection against Judgments Act of 1855, and the Mercantile Law Amendment Act of 1856. During the same period the Commons sent up to the Lords over four times as many bills as it received in return.[69]

That average of about 25 bills a year successfully introduced into the Lords remained reasonably steady through to 1900, once Provisional Order Confirmation bills and similar 'supplementary' bills are excluded. It fluctuated, of course: there were 35 in the 1890–1 session, only 14 in 1895, but in most years government

[65] Jupp, *British Politics*, 201–3; Adonis, *Making Aristocracy Work*, 52–60.
[66] Bagehot, *Collected Works*, vi, 14.
[67] May, *Treatise* (6th edn, 1873), 574–9.
[68] Bagehot, *Collected Works*, vi, 14.
[69] All figures are from *Alphabetical List of the Public Bills Introduced into the House of Commons*, *PP*, annual.

put 14 or 15 of its bills through the Lords, and other peers successfully introduced 10 or 11. Nor did the subject matter change. Bills affecting the legal system—courts pre-eminently, but matters such as bail and evidence also—tended to start in the Lords, reflecting the Lord Chancellor's position, minor measures affecting land or the Church, remedial bills retrospectively legitimizing marriages overseas, minor bills affecting colonial legislatures, or treaties with foreign powers, some law reform bills, often affecting commercial law, property, or lunacy, all these were the Lords' staple.

What did change was the success rate of Lords' bills in the Commons. During the 1870s about 80 per cent of government bills first passing the Lords went on to pass the Commons, but that rate fell during the Conservative administration of 1886 to 1892, and after 1896 barely half completed their legislative journey. Casualties would sit out a year or two and try again. Non-government measures fared even worse. During Gladstone's first ministry just over 60 per cent of bills successfully introduced into the Lords by peers outside the ministry also passed the Commons; by the end of the century less than 20 per cent did, and in the decade from 1903 there were only three years when the Commons passed any at all. Congestion in the Commons was no doubt the main reason, but in consequence there was no prospect of building up the Lords as an originating chamber even if governments had wanted to.[70] The Lords survived as a 'checking—not an originating chamber', Salisbury told Chamberlain when the latter wanted to revive its fortunes by having it launch a programme of social reforms and capture the working class from Gladstonian liberalism.[71]

Analysts from the brash colonialist Edward Gibbon Wakefield in the 1840s, to Bagehot in the 1860s and the Bryce Conference in 1917, agreed that the Lords had a revising role, distinct, Bagehot and the Conference said, from its (temporary) legislative veto.[72] 'Revision' was not a term of art. At one extreme some amendments merely filled in blanks left by the Commons, at the other revision shaded into rejection. Sometimes a bill would be extensively rewritten, especially if it were a private member's bill, sometimes to the very edge of disavowal by its originators, as with Gladstone's Compulsory Abolition of Church Rates bill 1868 or the Married Women's Property bill of 1870. In between the extremes lay a wide range of bills commonly designated 'of secondary importance', where careful attention might improve the intended purpose. But revision was not a differentiated

[70] Adonis, *Making Aristocracy Work*, 65.

[71] D. Steele, *Lord Salisbury* (1999), 281–2.

[72] For Wakefield, see 'Sir Charles Metcalfe in Canada' (1844), reprinted in E. M. Wrong, *Charles Buller and Responsible Government* (Oxford, 1926), 171, 180; *Conference on the Reform of the Second Chamber: Letter from Viscount Bryce to the Prime Minister*, PP 1918 (Cd. 9038), x, 569, 572; Adonis, *Making Aristocracy Work*, 60–9.

function that the Lords sought to develop, more just a consequence of being second in line. There was no attempt to institute a semi-professional scrutinizing role over public bills parallel to the Chairman of Committees' oversight of private bill legislation, where, aided by permanent counsel, he held autocratic sway over a bill's content. Nor in practice was there much time for systematic revision, since most bills tended to reach the Lords in a flood in the last few weeks of a session. At the end of the century, sittings before the last couple of months of a session were usually finished in 20 minutes.[73] The Commons, Liberals especially, saw no value in increasing the Lords' usefulness, as their rejection of proposals to carry unfinished business over from one session to the next shows.

So constructive engagement with Commons bills was necessarily rather modest. The *Journals* of the House of Commons show that from 1852/3 to 1857, and excluding money bills from the count, about a third of the Commons' bills passing into law had had Lords' amendments accepted by the Commons. In the 1870s the Lords offered amendments to about half the Commons bills, money bills again excluded, the vast majority being accepted by the Commons, and in the 1880s the figure varied from about a third to about a half. But although many bills were amended *in* the Lords, this is not to say that many were amended *by* the Lords. The major political bills included, for example, the various Irish land and church bills and the University Test bill. But Lord Salisbury, surveying the Lords' contribution to legislation in the 1887 session, considering bills originating in the Lords as well as bills sent from below, pointed out that in a year when 73 bills had been enacted, only two were of that high political nature.[74] Of the remainder, no fewer than 53 had passed through the Lords with no discussion whatsoever. Only a minister had spoken to them. Seven had been discussed by two members other than the minister, and a further three by one member and the minister. Eight others were bills that the Lords constitutionally could not amend. That, indeed, had been the pattern for a very long time.

Salisbury therefore supported a proposal, which he later credited to Lord Herschell, that the Lords institute standing committees for the systematic revision of these many bills of secondary importance.[75] But the experiment rapidly petered out, despite Herschell's opinion that during their first two years the two standing committees had significantly improved legislative quality.[76] The role, such as it was, did not match peers' interests or aptitudes. As one of them observed, government bills got government drafting and inter-departmental

[73] Smith, *House of Lords*, 160.
[74] *PD* 1889 (s3) 333: 1769.
[75] Crediting Herschell is at *PD* 1891 (s3) 349: 1138.
[76] Adonis, *Making Aristocracy Work*, 62–9.

scrutiny anyway, a point perhaps remembered by Herschell when he drew particular attention to private members' bills, which often had to pass the Commons
without a single word of discussion if they were to pass at all.[77] His ambition was
only the lawyer's modest hope of avoiding litigation by improving bills' technical quality, their clarity, and consistency. So the role of such standing committees reduced to acting as long-stop for government and as lawyerly scrutineer
of the thin flow of private members' bills. As Herschell himself noted, a sub-
committee of the Lord Chancellor and a couple of peers knowledgeable about
the subject-matter would sometimes be more suitable anyway, a step which could
be arranged informally without need for an apparatus of standing committees.
So the experiment faded away, as did all other proposals to revitalize the Lords
during the late 1880s and 1890s, leaving peers to propose amendments in the
chamber itself, if they felt so moved, and if they did not think that approaching
the minister informally would get the result sought.

The outcome was not the result of Lords' idleness or decadence.[78] Ministers'
control of the text of their bills had tightened to the point that systematic independent scrutiny was unlikely to bring rewards commensurate with the effort.
Lords' amendments had anyway to be accepted by the Commons, which in
practice meant the government, and it was rare for the Lords to persist with an
amendment after the Commons had sent up its reasons for rejecting it, highly
political bills aside. So significant amendment had to be proposed by government itself, with the pressure to do so being most usefully applied informally and
externally. Bills were not made in the chamber. That left only the lawyers' work
of superintending the draftsman, as it were, no more an interesting role in the
1890s for a House constituted by noble blood and great wealth than it had been
in 1867 when Bagehot saw a steady injection of life peerages as the Lords' only
possible salvation.[79] So far as routine legislation coming from the Commons was
concerned, and that was the great bulk of it, the only use of a second chamber
was to provide ministers and departments with an opportunity for last-minute
corrections.

The Lords' other role, the role that saw big attendances, long debate, public
interest, and full galleries, was oppositional. The Lords possessed the power to
reject Commons bills at large, restraint being purely political. Rejecting a private
member's bill, however far-reaching, was not the same as rejecting a government
bill. It was disappointing for Dissenters, for example, when three times between
1858 and 1867 the Lords rejected Commons' bills for the abolition of church rates,

---

[77] *PD* 1889 (s3) 333: 1774 (Cadogan); 1891 349: 1132–3 (Herschell).
[78] Adonis, *Making Aristocracy Work*, 50–83.
[79] *English Constitution, Collected Works* (ed. Stevas), v, 279–87.

but they did not say that something improper had happened or use the occasion to lobby for reform of the Lords. However, government bills from the Commons were seen by their supporters as having additional legitimacy, the more so as governments took on a greater part of the Commons legislative programme and hence a greater electoral responsibility. Further, government measures were party measures, and at least from the 1830s the Lords was as much a party assembly as the Commons. So as government responsibility for legislation increased, and as 'the people' became more respectable, the cry 'the peers against the people' became less of an obvious statement of the constitutional position of the House of Lords and more a political criticism for the Lords to sidestep wherever possible.

In the 1830s, when 'the Lords have been bowling down Bills like ninepins', it was only the Radicals who called for reduction of the Lords' powers, they who felt most strongly the link between the Commons, the government, and the people.[80] The Whigs, with just 87 supporters in a House of 430, lost bills concerning the Irish Church, Irish tithes, Irish municipal corporations, Jewish civil disabilities, Dissenters' entry to the universities, all central to their view of a reformed state, but retaliation against the powers of the landed aristocracy was not part of their creed.[81] The excitement diminished after Wellington coaxed the peers away from confrontation, and he repeated the service in 1846 when he led the Lords away from denying Peel his repeal of the corn laws. That issue split the Conservative party in the Lords as in the Commons, creating a small but generally reliable majority for the ensuing governments, until, in 1860 the Lords famously rejected Gladstone's bill to repeal the paper duties, again provoking Radical outrage. But it was well known that prime minister Palmerston himself disliked the bill, so though it was a money bill, and for all Gladstone's bluster, Palmerston could still treat it as an individual effort by a wilful Chancellor of the Exchequer.[82] The consequent Commons' resolutions restating what it regarded as its privileges were anodyne and unthreatening.[83] Any crisis that there might have been vanished the next year, when Gladstone dramatically increased the stakes by amalgamating all his financial proposals into one bill, successfully facing down the Lords by a ploy that Erskine May, a closet Gladstonian himself, later declared perfectly constitutional because it did no more than follow a precedent set by Mr Pitt.[84]

When a Conservative Lords was once again faced by a reforming Commons the political context had changed with the passage of the second Reform Act.

[80] Lord Greville, quoted by A. S. Turberville, *The House of Lords in the Age of Reform* (1958), 361.
[81] Lord Hatherton, quoted by Smith, *House of Lords*, 96.
[82] R. Shannon, *Gladstone: Peel's Inheritor, 1809–65* (1982), 416–18.
[83] (1860) 115 *House of Commons Journal*, 360.
[84] May, *Treatise* (6th edn), 583; D. Holland and D. Menhennet (eds), *Erskine May's Private Journal 1857–1882* (1972), 23.

Opposition, while not yet 'undemocratic', far more clearly offended the principle of the responsibility of representative government. Two constitutional rationali zations for opposition emerged, sometimes overlapping, ultimately conflicting. One contrasted the government with its supposed Commons majority, arguing that the Commons was not really agreed to the measure, merely pressured into acquiescing, a claim made the more plausible by chronic dissension among Liberal members, coupled with autocratic and remote cabinet style. For the true will of the Commons to be heard, it should be given a further chance to consider. Rejection of the Ballot bill in 1871 followed by its acceptance in the next session illustrates the point. It is the basis of Bagehot's distinction between 'genuine' and 'fictitious' majorities in the commons, the former to be heeded by the Lords however unpalatable, the latter open to temporary rejection while the Lords appealed from one session of Parliament to the next.[85] But Bagehot blurred his distinction, eliding a 'genuine' commons majority with the 'strong' and 'universal' opinion of the nation articulated independently of its representatives in Parliament.

Separate the two, and we have the second, far more potent, rationalization for Lords' obstruction: Lord Salisbury's well known 'mandate' principle. This was his antidote to electoral reform: 'the nation is our master, though the H of C is not: & [we should] yield our own opinion only when the judgement of the nation has been challenged at the polls, & decidedly expressed'.[86] The Lords could appeal from one Parliament to the next, perhaps even on each issue separately, with room for further interpretation of what should count as a decisive expression. It has been plausibly argued that Salisbury never lost sight of the political objective—that the Conservatives should win that election—hence that he chose a battle with much more discrimination than his supposed doctrine might suggest, and that if this principle did not suit him he was ready to adopt others that did.[87] Nonetheless, a constitutional gloss was thought necessary. Rejection and fundamental rewriting of Commons' bills were not advanced just on political grounds, and versions of his mandate principle can be found from the benches of the Lords to the pages of Dicey.[88]

As is well known, the Conservatives sought to defeat in the Lords measures on which the Liberals put much store, but which would not generate enough of a cry to sustain an election campaign. So the weak Liberal government of 1892–5 simply had to endure the loss of its Government of Ireland bill and the death

---

[85] Introduction to 2nd edn of *English Constitution*, *Collected Works* (ed. Stevas), v, 177.

[86] Quoted in full by Smith, *House of Lords*, 128; see also M. Bentley, *Lord Salisbury's World* (Cambridge, 2001), 169.

[87] Adonis, *Making Aristocracy Work*, 112–16, 124–5.

[88] *Ibid.*, 259–60, citing Dicey, *Introduction to the Law of the Constitution* (4th edn, 1893), 359 (which remained unchanged in the 8th edn, 1915, 427–8).

through mutilation of its Employers' Liability bill and Sea Fisheries Regulation (Scotland) bill. Such was the intensity of Conservative opposition in the Lords that within two years of the Liberal landslide victory in the 1906 election 'practically everything that could be done with the consent of the House of Lords had now been accomplished, and on all the major measures of Liberal policy—education, temperance reform, land reform, Welsh Disestablishment, Irish Home Rule—the road seemed to be hopelessly blocked'.[89] It was unblocked by the Lords' rejection of 'the people's budget' in 1909, a rejection taking the form of a denial by the old aristocracy of new liberalism's inroads into its landed privileges in the name of social progress, but with the underlying motive of blocking a politically strategic budget in order to keep alive the Conservatives' own strategic preference for tariff reform. Strategic to both sides, this was a measure on which an election could be fought.

In the constitutional crisis that followed, the Liberals finally opted for a simple, effective, and direct limitation upon the Lords' powers, a radical measure first suggested in the 1830s, but one which would also have been recognized by Bagehot as an enhanced codification of his own writings on the Lords in the late 1860s and early 1870s.[90] The House of Lords was not to be abolished, but nor was its hereditary composition to be molested, which might have strengthened it. Nor were there to be joint sittings of the two Houses to break deadlocks, nor meetings of delegates from them, though the idea came close to acceptance at the inter-party constitutional conference consequent upon the death of Edward VII.[91] In the 1910 election the Conservatives proposed the referendum as a means of resolving an impasse, but with their defeat the idea lapsed.

So with immense difficulty and prolonged drama the Liberals forced through the Parliament Act 1911, which reduced the Lords' powers over ordinary legislation to a suspensory veto, and to a token delay of one month for money bills. The Liberals insisted that identification of a money bill remained within the Commons; judges must not have a role in that.[92] According to the Speaker at the time, the narrow definition of money bills probably meant that only the 1860 precedent was reversed, not the 1909.[93] The main provision, that a public bill (other than one to prolong Parliament's life beyond five years) passing the Commons in the same form three times in not less than two years would become law without Lords' approval, had enough flexibility for all ordinary cases, since

[89] J. A. Spender, quoted by P. Rowland, *Last Liberal Governments*, i, 166.

[90] Smith, *House of Lords*, 137.

[91] C. C. Weston, 'The Liberal Leadership and the Lords' Veto, 1907–1910' (1968) 11 *Hist. J.* 508–37; J. D. Fair, *British Interparty Conferences* (Oxford, 1980), 77–102.

[92] J. Jaconelli, 'The Parliament Bill 1910–1911' (1991) 10 *Parl. Hist.* 277–96, 281, 286.

[93] Jenkins, *Poodle*, 188, citing Lord Ullswater, the former Mr Speaker Lowther.

a proviso to section 2(4) allowed amendments by agreement. The Lords would most likely accept proffered amendments as the best it was likely to get. As a balance to maintain accountability, the maximum duration of a Parliament was reduced from seven years to five.

Recent assessment of the Parliament Act has focused on its cumbrous procedures and the contribution they made to a general disillusion with the parliamentary process.[94] Yet the Act undoubtedly enabled the Liberals to govern in a way they had not before. Welsh disestablishment finally passed, so too a Scottish temperance measure, which would have passed under Parliament Act procedures but which was compromised to settle it a year early. Abolition of plural voting would also have passed, had its third journey through the Commons not been suspended for the war, and, particularly, the Government of Ireland bill was enacted. With Ulster arming, the Government of Ireland Act certainly did not solve the question of Irish home rule, and it has been argued that the Parliament Act's two-year suspensory period exacerbated the problem of finding an acceptable text.[95]

Yet a slicker process would hardly have reversed the momentum of Ulster separatism, and the paradoxical view that it would have been better to have had no Parliament Act at all, because then the Unionists would have abandoned their resistance to home rule on losing the next election, grossly underestimates their growing commitment to the northern counties.[96] Similarly, to argue that the Parliament Act's structure would give a reforming government 'immense problems' of 'two years in the deep freeze' is to exaggerate the Liberals' difficulty in clearing off their complex and long-delayed legislative backlog.[97] While the first passage of these controversial measures through the Commons took several months, their second and third were generally much quicker, aided by procedural orders designed to protect them from amendment, drafted with all the nicety of statutes themselves.[98] Thus the Established Church (Wales) bill began its second reading on 16 June 1913, passing the Commons on 8 July, and started its third reading on 20 April 1914, passing on 19 May. Much the same is true of the Temperance (Scotland) bill and the Plural Voting bill, each of which had an arduous first passage but a brisk second. Even the second passage of the Government of Ireland bill took only a month, though the third was protracted, acrimonious, and at times disorderly.

---

[94] D. Powell, *The Edwardian Crisis* (Basingstoke, 1996), 165–6; Adonis, *Making Aristocracy Work*, 159–60.

[95] Adonis, *Making Aristocracy Work*, 159–60.

[96] Paradoxical view: Adonis, *Making Aristocracy Work*, 159–60. Contrast R. F. Foster, *Modern Ireland 1600–1972* (1988), 456–93; N. Mansergh, *The Unresolved Question* (New Haven, 1991), 43–112.

[97] Deep freeze: Adonis, *Making Aristocracy Work*, 159.

[98] Jennings, *Parliament*, 426n.

These Parliament Act bills were all part of the Liberals' old agenda. The Conservatives knew better than to block the National Insurance bill 1911 and the Trade Union bill 1913, just as they had let the 1906 Trade Disputes Act pass the unreformed Lords. So it is difficult to tell for how long the Conservatives would have held to their belief that the Liberals had suspended the constitution by introducing what was tantamount to single chamber rule, and hence how often they would have held the Liberals to the full rigour of the Act. Certainly neither Liberals nor Conservatives thought the Act would be final. Its preamble implied an imminent reform and remodelling of the Lords that might include revisiting the suspensory veto, and the Liberals even began discussing the contours of Lords reform in 1912. Yet after the war, even though the political parties failed to agree upon reform of the Lords, the issue very quickly lost all its heat and the Conservatives did not bother to restore the status quo ante by repealing the Parliament Act.[99]

So in the event the Parliament Act did become final, and it proved to be particularly robust. It was used only three times in its first 80 years, as all students of constitutional law know, somewhat vindicating the prediction of its immediate progenitor, Sir Henry Campbell-Bannerman, that once the Commons had power to force through their measures the Lords would nearly always yield without delay.[100] The Act was not entrenched, and it contained no exceptions for 'organic' or constitutional measures, which had been urged by Conservatives but rejected by Liberals during the 1910 constitutional conference. Thus the very next reforming government was able to use the Act to amend itself, and hence reduce the two years to one.[101]

Since there was, deliberately, no role for the courts in judging its applicability, its mode of interpretation depended on the Speaker. He did not allow technicalities to delay the passage of the Government of Ireland bill or the Welsh Disestablishment bill when, on their second introduction into the Lords, they were merely adjourned rather than rejected. A perfectionist might say that adjourned bills could not be certified as 'not passing' until after the session was ended, and hence that they must wait until the start of the next to be enacted under the Parliament Act, but the Speaker took the practical view, certifying them so that they became law just before the prorogation.[102] An elected government able to hold its majority could, in principle, legislate as it wished.

[99] For interwar period: Jennings, *Parliament*, 434–53; P. A. Bromhead, *The House of Lords and Contemporary Politics* (1958), 259–65.

[100] J. Wilson, *CB: A Life of Sir Henry Campbell-Bannerman* (1973), 502; for the fourth time of its use see G. Ganz, 'The War Crimes Act 1991—why no constitutional crisis?' (1992) 55 *MLR* 87.

[101] Jennings *Parliament*, 428–34; Bromhead, *House of Lords*, 265–8.

[102] Jennings, *Parliament*, 427.

3. PRIVATE BILL LEGISLATION

Private bill legislation was one of the eighteenth-century parliaments' more business-like legacies. Blackstone's description had been very thin. Taking the law as a holistic entity he saw private Acts as a privilege, an exception to a rule rather than a rule itself. In the only context that interested him he treated estate Acts as a form of private deed rescuing estates from the incompetence or over-elaboration of conveyancers.[103] From about 1750, however, a sub-category that was to be formally recognized in 1798 as 'local and private Acts' came to pre-dominate, most of them authorizing various town improvements and, particu-larly, construction of infrastructure: new roads, canals, and harbours.[104]

Taking the whole category of private bill legislation together, in the unremark-able years of Wellington's administration, 1828 to 1830, some 250 petitions a year were producing just under 200 Acts a year.[105] Local initiative for town develop-ment did not relax, nor did that for the construction of roads. Gas and water promoters used the process, be they capitalist or some form of local not-for-profit enterprise. Railway promoters naturally used private bill legislation, both for the formation of companies and to acquire the multitude of powers necessary to acquire the land, build the line, and subsequently operate it. At best in the 1820s the process was semi-regulated, allowing for local initiative within reasonably well established precedents. At worst it was a form of legislative free for all, where rival promoters competed for the same local monopoly in the absence of criteria or pre-existing procedures for selection.

One set of pressures for change operated along a local initiative/central regu-lation axis. A second, concerning the Commons more than the Lords, paralleled the shifting balance of authority from non-official members to the government. How much should control of private bill process continue to rest with members as such? A third was for better quality law-making. If Parliament did retain the business, how could it be sure that it was well informed, that it was making the right choices? Finally, how was private bill legislation to be fitted into a parlia-mentary timetable barely adequate to cope with public business? From, say, 1867, how were parliamentary resources to be divided between these local affairs and the demands of a disciplined two-party system, where successful promotion of general legislation was essential to electoral appeal? The combined effect of these pressures was to shift much of the work to general legislation and to government agencies. But until nearly the end of our period local and private legislation of one form or another remained a substantial component of Parliament's work.

---

[103] Bl. Comm. i, 86; ii, 344.
[104] J. Innes, 'The Local Acts of a National Parliament' (1998) 17 *Parl. Hist.* 21–47.
[105] Jupp, *British Politics*, 181. Future references to private bill legislation 1828–30 are from this source.

The Extent of the Enterprise

Curiously perhaps, the volume of private bill legislation remained fairly steady throughout our period, boom years aside. This was despite the increasing domination of public general legislation, evermore the monopoly of central government, some of it directly power conferring, some of it adoptive legislation for localities to activate, and despite also the development of alternative procedures whereby commissions or ministries substituted for some of Parliament's role. The rough averages from 1828–30 of 250 bills and between 180 and 200 Acts are matched almost exactly by the official returns of bills deposited in the House of Commons Private Bill Office from 1850 to 1885 (though they may not include all bills started in the Lords).[106] There were some slack periods in the unsettled years of the early 1840s, also just after the Public Health Act 1848, but they did not persist. Again, for ten years from 1885 there was something of a reduction, to about 150 Acts a year from 200 petitions, until the numbers revived once more. Permanent decline began only from 1907.[107] Booms could be frighteningly intense but were usually short lived. With 364 petitions, 1825 stood out until an avalanche of 728 and 464 petitions hit the Commons in 1846 and 1847 respectively, and, finally, during a longer period from 1861 to 1867 petitions ran at over 470 a year and Acts over 300.

The truly personal bills—estate and divorce—began in the Lords, where they underwent direct or indirect judicial scrutiny. But even in the years 1828–30 they, with the other most personal category—naturalization—together numbered only some 30 or 40 annually, one-sixth or one-seventh of the total. They reduced to about ten a year from 1858 to 1871 as general legislation reduced their need, dwindling even further thereafter.[108] Land enclosure too, intermediate between public and private, had also generated about 30 petitions a year in 1828–30, but after 1845 it became almost entirely commissioners' business, though subject to varying degrees of parliamentary approval.[109] Individual enclosure bills then became rare. Instead the bulk of private bill legislation, about two-thirds in 1828–30, lay at the 'public' end of the spectrum, the steady petitions for transport

---

[106] If the *Account of Number of Petitions for Private Bills Presented to the House of Commons, 1825–29* at *PP* 1829 (311), xxi, 53 excludes House of Lords' bills the figures are reasonably consistent. Collated annual returns: *Return of number of private bills [etc]*, *PP* 1866 (467), lvi, 581; 1872 (68), xlvii, 37; 1878 (110), lxi, 27; 1880 (425), lvi, 51; 1890 (371), lvii, 107; 1898 (198), lxxii, 85.

[107] O. C. Williams, *The Historical Development of Private Bill Procedure and Standing Orders in the House of Commons* (1948), i, 236–7. Acts to confirm Provisional Orders should be subtracted from most published series. For example, the list of 291 local and private Acts passing in 1900 includes 56 confirmatory Acts, and the 176 local and private Acts passing in 1913 include 66 confirmatory Acts.

[108] *SC on Private Bills*, Report, *PP* 1847–8 (32), xvi, 221; *Return of Number of Private Bills [etc]*, *PP*, annual.

[109] 8 & 9 Vict. c. 118; 15 & 16 Vict. c. 79.

and local improvement bills. These quasi-public bills nearly always started in the Commons. Indeed, until 1858 bills levying money on the subject through rates, tolls, charges, had to—the Commons treating them as within its privilege of initiating money bills.[110]

Of these local and private bills, petitions for town improvement bills, understood broadly to include 'police' and local regulation, bills for works, be they court rooms, churches, markets, jails or whatever, bills for water or gas works, and bills for small debt courts, numbered some 57 a year in 1828–30, yielding an annual average of 37 Acts. There were fluctuations in the 1840s, but by the 1850s the average was up to about 42 Acts, increasing gently into the 1880s.[111] Classification became more difficult as local authorities took on more functions, but in the early twentieth century 55 to 65 bills of generally that nature passed annually, plus some relating to private gas and water enterprises.

The larger category, however, was always transport. There were boom years, of course, which panicked Parliament: 457 railway bills passing in the two sessions 1846–7, and 667 between 1864 and 1866. Generally, however, the average of 93 bills and 79 Acts a year from 1828 to 1830, aggregating road, canal, river, and railway transport, was typical for a much longer period. Again there were fluctuations. General legislation reduced the need for individual road bills, though bridges sometimes needed them through into the twentieth century. Railway Acts settled to a new plateau of about 65 a year from 1847 through to 1860, boomed again, settled, and then declined in the 1890s. In the early twentieth century there were still over 30 railway Acts a year, however, and numerous acts concerning tramways. Railway bills in particular had brought to Parliament contested and complex issues concerning competition, profit, monopoly, share subscriptions, borrowing powers, land acquisition, regulation, and accountability on a national scale.

The Early Nineteenth-Century Model

Parliamentarians' central assumption in the 1820s was that within broad limits the merits of local legislation were for local determination. Bills could be sought only by lodging a petition which, by the 1820s, promoters were required to publicize by alerting local landowners and occupiers individually and the local public through advertisement. The petition had to allege both the need for a bill and the suitability of the one proposed, but assessment rested with the local elite,

---

[110] It waived its privilege for bills authorizing fines for offences in 1849, and for tolls and charges in 1858: *Joint SC on Despatch of Business in Parliament*, Report, PP 1868–9 (386), vii, 171, 174; May, *Treatise* (11th edn, 1906), 579–80.

[111] *Return of Number of Private Bills*, PP, annual.

and especially with local members and with peers holding land locally. The latter's opposition would usually block a bill in the Lords. In the Commons local members would normally be entrusted with bringing in the private bills for their locality, and would always belong to the bill committees concerned. Their agreement and their ability to resolve any local difficulties, demonstrated by a lack of petitions opposing the bill, signalled to Parliament that a bill broadly fitting the established precedents should pass with minimal scrutiny. After all, securing local interests was what local members were for.[112] It was not disreputable that opposition had been silenced by payment; bill committees preferred private agreements to protective clauses in Acts.

An opposed bill was a trial of local and personal strength, to be won by influence and votes. In the early 1820s the first procedural step in the Commons was still the examination of the petition by an *ad hoc* committee, which would report on its *prima facie* truthfulness to the House, usually having heard just outline evidence from the promoters' side, usually without skirmish. A bill would then be brought in and receive a formal first reading. At second reading its preamble would be considered, an important matter because the preamble contained allegations of fact which, if accepted, would determine the bill's shape and extent. Formerly counsel had been heard at the bar of the Commons, but that practice had ended by the 1820s, perhaps in recognition that the process was political.[113] Personal canvassing by the parties was normal, and in fierce contests was disciplined enough to resemble whipping.[114]

If successful, the bill would proceed to a bill committee, again *ad hoc*, which would consider its clauses, hearing counsel for the bill and their evidence. That bill committee would also decide whether a bill's opponents had sufficient standing in the matter for counsel and evidence to be admitted against the bill. But this semblance of judicial procedure was often illusory. Committees were potentially large bodies, part microcosm of the House, part assembly of local members, but participation again turned on the politics of influence. Usually any member of the House could attend and vote, whether formally on the committee or not. Nor were they obliged to attend during the giving of evidence; being present to vote sufficed.[115] Report and third reading stages followed, where the bill's opponents

---

[112] F. O'Gorman, *Voters, Parties and Patrons: The Unreformed Electoral System of Hanoverian England 1734–1832* (Oxford, 1989), 51–2, 240, 252–3.

[113] F. Clifford, *A History of Private Bill Legislation* (1885), ii, 860–1; Williams, *Historical Development*, i, 57.

[114] *SC on Private Business*, Report, PP 1837–8 (679), xxiii, 405, 411–12; Jupp, *British Politics*, 183; Holdsworth, *HEL* xi, 343.

[115] *SC on Constitution of Committees on Private Bills*, Report, 1825–6 *House of Commons Journal*, App. E, 968; *SC on Private Business 1837–8*, Report (679), 413–15.

might try again, or where new clauses might be inserted, and then the bill went up to the Lords, to go through a similar though more streamlined procedure.

Mid-century: Reform of Parliamentary Process

Much of this process was reformed by about 1855, the result of changing sensibilities and changing context. It remained true that in constitutional theory these quasi-public private bills 'called for the suspension of some general law in a case alleged to be for the public good', but what was meant by public good began to change.[116] From being virtually synonymous with the predominant local interest it became an external standard against which that interest should be measured. It was to be determined not by the number of friends who could be mustered for a parliamentary vote, but by the verdict of neutrals having heard the interplay of 'argument' and 'evidence'. Much control of the content of bills shifted away from promoters, in face of increasing standardization and textual scrutiny of even unopposed bills. There was a progressive differentiation between the various stages of the legislative process, with an allocation of different functions to different sorts of body, consequently a shift of control and authority to specialists in each House.

Initial scrutiny of proposals drifted away from the House at large. In the Commons, petition committees had once had that role, but they became consumed with hearing proofs of compliance with Standing Orders, increasingly detailed in the notices they required promoters to serve. Non-compliance, often technical, gave opportunity to rival promoters to defeat a bill before its merits had even been considered, causing petition committees to become steadily more judicial in their deliberations.[117] In 1847 they became so congested with railway business, causing such expense for promoters and such embarrassment in the Commons that the task was delegated to salaried officials and the petition committees abolished.[118] Then just as examination of the petition was no longer a test of a bill's basic premises, so too proof of the preamble gradually shifted from the House at second reading, to the bill committees.[119] Indeed parliamentary agents repeatedly asserted the unfairness of seeking to defeat a bill on second reading, before its real merits had been investigated in committee.[120] So although

[116] *PD* 1826–7 (s2) 16: 152–3 (Littleton).

[117] Williams, *Historical Development*, i, 68–71.

[118] *SC on Standing Orders for Railroad Bills*, Report, PP 1836 (511), xxi, 221; Williams, *Historical Development*, i, 68–9, 276, 286.

[119] Williams, *Historical Development*, i, 57.

[120] D. L. Rydz, *The Parliamentary Agents* (1979), 86–93; cf. T. M. Sherwood, *A Treatise on the Proceedings to be Adopted by Members in Conducting Private Bills through the House of Commons* (1828), 30, 60.

second reading votes never disappeared, averaging about seven a year for the decade from 1847 to 1856, falling away sharply thereafter, that stage now affirmed just the 'principle', usually an empty matter.[121]

Instead initial scrutiny became a matter of textual detail and of personal authority. It began in the Lords in the mid-1820s when Lord Shaftesbury, Chairman of Committees, took upon himself the clause-by-clause scrutiny of all private bills, not allowing any to proceed to committee until, aided by his permanent counsel, he was satisfied with its content, a process often involving personal consultation.[122] The Commons' response was to try to improve its decision-making by having breviates prepared—summaries—for all members prior to second reading.[123] From 1840, however, in recognition of a public interest in even uncontested bills, and in partial imitation of the Lords, the Chairman of Ways and Means came to chair all unopposed bill committees, to prevent undesirable clauses slipping through.[124] By the end of the decade, with the breviate system failing, the Chairman of Ways and Means extended his responsibility to the preliminary scrutiny of all private bills and control of late amendments.[125] Thus only bills meeting the approval of these two powerful Chairmen would be allowed to proceed.

By then, however, most private bills had become in large measure standardized by the enactment of general template Acts. These were modelled upon the General Inclosure Act 1801, which had become the template for all subsequent private enclosure bills, and are known collectively as the clauses Acts. There were three such Acts in 1845, for railways, for companies for public purposes, and for land acquisition, all aimed at reducing costs, speeding scrutiny, and identifying novel proposals more easily. They turned the clauses usually found in private bills into templates for all future private bills in those classes, deemed to be incorporated so far as not expressly excluded. Bills which could once have taken 100 pages could now be fitted into ten.[126] At the instigation of Joseph Hume's Private Bills select committee, eight more clauses Acts were passed quickly in 1847, differing in theory in that they needed express incorporation into private bills, but much the same in practice.[127] Initial scrutiny then became a matter of inquiring into departures from the template.

---

[121] *Return Relative to Divisions of the House, PP*, annual.
[122] For examples, ultimately regrettable, see Clifford, *History*, i, 66–7; ii, 148n.
[123] *SC on the Public and Private Business of the House*, Report, *PP* 1837 (517), xiii, 293.
[124] *SC on Private Business*, Report, *PP* 1840 (463), xv, 207; Williams, *Historical Development*, i, 279.
[125] *SC on Private Bills* 1847–8, Report; *SC on Private Bills*, 1st Report, *PP* 1851 (35), x, 741, 752; Williams, *Historical Development*, i, 96, 101.
[126] *SC on Private Bills* 1847–8, Report, 243 (Palk); Clifford, *History*, i, 102–3, 221.
[127] *SC on Private Bills*, Report, *PP* 1846 (556), xii, 1; *SC on Private Bills* 1847–8, Report, 233 (Greene).

A bill's content thus came to rest upon a new triangle of authority, with the two Chairmen at its apex, their counsel at one corner, and the parliamentary agents at the third, for it was they who acted between client and official. Shaftesbury encouraged their monopoly of the conduct of private business, but used them also as a route to discipline. Through their medium in the early 1840s he peremptorily distributed model bills drafted by the Chairmen's counsel, a practice of unofficial law-making that foreshadowed passage of the clauses Acts and continued as a complement to them long afterwards.[128] In return for their co-operation the parliamentary agents acquired professional status. They became persistent lobbyists in their own interest and influential as witnesses before the many parliamentary committees seeking to improve private bill process.[129]

Contested bills still went to committee, to investigate both the purposes of the bill and the nature and capacity of the promoter, but those bill committees also changed. Again the first radical step was taken in the Lords, in 1837, when committees on opposed bills were reconstituted as judicial committees of just five disinterested peers, obliged to attend throughout and to decide only upon the evidence.[130] The unreformed Commons had flirted with similar ideas in the aftermath of the petitions boom of 1825, but had balked at insisting upon members' attendance. So all that could be achieved then was better representation of neutral members and abolition of the right of all-comers to attend.[131] True, Commons railway bill committees were brought under some control in 1836 by a requirement that they report specially on a long list of detailed matters concerning each bill, but arguments for fully 'judicial' committees from rationalizers such as Joseph Hume continually lost to members' constitutional right of involvement in local affairs, and their constituents' reciprocal right to have it.[132]

Only the torrent of railway bills in 1845/6 broke the dam, partly through force of numbers, partly through the logic of grouping competing bills together for joint investigation.[133] So the Commons reconstituted its railway bill committees on much the same lines as the Lords, and by contested stages all its other bill committees too.[134] Members arguing that they were needed in committee as a voice for constituents too poor to fee counsel were told to appear as witnesses,

---

[128] Rydz, *Parliamentary Agents*, 52–5; Williams, *Historical Development*, i, 105; May, *Treatise* (11th edn), 694.

[129] *SC on Private Business*, Report, PP 1840 (56), xvi, 57; Rydz, *Parliamentary Agents*, 93–109.

[130] Rydz, *Parliamentary Agents*, 93; *SC on Private Business* 1837–8, Report, 457, 461.

[131] *SC on Constitution of Committees on Private Bills* 1825–6; PD 1826–7 (s 2) 16: 152–63; Williams, *Historical Development*, i, 49–52, 271.

[132] PD 1836 (s3) 31: 1112–24; *SC on the Public and Private Business of the House* 1837, Report; PD 1839 (s3) 45: 963–77; *SC on Private Business* 1840, Report; PD 1844 (s3) 73: 516–28, 720–3.

[133] PD 1845 (s3) 78: 271–307.

[134] Williams, *Historical Development*, i, 76–91; PD 1847 (s3) 93: 701–10.

just like anyone else. And where once a bill committee would always have been chaired by a local member, from 1847 a Committee of Selection chose the chairman just as it chose all other members of each bill committee.[135]

Judicializing bill committees also hastened ordinary members' exclusion from meaningful debate at report and third reading stage. In a great 'battle of the gauges' in 1845 the Commons met to determine whether the broad gauge Great Western Railway should be allowed to expand into a rival's territory, as a bill committee had recommended, each company claiming the allegiance of many members. While some no doubt did vote for interest, the balance was held by members voting simply for what the committee had decided. Committee knowledge, painfully acquired through attention to counsel and evidence, was not to be gainsaid by members' ignorance or the results of 'personal canvass and private interests'.[136] From 1846, when there were six divisions at third reading stage, opposition at report or third reading stage became rare, usually affecting just one or two bills a year, sometimes none at all.[137]

Thus internal private bill procedure was becoming more public, yet also more differentiated and professionalized, more bureaucratic, more judicial. Officials and parliamentary agents, supervised more or less closely by the two Chairmen, shepherded bills through the long legislative process, where previously local members would have taken charge. In 1861 the two Chairmen negotiated directly with railway company representatives over points of friction, the outcome being translated into proposed model clauses by a committee of railway bill committee chairmen, a panel established in 1854 to encourage consistency between bill committees.[138] By 1863 it was even plausible to propose that bill committee chairmen be paid.[139] And committee membership was now a duty to the House, imposed on disinterested members with nothing better to do. In a rebuke unthinkable in the 1820s, in 1845 members forgetting to attend a new style bill committee were summoned by the House for explanation.[140]

Mid-century and Later: The Executive

Private bill legislation shared a weakness with social legislation initiated by private members, that Parliament could not be sure of its information. It had not

---

[135] Williams, *Historical Development*, ii, 138.

[136] *PD* 1845 (s3) 81: 973–98.

[137] *Returns of the Number of Divisions of the House of Commons*, PP, annual. And compare the House of Lords: *SC on Private Business* 1837–8, Report, 417.

[138] Clifford, *History*, i, 176.

[139] Williams, *Historical Development*, i, 132, 147.

[140] *PD* 1845 (s3) 79: 1056; see also Hastie's application: *Return of Number of Divisions*, PP 1850 (714), xlvi, 27, 45.

mattered when the ethos was that a locality wanting a statute should be given one, because whether it truly was a locality and truly did want one were issues that could be tested by a bill committee. But once 'the public good' became a yardstick in its own right some means of evaluation was needed. For public general legislation initiated by private members the member-initiated select committee provided the means, calling witnesses, recording their questioning, and making a report.[141] It was relatively unimportant that witnesses might be slanted and a report biased, because legislation was not expected to follow immediately, building opinion took time, there could always be other select committees, and there was ample opportunity for debate in both Houses. None of that was true for private bill legislation. As Joseph Hume, an habitual member of inquiries into private bill legislation, never tired of arguing, the 'line between public and private legislation has seldom been correctly drawn... in a large class of Bills, private in name, but often affecting important public interests, the existing mode of procedure before the legislature supplies no adequate means of obtaining knowledge of the real merits of the measure to other parties than those who promote or oppose them'.[142]

As Hume hinted, and as his own select committee on private bill legislation was to report in 1846, one solution was to enact public general legislation that would confer powers without need for individual application to Parliament.[143] His context was urban improvement, where some of the powers envisaged would interfere with property rights either directly, through forbidding or mandating particular uses of land, or indirectly by authorizing local bodies to levy rates and charges, and others would authorize the making of rules that would have the force of law. But local authorities would have to be created to wield those powers, and since they could hardly appoint themselves (if their powers were to be coercive) some agency must act as intermediary, and that agency must be armed with appropriate processes. The link with Chadwick's centralizing boards, the Poor Law Board and the General Board of Health, is very close.

Hume's precedent, however, was the less controversial arena of land enclosure. In 1844 Lord Worsley had obtained a select committee with the aim of speeding the final phase of enclosure by simply removing from the House business whose principles he thought no longer controversial.[144] Enclosure bills had long been standardized. So local inquiry before a competent inspector reporting to a responsible commission would suffice, he argued, on the model of the Tithe

---

[141] Jupp, *British Politics*, 210–15.

[142] *SC on Railway Acts Enactments*, 2nd Report, *PP* 1846 (687), xiv, 5, 7; cf. *SC on Private Bills* 1846, Report.

[143] *SC on Private Bills* 1846, Report.

[144] *SC on Commons Inclosure, PP* 1844 (583), v, 1.

Commission. That commission was credited with having resolved the difficult problem of tithe commutation with skill and tact.[145] Worsley's analogy and hence his purely executive model were accepted, but only with an important reservation.[146] For the sensitive matter of enclosure near towns executive enclosure orders were to be provisional only, to be effective when confirmed by Parliament in a statute after a report from the commissioners.[147] But otherwise executive authority operating under a public general Act laying down the rules would replace individual parliamentary decision. Hume recognized that that sort of structure would not always be appropriate. Even where it was not, similar personnel could use similar techniques of inquiry and validation to report to Parliament directly. The executive (in some guise or other) would thus be the supplier of information that would enable Parliament to assess the public interest in situations where individual application was still desirable.

The outcome was the Preliminary Inquiries Act 1846, which required that parliamentary consideration of town improvement bills be preceded by a local inquiry before an inspector—ideally an engineer or surveyor.[148] It was meant to be a cheap and accessible process for local people, but it failed, ostensibly because it was counter-productive. Two inquiries cost more than one, experts were cheaper to interview in London than in the locality, and the process caused unpredictable delays.[149] The Act worked well only where the bill impacted upon tidal waters, because then the preliminary report went first to Admiralty, which could produce a finality lacking in other cases by wielding the Crown's veto.

These utilitarian reasons masked deeper antipathies. The Act threatened the livelihood of the parliamentary agents, and it was they who marshalled much of the case against it.[150] The Act had owed something to Edwin Chadwick's lobbying for increased executive power, a theme within Hume's committee most obviously visible in its strong support for the Chadwick-inspired Health of Towns Commission.[151] Now Commons hostility to Chadwick's General Board of Health, which used a similar inspection/inquiry routine, found an easy surrogate target.[152] The Chadwickian alternative, that the preliminary inquiry should become final, was dismissed out of hand as too great a delegation of authority to the executive.

---

[145] E. J. Evans, *Tithes and the Tithe Commutation Act 1836* (1978).

[146] *Select Committee on Commons Inclosure*, Report, PP 1844 (583), v, 1.

[147] 8 & 9 Vict. c. 118.

[148] 9 & 10 Vict. c. 106, repealed and (in effect) re-enacted 11 & 12 Vict. c. 129.

[149] *SC on Local Acts (Preliminary Inquiries)*, Report, PP 1851 (582), xiii, 531.

[150] Rydz, *Parliamentary Agents*, 100–9.

[151] A. Brundage, *England's "Prussian Minister", Edwin Chadwick and the Politics of Government Growth 1832–1854* (Pennsylvania, 1988), 108–9.

[152] J. Prest, *Liberty and Locality* (Oxford, 1990), 39–40.

Save for bills affecting Admiralty matters the process was abolished in 1851.[153] At much the same time, and as part of the same abatement of the centralizing mood, the Inclosure Commissioners' ability to make final orders on their own account was removed. From 1852 a confirmatory statute would be required for all enclosures, whether in a sensitive area near a town or not.[154]

Railway bills raised the question of executive oversight even more acutely. Though private insofar as they interfere with property, said Gladstone, who was President of the Board of Trade at the time, they were public in their transport implications, hence public interests needed large representations in bill committees, somehow.[155] So from 1844 railway bills were sent for prior scrutiny to a Railways Board, a semi-autonomous branch of the Board of Trade.[156] But although the Commons directed much of the Board's investigation through detailed Standing Orders, the welter of competing bills impelled the Board to develop its own policy preferences, without having clear lines of responsibility. Inevitably its reports reflected its policies, and inevitably that conflicted with the Commons' other response to the increase in railway bills, the judicializing of bill committees. So the 'battle of the gauges' was a showdown for the Railways Board too, because it had reported against the Great Western Railway's expansion whereas the bill committee had reported in favour.

When the vote came, Peel and several other ministers were among the majority siding with the bill committee, some contrasting its open and thorough process with the Board's 'ex parte' receipt of information behind closed doors.[157] The Board's president, Lord Dalhousie, thereupon confronted Peel, his prime minister, with the argument that collective responsibility required all ministers to support the Board's recommendations. When Peel stood his ground the Board withdrew from scrutinizing bills altogether.[158] A differently constituted Railway Commission was created in 1846, the result of Hume's Railway Acts select committee, but neither it nor its successors gained a significant role in the scrutiny of bills, technical matters aside.[159] For all the expense of private bill legislation, railway companies disliked any closed process that might enable a rival to steal a march.[160] When the railway rush of the 1860s again led to some devolution, this

[153] 14 & 15 Vict. c. 49.

[154] *PD* 1845 (s3) 82: 33, 49–54; 15 & 16 Vict. c. 79.

[155] *PD* 1844 (s3) 73: 517.

[156] H. Parris, *Government and the Railways in Nineteenth Century Britain* (1965), 56–7. Some regulation was also imposed: Railway Regulation Act 1844, 7 & 8 Vict. c. 85.

[157] *PD* 1845 (s3) 81: 973–98.

[158] Parris, *Government and the Railways*, 84–8.

[159] *Ibid.*, 125–8, 158–62; Brundage, *England's 'Prussian Minister'*, 109–12.

[160] See also R. Kostal, *Law and English Railway Capitalism 1825–1875* (Oxford, 1994), 141–3, who sees the expense to small landowners of opposing a bill in Parliament as being the companies' reason for preferring that process.

time to a Court of Referees, the reaction when the rush was over was just the same—the House quickly clawed back questions of discretion and policy.[161]

Despite these well-known episodes of conflict, initiative was shifting from the House to the executive. The vehicle was the wonderfully ambiguous device of the provisional order, pioneered for enclosure bills in the Acts of 1846 and 1852. An executive agency would receive an application, inquire into it, and then make an order that would become binding when confirmed by a statute. So in form a provisional order was a recommendation to Parliament, which it could treat as it liked; in practice it was an executive decision that could be reopened by appeal to the Commons.[162] As with enclosure, it could be combined with clauses Acts to substitute for private bill applications, leaving Parliament the last word while freeing it from the necessity of having any other. Alternatively it could subtract from, and hence sugar, original grants of power to the executive. When the Public Health Act 1848 gave local bodies wide powers of drainage, sewage removal, water supply, and road maintenance, conditional only upon General Board of Health approval, some especially sensitive matters were reserved for parliamentary sanction via provisional order procedure—boundary adjustment (hence removal of jurisdiction) and conflict with existing private Acts. A decade later, when yet greater powers were conferred on local bodies, but the General Board and its suzerainty abolished, these reservations were maintained, and new ones added for use of the compulsory purchase sections of the Lands Clauses Consolidation Act and for borrowing money.[163]

A pattern was thereby set of allowing local bodies' powers to increase while entrenching a convention that deprivation of property required local inquiry followed by parliamentary consent.[164] Projects concerning piers, docks, and harbours followed in 1861, an easy extension of the preliminary inquiry system that had worked well in that context.[165] A 'provisional certificate' process was invented in 1864 to help with the rush in railway business, facilitating construction where all the necessary land could be obtained by agreement, empowering the raising of further capital, and enabling railway companies to reach joint management agreements.[166] Then, decisively, as part of the Gladstone ministry's reorientation of parliamentary resources towards government business, provisional

---

[161] Williams, *Historical Development*, i, 148–59.

[162] Parliament could amend a provisional order, not simply confirm or reject: May, *Treatise* (10th edn, 1893), 780–1.

[163] Local Government Act 1858, ss 75, 77, 78.

[164] For examples see Turnpike Trusts Relief Act 1851, Metropolitan Commons Act 1866, Sea Fisheries Act 1868, Land Drainage Act 1861, Sewage Utilization Act 1865, Elementary Education Act 1870.

[165] Piers and Harbours Act 1861; as with land drainage there was the inducement of public loans, under the Harbours and Passing Tolls etc Act 1861.

[166] Railway Construction Facilities Act 1864, Railways (Powers and Construction) Act 1870.

order procedure was made available in 1870 for gas, waterworks, and tramway projects.[167]

By the 1890s statutes ordaining this procedure could be counted in dozens.[168] In all cases notices had to be served, as for private bills, and local inquiries held, usually before an inspector appointed by a ministry.[169] Applications given provisional approval by the department would then be submitted to Parliament in batches, usually for express confirmation in an Act, but in 'provisional certificate' cases just for possible disallowance within a fixed time. The resulting certificate, or order incorporated in a statute, would automatically contain the relevant clauses from clauses Acts.

Parliament retained authority and oversight, because opposition to a confirmation bill before a parliamentary committee was always possible. Provisional certificate process was blocked at the outset if another railway or canal company gave notice of opposition, leaving the applicant to proceed by private bill, and a provisional order could always be opposed as if it were a private bill.[170] Further, the process was facilitative, not mandatory, constitutional principle demanding that even local bodies as impeccably statutory as county boroughs or local boards should have direct access to Parliament if they chose.[171] Large authorities, cities especially, continued to seek private legislation, not to the exclusion of provisional orders, but when their proposals straddled different provisional order procedures, or if they wanted powers different from those in the clauses Acts, or they found a department's policy irksome and wished to challenge it in committee.[172] So although provisional orders became numerous, averaging some 190 a year between 1882 and 1896, and although they expanded the opportunities available for local bodies by reducing costs, their effect within Parliament was to prevent an increase in local and private legislation, not significantly curtail it.[173]

Nonetheless the process necessarily ceded expertise and judgment to the executive, whose reports were influential even when provisional orders were contested.[174] The same had become true of local and private legislation. Where once the

---

[167] Gas and Waterworks Facilities Act 1870, Tramways Act 1870.

[168] May, *Treatise* (10th edn, 1893), 651–76; Clifford, *History*, ii, 676–709.

[169] Applications for private legislation by Scottish local authorities were shifted to provisional order procedure in 1899 to enable inquiries to be held locally rather than at Westminster: Private Legislation Procedure (Scotland) Act 1899.

[170] Clifford, *History*, ii, 676–715 gathers the data on opposition and its success; also *Joint Committee on Private Bill Legislation*, Report, PP 1888 (276), xvi, 1, App. O.

[171] Williams, *Historical Development*, i, 198; but unexpected doubts about the legality of paying for bills needed cure by the Municipal Corporations (Borough Funds) Act 1872; see below, pp. 441–2.

[172] Clifford, *History*, i, 246–7; ii, 709–15.

[173] Williams, *Historical Development*, i, 179; Office of Public Sector Information, *Chronological Table of Local Acts* (electronic: http://www.opsi.gov.uk/chron-tables/local/index.htm).

[174] *Joint Committee on Private Bill Legislation* 1888, Report, App. O.

Commons had kept ministries' opinions at arms' length, by 1902 a select committee was worried that waiting for them to arrive was delaying bills' progress.[175] In 1882, following a member's complaint of committee laxity and inconsistency, scrutiny of all local authority bills was shifted to a single select committee.[176] With a stable membership it soon became a committee of experts making minor policy decisions, from the optimum repayment period for local authority borrowing through to the precise circumstances in which gypsies could be moved on, sale of indecent prints suppressed, and verminous persons disinfected.[177]

The committee was fed by reports from the Local Government Board and the Home Office, on which it increasingly came to rely. It aligned its concept of public interest with these ministries' own, concerning itself as much with proposing changes to general legislation as with considering individual applications. Often it would delay an application in the hope of achieving a change to the law, though it would sometimes relent if its pressure failed.[178] There were occasions too when the committee would reject a clause for conflicting with the precedents and with ministry advice but encourage the applicant to try again when the confirmatory bill was before Parliament.[179] So as with provisional orders, the Commons gave an opportunity for scrutiny and appeal, but for the most part authority had shifted to a ministry.

The Role of Courts

Correspondingly the courts' role declined. From the 1820s through to 1870 judges toyed with notions that they had a role in safeguarding the public interest in private bill legislation. Often their intervention was rather fragile, based on majorities rather than consensus. It sputtered out in 1870, and by the 1890s judges disparaged the techniques used in the 1820s and 1830s, preferring simply to interpret statutes and enforce contracts without intruding their own public morality.

First, from about 1825 until a sudden reversal in 1853, they used a characterization of private procedure Acts that looked not just at the text but also at the

[175] SC on Private Business, Report, 1902 PP (378), vii, 321, 325.

[176] Named the Police and Sanitary Committee until 1908, from 1909 the Local Legislation Committee: Williams, Historical Development, i, 216–20; Clifford; History, ii, 536–42; J. Redlich and F. W. Hirst, Local Government in England (1903), ii, 276–301.

[177] SC on Police and Sanitary Bills, Special Report, PP 1884 (298), xv, 595, 599; SC on Local Legislation, Special Reports, PP 1914 (432), viii, 47; PP 1910 (323), vi, 521; PP 1912–13 (347), vii, 537. A wide range of powers impacting on civil liberties was discussed before the committee.

[178] SC on Local Legislation, Special Report, PP 1913 (267), vii, 41, 44.

[179] Ibid., 43 ('exceptional and important').

context. This differed from their approach to public general legislation. Private bill legislation, they said, was a contract between the promoters and either the public or Parliament, a bargain resting on representations made to secure a bill's passage. The notion may initially have done no more than justify a set of *contra proferentem* presumptions already well established, but in the 1830s it was extended in the public interest to pressure promoters into completing the projects they had undertaken.[180] Only when completed would the courts permit promoters to impose burdens upon the public.[181] From there, Lord Denman and Lord Campbell, successive chief justices of the King's Bench, indicated, it would be just a short and justifiable step to issue *mandamus* to compel completion of a scheme, all of it, even though the scheme might be a railway, and even though the Act might be worded permissively.[182]

Where Lord Denman would not allow a railway Act to be merely a 'boon [for] the projected company', however, and where Lord Campbell saw bargain theory as a deterrent to 'rough and reckless speculators', the Exchequer Chamber in 1853 saw only a statute to be given its plain meaning. Permissive words created no duty. Nor was that a bad thing, for 'by leaving the exercise of the powers to the company, the legislature adopts the safest check upon abuse...self interest'.[183] There was only text, to be interpreted.[184] Such a turn is consistent with a general tendency to a literally inclined 'ordinary meaning' canon of construction at that time, so it cannot be known how far it was also a response to the parliamentary disciplining of private promotions outlined above.[185]

[180] *Blakemore* v. *Glamorganshire Canal Co* (1832) 1 My. & Cr. 154; *Scales* v. *Pickering* (1828) 4 Bing. 448; *Barrett* v. *Stockton and Darlington Railway Co* (1840) 2 Man. & G. 134; and see the early example of *Gildart* v. *Gladstone* (1809) 11 East 675.

[181] *R* v. *Cumberworth* (1832) 3 B. & Ad. 108; *R* v. *Edge Lane* (1836) 4 Ad. & El. 723; *R* v. *Cumberworth (Branch Road)* (1836) 4 Ad. & El. 731.

[182] *R* v. *Eastern Counties Railway Co* (1839) 10 Ad. & El. 531; *R* v. *York and North Midland Railway Co* (1852) 1 E. & B. 178; *R* v. *Lancashire and Yorkshire Railway Co* (1852) 1 E. & B. 228 (reversed *ibid.*, 874); *R* .v. *Great Western Railway Co* (1852) 1 E. & B. 253; compare *Lee* v. *Milner* (1836) 2 M. & W. 824, but contrast *ibid.* (1837) 2 Y. & C. Ex. 611, 618–19. For Lord Denman's lack of sympathy with railway companies, see Kostal, *Law and English Railway Capitalism, passim.*

[183] *York and North Midland Railway Co* v. *R* (1853) 1 E. & B. 858; approved in *Edinburgh, Perth and Dundee Railway Co* v. *Philip* 2 Macq. 514 (HL); see also *Scottish and North Eastern Railway Co* v. *Stewart* 3 Macq. 382.

[184] Similarly, the *Cumberworth* principle was unavailable if the statute was worded disjunctively: external understandings might supplement the text, but could not contradict it: *Sidebottom* v. *Commissioners of Glossop Reservoirs* (1847) 1 Ex. 177 and 611; and see *R* v. *West Riding Justices* (1834) 5 B. & Ad. 1003.

[185] J. Wigram, *An Examination of the Rules of Law Respecting the Admission of Extrinsic Evidence in Aid of the Interpretation of Wills* (1831). For examples in that context, see *Roddy* v. *Fitzgerald* (1858) 6 H.L.C. 823; *Grey* v. *Pearson* (1857) 6 H.L.C. 61; *Abbott* v. *Middleton* (1858) 7 H.L.C. 68; *Smith* v. *Osborne* (1857) 6 H.L.C. 375; *Thellusson* v. *Rendlesham* (1859) 7 H.L.C. 429.

Secondly, some judges, not all, wanted courts to help preserve the integrity of parliamentary process. They would not directly enforce Standing Orders.[186] Nor, to Lord Campbell's regret, would a court hold a promoter to a representation in the plans deposited with a bill in Parliament, if the Act clearly authorized something different.[187] But, Lord Denman argued in the late 1830s, bargain theory might at least invalidate some agreements in which promoters paid landowners not to oppose a bill, a feature, particularly, of railway bill process, and one that from time to time caused acute public concern.[188] To Lord Denman such bargains were frauds to deceive Parliament about the true state of local opinion, especially where the noble landowner had a vote in Parliament.[189] Not so, replied Lord Cottenham, emphatically: since all opposition is based upon private interest, removing it actually serves the public.[190] Nor should peers lose freedoms possessed by other landowners. Only a bargain causing a deliberate misrepresentation of the true scheme would be invalidated, that and the purely hypothetical case where a bargain bought a peer's actual vote, a case so unimaginable to judges that only explicit words in a contract might persuade them of what less fastidious observers more readily believed.

An alternative route to invalidating non-opposition agreements with landowners was more successful, however. Starting from the same commercial premise that attracted Lord Cottenham it was argued that investors—shareholders buying into a company on the strength of its recently acquired statute, particularly into railway companies—were deceived by those secret undertakings which added so much to the costs of the project. The public estimates of costs required by Parliament as part of the private bill process never disclosed how much had been paid to buy off opposition. It may be a legitimate act of self-interest for landowners to surrender their opposition, but it could be beyond a company's statutory powers to pay them for it. Thus in the 1850s and 1860s the doctrine of *ultra vires*, seemingly technical but in fact based upon the conception that powers were given only in the public interest, for a time by-passed Lord Cottenham's doctrine, to

---

[186] *Edinburgh & Dalkeith Railway* v. *Wauchope* (1842) 8 Cl. & F. 710.

[187] *North British Railway* v. *Tod* (1846) 12 Cl. & F. 722; *Squire* v. *Campbell* (1836) 1 My. & Cr. 459; *Feofees of Heriot's Hospital* v. *Gibson* 2 Dow. 301; *Beardmer* v. *London and North-Western Railway Co* (1849) 1 Mac. & G. 112.

[188] Kostal, *Law and English Railway Capitalism*, 149–53, 161–75.

[189] *Lord Howden* v. *Simpson* (1839) 10 Ad. & El. 793; see also Lord Langdale in the same case ((1837) 1 Keen 583), and Plumer VC in *Vauxhall Bridge Co* v. *Earl Spencer* (1817) 2 Madd. 356, disavowed by Lord Eldon (1827) Jac. 64, 68.

[190] *Lord Howden* v. *Simpson* (1837) 3 My. & Cr. 97, (1842) 9 Cl. & F. 61; *Edwards* v. *Grand Junction Railway Co* (1836) 1 My. & Cr. 650; *Hawkes* v. *Eastern Counties Railway Co* (1852) 1 De G. M. & G. 737, 5 H.L.C. 331.

the palpable relief of judges who shared public indignation at the best known examples of landed greed.[191]

Technical doctrine begets technical solutions, however, particularly when the political climate changes. The weakness of this indirect enforcement of constitutional principle was that companies' powers were malleable. It was conventional that landowners parting with land to a railway company were compensated not just for the land but also for the inconvenience, hence that payment for inconvenience would be within a company's powers. It could therefore contract to compensate the estate concerned for inconvenience, in return for its owner not opposing the bill, conditionally only upon the bill passing. Eventually, in 1870, after disagreement in the lower courts, Lords Hatherley and Westbury indignantly refused to limit a company's powers by mere implication, refusing even to imply a term that the non-opposing landowner's land should ultimately have been required for the railway.[192] The public interest lay in enforcing contracts.

Shortly afterwards the cases requiring promoters to complete their project before beginning to levy charges on the public were overruled.[193] By then the legislative process was disciplined, both by party management and by the close involvement of officials in the preparatory vetting of bills. Courts saw no room for supplementing the words of statutes by contract theory. That was an 'old and extinct archaic class of cases', said Bowen LJ, looking back in 1893, mocking the patriarchal conceit that judges should ever think of telling railway companies what to do if Parliament had not.[194] Private interests were best managed by contracts; assessment of the public interest was for Parliament; in either case it was inappropriate for courts to interpret powers as duties or subject them to implied conditions.

---

[191] *Gage* v. *Newmarket Railway Co* (1852) 18 Q.B. 457; *Preston* v. *Liverpool, Manchester and Newcastle-upon-Tyne Railway Co* (1856) 5 H.L.C. 605; Kostal, *Law and English Railway Capitalism,* 150–1, 166; and cf. *Caledonian Railway Co* v. *Helensburgh Harbour Trustees* (1856) 2 Jur (NS) 695, using the law of pre-incorporation contracts to the same end. For the basis of *ultra vires* in the notion of public interest see for example *East Anglia Railways Co* v. *Eastern Counties Railway Co* (1851) 11 C.B. 775.

[192] *Taylor* v. *Chichester & Midhurst Railway Co* (1870) LR 4 HL 628; cp. (1867) LR 2 Ex 356.

[193] *R* v. *French* (1879) 4 QBD 507.

[194] *R* v. *Great Western Railway* (1893) 62 LJ KB 572.

II

Central Executive: The Legal Structure of State Institutions

1. INTRODUCTION

An account of how the central executive was structured in law, and how and why that changed, needs to begin by confronting a contradiction. On the one hand Paul Finn's perceptive account of nineteenth-century law and government deals dismissively with the eighteenth-century inheritance by saying that 'Customs, Excise and the Post Office apart, the central civil administration was a small affair indeed, bearing little on the everyday life of ordinary citizens', and then that 'not even the great officers of state—the Principal Secretaries of State, the Lord Treasurer and the like—were possessed of significant common law or statutory functions'.[1] By contrast John Brewer has shown that far from being complacent and ineffective, England's central administration created a fiscal-military state at least as powerful and efficient as any in Europe at what it chose to do.[2] While Finn has nothing more to say about customs, excise, and the post office, Brewer makes the excise commissioners central to his analysis. How can these descriptions be reconciled?

As for the army, it was of immense constitutional importance, and of practical significance too, that within England it was controlled neither by the king nor a general but by civilians responsible in some sense or other to Parliament.[3] Some small part of their powers would be statutory, under provisions in the Mutiny Acts, and after 1783 the Secretary-at-War's financial control was statutory too, but the broad issues of troop movements and disposition are best seen as involving civilian exercise of prerogative powers that had devolved to them

---

[1] P. Finn, *Law and Government in Colonial Australia* (Melbourne, 1987), 8.

[2] J. Brewer, *The Sinews of Power* (New York, 1989); for an early exposition of the same theme see Bl. Comm. Book 1 Ch. 8, 335–7.

[3] See Ch. IV below. Complex fragmentation of administration was another constitutional safeguard against an overbearing military: H. Strachan, *Wellington's Legacy* (Manchester, 1984), 234. Complete civilian control was seen as just as great a constitutional threat: J. Sweetman, *War and Administration* (Edinburgh, 1984), 21.

consequent upon the practice of permitting the king an army for but one year at a time.[4] Some of the more important functions were performed by the Secretaries of State, but their offices left a notoriously light footprint on the law. They were offices created by the sovereign of his own power, not statutory creations. By the end of the eighteenth century their duties (though capable of statutory addition) were largely a matter of convention, agreement, and the discretion of the Prime Minister.[5] Thus the big questions of control of the army at home, vital though they were to the character of the eighteenth-century polity, were a prerogative matter that had fallen into the hands of political officers whose existence and demarcation were also matters of prerogative or of politics. Legally, they had low visibility.

The same was sometimes true of the civil establishment. The government's ability to group and direct Crown servants allowed it to create central institutions that had considerable political significance while lacking independent legal personality. The Board of Trade was established by order in council in 1786, the Committee of the Privy Council on Education likewise in 1839. But the latter, though not unique in our period, was exceptional—an expedient for a government with support for its proposal in the Commons but without the votes to pass a bill through the Lords.[6]

By contrast the Commissioners of Excise controlled a large modern statutory agency, efficient and effective, which precociously satisfied all Max Weber's criteria for bureaucratic rationality.[7] In the writings of Sir Norman Chester and Paul Finn much is made of a transition undergone between the late eighteenth and mid-nineteenth centuries by public functionaries below the top rank, whose status changed from one of office holder to one of employee.[8] There was, they argue, a concomitant loss of autonomy and, importantly, a loss of public accountability through legal process, as private discipline through demotion and dismissal replaced older sanctions of fines and indictments. The excise Acts contained that transition within themselves from the beginning. The excisemen were treated as officers in relation to the public, and a range of statutory offences was created

---

[4] e.g. Mutiny Act 1799, 39 Geo. III c. 46; 23 Geo. III c. 50 (1783).

[5] *The Manual of Military Law* (6th edn, 1914), 161 dryly notes of the Secretary-at-War, 'his position and duties were vague'.

[6] The government tried the same ploy in 1837 to reform army administration but failed: Strachan, *Wellington's Legacy*, 250.

[7] Brewer, *Sinews of Power*, 66–8; J. Brewer, 'Servants of the Public—Servants of the Crown', in J. Brewer and E. Hellmuth, *Rethinking Leviathan* (Oxford, 1999), 140; Return of Establishments of Public Offices, PP 1833 (514), xxiii, 455; P. Jupp, *British Politics on the Eve of Reform* (1998), 109.

[8] N. Chester, *The English Administrative System 1780–1870* (Oxford, 1981), 12–30; Finn, *Law and Government*, 15–33.

applicable to the entire excise hierarchy from commissioners to doorkeepers, to
keep them in line. Functionally, however, the relationship between commissioners and excisemen was one of employment, with all the subjection to discipline
and direction that that entailed, and that relationship was acknowledged in the
statutes.[9] Brewers, distillers, and manufacturers of the myriad commodities bearing excise duty would be in no doubt exactly how their processes were to be conducted, policed, measured, and taxed, or which official would be responsible for
which aspect of tax-gathering. But nor would they doubt that every aspect of the
system operated under the direction of the commissioners through the printed
regulations they distributed to officers and through the systematic superintendence they exercised via supervisors and collectors.[10]

The minute particularity of these statutes leads, paradoxically, to much the same
result as the invisibility of the prerogative. Statute was tailor-made. The excise
management legislation was not like the customs legislation, and the post office
was different again.[11] These agencies had high legal visibility—copious statutes,
case law on many aspects of it—but their particularity discourages generalization,
and to writers in the common law tradition generalization is especially valued.

G. E. Aylmer famously remarked that late eighteenth-century administration
remained 'an extraordinary patchwork—of old and new, useless and efficient, corrupt and honest—mixed in together', and it follows from what has been written
above that its legal form was equally fragmented.[12] The general tension, though,
is reasonably clear. It was between an organization based upon prerogative (or
fact, or politics) and an organization based upon statute. The former stressed

---

[9] Excise Management Act 1827, 7 & 8 Geo. IV c. 53, consolidates the mass of earlier Acts (for
examples of 'employment' language see its s 4 and 10 Ann. c. 19, 12 Ann. stat. 2 c. 9, 33 Geo. II c. 9).
Excise pensions law likewise drew no distinction between officers and employees: 59 Geo. III c. 96,
replacing a contributory scheme endorsed by the Treasury, which was wound up by 52 Geo. III c. 81;
Chester, *English Administrative System*, 129. Brewer, *Sinews of Power*, 94, 101–3, and *Servants of the
Public*, shows how the employment relation worked in practice.

[10] This was explicitly recognized in the consolidation Act in 1827, Excise Management Act, 7 & 8
Geo. IV c. 53, s 6, where previously it had been taken for granted by 'under the management' clauses,
see for example 37 Geo. III c. 114, 39 & 40 Geo. III c. 23. Elaborate statutory provisions were needed
to square the commissioners' control with the vesting of legal powers in the excisemen, for example
56 Geo. III c. 104, s 15; 7 & 8 Geo. IV c. 53, s 61. For how the commissioners used their powers, see
generally the evidence appended to the *RC on Commissioners of Excise*, 3rd Report, *PP* 1834 [3], xxiv,
87. Where discretion was unavoidable, it was usually vested in the commissioners even when it concerned individual circumstances: e.g. 7 & 8 Geo. IV c. 52, ss 6, 20. Reported litigation is rare; see *R v.
Speller* (1847) 17 LJ MC 9, 1 Ex. 401; *A.-G. v. Bell* (1828) 2 Y. & J. 431, (1830) 1 C. & J. 237.

[11] Customs Management Act 6 Geo. IV c. 106; Excise Management Act, 7 & 8 Geo. IV c. 53; Post
Office Management Act 7 Will. IV & 1 Vict. c. 33; for differences between management of customs
and of excise see G. Smith, *Something to Declare: 1000 years of Customs and Excise* (1981), 87.

[12] G. E. Aylmer, 'From Office-holding to Civil Service: The Genesis of Modern Bureaucracy'
(1980) 30 *TRHS* (5th ser.), 91, 106.

the uniqueness and the exclusiveness of the Crown, the latter, when it could be generalized, invited comparison with the statutory agencies that exercised public functions in the localities. But differences of legal form did not necessarily connote differences of political substance. The excise commissioners surely resembled statutory local commissioners in their legal form, but they were Crown servants who quite early in the eighteenth century became subjected to a *de facto* Treasury superintendence that in due course was written into the law. Because statute was tailor-made the constitutional relations of a statutory agency could not be generalized; instead each was created anew and differently.

The sovereign's powers, the Crown's powers, were, of course, exercised by the government in the sovereign's name. How much say the sovereign had in that, if any, depended on the sovereign, the sovereign's consort, the ministers concerned, the subject-matter, the circumstances, and the time—but the law was blind to the question, just as it was blind to the question of which ministers the Prime Minister chose to involve in any particular exercise of a prerogative. But there was never any question of framing statutes so that they vested their new powers in the sovereign. That would have been undignified, or stretching the fiction too far, or, depending on the subject-matter, at risk of being taken seriously.[13]

Nor, to the regret of late twentieth-century theorists, was the 'state' given legal personality and made the repository of statutory power. Such an idea contradicted early and mid-nineteenth-century notions of responsibility and status. These cut two ways. On the one hand, through into the 1840s and, with some of them even into the early 1850s, ministers expected to attend to administrative detail. Powers were vested in them personally because they expected to exercise them personally. As late as 1865 the future Lord Salisbury was still expressing incredulity and hostility to the notion that a civil servant might in fact be exercising in his master's name the power that the law vested in a minister or a board, even though that had become conventional by at least a decade earlier.[14] Secondly, there was a mid-century reaction against the Whiggish notion that executive power was best vested in multi-member boards, the 'balanced constitution' in miniature, to favour instead a 'single seatedness' that would bring greater efficiency and accountability through individual responsibility.[15] Both currents

---

[13] See for example the embarrassment Cockburn CJ and Blackburn J. felt when discussing 'duty' and 'Her Majesty' in the same sentence: *R* v. *Lord Commissioners of the Treasury* (1872) LR 7 QB 387.

[14] *SC on Constitution of the Committee of Council on Education*, Report, *PP* 1865 (403), vi, 1, 15–16, 25–6; *SC on the Ecclesiastical Commission*, 1st Report, *PP* 1856 (174), xi, 1, qq. 577–81, 2263–8 cited by G. F. A. Best, *Temporal Pillars: Queen Anne's Bounty, the Ecclesiastical Commissioners and the Church of England* (Cambridge, 1964), 415–16.

[15] B. B. Schaffer, 'The Idea of the Ministerial Department: Bentham, Mill and Bagehot' (1957–8) 3 *Australian Jnl. of Politics and History* 60–78.

of thought militated against vesting power in an abstraction such as the Crown or the state.

The nearest that common legal form came to vesting powers impersonally was when statute conferred them on 'one of Her Majesty's principal Secretaries of State', leaving it to orders in council or patents of appointment to identify which Secretary of State would usually exercise them. In law it did not matter, for in law the principal Secretaries of State were interchangeable (save, as always has to be said, that a statute might stipulate just one of them). There was potential here for creation of a unified and abstract substitute for the monarch, but the intermediate stage would have seen an unpalatable concentration of statutory power—a prospect which lost Sir James Graham, Home Secretary from 1841 to 1846, many of his legislative proposals.[16]

For many reasons the usual nineteenth-century way was to create individual agencies by statute. Occasionally the initiative came from outside government, often new powers were needed too—it had long been settled that new coercive powers could not be created by prerogative—existing offices of a proprietary nature could not be abolished by prerogative.[17] Similarly it was common form for statute to authorize Secretaries of State and other ministers to appoint staff even though common law or prerogative powers should have been quite adequate.[18] For all this statutory activity, however, the offices at the peak of the political pyramid retained their legal character as creations of the prerogative (for lack of a better word), though some presided over departments that had been reorganized by statute. Just three of the 16 members of Palmerston's cabinet, 1855–8, held statutory posts, and only five of the 21 offices represented in the Conservative cabinets 1895–1905 were statutory.[19]

Through into the 1850s there was no consensus about the relation between this political elite and the holders of new statutory powers. When new powers were mooted or old ones consolidated the question of who was to wield them was approached along three lines. The first and most important was political. Should the powers vest in an existing power holder or in someone new? Then, to what extent and in what ways should that person be subject to, or free from,

---

[16] A. P. Donajgrodzki, 'Sir James Graham at the Home Office' (1977) 20 *Hist. J.* 97–120.

[17] Chester, *English Administrative System*, 13–40. Even when posts were not proprietary the Crown usually paid compensation for their abolition: M. Wright, *Treasury Control of the Civil Service 1854–1874* (Oxford, 1969), 331.

[18] e.g. Local Government Act 1858, s 79; New Ministries and Secretaries Act 1916, s 10.

[19] Palmerston: President of the Board of Control (33 Geo. III c. 52), Postmaster General (7 Will. IV & 1 Vict. c. 33, re-enacting 9 Ann. c. 10), and the First Commissioner of Works (14 & 15 Vict. c 42). Conservatives: add the presidents of the Board of Agriculture, the Board of Education (from 1899), and the Local Government Board, but subtract the President of the Board of Control, who had been replaced by the Secretary of State for India.

control by another, or have to account to another in some way? When should that other be Parliament (and in particular, the House of Commons), and when should it be a minister of the Crown? These were the most important issues through into the 1850s and 1860s, resulting in something of an orthodoxy that privileged ultimate control by a minister responsible to Parliament, and hence to the electorate.

The second line, closely related to the first, was the administrative. There was a pervasive and contestable concern for efficiency and economy. What was the ideal executive agency in the circumstances? Should it be a commission of several members or should all agencies be hierarchies with a single head able to command subordinates? Should the agency itself control the recruitment, payment, and pensioning of its staff, the provision of premises, the purchase of consumables, or should those functions be centralized (and hence controlled)? This is the history of the growth of the central civil service and the rise of the Treasury as its administrative controller.

The third line was legal: what legal characteristics should the power holder have? Statute could vest legal powers in any natural or artificial legal person, or in any group of persons. No particular designation was needed, no particular legal form.

2. STATUTORY AGENCIES: AUTONOMY AND INTEGRATION

Through into the 1840s, tailing off by the mid-1850s, the equation of 'the executive' with 'ministers of the Crown' was neither fully established nor fully accepted. Rather, the critical question for the reform Parliament of the 1830s was the degree of ministerial control there should be over the exercise of the new powers it was creating. The three new agencies, the factory inspectors, the Poor Law Commissioners, and the Tithe Commissioners were designed to no consistent pattern save that they received statutory powers in their own right, not by delegation from a Secretary of State. All began well distanced from ministers and day-to-day political control.

That did not necessarily leave them unaccountable to Parliament, since accountability of a sort could be achieved by other means. An agency might be kept on a short rein by having its powers granted for only a fixed, and short, duration, hence needing periodic renewal. Its funding might be annual, through the Appropriation Act. A more favoured agency might instead be given powers of indefinite duration and its funding charged on the consolidated fund. In addition, agencies might have a reporting obligation, which might occasion questions and debate in Parliament. The distinction was between, on the one hand, control by, and accountability through, a minister of the Crown, and, on the other, independence of government but some form of accountability to Parliament. Ministers could be just one sort of agency in a variably accountable set.

According to their constitutive Act in 1833, the factory inspectors were free to promulgate legally binding rules, either individually or collectively, to act as itinerant magistrates adjudicating upon the statute, and to control their subordinate staff, all of this without a suggestion that they were subject to anyone's direction. Indeed the only provision the Act made to encourage uniformity was to require the inspectors to meet together periodically for the purpose.[20] It is unsurprising that the Home Secretary should at first have refused the inspectors' request for supplies from H.M. Stationery Office on the ground that they were not part of the central administration.[21] Even so, they were not entirely independent. The initial appointment of their subordinate staff rested with the Secretary of State, and the inspectors' reporting obligations, collective and individual, were likewise to the Secretary of State—the Act said nothing about reporting to Parliament.

As for the Poor Law Commissioners, it is well known that its architect, Edwin Chadwick, sought an executive board of maximum independence insulated as far as possible from political influence. It was not to be under ministerial direction, nor could a minister (or indeed any Member of Parliament) serve concurrently as a commissioner, contrary to the initial preference of Lord Althorp, who as Chancellor of the Exchequer introduced the bill creating it.[22] Further, the commissioners could appoint their own staff, subject only to statutory maxima and Treasury control of salaries. Their accountability was to Parliament through annual reporting (directly, not through a minister), dependence on an annual vote of supply, and a five-year limitation of their powers.[23] But they too were not, quite, an independent statutory agency, since their General Orders needed submission to a Secretary of State and could be disallowed by His Majesty in Council, and they had an additional reporting obligation to the Secretary of State, including on each occasion that they failed to reach agreement.

The third of these pioneer agencies, the Tithe Commissioners, were modelled on the Poor Law Commission save that they were yet a degree more autonomous

---

[20] Factories Act 1833, 3 & 4 Will. IV c. 103, s 45.

[21] M. W. Thomas, *The Early Factory Legislation* (Westport Conn., 1948), 100.

[22] S. E. Finer, *The Life and Times of Sir Edwin Chadwick* (1952), 88–90; Chester, *English Administrative System*, 261.

[23] Poor Law Amendment Act 1834, 4 & 5 Will. IV c. 76, ss 1–9. Chadwick's claim that it was constructed on the same principle as governed the regulation of friendly societies (Finer, *Chadwick*, 90) is plausible, if at all, only if the principle is stated at a very general level: see 4 & 4 Will. IV c. 40 for the comparison, and E. J. Cleary, *The Building Society Movement* (1965), 31–2, 285 n.12 for a brief description.

through having their funding charged directly upon the consolidated fund.[24] They originally perhaps owed their greater independence to their character as a joint creation of church and state, the Archbishop of Canterbury having the appointment of one of the three commissioners, but they kept it when they were given the additional and wholly secular function of implementing copyhold commutation in 1841.[25]

Just as these three pioneer statutory agencies varied in their initial relations with Parliament and government so their susceptibility to review or reversal by the courts differed. The Factories Act 1833 was brief but definite: conviction whether by magistrates or inspectors were not to be appealed or removed by *certiorari* save in forgery cases.[26] As further judge-proofing, a short form for recording convictions was stipulated.[27] No means were provided for challenging the validity of orders and regulations the inspectors might make, though, exceptionally, their refusal to countersign an age certificate could be appealed to a magistrate.[28]

This favoured position was not copied for the Poor Law Commissioners. Their situation was different of course, in that their decisions affected individuals at one remove through their orders to local boards of guardians. Disputes were in a sense inter-governmental, local against central. The commissioners' statute provided that their rules, orders, and regulations could be challenged on *certiorari*, while adding, importantly, that until set aside instruments were valid and to be obeyed.[29] That had a useful side effect. The cabinet had denied Chadwick's request that the commissioners have their own direct powers of enforcement, so instead they had to proceed through courts by *mandamus*.[30] The Queen's Bench obligingly ruled, however, that the way the *certiorari* section was worded precluded

[24] Tithe Commutation Act 1836, 6 & 7 Will. IV c. 71. A precursor bill in 1834 (1834 *PP*, iv, 193), designed to facilitate voluntary commutation, limited central intervention to the appointment of surveyors by the Secretary of State, on the recommendation of local justices. In addition the administrative structure it envisaged involved quarter sessions, bishops, and locally appointed ecclesiastical commissioners. Centralization was far less complex. For an appreciation of the Tithe Commissioners' work, see E. J. Evans, *Tithes and the Tithe Commutation Act 1836* (1978).

[25] Copyhold Commutation Act 1841, 4 & 5 Vict. c. 35. Strictly, the commissions were separate but the commissioners were *ex officio* the same people. Accordingly they issued two annual reports, one under each Act, and they used the titles of Tithe Commissioners, Copyhold Commissioners, or Copyhold and Tithe Commissioners depending on the context.

[26] 3 & 4 Will. IV c. 103, s 42.

[27] See Ch. VI.2 below.

[28] Section 16.

[29] 4 & 5 Will. IV c. 76, s 105. The section also gave the commissioners some small procedural advantages over the usual *certiorari* procedure: R. J. and A. B. Corner, *The Practice on the Crown Side of the Court of Queen's Bench* (1844), 82–3.

[30] Finer, *Chadwick*, 90.

challenge to the validity of their orders at enforcement stage.[31] The commissioners did not win all their jurisdictional disputes, especially with unions already incorporated under Gilbert's Act or local statute, though they did preserve their discretion intact from judicial scrutiny.[32] But, whatever the results, the framework was significant. Guardians were not subordinates to be commanded, as Chadwick had wished, but legal entities subjected to a superior jurisdiction only to the extent that the statute provided, that question to be decided by a court.

The Tithe Commissioners were the most judicial of these three agencies, their aim clearly adjudicatory, their method inquisitorial.[33] Their Act provided that after a process of inquiry and adjudication, usually conducted by an assistant commissioner, the commissioners must consider whether to confirm the resulting draft order. Confirmed orders would be final and conclusive, their validity unaffected by errors of form.[34] *Certiorari* was barred, but appeals lay by streamlined process on factual issues or on points of law.[35] The commissioners were thus explicitly integrated into the legal system. That did not preclude further judicial supervision through writs of prohibition or *mandamus*, indeed the commissioners themselves seem to have encouraged the former at least, as the appropriate way to settle the limits of their statutory jurisdiction.[36] They argued nevertheless that courts should take a narrow view of what should count as jurisdictional error, and the courts duly obliged.[37] Other decisions respected the commissioners' discretion and accepted the finality of their orders.[38] The

---

[31] R v. *Churchwardens and Overseers of Bangor* (1847) 10 Q.B. 91; R v. *Overseers of Oldham* (1847) 10 Q.B. 700; R v. *Governors of the Poor of Bristol* (1849) 13 Q.B. 405 (aff'd *ibid.*, 414). A possible exception for 'manifest want of jurisdiction' was left open. See also R v. *Poor Law Commissioners (Allstonefield Incorporation)* (1840) 11 Ad. & El. 558.

[32] Defeats: R v. *Poor Law Commissioners* (1837) 6 Ad. & El. 1; R v. *Poor Law Commissioners* (1839) 9 Ad. & El. 901; R v. *Poor Law Commissioners* (1839) 9 Ad. & El. 911; R v. *Poor Law Commissioners* (1851) 17 Q.B. 445. Discretion: R v. *Poor Law Commissioners in re Newport Union* (1837) 6 Ad. & El. 54; *Frewin* v. *Lewis* (1838) 4 My. & Cr. 249.

[33] C. Stebbings, *Legal Foundations of Tribunals in Nineteenth Century England* (Cambridge, 2006), esp. 242–4.

[34] 6 & 7 Will. IV c. 71, ss 45, 95.

[35] 6 & 7 Will. IV c. 71, ss 46, 95 (and see also s 24). When the commissioners' jurisdiction was extended to settling parish boundaries *certiorari* was allowed back in for those decisions (only): 7 Will. IV & 1 Vict. c. 69, s 3. The point of that was so unclear that a further statute and litigation was needed: 2 & 3 Vict. c. 62, s 35; *In re Dent Tithe Commutation* (1845) 8 Q.B. 43; R v. *Merson* (1842) 3 Q.B. 895; R v. *Hobson* (1850) 19 LJ QB 262.

[36] *Barker* v. *Tithe Commissioners* (1843) 11 M. & W. 320; *In re Ystradgunlais Tithe Commutation* (1844) 8 Q.B. 32; R v. *Tithe Commissioners* (1843) 12 LJ QB 109; R v. *Tithe Commissioners* (1850) 15 Q.B. 620.

[37] *In re Appledore Tithe Commutation* (1845) 8 Q.B. 139; *In re Tithes of Crosby-upon-Eden* (1849) 13 Q.B. 761; *Bunbury* v. *Fuller* (1853) 9 Ex. 111; *Re Wintringham Tithes* (1862) 31 LJ CP 274; *Russell* v. *Tithe Commissioners* (1871) 40 LJ CP 265.

[38] Discretion: R v. *Merson* (1842) 3 Q.B. 895 (rather narrowly distinguished in the inclosure case, *Ex p Kelsey* (1850) 19 LJ QB 145); *Barker* v. *Tithe Commissioners* (1843) 11 M. & W. 320; R v. *Tithe*

one restriction on which the courts insisted was that the commissioners' jurisdiction concerned disputes between tithe-payers and tithe-owners, not disputes between rival claimants to the ownership of tithes.[39] Only in the context
of such matters of title can one find dicta casting doubt on the commissioners'
competence and suitability, thence a reading down of what was to count as
a 'difference', the key term on which the commissioners' ability to begin an
inquiry turned.[40] Still, the use the courts made of their statutory and common
law jurisdictions in relation to the commissioners matters less than the fact that
they were given the one and took the other.

Of the three agencies only the Tithe Commissioners retained their initial independence from government. The factory inspectors soon found that the difficulty
of performing their many roles and the opposition they met drew them closer to
the Home Secretary, and drew him into assuming an authority the Act did not
give. He ordered the abandonment of a practice he thought beyond the inspectors' powers, he required them to obtain the law officers' opinion before issuing
instructions under the Act, he directed them no longer to exercise their powers
as magistrates, and in the interests of uniformity the government instructed that
the inspectors agree on a single set of regulations.[41] Thus a different relationship evolved, confirmed when the 1844 Factories Act empowered the Secretary of
State to regulate the inspectors' duties, which were no longer to include acting as
magistrates or issuing regulations.[42] That explicit subordination reflected not just
the opposition of factory owners to the new regimen, but also a noticeable preference of Peel's administration for having matters under ministerial control.

How the new relationship worked out was not a matter of law, but of the attitudes
and aptitudes of successive Home Secretaries.[43] Similarly the related question of
how autonomous the inspectors should remain within the Home Office, and how

---

Commissioners (1849) 14 Q.B. 459. Finality: Clarke v. Yonge (1842) 5 Beav. 523; Walker v. Bentley (1852)
9 Hare 629 (contrast the much later inclosure case Jacomb v. Turner [1892] 1 QB 47 which used broad
jurisdictional theory to deny finality in a similar context. The statutes were different enough to justify different results, so it is difficult to say whether there had also been a change of attitude).

[39] Girdlestone v. Stanley (1839) 3 Y. & C. Ex. 421; Clarke v. Yonge (1842) 5 Beav. 523; R v. Tithe
Commissioners (1850) 15 Q.B. 620; Shepherd v. Marquis of Londonderry (1852) 18 Q.B. 145; R v. Tithe
Commissioners (1852) 18 Q.B. 156. The initial narrow reading of the commissioners' boundaries jur-
isdiction (In re Ystradgunlais Tithe Commutation (1844) 8 Q.B. 32) was renounced in In re Dent Tithe
Commutation (1845) 8 Q.B. 43.

[40] Girdlestone v. Stanley (1839) 3 Y. & C. Ex. 421 (Alderson B.); Shepherd v. Marquis of Londonderry
(1852) 18 Q.B. 145 (Coleridge J.).

[41] Thomas, Early Factory Legislation, 131–2, 142, 250–1. The last example might just possibly have
been warranted by s 45 of the Act of 7 & 8 Vict.

[42] 7 & 8 Vict. c. 15, s 6, which cautiously added that his regulation not be contrary to the Act.

[43] A. P. Donajgrodzki, 'Sir James Graham', 97; Thomas, Early Factory Legislation, 255–8; J. Pellew,
The Home Office 1848–1914 (1982), 145–9; P. W. J. Bartrip and S. B. Burman, The Wounded Soldiers of
Industry (Oxford, 1983), 54–68.

far become an integrated sub-department answerable to what level of permanent civil servant, would be answered by the dynamics of central government growth, Treasury control, and the attitudes of the inspectors themselves.[44] They resisted until 1878 suggestions that a chief inspector be appointed to rule on policy when consensus could not be achieved, but even before then statute was vesting powers of exemption and variation in the Secretary of State rather than in the inspectors directly, casting them as delegates and implying at least that someone in the department was acting as co-ordinator.[45] With their new role in 1844 came a realignment with the legal system. It alluded to possible liability in tort by extending the procedural protections of the Constables Protection Acts to them, but, more particularly, their exercise of their new power to classify machinery as dangerous could be contested through arbitration.[46] They thus lost autonomy on both fronts.

This new model of political and legal responsibility was copied for the later statutory inspectorates. On the one hand, inspectors could not impose penalties themselves, only through prosecution in the courts, and their administrative orders that might indirectly make factory operators liable could be contested through arbitration.[47] On the other, they were explicitly subordinated to a minister, even though it was often many years before administrative practice caught up with constitutional theory. Railway inspectors were responsible from the start to the Board of Trade, save for a brief interlude when they answered instead to railways commissioners.[48] As for inspectors of mines, the appointee under Ashley's Act of 1842 can be passed by lightly. More a standing commission of inquiry than an inspector, he received only the most general initial instructions from the Secretary of State and thereafter created his own role as social commentator and lobbyist.[49] In their second incarnation from 1850 the mines inspectors

---

[44] Pellew, *Home Office*, 123–32, 147–8, 151–64 178–82.

[45] Chief inspector: Thomas, *Early Factory Legislation*, 247, 259, 263–4, 281–3; Pellew, *Home Office*, 125–7, 151; Factory and Workshops Act 1878, s 67. Dispensing powers: Factory and Workshops Act 1871, 34 & 35 Vict. c. 104, a technique used extensively in the 1878 consolidation and amendment Act.

[46] 7 & 8 Vict. c. 15, ss 4, 43; Bartrip and Burman, *Wounded Soldiers*, 54–5. The immunity from judicial scrutiny the 1833 Act gave to convictions was carried forward in a new version (s 69), to the inspectors' embarrassment when they themselves wanted to bring a test case from magistrates before a court at Westminster: Thomas, *Early Factory Legislation*, 309–10.

[47] The mining legislation followed the Factories Acts in permitting inspectors to issue notices of dangerous installations, whereas the Alkali Acts relied solely upon prosecutions: Coal Mines Regulation Act 1872, ss 46, 49; Metalliferous Mines Regulation Act 1872, ss 18, 21; Coal Mines Regulation Act 1887, ss 42, 47 (and see s 53(3) for settling disputes over 'special rules'); Alkali Act 1863; Alkali Works Regulation Act 1881.

[48] 3 & 4 Vict. c. 97, 7 & 8 Vict. c. 85.

[49] 5 & 6 Vict. c. 100; A. Bryan, *The Evolution of Health and Safety in Mines* (Letchworth, 1975), 36–8; O. G. M. Macdonagh, 'Coal Mines Regulation: The first decade 1842–1852', in R. Robson

were always explicitly subordinated to the Secretary of State.[50] From the 1855 Act onwards powers that would in fact be exercised by the inspectors were vested in law in the Secretary of State, again implying delegation and control, even though at that time and for many years to come the inspectors in fact acted independently of him and of each other.[51] The powers of the Alkali Act inspectors were their own, though in matters of appointment, salary, and report they were subordinate to a ministry—first the Board of Trade, later the Local Government Board.[52] There was never a possibility of their having a legally autonomous status, however. As a royal commission considered it in 1878, the issue was only whether they should continue within a central department or be dispersed among local authorities.[53] The factory inspectors' early shift from putative autonomy to branch of a ministry thus set an important precedent.[54]

At first the second of the hallmark agencies of the reform Parliament, the Poor Law Commissioners, shrugged off the formal constraints on their autonomy. They found special or particular orders to be more practicable than general orders and just as lawful, while not needing political approval.[55] Lord John Russell, Home Secretary when the Act took effect and the man responsible for changing Althorp's mind, rapidly disavowed the implied power the reporting obligation gave him, saying its use would be an affront to the commissioners.[56] Then, in 1847, came its implosion and replacement, nominally by a Board but in fact by its President who, equipped also with a salaried parliamentary secretary, ran it

(ed.), *Ideas and Institutions of Victorian Britain* (1967), 58–86; Pellew, *Home Office*, 128; Bartrip and Burman, *Wounded Soldiers*, 83–92.

[50] 13 & 14 Vict. c. 99; Coal Mines Act 1855; Coal Mines Regulation Act 1872; Mines Act 1860; Metalliferous Mines Regulation Act 1872; Coal Mines Regulation Act 1887; Bryan, *Evolution of Health and Safety*, 54, 63–4; R. Church, *The History of the British Coal Industry* (Oxford, 1986), iii, 426 (quotation; Bartripp and Burman, *Wounded Soldiers*, 90–1).

[51] It was not until 1908 that His Majesty's Chief Inspector of Mines was appointed and the nucleus of a London headquarters created in the Home Office: Bryan, *Evolution of Health and Safety*, 90–1. Though subordinated to the Secretary of State, the inspectors kept their individual duty to report annually to Parliament, even through into the Coal Mines Act 1911, s 100, though by then it applied only to district inspectors. It is not known whether the Home Office screened their reports before submission to Parliament in the way that Home Secretaries had done from an early period with the factory inspectors' reports: Thomas, *Early Factory Legislation*, 255–8.

[52] Alkali Act 1863; Public Health Act 1872, s 35; R. M. McLeod, 'The Alkali Acts Administration: The Emergence of the Civil Scientist' (1965) 9 *Vict. St.* 87.

[53] *RC on Noxious Vapours*, Report, PP 1878 [C. 2159], xliv, 1, 31–6.

[54] For Home Office inspectorates see Pellew, *Home Office*. Local Government Board inspectors, important in the implementation of the Public Health Acts, were appointed by the Board in the same manner as other office staff and allocated work as the Board saw fit: Local Government Board Act 1871, ss 3, 6.

[55] *Report of the Poor Law Commissioners on the Continuance of the Poor Law Commission*, PP 1840 [226], xvii, 167, 193–7; S. and B. Webb, *English Poor Law Policy* (1910), 21–2. Their power to use particular orders to overrule or depart from general orders was removed by 5 & 6 Vict. c. 57, s 3.

[56] Finer, *Chadwick*, 121.

as though it were a ministry for which he alone was accountable to Parliament. The usual explanation, beginning with the memoirs of one of the commissioners, then on through the writing of Earl Grey and Bagehot into modern texts, is that without a minister to answer for them in the Commons the commissioners were fatally vulnerable to ill-informed and malevolent attack inspired by opposition to their policies.[57] Hence their demise has been treated as part of, and justification for, the concentration of executive power within ministries.

The same push came from within the Commission. Chadwick himself, the very engineer of the commission's independence, was quick to plead in aid the Secretary of State when he did not get his way with the commissioners, and as hostilities became intractable Lord John Russell and his Conservative successor in the 1840s, Sir James Graham, did have to use their control over the rule-making power to adjudicate on policy differences and to impose their own views.[58] The result was that though formally independent, under Peel's Conservative administration it came to function as though it were led by the Home Secretary.[59]

It might perhaps have evolved into a mixed board with a minister as a member, the form originally sought by Althorp and which became fashionable in the mid-1840s, were it not that a parliamentary inquiry into cruelty at the Andover workhouse turned into such a desperate contest for political survival between Chadwick and his major antagonist that the exasperated government determined to replace the entire commission with a different sort of board.[60] Even then the exact form of the new Poor Law Board was not concluded by its constitutive Act.[61] Usually such boards with a President and *ex officio* membership of senior politicians were a form of fiction, but the Act very carefully provided that this one might actually meet, and that for some of its activities the signatures of two were required.

The experience of the factory inspectors and the Poor Law Commissioners did not cause a wholesale shift to ministerial control. Rather the typical agency of the 1840s, if there was such a thing, was a mixed board that included a politician. He might inform parliamentary debate, but, not having legal control, he could not be held accountable for the board's decisions. As always there were variations

---

[57] Chester, *English Administrative System*, 261–2, relying on Sir G. Nicholls, *History of the English Poor Law* (1854), ii, 410–11; Henry, Earl Grey, *Parliamentary Government Considered with Reference to Reform* (2nd edn, 1864), 22–4; G. Kitson Clark, '"Statesmen in disguise": Reflexions on the History of the Neutrality of the Civil Service' (1959) 2 *Hist. Jnl.* 19–39 at 29–30; H. Parris, *Constitutional Bureaucracy* (1969), 90, following W. Bagehot, *English Constitution* (2nd edn, 1872), Ch. VI.

[58] P. Mandler, *Aristocratic Government in the Age of Reform* (Oxford, 1990), 173–7; Finer, *Chadwick*, 121, 137–9, 205.

[59] Finer, *Chadwick*, 207, 247–50.

[60] *Ibid.*, 257–91. George Nicholls, formerly a commissioner, became secretary to the new board.

[61] Poor Law Board Act 1847, 10 & 11 Vict. c. 109.

within the type. Most independent were the Railway Commissioners established by the Whigs in 1846. Their precursor had been a board constituted within the Board of Trade in 1844 to report on railway bills coming before Parliament, after Peel had rejected a Commons resolution that a wholly new department for railways was desirable.[62] That had been an uncomfortable compromise because formally all members of the board had an equal voice, though its president was Lord Dalhousie, the Vice-President of the Board of Trade, and the other members were his officials. One element in its quick collapse was that such a composition blurred responsibility in what was a most contentious area.

Yet the Whigs' solution was not an accountable minister but a 'mixed board, made up of people in high authority, or of high rank, with others to aid them', and they offered its presidency to Dalhousie, now in Opposition.[63] When he declined, a Member of Parliament became its president, and a member of the Lords joined the commission too, but it is clear that they were seen as spokesmen rather than as ministers or minister-substitutes who might be held accountable. As the commission was to take over the Board of Trade's regulatory and inspection powers this was a subtraction from political responsibility.

Similar to the railway commissioners were the Church Estates Commissioners, born out of the Ecclesiastical Commissioners in 1850.[64] Kitson Clark saw their creation as 'reducing to ministerial discipline...that part of the Ecclesiastical Commissioners whose work really interested Parliament, that part which dealt with the holding of land'.[65] On the face of the statute that might be true, since the Crown-appointed First Commissioner was to be salaried and to be capable of sitting in the Commons, which makes him look just like a minister. But the Earl of Chichester occupied the post through until 1878 irrespective of government changes, and though he might speak for the Commissioners in the Lords, so too in the Commons did successive (and salaried) Third Commissioners, nominees of the Archbishop of Canterbury. Only by accident did the Second Commissioner become the political post, and then only from 1859.[66] But though the work of the parent Ecclesiastical Commissioners, which was in part driven by the Church Estates Commissioners as a form of inner cabinet, often came under critical scrutiny in and out of Parliament, the Second Commissioner was never held accountable as a minister might be.[67]

---

[62] Parris, *Government and the Railways*, 61–3, 69, 82–9.

[63] *Ibid.*, 104; Railways Commissioners Act 1846, 9 & 10 Vict. c. 105.

[64] Ecclesiastical Commissioners Act 13 & 14 Vict. c. 94; Best, *Temporal Pillars*, 393–7.

[65] Kitson Clark, 'Statesmen in disguise', 30.

[66] Best, *Temporal Pillars*, 418–19.

[67] *Ibid.*, 419–21, 438–41. The Church Estates Commissioners were born out of such a concern: *ibid.*, 395.

The Tories were less keen to disperse power than the Whigs were. In 1844 they rejected as lacking proper political accountability Lord Worsley's original proposal for speeding enclosure of the remaining common land by giving a further jurisdiction to the autonomous Copyhold and Tithe Commissioners.[68] Instead the Tories' Inclosure Commissioners were to be a new board comprising the First Commissioner of Woods and Forests as its political head plus two other members appointed by the Home Secretary, the board as a whole reporting to him. Though their funding was charged on the consolidated fund their powers were of limited duration, hence needing periodic parliamentary renewal.[69] Further, the more sensitive of their schemes would need parliamentary confirmation through a provisional order system before being implemented. So too with the pressing question of the health of towns, the Tories' preference was for a new sanatory Act to be enforced by an inspectorate under the Home Secretary, while the Whigs wanted a board and Chadwick wanted either an independent commission or a single administrative post answerable to a committee of the Privy Council.[70] After considerable parliamentary haggling the Whigs got their board, to consist of a minister plus two members to be appointed by Her Majesty—hence not dependent on a single minister—one of whom could be salaried.[71] Accountability was thus seen as important, but in the 1840s it was contested and did not lead to a single template for executive agencies.

There was also one creation that was the purest example of independent statutory commissioners of them all, Lord Ashley's custom designed Commissioners in Lunacy. The Lunacy Act 1845 actually named the 11 men to be the first commissioners—five men of rank or authority, including Ashley himself, and six professionals, three each of physicians and lawyers.[72] The professionals were to be salaried and full time, intended to perform the commissioners' duties of inspection; all were to hold their office during good behaviour. Ashley served as their duly elected president right through until 1885. The commissioners did not have strong legal powers, and according to one commentator their role was principally as advisor and stimulator, co-ordinator and information bureau, though he records also that their inspection duties snowballed.[73] They issued general

[68] *PD* 1844 (s3) 80: 26 (Earl of Lincoln).

[69] Inclosure Act 1845, 8 & 9 Vict. c. 118.

[70] C. Hamlin, *Public Health and Social Justice in the Age of Chadwick* (Cambridge, 1998), 266–74; Finer, *Chadwick*, 304–5, 319; R. A. Lewis, *Edwin Chadwick and the Public Health Movement 1832–1854* (1952), 128; Sewerage, Drainage etc of Towns Bill, *PP* 1845 (574), v, 363.

[71] Public Health Act 1848, 11 & 12 Vict. c. 63.

[72] 8 & 9 Vict. c. 100, which also named the man to be appointed secretary. The Lord Chancellor was given power to fill vacancies. The Act is to be read with 8 & 9 Vict. c. 126.

[73] D. J. Mellett, 'Bureaucracy and Mental Illness: The Commissioners in Lunacy 1845–90' (1981) 25 *Medical History* 221–50.

regulations for the management of asylums, subject to the Home Secretary's approval (and initially at his insistence) and they made recommendations to the Home Secretary on local authority proposals to construct or expand asylums, often influentially.[74] They were, however, otherwise independent of the Home Secretary, who might choose to defend them if he wished but who was not responsible for them. Ashley might speak for them in Parliament, as might any other of the unpaid commissioners with a seat there, but on a strictly voluntary basis, again without responsibility; any commissioner might be detailed to lobby and cajole.[75] Yet this strange semi-executive, semi-advisory body survived until 1913, when it was transmuted into a stronger version of the same thing over the protests of those who thought an unelected and irresponsible body inappropriate.[76]

Of the mixed boards only the Church Estates Commissioners survived. The Board of Trade regained *de facto* regulatory authority over railways when its President and Vice-President came to occupy the two equivalent positions on the railways commission in 1848.[77] Principles of economy then led to the abolition of the commissioners and the retransfer of their powers to the Board of Trade in 1851.[78] Whatever the motivation, the result was a restoration of ministerial responsibility. The General Board of Health met similar political hostility to the Poor Law Commissioners and shared their fate. Rather than defending the board from sustained parliamentary attack in 1854, its ministerial member sided with its critics against his fellow members; he was a spokesman and informant, after all, not a controlling hand to be held responsible.[79] The board collapsed when the Commons withdrew its funding, to be replaced by what had become the legal model for a single-seated ministry, that is a board of political office holders, not intended to meet, headed by a salaried president with a seat in the Commons.[80]

By contrast the Inclosure Commissioners flourished. Their jurisdiction was soon significantly extended when they were given the administration of the

---

[74] A. Scull, *The Most Solitary of Afflictions* (New Haven, 1993), 280, 313; A. Scull, C. MacKenzie, and N. Hervey, *Masters of Bedlam* (Princeton, 1996), 174–81.

[75] N. Hervey, '"A Slavish Bowing Down": The Lunacy Commissioners and the Psychiatric Profession 1845–60', in W. Bynum, R. Porter, and N. Shepherd (eds), *The Anatomy of Madness* (1985), ii, 98–131.

[76] Mental Deficiency Act 1913, instituting the Board of Control; M. Thomson, *The Problem of Mental Deficiency: Eugenics, Democracy, and Social Policy in Britain c.1870–1959* (Oxford, 1998), 77–109.

[77] Parris, *Government and the Railways*, 105–9.

[78] 14 & 15 Vict. c. 64; Parris, *Government and the Railways*, 129.

[79] Finer, *Chadwick*, 463, 469–72.

[80] Public Health Act 1854. When its functions were reduced in 1858 to the point that a separate minister was no longer justified its remaining powers were transferred to the Home Secretary or the Privy Council and the board abolished: Public Health Act 1858, Local Government Act 1858.

Public Money Drainage Act, and it might have been expected that this, the clos-est of all the mixed boards to ministerial control, would in due course supplant the autonomous Copyhold and Tithe Commission, since their functions were similar.[81] In fact the reverse happened. When its ministerial head was restruc-tured out of existence in 1851, rather than getting a new one the commission had its functions transferred to the Copyhold and Tithe Commissioners (whose name was then even further extended) much as Worsley had originally wanted.[82] The Home Secretary duly declined to take political responsibility for their actions, though it was through him that they reported to Parliament.[83] On the other hand their accountability to Parliament was shortly afterwards increased by a require-ment that all their inclosure awards should use the provisional order procedure, and theirs was one of the many agencies whose funding was shifted off the con-solidated fund and on to the annual vote of supply in 1854 as the Commons tight-ened its grip on public expenditure.[84] They were operating more as a department of Parliament than as part of the Executive.

Perhaps in consequence—there was no talk of it—the courts subjected the Inclosure Commissioners to unusual scrutiny. As with the tithe legislation, appeals were possible at various stages of the inclosure process, but the courts exercised their review function as well. The commissioners did once argue that statutory confirmation of provisional orders brought statutory finality, but the court turned a deaf ear.[85] It could instead have taken a narrow view of its role,

---

[81] 9 & 10 Vict. c. 101.

[82] Inclosure Commissioners Act 1851, 14 & 15 Vict. c. 53. They retained their curious triple identity until 1882, when at last they were renamed Land Commissioners, with a single style and single seal, just seven years before they were wound up, their staff and (by then very extensive) functions being transferred to a new ministry, the Board of Agriculture: Settled Land Act 1882, s 2; Board of Agriculture Act 1889. Their extended functions can be traced through the Land Drainage Act 1861 and the Land Improvement Act 1864, and accounts of their work found in D. Spring, *The English Landed Estate* (Baltimore, 1963), 135–77, Stebbings, *Legal Foundations*, and Board of Agriculture, *Annual Report of Proceedings under the Inclosure Acts [etc]* [for 1892] 1893–4 PP [C. 6891], xxiii, 1.

[83] Spring, *English Landed Estate*, 138, 171–2 (the Home Secretary's subsequent endorsement of the parliamentary question to the commissioners and their reply to it are printed at PP 1865, xlvii, 429). The commission, which had its own premises and own staff, is not mentioned by Jill Pellew in her study of the Home Office.

[84] Inclosure Act 1852, 15 & 16 Vict. c. 79, s 1; Public Revenue and Consolidated Fund Act 1854. Their commissions continued to need periodic renewal by Parliament, a legal precariousness that contrasted with the solid permanence they had acquired as their land improvement functions mul-tiplied, and one that excluded them from the pensions available to members of the permanent civil service until special statutory provision was made: Inclosure Commissioners Continuation Act 1862, bringing them within the provisions of Superannuation Act 1859.

[85] *Turner* v. *Blaimire* (1853) 1 Drew. 402 (Kindersley VC: determination of what were commons was within commissioners' jurisdiction; statutory appeal process exclusive), 22 LJ Ch 766 (LJJ: com-missioners' determination correct on its facts).

as it did when refusing to intervene on any other provisional orders.[86] But in the inclosure context the judges instead entertained claims that the commissioners had lacked jurisdiction to include particular land in their order just as if there had been no statutory confirmation at all.[87] They once even went as far as prohibiting the commissioners from submitting a provisional order to Parliament, on the ground that the commissioners had mistaken what consents were required for their proposal to go ahead.[88] This was intrusive scrutiny, though it was on jurisdictional grounds only; the judges would not intervene on matters they characterized as fact or discretion.[89] The commissioners thus continued as a statutory agency free from ministerial control, but subject to close jurisdictional control by the courts, and subject also to close parliamentary scrutiny of some of their outputs, depending on whether it was inclosure, or commutation of tithes, or copyhold enfranchisement that was in issue.

In the 1950s B. B. Schaffer noted that autonomous statutory commissions had become invisible to the constitutional writers of the 1880s.[90] As Schaffer emphasized, that is probably explained by the impact of Bagehot's analysis of cabinet government and parliamentary accountability. The most flamboyant of the statutory agencies, the Poor Law Commission and the General Board of Health, had long since collapsed into ministries, the inspectorates had likewise become arms of ministerial departments, and all but one of the mixed boards had vanished. The surviving statutory agencies were a politically uninteresting miscellany, their number reducing as ministries expanded to take them over. The Patent Commissioners, established in 1851 to substitute bureaucratic process for prerogative grants, were abolished in 1883 and the Patent Office transferred to the Board of Trade.[91] The Land Commissioners, the renamed Copyhold, Inclosure and Tithe Commissioners, were folded into the new

---

[86] *Frewen v. Hastings Local Board of Health* (1865) 13 WR 678; see below, pp. 502–3.

[87] *Chilcote v. Youldon* (1860) 3 E. & E. 7, 2 LT (NS) 370; *Musgrave v. Forster* (1871) LR 6 QB 590; *Jacomb v. Turner* [1897] 1 QB 47; *Blackett v. Ridout* [1915] 2 KB 415; and for similar but less precisely directed sentiments see *Grubb v. Brown* (1858) 1 F. & F. 352 and re *Earl of Portsmouth, Partridge v. Inclosure Commissioners* (1861) 3 LT 779, 9 WR 336. The reports of *Chilcote v. Youldon* say nothing about the provisional order having been sanctioned by a statute, but it can hardly be doubted that it had, since 15 & 16 Vict. c. 79, s 1 forbade the commissioners to 'proceed with the inclosure' (which is what they were doing) without such sanction. The land was at Brixham, so probably the Act was Inclosures Act 1856. If so, the inclosure was still incomplete in 1865: 1865 *PP*, xlvii, 425.

[88] *Church v. Inclosure Commissioners* (1862) 11 C.B. (N.S.) 664.

[89] *Minet v. Leman* (1855) 24 LJ Ch. 545; *Harris v. Jose* (1866) 13 LT 699; *Lingwood v. Gyde* (1866) LR 2 CP 72. Compare *Reynolds v. Lord of the Manor of Woodham Walter* (1872) LR 7 CP 639 (what constituted hardship treated as a question of fact for copyhold commissioners).

[90] Schaffer, 'Idea of the Ministerial Department', 77–8.

[91] 15 & 16 Vict. c. 83; Patent, Designs, and Trade Marks Act 1883, ss 82–102; L. Bently and B. Sherman, *The Making of Modern Intellectual Property Law* (Oxford, 2001), 133–4.

Board of Agriculture in 1889.[92] Even the Charity Commissioners lost some of their functions to the newly established Board of Education.[93] It was possible, as Schaffer notes, to believe with Bagehot that ministers were answerable to the Commons in a real sense. High-Victorian orthodoxy required administrative agencies to answer to a minister of the Crown accountable in Parliament.

Only at the very end of our period were new statutory agencies created, as part of the new Liberal expansion of the state.[94] Insurance Commissioners, the Road Board, and the Development Commission represented an increasing tendency which needed careful scrutiny, reported the Machinery of Government Committee to the Ministry of Reconstruction in 1918, endorsing the pre-war Royal Commission on the Civil Service.[95] These inquiries were not dogmatic; as in the 1830s, there could be shades of accountability. The Development Commission might be acceptable because the grants it recommended the Treasury to make would be processed through departmental estimates that were subject to Commons' scrutiny, whereas the Road Board was suspect because its funding through grants-in-aid received only cursory parliamentary attention.[96] The Machinery of Government Committee thought the Medical Research Committee passed muster because it reported annually to Parliament and because the minister responsible for health insurance would answer for it, though it worried whether a generalist minister could speak usefully for such an expert and specialist body.[97]

These issues, so strikingly reminiscent of the late 1830s and 1840s, were thus played out again a century after they had first arisen, as boards proliferated, but this time against a background of party discipline that had deprived the Commons of its ability to act independently of government.[98] By then it was difficult to conceive of statutory agencies independent of government, or under loose supervision only, being responsible in meaningful ways to Parliament. That had been possible from the 1830s until about the early 1860s, but it had been overtaken then by centralization of powers into ministries and the growth of party government.[99]

[92] Land Commissioners: Settled Land Act 1882, s 2; Board of Agriculture Act 1889.

[93] Board of Education Act 1899, s 2; A. Bishop, *The Rise of a Central Authority for English Education* (Cambridge, 1971), 138, 238–58.

[94] F. M. G. Willson, 'Ministries and Boards: Some Aspects of Administrative Development since 1842' (1955) 33 *Public Administration* 43–58 at 55–6.

[95] Ministry of Reconstruction, *Report of the Machinery of Government Committee*, PP 1918 (Cd. 9230), xii, 1 esp. 11, 28–9, 34; *RC on the Civil Service*, 4th Report, PP 1914 (Cd. 7338), xvi, 1, 62, 76–9.

[96] *RC on the Civil Service*, 4th Report, 76–7.

[97] *Machinery of Government Committee*, 28–9.

[98] D. N. Chester, 'Public Corporations and the Classification of Administrative Bodies' (1953) 1 *Political Studies* 34–52; I. Jennings, *Parliament* (2nd edn, Cambridge, 1957), 341–54.

[99] Parris, *Constitutional Bureaucracy*, 84–93.

3. MINISTRIES AND OTHER CROWN AGENCIES

In principle the government did not need statutory authority to create new agencies. It could instead further divide the Secretaryship of State. Her Majesty had power to decide between how many office holders it should be split and what their responsibilities should be, and it was established law that one Secretary of State could stand in for any other. That was why the Place Acts had been passed, excluding Crown office-holders from the Commons, hence any new office intended to be political did need an enabling Act. So statutes were passed in 1855 when the Secretaryship of State for War and Colonies was divided into two, and in 1858 when a new post was created for India. [100] Nonetheless these Acts followed constitutional nicety meticulously. They did not create the new posts, or even authorize Her Majesty to create them—she needed no such authority. Instead they merely laid out the consequences if Her Majesty should graciously signify her pleasure. Such concern not to trespass upon the sovereign's prerogative survived even to the end of our period, when provision for the governance of the newly created air force followed the same form. [101]

Further, government could create a new agency not needing coercive powers just by redeploying Crown servants. On the small scale the Privy Council could be used as an institutionalized Crown either directly or through committees, the ultimate Ministry of Miscellaneous Affairs. It became the repository for homeless powers, though in those cases, of course, statute was needed to create and vest the powers. [102] That was not necessary for the Committee of the Privy Council on Education, which was founded upon the inherent power of the Crown to spend money voted by the Commons. In such a situation Commons control over finance substituted for control through law. From 1839 an appropriation Act would authorize the issue of a sum 'for public education', which would pass to a committee of privy councillors created by an order in council to superintend its application. [103] No more legal structure was needed than that.

The Education Committee remained in that state for 60 years, save for a laconic single-section statute in 1856 which authorized appointment of a salaried Vice-President of the committee who might sit in the Commons, the better, it was said,

---

[100] House of Commons Act 1855; Government of India Act 1858, s 4 (explained in House of Commons (Vacation of Seats) Act 1864); Chester, *English Administrative System*, 88, 150, 237–9.

[101] Air Force (Constitution) Act 1917.

[102] e.g. Public Health Act 1858. K. B. Smellie's memorable description of it as a 'kind of potting shed for new administrative plants' implies a prescience that was only sometimes true: *A Hundred Years of British Government* (1937), 90.

[103] e.g. 2 & 3 Vict. c. 89, s 17; *Copy of an Order in Council [etc]*, PP 1839 (287), xli, 256.

to secure accountability.[104] The committee immediately advised Her Majesty to appoint it a secretary, and shortly afterwards inspectors. [105] Thus a department was created, which grew in the ordinary way. There was of course a political storm, when those opposed to state encroachment on the Church's educational sphere objected also that the Whigs' chosen method unconstitutionally by-passed one legislative House.[106] From the political stand-off that followed between the government and the Church there emerged a concordat that cemented in place a system of denominational education subsidized by state grants, watched over by inspectors over whose appointment first the Church (in respect of Church schools), and later Dissent (in respect of Nonconformist schools), had an initial veto and a *de facto* power of removal.[107] The grants' purposes, the all-important conditions attached to them, and the functions of the inspectors were settled from time to time by Minutes of the Committee of Council, which were reported to Parliament together with a mass of circulars and letters from the secretary elaborating them, and also the inspectors' reports. So the legal structure might be exiguous, but political accountability certainly was not.

The Education Committee managed without statutory powers until 1870. It was politics, not law, that determined that the committee itself should become very largely ornamental and the real authority (and accountability) lie with the Lord President of Council, just as, later, it was politics that determined how far the Vice-President should wrest it away.[108] Similarly with the inspectors; they had power long before 1870—school managers and teachers never doubted that—and,

---

[104] Education Department Act 1856; Bishop, *Rise of a Central Authority*, 43–8; R. J. W. Selleck, *James Kay-Shuttleworth* (Ilford, 1994), 281. The Order in Council constituting the Vice-President of the Committee of Council on Education emphatically subordinates him to the Lord President: *SC on Constitution of the Committee of Council on Education*, Report, PP 1865 (403), vi, 1, 22, 465. Because he was a Privy Councillor, and subordinate to the Lord President, he found himself landed with Privy Council duties unrelated to education—the administration of the Contagious Diseases (Animals) Act 1867; for example: Bishop, *Rise of a Central Authority*, 122.

[105] For this and the rest of this paragraph, see N. Ball, *Her Majesty's Inspectorate 1839–1849* (Edinburgh, 1963), and J. Hurt, *Education in Evolution: Church, State, Society and Popular Education 1800–1870* (1971).

[106] e.g. PD 1839 (s3) 48: 229 (Lord Stanley), 1241–2, 1253–5 (Archbishop of Canterbury). The government's rebuff of its defeat in the Lords is at 49: 128.

[107] Ball, *Her Majesty's Inspectorate*, 45–62.

[108] As to the committee's composition see Hurt, *Education in Evolution*, 149; Bishop, *Rise of a Central Authority*, 124, 277–8. President: Ball, *Her Majesty's Inspectorate*, 24–5; *SC on Committee of Council*, 7, 20, 23 (Lingen), 50 (Bruce), 103–6 (Granville); G. Sutherland, *Policy-Making in Elementary Education 1870–1895* (Oxford, 1973), 14–19, 134, 151, 218, 227. Lingen, who was secretary, was clear that from 1856 the Lord President and Vice-President might together constitute a meeting of the committee. On the Vice-President see *SC on Committee of Council* evidence of Lingen, Lowe, Bruce, Adderley, and Granville; Hurt, *Education in Evolution*, 155 (1860s); Sutherland, *Policy-Making*, 228–32 (1880s). In the 1880s the Vice-President secured his choice for the vacant secretaryship ahead of the President's by threatening his resignation: Bishop, *Rise of a Central Authority*, 107.

as the Minutes became an increasingly prescriptive Code, the power the inspectors and the secretary shared could properly be seen as regulatory. But it was not a legal power.

Nor did the inspectors have a statutory status that might have clarified their relation with the department. They did have social status—they were 'most emphatically gentlemen', as one historian puts it.[109] That and the dual allegiance most of them owed to Church and state brought a degree of autonomy that secured them for a while a right to have their reports presented to Parliament free from departmental censorship. But that was contested by the secretary and Vice-President and, being necessarily a matter beyond legal control, varied with the climate within the department.[110] Similarly, the extent to which inspectors were consulted on policy or even on technical revisions of the Code was a matter for Vice-President and secretary to determine; the only law that applied was that these senior Crown servants might direct their subordinates.[111] Unsurprisingly, that was not changed when the 1870 Education Act began the secularization of elementary education. The committee was given a statutory name and a folio of powers, its Minutes gained indirect statutory status and were subjected to a formal requirement of being laid before Parliament, but its legal structure and personality remained untouched.[112]

There had always been those who thought its constitutional position at best quaint and at worst mystifying and inappropriate. Their concern for constitutional and administrative propriety led usually to the proposition that education should have a stand-alone ministry, which was justifiably seen as being apiece with their wish to aggrandize state education and, until 1870, fell with it.[113] After 1870 the issues were political of a different kind: whether education was important enough to warrant its own cabinet minister, what was the optimal size of cabinet, whether it was worth upsetting the Lord President of Council by reducing his

---

[109] Sutherland, *Policy-Making*, 56.

[110] For the early period see Ball, *Her Majesty's Inspectorate*, 205–9, 221; for tightening departmental control and the Commons' censure of Vice-President Robert Lowe in 1864, see J. E. Durnford, 'Robert Lowe and Inspectors' Reports' (1977) 25 *British Journal of Educational Studies* 155–69; H. G. Williams, 'Nation State versus National Identity: State and Inspectorate in Mid-Victorian Wales' (2000) 40 *History of Education Quarterly* 145–68; for that and examples of later outspokenness by inspectors, see Sutherland, *Policy-Making*, 68–9, 195–7, 201–2.

[111] Sutherland, *Policy-Making*, 68–9, 309; Bishop, *Rise of a Central Authority*, 7–78, 92–3, 104–5.

[112] Sections 3, 7(4), 97, 100 (and *passim* for powers). The name 'Education Department' was not itself new, attaching to the committee by the 1856 Order in Council appointing the Vice-President of Council: *SC on Committee of Council*, App. Since the Act itself also imposed conditions and limitations on education grants the department no longer had as free a hand in instituting change, but instead had sometimes to sponsor a statute: Sutherland, *Policy-Making*, 239–42; Education Code Act 1890.

[113] Bishop, *Rise of a Central Authority*, 43–8, 64–5 (low priority a further reason).

portfolio.[114] Only in 1899, when the Conservatives finally decided that elementary education, secondary education, and the Charity Commissioners' jurisdiction over endowed schools needed unified control, was the committee converted into a statutory ministry.[115]

Much less controversial, but showing that the education committee did not stand alone, were the emigration commissioners, created in 1843 as successors to the Agent-General for Emigration.[116] They may have looked like an autonomous agency, but as originally created they were in law simply a cluster of Crown servants lacking independent legal status and subject to control by the Secretary of State for War and Colonies. At first their functions combined the supervision of other Crown servants—the emigration officers who were charged with bringing prosecutions under the Passenger Acts—with selection and processing of emigrants to the Australasian colonies, and making the concomitant payments to the shippers. They thus had a *de facto* regulatory power over the conditions on emigrant ships to Australasia, but neither a statutory existence nor statutory powers.[117] For the Passenger Acts to work, however, coercive powers turned out to be needed, which had to be vested in someone, hence the empowering of emigration officers and commissioners.[118] That need not have changed the commissioners' legal status, and indeed in one sense it did not, for when eventually their role became obsolete and their statutory powers were transferred to the Board of Trade, the commissioners themselves still continued in office, falling back to being a branch of the Colonial Office until in 1878 their commission was revoked by simple executive decision.[119]

Were it not for one curious twist they could be seen simply as a convenient administrative device for the Colonial Office, which never lost political responsibility for them or power of command.[120] This twist was that the commissioners

---

[114] *Ibid.*, 99, 106, 109–11. In the Liberal government 1892–5 the Vice-President had sole charge of the department, the Lord President holding time-consuming additional offices: Bishop, *Rise of a Central Authority*, 126.

[115] Board of Education Act 1899.

[116] From at least as early as 1834 emigration business had been handled by a specialist clerk within the Colonial Office: R. C. Snelling and T. J. Barron, 'The Colonial Office: Its Permanent Officials 1801–1914', in G. Sutherland (ed.), *Studies in the Growth of Nineteenth-century Government* (1972), 139–66 at 150.

[117] R. Haines, 'Indigent Misfits or Shrewd Operators?' (1994) 48 *Population Studies*, 223–47; Colonial Land and Emigration Commissioners, Report, *PP* 1842 (567), xxv, 55.

[118] Passengers in Merchant Ships Act 1842, 5 & 6 Vict. c. 107; Passengers Act Amendment Act 1847, 11 & 12 Vict. c. 6; Passengers Act 1849, 12 & 13 Vict. c. 33. This process has become very familiar to administrative historians through the writing of O. MacDonagh: 'Emigration and the State 1833–55' (1955) 5 *Trans RHS* (5th ser.) 133–59, and *A Pattern of Government Growth* (1961).

[119] Merchant Shipping Act 1872, s 51; B. L. Blakeley, *The Colonial Office, 1868–1892* (Durham NC, 1972), 93, 109; MacDonagh, *Pattern of Government Growth*, 319.

[120] Passengers Act 1852, 15 & 16 Vict. c. 44, ss 34, 55; Passengers Act 1855, ss 37, 59; MacDonagh, *Pattern of Government Growth*, 224, 313; Blakeley, *Colonial Office*, 93, 109.

were given a quasi-corporate status enabling them to sue and be sued in their own right, free from personal liability.[121] Had this provision been litigated it would have raised questions about how far the commissioners had become a legally independent agency and whether they continued to enjoy various Crown immunities. More will be said about this below.[122]

The committee on education was an exceptional political expedient and the emigration commissioners a curiosity. A legal form was needed for activities that justified separate ministerial supervision but were too mundane to warrant the highest rank. The Secretaries of State retained a cachet that came from the breadth of the responsibilities still attaching to each of the subdivisions, and a substantially higher salary than accorded to other senior political posts. They were too grand for the everyday governmental purposes that slowly developed from the mid-century, from the crisis-ridden poor law in 1847 to the worthy but undoubtedly prosaic public works, reorganized along with woods and forests in 1851.[123]

The form chosen was a statutory board of high political office holders with a president who was to be the minister and to bear responsibility for the department—the form into which the Poor Law Board had fallen from the options left open by its constitutive statute. In its improved format from 1851 such a board was not expected to meet, and the statute was drafted so that the president could exercise its powers. However, a full board was needed, so the Chancellor of the Exchequer explained, so that someone could exercise its powers in lieu of the president, should he be absent or indisposed.[124] That became the conventional form, being used from 1854 for the last few years of the General Board of Health's existence, for the Local Government Board in 1871 and for the Board of Agriculture in 1889.[125]

In 1851 the fiction looked reasonably plausible. Secretaries of State, interchangeable in law, did occasionally stand in for each other in fact.[126] Ministers might still do some of a department's work themselves.[127] They did not generally

---

[121] Passengers Acts 1852 and 1855. The latter extended personal immunity to the emigration officers (s 7), who had been harassed by threats of legal action when they took it upon themselves to object to particular methods of stowage of iron cargo in the interests of safety: MacDonagh, *Pattern of Government Growth*, 249–51; *SC on Emigrant Ships*, 1st Report, PP 1854 (163), xiii, 1, 19, 29. Their power to hire was subject to the Secretary of State's consent.

[122] The Civil Service Commissioners are a third example, but looking inwards to the appointment of the Crown's own servants rather than outwards to the public. For them, see Wright, *Treasury Control*, 65–109 and Superannuation Act 1859, (Wright, *Treasury Control*, 306–28; Chester, *English Administrative System*, 164–6).

[123] Chester, *English Administrative System*, 150; Bishop, *Rise of a Central Authority*, 261.

[124] PD 1851 (s3) 118: 180.

[125] Public Health 1854; Local Government Board Act 1871; Board of Agriculture Act 1889; Board of Agriculture and Fisheries Act 1903.

[126] Donajgrodzki, 'Sir James Graham', 117.

[127] Parris, *Constitutional Bureaucracy*, 106–15.

have a deputy; the post of parliamentary secretary could have evolved that way but did not.[128] The anomalous office of the Vice-President of the Board of Trade, whose patent stated that he was the President when the President was absent, was converted into an orthodox parliamentary secretaryship in 1867.[129] The relationship between the Lord President of the Council and the Vice-President of the Committee of Council on Education might have been conceived as one of principal and deputy, but it did not function like that.[130] A department's permanent secretary could not formally have been his minister's deputy, at first because he was too lowly, later because that would have blurred the line between the political direction of a department and its neutral administration.

Nonetheless, by 1899 nearly all a department's work was done by the permanent civil servants in the minister's name, so it could not have seemed revolutionary to the draftsman of the bill needed to convert the Board of Education from being a committee of the Privy Council into its own statutory ministry when he proposed it be led by a single-seated minister rather than the president of an ornamental board. Within a week he had been corrected by the senior parliamentary counsel, Sir Courtney Ilbert, who saw no reason to change from the principles of 1851.[131] It took the wartime creation of new ministries on an unprecedented scale to bring legal form into line with function.[132]

4. THE COURTS AND THE CROWN; THE STILL-BIRTH OF PUBLIC LAW IN ENGLAND

Until the 1850s or early 1860s it was unclear how uniform the constitution of the central executive would be, what parts of it would be subject to political control through ministers and what parts would consist of autonomous or

---

[128] Chester, *English Administrative System*, 293; Parris, *Constitutional Bureaucracy*, 122–6.

[129] Board of Trade Act 1867, consequent upon a report from the Vice-President and the Financial Secretary to the Treasury: *Correspondence relative to the establishment of the Board of Trade, PP* 1867 (47), xxxix, 213, esp. at 228.

[130] There is a tortured passage in the evidence to the SC on the Constitution of the Committee of Council on Education in which Robert Lowe asserts a significant difference between the Vice-President of the Board of Trade (whose patent said he was the President in the President's absence) and the Vice-President of the Committee on Education (whose Order in Council said merely that he shall act for the President in his absence): *PP* 1865 (403), vi, 1, 48.

[131] Bishop, *Rise of a Central Authority*, 261; Board of Education Act 1899. The Education Department's Permanent Secretary believed that saving expense was the more likely explanation.

[132] Ministry of Munitions Act 1915; Ministry of Pensions Act 1916; New Ministries and Secretaries Act 1916; New Ministries Act 1917; Ministry of Health Act; Ministry of Transport Act 1919; Ministry of Agriculture and Fisheries Act 1919 (rather a strange, Janus-faced Act; for the argument that the Board of Agriculture needed to be brought into the Whitehall mainstream, see *RC on the Civil Service*, 4th Report, 64–5).

semi-autonomous statutory agencies whose responsibilities lay to Parliament rather than to government. The more prominent the role of statutory agencies, the more plausible would be a perception of a continuum of public executive entities without sharp demarcation between the local and the central, their statutory style and structure being similar. Something like that perception can be distilled without difficulty from themes in judicial reasoning vigorous in the 1820s, extant through into the late 1830s, but thereafter becoming less coherent until, in the mid-1860s, it was abandoned in favour of a sharp distinction between the Crown and the rest. Until that happened it would not have been fanciful to have claimed that England had a nascent public law, if conceptualization of that sort had been how mid-nineteenth century lawyers thought.

It had four linked elements. The first, relatively weak and general, was a conception of a public trust as a means of marking where private interest ended and public duty began. The second was that occupiers of property for public purposes were exempt from the liability to pay rates that attached to private occupiers. The third was that public servants were not vicariously liable for the torts of their subordinates or contractors as private employers would or might have been. The fourth strand was that office holders entering into contracts on behalf of the public did not attract personal liability as principals nor could they be sued as agents might be in private law. The reasoning used by judges when justifying and applying these rules generally treated central and local office holders alike.

The first strand, the notion of a public trust, was as much political or legislative as judicial. From the 1780s it underlay the administrative reforms that slowly abolished sinecure offices, fee taking, and irregular emoluments and pensions, and in their place substituted salaries, statutory pensions, accountability and, in due course, bureaucracy.[133] The principle articulated a difference between public service and private interest that could be carried over into judicial proceedings. In 1783 it was the essential foundation for the conviction of Charles Bembridge for corrupt accounting in the office of the receiver and paymaster-general of the forces, as it was for the failed prosecution of Sir Thomas Rumbold for the sale of offices in India.[134] Then, in the 1830s, the notion crossed over into local affairs when it was wielded rhetorically to justify reconceptualizing municipal corporations as public institutions rather than private persons.[135] Thence it was used as a legal tool to subject municipal corporations' spending decisions to Chancery

[133] P. Harling, *The Waning of 'Old Corruption'* (Oxford, 1996), 58–60, 107–8; J. Torrance, 'Sir George Harrison and the Growth of Bureaucracy in the Early Nineteenth Century' (1968) 83 *EHR* 52–88.

[134] 22 State Trials 1; preamble to bill of pains and penalties 22 Geo. III c. 59.

[135] See below, pp. 431–4.

scrutiny.[136] That placed municipal corporations on a continuum with statutory improvement commissioners, charitable trustees, and those statutory local utility commissioners whose empowering statutes did not permit a distribution of profits into private hands. In all these cases the notion of a public trust gave complainants the procedural advantages of suing through the Attorney-General in relator actions. At first there had been doubt whether this boon should be available only against commissioners whose statutory purposes were charitable, or whether perhaps all statutory public purposes were *ipso facto* charitable. Then in 1827 Lords Eldon and Redesdale ruled that it should be generally available against statutory commissioners, for the reason simply that the control was needed.[137]

This broad concept of a public trust was linked to the second relevant legal principle, that occupiers of premises for public purposes were not liable to pay poor rates. That immunity was made possible by the long-standing judicial reading that the Elizabethan Poor Law rated only 'beneficial' occupiers, a much-litigated gloss on the act. By the early nineteenth century, judges had constructed a general 'public purpose' category of non-beneficial occupation embracing occupation for Crown purposes and by 'public trustees'. By that they meant charitable trustees and their close cousins, those statutory commissioners who were bound to use their funds only for stipulated statutory purposes even though they charged tolls or fees for use of their facilities.[138] These were wide exemptions, defended by the judges against policy objections from at least as early as the 1750s.[139] As local not-for-profit enterprise expanded, so too did the immunity. It culminated in a decision in 1839 that brought municipal corporations within the exemption, the logical consequence of the public trust imposed upon their property and revenues by the 1835 reforms.[140] That particular decision was more than Parliament could

---

[136] *A.G.* v. *Aspinall* (1837) 2 My. & Cr. 613; *A.G.* v. *Wilson* (1837) 7 LJ Ch. 76.

[137] *R* v. *Brown* (1818) 1 Wils. Ch. 323, 1 Swan. 265; *A.G.* v. *Heelis* (1824) 2 Sim. & St. 67; *A.G.* v. *Mayor of Dublin* (1827) 1 Bli. (N.S.) 312; *A.G.* v. *Eastlake* (1853) 11 Hare 205.

[138] *R* v. *Terrott* (1803) 3 East 506; *Lord Amherst* v. *Lord Sommers* (1788) 2 T.R. 372; *R* v. *St. Luke's Hospital* (1759) 2 Burr. 1053 (contrast Lord Holt in *Anon.* (1702) 2 Salk. 527); *R* v. *Commissioners of Salter's Load Sluice* (1792) 4 T.R. 730. The latter must be consequent upon *R* v. *Cardington* (1777) 2 Cowp. 581 which rated sluices for the first time. Turnpike trustees were exempt by the General Turnpike Act 1773, 13 Geo. III c. 84, s 56, which provided, reciprocally, that keepers of toll gates did not gain a parochial settlement; it may perhaps codify previous practice. Not all occupation by Crown servants was exempt, only that for public purposes rather than personal advantage. For a synthesis see *Eckersall* v. *Briggs* (1790) 4 T.R. 6.

[139] *R* v. *St Luke's Hospital* (1759) 2 Burr. 1053.

[140] *R* v. *Liverpool* (1827) 7 B. & C. 61; *R* v. *Trustees of the River Weaver Navigation* (1827) 7 B. & C. 70n; *R* v. *Commissioners for Lighting Beverley* (1837) 6 Ad. & El. 645; *R* v. *Mayor of Liverpool* (1839) 9 Ad. & El. 435; and *R* v. *Exminster* (1840) 12 Ad. & El. 2.

stand, but as was usual with legislation stipulating exactly how public property should be rated, its reversal left the general principle intact.[141]

The third element in this conception of the 'public' was public officials' immunity from vicarious liability for the torts of their subordinates. This was the counterpart of the liability that both they and their subordinates had to accept for their own personal wrongdoing. Lord Mansfield's great decisions in *Money* v. *Leach* and *Mostyn* v. *Fabrigas* showed that Crown orders or Crown service afforded no defence.[142] Justices who without jurisdiction imprisoned someone or ordered the seizure of goods were routinely sued for trespassory torts. Commissioners who authorized street works beyond their statutory powers were liable for nuisance.[143] It was generally agreed that commissioners who went so far as directing their employees and contractors how to undertake a task could in suitable circumstances be treated as personally negligent.[144] These liabilities underlined a conception of power as personal, for which responsibility was to be met from the wrongdoer's own pocket. But where the wrongdoer was a subordinate to an official whose powers and duties existed for the public service, and not for his benefit, it would be an affront for the superior to have to pay for an act he neither directed nor profited from. In the late eighteenth and early nineteenth centuries the common theme of what later came to be seen more narrowly as 'Crown servant' cases was not a simple dogma about the nature of Crown service, but a generalized concern that men would be deterred from public service if made liable vicariously, and that the public service would suffer as a result.[145] Thus the reasoning used in *Whitfield* v. *Lord Despencer* to

---

[141] Municipal Corporations Poor Rates Act 1841, 4 & 5 Vict. c. 48, which clearly concedes the general principle. Churches had a statutory exemption that seems to codify common law, 3 & 4 Will. IV c. 30, and there is a list of exempted purposes in the Towns Improvement Clauses Act 1847, 10 & 11 Vict. c. 34, s 168. Shaftesbury's Lunatic Asylums Act 1853, s 35, fixed the rateable value of asylums at their value at the date of their acquisition, a technique tried rather more clumsily in a Taunton market Act of 1768, litigated in *R* v. *Badcock* (1845) 6 Q.B. 787. St Marylebone's paving Act of 1773, 10 Geo. III c. xxiii, s 105, explicitly subjected 'public buildings' to its improvement rate, allocating the burden to the owners: *Eckersall* v. *Briggs* (1790) 4 T.R. 6.

[142] For central government office-holders, see *Money* v. *Leach* (1765) 3 Burr. 1742; *Mostyn* v. *Fabrigas* (1774) 1 Cowp. 161; *Glynn* v. *Houston* (1841) 2 Man. & G.; and *Cobbett* v. *Grey* (1849) 4 Ex. 729.

[143] *Leader* v. *Moxton* (or *Moxon*) (1773) 3 Wils. K.B. 461, 2 W. Black. 924, was usually treated as the fount of the nuisance cases, if only to be distinguished on its facts.

[144] *Harris* v. *Baker* (1815) 4 M. & S. 27; *Humphreys* v. *Mears* (1827) 1 Man. & Ry. 187; *Grocers Company* v. *Donne* (1836) 3 Bing. N.C. 34, though all three found for the defendants.

[145] *Whitfield* v. *Lord Despencer* (1778) Cowp. 754; *Nicholson* v. *Mouncey* (1812) 15 East 384. The same reasoning justified the rule that a Crown servant entering a contract on behalf of the Crown would not be personally liable: *Macbeath* v. *Haldimand* (1786) 1 T.R. 172, a rule extended easily and naturally to immunize county justices from personal liability on a bridge building contract they had entered pursuant to a local Act: *Allen* v. *Waldegrave* (1818) 8 Taunt. 566. See too *Unwin* v. *Wolseley*

hold the Postmaster General immune from vicarious liability for his subordinates was in no way specific to Crown servants.[146] It was used in *Harris* v. *Baker* in 1815, a case about the liability of commissioners for nuisance, extended to turnpike trustees by Gibbs CJCP in 1815, and then to street improvement commissioners by Best CJCP in 1824.[147] He reiterated the need not to deter public service and noted that of all public officers only sheriffs were liable for the negligence of a subordinate.

Would it be possible to reconceptualize the situation by shifting liability on to some abstraction such as the state or the public purse? The approach was tried in *Attorney General* v. *Viscount Canterbury* in 1843, a critically important case against the Crown in which Lord Chancellor Lyndhurst refused to extend the process of petition of right to redress for tort.[148] Had he allowed it, litigants would then have side-stepped one of the obstacles to redress from the Crown, that the sovereign could not be sued in her own courts. But Lord Lyndhurst could not see an abstraction, only the very personal Victoria R. He raised two objections (among others) that went to the heart of her immunity. First, the sovereign had given up most of her personal income to the state in exchange for a civil list voted by Parliament, and hence, by implication, no more had personal funds to make good the defaults of her subordinates than public servants did. Secondly, in no real sense were the men whose negligence had caused the damage her servants. Rather they were employed by the Commissioners of Woods and Forests and hence, by implication, it was the commissioners' liability that needed attention. There was no statute in that case that could have been read as shifting liability on to the commissioners' public funds, but even if there had been judges at the beginning of our period were resistant to the idea. Best CJ rejected it in *Hall* v. *Smith* in 1824, for reasons that were generalized by Lord Cottenham in *Duncan* v. *Findlater* in 1839: if the action which harmed the plaintiff was authorized by the statute, then the remedy was through whatever compensation provisions the statute contained, but if the action was unauthorized, Parliament could not have meant the public fund to make good what was a 'private error or misconduct'.[149] If the rule were otherwise, Lord Campbell said when applying it to a claim against

---

(1787) 1 T.R. 674, another Crown immunity case justified on public service grounds. Though there was no crossover between the lines of cases there was a general concordance with a similar immunity for private trustees, who likewise were thought to fulfil a role of service: C. Stebbings, *The Private Trustee in Victorian England* (Cambridge, 2002), 116.

[146] (1778) Cowp. 754.

[147] *Harris* v. *Baker* (1815) 4 M. & S. 27; *Sutton* v. *Clark* (1815) 6 Taunt. 30; *Hall* v. *Smith* (1824) 2 Bing. 155.

[148] (1843) 1 Ph. 306.

[149] (1824) 2 Bing. 155; (1839) 6 Cl. & F. 894.

funds held by charitable trustees, 'the trustees would be indemnified against the consequences of their own misconduct and the real object of the charity would be defeated'.[150]

Thus through into the 1840s there was a general principle that individual responsibility required charitable trustees, voluntary commissioners, and Crown servants to compensate those whom their own negligence or misconduct harmed, but, since they acted either gratuitously or for reward that merely compensated for time and trouble, they were not to be vicariously liable lest good men be deterred from accepting office.[151] Nor would liability be thrown on to their funds. This was much the same range of persons who were immune from payment of the poor rate because their occupation of land was for public purposes.

The final legal principle, that office holders entering into contracts on behalf of the public did not attract the personal liability, is conventionally traced to *Macbeath* v. *Haldimand* in 1786.[152] As that case concerned a Crown servant, the rule itself was later attributed to the peculiarities of the Crown. It was generalized by Dallas CJCP in 1822 into a principle that in the absence of a personal tort, Crown officers could not be personally liable for anything done in their official capacity, this in the important case of *Gidley* v. *Lord Palmerston*, denying an assumpsit against the Secretary-at-War for payment of a pension.[153] But at the same time *Macbeath* v. *Haldimand* was also treated as illustrative of a general principle applicable as naturally to vestrymen and to county justices who entered a contract pursuant to statutory powers.[154] In all these cases the judges offered a broad public service justification to exempt defendants from personal liability, just as they were immune from vicarious liability in tort. Significantly, though, and unlike the rules for tort, churchwardens and statutory commissioners attracted a different rule. To the extent that they had, or at least at the relevant time had had, power to levy a rate to reimburse themselves, their contracts might be read as imposing personal liability.[155]

Retreat from the rates exemption had begun in the King's Bench in the 1830s, even as that court was expanding it. With little explanation Lord Denman's court narrowed what counted as 'public' occupation so as to exclude occupation for the

---

[150] *Feoffees of Heriot's Hospital* v. *Ross* (1846) 12 Cl. & F. 507.

[151] See also *Boulton* v. *Crowther* (1824) 2 B. & C. 703; *Humphreys* v. *Mears* (1827) 1 Man. & Ry. 187; *Grocers' Company* v. *Donne* (1836) 3 Bing. N.C. 34.

[152] (1786) 1 T.R. 172; the other leading 'Crown' cases were *Unwin* v. *Wolseley* (1787) 1 T.R. 674 and *Rice* v. *Chute* (1801) 1 East 579.

[153] (1822) 3 Brod. & Bing. 275.

[154] *Lanchester* v. *Frewer* (1824) 2 Bing. 361; *Sprott* v. *Powell* (1826) 3 Bing. 478; *Allen* v. *Waldegrave* (1818) 8 Taunt. 566.

[155] *Eaton* v. *Bell* (1821) 5 B. & Ald. 34; *Sprott* v. *Powell* (1826) 3 Bing. 478.

benefit of only a section of the public.[156] The resulting incoherence was reduced somewhat, in aspiration at least, by Denman's successor, Lord Campbell. He avowedly set about reducing the exemption by whatever manipulations of the precedents sufficed, to the point that his court managed to rate the municipal docks of Birkenhead and Newcastle in the teeth of an earlier decision exempting Liverpool's.[157] Newly created institutions such as local boards of health, which surely would have been treated as 'public' only a few years before, were construed as conferring sectional benefits only.[158] At the same time, however, county buildings, court rooms, and prisons were given the immunity, and though the decisions contain traces of a different sort of reasoning—that there was no 'occupation' at all that could be rated—the dominant justification still was that the occupation was for public purposes.[159] Similarly, most instances of occupation for central government purposes continued to be immune on general public purpose grounds.[160]

The denouement came in 1864–5 when the House of Lords revisited the Liverpool docks' exemption.[161] Of the judges advising the Lords only Byles J. would have opted to maintain the broad public purpose immunity spanning the Crown and other public institutions. Instead their lordships accepted Blackburn J.'s radical revision of two centuries of judicial gloss of the Elizabethan Poor Law, and abandoned altogether the rule that only beneficial occupation was

---

[156] *Governors of the Bristol Poor* v. *Wait* (1836) 5 Ad. & El. 1; *R* v. *Guardians of Wallingford Union* (1839) 10 Ad. & El. 259; *R* v. *Badcock* (1845) 6 Q.B. 787, interpreting *R* v. *Terrott* (1803) 3 East 506; *R* v. *Churchwardens of Longwood* (1849) 13 Q.B. 116. The Parochial Assessments Act 1836, 6 & 7 Will. IV c. 96, may perhaps have been an influence, in that its stipulation that rateable value be calculated from the notional rent a property might reasonably be expected to fetch emphasized that rates had to be paid even though the property might currently be put to an unremunerative use. There are traces of this reasoning in *R* v. *Sterry* (1840) 12 Ad. & El. 84, a charities case that otherwise fits comfortably in a line going back to *R* v. *Agar* (1811) 14 East 256 and *Robson* v. *Hyde* (1787) Cald. 310.

[157] *Mayor of Liverpool* v. *Overseers of West Derby* (1856) 6 E. & B. 704; *R* v. *Harrogate Improvement Commissioners* (1850) 15 Q.B. 1012; *R* v. *Temple* (1852) 2 E. & B. 160 ('there is no power, as yet, conferred on an individual to compel the ratepayers of the parish in which he wishes to found such an institution to contribute to it against their inclination'; contrast the values of Buller J. in *R* v. *Waldo* (1783) Cald. 358: 'do you mean to argue that if a man gives all he has in charity, he shall apply something more in charity?'); *Trustees of Birkenhead Docks* v. *Overseers of Birkenhead* (1852) 2 E. & B. 148; *Tyne Improvement Commissioners* v. *Chirton* (1859) 1 E. & E. 516.

[158] *R* v. *Hull Justices* (1854) 4 E. & B. 29.

[159] *R* v. *Worcestershire Justices* (1839) 11 Ad. & El. 57; *R* v. *Overseers of Manchester* (1854) 3 E. & B. 336; *Gambier* v. *Overseers of Lydford* (1854) 3 E. & B. 346; *Hodgson* v. *Carlisle LBH* (1857) 8 E. & B. 116; *Lancashire Justices* v. *Overseers of Stretford* (1858) E.B. & E. 225.

[160] *Smith* v. *Guardians of Birmingham* (1857) 7 E. & B. 483; *R* v. *Stewart* (1857) 8 E. & B. 360. The exception is the difficult case of *R* v. *Temple* (1852) 2 E. & B. 160, where the headmaster of the Committee of the Privy Council's model school for training teachers was held to be rateable. His receipt of fees was one element in holding that he had a beneficial occupation.

[161] *Mersey Docks and Harbour Board* v. *Cameron and Jones* (1864–5) 11 H.L.C. 443.

rateable.[162] This was not a turn to a literal reading of the Act for its own sake, for Blackburn J. carefully approved the judicial gloss that denied churchwardens discretion in their distribution of the burden of a rate, which a literal reading would have allowed. Rather it was a choice to maintain parishes' rateable base, denying relevant differences between an expanded 'public purpose' and private enterprise, stressing that both private and municipal docks took most of their powers from the same clauses Act, and asserting that there was no difference in principle between the one's distribution of dividends to shareholders and the other's payment of interest to bond holders.

Together with the exclusion, begun in the 1830s, of the purely local from what counted as the 'public', this assimilation of municipal activity with the private sphere made the concept of public purpose redundant.[163] That important general point to be taken from this 'great revolution' in rating law was emphasized by formulation of the exception, which was a Crown immunity premised not upon public utility but upon the formal proposition that the Crown was bound only by express statutory provision, absent from the rating statute.[164] By itself that proposition would prove too much, since it would remove the exemptions for courtrooms, prisons, and police stations. Blackburn J. finessed those as functions committed by the constitution to the sovereign though administered on her behalf by local agencies, an imaginative reinterpretation of the case law, but a seriously incomplete analysis of the relation between county or borough government and the Crown in the 1860s.[165]

Thus the line once drawn between the public and the private now had to be drawn in a different place, a place dictated by some constitutional principle known only to the judges. This was that for some functions local government acted as surrogate for the Crown whereas for others it did not. As one might expect, functions acquired by recent statute did not attract exemptions, but nor did general

---

[162] The property still had to be 'beneficial' in the different sense that it produced a notional net surplus after deduction of the usual outgoings. Blackburn J.'s advice was on behalf of himself and four others.

[163] *Governors of the Bristol Poor* v. *Wait* (1836) 5 Ad. & El. 1; *R* v. Overseers of West Derby (1875) LR 10 QB 283.

[164] *R* v. *St Martin's Leicester* (1867) LR 2 QB 493; *Greig* v. *University of Edinburgh* (1868) LR 1 Sc. & Div. 348. The argument by G. E. Robinson, *Public Authorities and Legal Liability* (1925), 21, adopted by J. M. Jacob, *The Republican Crown* (Aldershot, 1996), 63, that the judges' *objective* was to curtail Crown privileges, which has some plausibility when applied to the particular case of *R* v. *Temple* (1852) 2 E. & B. 160, as a generalization seems inconsistent with the initial breadth of the 'public purposes' rubric and its dismantling on two fronts—local commissioners *and* charitable trustees. There is no suggestion in the judges' reasoning, during either the construction of the concept or its demolition, that the scope of central government was the important issue.

[165] *Mersey Docks and Harbour Board* v. *Cameron* (1864–5) 11 H.L.C. 443; *Coomber* v. *Berkshire Justices* (1883) 9 App Cas 61.

local governmental purposes—shirehalls became rateable on their transfer from the county justices to the new county councils, though their function remained almost exactly the same, because justices could be seen as within the Crown's penumbra while county councils could not.[166] Doctrinally the shift was from a functional to what was mostly a formal test—Crown or not Crown—albeit with a residual functional fringe to cater for precedents thought too firmly entrenched to overrule. The unity inherent in 'public purposes' had gone.

The judges reached the same result with liability for torts, at the same time and in a case concerning the same defendant.[167] Again they left central government substantially untouched, to be conceptualized now simply as 'the Crown'. The shift began in the 1850s, its immediate cause being judges' increasing attention to the statutory structure of the body concerned, doctrinally a shift from joint office holding to corporate or quasi-corporate. The first and easiest case concerned municipal trading corporations, where there was neither the possibility that its members would have to pay damages from their own pockets nor that ratepayers would have to foot the bill for something apparently outside the ambit of the statute.[168] If a board was not incorporated it was usual for the Act to provide that its members could be sued in the name of their secretary, who was to be recompensed from the board's funds. It was sections like this that Best CJ and Lord Cottenham had thought insufficient in themselves to imply a quasi-corporate liability falling on the board's funds for the torts of its members or their contractors. It is not known when or by whose initiative local Acts began to add explicitly that members of local statutory boards and commissions who had acted *bona fide* should not be sued personally, but in 1848 both the Public Health Act and the Metropolitan Commissioners of Sewers Act had such a section.[169] Faced with this negation of their underlying principle, judges held that

---

[166] *Worcestershire County Council* v. *Worcester Union* [1897] 1 QB 480 (the same buildings exempted in *R* v. *Worcestershire Justices* (1839) 11 Ad. & El. 57); *Middlesex County Council* v. *Assessment Committee of St George's Union* [1897] 1 QB 64. 'Statutory functions': *R* v. *West Derby* (1875) LR 10 QB 283; *Tunnicliffe* v. *Overseers of Birkdale* (1888) 20 QBD 450; *Bray* v. *Lancashire Justices* (1889) 22 QBD 484. Prisons fared rather better, as did volunteer forces and, later, the territorial army: *Coomber* v. *Berkshire Justices* (1883) 9 App Cas 61; *Pearson* v. *Assessment Committee of Holborn Union* [1893] 1 QB 389; *Wixon* v. *Thomas (No. 2)* [1912] 1 KB 690.

[167] *Mersey Docks and Harbour Board* v. *Cameron* (1864–5) 11 H.L.C. 443; *Mersey Docks and Harbour Board* v. *Gibbs* (1865–6) 11 H.L.C. 686.

[168] *Scott* v. *Mayor of Manchester* (1856) 1 H. & N. 59; *Gibbs* v. *Trustees of Liverpool Docks* (1858) 3 H. & N. 164 (Exch. Ch.), though in this case the declaration to which the defendant demurred was compatible with both personal negligence by the statutory trustees and vicarious liability; *Mersey Docks and Harbour Board* v. *Penhallow* (1861) 7 H. & N. 329. Compare *Manley* v. *St Helens Canal* (1858) 2 H. & N. 840.

[169] 11 & 12 Vict. c. 63, s 140 and c. 112, s 128; contrast the rather less explicit Commissioners Clauses Act 1847, 10 & 11 Vict. c. 16, s 60. The explicit section in the Dartford & Crayford Navigation Act 1840, 3 & 4 Vict. c. lv, was litigated in *Allen* v. *Hayward* (1845) 7 Q.B. 960.

Parliament must have meant liability to fall on the public fund instead—even if it did not quite say so.[170] With some hesitation Lord Campbell concurred, adhering in principle to the sentiments of *Duncan* v. *Findlater* and *Feoffees of Heriot's Hospital* v. *Ross*, House of Lords cases both, but finding comfort in the supposition that an elected board did in a sense represent the ratepayers now footing the bill.[171]

By this route quasi-corporate liability superseded the restriction of vicarious liability, though not without judicial misgiving. Some judges required all those statutory elements to be present before they would concede that the combined principle of *Hall* v. *Smith* and *Duncan* v. *Findlater* had been abrogated.[172] By contrast Blackburn J. thought the mere statutory direction that commissioners could be sued in the name of their secretary was enough to raise the inference, and Bramwell B. disposed of *Duncan* v. *Findlater* by arguing, of a negligent act, that 'though in one sense unlawful, it is still a thing done within the general scope of the authority of the board'.[173]

The climax again featured the Mersey Docks and Harbours Board as defendant, a coincidence that Lord Wensleydale resignedly thought prevented retention of a full public service immunity linking Crown servants, public trustees, and corporations like the defendant. [174] The removal of its 'public purposes' rates immunity in *Cameron and Jones* stood decisively in the way, he said. Instead it was again Blackburn J.'s purposive rationalization offered as advice to the Lords that was accepted, and again he took the high road. Rather than arguing just that commercial quasi-corporations had to be liable vicariously if they were to be liable at all, Blackburn J. secured the wider point that Parliament should be taken to have meant public boards and trustees as a whole to be treated as though they were corporations. This was because they had some corporate features and because it was in the interests of plaintiffs to do so—which Parliament must surely have intended. That the Lords had indeed adopted such a wide rule was confirmed almost immediately, when counsel for defendant drainage commissioners who had won a case on public service grounds simply dropped that

---

[170] *Ward* v. *Lee* (1857) 7 E. & B. 426; *Ruck* v. *Williams* (1858) 3 H. & N. 308; *Southampton & Itchen Floating Bridge Co* v. *Southampton LBH* (1858) 8 E. & B. 801. A standard form section enabling the board to tender 'amends' gave colour to the argument.

[171] *Southampton & Itchen Floating Bridge Co* v. *Southampton LBH* (1858) 8 E. & B. 801.

[172] *Holliday* v. *Vestry of St Leonard, Shoreditch* (1861) 11 C.B.N.S. 192; *Coe* v. *Wise* (1864) 5 B. & S. 440 (Cockburn CJ and Mellor J., Blackburn J. diss.).

[173] *Coe* v. *Wise* (1864) 5 B. & S. 440; *Brownlow* v. *Metropolitan Board of Works* (1864) 16 C.B.N.S. 546.

[174] *Mersey Docks and Harbour Board* v. *Gibbs* (1865–6) 11 H.L.C. 686. Lord Cranworth agreed that *Cameron* was very nearly decisive.

defence on appeal.[175] Soon afterwards Blackburn J. himself decided that *Gibbs* had overruled the immunity that the Common Pleas had accorded to local boards of health in 1861.[176]

Thus together the two Mersey dock board cases worked a major reconfiguration of the law. In greatly broadening the liabilities of local public bodies they denied the relevance of the hitherto governing concepts of public occupation and public service, in each case leaving the Crown to continue with its immunities simply because it was the Crown. As recently as 1864 the Common Pleas had integrated Crown immunity from claims in tort with a general public service immunity from vicarious liability, but shorn of that prop there was now only the dogma that the Crown could do no wrong.[177]

This broadening of local bodies' tortious liability had depended upon their being reconceived as corporations or quasi-corporations and then upon judges' willingness to see the damages cast upon the rates, tolls, or charges. Much the same happened, and at much the same time, with the principle that protected local officials from personal liability on contracts. Municipal corporations contracted as corporations, not as groups of individuals, and though there might be argument about what processes were needed for a valid contract and about which of a corporation's funds were liable to meet what sorts of debts, individual liability was not an issue.[178] Nor was it in practice for local boards of health, for statute provided that those that were not corporations were to sue and be sued through their clerk, and their members were to be free from personal liability if they had acted in good faith.[179] Judges seem to have nudged statutory commissioners into much the same position, enabling creditors to bring an action against the commissioner's clerk and then have a *mandamus* to enforce the judgment.[180] That superseded the previous practice whereby commissioners could be sued to the extent that they were able to indemnify themselves from the rates.

It was the *mandamus* that was controversial, because usually the only way it could be obeyed was through levying a rate. That raised an issue similar to those

[175] *Coe* v. *Wise* (1864) B. & S. 440, (1866) LR 1 QB 711.

[176] *Foreman* v. *Mayor of Canterbury* (1871) LR 6 QB 214, holding the decision of the Common Pleas in *Holliday* v. *Vestry of St Leonard, Shoreditch* (1861) 11 C.B.N.S. 192 to have been overruled.

[177] *Tobin* v. *R* (1864) 16 C.B.N.S. 310 (essentially an affirmation of *Viscount Canterbury* v. *A.G.* (1843) 1 Ph. 306); contrast *Feather* v. *R* (1865) 6 B. & S. 257.

[178] See for example *Addison* v. *Mayor of Preston* (1852) 12 C.B. 108.

[179] Public Health Act 1848, 11 & 12 Vict. c. 63, ss 85, 138, 140. Public Health Act 1875 turned all local authorities (as defined in the Act) into corporations and continued the 1848 Act's protection for members: ss 7, 173–4, 265.

[180] *Kendall* v. *King* (1856) 17 C.B. 483; *Hall* v. *Taylor* (1858) E.B. & E. 107; *Bush* v. *Beavan* (1862) 1 H. & C. 500; *Bush* v. *Martin* (1863) 2 H. & C. 311. These were *mandamus* orders made under the Common Law Procedure Act as an adjunct to an action.

that deterred some judges from broadening local bodies' tortious liability, since often the rate would have to be 'retrospective', that is it would cast upon present ratepayers a cost which should have been met by their predecessors. There had been something of a principle that retrospective rates were not valid, but in 1848 the House of Lords denied there was any such rule, opening the way to a sometimes reluctant reconsideration of rating powers during which most judges swallowed their objections and enabled creditors to achieve satisfaction through a forced rate.[181] For local bodies, then, the result by the mid-1860s was a reasonably effective corporatizing of liability, both tortious and contractual.

By contrast Blackburn J. had characterized Crown servants as mere managers, no matter how senior.[182] They were liable for their own wrongs of course, but not for anyone else's, nor for the contracts they negotiated for Her Majesty. Her Majesty herself could do no wrong, she could not be sued in her own courts, and nor could a coercive remedy be issued against her. That barred actions in tort, save against the individual malefactor, and confined contract actions to the quasi-declaratory petition of right. That had been a cumbrous process, but it was streamlined in the aftermath of the Crimean war. A dispute over a provisioning contract so exposed its absurdity that the Crown itself negotiated in open court with the suppliant and the Lord Chancellor to modify the procedure in the suppliant's interest, leading very soon to a statutory modernization sponsored by the Conservative MP and commercial lawyer, William Bovill.[183] Such a reform, while certainly useful, emphasized the centrality of the Crown and, critically to the argument that is to follow, it explicitly left satisfaction of the plaintiff's right to the discretion of Parliament.[184]

The contrast looks complete. Formerly office had been perceived as personal, whether local or central, and though it carried personal liability for personal wrongs it also carried immunity from vicarious liability and on contracts. A notion of 'public purpose' unified the legal field. But now modern statutes had worked, or facilitated, a significant change. Where they existed, liability generally fell on a corporate or quasi-corporate entity, to be met from its public funds. Because the Crown was not a statutory body, this modernization did not apply to

---

[181] *Harrison* v. *Stickney* (1848) 2 H.L.C. 108; *R* v. *Rotherham LBH* (1858) 8 E. & B. 906; *Ward* v. *Lowndes* (1859) 1 E. & E. 940; *Burland* v. *Hull LBH* (1862) 3 B. & S. 271; *Worthington* v. *Hulton* (1865) LR 1 QB 63. Most of the cases concerned the interpretation of Public Health Act 1848, 11 & 12 Vict. c. 63, s 89. The later cases are reviewed in *Croydon Corporation* v. *Croydon RDC* [1908] 2 Ch 321.

[182] *Mersey Docks and Harbour Board* v. *Gibbs* (1865–6) 11 H.L.C. 686.

[183] Petitions of Right Act 1860, debated at *PD* 1859 (s3) 152: 1114 and 1544, (1860) 156: 545. The litigation is reported as *Ex p Frantzius* (1858) 2 De G. & J. 126, and the link is '*Suggestions for Amendment of the Law as to Petitions of Right: a Letter to William Bovill, Esq., M.P.*' (1859) by T. A. Archibald, junior counsel to the suppliant.

[184] Petitions of Right Act 1860, s 14.

it, and hence there was no longer room for a unifying concept of public purpose. But to rest there would be to ignore the statutory creation of new ministries and reorganization of old. If judges interpreted that statutory activity in the same way they had treated Acts creating local bodies, then departments of state too would have a corporate or quasi-corporate status, Blackburn J.'s analysis would not survive, and a way around Her Majesty's historic immunities from suit would have been found.

Some departments, those heavily involved in land transactions, certainly had been equipped with their own corporate or quasi-corporate personality that at least substituted ordinary liability in contract for the processes of the petition of right. The most prominent were the Commissioners of Woods and Forests, later reorganized as the Commissioners of Works and Public Buildings. Their legal position was complex, combining serial *ad hoc* incorporation and empowerment for particular projects—the construction of Regent Street, for example—with measures of general incorporation, until finally (one can almost hear the exasperation), the Works and Public Buildings Act 1874 ordained that they be 'a corporation to all intents and purposes'.[185] The earlier Acts typically empowered the commissioners to enter contracts, stipulated that they sue and be sued in the name of their Secretary, who was to be reimbursed from funds raised by virtue of the Acts, and absolved the commissioners from personal liability. Notwithstanding that the commissioners represented the Crown, judges held them subject to injunction and specific performance just as if they did not, and were willing to contemplate a *mandamus* against them.[186]

Though the Commissioners' statutes became less expansive, they could still have easily been read as allowing the same form of enterprise liability that befell

[185] The Commissioners of Woods and Forests' modern creation began with 26 & 27 Geo. III c. 87. Specific incorporations include 53 Geo. III c. 121, 7 Geo. IV c. 77, and Courts of Justice Concentration (Site) Act 1865. Crown Lands Act 1829, 10 Geo. IV c. 50, to some extent generalized that status. The commissioners were amalgamated with the Surveyor General of Works and Public Buildings by 2 & 3 Will. IV c. 1 (1832), but separated again by Crown Lands Act 1851, 14 & 15 Vict. c 42, which constituted the Commissioners of Works and Public Buildings as a government department with a corporate or quasi-corporate status and a political head (as the Commissioners of Woods and Forests had previously been) and the Commissioners of Woods and Forests as a revenue branch of the Treasury. Their corporate status was strengthened by 15 & 16 Vict. c. 28 (1852), consequent upon *Nurse* v. *Lord Seymour* (1851) 13 Beav. 254, and restated by Works and Public Buildings Act 1874.

[186] *Rankin* v. *Huskisson* (1830) 4 Sim. 13; *Thorn* v. *Commissioners of Works* (1862) 32 Beav. 490 (contract for sale of stone from old Westminster Bridge); *Corbett* v. *Commissioners of Works* (1868) 18 *LT* 548 (contract for sale of land); contrast *Nurse* v. *Lord Seymour* (1851) 13 Beav. 254, remedied by 15 & 16 Vict. c. 28 (1852); *R* v. *Commissioners of Woods and Forests, in re Budge* (1848) 17 LJ QB 341. And see Lindley LJ in *re Wood's Estate, ex p. Commissioners of Works and Public Buildings* (1886) 31 ChD 607, a costs case, displaying impatience with the notion that a corporation for particular statutory purposes should be treated as the Crown.

local bodies.[187] Indeed it happened: in *Dalton* v. *Angus* in 1881, though nobody at the time or since seems to have noticed.[188] Perhaps, like the emigration commissioners, whose statute was written in very similar style, everyone accepted that they were an anomaly.

There was no central department like them. The Admiralty's Act of 1864 was perhaps the nearest equivalent, but while it provided that the Admiralty was to be treated as a quasi-corporate entity and its litigation to be conducted as if between subjects, apart from a few ambivalent words here and there the context was limited to lands and works.[189] When one of the Admiralty's commercial contracts was litigated in 1865 nobody argued that it was anything other than a Crown contract.[190] Significantly, the court's main reason against implying a term that would have committed the Admiralty to provide work for the contractor was that that would have tended to undermine Commons' control of spending. That was fitting for a year nearing the climax of the Treasury's drive to refine and perfect its and the Commons' grip on all aspects of public expenditure.[191]

The Defence Acts were more limited still.[192] When counsel was adventurous enough to argue that his action was 'really against the War Department' rather than the Crown, Quain J.'s austere reply said it all: 'We do not know what the War Department means'.[193] Similarly the Post Office, from the outside perhaps the most business-like of all government departments, normally had its rates and terms of carriage proposed and negotiated by inter-departmental committees, got its uniforms through the War Office, and even looked to the Stationery Office for government-issue pens and paper.[194] Departmental legal autonomy was thus

[187] Courts of Justice Concentration (Site) Act 1865, s 4; and compare the order in *re Wood's Estate* (1886) 31 ChD 607, that the commissioners pay costs 'out of any money that may be appropriated by Parliament and put at their disposal for the purpose'.

[188] (1881) 6 App Cas 740.

[189] Admiralty Lands and Works Act 1864, esp. ss 11, 25. Its precursors were similar; according to Maule J. they did not confer corporate capacity but instead a 'collective capacity': *Williams* v. *Lords Commissioners of Admiralty* (1851) 20 LJ CP 245, 249, 16 Jur. 42, 43. The report at 11 C.B. 420 does not contain that phrase.

[190] *Churchward* v. *The Queen* (1865) LR 1 QB 173. Two appropriation Acts specifically excluded Churchward from receipt of the funds voted.

[191] The words are Chester's, *English Administrative System*, 362. The Exchequer and Audit Departments Act was passed just a year later.

[192] Defence Acts 1842 (5 & 6 Vict. c. 94) and 1860; Ordnance Board Transfer Act 1855; Defence Act Amendment Act 1864.

[193] *Thomas* v. *R* (1874) LR 10 QB 44.

[194] Land: Post Office Act 1840 (3 & 4 Vict. c. 96), Post Office Lands Act 1863, s 67, made less independent and more Crown-like by Post Office (Land) Act 1881; contracts: Post Office Management Act 1837, 7 Will. IV & 1 Vict. c. 33, s 7, Packet Service, Securities Act 1860, Post Office Lands Act 1863, s 6—none of them very clear; carriage of mails: Railways (Conveyance of Mails) Act, 1 & 2 Vict. c. 98 (1838), Regulation of Railways Act 1868, ss 36, 37, Regulation of Railways Act 1873, ss 18–20, Post

rather limited. When the House of Lords eventually pronounced that there was no such thing as a departmental liability on a contract it was just repeating the orthodoxy.[195]

Departmental liability for tort would have offended the same constitutional principle. The difference between local bodies and central departments was that judges had been willing to interpret local statutes as enabling local bodies to levy rates to meet tortious liability, substituting corporate liability for individual, whereas central departments were dependent on annual parliamentary votes of supply consequent upon submission of an estimate. For the spending departments this was a matter of high constitutional principle. Revenue-raising departments might once have claimed the ability to meet liabilities out of income, but that changed from the late 1840s, when the Commons began to insist that revenue be paid directly into the consolidated fund. Statutes in 1854 and 1866 completed the process.[196] Ministries thus had no funds of their own, nor the means of raising them.

The exception might be allowed to prove the rule. The Government of India Act 1858, as part of vesting sovereign powers in the Secretary of State in Council, empowered him (or it, or them) to enter contracts, and to sue and be sued as a body corporate, its members free from personal liability.[197] Significantly, the Act also provided that liabilities be met from the revenues of India. Further, those revenues went directly to the Secretary of State in Council without need for a parliamentary vote.[198] In a decision little known outside India this combination of circumstances allowed Barnes Peacock, then chief justice of the supreme court at Calcutta, to hold the Secretary of State in Council liable for a street accident caused by the negligence of employees at a government dockyard.[199] The facts, the reasoning, and the result reached are strikingly similar to the much better known case of *Blanco* a few years later, which is treated as the foundation of

Office Act 1875, Post Office (Parcels) Act 1882. For integration with Whitehall see M. J. Daunton, *Royal Mail: The Post Office since 1840* (1985), 121–34, 146, 178, 277, 317, but contrast C. R. Perry, *The Victorian Post Office* (1992), 32, 36, 41, 48, 206–7, 212, which suggests that from time to time the Post Office achieved rather more autonomy in its inland operations.

[195] A.G. v. *Great Southern & Western Railway Co of Ireland* [1925] AC 754.

[196] Public Revenue and Consolidated Fund Charges Act 1854, Consolidated Fund (Appropriation) Act 1866; Chester, *English Administrative System*, 140, 180–1, and compare 191–7. It was so scandalous in 1873 that the Second Secretary at the Post Office had diverted its revenue towards completing the nationalization of the telegraphs that the Postmaster General had to resign: Daunton, *Royal Mail*, 318–21; Perry, *Victorian Post Office*, 125–32; the culprit was deemed indispensable.

[197] Sections 39, 40, 65, 68, amended by Government of India Act 1859.

[198] Chester, *English Administrative System*, 241–4.

[199] *Peninsular and Oriental Steam Navigation Co* v. *Secretary of State for India*, Supreme Court of Calcutta, (1861) 5 Bom., App. A, and see *Secretary of State for India* v. *Moment* (1912) LR 40 IA 48. Peacock later became a salaried member of the judicial committee of the Privy Council.

state liability in French law.²⁰⁰ Peacock cited and distinguished the principles of tortious immunity discussed so far in this section, anticipated what the Mersey harbour board case was later to decide for local bodies, and then advanced a policy of state enterprise liability where private commercial operators would also be liable. This was not to say that everything that the Secretary of State in Council did that harmed an individual would be justiciable, for Peacock excluded things only a sovereign could do—such as making a treaty or seizing property during a war.²⁰¹ He thus laid a foundation from which a new public law could have been created in England as it was in France, if the statutory structure had been favourable.

The circumstances of the Secretary of State for India in Council were unique, however. For other departments the principles of prior approval of expenditure, Treasury scrutiny, and detailed parliamentary grant were vital to mid-Victorian politics, their centralizing tendency emphasizing the essential unity of what from the late 1850s was coming to be thought of as a single civil service.²⁰² In 1870 even the Defence Department and the Admiralty, the last of the recalcitrant and would-be autonomous departments, finally acknowledged Treasury suzerainty, completing its hegemony.²⁰³ In such a system Parliament was unlikely to confer as clear a corporate status on a department as it had done for the Secretary of State for India in Council, and judges equally unlikely to imply one.

As it happened, the litigation that might have done for central departments what *Gibbs* had done for local bodies came far too late, and the cases arose in the wrong order: weakest first. So in 1898 a case against the Admiralty was lost on general principles, and in 1906 a claim against the Postmaster General was also lost, though it concerned functions under the Telegraph Act 1868 that might plausibly have been read as imposing a corporate liability, the absence of an explicit statutory reference to a funded liability being decisive.²⁰⁴ The precedent value of these two cases was enough to win the Crown the third and

²⁰⁰ TC 8 February 1873; D. Fairgrieve, *State Liability in Tort* (Oxford, 2004), 12–13, 20–3; J. D. B. Mitchell, 'The Causes and Effects of the Absence of a System of Public Law in the United Kingdom' [1965] *PL* 95–118 at 105. The *P&O* case concerned a horse injured by metalwork being carried across a public road from one part of a government dockyard to another. Agnès Blanco was injured by a wagon crossing the road between different parts of a state-owned tobacco enterprise.

²⁰¹ There is thus no inconsistency with *Kinloch* v. *Secretary of State for India* (1882) 7 App Cas 619. There would have been if the Lords had endorsed James LJ's forthright opinion ((1880) 15 ChD 1) that the 'Secretary of State in Council' was a mere name or device, and not a legal person, but the lords who addressed the point seem clearly to have accepted his, or its, quasi-corporate existence. Contrast Grove J.'s decision in *Grant* v. *Secretary of State for India* (1877) 2 CPD 445, where an action for libel was dismissed in a judgment more instinctive than fully reasoned.

²⁰² Chester, *English Administrative System*, 152–66, 197–208, 298–311.

²⁰³ Wright, *Treasury Control*, 343–5.

²⁰⁴ *Raleigh* v. *Goschen* [1898] 1 Ch 73; *Bainbridge* v. *Postmaster General* [1906] 1 QB 178.

strongest case, Shearman J. holding that they bound him to rule that statutory incorporation ('to all intents and purposes') of the Commissioners of Works and Public Buildings did not entail independent liability for the torts of their officers.[205] The Crown settled with the plaintiff before an appeal was heard, but the most that could have been established by then was that these commissioners were an anomalous exception.

A similar judicial reluctance to order central government agencies to pay money can be seen in the *mandamus* cases. It was not that *mandamus* to pay money was seen as a general problem, since judges had steadily extended *mandamus* against statutory bodies for that purpose, provided that no suitable alternative remedy was available.[206] *Mandamus* did not ever lie against the Crown, but it would be issued against holders of offices under the Crown, provided that they owed legal duties to the public and, again, that there was no alternative remedy.[207] By extrapolation, then, it could have been issued to order a Crown servant to pay money owed under a public duty, and that seems to be just what the Queen's Bench did decide in 1835, for all the later reinterpretation and disavowal of that case.[208]

That decision to order the Lords of the Treasury to pay a former office holder arrears of a pension quickly came to be distinguished on two main lines of analysis, both indicative of judicial reluctance to enforce monetary payments against central departments. The first held that pensions remained intrinsically matters of grace even when authorized by statute, and even when money was appropriated to their payment.[209] On the one hand this was obvious deference to the government, allowing it to vary or revoke pensions just as it could vary or revoke salaries. On the other, by denying the Crown power to bind itself by granting pensions for life,

---

[205] *Roper* v. *Commissioners of Works* [1915] 1 KB 45. The law officers even attempted to deny the commissioners' independent contractual capacity, though unsuccessfully: *Graham* v. *Commissioners of Works* [1901] 2 KB 781. W. Harrison Moore recognized these commissioners as the most likely to have independent liability: 'Liability for Acts of Public Servants' (1907) 23 *LQR* 11, 23. *Dalton* v. *Angus* was forgotten.

[206] *R* v. *St Katharine's Dock* (1832) 4 B. &. Ad. 360; *R* v. *Nottingham Old Waterworks* (1837) 1 Nev. & P. KB. 480; *R* v. *Trustees of Swansea Harbour* (1839) 8 Ad. & El. 439; *R* v. *Deptford Pier Improvement Co* (1839) 8 Ad. & El. 272.

[207] *R* v. *Cookson* (1812) 16 East 376; *R* v. *Commissioners of Appeals in Matters of Excise* (1814) 3 M. & S. 133. Later: *R* v. *Arnaud* (1846) 9 Q.B. 806.

[208] *R* v. *Lords Commissioners of the Treasury* (1835) 4 Ad. & El. 286.

[209] *R* v. *Lords Commissioners of the Treasury* (1836) 4 Ad. & El. 976; *R* v. *Lords Commissioners of the Treasury* (1836) 4 Ad. & El. 984; *Ex p. Ricketts* (1836) 4 Ad. & El. 999; *Ex p. Napier* (1852) 18 Q.B. 692. The 1835 decision was explained away on the ground that the Treasury had formally acknowledged that it had ceased to hold the money preparatory to paying and instead held for the payee.

it maximized the power of the Commons to scrutinize and reduce expenditure.[210] This led into the second line of reasoning, which worked back from the constitutional arrangements for the annual voting of money. Thus for Littledale J. it was *because* the Commons voted money annually that the pensions legislation should be interpreted as not permitting the Treasury to grant pensions for life.[211] Similarly, the Queen's Bench in 1850 decided that because the Commissioners of Woods and Forests had only such money for a particular project as Parliament should vote them, so processes they had invoked under a compulsory purchase statute would be interpreted as not creating an obligation (since the commissioners could not be sure of meeting it) although virtually identical processes invoked by statutory companies did create enforceable obligations.[212]

These decisions still left the possibility that once the Commons had voted the money needed for performance of a legal obligation a department could be subjected to a *mandamus* to pay it over, but here a second line of constitutional reasoning cut in. This was that because it was the Crown to which the Commons voted money, and the Crown that then made it available to its servants for the performance of their various roles, Crown servants held such money subject only to a duty to account to the Crown for its proper use, not on duties to the public.[213] The Crown itself was not subject to a duty—in the 1870s the very idea made Cockburn CJ and Blackburn J. wince—and the old principle that *mandamus* would not lie against servants to perform duties they owed to their masters applied as much to Crown servants as to any others, so those judges held.[214] This notion was akin to Blackburn J.'s analysis in the Mersey harbour board cases of Crown servants as mere managers—he made that connection himself—and, as there, it served to insulate central departments from judicial interference even in cases where the judges were certain that departmental withholding of money was unlawful.[215]

---

[210] This is how I interpret Att.-Gen. Campbell's argument in *R v. Lords Commissioners of the Treasury* (1836) 4 Ad. & El. 984 that the statutory tendency has been to curtail the Crown's power to grant pensions for life.

[211] *R v. Lords Commissioners of the Treasury* (1836) 4 Ad. & El. 984.

[212] *R v. Commissioners of Woods and Forests ex p. Budge* (1850) 16 Q.B. 761, which was a further stage of *R v. Commissioners of Woods and Forests* (1848) 17 LJ QB 341.

[213] *In re Baron de Bode* (1838) 6 Dowl. 776.

[214] *R v. Lord Commissioners of the Treasury* (1872) LR 7 QB 387. The general principle is illustrated by *R v. Shaw* (1794) 5 T.R. 549; *R v. Bristow* (1795) 6 T.R. 168; *R v. Jeyes* (1835) 3 Ad. & El. 416. The exception made for a nominal defendant in *R v. Surveyors of Highways for Wood Ditton* (1849) 18 LJ MC 218, 13 Jur 680 (*sub. nom. Ex p Bottom*) seems not to have been developed, and certainly not so as to outflank the Treasury cases.

[215] *R v. Lord Commissioners of the Treasury* (1872) LR 7 QB 387; *R v. Postmaster General* (1873) 28 LT 337; see also *In re Lords Commissioners of the Treasury ex p. Walmsley* (1861) 1 B. & S. 81. A related

It seems clear that money orders were seen as the peculiar problem, since *mandamus* went against central departments to order performance of statutory duties other than the payment of money.[216] Further, the reasoning is heavily constitutional; the more mundane ground, that *mandamus* would not be issued against a party who could not get the means to satisfy it, if it appears at all is secondary or additional.[217]

Taken together with the cases refusing to extend to Crown agencies the principles of tortious liability affirmed in the 1860s for local authorities, and with the reasoning in the contract case of *Churchward* v. *The Queen*, there is thus a pattern of judicial unwillingness to order central government to pay money. The formalism invoked—that central government exists in law only as the Crown, that the Crown has always been immune from suit, and that Crown servants incur no more liabilities than any other servants—was certainly not out of step with the mid-century centralization of the civil service. But formal reasoning was only the façade. Judges saw financial control through Parliament and the Treasury as constitutionally vital, and as reasons why they should not themselves impose liabilities in the absence of the clearest statutory authority.

---

line of reasoning held that the Commissioners of Woods and Forests remained merely managers of Her Majesty's manors, despite their very extensive statutory powers, and had not become a statutory substitute for the lord. Hence *mandamus* would not lie to order admission of a copyhold tenant in a Crown manor: *R* v. *Powell* (1841) 1 Q.B. 352, and see also *Ex p. Reeve* (1837) 5 Dowl. 668 (same commissioners not occupiers in their own right and hence not compellable to pay rates).

[216] *R* v. *Local Government Board* (1874) LR 9 QB 148; *R* v. *Postmaster General* (1878) 3 QBD 428 ('judgment ought technically to be for the Crown, though in reality it is against the Crown, as the Postmaster General is the defendant', per Blackburn J.); *R* v. *Local Government Board* (1885) 15 QBD 70; and see *ex p. Matlock Bath District* (1862) 31 LJ QB 177 and *R* v. *Board of Trade* (1874) 22 WR 807 where *mandamus* was available on principle but denied on the merits. The marginal area concerned *mandamus* to boards of Crown servants under a statutory obligation to refund overpaid taxes. In the early cases the objection was either not taken or it was waived by the Crown: *R* v. *Commissioners of Stamps and Taxes* (1846) 9 Q.B. 637; *R* v. *Commissioners of Stamps and Taxes* (1849) 18 LJ QB 201; compare *R* v. *Commissioners of Excise* (1845) 6 Q.B. 975. The high point of judicial withdrawal came with *R* v. *Commissioners of Inland Revenue ex p Nathan* (1884) 12 QBD 461, where the Court of Appeal in a detailed judgment ruled that petitions of right were a suitable alternative remedy that barred *mandamus*. But shortly afterwards first the Court of Appeal and then the House of Lords abruptly reached the opposite conclusion: *R* v. *Commissioners for Special Purposes for Income Tax* (1888) 21 QBD 313; *Commissioners for Inland Revenue* v. *Pemsel* [1891] AC 531. Crown counsel seem not to have taken a general point from these reversals, since they continued to raise the objection and then waive it right through to the end of our period, even in very ordinary cases of *mandamus* to grant licences, where to a modern eye the context seems wholly statutory: *R* v. *Commissioners of Inland Revenue* (1888) 21 QBD 569; *R* v. *Commissioners of Inland Revenue* [1891] 1 QB 485; *R* v. *Commissioners of Inland Revenue ex p. Silvester* [1907] 1 KB 108. Except in *ex p. Nathan* the reasoning is too cursory to sustain much analysis.

[217] Cases illustrating the restriction are rare; *R* v. *Bristol and North Somerset Railway Co* (1877) 3 QBD 10 is a clear, if extreme, example.

III

The Church and the State

1. THE CHURCH AND ITS PRIVILEGES

This chapter considers the governance of the Church, particularly the role of the secular organs of the state. To isolate that one set of relationships from other aspects of the Church's complex integration with the state is artificial, and something must first be said about the establishment in a broader sense, the sense that outsiders might summarize as the privileges of the Church. So at the risk of gross over-simplification four well-worn facets of the Church's relation to the secular state need a brief narrative before the fifth, the establishment in its narrower, institutional, sense can be addressed. Formulation of these facets inevitably begs questions. To take a simple argumentative illustration, Anglicans' monopoly of entry to the University of Oxford and its colleges was attacked as a privilege, but defended as an aspect of property resting on an assertion of the historic truth that those bodies were as integral to the Church as canonries at a cathedral. There was no right answer to the question whether Oxford was a national or a Church institution, whether privilege or property was in issue. There was merely a political winner. An extensive modern literature treats these themes at length.[1]

The first facet of the Church-state relationship, made redundant in the generation before 1820, was the imposition of criminal penalties on public adherence to other churches. That was dismantled for Catholics in 1791 and for Unitarians in 1813.[2] Catholics willing to subscribe to an oath supporting the protestant succession and denying any temporal claims of the pope could thereafter worship in public on similar terms to protestant Trinitarian dissenters, that is in licensed

---

[1] O. Chadwick, *The Victorian Church*, 2 vols (1966–70); G. I. T. Machin, *Politics and the Churches in Great Britain 1832 to 1868* (Oxford, 1977), and *Politics and the Churches in Great Britain 1869 to 1921* (Oxford, 1987); P. T. Marsh, *The Victorian Church in Decline* (1969); F. Knight, *The Nineteenth-Century Church and English Society* (Cambridge, 1995); R. E. Rodes, *Law and Modernization in the Church of England* (Notre Dame, 1991).

[2] Roman Catholic Relief Act, 31 Geo. III c. 32, Doctrine of the Trinity Act, 53 Geo. III c. 160.

buildings before licensed priests.[3] Likewise they could enter the professions, though such was the equation of religion with education that masterships of schools and (of course) membership of the universities remained closed to them.

A second facet, of major political importance at the start of our period, excluded from civil power all who did not take the Anglican sacrament. Its impact on Dissenters had been mitigated for a long time by annual indemnity statutes, of sufficient practical importance for some Tories to regard the legislative barriers against Dissenters as being merely symbolic. The necessity the Whigs felt in 1835 to complete the job by radical reform of municipal corporations suggests that those Tories were right, though not for the reasons they gave. The repeal of those legislative barriers, the Test and Corporation Acts, in 1828 did not presage emancipation for Catholics, though that came the following year, the genesis and politics of the two reforms being quite different.[4] Nonetheless, the two together did signal a swift transition from an Anglican state via a protestant state to a Christian state. That led to recurrent pressure on the third facet of the relationship, the legally protected privileges of Anglicans (not all of them wholly exclusive) such as the use of only their parish registers for recording births and only their service at burials in the parish churchyard. Anglican privileges extended beyond the use of the parish church and its environs, notably to the universities of Oxford and Cambridge, and as elementary education became an increasingly important political question so too the Church's role in its provision came to be contested as both a privilege and as a barrier to progress. There was continuous pressure too on the fourth element of the relationship, the compulsory financing of the Church, be it through state grants in aid of new churches, or through tithes, or through the levying of church rates.

Transformation of these relations, from the Church as part of the constitution to the Church as nearly just another denomination, is a familiar theme of nineteenth-century history. One aspect, though, should be stressed here, which is best approached indirectly through recalling Dicey's famous but much derided assertion that the civil liberties of Englishmen were better protected by the ordinary law than they would have been by a written constitution, because the former is much harder to dismantle.[5] The Church was similarly woven into the political constitution. There was no one great redrawing of the pattern, but instead an

---

[3] The licensing was non-discretionary. A flurry of cases in 1812 which revealed the difficulties some justices had, or made, in assessing dissenting preachers' credentials led to a further statutory relaxation for them: 52 Geo. III c. 155; *R* v. *Denbighshire Justices* (1811) 14 East 285; *R* v. *Gloucestershire Justices* (1812) 15 East 577; *R* v. *Suffolk Justices* (1812) 15 East 590.

[4] Sacramental Test Act, 9 Geo. IV c. 17; Roman Catholic Relief Act, 10 Geo. IV c. 7.

[5] A. V. Dicey, *An Introduction to the Study of the Law of the Constitution* (10th edn, 1959, by E. C. S. Wade), 221–2, 238.

unpicking thread by thread, the timing and detail of each change dependent on all manner of contingencies.

That is obviously true of the piecemeal dismantling of Anglican privileges, but it is just as true of the admission of non-Anglicans to participation in the processes of political power. Toleration was important as a Whig state of mind and as a liberal principle, but it was just the backdrop to very specific political contests. Lord John Russell omitted the Jews from the bill repealing the Test and Corporation Acts, for example, whereafter they had to claw their way to civic equality step by step. A Christian oath required of electors to municipal corporations in 1828 barred Jews until 1835, and remained to exclude them from municipal office for a further decade, though the Quakers, Moravians, and Separatists broke that barrier in 1838—these being not heathens but merely protestants who objected to oaths.[6] A Christian oath also barred Jews elected to the Commons from taking their seats, and though the Liberal Commons when pressed by an actual case in point would have changed the law to accommodate him and his electorate's wishes, the Conservative Lords would not.[7] When the Lords reluctantly backed down in 1858 it was for fear of jeopardizing the minority Conservative government, allowing the Commons to go its own way, until in 1866 a uniform provision was enacted that was just enough to allow Jews entry to the Lords as well.[8]

As has often been pointed out, their achievement still did not establish a rule that belief was irrelevant as a qualification for entry to Parliament.[9] So a generation later both protestant and Christian constitutionalism, in the Commons and out of it, were important strands in preventing the atheist Charles Bradlaugh from taking his seat.[10] He was admitted only when the Speaker took advantage of the general swearing-in after a general election to allow him to take the oath,

---

[6] Sacramental Test Act 1828, 9 Geo. IV c. 17; Parliamentary Elections Act 1835, 5 & 6 Will. IV c. 36; Declarations by Quakers etc Act 1838, 1 & 2 Vict. c. 15; Municipal Offices Act 1845, 8 & 9 Vict. c. 52; A. Gilam, *The Emancipation of the Jews in England 1830–1860* (New York, 1982), 86–96; U. R. Q. Henriques, 'The Jewish Emancipation Controversy in Nineteenth-Century Britain' (1968) 40 *P & P* 126–46.

[7] For interpretation, see D. Feldman, *Englishmen and Jews: Social Relations and Political Culture 1840–1914* (New Haven, 1994), 28–47; Machin, *1832 to 1868*, 194–5, 292–4.

[8] Oaths of Allegiance etc and Relief of Jews Act 1858; Jews Relief Act 1858; Parliamentary Oaths Act 1866 (further consolidated and amended by Promissory Oaths Acts 1868 and 1871).

[9] Machin, *1832 to 1868*, 305; Rodes, *Law & Modernization*, 95.

[10] R. E. Quinault, 'The Fourth Party and the Conservative Opposition to Bradlaugh 1880–1886' (1976) 91 *EHR* 315–40; Machin, *1869 to 1921*, 133–41. The important judicial rulings were that the Commons' decisions not to allow Bradlaugh to take the oath prescribed by law were not justiciable (*Bradlaugh v. Gossett* (1884) 12 QBD 271), that he was not entitled to affirm (*Clarke v. Bradlaugh* (1881) 7 QBD 38), that subscription to a Christian oath by an unbeliever was void (*A.-G. v. Bradlaugh* (1885) 14 QBD 667), but that only the Crown could sue for the statutory penalty (*Clarke v. Bradlaugh* (1883) 8 App Cas 354).

nearly six years after his first election. Even then he functioned as a member only because of the Speaker's discretionary decision to swear him in and the government's forbearance to sue for a penalty for taking a false oath. Only after a further two years was a right enacted for anyone to affirm rather than swear, when Bradlaugh's own Oaths Act was passed in 1888.[11]

Similarly, emancipation of Catholics had been a begrudging affair, with many exceptions expressed in the 1829 Act itself or left extant from the previous law, to be removed step by step as opportunity arose. A steady diet of such questions took its place alongside major matters like the disestablishment of the Irish Church and the abolition of compulsory church rates to ensure that there was never a time when some aspect of the Church's relation with the state was not in issue.

The very substantial changes to the Church-state relationship in all the facets outlined above are the backdrop to consideration of the legal structure of establishment in its narrow sense, the power of the secular organs of the state in the governance of the Church, the power to appoint senior clerics, to make rules for the Church, and to adjudicate upon disputes within it. There was periodic external pressure for disestablishment of course, and widespread internal discomfort at the erosion of the Church's status. That shaded into acute dissatisfaction among some high-churchmen reacting against what they saw as the betrayal of the Church by Catholic emancipation in 1829, and the king's unwillingness to use his coronation oath to prevent it. They abhorred also such further manifestations of state power as the reduction of Irish bishoprics in 1833. But despite pressures for disestablishment or for a measure of self-government the Church's legal relationship with government and Parliament changed significantly in only one respect during our period, and that came with the permanent establishment of the Ecclesiastical Commissioners in 1836.

2. INTERNAL GOVERNMENT: THE CROWN AND THE CHURCH COMMISSIONERS

The Ecclesiastical Commissioners' ostensible role was to manage the Church's property. Deliberately to keep the Commons at arm's length, they were invested with delegated legislative power, to be implemented through Orders-in-Council that needed only to be laid before Parliament.[12] In law the commissioners

---

[11] It also reversed the holding in *Clarke* v. *Bradlaugh* (1881) 7 QBD 38 that an oath by an unbeliever was void.

[12] Machin, *1832 to 1868*, 51; Ecclesiastical Commissioners Act 1836 (also known as the Established Church Act) 6 & 7 Will IV c. 77, ss 10–15; Ecclesiastical Commissioners Act 1840 (also known as the Dean and Chapter Act) 3 & 4 Vict. c. 113, ss. 83–7.

possessed a set of statutory powers through which they could direct the various property-owning corporations that made up the Church of England. The effect, however, was to weld the Church into something like a single quasi-corporate entity, as the commissioners redistributed income and suppressed posts they thought no longer served the Church's spiritual mission.[13] Initially the commissioners' strategy bore Sir Robert Peel's imprint, their legitimacy executive rather than parliamentary. From 1843 the New Parishes Act directed their priorities towards the financing of new urban parishes at the expense of the augmentation of rural livings—legislative guidance, albeit one that again owed much to Peel.[14]

So to some extent the commissioners' vision of a rejuvenated Church had to be shared by Parliament, if the commissioners were to have the powers they wanted. But once the legislation was passed the commissioners enjoyed considerable autonomy to mould the structure of the Church as they wished. Their composition was therefore crucial. Initially the commissioners had been a small and select partnership of Church and state, essentially nominees of the executive and the archbishops.[15] High-church criticism, however, stimulated a very important reconstruction of the commission in 1840, by which it became a much larger body that included all the bishops.[16] So far as its assets went, the Church thus became an organizational unity, with administrative power centralized, in practice, in the bishops collectively and in the bureaucracy that they, as commissioners, generated. It remained dependent on Parliament for augmentation of the commissioners' statutory powers, but enjoyed substantial operational autonomy.

There was no similar autonomy over the appointment of Church leaders or, to that extent, over conformity to doctrine. The Crown continued to appoint bishops and archbishops much as it had always done. The Prime Minister made the decisions, led, abetted, or opposed, after the death of Prince Albert, by the Queen herself, who took her role as head of her Church very seriously. Melbourne was the last Prime Minister to make party political allegiance an explicit prerequisite for preferment, but political colour in a general sense continued as a relevant factor, weightier with some Prime Ministers than others.[17] More importantly, Prime Ministers could, and did, develop their own religious policy, which from time to

---

[13] Pluralities Act 1838, 1 & 2 Vict. c. 106; Ecclesiastical Commissioners Act 1860; K. A. Thompson, *Bureaucracy and Church Reform* (Oxford, 1970); G. F. A. Best, *Temporal Pillars: Queen Anne's Bounty, the Ecclesiastical Commissioners and the Church of England* (Cambridge, 1964).

[14] 6 & 7 Vict. c. 37; Chadwick, *Victorian Church*, i, 233; Machin, *1832 to 1868*, 85.

[15] 6 & 7 Will. IV c. 77. Founding members, including three laymen, were named in the Act; formal powers of dismissal and replacement were vested in the Crown.

[16] 3 & 4 Vict. c. 113, ss 78–81.

[17] Chadwick, *Victorian Church*, i, 121–6, 226, 472–4; ii, 328–40.

time might cause acute controversy, doctrinal divisions within the church being endemic.

In 1847 that raised an important question of law when high-church opponents of Lord John Russell's provocative nomination of Dr Hampden to the see of Hereford tried to wrest at least some of the process away from the secular state. They claimed that the penultimate step in the process, which was public confirmation of the appointment by the Archbishop of Canterbury in his court at Bow Church, should be an occasion for serious theological investigation of the nominee's credentials, not a mere formality.[18] Rebuffed by the archbishop's legal assessor, they sought a *mandamus* from the Queen's Bench that the archbishop must receive their objections to Dr Hampden and adjudicate. The claim was possible because the process was statutory, resting on the original Act of Henry VIII that removed the jurisdiction of the pope. If successful it might have seriously curtailed the Crown's freedom of choice. Two judges, Coleridge and Patteson JJ, accepted the argument, agreeing that the Act's silence in face of a long prior practice of spiritual confirmation by archbishops must be taken to have preserved it. Erle J. and Denman CJ, less unworldly, doubted that that was what Henry VIII had intended, and pointed also to the subsequent unbroken practice of unquestioning acceptance of Crown nominees.[19] This deadlock was enough to discharge the application and preserve the unchallengeable discretion of the Crown. When next the question arose, in 1902, the Queen's Bench refused the *mandamus* much more easily, in line with a general tendency by then to minimize the intrusion of common law courts.[20]

3. LEGISLATING FOR THE CHURCH: CONVOCATIONS AND PARLIAMENT

High-churchmen raised similar questions about the legislative branch. Parliament was, of course, omnicompetent. But long ago the two houses of Convocation legislated, making and amending canons for the Church. Inconveniently for advocates of autonomy, Convocation's Acts had needed Crown assent, just like those of the two Houses of Parliament. And like Parliament, it could meet only by royal summons and was subject to royal prorogation. Unlike Parliament, however, Convocation had neither the power of the purse nor representative legitimacy to gain even indirect control of those prerogatives. Consequently,

---

[18] *Ibid.*, i, 238–46; S. M. Waddams, *Law, Politics and the Church of England* (Cambridge, 1992), 303–8; *The History of the University of Oxford*, ed. M. G. Brock and M.C. Curthoys (Oxford, 1996), vi(1), 214–15, 222–31, 255–6.

[19] *R* v. *Archbishop of Canterbury* (1848) 11 Q.B. 483; Waddams, *Law, Politics*, 303–8.

[20] *R* v. *Archbishop of Canterbury* [1902] 2 KB 503.

after a particularly bitter session in 1717 it had been summoned only formally, thereafter existing in a state of serial prorogation save for an experimental session in 1741 and 1742.[21]

Nonetheless, Convocations did revive, albeit in a rather different form—one for each of the two provinces, rather than one for the whole Church. At first they met without Crown assent, a product of high-church outrage at the *Gorham* decision by the Judicial Committee of the Privy Council in 1850. Then they were legitimized by Lord Aberdeen, the Prime Minister, who from 1853 gave his cautious and circumscribed permission, initially for discussion only.[22] All three common law courts had refused to be a lever in this revival. In the course of the *Gorham* litigation high-churchmen had sought a prohibition from each of them, arguing that the Henrican legislation gave jurisdiction to resolve the dispute between the Reverend Gorham and his bishop to the upper house of Convocation—the bishops. Each court had ruled instead that it lay with the essentially secular Judicial Committee.[23]

Common law judges were also inclined to take a very narrow view of the legal effect of canons of the Church. It had long been established that canons bound neither the laity nor even the clergy in their temporal possessions.[24] But when, unusually, the Crown gave the revived Convocations permission to amend and replace four of the existing canons, some of the common law judges took an opportunity to say that the traditional common law view did not entail even that the canons bound the clergy on spiritual matters.[25]

Despite the revival of the Convocations, Parliament remained the unrivalled legislature for the Church on all matters, including changes to liturgy. True, some modest recognition of Convocations' existence and status could be detected by the contrast between the Clerical Subscription Act 1865, the Prayer Book (Table of Lessons) Act 1871, and the Act of Uniformity Amendment Act 1872. The first originated from a royal commission, and was taken directly to Parliament. The second also stemmed from a commission, but had in the meantime been taken to the revived Convocations for approval. The third went so far as to recite the role of the Convocations in its preamble, the Crown (i.e. the government) having

---

[21] P. Langford, *A Polite and Commercial People* (Oxford, 1989), 42.

[22] Chadwick, *Victorian Church*, i, 309–24.

[23] *Gorham* v. *Bishop of Exeter* (1850) 15 Q.B. 52; *ex p. Bishop of Exeter* (1850) 10 C.B. 102; *In re Gorham* v. *Bishop of Exeter* (1850) 5 Ex. 630. For a similar sentiment, see *Read* v. *Bishop of Lincoln* (1889) 14 PD 88.

[24] *Middleton* v. *Croft* (1736) 2 Stra. 1056 was the authority usually cited for this general rule, though it dates back much further.

[25] *Bishop of Exeter* v. *Marshall* (1866–8) LR 3 HL 17, per Blackburn J. (for himself Lush and Pigott JJ) and Willes J. advising the Lords. A contrary ruling would have been inconsistent with *Gorham* (1850) 14 Jur. 443.

empowered the Convocations to frame resolutions consequent on the royal commission's report.[26] The progression did not continue, however. The Public Worship Regulation Act of 1874, which was seen as an important measure of Church discipline, was passed without the Convocations' concurrence. Proposals to give the Convocations delegated legislative powers subject to parliamentary supervision failed.[27] Instead the Church had still to ask Parliament to legislate for it, and when it did 'government treated the Church's legislative requests like those of any other major but private interest'—they had no special priority, but must take their chance through the lottery of private members' bills.[28]

At the end of the 1890s, and through into the early years of the twentieth century, bills on ceremonial were still being introduced to Parliament without Church consent. None passed, but there was not yet a consensus that none ought to pass unless they had the Church's blessing. Substantial segments of the Commons retained the belief that the Church was a national institution to be guided by the people's lay representatives in Parliament.[29] Reform of internal Church deliberation through the addition of laity to the Convocations (Canterbury 1886, York 1892) was too half-hearted to make a difference. However, formation of a more broadly based Representative Church Council in 1904 did eventually lead to the archbishops appointing a commission on Church-state relations.[30] That in turn led to the establishment of a new Church Assembly in 1917 which, after the war, Parliament thought fit to endow with delegated legislative powers.[31] Parliamentary supremacy remained a reality long after our period ended, however, as demonstrated by the Commons' refusal in 1927 and 1928 to pass the Assembly's revised Prayer Book into law.

4. ADJUDICATION: COURTS SECULAR AND SPIRITUAL

The Church was not just established by law but structured by it too. Secular law and courts were fundamental to its operation in a way that they were not to the Catholic Church, which was authoritarian, or to the protestant dissenting churches, which were constructed on the voluntary principle. Of course, any religious society might find itself before a secular judge on a question of property, especially in cases of schism, and with serious consequences for the distribution

---

[26]　Chadwick, *Victorian Church*, ii, 132–3, 361.
[27]　*Ibid.*, ii, 322; Marsh, *Victorian Church*, 209–17, and cf. 264.
[28]　Marsh, *Victorian Church*, 281.
[29]　Machin, *1869 to 1921*, 237–8, 245–6, 253.
[30]　For this and what follows see Machin, *1869 to 1921*, 318–20, 329.
[31]　Church of England Assembly (Powers) Act 1919.

of spoils.[32] Opportunities for intervention in the Church of England's affairs were more numerous, however, and the intervention more intrusive. In part this was because the Henrican statutes establishing the Church conferred powers that like any other statutory powers were subject to jurisdictional control, as the challenge to Bishop Hampden's appointment showed. There was obvious danger to the Church here as the statutes were very old, and had not been much litigated, if at all. Judges had room for interpolation of context, as the division in the Hampden case also shows, perhaps also for individual doctrinal preferences.[33] Coleridge J., who would have held for the complainants, was known to be sympathetic to the Tractarians who were opposing Hampden.

Further, patrons of livings and holders of benefices had long been treated as having individual property rights. Patrons had a right to present qualified persons for induction.[34] Once inducted, an incumbent enjoyed his parish as of right. Of course, bishops also had a right and a duty to satisfy themselves that presentees really were qualified, but too stringent an understanding of what should count as a qualification would detract from patrons' rights. Bishops were responsible for the continuing orthodoxy of the ministers in their diocese, but, again, too rigorous an understanding of orthodoxy would subtract from the rights of incumbent and patron. These relationships were mediated through law in secular courts. A patron could bring a writ of *quare impedit* to a common law court if a bishop rejected his presentee, to have the adequacy of his reason tested.[35]

Such was the pervasiveness of law that it was possible to argue that since this was a national church the laity had rights too, especially to have the national liturgy performed (and none other).[36] Indeed parliamentary supremacy over the Church made little sense unless that was so. This is not to say that a structure of

[32] Important schism cases include *A.-G.* v. *Shore* (1842) 9 Cl. & F. 499; *A.G.* v. *Hardy* (1851) 1 Sim. (N.S.) 338; *Ward* v. *Hipwell* (1862) 3 Giff. 547; *General Assembly of the Free Church of Scotland* v. *Overtoun* [1904] AC 515 (see Rodger of Earlsferry, Lord, *The Courts, the Church and the Constitution* (Edinburgh, 2008), 97–104). The piecemeal nature of emancipation could create difficult questions of the validity of charities: *West* v. *Shuttleworth* (1835) 2 My. & K. 684; *Baker* v. *Lee* (1861) 8 H.L.C. 495; contrast *Re Michel's Trusts* (1860) 28 Beav. 39.

[33] For a particularly striking use of context see Martin B.'s dissenting judgment in *Miller* v. *Salomons* (1852) 7 Ex. 475, and contrast the textual orthodoxy of the Exchequer Chamber on appeal (1853) 8 Ex. 778.

[34] Parliamentary insistence (in 1711) that the same should apply to the presbyterian Church of Scotland was the underlying cause of the Disruption in 1843 which split that Church: Rodger, *Courts, Church*, 1–36. Derogation from the proper role of presbyteries was more deeply and more widely resented than derogation from the power of Anglican bishops, though in England it became Church policy to buy back rights of presentation whenever it could.

[35] *Bishop of Exeter* v. *Marshall* (1868) LR 3 HL 17; *Walsh* v. *Bishop of Lincoln* (1875) LR 10 CP 578.

[36] *R* v. *Bishop of Oxford* (1879) 4 QBD 245, reversed (1879) 4 QBD 525; Marsh, *Victorian Church*, 185.

rights necessarily extended to all members of the Church. As law was the foundation, the distribution of authority depended upon the will of Parliament as expressed through statute, which might instead confer discretion. That is how courts interpreted bishops' powers to license curates and lecturers (and *a fortiori* to admit applicants to holy orders), with the consequence that bishops could not be required to state their reasons for refusal, nor were their decisions subject to appeal to an ecclesiastical court.[37] But the courts were stern when rights were in issue, and not just when those were the property rights of patrons. They held that supplementary testimonials required by bishops from ministers seeking to transfer into their diocese were illegal, for example, undermining episcopal efforts to maintain purity of doctrine.[38]

There were, of course, the ecclesiastical courts, which, viewed from the outside were 'church courts'.[39] But from the inside they were courts; they administered law, not doctrine, and once appointed their judges were not amenable to episcopal (or any other) direction. In 1874 Archbishop Tait hoped to substitute episcopal authority for judicial in the matter of disciplining clergy, but failed.[40] So too the freedom of clergy to withhold the sacrament from persons whose morals they found offensive was limited by law, and when tested was construed strictly.[41] In this sense even the ecclesiastical courts were secular courts, the state's courts.

Those courts became a forum in which quite bitter disputes about the nature and direction of the Church, its structure of authority, and the nature of theological truth were fought out. Until 1832 the ultimate court of appeal from the network of local ecclesiastical courts was the High Court of Delegates. It had come to comprise some common law judges—none of whom knew any civil law—and a selection from whichever advocates from Doctors' Commons had not been involved in the cause as judge or counsel, inevitably the junior and out of work. It was an easy target for Henry Brougham in his great law reform speech in 1828.[42] Very few of its decisions, however, had had to address the relation between ecclesiastical law and theology that later became so contentious.[43] So no special provision was made for such cases when the court was abolished and its whole jurisdiction transferred to a redesigned Judicial Committee of the Privy

[37]   *R* v. *Archbishop of Canterbury* (1812) 15 East 117; *Poole* v. *Bishop of London* (1861) 14 Moo. P.C. 262. But bishops must follow the correct procedure: *R* v. *Archbishop of Canterbury* (1859) 1 E. & E. 545.

[38]   *Bishop of Exeter* v. *Marshall* (1868) LR 3 HL 17; cf. *Thompson* v. *Dibdin* [1912] AC 533.

[39]   See Pt 3, Ch. V.

[40]   Tait: Marsh, *Victorian Church*, 163–72, and see below.

[41]   *Jenkins* v. *Cook* (1876) LR 1 PD 80; *Bannister* v. *Thompson* [1908] PD 362.

[42]   P. A. Howell, 'The High Court of Delegates' [review] (1973) 16 *Hist. J.* 189, 193–4.

[43]   Marsh, *Victorian Church*, 121 (a maximum of 7 out of 177).

Council.[44] This was by any measure a secular court, a supreme court of appeal for miscellaneous causes to parallel the miscellany that was the executive Privy Council. The committee might have an ecclesiastical lawyer on its panel but was predominately a court of common law and equity specialists. In retrospect this institutional reform took on far greater significance than it had had at the time.

The Judicial Committee Act 1832 did contain a provision for summoning non-judicial privy councillors to attend a panel without being members of it. Later that was used as an expedient to allow the episcopal privy councillors to advise the judges in what were essentially heresy cases, but that use had not been a conscious part of the original design. It is more accurate, then, to see the Church Discipline Act 1840 as a new departure and not as the correction of an oversight.[45] This Act was meant to be the sole procedure for disciplining errant clergy. It provided that if such a case were to reach the Judicial Committee the episcopal privy councillors might be full members of the panel and at least one of them must be.[46] This was new. Prelates were not ecclesiastical lawyers. Indeed nobody who had held holy orders could even be an advocate in ecclesiastical courts.[47] The 1840 Act thus recognized that in times of heightened theological controversy more than law was in issue, more even than ecclesiastical law.[48]

Even before the celebrated *Gorham* case high-churchmen had been sceptical of the Crown's ecclesiastical courts. In 1847 and 1848 Bishop Blomfield, Bishop of London, tried to secure the wholesale replacement of secular judges by a bench of bishops in cases of doctrine, but his bills to that effect failed.[49] *Gorham* itself, a dispute about the effects of baptism, was not an action by a bishop against an incumbent, but one brought by Gorham against the bishop for refusing to approve his transfer to a new parish. The Court of Arches had virtually had to reinvent a process to enable a presentee himself to contest his rejection by a bishop, itself a sign of the ubiquity of law.[50] Because the dispute fell outside the Church Discipline Act it had to be decided by the wholly lay Judicial Committee, though the two archbishops and the bishop of London attended under the provisions of the Judicial

[44] Abolition: 2 & 3 Will. IV c. 92; reconstitution: Judicial Committee Act 1833, 3 & 4 Will. IV c. 41. For a full account, see P. A. Howell, *The Judicial Committee of the Privy Council 1833–1876* (Cambridge, 1979), 18–48.

[45] Chadwick, *Victorian Church*, i, 256–8; Machin, *1832–1868*, 30; Howell, 'High Court of Delegates', 194.

[46] 3 & 4 Vict. c. 86, s 16.

[47] *R* v. *Archbishop of Canterbury* (1807) 8 East 213; G. D. Squibb, *Doctors' Commons* (Oxford, 1977), 28, 42. The last time a bishop had sat on the High Court of Delegates was 1781: Howell, 'High Court of Delegates', 192.

[48] For the difficulty of the relation between theology and this branch of ecclesiastical law, see Waddams, *Law, Politics*, esp. 341–6.

[49] Machin, *1832 to 1868*, 204.

[50] (1849) 13 Jur. 238 (compare a similar revival of ancient process in *ex p. Read* (1888) 13 PD 1).

Committee Act.[51] The result was a thoroughgoing insistence on legal standards. Once presented by the patron, Gorham had a right to admission conditionally upon his being a fit person. To deny his fitness the bishop must point to precise statements by Gorham that clearly contradicted identified Church doctrine that had the force of law. How, then, was that to be identified? The court held narrowly that Gorham must be shown to have contradicted the Thirty-nine Articles or the 'dogmatical' parts of the Book of Common Prayer according to the usual principles of legal interpretation in penal cases.[52]

Allowing for differences in context, this was a decision in the tradition of *Entick* v. *Carrington* and *Leach* v. *Money*, and as important. Its substantive standard tended to a broad Church, since the designation of what materials were binding omitted a great deal of theological exegesis, leaving just the sixteenth-century prescriptions. Those were often compromises, worded with the latitude that compromises usually are. Anyway, they could hardly be expected to cover with the precision the court now demanded all the nice disputes that had subsequently arisen.

The procedural standards the court imposed in *Gorham* were important too. They led, particularly, to the exoneration in 1863 of the clerical authors of chapters in the *Essays and Reviews* collection. Here the Judicial Committee insisted that the authors could be charged only with what each individually had written, and that their errors be properly identified and put to them before condemnation. The 'meagre and disjointed extracts' cited were too equivocal to found a conviction, it held.[53] The contrast with the reaction of the Convocation of Canterbury is very clear. It established a committee which led both houses into condemning the book as a whole—to the scorn of the Lord Chancellor in the subsequent House of Lords debate, who once again emphasized the primacy of lawyers' values.[54]

---

[51] E. F. Moore, *The Case of the Rev. G. C. Gorham, against the Bishop of Exeter* (1852); (1850) 14 Jur. 443 (Marquis of Lansdowne (President)—who left after opening the proceedings—Lord Langdale, Lord Campbell, Knight-Bruce VC, Baron Parke, Dr Lushington, and Pemberton Leigh; with the Archbishops of Canterbury (Sumner) and York (Musgrave) and the Bishop of London (Blomfield) in attendance. For a contemporary account of the decision-making, see *The Greville Memoirs by Charles C. F. Greville*, ed. H. Reeve (1903), vi, 308–11, and for recent analysis Waddams, *Law, Politics*, 271–80. As the proceeding was by *duplex querela*, not under the Church Discipline Act 1840 (when the clerics would have been members of the court) Lord Langdale's advice distinguished carefully between Knight-Bruce who, as a member, dissented, and the Bishop of London who, as one merely attending, did not concur.

[52] *Heath* v. *Burder* (1862) 15 Moo. P.C. 1; *Williams* v. *Bishop of Salisbury* (1863) 2 Moo. P.C. (N.S.) 375; *Bishop of Exeter* v. *Marshall* (1868) LR 3 HL 17; *Sheppard* v. *Bennett* (1872) LR 4 PC 371; *Willis* v. *Bishop of Oxford* (1877) 2 PD 192.

[53] *Williams* v. *Bishop of Salisbury* (1863) 2 Moo. P.C. (N.S.) 375; Waddams, *Law, Politics*, 310–11; Chadwick, *Victorian Church*, ii, 75–84. There was no jurisdiction over the non-clerical authors.

[54] I. Ellis, *Seven Against Christ* (Leiden, 1980), 192–200.

For liberals, then, the *Gorham* decision stood as a barrier against persecution of opinion, and for Erastians such as Lord John Russell it affirmed the breadth necessary in a national church.[55] For high-churchmen, however, the criticism was that for all its protestations the court was in fact deciding doctrine, not law.[56] Some now acknowledged this as an inherent feature of an established church, and a reason to secede.[57] For others it was unacceptable only from a court so constituted. They sought a better way of determining what was the true doctrine of the Church, doctrine that its clergy should accept or, at least, not publicly contradict. The attendance of only the two archbishops and the bishop of London at Judicial Committee hearings excluded, or might exclude, influential or even dominant strands of doctrinal opinion, they thought. In the 1850s the preference of these high-church critics was that the Judicial Committee should be obliged to receive an authoritative statement of doctrine from the bishops as a whole, a proposal they had to abandon after rejection by the Lords.[58]

The revival of the Convocations suggested an alternative, that the clerics be withdrawn entirely from the Judicial Committee, leaving law to the lawyers and leaving the Convocations with the option of issuing corrective restatements of doctrine after the event.[59] That proposal eventually passed the Commons as part of the Supreme Court of Judicature Bill in 1873, but was rejected by the Lords after opposition from Archbishop Tait. The outcome was that full clerical membership of the Judicial Committee under the Church Discipline Act was indeed abolished, but that attendance by assessors in ecclesiastical cases was extended to include bishops who were not privy councillors.[60] That created a potentially more representative advisory panel, at least once the Archbishop of Canterbury and his bishops had negotiated a process for constituting it.[61] It was, however, only an advisory panel; the full members of the Judicial Committee made that clear by allowing the bishops to attend during the argument only, and not during the subsequent deliberations.[62]

---

[55] Chadwick, *Victorian Church*, i, 250–71; Machin, *1832–1868*, 204.

[56] P. B. Nockles, *The Oxford Movement in Context* (Cambridge, 1994), 93–103, 229–35; and consider *Sheppard* v. *Bennett* (1872) LR 4 PC 371 as an example of explicit restatement of doctrine.

[57] There are broad parallels with the Disruption in Scotland, though some of those seceding there hoped that the new Free Church would supplant the Church of Scotland as the established Church: see Rodger, *Courts, Church*, 96–8 for an outline.

[58] Chadwick, *Victorian Church*, i, 264.

[59] M. D. Stephen, 'Gladstone and the Composition of the Final Court in Ecclesiastical Causes, 1850–73' (1966) 9 *Hist. J.* 191–200.

[60] Appellate Jurisdiction Act 1876, ss 14 and 24, repealing and partly re-enacting Supreme Court of Judicature Act 1873, s 21.

[61] J. Bentley, *Ritualism and Politics in Victorian Britain* (Oxford, 1978), 99–100; Howell, *Judicial Committee*, 71, 216–17.

[62] Howell, *Judicial Committee*, 217.

In the 1870s increasing use of Roman-like ceremonial by high-churchmen during public worship threatened the latitude induced by *Gorham*. Ritual forced itself upon a congregation in a way that mere statements of belief by clergymen did not.[63] Reaction within Parliament led to the Public Worship Regulation Act 1874 which, while disappointing those who wanted a tightening of substantive ecclesiastical law, was significant for allowing individual complainants greater access to the prosecution process.[64] That brought a serious possibility that bishops might be pushed aside, if anti-ritualist associations brought prosecutions and the Judicial Committee were the ultimate arbiter. It also raised a series of difficult questions for the secular judges, be they members of the Privy Council or the common law courts.

The first difficulty was that the Judicial Committee was as divided as the Church itself on what ritual was permissible. Its façade of unity was maintained, however, by Lord Cairns. He first invoked, and in 1878 modernized, an ancient Order-in-Council that forbade overt dissent.[65] The second set of questions concerned the relation between the ecclesiastical courts and the courts of common law in the application of the new statute. Part of the difficulty was personal. The 1874 Act had insinuated a new judge into the ecclesiastical courts of Canterbury and York so as to achieve uniformity of application, but Lord Penzance, the judge appointed, took the view that his status was entirely statutory and owed nothing to the traditional constitution of the ecclesiastical courts. He therefore declined to take the oath the canons of the Church required of judges of ecclesiastical courts, arguing that there was no such requirement in the statute.[66] In a backhanded way the Queen's Bench supported him, to his embarrassment, by indicating that he had not acquired the usual ancillary powers adhering to ecclesiastical courts. It did not reverse that stance until 1881.[67] As a result of Lord Penzance's gesture the ritualists became openly contemptuous of his court, and very willing to attack it through writs of prohibition, *certiorari*, and *habeas corpus*, as their disobedience fructified into imprisonment.

---

[63]   Marsh, *Victorian Church*, 122 quoting *Sheppard* v. *Bennett* (1872) LR 4 PC 371, 404.

[64]   Machin, *1869 to 1921*, 69–77; Bentley, *Ritualism*, 93–6; Marsh, *Victorian Church*, 159–65; Chadwick, *Victorian Church*, ii, 322–5. The Act also introduced a more uniform procedure for prosecuting unlawful innovation. Archbishop Tait's original proposal was that the Archbishops should determine whether there had been an infraction, not a court.

[65]   Bentley, *Ritualism*, 98; D. B. Swinfen, 'The Single Judgment in the Privy Council 1833–1966' (1975) 20 *Jur. Rev.* 153–76.

[66]   Machin, *1869 to 1921*, 78.

[67]   *Serjeant* v. *Dale* (1877) 2 QBD 558 and *Hudson* v. *Tooth* (1877) 3 QBD 46, distinguished in *Dale's case* (1881) 6 QBD 376, where Coleridge LCJ was scornful of those who thought it mattered whether Lord Penzance had taken the oath required of Ecclesiastical Court judges (and agreeing that he was right not to have done); *Green* v. *Lord Penzance* (1881) 6 App Cas 657. As the sitting judges in the two provincial courts quickly made way for Lord Penzance, he became, so the common law courts held, the Official Principal of each.

The theory of prohibition is that common law courts have power to prevent other courts from exceeding the bounds of their jurisdiction, and for centuries they had exercised that power over ecclesiastical courts. But the statutory jurisdiction under attack was very modern, and there was also a modern appeal structure running up to the Judicial Committee. How should jurisdictional theory work in this new context? Some questions were easy, with judges at all levels agreed. In particular they had no difficulty holding that if an ecclesiastical court erred when deciding such matters as whether items of costume or acts of ceremonial were sufficiently 'like' one another to attract the same sanction, the remedy was to appeal, not to seek review from common law courts on jurisdictional grounds.[68]

They found it much harder to decide on the legality of the new coercive remedies that ecclesiastical courts found themselves developing to deal with ritualists' cases. Judges took radically different approaches until the House of Lords ruled that, though jurisdictional review would of course sometimes be possible, the innovations could be brought within a broad understanding of 'procedure', a category that was uncontentiously within the ecclesiastical courts' powers to determine.[69] These decisions did not abolish the ancient proposition that common law courts would review ecclesiastical court decisions for lack of jurisdiction, but they signalled, decisively in the end, that the concept of jurisdictional error would be kept narrow so as to maximize ecclesiastical courts' autonomy. How much that owed to the presence by then of regular law lords on the Judicial Committee or to the expanded attendance by bishops cannot be known.

Prosecution in the ecclesiastical courts did not deter the ritualists, instead it begat martyrs. Some were imprisoned, others released by the Queen's Bench for the sort of technical (but jurisdictional) defects in the proceedings that reflected well on nobody.[70] So bishops began to veto prosecutions systematically, and that too led to challenges in the common law courts.[71] Their result was a striking vindication of episcopal authority over the laity—in practice over the associations that sought out ritualists for prosecution. Left to itself, the Queen's Bench would not have conceded that. In both the *Julius* case (under the Church Discipline Act) and the *Bishop of London* litigation (under the Public Worship Regulation Act) it espoused a vision of the Church that accorded citizens a right to a legal form of worship wherever they might be, not to be denied by the discretion of

[68]   *Enraght* v. *Lord Penzance* (1881) 7 App Cas 240.
[69]   *Martin* v. *Mackonochie* (1878) 3 QBD 730, (1879) 4 QBD 697, (1881) 6 App Cas 424.
[70]   *Serjeant* v. *Dale* (1877) 2 QBD 558; *Hudson* v. *Tooth* (1877) 3 QBD 46; *Dale's Case* (1881) 6 QBD 376; *Ex p Cox* (1887) 19 QBD 307 (reversed (1887) 20 QBD 1, restored on jurisdictional grounds (1890) 15 App Cas 506); Machin, *1869 to 1921*, 77–8, 81–6 126–9; Chadwick, *Victorian Church*, ii, 322–5, 348–58.
[71]   Chadwick, *Victorian Church*, ii, 348–9.

any individual bishop.[72] Accordingly it read the former statute as imposing an enforceable duty on the bishop to prosecute and the latter as confining his discretion and subjecting it to review. By contrast the Lords expected parliament to have given bishops a discretion, and duly found it.[73] And though the Court of Appeal, Lord Esher MR particularly, would have inquired whether in reaching his decision the bishop had considered only factors the judges deemed legally relevant, the Lords were adamant that that standard was impermissibly intrusive.[74] It was not that these judges agreed with the bishops' decisions. Lord Bramwell was forthright that Bishop Mackarness had exercised his discretion wrongly in the *Julius* case; but he denied that that gave common law courts an entrance.[75]

As for those ecclesiastical courts, at very much the same time very much the same senior judges, sitting now in the Judicial Committee of the Privy Council, reiterated a principle first announced in 1877, that the Judicial Committee was not bound by its own previous decisions in ecclesiastical cases nearly as strictly as was usual for final appeal courts.[76] That enabled them to endorse the broadchurch policy of accommodating the Anglo-Catholics begun by Archbishop Tait and continued by his successor, Benson, and find ceremonial lawful that previously had been condemned.[77]

The judges in the Queen's Bench had operated on an underlying premise that a national church served its individual members and hence they saw a more important role for secular courts. The decisions of the senior judges, by contrast, supported episcopal authority—unsurprisingly, perhaps, for an episcopal foundation. Similarly the consequence of their decisions, as surely must have been intended, was to throw the responsibility of shaping the established Church back to parliament.[78] All these courts claimed, of course, that they were simply interpreting the statutory texts; but they saw the context very differently.

---

[72] *R* v. *Bishop of Oxford* (1879) 4 QBD 245 (compare the division of opinion in *R* v. *Bishop of Chichester* (1859) 2 E. & E. 209); *R* v. *Bishop of London* (1889) 23 QBD 414 (Pollock B. diss.).

[73] *Julius* v. *Bishop of Oxford* (1880) 5 App Cas 214 (it was a nice touch that the panel contained Lords Cairns, Penzance, and Selborne—spanning the ecclesiastical range.)

[74] *R* v. *Bishop of London* (1889) 24 QBD 213; *Allcroft* v. *Bishop of London* [1891] AC 666.

[75] *Allcroft* v. *Bishop of London* [1891] AC 666; he had heard *Julius* in the Court of Appeal: *R* v. *Bishop of Oxford* (1879) 4 QBD 525.

[76] *Read* v. *Bishop of Lincoln* [1892] AC 240, endorsing *Ridsdale* v. *Clifton* (1877) 2 PD 276. The panel in *Read* included Lord Halsbury.

[77] *Read* v. *Bishop of Lincoln* [1892] AC 240, departing from *Hebbert* v. *Purchas* (1871) LR 3 PC 605.

[78] For bills at this time to curb ritualism and/or remove the bishops' veto on proceedings see Machin, *1869 to 1921*, 234–55, 293–4.

IV

The Army

I N law the army was the king's, or queen's. Politically it had for long been controlled by ministers whose responsibilities had come to be owed to Parliament,
and Parliament had come to control its finance, but the extent of those controls,
the remaining role of the monarch, and the autonomy of the army high command, together formed a persistent if minor theme in Victorian and Edwardian
constitutionalism.[1] The army's prerogative status was used rhetorically from time
to time by army high command as a justification for autonomy from politicians,
and right to the end of our period it was possible for army officers, in times of
stress, to seek solace that the unpalatable orders they anticipated receiving had
the king's personal approval and were not merely the implementation of government policy.[2] Like the Church, the army had its own internal system of law. The
common law judges accorded it a high degree of autonomy, in part as a reflection
and reiteration of its prerogative status, but predominantly because they thought
external adjudication would prejudice good discipline. Though this attitude
was tested in the common law courts from time to time, it remained essentially
unchanged throughout our period.

1. THE CONTOURS OF CIVILIAN CONTROL

Through into the mid-century, command, control, and administration of the
army rested on an eighteenth-century Whiggish construct of checks and balances
that from the late 1820s politicians of both parties would like to have replaced
with a more centralized, rational, and cheaper system.[3] Broadly, command rested

---

[1] G. H. L. Le May, *The Victorian Constitution* (1979), 75–81.

[2] I. F. W. Beckett (ed.), *The Army and the Curragh Incident 1914* (1986), *passim*; P. Jalland, *The Liberals and Ireland* (New York, 1980), 207–47.

[3] This account draws particularly on H. Strachan, *Wellington's Legacy: The Reform of the British Army* (Manchester, 1984); J. Sweetman, *War and Administration: The Significance of the Crimean War for the British Army* (Edinburgh, 1984); H. Strachan, *The Politics of the British Army* (Oxford, 1997); G. Harries-Jenkins, *The Army in Victorian Society* (1977); W. S. Hamer, *The British Army: Civil and Military Relations 1885–1905* (Oxford, 1970); and E. M. Spiers, *The Army and Society 1815–1914* (1980).

with the military through the general commanding-in-chief, usually known as the Commander-in-Chief. For most of the nineteenth century his was in practice a joint appointment by the sovereign and the Prime Minister, for a period or for life, hence apolitical in the sense of not changing with each government. It was a prerogative post, a delegation of the sovereign's own powers as commander of his forces, a designation which, in the eyes of the Commander-in-Chief at least, could be taken to suggest that he owed his duties directly to the sovereign, not to be mediated through politicians.[4] With command went appointment, dismissal, and disciplining of officers, and it was fear of what might happen if those powers fell to politicians that explains why through until at least the 1860s proposals for 'direct subordination of the army to a civilian minister invited violent reaction from the Crown, military figures and political opinion', as John Sweetman put it.[5]

Command, however, had its limits. Disposition of the troops within the realm was controlled by the Secretary at War, later the Secretary of State for War, not the Commander-in-Chief.[6] Civilians also initiated the use of troops to quell civil unrest, in that their deployment depended first upon the magistrates to make a request, and then upon the Home Office (later the War Office, later still the Home Office again) to agree either in the specific instance or by general instructions.[7] How far civilian command extended to the disposition of troops once called out was a delicate question more suited to negotiation than to regulation. Statements of the official position ranged from Home Secretary Gathorne Hardy's in 1869, that disposition was for the officer in command, to Adjutant-General Sir Redvers Buller's in 1893 that if the magistrate was firm the commanding officer must obey, through to an inter-departmental committee's the following year that it was for the magistrate to formally commit the military to action but that thereafter the commanding officer's discretion was absolute.[8] Queen's Regulations (and the inter-departmental committee) stressed that detachments should ensure that a magistrate accompany them, but as was only too evident both to the military and to the committee of inquiry that Buller was addressing, the commanding officer

---

[4]   J. Chitty jun., A Treatise on the Law of the Prerogatives of the Crown (1820), 44–50.

[5]   Sweetman, War and Administration, 21.

[6]   C. M. Clode, The Military Forces of the Crown; their Administration and Government (1869), ii, 331–3.

[7]   Sweetman, War and Administration, 11; Clode, Military Forces, ii, 137–40; S. H. Palmer, 'Calling Out the Troops: The Military, the Law, and Public Order in England, 1650–1850' (1978) 56 Journal of the Society for Army Historical Research 198; F. C. Mather, Public Order in the Age of the Chartists (Manchester, 1959); and F. C. Mather, 'The Government and the Chartists', in A. Briggs (ed.), Chartist Studies (1959), 372–405.

[8]   Quoted by C. Townshend, 'Military Force and Civil Authority in the United Kingdom, 1914–1921' (1989) 28 J. Brit. Stud. 262–92, 265; Report of the Departmental Committee...into the Disturbances at Featherstone..., PP 1893–4 [C. 7234], xvii, 381, 521; Report of the Inter-departmental Committee on Riots, PP 1895 [C. 7650], xxxv, 605, 611.

could not insist. It was in any event a regulation only, and could be waived at will. In the midst of the very serious labour disputes of 1911 Home Secretary Churchill went one stage further by suspending the requirement for an initiating requisition from civil authorities: if the need existed, troops could call themselves out.[9]

Command was limited also by law, in the dual sense that an order had to be lawful before disobedience to it constituted an offence against army discipline— not a matter that was tested often in the nineteenth century—and, more significantly, that it was an almost axiomatic feature of military subordination to civil power that the civil authorities might insist on trying soldiers for offences against the general law irrespective of whether they were also offences against military law.[10] In the nineteenth century this principle was no longer disputed, but it did cause the military some concern when their duty to assist the suppression of civil disturbance exposed them to possible prosecution for the use of excessive force.

One response was to try to shift the moral responsibility to the magistracy: in 1835 the eighteenth-century guideline, that soldiers should fire only under orders from magistrates or in conditions of necessity, was tightened by amending King's Regulations to make a magistrate's order essential. [11] In the much calmer times of 1868 it was changed back again, but in 1893, in the aftermath of fatal shootings during the Featherstone colliery strike, Sir Redvers Buller testified that he could not recall an occasion of 'necessity'.[12] Nonetheless, necessity it presumably was that led the troops freed by Churchill to the shooting of two strikers at Llanelli in 1911. Another response in the 1890s through into the first decade of the new century was from the military for a reduction in personal responsibility when under civil command.[13] It was firmly rebuffed by Secretary of State Haldane, who undertook only to align the King's Regulations more precisely with the austere principles of the common law.[14] The symbol of submission to law was important;

---

[9]   P. Addison, *Churchill on the Home Front 1905–1955* (1992), 149; N. Rose, *Churchill, an Unruly Life* (1994), 78–9.

[10]   *Warden* v. *Bailey* (1811) 4 Taunt. 67 is a rare example of an unlawful order, though on a retrial the soldier's punishment was held lawful: (1815) 4 M. & S. 400; L. Radzinowicz, *A History of the English Criminal Law and its Administration from 1750* (1968), iv, 124–30; Clode, *Military Forces*, i, 159–60, 206–7; ii, 137–53; Townshend, 'Military Force'. The Mutiny Acts had a section preserving the 'ordinary process of law': Palmer, 'Calling Out the Troops', 209. The principle was codified as Army Act 1881, s 41 supported by s 39 (military offence not to surrender suspect to magistrate on request).

[11]   T. Hayter, *The Army and the Crowd in Mid-Georgian England* (1978), 20–35; Radzinowicz, *History of Criminal Law*, iv, 115–57, esp. 141–52.

[12]   Radzinowicz, *History of Criminal Law*, iv, 152; *Featherstone Inquiry*, 521.

[13]   Townshend, 'Military Force'.

[14]   *Select Committee on Employment of Military in Cases of Disturbance*, PP 1908 (236), vii, 365. *Manual of Military Law* (6th edn, 1914), 216–33, states the official view of the law, and includes extracts from Lord Bowen's statement of the law in the Featherstone inquiry and Haldane's undertaking.

in practice it could always be mitigated by prosecutor's discretion and the ability of the Attorney-General to enter a *nolle prosequi*, though this has not been systematically researched.

In the Whig model, command was balanced by administration. In 1820 administration was the function of civilians responsible to Parliament, principally through the Secretary of State for War and Colonies, the Secretary at War, and the Master-General of Ordnance, who was a soldier but a political appointment and member of the cabinet. The administrative side included supply, first of money, which was the business of the Commissariat (accountable to the Treasury, and responsible also for provisions and transport in the field), secondly of equipment, which was the responsibility of the Master-General of Ordnance and the Board of Ordnance, which also controlled the artillery, the engineers, the survey, and, from 1822, the barracks. Political control itself was thus fragmented, indeed all three Secretaries of State were involved in one way or another, plus the Treasury. Demarcation lines were vague, the precise duties of figures such as the Secretary at War and the Judge-Advocate General (another political appointment) difficult to state, and lines of responsibility were sometimes notional. But, as Hew Strachan writes, 'to unify the control of the army would increase its potential power in the state, whether as an independent pressure group applied to Parliament or as a further subject of Parliamentary sovereignty', so the system of dual control survived for fear of the alternatives and proposals for administrative rationalization were always resisted.[15]

Parliament legislated for the army annually, a regular opportunity for intervention in such internal matters as the nature of regimental courts martial and the use of flogging as a punishment. There was temptation also to use the occasion to pursue wider political goals, most spectacularly when the Conservative opposition in 1913 was known to be contemplating, but did not pursue, an amendment to prevent troops being used to force home rule on Ulster.[16] For the most part, however, the main thrust of the annual Mutiny Act was only to make lawful what statute and common law otherwise prohibited. It permitted the sovereign to maintain an army of specified size at home in peacetime, it gave power to enlist soldiers, to billet them, to discipline them outside the procedures of the common law, and to empress transport for their movement within the realm.[17] It did not say how the army was to be composed, commanded, controlled, directed,

---

[15] Strachan, *Wellington's Legacy*, 246.

[16] J. R. Dinwiddy, 'The Early Nineteenth-Century Campaigns against Flogging in the Army' (1982) 97 EHR 308–37; R. J. Q. Adam, *Bonar Law* (1999), 147–52.

[17] From 1830 it included provisions for payment for the quartering of troops, which by convention had previously required their own separate annual Act.

or equipped.[18] During Victoria's reign that territory was contested between Her Majesty's military servants, sometimes buttressing their claims to expertise with assertions of direct allegiance to the Crown—their interpretation of what it meant to fill a prerogative post—and Her Majesty's ministers of state, with their responsibility to Parliament. The Queen herself was a partisan for army autonomy and an opponent of Commons' intrusion. The Commons, of course, controlled the money. Its powers had been greatly strengthened by Burke's Act of 1783, which had brought regimental allowances into the annual estimates and increased the Commons' power of audit, giving ample opportunity for debate.[19]

Largely on the back of concerns about financial control, senior officials collected a medley of statutory powers concerning money and army property, the Secretary at War and the Ordnance Board especially.[20] Administrative reform remained politically difficult even when the shocks of the Crimean war broke much of the resistance to it, and when it came it appeared in the statute book as a minimalist transfer of powers, a matter of mere housekeeping. Neither the Ordnance Board Transfer Act 1855 nor Cardwell's War Office Act 1870 so much as mentioned the Commander-in-Chief, since his directive and command functions flowed from the prerogative rather than statute, though demarcation of his role and his relation to political authority were matters of supreme political concern. They were dealt with by prerogative instruments of one sort or another, studiously vague and not meant for public discussion.[21] In 1854/5 this resulted from the Queen's intervention. In 1854 a separate Secretary of State for War was created, who absorbed the duties of the Secretary at War and assumed responsibility for the Commissariat and the Ordnance department. He also took over control of the militia and other auxiliaries from the Home Secretary, a shift that had previously been resisted on constitutional grounds—that the function of the militia ought to be kept separate from that of the army, and its basis remain local rather than national.

This was a considerable centralization. But through pressure from the Queen the Commander-in-Chief's position remained separate, and he gained command of the military side of the Ordnance Board's activities—the Royal Artillery, the Royal Engineers, plus responsibility for various formerly semi-autonomous

---

[18] So too the Yeomanry Act 1804, 44 Geo. III c. 54, authorized His Majesty to accept and disband corps of volunteers on such terms as he saw fit. In the late 1850s the government could use the power (reluctantly) to instruct lord lieutenants of the counties to raise volunteers, but not to equip them at public expense: I. F. W. Beckett, *The Amateur Military Tradition 1558–1945* (Manchester, 1991), 165–8.

[19] Paymaster-General Act 1783, 23 Geo. III c. 50; Strachan, *Politics of the British Army*, 52.

[20] See e.g. the Schedule to the Secretary at War Abolition Act 1863.

[21] *Copy of Letters Patent etc, PP* 1857–8 (203), xxxvii, 179; *Copy of Order etc, PP* 1868–9 (75), xxxvi, 591.

agencies such as the medical department previously attached to the Board. There was thus a rationalization of both parts of the dual command, but thanks to the Queen there was no unifying board, nor did the Secretary of State have access to military advice other than through the filter of the Commander-in-Chief. The vagueness of the demarcation line with the Secretary of State was to work to the advantage of the Duke of Cambridge, the Queen's cousin, who was appointed Commander-in-Chief in 1856. The force of his personality and his ability to build on his relation to the Queen to reinforce the prerogative basis of the post enabled him to keep matters of command at arm's length from the Secretary of State for the next 40 years.[22] Formally his relation to the Secretary of State for War was settled in 1870, when as part of Cardwell's centralization of all administration under the War Office he accepted that, constitutionally, he advised the Secretary of State and not the Queen, and was responsible to him, though, again, there was no sign of this in the statute. Politics continued as normal, however; reconciliation of military expertise with party government could not be achieved merely by Acts of Parliament or orders-in-council, and in practice the Duke continued to claim a special constitutional relationship with the Queen that freed him from the normal constraints of a subordinate official.

When the Duke was finally persuaded to retire in 1895, his successor was moved into an amorphous supervisory role, the heads of his military sub-departments made directly responsible to the Secretary of State, and formal roles delineated for a War Office Consultative Council and an Army Board to propose promotions, senior appointments, and expenditure, all under the Secretary of State's suzerainty.[23] All this was done, as Gwyn Harries-Jenkins writes, with one stroke of the pen—by order-in-council, with an explanatory memorandum to follow.[24] It was, as he writes, just the first, if much belated organizational step in transforming the traditional military into the new military of an industrialized society. Legally all were simply rearrangements of Her Majesty's servants like many another.

---

[22]   There is a good short account in *ODNB*, 'George, Prince, Second Duke of Cambridge'.

[23]   *Order in Council...defining the duties of the Commander in Chief etc*, 1896 PP (59), li, 483; *Memorandum Showing the Duties of the Various Departments of the War Office, etc, ibid.*, 487.

[24]   Harries-Jenkins, *Army in Victorian Society*, 268–9. The single stroke of the pen that likewise ended the sale of commissions in 1871 was not an exercise of the prerogative but of an implied power in s 7 of the Sale of Offices Act 1809, 49 Geo. III c. 126. That section made sales of commissions lawful only on the terms contained in a royal warrant as it stood from time to time, which Crown lawyers interpreted as enabling the Crown to revoke the existing warrant and not replace it. Since the government's bill to abolish purchase had just been rejected in the Lords the political row was loud, but the culture was not, as it would have been a century later, such as to generate an immediate challenge by way of judicial review. The major point lost, the Lords allowed the passage of the Regulation of the Forces Act 1871, because without it compensation would not be payable: A. Bruce, *The Purchase System in the British Army 1660–1871* (1980), 141.

2. JUDICIAL PROCESS

Civilian Courts

Whoever wielded His Majesty's powers over his military servants was safe from judicial scrutiny. That is not to say that courts were not asked to adjudicate. Dismissal from the service might itself bring litigation, or it might be that the manner or cause left such a stain on an ex-officer's character that he sought redress as a matter of honour, or his concern might be for the consequences, such as loss of a pension, or its amount, or the recovery of accrued pay. Throughout our period, however, the courts were consistent: in Lord Esher's succinct summary, the Crown's military engagements were voluntary on its side (though binding, of course, on the other).[25]

It made no difference that the power concerned might plausibly be seen as resting on statute rather than the prerogative, or that deprivation of a pension or a retirement allowance could be seen as loss of property.[26] Provisions in the Mutiny Act that might have been interpreted as giving an officer a right to pay and allowances once accrued were interpreted instead merely as imposing sanctions upon paymasters.[27] Because the Crown could part with its military servants merely because it wished to, courts held themselves unable to inquire into the grounds of dismissal or the procedures used.[28] The courts treated the Crown's civil engagements as voluntary too, but in military cases they tended to use military justifications and, as will be seen below, their reticence led also to only the most rudimentary scrutiny of courts martial proceedings. In essence, the courts held that if the behaviour complained of affected only a soldier's military status, or the incidents that flowed from that status, redress was to be found solely through military channels, not at common law.[29] 'It would be a very lame application of the doctrine that military men are to dispose of military questions, to apply it only if it is proved by the result of a trial that a military question arises', said Willes J. in 1866.[30]

---

[25]   *Mitchell* v. *R.* (1890) [1896] 1 QB 121n, approving Mathew J.'s reasoning below: (1890) 6 TLR 181. For the corollary, see e.g. *R* v. *Cumming* (1887) 56 LJ QB 287.

[26]   *In re Tuffnell* (1876) 3 ChD 164; *ex p. Roberts, The Times*, 11 June 1879. Since *Flarty* v. *Odlum* (1790) 3 T.R. 68 the same principle applied to half pay.

[27]   *Ex p. Napier* (1852) 21 LJ QB 332.

[28]   *Barwis* v. *Keppel* (1766) 2 Wils. KB 314; *Oliver* v. *Lord Bentinck* (1811) 3 Taunt. 456; *Home* v. *Lord Bentinck* (1820) 2 Brod. & Bing. 130, 8 Price 225; *In re Tuffnell* (1876) 3 ChD 164. See also *Re Poe* (1835) 5 B. & Ad. 681 (and, for proceedings before the Lord Chancellor, *The Times*, 10 May 1834); in *re Mansergh* (1861) 1 B. & S. 400.

[29]   *Sutton* v. *Johnstone* (1786) 1 T.R. 493; (1787) 1 Bro. P.C. 76; *re Mansergh* (1861) 1 B. & S. 400.

[30]   *Dawkins* v. *Rokeby* (1866) 4 F. & F. 806, 837.

Litigants in dismissal cases tried two overlapping ways around that doctrine. First they alleged malice, which in common law theory was a claim that the defendant was acting from personal motives and not within the role allocated to him by law; hence that the harm he did to the plaintiff was not done as a soldier, hence he could not claim the benefit of the exclusive military code. This was the claim in the important eighteenth-century case, *Sutton* v. *Johnstone*, where the defendant was alleged to have maliciously exposed the plaintiff to a court martial.[31] The rule of law implications invoked by the plaintiff had attracted the court of Exchequer, only to be rejected by Lord Mansfield and Lord Loughborough, who feared the potential for making common law courts into general courts of appeal from courts martial. Officers, who alone stood between the subject and a licentious soldiery, were to be protected from harassment in the courts. Nonetheless, there is a case reported at *nisi prius* in 1843 where Cresswell J. nonsuited a plaintiff for failure to plead malice, and another going a stage further in 1865, when Erle CJCP let the question of malice go to a jury, so the principle of *Sutton* v. *Johnstone* may not have been deeply embedded.[32]

The second route to attracting common law attention and the hoped-for sympathies of a jury was to seek vindication for loss of reputation through an action for libel or slander. There was a range of targets, from the bringing of charges, through to things said at courts martial, or at courts of inquiry, or in reports, correspondence or public announcements. Common law privilege attached to courts martial and, so it was held, to the other situations as well, but it would be lost if the defendant had been malicious—and again that issue exposed the plaintiff's senior officers to scrutiny by a jury.[33] In 1806 Mansfield CJCP had echoed *Sutton* v. *Johnstone* in rejecting the applicability of common law altogether, hence ruling that malice could not even be put to the jury, but in 1820 Dallas CJCP was more equivocal.[34] Though in the circumstances of the case he held the communication under challenge to have been absolutely confidential, he left it unclear whether he too was rejecting the applicability of common law or finding a defence within it. In 1859, however, Lord Campbell CJ allowed military proceedings short of a court martial to be examined by a jury for malice, and in 1863 Cockburn CJ did the same, later justifying his view as necessary for the prevention of abuse, declaring his confidence in juries to do justice.[35]

[31] (1786) 1 T.R. 493; (1787) 1 Bro. P.C. 76.

[32] *Freer* v. *Marshall* (1865) 4 F. & F. 485; *Baillie* v. *Evans*, *The Times*, 4 December 1843.

[33] For an example of common law privilege proving decisive, see *Thorburn* v. *Crawford*, *The Times*, 21 November 1884.

[34] *Jekyll* v. *Moore* (1806) 6 Esp. 63, confirmed at (1806) 2 Bos. & P.N.R. 341; *Home* v. *Lord Bentinck* (1820) 2 Brod. & Bing. 130.

[35] *Dickson* v. *Earl of Wilton* (1859) 1 F. & F. 419; *Dickson* v. *Viscount Combermere* (1863) 3 F. & F. 527; *Dawkins* v. *Paulet* (1870) LR 5 QB 119.

It could be argued, then, that there was a shift under way from regarding the affairs of military men as beyond the remit of the common law courts. But Cockburn CJ failed to convince his own court, which endorsed instead a strong version of Lords Mansfield and Loughborough's analysis: relations between military men were wholly governed by an exclusive code of military law founded upon their presumed consent and the need to preserve discipline, a code providing its own means of redress through complaint to commanding officers.[36] In 1875 the Lords declined to decide between these analyses, but from then through to the end of our period the 'code' analysis of military law was orthodoxy up to and including Court of Appeal level.[37] It is possible that judges had a more interventionist attitude in the mid-century—the materials are too scanty to be sure—but if so it was only an interlude.[38]

Maintenance of Military Discipline

This was the legal background against which the maintenance of military discipline should be seen. Responsibility lay with the Commander-in-Chief, aided and regulated by the annual Mutiny Act and the Articles of War the Act authorized. Political responsibility for those codes, however, was the Secretary at War's, later the Secretary of State's, though in the 1860s (if not earlier) much of the work was done by the Judge-Advocate General.[39] Because the Act was annual there was scope for parliamentary pressure, as with attempts to reduce flogging, for example, and that could also impact on the articles, though formally they did not come Parliament's way.[40] At all times control of the formal disciplinary

[36] *Dawkins* v. *Paulet* (1870) LR 5 QB 119 (and see *Dawkins* v. *Rokeby* (1866) 4 F. & F. 806); the reference was to Articles of War 12–13, codified later as Army Act 1881, ss 42–3. The juridical weight of s 42 was meant to be tested in *Woods* v. *Lyttelton* (1909) 25 TLR 665, but the case went off on a pleading point.

[37] Lords: *Dawkins* v. *Lord Rokeby* (1875) LR 7 HL 744; *Fraser* v. *Balfour* [1918] WN 217; Exch. Ch and CA: *Dawkins* v. *Lord Rokeby* (1873) LR 8 QB 255; *Marks* v. *Frogley* [1898] 1 QB 888; *Fraser* v. *Hamilton* [1917] WN 13; see also *Grant* v. *Secretary of State for India in Council* (1877) 2 CPD 445; W. S. Holdsworth, 'The Case of *Sutton* v. *Johnstone*' (1903) 19 LQR 222. In 1919 the law was analysed at length by Macardie J. in *Heddon* v. *Evans*, 33 TLR 642, whose judgment was reprinted unabridged as a booklet with an introduction by R. O'Sullivan (*Military Law and the Supremacy of the Civil Courts*, 1921).

[38] Though the doctrine of *Sutton* v. *Johnstone* made senior officers unpromising defendants, a very lucky and tenacious plaintiff might still get them cross-examined if he could find a journalist to sue for defamatory reporting: *Edmondson* v. *Avery*, *The Times*, 26 January 1911 (consequent upon *Edmondson* v. *Rundle*, *The Times*, 26 March 1903), where the former Commander-in-Chief appeared as witness for the defence.

[39] Strachan, *Wellington's Legacy*, 10; *RC on Courts Martial in the Army*, 2nd Report, PP 1868–9 [4114–1], xii, 141, evidence at 310 (Mowbray), 320 (Cambridge).

[40] Dinwiddy, 'Flogging'.

codes thus rested with civilians—though presumably the War Office worked in co-operation with the military through the Adjutant-General, the head of the Commander-in-Chief's staff.[41]

Eighty years on, and a statutory consolidation later, Sir Henry Thring, parliamentary counsel and architect of the consolidation, saw the 1803 Mutiny Act as the culmination of a long process of replacing prerogative articles of war by statutory authorization, because it was the first to apply to the army wherever it might be.[42] This was a partial and formal truth only. It was true in that the sovereign needed legal authority to create offences punishable by death, flogging, or imprisonment, and to authorize their trial otherwise than by common law procedure, and true in that the most serious offences were delineated in the Mutiny Act, but it was not true that everything in the articles could be sourced back to the Act, save in the most general terms. The Act authorized articles to be made for the discipline of the army, and instructed judges to take notice of them, but that did not entail that articles were valid only to the extent that they elaborated some particular provision of the Act. Instead, as Vernon Lushington, Deputy Judge-Advocate General, explained to a royal commission in 1869, articles were valid unless positively contradicted by the Act, that is, they continued to be treated as though they were made under the prerogative.[43] Though this flexibility rather disconcerted some members of the royal commission, it was good law, or, at least, it was good military law; whether it was good common law was not tested.[44] It was certainly usual practice, as when the Common Pleas, in an unusually interventionist mood, had held that a soldier could not be imprisoned for disobeying an order to attend school, because the order was too remote from military concerns to be lawful, the response had been to amend the articles, not the Act.[45]

The articles duplicated much that was in the Act, and were thus much more compendious. Occasionally the codes were remodelled, in 1829 and again in 1860, and annual amendment seems to have been easy—the Act could be amended to introduce and then to fine-tune a statutory offence of stealing from a comrade, for example, or to validate some enlistments that had broken the rules.[46] The result was an increasing refinement of both codes, the articles in particular

[41]   Strachan, *Wellington's Legacy*, 231, speaks of general liaison between these two officials but research has not investigated its nature or extent in this context.

[42]   *Manual of Military Law*, 13–14.

[43]   *RC on Courts Martial*, 2nd Report, evidence at 156–9.

[44]   *RC on Courts Martial*, 2nd Report, evidence at 228–30, 309–11; (legal nature) T. F. Simmons, *Remarks on the Constitution and Practice of Courts Martial* (5th edn, 1863), 42.

[45]   *Warden* v. *Bailey* (1811) 4 Taunt. 67 (on a retrial the disobedience was proved to have taken on a more serious colour, justifying the imprisonment, so the King's Bench held, even if the order was 'not strictly legal': *Warden* v. *Bailey* (1815) 4 M. & S. 400); Article of War 36.

[46]   Simmons, *Courts Martial* (5th edn), 92–3; *SC on Mutiny Act*, Report, *PP* 1878 (316), x, 263, 313–14.

drawing praise from Cockburn CJ in 1867 for their elaboration and precision.[47] But while courts of common law treated only the Act and the articles as law, officers responsible for prosecuting breaches of military law needed familiarity with the Queen's Regulations, which detailed how the Act and articles were to be applied, and sometimes extended them and plugged their gaps, and with the numerous circulars and general orders issued in the Commander-in-Chief's name; for as the standard text on courts martial explained, in fixing the meaning of the articles the expressed pleasure of His Majesty was decisive.[48] Where all else failed there was still a role for military custom too; it was that, said Vernon Lushington, that must explain commanding officers' summary power of detention, since neither the Act nor the articles did.[49]

The royal commission accordingly recommended a statutory simplification and consolidation of the two codes into one, which materialized a decade later in the Army Discipline and Regulation Act 1879, shortly afterwards amended and further consolidated as the Army Act 1881.[50] Those Acts preserved the power to make articles—the Duke had insisted to the royal commission that they were necessary to preserve elasticity—and with touching constitutional precision that power was vested in the Queen, whereas the power to regulate procedure under the Act was vested in the Secretary of State.[51] It is unlikely that this difference would have affected how new rules of either description were generated within the War Office, but what happened next would differ, for procedural rules had to be laid before Parliament, whereas articles did not. In the event a detailed code of procedure soon covered every aspect of courts martial from arrest to confirmation of sentence, taking in along the way such minutiae as the seating of members and the swearing in of shorthand writers.[52] By contrast no articles were made, and the writers of the official manual that accompanied the reform henceforward

---

[47]   F. Cockburn (ed.), *Charge of the Lord Chief Justice of England to the Grand Jury at the Central Criminal Court in the Case of the Queen Against Nelson and Brand* (1867), 91.

[48]   Simmons, *Courts Martial* (5th edn), viii (from the preface to the 1st edn). For a good example see the evidence of Major-General I. L. A. Simmons to the royal commission, that the 'repeated circulars' on the meaning of 'disgraceful conduct' had been consolidated into a General Order by the Duke of Cambridge in 1856: *RC on Courts Martial*, 2nd Report, evidence at 358. Courts did not regard the Regulations as law: *Bradley* v. *Arthur* (1825) 4 B. & C. 292, 304.

[49]   Simmons, *Courts Martial* (5th edn), 37, 166n; *RC on Courts Martial*, 2nd Report, evidence at 159, 231.

[50]   *RC on Courts Martial*, 2nd Report, 145; Army Discipline and Regulation Act 1879, amended by Regulation of the Forces Act 1881 and then consolidated as Army Act 1881. The Army Act had no force of itself, needing the Army (Annual) Act (replacing the former Mutiny Act) for that, which also amended it from time to time.

[51]   Army Act 1881, ss 69, 71. *SC on Mutiny Act*, Report, 256–7. The power to issue Queen's Regulations was also given by s 71.

[52]   Rules of Procedure 1881, revised and reissued 1893, 1907.

treated the basis of military law as wholly statutory.[53] In that sense military law had lost its distinctive character as a blend of statute, prerogative, and custom.

Military law was administered by courts martial consisting of army officers. From 1829 there were three main types: general courts martial for the trial of commissioned officers and the most serious offences by soldiers, district or garrison courts martial for intermediate offences, and regimental courts martial. The long-term tendency was to diminish that last category: by the introduction of district courts martial in 1829 and by the later expansion of commanding officers' powers of summary punishment.[54] General courts martial were valid only if attended by a judge advocate, who was not a member of the court, but whose role, first by custom later by regulation, included advising the court on law and, until 1860, the settling of the charges to be brought. There was nothing quite like him in other courts, but clerks to justices of the peace were not entirely dissimilar. For important trials the Judge-Advocate General might send his permanent deputy if he had one, more usually he would appoint a judge advocate *ad hoc*; semi-permanent deputies were often appointed for garrisons or campaigns overseas. At first there was the same requirement for district courts martial, but it was quickly removed in 1830, the judge advocate's duties devolving instead to the court's president, its presiding officer.[55]

According to *Simmons on Courts Martial*, the leading text from the 1830s through to the 1870s, it was not unusual for civilian lawyers to have been appointed judge advocates before 1802, when a War Office circular insisted on military men only.[56] Thereafter judge advocates were officers who had trained themselves in military law, or, from the 1860s, had been trained at staff college.[57] By long tradition civilians were not allowed to speak for soldiers at a court martial.[58] There was no bar to a lawyer being the friend the accused was allowed to have with him to suggest questions he might ask or statements he might make—like a twentieth-century *Mackenzie* friend—indeed in the most difficult cases the judge advocate

[53] *Manual of Military Law*, 24.

[54] Two regimental commanding officers invited the royal commission to abolish regimental courts martial (which at that time ran at about 12,000 a year as against 8,000 district and general courts martial) because they only ever established them to secure severer punishment than they could impose themselves, and viewed an acquittal as undermining their authority. They were supported by two former Judge-Advocates General, but not by the Commander-in-Chief: *RC on Courts Martial*, 2nd Report, evidence at 255, 292, 312, 342; contrast the Duke of Cambridge at 318. Their summary powers were consolidated in Army Discipline & Regulation Act 1879, s 46.

[55] Simmons, *Courts Martial* (5th edn), 111n (the dating of the change to 1835 in Simmons's 2nd edn, p. 56n, is corrected in the 3rd, p. 63n).

[56] Simmons, *Courts Martial* (5th edn), 177n.

[57] G. R. Rubin, 'The Legal Education of British Army Officers 1860–1923' (1994) 15 *JLH* 223–51.

[58] A. F. T., Lord Woodhouselee, *An Essay on Military Law and the Practice of Courts Martial* (Edinburgh, 1800), 253.

sometimes had counsel sitting behind him to whisper advice; but the court itself should not have to suffer them.[59]

In the 1860s procedural changes were made to encourage greater legal regularity in courts martial.[60] Judge advocates had gradually shifted into a wholly neutral role at trials, with particular responsibility for summing up the evidence. In 1860 they shed the final vestigal traces of their former function as prosecutors, though the charges might still be drawn in the Judge-Advocate General's office.[61] In 1864 a deputy judge advocate was appointed for a five-year term for each of the three military regions of the British isles, to attend all general courts martial in their region and such district courts martial as they chose or were ordered to. There were possibilities for tension here; even before 1864 *Simmons* worried that courts martial tended to devolve too much to the judge advocate, whereas Thomas Headlam, who was Judge-Advocate General from 1859 to 1866, wanted the judge advocate's relation to the panel at a court martial to be 'almost' that of judge to jury.[62] Army ethos, however, was that trial should be by officers, so there were difficulties in formally elevating a judge advocate over a court's presiding officer, who would usually outrank him.[63] The sensitive balance reached in the 1860s survived through to the end of our period, by which time it was written into the statutory Rules of Procedure: on points of law and procedure 'the court should be guided by his [the judge advocate's] opinion, and not overrule it, except for very weighty reasons'—more an admonition, perhaps, than a rule.[64]

No court martial could pronounce sentence itself. In all cases it had first to be confirmed by the commanding officer of the troops concerned—which once

---

[59]   *RC on Courts Martial*, 2nd Report, evidence at 224, 226, 244, 254, 256, 257, 259, 321 (men of 'questionable propriety'); Simmons, *Courts Martial* (5th edn), 177n, 183–4.

[60]   Simmons, *Courts Martial* (5th edn), 181; *RC on Courts Martial*, 2nd Report, 143 and evidence at 252–3, 311, 318.

[61]   Simmons, *Courts Martial* (2nd edn, 1835), 160, (4th edn, 1852), 180–1, 210, (5th edn, 1863), 181. There are good accounts of judge-advocates' roles in Woodhouselee, *Military Law*, 356–71; W. Hough, *The Practice of Courts Martial* (2nd edn, 1825), 51–3; and V. Kennedy, *Practical Remarks on the Proceedings of General Courts-Martial* (1825), 243–62, who is particularly sensitive to the increasing delicacy of the role for relatively low-ranking judge-advocates now being called upon to display authority that might be taken for insubordination.

[62]   Simmons, *Courts Martial* (5th edn), 175–6; *RC on Courts Martial*, 2nd Report, evidence at 253–4.

[63]   *RC on Courts Martial*, 2nd Report, evidence at 265; Kennedy, *Practical Remarks*, 243–62.

[64]   *RC on Courts Martial*, 2nd Report, evidence at 253, 256, 257; Rules of Procedure (1907 version), 103(F). The admonitory part of the rule continued into an explanation of the consequences in terms that look to have come straight out of *Simmons*. Such seamless blending of rule and educational material in one text would look quite out of place in a statutory instrument governing procedure in a common law court but is typical of the different texture and orientation of military law even after the consolidation.

caused Sir Henry Thring to muse that courts martial might not be courts in the true sense at all—indeed until the consolidation in 1879 no court martial could even pronounce its verdict.[65] For general courts martial confirmation was by the sovereign personally, after receiving advice from the Judge-Advocate General as to whether the court had properly observed the law.[66] Commanding officers also scrutinized the sentence to ensure uniformity; where the sovereign was the confirming officer it was the Commander-in-Chief who advised on sentence. Some of this process was statutory, or partly statutory, but until the consolidation most rested simply on military custom. In addition to the confirmation process, the papers of district courts martial were sent to the Judge-Advocate General's office, where they were scrutinized for error.

These processes were important, but open to different interpretations. In parliamentary debates near the end of our period there was a strong current of opinion that the Judge-Advocate General was meant to protect soldiers from abuse, that this was a necessity given the harsh content of military law, and that it was also why he had (or, by then, ought once again to have) a seat in the Commons so that he could be held accountable. More cautiously, the Secretary of State, Arnold-Forster, added that the Judge-Advocate General also existed to protect courts martial from the illegality of exceeding their statutory powers—which historically has a truer ring to it, even if it had been giving way since the changes in 1860.[67] This debate was the sequel to a decade-long dispute within military administration from about 1876 over the proper role of the Judge-Advocate General, and, particularly, his independence. More will be said about that below, and about the confirmation and revision processes, but first it is necessary to consider the relation between military law and common law in this context, since Arnold-Forster's remark clearly implied that soldiers might seek redress if courts martial did exceed their powers. The general principle, it will be recalled, was that loss of purely military status or the incidents attached to it were not justiciable in a common law court.

There was no appeal from courts martial to common law courts, so the question was how far there might be review. Just as the Mutiny Act was needed to legalize physical punishments by courts martial so common law courts could issue a writ of prohibition to prevent or curtail a court martial that was proceeding on such a matter without jurisdiction. The law on that was clear; but the books

---

[65]   Simmons, *Courts Martial* (5th edn), 113, 117, 268–71; *SC on Mutiny Act*, Report, 365–7. By Army Discipline and Regulation Act 1879, s 54(3) courts martial got a limited power to announce acquittals on the spot.

[66]   The confirmation power could be delegated for troops overseas, and there were separate rules for India.

[67]   *PD* 1904 (s4) 131: 1479–92.

could find no examples of a successful application.[68] The courts could also award damages for the infliction of such punishments without jurisdiction.[69] Again the law was clear—in principle anyway—and, as Arnold-Foster may have known, military textbooks continued to hold it *in terrorem* over convenors of courts martial as an inducement to regularity.[70] Perhaps the books and the revision process were simply very effective, for the most recent mainstream example the books could find dated from 1811, and even that case was decided for the defendant on a retrial.[71] All but one of the others concerned impulsive behaviour towards civilians, and even the exception arose from breach of the rules when transporting a military prisoner from India to England rather than the conduct of his court martial itself.[72] Research in the War Office papers may perhaps uncover threats of litigation that were then settled, but there is no trace of them in the books.

Actions would be available for jurisdictional error only, which, apart from the obvious instances of purporting to apply military law to someone not legally subject to it, would include sentences imposed by courts improperly constituted. Though this was not a risk that *Simmons* had emphasized, after 1881 the Rules of Procedure ordained that the first step in any court martial must be a formal inquiry into and confirmation of its own constitution; but whether that resulted from a bad experience or just from increasing scrupulosity is not known.[73] If a court martial was properly constituted, the charge and the sentence within its jurisdiction, its members had nothing to fear from the common law. They were obliged to apply common law rules of evidence, and the royal commission in 1869 questioned its witnesses closely about how far the confirmation and revision

---

[68] *Grant* v. *Gould* (1792) 2 H. Bl. 69; *Sutton* v. *Johnstone* (1786) 1 T.R. 493, (1787) 1 Bro. P.C. 76; *Manual of Military Law*, 122. In 1892 the Queen's Bench contemplated issuing a prohibition against carrying out a sentence, but the applicant opted for a *certiorari* instead and lost on the facts: *In re Brown*, *The Times*, 3 November and 12 November 1892.

[69] *M'Intyre* v. *Layard*, *The Times*, 1 February 1825 (£200 awarded for imprisoning a soldier to keep him incommunicado from his co-conspirator in a rations fraud, pending the latter's court martial).

[70] *Barwis* v. *Keppel* (1766) 2 Wils. K.B. 314; Clode, *Military Forces of the Crown*, i, 176; Simmons, *Courts Martial* (5th edn), 175, 180; *Manual of Military Law*, 129–34, 630–1.

[71] *Warden* v. *Bailey* (1811) 4 Taunt. 67, (1815) 4 M. & S. 400. *Mann* v. *Owen* (1829) 9 B. & C. 595, a case on the naval discipline Act, may perhaps be the reason why, its analysis showing how well these statutes were drafted to catch behaviour that the authorities might wish to penalize.

[72] *Goodes* v. *Wheatly* (1808) 1 Camp. 231; *Glynn* v. *Houston* (1841) 2 Man. & G. 337; *Ricketts* v. *Walker* (1841) cited in *Manual of Military Law*, 130n. The exception is the Allen litigation, the sequels to *Allen's Case* (1861) 7 Jur (NS) 234: *Allen* v. *Duke of Cambridge*, *The Times*, 11 July 1861 and *Allen* v. *Boyle*, *the Times*, 4 March 1861 (against the governor of the military prison), cited in Simmons, *Courts Martial*, 283n, where Lieutenant Allen was awarded damages of £200 and £50 respectively for having been unlawfully returned to England to serve his sentence for manslaughter, rather than being left to serve it at Agra.

[73] Rules of Procedure clause 22 (1907 version); *Manual of Military Law*, 41–2.

processes went to ensure that they did.[74] But on the one reported occasion that a common law court had been invited to take an interest it had declined.[75] Prohibition might still have been a plausible remedy for unlawful admission or refusal of evidence, if sought between trial and confirmation, as might *certiorari*, if it lay at all to courts martial. In 1861 Cockburn CJ and perhaps Wightman J. indicated, obiter, that *certiorari* would lie to a court martial held in England if its sentence affected life, liberty, or property, though Cockburn CJ may later have thought better of it, and there is one reported instance from 1892 of the Queen's Bench issuing a rule *nisi* for a *certiorari* on an allegation a court martial lacked jurisdiction.[76] But that seems to be all.

In contrast to their treatment of summary convictions by magistrates—the other, and major, exception to the common law principle that trials should be by jury—eighteenth and nineteenth-century judges never laid down, or even had occasion to lay down, what must go into the 'record' of a court martial to make it lawful, or even whether it had a record in the technical sense.[77] So irregularities had no redress at common law, which is to say that common law judges never took it upon themselves to analyse exactly how common law principles should apply or be modified in the range of contexts covered by courts martial. And, for all that the texts might say about actions for damages, the judges said next to nothing about what errors were jurisdictional either, save that the person tried must be truly subject to military law. This was consistent with their general refusal to allow questions of military status to be litigated in the common law courts, and its consequence was to throw Judge-Advocates General back on to general principle and their own invention.

Because the common law intruded so little into the concerns of military law it is hazardous to make too much of the contrast between the two systems—there is no way of telling what common law judges would have made of the niceties of courts martial if they had been minded to extend their supervisory jurisdiction to them. Cornelius O'Dowd, for example, who as Deputy Judge-Advocate General should have known better, attributed a former Judge-Advocate General's heightened scrutiny of convictions for desertion to his insistence on a common

[74]   *RC on Courts Martial*, 2nd Report, evidence at 163, 235, 237.

[75]   *Grant* v. *Gould* (1792) 2 H. Bl. 69, which also took a relaxed view of a possible disparity between the charge brought and the conviction made.

[76]   *In re Mansergh* (1861) 1 B. & S. 400 (Compton and Blackburn JJ did not consider what would have been the position if the court martial had been in England rather than India). However, in *ex p. Roberts*, *The Times*, 11 June 1879, Cockburn CJ said that *certiorari* would not lie against the Judge-Advocate General, who had the papers in his custody, because he held them as a mere servant of the Crown. The allegation in *In re Brown*, *The Times*, 3 November (rule *nisi*) and 12 November 1892 (rule discharged on the facts) was of *autrefois acquit*.

[77]   *ex p Roberts*, *The Times*, 11 June 1879, implies that it did not.

law interpretation of the offence—but since precisely the same interpretation can be found earlier in *Simmons*, classically a book of military law, the supposed contrast evaporates.[78] Nonetheless, there was felt to be a general difference, encapsulated in the single word 'technicality', which the military deplored. The Duke of Cambridge's model court martial would be a court of honour under legal regulation but free from legal technicality.[79] Less idealistically, and with more sense of the difficulty, *Simmons* summarized it thus:

> As courts martial professedly discard mere technical formalities, it is…the more necessary to distinguish where form is essential to justice, and in this view, if in the practice of courts martial the spirit of the forms of civil courts of judicature can…be laid hold of without entailing the necessity of adherence to the subtile [sic] distinctions made by lawyers, a great point will be gained: and it must be under this restriction that precedents in the practice of civil courts of justice may be sought for, or admitted.[80]

No doubt this 'technicality' was one source of military men's antipathy to lawyers. It must underlie, though it does not wholly explain, the serious dispute that G. R. Rubin has shown to have existed between the Commander-in-Chief's department and the Judge-Advocate General in the decade from about 1876 over which had final authority to set aside verdicts of courts martial for irregularity.[81] Certainly the dispute was occasioned and subsequently fuelled by decisions of the Judge-Advocate General that deserved the epithet of 'subtile distinctions' and which departed from previous understandings of how military law worked.[82] In its strong form the Judge-Advocate General's claim was that he was akin to a judge, hence his decisions were beyond rejection by the Commander-in-Chief or appeal to the Attorney-General; in its weak form he claimed immunity only from the Commander-in-Chief. The military men took the opposite view: that they should be able to reject the Judge-Advocate General's decisions if harmful to military discipline, or, in the weak version, that they should have recourse to the Attorney-General if they thought him mistaken in law.

The difficulty is in knowing whether the dispute should be seen primarily as part of a general push by military men against civilian influence in military

---

[78] *SC on the Mutiny Act*, Report, 335–6; Simmons, *Courts Martial* (5th edn), 70–2.

[79] *RC on Courts Martial*, 2nd Report, evidence at 321.

[80] Simmons, *Courts Martial* (5th edn), 153 (in the context of considering what precision is needed for a charge; it is clear from his tone that he has a didactic purpose).

[81] G. R. Rubin, 'Parliament, Prerogative and Military Law' (1997) 18 *JLH* 45–84.

[82] The one that brought matters to a head in 1883 arose because the Judge-Advocate General thought that as the power conferred by s 48(9) of the Army Act to choose the members of a court martial was vested in a nominated officer it was not delegable (Rubin, 'Parliament, Prerogative and Military Law', 68) whereas army practice was to read it subject to Army Act 1881, s 171, which allowed delegation wherever it had been customary. That this particular delegation *was* customary can be seen from Simmons, *Courts Martial* (5th edn), 159–60.

administration, or as (over-)reaction by the military to expansionism by the Judge-Advocate General, or as the culmination of a long and unwelcome juridification of courts martial.[83] The first is well attested in general terms in the writings of the military historians.[84] In this particular context the Judge-Advocate General fitted awkwardly into Cardwell's centralization, remaining a political appointee with direct access to the sovereign, seemingly accountable to nobody but Parliament. It was not self-evident that his role in revising courts martial would not be better accomplished by a departmental official, who might be better located in the Commander-in-Chief's department where all the other army personnel matters were conducted. As for expansionism by Judge-Advocates General, that can easily be found in the evidence of former holders of the office to the 1869 royal commission that the position had been evolving towards that of a final appellate authority, and that that should be its destiny.[85] This was a big claim, and it is easy to see why it would be resisted, for there would be no checks: it had never been suggested that common law courts might review decisions of the Judge-Advocate General, nor had they even laid down a body of law that the Judge-Advocate General might follow—essentially it was a claim that the interpretation of military law was uniquely for the Judge-Advocate General.[86]

As for juridification of courts martial over a long period, that also can easily be established. Modern research has not investigated the process, but *Simmons* and the witnesses to the 1869 royal commission suggest that it was continuous rather than episodic. Regimental courts martial were required from 1805 to take oaths binding them to decide on the evidence and in accordance with the articles and the Act, an innovation that the Duke of Wellington subsequently fingered somewhat accusingly as converting them from courts of honour into courts of law.[87] District or garrison courts martial replaced the upper level of regimental

---

[83] Similarly the military men's claim that military discipline should take priority over law had overlapping functional and jurisdictional elements: that the Judge-Advocate General really was encouraging men to doubt their officers; and that as military law was a necessary part of military discipline it fell within the remit of the Commander-in-Chief's department ('discipline, training, recruiting, education, appointments and promotion': Hamer, *British Army*, 7n).

[84] Hamer, *British Army*, 9 and *passim*; Spiers, *Army and Society*, 177–200.

[85] *RC on Courts Martial*, 2nd Report, evidence at 312. This may explain the appointment of R. J. Phillimore in 1871, who was not an MP but the judge of the High Court of Admiralty. On his resignation normality was restored by the appointment of A. S. Ayrton MP.

[86] Simmons, *Courts Martial* (2nd edn), 136 had long since noticed that a judge-advocate was not responsible to any court of justice for the opinion he might give.

[87] Simmons, *Courts Martial* (5th edn), 166–8 (the oath was not completely assimilated to that in other courts martial until 1829: *ibid.*, 116); *RC on Military Punishments*, Report, *PP* 1836 [55], xxii, 1, 355 (an aside, perhaps, rather than a developed comment). Contrast eighteenth-century regimental courts martial: G. A. Steppler, *British Military Law, Discipline, and the Conduct of Regimental Courts Martial in the later Eighteenth Century* (1987) 102 *EHR* 859–96.

courts martial in 1829, ensuring that the officers who were to act as judges for the more serious offences that marked those courts' jurisdiction would not all be drawn from the same regiment, and applying to them the same centrally directed procedural requirements that attached to general courts martial.[88] Then there were the smaller testaments to the existence of something akin to a rule of law mentality: the order of the commanding officer at Simla in 1828 setting aside a conviction because one member of the court had participated in the verdict despite having been absent through illness for part of the hearing; the War Office circular in 1829 discouraging the bringing of 'disgraceful conduct' charges if more specific ones would lie; the decision by both the Judge-Advocate General and the confirming officer in 1830 to set aside a conviction for disgraceful conduct where the charge had not provided adequate detail; the War Office circular, also in 1830, that the officiating judge advocate must give the prisoner notice if it was intended to bring his previous convictions before the court; the setting aside of a well-merited conviction in 1839 because the judge advocate had not been properly appointed; and the decision by the Commander-in-Chief at Bombay in 1841 to set aside a conviction because the judge advocate had doubled as interpreter for the court, creating a possibility of bias.[89] In addition, there were the reforms in the 1860s that recast judge advocates as wholly neutral referees and advisors on the law, enjoined presidents of courts martial to adopt that same neutral posture in cases where an advocate general was not present, and established the three deputy judge advocates with regional responsibilities—a reform that both reflected and encouraged increased adherence to legal form.[90] Finally, the royal commission heard how the Queen's Regulations stipulated in exact detail who had what speaking rights at a court martial, and in what order.[91]

So, harsh though its content certainly was, military law clearly did come to embody the procedural virtues. It is not fully known, however, whether they were forced upon a reluctant military or whether they met easy acceptance. Some changes clearly did come from outside, as with the introduction of oaths into regimental courts martial.[92] Some officers did regret that law was so prominent and would have preferred courts martial to have remained as courts of honour.[93] Some evidence to the royal commission suggests that courts of inquiry were sometimes used instead of courts martial and that they did function as courts of honour, save that they forwarded their findings to the commanding officer rather

---

[88] Simmons, *Courts Martial* (5th edn), 110–13.
[89] *Ibid.*, 205, 93–4, 156–7, 177–8, 185n; and see his 2nd edn, 58.
[90] *RC on Courts Martial*, 2nd Report, evidence at 199, 318.
[91] *Ibid.*, evidence at 160.
[92] Dinwiddy, 'Flogging'.
[93] *RC on Courts Martial*, 2nd Report, evidence at 256.

than reaching a decision themselves.[94] Very few verdicts or sentences sent back to courts martial for reconsideration on proper legal lines were altered by the reconvened panel, which is why the royal commission sought a change of practice to allow confirming officers to make more of the decisions themselves.[95] Yet the royal commission also heard that commanding officers commonly sought the Judge-Advocate General's opinion before confirmation or when revisiting a conviction (the dispute Rubin documents began with just such an occasion), and the Adjutant-General ordered that before regional commanders confirmed any sentence of a district court martial the papers be sent to the regional deputy judge advocate for scrutiny.[96] The Duke of Cambridge wanted the revision system kept, though that was in 1869, and he had in mind the extreme cases— courts martial were capable of 'such extraordinary things, and sometimes such really unaccountable things'—not yet the technicalities that he was soon to find so unpalatable.[97]

It is certainly possible to see constitutional issues at stake in the dispute between the Judge-Advocate General and the department of the Commander-in-Chief, as some of the participants claimed. But a more modest analysis from within the public service was provided by the government's draftsman, Sir Henry Thring, to the select committee considering the consolidation of the Mutiny Act and the articles of war in 1878. He could not see his way to conferring on the Judge-Advocate General a statutory power to quash court martial decisions so, for him, it should remain just an 'administrative question'—that is, a matter of convenience for the Secretary of State to decide.[98]

In 1886 the Secretary of State did decide: the Judge-Advocate General's decisions on points of law should be final.[99] Whether that meant final only in relation to the Commander-in-Chief's department or free also from recourse to the Attorney-General does not appear, but it is probably significant in that respect that in 1893, when the office of Judge-Advocate General ceased being tenable by a politician, it was given to a sitting judge, Sir Francis Jeune, the President of the Probate, Divorce, and Admiralty Division. Because Jeune was not an MP, however, and because he drew no salary as Judge-Advocate General, his advice to the sovereign could not be questioned in the Commons, even though most of the

---

[94] *RC on Courts Martial*, 2nd Report, evidence at 221 and *passim*.

[95] *Ibid.*, 147–8 (2 out of 375 reversed, 48 punishments reduced).

[96] G. D'Aguilar, *Observations on the Practice and the Forms of District, Regimental, and Detachment Courts Martial* (Dublin, 6th edn, 1866), 244–6; for implementation in the Northern Region see *RC on Courts Martial*, 2nd Report, evidence at 163, 260–1.

[97] *RC on Courts Martial*, 2nd Report, evidence at 319.

[98] *SC on Mutiny Act*, Report, 371.

[99] Rubin, 'Parliament, Prerogative and Military Law', 72–4.

work was in fact done by his salaried deputy, Sir John Scott. So when Scott's death in 1904 coincided with Jeune's retirement (and continued anxiety about army reorganization after the South African war) there was further reconsideration designed to restore accountability.[100] Rather than re-creating the political office that had been abolished in 1893 the government turned it into a civil service post with responsibility to advise the Secretary of State, who in theory would take the final decisions (as in theory the sovereign had previously done) and answer for them in the Commons.[101] Whether the military men could, did, or ever wanted to intervene between the Judge-Advocate General's advice and the Secretary of State's decision is not known.

Without a study of what faults Judge-Advocates General over the years did and did not find vitiated a court martial, it is difficult to tell whether the 'subtile distinctions' *Simmons* feared did come to infest military law and, if they did, why. Their interventions were never numerous, but there is some evidence that they did increase.[102] Formally the 1879–81 consolidation did mark a great change. As the new oath taken by members of courts martial testified, military law was now contained in the Army Act alone, not in articles of war, not in custom.[103] The Rules of Procedure did not cover quite everything—the manner in which a confirming officer should consider commuting or mitigating sentence, for example, was detailed in the Queen's Regulations—but they did include in one code the practice that could previously have been found only in the pages of *Simmons*.[104] Military law had become more open to scrutiny.

How far the practice of courts martial changed is a different matter, and one that is almost completely unexplored. The consolidation made provision for civilian lawyers to appear for either side at general and district courts martial, but with restrictions on some of the questions they might ask and with a stern warning to show respect when cross-examining the accused's senior officer.[105] In 1918 Percy Winfield, sometime barrister, Cambridge law tutor, officer in the Cambridgeshire Regiment, published his impressions of the courts martial he

---

[100] *PD* 1904 (s4) 131: 1479–92. Sir John Scott (1841–1904), once a judge at Bombay, creator of a system of western-style justice for Egypt, had been appointed because cases built up during the South African war. He was generally regarded as very able.

[101] *PD* 1905 (s4) 148: 1448; 152: 492; Rubin, 'Parliament, Prerogative and Military Law', 84n., 108.

[102] In 1872 the Judge-Advocate General's office quashed 21 out of 7,238 proceedings (Rubin, 'Parliament, Prerogative and Military Law', 62); in 1904, out of 8820 proceedings scrutinized it quashed 45 outright, 75 in part, and found 'irregularities not necessitating interference' in 184—in addition military authorities had themselves quashed or withheld their confirmation from 69 convictions (*PD* 1905 (s4) 148: 770).

[103] Army Act, s 52.

[104] *Manual of Military Law*, 605.

[105] Rules of Procedure 87–94 (reprinted in *Manual of Military Law*).

had attended during the war.[106] By then, as he delicately pointed out, the experience of officers long familiar with the ethos of courts martial had been lost. What he portrayed was more an inquisitorial inquiry than a trial, where (if he sat) the deputy judge advocate kept the court punctiliously to the straight and narrow, where lawyers and their niceties were out of place, but where, Winfield wrote, fairness and the best traditions of British justice were upheld—he was not writing of field courts martial. This does sound like the system Thomas Headlam had aspired to in 1869, and, if so, the question that remains unanswered is whether it had become so with the consolidation of 1879–81 or only with the war; and whether Winfield was wholly accurate, perhaps.

[106]   P. H. Winfield, 'Courts-martial from the Lawyer's Point of View' (1918) 34 *LQR* 143–51.

V

Local Government

1. OVERVIEW

At the beginning of our period there was local authority, exercised through the key Hanoverian agencies of the justices of the peace and the officers of the parish vestries. In the counties this was the rule of landed property in legal form. Most urban areas with municipal corporations would have a separate magistracy; many had their own quarter sessions that excluded the county justices. In these towns rule, so far as it went, was usually in the hands of a local oligarchy of the more substantial tradesmen. Overlapping the municipal corporations were local improvement commissioners. These had been created under myriad local Acts of Parliament at the behest of the propertied citizens of each place, with functions that in a different political culture might have been exercised by the corporations. Improvement commissions, not usually the corporations, had been the vehicle for the eighteenth-century wave of town improvement. They were the prototype modern local authority.

At the end of the nineteenth century there was instead a network of local authorities of more or less stereotyped legal form, to a contested degree the agents of central government, more usually possessing considerable local autonomy and a legitimacy based on local election. This section of this volume traces that transition of institutional form and the alternatives that from time to time were possible. The driving force was population increase and its result-ing urbanization, which both redistributed political power and impacted on the perception of what counted as a problem to be solved. That gave primacy to the legal forms of the cities and towns. The institutions of the biggest city by far developed differently, however, so London will need a section to itself. Often, not quite always, the timing and the details turned on nice calculations of party political advantage.

The sharpest break with the past came with the radical reform of municipal corporations in 1835. It was not, however, an imposition of a standard form for all places, rather it was a reform of the then-existing corporations and a prescription for corporations that might be created for new places in the future. The new legal form was the product of two different ideas. One was the royal commissioners' pious hope in 1835 that reformed municipal corporations would become agents of good local government. The other was the politicians' fear that reformed corporations might have independent political strength. The combination fashioned an institution capable of development only as a bearer of statutory powers. The reform split the new borough councils off from borough magistrates (and their statutory administrative powers), and at the same time deprived the new councils of the power and independence that property ownership had brought their unreformed predecessors, in large measure at least. The new councils were left much like improvement commissioners, usually dependent on the power of Parliament to equip them with the wherewithal to alter their environment. Save for a requirement that all boroughs be policed, the initiative was with each corporation individually to seek a role or not, as it chose. That had dramatic results during the municipal renaissance of the 1860s.

In the 1830s and 1840s there were centralizers who did think much more in terms of creating a uniform system for the whole country. It was a system, however, that saw local government as local agency for a national authority, responsible upwards to the national community not outwards to the locality. Of the two local agencies they created, the boards of guardians and the local boards of health, the former came closer to the centralized ideal, but still fell well short. In 1858, however, the centre's control was much reduced, marking a return to valuing local initiative. The result was both a proliferation of agencies and a patchiness of cover that offended the results-oriented professionals, who were always more concerned with outcomes than with process. Their prescription was the public health legislation of the 1870s. That instituted a reasonably uniform network of local agencies—the sanitary authorities (which included the municipal councils and the surviving improvement commissioners)—and a more powerful central department, but still left considerable choice to the localities.

A rival model for reform failed for lack of political enthusiasm. It was process-oriented, and would have integrated all the major local agencies—parishes, guardians, sanitary authorities, borough councils, and counties—into something resembling a coherent pattern of representative and accountable local government for its own sake. That was the Liberal minister George Goschen's bill in 1871, one of only two attempts in the nineteenth century to systemize the whole spectrum of local government. The other also failed, in that its attempt to arrange local government into a hierarchy where an upper level supervised a lower was rejected by the localities and supported only weakly by the government departments whose powers would have been devolved. That was the Conservatives' proposal in 1888 and 1889, better remembered for what survived: the creation of county councils in place of the administrative side of county quarter sessions and the creation of a top tier of boroughs, the county boroughs, which possessed both borough powers and county council powers.

All these nineteenth-century creations were elected, which was their most novel and distinctive feature. By the late 1880s, however, the property-privileging franchises of the electors for the guardians and for the sanitary authorities lagged behind the parliamentary franchise, for men, that is. The Liberals finally removed plural voting in 1894. The sanitary authorities became district councils and, since this was a Liberal measure, a democratic gesture of largely symbolic importance was made in the face of the country gentlemen by the creation of parish councils and parish meetings in the rural areas.

In the result there was a network of distinctively modern institutions with the same legal features. They had legal personality, elected councils, salaried employees, committee structures, and were responsible to their ratepayers through law in the guise of judges and auditors as well as through election. The various types sometimes overlapped but essentially they existed in parallel, jealous of their boundaries both territorial and legal.

2. MUNICIPAL CORPORATIONS

Charters, Size, and Status

The municipal corporation came to be the legal form through which local self-government of cities and large towns was realized, its legal basis stemming from the Municipal Corporations Act 1835. Few new charters had been granted in the eighteenth century, and the Act created no new corporations for populous places. It listed 178 incorporated boroughs sufficiently distinguished by population size or continuing parliamentary representation to be worth reform, omitting a further 70 or 80 investigated by the commissioners, either as too trivial for modernization, or irrelevant to its purposes, or simply because they were overlooked.[1] The corporation of the City of London was the only substantial body to evade reform, the commissioners' separate report for it being delayed until after the reforming moment had passed.[2]

The Act's new regime covered about 60 per cent of the towns outside London listed as significant by modern urban historians, increasing to comfortably over 70 per cent by 1851 as towns took advantage of the Act's new procedure for

---

[1] *List of municipal corporations not incorporated under the Municipal Corporations Act 1835*, PP 1875 (441), lx, 647; RC on municipal corporations not subject to the Municipal Corporations Act, Report, *PP* 1880 (c. 2490), xxxi, 1.

[2] See below, pp.472–4.

petitioning the Crown for advancement to corporate status.[3] By 1854 the list of new corporations had grown to 26, all but four of them northern or midland industrial centres of rapid recent growth.[4] By 1888, when the Local Government Act made significant changes to municipal boroughs, it had become 105.[5] But 24 of that 105 were small, even tiny, ancient boroughs, their corporations left unreformed in 1835 but belatedly allowed into the fold consequent on the Municipal Corporations Act 1883, and a further six were small places that had taken a similar restorative step earlier.[6] Subtracting these leaves some 75 major towns or cities which between 1835 and 1888 had attained the highest status available to them.

If population size is used as a rough indicator of a town or city's significance, then borough status correlates reasonably well. The 1891 census shows that 112 of the 141 urban areas with a population exceeding 25,000 were chartered, very nearly 80 per cent.[7] Many of the unincorporated settlements in that size bracket were situated uncomfortably close to a neighbouring giant, well on their way to being swallowed up—places such as Tottenham, Handsworth, Walton-on-the Hill, and Moss Side. At the same time incorporation had a social cachet to it that must have made it seem quite proper that the aspiring new growth centre of Southend-on-Sea should seek, and even be granted, the status that brought it aldermen and his worship the mayor, while the South Wales growth area of Ystradyfodwg (as the Rhondda was then known), more than six times its size, should not. Southend was just one of 30 new boroughs created between 1888 and 1902, places taking their first step on the road to the coveted status of county borough that would bring them autonomy from the newly formed county councils.[8]

---

[3] P. Clarke (ed.), *The Cambridge Urban History of Britain*, (Cambridge, 2000), ii, Ch. 2 'England', and Ch. 3 'Wales' charts some 132 significant towns from early modern times through to the early nineteenth century, of which 78 are scheduled in the 1835 Act and a further 17 were incorporated by 1851. Those omitted tended to be either only marginally significant or to be boom towns without an established ruling class—Merthyr Tydfil being the extreme example.

[4] D. Fraser, *Power and Authority in the Victorian City* (Oxford, 1979), 150–1, which, however, omits Halifax (1847/8); *Incorporated Towns, Abstract of Returns*, PP 1840 (610), xli, 513, 514. Since, strictly, the 1835 Act, and other Acts referring to it, applied only to the corporations listed in its Schedule, further legislation was needed to assimilate post-1835 creations: Municipal Corporations Act 1853, ss 2, 3.

[5] *Return showing boroughs with populations of 50,000 etc*, PP 1888 (316), lxxxvi, 1.

[6] The 24 can be identified by comparing *Return of boroughs etc*, PP 1888 (316), lxxxvi, 1 with the 1883 Act; *RC on Municipal Corporations not subject to the Municipal Corporation Acts*. The six are Yeovil, Lewes, Aberavon (a borough by prescription), Honiton, Conway, and Hedon. Taunton (1877), Burton-on-Trent (1878), and Bangor (1883) had previously had corporations which had become defunct.

[7] *Census of England and Wales 1891 vol. II*, PP 1893–4 (c. 6948–1), cv, 1.

[8] *Return giving the name etc of every place which has applied for a municipal charter since 1888*, PP 1902 (284), lxxxviii, 341. Southend became a borough in 1892 and a county borough in 1914.

Inherited Legal Attributes

The post-1835 municipal corporation was a hybrid of the prerogative form that preceded it and its eighteenth-century alternative, the statutory local commission. The prerogative form itself was pregnant with what turned out to be unrealized possibilities. It gave continuing legal personality, an inherent power to make regulatory byelaws, and full property-owning capacity. Those powers and attributes were essentially common law matters, for late eighteenth-century law was clear: charters could curtail corporations' common law powers but could not extend them, no matter how wide their purported grant.[9] From that common law foundation an organic conception of local government entities could have developed, had there been the incentive. Corporations could then have developed their byelaws in step with the changing needs of their towns simply by virtue of their common law powers. Judges would have become the arbiters of validity after the event, upholding those 'reasonable' byelaws they thought properly fell within the changing ambit of municipal government allowed to corporations, just as they had long done with such well-established municipal functions as the regulation of local trade.[10] Where finance was needed for town improvements the critical step would have been validation of the power to levy rates. Historians do point to corporations rating in the early eighteenth century, though they are rarely explicit about its legal basis, which to modern eyes seems obscure.[11] If claims to levy rates without statutory authority had become widespread their resolution would have been a difficult matter, because for a charter to have empowered a rate on occupiers would have infringed the important post-revolution principle that the Crown cannot tax without parliamentary consent, charters owing their legal force to the prerogative and hence subject to that limitation.[12]

However, these possibilities latent in corporations' common law personality were stillborn, perhaps for two reasons. First, eighteenth-century municipal

[9] S. Kyd, *A Treatise on the Law of Corporations* (1793–4), ii, 109; J. W. Willcock, *The Law of Municipal Corporations* (1827), 95.

[10] Kyd, *Corporations*, ii, 102, 119, 131–8; Willcock, *Municipal Corporations*, 95, 100, 105, 141–2, 159. See below, pp. 518–21.

[11] M. Falkus, 'Lighting in the Dark Ages of English Economic History', in D. C. Coleman and A. H. John (eds), *Trade, Government and Economy in Pre-industrial England* (1976), 263, and see 264, 266; J. Innes, 'Local Acts of a National Parliament', in D. Dean and C. Jones (eds), *Parliament and Locality, 1660–1939* (Edinburgh, 1998), 23, 35–6; S. and B. Webb, *The Manor and the Borough* (1908), 703–4n. Bristol, used by the Webbs as an example, had long had statutory powers. Lynn, another example, had power by charter to rate for sea defences (*RC on Municipal Corporations*, 1st Report, *PP* 1835 (116), xxvi, 1, 312), which would have been valid at common law if seen as part of a bargain with the Crown for new privileges—compare *Lyme Regis Corporation* v. *Henley* (1834) 2 Cl. & F. 331.

[12] Kyd, *Corporations*, ii, 110; *Rutter* v. *Chapman* (1841) 1 M. & W. 1, 63 (Williams J.), 74 (Patteson J.).

corporations drifted into oligarchy. In many parliamentary boroughs they had become devices for securing party or factional control of the House of Commons, entailing a serious loss of local mana. Secondly, local elites had found superior solutions to local problems through Parliament. Statute was superior because Parliament's sovereignty was boundless, undoubted, and pre-emptive. General Acts of Parliament confirmed for towns with their own exclusive quarter sessions the power to levy a rate 'in the nature of a county rate' covering such functions as the maintenance of gaols, houses of correction, and some bridges, and sundry purposes ancillary to the Poor Law.[13] Local Acts of Parliament by their hundreds gave new powers, stipulated new procedures, and delineated new boundaries.[14] They too empowered the levying of rates, and enabled rates to be mortgaged to create a capital fund for development. They created new local offences and the procedures for their enforcement, obviating by-laws and avoiding their uncertainties: no thatched roofs, no projections over the highway, no football in the street, no beating carpets in the street after 8 a.m....and so on by unbroken succession into the clauses Acts of 1847.[15] Where once a corporation by-law might have required householders to light their street frontages with lanterns on dark evenings, now statutory regulation empowered the provision of rates-funded gas lamps.[16]

In towns where local opinion thought it appropriate the new powers were conferred on the municipal corporation. Much more usually local Acts gave power to *ad hoc* commissioners, though the mayor was often a commissioner *ex officio*, the Acts were often promoted by the corporation or with their assistance, and sometimes the commissioners were simply the councilmen in different guise.[17] Often, however, a portion of the commissioners was elected, or the status was open to any propertied resident.[18] Local Acts were not, as lawyers have sometimes been tempted to see them, weak or experimental substitutes for general legislation. They were modernized equivalents of royal charters, negotiated among local property owners and rooted in their consent.

[13] 13 Geo. 2 c. 18, s 7 extending 12 Geo. 2 c. 29; 55 Geo. 3 c. 51; *Weatherhead* v. *Drewry* (1809) 11 East 168; V. D. Lipman, *Local Government Areas 1834–1945* (Oxford, 1949), 5–15.

[14] J. Innes, 'Local Acts', 26–30.

[15] Falkus, 'Lighting', 267; Webbs, *Manor & Borough*, 145–6 (Wisbech); 412–15 (Penzance), 610 (City of London); Town Police Clauses Act 1847, 10 & 11 Vict. c. 89 ss 21–9, esp. s 28; Towns Improvement Clauses Act 1847, 10 & 11 Vict. c. 34, ss 99–108.

[16] Falkus, 'Lighting', generally. Some corporations instead took a common law approach, using corporation funds to buy the lights, then inducing frontagers to contract for their lighting and maintenance in lieu of their direct obligation.

[17] e.g. Newcastle-under-Lyme: *RC on Municipal Corporations*, PP 1835 (116), xxv, 1, 546.

[18] J. Innes and N. Rogers, 'Politics and Government 1700–1840', in Clark, *Cambridge Urban History*, ii, 536.

Corporations' general and inherent power to make by-laws was thus marginalized, though never entirely superseded. The Municipal Corporations Act 1835 did preserve an apparently unlimited power to make byelaws for the 'good rule and government of the borough, and for prevention and suppression of all … nuisances …'.[19] That led the Webbs to believe that corporations thereby acquired general powers, perhaps overlooking that the maximum penalty authorized by the section was just £5.[20] But the section was no more than a statutory variant of the common law or charter form, to be interpreted incrementally by the judges. Their instinct always was to treat the general words as descriptive rather than empowering, and to require a 'nuisance' or 'police' justification before holding a byelaw valid.[21] The 1835 Act did not herald a turning back to a common law conception of a corporation as a general governing entity. Powers and functions would continue to derive from Parliament, by general or local statute.[22]

Legal Attributes From 1835

As is well known the 1835 Act's immediate genesis was primarily political. Its aim was to break the mainly Tory, Anglican, oligarchic control of corporations so as to redistribute their patronage and, particularly, reduce their influence in parliamentary elections. That was a matter of continuing concern to the Whigs, given the relatively narrow reform of the parliamentary franchise in 1832 and the importance of local officials in the conduct of elections. The decision having been made, the Whig government appointed a royal commission to 'collect information respecting the defects in [the] constitution' of corporations, and then sought to legislate on the basis of its findings, only to be forced into compromise by Tory resistance in the House of Lords.[23] In the result there were to

---

[19]   5 & 6 Will. IV c. 76, s 90.

[20]   Webbs, *Manor & Borough*, 754–5. The real significance lay in s 91, making summary procedure generally available for prosecution of breach of byelaws. Section 14 abolished discriminatory trading by-laws.

[21]   *Elwood* v. *Bullock* (1844) 6 Q.B. 383; *Everett* v. *Grapes* (1861) 3 *LT* (NS) 669; *Johnson* v. *Mayor of Croydon* (1886) 16 QBD 708; *R* v. *Justices of Truro* (1884) 51 *LT* 92; *Munro* v. *Watson* (1887) 51 J.P. 660. After a particularly restrictive interpretation of the power in *Strickland* v. *Hayes* [1896] 1 QB 290, from which no appeal was possible, a special Divisional Court was convened, resulting in the well-known decision in *Kruse* v. *Johnson* [1898] 2 QB 91. But even that required an 'annoyance' before the byelaw would be valid. A warning from the Local Government Board to local boards about the public health legislation is apt: 'authorities cannot legally assume the power of making byelaws for carrying out the general objects of the Act'. *Local Government Board*, 7th Annual Report, *PP* 1878 (c. 2130), xxxvii(1), 1, 195.

[22]   See, generally, Innes, 'Local Acts'.

[23]   Fraser, *Power and Authority*, 3–21; W. Thomas, *The Philosophic Radicals* (Oxford, 1979), 264–8, 278–91.

be elected councillors for the corporations listed in the Act, who in turn would elect a mayor and aldermen. There was to be a ward system for boroughs with a population exceeding 6,000. The reformed corporations were given a statutory internal structure, a new property regime, and a new duty to police their area.

The franchise was confined to men who were householders resident within seven miles of the borough and who had paid the poor rate for 2½ years, excluding occupiers of mere tenements. How that operated in any particular borough would turn on its practice of rating or not rating small cottages, and on whether the local vestries could require landlords to pay in place of tenant. In places practising such 'compounding' the landlord's name would appear in the rate book, and the tenant would be disfranchised. In practice it was a franchise empowering the rate-paying middle class rather than the lower orders, men rather than women (an unusual feature for a local franchise at that time). Given those limitations, however, it was egalitarian, in that unlike the more widespread of the other local ratepayer and property-owner franchises created in the first half of the century it did not give burgesses multiple votes in proportion to the rateable value of their property.[24]

The franchise broadened after an adoptive Act of 1850 brought in many compounding tenants, the process seemingly being completed when the municipal franchise was extended to them all in 1858.[25] That settlement was disrupted, however, by the treatment of compounding in the 1867 Reform Act and not finally put to rest until 1878.[26] Female ratepayers were enfranchised in 1869 by an amendment slipped through without fanfare, though the Queen's Bench rather spoilt the effect by holding that married women still could not qualify, being ineligible to hold landed property at common law.[27] But for all these extensions, the theory of the franchise remained that it should be held by ratepayers only, even after the third Reform Act had abandoned that principle for parliamentary elections. Even the further shift towards democracy in 1888, by inclusion of the occupiers of premises worth £10 a year, excluded some parliamentary electors.[28]

---

[24] Elections for vestries (in most cases), boards of guardians, and local boards (of health) allowed multiple votes. Those for Commissioners of Lighting and Watching under general legislation, and for vestries under Hobhouse's Act (just a few, nearly all in London) did not.

[25]* 13 & 14 Vict. c. 99; Municipal Franchise Act 1858.

[26] B. Keith-Lucas, *The English Local Government Franchise* (Oxford, 1952), 55, 64–74.

[27] Municipal Franchise Act 1869; *R* v. *Harrald* (1872) LR 7 QB 361; L. Holcombe, *Wives and Property* (Oxford, 1983), 128, 212. The Act's main object was to reduce the qualifying period from two-and-a-half to one year.

[28] County Elections Act 1888, adding the £10 occupier from the (parliamentary) Registration Act 1885 to the existing simple ratepayer franchise of the Municipal Corporations Act 1882; Keith-Lucas, *English Local Government Franchise*, 74–5.

The new councils did not take over all that the unreformed corporations had enjoyed, far from it. On Tory insistence they were not to have judicial functions. Corporations lost their power of nomination or appointment to the borough bench, that being henceforward vested solely in the Crown—save that the mayor remained as a magistrate. Boroughs with (or wanting) a separate quarter sessions must have a Crown-appointed Recorder.

The Act also significantly curtailed corporations' common law capacities. The first significant reduction was that they lost control of borough charities.[29] This too was a Tory amendment forced on the Whigs, whose initial preference had been for the elected councils to choose trustees for borough charities each year.[30] Facing criticism that that would perpetuate political manipulation of charitable distributions, the Whigs then proposed a form of election designed to avoid a simple political replication of council elections: burgesses would elect but could cast only half as many votes as there were places to be filled.[31] Either proposal would have recognized the organic link between a corporation and its charities, many of which had been under corporation control for a century or more, some having always been of that character, others having been transferred when attrition of private trustees threatened a charity's survival. Recognizing that link might have led to substantive changes to the law, to develop a separate category of publicly administered local charities. There was, however, no incentive to look behind the condemnations of the municipal corporations commissioners and the reports of the charity commissioners on which they relied. The charity commissioners' role was to treat the law of charity as a given and as a constant, investigating charities to see that they measured up to its requirements, not whether the law of charity measured up to the requirements of the populations it served.[32] Nor were the municipal corporations commissioners interested in mitigating the 'defects' and 'abuses' they found.

Yet what the commissioners saw as diversion of charitable funds to unauthorized purposes could as well have been seen as reasonable municipal management in changing times. To pay ancient small dole charities producing, say, £5 a year into the poor's rate might well have been the best use for them, unlawful though it was. To sell the site of a derelict almshouse and use the proceeds for

---

[29] Municipal Corporations Act, s 71; Fraser, *Power and Authority*, 164; Innes and Rogers, 'Politics & Government', 572. Strictly speaking, it was the mayor, aldermen etc, individually, who were the trustees.

[30] *PP* 1835 (277), i, 497, 516 (cl. 56), 565 (cl. 63); *PD* (1835) (s3) 29: 232–44; *PD* (s3) 30: 645.

[31] Election of Charitable Trustees Bill, *PP* 1836 (307), i, 569; *PD* 1836 (s3) 34: 201–3; 35: 314–42, 638–49.

[32] R. Tompson, *The Charity Commission and the Age of Reform* (1979). Their final (32nd) report contains some procedural recommendations: *PP* 1837–8 (108), xxv, 1.

some similar purpose might benefit all concerned, though it would be unlawful because in their charitable capacity the trustees had no power to sell, even though they would have had if they had held the land in their corporate capacity. And if a school in a borough turned out to have been over-endowed, and its trustees were the mayor and so on, it is not self-evident that an expensive Chancery-initiated *cy-près* scheme for the surplus would be either more useful or more in accordance with the founders' intentions than an informal borough-initiated 'diversion' for other municipal purposes.[33] Similarly, it was common for corporations to pay charitable income into their general funds, but make compensatory payments out—perhaps not every year, but then perhaps of a greater amount in some years.

The charity commissioners were clear that such distributions could not mitigate the breach of trust, and that rather than being compensation they should be seen as voluntary donations. Lord Brougham, important in establishing both sets of commissioners, agreed, holding judicially that even if a corporation, after mixing charitable funds, spent them all on public purposes, without personal benefit, it was still a serious breach. Though 'it might relieve them from moral imputation, [it] could not exculpate them, in the eye of the law, from the charge of abusing their trust'.[34] Liability was strict, not excused by reasonableness or good faith. 'Charity' thus remained homogenous, to be administered by trustees deemed to be blinkered to any wider sense of responsibility. The only goal the Whigs had was to eradicate the use of charitable expenditure for political ends, of which there was considerable evidence.[35]

So Lord Lyndhurst's amendment to the Municipal Corporation bill was nicely calculated: the existing (mostly Tory) trustees should remain in office until the general measure of reform of charities administration promised by Lord Brougham should have been considered and carried. If no such reform was carried, the existing trustees should go out of office on 1 August 1836, to be replaced by whomever the Lord Chancellor should appoint—which is what happened.[36] The Chancellor's power was delegated to the Chancery Masters, whose discretion

[33]   These examples are taken from reports of the Charity Commissioners: *PP* 1826 (383), xiii, 1 (Lancaster, Bridgwater); 1828 (374), xi, 1 (Ipswich, Worcester); 1829 (19), vii, 1 (Nottingham), (349), viii, 1 (Newark). Compare *A.G.* v. *Kell* (1840) 2 Beav. 575.

[34]   *A.G.* v. *Mayor of Newbury* (1834) 3 My. & K. 647; *A.G.* v. *Mayor of Newbury* (1838) C.P. Coop. 72; see also *A.G.* v *Bailiffs of East Retford* (1832) 2 My. & K. 275.

[35]   e.g. *RC on Municipal Corporations*, App., *PP* 1835 (116), xxv, 1, 427 (Coventry); Webbs, *Manor & Borough*, 654–6 (Ipswich).

[36]   Municipal Corporations Act, s 71. Only creative interpretation by Parke B. saved this poorly drafted section from incoherence: *Doe d. Governors of Bristol Hospital* v. *Norton* (1843) 11 M. & W. 913; *Christ's Hospital* v. *Grainger* (1846) 16 Sim. 83, 102. For bills after 1835 seeking special status for borough charities, see Tompson, *Charity Commission*, 207–8.

was usually unchallengeable, whose proceedings went unreported, and whose initial decisions were thought to be obviously politically partisan.[37] At least sometimes Masters appointed new councillors as the first set of trustees after 1836, but those appointees stayed in office whatever subsequently became of the composition of the borough council. The council did not even have standing to propose new trustees to fill vacancies—not that there was anyway a principle that the original number of trustees should be kept up.

The organic link between corporations and what had been 'their' charities was thus broken, one result being that the new representative councils lost the management of ancient borough schools. Dealings a century or more old were revisited and found to have been unlawful. Litigation, local Acts of Parliament, and judicially brokered settlements completed the separation.[38] When, in 1853, a new Charity Commission was invented with power to propose schemes for charitable consolidation and rationalization, no different provision was made for corporation charities.

Nor could municipal corporations be as free with their own property after 1835 as they had been before. At common law municipal corporations were legal persons able to own property as they wished, subject only to the need for a licence in mortmain to hold land. They could mortgage, lease, or sell their corporate estate. They were free to spend their income as they saw fit. Doncaster spent £20,000 on its racecourse to generate further income, and lent extensively to turnpike trustees to improve local roads. Kidderminster mortgaged its market site and future tolls to finance market redevelopment. Carlisle put £1300 into shares in the local canal company and subscribed for £1000-worth of shares in the Newcastle to Carlisle railway, not, it explained, as a profitable speculation but to benefit the city, just as Lynn had spent £400 on shares in a local bridge.[39] For these and the scores of similar instances recorded by the municipal corporation commissioners in 1835 no statutory authorization had been needed.[40] For radicals and for

---

[37] 'Lord Chancellor Cottenham' (1851) 15 (s2) *LM* 280–8, at 287.

[38] *In re Norwich Charities* (1837) 2 My. & Cr. 275, affirmed *sub nom. Bignold* v. *Springfield* (1839) 7 Cl. & F. 71; *R.* v. *Mayor of Warwick* (1846) 15 LJ QB 306, 8 Q.B. 926, 930n; *In re Worcester Charities* (1847) 2 Ph. 284; *A.G.* v. *Corporation of Ludlow* (1848) 2 Ph. 685; *In re Shrewsbury Charities* (1849) 1 Mac. & G. 84; *In re Shrewsbury School* (1849) 1 Mac. & G. 85; *A.G.* v. *Corporation of Ludlow* (1849) 1 Hall & Tw. 216; *S.G.* v *Corporation of Bath* (1849) 18 LJ Ch 275; *A.G.* v. *Corporation of Newcastle* (1842) 5 Beav. 307; *A.G.* v *Corporation of Shrewsbury* (1843) 6 Beav. 220; *A.G.* v. *Corporation of Boston* (1846) 9 Jur. 838; *A.G.* v *Corporation of Plymouth* (1845) 9 Beav. 67; *In re Huntingdon Municipal Charities* (1859) 27 Beav. 214. See also *R.* v. *Mayor of Norwich (In re Beckwith)* (1842) 11 LJ QB 246.

[39] *RC on Municipal Corporations*, App., *PP* (116) 1835, xxv, 1, 69, 94, 473; xxvi, 1, 332.

[40] Statute might prohibit, of course: Corporate Property (Elections) Act 1832, 2 & 3 Will. IV c. 69, prohibited payments towards the expenses of candidates in parliamentary elections, a foretaste of what was to come.

the commissioners the independence that property brought was a problem. As the commissioners complained

Few Corporations admit any positive obligation to expend the surplus of their income for objects of public advantage. Such expenditure is regarded as a spontaneous act of private generosity, rather than a well-considered application of public revenue, and the credit to which the Corporation, in such cases, generally considers itself entitled, is not that of judicious administrators, but of liberal benefactors.[41]

Lord Eldon had ruled that municipal corporations did not hold their property on trust. 'In all corporations,' he said, 'there is somewhere vested an absolute, uncontrollable, power and discretion, without appeal', with the consequence that (the mainly Tory) corporations might lawfully spend their resources for the benefit of their political supporters.[42] By contrast the commissioners condemned as erroneous the 'strongly rooted opinion that the property of the corporations is held in trust solely for the benefit of the corporate body only, distinguishing that body from the community with which it is locally connected'.[43] From that premise careless management and extravagant expenditure became a 'defect' of proper public concern, even where the corporation had not succumbed to 'the opportunity afforded to them of obliging members of their own body, or the friends and relations of such members', and even when uninfluenced by 'party and sectarian purposes'.[44] Indeed some such notion as a public trust was essential to explain why subjecting corporations to the direction of elected councils would not sufficiently remedy the abuses the commissioners found.[45]

So the reformed boroughs with their elected councils were not to have the same freedom to deal with borough property that their oligarchic predecessors had enjoyed. Instead the 1835 Act and its amendments over the next two years limited their powers and subordinated them to an element of central control.[46] Sale or mortgage of any part of the corporate estate would be lawful now only with Treasury approval and after public advertisement in the borough. The terms

---

[41] *RC on Municipal Corporations*, Report, *PP* 1835 (116), xxiii, 1, para. 111.

[42] *Mayor etc of Colchester* v. *Lowten* (1813) 1 Ves. & B. 226, also *A.G.* v. *Corporation of Carmarthen* (1805) G. Coop. 30. There was no inherent common law limitation either: *Weatherhead* v. *Drewry* (1809) 11 East 168, 175; *Mayor of Southampton* v. *Graves* (1800) 8 T.R. 590 (corporation under no greater liability to disclose its books and papers to a litigant than a private person, reversing recent cases to the contrary; modified in *Harrison* v. *Williams* (1824) 4 Dow. & Ry. KB. 820, 3 B. & C. 161). Eldon's decision was uncritically adopted by subsequent judges (albeit when it no longer mattered); see e.g. *A.G.* v. *Mayor etc of Liverpool* (1835) 1 My. & Cr. 171, and *Davis* v. *Corporation of Leicester* [1894] 2 Ch. 208.

[43] *RC on Municipal Corporations*, Report, *PP* 1835 (116), xxiii, 1, para. 112.

[44] Report, paras 110, 111.

[45] Webbs, *Manor & Borough*, 731–7.

[46] 5 & 6 Will. IV c. 67, ss 94–7, 139; 6 & 7 Will. IV c. 104.

and maximum duration of leases were stipulated, subject again to variation only with Treasury consent. Advowsons held by corporations before the 1835 Act were to be sold, an important element in facilitating Dissenters' membership of borough councils. But the destination of the proceeds was not entrusted to the new councils: they were to be invested in government stock and the income carried to the borough's general account, renamed by the statute 'the borough fund'.

All the borough's income was to be paid into the borough fund. Expenditure from it was to go first on paying pre-1835 debts, then on the purposes of the 1835 Act itself—policing, especially, which was the major function expressly designated for councils, plus the costs of running elections, for example.[47] Councils could levy a rate for these purposes, should the corporation's income from its property be insufficient. Only if the borough fund produced a surplus after meeting these expenses without a rate having to be levied could the council spend the income for 'the public benefit of the inhabitants and the improvement of the Borough'—and not only 'could', but according to section 92 'shall'. That enacted the commission's broad notion of the nature of borough property.

In 1837 Lord Cottenham ruled that the structure of section 92 and its words of general purpose were such that 'in the hands of the new council the capital was unalienable, and the whole income was subject to certain public trusts'.[48] In the first cases Chancery judges allowed new councils to recover corporate property spirited away by their predecessors in the period between the Act's passing and the new councils' election.[49] But the reasoning entailed a litigable trust relationship between a council and its individual ratepayers that not only applied to the portion of the borough fund comprised of income from corporate property but extended also to that raised from levying rates.[50] It made no difference that these modern councils were chosen by a representative electorate, nor that council accounts were subject to audit by independent and elected auditors, nor that the Acts provided for appeals against rates, nor that they contained various explicit remedies that might plausibly be supposed to be exclusive, though all these points were argued. In the eyes of nearly all Chancery judges then and since, a private remedy for misuse of the fund was needed and none was as effective as Chancery's full jurisdiction to prevent or redress breach of trust, with its wide range of orders and declarations. Corporations were thus assimilated to statutory commissioners, whose rates funds had already been subjected to the

---

[47] Municipal Corporations Act, s 92.

[48] *A.G.* v. *Aspinall* (1837) 2 My. & Cr. 613, reversing Langdale MR (1836) 1 Keen 513; Webbs, *Manor and Borough*, 488–9.

[49] *A.G.* v. *Aspinall* (1837) 2 My. & Cr. 613, reversing Langdale MR (1836) 1 Keen 513; *A.G.* v. *Wilson* (1837) 7 LJ Ch. 76; see Fraser, *Power and Authority*, 55–8, 158.

[50] *Parr* v. *A.G.* (1842) 8 Cl. & F. 409, confirming 4 My. & Cr. 17, reversing 2 Keen 190.

same trusts analysis by Lord Eldon, in a case which counsel introduced as by far the most important he had known since beginning in Chancery practice.[51]

So even after a council had met its statutory responsibilities its spending decisions could be challenged at law, in Chancery based on a trusts analysis of section 92, or from 1837 in the Queen's Bench by *certiorari*, made possible by a rare statutory extension of that writ.[52] To be lawful, expenditure of a borough's surplus had to be for 'the public benefit of the inhabitants and the improvement of the Borough', and it is probable that judges always considered themselves the arbiter of that standard, despite some early dicta suggesting that the words be treated as saving all that would have been lawful before the Act.[53] Soon partisan expenditure of the sort Lord Eldon had previously found to be beyond judicial control was held unlawful.[54] In the next generation expenditure on conspicuous display features in the law reports—to be disallowed, except when it was associated with royalty.[55] By the end of the century serious policy choices were in issue. In one case Lord Shand indicated that he would not think it lawful for a council to spend a borough fund surplus on taking sides in legal contests between the police and brewers over public house licensing, in another Romer J. held that payment towards a university college's rent was not a public benefit.[56]

All this cramped boroughs' inherent spheres of activity and marked the freedom they had lost. But courts were careful to resist the argument that a surplus could be spent only on objects positively authorized by statute, so assimilation with statutory commissioners was not complete.[57] Moreover, with skill a wealthy

---

[51]   *R* v. *Brown* (1818) 1 Wils. Ch. 323, 1 Swan. 265. Counsel was John Leach, elevated to the vice-chancellorship later that same year. The logic was worked out through *A.G.* v. *Heelis* (1824) 2 Sim. & St. 67; *A.G.* v. *Mayor of Dublin* (1827) 1 Bli. N.S. 312; *A.G.* v. *Eastlake* (1853) 11 Hare 205; and *A.G.* v. *West Hartlepool Improvement Commissioners* (1870) LR 10 Eq 152.

[52]   7 Will. IV & 1 Vict. c.78, s 44; see below, pp. 498–9.

[53]   *A.G.* v. *Mayor of Norwich* (1848) 12 Jur. 424, 16 Sim. 225 (Shadwell VC). Section 92 was repealed and substantially re-enacted by Municipal Corporations Act 1882, ss 140–3.

[54]   *R* v. *Mayor of Leeds* (1843) 4 Q.B. 796 (Williams J.: 'It is nothing to the borough whether Potts or Richardson were elected'); *R* v. *Mayor of Bridgwater* (1839) 10 Ad. & El. 281; *R* v. *Paramore* (1839) 10 Ad. & El. 286.

[55]   *A.G.* v. *Mayor of Batley* (1872) 26 *LT* 392; C. Rawlinson, *The Municipal Corporations Act* (7th edn, 1881), 131n (celebrating visit by ex-President General Grant); *A.G.* v. *Corporation of Blackburn* (1887) 57 *LT* 385; *A.G.* v. *Corporation of Cardiff* [1894] 2 Ch. 337. The last two cases suggest that *ad hoc* inflation of the mayor's stipend was a conventional device for funding public celebrations. Chitty LJ's defence of his *Blackburn* decision in *A.G.* v. *Tynemouth Corporation* [1898] 1 QB 604, 620 indicates some embarrassment.

[56]   *A.G.* v. *Tynemouth Corporation* [1899] A.C. 293, 306; *A.G.* v. *Corporation of Cardiff* [1894] 2 Ch. 337.

[57]   *A.G.* v. *Mayor of Newcastle* (1889) 23 QBD 492, affd [1892] AC 568 (but Newcastle's 15-year contract for a toll free bridge, payable out of its surplus, was enforceable only to the extent that a surplus actually arose each year); *Leith Magistrates and Council* v. *Leith Harbour and Docks Commissioners* [1899] AC 508.

borough could preserve its surplus for such extra-statutory purposes even as it took on new functions. It could word its local acts to direct new developments to be funded out of a separate account—usually an 'improvement rate'—rather than out of the borough fund. This was a strategy employed by Newcastle, for example.[58] On the other hand, public general Acts could decree that specific new functions should be charged to the borough fund, and commonly did.[59]

Becoming the Dominant Form

In the result municipal corporations became less like private legal persons and more like statutory commissioners, but with a robust combination of a continuing legal personality and a statutory, representative, constitution. Policing powers were conferred by the 1835 Act, which terminated the watching and corresponding rating powers of local statutory commissioners in the scheduled boroughs. But commissioners' other powers were unaffected. Commissioners might still be more like a town government than the new borough councils were. The 1835 Act allowed commissioners to transfer their statutory powers to corporations by agreement, but after ten years fewer than a quarter had done so, and commissioners remained in every town that had had them before 1835.[60] Rivalry continued, sometimes with both institutions increasing their powers by acquiring new local Acts, though Parliament's preference became increasingly clear as it granted some individual councils comprehensive new improvement Acts that ended the authority of commissioners within their boroughs.[61]

When the issue of the public health of towns came to a head in the 1840s, Tory and Whig instincts diverged. Lord Lincoln's bill for the Tories in 1845 would have introduced town commissioners very much under central executive control even though elected by ratepayers. Borough councils would be reduced to sending nominees to afforce this board of commissioners, as would statutory commissioners in towns that had them, and the justices.[62] Lord Morpeth's bill for the Whigs in 1847 would have created town commissioners only in unincorporated

---

[58]   J. F. Gibson, *The Newcastle-upon-Tyne Improvement Acts and Byelaws 1837 to 1877* (Newcastle-upon-Tyne, 1881), p. lx, and *A.G.* v. *Mayor of Newcastle* (1889) 23 QBD 492, aff'd [1892] AC 568.

[59]   e.g. Education Act 1902. The effect on a borough's ability to spend its income was raised in the Newcastle litigation, above, but not decided.

[60]   *Abstract of the number of local trusts transferred to municipal corporations*, PP 1846 (713), xl, 55.

[61]   Leeds (1842): E. P. Hennock, *Fit and Proper Persons* (1973), 186–91; Liverpool (1846): B. D. White, *A History of the Corporation of Liverpool* (Liverpool, 1951), 41–3, 9 & 10 Vict. c. cxxvii; Macclesfield (1852): C. Hamlin, *Public Health and Social Justice in the Age of Chadwick* (Cambridge, 1998), 282, 15 Vict. c. x; and compare Birmingham (1851), a post-1835 incorporation: Hennock, *Fit and Proper Persons*, 19, 29–30, D. Fraser, *Urban Politics in Victorian England* (1976), 102.

[62]   Sewerage and Drainage of Towns Bill, PP 1845 (574), v, 363.

towns, one-third nominated by the Crown, two-thirds elected. In the corporate towns the borough councils would become the beneficiaries of what in essence would have been a huge empowerment measure.[63] Despite this sharp difference, the rival bills shared an assumption that lasted through until the 1870s, that institutions were not to be created generally, but only where particular need was shown. That is how local Acts of parliament were obtained, the petition alleging the need, the parliamentary committee or local inquiry validating the claim. In Lincoln's bill, and Morpeth's as first drafted, the trigger would have been an inquiry instituted by a centrally appointed inspector.

In the Public Health Act 1848 as it eventuated, the trigger was a petition from 10 per cent of the ratepayers followed by a local inquiry and an inspector's report. In a corporate town, if the inspector recommended the Act's adoption, and provided that he accepted the borough's boundary as the appropriate area for the Act, the borough council would simply become the local board of health.[64] In other towns existing statutory commissioners might likewise be given the Act's powers and responsibilities. Elsewhere a local board of health would be elected on a franchise allowing the wealthy up to six votes each as ratepayers and up to six as owners, markedly different from the 1835 Act's franchise.[65]

Significantly, if a town incorporated after the formation of a local board of health, the new borough council would supersede the board.[66] The Local Government Act 1858 took this one step further, effectively securing for councils the power to become sole governors of corporate towns. It provided that within their boundaries henceforward they alone could adopt its very extensive range of powers, and do it by simple resolution, albeit one requiring a two-thirds majority.[67] Finally, as the pendulum swung back towards centralized co-ordination and supervision, the Public Health Act 1872 authorized the newly created Local Government Board to dissolve any remaining improvement Act districts within boroughs and transfer their powers to the borough councils.[68] By 1878 only 49 improvement Act districts remained, dwindling to 28 a decade later, and only Cambridge retained both a corporation and statutory commissioners.[69]

---

[63] Health of Towns Bill, *PP* 1847 (244), i, 457.

[64] 11 & 12 Vict. c. 63, s 12. The jurisdictions remained separate, so the council had two different legal capacities. Where the inspector recommended an area extending beyond the borough's boundary a joint board was constituted; for an example of one in operation see B. S. Trinder, *Victorian Banbury* (Chichester, 1982), 95–7.

[65] 11 & 12 Vict. c. 63, s 20.

[66] 11 & 12 Vict. c. 63, s 33.

[67] Local Government Act 1858, ss 12, 15.

[68] Section 22(2).

[69] *Return...for each county...the names of the municipal boroughs [etc]*, PP 1878 (74), lxiv, 397; *Return of the counties [etc]*, PP 1888 (333), lxxxvi, 11.

Getting a Charter

Most of the larger improvement Act districts were among the towns that eventually petitioned to become chartered boroughs with their own borough councils. The 1835 Act sketched out the procedure, which was codified in 1877, but it stipulated no particular criteria.[70] The Privy Council would send down an inspector to hold an inquiry, scrutinize the petitions, determine where the weight of rate-paying opinion lay, assess what advantages a corporation might have over any existing statutory commissioners, what costs would ensue, and so forth—all matters of interpretation and judgement. In the early years, at least, petitioning for a municipal corporation often drew counter-petitions from traditional urban ruling élites and those who feared the likely outcome of the elections that would follow incorporation.[71] Wealthy men might petition against incorporation because they stood to lose the benefits of the multiple votes allowed by the Public Health Act and, often, local improvement Acts.[72] Women might petition against incorporation because the franchise under the Public Health Act or, commonly, local Acts was gender blind, unlike the municipal franchise before 1869.[73]

Assessment was entirely a matter for the Privy Council's discretion. Only when it decided to include in some new corporations' territory either a little more or a little less than the area covered by the supporting petitions was legislation hurriedly needed to make quite sure that that was lawful.[74] Still, the process was essentially simple, and soon came to have the added encouragement that a newly created municipal corporation could lawfully recover the cost of acquiring its charter by charging it to the borough rate—though that was something some boroughs had already assumed they could do.[75] A generation later the Privy Council was given power to endow newly created corporations with the powers

---

[70]   Municipal Corporations Act 1835, s 141, repealed and replaced by Municipal Corporations Act 1837 (1 Vict. c. 78), s 49; Municipal Corporations (New Charters) Act 1877, re-enacted as Municipal Corporations Act 1882, ss 210–18.

[71]   Fraser, *Power and Authority*, 82–6, 130–4, 139–40. The judges' contribution was to rule that there was a prior question of jurisdictional fact—whether the Crown had indeed received a petition qualifying as one from 'the inhabitant householders', as the Act required—which was ultimately one for a local jury: *Rutter* v. *Chapman* (1841) 1 M. & W. 1.

[72]   Brighton: *Return of towns etc*, PP 1852–3 (267), lxxviii, 335, 337; *Report... on petition of inhabitant householders of town of Brighton*, PP 1854 (231), lxiii, 563; Reigate: *Report... into expediency of granting charter of incorporation to borough of Reigate*, PP 1864 (77), l, 341; Municipal Corporations Act, s 9; Public Health Act 1848, s 20; Commissioners Clauses Act 1847, s 24 (which could be excluded from any particular local Act, of course).

[73]   Brighton, above; Municipal Franchise Act 1869.

[74]   Municipal Corporation (Incorporation) Acts 1848 and 1850, 11 & 12 Vict. c. 93, 13 & 14 Vict. c. 42. Compare *Return of Petitions for Charters*, PP 1852–3 (267), lxxviii, 335. Brighton needed its own validation Act: Incorporation of Brighton Act 1855.

[75]   13 & 14 Vict. c. 42, ss 2–3 (1850).

of any previous local authority in its area, including statutory improvement commissioners, though if its scheme were opposed by one twentieth of its electorate parliamentary approval was needed.[76] And, to add a much needed finality, from 1877 grants of charters were put beyond subsequent legal challenge.[77] It would not have been arguable that a Privy Council decision against incorporation was justiciable.

Adding Powers: The Convergence of Corporate and Non-corporate Towns

Corporations' powers came increasingly from general legislation. Some of it needed prior local adoption, some local applications needed executive approval and confirmation by provisional order, but, especially from the Public Health Act 1875, much of it was directly applicable. The need for local legislation correspondingly diminished, though some of the larger cities continued to rely heavily on it, others used it from time to time, and it was still used by utility companies, whose activities might impact significantly on corporations' ambitions.

Municipal expenditure on applying for a local Act of Parliament or resisting someone else's application was problematic. A corporation with a surplus could spend it on defending itself against hostile claims or bettering itself by seeking further powers from Parliament, indeed that seems an intrinsic part of its being.[78] Could a corporation without private means use its statutory power to levy a rate to the same ends? Defence was easier, for Chancery saw the situation as concerning the rights and duties of trustees. Hence it allowed expenditure from the rates in defence of an activity threatened by litigation or someone's promotion of a local bill, whether or not the activity was a statutory purpose, and whether the trustee was a corporation or a statutory board.[79] Common law judges were more particular, and certainly did not allow corporations to claim a general interest

---

[76] Municipal Corporations (New Charters) Act 1877, in this respect building on the powers of the Local Government Board under Public Health Act 1875, s 303, and, earlier, Public Health Act 1872, ss 22(2), 33. The 1877 Act had a costs provision relating to schemes, which P. J. Waller (*Town, City, and Nation* (Oxford, 1983), 243) mistook as an innovation allowing corporations to charge the costs of their incorporation to the rates, and hence as a possible explanation for what he saw as an accelerated rate of incorporation after 1877. But it was the 1850 Act that first allowed recovery of costs, the Privy Council's powers seem similar to those possessed by the Local Government Board since 1872, and if there was an acceleration it seems to have begun in 1876 rather than after the Act.

[77] Municipal Corporations (New Charters) Act 1877, s 9 (save on the ground that the charter had not been accepted).

[78] *A.G.* v. *Mayor of Brecon* (1878) 10 ChD 204; *Leith Magistrates and Council* v. *Leith Harbour and Docks Commissioners* [1899] AC 508.

[79] *Bright* v. *North* (1847) 2 Ph. 216; *A.G.* v. *Burgesses of Wigan* (1854) Kay 268 (Wood VC), 5 De G. M. & G. 52 (LJJ); *A.G.* v. *Mayor of Brecon* (1878) 10 ChD 204.

in safeguarding their inhabitants. So in 1846 Warwick was not allowed to spend money from the rates on applying for the replacement of the trustees of the borough's erstwhile charities, now in the hands of the council's political opponents who were no longer applying the large annual surplus towards the borough's lighting and watching.[80] Chancery judges might not have disagreed with that, but in 1871 a clear rift opened with the decision in *R* v. *Mayor of Sheffield*, which significantly narrowed what corporations could count as legitimate defence of their interests. [81] Here, in the interests of its inhabitants, the council had appeared before local magistrates to oppose an application by the local water company to increase its prices, winning a substantial concession, and had then opposed the company's application for a new Act, causing its withdrawal. The Queen's Bench disallowed both sets of expenditure.

As for obtaining new powers, not very long after the 1835 reforms and at a time when corporations were still dependent on local Acts for expanding their role, Chancery had ruled that councils could not fund applications for new local Acts from the rates.[82] At best, Chancery judges thought, such applications were mere speculations—and trustees must not speculate—and at worst they were jobs drummed up by professionals for sake of the fees. The ruling became conventional, surviving the changed status of municipal corporations after the Public Health Act 1858. It had not been inevitable, for as Page Wood VC later pointed out, to say that corporations held their property on a public trust was tantamount to saying the trusts were charitable, and it was established that trustees of charities could apply for a variation scheme, funded from the trust.[83] Its effect was limited, since local Acts incorporating the Towns Improvement Clauses Act 1847 could adopt a section allowing applications for subsequent amendment Acts to be charged to the rates, and as Page Wood VC again suggested, far-sighted councils could include a similar section in their own local Acts, which Parliament seems to have allowed.[84] Successful applications to Parliament nearly always contained a clause allowing costs recovery from the rates. But the financial risk of failure fell on councillors, who were vulnerable also to

---

[80] *R* v. *Mayor of Warwick* (1846) 8 Q.B. 926, 15 LJ QB 306; *A.G.* v. *Norwich Corporation* (1837) 2 My. & Cr. 406, affirming *R* v. *Corporation of Norwich* (1837) 1 Keen 700, may have been more generous to the council, but turned substantially on pleading points.

[81] (1871) LR 6 QB 652. For subsequent Chancery criticism see *A.G.* v *Mayor of Brecon* (1878) 10 Ch D 204 and the narrow defence of that case by Lord Halsbury in *Leith Magistrates and Council* v. *Leith Harbour and Docks Commissioners* [1899] AC 508.

[82] *A.G.* v. *Mayor of Norwich* (1848) 12 Jur 424, 16 Sim. 225.

[83] *A.G.* v. *Eastlake* (1853) 11 Hare 205.

[84] 10 & 11 Vict. c. 34, ss 132–3, 142 (expenditure was subject to ratepayer veto); *A.G.* v. *Eastlake* (1853) 11 Hare 205. E.g. Bolton Improvement Act 1854 (local), s 197 (provided General Board of Health approved the application); Borough Funds Act Amendment Act 1903.

injunctions forbidding council expenditure on the preliminary work necessary for an application.[85]

The outcome was the Borough Fund Act 1872, provoked by the *Sheffield* case. It introduced a general procedure for rates funding of litigation and the promotion and opposition of local bills in Parliament. Threading its way between the demands of ratepayer democracy and the protection of private property, it required prior approval from ratepayers for promotion of, or opposition to, bills in Parliament, did not extend to allowing rates funded applications for bills to rival existing gas or water companies, but was otherwise quite general in its ambit.[86] Despite its title it did not apply only to municipal corporations. The Chancery doctrine it replaced applied to all rates-funded bodies, be they councils, improvement commissioners, boards of guardians or whatever.[87] Similarly, the 1872 Act took its cue from the 1858 Local Government Act, bracketing together the major entities of urban administration—corporations, local boards of health, and improvement commissioners. Each, equally, was a power-bearing and a power-seeking entity, irrespective of legal form. This was no abstract point of constitutional theory, for although applications for local bills by local boards were not numerous, examples can be found in most years. Sometimes such a local Act was followed soon afterwards by promotion to corporate status—Barnsley, Rotherham and Kimberworth, Leamington Priors, Keighley, and Eastbourne are all examples.[88] Sometimes the Act was needed for a specific purpose like the purchase of an existing gas or waterworks, sometimes a local board's Act was indistinguishable from the sort of general improvement Act acquired by one of the smaller or medium sized boroughs.[89] So far as powers and the means of getting them were concerned, there was often little difference between a corporation and a local board.

---

[85] R v. *Mayor of Sheffield* (1871) LR 6 QB 652, noting otherwise unreported Chancery injunction; Fraser, *Power and Authority* 137 (Bradford in 1853); cf. J. Roebuck, *Urban Development in 19th-Century London* (1979), 92 (Lambeth vestry, 1888).

[86] The compromises necessary made it a difficult Act to work, needing clarification by Borough Funds Amendment Act 1903. Even then county councils needed their own Act: County Councils (Bills in Parliament) Act 1903. There is even a text: W. L. Williams, *Handbook on the Borough Funds Acts* (1904).

[87] A.G. v. *Southampton Guardians* (1849) 18 LJ Ch. 393; A.G. v. *Andrews* (1850) 2 Mac. & G. 225; A.G. v. *Eastlake* (1853) 11 Hare 205; A.G. v. *West Hartlepool Improvement Commissioners* (1870) LR 10 Eq. 152; *Cleverton* v. *Rural Sanitary Authority of St. Germain's Union* (1886) 56 LJ QB 83.

[88] Barnsley: local Act 1862, incorporated 1869; Rotherham and Kimberworth: local Acts 1863 and 1870, incorporated 1871; Leamington Priors: local Act 1868, incorporated 1875; Keighley: local Act 1869, incorporated 1882; Eastbourne: local Act 1879, incorporated 1883.

[89] Examples of water and gas Acts include Sowerby (1863), Tyldesley with Shakerley (1865), Cleckheaton (1870), and Dalton-in-Furness (1878). General purpose Acts include Wallasey (1861) and (1864), St. Mary Church (Devon) (1868), Melton Mowbray (1869), and Nelson (1879).

So far as by-laws were concerned, again there need be little difference between a corporation and a local board. Where the source of power was the same the procedure would be too, requiring byelaws to be submitted to a minister of the Crown for approval. For powers under the Public Health Act 1848 and the Local Government Act 1858 that meant the Local Government Act Office, which began to issue codes of model byelaws and to require good reason for departure from them.[90] After 1875 that scrutinizing function was transferred to the Local Government Board, whose secretary issued a somewhat stern circular in 1877 reminding all local boards (including borough councils acting as local boards) of the general legal requirements for byelaws, stating how the Board interpreted them, detailing the consultations it had made on technical detail, and appending a complex code.[91] Corporations' byelaws under the Municipal Corporations Act needed approval from the Home Secretary instead, but from 1875 the function was split, approval of those concerning the suppression of nuisances shifting to the Local Government Board.[92]

It may have been possible to evade some of this scrutiny by instead including byelaw-like material in the text of a local bill, and trusting to the laxer scrutiny of Parliament. That route, if available at all, would have been more likely to be taken by boroughs than by local boards. But whatever opportunity there was would have been lost after 1882, when the Commons established its Police and Sanitary Committee to tighten scrutiny, a committee that then built a close relationship with the Local Government Board.[93]

Power to approve local authority borrowing was more divided. If corporations borrowed under the Municipal Corporations Act 1835 they needed Treasury approval. In the eyes of its major critic at least, Treasury concerned itself only with procedural questions, seeking only to ensure that local opinion was in favour of the loan.[94] Nonetheless, from 1860 at the latest the Treasury was able to impose conditions to secure repayment and monitor progress, and could generally aid a corporation with its debt management.[95] The Treasury's critic, predictably, was

---

[90]   R. Lambert, 'Central and Local Relations in Mid-Victorian England: The Local Government Act Office, 1858–71' (1962) 6 *Vict. St.* 121, 130.

[91]   Public Health Act 1875, s 184; *Local Government Board*, 7th Report, *PP* 1878 (c. 2130), xxxvii(1), 1, 191–204. The process is described at *ibid.*, 99–106, and the codes are reprinted at *ibid.*, 204–307. There are annotations in *Knight's Annotated Model Byelaws of the Local Government Board* (1883) and W. Mackenzie and P. Handford, *Model Byelaws* (1899).

[92]   Public Health Act 1875, s 187; Municipal Corporations Act 1882, s 23; A. E. Lauder, *The Municipal Manual* (Westminster 1907), 27.

[93]   See above, pp. 337–8.

[94]   *Report of the General Board of Health on the Public Health Act 1848–54*, *PP* 1854 [1768], xxxv, 1, 52–3; cf. Hennock, *Fit and Proper Persons*, 6 (Treasury rejections occasional).

[95]   Municipal Corporations Mortgages Act 1860.

the General Board of Health. It was responsible for vetting applications under the Public Health Act 1848, and it prided itself on detailed scrutiny of both the projects and their costings.[96] Its successor, the Local Government Act Office, continued that detailed scrutiny of the project itself, if with rather less messianic self-belief, but still rejected some proposals and modified many.[97] There was no doubt a disparity here. It was resolved in the 1880s, like so many others, when the Local Government Act 1888 made the Local Government Board the only approving authority, save for loans under a couple of minor statutes, which appear to have been overlooked.[98]

Much more important, because this was the origin of most local authority borrowing, was the relative freedom conferred by powers in local Acts.[99] The powers needed parliamentary approval, of course, but there is no evidence of scrutiny of the sorts outlined above. A recommendation from a select committee in 1848 that no local Act should confer a borrowing power on a local authority without prior approval of a Secretary of State came to nothing.[100] This was the route taken by the boroughs, especially the large ones. But this too was reined back in the 1880s as model clauses extended the Local Government Board's control. By the early twentieth century it became usual for local Acts to delegate the settlement of the terms and technical detail of a loan to the Board, whereas previously they had been spelt out in the local Act itself.[101]

This was all a substantial convergence. There were still some differences. The franchise for borough councils and for local boards remained radically different until 1894. And, perhaps the last symbol of corporations' difference, their audit was essentially an internal matter whereas local boards (meaning now only those local boards that were not also borough councils) were subjected to the full external audit procedures of the poor law union auditors, which by stages became the district audit system.[102] But, those differences aside, by the 1880s local boards and all but the largest borough councils were substantially similar, similar enough

---

[96] *Report of General Board of Health 1848–54*; C. Hamlin, *Public Health*, 302–34.

[97] Lambert, 'Central and Local Relations', 131. For complaints about the system of lending to local boards, see *RC on Sanitary Laws*, 2nd Report, *PP* 1871 [c. 281], xxv, 1, 417–19.

[98] Local Government Act 1888, s 72. The Treasury's powers under the Burial Acts and the Baths and Washhouses Acts were not transferred until Local Authorities (Treasury Powers) Act 1906.

[99] M. Schulz, 'The Control of Local Authority Borrowing by Central Government', in C. H. Wilson (ed.), *Essays on Local Government* (Oxford, 1948), 167.

[100] Schulz, 'Control of Local Authority Borrowing', 170. By contrast the acquisition of additional borrowing powers under the Local Government Act 1858 did need the Secretary of State's approval (read: Local Government Act Office) before embodiment in a provisional order: s 78.

[101] Schulz, 'Control of Local Authority Borrowing', 175–6, 187–93.

[102] Poor Law Amendment Act 1844, 7 & 8 Vict. c. 101, s 32; Public Health Act 1848, 11 & 12 Vict. c. 63, s 122; Local Government Act 1858, s 60; Poor Law Amendment Act 1868, s 24; *RC on Sanitary Laws*, 2nd Report, 419–20. District Auditors Act 1879; Municipal Corporations Act 1882, ss 25–8

for the Conservatives to attempt to subordinate both to a new level of county government within a thorough restructuring of local government as a whole. To appreciate how that came about it is first necessary to consider local government outside the cities and the towns.

3. PARISHES, VESTRIES, AND LOCAL BOARDS

As a unit of local government the parish may have been old, nearly ubiquitous, and charged with administration of the all-important Poor Law, but it was ill-adapted to handle the changing economic and social conditions of the early and mid-nineteenth century. At the time of the Poor Law Commissioners' report in 1834 there were 14,353 English parishes supporting their own poor, and 1182 Welsh.[103] According to David Eastwood, some 63 per cent of English parishes had a population of less than 500, while only 17 per cent had more than 1000.[104]

The parish was essentially a rural institution, with a structure to match. Its organ of government, the vestry, was a meeting of inhabitants; it was not a legal person. It had no general executive, and it could not hold property other than through trustees. The vestry might nominate or elect parish officers each year— churchwardens and overseers, surveyor of the highways—but once in office the statutory powers were theirs individually. Ratepayers might bind themselves individually by their vote in vestry, but the majority could not bind the minority to any expenditure that the courts held to be beyond the traditionally narrow scope of the officers' authority.[105] This legal structure had been well suited to the Hanoverian rural parish, allowing domination by the substantial ratepayers, usually the farmers. It would perhaps have remained so while a parish's government remained nobody's concern but its own, though it needed adaptation if it was to suit the sprawling semi-urban areas or the non-corporate towns.

When rural disorder and continuing high levels of poor relief after the end of the French wars caused extreme anxiety, two reforming statutes were enacted to strengthen vestries by shifting them away from popular influence.[106] The first,

(substantially re-enacted in Local Government Act 1933, s 238, and see s 239. County Councils were subjected to the district audit system from their inception, Local Government Act 1888, s 71(3).

[103] *RC on Poor Laws*, Report, PP 1834 (44), xxvii, 1, 246–7.

[104] D. Eastwood, *Governing Rural England* (Oxford, 1994), 31. In the north of England, especially, the statute 13 & 14 Car. II c. 12, s 21 allowed the division of large ecclesiastical parishes into townships, for the administration of the poor law. 'Parish' was then conventionally taken to include all such townships, being defined in that way in numerous statutes including the Poor Law Amendment Act 1834.

[105] *R v. Glyde* (1813) 2 M. & S. 323; *R v. Gwyer and Manley* (1834) 2 Ad. & El. 216.

[106] A. Brundage, *The English Poor Laws 1700–1930* (Basingstoke, 2002), 50–2, and see 18–21 for the similar tendency of local Acts creating poor law unions.

Sturges Bourne's Vestries Act 1818, altered their constitution by instituting a system of plural voting.[107] It allowed ratepayers up to six votes each in proportion to the rateable value of the properties they occupied, and was amended in the following year to give the same scale of votes to property owners as well. That was a notable shift of power that survived in general principle until nearly the end of the century. Perhaps in close rural vestries this change made little difference. Historians seem to have found little evidence that it affected the usual run of business even in larger and more open parishes—though their sources may not be apt to disclose it—but in towns it was certainly used both for elections and for decisions controversial enough for a poll to be called.[108] Potentially it could apply to any vestry decision on any matter.

The second reforming statute, Sturges Bourne's Poor Relief Act 1819, armed each vestry with new powers to administer the Poor Law more effectively.[109] It gave them the ability to delegate their Poor Law policy making and administration to a management committee (a 'select vestry'), which was to meet at least fortnightly. That was a significant acknowledgement that even after the 1818 Act vestry meetings could be an inefficient and inappropriate means of maintaining close control. More than two thousand vestries quickly adopted this innovation, which might in time have become the basis of a general executive for all parishes, enabling them to develop into general purpose agencies.[110]

As is well known, the proposal originating from Edwin Chadwick and adopted by the Whig government to solve the Poor Law problem aimed for a fresh start institutionally as well as on the substantive question of paupers' eligibility for relief.[111] Decision making in individual cases was to be as rule bound as possible, removed from personal influence. Under the Poor Law Amendment Act 1834 parishes would be grouped into unions, each containing perhaps as many as 25 or 30 parishes, preferably centred on a market town. [112] While each parish would remain liable to pay for the relief given to its poor, the union's guardians and their employees would determine the extent and manner of that relief.

---

[107] 58 Geo. III c. 69, 59 Geo. III c. 85. Rated inhabitants who had failed to pay their rates were disqualified. In the context of a strong move to solve the Poor Law problem by abolishing it, the 1818 Act was a compromise: Eastwood, *Governing Rural England*, 127–31.

[108] J. P. Ellens, *Religious Routes to Gladstonian Liberalism* (University Park, PA, 1994), 14; J. Prest, *Liberty and Locality* (Oxford, 1990), 11n; Fraser, *Urban Politics*, 27–8, 30, 38–40, 46–7, 64, 96.

[109] 59 Geo. III c. 12.

[110] *SC on Poor Rate Returns*, PP 1822 (556), v, 517 (2145 select vestries in March 1821); *Abstract return of amount levied and expended in each county as assessment for poor rate and county rate 1833–34*, PP 1835 (284), xlvii, 453 (2259 on the eve of the new Poor Law).

[111] Brundage, *English Poor Laws*, 62–9.

[112] There is useful discussion of the geography of unions in F. Driver, *Power and Pauperism* (Cambridge, 1993), 32–57; on their formation see Brundage, *English Poor Laws*, 71–4.

They would be under close direction of the central Poor Law Commissioners in London, enforced by regulation, inspection, and audit. The parish ratepayer's role was reduced from participation to voting for however many guardians the Poor Law Commissioners allocated to the parish, and the vestry's role was reduced to levying and collecting the rate.[113] As David Eastwood writes, 'the old poor law was the defining social and political institution in rural England', so this revolution in local government eviscerated the rural vestry.[114]

Vestries were left with the far more mundane role of seeing to the upkeep of the highways, where as often as not the initiative in repairing a highway had come through insistence by the justices. The Highways Act 1835 affirmed petty sessions as the effective policy forming body. A generation later quarter sessions was empowered to group rural parishes into highway divisions, substituting divisional highway boards for vestries and confining the vestry to the election of its representative member.[115] Only six counties forswore that power entirely, while 18 amalgamated all or nearly all their parishes into districts.[116] From 1878 even that parochial involvement could be lost, if quarter sessions allowed a rural sanitation authority—the guardians of rural Poor Law unions in a different guise—to take over as the highway board for its area.[117]

It was a similar story with the removal of disease-causing filth. In rural areas and towns without an urban authority it was the union guardians that acquired the powers and duties in 1846, not the parish, and though that situation was reversed in 1855 it was reinstated in 1860.[118] Unions may not have been particularly effective, but unlike parishes their areas were large enough to justify the employment of salaried inspectors, and they were susceptible to central direction.[119]

As with the poor law, so with policing, parishes were offered the glimpse of a new dawn, but it came to nothing. What was wanted by the sort of opinion that

[113] 4 & 5 Will. IV c. 76, s 40. The voting scale for owners was that in Sturges Bourne's Vestries Act and its amendment, 58 Geo. III c. 69, 59 Geo. III c. 85, giving up to six votes each in steps of £25 rateable value, but for ratepayers the bands were much broader: up to three votes each in steps of £200 rateable value. If the PLC designated a parish as the appropriate unit, rather than a union, as it did with some large city parishes, it could still replace the vestry with guardians, *ibid.*, s 39.

[114] *Governing Rural England*, 166.

[115] Highway Act 1862, amended by Highway Act 1864.

[116] Lipman, *Local Government Areas*, 58–9; the remaining 18 used it for some parishes. A statutory immunity for places with local boards led to some opportunistic applications to adopt the Local Government Act, blocked by Local Government Amendment Act 1863, which confirmed local boards as urban agencies by reserving them for places with a population above 3000.

[117] Highways and Locomotives (Amendment) Act 1878.

[118] 9 & 10 Vict. c. 96; 11 & 12 Vict. c. 123; Nuisance Removal Acts 1855 and 1860; Cornish and Clark, *Law and Society*, 159.

[119] Poor Law Board, 13th Annual Report, *PP* 1861 [2820], xxvii, 1, 29, 31 (and compare 8th Annual Report, *PP* 1856 [2088], xxviii, 1, 14, 27); *RC on Sanitary Laws*, 2nd Report, 9, 21.

mattered, at county and at national level, was a new police, a police of surveil-lance, crime prevention and detection, the catching of criminals, the maintenance of public order. What existed at parish level was the constable, part-time, fee-earning, and reactive: the man who enforced the warrant after the victim had identified the criminal; an individual, where a system was wanted. Some par-ishes did aim for something more reliable, sometimes paying a stipend by volun-tary subscription, for courts were conservative about what could be charged to the rates.[120] Encouragement came through the Lighting and Watching Act 1830, remodelled and made easier for parishes to adopt by an Act of the same name in 1833, the work of Joseph Hume.[121] Essentially it was like a rather thin local Act of Parliament, but available for free to any parish whose ratepayers wanted it, provided only that two-thirds of those present voted in favour. Its policing pow-ers were attractive to some small unincorporated towns, and also to some rural parishes, which sometimes combined to form a joint force. Its adoptive nature and its reliance upon the continuing willingness of parish ratepayers to meet its costs, however, made it insufficient for the influential country gentlemen seeking something more widespread and malleable to their control.[122]

To the London-based politicians and reformers dreaming of centralized com-mand the Lighting and Watching Acts were an irrelevance. The adoptive County Police Act 1839 enabled county quarter sessions to create police forces at county or sub-county level, which would supersede or absorb any policing initiatives taken by parishes, transfer operational control to a chief constable, financial and policy control to the justices, and put the cost on the ratepayers.[123] In some coun-ties the justices were suspicious that the Act was perhaps just the thin end of a Whig wedge designed ultimately to replace them too by paid functionaries, and in some the justices were responsive to the outraged ratepayer opinion that pro-tested against this novel expense and loss of responsible control. For them the country Tories' Parish Constables Act 1842, offered an alternative, especially after its amendment in 1850. This measure preserved parish autonomy to the extent that a parish was willing to adopt the Lighting and Watching Act, but otherwise, as David Philips and Robert Storch relate, it too shifted authority away from the

---

[120]   R v. Bird (1819) 2 B. & Ald. 522.

[121]   11 Geo. IV & 1 Will. IV c. 217, 3 & 4 Will. IV c. 90; D. Philips and R. D. Storch, *Policing Provincial England, 1829–1856* (1999), 94–7; Prest, *Liberty and Locality*, 8–14.

[122]   Philips and Storch, *Policing Provincial England*, 94–7.

[123]   2 & 3 Vict. c. 93; A. Brundage, 'Ministers, Magistrates and Reformers: The Genesis of the Rural Constabulary Act 1839' (1986) 5 *Parl. Hist.* 56–64. Parish constables of the old style continued to be appointed until made optional by the Parish Constables Act 1872. Supersession of Lighting and Watching Act forces, or of forces established under local Acts, was at the discretion of the chief con-stables, who would be acting under instruction from Quarter Sessions: County Police Amendment Act 1840.

parish, this time to the justices in petty sessions, who gained the power to appoint the parish constables and to employ superintendents.[124] But parish involvement was almost wholly lost in 1856, when the superintendent system was abolished and county (and borough) forces became mandatory.[125] With the Poor Law centralized and administered through unions, with justices' supervision of highway maintenance becoming more direct and more intensive, and with responsibility for rural policing firmly in the hands of quarter sessions, rural vestries had become sickly institutions.

Urban vestries had also been tamed by Sturges Bourne's Acts, but in the 1830s and 1840s elections to parish offices often remained part of a town's political fabric. Party politics were often dominant, especially in the absence of other representative institutions—in the corporate towns before 1835, and in many others until the advent of local boards, described below.[126] The vestry's original function of voting a rate for the repair of the parish church could become bitterly controversial too as Dissenters sought to avoid this compulsory Anglican levy by contesting churchwardens' elections and seeking to control vestry rating meetings.[127] In towns where no accommodation had been reached between Anglicans and Dissenters that struggle kept vestry politics alive until abolition of compulsory church rating in 1868. It did nothing to further the case for the vestry as a suitable agency for local government. The situation was different in London, where the presence of the City and the absence of any other chartered corporations led to the vestries becoming general-purpose agencies with statutory powers. That is a special case, which will need separate discussion below. Elsewhere the same eighteenth- and early nineteenth-century local Acts which by-passed municipal corporations by-passed vestries as well.

The Lighting and Watching Acts described above continued that pattern, for though they used the parish as the unit of adoption, the parish ratepayers as the initiators, and the churchwardens as the ministerial agents for the adoption meeting, poll, and subsequent levying of rates, they were not vestry Acts. The executive they created was distinct from the vestry. Instead the ratepayers created 'inspectors', elected for three years on a franchise of one vote per ratepayer, reporting annually, their monthly meetings open to ratepayers. Other mid-century adoptive Acts did channel the initiating decision through a vestry meeting, usually requiring a two-thirds majority, but then again required the vestry to appoint commissioners to execute the adopted powers, parishes still not having a

---

[124] *Policing Provincial England*, 213–19; R. J. Olney, *Rural Society and County Government in Nineteenth-Century Lincolnshire* (Lincoln, 1979), 122–3.

[125] County Police Act 1856.

[126] Fraser, *Urban Politics*, 1–54.

[127] *Ibid.*, 31–54; Ellens, *Religious Routes*, 95–8, 113–20.

general executive body.[128] Unlike the Lighting and Watching Act, parishes rarely used them, the Burials Act aside.[129]

An urban vestry might still be responsible for its highways. Where that was the case the office of surveyor might continue as a minor political prize worth the contest, and if the parish's population exceeded 5000 the vestry might elect a parochial highways board to provide the continuous supervision needed.[130] But this too was vulnerable to take-over by local Act, especially after the clauses Acts of 1847 made that process easier, the Towns Improvement Clauses Act providing a template whereby town commissioners could simply become the surveyor for their area.[131]

This distancing from the vestry was accelerated by the (mostly) adoptive Public Health Act 1848, which again allowed for the continued use of the parish's geographical area where the inspector thought it appropriate, but substituted local boards of health for the vestry, with supervision by the General Board of Health.[132] The Act's very purpose was to bring order to the jumble of town authorities which in the eyes of the sanitary reformers impeded the application of true science to the most urgent problems of urbanization. Local government, writes Christopher Hamlin, became the hook which the General Board's inspectors used to persuade towns to adopt the Act, which is true in the sense that they were getting worthwhile powers, but is misleading if it suggests that the unincorporated towns were previously without governing institutions.[133] For those which previously had adopted the Lighting and Watching Act, or which were shifting away from improvement commissioners, the change was to a different form of representative institution with (probably) a different franchise. Elections to boards of health used the Vestries Acts' weighted scale of up to six votes for each

---

[128] Baths and Washhouses Act 1846, 9 & 10 Vict. c. 74; Lodging Houses for the Labouring Classes Act 1851, 14 & 15 Vict. c. 34 (available to parishes with a population exceeding 10,000); Burials Act 1853, s 7, extending Metropolitan Burials Act 1852, 15 & 16 Vict. c. 85. The Bakehouse Regulation Act 1863 adopted the mechanisms of the Nuisance Removal Acts. The Common Lodging Houses Act 1851, 14 & 15 Vict. c. 28, which used councils, improvement commissioners, and local boards of health where they existed, by-passed vestries altogether where they did not, using justices of the peace instead.

[129] Prest, *Liberty and Locality*, 182.

[130] Highways Act 1835; Fraser, *Urban Politics*, 103–11.

[131] 10 & 11 Vict. c. 34; in towns which adopted the Local Government Act 1858 (see below) the local board became the surveyor.

[132] The General Board could impose the Act on a place with a high death rate. Chadwick's preference had been for boards to consist only of crown appointees.

[133] *Public Health*, 289. For incorporated towns the Act's powers were the hook: in its first decade, before the abolition of the General Board, 62 municipal councils took up the Act, and seven more incorporated parts of it into their local Acts: *Return of the districts where the Public Health Act 1848 of the Local Government Act 1858 or both of them are in force*, PP 1867 (80), lix, 141.

ratepayer and each owner, but in steps of £50 rateable value rather than merely £25.[134] For other places the change was more radical, from the underdeveloped participatory politics of the vestry to the politics of elections.

The pace of adoption quickened after the General Board was abolished in 1854, removing what most of the biggest cities and many independently-minded small places saw as unwarranted central intrusion. The Local Government Act 1858 then extended the empowering provisions of the 1848 Act, enabling local boards of health and their successors, termed local boards, to float free, picking and choosing powers from an extensive legislative catalogue. A return in 1867 shows that 548 places had adopted all or part of these Acts by then.[135] Of them, some 450 had not been incorporated towns at the time of adoption, and so had no borough council, whether or not they had previously had Lighting and Watching Commissioners or local improvement commissioners. When combined with another return, almost contemporaneous but difficult to reconcile entirely, the figures suggest that about two-thirds of these non-corporate places chose a single existing parish or township as the appropriate territorial unit.[136] While many were obviously substantial towns, about 60 per cent had a population of 5000 or less, making them small for a town but large for a vestry to have managed. At that time too, a further 271 places had adopted the Lighting and Watching Act, some of them places only recently emerged from the fields, making their first gesture of independence.[137] So the parish as a geographic unit might live on in some of these urban or urbanizing environments, though in others local boards amalgamated or split parishes to form units suitable for draining and sewering, but in all of them the urban vestry and its participatory ethic had been superseded by these statutory elective boards.[138]

Of the three reasons for the decline of the vestry one was inescapable: the parish would often be too small a unit for the role envisaged by the framers of legislation. Thus any scheme that used the parish as its base would need elaborate provisions for uniting and subdividing parishes that might undermine the reasons for its choice. The other two reasons were political. One was fear of

[134]   11 & 12 Vict. c. 63, s 20. The constitution of improvement commissions varied. Some were already elected under a plural voting system.

[135]   1867 return (which records a further 16 towns which had incorporated parts of this legislation into their own local Acts).

[136]   *Return of the number of local boards etc*, PP 1867–8 (489), lviii, 789. The population figures, from the 1867 return, were for 1861, the latest census, and in many cases where the local board's territory did not coincide with the census unit they were clearly estimates. For other contemporaneous returns see Prest, *Liberty and Locality*, 182.

[137]   Prest, *Liberty and Locality,* 183.

[138]   The delicacy of questions about the burial of the dead preserved a minor role for the vestry: Local Government Act 1858, s 49, re-enacted by Public Health Act 1875, s 343 and Sch V, Pt III.

participation by the disfranchised and the lesser strata of ratepayers, both because of its inherent unruliness and its threat to property, and also—and in partial contradiction—because it led to unprincipled penny-pinching in face of pressing social problems. Linked to that was the third reason, a professionalizing ideology that saw administration by technical experts as the ideal. Administrative units should then be constituted in whatever way made their work most effective. The report of the Royal Sanitary Commission in 1871 expressed it well when proposing that the union guardians rather than the parish vestry become the new unified general purpose public authority outside the towns. The unions had organization, they had specialist staff, they were large enough to warrant the full-time employment of medical experts: 'to set up vestries as authorities under the new statute would involve a rare combination of inconveniences. For practical purposes they cannot be said to exist in many places.'[139]

Yet, contemporaneously, and with the quite different objective of extending popular control, Liberal ministers introduced two bills that had the parish and its vestry at their centre. The first was Foster's education bill of 1870, which proposed giving the local management of universal non-denominational elementary education to school boards elected by municipal councils where they existed, and everywhere else to vestries. In the complex denominational politics that followed the school boards were instead cast free from their local government moorings. They were to be directly elected, on a parochial basis where there were no borough councils, but not through the vestry.[140] The second Liberal proposal was Goschen's Rating and Local Government bill of 1871.[141] This was a complex and unwieldy measure, in part a technical reappraisal of rating procedures, in part a series of interlocking proposals for making local government more responsible, which modified the Royal Sanitary Commissions' proposals in the interests of making local government more representative. Its key elements were to be the revitalizing of the parish and the transfer of all administrative powers from the unelected county quarter sessions to new county boards. Each parish was to have an elected parochial board as its 'superintending authority', with the powers of the Nuisance Removal Act and the raft of less important adoptive Acts. If its population was 3000 or more its parochial board would also become the urban sanitary authority, with Local Government Act powers, ousting an existing local board if necessary (but not a borough council or improvement commissioners). Parochial boards were to be elected by ratepayers and owners, male and female, without plural voting. It was critical to the scheme that each parochial board was

<hr />

[139]   RC on Sanitary Laws, 2nd Report, 24.

[140]   Elementary Education Act 1870; Cornish and Clark, Law and Society, 445–7. The Board of Education could unite parishes and declare one parish to be contributory to another.

[141]   RC on Sanitary Laws, 2nd Report, 317.

to have a chairman, directly elected in the same way as the board, who would have his own statutory role in the board's management and who would provide the parish's link with other local government bodies—not exactly an executive mayor, but something of the same genus. With the other parochial board chairmen from his county he would choose which of their cohort would serve alongside an equal number of nominees of the justices on the new county boards, thus enabling those boards to have an element of responsible representation without being directly elected.[142] Outside the towns the parochial board chairmen would join the parishes' guardians as members of the new rural sanitary authority for the area, which would be the same territory as the poor law union though the sanitary board would be a separate entity from the union board of guardians.

These would have been significant extensions of representative local government, but the bill came to nothing. It reads like a twentieth-century departmental measure embodying a political principle on which the government insists, but modified at all points by compromises to reduce opposition from vested interests—a bill which could certainly be pressed through the Commons by sustained party discipline. But that was not the general style of Gladstone's ministry, which relied on ministers to inspire its supporters' enthusiasm by the merits of their proposals. This one was too much of a compromise to win positive Liberal support, while being too dangerous an incursion into the power of the county justices to remove their opposition. Goschen's parallel proposals to redistribute the costs of local expenditure met similar hostility from the landed interest and relative indifference from his supporters, and his bills were withdrawn after the introductory debate.[143]

The loss of Goschen's bills left the field to the bureaucratic, technocratic, model proposed by the Royal Sanitary Commission, which duly became the Public Health Act 1872. All places outside London were to be within the jurisdiction of a sanitary authority. That might be a borough, a local board or a board of improvement commissioners in towns, or the guardians of a union in rural areas, but not a vestry. Electoral franchises were not altered, so plural voting was retained. The newly created Local Government Board was empowered to constitute new urban districts by provisional order, and to extend some or all of the powers of urban districts to rural districts upon petition. No place could adopt the Local Government Act without permission from the Board. Shortly afterwards the final part of the Sanitary Commission's recommendations was enacted in the

---

[142] Because this proposal was made before the third Reform Act enfranchised farm labourers, direct election would have favoured the Tory farmers, which was not what Liberals wanted: J. Parry, *The Rise and Fall of Liberal Government in Victorian Britain* (New Haven, 1993), 242.

[143] Rating and House Tax Bill, *PP* 1871 (105), iii, 263; *PD* 1871 (s3) 205: 1115 *et seq.*, and see 1147; A. Offer, *Property and Politics 1870–1914* (Oxford, 1981), 176–9.

Public Health Act 1875. That greatly augmented the powers and responsibilities of the local sanitary authorities, repealed and re-enacted the provisions of the Local Government Act 1858 and extended them to all urban districts, and further embedded the Local Government Board as general supervisor.

This was now a uniform and efficient system of local government outside London, with no place for parish vestries. Apart from the incorporated boroughs, its forms and its boundaries were the product of centralized, professionalized, thinking. Surprisingly perhaps, the counter-current evident in Goschen's bill, that started instead by asking what was the most suitable unit to allow people to play a part in representative local government resurfaced in 1894, when parish councils were finally instituted for rural areas, though they looked rather out of place in the contemporary administrative world. Before discussing that, however, it is necessary to consider the justices, the other key element of Hanoverian local government.

4. GOVERNMENT OF THE COUNTIES

Justices and their System of County Government

Government in the counties meant rule by the justices, which in turn meant rule by the substantial landowners through an oligarchic co-optive system. Appointment was by the Lord Chancellor on the nomination of the county's lord lieutenant, who would use his own knowledge to vet applications from aspirants or would rely on the views of existing magistrates already most active at county or divisional level.[144] In the eighteenth century a shortfall between a county's need for active magistrates and the willingness of its landed elite to supply it had been met by appointing the wealthier stratum of the clergy. In 1831 they made up 26 per cent of the magistracy, falling to 13 per cent in 1842 after the Whig reform government advised lords lieutenants against recommending clerical magistrates—Tories as they mostly were—and down to 6 per cent

---

[144] A return in 1852–3 gives a total of 17,840 justices for England and Wales, of whom 7825 had taken out their *dedimus* and hence were qualified to act, not wholly reliable figures since some counties included in their return such honorary figures as judges and privy councillors while others did not: *Return of the number of justices in the commission of peace etc*, PP 1852–3 (558), lxxviii, 329. Fewer were active, especially at routine meetings of quarter sessions, but Foster calculates from a return in 1856, which shows generally that petty sessions attracted from two to four justices in most divisions in most counties, that nearly 80% of Hampshire justices who had taken out their *dedimus* could claim to be active: R. Foster, *The Politics of County Power; Wellington and the Hampshire Gentlemen 1820–52* (Hemel Hempstead, 1990), 41–2; *Return of the number of justices etc*, PP 1856 (110), l, 161.

in 1887.[145] Nonetheless, counties with sparsely populated areas and whose lord lieutenant resisted social dilution of the magistracy might continue to appoint clerics. Lincolnshire, which had 41 among its 92 active magistrates in 1807, had 70 among its 196 active magistrates in 1872.[146] Other counties found they had to include men from the lesser gentry if the bench was to be kept large enough to be efficient.[147] By mid-century, a few, driven by industrialization, were even admitting middle-class capitalists in significant numbers, preferably after they had retired from their business, but eventually even when they had not.[148] Thereafter businessmen appeared in small numbers on many benches, but everywhere the landowners held on, and in the agricultural counties they remained dominant through into the 1880s.[149]

For as long as the parish vestry had had civil functions the justices had had a supervisory role, a legal relationship matching the social, as the magnates and big landowners on the bench supervised the yeomen, tenant farmers, and independent tradesmen who typically constituted the vestries.[150] This was particularly true of the poor law, since there was scarcely a section in the statute of Elizabeth which did not confer some function or other on the justices, a feature which had been frequently amended by subsequent statutes and interpreted in numerous judicial decisions, all aiming to establish the boundaries between vestry, individual justice, and sessions, for the time being at least. The Elizabethan Act itself provided that justices appoint 'substantial householders' as overseers, conventionally on the nomination of the vestry.[151] Appeal lay to quarter sessions, which could control access to the King's Bench on review by choosing whether to state its reasons or merely give a bare decision.[152] So justices and benches could prevent the appointment of overseers of too low a

[145] J. V. Beckett, *The Aristocracy in England 1660–1914* (Oxford, 1986), 391; Olney, *Rural Society*, 98; Eastwood, *Governing Rural England*, 80–1.

[146] Olney, *Rural Society*, 101–3. Beckett, *Aristocracy*, 125, gives Sussex, Herefordshire, Essex and 'Yorkshire' as further examples, though the last does not seem borne out from the *Return of number of magistrates in holy orders*, PP 1861 (198), li, 665 and *Return of number of clergymen in commissions of peace*, PP 1863 (322), xlviii, 259 which would also add Norfolk, Suffolk, and Cumberland. The 1861 return lists 1357 clerical magistrates, but only some counties' returns indicate how many were qualified or active.

[147] Foster, *Politics of County Power*, 8–9.

[148] D. Philips, 'The Black Country Magistracy 1835–1860' (1976) 3 *Midland History*, 161–90; Beckett, *Aristocracy*, 122–7.

[149] Beckett, *Aristocracy*, 392.

[150] Eastwood, *Governing Rural England*, 31–4.

[151] 43 Eliz. c. 2, s 1.

[152] *R* v. *Gayer* (1757) 1 Burr. 245; *R* v. *Alice Stubbs* (1788) 2 T.R. 395. Rarely, appointment of someone legally ineligible might be set aside without the sessions having stated a case, the defect being jurisdictional.

social status if they wished, and David Eastwood has found evidence from the early 1830s that some did.[153]

Justices' direct role in rating questions had been limited by judicial decision and by a statute of 1743.[154] The same Act, however, elaborated the requirement that overseers' accounts be confirmed by a justice, with power to disallow illegal or exorbitant expenditure and to adjudicate on objections from ratepayers, with appeal to quarter sessions. In theory that gave justices ample scope to influence policy, but since there was no standard form for accounts, nor any obligation to produce the receipts and vouchers that would make for a full audit, disallowance was said not to have been much used in practice.[155] If it had been, quarter sessions' decisions would have been final, because a preclusive clause blocked access to *certiorari*. If, on the other hand, sessions allowed an item in the accounts a dissatisfied ratepayer did have access to the courts.[156] Though professing anxiety not to entrench upon quarter sessions' discretion, and declining to receive evidence of illegality by affidavit, the judges would still quash accounts unlawful upon their face.[157] In particular, the King's Bench would not sanction payment from the rates for salaried assistance to parish officers, no matter how clear the vestry's wish, how obvious the efficiency to be gained, or how willing the justices were to move away from traditional limitations.[158]

More directly, the Elizabethan Act was taken to authorize individual justices to hear appeals by paupers against an overseer's refusal of relief.[159] Quarter sessions could not overrule an overseer itself, nor did an appeal lie against a justice who ordered relief. Thus on the one hand an individual justice had power to procure the deference of his local vestry to his actual and anticipated rulings, and on the other a policy both general and consistent could be developed only if justices were willing to act collectively.[160] That is what happened in the 1790s in much of the south of England, when in response to prolonged economic crisis an allowance system was introduced whereby poor relief was used as a wage subsidy,

---

[153]   *Governing Rural England*, 39–40.
[154]   *R v. Dorchester Justices* (1721) 1 Stra. 393, 17 Geo. II c. 38, 50 Geo. III c. 49. The limits of the Dorchester decision were discussed in *R v. Hamstall Ridware* (1789) 3 T.R. 380.
[155]   *SC on Poor Rate Returns* 1822, 521.
[156]   *R v. Bird* (1819) 2 B. & Ald. 522.
[157]   *R v. James* (1814) 2 M. & S. 321.
[158]   *R v. Glyde* (1813) 2 M. & S. 323; *R v. Gwyer and Manley* (1834) 2 Ad. & El. 216.
[159]   *R v. Keer* (1793) 5 T.R. 159 (holding that the jurisdiction was excluded by a local Act, 4 Geo. 3 c. xc). Statutes prescribing particular modes of poor relief were careful to give (or preserve) a justice's power to award relief where overseers had refused: 3 Will. & Mar. c. 11, s 11; 22 Geo. 3. c. 83 (Gilbert's Act—which generally gave justices a large role, as might be expected of a measure encouraging action on a pan-parish scale). The general power was restated in 36 Geo. III c. 23.
[160]   *R v. Winship* (1770) 5 Burr. 2677; *R v. North Shields* (1780) 1 Dougl. 331.

based on scales originating from justices of the local petty sessions division—the well-known 'Speenhamland system'.[161]

In the 1830s reaction to this allowance system, the burden it was thought to be throwing on to the rates, and its affront to orthodox Malthusianism, was to sweep away both parish administration of the poor law and the discretionary, supervisory role of justices over it. There was a place for justices in the new system, as *ex officio* members of the boards of guardians, but there they would share power with the ratepayers' representatives, usually the tenant farmers who, as parish officers, had been under their supervision. Nonetheless, in many unions justices were prominent in the early years of the new system, when the important policy decisions were taken. Later, when it all became a matter of mere administration under regulation by the Poor Law Commission and its successor, the Poor Law Board, they tended to lose interest.[162] Central direction of a systemized and intrusive sort had replaced their piecemeal supervision.

As for quarter sessions itself, the statutory quarterly meetings of the county justices, its administrative functions changed significantly but within a relatively narrow compass. It never acquired public health functions, for example. Law and order in a general sense had long been the central concern, bridges and highways a distant second. These functions required an executive structure of sorts, something to give continuous attention and fill the gaps between meetings of sessions. By the end of the eighteenth century most counties had appointed a permanent Chairman of Quarter Sessions and formally separated their administrative from their judicial business.[163] Many devolved work to committees, both standing and *ad hoc*. There was potential legal difficulty here, for delegation was not (and is not) an inherent power of judicial bodies or those with discretionary powers, though it was always open for a committee to do the ground work and the sessions the deciding.[164] Something too could be achieved through use of adjournments.

So statutes that increased quarter sessions' functions would sometimes create additional machinery. The Gaols Act 1823 left rule-making to the sessions generally, but required a committee of visitors for monitoring and inspection, and the Lunatic Asylums Act 1845 vested many of its powers directly in a committee of visitors, often with only reporting responsibility to the parent body. On the other hand the County Police Acts left it up to the sessions itself, so that Hampshire

---

[161] Eastwood, *Governing Rural England*, 107–21, 134–46. The policy was legitimized by 36 Geo. III c. 23.

[162] A. Digby, *The Poor Law in Nineteenth Century England and Wales* (1982), 16; Olney, *Rural Society*, 134–5.

[163] Eastwood, *Governing Rural England*, 70–3; Foster, *Politics of County Power*, 48–50.

[164] For a nice example of delegation, cured by 'consent', see *R v. Northampton Justices* (1777) Cald. 30.

sessions did not feel it need create a police committee until 1872, though its police force was instituted in 1839.[165]

For the most part structure was minimal, and imposed by the justices themselves, but it served a county government that despite its political critics was often both efficient and economical.[166] As for capital, justices needing to borrow for the construction of county buildings—shire halls and the like—needed sanction from a local Act, until a general power for those purposes was granted in 1826.[167] Similarly, the Mortgages of County Rates Act 1825 allowed money to be raised for building prisons and asylums, and later statutes imposing new obligations also included the necessary borrowing powers.[168]

The major function gained by the justices was policing. Neither parish nor poor law union was to be the unit for local policing, nor was there to be a national police force. A quarter sessions that adopted the 1839 County Police Act necessarily proclaimed the power of magisterial government, be its force large or small. Adoption of the Parish Constables Act 1842 enhanced instead the role of the justices in their petty sessions divisions, and the 1856 County and Borough Police Act confirmed that the county was a natural unit for policing. But quarter sessions would have less authority than a borough watch committee. The latter could direct its police and hire and fire at all levels, whereas the 1839 Act created an independent operational role for the chief constable of a county, albeit subject in some rather uncertain way to the 'lawful orders' of sessions.[169] Counties thus felt the drive towards professionalism rather sooner than the boroughs did, mitigated to some extent by their ability to find their chief constables from among the gentry, and subject always to the power that came with financial control.[170]

So far as central influence is concerned, however, it is clear that at first the counties voluntarily adopting the 1839 Act were virtually free from it.[171] Compulsion changed that relationship, immediately in that the 1856 Act mandated both that there be a county police force and that it have a chief constable, and potentially through the grant in aid for forces declared efficient by Home Office inspectors.

---

[165] Foster, *Politics of County Power*, 47, 91–9.

[166] Eastwood, *Governing Rural England*, 74; Foster, *Politics of County Power*, 62–4, 156.

[167] County Buildings Act, 7 Geo. IV c. 63; Olney, *Rural Society*, 116–17. Local Acts were still occasionally needed to authorize works, e.g. Lancashire County Justices Act 1879 (local), and see Olney, *Rural Society*, 128.

[168] 6 Geo. IV c. 40; Lunatic Asylums Act 1845, 8 & 9 Vict. c. 126, ss 34–8.

[169] C. Steedman, *Policing the Victorian Community* (1984), 41–7.

[170] Steedman, *Policing*, 48–9. The critical question appears to be how far, if at all, divisional inspectors or superintendents were subject to direction by the justices of their petty sessional division, independently of the chief constable—on which there is too little evidence for a conclusion to be drawn: compare Steedman, *Policing*, 50, with Philips and Storch, *Policing Provincial England*, 223, 330 n110.

[171] Philips and Storch, *Policing Provincial England*, 220–3.

Their views on the appropriate size and structure of forces prevailed, and on matters of uniform and equipment. On other matters where inspectors would like to have seen a professionalized uniformity, however, the Home Office generally deferred to local autonomy.[172] Further, as Carolyn Steedman has pointed out, the very conception of policing in the first decades of the county forces had a magisterial hue to it. Counties were empowered to use their policemen for a range of administrative tasks that fell within quarter sessions' general remit, and they did so—using them for anything from assistant relieving officers, through inspectors of weights and measures, to ferrying prisoners to and from prison, until central pressure and the professional ethic began to cut away such ancillary roles in the 1870s.[173]

At about the same time the grant in aid was increased, bringing with it a further concern for value for money.[174] Its main focus, however, was on the police of the small boroughs, and the solutions, further consolidation of borough forces with the adjacent county, and a bar against newly created boroughs having their own police unless they had a population of 20,000 or more, enhanced the status of the county forces.[175] In 1888, when elected county councils replaced the administrative side of quarter sessions, county police forces were still so closely identified with the county bench that the question of their future governance was cast as being whether the justices should retain the whole control or have to share it with the elected representatives of the people.[176]

As policing was gained, prisons were lost. Quarter sessions had long acknowledged responsibility for provision of gaols and houses of correction. What changed was that Home Office supervision dictated both the programme for building and, by stages, the type of design that was acceptable and the penal regime employed. Peel's Gaols Act of 1823 required that a county's gaols be adequate for a punishment system that divided prisoners into five different categories.[177] Oxfordshire, which had just spent £3,187 modernizing the castle gaol, had to spend a further £2,985 as well as increasing the salaries of its gaoler and chaplain to meet their new responsibilities.[178] The quarter sessions for the

---

[172] Steedman, *Policing*, 29–30, 38–40.

[173] Steedman, *Policing*, 53–5; Foster, *Politics of County Power*, 58. Steedman argues that the Explosives Act 1875 and the Sale of Goods Act 1875 (which gave powers against purveyors of adulterated food) weakened this link by conferring significant administrative powers directly upon the police (*Policing*, 54).

[174] Police (Expenses) Act 1874.

[175] Municipal Corporations (New Charters) Act 1877; T. A. Critchley, *A History of the Police in England and Wales 1900–1966* (Letchworth, 1967), 126–9; Cornish and Clark, *Law and Society*, 594–5.

[176] Critchley, *History of the Police*, 133–8.

[177] 4 Geo. IV c. 63.

[178] Eastwood, *Governing Rural England*, 252, 255.

Lindsey division of Lincolnshire, which had improved its house of correction in 1808, now found that in addition it needed a gaol, which would cost £26,400.[179] Inspectors appointed by the Home Office under the Prisons Act 1835 accelerated the process, necessitating prison building programmes in Hampshire, Berkshire, and Lincoln for example.[180]

The gap between those who were designing and those who were paying was filled from 1846 by a system of grants in aid, though this made it easier for inspectors to press for the conversion of local prisons into forms that better suited current penal theory, and emphasized that policy was determined at national level.[181] Long before prisons were nationalized by Disraeli in 1877 as the easiest means of reducing the burden of county rates, even before the 1865 Prisons Act caused a second and even more extensive round of prison building and modification, magisterial autonomy had been permanently undermined.[182]

It was a similar story with pauper lunatic asylums, though the Lunacy Commissioners were much less peremptory than the inspectors of prisons. From 1808 quarter sessions had power to provide a county asylum for lunatic paupers, which some entrepreneurial counties turned into a successful trading enterprise catering for private patients and paupers from other counties.[183] In 1845 Shaftesbury's Lunatic Asylums Act made such provision compulsory, prescribed a management structure, and provoked another expensive round of building.[184] After a year in which the situation was doubtful, however, justices regained some control over admissions to the asylums, and were also able to use their role as statutory visitors to claim some autonomy in management.[185] Scholars contest how great that autonomy was, but it is clear that whatever authority quarter

---

[179] Olney, *Rural Society*, 105–6.

[180] 5 & 6 Will. IV c. 38 ('for effecting greater uniformity …'); Foster, *Politics of County Power*, 54; Eastwood, *Governing Rural England*, 259n; Olney, *Rural Society*, 115, 118–19; B. Forsythe, 'Centralisation and Local Autonomy: The Experience of English Prisons 1820–1877' (1991) 4 *J. Hist. Sociology* 317, 322–3.

[181] Cornish and Clark, *Law and Society*, 583–4; Eastwood, *Governing Rural England*, 259–60.

[182] Forsythe, 'Centralisation and Local Autonomy'; for an example of the impact of the 1865 Act, see Olney, *Rural Society*, 106–8.

[183] Lunatic Paupers or Criminals Act 1808, 48 Geo. 3 c. 96; L. D. Smith, 'The County Asylum in the Mixed Economy of Care', in J. Melling and B. Forsythe (eds), *Insanity, Institutions, and Society, 1800–1914* (1999), 33–47.

[184] 8 & 9 Vict. c. 126; A. Scull, *The Most Solitary of Afflictions: Madness and Society in Britain 1700–1900* (New Haven, 1993), 155–65, 267–8, 277–83; P. Bartlett, 'The Asylum and the Poor Law', in Melling and Forsythe, *Insanity*, 48, 52; Olney, *Rural Society*, 119–21.

[185] P. Bartlett; *The Poor Law of Lunacy* (1999), 98–101, 115–22; D. Wright, 'The Discharge of Pauper Lunatics from County Asylums in Mid-Victorian England', in Melling and Forsythe, *Insanity*, 93–108.

sessions retained, it had to be constantly negotiated with the agents of central government. [186]

Internal Hierarchies: Petty Sessions

Quarter sessions was only one forum where justices exercised administrative authority, of course. Counties had established divisions in the seventeenth century, and it was at their statutory 'special sessions' that the justices of each division saw to the maintenance of the highways under the Highways Act 1773, and licensed inns and alehouses under the Licensing Act 1753. Both gave important control, the former over the vestry and its surveyor, the latter over the number, quality, and characteristics of drinking places, often determined with reference to a general county policy. The statutory assignment of these functions to the divisions overlapped with the voluntary processes by which justices gradually created a court of petty sessions as the appropriate setting for the exercise of their more important judicial powers. Those processes had varied between counties, and could be regretted by justices holding to notions of individual jurisdiction, but they were reasonably complete by the start of our period.[187] The old-fashioned view, voiced by the royal commission on county rates in 1836, that petty sessions were merely voluntary meetings of magistrates, belied their regularity and legitimacy.[188] It did perhaps explain why as courts they were badly serviced, often reliant on rooms in inns for their location and on poor quality fee-taking clerks for their record keeping.

A first step towards bureaucratic rationalization of this home-grown system had been taken in 1828 with an Act providing quarter sessions with a process for settling divisional boundaries to provide certainty and notoriety, a process which required advance notice and allowed for objection by petition.[189] Each settlement was to last for 21 years, amenable to amendment only after ten, a limitation that had to be reduced to three in 1836 to enable, or encourage, counties to realign their sessional divisions with the new poor law unions.[190] The second step was proposed by Peel in 1829, only to be lost with the fall of Lord Liverpool's administration and never reintroduced. His bill 'for the better execution of the office of the Justice of the Peace in England' would have combined special and petty sessions into a

---

[186] B. Forsythe, J. Melling, and R. Adair, 'Politics of Lunacy: Central Regulation and the Devon Pauper Lunatic Asylum, 1845–1914', in Melling and Forsythe, *Insanity*, 68–92; A Scull, 'Rethinking the History of Asylumdom', in Melling and Forsythe, *ibid.*, 295, 301–2.

[187] Eastwood, *Governing Rural England*, 88–95.

[188] *PP* 1836 (58), xxvii, 1, 32, quoted by Eastwood, *Governing Rural England*, 89.

[189] 9 Geo. IV c. 43.

[190] 6 & 7 Will. IV c. 12.

new court of petty sessions, with a stipulated jurisdiction including all the justices'
administrative functions outside quarter sessions plus their more important judicial business.[191] Nonetheless, even without this neat tidying special and petty sessions did coalesce, if they had not already. Detailed returns in 1851 show that they
were everywhere being held at the same venue and attended by the same justices,
the same meeting often serving as both.[192]

So there was capacity for justices to rule their counties through their divisions
as well as centrally through quarter sessions, meeting more frequently than the
size of a county might easily allow, the better focused through an identity of local
interest. The possibilities were there, with the two major jurisdictions receiving
legislative makeovers which retained the divisional justices as the important
decision makers—Estcourt's Licensing Act 1828 and the Highways Act 1835. In
addition there was the bonus of divisional policing for those counties which
eschewed the County Police Act 1839 in favour of the Parish Constables Act 1842.
Of these, the last has already been mentioned: it was repealed when county policing became compulsory, shifting the locus of justices' control from divisional to
county level. The highways jurisdiction continued unreduced, a complex mix of
general and detailed powers to supervise the surveyor. It survived a bid by Edwin
Chadwick to shift it to the poor law unions ('the opinion appears to be gaining
ground, that the new unions are the most efficient bodies for the chief objects of
local administration'), and was extended in 1841 by an Act empowering the divisional justices to make parishes pay for the upkeep of turnpikes if the turnpike
trustees could not.[193] Chadwick was no doubt right, but the bureaucratic centralization of the Poor Law Board was too high a price to pay for making the coaches
run on time. It was to be 35 years before the poor law unions became the basis of
something beginning to look like a general purpose authority.

The third important jurisdiction vested in petty sessions, control of liquor
licensing, was seriously reduced between 1830 and 1869 by the Beer Act. That
freed beerhouses from the need for any but an excise licence, depriving the justices of a primary instrument for social control, as was its promoters' intention.[194]
Control was no longer to be by prior licensing, hence rationing and detailed individual scrutiny, but by general laws applicable to all and enforced through judicial

---

[191] *PP* 1829 (115, 277), i, 333, 365.

[192] *Return of the number of justices, etc* 1856, 161. Sometimes a joint 'special sessions' was held for
neighbouring divisions, so it seems.

[193] *Select Committee on the Highways Act*, Report, *PP* 1837–8 (463), xxiii, 253, 274 (repair of the
highway had long been associated with the Poor Law through the use of highway or quarry labour
as a form of outdoor relief); 4 & 5 Vict. c. 59.

[194] S. Anderson, 'Discretion and the Rule of Law: The Licensing of Drink in England *c*.1817–40'
(2002) 23 *JLH* 45–59.

process. That of course came back to the justices, but in their judicial capacity, which increasingly came to depend upon having police available as prosecutors.[195] None the less, justices continued to control the issue of new licences for the sale of wines and spirits, and their renewal. These were important jurisdictions as the temperance movement gained strength in the mid-century, forcing benches to decide whether 'need' should be a criterion in their divisional area. As debate polarized, with temperance advocates on one side and a diminishing cadre of free traders on the other, a middle ground supporting control through the justices gained cross-party support in Parliament.[196] Control would remain local, and could be made stricter, but neither working-class drinkers nor existing licensees would be put at the mercy of plebiscitary polls of the local ratepayers. Discretion over the critical matter of issuing new licences could be retained, but insulated. Other issues, principally the removal of existing licences, could be subjected to rules to be administered through judicial process—a form of centralization.

This compromise first appeared in the Wine and Beerhouse Act 1869, a Conservative private member's bill, which restored the licensing of beerhouses by making the requisite excise licence dependent on a certificate from divisional justices. Bruce's licensing bill of 1871 would have allowed a poll of ratepayers to reduce the number of liquor licences permitted for their area by the justices, but it was withdrawn after raising a political storm which effectively destroyed his political career. His 1872 bill, ultimately the Licensing Act 1872, introduced a general licensing regime for all on-sales, and the off-sales of wines and spirits, retaining the main features of both Estcourt's 1828 Act and the 1869 Act, but adding that new licences also required approval by a standing committee of quarter sessions.[197] These important powers signalled a confidence in the justices that had been lacking in the 1830s.

Other new jurisdictions, a miscellany of licensing and certificating functions, cast the justices more in the role of agents of an administrative state than as wielders of discretionary power. Perhaps the licensing of game dealers under the Game Act 1831 can be seen as an exercise of social power in legal form, but that is hardly true of the licensing of emigrant runners or the certificating of pawn-brokers, even less of the licensing of places for the storage of petroleum or for the

---

[195] Research has not yet uncovered how far divisional justices were able to direct their local inspector or superintendent in his policing—but if some of them did it was perhaps more by personal influence than through formal decision at a sessions.

[196] B. Harrison, *Drink and the Victorians* (2nd edn, Keele, Staffs, 1994), 242–73.

[197] The Beer Dealers Retail Licences (Amendment) Act 1882 completed the new regime by extending it to off-licences for the sale of beer.

manufacture or storage of explosive substances.[198] These were all useful functions, but there was nothing about them that needed them to be done by a justice,
nothing, as it were, to keep the justices in the business of unelected government.

Becoming Representative

As county rates expenditure increased there was a persistent reaction that greater
economy could be achieved if county government were representative instead,
even though most of the increase was driven by centrally imposed standards for
police, gaols, and asylums.[199] Proposals varied from Joseph Hume's radical outright substitution of election for nomination in 1836, through his bill for a joint
board of justices and representatives of the ratepayers in 1849, to a bill introduced
by various private members between 1851 and 1867/8 which would have established county financial boards consisting of a representative from each board of
poor law guardians to take over most of the administrative and financial powers
of quarter sessions. A variation on this theme became part of the first government
proposal to reform the counties, Goschen's Rating and Local Government bill in
1871. It proposed to substitute the chairmen of his proposed parish boards for
the poor law guardians as the electorate for county boards. All these bills failed.
They were opposed by the landed interest, of course, and also made to appear the
less necessary by the aptitude county elites developed for acquiring grants from
central taxation to alleviate the rates burden without having to make structural
change.[200] In part, also, the selectorates the bills proposed were unattractive—
but here the Liberals were in a quandary, for they had no wish to enfranchise the
Tory tenant farmers by introducing direct elections.

In the 1880s, however, the frame of reference changed. Gladstone saw reformed
county government as a means of decentralizing, not just the myriad minor
regulatory functions that had accreted to Whitehall but also the major role of
approving local applications for additional legal powers, up to the stage of promulgating the necessary provisional orders. After the third reform Act extended
the parliamentary franchise to agricultural labourers in 1884 the anomaly of
unrepresentative county government became inescapable. As it happened it was

[198]   Game Act 1831, 1 & 2 Will. IV c. 32; Passengers Act 1855, 18 & 19 Vict. c. 119; Pawnbrokers Act
1872; Petroleum Act 1871; Explosives Act 1875. In the towns the town council or local board typically
held these powers.

[199]   Keith-Lucas, *English Local Government Franchise*, 97–107; on central government's impact on
local expenditure, see Foster, *Politics of County Power*, 60; J. P. D. Dunbabin, 'Expectations of the
New County Councils and their Realisation' (1965) 8 *Hist. J.* 353, 373n.

[200]   From grants towards prosecution costs and county police forces in 1835 and 1856 respectively,
subventions for prisons from 1846 through to their wholesale transfer to the national exchequer by
Disraeli in 1877, and grants towards the maintenance of main roads from 1882.

a Conservative measure that did for county government what the 1835 Act had done for corporations, Lord Salisbury coaxing his reluctant party into passing a Local Government Act in 1888.[201] It created county councils on the now standard model—corporate personality, power to own land, committee structure, and so on. They were to be elected on a nearly-democratic franchise comprising ratepayers plus occupiers of rated property valued at £10 or more, but, like municipal corporations, with near-democracy tempered by the requirement that councils include a proportion of indirectly elected aldermen.[202] And, as in 1835, structural reform was accompanied by only meagre new powers. There was, of course, a transfer of the administrative functions of quarter sessions, save, significantly, that confirmation of new liquor licences remained with the justices and responsibility for policing was vested in watch committees comprising both councillors and justices. But governance of the poor law remained where it was, elementary education was not shifted from the school boards, indeed the only major new role that county councils were given was full responsibility for main roads.[203]

There was, however, an accompanying shift in authority away from the smaller incorporated boroughs, particularly those that had had their own quarter sessions. Previously the council of such a borough had enjoyed many powers which elsewhere were held by county quarter sessions, and the borough was immune from some or all of the county rate. Now if its population was less than 10,000 such a borough lost all those powers to the county, and became fully liable to the county rate. All boroughs with a population below that figure, whether they were quarter sessions boroughs or not, lost their police force to the county, and a variety of other statutory powers too. Small boroughs thus became, in terms of their powers, indistinguishable from local boards under the 1875 Public Health Act. They kept the name, trappings, and council of an incorporated borough, but were under the county council's jurisdiction just as if they had not been boroughs at all. At the other extreme, county boroughs, which will be discussed further below, were to stand outside the county's jurisdiction in all respects, whether or not they had previously had their own quarter sessions. In between, quarter sessions boroughs with a population above 10,000 but which did not qualify for the status of county borough kept all their statutory powers, and their police force, but became subject to the county council's jurisdiction over main roads and to various other county charges too. This pragmatic realignment of county and incorporated borough was the surviving element of a much grander scheme,

---

[201] D. Cannadine, *The Decline and Fall of the British Aristocracy* (New Haven, 1990), 157; J. P. D. Dunbabin, 'The Politics of the Establishment of County Councils' (1963) 6 *Hist. J.* 226.

[202] County Elections Act 1888, adding the £10 occupier from the (parliamentary) Registration Act 1885 to the existing simple ratepayer franchise of the Municipal Corporations Act 1882.

[203] Dunbabin, 'Expectations', 375; Olney, *Rural Society*, 139.

one which, on the one hand would have brought unity and system to local government, and on the other would have subordinated all but the greatest cities to the reformed counties.

5. CONTESTED ROLES FOR LOCAL GOVERNMENT

The 1880s: System, Devolution, Compromise

The Conservatives' 1888 Local Government bill envisaged a very significant devolution of power from central government to the new county councils. A raft of supervisory, ratifying, and appellate powers concerning local authorities were to be transferred from central government. County councils would also take over from the Local Government Board and the Board of Trade the inquiry and approval functions under the Gas and Water Facilities Act 1870 and the Tramways Act 1870, issuing provisional orders in their own name prior to inclusion in confirmatory Acts of Parliament. This supervisory role would subordinate nearly all other local authorities to the counties, and by including nearly all the urban authorities within counties' jurisdiction the bill also included their territories in the counties' rating base, providing part of the additional finance that would be needed.[204] Only the ten incorporated boroughs with a population exceeding 150,000 were to be allowed the status of county borough that treated them as if counties in their own right, outside the supervisory jurisdiction of county councils, free from the county rate, maintaining instead all their direct links with central government departments.

County councils would thus be sub-regional authorities combining urban and rural constituencies, only the few greatest provincial cities standing aside. The uproar that followed from the incorporated boroughs focused in part on the revenue transfer from town to country, as it was portrayed, and part on the loss of an historic or (for recently created boroughs) hard-won independence from county rule. Pressure in the Commons forced a cascade of concessions, resulting in county borough status being accorded to the 55 incorporated boroughs with a population above 50,000, plus six cathedral towns which had previously enjoyed the status of 'county of a city', and the dropping of the devolution proposals for a year.[205] When reintroduced in 1889 they were referred to a select committee, which heard evidence raising issues so complex, it said, that no report was possible, and the proposal was lost.[206] The President of the Tramways Institute

---

[204] The rest came from 'allocated taxes', see below.

[205] P. J. Waller, *Town, City, and Nation*, 246–52.

[206] *Select Committee on the Government Departments (Transfer of Powers) Provisional Order Bill*, Report, *PP* 1889 (275), xi, 1.

testified to the inveterate and unfounded hostility of the counties to the tramway companies, in contrast to the calm understanding of the Board of Trade. The town clerk of Morley, representing the Association of Municipal Corporations, raised every conceivable issue with immense persistence, pointing out that the lifeboat that had carried the lesser county boroughs to safety had condemned the remaining non-county boroughs to the sufferance of county councils a good deal more rurally biased than would otherwise have been the case. Those councils, he said, would be likely to have political divisions, local, perhaps, rather than party, in contrast to the benign neutrality of government departments. Predictably perhaps, those government departments were not wholly helpful to the bill. The Secretary of the Local Government Board insisted that county councils would have to employ their own technical experts, if they could find them, and not borrow his, though his department would of course help councils get legislative confirmation of their provisional orders. The Assistant Secretary for the Board of Trade promised counties copious advice and assistance on technical matters, but insisted that they find their own way of guiding their confirmatory bills through Parliament.

The upshot of this defeat can be seen from the structure of the Local Government Act 1894. This was a Liberal measure that completed what had always been intended in 1888 by rationalizing the district authorities, but without shifting power to the county elites. It reconstituted urban sanitary authorities as urban district councils, and rural sanitary authorities as rural district councils. They were to be elected on a single-vote franchise for ratepayers (male and female) plus non-ratepaying males who qualified for the parliamentary franchise. That ended the principle of Sturges Bourne's Vestries Act that had given extra votes to the wealthy. But there was no attempt to reintroduce the hierarchy of local units that had been rejected in 1889. County councils and district councils were to have separate powers, and to co-operate as best they could, with the supervisory powers remaining with the Local Government Board.

What had eventuated was not a reformulation of local government, but the substitution of county councils as the democratic equivalent of quarter sessions, and the rural district councils as the democratic equivalents of the administrative side of the petty sessions divisions. So rural district councils inherited most of the various licensing and minor regulatory powers held by petty sessions, though not liquor licensing. They became the local highway authority too. The justices were also removed from their *ex officio* positions on boards of guardians, the rural district councillors automatically becoming the guardians for rural parishes in a union, and the urban parishes electing theirs separately.

These were significant extensions of democracy into local government, but the Liberals aimed to go further by providing agricultural workers with a more direct and a more local participation. The rural districts were too big for that, being based on the rural parts of the poor law unions and covering perhaps 20 or 30 parishes. So the larger rural parishes were to have their own elected councils, and the smaller to have parish assemblies, these to operate below the rural district councils and the county councils. The Conservatives fought that proposal line by line, seeing it as a further attempt to reverse the proper social order in rural areas. They particularly resented clauses allowing parish councils to acquire land for allotments and to make provision for water supply. In the result what had been in any event a modest list of powers with weak financing became even less inspirational. Parish councils became a form of addendum to the structure of county and district councils, not the focal point they would have been if Goschen's bill had been enacted in 1871.

To 1914, and Beyond

Whereas up to 1888 institutional design and allocation of powers were the main points of political contention, from the 1890s political attention shifted to the financial relations between central government and the localities. Part of the Conservatives' devolutionary programme in 1888–9 was the replacement of the heterogeneous collection of grants in aid by a system of local taxation for local government to supplement the rates. It was not independence, since tax rates would be set nationally, and for ease of administration the taxes would continue to be collected centrally before distribution to the localities. However, there would be a measure of separation of local from central finance, signifying both that all of what local authorities spent was in some sense theirs by right and that they should live within their means.

This local connection applied at any rate to the revenue raised from excise licences henceforward to be allocated to local authorities—liquor, especially, but also such minor items as duties on carriages, male servants, shooting game, and carrying guns. In addition they were to receive 40 per cent of the revenue raised from probate duty, specifically a tax upon realized personalty, this to redress what in Conservative eyes was an imbalance in local taxation which penalized the landed interest. To make that point abundantly clear, distribution of the produce of these allocated taxes was not to be on the basis of population, which would have accorded with the localization rationale but would have benefited the metropolis and the county boroughs. Instead it was to be distributed in the same proportions as the superseded grants in aid, which favoured the counties.[207]

---

[207] Local Government Act 1888, s 22; Waller, *Town, City, and Nation*, 267; Offer, *Property and Politics*, 203.

Because some proposed new excise duties which would have been transferred to local authorities proved impracticable, the scheme was modified in 1890 by the creation of 'local taxation (customs and excise) duties', being a share of the beer tax and the product of an extra sixpence a gallon on spirits (hence its common name, 'the whisky money'), to be distributed according to the same formula as the other allocated taxes, some to be spent only on police superannuation, the rest steered, but not yet directed, towards technical education.[208]

The conceptual basis of the allocated revenues scheme survived Harcourt's Finance Act 1894, the Liberal measure creating a unified estate duty. It simply provided local authorities with a share of estate duty from personalty in place of probate duty. Carriage duties were extended to motor vehicle excise duties and became part of the local taxation cache in 1896.[209] In 1909 Lloyd George had to concede local authorities half the proceeds of his new land values tax, though in 1911 he managed to postpone payment for three years.[210]

The philosophy of separate revenues, however, was undermined from the beginning by the continuation of some grants in aid for education, which were almost immediately increased in 1891 by per capita fee grants to elementary schools willing to provide their service free.[211] As Liberals aimed to tax land more, so Conservatives reduced rates on agricultural land. They subsidised voluntary (chiefly Church of England) schools, and introduced another grant in aid as a sop, this time for the worst off board schools.[212] The dénouement came when the Conservatives rescued the ailing voluntary schools by restructuring elementary education entirely. They abolished the school boards, and shifted responsibility for all elementary schools to the counties and county boroughs, at the cost of a further annual grant in aid.[213] More grants for education followed from 1912 (medical services) and 1914 (school meals), also for road improvements from 1909.[214] At much the same time Treasury dislike of losing control of specific revenues led to two modifications. First the 1907 Finance Act substituted equivalent sums for the allocated taxes themselves, and then the 1909–10 Finance Act put a cap on some of the most significant.[215] There was continual wrangling over these

---

[208] Customs and Inland Revenue Act 1890, ss 4, 7; Local Taxation (Customs and Excise) Act 1890; (Technical Education Act 1889, extended by Technical Instruction Act 1891). From 1902 the whisky money, after the deduction for police superannuation, could be spent only on post-elementary education: Education Act 1902, s 2.

[209] Locomotives on Highways Act 1896, s 8.

[210] Finance Act 1909–10, s 91; Revenue Act 1911, s 16; Offer, *Property and Politics*, 385–6.

[211] Waller, *Town, City, and Nation*, 266; Finance Act 1894, s 19; Elementary Education Act 1891.

[212] Offer, *Property and Politics*, 207–17; Voluntary Schools Act 1897; Elementary Education Act 1897.

[213] Education Act 1902, s 10; Offer, *Property and Politics*, 216.

[214] Waller, *Town, City, and Nation*, 253, 271.

[215] Finance Act 1907, s 17; Finance Act 1909–10, ss 88–91.

details, just as much as there would have been if payment had been by grant in aid, some of what local authorities had lost being returned to them in 1911 when the payment of land value tax revenue was postponed.[216]

The crux of it all was that the nature of the central state was changing. The allocated taxes system had been predicated on a reasonably stable division of functions; but now the state was using the localities as its surrogate for the delivery of an increasingly expensive elementary education system.[217] It was taking a direct interest in main roads through the establishment of the Road Board in 1910. The introduction of labour exchanges, unemployment insurance, old age pensions, and national health insurance moved it into areas once paid for entirely from the rates that funded the poor law and the provision of district hospitals. Whereas a royal commission on local taxation in 1901 could conclude that the system was good and should be strengthened by allocating the inhabited houses duty to local authorities, albeit against the reasoned dissent of its chairman, a departmental committee chaired by the Comptroller and Auditor General in 1914 had very little difficulty in proposing it be swept aside in favour of a full return to grants in aid.[218]

The challenge was to find tax sources to fund all this increased state activity, to say nothing of the cost of armaments, and then to develop principles which could determine which functions should be treated as local and which national. The former led Lloyd George into the land taxes of his 1914 budget, the latter led the departmental committee to recognize a dilemma soluble only by politically inspired pragmatism: to maintain their vitality elected local authorities could not simply be the agents of central government, yet central government must always be able to graduate its supervision on a case-by-case basis, since the object must always be 'the best interests of the service'.[219]

The 'best interests of the service' had in fact for a long time dictated the structure of what became the lower levels of post-1918 local government—the poor law unions and rural sanitary authorities that became the rural district councils, and, up to a point, the urban sanitary authorities that became the urban district councils. Urban districts were to an extent self-identifying, in that the status of urban sanitary authority was given to local boards, and to have had a local board a place must first have applied for one. That could make for some odd contrasts when the composition and populations of the bigger rural districts were

[216]   The legislative trail includes Finance Act 1909–10, s 88(2); Revenue Act 1911, ss 17, 18.

[217]   Expenditure can be found in *Departmental Committee on Local Taxation*, Report, *PP* 1914 [Cd 7315], xl, 537.

[218]   *RC on Local Taxation*, Report, *PP* 1901 [Cd. 638], xxiv, 413; *Departmental Committee on Local Taxation*, Report.

[219]   Offer, *Property and Politics*, 384–400; *Departmental Committee on Local Taxation*, Report, 565.

compared with the smallest 'urban' areas.[220] But from 1875 the Local Government Board had been able to adjust boundaries, transfer areas, and give urban powers to suitable rural districts.[221] What central government and professional administrators regarded as historical anomalies were addressed in the post-war revision of local government. That required county councils to evaluate the boundaries and status of all its district councils, including non-county boroughs, and make proposals for change to the Ministry.[222]

The county boroughs, on the other hand, were the culmination of the 1835 Municipal Corporations Act's design. They were unitary general purpose authorities subordinate to no other. So long as there was a reasonably clear social and environmental division between town and country a sharp legal division between county and county borough did no harm. Landed proprietors remained the dominant influence in many counties to 1914, elected now to county councils rather than appointed to the bench. It was as inconceivable to Conservatives that the large towns should absorb their hinterlands as it was unacceptable to the ruling elites of the large towns, whatever their political complexion, that the hinterlands should dominate the towns.

The 1914–18 War was a watershed after which changing patterns of building and of transport made a sharp line much harder to maintain.[223] Boroughs had almost been designed to compete. Acquisition of borough status had been a reward for successful investment and growth, an acceptance of a duty to maximize the social returns of that investment, and a declaration of identity. By 1914 the list of county boroughs had grown from 61 to 80. Each one was capable of competing for territory, population, and wealth with its adjoining county, which, locked into its ancient boundaries, could only ever defend.[224] From the 1920s through into the 1950s the relationship became ever more acrimonious. Only with the Redcliffe-Maud report in 1969 was it possible to propose what in 1888 or even in 1914 would have been so out of keeping with social and political structure as to be unthinkable: that a thorough design for local government based upon its function in a national polity rather than upon existing forms would have to start with the abolition of the counties.[225]

---

[220] Olney, *Rural Society*, 141–2.
[221] Public Health Act 1875, ss 270–3, 276, 286.
[222] Local Government Act 1929.
[223] *RC on Local Government in England and Wales*, Research appendices, *PP* 1968–9 (Cmnd. 4040-II), xxxviii, 715, 735–8.
[224] Save for absorbing detached areas of other counties. There is an informative map of the distribution of county boroughs to 1914 in R. C. K. Ensor, *England 1870–1914* (Oxford, 1936), map 7, reprinted in Waller, *Town, City, and Nation*, 248.
[225] *RC on Local Government in England and Wales*, Report, *PP* 1968–9 (Cmnd. 4040), xxxviii, 29.

6. LONDON

London's difference was a compound, first of its great size, its piecemeal expansion over a long period, and the consequent adaptation of some of its parish vestries. Secondly, it was a consequence of the intransigent self-centredness of the Corporation of London (the 'City'), which had never sought to expand its territory and its representative institutions beyond the original square mile of the Norman city, but which guarded its ancient privileges tenaciously. It made all-London solutions to any problem difficult. Thirdly, it reflected London's great political importance as the capital and seat of government. In the 1840s especially, 'local' government almost by definition excluded London, which was the centre. After that moment passed there was still an administrative pull towards unified or centralized government but as the franchise broadened it was balanced by the realization that a strong administrative centre would also be a strong political centre. All late nineteenth-century reorganization of local government was political calculation, but the mark that left on London is particularly evident.

So although London's institutions had broad functional parallels elsewhere, the mix was always different. For most of the period from the 1820s to 1914 there were four types of institution in play, the relations between them frequently changing. There were those that operated at parish level or similar; there were those that had a full metropolitan jurisdiction; there was the City; and there was the central government. At the beginning, as in the country at large, local institutions predominated, their character and capacities very varied. At the end, again as in the country at large, there was a structured system of local government, kin to that elsewhere but heavily adapted to the circumstances of the capital, especially its political circumstances.

The Corporation of London (the 'City')

The City was the only significant municipal corporation to escape remodelling in 1835. The municipal commissioners' separate report on it was delayed until after the Whig government's reforming impetus had slowed.[226] So it kept its complex constitution replete with medieval survivals—its Court of Aldermen elected for life, its Court of Common Hall where liverymen of livery companies elected some of the City's officials.[227] Unlike the corporations of all other cities it kept

---

[226]   RC on Municipal Corporations, 2nd Report, PP 1837 (239), xxv, 1; I. G. Doolittle, The City of London and its Livery Companies (Salisbury, 1982), 22–4.

[227]   Terminology: 'City' was used promiscuously for both the Corporation and its territory, a usage followed here for convenience. Liverymen continued to enjoy the parliamentary franchise until 1918, in addition to whoever qualified under the general law: Representation of the People Act

full control of its property (and continued its feasting, celebrations, and political expenditure), did not surrender nomination of its magistracy to the Crown (and continued to combine executive and judicial authority in its aldermen), and did not have to institute a simple ratepayer franchise for its Common Council.[228] Unlike reformed corporations it kept its customs and byelaws restricting, for example, the privilege of retail trading within its territory to freemen, a privilege it enforced into the 1850s by requiring unfree traders to buy their freedom. However, it also kept its representative Court of Common Council, based upon a ward system which brought representative government down to the very local level, however unevenly it came to work as some wards lost their residential character.[229]

The difficulty for those outside the City was that while refusing to expand its territorial base, and hence extend its representative ward system beyond the square mile, it resolutely maintained its ancient privileges however far they reached. Its monopoly over markets extended well beyond its boundaries, leading to sharp conflict with the government in 1850 before the Corporation agreed to move the Smithfield live meat market from its central city site.[230] Likewise it took 20 years of 'repeated inquiry and animadversion' before in 1857 the Corporation was forced into sharing with the Crown the conservancy of the Thames and the revenues it had derived from riverside wharves.[231] Even then it dominated the reformed Thames Conservancy, defending it as a bastion against democracy until the beginning of the twentieth century.[232] It levied a duty of 13 pence on each chaldron of coal landed within an extended area around London—originally

1918, s 17(1), which substituted a business qualification. For accessible general accounts, see J. Davis, *Reforming London* (Oxford, 1988), 51–8; D. Owen, *The Government of Victorian London 1855–1889* (Cambridge, Mass., 1982), 226–59; Doolittle, *City of London*, 1–20.

[228] Only freemen householders held the City franchise until 1867, when in face of a rapidly declining population the Corporation itself substituted a £10-householder qualification, a more modest change than some reformers within the Corporation had hoped: City of London Municipal Elections Amendment Act 1867 (local); Doolittle, *City of London*, 85. The city's population stood at about 122,000 in 1831, peaking at about 130,000 in 1851 before crashing to some 75,000 in 1871 as commercial redevelopment took hold, and to 26,000 in 1901: *PP*, Census returns for census years.

[229] Doolittle, *City of London*, 25

[230] Owen, *Government of Victorian London*, 236, 244–5; *RC on Smithfield and other Meat Markets in London*, Report, PP 1850 [1217], xxxi, 355, and the Corporation's response in *Copies of letter addressed to the City Remembrancer*, PP 1850 (678), xxxiii, 623; Metropolitan Market Act, 14 & 15 Vict. c. 61 (1851) (statutory commissioners to make the shift and appropriate the tolls if Corporation would not).

[231] *SC on Thames Conservancy*, Report, *PP* (454) 1863, xii, 1; Thames Conservancy Act 1857 (local) (and see *Articles of Agreement*, PP 1857 (sess. 2) (41), xxix, 545); Thames Conservancy Act 1864; G. H. Porter, *The Thames Embankment* (Akron, Ohio, 1998), 137–41.

[232] B. Luckin, *Pollution and Control: A Social History of the Thames in the Nineteenth Century* (Bristol, 1986), 144–50. In particular, it barred representation of the Metropolitan Board of Works.

westwards as far as Staines, when coal came in by the Thames, then updated to take account of canal traffic, finally settled as a radius of 20 miles from the General Post Office.[233] Though nine of each of those 13 pence were dedicated by statute to the improvement of the approaches to London's bridges, so that the Corporation was in some sense a trustee, it saw the remaining four as its personal property, despite the fact that the impost was periodically renewable by Parliament. It might choose to spend most of it on road improvements within the square mile, but it need not.

It went without saying that the City would try to opt out of government-imposed centralization. It succeeded wholly in keeping out of the metropolitan police district, it retained its own Commission of Sewers when the rest of London's were amalgamated in 1847 (though with an obligation to pay towards some works), and it pre-empted the General Board of Health by acquiring its own public health statute in 1848, its own medical officer of health, and its own chief engineer.[234] For a government seeking an all-London solution to some perceived problem the Corporation of London was usually an irritant. Yet, as a system of local administration, even its critics admitted it operated at least reasonably well.[235]

Beyond the Square Mile

Because the City's boundaries were static, local elites had responded to the outwards wash of London's new housing in the classic eighteenth-century manner by acquiring local improvement and poor law management Acts for their districts.[236] Unusually, some of those empowered a parish vestry rather than creating independent commissioners. There were thus some highly centralized parishes, notably St Marylebone and St George's, Hanover Square. Other parishes were highly fragmented, most notoriously St Pancras, where poor law administration was vested by local Act in self-perpetuating trustees, and responsibility for

---

[233] For what follows see 8 & 9 Vict. c. 101 (1845) continuing London & Westminster Coal Trade Act 1838, 1 & 2 Vict. c. ci, which updated and continued London, Westminster & Home Counties Coal Trade Act 1831, 1 & 2 Will. IV c. lxxvi; RC on City of London, Report, PP 1854 [1772], xxvi, 1, 25, showing that of the £179,857 raised in 1852, the Corporation retained only £15,305 directly for its own use; 2 & 3 Vict. c. 80 (1839), 3 & 4 Vict. c. 87 (1840); 4 & 5 Vict. c. 12 (1841); 8 & 9 Vict. c. 101 (1845); 9 & 10 Vict. c. 34 (1846). A similar duty applied to wine.

[234] In addition to its own parallel public health Act it acquired a parallel police Act in 1839, again to head off amalgamation with the metropolitan force: City of London Police Act, 2 & 3 Vict. c. xciv.

[235] The report of the RC on the City of London praised the City's prison administration, e.g.: PP 1854 [1772], xxvi, 1, 18.

[236] For this paragraph see F. H. W. Sheppard, Local Government in St. Marylebone, 1688–1835 (1958), 158–60; Returns from the Vestry etc…[concerning] the paving, cleansing and lighting of each parish, PP 1854–5 (127), liii, 153; Owen, Government of Victorian London, 284, 286.

cleansing and paving rested with estate commissioners, 14 sets of them by 1819, three more by 1855. To offset this divided authority in 1817 an early measure of co-ordination equipped all commissioners and parochial authorities within the metropolitan area possessing statutory powers of street management with a uniform and comprehensive code of powers for use in addition to their own Act.[237] Its uptake and interpretation could vary greatly, of course, but in 1862 it was still thought worth extension.[238]

There was variety too in vestries' constitutions. Some parishes had retained their common law open vestries, others had responded to massive population increase by instituting self-perpetuating 'select vestries' (of the oligarchic sort), corrupt, extravagant, and incompetent, so it was said, while others had created annually elected management committees ('select vestries' of the Sturges Bourne type).[239] In 1831, however, Hobhouse's Vestries Act empowered ratepayers to demand a poll to shift from an oligarchic to a vestry elected on a gender-blind one-ratepayer one vote franchise, the first fruit of the Parliament that was to end by reforming itself.[240] St. Marylebone and St George's, Hanover Square managed the transition with a minimum of fuss, giving them much the same functional character that the reformed municipal corporations came to have elsewhere.[241] Three other London parishes adopted the Act, and at least one rejected it amid protests about improperly denied votes.[242] As the newly elected vestry of St. Pancras found, however, representative government might have little to do, since Hobhouse's Act did not affect the statutory commissioners either in their powers or their constitution.[243]

Fragmented authority thus remained fragmented.[244] Similarly, the Poor Law Amendment Act applied to London as it did elsewhere, shifting vestry control to the Poor Law Commissioners (later Board). Since there had already been a good deal of local reform and consolidation of small parishes into unions in some

---

[237] Metropolitan Paving Act, 57 Geo. 3 c. xxix (1817), extending to the area then covered by the bills of mortality plus St Marylebone and St Pancras, less St Mary, Islington, St John, Hackney, and a few estates.

[238] *Returns from the Vestry etc…1854–5*; Metropolis Management Amendment Act 1862, s 73.

[239] *SC on select vestries*, Report, *PP* 1830 (215), iv, 569 (and preliminary report 1830 (25), iv, 425).

[240] Vestries Act, 1 & 2 Will. IV c. 60; Keith-Lucas, *English Local Government Franchise*, 28–34.

[241] Owen, *Government of Victorian London*, 262–4.

[242] *Return of the Parishes…which have adopted the Act 1 & 2 Will. IV…*, *PP* 1842 (564), xxxiii, 569; *Return of the Churchwardens without Cripplegate*, *PP* 1831–2 (723), xliv, 83.

[243] Owen, *Government of Victorian London*, 286–9; cf. St. Leonard Shoreditch, F. Sheppard, in Owen, *Government of Victorian London*, 326–7; and see e.g. reform of Bethnal Green's paving and lighting commissioners (but still requiring a high property qualification of electors): *VCH Middlesex*, xi, 196–7; Bethnal Green & Shoreditch Improvement Act 1843, 6 & 7 Vict, c. xxxiv.

[244] See e.g. *Returns showing by what authority the municipal and parochial affairs of the City of Westminster [etc] are carried on*, *PP* 1833 (713), xxxi, 341.

parts of London, the relation between the Commissioners (and Board) and trus-tees under local Acts was particularly litigious.[245] This dispute between local and centralized authority was not finally settled in the Board's favour until 1867.[246]

The Pull of Central Government

There were some other significant centralized or consolidated authorities, pecu-liar to London. The Metropolitan Police was the most obvious, its commissioners appointed by and answerable to the Secretary of State. The mobs whose disorder was thought to threaten political stability did not observe parish boundaries, nor was the unreformed vestries strong enough (or even inclined) to resist this inno-vation in centralized policing—unlike the City, which did.[247] The police district from 1829 spanned a seven-mile radius from Charing Cross (bar the City), with extensions possible by Home Office order to places within 12 miles—a prospect that provoked distant Willesden to adopt the watching provisions of the Lighting and Watching Act in 1835 in an attempt to head off the unwelcome burden of the metropolitan police rate.[248] The radius for extensions was increased to 15 miles in 1839 and the power soon exercised, in the interests of unity and efficiency, as Radzinowicz puts it.[249] Local pleas for the adequacy of existing arrangements were disregarded. The contrast with policing elsewhere in the country was stark.

Roading was another activity that transcended local boundaries. The oldest and oddest of the consolidated authorities was the Metropolis Road Board, an institution that was self-perpetuating until 1863, when power to fill vacancies was transferred to the Treasury.[250] It was formed in 1826 to manage the arterial turnpikes north of the Thames, taking over from 14 existing turnpike trusts, and reporting annually to Parliament.[251] Its territory never extended south of the river, however, for the trusts there had resisted further amalgamation.[252] Then the advent of railways in the mid-1830s halted the consolidation movement that might perhaps have expanded the board into a general highways authority for

---

[245] Owen, *Government of Victorian London*, 276–9; F. Sheppard in Owen, *Government of Victorian London*, 296–8.

[246] Metropolitan Poor Act 1867, ss 73–8.

[247] See XIII, Pt 1, pp. 28, 34–5.

[248] 10 Geo. IV c. 44, s 34; *VCH* Middlesex, vii, 230.

[249] 2 & 3 Vict. c. 47, s 2 (1839); L. Radzinowicz, *A History of the English Criminal Law and its Administration from 1750* (1968), iv, 204–5.

[250] Metropolis Roads Act 1863, s 2.

[251] Metropolis Turnpike Roads North of the Thames Act 1826, 7 Geo. IV c. cxlii, extended by 10 Geo. IV c. 59 (1829). Its members were nominated in the Act, with power to fill vacancies themselves.

[252] T. F. Ordish, *History of Metropolitan Roads*, being App. H to *Report of the London Traffic Branch of the Board of Trade*, PP 1910 (Cd. 5472), xxxviii, 1, 183–6, 191.

London. Though the board created several important new turnpike roads, its policy of removing tolls from existing roads wherever possible worked in fact as a decentralization, since responsibility for their upkeep then fell on the parishes.[253] By contrast, devising and constructing new roads through the densely inhabited inner metropolitan areas needed a combination of powers and finance only Parliament could provide, and an agency that could not be found merely locally. A series of statutes therefore empowered the Commissioners of Woods and Forests—the government's public works department—who thereby gained a role in London's government that was to become influential.[254] Their broader jurisdiction began in 1844, with the supervision of building standards across the metropolis.[255]

So it was not quixotic for Edwin Chadwick to scheme in the 1840s for the creation of a single Crown-appointed commission to control the public health and sanitation of all London. That should replace the vestries just as local boards were to do in the country, a need all the more apparent in London where, it could be presented, ancient boundaries and fragmented authorities bore no relation to topography.[256] Science, not tradition, should shape the institutions required. Denial of the existence of genuinely local interests and a denigration of vestries and improvement commissioners were as much part of the reformers' stock-in-trade as was an insistence on small-bore sewer pipes and reticulated water supplies.[257] Local government in London was not to be local self-government, because there was no self.[258]

Chadwick could not sustain his principle. His first step was the replacement of the six sets of Crown-appointed commissioners of sewers with jurisdiction within the London area by a single Metropolitan Commission of Sewers, though (once again) the City had to be omitted since there the Corporation had the power of appointment.[259] Then the commissioners' powers were greatly extended, converting them from an agency managing surface water and flood prevention into a

---

[253] See Ordish, *History of Metropolitan Roads*, above, generally, and Metropolis Roads Act 1863. The board was wound up in 1872.

[254] Metropolitan Thoroughfares Act, 2 & 3 Vict. c. 80 (1839), extended in 1840, 1841 (twice) and 1844.

[255] Metropolitan Buildings Act, 7 & 8 Vict. c. 84 (1844) amended by 9 & 10 Vict. c. 5 (1846).

[256] S. E. Finer, *The Life and Times of Sir Edwin Chadwick* (1952) 308–10; R. A. Lewis, *Edwin Chadwick and the Public Health Movement 1832–54* (1952), 156–7.

[257] Hamlin, *Public Health*, 179–84.

[258] Lewis, *Edwin Chadwick*, 260–1, 272–3; special pleading, perhaps, since Chadwick disdained local self-government generally: A. Brundage, *England's 'Prussian Minister', Edwin Chadwick and the Politics of Government Growth 1832–1854* (Pennsylvania, 1988), 123–8.

[259] The City's Commissioners of Sewers were effectively a committee of Common Council.

drainage and sewering board.[260] But its political overlord, the First Commissioner of Woods and Forests, acknowledged that constitutional principle, or perhaps political expediency, required such an executive commission to include representatives of those who were to pay, albeit few, and Crown-appointed rather than elected. That brought a solitary (but loud) voice from the vestries on to the commission, and representatives of the City, since the City was to be precepted for works affecting it.[261] Despite this dilution of the pure executive principle the commission was potentially a powerful body.

Its complementary agency, the General Board of Health, also Chadwick-dominated, also answerable to the First Commissioner, was not designed to be strong in London. It had direct executive authority there in times of epidemic, but it lacked the institution-creating and supervisory powers it enjoyed elsewhere in the country, because the notion that local boards of health were appropriate in London ran counter to all that Chadwick believed.[262] So when Chadwick (and his supporters, and his enemies) were removed from the Metropolitan Commission of Sewers in 1849 because their mutual loathing made constructive work impossible, he found the General Board a difficult base from which to recapture London. He had to rely upon obtaining new legislation, and that at a time when the commission's fruitless expenditure and the board's dictatorial use of its epidemic powers had pushed the vestries into co-ordinated opposition to centralization in general.[263]

Chadwick's failure to redirect the General Board towards London has been well recounted.[264] The Treasury refused to fund the board's projected monopoly of human burial in the metropolis, and the water companies defeated its move to control London's water supply in aid of a great combined supply and sewerage scheme. Reaction then led to the non-renewal of the board's leasehold on power in 1854. It was coincidence that the re-reconstituted Metropolitan Commissioners of Sewers, now predominantly railway engineers, were perceived as having failed to stem the ravages of cholera, but the two things together ruled out any further attempt at centralization.[265] Yet the sanitary movement had nevertheless succeeded in its general aim of persuading government that sewerage schemes were

[260] Metropolitan Commissioners of Sewers Act, 11 & 12 Vict. c. 112 (1848); Hamlin, *Public Health*, 88, 241–2, 275, 310; Brundage, *England's 'Prussian Minister'*, 121–5, 137–40; Finer, *Chadwick*, 314–18.

[261] City: 11 & 12 Vict. c. 112, ss 4, 12, 116–17; vestries: Finer, *Chadwick*, 357; Lewis, *Edwin Chadwick*, 216–17; Brundage, *England's 'Prussian Minister'*, 124.

[262] Neither the Public Health Act 1848, 11 & 12 Vict. c. 63, nor the Local Government Act 1858 applied to the metropolis, where public health legislation was mostly to be found in the Metropolis Management Act and its amendments, down to the Public Health (London) Act 1891.

[263] Finer, *Chadwick*, 326–30, 379–81; Lewis, *Edwin Chadwick*, 235–7.

[264] Finer, *Chadwick*, 379–429; Lewis, *Edwin Chadwick*, 238–78.

[265] Owen, *Government of Victorian London*, 31–2.

the answer to the public health question, so the issue became how to devise institutions at once effective and acceptable.

The Tortuous Evolution of a Tiered System

The federal solution devised in 1855 by Sir Benjamin Hall, MP for St Marylebone, First Commissioner of Works in Palmerston's government, proved a good deal more resilient than its critics have allowed.[266] In a sort of contextual byway from its terms of reference, a royal commission on the Corporation of London—government irritation made manifest—had proposed that a City reformed on the lines of the 1835 Municipal Corporations Act be surrounded by sibling corporations, one for each of London's parliamentary constituencies, with a somewhat minimalist overarching metropolitan board to see to the mains drainage.[267] Hall accepted the board and its ostensibly minor role, but in what has aptly been described as a prime example of the art of the possible he rejected the constituency-based boroughs in favour of retaining the vestries, to be strengthened by turning them into copies of the admirable St Marylebone vestry itself.[268]

The reformed vestries took their constitution almost exactly from Hobhouse's Act—elective vestries on a ratepayer franchise, vestrymen to qualify by occupying property with a rateable value of £40 or more (but softened from Hobhouse's Act by reducing the figure to £25 in poor parishes), the maximum permitted size of the vestry, its quorum, even the details of the election process, all stemmed from the 1831 Act that had worked for St Marylebone.[269] This time, however, the vestry was to have no rivals. The local paving commissions were to be wound up, their powers transferred to the vestries. In addition the vestries were to receive

---

[266] Metropolitan Management Act 1855. Crown Lands Act, 14 & 15 Vict. c. 42 (1851), split the activities of the Commissioners of Woods and Forests. The First Commissioner was renamed the First Commissioner of Works, remaining a minister, sometimes with a seat in cabinet. His department, the Board of Works, was responsible for public works, which included the London parks and thoroughfares, and for the administration of most of the statutory powers previously vested in the Commissioners of Woods and Forests, including the Metropolitan Buildings Acts. His department was subordinate to the Treasury: M. Wright, *Treasury Control of the Civil Service 1854–74* (Oxford, 1969), p. xxiv. The remaining Commissioners of Woods and Forests continued as a revenue department of the Treasury under the direction of a Surveyor General, responsible for Crown lands and revenues. In due course the Commissioners of Works became the Ministry of Works, and the Commissioners of Woods and Forests became the Commissioners of Crown Lands.

[267] *RC on the Corporation of the City of London*, Report, PP 1854 [1772], xxvi, 1.

[268] Porter, *Thames Embankment*, 63; St Marylebone: South London Advertiser, quoted by Owen, *Government of Victorian London*, 215.

[269] The debt to Hobhouse's Act is noticed by Davis, *Reforming London*, 12. The major difference was that the 1855 Act required parishes with more than 2000 rated householders to be divided into wards.

street management powers, though much of that either copied or updated what was already in the Metropolitan Paving Act 1817, plus powers and duties to see to local drainage and sewerage.[270] At least these were the powers conferred on the vestries of the 23 largest parishes, which remained autonomous. A further 57 parishes were grouped into 16 districts, powers there to be exercised by district boards comprised of members chosen by and from the vestrymen elected to the component vestries. Apart from those special arrangements for conjoined parishes there is considerable convergence in this plan with the reformed municipal corporations and the local boards outside London, though some of the details differed reflecting the different raw materials. Once again the Corporation was left over to be dealt with separately.[271]

The independent vestries, the district boards, and the Corporation were each to elect representatives to serve on a Metropolitan Board of Works, which would take over from the Metropolitan Commissioners of Sewers the task of constructing the mains sewers. It would also take over administration of the Metropolitan Buildings Acts from the Commissioners of Works.[272] Further, a single but extremely important section empowered the new board to improve London's roads and streets, subject to the same need for parliamentary authorization for particular schemes that had applied to the Commissioners of Woods and Forests and their successor, the First Commissioner of Works.[273] Similarly the board's plans for mains sewers required the First Commissioner's approval, just as he had overseen the Crown-appointed Metropolitan Commissioners of Sewers. The board was therefore a constitutional novelty, pitched uneasily between being an agency of central government and a delegate of the vestries (and the City). When Sir Benjamin Hall asserted an authority to scrutinize both policy and detail three years of deadlock resulted.[274]

The Conservatives, returning to office just as the summer of the 'great stink' from the Thames encouraged creative thinking, broke the deadlock by freeing the board from this particular central control. Dale Porter has argued, however, that control recurred shortly afterwards under a different First Commissioner, so that in its early years the board can be seen as a substitute but essentially subordinate executive arm for the commissioner's own unambitious department, the Board of

---

[270]   In 1862 the Metropolis Management Amendment Act, s 73 extended the 1817 Act to all unpaved streets.

[271]   It duly evaded a succession of government proposals between 1854 and 1863 for its internal reform and reduction of its privileges: Doolittle, *City of London*, 51–68.

[272]   Metropolitan Buildings Act 1855.

[273]   Metropolis Management Act 1855, s 144.

[274]   Porter, *Thames Embankment*, 70, details Hall's involvement in the board's plans for its mains drainage.

Works.[275] That second occasion arose when the metropolitan board's chairman, John Thwaites, achieved a form of political partnership with William Cowper, the then First Commissioner, through which it was the board rather than a new or centralized agency that designed and built the Thames Embankment. That was a crowning achievement for the board, but it came on the condition that its plans were approved by the First Commissioner. This, however, was a power to veto, much less than the power to command that Hall had assumed and which the board had withstood. The need for the commissioner's approval might also have been premised upon the Crown's valuable property interest in the riverbed and foreshore justifying a measure of control over the Embankment's design.

Still, Porter's argument could be taken a step further, in that it was yet another First Commissioner, A. S. Ayrton, who, though he had no formal responsibility for the board, took upon himself in 1869 the role of persuading Parliament to restructure the board's finances so that it could borrow long term at low rates, thus enabling it to expand its capital-hungry projects for street improvements.[276] That reform also contained a veto, first in the shape of Treasury control, no different perhaps from that required of municipal corporations, but supplemented in 1875 by the stipulation that the board's annual borrowing requirement be embodied in statute.[277] That obliged the board to submit its annual capital works budget to Parliament much as if it were a central department, unless, perchance, it could fund a development without borrowing.[278]

If the board's relation with central government thus remained ambiguous, that ability to borrow advantageously ultimately strengthened its position *vis-à-vis* the vestries and district boards. Before then it had struggled to find an adequate financial base. From the beginning it could precept on parochial rates, though the 1855 Act had deliberately left open whether vestries and district boards should pay in proportion to their rateable value or in proportion to the benefits they received.[279] That uncertainty was removed as first the Conservatives' 1858 Act deemed the board's mains sewers to be of equal benefit to all parts of the metropolis, and then the Metropolis Management Amendment Act 1862 allowed precepts

---

[275] Metropolis Management Amendment Act 1858, s 1; Porter, *Thames Embankment*, 70, 84–5, 88; and see Owen, *Government of Victorian London*, 31–46.

[276] Metropolitan Board of Works (Loans) Act 1869; Owen, *Government of Victorian London*, 165–8. The Embankment was funded by the 9d coal duty (see above), fortuitously up for renewal and diverted by Parliament to the board's advantage, though the board later had to borrow additional money: Porter, *Thames Embankment*, 155–8.

[277] Metropolitan Board of Works (Loans) Acts 1869 and 1875.

[278] The LCC, which inherited this restriction from the board, did once hold out successfully from a parliamentary refusal, in 1935: D. N. Chester, *Central and Local Government* (1951), 150–1.

[279] Metropolis Management Act 1855, s 170.

only in proportion to rateable value.[280] This had a mild redistributive effect, and gave the board a characteristic of an independent municipal authority. However, since it was somewhat at odds with its status as only an indirectly elected entity it accentuated antagonism between vestries and the board, as each vestry and its representatives greeted each proposal for expenditure with a minute calculation of local benefit.[281] Parochial rates paid also for the metropolitan police, the poor law (including hospitals and dispensaries), vestry expenditure, and (from 1870) elementary schools, tending to discourage further expenditure.

Outside London municipal corporations frequently funded projects from the profits of water and gas supply, but the board's attempts to acquire those in the metropolitan area failed.[282] Some indirect relief came when, first, the Poor Law Board established the Metropolitan Common Poor Fund in 1867, to which parishes contributed in proportion to their rateable value, and then the Valuation (Metropolis) Act 1869 imposed a common system for the valuation of rateable property, preventing undervaluation by wealthy parishes, to the benefit of the board's precept.[283] Then in the same year its ability to fund street improvement projects was transformed by Ayrton's creation of consolidated loan stock, enabling it to borrow for long terms at low interest rates.[284] That coincided with a rise in property values, these reforms together generating a rate fund sufficient to service the loans. The new loans Act also authorized the board to lend to the vestries and district boards, enabling it to transfer the benefits of this efficient financing system to them.[285] By these means its financial position relative to the vestries and district boards was secured—the critical element in any federal system.

In parallel the board's powers increased. In part this was simply that as Parliament imposed regulation and sought local agency for its enforcement, the board became the repository of a miscellany of powers in the same way that local

[280]   Metropolis Management Amendment Act 1858, s 12; Metropolis Management Act 1862, s 5.

[281]   Owen, *Government of Victorian London*, 129, 267–70 (but contrast 318); Sheppard in Owen, *loc cit*, 295–6 (but contrast 337); Davis, *Reforming London*, 34–40, 44; J. Roebuck, *Urban Development in 19th-Century London* (1979), 85–7.

[282]   Owen, *Government of Victorian London*, 134–45; E. P. Hennock, *Finance and Politics in Urban Local Government in England, 1835–1900* (1963) 6 *Hist. J.* 212–25.

[283]   Metropolitan Poor Act 1867 (the London equivalent of the Union Chargeability Act 1865), building on Metropolitan Houseless Poor Act 1864, made permanent by Metropolitan Houseless Poor Act 1865; Valuation (Metropolis) Act 1869.

[284]   Metropolitan Board of Works (Loans) Act 1869; Owen, *Government of Victorian London*, 165–8; Porter *Thames Embankment*, 156–8. The novelty lay in the consolidation of loans, Treasury control, the easy negotiability of stock, and the 60-year period for repayment. Metropolis Management Act 1855, ss 183–90, had always enabled the board to borrow on the strength of its future rates income. From 1877 it was authorized to issue bills: Metropolitan Board of Works (Money) Act 1877.

[285]   From 1875 exercise of this power was subject to the same need for parliamentary approval as was the board's exercise of its borrowing power.

authorities and the county justices did—though to say that recognizes the board as a member of that same broad category.[286] In a similar way it became responsible for the capital's fire brigade.[287] But it was also that as both the board's and the vestries' local management powers increased, the board's superior role became ever more apparent. That began with the 1862 Metropolis Management Amendment Act, which emphasized throughout that on matters of sewerage, drainage, and street management the board was to supervise the vestries and set the appropriate standards.[288] The vestries and district boards thus became a lower tier of local government, rather than bodies operating in parallel to the board.

Vestrydom was subjected to much contemporary scorn, reinforced by some historians, but it has been pointed out that the vestries did construct the local sewers expected of them, and did manage their streets, just as the metropolitan board did construct the mains sewers and many new roads, in addition to the prestige project of the Embankment.[289] The doubts came as expectations increased in the next generation.[290] Then the vestries' perceived failure to make more than superficial inroads into the newly recognized problem of working-class housing, the failure of most vestries to make use of adoptive legislation at their disposal on such matters as the provision of public libraries, baths, and washhouses, the board's failure to acquire ownership of London's water supply, the endless bickering between board and vestries over the acquisition of land for parks and open spaces, and the general apathy they seemed to engender among the people of London, all suggested that Sir Benjamin Hall's legacy was two levels of government each too weak to manage the complexity of the metropolis of the 1880s.

From this point on the shape of London's government was determined by the dynamic of party politics. In terms simply of law and of institutional design the choices were fairly clear. There could be a unitary authority, or there could be tiers. If tiers, there could be a strong centre superior to relatively many small local units, or there could be a weak centre hemmed in by relatively few big corporation-like entities. The City could be brought into the system (and reformed)

---

[286] Owen, *Government of Victorian London*, 127, 153–5.

[287] *Ibid.*, 127–30; Metropolitan Fire Brigade Act 1869.

[288] Metropolis Management Act 1862, e.g. ss 32, 48, 72, 83; see too Metropolitan Building Act 1869.

[289] A. Clinton and P. Murray, 'Reassessing the Vestries: London Local Government, 1855–1900', in A. O'Day (ed.), *Government and Institutions in the post-1832 UK* (1995); and see generally, Owen, *Government of Victorian London*, esp. Chs 12, 13 (by F. Sheppard), 14, and 15 (by F. Sheppard).

[290] This paragraph and the next two draw heavily on Davis, *Reforming London*, though the interpretation is my own. See also F. M. L. Thompson, *Hampstead: Building a Borough 1650–1964* (1974), 167–8, 184–202, 329–34 for the difficulty of acquiring Hampstead Heath. Modern commentary on London's housing is kinder to the board: see Owen, *Government of London*, 115 and A. W. Wohl, *The Eternal Slum* (1977), 133–6.

or left out (and remain unreformed.) All of these were proposed at one time or another; none needed new legal techniques. Only one element was never questioned: in the new environment of the 1880s all these institutions must have a directly elected council. Quite apart from the logistics, however, the party political ramifications of any of these choices could become very complex.

Surprisingly, the vestries and district boards proved resilient. From the later 1880s they began to do all that their critics had said they were incapable of doing, and doing it without legislative change to their constitution.[291] The new mood seems to have begun before the directly elected London County Council replaced the indirectly elected Metropolitan Board, so the undoubted stimulus to local government growth that came from the Progressives' victory in the first LCC elections cannot have been the only cause. Sir Benjamin Hall's lower tier (as it had become) thus proved flexible enough to serve two quite different political cultures.[292] The board was less fortunate. As a type of local authority it lacked the usual base in electoral politics; as a substitute for a central department it lacked a minister responsible for it to Parliament. Hence it turned out to be more than usually dependent on individual leadership, which declined from the death of John Thwaites in 1870.[293] Its early achievements did not continue, and it ended in (but not because of) a scandal of systemic corruption on the part of its Chief Valuer and Assistant Surveyor.[294]

The board's replacement by the directly elected London County Council was the simplest outcome of the logic of county reform in 1888, given that an upper tier of metropolitan government be retained. The alternatives would have either multiplied tiers of government or bifurcated the functions of the new county councils of Middlesex, Surrey, and Kent. So the board's replacement was in itself uncontroversial. It was uncontroversial also that ward boundaries for the new elections would follow the new parliamentary constituencies created after the third Reform Act, all 59 of them. However, Charles Ritchie, Conservative president of the Local Government Board and the architect of the 1888 Act, had hoped to replace the vestries and district boards as well, with larger, more powerful district councils that could take powers away from the LCC.[295] That proposal

[291]   Davis, *Reforming London*, 158–68.

[292]   Disaggregation of district boards to reflect population growth in their constituent parishes came surprisingly late: Metropolis Management Amendment Act 1885, Metropolis Management (Battersea and Westminster) Act 1887. For an earlier informal separation, see Roebuck, *Urban Development*, 58.

[293]   Owen, *Governing Victorian London*, 157–8.

[294]   *Ibid.*, 169–92. To the end, though, it was acquiring new functions: London Parks and Works Act 1887 transferred responsibility for several London parks to it from the Commissioners of Works.

[295]   Davis, *Reforming London*, 101–8.

foundered for fear that it would threaten the City's privileges.[296] The result left a powerful LCC, with a profile unlike that of any other county council. It had far more extensive public health and road management powers, though it lacked even the partial and indirect influence over policing enjoyed in the counties proper.[297] It had quite a different financial relation with the local units, and the central controls over its borrowing remained different from those over counties proper.

The Progressives dominated the LCC; the Liberals, returning briefly to office, extended the vestry franchise to those (male) inhabitants who did not qualify as ratepayers but were on the parliamentary roll, and also passed a modest redistribution measure levying the richer parishes and the City for the benefit of the poorer.[298] The Conservatives were in a bind. To curtail Progressive influence, satisfy the localist emotions of local government representatives, protect the City from amalgamation, and insulate the wealthy West End vestries from importunate demands on their rates by the slum districts all pointed to secession or extensive devolution.[299] But that would harm suburban Conservatives intent on developing their areas by claiming on the general wealth of the metropolis, and meet opposition in Whitehall from bureaucrats who doubted that the outcome would be sustainable and manageable.

In the result the London Government Act 1899 was something of a cross-party measure.[300] Finally it created metropolitan boroughs. But like the 1855 Act it took parishes as its basic unit; the 15 largest became metropolitan boroughs in their own right, to be joined by 13 more formed by aggregating smaller parishes.[301] It was an intermediate reform of the sort attractive to administrators. The Act transferred only a few very minor powers from the LCC to the new metropolitan boroughs; anything more substantial would need the LCC's consent. For the rest of our period central control of local government in London turned, as it did elsewhere, not on further changing the institutional design but on funding.

---

[296] The City survived as a county in its own right for judicial purposes, and as if it were a quarter sessions borough (not a county borough) for the purposes of dividing its justices' administrative functions between the Common Council and the LCC, in each case with some adaptations: Local Government Act 1888, ss 40(3), 41.

[297] London's public health legislation was consolidated into the Public Health (London) Act 1891, aligning its substance more closely with the rest of the country's.

[298] Local Government Act 1894, ss 2, 31; London (Equalization of Rates) Act 1894; Davis, *Reforming London*, 168–75.

[299] For Liberal proposals to amalgamate the City with the LCC see Davis, *Reforming London*, 176–84, 195–8; Doolittle, *City of London*, 122–9.

[300] Davis, *Reforming London*, 243.

[301] London Government Act 1899; Woolwich and South Hornsey were brought into the metropolitan area for the first time, the latter as part of Stoke Newington.

VI
Judicial Review

PREVIOUS chapters contain numerous instances of courts passing judgment on the legality of decisions, regulations, and actions made in pursuance of statutory authority, which together constitute the division of law in the twentieth century called judicial review or, in one of its senses, administrative law.[1] The twentieth-century texts by S. A. de Smith or H. W. R. Wade have no nineteenth-century counterparts, however, because to have such a general concept of review depends on a perception of state or official power which itself transcends the particular context of its exercise.[2] That was twentieth-century thinking, rooted, in England, in the politics that followed the third Reform Act, 1884. In the nineteenth century legal writers embedded their analysis of courts' powers to determine legality within an account of a particular context—summary convictions, railways, corporations, public health, for example.[3] In addition there was a thin literature on particular legal processes. *Mandamus* attracted the most because, lying to compel the performance of any public duty, it spanned a broad range of contexts.[4] Prohibition, which was used most often to prevent ecclesiastical and admiralty courts encroaching on to common law territory, had a single text.[5]

There were public lawyers before there was public law. Robert Pashley had a large presence in reported litigation in the 1840s, noticeable in marginal decisions, Robert Vaughan Richards likewise, as Nicholas Fazakerley had had

---

[1] For its different sense, the law made by administrators, see C. T. Carr, *Concerning English Administrative Law* (1941) and H. W. Arthurs, '*Without the Law*' (Toronto 1985). F. J. Port, *Administrative Law* (1929) and J. A. G. Griffith and H. Street, *Principles of Administrative Law* (1957) combine the genres.

[2] S. A. de Smith, *Judicial Review of Administrative Action* (1954); H. W. R. Wade, *Administrative Law* (1961).

[3] W. Paley's *Law and Practice of Summary Convictions* (1814) has a claim to being the first text with judicial review as a major theme.

[4] W. J. Impey, *A Treatise on the Law and Practice of Mandamus* (1826); T. Tapping, *The Law and Practice of the High Prerogative Writ of Mandamus* (1848). Later there is some broadening: J. Shortt, *Informations (Criminal and Quo Warranto), Mandamus and Prohibition* (1887).

[5] M. Lloyd, *A Treatise on the Law of Prohibition* (1849). Prohibition was becoming used then to determine the limits of county court jurisdiction.

during a formative period a century earlier.[6] Their staple was the stream of local decisions emanating from justices, whether by an order, or by a summary conviction, or through quarter sessions. That had an extensive literature, traditionally in the form of compendia that immediately break down the promise of generality into specialized subsections. These included primary jurisdictions, where justices made and enforced their own orders, but also important secondary jurisdictions to enforce orders made by local commissioners and local boards who, through into the mid-century tended not to have their own enforcement powers. Questions would then arise whether justices had a supervisory jurisdiction over the commissioners' and boards' orders they were asked to enforce, which might themselves be reviewed by a superior court. The law on all this became extensive and homogeneous enough to generate a text by Scholefield and Hill in 1902 on how justices' 'proceedings and acts may be supervised and controlled'.[7] Within its limited context it is a recognizable forerunner of de Smith and Wade.

Justices had no political responsibility, but the local boards and councils that took over local governance from them did, and ministers of the Crown more so. It takes a degree of abstraction and some political predisposition to bracket them together as 'persons exercising statutory powers', hence equally subject to judicial review. Judges could never escape asking whether political accountability should make a difference or whether that was a matter for Parliament to make explicit. They would sometimes struggle, as they did in the 1830s while deciding that though mandamus would not lie against the Crown it would against even the most senior political office holder, though (retreating) only in respect of duties owed to an individual, not duties owed to the Crown.[8] But challenges to ministerial decisions were few. Those to the Local Government Board were directly authorized by statute, the Board being the successor to the Poor Law Commissioners, whose orders were amenable to statutory certiorari, and those at the end of our period that were enveloped in political controversy concerned appeals to central ministries from local bodies, where at least some of the difficulty arose from the ministries' ambiguous dual role.

This chapter offers a framework for the instances of review raised in previous chapters. It begins with the world of Pashley and Richards and ends with Rice, Arlidge, and the cases tentatively asserting judicial control over discretionary

---

[6] Pashley and Fazakerley have entries in ODNB.

[7] J. Scholefield and G. R. Hill, Appeals from Justices (1902), 3.

[8] R v. Commissioners of Appeals in Matters of Excise (1814) 3 M. & S. 133; R v. Lords Commissioners of the Treasury (1835) 4 Ad. & El. 286, R v. Lords Commissioners of the Treasury (1836) 4 Ad. & El. 976, R v. Lords Commissioners of the Treasury (1836) 4 Ad. & El. 984; Ex p. Ricketts (1836) 4 Ad. & El. 999. See above, pp. 382–3.

decisions.[9] Scholefield and Hill's book did not go into further editions—which practically any law book does that sells. Instead, when F. J. Port wrote his pioneering study in 1929 his focus was on centralized authority.[10] His book was different in another respect too, in that it was a product of a university rather than the bar, which may suggest another reason why there was no general administrative law until well into the twentieth century.

1. EIGHTEENTH-CENTURY FOUNDATIONS

In addition to *mandamus* and prohibition there was *certiorari*, which brought inferior courts' records into the King's Bench, freezing the lower court's process and awaiting the bench's own exercise of authority. That might be simply a matter of judicial administration—shifting the venue of a trial or enabling enforcement through the King's Bench of a local civil court's order against a defendant who had skipped its jurisdiction. Importantly, it was *certiorari* that brought to Westminster the many special cases stated for its opinion by quarter sessions, a voluntary substitute for appeal on point of law about which more will be said below. But it might also be to scrutinize the record for unlawfulness, a power the King's Bench held to be within its own inherent jurisdiction.

Such reviewable unlawfulness might be a deficiency of jurisdiction or it might be an error of law within jurisdiction.[11] Jurisdiction signified legal authority within a denoted sphere, a competence dependent on person, place, subject-matter, and, to an extent, process. Review to check that those preconditions were satisfied was uncontroversial in principle, to the point that no-*certiorari* clauses in statutes did not prevent it.[12] For some legal processes judges required applicants to show that the error affecting a decision was jurisdictional, for example if they were seeking damages for its consequences or wanted a *mandamus* to compel a (re)hearing. But *certiorari* and prohibition were broader, subject, however, to the

---

[9] *Board of Education* v. *Rice* [1911] AC 179; *Local Government Board* v. *Arlidge* [1915] AC 120.

[10] *Administrative Law.*

[11] A. Rubinstein, *Jurisdiction and Illegality* (Oxford, 1965); de Smith, *Judicial Review* (3rd edn, 1973), 95n. This reading of the reported cases avoids the contortions attributed to jurisdiction theory. For the opposing view see L. L. Jaffe and E. Henderson, 'Judicial Review and the Rule of Law: Historical Origins' (1956) 72 *LQR* 345–64; E. Henderson. *Foundations of English Administrative Law* (Cambridge, Mass., 1963); D. M. Gordon, 'Conditional or Contingent Jurisdiction of Tribunals' (1960) 1 *U.B.C. Law Rev.* 185–228.

[12] *R* v. *Justices of Derbyshire* (1759) 2 Keny. 299; *R* v. *West Riding Justices* (1794) 5 T.R. 629 (and sequel, 701); *R* v. *Somersetshire Justices* (1826) 5 B. & C. 816; *R* v. *North Riding Justices* (1827) 6 B. & C. 152; *R* v. *Sheffield Railway* (1839) 11 Ad. & El. 194; *Ex p. Hopwood* (1850) 15 Q.B. 121. All concern orders, not convictions, but see also Paley, *Summary Convictions* (1st edn), 212–15.

need for the error of law to be demonstrable from the formal record.[13] Indeed, for review of summary convictions on *certiorari* the difference between juris-dictional and non-jurisdictional error was insignificant, since very probably no error was reviewable unless it was disclosed by the record.[14] Justices returning a mere order in response to a *certiorari*, however, were not required to produce a full record of their proceedings, and in that case the rule was different: lack of jurisdiction could be proved by affidavit, though error within jurisdiction could not.[15]

It was axiomatic that a decision of an inferior court or executive officer made without legal power—without jurisdiction—was a nullity. If its execu-tion had led to imprisonment, or a fine, or to sale or impounding of goods a chain of tortious liability arose, spanning those who did the seizing back to those who made the null order. This was a central element in the eighteenth-century rule of law. It meant that this form of unlawfulness could be tested by action before a jury, which judges would sometimes think preferable to proceedings by *certiorari*.[16] Constables and other process servers enforcing apparently valid warrants had been given statutory immunity in 1751, and the issuing and enforcing justices given procedural protections designed to allow them to make graceful amends where they had transgressed.[17] The basic prin-ciple, however, remained.

It was axiomatic too that anyone exercising a judicial power, which in this context included justices in all they did, must not have an interest in the subject-matter.[18] If they, or just one of them, did the decision was void.[19] It was a principle easily carried over to statutory commissioners.[20] Equally, however, it was one that statute might adjust to allow leading local figures to hold positions on bodies whose interests the judges might think conflicted.[21]

---

[13] For the breadth of prohibition see *Gould* v. *Gapper* (1804) 5 East 345 and *Veley* v. *Burder* (1841) 12 Ad. & El. 265. There had been doubters: Buller J. in *Lord Camden* v. *Home* (1791) 4 T.R. 382 and Patteson J. in *Blunt* v. *Harwood* (1838) 8 Ad. & El. 610, the latter recanting in *Burder* v. *Veley* (1840) 12 Ad. & El. 233, 264.

[14] Paley, *Summary Convictions* (2nd edn, 1827), 320–2; *Anon.* (1830) 1 B. & Ad. 382.

[15] *R* v. *Great Marlow* (1802) 2 East 244; *R* v. *James* (1814) 2 M. & S. 321; *R* v. *Standard Hill* (1815) 4 M. & S. 378; *R* v. *North Riding Justices* (1827) 6 B. & C. 152; *R* v. *Cheshire Justices* (1838) 8 Ad. & El. 398.

[16] e.g. *R* v. *Cambridgeshire Justices* (1835) 4 Ad. & El. 111 (Williams J.); *R* v. *Bristol Railway* (1838) 11 Ad. & El. 202n.

[17] Constables Protection Act 1751, 24 Geo. II c. 44; Paley, *Summary Convictions* (1st edn), 248–53, 257–62.

[18] *R* v. *Rishton* (1813) 1 Q.B. 480n; *R* v. *Hertfordshire Justices* (1845) 6 Q.B. 753.

[19] *Dimes* v. *Grand Junction Canal* (1852) 3 H.L.C. 759.

[20] *R* v. *Cheltenham Commissioners* (1841) 1 Q.B. 467.

[21] S. Stone, *The Justices' Manual* (11th edn, 1865), 394.

A second central element of the eighteenth-century rule of law, fading by the time our period begins, vigorous then only in perennial complaints about the arbitrary enforcement of the Game Laws, was that the process of summary conviction by justices needed close judicial supervision from Westminster. It had been achieved by expanding what a record of conviction required—with the concomitant understanding that justices need write it up only when summoned by *certiorari*.[22] Over the century the King's Bench had seized upon what they held to be critical omissions from records so as to construct an ever more detailed law of summary criminal procedure in the interests of the accused.[23] Justices must show that there had been credible evidence underlying the conviction, that it was given in the presence of the accused, that it had not been given by someone with a pecuniary interest in a conviction, that it met the elements of the offence (properly understood), that it was admissible in law ... and so on to the point where late in the century they were required to detail also the evidence for the defence.[24] A full 'speaking' record came to be a formidable document, scrutiny for error of law correspondingly intense.[25]

It seems that these two elements of liability and intensifying scrutiny interacted. In theory they ought not to have done. From the *Case of the Marshalsea* in 1616, at the latest, only a decision made without jurisdiction was actionable, not one that was merely erroneous.[26] The difficulty seems to have been with the mechanics of *certiorari*. If a record of conviction had been removed to Westminster and quashed, and the accused who had suffered a penalty now sued the justice for redress, there was no formal record that could be proffered in defence whether or not the error had been jurisdictional—the reason would not appear on the absence of record, as it were.[27] This explains the Justices Protection Act 1803, a statute which, while influential, was sometimes treated as mysterious.[28] It provided that if a conviction had been quashed the plaintiff in a subsequent action could recover no more than the return of any penalty plus twopence damages unless he could prove malice and lack of probable cause.[29] If the defending justice

---

[22] Paley, *Summary Convictions* (1st edn), 227–8.

[23] Paley, *Summary Convictions*; W. Boscawen, *A Treatise on Convictions on Penal Statutes* (1792).

[24] *R* v. *Clarke* (1799) 8 T.R. 220; *R* v. *Rix* (1824) 4 Dow. & Ry. KB. 352; *R* v. *Warnford* (1825) 5 Dow. & Ry. KB 489.

[25] See R. Burn, *The Justice of the Peace* (21st edn, 1810), i, 555–9 for the template; the consolidation in Summary Procedure Act 1822, 6 & 7 Geo. IV c. 20, preserved the spirit of these rules.

[26] 10 Co. Rep. 68b; Rubinstein, *Jurisdiction and Illegality*, 56–61.

[27] Paley, *Summary Convictions* (1st edn), 246.

[28] 43 Geo. III c. 141; *Massey* v. *Johnson* (1809) 12 East 67; *Gray* v. *Cookson* (1812) 16 East 13. J. F. Archbold, *Jervis's Acts* (1848), 182n.

[29] Hence 'the twopenny act': J. Adolphus, *Observations on the Vagrant Act* (1824), 99.

proved that the plaintiff was guilty of the offence he would receive nothing at
all, for all that the conviction had been quashed. Contemporary understanding,
according to Burn's *Justice of the Peace*, was that the first of those provisions, at
least, was limited in its conception. It applied 'to those cases only where the justice
improperly convicts', that is, only where the mistake was within jurisdiction.[30]

That reasoning explains why the 1803 Act applied only to convictions, and not
to the many sorts of order justices could also make. Quashing mere orders for
error within jurisdiction was rare because for them speaking records were not
required. Successive chief justices in the 1720s and 1730s had tried to persuade
their puisnes that records of orders should be made to speak in similar detail
to convictions, but they had failed.[31] The policy that had required close scrutiny
of summary convictions was not carried over. So although an order would be
set aside for error of law within jurisdiction if the justices chose to disclose it,
they could not be required to provide the wherewithal for such scrutiny.[32] This
important limiting feature of *certiorari* lasted throughout our period.

That deficit in scrutiny of orders was made good in practice by the customary jurisdiction of quarter sessions to state a case for the opinion of the King's
Bench.[33] For it to arise a magistrate's order had first to be appealable to the sessions, which needed express statutory provision. And there needed not to be a
no-*certiorari* clause in the statute, since that writ was necessary to remove the
proceedings into the King's Bench.[34] Appeal rights from justices were common,
however, both in civil and criminal matters, though the practical details differed
so greatly from statute to statute that John Stone, whose work on petty sessions
became a standard, wondered whether Parliament's intention was deliberately to
deter their use.[35]

Once seised the sessions could state the facts for the opinion of the King's
Bench and seek a decision on the application of the law. That was just like an
appeal on a point of law save, importantly, that it was voluntary. Sessions could
not be required to submit a case to the King's Bench, no matter how clear it was

---

[30] Burn, *Justice of the Peace* (21st edn), iii, 40. Paley, *Summary Convictions*, (1st edn), 243, 247n;
Groome v. *Forester* (1816) 5 M. & S. 314.

[31] *R* v. *Cleg* (1722) 1 Stra. 475; *R* v. *Venables* (1725) 2 Ld. Ray. 1405; *R* v. *Austin* (1732) 2 Barn. KB
203; *R* v. *Ames* (1733) W. Kel. 128; *R* v. *Trustees of Kingston Turnpike* (1733) 2 Barn. KB 288; *R*. v. *Lloyd*
(1734) 2 Barn. KB 310, 466, Cun. 84, 183; *R* v. *Bissex* (1756) Say. 304; and see e.g. *R* v. *South Lynn* (1815)
4 M. & S. 354.

[32] e.g. *R* v. *James* (1814) 2 M. & S. 321; *R* v. *Glyde* (1813) reported as a note to it, and *R* v. *Townrow*
(1830) 1 B. & Ad. 465.

[33] A full but succinct account can be found in W. Dickinson, *A Practical Guide to the Quarter
Sessions* (4th edn, 1836, by Talfourd), 828–36.

[34] *R* v. *Middlesex Justices* (1826) 8 Dow. & Ry. KB. 117.

[35] J. Stone, *The Practice of Petty Sessions* (3rd edn, 1839), 122–3.

to counsel or King's Bench that they ought to.[36] 'The facility with which these cases are granted varies very much in different Courts ...', wrote one commentator.[37] Nonetheless use was common, especially for the Poor Law settlement cases and the various rating questions that together made up the bulk of non-criminal work at most sessions.[38] As a later writer put it, it was a means whereby a sessions could choose to make its order speak.[39] It was required, however, that the sessions did find the facts; judges would become tetchy if they thought that that buck was being passed to them.[40] Fact-finding was pre-eminently part of the 'merits', reviewable only by appeal, for which an express statutory jurisdiction was necessary.

2. DISMANTLING AND REBUILDING: THE DECLINE OF REVIEW AND THE RISE OF APPEAL

Opportunity to challenge summary convictions had eroded before the 1820s. William Paley complained in 1814 that no-*certiorari* clauses and statutory short forms of conviction, which relieved justices of the need to demonstrate full legality, were encouraging injustice from haste, mistake, and preconception.[41] John Adolphus, leader of the Old Bailey bar, wrote caustically of the ' "holiday and lady terms" better fitted to the pages of a romance than an act of parliament' in the Summary Proceedings Act 1822, which aimed to neuter *certiorari* by instructing judges to ignore defects of form after a conviction.[42] Peel's statutes in the late 1820s consolidating the criminal law instituted short forms and barred *certiorari*, usually substituting an appeal to quarter sessions.[43] Protection was being frittered away by the short forms, said Bolland B.[44] In the mid-1830s Stone thought it not worthwhile explaining review on *certiorari* 'on account of the unfrequency with which summary convictions are now brought under the notice of judges'.[45]

---

[36]   *R* v. *Carnarvon Justices* (1820) 4 B. & Ald. 86.

[37]   J. F. Archbold, *The Jurisdiction and Practice of the Court of Quarter Sessions* (1836), 48.

[38]   R. Foster, *The Politics of County Power* (Hemel Hempstead, 1990), 50.

[39]   F. H. Short, *The Practice on the Crown Side of the Queen's Bench Division* (1890), 165–6. In 1878 the House of Lords rooted the practice in *certiorari*, the better to secure a right of appeal from the Queen's Bench: *Overseers of Walsall* v. *London & North Western Rwy* (1878) 4 App. Cas. 30.

[40]   Dickinson, *Quarter Sessions* (4th edn), 830–2.

[41]   *Summary Convictions* (1st edn), pp. xxxi–xxxii.

[42]   *Observations*, 105; 3 Geo. IV c. 23, s 3.

[43]   Larceny Act 1827, 7 & 8 Geo. IV c. 29, ss 71–3; Malicious Injuries Act 1827, 7 & 8 Geo. IV c. 30, ss 37–9; Offences against the Person Act 1828, 9 Geo. IV c. 31, ss 35–6; cf. Game Act 1831, 1 & 2 Will. IV c. 32, ss 39, 44–5.

[44]   *Wilkins* v. *Wright* (1833) 2 C. & M. 191, 209.

[45]   *Petty Sessions* (3rd edn), 127.

Nor would judges allow this stunting of *certiorari* to be sidestepped by shifting into tort. They would not let defects that would have been revealed, had a speaking record been available, be brought up in an action against the justice—for example that there was no evidence to sustain his decision on a matter properly before him. That was reasserted in *Brittain* v. *Kinnaird* in 1819, a decision 'oftener recognized than almost any modern case', according to Coleridge J. in 1844.[46]

There are suggestions that challenge was taking a different route. Stone thought it more usual for defendants believing themselves improperly dealt with to attack instead the subsequent warrant of commitment or distress by an action against the issuing magistrate—who may or may not have made the conviction.[47] They might allege a mistake in the warrant (there was room for pickiness here) or a jurisdictional defect in the conviction. Judges could show sympathy; in 1825 the Common Pleas reiterated that justices received ample procedural protection against surprise actions, and that it was only proper that those who had made errors should make amends.[48] Stone was sceptical, preferring the sections in Peel's Acts that protected justices in those circumstances and regretting that recent legislation such as the Poor Law Amendment Act and the General Highways Act had not followed suit.[49] Archbold thought that justices were often intimidated by open threats of actions when called upon to issue warrants.[50]

The reasoning applied equally to the issue of distress warrants to collect rates and other civic liabilities.[51] Parke B. explained the theory later: because justices did not *adjudicate* upon the validity of the prior conviction or order, its validity must be a precondition to the exercise of their enforcement authority.[52] That was an aspect of the eighteenth-century conception of the rule of law. Since there was ample room for disagreement about the interpretation of the statutes that created the offence or imposed the liability, as also about which elements were jurisdictional, there was risk enough to enforcing justices for the King's Bench to show caution. If in a marginal case the justices declined to issue a warrant the court

---

[46] (1819) 1 B. & B. 432 (see 2 Geo. III c. 28, s 11 for the very short statutory form of conviction); *Mould* v. *Williams* (1844) 5 Q.B. 469, 473.

[47] *Petty Sessions* (3rd edn), 111. For reported examples see *Rogers* v. *Jones* (1824) 1 B. & C. 409; *Wickes* v. *Clutterbuck* (1825) 2 Bing. 484; *Gimbert* v. *Coyney* (1825) M'Cle. & Yo. 469.

[48] *Wickes* v. *Clutterbuck* (1825) 2 Bing. 484.

[49] *Petty Sessions* (3rd edn), 110–11; for an example of protection see *Daniell* v. *Philipps* (1835) 1 C. M. & R. 662. The Highways Act did, however, immunize issuers of distress warrants: 5 & 6 Will. IV c. 108, s 105.

[50] Archbold, *Jervis's Acts*, 186.

[51] *Weaver* v. *Price* (1832) 3 B. & Ad. 409; *Fernley* v. *Worthington* (1840) 1 Man. & G. 491.

[52] *Newbould* v. *Coltman* (1851) 6 Ex. 189.

would not order them to do so by *mandamus*.[53] The opinion of even the bench in *mandamus* would not validate that which was void.

These elements of liability, these possibilities for review, were removed in the 1840s. Archbold drafted a section for the Mandamus Act in 1843 immunizing justices who obeyed a *mandamus* from subsequent liability, removing their excuse for inaction.[54] In 1848 that provision was carried forward into a new streamlined statutory alternative to *mandamus*—just to justices—which was part of a systematic consolidation and rationalization of summary jurisdiction.[55] That was the work of John Jervis, then attorney-general, and spanned three Acts that collectively bear his name.[56] In short, having spelled out magistrates' manner of exercising summary jurisdiction, his Acts made appeal to quarter sessions virtually the only practicable redress, save for jurisdictional error narrowly conceived. To that end they stipulated a standard short form of conviction, albeit one that was a little more informative than the skeletal versions that had sometimes found their way into law.[57] More importantly perhaps, since particular statutory short forms had been common for some time, Jervis's third Act, the Justices Protection Act, snuffed out most uses of actions to raise issues of validity.

That Act rewrote its precursor of 1803 in more rational terms, extended it to orders as well as convictions, provided that defects in pre-trial warrants would usually be cured by conviction and that defects in post-trial coercive orders would be immaterial if their substance could be sustained by a prior, lawful, conviction or order. Justices issuing commitment or distress warrants consequent upon an order or conviction by another justice were not to be liable for its invalidity at all. Nor any longer could liability for a Poor Law rate be tested by bringing an action against the justice who issued the distress warrant.[58] Justices remained liable for the consequences of their own acts done without jurisdiction, but with the new requirement that the offending conviction or order should first have been quashed on appeal or review. Likewise, justices remained liable for malicious acts done within jurisdiction. So, to facilitate settlement and to protect justices from

---

[53]   e.g. *R* v. *Dayrell* (1823) 1 B. & C. 485; *R* v. *Broderip* (1826) 5 B. & C. 239; *R* v. *Mirehouse* (1835) 2 Ad. & El. 632; Tapping, *Mandamus*, 224, 240–2.

[54]   Mandamus Act, 6 & 7 Vict. c. 67, s 3; Archbold, *Jervis's Acts*, 186.

[55]   11 & 12 Vict. c. 44, s 5.

[56]   11 & 12 Vict. cc. 42, 43, 44; D. Freestone and J. C. Richardson, 'The Making of English Criminal Law: Sir John Jervis and his Acts' [1980] *Crim. Law Rev.* 5–16.

[57]   Archbold, *Jervis's Acts*, 137–8.

[58]   Replevin remained available; being an action in rem it was not an action 'against' anyone (and the Elizabethan poor law explicitly said it lay). Judges agreed that it lay if the alleged ratepayer was not an 'occupier', but disagreed whether it lay if the defence were that an admitted occupation was not 'beneficial'. The current of decision was against that use, with the result that the test case repealing that criterion nearly foundered on procedural grounds: *Mersey Docks and Harbour Board* v. *Cameron* (1861) 30 LJ MC 194, point waived at (1865) 35 LJ MC 1, 6.

publicity, the Act also re enacted the procedural protections justices had enjoyed since 1751.

Thus Jervis's Acts finally stultified *certiorari* as a means to address errors of law within jurisdiction and removed most of the opportunities to use tort actions against enforcers to reopen the validity of upstream decisions. Contemporaneously Baines's Act, the Poor Law Procedure Act 1848, made quarter sessions the sole judge of the sufficiency of the paperwork that had brought appeals on removal orders to it.[59] Previously, its preamble claimed, disputes over what details should have been included in what notices had produced 'much expensive and useless litigation...so that few cases of appeals against such orders are now decided upon the merits', with the added baleful consequence that such disputes were going a further round by case stated to the Queen's Bench. Now all that would be stopped; it was, as his friends put it, an 'act for the better suppression of Pashley', leader of that part of the bar.[60] A year later the Quarter Sessions Act applied these rules to appeals to sessions in nearly all other matters too and standardized appellate procedures—where the originating Act gave an appeal.[61] Together all this legislation replaced an eighteenth-century conception of legalism, in which each step in a coercive process had to be independently valid, with instead an efficient appeal on the merits (if one lay at all) which, if the sessions could see that nobody had been substantially disadvantaged, would cure many errors or oversights en route.

Where no appeal lay there was room for review on narrow jurisdictional grounds only. That, however, was much in line with judges' own preferences, as two well-known examples show. The first was the sequel to *Stockdale* v. *Hansard*, where, in 1839, the Queen's Bench had determined that, whatever the outrage the House of Commons displayed, a resolution of a single House of Parliament was not 'law' enough to justify a libel outside the House.[62] But when the Speaker ordered the two men who held the office of sheriff of Middlesex to be detained for contempt of Parliament—not saying in the warrant that the cause was their role in enforcing the courts' orders contrary to the wish of the Commons—the court declined to release them.[63] The Speaker had a lawful jurisdiction to detain; if he chose not to let his order speak the court would not look behind its face.

In the second example, also in 1839, Coleridge J. allowed a *certiorari* to bring up a justices' order giving parish officials possession of a house, because the parties

---

[59] 11 & 12 Vict. c. 31.

[60] 'Robert Pashley', *ODNB*.

[61] Quarter Sessions Act 1849, 12 & 13 Vict. c. 45; Customs, Excise, Stamps and Taxes were the conspicuous exclusions, and removal orders and bastardy orders were also excluded from some provisions.

[62] *Stockdale* v. *Hansard* (1839) 9 Ad. & El. 1.

[63] *Sheriff of Middlesex's Case* (1840) 11 Ad. & El. 273.

appeared to agree that the man being evicted was a tenant, whereas the justices' process lay only against pauper licensees.[64] By the time the full Queen's Bench heard argument on the order's validity the parties' apparent agreement had evaporated, their affidavits were irreconcilable, and since this was an order there was no record of the justices' findings. The court declined to re-try the facts. Invoking *Brittain* v. *Kinnaird*, it held that matters such as this man's status were to be taken as being within the justices' jurisdiction to decide, and since their order was regular on its face it was valid. This is *R* v. *Bolton*, which has been argued over ever since; it would have been surprising if, in 1841, the decision had been otherwise.[65] In the following year Pashley induced the Queen's Bench to order justices to send up their examination of witnesses in a settlement dispute though no case had been stated—a transparent evasion of the principle that a speaking record could not be required for a mere order—only to be rebuked when he tried it again.[66] Such a speculative novelty must not be repeated, the court said.

The problem in *R* v. *Bolton*, as the applicant told the court, was that the statute did not provide an appeal to quarter sessions. Where one did lie the Quarter Sessions Act 1849 provided, cautiously, that if both parties to a justice's summary decision agreed, they could lodge an appeal to sessions but then state a case to a superior court at Westminster, ultimately enrolling the result in the sessions' records as though it were a judgment of that court.[67] It became a common way of testing legal liability to rates.

The change away from begrudging access to the Westminster courts came in the more relaxed years of the 1850s, with the Summary Jurisdiction Act 1857, a government measure passed with no recorded discussion.[68] It enabled any party to a summary adjudication to waive appeal to the sessions and unilaterally apply by case stated to a superior court. It was limited to determinations upon information or complaint, and applicants had to move fast: the time limit was three days. But this unilateral power was new in this context, and the form was modern too—the Act explicitly said that *certiorari* was not needed to take the special case to Westminster. Prior to this Act, said Lord Campbell a year later, the

---

[64] *R* v. *Middlesex Justices* (1839) 7 Dowl. 767. He was sitting in the Bail Court, where applications for *certiorari* were heard by a single judge: R. J. Corner and A. B. Corner, *The Practice of the Crown Side of the Court of Queen's Bench* (1844), 5.

[65] 6 Q.B. 66; for its rejection in Ireland see K. Costello, '*R (Martin) v Mahony*: the History of a Classical Certiorari Authority' (2006) 27 JLH 267–87.

[66] *R* v. *Rotherham* (1842) 3 Q.B. 776, *Ex p. Tollerton Overseers* (1842) 3 Q.B. 792; see also *R* v. *Buckinghamshire Justices* (1843) 3 Q.B. 800; *R* v. *Kesteven Justices* (1844) 3 Q.B. 810.

[67] 11 & 12 Vict. c. 31, s 11 (with exclusions for bastardy orders and revenue cases); *Guardians of Holborn Union* v. *Guardians of Chertsey Union* (1885) 15 QBD 76.

[68] 20 & 21 Vict. c. 43; G. Tayler, *The Law of Appeals to the Superior Courts of Law by Appeal Case* (1865).

Queen's Bench could not get at the merits of a decision within jurisdiction, and he then proceeded to do what the eighteenth-century court would have done on *certiorari* with a speaking record: assess whether the facts stated amounted to the offence charged.[69]

From the 1849 and 1857 Acts together there followed numerous reported decisions on the validity of rates, on liability to market tolls and on similar issues requiring interpretation of local legislation, on the construction of the Public Health legislation and the validity of byelaws and orders made under it, as well as cases arising under the master and servant legislation and the Factories Acts. In 1879 the facility to appeal by case stated was extended to all convictions, orders, determinations, or other processes of any court of summary jurisdiction—closing the gaps in the 1857 Act—and by Order made under the Judicature Act the previous tight time limit of three days was relaxed to seven.[70] This was a nineteenth-century rule of law, pressing enforcement through justices and then integrating them with the Westminster courts.

Where enforcement or adjudication was not through justices, but through a new statutory agency then explicit statutory provision needed to be made if this, or any, process for taking points of law to superior courts were to be available. On principle, perhaps, *certiorari* would be available; but without a speaking record the Queen's Bench could address only jurisdictional errors. There was an eighteenth-century precedent for statutory case stated, however, from the commissioners for house and window duties, interesting for not requiring the commissioners' consent, and though such a provision was not universal even in taxing statutes it was copied frequently enough for Chantal Stebbings to conclude in a recent study that nearly all nineteenth-century statutory adjudicative tribunals had something like it, from the tithe and copyhold commissioners onwards.[71] The technique was carried forward, with variations, into legislation such as the Housing of the Working Classes Act 1890 and (as a reluctant political concession) its reinforcement, the Housing and Town Planning Act 1909, where it applied to decisions of the Local Government Board on appeal against closure and demolition orders.[72]

Case stated was obviously apt to raise questions of statutory application, but it was used also to determine how far a justice called upon to enforce an order made by some other agency could inquire into its validity or wisdom. This was

[69] *Flannagan* v. *Bishopswearmouth Overseers* (1857) 27 LJ MC 46.

[70] Summary Jurisdiction Act 1879, s 33; Summary Jurisdiction Rules 1880, r 17. The jurisdiction was given a broad reading in *Sandgate Local Board* v. *Pledge* (1885) 14 QBD 730.

[71] 20 Geo. II c. 10, s 10; C. Stebbings, 'The Appeal by Case Stated from Determinations of General Commissioners of Income Tax' (1996) 6 *BTR* 611–18; C. Stebbings, *Legal Foundations of Tribunals in the Nineteenth Century* (Cambridge, 2006), 237–50.

[72] Housing of the Working Classes Act 1890, s 35; Housing and Town Planning Act 1909, s 39.

important as the powers of local boards on matters of public health grew, where justices' sympathies might not align with the boards'. Generally the Westminster courts reduced justices' supervisory role. Thus in the 1860s the Queen's Bench held that justices called upon to enforce a local board of health's order that a privy be replaced by a water closet could not revisit the board's opinion that the change was 'necessary'—though Blackburn J.'s doubts show that the statute could have been read to allow such a check.[73] A ratepayer could not argue that the rate levied under the Public Health Act was for works insufficiently 'permanent' to qualify, or that it was only other people who benefited.[74] A justice or arbitrator required to settle or enforce an apportionment order of the costs incurred in works compulsorily implemented under the Public Health Act must not inquire into its reasonableness, Erle CJ stressing the trustworthiness of an elected, responsible authority publicly audited.[75] With much greater difficulty, but similar result in the end, finality was likewise given to urban building lines prescribed by boards of works and their architects—there is nothing unjust about such a skilled public officer indirectly affecting property rights, said Lord Selborne in the decisive case, ending 20 years of judicial disagreement.[76] There was no appeal route against prescription of a building line, a fact that had weighed with some of the earlier courts, so this decision was particularly important.[77]

3. ACCOMMODATING THE NEW

Statutory Review

The reforming legislation of the 1830s often provided tailored access to the courts, sometimes using *certiorari*.[78] The Poor Law Amendment Act 1834 enabled any rule, order, or regulation of the Poor Law Commissioners to be challenged by that route but provided that anything removed by *certiorari* should remain enforceable until actually quashed.[79] It brought into the Queen's Bench several bitterly fought contests for local control between the commissioners and, especially, the guardians of existing statutory unions. A decade later the Poor Law audit process was also linked to the courts through *certiorari*, this time enabling anyone

---

[73] *Hargreaves* v. *Taylor* (1863) 3 B. & S. 613; *St Luke's Vestry* v. *Lewis* (1862) 1 B. & S. 865; *Robinson* v. *Sunderland Corp* [1899] 1 QB 751.

[74] *Luton LBH* v. *Davies* (1860) 29 LJ MC 173; *R* v. *Newman* (1860) 29 LJ MC 117.

[75] *Bayley* v. *Wilkinson* (1864) 16 C.B. (N.S.) 161; *Cook* v. *Ipswich LBH* (1871) LR 6 QB 451; *R* v. *Recorder of Sheffield* (1883) 53 LJ MC 1.

[76] *Spackman* v. *Plumstead DBW* (1885) 10 App Cas 229.

[77] Contrast *Simpson* v. *Smith* (1871) LR 6 CP 87, which was overruled.

[78] Stebbings, *Legal Foundations*, 229–72.

[79] 4 & 5 Will. IV c. 76, ss 105–8.

dissatisfied by an allowance, disallowance, or surcharge to make the auditor state his reason and then complain to the court that it was 'erroneous'. The Tithe Commissioners' statute had explicitly excluded *certiorari* in favour of other forms of court access, but in 1837 an amendment made exception for boundary decisions.[80] Also in 1837 the Municipal Corporations Act laconically provided that *certiorari* could move any order for the payment of money into the King's Bench for review.[81] There was a similar non-statutory power over the spending decisions of quarter sessions, but this one needed spelling out, no doubt, because municipal councils were not even colourably courts.

Though these statutes enabled these new decisions to be moved into court, often they said little about what the court was to do next. Context made it clear that the *certiorari* to an assistant tithe commissioner on a question of fixing boundaries constituted the Queen's Bench an appeal court on the merits of that matter, but, once issued, did it also open his award to everything else that could normally be argued on *certiorari*, the parent Act having assiduously removed the writ? 'Probably the framers of the Act did not know what a *certiorari* meant ...', said Patteson J., holding that the answer was 'yes'.[82] Likewise the requirement that an auditor state his reasons made that inquiry more like a review of a speaking record than the search for jurisdictional fault that had come to characterize common law *certiorari*. But did the court's statutory ability to quash an auditor's 'erroneous' decision authorize it to consider the merits and weigh the auditor's judgement? Towards the end of the century and into the next, as councils' activities became more complex, and so conflict between their discretion and auditors' assessment of it became more likely, so courts began to construe this power as though it were like an appeal.[83] By contrast the very bare provision enabling *certiorari* to the Poor Law Commissioners' orders gave no such leverage, so once their power in a particular matter was admitted the court would not look at their exercise of discretion.[84]

These jurisdictions all survived, but only that over public auditors expanded, as the audit process itself was applied to the new forms of local authority.[85] Statutory *certiorari* never became a norm, perhaps because it did open up anything the Queen's Bench took to be an error of law.

[80] 1 Vict. c. 69, s 3. All other decisions by assistant tithe commissioners were routed through a 'feigned action', a regular trial process before judge and jury but on reduced pleadings.

[81] 1 Vict. c. 78, s 44.

[82] *Re Dent Tithe Commutation* (1845) 8 Q.B. 43. The same result was reached for the Poor Law Commissioners: *In re Westbury upon Severn Union* (1854) 4 E. & B. 314.

[83] *R* v. *Haselhurst* (1887) 51 JP 645; *R.* v. *Carson Roberts* [1908] 1 KB 407.

[84] *R* v. *Poor Law Commissioners in re Newport Union* (1837) 6 Ad. & El. 54.

[85] See above, p. 444.

Adapting Common Law Process

There thus remained room for common law *certiorari* to new institutions, though given that so much regulatory legislation used justices as enforcers, opening the way to a superior court through case stated, and that statutory *certiorari* was available in the contexts outlined above, it was residual. The easiest translation was to the many inquisitions by sheriffs' juries assessing compensation for land taken compulsorily for the building of railways, because those too were 'courts', and clearly 'inferior'. There was a difficulty, that the template statute for compulsory land acquisition, Lands Clauses Consolidation Act 1845, contained a no-*certiorari* clause.[86] Conventionally, however, no-*certiorari* clauses were construed as not excluding review for jurisdictional error, so by exploiting the concept of excess of jurisdiction, and by allowing complainants to demonstrate such a defect by affidavit, rather than having to rely upon the face of the jury's verdict, the King's Bench asserted firm control over what types of loss were or were not compensable.[87] Great practical injustice would be caused otherwise, said Coleridge J. in 1849, knowing, no doubt, that juries' vulnerability to bullying from railway companies and landowners alike was causing considerable public heat.[88]

Not many new contexts were so obviously court-like, and it had been understood that *certiorari* even to justices would not bring up merely ministerial decisions. The same two eighteenth-century cases tended to be cited for that proposition, however, neither of them receiving any development that can be detected.[89] 'Ministerial' seems to have been taken as Stone took it, to encompass mainly steps preliminary to some more structured disposition, steps requiring 'no discretionary or judicial consideration'.[90] It was not equated with 'administrative'. Justices' orders allowing items in accounts, or confirming appointments, or stopping highways, or instructing their clerk not to take fees, or—on a grander scale—charging a neighbouring borough for use of the county prison were all held to be amenable to *certiorari* in the 1830s through to the 1850s.[91]

---

[86] 8 & 9 Vict. c. 18, s 145.

[87] *R* v. *South Wales Railway* (1849) 13 Q.B. 988; *R* v. *London & NW Railway* (1854) 3 E. & B. 443; *re Penny* (1857) 7 E. & B. 660.

[88] *R* v. *South Wales Railway* (1849) 13 Q.B. 988; R. Kostal, *Law and English Railway Capitalism 1825–1875* (Oxford, 1994), 154–61.

[89] *R* v. *Lediard* (1751) Say. 6; *R* v. *Lloyd* (1783) Cald. 309. Where *certiorari* was convenient to both parties these rulings were ignored: *R* v. *James* (1863) 3 B. & S. 901.

[90] Stone, *Practice of Petty Sessions* (3rd edn), 195.

[91] Accounts: *R* v. *Johnson* (1836) 5 Ad. & El. 340; *R* v. *Saunders* (1854) 3 E. & B. 763. Highways: e.g. *R* v. *Jones* (1840) 12 Ad. & El. 684, *R* v. *Arkwright* (1848) 12 Q.B. 960. Appointments: *In re the Constables of Hipperholme* (1847) 5 Dow. & L. 79, 2 B.C.R. 98 (contrast the initial nomination by the vestry); *R* v. *Standard Hill* (1815) 4 M. & S. 378; *R* v. *Jones* (1840) 12 Ad. & El. 684; *R* v. *Jarvis* (1854) 3 E. & B. 640; *R*

There was an exception for licensing, but it is difficult to gauge its extent or significance. It was not much litigated in the mid-century, perhaps because the Beer Act 1830 had removed licensing of beerhouses from justices' discretionary overview, not restored until 1869. The two cases usually cited were failed challenges to grants of licences, not to refusals, and in the first counsel pointed out that if, as the applicant said, there were fault enough for the court to quash the licence he could (and should) just treat it as void anyway.[92] Nonetheless in each the court treated it as axiomatic that licensing was not judicial, and that *certiorari* lay for judicial decisions only. It may not have mattered greatly, since refusals of a licence could often be appealed and made the subject of a case stated.[93] Further, if it could be made out that the justices' error was so significant that they had not in law addressed the right question, their first supposed decision could simply be ignored and a *mandamus* issued to require them to hear and determine.[94] Potentially, however, the principle was important if it denied that a discretionary decision in a judicial setting could be reached by *certiorari*.

After beerhouse licensing was reinstated, and control of drinking places became a noisy political issue locally and nationally, generating many disputes at licensing sessions, *certiorari* does seem to have been one of the means used to press questions upon the Westminster judges. Cockburn CJ said as much in 1880, and counsel in 1898 claimed it had been the usual practice.[95] He was reacting, however, to a Lords' ruling that licensing justices were not a court for the purposes of awarding costs against objectors—the political sense of that can be gauged easily enough—from which it was deduced that they were not courts at all.[96] There followed a decade of doubt during which *mandamus* was used to fill the gap instead, until in 1906 a Court of Appeal restored the previous practice by ruling that, court or not, liquor licensing decisions were judicial for purposes of *certiorari*.[97] As with the earlier experience of sheriffs' juries, it was difficult to turn such a continuously contentious source of dispute away. At the same time, however, judges were asserting how broad the licensing discretion was, so the significance of the decision was that however wide the discretion, if it must be decided in a 'judicial spirit', hearing applicants fairly, acknowledging the legal

---

v. *Cousins* (1864) 4 B. & S. 849. Clerk: *R* v. *Coles* (1844) 8 Q.B. 74. Prison: *R* v. *Lancashire Justices* (1839) 11 Ad. & El. 144; strictly it was a motion directing its visiting justices to contract with the borough.

[92] *R* v. *Salford Overseers* (1852) 18 Q.B. 687; *R* v. *Lucey* (1897) 66 LJ QB 308 (*sub nom. R* v. *Co. of Watermen* [1897] 1 QB 659).

[93] e.g. *R* v. *Sylvester* (1862) 31 LJ MC 93.

[94] *R* v. *Middlesex Justices* (1871) LR 6 QB 781; *R* v. *De Rutzen* (1875) 1 QBD 55.

[95] *R* v. *Kent Justices* (1880) 44 JP 298; *R* v. *Bowman* [1898] 1 QB 663.

[96] *Boulter* v. *Kent Justices* [1897] AC 569; *R* v. *Sharman* [1898] 1 QB 578.

[97] *R* v. *Woodhouse* [1906] 2 KB 501, citing *Sharp* v. *Wakefield* [1891] AC 173 (see below, pp. 516–17).

framework in which the discretion was embedded, then *certiorari* would lie to bring up the decision for review.

For all that, however, subtract the cases of statutory *certiorari* and there were few reported instances of *certiorari* to modern statutory bodies.[98] Rarely an administrative decision of statutory commissioners might be reached, as when a consent given by canal commissioners to a landowner to bridge the canal was quashed for conflict of interest, but usually there was no need.[99] Instead the challenge would come against the subsequent enforcement order or conviction by the justices, be that through *certiorari* or, more usually, case stated.[100] In the 1890s a *certiorari* brought up a chief gas examiner's adverse report on the illuminating power of a company's gas, and one issued to bring up a certificate by the Board of Agriculture that some tithes had been redeemed.[101] In 1904 it lay for the first time to the General Commissioners of Income Tax.[102] This was not much, though, with one exception, there was nothing to the contrary.

The exception was important, though strictly the process was prohibition rather than *certiorari*. In *Frewen* v. *Hastings Board of Health* in 1865 the Queen's Bench held that a provisional order to acquire land for road widening could not be reviewed.[103] Narrowly, the Secretary of State who was submitting the order for confirmation to Parliament was not acting judicially, nor was the order determinative of rights. More broadly, however, review would trespass against Parliament, partly because submission of the order could be seen as a report to the House for its consideration, partly because the provisional order process was a substitute for the early stages of private bill procedure, so an aggrieved party's remedy remained political—he should petition to stop confirmation. Chancery similarly showed the greatest reluctance to issue an injunction against seeking a private Act.[104]

---

[98] *R* v. *Local Government Board* (1873) LR 8 QB 227; *R* v. *Local Government Board* [1901] 1 QB 210; *R* v. *Local Government Board ex p Arlidge* [1915] AC 120 are all statutory *certioraris*. Commissioners of sewers were a statutory body amenable to common law *certiorari*, but they qualified comfortably as 'courts'.

[99] *R* v. *Aberdare Canal Co* (1850) 14 Q.B. 854.

[100] e.g. *R* v. *Arkwright* (1848) 12 Q.B. 960.

[101] *R* v. *London County Council ex p. Commercial Gas* (1895) 11 TLR 337; *R* v. *Board of Agriculture* (1899) 15 TLR 176.

[102] *R* v. *Commissioners of Income Tax* (1904) 91 *LT* 94; C. Stebbings, 'The Origins of Certiorari to the General Commissioners of Income Tax' [1997] *BTR* 119–30.

[103] The full facts and argument require all the reports: (1865) 13 WR 678, 34 LJ QB 159, 11 Jur (NS) 670, 12 *LT* 346, 29 JP 711, 6 B. & S. 401 (*sub nom. R* v. *Hastings LBH*).

[104] *Lancaster & Carlisle Railway Co* v. *North-Western Railway Co* (1856) 2 K. & J. 293; *Steele* v. *Northern Metropolitan Railway Co* (1867) LR 2 Ch 237; *Re London, Chatham and Dover Railway Arrangement Act* (1869) LR 5 Ch 671. Contrast *Telford* v. *Metropolitan Board of Works* (1872) LR 13 Eq 574, where an injunction went to stop an application made in breach of contract.

There was congruence here with the refusal to assist the atheist Charles Bradlaugh in his efforts to take his seat in the Commons: a Commons resolution cannot change the law, but a court cannot enjoin the Serjeant-at-Arms from acting upon it.[105] A decade later Lords Herschell and Watson held that rules made by the Board of Trade, and taken to have been approved by having been laid before Parliament, must, as the statute said, be taken to have been made in pursuance of it.[106] That is, they were put beyond judicial challenge. This would become a significant limitation on courts' powers in the interwar years. It is curious, all the same, that none of this deference had been shown when the Inclosure Commissioners proposed provisional orders for confirmation; there was no hesitation then to assess conformity with the parent legislation.[107]

The gentle trend to let *certiorari* issue to central departments was confirmed in the highly charged litigation reported finally as *Board of Education* v. *Rice*.[108] That was a fierce and protracted contest between Church and state, between Conservative and Liberal, over ratepayer funding to a Church of England school in nonconformist Swansea, where the Liberals controlled the city council.[109] Public funding was mandatory under the Conservatives' Education Act 1902, but the council's response had been to continue paying Church-school teachers only what they received before 1902, which was less than the scale for council schools. The Church found itself having to make up the difference, which it said was contrary to the Act. Nationally the Liberals were in government, but had remained unwillingly saddled with the 1902 Act because the Conservatives were blocking their education bills in the Lords. So when the Board of Education rejected an appeal from the school's managers, persisting despite a report in the managers' favour from a government-appointed lawyer, the suspicion was that the board was legislating in the guise of administrative action. The Swansea question became an open political sore. Eventually all three levels of court held that the statute cast the department in an appellate role to which *certiorari* lay, and that as it had not addressed the correct legal question its decision must be quashed.[110]

The courts, of course, presented their decision as the natural continuation of their centuries of supervision of inferior jurisdictions; Farwell LJ said as much and the rest took it for granted. Nonetheless, it was the first fully considered use of a

[105] *Bradlaugh* v. *Gossett* (1884) 12 QBD 271; see pp. 387–8, above.

[106] *Institute of Patent Agents* v. *Lockwood* [1894] AC 347, Lord Morris dissented on this point.

[107] *Church* v. *Inclosure Commissioners* (1862) 11 C.B. (N.S.) 664; see above, pp. 358–9.

[108] [1911] AC 179 (HL), *sub nom. R* v. *Board of Education* [1909] 2 KB 1045 (KB), [1910] 2 KB 165 (CA).

[109] G. R. Searle, *A New England* (Oxford, 2004), 329–34; K. O. Morgan, *Rebirth of a Nation* (New York, 1981), 37–8, 111–12, 140.

[110] The Board duly passed the buck to Swansea council, which capitulated: *The Times*, 18 May 1911.

common law *certiorari* to enable the quashing of a central department's decision, and it came at a time of great political tension over the Liberals' redistributive policies, the future of the legislative House of Lords, and the rise of 'administrative justice' that reserved increasing discretion to the executive. Considerable hostility to a tendency within Whitehall to see departmental decisions as unreviewable was being voiced in and through *The Times*, a supporter of the Conservatives.[111] The Lord Chief Justice himself—Alverstone, a former Conservative attorney-general—was alarmed enough to say publicly that he hoped the time would never come when the executive government was to be its own interpreter of Acts of Parliament.[112] Some prominent Liberal lawyers took the same view; Rupert Isaacs and Stanley Buckmaster both spoke out during the report stage of the Finance Bill 1909—a protracted political struggle of extraordinary intensity—against immunizing decisions on liability to the proposed land valuation tax from all but executive scrutiny.[113] They won what *The Times* begrudgingly called a quasi-concession from Lloyd George, whose bill it was.[114] In this context *Board of Education* v. *Rice* was an important assertion of the courts' powers.

Declaration: A New Remedy for the Times

The Liberals' new land taxes spawned new forms to be filled, hence more opposition, which in 1911 generated the decision in *Dyson* v. *Attorney-General* that further changed the dynamic of judicial review.[115] Against arguments that a taxpayer declining to fill out his hated Form IV should wait until prosecuted to make his defence, and that the law officers were far too busy to have so many potential litigants suing them, the Court of Appeal allowed a taxpayer to seek a pre-emptive declaratory judgment that the form was unlawful for not accurately following the enabling Act.[116]

As always, much of the reasoning stressed continuity, even inevitability, but again Farwell LJ addressed the mood as well. Comparing the attorney-general's claim to that of Stuart kings, he lamented a trend visible through recent litigation for departments to think themselves above the law, pointed out that in one of those cases formal questions in the Commons had failed to elicit even an answer

---

[111]   e.g. *The Times*, 8 January 1908 (letter from W. A. Spooner); 6 February 1908; 22, 23, 25, 29, 30 December 1908; 2 January 1909; 8, 31 July 1909; 2 September 1909. See also 'Departmental Interference with the Execution of Warrants of Arrest' (1911) 75 *JP* 385, linking an individual instance to a perceived trend across central departments.

[112]   *The Times*, 19 June 1909.

[113]   *PD* 1909 (s5 HC) 7: 1076–9, 1086–7, 1096.

[114]   *The Times*, 8 July 1909.

[115]   [1911] 1 KB 410.

[116]   For Form IV see A. Offer, *Property and Politics* (Cambridge, 1981), 363–9.

on the relevant point, and concluded that since ministerial responsibility was now merely the 'shadow of a name' the courts alone stood between the subject and departmental aggression.[117] *The Times*, lapping all this up, said that what should have been a platitude was now an imperilled truth.[118]

The declaratory remedy—quite new in this context—was triply significant. It allowed citizens to take the initiative, it freed the subsequent analysis from the technicalities of *certiorari*, and it provided a new route into courts for determining questions of law where previously no appeal lay. Putting limits to that would come later, of course. Its potency was soon shown by a trilogy of decisions declaring first Form IV invalid, then Form VIII, and then that taxpayers who had nonetheless completed Form IV could not be penalized for inaccuracies in their return—the latter two cases being brought by the Land Union, an alliance of landowners and Conservative politicians.[119]

As noted above, *certiorari* to orders did not demand that decision makers produce a speaking record, so it could not reach an undisclosed error of law within jurisdiction. The new declaratory remedy was a declaration of invalidity, so that too left room for authorities to make errors of law within jurisdiction but escape review. The gap could be closed, however. In the *Rice* litigation Farwell LJ had adopted a technique found particularly in cases of *mandamus* to licensing justices, whose discretion was unreviewable provided not only that they addressed the right legal question but also that they did not take into account legally irrelevant matters. In the new context of reviewing central departments those might include departmental policy and the politics of the situation, but they could stretch to anything induced by a misreading of law. There was obvious room for expansive judicial oversight here, and it may be significant that when the Attorney-General took what looked a hopeless appeal to the Lords it was Farwell LJ's judgment that he particularly attacked.[120]

Taking *Dyson* and *Rice* together, judges had secured what they saw as their constitutional role as interpreters of the statutory law, given that the point of law in question could be seen as jurisdictional. More immediately, however, that step now exposed them to party conflict, given the changed nature of politics and the expanding intrusive role of central government. *The Times* recognized

---

[117] Citing *Re Weir Hospital* [1910] 2 Ch 124; *Re Hardy's Crown Brewery* [1910] 2 KB 257; and the Swansea case, which had passed through the Court of Appeal but not yet reached the House of Lords. *Wilford* v. *West Riding CC* [1908] 1 KB 685 was another case used by Conservatives as evidence of Liberal officialism.

[118] *The Times*, 12 December 1910.

[119] *Dyson* v. *A.G.* [1912] 1 Ch 158; *Burghes* v. *A.G.* [1912] 1 Ch 173; *A.G.* v. *Foran* [1916] 2 AC 128; Offer, *Property and Politics*, 367–9; R. B. Yardley, *Land Value Taxation and Rating* (n.d. [London, 1930]), 652–5.

[120] *Board of Education* v. *Rice*, *The Times*, 25 February 1911.

that at once; though it clearly enjoyed seeing Farwell LJ flaying the Executive it cautioned now that judges should not stray from the legal point nor indulge themselves in 'picturesque, incisive, and unguarded words'.[121] That would become a familiar theme in twentieth-century commentary.

4. THE VIRTUE OF FAIR PROCEDURE

Judges likewise showed a persistent assumption that the common law contained principles of procedural fairness that would apply to new forms of decision making too. They had long since imposed their values on the processes of summary conviction. As Paley wrote in 1814:

...even where the statutes are silent, as to any particular mode of proceeding, the law declares, that the magistrates to whom cognizance of offences is referred, are nevertheless bound to observe the rules of natural justice, one of which is, that the accused should have an opportunity of being heard before he is condemned. This is indispensably required....[122]

In the 1790s Lord Kenyon CJ insisted that that rule apply also to justices issuing distress warrants to recover unpaid parish rates, against what seems to have been previous practice.[123] Given that in the mid-century so much enforcement was routed through justices, it was only a short but very significant step to hold, as the King's Bench did in *Painter* v. *Liverpool Oil Gas Light Co* in 1836, that a justices' distress warrant issued under a modern statute to a statutory utility company to recover an unpaid account was lawful only if the parties had first been summoned.[124] Further, just as a justice whose disregard for procedural requirements would be liable for damages in tort, so too was the gas company for originating and executing this unjudicial process.[125] Though a trivial error might be classed as a 'mere irregularity', a breach of natural justice took the perpetrator outside jurisdiction.

---

[121] *The Times*, 18 November 1911. B. Abel-Smith and R. Stevens, *Lawyers and the Courts* (1967), 126–7, claimed that at about this time judges reactivated contempt of court to punish seriously derogatory comments about themselves and took pleasure in using it. While the former is true (*R* v. *Gray* [1900] 2 QB 36) they produced no evidence of any other such prosecutions, and use of that particular aspect of contempt of court was denied by *The Times*, 9 November 1910. *The Times* did, however, concede that the possibility of such a prosecution might explain the restraint it now saw in press comments.

[122] Paley, *Summary Convictions* (1st edn), 16–17.

[123] *R* v. *Benn* (1795) 6 T.R. 198; see also *Harper* v. *Carr* (1797) 7 T.R. 270.

[124] (1836) 3 Ad. & El. 433, see also *R* v. *Hughes* (1835) 3 Ad. & El. 425 (statutory paving commissioners).

[125] e.g. *Caudle* v. *Seymour* (1841) 1 Q.B. 889; *Bridgett* v. *Coyney* (1827) 1 Man. & Ry. 211.

The common law principle requiring a hearing before deciding had been applied to a much wider range of decision makers than merely the justices; *Bagg's Case* (1615), which was a disfranchising of a borough freeman, and *Bentley's Case* (1723), which was a deprivation of university degrees, were cited from time to time in nineteenth-century litigation just as they are in twentieth-century textbooks.[126] Lord Lyndhurst's Exchequer applied the principle in 1832 to the sequestration of a benefice by the Bishop of London for the incumbent's neglect of his parish—an important incursion into Church discipline at a sensitive time, but one justified both on principle, the court said, and by implication from the statute: a penalty for cause implied a hearing to determine the true facts.[127]

Alderson B. later doubted that decision, because the statute enabled the bishop to decide of his own knowledge, but his lead was not followed.[128] Instead the line was drawn at offices held merely at pleasure, a function of the judges' general unwillingness to be drawn into questions of discretion—of which more will be said below. The upper master of Darlington School, dismissed by the trustees in 1840, the relieving officer of Godstone Union, dismissed by the Poor Law Commissioners in 1849, Dr Hayman, headmaster of Rugby School dismissed in 1873, and the district surveyor of Bethnal Green, dismissed by the London County Council in 1915 all found themselves in this category, though in all cases there was no doubt something they could have said in their defence if given the chance.[129]

In the twentieth century those cases might be seen as instances of employment, with the line to be drawn between contract and office. In the nineteenth all were seen as offices; whether they were terminable at will or only for cause depended on the statute or instrument that created them. Nor do judges seem to have brought social assumptions to bear on that question of interpretation.[130] Alfred Poole was but a junior curate at the Anglo-Catholic chapel at Pimlico when he antagonized parishioners of a lower-church persuasion by asking young women indelicate questions when hearing their confessions, but, the Queen's Bench held, the Archbishop of Canterbury was nonetheless wrong to confirm the bishop's revocation of his curate's licence without giving him full opportunity to

---

[126] 11 Co. Rep. 93b, 1 Str. 557.

[127] *Capel* v. *Child* (1832) 2 C. & J. 558. The sequestration was of the benefice's income, sufficient to pay the curate the bishop had appointed to do the necessary work.

[128] *Re Hammersmith Rentcharge* (1849) 4 Ex. 87, contrast *Bonaker* v. *Evans* (1850) 16 Q.B. 162.

[129] *R* v. *Governors of Darlington School* (1844) 6 Q.B. 682; *R* v. *Poor Law Commissioners* (1850) 19 LJ MC 70; *Hayman* v. *Governors of Rugby School* (1874) LR 18 Eq 28; *Notley* v. *London CC* [1915] 3 KB 580.

[130] For a stark example see *R* v. *Smith* (1844) 5 Q.B. 614.

present his case.[131] The statute said nothing about process, and enabled the archbishop to decide as 'shall appear to him just and proper', but the court cast the function as appellate, hence requiring a 'hearing' at which the appellant could contest the evidence and produce his own.

The principle carried over into justices' decisions that might be labelled administrative, most notably in *R* v. *Totnes Union* in 1845, where justices had ordered the union to maintain an elderly woman at home rather than in the workhouse without having summoned the guardians or an officer.[132] And in a similar way mid-century judges decided that because orders by commissioners of bankruptcy were not judicial, and hence could be made *ex parte*, they could not be final in law.[133] That reasoning was to recur in the building line cases mentioned above, where one reason judges gave for allowing justices to reopen the question at enforcement stage was that district surveyors did not have an obligation to hear before deciding, whereas one reason for ultimately deciding that their line was final was that surveyors (and judges) now agreed that they did.[134] At its broadest, in the loose words reported in *R* v. *Totnes Union*, the obligation attached to any order that 'affects the interests of persons in some way' even though not a penalty or 'direct burden'.

The principle's breadth and the heterogeneity of the situations to which it was being applied may explain why the decision in *Cooper* v. *Wandsworth Board of Works* in 1863, which a century later became an obligatory point of reference, caused no excitement at the time.[135] The statute, Metropolis Local Management Act 1855, gave power to demolish houses, and said nothing about according a hearing, but it nonetheless seemed orthodox to require the Board first to tell Cooper of its intention and why—he had failed to give the statutory advance notice of construction that enabled the Board to check compliance with building regulations—and give him a chance to dissuade it. None of the judges doubted the importance of building regulation, or that the power to demolish existed in the circumstances, but those were not reasons for excusing the Board from a basic obligation that would cause it no discernible harm. The decision was quickly absorbed into textbooks on subjects as varied as partnership, arbitration, and local authority by-laws, but the 'of course' with which the editor of *Addison*

---

[131] *R* v. *Archbishop of Canterbury* (1859) 1 E. & E. 545. The archbishop reached the same conclusion on a (re)hearing (*The Times*, 24 March 1859). For the scandal see *The Times*, 11 June 1858 and N. Yates, *Anglican Ritualism in Victorian Britain* (Oxford, 1999), 164, 210–11.

[132] (1845) 7 Q.B. 690.

[133] *Graham* v. *Furber* (1853) 14 C.B. 134.

[134] *Simpson* v. *Smith* (1871) LR 6 CP 87; *Spackman* v. *Plumstead DBW* (1885) 10 App Cas 229.

[135] (1863) 14 C.B. (N.S.) 180, followed on similar facts in *Masters* v. *Pontypool LGB* (1878) 9 Ch D 677; *Hopkins* v. *Smethwick LBH* (1890) 24 QBD 712.

on Wrongs greeted it speaks for them all.[136] Like the gas company in *Painter*, the Board had to pay damages for its unjustified trespass.

At least one local authority took the point and drafted its surveyors' emergency statutory powers explicitly to exclude need for 'presentment, notice or other formality', which the Common Pleas took entirely at face value just as the Queen's Bench had taken offices terminable at will in the *Darlington School* case.[137] More usually, and more importantly, a middle way evolved of providing an appeal to an administrative authority. It was used in public health legislation, where, rather than presenting a need to a justice, who would then hear and decide, an official might serve a notice requiring work to be done, with a short time limit, after which the authority might do the work itself and charge for it, or perhaps make a closing order or some such.[138] There was no statutory provision for the surveyor or authority to hear the property owner, but an appeal lay to the Local Government Board.[139] Meeting a similar power for the first time in 1889 Field J. said he hardly knew how to go about classifying it.[140] In 1890, however, the Queen's Bench revisited *Cooper*, found that it did not mandate a particular style of fair procedure, and held that the opportunity for a hearing before the appellate authority sufficed without need for the authority to 'hear' as well.[141]

The critical question then became how much of what the courts had imposed upon justices they would now impose on these new administrative appellant authorities. They had not previously been inflexible. The reform of municipal corporations in 1835 had entailed the removal of office-holders, some of whom were to be compensated by the new councils. Anticipating disputes, the Act gave a right of appeal to the Lords Commissioners of the Treasury. The Queen's Bench eventually decided that that august body's unsuitability to find facts or apply law made it unlikely Parliament meant it to adjudicate whether a town clerk was a victim of the Act (as he claimed) or had been dismissed for misconduct (as the council claimed), and that therefore the Treasury's role was confined to valuing

[136] N. Lindley, *Treatise on the Law of Partnership* (4th edn, 1881), 845; H. F. A. Davis, *The Law and Practice of Friendly Societies and Trade Unions* (1876), 149–51; W. G. Lumley, *An Essay on By Laws* (1877), 204–5; C. G. Addison, *Wrongs and their Remedies* (4th edn, 1870), 684 (see also 284, 1057); P. B. Maxwell, *On Interpretation of Statutes* (1875), 325–30.

[137] Manchester Waterworks and Improvement Act 1867 (local); *Cheetham* v. *Mayor of Manchester* (1875) LR 10 CP 249 (declining to hold surveyor's decision not conclusive).

[138] Allowing public authorities direct powers of enforcement exposed them to the same liability that justices had (as in *Cooper*), leading to extension of the procedural protections justices had enjoyed since 1751 to all public authorities: Public Authorities Protection Act 1893.

[139] Public Health Act 1875, s 268.

[140] *Parsons* v. *Lakenheath School Board* (1889) 58 LJ QB 371.

[141] *Vestry of St James, Clerkenwell* v. *Feary* (1890) 24 QBD 703; also *A.G.* v. *Hooper* [1893] 3 Ch 483; *Robinson* v. *Sunderland Corp.* [1899] 1 QB 751.

the office.[142] However, on the assumption that the Commissioners did have jurisdiction they could decide on the papers and not, as the applicant wanted, only
after a hearing adorned by counsel and witnesses.[143] Similarly, when the Queen's
Bench had ordered the archbishop to hear the curate, Alfred Poole, it had pointedly left the manner of hearing to his discretion—it too might be done on the
papers, Lord Campbell suggested.[144]

Like *Board of Education* v. *Rice*, the litigation that was to determine the courts'
general approach for a generation or more arose from the heated politics of the
Liberals' new agenda. It concerned the Housing and Town Planning Act 1909,
which introduced planning controls and council housing for the first time, and
in addition strengthened local authorities' powers to order closure or demolition
of houses deemed unfit for habitation. That latter objective included replacing
appeals to quarter sessions with an appeal to the Local Government Board.
Opposing the bill almost line by line, the Conservatives used their majority in the
Lords to force numerous amendments, one of which allowed appeal to a county
court as an alternative.[145] When the government rejected that, a compromise was
reached deleting the amendment but requiring a public local inquiry by a Board-
appointed inspector before the Board could dismiss an appeal.[146] John Burns, the
independent socialist who was the President of the Local Government Board,
conceded also that the Board should have power to state a case on a point of law
to a superior court. The Conservatives did not release the pressure however, since
tarring the Liberals with arrogant and unchecked use of state power seemed good
politics. Thus the appeal right was politicized from the beginning.

The following year a London landlord, William Arlidge, won an appeal against
closure of houses, but only after a three-day inquiry for which, though victorious,
the Board denied him his costs, as it also denied him a copy of the inspector's
report.[147] In retaliation Arlidge lobbied several London borough councils to agi-
tate for a restoration of appeals to a court, successfully enough for a Conservative
MP to use the boroughs' complaints to harry Burns in the Commons.[148] In
reply to a formal question the President refused to release inspectors' reports.[149]

[142]   *R* v. *Warwick Corporation* (1840) 10 Ad. & El. 386.
[143]   *R* v. *Treasury Commissioners in re Tibbits* (1839) 10 Ad. & El. 374.
[144]   *R* v. *Archbishop of Canterbury* (1859) 1 E. & E. 545, 559, 561.
[145]   *PD* 1909 (s5 HL) 3: 138–52.
[146]   *PD* 1909 (s5 HC) 12: 1498–1509; (s5 HL) 3: 667–79.
[147]   Letter from his solicitor, J. S. Rubinstein, to *The Times*, 9 December 1910. Arlidge may have
been gearing up to sue the alderman who proposed the closure motion, and who had incautiously
labelled him a slum landlord in the local newspaper: *The Times*, 17, 18 November 1911; *PD* 1911 (s5
HC) 32: 1409, 1887.
[148]   *The Times*, 22 March 1911; *PD* 1911 (s5 HC) 22: 517–18W; see also 25: 1000–1W.
[149]   (1911) 75 *JP* 101, 114; *PD* 1911 (s5 HC) 32: 2835.

Further, the Board adopted a process whereby one official served as inspector at the inquiry, viewing the properties, hearing argument, and writing a report, but a different official made the decision in the Board's name.[150] Under pressure from yet another Conservative Question the President declined to identify which officials decided, but—assuring his questioner of the seriousness of the enterprise—said that sometimes it was he or his Parliamentary Secretary, which might suggest that more than a simple inquiry into the facts was involved.[151] A few days later an inquiry began on an appeal by Arlidge against the closure of another of his houses. He lost, and took his case to court by *certiorari*. By then every issue he would raise had been raised already in the Commons, where the President defended the Board on the ground—put shortly—that it was implicit in rejection of the Conservative amendment in 1909 that its procedure was not that of a court.[152]

The judges need not have agreed. A majority in the Court of Appeal sided with Arlidge, but none in the Queen's Bench or the Lords. The two who did saw the Board as the decider of a judicial question and the inspector's report as evidence, hence the latter should certainly be disclosed and the former should be open to an oral hearing if the appellant requested it. But the eight others saw the report simply as a statement of proceedings at the inquiry, at which the appellant could appear and be represented, and they saw no unfairness in the Board deciding on the papers. Among them was Hamilton LJ, who had been the inspector in the Swansea case, and whose judgment demonstrated at length how well Parliament must have known that this was how administrative appeals worked, pointing out too that there were occasions within judicial structures when decisions were made without a formal hearing. The Lords agreed: there must be a hearing, and it must accord with the judicial spirit (left undefined) but what had happened was comfortably within what Parliament had intended. Lord Loreburn had sketched out much the same thing in *Board of Education* v. *Rice*, and Lord Selborne in the leading building line case, showing how general this understanding was.[153] Nor was there a difficulty with an official deciding on behalf of the Board—how else could departments run? For Lord Parmoor it would be pointless for the inspector's report to be public; for Lord Moulton it would be mischievous.

---

[150] (1911) 75 JP 567–8. The procedure was suggested in debate on the bill, and was meant to secure uniformity: *PD* 1909 (s5 HC) 12: 1504–8.

[151] *PD* 1911 (s5 HC) 25: 1000–1W; see also 23: 891–2; 24: 867–7. Burns hinted at personal antagonism to Arlidge, but when challenged evaded the point: *PD* 1911 (s5 HC) 28: 678–9; 29: 568–9, 629–33, 650–1.

[152] In addition to the references cited, see *PD* 1911 (s5 HC) 21: 1200–1W.

[153] *Spackman* v. *Plumstead DBW* (1885) 10 App Cas 229.

Dicey's immediate reaction to this decision was that it was what Parliament intended.[154] He worried that departments could now use the secrecy of their deliberations to smuggle political factors into their decisions, but, reading the case in conjunction with *Board of Education* v. *Rice*, he was confident that courts could still keep departments within the legal framework established by the statute. He was aware that he was witnessing new law, as courts came to terms with new administrative and political developments. Sir Frederick Pollock, thinking as a private lawyer and asking what would be expected of an arbitrator, could see no argument for Arlidge.[155] And though it was not put this way, the judges' refusal to characterize the inspector's report as a public document fits a longstanding reluctance to require a speaking record outside summary convictions.

So although many commentators 50 or 60 years on will have agreed with Robert Stevens that *Arlidge* marked a judicial retreat (without being very clear what it was a retreat from), even that it was the foundation of the inter-war 'tragedy of public law', that reaction does not seem discernible at the time.[156] There were warning voices too, that any greater intervention would be seen as politically motivated; Ivor Jennings wrote that the Court of Appeal had been making 'an effort...to hamstring the whole administrative process'.[157]

5. THE REVIEW OF DISCRETION

Decisions

At the start of our period counsel manoeuvred into conceding that a power was discretionary had all but lost the case; only the long shot of showing that the decision could not fall within its terms remained.[158] It is an 'invariable rule that we do not interfere' with quarter sessions' exercise of discretion, said Bayley J. in 1822.[159] There was a glimmer of an exception, when the King's Bench treated as unreasonable a sessions' decision about what notices had to be given before it would hear a settlement appeal, Lord Ellenborough claiming a 'kind of visitatorial jurisdiction' in such cases.[160] By the 1830s, however, the court was stressing the inviolability of justices' discretion, looking only to see that a sessions had

[154] A. V. Dicey, 'The Development of Administrative law in England' (1915) 31 *LQR* 148–53.
[155] (1913) 29 *LQR* 253.
[156] R. Stevens, *Law and Politics* (1979), 197–8, 252.
[157] W. I. Jennings, 'Courts and Administrative Law' (1936) 49 *HLR* 426–54 at 443.
[158] e.g. *R* v. *Mills* (1831) 2 B. & Ad. 578.
[159] *R* v. *Norfolk Justices* (1822) 1 Dow. & Ry. KB. 69.
[160] *R* v. *Wiltshire Justices* (1808) 10 East 404; *R* v. *Lancashire Justices* (1828) 7 B. & C. 691.

not adopted an unlawful rule.[161] On a matter like whether Joe's Coffee House, off Fleet Street, should have its licence renewed the justices' sway was unchallengeable, and without hesitation the judges carried the same immunity over to the Poor Law Commissioners' decisions that Newport and Holborn needed new workhouses.[162] 'This court cannot entertain such a question', said Lord Denman.[163]

Such direct challenges as there were usually sought a *mandamus* to order a sessions to hear and decide, arguing that the decision it had already made was vitiated by legal error and hence was no decision in law. Martin Stapylton, a North Riding justice appalled by his bench's prison policy, had to argue that a diet of bread and water cannot be 'plain and wholesome food' within the meaning of the statute, hence that it was a breach of duty to provide only that diet to a remand prisoner who refused to work for his meals by walking the prison treadmill, hence that the bench had not yet reached a decision on his report to it—where in fact the bench had rejected it.[164] The true issue was the inhumanity of subjecting remand prisoners in the guise of work to an ordeal regarded as harsh for convicts. But the court was clear that the nature of work to be provided was discretionary, just as 'plain and wholesome' was for the justices' judgment. Stapylton had to take his complaint to Parliament, where he got the law changed.[165] It is rare to find a case such as Stapylton's, and as his counsel seem to have found no precedents on which to base their argument it may be that his eye always was on Parliament.

In the twentieth century a jurisdiction to review discretionary decisions for unreasonableness was rooted in *Rooke's Case* (1598), then, with a hop and skip to any intervening case that happened to use the word, a principle was constructed and portrayed as having been in general use.[166] There was no such usage until the very end of the nineteenth century, and then only tentatively, save for a jurisdiction over byelaws, which will be discussed further below. *Rooke's Case* was not treated as holding that a decision to charge the whole of a rate for repairing a riverbank on just one ratepayer was unreasonable—as a similar

---

[161] R v. Wilts. Justices (1828) 8 B. & C. 380; R v. Frieston (1833) 5 B. & Ad. 597; R v. West Riding Justices (1833) 5 B. & Ad. 668; R v. Norfolk Justices (1834) 5 B. & Ad. 990.

[162] R v. Farringdon Licensing Justices (1824) 4 Dow. & Ry. KB 735; cf. Shaw v. Pope (1831) 2 B. & Ad. 465; R v. Poor Law Commissioners in re Newport Union (1837) 6 Ad. & El. 54; Frewin v. Wood (1838) 4 My. & Cr. 249.

[163] R v. Poor Law Commissioners (1837) 6 Ad. & El. 54.

[164] R v. North Riding Justices (1823) 2 B. & C. 286.

[165] Northallerton Gaol, Copy of Orders, PP 1824 (68), xix, 133; Treadwheels, Copy of Correspondence, ibid. (45) 147; Statement Respecting Treadmills, ibid. (247) 165; PD 1824 (s2) 10: 138–41; 11: 509–24; The Times, 25 May 1824; Gaols Act 1824, 5 Geo. IV c. 85, s 16.

[166] 5 Co. Rep. 99b; Wade, Administrative Law (5th edn, 1982), 353–4.

twentieth-century case would be—but as illustrating a common law rule that rates can be charged only on owners who will benefit from the work to be done, or, put more broadly, a rule that rates must be 'equal'.[167] That preserved the outcome of *Rooke's case*, enabled a set of rules to be developed for different contexts, but prevented it becoming a precedent for any other inquiry into the exercise of discretion. The technique was to constrain the power by boundary rules of law, not to evaluate decisions within jurisdiction. 'What difference is there', asked Tindal CJ rhetorically in the *Darlington School* case, where, unusually, counsel had cited *Rooke's Case*, 'between power to remove at discretion, and at will?'[168]

The same techniques were used in Chancery, where disputes were taken about the acquisition of land under statutory powers and about the use made of statutory powers to erect works that interfered with a landowner's previous enjoyment of his property. A power to acquire land for one purpose could not be used to acquire it for another, but, so the courts held, where the power allowed, say, a railway company to acquire whatever land it deemed 'necessary' for the statutory purpose the court would inquire no further into the necessity than that the opinion was honestly held.[169] In 1888 Stirling J. carried that minimal standard over into acquisitions by local boards of health, the more readily, he said, because boards performed important public duties and acted for the benefit of the whole community.[170] It mattered not how many eminent engineers the complainant produced to testify that they would have found an alternative way. In 1865 Kindersley VC had suggested a tougher standard, saying that railway company surveyors needed to give their reasons so that they could be scrutinized to make sure there really was a necessity, but that was quickly disavowed for fear of a deluge of affidavits.[171]

In the second situation common in Chancery the argument was that with no harm to itself the statutory undertaker could have built its pier, or situated its urinal, or put the fuse-box for its tramway just a little further away, and

---

[167] *R v. Commissioners of Sewers for Tower Hamlets* (1829) 9 B. & C. 517; *Soady v. Wilson* (1835) 3 Ad. & El. 248; *Hammersmith Bridge Co v. Hammersmith Overseers* (1871) LR 6 QB 230; contrast *Mackenzie District Council v. Electricorp* [1992] 3 NZLR 41. A computer search of the English Reports shows counsel using *Rooke's Case* in what becomes the twentieth-century way in *Doswell v. Impey* (1823) 1 B. & C. 162; *De Beauvoir v. Welch* (1827) 7 B. & C. 266; *R v. Governors of Darlington School* (1844) 6 Q.B. 682, all unsuccessfully, then with some success in *R v. Boteler* (1864) 4 B. & S. 959.

[168] *R v. Governors of Darlington School* (1844) 6 Q.B. 682, 701.

[169] *Dodd v. Salisbury & Yeovil Railway* (1859) 1 Giff. 158; *Stockton & Darlington Railway v. Brown* (1860) 9 H.L.C. 746.

[170] *Lewis v. Weston-super-Mare Local Board* (1888) 40 Ch D 55.

[171] *Flower v. London, Brighton & South Coast Railway* (1865) 2 Dr. & Sm. 330; *Beauchamp v. Great Western Railway* (1868) LR 3 Ch App 745; *Kemp v. South-Eastern Railway* (1872) LR 7 Ch App 364; *Wilkinson v. Hull Railway & Dock Co* (1882) 20 Ch D 323.

thus avoided harm to the adjoining landowner.[172] If the landowner was being victimized—deliberately harmed for some collateral purpose—then an injunction would lie.[173] But otherwise the Chancery judges approached the issue through boundary rules rather than through assessing the reasonableness of the decision. They asked whether the Act authorized a nuisance; if it did (as in all the cases just cited), there could be no complaint that by doing things differently the nuisance would have been avoided, again no matter how many engineers said that that would have been their way.

In addition, however, to the constraints of using a power only for its authorized purpose, and of acting honestly (which were sometimes conflated), judges held that a power to decide did not imply a power to make a rule.[174] The King's Bench had applied that principle to quarter sessions in preference to Lord Ellenborough's more intrusive visitatorial jurisdiction: the discretion was the justices', but they must exercise it with a view to the particular circumstances.[175] Carried over into modern statutory jurisdictions the principle could be severely limiting. Wandsworth Board of Works could not lawfully decide that all the privies in its district must be converted to water closets, but must consider them one by one.[176] Abingdon licensing justices could not clamp down on lower-class drinking by re-licensing pubs only if they took out an excise licence for selling spirits as well.[177] Then, into the twentieth century, the Metropolitan Police Commissioner could not decide that no one still paying for his vehicle on hire purchase could have a cab licence.[178] The principle seems not to have changed throughout.

Further, it could be generalized: a duty to assess the individual circumstances ruled out pre-commitment to an outcome. Two situations in particular tended to recur. The principle that in a judicial context held that an individual justice might become so identified with a prosecutor as to become disqualified for bias reached over into licensing applications. So Nonconformist magistrates who belonged to temperance societies could not participate in licensing decisions where the society opposed, however discretionary the decision might be.[179]

---

[172] *A.G.* v. *Thames Conservators* (1862) 1 H. & M. 1; *Biddulph* v. *Vestry of St George Hanover Square* (1863) 33 LJ Ch. 411; *Vernon* v. *Vestry of St. James, Westminster* (1880) 16 Ch D 449; *Goldberg* v. *Mayor of Liverpool* (1900) 82 LT 362; *Chaplin* v. *Mayor of Westminster* [1901] 2 Ch 329.

[173] *Goldberg* v. *Mayor of Liverpool* (1900) 82 LT 362.

[174] For a conflation see *Wilkinson* v. *Hull Railway & Dock Co* (1882) 20 Ch D 323.

[175] *R* v. *West Riding Justices* (1833) 5 B. & Ad. 668; *R.* v. *Norfolk Justices* (1834) 5 B. & Ad. 990.

[176] *Tinkler* v. *Wandsworth Board of Works* (1858) 2 De G. & J. 261.

[177] *R* v. *Sylvester* (1862) 31 LJ MC 93; see also *Macbeth* v. *Ashley* (1874) LR 2 Sc & Div 352.

[178] *Ex p. Randall* (1911) 27 TLR 505.

[179] *R* v. *Fraser* (1893) 9 TLR 613; *R* v. *London County Council* [1892] 1 QB 190; cf. *R* v. *Allan* (1864) 4 B. & S. 915.

Secondly, an authority could not contract to dispose of surplus lands before exercising its power to acquire them, even though that might be a common way of
funding part of the development that otherwise might fall on the rates.[180] Courts
regarded the principle as obvious, but it could cause difficulty if several authorities with different powers had to work together. It is the reason why Cordings'
charming shop front on Piccadilly had to be embedded in Sir Norman Shaw's
grand design: Westminster Corporation, a cipher in the dealings of the Crown,
the London County Council, and the Piccadilly Hotel Company, had considered
only its contract, not the merits, so its decision to acquire that part of the site was
quashed.[181]

Nonetheless, through into the 1880s and 1890s judges would sometimes give
the uncontrollable nature of the discretion as a reason for reading legislation
down. The power that authorities had in London to acquire land compulsorily
for street widening extended only to the strip needed, the Court of Appeal held
in 1885, not to the whole plot of which it formed part; otherwise, said Bowen LJ,
an authority needing a few feet to widen Threadneedle Street could pull down the
Bank of England, which cannot have been what Parliament intended.[182] He gave
no indication that a broad power could be satisfactorily controlled by assessing
the reasonableness of a decision, though that might have worked just as well as the
tangle of rules that resulted.[183] Likewise Cave and Field JJ denied that Newcastle-
upon-Tyne Corporation's statutory powers, properly read, allowed it to reject a
building application for lowering the tone of a neighbourhood—there were no
discernible legal criteria a court could use to control such a discretion, and 'economical' ones would be unsuitable for both it and an appellate magistrate, so
again Parliament must have intended a different reading.[184] Coleridge LCJ took
the same approach to bishops' powers under the Public Worship Regulation Act,
but was reversed on appeal.[185]

That was the point Lord Halsbury was addressing in *Sharp* v. *Wakefield* in
1891 when he summarized the constraints judges had placed around the edges of

---

[180] *Galloway* v. *Corporation of London* (1864) 2 De G. J. & Sm. 211 (reversed on the statute (1866)
LR 1 HL 34); *Carrington* v. *Wycombe Railway* (1868) LR 3 Ch App 377.

[181] *Denman* v. *Westminster Corporation* [1906] 1 Ch 464; F. H. W. Sheppard (Gen. Ed.) *Survey of
London*, vol. 31 (1963), 85–100.

[182] *Gard* v. *Commissioners of Sewers of the City of London* (1885) 28 Ch D 486; see also *Lynch* v.
Commissioners of Sewers (1886) 32 Ch D 72 (where there is a dictum about reasonable evidence).

[183] *Gordon* v. *Vestry of St Mary Abbotts* [1894] 2 QB 742; *Aldis* v. *London Corporation* [1899] 2 Ch
169; *Gibbon* v. *Paddington Vestry* [1900] 2 Ch 794; *Pescod* v. *Westminster Corporation* [1905] 2 Ch 475;
Green v. *Hackney Corporation* [1910] 2 Ch 105; *Davis* v. *Corporation of City of London* [1913] 1 Ch 415.

[184] *R* v. *Mayor of Newcastle* (1889) 60 *LT* 963.

[185] *R* v. *Bishop of London* (1889) 24 QBD 414, reversed in *Allcroft* v. *Bishop of London* [1891] AC
666; compare *Julius* v. *Bishop of Oxford* (1880) 5 App Cas 214 and *Marquis of Abergavenny* v. *Bishop
of Llandaff* (1888) 20 QBD 460. See above, pp. 399–400.

discretion, emphasizing their potency.[186] The case was a climax in a long struggle between the brewers and the temperance movement, the one defending existing liquor licences, the other seeking at least a wholesale reduction in their number. It decided, as some earlier cases in lower courts had done, that licensing justices had the same discretion to decline applications to renew existing licences as they had to decline first-time applications. That was potentially crushing for the brewers, the more so because nearly all the judges stressed that the discretion was absolute.[187] The impact was delayed while governments unsuccessfully sought a solution broad enough to win support, but then it was magnified by a further judicial decision.[188] This came in *Smith* v. *Farnham Licensing Justices* in 1902, when the Court of Appeal held that though the justices could not just apply a rule there was no objection to their having a fixed policy of reducing existing licences, provided, as had happened, that they then considered each applicant individually.[189] The decision was the immediate cause of the 1904 Licensing Act, in which the Conservatives finally put licensing on to a new basis.

Sharp v. *Wakefield*, however, must have put Lord Halsbury, the Conservative Lord Chancellor, into an embarrassing position. 'Large interests are involved in the decision of this case', Lord Esher had begun in the lower court, which included, for the brewers, a very much closer political association with the Conservatives than with the Liberals.[190] Perhaps that is why Halsbury softened the blow. Because licensing justices must consider the merits and not act on a rule, and because they must act as honest and competent men would, and because they could not be arbitrary, vague, or fanciful (citing *Rooke's Case*), it was quite probable that Parliament did mean them (back in 1828) to have this discretion, he said. Lord Hannen went with him on the first of those restrictions, Wills J. in the Queen's Bench had said justices could not deny a licence for wearing a blue coat or a white hat, but most, including Lords Herschell and Bramwell, said simply that the discretion was unfettered.

Halsbury's general statement, based on very little decided case law, drawn from widely different contexts, was something new.[191] Its fragility was shown

---

[186] [1891] AC 173.

[187] D. W. Gutzke, *Protecting the Pub* (1989) (and see untitled review by D. M. Fahey (1991) 34 *Vict. St.* 514–15); D. M. Fahey, 'Brewers, Publicans and Working-class drinkers' (1980) 13 *Histoire Sociale* 85–103.

[188] Gutzke, *Protecting the Pub*, 153.

[189] [1902] 2 KB 363. For the limit to the decision see *Raven* v. *Southampton Justices* [1904] 1 KB 430, and compare *R* v. *Bowman* [1898] 1 QB 663.

[190] The complexity of the relationship is well described in Gutzke, *Protecting the Pub*.

[191] *R* v. *Boteler* (1864) 4 B. & S. 959 (justices' power to enforce rate on overseer), perhaps *Ex p. Prater* (1864) 5 B. & S. 299; *R* v. *Adamson* (1875) 1 QBD 201 (justices' power to issue summons). Lopes LJ went part way in *R* v. *Bishop of London* (1889) 24 QBD 213, while making it very clear that he was thinking only of cases where the decision maker defied the law.

when Farwell LJ in the *Rice* litigation applied its reasoning to central government too, in that instance to the deliberations of the Board of Education, where avoiding extraneous and improper considerations would mean keeping politics out of the decision.[192] His judgment was particularly attacked by the Attorney-General on further appeal, who won not a condemnation, but a markedly narrower statement of the Board's obligations.[193]

It was surprising, therefore, when in 1905 Lord Macnaghten not only said that statutory powers must be exercised reasonably but went ahead to apply his standard, though he concluded for the authority.[194] He understood reasonableness to require the decision maker to act with 'judgment and discretion' and credited it to Turner LJ in 'a well-known case'. But though Turner had used his formulation to condemn a land-acquisition decision on the basis that the authority had improperly fettered itself by a prior contract, he had been reversed in the Lords on his reading of the relevant statute and, with one exception, his method had not taken root.[195] The exception was Macnaghten himself, in a Privy Council case in 1902.[196] When in 1906 counsel argued unreasonableness to the King's Bench, where most review cases would start, Lord Alverstone acknowledged Turner's usage, declined to commit himself, and grounded the case elsewhere.[197] Macnaghten was sure of his principle, however, and in 1911 explicitly used unreasonableness as the Privy Council's ground for invalidating a superannuation decision made by the New South Wales Public Service Board.[198] Much was to come of this idea later in the century, though when it did Lord Macnaghten was not generally recognized as its progenitor.[199] Lord Halsbury's formulation, however, did take root.[200]

Byelaws

While reasonableness was a novel criterion for validity of a decision, it was a well-established yardstick for assessing byelaws, where its origin lay in the

---

[192]   *R* v. *Board of Education* [1910] 2 KB 165.

[193]   *The Times*, 25 February 1911; *Board of Education* v. *Rice* [1911] AC 179. Similarly, Sir Samuel Hall's use of a Halsbury-like formula in *Goldberg* v. *Mayor of Liverpool* (1900) 82 *LT* 362, the fuse-box case mentioned above, was replaced on appeal by a conventional analysis based on boundary rules.

[194]   *Westminster Corporation* v. *London & North-western Railway* [1905] AC 426.

[195]   *Galloway* v. *Corporation of London* (1864) 2 De G. J. & Sm. 211 (LJJ); (1866) LR 1 HL 34.

[196]   *Mayor of East Freemantle* v. *Annois* [1902] AC 213.

[197]   *R* v. *Mayor of Brighton* (1906) 95 *LT* 391. Counsel seems to have mis-identified Turner LJ's case as *A.G.* v. *Wigan* (1854) 5 De G. M. & G. 52.

[198]   *Williams* v. *Giddy* [1911] AC 381.

[199]   *Roberts* v. *Hopwood* [1925] AC 578; *Associated Provincial Picture Houses* v. *Wednesbury Corporation* [1948] 1 KB 223.

[200]   *R* v. *London County Council* [1915] 2 KB 466; *Roberts* v. *Hopwood* [1925] AC 578.

ancient law of corporations.[201] Its application was not always clearly demarcated from its twin requirement of lawfulness, since provisions in charters or old statutes were often skeletal and the constraints judges added took on the appearance of rules. There came to be many such rules about byelaws affecting corporations' constitutions—their elections, offices, disqualifications. Many more byelaws concerned the regulation of local trade, where judges drew a line between forbidden restraint and permitted regulation, often using reasonableness as a criterion. To that extent reasonableness was internalized into a set of common law rules rather than functioning as an independent test. Outside the City of London most of this law became obsolete in 1835, when the Municipal Corporations Act gave the reformed corporations a statutory constitution, repealed all trading byelaws that had excluded outsiders, and granted new powers to make byelaws restricted to the suppression of nuisances and the appointment of stipendiary magistrates.[202]

The jurisdiction was so much a part of corporations law, however, that it carried over without serious question into the activities of the reformed municipal corporations, and the railway companies, and likewise into byelaws made under the new public health legislation.[203] It made no difference, said Lord Campbell CJ, that modern statutory byelaws needed approval, in this case by the Secretary of State: courts say what is legal. That was a case of straightforward *ultra vires*: a power requiring removal of nuisances cannot require householders to clear away snow.[204] Other cases are more ambiguous. In *Everett* v. *Grapes*, for example, Newport's byelaw prohibiting keeping swine in the borough might have been invalid as unreasonably broad or as exceeding a power restricted to the suppression of nuisances.[205] With more far-reaching consequences, the invalidation of a byelaw requiring a month's notice before commencing building and another allowing demolition of houses for a wide range of breaches, seem to have been based upon unreasonableness, though the judgments are so cursory that it is difficult to be sure.[206] Certainly it is unusual to find a judge in the 1860s arguing strongly that public authorities should be allowed latitude; Erle CJ is an exception

---

[201] S. Kyd, *A Treatise on the Law of Corporations* (1794), ii, 107–37; J. Grant, *A Practical Treatise on the Law of Corporations* (1850), 76–97.

[202] 5 & 6 Will. IV c. 76, ss 14, 90, 99. For its continuation in the affairs of the livery companies, see *R* v. *Saddlers' Company* (1863) 10 H.L.C. 404.

[203] *Elwood* v. *Bullock* (1844) 6 Q.B. 383; *Chilton* v. *London & Croydon Railway* (1847) 16 M. & W. 212.

[204] *R* v. *Wood* (1855) 8 E. & B. 49.

[205] (1861) 3 L.T. (N.S.) 669.

[206] *Hattersley* v. *Burr* (1866) 4 H. & C. 523; *Young* v. *Edwards* (1864) 33 LJ MC 227; and see *Waite* v. *Garston Local Board* (1867) 37 LJ MC 19. Legislation was needed: Lumley, *By Laws*, 143–4.

but, perhaps significantly, his was a market regulation case, not one involving property rights.[207]

In the 1870s there was a change of judicial mood. Wanstead's prohibition on keeping pigs near dwelling houses was upheld, Blackburn J. saying that if the place was so rural as not to need such a byelaw the Home Secretary should be petitioned before approval—a remark that was to be ignored a decade later.[208] Byelaws requiring advance notice of building and allowing demolition for breach were now upheld too.[209] The published correspondence of the Local Government Board still shows nervousness that byelaws insufficiently concentrated on an identifiable target would be held unreasonably broad, so it may be that the Board was intercepting suspect rules before they could get to court.[210] However, in 1888, the Privy Council dismissed an argument that a byelaw prohibiting burials within 100 yards of buildings should be invalidated because it did not contain the exceptions usually found in such rules, saying that only extreme cases should be held unreasonable, cases where the byelaw was capricious or oppressive.[211] It looks as though the standard for byelaws might have been shifting towards that for decisions.

If so, it would be easy to read *Kruse* v. *Johnson* in 1898 as confirmation.[212] It was decided by a majority of six judges to one, in a Divisional Court especially strengthened to act as though it were an appeal court from its own previous decisions—there being no other way to appeal a criminal case from it. The occasion was a conviction on a byelaw prohibiting singing in the street, a charge most notoriously brought against members of the Salvation Army. A decade previously there had been frequent riots in southern towns against their aggressive presence, causing local authorities to use byelaws against street music to remove them before the fighting began.[213] The byelaws varied, of course, but some judges were willing to invalidate some for unreasonableness, and the differences were difficult to reconcile.[214] The outcome was a strong statement that judges should respect the legitimacy that local councils' byelaws had through their political

---

[207] *Savage* v. *Brook* (1863) 15 C.B. (N.S.) 264; but see *Wortley* v. *Nottingham Local Board* (1870) 21 LT (NS) 582 for a less sympathetic judgment on market by-laws.

[208] *Wanstead Local Board* v. *Wooster* (1874) 38 JP 21 (and see *Tong Street Local Board* v. *Seed*, *ibid.*, 757); *Heap* v. *Burnley Union* (1884) 12 QBD 617.

[209] *Baker* v. *Mayor of Portsmouth* (1878) 3 ExD 157; *Hall* v. *Nixon* (1875) LR 10 QB 152.

[210] Local Government Board, *Selections from Correspondence* (1880–1), ii, 127–8, 179, 204.

[211] *Slattery* v. *Naylor* (1888) 13 App Cas 446; cf. *Shrike* v. *Collins* (1886) 51 LT (NS) 182; *Simmons* v. *Malling RDC* [1897] 2 QB 433.

[212] [1898] 2 QB 91, see also *Burnett* v. *Berry* [1896] 1 QB 641.

[213] V. Bailey, 'Salvation Army Riots, the "Skeleton Army" and Legal Authority in the Provincial Town', in A. Donajgrodski (ed.), *Social Control in Nineteenth-century Britain* (1977), 231–53 at 245–6.

[214] *R* v. *Powell* (1884) 51 LT (NS) 92; *Johnson* v. *Mayor of Croydon* (1886) 16 QBD 708; *Munro* v. *Watson* (1887) 51 JP 660.

process, and they should recognize too that reasonableness was a matter of opinion lacking definite standard. In the years immediately after the decision, judicial statements are common that policing and moral matters should be left to local authority.[215]

This denial of a strong role for a reasonableness criterion for validity of a byelaw was not the final word, however. From 1904 three Islington byelaws regulating lodging houses were invalidated, initially for imposing penalties without giving notice of breach, then, after they had been rewritten, for requiring compliance by a landlord who might not have had a legal right of entry.[216] It was also unreasonable, said Wills J., to require cleansing to be done in the first week of April—as the byelaw initially did—because when Easter fell then landlords would have difficulty finding labour.[217] This looks a more intrusive scrutiny than *Kruse* v. *Johnson* recommended, reminiscent of the cases in the 1860s, explicable perhaps by the context—though that had not been so in the 1870s—but capable of being linked to the standard Lord Macnaghten was developing for individual discretionary decisions.

Postscript

Perhaps the most significant feature of this narrative is that judges took for granted that principles of legality and fair procedure existed and that they should apply to new decision makers, however exalted. Procedural obstacles were minimized. It could not clearly be predicted, however, how review of centralized discretionary power would evolve after 1914; techniques were there for constraining discretion, even to the point of strangulation if pursued, and the statements from Lords Halsbury and Macnaghten were there to be exploited. But none of that was well established, and it was all vulnerable to prophylactic techniques of statutory drafting.

Further, judges showed deference to the chambers of parliament. Statutory rules laid before Parliament were not treated like byelaws; provided only that the rules fell within the broad subject-matter authorized the courts would not inquire into their reasonableness.[218] Save in the very rarest cases, courts would not intervene to intercept presentation of a rule to Parliament for approval. Decisions fell

---

[215] *White* v. *Morley* [1899] 2 QB 34; *Thomas* v. *Salters* [1900] 1 Ch. 10; *Gentel* v. *Rapps* [1902] 1 KB 160; *London County Council* v. *Bermondsey Bioscope* [1911] 1 KB 445; see also *Clayton* v. *Peirse* [1904] 1 KB 424, but contrast the divided opinions in *Scott* v. *Pilliner* [1904] 2 KB 855.

[216] *Nokes* v. *Islington Borough Council* (1904) 90 LT 22; *Stiles* v. *Galinski* [1904] 1 KB 615; *Arlidge* v. *Islington Corporation* [1909] 2 KB 127.

[217] *Stiles* v. *Galinski* [1904] 1 KB 615.

[218] *Institute of Patent Agents* v. *Lockwood* [1894] AC 347.

more clearly into the realm of the Executive, however, and could not claim privilege from political association. Nor could the rules of local authorities, who were to become subject to a similar range of review experienced previously by justices. It would take a great deal more litigation, however, before anyone could plausibly claim to find patterns in the application of these very general principles.

Part Three

THE COURTS OF LAW

I
General Introduction

I F a regency lawyer had fallen asleep just after Napoleon's exile to Elba and, in the manner of Rip van Winkle, had awoken just before the outbreak of the Great War, he would have found that after the passage of a century much had changed in the courts but much remained familiar. Indeed in comparison with the momentous changes in economic and social life the structures of the law, like those of government, would perhaps seem more notable for what had been preserved than for what had been replaced or transformed.

True the superior courts of law had deserted Westminster Hall for a splendid edifice in the Strand (albeit one whose gothic style looked to the past rather than the future). True also that two of the three historic courts of common law, the Common Pleas and Exchequer, had passed into history while the third, the King's Bench, had been relegated to the status of a mere division in a new entity, a 'Supreme Court of Judicature' (SCJ). A similar fate had befallen the court of Chancery, while a third division comprised in incongruous cohabitation the former court of Admiralty and those of Probate and Divorce, two courts unknown in 1814 and whose independent existence, dating from 1857, had been short-lived. Both had been hived off from the ecclesiastical courts and these, though they still survived, had been shorn of almost all their jurisdiction over laymen. All three divisions were empowered to dispense law and equity alike, though they remained distinct doctrinal sources. Equally, with a few exceptions all divisions might in theory hear any sort of case, but in practice the allocation of business was very much on pre-Judicature Act lines.

Above the divisions was a further novelty, a Court of Appeal hearing appeals from all three of them. However, the whole of the SCJ remained subject to a further appeal to the House of Lords. Admittedly the House's appellate functions were now performed chiefly by professional judges ('lords of appeal in ordinary') who were life peers only, and who also sat in a new 'Judicial Committee' of the Privy Council to hear appeals from the empire, the ecclesiastical courts and sundry other bodies. Nevertheless, the continuance of the Lords as a court of law, which had come very close to being ended in the 1870s, was one of the most striking continuities. Another institution which had endured was the Assizes, and here the changes in circuits and venues were relatively small, with the notable exception that Wales had been incorporated into the system in place of its own great sessions.

Below the level of the SCJ the changes were, at least on the civil side, more drastic, though criminal justice continued to be dispensed chiefly by the lay justices of the peace either in quarter or petty sessions; stipendiary magistrates, already known in 1814, were to be found only in a few places outside London. But what would have appeared to our observer at first glance as exhibiting a similar continuity on the civil side—county courts as the forum for the great majority of smaller disputes—was entirely deceptive. These courts were something new, products of mid-century legislation and named after the ancient county courts to provide a spurious pedigree. The ancient county courts, along with most others—manor and hundred, borough and franchise courts—had either been formally abolished or had become entirely inactive, leaving only a handful to spoil the simplicity of the picture. Even the courts of requests, which our observer might have expected to continue the rapid spread he had recently observed, were gone, liquidated to give the new county courts a clear run.

Within the courts a similar mixture of continuity and change might be found. Judges were still drawn exclusively from the bar even in the lower courts, though they no longer sat in banc at common law, adopting instead the equity practice of a single judge. The jury (and the special jury) survived, as rather precariously, did the grand jury. But while the petty jury remained the only mode of trial for serious criminal offences, civil litigants now had a choice. In county courts the jury was a rarity and in the King's Bench, though still holding its own, it was no longer the normal mode of trial. The bar still had exclusive audience in the higher courts but the ancient race of serjeants had passed into history, leaving the king's counsel masters of the field. Gone too was Doctors' Commons with the civilians and proctors, and gone also were the inns of Chancery. So were attorneys, done away with by Act of Parliament, but they had all become solicitors instead. And one thing was quite unchanged: all the judges and lawyers were still men.

Much had been altered in procedure. No longer was it a laborious business to hale a defendant into a common law court; instead judgment by default now enabled the High Court to process undefended cases with great rapidity. That change undercut the need for imprisonment upon mesne process and it had been duly ended in 1838 as (30 years on) was imprisonment for non-compliance with a judgment debt, save that in county courts it survived controversially as a species of contempt of court. The art of the common law special pleader had been rendered redundant and they had died out along with John Doe, Richard Roe, and the forms of action, while the Chancery bill had ceased to be the monstrosity of Eldon's day. Pleadings were comparatively simple, and readily amended, but the route to trial was so readily obstructed by interlocutory pleas, especially for interrogatories and discovery, that in the King's Bench things went no more quickly than of old. Not surprisingly therefore, our observer would have found that, while the legal professions for the most part boasted of the superiority of English justice over foreign systems, there was—as ever—very vocal criticism from laymen, centering on the traditional evils of cost and delay, now exacerbated by the facility for appeals.

If he looked more closely our observer would have found one innovation that was beginning to cause disquiet among lawyers. Alongside the courts had come into being boards, commissions and tribunals exercising dispute adjudication functions, performing in fact the same role as the courts themselves, though in limited spheres. They were not quite unknown in the regency, for commissioners of the land and assessed taxes and the more recent special and general commissioners of Pitt's hated income tax had this role. In the early Victorian period several commissions dealing with aspects of land reform—tithes, enclosures and copyhold enfranchisement—had also been given 'quasi-judicial' functions and later a Railway and Canal Commission had been added. These bodies differed widely in organization, powers, and procedures. The Railway Commission looked very like a court, headed as it was by a High Court judge, while the land commissions were more like administrative departments, for which adjudication was a minor function. These bodies had not been opposed in principle by judges and lawyers, and they were, after all, subject to control by the prerogative writs.[1]

However, some theorists, notably A. V. Dicey, had seen a nascent threat to the constitution in the power to adjudicate disputes being given to the very body responsible for making the administrative decisions which gave rise to the dispute, and with the advent in 1905 of a Liberal government of strongly reformist bent, Dicey ceased to be a lone voice. Exasperated with the ponderous and costly procedures of the courts and suspicious of their lack of sympathy towards the objectives of some of the new legislation, the ministries of Campbell-Bannerman and Asquith uncompromisingly assigned adjudication of disputes under national insurance, old age pensions and land valuation and taxation to agencies of government or tribunals, often with minimal scope for judicial supervision. This provoked anxious discussions of 'our new judiciary' which would intensify during the following decades.[2]

---

[1] C. Stebbings, *Legal Foundations of Tribunals in Nineteenth Century England* (Cambridge, 2006), and see above, pp. 487–517.

[2] e.g. W. J. L. Ambrose, 'The New Judiciary' (1910) 26 *LQR* 203–14. For post-War developments, see R. M. Jackson, *The Machinery of Justice in England* (1940) and W. A. Robson, *Justice and Administrative Law* (1928).

II

The Judicial Roles of the House of Lords and Privy Council, 1820–1914

1. THE HOUSE OF LORDS[1]

The Era of Lord Eldon

In the last years of Eldon's Chancellorship, both of the courts over which he presided experienced a crisis of arrears. Critics of both Chancery and the House of Lords directed their fire chiefly at delays in getting causes heard once they were set down, but whereas in Chancery that was attributed largely to Eldon's judicial style and insistence on retaining bankruptcy business, it was generally acknowledged that the problems of the Lords did not arise from his defects as a judge. The basic cause was clear to everyone, including select committees, namely an increase in appeals, particularly from Scotland, which outstripped inadequate judicial resources. Earlier remedies had plainly proved insufficient and in 1823 Eldon supported a fresh inquiry.[2]

Unlike Chancery, the malaise in the Lords was not a product of deep-rooted and complex structural and procedural defects. The residue of their original jurisdiction—peerage claims, privilege matters, criminal trials of peers etc—was never numerous enough to cause delays and the last impeachment, Lord Melville's, had taken place in 1805.[3] The procedure in appeals, though it differed according to whether the cause was an English or Irish equity appeal, a Scottish appeal or a writ of error from the common law courts, was comparatively straightforward, albeit embodied in standing orders which were not collected or

---

[1] On the House of Lords generally the fullest accounts are still the two books by A. S. Turberville: *The House of Lords in the Eighteenth Century* (1927) and *The House of Lords in the Age of Reform* (1958). For its judicial work, see R. Stevens, *Law and Politics: The House of Lords as a Judicial Body* (1979) and L. Blom-Cooper and G. Drewry, *Final Appeal* (Oxford, 1972); also Turberville, 'The House of Lords as a Court of Law, 1784–1837' (1936) 52 *LQR* 189–213.

[2] Stevens, *Law and Politics*, 14–18. In the regency Scottish appeals made up some 80% of the total: Lord Brodie, 'Regional and Historical Perspectives—Scotland', in L. Blom-Cooper, B. Dickson, and G. Drewry, *The Judicial House of Lords* (Oxford, 2009).

[3] Holdsworth, *HEL*, i, 379–94.

arranged in accessible form.[4] In equity appeals, for example, though every party to the cause below must be a party to the appeal, they were not obliged to take a full and separate part in the proceedings, so this did not have the ill-effects it had in Chancery.[5]

What kept the process from dragging out was the Lords' firm stand against examining witnesses or receiving new written evidence.[6] They might remit the cause to the court below if important new evidence was brought forward, but in *Attwood* v. *Small* Brougham insisted that even that should be done sparingly.[7] As a result, interlocutory applications were comparatively sparse and since 1812 had been referred to an appeals committee consisting of the 'law lords', whose recommendation was invariably adopted.[8]

As in other courts, many causes never reached the hearing stage. Between 1791 and 1800 there were 290 set down and 152 heard; in the next decade 492 and 130, so that figures showing an unmanageable number of causes depending could be misleading.[9] Cooper speculated that many 'melted away' in the long interval before a hearing because of deaths or changes of circumstances,[10] but some, especially in Scotland, were brought merely for delay, since until 1808 even the presentation of a petition suspended the execution of a judgment.[11] It was plausibly suggested that while the long delay in obtaining a hearing tended to discourage genuine appeals, it positively encouraged these bogus ones.[12] Aware of the possibility of abuses, in *Way* v. *Foy* (1812) Eldon had reinforced the requirement that counsel sign the petition by demanding a declaration that there was reasonable cause.[13] This, however, was little more than symbolic since the purely tactical appeals were withdrawn once the hearing date became imminent.[14]

The House was not unduly indulgent to appellants. It consistently refused to enlarge the two-year time limit on equity appeals, and requests for extra time to submit the printed case were not granted as a matter of course.[15] It was a fixed rule that the appellant would not be awarded costs if successful, since that would be unfair to a respondent relying in good faith on the judgment of a competent

---

[4] J. F. MacQueen, *A Practical Treatise on the Jurisdiction of the House of Lords etc.* (1842) reproduces 26 standing orders, made between 1661 and 1835 in App. 1.

[5] *Ibid.*, 123–5.   [6] *Ibid.*, 171–81.   [7] (1838) 6 Cl. & F. 280.

[8] Stevens, *Law and Politics*, 17. The term 'law lords' had no technical meaning, but is used here to denote those peers who held, or had held, high judicial office.

[9] C. P. Cooper, *A Brief Account of Some of the Most Important Proceedings Relative to the Defects in the Administration of Justice...* (1828), 170.

[10] *Ibid.*, 170–2.

[11] Administration of Justice (Scotland) Act 1808 (48 Geo. III c.151) permitted interim execution: MacQueen, *Practical Treatise*, 322–30.

[12] Cooper, *Brief Account*, 172.   [13] 18 Ves. Jun. 453. SO 58 of 1697.

[14] Cooper, *Brief Account*, 171.   [15] MacQueen, *Practical Treatise*, 107–17, 192–3.

court below,[16] and there was no automatic stay of proceedings in the lower court if the appeal was from an interlocutory order.[17] There was also the barrier of cost. The recognizance was not a major obstacle, for it was considered that appeal was a constitutional right and recognizances might not be disputed on the grounds that the appellant would be unable to make them good.[18] However, sizeable sums needed to be laid out during the proceedings, including the expense of 500 copies of the printed case, often bulked out with supporting documents. [19]

But neither this, nor the measures taken to discourage Scottish appeals had made much impact,[20] and not only did the Scottish litigants persist, but Irish cases grew in number and even writs of error from English courts showed an increase.[21] Because it was in cases of error that the Lords most frequently summoned the judges for their opinions, that would add to delays,[22] but for the time being it was the Scots who posed the main problem. The select committee found 225 cases in the queue, 151 from Scotland,[23] and sought to tackle the problem from both ends. Further measures were proposed to reduce Scottish appeals, some of which were considered frivolous or trivial, and suggestions were made to reduce the demands of Chancery upon the Lord Chancellor.[24] Judicial sittings were extended from three to five mornings a week, but the difficulty lay in finding manpower for them. With more than 300 peers, making up a quorum of three should have been easy, but Scottish law appeals did not offer much entertainment and lay peers had become reluctant to exhibit that 'delicacy of sentiment so peculiar to noble birth' which Blackstone had claimed made them such scrupulously honest judges.[25] The peers had no desire to relinquish their appellate role, jealously cherishing their place in the mixed polity of King, Lords, and Commons.

---

[16] *Ibid.*, 267–9. Incidental costs and, on occasion, costs of the action in the court below, might be awarded.

[17] A practice debated later in several memoranda in NA PRO LCO 2/1007.

[18] MacQueen, *Practical Treatise*, 145. McQueen inferred that the object of the recognizance was to subject the litigant to Exchequer process if he defaulted, the House having no direct process of its own to issue against him.

[19] By the 1870s, counsel's fees were considerably the largest element: *HLSC on Appellate Jurisdiction 1872, Report*, PP 1872 (325) VII, D. McLaurin, qq. 646 ff.

[20] Stevens, *Law and Politics*, 16–18; Brodie, 'Regional and Historical Perspectives'.

[21] Stevens, *Law and Politics*, 18. Irish appeals had returned to Westminster after the end of the Irish Parliament in 1801.

[22] Between 1833 and 1865 the judges were summoned in almost 70% of cases upon writs of error: Blom-Cooper and Drewry, *Final Appeal*, table 1. They were summoned less frequently for equity appeals and the English judges were occasionally called upon in Scottish cases, e.g. *Baillie* v. *Grant* (1832) 6 Wilson & Shaw 40.

[23] Stevens, *Law and Politics*, 18 n.67.

[24] *HLSC on Appellate Jurisidiction, First Report*, HLSP 1823 (65).

[25] Quoted by J. F. MacQueen without apparent irony in his *Letter to Lord Lyndhurst on the Houses of Parliament in its Judicial Character* (1855), reviewed in (1856) 104 *Edin. Rev.* 209–29.

Rather, they were content that the Chancellor or other law lords should take the lead in ordinary cases, obtaining the opinions of the judges where necessary, and that their views should normally prevail. There were still instances, however, where even Eldon's authoritative opinion was rejected by the House,[26] and on occasion, in the unexpected absence of any law lords, lay peers would take the decision unaided, albeit advised by the judges.[27]

That, however, was unusual. At least one law lord was practically indispensable, and that created problems, for as a result of Eldon's interminable hold on the great seal there were no former Chancellors in the House. Abbott, the Chief Justice of the King's Bench, was not given a peerage until 1827,[28] and then was usually too busy in his own court to afford much help, so apart from Gifford MR Eldon had regular assistance only from Lord Redesdale.[29] Eldon himself could not be faulted, having taken infinite pains to familiarize himself with Scottish law, and the quality of decisions, now properly reported, was generally high.[30] Unfortunately, however, beyond making Gifford deputy speaker, Eldon was bereft of constructive ideas for expediting hearings

The Select Committee had no desire to dilute the peerage by adding to the judicial peers, but to ensure that hearings were not delayed for want of lay peers it recommended a rota of attendance for all able-bodied peers, with fines for non-compliance.[31] In 1824 and 1825 the House rattled through 82 and 86 cases respectively and the immediate crisis was averted, but Eldon's resignation led to a further innovation. His successor, Lyndhurst, was still getting to grips with equity and had no intention of grappling with Scots law too. Lyndhurst persuaded the peers to accept two deputy speakers, not members of the House, to preside over appeals, and in reality to decide them; Alexander CB would handle the Scots, Leach MR the equity cases, while Lyndhurst himself coped with the remainder.[32]

These expedients carried a price. Both the rota and the deputy speakers exposed the pretence that the peers were acting as a bench of judges. Lord King mercilessly quizzed the House on just what was expected of him when he

[26] *Fletcher* v. *Earl Sondes* (1826) 2 Bing. 501.

[27] The last instance was in 1834: T. Beven, 'The Appellate Jurisdiction of the House of Lords, part two' (1901) 17 *LQR* 357–71 at 369.

[28] The delay was because he lacked the means to sustain the dignity: R. A. Melikan, *John Scott, Lord Eldon, the Duty of Loyalty* (Cambridge, 1999), 200–1.

[29] Lord Chancellor of Ireland 1802–6, and the author of a much praised work on Chancery pleadings.

[30] Holdsworth, *HEL*, xii, 104–5.

[31] Stevens, *Law and Politics*, 19.

[32] T. B. Martin, *A Life of Lord Lyndhurst* (2nd edn, 1884), 220–1; John, Lord Campbell, *Lives of the Lord Chancellors*, 8 vols (1869), viii, 52; *PD* 1827 (s2) 17: 573–6.

sat, perhaps on a part-heard appeal,[33] and Lord Holland deplored the fact that '[e]very man in the country was now informed of the manner in which this business was now managed'. Though Holland 'knew no distinction between learned and unlearned Lords', it was not that the latter were expected to play only a ceremonial role in judicial proceedings that upset him: 'what he objected to was the exposure'.[34] Holland also deplored the resort to deputy speakers, which had indeed elements of farce since they were not allowed to address the House but must whisper their opinions to a compliant peer for him to voice.[35] The peers were in a touchy and suspicious mood as the collapse of the old constitution put their own place in the constitution in doubt. Their judicial role was of very minor importance in the wider constitutional frame, but they were not prepared formally to hand it over to the judges.

From Brougham to the Judicature Commission

When Brougham became Lord Chancellor in 1830 he did not have the Lords near the top of his ambitious list of institutional reforms, which included important alterations to other appeal fora. He also revelled in the chance to display his learning in Scottish law and breezed through the Lords appeals at great speed, deciding 129 in 1830 and 1831.[36] Arrears were cleared, the government was persuaded to make Chief Justice Denman a peer,[37] and with Lyndhurst, the Irish Chancellor Plunket and that borderline law lord the Earl of Devon often available, the indignity of the rota was ended.[38] With the Lords now looking more like a court of law, reform was no longer a necessity, which would make its accomplishment more difficult.

Melbourne resigned before Brougham's own plan, which was in effect to divert all appeals to the Lords to his Judicial Committee of the Privy Council, could even be debated, and other ambitious schemes for remodelling the role of the Lord Chancellor and the highest courts never got off the ground.[39] The only one

[33] *PD* 1827 (s2) 17: 573–6 and see also Stevens, *Law and Politics*, 21–2.

[34] *Ibid.*, quoted in Cooper, *Brief Account…*, 13.

[35] Stevens, *Law and Politics*, 21–2.

[36] *Ibid.*, 25.

[37] Sir J. Arnould, *A Memoir of Thomas, First Lord Denman*, 2 vols (1873), ii, 2–3. They also ennobled the undistinguished Best CJCP as Lord Wynford and later the Master of the Rolls, Bickersteth, as Lord Langdale.

[38] Stevens, *Law and Politics*, 29–30. William Courtenay was, largely through Brougham's agency, able to lay claim to the earldom of Devon in 1835. Having been successively a commissioner of bankrupts, a master in Chancery and clerk assistant to the parliaments, he was treated as a law lord. His vote effectively decided the great case of *Attwood* v. *Small*: H. Reeve (ed.), *The Greville Memoirs* (1874, edn of 1888, 4 vols), iv, 84.

[39] *Ibid.*, 28.

with tentative government support was Cottenham's, which would have taken the Chancellor out of Chancery and made him president of the Judicial Committee, but even a modest bill enabling the Lords to hear appeals outside the parliamentary session, encountered too much resistance to pass.[40] Campbell also tried to achieve that in 1841, but by linking it with the merger of the two bodies ruined its chances.[41] The peers were disinclined to part with their jurisdiction or to become more like other courts, even though some distinctive features, such as the flexibility in the order in which appeals were heard, which encouraged lobbying, the delays in delivering judgments[42] and the occasionally wayward decisions occasioned by ignorance of the relevant law caused discontent.[43] Their conservatism left two key questions unresolved.

The first was whether lay peers might still vote on an appeal. In 1844 a writ of error was brought by Daniel O'Connell to overturn his conviction for conspiracy in the Queen's Bench of Ireland. Against the opinion of the judges, three law lords (all sound Whigs) outvoted Lyndhurst and Brougham in O'Connell's favour.[44] Although the decision seemed to owe as much to politics as to law, the party's leaders gave no countenance to Conservative peers who were disposed to insist on voting, and tactful interventions by Wharncliffe and Lyndhurst dissuaded them from the attempt.[45] In yielding to these moderate counsels the dissident peers effectively gave up the principle, and with each passing year it became less likely that lay votes would be attempted, though several witnesses to the select committee in 1856 maintained that they were still legitimate and might sometimes be desirable.[46]

However, if the Lords had become essentially a court of appeal composed of lawyers, it needed enough of them to do the job. That was no problem in the 1840s. Cottenham, Lyndhurst, Brougham, and Campbell were well able to cope

---

[40] *PD* 1836 (s3) 34: 413–86. Lyndhurst, stating that appeals averaged 47 a year, of which 20% never reached a hearing, and sittings occupied 70 sitting days, argued that no enlargement was necessary (427–40). Langdale, in the course of a long speech advocating his own, quite different reforms, also resisted the continuation of appeal hearings after a dissolution (469).

[41] Stevens, *Law and Politics*, 31; 'Lord Campbell's Proposed Reform of the Appellate Jurisdiction' (1842) 27 *LM* 402–7.

[42] J. Miller, *On the Present Unsettled Condition of the Law and its Administration* (1839), 109, 138, 151. Miller did approve the adoption of written judgments, noting how superior Stowell's were (who used this mode) to Eldon's, who had often delivered his verbally.

[43] Scottish lawyers were particularly disgruntled. For example, Wynford blundered embarrassingly in *McGavin* v. *Stewart* (1831) 5 Wilson & Shaw 807 in directing a retrial before a special jury, an institution unknown in Scotland: Stevens, *Law and Politics*, 80. Complaints about the 'anglicization' of Scottish law are appraised in Lord Brodie, 'Regional and Historical Perspectives'.

[44] *O'Connell* v. *R* (1844) 11 Cl. & F 155.

[45] Stevens, *Law and Politics*, 32–3.

[46] HLSC on Appellate Jurisdiction, *PP* 1856 (264), vii: evidence of St. Leonards, Stuart VC and Lord Abinger.

with around 35 cases a year, still mostly Scottish, which occupied them for about 50 days.[47] However, there was a period after 1850 when Brougham, with nominal assistance from a couple of lay peers, acted as a one-man court, more to his own satisfaction than others',[48] and when he was reinforced by St. Leonards and Cranworth matters were not much improved, since the trio were often at odds, which created an undignified atmosphere and, when one was absent, frequently resulted in the decision of the court below being affirmed because their differences could not be resolved.[49] With the superior courts undergoing investigation and reform, it was inevitable that the defects of the highest court should also attract criticism. The situation demanded a temporary increase in manpower and an inquiry into procedural questions. Instead, Palmerston failed to restrain his headstrong Solicitor-General Bethell from averring that the law lords were comporting themselves 'in a manner which would disgrace the lowest court of justice in the kingdom',[50] and pushing the government into a hasty and ill-considered course of action.

They proposed to create life peerages, offered first to Sir James Parke, then the more cautious Sir Stephen Lushington.[51] This idea had been mooted in the 1830s and revived in 1851, when Russell had offered such a peerage to Lushington, and Redesdale had suggested time-limited peerages for lawyers.[52] It removed a big obstacle to raising judges to the peerage, which was that many of those with issue, such as the philoprogenitive Chief Baron Pollock, could not leave them enough money to sustain the living standard expected of a peer. But both the choice of Parke and the timing of the proposal were spectacularly inept. Since Parke was elderly and childless, the offer of a mere life peerage fuelled suspicions that this was a precedent for the infiltration of eminent professionals and scientists into the House, as Prince Albert was believed to want,[53] and that it was welcomed by the maverick Whig Sir George Grey and the radical Administrative Reform

[47] Over the whole period 1833–65 the average was 32–3 (including four writs of error); more than 60% were from Scotland: Blom-Cooper and Drewry, *Final Appeal*, table 1. For the sittings of these peers in the late 1840s see Stevens, *Law and Politics*, 37 n.1.

[48] Campbell, *Lives of the Lord Chancellors*, viii, 566–8. Figures are in Stevens, *Law and Politics*, 39.

[49] Stevens, *Law and Politics*, 39; Campbell, *Lives of the Lord Chancellors*, viii, 578.

[50] *PD* 1855 (s3) 139: 2117; J. B. Atlay, *The Victorian Chancellors*, 2 vols (1908), 73; T. A. Nash, *A Life of Lord Westbury*, 2 vols (1888), i, 177–81.

[51] M. S. Hardcastle (ed.), *The Life of Lord Campbell*, 2 vols (1881), ii, 338–9; S. M. Waddams, *Law, Politics and the Church of England* (Cambridge, 1992), 48–50.

[52] Waddams, *Law, Politics and the Church of England*, 46–8; O. Anderson, 'The Wensleydale Peerage Case and the Position of the House of Lords in the Mid-Nineteenth Century' (1967) 82 *EHR* 486–502 at 488–9.

[53] Anderson, 'Wensleydale Peerage Case', 488, 491. See e.g. W. D. Lewis, 'Peerages for Life' (1856) *Papers Read to the Juridical Society*, 141–72.

Association only aggravated hostility among conservatives.[54] Furthermore, Cranworth and Bethell inexcusably failed to consult their own profession and reaped a harvest of indignant protests, not least a weighty intervention from Lyndhurst, at this supposed slight on lawyers.

The ministry was unable to persuade Parliament either to agree that life peers could be made by prerogative or to do it by legislation. Instead, they had to accept a call for an inquiry from Derby, who had criticized the workings of the appellate process.[55] That Committee endured some bruising exchanges between Bethell and the law lords, who insisted on unconvincing vindications of their recent record, and it had to be manoeuvered into endorsing some of Derby's criticisms to provide the basis for a compromise between the parties.[56] The Committee agreed that the sittings should no longer be held only when Parliament was in session, resurrected the old expedient of paid deputy speakers from the judiciary, and proposed a higher quorum, of five, but its middle course served only to attract opposition from conservatives and reformers alike and a bill based upon its recommendations had to be abandoned.[57]

So the House continued to operate only through the services of past and present Lord Chancellors and a variable number of other peers with judicial experience. It managed because appeals seldom rose much above 40 a year, and the political carousel deposited further ex-Chancellors in Chelmsford and Westbury. The legal membership of the House was further enlarged by peerages given to Lord Colonsay, the former Lord President McNeill (Scottish witnesses before the Select Committee had been divided on whether they should have a Scottish law lord[58]), and Pemberton-Leigh, as Lord Kingsdown.[59] The end of divorce bills in 1857 also increased the time the law lords could give to appeals.

The Judicature Commission

In 1867 Disraeli's momentous 'leap in the dark' doubled the electorate. In the narrower world of the law the Judicature Commission was set up, and though the Lords and Privy Council were outside its terms of reference (a separate

[54] Anderson, 'Wensleydale Peerage Case', 493–5. Lyndhurst had once been an advocate of such peerages and was still favourable in private.

[55] Campbell called this an 'indiscreet harangue': *Lives of the Lord Chancellors*, viii, 194.

[56] *HLSC on Appellate Jurisdiction 1856*; Stevens, *Law and Politics*, 42–3 (his view of these events is different from Anderson's).

[57] Anderson, 'Wensleydale Peerage Case', 498–502; Stevens, *Law and Politics*, 43–4. For examples of contemporary criticism see (1856) 104 *Edin. Rev.* 209–29 and 'Appellate Judicature' (1856–7) 2 (s3) *LM & LR*, 368–85.

[58] *HLSC on Appellate Jurisdiction 1856*.

[59] He was said to have turned down a life peerage in 1855: Stevens, *Law and Politics*, 40 n.12.

commission was sitting for Scotland), they could not be unaffected by its deliberations. There was now the prospect of what Bagehot sought, that '[t]he supreme
court of the English people ought to be a great conspicuous tribunal...ought not
to be hidden beneath the robes of a legislative assembly'.[60] What could scarcely
have been foreseen, however, was that instead of a leap in the dark there would
be a decade of trips, stumbles, and falls, and that instead of a 'great conspicuous
tribunal' the outcome would be that the two existing bodies would still share
separately the role of a court of final appeal.

What Stevens called 'a story of intrigue, legislation and counter-legislation
that virtually defies unravelling'[61] has since been meticulously pieced together
by Steele and need only be summarized here.[62] In the first stage, Hatherley made
two characteristically unskilful attempts to improve the appeals structure. The
first, in 1870, was part of his ill-fated bill to implement the Commission's first
report and went too far for the peers by providing for commoner privy councillors to form a minority of an annually chosen 'judicial committee'; the second, in
1871, aimed to unite the Lords and Judicial Committee but made little headway.[63]
Between the two Hatherley had been compelled to add paid judges to the Privy
Council as a temporary measure.[64]

A select committee set up in response to the second Hatherley bill by a bare
majority recommended the amalgamation of Judicial Committee and Lords for
judicial purposes; reinforced by four professional law lords (lords of appeal),
who would be life peers, this tribunal would be able to sit all year and in divisions.[65] But the new Lord Chancellor, Selborne, scorned the Lords as a court of
law and produced a far bolder plan for a large and powerful court of appeal which
would be the final tribunal for appeals from English courts (other than ecclesiastical courts), and for colonial appeals, these latter by reference from the Privy
Council, to which they would continue to be addressed. Selborne was too prudent to propose sending Scottish and Irish appeals to his new court immediately
but expected they would eventually follow the English route; his bill made their
counsel eligible for appointment as its judges.

---

[60] *The English Constitution*, quoted in Stevens, *Law and Politics*, 46.

[61] *Law and Politics*, 57.

[62] D. Steele, 'The Judicial House of Lords, Abolition and Restoration 1873–1876', in Blom-Cooper
et al., *Judicial House of Lords*.

[63] *Law and Politics*, 48–50. For Hatherley's wider proposals, see P. Polden, 'Mingling the Waters'
(2002) 61 *CLJ* 575–611 at 576–9.

[64] Judicial Committee of the Privy Council Act 1871 (c. 91). See below pp. 560-1.

[65] *PP* 1872 (325), vii. Evidently feeling that it possessed sufficient knowledge of the workings of
the House in English appeals, it called only one English witness, the eminent solicitor J. W. Farrer,
for that purpose.

Selborne was a strong opponent of the 'double appeal', especially while the common law divisions doggedly persisted in preserving the banc system, and he had the advantage over Hatherley in that Cairns was generally in sympathy with his proposals, though Cairns would have preferred a gradualist approach, 'choking off' appeals to the Lords by imposing monetary and other restrictions.

Selborne's bill had an easy passage through the Lords and only hit trouble in the Commons because Gladstone tried to extend it to Scottish and Irish appeals in precisely the way its author had forborne to do.[66] The appeal sections of the bill, however, never became operative. Gladstone's 'row of extinct volcanoes' lost power at the general election of 1874 and Selborne, far from extinct, was left to rumble and steam as his handiwork was undone. This was not Cairns' doing, but in a lengthy passage of politicking he lost a battle within his own party to reactionary elements which became a highly effective 'Committee for Preserving the House of Lords' headed by Redesdale in the Lords and W. T. Charley and Sir George Bowyer in the Commons.[67] Cairns might have been wiser not to have pressed Selborne's proposals to their logical conclusion as his 1874 bill did, for by sending the Scots and Irish to the new 'Imperial Court of Appeal' he aroused opposition in those quarters.[68] Disraeli, with characteristic 'naked opportunism' was anxious only that 'the impotence of the government should be demonstrated to the country'[69] and readily yielded to the clamour from the Committee and its supporters, forcing Cairns to substitute a measure which preserved the double appeal for British courts, left the Judicial Committee alone and reinstated the appellate jurisdiction of the House of Lords.[70]

The triumph of the conservatives was not complete however. Like the Judicial Committee, the Lords was now to have professional judges, the lords of appeal in ordinary, who were peers only while they continued in that office. How far this protected the role of the Upper House in the constitution was a moot point. While some observers saw a classic example of the English genius for adapting venerable institutions to changing times, others who had favoured the retention of a second appeal would not have chosen this expensive and anachronistic forum.[71]

[66] Supreme Court of Judicature Act 1873 c.66; Stevens, *Law and Politics*, 52–6. Selborne's own account is in *Memoirs Personal and Political*, 2 vols (1896), ii, 304–15.

[67] Stevens, *Law and Politics*, 57–67.

[68] SCJ Act (1873) Amendment Bill 1874. Cairns hoped they would be placated by the provision that their appeals should go to the 'First Division', which was to have five judges as opposed to the three in the other two divisions.

[69] Steele, 'Abolition and Restoration'.

[70] Appellate Jurisdiction Act 1876 c.59; Stevens, *Law and Politics*, 57–67. Cairns's case was not helped by the criticisms directed at the operation of the Court of Appeal which he had introduced in the Supreme Court of Judicature Act 1875 (c. 77): Polden, 'Mingling the Waters', 595–6.

[71] Stevens, *Law and Politics*, 67.

The House of Lords, 1876–1914[72]

PERSONNEL

The Appellate Jurisdiction Act was shorn even of the modifications to the work-ing of the House that Cairns had envisaged, for it neither created a judicial com-mittee nor excluded lay peers from participating in judicial work.[73] The latter was achieved in practice, but only with characteristic indirectness in the bitterly con-troversial *Bradlaugh* case when Lord Denman, unabashed by rebuffs in earlier cases, sought to add his dissent to Blackburn's but was once again ignored and unsupported.[74]

The 1876 Act did ensure that any appeal would be heard by a minimum of three peers drawn from prescribed categories, namely the Lord Chancellor (who when present would chair their deliberations[75]), the new lords of appeal in ordi-nary, and peers who had held specified 'high judicial offices' for a minimum of two years; this restriction was presumably a safeguard against another 'Colliery explosion',[76] but since the lords of appeal might be appointed direct from the bar it does not seem a very necessary precaution.[77]

The lords of appeal in ordinary were given non-hereditary baronies and sat in the Lords only while they held office. They were paid £6,000 per annum, with a pension of £3,750 if they had accumulated 15 years' judicial service.[78] Initially restricted to two, they might be augmented when successive pairs of the four salaried members of the Judicial Committee of the Privy Council (JCPC) retired or died.[79] This was presumably an economy measure, and even the initial appointments—Blackburn and Gordon—were delayed for several months.[80] The third law lord (Fitzgerald) was appointed in 1882 and the fourth (Hannen) in 1891. This balance, two from the English bench or bar, one apiece from Scotland and Ireland, was more or less maintained, Macnaghten succeeding Blackburn and Hannen being followed in rapid succession by Bowen, Russell, and Davey.[81]

---

[72] For a more extended treatment, see P. Polden, 'The House of Lords 1876–1914', in Blom-Cooper et al., The *Judicial House of Lords*.

[73] Stevens, *Law and Politics*, 69 n.190.

[74] *Bradlaugh* v. *Clarke* (1883) AC 354. Eccentric son of the Lord Chief Justice, he was called from Lincoln's Inn but never practised at the bar: *ODNB* 15: 804. See his speeches in the debates on the Appellate Jurisdiction Bill 1887: *PD* 1887 (s3) 310.

[75] To judge from reported cases, Lord Chancellors gave a high priority to this duty.

[76] See below, p. 561.

[77] Administration of Justice Act 1876, ss 5, 6. Charley's committee had sought unsuccessfully to restrict the lords of appeal to those who were already members of the House.

[78] *Ibid.*, ss 6, 7.   [79] *Ibid.*, s 14.   [80] Stevens, *Law and Politics*, 67

[81] *Ibid.*, 110. He offers appraisals on 107–32 and there is an alphabetical list of law lords in Blom-Cooper and Drewry, *Final Appeal*, table 13. Macnaghten, appointed directly from the bar, was per-haps the ablest lord of appeal of his time: see W. R. Kennedy (1911–12) 37 (s5) *LM & R* 455–60.

Davey was a considerable presence from 1894 to 1907[82] but his successors, Collins and Robson, were both ailing and short-lived.[83] Moulton followed Robson in 1912 and in the next year, when Parker replaced Macnaghten, two new lords of appeal (Sumner and Dunedin) were added in fulfilment of a promise to strengthen the JCPC.[84] After Gordon, Scottish representation was in the distinguished person of Watson from 1899, then the much less imposing Robertson and later (from 1909) the exigent and unpopular Shaw.[85] Neither of Fitzgerald's successors—Morris and Atkinson—was in the top rank and between 1899 and 1905 there was no representative of the Irish bar, for Lindley had been elevated from Master of the Rolls to accommodate Webster.[86]

After 1880 only the Lord Chancellor and the Lord Chief Justice among the English judges automatically received a peerage, so the government of the day had a considerable discretion in the composition of the Lords' judicial element. No one could cavil about the first judge to be made a peer, Sir George Bramwell in 1882, but though Gorell and Mersey were respectable choices, Lopes was mediocre and Field deaf and irascible, while to make Henry Hawkins Lord Brampton, was questionable, since he interested himself only in criminal cases, which did not reach the House anyway.[87] Two Scottish judges, Shand and Kinnear, were more useful additions, and though none was appointed from the Irish bench, two Irish Lord Chancellors in O'Hagan and Ashbourne sat with some regularity.

Experience soon suggested that the eligible categories needed to be extended, and in 1887 they were expanded to include retired lords of appeal, so retaining Blackburn's services.[88] During the bill's passage Selborne procured a further

[82] Stevens *Law and Politics*, 118 is rather ungenerous to Davey. His appointment did something to restore the balance between common lawyers and equity men, particularly important since Halsbury's ignorance of equitable doctrines was sometimes very obvious—see e.g. *Smith* v. *Coke* [1891] AC 297. Even so, the equity element was undesirably weak.

[83] Stevens, *Law and Politics*, 113.

[84] See below, p. 562. It was rumoured that one would be appointed from supporters of the Labour party and the other from those of the Irish Nationalists: *PD* 1913 (s5 HC) 56: 2201 (J. M. Hogge).

[85] Stevens, *Law and Politics*, 130–2, 246–53; A. A. Paterson, 'Scottish Lords of Appeal, 1876–1988' [1988] *JR* 235–54.

[86] Stevens, *Law and Politics*, 109, 112, but cf. the more benign views of Lord Lowry, 'The Irish Lords of Appeal in Ordinary', in D. S. Greer and N. M. Dawson (eds), *Mysteries and Solutions in Irish Legal History* (Dublin, 2001), 193–216. The Ulsterman Macnaghten was an equity lawyer from the English bar.

[87] Stevens, *Law and Politics*, 111, 113–14, 127–9. It is said that this was done to remove Hawkins from the trial courts.

[88] Appellate Jurisdiction Act 1887, c. 70, s 2. The debates (*PD* 1887 (s3) 310) record a fulsome tribute to Blackburn by Fitzgerald (747).

enlargement, to unpaid members of the Judicial Committee, which accommodated Hobhouse, and later Sir Henry James.[89]

These arrangements meant that the judicial complement of the House fluctuated. The *Law List* named 10 in 1883, 12 in 1893, 11 in 1903 and again in 1913. The figure is not very meaningful, however, since there were always some qualified peers who were too elderly or infirm to sit or (like Lord Ashbourne) were regarded as a liability.[90]

No provision was made for the Lords to sit in divisions and no firm convention emerged as to the appropriate number of judges. Some critics had felt the minimum too low,[91] but in the first decade a bench of only three or four was common, though later five seems to have become the most usual number, with seven in particularly important cases.[92] This latitude lent itself to manipulation by the Lord Chancellor and this may have become more frequent as the number of appeals with a controversial political element rose. Halsbury and Loreburn both seem to have sought favourable panels in such cases,[93] but, as Heuston's painstaking analysis of Halsbury's manoeuvres in *Quinn* v. *Leathem*[94] shows, it is dangerous to infer it too readily simply from the composition of the House.[95] The great trade union cases of *Allen* v. *Flood* and *Quinn* v. *Leathem* give a misleading impression of the Lords as a tribunal where divided opinions were common, for in fact, at least in the 1880s, it was 'a remarkably unanimous body'.[96] It was also one in which the appellant's prospects were none too good, studies suggesting that fewer than one-third of those from England would succeed, though Scots and Irish fared somewhat better.[97]

JURISDICTION AND BUSINESS

The 1876 Act made no attempt to restrict appeals, though neither did it provide any facility to 'leapfrog' the new 'Intermediate Court of Appeal' as had been

---

[89] Appellate Jurisdiction Act 1887, s 5. In fact Hobhouse seldom sat in the Lords but devoted his services to the Privy Council.

[90] Stevens, *Law and Politics*, 112 n.29.

[91] e.g. W. F. Finlason, *An Exposition of our Judicial System and Civil Procedure . . .* (1877), 257.

[92] R. E. Megarry, *A Second Miscellany-at-Law* (1973), 61. This is my impression from a cursory examination of the law reports, but the reported cases may tend to exaggerate the proportion of larger benches.

[93] Stevens, *Law and Politics*, 85–6.

[94] [1901] AC 513.

[95] R. F. V. Heuston, 'Judicial Prosopography' (1984) 100 *LQR* 90–113.

[96] Stevens, *Law and Politics*, 70 n.197, and noted by C. A. Heresch, 'Dissenting Opinions' (1906–7) 32 (5s) *LM & R* 54–64.

[97] Blom-Cooper and Drewry, *Final Appeal*, table 2B; Civil Judicial Statistics 1894, *PP* 1896 (C. 8263), xciv; 1905, *PP* 1907 (Cd. 3477), xcviii. Halsbury's notorious reluctance to interfere with jury verdicts was one obstacle to appellants.

possible with the court of Appeals in Chancery.[98] Apart from divorce, where appeals were confined to questions of law, and bankruptcy, all major civil actions might be taken to the final appeal,[99] though the criminal jurisdiction was not bestowed until 1907, with the first appeal in 1910.[100] A few statutes expressly ousted or restricted an appeal,[101] but more important were limits imposed by the House itself, which would not entertain an appeal from an order for costs *simpliciter*, nor a question of practice unless it caused serious injustice.[102] With no effective sifting mechanism other than the expense of proceedings, it remained a matter for frequent grumbling among the law lords that many appeals before them were trivial or simply questions of fact.[103]

During the 1870s, probably partly on account of the creation of a Scottish appeal court, England overtook Scotland as the chief source of business. For a time there were still years when the latter predominated, but averaging cases over the years 1876–80 England supplied 31.2 out of 60 a year; across 1896–1900, 50.4 of 71.2; and from 1906 through to 1910, 63.6 of 90.[104] Of the 89 appeals presented in 1910, 64 were English, 18 Scottish and 7 Irish.[105] There was no dramatic rise in the overall number of appeals, and in the 1890s it was estimated that only 7 per cent of Court of Appeal judgments were appealed.[106] There were appreciable fluctuations in the level of business (only 63 cases were heard in 1913 as against 108 in 1909) but overall it began to rise sufficiently to cause delays when combined with a similar increase in the Privy Council.[107] Even so, since the House sat on fewer than 100 days a year, there was plenty of scepticism among MPs when the two extra law lords were demanded in 1913.[108]

The substance of the appeals changed too. Among the English cases common law matters became much more prominent, presumably because of the greater facility for appeal now that it had no longer to be grounded in a writ of error. Statutory interpretation, mostly of local and private acts, was increasingly at issue, and whereas at the end of the century the bulk were family or commercial matters, by 1910 there was a marked rise in contractual disputes and torts,

---

[98] *HLSC on Appellate Jurisdiction 1872*, W. J. Farrer, qq.723, 772. This was not introduced until the Administration of Justice Act 1969 (c. 58).

[99] Stevens, *Law and Politics*, 71–2.

[100] *R v. Ball* [1911] AC 47. In theory a writ of error had lain, but that was obsolete.

[101] Examples are in Stevens, *Law and Politics*, 71 n.201.

[102] C. M. Denison and C. H. Scott, *The Practice of the House of Lords in English, Scottish and Irish Appeal Cases...* (1879), 71.

[103] Blom-Cooper and Drewry, *Final Appeal*, 33–4.

[104] Stevens, *Law and Politics*, 70. Figures are of appeals presented, not cases heard.

[105] Blom-Cooper and Drewry, *Final Appeal*, table 2A.

[106] *Civil Judicial Statistics 1894*.

[107] Stevens, *Law and Politics*, 71–3.

[108] *PD* 1913 (s5 HC) 53: 141–55, 173–218.

especially workmen's compensation. Corporations and public authorities were increasingly prominent among litigants, and tax cases were becoming a more regular part of their lordships' workload.[109]

ORGANIZATION AND PROCEDURE

The hybrid features of the jurisdiction were replicated in its clerical arrangements. The Judicial Office was part of the House's clerical establishment, and comprised a chief clerk (in effect the registrar) and three juniors not employed exclusively on judicial work.[110] They were appointed by the clerk of the parliaments, Sir H. J. L. Graham for 31 years from 1885. A former master in lunacy, Graham had also been the Lord Chancellor's principal secretary and he ensured that the potential friction inherent in a situation where the Lord Chancellor necessarily exercised a practical dominion over the Judicial Office while the clerk retained formal authority was minimized.[111] Nevertheless, it exasperated Muir McKenzie, whose efforts to 'confer Home Rule on the Judicial Office' were fruitless,[112] since the forces of conservatism at this level were too strong for any Lord Chancellor.[113]

There were some significant changes in procedure following the 1876 Act, when the standing orders were consolidated.[114] At last hearings could be held when Parliament was prorogued or dissolved and the delivery of judgments were no longer liable to be delayed by those interruptions.[115] Writs of error, save in criminal cases, were abolished and all English appeals were to be made by petition.[116] All would henceforth be subject to the requirement for security, which was given teeth by adding to the ineffective £500 recognizance the need for a bond or cash deposit of £200.[117] A side-effect of that, however, was more attempts to invoke the *in forma pauperis* procedure. Cairns had strongly attacked abuses in this procedure in 1874,[118] but it was Herschell, following a

[109] Based upon an examination of cases in the Law Reports at five-year intervals from 1877–8 and Stevens, *Law and Politics*, 69–72.

[110] Denison and Scott, *Practice of the House of Lords*, 27; Lord Donoughmore to Lord Curzon, 17 February 1917, LCO 2/387. This 'cave of mystery' is now illuminated by J. V. White, 'The Judicial Office' in Blom-Cooper et al., *The Judicial House of Lords*, who notes the first reference to it in 1854.

[111] Graham to Lord Chancellor, February 1917; Schuster's memorandum, February 1917, LCO 2/387.

[112] Donoughmore to Curzon, 17 February 1917, *ibid.*

[113] Finlay LC to Lord President, 21 February 1917, *ibid.*

[114] Denison and Scott, *Practice of the House of Lords*, 221.

[115] *Ibid.*, 117–25; Appellate Jurisdiction Act 1876, ss 8, 9.

[116] Section 4.

[117] Denison and Scott, *Practice of the House of Lords*, 48–52.

[118] *Davis* v. *Lewis*: see A. Munns to Lord Chancellor, 15 February 1876, LCO 1/3.

collective protest in *Blair v. North British Insurance Co*,[119] who put through a short Act in 1893 referring all such applications to the House's appeal committee for preliminary scrutiny.[120]

There were two other notable changes. One was that the judges ceased to be summoned for their opinion. This seemed to be slipping into obsolescence in the 1870s but was revived in the great case of *Dalton v. Angus & Co* in 1880[121] and for the last time, with very questionable motives and propriety, at Halsbury's insistence in *Allen v. Flood*.[122] The second change was that the House relaxed its stance against granting costs to a successful appellant. What Westbury had began, with surprising casualness in 1871,[123] became well established in 1877, though never a settled practice.[124] The cost of taking a case to the Lords remained high, however, partly through the continued insistence on multiple copies of printed cases (which grew longer as the documentation in commercial cases expanded) and partly because of the insistence on employing the most fashionable counsel at inflated fees. In 1900 the averaged taxed cost of an appeal allowed to a successful party was £354, but by 1910 it had risen to £448. The full cost was considerably higher.[125]

As in the High Court, cases were beginning to take longer, and by 1914 the average time was creeping up from one-and-a-half days to two.[126] In some respects the Lords were decidedly brisk; in particular they frequently denied the respondent's counsel his opportunity, convinced that the appellant had failed to make his case.[127] Against that, however, they developed a tendency to interrupt and sometimes harass counsel. Herschell was the most notorious exponent, leading to Lord Morris's celebrated aside that he now understood what was meant by molesting a man in his trade.[128] Watson was another offender,[129] and there was relief when under Haldane the court became once more a 'listening' one.

---

[119] (1890) 15 AC 405.

[120] Appeals (Forma Pauperis) Act 1893 c.22. For background, see P. Polden, 'Doctor in Trouble' (2001) 22 *JLH* 37–68 at 54–9.

[121] (1881) 6 App Cas 740. There had been only two other instances after the 1876 Act: V. V. Veeder, 'Advisory Opinions of the Judges of England (1899–1900)' 13 *HLR* 358–70.

[122] [1898] AC 1; Stevens, *Law and Politics*, 92–4.

[123] *English and Foreign Credit Co. v. Arduin* (unreported).

[124] Denison and Scott, *Practice of the House of Lords*, 141–69.

[125] Civil Judicial Statistics 1900, *PP* 1902 [Cd. 1115], cxvii and 1910, *PP* 1912–13 [Cd. 6047], cx.

[126] Stevens, *Law and Politics*, 187; A. A. Paterson, *The Law Lords* (1982), 68.

[127] This was not new; Sir John Shaw-Lefevre told the Select Committee of 1872 that it had been done in 43 of 190 cases (q. 886).

[128] Atlay, *Victorian Chancellors*, ii, 461. That was, of course, the point at issue in the case.

[129] E. Manson, *Builders of Our Law in the Reign of Queen Victoria* (1895, edn of 1904), 440–8; KCL library, Lord Lindley's Autobiography, 123.

Reserving judgment became much commoner, the House following the Court of Appeal in adopting written judgments; judgment was reserved in about half the reported cases (which perhaps exaggerate its prevalence) in 1914. [130]

JUDGMENTS AND JURISPRUDENCE

Little is known about how the Lords went about framing their judgments.[131] It gradually became commoner for a panel member simply to record his concurrence in the judgment, either of a particular colleague or generally.[132] In 1877–8 only Gordon regularly did so (probably because of ill-health), but in 1908 there were instances in 33 out of 41 reported cases, and it had become common for just one substantive speech to be given.[133] Even those who have been named as frequent dissenters—Bramwell, Morris, and Davey for instance[134]—did so relatively seldom. Cases in which their lordships were evenly, or almost evenly, divided are strikingly few,[135] though sometimes judges indicated disagreement without actually registering a dissent, like Blackburn in *Foakes* v. *Beer*[136]and Morris in *Comber* v. *Leyland*.[137] Experience in the Judicial Committee, where dissenting opinions could not be given, may have had some influence on the little-studied evolution of this practice.

Since the Lords did not sit in plenary session but with a fluctuating body of judges, it could not be expected to produce a coherent jurisprudence, especially since its caseload was a haphazard mixture of the portentous and the trivial; thus in 1898, the Law Reports volume which features *Allen* v. *Flood* and *London*

---

[130] According to Davey, they were not the rule in Selborne's day: Selborne, *Memorials, Personal and Political*, ii, 83. Lord Hatherley, whose sight was poor, complained that to write judgments was injurious to his health: D. Pannick, *Judges* (Oxford, 1987), 6. Halsbury tended to give *extempore* judgments: Stevens, *Law and Politics*, 121.

[131] Dissenting opinions were circulated, though Halsbury refused to do so in *Allen* v. *Flood*; Stevens, *Law and Politics*, 87 n.93.

[132] Lindley sometimes read out his concurring judgment, 'avoiding all suspicion of laziness': *Autobiography*, 128.

[133] In *Refuge Assurance Co* v. *Kettlewell* [1909] AC 243, there was no reasoned judgment at all, Loreburn moving to affirm and Ashbourne, James, and Macnaghten concurring: Megarry, *Second Miscellany-at-Law*, 64.

[134] V. V. Veeder, 'A Century of Judicature', Committee of American Law Schools (ed.), *Select Essays in Anglo-American Legal History*, 3 vols (Boston USA, reprint of 1968, London), iii, 730–836 at 831; Stevens, *Law and Politics*, 109, 118. Hobhouse dissented in two of the only three cases in which he participated.

[135] Just three instances in a sample of six years: *General Accident* v. *McGowan* [1908] AC 207: 4:3; *Allen* v. *Flood* [1898] AC 1: 6:3, and *Costello* v. *The Owners of 'The Pigeon'* [AC] 1913: 3:2. In *Harris* v. *Earl of Chesterfield* [1914] AC 623 the 3:3 tie was eventually broken when Loreburn announced that Kinnear, who had heard the arguments but missed the speeches, favoured affirming the respondent.

[136] (1884) 9 App Cas 605.

[137] [1898] AC 524.

Tramways Co v. *LCC*[138] also contains minor cases on party walls, sewers and parish settlements.[139]

However, there were variations in the Lords' outlook over time which reflect changes in membership.[140] In the 1870s, dominated by past and present Lord Chancellors, it was inclined to eschew the detailed examination of facts and decided where possible upon principle, fitting in the previous decisions with more (Selborne and Hatherley) or less (Cairns) meticulousness.[141] This court would have enmeshed companies and other businesses within a framework of equitable obligations,[142] but it was soon succeeded by one dominated by common lawyers, who in *Salomon and Co* v. *Salomon* and *Derry* v. *Peek* reasserted the primacy of the common law's particularist approach.[143] In turn this period in which laissez-faire and freedom of contract held sway gave way to one in which the Edwardian judges were readier to imply terms in commercial contracts.[144]

Another trend is unmistakable: the Lords were conducting a dignified retreat from any openly acknowledged law-making role. Judicial reticence probably owed something to a collective unease; after the Third Reform Act in 1885 the legitimacy of unelected judges as law-makers was highly questionable. The controversies aroused by their decisions in the great sequence of trade union cases may well have strengthened this feeling: the constitutional crisis of 1911 almost certainly did.

One manifestation of this concern was an ostensible, and sometimes ostentatious, adherence to the strict affirmation in *London Tramways* of the self-denying ordinance that the Lords would not overturn their earlier decisions.[145] The case is actually a rather flimsy basis for such a portentous doctrine[146] and it was widely regarded as merely endorsing a position held since 1860 if not earlier, albeit with exceptions, although judges had from time to time bemoaned their inability to overturn inconvenient precedents.[147]

---

[138] At 1, 375.

[139] *Bethnal Green Vestry* v. *London School Board*, 190; *Pasmore* v. *Oswaldthwaite UDC* (1898), 387; *Plymouth Poor Guardians* v. *Axminster Poor Guardians* (1898), 586.

[140] This section draws heavily on Stevens, *Law and Politics,* and P. S. Atiyah, *The Rise and Fall of Freedom of Contract* (Oxford, 1979).

[141] Atiyah, *Rise and Fall*, 671–4, Stevens, *Law and Politics*, 114–16.

[142] e.g. *Erlanger* v. *New Sombrero Phosphate Co* (1878) 3 App Cas 136.

[143] [1896] AC 22; (1889) 14 App Cas 337.

[144] Stevens, *Law and Politics*, 143–6.

[145] [1898] AC 375.

[146] D. Pugsley, 'London Tramways 1898' (1996) *JLH* 172–84, discusses the background and the implicit rebuff to Sir F. M. Pollock.

[147] *Bradley* v. *Carritt* [1903] AC 253 (Lindley); *Samuel* v. *Jarrah Timber and Wood Paving Corporation* [1901] AC 323 (Macnaghten); *Foakes* v. *Beer* (1884) 9 App Cas 605 (Blackburn).

In reality the doctrine of *stare decisis* was never operated in so rigid a fashion as Halsbury's formulation would suggest: indeed no one was more adept and unscrupulous in escaping the chains of precedents as Halsbury himself.[148] Others were more subtle but equally effective, culminating in the sophistry of Haldane's reshaping of the law of collateral advantages in mortgages in *Kreglinger (G & C) v. New Patagonia Meat and Cold Storage Co.*[149] The importance of *London Tramways*, however, is its unequivocal avowal that the law lords did not make law: they only ascertained it, and once discovered it could not be altered save by Parliament.[150]

The second manifestation of this reticence was in the construction of statutes, where the dominant approach was increasingly to disclaim any attempt to uncover and implement the underlying policy of an enactment, but rather to apply the so-called 'golden rule', giving each word and phrase its 'normal' or 'natural' meaning, though in practice this distinction was often unworkable and probably no judge was rigidly consistent in applying it. However, in workmen's compensation, although differing attitudes could be distinguished,[151] in general the Lords were more prone to adopt a purposive construction than Collins MR's rigidly literalist division of the Court of Appeal.[152] In contrast, there were signs that an initially even-handed approach to tax statutes was yielding to one which insisted that the revenue must bring the taxpayer within the narrowest, most literal reading of the statute in order to exact tax.[153] In general the law lords' public stance was that they were not junior partners in the legislative process, but disinterested, dispassionate technicians. Indeed, when the legislature positively invited judges to develop the law, as with the 'just and reasonable' charges clauses of the Railway and Canal Traffic Acts, some of the most eminent recoiled with almost comical dismay.[154]

This attitude reflected a gradual retreat from the boldness, and sometimes dogmatism, of some High Victorian judges into a substantive formalism which treated the common law as 'a self-contained objective system of rules'.[155] Equity's

---

[148] Stevens, *Law and Politics*, 90–2. Like others, Halsbury was apt to declare that inconvenient precedents turned on a question of fact rather than law.

[149] [1914] AC 25; *Law and Politics*, 97–100. See also *Nocton v. Ashburton* [1914] AC 932 in which Haldane led the Lords in deliberately undoing much of the mischief wrought by *Derry v. Peek: The Correspondence of Mr. Justice Holmes and Sir Frederick Pollock*, ed. M de Wolfe Howe, 2 vols, (2nd edn, Cambridge, Mass., 1962), i, 215.

[150] Herschell was a particularly strenuous advocate of this viewpoint: Stevens, *Law and Politics*, 122; Atiyah, *Rise and Fall*, 831–4.

[151] As later expounded by Lord Dunedin: Stevens, *Law and Politics*, 169.

[152] *Ibid.*, 165–70; P. W. J. Bartrip, *Workmen's Compensation in Twentieth Century Britain* (1987), 62–3.

[153] Stevens, *Law and Politics*, 170–6.

[154] Atiyah, *Rise and Fall*, 558–9.

[155] Stevens, *Independence of the Judiciary*, 22. On the changing content of judgments, see S. Hedley, '"Words, Words, Words"…Making Sense of Legal Judgments', in C. Stebbings (ed.), *Law Reporting in England* (1995), 169–86.

'capacity for parthogenesis' withered, the potential of the adventurous decision in *Hughes* v. *Metropolitan Railway*[156] remaining to be exploited by Lord Denning. Inasmuch as considerations of public policy openly informed decisions at all, they usually embodied a rather outmoded adherence to laissez-faire, a stance which allowed cartels to strangle rivals[157] and gave anti-competitive arrangements in restraint of trade free rein.[158] In tort the same thinking informed a drift towards insistence that liability should be fault-based[159] and a narrow view of the scope of fraud.[160] There were of course cases which invited a broad statement of the law—Macnaghten's abiding re-ordering of 'the wilderness of legal charity' into four categories is an example[161]—but the House did not actively seek such ambitious tasks. [162]

In the light of the above, there was also a predictable reluctance to engage in any supervisory review of executive power. In *Metropolitan Asylum District* v. *Hill* the Lords took a narrow view of the scope of delegated powers of a public body where they encroached upon private property rights,[163] but when it came to reviewing decisions made under delegated powers the furthest they would go was to enforce procedural due process, declining to investigate the propriety of actual decisions.[164] Haldane aspired to separate law from politics altogether[165] and with their almost complete abdication in *Local Government Board* v. *Arlidge*,[166] the law lords took a long step towards doing so.

2. THE PRIVY COUNCIL

The Creation of the Judicial Committee

The Judicial Committee of the Privy Council is an enduring monument to the law reforming zeal of Henry Brougham.[167] Brougham was temperamentally

---

[156] (1877) 2 App Cas 439; Atiyah, *Rise and Fall*, 671–2; Stevens, *Law and Politics*, 138.

[157] *Mogul Steamship Company* v. *McGregor* [1892] AC 25; Atiyah, *Rise and Fall*, 697; Stevens, *Law and Politics*, 158–9.

[158] *Nordenfelt* v. *Maxim Nordenfelt Guns and Ammunition Company* [1894] AC 535; Atiyah, *Rise and Fall*, 697.

[159] Stevens, *Law and Politics*, 151–4.

[160] Ibid., 156–7.

[161] *Commissioners for Special Purposes of Income Tax* v. *Pemsel* [1891] AC 531. Halsbury delayed this decision for over a year because he found himself in a minority.

[162] Despite the urging of Brett MR: (1889–90) 34 *Sol. J.* 2.

[163] (1881) 6 App Cas 193; Stevens, *Law and Politics*, 160–1.

[164] The position taken up in *Board of Education* v. *Rice* [1911] AC 179; Stevens, *Law and Politics*, 178–9.

[165] Stevens, *Law and Politics*, 219.

[166] [1915] AC 120.

[167] D. B. Swinfen, 'Henry Brougham and the Judicial Committee of the Privy Council' (1974) 90 LQR 396–411; P. A. Howell, *The Judicial Committee of the Privy Council 1833–1876* (Cambridge, 1979).

and intellectually better suited to sweeping schemes for new or remodelled institutions than to the careful reorganization of complex ones like the court of Chancery, and his plans for the Privy Council were characteristically bold. He envisaged a body having the characteristics of a court of law while retaining those features indispensable to its status as a committee of the Privy Council.[168] It would handle not only appeals from overseas possessions but also from the court of Admiralty and the ecclesiastical courts, which presently lay to the court of Delegates, and would be able to grant full divorces (*a vinculo*).[169] Brougham did not achieve all his objectives; the divorce proposal was altogether too ambitious and the Privy Council's judicial hearings would not be conducted exclusively by legally trained privy councillors; nor would its membership include salaried judges. Nevertheless, it was one of his biggest achievements in law reform.

Brougham had attacked the Privy Council and the court of Delegates in their judicial capacities in his great law reform speech of February 1828,[170] and though thwarted in his proposal for an all-embracing investigation into the administration of justice, he secured a commission to examine the church courts, and once he became Lord Chancellor persuaded it to issue a preliminary report which condemned the Delegates and recommended the Privy Council, if suitably provided with men 'conversant with legal principles' and with adequate sitting days, as its replacement.[171]

Yet Brougham had unsparingly exposed many defects in the Privy Council. Appeals were heard by an open committee with no guarantee that it would be guided by legally qualified councillors. Few such men sat regularly and the Master of the Rolls, with fewer commitments than other judges, had emerged as the dominating figure. The standing order prescribing its sittings had long been abandoned and it sat infrequently, usually only when the courts were not in session. There was no distinct bar, and Brougham was one of the few to appear regularly.[172] Such a body could only function satisfactorily while business remained modest and the Master of the Rolls generally respected, and in the 1820s that was no longer the case.

Weaknesses had been masked while Sir William Grant was Master of the Rolls by his exceptional knowledge and understanding of the civilian laws which were

---

[168] For the evolution of jurisdiction which stemmed from the Crown's prerogatives in relation to overseas possessions, see XI, Pt 1, Ch. VII.

[169] For the course of divorce reform, see XIII, pp. 781–4.

[170] *PD* 1828 (s2) 18: 155–60.

[171] Special Report, *PP* 1831–2 (199), xxiv, 6–7. And see below, p. 557.

[172] *PD* 1828 (s2)18: 155–60; Howell, *Judicial Committee*, 15–16; C. P. Cooper, *A Brief Account of Some of the Most Important Proceedings in Parliament…* (1828), 225–6.

often in issue and his capacity to decide quickly and satisfactorily.[173] His successors, Plumer and Gifford, were second rate in comparison and Leach exposed his own and the court's deficiencies. In two well publicized cases Leach disarmingly confessed his own (pardonable) ignorance of the applicable laws, and privately sought and adopted the views of foreign jurists.[174] Further, he openly deplored and rejected Knapp's published reports, declaring that 'the decisions of the privy council could not be considered as a correct exposition [of the law]…'.[175] Grant's departure was also followed by a marked rise in actual and potential business. Just when the courts were beginning to recover from the deep trough in litigation the Privy Council suddenly lost a major source of appeals, the American colonies. However, it soon began to acquire new sources. More than 20 territories were hoovered up during the French wars, and between 1815 and 1826 appeals came in from a forbidding range of legal systems: French, Spanish, Dutch, Danish, Hindu, Mohammedan, and Buddhist. Coupled with the peculiarities of the lesser islands of the British Isles, they made a daunting proposition for even the best informed court.[176]

Returns bolstered Brougham's argument that the Committee was unable to dispose of cases with reasonable dispatch. Of 517 appeals lodged between 1814 and 1826, only 243 had been disposed of, and of those only 129 had been actually heard.[177] Moreover, the rate at which they were disposed of (319 in 120 sitting days) supported Brougham's claim that they were sometimes heard 'in a manner the most summary that can be conceived in this country', hardly surprising if the notoriously hasty Leach was in charge.[178] Indian appeals were the immediate cause for concern, for although they constituted little more than 10 per cent of the total, they were disproportionately represented among the undisposed of causes. To blame suitors for failing to set the appeal effectively in motion by appointing agents and putting them in funds, made no allowance for conditions in India, and did not explain scandalous cases like that of the revenues of the Ranee of Ramnad, an appeal pending since 1814 which paralysed a large territory because of the uncertainty over property rights.[179]

---

[173] Howell, *Judicial Committee*, 9–11.

[174] *Ibid.*, 11–13; *Freyhaus* v. *Forbes* (1827) 1 Knapp 117; *Quelin* v. *Moisson* (1827) 1 Knapp 266.

[175] *Ibid.*, 17–18.

[176] *Ibid.*, 9–10; Cooper, *Brief Account of Proceedings in Parliament*, 228–30. By 1914 the jurisdiction encompassed around one-quarter of the world's land mass and population: K. Keith, 'The Interplay with the Judicial Committee of the Privy Council', in Blom-Cooper et al., *Judicial House of Lords*. Keith provides a concise appraisal of the performance of the Committee in imperial appeals.

[177] *PD* 1828 (s2) 18: 156–7.

[178] *Ibid.*, 158.

[179] *Ibid.*, 158. This case was raised by Lansdowne in the Lords: *PD* 1827 (s2) 17: 152–7.

The Tory administrations responded to criticism by persuading eminent judges to attend more frequently,[180] but business in Chancery and King's Bench was already outstripping the available judge-power. Moreover, by transferring the appellate work of the Delegates to the Privy Council, Brougham used the addition of this important and abstruse business as a further argument for reforming the latter,[181] and when he presented his grand scheme the only question was whether, as the Lord President (Lansdowne) doubted, it was 'necessary to the purpose to *create* a new court of an anomalous character' or whether further steps to boost the attendance of judges might suffice.[182] Lansdowne was urged to oppose Brougham's plans by the clerk to the Council, Charles Greville, backed by 'Mr Over-Secretary Stephen' of the Colonial Office, both driven partly by selfish motives.[183] Other cabinet members mistrusted Brougham, suspecting that he had even more expansive plans to enhance his own position. They also resisted the complete judicialization of the Council for policy reasons, wishing to retain some means of influencing decisions on appeals with a public interest element or involving imperial policy.[184] Brougham had to retreat from requiring the Lord Chancellor's attendance at hearings and had to preserve a lay element in the shape of present and past lord presidents. More important in the long term was the substitution for his four salaried judges of the offer of an enhanced pension for any four retired judges willing to undertake regular attendance. Nevertheless, it is striking how much of Brougham's scheme was left intact and how little parliamentary attention it received during its passage.[185]

Jurisdiction and Business

Safford and Wheeler's manual of Judicial Committee practice of 1901 ran to 1194 pages, many of them setting out the regulations governing appeals from the greatly expanded British Empire.[186] No serious attempt had been made to harmonize these regulations, which sometimes originated with the governments of the

---

[180] Howell, *Judicial Committee*, 17–18.

[181] *Ibid.*, 18–22; Privy Council Appeals Act 1832 (2 & 3 Will. IV c. 92).

[182] Lansdowne to Brougham, January 1833, quoted in Swinfen, 'Brougham and the Judicial Committee', 401.

[183] *Ibid.*, 400–4; Howell, *Judicial Committee*, 23–7.

[184] Howell, *Judicial Committee*, 24, 27.

[185] Much to Greville's disgust: *Memoirs*, ii, 350–2, 373. Howell (*Judicial Committee*, 27–8) and Swinfen (Brougham and the Judicial Committee, 403–4) offer rather different interpretations of Brougham's handling of the bill.

[186] F. Safford and G. Wheeler, *The Practice of the Privy Council in Judicial Matters* (1901); Howell, *Judicial Committee*, 78. The previous standard work, MacPherson's of 1860, was much more compact.

territory and sometimes with the Colonial Office or Foreign Office; the Judicial Committee was seldom consulted.[187] The results reflected little credit on imperial administration, being marked not only by irrational distinctions but by glaring omissions and occasional outright blunders. Thus the inhabitants of Heligoland, taken from the Danes in 1807, had no right of appeal until 1856 and the inhabitants of New South Wales were inadvertently deprived of theirs between 1828 and 1850.[188]

The only general enactment on colonial appeals was the Judicial Committee Act 1844, which remedied injustices arising from the requirement in most territories that appeals lay only from the local court of error or appeal. This usually comprised the governor and his executive council, in some places sitting infrequently and in others of questionable integrity.[189]

There were two common restrictions upon the right to appeal. Save for Bengal, Bombay, and Madras, no appeal lay as of right from interlocutory orders, and few colonies permitted appeals in criminal cases.[190] Other restrictions mostly involved money limits, time limits, and security for costs. Minimum figures for sums at issue varied widely and with no discernible pattern, but £500 was common and some were much lower.[191] There were similar variations in the requirement for security, sometimes within the discretion of the local judges, which could lead to abuses.[192] Time limits were more standard, usually requiring notice to be given to the local court within 14 days and the appeal to be prosecuted by lodging papers with the Privy Council office within a year and a day.[193]

These rules, however, might be set aside by the Judicial Committee granting an application for 'special leave'.[194] No general rules were laid down, but leave was commonly given where there was no appeal as of right (as in New South Wales between 1828 and in 1850), where the sums at issue were below the minimum required but there was an important issue at stake; or to ensure the trial of matters touching on statutory construction, jurisdiction, or otherwise of public importance. It was also generally given where there was a credible allegation of an abuse in the administration of justice.[195] The Committee was less

---

[187] Howell, *Judicial Committee*, 73–6.　　　　[188] *Ibid.*, 83–6.

[189] 7 & 8 Vict. c. 69, s 1; Howell, *Judicial Committee*, 55.　　　[190] *Ibid.*, 92–3.

[191] Thus in New South Wales the limit was first raised from £300 to £3000 in 1814 (the governor had wanted £6000), then lowered to £2000 in 1823 against local wishes. The litigiousness of the inhabitants probably explains the exceptionally high limit of £5000 in Bengal: *ibid.*, 76–7, 80–1.

[192] *Ibid.*, 77. For an example from Tobago in the 1890s see P. Polden, 'Doctor in Trouble' (2001) 22 *JLH* 37–68, at 43.

[193] Howell, *Judicial Committee*, 76–7.

[194] *Ibid.*, 94–109; W. MacPherson, *The Practice of the Judicial Committee of her Majesty's Most Honourable Privy Council* (1860), 19–52.

[195] Howell, *Judicial Committee*, 94–6.

easily persuaded to waive time limits where the appellant had been remiss,[196] and was staunch against granting special leave to appeal from a criminal conviction, from a well-grounded apprehension that such applications would become routine, especially in capital cases. Exceptional cases from the Falkland Islands in 1863 and New South Wales in 1867 made a breach and were followed by a steady trickle.[197] This willingness to entertain criminal appeals produced indignation in Australia,[198] and when the possibility of an appeal from the rebel Louis Riel arose, the Canadian response was to ban such appeals in their criminal code of 1888, though it was subsequently declared unenforceable.[199]

In fact the Canadians had contemplated a drastic curb on appeals generally, which some felt were abused by corporations. A bill of 1875 for the establishment of a supreme court for the whole dominion included a clause barring appeals of right from its decisions, leaving open those accepted by prerogative. It was probably intended to exclude any role for Selborne's proposed 'imperial court of appeal' and suggests confusion over the nature of 'special leave' appeals, but it was strongly opposed by Cairns, and the Privy Council registrar wrote a vigorous defence of the right of appeal.[200] The Colonial Office was less resolute and the act was not disallowed, but the clause was ineffective against grants of special leave, which was freely given in a series of cases which strengthened hostility to the Judicial Committee in some quarters. An initial decision in favour of the federal government[201] was followed by several cases in which the Committee, piloted by Lord Watson and later by Haldane, interpreted the British North America Act in favour of provincial governments, and though no further attempt was made to abolish the right of appeal there was little enthusiasm for it either.[202]

In Australia too there were moves to impose restrictions in conjunction with the creation of a high court for the whole territory. A bill brought to London in 1897 provided that '[n]o appeal shall be permitted to the Queen in Council in any matter involving the interpretation of this Constitution or of the Constitution of a State, unless the public interests of some part of Her Majesty's Dominions,

---

[196] *Ibid.*, 99–101. See particularly *Laing* v. *Ingham* (1839) 3 Moo. P.C. 26–8.

[197] *Ibid.*, 103–8; *Falkland Islands Co* v. *The Queen* (1863) 1 Moo. N.S. 299; *R* v. *Bertrand* (1867) LR 1 PC 520.

[198] Howell, *Judicial Committee*, 226.

[199] *Ex p Riel* [1885] 10 App Cas 675; *Nadan* v. *The King* [1926] AC 482. The *Connors* case, also in 1885, created further controversy: R. Stevens, *The Independence of the Judiciary* (Oxford, 1992), 17.

[200] D. B. Swinfen, *Imperial Appeal* (Manchester, 1987), 27–45; C. G. Pierson, *Canada and the Privy Council* (1960).

[201] *Russell* v. *The Queen* [1882] 7 App Cas 829.

[202] Swinfen, *Imperial Appeal*, 46–9. Not all Canadians would have agreed with Haldane that Watson's work had 'produced a new contentment in Canada with the constitution they had got': 'The Work for the Empire of the Judicial Committee of the Privy Council' (1923) 1 *CLJ* 143–55 at 148–50.

other than the Commonwealth or a State, are involved...'.[203] Determined opposition by Chamberlain as Colonial Secretary drastically narrowed the range of excluded appeals, but more importantly, it impelled him to hold out the possibility of a 'great Imperial Tribunal', a chimera which made its appearance at a succession of imperial conferences.[204]

The Committee's jurisdiction in domestic matters underwent significant changes. Brougham's renewed attempts to add divorce, particularly in 1844, never succeeded,[205] but Admiralty work remained, together with appeals from the Prize court, which Brougham had added in 1833.[206] Acts of 1835 and 1839 granted and enlarged powers to extend the life of a patent and Brougham later consolidated the jurisdiction.[207] Lyndhurst granted the Judicial Committee a more limited role in copyright, to license republication of books by a deceased author where the copyright owner refused permission.[208] A harbinger of things to come—the Judicial Committee as a repository for appeals lacking a suitable home—was the Endowed Schools Amendment Act 1873.[209] However, in 1876 Admiralty appeals were removed to the House of Lords (though Prize appeals remained) and the patent jurisdiction was taken away in 1907, leaving a greater emphasis on its imperial role.

Overseas cases generally held little interest for the British public, but the Judicial Committee's role in the religious controversies of the mid-nineteenth century brought it inescapably into the public eye.[210] No one had foreseen that the Privy Council would become a forum for theological dispute since the Delegates had seldom been one.[211] Nevertheless it became the final court of appeal for cases

---

[203] Swinfen, *Imperial Appeal*, 59. See the anxieties of R. B. Haldane, 'The Appellate Courts of the Empire' (1900) 12 *JR* 1–14.

[204] *Ibid.*, 54–87. The South Africa Act 1910 allowed appeals from the Supreme Court only by special leave: Keith, 'Interplay with the Judicial Committee'.

[205] Howell, *Judicial Committee*, 48, 54, 57, 60.

[206] *Ibid.*, 34–5, 58.

[207] *Ibid.*, 49, 57; Letters Patent for Inventions Act 1835 (5 & 6 Will. IV c. 83), s 2, also promoted by Brougham; Judicial Committee Act 1844, ss 2–7; MacPherson, *Practice of the Judicial Committee*, 242–75.

[208] Copyright Act 1842 (5 & 6 Vict. c. 45), s. 5.

[209] Howell, *Judicial Committee*, 68. It also acquired supervisory jurisdiction over certain universities by the Universities (Scotland) Act 1858 (21 & 22 Vict. c. 83).

[210] R. E. Rodes jnr, *Law and Modernization in the Church of England* (Notre Dame, Indiana, 1991), 323–31. They coincided in the sensational case of the deposed bishop of Natal, J. W. Colenso, in 1865: *In re Lord Bishop of Natal* 3 Moore (N.S.) 115. See also *Long* v. *Bishop of Capetown* 1 Moore (N.S.) 411. See above, pp. 392–400.

[211] *RC on Ecclesiastical Courts*, PP 1883 [C-3760], xxiv.1, xliii–xlv; Rothery's return, App. In 1844 Philpotts, Bishop of Exeter, mindful that his dispute with Gorham seemed likely to come ultimately to the Privy Council, had protested that it had surely never been intended that it should be the forum for heresy cases: *PD* 1844 (s3) 73: 715–17.

of clerical misconduct under the Church Discipline Act 1840 and the Clergy Discipline Act 1892.[212] It had a similar role under the Public Worship Regulation Act 1874, Archbishop Tait's misguided attempt to streamline the process for prosecuting allegations of liturgical heterodoxy.[213] Accusations that clergymen used bad language or solicited alms under false pretences were manageable,[214] but in judging the compatibility of their beliefs, writings, or liturgical practices with the teachings of the Church of England as the *Gorham* case required, the Judicial Committee was on a hiding to nothing.[215] The line between law and theology could not easily be drawn[216] and such was the intensity of the religious controversies of the mid-nineteenth century that a losing party before the court of Arches, buoyed by the prospect of financial support from high or low church organizations, would readily mount a challenge,[217] and neither side would gracefully accept an adverse verdict from a 'pseudo-ecclesiastical tribunal' like the Judicial Committee.[218]

The result was a whole series of high profile cases which constitute 'some of the oddest litigations in English history', among them the *Essays and Reviews* case in which famously if inaccurately Lord Westbury was said to have 'dismissed Hell with costs and [taken] away from orthodox members of the Church of England their last hope of eternal damnation'.[219] *Gorham* was reported at a length of 277 pages and gave rise to an outpouring of over 140 pamphlets.[220] It was followed, inter alia, by *Denison, Bennett* and, the most celebrated, '*Essays and Reviews*'.[221] Cases turning on pure doctrine came to an end with *Voysey* in 1871,[222] but were

---

[212] Rodes, *Law and Modernization in the Church of England*, 212–21; J. Bentley, *Ritualism and Politics in Victorian Britain* (Oxford, 1978).

[213] Rodes, *Law and Modernization in the Church of England*, 255–8; P. T. Marsh, *The Victorian Church in Decline* (1969), 158–92, and see above, p. 398.

[214] Rodes, *Law and Modernization in the Church of England*, 219; *Fitzmaurice* v. *Hesketh* [1904] AC 266; *Moore* v. *Bishop of Oxford* [1904] AC 283.

[215] *Gorham* v. *Bishop of Exeter* (1850), Brodrick and Fremantle, 64 and see above, pp. 395–7.

[216] S. M. Waddams, *Law, Politics and the Church of England* (Cambridge, 1992), 274. For the role of the bishops in the deliberations of the Judicial Committee see above, pp. 395–7.

[217] Rodes, *Law and Modernization in the Church of England*, 267; Marsh, *Victorian Church in Decline*, 124–5. The English Church Union backed high churchmen; the Church Association, low churchmen.

[218] M. D. Stephen, 'Gladstone and the Composition of the Final Court in Ecclesiastical Causes' (1966) 9 *Hist. J.* 191–200.

[219] Quoted, inter alia, in Atlay, *Victorian Chancellors*, ii, 264.

[220] Rodes, *Law and Modernization in the Church of England*, 267–71; Waddams, *Law, Politics and the Church of England*, 271–80; Marsh, *Victorian Church in Decline*, 111–34.

[221] *Ditcher* v. *Denison* (1857) 11 Moo. P.C. 324; *Sheppard* v. *Bennett* (1869) LR 2 PC 450, (1871–2) LR 4 PC 371; *Williams* v. *Bishop of Salisbury* (1863) 2 Moore (N.S.) 375; Rodes, *Law and Modernization in the Church of England*, 263–75; Waddams, *Law, Politics and the Church of England*, 280–8, 310–47.

[222] *Voysey* v. *Noble* (1870–1) 7 Moore (N.S.) 167; Rodes, *Law and Modernization in the Church of England*, 262–3.

succeeded by fierce quarrels about liturgy and ritual.[223] That notorious stronghold of ritualism St. Barnabas, Pimlico, had already been the subject of litigation over a stone altar and other disputable furnishings in 1857,[224] and now candles, confessions, denial of access to the sacraments, the 'eastward' position of the priest celebrating the Eucharist, and an assortment of esoteric but controversial ecclesiological questions were contested, most famously in the long-running attempt to bring the indomitable Alexander Mackonochie into line.[225] Privy Council judges were doubtless thankful that after the case against Bishop King in 1892[226] they finally petered out, though still arousing fierce local passions. And appeals still came from the Ecclesiastical Commissioners' decisions to unite benefices under an Act of 1860.[227]

High churchmen were angered by what they saw as the laxity of the early decisions as to doctrine, and were strongly critical of the Judicial Committee. Their resentment grew when the Committee seemed inclined to greater strictness over ritual and liturgy and it was strengthened when, over the opposition of Archbishop Tait, the prelates were relegated to assessors in the Appellate Jurisdiction Act 1876.[228] The Ecclesiastical Courts Commission a few years later summed up these criticisms: 'that the decisions have been dictated by policy; that they have been rigid in the enforcement of a particular standard of ritual conformity, lax in reproving heresy; and opposed to clear principles of theological interpretation'.[229] The proposal of the majority for a court of lawyer-judges, who must be Anglicans, summoned in strict rotation to serve on a panel of five was never likely to be acceptable[230] and though the Judicial Committee's record in ecclesiastical cases was undistinguished, no other tribunal would have fared much better.

For the first 25 years or so of its existence the flow of business was fairly constant at between 40 and 60 cases a year. Between 30 and 40 per cent came from the British Isles, with ecclesiastical causes somewhat outnumbering

---

[223] See above, pp. 398–400.

[224] *Liddell* v. *Westerton*, Brodrick and Fremantle 125; Waddams, *Law, Politics and the Church of England*, 288–97

[225] C. Smith, 'Martin v. Mackonochie/Mackonochie v. Penzance' (2003) 24 *JLH* 250–72. The later cases, brought under the Public Worship Regulation Act and beginning with *Ridsdale* v. *Clifton* ((1876–7) 2 PD 276) are summed up in the title of Marsh's chapter, 'The Failure to Put Down Ritualism' (218–41).

[226] *Read* v. *Bishop of Lincoln* [1892] AC 644; Rodes, *Law and Modernization in the Church of England*, 306–12.

[227] Union of Benefices Act 1860 (23 & 24 Vict. c. 142); Rodes, *Law and Modernization in the Church of England*, 170–1.

[228] Marsh, *Victorian Church in Decline*, 129–32.

[229] *Report*, v.

[230] *Ibid.*, lvii.

patents and Admiralty cases. Business from the church courts predictably fell away after 1857, however, whereas Admiralty and (especially) Prize cases were boosted by the Crimean War. Among overseas providers, India was always the biggest, with roughly ten a year as against around 18 from all other possessions put together.[231] The others began to rise in the 1870s, Canada and Australia featuring more strongly while West Indian appeals, a major component of the Privy Council's business early in the century, declined along with the prosperity of the islands, falling as low as three a year in the 1890s.[232] Matters relating to commerce and financial services became more prominent, though land disputes remained the biggest category.[233] As the surge in Indian appeals had highlighted the necessity for reform in the 1820s, a further, more dramatic rise in the 1860s and 1870s precipitated demands for further changes. Bengal was the source, its appeals rising tenfold over a short period to make up over half of the Judicial Committee's workload. This was largely the consequence of oppressive administration by the state government, aggravated by well-intentioned changes to the substantive law and the court system. Remarkably, appeals were brought from the Bengal High Court in nearly a third of those cases where the value of property at stake was high enough to allow them. In 1868 the annual number of Privy Council suits had reached 100 and arrears were mounting alarmingly, aggravated by the tendency of Indian cases to take longer than others.[234]

The crisis was resolved by the addition of permanent judges.[235] The annual average of appeals entered fell from 134 (1868–72) to 69 (1878–82) and then rose only gently. MacDonell noted large increases in the share of the Privy Council's business taken by colonial and Indian appeals, which had risen from 27 to 48.3 per cent and 30.15 to 51.7 per cent respectively over 30 years. In relation to their populations, Canada and (even more) the Australian colonies, contributed disproportionately, contrasting with a precipitate decline in West Indian (especially Jamaican) appeals and an equally marked, less readily explicable, fall to negligible numbers from the Channel Islands and the Isle of Man.[236]

---

[231] Howell, *Judicial Committee*, table 1.

[232] *Ibid.*, 111; Civil Judicial Statistics 1894, *PP* 1896 [C. 8263], xciv.

[233] Howell, *Judicial Committee*, 111.

[234] *Ibid.*, 112–17. For a critical appraisal of the handling of Indian appeals, see C. Collett, 'The Judicial Committee of the Privy Council with Special Reference to India' (1872) 1 (n.s.) *LM & R* 14–23.

[235] See below, p. 561. An order in council 'of a peculiar character' specially aimed at clearing the Indian backlog also helped: RC on the Legal Departments, Evidence, *PP* 1875 (C. 1245), xxx, Reeve, q. 8702.

[236] *Civil Judicial Statistics 1894*. Some 1913 cases are described in A. Page, 'The Privy Council and the Empire' (1913) 194 *Blackwood's Mag.* 838–49.

The same broad trends continued, with a peak of 132 cases heard in 1912, though they fell to 93 in 1913. For the most part the Judicial Committee could still get through its business in the 100–120 days Reeve had estimated it would need;[237] the problem was that the overlap in membership between the Committee and the House of Lords, where business was also rising, meant the same judges were often wanted for both.[238]

Composition

Brougham had wanted 'men of the largest legal and general information, accustomed to study other systems of law besides our own, and associated with lawyers who have practised or presided in the Colonial courts'.[239] The actual composition of the new Committee fell well short of this ideal.[240] It was to comprise all who were or had been Lord President, Lord Chancellor, Master of the Rolls, Vice-Chancellor, or a chief judge of any of the superior courts including (much to Eldon's disgust) the chief judge of Brougham's new Bankruptcy court.[241] In addition, two men might be made privy councillors at any time with a place on the Committee.

Despite Brougham's attempts to reduce it to three, the quorum was four until 1851, when it became three exclusive of the Lord President.[242] The quorum excluded the 'assessors', former colonial or Indian judges who, by virtue of the mangled remains of Brougham's grander plan, were (if privy councillors) awarded an enhanced pension for attending the Judicial Committee. Sir Edward Hyde East and Sir Alexander Johnston were immediately appointed, and because the latter refused the remuneration, the government was able to add Sir Edward Ryan; two of them usually attended Indian appeals. However, East and Johnston were not immediately replaced when they died in the late 1840s. Perhaps with Ryan becoming a full member of the Committee in 1850 they were felt superfluous, but when two capable chief justices of Calcutta, Sir Lawrence Peel and Sir James Colvile, later became eligible they were promptly added. The way the

---

[237] *HLSC on Appellate Jurisdiction, Report 1872*, q. 137.

[238] Haldane complained that the Judicial Committee was often left with only a 'scratch collection of three members' for important cases: 'Appellate Courts of the Empire', 10.

[239] *PD* 1828 (s2) 18: 158. Cf. the similar prescription of William Burge of the Privy Council bar: 'H', 'Supreme Courts of Appeal' (1841) 25 *LM* 373–80, at 373. For Burge's exhaustive treatise on the conflict of laws see above, p. 281.

[240] Howell, *Judicial Committee*, 28. There is a useful short summary of the changes in W. C. Petheram, 'English Judges and Hindu Law' (1900) 16 *LQR* 392–6.

[241] Judicial Committee of the Privy Council Act 1833, s. 1; Eldon to Stowell, April 1833, quoted in Swinfen, 'Henry Brougham and the Judicial Committee', 401.

[242] Court of Chancery Act (14 & 15 Vict. c. 83), ss 5, 15–16; Howell, *Judicial Committee*, 53, 58.

Committee operated makes the part played by the assessors hard to ascertain, but they were probably helpful in expounding the intricacies of Indian law.[243]

The Act also authorized the summoning of other privy councillors to meetings at discretion.[244] This provision probably met two needs. One was to avoid a deadlock when four legal members were equally divided, and in such cases it was always other Judicial Committee members who were summoned. The other was to enable a departmental minister to ensure that in cases with political implications, his position could be put directly to the judges. At the behest of the Lord President it was also invoked in a few controversial religious cases to enable prelates who were privy councillors to provide guidance on doctrine.[245]

Though Brougham did his best to keep the Lord President away from the Committee's sittings, the sheer difficulty of making up a quorum meant that Lansdowne and his successors were sometimes needed. To those who criticized this, Reeve retorted that Indian litigants would probably be gratified to note that a grandee such as the Duke of Buccleuch had lent his distinguished presence to their appeal, even though his role was purely ornamental.[246]

Despite the reforms of 1833 the Judicial Committee was a court of part-time judges, and it lacked a suitably authoritative judicial chief. Law reformers found this unsatisfactory and repeated attempts were made to remedy the perceived shortcoming.[247] Ambitious schemes to amalgamate the two highest appeal courts and/or to reconstruct the role of Lord Chancellor came to nothing[248] and even more modest proposals such as Sugden and Pemberton-Leigh's to create 'lords assistant' and Cranworth's for a salaried vice-president failed.[249] The idea of a vice-president was not new. In 1841 Lyndhurst had vainly urged Brougham to accept the post (unpaid) and in 1844 Brougham presented a bill which would have created a vice-president on £2000 and two salaried puisnes. This encountered resistance and ridicule, his enemies claiming Brougham wanted it for himself, and it became impossible to pass. On this occasion Brougham was probably treated unfairly; if he had any ulterior motive, it was probably to help his hard-up protégé the Earl of Devon, and the government's clumsiness was more blameworthy for the debacle than he was. Even so, its failure was a blow to his hopes for a wider role for the Committee.[250]

---

[243] Howell, *Judicial Committee*, 156–8.

[244] Section 5.   [245] Howell, *Judicial Committee*, 32–4, 50–1.

[246] *Ibid.*, 123, 129; *SC on Appellate Jurisdiction, Report 1872*, q. 119.

[247] See for instance the criticisms by Lord John Russell and Sir Edward Sugden quoted in 'H', 'Supreme Courts of Appeal'.

[248] See below, pp. 656–7.   [249] Howell, *Judicial Committee*, 61–2.

[250] Swinfen, 'Brougham and the Judicial Committee, 406–11; M. J. Lobban, 'Henry Brougham and Law Reform' (2000) 115 *EHR* 1184–215, at 1201–2. Cottenham made a particularly outspoken

In fact, additions to the Judicial Committee's strength came about through reforms to the court of Chancery rather than by direct measures. In 1841 the two new vice-chancellors were made privy councillors, though not *ex officio*, and not all of their successors were similarly honoured.[251] In 1852, when the court of Appeals in Chancery was created, its members would, if privy councillors, belong to the Judicial Committee; all of them were, and did. [252]

Eighty members of the Judicial Committee actually attended at least one meeting between 1833 and 1876, but in practice the Committee was quite a compact body.[253] Ten of the 20 originally qualified and 16 subsequent potential members never attended, the most notable being Lord St. Leonards, who objected to the convention of not disclosing dissents.[254] Most members were there *ex officio*, but the power to appoint judges or lawyers to the Privy Council was regularly exercised. In the early instances of Graham and Bayley, it was probably an inducement to retire and they never sat on the Judicial Committee, but Patteson, J. T. Coleridge, Williams, Kindersley, and Keating were all diligent members.

Just five men were appointed under the 'any two other persons' provision of section 1. It was one of several rewards extorted from Whig administrations by Campbell and political considerations also dictated the appointment of Sir Joseph ('Holy Joe') Napier in 1868; his deafness was already a handicap and he was finally made to resign in 1881, almost a decade after he had last participated in a hearing.[255] Two of the others were Indians, the mediocre Ryan and the capable Colvile. The outstanding success, however, was Thomas Pemberton-Leigh, later Lord Kingsdown. Pemberton-Leigh was one of the foremost counsel of his day, not least in the Privy Council, but ample means and temperamental disinclination led him to resist every offer of judicial preferment. He was with difficulty persuaded to agree that he would join the Privy Council when he retired from the bar, and demonstrated his anger when the honour was bestowed prematurely in 1843 by continuing to practise before the House of Lords and the Master of the Rolls for some months afterwards.[256] Kingsdown was the most regular member of the Committee for the next 22 years (hearing 704 cases in all) and was

attack on the clause allowing any matter to be referred to the Judicial Committee: *PD* 1844 (s3) 73: 701–14.

[251] Administration of Justice Act 1841 (5 Vict. c. 5). Stuart and Malins were not.

[252] Court of Chancery Act 1851, ss 15–16.

[253] Howell, *Judicial Committee*, App.

[254] *Ibid.*, 126–7.

[255] *Ibid.*, 128–33; A. C. Ewell, *The Life of Sir Joseph Napier, bart.* (1887), 300, 411.

[256] E. L. Pemberton (ed.), *Lord Kingsdown's Recollections* (1868), 126. Kingsdown's assiduous work on the intricacies of Indian land rights was invaluable in enabling the Privy Council to cope with an intractable problem.

the outstanding figure in its deliberations, drafting innumerable judgments and refining its jurisprudence.[257]

The usual pattern was that in any given year between nine and 14 members would sit, a few of whom would make only a handful of appearances while a hard core would be regulars, that core growing over time from four to seven.[258] In the 1830s Brougham, who remained active and zealous until 1850 when he gave up sitting, perhaps in exasperation at Ryan's appointment, Sir James Parke, Sir John Bosanquet, and Sir Thomas Erskine were the most assiduous attenders. In the 1840s Stephen Lushington, who had come onto the Committee as Admiralty judge in 1838, began that conscientious attendance that he continued until his resignation in 1866, accumulating more appearances than anyone save Kingsdown.[259] Apart from Kingsdown and Brougham, Langdale, Campbell, and Knight-Bruce were Lushington's most frequent colleagues, and from the 1850s the equity side tended to dominate as the vice-chancellors and lords justices of appeal were now eligible while the common law chiefs were too busy. Patteson, J. T. Coleridge, and Williams were the leading representatives of the common lawyers while from Chancery the most regular were Turner and Knight-Bruce. Lord Chelmsford, a common lawyer who became Lord Chancellor, spanned both categories. No other civilian approached Lushington's record, but the judges from India, Ryan and especially Colvile, were regulars.[260]

Until the torrent of Bengal appeals threatened to overwhelm its resources, the Judicial Committee seemed to be running satisfactorily. That crisis came at a particularly inconvenient time for Gladstone's administration, since the Judicature Commission, whose remit excluded the House of Lords and Privy Council but did cover appeals at a lower level, had issued its first report.[261] The provisions for appeals in the bill which Hatherley introduced in 1870 were unacceptable to the judges and many peers, and to add to Hatherley's woes, Westbury now tabled a motion demanding urgent measures to deal with the backlog in the Judicial Committee. The Chancellor, having failed to fob him off with the possibility of adding to the unpaid membership, reluctantly responded with a more plausible proposal, but under a Prime Minister who wanted to reduce judicial salaries, his offering was necessarily ungenerous.[262] It drew upon three sources of additional manpower. Two former Indian judges would be paid £1000 to attend; two former colonial judges or English barristers of 15 years' standing might be appointed at £2500; and any retired English judge who undertook to sit regularly might have

[257] Howell, *Judicial Committee*, 130–3.   [258] *Ibid.*, App.

[259] Waddams, *Law, Politics and the Church of England*, 238–48.

[260] Howell, App. and 120–59.   [261] See below, Ch. VI.

[262] Howell, *Judicial Committee*, 62–7; Nash, *Life of Lord Westbury*, ii, 219–34.

up to £500 per annum. With the law officers pointedly declining to help the bill through the Commons, and the bar indignant at what it deemed an insult to the profession, the disclosure that the 'Indian' members would be paid out of Indian revenues, seemingly in violation of the Government of India Act 1858, doomed it to failure.[263]

Next session, Hatherley returned with a temporary expedient pending a further attempt at a comprehensive solution to the overall problem of appeals.[264] Though somewhat more generous, it was still redolent of economy. Two former Indian chief justices and two former judges of English superior courts would have £5000 (including, however, any pension they received). Colvile was promoted from assessor to judge and Montagu Smith was eager to be relieved of the circuit duty which caused him suffering, but Gladstone and Hatherley had overlooked the fact that English judges accepting this position would lose financially unless they cast adrift their clerks, who were paid by the Exchequer. After three rebuffs they blundered into the 'Colliery explosion', making a compliant Attorney-General a judge of Common Pleas for a couple of days to meet the letter of their own Act and bringing down a storm of reproach, rupturing relations with eminent judges for want of tact and common sense.[265]

Their other appointment, Sir Barnes Peacock, was also controversial, since many of the outstanding appeals were from his decisions in Bengal, and they had to accept an amendment barring him from sitting on them.[266] It was a sorry business, which rather obscured the significant change whereby the Judicial Committee had at last rather fortuitously acquired full-time judges and therefore become able to hold sittings without interruption throughout the legal year.

The Judicial Committee Act 1871 was intended as a stop-gap measure and so it proved. By the Appellate Jurisdiction Act 1876 the four salaried members were to be succeeded in due course by four lords of appeal in ordinary sitting in the Judicial Committee when their primary duties permitted.[267] Howell's view that they dominated the Committee numerically was not true of 1895—at least not in reported non-Indian appeals—for although Lords Macnaghten and Watson attended most frequently, the Lord Chancellor, Lords Hobhouse and Shand, and Sir Richard Couch were the next most regular. However, in 1913 Halsbury was the only regular attender apart from the lords of appeal in ordinary.[268]

[263] Howell, *Judicial Committee*, 62–7.

[264] *Ibid.*, 67–8.   [265] *Ibid.*, 151–3.   [266] *Ibid.*, 65–6, 153–4.

[267] See above, p. 538. The Appellate Jurisdiction Act 1887 (c. 70) reduced the former Indian judges to one.

[268] Howell, *Judicial Committee*, 156. The figures for 1895 and 1913 are based only on the cases reported in the Law Reports for those years. Non-judicial privy councillors evidently still sat on cases of particular sensitivity; Haldane instanced a Jersey case (unnamed) argued before the Prime

In both 1895 and 1913 the composition of the Committee was enlarged by statute, under pressure from Canada and Australia, and later South Africa. With
the British government rightly regarding the creation of an 'Imperial Court of
Appeal' as not practical politics, efforts were made to ensure that the Judicial
Committee had as impressive an array of judicial talent as possible, which became
more difficult as the demands made on the lords of appeal by both courts grew,
hearings becoming longer and cases more numerous.[269]

In 1895 provision was made for up to five judges of the superior courts of
Canada, Australia, and South Africa to be chosen as members.[270] Before the
imperial conference of 1901 it was proposed to offer to double the number of lords
of appeal, with the four additional members (presumably men appointed under
the 1895 Act) limited to seven-year terms.[271] However, none of the conferences
could reach agreement on the future arrangements for imperial appeals, and so
the Judicial Committee continued as their forum. As promised by Loreburn at
the 1911 conference, two lords of appeal were added in 1913.[272] The reinforcement
was badly needed, for whereas in 1895 the Committee had frequently mustered
between six and eight, in 1913 five was only reached five times out of 19 and quite
often there were just three; moreover, even that sometimes included a law lord
attempting to sit simultaneously in both courts.[273] Indian appeals were probably
even worse served, for the priority given to finding a 'strong' panel for the white
dominions which became notorious after the Committee was authorized to sit in
two divisions in 1915, was probably evident before then.[274]

Organization and Procedure

Like the Lords, the Privy Council as a court lacked a dedicated clerical staff.
However, though there were two clerks of the Council, the judicial work was performed almost wholly by one, initially C. F. Greville, with the assistance of a

---

Minister, a bishop, two lay privy councillors, the Lord Chancellor, two former Lord Chancellors and
four law lords: 'Appellate Courts of the Empire', 12–14.

[269] Stevens, *Independence of the Judiciary*, 17–21.

[270] Appellate Jurisdiction Act 1895 c. 44. The range and number of eligible colonial judges was
extended by Administration of Justice Act 1908 c. 51 but this was 'a dead letter': Swinfen, *Imperial
Appeal*, 77.

[271] Stevens, *Independence of the Judiciary*, 18–19; Swinfen, *Imperial Appeal*, 60–6.

[272] See above, p. 539.

[273] Law Reports Appeal Cases. It does not include Indian appeals, which were reported in a separate volume.

[274] G. R. Lowndes to Lord Chancellor, 29 October 1918, LCO 2/3464. W. C. Petheram, 'English
Judges and Hindu Law' (1900) 16 *LQR* 77–87, complained that after Peacock's death Sir Richard
Crouch (appointed 1880) was the only expert in Indian law, and that this led to decisions such as
Sartaj Khan v. *Deoruj Khan* (1878) 15 *Indian Appeals* 51, which caused great dissatisfaction in India.

clerk of appeals.[275] Greville is better known as a diarist and society figure than an administrator and was no enthusiast for change in general or Brougham's creation in particular.[276] He was capable enough but at least once abused his position (unsuccessfully) on behalf of one of the parties in a nullity case (*Swift* v. *Kelly*, 1835) and his opinions of the Committee members are not dependable.[277] Fortunately for the Committee, when the clerk of appeals died in 1837, the Lord President made an inspired choice of replacement in the youthful Henry Reeve. Brougham was displeased but in 50 years at the Council Reeve proved his worth. Imposing and dignified, he was also hard-working, skilful in his management of the judges, and instrumental in effecting procedural reforms which appreciably reduced the cost of suits.[278]

In 1853 Reeve was made registrar, a post created in 1833 but not previously filled.[279] It was hoped that firmer case management would prevent the growth of arrears, and with a higher salary (£1000) went greater responsibilities; the registrar could administer oaths, take affidavits and depositions, and issue routine interlocutory orders.[280] By sifting the parties' transcripts and eliminating their recital of unnecessary facts Reeve reduced their length, and therefore their cost, and helped the Committee to focus on the issues of law.[281] Reeve was also given more clerical support and though repeatedly passed over for promotion to clerk of the Council, he continued until 1887 to enjoy a role that gave him time to edit *The Edinburgh Review*.[282]

The leading members of the Judicial Committee turned down Brougham's attempt to create a new code of rules and perpetuated existing distinctions. Thus for cases from the civilian courts the Admiralty registrar would attend to ensure conformity to existing practice and the proctors had exclusive rights to act as agents. True, some changes were imposed: new evidence was not generally received and, unlike the Delegates, the Judicial Committee gave reasons for its judgments; but all the intermediate stages followed the practice of Doctors'

[275] Howell, *Judicial Committee*, 159–60. When Greville retired in 1859 he was not replaced. So long as Reeve remained registrar the clerk of the Council had little to do with it.

[276] *ODNB* 23: 780. Reeve published Greville's diaries and so earned the gratitude of historians and the disapproval of the Queen.

[277] Howell, *Judicial Committee*, 160–2.

[278] Ibid., 163–7. See his evidence to the *SC on Appellate Jurisdiction 1872* and the *RC on Ecclesiastical Courts 1883*, and *Memoirs of Henry Reeve*, ed. J. K. Laughton (1898).

[279] Section 18.

[280] Howell, *Judicial Committee*, 165.

[281] *SC on Appellate Jurisdiction 1872*, qq. 139–46.

[282] Howell, *Judicial Committee*, 165–7. In 1923 Schuster, presumably referring to Reeve's successors, wrote that 'appointments to [registrar] in the past...have been made without any regard to the previous experience of those appointed to the duties which they have to perform'. The Lord President still made these appointments: memorandum of 10 July 1923, LCO 2/3464.

Commons and were usually handled by surrogates. In 1865 the proctors lost their monopoly and the surrogates their powers, and certain other civilian procedures were ended.[283]

Appeals from outside the British Isles in general followed the practice evolved by the old conciliar appeals committee.[284] First the appellant must give notice to the court appealed from, providing the security required by that court to prosecute his appeal and pay costs. He must send a transcript of the court's proceedings to the Council office, along with his petition, comprising a short summary of events and a prayer for reversal of the decision. A much more detailed, printed, version of his case had to follow, and the respondent would reply in kind. From 1838, to save duplication, the parties were required, where possible, to combine in producing an agreed appendix of the documentary material accompanying the printed case.[285]

There were no time limits for most of these stages, but either party might move for the other to speed the cause and, in default, to secure either dismissal of the case or an *ex parte* hearing.[286] Though the Committee might examine witnesses *viva voce*, it seldom did so except in patent cases, which were closer to an initial hearing than an appeal;[287] indeed it was reluctant to accept any new evidence without some special reason.[288] It would if necessary try issues of fact not tried below, for time and distance made it reluctant to remit cases for re-hearing, but would not allow itself to become in effect a court of first instance.[289] It also gained a reputation for being impatient with narrowly technical arguments.[290]

According to Reeve, about two-thirds of appeals proceeded to a hearing.[291] The Committee sat in the council chamber overlooking Downing Street, an unimpressive venue which bemused visitors expecting something in keeping with its imperial role. The judges were seated around a table and the atmosphere was

---

[283] Howell, *Judicial Committee*, 181–4.

[284] *Ibid.*, 185.

[285] J. F. MacQueen, *A Practical Treatise on the Jurisdiction of the House of Lords etc.* (1842), 712.

[286] Howell, *Judicial Committee*, 187–8. As MacQueen pointed out (*Practical Treatise on the Jurisdiction of the House of Lords etc*, 719) the insistence that the respondent produce his printed case before taking this step was productive of unnecessary expense. 'JPT', 'Practice of the Superior Courts of Appeal' (1843) 29 *LM* 1–21, at 18–19.

[287] Judicial Committee of the Privy Council Act 1833, s 7; Howell, *Judicial Committee*, 195–7.

[288] Howell, *Judicial Committee*, 194.

[289] *Ibid.*; N. Bentwich, *The Practice of the Privy Council in Judicial Matters* (1912), 316–17. There was, however, criticism in the 1870s that they had recently abandoned their practice of not usually overturning findings of fact: Keith, 'Interplay with the Judicial Committee'.

[290] Howell, *Judicial Committee*, 194; Bentwich, *Practice of the Privy Council*, 320.

[291] *HLSC on Appellate Jurisdiction 1872*, q.22.

usually sedate.[292] The clerk or registrar generally arranged the cause lists and Reeve claimed to ensure that urgent matters, such as many Admiralty appeals, and colonial appeals were given priority over the mass of Bengal cases, many of which he felt could be put off without injustice.[293]

Though privy councillors probably had no right to insist on attending,[294] it was the practice to allow anyone to sit who wished to, and the Committee occasionally had as many as ten or 11—even more on some special references, such as the *Serjeants' Case*.[295] The power to sit with just three was seldom used before 1900, and tied votes on a four-man panel were resolved by ordering a re-argument before a new panel.[296] Formally the Lord President chose the panel, and some took an active part, but from the 1870s he generally relinquished this task to the Lord Chancellor. Some suspected that Reeve enjoyed more freedom than was warranted, but he was vigorously defended by Cairns and Selborne.[297]

The rash of ecclesiastical appeals focused attention on the composition of the panels, and to meet the suspicion that they were manipulated to ensure the desired outcome, Hatherley and Lord President Ripon began the practice of having all active members summoned to such hearings, though all were not expected to attend.[298] It was always sought to have someone on the panel with particular expertise in the subject of the appeal, so that Hobhouse, for example, would usually be found on Indian appeals; other members were probably grateful for anyone willing to endure a diet of what Westbury disparaged as 'curry and chutnee' cases.[299]

In 1871 Sir Henry James insisted on a formal bar on members from sitting on appeals from their own decisions.[300] This probably only reinforced a customary prohibition, but there was certainly a remarkable earlier instance where Lushington (with Brougham's backing) had been prepared, if no objection was

---

[292] Affectionately described by Haldane ('Work for the Empire of the Judicial Committee of the Privy Council') and in detail by Howell, *Judicial Committee*, 168–80.

[293] *HLSC on Appellate Jurisdiction, Report 1872*, q. 173. John Miller, who practised before the Privy Council, complained in 1839 of the latitude the officials exercised in making up the lists: *On the Present Unsettled Condition of the Law and its Administration* (1839), 111.

[294] A question raised in the hearings of the select committee in 1872 (see q. 101).

[295] Howell, *Judicial Committee*, 189–90.

[296] It had happened two or three times: Reeve's evidence to *SC on Appellate Jurisdiction Report, 1872*, q. 220.

[297] Ibid., qq. 75–108; *RC on the Ecclesiastical Courts, Report*, q. 6760.

[298] *RC on the Ecclesiastical Courts, Report*, q. 6773.

[299] Ibid., q. 6800; L. T. Hobhouse and J. L. Hammond, *Lord Hobhouse, a Memoir* (1905), 210–11; Atlay, *Victorian Chancellors*, ii, 261. See *Greville Memoirs*, iii, 307–11, 330, for attempts to ensure there was a common law judge on the panel for the *Gorham* case.

[300] *PD* 1871 (s3) 103: 1715–16; Judicial Committee Act 1871, s 1.

taken, to sit on a case with a great inheritance at stake in which he had been a counsel at an earlier stage. There is also evidence that the Committee eschewed strict orthodoxy in other respects, judges whose decisions were under appeal being consulted by correspondence.[301]

The Judicial Committee attracted a powerful bar, because until after 1871 it sat mostly in vacations and did not interfere with regular practice in the superior courts.[302] A select handful made it a speciality as J. D. Mayne did with Indian appeals,[303] and it suited the quiet precision of a Pemberton-Leigh or Haldane. As steam succeeded sail it became more feasible for colonial barristers to appear and they became progressively more common in the council chamber.[304]

A unique feature of the Judicial Committee was the nature of the judgment, which was not, in form, a judgment at all, but simply a recommendation to the sovereign, which had to be given the effect of a judgment by the full Council.[305] For this reason some argued that the Judicial Committee was not truly a court at all. Cairns persuaded Selborne of this thesis, but it has rightly been termed 'carrying pedantry to extreme lengths'[306] and would have been an arid debating point had it not appealed to churchmen wishing to contest its authority as a forum for matters spiritual. [307]

Unlike the Lords, the Committee declined to be bound by its previous decisions.[308] The reasoned judgment delivered in writing by the Committee was read by one of the members, and no dissenting opinion might be delivered. The judgment was often a collective enterprise, which emerged from a draft circulated by whoever had assumed the task of drawing it up.[309] The prohibition on dissents was felt by those of the Committee who discussed the question in 1837 to be consistent with a resolution of 1627, but conviction, as much as this shaky authority, sustained it.[310] Several times a member was allowed to make public the fact of his dissent, indeed it would have been impossible to restrain the wilful Knight-Bruce from doing so in the *Gorham* case,[311] but there was no direct challenge to the convention until the early 1870s, when Peacock's desire to proclaim

---

[301] Waddams, *Law, Politics and the Church of England*, 239–40.

[302] Howell, *Judicial Committee*, 192–3.

[303] Hobhouse, and Hammond, *Memoir of Lord Hobhouse*, 199.

[304] G. Alexander, *The Temple of the Nineties* (1938), 168–75; Howell, *Judicial Committee*, 214–15.

[305] Reeve had great difficulty explaining this to the Ecclesiastical Courts Commission in 1883.

[306] Howell, *Judicial Committee*, 36.

[307] *RC on the Ecclesiastical Courts, Report 1883*.

[308] Keith, 'Interplay with the Judicial Committee'.

[309] Howell, *Judicial Committee*, 198–9; Waddams, *Law, Politics and the Church of England*, 242–3.

[310] D. B. Swinfen, *The Single Judgment in the Privy Council* (1975) JR 153–76, at 155–7.

[311] Howell, *Judicial Committee*, 201–3; *Greville Memoirs*, iii, 311.

his dissent in Admiralty cases had to be repressed.[312] The immediate concern, forcefully expressed by Reeve, was the ill-effect any dissents in ecclesiastical cases would have, and one such, *Ridsdale v. Clifton* in 1877, brought it into the spotlight. Sir Fitzroy Kelly, if not 'in his dotage' as Cairns claimed then at least grown careless of niceties, rashly disclosed his minority view in an interview, and when he proved unrepentant Cairns obtained what the high churchman Lord Grimthorpe indignantly termed an 'illegal muzzling order' to give the practice formal status.[313]

In later years it was claimed that disclosure of minority opinions would weaken the authority of the Committee's decisions overseas and would prove especially mischievous in India. This argument, however, became vulnerable when colonial opinion seemed to shift towards disclosure, starting in Australia. The question surfaced at successive imperial conferences, and in 1911 the majority of the dominions seemed to be in favour. Since Loreburn held the same view he held out the prospect of an accommodation but first delayed and then produced a compromise proposal for a single judgment accompanied by a facility for a reasoned dissent. By then most dominions, led by Canada, had had second thoughts, leaving South Africa (which generated few appeals anyway) isolated, and the *status quo* was preserved for a further 55 years.[314]

It was probably from a desire to improve the prestige of the Judicial Committee in the dominions that a long overdue overhaul of the rules was undertaken in 1908. The Judicial Committee had escaped the rule-making of 1883 and operated under a succession of orders in council. The new set of 88 rules made a few useful improvements, particularly in simplifying the procedures for withdrawing and dismissing appeals and petitions and removing the useless issue of appearance orders on defendants, but it was essentially a consolidation.[315] It did not tackle the chief criticism, which was cost. Although much cheaper than the Lords—in 1904 the average of bills taxed was £328, with £263 allowed, as compared to £538 and £363—it was still daunting for many.[316] Court fees were low,[317] but though Reeve had forcefully championed the virtues of printing over manual copying, it was still costly to produce multiple copies,[318] and parties further inflated costs by insisting on expensive counsel.[319]

---

[312] Swinfen, 'Single Judgment in the Privy Council', 157–8.

[313] *Ibid.*, 166–75.

[314] *Ibid.*

[315] 'The New Judicial Committee Rules' (1908) 125 *LT* 50.

[316] Civil Judicial Statistics 1904, *PP* 1906 (Cd. 2945), cxxxv.

[317] *SC on Appellate Jurisdiction, Report 1872*, Reeve, qq. 155–8.

[318] (1902) 113 *LT* 26. *SC on Appellate Jurisdiction Report 1872*, Reeve, qq. 141–64; *RC on the Legal Departments, Evidence 1874*, Reeve qq. 8707–23.

[319] *SC on Appellate Jurisdiction, Report 1872*, Reeve q. 153.

Initially the Judicial Committee followed the House of Lords in refusing in general to award costs to a successful appellant except where (as in the Delegates) it had been the usual practice. However, they were always readier to make exceptions and rule changes in 1853 left them with an unfettered discretion. It seems at first to have been exercised with some caution but Bentwich in 1912 was unable to offer any clear guidelines.[320]

---

[320] MacPherson, *Practice of the Judicial Committee*, 228–41; Bentwich, *Practice of the Privy Council in Judicial Matters*, 332–40.

III

The Superior Courts of Common Law

1. PRACTICE AND PROCEDURE[1]

The Pre-trial Stage

INITIATING PROCEEDINGS

The writ system through which a plaintiff activated the superior courts had developed by offering a particular writ, issuing out of the Chancery, for every recognized cause of action, and choice of the correct writ was crucial. In the 1820s there were still actions, the real actions for the recovery of dower and advowsons for example, for which this traditional course had to be followed, and others where it might sometimes be prudent; thus it was unwise to employ a *latitat* in the King's Bench against a defendant with the determination and means to resist, for he could take an adverse verdict direct to the House of Lords by a writ of error, bypassing the Exchequer Chamber. However, over the centuries the original writs had in many cases been superseded or circumvented by various devices, and the Common Law Commissioners identified 17 ways of commencing an action in the common law courts.[2]

This proliferation of procedural devices had three sources. Some were privileges granted to officers of the court (including its attorneys) to sue or be sued in their own court; others sprang from the determination of the King's Bench and Exchequer to acquire business properly belonging to the Common Pleas; still others were attempts to reduce the complexity and expense associated with the writs themselves, some of which, including popular actions of trespass and *assumpsit*, demanded the expertise of a special pleader. Fortunately the older writs for land recovery had, with few exceptions, been superseded by the fiction-laden action of ejectment.[3]

---

[1] For criminal trials and procedure see XIII, Pt 1, Ch. III.

[2] *RC on the Common Law, First Report, PP* 1829 (46), ix (hereafter *First Report 1829*), 72–4; Holdsworth, *HEL*, ii, 512, 520–1.

[3] *First Report 1829*, 75. A. W. B. Simpson, *An Introduction to the History of the Land Law* (2nd edn, Oxford, 1986), 140.

In volume the personal actions of *latitat* and the bill of Middlesex dominated the King's Bench, numbering 38,138 and 17,913 respectively of 66,549 cases commenced in 1827 (there were also 1647 ejectments). In Common Pleas the *capias ad respondendum*, with 16,794 out of 18,529, was even more dominant, while in the torpid Exchequer *quominus* accounted for 6618 of 8397 actions.[4] A further complication was that while most original process took the form of an instruction to the defendant to appear in court, the majority (*capias* in particular) could also be sued out in bailable form, that is, as a command to the sheriff to arrest the defendant and secure his appearance by keeping him locked up or insisting on adequate bail.[5]

Such complexities, which bulked large in practice books such as Tidd's[6] and had only an historical rationale, had few defenders. The King's Bench filazers, with ineffable complacency, airily declared that 'we are not aware of any inconvenience attending the practice of commencing actions by original writs',[7] but even the Common Pleas prothonotaries felt rationalization would be desirable and practitioners were virtually unanimous in condemnation.[8]

Hence the Commissioners might expect little criticism if they proposed a radical simplification.[9] Concerning the real actions they were in agreement with the Real Property Commissioners in recommending the abolition of most of them as being usually the resort of unscrupulous practitioners with unmeritorious clients who were almost invariably foiled by hostile judges insisting on the most minute exactitude in their deployment.[10] The Real Property Limitations Act 1833 preserved only writs of dower and *quare impedit*, which survived as relics of feudalism until 1860,[11] though the Commissioners' proposal to convert ejectment into a more straightforward plea of land was not carried out. Ejectment was later amended and the fictions dispensed with but, unlike the earlier proposal, this confined the point at issue to a pure question of who had the better title.[12]

---

[4] *First Report 1829*, tables 1–3.

[5] *Ibid.*, 85–93.

[6] *Ibid.*, 78. According to Richard Whitcombe, writing of the great sessions of Wales, 'Mr. Tidd's Book of Practice is the authority to which...we are constantly in the habit of referring', *First Report 1829*, App. E, 50 at A1. Readers of *David Copperfield* will remember Uriah Heep's encomium.

[7] *Ibid.*, App. A, 497. The filazers filed writs and issued process.

[8] *Ibid.*, App. A, 500 and *passim*.

[9] The original Commissioners were five barristers: J. B. Bosanquet, E. H. Alderson, H. J. Stephen, J. Parke, and J. Patteson. All but Stephen became judges. J. F. Pollock, T. Starkie, J. Evans and W. Wightman were subsequently added.

[10] 'The Real Property Commission Report' (1829–30) 3 *LM* 1–71, at 52–3.

[11] 3 & 4 Will. IV c. 27; *RC on the Common Law, Second Report, PP* 1830 (123), xi (hereafter *Second Report 1830*), 7; *Third Report*, PP 1831 (92), x (hereafter *Third Report 1831*), 7; Common Law Procedure Act 1860 (23 & 24 Vict. c. 126), ss 26, 27.

[12] *Second Report 1830*, 13–16; *RC on the Common Law Courts, First Report, PP* 1851 [1389], xxii (hereafter *First Report 1851*), 55–60; Common Law Procedure Act 1852 (15 & 16 Vict. c.76), ss 168–221. The action was still styled ejectment.

Uncertainty about the future of imprisonment on mesne process obstructed a single form of personal action.[13] While the Commissioners' recommendation for a very simple writ of summons was adopted, suitors were given the alternative of a simplified form of *capias* to preserve the option of bailable process.[14] The value of the uniform process was slightly diminished by the judges' decision (contrary to the promoters' ideas) to restrict its scope to the county named in the writ, but this limitation, and the superfluous requirement to name the subject-matter of the action, were removed in 1852.[15]

JOINDER OF PARTIES

An action had to be brought in the name of all parties with legal title to sue and only those parties. In contract-based forms of action the omission of a plaintiff or a wrong joinder each caused the action to fail and although in torts that omission only entitled the defendant to plead in abatement, a wrong joinder was fatal to the action. As for defendants, wrong joinders in contract were fatal and omissions of parties gave rise to pleas in abatement; in tort, however, neither was of much moment.[16]

The first Common Law Commissioners recognized the difficulties which were experienced in identifying the correct parties, but regarding the general rules as 'not practicable to simplify',[17] and being especially alert to misjoinders being mis-used to keep a dangerous witness off the stand, they recommended only minor changes.[18]

The second Commissioners were bolder, and most of the penal rules were relaxed in 1852 by giving the court a large power before or at trial to allow amend-ment as to parties and to do likewise if a plea of abatement was entered.[19] This did not help where it was unclear who had legal title, where a mistake continued to create 'a very costly defeat'.[20] The Commissioners tackled this in their third report and in 1860 provisions already made for ejectment were extended by allowing a plaintiff to act in the names of everyone he thought might have legal title and empowering the court to pronounce judgment in favour of those among them

---

[13] See below, pp. 575–9.

[14] Uniformity of Process Act 1832 (2 & 3 Will. IV c. 39).

[15] *First Report 1851*, 2–4; Common Law Procedure Act 1852, ss 2, 3.

[16] Holdsworth, *HEL*, xv, 107.

[17] *Third Report 1831*, 9.

[18] *Ibid.*, 9–11. Consultees were generally more favourable to relaxing the rules for wrong or non-joinder of defendants than for plaintiffs (see replies to questions 16 and 17) and the Commission's proposals reflected this.

[19] *First Report 1851*, 9–11; Common Law Procedure Act 1852, ss 34–7.

[20] *RC on the Common Law Courts, Third Report*, PP 1860 [2614], xxxi (hereafter *Third Report 1860*), 6.

who actually had, the defendant being safeguarded by an entitlement to costs incurred through unnecessary joinders.[21]

The Common Law Procedure Acts also improved the position when an action was interrupted by a party's death, bankruptcy, or marriage. This formerly involved the complications and expense of a writ of revivor, but henceforth the plaintiff or his successor had merely to enter a note on the record. The same applied to the representative of a defendant; from 1854 the surviving or representative defendant was permitted to demand that the plaintiff either continue or terminate the action.[22]

SERVICE AND APPEARANCE

Before 1725 litigants, particularly those pursuing a debtor with no real defence, were often frustrated by the court's insistence on the defendant entering an appearance to the action before any further proceedings could take place: 'medieval process involved two struggles: one between the state and the defendant: the second between the plaintiff and the defendant. Only when the state had won the first could the second occur.'[23] The move to a procedure which, once initiated by service of the plaintiff's claim, proceeds remorselessly to judgment and execution unless the defendant intervenes is a critical one if the courts are to serve the needs of a credit-based, commercial society.[24]

Judgment in default of appearance was essentially confined to the real actions (and even then the defendant was permitted subsequently to dispute the outcome) and made a first, tentative appearance in personal actions in 1725.[25] A plaintiff, on presenting an affidavit of personal service on the defendant, might enter an appearance on the latter's behalf and so drive the action forward. The Act's scope, however, was limited—a plaintiff claiming more than £10 could still resort to arrest—and preserved the fiction that the defendant had submitted to the court's jurisdiction. It was enlarged in 1828[26] and the difficulties frequently experienced in effecting service inclined the Common Law Commissioners to extend it to cases where service had proved impossible.[27] Many of those who gave

---

[21] Common Law Procedure Act 1860, ss 19–21.

[22] *Ibid.*, s 92.

[23] S. C. Yeazell, 'Default and Modern Process', in W. M. Gordon and T. D. Fergus (eds), *Legal History in the Making* (1991), 125–44 at 142.

[24] C. Crifo, 'The "Creation" of the Default Judgment in Nineteenth Century English Procedural Reforms', in A.Lewis et al., *Law in the City* (Dublin, 2007), 181–205.

[25] An Act to prevent Frivolous and Vexatious Actions (12 Geo. I c. 29); Yeazell, 'Default and Modern Process', 126–31.

[26] 7 & 8 Geo. IV c. 71 extended it to process excluded from the original Act.

[27] *First Report 1829*, 94–5.

evidence to them, however, were wary of dispensing with personal service as a prerequisite to judgment, so the measure was quite modest.[28]

The 1832 Act[29] still preserved the fiction of a real appearance and, while making the facility generally available, with appearance entered eight days after service, it was only permitted (when service had not been achieved) with safeguards. Thus, where service had been effected at the defendant's abode, through wife or servants, it was necessary to issue a *distringas* before the eight-day period could commence.[30] In the growing number of instances where the defendant was believed to be out of the jurisdiction (or had no known abode, nor property to distrain upon) application had to be made to a judge to authorize publication of the writ of summons and subsequently the entry of appearance.

These limitations ensured that the older means of securing an appearance would not become obsolete overnight. Arrest was the most controversial, but distraint, attachment and outlawry also had their users. The writ *distringas* operated in two forms. The older, common law one involved a sequence of writs each authorizing the sheriff to seize a portion of the defendant's goods until he submitted to appear.[31] It remained the only form available against corporations, but it had been intended to be otherwise superseded by statutory forms. However, the court of Exchequer, 'notwithstanding an apparent prohibition in the Act' had interpreted it as preserving the option of the older form, and the courts had also severely curtailed the statute's utility. In particular, they insisted upon an affidavit averring that at least three attempts had been made to serve it on the defendant at his abode and that he was believed to be keeping out of the way to avoid being served. In consequence, 'the mode of proceeding devised by the statute is beset with so many difficulties, that plaintiffs often adopt by preference the old method of distress infinite'.[32] Since the Commissioners wanted to use *distringas* in cases where service was proving difficult, it clearly needed further reforms.

They found little use for the other coercive measures. Attachment and commission of rebellion upon subpoena in the Exchequer they pronounced 'highly objectionable in its character'.[33] If the sheriff's men found the defendant he was imprisoned until he became compliant, but he seldom was found, necessitating a commission of rebellion enabling his house to be entered forcibly. Since there was every chance that he had not learned of the proceedings against him this might cause injustice and it was too elaborate and costly for everyday litigation between subjects.

---

[28] *Ibid.*, App.G, esp. J. F. Archbold (13).
[30] Section 3.
[32] *Ibid.*, 87.

[29] Uniformity of Process Act 1832 c. 39.
[31] *First Report 1829*, 86.
[33] *Ibid.*, 88.

The same objections were even stronger with outlawry. It was employed chiefly where a partner was abroad or had gone missing when an action was brought, thereby halting it in its tracks. Outlawry was dramatic and punitive, and so judges had enmeshed it in technicalities to prevent oppression.[34] It had become an expensive, dilatory and inconvenient proceeding, which amassed costs of at least £17 and at its speediest took six months, more often a year, before the frustrated plaintiff could proceed with his suit.[35] Being used mostly against Englishmen abroad, who might well be ignorant of the suit, it also had the potential for injustice to defendants; hence the ease with which it might be set aside. Apart from those who opposed all change, few witnesses had a good word to say for outlawry, and the Commissioners were for sweeping it away.[36]

That reform had to await the condemnation of a further royal commission: '[f]rom beginning to end the proceedings to outlawry on mesne process are founded on fiction and built up of technical forms...It seems to us that the principles on which this proceeding is founded are wholly false, and unworthy of the jurisprudence of a civilised country.'[37] Less cautious than their predecessors, and concerned more with the needs of creditors than the plight of debtors, these Commissioners were also prepared to dispense with the *distringas*: 'in substance...an attempt to give notice to the defendant to appear',[38] and an expensive one at that. Though personal service remained the rule, a plaintiff who could demonstrate that the defendant knew of the writ or was evading service might now proceed by way of a court order 'as if personal service had been effected'.[39] If he served a specially endorsed writ to which the defendant failed to appear he might enter judgment after eight days, although the defendant could still seek to persuade the court to re-open the judgment.[40]

The inception of default judgment in essentially its modern form gave the superior courts an invaluable weapon against the drift of unopposed debt claims to the county courts, which were persistently denied the same power.[41] It dramatically reduced the costs of debt collection and was welcomed by most lawyers and commercial interests.[42] For those wishing to bring actions on bills of exchange or promissory notes, however, it did not go far enough, and they were able to profit from a political climate sympathetic to the needs of commercial creditors to obtain

---

[34] Yeazell, 'Default and Modern Process', 128–9; Holdsworth, *HEL*, ix, 254–5.

[35] *First Report 1829*, 90–2.

[36] A predictable exception were the King's Bench filazers (App. G7).

[37] *First Report 1851*, 5–6.

[38] *Ibid*, 4. The Act (ss 18–19) also greatly facilitated service on a defendant abroad.

[39] Common Law Procedure Act 1852, s 17. He had otherwise to give the defendant eight days' notice to plead, s 28. A similar procedure was instituted in Chancery by the Chancery Procedure Act 1852 (15 & 16 Vict. c. 86), s 15.

[40] Section 27.   [41] See below, pp. 896–7.   [42] Crifo, 'Default Judgment', 198.

a further concession. It had long been a complaint that debtors upon such instruments were able to postpone judgment by resorting to pleading fanciful or downright fictitious defences.[43] In Brougham's celebrated law reform speech in 1828 he had advocated the adoption of the expedited procedures available in Scotland as a preferable alternative to the cumbersome confession of judgment (*cognovit*) by warrant of attorney.[44] In 1853, in a more favourable climate, he returned to the charge with a bill which passed the Lords before stalling in the Commons.[45] It was revived the next year, but now went forward alongside a rival bill presented by a barrister, H. S. Keating.[46] The achilles heel of Brougham's scheme was that it involved registration of protested bills, which would be effected through notaries. The former, as bringing in fees, bureaucracy, and patronage, aroused misgivings in some quarters and the latter ensured the hostility of the solicitors,[47] and from a select committee of lawyers and businessmen it was Keating's bill which emerged triumphant.[48] The Act of 1855 created a specially indorsed writ available only for bills of exchange and promissory notes on which judgment might be entered after 12 days unless the defendant had persuaded a judge that he had a plausible defence.[49] Taken together, these two measures represented a significant departure from the stately course of an action at law and a marked shift in favour of creditors.

IMPRISONMENT UPON MESNE PROCESS

A writ might be made bailable or serviceable. The former was much more drastic for the defendant, requiring the sheriff's officer (in practice a bailiff) to take him to prison to ensure he entered appearance and would be on hand to obey any judgment given against him. Because it was a draconian measure, ostensibly aimed at preventing defendants from taking flight, statutory safeguards had been introduced and from 1825 it could be used only in claims of at least £20 (£50 if the writ was to be carried into Wales or a palatinate) except where ordered by a judge.[50]

Defenders of the process argued that any harshness was more apparent than real, since a defendant could avoid prison simply by offering bail. An alternative

---

[43] L. J. Bauman, 'Evolution of the Summary Judgment Procedure' (1955–6) 31 *Indiana LJ*, 329–56 at 334.

[44] *PD* 1828 (s2) 18: 127.

[45] 'Bills of Exchange and Promissory Notes—Lord Brougham's Bill' (1855) 23 (s2) *LM* 77–114.

[46] A future judge of Common Pleas: *ODNB* 30: 977.

[47] 'Bills of Exchange and Promissory Notes', esp. 108–12. Bankers were opposed to entrusting solicitors with this responsibility.

[48] Bauman, 'Evolution of Summary Judgment Procedure', 337–9.

[49] Bills of Exchange 1855 (18 & 19 Vict. c. 67), usually known as Keating's Act.

[50] Arrest on Mesne Process Act (7 & 8 Geo. IV c. 71).

of paying the full amount claimed and costs into court was little used.[51] Though used rather less than serviceable process (over a five-year period 256,901 writs were serviceable, 174,495 bailable[52]) bailable process was very common. It had, however, become a target for reformers. Joseph Hume brought in a bill to abolish it in 1827, then combined with Brougham in another, aimed at restricting its compass.[53] Shortly afterwards Scarlett, as Attorney-General, initially included in his Administration of Justice Bill a clause limiting it to debts over £100, but dropped it as too controversial.[54]

By then the subject had come before the Common Law Commissioners, but when their initial investigations found no consensus among interested parties they prudently decided that it raised questions about the substance of the law itself and therefore fell outside their remit.[55] They did, however, draft regulations to improve the operation of the bail system, which they held 'abounds in inconveniences and abuses...it is an extremely complex and cumbrous method, overloaded with rules and distinctions, and (as a natural consequence) highly embarrassing and troublesome in its operation. It may truly be said, indeed, to give rise to more contentions upon the method of proceeding, to expose the practitioner to more petty miscarriages, and to consume more of the time of the Court, in proportion to the real importance of the points in dispute, than any other branch of the ordinary practice of a suit at law.'[56]

The defendant could not appear until he had provided both 'bail below' to the sheriff and 'bail above' to the action, each needing two sureties. If the plaintiff excepted to the latter bail on the ground of insufficiency, the defendant had to justify it; if he made no attempt to do so, or if the bail were held insufficient, the action ground to a halt, leaving the plaintiff to bring actions against the sheriff or the bail below and occasioning considerable delay.[57]

The whole process was over-elaborate. It involved at least four parties— the suitors, the sheriff, and the bail/sureties—commonly five if the bail below did not also become the bail above. As it was often inconvenient for defendants to find adequate sureties immediately they resorted to 'sham bail'—men

---

[51] *First Report 1829*, 102. Perhaps because costs of £10 were payable.

[52] *Ibid.*, table 17.

[53] B. Kercher, 'The Transformation of Imprisonment for Debt in England, 1828–1838' (1984) 2 *Australian Journal of Law and Society* 60–109 at 71–4.

[54] M. J. Lobban, 'Henry Brougham and Law Reform' (2000) *EHR* 1184–215 at 1198. This was characteristic of the uncoordinated approach to implementation of law reform proposals which prevailed at that time: 'JWD', 'History of Law Reform' (1832) 3 *Jurist* 55–94.

[55] *First Report 1829*, 71. Their comments suggested that they did not favour abolition.

[56] *Ibid.*, 88–90, 101–3.

[57] *Ibid.*, 89–90.

to be found lounging outside Serjeants' Inn[58]—and substituting men of more substance (supposed to be householders with a net worth, clear of debts, double the sum claimed or £1000 if it exceeded that), only if the action were not settled. Consequently it also became routine for plaintiffs to except to the bail, so a judge had to hear justifications which were mostly purely formal. This took a whole day each term in the King's Bench and yet of one cluster of 381 justifications only 82 were opposed and just two of those 82 succeeded, unsurprisingly since the plaintiff had minimal information about the sureties.

This in turn left the sheriff in a vulnerable position. Illogically and unfairly, the law held him responsible to the plaintiff if the bail defaulted, though he had no real control over the acceptance of the bail above. Sheriffs secured their position by taking indemnities from the under-sheriff in return for the profits of the process and they in turn deflected responsibility onto the bailiffs.

Temptations abounded for bailiffs. Their legitimate fees from defendants had not been raised for centuries and were wholly inadequate, except perhaps in London where higher fees had some official sanction. The actual fees were exacted according to no authorized scale and defendants bought freedom from imprisonment without bail bonds, but rather on their attorney's undertaking supported by payments to the bailiffs. Furthermore the bailiffs had an effectively unconstrained discretion to reject sureties offered for bail below and sometimes extorted bribes for accepting them.

The Commissioners pessimistically declared that 'the causes of this complexity are in great measure of a permanent kind, and such as to defy remedy'. They acknowledged the anomaly of the sheriff's liability but felt that its practical advantages over either empowering the plaintiff to detain the defendant while he investigated the proffered bail or allowing the defendant to remain at large outweighed logic.[59]

They did, however, propose simplifications. Instead of a bail bond, the defendant and his sureties were to execute an indemnity promising either to pay the plaintiff what was found due or to return the defendant into custody and to indemnify the sheriff if he did not. The sureties, and any substituted sureties for the bail below, must file affidavits of sufficiency, providing material for the plaintiff to except to, and justifications might be heard by a judge of any superior court sitting for that purpose or by an appointed officer. Sundry other improvements were proposed and the Commissioners pronounced their system 'very superior in clearness and simplicity'.[60]

---

[58] See C. Dickens, *The Posthumous Papers of the Pickwick Club*, serialized in 1836–7, Ch. 40.

[59] *First Report 1829*, 103–6.

[60] *Ibid.*, 108–13 and Regulations.

In 1831 renewed and enlarged instructions expressly empowered the Commission to investigate imprisonment for debt, both on mesne process and final judgment. The investigation was thorough, taking written evidence from more than 400 lawyers and businessmen and a few incarcerated debtors, interviewing 38 witnesses and looking at other jurisdictions.[61] Although the balance of these opinions was strongly in favour of retaining imprisonment on mesne process, the Commissioners sided with the minority.[62] They agreed that it was necessary in the fairly infrequent cases where there was a real risk of the defendant absconding, but otherwise it was 'a singular inversion of the usual course of justice...inconsistent with reason and natural justice' to presume that a defendant not only owed the full sum claimed but could not be trusted to appear and await judgment, and the safeguards against abuse were inadequate.[63]

Besides the objection in principle, the Commissioners felt pre-judgment imprisonment had other pernicious consequences. '[F]rom the unrestrained power of arrest, facility of credit, crowded gaols, and a Court of Discharge are successive and necessary consequences.'[64] Even in achieving its (questionable) aim of extracting the alleged debt through the threat of gaol it was inefficient and expensive; results suggested success in only one-quarter of cases without resort either to imprisonment or bail to the action, and it was more expensive than serviceable process. Moreover, when money was forthcoming it was often extorted from the defendant's family or friends.[65] The report ignored the reforms proposed in the first report and reiterated the complaints that the bail system invited corruption among the bailiffs and made inevitable the 'hired bail', since few reputable men would risk a public examination on their own credit.[66] For the Commissioners, imprisonment on mesne process except where flight was apprehended was indefensible in principle and unnecessary in practice.

One of them, Henry Stephen, penned a lengthy and elaborate dissent. Stephen skilfully marshalled the opinions of witnesses and consultees in support of the existing system, but his argument was premised almost exclusively on the importance of sanctions to underpin the essential credit structure of the economy. Stephen was prepared to assume from the plaintiff's affidavit that he had a good claim to the whole sum demanded and that the defendant was *prima facie* in wilful default, justifying coercive measures to make him meet his obligations.[67]

Given the sharp differences of opinion, it is unsurprising that legislation was delayed. From 1833 on, bills presented first by Campbell and latterly by Cottenham

---

[61] RC on the Common Law, PP 1832 (239), xxv.i (hereafter Fourth Report 1832).
[62] Kercher, 'Transformation of Imprisonment for Debt', 75–9.
[63] Fourth Report 1832, 27.   [64] Ibid., 11.
[65] Ibid., 12–13.   [66] Ibid., 22.
[67] Ibid., 46–86; Kercher, 'Transformation of Imprisonment for Debt', 78–9. Stephen's stance was supported in 'Fourth Report of the Common Law Commissioners' (1832) 8 LM 70–122.

proposed to restrict access to the debtor's person in exchange for improved access to his property, but until 1838 each bill foundered, usually in the Lords, where the dominating figure of Lyndhurst defended imprisonment on mesne process as harsh but necessary.[68] It was only by jettisoning wider proposals on post-judgment imprisonment and accepting that imprisonment on mesne process might continue on the basis of a judicial order rather than the plaintiff's affidavit, that a bill was finally passed.[69] Pre-judgment imprisonment was restricted essentially to cases where flight was feared, and then with the alternative of giving bail not exceeding the amount claimed (sections 1–3, 21).

The effect seemed to justify the reformers' contentions, for committals dropped rapidly from more than 4070 in 1838 to between 100 and 200.[70] Another commission, in 1840, felt it would be safe to abolish it completely, but that did not come about until 1869; however, as a means of securing appearance to answer a writ, bailable process was of minimal importance after 1838.[71]

PAYMENT INTO COURT

If plaintiffs were to benefit from judgment in default of appearance, those who admitted liability but contested its extent also deserved help. It was already open to a defendant to tender the amount he acknowledged to be due before an action was begun, or to pay that sum (and the costs of the action to that point) into court after the plaintiff's declaration, and in either case a plaintiff who declined the offer was at risk of all subsequent costs if he failed to establish his claim to a bigger sum. This facility, however, was only available for 'debts strictly so called'[72] and there were objections to making it general lest it enable rich men to buy off poor victims of their own culpability in offences with a strong moral flavour.[73] The Commissioners concurred that that would be 'contrary to every principle of justice', and while favouring a broader 'privilege', excluded it in cases of assault and battery, false imprisonment, libel, slander, malicious prosecution, criminal conversation, and seduction.[74]

[68] Kercher, 'Transformation of Imprisonment for Debt', 87–93; V. M. Lester, *Victorian Insolvency* (Oxford, 1995), 111–14. Lord Ashburton tellingly pointed out that barristers, unlike solicitors, were shielded from the realities of debt collection.

[69] Abolition of Imprisonment on Mesne Process Act 1838 (1 & 2 Vict. c. 100).

[70] Kercher, 'Transformation of Imprisonment for Debt', table on 95.

[71] *PP* 1841 (289), xii, 25.

[72] *Second Report 1830*, 52. There were statutory extensions in favour of magistrates and in cases of involuntary trespasses to land.

[73] See e.g. Serjeant Peake's evidence, *ibid.*, App. A9.

[74] *Ibid.*, 52–3. Brougham's law reform speech of 1828 had urged extension: *PD* 1828 (s2) 18: 127–233 at 189. Scarlett's suggestion that defendants should, in effect, be able to offer to pay in three months (providing sureties for performance) did not find favour: *First Report 1829*, evidence L31.

Defamation was a difficult case, for it was arguable that allowing payments in would keep unmeritorious cases out of court, and it was included in the special protection offered to newspapers and journals in 1843.[75] There were also doubts on whether a tender of payment in did, or should, constitute an admission and so deny the defendant the right to plead a defence. The Commissioners felt that it did, but offered a procedure which would circumvent this difficulty: a defendant might accompany his payment by a notice declaring that if his defence failed, he would propose damages at that same figure, and if the award proved to be lower, the plaintiff would become liable for the costs of assessing the damages.[76]

The topic was cursorily examined by the second commission, which suggested that in the excluded torts the judge might allow payment in if he chose,[77] but that was omitted from the Common Law Procedure Act which gave substantial effect to the original proposals.[78] In 1860 the facility was extended to detinue and conditional bonds[79] but it became most significant in personal injury claims, which had scarcely featured in the earlier discussions; the Commission report of 1853 had declared that most plaintiffs had as their object 'not merely compensation in damages, but vindication of honour or character'.[80]

Pleadings

THE NATURE OF COMMON LAW PLEADINGS

One of the most distinctive and controversial features of common law procedure was the role played by pleadings.[81] Pleadings began with the plaintiff's declaration, setting forth the essential features of his claim, and continued through a sequence of written exchanges between the parties which aimed to identify and define the disputed issues of fact and/or law which were essential to the resolution of the claim and to discard everything which was not directly relevant. This process was usually completed within three or four stages (declaration, plea, replication, rejoinder), and more summarily if the defendant demurred to the declaration on a point of law. It might, however, wend a tortuous course via surrejoinder, rebutter, and surrebutter, occasionally venturing into territory where the pleadings had no names.[82] At some point, however, the strict rules which governed each pleading ensured that the parties would be driven to joinder in

---

[75] Libel Act 1843 (6 & 7 Vict. c. 96).   [76] *Second Report 1830*, 52–4, 97.

[77] *Ibid.*, 33.   [78] Sections 70–3.

[79] Common Law Procedure Act 1860, s 25.

[80] *RC on the Common Law Courts*, PP 1852–3 [1626], xl (hereafter *Second Report 1853*), 33–4.

[81] Holdsworth, *HEL*, ix, 262–315; *Second Report 1830*.

[82] 'Principles and Practice of Pleading' (1828–9) 1 *LM* 1–32 at 9.

issue and thence to a trial before a jury (if there were facts in dispute), or before the judges in banc if it were a pure question of law.

In a system where the judge took an essentially passive part, such a deployment of pleadings, especially 'special pleadings', which discriminated more carefully between law and fact and ruthlessly pared down the issues, was convenient and economical. It spared the parties the expense of unnecessary witnesses and documentary proofs and enabled counsel to argue concisely on the relevant law. It made for short trials and could therefore be managed by a small number of judges.

Some commentators argued that besides this unglamorous and utilitarian function, pleadings fulfilled a further, more elevated one. They were said to underpin the logical and scientific structure which could apparently be found beneath the luxuriant wilderness of common law doctrine and practice.[83] Such a view became plausible once systematic studies of the rules and role of pleadings appeared, beginning with Gilbert's *History and Practice of Civil Actions* in 1737, and the few who delved into John Reeves's *History of English Law* would find ample evidence of the crucial part played by pleadings in the incremental development of substantive law.[84] Further publications, notably Chitty's popular *Treatise on Pleadings and the Parties to Actions* (1817), attested to the importance the profession attached to the subject and they culminated in Henry Stephen's highly influential *Treatise on the Principles of Pleadings in Civil Actions* (1824).[85]

Stephen and other enthusiasts for special pleading argued that one of its most valuable characteristics was in ensuring that separation of fact and law which corresponded to the respective functions of jury and judge, thereby eliminating the impurity of unreasoned jury discretion.[86] Properly deployed, it also assisted the common law's proper focus on remedies, making for an orderly development of each distinct form of action. Special pleading might therefore be seen as a conservative element which fitted into a conception of the common law no less 'scientific', but quite different from that produced by Blackstone.[87] Some legal theorists 'even raised [it] on a pedestal',[88] drawing analogies with algebraical equations, Euclidian geometry, or 'the strictest rules of pure dialectic'.[89]

Runnington admitted that some did not understand special pleading and affected to despise it,[90] but whether they understood it or not, few laymen shared the profession's pleasure in its logical perfection. Where enthusiasts saw a

---

[83] M. J. Lobban, *The Common Law and English Jurisprudence 1760–1850* (Oxford, 1991), 61–79.
[84] *Ibid.*, 61–3.
[85] Holdsworth, *HEL*, ix, 312.
[86] Lobban, *Common Law and English Jurisprudence*, 61.
[87] *Ibid.*, 207–9.
[88] *Ibid.*, 65.
[89] *Ibid.*, 65 (Charles Runnington).
[90] Holdsworth, *HEL*, ix, 312.

science, they saw unwieldy and arbitrary rules, many divorced from their original rationale, which were unintelligible to the unitiated and a trap even for the knowledgeable. The Common Law Commissioners admitted that 'considerable misapprehension popularly prevails upon the subject'[91] and the first article of the new *Law Magazine* conceded that it was 'universally condemned' outside the profession.[92]

And not only outside the profession. Brougham's great speech had included some strong condemnation of pleadings in action[93] and some of the severest critics were Bentham and his followers. Bentham was a devotee of a 'natural procedure' in which the parties would appear in person before the judge and orally explain their respective positions, though he also envisaged very simple written pleadings based on standard forms.[94] Bentham was not so much opposed to precision in pleadings as to the insistence on strict formality and restrictive rules which could easily defeat the ends of justice, especially in criminal cases, and to the complexities which necessitated the employment of specialists for even simple ones.[95] However, since the Benthamite ideal of pleadings really presumed the existence of a law code and a whole network of local courts, it was never a serious proposition and it was quite easy for a conservative critic to demolish James Mill's *Encyclopaedia Britannica* entry on pleading as visionary,[96] whereas the less radical reforms urged by George Graham in *The Westminster Review* were closer to the mainstream of critical opinion.[97]

Almost all critics were agreed that a vice of special pleading was the fictions which permeated it,[98] but the fictions were only the scarcely defensible outworks of the citadel. Closer to its heart were limitations on what a party might plead; rules which forbad duplicity and argumentativeness and enjoined certainty, sensible in principle but apt to be applied too narrowly, with mischievous consequences. These and other traps for the unwary generated devices designed to circumvent their mischief, such as colour and special traverses, and these in turn

---

[91] *Second Report 1830*, 45.   [92] 'Principles and Practice of Pleading', 1.
[93] *PD* 1828 (s2) 18: 202–12.
[94] Lobban, *Common Law and English Jurisprudence*, 127–31, 146–51.
[95] *Ibid.*   [96] 'Principles and Practice of Pleading', 2.
[97] [G.J. Graham] 'Law Abuses—Pleading' (1825) 4 *Westminster Rev.* 60–88.
[98] Even a defender asked rhetorically, '[h]ow happens it that so many absurd fictions are retained? Why, in one court, is it falsely said at the commencement, that the defendant is in the custody of the marshal? In another, that the plaintiff is indebted to the king? Why, in actions of assumpsit, are time and paper wasted in stating promises never made and never cared for in the proof? Why, in actions to recover property improperly detained, is it invariably asserted, that the goods came to the possession of the party by finding, without regard to the real manner of acquiring them? And why are Doe and Roe eternally appearing, whenever an expulsion is complained of, with a long story about a lease and an ouster, of which no-one believes a syllable?': 'Principles and Practice of Pleading', 13–14.

gave rise to a sticky web of rules governing their use.[99] Most of the rules could
be justified in the logic of the system and could be manipulated by the skilful
pleader, but the logic was an interior one which frequently led only to disputes
which were 'the merest legal conundrums which bore no relation to the merits of
any controversies except those of pedants'.[100] Even if the essential structure were
sound, it was strongly argued that it needed purging of obsolete, fictional and
otiose matter and the justification for each rule subjected to narrow scrutiny.

The current state of pleadings was also criticized from an opposite perspective however. Some argued that despite its apparent precision and logic, it did
not deliver its promises. This was because of measures taken by Parliament and
judges to palliate the injustices wrought by the strictness of the rules. Most of the
statutes were timid affairs; thus the statutes of jeofail, intended to allow technical errors to be remedied by amendment, were interpreted very narrowly, while
another act of Queen Anne's reign allowing defendants to plead more than one
defence merely transferred the injustice to the plaintiff.[101]

However, two devices, both common law inventions (though one was augmented by statutes) proved really damaging to the exquisite theory of special
pleading. The first was intended to counter the injustice of requiring the plaintiff
to provide precise details of his case in the declaration, details which must prove
to be consistent with the evidence led at trial. Any material variance between the
two, because it created an intolerable inconsistency on the record, was fatal to his
case even if he had succeeded at trial.[102]

The only statutory mitigation was an Act introduced by Tenterden in 1829
enabling variances between recitals of documents in pleadings and the originals to be corrected at trial.[103] Pleaders, however, had long been exercising their
ingenuity and inserted as many different counts as were necessary to cover all
the likely evidential outcomes, the same transaction being described in 15 to
20 ways with only minor differences. The Commissioners found attorneys a

---

[99] Holdsworth, *HEL*, ix, 262–307.

[100] Sir C. S. Bowen, 'Progess in the Administration of Justice During the Reign of Queen
Victoria', Committee of American Law Schools (ed.), *Select Essays in Anglo-American Law*, 3 vols
(Boston, USA, 1907, repr. of 1968), i, 516–57, 526. Lord Abinger CB claimed he had never known a
civil case decided from beginning to end on its merits: [J. G. Phillimore], 'The Progress of English
Jurisprudence' (1857) 12 ns *Westminster Rev.*, 511–32, at 530n.

[101] Holdsworth, *HEL*, ix, 315–17.

[102] *Ibid.*, 304–6; *Second Report 1830*, 34–44. An example given by the Commissioners was a felony
case which failed because the title of a justice was given as baron Waterpark 'of Waterfork' instead
of 'of Waterpark': *Second Report 1830*, 35. Littledale J. upheld a demurrer to a declaration on a bill of
exchange because it read 'A.D. 1834' instead of 'in the year of our Lord 1834': S. Warren, *The Moral,
Social and Professional Duties of Attornies and Solicitors* (1848), 195.

[103] *Second Report 1830*, 38; An Act to Prevent Failures of Justice on account of Variances, 9 Geo.
IV c. 15.

convenient scapegoat for this practice, maintaining that they had become too lazy to discover and acquaint the pleader with the full facts, but no doubt the pleaders' own self-interest had some part to play. Whatever the cause, the outcome was an expanded record, made even bulkier when the defendant retorted with multiple pleas of his own in answer to each count (it being a rigid rule of pleading that a plea must deal with each count). The unwieldy set of pleadings was only too likely to confuse a judge, lengthen the trial and give scope for captious technical objections.[104] Chief Justice Best was one of many witnesses/consultees who hankered for a return to 'the practice of our ancestors',[105] though quite when his golden age of pleadings existed he wisely left unsaid. Certainly the practice of the more scientific age was found wanting, for despite the inconvenience of multiple counts variances were still one of the most common causes for the failure of an action.[106]

These practices were easy to condemn but hard to remedy. The Commissioners considered various ways of discouraging plaintiffs, from costs sanctions through supplementary statements of agreed facts to a simple restriction on the number of counts, pronouncing the last the least objectionable and most practicable.[107] However, they sensibly preferred to focus on reducing the damage of variances, recommending that those which were not logically fatal to the plaintiff's case should either be treated as immaterial or allowed to be corrected at the trial.[108]

If the multiplication of counts was a response from plaintiffs to the rigours of special pleading, the general issue was a safeguard for defendants, especially when faced with the ineluctable choice between a plea and a demurrer, but in the eyes of Stephen and his allies, this was even more damaging. By pleading the general issue the defendant maintained a blanket denial of liability without disclosing the nature of his defence. This was the antithesis of special pleading, which was supposed to inform each party of the other's case, and the willingness of the courts to allow it an extended scope testifies to the judges' mistrust of the pleading system.[109]

---

[104] *Ibid.*, 36. Best CJ, in a typically forceful submission to the Commission, instanced two recent cases in his own court; in *Gully* v. *Bishop of Exeter* there were 43 separate issues before the court on the construction of the conveyance of an advowson, while in *Kingsbury* v. *Collins*, a case about emblements worth a trifling amount, the pleadings covered 38 brief sheets: *ibid.*, App. B2.

[105] *Ibid.*, App. B2.

[106] *Ibid.*, see e.g. evidence of J. L. Dampier and A. J. Wallace (App. A10, 11).

[107] *Ibid.*, 36–8.   [108] *Ibid.*, 38–44.

[109] *Ibid.*, 44–7; Holdsworth, *HEL*, ix, 270–1, 319–25, quoting Blackstone at 321: 'the science of special pleading, having been frequently perverted to the purposes of chicane and delay, the courts have of late in some instances, and the legislature in many more, permitted the general issue to be pleaded, which leaves everything open, the fact, the law and the equity of the case; and have allowed special matter to be given in evidence at the trial'.

In a succession of local and private Acts which expressly permitted various public officials to plead the general issue, Parliament had given the device its blessing and it had become popular with defendants of all sorts; it was apparently the uniform practice in ejectment and in cases on bills of exchange and insurance and was common in *assumpsit*.[110] But its popularity did nothing to endear it to the Commissioners. While they acknowledged a strong minority view that it should be encouraged and extended,[111] they correctly noted that most respondents shared their own opinion that the general issue was the biggest single obstacle to the effective operation of pleadings and the one most responsible for inflating costs and creating delays. It was wasteful because it led to unnecessary trials where there was no material fact in dispute; those trials were expensive because witnesses had to be at hand to prove matters which did not require to be proved; they were unsatisfactory because the *nisi prius* judge had to sort out the real issues on the day and present those which were for the jury to them intelligibly and accurately, while ruling on questions of law without the opportunity to consult his books or his brethren. Unsatisfactory trials led to more motions for new trials, which was an undesirable departure from the common law assumption that the trial verdict ought ordinarily to be final and had serious practical consequences for the administration of the courts: 'we know of no existing abuse of which the influence is so wide and the pressure so intolerable' reported the Commissioners.[112] It was very difficult for the court to decide the merits of applications for a new trial on the limited materials available and these motions were clogging them up; 99 were in King's Bench alone in Michaelmas term 1829, of which 53 were granted, the fresh trials having to be squeezed in alongside new business. And each new trial meant extra costs for the parties and vexation for the one successful at the first trial.[113]

THE NEW PLEADING RULES OF HILARY TERM 1834

In comparison with the evils produced by the general issue, the Commission found those of special pleading 'insignificant'.[114] Though they fought shy of suggesting that the statutory right to the general issue be abolished, for those outside that protective umbrella the scope of the general issue was to be severely curtailed. The plea of *non debet* in debt was to be abolished altogether; '*non assumpsit*' would no longer cover all sorts of reasons but would be a direct denial of the alleged promise—and would be inapplicable henceforth to negotiable instruments; 'not guilty' in any case was to be simply a denial of the wrongful act or omission and similar restrictions were suggested in trespass.[115]

---

[110] Holdsworth, *HEL*, ix, 321–2.
[111] e.g. A. J. Wallace, *Second Report 1830*, App. A11.
[112] *Ibid.*, 46.
[113] *Ibid.*, 46–7.
[114] *Ibid.*, 47.
[115] *Ibid.*, recommendations, 89–90.

The Commissioners also suggested 'the abridgement, in many cases, of the forms and language of pleading'.[116] They offered more succint specimen forms,[117] proposed to remove many formal entries (continuances) from the record, and to dispense with many reiterations. Pleadings were to be able to be filed during the vacation, with time running from the actual date of filing rather than from the start of the next term.[118] They proposed to curtail the abuse of sham demurrers and pleas, though evidently without great faith in the means proposed. They sought the abolition of the necessity for rules to declare, plead, etc. and the substitution of simple time limits;[119] and they suggested improvements to individual forms of action.[120] However, the Commissioners' energies were devoted mostly to multiple counts and the general issue and their approach to other parts of the subject was cautious if not timid. In particular, most of the fictions remained intact and it was still open for a party to take an objection to a defective pleading after the trial verdict.

Now special pleading was to be given full rein with many of the features which made it unintelligible to laymen and formidably difficult to lawyers intact; as Chitty pointed out, it would be necessary to employ a pleader for any but the most straightforward case.[121] In Holdsworth's view the Commissioners had fallen under the sway of Stephen.[122] However, there is no direct evidence for this, nor is it necessary to explain the outcome of their deliberations. Those they consulted were mostly of the same opinion and the questions that were circulated show that they were headed in that direction from the outset.[123] They recommended what most lawyers wanted, and it evidently met the views of the judges, since they used a new statutory power to adopt the recommendations wholesale in the new pleading rules issued in Hilary term 1834.[124]

These rules gave special pleading the chance to demonstrate that it did indeed possess the virtues claimed for it. Unfortunately the outcome was very different. The apotheosis of special pleading lasted fewer than 20 years until another Commission pronounced a damning verdict. The system was

entitled to great admiration and praise for its simplicity and usefulness [but] on a system so simple and sound in principle defects and abuses have been engrafted which have gone

---

[116] *First Report 1829*, 7.

[117] *Second Report 1830*, Examples of Pleadings, 90–101.

[118] *Ibid.*, 81–4.

[119] *Third Report 1831*, 30, 48–50 and recommendation 11; Holdsworth, *HEL*, ix, 306–7.

[120] *Third Report 1831*, 43–5 and recommendations 51–63.

[121] *Second Report 1830*, App. B4, and see 'Second Common Law Report' (1829) 3 *LM* 438–80 at 460.

[122] 'The New Rules of Pleading of the Hilary Term 1834' (1921) 1 *CLJ* 261–78.

[123] *Second Report 1830*, App. A1; see especially q. 1 on the general issue; Lobban, *Common Law and English Jurisprudence*, 207–16.

[124] An Act for the Further Amendment of the Law (3 & 4 Will. IV c. 42), s 1.

far to destroy its utility. This has arisen in great measure from an over-anxiety to ensure exact precision and certainty, and from the rigorous character of the rules introduced for the attainment of these objects.... But unhappily the rules framed to prevent...mischiefs have been abused, and they and certain arbitrary regulations and forms have caused the existence of...objections to the practice of special pleading, the justice of which we thoroughly feel.[125]

The Commissioners identified three major complaints about the new pleading rules. First, pleadings were still long and prolix,[126] evidently the attack on multiple counts had been at best a partial success. Secondly, what generated the most complaint was 'the requirement of unnecessary precision'.[127] Long-established rules as to certainty of time, place etc. (partly met by the device of the videlicet, which satisfied the formal requirements at the expense of truth and brevity), argumentativeness and duplicity, had formerly been capable of evasion by the general issue; now they were rigorously enforced the difficulty of complying with them was much more deeply felt. The third big complaint was the power of a party to withhold his objections to pleading defects until after the trial.[128]

Those responsible for the new pleading rules had badly misjudged their effect, for one scholar suggests that the number of cases which turned on points of pleading rather than substance rose from one in six to one in four.[129] Yet the first Commission had been sanguine indeed: 'the principles of the science of special pleading have been so successfully cultivated, and are at the present day so well understood, that the extent of such embarrassment would probably be small, and we should expect the whole law on this subject to be permanently settled within a short period, and at the expense of a few adjudged cases'.[130]

Stephen and company were confident in lawyers' ability to pick their way unscathed through the thorny thickets of the pleading rules and to formulate accurate pleadings with scientific precision, but in their entrancement with the science they neglected history. The ready resort to what they characterized as abuses—multiple counts and the general issue, unlike for example sham pleadings which were purely delaying tactics—was the best evidence of how unsatisfactory the rules were. Those very expedients were presumably most freely adopted in difficult cases, thereby masking the perils of true special pleading, especially along that crucial boundary between trespass and case. The new pleading rules actually reinforced the distinctions between forms of action which Tindal CJ had

---

[125] *First Report 1851*, 12.

[126] 'in great measure to be ascribed to the rigour with which pleadings are construed, which has introduced verbosity and length, from a desire to omit nothing, to be strictly precise, and to put everything in so many shapes that some one at least shall be found to square with the facts': *ibid.*, 17.

[127] *Ibid.*, 13.   [128] *Ibid.*, 19.

[129] Holdsworth, *HEL*, ix, 325.   [130] *Second Report 1830*, 51.

recently relaxed[131] and with ever more novel factual matrices in disputes it is no wonder that anxious pleaders sought safety in saturation pleading or that the range of potential challenges on essentially technical grounds was so large.

Moreover the Commissioners did not allow for the fact that attorneys and pleaders were not scientists engaged in a disinterested common endeavour to give the court an accurate version of their dispute, but partisans eager to deploy their arcane arts on behalf of their clients.[132]

For this sorry state of affairs the judges must take some responsibility. Many of them had been trained as special pleaders, though that did not necessarily make them pedantic. Maule for one was always 'ingenious to defeat technicalities',[133] but it is significant that in 1851 the *Law Magazine* expressed relief that less technically minded judges were being appointed.[134] The epitome of the pedantic sort was James Parke, Lord Wensleydale, immortalized as Baron Surrebutter in Hayes's *Dialogue*.[135] Parke more than anyone was responsible for that 'extreme refinement... [which] has resulted in tediousness, formality and chicane...'.[136] When technical points were not in issue Parke was capable of bringing broad principles, and not just of law, to bear on a problem, but he was indifferent, if not gratified, when a suitor was non-suited on a purely formal defect.[137] Belatedly, the judges began to realize that formality and strictness had been carried too far and sought to palliate it by allowing the extensive use of the replication *de injuria*, which 'was made to perform somewhat the same service as the general issue',[138] but that only complicated matters further.

Dissatisfaction grew steadily during the 1840s. In 1841 the *Law Magazine* could still describe the system as being in 'a high state of perfection',[139] but public

---

[131] *Williams* v. *Holland* (1833) 10 Bing. 112, described by J. Getzler, 'Patterns of Fusion', in P. Birks (ed.), *The Classification of Obligations* (Oxford, 1997), 157–92 at 173 n.76, as 'a long step towards burying the forms of action'.

[132] The chicanery Blackstone had condemned did not vanish: 'defendants who had no real defence availed themselves of the chance of a temporary success by pleading subtle and tricky pleas to write special demurrers for the mere purposes of delay... The reports abound in instances of objections of the most technical description, which have been held fatal on special demurrer, and the subtlety and ingenuity of pleaders are constantly exercised in raising points of a purely formal nature, more especially when it is desired to evade a substantial issue in fact': *First Report 1851*, 20. Examples are in R. E. Megarry, *A Miscellany-at-Law* (1955), 43.

[133] 'Common Law Reforms' (1851) 15 (s2) *LM* 121–40, at 139–40.

[134] *Ibid.*, 140.

[135] *Crogate's Case: A Dialogue in the Shades on Special Pleading Reform*, reprinted as appendix to Holdsworth, *HEL*, ix.

[136] 'Reforms in Common Law Procedure' (1850–1) 13 *LR* 327–54 at 344.

[137] C. H. S. Fifoot, *English Law and its Background* (1932), 154–5; Lord Coleridge, 'The Law in 1847 and the Law in 1889' (1890) 57 *Contemp. Rev.* 797–807, at 799–801.

[138] Holdsworth, *HEL*, ix, 326 n4.

[139] 'The New Local Court Bill' (1841) 25 *LM* 310–44, 326.

opinion was exasperated by high profile criminal cases where the prosecution failed on abstruse technicalities. Among the beneficiaries were Daniel O'Connell and Feargus O'Connor and other chartist ringleaders in the Plug Riots of 1842, and if some of the attacks on the pleading rules which followed were intemperate and exaggerated, forceful complaints by pamphleteers like J. G. Phillimore could not lightly be dismissed.[140]

Moreover, it could no longer be contended that pleadings in the English style were essential for the common law to operate effectively. The New York State Code, with pleadings stripped down to essentials, received wide and generally favourable publicity in England, especially through the proselytizing visit of its chief author D. D. Field.[141] The less daring revised pleading rules of Bengal (1849) helped maintain the momentum for change[142] and the Law Amendment Society produced a set of its own, an initiative commended in *The Times*.[143]

The most influential innovation was the procedure of the new county courts. Except for a few actions, the plaintiff was required to give only the barest information about his case and the defendant usually none at all about his defence. It was acknowledged that this could lead to the same problems at trial as the general issue and would be unsuitable for complicated commercial and land disputes, but the unpalatable fact was that county courts were taking large quantities of straightforward business, particularly simple contract debts, from the superior courts, and that litigants' dissatisfaction with their quality of justice was on the whole outweighed by its speed and cheapness.[144] The immediate response was an Act promoted by Lord Campbell in 1850, enlarging the judges' powers to make procedural rules,[145] and by then another commission on the common law courts was sitting.[146]

THE REMODELLING OF PLEADINGS

Pleadings were 'by far the most difficult and anxious' part of the new Commission's deliberations.[147] As noticed above, the Commission deplored the technicalities which disfigured pleadings, but was not prepared to recommend a radical

---

[140] See e.g. reviews in 'Special Pleading and Special Pleaders' (1847) 7(s2) *LM* 85–96 and 'Reform of the Law' (1846) 6(s2) *LM* 42–58.

[141] 'The Code of Civil Procedure in the State of New York' (1850) 12 *LR* 366–98, (1851) 13 *LR* 65–87; 'History of the New York Code and its Applicability to this Country' (1850–1) 13 *LR* 213–50; 'RF', 'The New Code of Procedure of New York' (1851) 14 (s2) *LM* 1–18.

[142] 'Special Pleading Reform' (1850) 12 *LR* 27–49.

[143] 'Reforms in Common Law Procedure', 327–54.

[144] See below, Ch. XII.

[145] Administration of Justice Act 1850 (13 & 14 Vict. c. 16).

[146] Instructions issued 13 May 1850 with Sir John Jervis as chairman.

[147] *First Report 1851*, 11

departure from the system; nor, wisely, did it adopt the suggestion that the draw-ing of pleadings should become the responsibility of a court official.[148] However, its approach was much more robust than its predecessor, some of whose unim-plemented proposals it adopted and extended. The most important change was one of the simplest. The several powers the courts possessed to allow amendment to pleadings were replaced by a sweeping general power applying to any proceed-ing, at a stroke relieving the parties of the fear that a minor slip would be fatal to their cause.[149]

Likewise, the obstructive possibilities of special demurrers were drastically reduced by a provision that whenever issue was joined on one, the court would give judgment on the substantive law at issue, disregarding defects of form and inessential omissions.[150] Objections based on uncertainty and the rules which grew out of it (duplicity etc.) were to be taken before a judge upon summons, though it was hoped that this would seldom prove necessary 'at least where the parties mean fairly'.[151] A mass of obsolete and unnecessary matter was simply abolished: most of the fictional statements; profert and oyer of deeds; express colour; special traverses; formal defences and conclusions all got their *quietus*.[152] The unimplemented recommendation of 1830 that the requirement of a rule to plead should be removed was carried out this time: '[i]t is inconceivable how this vexatious practice can have subsisted so long'.[153]

The general issue was not reinstated, though contrary to the Commissioners' recommendations its statutory manifestations were not removed,[154] but inconven-ient restrictions on the scope of pleadings were lifted. By leave of the court either party could now both plead and demur; some pleas could with leave be combined, and several matters could be pleaded together at any point in the exchanges.[155]

One intractable problem remained: the right of the losing party to bring the writ *non obstante veredicto* after trial, 'a great scandal and demands reform'.[156] The first Commissioners had suggested discouraging it by a costs sanction and their successors went further, proposing to enable the court to correct the record

---

[148] *First Report 1851*, 13–21.

[149] Common Law Procedure Act 1852, s 222, based on *First Report 1851*, 54.

[150] This, it was hoped, would 'at once put an end to all captious objections in respect of trivial slips, words left out, formal matter omitted, and other faults which, although quite immaterial to the merits of the case, and of no prejudice to the opposite party, are, nevertheless, at present ground of special demurrer': Recommendation 33, becoming Common Law Procedure Act, s 50.

[151] *First Report 1851*, 23.

[152] Common Law Procedure Act 1852, ss 49–90.

[153] Section 62; *First Report 1851*, 39.

[154] *First Report 1851*, 24; Rules of Trinity Term 1853, r 21. The privilege of pleading the general issue conferred by local Acts was repealed by Pollock's Act (5 & 6 Vict. c. 97), s 3.

[155] Common Law Procedure Act 1852, ss 80–4.

[156] *First Report 1851*, 52.

from the judge's trial notes or evidence produced at the hearing by the party whose verdict was challenged.[157]

As a pessimistic defender of special pleading had foreseen, the Commission's wish to retain it, albeit with large modifications, was unpopular with laymen[158] and further ground had to be conceded in the Commons, notably on special demurrers, requiring only that a pleading be 'good in substance'.[159] Even so, what was accomplished through the Common Law Procedure Acts and the judges' rules was a simplification and pruning of the system of pleading rather than a fundamental revision. Its pretensions to embody logic and science were no longer paraded and it was made more forgiving to errors which were now allowed to be inevitable. It was a long step towards the loose, Chancery-based model adopted after the Judicature Acts, and in its 20 years of operation it seems to have worked satisfactorily.[160] It is therefore not surprising that common lawyers were later inclined to proclaim its superiority and lament its demise.[161]

The Trial

VENUE

The Common Law Commission found 'the Rules relating to venue, and the whole doctrine connected with that subject…greatly in need…of revision. A reference to the books of practice will satisfy any inquirer of the intricacy and minuteness of the distinctions which the law of venue, and of change of venue, involves; and also of the inutility of the greater part of those distinctions. But it is open to other censure also. It affords to the defendant the means of vexation and delay; for it is notorious that the motion to change the venue is generally made with a dilatory or unfair purpose.'[162]

The rules distinguished between 'local' actions (mostly those involving claims to land or injuries to it) and 'transitory' ones. The latter afforded the defendant the greater opportunity for mischief, since by the 'common affidavit' he could obtain an order of course to remove the action into the county in which he claimed the cause originated. The plaintiff might restore it to his own preferred venue, but

---

[157] Ibid., 51–3; Third Report 1831, 28. It was the fundamental principle that the record must show a good cause of action or defence which meant that a verdict which was not formally justifiable could not be countenanced.

[158] 'H', 'Common Law Reform' (1851) 15 (s2) LM 121–41 at 128.

[159] Sections 50–1. Though Pollock CB upbraided draftsmen for not following the specimen forms provided, the Queen's Bench at least rapidly adopted a very broad interpretation of what was acceptable: 'JP', 'Pleadings at Common Law—Must They Be Good in Substance?' (1855) 22 (s2) LM 201–15.

[160] See e.g. Third Report 1860, 6.

[161] Holdsworth, HEL, xv, 108–10; Third Report 1860, 6.

[162] Third Report 1831, 14.

only on undertaking to produce 'material evidence' in his chosen county at trial, and at the peril of nonsuit if he did not. The Commissioners wanted to abolish transfers of course, requiring instead that the defendant show a particular reason, such as prejudice to a fair trial or the expense of many witnesses having to travel long distances. They also proposed, contrarywise, that local actions, which at that time could not be removed, should become removable as a matter of course into the county where the property was situated.[163]

When action was taken upon these recommendations, in the rules of 1853, it was in a very succint form: '[n]o venue shall be changed without a special order of the court, or a judge, without consent of the parties'.[164] There followed a period of uncertainty, for Parke and Wightman, charged with settling practice under the rule, promulgated the very conservative view that in transitory actions the defendant's common affidavit still raised a *prima facie* case for transfer which had to be rebutted by the plaintiff, and the Exchequer judges added a further gloss restricting it to actions which might be transferred under the existing rules.[165] Willes J., however, said that this was just a suggestion to which the judges had not agreed,[166] and according to Day 'the only rule observed in practice is that, after issue joined, the judge will take into consideration all the circumstances of the case, and use his discretion..., and that the court will very rarely interfere with the discretion so exercised'.[167]

SPECIAL CASE, ACCOUNTS, AND ARBITRATION

In some cases the parties had no dispute over the facts and could readily formulate the question of law dividing them. An Act of 1833 enabled them, after issue was joined, to take a special case direct to the court for a judgment, a more expeditious mode than first having the jury return a special verdict.[168] Until 1854 it had the drawback of allowing no scope for a writ of error (since the record disclosed none),[169] but was improved by removing the need for pleadings to be drawn up and a similar provision allowed a purely factual dispute to be taken directly to a jury.[170] Neither of these extended facilities was much used, perhaps because the simplification of pleadings reduced their attractions.[171]

---

[163] *Ibid.*   [164] Rule 18.

[165] J. C. F. S. Day, *The Common Law Procedure Acts* (1861, 1872 edn), 94–7; *De Rothschild* v. *Shilston* (1853) 8 Ex. 503, and see *Smith* v. *O'Brien* (1857) LJ 26 Ex. 30.

[166] *Church* v. *Barnett* (1870–1) LR 6 CP 119.   [167] *Common Law Procedure Acts*, 95.

[168] Law Amendment Act 1833 (3 & 4 Will. IV c. 42), s 25, on which see Lord Wynford in *MP* (1833), 2: 1234–5.

[169] *Second Report 1853*, 26–7.

[170] Common Law Procedure Act 1852, ss 42–8. The proposals were welcomed in 'H', 'Common Law Reform', 130.

[171] Day, *Common Law Procedure Acts*, 6.

There were cases unfit for jury trial because the question involved the examination of disputed accounts too complicated for jurymen. The old common law action of account had become so mired in technicality that it was obsolete, the auxiliary jurisdiction of Chancery being the usual recourse.[172] Instead, judges were often ready, usually with the connivance of counsel, to suggest a reference to arbitration by a barrister, and such suggestions were apt to become quite coercive.[173] When the Commissioners suggested that a judge be empowered to insist upon arbitration either before trial upon the application of either party or at trial of his own motion, they were going against a sizeable body of professional opinion which feared this power would be too freely used, especially at Assize. It was said that arbitration was inclined to be slow (because the arbitrator would not give it a high priority), expensive and, since barristers were often unfamiliar with mercantile accounts, inexpert.[174] Nevertheless, the proposal was repeated by the second Commissioners, coupled with recommendations to abolish the frequent adjournments which were the bane of arbitrations.[175] It was more acceptable now that there were masters to whom the reference could be made, though the parties might choose their own arbitrator instead.[176] County court judges outside London were indignant at also being given this role and quickly secured the unpalatable provision's repeal.[177] The masters were initially overwhelmed by references and had to resort to the bar for assistance, and since the masters themselves were not always competent to unravel commercial accounts, businessmen remained dissatisfied with the quality of the service they received.[178]

SUMMONING THE JURY

This was also encumbered with obsolete practice, pithily denounced by the second Commission as entailing 'forms useless and expensive, and a source of irregularities which sometimes defeat justice'.[179] In the Common Law Procedure Act 1852, section 104 the old writs of *distringas* (Queen's Bench) and *habeas corpora* (Common

---

[172] *Second Report 1830*, 25. For the history of this action, see S. F. C. Milsom, *Historical Foundations of the Common Law* (2nd edn, 1981), 275–82.

[173] *Second Report 1830*, App. A 6, 10, answers of G. Long and J. L. Dampier; and see C. Hanly, 'The Decline of Civil Jury Trial in Nineteenth Century England' (2005) 26 *JLH* 253–78, at 259 n38.

[174] *Second Report 1830*, 25, 77–8 and App. A, answers to q. 23; C. Jay, *The Law* (1868), 328–30. For sarcastic comment on the 'briefless barristers' given references 'simply because the judge prefers grouse to arithmetic', see 'The New Procedure Act' (1854) 21 (s2) *LM* 121–41 at 123.

[175] *Second Report 1853*, 4–6.

[176] Common Law Procedure Act 1854 (17 & 18 Vict. c. 125), ss 3, 6.

[177] *Ibid.*

[178] 'Results of the Common Law Procedure Acts, 1852 and 1854' (1858–9) 6 (s3) *LM & LR* 248–59, at 256. See below.

[179] *Third Report 1831*, 64–5; see also *First Report 1851*, 12–13. Unauthorized customary practices persisted: J. F. Cleave, 'On the Summoning of a Jury' (1910–11) 36 (s5) *LM & R* 308–15.

Pleas), which were issued contemporaneously with the *venire* and premised on its failure to take effect, were replaced by a simple precept to the sheriff.

The *nisi prius* record was also unduly cumbersome, though here the complaint was of expense alone. In theory the record was made up as the pleadings were exchanged and entered, and when the parties joined issue a copy, which had to be 'passed' (certified as accurate), was made for use at the trial. The reality had long been that the parties' attorneys undertook these duties and did not even produce the original until issue was joined, when both original and copy were made together; appearances were preserved by rules requiring the original to be in place before the copy.[180] The expensive ceremony of passing the record continued purely for the benefit of officers entitled to the fees; one case in the King's Bench was instanced which cost £20–13s-6d, and even a record of only 30 sides cost £1 6s,[181] in addition to the attorney's charges for doing the real work. The second Commission felt that the copy itself was of value as a record of the pleadings, but from 1852 it had merely to be entered without the ritual of passing and sealing.

TRIALS

Successive Commissions were concerned with the unfairness which frequently resulted from the established order of trial proceedings. The plaintiff's counsel[182] would open his case and call his evidence; then the defendant would either follow suit or, if he declined to call any evidence, would attack the plaintiff's case. The choice for the defendant was both important and difficult. If he called evidence, he would have no chance later to smooth out inconsistencies or put the best gloss on his witnesses; instead, the plaintiff would have the right to reply, and would highlight the weaknesses in the defence case. If the defendant called no witnesses, he could instead mount a damaging attack on the plaintiff's evidence without affording him the chance to reply.[183] A large body of professional opinion emphasizing the practical benefit of this arrangement in keeping down the length of cases, placed great weight (rather questionably) on the judge's summing-up in holding the balance.[184]

However, the injustice of the restrictions became more manifest with the admission of the parties to give evidence and so expose themselves to cross-examination and unanswered animadversions,[185] and with the Commissioners

---

[180] Holdsworth, *HEL*, ix, 258–9.

[181] *Third Report 1831*, App. E1.

[182] Usually; in fact whichever party would be entitled to a verdict if no evidence were given on the opposite side: Day, *Common Law Procedure Acts*, 259–60.

[183] *Third Report 1831*, 68–9; *Second Report 1853*, 8–9.

[184] *Third Report 1831*, App.B, answers of barristers to q. 25.

[185] *Second Report 1853*, 8.

optimistic that counsel would confine themselves to a brief opening if their opportunities were enlarged the inconvenience of lengthening trials yielded to 'justice' [186] and by the Common Law Procedure Act 1854 a defendant who called evidence was allowed to sum up in conclusion; if he did not, the plaintiff was to be allowed the same privilege at the end of his own evidence.[187] This may have led to tedious speechifying[188] but there would be no going back.

The same Act rectified an indefensible omission, empowering the judge to adjourn the trial where a party was surprised by unexpected evidence. Hitherto a jury trial had proceeded unstoppably and the disconcerted party had to submit to a nonsuit or an adverse verdict and commence further proceedings.[189]

THE COMMON JURY

The nineteenth-century civil jury was an institution in decline, but neither the extent of the decline nor its rapidity should be overstated.[190] Following a centuries-long process whereby the judge gradually circumscribed the role of the jury, '[t]he emasculation or diminution of the civil jury was then followed in the second stage by its elimination'.[191] The second stage is of course easier to chart, but land-mark decisions signpost the encroachments of judges quite clearly. For instance, the 'active model' of the special jury of merchants described by Oldham[192] had presumably ceased by the time Parke and Tindal insisted that expert knowledge was the province of witnesses not jurymen.[193] Contemporary writings also help to pinpoint the position at particular moments in time.[194]

Judges had curtailed that rough, common sense equity that juries brought to the judicial process by enlarging the scope for applications for new trials on the grounds that the jury's finding was against the weight of the evidence (in effect against the judge's own view). They remorselessly turned questions of fact,

---

[186] *Ibid.*, 10.

[187] Section 18.

[188] *Results of the Common Law Procedure Acts 1852 and 1854*, 256

[189] Section 19; *Second Report 1853*, 10.

[190] M. J. Lobban, 'The Strange Life of the English Civil Jury, 1837–1914', in J. W. Cairns and G. McLeod (eds), *The Dearest Birth Right of the People of England* (Oxford, 2002), 173–-215; Hanly, Decline of Civil Jury Trial'. For the jury in criminal trials see Vol. XIII, pp. 115–21.

[191] J. Getzler, 'The Fate of the Jury in Late Victorian England: Malicious Prosecution as a Test Case', in *Dearest Birth Right of the People of England*, 218–37 at 218.

[192] J. C. Oldham, 'Jury Research in the English Reports in CD-ROM', in *Dearest Birth Right of the People of England*, 131–53, at 136.

[193] R v. *Frederick Rosser* (1836) 7 Car. & P. 648; *Manley* v. *Shaw* (1840) C. & M. 361; see Lobban, 'Strange Life of the English Civil Jury', 173.

[194] Notably 'The Province of the Judge Distinguished from the Province of the Jury' (1834) 12 *LM* 53–74; [T. Starkie], 'Of the Distinction Between Law and Fact' (1844) 1 *LR* 37–61; 'Of the Functions of the Judge as distinguished from those of the Jury' (1845) 2 *LR* 27–44; W. Forsyth, *History of Trial by Jury* (1852).

especially in contract cases, into questions of law for their own decision and narrowed the questions of fact which were put to the jury, and the new pleading rules
of 1834 reinforced this trend by drastically curtailing the use of the general issue.
When the resulting need to synthesize, arrange, and present the facts in a suitably clear-cut form threatened to overwhelm the available judge-power a marked
trend towards objectification of intention set in which enabled much of the more
instance-specific and witness-heavy fact-finding to be dispensed with.[195]

The attractive view that this phenomenon, found in the United States as well as
England, had an ideological basis, that '[t]hus did the political economy of the law
vanquish the moral economy of the jury',[196] has fallen out of favour. It seems more
plausible to postulate that judges wished rather to improve the consistency and
'correctness' of decisions at law, increasing predictability and enabling disputes
to be resolved by reference to a law book rather than a court while disarming critics of uncodified law's 'primitive' state.[197]

The degree of control obtained by judges must not be exaggerated. The egregious examples of 'perverse' jury verdicts exposed in the newspapers were probably the tip of a considerable iceberg.[198] They were sometimes attributed to sheer
ignorance and stupidity, but common juries were believed to be endemically
prejudiced for and against certain types of litigant: favourable to shopkeepers
and traders, hostile to attorneys and railway companies.[199] Juries were not always
helped by judges, some of whom (like Abinger CB) courted rebuffs by blatant
attempts to lead them down the path they favoured while others, like Littledale,
offered them too little guidance.[200] Juries were seldom found in the courts of
requests and few litigants chose the jury option in the county courts.[201] The
common jury seemed to many hard to defend on logical or practical grounds.[202]
Laymen no longer felt the jury a necessary or effective safeguard against waywardness, bias, or politics in judges and many lawyers were impatient with the
involvement of non-professionals in the trial process.[203]

[195] Getzler, 'Fate of the Jury in Late Victorian England', 218–24.
[196] *Ibid.*, 219.
[197] *Ibid.*, 219–20.
[198] For examples, see Lobban, 'Strange Life of the English Civil Jury', 174–5 and for the notoriously
independent Welsh juries, R. W. Ireland, 'Putting Oneself on Whose Country? Carmarthenshire
Juries in the Mid-Nineteenth Century', in T. G. Watkin (ed.), *Legal Wales: its Past, its Future* (Cardiff,
2001), 63–88.
[199] Lobban, 'Strange Life of the English Civil Jury', 175.
[200] 'J.F.', 'Trial Without Jury' (1855) 22(s2) *LM* 8–17.
[201] See below, p. 899.
[202] Lobban, 'Strange Life of the English Civil Jury', 175–9. One of the best-known attacks was J.
Brown, *The Dark Side of Trial by Jury* (1859), summarized in 'The Jury System in England' (1859) 7
(s3) *LM & LR* 318–43.
[203] Hanly, 'Decline of Civil Jury Trial', 269–74.

Yet the critics did not have things all their own way. Even within the Law Amendment Society opinion was divided over the merits of jury trial, and the Society went no further than wanting it made optional.[204] The jury was defended upon several grounds. Some commentators, such as William Forsyth, while deploring its attenuated role, nevertheless argued that allowing citizens to participate directly in the judicial process had an educational and constitutional role,[205] though the level of participation outside a few places and a few groups who served as special jurors, was so low that 'it was hardly a democratic institution'.[206] The second Commissioners urged more practical considerations, some running counter to the limitations judges were busily creating. They applauded the fact that 'the merchant, the man of business, the agriculturalist, the man of the world, the man of science, bring each his peculiar knowledge and experience to assist in determining the varied questions which arise…', though it had by then been ruled that special knowledge should not to be shared with other jurors.[207] Likewise, welcoming the way 'the tendency of the professional judge to look only to the strict letter of the law, is corrected and tempered by the opposite tendency of the jury to take a more enlarged and liberal view, according to the morality and equity of the case', was to adopt a view of the jury's function which was widely criticized.[208]

Aside from cases involving complicated accounts[209] the Commissioners recommended the retention of jury trial as the standard mode, while enabling the parties to elect for trial by a judge alone.[210] Disappointed reformers and conservatives alike rightly predicted that it would prove a dead letter;[211] until 1883 more than 90 per cent of eligible cases continued to be tried by a jury and the notion that the 1854 Act was a major landmark in the history of jury trial is misleading.[212]

However the Commissioners felt the force of criticisms of country juries' quality and suggested that the property qualification in country districts (which Peel's Act of 1825 had set at premises of £10 freehold or £20 leasehold annual

---

[204] Lobban 'Strange Life of the English Civil Jury', 178–9.

[205] Forsyth, *History of Trial by Jury*, Chapter 18, 'The Jury as an Institution'.

[206] Lobban, 'Strange Life of the English Civil Jury', 193–8 at 195.

[207] *Second Report 1853*, 4; see above, p. 595.   [208] *Ibid.*   [209] See above, pp. 592–3.

[210] *Ibid.*, 5; Common Law Procedure Act 1854, s 1. It was subject to the judge's permission, and the judges never made the rules envisaged in the statute prescribing types of case in which express permission would not be required.

[211] 'J.F.', 'Trial Without Jury'; 'Results of the Common Law Procedure Acts', 248–59, at 256. Campbell claimed the credit for introducing qualifications and conditions which effectively annulled it (M. S. Hardcastle (ed.), *Life of John, Lord Campbell*, 2 vols (1861), ii, 328). Pollock CB would not dispense with one where essential facts were in dispute: C. Fairfield, *Some Account of George William Willshere, Baron Bramwell of Hever and his Opinions* (1090), 39.

[212] R. M. Jackson, 'The Incidence of Jury Trial During the Past Century' (1938) 1 *MLR* 132–44, at 139; Hanly, 'Decline of Civil Jury Trial', 253.

value) should be raised.[213] This found its way into the Common Law Procedure Bill of 1853 but was withdrawn because of fears that it would seriously diminish the pool of jurors. The same argument defeated attempts in 1869 and 1870 to raise the lower limit to £30 rateable value, £50 in the larger towns.[214]

The Commissioners also tried to improve the jury by enforcing the neglected rule that special jurors were eligible to serve on a common jury, yet under-sheriffs went on in their accustomed way.[215] Coleridge's reform proposals in the 1870s included a provision that each common jury should contain at least one special juror but it fell to the argument that the disparity between the payments they received would cause friction on the jury.[216]

In other respects the second Commissioners were less reform-minded than their predecessors, surprisingly given that criticism of the jury was by then more widespread and vigorous. The first Commissioners were greatly concerned about the requirement for unanimity and the crude coercive measures—deprivation of fire and food—inflicted on jurors to bring that unanimity about. Their remedy was surprisingly radical: at the end of 12 hours, unless the jury sought more time, a majority verdict of 9–3 was to be acceptable.[217] Evidently it was too radical for the time.

The second Commissioners were also embarrassed by the locking up of juries, but did not advocate majority verdicts, holding that the present system ensured a 'full and complete discussion' (not a view every commentator would have endorsed) and that it would encourage more applications for a new trial ('which might, not unreasonably, be entertained').[218] Informed opinion was divided about majority verdicts.[219] Cranworth preferred the Commission's less drastic proposal that after 12 hours the jury should be discharged and though Campbell LCJ persuaded the Lords to adopt majority verdicts the clause was lost in the Commons, where fears that it would be extended to criminal trials were too strong.[220] Campbell tried again in 1859, provoked by his personal experience of a hung jury in *Smith* v. *GNR*, but strong opposition led by Lyndhurst defeated him. It was therefore most unwise of Coleridge to propose a smaller jury of seven,

---

[213] *Second Report 1853*, 6. Peel was seeking to increase the number of potential jurors and was supported by Scarlett and Brougham: *PD* 1825 (s2) 13: 798–801.

[214] Lobban, 'Strange Life of the English Civil Jury', 198–9.

[215] *Second Report 1853*, 6; *Third Report 1860*, 8.

[216] Lobban, 'Strange Life of the English Civil Jury', 203–4. Special jurors were paid a guinea, common jurors a shilling.

[217] *Third Report 1831*, 69–70.

[218] *Second Report 1853*, 6–8.

[219] For opposition, see G. Rochefort Clarke, *Unanimity in Trial by Jury Defended* (1859).

[220] Lobban, 'Strange Life of the English Civil Jury', 205–6; Hardcastle, *Life of Lord Campbell*, ii, 324.

or even five, with provision for a majority verdict, and to apply both to all but the most serious criminal offences. He failed in 1872 and again in 1874, even though this time he had uncoupled it from the criminal side; evidently it lacked general support.[221]

SPECIAL JURIES

Although the term special jury bore several meanings and was most accurately used to describe a 'struck jury',[222] it was particularly associated with the juries of London merchants and businessmen on whose mercantile experience Lord Mansfield drew extensively in creating a coherent body of commercial law. The special jury was not confined to commercial cases however, and if, as seems likely, Mansfield manipulated the process to secure suitable juries for his laudable purposes, jury packing was also said to occur in the much less benign context of state trials, like Wooler's for seditious libel in 1817.[223]

Such complaints were voiced with characteristic vehemence by Bentham in a pamphlet of 1808 prudently left unpublished until 1821.[224] Bentham was disappointed with Peel's reforms in the County Juries Act of 1825, an attempt to improve the quality of the special jury (often well short of Mansfield's 'knowing and considerable merchants'[225]) by confining eligibility to merchants, bankers, and esquires. Peel also tried to reduce the likelihood of gerrymandering by replacing the selection of names for the panel by the sheriff and ordinary by ballotting.[226]

In specifying qualifications the Act was a failure. The terms were not defined, so giving local officials discretion. Busy and successful businessmen anxious to avoid jury duty could sometimes get themselves downgraded to the common jury list where the chances of being called were much smaller, while men for whom a guinea a trial was attractive insinuated themselves onto the list; exponents of this 'guinea trade' hung around the courts in the hope of being co-opted as talesmen when the jury was incomplete.[227]

---

[221] Lobban, 'Strange Life of the English Civil Jury', 206.

[222] One which was the outcome of a special procedure whereby the parties were allowed to strike names off a longer than usual list of jurors.

[223] J. C. Oldham, 'Special Juries in England: Nineteenth Century Usage and Reform' (1987) 8 *JLH* 148–62 at 148–50.

[224] *The Elements of the Art of Packing, as Applied to Special Juries, Particularly in Cases of Libel Law* (1821).

[225] *Lewis v. Rucker* (1761) 2 Burr. 1167, 1168, quoted in Oldham, 'Special Juries in England' 149.

[226] 6 Geo. IV c. 50, ss 31–2; Oldham, 'Special Juries in England' 155–6.

[227] *Ibid.*, 156–8.

As that suggests, the special jury was in frequent demand, sometimes for discreditable reasons. Securing a different panel for each trial was costly to litigants and burdensome to jurors, making up half of the £24 a special jury usually cost.[228] It bred delays, so defendants with no case were liable to demand it on that account.[229] Even when sought with more legitimate motives it was less often for any commercial expertise than for social reasons: what was wanted was 'their more cultivated minds and superior intelligence'.[230] In some places the pressure on a comparatively small number of special jurors led them to complain;[231] for example in 1865 there were 190 special jury trials in London and 111 in Middlesex, with only 4100 and 1000 special jurors respectively;[232] one enterprising official ran a profitable sideline in arranging false excuses.[233] Following adverse press comment and an influential pamphlet by T. W. Erle, the associate of the Common Pleas, matters came to a head at the Queen's Bench *nisi prius* sittings of February 1867, when every special jury case had to be put off because the jury was incomplete. Mr Justice Shee's dismayed plea for legislative action brought about an enquiry.[234]

The fruits of that enquiry, the Juries Act 1870, extended to London and Middlesex the procedure established for the rest of the country in 1852 on the recommendation of the second Common Law Commissioners, namely, a single panel for all trials at a sessions or Assize.[235] The pool of qualified jurors was enlarged and any pretence that commercial or other special knowledge was their distinguishing feature was abandoned by creating as alternative qualifications the occupation of a dwelling house rated above £100 in towns and £50 elsewhere; or of a farm rated at £300; or of other premises rated at £100.[236] The Act, however, did nothing to improve the accuracy of the lists, from which many eligible persons (several thousand in Middlesex) were omitted through the deliberate act or indolence of the overseers.

---

[228] *First Report 1851*, 43. The rest went in jurymen's expenses.

[229] Oldham, 'Special Juries in England', 158–9. Lobban, 'Strange Life of the English Civil Jury', 192, points out that the delaying potential was reduced after 1852 (1870 in London and Middlesex) once it was no longer necessary to empanel a new special jury for each case.

[230] Quoted in Oldham, 'Special Juries in England', 151.

[231] Lobban, 'Strange Life of the English Civil Jury', 199–200.

[232] *Ibid.*, 196. These made up 22.3% of the civil suits heard in the superior courts in London and Westminster. For earlier figures see Oldham 'Special Juries in England', 152.

[233] Lobban, 'Strange Life of the English Civil Jury', 200.

[234] *Ibid.*, 199–200.

[235] Juries Act 1870 c. 77, ss 11–15, 17, 19; Common Law Procedure Act 1852, s 108, based upon *First Report 1851*, 43. London and Westminster were exempted following representations from City merchants that being kept away from their business for a week or more would be more inconvenient than more frequent absences to try single cases.

[236] Juries Act 1870, s 6.

Post-trial Proceedings

'APPEALS'

The procedures by which a judgment of one of the courts of common law might be challenged were characterized by utter incoherence.[237] The most venerable (and expensive) was a writ of error, which offered fresh proceedings rather than a correction and required an error visible on the face of the record. If no error was visible—if, for example, the judge had wrongly refused to admit evidence—there could be no writ of error, whereas even an error immaterial to the outcome of the trial would secure a verdict for a new trial.

The location of this corrective mechanism depended upon the court in which the error occurred. The King's Bench had jurisdiction over errors in Common Pleas but not over the Exchequer, which had an internal 'appeal court', known as the Exchequer Chamber. In 1585 a differently constituted court confusingly bearing the same name (this one comprising the Exchequer barons and the judges of the Common Pleas) had been given jurisdiction over writs of error from the King's Bench.[238]

A means of challenging verdicts with no error on the record was the bill of exceptions created by the Statute of Westminster 1285. The bill covered, inter alia, 'improper rejection or admission of evidence, or...erroneous direction in point of law',[239] but did not lie against the Crown. It issued directly to the Exchequer Chamber, by-passing the sitting of the court in banc, and was as rigid as the writ of error in not allowing any distinction between material errors and others.[240]

Finally, there was the possibility of a motion for a new trial, evolved by the courts themselves and urged by Mansfield in 1757 as a necessary corrective to the waywardness of juries.[241] Unlike the bill of exceptions, the motion carried the case to the originating court in banc, with the trial judge sitting alongside his colleagues. The decision of that court was final, though a disappointed applicant might still be able to resort to a bill of error. To dissuade parties from resorting to bills of exceptions the courts at one time followed on these motions the practice on bills of exceptions in granting a new trial automatically if an error was shown, but by the 1860s they were adopting a more flexible approach, altering the verdict when the case was clear enough to warrant it.

Though this state of affairs was evidently unsatisfactory, improvements were slow and hesitant, perhaps because common law practitioners and judges reposed great confidence in verdicts in banc and reprobated the want of finality

---

[237] Holdsworth, *HEL*, i, 213–18, 222–4. For the court of Crown Cases Reserved and the later Court of Criminal Appeal, see Ch. VIII.

[238] *Ibid.*, 242–5.

[239] *Second Report 1853*, 28.

[240] Holdsworth, *HEL*, i, 223–4.

[241] *Ibid.*, 225–6.

in Chancery. In 1830 Brougham's measure combined the two differently constituted versions of the court of Exchequer Chamber in a single court comprising the judges of all three common law courts, those from the court where a case originated not sitting.[242] The procedure for taking a case there, however, remained notable for 'unnecessary delay, expense and complexity'[243] until the Common Law Procedure Act 1852 substituted for the writ of error a simple memorandum to a master; it also removed other inconvenient features, notably by enabling the court to alter the verdict rather than simply direct a new trial.[244]

The other two 'appeals' were improved by the 1854 Act. Motions for new trials were no longer confined to the originating court sitting in banc but might be taken to the Exchequer Chamber by way of error unless the decision of the court below was unanimous and it refused consent.[245] The same applied to the procedure by special case stated, which had hitherto been unable to reach a court of error because it showed no error on the record.[246] The Commission hoped that these changes would almost end bills of exceptions, but decided against recommending their abolition because of one circumstance in which the procedure might still be useful: where the court below was bound by a previous ruling of its own, a bill of exceptions took the case direct to the Exchequer Chamber, where it was open for reversal.[247]

Despite these changes, the common law appeals process remained unsatisfactory and untidy until the Judicature Acts.[248] Nor, in the short term, do they seem to have offered litigants much more encouragement to appeal. The number of appeal and error cases set down in the Queen's Bench was the same (15) in 1856 as in 1843, though they had risen somewhat in the other two courts. Motions 'for new trials, to enter verdicts and the like' were considerably fewer in the Exchequer and Queen's Bench and slightly fewer in Common Pleas.[249]

---

[242] Administration of Justice Act 1830 (11 Geo. IV and I Will. IV c.70).

[243] *Third Report 1831*, 32.

[244] Sections 32–6, based on *Second Report 1853*, 53–4.

[245] Sections 34–6.

[246] Section 32; Day, *Common Law Procedure Acts*, 16.

[247] *Second Report 1853*, 30. Day in *Common Law Procedure Acts*, 17 said that bills of exception had become rare.

[248] Holdsworth, *HEL*, i, 246.

[249] *RC on the Common Law (Judicial Business)*, PP 1857 (2268), xxi, sess. 2, returns of business, though Bramwell (q. 18) felt that the recent changes had much increased the sittings of the court of error. Original writs of summons in Common Pleas and Exchequer were at much the same level in 1843 and 1856; those in Queen's Bench had fallen appreciably, having been inflated by railway business. According to 'Judicial Statistics of 1862—Annals of the Civil Courts' (1864) 17(s3) *LM & LR*, the Exchequer Chamber had a strong tendency to affirm judgments (35).

JUDGMENT AND EXECUTION

One of the biggest frustrations for plaintiffs was that proceedings ground to a halt when the vacation started. It was particularly unfortunate for a man who had succeeded at trial but had been unable to enter judgment before the long vacation, for while the formal giving of judgment in open court had ceased long ago, a judgment entered in vacation would be dated in the next term and could not be enforced until then.[250] The same applied to judgments awaiting execution, and in the interim the defendant might have absconded or become insolvent; in the case of an ejectment he might remain in possession and exploit the land.[251]

This state of affairs was defended on two specious grounds: as giving the defendant a breathing space to find the money, and encouraging the parties to find a compromise. This, however, was purely fortuitous, and actually encouraged plaintiffs to hasten on with the suit to avoid running into the vacation. It was also said that allowing business to be done in vacation encroached upon the lawyers' necessary recuperation, though this scarcely applied to execution. The first Common Law Commissioners rejected both arguments, but the immediate fruits of their recommendations were limited to an act enabling the trial judge to direct immediate execution if he thought fit.[252] In the absence of any guidelines, judges varied widely in their attitude to such requests, and the second Commissioners disapproving of these inconsistencies, it was enacted in the Common Law Procedure Act 1852 that an execution from a trial in vacation should be issued after 14 days unless an application for earlier or deferred execution was granted.[253]

The 1852 Act also abolished ground writs ('which ought to have been effected long since'[254]) and simplified the procedure for reviving an execution which had lapsed because more than a year and a day had passed without it being carried out or because one of the parties had died. Hitherto it had been necessary to obtain a writ of *scire facias*, which set in motion a tedious and expensive formal process, but henceforth (following the precedent of the Joint Stock Companies

---

[250] See XIII, Pt. 1, pp. 83–115.

[251] *First Report, 1829*, 26–7; Holdsworth, *HEL*, ix, 259.

[252] *Ibid.*, 28–9; an Act for More Speedy Judgment and Execution (1 Will. IV c. 7), s 2.

[253] *First Report 1851*, 46–7; Common Law Procedure Act 1852, s 120. It became the general practice to allow 'immediate' execution (usually after four days) in ejectment and undefended debt cases: Day, *Common Law Procedure Acts*, 142–4.

[254] *First Report 1851*, 47; Common Law Procedure Act 1852, ss 121–2. The ground writ was a needless preliminary, usually ignored, before a writ could issue to the sheriff of the county where the property to be levied upon was.

Act[255]) the judgment would remain enforceable for six years and in case of a death a writ of revivor or a suggestion on the roll would suffice.[256]

2. THE LAW OF EVIDENCE IN CIVIL CAUSES[257]

Nineteenth-century Developments

In the mid-1820s two of Bentham's works on evidence appeared: the *Traité des Preuves Judiciares* in 1823 and the massive *Rationale of Judicial Evidence* in 1827.[258] They were more ambitious than his earlier writings on the subject and attracted more attention.[259] The *Rationale* in particular developed its attack on the English system of evidence at forbidding length, and had three main objectives: to establish the principle of non-exclusion; to suggest means for securing the availability and trustworthiness of evidence; and to provide guidance for the judge in assessing the weight of evidence. One of Bentham's most fruitful suggestions was to procure where possible 'pre-appointed evidence' through registration systems,[260] but the heart of his plans was a 'natural' system with few of the technicalities of the existing one, which he considered was calculated to further the interests of 'Judge & Co' by maximizing their opportunities to extract fees from litigants. In Bentham's world no potential evidence would be excluded unless on a utilitarian calculation its admission would cause undue delay, expense, or vexation.[261]

The extent of Bentham's influence on developments in evidence is much debated.[262] While many agreed with him in damning most of the exclusionary rules and improving the availability of evidence by registration, very few reformers supported a wholesale transformation along the lines he proposed. Bentham's works, and Bentham's disciples, were an important influence on this branch of the law, but only one of several such influences.

After Bentham the only important attempt to redraw the map of evidence was by J. F. Stephen. Largely responsible for the recent Indian code of evidence, Stephen was asked by the Attorney-General, Sir John Coleridge, to produce one

---

[255]   7 & 8 Vict. c. 110, s 68.

[256]   *First Report 1851*, 49–51; Common Law Procedure Act 1852, ss 128–9.

[257]   For evidence in criminal cases see XIII, Pt. 1, pp. 83–115.

[258]   An English translation of the *Traité* appeared in 1825. For his earlier writings on the subject see C. Allen, *The Law of Evidence in Victorian England* (Cambridge, 1997), 20.

[259]   There was a long review of the *Traité* by Thomas Denman in (1824) 40 *Edin. Rev.* 169–206 and of the *Rationale*, attributed to William Empson, in (1828) 48 *Edin. Rev.* 457–520. For these and other reviews, see W. L. Twining, *Theories of Evidence: Bentham and Wigmore* (1975), 100–9.

[260]   Twining, *Theories of Evidence*, 31–2.

[261]   Allen, *Law of Evidence in Victorian England*, 8–10; Twining, *Theories of Evidence*, 47–52.

[262]   For a summary, see Allen, *Law of Evidence in Victorian England*, 4–8.

for the home country in 1872. But Coleridge soon got cold feet and no other leading minister or judge was willing to promote the project, which did not even reach the publication stage.[263] Stephen's code was very much less radical than Bentham's, for its author regarded the existing law, however ill-organized, as 'full of the most vigorous sense...the result of great sagacity applied to vast and varied experience'.[264] His attempt to claim 'relevancy' as its ruling principle did not impress all critics, but his endeavours had his characteristic virtue of great clarity and the *Digest of the Law of Evidence* (1879) which Stephen derived from them became the standard resort for generations of bar students.[265]

Overall, English writings on evidence compared unfavourably with their American counterparts, for Wigmore produced the most erudite and authoritative account of its evolution and Thayer provided the most acute critical analysis.[266] There was no shortage of textbooks and treatises in England. S. M. Phillipps, Thomas Starkie, W. M. Best and John Pitt Taylor all produced substantial volumes,[267] which expanded through successive editions, displacing the smaller work of Sir Jeffrey Gilbert which had provided the foundation for evidence as a distinct legal subject.[268] None quite succeeded in achieving canonical status (Taylor probably came nearest[269]) and from 1892 they were rivalled by Phipson's work.[270] Their success, alongside a host of smaller works or ones restricted to criminal evidence, suggests a substantial market among practitioners, which owed much to two related trends.[271] One was that reported decisions hardened into rules carrying the authority of precedent. The relative freedom a judge had possessed in deciding what evidence to admit and what weight the jury ought to give to it was steadily narrowed between c.1780 and 1830 as rules of evidence assumed a clearer and more rigid form. Wigmore and others believed

---

[263] *Ibid.*, 27–9.

[264] K. J. M. Smith, *James Fitzjames Stephen, Portrait of a Victorian Rationalist* (Cambridge, 1988), 85.

[265] *Ibid.*, 84–8; J. B. Thayer, *A Preliminary Treatise on Evidence* (Boston, USA, 1898), 266–8. Regarded as a barrister's subject, evidence was not studied for solicitors' examinations nor in most law degrees: Twining, *Theories of Evidence*, 5 n.44.

[266] J. H. Wigmore, *A Treatise on the System of Evidence in Trials at Common Law* (Boston, USA, 1904–5); Thayer, *Preliminary Treatise on Evidence*. Holdsworth drew heavily on both works, especially Wigmore's, for his account in *HEL*, ix, 127–222.

[267] For details see Allen, *Law of Evidence in Victorian England*, 14–25.

[268] *The Law of Evidence* (Dublin, 1754). The 3rd edn (London, 1769) became a standard reference point. Lord Bathurst's *Theory of Evidence* was incorporated by Sir Francis Buller into his much-used *Introduction to the Law Relative to Trials at Nisi Prius* (1772).

[269] Thayer (*Preliminary Treatise on Evidence*, 511) described it as 'the chief English book on evidence'. It borrowed heavily from an American work, S. Greenleaf, *A Treatise on the Law of Evidence*; Twining, *Theories of Evidence*, 5.

[270] S. L. Phipson, *The Law of Evidence*. It is now in its 15th edition.

[271] Allen, *Law of Evidence in Victorian England*, 25.

that originated in civil trials, where counsel were present to argue from precedent and there was scope for appeals, and spread to criminal trials as counsel began to appear in them more regularly, but this has been questioned and the reverse chronology suggested, with the more assertive Old Bailey counsel carrying the challenges into the civil courts.[272]

Nisi prius reporting also contributed.[273] Some judges resented reports of decisions made in haste and often without hearing full argument,[274] and that the body of case law built upon such insecure foundations was notable more for increasing bulk than coherence. Ellenborough had declared that 'the rules of evidence must expand according to the exigencies of society'[275] but would probably have deplored the unselective accretion of cases which filled the textbooks. Writers zealously collected decisions, but most failed to meet the prescription that their works 'should be expositions of principles, not strings of cases'.[276] Through the regular citation of cases and treatises, however, differences in practice between circuits and between the common law courts gradually ceased and the law of evidence became a distinct, if not highly regarded, legal category.[277]

It was almost entirely a product of the common law courts. Equity judges claimed that, with certain exceptions, they followed the same rules, and equity counsel certainly argued that material included in depositions and affidavits should be excluded for contravening those rules;[278] indeed, one of Brougham's blunders as Lord Chancellor was to proclaim that he had read the evidence in advance without taking account of this.[279] However, the most important exclusionary rules essentially covered witness testimony and made little sense in a court without a jury and considering testimony at one remove from the witness's examination.[280] Through orders for inspection of documents and bills of

---

[272] T. P. Gallanis, 'The Rise of Modern Evidence Law' (1999) 84 *Iowa Law Rev.* 499–559.

[273] J. C. Oldham, *Law Making at Nisi Prius in the Early 1800s* (2004) 25 *JLH*, 221–48.

[274] See below, pp. 1212–13.

[275] *Pritt* v. *Fairclough* (1812) 3 Camp. 305, quoted in Allen, *Law of Evidence in Victorian England*, 31.

[276] Review of H. Roscoe's *Digest of the Law Evidence* (1844) n.s. 2, 201, quoted in Allen, *Law of Evidence in Victorian England*, 15. Thayer, *Preliminary Treatise on Evidence*, 511, noted that the most recent edition of Taylor's work extended to 1234 pages. Taylor himself had felt obliged to add at least 1300 more cases to his 2nd edition of 1855: Allen, *Law of Evidence in Victorian England*, 25.

[277] Allen, *Law of Evidence in Victorian England*, 25; G. Pitt-Lewis, *Commissioner Kerr, an Individuality* (1903) 51; F. J. Wrottesley, *On the Examination of Witnesses* (1919), 33.

[278] However, the rules were much less extensive than those at law: review of R. N. Gresley, *A Treatise on the Law of Evidence in the Courts of Equity* in (1837) 18 *LM* 133–52 at 135. There are different views of how closely equity followed the law: compare Holdsworth, ix, 127, quoting Hardwicke LC in *Manning* v. *Lechmere* (1737) 1 Atk. 453 ('the rules as to evidence are the same in equity as at law') with the 'wide variations' claimed by Keeton and Marshall (quoted in Twining, *Theories of Evidence*, 22).

[279] (1837) 18 *LM* 137.

[280] Thayer, *Preliminary Treatise on Evidence*, 529.

discovery equity provided facilities to bring evidence before common law courts which their own procedures did not allow, though reforms of the 1850s, giving these powers to common law and conversely allowing oral examination in equity narrowed the distinctions.[281] In general, equity judges seem to have been more relaxed about the admission of witness evidence and, in will cases particularly, more ready to accept parol evidence in the construction of documents.[282]

The textbooks swelled not only because of the proliferation of law reports but because they included matter which a rigorous analyst like Thayer regarded as extraneous.[283] Because the law of evidence lacked a clear theoretical basis, its boundaries were hazy, and books often included such topics as judicial notice, estoppel, rules of document construction, presumptions, and the burden of proof.[284] Attempts to set their topics within an overall body of principles seldom transcended the banal or the obvious. Even Best, the most 'Benthamite' among them, clung to the 'best evidence' rule which Gilbert had grounded explicitly in his Lockean philosophy, though he was driven to admit that it was 'more easily conceived than described'.[285]

The best evidence principle was not free from ambiguity. It might be presented as an exclusionary principle, demanding that all evidence meet a high standard of probative value, but it might also be interpreted in a much more generous way, enabling the party to rely on the best he could produce in the circumstances of the case. It had three particular applications: a potential witness should be called rather than having his evidence reported at second hand (the rule against hearsay); where a document was attested, the attesting witness should be called; where a document was relied upon, the original should be produced. These were sound rules, but they could exist independently of any unifying principle and the great shortcoming of the best evidence rule as an overarching principle was that the best evidence a party could produce in the circumstances would not always be accepted. [286]

The law of evidence as developed in the nineteenth century comprised several exclusionary rules along with others which were arguably not truly part of the subject at all and helped to obscure its central premises. Thayer excoriated the 'bastard sort of technicality' this engendered and felt that '[t]he few principles

---

[281] Holdsworth, *HEL*, xv, 141.

[282] Thayer, *Preliminary Treatise on Evidence*, 429–36. An example of the differences of approach between an equity judge (Romilly MR) and one whose experience was essentially at common law (Campbell LC) is in Allen, *Law of Evidence in Victorian England*, 38–9, discussing *Bright* v. *Legerton (No. 1)* (1860) 29 Beav. 60.

[283] *Preliminary Treatise on Evidence*, prefatory note.

[284] This was also true of *Halsbury's Laws of England*, xiii (1910).

[285] For Best see Thayer, *Preliminary Treatise on Evidence*, 488. For Gilbert, see Twining, *Theories of Evidence*, 1–2; Thayer, 490–1, and Gallanis, 'Rise of Modern Evidence Law' esp. 506.

[286] Thayer, *Preliminary Treatise on Evidence*, 484–507.

which underlie this elaborate mass of matter are clear, simple and sound. But they have been run out into a great refinement of discrimination and exception, difficult to discover and apply; and have been overlaid by a vast body of rulings at nisi prius and decisions in banc, impossible to harmonize or to fit into any consistent and worthy scheme.'[287] Nothing ambitious was attempted in the rules of court produced for the new SCJ,[288] and the express authorization in the Judicature Act 1894 for the Rule Committee to 'regulat[e] the means by which particular facts may be proven and the mode in which such evidence may be given' was practically a dead letter, since the only such rule made was given the narrowest of constructions by a judge of the Chancery division.[289]

Witness Evidence

EXCLUSION FOR INTEREST AND INFAMY

The most heavily criticized manifestation of the exclusionary principle was that which prevented certain witnesses from testifying, their incapacity resting upon either natural or artificial disqualifications. The former excluded persons whose testimony was reckoned unreliable either because of youth or mental incapacity or illness. This remained in the discretion of the judge, and although Sir Edward Clarke expressed misgivings at the judges' tendency to accept the testimony of very young children, especially in criminal cases, it received little scholarly or public attention.[290]

It was otherwise with artificial incapacity, which had two branches. One was disqualification through infamy, where conviction of certain offences branded a person too untrustworthy to give evidence;[291] the other was where a prospective witness had some material interest in the outcome of the proceedings. Though it may have originated in a desire to avoid a verdict imputing that a man of good social standing had given false evidence, it was usually predicated on the inherent unreliability of an interested witness.[292]

---

[287] *Ibid.*, 273, 511.

[288] The Judicature Act 1875, s 20 expressly provided that the new rules would not affect the law of evidence. RSC order 37, headed 'evidence generally' had a very narrow scope.

[289] Section 3. C. Mullins, *In Quest of Justice* (1931), 249–50, referring to *Rainbow* v. *Kettle* (1916) 140 *LT* 412. This was the more unfortunate as in 1895 the Court of Appeal had held that the power to dispense with technicalities could only be exercised under that statutory provision: *Baerlein* v. *Chartered Mercantile Bank* (1895) 2 Ch. 488.

[290] *Halsbury's Laws of England*, xiii, 569–70; *PD* 1888 (s3) 323: 1230. He may have had in mind cases under the Criminal Law Amendment Act 1885, see D. J. Bentley, *English Criminal Justice in the Nineteenth Century* (1998), 259.

[291] Allen, *Law of Evidence in Victorian England*, 95–6.

[292] *Ibid.*, 96–8. Its scope extended only to vested interests and Brougham pointed out the anomalies springing from accepting the testimony of those with contingent interests and from heirs apparent or expectant.

Although it was widely acknowledged that these rules often led to injustice they had become too deeply entrenched to be altered by the judges even had they wished to do so.[293] Instead, they were removed in stages by legislation, beginning in a very modest way with an Act of 1833 which lifted the bar on a witness for whom the outcome of the proceedings would be admissible as evidence in other proceedings, retaining as a safeguard that the verdict for or against the party on whose behalf he testified would be inadmissible in evidence for or against the witness.[294]

A bigger step was taken in 1842 when Denman, assured of the support of fellow judges, brought in a bill to abolish both types of incompetency.[295] The anomalies in the case of infamy were so gross that it found few defenders, and though delayed by parliamentary manoeuvering the bill became law in 1843 with both elements intact.[296] The admission of interested witnesses undercut arguments against allowing the parties themselves to give evidence, though Denman still shied away from that. The law on interest had grown so elaborate that it occupied 80 pages of Phillipps' treatise,[297] and though defenders argued that repeal would increase perjury the provision passed unopposed.[298]

When it came to admitting the parties' evidence, however, opposition was stronger. This was an article of faith with true Benthamites, and with Brougham, though his bill in 1845 rapidly emptied the House of Lords.[299] By then Denman had been converted and the Law Amendment Society produced a bill drafted by Pitt Taylor.[300] However, most judges were opposed, fearing perjury and longer trials; so was Lord Chancellor Truro and, surprisingly perhaps, the Law Society.[301]

What probably tipped the scales was the hard fact that the parties' testimony was admitted in other courts with encouraging results. Chancery might be discounted as essentially different but in the new county courts the parties were

[293] Hollams cites an instance concerning dues of the Port of London where every potential witness was disqualified by having a minute interest in the outcome: J. Hollams, *Jottings of an Old Solicitor* (1906), 13.

[294] Law Amendment Act 1833, s 26.

[295] Allen, *Law of Evidence in Victorian England*, 106; J. N. Bodansky, 'The Abolition of the Party-Witness Disqualification' (1981–2) 70 *Kentucky Law Rev.* 91–130.

[296] Bodansky, 'Abolition of Party-Witness Disqualification', 95–6, 107; 6 & 7 Vict. c. 85, often known as Denman's Act. Curiously, Denman had feared more opposition to this repeal than the disqualification for interest.

[297] (1843) 7 *Jur.* 296–7.

[298] Allen, *Law of Evidence in Victorian England*, 108–9, citing in particular a pamphlet by John Lowndes.

[299] *Ibid.*, 101.

[300] *Ibid.*, 115. Pitt Taylor was one of the first batch of county court judges, so he had some experience of hearing parties' evidence.

[301] Hardcastle, *Life of Lord Campbell*, ii, 292; C. Alderson, *Selections from the Charges…of Baron Alderson* (1858), 130; Allen, *Law of Evidence in Victorian England*, 117–18; Bodansky, 'Abolition of Party-Witness Disqualification', 103.

usually witnesses and often the only ones.[302] The Law Amendment Society clev-
erly polled the county court judges and almost without exception they declared
that, while perjury did abound, the greater facility for getting at the truth far
outweighed it.[303] Superior court judges may not have been convinced by argument, but the flight of litigants into the county courts was telling, and the big
London solicitors who ran the Law Society probably did not represent the views
of the profession.[304]

Brougham's Act passed with relatively little opposition, helped by an amendment which excluded actions for breach of promise and those stemming from
adultery.[305] When spouses were made competent and compellable in 1853 it was
subject to the latter exception[306] and both exceptions otherwise remained until
1869.[307] Thereafter the only limitation in civil cases was that communications
made during a marriage were privileged. Initially some judges were said to signal
their dislike of Brougham's Act by obstructive interpretation,[308] but the Common
Law Commissioners soon pronounced it to work admirably, complacently summing up the changes: '[s]uch is the gradual progress of opinion and intelligence.
A quarter of a century ago such a measure, if proposed, would doubtless have
been treated as a wild and dangerous innovation, altogether unfit to be entertained by the legislature.'[309]

OATHS

Removing the disqualification of witnesses for 'defect of religious principle'[310]
was a lengthier and more contentious process, for whereas the other forms of disqualification were of little interest to the general public, the judicial oath touched
religious sensibilities and became part of a wider debate on the place of the oath
in public life which culminated in the controversy over Charles Bradlaugh's
refusal to take the oath required of a Member of Parliament.[311]

---

[302] County Courts Act 1846 (9 & 10 Vict. c. 95), s 83, and see J. E. Davis, *A Manual of the Law of Evidence in the New County Courts* (1848). The clause seems not to have been debated: (1846) 33 *Leg. ob.* 409.

[303] (1850–1) 13 *LR* 395–418. One judge, Andrew Amos, an acknowledged expert on evidence, weighed in with a pamphlet, *On the Expediency of Admitting the Testimony of Parties to Suits* (Cambridge, 1850).

[304] Amos explicitly argued that it would help stem the exodus.

[305] 14 & 15 Vict. c. 99, ss 2–4. Allen, *Law of Evidence in Victorian England*, 103–4.

[306] Evidence Amendment Act 1853 (16 & 17 Vict. c. 83).

[307] Evidence (Further Amendment) Act 1869, c. 68.

[308] See below, pp. 616–17.

[309] *Second Report 1852*, 11.

[310] Phillipps, *Treatise on the Law of Evidence*, quoted by Allen, *Law of Evidence in Victorian England*, 50.

[311] W. L. Arnstein, *The Bradlaugh Case: A Study in Late Victorian Politics and Opinion* (Oxford, 1965) is a thorough account.

In the face of commercial realities the courts had already retreated from Coke's position that only Christians could be competent witnesses.[312] *Omichund v. Barker* in 1744[313] had allowed in the testimony of any heathen prepared to swear an oath in terms appropriate to his religion, provided that religion acknowledged a god with the capacity and willingness to punish falsehood on earth or in the hereafter.[314] However, difficulties arose with Christian sects whose tenets forbade the swearing of oaths. Quakers and Moravians already enjoyed a measure of relief (extended to criminal proceedings in 1828[315]) which was extended to Separatists in 1833,[316] a solemn affirmation being substituted for the oath. Still excluded were Christians outside the exempted sects who were unwilling to swear an oath and, lurking in the background, an uncertain number of acknowledged atheists.[317]

Bentham had stopped just short of calling for the outright abolition of the witness oath, but several of his followers went beyond him.[318] Some claimed that it promoted a double standard of truth-telling, and that the additional force of the divine sanction on top of the ethical and practical sanctions against falsehood added nothing to a witness's credibility.[319] Others said its weight was diminished by the undignified and slovenly manner in which the oath was often administered[320] and by the artifices whereby some witnesses evaded (as they thought) its effect.[321] It seriously hindered both criminal and civil justice by excluding the potential witnesses least likely to perjure themselves.[322] Nevertheless, although there were advocates of substituting affirmation for all civic oaths, citing the Indian Code of Evidence and the report of a royal commission on non-judicial

---

[312] Allen, *Law of Evidence in Victorian England*, 51.

[313] (1744) 1 Atk. 21, described by Brett MR in *A-G v. Bradlaugh* (1885) 14 QBD 667 at 697 as 'the most prominent and satisfactory judgment' on the subject. See also [W. Empson] 'Tyler on Oaths' (1834) 59 *Edin. Rev.* 446–74 and 'L', 'Origin, Nature and History of Oaths' (1834) 12 *LM* 169–87.

[314] For the test, see *R v. Taylor* (1790) Peake 14.

[315] Evidence Amendment Act 1828 (9 Geo. IV c. 32); Allen, *Law of Evidence in Victorian England*, 56–7.

[316] Oaths Act 1833 (3 & 4 Will. IV c. 8). The Separatists, later Congregationalists, eventually merged with Presbyterians to form the United Reformed Church.

[317] Allen, *Law of Evidence in Victorian England*, 81.

[318] *Ibid.*, 52–6.

[319] *Ibid.*, 85–6.

[320] A House of Lords committee in 1834 deplored the 'indecent mode of administering oaths, and the consequent want of reverence in taking them, which too often disgrace our Courts of Justice'; quoted in F. S. Reilly, 'Judicial Oaths', *Papers Read Before the Juridical Society 1855–1858*, 435–55, at 454–5.

[321] Instances were given in the debates on Bradlaugh's Oaths Bill: *PD* 1888 (s3) 323: 1182–236.

[322] Reilly ('Judicial Oaths', 450) cites the author ('A Barrister') of *A Letter to... Sir Robert Peel on a Scheme of Affirmation etc.* to the effect that a perjurer is unlikely to want to draw attention to himself by affecting scruples over the oath.

oaths in 1867,[323] that never became a serious proposition. In the 1830s Denman and other reformers were taught by experience to be modest and incremental, and even so the only fruit of their labours was a single clause bill enabling witnesses to swear in the form they regarded as binding on their consciences.[324] Wider proposals were opposed (by the judges among others[325]) as opening the way for unscrupulous persons to claim the right to affirm and so give false testimony without (as they might think) incurring divine wrath; no doubt it was also feared that it would lead the irreligious to claim the right to affirm.[326]

The Common Law Commissioners offered strong arguments in favour of a limited extension to those with a religious objection to swearing (the imprisonment for contempt of some of those was a particular embarrassment)[327] and this went into the Common Law Procedure Act 1854 despite opposition led by St. Leonards.[328] The Commission was divided on further enlarging eligibility to affirm. While acknowledging the force of the complaint that the exclusion of witnesses injured both victims of crime and sufferers of civil wrongs, it shared the view of many practising lawyers (including Brougham[329]) that many witnesses did fear the supernatural sanction and that its removal would increase perjury in the courts.[330] The Commission passed over another common argument, that atheists could not be trusted to tell the truth, often being republicans and revolutionaries besides. Many felt the social stability of the country was bound up with the maintenance of christianity in its institutions and rejected explicit recognition of unbelief as a permissible basis for full citizenship. Unsurprisingly, Sir John Trelawney's bills of the early 1860s to extend affirmation to professed unbelievers failed:[331] it is more difficult to explain (and it bemused Trelawny) why George Denman's similar measure of 1869 passed with little opposition.[332] Henceforth affirmation might be substituted for an oath

---

[323] *PP* 1867 (3885), xxxi. For earlier advocacy of this position see e.g. 'L', 'Origin, Nature and History of Oaths'.

[324] Oaths Validity Act 1838, 1 & 2 Vict. c. 105; Allen, *Law of Evidence in Victorian England*, 57–8.

[325] Sir J. Arnould, *A Memoir of Thomas, First Lord Denman*, 2 vols (1873), ii, 92–4. Abinger CB led the opposition.

[326] Allen, *Law of Evidence in Victorian England*, 57–9.

[327] *Second Report 1852*, 14–15.

[328] Section 20; *PD* 1854 (s3) 133: 787–92.

[329] For Brougham's opposition, see Allen, *Law of Evidence in Victorian England*, 79.

[330] *Second Report 1852*, 14–15.

[331] Allen, *Law of Evidence in Victorian England*, 81–4.

[332] *Ibid.*, 60–1. Evidence Further Amendment Act 1869 c. 68, s 4. It was amended by the Evidence Further Amendment Act 1870 c. 49 to meet the *lacuna* revealed by *Bradlaugh* v. *de Rin* (1870) 5 WN 9. Defects in the law were glaringly exposed in *Maden* v. *Catanach* (1861) 7 H. & N. 360, and perhaps the opinion of E. Gardner that juries were seldom influenced by whether evidence was given on oath or by affirmation had gained ground: 'On the Utility of Oaths' (1867–8) 24 (s3) *LM & LR* 265–77.

whenever a witness could satisfy the judge that an oath would have no binding effect on his conscience.[333]

There were few complaints about the working of the Act. A gradual shift in public opinion brought about a recognition that society was too resilient to crumble if no longer buttressed by religious tests, but it is clear from the debates on Bradlaugh's Oaths Act in 1888 (and from the extra-parliamentary opposition to Bradlaugh) that many still regretted the concession;[334] Halsbury was among those opposed to allowing atheists to serve on juries,[335] and not all were satisfied with the verbal concession obtained by Sir Edward Clarke which made the affirmation 'solemn'.[336] Even then practical problems over the manner in which the oath was administered required further legislation in 1909, when the oath itself assumed the form of words (suggested by Alverstone LCJ) which became familiar to succeeding generations.[337]

WITNESS EXAMINATION

The gradual relaxation of exclusionary rules as to persons naturally placed more emphasis on the role of examination and, particularly, cross-examination in elucidating the truth from witnesses. This was generally welcomed by the common law bar, for it enlarged their role in the trial and underlined its adversarial nature. Advocates became celebrated for their skill as examiners or cross-examiners, though they still tended to leave examination-in-chief to a junior.[338] Scarlett was one of the first and others with a great reputation, in a variety of styles, included Follett, Hawkins, and Russell.[339] Cross-examination was exalted as the most perfect engine for the discovery of truth yet invented[340] and reached its apogee in Coleridge's prolonged cross-examination of the Tichborne claimant—though some felt that Hawkins would have accomplished the task less suavely but much

[333] Inserted in the Lords, where Lord Penzance admitted the bill was worded in a more liberal way than had been intended.

[334] *PD* 1888 (s3) 323: 1182–236; Arnstein, *Bradlaugh Case*, 312–18.

[335] *PD* 1888 (s3) 330: 1013–26 at 1018.

[336] The main purpose of the bill was to ensure that atheists on juries and in coroners' courts might affirm, but Bradlaugh also contended that the 1869 Act contained some passages 'so peculiar that it had given rise to a variety of practices' (323: 1186). He instanced *Ex p. Lennard* (QBD 1875, unreported).

[337] Oaths Act 1909 c. 39. In LCO 2/238 the 1888 Act is described as a 'dead letter'. See also criticisms in (1909–10) 54 *Sol. J.*, esp. 24, 243.

[338] Wrottesley, *On The Examination of Witnesses*, 51.

[339] *Ibid.*, 51, 61 and 84; R. B. O'Brien, *The Life of Lord Russell of Killowen* (1901), 272; 'Circuit Tramp' [J. A. Foote], *Pie-Powder* (1911), 170.

[340] W. E. Schneider, '"Perjurious Albion": Perjury Prosecutions and the Victorian Trial', in A. D. E. Lewis and M. J. Lobban (eds), *Law and History* (Oxford, 2003), 343–74 at 350; Bodansky, 'Abolition of Party-Witness Disqualification' 96. Bentham also stressed its value: Twining, *Theories of Evidence*, 31.

more rapidly.[341] But cross-examination, particularly in criminal trials, could easily degenerate into brutal browbeating and by the 1890s public disapproval of
such exhibitions contributed to bringing a less abrasive style into favour.[342]

The rules governing examination of witnesses grew more elaborate as the trial
judge's discretion became fettered by counsel's insistence on relegating him to
referee in their contest. A judge still retained considerable latitude, in ruling on
leading questions for example, but he was increasingly circumscribed over the
admission of hearsay, corroboration and character evidence. Stephen characterized the particular rules as 'too much matters of common practice to need
authority for the main principles laid down',[343] but reported cases on their application continued to swell the practice books.[344]

A few questions were resolved by statute, notably the Common Law Procedure
Act 1854, sections 22–5, provisions having their origin in the second report of
the Common Law Commissioners.[345] They had to decide between well-matched
arguments on whether a party might seek to discredit his own witness whose
testimony proved unfavourable. Denman and Bolland had been deadlocked in
Wright v. *Beckett*[346] and the Commissioners sided with Denman; not indeed to
the extent of allowing general evidence of untrustworthiness, but, where the
judge ruled that this was an adverse witness, permitting evidence to contradict his
statements or to show that he had previously told a different tale.[347] They adopted
Parke's view that where a witness, without positively denying making an earlier
statement at odds with his evidence, did not admit to it, evidence of the statement might be adduced, something Tindal CJ and Abinger CB had refused.[348]
The rule in *The Queen's Case*,[349] much complained of by Brougham, that where
such an earlier statement was in writing, it must be given to the witness before
he was questioned upon it, was now modified, allowing him only notice of the
writing's existence but allowing the judge to see and use the whole document if
he wished.[350]

[341] E. Graham, *Fifty Famous Judges* (1930), 9–30.

[342] Sir Frank Lockwood in Wrottesley, *On The Examination of Witnesses*, 91.

[343] J. F. Stephen, *A Digest of the Law of Evidence* (1876), 163.

[344] E. D. Purcell said that the rules of evidence were constantly changing: *Forty Years at the
Criminal Bar* (1916), 46–8.

[345] At pp. 15–22.

[346] (1833) 1 M. & Rob. 414.

[347] *Second Report 1852*, 15–18, Common Law Procedure Act 1854, s 22.

[348] Section 23; *Second Report 1852*, 18–19. See *Crowley* v. *Page* (1837) 7 Car. & P. 791 (Parke); *Pain* v.
Beeston (1830) 1 Mo. & R. 20 (Tindal), *Long* v. *Hitchcock* (1840) 9 Car. & P. 619 (Abinger).

[349] (1820) 2 B. & B. 286. For its impact in criminal cases see Bentley, *English Criminal Justice in the
Nineteenth Century*, 144–6.

[350] Section 24; *Second Report 1852*, 19–21.

The most intractable of the problems considered by the Commissioners was whether a witness might be questioned about previous convictions or other past events tending to degrade his character in the eyes of the jury and so devalue his evidence, a problem aggravated by ending the exclusionary rule based on infamy.[351] The Commissioners came down on the side of the witness, recommending that only convictions for perjury and cognate offences should be provable in rebuttal of his denial,[352] but the Act went further, extending to any felony or misdemeanour. It was, however, in criminal trials that the wider question of character evidence assumed major importance.[353]

EXPERT WITNESSES

By the 1820s, if not earlier,[354] there was general acceptance of Lord Mansfield's *dicta* in *Carter* v. *Boehm* and, especially, in *Folkes* v. *Chadd*,[355] suggesting that evidence of opinion was admissible only in exceptional categories of case, chiefly where a witness was called to provide the jury with specially authoritative knowledge on some art, science, or trade needing particular training or expertise. What qualified that witness was not necessarily a professional education or qualification, but expertise however acquired, so that, for instance, a bill broker might pronounce on the law of a foreign country or a solicitor on handwriting.[356]

While medical knowledge continued to provide the commonest scope for expert witnesses (most sensationally in murder trials, especially for poisoning[357]), the range expanded incrementally: accountants and actuaries, engineers and shipbuilders, underwriters and shopkeepers all made their appearance[358] and there was no attempt at a judicial definition of a specialist subject for this purpose.[359] Nor in England was there much discussion about what Learned Hand viewed as the contradiction at the heart of expert evidence—the admission of opinions (often contradictory opinions at that) which a jury must evaluate without, *ex hypothesi*, possessing the knowledge to do so.[360] In general, English judges

---

[351] See above, and Bentley, *English Criminal Justice in the Nineteenth Century*, 140–2.

[352] *Second Report 1852*, 21–2.

[353] Section 25. It was, of course, most often in issue in relation to the defendant rather than witnesses: see XIII, Pt 1, Ch. III esp. pp. 88–90.

[354] As argued in T. Hodgkinson, *Expert Evidence: Law and Practice* (1990), 7–8.

[355] (1766) 3 Burr. 1905; (1782) 3 Doug. 157.

[356] *Van der Donckt* v. *Thellusson* (1849) 8 C.B. 812; *R* v. *Silverlock* [1894] 2 QB 766.

[357] See Ch. XIV.

[358] *Halsbury's Laws of England*, xiii, 480–1.

[359] Hodgkinson, *Expert Evidence*, 131–2.

[360] 'Historical and Practical Considerations Regarding Expert Testimony' (1901) 15 *Harvard LR* 40–58.

seem to have taken a relaxed attitude to admitting expert evidence, according it more or less weight as it appeared more or less persuasive.

Handwriting posed particular difficulties. It was arguable that at least where there were specimens of the genuine writing of the author or signatory of a disputed document available, the jury was competent to judge for itself, but it had long been the custom to allow testimony from those who were familiar with his writing.[361] Unfortunately the want of a clear notion of the function and limits of opinion evidence had created a muddle, with the Exchequer and the Queen's Bench at odds on whether a document not related to the cause might be used to test a witness's accuracy in identifying handwriting.[362] Judges had also differed on whether to admit the evidence of an expert who had formed his opinion from signed documents rather than seeing the signatures made or having them in correspondence.[363] The Common Law Commissioners favoured allowing any document the judge accepted as genuine to be used as the basis for witness evidence on handwriting.[364]

THE PROBLEM OF PERJURY

One of Bentham's responses to criticisms that his inclusive policy on evidence would greatly increase falsehood was to propose a strengthening of the criminal law sanction against perjury ('mendacity', he called it).[365] Perjury trials were then uncommon, but increased significantly after the County Courts Act 1846. County court judges admitted that it was a serious problem, but reformers intent on admitting the testimony of parties in the superior courts downplayed the likelihood of an explosion of false testimony. Presumably because the tacit admission would have damaged their case, they did not propose any strengthening of the criminal sanction, but Lord Campbell CJ, backed by fellow judges, pressed through Parliament almost in tandem with the Evidence Bill an Act to facilitate prosecutions for perjury committed in the lower courts.[366]

In the superior courts some judges showed such a strong inclination to commit the losing party for perjury that it was suspected that they were out to sabotage Brougham's Act, but they soon concluded that they were simply making a rod for their own backs and, as reformers had predicted, afterwards showed

[361] *Second Report 1852*, 24. These were not, of course, expert witnesses.

[362] The Exchequer, in *Young* v. *Honner* (1843) 2 M. & R. 536, declined to follow the Queen's Bench ruling in *Griffits* v. *Ivery* (1840) 11 Ad. & El. 322.

[363] *Second Report 1852*, 24. The Queen's Bench divided equally on this in *Doe d. Mudd* v. *Suckermore* (1835) 5 A. & El. 703. The Lords' committee of privileges rejected such evidence in the Fitzwalter peerage case (1843) 10 Cl. & F. 193.

[364] Common Law Procedure Act 1854, s 27.

[365] Schneider, 'Perjurious Albion', 345.

[366] *Ibid.*, 346–52; 14 & 15 Vict. c. 100.

little inclination to find perjury in their own courts.[367] A startling initial rise in perjury prosecutions was followed by a steady decline overall. Most were cases from lower courts, with a marked concentration within a narrow range of actions (game laws, affiliation, licensing); moreover a surprising number of cases ended in a directed acquittal. And when one obstacle to prosecution was removed by the appointment in 1879 of a Director of Public Prosecutions, he was strongly criticized for his highly selective policy on prosecutions, a pragmatic recognition of the difficulty in securing convictions from juries.[368]

It is unlikely that there was any decline in perjury in civil courts.[369] It was most notorious in the divorce court and the Queen's proctor was a not very effectual safeguard.[370] Chalmers was eloquent on its pervasiveness in county courts and other judges echoed his views, albeit sometimes with a tendency to single out the Welsh and the Jews.[371] Perjurers seldom faced prosecution unless they were detected in a conspiracy to pervert justice.[372]

DOCUMENTARY EVIDENCE

Documents had long been admitted as evidence, first deeds and later informal writings too; indeed the Statute of Frauds was passed precisely because reliance upon witness testimony was sometimes unsatisfactory.[373] In keeping with the policy of that statute, the circumstances in which parol evidence was admitted to construe the meaning of a document were severely restricted, though courts of equity were markedly more generous in this regard.[374] Common law rules still bore traces of the older practice whereby a deed might operate to estop a claim rather than merely as evidence bearing on its validity, and until 1852 a rule of pleading, profert, required a party who relied upon a deed in his possession to set it forth in full in his pleadings.[375]

Proof was always required of the genuineness of a document, and if attested by witnesses, they had to be called or their absence justified.[376] Since if the witnesses

---

[367] *Ibid.*, 347–51. At first they also insisted that even a party must leave the court if he might give evidence, but this was soon abandoned: Hollams, *Jottings of an Old Solicitor*, 41–2.

[368] Schneider, 'Perjurious Albion' 365–70.

[369] Wrottesley, *Examination of Witnesses*, 81, who considered it less common than was usually thought, was in the minority; compare e.g. J. A. Strahan, *The Bench and Bar of England* (1919), 57.

[370] See below, pp. 751–3.

[371] 'Petty Perjury' (1895) 11 *LQR* 217–22; P. Polden, *A History of the County Court, 1846–1971* (Cambridge, 1999), 99–100; J. Cooper, *Pride Versus Prejudice* (Oxford, 2003), 136–43.

[372] *Report of the DPP, PP* 1894 (73), lxxi.

[373] Holdsworth, *HEL*, vi, 388–90; ix, 163–77. In Gilbert's time documentary evidence was still the most important sort: Gallanis, 'Rise of Modern Evidence Law', 509–11.

[374] Thayer, *Preliminary Treatise On Evidence*, 429–39.

[375] Holdsworth, *HEL*, ix, 155–6, 171–2; *First Report 1829*; Common Law Procedure Act 1852, s.55.

[376] Holdsworth, *HEL*, ix, 169.

denied their signatures or affected not to recall the transaction other evidence was sometimes admissible to prove the document, this requirement was perhaps otiose,[377] but it was peremptorily affirmed by Lord Ellenborough[378] and thereafter could be modified only by legislation, the Common Law Procedure Act 1854. Thenceforth attesting witnesses were called only where the law or the parties had made attestation a condition.[379]

That reform was the only one suggested by the Common Law Commissioners, who declared that '[t]he great improvements which have been made by recent legislation in the matter of documentary evidence leave us but little to suggest in this respect.'[380] The rules were certainly elaborate, sometimes necessarily, as where it was sought to substitute secondary evidence of a document for production of the original, but an invaluable simplification had been made in the Documentary Evidence Act 1845, an early achievement of the Law Amendment Society.[381] A large number of public or quasi-public documents had already been made admissible as evidence by individual statutes, public, local, or personal. They included certificates of conviction and of discharge from bankruptcy or insolvency; licences to practise, e.g. as an apothecary; registers, e.g. of copyrights, and bye-laws.[382] In fact, 'there is scarcely a single railway act, canal act, dock, harbour or town improvement act, or, in fact, any act giving powers to joint-stock companies, which does not contain [such] clauses'.[383]

With no statutory template the result was untidy and inconvenient. Some Acts exempted documents from the strict common law requirements of proof altogether, others in part, some not at all. Courts were not always sympathetic to the draftsman's efforts; an amending Act to make a certificate under the Apothecaries Acts admissible provided that it bore the company's seal was rendered useless by a decision that the genuineness of the seal had still to be proved.[384] Given the improbability of successful forgeries of most of these instruments, the additional security came at a wholly disproportionate cost to litigants and it was a great improvement to make documents admissible provided only that they complied upon their face with the formalities prescribed by the Act which established them.[385] It was a timely reform, for documentary evidence was becoming progressively more important in civil cases.

[377] *Second Report 1853*, 23.			[378] *R* v. *Harringworth* (1815) 4 M. & S. 354.

[379] Section 26.					[380] *Second Report 1852*, 22.

[381] 8 & 9 Vict. c. 113.

[382] 'Documentary Evidence Act' (1845–6) 3 *LR* 16–27, 171–8, taken from the LAS Common Law Committee's Report.

[383] *Ibid.*, 21.

[384] 6 Geo. IV c. 133; *Chadwick* v. *Bunning* (1825) Ry. & Moo. 306.

[385] Documentary Evidence Act 1845, s 1. Section 3 simplified the putting in evidence of statutes, the journals of Lords and Commons and royal proclamations.

3. ORGANIZATION AND BUSINESS

Jurisdiction and Business

The three courts of common law preserved elements of their original functional separation. The King's Bench alone had a general criminal jurisdiction, and was also the forum in which decisions of lesser courts and public officers and bodies could be challenged through the prerogative writs (though the Common Pleas could also hear habeas corpus applications). The Exchequer still heard disputes arising out the Crown's revenue claims, while it was in the Common Pleas that attempts to use the old real and mixed actions had to be made.[386]

However, where subject fought against subject, most litigants could choose their forum. This was the result of encroachments by the King's Bench (via *latitat* and bills of Middlesex) and the Exchequer (via *quominus*) on the jurisdiction of the Common Pleas, whose attempts to emulate the attractive features of their rivals had only limited success.[387] By the 1820s suitors' preferences had created an embarrassing imbalance in their workloads: in five years to the end of 1827 the King's Bench saw 281,109 actions commenced; the Common Pleas 80,158, and the Exchequer 37,197.[388] Thus King's Bench judges were 'immoderately over-burthened'[389] and in arrears while the other courts, with the same number of judges and essentially the same facilities, were comparatively—and in the case of the Exchequer absolutely—underused. It was to the dispatch of business that the Common Law Commissioners first directed their attention.

At either extreme were two solutions favoured only by the most, and least, radical thinkers respectively. One was to allow the market forces which had created this situation to resolve it: beyond a certain point, delays in the King's Bench would drive suitors to seek relief elsewhere. On the other hand, the separate existence of the courts could be ended and a single *curia regis* be re-established, but no one who came before the Commission was willing to embrace that. The outer limit of practical politics was to direct certain types of business, or business from a particular locality, into one court or to allot suits to each court in rotation. The Commissioners rejected all these, though their grounds for rejecting a rota—that

---

[386] Holdsworth, *HEL*, i, 194–240.

[387] This 'emulation' was praised by Adam Smith: *An Inquiry into the Nature and Causes of the Wealth of Nations* (1776) quoted in A. H. Manchester, *Sources of English Legal History* (1984), 77. On this 'dynamic market competition', see C. W. Francis, 'Practice, Strategy and Institution: Debt Collection in the English Common Law Courts, 1740–1840' (1986) 80 *North-Western University Law Rev.* 808–954 at 847–9.

[388] *First Report 1829*, 11.

[389] *Ibid.*, 17.

it would be easily evaded by suitors using sham writs—were flimsy.[390] However, without endorsing Sir Robert Graham's remarkable assertion that any restriction on choice of court was 'an invasion of the privileges of the subject', they did deem it 'a fair and valuable privilege' and one which should be infringed only as a last resort.[391]

The congestion in the King's Bench could not be relieved by isolated expedients, for several had already been tried with (at best) limited success. Vacation sittings to complete term business, introduced by Ellenborough in 1813 and later given statutory authority,[392] and extending the time for the Middlesex court sittings in vacation only encouraged more business at *nisi prius* without providing facilities for handling the additional motions in banc that would be generated, while an Act of 1821 which permitted parallel *nisi prius* sittings by the Chief Justice and one of the puisnes was quickly abandoned because of the difficulty of securing counsel's attendance when they might be wanted in two places at once.[393] Besides such practical considerations, the feeling of the profession was that judgments given in banc while the Chief Justice was sitting at *nisi prius* lacked authority; no one was yet prepared to argue that the banc system became inherently problematic when litigation grew beyond a certain point.[394]

An obvious shift, to borrow underemployed judges from the Exchequer, was exposed to the same objection, and would still be insufficient to cope with the influx of business.[395] The causes of the disparity had to be tackled at source, and this required changes at three levels. One was the calibre of the judges, for it was generally acknowledged that there was a distinct hierarchy and that some of the appointments to the Exchequer and Common Pleas were hardly calculated to commend them to litigants' attorneys.[396]

The second change was to remove constraints which discouraged attorneys from using the Common Pleas and Exchequer. Two measures were proposed to

---

[390] *Ibid.*, 22–3. Such a rota was introduced into the Irish courts by the Common Law Procedure Act (Ireland) 1852.

[391] *Ibid.*, 22–3 and App. A12, q. 11. They recommended that suits brought by common informers and cases reserved from quarter sessions should be directed into the Exchequer: 30.

[392] *Ibid.*, 17–19; An Act for the Further Facilitation of the Despatch of Business in the King's Bench 1821 and an Act to make Further Provision for the Despatch of Business in the King's Bench (1822) 1 & 2 Geo. IV c. 16, 3 Geo. IV c. 102.

[393] *Ibid.*, 19–20; Trial of Causes in Vacation Act 1821 (1 Geo. IV c. 65); Trial of Causes at Nisi Prius Act 1821 (1 Geo. IV c. 6).

[394] *Ibid.*, 17–21. John Miller' s *Inquiry* criticized this practice: 'The Constitution and Practice of the English Courts of Civil Law' (1828) 1 *LM* 185–219 at 213.

[395] *First Report 1829*, 21–2.

[396] See below, pp. 984–5. In the Exchequer ('an asylum for age and infirmity' according to 'Proposed Alterations in the Courts of Common Pleas and Exchequer' (1827) 1 *Jurist* 99–107 at 100), examples are Vaughan (Exchequer 1827) and Bolland (Exchequer 1829).

enhance the Exchequer's attractions. One—not immediately carried out—was to separate the equity jurisdiction from the plea side and have all its judges sitting in banc.[397] The other was to end the monopoly of the four sworn attorneys and their 16 clerks, who had to be paid by the suitors' own attorneys, and allow all attorneys to be enrolled. [398]

The Common Pleas monopoly, however, was a bar monopoly and so received more tender treatment. The Commissioners proposed only minor changes to the position of the serjeants, justifying their privilege on the shaky ground that a concentration of senior counsel helped to secure their regular attendance.[399] This hardly sat well with the attempt to encourage suitors to use the Exchequer and ignored the objection that the serjeants were a mediocre bunch when compared with the King's Counsel. The serjeants' monopoly was in effect abolished by Brougham and its restoration following the Serjeants' Case in 1840 was short-lived.[400]

Besides those obvious obstacles to parity of esteem, the Commissioners took aim at other differences, in procedure, practice etc., seeking to put the three courts as nearly as possible on an identical footing. Gaselee had hoped to induce Littledale and Hullock to join him in an informal standing committee to revise and consolidate practice but Hullock's death had aborted that initiative.[401] In 1832, however, the Uniformity of Process Act, section 8 enabled the common law judges to make rules for all the courts and the work of the Fees Committee enabled them to create a common structure which made it easier for counsel to operate in all courts.[402]

Viewed from a lay perspective the inability of the courts to handle a rising workload was largely because there were so many days on which they did not sit. Besides the many holidays,[403] there were the three vacations, especially the long vacation stretching from August to October, with four short terms sandwiched in between. But the long vacation was fiercely defended by judges and lawyers and although various minor changes, and the move to fixed dates for terms, enabled

---

[397] *First Report 1829*, 23.

[398] *Ibid.*

[399] *Ibid.*, 24–7.

[400] See below. Another drawback to the Common Pleas was that the fees were higher and the prothonotaries demanded more money in advance from attorneys: Francis, 'Practice, Strategy, and Institution' 850.

[401] (1829–30) 3 *LM* 595.

[402] Byles was the last leading counsel to confine his practice to a single court: 'Baron Bramwell, the Press and the Bar' (1859–60) 8 (s3) *LM & LR* 1–12.

[403] See the list by C. Short, *Common Law Commission First Report 1829*, App. L. The Commission recommended the discontinuance of most of them (31) and this was effected by the Law Amendment Act 1833, s 43.

more productive use to be made of the available time, the case for more judges was compelling.[404]

The changes made in the 1830s were successful in redistributing common law business and in keeping it to a manageable amount in each court. By 1845 the Exchequer had overtaken the Queen's Bench[405] and though the Common Pleas persistently lagged in popularity even after the serjeants' monopoly was ended, it still claimed around 20 per cent of the total.[406] Business arrangements were still far from perfect,[407] but at least some of the chiefs now showed an interest in tackling them[408] and except when the influx of a 'vicious cross-fire of lawsuits'[409] in the wake of the railway crash of 1845 threatened to overwhelm their resources, arrears did not approach the levels experienced in the King's Bench in the late 1820s. In fact no sooner had that 'hurricane of litigation'[410] passed than practitioners at Westminster Hall were thrown into a panic by the threat of business being sucked away by the new county courts. Many of the junior bar desponded at their prospects and the immediate success of this forum for that 'cheap law' which the public demanded and the superior courts had been unable or unwilling to supply, seemed to justify their worst fears.[411] Indeed, following the increase in county court jurisdiction to £50 in 1850 the Common Pleas actually had to close early a couple of times through lack of business and it was even suggested that the courts could operate with fewer judges.[412]

It was never likely that any Commission dominated by judges and barristers would support that idea, and business soon picked up again.[413] Even so, the

---

[404] *First Report 1829*, 27–34.

[405] Francis, 'Practice, Strategy and Institution', App. 3.

[406] *RC on the Common Law (Judicial Business), Report 1857*, q. 44 and App. Common Pleas still trailed the other courts in 1862, attributed to 'the force of old habits' in 'Judicial Statistics 1862' (1864) 17(s3) *LM & LR* 28–46 at 31.

[407] 'C', 'Business Arrangements of the Courts' (1845) 2 (s2) *LM* 240–7; (1845) 3 (s2) *LM* 102–5.

[408] Thus Denman was responsible for an Act of 1838 (1 & 2 Vict. c. 32) to restore their power to hold sittings in banc during the vacation: Arnould, *Memoir of Lord Denman*, ii, 94. He had this achievement, which he calculated to have added two years' worth of sittings by 1850, inscribed on his tombstone in Stoke Albany churchyard. Pollock introduced double sittings in the Exchequer to avoid remanets, which succeeded despite teething troubles: (1849) 11 (s2) *LM* 202; *RC on the Common Law (Judicial Business), Report 1857*, evidence, q. 589.

[409] R. W. Kostal, *Law and English Railway Capitalism* (Oxford, 1994), 53. Denman claimed to have disposed of King's Bench arrears he had inherited: Arnould, *Memoir of Lord Denman*, i, 430.

[410] Kostal, *Law and English Railway Capitalism*, Ch. 2.

[411] See below and Polden, *History of the County Court*, 43–5, 51–2.

[412] (1852) 16 (s2) *LM* 156. Instructions to the royal commission on the courts in December 1856 included 'whether any reduction may be made in the present number of judges'. Headed by Campbell CJ, it included Wensleydale (the former Baron Parke), Alderson, and Cresswell. Martin was added later.

[413] Especially judges: Baron Alderson wrote of the 1844 Circuit Commission that he, Parke, and Coleridge were 'to be at the head' of it, 'assisted by four barristers and three gentlemen of the country': Alderson, *Selections from the papers of Baron Alderson*, 98.

annual average of causes tried on circuit in the ten years ending 1844 had been 1394 and for the next 12 years to 1856 was only 1094, though criminal trials had risen from 3941 to 4305.[414] The superior courts retained important advantages for creditors. They offered judgment by default, which was persistently denied to county courts;[415] execution by the sheriff's officers was generally more efficient than by bailiffs; and the county courts had to set fees at a level which made them self-supporting. These advantages ensured that they kept, or recovered, some of the debt recovery cases which were the staple of common law courts.[416] However, there were important changes in the type and course of business.

County courts had indeed taken away many routine, uncomplicated small debt recovery cases. The master of the Crown Office said that 'all the light cases have gone away', and others agreed.[417] The proportion of more demanding cases, like those involving joint stock companies and railways, had grown markedly.[418] There were more cases with a commercial background, especially since the balance of work tilted in favour of northern England.[419] The jury trials of 1860 were mostly contract suits, especially in town causes, but there was a considerable proportion of torts, the vastly greater tendency of contract cases to be settled before trial or to go to judgment by default greatly reducing their dominance in the later stages.[420] In 1869 the largest categories were actions for goods sold and delivered (297), promissory notes, bills of exchange etc. (251), breach of contract (167), work and labour (108); among the torts Fatal Accidents Acts cases (137) far outnumbered other negligence suits (41). Libel (37), slander (38), and trespass to land (54) were also prominent.[421]

Even worse for the junior bar, the motions of course and suchlike which had sustained newcomers had all but dried up as a result of reforms to fees and

---

[414] *RC on the Common Law (Judicial Business), Report 1857*, App., table 1. The same trend affected all three courts: Francis, 'Practice, Strategy and Institution', App. 3.

[415] In 1856 some 30% of superior court proceedings ended with a default judgment: *RC on the Common Law (Judicial Business), Report 1857*, App.

[416] In 750 of 1610 cases in 1869 the plaintiff recovered no more than £50, and more than £100 in only 551: *RC on the Judicature, Second Report*, PP 1872 [C. 631–1], xx, App., 465. In Queen's Bench cases in 1840 more than £50 had been recovered in 60%: Francis, 'Practice, Strategy and Institution, App. 13.

[417] *RC on the Common Law (Judicial Business), Report 1857*, qq. 551–70 (C. F. Robinson). Crown Office business was atypical, but Robinson noted how 'easy' settlement cases had been replaced by more complex matters. J. H. Cancellor, a master of the Common Pleas, testified to similar effect (q. 577) and the Commission agreed (p. xi).

[418] *Ibid.*, xi. The jurisdiction over railway matters given to the Common Pleas by an Act of 1854 was seldom invoked: C. Stebbings, *Legal Foundations of Tribunals in Nineteenth Century England* (Cambridge, 2006), 52–7.

[419] C. W. Brooks, 'Litigation and Society in England, 1200–1996', in *Lawyers, Litigation and English Society since 1450* (1998), 63–128 at 110.

[420] Lobban, 'Strange Life of the English Civil Jury', tables 5 and 6.

[421] *RC on the Judicature, Second Report 1872*, App., 465.

procedures, first in 1838 and then in 1852.[422] There was still plenty of interlocutory business, but much went before a judge in chambers, where counsel's attendance was the exception rather than the rule. Procedure by summons and order was cheaper and more straightforward than by motion and rule.[423] Chambers arrangements still attracted much criticism.[424] Conditions in Serjeants' Inn, where they were held, were such that 'no respectable attorney can give his attendance',[425] so they sent their clerks, not all of them capable or experienced: no wonder the chiefs claimed to be excused from taking their share of the long vacation rota.[426] In term the 'out judge', who was supposed to arrive at 3 pm, was often delayed by his other obligations,[427] making for a frantic and unseemly scramble when he did arrive and was 'pestered to death',[428] sometimes amid uproarious scenes.[429]

Some of the 'quasi-judicial' work of the courts was now done by the masters. Besides attending in court they taxed costs and examined witnesses who would be unavailable at the trial.[430] Their handling of references did not always give satisfaction, however, and it was felt that judges too readily sent complicated commercial accounts their way.[431]

One change was the speed at which trials now came on in comparison with more leisurely times. 'When I first went into the City', Germain Lavie told the Commission, 'an action was brought, and there was no pleading required, merely the general issue, and the parties came to issue and the cause was set down. In my office we never used to look at those papers for a year, we never thought it necessary at all to look at them till we knew the cause was likely to be tried.'[432] By the 1850s attorneys were regularly asking for postponements of trials because they were unprepared rather than as a delaying tactic.[433]

---

[422] R. Abel-Smith and R. Stevens, *Lawyers and the Courts* (1967), 41. The number of rules granted fell from 38,009 to 3,081 over a nine-month period in 1852–3: *RC on Common Law, Third Report 1860*, 6.

[423] A. S. Diamond, 'The Queen's Bench Masters' (1960) 76 *LQR* 504–20 at 507–8.

[424] *RC on Common Law, Third Report 1831*, 42–3 and evidence of Jones and Ward (C. 31), C. Shearman (C. 41), B. Austen (C. 36), and W. Fisher (C. 52).

[425] *Ibid.*, B. Austen (C. 36).

[426] (1848) 9 (s2) *LM* 257; *RC on the Common Law (Judicial Business), Report 1857*, Bramwell q.32.

[427] *RC on Common Law, First Report 1851*, 63.

[428] *SC on Official Salaries*, PP 1850 (611), xv, Sir John Jervis AG, q. 1723.

[429] (1860) 9 (s3) *LM & LR* 171.

[430] Sir W. F. Pollock, *Personal Reminiscences*, 2 vols (1887), ii, 240–1 uses this expression to describe his work as an Exchequer master from 1847. A concise account of the masters' duties is in *RC on Chancery and Common Law Courts of England and Ireland*, PP 1866 [3674], xvii, App. I.

[431] (1859) 9 (s3) *LM & LR* 172–4.

[432] *RC on the Common Law (Judicial Business), Report 1857*, q. 612.

[433] *Ibid.*, Sir J. T. Coleridge, q. 526.

An even greater change had come over the trial itself. The changes to the rules of evidence were bound to prolong proceedings, not least because interested parties, and the parties themselves, were susceptible to more searching cross-examination than other witnesses.[434] The greater facility for counsel to sum up had a similar effect, and encouraged the employment of more counsel, with the juniors having a more active part.[435] Counsel were tending to become more prolix[436] and while judges varied enormously in the latitude they allowed, there were fewer Ellenboroughs and more Tindals on the bench.[437] It would no longer be possible to claim that a courtroom must be able to accommodate six trials a day.[438]

Fees, Costs and Organization

There were differences among the clerical organizations of the common law courts and in the nomenclature of officials performing similar functions, predictably since all were of ancient origin and none had been radically overhauled since the sixteenth century. Organic and unsystematic growth created structures that were untidy, irrational, and inefficient, but more notable than the differences were the similarities.[439]

Apart from judges' salaries, the courts were funded almost entirely from suitors' fees. These fees were mostly paid directly to the official performing the function for which the fee was charged (though he might not in reality perform it) or to another acting on his behalf, rather than to an office dedicated to the receipt of fees. The fee did not go into a common fund but directly remunerated the recipient or his superior. Many of the fees were demanded on no better authority

---

[434] '[C]auses are now tried of as grave a character, and lasting as long, in Term time as in the sittings after Term, and by that means, and by that only, you get through the business, which has been enormously prolonged both from the modern manner of trying causes, and from the habit of hearing them out instead of disposing of them as they used to do in a very summary way. A cause is now enormously prolonged by an accumulation of speeches, which are allowed, very properly I dare say, under the last Common Law Procedure Act, and also by allowing parties to be allowed as witnesses, which imposes on every Defendant the necessity of getting into the witness box, and when he has once taken the plunge of appearing as a witness himself, of course he brings others to support him if he can', *ibid.*, Sir C. Cresswell, q. 36.

[435] Criminal trials were lengthened by the increasing employment of counsel for the defence: Bentley, *English Criminal Justice*, 107, and see XIII, Pt. 1, pp. 71–81.

[436] 'Third Common Law Report' (1831–2) 6 *LM* 249–348 at 323; (1842) 27 *LM* 485; (1848) 8 (s2) *LM* 162.

[437] 'Chief Justice Tindal' (1846) 5 (s2) *LM* 105–11. The judge taking a note of the evidence, which became the normal practice, may also have slowed down the trial: (1857–8) 2 *Sol. J.* 1037.

[438] 'Courts in Westminster Hall' (1830) 4 *LM* 230–6.

[439] Holdsworth, *HEL*, i, 246–64.

than established user.[440] Most court offices were held not during pleasure or good behaviour but for the equivalent of a freehold estate in land, for life most commonly but sometimes in tail or in fee, and so closely had these offices been assimilated to real property that they followed most of its rules of transmission and were commonly granted in reversion.[441] Though disconcerting, it is not altogether inapt to describe the organization of the courts as feudal.

This state of affairs had several deleterious effects. First, it meant that if an office became redundant, like those of the clerk of the King's Bench or *custos brevum* of the Common Pleas, it would not cease. Secondly, it had encouraged Tudor and Stuart monarchs to create superfluous offices for their favourites at no cost to themselves. Thirdly, when an officeholder found his work beneath his dignity or too onerous, he would appoint a deputy to do it; the filazer exigenter and clerk of the outlawries of the King's Bench was noted as having managed to get his work done for less than £600 per annum while pocketing a balance of £4500. This practice, akin to subinfeudation, could be replicated by the deputy. Fourthly, there were officials, such as the common pleas prothonotaries, who continued to perform some of their duties, but had managed to pass off others onto the parties' attorneys, who handed over fees for work they were doing themselves.[442]

It is possible to see within this apparently irrational and haphazard structure a well-founded strategy for securing the interests of the officers. As pressure on limited judicial resources grew, so the cost of the trial stage of a lawsuit was increased, keeping the number of cases reaching that stage just within manageable limits while benefitting the officials who mostly derived their incomes from the earlier stages. Whether this was achieved through deliberate manipulation of particular fees is however speculative.[443]

Hanoverian parliaments had shown little interest in these matters, partly because the levying of fees ensured that the courts made no large demands on the public purse. The expense of litigation was a frequent complaint, but the only major investigation, in the 1730s, simply petered out.[444] However, the movement for economical reform, which targeted sinecures and sales of public office because they were thought to bolster the influence of the Crown, at length turned

---

[440] '[c]onstant receipt by the present officers and the information as to a similar receipt by their predecessors, derived either verbally or from books of accounts or written memoranda, are for the most part the grounds on which the officers at the present time have acted in regard to the amount of the fees they have severally received': *RC on Fees in the Courts of Justice, 1818*, quoted in Holdsworth, *HEL*, i, 256.

[441] Holdsworth, *HEL*, i, 246–51.

[442] *Ibid.*, 257–9.

[443] Francis, 'Practice, Stratgey and Institution' 843–6, at 863–5.

[444] *RC on the Legal Departments, Second Report 1874*, 1–3.

the spotlight on the courts in 1810,[445] and a commission produced three detailed reports on the common law courts between 1818 and 1821 which revealed a situation difficult to defend.[446]

It was also a situation which was difficult to change. Opposition Whigs yielded little to Tories in their veneration for private property, so vested interests must either be bought out or allowed to lapse. Moreover, the emoluments of the judges, particularly the chiefs, were partly derived from the patronage they held until three Acts of 1825 prospectively ended the sale of the offices which were in their gift or in the gift of officers appointed by them and raised their salaries as recompense.[447] Officers would still be appointed by the chiefs[448] but their tenure would henceforth be during good behaviour and the use of deputies was restricted.[449]

The patent officers had no intention of being ousted without hefty compensation and successfully obstructed the revamping of county courts which threatened their incomes,[450] forcing Peel to promote a general Act in 1830 'for better regulating the receipt and future appropriation of fees...'.[451]

This smoothed the path for a reorganization of the court offices, beginning with the plea side of the Exchequer in 1832[452] which served as a model for the wider changes implemented in 1838. The statute carried out its declared aim, to 'make provision for a more effective and uniform establishment of officers' by abolishing many sinecures and placing most of the establishments on salaries with provision for retirement pensions.[453] The key figures in the new establishments were to be five masters in each court, barristers, pleaders, or attorneys of

---

[445] RC on Saleable Offices in Courts of Law, PP 1810 (358), ix. Those in the King's Bench are reproduced in Manchester, Sources of English Legal History, 77.

[446] Summarized in the RC on the Legal Departments, Second Report 1874, 3–4.

[447] Acts to Abolish the Sale of Offices in the King's Bench and Common Pleas, and to Augment the Salaries of the Judges, 6 Geo. IV cc. 82, 83, 84.

[448] Puisne judges had little patronage, but valued the chance to appoint to Clerkships of Assize, which lay within the gift of the senior judge on the circuit at the time a vacancy occurred. One judge went the same circuit year after year in hopes of an opportunity only to be thwarted by a clerk who lived to be 90: SC on Fees in Courts of Law and Equity, PP 1847 (643), viii, qq. 105–8 (R. Hankins).

[449] 6 Geo. IV c. 89 empowered the Treasury to purchase two sinecure offices, but the most notorious, the receiver and comptroller of the seals of the courts, entailed upon the Dukes of Grafton by Charles II, was not bought out until 1845: RC on the Legal Departments, Second Report 1874, 6.

[450] See below, p. 858.

[451] Geo. IV & 1 Will. IV c. 58. No new offices were to be created without Treasury consent. Existing fee collectors were to account for their receipts and would henceforth receive (in most cases) the average of their last ten years' receipts, the balance going into the consolidated fund, which would also meet any shortfall. No future officers would be entitled to compensation if their post were abolished and existing ones might receive up to three-quarters of its average value by way of compensation for the loss of the right to sell it.

[452] Offices on the Plea Side of the Exchequer Act (2 & 3 Will. IV c. 110); necessitated by increased business after the abolition of the great sessions of Wales and Chester.

[453] Courts of Common Law (Offices) Act 1837 (Will. IV & 1 Vict. c. 30).

five years' standing, on salaries of £1000 and holding during good behaviour.[454] They might appoint as many clerks as were needed (subject to the approval of the chief judge), and clerks were strictly forbidden to take fees or gratuities.[455]

The Act was not comprehensive. The Crown Office was similarly reformed in 1845[456] and in 1852 the *nisi prius* and Assize officers were rationalized, following bitter and justified complaints about the fees charged for their services.[457] The associates, appointed by the chiefs, were to fill the role played elsewhere by the masters, with up to two clerks each.[458] The same Act dealt with the more delicate position of the judges' clerks. These did very well out of the fee system, especially when their master did chambers business in town during the circuits; it yielded £2000 in six weeks to one pair.[459] Judges continued to appoint their own two personal clerks (three for the chiefs) and also the ushers and subordinate trial officers, though the Treasury fixed their salaries. Court establishments were modest, with 23 clerks in the Queen's Bench, 18 in the Exchequer, and 14 in the Common Pleas, and each had functional divisions. Each court had three associates, each with three clerks, and there was a separate establishment for the Crown Office in the Queen's Bench, headed by the queen's coroner and a master, whose duties were nearly identical.[460]

Although it has been argued that the 'debt-recovery packages' offered to creditors by the superior courts were highly attractive, providing a good chance of full or at least substantial recovery at the ultimate expense of the debtor,[461] there was widespread criticism of the cost of bringing an action to recover a small sum. In 1823 a select committee was told that no prudent tradesman would bring an action for less than £15, a larger sum than the average award at a Lancaster Assize Brougham attended.[462] The average sum sought in actions using bailable process in 1830/1 was just £36 and it has been calculated that successful contract actions

[454] Ss.3, 5, 10; Diamond, *Queen's Bench Masters*, 510–11. D.W. Harvey attacked two of the chiefs for appointing their nephews : *PD* 1838 (s3) 38: 1244, 1671.

[455] Sections 12, 19. No vacancy would be filled without a certificate that it was necessary, s 11.

[456] Abolition of Offices and Regulation of the Crown Office Act (6 & 7 Vict. c. 20). Its omission had been criticized (*PD* 1838 (s3) 38: 1673); *RC on the Legal Departments, Second Report 1874*, 7.

[457] *First Report 1851*, 61–5. Goulburn, chairman of the Treasury committee of the 1830s, had intended to include them in a second bill but lost his seat: *SC on Fees, Report 1847*, q. 170 (R. Hankins).

[458] An Act to make provision for the establishment of *nisi prius* offices (15 & 16 Vict. c.73).

[459] *First Report 1851*, 62. Tenterden's clerk was said to have cleared £3000 in a year: *SC on Fees, Report 1847*, q. 169 (Hankins). Until 1830, after which he was required to deliver accounts, he simply kept one bowl for gold and one for silver: q. 126.

[460] *RC on the Legal Departments, Second Report 1874*, 8–17, summarized in Holdsworth, *HEL*, i, 262–4.

[461] Francis, 'Practice, Strategy and institution', esp. 810–34.

[462] *SC on the Recovery of Small Debts, PP* 1823 (386), iv, 1; *PD* 1830 (s3), 1: 719–20.

tried in the Common Pleas between 1740 and 1840 cost 6.3 times the sum at stake, and 7.1 times in the King's Bench.[463] Since costs were frontloaded and actions which went to trial tended to be the larger ones, these are probably lower than the figures for all actions. The cost of going to law had risen sharply during the first half of the eighteenth century and had not since been reduced.[464]

Between one-quarter and one-third of the costs was directly attributable to court fees levied at various points—'tollgates' as Francis calls them—along the highway of a suit—no fewer than 40 points in the King's Bench.[465] Most of the remainder were attorneys' charges, but attorneys were locked into the fee structure. Their charges had been mostly frozen by the taxing masters and they could only make litigation profitable by manipulating the system, elaborating and multiplying the steps they took in connection with the court's process and for which they were allowed to charge.[466] It is not surprising that some of them strongly attacked the whole fee-taking structure.[467]

Mansfield apart, the common law chiefs had made no real effort to improve the workings of their own courts and ignored the power given them in 1823 to revise the fees, a dereliction tactfully ascribed in a later statute to their 'numerous and important Duties and Avocations'.[468] The Common Law Commission gave priority to tackling the causes of delays and congestion in the courts—a sensible course since to encourage extra business by cheapening the service would have aggravated existing problems—but the Treasury was authorized to create another inquiry to advise on fees and offices.[469]

This small body, which included no judges,[470] caused an immediate outcry from the officers when it emerged that they intended to reduce fees to the level reported in 1730 wherever (as in most cases) no authority could be shown for subsequent increases. Tenterden promptly came to the rescue of his staff and obtained an Act recognizing 50 years' unchallenged receipt as establishing a

---

[463] Francis, 'Practice, Strategy and Insitution', 857–8.

[464] Brooks, 'Interpersonal Conflict and Social Tension: Civil Litigation in England 1640–1830', in *Lawyers, Litigation and English Society*, 27–62, 45–7.

[465] Francis, 'Practice, Strategy and Institution', 859–60.

[466] *Ibid.*, 865–7. As Brougham put it, 'the necessary consequence of not suffering an attorney to be paid what he ought to receive for certain things, is that he is driven to do a number of needless things which he knows are allowed as a matter of course; and the expense is thus increased to the client far beyond the mere gain which the attorney derives from it' (quoted in M. Birks, *Gentlemen of the Law* (1960), 209–10).

[467] *Third Report 1831*, Apps C and E.

[468] An Act to Enable Judges to Make Regulations 1822 (3 Geo. IV c. 69); Courts of Common Law (Offices) Act 1837.

[469] Courts of Common Law (Offices) Act 1838, s 6.

[470] Serjeant Edward Goulburn, Sir Fortunatus Dwarris, Matthew Davenport Hill, and T. E. Dickinson.

lawful right[471] and peace was restored through hefty compensation to officers who lost their jobs in the rationalization that was a necessary prerequisite to a revised schedule of fees.[472]

Accordingly, in 1838 46 offices were suppressed and a new fees table created.[473] It was intended that the fees should be only sufficient to cover officers' salaries and running expenses but they produced surpluses which were quietly applied to the compensation claims.[474] Some favoured high charges to deter unnecessary litigation[475] while others optimistically argued that court costs should be borne by the public at large through taxation,[476] but neither view came close to being adopted. However, although the number of fees had been reduced to around 25, a handful of which (affidavits, summonses, orders, office copies of interrogatories, and depositions) produced the great bulk of the income,[477] the arrangements at *nisi prius* and Assizes had not been included and generated strong complaints until they were tackled.[478]

The government's inability to deny that it was still unprofitable to collect a £50 debt in the superior courts was a factor in the passage of Fitzroy's bill in 1850 raising the county court jurisdiction to that level.[479] Lyndhurst claimed that the Common Law Procedure Bill would reduce the costs of undefended actions below £3[480] and perhaps he was right, and that judgment by default in particular cheapened the cost of recovery, for superior court costs, unlike those in county courts, were seldom discussed thereafter.[481]

Governments and inquiries shied away from the problem of creating a fair remuneration structure for attorneys in litigation. Their position was worsened by the removal of unnecessary forms and procedures for which they could charge and the small gestures in the direction of greater liberality on the part of taxing masters did not go far to offset the losses.[482]

---

[471] Hankins' evidence: *SC on Fees, Report 1847*, especially. qq. 84–7. Short, a King's Bench clerk, complained that his income would be reduced from £5000 to £2000. Compensation provisions were set out in Fees in Superior Courts Act 1830.

[472] *RC on the Consolidation of Offices*, PP 1835 (314), xlvi. It also suggested that judges should be empowered to transfer staff between the courts.

[473] Courts of Common Law (Offices) Act 1837.

[474] *First Report 1851*, 54. The surplus over the previous four years had never been less than £9500.

[475] See e.g. the discussion in (1837) 18 *LM* 491. Lord Ellenborough had been of this opinion.

[476] *First Report 1851*, 54.

[477] The fees table is reproduced in (1838) 19 *LM* 230.

[478] See e.g. 'H', *Common Law Reform*, 135–6, and *First Report 1851*, 60.

[479] Polden, *History of the County Court*, 53.

[480] *PD* 1852 (s3) 121: 982. However, 'WDC', in 'Law Reform and its Prospects' (1853) 18 (s2) *LM* 87–117 at 92, noticed that the revised fees had actually been raised overall.

[481] Though a remonstrance of the Law Society is reproduced in (1858) 5 (s3) *LM & LR* 160–76.

[482] Birks, *Gentlemen of the Law*, 210–11, 222–5. Evidence to the Judicature Commission suggested that the plaintiff's taxed costs alone amounted on average to 22% of the sum awarded in judgment:

4. THE GREAT SESSIONS OF WALES

The Common Law Commissioners were diverted from their investigation and asked to give priority to considering the unique arrangements for the principality of Wales and the palatinate of Chester.[483] These dated from the reign of Henry VIII and comprised four circuits (Chester, Anglesey, Brecknock, and Carmarthen), each served by a chief justice and a puisne, together with an administrative and clerical staff which replicated the English courts in miniature.[484] The sessions were held twice a year, the two judges spending six days at each county town. They dispensed both law and equity and condensed into the sessions were all the stages of a law suit from the issue of proceedings to the trial and judgment, so that it united the functions of a law term and an Assize.[485]

The sessions had been a matter of controversy for some years. A Commons select committee of 1817 had been partly converted from initial hostility and in an abbreviated report following the untimely death of its chairman and moving spirit George Ponsonby, pronounced that 'notwithstanding some imperfections, it has much to recommend it, from the cheapness and expedition with which it administers justice'.[486] However, a further inquiry was chaired by a determined abolitionist, the Hon. J. F. Campbell, whose management ensured that the report would conclude that the defects, particularly in the equity administration, were irremediable.[487] An Act of 1824, the work of Sir John Jones, corrected several of the exposed deficiencies, but critics were unappeased.[488] Brougham included the sessions among the targets of his compendious speech of reform and Campbell

---

Second Report 1872, App., p. 468. Material for a rationalization of the rules on costs had by then been provided in the *RC on Common Law and Chancery, Second Report*, PP 1866 [3674], xvii.

[483] (1828–9) 1 *LM* 446.

[484] W. R. Williams, *The History of the Great Sessions in Wales* (Brecknock, 1899); T. G. Watkin, *The Legal History of Wales* (Cardiff, 2007), 145–67. There were some differences between the great sessions of the county palatine and those of Wales; in the latter alone issues arising from suits at Westminster might be tried by *mittimus*; defendants living in Wales enjoyed some protection from being sued in England; an Act of 1824 granting the right to apply by motion to a common law court at Westminster for a new trial was confined to the Welsh sessions, and the Chester sessions had no equity jurisdiction. Nevertheless, the Commissioners dealt with both together: *First Report 1829*, 35–6.

[485] The Carmarthen and Brecknockshire circuit was timed to allow the Oxford circuit bar to continue into Wales: 'An Old Circuit Leader, John Jones of Ystrad' (1869) 27 (s3) *LM & LR* 31–8.

[486] *SC on the Administration of Justice in Wales*, PP 1818 (109), 1. For critical accounts of the select committees, see *First Report 1829*, evidence of John Jones MP (App. E 12 at A.9) and Serjeant Edward Goulburn, a judge on the Carmarthen circuit, E 54 at A.29). Edmund Burke had advocated abolition in 1780 as part of the movement for economical reform in government: Williams, *Great Sessions of Wales*, 26–7.

[487] *SC on the Administration of Justice in Wales*, PP 1820 (273), ii and 1821 (662), iv.

[488] An Act to enlarge the Powers of the Judges of Great Sessions 1824 (5 Geo. IV c. 106).

(now Lord Cawdor) returned to the charge with a pamphlet attack which received considerable publicity.[489]

Even defenders of the system conceded that it had glaring defects, the most general dissatisfaction concerning the selection and tenure of its judges, which the Commissioners attacked on three grounds.[490] The first was that they were part-time, though it was pointed out that English towns had their recorders, and that serjeants were sent on Assize from time to time. The second was that they were eligible to sit in the House of Commons, though only one was an MP at that time and the same was true of the Master of the Rolls and the judge of Admiralty in England. The third was that because these judges went the same circuit year after year they were likely to become too well integrated into the local community, raising suspicions of partiality.[491] The same charge was to be levelled against county court judges.

Curiously, the Commissioners ignored the complaints which their consultees and other critics felt most serious. These appointments, decently rewarded, were in high demand because they were compatible with practice at the English bar and with other part-time appointments.[492] They had become highly politicized appointments, and the most lucrative, the Chief Justice of Chester, was a notorious 'rat run' for defecting opposition lawyers; the particularly blatant case of Charles Warren in 1819 had been the trigger for a renewed inquiry into the courts.[493] But the most common complaint in the evidence to the Commission was that even when they were good appointments—and some very eminent men had been found in their ranks—the absence of any provision for retiring pensions persuaded those who did not move on upwards (and therefore usually the less able) to cling to office too long.[494] Among the long-serving judges were Abel Moysey, who was on the Brecknock circuit for 42 years and Francis Burton, 29 years on the Chester.[495]

---

[489] PD 1828 (s2) 18: 146–7; A Letter to the Lord Chancellor... (1828). Criticism of the pamphlet by [C. E. Dodd?], 'Common Law Reforms' (1830) 42 Quart. Rev. 181–228 was answered in (1829–30) 3 LM 283–90. See also (1828–9) 1 LM 185–219, at 213–14.

[490] First Report 1829, 38–9.

[491] See e.g. Edward Lloyd (App. E 6) and Evan Thomas (App. E 14). Judges on the Carmarthen circuit enjoyed the lavish hospitality of the circuit leader, John Jones: An Old Circuit Leader, 35–6.

[492] Williams (History of the Great Sessions of Wales, 25–7) reckons only 30 of the 217 judges were Welsh. Salaries ranged from £1630 for the Chief Justice of Chester to £1150, but the chief justices also benefitted from fees. There was also an attorney-general for each circuit, who had to be retained in any case affecting the Crown, and was accompanied by a second counsel: First Report 1829, evidence of E. Thomas, App. E 14; SC on the Administration of Justice in Wales, Report 1818, evidence of Sir William Owen (p. 43) and S. Y. Benyon (p. 16).

[493] Williams, Great Sessions of Wales, 29; (1829) 2 LM 710–12.

[494] See e.g. E. V. Williams, App. E 44 at A.28; Sir W. Owen bart., App. E 40 at A.1, A.28.

[495] Williams, Great Sessions of Wales, 68, 143.

A more intractable obstruction to justice was the invincible partiality of the juries in some parts of Wales, which the recent introduction of the special jury was doing little to improve.[496] It was owned on all sides that there were places in which 'the spirit of party' ran so high, and types of suit in which popular opinion was so bigoted that there was little a judge could do.[497] The original arrangements had given the plaintiff an alternative; he might either bring his case in England or have the trial held in one of the English border counties.[498] However, since that in turn was productive of oppression to poor defendants it had been curtailed by the imposition in personal or transitory actions of a costs sanction and a nonsuit if the plaintiff were awarded less than £10, unless (in the case where the trial alone was held in England) the judge was prepared to certify that a freehold title was in question or 'that the cause was proper to be tried in England'.[499] Jones's Act strengthened the sanction by raising the limit to £50, though this was offset by allowing the parties to seek an order for a new trial from any of the common law courts.[500] As defenders of the system argued, substituting an Assize for the sessions would do nothing to alter the stubbornness of Welsh juries and would deprive suitors of any recourse to English courts.

Among other criticisms it was said that the leisurely character of the circuits, which allowed six days for each town, encouraged pettyfogging attorneys (some thought Wales had more than its share of that breed) to foment lawsuits among the farmers and landowners gathered for jury service and for existing suits.[501] On the other hand, it was also claimed that the period was often too short to allow the proper preparation for the trial, especially on the part of the defendant. Special pleading was hardly possible, especially given the fewness of practitioners of that recondite art on the circuit, so the general issue was the usual recourse.[502]

[496] *First Report 1829*, 41, noting that the practice of challenging the jury, almost unknown in England, was common in Wales. See also *SC on the Administration of Justice in Wales, Report 1818*, W. Owen, p. 43 and *SC Report 1820*, W. Evans, p.38.

[497] Evidence of W. E. Taunton, App. E 49 at A.15; J. Wilson, App. E 55 at A.15.

[498] Holdsworth, *HEL*, i, 130–1. There is a lengthy, and partisan, account in the evidence of William Owen KC in *First Report 1829*, App. E 56.

[499] 'An Act to Discourage Frivolous and Vexatious Suits…1773' (13 Geo. III c. 51). According to W. Owen (App. E 56) judges were wholly unwilling to certify on the second ground.

[500] Judges of Great Sessions Act 1824, ss 2, 21. There had been widespread unease that a new trial could only be had from the trial judge: see e.g. *SC on the Administration of Justice in Wales, Report 1818*, evidence of C. Temple, 50.

[501] *First Report 1829*, 39; E. Thomas, App. E 14, T. Wood, App. E 1. See also *SC on the Administration of Justice in Wales, Report 1818*, Lord Bulkeley, 114; *SC on the Administration of Justice in Wales Report 1820*, evidence of H. Rees, 42; *SC on the Administration of Justice in Wales, Report 1821*, evidence of R. N. Thomas, 27. Several Select Committee witnesses attributed this to the stamp duty on practising certificates being half the English rate.

[502] *SC on the Administration of Justice in Wales, Report 1818*, evidence of G. Roberts, 30; *SC on the Administration of Justice in Wales, Report 1821*, evidence of R. N. Thomas, 26.

On the busiest (Carmarthen) circuit, Chief Justice Heywood introduced a rule which had the effect of putting complicated cases back to the next sessions,[503] but that gave further substance to another complaint, that practice varied between circuits.[504]

And even if the quality of justice was satisfactory, the machinery, when compared with that in parts of England, seemed extravagant. After all, in 1823 there were only 2039 actions commenced in Wales as opposed to 63,241 in Westminster, and though the number was rising (3052 in 1827), the proportion was not. Even the heaviest circuit (Carmarthen) produced only 1231 in 1827, and trials were still fewer than 100 in that year (89, out of 166 entered for trial). Despite the *mittimus* facility, the palatinate was no busier, with just 324 writs in 1827.[505]

There were solid grounds for criticism therefore, but as Elias Taunton (an Englishman) wrote, many of the objections were 'of a vague, frivolous and exaggerated description, and very few of a direct and tangible nature'.[506] Some correspondents, like the Marquis of Bute, simply argued that any observer at a great sessions sitting would be 'struck with the general character of an inferior jurisdiction, which it presents'.[507] Such generalities were difficult to rebut, though defenders did point to the illustrious lawyers who had figured among the Welsh judges.[508]

The advantages claimed for the great sessions did not impress the Commissioners. The action *concessit solvere*, which was said to provide a cheap and rapid form of debt recovery, would lose one of its advantages (the brevity of the declaration) if a similarly abbreviated count were introduced for other common law actions, and was also felt objectionable as commencing by notice rather than writ.[509] Proceedings conducted solely in Wales might be expected to be cheaper because there was no need to employ a London agent and because 'forms of office and the niceties of practice are less complicated and obscure'.[510] 'Everything is on a smaller scale', including attorneys' charges and counsels' fees according to one well-informed consultee,[511] but the Commissioners rather

---

[503] *SC on the Administration of Justice in Wales, Report 1820*, 8–9.

[504] *SC on the Administration of Justice in Wales, Report 1818*, evidence of Heywood, 39, 43, W. O. Russel, 45. Abuse of *certiorari* for delay on the Brecknock circuit was singled out for condemnation by the second select committee (*Report 1821*, 4).

[505] *First Report 1829*, table 17.

[506] *Ibid.*, App. E 49 at A.27.

[507] *Ibid.*, App. E 24 at A.9.

[508] *Ibid.*, e.g. John Jones, App. E 12. William Kenrick (App. E 41) cited Hugh Leycester, who had turned down a superior court judgeship, as a model judge.

[509] *Ibid.*, 36–7. It was also available in Bristol and in the courts of the City of London.

[510] *Ibid.*, W. E. Taunton, App. E 49 at A.9.

[511] *Ibid.* There had been laxity in the regulation of court fees, however. It was suspected that on one circuit the attorneys and prothonotary had struck a bargain whereby he would raise his fees and

questionably pronounced the evidence on costs 'somewhat contradictory'. By comparing the cost of Welsh actions with those at Westminster after the reforms they proposed should be implemented, they were able to conclude that the latter would ultimately be cheaper.[512]

Defenders of the system were faced with an uphill task, for the Commissioners' standpoint was that '[u]nless the course of proceeding applicable to remote counties, such as Cornwall and Northumberland, should be less capable of application to the principality of Wales, or vice versa, we can see no sound reason why a difference of system should continue to prevail'.[513] Moreover, in marked contrast to the approach which judge-dominated inquiries usually took in relation to England, they gave greater weight to lay opinion than professional. They found 'a very general desire expressed by persons of property and intelligence resident in Wales' for assimilation.[514] The contrary opinion of most of the lawyers consulted was delicately discounted, they being 'supposed to feel a partiality for the system in which they are, or have been engaged', though some were still in active practice at the common law bar.[515]

In truth, whatever the merits of the change, the outcome seems to have been a foregone conclusion.[516] The inclusion of a question inviting views on the 'progress' of Welsh manners, the desirability of the assimilation of Welsh habits to English ones, and the potential contribution of a union of judicatures thereto, is significant.[517] Even if this was not, as Serjeant Goulburn asserted, 'a mere party question',[518] it was more a political one than a legal one. The Commissioners, none of whom was Welsh, were anxious that the full panoply of justice as known in Westminster Hall should be extended to the backward Welsh and without awaiting the outcome of the reforms to the English system which were their main task.

It only remained to work out how the six circuits could be made into seven, a task which devolved chiefly upon Bosanquet.[519] His plan was to annex roughly

allow them more generous costs: *SC on the Administration of Justice in Wales, Report 1818*, evidence of J. Hutchinson, 18, G. Roberts, 30.

[512] *Ibid.*, 37 and App. M. The relative cheapness of the great sessions had been the subject of much disagreement among witnesses to the select committees.

[513] *Ibid.*, 36. Criticised in [Dodd], 'Common Law Reforms', 212.

[514] *Ibid.*, 39. Two great landed proprietors, the Marquis of Bute and Earl Grosvenor, favoured abolition.

[515] *Ibid.*, 38. Among the well-known lawyers were J. Raine KC, W.E. Taunton (shortly to become a superior court judge), Serjeants Goulburn and Russell, and E. V. Williams.

[516] Law Terms Act 1830 (11 Geo. IV and 1 Will. IV c.70). For some years Welsh judges had been appointed on the understanding that they would have no right to compensation if the sessions were abolished: Williams, *Great Sessions of Wales*, 27.

[517] *First Report 1829*, second set (App. E.38), Q.3.

[518] *Ibid.*, App. E 54 at A.24.

[519] Cawdor seems to have been involved too, see his letter of 7 November 1828, *ibid*, App. E 33.

one-fifth of the principality to the adjacent English circuit towns, mostly to Chester and Hereford, and to form the remainder into four, Carmarthen, Neath, Dolgellau, and Bangor. These were to become part of the Oxford circuit, and two judges were to go thence into the north Wales districts and two into the south.[520] In the event this scheme was frustrated by a combination of financial considerations and the uproar it created in the principality[521] and instead the judges divided a new Welsh circuit, which was practicable since the volume of business was modest. In the decade ending 1844 the average number of criminal trials was 109 in south Wales and 63 in the north, though much higher (162) in Chester.[522] *Nisi prius* trials were many fewer—only 15 in the north (though Chester had 34) and 57 in the south.[523] By the mid-1850s, however, the rising amount of business of both kinds from the industrial and commercial centres of south-east Wales was making the single judge visit unsatisfactory, while complaints were heard of the waste of judicial and official time in visits to small town in other parts of Wales which barely merited a county court.[524] The Common Law (Judicial Business) Commission was probably voicing an optimism it did not truly feel in suggesting that local opinion would be prepared to accept a certain amount of grouping of counties and alternation of their Assize towns.[525] It was on safer ground in urging that two judges should visit Cardiff and Swansea.[526] The problem of the extravagant use of superior court judges which arose from the imposition almost unadapted of the English circuit system on a less populous and wealthy country was to prove a stubborn one.

5. THE ASSIZES

Few aspects of the judicial system were so unsatisfactory as the delivery of justice by means of the Assizes and few were so resistant to effective reform, let alone to abolition. The nineteenth century saw inquiry after inquiry yet the system in 1914 differed very little in essentials from that of 1814.

---

[520] *Ibid.*, 42–51.

[521] *RC on Circuit Regulation*, PP 1845 [638], xiv, 6; *RC on the Common Law (Judicial Business)*, *Report 1857*, xviii and evidence of Sir J. T. Coleridge, qq. 503–4; [Dodd], 'Common Law Reforms', 214–15.

[522] The growth of Stockport was held responsible for the rise in crimes tried at Chester: *SC on the Administration of Justice in Wales, Report 1818*, evidence of Sir J. Mansfield, 56 and Francis Burton, 7.

[523] *RC on the Common Law (Judicial Business), Report 1857*, returns, 121.

[524] *Ibid.*, xvi, xviii. The Commission's own figures do not fully support the growth of Glamorganshire business, for while criminal trials did increase (it was given a winter Assize in 1855), *nisi prius* trials were actually fewer in 1856 than in 1845.

[525] At p. xviii. They had not found time to consult the local authorities. Cresswell and Wensleydale opposed the recommendation.

[526] *Ibid.*, p. xvii.

The two biggest changes occurred near the start of the era of systematic law reform. A pertinacious campaign by M. A. Taylor succeeded in extending the Lent Assize to the four northernmost counties and, much more contentiously, Wales was brought into the system in 1830. That increased the number of circuits to seven and (with the exception of London and Middlesex) made their scope comprehensive in place and equal in time.[527] There was never a complete symmetry, however, because from 1822 an additional commission issued for the trial of criminal cases on the home circuit.[528]

This expedient underlined one of the biggest structural flaws in the Assize system, the increasingly divergent demands of criminal and civil justice, the latter requiring longer sittings in the big towns, the former frequent visits to many more places. Each, however, suffered seriously from another flaw, the asymmetrical arrangement of the legal calendar. Assizes fitted into the intervals between Trinity and Michaelmas term (July and early August) and between the Hilary and Easter terms (late February and March), so that the intervals were grossly unequal. If a trial could not be ready for the Summer Assize a period of almost eight months must elapse, during which alleged criminals must languish in gaol and debtors might set their creditors at defiance. Humanitarian reformers and impatient businessmen alike found this anomalous and unacceptable.[529]

Like the structure of the legal year, the geography of the Assize had hardened into a shape which would be hard to change. It was based on the simple principle that one town in each county must be visited on every Assize, and while changes to the Assize towns were not unknown, they were likely to be fiercely resisted by the loser.[530] The disjunction between population centres and representation was not so spectacular as in the House of Commons, but the rapid growth of great industrial towns made the solemn spectacle of the 'red judges' and their entourage entering Oakham and Appleby to try a handful of cases while Manchester, Liverpool, and Birmingham went unvisited increasingly difficult to defend.[531] These, then, were the two issues which proved so intractable: how many Assizes

[527] The circuits were the home, western, midland, Oxford, northern, and Norfolk.

[528] PD 1819, 39: 293–6; 40: 1067–77; 1822 (s2) 6: 1317–26; Bentley, English Criminal Justice in the Nineteenth Century, 52–3.

[529] Bentley, English Criminal Justice, 53–4; RC on the Common Law, Fifth Report (hereafter Fifth Report 1833), PP 1833 (247), xxii, 15. Delays were somewhat alleviated by the extension of summary jurisdiction, see Vol. XIII, pp. 115–21.

[530] Even the order of visits had become fixed: J. S. Cockburn, 'The Northern Assize Circuit', (1968) 3 Northern History, 118–30.

[531] J. S. Cockburn, A History of English Assizes 1558–1714 (Cambridge, 1972), 23–48. Changes to Assize towns had once been quite frequent, especially on the home circuit, but they had become less common. There is a list in First Report 1829, 66–9. R. Walton, Random Reminiscences of the Midland Circuit (1869), 146–7, recalled great excitement in Oakham when it was rumoured that there would be two causes and three criminal trials at the Assize.

should there be, and when should they be held? Which towns should be the Assize towns? There were, of course, a few brave souls within the legal profession, and a good many outside it, who advocated a partial or complete dismantling of the Assize system in favour of permanent courts located in the major cities, but this was kept resolutely off the agenda of each inquiry.[532]

The desirability of a full-scale third Assize was regularly canvassed,[533] but it never obtained much support from those judges and practitioners who dominated the inquiries and was either ignored or perfunctorily dismissed in a few lines.[534] The 1845 inquiry placed a good deal of faith in equalizing the interval between the assizes, proposing to bring the Hilary term forward so that it would end at christmas, allowing a genuine Winter Assize in January, but that fell on stony ground.[535] This Commission had disapproved of the special commissions which, after being ended by Brougham in 1834,[536] had had to be revived and extended beyond the home circuit to several of the larger counties in 1843, objecting to the single judge, the incomplete bar accompanying him, and the inconvenience to sheriffs etc. However, by 1857 these had become indispensable and the Commission of that year, while opposed to a full third Assize, felt compelled to expand the special commissions to the civil side, suggesting that 'in effect a third assize' should go to the great cities of the north and a few other places where the demand was irresistible.[537] It was a strategy of make do and mend.

A similar outlook prevailed when it came to considering the location of Assize towns. Three considerations were allowed severely to limit a rational re-ordering to suit the age of the railway. The first was that the number of judges did not permit the circuits to be expanded beyond seven. The second was that in order to fit into the legal calendar, the length of each circuit had to be restricted to a maximum of 42 days and eight towns.[538] The third was that the county should remain the essential unit. It could not be sustained in the case of Lancashire, which had to be divided into three, and later for Yorkshire, but it was for this reason that Lancaster's enterprising bid to annex places in adjacent counties was briskly rejected and that Rutland and Westmoreland were sure of keeping their place.[539]

Even within these constraints, which made it difficult simply to add new places to the circuits, it was in theory possible to replace an existing town with one

---

[532] An example from *The Jurist* is criticized in (1828–9) 1 *LM* 185–218 at 198.

[533] *RC on the Common Law (Judicial Business), Report 1857*, evidence of G. Lavie, W. Murray, and W. Sharpe.

[534] *Ibid.*, xvi; *Fifth Report 1833*, 17; *RC on Circuits, Report 1845*, 3

[535] At pp. 3–4.   [536] Bentley, *English Criminal Justice*, 53.

[537] At p. xvi.   [538] *First Report 1829*, 48.

[539] *RC on the Common Law (Judicial Business), Report 1857*, xiii.

better situated for transport, better provided with facilities such as gaols and courthouses, or more populous. In practice, Commissioners were reluctant to recommend changes and ministers did not welcome the political row they would inevitably cause. Liverpool was added in 1833, ten years after the corporation first petitioned,[540] but Manchester had to wait until 1864, after an enquiry had reluctantly accepted that its claims were undeniable.[541] Leeds was given an Assize in the same year,[542] but Birmingham failed to persuade inquiries that it should displace Warwick or carve out a territory of its own. [543]

The proportion of civil business which went for trial in the country rather than in town was just under 40 per cent in the late 1820s.[544] It might have been expected that the competition from county courts and improved communications by post and rail would have hit the circuits hard, and this appears to have been the case,[545] but their experience varied considerably.[546] For criminal trials in the decade ending 1844 the Oxford was more than twice as busy as the Norfolk, whereas civil trials were far more numerous on the northern than anywhere else. Over the next decade or so civil trials were lower everywhere except the home, and fell most steeply on the midland, whereas crime grew substantially on the northern and more modestly everywhere save the western and the Oxford, where it fell slightly.[547] Some lighter circuits were desirable for the most elderly judges, but these discrepancies were altogether too large for comfort and the Norfolk in particular was doing very little business of any sort.

The great problem was the northern, which was swollen by the addition of new centres and was generating litigation which alike in quantity and complexity

---

[540] B. Nield, *Farewell to the Assizes* (1972), 105. An Act for the Appointment of Convenient Places for Holding Assizes 1833 (3 & 4 Will. IV c. 71), following the report of a select committee (*PP* 1831–2 (621), xxxv).

[541] *RC on the Common Law (Judicial Business), Report 1857*, xii–xiii. It had been recommended by the first Common Law Commission (*First Report 1829*, 50–2).

[542] Leeds and Wakefield tussled strenuously for the privilege. Wakefield had brought forward an impressively supported petition in 1821 (*First Report 1829*, 53 and App. F) and in 1857 obtained the support of a minority of the later Commission, which unanimously rejected Leeds (xiii–xiv).

[543] The Commission of 1857 were split 4–4 on this proposal: xiv–xv.

[544] *First Report 1829*, App., table 1.

[545] Even before these improvements had made much impact, Francis suggests that attorneys were opting more frequently for trial in London: 'Practice, Strategy and Institution', 880–1.

[546] Hardcastle, *Life of Lord Campbell*, ii, 350. A thoughtful examination of the records of the Oxford circuit in 1851 attributed its decline, inter alia, to the *nisi prius* rules of 1833; the power given to the sheriffs to try small causes in 1834, and to Denman's Act of 1840 denying plaintiffs in tort costs if they recovered less than 40s as well as to the county courts. The author also detected a decline in litigiousness and a reduction in torts relating to land as a result of reforms to the land law: 'J.E.D.', 'The Cause Lists of the Oxford Circuit, Past, Present and Future' (1851) 14 (s2) *LM* 217–28.

[547] *RC on Circuits, Report 1845*, App., 122.

dwarfed some of the other circuits.[548] Rumours that it would be divided were current in the early 1840s[549] but the 1845 Commission had a majority opposed to that.[550] If it had to be done they favoured making Yorkshire into a new circuit but served by the judges of the Norfolk, but their successors, now accepting (with the exception of Sir Cresswell Cresswell[551]) that some such arrangement was inevitable, preferred attaching it to the midland, with consequent musical chairs on the adjoining circuits in an attempt to rebalance the workloads. This avoided the creation of an extra circuit, which as needing additional judges was outside the Commission's remit,[552] but made for a rather strange itinerary.

6. THE CENTRAL CRIMINAL COURT

The Central Criminal Court (CCC) came into being through an Act of 1834.[553] Responsibility for the Act is unclear, and as so often, Brougham's admirers gave him all the credit, while his detractors denied him any.[554] In any event, some felt little credit was due, since the new court was no more than a restyled and extended Old Bailey sessions.[555]

A reform of the arrangements for London's criminal trials was badly needed and so far as it went, the Act was useful. Since 1800 the number of Old Bailey trials had tripled and even with each sessions lengthened from five to ten days the court was struggling to cope.[556] This court was a curious hybrid. Though there was no Assize for London and Middlesex, a separate commission of oyer and terminer and a gaol delivery commission issued for each and they shared Newgate prison. The judges' sittings were combined with the City quarter sessions, and had risen to eight a year.[557] The commission named not only all the common law judges (like the Assizes only two attended), but also the lord mayor, who

---

[548] The average number of civil trials on the northern for the ten years ending in 1844 was 465; the next biggest, the home, had 241. Because the northern did not generally try minor criminal offences, direct comparisons of that business cannot be made: *RC on Circuits, Report 1845*, 5 and n.3.

[549] (1841) 25 *LM* 472; (1842) 27 *LM* 244.

[550] At p. 5.

[551] Cresswell was at least consistent. He rejected every proposed change the Commission discussed, even the belated and partial rectification of the anomaly that Bristol had no criminal Assize and only a single civil one. The rest of the Commission favoured adding another civil one, but were evenly split on the criminal Assize (xvii–xviii).

[552] Explicitly in the case of the Circuit Commission, implicitly in the case of the Judicial Business Commission, whose principal remit was to investigate the feasibility of reducing the number of judges.

[553] Central Criminal Court Act, 4 & 5 Will. IV c. 36.

[554] A. N. May, *The Bar and the Old Bailey* (Chapel Hill, 2003), 147.

[555] 'Central Criminal Court' (1835) 22 *Westminster Rev.* 195–212, 197.

[556] May, *Bar and Old Bailey*, 146; Bentley, *English Criminal Justice in the Nineteenth Century*, 55.

[557] May, *Bar and Old Bailey*, 14–16.

notionally presided, and the aldermen, along with two City judges, the Recorder of London and (since 1790) the common serjeant;[558] a third City judge was added in 1824. The 1834 Act disappointed more thoroughgoing reformers by preserving all the City's privileges in relation to the court, even the requirement that an alderman must sit alongside the judge, though with the decline in the status of the aldermanic office it was becoming much less common for his opinion on the appropriate sentence to be sought. [559]

There would now be 12 sessions a year, with cases brought from parts of counties adjoining the metropolis which had been overwhelmed by the march of bricks and mortar. Many applauded the consequent removal of business from the Middlesex sessions at Clerkenwell, since the magistrates who sat there (particularly the chairman) were frequently criticized.[560]

The City had added an extra courtroom in 1824 but the courthouse was not extended along with the jurisdiction.[561] When further courtrooms were added in 1848 and the grand jury room subsequently pressed into service, it increased congestion in the lobbies where lawyers, witnesses, and members of the public mingled promiscuously, and facilities for counsel were wholly inadequate.[562] Worse, the ill-ventilated premises were a health hazard, said to have claimed the life of Mr Justice Coltman in 1849.[563] Public interest in sensational murder trials, such as Courvoisier's and Palmer's, far exceeded the public seating and enabled the lesser officers (and the sheriffs) to profit handsomely from would-be spectators without influence and connections.[564]

As noted elsewhere, the Old Bailey bar could not shake off the bad reputation it had acquired early in its distinct existence and which was perpetuated in the reminiscences of Hawkins, Ballantine, and others.[565] The reputation may have been unfair[566] but it was not without foundation. The less successful members included some who were unprincipled or desperate enough to flout the

---

[558] *Ibid.*, 146.

[559] *Central Criminal Court*, 199, 210; Bentley, *English Criminal Justice*, 55.

[560] *Central Criminal Court*, 197. For later extensions, see *Halsbury's Laws of England*, ix (1909) and G. G. Alexander, *The Administration of Criminal Justice in England* (1919 edn), 88.

[561] May, *Bar and Old Bailey*, 146. She describes the old courtroom on 17–19.

[562] Bentley, *English Criminal Justice*, 56; J. R. Lewis, *The Victorian Bar* (1982), 20–2. Witnesses were said to get drunk while waiting: *Central Criminal Court*, 202. This lack of separation was out of line with trends in courthouse building; see below, p. 780.

[563] Lewis, *Victorian Bar*, 18–19.

[564] *Ibid.*, 13.

[565] See below, pp. 969–70. R. Harris (ed.), *Reminiscences of Henry Hawkins, Baron Brampton* (1904); W. S. Ballantine, *Some Experiences of a Barrister's Life* (1883). According to 'The Old Bailey and its Practices' (1872) 1 (ns) *LM & R* 326–34, at 326, 'The Old Bailey bar has long possessed an unenviable notoriety'.

[566] This is May's view (*Bar and Old Bailey*, 33). For a contemporary defence see *Central Criminal Court*, 200.

conventions of the profession by undercutting or seeking instructions direct from prosecutor or prisoner, and this persisted after the more striking manifestations of unprofessional conduct (literally striking in Adolphus's duel with Alley and his umbrella scuffle with Andrews) had ceased. H. K. Avory, the clerk of arraigns, made repeated efforts to introduce order into the distribution of 'soup' to the indigent and exigent and to curb malpractices, but only the creation of a mess in 1891 and the stern rule of the puritanical R. D. Muir raised professional standards close to those in other courts. [567]

Old Bailey practitioners suffered especially from the widespread public perception of barristers as unscrupulous hirelings, which persisted after the debate provoked by the Courvoisier case,[568] and their methods laid them open to criticism. Though cross-examination became 'the most popular work and that which dazzles most bystanders',[569] it was seldom conducted with the surgical precision of a Garrow. Many of his imitators wielded a bludgeon rather than a scalpel, hectoring and bullying witnesses to an extent which occasionally provoked even the jury to protest, and the high rhetoric of an Erskine became bathos in many a sentimental address to the jury.[570] Outside the state trials prosecuting counsel had generally exercised restraint when faced with an unrepresented defendant,[571] but with defence counsel becoming more common and (after the Prisoners' Counsel Act) allowed to play a larger role, they retaliated in kind, adopting a 'vicious system of vindictive prosecutions'.[572]

Credit for ending that system, at least in public prosecutions, belongs mainly to H. B. Poland, Treasury counsel from 1865.[573] Poland's more dispassionate approach was by and large followed by his successors, though Muir was felt to be over-zealous in seeking convictions. Defence counsel were less inhibited but gradually the florid style epitomized by Gerald Geogeghan fell out of favour, and slowly the ignorant 'Old Bailey hack' became a less characteristic figure.[574]

---

[567] See S. T. Felstead and Lady Muir, *Sir Richard Muir* (1927), 154–6.

[568] During Courvoisier's sensational trial in 1840 for the murder of his employer, Lord William Russell, he disclosed to his counsel, Charles Phillips, that he was guilty. Phillips consulted Baron Parke, one of the trial judges, and reluctantly continued with the defence. His action aroused fierce controversy, with professional and public opinion sharply divided: May, *Bar and Old Bailey*, 202–36.

[569] [T. N. Talfourd], 'On the Profession of the Bar' (1825) n.s. 1 *London Magazine & Review* 323–38, at 327.

[570] May, *Bar and Old Bailey*, 40–2; B. W. Kelly, *Famous Advocates and their Speeches* (1921), 1–28.

[571] May, *Bar and Old Bailey*, 187–94.

[572] Sir C. Biron, *Without Prejudice* (1936), 106. Cross-examinations had been criticized even in the 18th century: May, *Bar and Old Bailey*, 124–45.

[573] See T. Humphreys, *Criminal Days* (1946), 67–89.

[574] Strahan, *Bench and Bar of England*, 94–9; A. Crew, *The Old Bailey* (1933), 78.

Much less is known about the attorneys and solicitors practising at the Bailey. Most reputable firms shunned criminal work and, as the Crouch affair of 1844 demonstrated, most of the 'respectable' business was handled by a few specialist firms who regularly employed the same leaders.[575] The leaders in turn farmed out much of the work to less fortunate brethren but others—unless they followed Crouch's lead in taking instructions directly from the prosecutor or prisoner— had to deal with shadier (and sometimes unqualified) attorneys who defied attempts to curb their dubious methods.[576]

However, what most damaged the reputation of the CCC was the behaviour of its judges. Lawyers found little fault with the common law judges, but they mostly tried the more important cases and few sat regularly (Hawkins was an exception).[577] Most cases were tried by the City judges, apparently to the disapproval of some prisoners.[578] Since the positions of Recorder and common serjeant were much coveted (past recorders included some Illustrious names), they might have been eminent barristers;[579] indeed even the less coveted third judgeship attracted good candidates.[580] Unfortunately the City corporation preferred a regular arrangement whereby one of the four City pleaders, who had usually bought their position, was elected common serjeant and then succeeded to the recordership. The City thereby secured a man of their own (Tory) persuasion and one likely to oppose any relaxation in the penal laws.[581] The results were unhappy. Sir John Silvester, the first such, had an unsavoury reputation;[582] Newman Knowlys had to resign after issuing a warrant for the execution of a pardoned prisoner;[583] John Mirehouse was notorious for excessive dispatch;[584] and C. E. Law, though

[575] May, Bar and Old Bailey, 80–4, and below, pp. 1135–6.

[576] H. K. Avory made persistent attempts to control such practitioners but 'as fast as one set of abuses has been got rid of, another has made its appearance': Old Bailey and its Practices, 333.

[577] Before the 1880s the other common law judge often sat on the bench with the trial judge, as Parke did with Tindal in the Courvoisier case. He would read the depositions for the next case: Bentley, English Criminal Justice, 55; E. Bowen Rowlands, Seventy-two Years at the Bar (1924), 21.

[578] 'L', 'Old Bailey Experience' (1833) 10 LM 259–96, 275–6. In the mid-1830s, the City judges were trying about 80% of cases: May, Bar and Old Bailey, 167.

[579] May, Bar and Old Bailey, 153. Salaries of the Recorder and common serjeant (£1000 and £550 respectively) were raised by £500 in 1837 in consideration of the increased workload. By 1900 they were earning £4000 and £3000, making them easily the best paid judges outside the SCJ: Bentley, English Criminal Justice, 69.

[580] The candidates in 1859 included W. F. Finlason, Serjeant Alexander Pulling and C. R. Kennedy: Pitt-Lewis, Mr. Commissioner Kerr, 98–100.

[581] May, Bar and Old Bailey, 150–67.

[582] Ibid., 36–40, 150–2.

[583] Ibid., 152–4, 158–9.

[584] Ibid., 159–66. One trial (R v. Jones) was said to have been timed at 2 minutes 53 seconds: Lewis, Victorian Bar, 17–18 (wrongly naming him Muirhouse).

conscientious, inherited little of his illustrious father's legal ability.[585] A team of Law, Mirehouse, and William Arabin (whose verbal eccentricities were cherished and collected) hardly inspired confidence in a court from which there was scarcely the possibility of an appeal. The succession was challenged by radicals on the common council, successfully in 1822, when they installed Denman as common serjeant instead of Bolland, but their candidate in subsequent elections, M. D. Hill, was defeated.[586]

Fortunately, Law's successor as Recorder, Russell Gurney was, in the view of one Old Bailey regular, 'the very best criminal judge that ever sat on the bench',[587] and 'Weeping Tommy' Chambers was also well regarded.[588] Even 'Commissioner' Kerr, though eccentric to a fault, was far better than the undignified Michael Prendergast.[589] But Sir William Charley's shortcomings ('How he ever...came to be common serjeant is a mystery'[590]) fatally discredited the elective system and in 1888 he was retired on full pay and the appointment of common serjeant given to the Lord Chancellor.[591] The Lord Chancellor's choices were not always approved[592]—some thought F. A. Bosanquet was ill-suited to the position[593]—but they were no worse than some county court appointments.

Not all the injustices perpetrated at the CCC were attributable to the defects of individual judges. Pressure of business in the 1830s led to trials being conducted with a briskness which, it was said, sometimes meant that the slower-witted prisoners left the dock unaware that it was over.[594] Wontner put the average trial at 8½ minutes, but even a critic's correction to 22 minutes implied that many were very short.[595] The growth of representation and the Prisoners Counsel Act must

[585] May, *Bar and Old Bailey*, 157–9, 164–5.

[586] *Ibid.*, 154–63. Curiously, the Whig-dominated Municipal Corporations Commission did not condemn the City's practice and pronounced that elections were not politically driven.

[587] M. Williams, *Leaves of a Life*, 2 vols (1890), 41–2. He was J. F. Stephen's cousin.

[588] *ODNB* 10: 996. Common serjeant 1857, Recorder 1878–91. City politics evidently underwent some changes, for the Liberal and moderate penal reformer Chambers was preferred to the Conservative J. F. Stephen. His nickname was the result of an eye condition.

[589] Polden, *History of the County Court*, App. 1. For Prendergast, see Ballantine, *Some Experiences*, 30.

[590] Biron, *Without Prejudice*, 108.

[591] *Ibid.*, 109.

[592] Polden, *History of the County Court*, App. 1.

[593] Biron, *Without Prejudice*, 120; A. C. Plowden, *Grain or Chaff? The Autobiography of a Police Magistrate* (1903), 133.

[594] T. Wontner, *Old Bailey Experiences* (1833). 'L', reviewing it for the *Law Magazine* ((1833) 10, 259–96, at 275–6) agreed but the reviewer in the *Westminster Review* ((1834) 20, 142–51, at 148) differed.

[595] 'Old Bailey Experience' (1834) 20 *Westminster Rev.* 142–51 at 146–7. Wontner's view of the rapidity of proceedings is supported by many anecdotes in memoirs etc. It should, however, be borne in mind that trials at sessions and *nisi prius* and on Assize at that time were often much

have prolonged proceedings, however, and complaints of excessive speed became less frequent. A major improvement was the ending of evening sessions. Until 1844 the court had sat from 9 am to 9 pm, the judges changing at 5 pm, and the day was punctuated by two hearty dinners. When the City judges commenced the evening shift they (and some counsel) were often well-lubricated and the quality of justice suffered.[596] The more fastidious Victorians found this Augustan practice whereby 'eating and drinking, transporting and hanging, were shuffled together'[597] repellent and when the dinners were temporarily stopped after a fire in 1877, the High Court judges declined to have them reinstated.[598]

Serjeant Robinson felt that serious injustice was prevented by the benign influence of the clerks.[599] Certainly at least two clerks of arraigns were men of impressive learning; Thomas Shelton was 'perhaps the most accomplished criminal lawyer of his day'[600] and Henry Avory 'knew more law than all the Bench of Judges put together'.[601]

The criminal trial underwent a major change with the Prisoners Evidence Act 1898 and, indirectly, with the creation of the court of Criminal Appeal in 1907, and the Old Bailey's physical environment changed too, with Newgate prison demolished in 1902 and the courts replaced by new buildings in 1907.[602] More of the serious cases were in the hands of the DPP[603] and a new generation of barristers such as Edward Marshall Hall was achieving national fame through murder trials.

shorter than the Edwardian amplitude which was causing such problems towards the end of the period (see below, pp. 821–2).

[596] May, *Bar and Old Bailey*, 170–1. Among many contemporary or near-contemporary descriptions, see T. Walker, 'The Original' (1836) 55 *Quarterly Rev.* 474–5, and the reminiscences of Serjeant Robinson and Montagu Williams.

[597] Ballantine's words, quoted in May, *Bar and Old Bailey*, 171.

[598] (1879–80) 24 *Sol. J.* 140.

[599] 'Steady, responsible men, well versed in criminal law and practice': *Reminiscences*, 47, and see Jay, *The Law*, 260–4.

[600] 'Mr. Baron Garrow' (1844–5) 1 *LR*, 318–28 at 318. His draft bill was later used in the preparation of the Central Criminal Court Act 1836: May, *Bar and Old Bailey*, 147.

[601] G. Lang, *Mr. Justice Avory* (1935), 40 and see Williams, *Leaves of a Life*, 60. He was the father of Horace Avory and had been clerk of indictments, the assistant to the clerk of arraigns. Before the Indictments Act 1915, the arcane technicalities of the indictment represented one of the biggest traps for prosecutors (Bentley, *English Criminal Justice*, 134–7). There were specialists, equivalent to special pleaders, to draw them up, one of whom, J. H. Tickell, joined the Old Bailey staff (T. Humphreys, *Criminal Days* (1948), 83–5). As junior Treasury counsel, Montagu Williams managed to get his done by the clerk of indictments, hence perhaps his fulsome praise for the Old Bailey officials: Purcell, *Forty Years at the Criminal Bar*, 25; Williams, *Leaves of a Life*, 6.

[602] See below, pp. 805–8 and XIII, Pt 1, pp. 102–7.

[603] C. Whiteley, *A Brief Life* (1942), 17.

IV

The Court of Chancery, 1820–1875

1. LORD ELDON'S CHANCERY

After 20 years of Lord Eldon's stewardship Chancery was a court in crisis, with both court and Chancellor being subjected to severe criticism. Attacks begun in 1810, which had led to the creation of a Vice-Chancellor to ease the Chancellor's burdens, were renewed by that most persistent critic, the Whig barrister M. A. Taylor, and scarcely abated during the rest of Eldon's tenure.[1] The critics charged the court with the terrible twins of the law, delay and cost, and attributed the delay largely to Eldon, but far from abating with Eldon's resignation in 1827, complaints about Chancery continued almost without pause, finding their most vivid expression in Charles Dickens' *Bleak House* in 1852.[2] The novel provoked plaintive remonstrances from the court's defenders, who correctly pointed out that some of the ills it described, notably the treatment of those imprisoned for contempt, had been remedied.[3] However, the court was further damaged by inaccurate revelations about the Jennens litigation, cited by Dickens in support of his indictment, and the revelation in 1856 that the fabulous Thellusson fortune had been so sweated in Chancery as to barely exceed the amount it had begun with 60 years earlier.[4]

Criticism of Chancery was nothing new. It had been a favourite target for reformers in the seventeenth century and had continued to attract complaints

---

[1] The best account is M. J. Lobban, 'Preparing for Fusion: Reforming the Nineteenth-Century Court of Chancery, Part One' (2004) 22 *LHR* 389–427. A useful summary is in D. M. Kerly, *An Historical Sketch of the Equitable Jurisdiction of the Court of Chancery* (Cambridge, 1890), and see A. Birrell, 'Changes in Equity, Procedure and Principles', in Council of Legal Education (eds), *A Century of Law Reform* (1901), 177–202.

[2] W. S. Holdsworth, *Charles Dickens as a Legal Historian* (1927), 79–115.

[3] *Ibid.* See the preface to the first edition of *Bleak House* (August 1853). Dickens had recently been criticized by Sir Edward Sugden in a letter to *The Times* for an article, 'The Martyrs of Chancery', in *Household Words* (December 1850). For the reform of the contempt process see below.

[4] P. Polden, 'Stranger than Fiction? The Jennens Inheritance in Fact and Fiction' (2003) 32 *Common Law World Rev.* 211–47, 338–67; P. Polden, *Peter Thellusson's Will and its Consequences on Chancery Law* (Lewiston, NY, 2002).

in the eighteenth.[5] However exaggerated Jarndyce and Jarndyce might be, there was ample testimony from more knowledgeable and dispassionate observers to support Dickens' condemnation. As for delay, George Spence declared that '[n]o man, as things stand, can enter into a Chancery suit with any reasonable hope of being alive at its termination, if he has a determined adversary',[6] while for a leading London solicitor, John Forster, its 'modes of proceeding... [are] as little adapted to the ordinary duration of human life as they are calculated for the determination of differences and the quiet of possession'.[7] Forster also testified to the excessive cost of a Chancery suit: 'for great estates, and great fortunes, there is no security so good, and no trustee so safe, as the court of Chancery, but to little fortunes it is ruin', and Henry Bickersteth claimed to have encountered cases like Jarndyce and Jarndyce, where the whole sum in dispute was consumed in costs.[8]

It took a succession of official inquiries, which provided a wealth of anecdotal and statistical evidence, and a series of statutes and orders to furnish Chancery with an adequate judicial staff, an efficient and uncorrupt clerical organization and a set of procedures adapted to the needs of litigants rather than officials and practitioners.[9]

The accurate diagnosis of the source of the problems was obscured by arguments over Eldon's own judicial style and the burdens he shouldered as Chancellor. Some complained that Eldon devoted too much time to his political duties, deserting the courtroom for the cabinet; others that he was preoccupied with the judicial sittings of the House of Lords. The most wounding allegation was that he gave preference to bankruptcy cases because of the fees they brought him. Finally, his notorious 'cunctative habit', his obsessive concern with perfect justice, willingness to allow re-hearings and tendency to take home and pore over case papers (which gave him the nickname 'Lord Endless') were said to be a major cause of the delays in reaching cases which had been set down for hearing; those delays were the main subject of criticism.[10]

---

[5] Holdsworth, *HEL*, i, 416–45; B. Shapiro, 'Law Reform in Seventeenth Century England' (1975) *AJLH* 280–311; W. Prest, 'Law Reform in Eighteenth Century England', in P. Birks (ed.), *The Life of the Law* (1993), 113–25.

[6] *An Address to the Public... on the Present Unsatisfactory State of the Court of Chancery...* (1839), much quoted, e.g. by Sir Charles Bowen, 'Progress in the Administration of Justice in the Victorian Era', in Committee of American Law Schools (eds), *Select Essays in Anglo-American Legal History*, 3 vols (Boston, 1907), i, 516–57 at 529.

[7] *RC on the Court of Chancery, PP* 1826 (143), xv, App. A16, q. 83. An erstwhile partner of Forster's, H. H. Oddie, had been a protagonist in the Thellusson case.

[8] *Ibid.* 302, App. A10, q. 271.

[9] Lobban, 'Preparing for Fusion, Part One', gives a succint account.

[10] The criticisms are summarized and appraised in R. A. Melikan, *John Scott, Lord Eldon, the Duty of Loyalty* (Cambridge, 1999), 295–325. The most elaborate defence of Eldon is in H. Twiss, *The Life of Lord Chancellor Eldon*, 2 vols (1846 edn), ii, 396–503.

Both critics and defenders drew extensively on statistics, but because they seldom searched back beyond the Chancellorship of Lord Hardwicke, 'the golden age of equity'[11] they acquired a distorted perspective on the court's history.[12] It enabled critics to claim that, since the number of bills filed each year was not substantially greater than under Hardwicke, three judges should be able to cope with the business; however, the great litigation decline in Chancery had bottomed out in the 1780s, so defenders could point to an increase in bills during Eldon's time. Other indicators were equally slippery. Causes set down did not distinguish short causes from those needing a full hearing. Motions had undoubtedly increased greatly—from 37,880 (1745–55) to 57,063 (1806–16)—but it was not clear how much was due to the multiplication of motions of course. There were many more appeals outstanding than formerly, but it was disputed whether that was a natural result of the creation of a Vice-Chancellor or was aggravated by Eldon's notorious susceptibility to encourage appeals even from his own judgments. The evidence was too crude, and its deployment too unsophisticated and partisan, to be conclusive.[13]

In suggesting remedies both parties were also on shaky ground. The Whigs never developed a coherent and consistent reform plan. Sometimes Brougham and others argued that three decisive judges could clear the arrears and handle future business; Leach's celerity encouraged that view. At other times they said that the bankruptcy business should be removed or an appeal court formed.[14] Eldon's defenders were awkwardly placed too, since if they argued that arrears were a consequence of increased business they were confronted with Eldon's reluctance to give up any of the work or reform the procedures of his court.

Some criticisms were certainly unjust. D. W. Harvey had to confess that he had vastly exaggerated the fees Eldon took from bankruptcy,[15] while it was irresponsible and impractical of others airily to dismiss the need for the Chancellor's presence when the Lords were sitting as a court. It was also unreasonable to expect him to give judicial work priority over cabinet meetings unless the critics were prepared to argue for a redefinition of the Chancellor's office. Yet there was a hard kernel of truth at the heart of these accusations. Eldon *was* desperately and unnecessarily slow in deciding cases, and blind to the fact that such painstaking

---

[11] *PD* 1836 (s3) 33: 403 (Lord Cottenham).

[12] H. Horwitz and P. Polden, 'Continuity or Change in the Court of Chancery in the Seventeenth and Eighteenth Centuries?' (1996) 35 *JBS* 24–57.

[13] Lobban, 'Preparing for Fusion, Part One', 398–409; J. C. Oldham, 'A Profusion of Chancery Reform' (2004) 22 *LHR* 609–14. For contemporary acknowledgments of its problematical nature, see 'Observations on the Judges of the Court of Chancery' (1823–4) 30 *Quart. Rev.* 272–91 at 280, and 'Substance of a Speech of Mr. M.A. Taylor' (1824–5) 41 *Edin. Rev.* 410–27 at 421.

[14] Lobban, 'Preparing for Fusion, Part One', 408–9, 415–16.

[15] Melikan, *John Scott, Lord Eldon*, 308, 316.

deliberations created unacceptable delays for some litigants and deterred others altogether. It was Redesdale who wrote that: '[i]n very few cases comparatively ought the parties litigating to be considered as the only persons interested in the result... expense and delay are evils often severely felt by the litigating parties; but they may be evils suffered for the public good',[16] but Eldon's practice came to much the same thing. His defence to criticism was that he aspired to deliver perfect justice and worked very hard, so hard that he had not the time to examine how the delays and costs afflicting suitors might be alleviated.[17] It is notable that among the great legacy of equitable doctrines Eldon bequeathed there is no set of general orders for the court.[18] He acknowledged that '[m]uch of modern practice will, I fear, be found inconsistent with subsisting orders, without any contradiction of them by subsequent orders; and, upon principle, repeated decisions, forming a series of practice, as it must be, against an order, may with safety be taken to amount to a reversal of that order'.[19] Yet he took no action. Not until Lord Chelmsford commissioned J. W. Smith and H. Cadman Jones to consolidate the orders in 1859 did practitioners have something more authoritative than the collections of Beames and Sanders.[20]

Eldon undoubtedly contributed to the crisis of Chancery, but institutional causes were at work too; outmoded and corrupt financial and clerical structures, and baroque practices and pleadings which were badly exposed by changes in the volume and character of business. Commentators on the growth of Chancery business tended to attribute it rather unspecifically to the general expansion of commerce and national wealth.[21] They complained of its inability to deal effectively with complex business organizations and in the mid-century business interests were certainly among the most vocal critics,[22] but a sample of Chancery cases in 1819 suggests that only around a quarter (one-sixth without including consumer debt cases) arose from commercial dealings.[23] Most of the cases

---

[16] Quoted from *The Times*, 31 August 1826, in J. Parkes, *History of the Court of Chancery* (1828), App. 6, 520.

[17] Twiss, *Life of Lord Eldon*, adopts this view. Melikan, *John Scott, Lord Eldon*, is more balanced.

[18] *RC on Chancery, Report 1826*, App. B1 (Master Stratford).

[19] *Boehm* v. *De Tastet* (1813) 1 Ves. & Beam. 324, 328.

[20] *Consolidated General Orders of the High Court of Chancery* (1860); J. Beames, *General Orders of the High Court of Chancery* (1815); G. W. Sanders, *Orders of the High Court of Chancery* (1845).

[21] 'Observations on the Judges', 280; *PD* 1824 (s2) 10: 305 (Sir R. Peel); *MP* 1828, 1: 144–5 (R. C. Ferguson).

[22] e.g. *PD* 1851 (s3) 118: 568 (R. A. Slaney). As F. B. Burns points out, Kostal's study of the railway industry and the law hardly mentions Chancery, but it is likely that its slowness, expense, and unfavourable decisions like *Edwards* v. *Grand Junction Railway* (1836) 2 My. & Cr. 650 will have exasperated the railway interest: 'Lord Cottenham and the Court of Chancery' (2003) 24 *JLH* 187–214, at 195–7.

[23] This sample was used in Horwitz and Polden, 'Continuity or Change in Chancery?'. It comprises bills (including bills of revivor and/or supplement and cross bills) filed in the legal year 1818/19

concerned partnerships and among them is one concerning a copper company which was both drawn out and complicated—very much the sort of matter which would expose the court's shortcomings.[24] But it is only one case; most of the other partnerships were rather modest in scale and several of the commercial cases were brought only to invoke equity's auxiliary jurisdiction, to examine witnesses overseas or take accounts. The non-partnership cases do include two substantial and protracted matters, arising out of the business difficulties of Hamilton Murray, a London builder,[25] and the sons of a well-known entrepreneur, John Bell.[26] Most of the debt cases are simply actions for an injunction to halt proceedings at law and from this sample commercial disputes seem unlikely to have been primarily responsible for the court's mounting arrears.

Disputes over land form a larger category, nearly one-third of the sample.[27] They were a staple for equity courts, which offered the crucial remedy of specific performance, and the fully developed equity of redemption made them the chief forum for sorting out mortgage debts. The Chancery Commission rightly identified the intricacies of conveyancing law as the source of many suits and much expense and one of its most fruitful recommendations was that a further commission should investigate that subject.[28] Most of the 'land' cases were either suits for specific performance or concerned mortgages or annuities charged on land. Among the former it is difficult to distinguish between friendly and hostile actions, but it is striking that in only a quarter of them was the land worth more than £1000 and the median is around £500. *Mellish* v. *Assender*,[29] concerning the purchase of a black varnish factory at Poplar (a Dickensian echo), illustrates the pitfalls of the 'old conveyancing'; after two years there were still uncertainties about lost documents, an outstanding legal estate and an unregistered deed. Most, however, were relatively uncomplicated, though in relation to the purchase price the costs of a Chancery suit will have been significant.

The mortgage loans in issue were also mostly between £500 and £1000, with two of £3000. In this sample, however, mortgage actions (mostly foreclosures) were the least likely of the common types of suit to get beyond the pleading stage—just four of 17 proceeded to judgment. It was just as well, for a seemingly

---

with first plaintiffs' names beginning with M. It therefore excludes charity matters brought in the name of the Attorney-General.

[24] *Mills* v. *Roe*, arising out of *Hawkins* v. *Roe*, NA PRO C 13/239/21.

[25] *Murray* v. *Rumball* (revivor); original bill 1801, C 13/588/22.

[26] *Millett* v. *Taber* (supplementary), original *Bell* v. *Taber*, 1811, C 13/2108/12.

[27] Categories are, of course, problematic. For discussion see Horwitz and Polden, 'Continuity or Change?', 32–7 and the different classification of M. McNair, 'The Court of Exchequer and Equity' (2001) 22 *JLH* 78–81.

[28] *RC on Chancery, Report 1826*, 34.

[29] C 13/1699/23.

friendly suit (*MacDonald* v. *Jackson*) took seven years to reach its conclusion[30] while *Montgomery* v. *Calland* provides a grim illustration of Chancery's ponderousness when confronted with a wily and determined defendant, for it took 25 years to recover the property.[31] It was not only mortgage cases that could take an unconscionable time. In a very straightforward action for waste, *Colyear* v. *Lord Portmore*, it took almost seven years for Master Cox to produce his definitive valuation report, and for this verdict of £250 the plaintiff's costs were taxed at £418.[32]

Bleak House has associated the court of Chancery imperishably with cases about wills, but they were never a numerical majority of suits, and samples suggest that the proportion actually fell from over 40 per cent in 1785 to 32 per cent in 1819 while cases concerning *inter vivos* trusts rose from 6 per cent to 10 per cent; given the almost universal adoption of settlements among landowners the latter figure is surprisingly low.[33] Most of the *inter vivos* cases of 1819 involved marriage settlements, with bills mostly framed in terms of breach of trust or failure to implement covenants to settle property.[34] Some are no doubt collusive suits, but a high proportion proceeded to a substantive hearing.

The classic administration suit, brought before the distribution of the estate, forms only a minority of the will cases. A large proportion went to trial, perhaps because compromise was impossible with infant and unborn beneficiaries, and only two or three seem to feature those small estates which could not bear the cost of Chancery.[35] Those are more numerous among the cases arising from more remote deaths—several more than 20 years earlier. Though most of these followed the death of a life tenant or annuitant, some are for the appointment of a new trustee or a guardian. Taking the estate cases as a whole there are some which needed a decision on a question of construction (several were felt worth reporting[36]) and several others where circumstances such as an insufficiency of assets, the need to wind up a family business, or the insanity or disappearance

---

[30] C 13/254/30.

[31] C 13/252. A very complicated matter which had its origins in a mortgage of 1780 and seems finally to have ended with a decree of 1845.

[32] C 13/157/3 (1813), revivor as *Viscount Milsinton* v. *Lord Portmore*.

[33] Horwitz and Polden, 'Continuity or Change?', table 6.

[34] Chancery's severe attitude towards trustees, and the virtual absence of a limitation period for breach of trust claims, encouraged claims stemming from many years before and these were apt to be complicated and time consuming. Thus the Milsinton trustees were harassed with two suits, one concerning land purchases in 1801 and the other failure to renew leases a few years later: C 13/2524, 2534.

[35] e.g. *Murrell* v. *Tate* (C 13/735/30) was a claim for a £50 legacy.

[36] e.g. *Matthews* v. *Paul* (1819) 1 Swans, 328; *Evans* v. *Shaw-Hellier* (1837) 5 Cl. & F.114; *Murray* v. *Addenbrook* (1830) 4 Russ. 408.

of a beneficiary made it prudent for the executors or trustees to seek safety in the court. For some there is no obvious explanation.

Although the estate and settlement cases were a minority of those coming into Chancery, they exerted a powerful influence. Some were the sort of suits which, as the Commissioners explained 'might usefully endure for half a century'.[37] The Thellusson will was no doubt exceptional in generating more than 950 orders and 780 reports over 60 years, but among the sample is *Morison* v. *Morison*, which began in 1815 and was still going in 1858 after more than 100 orders.[38] When Chancery lost business in the eighteenth century its fee-dependent officers seem to have elaborated procedures so as to extract more from the business which remained and when business began to revive there was no attempt to prune the luxuriant growth. With a higher proportion of matters involving multiple parties (well over half in 1819), more going beyond the pleadings stage and more needing to be referred to a master for the taking of accounts, the settling of a title etc., the court was becoming clogged up. Disregarding the cases (about 22 per cent, and fairly constant) which did not get beyond the bill, more than 40 per cent were lasting more than two years, and above one-sixth more than five.[39] This alone was not necessarily a ground for criticism but the strain on resources meant that it was taking six or seven years to extract a simple legacy.[40] Eldon responded to the backlog by making time for urgent matters at the expense of the regular list, but that was hardly a solution.[41] The court's problem was not so much with new sorts of business for which it was ill-equipped as that more business of a familiar sort was overloading it.

2. THE CHANCERY COMMISSION

In 1823 the attacks on Eldon took on a sharper and more personal tone through pamphlets, articles in the *Edinburgh Review* and combative attacks in the Commons by 'Johnny' Williams, who offered several instances of apparently unconscionable delays on the Chancellor's part.[42] Some of Eldon's cabinet colleagues (Peel, who wanted Eldon's support for his own criminal law reforms, was an exception) had become noticeably lukewarm in continuing to defend

---

[37] *RC on Chancery, Report 1826*, at 9.
[38] Reported at various stages, e.g. in (1838) 4 My. & Cr. 215. The list of parties occupies 27 lines.
[39] Horwitz and Polden, 'Continuity or Change?', 29–32, 53–6.
[40] Taylor's assertions (*MP* 1828, 1: 141, 1087) were not challenged.
[41] *RC on Chancery, Report 1826*, App. A1, q. 363 (John Bell) .
[42] *PD* 1823 (s2) 9: 706–94; 1824 (s2) 10: 372–437; 'Observations on the Judges of the Court of Chancery and the Practice and Delays Complained of in that Court..., and Observations on the Delays Complained of in the Court of Chancery and House of Lords...' (1823–4) 39 *Edin. Rev.* 246–60, 432–57. The cases are dealt with at length in Twiss, *Life of Lord Eldon*, ii, 402–12.

him from criticisms they privately felt were partly justified, and notwithstanding that a Lords' select committee had only recently reviewed the arrears in their own House and in Chancery, in February 1824 an inquiry was conceded, Peel acknowledging 'an increase of business...too great for human strength to cope with'.[43] It was not, however, to be the select committee the opposition wanted, but a royal commission with Eldon himself at its head.

The appointment of the Commission was a sound political tactic. It saved face for Eldon, who could claim that he had himself urged such an inquiry, and temporarily disarmed the critics. Moreover its terms of reference and membership suggested that it would not damage the Chancellor.[44] It was precluded from considering large questions such as fusion with the common law courts and provincial courts of equity and from examining the most sensitive issue, the multiple functions of the Lord Chancellor.[45] It included both Chancery judges, two masters and Eldon's ally Lord Redesdale, but no solicitors.[46] Neither Taylor nor other critics were included and since only Lushington, a civilian, and R. P. Smith could be classed as belonging to the opposition a whitewash seemed all too likely.[47]

Since the Commission's progress was leisurely, the critics were not quietened for long and when Eldon lamented that a motion of Burdett's calling for returns in a manner that reflected on his methods had not been opposed, Liverpool made it clear that the government was impatient for the report, which was at length produced on 28 February 1826.[48]

As a political expedient the Commission was a great success. The report was lengthy and being accompanied by acres of evidence and statistics it had the air of a comprehensive inquiry, with a focus on the minutiae of Chancery practice which made it rebarbative reading.[49] Though Eldon had not drafted it,[50] nor taken part in examining witnesses, critics claimed to see his hand throughout.[51] Lushington, no supporter of Eldon, rebutted accusations that the Chancellor had

[43] *PD* 1824 (s2) 10: 403–18.

[44] Eldon to Lady Bankes, 25 February 1824, Twiss, *Life of Lord Eldon*, ii, 90.

[45] *RC on Chancery, Report 1826*, instructions, 25 April 1824. The Commission was, however, empowered to suggest types of business which might be removed.

[46] There were 14 members in all, but Joseph Littledale was appointed a judge of the King's Bench during the proceedings and ceased to take any part.

[47] 'Substance of a Speech', 413–14; Lobban, 'Preparing for Fusion, Part One', 409. On Lushington see below, Ch. V, pp. 720–2. Smith was MP for Lincoln.

[48] Eldon to Liverpool (draft) and reply of 16 November 1825, Twiss, *Life of Lord Eldon*, ii, 140–3. Eldon was 'very nice and touchy about my judicial fame' (to Lady Bankes, 25 May 1825, *ibid.*, 235).

[49] See e.g. *The Times*, 14 September 1826, quoted in Parkes, *History of the Court of Chancery*, 529.

[50] Attributed to John Beames and J. H. Merivale (*The Times*, 27 December 1826, in Parkes, *History of the Court of Chancery*, 580). Brougham wrote *The Times* articles.

[51] e.g. Brougham's speech on Taylor's motion, 27 February 1827, *PD* 1827 (s2) 16: 727–30.

played a decisive role in their deliberations,[52] but Eldon probably had no need to do so; other Commissioners questioned witnesses so as to protect him from criticism[53] and the report's repeated insistence on a cautious and incremental approach was characteristically Eldonian.[54] The report concentrated on the early stages of a Chancery suit and when it did approach the reasons for delays after causes had been set down for hearing, it shied away from any close examination on the specious ground that the court's records did not give a full picture of the Chancellor's activities.[55] The verdict of a later inquiry that it was 'replete with information and has many suggestions, but in the main it is an elaborate defence of the status quo'[56] is understandable.

If the report was not the condemnation of the Chancellor that his critics had been seeking, it certainly did not vindicate his court, and by implication (though nowhere overtly), it criticized his slackness in not revising the court's procedures to cope with increasing business.[57] Even Williams later conceded that the report was useful, and it reshaped the debate on Chancery into a more fruitful form, albeit one which did not eliminate areas of political dispute.[58] It may be somewhat overstating the case to claim that the more critical element in the Commission (notably Lushington and Merivale) began to get the upper hand,[59] but the summoning of witnesses likely to be critical of the court—the boastful solicitor James Lowe and his more discreet fellows William Vizard, James Winter, and John Forster, along with the Benthamite barrister Henry Bickersteth—does suggest a more open-minded approach than might have been predicted. It was too adventurous for Redesdale, who did not sign the report and voiced his dissent through a pamphlet rather than a note to the report itself.[60]

The most impressive feature of the Commission's report is the concluding list of no fewer than 187 propositions, though a detailed perusal rather detracts from this imposing corpus, revealing some to be very minor.[61] The sum of the whole, if

[52] *Ibid.*, 13: 1085.

[53] Melikan, *John Scott, Lord Eldon*, 320–1.

[54] e.g. at 8: 'The wisdom of an established rule is frequently not discovered, until a new one is attempted to be carried into effect; and it is impossible, in every instance, to foresee all the effects upon an existing system which may result from the introduction of any change…'.

[55] At pp. 15–16.

[56] *RC on the Legal Departments, Second Report, PP* 1874 (C. 1107), xxiv, 29.

[57] At p. 10, and see evidence of Master Stratford, App. B1, 507.

[58] Lobban, 'Preparing for Fusion, Part One', 410, 414.

[59] *Ibid.*, 410. Leach's illness may have had some effect: T. D. Hardy, *A Memoir of the Life of the R.H. Lord Langdale*, 2 vols (1852), i, 353.

[60] *Considerations Suggested by the Report…Respecting the Court of Chancery* (1826), criticised in *The Times*, 31 August 1826 (Parkes, *History of the Court of Chancery*, 516–28).

[61] e.g. number 45, 'that the last Interrogatory, now commonly in use, be altered, by omitting the words, "which may be of any benefit or advantage or material to the said complainant (or defendant)"; and inserting, in lieu thereof, "material to the subject of this your examination"'.

not so trivial as critics alleged, fell far short of a revolution in Chancery practice. While correctly maintaining that 'although some of the alterations which we propose may appear at first sight minute, yet it is upon the operation of the system of practice made up of numerous minute regulations, that the dispatch or delay and the expense of a Chancery suit, so far as can be effected by any precise rules, must in a great degree depend',[62] the Commissioners displayed a marked reluctance to prescribe changes in practice rather than merely to commend them to practitioners. That was hardly bold enough if, as they alleged, much of the court's delay was 'imputable, neither to the Court, nor to its established rules of practice; but to the carelessness of some parties, the obstinacy or knavery of others, or the inattention or ignorance of agents'.[63] As for removing business, it was never on the cards that they would contest Eldon's insistence that bankruptcy appeals must remain,[64] and having noticed that lunacy occupied much of the masters' time as well as the Chancellor's, they conspicuously ignored it in their subsequent discussion of possible burdens to be shed, contenting themselves with following the Lords' committee in advocating that judicial functions imposed by new statutes should in future be entrusted to the Exchequer rather than Chancery.[65]

It was never likely that the Commission's report would silence Eldon's critics, but within a year of its publication he finally relinquished the great seal. 1827 marked the effective beginning of more than 30 years of intermittent reform of Chancery, enlarging its judiciary, remodelling its procedures, and modernizing its financial and bureaucratic structure.

3. JUDICIAL MANPOWER

Uncertainty over how much Eldon's judicial style contributed to delays so obscured the picture that Chancery's judge-power needs could hardly be assessed while he remained on the Woolsack. It was compounded by two wider considerations; what the proper role of the Lord Chancellor should be, and the future of the equity side of the Exchequer.

The Commission was not entrusted with considering judge-power other than obliquely, by ascertaining whether any business (particularly bankruptcy) might be removed; nevertheless several witnesses strayed onto the topic, notably when Lancelot Shadwell gave his much-quoted view that the quantity of business was such that 'I think if you had three angels they could not get through it'.[66] The Commission contented itself with suggesting that restrictions upon the Vice-Chancellor's court be removed[67] and that the 'unceremonious mode' of appeal

---

[62] At p. 10.   [63] At p. 9.   [64] At pp. 35–7.
[65] At pp. 7, 37.   [66] At q. 286.   [67] At p. 37.

from the Master of the Rolls or Vice-Chancellor to the Lord Chancellor by motion should be discouraged. They were too timid to propose removing the facility altogether and their proposed safeguard against abuse was flimsy.[68]

Even after Eldon's departure, opinion remained divided over the need for more judges. Eldon himself felt that it would be sufficient if the facility to obtain temporary assistance from common law judges or Chancery masters were restored. Lyndhurst, unwilling to overtax his strength by exhausting sessions on the bench, wanted an additional judge, while Brougham was initially anxious to demonstrate that his energy and intellect could clear the arrears and prevent new ones from arising. However, having proved that (to his own satisfaction at least) he became more concerned to avoid being detained in Chancery when he wished to be elsewhere.[69]

In 1829 Lyndhurst, endorsing the Common Law Commissioners' recommendation that the Exchequer should lose its equity business, proposed a fourth Chancery judge to conduct it, but not only found Peel doubtful because of the compensation claims it might generate, but to his annoyance, was also opposed by Leach MR and Shadwell VC. Leach's obstructiveness extended to resisting provisions designed to make the Master of the Rolls devote more time to Chancery with such success that the most Lyndhurst could achieve was to induce him to replace his evening sittings with morning ones.[70] Brougham reduced the workload by sending bankruptcy appeals to his new court but his ideas for a court of masters and a court of Chancery appeals both came to nothing, and the impetus for change was lost.[71]

Thereafter the remodelling of the equity bench tended to be driven mostly by sporadic panics over pressure of business, usually aggravated by the illness of the Lord Chancellor, resulting in remedies for the immediate problems rather than any direct grappling with the intractable question of the Chancellor's place in courts and cabinets. Whenever that was considered, in the mid-1830s, around 1840, and again around 1850, it proved impossible to arrive at any solution commanding a sufficient consensus among politicians and lawyers to be practicable. No one who became Lord Chancellor, or who had ambitions in that direction, would sacrifice the Chancellor's place in government and Parliament for him to become a judge pure and simple, while Chancery lawyers were equally unwilling

---

[68]   At pp. 37–8.

[69]   Lobban, 'Preparing for Fusion, Part One', 414–17.

[70]   *Ibid*. Leach was aggrieved at being passed over to succeed Eldon. Because the Master of the Rolls was still regarded as the Lord Chancellor's deputy, he did not sit on those evenings on which the latter had formerly done so. His sittings totalled only 120 days of four hours a day. For other restrictions, see Sir R. E. Megarry, 'The Vice-Chancellors' (1982) 98 *LQR* 370–405 at 371–2.

[71]   M. J. Lobban, 'Henry Brougham and Law Reform' (2000) *EHR* 1184–215 at 1195–7.

to have a 'political' Chancellor (or equivalent) as head of the court but removed from the bench in order to concentrate on the political and judicial functions of the House of Lords. No Chancellor wanted to admit that the workload was already more than he could handle and none would recognize that in a society whose population and commercial activity were visibly growing, Chancery business would outgrow his capacity to deal with it. Provincial courts of equity were regarded with horror by most equity lawyers, yet a court which could cope only because its own delays and costs artificially dampened demand, as James Wigram pointed out in 1840, was hardly defensible.[72] This created a deadlock. Proposals to reconstruct the Chancellor's role, whether, like Brougham's in 1833 and Cottenham's in 1836, they envisaged taking him out of Chancery or, like Langdale's in 1836 and the Russell ministry's in 1850, they sought to confine him there, were never practical politics.[73]

When delays in Chancery again became an issue in 1839 less ambitious solutions to the shortage of judge-power were advanced. Cottenham justified the proposed addition of two judges by the abolition of the equity side of the Exchequer and the installation of the Master of the Rolls as vice-president of the Judicial Committee of the Privy Council, but he had not prepared the ground properly. Sir Edward Sugden made Cottenham's failure to consider the impact on appeals to the Lords a plausible excuse for opposing the expansion of the judiciary generally, and the Chief Baron predictably led opposition to the dismemberment of his court.[74]

Abinger found little support for his 'bastard court' as Pemberton called it.[75] Although Lyndhurst, in whose time as Chief Baron the common law side had begun a remarkable revival, advocated two new equity judges, one apiece for Chancery and Exchequer, the features which put solicitors off the Exchequer had not been tackled; the suggestion that new types of statutory business should be sent there rather than to Chancery had never been implemented, and the Tithe Commutation Act 1836 virtually ended the only branch of business where it was routinely preferred to Chancery.[76] When the Whig bill, shorn of the Master of the Rolls clauses, was referred to a select committee in 1840 the antipathy of the legal profession came across strongly in evidence and although it seemed a paradoxical response to cure delays in one court by abolishing another, the equity

---

[72] Lobban, 'Preparing for Fusion, Part One', 419–20.

[73] *Ibid.*, 421–3.

[74] *Ibid.*, 421; J. B. Atlay, *The Victorian Chancellors*, 2 vols (1908), i, 139.

[75] *PD* 1839 (s3) 45: 499–500.

[76] H. Horwitz, *Exchequer Equity Records and Proceedings 1689–1841* (2001), 38–9 and 'Chancery's Younger Sister: The Court of Exchequer and its Equity Jurisdiction, 1689–1841' (1999) 72 *Hist. Research* 160–82, 169–70.

side of the Exchequer was condemned almost without debate in the Lords. In the Commons Sugden maintained his opposition, disputing the statistical evidence furnished to the Select Committee by E. W. Field, but without finding much support.[77]

This infusion of Exchequer business was the justification for giving Chancery two extra vice-chancellors, but the Whig administration fell and Lyndhurst, who took up the bill, gave ground; one vice-chancellorship would be renewable on the death or resignation of the incumbent, while the other would lapse on a vacancy. In October 1841 James Knight-Bruce and James Wigram became first and second vice-chancellor, respectively; Henry Jacob, who would have been a strong candidate, had recently died.[78] This enlarged judiciary enabled Chancery to cope with a considerable increase in business, from some 7300 'matters in total' to 8450, for most of the 1840s, though the railway mania of 1845–6 strained its capacity.[79] While Lyndhurst was Chancellor there was general harmony among the judges. He sat almost exclusively on appeals and generally endorsed the decisions of his juniors,[80] but when Cottenham returned in 1846 he proved almost equally prone to reverse them, especially Knight-Bruce.[81] It became established that suitors were allowed to choose their court, while the leaders limited themselves to a single one.[82] This had the potential to unbalance the workload and initially some of Shadwell's cases were transferred to Knight-Bruce to ease his burdens; otherwise it seems to have worked fairly well.

The great weakness in the new structure was that there were now four judges from whom an almost unrestricted appeal lay to the Chancellor. With a Chancellor like Cottenham, known to be ever ready to re-examine a case from first principles,[83] and a court which allowed great latitude to counsel in the way of long speeches,[84] this could create acute congestion at the appeal stage, as it did when Cottenham became gravely ill.

---

[77] *PD* 1840 (s3) 53: 1334–67; 54: 763–8; 55: 1304–44 and (1840) 72 *HLJ* App. 3, 117–53.

[78] Lobban, 'Preparing for Fusion, Part One', 421; Megarry, 'Vice-Chancellors', 377–8; Administration of Justice Act 1841 (5 Vict. c. 5); E. R. Daniell, 'Considerations on Reforms in Chancery' (1842) 27 *LM* 102–13, at 104–5.

[79] Lord John Russell, *PD* (s3) 115: 685. Petitions had risen from 2715 in 1843 to 3724 in 1850.

[80] Atlay, *Victorian Chancellors*, i, 142; J. Rolt, *The Memoirs of the Rt Hon. Sir John Rolt* (1939), 84–9.

[81] Atlay, *Victorian Chancellors*, i, 412–13.

[82] Lyndhurst had promised orders which would largely confine leaders to a single court (*MP* 1828, 1: 1094; 1829, 2: 1573). Rolt (*Memoirs*, 116) said that it was not such a rigid rule in the 1840s as it later became. The facility of choice was criticized by Daniell, 'Considerations on Reform in Chancery', 102–13 and in (1844) 8 *Jur.* 429.

[83] Burns, 'Lord Cottenham and the Court of Chancery', 199–203.

[84] Twiss, *Life of Lord Eldon*, ii, 444; Lord Redesdale, *MP* 1829, 2: 1752; 'Chancery Reform' (1835) 16 *LM* 1–23, at 21.

When Cottenham resigned in June 1850 the great seal was put into commission while new arrangements were considered,[85] but further complications soon arose with the death of Shadwell, the Vice-Chancellor of England, and the resignation through ill-health of Wigram, 'the second Vice-Chancellor'. These vacancies opened the way for the sort of ambitious restructuring that Bethell and others advocated, but the same lack of consensus which had stifled reforms in the mid-1830s prevailed and anxiety to prevent arrears from mounting led the government into expedients. Shadwell's vacancy was filled by the transfer of Mouncey Rolfe from the Exchequer and a bill was hastily passed to enable the other vacancy to be filled with a further 'one-off' appointment, George Turner in April 1851.[86]

Since Sir Thomas Wilde (Lord Truro), who became Chancellor in July 1850, was no more willing than his predecessors to break up the office, the government's initial idea, to relieve the Chancellor of sitting in Chancery and create a new judge for that purpose, had to be dropped and Russell reverted instead to the idea of a court of appeal for Chancery. Brougham had already dusted off his old bill, which likewise envisaged a court composed of existing judges: the Chancellor, the Master of the Rolls, and a common law judge, with the latter pair able to sit without the Chancellor.[87] The great merit of courts like these (such as the Exchequer Chamber on the common law side) was economy in manpower, but their concomitant drawback was that suitors would find courts of first instance, especially the Rolls, closed for business while the judge sat on appeals.[88] In the face of a rising tide of complaint about hearing delays that would be very impolitic, and finding the House of Commons in an unusually generous frame of mind, Russell presented a revised bill establishing a court with two wholly new judges, styled lords justices of the court of Appeals in Chancery. They might sit together, or one or both of them with the Chancellor, and though the Chancellor's own appellate jurisdiction was not displaced, it was expected that a common lawyer like Truro would welcome the assistance of at least one lord justice.[89]

[85] The commissioners were Lord Langdale MR, Shadwell VC, and Rolfe B. Shadwell had been a commissioner, along with Pepys MR and Bosanquet B., when Melbourne resorted to the same expedient in 1835. It was then severely criticised, especially by Sir Edward Sugden (*A Letter to ... Lord Melbourne ... on the Present State of the Court of Chancery* (1835)).

[86] Lobban, 'Preparing for Fusion, Part One', 422–4; Megarry, 'Vice-Chancellors', 382–4; Appointment of Vice-Chancellor Act (14 & 15 Vict. c. 4). Shadwell's successors were simply styled vice-chancellor.

[87] Lobban, 'Preparing for Fusion, Part One', 423. Atlay felt that 'the existence in its full integrity of the historical office of Lord Chancellor was never in greater peril': *Victorian Chancellors*, i, 450.

[88] This had been a cause for complaint when the seal was in commission. Earl Grey suggested this might be overcome by adding two further vice-chancellors, enabling four trial courts and an appeal court to sit simultaneously: note of 20 May 1851, JHB MS 439.

[89] Lobban, 'Preparing for Fusion, Part One', 243–4; Megarry, 'Vice–Chancellors', 379–80. Roundell Palmer later claimed that the intention had been that it would usually sit as a full court: 'JHP', 'Remarks on the Court of Appeal in Chancery' (1867–8) 24 (s3) *LM & LR* 202–12 at 208.

This arrangement enabled two co-eval courts of appeal to sit simultaneously. The decision on their composition lay with the Lord Chancellor, though it was open for the appellant to request a full court. Rolfe and Knight- Bruce were promoted to lords justices and when Rolfe (as Lord Cranworth) soon afterwards became Chancellor, he frequently sat in a full court at first; however this practice soon ceased and was only revived on a regular basis by Campbell, a pure common lawyer. Masterful equity Chancellors like St. Leonards and Westbury spurned assistance and would not brook contradiction, with the consequence that parallel sittings became usual.[90] In 1867 provision was made for a single judge of the court to hear many classes of appeal, which caused some concern in the profession when Giffard LJC several times overruled the Master of the Rolls during a protracted vacancy in the other lord justiceship.[91]

Between 1853 and 1866, while there was a rapid turnover of Lord Chancellors,[92] Chancery experienced a period of unusual stability among its other judges. Sir John Romilly had succeeded Langdale in 1851 and remained Master of the Rolls until 1873; Knight-Bruce and Turner were lord justices from 1853 until 1866; Kindersley, Stuart, and Page Wood were vice-chancellors until Kindersley's resignation in November 1866, Page Wood having succeeded Turner as vice-chancellor under the terms of an Act which, unlike its predecessor, made the position permanent.[93] Whatever its other defects, Chancery had become a court with an adequate number of judges, mostly chosen from the handful of leaders who dominated a close-knit bar, and sometimes bullied the less assertive judges too.

4. PROCEDURE: THE PRE-TRIAL STAGE

Among the defects of Chancery was the cumbersome and elaborate procedure which it imposed upon cases of every sort. Designed for real disputes, where the plaintiff needed to be able to quiz the defendant and to compel full responses from men who might be dishonest and evasive, and where the defendant needed strong safeguards against abuse of process and ample time to shape an appropriate response, it was applied also, with little variation, to uncontentious matters; to plaintiffs seeking an authoritative ruling on the construction of a document; to schemes for charitable bequests; to the appointment of a new trustee; to the dissolution of a partnership and the taking of accounts. True, when these reached

---

[90] Megarry, 'Vice-Chancellors', 380–1. It was said that Knight-Bruce found being relegated from presiding judge irksome.

[91] Court of Appeal in Chancery (Despatch of Business) Act 1867 (30 & 31 Vict. c. 64); (1869) 4 *LJ* 647; (1870) 5 *LJ* 146, 272, 311, 341.

[92] Truro, St. Leonards, Cranworth, Chelmsford, Campbell, Westbury, and Hatherley.

[93] Megarry, 'Vice-Chancellors', 383–6; Masters in Chancery Act 1852 (15 & 16 Vict. c. 80), s 52.

the hearing stage some might be disposed of fairly rapidly as short causes, but the time and expense taken to reach that stage was quite disproportionate.[94]

Eldon's Commission proposed only a timid remedy, a minor enlargement to the Legacy Act, and rejected the complaint that it had become the almost invariable practice for questions of construction in a will or settlement to be dealt with by an order for the administration of the estate in court, maintaining that this was usually because the executor/trustee desired it for his own security.[95]

Most proceedings in Chancery were commenced by a bill, which had achieved such a degree of ill-fame, partly through Bentham's celebrated scathing description of it as 'a volume of notorious lies'[96] that even one of its ablest defenders, Sir John Mitford, acknowledged that it was 'a common reproach to practitioners in this line that every bill contains the same story three times told'.[97] A bill was divided into nine parts, and it was the charging and interrogating parts which gave rise to the 'thrice told' gibe. Not only was it prolix and repetitious, it was necessarily deceitful in charging the defendant with a fraud even when the suit was amicable and in contested cases the pleader routinely inserted allegations he knew to be false as a means of extracting information.[98] Some bills were, as the solicitor James Lowe admitted, pure 'fishing bills' while bills for injunctions were frequently bereft of any semblance of truth.[99]

Here again, the Commission recoiled from any interference with the pleader's art. In their view 'terms of strong recommendation are...all that can be safely or usefully applied to the prevention of unnecessary prolixity'.[100] The Chancery leaders, Bell and Heald, were strong defenders of the status quo and even for common injunction bills the Commission was persuaded that no affidavit of truthfulness should be demanded of the client, only one from him and his solicitor affirming that it was not brought merely for delay.[101]

A subpoena obliged the defendant to collect an office copy of the bill, and an elaborate sequence of sanctions—from attachment through to sequestration—had evolved to compel his appearance; another complicated series of steps dealt with the defendant who was reluctant to put in his answer.[102] Declaring that their

---

[94] Holdsworth, *HEL*, i, 335–408. See also the briefer, characteristically elegant, account by Lord Bowen, 'Progress in the Administration of Justice', 523–31.

[95] *RC on Chancery, Report 1826*, 27–8.

[96] *Rationale of Judicial Evidence* (1827), quoted in Parkes, *History of the Court of Chancery*, 444.

[97] Holdsworth, *HEL*, i, 398. For a robust defence, see 'Lord Campbell's Notions of Equity Procedure...', (1841) 26 *LM* 241–66.

[98] Holdsworth, *HEL*, i, 401.

[99] *RC on Chancery Report 1826*, 30 and App. A13, q. 67.

[100] *Ibid.*, 26.

[101] *Ibid.*, 30 and Apps A1, 29, 30.

[102] *Ibid.*, App A10; Holdsworth, *HEL*, ix, 348–53.

objective was 'to provide that every party should be compelled to take that step in a suit, which the nature of the proceeding calls for, in as short a time as will enable him to be fully advised with respect to the particular act, and to perform what is required of him',[103] the Commission plunged into this labyrinth with some fortitude. They proposed to remove one or two stages and to simplify the granting of time to answer, substituting an eight-week period (15 for a country defendant) for the existing practice involving several orders of course.[104]

However, many plaintiffs were faced with several defendants, all of whom had to be served and answer before the suit could proceed. The doctrine of 'necessary party' lay at the heart of equity's mission to deliver comprehensive justice and required everyone with an interest in the property in question, however remote, to become a party to the suit;[105] as John Jarndyce gloomily remarked, 'we are made parties to it, and *must be* parties to it, whether we like it or not'.[106] Occasionally, mostly in cases involving large industrial or commercial concerns, Eldon had relaxed the rule because it was simply impracticable, and the Commission contented itself with the pious wish that this dispensation should be extended, without feeling able 'to specify particular instances'.[107] For technical reasons connected with pleadings it was the common practice to have only a single plaintiff, making all other parties co-defendants, which aggravated the problem of securing prompt answers.[108]

It was all too easy for the plaintiff to overlook someone, especially where his knowledge of the defendants was limited; thus in one of the many Jennens suits the plaintiffs, in a hurry because several of their key witnesses were very old, were frustrated when the defendants objected to the absence of a personal representative of the long dead Lady Andover, forcing them to file a supplemental bill against a dummy defendant who had taken out a grant for this purpose.[109]

Another frustrating possibility was that at some point one of the parties would die, or marry, that someone would be 'born into the suit' or that in some other way the interests to be represented would change. Such a change would necessitate a bill of revivor, or supplement, or both, enabling a recalcitrant opponent to employ the full range of delaying tactics. Except where the suit had already

---

[103] *Ibid.*, 10.

[104] *Ibid.*, 13.

[105] For the growing rigidity of the rule, and the failure of Eldon's attempt to limit it in *Cockburn* v. *Thompson* (1809) 16 Ves. Jun. 321, see G. C. Hazard, 'Indispensable Party: The Historical Origin of a Procedural Phantom' (1961) 61(2) *Columbia Law Rev.* 1254–89.

[106] *Bleak House*, Ch. 8.

[107] At pp. 26–7.

[108] Holdsworth, *HEL*, i, 344–5.

[109] Polden, 'Stranger Than Fiction?, Part One', 228–30. For an extreme example given by Sir R. W. Bulkeley see *PD* 1852 (s3) 119: 66–7.

been referred to a master the Commission did not feel able to curb such obstructiveness.[110] Without quite matching the elaboration of common law pleadings, the rules governing the use of bills, including the cross-bill which a defendant needed to file if he sought relief or discovery on his own account, had accumulated enough fine distinctions to make the choice of the appropriate bill a matter of careful consideration.[111]

As at law, a defendant might demur or plead rather than answer and here too great complexities had developed.[112] Bills were so artfully drawn that although the defendant was allowed to demur or plead to part and answer the remainder, any plea that touched upon the truthfulness of the bill invalidated the whole plea. Pleaders had become so adept that some thought it impossible successfully to counter the prayer for discovery by a plea, nor by any answer to obviate the need to disclose documents (such as lengthy accounts) which might be ruinously expensive.[113] The Commission tentatively sketched a rule change to make things easier for the defendant but with little faith in its efficacy;[114] in truth, equity did not favour pleas and demurrers and had made their employment very difficult.[115]

Once the answers were in there remained ample opportunities for delays and obstructions on both sides and some of these the Commission endeavoured to reduce. *The Law Magazine* summed up the main ones:

The plaintiff is allowed two terms, with the vacations (about three quarters of a year) to file exceptions, that is, to object to the sufficiency of the answer. To these exceptions the defendant either submits, in which case he is allowed six weeks to put in a better answer, or he suffers them to be referred to the master, who hears the parties by their counsel, and reports his opinion upon the question to the court—from this decision an appeal lies to the court itself. The second answer, which may also be excepted to, having been put in, the plaintiff is allowed to amend: for this no period is limited, and he may in fact do so at any time before the bill is open to dismissal for want of prosecution..., by a simple allegation that he is advised to amend. In some cases he may, even after replication, move for leave to withdraw his replication and amend, though nearly six terms have elapsed since the answer. Amendments generally require a further answer, and are a repetition of the proceedings above noticed. After the bill has been fully answered, although no step be taken by the plaintiff, the defendant is not entitled to call for a dismissal of the bill until the expiration of a period of three-quarters of a year; the plaintiff may then, by filing a replication, gain a further delay of equal duration; after which he undertakes to 'speed his

---

[110] *RC on Chancery, Report 1826*, 20.

[111] Holdsworth, *HEL*, i, 343–7.

[112] For common law pleadings see above, pp. 580–91.

[113] Holdsworth, *HEL*, i, 393; *RC on Chancery, Report 1826*, 29.

[114] *RC on Chancery, Report 1826*, 30.

[115] See e.g. Lord Redesdale, quoted in Holdsworth, *HEL*, ix, 393.

cause', and at the expiration of another term, 'to speed his cause with effect', and not until then is he compelled to proceed, or lose the benefit of his suit.[116]

The procedural changes which followed the Commission's report did little to counter continuing criticisms, but when the Lord Chancellor was given renewed powers to make general orders the small standing committee created by Cottenham drafted a set which made significant changes.[117] Among other improvements, the writ of attachment with proclamation and writ of rebellion were removed from the succession of stages compelling appearance, which was also simplified in other respects; moreover after service of a subpoena the plaintiff might enter an appearance for the defendant and continue with the suit.[118] The committee also grappled with necessary party. In future purely formal parties (other than infants) against whom no relief was sought, might choose not to take part in the suit, which promised 'a saving under that formidable head "Costs out of the estate" '.[119] The orders were nothing if not ambitious, proposing 'to prevent vexatious delays, unnecessary expense, and proceedings not really required by the occasion; to increase the prospect of bringing litigation to a speedy issue; to facilitate the prosecution of a suit from its commencement to its termination; to throw expense, not duly created, upon those who cause it; to deprive suitors of unfair advantages, and to check tricks and contrivances, which bring as much discredit upon the Court and practitioners, as mischief and heart-burnings upon the suitors'.[120] They evidently fell far short of these noble objectives, for in 1850 another royal commission listed many of the defects noted by its predecessor.[121]

The legislation which followed that second Commission's report transformed the pre-hearing stages of a Chancery suit in three main ways. First, it provided the summary procedures which solicitor witnesses had wanted in 1824 and which had been insistently demanded since then;[122] secondly, it greatly simplified

---

[116] 'Reforms in Chancery' (1828–9) 1 *LM* 32–45 at 35. For exceptions, see Holdsworth, *HEL*, ix, 387, and for the tactical use of amendments Lowe's evidence (App. A13).

[117] Administration of Justice in Chancery Act 1840 (3 & 4 Vict. c. 94), s 1; M. J. Lobban, 'Preparing for Fusion, Part Two' 22 *L & HR* (2004) 566–99 at 568. The most important are summarized in 'The New Orders in Chancery' (1841) 26 *LM* 241–66 at 260–6. The Committee comprised Lord Langdale MR, James Wigram, Thomas Pemberton, and Sutton Sharpe.

[118] Orders 6, 7, and 8.

[119] *New Orders in Chancery*, 262; Orders 23–9.

[120] *New Orders in Chancery*, 264.

[121] *RC on Chancery, First Report* (hereafter *First Report 1852) PP* 1852 [1437], xxi. The rule relieving formal parties from joining in the suit for example was undermined by 'some doubts and difficulties in applying it, and the expense of serving examined copies of the Bill, and the necessity of serving them again after every amendment', 16.

[122] Law Society Report to Chancery Commission, *PP* 1852 (216), xlii, 7.

the pleadings and process in cases which were still to start by a bill; thirdly, it drastically pruned the doctrine of necessary party.

Summary process had in fact been creeping in for some time. A succession of statutes, beginning with Romilly's Act of 1812 in charity cases[123] and extending through Sugden's of 1831[124] and Cottenham's Trustees' Relief Acts of 1847 and 1849[125] (both extensively used) had introduced proceedings by petition, which were also adopted in the Trustee Act 1850 for the appointment of new trustees.[126] Turner's Act of 1850 carried matters further, by providing a procedure by way of special case for executors and administrators who wanted to ascertain the estate's liabilities.[127] More wide-ranging than any of these was Cottenham's introduction of a procedure by claim which dispensed with pleadings altogether and was heard on affidavits.[128] This was available in a wide range of cases and proved instantly popular, used for almost 2000 suits in 18 months.[129] It had, however, unfortunate drawbacks, for when employed in inappropriate cases, where the form of the claim and summons gave insufficient information, the affidavits on each side had to serve the function of pleadings, for which they were ill-adapted.[130] Furthermore, claims, petitions, and special cases alike had the common disadvantage of not giving any facility for compelling the production of evidence.[131]

Despite these drawbacks the Commissioners were anxious 'to substitute in every case which admits of it the shortest and most summary process, with the least amount of preliminary written pleadings, and to bring the parties, by themselves or their counsel, to state their cases with as little delay as possible...'.[132] Accordingly, they proposed a procedure by originating summons, enabling a next of kin, legatee or creditor to seek in chambers an order that the personal representative administer the personal estate. Real estate was less straightforward, but the same procedure could be invoked where it was held by trustees with a power of sale,[133] and it was also available, and much used, when a guardian or maintenance for infants was sought in an original proceeding.[134]

---

[123] Charitable Trusts Act 1812 (52 Geo. III c. 101).

[124] Charitable Trusts Act 1831(1 & 2 Will. IV c. 50).

[125] 10 & 11 Vict. c. 96; 12 & 13 Vict. c. 74.

[126] C. Stebbings, *The Private Trustee in Victorian England* (Cambridge, 2002), 51, noting an instance of 1847 in which an undisputed application had taken three years and cost £337.

[127] Chancery Proceedings Act 1850 (13 & 14 Vict. c. 35). Turner's bill was originally more ambitious: Lobban 'Preparing for Fusion, Part Two', 578–9.

[128] General Orders of May 1850. See (1850) 15 *LT* 124.

[129] *First Report 1852*, 13.   [130] *Ibid.*, 13–14.

[131] *Ibid.*, 13.   [132] *Ibid.*, 14.

[133] *Ibid.*, 38, enacted in Chancery Amendment Act 1852 (15 & 16 Vict. c. 86), ss 45–7. The provision as to trustees of land was an extension of the General Order of August 1841 (*First Report 1852*, 115).

[134] *RC on Courts of Common Law and Chancery, First Report*, PP 1863 [3238], xv, Schedule; Barber's statement at 66.

Alongside the summons, the special case was retained for the purposes envisaged in Turner's Act, that is for obtaining a ruling on a question of construction, but this apparently became less popular, perhaps because it did not meet the greatest need, a procedure short of full administration. [135]

Despite these innovations many suits would still follow the traditional course of bill and answer, but it would be a very different bill from Bentham's monstrosity, printed in numbered paragraphs and shorn of its interrogatories.[136] Served on the defendants, it would displace the apparatus of subpoenas and would not require an answer unless accompanied or followed by interrogatories in a separate paper.[137] The complexities of rules governing appearance were simplified by substituting a straightforward eight days, though in practice solicitors' undertakings were apparently often accepted in lieu of formal service.[138] The answer must still deal fully with all matters raised in the bill and interrogatories, and exceptions might be filed for insufficiency, but no longer for impertinence.[139] After any further pleadings or amendments—the use of supplemental bills to update the original bill being also discontinued—the plaintiff would as before file his replication,[140] but the Chancery Amendment Act 1852[141] offered him an alternative which proved popular, that is, to file a motion for a decree, which would be set down after a month on the evidence of the pleadings and affidavits listed on the notice; the defendant had two weeks to file affidavits of his own and the plaintiff one further week for affidavits in response.[142]

In the view of the Commissioners, '[t]here is probably nothing in Chancery procedure which has tended so much to augment expense and delay as the rules of the Court as to parties'.[143] So far the only statutory modification of the rigid 'necessary party' rule was in the Winding-Up Act, which dealt with partnerships of more than six,[144] but with Cottenham's order 'falling more and more into disuse'[145] it was now to be put on a statutory basis and broadened. In suits for administration or concerning trusts and in injunctions for preserving property

---

[135] *Ibid.*, 67; Holdsworth, *HEL*, ix, 376.

[136] As recommended by the Commissioners (*First Report 1852*, 40–1) and enacted in Chancery Amendment Act 1852, ss 1, 10.

[137] *First Report 1852*, 40–1; Chancery Amendment Act 1852, ss 2–4.

[138] *RC on Common Law and Chancery, Report 1863*, Schedule; Barber's statement, 58.

[139] *Ibid.*, Barber's statement, 60.

[140] Chancery Amendment Act 1852, s 26.

[141] Section 15.

[142] Barber's statement (*RC on Common Law and Chancery, Report 1863*, Schedule, 60) says it was frequently adopted. In the 1860s more than 1000 such motions were filed each year.

[143] *First Report 1852*, 18.

[144] 7 & 8 Vict. c. 3.

[145] *First Report 1852*, 18, and see above.

or preventing waste no objection for want of parties could be taken.[146] Trustees might now represent their *cestuis que trust* just as personal representatives did the beneficiaries and instead of being made parties to a suit, 'formal parties' might merely be served notice that they would be bound by proceedings unless they wished to join the action.[147] This latter provision was not much used, since the removal of the requirement that all parties must put in an answer served much the same purpose in distinguishing the real parties from others.[148] The thorniest problem was mortgages, where both redemption and foreclosure suits often involved a whole mass of competing interests. It was not felt possible to dispense generally with the participation of them all, but anyone interested in the equity of redemption might seek an order for sale during foreclosure proceedings.[149]

These were only the most important of the procedural reforms to the preliminary stages of a Chancery suit brought about by the Act of 1852. It is a mark of how things had changed that the Commission's report attracted little criticism from conservatives and the bill as little opposition in Parliament.

5. EVIDENCE

Holdsworth pronounced that 'it may safely be said that a more futile method of getting at the facts of the case, than the system in use in the court of Chancery from the seventeenth century onwards, never existed in any mature legal system'.[150] It differed fundamentally from common law in two respects; first, Chancery not only allowed, but required, testimony from interested parties, including the parties themselves; secondly, that evidence was almost invariably in written form.[151]

This second feature attracted strong criticism, and not only from Bentham and other proponents of rationality. In 1799 Lord Alvanley MR said 'it is impossible to sit here any time without seeing, that a *viva voce* examination of witnesses is much more satisfactory than depositions, where a possibility of doubt can be raised',[152] but such a change was already too late in Hardwicke's day.[153] Even within the inherent limitations of written testimony, however, Chancery practice managed to combine costliness, delay, and inefficiency in a most discreditable fashion.

---

[146] Chancery Procedure Act 1852, ss 42–3. [147] *Ibid.*, s 42; rr 8, 9.
[148] *RC on Common Law and Chancery, Report 1863*, Schedule, Barber's statement, 58.
[149] Section 48; *First Report 1852*, 19. [150] *HEL*, ix, 353.
[151] *Ibid.*, 353–8. [152] *Binford* v. *Dommitt* (1799) 4 Ves. Jun. 756, 762.
[153] In *Graves* v. *Eustace Budgel* (1737) 1 Atk. 445, Hardwicke said, 'the constant and established proceedings of this court are upon written evidence like the proceedings upon the civil or canon law...There never was yet a case where witnesses have been allowed to be examined at large at the hearing; and though it might be desirable to allow this, yet the fixed and settled proceedings of the court cannot be broke through for it' (quoted in Holdsworth, *HEL*, ix, 354).

Witnesses in London and its environs gave their evidence to one of the court's examiners. He administered a series of questions drawn up by counsel for the party calling the witness and, if they chose, by counsel for other parties. The examination was in private with neither lawyers nor parties in attendance, and from the witness's answers the examiner produced a narrative of events. Country witnesses attended four examiners chosen by the parties, each nominating four persons from whom the other side would strike out two names. The examiners and a clerk would quarter themselves at an inn and conduct the examination along London lines. In either case the depositions would be sealed, and when all the examinations had been completed the plaintiff would obtain an order for them to be opened ('publication'), after which a trial date could be sought. There was, however, ample opportunity for interlocutory proceedings by way of motions to strike out evidence alleged to be inadmissible and to extend the time for more evidence to be taken.

Like most aspects of Chancery procedure, the time allowed for taking evidence was generous and where one party was in no hurry he had ample opportunity for tactical delay. It was also expensive, in particular in the country, where, as the commissioners were paid two guineas a day plus living expenses, their sitting day tended to be very short.[154] Worse, it was strikingly inefficient. First, since solicitors could not be certain what a witness's testimony would be, they had to cover any potentially fatal gap in their evidence by calling several witnesses, even to establish the provenance of a document or entry in a register.[155] Secondly, because the interrogatories had to be drawn up in advance, the draftsman had to provide against a range of initial answers, so the interrogatories were lengthy and often irrelevant. Effective cross-examination was not only difficult but potentially dangerous, since a line of questioning could not be curtailed if it was eliciting unfavourable testimony; it was therefore seldom used, and witnesses' statements tended to go unchallenged.[156] Furthermore, the questions were often phrased in technical language; their meaning might be unclear to the witness and since the examiners, prudently perhaps, did not usually consider it their duty to offer explanations, the 'wrong' answer might be given.[157] As Lancelot Shadwell commented, 'you are almost morally sure that you have not got upon the written deposition the answers the witness gave'.[158] The quality and style of the narrative varied and in country cases might be the product of wrangling and compromise.[159]

[154] *RC on Chancery, Report 1826*, evidence of Ralph Barnes, an Exeter solicitor, App. A37.
[155] *Ibid.*, William Vizard, App. A2.
[156] Holdsworth, *HEL*, ix, 355.
[157] See the example given by Vizard at q. 155.
[158] App. A14, q. 196.
[159] Barnes, App. A37, q. 8.

The Commissioners were palpably uneasy with this subject. They could not advocate a wholesale move to oral evidence, since that would require fundamental changes in procedure and by prolonging hearings would aggravate delays at the trial stage. However, they virtually acknowledged the inadequacy of the existing practice by pointing to the facility of sending feigned issues to be tried at law.[160] Equity judges had been increasingly resorting to this device, which enabled them to obtain a common law jury verdict on a disputed matter of fact, but as it increased cost and delay it was hardly satisfactory.[161] The Commissioners' only concession was to give masters the power to hear evidence *viva voce* on certain matters.[162]

The Commissioners followed leading counsels' unconvincing assertions that injustice was seldom done by the defective mode of taking evidence,[163] but if so, it was only because those same counsel and experienced solicitors had learned to seek what they wanted from another source. Complaints that the interrogatories in a Chancery bill were otiose overlooked the fact that they had been elaborated precisely to fill the gap left by relinquishing oral evidence. Heald admitted that they were unnecessary in simple cases, but he and the ultra-conservative Bell were right to claim that interrogatories were usually needed;[164] as Lowe boasted, it was through these that he could 'scrape the defendant's conscience', driving him to admit unpalatable facts.[165]

The Commissioners' suggestions for improvement were limited to reducing the time limits for examinations and curbing the extravagance of country commissions. They also hoped to raise standards by requiring that examiners, and at least one Commissioner on each side, must be barristers of ten years' standing.[166] The report of the Chancery Commission 25 years on suggests those recommendations which were implemented accomplished little. Cottenham's orders made some improvement in interrogatories, requiring them to be numbered and directed at only those parties with knowledge of the matter under question,[167] but the role of the examiners and the taking of evidence were at the forefront of the new Commission's instructions.

The Law Society claimed that 'it is admitted on all hands, that the present mode of taking evidence in Chancery, by written interrogatories before an officer of the court, is extremely defective and unsatisfactory'.[168] Its proposals formed the basis

[160] *RC on Chancery, Report 1826*, 12–15.
[161] Holdsworth, *HEL*, ix, 357. Leach's rapid disposal of business was attributable in part to his ready resort to this expedient: *ODNB* 32: 953.
[162] Proposition 92.   [163] At p. 14.
[164] Apps A (Bell), 29 (Heald).   [165] App. A13, esp. q. 63.
[166] Propositions 40 to 52.   [167] 'W', 'Chancery Practice', (1845) 2 (s2) *LM* 58–86 at 82.
[168] *Law Society Report to Chancery Commission*, 13.

of the Commission's recommendations, but such was the delicacy and complexity of the issue that the revised system was twice investigated, and twice altered, within the same decade. There was widespread support for change, but not all equity lawyers favoured aligning their practice as closely with the common law as enthusiasts for procedural fusion wished. The Commission itself maintained the old position that a wholesale move to *viva voce* examination in open court was impossible without more judges.[169] Instead, noting that affidavit evidence was now the dominant mode in interlocutory proceedings, and that in practice many cases were effectively determined on motions, they proposed to encourage affidavits in final hearings too. The defects of affidavits were acknowledged—coaching of witnesses, prolixity, and the inclusion of inadmissible matter among them— but it was felt that the way interrogatories were taken was in practice little better, as well as being a great deal slower and costlier. To meet the needs of the minority of cases where a witness's testimony was contested, any of the parties might require him to give oral evidence instead, or to be examined or cross-examined on his affidavit; it was felt that the prospect of this would do much to ensure honesty in affidavits. As a fallback the judge might himself require *viva voce* evidence at the hearing.[170] Examinations before the hearing, where demanded, would still take place, but before a 'Master or other competent person accustomed to the examination of witnesses and practically conversant with the law of evidence'; he would sit in public, in the presence of the parties, their solicitors and counsel, and it was the last-named who would do the questioning. The examiner would still present the evidence in narrative form as hitherto and would rule on admissibility.[171] As for the evidence of the parties themselves, the interrogatories were removed from the bill and must be administered separately in a more straightforward format.

Within a couple of years pressure from within the legal profession forced the Commissioners to review the working of the new system. In the end the examiners had not been abolished and it was alleged that there were long delays in getting appointments with them, partly because many parties failed to show up for theirs, having presumably settled out of court. Evidence taken in this fashion was felt unsatisfactory because the judge could not see the demeanour of the witness, and there was uncertainty over the line where inadmissibility (which the examiner could rule on) met materiality (on which he could not).[172] The Commission sought some changes (implemented through a general order early

[169] *First Report 1852*, 21.
[170] *Ibid.*, 21–3.
[171] *Ibid.*, 22; Chancery Procedure Act 1852, ss 28–41.
[172] *Ibid.*, App. A (memorandum, 23–4) and Apps B, 25–73 and C, 128–93.

in 1855), notably encouraging even the parties to give their evidence by affidavit, but without acceding to the pressure for a more decisive shift towards orality.[173] Still dissatisfied, the reformers pressed for a further investigation. Lyndhurst claimed that too many affidavits were 'cooked', Chelmsford that the retention of the examiners had been a mistake.[174] It was said, no doubt with some truth, that certain judges were reluctant to have *viva voce* evidence in their court, or to call a jury to resolve disputes (still preferring to send it to law by an issue), while the equity bar disliked conducting cross-examination.[175]

Yet another investigation was started, and duly recommended that *viva voce* examinations should henceforth be held before the judge or a jury, as indeed should cross-examination on affidavits. The role of the examiners would be restricted to taking *ex parte* examinations and those for which the parties agreed to use their services. It appears, however, that practitioners were tenacious of the old ways and general orders to this effect seem not have had the intended effect. In the matter of taking evidence Chancery had edged towards the common law without embracing it.[176]

6. THE TRIAL STAGE

Criticism of Eldon's court was chiefly concentrated on the delays in hearing causes which had been set down. Arguments over the extent of these delays continued— not every cause set down was in fact ready to be heard—but delays were real and serious and especially bad when a cause was referred to a master and had to climb up the lists twice; in 1840 Cottenham LC reckoned this would take three years though, like Leach before him, Cottenham was said to be particularly prone to order references almost as a matter of course.[177]

The leisurely course of Chancery proceedings had a bad effect on solicitors who regularly practised there.[178] In some it induced a corresponding lethargy, while others followed the example of Mr Vholes in *Bleak House* and manufactured interlocutory business to persuade their clients of their zeal, so that to revivors and supplements necessitated by the occurrences of everyday life were added

---

[173] Lobban, 'Preparing for Fusion, Part Two', 588.

[174] *PD* 1859 (s3) 154: 1027, 1033.

[175] See debate on the Chancery Amendment Bill 1858, *PD* 1858 (s3) 149: 1161–72.

[176] Lobban, 'Preparing for Fusion, Part Two', 589. In 1859–60 415 witnesses appeared before the examiners; in 1869–70 540 did so: *PP* 1871 [C. 442], lxiv.

[177] *PD* 1840 (s3) 53: 1334; 'A Sketch of Lord Cottenham as a Judge' (1869) 23 (s3) *LM & LR* 264–72 at 271.

[178] 'JGP', 'Lord Eldon, his Biography and its Reviewers' (1845) 2 (s2) *LM* 347–76 at 365, quoting Sir Samuel Romilly.

motions and petitions of doubtful value.[179] The materials were readily to hand. Maddock's practice book listed an inviting number of motions[180] and the growing resort to them is illustrated by their rise from 4684 to 6730 in Eldon's first decade as Chancellor.[181] Many were simply motions of course, but those overflowed the time allotted to them, giving rise to further discontent because of the practice, adopted by the bar with the acquiescence of the judges, of allowing counsel to bring forward motions in order of seniority rather than the order in which they were filed. This obliged solicitors and barristers to hang about in court in a state of uncertainty and encouraged resort to expensive leaders to ensure progress. The number of motions each counsel might make in his turn was eventually restricted, but it remained a grievance.[182]

A more helpful trend (particularly useful in friendly suits) which Eldon had encouraged was the use of motions as a short cut to obtain an opinion.[183] By contrast Cottenham was said to have been scrupulous to avoid touching on the merits of a suit at any interlocutory stage and was unwilling to offer any short cuts; his system 'held out till very lately, the practitioners priding themselves much less in justice than in technicalities'. [184]

Even after the hearing of a cause there was always the possibility of a re-hearing or an appeal. Much of the argument over the creation of a Vice-Chancellor centred upon whether, as opponents claimed, any benefit would be nullified by a proliferation of appeals from his decisions.[185] Reviving the debate in 1819, Taylor claimed that their predictions had been fulfilled, with serious arrears at the appeal stage, and though estimates of the scale of the problem varied widely, it became common ground that, whatever the merits of the establishment of the Vice-Chancellorship, appeals from him made an appreciable addition to the Lord Chancellor's burdens.[186] The propensity of unsuccessful litigants to appeal was encouraged by several factors. Decisions of the first Vice-Chancellors, Plumer, Leach and Shadwell, failed to give satisfaction, Plumer because his appointment was criticized and he started with a poor reputation, Leach because of his notorious haste, and Shadwell because he was in thrall to a succession of powerful

---

[179] *PD* 1839 (s3) 48: 40–56 (Lord Lyndhurst).

[180] Holdsworth, *HEL*, ix, 359.

[181] Melikan, *John Scott, Lord Eldon*, table 16.1, 311.

[182] *RC on Chancery, Report 1826*, 32–3; W. F. Finlason, 'Illustrations of our Judicial System, Part Two' (1873) 2 *LM & LR* 1053–82 at 1066.

[183] See *Bonner* v. *Johnston* (1816) 4 Mer. 709.

[184] 'Sketch of Lord Cottenham as a Judge', 270. 'Observations on the Judges of the Court of Chancery', 290 notes also the saving of costs.

[185] Lobban, 'Preparing for Fusion, Part One', 402–5.

[186] *Ibid.*, 405–6.

leaders.[187] Eldon so lacked confidence in his own judgments that he positively invited rehearings and appeals, even when the latter were in effect, as critics maintained, appeals from the Chancellor in his own court to the Chancellor and two mute lay peers in the House of Lords.[188] His reputation for minute scrutiny of documents also encouraged the hope that he would find something overlooked by the trial judge,[189] though he was provoked into uncharacteristic imprudence when James Abercromby was reported as having said that he admitted new evidence on appeals.[190] It was, however, open to the judge to look at evidence available at the hearing but not referred to. On appeals from interlocutory decisions upon motion there was no restriction at all. [191]

In fact the court was remarkably generous in reviewing decisions. Even when the court of Appeals in Chancery was set up it remained possible for the suitor to have his cause reheard by the judge first and it was not until 1852 that orders imposed a time limit of five years from the order or decree;[192] until then only the doctrine of laches set any bounds to appeals. It is no wonder that nothing was ever considered final in Chancery. The only safeguard against frivolous or vexatious appeals was the requirement that the petition be signed by counsel and £20 be deposited as security for costs, and that was probably ineffective.[193] Moreover, with an increasing amount of Chancery business involving a fund in court appellants were comforted by the knowledge that the costs of the appeal would generally be directed to be met from that source.

Few Chancery barristers supported restrictions upon the right of appeal, not just from interested motives but because they saw appeals as an essential security for the coherence of equitable doctrines, always vulnerable to the old jibes about their arbitrary and whimsical character. Moreover, with no juries, all decisions were reasoned decisions whose flaws, if not exposed, might form the basis for further errors.

If Chancery was much criticised for slowness in producing a verdict and generosity in allowing it to be challenged, it also came under strong attack for the treatment of those who disobeyed an order of the court. The process of enforcing orders was, like so much else in Chancery, ponderous and stately, but if it progressed to a writ of sequestration and the contemnor had no property to

[187] Megarry, 'The Vice-Chancellors', 374–7. Sir Anthony Hart was fleetingly Vice-Chancellor in 1827.

[188] See above, pp. 530–2.

[189] Examples are in Twiss, *Life of Lord Eldon*, ii, 417–19.

[190] *Ibid.*, 370–1.

[191] *RC on Common Law and Chancery, Report 1863*, Barber's statement, 72–3.

[192] Order 1, August 1852.

[193] *RC on Chancery, Report 1826*, 38.

sequestrate, then he might be imprisoned indefinitely if no one would purge his contempt.[194] Lyndhurst attempted to alleviate the plight of such persons, which had been well publicized and perhaps rather exaggerated but there were doubts whether it was lawful to do so through orders, so Sugden successfully introduced a bill which prescribed a quarterly return from the warden of the Fleet and examination by a master which might result in a discharge upon terms.[195] This reform did not prevent Dickens from excoriating the court in *The Martyrs of Chancery* and again in *Bleak House*,[196] unfairly perhaps but to good effect, for the procedures were improved in 1860 with the institution of a quarterly visit by a court official who would report to the Lord Chancellor. [197]

7. ORGANIZATION: MASTERS AND REGISTRARS

The ten masters in Chancery played an increasingly important role in the court as a fact-finding agency to whom judges referred a whole range of matters germane to the outcome of a suit but too time-consuming or mundane to warrant investigation in open court.[198] Their duties included: taking accounts of executors, trustees, mortgagees, partners, agents etc.; appointing receivers, guardians, and trustees; dealing with maintenance and advancement; arranging sales of land and settling schemes to administer charities.[199] As the proportion of Chancery business from wills and settlements, sales and mortgages of land and partnerships and other multi-party commercial transactions and from charitable endowments, grew at the expense of bonds and straightforward commercial disputes, so did the number and complexity of references. A crude index is the number of volumes of their reports, which rose from 245 (1701–50), to 335 (1750–1800) and 1400 (1800–52). This represents a much faster rate of increase than causes, and indicates also a change in practice, with parties increasingly seeking interim reports on a particular issue and delaying the final report, sometimes to settle an urgent matter, sometimes to procrastinate.

The masters practised out of the public gaze and initially it was only their fees (particularly from office copies) that engaged parliamentary attention.[200] However, the Chancery Commission also delved into the ways in which delays

---

[194] *RC on Chancery, Report 1826*, App. A q. 10 (Bickersteth); Holdsworth, *HEL*, ix, 352–3.

[195] 'Sugden's Acts' (1830) 4 *LM* 409–17; *MP* 1830, 1: 134–7; Equity (Contempt) Act 1830 (11 Geo. IV & 1 Will. IV c. 36).

[196] Holdsworth, *Charles Dickens as a Legal Historian*.

[197] Court of Chancery Act 1860 (23 & 24 Vict. c. 149), ss 2–4.

[198] E. Heward, *Masters in Ordinary* (Chichester, 1990); Holdsworth, *HEL*, i, 416–27, 439–42.

[199] Heward, *Masters in Ordinary*, 63, from the *First Report 1852*. At 14 he provides a list from an earlier commission, of 1734.

[200] Parkes, *History of the Court of Chancery*, 510–16.

and expense in the masters' offices contributed to the court's bad reputation. Some masters freely acknowledged that 'those evils exist, and to a very great extent',[201] but denied that they were at fault, blaming the parties and their solicitors for such systemic weaknesses as were not, in their view, an unavoidable consequence of the equity jurisdiction and the sort of business that came into Chancery.[202] With two of their number on the Commission, it was always likely that this view would be adopted,[203] and in any event, the masters had a plausible case. There were suits brought by a 'friendly' creditor purely to obstruct the real creditors and where inactivity was the whole purpose.[204] It was also common for executors or those entitled to the residue of an estate to delay paying simple contract debts and legacies (which carried no interest) in order to accumulate income for themselves.[205]

Most commonly, however, proceedings were leisurely because solicitors' clients were either indifferent to haste or unable to penetrate the obfuscation of their solicitor—and the worse Chancery's reputation for delay, the more plausibly the solicitor could blame the court. Solicitors and counsel operated a 'system of accommodation',[206] where none would complain of another's absence from a master's appointment or failure to produce material for it in order to ensure the like indulgence when he needed it. Attendance was often through a clerk, and not always the expert managing clerk whom most of the bigger firms employed, but a junior without the knowledge or authority to progress the suit.[207] When faced with the absence of the representative of one or more parties the master would usually adjourn rather than proceed *ex parte*. The party with conduct of the suit determined its pace, and if he allowed it to lag he seldom faced the serious consequences that would arise at common law. In theory another party might petition to have 'carriage of the suit' transferred to him, but the solicitors' mutual courtesy, the cost and the onerous nature of the burden in administration cases combined to make such applications a rarity.[208]

Accordingly, the masters claimed to be helpless to accelerate the progress of causes. Even Stephen, one of the more enterprising, told the Commission at length of his experience in *Silcox v. Bell*, an inheritance suit with over 100 claimants, many of them poor Dorset folk, which had slumbered from 1811 to 1820 because

---

[201] *RC on Chancery, Report 1826*, App. B6, return of Master James Stephen.

[202] All the masters sent in a return to the Commission (App. B).

[203] William Courtenay, later Earl of Devon, and Samuel C. Cox. According to *The Times*, 27 December 1826 (quoted in Parkes, *History of the Court of Chancery*, 580), Cox was too busy to attend many sittings, and the Commission relied heavily on the views of Courtenay and Stephen. It was said in 'The New Chancery Orders' (1828) 2 *Jurist* 137–79, that the orders largely incorporated Courtenay's views.

[204] *RC on Chancery, Report 1826*, App. B9, Master J. E. Dowdeswell.

[205] *Ibid.*, App. B8 (Stephen).   [206] *Ibid.*, App. B9 (Dowdeswell).

[207] *Ibid.*   [208] *Ibid.*, App. B9 (Stephen).

(he inferred) the previously active solicitor had become too prosperous and busy to pursue it. Some of the bewildered claimants had journeyed to London to see the master, who could offer little but sympathy.[209]

Not surprisingly, Stephen's bewildered claimants could not grasp the notion that a judge was helpless in his own court, and indeed the blame for this state of affairs did not rest wholly with the solicitors and parties. The masters had become too detached from their judges. In part this was geographical, for they had moved their offices to Southampton Buildings in 1795,[210] and in part procedural, for after 1826 they no longer attended in court to hear the reference being drawn, and so lacked knowledge of the case.[211] Successive Chancellors had made no attempt to improve their operations—Master Stratford more or less openly deplored Eldon's neglect to do so[212]—and without effective supervision practices had grown up which aggravated delays and increased costs. For example, in only one office was the first warrant to attend treated as peremptory, and as new masters felt unable to adopt that more demanding practice the laxer one spread.[213]

More serious was the standard use of hourly warrants. Even if the full hour was used, that often left barely time for the master to remind himself of the state of the case and make progress; often however, less than the full hour was used, for it had become customary to allow the parties up to half-an-hour's grace.[214] The office opening hours were short, and it was only a partial answer that the masters worked on their papers outside those hours. Unlike the court, the offices shut during the vacation, leaving only one or two masters available for urgent business.[215]

There were also complaints about the quality of their work. Some were undoubtedly able, Thomson and Alexander became Chief Barons of the Exchequer,[216] but Eldon's choices were not all welcomed; Eden, Farrer and, particularly, Francis Cross, a former militia officer said to have held few briefs, were singled out for criticism.[217] Their ability (in reality often that of their chief clerks) to master

[209] Ibid.

[210] Heward, Masters in Ordinary, 19–20.

[211] In 1798 three masters sat with the Lord Chancellor in term time and two out of term; two sat with the Master of the Rolls: ibid., 12. Eldon ended this practice: Rolt, Memoirs of Rolt, 205.

[212] RC on Chancery, Report 1826, App. B1.

[213] Ibid., App. B8. Several masters (e.g. W. Wingfield, App. B15) complained of want of uniformity.

[214] Ibid., App. B8 (Stephen).

[215] For a defence see the anonymous master quoted in 'H', 'The Masters' Offices' (1841) 25 LM 97–117 at 106–7.

[216] ODNB 54: 483; E. Foss, The Judges of England, 9 vols (1848–64), ix, 74–5.

[217] The Times, 27 December 1826, letter of 'AB', quoted in Parkes, History of the Court of Chancery, 583–4. Cross was called in 1813, appointed in 1821. Eden (later Lord Henley), called in 1814, was a commissioner of bankruptcy and king's serjeant of the Duchy of Lancaster 1825–6, when appointed

complicated commercial accounts was scouted by some businessmen—but this was an old complaint and not easily addressed.[218] Moreover, their judgments were not trusted. Every report was open to exceptions and the reports were just that; all returned to the judge to be converted into orders.

The Commission's proposals, mostly suggested by Master Courtenay, were unambitious. The master was to keep a record of each case and set a date for an initial hearing at which a timetable would be set for the various inquiries.[219] There would be no sanctions for non-compliance but it was hoped that this would induce reputable solicitors to be more diligent.[220] Only well-qualified solicitors' clerks, registered with a master, were to be allowed to appear;[221] transfer of carriage was to be made easier,[222] and a master's decision on objections that an affidavit, state of facts etc. contained scandalous or impertinent matter, was to be final.[223] The general idea was to encourage, rather than compel, parties to be more prompt and masters more pro-active. Lyndhurst implemented most of the recommendations by order, though Redesdale and his allies succeeded in getting even the minor curb on appeals dropped.[224] George Spence's bill proposed more drastic changes but was subsumed in Brougham's projects, which put the masters on a salary and removed the Lord Chancellor's personal patronage without improving the way business was conducted.[225]

The number of references continued to grow; in one office the number of reports and certificates rose from 371 to 584 in the 15 years to 1840.[226] As a rather inadequate substitute for fees as an incentive to urgency, the masters were required to produce an annual return, but it was too bald to be very revealing.[227] E. W. Field published an influential critique of the masters' offices in 1840, acknowledging that his own profession was largely to blame for delays but ramming home the old points about short hours, short terms, and inefficient procedures.[228]

---

master. He was also MP for Fowey (1826–30): Heward, *Masters in Ordinary*, 121, 139. Eldon had earlier yielded to the Prince Regent's importunities in appointing Jekyll a master, and to his own wife's in favour of Farrer: Twiss, *Life of Lord Eldon*, ii, 533; W.E. Surtees, *A Sketch of the Lives of Lords Stowell and Eldon* (1846), 148–54.

[218] Lord Northington's criticism was often quoted, e.g. in 'Reforms in Chancery' (1828–9) 1 *LM* 32–45 at 41, and even the Chancery Commission thought much could be improved: *RC on Chancery, Report 1826*, 22.

[219] *RC on Chancery, Report 1826*, 20.   [220] *Ibid.*, 21.

[221] *Ibid.*, 22–3, propositions 106–8.   [222] *Ibid.*, 23.

[223] *Ibid.*, proposition 97.

[224] Redesdale denounced this in his pamphlet (Parkes, *History of the Court of Chancery*, 521); *PD* 1827 (s2) 16: 701.

[225] Lobban, 'Henry Brougham and Law Reform', 1193–7; *MP* 1830, 2: 1432.

[226] *Facts and Suggestions Respecting the Masters' Offices*, quoted in *The Masters' Offices*, 106.

[227] Pemberton's speech, *PD* 1840 (s3) 55: 1317.

[228] *Observations of a Solicitor… on the Defects of… the Equity Courts* (1840).

In the Commons, Pemberton made powerful use of this material and he, like others, attributed much of the problem to the masters sitting in private.[229] Masters defended their order, but following the creation of the extra vice-chancellors and the abolition of the six clerks the masters became the primary target for reformers.[230]

When the Chancery Commission summoned Masters J. W. Farrer and William Brougham to give evidence in 1851 it found that many of the familiar flaws persisted; solicitors' 'courtesy' made them still reluctant to ask for conduct of a suit to be transferred, and the masters still adopted an essentially passive role;[231] Farrer's 27 years of pondering an effective means to compel the attendance of solicitors left him unable to think of any, and his one tentative experiment in imposing a costs penalty he felt sure would be ineffective.[232]

This Commission had not originally been intended to tackle the masters' offices at all. Its extended remit (reinforced by two laymen, Sir James Graham and J. W. Henley) was the result of stinging parliamentary criticisms of 'the Augean stables in Southampton Buildings'.[233] That was hyperbole, but the Solicitor-General admitted that they had been trying to get the masters onto a more satisfactory footing for a decade[234] and cross-party support for a further attempt was strong, the Conservative Sugden having long identified them as the greatest weakness in Chancery.[235]

Moves were afoot for the most drastic measure—the entire abolition of the masters and the transfer of their business to the judges in chambers assisted by chief clerks. This idea seems to have originated with a bankruptcy commissioner, Fane, in 1840.[236] William Brougham put it to Langdale, but though his Chancery committee discussed the masters' offices at length they evidently found the subject intractable.[237] The plan appealed to those who wanted to see courts of equity become more like those of common law, but there were two practical obstacles besides the sensitivity of proposing compensation in the light of the row over the six clerks' pay-off; one was that there might need to be more judges if they

---

[229] PD 1840 (s3) 55: 1305–26. See also Daniell, 'Considerations', 110–11.

[230] A. H. Lynch in Parliament (PD 1840 (s3) 55: 1330) and the anonymous author of the pamphlet reviewed in the Law Magazine (above, n.226).

[231] First Report 1852, 28–31.

[232] First Report 1852, App. A, qq. 22–3.

[233] J. Evans, PD 1850 (s3) 117: 1371, in the debate on Stuart's motion. The addition of the two laymen was announced by Palmerston a few days afterwards: 118: 350; Lobban, 'Preparing for Fusion, Part Two', 580.

[234] PD 1850 (s3) 111: 1137.

[235] e.g. PD 1841 (s3) 56: 193–4.

[236] Lobban, 'Preparing for Fusion, Part Two', 577.

[237] Ibid., 577 n.53.

were to work in chambers; the other was that some judges would not accept this imposition.[238]

These difficulties led some reformers, notably Henry Brougham, to seek less satisfactory, but more practicable solutions. Most of these gave masters the powers of judges, by enabling suitors to take certain classes of business directly to the master or otherwise streamlining the procedure by which they came into his office.[239] From 1848 the winding-up of joint stock companies was treated in this way ('a tormenting sort of proceeding' in Farrar's eyes)[240] and even if relatively rarely used, it was an influential precedent.[241] If advocates of this sort of reform had united behind a single proposal it might have been more persuasive, though probably not to Cottenham. He had his own, conservative, views, which found expression in his orders of May 1850, designed to make the existing system work better and so head off radical change. Whether Cottenham's orders would have transformed the culture of the masters' offices where previous attempts had failed would never be known, for they were not given enough time.[242] Solicitors certainly complained that the most drastic step, the abolition of hourly warrants and the instruction that matters should normally be heard *de die en diem,* condemned them to lengthy and unproductive waits,[243] but most critics were out of patience with incremental reform; Page Wood for instance claimed that 888 warrants had been issued in one matter and the average was over 50.[244] Few of the Commission's witnesses felt the current regulations sufficient and the choice plainly lay between giving the masters primary jurisdiction, probably along the lines of the Metropolitan and Provincial Law Association bill of 1848, and transferring their functions to the judges in chambers.

The latter became more practicable once the Master of the Rolls and Sir George Turner expressed their willingness to sit in chambers and the judges made no representations about needing to expand their numbers; the proposed court of Appeals in Chancery would remove Knight-Bruce VC, whose resistance to chambers sittings was no secret.[245] Despite the firm recommendation of the

---

[238] See e.g. Brougham in *Law Society Report to Chancery Commission*, at 16. These practical considerations underlay some of the confused and confusing changes of position noted by Lobban, 'Preparing for Fusion, Part Two', 577–81.

[239] *Ibid.*, 575–8. Proposals to send purely administrative suits direct to the masters were made in the 1820s.

[240] *First Report 1852*, App. A, q. 13.

[241] V. M. Lester, *Victorian Insolvency* (Oxford, 1995), 223–4.

[242] PD 1852 (s3) 119: 1468 (J. Stuart). They were scarcely mentioned by the Law Society or the Chancery Commission.

[243] *Law Society Report to Chancery Commission*, 18.

[244] PD 1850 (s3) 111: 1138–9.

[245] Lobban, 'Preparing for Fusion, Part Two', 581.

Commission, Truro hesitated but on the fall of Russell's government he was replaced by St. Leonards, a long time advocate of the change.[246] By the Masters Abolition Act 1852 four masters were to retire on full salary (one post had been left vacant for some time) while the remaining five worked their way through the existing references.[247] Each first instance judge would have two chief clerks, holding office during good behaviour. Existing masters' clerks, along with solicitors or attorneys of ten years' standing, were eligible and those belonging to the vacated masterships were the first appointees.[248]

The new system envisaged judges deciding legal questions while the chief clerks dealt with administrative matters.[249] Unsurprisingly it did not work perfectly. There was criticism of the slowness with which the masters got through their remaining business[250] and a bill tidying up omissions and errors in 1860 (when the last three masters finally retired)[251] had to be withdrawn because it also authorized additional chief clerks.[252] In 1862 Selwyn argued that the chambers practice was still the weak point in Chancery.[253] Delays occurred when levels of incoming business rose or when a judge was ill,[254] and Graham was not alone in feeling that some judges (Romilly MR was one[255]) were too ready to delegate matters which they should have been deciding themselves. This had been one of the more serious objections to the new system[256] and a later critic complained that 'unsupported and unchecked by the pressure of the Bar, the Clerks in Chief

    [246] First Report 1852, 42–3.
    [247] Farrer and Brougham were retired by s 3. The others were to be released by the Lord Chancellor as business permitted, the opportunity to be offered in order of seniority on each occasion.
    [248] Section 17. As the diary of Charles Pugh, who filled one of the vacancies, reveals, they could scarcely believe their good fortune: Lobban, 'Preparing for Fusion, Part Two', 581–2.
    [249] Section 26 listed certain matters to be disposed of in chambers and provided for other matters to be added by general order of the Lord Chancellor or 'as each Judge may from Time to Time see fit'. Section 29 empowered each judge to allocate work between himself and his chief clerks, subject to rules made by the Lord Chancellor with the advice or assistance of any two of the judges. Cranworth made a curious last minute bid to divert the clerks' function to the registrars but found no supporters: PD 1852 (s3) 121: 418.
    [250] PD 1854 (s3) 134: 1019–27.
    [251] R. E. Ball, 'The Chancery Masters' (1961) 77 LQR 331–57 at 343.
    [252] PD 1860 (s3) 156: 155; 159: 1634–7; (1859–60) 4 Sol. J. 617.
    [253] PD 1862 (s3) 166: 115.
    [254] PD 1867 (s3) 188: 492–5; RC on the Legal Departments, Evidence: PP 1875 [C. 1245], xxx, 248–55, E. B. Church.
    [255] Lobban, 'Preparing for Fusion, Part Two', 583. He complained, however, that appeals were routinely brought from their decisions where the matter had never been properly put forward: Finlason, 'Illustrations of our Judicial System, Part Two', 1075–7.
    [256] PD 1860 (s3)160: 1635; (1857) 1 Sol. J. 593. St. Leonards had been anxious to get the chief clerks out of Southampton Buildings lest they start to behave as independent judges like the masters: PD 1852 (s3) 120: 798–802.

administer a rough kind of justice'.[257] The clerks had no complaints about the extent of their responsibilities, only about their workload, and criticisms were neither so frequent nor so widespread as those which had assailed the masters in the 1840s.

The registrars were another obvious target for scrutiny, and Williams had singled them out, instancing *Chinnery* v. *Chinnery* as an example of their excessive charges.[258] The registrar was a sinecurist whose deputies and their chief clerks performed the duties.[259] A deputy registrar was always in court to advise on practice matters but he no longer prepared the judge's order in court at the end of the hearing but instead made a note or minute. The order was drawn up through a lengthy series of steps and was usually based not upon the registrar's note but that of counsel for the party whose solicitor 'bespoke' it.[260] Disputes over what precisely had been ordered were common and because the same registrar was not always in attendance throughout the hearing the official note was not always more dependable than counsel's, which sometimes necessitated a further hearing to clarify the outcome of the first one.[261] The leisurely timetable afforded opportunities for the clerks to favour certain solicitors and Lowe said (as did others more temperately) that favour was earned by taking extra copies.[262] The clerks had also become adept at spinning out the reports by lengthy recitals, which in turn aggravated the delays. The Commissioners shied away from probing these accusations, which were naturally denied, and instead suggested adding two more registrars to take account of the creation of the Vice-Chancellor.[263] That proposal was doomed because it was coupled with another, that the deputy registrars should henceforth be recruited from barristers of ten years' standing rather than their own clerks, which would involve compensating the clerks for loss of expectations.[264]

The Chancery Regulation Act 1833 did away with the ornamental chief and substituted six working registrars (two for each judge) and eight chief clerks.[265] Their number was enlarged to complement successive expansions of the judiciary and in 1859 they were given assistant clerks to make appointments, give in, and hand out papers etc.[266] A later investigation felt the assistants were too many and

[257] 'The Reform of the Procedure of the English Courts' (1871) 31 (s3) *LM & LR*, 72–87 at 85.
[258] *PD* 1824 (s2) 10: 394.
[259] *RC on Chancery Courts, Third Report* (hereafter *Third Report 1856*), *PP* 1856 [2064], xxii, 5.
[260] *Ibid.*, 7–8.
[261] *Ibid.*, and see Holdsworth, *HEL*, i, 566–8.
[262] *RC on Chancery, Report 1826*, App. A13, qq. 94–106.
[263] *Ibid.*, 17.
[264] *Ibid.*; *The Times*, 17 September 1826, quoted in Parkes, *History of the Court of Chancery*, 526.
[265] 3 & 4 Will. IV c. 94.
[266] 5 Vict. c. 5; Court of Chancery and Judicial Committee Act 1851 (14 & 15 Vict. c. 3); *RC on Legal Departments, Second Report 1874*, 51.

too well paid for their duties, and with this expansion the registrars were bulging out of their Chancery Lane offices.[267]

The larger complement was matched by a growth in the number of orders but not by any great improvement in speed or efficiency.[268] In fact, despite regular complaints from users no part of Chancery proved more resistant to change than the registrars' offices. They retained essentially intact three vulnerable features of their practice. Largely through the support of the judges, they kept their place in the courtroom in the face of justified scepticism whether their role as 'a finger post to the court in matters of practice'[269] really warranted their continuous presence there. They successfully fought off suggestions that solicitors should draft the orders and bring them to the office, defending a process which (except when by-passed for urgent injunctions) took at least ten days and often much longer.[270] Only at the prompting of the Chancery Commission did they abandon their rigid practice of allocating decretal orders to the registrars and interlocutory ones to their chief clerks, however simple or complicated each might be; from the late 1850s the clerks normally drew all reports for the registrars' approval.[271] And against the emergent canons of public administration, they protected their closed shop, whereby a clerk—he needed to be a solicitor and was usually articled to a registrar for five years—would, if he lived long enough, ultimately succeed to a vacancy for registrar, promotion being purely according to seniority.[272]

8. ORGANIZATION: FEES AND OFFICES

Forster's condemnation of Chancery's expense[273] was embarrassing for the Commissioners, for though they had been charged with tackling expense as well as delay, they concentrated on the latter, treating the reduction of costs almost as a by-product of proposals for shortening proceedings.[274] This was justifiable inasmuch as recent agitation had also focused on delays, whereas fees had already undergone an investigation by a Commons select committee in 1816.[275] That had

[267] *Third Report 1856*, 6, 13–14.

[268] 11,546 in year ending 31 October 1854 (*ibid.*, 7).

[269] *RC on the Legal Departments, Second Report 1874*, 48, quoting Registrar R. H. Leach.

[270] *Third Report 1856*, 8, 13; *RC on the Legal Departments, Second Report 1874*, 49.

[271] *Third Report 1856*, 13. As the Legal Departments Commission noted, two-thirds of orders were by then coming from chambers and were based on the minute of the judge's chief clerk, prompting the thought that many of the simpler ones might as well be drawn up by the latter: *Second Report 1874*, 50.

[272] *Third Report 1856*, 14–15. The Legal Departments Commission (*Second Report 1874*, 49) wished to end the automatic right of succession.

[273] Above. Brougham said no one would bring an action for less than £100: *PD 1824* (s2) 10: 782.

[274] *RC on Chancery, Report 1826*, 12, 22.

[275] *PP 1816* (428) viii, 91; extract in Parkes, *History of the Court of Chancery*, App. 6.

been a cursory affair, however, disgusting reformers by its refusal to condemn fees which were authorized neither by Hardwicke's general order of 1743 (revised by Erskine in 1807) or any express rule or enactment. While formally denying that mere custom was sufficient warrant, the committee allowed that 20 years' user and evidence of some function performed for the fee would be justification enough.[276]

Like other courts, Chancery was funded chiefly through suitors' fees. Like them it had sinecure offices, and as with other sinecures the patrons (mostly the Lord Chancellor), often filled them from their own family; the lucrative positions held by Eldon's son did not go unnoticed.[277] But none of these sinecurists was summoned to give evidence to the Commission and it needed a close scrutiny of the report to uncover their existence.[278]

The recent Lords' select committee had suggested changes to the fees structure, but the Commission studiously ignored this possibility.[279] However, this awkward subject could not be altogether avoided, since while the judges were salaried most of the officers were remunerated directly or indirectly by suitors' fees. The masters were partly fee-dependent, so changes to the workings of their offices were likely to affect their incomes.[280]

There were two general issues of public administration besides the political controversy over 'old corruption'.[281] Ought public servants to be paid by salary or out of fees, and should the costs of the courts be met by the suitors or by the public at large? The Commissioners did not engage directly with either issue, but at one point conflated them: 'there is no doubt that the suitor would be materially relieved, if the whole of the fees were discontinued, and the Masters were in future paid wholly by salary; but we have had no hesitation in rejecting this solution, as unjust to the public'.[282] The inescapable immediate problem, however, was that the principal source of the fees in the masters' offices was charges for copies of documents, which were the subject of trenchant public criticism.

Such complaints had a long history. Lord Keeper Coventry's orders of 1635 show that reports were being lengthened by needless recitals and the same allegation

---

[276] *Ibid.*

[277] W. H. J. Scott was receiver of fines, registrar of affidavits, clerk of letters patent. In addition, he held the reversion of two sinecures held by the Rev. Thomas Thurlow: J. Wade, *The Extraordinary Black Book* (1833 edn), 568.

[278] As Parkes conceded, some were technically not sinecurists as they had duties to perform, but did so by deputy: *History of the Court of Chancery*, 579.

[279] Melikan, *John Scott, Lord Eldon*, 302–3.

[280] Lobban, 'Preparing for Fusion, Part One', 394–5.

[281] The fullest, not entirely satisfactory, treatment of this issue is P. Harling, *The Waning of 'Old Corruption'* (Oxford, 1996), but his references to the courts are meagre and perfunctory.

[282] *RC on Chancery, Report 1826*, 23.

was made to the Commission, with the addition that documents were generously spaced, stretched thinly across folios.[283] Parties had to take copies they did
not want simply because once a document was filed it was copied for the fee.
Such 'dead copies' often had no actual existence, and it was believed that generosity in taking copies oiled the wheels if it was desired to expedite a cause.[284]
The Commission righteously exculpated the masters themselves of any suspicion that they engaged in practices designed to boost their income, but conceded
that copying charges were excessive and insisted they be dropped to the 'normal'
level.[285] By expressly forbidding gratuities (clerks should have 'a liberal allowance'
to make good the loss) and explicitly barring any obligation for parties to take an
office copy they virtually admitted that much was wrong. Even so, they put aside
the other fees in the masters' offices as too small to warrant full examination and
ignored other abuses such as the practice of solicitors and clerks colluding in
working out how many warrants a particular suit would be allowed on taxation
and taking out the whole number forthwith.[286] Consideration of the lesser fees
was to await the ascertainment of how much the masters lost by the proposals,
since this would need to be made good by salary or other fees. [287]

The masters' offices were not alone in exploiting the potential of a system where
income was linked to the number and size of documents generated. It made for
delay (fee takers would not reduce their own profits by expanding the copying
staff if work increased) and complexity, and gave plausibility to criticisms that the
court was no more than a machine for extracting money. The commonest targets
for complaints by lawyers were the six clerks and the sworn clerks (or clerks in
court), not so much for their manipulation of the system as because they charged
fees for services which were either overpriced or redundant.[288]

The six clerks had once been the solicitors for Chancery suitors but had yielded
these functions to their own clerks, known as the sworn clerks or sometimes the
sixty.[289] Demarcation disputes occasionally broke out over money, most recently
in the 1780s, but by then it was accepted that the principal function of the six
clerks was as record-keepers.[290] In evidence Francis Vesey could not conceal that

---

[283] Holdsworth, *HEL*, ix, 362; i, 427.

[284] *Ibid.* i, 441; *RC on Chancery, Report 1826*, App. A11, especially q. 41 (James Winter) and A13,
qq. 96–103 (James Lowe);

[285] *RC on Chancery, Report 1826*, 23.

[286] *The Times*, 20 September 1826, in Parkes, *History of the Court of Chancery*, 539.

[287] *Ibid.*, 24; *RC on Chancery, Report 1826*, 24.

[288] *Ibid.*, App. A2 (Vizard), A4 (Thomas Hamilton), A13 (Lowe).

[289] Lobban, 'Preparing for Fusion, Part One', 395–7. Serving them were 'waiting clerks' whose
precise position was 'not quite clear': T. W. Braithwaite, *The Six Clerks in Chancery* (1879), 16.

[290] *Ex p the Six Clerks* (1798) 3 Ves. Jnr. 589; H. Horwitz, 'Record Keepers in the Court of Chancery
and their "Record of Accomplishment" in the Seventeenth and Eighteenth Centuries' (1997) 70
Historical Research 34–51.

they were too many for this duty—indeed since 1785 they had done it by rota, two months at a time[291]—and his attempts to demonstrate that they were not idle the rest of the time verged on the comical.[292] In time the sworn clerks had also become superfluous to their original function. In 1729 solicitors were allowed to play the same role in Chancery as attorneys in common law courts and this, with the general fall in business, so diminished the role of the sworn clerks that their number declined to just 18.[293] Solicitor witnesses disparaged their learning[294] and by continuing to perform the formal part of their old functions the clerks essentially duplicated the work of the party's solicitor; William Vizard calculated that £61 out of a sworn clerk's fees of £85 for one matter was superfluous.[295] Reactionaries like Redesdale attributed most of the court's failings to the incursion of the solicitors, but that only betrayed his ignorance of the court's history and there was no realistic chance (as he admitted, albeit giving the wrong reason, the political influence of the solicitors) of a return to his prelapsarian Eden.[296] In view of the damning evidence, the Commission's benign treatment of both sets of clerks is remarkable. Since the six clerks had too little to do they were to tax bills in place of the masters, while the sworn clerks were left untouched on the basis that their fees did not bear hardly on suitors.[297]

The court of Chancery was a sizeable and complex organization, which formed part of the Chancery itself. Since reformers were impatient to tackle the most glaring defects and defenders were prone to offer only the most trivial concessions, it is not surprising that reforms in its finances and clerical structure took place piecemeal over several decades. The court was inquired into with wearisome frequency and as Russell complained despairingly, its practitioners were always formidably equipped with objections to any reform they disliked.[298]

Even Henry Brougham's plans were wide ranging rather than comprehensive, and despite the assistance of Vizard, Courtenay, and C. P. Cooper, and the services of the capable George Spence as draftsman, he found the practicalities of legislation irksomely intricate. Larger bills had to be divided into more manageable ones and compensation was often a bugbear; Eldon and Leach were always

[291] RC on Chancery, Report 1826, App. A9.

[292] Ibid., and see the exchange quoted from The Times, 27 December 1826, in Parkes, History of the Court of Chancery, 576–7.

[293] 'Reforms in Chancery', 34.

[294] RC on Chancery, Report 1826, App. A13; 'Recent Reforms in Chancery' (1843) 29 LM 308–35 at 311.

[295] Lobban, 'Preparing for Fusion, Part One', 396.

[296] The Times, 31 August 1826, in Parkes, History of the Court of Chancery, 516–28.

[297] RC on Chancery, Report 1826, 33. One member later implied that they had been misled by the sworn clerk who produced the figures on this point. The Commission's secretary, George Jackson, was himself a sworn clerk: Lobban, 'Preparing for Fusion, Part One', 413.

[298] PD 1840 (s3) 55: 1326–30.

prone to defend the status quo and political factors, particularly over patronage, insistently intruded. [299]

Nevertheless, Brougham did sweep away an impressive number of sine-cures and made important reforms, particularly in the masters' and registrars' offices.[300] However, the six and sworn clerks escaped his grasp and enjoyed another few years of existence, very prosperous years for some sworn clerks. Brougham had wanted to abolish both, but the sworn clerks mounted a deter-mined defence and opposition from Eldon and Leach protected the six clerks, though vacancies were now not to be filled up until their number was reduced to two.[301] So matters remained until Field's pamphlet, which made deadly use of statistics, gave Pemberton the ammunition for an unanswerable parliamentary attack in 1840.[302] Cottenham set his informal committee to work and the Court of Chancery Offices Abolition Act 1841 put an end to both sets of clerks and several other unnecessary offices.[303] The clerical staff from these offices were reconfig-ured into a record and writ department[304] and taxation was entrusted to a new body of six taxing masters, solicitors with 12 years in practice, each assisted by two clerks.[305] The masters' chief clerks were also empowered to tax bills but were generally too busy.

Few mourned the passing of the six and sworn clerks, but their compensation attracted strong and damaging criticism. Some was unfair: several sworn clerks had to pay a substantial proportion of theirs to those who had sold them the office and figures which suggested a great hike in fees to fund the compensation exaggerated the real increase.[306] Nevertheless the awards were breathtakingly generous. Even a sympathetic critic admitted that 'the statute teems with com-pensation'[307] and it was difficult to defend a deal which saw George Gatty receive more than £5000 per annum in compensation while earning £2000 as a taxing master.[308] Moreover, fee increases which were supposed to produce only enough to avoid any compensation burden falling upon the Treasury actually yielded considerably more, perhaps the result of abolishing the term fee and raising those

---

[299] Lobban, 'Henry Brougham and Law Reform', 1192–7.
[300] Chancery Offices Regulation Act 1833.
[301] Lobban, 'Henry Brougham and Law Reform', 1197.
[302] Lobban, 'Preparing for Fusion, Part Two', 569–70; PD 1840 (s3) 55: 1305–26.
[303] 5 & 6 Vict. c. 103.
[304] There is a useful summary of successive changes in the RC on the Legal Departments, Second Report 1874, 29–33.
[305] A seventh had to be added in 1858: ibid., 54–8; RC on the Legal Departments, Evidence 1875, 361–7, Master Bloxham.
[306] Lobban, 'Preparing for Fusion, Part Two', 570–2.
[307] 'Recent Reforms in Chancery', 310.
[308] Lobban, 'Preparing for Fusion, Part Two', 570.

on pleadings and taxations, which were more responsive to changes in levels of business.[309] Whatever the cause, the outcry forced a Commons select committee in 1847.

That Committee and its successor found relatively few officers still paid by fees, their remuneration totalling only £5000 per annum as against £142,000 for salaried officers.[310] Nevertheless some fee-related abuses were believed to linger in the shape of 'excuse copies', gratuities and expedition money. The fees were still nowhere tabulated and those for office copies varied between different offices.[311] Fees were levied at various stages of a suit, thereby discouraging any notion of making procedure less cumbersome; it was calculated that there were more than 180 different orders of course and that in one suit 102 different fees had been paid.[312]

Besides questions of efficiency, the burden of fees raised questions of justice. Field, Langdale, and others argued that they unfairly penalized poorer litigants and that the cost of Chancery should be borne by the community at large.[313] This need not, as might be feared, require an increase in general taxation beyond that needed to pay the judges' salaries out of the Consolidated Fund, for there was a further internal source available in the suitors' fund.

The suitors' fund had been established after the scandals of the masters' loss of suitors' money in the South Sea Bubble, and its mushrooming growth had greatly impressed participants in the debates of the 1820s; from less than £4.7 million in 1756 it had swollen to more than £33 million in 1818 and continued to increase rapidly.[314] The interest on such component parts of the fund as was not payable to the recipients was already used to pay the salaries of the Lord Chancellor and the two newer vice-chancellors, and reformers calculated that (relieved of that charge) it could cover most of the court's running costs.[315]

That dream foundered on the Treasury's insistence on raiding the suitors' fund to finance the building of the new law courts, and not all the Select Committee's recommendations for rationalizing the fees were implemented.[316] However, big changes were made, mostly by the well-named Suitors in Chancery Relief Act

[309] 'Recent Reforms in Chancery', 324–6.

[310] *SC on Fees*, PP 1849 (559), viii, pp. v–vii.

[311] *Ibid.*

[312] *Ibid.*, x, xvi.

[313] Lobban, 'Preparing for Fusion, Part Two', 571–2.

[314] Parkes, *History of the Court of Chancery*, 291–300, 425. The history of the suitors' fund is outlined in the report of the *RC on Chancery Funds*, PP 1864 [3280], xxix.

[315] Lobban, 'Preparing for Fusion, Part Two', 523–4.

[316] *RC on Chancery Funds, Report 1864*, xxxviii–ix. The Select Committee had modified some of its predecessor's recommendations: *Report 1849*, xx–xxi.

1852.[317] No officers were henceforth to be remunerated directly from fees, and the old problem of providing an incentive for lesser officials to offer a good service was, in theory at least, to be solved by a bureaucratic apparatus of promotions, inspections, and annual reports to the Lord Chancellor.[318] Gratuities were expressly forbidden. Offices were abolished and duties consolidated, the separate subpoena office and affidavit office being absorbed by the clerks of records and writs.[319]

The last redoubt of old corruption in Chancery was the accountant-general's office, where gratuities had persisted despite condemnation in 1826 and the collection of fees, some resting on no secure legal foundation, was subject to no satisfactory checks.[320] Even when these defects were remedied, however, paying money into the suitors' fund and extracting it was unconscionably slow and expensive.[321] The system had been created with a view to impregnable security against fraud and with little regard to convenience, and while its operations had expanded enormously—35 clerks dealt with £56 million in the early 1860s—law societies complained that its procedures had never been updated[322] and a select committee in 1850 agreed that the whole system needed revision.[323] Though one of the twin pillars of security, the report office account with the Bank of England, had been done away with, the Chancery Funds Commission a decade later found plenty of scope for further simplifications, hardly surprising when it cost at least £5, and took a fortnight, to make a deposit;[324] when those entitled to very small legacies were advised by their solicitors that the cost of applying for them would exceed the legacy, and when the office was closed for 13 weeks a year.[325] Bank officials scorned the unwieldy safeguards that the highly paid head of the office tried unconvincingly to defend,[326] and by 32 & 33 Vict. c. 91 the funds themselves were transferred to the National Debt Commissioners. In 1873 the accountant-general was replaced by a less august personage, the assistant paymaster-general for Chancery (the office becoming the Chancery pay office), suitors' money was put

[317] 15 & 16 Vict. c. 87. Some fees were reduced ahead of the Act: PD 1852 (s3) 119: 201–5.

[318] Section 1. Recommended by the SC on Fees in the Courts of Justice, Second Report, PP 1847–8 (307), xv, 3–4.

[319] Sections 3, 28–9.

[320] RC on Chancery, Report 1826, 25; SC on Fees in the Courts of Justice, First Report, PP 1847–8 (158), xv, evidence of S. Parkinson, 138–46.

[321] RC on Chancery Funds, Report 1864, Objections and Improvements Suggested by the Law Societies, xlvii.

[322] Ibid., 47–50.

[323] SC on Official Salaries, PP 1850 (611), xv, p. vii. Lyndhurst presented a petition from the MPLA asking that the accountant-general be abolished: PD 1852 (s3) 122: 1131.

[324] RC on Chancery Funds, Report 1864, Objections and Improvements, xviii–xx.

[325] RC on the Legal Departments, Second Report 1874, 53.

[326] RC on Chancery Funds, Report 1864, App. XX, pp. l–lii.

on deposit at 2 per cent unless otherwise directed and small amounts could be paid over at the office itself.[327] The increase in facilities and business—over 30,000 accounts when the Lisgar Commission reported in 1874—suggested a need for more clerks but the Commission declined to sanction any increase until greater attempts had been made to streamline procedures further; in comparison with the Paymaster-General's Office, the Chancery pay office was heavily overmanned and its procedure for drawing cheques unduly cumbersome.[328]

9. CHANCERY IN THE 1860s

At each end of the 1840s Chancery judges and practitioners were apt to respond to complaints about delays by blaming an influx of 'foreign' business, chiefly from railways; in 1840 Cottenham called it 'immense' and Brougham later remarked that it was particularly 'operose'.[329] Summary proceedings seeking to extract contributions from shareholders in failed companies swamped the vice-chancellors in 1850 and Cranworth complained that land compensation actions (also mostly concerning railways) were very heavy.[330] Winding-up actions also made disproportionate demands upon resources, especially on the masters and subsequently chambers clerks who had to take the complicated accounts, and these together were a substantial set off against the relief brought by the removal of bankruptcy from the Lord Chancellor.[331] Such business was extremely lucrative and was therefore welcomed by many at the bar but conservatives like John Stuart and judges who found it unfamiliar and uncomfortable affected to regard it as an unwanted intrusion upon the 'proper' business of the court.[332]

There were other intruders. 'Fusion', long a favourite among jurists and the more daring reformers, became a serious practical threat in the 1850s.[333] There were three sorts of proposition that traditionalists found unacceptable. One, already noticed, was the idea that equity should adopt common law practices in relation to evidence, in particular *viva voce* examinations.[334] Another was the encroachment of common law courts on equitable preserves, particularly the auxiliary jurisdiction to grant injunctions and specific performance, which threatened both to take away business and to erode the distinctive sphere of

[327] Hitherto the practice had been not to invest the money unless the suitor so requested.
[328] *RC on the Legal Departments, Second Report 1874*, 53.
[329] *PD* 1840 (s3) 53: 1339; 1851(s3) 114: 835.
[330] *PD* 1851 (s3) 114: 836–7.
[331] They were especially heavy in the aftermath of the Overend Gurney crash in 1866: (1867) 2 *LJ* 347.
[332] *PD* 1851 (s3) 117: 712 (A. H. Lynch); 1841 (s3) 56: 200–2.
[333] See below, pp. 757–60.
[334] See above, pp. 670–1.

equity.[335] The converse was that equity courts should decide for themselves (with the aid of a jury where appropriate) questions they had been accustomed to send to law. That was disliked for the inconvenience of jury trials, their impact on advocacy styles and the role of the judge, the novel need to assess damages, and the fear that it might be a staging post on the road to complete procedural fusion.[336]

Nevertheless, in 1852 Chancery judges were empowered to determine common law matters for themselves.[337] Soon afterwards the Chancery Commissioners, faced with the adoption in the Common Law Procedure Act 1854 of the more aggressive approach of their common law counterparts, felt obliged to recommend that Chancery should be able to award damages and hold jury trials.[338] Most of the judges, evidently with the support of the bar, ignored their new powers; only eight jury trials were held in 1859–60 and none at all in 1869–70.[339] Furthermore, they undermined the counterpart power given to their common law brethren to hear and pronounce upon equitable defences by interpreting the Act as still allowing defendants to resort to equity.[340] And when John Rolt tried to make it compulsory for them to decide questions of law his efforts were all but negated by an amendment which preserved the discretion to send such questions to the assizes.[341] It is therefore unlikely that these measures significantly affected either the quantity or the make-up of Chancery business.

One little studied factor which may have done so was the level of solicitors' costs. At all events, when the *Westminster Review* alleged that solicitors inveigled people into Chancery, the *Solicitors' Journal* retorted that until the recent increases in costs it had scarcely been profitable to do so where less than £1000 was at stake, and that even the new scale was ungenerous.[342]

The actual quantity of business was published in the annual civil judicial statistics from the 1860s but they do not reveal its nature. In the early 1860s around 2200 bills a year were filed, rising to nearly 2500 by the end of the decade.[343] Other indicators also show a substantial increase: 3498 orders and references for taxation of bills were made as against 3335; 479 originating summonses were issued

[335] Lobban, 'Preparing for Fusion, Part Two', 586–7.

[336] *Ibid.*

[337] Chancery Amendment Act 1852, s 62.

[338] *Third Report 1856*, 2, 4. For the earlier position on damages, see P. McDermott, 'The Jurisdiction of the Court of Chancery to Award Damages' (1992) 108 *LQR* 652–73.

[339] *Civil Judicial Staistics 1860*, PP 1861 [2860], lx; *1870*, PP 1871 [C. 442], lxiv.i; (1867) 2 *LJ* 188–9.

[340] Lobban, 'Preparing for Fusion, Part Two', 590.

[341] *Ibid.*, 593.

[342] (1857) 1 *Sol. J.* 125.

[343] *Civil Judicial Statistics.* These take the form of returns from the several offices in Chancery, with little attempt to link them up.

from chambers against 420, and 26,644 other summonses as against 16,481. The rate of disposal during the year was calculated at about 82 per cent in each case, suggesting that the court was able to keep abreast of a rising workload. The statistics however do not, for the most part, enable different types of business to be distinguished, nor are they enlightening on matters such as the sums involved and the time taken to deal with a matter from start to finish. Nevertheless, if at the end of its independent existence Chancery still had a forbidding reputation, it was no longer a national scandal.

V

The Civilian Courts and the Probate, Divorce, and Admiralty Division[1]

1. THE ECCLESIASTICAL COURTS

The Ecclesiastical Courts and their Critics

There were more than 300 ecclesiastical courts across the land. The highest courts in the province of Canterbury were the Prerogative (or Testamentary) court (PCC), which did most of the probate work, and the court of Arches, which was a court of first instance for other types of business and an appeal court for the lower courts. Their counterparts in York were the Prerogative court and the Chancery court respectively, but with only four dioceses against Canterbury's 22, York was much less important. Each diocese had its consistory court and archdeacon's courts and some also had commissary courts carved out of the outlying parts of the diocese. Outside the jurisdiction of the bishop in whose diocese they lay were various kinds of peculiars, mostly doing little business and ranging from royal peculiars to vicarial, with 'some of so anomalous a nature as scarcely to admit of accurate description'.[2] In the province of Canterbury a court of Peculiars heard appeals from the 13 peculiars of the diocese of London, but appeals from some of the other peculiars, and from the provincial courts, lay to the high court of Delegates.

The clergy had long lost their right to be tried in their own courts for criminal offences, and benefit of clergy itself was abolished in 1827,[3] but church courts still exercised disciplinary powers over wayward clerics.[4] Their powers over laymen

---

[1] This chapter is greatly indebted to Dr Brian Hutton's Ph.D. thesis, 'The Reform of the Testamentary Jurisdiction of the Ecclesiastical Courts, 1830–1857' (Brunel Univ., 2003).

[2] Holdsworth, *HEL*, i, 580–632, 600. R. B. Outhwaite, *The Rise and Fall of the English Ecclesiastical Courts 1500–1860* (Cambridge, 2006) offers the most conveniently accessible account of the evolution and workings of these courts.

[3] Holdsworth, *HEL*, i, 293–302.

[4] For the role of these courts in church affairs, see Pt 2, Ch. III.

had been steadily eroded,[5] some (such as charges of heresy) having fallen into disuse, while secular courts elbowed them out of others, establishing the rule that matters over which they gained jurisdiction ceased to be justiciable in the church courts.[6] Even so, there were areas of everyday life where their writ still ran. First, rare and parochial in the 1820s, disputes over the fabric and ordering of church buildings later became matters of bitter controversy.[7] Secondly, they retained sanctions against brawling in church, incest, defamation, and other immoral conduct.[8] Thirdly, they were the forum for pursuing those who failed to pay the church's taxes, principally tithe and church rates, in cases where the right to levy was not in dispute.[9] Fourthly, they dealt with matrimonial causes. Though unable to grant a full divorce, church courts could decree divorce a *mensa et thoro*, which was a necessary prerequisite to a parliamentary divorce, and also entertained suits for nullity and the restitution of conjugal rights.[10] However, what really sustained the church courts was the grant of probate or letters of administration to decedents' estates. Chancery had wrested from them their wider jurisdiction over the distribution of estates and the conduct of executors and administrators, and they were not able to decide on the interpretation of wills, but most wills were non-contentious and the grant of probate was an essentially administrative act.[11]

Procedure in these courts was based on Roman civil and canon law. An action commenced with a citation and the pleadings, beginning with the plaintiff's libel and the defendant's answer and continuing with their respective responsive allegations, were closer to Chancery than common law, though they fortunately had not acquired the layers of conventional allegation and denial that made Chancery pleadings so elaborate and misleading. Evidence was taken in writing by a court

[5] Outhwaite, *Rise and Fall of English Ecclesiastical Courts*, 84 *et seq*. R. E. Rodes, *Law and Modernization in the Church of England* (Notre Dame, Indiana, 1991), presents this as 'a new rapprochement between the two systems', rather than an acquisitive strategy on the part of the common lawyers.

[6] Holdsworth, *HEL*, i, 618–21; *Phillimore v. Machon* (1876) 1 PD 481. The same applied to statutory intervention unless the statute contained an express saving for the church courts.

[7] Holdsworth, *HEL*, i, 614–32; xii, 690–1 and *RC on the Ecclesiastical Courts, General Report*, PP 1831–2 (199), xxiv.

[8] Holdsworth, *HEL*, xii, 689. For incest see XIII, Pt 1, Ch. I. For defamation see S. M. Waddams, *Sexual Slander in Nineteenth Century England, 1815–1855* (Toronto, 2000). Brawling was more common than might be expected, since it extended to vestry rooms where contentious local matters were discussed: S. M. Waddams, *Law, Politics and the Church of England, the Career of Stephen Lushington, 1782–1873* (Cambridge, 1992), 170–1.

[9] Holdsworth, xii, 690. Statistical returns for the early 1840s are in *PP* 1844 (354), xxxviii.

[10] The London consistory court was the most frequently resorted to for this purpose: Waddams, *Law, Politics and the Church of England*, 161–3.

[11] Outhwaite, *Rise and Fall of the English Ecclesiastical Courts*, 89–90 and table at 93.

examiner, but at an earlier stage than in Chancery and on points on which the witness was informed in advance; even so, one writer compared it to 'a duel with hatchets in the dark'.[12] Trials were held before a single judge with no jury. Reasoned judgments were given but case reporting was less developed than at common law and precedent less compelling. A major weakness was the process of enforcement which, especially after an Act of 1813 reduced the effectiveness of excommunication, depended on invoking the aid of the sheriff by recourse to a writ out of Chancery and was 'slow, clumsy and expensive'.[13] As Holdsworth concluded, although the procedure shared the deficiencies of the secular courts in being expensive and leisurely, it was better in several respects, particularly the way the judge kept the parties and their lawyers under closer superintendence. This was possible because the ecclesiastical courts were not especially busy, with fewer of the delays which beset Chancery and King's Bench.[14]

With the passing of the confessional state and the rising numbers and influence of dissenters the role of church institutions was inevitably a matter for controversy. Dissenters were particularly aggrieved at their liability for church rates[15] and farmers of every denomination and none chafed at the imposition of tithe.[16] But even the church's keenest supporters were finding it difficult to deny that its courts had serious faults, sharing certain unacceptable characteristics of secular courts along with some peculiar to themselves. Their judges were chosen by bishops and generally possessed no legal qualifications, relying upon their untutored reading of a handful of unsatisfactory or dated treatises and practice books and the practical know-how of their registrar (or his deputy, since most registrars, and some judges, were absentee sinecurists).[17] The active registrars were mostly country lawyers who doubled as proctors without serving the long formal apprenticeship demanded of London proctors, for outside Doctors' Commons there was no scope for a specialist bar or full-time proctors.[18] Under the circumstances it is not surprising that wills in the custody of these courts were often kept in insecure and unsatisfactory conditions.[19]

---

[12] [J. Paget], 'The English Law of Divorce' (1856) 65 *Westminster Rev.* 338–55, at 343.

[13] L. Stone, *The Road to Divorce in England, 1530–1857* (Oxford, 1987), 196.

[14] Holdsworth, *HEL*, xii, 678–82.

[15] Waddams, *Law, Politics and the Church of England*, 249–70.

[16] For tithe reform, especially the Act of 1836 (6 & 7 Will. IV c. 71) see E. J. Evans, *The Contentious Tithe* (1976). The work of the tithe commissioners is discussed in C. Stebbings, *Legal Foundations of Tribunals in Nineteenth Century England* (Cambridge, 2006).

[17] Hutton, *Reform of the Testamentary Jurisdiction*, 43–4; S. M. Waddams, 'English Matrimonial Law on the Eve of Reform' (2000) 21 *JLH* 59–82 at 60–2. For example George Marriott, the Chancellor of St. David's, employed surrogates for all three of his courts, while the judge and principal registrar at York were father and son.

[18] *HEL*, xii, 75—7, and see below, pp. 698–701.

[19] Hutton, *Reform of the Testamentary Jurisdiction*, 32–47.

Things were quite different in Doctors' Commons, although it was a matter of acute concern that the will repository was essentially the private domain of an absentee registrar.[20] Here were learned judges, Nicholl in Arches and the Prerogative court and Lushington in the London consistory court, sharing a courtroom with the Admiralty court and the Delegates.[21] These courts were served by a small specialist set of advocates[22] and around 100 proctors. Such a small, geographically concentrated group hardly needed law reports or treatises and Doctors' Commons had evolved into that 'cosy family party' made so notorious by Dickens, a network of inter-related Jenners, Phillimores, and Nichollses, exchanging roles, taxing each others bills etc.[23]

Everyone in Doctors' Commons and the other church courts, from clerks to judges, was remunerated by fees, many recently exposed as resting on no more secure foundation than custom and practice, the last full-scale revision having been in 1604.[24] They generally produced enough to fund sinecures performed by deputy, the most lucrative being the registrarship of the PCC, which was used as outdoor relief for the families of successive primates. The tacit understanding which governed its succession broke down embarrassingly in 1829, necessitating a private bill for the benefit of the Manners Suttons which exposed it to scathing criticism in the House of Commons.[25]

It was not the first nineteenth-century parliamentary attack on the church courts. In 1812 the scandalous case of Mary Dix had pushed a reluctant Sir William Scott into an unwonted display of reformist activity, only for the bishops to demolish most of his bill.[26] Then in 1824 Joseph Hume began a series of attacks, drawing upon complaints against Sir John Nicholl's handling of *Peddle* v. *Evans*.[27] Concerns about the safe storage of wills and the long-running attempt to discipline Dr Free also spotlighted the church courts and Brougham weighed in,

---

[20] *Ibid.*, 9.

[21] For Nicholl see B. G. Hutton, 'Sir John Nicholl of Merthyr Mawr' (2001) 1 *Welsh Legal History Society*, 99–101; for Lushington, Waddams, *Law, Politics and the Church of England*.

[22] See below, pp. 696–8.

[23] *David Copperfield*, Chs 23, 26. It was later called 'the court of the Jenners' in *The Times*: Waddams, *English Matrimonial Law on the Eve of Reform*, 60 n. 8. Since none of the judges sat full time they were not barred from practice and with several courts sharing the courtroom judges and advocates frequently changed roles (like actors in a play as Dickens saw it), especially since the leading advocates regularly sat as surrogates for the judges.

[24] *RC on Fees in the Courts of Justice*, PP 1823 (462), vii; 1824 (43) (240), ix.

[25] *SC on Fees in the Courts of Justice, Second Report*, PP 1850 (711), xiii, p.iv.

[26] Outhwaite, *Rise and Fall of English Ecclesiastical Courts*, 126–7. The Better Regulation of Ecclesiastical Courts Act (53 Geo. III c. 127) removed the immediate grievance in *Dix's Case*, ending the power to imprison for contempt on the writ *de excommunicatio capiendo*. It also amended procedures for the recovery of church rates and tithes and imposed penalties on unqualified proctors.

[27] Hutton, *Reform of the Testamentary Jurisdiction*, 8–9.

directing his fire particularly at the court of Delegates.[28] Peel's modest measure to address the Fees Commission's recommendations essentially went only to revise and harmonize the fees of the courts of Doctors' Commons, display them and insist on legal qualifications and personal performance by the deputy registrars and clerks of the seats in the PCC. Nevertheless it encountered enough hostility for Peel, who had a genuine and sustained commitment to putting the church into a better shape to resist its enemies, to decide that, like the courts of Chancery and common law, these courts should be scrutinized by a royal commission.[29]

The Civilian Lawyers

The advocates were a very small group. Just 17 were named when they were incorporated in 1768 and though the opportunities in Admiralty and Prize presented by the American and French wars may have encouraged a modest expansion, there were only 30 admitted between 1820 and 1860.[30] There were 46 members of Doctors' Commons in 1830, falling to 30 by 1850, but the number in practice was between 20 and 26.[31]

It was not an easy profession to enter. It took at least eight years to acquire the DCL from Oxford or Cambridge University. This was the essential qualification for the Archbishop of Canterbury's fiat which admitted a man to plead in the court of Arches and would enable him to be elected to Doctors' Commons.[32] During their time at university some, like William Adams, followed the 'high road to the common law practice' by study with a special pleader[33] and an increasing number pursued the parallel route to the bar through the inns of court. However, before being admitted an advocate must endure a 'year of silence' sitting in the court. The most obvious result of this lengthy preparation was that advocates were mostly approaching 30 before their career really began. Indeed, there was a slight increase in the starting age, for whereas Jenner had been 25, Lushington and Nicholl 26 (and the reporter John Haggard just 24), no one admitted after

---

[28] *Ibid.*, 8–10. The Free case is explored in R. B. Outhwaite, *Scandal in the Church: Dr. Edward Drax Free, 1764–1843* (1997).

[29] Hutton, *Reform of the Testamentary Jurisdiction*, 8–12; Ecclesiastical Courts (Officers) Act 1829 (10 Geo. IV c. 53).

[30] G. D. Squibb, *Doctors' Commons*, (Oxford, 1977), 53 and App. III.

[31] Hutton, *Reform of the Testamentary Jurisdiction*, 1. In 1850 Lushington put the number at 23: *SC on Official Salaries 1850*, q. 2053.

[32] F. L. Wiswall, *The Development of Admiralty Jurisdiction and Practice Since 1800* (Cambridge, 1970), 77. Hume's motion that London University DCLs should also be accepted was carried by 67–0, but no case arose: *PD* 1839 (s3) 49: 1126–7.

[33] *SC on the Admiralty Court, Report 1833*, PP 1833 (670), xi, q. 1059. Adams was admitted in 1799.

1820 was younger than 27 and the best known, Harding and Robert Phillimore (28), Twiss (32), and Tristram (30) were older.[34]

Another marked effect was upon the social composition of Doctors' Commons. In view of the repeated charges of nepotism levelled at the institution,[35] it is not surprising to find that almost one-third of members' fathers were in the law[36] (the great majority from within the civilian courts), though there is an interesting decline in the number of proctors' sons, perhaps reflecting a want of confidence in the prospects of the profession.[37] Of the remainder, more than a third were sons of (self-described) peers, gentlemen, or esquires, and together with clergy these categories made up three-quarters of the members during its final 80 years.[38] Trade and commerce, never strongly represented, were actually diminishing; of the 30 post-1819 entrants just one was a merchant's son,[39] and the last from the lower trading occupations, sons of a draper, bookseller, and watchmaker respectively, were admitted in the 1780s. In fact the financial demands made entry hard even for the son of a poor clergyman like Christopher Robinson, whose father could afford only £20 and some law books and who needed the assistance of Sir William Scott and a good marriage.[40] As this background would suggest, a considerable proportion had been educated at the old public schools, with Westminster increasingly prominent. No longer was Doctors' Commons 'the offspring of Trinity Hall',[41] and Oxford became a bigger provider than Cambridge. In the last 80 years of Doctors' Commons its members included just two Welshmen, two Scots, and no Irishmen, with G. W. Dasent from St. Vincent as the only exotic implant.[42]

Prospects for the advocates were usually good. They were eligible for a substantial number of fee-generating offices in the ecclesiastical courts and could act as surrogates for the judges of the major courts.[43] The more eminent might

---

[34] Squibb, *Doctors' Commons*, App. III. The oldest was F. T. Pratt at 38.

[35] See below, p. 708.

[36] Squibb, *Doctors' Commons*, App. III, and see his examples of family connections at 34.

[37] From six among those admitted 1780–1819 to two between 1820 and 1860.

[38] Clergymen were barred from membership (*R v. Archbishop of Canterbury* (1807) 8 East 213) and an advocate had to resign if he subsequently took holy orders (e.g. William Herbert in 1815).

[39] C. R. Prinsep, who was in fact the only man practising in this period other than (perhaps) Richard Hey (admitted 1778, died 1835) admitted to the court of Arches but not a member of Doctors' Commons. Prinsep was unique in going to India to practise: Squibb, *Doctors' Commons*, App. IV.

[40] *ODNB* 47: 314. The tradition that each member's coat of arms be displayed in the courtroom (Squibb, *Doctors' Commons*, 73) is instructive.

[41] Wiswall, *Admiralty Jurisdiction*, 76.

[42] Dasent was the son of the attorney-general of St. Vincent. One Scot, W. W. Moncrieff (1807) was probably an honorary member. The other, Sir D. K. Sandford, son of a Scottish bishop, did not practise and his qualification is not mentioned in his *ODNB* entry (48: 1890).

[43] In 1840 they lost this privilege in the Admiralty court: Wiswall, *Admiralty Jurisdiction*, 80.

be called upon by the Foreign Office for opinions on international law and, occasionally, diplomatic missions.[44] It is such activities, and a whole range of scholarly and cultural ones, that explain their remarkable representation in the *DNB* and its successor.[45] It seems that the profession could offer a comfortable living without demanding the concentrated and exhausting workload of the leading common law barristers; Travers Twiss, for example, was 'eminent as a university teacher, a scholar and a practitioner'.[46] In addition, an increasing number were also members of the bar, six of the 13 admitted after 1839. Since Mansfield's day the common law courts had allowed advocates to appear in shipping and other cases where their expertise might be of assistance, but presumably these barrister/advocates wanted to be able to practise generally. [47]

There is little information about the earnings of the advocates. Lushington refused to make a guess, though he said that in peacetime the leaders did not equal their counterparts at the common law bar, which fits with the £5000 to £7000 for leaders given by the Solicitor-General in 1839.[48] The prize of the profession, Queen's Advocate, brought Dodson £3000 aside from practice, but there was no equivalent to the rank of QC. In 1858, however, when the advocates lost their monopoly, four leading men (Deane, Harding, Twiss, and R. J. Phillimore) were given that rank.[49]

There were evidently some who specialized in Admiralty law, since there were said to be barely half a dozen active in that field,[50] but none of the advocates ventured into the provincial courts. Even York's three regular advocates were barristers, and elsewhere it was the proctors who performed the advocate's role unless a barrister was brought in for the purpose.[51]

Much less is known about the proctors. They were more numerous, somewhere around 100 to 120[52] and, like solicitors, they were a mixture of sole practitioners and small partnerships; those who received compensation in 1858 were

---

[44] *Ibid.*, 79.

[45] Of 36 men admitted between 1780 and 1819, 14 were in the *DNB*, along with 7 of the 30 between 1820 and 1860. The descriptions include 'antiquary and astronomer' (John Lee); 'antiquary and historian of arms' (Sir Samuel Meyrick), 'Scandinavian scholar' (G. W. Dasent), and 'cricketer' (Herbert Jenner-Fust).

[46] *ODNB*: 55: 736.

[47] Wiswall, *Admiralty Jurisdiction*, 79.

[48] *SC on Official Salaries 1850*, qq. 2054–7; *PD* 1839 (s3) 49: 1109.

[49] *SC on Official Salaries 1850*, q. 2060; Sir J.C. Sainty, *A History of English Law Officers, King's Counsel and Holders of Patents of Precedence* (1987), 116–17.

[50] *SC on the Admiralty Court, Report 1833*, Lushington, q. 492.

[51] *RC on the Ecclesiastical Courts, General Report 1832*, App. B.

[52] *SC on the Admiralty Court, Report 1833*, H. B. Swabey, qq. 641–6; *RC on the Court of Chancery, Second Report*, PP 1854 [1731], xxiv, W. Fox, q. 395.

43 individuals, 21 two-man partnerships, and nine firms with three partners.[53] They employed a 'large body of clerks'[54] and only those clerks listed in the court's registry book were allowed to transact business in court, though much of their duties consisted of routine copying in the office.[55]

Though the route was very different, becoming a proctor was almost as lengthy a process as becoming an advocate.[56] It demanded a seven-year term of articles, for which the premiums might be very high[57] since only the most senior 34 proctors were entitled to have an articled clerk, and then only one at a time.[58] According to an embittered John Rolt, the proctors enjoyed 'the wicked pre-eminence [in] ... its assertion of class-exclusion', since no one who had been employed as a clerk was permitted to join their ranks.[59] On completing articles he was admitted as a notary by the Archbishop of Canterbury, whose fiat to the Dean of Arches procured him admission as a supernumary.[60]

A small number of proctors, 19 in 1833 but almost doubling by 1855, specialized in Admiralty work,[61] and perhaps others in divorce, but the great majority depended almost exclusively upon probate, in particular non-contentious probate: it was estimated that the 1857 Act would rob them of 77 per cent of their business.[62] They had already suffered through the introduction of stamps, which ended the favourable and easy-going practice whereby they paid outstanding court fees months in arrear instead of being obliged to carry the costs during the suit.[63] Unlike solicitors they were allowed to address the court on points of practice[64] and claimed that because they were few enough to be 'almost personally known to the judge',[65] their integrity and vigilance over forgeries and fraud were

---

[53] *Returns from the Ecclesiastical Courts*, PP 1859 s 1 (194), xxii.

[54] *SC on the Admiralty Court, Report 1833*, H. B. Swabey, q. 647.

[55] *Ibid.*, W. Fox, q. 680; H. C. Rothery, quoted in Wiswall, *Admiralty Jurisdiction*, 85.

[56] There was no effective regulation before the Ecclesiastical Courts Act 1813 (see above).

[57] Wiswall, *Admiralty Jurisdiction*, 87. Fox once managed to extract 800 guineas, though that was in wartime: *RC on Chancery, Second Report 1854*, q. 479. In addition, there was the stamp duty of £120 on articles and £25 stamps on admission to the courts of Arches and Admiralty: *SC on the Admiralty Court, Report 1833*, Fox, q. 679

[58] Holdsworth, *HEL*, xii, 75–7. Based on an ordinance of 1696, all the other proctors being technically 'supernumary'. The clerk had to start articles between 14 and 18 years of age and the principal could take on a second when the first had been with him for five years.

[59] *SC on the Admiralty Court, Report*, q. 468; Sir J. Rolt, *Memoirs of Sir John Rolt* (1939), 42–3.

[60] Holdsworth, *HEL*, xii, 75–7.

[61] Wiswall, *Admiralty Jurisdiction*, 80. An example is the firm of Dyke and Stokes, from whom Richard Webster had a number of briefs: Lord Alverstone, *Recollections of Bar and Bench* (1914), 20.

[62] Hutton, *Reform of the Testamentary Jurisdiction*, 332. A reluctant G. S. Heales said that one-sixth to one-eighth came from contested matters: *RC on Chancery, Second Report 1854*, qq. 667–8.

[63] Wiswall, *Admiralty Jurisdiction*, 83.

[64] *RC on Chancery, Second Report 1854*, Fox, q. 400.

[65] *Ibid.*, q. 397.

almost guaranteed. It was not entirely so, however,[66] and they were particularly vulnerable to accusations that in the absence of a regular facility for taxation of costs, they could overcharge their clients.[67]

By the 1840s the London proctors had a committee, perhaps a development provoked by the threat to their livelihood, but it does not seem to have had, or sought, any formal status and there was no attempt to broaden their training by examinations or to acquire disciplinary functions.[68] Most of their clients came to them through solicitors, but it was not until after the great upheaval of 1857 that any firm operated as both.[69] The compensation figures of 1858, while needing caution in relation to earnings, offer an interesting snapshot of the proctors at that time.[70]

Some 18 firms or individuals received annuities of more than £1000. The highest, Slade, Wadeson, and Appach, just passed £2000, though *per capita* this fell well short of W. Rothery (£1342), F. Robarts (£1309), and E. W. Crosse (£1358). The 20 firms making less than £200 (excluding those who were compensated instead partly by being given court offices) were struggling indeed, though most were young men perhaps newly in practice. However, some incomes must have been considerably augmented by office-holding and Admiralty work.

Outside London, except in the nearby diocese of Rochester and in the courts of Canterbury which were served by the London proctors, the position was quite different. There were dioceses which insisted that a man must serve five years articled to a proctor (or sometimes a deputy registrar) before being permitted to act;[71] and some which fixed a maximum number.[72] Most had no maximum, and several had no set qualification to fetter the bishop's discretion.[73] In almost all cases, however, the proctor was also a solicitor (or occasionally a notary) and

---

[66] Two were suspended for misconduct (*ibid.*, q. 634) and two others are known to have been mulcted in costs in the Admiralty court (Wiswall, *Admiralty Jurisdiction*, 83). Several proctors were deceived in the celebrated Fletcher-Barber forgeries of the 1840s. The court's inherent jurisdiction to discipline proctors was confirmed in *Piddle v. Toller* (1830) 3 Hagg. Ecc. 286 (Holdsworth, *HEL*, xii, 77).

[67] Their witnesses were pressed upon this point by both the Ecclesiastical Commission and the Chancery Commission, and it was also complained of in parliament.

[68] Hutton, *Reform of the Testamentary Jurisdiction*, 152.

[69] *RC on Chancery, Second Report 1854*, J. Iggulden and W. Fox, q. 475. Some acted as notaries, among them William Pritchard: Rolt, *Memoirs*, 39.

[70] *Returns from Ecclesiastical Courts 1859*. Compensation was paid at the rate of half the net profits from probate practice in the ecclesiastical courts over the previous five years: Probate Act 1857, s 105. The age profile is: under 30, 13; 30–9, 22; 40–9; 23; 50–9, 15; 60–9, 22; over 70, 6.

[71] *RC on the Ecclesiastical Courts, General Report 1832*, App. B. Examples are Hereford and Worcester.

[72] Six in Durham and Lichfield, eight at York: *ibid*.

[73] e.g. Lincoln and Llandaff: *ibid*. Some adopted intermediate positions; in Blandford (Bristol), the proctor must either have been articled to an attorney 'or otherwise qualified himself by a study of the law'.

his articles presumably served as a concurrent qualifying period for both pro-fessions.[74] In 1831 most dioceses had between three and eight, but Ely had none and in St. David's 'proctors only are allowed to act; and the professional men here conceiving that they may be liable to penalties unless they are admitted as notaries, have ceased altogether to act in the court'.[75] At the other extreme, Exeter boasted eight, as many as York.[76] In view of the fact that Coote in 1860 claimed that there had been no need for a treatise on probate practice before his, it is hardy surprising that the conduct of cases in the country was much said to be less strict than in town.[77] It was the fact of the proctors being also country solicitors (and of course in many instances such as the militant Robert Swan, court officials too) that gave them the influence to protect their interests so effectively in the reform controversies.[78]

The country proctors also became entitled to compensation, which provides some idea of the shape and profitability of this branch in the late 1850s. As might be expected, the York proctors were in a class of their own. Two two-man part-nerships received £1268 and £567 respectively and six individuals between £201 and £899.[79] The only other four-figure award was in Lichfield, whose three prac-titioners were all evidently prospering.[80] Elsewhere most sums are much smaller, with only one, in Worcester, above £300. No proctor in Wales received more than £100 and only two of the many in Exeter did.

Proctors firms survived the end of Doctors' Commons, at least in London, but by the 1870s it was said that most of the probate business was done by solicitors[81] and some, like Rolt's old employer William Pritchard's firm, had merged into solicitors' practices.[82]

---

[74] York's proctors seem to have been an exception, as, according to Stokes, were Chester's: *RC on Chancery, Second Report 1854*, q. 733. Lichfield's deputy registrar was unusual in having been a London proctor: Hutton, *Reform of the Ecclesiastical Courts*, 74.

[75] *RC on the Ecclesiastical Courts, General Report 1832*, App. B. They evidently overcame their caution, since three were compensated in 1858.

[76] Exeter continued to have a much bigger number than other dioceses. 10 received compen-sation for earnings from its consistorial court, four from the archdeaconry court, six from the archdeaconry court of Barnstaple and three from that of Cornwall.

[77] H.C. Coote, *The Practice of the Court of Probate* (3rd edn, 1860), vii; *RC on Chancery, Second Report 1854*, H. G. Stokes, qq. 726, 729.

[78] See below, pp. 704–13.

[79] *Returns from Ecclesiastical Courts 1859*. Figures ignore shillings and pence and must be doubled to give the average profit over the previous five years.

[80] They received £527, £726, and £1121 respectively: *ibid.*

[81] *RC on the Legal Departments, Evidence, PP* 1875 [C. 1245], xxx, H. A. Bathurst, q. 8940. Bathurst himself was the last proctor to become an Admiralty registrar, in 1890: G. H. M. Thompson, *Admiralty Registrars, some Historical Notes* (ed. K. C. McGuffie, Belfast, 1958), 20–1.

[82] Rolt, *Memoirs*, 39–40. London proctors ceased to have a separate entry in *The Law List* after 1860 and were listed under Solicitors and Proctors until 1939. Provincial proctors were never given a separate list.

The Ecclesiastical Courts Commission

The Commission, announced in February 1830, initially comprised a mixture of prelates (Howley, the Archbishop of Canterbury, and four bishops), judges (the common law chiefs and Lord Wynford, formerly Best CJCP), and civilians (the three judges of the leading civilian courts and Sir Herbert Jenner, who was also Queen's Advocate). When the Commission was renewed following the King's death the bishop of Gloucester and two barrister MPs were added. There were two notable omissions. None of the more outspoken critics of the church courts, such as Hume, was included, and neither was any Chancery judge, though they handled most disputes arising from probated wills. The Chancellor, Lyndhurst, conspicuously held himself aloof.[83]

The Commission's terms were wide and general.[84] They were soon extended to Wales and the Commissioners were given extra powers and required to produce a report within two years. Besides using existing materials, notably the report of the fees inquiry, the Commissioners circulated a questionnaire designed mostly to elicit information rather than opinions, the latter being furnished by 34 witnesses, including judges and officers of all sorts of ecclesiastical courts, professional users, solicitors, and antiquarians. However, with comparatively few drawn from the country courts there was a marked imbalance, all the more notable because the Commissioners were more familiar with Doctors' Commons. Late in their proceedings they also interviewed members of the Common Law and Real Property Commissions.[85]

The Commissioners' deliberations were diverted by Brougham's request to produce a separate and early report on the court of Delegates.[86] Questioning of one of its deputy registrars, H. B. Swabey, confirmed critical comments by other witnesses and earlier complaints in Parliament and the press, and the report (January 1831) endorsed Brougham's own proposal to transfer the appellate jurisdiction to the Privy Council.[87] Because the Delegates had no permanent judges or officers, this was a straightforward undertaking, unbedevilled by patronage and compensation and without serious implications for church-state relationships. In these respects it was quite unlike the main work of the Commissioners.

Although the Commissioners readily divided the church courts' business, other than their criminal jurisdiction, into 'temporal' (probate and matrimonial),

---

[83] Hutton, *Reform of the Testamentary Jurisdiction*, 16–31.
[84] *RC on Ecclesiastical Courts, General Report 1832*, 3–4.
[85] Hutton, *Reform of the Testamentary Jurisdiction*, 32–50.
[86] *Ibid.*, 53; P. A. Howell, *The Judicial Committee of the Privy Council 1833–1876* (Cambridge, 1979), 14–22.
[87] Hutton, *Reform of the Testamentary Jurisdiction*, 51–8.

'spiritual' (clergy discipline) and 'mixed' (church rates etc.), that classification did not directly determine their approach.[88] Through a long series of meetings it was first decided that the peculiars and other inferior courts should be abolished; they had few disinterested defenders so that was hardly controversial.[89] A little more hesitantly they agreed that non-contentious probate business should be concentrated in diocesan courts. The next step was to determine the allocation of contentious probate business, but in the absence of the Archbishop of York, who was not a member, the Commission would not follow most of its more active members in confining it to the PCC. Instead the report left it to be inferred that this was the better solution without making a positive recommendation.[90]

Another thorny question was the doctrine of *bona notabilia*, whereby if a testator's personal estate included goods valued above £5 in more than one diocese the probate must issue from the provincial rather than the diocesan court. This greatly favoured the PCC and not surprisingly its abolition was one of the chief aims of country courts. It was tackled for the Commission by Nicholl (awkwardly placed as a Doctors' Commons man), whose pragmatic solution was to allocate the business equitably among the courts through some sort of financial limits. This was difficult to justify on logical grounds, but the compromise might have been acceptable to the country registrars and proctors had not Lushington persuaded the Commission to the more confrontational course of restricting the business entirely to the provincial courts.[91] Lushington also successfully pressed for major changes to procedure in the provincial courts, opening them up to oral evidence and jury trials,[92] hoping that these reforms would strengthen the case for the church courts retaining a wide jurisdiction over the laity. They were to lose their jurisdiction over slanders and brawling in churchyards, which had become impossible to defend,[93] and changes were proposed to the machinery for disciplining errant clergymen, since the prolonged farce of the Free case had exposed the existing process as hopelessly defective.[94] On the other hand, the most active members of the Commission had in mind to expand the courts' role in probate.

The Commissioners could not ignore widespread criticism of the inconvenience arising from the need for the validity of a will dealing with both personal and real property to be determined by different courts under different rules, occasionally

---

[88] *RC on Ecclesiastical Courts, General Report 1832*, 12–13.

[89] *Ibid.*, 22.

[90] Hutton, *Reform of the Testamentary Jurisdiction*, 42–4, 60–2. The Archbishop was then invited to meet the Commissioners and approved their proceedings up to that point.

[91] *Ibid.*, 61–2.

[92] *RC on Ecclesiastical Courts, General Report 1832*, 31–2.

[93] Waddams, *Sexual Slander in Nineteenth Century England*, 3–13.

[94] *RC on Ecclesiastical Courts, General Report 1832*, 53–61.

leading to different conclusions, the law governing testamentary formalities also being different for land and personalty.[95] Lord Tenterden CJ would not accept an ecclesiastical judge ruling on the validity of a will of realty alone, though he was surprisingly generous in conceding that a mixed will might be so determined. The report represented this position in terms either clumsy or calculated to be misleading.[96]

Away from these, the most contentious areas, the report proposed a remod-elling of the surviving courts which was likely to find widespread acceptance. Their judges would be confirmed by the Crown (so leaving the bishops' patronage formally intact), and would be salaried from a general fee fund which would also compensate officers displaced in the abolition of courts, though not practition-ers whose livelihoods would be affected by the changes.[97] All officers would be required to perform their duties in person and the registrars (no longer sinecur-ists) would cease to treat their repositories as private facilities. There would now be a central registry, though if the York Prerogative court was retained it would not be the comprehensive one the Commission really wanted.[98]

Unlike the Common Law and Chancery Commissions, the Ecclesiastical Courts Commissioners had concentrated chiefly on where business was to be done rather than how. Discussions on fees, procedure, evidence, and practice took second place to re-arranging, and in some cases abolishing, jurisdiction. The proposals for the core business of the courts envisaged a higher degree of concentration than might have been expected, such as would make some dioc-esan courts scarcely viable. More predictably in view of its composition, the Commission did not propose the secularization of most of that business and one important class, matrimonial causes, was circumspectly left for Parliament.[99]

The Struggle to Reform the Ecclesiastical Courts

Grey's ministry was in no haste to implement the Commission's proposals. There were many more urgent matters and Brougham, the driving force behind their legal reforms, was occupied with bankruptcy and local courts.[100] It also had to consider whether the Real Property Commission, whose remit included wills

---

[95] *Ibid.*, 31; Hutton, *Reform of the Testamentary Jurisdiction*, 63–5.
[96] Hutton, *Reform of the Testamentary Jurisdiction*, 64.
[97] *Ibid.*, 64–9.
[98] *Ibid.*, 42.
[99] *Ibid.*, 43–4. It was recommended that they should be removed from lower courts to the provincial courts.
[100] *Ibid.*, 71–9. Brougham, Bellenden Ker, and Lushington cobbled together a bill, but no serious attempt was made to promote it.

and inheritance, might propose rather different solutions, as indeed their fourth report (April 1833) did.[101] This proposed a system of registration of wills and favoured Chancery as the forum for testamentary disputes. The stark conclusion was that '[p]robate of Wills [should] be discontinued and the whole Testamentary Jurisdiction of the Spiritual Courts, contentious and voluntary [should] be abolished'.[102]

The choice between the two sets of recommendations was made not on their intrinsic merits but as a by-product of the need to remodel the Admiralty court. Sir James Graham had already decided that the death of Sir Christopher Robinson would be the occasion for this and obtained a Commons select committee in June 1833.[103] If the Real Property Commissioners had their way, not only would the ecclesiastical courts lose their viability but the peacetime Admiralty too, since Doctors' Commons depended upon non-contentious probate for its survival. The Select Committee was heavily weighted towards the civilians and, as Graham wished, preferred the Ecclesiastical Commissioners' views.[104]

That verdict set the terms of the debate for the next 20 years.[105] What was first proposed was a new court called the court of Arches, with exclusive jurisdiction over the descent of realty as well as personalty, and with only small probates and the preliminary stages of bigger ones handled by country commissioners.[106] Before the bill was presented, potentially controversial elements dealing with clergy discipline, sequestrations, and the moral offences were removed, but as Graham warned Peel, the centralizing thrust of the main sections were its most vulnerable point.[107] That made it likely that common lawyers would be at best lukewarm in support and guaranteed determined opposition from lawyers who made their living in the country courts, as well as the bishops who would lose their patronage. This opposition, mobilizing the techniques of extra-parliamentary pressure which had recently become familiar, blocked measures brought forward first by Peel's and then by Melbourne's administrations and the next bill emerged from a Lords' select committee in 1836 with substantial concessions to localism. However, neither that bill, nor one by Jervis and Goulburn, more favourable to the diocesan courts, made much progress.[108] Besides the general listlessness of

---

[101] *PP* 1833 (226), vii.

[102] Quoted in Hutton, *Reform of the Testamentary Jurisdiction*, 79.

[103] Below, pp. 713–14.

[104] Hutton, *Reform of the Testamentary Jurisdiction*, 80–5.

[105] Outhwaite, *Rise and Fall of English Ecclesiastical Courts*, 145–56. There is a useful brief account by B. G. Hutton, 'The Ecclesiastical Courts are the Sebastopol of the Tribunes. Will they ever be taken?', in 'Legal Cultures, Legal Doctrine' (2002) *Cambrian Law Rev.* 93–100.

[106] Hutton, *Reform of the Testamentary Jurisdiction*, 102.

[107] *Ibid.*, 102–3.

[108] *Ibid.*, 100–31.

Melbourne's administration it had more important church issues to deal with and was faced with Lyndhurst's spoiling tactics in the upper house. Sensibly in view of the acute sensitivity surrounding all interference with the church, the government resolved to deal separately with clergy discipline and not until 1840 was the Church Discipline Act passed. By offering the bishop an alternative to proceeding in the provincial courts it removed one obstacle to reforming the structure of church courts.[109]

Unlike the Whigs, Peel made determined efforts to pass an ecclesiastical courts bill. Responsibility was given to the judge-advocate general Dr John Nicholl, son of Sir John, knowledgeable and diligent but handicapped by his junior position in the government and his professional connection with Doctors' Commons.[110] Nicholl tried painstakingly to conciliate vested interests. His 1843 bill offered substantial concessions to country solicitors,[111] but they were soon shown to be wholly insufficient. The country solicitors, under the intransigent leadership of Robert Swan,[112] mounted a formidable campaign of pamphleteering, letters to the press and, especially, petitioning; by the time the bill was abandoned after an acrimonious debate on the second reading, Parliament had received 152 petitions against, with just one in favour.[113]

The lesson Home Secretary Graham drew from that experience was that the forces of localism were too strong to be confronted head on as he and Peel had hitherto been determined to do. To improve the bill's prospects a reluctant Nicholl was instructed to make more concessions.[114] The bill was to be introduced in the Lords, where Lyndhurst openly pronounced it a bill 'framed to pass'.[115] And indeed it did pass the Lords, though not without strong opposition. It also passed its second reading in the Commons, but 158–89 was not a comfortable margin and the opening exchanges of the committee stage showed that it would take all

---

[109] 3 & 4 Vict. c. 6; W. L. Mathieson, *English Church Reform, 1815–1840* (1923), 161–5.

[110] Hutton, *Reform of the Testamentary Jurisdiction*, 133–5. His shorter published account of the abortive 1840s' legislation is in 'Dr. John Nicholl of Merthyr Mawr', in T. G. Watkin (ed.), *The Trial of Dic Penderyn* (Cardiff, 2003), 128–50.

[111] Hutton, *Reform of the Testamentary Jurisdiction*, 133–45. The diocesan registries would now be branches of the new 'court of Arches', enabled to keep original wills and to grant probates for estates not exceeding £300; their proctors would also be able to practise in the London court if they preferred to give up their solicitors' practice.

[112] Registrar of the Lincoln consistory court. He had been active in defending the diocesan courts from the time the report issued: *ibid.*, 75.

[113] *Ibid.*, 150–98.

[114] *Ibid.* Some were in favour of the courts of the Archbishop of York, whose uncertain place in the new scheme had always been a source of vulnerability. They were now to be reorganized and put on an equal footing with those of Canterbury. More was given to the diocesan courts too; in particular they might now handle contentious as well as common form probate.

[115] *Ibid.*, 202.

the government's will, and a great deal of its time, to force it through its remaining stages. Beset by more urgent problems, Peel had neither the time nor the will and the bill was dropped.[116]

These sessions showed that any worthwhile measure would have few true friends and many implacable enemies. The most serious and unyielding obstacle continued to be the country solicitors, whom every concession seemed only to make more exigent.[117] They, it seemed, would be satisfied only with full concurrent jurisdiction coupled with the abolition of the *bona notabilia* rule, which would expand their role. Their strength came from their ability to tap into the widespread suspicion of any extension or centralization of government functions. This attitude spanned the political spectrum and its adherents could point out, with at least superficial logic, that the plans for probate were inconsistent with the commitment of both political parties to introducing new or reformed local courts.[118] Yet if the principle of local justice were conceded, the demands of advocates of localism were not easy to satisfy, since there were competing interests at different levels: archdeaconal, diocesan, and provincial.

Elsewhere in the judicial system, in bankruptcy and common law, forces pressing for local courts were powerfully countered by the centripetal interests of the bar and the London solicitors, but neither had any enthusiasm for a project which denied them access to lucrative business and further entrenched the civilians' monopoly. In fact the Law Society and the professional press became insistent that the new court should be opened up to common lawyers[119] and it is notable that few barristers, who usually dominated parliamentary debates on law reforms, took a major part in these. Even the law officers were half-hearted and law reformers were disappointed that provisions to combine the jurisdiction over wills of realty and personalty in a single forum were dropped, especially as testamentary formalities had been harmonized in 1837.[120] Some dissenters, T. S. Duncombe was one, preferred the church courts were deprived of jurisdiction altogether than see it consolidated and reformed,[121] and any proposal that could unite Duncombe and the magnificently reactionary Colonel Sibthorp in opposition was a measure in difficulties.

---

[116] *Ibid.*, 202–21.

[117] They had even opposed the general fee fund on the grounds that it was only fair in the PCC, where the officers were full-time.

[118] See e.g. the speeches of John Jervis and Sir Robert Inglis on the second reading of the 1843 bill: *PD* 1843 (s3) 66: 325–32.

[119] Hutton, *Reform of the Testamentary Jurisdiction*, 166.

[120] See e.g. the criticisms of Sir George Grey and Howard Elphinstone on the second reading of the 1844 bill: *PD* 1844 (s3) 68: 1031–40, 1057–66.

[121] Hutton, *Reform of the Testamentary Jurisdiction*, 179.

In fact the misguided concessions embodied in the 1844 bill had the unwanted effect of turning what Peel insisted was a non-partisan law reform into a party question, for the leading Whigs came out against it and in 1845 resurrected a bill modelled on that of 1836. It did not get far, but muddied the waters and might have been expected to form the basis for a legislative initiative by Lord John Russell's administration. However, in five years of half-promises and evasions nothing of the sort appeared.[122]

However, although the church courts continued to escape reforms imposed from outside, their failure to reform themselves left them increasingly vulnerable. The Reverend Edward Muscott founded his 'Society for the Abolition of the Ecclesiastical Courts' in 1845 and he and Sir Benjamin Hall attacked the courts in public speeches and in pamphlets.[123] The tentacular hold of the Jenner clan on the PCC and court of Arches drew a complaint in court from an eminent advocate and was denounced in the press and in the Commons by an unsuccessful litigant and his supporters.[124] *The Law Review* and *The Law Magazine* kept them near the top of the law reformers' agenda,[125] and from 1850 returns to Parliament disclosed their business and the earnings and tenures of their officers.[126]

The most damaging publicity was the second report of the Fees Committee. Chaired with relish by a well-known enemy, Pleydell Bouverie, the Committee was trenchantly critical of both the PCC and the country courts.[127] It revealed that the new archbishop, Sumner, had promptly, and with doubtful legality, appointed his son to the reversion of the sinecure registrarship of the PCC after Howley had allowed an opportunity to lapse.[128] It condemned the way the taxpayer had to pay double the going rate for the Inland Revenue to procure copies of wills, and how the clerks of the seat, in plain defiance of an 1830 statute, did not carry out their duties in person, a long-known and still uncorrected abuse.[129] In the other provincial court at York the judge pocketed £1400 in fees for perhaps five half-day sessions a year.[130]

As for the diocesan registries, in the busiest, Chester, the table of fees appeared 'to have fallen into entire oblivion' and the registry had casually introduced a requirement that applicants provide and pay for a copy of a will. In Durham the deputy registrars smuggled in fees payable to themselves on top of those due to the registrar, an absentee clergyman living in the south of England.[131] In Bath and

---

[122] *Ibid.*, 203–11.   [123] *Ibid.*, 234–5, 242–4, 253–4.

[124] *Ibid.*, 236–7; Hutton, 'Dr. John Nicholl of Merthyr Mawr', 149.

[125] 'H.J.H.', 'The Jurisdiction of the Ecclesiastical Courts' (1848) 9 (s2) *LM* 59–83, 179–97; (1848) 8 *LR*, 347; 9 *LR*, 216–17.

[126] (1850) 105 *Commons Journals*, 303, 450.

[127] Bouverie had moved for the abolition of the ecclesiastical courts: *PD* 1848 (s3) 99: 100–27.

[128] *PP* 1850 (711), xiii, p.iv.   [129] p. v.

[130] p. vii.   [131] p. vi.

Wells the registrar, W. F. Beadon, was a London police magistrate; the judge, 'who is stated to have sat in court once or twice' took most of the fees while his deputy, the father of the deputy registrar, did the work; the deaconal court featured as its registrar a lady who was appointed when just five years old.[132] With officers such as these it was no wonder that judges increased the fees on their own motion, blithely ignorant of *Gifford's Case*, which had ruled this unlawful,[133] nor that the fees sometimes rested on no better authority than the *ipse dixit* of the officers.

Not all those associated with the courts were complacent. Robert Phillimore for instance put forward plans for moderate reforms which might have been acceptable 20 years before but were now too little and too late.[134] When in November 1852 a new Chancellor, Lord St. Leonards, announced that the Chancery Commission would be expanded by the inclusion of three civilians and its remit extended to the ecclesiastical courts, there could be little doubt about the outcome.[135]

The Achievement of Reform

Meanwhile the future of the church courts had been complicated by the need to tackle the acutely sensitive issue of matrimonial causes. A decree of divorce *a mensa et thoro* from a diocesan or provincial court was a necessary preliminary to a parliamentary divorce as well as an independent remedy. In the wake of the controversial Ellenborough divorce bill of 1830, Phillimore had presented a bill to enable the ecclesiastical courts to grant full divorce but had found little enthusiasm for widening their powers[136] and the Ecclesiastical Commission went no further than to recommend that the jurisdiction be restricted to the provincial courts.[137]

Only two courts handled a significant number of matrimonial causes, the court of Arches and, most popular, the London consistory court (LCC). Presided over by Lushington between 1828 and 1858, the LCC handled almost half of all matrimonial causes and they provided around 60 per cent of its workload, some 15 to 20 suits a year.[138] Divorce petitions easily predominated and women were

[132] pp. vii–viii.

[133] (1701) 1 Salk. 333.

[134] *The Practice and Courts of Civil and Ecclesiastical Law... Examined* (1848).

[135] Hutton, *Reform of the Testamentary Jurisdiction*, 524. They were Sir John Dodson, dean of Arches; Stephen Lushington, judge of Admiralty and the London consistory court; and Dorney Harding, Queen's Advocate. Derby had promised government action when the government accepted a bill abolishing the criminal jurisdiction of the ecclesiastical courts in the previous session.

[136] Stone, *Road to Divorce*, 364–6.

[137] *RC on Ecclesiastical Courts, General Report 1832*, 43–4.

[138] Stone, *Road to Divorce*, 183–211; Waddams, 'English Matrimonial Courts on the Eve of Reform', *passim* and *Law, Politics and the Church of England*, 160–8, 172–88. The London courts drew business

as likely to be initiators of those and nullity claims as men and twice as likely to seek restitution of conjugal rights. Many were unopposed—collusive in fact, especially where intended as preliminaries to a parliamentary divorce—and could be processed in a couple of months, but contested cases might last two years and more.[139]

Dissatisfaction with the limited availability of divorce led to the establishment of a royal commission in 1850. It reported around the same time as the Chancery Commission pronounced on the ecclesiastical courts, and to much the same effect.[140] There was much less opposition to the removal of matrimonial causes from ecclesiastical courts than probate. Outside the LCC they were relatively unimportant and even after the admission of oral evidence in 1855[141] it was difficult to argue that unreformed diocesan courts were a satisfactory forum for such delicate matters.[142]

The last stage in the wearisome process of reforming the probate jurisdiction, and so determining the future of the ecclesiastical courts, therefore had to take place in conjunction with the reform of divorce and also clergy discipline, and it began before the Chancery Commission issued its report. In April 1853 the Solicitor-General announced proposals for legislation on testamentary causes.[143] Bethell and Lord Chancellor Cranworth were keen to pre-empt the report because they had failed to persuade the Commission to adopt their own preferred solution, giving the testamentary jurisdiction to Chancery with only very limited local facilities. This was a logical move, since Chancery possessed an elaborate administrative apparatus and was the forum for deciding the construction of wills, and it might also overcome objections to another aim, to bring the descent of real property into the probate system. Furthermore, as Cranworth pointed out, it was economical to use an existing court rather than creating a new one whose business might not be sufficient to occupy a full-time professional judge.[144] They proposed the same solution for divorce.

Chancery was not the only option, however. R. P. Collier responded to Bethell's proposal with one which simply transferred probate to the common law courts, sending small estates to the county courts.[145] The Chancery Commission espoused

---

from the country by means of a 'legal loophole' allowing country suitors to claim residence: Stone, *Road to Divorce*, 185.

[139] Waddams, *Law, Politics and the Church of England*, 163 and tables 4, 5, 6.
[140] *RC on Divorce and Matrimonial Causes*, PP 1852–3 [1604], xl. And see XIII, pp. 781–4.
[141] See below, p. 711.
[142] *RC on Divorce, Report 1853*, 18–21.
[143] Hutton, *Reform of the Testamentary Jurisdiction*, 264.
[144] *Ibid.*, 286.
[145] *Ibid.*, 268–9.

neither solution, preferring a wholly new court with district offices to handle common form probates up to £1500. Like Bethell's, this was essentially a centralizing measure, the Commission concluding that the high degree of consistency of practice they felt desirable would not be obtained without a self-contained court with specialist practitioners.[146]

Defenders of the ecclesiastical courts did not give up the struggle. The Phillimores persevered with bills designed to make them more acceptable, and Robert succeeded in passing an Act to introduce common law modes of evidence in 1855.[147] A new champion in the commons, the future Chancery judge Richard Malins, led a spirited resistance to the loss of the crucial testamentary business, but could prevail only while the secularist reformers remained unable to agree on the crucial issues: a London testamentary court; the degree of local delegation; and how to compensate displaced officers and, perhaps, practitioners.

To reach such agreement took four sessions of Parliament.[148] Besides the usual distractions of other business, a change of ministry and the overriding preoccupation with the Crimean War, the probate bill needed to be synchronized with another dealing with matrimonial causes. Personal animosities among the law officers and Lord Chancellor, coupled with the very different, but equally damaging, shortcomings of Bethell and Cranworth as parliamentarians, contributed to the tortuous passage of the legislation.[149]

Delays and vacillations allowed opposition time to organize and lobby and resulted in yet another rival bill, Fitzroy Kelly's of 1856, which went much further in the direction of localism than the government's own.[150] In a series of reluctant concessions, Bethell and Cranworth were driven from their initial positions on several key issues and struggled to create an acceptable compromise. From being an integral part of Chancery, via a semi-independent court presided over by a vice-chancellor but sending all issues of fact to be determined at law, the testamentary court became the independent, fully competent court the Commission had suggested.[151] After much uncertainty appeals were to go not to the court of Appeals

---

[146] *RC on Chancery, Second Report 1854*, 15–16.

[147] Evidence in Ecclesiastical Courts Act 1855 (17 & 18 Vict. c. 47). The Ecclesiastical Courts Commission had been divided on the merits of introducing oral evidence and recommended that it should be used only where the validity of a will was disputed and in other cases at the discretion of the judge (*General Report 1832*, 31). A leading civilian, Dr Spinks, felt the Act would obviate one of the two main complaints about the courts, the other being delay: S. M. Waddams, 'Evidence of Witnesses in the Ecclesiastical Courts, 1830–1857', in C. H. Van Rhee (ed.), *The Law's Delay* (Antwerp, 2004), 343–60.

[148] Hutton, *Reform of the Testamentary Jurisdiction*, 275–355.

[149] *Ibid.*, 287.

[150] *Ibid.*, 312.

[151] *Ibid.*, 279–84, 297–8, 309–11, 316–17. The veteran dean of Arches, Sir John Dodson, declined to be its judge because its procedures would be drawn in part from common law.

in Chancery but to the House of Lords.[152] The country proctors were unable to preserve their diocesan courts, but local facilities were successively expanded, from glorified post offices to district registries capable of making grants themselves and retaining original wills. Their number was almost doubled from what Cranworth originally wanted, and at the last (through Palmerston's dramatic intervention in debate and Bethell's humiliation). Yorkshire interests secured the removal of the upper monetary limit and the requirement of a metropolitan probate for stocks and shares.[153] Since they had earlier yielded to Collier (whose own proposal they had effectively blocked by having Campbell declare the common law judges too busy to take on extra work[154]) in giving county courts contested jurisdiction over small estates,[155] the balance between centralization, which had been the main plank of reformers since the Ecclesiastical Commissioners' report in 1832, and localism was tilted towards the latter, with the crucial exception that contested probates of substantial estates would be handled only in the new court. *Bona notabilia* vanished, but grants out of district registries were limited to the estates of decedents who had been lately residing in the district.

These changes necessarily affected plans to alleviate the plight of victims of the near annihilation of the ecclesiastical courts. There were three main possibilities: to find places for them in the new arrangements; allow them exclusive rights to practise; or to pay them compensation. A new court could more easily accommodate the 'efficient' officers of the PCC, and with most diocesan registries now becoming district registries something similar could be done for the registrars and deputy registrars, though the exigent claims of the Chester deputy registrar caused friction.[156] Exclusive rights (whether temporary or permanent) to deal in non-contentious probate were initially favoured for the London proctors, but could hardly be given to the solicitor-proctors elsewhere and although initially Bethell and Cranworth were adamantly opposed to compensation for loss of profits, that position had to be abandoned in 1856, when the proctors ultimately preferred to yield up a monopoly now of uncertain value in exchange for generous compensation.[157] The advocates, who had been partly shielded by the temporary revival of the Prize court and the certainty that Admiralty at least would continue as a civilian court, held aloof, counting on exploiting their collective ownership of Doctors' Commons.[158]

It was thanks to Palmerston's strong position after the 1857 election and his determination to override the desires of his own law officers and Lord Chancellor

---

[152] *Ibid.*, 311–12, 316, 331–2. [153] *Ibid.*, pp. 264, 279, 297, 311–12, 316, 328, 337–40.
[154] *Ibid.*, 335.   [155] *Ibid.*, 328.   [156] *Ibid.*, 342.
[157] *Ibid.*, 264, 279, 281, 299, 309–11, 312, 328–9, 334, 340–3. For the compensation see above.
[158] *Ibid.*, 285, 343–4.

by making whatever concessions to local and vested interests were needful that the interminable siege of Doctors' Commons was ended. That determination was even more in evidence in the shorter battle for the creation of a divorce court.[159]

Although the two measures were interrelated, the obstacles they encountered were different. True, in both cases the inveterate suspicion of Chancery forced the government to abandon plans to bestow jurisdiction there, and both raised similar issues about the identity and powers of a new court's judges. However, apart from the largely unsuccessful attempt to draw succession to land into the probate system, opposition to the testamentary proposals did not go to the principle but to the practicalities, whereas judicial divorce was opposed outright by Gladstone and others and issues of women's property rights and the 'double standard' came to dominate the discussions. The outcome was different too: the centralization that was successfully resisted in probate was a main feature in divorce.

So at last the 'Sebastopol' among courts was overthrown. More flexibility, accepting the sort of moderate reforms and prudent concessions that Peel was fond of urging on the church, and which were made elsewhere in the 1830s, might have preserved them for longer. Equally, however, if Graham had not preferred the recommendations of the Ecclesiastical Courts Commission to the Real Property Commission's, the probate system might have been secularized much sooner.

Aftermath

The Acts of 1857 did not put an end to Doctors' Commons. Indeed the new courts used its premises for several years until the advocates, not with one voice, decided to sell up the place in 1865.[160] Nor of course were the ecclesiastical courts abolished, but their place in the nation's life was marginalized. Other functions which the Ecclesiastical Courts Commission had long before identified as secular— such as defamation and brawling in church—were removed,[161] and the eventual outcome of the great Braintree case was that they could not enforce the setting, as opposed to the enforcement, of a church rate; with the abolition of compulsory church rates in 1868 there would be no more 'martyrs' to that cause.[162]

---

[159] Stone, *Road to Divorce*, 368–82. There are several accounts of the passage of the divorce legislation from different scholarly perspectives. And see XIII, pp. 783–4.

[160] The sale produced £84,000. The corporation was not dissolved and the last survivor, T. H. Tristram, died in 1912: Squibb, *Doctors' Commons*, 102–11.

[161] Ecclesiastical Courts Jurisdiction Acts 1855 (18 & 19 Vict. c. 41), 1861 (23 & 24 Vict. c. 32).

[162] Church Rates Abolition Act 1868 c. 109; Waddams, *Law, Politics and the Church of England*, 249–69.

What remained was their jurisdiction over the ordering of churches and the conduct of the clergy, which became bitterly contentious.[163] The courts were still funded by fees and their procedure was not further altered.[164] The confusing terms of the ill-advised Public Worship Regulation Act of 1874 (c. 85) were eventually held not to create a new court but only to render the operations of the provincial courts under their new judge subject to its prescribed limitations and directions when dealing with cases brought under the Act.[165] The use of that Act, and the authority of Lord Penzance, were strenuously contested by the high church party and the opportunity for a general overhaul of the church courts presented by Tait's royal commission in 1881 proved illusory. The Commissioners duly condemned their condition as 'antiquated, cumbersome, expensive and unsuited to the requirements of the present day',[166] but were unable to reconcile their own deep differences to produce a consensual blueprint for reform. The report did recommend procedural changes and a greatly enlarged role for the bishops in diocesan courts, but its authority was weakened by a trail of dissents and Tait's successors had neither the drive nor the influence to persuade government to find space for legislation.[167] The practice of appointing the same man to be judge of several dioceses,[168] and bringing of the provincial courts under the same judge probably improved the quality of the justice they dispensed, but serious defects would remain unaddressed for many years.[169]

2. THE COURT OF ADMIRALTY

Jurisdiction and Business

The Admiralty judge presided over the instance court and, in wartime, the Prize court. The volume and importance of business in the latter had swollen

---

[163] O. Chadwick, *The Victorian Church*, 2 vols (3rd edn, 1966–70), 491–505; Rodes, *Law and Modernization in the Church of England*, 243–316. And see above, pp. 397–400.

[164] Ecclesiastical Jurisdiction Act 1847 (10 & 11 Vict. c. 98); Ecclesiastical Fees Acts 1867 (c. 135) and 1875 (c. 76).

[165] *Green* v. *Lord Penzance* (1881) LR 6 App Cas 651; J. Bentley, *Ritualism and Politics in Victorian Britain* (Oxford, 1978); C. Smith, 'Martin v. Mackonochie/Mackonochie v. Penzance: A Crisis of Character and Identity in the Court of Arches?' (2003) 24 *JLH* 250–72. And see above, pp. 397–400.

[166] *RC on Ecclesiastical Courts, Report, PP* 1883 [C. 3760], xxiv, vii.

[167] P. T. Marsh, *The Victorian Church in Decline: Archbishop Tait and the Church of England* (1969), 264–89; A. Robertson, 'The Jurisdiction of the Ecclesiastical Courts in England' (1883–4) 9 (s4) *LM & R* 404–41.

[168] e.g. T. H. Tristram (London, Ripon, Hereford, Wakefield, and Canterbury). Tristram adhered closely to precedent and angered ritualists by his approach: *Thomas Hutchinson Tristram, for Forty Years Chancellor of London, a Memoir* (1916), 85, 92.

[169] Rodes, *Law and Modernization in the Church of England*, 359–62. Reform was finally effected in the Ecclesiastical Jurisdiction Measure 1963.

to unprecedented levels during two decades of war and when peace came the instance court was exposed as an 'idle, backwater Court'.[170]

On paper the instance jurisdiction was impressively wide: salvage and droits of Admiralty; torts at sea; actions for seamen's wages; enforcement of liens for payment of freight; bottomry bonds and the supply of necessaries; contracts upon the sea and appeals from colonial vice-admiralty courts.[171] In reality, however, many of these categories had become very circumscribed after centuries of unrelenting hostility from the common lawyers, whose encroachments through the exploitation of legal fictions were consolidated by prohibitions.[172] As a result, most instance causes involved petty disputes between shipowners, and not many of those; in 1822 the court sat for just 38 days and heard 64 causes, in 1832 for just 28 days and 37 causes.[173] Aware that such levels of business made the court vulnerable to criticism, its defenders argued that some of the cases were lengthy, citing the three-day hearing in *Thetis*, but it was a feeble defence.[174]

For all his judicial fame, Stowell had been so very cautious in seeking to recover lost ground that not one prohibition was issued against his decisions.[175] Yet his reputation did provide a basis for future attempts and the instance court had real potential attractions, in particular, its unique facility for actions *in rem*, while the very shortage of business meant suitors need not suffer the delays plaguing the King's Bench. There were already signs that the hostility of the common lawyers was diminishing now that the Admiralty was no longer a serious rival; indeed an encroachment in respect of seamen's wages had caused them such difficulties that it had to be relinquished.[176] True, when shipowners' liability for cargo loss was further restricted by statute in 1813, Chancery, not Admiralty, was awarded sole jurisdiction, but several other statutes between 1813 and 1825 made minor augmentations to Admiralty jurisdiction, and though none was very significant, it was encouraging that they did not meet opposition.[177]

Against this background civilian witnesses (William Adams and, more cautiously, Stephen Lushington) felt able to urge the Select Committee of 1833

[170] H. J. Bourguignon, *Sir William Scott, Lord Stowell* (Cambridge, 1987), 60.

[171] F. L. Wiswall, *The Development of Admiralty Jurisdiction and Practice since 1800* (Cambridge, 1970), 9–11.

[172] Bourguignon, *Sir William Scott, Lord Stowell*, 1–30.

[173] *Ibid.*, 61; Wiswall, *Admiralty Jurisdiction*, 11.

[174] *SC on the Admiralty Court*, PP 1833 (670), vii, Sir John Nicholl, qq. 88–9.

[175] Bourguignon, *Sir William Scott, Lord Stowell*, 251. See e.g. *The Atlas (Clark)* (1827) 2 Hay 48, discussed at 91–2.

[176] Wiswall, *Admiralty Jurisdiction*, 25–6.

[177] *Ibid.*, 22–3, citing Frauds by Boatmen Act 1813 (53 Geo. III c. 67); Wages of Seamen Act 1819 (59 Geo. III c. 58); Cinque Ports Act 1821 (1 & 2 Geo. IV c. 76); Slave Trade Act 1824 (5 Geo. IV c. 113); Act for Regulating British Vessels 1825 (6 Geo. IV c. 110).

towards a modest enlargement of its powers.[178] Tindal CJCP, was also favourable, though rather at the expense of Chancery than common law, and the Committee was surprisingly generous, recommending concurrent jurisdiction over seamen's special contracts, 'demands of nautical men and of mortgagees when the vessel has been arrested, or the proceeds are in the registry' and perhaps questions of title to vessels and their freight.[179]

This 'great triumph for the civilians',[180] was not translated into legislation until Lushington became judge and then only in part. Ship mortgages in actions *in rem*; title and the division of proceeds of sale in possession actions; salvage claims for service; and necessaries and claims for towage were all conceded, but restrictions on contracts, freight, and charter-party remained.[181] The Act helped to revive business but the recovery of the instance court owed less to institutional changes than to increases in shipping, particularly the coming of the steamship, which contributed to a plentiful crop of collision cases.[182]

Procedural weaknesses still deterred potential suitors; for instance, the action by plea and proof, usual in more serious cases, was subject to interminable obstruction by a defendant.[183] However, the changes made in 1855 and especially 1859 probably enhanced the court's attractions[184] and Lushington showed real concern to keep down suitors' expenses.[185] Like Stowell, he was nervous of prohibitions but there were further statutory additions to jurisdiction. The Wreck and Salvage Act 1846, though narrowly interpreted, extended salvage claims to incidents where life, as well as property, was preserved,[186] and there were minor additions in the Merchant Shipping Act 1854, though that Act also sent seamen's wages claims to the magistrates unless they were above £50.[187] The biggest increase in business, however, arose from collisions, which gradually overtook salvage cases; from fewer than one-quarter in 1841 they rose to almost 40 per cent in 1861.[188] Overall, final decrees rose from 82 to 199 over that period, justifying the Lord Chancellor's claim that it 'had now become one of the most important tribunals in the country for the determination of civil causes.'[189]

[178] *SC on Admiralty Court, Report 1833*, qq. 511, 1126.
[179] *Ibid.*, 4 and qq. 1423–4.
[180] Wiswall, *Admiralty Jurisdiction*, 38.
[181] Admiralty Court Act 1840 (3 & 4 Vict. c. 65).
[182] W. Senior, *Doctors' Commons and the Old Court of Admiralty* (1922), 109.
[183] *Admiralty Court Returns*, PP 1867 (375), lvii, 5.
[184] See below, pp. 729–30.
[185] Waddams, *Law, Politics and the Church of England*, 197–8.
[186] 9 & 10 Vict. c. 99; Wiswall, *Admiralty Jurisdiction*, 43–4 .
[187] 17 & 18 Vict. c. 104.
[188] *Admiralty Court Returns*, PP 1867 (359), lvii.
[189] PD 1861 (s3) 161: 1394–5.

The opening of the court (now a court of record) to the common lawyers paved the way for a further extension in its jurisdiction.[190] Diehards still objected to the absence of a jury, but they could not stop the passage of an important Act in 1861.[191] Besides section 7, which by giving jurisdiction over any damage caused by any ship, opened up great possibilities,[192] its chief features were improvements to interlocutory and remedial facilities, notably in discovery, counter-claims, enforcement of judgments, and appeals. As the Admiralty became more like other superior courts, however, it also became slower and more expensive which led to the removal of smaller cases to cheaper local courts.[193] In 1862 the justices' jurisdiction over salvage claims, fixed at £200 in 1854, was raised to £1000.[194] Much more contentiously, some county courts in coastal towns were given Admiralty jurisdiction up to £300. This bill was fought strenuously by certain commercial interests and those opposed to devolution generally, but they managed only to reduce the money limit and the number of courts included.[195] Between 300 and 400 Admiralty cases a year were heard in county courts, roughly the same number as in the High Court, and the Mayor's court and Liverpool court of Passage also took a share; Admiralty court cases, while numerically more or less stationary, were becoming heavier in substance.[196]

Rothery's returns argued the case for preserving and expanding an independent jurisdiction.[197] Besides stressing the recent reforms, he marshalled statistics to demonstrate its 'progress' between 1841 and 1866.[198] With plaintiffs five times as successful as defendants[199] it should have appealed to potential suitors, but the Judicature Commissioners noted that, like other courts, it was often unable to offer a complete remedy and that there were undesirable conflicts of principle (notably over the basis for assessing damages in collision cases) between Admiralty and common law. Even so, they felt its *in rem* procedure would give it an advantage

[190] Admiralty Court Act 1861 (24 & 25 Vict. c. 10), s 14.
[191] e.g. 'The Prospects of the Admiralty Court' (1861) 10 (s3) *LM & LR* 262–7.
[192] Wiswall, *Admiralty Jurisdiction*, 59.
[193] e.g. E. E. Wendt, *Papers on Maritime Legislation* (1868), ix.
[194] Merchant Shipping Amendment Act 1862 (25 & 26 Vict. c. 63), s 49.
[195] County Courts Admiralty Jurisdiction Act 1868 (c. 71); County Court Admiralty Jurisdiction Amendment Act 1869 (c. 51); *PD* 1867–8 (s3) 190: 1828–9; 191: 161–71, 1553–4.
[196] *RC on the Legal Departments, Evidence 1874*, H. A. Bathurst q. 8913.
[197] *Admiralty Court Returns*, PP1867 (359) (365) (375), vii. For an opposing view see 'The Barristers' Petition', in Wendt, *Papers on Maritime Legislation*, 82–6.
[198] 147 sitting days against 38; 53 references to the registrar against 2; 247 taxed bills against 58; an average of £1592 at stake in salvage cases against £612, with £2323 in damage cases against £569; 137 cases above £2000 against 11.
[199] *Admiralty Court Third Return 1867*, 3. In 1861 Lord Chelmsford said plaintiffs won 99 times out of 100 in collision actions: *PD* 1861 (s3) 161: 1396.

over the common law courts.[200] In fact, considering its lack of political muscle, the Admiralty did rather well out of the Judicature Acts. All limitation of liability cases were acquired from Chancery;[201] its rule on damages was preferred to the common law's;[202] and because all branches of the High Court possessed concurrent jurisdiction, there could be no further prohibitions.[203] The rules of 1883 provided that all matters which would have gone to the Admiralty court before the Acts should be sent to the Probate, Divorce, and Admiralty Division, and its judges battled tenaciously and with some success to hold onto the mixed contracts and other business that might have formerly belonged to either civilian or common law courts.[204]

Levels of business did not alter very much through the upheaval of the 1870s, remaining at around 400 a year. Thanks to Brett it eventually lost some of the Fatal Accidents Acts claims,[205] but gained appeals under the Shipping Casualties Investigations Act 1879[206] and the great consolidation effected by the Merchant Shipping Act 1894 not only tidied up its powers but also added to them.[207] None of the additions, however, substantially altered either the quantum or the profile of its work.

MacDonell's analysis of 1901 showed that while writs had remained stationary since 1880, most measures of business—trials, taxed bills, costs—had risen by about 30 per cent despite a slight reduction in the merchant marine.[208] The caseload fell slightly in the 1900s despite Barnes's introduction of short cause rules in 1908 to encourage suitors, and by 1914 it was felt that salvage cases in particular were being lost to arbitration.[209] Salvage remained one of the major components in its caseload.[210] The striking feature is the growing dominance of collisions and salvage, especially the former, together making 366 out of 544 in 1913; bottomry bonds had not been seen in court for several years.[211]

Like the civil work of the instance court, Admiralty's criminal business had been eroded by the common lawyers and in a similar slackening of hostility Ellenborough's Act was held to apply to Admiralty, thereby extending its

---

[200] *RC on the Judicature, First Report, PP* 1868–9 [4130], xxv, 7–8.

[201] Supreme Court of Judicature Act 1873 (c. 83), s. 42; Wiswall, *Admiralty Jurisdiction*, 104–5.

[202] Section 25(9).   [203] One of the last was *Smith* v. *Brown* (1871) LR 6 QB 729.

[204] RSC 1883 Ord. 5 r 5; Wiswall, *Admiralty Jurisdiction*, 126.

[205] See below, see p. 723.   [206] c. 72.   [207] c. 60.

[208] *Civil Judicial Statistics, PP* 1903 [Cd. 1588], lxxxiii.

[209] *Civil Judicial Statistics 1913, PP* 1914–16 [Cd. 7807], lxxxii; *RC on the Civil Service, Evidence, PP* 1914–16 (Cd. 8130), xii, qq. 49,502–12 (Roscoe) and 50,870–1 (B. Aspinall).

[210] In 1870 it had comprised: collisions 159, salvage 62, bottomry bonds 23, necessaries 24, co-ownership disputes 25, damage to cargo 18, masters' claims for wages etc. 18, seamen's wages 11, limitations 2, others 21 (363). In 1896 the equivalents were 292, 102, 2, 12, 8, 1, 5, 3, 7, 39 (471): *Civil Judicial Statistics, PP* 1872 [C. 600], xxx; *PP* 1898 [C. 8838], liii.

[211] *PP* 1914–16 [Cd. 7807], lxxxiii; *RC on the Civil Service, Evidence*, Roscoe, q. 49,402.

scope to offences against the person.[212] However, unlike the civil actions, there was no recovery, and the special Admiralty sessions at the Old Bailey, where the Admiralty judge sat with two common law judges who conducted the trial,[213] slipped into an almost unnoticed oblivion after the offences were made triable at common law.[214] In 1902 a leading textbook declared the criminal jurisdiction virtually obsolete and no one seems to have wanted to revive it.[215]

Bench and Bar

The Admiralty judge ranked below the judge of the court of Arches and the judge of the PCC, but as judge of the Prize court in wartime he was busier and more important than either. At need he could command the assistance of a surrogate from the advocates of Doctors' Commons,[216] but after 1815 Stowell needed no assistance with the trickle of instance business. With his fortune made and his reputation secure this altered state of affairs scarcely fretted him even though the judge's income, largely derived from suitors' fees, fell to a level which would make it difficult to attract the leading civilians.[217] Stowell had also profited from being judge of the consistory court of London until 1821, and it was his protege and successor in that post, Sir Christopher Robinson, who became Admiralty judge on Stowell's retirement in 1828.[218]

Unlike Stowell, Robinson (already 62) had time to build neither a fortune nor a reputation in the five years[219] before his death in April 1833. By then the civilian courts were undergoing a searching inquiry, and the position of the Admiralty judge was proving particularly problematic. The Select Committee on Admiralty felt that under its proposals for reforming the jurisdiction of the higher ecclesiastical courts, a single judge would be able to combine their business with that of Admiralty, at any rate in peacetime.[220] The Admiralty side could hardly contend that the instance business now warranted a full-time judge, but had three

---

[212] By virtue of 1 Geo. IV c. 90; Holdsworth, *HEL*, xiii, 392–3.

[213] Described in Jenner's evidence: *SC on Admiralty Court, Report 1833*, qq. 296–309. Lushington (qq. 564–9) opposed its abolition and the committee's report makes no recommendation.

[214] Central Criminal Court Act 1834 (4 & 5 Will. IV c. 36), s 22; Admiralty Offences Act 1844 (7 Vict. c. 2).

[215] R. G. Williams and Sir G. Bruce, *A Treatise on the Jurisdiction and Practice of the English Courts in Admiralty Actions and Appeals* (3rd edn, 1902), 2. Noting *R v. Coelho* (1914) the *Law Times* commented on the rarity of such cases: (1914) 137 *LT*, 68.

[216] Bourguignon, *Sir William Scott, Lord Stowell*, 56.

[217] The judge had £2500 paid out of the navy estimates. By 1833 he was receiving only £200–£250 in fees: *RC on the Court of Admiralty, PP* 1824 (240), ix, 3.

[218] *ODNB* 47: 314–15.

[219] He left less than £1000 (*ibid.*). Holdsworth, *HEL*, xiii, 689–90.

[220] *SC on Admiralty Court, Report 1833*, 4.

powerful objections; first, in wartime the judge would be unable to cope (indeed Sir John Nicholl, who had become the Admiralty judge and was holding all three of the major judgeships, was unwilling to continue combining them even in peacetime);[221] secondly, there would be a danger of discouraging that learning in international law which was sometimes wanted by the government and which only civilians possessed;[222] thirdly, there was the problem of appeals.

Until Brougham came on the scene Prize appeals went to a commission comprising all privy councillors and the common law judges, while instance appeals were to the court of Delegates, made up of three common law judges and three or more civilians.[223] Brougham had denounced the latter as 'one of the worst constituted courts that ever was appointed',[224] since the common law judges knew no maritime law and the only civilians usually available were the least experienced and least successful. In 1833 both sets of appeals were transferred to Brougham's remodelled Judicial Committee of the Privy Council, of which the judge in Admiralty was an *ex officio* member.[225] As witnesses to the Select Committee pointed out, there must be two civilian judges so that the Judicial Committee might have appropriate expertise when hearing an appeal from the Admiralty judge.[226]

The Committee held to its view that a single judge would suffice, but yielded ground by stipulating that if two were felt preferable they should have interchangeable jurisdiction. It also endorsed an earlier recommendation of Brougham's, that the judge should be salaried instead of fee-dependent, and concluded that he should not sit in the Commons as Scott and Robinson had done and Nicholl was still doing.[227]

Because of the deadlock over the church courts the report was not implemented. In 1838 Nicholl retired and was replaced by Stephen Lushington, eminent as a civilian, judge of the London consistory court since 1828 and Whig MP for Tower Hamlets.[228] This appointment ensured the continuance of an exclusive judge of Admiralty and Lushington seems to have been promised at least some of the enlarged jurisdiction suggested in 1833. But two aspects of Lushington's appointment proved controversial and both were picked up by Brougham, whose

[221] *Ibid.*, q. 104; Holdsworth, *HEL*, xiii, 691–6; Wiswall, *Admiralty Jurisdiction*, 38–9.

[222] *SC on Admiralty Court, Report 1833*, e.g. q. 1316 (J. W. Freshfield), qq. 1388–9 (Tindal CJCP).

[223] For this court see G. I. O Duncan, *The High Court of Delegates* (Cambridge, 1971) and Howell, *Judicial Committee of the Privy Council*, 18–20 .

[224] Quoted in Howell, *Judicial Committee of the Privy Council*, 19.

[225] *Ibid.*, 20–2, 34–5; Privy Council Act 1833 (3 & 4 Will. IV c. 41).

[226] *SC on Admiralty Court, Report 1833*, 5 and evidence of William Adams (q. 1075) and Nicholl (q. 104).

[227] *Ibid.*, 5–6.

[228] Waddams, *Law, Politics and the Church of England*, 41.

opposition held up the reforming bill in 1839.[229] The government readily gave way on remuneration, offering £4000 in lieu of fees; since the leaders in Doctors' Commons made between £5000 and £7000 per annum it was not overgenerous, but that arch-economizer Joseph Hume objected that the Select Committee had proposed only £3000.[230] The Whigs also had to concede that the judge should no longer be eligible to sit in the Commons,[231] a disappointment to Lushington, who had gone to the trouble of getting himself re-elected after assurances from Russell.[232]

During almost 30 years Lushington contributed a very substantial mass of judgments to the court's jurisprudence and the Crimean War even gave him an opportunity to supplement and refine Stowell's doctrines of Prize law.[233] Like Stowell he drew upon a mass of unwritten learning which he had absorbed while an advocate,[234] but by this time regular reports were published, which met the criticism of common lawyers that the civilians drew upon a secret store of learning to preserve their own exclusiveness.[235] If Stowell was readier to draw upon decided cases than was often claimed,[236] both he and Lushington were very much in the civilian tradition of flexible application of principle rather than rigid adherence to precedent.[237] While careful to disclaim any systematic use of equitable doctrines—used only, 'as it were, incidentally and of necessity'[238]—Lushington's leaning towards equitable principles probably gave some substance to critics' claims that he was sometimes inconsistent in his rulings.[239]

During the 1840s Lushington was content to operate the court essentially along traditional lines, but in the 1850s he and the new registrar H. C. Rothery, using powers conferred in the 1840 Act,[240] placed the rules of the court on a more systematic footing. External pressures compelled this modernization. The admission of testimony of interested witnesses at common law, the great changes wrought by the Common Law Procedure Acts and their Chancery counterparts,

---

[229] *Ibid.*, 39–43.

[230] *PD* 1839 (s3) 49: 348–53, 1107–12, 1272; 1840 (s3) 53: 242–5, 1069–72.

[231] *PD* 1839 (s3) 45: 257–61; 49: 1113–26; 1840 (s3) 53: 1072–4; 54: 1410–11.

[232] Waddams, *Law, Politics and the Church of England*, 41–3.

[233] *Ibid.*, 194–237.

[234] *Ibid.*, 227; Bourguignon, *Sir William Scott, Lord Stowell*, 79–80.

[235] Holdsworth, *HEL*, xii, 51; xv, 262–3.

[236] Bourguignon, *Sir William Scott, Lord Stowell*, 244.

[237] Waddams, *Law, Politics and the Church of England*, 201–2.

[238] H. C. Coote, *The New Practice of the High Court of Admiralty of England* (1860), 9, quoting *The Saracen* (1847) 4 Notes of Cases, at 504. On appeal Lord Langdale MR stressed that the Admiralty was not a court of equity (6 Moore 74).

[239] Compare Wiswall, *Admiralty Jurisdiction*, 67–74 with Waddams, *Law, Politics and the Church of England*, 201–8.

[240] Admiralty Court Act 1840, s 18.

the imminent overthrow of the ecclesiastical courts and, above all, the dissolution of Doctors' Commons and the opening up of the court to the common law bar in 1858, all indicated a major overhaul.[241] Lushington had not been opposed to opening up the court in the 1830s and long experience and high reputation made him well placed to preside over the transition.[242]

The infiltration of the common lawyers was gradual. Some proctors still operated alongside the solicitors, though the big steamship companies were mostly represented by the latter[243] and in the cramped quarters of the 'cockloft' to which the court decamped the leaders of the last generation of advocates, Travers Twiss and J. P. Deane, contended against Brett, Butt, and Bruce.[244] Few of the newcomers limited themselves to Admiralty but Webster was one of several juniors who found it a useful staging post; the grant of Admiralty jurisdiction to the City of London court and county courts gave him openings as junior to Butt when established men demanded excessive fees.[245]

Lushington retired in 1867. The Probate Act of 1857 had provided that on the next vacancy in either judgeship they might be combined, with a salary enhanced by £1000, and allowed each judge to sit for the other, but it was soon superseded by the Divorce Act, which united the Probate judgeship with the Divorce court.[246] On the eve of Lushington's retirement a bill was floated which would create a chief judge on £5000 and two puisnes on £4000 each to cover all three of the courts, the puisnes also going circuit, but projected reconstructions were overtaken by the appointment of the Judicature Commission.[247] Lushington was succeeded both as Admiralty judge and Dean of Arches by Robert Phillimore. A transitional figure, Phillimore trained as a civilian, then went to the bar and later became a QC. His qualifications for the Admiralty were impressive: judge of Admiralty in the Cinque Ports court, Admiralty advocate, Queen's advocate and judge-advocate general; he had also written a learned treatise on international law.[248] It fell to Phillimore to defend the Admiralty court from serious external threats. He was unable to prevent the county courts from being given a limited jurisdiction but

[241] Wiswall, *Admiralty Jurisdiction*, 52–8.

[242] *SC on Admiralty Court Report 1833*, q. 501.

[243] *RC on Legal Departments, Evidence*, Bathurst, q. 8940.

[244] E. S. Roscoe, *Studies in the History of the Admiralty and Prize Courts* (1932), 8–11.

[245] Lord Alverstone, *Recollections of Bar and Bench* (1914), 20–2.

[246] Probate Act 1857, s 5; Divorce Act 1857, ss 8, 9. The Admiralty judge was one of several empowered to substitute for the divorce judge.

[247] Wendt, *Papers on Maritime Legislation*, 79–81.

[248] E. Manson, *Builders of our Law in the Reign of Queen Victoria* (2nd edn, 1904), 234–41; J. H. Baker, 'Sir Robert Phillimore, QC, DCL…and the Last Practising Doctors of Law' (1996–7) 4 *Journal of Ecclesiastical Law* 709–19.

a few months into the job he was added to the Judicature Commission, whose terms of reference endangered its very existence.

The Admiralty, Probate and Divorce courts proved difficult to fit into the unified structure favoured by the Commissioners. At one time it was proposed to join Admiralty with the Chancery division, leaving the Probate and Divorce judge as a non-divisional anomaly,[249] but ultimately Hatherley's original proposal to combine them in a distinct division was adopted.[250] The status and relationship of the judges within the PDA remained untidy for some years. The President created by the Judicature Act 1873, section 31 was Sir James Hannen, presumably because the judge ordinary ranked above the judge of Admiralty, though Hannen was junior to Phillimore both in service on the bench and in the Privy Council.[251] Yet Phillimore appointed the registrar and assistant registrar, which the Judicature Act 1875 reserved for the President, and he continued to be, in fact if not name, the Admiralty judge.[252] In this capacity he 'discharged his Office with a wisdom and diligence which by no means suffers in comparison with the erratic brilliance of his predecessor'.[253] He was more often reversed in the Privy Council than Lushington, but that may reflect changes in that body rather than his own shortcomings.[254] Inevitably, however, with no Prize cases and the solid (and by now well-reported) foundations of his predecessors to build upon, his contribution to Admiralty law is less impressive.

Phillimore was very successful in safeguarding the traditions, practices, and rules of his court during the great upheaval of the 1870s, but he and the shipping interest could not prevent the transfer of appeals from the Judicial Committee to the House of Lords.[255] However, the new Court of Appeal rather than the Lords proved the biggest curb on Admiralty jurisdiction now that prohibitions could no longer issue from the common law courts. Curiously, this atavistic hostility came mostly from Brett, who had made his name in shipping cases. In *R* v. *Judge of the City of London Court*, he pronounced 'I for one will not reopen the floodgates of Admiralty Jurisdiction upon the people of this country'.[256] Brett went to great lengths, resorting to some dubious law, to overturn decisions which enabled *in rem* actions under the Fatal Accidents Acts to be brought in Admiralty.[257]

Phillimore retired in 1881 and although he was the last true Admiralty judge, the concerns of the shippers that their affairs should continue to be handled by

[249] *PD* 1873 (s3) 214: 343 (Lord Selborne).
[250] *PD* 1870 (s3) 200: 169–72; 1873 (s3) 216: 878–85.
[251] Sir W. Phillimore to C. Schuster, 11 June 1920, LCO 2/460.
[252] Wiswall, *Admiralty Jurisdiction*, 107–8.
[253] *Ibid.*, 112.   [254] Holdsworth, *HEL*, xvi, 146–8.
[255] Wiswall, *Admiralty Jurisdiction*, 105–6.   [256] (1892) 1 QB 273, 310.
[257] Wiswall, *Admiralty Jurisdiction*, 124–5, 129–30.

a judge versed in maritime concerns was met by appointing C. P. Butt from the Admiralty bar. Butt's irrepressible love of facetiousness was quite out of keeping with the preternatural gravity of Hannen's Divorce court[258] and it was assumed that they would preserve a strict division of labour. The Admiralty clients made their displeasure known when the President insisted on taking some Admiralty cases himself.[259] He soon desisted, however, and the shipping interest had reason to be grateful to him, for he successfully supported Butt's appeals to be released from circuit duty[260] and decreed that the new forms provided by the RSC in 1883 'need not be slavishly adhered to', thereby encouraging the continuation of established practice.[261]

The Judicature Acts introduced a divisional court in the PDA, which in Admiralty was used mostly for county court and justices' salvage appeals.[262] It often had to be made up with a judge from the QBD, which also had sometimes to provide a judge to hear cases at first instance, especially when Barnes was incapacitated for long periods in 1894 and 1902. Unfortunately this was often Gainsford Bruce, one of Halsbury's more questionable appointments. Bruce had plenty of experience of maritime law (hence the joke at the expense of his distinctive physiognomy that in Admiralty this was 'putting the chart before the horse') but his 'friendly blunders' were unfortunate;[263] the court was better served when Bucknill was seconded.[264]

In 1891–2 the team of Hannen and Butt was succeeded by R. Gorell Barnes and F. H. Jeune, the latter as President.[265] Jeune came to be regarded as a sound Admiralty judge but his inexperience resulted in some decisions, particularly *The Dictator*[266] making important and controversial changes; indeed he is said to have exerted 'a greater influence upon the doctrines of the Law of Admiralty than any single common lawyer since Coke'.[267] Though Barnes had done plenty of shipping

[258] *ODNB* 9: 247; H. E. Fenn, *Thirty Years in the Divorce Court* [n.d.], 22–6.

[259] Wiswall, *Admiralty Jurisdiction*, 122. Though Hannen's name was on a treatise on Admiralty practice, Fenn relates an (unreliable) anecdote that he picked up his Admiralty law from the court usher (*Thirty Years in the Divorce Court*, 20).

[260] P. Polden, *Mingling the Waters* (2002) 61 *CLJ* 575–611, 607–8.

[261] Wiswall, *Admiralty Jurisdiction*, 119.

[262] Other instances are given in Williams and Bruce, *Treatise on Admiralty Actions*, 441.

[263] Wiswall, *Admiralty Jurisdiction*, 124–6. He was co-author of the treatise mentioned in n. 215 above.

[264] He had been a leader at the Admiralty bar: J. E. G. De Montmorency, *John Gorell Barnes, First Lord Gorell* (1920), 65.

[265] Hannen became a lord of appeal in January 1891 and was succeeded as President by Butt, who died in May 1892. Jeune had replaced Butt as puisne. For Jeune (Lord St. Helier) see *ODNB* 30: 97–9.

[266] [1892] P64, 304.

[267] Wiswall, *Admiralty Jurisdiction*, 132.

cases neither was from the Admiralty bar, which continued to have a distinct existence and despite its small size could be a pathway to the bench; though when its leader, Walter Phillimore, was made a judge in 1897, it was of the QBD because he had a principled opposition to divorce.[268] Barnes did more Admiralty cases than Jeune and went out of his way to boost the work of the division by announcing his willingness to take insurance cases, with no opposition from the judges of the Queen's Bench.[269] He later instituted the short cause rules with a similar object, and was also instrumental in overhauling the Prize rules.[270]

Barnes became President in 1905[271] and though the choice of Bargrave Deane as the junior judge caused grumbling at the bar, critics probably overlooked the fact that before committing himself to the divorce bar he had experience in shipping cases and had written on blockade.[272] He proved decently capable, but was evidently not considered good enough to be promoted, for in 1910 Bigham (created Lord Mersey) was transferred from the KBD to succeed Barnes (now Lord Gorell), and when Mersey pleaded ill-health after less than one (turbulent) year, Deane was again passed over, this time for the Solicitor-General Sir Samuel Evans. It was an unpopular appointment at the bar but Evans, another with no love for divorce, worked assiduously to learn the Admiralty business and when the war brought in Prize cases he seized his chance to devote himself to that branch.[273]

Procedure and Organization

Procedure in the instance court bore a marked similarity to the ecclesiastical courts[274] and in some respects also resembled Chancery, but it had features which were unlike either. The most important of these was the facility for suitors in many actions to choose between actions *in personam* against individuals and actions *in rem*, the latter giving rise to a 'maritime lien' which bore little resemblance to liens known to the common law and equity.[275] In effect, the suitor could seek to have his claim satisfied against the vessel from whose activities it

---

[268] Alverstone, *Recollections of Bar and Bench*, 33; Fenn, *Thirty Years in the Divorce Court*, 14, 56; Phillimore to Schuster, 11 June 1920, LCO 2/460.

[269] De Montmorency, *Lord Gorell*, 78. The short-term effect was very marked: G. Alexander, *The Temple of the Nineties* (1938), 231.

[270] Wiswall, *Admiralty Jurisdiction*, 136.

[271] Oddly, it was first offered to Sir Edward Carson: E. Marjoribanks, *Life of Lord Carson*, (2 vols (1932), i, 324.

[272] Fenn, *Thirty Years in the Divorce Court*, 50–88.

[273] Roscoe, *Studies in the History of the Admiralty and Prize Courts*, 40–55; ODNB 18: 750–1.

[274] Holdsworth, *HEL*, xiii, 678–85, combines them in a single section.

[275] Wiswall, *Admiralty Jurisdiction*, 12–16, 155–208.

arose. Since ships were usually worth much more than the amount claimed and did not go bankrupt, most plaintiffs elected that route—indeed Lushington at one point prematurely declared the *in personam* action obsolete.[276]

In an *in rem* action the entry of the plaintiff's action in the registry was followed by a warrant to the marshal to arrest the vessel in the traditional way, nailing the writ to its mainmast. It had to remain in port unless bail were given and if the plaintiff's claim was upheld and his judgment not satisfied, then by means of further process and the legal fiction of 'perishable condition' he might have it sold. He would be paid from the proceeds after satisfaction of any prior 'latent demands' which had been notified by incumbrancers.[277] This meant that the court always possessed a substantial amount of money arising from the sales and awaiting distribution.

If the claim was disputed the usual process was by plea and proof. Admiralty pleadings bore some resemblance to Chancery's in being detailed and circumstantial and not aiming at defining the precise legal point at issue, but they were less elaborate. The plaintiff's 'libel' might be met by a general concession, a general denial or exceptions, and unless the parties agreed that their pleadings alone should form the material for the trial, witnesses had next to be examined.[278] As in Chancery these examinations were carried out in private by officers of the court—in theory by the deputy registrars but in practice by examiners chosen by the registrars from the proctors;[279] in the country commissions were issued to local solicitors or merchants. However, in Admiralty the defendant was informed of the witnesses' identity and what they were being called to prove, so he could frame cross-examination interrogatories to be administered after the examination-in-chief. The examinations were reduced to a narrative by the examiner and were then the subject of the defendant's 'responsive allegations'.[280] A similar process occurred with the defendant's witnesses and following the disclosures either party might call further witnesses. It was theoretically possible to examine *viva voce* in court but in 1823 no one could recall the last occasion.[281] Rothery was scathing about the whole pre-trial procedure, which he described as 'in many cases a mere mockery of justice, the delays were almost

---

[276] *Ibid.*, 62. In his treatise of 1860 Coote devoted only nine pages to the *in personam* action against 120 to the action *in rem*.

[277] Wiswall, *Admiralty Jurisdiction*, 12–16.

[278] *Ibid.*, 14–15; Holdsworth, *HEL*, xiii, 679–80.

[279] Wiswall, *Admiralty Jurisdiction*, 15; *RC on the Court of Admiralty 1824*, 9. Unlike Chancery, the parties' proctors were allowed to be present.

[280] Wiswall, *Admiralty Jurisdiction*, 15. Rothery's pamphlet (see below) has a detailed account of the process.

[281] *RC on Admiralty Court Report 1824*, 9.

interminable, and the result arrived at often far from satisfactory'.[282] However, although it certainly offered plenty of scope for deliberate delays, especially while the court offered only four motion days a term, Rothery was probably overstating the shortcomings in order to emphasize the improvements he and Lushington had made.

As in Chancery, many cases were concluded upon motion,[283] but for those which went to trial the judge sat without a jury, often assisted by two nautical assessors drawn from the Elder Brethren of Trinity House. Their role, much criticized by common law purists, was to advise the judge,[284] drawing on their experience of the ways of the sea and ships.[285] Their views were not decisive but even that champion of the common law Baron Parke said: '[w]e certainly are not bound, any more than the learned judge of the Admiralty Court was, by the opinion of the Trinity Masters; but we of course give great weight to their nautical experience, and we do not see any ground for being dissatisfied with the opinion that they have formed'.[286]

The ways of the court were thoroughly familiar to the close corporation of Doctors' Commons, but an outsider would have been hard put to find them out. There were no published sets of rules and although Arthur Browne had produced an admirable treatise on the law of Admiralty in 1802, there was no modern practice book; a new edition of *Clerks' Praxis* which rather oddly emerged in 1829 was little help, being no more than a reprint of an edition from the previous century.[287]

The key figure in interpreting and developing practice was the deputy registrar. The principal was a sinecurist. Lord Arden enjoyed this lucrative place (for which he had spent 26 years waiting for the reversion to fall in) and three deputies did the work.[288] Aided by a small clerical staff which, since both staff and office expenses were met by the registrar, was never likely to become extravagant,[289] they performed functions which in busier courts were parcelled out among several officials. They oversaw the preparation of warrants and other process;

[282] *Admiralty Court Third Return 1867*, 5.

[283] *SC on Admiralty Court, Report 1833*, Swabey, q. 636.

[284] e.g. 'On the Evidence Receivable in the Court of Admiralty' (1853) 30 (s3) *LM* 57–74.

[285] See Lushington's explanation in *The Speed* (1844) 2 W. Rob. 225. He much preferred their assistance to the submission of expert evidence by the parties: Waddams, *Law, Politics and the Church of England*, 199.

[286] *The Christiana*, 4 Notes of Cases 47, quoted in *Evidence Receivable in the Court of Admiralty*, 71. Lord Kingsdown explained the way it operated: *PD* 1861 (s3) 161: 1396.

[287] G. Browne, *A Compendious View of the Civil Law and the High Court of the Admiralty*, 2 vols; F. Clerke, *The Practice of the High Court of Admiralty*. They are discussed by Wiswall, *Admiralty Jurisdiction*, 7–8, 35–6.

[288] G. H. M. Thompson, *Admiralty Registrars* (ed. K. C. M. McGuffie, Belfast, 1958), 13–14.

[289] *RC on Admiralty Court, Report 1824*, 9–11.

sat in court to advise on practice; drew decrees and orders; taxed bills (costs in Admiralty were in the judge's discretion[290]), and arranged the lists.[291] On occasion, though not yet a regular practice, the judge referred to the registrar the computation of damages.[292]

The only other significant clerical officer was the marshal, and in the 1820s he too acted mostly through a deputy.[293] In 1805 the marshal's greed in levying exorbitant brokerage had forced Stowell to intervene, but in general he had no interest in checking abuses, maintaining that even if they existed any inquiry would damage the confidence of suitors.[294] The office of registrar had been ineffectually regulated by two Acts, 1810 and 1813, the first to prohibit it being granted in reversion and to compel personal performance, the second to limit the amount of public and suitors' money the registrar could hold, but to avoid compensation claims; neither was to take effect until Arden's death.[295]

A fuller inquiry in 1823 revealed almost 250 different fees in the three courts.[296] Lushington later expressed disappointment that this Commission had recommended continuing fees which had an historical legitimacy rather than a functional justification[297] and although the Prize fees (which tended to be higher) were somewhat reduced, no rationalization was attempted.[298] In the 1840s one clerk was employed full time in recording the fees, which were collected in arrear (sometimes considerably so) from the proctors.[299]

Arden's death in 1840 finally opened the way to place the court officials on salaries, the fees being paid into the consolidated fund.[300] The report of 1824 had expressed concerns at the lax accounting system which allowed the registrar to handle large sums without any adequate check and to profit from balances in his private account—suitors' money was invested only by express request.[301] Their concern was dramatically justified in 1853 when Arden's long-serving senior deputy and successor H. B. Swabey decamped leaving some £75,000 of suitors' and

[290]   Williams and Bruce, *Admiralty Jurisdiction*, 467.

[291]   *RC on Admiralty Court, Report 1824*, 10.

[292]   Wiswall, *Admiralty Jurisdiction*, 48–9.

[293]   *RC on Admiralty Court, Report 1824*, 53.

[294]   Bourguignon, *Sir William Scott, Lord Stowell*, 273–5.

[295]   Registrars of Admiralty and Prize Court Acts 1810 (50 Geo. III c. 118) and 1813 (53 Geo. III c. 151); *RC on Admiralty Court, Report 1824*, 13–15.

[296]   *RC on Admiralty Court, Report 1824*. It covered Admiralty, Prize, and the Delegates.

[297]   *SC on Admiralty Court, Report 1833*, qq. 570–1.

[298]   *Ibid.*, H.B. Swabey, qq. 593–6.

[299]   K. C. McGuffie, *Notes on Four Admiralty Registry Letter Books* (1964), 26, 68.

[300]   High Court of Admiralty (Fees) Act 1840, 3 & 4 Vict. c. 66.

[301]   *RC on Admiralty Court, Report 1824*, 12–14.

public money unaccounted for. Reform of the court's finances could no longer be deferred.[302]

It was not the only reform that was needed. Lushington had already made some practice changes. References to the registrar on the calculation of damages became the norm, and he greatly favoured the use of near-contemporary documentary evidence such as the 'Protest' in collision cases.[303] However, though the 1840 Act had expanded the possibility of using oral testimony, it was seldom invoked, while the facility to direct an issue to a jury was simply ignored.[304] A court which remained essentially unchanged when others were undergoing radical reforms was in danger of seeming as old-fashioned as the ecclesiastical courts.

The prime mover in bringing about reforms was H. C. Rothery, Swabey's successor, who had recently published a pamphlet on the subject.[305] Some of Rothery's propositions, notably a general move to printing documents, were not approved by all the proctors,[306] but he was in general strongly supported by the judge and had his way on essentials. To meet the immediate problem exposed by Swabey, stamps were introduced as a security and the fees were overhauled at the same time. Suitors complained they were too heavy while the Treasury was disappointed that they did not, as calculated, cover the costs of running the court.[307]

The same Act of 1854 made changes to the procedure for taking evidence, and rules of 1855 successfully encouraged the general use of oral testimony. Lushington retained a civilian's preference for writing, however, and one of his innovations was the 'Preliminary Act', by which in collision cases each party had to deposit, ahead of his pleadings, a sealed statement setting forth the basic details of the accident, from which he could not easily depart when subsequently framing his case.[308]

The intrusion of the common law bar necessitated more drastic reforms, for 'what was cramped in the old procedure, but had become easy of application to

---

[302] SC on the Defalcations in the Admiralty Registry, PP 1854 (351), xlii; Wiswall, Admiralty Jurisdiction, 51–2.

[303] On the Evidence Receivable in Admiralty (1853), 66–8. The 'Protest' was a statutory declaration of master and crew drawn up soon after the incident it describes.

[304] Williams and Bruce, Treatise on Admiralty Actions, 449; Waddams, Law, Politics and the Church of England, 198.

[305] Suggestions for an Improved Mode of Pleading (1853).

[306] Wiswall, Admiralty Jurisdiction, 83–5, and see also McGuffie, Admiralty Registry Letter Books.

[307] McGuffie, Admiralty Registry Letter Books, 25–30, 41–3, 68; Admiralty Court Act 1854 (17 & 18 Vict. c. 78) and rules, 1854; RC on Legal Departments, Evidence 1874, Bathurst, q. 8945.

[308] 'The Admiralty Court and its Reforms' (1858) 5 (s3) LM & LR 34–45, 40–4.

gentlemen who had passed their lives in acquiring this knowledge, threatened to become as noxious as it was imperfect, if it were made compulsory upon those who had not given to it the steady and enduring affection of the practitioner of the older school'.[309] In 1859 pleading by petition and answer was introduced alongside rules which, while 'approximating the practice of the Admiralty to the more elastic procedure of Common Law, preserved those original peculiarities of the court which were its excellencies and its boast'.[310] Perhaps the most useful improvement was to substitute a new default procedure for one which was clumsy and artificial.[311]

The rules were very shortly followed by an Act of 1861, which empowered the court to make orders for pre-trial discovery, greatly facilitated cross-actions and counter-claims and allowed actions to be brought *in personam* in all matters over which the Act conferred jurisdiction.[312] Roscoe viewed these several enactments as 'entirely altering the whole previous practice of the Court',[313] though this exaggerates their impact; it was still possible for pleadings to be tactically prolonged for example.[314] Greater elaboration led to more business being done in chambers, and to heavier costs.[315] Liverpool's shipping interest and law society brought in a bill to give its district registrar considerable devolved power in Admiralty, but it was emasculated in the Commons, leaving him with only the power to hear references.[316] The experiment, as the Legal Departments Commission described it,[317] was not extended, and of the district registries serving the High Court only Liverpool and to a lesser extent Cardiff provided significant business.

The Judicature Acts threw the court's staffing and organization into the melting pot, but Rothery had recently been appointed Wreck Commissioner and was therefore able to be dispassionate in appraising the position of Admiralty staff in the new structure.[318] Unlike most of the officials, he did not exaggerate the mysteries of his office and, subject to safeguards, was amenable to the absorption

---

[309] 'The High Court of Admiralty' (1859–60) 9 (s3) *LM & LR* 351–60 at 353.

[310] Coote, *High Court of Admiralty*, vii.

[311] Wiswall, *Admiralty Jurisdiction*, 56.

[312] *Ibid.*, 58–60. In 1896 17% of actions were *in personam*: *Civil Judicial Statistics 1896*.

[313] E. S. Roscoe, *A Treatise on the Admiralty Jurisdiction and Practice of the High Court of Justice* 3rd edn, 1903), 62.

[314] Wiswall, *Admiralty Jurisdiction*, 56–7.

[315] Bathurst's evidence to the Judicature Commission describes chambers practice (*Appendix to Fourth Report*, PP 1874 [C. 984], xxiv, 73). Rothery was able to obtain an assistant as a result: *RC on Legal Departments, Evidence 1874*, Bathurst, q. 8893.

[316] *Ibid.*, evidence of Bathurst (q. 8931) and F. D. Lowndes, qq. 9139–9226. District Registrars (Admiralty) Act 1870, c. 45.

[317] *RC on the Judicature, Second Report*, PP 1872 [C. 631], xx, 89.

[318] *DC on the Judicature Acts (Legal Offices)*, PP 1878 [C. 2067], xxv, q. 75. Rothery was highly regarded (see e.g. Aspinall, *RC on the Civil Service, Evidence*, q. 50,838, 'remarkably able', and

of the registry within the new central office.[319] The Jessel Committee proposed this, making the registrar a master of the Supreme Court,[320] but presumably Hannen, no doubt urged by Rothery's more conservative successor Bathurst (the last proctor-registrar), defeated it;[321] in fact the registry, which absorbed the marshal's office in 1896, even managed to retain control of taxations in the shake-up of 1901.[322] E. S. Roscoe told the Civil Service Commission that he was less often in court than formerly (and he was no longer able to sit as a surrogate[323]), his most important duty being references, while his assistant concentrated on taxations.[324] It was a cosy office, clerks mostly being promoted through seniority, and served a notably conservative bar and a body of specialist solicitors who had no desire for sweeping changes in the way it did its business.[325]

The same conservatism extended to practice and procedure, for the Judicature Acts had only a modest impact on everyday litigation. Phillimore had contended strongly for the preservation of a jurisdiction whose pleadings had been recast into a form closer to what the Commissioners favoured than any of the other courts,[326] and despite changes of form in the new pleadings the leading textbook continued to explain the leading principles of the old, 'more especially as the same principles continue to be followed in the Admiralty division'.[327] The comprehensive revision of rules in 1883 did bring significant changes; defendants putting in a belated appearance were no longer treated so indulgently for example, and procedures governing arrest of ships were considerably altered; but more often it either reproduced old rules in substance; where it did not, reliance could be placed on a 'preservation clause' which retained existing practices and procedures unless expressly displaced.[328] This clause was invoked to such effect that even the commencement of actions by *praecipe* was continued, and orders

Thompson, *Admiralty Registrars*, 19) and obtained an establishment the Treasury thought extravagant: LCO 1/87.

[319] *Ibid.*, qq. 1–122.

[320] *Ibid.*, 7, 9.

[321] Thompson, *Admiralty Registrars*, 20.

[322] See below, p. 791. *RC on the Civil Service Evidence*, qq. 49,432, 49,506.

[323] Thompson, *Admiralty Registrars*, 32, says the last occasion the registrar did this was in *The Vladimir* (1874).

[324] *RC on the Civil Service, Evidence*, qq. 49,395–49,545. The assistant registrar, Stokes, was a particular expert in this field: Thompson, *Admiralty Registrars*, 24–5.

[325] In 1922, for example, Roscoe said that the bar regarded references as a profitable preserve of their own and would oppose anything which threatened it: to C. Schuster, 28 March 1922, LCO 2/505

[326] *RC on the Judicature, First Report 1869*, 25. He later wrote that the High Court pleading rules were 'modelled on that in use in the Admiralty Court': quoted in Holdsworth, *HEL*, xii, 684.

[327] Williams and Bruce, *Treatise on Admiralty Actions*, 352.

[328] RSC 1883 , Ord. 5, rr 16–17.

for sale before trial were made despite a rule which seemed to confine them to the hearing.[329] By tortuous reasoning even the right to appear under protest was retained.[330]

After 1883 the Rule Committee seldom exercised its power to alter Admiralty rules and rule-making power was effectively left to the President.[331] Apart from the Short Cause Rules of 1908 changes were few, though of course practice did evolve over time. The monition as a means of enforcing judgment gave way to *fieri fascia*,[332] oral evidence came to predominate and the general use of informal motions in chambers lost favour to applications in open court.[333] However, the distinctive features of Admiralty actions remained largely intact. No jury was ever seen, and although there was very occasional resort to the assessors made available by the Judicature Acts, judges mostly preferred to use the Trinity House Brethren to aid their deliberations,[334] while the registrar drew on his panel of merchants in the assessment of damages.[335] As though to emphasize continuity with the past, Jeune even resuscitated the practice of having the silver oar borne in the judges' annual procession.[336]

The Prize Court

The Prize court was active only briefly during this period, the Crimean War providing the only worthwhile opportunity for captures.[337] The Naval Prizes Act 1864 (c. 25) tidied up a few debatable matters which had arisen from Lushington's 200 and more cases and in 1898 the rules were consolidated.[338] By then, however, developments in international relations and law made a more thorough revision desirable and although a bill of 1901 stalled so badly that it was finally abandoned,[339] Gorell recast the rules in the light of the Hague Convention and Declaration of London. Designed to bring the Prize court as nearly as possible, into line with Admiralty practice they were completed just in time, in August 1914.[340]

---

[329] Wiswall, *Admiralty Jurisdiction*, 103–4 (on rules of 1873, 1875), 116–21.

[330] Williams and Bruce, *Treatise on Admiralty Actions*, 276–7.

[331] C. Schuster to Sir K. Muir McKenzie, 17 May 1920, LCO 2/469. Thus rr 8 and 9 of 1901 were expressly stated not to interfere with Admiralty practice: Williams and Bruce, *Treatise on Admiralty Actions*, 424.

[332] Wiswall, *Admiralty Jurisdiction*, 20.   [333] *Ibid.*, 121.

[334] Williams and Bruce, *Admiralty Jurisdiction*, 442, 449.

[335] *RC on the Civil Service Commission, Evidence*, Aspinall, qq. 50, 818–50, 825.

[336] Fenn, *Thirty Years in the Divorce Court*, 31.

[337] Waddams, *Law, Politics and the Church of England*, 219–30. Lushington also decided the unique *Banda and Kirwee Booty Case* (1866) LR 1 Ad. & El. 109.

[338] Holdsworth, *HEL*, xiii, 683.   [339] LCO 2/146

[340] Roscoe, *Studies in the History of the Admiralty Courts*, 66–77; Report of the Admiralty Registry Committee, LCO 2/505.

3. THE COURT OF PROBATE

The Court

The new court was a court of record which assumed the entire testamentary juris-diction of the PCC other than suits to recover legacies or distribute the residue.[341] Its jurisdiction in contentious matters was exclusive, save that county courts out-side London could handle cases where the personal estate did not exceed £200 and the realty £300.[342] Proctors in practice in the ecclesiastical courts became entitled to be admitted as solicitors and to practise in the court alongside them, and advocates and barristers both had rights of audience.[343] Fees were set by the judge with Treasury concurrence and were in addition to the stamp duty on grants.[344] There were grumbles in the press at the cost of the court, but the fee yield in the 1870s was over £100,000 and only the hefty burden of compensations (over £200,000 initially) made it seem expensive.[345]

Unlike the Divorce court, there was no serious contention that a single judge would not be suitable to handle probate cases.[346] The problem was rather whether there would be enough work to occupy a full-time judge, and as noted above, the government's solution was to provide for a combined appointment, first with Admiralty and then with Divorce.[347] Like the Divorce judge, the Probate judge was empowered to call upon one or more common law judges to sit with him, but it is unlikely that he ever did so.[348]

Since they were to be operated by the same officers, and perhaps the same judge, and were driven through Parliament in tandem, it is not surprising that the rules, procedure, and practice of the Probate and Divorce courts were similar in many respects.[349] Some of the differences arose necessarily from the peculi-arities of their work. Thus while evidence was usually to be given orally in open court, the Probate judge faced none of the anxieties about collusion which pro-duced such complications in divorce, whereas he found it necessary to adopt a

---

[341] Court of Probate Act 1857, ss 3, 4, 23; Holdsworth, *HEL*, xv, 203–4. J. B. Langhorne claimed to have been the principal draftsman: *RC on the Legal Departments, Evidence 1874*, q. 8045.

[342] Sections 54, 58. An appeal on points of law lay to the Court of Probate.

[343] Sections 40–3.

[344] Sections 92, 95.

[345] *RC on Legal Departments, Evidence 1874*, Langhorne at qq. 8128–33. A departmental commit-tee report in 1893 concluded there was no public pressure to reduce fees: LCO 2/26. The stamp duty yield on grants was substantial, £5,400,000 in 1891.

[346] Hutton, *Reform of the Testamentary Jurisdiction*, 335.

[347] Court of Probate Act 1857, s 10; Matrimonial Causes Act 1857, s 65.

[348] Court of Probate Act 1857, s 34. Sir John Dodson was given a pension of £2000 a year as compensation for the loss of the probate business: s 109.

[349] Some of the sections of the two Acts are identical.

more expansive view of his power to order discovery of documents, particularly in cases turning on incapacity or undue influence.[350]

Practice was based on rules issued in 1862,[351] which preserved several leading features of the PCC. It was open to any interested party to enter a *caveat* obtained from any probate registry to prevent a grant being made in common form. On appearance being entered by someone set on obtaining a grant the matter would be entered in the court books.[352] If no *caveat* had been lodged, the person seeking to propound the will[353] issued a citation (along with a *caveat* in the registry covering the place where the testator last resided) to interested parties to appear.[354] Uniquely to the Probate court, all the parties were also required to submit an affidavit as to 'scripts', that is, to identify all known testamentary papers and to send those in their custody to the registry.[355]

Pleadings took the form of a declaration by the person propounding the will and a plea, which must not be merely a general denial, by those opposing him. The difficulties created by the retention of a different succession regime for real property were met by requiring the heir-at-law and any devisee or other person interested in realty of which the will purported to dispose to be made a party; if they were not cited they were not bound. The Act also perpetuated the right of persons interested in the realty to intervene to protect their interest before being made parties.[356]

Interlocutory business was brought before the court by petition or, from 1858, by summons in chambers.[357] The heir-at-law alone could demand jury trial; others might ask for a jury, and the Probate judge usually granted it in cases of fraud, undue influence, and incapacity.[358] In 1871 there were twice as many trials by judge alone as with a jury, and by 1881 (by which time special juries were generally

---

[350] T. H. Tristram, *The Contentious Practice of the High Court of Justice in Respect of Grants of Probate and Administrations* (1881), 195.

[351] Court of Probate Act 1857, ss 29, 30. The first rules were to be made by the Lord Chancellor with the concurrence of the judge and the Chief Justice of the Queen's Bench, with subsequent alterations made by the judge with their concurrence. The practice of the court was to be 'of the most simple and expeditious Character'. Rules of 1857, modified in 1858, were superseded by those of 1862.

[352] Rules 1862, 7–12; *Tristram on Contentious Probate*, 46–53.

[353] For convenience this discussion refers to instances where a will was in issue; *mutatis mutandis* a similar process governed applications for grants to the estate of an intestate, which constituted about one-third of all grants.

[354] Rules 1862, 13–22; *Tristram on Contentious Probate*, 54–61.

[355] Court of Probate Act 1857, s 26; rules 1862, 30–2; *Tristram on Contentious Probate*, 109–11.

[356] Sections 61–4; rules 1862, 6; *Tristram on Contentious Probate*, 112–16.

[357] Rules 1862, 64–70, 98–106. The same *lacuna* as to chambers existed in divorce and each was filled by an Act in 1858, in this case Court of Probate Act 1858, ss 3–5. The Act also made other changes to procedure.

[358] Court of Probate Act 1857, s 35; *Tristram on Contentious Probate*, 237.

preferred to common juries) the proportion was higher.[359] The judge also had discretion to send an issue to be tried at Assizes and would generally do so if it would be cheaper unless the party objecting was prepared to make up the difference.[360]

The Judicature Acts had little impact on the way the court of Probate operated. Probate business was preserved exclusively to the new division and Probate rules were left intact except where expressly altered.[361] Names changed (writs of summons replaced citations, statements of claim replaced declarations[362]) but the substance was generally similar. Business too remained at a surprisingly constant level. Despite an increasing number of grants, contentious matters never reached a level to justify a dedicated Probate judge, nor were they sufficient to create a specialist bar.[363] Around 200 actions a year were commenced, less than one-fifth of the division's workload, though a high proportion—some 60 per cent—went to trial. The judges shared probate work amicably, but despite a sprinkling of sensational cases it was not a field to make or mar reputations.[364] The court was generally uncontroversial and avoided official investigation.

The Principal Probate Registry (PPR)

The registry was headed by four registrars[365] with the senior having an ill-defined supervisory role. They performed four functions in rotation among themselves; one sat in court; another presided over the common form business; a third handled correspondence from the district registrars; and the fourth taxed costs in probate and divorce and dealt with references.[366] Registry clerks might become registrars directly, like Musgrave, or, like Owen and Inderwick, after a turn as district registrar.[367] The registrars held office during good behaviour, and while

---

[359] *Civil Judicial Statistics.* The figures for 1861 give only 17 judge-only trials against 23 by jury, perhaps reflecting a preference on Cresswell's part.

[360] Court of Probate Act 1857, s 38; *Tristram on Contentious Probate*, 238.

[361] Judicature Act 1873, ss 33–4.

[362] Citations were, however, preserved for some purposes: *Tristram on Contentious Probate*, 54.

[363] Only around 20% of the population left property to be administered: 'The Progress and Procedure of the Civil Courts of England' (1897) 185 *Edin. Rev.* 156–82 at 161–2. In the 1870s one-quarter of probated wills were 'tolerably long' and the average length was 11 folios of 90 words each: *RC on the Legal Departments, Evidence 1874*, C.J. Middleton, qq. 7718–19.

[364] *Civil Judicial Statistics*; Fenn, *Thirty Years in the Divorce Court*, 14. Accounts of judges' careers usually mention a few of the most celebrated cases.

[365] Court of Probate Act 1857, s 107. The fourth registrar was added in 1858 with the influx of divorce business. The first three had been deputy registrars of the PCC (s 15).

[366] *RC on the Legal Departments, Second Report 1874*, 78; *RC on the Civil Service, Sixth Report*, PP 1914–16 [Cd. 7832], xii, App. xcv. The Treasury wanted them made masters in the reorganization of 1882, when the starting salary was set at £1,200: LCO 1/76.

[367] Court of Probate Act 1858, s 8, replacing Court of Probate Act 1857, s 20; *RC on the Civil Service, Evidence*, A. Musgrave, qq. 44,488, 44,572.

Jenkins (whom Muir McKenzie considered the most able), retired at 70 on principle, one was still clinging on at 86.[368]

The registrars presided over what was by the standards of the day a considerable bureaucracy of around 150 clerks, copyists etc.[369] Since the PCC clerks had to be found positions as similar as possible to their existing ones, some men were clearly overpaid and there was confusion over conditions of service and entitlements.[370] On the other hand, some former PPR and proctors' clerks complained they had to become copyists with little hope of promotion.[371] They and newcomers, who needed a civil service certificate[372] and were invariably appointed to the lowest grade, found promotion was discouragingly slow and some of the abler clerks never did rise above the overcrowded third class,[373] which was particularly frustrating for university men or qualified barristers or solicitors.[374] Moreover, the exercise of judicial patronage in the registry exacerbated the tensions between PCC clerks and newcomers, which were further aggravated by some unpleasant manifestations of social snobbery on the part of some of the latter.[375] In 1905 Jeune improved matters somewhat through a purge of several of the oldest men, leaving only a few over 65,[376] but the registry was firmly wedded to the old ways, abhorring open competition, promotion by merit, and the employment of women; even by the standards of the SCJ it was old-fashioned.[377]

The registry occupied several houses in Doctors' Commons until it moved into Somerset House in the early 1870s.[378] This detachment from the core of the Supreme Court offices, and from its own judge (who was never seen there) was one

---

[368] *RC on the Civil Service, Evidence*, qq. 44,118, 46,399–404 (Musgrave); 60,850 (Sir S. Evans P).

[369] The Legal Departments Commission numbered it at 162, plus 31 supernumerary clerks and copyists. In 1914 there were 98 clerks, but this figure excludes, inter alia, the copyists and typists in the scrivenery department.

[370] Court of Probate Act 1857, s 16; *RC on the Legal Departments, Second Report 1874*, App. 14. A return to the Commission noted that 'many seeming discrepancies present themselves on the face of this return': *Evidence 1874*, App. at 557.

[371] *RC on the Legal Departments, Second Report 1874*, App. 15.

[372] Not a formality, since some nominees failed the examination: *RC on the Legal Departments, Evidence, 1874*, Middleton, q. 7666.

[373] *Ibid.*, Middleton, qq. 7670–1; *RC on the Civil Service, Evidence*, L. Churton Collins and E. W. Leader, qq. 46,532–618. The clerks had protested about the reorganization, which left two-thirds of them in the third class: LCO 1/76, 23 March 1882.

[374] In 1914 about ten had degrees and there were seven barristers and two or three solicitors: *RC on the Civil Service, Evidence*, Churton Collins and Leader, qq. 46,702–4, Musgrave, q. 46,513.

[375] 'Lynx' [W.B. Wilson], *A Plea for the Entire Suppression of Patronage, the Bane of H.M.'s Civil Service* (?1874).

[376] *Ibid.*, Musgrave, qq. 44,682–7, Churton Collins and Leader, qq. 46,613–16.

[377] *Ibid.*, evidence of Sir S. Evans and Musgrave and *Sixth Report 1915*, 29–30.

[378] *RC on the Legal Departments, Second Report 1874*, 79. Rumours of a further move proved ill-founded: (1901) 111 *LT* 344.

factor contributing to the minor slackness which pervaded the establishment.[379] It was originally divided into nine departments[380] and a tenth, the personal applications department, was added in 1862 to cater for individuals who presented themselves in person rather than employing a solicitor or other agent. Intended to accommodate the poor, they were a minority of its users, who became numerous enough for it to need more space.[381]

The procedure for obtaining a grant in common form was elaborate and often entailed several visits to the registry.[382] The central figures in the process were the four clerks of the seats, each assisted by six clerks, who prepared the grants for the registrar's signature.[383] It was claimed in the 1870s that their work was more demanding than in the old PCC because instead of dealing only with knowledgeable proctors they received papers from solicitors, whose mistakes were frequent; however, the Lisgar Commission was rather sceptical that London solicitors were still generally unfamiliar with probate forms.[384]

Unsurprisingly given the circumstances of its creation, the registry was admitted to be top-heavy and struck outsiders as overmanned.[385] Pemberton thought it could be trimmed by 20, but Hannen was pressed by the senior registrar to keep up the establishment as applications began to rise faster in the late 1870s.[386] The Lisgar Commission felt there was room for a substantial simplification and consolidation of duties but in fact because arrears in the copying of wills accumulated extra copyists had several times to be recruited.[387] The staff were reorganized in 1882 and modest changes in practice introduced, but with grants rising from 19,262 in 1879 to 28,649 in 1892 delays developed in the examining of wills and calendaring of documents which were investigated by a small committee in 1893.[388]

[379] e.g. the registrars' clerks did not always sign the attendance book and up to ten minutes' lateness was tolerated: *RC on the Civil Service, Evidence*, Evans (q. 60,782), Musgrave (qq. 46,428–32).

[380] Described in the *RC on the Legal Departments, Second Report 1874*, 78–9 and *RC on the Civil Service 1915*, App. xcv.

[381] *RC on the Legal Departments, Evidence 1874*, Middleton, qq. 7753–62; *Civil Service Commission Sixth Report 1915*, App. xcv. For the solicitors' unavailing attempt to keep out the law stationers see Abel-Smith and Stevens, *Lawyers and the Courts*, 206.

[382] It is conveniently described in H. C. Coote, *The Practice of the Court of Probate* (3rd edn, 1860), Ch. 11.

[383] 'A functionary of great importance' (*ibid.*, 186). Hannen successfully defended their high salaries, Hannen to Selborne, 27 June 1881: LCO 1/76.

[384] *RC on the Legal Departments, Second Report 1874*, 79.

[385] *Ibid*, 82; *Evidence 1874*, Middleton q. 7671. In that same year W. B. Wilson (as 'Lynx') attacked the continued tendency to nepotism in the registry, instancing Jenners, Middletons, Owens, and other families: Squibb, *Doctors' Commons*, 35–6.

[386] Pemberton's report, 13 July 1881; Hannen to Selborne, 27 June 1881: LCO 1/76.

[387] Middleton to Treasury, 29 April 1886: *ibid.*

[388] *RC on the Legal Departments, Second Report 1874*, 82. It was chaired by a registrar, R. Pritchard, and its limited importance is suggested by the fact that LCO representation was entrusted to Muir McKenzie's assistant, Adolphus Liddell: LCO 2/26.

The outcome was the creation of a scrivenery department along with a cautious degree of modernization, which fell well short of what Muir McKenzie had hoped for:[389] parchment gave way to paper and there was a cautious move towards typing. The 'very embarrassing' fact that some clerks worked a very short day[390] was intractable because of the likelihood of compensation claims, and the abandonment of the Judicature Bill of 1893 limited what changes could be accomplished.[391] Even the lengthening of opening hours from 11 am to 3 pm to 10 am to 4 pm in vacations was quietly abandoned with the connivance of solicitors.[392] As a later investigation showed, changes would seldom be initiated from within, for there had been no extension of typing, no innovations in indexing or record-keeping, and no provision for postal applications.

The District Probate Registries

The 30 or so district registries Cranworth had envisaged were expanded to 41 during the bill's passage. They included all but a few diocesan registries and some large cities—Newcastle, Birmingham, Manchester, Liverpool, and Wakefield—were added after strenuous lobbying.[393] Diocesan registrars or their deputies who were executing their duties in person and not deemed incompetent by reason of age, ill-health etc., were entitled to be made district registrar; otherwise the registrar was to be a barrister, solicitor, proctor, advocate, clerk to a proctor of Doctors' Commons, officer or clerk of the PCC, or the Prerogative court of York or of a diocesan court.[394] It was said in the 1870s that most registrars were solicitors in good practice, but Penzance refused to appoint men with local business connections and preferred clerks from the PPR. This alleviated a promotions block at Somerset House, but the smaller registries were not always an attractive proposition; Northampton for instance had to be hawked around the senior clerks.[395]

Barnes followed Penzance's approach but Jeune and Evans sometimes chose solicitors who would undertake not to practise in the district. Evans was sympathetic to representations from local law societies and, though wishing all

[389] Pencil annotations (probably by Muir McKenzie) on copy of the report in LCO 2/26.

[390] *Ibid.*, Herschell to Jeune P., 30 August 1893.

[391] Jeune P. to Herschell, 4 September 1893 and reply of 21 September 1893, *ibid.*

[392] *RC on the Civil Service, Sixth Report 1915*, 29–30; *Evidence*, Musgrave, qq. 44,642–5. Short hours had been criticized in the *Pall Mall Gazette*: (1892–3) 37 *Sol. J.* 776.

[393] Hutton, *Reform of the Testamentary Jurisdiction* 335–6, 345; *RC on the Legal Departments, Evidence, 1874*, Langhorne at qq. 8043–5.

[394] Court of Probate Act 1857, s 17.

[395] *RC on the Legal Departments, Evidence, 1874*, Langhorne at q. 8103, Middleton at q. 7923; *RC on the Civil Service, Evidence*, Churton Collins and Leader, qq. 46,600–1.

registrars to be whole timers, accepted that in the smaller places it was impracticable.[396] Even so, nearly two-thirds of the registrars in 1914 were from Somerset House.

The registrars were initially remunerated by fees[397] but in 1866 Penzance and the Treasury substituted salaries based on the number of grants and ranging from £1200 at Wakefield to just £200 at Bury St. Edmunds and Chichester. Unfortunately they made no provision for reviews, and anomalies developed; thus by 1914 the Exeter registrar had £1000 per annum for his 1116 grants while his Durham colleague issued 1713 and received only £500.[398] Most registrars supplemented their salary by 'agency fees'. There was no formal facility for postal applications but the registries prepared them for solicitors; this was often done by clerks at home (sharing the fees with the registrar) and since the charges were unregulated some registrars made more than their salary. Evans frowned on the practice but had not taken action, and the Civil Service Commission urged an end to it.[399]

Some registrars (and the Lisgar Commission) regretted that they had not been given a lump sum allowance for clerical staff, though county court experience suggested that it did not eliminate all the problems associated with the employment of clerks who occupied a position somewhere between public servants and private employees.[400] The Act (section 110) required the judge to fix both the number and the salaries of clerks he needed,[401] but it proved difficult to apply civil service regulations to these tiny establishments and the arrangements 'seem to have given rise to general discontent'.[402] District registry clerks complained that their salaries were mostly lower than those in the PPR, and were aggrieved at variations between registries.[403] Their biggest grievance, however, was they were not pensionable. Although the legal position was highly uncertain the Treasury persisted in this line despite the clerks' argument that the Judicature Act 1883 had

[396] *RC on the Civil Service, Sixth Report 1915*, 16; *Evidence*, Sir S. Evans, qq. 60,764–70, Musgrave, qq. 44,611–12 and App. C.

[397] Court of Probate Act 1857, ss 18, 111.

[398] *RC on the Civil Service, Sixth Report 1915*, 46 and *Evidence*, App. C. The inflexibility was regretted by the Childers Committee: *SC on Civil Service Expenditure, PP* 1873 (248), vii.

[399] *RC on the Civil Service, Sixth Report 1915*, 12, 30; *Evidence*, Sir S. Evans, qq. 60,786–99; and R. H. Mais, qq. 52,616–22. For defences of the practice see E. Alms and W. H. Shadwell, qq. 52,938–70 and A. E. Davis, qq. 53,164–86.

[400] *RC on the Legal Departments, Second Report 1874*, 85 and *Evidence, 1874*, Langhorne, q. 8055 and B. H. Hunt, qq. 8174–86.

[401] There were 162 clerks in 1914, 88 of whom had served more than 20 years: *RC on the Civil Service, Evidence*, District Registry Clerks, q.53,122.

[402] *RC on the Legal Departments, Second Report 1874*, 85. For the working of the scale see Langborne's evidence at qq. 8078–84.

[403] *Ibid*, 85 and App. at 148; *Evidence, 1874*, C. H. Turner, q. 8523.

made them civil servants.[404] One result was that, as in the county courts, veterans like a 95-year-old Chester clerk hung on grimly to their jobs.[405]

Though free of financial limits, district registries were subject to two others. First, they were strictly limited to non-contentious grants and must refer any query or doubt to Somerset House. This rule was strictly maintained and the policy behind it was never questioned, even when county court and Divorce registrars were given wider responsibilities.[406] The other, geographical, restriction was a bigger irritation. Registries could make a grant only where the deceased had an abode within the district, whereas the PPR was open to everyone.[407] It was highly inconvenient that the will of a Liverpool merchant who had lived in Birkenhead could be proved only in London or at Chester, and the Civil Service Commission recommended that the territorial limit be abolished.[408]

Even with these limitations the district registries proved popular. Initially they issued more grants than the PPR, and some attributed the gradual increase of London grants at their expense to their more costly process.[409] In addition, some were much resorted to for search purposes, more than 1000 a year at Wakefield,[410] and the registries were still custodians (sometimes reluctant ones) of old wills.[411]

It was inevitable, however, that a distribution which owed more to expediency than to logic would come under criticism during ambitious attempts to rationalize the whole judicial system. The Lisgar Commission was incredulous at the insistence of registrars of places issuing barely one grant a day that their clerks were fully occupied, and besides, the probate registries did not fit neatly either with structure of Assizes or county courts or with district registries of a new High Court, which would be located in many fewer places. The Judicature Commission wanted them absorbed into their proposed central county courts[412] and the Lisgar Commission, finding that project unlikely to be realized, favoured reducing

---

[404] *RC on the Legal Departments, Second Report 1874*; a clause in the 1858 bill which would have made them pensionable was dropped: *Evidence*, Langhorne, q. 8057. *RC on the Civil Service, Sixth Report 1915*, 46–7.

[405] *RC on the Civil Service, Evidence*, R. W. Jones, q. 53,120.

[406] Court of Probate Act 1857, ss 48, 50; *RC on the Legal Departments, Evidence 1874*, Turner, q. 8503.

[407] Court of Probate Act 1857, s 46.

[408] *Sixth Report 1915*, 47; see also *Evidence*, C. H. Morton, q. 52,692.

[409] *RC on the Civil Service, Evidence*, Alms et al., qq. 52,897–906. In 1871 district registries made 16,895 grants of probate and 6478 letters of administration as against 10,263 and 5036 from the PPR. In 1914, 37,578 grants issued from the PPR as against 34,489 from the rest.

[410] *RC on the Legal Departments, Evidence 1874*, Langhorne, q. 8023.

[411] *RC on the Civil Service, Evidence*, Mais, qq. 52,544–9.

[412] *Second Report 1874*, 14, 19.

their number, combining a smaller place like Lewes with one of its neighbours, Chichester or Canterbury.[413]

Defenders of the status quo had two practical, and related, arguments, besides pointing out that the principle of localism was fundamental to the Act. The first was that district registries provided a 'full service'[414] to applicants in person, who were frequently poor and, as one registrar described his Sussex people, 'very slow'.[415] The second was that other agencies could not match this. A recent Act instigated by Lord Chelmsford and Sir Richard Baggallay had enabled county court regis-trars to complete forms for letters of administration for small estates and transmit them to the district registry,[416] and the probate registrars triumphantly declared that the forms came riddled with errors, justifying their claim that probate was a complicated business which non-specialists would not be able to master.[417]

Much the same arguments were made to the Civil Service Commission 40 years on and it was equally unimpressed.[418] What spared the district registries in the 1870s,[419] was neither those arguments nor the more persuasive political threat that the forces of localism which had been mobilized to defeat the central-ist thrust in the 1850s would be aroused again.[420] Rather, as Muir McKenzie wryly admitted, it was patronage that defeated reforms.[421] He had wanted to amalga-mate the probate registries with district registries, but successive Presidents of the PDA had no intention of relinquishing their empire, nor would they reduce the number of registries.[422] They could take this stance with impunity because even the smallest district registry made a profit for the Treasury,[423] so that attempted reforms would bring into question the level of probate fees generally. Most witnesses to the Civil Service Commission recognized that the extravagant provision had become indefensible, but it remained to be seen whether the robust

---

[413] *Ibid.*, 83–4.

[414] G. R. Harman (Norwich), q. 8436; C. H. Turner (Exeter), qq. 8480–2.

[415] B. H. Hunt (Lewes), q. 8180. Personal applications ranged from 1/4 to 1/15th in the courts whose registrars gave evidence.

[416] Intestacy Act 1873 c. 52; for background see Langhorne's evidence, q. 8020.

[417] Evidence of Turner and T. Holt, q. 8489; Langborne, qq. 8111–13. Not everyone shared this view, see e.g. Hunt, q. 8202 and Harman, q. 8412.

[418] *Sixth Report 1915*, 47.

[419] The Intestacy Bill (above) had allowed them to make grants for estates worth less than £100, but the registrars got the clause removed: *RC on the Legal Departments, Evidence 1874*, Langborne, q. 8111.

[420] *Ibid.*, Turner, q. 8480; Langborne, q. 8009.

[421] *RC on the Civil Service, Evidence*, q. 43,146.

[422] Mais served on a small inquiry which seems to have had this object, evidently without success: *ibid.*, qq. 52,532–5.

[423] Even Bury St. Edmunds, with only 180 grants in 1874 was said by its registrar to be profitable: C. Wodehouse, q. 8230.

recommendation for the probate registries to be pruned and absorbed within the district or county court registries would prevail.[424]

4. THE DIVORCE COURT

Jurisdiction and Business

The Divorce court acquired its jurisdiction from three quarters. From the ecclesiastical courts came the power to make orders for the restitution of conjugal rights, to annul marriages, and to grant decrees of judicial separation (replacing divorce *a mensa et thoro*); the obsolescent suit for jactitation of marriage, due for abolition in the bill, was also preserved.[425] From the House of Lords came the power to grant full divorces, and from the common law courts came the controversial action for criminal conversation, transformed into an action for damages which might be brought in conjunction with a divorce suit or as an independent action.[426]

There was general uncertainty as to the likely volume of business; indeed the bill's supporters were in the awkward position of having simultaneously to deny that demand would be very great while insisting that a cheaper and simpler provision was necessary to meet unsatisfied need. From the outset petitioners were numbered in hundreds rather than tens and the great majority were seeking a divorce. The annual averages for the quinquennium 1859–63 were: divorce 204, judicial separation 53, nullity 4, restitution of conjugal rights 11, others 2, a total of 274 petitions. Fifty years later divorces had mounted to 787, judicial separations were 93, nullity 31, restitution 72, with one 'other'.[427]

Petitions for judicial separation therefore formed a significant part of the court's workload. This new action gave the court advantages over its predecessor; it might grant custody or provision for the maintenance and education of children, had wider powers of alimony, and gave the wife (who was almost invariably the petitioner) the position of a femme sole, enabling her to contract independently of her husband.[428] The commonest ground was cruelty, and Wilde's decision in *Kelly* v. *Kelly* signalled a less restrictive approach than had been taken by the

---

[424] *RC on the Civil Service, Sixth Report*, 1915, 47. It took a full decade to make significant changes: P. Polden *Guide to the Records of the Lord Chancellor's Department* (1988), 102–3.

[425] S. M. Cretney, *Family Law in the Twentieth Century* (Oxford, 2003), 142–3.

[426] Matrimonial Causes Act 1857, s. 59; Cretney, *Family*, 152–3. For the laws of divorce see XIII, pp. 724–6.

[427] *RC on Divorce, Report* (PP 1912–13 [Cd. 6478], xviii) and *Evidence* [Cd. 6479, 6480], vol. 3, App. iii, table 1.

[428] Matrimonial Causes Act 1857, ss. 24–6, 35; Cretney, *Family*, 149–50.

ecclesiastical courts.[429] However, the extension of magistrates' courts jurisdiction in this field, offering a cheaper remedy, diminished its relative popularity.[430] The decline pleased the Gorell Commission, which described it as 'an unnatural and unsatisfactory remedy, leading to evil consequences'.[431]

Nullity suits, which provided the court with some of its most difficult and 'sordid' cases, never made up much above 4 per cent of its caseload.[432] There was a marked increase in suits for restitution of conjugal rights from about 1901 onwards, but contemporaries felt that many were a preliminary step to a divorce.[433]

Divorce was always the court's staple business and those who had predicted that the new forum would make divorce more attractive even if the grounds were not widened felt vindicated. Hopes that the initial surge represented pent up demand were undermined by figures in 1862 which showed that while some suits were grounded upon adulteries of long ago, half of them alleged acts which had taken place since the Act.[434] The fact—unpalatable to many—was that the demand for divorce had been underestimated. And the phenomenon proved lasting: the number of petitions rose almost uninterruptedly (reaching 1000 in 1913) not just absolutely but as a proportion of the married population.[435] The number of petitions from wives was much remarked upon, though they had been considerable from the first (37 per cent in 1859–63), so that an increase to 44 per cent in 1908 was hardly spectacular.[436]

This rise in petitions owed little to judicial activism or legislative initiatives.[437] Subsequent statutory authority to question the parties about adultery in 1869 has been suggested as one cause for the more rapid increase in petitions in the early 1870s, along, less convincingly, with a suggested lessening of the stigma associated with the Divorce court following the Prince of Wales' well publicized appearance on the witness stand in the Mordaunt divorce.[438] A more clear-cut case is the swift

---

[429] (1870) LR 2 P & D 59; see XIII, pp. 789–92.

[430] *RC on Divorce, Evidence*, vol. 3, App. iii, table 1; *Civil Judicial Statistics 1896*.

[431] *RC on Divorce, Report 1912*, para. 226; *Evidence*, i, Sir B. Deane, qq. 826, 1122–31.

[432] *RC on Divorce, Evidence*, vol. 3, App. iii, table 1; Cretney, *Family*, 74–82. The suits alleging physical incapacity to consummate produced the most intimate details.

[433] See below, p. 744.

[434] PP 1862 (99), xliv, reprinted in A. Horstman, *Victorian Divorce* (1985), 88. Returns were also presented in 1859 and 1861.

[435] G. Rowntree and N. H. Carrier, 'The Resort to Divorce in England and Wales, 1858–1957', (1958) 11 *Population Studies* 188–233, table 2. The table includes petitions for nullity. The divorce rate, as measured in relation to married women aged 15–49, increased from 0.83 for 1861–5 to 2.03 in 1913.

[436] Horstman, *Victorian Divorce*, 85–6, and see MacDonell's introduction to *Civil Judicial Statistics* for 1896 and 1913.

[437] Rowntree and Carrier, 'Resort to Divorce', is the most detailed study. Sir John MacDonell was notably cautious about the causes: *RC on Divorce, Evidence*, vol.1, qq. 219–565.

[438] Horstman, *Victorian Divorce*, 145. See XIII, p. 786.

legislative response to Hannen's reluctant admission that he had no choice but to enforce a decree for restitution of conjugal rights by committal if necessary.[439] Solicitors seem to have been puzzlingly slow to appreciate that the so-called 'Weldon relief Act' of 1884[440] offered women a route which dispensed with the need to prove cruelty, but once they did, the number of suits increased.[441] Some judicial decisions may also have afforded encouragement, such as Penzance's less narrow view of cruelty (for wives) and his less rigorous demands for security and interim alimony (for husbands).[442] However, none of the judges showed any consistent desire to make the petitioner's task easier.

Indeed this was a court rather set upon discouraging business than otherwise. True, it was encouraging for petitioners that most petitions succeeded, that there were few appeals and no serious delays.[443] However, divorce remained such a costly process that for many it was out of reach, and there was little attempt to make it affordable. For example, while the statute allowed the court to sit outside London, it never did (and was probably never really intended to).[444] The effects showed in the profile of male petitioners for 1871; of the 77 per cent whose occupations are known, 41 per cent were gentry, professionals, or managers, 13 per cent farmers and shopkeepers, 6 per cent black-coated workers, and 17 per cent working men, mostly skilled artisans.[445] Although the last-named are surprisingly numerous, it seems that except on the improbable assumption that matrimonial misery was greatest higher up the social scale, there was a mass of what would later be called unmet need.[446] Moreover, many more of the suits commenced by petitioners of modest means foundered, often through a husband's inability to meet a demand for security and alimony pending suit.[447] Usually between 60 and 70 per cent of suits were successful, but the percentage only rose into the 80s in the 1900s.[448]

---

[439] Weldon v. Weldon (1883) 9 PD 52.

[440] Matrimonial Causes Act 1884, c. 16.

[441] RC on Divorce, Report 1912, para. 102, drawing on the evidence of Sir George Lewis; Cretney, Family, 145–6.

[442] Horstman, Victorian Divorce, 145.

[443] RC on Divorce, Evidence, vol. 3, App. iii, table 3. Other judges had occasionally to be brought in to help, perhaps not always with satisfactory results: C. Willcock, vol. 1, q. 4756.

[444] Matrimonial Causes Act 1857, s. 12. O. R. McGregor, Divorce in England (1957), 18. When it was pointed out that for the full court to travel was hardly feasible a shake of the Attorney-General's head was understood to convey that it was not intended to do so: PD 1857 (s3) 146: 1153–82, 1192.

[445] Rowntree and Carrier, 'Resort to Divorce', table 11. Compare RC on Divorce, Report 1912, 39, and see MacDonell's explanation of the difficulties of such classifications (Evidence, vol. 1, q. 439).

[446] Not, of course, universally acknowledged. See e.g. 'The Progress and Procedure of the Civil Courts of England' (1897) 185 Edin. Rev. 156–82: 'Divorces at the present time can be obtained without undue expense and with reasonable facility' (161).

[447] Horstman, Victorian Divorce, 148.

[448] RC on Divorce, Evidence, vol. 3, App. iii, table 3. Few trials ended in favour of the respondent and there was a big increase in the proportion of decrees nisi made absolute, from 73% (1868–72) to 99% (1894): Civil Judicial Statistics 1896.

Though cost was the biggest, it was not the only, discouragement. One was the fear of the Queen's proctor's intervention, another the inability of the court to prevent the publication of salacious newspaper reports.[449] Moreover, where the judges had been expressly given discretion, in the so-called discretionary bars, they generally adopted a rather restrictive approach. In cases such as *Clarke*, *Wyke*, and *Churchward*[450] their criteria for not letting the petitioner's adultery prevent the grant of a decree left little scope for the discretion to operate at all; no wonder that it was later claimed that only 64 petitioners in the first 50 years even asked for it to be exercised.[451] If divorce petitions increased unrelentingly it was certainly not through any judicial encouragement. A handful of judges, supported by a close-knit bar and seldom hampered by the waywardness of a jury, were able to establish norms which did not always find a clear expression in reported cases and were seldom disturbed upon appeal.[452] And those norms were mostly conservative.

Judges and Officers

An unusual feature of the Divorce court as originally established was that the judge ordinary was empowered to sit alone in any suit except for divorce. In divorce he would deal with the pre-trial stages but the trial was reserved for the full court, in which he would sit alongside two others from the most senior judges of the common law courts and the Lord Chancellor.[453] This was not one of the 'eccentricities of the Act of foundation'.[454] The bill followed the Campbell Commission in favouring a bench of three and its composition reflected the gravity with which divorce was to be regarded.[455] Furthermore three judges were thought more likely to detect collusion, and reinforced the fact that this was a court of common law, where the practice was for decisions by judges in banc, rather than an ecclesiastical court, where a single judge was customary.

During the long and exhausting debates on the bill several MPs had pointed out that a court so composed would be unable to deal with a large caseload without disrupting the common law courts, and though the government added the three senior common law puisnes, the critics were quickly vindicated, and the

---

[449] See below, pp. 752–3.

[450] *Clarke* v. *Clarke & Clarke* (1865) 34 LJ (PA & M) 94; *Wyke* v. *Wyke* [1904] P 149; *Churchward* v. *Churchward and Holliday* [1895] P 7. See also XIII, p. 794.

[451] *RC on Divorce, Report 1912*, para. 368; Cretney, *Family*, 193.

[452] Cretney, *Family* , 400–1.

[453] Matrimonial Causes Act 1857, c. 85, ss. 8, 9.

[454] P. W. J. Bartrip, 'County Court and Superior Court Registrars 1820–1875, the Making of a Judicial Official', in D. Sugarman and G. R. Rubin (eds), *Law, Economy and Society* (Abingdon, 1984), 349–79 at 373.

[455] *PD* 1857 (s3) 145: 483–92.

next concession, extending to all common law judges, also proved inadequate.[456]
The obvious solution was adopted in 1860, entrusting full jurisdiction to the
judge ordinary; and while St. Leonards was justified in remonstrating that the
divorce bill would never have passed on that basis, he had no practicable alternative to offer.[457] The Act contained placatory gestures, allowing the judge ordinary
to summon another judge to assist him and/or to refer a case to the full court.
They were probably never envisaged as regular occurrences and in fact the first
was never done and the second very seldom; in 1871 the full court sat just thrice
as against 227 trials before the judge ordinary.[458]

The 1860 Act was a vote of confidence in the judge ordinary, Sir Cresswell
Cresswell. Though not the first choice he proved a very satisfactory one.[459] The
imperious and overbearing demeanour which made him an uncomfortable and
unpopular colleague in the Common Pleas was equally evident in his new court
where 'the discipline he enforced was perhaps too much that of a martinet',[460]
but it created a solemn courtroom atmosphere which reassured doubters, and
the judge made himself a master of the law as well as of the court. However, by
the time his life was abruptly terminated by an accident he was finding the work
'irksome and oppressive'[461] and it did not seem likely to attract the best men.
Cresswell was followed in 1863 by an Exchequer puisne, J. P. Wilde, less forceful and with more liberal inclinations. These, however, found more expression
in debates in the Lords after he was created Lord Penzance in 1869 than on the
bench. Penzance sat on the Judicature Commission, capably protecting his own
court, but before it had concluded its deliberations he retired through ill-health,
though since he became a judge of ecclesiastical courts and lived until 1899, his
retirement seems rather premature.[462]

The first choice as successor, J. D. Coleridge, declined but Sir James Hannen
was happy to leave the Queen's Bench, where Cockburn and Blackburn gave
little scope to the junior puisnes.[463] Hannen presided over the court for nearly

---

[456] *PD* 1857 (s3) 145: 795; 146: 1153–82; 155: 141–2; Matrimonial Causes Act 1859, s. 1.

[457] *PD* 1860 (s3) 157: 815, 1873–83; 158: 126–34; Matrimonial Causes Act 1860, s 1. St. Leonards proposed that a single common law puisne should sit with the judge ordinary, but a strong representation from the Chief Justice of the Queen's Bench was read to Parliament decrying the depletion of
his court for divorce hearings and describing it as a 'pure waste'.

[458] Civil Judicial Statistics 1871, *PP* 1872 [C. 600], xxx.

[459] It was turned down by Bethell and Sir William Erle: T. A. Nash, *Life of Lord Westbury*, 2 vols
(1888), ii, 61; Fenn, *Thirty Years in the Divorce Court*, 15.

[460] W. Forsyth, 'Sir Cresswell Cresswell' (1865–6) 20 (s3) *LM & LR* 179–88 at 186. See also Manson,
Builders of our Law, 124–32.

[461] Forsyth, *Sir Cresswell Cresswell*, 185.

[462] *ODNB* 58: 904–5.

[463] Coleridge to his father, 11 November 1872, E. H. Coleridge, *The Life and Correspondence of John
Duke Coleridge*, 2 vols (1904), ii, 214; *ODNB* 25: 79.

20 years and was the first President of the division. Coleridge may have exaggerated in claiming that he had seen no greater judge than Hannen[464] but he was unquestionably an extremely able one. However, as Jeune said, it was not so much for his decisions that he was held in such high regard as for his 'careful…independent, and…decorous administration day by day'.[465] Hannen may have carried the austerity and sobriety of the Divorce court too far for some tastes,[466] but he repressed the ever-likely outbreaks of levity, prurience, and cynicism inherent in its business, and his frigid but even-tempered demeanour, added to his decisiveness in imposing his own views on practice and rules and the polished clarity of his judgments made him, in the eyes of some contemporaries, 'a judicial ideal'.[467]

The Divorce bar took its character from the judges. A separate bar began to form once it became clear there was enough divorce to make it feasible, and in time solicitors who, unlike many of the best firms, were not too fastidious to take on divorce, notably Lewis and Lewis, Wontners and Charles Russell and Co, also became known.[468] In Hannen's time the barristers tended towards obsequiousness in court and affected a portentious gravity that echoed the judge's own.[469] They were required to tread an often delicate ethical line in cases with facts which neither party wished to disclose and which if revealed would jeopardize the decree. They were scrupulous in bringing forward inconvenient facts which had been incautiously disclosed to them and they, and their judges, argued that this was essential to the integrity of the divorce process; ordinary barristers, and especially country solicitors, could not be relied upon to meet the same exacting standards.[470] Hence the Divorce bar opposed devolution and provided the Gorell Commission with materials favouring their stance.[471]

The first leader of the bar after the Judicature Acts, F. A. Inderwick, was regularly passed over for the bench,[472] but Bargrave Deane was more fortunate. After Butt's brief presidency the Divorce court resumed its accustomed ways under Sir Francis Jeune, who, like his predecessors, held aloof from public arguments

---

[464] Quoted in *ODNB* 25: 79.

[465] *Ibid.*

[466] Hence the story that when he rebuked an outbreak of laughter with 'this is not a theatre, Charles Butt retorted *sotto voce*, 'no, and it isn't a church either'.

[467] See below, p. 988.

[468] J. Juxon, *Lewis and Lewis* (1983), 306.

[469] 'E' [Bowen Rowlands], 'Leaders of the Bar' (1896) 12 *Strand Mag.* 559–71 at 561.

[470] See e.g. *RC on Divorce, Evidence*, vol. 1, qq. 1339–40 (Lord Mersey); Bar Council (W. English Harrison) and Divorce bar (W. T. Barnard, J. C. Priestley, and C. J. Willcock).

[471] P. Polden, *A History of the County Court, 1846–1971* (Cambridge, 1999), 108–9.

[472] Fenn, *Thirty Years in the Divorce Court*, 60. His son became a registrar.

about the working of the divorce laws. Gorell Barnes, however, made a deliberate and considered attempt, in *Dodd* v. *Dodd*[473] to bring their deficiencies before the public.[474] Subsequently Barnes had to chair a royal commission where he found his preference for extending divorce facilities strongly opposed by his own bar. The bar prevailed, and having survived first the brief incursion of Lord Mersey, who 'brought the spirit of the commercial court to the trial of matrimonial causes',[475] and then the arrival of Evans, impatient and irritable, prospered in a wartime boom in business.

Since the Divorce court was not expected to need much clerical support, it was to be serviced by the new principal probate registry.[476] The registrars seem to have sat in rotation in court and as in other courts, gradually acquired extra powers and duties.[477] From the outset they were to settle the questions for the jury,[478] and in 1858 were required to tax costs.[479] They could hear minor motions (and more substantial ones which arose in the vacations)[480] and in 1865 Wilde gave them important further duties, particularly to investigate the financial position of the parties as disclosed in the pleadings for subsequent proceedings about maintenance and marriage settlements.[481] This ancillary business was taking increasing court time and before the Judicature Commission the judge, the author of the standard textbook,[482] the solicitor W. T. Pritchard, and the senior registrar Middleton all agreed more business needed to be devolved, though Pritchard felt an extra registrar would be needed and he and Hannen wanted to remove the divorce registrar from Somerset House to a more convenient location.[483] It was presumably as a result of this that in 1875 a new rule (191) made the registrar the person to decide (subject to appeal) on claims for both alimony pending suit and permanent maintenance.[484] Thenceforth the registrar was as much a junior judge as an administrator, and further judicial duties were given to him.[485] There was, however, no call for a separate divorce registry.

---

[473] [1906] P. 189; Cretney, *Family*, 200–11.

[474] De Montmorency, *Lord Gorell*, 11–12, introduction by Ronald Gorell. See XIII, pp. 799–801.

[475] *ODNB* 5: 702–4.

[476] Matrimonial Causes Act 1857, s. 14.

[477] *RC on the Judicature, Fourth Report 1874*, 92, evidence of Clarkson, Son & Greenwell; P. W. J. Bartrip, 'An Historical Account of the Evolution of the Registrars' Jurisdiction in Matrimonial Causes', in W. B. Baker et al., *The Matrimonial Jurisdiction of Registrars* (1977), 95–108.

[478] G. Browne, *A Treatise on the Principles and Practice of the Court for Divorce and Matrimonial Causes* (3rd edn, 1876), 233.

[479] Matrimonial Causes Act 1858, s 13.

[480] *Browne on Divorce*, 253–4.   [481] Bartrip, 'Evolution of Registrars' Jurisdiction', 99.

[482] George Browne, see above.   [483] *Fourth Report 1874*, Evidence, 72–92.

[484] Bartrip, 'Evolution of Registrars' Jurisdiction', 99.

[485] *Ibid.*, 100.

Procedure and Practice

Outside divorce, the court was to act 'on principles and rules...which shall be as nearly as may be conformable [to those] on which the Ecclesiastical Courts have heretofore acted and given relief'.[486] The rules accompanying the Act were heavily amended in 1866 but the Judicature Acts excepted the divorce court rules from the RSC save where specifically altered and few changes were made before the Gorell Commission.[487]

Pleadings commenced with a petition setting out the full facts upon which the petitioner relied (but not supporting evidence) and a claim for relief;[488] as noted above, a claim for damages against an adulterer might be included, or be mounted separately.[489] Originally a petitioner need select only one or more from several alleged adulterers as co-respondents, but that was soon disapproved by the court and the 1866 rules required all those against whom allegations were made to be made parties unless the judge directed;[490] this, of course, created problems of identification which generated a complex set of sub-rules and practices.[491] Unnecessary delays and costs were occasioned by the common practice of allowing a general charge of adultery to be tacked onto the specific ones, obliging the respondent to seek further particulars.[492]

Service had usually to be in person and a citation required the respondent to enter an appearance, usually within eight days.[493] However, judgment by default was not available because of the obvious danger of collusion: the requirement that the petitioner prove his case 'will be found to pervade the entire practice of the Court, and to cause very important deviations from the course pursued in other Courts'.[494] If the respondent did not appear, judgment was pursued through a motion and supporting affidavit.[495] Unless they were confined to a pure denial, answers also had to be accompanied by an affidavit,[496] and although Lyndhurst had hoped to see 'no labyrinths of that description'[497] there was scope for

---

[486] Matrimonial Causes Act 1857, s 22.

[487] Judicature Act 1873, s 18; *Wilson's Judicature Acts, Rules, Forms &c* (5th edn, by M. Muir McKenzie and C. Arnold Wilson, 1886), 118.

[488] Rule 1 of 1866; *Browne on Divorce*, 195–203.

[489] The civil judicial statistics did not distinguish such actions. By 1956 separate actions had become uncommon: Cretney, *Family*, 156.

[490] Rule 4 of 1866, following *Carryer* v. *Carryer* (1864–5) 34 LJ (PMA) 47 rather than *Hunter* v. *Hunter* (1859) 28 LJ (PC PD & Ad. M. Eccles.), 3.

[491] *Browne on Divorce*, 204–5.   [492] *RC on Divorce, Report 1912*, para. 429.

[493] Rule 10 of 1866; *Browne on Divorce*, 209.   [494] *Browne on Divorce*, 218.

[495] *Ibid.*, 218–19.

[496] Rules 28, 30 of 1866. Answers had to be delivered within 21 days after the service of the citation.

[497] *PD* 1857 (s3) 145: 499.

replications and rejoinders, though once a pleading denied an allegation in the petition the parties were regarded as being joined in issue.[498] In practice divorce pleadings tended to be short and straightforward,[499] but these rules escaped critical examination until the Gorell Commission, which saw no reason why the normal procedure by writ should not be adopted here, as elsewhere in the division, and felt the accompanying affidavits served no useful purpose.[500] In suits for a divorce *a mensa et thoro* the ecclesiastical courts had been generous in allowing amendments to the petition, but the Divorce court became less ready to admit fresh claims of pre-petition adultery or cruelty, and the practice changed, such allegations usually having to be made in a supplementary petition instead.[501]

Interlocutory proceedings were by summons for minor matters and motions for the more important.[502] In 1858 the judge was empowered to sit in chambers, where motions were usually heard, with a pointless and almost unused appeal from the judge in chambers to the judge in court.[503] One indispensable motion was for directions as to the mode of trial. From the 1870s the court used its power to direct an issue to be tried at the Assizes only in exceptional circumstances,[504] but it always had to decide whether to have a jury trial. Only in suits for damages was a jury mandatory, and judges felt that their awards showed disquieting variations.[505] In divorce suits either party might require one, otherwise it was within the judge's discretion.[506] Though Hannen claimed not to be opposed to having a jury in suitable cases,[507] by 1896 only one trial in seven was a jury trial and the proportion declined further;[508] the bar was more convinced of its merits than the judges.[509]

The most time-consuming of the common interlocutory applications was the wife's claim to alimony pending suit and sometimes security for costs. This was originally heard in open court with the parties present, but the view of a leading practitioner that: 'it seems hardly possible to conceive a worse tribunal for adjusting complicated accounts than an oral examination of witnesses in

---

[498] Rule 32 of 1866; *Browne on Divorce*, 228.

[499] *DC on the Judicature Acts (Legal Offices) Report 1878*, q. 224 (C. J. Middleton).

[500] *RC on Divorce, Report 1912*, paras 425–6.   [501] *Browne on Divorce*, 239–40.

[502] *Ibid.*, 250–5.

[503] Matrimonial Causes Act 1858, s 1; *RC on the Judicature, Fourth Report 1874*, registrars' evidence, 72–4.

[504] Matrimonial Causes Act 1857, s 40; E. S. P. Haynes, *Divorce Problems of Today* (1910), 47, citing the refusal in *Snowball* v. *Snowball* (1871) in contrast to *Richards* v. *Richards* (1861).

[505] Matrimonial Causes Act 1857, s 33; *RC on Divorce, Evidence*, vol. 1, q. 875 (Deane); Cretney, *Family*, 155 n.87.

[506] Section 28.

[507] (1886–7) 31 *Sol. J.* 14.

[508] *Civil Judicial Statistics 1896, 1913*. See also *RC on Divorce, Report 1912*, paras 397–405.

[509] *RC on Divorce, Evidence*, vol. 1, qq. 1056 (Deane), 1276–81 (Mersey), 4100–9 (Barnard).

open court'[510] prevailed and from 1866 these applications were referred to the registrar.[511]

The most difficult problem was with evidence. Although its proceedings were generally to be governed by the recently reformed rules of common law, applying general principles to matrimonial causes posed several special problems.[512] First, it was felt necessary to exempt the petitioner from having to answer questions about his own adultery unless he had expressly denied it in his pleadings.[513] Perhaps a precaution against requiring him to commit a still punishable offence under ecclesiastical law, it presented a serious obstacle to the court's battles against collusion but it was not modified when the Evidence Further Amendment Act 1869 (c.68) removed other limitations, ending the necessity for an earlier provision making both parties competent and compellable on a wife's petition to give evidence of cruelty or desertion.[514] Even so, the rules of evidence in divorce could produce outcomes which, as in the *Dilke* case, seemed puzzling and absurd to the lay public.[515]

Oral evidence was the preferred mode and many witnesses before the Gorell Commission were emphatic on the desirability of the judge seeing the witness in open court.[516] The broad powers intended to be given to the court to accept affidavit evidence had been regarded with suspicion, and that which allowed the parties 'to verify their cases in whole or in part by affidavit' was very sparingly exercised—denied where witnesses were difficult to bring to London, where there would be a great saving of expense, and where the petitioner was poor.[517]

Even with the witnesses before them, however, the court was often uneasy, fearing collusion, either in the narrower sense, of some agreement between the parties to arrange the financing, conduct, and terms of a divorce, or more broadly, the concoction of a false case or mutual concealment of a material fact that would jeopardize their suit.[518] For this reason the court had been enabled to appoint a counsel for a party who did not appear,[519] but that did not allay fears that there were insufficient means to detect collusion.[520] Brougham's solution was to make the Attorney-General or some other public officer a party to all matrimonial

[510] *Browne on Divorce*, 157–72 at 158.
[511] Rule 191 of 1866.
[512] Matrimonial Causes Act 1857, s 48.
[513] Section 43.
[514] *RC on Divorce, Report 1912*, paras 101, 384.
[515] Cretney, *Family*, 175.
[516] Matrimonial Causes Act 1857, s 46; *RC on Divorce, Evidence*, Sir George Lewis, Lord Mersey, and Sir Bargrave Deane, vol. 1, qq. 1622, 754, 813.

[517] Section 46 and rr 51–5 of 1866; *PD* 1857 (s3) 157: 1755; *Browne on Divorce*, 260–1.

[518] Cretney, *Family*, 166–8. As the evidence to the Gorell Commission shows, the wider and narrower usages were liable to confuse discussions.

[519] Matrimonial Causes Act 1860, s 5.

[520] *PD* 1857 (s3) 147, especially 1695–1702, 1717–27, and see e.g. the sceptical view in (1859–60) 4 *Sol. J.* 443.

suits[521] and this was taken up by the government in 1859, amid criticisms that undefended cases were being processed with the rapidity of a judgment summons, the inference being that no serious attempt was being made to sniff out collusion.[522] However, the Commons struck out the clause, rightly sceptical that a law officer would find time for this duty,[523] and the 1860 bill substituted a more obscure official, the Queen's proctor, coupled with a suggestion of Cranworth's, to divide the granting of the decree into two stages, with three months following a decree nisi in which the Queen's proctor or any member of the public might challenge it.[524] Cranworth's other idea, for a sort of banns in reverse, to be called in the couple's locality, was left out and how the Queen's proctor would obtain information was allowed to remain rather mysterious, presumably to create the impression of more effective means than really existed.[525]

To extend the Queen's proctor's opportunities for intervention the interval between the decree nisi and the decree absolute was extended to six months in 1866 and his jurisdiction to nullity cases in 1878.[526] No one really knew how widespread collusion was nor how effective the Queen's proctor was in combatting it. Many felt with Lord Ludlow, that the court was brimful of collusion, but Ludlow found himself unable to detect any when he came to sit there.[527] Hannen had complained that he lacked the time to investigate all the undefendeds with due care, and suggested that a recent enactment had made the Queen's proctor more wary of intervening.[528] Originally, though the proctor was awarded costs if he proved collusion, he was not liable to pay them if he failed, and when this changed in 1878 he became more cautious.[529] Lord Alverstone testified that in his time as Attorney-General he authorized only interventions which were certain of

[521] 'Remarks on Certain Defects in the Procedure of the Divorce Court' (1858–9) 6 (s3) *LM & LR* 380–6.

[522] *PD* 1858 (s3) 150: 2194–5; 151: 157–61. J. F. MacQueen, in *A Practical Treatise on the Law of Marriage, Divorce and Legitimacy* (2nd edn, 1860) drew attention to this.

[523] *PD* 1859 (s3) 155: 141–50, 510–17.

[524] *PD* 1860 (s3) 157: 126–34, 1734–51; Matrimonial Causes Act 1860, s 7. The Treasury solicitor acted as Queen's proctor: see G. L. Savage, 'The Divorce Court and the Queen's/King's Proctor: Legal Patriarchy and the Sanctity of Marriage in England, 1861–1937' (1989) *Historical Papers, Quebec*, 210–27.

[525] *PD* 1859 (s3) 155: 145. The best contemporary account is in Lord Desart's evidence to the Gorell Commission, vol. 2, qq. 15,745—16,014. See also Savage, 'Divorce Court and the Queen's/King's Proctor', 224–5 and Select Committee on the Legal Business of Government, First Report, *PP* 1877 (199), xxvii.1, qq. 283–442, evidence of Sir F. Hart Dyke.

[526] Matrimonial Causes Act 1866, s 3, Matrimonial Causes Act 1878, s 2. For returns see *PP* 1873 (303), liv and *PP* 1877 (14, 164), lxix.

[527] *RC on Divorce, Evidence*, vol. 1, q. 915 (Deane). Ludlow (formerly Lopes LJ) was presumably assisting the court when one of its judges was ill.

[528] (1879–80) 24 *Sol. J.* 113.

[529] Matrimonial Causes Act 1878, s 2 gave the court full discretion in these circumstances, overturning cases such as *Rogers* v. *Rogers* (1862) 31 LJ (PMA) 101.

success, so that while the Queen's proctor examined all undefendeds (anywhere between 306 and 631 cases a year), his interventions numbered only 11 to 34, and it was reckoned that he thwarted only 5 per cent of petitioners.[530]

Very different views on the extent of collusion and the operations of the Queen's proctor were presented to the Gorell Commission. The former incumbent, Lord Desart, indignantly denied accusations that the proctor concentrated on the poor[531] (sometimes with catastrophic results for a petitioner who was caught out[532]), but then the rich and well advised could better conceal their adulteries. Alverstone felt that not 10 per cent of the 'misconduct' cases were detected and very few of the true collusions[533] and Sir George Lewis's view that there were relatively few was flatly opposed to that of Sir Edward Clarke.[534] The Commission wisely declined to form a conclusion.

An unfortunate side-effect of the change from written to oral evidence was that the Divorce court soon became a place for salacious public entertainment.[535] Worse, newspaper proprietors declined to join a high-minded self-denying ordinance proposed by Delane of *The Times*,[536] ensuring that the juicier items, 'more suggestive than actually indecent',[537] gained a wider circulation. The Queen was appalled that 'what is daily brought and laid upon the breakfast-table of every educated family in England' was more scandalous than the worst French novels.[538] Her ministers agreed, but the Attorney-General's clause enabling the court to sit in camera in divorce cases[539] was rejected by the Commons,[540] and several subsequent attempts to curb reporting failed.[541]

---

[530] Horstman, *Victorian Divorce*, 102; *RC on Divorce, Evidence*, vol. 2, qq. 15,493, 16,002, and figures in the Report, at 54. Alverstone complained that a recent decision of the Court of Appeal had increased the vulnerability of the proctor to costs awards, but Mersey claimed to be pleased that his decision had been reversed: vol. 1, q. 568; vol. 2 q. 15,508.

[531] Volume 2, q. 15,745. Freke Palmer's criticism (q. 14,974) was echoed by Haynes, *Divorce Problems of Today*, 67–71. A sample of cases studied by Savage ('Divorce Court and the Queen's/King's Proctor', 223) suggests that these criticisms were unfounded.

[532] e.g. F. Rowland (q. 15,792) and Arthur Newton (q. 15,372) and Savage, 'Divorce Court and the Queen's/King's Proctor', 219–24.

[533] Volume 2, q. 15,494. [534] Volume 1, q. 1677; vol. 3, q. 42,158.

[535] S. M. Cretney, '"Disgusted, Buckingham Palace...": Divorce, Indecency and the Press, 1926', in *Law, Law Reform and the Family* (Oxford, 1998), 91–114 at 94–5.

[536] *RC on Divorce, Evidence*, vol. 3, q. 42,261 (T. H. Tristram).

[537] *RC on Divorce, Report 1912*, para. 474. [538] *Ibid.*, para. 477.

[539] The position in nullity was less clear cut. After some uncertainty s 22 of the 1857 Act, which required the court to follow the practice of the ecclesiastical courts, was held to permit sittings in camera and this discretion was frequently exercised: *A v. A* (1875) 44 LJ (P&M) 15; *Browne on Divorce*, 256; W. R. Rayden, *Practice and Law...in the Divorce Division of the High Court* (1910), 6.

[540] *PD* 1859 (s3) 155: 141–50, 510–15, 1367–75. Bethell said the clause was suggested by the judge ordinary, but apparently the other judges of the court were unfavourable: *RC on Divorce, Evidence*, vol. 3, q. 42261 (Tristram).

[541] *RC on Divorce, Report 1912*, para. 478.

The Gorell Commission was concerned enough to supplement extensive testimony with some research into press coverage.[542] The Commission came out decidedly in favour of imposing restraints,[543] but not all were convinced, and when Bargrave Deane overstepped the bounds of his contempt powers in seeking to prevent one undesirable publication, the House of Lords resoundingly reaffirmed their view that open justice outweighed the dissemination of intimate sexual details.[544]

However, by far the biggest brake upon the resort to divorce was its cost. Estimates varied, but there was a widespread view that even an undefended divorce with local witnesses would cost £30 to £40,[545] a defended action at least £100.[546] There were plenty of cases of men who had saved for ten years for the purpose, sometimes to find themselves defeated by a demand—often unmeritorious—for security for costs, or even by the court's own schedule if their case went into a second day.[547] Gorell claimed that he had done something to reduce both those obstacles,[548] but in 50 years the court did little else to make its proceedings more affordable; it was left to a solicitor to suggest modest procedural changes which would trim several pounds off the court fees.[549]

In theory the truly poor could use the *in forma pauperis* procedure (section 54), but in practice there were such discouragements that barely one-tenth of cases in 1890 were brought under its aegis and later only ten to 15 a year.[550] One big drawback was that at least from 1890 the court declined to assign a solicitor and counsel to act,[551] and since the registry officials were not reputed very helpful, few poor petitioners dared dispense with a solicitor, so even an *in forma pauperis* case would cost 25 guineas.[552] No wonder the poor flocked to the police courts, where a separation order could be had for as little as six shillings.[553]

[542] *Ibid*, paras 471–520; the analysis is in 475.

[543] *Ibid.*, paras 518–19.

[544] *Scott* v. *Scott* [1913] AC 417. Reporting was eventually curbed in 1926 after complaints by George V, initially provoked by *Russell* v. *Russell*: Cretney, 'Disgusted, Buckingham Palace'.

[545] Registrar Musgrave's estimate was adopted by the Gorell Commission (*Report 1912*, para. 69) and witnesses generally agreed it was out of reach of the working man (para. 74). Similar evidence had persuaded the Gorell Committee on County Courts.

[546] *Ibid, Evidence*, vol. 2, Freke Palmer, q. 14,827.

[547] *Ibid*, vol. 1, Deane, q. 798.

[548] *Ibid*, vol. 2, Palmer, q. 14,912; W. E. Hume Williams, q. 17,259.

[549] *Ibid.*, vol. 1, T. Smith Curtis, q. 4035.

[550] Petitioners filed 50 to 60 suits a year between 1907 and 1909 (*RC on Divorce, Report 1912*, paras 69, 73); Horstman, *Victorian Divorce*, 148–51.

[551] (1905) 119 *LT* 28; *RC on Divorce, Evidence*, vol. 2, Palmer, q. 14,832.

[552] *RC on Divorce, Evidence*, vol. 2, Palmer, q. 14,822. A personal application department like that in the probate registry was suggested by one official: W. Waterton, *Report*, App. 21.

[553] *Civil Judicial Statistics 1896*, introduction; G. K. Behlmer, *Friends of the Family, The English Home and its Guardians, 1850–1940* (Stamford, Cal. 1998), 181–230.

The exclusion of the poor had been a complaint from the beginning. Although almost any forum and procedure would have been cheaper than a private bill,[554] the Divorce court had been presented as affordable to persons of modest means, though many government supporters must have privately echoed Macaulay's scornful denunciation of that 'claptrap observation'.[555] Not only did the expense give ammunition to those who wanted to extend divorce facilities to county courts, but it enabled out-and-out opponents of divorce like Gladstone to make mischief by pointing out that the existing provincial facility (albeit not for full divorce) was being replaced by one which most could not afford.[556] As an inadequate response to these points Bethell produced a clause enabling judges at Assize to grant orders for judicial separation and restitution of conjugal rights, but he ensured it was repealed at the first opportunity.[557] Devolution of matrimonial causes, even to superior court judges, was strictly eschewed.

The county court solution to a problem which was becoming difficult to ignore reappeared rather unexpectedly as a proposal of Gorell's Committee on County Courts, and the ensuing Divorce Commission, while stopping well short of that drastic move, did propose to devolve divorce to selected county court judges sitting in borrowed plumage as commissioners for divorce in a few provincial centres.[558] The Commissioners preferred this to any large-scale attempt to fund impecunious litigants in the Divorce court, though it suggested small improvements to the *in forma pauperis* procedure.[559] That scheme, renamed the Poor Persons' Procedure, soon afterwards underwent a thorough revision and was imposed upon the PDA just before the war despite the petulant opposition of the President to this unfamiliar 'meddling with my little division'.[560] Many thought that some meddling was rather overdue.

Since the court regarded the granting of a decree as its principal function, it postponed consideration of ancillary relief—decisions on the custody of children and financial provision—until after the decree.[561] However, it was often necessary to consider at an earlier stage applications for alimony pending suit and

---

[554] Though the Divorce Commission exaggerated the cost: J. S. Anderson, 'Legislative Divorce: Law for the Aristocracy?', *Law, Economy and Society*, 412–44 at 436–42.

[555] *PD* 1857 (s3) 147: 1182.

[556] *PD* 1857, esp. 146: 1068–77; 147: 1170–84, 1236–57.

[557] *PD* 1857 (s3) 147: 1843–51; Matrimonial Causes Act 1857, s 10; Matrimonial Causes Act 1858, s 19. The Gorell Commission was puzzled at this turn of events: *Evidence*, vol. 1, Deane, qq. 959–62.

[558] Polden, *History of the County Court*, 107–8. Public attention was aroused by the six-judge hearing in *Harrman*: Haynes, *Divorce Problems of Today*, 55.

[559] *Report*, paras 409–20.

[560] Evans to Haldane, 18 December 1913, LCO 2/320. He had initially refused to accept them.

[561] Cretney, *Family*, 395–414 at 402.

sometimes interim custody too.[562] The court had a very broad discretion over how much maintenance or alimony it could direct, though it developed norms which probably followed fairly closely the practice of the ecclesiastical courts.[563] Its powers were, however, limited to making a secured provision and only from 1907 could unsecured periodical payments be ordered.[564] Under the 1866 rules the registrar became a key figure, hearing these applications (which required a fresh petition) in the presence of the parties and submitting a report to the court. Unless exceptions were taken, the report was invariably adopted and in many cases the terms had doubtless been agreed between the parties, though with the caution necessary to avoid a possible accusation of collusion.[565]

Until the Judicature Acts the losing party in a suit heard by the judge ordinary had the absolute right to appeal within three months to the full court,[566] and from there lay a further appeal to the House of Lords.[567] This was a presumed oversight in the Judicature Act 1873, section 18, which omitted to bring divorce within the scope of the new Court of Appeal, and was rectified in 1881.[568] The PDA divisional court handled a variety of matters, the biggest caseload being appeals from separation orders made by magistrates, but had no role in appeals from the judge in the Divorce court.[569]

[562] Above, and *Browne on Divorce*, 150, 157–72.

[563] Cretney, *Family*, 400, 409–11. Maintenance was the term properly used in divorce, alimony in judicial separation.

[564] Matrimonial Causes Act 1857, s 32, Matrimonial Causes Act 1907, c. 12.

[565] Rules 189–92.

[566] Judicature Act 1873, s 55. Described by Dr Spinks in 1874 as 'a mockery, a delusion and a snare', only ever used to gain time since the common law puisnes who usually made up the full court were almost never known to reverse the judge ordinary: *RC on the Judicature, Fourth Report 1874*, 75.

[567] Section 56, extended to nullity cases (for the avoidance of doubt) by Matrimonial Causes Act 1858, s 17.

[568] Judicature Act 1881, s 9. See the note in *Wilson's Supreme Court of Judicature Acts, Rules and Forms*, 158.

[569] For a list of its functions see *Rayden on Divorce*, 4–5.

VI

The Judicature Acts

1. FUSION BY CONVERGENCE

In Eldon's time there were signs of doctrinal convergence between law and equity. His approbation of remarks by Lord de Grey CJ and Lord Mansfield that they never liked equity so much as when it resembled the law and vice-versa[1] were consonant with his own notions of equity[2] and although equity occasionally displayed its continuing capacity for parthenogenesis—the restrictive covenant and the curious equitable tort of breach of confidence both emerged under the procedurally conservative Lord Cottenham[3]—it was not, in general, expansive. The common law was gradually coming to exhibit a more broadly equitable approach, at least inasmuch as through reforms to the law of evidence and pleadings and a greater control over jury verdicts judges fine-tuned their decision-making in the light of a fuller knowledge of the factual matrix.[4]

In institutions and personnel, however, the separation became more complete.[5] Chancery barristers ceased to go circuit and the court sat more often in Lincoln's Inn. The Exchequer, which had dispensed both law and equity (albeit impermeable to their interpenetration[6]), lost its equity side in 1841. The great sessions of Wales, on which judges dispensed both law and equity, had already been abolished and the courts of requests, licensed to deal out rough and ready equity, were replaced by county courts which did not acquire an equitable jurisdiction until 1865.[7]

The 'fusion' of law and equity, whether in its most ambitious form of a code combining their doctrines, or in the narrower sense of enabling each be to dispensed

---

[1] *Dursley* v. *Fitzhardinge Berkeley* (1801) 6 Ves. Jun. 252, 260; A. L Lincoln and R. L. McEwen (eds), *Lord Eldon's Anecdote Book* (1960), 162.

[2] Though he was by no means inflexible: D. Klinck, 'Lord Eldon on "Equity"' (1999) 20 *JLH* 51–74.

[3] *Tulk* v. *Moxhay* (1848) 18 LJ Ch. 88; *Prince Albert* v. *Strange* (1849) 1 Mac. & G. 24; F. R. Burns, 'Lord Cottenham and the Court of Chancery' (2003) 24 *JLH* 187–214.

[4] J. Getzler 'Patterns of Fusion' in P. Birks (ed.), *The Classification of Obligations* (Oxford, 1997), 157–92 at 185–90.

[5] Selborne felt this was harmful to equity: P. Polden, 'Mingling the Waters' (2002) 61 *CLJ* 575–611 at 581.

[6] Sir John Romilly MR, *PD* 1870 (s3) 200: 187.   [7] See below, p. 878.

within the same court, did not feature on the reformist agendas of practical men until around 1850. It then emerged onto centre stage through a combination of negative publicity for the divided system and the favourable reception given to the code of New York expounded by David Dudley Field on his two visits to Britain.[8]

These events coincided with (and helped to produce) renewed investigations into the superior courts. The law officers rejected the opportunity to stage a wider inquiry[9] and the parallel operations of separate commissions on common law and Chancery greatly influenced the approach to fusion. Once each commission had completed its review of the major remaining defects of procedure and organization, it turned to those caused by the want of remedies, procedures, and facilities which belonged to the other side—with a view to remedying the complaint that recourse to two courts was often needed to obtain justice.[10] The Chancery Commission cautioned that to achieve doctrinal fusion would require an entire revision of the law and that 'to blend the courts into one Court of universal jurisdiction'[11] was a change of such magnitude that it required fuller consideration, but concluded that most of the practical complaints could be met by endowing each court with the full armoury of legal and equitable remedies. It did postulate a major functional difference between the types of case for which each court was best suited, but while admitting that the common ground, where litigants might choose either a court of law or one of equity, would be enlarged by these facilities, denied that this would cause any difficulty, instancing fraud, account, and debts of deceased persons as existing areas where this created few problems.[12]

In furtherance of this approach, Chancery was given the power to decide common law questions without reference to common law judges; to hold oral examinations of witnesses; to assemble a jury to determine disputed questions of fact; and to award damages in lieu of injunction or specific performance.[13] Few of these additions were either sought or welcomed by the judges, most of whom continued in the old ways and shunned the new.

Parallel developments took place across the divide. The first Common Law Commissioners had argued for expanded facilities to compel the production of documents and for the pre-trial discovery of facts, and these were conceded 'very partially' in 1852.[14] The courts also obtained new or extended powers to

    [8] M. Lobban, 'Preparing for Fusion: Reforming the Nineteenth-Century Court of Chancery, Part II' (2004) 22 *LHR* 565–99 at 584–5.

    [9] *Ibid*, 586.

    [10] 'Equity sends questions to Law; Law sends questions back to Equity; Law finds it can't do this; Equity finds it can't do that…' *Bleak House* (1853), Ch. 8.

    [11] *RC on Chancery, First Report*, PP 1852 [1437], xxi, 2.   [12] *Ibid.*, 3.

    [13] See above, Ch. IV, and M. J. Lobban, 'Preparing for Fusion, Part Two', 586–9.

    [14] *RC on the Common Law, Second Report*, PP 1831–2 (239), xxv, 20–3; *RC on Common Law Courts*, PP 1852–3 [1626], xl, 34.

grant injunctions, relieve against forfeiture, admit interpleaders, and hear and decide upon equitable defences.[15] Some of the older common law judges had little enthusiasm for these innovations,[16] but a new generation had a more adventurous outlook and its representatives on the Commission were impatient with the limitations on their new powers.[17] They agreed with the Chancery Commissioners on the desirability of co-ordinated jurisdiction, but expressed themselves more boldly: 'the courts of common law, to be able satisfactorily to administer justice, ought to possess in all matters within their jurisdiction the power to give all the redress necessary to protect and vindicate common law rights and to prevent wrongs, whether existing or likely to happen unless prevented'.[18]

The premise seemed unimpeachable, yet the Commission's demands, in particular for injunctions against threatened wrongs and for specific performance, met with opposition. The equity judges denounced them as unacceptable[19] and they had to be stripped from Campbell's bill before it could pass.[20] The Commissioners had, with a mixture of arrogance and naïveté, overreached themselves. They might disclaim any ambition 'to extend, for the mere sake of extending, the field in which the courts have common jurisdiction, by giving to the Common Law Courts powers which may be exercised with equal benefit in the Court of Chancery',[21] but their real intention was just as unacceptable to equity lawyers and judges, being to create '[a] contrary and more effectual mode of putting an end to the contest between Courts of Common Law and Chancery by so distributing their jurisdiction as to render their interference with one another impossible'.[22] The aim was all too clear: to confine Chancery to those areas 'entirely outside the pale of the common law jurisdiction'[23] and to recapture exclusive jurisdiction over all areas within its own purview. From the tone of their brief comment on ejectment it is evident that they regretted the separate existence of equitable estates in land, and they envisaged taking back even so central a part of equity as mortgage actions.[24]

[15] Common Law Procedure Act 1854, ss 79, 83; Common Law Procedure Act 1860, ss 1–18; Lobban, 'Preparing for Fusion, Part Two', 589.

[16] e.g. Lord Wensleydale, *PD* 1860 (s3) 158: 18.

[17] Jervis was the only judge on the original commission, but Martin, Bramwell, Willes, and Cockburn were all raised to the bench during its deliberations.

[18] *RC on the Common Law, Third Report*, PP 1860 [2614], xxxi, 5–6.

[19] (1859–60) 4 *Sol. J.* 408. The reply of the three common law judges who were members of the Commission is at 639.

[20] *PD* 1860 (s3) 158: 1–21; 159: 834, 1616; Lobban, 'Preparing for Fusion, Part Two', 590–1.

[21] *RC on Common Law, Third Report 1860*, 13.   [22] *Ibid.*, 14.

[23] *RC on Common Law, Second Report 1853*, 38.

[24] *RC on Common Law, Third Report 1860*, 12. The *Solicitors' Journal* (1859–60) 4, 358, asserted that 'if carried, [the bill] will revolutionise, for good or evil, the whole juridical system of England'.

Though this was obviously a turf war, there were more presentable reasons for Chancery men to object. Chancery judges often exaggerated the importance of the common law courts' want of their own elaborate machinery for handling complex accounts and ongoing administrations, but there were legitimate doubts about the ability of a common law judge at *nisi prius*, unassisted by the Chancery bar, to handle sophisticated and unfamiliar equitable doctrines. Some judges were not only ignorant of these equitable doctrines but disparaged them; Commissioners Bramwell and Martin were notorious for this, while Cockburn would later argue that once the common law adopted those equitable glosses which its rigidities had made necessary, distinct equity courts would be almost redundant.[25]

Even the idea that courts of law and equity might simply compete for litigants within their concurrent jurisdiction ignored the fact that inconsistent pronouncements on law by Chancery judges and on equity by their common law counterparts would only confuse both branches, leaving the unsatisfactory forum of the House of Lords to decide between them.[26] The defeat of Campbell's proposals marked the end of this route to fusion, and there followed a lull during Westbury's Chancellorship—oddly, for he had been a very vocal advocate of fusion.[27] Fusion was resurrected by Gladstone's Attorney-General Sir Roundell Palmer, whose royal commission was novel in comprehending the organization and jurisdiction of all the superior courts, common law, equity, and civilian.[28] The membership was as wide as the remit (though like its predecessors it was a judge and lawyer-dominated body) and Palmer's choice of Sir Hugh Cairns, eminent both as a Chancery lawyer and a Conservative politician, as chairman was shrewd. Equally significant was the omission of all three chiefs, Cockburn, Kelly, and Bovill.

2. THE JUDICATURE COMMISSION AND THE JUDICATURE ACTS

The Commission's deliberations stretched over almost seven years and resulted in five reports. Its remit was expanded first to embrace inferior and local courts and then to consider the desirability of tribunals of commerce, and its membership also grew, notably on the common law side, the chiefs being added when tribunals

---

[25] Polden, 'Mingling the Waters', 581–2; Sir A. E. Cockburn, *Our Judicial System* (1860), 20–1.

[26] Common law practitioners feared, or affected to fear, that unscrupulous solicitors would send common law cases into Chancery in the hope of extracting a favourable decision from an inexpert judge: Lobban, 'Preparing for Fusion, Part Two', 593.

[27] *Ibid.*, 584–5.

[28] *PP* 1868–9 [4130], xxv. The Commission was issued on 18 September 1867.

of commerce came into question. The final strength of 27 was far too large for effective deliberations and no doubt a few members took the major part.[29]

All the Commission's really important work was contained in its first two reports, but while the first was largely carried into effect, key parts of the second were not.[30] As the trail of dissents and caveats to the second report shows, the Commission struggled for an agreement on the crucial matters of the delivery of justice in the provinces and the relationship between the superior and inferior courts, whereas its composition almost guaranteed that it would dismiss the demand for tribunals of commerce.[31] Investigations into chamber practice— where it did little more than print evidence[32]—and public prosecutors (delegated to a committee and doubtfully within the terms of the Commission) followed. However, instead of fulfilling its promise to grapple further with the vexed question of Assizes, the Commission wound up anticlimactically with the tame conclusion that it would be 'inexpedient to prolong our inquiry into these matters'.[33]

The achievements of the Commission have been valued very differently.[34] The Judicature Acts are described by Stevens as 'the most sweeping reform in the history of the English courts',[35] while for Manchester they were 'little more than a useful...summation of a piecemeal, evolutionary process which had taken far too many years to achieve; above all, an opportunity to make a radical overhaul of the whole system was missed'.[36] Sir Jack Jacob, acknowledging that they were 'a turning point in English legal history', found them 'in many respects...short-sighted and even myopic about the needs of the administration of justice'.[37] Those disposed to belittle the reforms of the 1870s can cite the failure to effect a doctrinal fusion of law and equity; the over-elaborate structure of appeals, and the survival of the Assizes. The last two at least demonstrated the obstacles to any radical reform posed by vested interests and entrenched prejudices. The collapse of other legal reforms of the time—the attempt to codify the criminal law and to modernize lawyers' education and the inns of court—underlines just how formidable those obstacles were, especially when coupled with the distractions of more

---

[29] Selborne named Hatherley, James, Cairns, and Hollams: *Memorials, Personal and Political*, 2 vols (1898), i, 46. Sir J. Hollams, *Jottings of an Old Solicitor* (1906), 242–3, mentions James and Quain.

[30] *PP* 1868–9 [4130], xxv; *PP* 1872 [C. 631], xx.

[31] *PP* 1874 [C. 957], xxiv.   [32] *PP* 1874 [C. 984], xxiv.

[33] *PP* 1874 [C. 1090], xxix, ix. Cockburn wrote to Cairns that it made a rather ignominious conclusion to their work: 4 August 1874, NA PRO Cairns Mss PRO 30/51/10.

[34] Selborne's own account is in his *Memorials, Personal and Political*, i, 298–315. The appeals controversy is fully explored in R. Stevens, *Final Appeal: The House of Lords as a Judicial Body* (1979) and some aspects of the making and working of the legislation in Polden, 'Mingling the Waters'.

[35] Stevens, *Final Appeal*, 351.

[36] A. H. Manchester, 'Law Reform in England and Wales 1840–80' [1977] *Acta Juridica*, 189–202 at 193.

[37] Sir J. I. H. Jacob, 'The Judicature Acts 1873–1875—Vision and Reality', *The Reform of Civil Procedural Law and Other Essays in Civil Procedure* (1982), 301–22 at 301, 302.

pressing or 'popular' business in Parliament (the Public Worship Regulation Bill in 1874 and the Eastern Question in 1878 for example) and make what was achieved as impressive as it was undoubtedly limited. Moreover, what was then put into place provided a platform for further reforms, though politics and personalities ensured they did not follow.

The Commission was emphatic in its conviction that a continuation of piecemeal reforms would be insufficient to remedy the 'evils' stemming from a divided judicature. It insisted that the remedy lay in creating a single court with judges dealing out common law or equity as appropriate. True, this full court would seldom sit, save where its judges made up the court for Crown Cases Reserved, but each judge would be competent to hear cases in any of the chambers or divisions into which the court would be divided for administrative convenience. This radicalism was sensibly tempered by the recognition that it would be prudent to 'facilitate the transition from the old to the new system' by initially retaining the identities of the existing courts as distinct divisions and distributing business among them more or less on the existing footing.[38]

Even with these concessions there was enough that was threatening to traditionalists on both sides of the law/equity divide to provoke strident opposition. On the common law side the most influential critic was Chief Justice Cockburn. He suggested that the common lawyers on the Commission had only accepted its proposals for fear of more drastic ones,[39] and certainly the threat to fundamental features of common law practice—to pleadings, juries, and sittings in banc—warranted concern. But Cockburn's chief fear was a loss of independence and the subjection of his and other common law courts to the Lord Chancellor, anxieties the structure of the proposed court hardly supported.[40] Many on the equity side were equally alarmed and with at least as much reason. They would be a small minority in the new court, their distinctive jurisprudence (whose rarefied sophistication they were liable to exaggerate[41]) threatened by common lawyers who neither understood it nor respected it.[42] Since the proposed reforms also fell short of what more radical reformers, such as the Master of the Rolls, wanted,[43] it should have been clear that a bill to implement those proposals would need the most delicate and diplomatic management.

From Lord Hatherley (a member of the Commission) it received neither. He took too little trouble to conciliate the judges, and seems not to have consulted Cairns, a pivotal figure, with the result that Cockburn presented a petition from the judges

---

[38] *First Report 1869*, 9.   [39] *Our Judicial System*, 4.
[40] Polden, 'Mingling the Waters', 579–82.
[41] See e.g. the scornful response of Sir John Holker quoted in *ibid.*, 581.
[42] Lobban, 'Preparing for Fusion, Part Two', 593–9.   [43] *PD* 1872–3 (s3) 214: 725.

against one key aspect of the reforms[44] and not only Cairns but two former Lord Chancellors in Westbury and Chelmsford were severely critical.[45] Worse, the bill itself was a mere skeleton, and by leaving most of the sensitive questions to be dealt with in rules it only confirmed the worst fears of partisans of law and equity alike. Despite substantial concessions it had to be abandoned and reform stalled until Palmer returned from his self-imposed exile to become Lord Chancellor Selborne.[46] Selborne learned from his predecessor's experience. His bill was accompanied by the rules, Cairns' general approval was gained[47] and further necessary concessions were made. The divisions kept their old names, with the Queen's Bench tactfully listed first, ahead of Chancery.[48] The Chief Justice of the Common Pleas and Chief Baron were named among the 'presidents' of divisions alongside the Lord Chancellor and Chief Justice of the Queen's Bench. That, along with the requirement for approval by the new 'judges' council', virtually guaranteed that the power to remodel the divisions would not be exercised while those chiefs lived.[49] The allocation of business was set out in the bill and the Queen's Bench was assured of its exclusive criminal jurisdiction.[50] The equity bar's concerns about being swamped were hardly allayed, but Selborne could at least point to the 'prevalence of equity' clause which gave equitable rules priority in the event of conflicts.[51]

This was the structure which finally emerged in 1875.[52] Though the newest of the chiefs, Coleridge, came to wish he had fought to keep the old courts as separate entities,[53] he could not resist the logic of consolidation when the departures of Cockburn and Kelly finally opened the way in 1880.[54] Only the most conservative

---

[44] They declined to assist with the other bill, on appellate jurisdiction: *HLSP* 1870 (309), xiii.

[45] Polden, 'Mingling the Waters', 579.

[46] *Ibid*. Selborne had refused the great seal because he opposed disestablishment of the Church of Ireland. With that a *fait accompli* he accepted it.

[47] Cairns to Selborne, 3 February 1873, Lambeth Palace Library, Selborne Mss vol. 1865, f. 209. Selborne described the bill as 'the work of my own hands': *Memorials, Personal and Political*, i, 298.

[48] Polden, 'Mingling the Waters', 583.

[49] *Ibid*.   [50] Judicature Act 1873, ss 32–6.

[51] Selborne only claimed to have 'disarmed active opposition…from that quarter' (*Memorials Personal and Political*, i, 301). Sir Richard Malins VC was the only judge openly to oppose the 1870 bill: (1870–1) 15 *Sol. J.* 67.

[52] By a rather circuitous route. The 1873 Act was due to come into force in November 1874 but the Conservative government would not implement its appeal provisions. A suspending Act was passed and then a further Judicature Act in 1875, which also brought the unamended provisions of the 1873 Act into force on 1 November 1875. In debates on the Appellate Jurisdiction Bill 1876 Disraeli provided a masterly but disingenuous account of these proceedings: *PD* 1876 (s3) 229: 1680–93.

[53] Coleridge to his father, 8 July 1875, E. H. Coleridge, *The Life and Correspondence of Sir John Duke Coleridge*, 2 vols (1904), ii, 251.

[54] Polden, 'Mingling the Waters', 590–1. The initiative was evidently Selborne's, for Gladstone wrote that he was 'no lover of old offices being abolished' (to Selborne, 20 September 1880, Selborne Mss, vol. 1867, f. 116). Perhaps he regretted the loss of patronage.

judges joined in him voting against,[55] and though they found some unlikely allies in the House of Commons,[56] in January 1881 the Exchequer and Common Pleas ended their long existence, giving the High Court a shape that would endure for 90 years.

The retention of the three common law divisions was one reason why the reduction in judges, which some felt was the principal aim of the Commission, was not achieved.[57] Selborne and Gladstone, like Hatherley, were keen that there should be a 'free circulation of judges', enabling resources to be targeted on busy areas[58] and Selborne's Act envisaged that common law puisnes would be reduced from 15 to 12 through unfilled vacancies arising from immediate appointments to the new Court of Appeal.[59] This was justified on the ground that the election petitions which had prompted an expansion in 1868 had proved to be fewer than expected,[60] but the reduction was unpopular with the legal profession and was abandoned by Cairns in 1875.[61] Under persistent pressure the government conceded the appointment of a new judge to the Chancery Division in 1877[62] and in 1881 replaced the two chiefs with two puisnes. With overall levels of business more or less static, the High Court should have been able to cope.

3. MAKING THE RULES

Hatherley's original notion was that the court should make its own rules, through which 'the procedure in each divisional or other court shall so far as is possible be assimilated'.[63] In the event a small group consisting of Bramwell, Quain, Sir William James, and Hollams was given the task and their handiwork became the foundation for the rules embedded in the 1873 Act.[64] Always intended as

[55] The minority of five included Coleridge, who claimed the credit for saving these 'prizes of the profession' in 1873: to his father, 16 July 1873, Coleridge, *Life and Correspondence of Coleridge*, 218.

[56] e.g. Sir Assheton Cross and Henry Fowler, *PD* 1881 (s3) 258: 572–612. The vote was 178 : 110. More predictably, the bar petitioned against their abolition; Polden, 'Mingling the Waters', 591

[57] e.g. W. E. Finlason, *Our Judicial System* (1877), 50. Introducing the 1873 bill, Selborne had mentioned his hopes for a future reduction: *PD* 1873 (s3) 214: 338.

[58] *PD* 1870 (s3) 200: 170 (Hatherley); Gladstone to Selborne, 4 January 1873, H. C. G. Matthew (ed.), *The Gladstone Diaries*, vol. 8 (Oxford, 1982), 343.

[59] Judicature Act 1873, s 6; Polden, 'Mingling the Waters', 585. Hatherley's bill had simply set a maximum of 22 in the High Court.

[60] Election Petitions Act 1868 c.125, s 11(8); *PD* 1873 (s3) 216: 650 (Sir J. Coleridge).

[61] Not expedient 'for the present', Judicature Act 1875, s 3; Polden, 'Mingling the Waters', 588–9.

[62] *Ibid.*, 590. Sir Edward Fry was the first Chancery judge to be styled 'Mr Justice'.

[63] *HLSP* 1870 (32), iv, cl.13. This clause was changed several times. At one point Hatherley offered a Privy Council committee, which was scorned by Cairns (*PD* 1870 (s3) 200: 2034; 201: 1569). By the report stage any four from a group comprising the most senior judges had become the rule-making authority (*HLSP* 1870 (72d), iv, cl.16).

[64] Hatherley seems to have wanted to create a 'uniform code of procedure' (James to Selborne, 5 October 1872, Selborne Mss vol. 1865, f. 60) in a Procedure Bill (Coleridge to Selborne, 25 December

temporary, these rules were superseded in the 1875 Act,[65] and a rule committee was established to continue the work.[66]

The workings of the Judicature Acts and rules came under sustained criticism, especially for making litigation more, rather than less, expensive, and in 1881 Selborne charged a committee headed by the LCJ with considering how they might be improved. Their report met with a mixed response.[67] By recommending a lower scale of costs where the sum claimed did not exceed £200 it upset solicitors;[68] suggestions that pleadings were usually unnecessary and that the use of juries might be limited antagonized many lawyers and their proposal that a single master handle all interlocutory applications in a cause was not welcomed by the masters.[69] Some felt their suggestions, especially for appeals, favoured the divisional courts over the Court of Appeal. On the other hand, at least some lay opinion was favourable.[70]

It was to be expected that the new rules of 1883 would also be attacked, though in fact they were less radical than the report,[71] the 'barbarous proposal to abolish pleadings' being a notable casualty.[72] Giffard complained in Parliament that there had been insufficient time for consultation and that their 'tone and tendency...was to make HM's judges absolute despots in the Courts of Law',[73] an absurd exaggeration, though judges were given some new powers, e.g. to intervene in cross-examination.[74] Conservatives might lament the demise of the

1872, *ibid.*, f. 196). Characteristically, he antagonized the law officers by not consulting them and then postponed the bill while attempting to sort out appeals.

[65] Selborne used a small committee comprising H. Cadman Jones (Chancery), A. Wilson (common law), and T. H. Tristram (civilian), commending the Common Law Procedure Acts rules drafted by Master Walton. Their handiwork was to be reviewed by a judges' committee (draft instructions, 26 November 1873, Selborne Mss vol.1866, ff. 75–8) and see *PD* 1874 (s3) 219: 1158–9. However, Jessel played an important part and Selborne personally scrutinized all the rules and himself settled the forms and costs: *Memorials, Personal and Political*, ii, 93.

[66] The 1875 Act (s.17) left it to 'a sort of general council of the Bench' (S. Rosenbaum, 'Studies in English Civil Procedure, II: The Rule-Making Authority' (1915) 63 *University of Pennsylvania LR* 151–82 at 165), but the Appellate Jurisdiction Act 1876, s 17 substituted a rule committee of six judges. It was increased to eight in 1881 (see below).

[67] Reproduced in (1880–1) 25 *Sol. J.* 911.

[68] (1881) 71 *LT* 382.

[69] *Ibid.*, 381–2, 400–1; (1881–2) 26 *Sol. J.* 53.

[70] See e.g. *The Saturday Review*, quoted in a hostile *Law Times*: (1871) 71 *LT* 412.

[71] (1883) 10 *Pump Court*, June, 10, suggested that the death of Jessel, whose views were radical and manner forceful, would contribute to this.

[72] (1882–3) 27 *Sol. J.* 610. This evidently gave great difficulty to the Rule Committee, see Coleridge to Selborne, 11 February1883, LCO 1/88.

[73] *PD* 1883 (s3) 283: 145–58.

[74] (1883) 75 *LT* 199–200; F. Lockwood, 'The New Rules' (1883) *TNAPSS* 189. Perhaps Giffard had in mind the extensive discretion conferred on the judge by Order lix.

demurrer, but Order 25 was an effective replacement;[75] some worried about the repeal of Keating's Act, but Order 14 with its much wider application offered 'the most effective weapon the law has ever had in its armoury';[76] there was some outcry over the supposed violation of the right to jury trial, but the practical effect of the change was very slight.[77] There were to be restrictions on applications for discovery and on interrogatories, and hopes were pinned on the new 'notice to admit', though there was scepticism about these measures.[78] Despite the masters' grumblings, the proposal to allot each cause to one of their number was implemented and they were charged with operating the new 'summons for directions', an innovation admirable in theory but which was to have a long and disappointing history.[79] The rules had plentiful defects and were not comprehensive,[80] but there was general approval that there now existed a single code which, if it fell short of the ambition of unifying procedure in courts administering law and equity, at least brought those procedures into one set of rules.[81]

4. TEETHING TROUBLES

In February 1881 Henry Fowler, a persistent and well-informed critic of the legal system,[82] deplored the 'breakdown of the Judicature Acts'. Two years later he claimed that costs and delays had soared.[83] Many agreed, and even the Acts' most enthusiastic supporters conceded that results had fallen well short of expectations.[84]

Various explanations were given. Serious delays in Chancery in 1876 and again in the early 1880s arose partly from the move to *viva voce* evidence, with which judges and practitioners were unfamiliar, and (according to some) to an influx

---

[75] *PD* 1883 (s3) 283: 145–87; Lockwood, *New Rules*, 189.

[76] T. E. Snow, 'Special Indorsement or Originating Summons?' (1893) 9 *LQR* 31–5 at 33; cf. Lockwood, *New Rules*, 188. Hollams, who had suggested the extension of Keating's Act to the Judicature Commission, felt that it had been taken further than originally intended: *Jottings of an Old Solicitor*, 143–4.

[77] M. Lobban, 'The Strange Life of the English Civil Jury, 1837–1914', in J. W. Cairns and G. McLeod (eds), *The Dearest Birth Right of the People of England* (Oxford, 2002), 173–215 at 186.

[78] Lockwood, *New Rules*, 190–1; (1882–3) 27 *Sol. J.* 631.

[79] Lockwood, *New Rules*, 189–90; (1882–3) 27 *Sol. J.* 646; (1883) 75 *LT* 403.

[80] Exceptions are listed in Rosenbaum, *Rule-Making Authority*, 166. The most important was the PDA: see above, pp. 731–2.

[81] According to (1883) 10 *Pump Court*, June, 10, they were drafted by Courtenay Ilbert. However, (1882–3) 27 *Sol. J.* 604 attributes them to G. B. Allen, H. S. Theobald and M. D. Chalmers and says that the biggest burden fell upon the brothers Muir McKenzie.

[82] See under solicitors.

[83] *PD* 1881 (s3) 258: 573; (1883) (s3) 283: 168.

[84] V. V. Veeder, 'A Century of Judicature', in Committee of American Law Schools (ed.), *Select Essays in Anglo-American Law* , 3 vols (1968 rep. of 1907), i, 730–836, 807.

of common law business, perhaps attracted by a more liberal costs regime.[85] At common law the reasons were more complicated, but there too procedural changes undoubtedly contributed.

One factor was the growth of interlocutory motions in chambers. In 1867 the common law courts had been authorized to delegate some chambers work to the masters, which 'relieved the judges from doing a great deal of rubbishy business'.[86] Three masters sat in rotation in the chambers of one of the judges, who came (often late) to handle the more sensitive and complicated matters.[87] Though the masters claimed that the arrangement was a great success, the organization of chambers business was chaotic (they were known as the beargarden)[88] until reformed (and the masters' jurisdiction extended) along the lines suggested by a judges' committee in 1878.[89] But even though some judges sought to restrict the resort to discovery and interrogatories, the latter came to be sought routinely and discovery, though useful, was undoubtedly expensive.[90] Both were abused and their increasing volume gave rise to unfortunate delays, particularly affecting the masters' role in handling references.[91] It remained to be seen whether the important changes of 1883 would improve the position.[92]

To compound these delays at the interlocutory stage, there was a double appeal from the master, first to a single judge and thence to the judges in banc. The Judges' Committee was dissuaded from recommending that appeal should lie straight to the latter by evidence that most litigants did not pursue appeals beyond the initial level;[93] indeed it was argued that except in term time the appeal to the divisional court was hardly feasible.[94]

---

[85] See below, pp. 813–17.

[86] Master Dodgson, *RC on the Judicature, Fourth Report 1874*, evidence, 10; Chambers (Despatch of Business) Act 1867 c. 68.

[87] *Fourth Report 1874*, evidence of masters.

[88] (1875–6) 20 *Sol. J.* 539, and see the several complaints in vol. 21 (1876–7).

[89] Judges' Committee on Chambers Report, *PP* 1878 [C. 2064], xxv, chaired by Cockburn CJ. As noted above, the Judicature Commission report of 1874 made no recommendations other than for the chambers procedure at common law and in Chancery to be harmonized.

[90] A. Robertson, 'The Judicature Acts and the Administration of Justice in England' (1886–7) 12 (s5) *LM & LR*, 123–43, 127. Sir John Holker claimed that no one had been able to suggest a remedy: *PD* 1878–9 (s3) 244: 1479–81.

[91] *RC on the Judicature, Fourth Report 1874*, evidence of F. Herschell, F. T. Streeten, 15, 111; *PD* 1878–9 (s3) 244: 1438–47 (H. James).

[92] Mr Justice Grove complained of the 'scandalous waste of judicial time and heavy expense to litigants caused by the present system of interlocutory proceedings', claiming that three-quarters of the time of the divisional court was occupied with appeals from chambers, many of them frivolous: to Selborne, 16 May 1883, LCO 1/5.

[93] *Judges Committee on Chambers, Report 1878*, 2.

[94] *RC on the Judicature, Fourth Report 1874*, evidence of Gainsford Bruce, 17.

However, some difficulties on the common law side were of the judges' own making. In particular, as Selborne and Cairns repeatedly pointed out, they ignored the Judicature Commission's measured conclusion that the single judge system should become the norm.[95] Even Blackburn, a member of the Commission, affected to assume that banc sittings would remain the general rule, and Cockburn was wedded to them.[96] Selborne had conceded to Cockburn that there should be banc hearings for 'such matters as are not proper to be heard by a single judge', though he offset this by a further proviso allowing a two-man divisional court where 'through pressure of business or other cause [three] may not conveniently be found practicable'.[97] An attempt to strengthen the presumption in favour of a single judge in 1876[98] was unsuccessful and the Queen's Bench divisional court continued to serve both as an appeal court and as a substitute for banc.[99]

It was much more difficult to accommodate banc sittings within a legal year which now required continuous sittings (save in vacation), and had a fourth Assize. Such adaptations needed both goodwill and organizational skills, and the veteran chiefs possessed neither, while Coleridge soon began to hanker after the old ways.[100] The legal press was scathing in denouncing the confusion that existed at times[101] and Fowler opposed the abolition of the chiefs for fear an enlarged QBD would be even less well administered.[102] In fairness to the chiefs, however, until the opening of the new courts in 1882 rational organization was greatly hampered by the way the courts, offices, and chambers were scattered around Westminster.[103]

Nevertheless, it was hardly unfair if 'outdoors it was asserted too frequently that the Judges had not really shown that anxious desire to accommodate them-selves and the business of their Courts to the new system which might fairly have been expected'.[104] One judge was quoted as saying, 'the beauty of the bill

---

[95] First Report 1869, 10; Polden, 'Mingling the Waters', 584–5. It was proposed that for a transitional period a single judge should only sit on matters specified in general orders or with the parties' consent.

[96] PD 1881 (s3) 258: 587–92 (Sir H. James AG); Blackburn to Selborne, 31 March 1873, Selborne Mss vol. 1865, f. 257. It was claimed that the common law judges had been becoming steadily more unwilling to decide any but the most straightforward cases at nisi prius: Finlason, Our Judicial System, vii.

[97] Judicature Act 1873, s 40.

[98] 'So far as is practicable and convenient', Appellate Jurisdiction Act 1876, s 17. There were vigorous debates on the clause, notably in the Lords on 10 August, where Cairns described banc as 'little more than a phantom' PD 1876 (s3) 231: 962.

[99] Cockburn continued to insist on a three-man divisional court for new trial motions: (1877–8) 22 Sol. J. 345–6. See also Finlason, Our Judicial System, 224–6.

[100] See e.g. his speech on the Judicature Bill 1876, PD 1876 (s3) 231: 949–58.

[101] (1878) 13 LJ 459. Cockburn confessed that 'this winter Assize has brought the whole of our proceedings into a state of confusion': (1879) 14 LJ 33.

[102] PD 1881 (s3) 258: 572–85.   [103] Jacob, Judicature Acts, 306.

[104] Charles Norwood, PD 1876 (s3) 231: 865. Norwood was prominent in the Association of Chambers of Commerce and introduced a bill to extend county court jurisdiction.

[of 1873] is, that it seems to do so much, and does so little; it looks as if we were all to be transmogrified, but it is only the difference between "as you was" and "as you were" '.[105] Chief Justice Bovill was reconciled to it only because it did not seem to require much change,[106] and this negative outlook was not confined to the older generation either; for among the most outspoken dissidents were Henry Manisty and Fitzjames Stephen, appointed in 1876 and 1879 respectively, and when attempts were made to diminish the two most distinctive common law features, jury trial and banc, Coleridge CJCP railed at the 'absolute destruction of the old system of common law' and quoted a letter in which Brett J. wildly exaggerated the impact of proposed reforms.[107]

Such attitudes inevitably coloured the judges' approach to their job. Even the reactionary barrister/MP Warton pithily remarked that they 'came late, lunched long, tried slowly, and rose early'.[108] The attachment of bar and bench to the long vacation was invincible and the judges' council managed to confine a proposed reduction to a few days.[109] Their opposition extended to longer court hours and vacation office hours,[110] and to many laymen the protracted closures of the courts remained a scandal.[111]

As with banc, the common lawyers fought a rearguard action for the civil jury. The Judicature Commission had envisaged that jury trials would become just one of several modes and that it would often be displaced by a preference for the official referees or judge only;[112] but Cockburn led a successful resistance and it was only in 1883 that the Coleridge Committee proposal, watering down the right to jury trial in any common law action (which cases such as *Sugg* v. *Silber*[113] had shown capable of absurd results), was implemented and judge-only trial became the standard form.[114]

Similar attitudes affected other innovations. It was said that Quain, one of the draftsmen of the original rules, would hardly give the new pleading rules a fair chance and other judges did their best to restore or preserve old forms.[115] The provisions about discovery were narrowly construed and interrogatories

---

[105] A. E. Miller, 'The Judicature Acts' (1876) *TNAPSS* 227–41 at 227.

[106] Bovill to Selborne, 7 February 1873, Selborne Mss, vol. 1865, f. 213.

[107] *PD* 1876 (s3) 231: 949–58.   [108] *PD* 1881 (s3) 265: 745–52, 754–6.

[109] (1881–2) 26 *Sol. J.* 119, 135. The common law judges also contrived to enlarge the interval between the Hilary and Easter terms. The Chancery judges followed suit: *PD* 1882 (s3) 267: 377.

[110] (1879–80) 24 *Sol. J.* 139; (1883–4) 28 *Sol. J.* 113, 119. Perhaps they shared the view of C. E. Lewis that 'it really encouraged unnecessary litigation by making the Courts too readily accessible at all times': *PD* 1873 (s3) 217: 1803.

[111] See e.g. C. C. Deane, 'The Judicature Acts' (1876) *TNAPSS* 254; *The Times*, quoted in (1880) 69 *LT* 262.

[112] *First Report 1869*, 18–20.   [113] (1875–6) 1 QB 362.

[114] Lobban, 'Strange Life of the English Civil Jury', 184–6.

[115] (1875–6) 20 *Sol. J.* 151; Miller, *Judicature Acts*, 228–9.

were routinely refused as premature until the opposing party's case had been disclosed, contrary to the purpose for which they were envisaged.[116]

The common law side was not uniquely conservative. Chancery judges were equally prone to pervert the pleading rules, with two vice-chancellors attempting to make affidavit evidence the normal mode in their courts.[117] Most glaring of all, Jessel MR, that daring advocate of substantive fusion, breezed through his list by invariably remitting issues of fact to be tried at Assize. When Baron Huddleston refused to try one such case, Coleridge denounced Jessel's practice as 'contrary to the whole spirit of the legislation' and Selborne and Cairns agreed with him, for it disrupted the scheduling of cases on circuit and its implications were profoundly divisive.[118]

5. 'FUSION'

The main purpose of the Judicature Acts was to effect a fusion of courts, not a fusion of law: on that Selborne and Cairns were in full accord. It had been assumed in some quarters that if the organization and procedure of the two systems were brought together, 'equity and the common law will intertwine and become one growth'.[119] However, once the implementation of the Commission's proposals got under way doubts became more widespread and the common law judges argued for at least the basic principles to be set out in the Act. The 'prevalence of equity' clause which Lord Penzance had first introduced into Hatherley's bill was finally transmuted into distinct provisions to resolve clashes between legal and equitable rules, concluded by a general clause (section 25). These provisions generated surprisingly little debate.[120]

The effect of this 'safety-net' at the end (section 25(11)), which stated that where the two were in conflict or at variance 'with reference to the same matter' equity was to prevail, remained to be worked out.[121] It most evidently applied where

---

[116] R. M. Pankhurst, 'The Judicature Acts' (1876) *TNAPSS* 249–51; Finlason, *Our Judicial System*, 309–12.

[117] Miller, *Judicature Acts*, 229–30; (1875–6) 20 *Sol. J.* 330.

[118] Polden, 'Mingling the Waters', 603.

[119] [F.W. Rowsell], 'The Progress of Law Reform in England' (1875) 141 *Edin. Rev.* 179–209 at 179.

[120] Lobban, 'Preparing for Fusion, Part Two', 593–9. Section 25(1–8 and 10) covered the administration of insolvent estates; the limitation period for actions by trust beneficiaries; the degree of waste permitted to life tenants of legal estates; merger or extinction of estates; mortgagors' actions to recover the secured property; assignment of debts and choses in action; time stipulations in contracts; injunctions and receivers, and custody and education of infants.

[121] There is a quite extensive literature on the extent to which the Acts did, or at least had the potential to bring about any substantive fusion of legal and equitable doctrines. It includes, inter alia, Getzler, 'Patterns of Fusion'; Sir R. Evershed, 'Reflections on the Fusion of Law and Equity after Seventy-Five Years' (1954) 70 *LQR* 326–41; P. V. Baker, 'The Future of Equity' (1977) 93 *LQR* 529–40; T. G. Watkin, 'The Spirit of the Seventies' (1977) 6 *AALR* 119–27; P. Sparkes, 'Walsh v.

contradictory rules of each jurisdiction were shown already to exist. Beyond this, courts would sometimes be tempted by counsel to favour a new extension, restriction, or qualification of the former law, whether that earlier rule was from common law or equity, as a result of 'fusion into one law'. On the whole, however, they resisted such invitations, adhering to the standard answer, given often enough, that the new judicature was only a matter of court administration.[122]

Let us take one example where 'fusion' made no difference (damages for negligent misrepresentation); and another where it did, but only in very particular circumstances (the effect of a contract to grant a lease). During the 1880s a much debated question was whether innocent misrepresentations could be compensated in common law damages, or whether the only remedy lay in an equitable order for *restitutio in integrum*, in so far as that remained practicable.[123] In 1889, as will be discussed elsewhere, the House of Lords would uphold the refusal of common law courts to expand the tort of deceit to encompass negligent misstatements.[124] The reasons given were mainly based on the weight of the precedents; but the inexpediency of increasing the scope of an action for damages also crept in.[125] However controversial the result, it did not turn on some loose argument that 'fusion' demanded the opposite conclusion.

The instance which gave rise to most speculation about fusion was *Walsh v. Lonsdale*,[126] where the owner of a spinning factory had contracted to lease it to a tenant under specified terms. The tenant had been permitted to occupy the

Lonsdale—the Non-Fusion Fallacy' (1988) 8 *OJLS* 350–63; P. M. Perell, *The Fusion of Law and Equity* (Toronto and Vancouver, 1990), 19–33; B. Mason, 'The Place of Equity and Equitable Remedies in the Contemporary Common Law World' (1994) 110 *LQR* 238–59, and A. S. Burrows, 'We do this at Common Law and that in Equity' (2002) 22 *OJLS* 1–16. Useful contemporary views are C. S. Drewry, 'The "Fusion" of Law and Equity under the Judicature Acts' (1876) 1 (s4) *LM & LR* 112–22 and C. F. Trower, 'The Growth of the "Prevalence" of Equity' (1879–8) 5 (s4) *LM & LR* 127–47.

[122] See e.g. Lord Watson, *Inde Coope v. Emmerson* (1887) 12 AC 300, 309: The Judicature Act 'was not intended to affect, and does not affect the quality of the rights and claims which…bring to court'. On occasion Jessel MR would put the matter in just these terms: *Salt v. Cooper* (1880) 16 Ch D 544, 549. For later affirmations, see R.P. Meagher et al., *Equity: Doctrines and Remedies* (4th edn, 2002), paras 2-200–229, where the determination to root out 'the fusion fallacy' is pursued with a terrier-like tenacity.

[123] In *Redgrave v. Hurd* (1881) 20 Ch D 1, 12, Jessel MR considered that the Judicature Act had eliminated the difference between the common law and equity rules, 'which makes the rules of equity prevail'. But Lord Blackburn in effect rejected any qualification on the need to show deliberate intent to deceive: *Smith v. Chadwick* (1884) 9 App. Cas. 187, 196.

[124] *Derry v. Peek* (1889) 14 App. Cas. 337.

[125] See e.g. Lord Bramwell, 'to say that there is a "right to have true statements only made", I cannot agree, and I think it would be much to be regretted if there was any such right. Mercantile men, as Stirling J says, would indeed cry out' (p. 350).

[126] (1882) 21 Ch D 9, 14–15. In *Joseph v. Lyons* (1884) 15 QBD 280, Huddleston B held that an equitable interest in goods conferred on the grantee of a bill of sale had been converted, by the Judicature Act 1873, s. 25(11) into a legal interest that would have priority over any later transfer of the grantor's

factory for some months even though a lease in proper form had not been executed. At common law, the tenant's entry gave rise to a tenancy from year to year, payable in arrears; if that was the extent of his liability, he had paid the rent due and so was not liable to suffer a distraint of his goods on the premises. Had the lease been executed, it would have required payment of rent in advance and the non-payment would have justified the distress that the landlord levied. The reported interlocutory proceedings concerned whether money should be paid into court in order to ensure satisfaction if at trial he should succeed in establishing that the contractual terms of the lease were already in effect. The nub of his argument, which Jessel accepted, concerned whether the maxim by which equity regards as done what ought to be done gave a right to enforce the contractual terms intended for the lease, despite the fact that the lease itself had not been executed. Jessel went so far as to pronounce that:

There are not two estates as there were formerly, one estate at common law by reason of the payment of the rent from year to year, and an estate in equity under the agreement. There is only one Court, and the equity rules prevail in it.[127]

F. W. Maitland insisted that, whatever else might be the consequence of Jessel's variety of 'fusion', it could not be a reason for holding the intended lessee entitled at law against a third party, such as a later innocent purchaser of the freehold or grantee of a lease in proper form.[128] That would overturn the distinction in nature between equitable and legal interests in land. The requirement to grant leases in set form led to conveyancing practices which limited the searches that the purchaser or lessee had to carry out—an arrangement that gave order to the distribution of the transaction costs between the two parties. What could be the practical advantage of changing such basic classificatory rules? After the 1880s arguments that substantive rights were affected by the general nature of the Judicature Act, coalescence become rarer. That is probably because they are inherently weak, seeking to cast a gloss over a development of the law that a judge wishes to make for more specific reasons.

As for procedure, if not 'a mere paper fusion' as one disillusioned MP called it,[129] the effect of the Acts was modest. The temporary divisional structure

---

interest—even that of a bona fide pledgee, but the CA held that the subsection was not intended to have any such effect.

[127] One issue was whether equity would have granted specific performance of the lease as of right, as distinct from investigating whether the court would first consider the particular circumstances of the transaction—this being an equitable remedy. In the Walsh case, counsel for the defendant conceded that specific performance would be available: see pp. 14–15, so the judgment arguably set a precedent of very narrow dimensions.

[128] *Equity* (Cambridge, 1909), Ch.12, esp. 159–62.

[129] Sir G. O. Morgan, *PD* 1873 (s3) 216: 666.

rapidly hardened into permanence and after several early appointments from the Chancery bar to the common law divisions and transfers between divisions, Hatherley's 'free circulation of judges' did not materialize.[130] However, the judges now sat under the same roof, operated under a common code of rules and were subject to a common appeal structure. Those changes should have gone a long way to curing the twin vices of the law, expense and delay, but they did not. Combining those features of each system which the reformers felt best—the common law's use of oral evidence, equity's preference for a single judge and facility of non-jury trial—and developing a single code of pleading and interlocutory facilities probably improved the quality of dispute resolution, but save for undefended liquidated demands it did not streamline it, nor make it cheaper. The challenge to the Supreme Court of Judicature in its new home in the Strand would be to make its services available at an affordable price to litigants and at an acceptable cost to the public.

6. TRIBUNALS OF COMMERCE

After their second report, Selborne had the Commissioners turn their attention to proposals for tribunals of commerce embodied in a bill presented on behalf of the Association of Chambers of Commerce.[131] It was a convenient way of disposing of an unwelcome bill, and one which presented some danger, since the idea had earlier obtained the backing of a partisan Commons select committee.[132]

That committee had acknowledged 'general dissatisfaction existing among the mercantile community' with the superior and county courts.[133] Most businessmen had long resented the cost, slowness, and technicality of common law adjudication, but there was now a substantial body of opinion that objected also to the rigorous application of legal doctrines and hankered after a court which would apply their own customs and usages in a pragmatic, commonsense way. They thought they saw tribunals in France, Belgium, Germany and elsewhere which did precisely that, and now sought to import foreign models, whose very foreignness set off the latent Podsnappery in many lawyers, just as Brougham's ill-fated 'courts of reconciliation' always had.[134]

---

[130] Polden, 'Mingling the Waters', 586–92.

[131] A. R. Ilersic and P. F. B. Liddle, *The Parliament of Commerce* (1960), 85. The bill was closely modelled upon the County Courts (Admiralty Jurisdiction) Act 1868: SC on Tribunals of Commerce, Report, *PP* 1871 (409), xii, Jacob Behrens's evidence, qq. 568–9.

[132] SC on Tribunals of Commerce, Report 1871. It drew on the evidence taken by an earlier select committee, *PP* 1858 (413), xvi.

[133] *Ibid.*, 1.

[134] P. Polden, *A History of the County Court, 1846–1971* (Cambridge, 1999), 19–20. The Brussels arbitration tribunal was featured in (1862) 13 (s3) *LM & LR* 349–57.

Of course businessmen could avoid the courts altogether if they agreed, either in their initial bargain or during their dispute, to resort to arbitration. Locke's Act of 1698[135] had given encouragement to this and although in the great case of *Scott* v. *Avery*[136] Lord Campbell was misled by poor reporting of two of Hardwicke's decisions into suggesting that Georgian judges had been antipathetic to arbitration, in fact the resort to the courts to enforce arbitration agreements or awards grew in popularity not only in Mansfield's busy King's Bench but in the less frequented Common Pleas, and lawyers were increasingly chosen as arbitrators.[137]

On the basis of recommendations from the Common Law Commissioners, gaps in the powers of arbitrators were filled in 1833[138] and 1854.[139] True, the judges exacted a price for lending their services to facilitate arbitration, extending their supervision to cover not only fraud and procedural irregularity but, to a rather uncertain extent, departures from the common law rules themselves,[140] but still it became a credible alternative to litigation.[141]

How popular it was is necessarily uncertain. Even institutional arbitrations by trade organizations are not very fully studied, but they were probably most successful when used within a particular, close-knit trade rather than within a defined locality.[142] The first Common Law Commission had suggested giving judges the power to direct an arbitration where a case was unsuited to jury trial, but that was not enacted until 1854, and then it was confined to matters of account.[143] However, judges freely invited parties to go to arbitration, and the Judicature Commissioners had already cast a disapproving eye over such arbitrations. If conducted by a layman they were liable to be flawed in reception

---

[135] 9 & 10 Will. III c. 15.

[136] (1856) 5 H.L.C. 811. See the contrasting interpretations in H. W. Arthurs, *'Without the Law': Administrative Justice and Legal Pluralism in Nineteenth-Century England* (Toronto, 1985), 85–6 and H. Horwitz and J. Oldham, 'John Locke, Lord Mansfield and Arbitration during the Eighteenth Century' (1993) 36 *Hist. J.* 137–59 at 146. A concise account of the history of arbitration is in Holdsworth, *HEL*, xiv, 182–98.

[137] Horwitz and Oldham, 'Locke, Mansfield and Arbitration', 148–55.

[138] Law Amendment Act 1833 (3 & 4 Will. IV c. 42 ss 39–42), giving court-appointed or approved arbitrators power to call witnesses and administer oaths and making such arbitration agreements irrevocable without the court's consent: based on *RC on Common Law, Second Report 1830*, 25–7.

[139] Common Law Procedure Act 1854, ss 11–17, allowed the court to stay an action to enforce an agreement to arbitrate, to nominate or replace an arbitrator when necessary to prevent an agreement being frustrated; enabled any agreement not providing to the contrary to be made a rule of court and empowered an arbitrator to submit his award for the court's opinion by special case. These provisions featured in Brougham's bill of the same session: (1854) 23 *LT* 50. Brougham would have enabled county court judges to be nominated as arbitrators, and some did act in that capacity: Polden, *History of the County Court*, 38–9.

[140] Arthurs, *'Without the Law'*, 68–77.   [141] *Ibid.*, 68.

[142] *Ibid.*, 62–7.   [143] *Second Report 1830*, 25–7; Common Law Procedure Act 1854, ss 3–10.

of inadmissible evidence, while lawyers were too apt to adjourn the hearing to attend their other commitments. Arbitrators' fees were pretty much at large and sometimes outrageous[144] and the Commission felt that control over the proceedings and challenges to the outcome were alike inadequate.[145]

But if lawyers were unenthusiastic about court-directed arbitrations, many businessmen were much more so. The Liverpool chamber of commerce originated the campaign for mercantile tribunals[146] and it was rapidly taken up by the Association of Chambers of Commerce, which passed regular resolutions.[147] A select committee in 1858, a bill to set up a merchant shipping tribunal in Newcastle (1865), and a deputation to the President of the Board of Trade all proved abortive,[148] but Manchester eventually went ahead with its own tribunal, the common council of the City of London had one under discussion, and there was even a private enterprise speculation.[149]

Yet there was never really any chance that the Judicature Commission, even with Sir Sidney Waterlow added to represent the world of business, would be sympathetic to a cause even the Law Amendment Society opposed.[150] The legal profession in general was hostile to the creation of specialist tribunals, whether for patents, railways, or personal injuries, and saw nothing about commerce which made it a special case.[151] Opposition was made all the easier because the foreign tribunals differed widely in fundamental features and proponents of tribunals could not agree on a scheme.[152] There were difficult practical questions to be resolved: the geographical reach of tribunals; the types of disputes they could hear; their powers to enforce decisions; the rules of evidence; the right to representation; and the facility for appeals. But the majority of the Commission, and all the lawyers except Lord Penzance, also urged the importance of consistent and principled (or at any rate rule-based) decisions, attributing far greater value than most business men did to legal certainty: '[I]t is of the utmost importance to the commercial community that the decisions of the Courts of Law should on all

[144] See e.g. the case cited in (1857) 1 *Sol. J.* 847, 853.

[145] *First Report 1869*, 13; C. Stebbings, *Legal Foundations of Tribunals in Nineteenth Century England* (Cambridge, 2006), 61.

[146] Arthurs, '*Without the Law*', 57. It initiated the Commons debate which led to the select committee of 1858: (1857–8) 2 *Sol. J.* 498 and see E. Heath's paper to the Social Science Congress (1857) *TNAPSS* 153–9. A further debate at the Congress in 1870 disclosed considerable support for tribunals: (1870) *TNAPSS* 191–208.

[147] Arthurs, '*Without the Law*', 57.

[148] Ilersic and Liddle, *Parliament of Commerce*, 83–4.

[149] B. Abel-Smith and R. Stevens, *Lawyers and the Courts* (1967), 52, 87; (1876–7) 21 *Sol. J.* 853; (1868–9) 26 (s3) *LM & LR* 365.

[150] Arthurs, '*Without the Law*', 57.

[151] (1881–2) 26 *Sol. J.* 87; T. Ryalls (1875) *TNAPSS* 225–34.

[152] *RC on the Judicature, Third Report 1873*, 7–8.

questions of principle be, as far as possible, uniform, thus affording precedents for the conduct of those engaged in the ordinary transactions of trade.'[153] If commercial expertise was wanting in the court (now that special juries could no longer be held out as providing it) the judge could be enabled to appoint expert assessors to sit with him as in Admiralty,[154] though given judges' neglect of the power to refer a technical matter for an expert opinion, there was justified scepticism about that.[155] Bramwell alone was prepared to countenance a limited experiment, and was criticized for it.[156] The report was predictably dismissive and though the idea resurfaced from time to time, it was never a practical proposition.[157]

7. PROVINCIAL JUSTICE

The creation of a coherent and efficient structure for civil justice outside the metropolis was an altogether more complicated task than reorganizing the courts in London, involving as it did both criminal and civil matters, and the relationship between the superior court judges on Assize, the county court, sundry surviving local courts, and the quarter sessions. It is not surprising that such a thoroughgoing reform was not accomplished.

The original instructions of the Judicature Commission were not so ambitious, though they did require the Commissioners to examine the Assizes.[158] However, even the relatively modest proposals in the first report would have had a momentous impact on the professions, and in particular on the bar. The suggested change in the rules for venue, shifting the place where the dispute arose as the normal place for its trial to one chosen by the plaintiff, would accentuate the drift of business to London.[159] Continuous sittings at *nisi prius* in London and Middlesex would oblige barristers to choose between remaining in town and going circuit.[160] Rearranging the circuits on the basis of an equal volume of business and convenience of travel ('a matter of Bradshaw' was the phrase popularized by

---

[153] *Ibid.*, 8 and Penzance's note at 11. Waterlow and Ayrton's dissents repudiated the idea that businessmen set great store by legal certainty.

[154] *Ibid.*, 8. This was not done until 1891. However, the ACC had attacked the court of Admiralty as 'a serious evil to the mercantile marine of Great Britain and of all foreign nations, in consequence of the great expense of prosecuting or defending a suit, and of the long delay . . . that is incurred before a decision is given'. This drew a caustic reply from the registrar: (1871) 32 (s3) *LM & LR* 189–94.

[155] Judicature Act 1873, s 56. According to (1880–1) 25 *Sol. J.* 65, the first use of this power was in 1880 when Williams J. called upon an engineer.

[156] Arthurs, '*Without the Law*', 58 n.39; (1884–5) 29 *Sol. J.* 3.

[157] *Third Report 1873*; Ilersic and Liddle, *Parliament of Commerce*, 85.

[158] Instructions, *First Report 1869*, 4. Ayrton was unsuccessful in his attempt to persuade them to endorse his preference for all civil causes to be commenced in the county court (note at 26).

[159] P.17. The old rules were in Common Law Procedure Act 1852, s 59.

[160] P.16; R. J. C. Cocks, *Foundations of the Modern Bar* (1983), 136.

Bramwell[161]) threatened traditions going back hundreds of years;[162] the abolition of the home circuit, which was particularly vulnerable to criticism for forcing suburban matters to be tried at Assize when the Westminster courts were nearer and more convenient, was a notably brutal instance of utilitarianism prevailing over tradition.[163]

Opposition to some of these proposals, which forced Hatherley to retreat a long way, signalled that anything more wide-reaching which emerged from the extended remit of an enlarged Commission would face a very rough ride.[164] In fact the Commissioners had disagreements among themselves. It was one thing to identify three different classes of civil action, needing three different sorts of forum,[165] but quite another to translate this into a structure which would satisfy the various professional and political interests. One solution which was firmly rejected was the creation of permanent provincial branches of the superior courts in the largest cities.[166] This had considerable support in those places but was generally disliked by the lawyers (except solicitors in the big cities who aspired to create an agency role for themselves)[167] and was abhorrent to the judges.[168] Instead, the Commission—not without some dissenting voices[169]—opted for an enhanced role for the county courts, which would be integrated with the superior courts in the new Supreme Court of Judicature. Small cases would henceforth be tried largely by their registrars and a plaintiff whose claim exceeded the £50 limit could commence his case there, his opponent having the right to remove it to a higher court. These bigger cases would be tried in the larger centres with better

---

[161] Hollams, *Jottings of an Old Solicitor*, 78, claims to have originated the phrase, which alludes to the popular railway timetable. It remained in common currency in legal circles for many years and was still used by witnesses at the KBD Commission in 1913.

[162] *First Report 1869*, 16–17. The Commissioners saw no need to increase the number of circuits.

[163] *First Report 1869*, 16; Cocks, *Foundations of the Modern Bar*, 136; Hollams, *Jottings of an Old Solicitor*, 77–9. During the Assizes at Kingston a special train from Waterloo carried most of the participants there and back, many from their homes in the Surrey suburbs.

[164] Cocks, *Foundations of the Modern Bar*, 136–9.

[165] '[T]here are two classes at least of the subject matter of litigation—those which can bear the expense of being tried before an elaborate and central tribunal, and those which require a cheap, simple and local procedure and trial. But there is a third or intermediate class of cases, which frequently involve questions of complexity, and of serious importance to the parties interested, yet the expense of taking the parties and witnesses to any considerable distance from the place where the cause of actions arose, and they probably dwell, is generally wholly disproportionate to the value of the matter in dispute.' *Second Report 1872*, 10.

[166] Cocks, *Foundations of the Modern Bar*, 140, 142.

[167] They also aspired to this role if certain county courts were given an enlarged jurisdiction: Polden, *History of the County Court*, 82.

[168] Judges found the idea of having to live in industrial districts unthinkable: (1883) 18 *LJ* 110.

[169] Quain, Moffatt, Penzance, Blackburn, and Collier.

administrative facilities, where the judge would spend most of his time. The extravagant provision of courts and districts would be cut back, the expensive 'banking function' curtailed and the judges paid more in the hope of improving their calibre.[170] The remaining local courts would be abolished.[171]

The Commissioners admitted that this would reduce the civil business at Assize, but except for awarding a fourth Assize to Manchester and Liverpool as compensation for denying them full courts of their own, they left the future shape and functions of Assizes and quarter sessions to be worked out subsequently, their unwillingness to grapple with details attracting some criticism.[172]

Even without a change of government, and even if the arguments over the role of the House of Lords in the new judicature had not absorbed most of the time and energy which could be given to law reform, it is unlikely that this programme could have been carried out. Most of the practising bar was strongly opposed to it. Some circuits were already desperately short of business and any further loss would make some of them hardly worth following and would encourage the growth of provincial chambers.[173] The bar took its cue from Mr Justice Blackburn, who insisted that the 'great central bar of England' must be preserved inviolate as a bulwark against judicial tyranny and government corruption. That became the banner under which the bar marched, and in the process it took almost by default the crucial decision to defend its traditional central organization.[174] By casting themselves in this romantic constitutional role (one which continued to be played with increasing implausibility) they conveniently favoured a forum giving them exclusive audience over one where they had to compete with solicitors.

The bar's opposition was not offset by the support of the solicitors' professional bodies. The Law Society and several provincial law societies in the bigger cities identified their interests more readily with the bar than with the smaller fry in their own profession and the Law Society feared a reversal of the inflow of provincial litigation to London.[175] Moreover, any threat to the right of the Rutlands, Westmorelands, and Huntingdonshires to their own Assize would be resisted by their MPs and other members anxious about the future of Assize towns. The most Selborne could include in the 1873 Act was the new venue rule.

The revision of circuits was left to be arranged by a committee of judges and when the Commissioners returned to this issue they lacked the will to engage with it. Their final report merely endorsed the general principles laid down earlier, much to the annoyance of those members who regarded this as a dereliction

---

[170] *Second Report 1872*, 10–18; Polden, *History of the County Court*, 75–7.

[171] *Second Report 1872*, 18.   [172] e.g. (1871–2) 16 *Sol. J.* 785, 798–800.

[173] 'The paucity or absence of causes on all the circuits has been beyond precedent. The Norfolk and Oxford circuits have been a complete farce': (1871) 6 *LJ* 189, and see also 566.

[174] *Second Report 1872*, 26.   [175] Polden, *History of the County Court*, 81–2.

of duty.[176] The Conservative government left the contentious question of an expanded role for county courts alone, declining to adopt any of several private members' bills and leaving them to be roughly handled by a hostile select committee.[177] The suggestion that the jurisdiction of quarter sessions might be modestly extended was also ignored[178] and the handful of active local courts were left intact.[179] In essence, the role of the Assizes remained scarcely damaged.

What remained was a tidying-up operation to enable Assizes to function more efficiently. Integrating them with continuous London sittings proved so awkward that it absorbed much time and energy on the part of judges and ministers.[180] Pessimistic predictions that 'the abolition of Assizes is a mere matter of time'[181] proved well wide of the mark. Even Surrey preserved its Assize, albeit in a rather truncated form,[182] and though the home circuit was amalgamated with the Norfolk to form the south-eastern, the division of the northern counties kept the number of circuits the same as before.[183] The county remained the unit, but a price was exacted for this in the grouping of several counties so that each Assize did not have to visit every Assize town.

Introduced by the Home Secretary, R. A. Cross, grouping was strongly attacked by a committee of judges but survived the immediate threat, albeit in a modified form.[184] The judges were even more averse to Cross's other innovation, the fourth Assize. This was a response to widespread complaints that innocent prisoners were still languishing too long in prison before the red judge came to town.[185] Judges were sceptical about the innocence of many of those who were acquitted and argued that in any event their sufferings were outweighed by the problems the new Assize caused for others and the adverse effect on themselves of too much travelling, especially in winter. They felt it would be catastrophic if leaders of the bar

---

[176] *Fifth Report 1874*, ix–x, and notes by Moffatt and Hollams. Even then, by repeating its former recommendation for grouping of counties and abolition of the home circuit, it attracted a dissent by Coleridge CJ.

[177] Polden, *History of the County Court*, 77–80. The report is *PP* 1878 (267), xi.

[178] The first report (17) had suggested they be allowed to try burglaries.

[179] See below, pp. 866–71.

[180] Abel-Smith and Stevens, *Lawyers and the Courts*, 84–7; R. Stevens, *The Independence of the Judiciary* (Oxford, 1993), 13–17.

[181] (1877) 62 *LT* 343.

[182] Cocks, *Foundations of the Modern Bar*, 142–6. For controversy over the workings of the revised arrangements see (1879) 14 *LJ* 475–7.

[183] *Ibid.*, 142–6. The judges' report is in LCO 1/4. One member, Mellor, was opposed to almost every suggested change.

[184] *The Judges' Report on Circuits*, *PP* 1878 (311), lxiii, 2–3 and Cross's reply, 10. In Parliament he admitted that grouping had been carried too far in some places: *PD* 1878 (s3) 240: 39–40.

[185] Winter Assizes Act 1876 c. 57; D. J. Bentley, *English Criminal Justice in the Nineteenth Century* (1998), 53–4.

declined judgeships on this account, yet were also hostile to allowing county court judges to take criminal trials or to expanding the role of the quarter sessions.[186]

The extra duty undoubtedly stretched judicial resources, and the relief provided by making judges from the other divisions and the Court of Appeal undertake circuit duty was short-lived; the disruption to the High Court and a few unfortunate instances of glaring ignorance of the criminal law and practice forced Selborne to end that experiment in fusion in 1884.[187] When he left office the following year he was entitled to great credit for the creation of the SCJ, but was not well satisfied with the limited improvements to provincial justice.

8. THE ROYAL COURTS OF JUSTICE

The creation of a vice-chancellor in 1813 gave the impetus for an overdue reconstruction of the courts in Westminster Hall, the chief venue for all the superior courts except the civilians of Doctors' Commons.[188] Sir John Soane's characteristically ingenious additions and alterations, mostly to the west side of the medieval hall, presaged the shape of courtrooms to come in their emphasis on the separation of public, lawyers, officials, and judges,[189] but were mutilated by a Parliament suddenly enamoured of the beauties of the old gothic structure.[190] The hall would anyway have been unable to accommodate successive additions to the numbers of judges of common law and equity, with new courts of bankruptcy and Chancery appeals and new or expanded registries, e.g. for judgment orders, land charges, and land registration.[191] The consequence was an unplanned and 'fantastic diffusion of the courts and offices'.[192]

Though veterans like the teak-tough Jack Campbell extolled the virtues of a brisk walk from the Temple to Westminster Hall, juniors perpetually struggling

---

[186] Judges' Report on Circuits 1878, 5–6, and see the rejection of Stephen J.'s proposal for single judge Assizes at 4. The Committee (chaired by Coleridge) considered that proposal and several cognate matters.

[187] Polden, 'Mingling the Waters', 598–610.

[188] For descriptions of the hall see J. M. Crook and M. H. Port, *The History of the King's Works*, vol. 6, 1782–1851 (1973), 497–503 and D. B. Brownlee, *The Law Courts: The Architecture of George Edmund Street* (Cambridge, Mass., 1984), 47–50.

[189] Brownlee, *Law Courts*, 48–9. The transformation of courts of law from largely undifferentiated public spaces to more complex structures affording greater privacy to judges and officers and providing the opportunity for a more rehearsed and controlled spectacle is explored in C. Graham, *Ordering Law* (Aldershot, 2003), 115–56.

[190] The attack was orchestrated by the 'mischievous' Henry Bankes (*History of the King's Works*, 506) through a carefully chosen select committee: PP 1824 (307), vi.

[191] Brownlee, *Law Courts*, 50–1.

[192] RC on Sites for the Law Courts, Report, *PP* 1860 (2710), xxxi, vii, quoted in Brownlee, *Law Courts*, 51.

between judges' chambers and the courts differed;[193] and with Chancery courts sitting increasingly in Lincoln's Inn and Chancery Lane, the separation of equity and common law bars was accentuated.[194] Solicitors and their clerks were greater sufferers, having to attend at both offices and courts while keeping their own premises manned as well.[195]

Laymen and lawyers suffered from the primitive and inadequate accommodation in the courts and offices. The equity courts in Lincoln's Inn were 'wretched sheds'[196] and the masters and registrars did business in cramped, noisy, chaotic conditions, while 26 clerks were crammed into the accountant-general's office which originally held just four.[197] Westminster Hall was worse.[198] The bar complained of the lack of a library (Sir Thomas Wilde was seen heading for court followed by two hackney carriages full of books)[199] and a hopeless shortage of consulting rooms. Solicitors were reduced to using their hats as writing desks in corridors thronged with people. Reporters elbowed students out of their box, while jurors awaiting their turn could find no seats and witnesses arrived in the box breathless and shaken from having barged through the crowd, a state hardly conducive to cool recollection.[200] Even judges were uncomfortable, especially those forced into the 'almost incredibly sordid'[201] rooms improvised to house extra courts and judges and known as the cock loft and the dog hole.[202]

As the imperial capital was gradually embellished with splendid public buildings suited to its pretensions the picturesque but undignified quarters of the law became more anomalous,[203] especially once ambitious provincial cities—Liverpool and Manchester, Birmingham and Leeds—invested in monumental court buildings.[204]

Many judges and barristers were deeply attached to Westminster Hall. Some, like Scarlett, were unabashedly sentimental[205] while others like Denman purported to find at least a symbolical importance in the juxtaposition of legislature

---

[193] 'H', 'Removal of the Courts from Westminster' (1843) 29 *LM* 162–83, 166, quoting evidence of Samuel Martin to the select committee of 1842 (*PP* 1842 (476), x, i).

[194] *Ibid.*, 175, quoting Sutton Sharpe's evidence.

[195] *Ibid.*, 169, 175, quoting evidence of E. W. Field and Bryan Holme. For similar problems at a later date, see E. F. Spence, *Bar and Buskin* (1930), 36–7.

[196] A. J. Ashton, *As I Went On My Way* (1924), 124.

[197] 'Courts of Law at Temple Bar' (1845–6) 4 (s2) *LM* 34–45 at 38–9.

[198] Nostalgically described by W. Willis, 'The Courts of Westminster' (1907) *Cornhill Mag.* 319–34, less uncritically by Ashton, *As I Went On My Way*, 115–22.

[199] 'H', 'Removal of the Courts from Westminster', 166, quoting M. D. Hill.

[200] *Ibid.*, 163–8.   [201] Ashton, *As I Went on My Way*, 118.

[202] Brownlee, *Law Courts*, 51.   [203] *Ibid.*, 58–9.

[204] Graham, *Ordering Law*, 97–8, 277–307.

[205] Evidence to select committee, 1842, quoted in 'H', 'Removal of the Courts from Westminster', 181–2.

and courts.[206] But they found Charles Barry adamant that his new Parliament buildings could not incorporate a major expansion of law courts,[207] and the Law Society (solicitors being less devoted to a site which held fewer associations and was less conveniently located for them)[208] shrewdly commissioned Barry to sketch a plan for their own favoured location in Lincoln's Inn Fields.[209] Driven by E. W. Field and supported by the Attorney-General Sir Thomas Wilde (a former solicitor), they secured select committees in 1842 and 1845 which published evidence overwhelmingly in favour of concentrating the courts and offices on a new site, though preference shifted to a warren of overcrowded, unhealthy, and immoral streets lying between Carey Street and the Strand, just behind the Law Society's hall in Chancery Lane.[210]

Not everyone favoured concentration. Lincoln's Inn offered to provide superior accommodation for Chancery alone, partly from financial self-interest but also from fears that the concentration of courts was linked to a fusion of law and equity,[211] as indeed some of its supporters openly avowed.[212] St. Leonards and other opponents of concentration also objected to the principal source of financing for the move, utilizing suitors' funds in Chancery; inability to tap that source would almost certainly doom such an expensive project.[213]

Despite energetic lobbying by the Law Amendment Society and law societies, the project made no headway until Attorney-General Bethell persuaded Palmerston to appoint a royal commission under Sir J. T. Coleridge. The Coleridge report was the turning point in the struggle, endorsing the Carey Street site and, by a majority, the raid on Chancery funds.[214] Equity judges continued to oppose the latter, and it took several years to translate the report into legislation, its

---

[206] Quoted in Brownlee, *Law Courts*, 60.

[207] SC on Courts of Law and Equity, Report, *PP* 1845 (608), xii, qq. 1–106. For a defiant riposte see 'Removal of Courts from Westminster' (1845–6) 3 *LR* 305–19.

[208] See evidence of W. Wright to the select committee of 1842, quoted in 'Removal of the Courts from Westminster', showing the concentration of solicitors and in particular agency firms around Chancery Lane and Lincoln's Inn Fields.

[209] Brownlee, *Law Courts*, 52–3. It was one of the first causes to be taken up by the Law Society. In 1830 Brougham had unavailingly presented a petition from 250 solicitors complaining about the condition of the courts.

[210] SCs on Courts of Law and Equity 1842 and *PP* 1845 (608), xii. Brownlee, *Law Courts*, 52–61. M. D. Hill was apparently the first to suggest this site: '"Where Shall the New Law Courts Be Built?"' (1849) 10 (s2) *LM* 341–55.

[211] Brownlee, *Courts of Law*, 63–5. Charles Selwyn led the Lincoln's Inn faction: Selborne, *Memorials Part Two, Personal and Political*, i, 22.

[212] Brownlee, *Law Courts*, 60–1; 'Observations on the Concentration of the Courts of Justice' (1858–9) 6 (s3) *LM & LR* 353–68, reviewing a pamphlet with that title.

[213] 'Observations on the Concentration of the Law Courts', 356–68.

[214] Brownlee, *Law Courts*, 63–5; *RC on Sites for Court of Law, Report 1860*.

prospects particularly damaged by Gladstone's alarmist prediction of cost over-runs in 1861. Gladstone actually favoured the new courts but Field's two bills only finally passed in 1865 (just before Bethell's disgrace)[215] after Gladstone had assembled a less controversial funding package.

The choice of an architect and a design was entrusted to an unusually large royal commission under Cranworth which included virtually the whole of the legal establishment either in person or by representation.[216] Despite its careful attempts to avoid the pitfalls exposed by previous competitions, it contrived 'the worst conducted architectural competition of all time'.[217] The judges it had entrusted with the final choice were unable to decide, and proposed an impossible solution requiring E. M. Barry and G. E. Street to collaborate. Eventually the Treasury nominated Street, who endured years of frustration and had to make endless alterations to his 'grand design'.[218]

Delays arose partly from the determined efforts of the First Commissioner of Works, Austen Layard, abetted by the Chancellor of the Exchequer, Robert Lowe and most of the barristers of the Temple, to jettison Carey Street for a site on the newly embanked riverside. With the government itself divided, this 'battle of the sites' had to be fought before a select committee and when the embankment site was finally scotched[219] Street had repeatedly to pare down his plans to meet the demands of both Lowe and also Layard's successor, the philistine Acton Ayrton, two of Gladstone's most economy-minded disciples.[220]

The plan which was finally accepted (though the architect did not live to see it completed[221]) fell short of the grandeur and scale of the original and did not accommodate all the offices; probate, lunacy, and the land registry were all housed elsewhere. The delays did have the fortuitous effect of ensuring that the building had electric lighting,[222] though it lacked lifts.[223] The most serious practical defect,

---

[215] Courts of Justice Building Act 1865 (c. 48) and Courts of Justice (Concentration) Site Act 1865 (c. 49); Brownlee, *Law Courts*, 65–74; Nash, *Life of Lord Westbury*, ii, 92–9.

[216] Brownlee, *Law Courts*, 77–9. Instructions to Architects, *PP* 1866 (325), lviii; Report, *PP* 1871 [C.290], xx, i. Summary in 'The Courts of Justice Commission' (1866) 21 (s3) *LM & LR*, 77–93.

[217] Abel-Smith and Stevens, *Lawyers and the Courts*, 80.

[218] Brownlee, *Law Courts*, 85–169. The most striking designs were by Alfred Waterhouse, whose Manchester law courts were highly praised, and that most romantic and lavish of goths William Burges. Both these and others had some influence on Street's final version.

[219] *Ibid.*, 181–203; Selborne, *Memorials Part Two, Personal and Political*, i, 23–5.

[220] Brownlee, *Law Courts*, 204–63.

[221] Street died on 15 December 1881. His son Arthur and A. W. Blomfield completed the building.

[222] Brownlee, *Law Courts*, 348–50.

[223] See the petition of the Solicitors' Managing Clerks Association in (1897–8) 42 *Sol. J.* 517, and earlier complaints in (1891–2) 36 *Sol. J.* 2.

however, was that many of the courtrooms had dreadful acoustics.[224] During its long gestation the ruling taste in public architecture had passed from the classical of Barry's original design for Lincoln's Inn Fields to the high gothic which all the competing architects had felt necessary to adopt, but when Street's masterpiece in that style was opened in 1882 gothic was already passé. Some advanced thinkers felt the conservatism of legal institutions was fittingly represented in an old-fashioned style.[225]

[224] Abel-Smith and Stevens, *Lawyers and the Courts*, 80 quote Baron Huddleston: 'the Courts were constructed so that counsel could not hear the judge, the judge could not hear the witness, and the jury could hear neither'.

[225] Brownlee, *Law Courts*, 369–74. According to (1885–6) 30 *Sol. J.* 415, Ayrton's cheeseparing had left it already short of courtrooms. A western extension was opened in 1908. E. W. Mountford's Central Criminal Court (1907) was in Neo-English Baroque.

VII

The Government and Organization of the Supreme Court of Judicature

1. THE INSTITUTIONS OF GOVERNMENT

The Lord Chancellor's Office

The nineteenth-century Lord Chancellor was in two senses 'a minister without a ministry'.[1] He had no team of civil servants nor accommodation dedicated solely to his executive functions. In the early part of the century he and his small retinue of secretaries and officers arrived in a coach each morning to conduct his business in his own court at the top of the steps at the south end of Westminster Hall. No permanent corpus of departmental records was kept and the papers belonging to an outgoing Chancellor were removed and usually destroyed.[2]

The Chancellor had officials serving him in his various capacities, but most of those belonging to the court of Chancery were not available to him for non-judicial work and those belonging to the great seal were reduced and remodelled in the 1870s.[3] Besides his retinue of body officers, some of whom were also employed on clerical duties[4] the Chancellor had three secretaries: a secretary of presentations for ecclesiastical patronage; a secretary of commissions for the magistracy; and a principal secretary who was a general factotum.[5] By the 1860s

---

[1] N. Underhill, *The Lord Chancellor* (Lavenham, 1978), 188.

[2] Even their personal papers are scarce, especially those between Lyndhurst and Selborne. For the early records of the LCO see P. Polden, *Guide to the Records of the LCD* (1988), xxv–xvii. Cairns thanked Selborne for leaving so many papers behind: Cairns to Selborne, 11 February 1874, Lambeth Palace Library, Selborne Mss. vol. 1866 f. 107.

[3] Westbury complained that he had no one whom he could use to do the preparatory work on a bill (quoted in Underhill, *Lord Chancellor*, 188).

[4] e.g. the mace-bearer and purse-bearer, usually by virtue of being appointed to undemanding offices in the House of Lords: R. F. V. Heuston, *Lives of the Lord Chancellors, 1885–1940* (Oxford, 1964), xx.

[5] D. Woodhouse, *The Office of Lord Chancellor* (Oxford, 2001), 41–7 and Polden, *Guide to the Records of the LCD*, 13–17. There is a contemporary account in the *RC on the Legal Departments, Second Report, PP* 1874 [C 1107], xxiv, 33–40.

all were quartered in the House of Lords, except a couple of outlying clerks in Quality Court, off Chancery Lane.[6]

At the same time that the Judicature Commissioners were seeking to remodel their structure, there were moves afoot to reduce the autonomy which the courts enjoyed and integrate the legal departments more closely with the rest of the public service. An Act of 1869 laid down the principle that the expenditure on the courts should be met from the consolidated fund; some of the suitors' funds in Chancery and bankruptcy were transferred to the exchequer and Treasury supervision over monies in court was strengthened.[7] In 1873, pursuant to the recommendations of the Childers Committee, all new appointees not permanently attached to a judge were 'deemed to be civil servants' and that same Committee expressed the need for 'some Department of the Government directly responsible to Parliament [to have] the power to administer and organise those officers in such a manner as to ensure the greatest amount of efficiency, combined with all practicable economy'.[8] Selborne persuaded the Committee not to recommend that this 'Ministry of Justice' be located in the Home Office, but it was due more to the reluctance of the government to embark on a major and (as involving patronage) controversial legislative initiative than to any convincing constitutional or administrative arguments that the Lord Chancellor became not only the president of the SCJ but also the responsible minister for its finances and organization.[9]

When, as had to be conceded, the legal offices were investigated by the Lisgar Commission, Selborne and Cairns agreed (as did the Commissioners) that the principal secretary should not be converted into a permanent official but should, like the other secretaries, continue to come in and go out with his master.[10] By 1882, however, the labour of implementing the Judicature Acts and the prospect of an ongoing supervision of the Supreme Court had convinced both men that this was no longer viable.[11] The last fruit of their co-operation in law reform was to combine in the person of Kenneth Muir McKenzie a new permanent secretaryship with the dignified and largely honorific office of clerk of the Crown in Chancery. The other secretaryships were continued and in 1886 Halsbury gave Muir McKenzie a chief clerk.[12]

---

[6] Polden, *Guide to the Records of the LCD*, 14; *DC Report on the Legal Offices*, PP 1878 [C. 2067], xxv, App. C.

[7] Courts of Justice Act 1869 c. 91.

[8] Judicature Act 1873, s 85; *SC on Civil Service Expenditure, Report 1873*, PP (248), vii, 104.

[9] Polden, *Guide to the Records of the LCD*, 15. For the revival of the Ministry of Justice project in 1918 see G. Drewry, 'Lord Haldane's Ministry of Justice—Stillborn or Strangled at Birth?' (1983) 61 *Public Administration* 396–414.

[10] *RC on the Legal Departments, Second Report 1874*, 34.

[11] R. Stevens, *The Independence of the Judiciary* (Oxford, 1992), 8.

[12] Polden, *Guide to the Records of the LCD*, 17.

This small department was now entirely concentrated at the House of Lords and for the next 30 years Muir McKenzie was, for all practical purposes, 'the Lord Chancellor's Office'. It was characteristic of the man that he chose for his assistant Adolphus Liddell, an unsuccessful barrister with no professional ambition, polished manners, and an amiable disposition.[13] Muir McKenzie is an elusive figure whose secretive working methods makes his influence difficult to follow.[14] For all his detestation of patronage,[15] he was rumoured to enjoy a considerable backstairs influence on judicial offices and, as befitted a political radical, he was at first a vigorous proponent of reforms in the legal system. Unfortunately for him, the Chancellor for most of that time was Halsbury, conservative in politics and administrative reform alike, and by the time a genuine reformer in Haldane arrived, Muir McKenzie had lost much of his earlier zeal.[16]

Haldane was astonished by the working practices and organization of the office, which he described as 'not far removed from being an interesting little museum', but he took no immediate action, perhaps waiting for Muir McKenzie to retire.[17] The only resource Muir McKenzie hankered after was a junior minister in the Commons, where LCO measures were inadequately promoted by Treasury ministers or law officers.[18] He was content with an office in which record-keeping was sparse and imperfect and which was wholly dependent upon his own memory and knowledge.[19] Though his contribution to reforming the courts was generously acknowledged by the Civil Service Commission,[20] it was clear that substantial changes in the LCO as well as the courts it supervised were badly overdue.

---

[13] Liddell became assistant secretary in 1888 and outlasted Muir McKenzie, retiring in 1919. His reminiscences, *Notes From the Life of an Ordinary Mortal* (1911) are for the most part unrevealing about the office.

[14] Evidently not a man to be taken lightly: see e.g. Master Chitty's evidence to the *RC on Delays in the King's Bench Division*, PP 1913 [Cd. 6761, 6762], xxx; 1914 [Cd. 7177, 7178], xxxvii: '[o]ne wishes to be particularly careful not to suggest anything against Sir Kenneth Muir McKenzie in any possible shape or form' (C. 6762, *Evidence I*, q. 425). An obituarist described him as 'a difficult man to know and a dangerous man to thwart or underestimate': *The Times*, 23 May 1930.

[15] He 'abstained almost ostentatiously from taking any part either in the work relating to magistrates or in that relating to the ecclesiastical patronage', Sir Claud Schuster's memorandum of 1943 in NA PRO LCO 2/3630.

[16] Stevens, *Independence of the Judiciary*, 10–12; Polden, *Guide to the Records of the LCD*, 18–21. He had an extraordinary late-flowering political career, becoming (under Labour) the oldest person to attain government office in the twentieth century.

[17] He did so in 1915, aged 70. His successor was that legendary figure Claud Schuster, permanent secretary until 1944 and, like his predecessor, raised to the peerage.

[18] Polden, *Guide to the Records of the LCD*, 21.

[19] Ibid., 18–19.

[20] *RC on the Civil Service, Sixth Report*, PP 1914–16 [Cd. 7832], xii, 9–10.

The Council of Judges

One of the permanent secretary's roles was as secretary to the Judges' Council. This body, comprising all the judges of the SCJ, originated in a concession to Cockburn and his allies.[21] It had an imposingly wide remit[22] and was to meet at least annually, reporting to the Home Secretary.[23] Although the Lord Chancellor was a member, he did not usually attend, leaving it to be chaired by the Lord Chief Justice.

As has been remarked, the Council had considerable potential for reformist activities but it was never fulfilled.[24] It seems that the official report to the Home Office was made on just three occasions (in 1880, 1884, and 1892) and the KBD Commission in 1912 was told that it had met only three times in 33 years.[25] This is a misleading figure, however. In fact what was described as the Council met regularly until 1889 and debated several important subjects: appeals from the benchers of the inns of court; rules for district registries; the proposal for continuous provincial sittings; sentences in criminal cases; and the long vacation.[26] Above all they held repeated discussions on the vexed question of circuits and Assizes.[27] If the Council was to become the main forum for dealing with the organization and procedures of the SCJ, it was essential that its *de facto* head should be in broad sympathy with the Lord Chancellor, but Coleridge had come to resent what he felt was the expansion of the Lord Chancellor's power at the expense of his own office, bemoaning 'the enthroning of the Lord Chancellor upon the neck of all of us' and finding 'the great traditional influences of the Chief Justice and the deference to him lessened materially, in every way, year by year'.[28] Coleridge became a defender of the old system and led the opposition to key changes—the fourth Assize and grouping in particular. In 1887 he was the beneficiary of a remarkable act of deference on Halsbury's part.

---

[21] It was not in the bill of 1870 but appeared as cl.75 in that of 1873.

[22] '...for the purpose of considering the operation of the Act and of the Rules of Court for the time being in force, and also the working of the several offices and the arrangements relative to the duties of the officers of the said Court respectively, and of enquiring and examining into any defects which may appear to exist in the system of procedure or the administration of the law in the said High Court of Justice or the said Court of Appeal...' (Judicature Act 1873, s 75).

[23] Presumably because the Lord Chancellor then lacked any permanent secretariat. That was the reason given by the Home Office for preparing orders in council concerning Assize arrangements: H. Leigh Pemberton to K. Muir McKenzie, 1 January 1886, PRO LCO 1/7.

[24] The view e.g. of S. Rosenbaum, 'Studies in English Civil Procedure, II' (1915) 63 *University of Pennsylvania Law Rev.* 151–82, 160 n.31, and C. Mullins, *In Quest of Justice* (1931), 194–5.

[25] LCO 2/602; *RC on the KB Division, Second Report 1913* [C. 7177], 42.

[26] Polden, *Guide to the Records of the LCD*, 86–7; LCO 1/4–7, 54. Other than 2/242, which is dated 1906–10, 1/54 is the only pre-Schuster file with this title, and it is not an original file but a miscellany made up by Liddell.

[27] See pp. 779–80, 825–8.

[28] Coleridge to Lindley, 17 September 1889, Coleridge, *Life and Correspondence of John Duke, Lord Coleridge*, 2 vols (1904), ii, 359.

Comprehensively outvoted on a proposal to impose extensive grouping for civil matters and to have home counties litigation heard in London in exchange for the end of the hated fourth Assize, Coleridge nevertheless backed the reactionary diatribes of Grantham J. with a 'bizarre outburst' of his own.[29]

Halsbury gave way but the episode probably left him disenchanted with the Council. At all events, its regular meetings ceased not long afterwards and the only time he summoned one after 1890 was to fend off demands for a royal commission.[30] After 1892 it did not meet again until 1904, when it considered proposals to alter the long vacation; there was a meeting in 1907 for the same purpose.[31] Loreburn and Haldane disparaged the Council and Schuster's reading of the papers (and perhaps a briefing by Muir McKenzie) suggested to him that 'the proceedings on each occasion have not been such as to encourage those present to come together again with any lively hopes of any good result'.[32] Brief revivals between the wars confirmed that view and it was at length abolished in 1981.

The Rule Committee

As established in 1881 the Rule Committee comprised the heads of the divisions and the Court of Appeal, plus four judges.[33] The judges were in practice nominated by the chiefs, two from the QBD and one apiece from Chancery and the Court of Appeal.[34] Though Halsbury had rebuffed the professional bodies' call for formal consultative status, in 1894 Herschell expanded the Committee to include the president of the Law Society *ex officio* and a further two persons, at least one a practising barrister.[35] Given the shortness of the president's term and his other commitments this hardly provided effective representation of solicitors, and in 1909 it was modified. Henceforth both bar and solicitors were to have two representatives, a silk and a junior nominated by the Bar Council, a London solicitor named by the Law Society and a provincial one chosen by the Lord Chancellor.[36] The

---

[29] Stevens, *Independence of the Judiciary*, 16; Polden, *Guide to the Records of the LCD*, 114.

[30] See below. There is a list of meetings from 1885 in LCO 2/242. Perhaps the omission to send the statutory report about most of the meetings is an example of what Schuster described as Muir McKenzie's compete unscrupulousness in interpreting statutes: Stevens, *Independence of the Judiciary*, 12.

[31] LCO 2/242.

[32] Schuster to Lord Reading CJ, 23 June 1919, LCO 2/442.

[33] Judicature Act 1881, s 19. See Rosenbaum, 'Studies in English Civil Procedure', 165–75; Polden, *Guide to the Records of the LCD*, 57–75.

[34] Polden, *Guide to the Records of the LCD*, 58. The nominations lay with the Lord Chancellor and at least from 1921, the Committee was formally reconstituted annually.

[35] *Ibid.*, 58; Judicature Act (Procedure) 1894 c. 16, s 4.

[36] Rule Committee Act 1909 c. 11; Rosenbaum, 'Studies in English Civil Procedure', 165. The London Chamber of Commerce's request for representation was refused: LCO 2/250.

full Committee of 12 was rather unwieldy and it was seldom that everyone attended. Most judges sat for only a few years but a few made substantial contributions, examples being Lindley and Chitty in the early years and Channell in the 1900s.[37] No rule was ever annulled under the parliamentary procedure, but dissents were now and then recorded.[38]

It was sometimes suggested that the Committee would benefit from having a master as a member, and the impressive contribution made by Master Chitty to rule-making after the First World War lends substance to this argument.[39] It was, after all, from the masters (who held monthly meetings) that most suggestions for amendment came.[40] The law societies were another frequent source (more so than the Bar Council, though that was very active in criticizing the new *in forma pauperis* rules which dominated the Committee's meetings from 1910 to 1914[41]). Much of the Committee's business, however, arose from new statutes.[42]

At intervals in the 1890s the Committee's composition and activities came under strong criticism.[43] No one denied its industry (it usually held two or three meetings a year) or productivity; 24 sets of rules were said to have been added to the 1883 code by 1894 and a further six between 1896 and 1899.[44] The quality of the drafting, however, left much to be desired. Order 30 (the summons for directions) proved a particular embarrassment. Rule changes of 1894 needed a six-strong Court of Appeal to interpret and then a further rule to remedy the consequences of their decision.[45] Furthermore, despite the abundance of rules they did not cover all details of practice and were supplemented by a growing body of practice directions issued by the chiefs.[46] These contributed to swell the *Supreme Court Practice* (the 'White Book'), which had reached 2400 pages with an index of 332 by 1914,[47] and which it was said only Chitty and perhaps Bray J.

---

[37] For the meetings see Polden, *Guide to the Records of the LCD*, 62–3.

[38] e.g. Vaughan Williams J.'s dissent on the Companies Act rules of 1903 (LCO 2/177).

[39] E. A. Bell, *Those Meddlesome Attorneys* (1939), 104. C. H. Morton, commenting on Chitty's suggestion, said there seemed to be a feeling against it on the Committee but he did not know why: *RC on the KB Division, Evidence I*, q. 423.

[40] Rosenbaum, 'Studies in English Civil Procedure', 166–7. The Evershed Committee in the 1950s also felt the Committee still lacking in practical expertise.

[41] e.g. PRO LCO 2/250. For these rules see S. M. Cretney, *Family Law in the Twentieth Century* (Oxford, 2003), 306–9.

[42] e.g. the Finance Acts from 1894 and the Patents Act 1907.

[43] (1889–90) 34 *Sol. J.* 784 (reporting the annual provincial meeting of the Law Society); (1894–5) 39 *Sol. J.* 5; (1898–9) 43 *Sol. J.* 310.

[44] (1898–9) 43 *Sol. J.* 326.

[45] (1892–3) 37 *Sol. J.* 124; (1893–4) 38 *Sol. J.* 378; *Re Holloway (a Solicitor)* [1894] 2 QB 163; (1894–5) 39 *Sol. J.* 5.

[46] Polden, *Guide to the Records of the LCD*, 59.

[47] F. H. Newbolt, 'The Rule Committee and its Work' (1914–15) 40 (s5) *LM & LR* 129–38. In an after-dinner speech in 1899 Lord Chief Justice Russell said they should burn the White Book: (1899) 18 *LN* 163.

fully mastered.[48] Its intimidating bulk was a measure of how far the hoped-for simplicity of the Judicature Acts had become encrusted with procedural niceties and complications,[49] and the only attempt the Committee made to consolidate the rules, in the mid- 1890s, was left incomplete.[50]

2. ORGANIZATION AND STAFF

The Lisgar Sub-Commission recommended that the common law offices should be amalgamated into a 'central Masters' department for the Common Law Divisions of the High Court of Justice, which shall provide all the official and clerical power required for the administration of civil and criminal justice in London and on circuit'.[51] The Jessel Committee was more ambitious, and proposed integrating almost all departments within the central office, the principal exceptions being the Chancery registrars and taxing office and the non-contentious business staff of the PDA, who alone among the officers were not to be relocated in the Strand but would remain in Somerset House.[52] In the event, the whole of the PDA and both the Chancery registrars and taxing masters preserved their independence.

A number of departments were created within the central office (eight of them in 1914). Besides those Chancery and PDA offices which retained their independence, there were added several others. The London Bankruptcy court staff were transferred in 1883, a Supreme Court pay office was created in 1884, a central scrivenery department in 1891, a companies winding-up department in the same year, and an office for the Court of Criminal Appeal in 1908. The only further amalgamation of offices to offset this proliferation was the central taxing office in 1901. All but the probate registry were housed in or adjacent to the RCJ.

Many of these offices were overmanned at the outset, and the central office nevertheless contrived also to offer a poor service to litigants, whose complaints

---

[48] T. Humphreys, *Criminal Days* (1946), 22. See also Polden, *Guide to the Records of the LCD*, 61.

[49] *The Last Serjeant: The Memoirs of A.M. Sullivan Q.C.* (1952), 280–3. Newbolt instanced Order lxv (costs), covering 90 lines with 114 pages of explanatory notes, yet with 115 other rules touching the subject: 'Rule Committee and its Work'.

[50] The work of Lindley, Charles, and Kay, who went beyond the remit given by Herschell of tidying-up the 1883 rules and sought, among other things, to incorporate the various sets which stood as separate rules and to extend the operations of the Commercial Court: LCO 2/126, especially Lindley to Halsbury, 5 August 1896, Halsbury to Rule Committee, 30 November 1896. The 'lost revision' was noted e.g. in (1896–7) 41 *Sol. J.* 286 and S. Rosenbaum, 'The Rule Committee and its Work' (1914–15) 40 (s5) *LM* 138–51. Lindley was furious: KCL Library, *Autobiography of Lord Lindley*, 114–15.

[51] *Second Report 1874*, 23.

[52] *DC on Legal Offices, Report 1878*, 7. According to Muir McKenzie, it was the intimate association between the probate registry and the revenue departments that dictated keeping them in the same location: *RC on the Civil Service, Evidence*, q. 43,905.

led to the setting up of a committee under the LCJ in 1886.[53] Overmanning was inevitable if all the staff of the old courts were kept on, for as the Chancellor of the Exchequer ruefully told the Childers Committee, 'I have never seen yet that we were able to get any great improvement in the law without paying smart money for it in some way.'[54] Government witnesses faced sharp questioning from the Committee over the generous compensation recently awarded to the redundant commissioners in bankruptcy and the accountant-general of Chancery, and there was no intention of incurring further expense and criticism by buying out court clerks and masters.

Consequently the Judicature Act 1873, section 77 enabled the court staff to 'continue to perform the same duties as nearly as may be', preserving their salaries, tenure, and pension rights. Only on a vacancy were the Lord Chancellor and the Treasury empowered to make a saving by leaving a post unfilled.[55] Since attempts to persuade surplus clerks to retire on less than their full salary were for the most part unavailing,[56] the departments created by the amalgamation of offices were manned rather according to the existing expertise of clerks (often very specialized) than to the number needed to carry out the work.[57] The reconstruction was all the more difficult because the RCJ buildings were not well adapted and the establishment was top-heavy with senior clerks; ultimately some half-a-dozen 'redundants' who could not be fitted in anywhere were pensioned off on full salary.[58] Only very gradually was the complement reduced to an appropriate level.[59]

The delicate task of fitting these clerks into their new departments was given by the Lord Chancellor to the official solicitor, H. Leigh Pemberton, for the Lisgar Commission's recommendation to create a superintendent was dropped.[60] The

---

[53] There was also a committee investigating the Chancery offices: see below, pp. 839–43.

[54] SC on Civil Service Expenditure, Report 1873, q. 4615.

[55] These provisions were strengthened by Judicature Act 1881, s 21, but the LCJ nevertheless filled a vacancy in a post the Lord Chancellor felt redundant: LCO 1/30.

[56] H. Leigh Pemberton to W.O. Law, 8 March 1880, LCO 1/27.

[57] DC on the Central Office, PP 1887 (181), lxi, iv. For examples see P. E. Vizard (q. 578), F. Gardener (qq.1133–4).

[58] Ibid., Master W. F. Pollock, q. 288, Master G. T. Jenkins, qq. 150, 268.

[59] The Central Office Committee hoped to reduce the central office clerks from 92 to 74 by natural wastage.

[60] DC on Legal Offices, Report 1878, 11. This curious official performed a range of functions, being 'a confidential adviser to the Court in matters where a solicitor's assistance is required' (RC on the Civil Service, Sixth Report 1915, 38), but mostly acted for lunatics and infants. He was allowed to continue in private practice and by 1913 his earnings from his official work came to £1800. He employed his own clerks, whose status was anomalous. Leigh Pemberton was succeeded in 1895 by W. H. Winterbotham, whom Muir McKenzie kept very much at arm's length. Descriptions of his duties are in LCO 1/61, RC on the Civil Service, Sixth Report 1915, 38–9 and Evidence, Winterbotham, qq. 49,857–50,056. See also Polden, Guide to the Records of the LCD, 80 and (on Pemberton) (1894–5) 39 Sol. J. 374.

Central Office Committee, and the senior master, felt this should have been entrusted to the masters, but they were a major part of the problem.[61] Initially they were too many[62] and most of them preferred their judicial role to the managerial.[63] The negotiations over establishment revealed them as conservative and eager to protect their own staff, and some were obstructive towards procedural innovations.[64] Some adopted such an unhelpful attitude that they drove solicitors to their more amenable colleagues, so unbalancing the workload,[65] and because they were too many for their duties they covertly arranged a rota of unauthorized absences.[66] After the Coleridge Report a 'committee of control' was set up with the senior master and two elected masters, but it seems to have achieved little.[67]

The whole hierarchy of oversight and control was weak. The Lord Chancellor had virtually no power over the PDA and there were doubts about the basis for the authority he exercised over the central office.[68] Heads of division mostly knew little about the running of their courts and the masters at the head of each department were really no more than 'primus inter pares'.[69] Not surprisingly, the result was a very conservative institution, which was only reluctantly embracing the typewriter—a reluctance compounded by the necessity of employing women to use it[70]—and the telephone[71] and in which the stated objectives of the 1879 Act, 'the assimilation of duties and places...homogeneity and co-operation'[72] had scarcely been fulfilled.

In 1893 Herschell, supported by the Treasury, sought to strengthen the Lord Chancellor's powers and align them more closely with those of other departmental ministers. But the judges were not deceived by the artless description of the clause as simply intended 'to strengthen the safeguards in the existing law

---

[61] Report, 1886, pp. iv–v and Master Pollock's evidence, q. 251.

[62] The number was reduced from 22 to 18 by the SCJ (Officers) Act 1879 c. 78 and the Committee felt that 15 would probably be enough (Report 1878, viii).

[63] In this respect MacDonell (RC on the Civil Service, Evidence, q. 4571) was probably more typical than Chitty (RC on the KB Division, Evidence I, q. 274). A. L Diamond, 'The Queen's Bench Master' (1960) 76 LQR 504–20, gives only one line to the management function.

[64] LCO 1/24, 27–35.

[65] DC on the Central Office, Report 1886, W. G. Andrews (qq. 1675–80) and C. L. Simpson (qq. 1746–9). The Committee, while disclaiming an intention to criticize, in fact made clear its disapproval at some of the masters' conduct (vi–viii).

[66] Ibid., Andrews, qq. 1665–72.   [67] Ibid., v.

[68] RC on the Civil Service, Sixth Report 1915, 8–9.

[69] Ibid., 21; DC on the Central Office, Report 1886, Pollock, q. 266. The senior master was chosen by length of service. Schuster later commented that Chitty was exceptional and no one was really fit to succeed him: to Sir W. Fisher, 6 August 1924, LCO 12/40.

[70] RC on the Civil Service, Sixth Report 1915, 26–7. There was only one female typist in the RCJ in 1914 and all copying was done by hand by 43 writers paid by piecework.

[71] As late as 1938 the Chancery division did not provide a telephone number for litigants.

[72] DC on the Central Office, Report 1886, iv.

in matters of unnecessary appointments'.[73] They reacted forcefully and unanimously, a committee claiming that the bill 'practically vests the whole control of the subordinate officers administering the law, whose numbers exceed 500, in [the Lord Chancellor]' and that it would be 'prejudicial to the due administration of justice', sacrificing 'much of the independence of the great tribunals of this country'.[74] Faced with this assertion that the independence of the judiciary was threatened and without (seemingly) Halsbury's support, Herschell abandoned the offending clause and draft regulations.[75]

It was not until 1913 that a further general scrutiny of the SCJ took place, as part of a wider inquiry into the civil service. This investigation, like the Childers Committee of 40 years before, found that the legal departments lagged badly behind the rest of the civil service in their working practices: in office hours, promotion and transfer, retirement, and above all in that most sensitive matter of recruitment. The Lisgar Committee had been split on the issue of whether all clerks other than the judges' body clerks should be appointed by the Lord Chancellor or some other 'Minister of Justice' and Selborne and Cairns had no wish to provoke unnecessary opposition to their proposals.[76] The Judicature Act 1873 provided that while the Lord Chancellor and the Treasury would determine the number of officials, and the former would appoint to all the non-divisional offices, divisional staff would be chosen by the head of the division.[77] This favoured the President of the PDA, whose staff were all outside the central office, but when the common law divisions were amalgamated it was felt undesirable to concentrate the patronage of the central office in the Lord Chief Justice so a rota was introduced which gave him, the Lord Chancellor, and the Master of the Rolls nominations in turn.[78] From the creation of the combined taxing office in 1902 a different rota applied to masters' appointments, the Lord Chancellor choosing taxing masters and the Master of the Rolls and Lord Chief Justice nominating alternately to the others.[79]

[73] Supreme Court of Judicature (Officers) Bill 1894, LCO 2/93, describing cl. 1. The provisions had been dropped from the SCJ Bill 1893 when they threatened to derail its less contentious changes to appeals.

[74] LCO 2/138. This response (16 May 1895) was published in *The Times* and the legal press.

[75] *RC on the Civil Service, Sixth Report 1915*, 23; LCO 2/91, 138. The provisions were also opposed in the legal press and some felt they showed that the Lord Chancellor and his permanent secretary had lost touch with the bar and the public: [E. S. Roscoe], 'The Progress and Procedure of the Civil Courts of England' (1897) 185 *Edin. Rev.* 156–82, at 180.

[76] Polden, 'Mingling the Waters', 578–9; *RC on the Legal Departments, Evidence, PP* 1875 [C. 1245], xxx, Selborne, 513–17 and supplementary report. See also *PD* 1873 (s3) 217: 223–6.

[77] Section 84.

[78] *RC on the Civil Service, Sixth Report 1915*, 13. See also *PD* 1881 (s3) 258: 604 and (1880–1) 25 *Sol. J.* 348, 714, 736, 749, 750.

[79] *RC on the Civil Service Evidence*, Muir McKenzie, q. 44,407.

'The case of clerks of assize', as the Civil Service Commission reported, stands by itself.[80] Here the judges still had the patronage, exercised by the senior judge going the summer circuit immediately preceding a vacancy.[81] Some judges were very keen to have this chance, so that Grantham and J. C. Lawrance doggedly went on the northern until the former won the prize for his son.[82] Indeed the prize was all too often awarded to one of the judge's relations; in 1914 five of the eight clerks were sons of judges, and not all were satisfactory.[83] Wilde had ceased to attend the Oxford circuit altogether and it was no radical critic but a King's Bench master who averred that 'it is common ground that the appointment of Coleridge and Lawford was a public scandal, solely directed to finding an occupation and livelihood for two of LCJ Coleridge's relations'.[84] Nepotism also flourished among the masters, where six or seven out of nine were related to judges.[85]

The 'influence' the Commission felt sure was at work here was less important for clerkships, which were, as Loreburn put it, 'not an object of very great ambition'.[86] Even so, appointment by nomination was unsatisfactory, if only because posts were not advertised, so giving those with connections in the courts early notice and the chance to push their case.[87] Muir McKenzie dispensed the Lord Chancellor's patronage and no one could have been more scrupulous, but even then, though his candidates had stronger educational qualifications than those chosen by the Lord Chief Justice, they were still below general civil service standard. Judges and lawyers had little faith in the civil service examination, nor in competitive entry (though it was acknowledged by some as desirable in principle), and even restricting the choice, as Muir McKenzie did, to men from

---

[80] *Sixth Report*, 1915, p. 13. Their work is described in G.P. Bancroft, *Stage and Bar* [1939], 214–20.

[81] Judicature Act 1884, s 21 put the existing practice as to the Clerks of Assize on a statutory footing but, to their annoyance, transferred the right to appoint their staff to the judges: *RC on the Civil Service, Evidence*, Arthur Denman, q. 51,445.

[82] Sir R. Bosanquet, *The Oxford Circuit* (1951), 15–16. Lawrance's son became registrar of the court of Criminal Appeal.

[83] *RC on the Civil Service, Sixth Report 1915*, 13.

[84] *RC on the KB Division, Evidence II*, J. L. Matthews, qq. 2074–80; Master Bonner to Schuster, 19 June 1928, LCO 2/1012. See also LCO 4/70 and Arthur Denman's evidence to the Civil Service Commission (*Evidence* qq. 51,445, 51,452). Denman said that the select committee on circuit officers in 1869 had been a result of Bovill giving his son, a soldier, a circuit appointment.

[85] *RC on the Civil Service, Sixth Report 1915*, 13.

[86] *Ibid*. Nevertheless, Jessel MR made his butler a messenger (Bell, *Those Meddlesome Attorneys*, 52) and Coleridge LCJ protested when the introduction of a five-year service rule threatened his patronage: Coleridge to Herschell, 18 June 1886, LCO 2/48. Moreover, Loreburn himself complained that he had 'come under a good deal of...political pressure' (*RC on the Civil Service, Evidence*, q. 50,542).

[87] Thus J. F. Townsend attributed his selection to his father having been at college with the Chief Baron's son and Francis Stringer, who got his own son appointed, claimed that his family had been in the courts for generations and that among the senior clerical staff it was seen as a perk ('they think there is something in heredity'), as well they might: *ibid.*, qq. 52,368, 49,798.

solicitors' offices or university men, the number was still overwhelming, with very little to choose between the better ones.[88]

Largely through Muir McKenzie's resolve and persistence, a uniform grading and salary structure was substituted for the mass of different ones.[89] Salaries were harmonized, for the most part by levelling up, and a threefold classification of clerks introduced, rather top-heavy at first, since it had to reflect the existing positions clerks held rather than the needs of the courts.[90] All clerks were to enter at the lowest grade, which 'to some extent mitigated the evils of a diffused patronage'[91] and all were eligible for promotion, though with few exceptions[92] the highest, quasi-judicial, positions remained barred to those without legal qualifications. Promotions were in theory according to merit, as the Central Office Committee had recommended, but the creation of a committee of control from among the masters only strengthened the tendency for seniority to be the almost invariable rule.[93]

It is difficult to escape the impression that the SCJ gradually settled into a rut after the completion of its organization, and perhaps the failure to create a superintendent was partly responsible. The threefold classification did not correspond with the work the clerks actually did; too many first-class clerks were employed on routine tasks and there was little interchange between some of the departments.[94] Indeed, the taxing masters each had their own set of clerks whose separate establishment they jealously guarded.[95] The bigger departments, not under the immediate eye of a master, lacked any intermediate authority to enforce the regulations governing attendance and to insure against slackness. In the early days after the amalgamation this was not surprising. Master Jenkins described the clerks as 'a very special and peculiar staff to deal with' and called the writers 'a very troublesome set of men to manage'.[96] The clerks' vehement resistance to an attendance book prevailed in parts of the central office for some years, and even where one was kept it was often ignored.[97]

---

[88] *RC on the Civil Service, Sixth Report 1915*, 15–18.   [89] *Ibid.*, 9–10.

[90] *DC on the Central Office, Report 1886*, iv; SCJ (Officers) Act 1879, modified by order in 1882: *RC on the Civil Service, Sixth Report 1915*, 7.

[91] *RC on the Civil Service, Sixth Report 1915*, 10.   [92] Chancery and probate registrars.

[93] *DC on the Central Office, Report 1886*, v; *RC on the Civil Service, Sixth Report 1915*, 18–20. Surprisingly, Haldane's War Office experience led him to favour seniority 'tempered by selection': *Evidence*, qq. 60,922–3.

[94] *RC on the Civil Service, Sixth Report 1915*, 20–2.

[95] *Ibid., Evidence*, Master Baker, qq. 45,770–4.

[96] *DC on the Central Office, Report 1886*, qq. 286, 126.

[97] *Ibid.*, q. 286, and see E. H. Aldridge at q. 476. *RC on the Civil Service, Sixth Report 1915*, 24, shows that laxity still prevailed.

Similarly, there had been a struggle to impose the six-hour day in the courts, and for some years the taxing office allowed the older clerks, many of whom 'lived in the country' to continue to arrive at 11 am as they had been used to doing,[98] yet by 1914 the general civil service had gone over to seven hours.[99] In addition to their shorter hours, the clerks (especially those in lunacy, Chancery and taxing offices, who enjoyed the whole of the long vacation) had longer holidays, so that '[f]or nearly one-third of the year the taxpayer receives little return for the sums expended upon salaries'.[100] Since it proved impracticable to make use of the circuit officers in London in between Assizes, or conversely, to send clerks from the associate's department to do circuit business, the former were idle half the year.[101]

Once appointed, a clerk had a job for life.[102] Despite criticism from outside,[103] recommendations for compulsory retirement were ignored, no doubt because they extended to masters and the judges feared that they would be exposed to a similar demand.[104] The result of course was that masters, registrars, and clerks alike were shielded by their colleagues when they became incapable of effective work.[105] James Brougham was a senior registrar until the age of 88 and he was by no means the only octogenarian in the SCJ.[106]

In all these areas—appointments, hours of work, promotions, retirement— the Civil Service Commission found the SCJ and other legal departments no longer abreast of developments in the public service. Like the Childers and Lisgar reports 30 years before, its publication was the beginning of a process of reform which proved lengthy, encountered stiff resistance and ended incomplete.[107]

---

[98] *DC on the Central Office, Report 1886*, A.G. Lovell, qq. 686–90, and cf. P. E. Vizard, q. 566.

[99] *RC on the Civil Service, Sixth Report 1915*, 23–4.

[100] *Ibid.*, 23.   [101] *Ibid.*, 39–40; *Evidence*, Muir McKenzie, qq. 44,242–7.

[102] Clerks were occasionally dismissed (Master Baker instanced one, *RC on the Civil Service Evidence*, q. 45,815) but the chief of the pay office (which came under Treasury regulations) complained that it was difficult to get rid of men who made mistakes: *ibid.*, evidence of J. P. Paulton.

[103] e.g. in *The Times*, see (1900–1) 111 *LT* 558.

[104] *DC on the Central Office, Report 1886*, v, vii.

[105] *RC on the Civil Service, Evidence*, Muir McKenzie, q. 44,183. Pollock and Jenkins admitted to the Central Office Committee that some of their fellow masters were too old (q. 383) and the Committee strongly urged retirement on such men (vii). Most witnesses to the Civil Service Commission opposed compulsory retirement, but Townsend and Brocklesby admitted that their younger colleagues favoured it.

[106] *RC on the Civil Service, Sixth Report 1915*, 25. The Central Office Committee examined W. R. Kemp, chief clerk in the summons and order department, who had been in the courts since 1827. His attempt to claim that his department was overworked was met with incredulity (see q. 1280).

[107] For the proceedings of the Tomlin Committee, see Polden, *Guide to the Records of the LCD*, 52–3.

VIII
The Courts of Appeal

1. THE COURT OF APPEAL

Jurisdiction

The Court of Appeal was almost exclusively an appeal court.[1] It absorbed the appellate jurisdiction of the court of Appeals in Chancery, the court of Exchequer Chamber, and various others, though it did not cover Divorce and Prize appeals until 1881 and 1891 respectively.[2] Appeals expressly assigned to a divisional court and other instances where appeals were limited or excluded altogether (such as most decisions on costs and criminal trials) were outside its competence.[3] Appeals from chambers and from a divisional court hearing an appeal from an inferior court reached the Court of Appeal only with special leave.[4]

The Appellate Jurisdiction Act 1876 offered a further appeal to the House of Lords in most cases. For a while it was thought that the double appeal might be abolished for English cases and the two appeal courts amalgamated,[5] but it gradually became clear that this was not practical politics and only the most optimistic reformers continued to argue for it.[6]

Instead, since the multiplicity of appeals was a much criticized feature of the remodelled judicature, attention became focused on the relation between divisional courts and the Court of Appeal. Divisional courts were preserved, and even extended to Chancery, Probate, and Admiralty, for 'such causes as are not proper to be heard by a single judge'.[7] This was Selborne's concession to the common

---

[1] Its very restricted original jurisdiction is described in *Halsbury's Laws of England* viii (1909), 63, para. 134.

[2] Judicature Act 1881, c.68, s. 9; Judicature Act 1891 c. 53, s. 4.

[3] M. J. M. Muir McKenzie and C. A. White (eds), *Wilson's Supreme Court of Judicature Acts and Rules* (5th edn, 1886), 13–17.

[4] Judicature Act 1873, c.25, ss 45, 50.

[5] e.g. Sir C. Bowen, 'The Law Courts Under the Judicature Acts' (1886) 2 *LQR* 1–11 at 11.

[6] e.g. T. Snow, 'The Reform of Legal Administration, an Unauthorised Programme' (1893) 9 *LQR* 129–35.

[7] Judicature Act 1873, s 40. For the PDA divisional court see above, p. 724; the Chancery court was abolished by the Statute Law Revision Act 1883 c 49.

lawyers' dislike to the 'single judge system',[8] but the number of judges in banc was reduced from four to three, or even two if there was difficulty in assembling a court.[9] Cockburn's Queen's Bench in particular stuck to its traditions[10] and the Coleridge Committee in 1881, while denying any intention of preserving sittings in banc under the guise of the divisional court, proposed to expand its role. The divisional court was to keep appeals from inferior courts, with further appeal only by leave; it was also to be available to suitors in a range of important public law matters and, most important, was to be the final forum for applications for a new trial in jury cases except (1) where special leave was granted; (2) where a difference of opinion emerged within the divisional court; or (3) where the sum at stake exceeded £500. The justification for this last category was curious; without these matters it was felt the common law judges might be underworked between circuits and the Court of Appeal overburdened. Presumably the same reasoning underpinned the proposal that chambers appeals—where section 9 allowed them at all—should not go beyond the divisional court without special leave.[11]

Selborne had little time for the divisional courts, and Muir McKenzie would later scorn them as an 'antediluvian fatuity',[12] while the legal press condemned the Committee's transparent attempt to put the clock back.[13] Nonetheless, many of its recommendations were embodied in the 1883 rules.[14] However, as Bowen pointed out, divisional courts worked by a rotation of judges were a poor substitute for hearings in banc and Coleridge impotently lamented the decline of banc.[15] At least initially official policy favoured the Court of Appeal; the Judicature Act 1890 (c. 44) moved chambers appeals and applications for new trials there and the Act of 1894 (c. 16) imposed some restrictions on interlocutory appeals and sent all practice matters direct to the Court of Appeal.[16]

Membership

The membership of the projected Court of Appeal was the subject of much variation, ranged in the several bills of the 1870s between eight and 11.[17] All the proposals

---

[8] See above, pp. 767–8.

[9] Recommended by the Judicature Commission, *First Report 1869*, 10.

[10] See above, p. 768.   [11] (1880–1) 25 *Sol. J.* 893, 937.

[12] To H. A. McCardie, 11 July 1913, NA PRO LCO 2/321.

[13] (1881–2) 71 *LT* 412; (1880–1) 25 *Sol. J.* 937–8.   [14] RSC 1883 Ord. 59.

[15] Bowen, 'Law Courts Under the Judicature Acts', 8–9; Coleridge to Lindley, 22 September 1889: E. H. Coleridge, *The Life and Correspondence of John Duke, Lord Coleridge*, 2 vols (1904), ii, 361.

[16] In 1901 a bill redistributing certain statutory appeals to the divisional court and sending certain other appeals from the divisional court direct to the House of Lords was dropped: (1901) 111 *LT* 197.

[17] P. Polden, 'Mingling the Waters: Personalities, Politics and the Making of the Supreme Court of Judicature' (2002) 61 *CLJ* 575–611 at 593.

included *ex officio* the Lord Chancellor (who was not expected to sit regularly[18]), the three common law chiefs, the Master of the Rolls, and the two lords justices of appeal in Chancery. The court set up in 1875 also included a single justice of appeal (Sir Richard Baggallay), but it never met, overtaken by the decision to preserve the Lords' appellate role which, of course, diminished the new appeal court to an 'intermediate court of appeal'.[19] Its composition was also changed, emerging with three lords justices (so styled from 1877[20]), and so comprising six permanent judges plus five *ex officio*. Each lord justice was paid £5000 and given his own clerk.[21]

Its existence in this shape was also brief, for in 1881 Selborne used the opportunity created by the abolition of two chiefs to remodel it, making the Master of the Rolls its president and exclusively a judge of appeal and adding the President of the PDA; the lord justices were reduced to five, making the full complement nine.[22] Selborne had also intended to expand the role of puisne judges in the court. In 1875 the Lord Chancellor had been empowered to call on them at need, which was done by rotation and in order of seniority to avoid invidious reflections on aptitude.[23] Now Selborne substituted 'journeymen judges'[24]—three judges to be selected annually by their brethren and to sit in the court when business in their own courts allowed—but they did not survive a hostile reception from Cairns, who argued that they would not be available when most needed, during Assizes, and that not all were of the right calibre.[25] At the beginning of the 1890s, when arrears were beginning to create difficulties, all former Lord Chancellors were added to the court, sitting at the Lord Chancellor's request if they consented, though there was little opportunity for this to be invoked.[26] Despite suggestions that the court needed more permanent judges there was no increase until 1938.[27]

Organization

One of the contentious issues was whether the appeal court should sit in banc or in divisions. The Judicature Commission took the latter view and although some common lawyers objected, arguing that a three-man court would lack authority if it reversed the decision of a four-strong common law court in banc, it was hardly practicable to do otherwise.[28] Cairns and Selborne were in agreement on

---

[18] Selborne to Gladstone, 2 October 1881, Lambeth Palace Library, Selborne Mss, 1867 f. 190.

[19] So described in the debates on the Appellate Jurisdiction Bill: Polden, 'Mingling the Waters', 595–6.

[20] Judicature Act 1877 c. 9, s 4.   [21] Judicature Act 1873, ss 13, 79.

[22] Polden, 'Mingling the Waters', 597; Judicature Act 1881, ss 2–4.

[23] *PD* 1876 (s3) 227: 909–12, 925.   [24] (1881–2) 26 *Sol. J.* 541.

[25] *PD* 1881 (s3) 263: 9–14, 629–32.   [26] Judicature Act 1891, s. 1. Herschell sat at least once.

[27] (1902–3) 114 *LT* 52.

[28] *First Report* 1869, 20; Polden, 'Mingling the Waters', 593; (1875–6) 20 *Sol. J.* 20.

this, and offered only the concession that it might enlarge itself if differences of opinion emerged.[29] It mustered eight in *Bustros* v. *White*, six in *Vagliano* v. *Bank of England* and *Re Holloway*[30] but this was rare, and the Coleridge Committee's proposal that an appeal from a divisional court by special leave should be heard by at least five was ignored.[31]

In theory the court had enough members for a third division, and in 1902 this was authorized, though it does not seem to have been a regular occurrence.[32] What the LCO really wanted was for the court to be able to sit with just two judges. The 1875 Act had authorized this only in appeals from interlocutory decisions, thereby generating a considerable body of case law on which appeals qualified.[33] From 1899 it was permitted in any case where the parties consented, but even then, if the judges differed it must be re-argued before a three-man panel.[34] The Bar Council had opposed that extension and was joined by the Law Society in a successful resistance to a further one in 1907.[35]

Practice

In contrast to the Lords' costly and elaborate mechanism, the Court of Appeal was regarded as 'simple and satisfactory'.[36] All appeals were by way of re-hearing and commenced by notice of motion in a summary way,[37] but this concealed a distinction between appeals from interlocutory decisions, in which new evidence was readily admitted, and others, where fresh evidence needed special leave and the process was essentially a review.[38] Counsel were limited to two for each party[39] and the court normally relied upon the judges' notes, accepting shorthand notes only if there was good cause.[40] The court resisted attempts to deny it the routine service of a registrar in court[41] and Kay was credited with introducing the practice of issuing a written judgment as a matter of course.[42]

There were some criticisms of the court's methods. It was said to rise earlier for the long vacation than the other courts[43] and efforts to discourage long speeches

---

[29] Judicature Act 1873, s. 53.

[30] (1875–6) 1 QBD 423, (1875–6) 20 *Sol. J.* 378; (1889) 23 QBD 243, Lord Alverstone, *Recollections of Bar and Bench* (1914) 157–9; [1894] 2 QBD 163, (1893–4) 38 *Sol. J.* 378.

[31] (1881) 71 *LT* 385—8.   [32] Judicature Act 1902 c. 31, s. 1.

[33] *Wilson's Judicature Acts*, 64, 109, 525.   [34] Judicature Act 1899 c. 6, s 1.

[35] LCO 2/140, 270.

[36] T. Snow, 'The Near Future of Law Reform' (1900) 16 *LQR* 229–40 at 239.

[37] RSC 1883 Ord. 58, r 1.

[38] Order 58, r 4; *Wilson's Judicature Acts* 526–7. Hence the label 're-hearing' is 'ill-conceived': G. Drewry et al., *The Court of Appeal* (Oxford, 2007), 17.

[39] *Wilson's Judicature Acts*, 525.   [40] *Ibid.*, 529.

[41] (1889–90) 34 *Sol. J.* 571.   [42] (1899–1900) 44 *Sol. J.* 566.

[43] (1900–1) 45 *Sol. J.* 417.

from counsel, especially in patent cases, seem to have met with little success;[44] indeed the reading of increasingly prolix judgments lengthened trials and some judges were too prone to interrupt counsel.[45]

The court did make some attempt to discourage appeals. They made it known in the 1880s that they would seldom interfere with a judge's discretion on matters such as whether to require pleadings and were reluctant to reverse a judgment where the judge had heard and formed an opinion of witness evidence.[46] It became notorious that in Esher's division it was almost a waste of time to challenge a jury verdict;[47] in fact after Esher's retirement, his junior colleague Lopes acknowledged that reverence for the jury had been carried too far.[48] If Hollams was right, there was a noticeable change in the new century, for he claimed the court was by then very ready to reverse judges and grant new trials and that this contributed to that spirit of treating litigation as a gamble which drove many commercial disputants to arbitration.[49]

Hollams' severest criticism, however, was that the court espoused from the beginning the principle that the loser must pay the costs both of the appeal and the original trial.[50] This was not inevitable, for it had a broad discretion to 'make such order...as may be just'[51] and practice in the Exchequer Chamber had been apt to burden the party who claimed that the verdict was against the weight of the evidence with costs. Whether the practice with regard to costs did, as Hollams and others suggested, encourage appeals remains unexplored.[52]

Jurisprudence

The ideal of a unitary court with members drawn from law and equity and hearing appeals from both indifferently did not survive the concerns of the respective bars that their doctrines would be at the mercy of ignorant appeal judges from the other.[53] These had to be allayed by making provision for common law puisnes to sit on appeals[54] and, more importantly, by conceding that each division of the court

---

[44] (1887–8) 32 *Sol. J.* 553 (*Erlich* v. *Ihlee*); (1898–9) 43 *Sol. J.* 55.

[45] (1907–8) 52 *Sol. J.* 681; [J.A. Foote], *Pie-Powder* (1911), 92.

[46] *Wilson's Judicature Acts*, 16–17.

[47] E. Manson, *Builders of our Law in the Reign of Queen Victoria* (2nd edn, 1904), 392–4; A. R. Jelf, 'In Memoriam Viscount Esher, MR' (1898–9) 24 (s5) *LM & LR* 395–404 at 400.

[48] (1896–7) 41 *Sol. J.* 234. Esher's court was said to be 'almost a public scandal': (1897) 16 *LN* 323.

[49] *Jottings of an Old Solicitor* (1906), 75.

[50] *Ibid.*, 65–8 ; *Olivant* v. *Wright* (1875–6) 1 Ch D 41; (1875–6) 20 *Sol. J.* 69.

[51] RSC Ord. 58, r 4.

[52] Hollams, *Jottings of an Old Solicitor*, 67; C. Mullins, *In Quest of Justice* (1931), 143.

[53] Polden, 'Mingling the Waters', 594–5.

[54] See above pp. 799–800.

would comprise a mixture of common law and equity judges, with appeals from equity handled by the division with a preponderance of the latter, and vice-versa.[55] How this was actually worked in the early years is uncertain, as there are puzzling variations in the composition, and indeed size, of the divisional sittings, and nor did it bed down easily. Cotton had to be allowed to confine himself to Chancery cases, Bramwell occasionally vented his robust dislike of equity and Lush was palpably unhappy outside the common law.[56] Sir William James complained of having a common lawyer (Brett) sitting on an equity appeal, but Brett soon got his own back. He claimed that Jessel MR had been given the task of implementing doctrinal fusion through the Court of Appeal and after Jessel's early death, when Selborne disregarded Sir Henry James' plea to keep the rolls as the preserve of the equity bar and made Brett MR, the latter set himself to foil any movement of that sort. [57]

The accepted view is that Brett's division of the court tended to dispense common law rather than equity in cases, such as contract disputes, where the two approaches came into conflict although Lindley was something of a counterweight.[58] This was particularly important because, as Bowen put it, the Court of Appeal had become 'the pivot of the system'[59] and the chief source of judicial law-making. Broadly speaking, the balance between equity and common law in membership was retained, though the equity bar was angered when A. L. Smith succeeded Fry in 1892, and in 1900 it was suggested that it should lobby for a stronger representation.[60]

It is not clear how business was allocated between the divisions, since if they sat more or less the same number of days[61] that would suppose a broad equality of appeals proceeding from the QBD on the one side and the Chancery and PDA on the other, which statistics do not bear out. Presumably a steadily rising number of appeals under various statutes helped to balance the workload. The Master of the Rolls and the most senior lord justice headed the divisions, an arrangement which had caused Kelly and Coleridge to mutiny because Jessel and James were both from equity,[62] and one which did not always work out well. Much clearly depended upon the management style and personality of the chief of division. Thus Brett gave his division a reputation for being 'very robust' and unpleasant for senior counsel to argue before and for being cavalier with precedents.[63] When

[55] PD 1873 (s3) 216: 1734 (Jessel S-G).
[56] Polden, 'Mingling the Waters', 596–7; [W. D. I. Foulkes], A Generation of Judges (1886), 21–9.
[57] Polden, 'Mingling the Waters', 596–8; G. R. Askwith, Lord James of Hereford (1930), 116.
[58] P. S. Atiyah, The Rise and Fall of Freedom of Contract (Oxford, 1979), 671–4.
[59] Bowen, 'Law Courts Under the Judicature Acts', 9.
[60] Polden, 'Mingling the Waters', 597; (1899–1900) 44 Sol. J. 461.
[61] As they did in 1890: T. Snow, 'The Waste of Judicial Manpower' (1891) 7 LQR 256–61 at 259.
[62] Polden, 'Mingling the Waters', 596.
[63] G. Alexander, The Temple of the Nineties (1938), 176–8; J. G. Witt, A Life in the Law (1906), 106–7.

A. L. Smith took over that character changed, though it was then thought unduly narrow in workmen's compensation cases.[64] The worst court was Vaughan Williams's. He drove counsel and fellow judges alike to distraction by his garrulousness, impelling Romer, a very able judge, into premature retirement.[65] Fletcher Moulton became notorious for the frequency of his dissents and the length of his speeches, and when Eady joined the court his frigid sarcasm hardly improved matters.[66] There is, however, need for a fuller study.[67]

2. CRIMINAL APPEALS

The Court for Crown Cases Reserved

As explained elsewhere, growing demands to provide a more extensive and effective appeal procedure for those convicted upon indictment led to the establishment of the Court for Crown Cases Reserved in 1848.[68] However, the court was intended by its promoter, Lord Campbell, to deflect those demands into a narrower, less contentious channel, and really only gave institutional form to an existing process whereby a trial judge at Assize or the Old Bailey might refer a point of law to the collective deliberation of the common law judges.[69]

Those private and informal proceedings would now be heard in public, with judgments which might be properly reported.[70] The court would have power to quash verdicts or arrest a judgment, though not to order a new trial, and would take references from quarter sessions.[71] It would not be necessary for the full court to

[64] Alexander, *Temple of the Nineties*, 178–80; P. W. J. Bartrip, *Workmen's Compensation in Twentieth Century Britain* (Aldershot, 1987), 23–5.

[65] G. Rentoul, *This Is My Case* [?1944], 60–1; E. A. Bell, *Those Meddlesome Attorneys* (1939), 59; *ODNB* 47: 660. Sir Frederick Pollock, whose view of the court was unflattering, regarded Romer as its best judge: Pollock to Holmes, 6 July 1903, M de Wolfe (ed.), *The Correspondence of Justice Holmes and Sir Frederick Pollock*, 2 vols (2nd edn, Cambridge, Mass., 1961), i, 113.

[66] H. F. Moulton, *The Life of Lord Moulton* (1922), 64; Rentoul, *This Is My Case*, 61.

[67] Academic neglect was remarked on by Drewry et al., *The Court of Appeal*, 2.

[68] Criminal Law Administration Amendment Act 1848 (11 & 12 Vict. c. 78). In contemporary literature and law reports it was frequently called 'The Court of Criminal Appeal'.

[69] *Select Cases From The Notebooks of the Twelve Judges*, ed. D. Bentley (1997), introduction. If the trial judge was one of the 12, he usually participated in the proceedings.

[70] *Select Cases*, 49–52; J. F. Stephen, *A History of the Criminal Law*, 3 vols (1883), i, 308–18. A very brief set of rules was issued in 1850: (1850) 15 *LT* 268. In a sample of 33 cases reported in *Cox's Criminal Cases*, vol. 14 (1877–82) counsel appeared on both sides in 15, for the appellant only in three, for the prosecution only in six, and on neither side in nine.

[71] Several of the judges consulted by the Lords select committee on criminal administration opposed the quarter sessions provision (*PP* 1847–8 (523), xvi), but all preferred it to the original proposal to send such references first to an Assize judge. Lord Denman CJ, who had 'never heard of any Dissatisfaction touching Convictions at Quarter Sessions', argued that the burden upon judges

sit, a quorum being set at five, headed by one of the common law chiefs.[72] However, with no provision for majority decisions, any irreconcilable disagreements would require further argument before the full court.[73] The inconvenience of this was spectacularly demonstrated in the *Franconia* case in 1876, where the difficulties experienced were compounded by uncertainties about the appropriate composition of the full court following changes made in the Judicature Act 1873.[74]

Full hearings were in fact rare (one or two a year)[75] and business was never large,[76] perhaps because the decision to refer remained in the unfettered discretion of the trial judge and (for much of its history at least) chairmen of quarter sessions proved reluctant to do so.[77] Because of its narrow remit, the court did not meet the demands for a court of criminal appeal.

The Court of Criminal Appeal

In the teeth of tenacious opposition, including that of most KBD judges, a right of appeal from conviction and/or sentence for an indictable offence was at length established in 1907 and the new court began its sittings in 1908.[78] Since it was not part of the SCJ, separate provision for rules was needed, entrusted to the Lord Chief Justice and at least three of the court's judges with the advice of a committee. The committee, on which no judges sat, actually produced the rules, and then went into

would be impossible (qq. 287–8): R. Pattenden, *English Criminal Appeals: Appeals against Conviction and Sentence in England and Wales* (Oxford, 1996), 8.

[72] Section 3. This reduction was generally approved by the judges, especially by Denman, who complained of 'a great Scattering of Responsibility, and some Want of Decorum' in the existing arrangement (*HLSC on Criminal Law Administration Amendment Bill 1847*, q. 298). After the abolition of the other chiefs the Lord Chief Justice presided (Judicature Act 1881, s. 15). The QBD judges arranged a rota and five seems to have been the invariable number.

[73] At the instigation of any one of the panel. Stephen felt this had not been the intention: *History of the Criminal Law*, i, 312.

[74] *R* v. *Keyn* (1876) 2 Ex D 63, discussed at pp. 272–3 above. The Judicature Act 1873, s. 47 made all High Court judges members of the CFCCR and the six-man panel which heard Keyn's appeal included the Admiralty judge, Sir R. Phillimore. When their divisions became apparent, Lord Chancellor Cairns intended to sit in the full court but was dissuaded by Cockburn. The fuller court (probably chosen by Cairns) comprised 14 of a possible 28 members, all but Phillimore from common law divisions. Counsel were harassed by frequent interruptions from the bench, one judge (Archibald) died during the proceedings and the remainder divided 7–6 against the Crown: G. Marston, 'The Centenary of the Franconia Case—the Prosecution of Ferdinand Keyn' (1976) 92 *LQR* 93–107.

[75] *Select Cases*, 51.

[76] A maximum of 36 in 1857, a minimum of three in 1899, and never more than 20 after 1877: *Select Cases*, App. 3. The court mostly sat on Saturdays and three or four sittings a year usually sufficed: Stephen, *History of the Criminal Law*, i, 312. It does not seem to have been given a dedicated clerical staff.

[77] Pattenden, *English Criminal Appeals*, 9.

[78] A new series of reports, edited by H. Cohen, recorded its activities: D. Seabourne Davies, 'The Court of Criminal Appeal: The First Forty Years' (1951) 1 (ns) *JSPTL* 425–41 at 425–6.

abeyance for the next 30 years.[79] Its handiwork, necessarily bulky to cope with all contingencies, was well received and generally proved soundly constructed.[80]

The Criminal Appeals Act appointed as judges eight puisnes from the KBD, chosen by the court's president, the Lord Chief Justice, but this was soon extended to all the division's judges.[81] They would sit as an odd number with a minimum of three, which became the norm, a five-man court being assembled only where disagreements had emerged, where the point at issue was clearly both important and difficult, or where it was contemplated that one or more previous decisions of the court would be departed from.[82] Since judges sat in rotation only a handful of the longest serving, beginning with Darling, played a substantial part in shaping the court's jurisprudence and it rightly came to be perceived as the Lord Chief Justice's court.[83] This had important consequences, enabling Alverstone, who had strongly resisted its establishment, to influence the court's approach.[84]

Cases reached the court by several routes. It remained open for a trial judge to halt the proceedings while he sought a ruling on a question of law by way of a case stated.[85] Alternatively, at the conclusion of the trial he might send up an appeal on his own certificate.[86] Equally, the Home Secretary might refer a prisoner's petition to the court.[87] Yet these routes accounted for only a handful of cases a year, the vast majority stemming from the convicted men themselves. Only those who appealed solely on a point of law had an unrestricted right of access to the court,[88] the others needing either the trial judge's certificate or leave from the court itself. Applications for leave went first to the registrar, and unless clearly admissible were scrutinized by a single judge in chambers, who might decline to decide but

---

[79] Criminal Appeals Act 1907 c. 23, s 18; LCO 2/233; P. Polden, *A Guide to the Records of the LCD* (1988), 93–4.

[80] Criminal Appeal Rules 1908 (227/L6 and 277/L 10); Rule Committee report to the LCJ, 11 February 1908, LCO 2/233; 'The Criminal Appeal Rules 1908' (1907–8) 52 *Sol. J.* 366–7, 389–91.

[81] Criminal Appeals Act 1907, s. 1(1); Criminal Appeals (Amendment) Act 1908 c. 46, s. 1.

[82] Davies, 'Court of Criminal Appeal', 438–9. The court was empowered to sit in two divisions and to sit outside London, but initially seems to have done neither. No convention emerged to prevent the trial judge from sitting on an appeal, and this was criticized: (1913) 135 *LT* 399.

[83] Davies, 'Court of Criminal Appeal', 438.

[84] See XIII, Pt 1, pp. 127–9, 135–7 and 'The Opening of the Court of Criminal Appeal' (1907–8) 52 *Sol. J.* 512–13.

[85] Criminal Appeals Act 1907, s 20(4); D.A. Thomas, 'Case Stated in the Court of Criminal Appeal' [1962] *Crim. Law Rev.* 820–7. The CCA might itself require an appeal purely on law to be so dealt with, but it never did: Pattenden, *English Criminal Appeals*, 50–1.

[86] Section 1(2). Pattenden (*English Criminal Appeals*, 95–6) suggests that the CCA's clearly stated attitude towards jury verdicts may have ensured few judges did so.

[87] Section 19; Pattenden, *English Criminal Appeals*, 356–67, noting two 1909 cases at 363. Some time after *R v. Rodda* ((1910) 5 Cr App R 85) it became Home Office practice not to accept a petition until the right of appeal had been exhausted.

[88] Section 3.

remit the case directly to the court with no recommendation.[89] There was an appeal from his refusal to grant leave, which the KBD Commission contemplated removing to save on judicial resources; they desisted on finding that although the appeal from a refusal was overturned in only 2 per cent of cases, in 12.6 per cent of those the appellant won his substantive appeal.[90]

It fell to the registrar,[91] his assistant, and a small clerical staff to prepare the papers for an appeal, and these could be voluminous—Alverstone estimated that it took five or six hours to read through a case.[92] This was because all trials on indictment had a shorthand writer, whose transcript, along with the judge's notes and report, formed the basic material for the appeal.[93] It was open to the CCA to supplement these by admitting fresh evidence, but though the powers were widely drawn they were interpreted very narrowly.[94] Unable to order a new trial (a regular subject of complaint[95]) the court showed no inclination actively to investigate miscarriages of justice.[96]

Many appellants were incapable of furnishing the court with any coherent statement of their claim and few of them could afford legal representation.[97] The Act therefore provided for them to have professional assistance where necessary and the rules directed the registrar to facilitate its provision.[98] Clerks of Assize and quarter sessions were to seek out solicitors and barristers willing to undertake this service, but even so, many applications were unassisted and many hearings unattended by counsel, adding to the judges' burdens.[99] The rule-makers had sensibly left the court to sort out its own procedures and it adopted a flexible

---

[89] Pattenden, *English Criminal Appeals*, 96–7; *RC on the King's Bench Division, Second Report*, PP 1914 [Cd. 7177], xxx, para. 45; 'Opening of the CCA', 512–13.

[90] *RC on the KB Division, Second Report 1913*, para. 45 and App. 4.

[91] Criminal Appeal (Amendment) Act 1908, s 2 substituted the master of the Crown Office for the senior KBD master as registrar following representations from the masters (memorandum of 1 June 1908, LCO 2/234). L.W. Kershaw (assistant registrar 1908, registrar 1912) felt the combination of posts did not work well: *RC on the Civil Service, Evidence*, PP 1914–16 [Cd. 8130], xii, qq. 53,245–321.

[92] *RC on the King's Bench Division, Evidence*, PP 1913 [Cd. 6762], xxx, q. 30, and *Second Report 1913*, para. 45.

[93] Rule 5. Shorthand writers were recommended by the Bar Council: report of June 1907: LCO 2/232 and required some hasty improvisation at Assizes: W. L. Woodland, *Assize Pageant* (1952), 15–16. The judge's report was not disclosed to the appellant save by leave, a rule criticized in (1907–8) 52 *Sol. J.* 347.

[94] Section 9; Pattenden, *English Criminal Appeals*, 130–2. There were exceptions, such as a case in 1912 where eight new witnesses were heard: (1912) 133 *LT* 390.

[95] Pattenden, *English Criminal Appeals*, 190–1. Recommended in *RC on the KB Division, Second Report 1913*, para. 44.

[96] XIII, Pt 1, pp. 135–7.

[97] 90% of applicants were unrepresented: *RC on the Civil Service, Evidence 1915*, Kershaw, q. 53,297.

[98] Section 15, rr 30, 37–8. The Law Society advertised for volunteers: (1907–8) 52 *Sol. J.* 422.

[99] Since private prosecutors could not be expected to take any part in an appeal, the duty fell to the DPP (rr 27–8). Desart had protested at this imposition: undated memo in LCO 2/232.

approach in which citation of precedent was discouraged.[100] Rather curiously, the Act itself prescribed a single judgment, except on questions of law where the court felt it more convenient to issue separate ones.[101] Since the court took rather a narrow view of its functions, it seldom invoked this provision, and to the disappointment of some of its supporters, the CCA made little attempt to harmonize sentencing practices or to provide learned disquisitions in the more arcane reaches of the criminal law.[102] Its jurisprudence did over time exercise a profound and usually benign influence on the conduct of criminal trials, but that was rather a by-product of its activities than a core function.

The two greatest—and connected—fears voiced by opponents of an appeal on fact, which after the *Beck* case had become hard to deny, were that jury verdicts would be regularly overturned and that consequently the court would be overwhelmed with applications.[103] Neither happened. Even Chalmers' Home Office estimate of 2000 applications a year proved very pessimistic, for they numbered only 500 to 600, and only a minority survived the 'filtering' process.[104] Alverstone ensured that both the verdict of the jury and the sentence of the judge remained inviolate except where they proved indefensible.[105] That approach, rather than the threat of increased sentences,[106] probably did most to discourage frivolous appeals. Even so, the workload (Alverstone reckoned 120 judge-days a year) did cause extra problems for the KBD.[107] The Act also opened up the possibility of a further appeal to the House of Lords, which had been all but impossible hitherto,[108] but although the court was not uniformly strict they remained rare.[109]

---

[100] Rule Committee memo, 11 February 1908, LCO 2/233; Pattenden, *English Criminal Appeals*, 119–22.

[101] Section 1(5); Davies, 'Court of Criminal Appeal', 440.

[102] Davies, 'Court of Criminal Appeal', 434–8. *The Times* encouraged the court to offer more guidance: (1914) 136 *LT* 221, but Thomas ('Case Stated in the Court of Criminal Appeal'), suggests that the form in which most cases reached the court militated against it.

[103] Pattenden, *English Criminal Appeals*, 93

[104] Undated memo [1906] in LCO 2/232. Only 6% of those eligible appealed in 1912, and in its first four years and nine months 2704 applied and 843 were set down, 17 of which were abandoned; 150 had sentences reduced, and 141 verdicts were quashed: G. G. Alexander, *The Administration of Justice in Criminal Matters* (Cambridge, 1919 edn), 128–9.

[105] Pattenden, *English Criminal Appeals*, 141, 166. Perhaps unexpectedly, the court did not make extensive use of the proviso enabling them to reject an appeal 'if they consider that no substantial miscarriage of justice has actually occurred' (s 4(1)): E. H. Pickersgill, 'The Proviso in the Criminal Appeals Act' (1907–8) 52 *Sol. J.* 530, on *R* v. *Dyson* (1908) 1 Cr App R 13.

[106] Section 4(3).

[107] *RC on the KB Division, Second Report 1913*, para. 45. Judges read the papers on Saturdays for hearings on Monday mornings.

[108] Above, p. 541.

[109] The first was *R* v. *Ball* (1910) 6 Cr App R 31; [1911] AC 47. See also *R* v. *Thompson* [1918] AC 221, in 'Appeals to the House of Lords' [1957] *Crim Law Rev.* 566–76.

IX
The King's/Queen's Bench Division

1. THE PROBLEMS OF THE DIVISION

Within a decade of the completion of the new structure, the two most senior judges had each called upon the Lord Chancellor to set up another royal commission on the judicature to remedy serious deficiencies in its working. The Master of the Rolls was particularly concerned with delays in the Queen's Bench and the proliferation of interlocutory motions and appeals, which he attributed to Jessel engrafting inapposite Chancery devices onto common law procedure,[1] while the Lord Chief Justice listed five issues needing urgent attention.[2] Halsbury was no enthusiast for another bout of reforming—he was making speeches extolling the virtues of special pleading and the circuit system[3]—but he could not ignore Coleridge's plea, which reflected widespread dissatisfaction within and without the legal profession. Lawyers denounced delays, costs, and lack of finality, their journals highlighting the excessive use of interrogatories, great inconsistencies in rulings in chambers,[4] incompetent case listing, and judges starting the long vacation early.[5] Even the Law Society and Bar Committee were sufficiently united to set up a joint committee.[6] Outside the profession, it was not just *The Times* which

---

[1] Brett to Halsbury, 9 June 1890, NA PRO LCO 2/47 and *PD* 1890 (s3) 347: 32–65. He was supported by the Law Society's APM: (1889–90) 34 *Sol. J.* 784.

[2] The cost of appeals; the backlog in Chancery; the expense of litigation; appeals in criminal cases; the flight of commercial suitors: to Halsbury, 28 December 1891, LCO 2/242; R. Stevens, *The Independence of the Judiciary* (Oxford, 1992), 13. Bowen and Mathew were instrumental in this initiative.

[3] (1891–2) 36 *Sol. J.* 399.

[4] Lush J. was praised for having shaped chambers practice after the Judicature Acts ([W. D. I. Foulkes], *A Generation of Judges* (1886), 22–30), but thereafter it was less satisfactory. A few judges, such as Field, were regarded as specialists (*RC on Delays in the King's Bench Division, Evidence*, PP 1914 [Cd. 6762], xxx, T. Chitty, q. 368) but others were less adept; Alverstone, for instance, was reputed to rely heavily on his clerk (E. A. Bell, *Those Meddlesome Attorneys* (1939), 53), and they had predictable attitudes which made the right selection important (J. G. Witt, *A Life in the Law* (1906), 37–8; J. E. G. de Montmorency, *John Gorell Barnes, Lord Gorell, a Memoir* (1920), 63–4). Decisions were not passed down to the masters, so that only in the divisional court was consistency imposed ((1891–2) 36 *Sol. J.* 320, 339). It was also notorious that the clerks decided whom to hear first and had favourites (see solicitors).

[5] e.g. (1891–2) 36 *Sol. J.* 320, 339; (1887–8) 32 *Sol. J.* 1; (1890–1) 35 *Sol. J.* 689.

[6] (1887–8) 32 *Sol. J.* 556, 589.

thundered criticisms.[7] The chambers of commerce renewed their campaign for more localized justice, including the enlargement of county court jurisdiction, a particular *bête noire* of Halsbury's.[8] Businessmen were deserting the courts for arbitration and the establishment of a London Chamber of Arbitration caused great fluttering in the legal dovecotes.[9]

Instead of a commission, Halsbury invited the Council of Judges to investigate, to the disappointment of his permanent secretary and scepticism of others.[10] Unfortunately the Council did not have the benefit of the first set of civil judicial statistics issued under the auspices of Master Macdonell, whose penetrating analyses provided a fuller picture than the hitherto unimaginative compilations.[11] They showed that both original actions and appeals were fewer than in the early 1880s and even interlocutory motions, which had greatly increased after the Judicature Acts, had fallen back somewhat.[12] A decline in the number of small claims in the QBD was accompanied by a higher proportion of defendants entering an appearance, but that was offset by the increasing use of Order 14. 'Notwithstanding the objection of judges to try in this manner cases presenting complexity', in 1898 they formed more than 15 per cent of actions tried in town.[13] A reduction in jury trials, from over 90 per cent of trials before 1883, to around 50 per cent, also saved time and costs.[14] The problems of the division were essentially London ones, with more provincial cases being brought to town, and too few judges there to cope with them.[15]

So although it proposed curbs on appeals, the Council rightly focused on the QBD, which *The Times* was comparing with Eldon's Chancery.[16] Its report suggested improvements to the listing arrangements and sundry procedural changes, including the establishment of a special list purely for commercial cases and drastic amendments to the circuits to ensure that the capital had enough judges.[17]

The circuit proposals were never implemented and criticism did not abate. Atherley Jones supported his motion by claiming that the English judicature was more extravagant than any bar the French and made play with the short hours,

---

[7] (1891–2) 36 *Sol. J.* 194, and see [E. S. Roscoe] 'The Judicial System' (1891) 173 *Edin. Rev.* 360–75.

[8] A. R. Ilersic and P. F. B. Liddle, *The Parliament of Commerce* (1960), 87, and see below pp. 882–3.

[9] Enthusiastically described by E. Manson in (1893) 9 *LQR* 86.

[10] Stevens, *Independence of the Judiciary*, 13. The Council had been suspected of a tendency to 'push their class interests': (1881–2) 26 *Sol. J.* 713, and see (1891–2) 36 *Sol. J.* 157.

[11] C. W. Brooks, 'Litigation and Society in England, 1200–1996', in his *Lawyers, Litigation and English Society since 1450* (Cambridge, 1998), 63–128 at 108–13. The first set, for 1894, were issued in 1896: *PP* 1896 [C. 8263], xciv. MacDonell is described in Bell, *Those Meddlesome Attorneys*, 109–11.

[12] *Civil Judicial Statistics 1894.*   [13] *Civil Judicial Statistics 1898, PP* 1900 [Cd. 181], ciii.

[14] *Ibid.*   [15] *Ibid.*   [16] (1893–4) 38 *Sol. J.* 609.

[17] For the report see (1891–2) 36 *Sol. J.* 708–10, 727. Bowen wrote two pseudonymous commentaries in *The Times*: Sir H. S. Cunningham, *Lord Bowen, a Biographical Sketch* (1897), 172–4.

large salaries, and long holidays of the judges,[18] though litigants, and the profession generally, complained more of its costs and delays.[19] The appointment of an extra Chancery judge in 1899 and the adoption of the linked judges system did much to improve that division,[20] but the QBD was hopelessly in arrears, doing its best 'to court extinction' as one journal put it.[21]

This was not because business was expanding. MacDonell's first commentary had noted that 'the drift of business is distinctly towards the county courts'[22] and the High Court continued to remit more than 1,000 cases a year to them. The fall in the QBD's workload was clear from quinquennial averages of writs and trials:

1882–6	80,018.2	2,429.2
1887–91	71,903.8	2,198.4
1892–6	71,493	2,353.4
1897–1901	70,284	2,598.2
1902–6	69,172.6	2,180.8

In 1909 writs of summons issued from the QBD (62,916) were at their lowest level since the creation of the SCJ, and the decline continued, to 60,511 in 1913.[23] Furthermore, many cases were either undefended or were despatched with acceptable expedition and expense under Order 14; for the years 1891–4 judgment in default of appearance was given in 63.5 per cent of cases, with Order 14 judgments accounting for a further 22.4 per cent.[24]

MacDonell concluded that 'a larger proportion of the actions that come into court turn on real disputes',[25] but most concerned comparatively small sums; in 1904 69 per cent of verdicts or judgments in London and Middlesex and 54.3 per cent of those on circuit were for £100 or less.[26]

Yet still the division was slowing down. Figures for 1898 suggested that the whole process, from writ to trial, averaged 194 days, with a lapse of 51 days between entry in the lists and the trial, and it was getting worse.[27] The press may sometimes have exaggerated the delays, but by and large legal commentators

[18] *PD* 1897 (s4) 46: 987–1013.
[19] e.g. the reports of the Bar Council and Law Society in (1898) 42 *Sol. J.* 266.
[20] See below pp. 838–9.
[21] R. Abel-Smith and R. Stevens, *Lawyers and the Courts* (1967), 94.
[22] *Civil Judicial Statistics 1894*, and see T. Snagge, *The Evolution of the County Court* (1904), 28–33.
[23] *Civil Judicial Statistics 1909* (PP 1911 [Cd. 5501], cii) and 1913 (*PP* 1914–16 [Cd. 7807], lxxxii).
[24] *Civil Judicial Statistics 1894.*   [25] *Civil Judicial Statistics 1903, PP* 1905 [Cd. 2403], xcix.
[26] *Civil Judicial Statistics 1904, PP* 1906 [Cd. 2945], cxxxv.
[27] *Civil Judicial Statistics 1898.* This disclosure prompted the LCJ to ensure that it was reported in *The Times* that many of the delays originated with the parties (25 January 1900).

concurred.[28] Some delays arose from the extensive resort, sometimes for tactical reasons, to interlocutory proceedings, especially discovery.[29] The omnibus summons for directions was a failure[30] and interlocutory orders further clogged up the system by their propensity to generate appeals. They comprised around half of all appeals from the KBD in 1901 and with over 40 per cent of appeals from masters and district registrars succeeding there was every incentive to appeal.[31]

A gradual change in the type of business may also have been a factor, though MacDonell found it hard to make out the subject-matter from the writs.[32] Slander and libel remained surprisingly persistent: 12½ per cent of actions on circuit in 1898 and more than 16 per cent in 1908, compared with 9 per cent in London.[33] Since defamation involved a jury and usually several witnesses, it tended to be a slow business. Torts were still a minority of actions (fewer than 10 per cent were personal injury claims[34]), whereas more than 70 per cent were money claims.[35] However, some contract claims were more complex than before. The issuing of new rules governing service of proceedings on firms in 1891 signalled the growing prominence of limited companies in litigation, and by 1900 they were involved in 45 per cent of actions.[36] Many cases involving corporations were, no doubt, no different from those involving individuals, but they included a growing number of altogether more complex matters, involving masses of correspondence and sometimes quantities of peripheral matter unearthed by discovery.[37] Revenue actions, though comparatively few, were also notoriously complex.

Changes in procedure and business were not adequately met by adaptations in organization and arrangements and ongoing dissatisfaction with the KBD led to a series of inquiries beginning with the Gorell Committee on county court

---

[28] (1907–8) 52 *Sol. J.* 809, (1910) 129 *LT* 76.

[29] Roscoe, 'The Judicial System', 365; *RC on the KB Division, Evidence I*, T. W. Chitty q. 321; *PP* 1914 [Cd. 7178], xxxvii (*Evidence II*), Channell J., q. 2,265.

[30] See below, pp. 819–20.

[31] Interlocutory appeals were almost double those from the Chancery division: *Civil Judicial Statistics 1901, PP* 1903 [Cd. 1588], lxxxiii.

[32] *Ibid.*

[33] *Civil Judicial Statistics 1898,* 1908 (*PP* 1910 [Cd. 5097], cxi) and see [J. A. Foote], *Pie-Powder* (1911), 77.

[34] Workmen's compensation claims under the Acts of 1897 and 1906 were not brought in the High Court.

[35] Brooks, 'Litigation and Society', 110–12. Montague Shearman said running down cases had become common, but he also claimed an increase of claims involving moneylenders: *RC on the KB Division, Evidence I*, q. 857.

[36] (1890–1) 35 *Sol. J.* 588; *Civil Judicial Statistics 1898,* 1900 (*PP* 1902 [Cd. 1115], cxvii). E. S.Roscoe, 'Progress and Procedure of the Civil Courts of England' (1897) 185 *Edin. Rev.* 156–82, suggests the agricultural depression reduced litigation by farmers.

[37] Witt, *Life in the Law*, 98–9; Foote, *Pie-Powder*, 90–1; E. F. Spence, *Bar and Buskin* (1930) 160–4; *RC on the Civil Service, Evidence, PP* 1914–16 [Cd. 8130], xii, MacDonell at q. 5550. Thus *Wyler v. Lewis* occupied 33 days in the KBD and 18 in the Court of Appeal: G. Rentoul, *This Is My Case* (1944), 48–9.

jurisdiction in 1906. Its composition made it unlikely that a major devolution of business would be recommended, but it acknowledged that the status quo was only tenable if the KBD put its house in order, and in particular if it reformed the Assizes so as to improve facilities in London.[38] Because of Gorell's startling recommendations to devolve divorce, that report generated an inquiry into divorce which embraced the capacity of the KBD to take on some of that work.[39] The Lord Chief Justice's response to criticism was (reasonably enough) to demand more judges, but that meant legislation, which in turn necessitated an inquiry into his division. A joint select committee's deliberations were abruptly curtailed by the calling of a general election in 1911 and it issued the briefest of reports, recommending two extra judges as a temporary measure and that 'in the meantime and without delay, certain reforms, which have been suggested to them for the better organization of business in London and on circuit, should be considered with a view to such of them as are found to be practicable and desirable being carried into effect'.[40]

It is hardly surprising that the Lord Chief Justice professed to be unable to understand exactly what the report had recommended,[41] so Loreburn had to set up yet another inquiry, this time a royal commission. Concurrently, a departmental committee under Lord Mersey conducted an overdue examination of the jury system,[42] and with the Civil Service Commission turning its attention to the legal departments, the KBD experienced a relentless and often uncomfortable scrutiny. It was not, however, a very productive one. It was easy to identify weaknesses, but to suggest remedies which were politically practicable and administratively feasible was another matter when, as an earlier writer had observed, '[j]udges cannot be ordered about like clerks in an office'.[43] This applied both to cheapening High Court litigation and speeding it up.

2. THE QUESTION OF COSTS

It was soon alleged that the Judicature Acts had actually increased the costs of litigation,[44] and despite the harmonization which all but ended the higher scale which had been almost the norm in Chancery,[45] little was done to make

---

[38] *SC on County Court Procedure*, PP 1909 (71), lxxii, 11–21; and see P. Polden, *A History of the County Court 1846–1971* (Cambridge, 1999), 106–8.

[39] See below, p. 755.   [40] *JSC on the KB Division*, PP 1909 (333), viii, 5.

[41] *RC on the KB Division, Evidence I*, q. 65.   [42] See below, pp. 823–5.

[43] Roscoe, 'The Judicial System', 361.

[44] See above, pp. 766–7. Statistical evidence was scarce even in the 1930s: R. M. Jackson, *The Machinery of Justice in England* (Cambridge, 1940), 246; C. Mullins, *In Quest of Justice* (1931), 202–15. In 1900 50 bills after trial in the QBD averaged £149, with £115 allowed on taxation; 50 solicitor and client bills averaged £105, with £87 allowed: *Civil Judicial Statistics 1900*.

[45] According to Hannen P. in 'The Horace' (1884) 50 LT 595, the higher scale was invariably awarded in Chancery for claims above £1000 but seldom allowed in the common law courts, where

it cheaper.[46] True, the provision in Order 65, r 11 which so aggrieved solicitors was sometimes invoked to deny them their costs[47] and rigorous taxation took off an average of 25–30 per cent of bills.[48] Even so, the gap between costs allowed to the successful party on a party-and-party basis and actual costs incurred on an indemnity (solicitor and own client) basis remained a standing grievance.[49] The Judges' Council in 1892 had recommended that 'costs allowed in litigious matters shall be all those which have been reasonably incurred by the client'[50] and in 1897 Halsbury and the law officers professed themselves eager to implement it, but although it was hoped that the rules adopted on the unification of the taxing offices would have this effect, the distinction proved too deeply embedded to be removed.[51]

Judges might have done something to reduce costs, but some were reluctant to permit short cuts in procedure and evidence which would have been economical. One Chancery judge would not allow the simpler method of extracting money from the court, by summons, to be used for sums above £1000 while the Rule Committee scarcely made use of the power given it in 1894 to simplify the rules of evidence, and even in the Commercial court an attempt to 'dispense with the technical rules of evidence' was quashed by the Court of Appeal.[52]

Since bench and bar were usually keen to emphasize that proper justice could not be had in the less expensive inferior courts, it is unsurprising that few of them displayed much zeal for economy. Judges were insulated from, and often ignorant of the way costs accumulated,[53] and the rules still encouraged solicitors to do unnecessary things, such as extravagant use of interlocutories, to recompense

the 'special grounds' which justified the higher scale payment were interpreted very restrictively: (1891–2) 36 *Sol. J.* 705; (1900–1) 45 *Sol. J.* 605 and see *Grafton* v. *Watson* (1884–5) 51 *LT* 141.

[46] Order 65, rr 8–10, based upon the report of the Legal Procedure Committee 1881. Some differences between the divisions and between individual QB masters persisted at least until the amalgamation of the taxing offices in 1900 (*Civil Judicial Statistics 1901;* (1893) 12 *LN* 228) and some solicitors remained aggrieved at losing the more generous Chancery approach: see e.g. J. Rawlinson (1900–1) 45 *Sol. J.* 601.

[47] E.g. Report of ILS APM in (1891–2), 36 *Sol. J.* 801–19.

[48] 28.97% in the KBD in 1901: *Civil Judicial Statistics 1901.* Arguably, however, this merely transferred the burden to the winner: Roscoe, *Progress and Procedure of Civil Courts,* 178.

[49] (1901) 111 *LT* 195; Jackson, *Machinery of Justice,* 241–6.

[50] (1895–6) 40 *Sol. J.* 471.

[51] *PD* 1897 (s4) 46: 1007 (F. Lockwood); (1900–1) 45 *Sol. J.* 731, (1901–2) 112 *LT* 205. Order 65, r 27 effectively preserved the distinction by disallowing party and party costs where costs were incurred or increased through over-caution, negligence, or mistake, or as special fees to counsel, or special charges or expenses by witnesses or other persons, or by other unusual expenses.

[52] Mullins, *In Quest of Justice,* 189, 249. Russell LCJ acknowledged that the streamlined procedures in the Commercial court denied solicitors a proper reward (1895–6) 40 *Sol. J.* 365; for expedients to remedy this see (1900–1) 45 *Sol. J.* 804.

[53] Spence, *Bar and Buskin,* 159–60.

themselves for the necessary ones which were not remunerated.[54] Even so, their charges probably did not soar like the fees of the leading counsel.[55] Moreover barristers found other ways of enlarging their income. Taxing masters were persuaded to be generous in allowing three counsel,[56] accepted the 2/3rds rule for juniors and, despite solicitors' objections, did nothing to stop the growth of refreshers.[57] Refreshers were particularly pernicious, providing a perverse incentive to prolong trials, and so contributing to delays as well as expense.

It was, however, the judges who perpetuated the general rule that costs follow the event. The wide discretion offered in the original Judicature bills was narrowed for jury cases by a Commons amendment during the 1873 bill's passage and judges understandably sought the security of the simple rule in other cases too.[58] In fact they actually extended it. Before 1875 a successful common law appellant had to bear his own costs, but that was altered by the Court of Appeal, giving rise to what Hollams and others criticized as a 'gambling system' which encouraged appeals in the hope that an ultimately favourable decision would carry the costs of the entire suit with it.[59]

Few successful barristers were interested in cheapening litigation. W. J. Disturnal airily told the KBD Commission that '[t]he question of cost does not appeal to me, so much as the manner in which business is done',[60] but in advocating the appointment of several extra judges he was necessarily also suggesting an increase in court fees. This was because, while Lord Chancellors had successfully fought off Treasury demands that the SCJ be entirely self-supporting, they had had to concede that fees should cover all public expenses save the salaries of the judges; even the costs of building the courts in the Strand were to be recovered out of litigants' fees.[61] This compromise was embedded in the Fees Order of 1883 and it was fortunate that the yield from uncontested probates enabled the High Court (unlike the county courts) to turn a profit. This meant freedom from Treasury pressure to increase fees, but also that any extra judges would have to be fought for.

---

[54] Bramwell was one who suggested a move to lump sum charges ((1880–1) 25 *Sol. J.* 331, but although it had other advocates (e.g. (1913) 135 *LT* 199), it was never given serious consideration. It is not surprising that laymen's criticism of solicitors' bills was sometimes ill-informed, e.g. (1905–6) 120 *LT* 25.

[55] Jackson, *Machinery of Justice*, 249–50. [56] (1877–8) 22 *Sol. J.* 678.

[57] Abel-Smith and Stevens, *Lawyers and the Courts*, 213, 223–5, and see below.

[58] J. Hollams, *Jottings of an Old Solicitor* (1906), 73–5.

[59] *Ibid.*, 65–7; *Olivant* v. *Wright* (1875–6) 45 LJ Ch. 1 and memorandum of James LJ (1875–6) 1 Ch D 41.

[60] *Evidence I*, q. 946. Jackson, *Machinery of Justice* noted that the subject received little attention in legal writings or in education for the bar, which was also true of the earlier period.

[61] Jackson, *Machinery of Justice*, 239–41; LCO 1/44, 83–4.

The High Court was beyond the means of many. The *in forma pauperis* procedure which offered the impecunious access was very narrow in scope and had been confined to plaintiffs by the Judicature Acts.[62] The gap was only partly filled by the charitable exertions of Poor Man's Lawyer schemes and there was concern at the activities of unscrupulous ambulance-chasing solicitors and 'legal aid societies'.[63] The creation of a Poor Persons' Procedure was the major preoccupation of the Rule Committee between 1909 and its introduction in 1914.[64]

One unwanted consequence of the High Court being so costly was that some determined or desperate men and women dispensed with the services of lawyers and the courts began to be infested with litigants in person.[65] Of course, the county courts had always had to grapple with individuals presenting their case in person and their procedure was designed with that in mind,[66] but before the procedural reforms of the 1850s only the most sanguine or foolhardy litigant would plunge into the procedural thickets that protected the courtrooms of the superior courts.[67] There had always been men and women who brought actions which were either frivolous or vexatious or both, and Denman's Act[68] had strengthened the powers of the courts to deal summarily with those, though no legislation could entirely suppress the urge to go to law where there was believed to be a huge potential reward (as with the interminable attempts to get at William Jennens' fortune[69]) or where the plaintiff made it a matter of principle.

However, the legal press noticed a significant increase in the number of litigants in person. Some, probably the majority, could not afford counsel, while others had a usually unfounded confidence in their own forensic aptitude.[70] 'Amateur litigation of this class appeared to have reached epidemic proportions' wrote one barrister,[71] and Mr Justice Chitty had to deal with three in the same week.[72] Besides resenting these incursions into their cosy quasi-private courts, judges and lawyers had a more legitimate concern with the way laymen protracted proceedings. They experienced particular problems with 'the gentle sex', which provided

---

[62] *Civil Judicial Statistics 1907, PP* 1908 [Cd. 4424], cxxiii.   [63] (1912) 31 *LN* 33.

[64] Above, pp. 755–6, 790.

[65] 'It is impossible to conceal the fact that the litigant in person is fast becoming a serious nuisance in the court': (1877–8) 22 *Sol. J.* 85.

[66] Polden, *History of the County Court*, 46–8.

[67] For a rare example see F. Pollock, *The Personal Reminiscences of Sir Frederick Pollock*, 2 vols (1887), i, 36. He was nonsuited.

[68] Costs in Frivolous Suits Act 1840 (3 & 4 Vict. c. 24).

[69] P. Polden, 'Stranger than Fiction: The Jennens Inheritance in Fact and Fiction' (2003) 32 *Common Law World Law Review* 211–47, 338–67, esp. 345–7, 364–7.

[70] P. Polden, 'Doctor in Trouble: *Anderson v. Gorrie* and the Extension of Judicial Immunity from Suit in the 1890s' (2001) *JLH* 38–68 at 55–6.

[71] Foote, *Pie-Powder*, 191.   [72] (1895–6) 40 *Sol. J.* 59.

some of the most pertinacious litigants in person. Some were far from gentle[73] but others skilfully exploited the conventions of a patriarchal society. Judges like Lord Esher, habitually brusque and intimidating to counsel, were disarmed by feminine charms and wholly unable to maintain control of the pace of the trial.[74] 'We are at your mercy', lamented Lord Coleridge, and Lord Hatherley bemoaned the fact that Miss Shedden had consumed 28 days of the House of Lords' judicial time.[75] Rosanna Fray was styled 'the queen of lady litigants', but the most prolific and successful serial litigant was the celebrated Georgina Weldon.[76]

For a time Mrs Weldon was assisted by Alexander Chaffers, whose notoriety, in legal circles at any rate, equalled her own. Chaffers' melodramatic persecution of Lady Twiss in 1872 cost him his profession, his reputation, and his livelihood and as with many a litigant in person his grievances ripened into obsessions and drove him to fire off writs against judges, politicians, archbishops, and all sorts; most piquantly, he even sued Pym Yeatman, a barrister so combustible and litigious that newcomers to the midland circuit were warned to avoid him.[77] The judges pressed their inherent jurisdiction to its limits through *Grepe* v. *Loam* orders, and occasionally beyond,[78] but faced with Chaffers, Yeatman and their like, who seemed disposed to plague the courts with accusations against the judges themselves, Halsbury resorted to statute. The Vexatious Actions Act 1896 (c. 51) enabled the court to create a list of persons who would be unable to bring any action without express permission; Chaffers had the dubious distinction of being the first on the list.[79]

The 1896 Act only removed the menace of the most extreme litigant in person. Others continued to prolong trials and a few, like Horatio Bottomley, appeared with some regularity.[80] 'If you could find some way of dealing with the lady litigant we should all be grateful', said Scrutton[81] and the senior master said that his correspondence with solicitors over cases involving litigants in person was steadily growing.[82]

---

[73] Polden, 'Doctor in Trouble', 56.

[74] M. J. Taggart, 'Alexander Chaffers and the Genesis of the Vexatious Litigants Act 1896' (2004) 63 *CLJ* 656–84, 663.

[75] Polden, 'Doctor in Trouble', 56.

[76] 'Lady Litigants' (1890) 1 *LG* 123; Taggart, 'Alexander Chaffers', 662–3.

[77] Taggart, 'Alexander Chaffers'; Polden, 'Doctor in Trouble', 37–40, 49–54.

[78] Polden, 'Doctor in Trouble', 57, Taggart, 'Alexander Chaffers', 677–81.

[79] Taggart, 'Alexander Chaffers', 677–81.

[80] Foote, *Pie-Powder*, 191.

[81] *RC on the KB Division, Evidence II*, q. 3141. He had particularly in mind Miss Lind-af-Hageby, who had engaged the court for three weeks: *ibid.*, Rowlatt J., q. 3411.

[82] *RC on the Civil Service, Evidence*, q. 45,291.

3. PRE-TRIAL PROCEEDINGS

The draftsmen of the SCJ rules had wanted to create a uniform procedural frame-work across the divisions, all actions being commenced with a writ of summons. The revenue departments, however, succeeded in retaining their antiquated procedure by way of English information[83] and the 1883 rules restored to the Chancery division the originating summons omitted from those of 1875. This provided a short cut for parties in cases where only a decision on the construction of a document, such as a will, was sought, the facts being set out in rival affida-vits and the decision often given in chambers. It became so popular that it was extended to the QBD in 1893 even though many common lawyers (and seemingly the masters) disliked it, arguing that a similar result could be better obtained through a specially endorsed writ coupled with minor modifications to the Order 14 procedure.[84] Not surprisingly, the originating summons never caught on out-side its original home.[85]

With pardonable exaggeration, Bowen 'asserted without fear of contradic-tion that it is not possible in the year 1887 for an honest litigant in her Majesty's Supreme Court to be defeated by any mere technicality, any slip, any mistaken step in his litigation'.[86] Elsewhere he conceded that this achievement came at a price. 'What was believed ten years ago by the authors of the Judicature Rules to be a simplification of pleading and an abolition of pleading technicalities has turned out to be the introduction of a mode of pleading so confused and inart-istic as to be in many instances only a source of embarrassment and expense.'[87] Carelessness was encouraged by the awareness that the liberal power to allow amendments up to and including the trial was being generously exercised,[88] and that even the power to strike out pleadings which disclosed no cause of action or

---

[83] *RC on the KBD, Evidence I*, Cozens-Hardy MR at q. 482.

[84] T. Snow, 'Special Endorsement or Originating Summons?' (1893) 9 *LQR* 31–5. It was said that QB officers would not use it: (1890–1) 35 *Sol. J.* 216.

[85] 'Procedure by Originating Summons' (1895–6) 40 *Sol. J.* 4, and see also 26, 254, 271, 290.

[86] 'Progress in the Administration of Justice during the Victorian Period', in Committee of American Law Schools (eds), *Select Essays in Anglo-American Legal History*, 3 vols (Boston 1907, repr. 1968), i, 516–17, 541. Since Bowen was responsible for many of the judges' resolutions on pro-cedure, he wrote with some authority: Cunningham, *Lord Bowen*, 157. This feature impressed the American scholar W. B. Perkins: 'The English Judicature Act of 1873' (1913–14) 12 *Michigan Law Rev.* 277–92.

[87] 'The Law Courts Under the Judicature Acts' (1886) 2 *LQR* 1–11, 8. Cf. H. F. Dickens, *The Recollections of Sir Henry Dickens KC* (1934), 136.

[88] Order 28. M. Muir McKenzie and C. A. White, *Wilson's Supreme Court of Judicature Acts* (5th edn, 1886), 311, esp. *Tildesley* v. *Harper* (1878–9) 10 Ch D 393.

defence was only used where it was 'plain and obvious'.[89] Even the general denial, seemingly specifically outlawed by rule, made a reappearance in 1893.[90]

Since the Coleridge Committee had pronounced that 'as a general rule, the questions in controversy between litigants may be ascertained without pleadings',[91] the rules enabled parties to dispense with them, but this never became widespread. It was later rumoured that the Council of Judges would recommend the abolition of pleadings[92] but the rule made in 1897 instead required permission for pleadings to be used, and that proved futile, since permission was given as a matter of course.[93] Pleadings remained, but the days of Bullen and Leake which some hankered after[94] would never return, and neither would the speedy identification and resolution of issues which old-style pleadings had promoted. It became common for parties to seek further and better particulars; sometimes justified by the looseness of the pleadings, they nevertheless developed into an abuse which Esher denounced as 'expensive, oppressive, and [liable] to cause infinite delay' and which the Gorell Committee agreed required curbing.[95]

The Coleridge Committee had intended that the dangers posed by looser pleadings and greater facilities for discovery etc. should be curbed by 'a change in procedure which would enable the court, at an early stage of litigation, to obtain control over the suit, and exercise a close supervision over the proceedings'.[96] The vehicle for this supervision was the summons for directions, but while it was clearly intended to supersede the previous practice, it proved a complete failure.[97] A major reason was hostility to this 'foisting of the Chancery principle upon the

---

[89] *Hubbuck* v. *Wilkinson* [1899] 1 QB 86, 91, quoted in R. W. Millar, *Civil Procedure of the Trial Court in Historical Perspective* (New York, 1952), 188. Looseness in pleading was occasionally criticized (e.g. *Clydesdale Bank* v. *Paton* [1896] AC 381), but in general the judges welcomed the liberal powers of amendment: *ibid.*, 175, and see C. H. S. Fifoot, *English Law in its Background* (1932), 161.

[90] *Adkins* v. *North American Tramway Co* (1893) 10 TLR 173, cited in J. I. H. Jacob, 'The Present Importance of Pleadings', in *The Reform of Civil Procedural Law* (1982), 243–58, 253. Similarly, Chitty J. had said that the rule-makers 'could not have intended to abolish demurrers by the right hand and restore them by the left': *Republic of Peru* v. *Peruvian Guano Co* (1886) 36 Ch D, 489, 495; Millar, *Civil Procedure of the Trial Court*, 188.

[91] Quoted in Jacob, 'Present Importance of Pleadings', 248.

[92] (1891–2) 36 *Sol. J.* 586.

[93] Jacob, 'Present Importance of Pleadings', 248.

[94] See e.g. the exchange between Darling J. and Master Chitty before the KBD Commission: *Evidence I*, q. 292.

[95] *PD* 1890 (s3) 347: 38; *DC on County Court Procedure Report 1909*, 21; *RC on the KB Division Evidence I*, Chitty, q. 321.

[96] Quoted in S. Rosenbaum, 'Studies in English Civil Procedure, II: The Rule-Making Authority' (1915) 63 *University of Pennsylvania Law Rev.* 151–82, 273–304 at 296.

[97] Order 30; Wilson, *Judicature Acts*, 319.

common law'.[98] Because the Law Society and most of the bar were antagonistic to the whole notion of interference with the parties' freedom to control the pace and direction of a suit, it had not seemed feasible to make it compulsory and it was generally shunned.[99]

The last of Mathew's rule-making contributions was to strengthen the summons for directions,[100] but consultations in 1896 showed that, as well as lawyers, many judges were hostile; Bruce felt it would mean 'the abolition of all settled procedure'[101] and Wright produced alarmist calculations suggesting a judge would have 150 to deal with per day.[102] If it were to be imposed, insisted the QBD judges, it must be by masters with an appeal to the judge to whom the case was allocated, and on that basis the rules were again amended in 1897.[103] Advancing it to an earlier stage in the proceedings as in the Commercial court seems only to have made it less effective. The solicitors' clerks who attended often knew too little about their case to be helpful, especially in country cases sent to London, so it became formulaic and made no substantial impact upon the volume of applications for discovery, interrogatories etc.[104] It continued to attract devotees of procedural reform[105] but was too inconsistent with the way the profession and the courts preferred to operate to make much impact upon the problems of the QBD, especially those stemming from the lavish use of interlocutories.[106]

Since the summons for directions was ineffective, there was little to restrain parties from fully exploiting the facilities the Judicature Acts provided. The results were unfortunate. 'Discovery of documents and interrogatories, the theoretical value of which is evident, and which occasionally in practice are essential to the attainment of truth, in very many instances only added to the costs of the action without any commensurate benefits to the suitor.'[107] The main benefit was often to solicitors in generating additional costs at little expense in time

[98] C. L. Simpson, *DC on SC Procedure 1881*, q. 1758, and cf. W. G. Andrews, q. 1696. Both were experienced managing clerks with big London firms.

[99] Rosenbaum, 'Studies in English Civil Procedure', 299.

[100] *RC on the KB Division, Evidence I*, Phillimore J., q. 1141.

[101] Bruce to Halsbury, 30 November 1896, LCO 2/126.

[102] To Halsbury, 30 November 1896, *ibid.*

[103] Report of divisional meeting, 5 December 1896, *ibid.* Commentary in (1896–7) 41 *Sol. J.* 815, 836, 857; (1897–8) 42 *Sol. J.* 4.

[104] *RC on the KB Division, Evidence I*, Chitty, q. 282, and see the exchange between MacDonell and C. A. Coward in *RC on the Civil Service Evidence*, qq. 45,434–7.

[105] The Gorell Committee urged that it be made more useful (*Report 1909*, 20) and the 'robust summons for directions' attracted the Evershed Committee in the early 1950s.

[106] It did not substantially reduce the number of other interlocutory orders: *Civil Judicial Statistics 1900*, suggested an overall fall of only 3%.

[107] Bowen, 'Law Courts Under the Judicature Acts', 8.

and effort.[108] Consequently restrictions had to be considered, though opponents argued that the ready resort to information about the other side's case frequently brought about a settlement.[109] Leave was already required for interrogatories in most cases, and from 1893 they were to be allowed only where 'necessary either for disposing fairly of the cause or matter or for saving costs'.[110] It would seem, however, that they were still freely sought and granted.[111]

On the common law side discovery of documents was even more eagerly embraced, and when the Judges' Council proposed stricter rules strong professional opposition prevailed.[112] Like interrogatories, discovery sometimes operated to terminate a suit, but where it did not, it often inundated the trial with documents, some of doubtful relevance.

4. THE TRIAL OF CIVIL ACTIONS[113]

The whole pre-trial process had therefore become greatly extended and complicated,[114] and it was commonly believed that another problem was 'the more elaborate manner in which cases are contested'.[115] Changes in the law of evidence no doubt contributed to lengthening criminal trials[116] and Hollams felt the increasing reliance on expert witnesses had a similar effect on civil trials.[117] Counsel's speeches were said to be growing longer[118] and, increasingly anxious about appeals, judges contributed to the lengthening of trials, both by permitting counsel to read long documents to the court, and by elaborating their own summings up and judgments.[119] What may also have contributed was the failure of a new mode of trial, before an official referee, and the tenacity of an old one, trial by jury.

One of the innovations suggested by the Judicature Commissioners was that a plaintiff should be able to elect for trial before a referee, preferably one of the new, full-time official referees. It would also be open to a judge to direct a referee

---

[108] G. Alexander, *The Temple of the Nineties* (1938), 27; A. J. Ashton, *As I Went On My Way* (1924), 138.

[109] Rosenbaum, 'Studies in English Civil Procedure', 297–8. It was for this reason that Cotton LJ thought interrogatories should be encouraged: *AG* v. *Gaskill* (1882) 20 Ch D 510, 528, quoted in Jacob, 'Present Importance of Pleadings', 256.

[110] Order 31, r 2.   [111] *RC on the KB Division, Evidence I*, W. Disturnal, q. 871.

[112] T. Snow, 'The New Rules of the Supreme Court' (1894) 10 *LQR* 78–84.

[113] For criminal trials XIII, Pt 1, Ch. III.

[114] *RC on the KB Division, Evidence I*, C. L. Samson, q. 644.

[115] *DC on County Court Procedure, Report 1909*, 13.

[116] The Gorell Committee was told that the Prisoners' Evidence Act lengthened trials by one-quarter: *Report 1909*, 13.

[117] Hollams, *Jottings of an Old Solicitor*, 72–3.   [118] (1906–7) 51 *Sol. J.* 788.

[119] Reported judgments in the division expanded fourfold between 1875 and 1940: S. Hedley, 'Words, Words, Words: Making Sense of Legal Judgments, 1875–1940', in C. Stebbings (ed.), *Law Reporting in Britain* (1995), 169–86 at 169.

to handle either the cause itself or any matter in connexion therewith.[120] Despite resistance to giving the judges this power the official referees were created by sections 56–7 of the 1873 Act.[121]

The first referees were appointed in 1875[122] but it was soon noticed that they were not being used to any extent and in February 1877 the Attorney-General admitted that they were such a failure, that judges and litigants were preferring the 'special referees' also allowed by the Act.[123] If the official referees were to be credible that they needed to be men of some repute yet the salary was only £1500 and the first appointments were tainted and discredited by jobbery.[124] One referee, H. W. Verey, was the subject of personal attacks in Parliament and the press[125] and others had no pretensions to such positions. These weak choices were all the more damaging because the Lord Chancellor and Lord Chief Justice had successfully fought the Treasury to get them something akin to judicial tenure, and since they had to serve 25 years for a full pension there was no getting rid of them.[126]

Lack of confidence in the referees may have disposed the judges to a very narrow interpretation of their powers, denying them the right to pronounce judgment or to try a case as opposed to an issue.[127] This was rectified in 1884 but still business was slack,[128] and as well as substituting an hourly fee for a flat one (the size of the fee was said to have been another deterrent[129]) the Lord Chancellor ordered an inquiry into whether they could be made useful in other ways.[130] This may have succeeded, for in 1897 one referee was described as 'the hard-working official, the bearer of so many heavy burdens of the High Court judges'.[131] It was ironic that he was also praised as 'a conscientious worker in the discharge of a duty from which almost every Queen's Bench judge draws back as wearisome

---

[120] *First Report 1869*, 13.   [121] *PD* 1873 (s3) 217: 173–81.

[122] By Judicature Act 1873, s 83 the Lord Chancellor, with the concurrence of the heads of division and the sanction of the Treasury, would determine their number, tenure, and qualifications. Cairns appointed four.

[123] A. E. Miller, 'What Has Been the Effects of the Judicature Acts?' (1876) *TNAPSS* 233; *PD* 1877 (s3) 235: 1288; (1876–7) 21 *Sol. J.* 785; (1877–8) 22 *Sol. J.* 947.

[124] (1879–80) 24 *Sol. J.* 685.

[125] (1875–6) 20 *Sol. J.* 289; Ashton, *As I Went On My Way*, 139. Watkin Williams, in defending Verey as the best of them, called all four unsuitable: *PD* 1876 (s3) 227: 1847–50.

[126] LCO 1/73; P. Polden, *A Guide to the Records of the Lord Chancellor's Department* (1988), 79–80.

[127] Wilson, *Judicature Acts*, 382–4.

[128] Judicature Act 1884, s. 9. They were said to be handling only 18 to 20 cases a year each: LCO 1/73.

[129] Fees Order 1877; LCO 1/84; Miller, *Judicature Acts*, 233.

[130] *Report of the DC on Official Referees*, 30 January 1889, LCO 2/28.

[131] R. F. V. Heuston, *Lives of the Lord Chancellors* (Oxford, 1964), 51, quoting (1897) 102 *LT* 572. According to *Civil Judicial Statistics 1894*, they tried 255 cases, but this may include references confined to sorting out accounts.

and unpleasant',[132] for if that duty was examining judgment debtors, the referee in question, Edward Ridley, made a great fuss about having to do it.[133]

Ridley had been appointed by Halsbury when it was at least arguable that the referees should be reduced in number, and in 1897 he was further favoured by promotion to the High Court, one of Halsbury's worst appointments. His replacement, G. W. Hemming, was not held in high regard and was said to eke out his work, which was perhaps one reason why hearings before the referees lengthened like those before judges.[134] The referees' court was not popular with the bar,[135] and when Montague Muir McKenzie, known as 'the bankruptcy attorney-general', became a referee his greater aptitude with complicated accounts caused many parties to seek dispensation from the rota of business to obtain his services.[136] By that time the official referees were performing a useful function, but their role fell well short of what the Judicature Commissioners had envisaged, and in the inquiries into the arrears in the KB Division they were neither consulted nor seen as a possible source of relief.[137]

A sharp fall in jury trials following the 1883 rules quickly levelled out at around half of civil trials and in 1910 had recovered from 54 to 62 per cent. It was always higher on circuit,[138] but was above half in town too, though Chitty said they were sometimes sought just to delay a trial.[139] Even the special jury, though often very far from special, was still in vogue.[140] That juries were invincibly prejudiced in certain types of case, particularly where the defendant's insurance exercised a 'corrupting influence', was widely recognized,[141] but they still had many defenders.

More than 40 years after Coleridge's attempt to remodel the jury, a Home Office committee under Lord Mersey sat to overhaul the law and practice. Contained in over 30 statutes, supplemented by custom and practice which varied from place to

---

[132] *Ibid.*   [133] LCO 2/28.

[134] Alexander, *Temple of the Nineties*, 102; (1906–7) 51 *Sol. J.* 107.

[135] B. Lailey, *Jottings From a Fee Book* (Portsmouth, 1932), 67, 71.

[136] Bell, *Those Meddlesome Attorneys*, 97. He was the brother of the permanent secretary to the Lord Chancellor. Cases were allocated in rotation (Ord. 50, r 45) unless the judge ordered otherwise (r 47).

[137] Edward Pollock, who became a referee in 1897 when his voice failed after an operation, improved their standing: Dickens, *Recollections of Sir Henry Dickens*, 136; Sir R. Bosanquet, *The Oxford Circuit* (1951), 81.

[138] *DC on Jury Law and Practice Report*, PP 1913 [Cd. 6817], xxx, and *Evidence* [Cd. 6818], App. 2. Consistently at or above 60% since 1895, it was above 70% for the period 1906–10. Lobban plausibly attributes this to the higher proportion of tort actions on circuit: 'The Strange Life of the English Civil Jury', in J. W. Cairns and G. McLeod (eds), *The Dearest Birth Right of the People of England* (Oxford, 2002), 190–2.

[139] *RC on the KB Division, Evidence I*, q. 359, and see the criticisms summarized in the *DC on Juries, Report 1913*, paras 156–91. Channell J. told that Committee that some asked for a jury in case they got a judge they felt unfavourable (q. 1,589).

[140] See below, pp. 824–5.   [141] *RC on the KB Division, Evidence I*, Cozens-Hardy MR, q. 593.

place, it was badly in need of tidying-up and there was a steady volume of complaint about the treatment of jurors and the quality of the justice they delivered.[142]

Aside from rationalizing and improving the processes by which jury lists were compiled and entered into the jury book and jurors summoned and selected, there were several more fundamental issues: qualifications for jury service; the future of the special jury; the payment of jurors and, most fundamental, the right to jury trial. The barristers on the Committee argued that its reference did not extend to the dangerous ground of curtailing the right to jury trial but the chairman ruled that a partial exclusion was within their terms.[143] Other questions which had been extensively debated in the 1870s—majority verdicts and smaller juries—received only cursory examination this time.[144]

The Committee was split on the desirability of democratizing the jury. Most members were not convinced that it was necessary in order to meet the feeling in the labouring classes (especially among trade unionists) that juries brought middle-class prejudices into the box,[145] and while making the optimistic prediction that 'the amount of education to be found among all classes is steadily and progressively increasing, [and] it is obviously permissible to anticipate a corresponding advance in the standard of intelligence of the common juror',[146] wanted to retain a property qualification as a surrogate for intelligence and responsibility. The report suggested a reduction to £15 rateable value, £20 in Middlesex[147] and proposed raising the maximum age from 60 to 65.

The inquiry also reprieved the special jury, though a minority dissented, describing it as 'a class jury chosen by reason of the wealth of its members'.[148] It had, however, been attacked from the opposite viewpoint; the London special juries in particular were said to be of very poor quality, often with a disproportionate number of publicans.[149] This was met by recommending higher property qualifications and abandoning the pretence that special jurors were 'bankers, merchants or esquires'.[150]

---

[142] e.g. S. L. Holland, 'Grievances of Jurors' (1895–6) 21 (s4) LM & LR 221–32. Tudor Rees claimed the inquiry stemmed from his agitation about payment to jurors: J. T. Rees, Reserved Judgment (1956), 36–7.

[143] Memorandum of W. English Harrison and Rupert S. Gwynne, Report 1913, 50–1.

[144] Report 1913, 36.

[145] Ibid., 30–1. Some felt that prejudice was usually in favour of a poor plaintiff.

[146] Ibid., 28. The standard of the common jury, at least in London, was thought by most witnesses to have improved, but see the contrary view of Lord Alverstone in (1911) 30 LN 98.

[147] Ibid., 38–9. The qualification in the City of London was not to be altered from £30.

[148] Minority Report of P. Snowden, E. W. Davies and Judge Parry, 54–6.

[149] T. E. Crispe, Memories of a KC (2nd edn, 1909), 250; Hollams, Jottings of an Old Solicitor, 379; DC on Juries, Report 1913, 29–35, and see the occupational breakdown of the special jury in Royal Exchange v. Cornfoot (1903) by C. A. Coward at q. 3550.

[150] DC on Juries, Report 1913, 39–40.

Payment of jurors had long been a sore point, especially since special jurors received a guinea a day, while common jurors received only a shilling per case (eight pence on circuit).[151] This was obviously bound up with the issue of qualifications and it was probably impracticable to make any recommendation entailing substantial public expenditure. As it was, the Committee suggested a modest allowance for travel and subsistence (and, where necessary, accommodation) hoping the cost would not exceed £40,000 per annum.[152]

The most delicate question was, of course, whether the right to jury trial in civil cases should be curtailed. The representatives of the bar were stoutly opposed and were content to repeat the views of previous Chief Justices and a 50-year old Commission.[153] The others differed and the KBD Commission sided with them.[154] The Mersey Committee recommended that while the right to jury trial was to remain absolute where character was at stake or where all parties desired, it should otherwise be at the discretion of the judge, as would any request for a special jury.[155] But the Mersey report was overtaken by events, and the right to jury trial in civil actions, curtailed near the end of the War and restored in 1925, survived until 1933.[156]

5. THE ASSIZES

The shift in business from the provinces to the capital was noticeable in the 1890s and Webster's optimistic notion that the summons for directions, by giving the master or judge the power to decide where trial should take place, would undo the damage done by the abolition of the venue rule and restore business to the smaller Assize towns, was soon dispelled.[157] On the contrary, it became more pronounced, so that by 1909 there were 2320 actions set down in London and Middlesex against 935 elsewhere.[158] The disproportion in trials was not so great (1,249 against 699), but the respective amounts recovered, £533,211 against £120,211, suggest that

---

[151] See above, pp. 599–600. A custom, said to have originated in the *Tichborne* case, had developed of special juries asking the parties for extra payment if the case went into a second day: Hollams, *Jottings of an Old Solicitor*, 60–2; *DC on Juries, Evidence*, Channell, q. 1764, T. W. Reed, q. 112.

[152] *DC on Juries, Report 1913*, 19, 46. The Committee recommended retention of the special jurors' allowance as they bore a double burden, though many under-sheriffs omitted special jurors from the common jurors list, despite repeated remonstrances, e.g. by Bramwell B. in 1878 ((1877–8) 22 *Sol. J.* 472).

[153] Memorandum by Gwynne and Harrison, *Report 1913*, 50–1.

[154] *RC on the King's Bench Division, Second Report*, PP 1914 [Cd. 7177], xxxvii, para. 46. Supporters of restrictions included Loreburn and Haldane.

[155] *Report 1913*, 35–6.

[156] R. M. Jackson, 'The Incidence of Jury Trials During the Present Century' (1937–8) 1 *MLR* 132–44 at 140–2.

[157] *PD* 1897 (s4) 46: 1004.

[158] *Civil Judicial Statistics 1909*, cii. and see introduction to those of 1894.

the metropolitan drift was most pronounced in the heavier cases. As the KBD Commission reported in Benthamic language, '[i]f the greatest good of the greatest number is to be studied', then in the 'long continued struggle between London and the provinces for the time of judges', London was getting a raw deal.[159]

The beneficiaries were small Assize towns which MacDonell's annual statistics regularly named and shamed. In 1911 715 criminal cases were tried in five places outside London, another 51 places mustering just 1,752.[160] In civil cases the disparity was even more glaring, for of 620 circuit trials in 1906 no fewer than 270 were held in Liverpool, Manchester, and Leeds.[161] Support for the Provincial Sittings Bill of 1885[162] and the extension of county court jurisdiction was strongest in the big cities. As Lewis Cave pointed out, 'the maintenance of the Circuit System in unimpaired efficiency is a condition of the courts in London',[163] but the strength of vested political and legal interests limited circuit changes to little more than tinkering.

Even the changes made by Cross[164] were soon undone by strenuous judicial lobbying. The hated fourth Assize was jettisoned save for Liverpool, Manchester, and Leeds, as was grouping of counties for criminal business. Moreover, the proposal to transfer all home counties litigation to London was effectively vetoed by the Lord Chief Justice.[165] In 1888 the Judges' Council resolved that 'grouping for civil business is the only answer...[but] they understand from the Lord Chancellor that such grouping is at present impracticable'.[166] Reactionary judges like Day and Grantham could not restore the days when the courts at Westminster Hall closed down while men went on circuit; indeed the quality, and on some circuits the numbers, declined.[167] The great leaders were seldom seen except on special retainer and it was becoming hard to brief a good man for a single case in a small town.[168]

Nevertheless, the circuits survived more or less intact. In the early 1890s the judges brought forward a proposal for a drastic cull of the towns where civil business was done, reducing them to just 18, but neither then, nor in 1896 when they tentatively proferred a much less extensive scheme, was any step actually

---

[159] *Second Report 1913*, 15.   [160] *Ibid.*, 16.

[161] *Civil Judicial Statistics 1906*, PP 1908 [Cd. 4029], cxxiii.

[162] Emphatically rejected by the Judges' Council, report of 26 February 1885.

[163] Dissenting note to Judges' Council report, 23 June 1888, LCO 1/10. The judges presented Cave with a silver bowl to mark their appreciation of his circuit scheme, but did not adopt it: *RC on the KB Division, Evidence I*, Alverstone LCJ, q. 100.

[164] See above, pp. 779–80.

[165] Above, and Stevens, *Independence of the Judiciary*, 13–16.

[166] Report of 30 June 1888, LCO 1/54. Halsbury rather acidly pointed to the fate of the earlier proposals in replying to Esher's complaint that grouping had not been carried out: *PD* 1890 (s3) 347: 52.

[167] R. J. C. Cocks, *Foundations of the Modern Bar* (1983), 166–74.

[168] *DC on County Court Procedure Report 1909*, 12–13; *RC on the KB Division, Second Report 1913*, 16 and *Evidence II*, Rowlatt J., q. 3434.

taken.[169] The chief obstacle was political. Neither party was prepared to face down the intense opposition to the loss of their Assize towns from its own supporters. Balfour's government refused a royal commission on Assizes in 1900[170] and the Liberals knew their Welsh strongholds must be among the biggest losers in any shake-up of the 'rotten boroughs' of the legal system.[171] Predictably, when an inquiry consulted representatives of the least busy Assize towns, their 'evidence…practically consisted of strong opposition to any alteration in the existing circuit system'.[172]

With neither such a cull nor a reversion to large-scale grouping (which most judges still opposed[173]), the problem of serving London and the provinces adequately with the existing number of judges was, as one judge admitted, insoluble.[174] Some of his colleagues brought assiduity and ingenuity to bear in devising novel permutations, and several were submitted to the KBD Commission, but none commanded general assent.[175] The Commission was not persuaded by the attempts of Alverstone and Phillimore to demonstrate that the system was efficient—'the waste of time is astonishing', interjected the chairman at one point[176]—but acknowledged the limitations within which they had to work. Alverstone was more diligent than Coleridge and had to his credit a modest measure enabling an Assize town to be by-passed if no business had been notified,[177] but he could not ensure that magistrates gave the intended effect to an earlier measure, the Assize Relief Act 1889 (c. 41).[178] This was to have ensured that prisoners triable at quarter sessions should await trial at the next Assize unless there was a 'special reason'. Judges opposed to the Act ensured the justices knew that they regarded the very proximity of an Assize as a 'special reason' and Home Office circulars to justices

[169] *DC on County Court Procedure, Report 1909*, 14; Abel-Smith and Stevens, *Lawyers and the Courts*, 89. According to the KBD Commission, 'no explanation or reason has been given for the disregard of its recommendations' (*Second Report 1913*, 19). Sir Kenneth Muir McKenzie could no doubt have enlightened them.

[170] Abel-Smith and Stevens, *Lawyers and the Courts*, 90.

[171] This fate befell reforms mooted in 1919: LCO 2/442. Muir McKenzie was discouraging when the union of the two Welsh circuits was suggested by S. Coleridge in 1893: LCO 2/55. Alverstone and other defenders of the circuits triumphantly produced to the KBD Commission isolated instances of substantial cases at the small Welsh towns, but they more often yielded none at all.

[172] *RC on the KB Division, Second Report 1913*, 12.

[173] Report of KBD judges on the royal commission report, 12 January 1914, LCO 2/324.

[174] *RC on the KB Division Commission, Evidence II*, Hamilton, q. 2839.

[175] *Second Report 1913*, 6. The Law Society was unable to produce a scheme.

[176] *Evidence I*, q. 1084. Alverstone was a sick man and did not complete his evidence. He rather ineptly defended 'the principle of counties', which Haldane dismissed as 'superstition' (q. 91, *Evidence II*, q. 4773).

[177] Quarter Sessions Act 1908 c. 41; *RC on the KB Division, Second Report 1913*, 17, and *Evidence I*, q. 66.

[178] Section 1(1).

proved ineffective; hence at the Leeds winter Assizes in 1912 some 60 out of 80 cases were of this sort.[179]

Rightly sceptical of any likely reforms, Liverpool and Manchester mounted a successful campaign to improve their own situation.[180] The KBD Commission 'consider[ed] it idle to suggest remedies which we do not consider could be applied' and their proposals, apart from recommending the abolition of the grand jury, were accordingly very modest.[181]

6. ARRANGEMENTS FOR TRIALS IN LONDON

Even without the problems caused by the circuits, arrangements for trials in London left much room for improvement and had led to a flight of litigants. Even Coleridge was anxious to recapture commercial litigation, but reinstating the Guildhall sittings proved a failure.[182] A more successful response was the creation of the commercial list in the QBD, rather grandiosely called the Commercial court. This had been suggested by a joint Law Society/Bar Committee initiative,[183] and when Barnes, a pupil of Mathew, became an Admiralty judge, he quickly offered commercial suitors a more attractive regime there.[184] Coleridge blocked such initiatives in the QBD and rejected successive resolutions of the judges,[185] but the inadequacy of existing arrangements was embarrassingly demonstrated by the wretched performance of Lawrance J. in a general average case,[186] and after Coleridge's retirement a third resolution was implemented; not without difficulty, for the Rule Committee was unable to agree on a definition of a 'commercial cause', but eventually Mathew and his allies by-passed it by a simple direction grounded in the court's inherent jurisdiction.[187]

The advantages offered by the new 'court' included a judge familiar with business (Mathew presided initially and Scrutton was among his successors); the hearing of a summons for directions and all subsequent interlocutory applications by that judge;[188] a fixed and early date for the trial, usually without pleadings; and a

---

[179] *RC on the KB Division, Second Report 1913*, 17–18 and *Evidence II*, Channell J., q. 2140. According to Muir McKenzie, the response of the judges to the report's suggestion that the Act should be more fully implemented 'nullifies the Assize Relief Act': LCO 2/324.

[180] LCO 2/242. An earlier deputation in 1896 had been less successful: (1895–6) 40 *Sol. J.* 287.

[181] *Second Report 1913*, 30.

[182] SCJ (London Causes) Act 1891 c.14; (1890–1) 35 *Sol. J.* 717; (1894–5) 39 *Sol. J.* 159. For their earlier features see de Montmorency, *Lord Gorell*, 50–1.

[183] (1891–2) 35 *Sol. J.* 194, 203.   [184] See above, p. 725.

[185] E. H. Coleridge, *The Life and Correspondence of John Duke, Lord Coleridge*, 2 vols (1904), ii, App. 2 (Mathew); A. D. Colman, *Mathew's Practice of the Commercial Court* (2nd edn, 1967), 5–6.

[186] *Rose v. Bank of Australasia* [1894] AC 687: see F. D. M[cKinnon] in (1944) 60 *LQR* 324.

[187] Colman, *Mathew's Practice of the Commercial Court*, 6–7.

[188] 'We have abolished the master altogether': *RC on the KB Division, Evidence II*, Scrutton, q. 3163.

better jury list.[189] In its early years the volume of business was fairly modest (around 200 actions entered), but the proportion actually tried, about 70 per cent, was much higher than in the general list and formed about 8–10 per cent of London trials.[190]

The commercial list did something to stem the exodus from courts to arbitration in London[191] but 20 years later the president of the Law Society said that clients constantly inserted into contracts that '[e]very dispute under this contract shall be referred to arbitration, and no solicitor or counsel shall be employed'.[192] Through the Arbitration Act 1889 the courts could limit the extent of such contracting out by empowering either party to insist on the arbitrator stating a point of law to the court, but solicitors were understandably concerned at being shut out of potentially lucrative business.[193] However, in some big arbitrations a whole array of eminent counsel were engaged at great expense; Fletcher Moulton was in a Welsh one which dragged on for 11 years and Hawkins, who had done wondrously well out of them, jocularly referred to the Surveyors' Institute, where most of the big London ones were held, as 'the gold mine'.[194] Balfour Browne also figured regularly, but his record earnings of £25,000 were beaten by Danckwerts in the Bell Telephone arbitration.[195] Railways and utilities could well afford the expense, but Higgin QC was said to have almost extinguished arbitrations in Manchester by his charges and slowness. [196]

Plaintiffs who were neither on the commercial list nor on the short cause list continued to complain about the delays and uncertainties in getting their cases tried.[197] Alverstone attributed both to a shortage of judges and pointed out that his division had to man the Central Criminal Court and provide judges for special jurisdictions, such as bankruptcy and the railway commission;[198] it had

---

[189] Colman, *Mathew's Practice of the Commercial Court*, 7–9. Juries, however, were rare in the Commercial court: *RC on the KB Division, Evidence I*, Shearman, qq. 773–4; *DC on Juries, Report 1913*, Reed, qq. 104–5.

[190] *Civil Judicial Statistics 1898*.

[191] Sir Alfred Jones, for the Liverpool Chamber of Commerce, told Loreburn that they had been obliged to set up their own arbitration procedure: report of deputation, 5 May 1909. Loreburn in turn told the KBD Commission that businessmen were driven to arbitration by the 'confusion and uncertainty' in the KBD: *Second Report 1913*, 4.

[192] *RC on the KB Division, Evidence I*, C. L. Samson, q. 695. For its spread in some industries see *DC on Juries, Evidence*, Sir W. J. Crump, q. 4045.

[193] H. W. Arthurs, *'Without the Law'* (Toronto, 1985), 75–7.

[194] H. F. Moulton, *The Life of Lord Moulton* (1922), 58; J. H. B. Browne, *Forty Years at the Bar* (1916), 203–16. See also G. W. Keeton, *A Liberal Attorney-General* (1949), 50.

[195] F. Pearson, *Memories of a KC's Clerk* (1935), 73.

[196] Spence, *Bar and Buskin*, 56–7; E. A. Parry, *What the Judge Saw* (1912), 98–101.

[197] e.g. (1901) 111 *LT* 197; (1904) 117 *LT* 211, 234, 258; (1905–6) 120 *LT* 260. Complaints were 'fully justified': *RC on the KB Division, Second Report 1913*, 17.

[198] The latter was particularly awkward since a judge had to be appointed for five years: *RC on the KB Division, Evidence II*, Rowlatt J., q. 3433.

occasionally to help out the Court of Appeal and the PDA and had now to man the Court of Criminal Appeal.[199]

A further complication was the divisional court. Though some advocated the abolition of this 'excrescence upon the general structure',[200] it still handled appeals from county and other inferior courts as well as applications for the prerogative writs and other orders. In 1910 336 appeals were argued (210 from county courts), plus 226 applications and a further 59 rules nisi, together making a significant demand upon the division's resources.[201] For reasons of history rather than logic, it was divided into two lists, a civil paper and a Crown paper, and the latter was manned by three judges, rather wastefully since in some instances a further appeal lay to the Court of Appeal.[202]

Coleridge had been unwilling to grapple with the problem of creating reliable trial lists.[203] Some were 'utterly unreliable', and in 1893 complaints from the professional bodies led to an overambitious attempt to produce a daily, rather than a weekly, list.[204] More successful was the short cause list started in 1894 and designed to secure the rapid trial of undefended and Order 14 actions on Saturday mornings. With trials coming on a month after the writ as opposed to five months in ordinary cases, it proved popular and by 1898 some 15 per cent of trials were handled in this way.[205]

Because of the circuits and the division's commitments, Alverstone insisted that it was impossible to emulate the Chancery division in creating lists for judges individually or in pairs. As proof he explained that a recent scheme prepared by Bray and Channell had collapsed because it had no spare capacity to accommodate absences through sickness and had only been possible by abandoning the judge in chambers; this had provoked a 'storm of opposition'[206] from the junior bar which brought about its withdrawal.[207]

---

[199] *Ibid., Evidence I*, q. 19 and App. 2.

[200] (1891–2) 36 *Sol. J.* 360. Abolition was suggested by a joint committee of the Law Society and Bar Committee in 1888 ((1887–8) 32 *Sol. J.* 556) and by T. E. Snow, 'The Reform of Legal Administration: An Unauthorised Programme' (1892) 8 *LQR* 129–39.

[201] *Civil Judicial Statistics 1910, PP* 1912–13 [Cd. 6047], cx.

[202] *RC on the KB Division, Second Report 1913*, 26–7.

[203] Coleridge, *Life and Correspondence of Lord Coleridge*, ii, App. 2 (Mathew). 'The fact, briefly stated, is that the judges of the Queen's Bench Division never really settle down to work in an organised and systematic manner': *The Judicial System*, 866.

[204] (1887–8) 32 *Sol. J.* 556, 589; (1893–4) 38 *Sol. J.* 524.

[205] *Civil Judicial Statistics 1898.*

[206] *RC on the KB Division, Evidence II*, Bankes J. q. 3705.

[207] The scheme had been modelled upon the procedure of the Commercial court: *ibid, I*, qq. 137 (Master Lawford), 1225 (Phillimore J.); *II*, 2193 (Channell). See also (1908–9) 53 *Sol. J.* 847. Loreburn (*Evidence II*, q. 4234) regretted the abandonment, feeling that the judge in chambers was underoccupied.

Yet many of the judges were adamant that only by entrusting them with their own list could cases be dispatched efficiently and timeously, and not all of them shared their chief's pessimism, although it was argued (and conceded by the Commission) that this would require a modest increase in their number.[208]

Demands for more judges when their workload—at least as measured in simple numbers of actions—was static inevitably invited a suspicious scrutiny of how long and hard they worked.[209] Alverstone was indignant at the sceptical views voiced in the Commons but they were hardly surprising.[210] Haldane showed that it was only by stretching the definition of a working day that the judges could claim they sat on up to 200 a year, yet one well-informed official claimed that 215 days would enable even 16 judges to handle their caseload.[211]

That naturally revived the question of the long vacation, which Bonner called 'the old man of the sea on the back of our whole legal system'.[212] While one Chancery judge had the hardihood to argue that the other vacations were too short,[213] and his colleagues lamented the modest trimmings of the long vacation,[214] Loreburn was 'almost revolutionary' on the subject and Haldane was prepared to have the courts operate uninterruptedly.[215] It was fortunate for the judges that their privileges were supported by the bar,[216] but some of them felt it prudent to admit that a further two weeks might be cut without complete disaster.[217] Even so,

---

[208] Second Report 1913, 5, 27–32. The Commissioners were clearly unimpressed with the defeatist attitude of Alverstone and Lawford, who drew up the lists.

[209] The only tangible fruit of the Select Committee's deliberations was a single clause Act of 1910 permitting the appointment of two additional judges (Judicature Act 1910 c. 12). One was duly made and Alverstone felt the Division could cope, but the death of Grantham and incapacity of Lawrance undermined the attempt to tackle arrears. The Commission's first report accepted the need for another judge to bring the total to 18.

[210] Memorandum of 16 May 1910, LCO 2/269.

[211] RC on the KB Division, Evidence II, q. 47,433; Master Bonner to Haldane, 28 May 1913, LCO 2/324.

[212] Bonner to Haldane, 28 May 1913, LCO 2/324. Bonner later became senior master in succession to Chitty.

[213] RC on the KB Division, Evidence I, M. Ingle Joyce, q. 540. Besides Sundays and public holidays the judges enjoyed a total of 115 days' vacation.

[214] In 1875 it ran from 8 August to 2 November. Despite opposition from the Council of Judges ((1881–2) 26 Sol. J. 119) it was reduced in 1883 to 12 August to 24 October. A Council of Judges' meeting in 1904 rejected any further cut but in 1907 it was moved forward to 1 August to 12 October: RC on the KB Division, Second Report 1913, 36–8; (1904) 117 LT 25.

[215] Evidence II, qq. 4321, 4690.

[216] Solicitors were divided on the question in the mid-1890s: ((1895–6) 40 Sol. J. 432, 461) but in 1898 the Law Society tried unsuccessfully to persuade the Bar Council to join them in lobbying for a reduction: (1897–98) 42 Sol. J. 671. The two bodies adhered to these positions before the KBD Commission: Second Report 1913, 7–8.

[217] The position taken by the Commission (Second Report 1913, 36–8). Alverstone had been reluctant to discuss the long vacation, arguing that it was not a question confined to the KBD (Evidence I, q. 118). The Chancery division and Court of Appeal were consulted and also opposed any shortening. The

claims that a long break was necessary for elderly men to recuperate invited the retort that there should be a retiring age for judges.[218]

Furthermore, the courts had shortened their sitting day to 10.30 am to 4 pm,[219] and if the judge sometimes sat later to finish a case, he more often rose early,[220] and some arrived late, Coleridge having set a bad example.[221] Saturday morning sittings were often exiguous, judges decamping briskly instead of seeking out other short list cases as they were supposed to, at least until Darling took them to task.[222] Alverstone did not keep his judges on a tight rein,[223] nor did he tackle those who were too ready to accommodate fashionable counsel at the expense of other litigants, disregarding a resolution made in Russell's time.[224]

This flurry of investigations into the High Court, and particularly the KBD, produced little significant change. The KBD Commission report of 1913 was very unambitious, the Commission eschewing 'sweeping changes' and 'confin[ing] our recommendations to such reforms as may meet the actual necessities of the case'.[225] These were minor changes to circuit arrangements: the long vacation reduced to two months; judges in London each to work through his own list; grand juries to be abolished and judges to retire at 72. Few of the recommendations were implemented, partly because of the distractions of war and the great

Commission also proposed that the court offices should be re-opened ahead of the new session. A previous attempt at this had been halted by fierce protests from the masters and registrars: LCO 2/248.

[218] As was in fact proposed: see below. Channell attributed his longevity to the long vacation: H. L. Cancellor, *The Life of a London Beak* (1930), 246.

[219] 11 am on Mondays, a concession made by Russell to jurors which persisted despite improvements in public transport: *RC on the KB Division, Evidence I*, Lawford, qq. 193–9; Abel-Smith and Stevens, *Lawyers and the Courts*, 88.

[220] Bankes kept a record which showed this: *RC on the KB Division, Second Report 1913*, 39.

[221] Coleridge, *Life and Correspondence of Coleridge*, ii, App. 2 (Mathew).

[222] The press waxed satirical about this: (1907–8) 52 *Sol. J.* 123, and Rowlatt admitted his early departure had caused a scandal: *RC on the KB Division, Evidence II*, q. 3462. Loreburn had allowed the Chancery division to abandon Saturday sittings in exchange for an extra half hour on weekdays (*ibid.*, I, Alverstone, q. 34) and the Commercial court had never sat on Saturdays, which was unpopular with its clientele. In fact it was a losing battle to hold onto Saturday sittings against the irresistible trend towards making it a holiday: see e.g. *RC on the KB Division, Evidence I*, Alverstone (q. 35), Phillimore (q. 1136), Eady (q. 1251) and *Evidence II*, Buckmaster (q. 2867).

[223] As he more or less admitted: *ibid.*, q. 65. Coleridge had been apprehensive about handling judges who resented the amalgamation of courts: to E. Yarnall, 12 March 1881, E. Yarnall (ed.), *Fifty Years of Friendship* (1911), 194. The older judges were the most disgruntled (KCL Library, t/s of Lord Lindley's Autobiography, 88), and according to J. B. Atlay, *The Victorian Chancellors*, 2 vols (1908), ii, 417, the amalgamation caused their slackness.

[224] *RC on the KB Division, Evidence II*, Bankes, q. 3828, Channell, q. 2284.

[225] *Second Report 1913*, 13, 14. The Commission was, for once, not dominated by judges, of whom only Darling sat, but there was a majority of lawyers. F. Newbolt, 'Delay in the KBD' (1913–14) 39 (s5) *LM & LR* 257–67, felt the practising bar was under-represented.

fall in litigation.[226] It nevertheless remains striking how closely the complaints which led to the next round of inquiries and proposals, in the 1930s, echo the earlier ones. And in comparison with the dynamism of procedural and institutional reform in the half century leading up to the Judicature Acts the following 60 years are characterized by timidity and conservatism,[227] grounded in a complacency expressed in the Gorell Report: 'notwithstanding the defects in our system which undoubtedly exist...the fact remains that the administration of justice in civil as well as criminal cases is more satisfactory than in any other country in the world'.[228]

[226] Brooks, 'Litigation and Society', table 4.9, 114.
[227] Abel-Smith and Stevens, *Lawyers and the Courts*, 100–10.
[228] At pp. 1, 35.

X

The Chancery Division

1. BUSINESS

The Judicature Act 1873 protected the Chancery division by specifically assigning to it the core areas of Chancery business: administration of estates, mortgages, partnerships, trusts (including charities), land contracts, and wardship.[1] Business was brisk, with total proceedings rising steeply from an average of 4,633 between 1871 and 1876 to 7,014 in the next quinquennium and continuing to rise thereafter, though more gently.[2] This necessitated the appointment of an extra judge in 1877 and by 1883 cases were being transferred to the QBD to meet complaints of delays.[3] Some judges blamed solicitors for bringing *nisi prius* type actions in Chancery because of its greater generosity with costs, and the Esher Committee accepted that another judge was needed to assist with the growing number of lengthy witness actions.[4]

When the sixth judge was added, in 1899, business was already in decline. With the exception of 1896–1900 the number of actions commenced fell in every quinquennium after 1886, a trend regularly noted in MacDonell's annual review. Yet although he described it as 'one of the most striking facts in the returns of recent years',[5] he made little attempt to explain it.

There is in fact no easy explanation, for the fall does not match the general trend of civil litigation.[6] Even after the costs in the two divisions were aligned it does not seem that plaintiffs who had the option chose the QBD,[7] while the county courts did not attract more equity business in the period of Chancery's decline.[8] Company winding-up petitions were transferred to Vaughan Williams J. 'as an additional judge of the Chancery division' in 1892, but were restored to the division

---

[1] Section 34(3). It was also given all the statutory matters belonging to Chancery, other than county court appeals.

[2] Civil Judicial Statistics 1894, *PP* 1896 [C. 8263], xciv.

[3] Judicature Act 1877 c. 9. *DC on Business in the Chancery Division*, *PP* 1886 (sess. 1) (92), liii, 5.

[4] *Ibid.*; Kay J. to Halsbury, 28 November 1888, NA PRO LCO 2/9.

[5] Civil Judicial Statistics 1910, *PP* 1912–13 [Cd. 6047], cx, introduction.

[6] C. W. Brooks, 'Litigation and Society in Britain, 1200–1996', in *Lawyers, Litigants and English Society Since 1450* (Cambridge, 1998), 63–128, figs 4.7, 4.8.

[7] See above, Ch. IX.

[8] P. Polden, *A History of the County Court, 1846–1971* (Cambridge, 1999), App. 3.

in December 1901.[9] It managed, however, to reject the resumption of bankruptcy, which had been the responsibility of Vice-Chancellor Bacon until 1884, when it was transferred to the QBD.[10] The removal of bankruptcy made a considerable dent in Chancery business while the restoration of company matters did little to offset the decline elsewhere. By an Act of 1907 patents were also made the responsibility of a Chancery judge, without much impact on the volume of business.

In the absence of detailed studies, a profile of Chancery litigation, albeit of questionable accuracy, can be derived from the Law Reports.[11] The principal categories in 1883 and 1913 respectively were:

	1883	1913
Wills	(including nine administration suits)	(including two administration suits)
	28 (17%)	23 (19%)
Trusts and Settlements	19 (11%)	14 (12%)
Charities	2 (1%)	5 (4%)
Settled Land Act	12 (7%)	7 (6%)
Land (including Vendor and Purchaser Act)	22 (13%)	16 (13%)
Mortgages	6 (4%)	8 (7%)
Company and Partnership	11 (6%)	10 (8%)
Winding-up	14 (9%)	13 (11%)
Bankruptcy	15 (9%)	Nil
Patents, Copyright, Trade marks, Passing Off	6 (4%)	7 (6%)
Bills of Sale	5 (3%)	Nil
Land Clauses Acts	3 (2%)	2 (2%)
Building Societies Acts	3 (2%)	1 (1%)
Exercise of statutory powers Nil		3 (3%)
Taxation	1 (1%)	4 (3%)
Other	19 (11%)	7 (5%)

[9] The *Solicitors Journal* protested that the transfer cast a slur on the judges and officers of the Chancery division: (1892) 37 *Sol. J.* 387.

[10] Bankruptcy Act 1883 c. 52, ss 92–4; LCO 2/107, file 835/9A.

[11] (1883) LR 23, 24 Ch D; [1913] 1 & 2 Ch D. Cases include Chancery appeals in these volumes but omit a few reports on procedural or practice questions where no subject-matter is indicated. The sample could be enlarged by including cases reported in *Weekly Notes*, in other series, and in *The Times*, but would not necessarily be more accurate. To the distortions produced by the reporters' selection must be added those inevitable in any categorization.

The similarities are more striking than the differences. Indeed the only substantial business other than bankruptcy which vanished was that occasioned by the controversial Bills of Sale Acts and which was probably ephemeral. On the other hand, tax cases were beginning to appear and disputes arising from the exercise of statutory powers by public bodies and utilities were becoming more prominent. Nevertheless, the decline looks to be spread across the staples of business rather than particular areas.

Such fluctuations are often attributable to changes in the economy and society, but legislation and a court's reputation also play a part. So with land transactions: their volume and value, at any rate in towns, followed long cyclical movements, one of which reached its peak in 1899 and then fell away steadily until the First World War,[12] but their capacity to generate disputes may have diminished. The first Chancery Commission had partly blamed the complexity of the land law for causing delays in Chancery[13] and although a comprehensive overhaul only took place in the 1920s, earlier amendments, especially the Conveyancing Act 1881, certainly effected considerable simplifications.[14] Against that, however, Chancery became a less forbidding venue for land disputes. From 1854 six eminent conveyancers were retained to sort out tangled titles[15] and the Vendor and Purchaser Act 1874 (c.78) introduced a more user-friendly procedure for resolving single questions.

No comparable economic trends or legislative reforms affected wills and estate administration but there was a major change in how they were handled. Judges in the 1880s were still despondent at 'the suffering and ruin occasioned by the delay and expense of chancery proceedings'[16] and small estates were still swallowed up in costs; Kay instanced *Brown* v. *Burdett*, in which a £4000 estate was consumed by the costs of probate (£1500) and an administration suit (£3000).[17] As late as 1895 the Trusts Administration Committee ruefully accepted that any form of official trusteeship must avoid any association with Chancery—indeed the judicial trustees borrowed from Scotland failed partly through that very taint.[18] By then, however, the court's ill-repute was less deserved, for in 1883 the new RSC (Order 55, rule 10) had at last created a simpler procedure; this avoided the full-blown

[12] A. Offer, *Property and Politics, 1870–1914* (Cambridge, 1981), 49–55, esp. fig. 4.2 on 52.

[13] See above, p. 650.

[14] J. S. Anderson, *Lawyers and the Making of English Land Law, 1832–1940* (Oxford, 1992), 146–56.

[15] *Ibid.*, 6.

[16] Kay J. to Halsbury, 17 December 1888, LCO 2/9. See also Pearson J. to Halsbury, 6 November 1885, LCO 1/35.

[17] *Ibid.* (1882) 21 Ch D 667.

[18] *SC on Trusts Administration*, PP 1895 (248), xiii; P. Polden, 'The Public Trustee in England, 1906–1986: A Study in Failure?' (1989) 10 *JLH* 228–55, 228–31.

administration action which, though not obsolete, quite quickly became a comparative rarity.[19]

As noticed above, the rules of 'necessary party' which had bedevilled both wills and trusts had been much modified in the mid-century. Moreover, alterations to settlements of land, hitherto only possible by a private Act of Parliament, were brought within the jurisdiction of the court, especially by the Settled Land Act 1882, and applications for that purpose were quite numerous.[20] Trustees of other settlements, however, found their position so onerous as to produce a crisis of trusteeship towards the end of the century, for despite the Trustee Relief Acts there continued to be a steady flow of disputes arising out of the clash between beneficiaries' desire to profit from the widening range of investment opportunities and the court's strict and narrow view of what was permissible.[21]

2. THE JUDGES

Sir Charles Hall, who filled the vacancy left by Wickens' retirement in 1873,[22] was the last of the vice-chancellors in this incarnation, for though they kept their title under the Judicature Act 1875, future Chancery division judges were styled justices of the High Court; the last vice-chancellor, Sir James Bacon, retired at 88 in 1886.[23] Unlike the vice-chancellors, their successors were not initially exempted from circuit duty, which was one factor in the 'block in Chancery' until they were relieved of it in 1884.[24] By then the Master of the Rolls had been made a purely appellate judge and replaced by a further puisne,[25] and although this left the division without a resident head, that seems not to have concerned the judges, while the Lord Chancellor and his permanent secretary probably preferred not to have an intermediate authority through whom reforms of the organization must be negotiated. Certainly Muir McKenzie would claim that more 'leapfrogging' occurred in promotions among the clerks in Chancery, where he kept a closer eye on such matters, than elsewhere and the division was the last to have a committee for staff appointments and promotions.[26]

Just as before, 'the Division functioned more as a collection of separate courts than as a unitary Division'.[27] Apart from the most junior, each judge had three

---

[19] *Civil Judicial Statistics 1894.*   [20] See XII, pp 91–4.

[21] C. Stebbings, *The Private Trustee in Nineteenth Century England* (Cambridge, 2002), 128–62.

[22] P. Polden, 'Mingling the Waters: Personalities, Politics and the Making of the Supreme Court of Judicature' (2002) 61 *CLJ* 575–611 at 586–8.

[23] Sir R. E. Megarry, 'The Vice-Chancellors' (1982) 98 *LQR* 370–405, 388–95.

[24] Polden, 'Mingling the Waters', 599–610.   [25] Judicature Act 1881, c. 68, s 2.

[26] *RC on the Civil Service, Evidence, PP* 1914–16 [Cd. 8130], xii, Muir McKenzie, q. 44,104.

[27] Megarry, 'Vice-Chancellors', 396.

chief clerks, with their junior clerks, attached to his chambers and each judge combined hearing witness actions and motions with chambers work.[28] Each had leaders who practised (unless on special retainer) only in his court and until 1883 suitors still chose their judge, creating workload imbalances which had to be redressed by periodic transfers of business to the less favoured judges.[29] The junior judge had no chambers staff and dealt only with witness actions and business coming from district registries. With the exception of Manchester and Liverpool, the district registries did not account for many actions,[30] and although it was suggested that Liverpool originated 1/6th of Chancery actions and Manchester almost 500, the only concession to their insistent demand for devolution was extended sittings at the Assizes; even then, provisions protecting the Duchy of Lancaster court limited their applicability.[31] That apart, Chancery remained essentially a metropolitan court.

The division did not cope well with the rapid increase in witness actions and the unexpected enthusiasm of solicitors for originating summonses under various statutes.[32] Jessel's ruthless abuse of the power to send cases to Assizes for trial could not be copied by the other judges[33] and a chorus of complaints led to the setting up of the Esher Committee. The Committee's proposals for remodelling practice were predicated on the addition of a sixth judge,[34] business slackened soon afterwards and the new rules probably improved matters. Lord Chancellors found the Treasury unaccommodating, which in turn hampered some of the economies the reorganization promised.[35] The new judge finally arrived in 1899, and two years later a scheme first suggested by Horace Davey was implemented, whose principal feature was to combine judges in pairs. Each new action was assigned to a pair, one of whom heard witness actions while the other did interlocutory and chamber work, each pair being assisted by four masters and their clerks.[36] The system seems

---

[28] *DC on the Chancery Division, Report 1886*, 1–6.

[29] *Ibid.*; Polden, 'Mingling the Waters', 605, wrongly gives it as 1882. There is a good description of the attempts to circumvent the ballot which was then instituted in E. A. Bell, *Those Meddlesome Attorneys* (1939), 211–13.

[30] Civil Judicial Statistics 1900, *PP* 1902 [Cd. 1115], cxvii.

[31] *DC on the Chancery Division, Report 1886*, evidence of Francis Hampson (Manchester ILS) and I. H. E. Gill (Liverpool ILS).

[32] *RC on the Legal Departments, Evidence, PP* 1875 (C. 1245), xxx, esp. R. H. Leach, q. 3509; *DC on the Chancery Division, Report 1886*, esp. J. W. Hawkins, q. 640, citing summonses under the Settled Land Acts, Lands Clauses Acts, Married Women's Property Act etc.

[33] Polden, 'Mingling the Waters', 603.

[34] *DC on the Chancery Division, Report 1886*, resolutions, 17–19, esp. number 7. They offered as a fallback a plan by Pearson J.

[35] The Esher Committee plan was endorsed by a small committee headed by Sir Charles Bowen in 1889 (LCO 2/32); M. Hicks Beach to Halsbury, December 1895 (*ibid.*).

[36] LCO 2/107.

to have worked well, at least while business remained relatively slack, and it enabled them to retain their cherished 'closed shop' among the Chancery leaders.[37]

3. OFFICES

For the Childers Committee the Judicature Acts were an unmissable opportunity to rationalize and economize on the offices of the courts, combining most
of the clerical departments, so when the Jessel Committee was charged with
putting this administrative reorganization into effect, the separate existence of
all Chancery offices—the chambers staff, the registrars, the taxing masters, the
pay office, and the office of records and writs—was threatened.[38] In fact, however,
the integration was both gradual and incomplete.

The Chief Clerks in Chambers [Masters]

In 1874 the chief clerks in chambers were described as being 'among the hardest
worked men in the State service'.[39] Pressure on them was growing as statutes sent
new types of business their way and solicitors awoke to the possibility of getting
things done more cheaply and quickly.[40] Some judges, notably Sir John Romilly
MR and his successor Sir George Jessel, delegated matters so freely that some
lawyers, and at least one judge, felt they had gone rather too far.[41] A troubling
diversity of practice arose between different chambers, so that '[t]he practitioner,
instead of being able to conduct his business according to one uniform method,
must endeavour to learn the different mode of treatment in each Court and set of
chambers. The difficulty of doing so leads to mistake, and mistake causes delay
and expense.'[42] The problem was that RSC Order 55, rule 15 empowered each
judge '[s]ubject to these Rules, to order what matters shall be heard and investigated by their Chief Clerks, either with or without their direction, during their
progress', leaving ample scope for divergence.[43]

---

[37] Chancery judges to Halsbury, 15 March1900, *ibid.*
[38] *DC on Legal Offices, PP* 1878 [C. 2067], xxv. The brevity of the report is characteristic of the
chairman.
[39] *RC on the Legal Departments, Second Report 1874*, 59.
[40] *Ibid.* Useful later descriptions are R. E Ball, 'The Chancery Masters' (1961) 77 *LQR* 331–57 and
E. Heward, *Masters in Ordinary* (Chichester, 1990), 67–73.
[41] *RC on the Civil Service, Evidence*, Master Fox; H. M. Humphry, 'The Judges' Report on Practice
from a Chancery Point of View' (1892) 32 *LQR* 289–300; *DC on the Chancery Division, Report 1886*,
Chitty J., qq. 2110–11.
[42] *DC on the Chancery Division, Report 1886*, 3.
[43] A particular generous delegation was disapproved in *Re Pickel* (1886–7) 31 *Sol. J.* 311 (CA):
'Mr. Burney's Proposed Scheme for the Amalgamation of the Administrative Staff of the Chancery
Division', LCO 1/35.

That the chief clerks got through a great quantity of business was not in doubt,[44] but they might have done more, and done it better, had solicitors been less inclined to send inexperienced or incapable clerks and had the snobbery of the bar not precluded counsel from condescending to argue before a mere clerk.[45] Nevertheless, the Esher Committee recommended that their authority be enlarged to allow them to draw up certain kinds of order and that they should gradually absorb the registrars and taxing masters.[46] Some Chancery judges feared that these proposals would weaken the principle that the judge was to draw his own orders in chambers rather than referring matters to independent minor judges,[47] but in practice, 'either immediately or by degrees, the [clerks] came to do practically everything that their predecessors had done in the exercise of their judicial functions'.[48] Many of them disliked winding-up, which was subject to extensive fluctuations and could disrupt their timetable and they were relieved when it was shifted to the registrars in bankruptcy in 1892 as a non-divisional winding-up department.[49] Even when business fell away, leaving the chambers vulnerable to accusations of over-manning, they resisted taking on lunacy work as a royal commission suggested,[50] and also successfully fought off an attempt to reduce the complement for each pair of judges from four to three.[51]

In 1897 the chief clerks were metamorphosed into masters—according to the oral tradition of the bar after one of their number had been refused membership of the Athenaeum because of his lowly title.[52] It affected neither their precedence nor their salaries, but may have made the position more attractive to barristers. This was a concern of the Law Society but in 1914 all but one were still solicitors.[53] Appointed by the Lord Chancellor, they headed watertight compartments. Muir McKenzie effectively chose their clerks, who were drawn from solicitors' offices; the introduction of a masters' committee by Haldane, however, ensured that most promotions would be by seniority.[54]

---

[44] In 1890 2183 matters were brought into chambers, plus 138 in winding-up. 89,265 applications were disposed of, 3173 certificates issued, 9662 orders drawn up, 1185 receivers' accounts, and 1278 others, passed and 579 sales made: *Civil Judicial Statistics 1890, PP* 1890–1 [C. 6443], xciii.i.

[45] *DC on the Chancery Division, Report 1886*, observations of F. Mowatt, 13–15; *RC on the Legal Departments, Second Report, PP* 1874 (C. 1107), 59; *Evidence*, C. Milne, q. 6888.

[46] Resolution 28.

[47] *Ibid.*, observations of Sir E. E. Kay, 11, and see his questions to H. J. Francis, qq. 1270–7.

[48] Ball, 'Chancery Masters', 344.

[49] *RC on the Legal Departments, Evidence*, E. B. Church; Heward, *Masters in Ordinary*, 71.

[50] *RC on the Civil Service, Evidence*, Master Fox and App. xci, Cozens-Hardy Committee Report, 1910.

[51] *Ibid.* For an earlier proposal see LCO 2/107.   [52] Ball, 'Chancery Masters', 343.

[53] (1896–7) 41 *Sol. J.* 305.

[54] *RC on the Civil Service, Sixth Report, PP* 1914–16 [C. 7832], xii, 30–1, and *Evidence*, Muir McKenzie and Master Romer.

Record and Writs Clerks, Enrolment, and Report Offices

These offices were obvious candidates for absorption into the new central office. They were overmanned[55] and solicitors had complained of the pedantry of the clerks and that the heads of each division secreted themselves in their offices appearing to do very little.[56] Selborne's apology for having filled a vacancy unnecessarily confirmed the impression that these offices were inadequately supervised and they were duly absorbed into the central office.[57]

The Pay Office

Despite earlier reforms, the pay office remained a byword for circumlocution among solicitors,[58] who hoped that an outsider, Sir George Kellner, 'untrammelled by its traditions' as its new head would lead to an improvement.[59] Kellner was to head a larger unit, the Supreme Court pay office, established under the Supreme Court (Funds) Act 1883 (c. 29)[60] under Treasury control, but although its operations covered all divisions, it was essentially the old Chancery pay office writ large and the Civil Service Commission noted disapprovingly that the higher positions were filled by political patronage.[61]

Taxing Masters

Though the Lisgar Commission had found the taxing masters overpaid and the structure top heavy an eighth master had to be appointed in 1878 to meet complaints about delays.[62] They preserved their separate existence because the Jessel Committee saw no advantage in an amalgamation since so much of their work was done on a different basis—solicitor and client comprising 58 per cent of the bills taxed.[63] Some of the masters favoured becoming attached to individual judges like the chief clerks, perhaps to forestall the alarming prospect raised by the Esher Committee that they should be phased out and their duties

---

[55] RC on the Legal Departments, Second Report 1874, 43–7.

[56] It was alleged that if the clerks felt the paper used for an affidavit was too thin, it was rejected and the solicitor had to go before a judge for a ruling: ibid., Evidence, W. Crossman, q. 7298.

[57] Ibid., q. 9590; DC on the Legal Offices, Report 1878, 8; Supreme Court (Officers) Act 1879 c. 78.

[58] LCO 1/28, ILS memo., 1880.   [59] (1883–4) 28 Sol. J. 283.

[60] For discussions about the arrangements see LCO 1/75.

[61] Sixth Report 1915, 38.

[62] RC on the Legal Departments, Second Report 1874, 54–8; (1877–8) 22 Sol. J. 724; (1878–9) 23 Sol. J. 283, 294.

[63] DC on the Legal Offices Report 1878, 9; DC on Taxing Officers Report 1901, LCO 2/192. Upwards of 66% of taxations in 1900 were for costs to come out of a fund in court: Civil Judicial Statistics 1900.

performed by clerks attached to judges' chambers.[64] The LCO preferred a single taxing office for the SCJ, but a committee of Queen's Bench and Chancery masters could not reach agreement[65] and even when it came about, in 1901, the PDA was excluded 'temporarily', because of difficulties 'as to immediate expense and vested interests'.[66] Lunacy taxations had been hived off to a chief clerk in the office of the masters in lunacy in 1889,[67] but the costs taxed in the Chancery division still far exceeded those in both other divisions together.[68]

Registrars

The registrars were the great survivors, owing this largely to the support of judges and practitioners, who helped them see off repeated threats, particularly from Muir McKenzie. The permanent secretary quickly formed an unfavourable impression of the registrars as 'always obstructive and old-fashioned',[69] and their offices as 'established on a scale quite unknown in any other part of the public service, and even in the other divisions of the High Court itself. [Whereas] officers are usually graduated like a pyramid, here the pyramid stands on its apex.' 'The attachment of two full Registrars to every Court', he declared, 'is magnificent, but it is not business.'[70] Perhaps the registrars were old-fashioned because they were old, for a structure in which a man became a registrar by seniority in a hermetically sealed office was liable to encourage conservatism.[71] They were certainly no innovators: their representative told one inquiry he was unable to think of any improvement in their operations[72] and the senior registrar was hardly more imaginative before the Civil Service Commission.[73]

The Esher Committee was the first to threaten them with amalgamation with chambers clerks, a proposition endorsed by the Judges' Council in 1892.[74] Shortly before that meeting, Chitty J. proposed that the registrars should help the hard-pressed chief clerks, but two of his colleagues opposed that as the thin end of the amalgamation wedge, the clerks were jealous of handing over any of their work, and Halsbury withdrew it from the Rule Committee, fearing lest it

---

[64] Master Longbourne to Muir McKenzie, 11, 18 January 1889, LCO 2/9; *DC on the Chancery Division Report 1886*, 10.

[65] LCO 2/46.   [66] Halsbury to Alverstone LCJ, 5 July 1901, LCO 2/192; RSC 1902 Ord. 2.

[67] LCO 2/9.   [68] *DC on Taxing Officers, Report 1901*.

[69] Note on the back of an envelope marked 'draft of amended supreme court funds rules', undated in LCO 1/85.

[70] Memorandum prepared for the DC on Registrars, 1906, reprinted as App. xcii to the *RC on the Civil Service Evidence*.

[71] e.g. the senior registrar P. J. King had been in the office for 46 years when he retired in 1886: (1886–7) 21 *Sol. J.* 807.

[72] *DC on the Chancery Division, Report 1886*, L. L. Pemberton, q. 838.

[73] *RC on the Civil Service, Evidence*, C. E. Farmer, qq. 45, 168–245.

[74] *DC on the Chancery Division, Report 1886*, 10; Humphry, *Judges' Report*, 29.

put the registrars 'in a position which would make them more difficult to deal with than they are now, when any amalgamation of Chancery Departments was attempted'.[75]

It was a tactical error, for Muir McKenzie's next attempt, via the Kekewich Committee in 1907, failed.[76] The Committee was split over almost everything and the dissents weakened its authority. Registrars were to keep their separate identity (reluctantly on the part of half of the members[77]), but their chief clerks might substitute for them in court. Registrars, like the masters, should be attached to a particular pair of judges and the senior registrar should have more clearly defined authority.[78] However, registrars and judges combined to preserve the status quo as nearly as possible. Judges restricted the cases in which a clerk could be in court and gave a very narrow interpretation to the Esher Committee's recommendation as to which orders could be drawn up in chambers, so protecting the registrars from the full impact of declining business.[79] The registrars also battled to preserve their unreconstructed clerical structure. Farmer maintained that the Act of 1841,[80] never repealed, meant that only one of their clerks could be made a registrar, and he had undercut the clear notice given to more recent appointees that they acquired no vested rights by a 'tacit understanding' that the old practice would be followed.[81]

Nevertheless, reductions in staff were made and the number of registrars fell from 12 to nine and then, during the war, to the six which Muir McKenzie had suggested as sufficient.[82] But though battered, the survivors were unbowed. The Civil Service Commission was unimpressed with the case they advanced, noting the fall in business, that their counterparts in winding-up did not sit in court and that Seton's *Decrees* and the changing character of business dissolved some of the mysteries of the Chancery order.[83] Yet it was vain for the Commission to renew the recommendation for amalgamation, for when the Oliver Committee examined Chancery in 1981 it found the registrars still entrenched, dinosaurs of the courts.[84]

---

[75] Lord Chancellor to Chitty, 16 August 1892, LCO 2/79. The file has the views of the Chancery judges (December 1891) and observations of the chief clerks.

[76] LCO 2/201. The unpublished report is in App. xcii to the *RC on the Civil Service, Evidence*.

[77] The prominent solicitor Roger Gregory, the official solicitor, W. H. Winterbotham, and the Public Trustee, Charles Stewart.

[78] Kekewich and the barrister C. James dissented from this. Gregory and Winterbotham also opposed the recommendation that the position of registrar be open to barristers.

[79] *RC on the Civil Service Sixth Report 1915*, 31–2 and *Evidence*, Master Fox and C. E. Farmer. Nevertheless, by then half the orders were being made in chambers.

[80] Administration of Justice Act 1841 (4 & 5 Vict. c. 5).

[81] *RC on the Civil Service, Sixth Report 1915*, 31–2.

[82] Farmer to Muir McKenzie, 24 July 1907, LCO 2/201; C. Schuster to Master Fox, 26 July 1921, LCO 2/464.

[83] *RC on the Civil Service, Sixth Report 1915*, 31–3.

[84] Heward, *Masters in Ordinary*, 68.

4. PRACTICE AND PROCEDURE

Throughout the 1870s and 1880s aspects of Chancery's rules and practices came under fire for the old reasons, delay and expense, leading to committees under Lord Esher and Lord Bowen. Thereafter there was a marked lessening in the frequency of complaints in the professional press and Parliament. Apart from the Kekewich Committee[85] there were no further inquiries, and although the Rule Committee made some changes, its contributions are unlikely to have been the only reason for this respite. It seems likely that the decline in administration actions and the removal of winding-up, by making the costliest and most complained-of types of work less prominent, coupled with the decline in overall workload, were as much responsible as improvements to practice and procedure generally, though this remains to be tested.[86]

The traditional Chancery pleadings, by way of bill and answer, came to an end with the Judicature Acts.[87] Unlike their common law brethren, the Chancery bench and bar do not seem to have bemoaned the loss, nor did the suitors. Not everything changed however. Although the time limits for appearing, replying, and so on were reasonably strict, they were not stringently enforced, so that it was usually months rather than weeks, before the pleadings closed.[88] Until they were curbed, interrogatories were a particularly fruitful source of delay.[89]

One of the biggest changes was the increasing resort to originating summons. Some felt they were used in cases whose complexity made them unsuitable,[90] but their popularity steadily grew, especially in the core business of administration of estates. It was not before time. One judge summed up his dilemma thus: '[a]t present applications are constantly made by persons who are entirely unable to bear the cost of the proceedings to have such estates administered in Chancery. The judge feels that if the order is made the costs will swallow up the estate. On the other hand, if the order be not made the executor or trustee against whom it is sought may apply a great part of the estate for his own purposes and may be an impecunious person unable to answer the costs. Consequently in such cases the court constantly finds that it is compelled in the result to apply the whole estate

---

[85] See above, p. 843.

[86] Some rule changes did have a marked effect; summonses for a time fell away dramatically after one such change: *Civil Judicial Statistics 1895*, *PP* 1897 [C. 8536], c.

[87] Proceedings were henceforth to be styled actions and commenced by a writ of summons: RSC 1883 Ords 1, 2.

[88] Humphry, *Judges Report*, 294–5.

[89] *DC on the Chancery Division, Report 1886*, J. W. Hawkins, qq. 327–8; T. Snow, 'The New Rules of the Supreme Court' (1894) 10 *LQR* 78–84 at 79.

[90] *DC on the Chancery Division, Report 1886*, H. J. Francis, q. 1248; Humphry, *Judges' Report*, 297.

in payment of the costs.'[91] Only a handful of suitors each year met the criteria for *in forma pauperis* assistance.[92]

Judges like Pearson and Kay strove hard to mitigate the consumptive effects of the traditional administration suit, lasting six or seven years and swallowing small estates,[93] but only the creation of Order 55, rule 10 offered a real alternative. Thenceforth only a judge could make an administration order and it soon became known that most of them were reluctant to do so.[94] There might still be a few families whom, as Cozens-Hardy said, manufactured doubts to obtain the security of administration in court, but the great majority preferred the simpler, cheaper method; indeed the Judges' Council was so impressed that it recommended an extension to all disputes over the construction of a document.[95] And while the Law Society claimed that the proliferation of originating summonses created more work for judges and chief clerks,[96] it was plausibly argued that the latter became less burdened with the regular applications generated in administration actions.[97]

Not all actions were friendly, and handling the genuine disputes gave the Chancery division most difficulties in adapting to the new regime. Though two of the vice-chancellors were said to have promoted affidavit evidence as the general rule, parties increasingly preferred witness actions.[98] Judges effectively froze jury trials out of their court,[99] but they experienced such problems in accommodating trials with witnesses that long delays arose after an action was set down and many had to be adjourned part-heard, to the legitimate dissatisfaction of litigants.[100] The delays only added to the attractions of witness actions for the less scrupulous litigants and their lawyers, and their tactical choice may often have paid off, for in 1900 barely half of actions set down were actually heard.[101] Even more upright solicitors were tempted to manufacture unnecessary interlocutory motions to demonstrate their zeal for the client.[102]

---

[91] Kay J. to Lord Chancellor, 26 November 1885, LCO 1/35.

[92] *Civil Judicial Statistics 1890.*

[93] (1881–2) 26 *Sol. J.* 208 (*Meyrick* v. *Jones*); (1884–5) 29 *Sol. J.* 229 (*Evans* v. *Nicholls*).

[94] *SC on Trusts Administration Report 1895*, H. H. Cozens-Hardy, q. 1548.

[95] *Ibid.*; Snow, 'New Rules', 80–1.

[96] 'Some Reasons for the Appointment of a New Judge in the Chancery Division', 28 February 1891, LCO 2/32.

[97] *SC on Trusts Administration Report 1895*, Cozens-Hardy, q. 1548.

[98] (1875–6) 20 *Sol. J.* 330, 409.

[99] (1876–7) 21 *Sol. J.* 215; (1877–8) 22 *Sol. J.* 524. In 1875 there were just two jury trials: *Civil Judicial Statistics 1875*, PP 1876 [C. 1595], lxxix.i.

[100] Sir C. S. Bowen, 'The Law Courts Under the Judicature Acts' (1886) 2 *LQR*, 1–11 at 6.

[101] 'It is the common talk of the profession that any defendant seeking delay refuses to have it heard as a non-witness action': *DC on the Chancery Division, Report 1886*, T. Rawle, q. 1599; *Civil Judicial Statistics 1900.*

[102] Humphry, *Judges' Report*, 29.

Complaints about witness actions were largely responsible for the creation of the Esher Committee, and though its suggestions could not be fully implemented until the extra judge was in post, the judges did manage to re-arrange business so as to alleviate the delays, albeit perhaps at the expense of their other duties.[103] By 1900, however, the worst of these problems had been solved and witness actions continued greatly to outnumber others.[104]

The Esher Committee also had within its remit the arrangements for chambers business, another source of dissatisfaction. As was often the case with such inquiries, it was only outsiders, this time the Treasury's Frank Mowatt, who pointed to one of the main inefficiencies, that chambers dealt only with vacation business for more than 100 days in the year. Solicitors testifying to a subsequent inquiry, while not questioning the sanctity of the long vacation, complained that some masters had a vary narrow definition of vacation business.[105]

Even without that, however, there was plenty for the Esher Committee to criticize. Judges mostly fitted in their chambers appointments at the end of their day, with predictably unsatisfactory results.[106] Uncertainty about whether counsel should appear in chambers meant that matters were sometimes expensively adjourned into court to give the judge the benefit of counsel's wisdom.[107] As for the chief clerks, their system of 'long appointments', while not reproducing the worst inefficiencies of the old hourly warrants, too often left a matter unfinished.[108] The Committee's proposals that matters should be taken in strict rotation and without regard to which judge's court they came from, and that the chief clerks should generally deal with them *de die en diem*,[109] was condemned in one journal as 'utterly unworkable' and seemingly lawyers and officials combined to make it so, for the next enquiry found that it had not been implemented.[110]

Not all the deficiencies in chambers proceedings could be blamed on officials, however. One chief clerk claimed to have insistently complained that the proce-

[103] (1898–9) 43 *Sol. J.* 22. In 1891 the Law Society claimed that more than 500 witness actions were waiting for a hearing and that on average only 290 were heard in a year: 'Some Reasons…', LCO 2/32.

[104] In 1902 they were eight times the non-witness actions and the gap was widening: *Civil Judicial Statistics 1902*, PP 1904 [Cd. 2040], cvii.

[105] *DC on the Chancery Division, Report 1886*, 'Observations', 13–15; *RC on the Civil Service, Evidence*, R. Gregory and E. R. Cook.

[106] *DC on the Chancery Division, Report 1886*, 4. Chitty J. gave a breakdown of the structure of his week, q. 2058.

[107] *Ibid.*, Hawkins, q. 454.

[108] *Ibid.*, 3. 'Long appointments' were made in advance for an hour or two hours.

[109] Hawkins claimed that Vice-Chancellor Kindersley had ordered his chief clerks to do this, but it soon broke down: *ibid.*, q. 364.

[110] (1885–6) 30 *Sol. J.* 315; Report, LCO 2/32. It was noted, however, that some judges were now allowing a full day to chambers work.

dure for auction sales was unduly elaborate[111] (a solicitor witness agreed that the auctioneer's affidavit of fitness was 'a pure waste of money and an absurdity'[112]), while the method of taking accounts also left much to be desired—rather damagingly, as the number of accounts to be passed rose steadily in the 1890s.[113]

After judgment (and sometimes at an interlocutory stage) there would be an encounter with the registrars' office, where reluctance to streamline procedures was equal to the resistance to organizational change; despite the fall in business it was only an instruction issued on the recommendation of the Kekewich Committee that orders be drawn within 14 days that put an end to delays.[114]

Costs in Chancery were still a big problem in the 1870s; indeed the court was so sensitive to the exactions in winding-up that it allowed orders to be drawn up in chambers to avoid the additional expenses of the registrars' office.[115] As noted, the most acute difficulties, however, were with small estates, and in the judges' view the problem lay not with court fees, but with solicitors' charges. Attempts were made to lessen the near-automatic allowance of costs out of the estate, but that was only a palliative.[116] Kay in particular gained a reputation for his 'solicitor-baiting' orders,[117] but the solution he and others favoured, a move to allowing a percentage fee on the value at stake, was felt too difficult to accomplish.[118] Changes in 1889 displeased the Law Society, but whether they did much to reducing charges is unclear.[119] Herschell admitted to the Trusts Committee in 1895 that although a less costly procedure was now in place the problem of small estates remained unsolved,[120] but public complaint about the cost of Chancery was much diminished.[121]

---

[111] *DC on the Chancery Division, Report 1886*, Hawkins, q. 553.

[112] *Ibid*, T. Rawle, q. 1506. The Committee proposed simplifications.

[113] *Civil Judicial Statistics 1895*, *PP* 1897 [C. 8536], c.

[114] *RC on the Civil Service, Evidence*, W. G. Oakeshott.

[115] *RC on the Legal Departments, Evidence*, Leach and Milne, q. 3763.

[116] (1891–2) 36 *Sol. J.* 706; Humphry, *Judges' Report*, 295–6.

[117] (1888–9) 33 *Sol. J.* 434.

[118] Kay to Halsbury, 17 December 1888. Muir McKenzie had been attracted by the idea: note of 6 November 1885, LCO 1/35.

[119] Correspondence of Law Society and Muir McKenzie, May–June 1889, LCO 2/9. Taxations took off about 15–20% of a bill (*Civil Judicial Statistics 1900*) and the average sum in taxed bills fell from £133 to £97 between 1876 and 1894: *Civil Judicial Statistics 1895*.

[120] *Report*, Herschell's evidence at q. 83.

[121] Though see e.g. H. J. Randall, 'The Cost of a Law Suit' (1904) 19 *LQR* 430–4.

XI
Local Courts

1. INTRODUCTION

There was no shortage of courts which were, in theory at least, open to the person wishing to collect a debt or seek damages for loss or injury. There was in fact 'a curious array of Courts above Courts, and jurisdictions within jurisdictions'.[1] Alongside the historic units of county and hundred (or wapentake), manor and borough, stood assorted franchises, liberties, and so forth, and even attorneys claimed familiarity with only a few of those in their own county.[2] No one knew how many courts there were and little is known of how they dealt with such business as came before them.[3]

2. THE OLD ENGLISH LOCAL COURTS

County Courts

The county court was an ancient and imposing institution in terminal decline. Though practice books were still being written[4] and its officers staunchly defended it,[5] in many counties suitors had long ago deserted it, leaving Blackstone and other conservatives to lament its moribund condition.[6] The Common Law Commissioners were severe:

The limitation in point of amount; the annual change of the officers who preside in these Courts; the want of competent juries; the lengthened pleadings, heavy costs,

---

[1] S. and B. Webb, *English Local Government from the Revolution to the Municipal Corporations Act: The Manor and the Borough, Part One* (1908), 32.

[2] For a valuable analysis from an earlier period see L. Knafla, *Kent at Law* (1994).

[3] *RC on the Common Law, Fifth Report*, PP 1833 (247), xxii (hereafter *Fifth Report 1833*), App. A. Successive official inquiries in 1823, the early 1830s and 1839 cast some light and see also W. A. Champion, 'Recourse to Law and the Meaning of the Great Litigation Decline: Some Clues from the Shrewsbury Local Courts', in C. W. Brooks and M. J. Lobban (eds), *Courts and Communities in Britain, 1150–1900* (1998), 179–198.

[4] S. Webb and B. Webb, *English Local Government from the Revolution to the Municipal Corporations Act: The Parish and the County* (1906), 290.

[5] e.g. G. Keen, clerk of the peace for Staffs., *Fifth Report 1833* App., no. 1.

[6] Holdsworth, *HEL*, i, 69–82, at 74.

unnecessary delay, and a vicious system of practice, attended with enormous abuse and oppression committed by bailiffs in the execution of process by improper agents, render these Courts inefficient for the administration of justice, and the subject of general complaint.[7]

To take these points in turn: unless the suitor put himself to the expense of procuring the writ *justicies*, the money limit was a mere 40s. The under-sheriff who presided was usually a local attorney, chosen only for a year, though in practice he often served for long periods.[8] Frequently doubling as the county clerk, he often exercised a powerful influence over the jury,[9] which itself sometimes consisted of men 'who made almost a trade of it'.[10] Pleadings 'in point of length and expense [fell] little short of those used in the superior Courts'[11] and the full range of formal objections could be taken. Costs were heavy because there was no discouragement to the employment of lawyers. The Commissioners were particularly concerned at the practice of compelling the defendant to appear, without prior notice, by seizing his goods, sometimes 'not by regular bailiffs, but by casual agents of the lowest description... frequently... in a violent and oppressive manner'.[12] Moreover, as a forum for local justice the county court was inherently defective so long as it persisted in sitting only in the county town.[13] It was perhaps in the interests of justice, but hardly of expedition or economy, that by the writ *pone* a case could be removed to the superior courts.[14]

In the two counties where demand was greatest, statutory modifications had made the county court more user-friendly. From 1750 the county clerk of Middlesex (a barrister) held a small debts court in every hundred with simplified process and a jury, but the judge himself did not feel it was a suitable model for cases above 40s.[15] Under an Act of 1794 the Lancaster court sat not only at Preston but in Manchester, simplified its procedure, and appointed a barrister as assessor. *Justicies* was more cheaply available in the Duchy and the Act made it difficult for defendants to remove a suit under £10 into the superior courts.[16] These provisions were effective enough for the court to have 9000 suits by 1830, double that of Yorkshire and far more than Warwickshire (162), Northumberland (2755) and

---

[7] *Fifth Report 1833*, 6.   [8] Webb and Webb, *Parish and County*, 287–8.

[9] *SC on County Courts*, PP 1823 (386), iv, 7.

[10] *Fifth Report 1833*, App., 2nd series, G. Walters, no. 3, q. 7.

[11] *Ibid*, 9.   [12] *Ibid*, 8–9.

[13] *Ibid*, 6. In particular, it added substantially to the expense of trials through the cost of bringing witnesses from a distance.

[14] Holdsworth, *HEL*, i, 73.

[15] *Ibid*, 191; *SC on County Courts Report 1823*, 5–6. Serjeant Heath gave evidence to similar effect to the Commissioners: *Fifth Report 1833*, App. B, no. 5.

[16] *SC on County Courts 1823*, 6; *Fifth Report 1833*, 7; Duchy of Lancaster Court of Common Pleas Act 1794 (34 Geo. III c. 58).

Nottinghamshire (260). Nevertheless it shared some of the drawbacks of the others and costs were still heavy.[17]

Hundred Courts and Courts Baron

The hundred court, held by a deputy of the sheriff, had much the same jurisdiction as the county court and similar drawbacks.[18] It was also damned by the Common Law Commissioners: '[i]ncompetent juries, an ill-regulated course of pleading, and the practice of allowing costs wholly disproportioned to the cause of action...render these courts inoperative for any useful purpose'.[19] With a few exceptions, such as Salford and the Wirral, which embraced Birkenhead and was lucrative enough for a Liverpool attorney to purchase for £500 in 1820, they were entirely inactive.[20] A few other courts of varying origin and also covering several manors were still active, notably the Peveril court and the court baron of the Honour of Pontefract, which covered Leeds, Bradford, and Huddersfield.[21]

A good many manorial courts (courts baron) were still trying small debt actions.[22] One, the court of the manor of Wakefield, had combined with the Pontefract Honour court to extend its area and raise its money limit to £5,[23] but as in most other local courts the parties' expenses were proportionately very large—£9 to £18 for plaintiffs, £6 to £12 for defendants—and this, along with the infrequent sittings, led the Commissioners to conclude that their extension had produced 'very little advantage to the public', notwithstanding that 5171 suits were brought in the Pontefract court in 1830/1.[24]

Borough Courts

Borough courts were extremely numerous, and very various not merely in their colourful profusion of names but more importantly in jurisdiction, judges, and procedure.[25] A handful, such as the Liverpool court of Passage and the Bristol Tolzey court, were much used, but the great majority were pretty inactive. In Kent, for example, Canterbury's was 'not held very often'; Queenborough's 'discontinued'

---

[17] *RC on the Common Law, Fourth Report*, PP 1831–2 (239), xxv, App. I.; *Fifth Report 1833*, 7.

[18] Holdsworth, *HEL*, i, 70–1.

[19] *Fifth Report 1833*, 9. The appendix gives examples, notably from the Amounderness Wapentake court, whose juries comprised 'the dregs of society' (Edward Rishton, A 45).

[20] Webb, *Manor and Borough*, 61.   [21] *Ibid.*, 62–3; *Fifth Report 1833*, 9–10.

[22] Webb, *Manor and Borough*, 119–20; Holdsworth, *HEL*, i, 184–5.

[23] *Fifth Report 1833*, 9 and App. A 24 (J. P. Heywood).

[24] *Ibid*, 9 and see App. A 24, 64, 73 and 2nd series A52, 116; *RC on Common Law. Fourth Report 1832*, Apps I, V.

[25] Webb, *Manor and Borough*, 339–44; Holdsworth, *HEL*, i, 148–51.

and Maidstone's court of pleas, inaugurated under a charter of George II, '[n]ot used, being as expensive as the courts of Westminster Hall'.[26] That last comment points to one of their big weaknesses; in Newark the plaintiff's taxed costs to recover a debt of £2 11s were £13 16s 6d; '[t]he allowance of costs being seldom regulated by Act of Parliament or the Charter...is usually arbitrary'.[27] Procedure was often archaic—in New Romney's it was 'equally perplexed and vexatious as in the Superior Courts'.[28] Geographical limits were inconveniently narrow and the superior courts reduced their utility by freely granting *certiorari* and prohibition. Local pride and self-interest supplied even the least used with defenders,[29] and in some towns efforts were under way to revive them.[30] However, many boroughs had preferred to seek new machinery for the enforcement of obligations, particularly small debts, and these took the form of courts of requests.

3. COURTS OF REQUESTS

Origins and Development

Since the promoters of courts of requests (initially styled courts of conscience) prudently avoided seeking to abolish an existing local court, their creation added to the complexity of the juridical landscape, but they became numerous and popular (with creditors at any rate) and some practically eclipsed an older court altogether.[31]

From about 1750 expansion took place in fits and starts, especially between 1805 and 1810, and by 1830 more than 100 Acts had been passed and courts were held in over 250 places.[32] Their distribution was highly uneven; in Kent there were courts for the hundred of Blackheath, for several hundreds around Tonbridge and for eight towns, yet the big counties of Buckinghamshire and Devon had none at all.[33] Not all succeeded in attracting business; in Kent in 1830/1 Folkestone had only 65 actions and Deal 121, while Gravesend and Sandwich mustered more than 500

---

[26] (1823) *HCJ* 78, 126.   [27] *Fifth Report 1833*, 11.

[28] *Ibid.*, App. A 117 (William Stringer).

[29] *Ibid.*, App. A 103 (W. Waterman, Tenterden),111 (C.C. Bartlett, Wareham).

[30] *Ibid.*, App. A 59 (A. Taylor, Thetford, B 10 (Serjeant Talfourd, Banbury).

[31] The standard account is still W. H. D. Winder, 'The Courts of Requests' (1936) 52 *LQR* 369–94. See also H. W. Arthurs, 'Without the Law': *Administrative Justice and Legal Pluralism in Nineteenth-Century England* (Toronto, 1985), 25–34 and '"Without the Law": Courts of Local and Special Jurisdiction in 19th Century England' (1984) 5 *JLH* 130–49. Fresh light on their operation is given by M. C. Finn, *The Character of Credit* (Cambridge, 2003, edn of 2007).

[32] Winder, 'Courts of Requests', 370–4; C. W. Brooks, 'Interpersonal Tension and Social Conflict: Civil Litigation in England, 1640–1830', in *Lawyers, Litigation and English Society Since 1450* (Cambridge, 1998), 27–62 at 41; Arthurs, 'Without the Law', 26; *Fifth Report 1833*, App. B3 (Sir John Cross).

[33] *RC on Common Law, Fourth Report 1832*, App. (I). The list in Holdsworth, *HEL*, i, App. xxviii, differs, showing that by then Exeter and Plymouth had acquired courts.

each and Blackheath over 5000. Elsewhere some were much busier; 28,000 actions were commenced in Tower Hamlets while Halifax and Liverpool each exceeded 20,000.[34] In all, the courts of requests entertained over 200,000 suits, some 2.5 times the figure for the superior courts, and it is little exaggeration to say that 'for most Englishmen civil justice was the justice of the courts of requests (and other local courts), not the justice of the superior courts and the common law'. [35]

Jurisdiction

Most courts of requests were sought by towns and their jurisdiction was limited accordingly, so that populous suburbs of rapidly expanding cities such as Birmingham and Newcastle fell outside the court's reach, leading some, such as Bristol, to seek supplementary Acts to enlarge their area.[36] Some courts had one or more hundreds for their area, like that established in 1808 for 'the hundreds of Codsheath, Somerden, Westerham and Edenbridge, Westham, Brenchley and Horsmonden, Washingstone, the Lowey of Tonbridge and the Ville and Liberty of Brasted'.[37] Some Acts expressly provided for sessions to be held in different places, while others gave the commissioners freedom to arrange the locations for themselves. In some rural counties like Lincolnshire almost the whole county was within the jurisdiction of one or another court of requests.[38]

The early Acts mostly required that all parties to a suit should reside or be engaged in business within the limits of the court, but this was found unduly restrictive and later Acts made only the defendant's residence necessary to found jurisdiction.[39] There was no single formula and challenges to jurisdiction were not infrequent. The superior courts, always jealous of rivals, tended to construe the limits narrowly even if, as in *Meredith* v. *Drew*,[40] that might make a trader or professional man practically immune from suit in any court of requests. Most courts were open to plaintiffs from outside its area, and in Bath changes in their occupational file suggest outsiders were increasing.[41]

The early courts of requests had the same limit of 40*s* as existing local courts, but in 1805 Bath obtained an Act with a £10 limit and a few months later Grimsby had one for £5; £5 immediately became the standard[42] and from the same time the suits

---

[34] *RC on Common Law, Fourth Report 1832*, App. (I).

[35] Arthurs, 'Without the Law', 132; Brooks, 'Civil Litigation in England', 141–2.

[36] Winder, 'Courts of Requests', 384.   [37] *RC on Common Law, Fourth Report 1832*, App. (I).

[38] Winder, 'Courts of Requests', 385–6.   [39] *Ibid.*, 387.

[40] (1832) 2 Moore & Scott, 116, 8 Bing. 141.

[41] M. Finn, 'Debt and Credit in Bath's Court of Requests' (1994) 21 *Urban History*, 211–36.

[42] Winder, 'Courts of Requests', 387–8. It was, however, common for suitors to abandon the excess of their claim in order to sue in the court.

which could typically be brought were extended from debts to 'all cases of assumpsit, and insimul computasset, and in all causes or actions of trover and conversion, and in all causes or actions of trespass or detinue for goods and chattels taken or detained'.[43] Only money claims which involved the title to land were excluded.

Judges and Procedure

The only general statute ever enacted for courts of requests laid down minimum property requirements for the commissioners (judges): realty in the district worth £20 per annum or personalty worth at least £500, though this may not have been scrupulously observed,[44] and some Acts imposed higher requirements.

There was, however, no uniformity in numbers or service. Canterbury's were supposed to be chosen every three months, while Birmingham in 1787 had 72 commissioners from whom ten were struck off by ballot and replaced every other year; some early Acts confined them to aldermen and councillors, yet Southwark's enabled it to have 152 at one time.[45] No doubt their arrangements for sittings were equally varied, but Birmingham was probably typical in having a small number who sat regularly, with the (sometimes doubtful) assistance of others who participated occasionally. Only a few had appointed a barrister as an assessor to inform their deliberations, others relying to differing extents on their clerk, a local attorney.[46]

Lawyers were sometimes formally excluded but more often, though permitted, were discouraged by being allowed only minimal costs.[47] Local 'low attorneys' were not infrequently to be found, however, engaged in vigorous competition with 'agents' and 'accountants'. However, in most courts judges generally dealt with the parties themselves or the defendants' wives or family members.[48] There were no juries, the commissioners being sole judges of law and fact, and the rules of evidence were probably ignored—indeed any attempt to adhere strictly to them would have raised the cost of proceedings beyond what suitors were prepared to pay. Hutton in Birmingham seems to have come quite close to the Benthamite ideal of oral pleading by the parties in person and examination of the parties was normal practice.[49] These courts were the site of negotiation and broad, discretionary justice rather than agencies rigidly enforcing the common

---

[43] Bath Court of Requests Act 1805 (45 Geo. III c. lxvii), s 16, quoted by Winder, 'Courts of Requests', 389.

[44] *Ibid.*, 376. In Manchester they needed property of £1000 and a house within the town: *Fifth Report 1833*, App. B 1 (Samuel Kay).

[45] Winder, 'Courts of Requests', 375–6. [46] *Ibid.*, 377.

[47] Arthurs, 'Without the Law', 131. [48] Finn, *Character of Credit*, 238–40.

[49] Winder, 'Courts of Requests', 389–90; *Fifth Report 1833*, App. B, 1 and 3 (S. Kay and Sir J. Cross on the Manchester court).

law. Indeed, courts of requests were enjoined by their statutes to decide cases according to 'equity and good conscience'. There is little evidence to evaluate the use they made of this freedom, but it might be used to support local customs and to give effect to defences not recognized at law.[50]

Business

While the main attraction of courts of requests for urban elites was to facilitate the cheap and speedy recovery of small debts, they were not used exclusively by creditors pursuing labourers and artisans. In Bath farmers and yeoman frequently appeared either as plaintiff or defendant (over 9 per cent of each in 1829), while in Bristol in 1830 merchants and manufacturers made up 57 per cent of plaintiffs and 34 per cent of defendants.[51] The use of these courts to resolve disputes between the town's better-off citizens suggest confidence in their judges and process. Nor were the disputes a monotonous procession of 'goods sold and delivered', although those made up 70 per cent of Sheffield cases, more than in Bristol. Bristol figures also demonstrate the importance of the increased monetary limit: only 55 per cent were for £5 or less.[52]

Business was not static. The rural element in Bath was declining and they were increasingly used by regular suitors pursuing the poor.[53] Some traders were operating regionally if not nationally and the tallyman and 'Scotch draper' who became so familiar to county court judges were already in evidence.

Courts of Requests and their Critics

Those professionally concerned with provincial justice usually acknowledged the useful role played by these courts, but few felt them a suitable model for a national system. The Select Committee of 1823 declared that 'the process for recovery [of small debts] is very cheap, and their decisions give general satisfaction', but claimed they had two serious flaws. First, except for small claims the absence of the jury was unacceptable, and while in the bigger towns 'it is very easy to find intelligent and respectable men, well qualified to perform the duties of commissioners, it would be impossible to do so in more thinly peopled and less opulent districts'.[54] This was the reverse of the problem experienced with magistrates, where it was industrial towns which were short of suitable gentlemen.

---

[50] Winder, 'Courts of Requests', 389–90; Arthurs, 'Without the Law', 29–31. The only substantial contemporary account is William Hutton, *Courts of Requests* (Birmingham, 1787).

[51] Finn, 'Debt and Credit in Bath's Court of Requests', 216–22; Arthurs, 'Without the Law', 130–5.

[52] Arthurs, 'Without the Law', 132–4.

[53] Finn, 'Debt and Credit in Bath's Court of Requests', 220–1; Finn, *Character of Credit*, 248–51.

[54] *SC on County Courts 1823*, 4.

Brougham, who also admitted their value, had far more ambitious plans, and the more detailed investigation by the Common Law Commissioners in 1833 (unlike the Select Committee they were all barristers) lumped them with other local courts, whose 'defects [are] so numerous and complicated, that it is easier to devise new institutions than to introduce effectual improvements in those which exist'.[55]

The Commissioners' main objection to courts of requests was their judges. They quoted Blackstone's censure that 'with methods of proceeding entirely in derogation of the Common Law, and whose large discretionary powers make a petty tyranny in a set of standing Commissioners', adding that his doubts 'have not been removed by experience'.[56] It was thought that the shopkeepers and tradesmen with little business who alone would have the time and inclination to sit as commissioners would exhibit a pro-creditor bias, but they received little evidence to justify the suspicion 'that their decisions are often wanting in impartiality', which they admitted was 'difficult to determine'.[57] The most circumstantial accusation, the so-called 'Hackney map case' was at best unproven[58] and criticisms were generally muted compared with those levelled at some of the older courts.[59] Nevertheless the constitution of these courts meant that even a good one could easily fall from grace; Hutton's old court at Birmingham was in such a state by 1828 that Joseph Parkes and others constituted themselves a self-appointed group of reformers.[60]

A particular source of disquiet for the Commissioners was that these lay judges had extensive powers to commit debtors to prison. Such concerns were not new. They had been instrumental in bringing about legislation in the 1780s which limited the length of the imprisonment and established that it operated to clear the debt. By the 1830s cross-currents in the debates over committals and local justice confused and hindered initiatives to reform each of them. The Commissioners were fresh from reporting on the use of imprisonment for debt and the majority tended towards the school of thought which held that too effective punitive sanctions against debtors encouraged both irresponsible lending and incautious borrowing rather than that which insisted that such sanctions were indispensable to the operation of the credit system which was necessary for the country's prosperity. In the parallel debate over the shape and working of the courts, the latter view

---

[55] *Fifth Report 1833*, 18.   [56] *Ibid.*, 11.   [57] *Ibid.*, 12.

[58] *Ibid.*, App. B, 6 (Thomas Starling) and 12 (Thomas Offor and Benjamin Hammuck).

[59] For critics see e.g. *Fifth Report 1833*, App. A 54, 123. Wilson and Harrison of Kendal complained that 'there is no uniformity of decision, no record of its proceedings, and consequently on means of anticipating its decision in any particular case; no respectable professional man ever practises in it'.

[60] Winder, 'Courts of Requests', 380. Contrasting views of its condition a few years later are in *Fifth Report 1833*, App. A (2nd sess.), 102 (W. Beale) and 104 (J. Turner).

translated into support for courts with professional judges rigidly enforcing legal rules sanctifying bargains rather than exercising older forms of discretionary justice.

Though the courts of requests lacked the superior courts' powers of execution against the body in mesne process, some used it rather freely to enforce judgments, especially after the types of personal property against which execution could be levied had been greatly reduced.[61] In Bath in 1830–1 9.6 per cent of the 3711 suits produced orders for execution against debtors' bodies and 3 per cent of debtors in that year actually underwent imprisonment for failure to meet judgments.[62] These figures were on an upward curve and Bath was certainly not alone in its frequent resort to the prison, for the Liverpool court imprisoned 1064 and the City of London court 470.[63]

Courts of requests were not in general harsh towards poor debtors. They pioneered the practice of ordering payment by instalments and used the power chiefly to assist poor defendants—labourers, spinsters, and widows.[64] Unfortunately the use of instalments could actually increase the resort to imprisonment, a single lapse in repayments being treated as contumelious where the court had already established that the debtor had the means to pay.[65] Moreover the Commissioners felt that the ease of obtaining execution, whether against goods or persons, had the effect of encouraging irresponsibility in seeking and granting credit.[66]

The Commissioners' recommendation for a network of small debt courts temporarily halted the spread of courts of requests, but once it became clear that it would not soon be implemented petitions resumed, no fewer than 49 Acts being passed between 1835 and 1846.[67] Some still conferred those 'large discretionary powers' to dispense the loose and informal equity that Blackstone had deplored, but others now prescribed adherence to the common law.[68] New courts were designed to disarm other objections. They usually had a barrister as assessor;[69] were wider in their geographical coverage, and tended to offer either party the

---

[61] *Fifth Report 1833*, 12; Finn, 'Debt and Credit in Bath's Court of Requests', 213–14.

[62] Finn, 'Debt and Credit in Bath's Court of Requests', 214–15.

[63] *RC on Common Law Fourth Report 1832*, App. (I).

[64] Finn, 'Debt and Credit in Bath's Court of Requests', 218–19.

[65] Courts' willingness to commit debtors for breaches varied, but enforcement could be 'rapacious, arrogant, arbitrary and illegal': Finn, *Character of Credit*, 234, and see 242–5.

[66] *Fifth Report 1833*, 12.

[67] Winder, 'Courts of Requests', 381. Peel's 1827 bill may have had a similar effect; it dissuaded Faversham from proceeding with a bill for enlarged jurisdiction: *Fifth Report 1833*, App. A 142 (J. G. Shepherd).

[68] Winder, 'Courts of Requests', 375; Arthurs, *Without the Law*, 26, 42.

[69] Sometimes leading to animated politicking, e.g. in Bristol: G. Bush, *Bristol and its Municipal Government, 1820–1851* (Gateshead, 1976), 150.

option of a jury in cases above £5. They therefore became more like conventional law courts, perhaps as a condition of their passage.[70]

In the early 1840s the courts of requests were thriving. The number of suits is estimated to have risen to over 400,000, which in some cases may have made it difficult to deal with them speedily and effectively.[71] Their achilles heel continued to be the reliance upon imprisonment to enforce judgments which, by a strange chain of circumstances, brought about their abrupt and unexpected demise.

4. THE MOVEMENT FOR REFORM

Althorp and Peel

In the early 1820s two men with opposite political views presented bills aimed at remedying the deficiencies of the old county court: the arch-Tory Lord Redesdale in 1820 and the rising Whig Lord Althorp in 1821. Althorp's bill became the basis for a protracted and ultimately fruitless campaign.[72]

Althorp proposed to raise county court jurisdiction from 40s to £15 and to give the sheriff a legally trained assessor who would make a quarterly circuit of towns nominated by the justices at quarter sessions. Lawyers would only be allowed to address the court on points of law and trials would be by jury.[73] Discouraged by a cool reception, Althorp tried again in 1823 by the longer route of a select committee which he had fully primed with evidence on the courts' failure to support the growing volume of credit trading.[74] Discarding the possibility of enlarging the money limits of the courts of requests, the Committee endorsed Althorp's proposal, though only to £10, substituting a salaried commissioner as judge, appointed by the *custos rotulorum* to avoid giving patronage to the government. Procedure would be simplified and the court enabled to direct payment by instalments; appeals would be restricted and, to placate those who predicted that better facilities for recovering debts would make traders irresponsible in granting credit, there was to be a two-year limitation period.[75] A bill based on this report

---

[70] Winder, 'Courts of Requests', 381. Yet apparently when Southwark sought a new Act they were obliged to exclude lawyers: *Fifth Report*, App. B 12 (Offor and Hammuck). Finn, *Character of Credit*, 237–8, is less persuaded of a marked trend to embrace lawyers' values than Arthurs.

[71] Arthurs, 'Without the Law', 132.

[72] P. Polden, *A History of the County Court, 1846–1971* (Cambridge, 1999), 13. See also A. L. Cross, 'Old English Local Courts and the Movement for their Reform' (1942) 30 *Michigan Law Rev.* 369–85.

[73] PP 1821 (85, 233), i.

[74] The radical William Hone collected information for him. The bills of 1824 and 1825 were supported by many petitions, probably orchestrated: *HCJ* 79, 80.

[75] *PP* 1823 (386), iv.

was presented in 1824 and though opposed by some lawyers (who argued that the bar would be corrupted by the lure of judgeships) and by members concerned for the county rate, it made good progress until halted by an unforeseen objection.[76]

Sinecure office-holders in the superior courts, who had paid for their offices (or had them purchased for them) demanded compensation on a novel ground— not that the existence of their offices was threatened, but that their profits would be diminished by the loss of business to the revitalized county courts, which they estimated at one quarter.[77] No government could accept that without cre- ating a damaging precedent across the public service, but it was seized on by the bill's opponents and wrecked its chances. Althorp then persuaded Peel, who had acquired a reputation for modest, consensual law reforms, to adopt it.[78] Peel made amendments appropriate to his programme of judicious modernization of ancient institutions. His Small Debts Recovery Bill of 1827 avoided creating permanent judges and side-stepped the patronage question by merely empower- ing the sheriff (in reality the under-sheriff) to appoint an assessor at need. The jury was reduced to five and there was to be no power to seize the debtor's person, only his goods; safeguards were added to meet recurrent complaints about the misconduct of county court bailiffs.[79]

It was a typical measure of Liberal Toryism, economical and conservative, and with Althorp generously greeting it as an improvement on his own, its chances looked good. Unfortunately by the time Peel had removed the obstacle of the patent officers by a general reform of court offices,[80] the Whigs had finally secured their turn in government, but it was not their Home Secretary who tackled the problem of local justice but the new Lord Chancellor, Henry Brougham, whose ideas were very different.

Brougham and the Common Law Commissioners

Brougham abandoned the reform of moribund courts in favour of 'forming a Court, new in its kind, but modelled upon ancient principles'.[81] These 'Courts of Local or Ordinary Jurisdiction' would ultimately, but not immediately, have exclusive jurisdiction over matters within their competence and older local courts would eventually be abolished. The new courts would be served by well paid full-time judges (£1500 per annum plus £500 from fees) assisted by a regis- trar (£400 per annum plus up to £300 from fees).

---

[76] *PD* 1824 (s2) 10: 210–12, 303–4, 728–9, 1425–42; 11: 852–6.

[77] A particularly intemperate attack was launched by Lord Ellenborough, son of the former Lord Chief Justice, who held a sinecure worth £9000 a year in the King's Bench.

[78] Polden, *History of the County Court*, 15–16.   [79] *PP* 1826–7 (535), ii; *PD* (s2), 17: 1350–8.

[80] Fees Act 1830 (11 Geo. IV & 1 Will. IV c. 58).   [81] *PD* 1830 (s3), 1: 727.

The versatile judge would earn his money. Within the county he would hold courts at least monthly in such towns as he chose, trying matters up to £50 in tort and up to £100 in debt, contract, trespass to goods, trover, and small legacies; if both consented the money limit could be waived. As a small claims judge he could try cases without a jury, and he would also be a magistrate, would take arbitrations and—a particular favourite of Brougham's which he vainly endeavoured to foist upon the invincibly insular English until almost the end of his long life—would hold 'courts of reconcilement' on continental models.[82] Each different function needed different rules of practice, costs, and fees and with characteristic impatience Brougham had not given his helpmates time to incorporate these in the bill, allowing his critics to argue that without knowing the financial arrangements it was impossible to appraise the scheme.[83]

Brougham's scheme was far bolder than Peel's, something he acknowledged by proposing to use Kent and Northumberland as test beds to iron out any flaws. True, Bentham and his acolytes claimed that it was a mere tinkering with 'matchless constitution', but their visionary ideals were far removed from practical politics.[84] For everyone else Brougham had dramatically raised the stakes and it quickly became apparent that his bill did not command a consensus. The 'respectable' and influential elements of the legal professions were uncompromisingly hostile, especially the bar and the London agency solicitors. The first issues of the new *Legal Observer* contained almost all the objections that would be persistently made over the next 15 years; the scheme would encourage litigation fomented by rascally local attorneys; it would be costly to run and would give a dangerous quantity of patronage to the government; it would enable creditors to oppress poor debtors; by taking business from Westminster Hall, it would weaken the integrity and consistency of the common law and imperil that invaluable safeguard against tyranny, the great central bar of England.

Brougham, struggling to fulfil his boast to clear the Chancery arrears and deeply involved in the battle for the reform bill, gratefully accepted Lyndhurst's suggestion that the whole question of local courts be referred to the Common Law Commissioners under terms of reference that left open both a reconstruction of old courts and the creation of new ones. Although Brougham added three Commissioners of his choosing,[85] conservatives felt reasonably secure that they would espouse moderate, piecemeal reform.

---

[82] *PD* 1830 (568, 569), i. Thomas Denman and M. A. Taylor were among those who helped frame the bill.

[83] See e.g. (1831) 5 *LM* 1–49; (1830–1) 1 *Leg. O. passim.*

[84] [J. Bentham and others], 'Mr. Brougham and Local Judicatories' (1830) 13 *Westminster Rev.* 420–57.

[85] J. Evans, T. Starkie, and W. Wightman.

The Commissioners had been impressed with evidence about the use in local courts of arrest following judgment, which may have contributed to their severe verdict.[86] They made no explicit reference to existing reform proposals, but to the surprise and dismay of conservatives, pronounced that none of the changes made or contemplated for the superior courts would equip them to try small actions and that the only solution was a national network of local courts.[87]

There were important differences between the Commissioners' proposals and Brougham's. In some respects the Commissioners were more radical. They envisaged the immediate closure of local courts and abandoned the county as a unit, preferring a distribution which would ensure that no litigant should need to travel more than 20 or 25 miles and that each market town of 20,000 people should have its court. In other ways they were less ambitious: no courts of reconcilement and jurisdiction limited to £20, with a separate procedure for claims up to £5. For all the Commissioners' disapproval of courts of requests, they borrowed some of their most distinctive features; thus the venue would be the residence of the defendant; parties might be examined; payment in instalments might be ordered; and the procedure was to be greatly simplified, especially for small claims. There would be a jury, of six, but no special pleading. However, the Commissioners were anxious not to discourage 'intelligent and respectable' attorneys lest the new courts become the haunt of 'incompetent or dishonest persons'; hence though no legal costs were allowed in the smallest suits, those above £5 should afford 'a fair remuneration', considered possible if process were made very simple.[88]

The proposals were sufficiently close to Brougham's to meet opposition from the same quarters, but sufficiently different to gain support from those who recognized change as inevitable but could not stomach it coming from Brougham. Some affected to credit the reform wholly to the Commissioners, marginalizing Brougham's contribution just as his supporters exaggerated it. The Whig ministry maintained an equivocal line on whether the revised bill Brougham introduced in the Lords in 1833 was a government measure but Lyndhurst made it a party question with a vengeance, seizing an opportunity to demonstrate that the peers were not cowed by the passing of the Reform Act. The London agency firms provided him with ammunition and the revised bill still had plentiful drafting deficiencies for captious objections. In the third reading debate Lyndhurst's masterful display of wholly destructive oratory won the day in an impressively full house, and in Hansard's inelegant phrase, the bill was 'thrown out'.[89] Soon Brougham was thrown out too—of the cabinet, having finally exasperated Grey

---

[86] *Fifth Report 1833*, 1.   [87] *Ibid.*, 17.   [88] *Ibid.*, 18–30.
[89] Polden, *History of the County Court*, 24–7.

by his intolerably wilful conduct, and though Althorp tested the water in the next session he mournfully gave up the bill.[90]

Reform Stalled

For the rest of the 1830s the reform of local justice marked time. Bills from various quarters were either promised or made only fleeting appearances, justifying the claim that 'all is rumour and conjecture'.[91] Numerous bills for new courts of requests came forward and an added complication was Sir William Follett's clause in the Municipal Corporations Bill encouraging the revival of borough courts by raising their jurisdiction to £20 and enabling them to make new procedural rules.[92] Some diehard opponents argued that these provisions obviated the need for a nationwide scheme of local courts, but others reluctantly concluded that a network of courts which at least approximated to the lawyers' conception of a judicial body might be preferable to municipal courts and courts of requests far removed from that ideal.[93]

Lord Cottenham had little liking for local courts and hoped that enlarging the existing power of the superior courts to remit claims up to £50 to the county court would suffice,[94] but Lord John Russell, the Home Secretary, brought forward a more ambitious proposal in 1837. Russell ill-advisedly combined his plans for civil justice with a controversial reform of quarter and petty sessions. His bill gave the justices at quarter sessions jurisdiction over debts up to £10, with a legally qualified judge if they wanted one, and a small jury.[95] The supposed encroachments made by other parts of the bill upon the sessions, which country gentlemen regarded as peculiarly their own preserve, met fierce resistance and a residue of hostility awaited the revised bill Russell produced in 1838. Although uncoupled from the reform of the sessions it still threatened to throw the burden of a judge's salary onto the county rate if fees fell short.[96] A Commons select committee exposed further sharp differences: over the power to imprison for non-payment of judgment debts; over the future of existing local courts; and, as usual, over patronage.[97] Despairing of progress, Russell readily agreed to Cottenham's urging that the bill be put off until he had tackled the even more intractable problem of insolvent debtors.[98]

---

[90] *PD* 1834 (s3) 21: 210.

[91] (1836–7) 13 *Leg. Ob.* 273. There is a summary in (1838–9) 17 *Leg. Ob.* 401.

[92] 5 & 6 Will. IV c. 76 ss. 98–9. Russell had originally proposed to give each municipal borough a court of requests: R. Russell (ed.), *The Early Correspondence of Lord John Russell, 1805–1840*, 2 vols (1913), ii, 110 (cl. 17).

[93] e.g. (1838–9) 17 *Leg. Ob.* 401.   [94] *PD* 1837–8 (s3) 41: 339–40.

[95] *Ibid.*, 332–44.   [96] *Ibid.*, 1838–9 (s3) 45: 221.

[97] *SC on the County Courts Bill*, *PP* 1839 (387–II), xiii.

[98] *PD* 1838–9 (s3) 49: 519; 1839–40 (s3) 52: 1080.

The Making of the New County Courts

When the Melbourne ministry's Small Debts Courts Bill finally appeared in February 1841, it was linked with a bankruptcy bill because the judges were also intended to have jurisdiction in bankruptcy and insolvency.[99] The bill was presented as being essentially based on the select committee's deliberations. Twenty-five judges appointed by the Lord Chancellor would be paid between £800 and £1500 per anum, would be barred from practice, and must be resident in their district. They would handle torts, contracts, and debts up to £20, and ejectments from tenements valued at not more than £20 per anum. Pleas would be determined 'in a summary way' through very spare pleadings, with a jury available on request only in the larger cases. The judge would make 'such orders and decrees as shall appear to him to be just and agreeable to equity and good conscience', explicitly including payment by instalments; appeals were restricted to cases for £5 or more. The courts of requests would be abolished and costs in a superior court action for a claim within the Small Debt court limit would be disallowed unless the plaintiff recovered at least £20 or the judge certified that he had good cause to think he would do so.[100] The bill was a hybrid, borrowing elements from courts of requests, from Brougham, from the Commissioners, and from the Irish Small Debts courts. That its introduction was entrusted to an under-secretary hardly suggested confidence, and powerful opposition had been signalled before the ministry's fall brought it down.[101]

The Whig bill, reintroduced by Cottenham in the autumn of 1841, did not appeal to the Conservative administration. Several party-leaders, notably the Lord Chancellor (Lyndhurst) and the Duke of Wellington, opposed the whole idea.[102] Peel, having sponsored local courts bills in the 1820s, differed, insisting on 'the necessity of a universal arrangement with regard to the facilities for the recovery of small debts'[103] and one was duly produced.[104] Lyndhurst claimed that it avoided the biggest evil, judges who resided in the court's locality, by having them undertake circuits round their district, and it fell short of previous proposals in providing for the creation of new courts only upon the request of the local quarter sessions. But professional opinion noted that it also provided for existing courts of requests to be made into 'county courts' and included many of their

---

[99] *PP* 1841 (43), (153), i; *PP* 1841 (44), i.

[100] *PD* 1840–1 (s3) 56: 472–6.

[101] *Ibid.*, 1840–1 (s3) 57: 172–93; 'The New Local Courts Bill' (1841) 25 *LM* 310–44.

[102] Polden, *History of the County Court*, 30.

[103] Peel to Graham, 12 October 1842, C. S. Parker, *The Life and Letters of Sir James Graham*, 2 vols (1907), ii, 333.

[104] *HLSP* 1842 (39, 215), ii: *PP* 1842 (498) (531) (550), i.

objectionable features.[105] It was the most limited plan that stood a chance of being accepted, but though Cottenham and Brougham gave it grudging support, the government's own timetable could not accommodate it.[106]

To ease its passage in 1843 both the number of courts and the limit of their jurisdiction were reduced, but Graham was suspiciously ready to withdraw it when John Jervis and others brought out a rival scheme.[107] Jervis's scheme, embodied in two bills, was a last-ditch effort by lawyers to defeat the project for local courts. One bill expanded the facilities for remitting actions to sheriffs' assessors, while the other gave justices of the peace at petty sessions power to deal with cases of debt up to £5.[108] Next session Graham offered to incorporate the remitted actions provisions in the government bill but declared that 'a worse tribunal for the purpose than the justices he could not imagine'.[109] While some opponents were prepared to accept the government bill as the least harmful on offer, others maintained a hostility increasingly tinged with desperation. The newly-founded *Law Times* shrilly denounced it as a 'Bill for the promotion of quarrelling, the establishment and protection of pettifoggers, the dissemination of cheap injustice, the encouragement of perjury, and the unlimited increase of debtors' prisons'.[110] The bill had been introduced too late in the session to pass and the last of the *Law Times* accusations started the chain of events which finally overcame the obstacles to its passage.

Both Whig and Conservative bills had contained powers of varying width for the courts to enforce their judgments by imprisonment, but the extensive use of imprisonment by existing local courts, and the frightful state of the gaols in which debtors were incarcerated, were under increasing fire.[111] The session of 1844 had seen yet another round in the everlasting tinkering with insolvency, bedevilled by personal antipathy between Cottenham and Brougham and Lyndhurst's cynical detachment. The outcome was an Execution Bill intended to clarify uncertainties in the power to imprison debtors,[112] and in its hasty progress at the end of the session the Duke of Richmond seized the opportunity afforded by an almost deserted Parliament and incompetent government management to insert a clause abolishing imprisonment for debts not exceeding £20 except in cases of fraud.[113]

---

[105] *PD* 1841–2 (s3) 65: 230–2; (1841–2) 23 *Leg. Ob.* (1842) 24 *Leg. Ob.*, *passim*.

[106] *PD* 1841–2 (s3) 65: 224–41, 1182. There was strong local opposition too: Bristol sent a petition with 1500 signatures: Bush, *Bristol and its Municipal Government*, 161.

[107] *PP* 1843 (198), i; *PD* 1842–3 (s3) 68: 973.   [108] *PP* 1843 (214), ii; (232), iv.

[109] *PD* 1844 (s3) 72: 683.   [110] (1844) 3 *LT* 150.

[111] Polden, *History of the County Court*, 31–2.

[112] M. J. Lobban, *Henry Brougham and Law Reform* (2000) 115 *EHR*, 1184–1215, 1200; V. M. Lester, *Victorian Insolvency* (Oxford, 1995), 113–16; *PD* 1844 (s3) 74: 442–72; 76: 1173–1204, 1387–1411; 76: 1623–41, 1706–13, 1847.

[113] 7 & 8 Vict. c. 96; (1845) 5 *LT* 420, 47. The categories of fraud had, however, recently been widened: Finn, *Culture of Credit*, 173.

The trading community and their attorneys reacted with outrage and disbelief.
An orchestrated campaign ensured that petitions covered the Lords' table when
they reassembled in the autumn and a hastily arranged select committee was easily persuaded that the change would lead to a massive increase in uncollectable
debts.[114] Amid squabbles over whose fault it had been, Brougham cobbled together
a short amending bill to restore the power of imprisonment in certain situations,
but in the course of its headlong passage through the Commons it was transformed by the wholesale addition of clauses expanding the powers of courts of
requests. Brougham's bill restricted the power to imprison to courts with a legally
qualified judge, and towns argued that they could only afford to pay a judge if the
monetary limit of their court was high enough to generate an adequate fee yield.
Their lobbying succeeded: by the Small Debts Recovery Act, section 72 the Privy
Council was authorized to raise to £20 the jurisdiction of any court of requests
which was prepared to appoint a suitably qualified assessor. Unable to justify the
course taken by the bill, Lyndhurst disingenuously attempted to deny that it was
a government bill at all, but the session was running out and it was unthinkable
to leave the creditors' demands for the restoration of imprisonment unmet, so the
peers reluctantly swallowed the bill whole.[115]

Now lawyers were outraged. This expansion of 'courts of requests law' was
worse than the threatened creation of new courts and they protested loud, long,
and to good effect. To the frustration of towns eager to obtain their expanded
jurisdiction their petitions gathered dust in the Privy Council office and it was
eventually intimated that none would be granted; instead another attempt to pass
a local courts bill would be made.[116] The history of that bill suggests that a consensus had gradually evolved, for it had not progressed far in the Lords when Peel
resigned, yet the Whigs, Cottenham in particular, rescued it and, with relatively
minor modifications, saw it onto the statute book. One attempt to appease conservatives was the pretence that the small debt courts were a part of the ancient
county court: what was in reality a new institution was dressed up as an old one
in modern garb. The hallowed name dignified what were intended to be basically
debt collection agencies and suggested a spurious continuity.[117] With Parliament
absorbed by the recent political turmoil and profoundly weary of the endless
sequence of small debt bills lawyers practically monopolized the debates and as
usual the most vigorously contested issue was patronage. Unlike some previous
proposals, the judges of the courts of requests would not be entitled to be judges

---

[114] Polden, *History of the County Court*, 32.

[115] *Ibid.*, 33–5; 8 & 9 Vict. c. 127.

[116] D. D. K[eane] 'The Small Debts Act' (1846) 5(s2) *LM* 189–255, 204.

[117] The Act (9 & 10 Vict. c. 95) had a more prosaic title, 'An Act for the More Easy Recovery of
Small Debts'.

of the new courts but were specifically made eligible for appointment. Its judges would not be made by the lord-lieutenants as the Conservative bill had proposed, but by the Lord Chancellor. It was understood that they would be used for party purposes, but no one could come up with anything more satisfactory.[118]

For the rest, the new county courts embodied features of earlier bills. A small jury would be available for bigger claims upon request; pleadings would be succint, with no special pleading allowed; the parties themselves might be examined; payment in instalments could be ordered. Lawyers, and lawyers alone, would have the right to appear for clients but their costs were set at a level calculated to discourage them. One concession which the bar had become increasingly anxious to obtain was that the new courts' jurisdiction would be concurrent with the superior courts, but bringing small cases in the latter would be discouraged by the risk of disallowed costs. Courts of requests would be swept away but the other, older local courts were to remain. The bar was further propitiated by sacrificing the attorneys; barristers alone would be eligible to be judges. But the bar did not persuade the Whigs to lower the ceiling on claims from £20, the figure adopted in successive proposals. The biggest uncertainty remaining after the Act for the More Easy Recovery of Small Debts received the royal assent on 28 August 1846 was how many courts and judges there would be, for despite their name the Act did not envisage the county as the unit, but rather provided for each to be divided into districts by order in council.[119]

5. LOCAL COURTS AFTER 1846

The Survivors

The County Courts Act killed off the courts of requests but left other local courts intact. However, two of them attracted sufficient opprobrium to be abolished soon afterwards. The Palace court of Westminster had been praised by the Common Law Commissioners as 'a very useful and effectual court for the trial of causes below the amount of £20',[120] but its less appealing side was exposed first by an unedifying squabble between officials and then by an outraged litigant, M. J Higgins ('Jacob Omnium'), publicized in Thackeray's verses.[121] Further

---

[118] Polden, *History of the County Court*, 34–7. The *Law Magazine* ((1846) 5 (s2), 157–8) rather optimistically suggested the chief justices of the common law courts.

[119] Polden, *History of the County Court*, 35–7.

[120] *Fifth Report 1833*, 10. The praise was repeated in returns relating to courts of requests etc., *PP* 1840 (619), xli.

[121] T. Mathew, 'The Mayor's Court, the Sheriffs' Courts and the Palace Court' (1919) 31 *JR* 134–51 at 139–51, and see *For Lawyers and Others* (1937), 32–52.

damning stories about this 'wicked little tribunal'[122] followed, and the fact that six attorneys and four barristers held monopolies of its business acquired by purchase was by now unacceptable.[123] Down with the Palace court went the Peveril Honour court, which also had an unsavoury reputation.[124]

Apart from two surviving hundred courts,[125] there were no further closures for some years. However, from 1852 any town council, or a majority of ratepayers, might petition the Privy Council to exclude from the jurisdiction of a local court all cases within the cognisance of the county court. Birmingham and Worcester were among the first, and several towns removed themselves from the Salford Hundred court.[126] Most other borough courts which were still active in the 1840s fell into complete disuse, but a few remained popular; according to the Romilly Commission because of 'the ancient mode of proceeding [which] is preserved in these courts, not for the benefit of the public, but for the profit of those who practise there';[127] being more expensive to the suitor they should, it recommended, be subjected to the same costs sanction as the superior courts.

Aside from the palatinate courts,[128] some half dozen assorted hundred, wapentake etc. courts and 26 borough courts were still doing significant business, though few were busy and some of these were struggling: Preston had to reduce the remuneration of its judge;[129] Northampton was embroiled in a scandal involving its registrar;[130] and Digby Seymour defended himself from accusations of neglecting his duties as judge of the Newcastle Burgess and Non-Burgess courts by disparaging their 'trivial business' which made his appearances 'some public pantomime'.[131] Only the Lord Mayor's and Sheriffs' courts in London, the Manchester court of Record and Salford Hundred court (which amalgamated in 1868)[132] and the Liverpool court of Passage were really busy.

Salford apart, the hundred courts practically vanished after the County Courts Act 1867, section 28 deprived inferior courts other than courts of record of any matter which could be brought in a county court. The successful borough courts, however, put forward to the Judicature Commission a plausible case for their survival.

---

[122] *Ibid.*, 139.

[123] Mathew, 'Mayor's Court', 149–51. A measured criticism by 'K' is in (1849) 10 (s2) *LM* 128–44.

[124] County Courts Act 1849 (12 & 13 Vict. c. 101), s. 13. For the Peveril court see *Fifth Report 1833*, App., no. 136, J. W. Lee.

[125] Offlow and Hemlingford: County Courts Act 1852, s 11.

[126] *Halsbury's Laws of England*, ix (1909), paras 293–480.

[127] *RC on County Courts*, PP 1854–5 [1914], xviii, 50.   [128] See below, pp. 872–5.

[129] *Addison* v. *Mayor etc. of Preston* (1852) 12 C.B. 108 at 120.

[130] (1857–8) 30 *LT* 206, 213, 328.

[131] *Newcastle Daily Chronicle*, 17 October 1867. The town council had debated formally amalgamating the courts: *Northern Daily Express*, 5 January 1865.

[132] Salford Hundred Court of Record Act (31 & 32 Vict. c. cxxx).

They attributed their appeal to the facility for full jury trial, better quality judges, and a regular bar; their fees were lower than the county courts and their judgments easier to enforce.[133] That last claim may have worked against them, for Law Society witnesses averred that their chief attraction was to wholesale firms wanting default judgments;[134] a reputation for being less protective to the poor was not calculated to create a favourable impression.

The Commissioners felt these courts were now anomalous: 'if they did not exist no one would think of establishing them';[135] they believed it undesirable for municipalities to profit from justice and to appoint judges, and deprecated competition for business.[136] Like the Romilly Commission, they believed the real attraction of local courts was the higher costs they allowed solicitors, and briskly consigned them all to the dustbin of history.

The City of London Courts

There was, however, one significant gap in the geographical coverage of the county courts.[137] The City of London had ensured that there was none within its limits and argued that two of its courts adequately met litigants' needs. The Sheriffs' court had sat in two locations, at the Poultry and the Giltspur, before different judges until the 1830s when one post was left unfilled. It had jurisdiction over debt and personal actions arising within the City and its liberties and adopted the pleadings and rules of the superior courts.[138] In the 1840s the judge was William Arabin, whose eccentricities provided the bar with a fund of entertainment and anecdote.[139]

In 1835 the City had succumbed to the fashion for courts of requests and a few months after the County Courts Act it opened a small debts court modelled on the new county courts. In 1852 this became the City of London Small Debts court, presided over by the judge of the Sheriffs' court, which thereafter had only a formal existence. The Small Debts court obtained powers denied to county courts: a costs sanction against plaintiffs unjustifiably bringing actions in the superior courts and recovering less than £50; the facility to commence actions where any

---

[133] *Second Report 1872*, App., esp. 141–51 and evidence of W. Brandon, R. Gurney, Sir J. Heron, J. Mountain, J. Fleet, J. Rayner.

[134] *Ibid.*, qq. 6128–30.   [135] *Second Report 1872*, 19.

[136] *Ibid.*, 18–19. George Moffatt was for saving the Liverpool, Salford and Mayor's courts, Cairns demurred to immediately abolishing those of the Duchy of Lancaster.

[137] The City was a special case in other respects, in its criminal courts and in having its own police force for example: see XIII, Pt 1, pp. 23–35.

[138] Mathew, 'Mayor's Court', 137–9; G. Pitt-Lewis, *Commissioner Kerr, an Individuality* (1903), 76–7; memo. by H. Jenkyns, n.d., NA PRO LCO 2/14.

[139] R. E. Megarry, *An Arabinesque at Law* (1969).

part of the cause arose within the City; and jurisdiction over any defendant who had been employed in the City within the previous six months.[140]

The judge was elected by the corporation and in a stirring contest in 1859 Robert Malcolm Kerr won by just two votes out of 202.[141] It was a fateful decision, for the victor held onto his post for more than 40 years, frequently in acrimonious relations with his paymasters.

'Commissioner' Kerr (he was also *ex officio* in the commission for the Old Bailey) was 'an individuality'.[142] His manner on the bench was frequently rough and brutal; he was opinionated and stubborn, avaricious, and self-righteous. Autocratic with juries and hostile to moneylenders, he became notorious for his abrasive attitude towards solicitors and his meanness over their costs.[143] '[H]e possessed many of the qualities that go to make up a good judge, but, owing to certain idiosyncrasies, it is impossible to say that he ever attained that end.'[144]

Kerr clashed repeatedly with the corporation and with the superior courts, but he effected some useful reforms in the court.[145] From 1867 in all future Acts the words 'county courts' were to include the City of London court,[146] but the section was so loosely drawn that it generated a series of disputes,[147] some of Kerr's own making. But despite these distractions the City court prospered, receiving a good many remitted actions and Admiralty cases.[148] The corporation became ambitious,[149] and when they finally bribed Kerr into retirement in 1901 they sought two judges, one an Admiralty specialist. But there were no longer elections,[150] and Halsbury characteristically balanced the competing claims of judicial quality and political patronage by choosing an excellent county court judge (Lumley Smith from Westminster) and the man the corporation was particularly anxious to avoid, the needy Unionist MP J. A. Rentoul.[151] For all his good

---

[140] London (City) Small Debts Acts 1847 (10 & 11 Vict. c. lxxi) and 1848 (11 & 12 Vict. c. clii); London (City) Small Debts Extension Act 1852 (15 & 16 Vict. c. lxxvii); G. M. W[eatherfield], 'The City Courts' (1870) 28 (s3) *LM & LR* 208–15.

[141] A. N. May, *The Bar and the Old Bailey* (Chapel Hill NC, 2003), 175; Pitt-Lewis, *Commissioner Kerr*, 76–7.

[142] Pitt-Lewis, *Commissioner Kerr*.

[143] *Ibid.*, 121–6, 227–8. He could be immovably wrong-headed: (1932) 174 *LT* 90.

[144] (1901) 111 *LT* 491.

[145] Pitt-Lewis, *Commissioner Kerr*, 121–88, a partisan account.

[146] County Courts Act 1867, s 35.

[147] See e.g. *Osgoode* v. *Nelson* (1871–2) LR 5 HL 636 and *Blades* v. *Lawrence* (1873–4) 9 QB 374.

[148] (1902–3) 47 *Sol. J.* 95

[149] Pitt-Lewis, *Commissioner Kerr*, 350–64; Corporation memo., n.d. [1919], LCO 2/461.

[150] The Local Government Act 1888 had transferred appointments to the Lord Chancellor. The legality of creating two judges was questionable: C. Schuster to Solicitor-General, 8 July 1920, LCO 2/461.

[151] (1898) 33 *LJ* 421; (1901–2) 112 *LT* 1.

intentions Rentoul damaged the court's popularity by his protective attitude to debtors and attacks on solicitors[152] and when Lumley Smith retired in 1913 the Liberals provided a successor just as bad as Rentoul, the vain and complacent radical MP Atherley Jones.[153]

The corporation's other court was the Mayor's court.[154] The Judicature Commissioners had acknowledged that the abolition of local courts might 'meet with opposition from some of the powerful corporations interested in their maintenance',[155] and the corporation's determination to preserve the Mayor's court probably saved the others too.[156] Presided over by the Recorder, or in his absence the common serjeant, it had a long and complicated history, with jurisdiction over all common law actions (save replevin) arising within the City, as well as equity and City customs. An Act of 1857[157] modernized some of its procedures, though it maintained ancient and obsolescent forms such as *concessit solvere*.[158] It grew in popularity once it removed the monopoly enjoyed by four barristers and four attorneys in 1853[159] and suitors found especially attractive its customary remedy of foreign attachment and its rule that no defendant who had been dwelling or trading within the City within the six months preceding an action could plead to the jurisdiction in cases not above £50. Very much a plaintiff's court, its business doubled in the 1860s to more than 6000 cases.[160]

The court's pretensions to a special status were denied by the House of Lords in *London Corporation v. Cox* in 1867[161] and it was further damaged by rulings that foreign attachment could not be used against corporations[162] and by prohibitions enforcing the rule that the whole cause of action had to originate in the City.[163] Nevertheless despite the 'barbarous and severely technical procedure'[164] the court remained popular enough to need a regular assistant judge and it was only the financial losses incurred by both City courts during the war that prompted their amalgamation in 1921.[165]

---

[152] Polden, *History of the County Court*, 324.   [153] *Ibid.*

[154] *Ibid.* Popular enough for several practice books, the fullest by W. Brandon, *Notes of the Practice of the Lord Mayor's Court...in Ordinary Actions* (1864), it merited an individual entry in the first four editions of *Halsbury's Laws of England*.

[155] RC on the Judicature, Second Report, PP [C. 631], xx, 18.

[156] Nicol to Muir McKenzie, 8 May 1894, LCO 2/75.

[157] Mayor's Court of London Procedure Act 1857.

[158] *Halsbury's Laws of England*, xx (1911), 283–302.

[159] RC on the Judicature, Second Report 1872, App., 145, W. Brandon.

[160] (1865–6) 41 *LT* 829; (1870) 5 *LJ* 508.   [161] (1867) 2 LR HL 239.

[162] *London Corporation v. London Joint Stock Bank* (1880–81) 6 App Cas (HL) 393.

[163] (1874) 9 *LJ* 315, 488; (1874–5) 1 *The Law* 34–9, 205–12.   [164] (1878) 26 *CCC*, 411.

[165] Mayor's and City Court Act 1920 c. cxxxiv.

The Judicature Commission and After

In view of the Judicature Commission's report it is remarkable that very shortly afterwards Parliament passed an 'Act to amend the law relating to Borough and other Local Courts of Record', seemingly without debate.[166] The Act is something of a mystery, though Lord Redesdale may have promoted it in preference to provisions slipped into local bills.[167]

Selborne was embarrassed and annoyed at being confronted with immediate requests from the Mayor's court, Bristol, Hull, York, and Scarborough for some of the powers which could now be conferred by order in council,[168] several of which were highly objectionable as not being possessed by county courts. Some were already exercised in Liverpool, in Salford, and in the Mayor's court;[169] extend them to the supplicant courts and they could scarcely be denied to all and sundry.[170] The combination of interpleader, one of Hull's main objectives and already abused in the Mayor's court,[171] and the facility to serve process anywhere raised the spectre of persons being haled from one end of the country to the other to defend their title to goods. The liberal power to appoint deputies was also objectionable unless strictly confined to barristers of seven years' standing, and the unlimited power to revise fees might lead to fee structures designed to lure suitors from the county courts.[172]

Selborne ensured that no orders granting the objectionable powers were made and persuaded the High Court judges to follow suit when presented with draft rules for approval. In 1883 the Statute Law Revision Act empowered the Privy Council to give the new RSC to local courts, but only the *sui generis* Oxford Vice-Chancellor's court was so favoured,[173] and in 1884 Selborne brought all inferior court rules, including those of the county courts, under the supervision of the Rule Committee.[174]

Forty-two unused courts were abolished by statute in 1883[175] and the number of active ones slowly diminished; only 24 appear in the *Civil Judicial Statistics* between 1865 and 1908. Though only one further court, the Stannaries, was actually abolished,[176] attempts to revive moribund courts like Plymouth and

[166] 'A curiosity of legislation': G. M. W[etherfield], 'The City Courts' (1872) 1 (ns) *LM & LR* 915–19, 915.

[167] Selborne to H. A. Bruce, 20 January 1873 and Nicol's attached memo.: LCO 1/48; T. Falconer, 'Salford and Other Local Courts' (1878) 65 *LT* 245–7.

[168] Selborne to Bruce, 20 January 1873, LCO 1/48.

[169] Town clerk of Hull to Bruce, 15 April 1873, *ibid.*

[170] Selborne to Bruce, 20 January 1873, *ibid.*   [171] Nicol's memo., *ibid.*

[172] *Ibid.*   [173] Only in relation to appeals: *Halsbury's Laws of England*, ix, 133.

[174] Circular to judges, 8 March 1884 and replies, LCO 1/49; Judicature Act 1884 c. 61, s 24.

[175] Municipal Corporations Act 1883 c. 18.

[176] Holdsworth, *HEL*, i, 156–65; Stannaries Court (Abolition) Act 1896 (c. 45). The Stannaries courts had been reformed by statute in 1836 and the Lord Warden's appellate jurisdiction was transferred to the Court of Appeal by the Judicature Act 1873, s 18. The 1896 Act transferred the original jurisdiction of the Vice-Warden's court to the county court.

Bideford were unsuccessful.[177] Denied the extra powers for which they importuned, Hull, Newcastle, and other moderately used ones declined,[178] and the LCO held to the policy that new rules must be based on those of county courts:[179] modelling themselves on the RSC would be 'too aspiring'.[180] The confusing array of rules ancient and modern found among the local courts became a useful barrier against outsiders for those who regularly practised there.

Importunities continued and eventually in 1894, disconcerted perhaps by the discovery that the Salford and Bristol courts had inadvertently been allowed some of the jealously guarded powers,[181] Halsbury referred the general question to a Rule Committee sub-committee under Baron Pollock. Surprisingly, it recommended that local courts should be allowed the much sought Order 14, since 'to sanction borough courts and withhold from them this procedure would be to cripple their efficiency'.[182] Gradually, and subject to safeguards, the leading local courts acquired this crucial power.

By 1914, however, barely half-a-dozen were transacting substantial business. The Norwich Guildhall court was in gentle decline[183] but the Bristol Tolzey court retained a certain popularity by offering plaintiffs the rare facility of foreign attachment and incorporating most of the RSC.[184] The most highly regarded, however, was the Liverpool court of Passage.[185] Though denied equity jurisdiction, let alone its aspiration to become a branch of the High Court,[186] it had prospered under highly regarded judges—Henry Roscoe (1834–6), Charles Crompton (1836–52), and Edward James (1852–67)—and attracted a talented bar, including rising men like Russell and Herschell.[187] However, 'towards the end of the nineteenth century the Court of Passage fell upon evil days'.[188] T. H. Baylis (1876–1903) was a less distinguished judge,[189] but perhaps more important was the unexpected

---

[177] LCO 2/24, 71, 124; *Halsbury's Laws of England*, ix, para. 423.

[178] *Halsbury's Laws of England*, ix, paras 372, 410; LCO 1/52 (Newcastle), 2/50, 75 (Hull).

[179] e.g. K. Muir McKenzie to C. G. Prideaux, 12 February 1890, LCO 2/23.

[180] C. E. Pollock to K. Muir McKenzie, 19 April 1886, LCO 1/52.

[181] Report of sub-committee, 2 June 1894, LCO 2/76.

[182] *Ibid.* Order 14 afforded judgment in default of appearance.

[183] M. Slatter, 'The Norwich Court of Requests—a Tradition Continued' (1984) 5 *JLH* 97–107.

[184] W. V. Veale, 'The Bristol Tolzey Court' (1939) *JSPTL* 20–9; *Halsbury's Laws of England*, ix para. 318. When new rules were submitted in 1890, however, the judge was told they should resemble those of the county court.

[185] W. Peel, *The Jurisdiction of the Liverpool Court of Passage* (Liverpool, 1909) and *The Liverpool Court of Passage* (reprint, 1918, from Transactions of the Historic Society of Liverpool and Chester); (1955) 220 *LT* 236–7. See also *RC on the Judicature, Second Report, 1872*, qq. 1224–1710 and P. H. Williams, *A Gentleman's Calling* (Liverpool, 1980), 45–57.

[186] T. H. Baylis to Cairns, 22 December 1876, LCO 1/51.

[187] R. B. O'Brien, *Life of Lord Russell of Killowen* (1902 edn), 81.

[188] Peel, *Liverpool Court of Passage*, 10.

[189] The corporation preferred him to Russell: O'Brien, *Life of Lord Russell*, 127.

deprivation of the judgment by default process through Wills J.'s decision in
Speers v. *Daggers* in 1885.[190] It took a long time to recover the power[191] but the
court soon revived under a long-serving and popular judge W. Kyffin Taylor, and
in 1920 was too well regarded to be touched.[192]

Equally busy, but with a more equivocal reputation, was the Salford Hundred
court. Its judges, one of whom was the Recorder of Manchester *ex officio*, were barristers of ten years standing (two became county court judges), but with a money
limit of £50 it was essentially a small debts court. Barristers liked it because they
had exclusive audience, solicitors because it was relatively generous with costs, and
creditors because it sat frequently and did not use instalment orders.[193] Critics, however, said its 'elaborate and expensive' procedure made it costly for claims above
£20.[194] Nearby local authorities began to demand exclusion from its jurisdiction by
order in council, and in 1910, with Stockport, Heywood, and Todmorden all petitioning, a committee was appointed to improve its working. The Mersey report
conceded that its area should be limited to the two county courts of Manchester
and Salford (it had originally embraced eight county courts) and that leave to
serve process out of the jurisdiction should be less readily granted.[195] The court
was spared less by its merits (it was reputed not to 'temper the wind to the shorn
lamb'[196]) than by saving the salaries of at least two more county court judges.

The real black sheep, however, was Derby, whose popularity with Nottingham
moneylenders suggested it was even less accommodating to debtors. Criticized
by the Law Society and a select committee in the 1920s, it was forced into changes
which rapidly reduced it to inactivity.[197]

The Lancaster and Durham Courts

The Chancery courts of the palatinates of Lancaster and Durham stood on a
rather different footing from other local courts.[198] Both also had a court of pleas,

---

[190] Unreported. The 'ne plus ultra of legal anomaly', according to a Rule Committee report
(26 March 1885, LCO 1/49). Wills consulted Muir McKenzie on his draft judgment: LCO 1/51.

[191] LCO 1/51, 2/18, 73. Its proceedings and constitution were amended by two Liverpool Court of
Passage Acts 1893 c. 37, 1896 c. 21 and rules of 1903 and 1909.

[192] Schuster to F. W. Hirst, 29 January 1921, LCO 2/548. For Taylor (Lord Maenan) see *The Times*,
24 September 1951.

[193] *RC on the Judicature, Second Report 1872*, evidence of J. Kay and H. W. West, and Sir J. Heron,
App., 148–51.

[194] Falconer, 'Salford and other Local Courts', 261.

[195] *DC on the Salford Hundred Court, PP* 1911 (Cd. 5530), xl.

[196] Notes of 25 March 1936, LCO 2/1821.

[197] LCO 2/1089–90; *JSC on the Moneylenders Bill, PP* 1924–5 (Cmd. 153), viii. Earlier complaints
are in LCO 1/50, 2/121, 303.

[198] K. Emsley and C. M. Fraser, *The Courts of the County Palatine of Durham* (Durham, 1984).

but Durham's was underused and though re-organized in 1839 and subsequently, it remained unpopular and was absorbed into the High Court in 1873.[199]

The Duchy of Lancaster's courts were much busier and more important.[200] The court of Common Pleas was held during the Assizes at Lancaster by the northern circuit judges and was served by a prothonotary at Preston.[201] A 'superior court of general jurisdiction',[202] it had exclusive jurisdiction over pleas of land within the county palatine, actions against corporations in the county, and suits for less than £20 on which the defendant was liable to arrest if within the jurisdiction.[203] In 1830 it was commended for its 'facility, expedition and cheapness',[204] which evidently endeared it to local attorneys, and procedural improvements were made in 1834.[205] However, although enabled to sit at Liverpool (1835) and Manchester (1864), business fell away because Preston was inconvenient to attorneys in the populous parts.[206] The creation of district registries at Liverpool and Manchester in 1869 'galvanized [the court] into life':[207] between 1867 and 1869 only 140 of 1336 actions entered for trial in Lancashire were for the palatinate court; over the next three years they rose to 772 out of 1333.[208] The renaissance was abruptly curtailed by the Judicature Act 1873, which ended the court's independent existence.[209]

The palatinate Chancery courts exercised concurrent jurisdiction with the court of Chancery, but limited to persons residing within their geographical

---

[199] Ibid,, 39–45. See also RC on the Common Law First Report, PP 1829 (46), ix, App. C.

[200] In 1827 3845 actions were brought in the Lancaster Common Pleas as against 527 in Durham (RC on the Common Law, First Report 1829, App. A, tables 5 and 6).

[201] RC on the Legal Departments, Evidence, T. E. Paget (prothonotary), q. 9504. He usually acted by deputy: J. G. D. Engleheart, q. 9454.

[202] Paget's description, ibid., q. 9537.

[203] R. Somerville, History of the Duchy of Lancaster, 1603–1965 (1970), ii, 221–2. The only practice book, by Sir W. D. Evans (1813) was 'compiled in a very slovenly way…from loose rules and memorandums supplied by some professional gentlemen in Preston' (RC on the Common Law, First Report 1829, J. Gardner, App. B 11).

[204] RC on Lancaster Assizes and Common Pleas, PP 1831–2 (621), xxv, 201, quoted in Somerville, History of the Duchy of Lancaster, ii, 422. Practitioners consulted by the Common Law Commissioners were generally favourable (First Report 1829, App. B) and it was also praised by the Manchester chamber of commerce in 1834 for its 'dispatch and economy' (Arthurs, 'Without the Law', 17 n.23). For a less enthusiastic view see 'H', 'Lancaster Courts and Assizes' (1833) 9 LM 148–64.

[205] Court of Common Pleas of Lancaster Act 1834 (4 & 5 Will. IV c. 62); Somerville, History of the Duchy of Lancaster, ii, 422–3.

[206] Somerville, History of the Duchy of Lancaster, ii, 423.

[207] Second Report 1872, R. B. Kerr (disapprovingly) q. 1893; Court of Common Pleas (County Palatine of Lancaster) Act 1869 c. 37.

[208] RC on the Legal Departments, Evidence, Paget, q. 9529. The immediate influx was inflated by practitioners' erroneous belief that s. 15 had removed one of the court's main drawbacks, the inability to bring actions against defendants not resident within the jurisdiction: ibid., q. 9551 and see RC on the Judicature, Second Report 1872, Manchester and Liverpool Law Societies, qq. 5959–62.

[209] Judicature Act 1873, s. 16.

limits.[210] The general decline in litigation in the eighteenth century was probably worsened in the case of Lancaster by a long-serving but inept vice-chancellor in William Swinnerton.[211] An abler successor in J. A. Park may have contributed to a modest revival,[212] but despite a succession of notable vice-chancellors, the Durham court remained unattractive to suitors and was therefore vulnerable when the government suggested that the courts should be abolished. Finding powerful allies in Eldon (for the Chancery), and Lyndhurst (for the Common Pleas) they survived for the time, but the bishop's jurisdiction was transferred to the Crown 'as a separate Franchise and Royalty'.[213]

The Duchy court sat at Lancaster during the Assizes and held a sitting at Preston in between.[214] There was never enough business to warrant a full-time judge and a registrar performed most of the functions which in Chancery were divided among masters, registrars, examiners, and accountant-general.[215] Since its procedures were closely modelled upon Chancery, it was not much cheaper and although given a rather perfunctory approval in 1830, it needed similar reforms to those adopted in Chancery.[216] Those which needed legislation began after Page Wood became vice-chancellor in 1849[217] and they also enabled the court to rid itself of clerks in court, created district registries in Liverpool and Manchester, and substituted an appellate tribunal comprising the Chancellor of the Duchy and two of the lords justices of appeal in Chancery for the Duchy Chamber.[218]

With these changes business revived. It survived the Judicature Commission seemingly unscathed, though appeals were brought within the new framework and rules were harmonized with those of the Chancery division.[219] Further

---

[210] Halsbury's Laws of England, ix, paras 254–62; Emsley and Fraser, Courts of the County Palatine of Durham, 83–6; Somerville, History of the Duchy of Lancaster, ii, 217–26.

[211] H. Horwitz and P. Polden, Continuity or Change in the Court of Chancery in the Seventeenth and Eighteenth Centuries? (1996) 35 JBS 24–57, 52; Somerville, History of the Duchy of Lancaster, ii, 225.

[212] Later a judge of the Common Pleas. The Vice-Chancellor was the only judge of the court. Appointed by the Chancellor of the Duchy, he held office during pleasure, and despite proposals to alter this in 1890 (LCO 2/21) it was not changed to good behaviour until 1927 (LCO 2/785).

[213] Emsley and Fraser, Courts of the County Palatine of Durham, 83–6.

[214] Somerville, History of the Duchy of Lancaster, ii, 436 n.14.

[215] Ibid., ii, 436 n.13. The Chancellor did not perform judicial functions.

[216] Ibid., ii, 424–5.

[217] Ibid., ii, 302, 425; W. R. W. Stephens, A Memoir of the R.H. William Page Wood, Baron Hatherley, 2 vols (1883), 81–2; Court of Chancery of Lancaster Acts 1850 (13 & 14 Vict. c. 43); 1854; 1858.

[218] Somerville, History of the Duchy of Lancaster, ii, 426–7. The Duchy Chamber remained in existence, but was inactive: Halsbury's Laws of England, ix, para. 254.

[219] Judicature Act 1873 c. 66, s 18. Though expressly included in the recommended abolition of local courts, Cairns' dissent meant that it was in little danger. Chamber practice in both palatinate Chancery courts is described in the Commission's fourth report: PP 1874 [C. 984], xxiv, App., part 7.

changes to Chancery practice necessitated new statutes. Durham's Act of 1889[220] extended the powers of the Vice-Chancellor and at last gave the court effective power to enforce its decrees against persons outside the jurisdiction.[221] Lancaster's turn came the next year, but an attempt to obtain jurisdiction over patents was rebuffed.[222] Lancaster remained a locally popular alternative to the Chancery division, though the attractions to solicitors may have included a more generous costs regime, leading to complaints and an inquiry in 1916.[223]

The reform of local courts was a process quite unlike that of the superior courts. Instead of a progressive adaptation of existing courts followed by their combination in a unified structure, it took the form of dismantling traditional institutions and the court of requests, which represented a different and plausible model of local justice. They were replaced, after a wearisome struggle, by a new set of courts with a name misleadingly suggestive of continuity. And it was characteristic of the untidiness which local and professional influences often produced that neither were these 'county courts' integrated into the post-Judicature Act structure nor were all the surviving local courts extinguished.

[220] Palatine Court of Durham Act 1889 c. 47; LCO 2/22. A later bill of 1898–1900 (LCO 2/134) seems never to have been enacted.

[221] Sir Samuel Romilly had felt this was why the court was not popular: Emsley & Fraser, *Courts of Durham*, 84–6. Business remained insignificant at around 30–40 suits in the 1890s.

[222] Chancery Court of Lancaster Act 1890 c. 23; Lord Chancellor to President of the Board of Trade, 10 July 1888, LCO 2/21.

[223] Business had trebled over 30 years to an average of between 700 and 800 suits a year, though in proportion to population it fell far short of use made of the Chancery division. By the time of the complaints (LCO 2/406), the court was in financial difficulties: Somerville, *History of the Duchy of Lancaster*, ii, 450–1.

XII

The County Courts

1. JURISDICTION

The original limit of the jurisdiction of the county courts in personal actions was £20, and attempts to enlarge it indirectly by 'splitting the demand' were struck down, although a plaintiff might abandon the excess of his claim above £20.[1]

However, the pessimists who said that the county courts would be soon be expanded were justified. It was an era of weak governments and Henry Fitzroy's County Courts Extension Bill exposed Russell's to humiliating rebuffs in the Commons. It was left to the Lords, and in particular Brougham, to dilute its more adventurous provisions, in particular keeping the concurrent jurisdiction of the superior courts in cases over £20 free from any financial disincentive to the plaintiff. Though enthusiasts for expansion were disappointed, an extension of common law actions to £50 was a considerable step. However, despite lamentations that it would be the end of the bar and the prelude to further encroachments it was the last such increase for 50 years.[2]

Few contemporaries would have predicted that. Brougham's fecundity in legislative initiatives generated a succession of bills (some of them mere sketches).[3] One of them passed in mangled form, 'a complete mess of confusion'.[4] Vexed by several others—the Equitable Jurisdiction, Further Extension, and Arbitration Law Amendment Bills—in the session 1852–3, a harassed Lord Chancellor Cranworth charged a royal commission with enquiring, inter alia, whether 'any further business can be profitably transferred' to them.[5]

The investigation carried out by Sir John Romilly's Commission was not very searching and its report is uninspiring. The county courts were praised for their

---

[1] 'New County Courts' (1847) 7 (s2) *LM* 201–16; County Courts Act 1846 (9 & 10 Vict. c. 95), s. 63; (1847) 9 *LT* 205.

[2] P. Polden, *A History of the County Court, 1846–1971* (Cambridge, 1999), 53–4.

[3] For Brougham's role in law reform see M. Lobban, 'Henry Brougham and Law Reform', (2000) *HER*, 1184–215. .

[4] County Courts Further Extension Act 1852 (15 & 16 Vict. c. 54). The phrase is J. R. Mullings' (*PD* 1852–3 (s3) 120: 796).

[5] *PP* 1854–5 [1914], xviii, instructions.

'simple, prompt and inexpensive procedures; the experiment has been eminently successful, and benefits have been conferred on the community by means of these courts, which it is perhaps difficult to exaggerate'.[6] The Commission's enthusiasm, however, fell short of recommending a substantially enlarged jurisdiction. They should be given one of the 'excluded torts', (malicious prosecution); a wider jurisdiction by consent and a minor extension to ejectment actions, but even these modest gains were offset by making it easier for the defendant to remove a case within the concurrent jurisdiction into the superior courts.[7] Moreover, as John Pitt Taylor pointed out in his 'observations', the consent jurisdiction would remain illusory while it depended upon the express consent of both parties.[8]

Pitt Taylor advocated a change which continued to be strongly urged whenever reforms were under discussion: that the plaintiff might choose his forum subject to the defendant's right (either absolute, or more radically, exercisable only on showing cause) to remove the case into a higher court.[9] It alarmed the bar and its allies and was never enacted; instead there was repeated tinkering with the so-called 'costs sanction', the rule whereby a plaintiff who failed to recover more than £20 in contract or £5 in tort in a superior court action was liable to be deprived of his costs.[10] Despite Pitt Taylor's supposed influence over Cranworth, the ensuing legislation mostly followed the report. It denied the plaintiff costs in cases within the sanction where the defendant submitted to judgment by default, but since the costs to that point were small that may actually have encouraged plaintiffs to resort to the superior courts' default procedure and allegedly superior machinery for enforcement.[11]

Ten years later the costs sanction was rather timidly raised to £10 in torts. To the alarm of lawyers, the 1867 Act also entitled the defendant in a superior court action within the concurrent jurisdiction to have it remitted to the county court unless the plaintiff showed good cause.[12] 'Not a reform but almost a revolution', announced the *County Courts Chronicle*,[13] but this was a wild exaggeration, for relatively few defendants wanted to change the forum and judges took little persuading that there was good cause to retain the action.[14]

---

[6] *Ibid.*, 25, 37.   [7] *Ibid.*, 25–9.

[8] *Ibid.*, unpaginated at end, and see A. J. Johnes, 'County Courts' (1854) 21 *LR* 257–71. Pitt Taylor was judge at Greenwich and Lambeth 1852–85 and a noted authority on evidence.

[9] *RC on County Courts 1855*, at end. Recommended eg by the Judicature Commission, in the debates on the 1888 County Courts Bill, in the Gorell Report, and included in the bills of 1909 and 1911.

[10] *Ibid.*, 25. Initially in County Courts Act 1846 ss.128–9.

[11] County Court Amendment Act 1856 (19 & 20 Vict. c. 108), s. 30. For Campbell's allegation about Pitt Taylor's influence see *PD* 1855 (s3) 141: 5.

[12] County Courts Act 1867 c. 142, ss. 5, 7; (1867–8) 12 *Sol. J.* 110.   [13] (1867) 20 *CCC* 249.

[14] The 1867 Act enlarged previous powers. Remitted actions had already risen sharply from 146 in 1865 to 244 in 1866. In the 1870s they ranged from 548 to 767 per annum (Polden, *History of the County Court*, App. 2). For their impact see below.

The Romilly Commission never delivered its promised further report on equitable jurisdiction.[15] Nevertheless, over the following decade the county courts steadily acquired additional powers which (with the notable exception of divorce) came close to making it a court of complete civil jurisdiction.[16] Small probates arrived in 1858,[17] but much more important was the reconstruction of insolvency law and practice in 1861. From their inception the county courts had had some jurisdiction over insolvent debtors,[18] but with the amalgamation of the separate regimes for bankruptcy and insolvency, judges and registrars in selected provincial towns were given jurisdiction in bankruptcy, something the Walpole Commission had rejected in 1854[19] and which barely scraped through the Upper House.[20] Since there was no limit to the size of the estates they could handle, this created an anomalous situation whereby the county courts were trusted to handle estates worth thousands of pounds while contractual disputes and accident claims for less than £100 were regarded as beyond their capacity.[21] It was well used too; in 1869 nearly 5000 bankruptcies, involving nearly £70,000 of property, went through the county court.[22]

Equity jurisdiction over claims up to £500 finally arrived in 1865 after a rearguard action led by Lord St. Leonards. Opponents made some pertinent objections, in particular about the administrative machinery Chancery suits often needed, but the clamour for a forum where small estates would not be consumed in costs was ultimately unanswerable. In expectation of a considerable accession of business the Treasury agreed to raise the judges' salaries by £300 and was unamused (others were puzzled) when it amounted to fewer than 800 suits a year.[23]

The final addition in the 1860s was Admiralty, but Admiralty practitioners and officers were successful in restricting the devolution to 22 named courts and the maximum at stake to £300.[24]

---

[15] *RC on County Courts 1855*, 24.

[16] It was occasionally suggested that they should exercise a criminal jurisdiction, see e.g. 'County Courts and their Claims' (1853) 17 *LR* 265–78 and (1871) 6 *LJ* 798 (Eardley Wilmot).

[17] Personalty under £200 and realty under £300: Courts of Probate Act 1857 (20 & 21 Vict. c. 77), ss 54, 58; Holdsworth, *HEL*, xv, 203–5. The Royal Commission on the Legal Departments considered the possibility of transferring some district probate registry business to county court registrars.

[18] P. W. J. Bartrip, 'County Court and Superior Court Registrars 1825–1875: The Making of a Judicial Official', in D. Sugarman and G. R. Rubin (eds), *Law, Economy and Society, 1750–1914* (Abingdon, 1984), 349–79 at 349–50, 359–61.

[19] *RC on Bankruptcy*, PP 1854 [1770], xxiii.

[20] Polden, *History of the County Court*, 59; V. M. Lester, *Victorian Insolvency* (Oxford, 1995), 133–46.

[21] Bartrip, 'Registrars', 361.   [22] County Court Returns, PP 1870 (224), lvii.

[23] Polden, *History of the County Court*, 59 and App. 2; (1869) 47 *LT* 75. The *County Courts Chronicle* started a regular section on equity, but it soon petered out.

[24] County Courts Admiralty Jurisdiction Act 1868 c. 71; Polden, *History of the County Court*, 60. The Select Committee on Tribunals of Commerce (*PP* 1871 (409), xii) reported that the Act gave general satisfaction.

Notwithstanding these accretions, county court business continued to be dominated by common law actions, and even tort claims were fewer than might have been expected in the age of the railway and the factory.[25] Furthermore, most claims were still for small sums: of 940,342 plaints in 1869, only 12,029 were above £20 (just 28 over £50, under the consent provisions).[26] A professional journal could still sneer that 'at present the county courts furnish a mere machinery for the recovery of trumpery debts, indeed, are a kind of collecting agency for the tallyman and other small dealers'.[27] Such bluster, however, often concealed unease at their potential impact, and particular anxiety over what the Judicature Commission might propose.

The questions it circulated suggest the Judicature Commission was predisposed to recast the county courts into fewer districts, each with a judge sitting mostly at a major trial centre and making forays to the satellite towns at need. The judge would probably handle some cases above the existing money limit, leaving his registrar to deal with small debts in the lesser towns.[28] The 'central courts' which its report envisaged were intended to deal with an 'intermediate class of cases, which frequently involve questions of complexity, and of serious importance to the parties interested, yet the expense of taking the parties and witnesses to any considerable distance from the place where the cause of action arose, and they probably dwell, is generally wholly disproportionate to the value of the matter in dispute'.[29] Like so many reformers before and after, the Commissioners favoured a jurisdiction unlimited by amount (and augmented by the remaining excluded torts) but with the defendant able to remove it upwards as of right; the judges would be freed for this work by giving the registrars jurisdiction in all cases up to £5.[30]

Since this change would 'necessarily cause a considerable diminution in the civil business of the assizes',[31] fierce opposition could be expected from traditionalists, and the delay in issuing the report, and its trail of dissents and reservations, considerably weakened its authority. Although Cairns (as would appear) had ambitious views of his own, he made no effort to enact the recommendations.[32]

Impatient reformers brought forward their own proposals and in 1878 three bills, differing in their scope, and sponsored respectively by the radical Joseph Cowan, Sir John Eardley Wilmot, an ardent follower of Brougham, and Charles Norwood,[33] were forwarded to a Commons' select committee. It revisited the questions so recently examined by the Commissioners but in a very different

[25] See below, p. 886. [26] Polden, *History of the County Court*, App.1.
[27] (1867) 2 *LJ* 515.
[28] *Second Report*, PP 1872 (C. 631), xx, App. The questions and accompanying memorandum were the work of a sub-committee under Ward Hunt: (1869–70) 14 *SJ* 751.
[29] *Second Report 1872*, 10. [30] *Ibid.*, 11–17. [31] *Ibid.*, 21.
[32] For Cairns' reservations see above, p. 874. [33] Polden, *History of the County Court*, 77–8.

atmosphere. Eardley Wilmot was a partisan and unskilful chairman and some members had entrenched opinions impervious to evidence. The chairman could not carry the Committee with him; his own bill was roughly handled, and even Norwood's modest measure, which (somewhat revised) became the reformers' choice, would clearly not have an easy passage.[34]

Out of the blue Cairns produced a bill more radical than Norwood's, seizing on severe congestion in the QBD as demanding several solutions: the unlimited county court jurisdiction, plus a higher limit for equity suits; an increase in the 'costs protected' limit to £200; and measures to encourage more remitted actions.[35] The failure of Cairns's bill remains something of a mystery. Curiously, it was attacked by Selborne (who had signed the Commission's report) and Hatherley, and though it reached the Commons in a modified form, it was withdrawn without explanation.[36] The following year (1880) the ministry fell and the bill never resurfaced. Norwood's made token appearances for a few years but it became apparent that the movement to reform local justice was stalled.

There were several reasons for a failure which marks a watershed in the history of the county courts. Seemingly Cairns and Selborne found co-operation on this more difficult than on reforming Westminster Hall, and the Treasury's veto on raising judges' salaries (understandable after the equity jurisdiction episode) was a problem.[37] So too were the divisions among those, especially commercial interests, who wanted better local justice. A widespread preference for tribunals of commerce or provincial branches of the High Court weakened the lobbying for expanded county courts.[38] Moreover even the most ardent advocates for county courts could not deny that they had serious defects. They lamented judges whose claims could only stem from connection, men who had made no mark at the bar. They deprecated the antics of others like J. W. Smith, W. H. Cooke, T. E. P. Lefroy and Crompton Hutton whose idiosyncratic interpretations of law, despotic courtroom manners, or sheer indolence brought the whole bench into disrepute. They admitted there were doubts over whether some of the country registrars could be trusted with judicial functions, and there was the undeniable fact that many liberals deplored the courts' reliance on imprisoning poor debtors to enforce its judgments.[39]

Perhaps the most powerful factor, however, was the attitude of the legal profession, particularly the higher judiciary, the bar and the Law Society. The bar was over-represented in Parliament and solicitously protected by the law officers; it

---

[34] *Ibid*, 78–9; proceedings are in *PP* 1878 (100), i.   [35] *PP* 1878–9 (45, 91), i.

[36] *HLJ* 125, *passim*; *PD* 1878–9 (s3) 245: 258, 1239; (1878–9) 67 *LT* 23–4. Muir McKenzie drew Halsbury's attention to this bill when he became Lord Chancellor: BL Add. Mss. 56,370, f. 18 (20 October 1885).

[37] (1877–8) 22 *SJ* 758.   [38] See Ch. VI.

[39] Polden, *History of the County Court*, 80–5.

gratefully echoed Lord Blackburn's warning that 'the great central bar of England', a necessary safeguard against judicial tyranny, would be irreversibly damaged if the Assizes were weakened by provincial courts or enlarged county courts.[40]

From the 1880s these conservative forces had a staunch ally in Lord Halsbury. In and out of office Halsbury was a doughty champion of the High Court and the Assizes and an immovable opponent of county court encroachments.[41] His unwillingness to bring forward even minor procedural improvements was probably influenced by a disagreeable experience with the consolidation bill of 1888. Such a measure was badly overdue and though Halsbury had dropped the accompanying amending bill[42] and insisted that it should not become a vehicle for changes, the government was hard pressed on several important amendments; one sought to raise the money limit to £150; another to create unlimited jurisdiction subject to removal on showing good cause, and a third raised the costs—protected figure in contract from £20 to £50.[43] As it was, Halsbury had to accept several unpalatable minor changes; in particular, registrars were given jurisdiction in contested personal actions up to £2[44] and the ill-drafted section 65, which Cave J. was 'unable to put any meaning on'[45] required contract actions for £100 or less to be remitted from the High Court 'unless good cause is shown to the contrary'; since 30 per cent of defended QBD actions already fell within the scope of remitted actions, section 65 had the potential to displace a lot of business into the county courts.[46]

Halsbury's hostility to county courts did not extend to new statutory duties. These were numerous, but few created much work, even when expected to do so, like the Employer's Liability Act 1880.[47] Ironically, the next statutory initiative covering industrial accidents, Chamberlain's Workmen's Compensation Act 1897, which its author intended to be as judge proof as possible, gave county

---

[40] *Ibid.*

[41] An early example is his speech as Solicitor-General on Norwood's bill: *PD* 1880 (s3) 20: 1408.

[42] Polden, *History of the County Court*, 89. The Judicature Commissioners had prepared a consolidation bill, but Halsbury's was based on one presented in 1886 with the promise of an amending bill (already prepared) to accompany it.

[43] *Ibid.*, 89. There is a good summary by M. D. Chalmers, 'The County Courts Amendment Act 1888' (1889) 5 *LQR* 1–10.

[44] County Courts Act 1888 c. 43, s 92. Bartrip, 'Registrars'; Polden, *History of the County Court*, 276–7. The Act imposed a qualification of five years' standing.

[45] *Parsons* v. *Lakenheath School Board* (1889) 32 *CCC* 124, 128–9, and see discussion in (1889) 24 *LJ* 731–2.

[46] F. K. Munton, 'County Court Reforms' (1889) 5 *LQR* 134–9, at 135. According to (1888) 23 *LJ* 309, the proposed section would denude the High Court of half its business.

[47] An early list is in 'The County Courts' (1855) 21 *LR* 255–63. In 1880 Charles Norwood claimed that 32 statutes had imposed duties on the county courts: *PD* 1880 (s3) 250: 255–63. The Pollution of Rivers Act was one which had fallen short of expectations (*SC on County Court Bills 1878*, Judge Motteram at q. 2076).

courts more work than any special jurisdiction before the Rent Acts. County court judges were by far the most popular choice among the arbitrators listed in the Act and after the protective regime was extended to most trades in 1906 their caseload rose from 1046 in 1900 to 5289 in 1913,[48] while registrars had the duty of appraising the adequacy of voluntary settlements presented to the court for approval and in managing funds deposited for infants and widows.[49] Judges found their role a taxing one, since besides the notorious difficulty of interpreting key words and phrases in the legislation, the parties tended to be supported by trade unions and insurance companies who funded professional representation, and showed a willingness to appeal hitherto confined to railway companies.[50]

Until 1902 Halsbury easily fended off demands for wider common law jurisdiction. The Association of British Chambers of Commerce began a new campaign in the 1890s[51] but bills presented from 1897 onwards to raise the money limit to £1000 (cases above £100 being removable on good cause) and designate 'special courts' on the busiest circuits with better paid judges whose registrars would hear cases up to £20, were given short shrift.[52] Still, there was rising dissatisfaction with the QBD and though many resorted to arbitration even some with little love for county courts were driven to support their enlargement as a palliative.[53] When a former county court registrar, Sir Albert Rollit, took up the cause in 1902 the government was thrown onto the defensive. Rollit persuaded the chambers of commerce and the Law Society to support a less ambitious scheme, giving registrars jurisdiction up to £5 and doubling the upper limit in tort and contract to £100. He neatly sidestepped the usual objection—that county courts were overworked and lacked the facilities to handle larger cases—by stipulating that those should be heard only in courts designated as suitable by order in council.[54]

Halsbury had the backing of the Treasury (which feared having to pay judges bigger salaries) in resisting Rollit[55] and he was characteristically scornful of the 'marvellous ignorance' of the bill's supporters.[56] However, the ministry badly misjudged the temper of the Commons and suffered humiliating defeats.[57] Even then Halsbury would not yield, but nearly two years of clumsy manoeuvering

---

[48] Polden, *History of the County Court*, 93–5 and table 2a. A fuller account is in P. W. J. Bartrip, *Workmen's Compensation in Twentieth Century Britain* (Aldershot, 1987).

[49] Polden, *History of the County Court*, 95, 277.

[50] Bartrip, *Workmen's Compensation*, 58–74 and table 4.3.

[51] A. R. Ilersic and P. F. B. Liddle, *The Parliament of Commerce* (1960), 86–90.

[52] Polden, *History of the County Court*, 100.

[53] R. Abel-Smith and R. Stevens, *Lawyers and the Courts* (1967), 87–9.

[54] Polden, *History of the County Court*, 100.

[55] *Ibid.*, 101; NA PRO LCO 2/153.   [56] *PD* 1903 (s4) 126: 826–8.

[57] *Ibid.*, (s4) 118: 1016–26; 124: 665–84. The announcement of the numbers in the last division was greeted with laughter: (1903) 115 *LT* 216.

to emasculate the unwanted measure ended in failure. The Act Halsbury had denounced as unworkable was found to be quite straightforward, but in the acrimony and blundering opportunities were lost for much needed procedural reforms and the indignant judges were left unrewarded. [58]

This measure, which one opponent had claimed 'would practically wreck the ancient system of the administration of civil justice in the country',[59] did nothing of the sort. Nevertheless it was fairly successful, leading to more than 2000 suits a year over £100. Even so the KBD was still unable to cope, but Halsbury proved no less dogmatic in opposition and Loreburn had problems enough in persuading the whips to find room for county courts in a crowded legislative programme without the likelihood of opposition in an Upper House with a big Conservative majority. Loreburn set up a committee under Lord Gorell to investigate relations between High Court and county court and was disappointed with the conservative tenor of its report.[60] The Committee was more concerned to improve the workings of the High Court than to remove business from it,[61] but since it could not ignore the exasperation of commercial litigants it reluctantly revived the old suggestion that it should be open to the plaintiff to start almost any case in the county court, the defendant being able to remove it simply by entering an appearance in the High Court. Cases above the county court money limit would be confined to special county courts and the bar would have exclusive audience.[62] Even this measure would not be brought in until its proposed remedial measures in the KBD had been implemented.[63]

However, the Gorell Report contained one unexpectedly radical recommendation. It felt that the only economical way to meet pent up demand for divorce from the poor was in the county court, though here again the bar was to have exclusive audience to preserve dignity and propriety.[64] This was altogether too controversial for the government, which made Gorell chairman of a commission to investigate divorce law and practice generally. The Commission suggested instead that county court judges might be made Commissioners of Assize and handle divorce in that capacity, but that was shelved too.[65]

Meanwhile Loreburn's officials assembled a County Courts Bill comprising a mixture of long-standing reform suggestions and the Gorell Committee's other proposal. The unlimited jurisdiction was boldly placed at the head of the bill

---

[58] Polden, *History of the County Court*, 101–2.

[59] H. E. Duke, later Lord Merrivale P., *PD* 1903 (s4) 124: 676.

[60] *PP* 1909 (71), lxxii.   [61] *Ibid.*, 15–21.   [62] *Ibid.*, 17.

[63] The illogicality of this was pointed out in (1908–9) 53 *Sol. J.* 442–3 and (1909) 44 *LJ* 227.

[64] *DC on County Court Procedure*, *PP* 1909 (71), lxxii, 23–6. For an earlier proposal see Henry Broadhurst's County Courts (Divorce) Bill 1885, *PP* 1884–5 (77), i.

[65] *PD* 1909 (s5 HL) 2: 473–507; *RC on Divorce etc. 1912*, *PP* 1912–13 [Cd. 6478], xviii, paras 52–7.

but in a thin House of Lords Halsbury mustered 37 votes to the government's 32; Loreburn would not have the bill without its centrepiece and it was therefore withdrawn.[66] It was reintroduced in 1911 under the shadow of the Parliament Bill but the opposition of several eminent judges and lawyers delayed it in the Lords long enough for it to fail for lack of time.[67] It is probable that Haldane, who succeeded Loreburn, could have forced it through if it had been his top priority, but his interests lay elsewhere and Muir McKenzie told the Civil Service Commission a melancholy tale of bills regularly slaughtered for want of time and energetic backing.[68] In fact, remitted actions apart, Rollit's Act was the only substantial change to the common law jurisdiction of the county courts between the Romilly Commission and the First World War.

2. BUSINESS

Denunciations of this 'ruinous piece of experimental quackery'[69] concealed fears that it would be only too successful, and so it proved. Even before the money limit was raised in 1850 almost half a million plaints a year were being entered and by 1860 there were more than three-quarters of a million.[70] The initial impetus came from the release of a pent-up demand, but later trends probably owed more to economic and social changes than to developments within the legal system.[71] Plaint numbers passed 900,000 in 1861 and then fell quite steeply, recovering from 1865 to peak in 1868 before dropping from 975,373 to 865,040 in 1874. Another rise carried them past the million mark in 1877 and they remained pretty stable, between 900,000 and 1,100,000, until the end of the 1890s, rising thereafter to a peak of 1,338,732 in 1904. Shortly before the War they had begun to fall significantly, dropping below 1,200,000 and then they fell precipitously.[72] Set against changes in the size of the population, however, these fluctuations look less notable. There was certainly a substantial rise in the 1850s and early 1860s but thereafter the picture is one of general stability, with a gentle decline in litigiousness overall.[73]

[66] *PD* 1909 (s5 HL) 2: 239–50, 729–50; Muir McKenzie to President of the Law Society, 28 July 1909, LCO 2/207.

[67] Polden, *History of the County Court*, 108–9.

[68] *RC on the Civil Service, Evidence*, PP 1914–16 [Cd. 8130], xii, qq. 44,234–5.

[69] (1847) 34 *Leg. Ob.* 557.

[70] Polden, *History of the County Court*, table 1.

[71] C. W. Brooks, 'Litigation and Society in England, 1200–1996', in *Lawyers, Litigation and English Society Since 1450* (1998), 63–128, at 104–13; P. Johnson, 'Small Debts and Economic Distress in England and Wales, 1857–1913' (1993) 46 *Econ. Hist. Rev.* 67–87.

[72] Polden, *History of the County Courts*, table 1.

[73] Brooks, 'Litigation and Society', 108–10.

Since the county courts were highly dependent upon one class of business—contractual debts—the volume of business might be expected to vary noticeably in line with economic fluctuations. Actions for debt recovery arose from two circumstances. The working class (against whom they were chiefly brought) was more likely to seek 'premeditated' credit for consumer goods in good times, when they were also less likely to need 'crisis' credit for life's necessities. In bad times the converse would be true, but they would then be more likely to default, though some creditors might be more forbearing for humanitarian or practical reasons.[74] The most detailed study suggests variations in plaint numbers 'strongly related to specific short-term fluctuations in the labour market and labour income'[75] and, as was noticed in the 1890s, trends were often far from uniform across the country;[76] courts in areas prone to violent cycles of prosperity and misery experienced correspondingly sharper fluctuations in business.

Within these fluctuations one remarkably constant feature was that county courts remained principally institutions for the recovery of small debts. The average plaint value between 1858 and 1862 was £2 8s 10d; in 1893–4 it was £3 1s,[77] and the typical action was for even smaller sums; 70 per cent of judgments issued in 1865 were for £2 or less, 90 per cent for no more than £5, while in 1913 more than 98 per cent of plaints were for less than £20.[78] The proportion of larger cases hardly increased during the period although in sheer numbers they were not unimpressive; in 1913 some 16,000 plaints above £20 were issued, nearly 3000 of them above £50.[79]

Nevertheless, numerically the county courts dwarfed the High Court, generally accounting for between 80 and 90 per cent of the total, and at times when the QBD/KBD was particularly beset by delays there was a distinct decrease in its share.[80] However, KBD business was much more mixed; torts made up around a quarter, whereas in county courts they were comparatively unimportant.

This was partly a result of the deliberate exclusion of certain torts from the county court jurisdiction.[81] Though subsequently removed for several, the prohibition remained for the only ones likely to produce substantial business—libel and slander. Though other reasons were sometimes adduced—the doubtful quality of

[74] Johnson, 'Small Debts and Economic Distress', 69–70, and see the introduction to Civil Judicial Statistics 1912, PP 1914 [Cd. 7267], xii.

[75] Johnson, 'Small Debts and Economic Distress', 86.

[76] Civil Judicial Statistics 1894, PP 1896 [C. 8263], xciv.

[77] Ibid.

[78] Johnson, 'Small Debts and Economic Distress', 68.

[79] Polden, History of the County Courts, table 1.

[80] Civil Judicial Statistics 1894, table 20.

[81] County Courts Act 1846, s. 58, excluding malicious prosecution, libel or slander, criminal conversation, seduction or breach of promise.

the county court jury and congestion in the courts[82]—the main reason, openly avowed by the Gorell Committee, was simply that 'it is not desirable to encourage them'.[83] Most county court judges probably shared these sentiments, but this came perilously close to 'class law': the 'pothouse slander' was to be shrugged off, the defamatory utterance in a gentleman's club might be pursued in the High Court.

Even allowing for the excluded torts, however, observers have been struck by the relative paucity of accident claims in county courts,[84] for given the number of accidents on railways, in factories and in the streets, it was potentially a fertile field. Yet when Judge Kettle described and disparaged the torts brought before him in the industrial west midlands in 1878, he might have been describing a rustic community. There are several possible explanations. Certainly, as opponents of wider jurisdiction pointed out, the county court lacked the full apparatus of pleadings and interlocutories, but that defect was often exaggerated. Then too, it might be difficult to obtain trial by jury and, more important, the venue was likely to be the defendant's place of business—inconvenient for anyone suing a railway company. The upper limit on damages was a drawback too, though average awards in the higher courts were below £50. And for solicitors the High Court offered more generous costs; with the costs sanction in torts kept very low there was no real disincentive to take one's chance in the more promising forum.[85]

Sometimes torts were remitted to a county court from above. Numerically unimportant—they never reached 2000 and by 1914 were little over 1000 a year—their impact was sometimes serious. They were not evenly distributed around the country but were concentrated disproportionately in the London courts[86] where they disrupted judges' listing arrangements and were likely to take longer than a run-of-the-mill case.[87] For these reasons some county court judges vented their irritation in the courtroom or in print.[88]

Though personal actions greatly predominated, others were important for making greater demands upon time and resources. Thus, although the equity jurisdiction was generally seen as a failure, it generated between 600 and 900 cases a year (a remarkably consistent figure), while bankruptcy work, except between 1869 and 1883, was considerably heavier, usually in the 3000s; administration orders, though never so popular as had been hoped, also amounted to several

---

[82] e.g. (1887–8) 32 *Sol. J.* 519.

[83] *DC on County Courts 1909*, 21. A similar stance was taken by the *SC on County Court Bills 1878*, 8.

[84] H. Smith, 'The Resurgent County Court in Victorian Britain' (1969) 13 *AJLH* 126–37.

[85] Polden, *History of the County Court*, 90–2. R. W. Kostal's detailed study of accident claims against the London and North-Western Railway (*Law and English Railway Capitalism* (Oxford, 1994) App.) makes no reference to county courts.

[86] *SC on County Court Bills 1878*, Judge Dasent, q. 419; (1888–9) 33 *Sol. J.* 639.

[87] For examples see Polden, *History of the County Court*, 62.

[88] (1903) 38 *LJ* 42; E. Bowen Rowlands, 'County Court Judges and their Jurisdiction' (1902) 18 *LQR* 237–46, at 241.

thousand a year. The Workmen's Compensation Acts also kept both judges and registrars busy, with 9000 arbitrations in 1913 and 30,000 memoranda registered (often, but by no means always, a formality).[89]

3. CENTRAL ORGANIZATION

Responsibility for the county courts was initially divided among three government departments. The Lord Chancellor chose the judges and, if it became necessary, removed them, while the Treasury oversaw the financial administration. The main burden fell upon the Home Office, which had general responsibility for organization and operations, including finding courtrooms, arranging the districts and handling complaints, but it was indifferent towards its new charge, and in 1868, with the Judicature Commissioners already deliberating on the future of civil justice, it willingly ceded its responsibilities to the Lord Chancellor, though without any transfer of resources.[90]

In practice the running of the county courts had for some years devolved upon Henry Nicol.[91] Nicol was a relatively junior Treasury official, given charge of its new 'county courts department' in 1861. He became 'a kind of Secretary to [the Lord Chancellor] for regulating the offices of the County Courts', whose importance belied his modest position and made his attempts at self-depreciation unconvincing. Until a permanent secretary arrived in the mid-1880s he had direct access to the Lord Chancellor and his great experience made him the indispensable factotum in county court matters.[92]

After Nicol's retirement in 1892 his successors in the county court department enjoyed nothing like the same influence. Muir McKenzie kept things within his own grasp and dealt directly with his Treasury opposite numbers while the county courts department still carried out the 'accountant' duties, along with 'certain duties not strictly financial' which arose from the inspections carried out by its examiners.[93] The superintendent exercised day-to-day supervision over registrars and their staffs and B. J. Bridgeman (superintendent between 1896–1922) was felt by many registrars to have a narrow and economy-driven outlook. Bridgeman made no secret of his low opinion of many judges, and of registrars and clerks generally, and the registrars came to regard him as their enemy. His entrenched opposition to change also made him unpopular with the LCO and he continually obstructed necessary reforms.[94]

---

[89] Polden, *History of the County Court*, table 2a.   [90] *Ibid.*, 198–9.

[91] *RC on the Legal Departments, Evidence*, qq. 7366–8.

[92] Polden, *History of the County Court*, 199; P. Polden, 'Judicial Independence and Executive Responsibilities, Part One' (1996) 25 *Anglo-Am. Law Rev.* 1–38, at 4. Starting as a second-class clerk in the law clerk's department, he retired with a CB and a pension of £700 per annum.

[93] *RC on the Civil Service, Evidence*, Bridgeman, qq. 51,630, 51,633.

[94] Polden, *History of the County Court*, 202–3.

One intractable problem in providing a public forum for disputes over small sums is that the cost of providing the facilities will be disproportionate to the amount in dispute. The balance between charging the suitors (which in the superior courts system essentially meant the losing party) and meeting the cost out of general taxation has always been difficult; indeed courts of requests were popular because without paid judges and costly courtrooms their fees could be set very low.

The Common Law Commissioners had optimistically pronounced that 'very moderate fees, to be paid in each cause, would supply a fund sufficient to defray every expense attendant on the establishment of Local Courts'[95] and that was the principle adopted in 1846, though the fees were hardly moderate and were supplemented by a temporary 'tax on suitors' to defray the cost of setting up offices and courthouses.[96] Despite a reduction in 1850, the level of fees was the subject of wide and persistent complaint[97] and with a healthy surplus flowing into Treasury coffers the pressure intensified.[98] One of the questions asked of the Romilly Commission therefore was 'whether the fees can be made reduced, or levied in a less burthensome manner'.[99]

That lawyer-dominated body rose easily to that challenge and after a superficial examination produced a draft fees table which abandoned the premise that the courts must be self-financing, assuming that the state should meet the cost of judges and buildings with the suitors paying the rest of the expenses. On that footing, and with the sanguine view that 'experience renders deficit improbable',[100] the Commission had no difficulty in suggesting substantial reductions. This more generous funding arrangement was duly implemented in 1856[101] but the Commission's optimism proved unjustified and fees had to rise in 1864. The financial arrangements then came under fire from two inquiries. The Judicature Commissioners found that fees were sometimes oppressive and recommended simplifications in procedure (notably the curtailment of the 'banking function') with a view to effect a reduction in fees for the benefit of suitors,[102] while the Childers Committee invoked the taxpayers' interests; with the net charge reaching £175,000 per annum it found the provision of judges, officials, and courts extravagant.[103]

---

[95] *RC on the Common Law, Fifth Report*, PP 1833 (247), xxii, 21.

[96] County Courts Act 1846, ss. 50–4, 77, and Schedules.

[97] Within a few months of the opening of the courts the fees were denounced at a big public meeting in Sheffield: (1847) 9 *LT* 541.

[98] County Court Returns in *PP* 1854–5 (350), xlii.

[99] *RC on County Courts 1855*, 38–44, at 44.   [100] *Ibid.*, sidenote to 44.

[101] See the calculations in *New Charges on the Exchequer...*, PP 1856 (340), l.

[102] *Second Report*, PP 1872 (C. 631), xx, 20; Polden, *History of the County Court*, 75–7.

[103] *SC on Civil Service Expenditure, Second Report*, PP 1873 (248), vii, 'recommendations'; *RC on the Legal Departments*, PP 1874 (C. 1107), xxiv, 97–100.

Economies had already been effected by the abolition of district treasurers and most high bailiffs,[104] but when in 1872 the Treasury made a unilateral hamfisted attempt at economy by curbing the judges' travelling allowances it was forced into an undignified retreat by strident criticism from the judges and lawyers.[105] Nicol was given a hard time by successive inquiries probing the hitherto ineffectual efforts to streamline and modernize the district structure[106] but Selborne, while admitting his failure to reduce judges and districts, insisted that 'it is clearly not the intention of the Constitution that the Treasury should have the control over the legal departments'.[107]

Once the external pressures were relaxed the Treasury and the LCO reached a tacit understanding. The Treasury would not seriously press for major economies while the LCO would not push for higher judicial salaries nor give any encouragement to campaigners for lower fees. The fees agitation resurfaced in the early 1890s, when Henry Fowler described them as 'enormous'[108] and returns showed that at 5s 2d in every pound recovered they were a little higher than for 1858–62, albeit the rise in legal costs over that period from 10d to 1s 10d, was much greater.[109] The Law Society won enough influential support to force an internal inquiry, but it only resulted in redistribution, not significant reductions.[110] The usual defence to the professions' complaint that High Court costs in small cases were much lower was that the county court plaintiff got a fuller service for his money, but many plaintiffs would have been very willing to forgo that.[111] They were probably even less impressed by a government spokesman's defence that high recovery fees helped to discourage the irresponsible granting of credit.[112]

The demand for lower fees remained at the top of the shopping lists of reforms presented by creditors' organizations, fuelled by such annual statistics as those of 1906 showing fees making up 25 per cent of the total monies recovered,[113] and in 1913 the Law Society renewed its campaign. There was little hope of success however. The Treasury was showing a 'profit' in most years and the LCO would not jeopardize a subsidy of £100,000 a year.[114] Only in a post-war overhaul of the whole structure was a financial re-settlement practical politics.

[104] For treasurers see Polden, *History of the County Court*, 63; for high bailiffs see below, pp. 902–3.
[105] Polden, 'Judicial Independence and Executive Responsibilities, Part One', 11–12.
[106] *SC on Civil Service Expenditure, Second Report 1873*, qq. 1791–2110, *RC on the Legal Departments, Evidence, PP* 1875 (C. 1245), xxx, qq. 7364–565.
[107] *RC on the Legal Departments, Evidence*, q. 9594.
[108] *PD* 1893–4 (s4) 17: 1383.   [109] *Civil Judicial Statistics 1894*.
[110] Polden, *History of the County Court*, 228–9. An inquiry was also recommended by the House of Lords Select Committee on the Debtors Act (1893–4), *HLJ* 125 para. 18.
[111] e.g. *DC on County Courts, Report 1909*, 31.
[112] Hanbury, a Treasury under-secretary: *PD* 1899 (s4) 68: 192.
[113] Noted in (1906) 121 *LT* 380.
[114] Polden, *History of the County Court*, 230.

4. LOCAL ORGANIZATION AND STAFF

The 1846 Act set no limit to the number of judges and courts and, after consultation with local leaders and lobbying from towns, the scheme drafted by Drinkwater Bethune for the Home Office employed 60 judges. Each had a district[115] which (outside the metropolitan courts) ranged in population size from 202,000 in mid-Wales to 312,000 in Hampshire.[116] *R* v. *Parham*[117] confirmed that the Act should be read as allowing one judge per district rather than one per court, which was just as well, for the provision was generous if not downright lavish, with no fewer than 491 courts, some in places which even Bethune called 'inconsiderable'.[118] He followed instructions that no one should be more than seven or eight miles from a court, which was an admirable prescription for local justice in the age of the stagecoach but soon looked extravagant in the age of the railway.[119]

The power to add or remove towns by order in council was soon exercised: Henley and Woolwich were added, Clutton (Somerset) and Boston (Yorkshire) removed.[120] Though it was also possible to alter or abolish whole districts, express statutory authority was obtained to give Liverpool a second judge at the expense of an underused district.[121] Once it had become clear that over 300 courts would not pay their way, Nicol prepared schemes for drastic reductions, but local opposition frustrated a plan to close 100 or so in 1849 and half that number in 1857.[122] Though Nicol kept a list of 60 for possible closure, political considerations continued to make major alterations impossible[123] and even minor ones could be thwarted, as in Sussex in 1877.[124]

Similarly, attempts to equalize the workload between districts, strongly urged by inquiries in the 1860s and 1870s, proved tricky. Travelling times had to be taken into account and there were unforeseen obstacles. When a judge in the Manchester district found that courts had been transferred to him he promptly reduced the frequency of his sittings in others to keep his working days at their previous number, and this embarrassing outcome made Nicol wary of further attempts.[125]

As that incident suggests, judges had considerable autonomy in managing their districts. They were supposed to hold court at least monthly in each town but on

---

[115] From the outset districts were often referred to as circuits.

[116] Polden, *History of the County Court*, 210–12. Nicol was one of Bethune's assistants.

[117] (1849) 13 Q.B. 858.   [118] Bellingham (Northumberland), LCO 8/1.

[119] *Ibid.*   [120] LCO 8/1.

[121] County Courts Districts Act 1858 (21 & 22 Vict. c. 74), s. 3. This Act limited the number to 60, the 1846 Act merely specifying 'as many fit persons as are needed'.

[122] *SC on County Court Bills Report 1878*, Nicol's evidence, q. 5055.

[123] *Judicature Commission Second Report 1872*, q. 2718; *RC on the Legal Departments, Evidence*, q. 7402.

[124] (1877) 26 CCC 203.   [125] Polden, *History of the County Court*, 219.

finding little or no business some reduced the frequency even before statutory authority was obtained in 1858.[126] They found the Lord Chancellor a good deal more liberal in this than the Home Office had been but there were still occasions when a judge would arrive to find no business, like Martineau on three successive visits to East Grinstead.[127] Official statistics exposed glaring variations in the judges' number of sitting days; in 1864 three sat more than 165 days, three others less than 110; their average of 135 days in 1873 was well short of the 200 of superior court judges.[128] Some also made rather liberal use of the power to appoint a deputy in case of 'illness or unavoidable absence', so that had to be more strictly regulated in 1888.[129] Opponents of a wider jurisdiction argued that the judges could not cope with extra work, but though London judges were generally acknowledged to be hard working, Loreburn and Bridgeman felt many had a rather easy life.[130]

Halsbury and his successors preferred to avoid stirring up the question of county court organization generally, and apart from a remodelling of the London courts in 1893 no major changes in distribution or numbers were sought until after the First World War.[131] New courts were opened, underused ones closed, but the number was practically the same in 1914 as in 1847 and the district organization and number of judges was likewise little altered. That may be regarded either as a tribute to Bethune's well-crafted scheme or an indication of how difficult it was to change the institutions of the law.

5. REGISTRARS

Each court had its clerk, soon styled registrar.[132] Registrars were required to be solicitors, appointed by the judge subject to the Lord Chancellor's approval. The Act allowed pluralism and some judges carried this to extremes, as in district 57 where J. M. Carew had charge of all 13 courts.[133] Criticisms of a similar position in west Wales, where Morris of Carmarthen had ten courts in his keeping,[134] soon led to restrictions; unless the Lord Chancellor gave his sanction, it was to be one

---

[126] Polden, 'Judicial Independence and Executive Responsibilities, Part One', 5–6.

[127] *SC on County Court Bills, Report 1878*, Martineau, q. 1859.

[128] Polden, *History of the County Court*, 270–1; Polden, 'Judicial Independence and Executive Responsibilities, Part One', 11 n.39.

[129] County Courts Act 1846, s. 20, County Courts Act 1888, s. 18; Polden, 'Judicial Independence and Executive Responsibilities, Part One', 20–1.

[130] Polden, *History of the County Court*, 110, 220–1. The argument that the courts would be unable to cope with the extra work had to be abandoned when the LCO's own inquiries showed it to be unfounded. A concern voiced in the Gorell Report (p. 10), it was pressed strongly against the government bills of 1909 and 1911.

[131] Polden, *History of the County Court*, 213.

[132] *Ibid.*, 281–92 ; Bartrip, 'Registrars', 349–79.

[133] County Court Returns, *PP* 1850 (743), xlvi.

[134] (1856) 27 *LT* 151.

registrar, one court and few exceptions were made;[135] and in theory at least, registrars had to attend at offices where a day with even a single plaint to be entered was the exception rather than the rule.[136] Numbering almost 500, registrars were able to form their own association with a sizeable membership and it played an active and constructive role in regularizing practice. [137]

Most registrars were paid by fees. A few made a good thing out of it, but three-quarters were getting less than the statutory minimum of £100 and in small courts the rewards proved insufficient to attract the better class of solicitor.[138] Part-timers had therefore to be allowed, which became a problem when it was wished to give them judicial powers: there was disquiet at the notion of a man sitting in judgment over litigants who were also clients of his. There were instances where a registrar acted as a judge in his own cause[139] but more commonly there was a suspicion of bias towards one party, which was hard to test.[140] Although their common law jurisdiction was limited to undefended cases, it was notorious that many registrars helped the judge get through the mass of small debt actions of all sorts[141] and in 1888, with formal extension to defended cases under discussion, the government was hard pressed to defeat an amendment making all registrars whole-time.[142] It was, however, unthinkable to instigate a mass closure of all the smaller courts and the solution eventually adopted was a gradual return to controlled pluralism under the guise of 'grouping' courts, though this had not been carried far by 1914.[143]

As a rule the judge's field of choice was rather narrow and in smaller towns the office tended to become the perquisite of one or two of the leading firms, sometimes passing from father to son as it did with the Tassells in Faversham.[144] Some judges resorted to nepotism, a particularly bad example being Pitt Taylor's appointment of his newly qualified son.[145] Not all incestuous choices turned out badly, however—T. H. Marshall of Leeds was widely reckoned an abler man than his father the judge.[146] The practice of a judge bringing in a registrar from outside, as when Woodfall took F. B. McFea to Plymouth, probably became commoner in the big courts after the changes in remuneration made in 1888, but was always unpopular with local practitioners.[147]

---

[135] County Courts Act 1852, ss 1, 14, 17. The County Courts Act 1856, s 9 empowered the Lord Chancellor to terminate existing plural holdings.

[136] Bartrip, 'Registrars', 357.   [137] Polden, *History of the County Court*, 290–2.

[138] *RC on County Courts, Report 1855*, 44.   [139] e.g. *McGachen* v. *Cooke* (1875/6)22 *Sol. J.* 451.

[140] The Swift Committee on county court staff took this point: *PP* 1920 [Cmd. 1049], xx, 8.

[141] Bartrip, 'Registrars', 363–4.   [142] See above, p. 881.

[143] Polden, *History of the County Court*, 282.   [144] *Ibid.*, 284.

[145] *Ibid.*, 283. From 1888 five years from qualification was required.

[146] (1909–10) 53 *Sol. J.* 266. Marshall was a long-serving president of the Association of County Court Registrars.

[147] Polden, *History of the County Court*, 283.

Remuneration continued to pose an intractable difficulty. It had always been possible for a registrar to be paid a fixed salary (up to £600, raised to £700 in 1856), but the Treasury had seldom been persuaded.[148] A new structure was created after the Romilly Report with three different formulae depending upon the business level in the court, but although fees henceforth went to the Treasury, most registrars' income was still tied to the number of plaints, or subsequently regulated by a more complicated formula.[149] The registrars' peculiar hybrid status puzzled the Lisgar Commission[150] and matters were further complicated when two overlapping provisions in the 1888 Act empowered the Lord Chancellor to exclude registrars from practice and make them salaried civil servants. Only 22 cases had occurred by 1914 (more than 40 other registrars undertook not to practise as a condition of appointment) but it had become a widespread aspiration.[151] Bridgeman and the Treasury still preferred a system with an element of payment by results, but it was increasingly criticized as anomalous and overcomplicated: as Chalmers wrote, '[f]rom a Treasury point of view there is a good deal to be said for the system of payment by results, but as a question of public morality the system is abominable'.[152] Besides the potential for conflicts of interest, it encouraged registrars to stay in post when their physical and sometimes mental condition had deteriorated; Nuneaton's first registrar, Henry Dawes, was there for 60 years and another arthritic veteran's contorted progress to the office provided public entertainment.[153] Both consequences provided legitimate grounds for objecting to the increase in registrars' judicial powers proposed in successive government bills.

The registrars' discontent with their terms of employment was greatly exceeded by their clerks. To keep costs down and enable changes to courts and districts to be made without generating claims to compensation, the registrar's clerks were supposed to be his own employees, and he was financially responsible for losses caused by their carelessness or fraud. Often drawn from his own firm, they were seldom well paid (and sometimes badly treated) and save in a few busy courts (Birmingham was exceptional in having over 50 clerks and ushers) they had minimal prospects of promotion. Lacking any pension scheme, they were even more prone than the registrar to cling on at their desks despite age and infirmity and many registrars were too compassionate to dismiss them, with unfortunate results for efficiency. The clerks formed associations to press their demand for civil service status and pensions, but scattered and vulnerable as they were,

---

[148] Bartrip, 'Registrars', 357.   [149] Polden, *History of the County Court*, 285.

[150] *RC on the Legal Departments, Evidence*, Nicol, qq. 7540–5.

[151] Polden, *History of the County Court*, 285–6. Section 25 was never used, all appointments being made under s. 45.

[152] 'The County Courts Act 1888' (1889) 5 *LQR* 1–10 at 7.

[153] (1907) 41 *CCC* 191; G. F. Bamford, 'I Remember' (1956) 33 *County Court Officer*, 17.

they were unable to move the Treasury, which did not even know how many they were.[154]

6. PRACTICE AND PROCEDURE

In their first quarter century a dozen further county courts Acts, of widely varying size and importance, were passed. The consolidation Act of 1888 was therefore both desirable and overdue, but as the 1903 Act was the only substantial measure before 1919 no further consolidation was necessary until the 1920s.

The 1846 Act was supplemented by a rather sketchy set of rules drawn by a group of superior court judges[155] and in 1850 this code was expanded from 52 to 210 by a newly established rule committee comprising five county court judges.[156] Initially the Lord Chancellor might (and did) alter its composition at will, but from 1856 his power was limited to filling vacancies.[157] The rule-making power was broad and vague and the Committee's efforts were often criticized.[158] Its most demanding task was dealing with costs, and the first attempt was rejected as too generous by the superior court judges charged with oversight of the Committee.[159] The Committee also made itself unpopular in some quarters a few years later, when it was rather unfairly told to investigate the use of committals; it prudently sought, and essentially adopted, the views of most county court judges, who favoured only minor changes.[160]

The superior court judges' oversight was removed in 1856, only the concurrence of the Lord Chancellor being required, but from 1884 the newly established SCRC scrutinized the rules in draft. It soon found itself with plenty to do.[161] The rules had steadily been expanding as new duties were imposed and the initial simplicity of procedure became encumbered with interlocutory facilities etc.[162] In 1886 a much-needed revision was undertaken, mostly the work of the new Birmingham judge McKenzie Chalmers and G. W. Heywood, author of practitioners' works.[163] The rules were recast along the lines of the supreme court rules, and by section 164 of the consolidation Act the High Court practice was to apply in default of any rule inconsistent with it.[164]

---

[154] Polden, *History of the County Court*, 292–8.   [155] County Courts Act 1846, s 78.
[156] Polden, *History of the County Court*, 216.   [157] County Courts Act 1856, s 32.
[158] Polden, *History of the County Court*, 217.
[159] *Ibid.* Solicitors suspected, probably rightly, that they had been influenced by their self-interested taxing masters.
[160] Not printed until 1867 (*PP* (209), lvii).
[161] County Courts Act 1856, s 32; S. Rosenbaum, 'Rule Making in the County Courts', (1915) 31 *LQR* 304–13.
[162] See e.g. (1867–8) 12 *Sol. J.* 211.
[163] There is a useful summary in (1885–6) 30 *Sol. J.* 334–5 *et seq.*
[164] *Halsbury's Laws of England*, viii (1909), paras 1479–81.

The consolidation was urged by Muir McKenzie, and after Nicol retired he and the chairman Lucius Selfe were the dominant force on the Committee. Under their guidance, and with the assistance of several able and long-serving members, the Committee settled into a pattern of productivity (or at least unceasing activity), making or altering at least one set of rules each year. Some were responses to new Acts—the Workmen's Compensation Acts alone required 100 rules and 80 forms—or decisions of the higher courts, others the result of suggestions received or the members' own initiatives. Though the rules usually had their critics and were occasionally argued to be *ultra vires*, most were uncontentious.[165] However, the Committee once blundered rather badly. Since recent High Court decisions, especially *Northey, Stone & Co v. Gidney*,[166] had so encouraged bulk plaintiffs by a generous interpretation of section 74 of the 1888 Act (which enabled defendants to be sued 'in the district within which the cause of action or claim wholly or in part arose' in certain circumstances) that 10 per cent of actions were now being brought under the section, they made the governing rule (Order 5, rule 9) much narrower to curb the practice. The Committee badly underestimated the influence of the credit traders and solicitors and the rule had to be embarrassingly withdrawn.[167]

Such was the Committee's diligence, and the extra duties imposed on the courts, that the rules—consolidated again by Selfe in 1903—had passed 1000 by 1914. The Committee accepted, however, that it was usually beyond them to impose uniform interpretations and practice on the judges,[168] though the Association of County Court Registrars, besides being the most useful source of suggestions for rule changes, issued helpful practice notes from 1907. Its president, A. L. Lowe, was regularly consulted on draft rules[169] and many felt the Rule Committee would benefit from the inclusion of a registrar, since judges were less exposed to the direct consequences of some rule changes.[170] However, some judges were themselves aggrieved at not being consulted; since their own meetings were thinly attended this grievance was perhaps imaginary.[171] In 1919 the Committee was expanded to include a registrar, and also a barrister and solicitor.

To provide speedy and cheap justice the county courts would necessarily be shorn of many of the trappings of the superior courts and could not be expected to match their quality of justice; as one High Court judge rather superciliously

---

[165] Polden, *History of the County Court*, 218–19; Rosenbaum, 'Rule Making in the County Courts', 310–12.

[166] [1894] 1 QB 99.   [167] Polden, *History of the County Court*, 219.

[168] *Ibid.*

[169] *Ibid.*, 290–1. Lowe was registrar at Birmingham and joined the Rule Committee in 1920.

[170] (1900–1) 110 *LT* 230.

[171] *SC on Moneylending, Second Report*, PP 1898 (260), xi, q. 4442 (Judge Owen). *HLSC on the Debtors Act, Report 1894*, q. 749 (Sir R. Harington).

put it, they were 'usefully administering summary, imperfect justice'.[172] From the outset, however, there were tensions between their role in serving commercial creditors recovering small consumer debts, and protecting defendants of limited means and usually without lawyers. As one critic wrote: '[t]he original founders of the County Courts started with a procedure that can only be called paternal. They treated suitors as children, young and inexperienced in the ways of the world.'[173] Inevitably, they often failed those who were anything but inexperienced, and they complained loudly and often of the paternalistic and officious procedures that limited the court's effectiveness.[174]

One instance was the difficulty in serving process on the defendant. Initially all process had to be served by the court's bailiffs—the Attorney-General withdrew a clause in the 1850 bill enabling parties to effect service themselves[175]—and in 1860 10–15 per cent of summonses in Manchester and Liverpool were returned 'not served'.[176] Plaintiffs believed that the bailiffs, lacking any financial incentive, made little effort, and repeated attempts to improve on the record suggest the problem was real and stubborn.[177] The Judicature Commissioners evidently agreed, for they recommended that service by the parties should become the normal route,[178] but bailiff service remained the general rule and the complaints continued, evidently with some justification, for in 1898 a *Daily Mail* investigation of London courts unearthed compelling evidence that bailiffs were open to inducements to be more—or less—zealous in effecting service.[179]

When the county courts were set up the superior courts were still struggling in the grip of new pleading rules of 1834 and the contrast between their labyrinthine special pleading and the pared down equivalent below was very striking. A county court plaintiff had only to disclose 'the substance of the action' on a simple form[180] and unless he wished to rely upon one of a handful of defences named in the Act the defendant need not answer at all but might simply turn up for the trial and make his defence there.[181] Plaintiffs naturally resented this indulgence, which put them to the expense of preparing to meet any possible defence; worse, many defendants did not come, so the expense of trial preparation, especially the cost of witnesses, was thrown away. Bulk plaintiffs therefore demanded for the county courts the superior courts' facility for judgment in default of appearance.[182] The

[172] Grove J., 'County Court Appeals' (1875–6) 20 *Sol. J.* 641.
[173] 'The County Court System' (1878–9) 66 *LT* 203.
[174] Polden, *History of the County Court*, 52, 68–71.   [175] *PD* 1849–50 (s3) 111: 1163.
[176] Returns from Liverpool and Manchester, *PP* 1860 (322), lvii.
[177] Polden, *History of the County Court*, 305–7.   [178] *Second Report 1872*, 16.
[179] Polden, *History of the County Court*, 307–8.   [180] County Courts Act 1846, s. 59.
[181] *Ibid.*, s 76; Polden, *History of the County Court*, 46.
[182] Polden, *History of the County Court*, 70.

Romilly Commission recommended it in cases above £20 but when provided in 1867 it was only for goods sold in the way of trade.[183] Though the Judicature Commission recommended its wider use (with safeguards in small debt cases), Nicol claimed that it could not be done[184] and it remained 'rudimentary and imperfect'.[185] The Law Society ensured it was discussed during the passage of the 1888 bill but it remained hedged about with protections for working men and small debtors even though Chalmers claimed that 80 per cent of all 'defences' were merely mounted to delay judgment.[186] The judges were adamant that such safeguards were needed and the Gorell Committee, while suggesting minor improvements, agreed they should remain.[187] As a result the High Court remained attractive for the suitor who was sure of an unopposed claim.

Another source of complaint was the rule on venue of actions, which had normally to be brought in the defendant's home court.[188] Though described in 1848 as 'a nuisance so perfectly intolerable that it is idle to suppose it can be suffered long to exist',[189] it was a very necessary protection for the poor from creditors operating on a regional or national scale. Creditors felt that the provision for leave (modified in 1856 and 1867) remained insufficient since most judges were unwilling to use their discretion.[190]

The High Court proved more sympathetic to plaintiffs in its interpretations of the provision and by 1914 there was criticism of the routine granting of leave to sue out of the jurisdiction.[191] It did not escape notice that registrars had a vested interest in issuing plaints.[192]

Venue was only one crucial matter on which the county court judge had great autonomy in his courtroom. He controlled the order in which cases were heard, largely dictated who might appear and what evidence might be presented. Lawyers alone had the right of audience and judges used more or less latitude both in accepting the 'attorney-advocates' who had been outlawed by statute,[193] and also

---

[183] *RC on County Courts, Report 1855*, 37; County Courts Act 1867, s 2. By County Courts Act 1856, s 28 in cases above £20 a defendant might be required to serve notice of intention to defend.

[184] *Second Report 1872*, 16; *SC on County Court Bills, Report 1878*, qq. 5075, 5083.

[185] M. D. Chalmers, 'The County Court System' (1887) 3 *LQR* 1–13 at 11. Differences between the two procedures are outlined in (1881–2) 28 *CCC* 33.

[186] M. D. Chalmers, 'The County Courts Consolidation Act 1888' (1889) 5 *LQR* 1–10 at 7–8.

[187] *DC on County Courts 1909*, 30.

[188] County Courts Act 1846, s 60, which also provided for service in the district where the cause of action arose, but only by leave.

[189] (1847–8) 7 *LR* 248.

[190] County Courts Act 1856, s 15, County Courts Act 1867, s 1; (1870–2) 22 *CCC* 245–7.

[191] (1911) 46 *LJ* 356 (Judge Rentoul in the City court; the journal agreed with him); DC on County Courts, *PP* 1919 [Cmd. 431], xiiia, 3.

[192] *HLSC on the Debtors Act Report 1894*, Judge Sir R. Harington at q. 683.

[193] See below, p. 1134.

solicitors' managing clerks, many of them admitted solicitors who were nevertheless outside the statutory right of audience.[194] Judges had discretion to admit others, those agents or accountants whom regular users often preferred to employ, and their attitudes to such men differed widely. There was no attempt at central direction: indeed when Eardley-Wilmot sought advice from the Lord Chancellor, he declined to offer it.[195] Few defendants could afford professional representation and judges, like their predecessors in the courts of requests, more often had to deal with the defendant in person or his wife. Though their effectiveness should not be underestimated, it required a degree of patience, common sense, and understanding not readily acquired at the bar for a judge to do justice to them, and it is no wonder that many judges, particularly in the industrial areas, leaned heavily on the plaintiffs' attorneys and agents to get through their list.[196]

There were similar variations in the admissibility of evidence. Except when they wished to make life difficult for certain classes of plaintiff, judges seem by and large to have been very liberal in what they would accept,[197] though it was rather indiscreet of the president of the registrars' association to announce publicly that 'no registrar who knew his business thought of insisting on the rules of evidence'.[198] The founding Act resolved one crucial question by expressly allowing the parties to give evidence, and when the judges were asked for their views five years later they were all but unanimous that, despite its drawbacks, it offered such important facilities for getting at the truth that to dispense with it would be unthinkable.[199] The principal drawback, of course, was the encouragement it gave for perjury, forecast by opponents and readily acknowledged to occur on a large scale.[200] Some judges openly denounced litigants in their courts. When French summed up one case in the phrase, 'Gentlemen, if you can believe either the plaintiff or the defendant, or any of the witnesses for either...you will find accordingly',[201] he was only saying openly what many of his brethren felt, though few were so extreme as Owen, who longed 'to keep the Court-house purified from the squalid herd who so often pollute it'.[202]

---

[194] An unsuccessful bill of 1897 attempted to give audience to both: *PP* 1897 (126), i. Bacon at Bloomsbury was one who vexed solicitors by his refusal to hear their clerks: (1903) 38 *LJ* 77.

[195] (1858–9) 3 *Sol. J.* 249; Polden, *History of the County Court*, 45–6.

[196] M. C. Finn, *The Character of Credit* (Cambridge, 2003, edn of 2007), 238–40, 252–8. In this, as other respects, the distinction between the courts of requests and county courts may have been less clear than lawyers would have cared to admit. Moreover, among the first generation of judges were many from the courts of requests (see below, p. 992).

[197] The reviewer of the 3rd edition of J. E. Davis, *Manual of the Law of Evidence on Trial of Actions in the County Court* agreed with the author on this: (1864) 18 *LM* 177.

[198] Thomas Marshall (1905) 119 *LT* 159–60.

[199] Polden, *History of the County Court*, 47.   [200] *Ibid.*, 99–100; above, pp. 609–10, 616–17.

[201] (1901–2) 38 *CCC* 569.

[202] 'The Re-organization of Provincial Justice' (1893) 9 *LQR* 321–30 at 329.

The case before French was unusual in having a jury. The 1846 Act gave the parties the option as of right only in cases above £20; in smaller cases the judge might grant one if he chose.[203] Jury trials were very scarce, though the statistics do not reveal how many were sought but denied; indeed some judges (J. W. Smith was notorious for this) not only refused them in discretionary cases but discouraged litigants from exercising their unqualified right by punitive scheduling and unconcealed disapproval.[204] They had some excuse for this attitude, since a single prolonged jury case in a country district could completely disrupt the day.[205] Even so, the rarity of jury trials suggests that few people wanted them; between 1884 and 1901 they ranged from 1001 to 1505, compared with between 576,394 and 732,094 tried by judge alone.[206] In 1903 the size of the jury was raised from five to eight but between 1902 to 1914 jury trials never reached four figures while non-juries never fell below 780,000, suggesting that the change had little effect.[207]

Thus the judge was, in most cases, the arbiter of fact as well as law. It was often an unenviable task, though when Edward Parry, the best-known judge of his time, described it as 'a life too often dull, wearisome and painful' he was deliberately seeking to counter the popular view that it regularly involved encounters with colourful characters in a lively atmosphere.[208] True the atmosphere could be lively, especially in urban courts where parties and witnesses observed none of the decorum of Westminster Hall,[209] but courtrooms were often inconvenient and crowded,[210] metropolitan courts were frequently overloaded with business and Owen was not the only one to 'turn away with loathing' from 'the motley herd of thieves and beggars'.[211]

Often without the aid of counsel, seldom well provided with books and invariably sitting alone, judges could hardly be expected to maintain a high standard of correct adjudication, though some were well up to High Court level and others acquired a shrewd judgment of human nature which was probably more useful than any book learning. They could indulge their idiosyncratic notions of justice rather freely, though restrained somewhat by local solicitors and the scrutiny

---

[203] Section 69.

[204] Polden, 'Judicial Independence and Executive Responsibilities, Part One', 29–30. The judge in Oldham never allowed them in discretionary cases: SC on County Court Bills Report 1878, S. Wall, q. 5411.

[205] For an example in Bath, see (1868) 3 LJ 314.

[206] Polden, History of the County Court, table 3.

[207] Ibid.; County Courts Act 1903 c. 42, s 4.

[208] 'The Insolvent Poor' (1898) 69 (os) Fortnightly Rev. 797–804, at 797.

[209] Polden, History of the County Court, 48.

[210] Ibid., 316–18.

[211] Owen, Re-organization of Provincial Justice, 326. According to (1892–3) 6 LG 369, the court at Churston Ferrers was held in the room of a wayside inn half a mile from any houses and was full of smelly Brixham fishermen with a propensity for drunkenness.

of the press.[212] J. W. Smith insisted that he should be dispensing 'justice, moral right and public policy';[213] others brazenly discriminated against tallymen and moneylenders, strained the law to aid the poor or were notoriously susceptible to sentimental pleadings.[214] Some were painstakingly slow while others rattled through their cases at extraordinary speed; in 1866 one got through just 55 a day, another 222.[215] Since a high degree of independence was one of the attractions of the job, they were seldom concerned to adopt a common approach and a judge who remained a long time in one district (as many did) could give local justice that distinctiveness which critics always claimed would be a serious concern if provincial courts replaced the Assizes.

Despite pressure from lawyers, the original Act contained no provisions for appeals and the superior court judges, especially in the Exchequer, thought to be particularly ill-disposed to the new courts, did their rather ineffectual best to fill the gap by freely granting prohibition and *certiorari*,[216] much to the resentment of some county court judges.[217] The extension of jurisdiction in 1850 included a provision for appeal by way of case stated, but where the amount in issue was not above £5 it required the judge's leave, and it was confined to mistakes of law.[218] Some judges were openly and notoriously hostile to appeals and discouraged would-be appellants or, if that failed, dressed up a finding of law as one of fact,[219] so their claims and those of their obituarists that they were rarely appealed from cannot be taken at face value.[220]

Dissatisfaction with the appeal provision led to the provision of an alternative in 1875 whereby a party might require the judge to take a note as the case progressed, the note forming the material for a possible appeal.[221] This led to a prolonged and at times farcical and undignified 'battle of the notes' between 'Commissioner' Kerr in the City court and the higher judiciary.[222] Other judges were less openly confrontational but more effective in sabotaging appeals. Moreover the provision was genuinely difficult to operate and Fisher's exasperation—'if I were to take a

[212] P. Polden, 'Judicial Selkirks: The County Court Judges and the Press, 1847–80', in C. W. Brooks and M. Lobban (eds), *Communities and Courts in Britain, 1150–1900* (1997), 245–62.

[213] (1876–7) 21 *Sol. J.* 333–4.

[214] Polden, 'Judicial Independence and Executive Responsibilities, Part One', 29–30.

[215] County Court Returns, *PP* 1867 (244), lvii

[216] (1850–1) 16 *LT* 348; (1857–8) 2 *Sol. J.* 757. Returns are in (1851) *HLSP* 1851 (25), i and (161), xi.

[217] A. J. Johnes, 'On the Union of Law and Equity in Relation to the County Courts' (1851–2) 15 *LR* 313–26.

[218] County Courts Extension Act 1850 (13 & 14 Vict. c. 51), s 14.

[219] Polden, 'Judicial Independence and Executive Responsibilities, Part One', 31–2.

[220] *Ibid.*, and see the contrasting views of Judge Motteram, J. K. Wright and Judge Bristowe in (1881) *TNAPSS* 184–206. According to Motteram, of 90 appeals, only 19 succeeded.

[221] County Courts Act 1875 c. 50, s 6; (1879) 14 *LJ* 691–2.

[222] Pitt-Lewis, *Commissioner Kerr*, 173–86.

note in every case I should sit until Doomsday'—is understandable.[223] Supervision exercised through the appeals process was not entirely ineffectual. *Evans* v. *Wills* was one instance where it compelled a significant change of practice concerning committals,[224] but even after the provisions had been re-drafted with the aid of Coleridge LCJ in 1888[225] they remained for some years 'uncertain and confused to the last degree'.[226] The limited scope of appeals was often cited in opposition to further extensions to the jurisdiction and the Gorell Report recommended allowing an appeal on questions of fact at least in cases above £50 if not above £20.[227] Like its other proposals, this was not carried out.

7. THE ENFORCEMENT OF JUDGMENTS

Plaintiffs had an even better success rate in the county courts than in the superior courts: 96 per cent according to a contemporary source in 1871, 98 per cent in small debt cases according to a recent study.[228] Most plaintiffs who regularly pursued debtors expected to get judgment as a matter of course; what concerned them more was the enforcement of those judgments. In the superior courts judgment was for the full amount, payable forthwith, and was exacted by the under-sheriff and his men, who were paid by results; in the county courts judges might order payment in instalments and collection was in the hands of the court's bailiffs.

The routine use of instalment orders was a regularly rehearsed grievance.[229] Some judges did not confine them to poor consumer debtors but made them against traders too, though this was not generally approved.[230] Some took into consideration—usually covertly but the bolder ones quite openly—not only the debtor's means but the person and conduct of the creditor, making tiny orders over long periods to discourage tallymen and Scotch drapers from plying their trade in the district.[231] Such plaintiffs were responsible for a large proportion of the caseload, credit drapers alone increasing from 9459 in 1831 to 69,347 in 1911. They organized themselves into trade associations and trade protection societies which sought to routinize debt collection through the courts by issuing bulk

---

[223] *Wray* v. *Clements* (1876–7) 62 *LT* 10. On differing note-taking practices see the evidence of judges to the Select Committee of 1878.

[224] (1875–6) 1 CPD 229; (1876) 61 *LT* 51.

[225] County Courts Act 1888, ss 120–1; (1888) 23 *LJ* 262–3. Appeal lay to the divisional court of the QBD.

[226] (1898–9) 106 *LT* 430.   [227] At p. 33.

[228] (1871) 6 *LJ* 657; Johnson, 'Small Debts and Economic Distress', 67.

[229] An early example is (1847–8) 10 *LT* 317.

[230] *SC on Tribunals of Commerce*, PP 1871 (409), xii, Judge Kettle qq. 1608–10.

[231] G. R. Rubin, 'The County Courts and the Tally Trade, 1846–1914', in Sugarman and Rubin, *Law, Economy and Society*, 321–48 at 328–30.

summonses and using experienced attorneys or agents. Some of these bodies were highly successful, but much depended upon the willingness of the judge to accept their evidence of the defendant's means and—in many cases—to adopt a broad view of the wife's agency to pledge her husband's credit. Many judges were resistant, whether from dislike of the credit system, humanitarian leanings, or a lawyerly view of due process and strict proof. However, even where the judge wished to be strictly impartial, the speed at which he often had to proceed, the flimsy evidence of means he had before him and, in some cases, a lack of familiarity with the local industries to enable him to gauge how realistic a proposed figure was, inevitably made fixing instalments a hit-and-miss affair.[232]

Creditors also complained that all payments of judgment debts had to be made through the court, adding appreciably to the costs and causing delays. The 'banking system' was recommended for abolition by the Judicature Commissioners but in the LCO it was considered a necessary check upon creditors' harassment of debtors and the only secure way of keeping accounts.[233] And one facility the county courts provided to creditors had no counterpart in the superior courts: the register of county court judgments created in 1852 and maintained at public expense. At some point it was very discreetly made more accessible by opening it to the proprietors of *Stubbs' Gazette*, who paid for the right to publish it.[234]

The chief complaint of judgment creditors, however, was that the means of enforcing the judgment were so defective. Initially each court had its own high bailiff, employing clerks and under-bailiffs. As with the registrars' clerks, this minimized claims on the public purse, though unlike the registrars, high bailiffs remained able to serve several courts. Before long the separate bailiff organization was perceived as an extravagance and although most judges favoured its retention, from 1866 on, the next vacancy was filled only in those courts where the level of business justified it. Elsewhere the high bailiff and registrar were amalgamated, and separate high bailiffs had dwindled to 51 by 1914.[235] Bailiffs were either full or part time and in the biggest courts were divided into process servers and warrant officers. Getting the right sort of man was difficult, for the pay (few earned more than £80 a year) was low and could hardly be raised without increasing the expense of enforcement. There were inevitably cases of corruption, even in Birmingham, which had a reputation for efficiency, and it was sensible to employ retired policemen and soldiers whose pension supplemented

---

[232] G. R. Rubin, 'Law, Poverty and Imprisonment for Debt, 1869–1914', in Sugarman and Rubin, *Law, Economy and Society*, 241–299, at 256–61. Finn, *Character of Credit*, 306–13.

[233] *Second Report 1872*, 14, 20; *RC on Legal Departments, Evidence*, Nicol at q. 7446.

[234] Polden, *History of the County Court*, 233–5.

[235] *Ibid.*; County Courts Act 1866 c. 14, s 11.

their earnings and lessened their vulnerability to temptation. However, they were often elderly and, so creditors claimed, lacked vigour and initiative.[236]

The main work of the warrant officers was in levying—or more often threatening to levy—execution against the debtors' goods. In 1858, almost 100,000 warrants were issued, and in 1871 they topped 180,000. Through the 1870s they mounted to 240,000 and after plateauing somewhat below that level, rose again around 1900, reaching an all-time peak of 352,308 in 1909. The theory was that execution was followed by seizure and sale of goods out of which the debt was paid, but in practice execution was almost always coercive. The number of sales fluctuated between 3000 and 6000 per annum until 1912, when it fell into the 2000s.[237] Creditors, though they used execution so freely, insisted that it was ineffective and that the bailiffs were lethargic and soft-hearted.[238] They tended to underestimate the bailiffs' difficulties. The law of interpleader was notoriously complicated and the task became steadily trickier as hire purchase, first noticed in the reports of cases in the 1870s, spread its temptations ever wider.[239] Moreover some judges felt that breaking up a poor man's home was worse than putting him in prison and the bailiffs no doubt took their cue from the judge.

Committals were the only real alternative for the creditor, since they showed no interest in pressing for attachment of earnings and the 'poor man's bankruptcy'—administration orders under section 122 of the Bankruptcy Act 1883—proved dismally ineffective.[240] As described, in 1845 Parliament had hastily backtracked from its abolition of imprisonment for judgment debts of small amounts and committal was still a threat to any debtor who could be said to have contracted the debt without having had the means to pay it. Moreover, where previously imprisonment had been punitive and had the effect of discharging the debt, it now became purely coercive, leaving the judgment still outstanding.[241] Creditors made liberal use of the threat: in five years from 1854 orders doubled to 30,000 and one-third of them were carried into effect.[242] Not surprisingly, this caused an outcry, prompted by a county court treasurer J. A. Busfield and pursued, inter alia,

---

[236] Polden, *History of the County Court*, 304–9.   [237] *Ibid.*, table 5.

[238] Rubin, *Law, Poverty and Imprisonment for Debt*, 276–8. Examples of criticisms are (1867–8) 44 *LT* 185 and (1880) 27 *CCC* 431–2 ('a chorus of complaint'). For an example of negligent execution see Stonor's judgment in *Drayton* v. *Dalton and wife* (1892) 93 *LT* 276.

[239] Polden, *History of the County Court*, 71. The leading hire purchase case of *Helby* v. *Matthews* [1895] AC 471, began in the county court and the Pickersgill Report noted that the efficacy of executions had been lessened by the growth of hire purchase and the practice of putting goods into the wife's name: *SC on Debtors, Second Report, PP* 1909 (239), vii.

[240] Polden, *History of the County Court*, 103–4. See XII, pp. 844–8.

[241] The maximum was 40 days. Rubin, *Law, Poverty and Imprisonment for Debt*, 244–6.

[242] Polden, *History of the County Court*, table 5.

by the Law Amendment Society,[243] whose patron Brougham highlighted another disquieting feature, the very marked variations between districts.[244] The judges were consulted and most came out in favour of retaining the power to commit; then, as later, they insisted that they were scrupulously careful in using it and that it was a necessary weapon against a minority of recalcitrant debtors.[245]

Immediate reform was fended off, but the extension of bankruptcy to non-traders in 1861 strengthened the impression that this was 'class law'[246] and the Liberals passed the Debtors Act 1869, which purported to abolish imprisonment for debt with only minor exceptions.[247] But one proved anything but minor. Section 5 preserved the right to commit a judgment debtor who defaulted, either having, or having had, the means to pay at some point after judgment. As in the courts of requests, the routine use of instalment orders could have an unfortunate effect. A judge might well take the view that where he had set instalments following an examination of means, any failure to meet them which could not be explained by unavoidable loss of employment or cuts in wages must be culpable. This showed little regard for the precarious realities of working-class life and demanded of the poor a provident and capable handling of their money that, as critics pointed out, was often lacking in their betters.[248]

The basis for committal orders was uncertain. They were often described as being for contempt of the court's order, but unlike contempt orders did not purge the contempt; yet they could no longer be, as formerly, simply coercive. Various rationales were advanced but none was very convincing.[249] In *Horsnail* v. *Bruce*[250] the Common Pleas confirmed that a debtor could be imprisoned only once for each default but an *obiter dictum* validated a common practice, an immediate committal order, suspended while instalment payments were kept up, and this was confirmed by the House of Lords in *Stonor* v. *Fowle*.[251] Whatever their basis, committals were extensively used and even the minority of judges and registrars who favoured abolition admitted that they alone ensured the credit which underpinned working-class lives, albeit the minority were anxious to see that access to credit curtailed.[252] A Commons committee was prevailed upon to

---

[243] *Ibid.*, 71–2.   [244] *PD* 1859 (s3) 155: 140.

[245] Answers of the Judges, *PP* 1867 (209), lvii.

[246] (1869) 4 *LJ* 149. Historians tend to agree: Rubin, *Law, Poverty and Imprisonment for Debt*, 275–6; P. Johnson, 'Class Law in Victorian England' (1993) 141 *P & P* 147–69.

[247] c. 62; Rubin, *Law, Poverty and Imprisonment for Debt*, 246–9.

[248] Rubin, *Law, Poverty and Imprisonment for Debt*, 256–61, and see e.g. the view of Judge Parry quoted on 248.

[249] *Ibid.*, 252–6.   [250] (1872–3) 8 CP 378.   [251] (1888) 13 AC 20.

[252] Judges' evidence to successive inquiries, in 1859, 1873, 1893, and 1908, shows little shift in attitudes.

recommend abolition in 1873[253] but a succession of bills promoted by Michael Bass was defeated and the issue went quiet again. Nevertheless, the identification of the county court judges with what many Victorians saw as a distasteful feature of contemporary life probably weakened the campaign to give these courts wider jurisdiction.

Barely ten years after the Debtors Act, the number of committal orders made passed the pre-1869 level and more than 5000 people a year were being put in prison, mostly under section 5. Twice more before 1914 an official inquiry was held: a Lords committee in 1893, then the Pickersgill Committee, encouraged by Loreburn with the hope that it would decisively recommend abolition.[254] The arguments had barely changed since the Walpole Report and neither had the positions of the antagonists. Credit traders were well organized and debtors had no counterpart, for trade unions were quite indifferent to this issue.[255] Opposition to repeal was supported by a clear majority of county court judges (the registrars were even more emphatic). Some judges worked on what Chalmers called 'the screw theory', that the debtor himself or a relation or friend would usually come forward to keep him out, or get him out, of gaol, while others prided themselves on adapting their methods to their district.[256] Deliberate strategies partly accounted for embarrassing discrepancies; at one time Nottingham was notorious for its severity, and in 1913 just five districts out of 54 accounted for more than one-third of all committals.[257] Most judges did not even see consistency among themselves as important and piqued themselves on their individual practice.

The Pickersgill Committee disappointed both Loreburn and its chairman, who could only persuade it to recommend that prison should not be available to the tallyman, but should be limited to cases of 'necessaries', the goods for which a wife might pledge her husband's credit.[258] That was objectionable to the Board of Trade[259] and nothing was done, though awareness of the strength of public opinion made judges more selective in sending men to gaol; while the number of

---

[253] SC on Imprisonment for Debts, PP 1873 (348), xv.

[254] Polden, History of the County Court, 103–5. Loreburn announced that he wanted to bring in a bill to repeal or amend the section in a circular to the judges seeking their views: 30 November 1906, LCO 2/211

[255] Rubin, Law, Poverty and Imprisonment for Debt, 281–5.

[256] Ibid, 249–51, 261–5.

[257] Ibid, 261–5; SC on Debtors Imprisonment, Second Report, PP 1909 (239), vii, viii.

[258] SC on Debtors' Imprisonment, ix. It also recommended, inter alia, reducing the maximum period to 21 days, suspending the original instalment order when a committal order was made and (save for non-manual workers) requiring the debtor to have some means in hand or falling due out of which payment might be made.

[259] NA PRO BT 37/22.

committal orders did not change very markedly, the number actually enforced halved from its peak of almost 11,000 in 1906. Parry and other humanitarians on and off the bench continued to inveigh against committals, but it would be half a century before the prison ceased to be a routine weapon in the pursuit of the judgment debtor.[260]

[260] Polden, *History of the County Court*, 105.

XIII
Justices of the Peace and their Courts

1. JUSTICES OF THE PEACE

The county bench in the 1820s was anglican, landed, and Tory.[1] The first was inevitable while the penal laws hampered the recruitment of dissenters; the second was partly the consequence of a property qualification,[2] and the third reflected the politics of the lesser gentry and a long Tory ascendancy. Over the following 100 years the first two characteristics became gradually less marked, while the persistence of the third became a matter of acute political controversy.

Changing the social composition and political complexion of the county magistracy was a slow and difficult process because, outside the Duchy of Lancaster (where the Crown's patronage was exercised by its Chancellor), appointments were generally made upon the recommendation of the lord-lieutenant in his capacity as *custos rotulorum*.[3] The *custos* usually took advice from chairmen of quarter sessions, clerks of the peace or senior magistrates, but although a few, like the Duke of Ancaster in Lincolnshire, merely transmitted their recommendations, most matched his successor Lord Brownlow in filtering them through their own criteria.[4] Even so, it was necessary to have regard to magistrates' susceptibilities. There was a notorious incident in 1830s Merioneth, whose justices 'went on strike' over the supposed degradation of their bench with an appointee who had kept a draper's shop and was a dissenter to boot, while 60 years later the Duke of

---

[1] For general descriptions see S. and B. Webb, *English Local Government vol. 1, The Parish and the County* (revised edn, 1963), 319–86; Sir W. T. C. Skyrme, *A History of the Justices of the Peace*, 2 vols (Chichester, 1991), ii, 21–37; D. Eastwood, *Governing Rural England* (Oxford, 1994), 76–82.

[2] The Justices Qualification Acts 1732 (7 Geo. II c. 18) and 1774 (4 Geo. III c. 47) prescribed an estate in freehold, copyhold, or customary fee worth £100 per annum or occupation of property rated at £100. It is estimated that in Hampshire in 1821 some 900 men qualified for the commission of the peace but only 238 were in it: D. Eastwood, *Government and Community in the English Provinces, 1700–1870* (Basingstoke, 1997), 95.

[3] The two offices were almost invariably combined, and the distinction between the powers exercisable through each was often disregarded: Skyrme, *History of Justices of the Peace*, ii, 21–2, 228–9. There were also *ex-officio* justices, including high officers of state and judges: see G. C. Alexander, *The Administration of Justice in Criminal Matters in England and Wales* (Cambridge 1915, re-issue of 1919), 7.

[4] Webb and Webb, *Parish and County*, 382; R. J. Olney, *Rural Society and County Government in Nineteenth Century Lincolnshire* (Lincoln, 1979), 11.

Devonshire was claimed to feel unable to put millers, maltsters, and suchlike into the commission against the opposition of the justices.[5]

Most of the territorial magnates subscribed to the Duke of Wellington's ideal of a justice: 'magistrates must be gentlemen of wealth, worth, consideration and education; that they should have been educated for the bar, if possible; and that, above all, they should be associated with, and be respected by the gentry of the county'.[6] It is no wonder that admission to the bench was 'possibly the most clear-cut evidence of social acceptance',[7] but it became increasingly difficult to impose such an exalted standard except at the cost of an inconveniently small bench.[8]

Filling the bench was all the more difficult because many men of the right social rank were reluctant either to accept the nomination or, if they did, to take out the *dedimus* which entitled them to perform its duties. Some counties were better served than others.[9] In the middle of the century it is reckoned that 80 per cent of those who took out their *dedimus* in Hampshire became active to some degree,[10] but nationwide it has been calculated that fewer than half were even formally qualified and barely a third were active.[11]

The most common expedient to supply the deficiency was to appoint anglican clergymen, and though this was unknown in a few counties (e.g. Derbyshire and Sussex), they made up one quarter of the bench in 1831. What is more, they tended to be among the most zealous and conscientious magistrates and so were even more prominent in county affairs than their numbers would suggest; for example, of six county magistrates acting in the vicinity of Wolverhampton in 1827, four were clergymen and in the same decade four of the eight petty sessions chairmen in Northamptonshire were clergymen.[12] The Whig administrations of the 1830s,

---

[5] Webb and Webb, *County and Parish*, 385–6; *PD* 1893 (s4) 12: 258 (Sir C. Dilke).

[6] C. H. E. Zangerl, 'The Social Composition of the County Magistracy in England and Wales, 1831–1887' (1971) 11 *JBS* 113–25, at 117, quoting a Lords' debate of 1838.

[7] J. V. Beckett, *The Aristocracy in England* (1989), 122.

[8] Lincolnshire, where Brownlow wanted men with land worth at least £2000 per annum within the county, had 111 magistrates in 1831, many fewer than comparable counties; moreover 52 of them were clergy: Olney, *Rural Society in Nineteenth Century Lincolnshire*, 99–100. The proverbially snobbish Dukes of Buckingham seem to have fared better: D. Cannadine, *The Decline and Fall of the British Aristocracy* (rev. edn, 1992), 154; Beckett, *Aristocracy in England*, 122–5.

[9] E. Moir, *The Justice of the Peace* (1969), 162.

[10] Above, p. 454.

[11] Eastwood, *Governing Rural England*, 77–8. An official return of 1831 (*PP* 1831–2 (498), xxv) gives 4496 in the English counties, but, like other such returns, has serious inaccuracies. However, it has been claimed that gentry 'flocked back to the bench' in alarm following the widespread social unrest of 1830: Beckett, *Aristocracy in England*, 391.

[12] R. Swift, 'The English Urban Magistracy and the Administration of Justice during the Early Nineteenth Century: Wolverhampton 1815–1860' (1992) 17 *Midland History* 75–92, 77; R. W. Shorthouse, 'Justices of the Peace in Northamptonshire, 1830–1845' (1975) 5 *Northamptonshire Past and Present* 129–40, 243–51, 244. The Northants figure is the more striking in that the county

and especially the Home Secretary, Lord John Russell, disapproved of clerical justices and rejected nominations unless the lord-lieutenant was able to make an exceptionally strong case.[13] However, because justices had become in practice irremovable save for a criminal conviction,[14] a strong clerical element persisted in several counties.[15] By then it had become possible to appoint dissenters, but there was still a prejudice against them in many counties and the Duke of Newcastle maintained his objections so insolently that he was dismissed from the lieutenancy.[16]

Though the Whigs gradually succeeded in laicizing the county bench they found it much more difficult to redress the political balance. Brougham was eager to challenge 'the present strict and absurd rule which really subjects the Government to its own deputies',[17] but although his successors' efforts provoked protests in Parliament from several lord-lieutenants,[18] there could be no wholesale change while the Whigs resisted a social broadening of the magistracy. In some industrializing districts even a resolutely conservative *custos* like Lord Talbot (Staffordshire 1812–49) could not hold the line, for the few resident gentry took flight just as social unrest, crime, labour disputes, and political agitation demanded a large and active magistracy.[19] Talbot and his like had set their faces resolutely against ironmasters and other industrialists, even as the Chancellors of the Duchy had kept out the cotton masters of south Lancashire.[20] Even Russell agreed that there were solid objections to factory owners upon the bench,[21] and

---

bench was 'one of the most socially exclusive in the country' (131). On the role of clerical magistrates generally see Moir, *Justice of the Peace*, 106–9, Skyrme, *History of the Justices of the Peace*, ii, 29–36; Eastwood, *Governing Rural England*, 79–82.

[13] D. Philips, 'The Black Country Magistracy 1835–1860: A Changing Elite and the Exercise of its Power' (1976) 3 *Midland History* 161–90, 172; Olney, *Rural Society in Nineteenth Century Lincolnshire*, 98.

[14] A policy perhaps initiated, and certainly maintained, by Eldon and adhered to by all Lord Chancellors: Webb and Webb, *Parish and County*, 380

[15] In Wiltshire in 1875 there were still 24: R. A. Lewis, 'County Government Since 1835', *VCH Wiltshire* (1957), v, 231–95, 232. See also the discussion 'Administration of Criminal Justice' in *TNAPSS* (1862), 254–69. For the 'squarsons' see T. Cockerill, 'The English Squarson (or the black squires of England)' (2008) 41 *Ecclesiology Today* 29–46.

[16] Moir, *Justice of the Peace*, 161–2; J. B. Atlay, *The Victorian Chancellors*, 2 vols (1908), i, 404. As late as 1873 there were no nonconformists on the Huntingdonshire bench (J. R. Vincent, *The Formation of the British Liberal Party* (1972 edn),166) and there were loud complaints from Wales on this score (e.g. T. P. Lewis, *PD* 1893 (s4) 12: 272–4).

[17] To Lord Grey, 30 December 1832, H.P., Lord Brougham, *Life and Times*, 3 vols (1871), iii, 258

[18] Atlay, *Victorian Chancellors*, i, 403–4

[19] Philips, 'Black Country Magistracy', 168–73; Swift, 'English Urban Magistracy', 77–85.

[20] Philips, Black Country Magistracy', 172–3. Lord Bexley as Chancellor insisted on no connexion with trade: D. Foster, 'Class and County Government in Early Nineteenth Century Lancashire' (1974) 9 *Northern History* 48–61 at 49.

[21] As Home Secretary Melbourne had been content to maintain the restriction: Philips, 'Black Country Magistracy', 169–71.

the fear that they would not be impartial in master–servant disputes proved well justified;[22] but there was no realistic alternative, and since they included many staunch Whig supporters there was every incentive for the Whigs to dilute the policy of exclusion.[23] Inevitably and with great rapidity the character of the bench in the potteries, the black country, and south Lancashire changed, the landed interest ceasing to dominate numerically, though they may have continued to feature most strongly in 'county' business as opposed to criminal justice.[24] The same trend can be detected in other industrial areas,[25] though in several places the bench had to be supplemented by stipendiaries.[26]

Outside the counties of mines and factories change was slower. It was long before farmers were accepted in Lincolnshire, and solicitors were still excluded in many counties, but by the mid-century new purchasers of landed estates, retired from business or professions, rather than their sons, became acceptable,[27] and in the next generation active businessmen and doctors were put into the commission. From 16 per cent of new appointments the proportion of 'middle class' ones grew to 30 per cent in the 1880s, though some counties the bench might still be described as 'patrician'.[28]

The borough magistracy had a rather different history. The power of appointing magistrates in towns with their own commission of the peace was exercised by the corporation with little effectual check by a Lord Chancellor without personal knowledge or reliable informants. In many boroughs the justices were either the corporation themselves or their relations and cronies and they exhibited a 'tendency…to develop into a small, self-perpetuating oligarchy'.[29] Numbers were small—Southampton's 11 was exceptional—and with no property qualification social standing was often modest. Though some had a good reputation (in Leeds

---

[22] The justification given by Earl Bathurst in 1813 for his policy of excluding industrialists from the Duchy bench: Webb and Webb, *Parish and County*, 383. See below, pp. 927–8.

[23] In Lancashire G. W. Wood as the Chancellor's chief adviser on appointments ensured that party affiliations would come to the fore: Foster, 'Class and County Government', 54–5.

[24] Foster, 'Class and County Government', 52; Swift, 'English Urban Magistracy', 83–4; Philips, 'Black Country Magistracy', 166–7; D. Hay, 'England 1562–1875, the Law and its Uses', in D. Hay and P. Craven (eds), *Masters, Servants and Magistrates in Britain and the Empire 1562–1955* (2004), 59–116, at 100.

[25] e.g. in the West Riding of Yorkshire: Cannadine, *Decline and Fall of the British Aristocracy*, 154.

[26] See below, pp. 1012–15.

[27] F. M. L. Thompson, *English Landed Society in the Nineteenth Century* (1963), 128.

[28] Cannadine, *Decline and Fall of the British Aristocracy*, 154–6. National patterns conceal significant local variations; in Cheshire, where the number of active magistrates doubled between 1846 and 1886, there emerged 'rule by a class of successful business people presided over by the great landowners': J. M. Lee, *Social Leaders and Public Persons* (Oxford, 1963), 22.

[29] Moir, *Justices of the Peace*, 170. Leeds was an example: D. Fraser *Power and Authority in the Victorian City* (Oxford, 1979), 51–2. There were also *ex officio* magistrates, notably the Recorder, the mayor, and his immediate predecessor for one year (unless a woman).

'their impartial conduct as justices were universally acknowledged'[30]), in general the Municipal Corporations Commissioners reported 'a distrust of the Municipal Magistracy, tainting with suspicion the local administration of justice, and often accompanied with contempt of the persons by whom the law is administered'.[31]

The Commissioners' solution, adopted by Melbourne's administration, was to make the Lord Chancellor responsible for appointments, though in practice the Home Secretary took the bigger part.[32] In some industrial towns there followed a very rapid change in the social composition of the magistracy, as in Wolverhampton, where within a few years of its charter two-thirds of the justices were ironmasters.[33] Change was much slower in older, slower growing towns such as Exeter, Lincoln, and York,[34] but by the mid-1880s most had become 'middle-class bailiwicks', with landed representation declining from around half in 1841 to around a quarter in 1885.[35]

These changes were the outcome of an intensely politicized process.[36] Both parties were unscrupulous in disregarding the personal qualities of candidates and the wishes of the inhabitants to boost their own numbers, injecting party animosity even in a town like Chester where the local leaders wished to moderate it.[37] After something of a lull, the appointment of magistrates again became a matter of sharp party controversy in the 1880s. Conservative peers had seen off Lord Albermarle's attempt to remove the property qualification in 1875[38] but the demand to introduce an elective element into county government was irresistible and Salisbury promoted the County Councils Act 1888 to limit the damage to Conservative interests. Removing the magistrates' local government function might have tended to de-politicize appointments to the bench, but they were still valued as political patronage, whose distribution in the counties was a very sore point with Liberals.

---

[30] Fraser, *Power and Authority in the Victorian City*, 53, quoting commissioners of 1833.

[31] *RC on Municipal Corporations Report*, *PP* 1835 (116), xxiii, 49. The verdicts of the Commissioners must be treated with caution in view of their political stance and objectives: G. B. A. M. Finlayson, 'The Politics of Municipal Reform' (1966) 81 *EHR* 673–92.

[32] 5 & 6 Will. IV c. 76, s 98, repeated in Municipal Corporations Act 1882 (c. 50), s 157(1); *PD* 1842 (s3) 63: 125–6 (Sir James Graham), 180 (Lord John Russell). This may have changed later, for Lord Chancellor Westbury outlined his policy as balancing Conservatives and Liberals with a slight preponderance to the latter and never (unless no others could be found) appointing clergymen, attorneys, vintners, brewers, or owners of public houses: to Moncrieff, (initials not given in source): 1862–3, T. A. Nash, *Life of Richard, Lord Westbury*, 2 vols (1888), ii, 49.

[33] Swift, 'English Urban Magistracy', 88.   [34] *Ibid.*, 90.

[35] Zangerl, *Social Composition of the County Magistracy*, 116.

[36] Vincent, *Formation of the Liberal Party*, 161–72.

[37] *PD* 1842 (s3) 63: 116–91 (W. Hutt's motion). The affiliations of all but a few magistrates were known, and Graham claimed to have reduced the Whig preponderance from 743:226 to 743:625.

[38] Zangerl, *Social Composition of the County Magistracy*, 121.

The drift of the landed classes into Conservatism would in any event have made it difficult to ensure an equal balance between the parties, but the seismic shift in British politics over home rule for Ireland dramatically aggravated the imbalance. Gladstone was left with just three lord-lieutenants out of 42[39] and the Conservatives ruthlessly exploited their advantage. Between 1886 and 1906 36 lieutenancies fell vacant and most were filled with youthful Conservative noblemen, threatening to perpetuate a Conservative monopoly of the bench for the foreseeable future, since it was now 'long established and inviolable usage' that a lord-lieutenant's recommendation would not be questioned unless it was objectionable on the face of it.[40] Not surprisingly, some Liberals were attracted to an elected or professionalized magistracy[41] and when they returned to power in 1892 they expected the Lord Chancellor to redress the balance, Dilke's resolution having urged that the lord-lieutenant's recommendation no longer be the basis for appointment.[42]

In the Duchy James Bryce tore up the Dufferin agreement and did just that,[43] but Herschell proved much too cautious for his party's liking.[44] Another ten years of Halsbury, which left Shropshire with just ten Liberal justices against 240 Conservatives, ensured that Loreburn would face even more exigent demands, especially from Wales, where party antagonisms were unpleasantly sharpened by religion and nationalism.[45]

Loreburn made a promising beginning by removing the property qualification,[46] but importunate MPs and whips found him even less pliant than Herschell in refusing to 'job the judicial bench'[47] by adopting 'the snobs and the hacks whom

---

[39] Earl Powis would hold the Shropshire lieutenancy from 1896 to 1951. J. M. Lee, 'Parliament and the Appointment of Magistrates' (1959–60) 13 *Parliamentary Affairs* 85–94 at 88.

[40] Sir Henry Hope to S. K. MacDonnell, 1892, quoted in R. F. V. Heuston, *Lives of the Lord Chancellors 1885–1940* (Oxford, 1964), 114.

[41] *Ibid.*, 219. In 1832 the Whigs had been forced to drop an ambitious scheme for a nationwide system of stipendiaries in charge of local police forces: Eastwood, *Government and Community in the English Provinces*, 143–4.

[42] *PD* 1893 (s4) 12: 258–99. Balfour acutely pinpointed the central flaw in the Liberal position: they objected to the consequences of a politicized appointments system but their proposed cure would make it more nakedly political (289–93). Asquith unrealistically offered to de-politicise it once parity had been achieved (284–9).

[43] The agreement of 1870 had transferred appointments to the lord-lieutenant. Bryce put a number of working men into borough commissions and in all added 257 names in two years: J. Shepherd, 'James Bryce and the Recruitment of Working-Class Magistrates in Lancashire, 1892–4' (1979) 52 *BIHR* 156–69.

[44] Heuston, *Lives of the Lord Chancellors 1885–1940*, 114–16.

[45] Cannadine, *Decline and Fall of the British Aristocracy*, 154–6.

[46] Justices of the Peace Act 1906 (c. 16). The same Act relaxed the restrictions on solicitors as magistrates.

[47] Loreburn to G. Whiteley, 10 December 1909, Heuston, *Lives of the Lord Chancellors 1885–1940*, 156.

[MPs] wish to reward'.[48] His principled stance led to private members' bills for justices to be elected by county and borough councils,[49] and despite Loreburn's protestation that he had 'appointed twice as many as have been appointed in any single year, the vast majority being Liberals', it was awkward that eight of the fifteen newcomers to that bluest of benches, Shropshire, were Conservatives.[50]

Loreburn's solution was a royal commission under a trusted ally, Lord James of Hereford, which readily adopted Loreburn's position of adapting the existing system rather than making radical change. Each county or borough would have an advisory committee chosen by the Lord Chancellor and this would be the source of nominations.[51] Loreburn set up the committees without even waiting for parliamentary approval, but they worked very differently from the way the Commission had hoped.[52] It envisaged a broader social mix among the magistracy and the lessening of party political influences, but though there was soon evidence of the former—'rapid and dramatic' in Wales[53]—party politics became entrenched in the new system. Selection committees, initially chosen for life,[54] had a predominantly political character and rather than a source of informed and dispassionate intelligence about likely candidates they became a forum for party bargaining, worsening the ill they were supposed to cure.[55]

Loreburn's defence of the number he had appointed was well justified, and since Halsbury had been no slouch, no fewer than 7267 were added to the bench between 1902 and 1908. By 1911 there were 23, 039 in all (including 2171 in Wales), though the number who were active is uncertain.[56] However, they were by then distributed more evenly and were probably numerically sufficient for the duties they had to perform.

---

[48] Loreburn to Ponsonby, 22 November 1906, *ibid.*, 155.

[49] Lee, 'Parliament and the Appointment of Magistrates', 90.

[50] Loreburn to Ponsonby, 22 November 1906; Whiteley to Loreburn, 11 December 1909; Heuston, *Lives of the Lord Chancellors 1885–1940*, 155–6. In all it was reckoned that he selected 3197 Liberals out of some 7000. However, as Frederic Harrison, a JP himself and a critic of the Conservative monopoly, acknowledged, it was difficult to find men of education and leisure who were not Conservatives: *Autobiographic Memoirs*, 2 vols (1911), ii, 244–50.

[51] *PP* 1910 (Cd. 5250), xxxvii. Loreburn had been impressed with existing local advisory committees.

[52] Skyrme, *History of the Justices of the Peace*, ii, 223–9.

[53] Cannadine, *Decline and Fall of the British Aristocracy*, 156.

[54] In 1927 Lord Chancellor Cave imposed a six-year term, but continued Loreburn's practice of making the lord-lieutenant chairman of county committees.

[55] Skyrme, *History of the Justices of the Peace*, ii, 227–30. The vexed question of the political parties' involvement in the selection of justices divided the next royal commission, set up in 1946: *ibid.*, 287–91.

[56] This represented a very big increase since 1862, when one calculation put their number at 9600: 'Administration of Criminal Justice', *TNAPSS*, 254–68, 262.

2. QUARTER SESSIONS

Time and Place

Each county[57] was obliged to hold a general sessions at least four times a year and these naturally became known as quarter sessions. Dates were fixed in 1830,[58] but by the Assizes and Quarter Sessions Act 1908 (c. 41) justices at a specially convened meeting might postpone or advance the date by up to 14 days. This was to facilitate a better synchronicity with the Assizes, and the same Act permitted the cancellation of a scheduled meeting if no business was known to the clerk of the peace.[59]

By the 1820s some counties were holding their quarter sessions at several different locations.[60] In Suffolk and Sussex this reflected recognized county subdivisions;[61] in Kent it arose out of irreconcilable intra-county quarrels,[62] while in Wiltshire, it was a conscious attempt to involve the whole county community.[63] Others counties preferred always to meet at one town (e.g. the West Riding of Yorkshire at Pontefract) but routinely adjourned to others.[64] Both practices had the drawback of a smaller attendance, making general policy decisions difficult, but this might reflect an understanding that major decisions would be made only at a particular central sessions.[65]

Roads were so poor in some places that spreading the sessions around the county was the only way to secure a good attendance. In theory the sessions were a grand affair, featuring a full turnout of the county's great men and high officers and a ceremonial display like a lesser Assize.[66] The reality was usually very different. In the winter sessions in particular, attendance was often small and the pomp and circumstance very muted.[67] But the turnout had begun to improve, perhaps

---

[57] As the Webbs remarked, '[i]t is not easy to determine exactly what constituted a county jurisdiction, nor how many counties there were', *Parish and County*, 310, and see 310–18. Yorkshire and Lincolnshire were each divided into three and there were anomalous areas such as the Isle of Ely. London became a county in 1889 and the Isle of Wight was given a distinct county sessions in 1890.

[58] Law Terms Act 1830 (11 Geo. IV & 1 Will. IV c. 70), s. 35. An attempt to bring the winter sessions forward a few days foundered on the opposition of the bar, who feared it would conflict with the law term: (1848) 7 (s2) *LM* 162.

[59] See above, pp. 827–8.   [60] Webb and Webb, *Parish and County*, 425–33.

[61] Formally recognized in the Local Government Act 1888 and the County of Sussex Act 1865 (c. 37), respectively.

[62] Webb and Webb, *Parish and County*, 427 n.2.

[63] *Ibid.*, 430.   [64] *Ibid.*, 426.

[65] *Ibid.*, 430–3; W. R. Ward, 'County Government 1660–1835', *VCH Wiltshire*, v, (1957) 170–94 at 177–8.

[66] Webb and Webb, *Parish and County*, 421–2.

[67] Five or six was not unusual (Skyrme, *History of the Justices of the Peace*, ii, 42) but Cottu's impression was 12 to 15 (C. Cottu, *On the Administration of Criminal Justice in England* (trans. of 1822), 26) and later on numbers were usually considerably larger: 25 to 35 in Wiltshire and around

partly because of the growing fiscal demands issuing to landowners from quarter sessions, and on special occasions, as when a county officer was to be elected and political passions were aroused, a veritable swarm of justices might descend.[68] The justices who did come were having to stay for longer to get through their business, and more often had to adjourn or hold supplementary meetings; even monthly meetings had become not uncommon.[69]

Business

Quarter sessions undertook a vast range of miscellaneous business, embracing both criminal trials and appeals and 'administrative' business. Longer and more frequent sittings were the consequence of a formidable increase in both.[70] The criminal work is more easily measured, at least for illustrative purposes. In Warwickshire convictions for larceny, theft or fraud, which between 1775 and 1788 had averaged only eight a year, had risen to 245.7 between 1823 and 1832, and the number of prisoners in the county gaol rose from 41 in 1775 to 351 in 1835. Warwickshire saw rapid population growth and industrialization, but even in more rural counties criminal business grew alarmingly; committals in Oxfordshire rose from 38 in 1805 to 271 in 1835.[71]

Administrative business admits of no straightforward measure. Some burdens were reduced after Waterloo, militia and volunteers ceasing to be a concern, and though fear of disorder remained potent, the Regency preoccupation with internal security faded.[72] The archaic powers to regulate aspects of economic life to which some justices had clung tenaciously in defiance of the teaching of Scottish economists had also to be relinquished; the last, the Assize of bread, was finally abandoned in 1836.[73]

In other respects, however, the justices at sessions became ever busier as the nearest approach to a county government, sometimes of their own initiative, sometimes under pressure from above. After Peel's Act of 1823 the building and

30 in Shropshire (Lewis, 'County Government 1835–1888', 232–3; G. C. Baugh, 'County Government 1834–89', *VCH Shropshire* (1982), iii, 135–66 at 137.

[68] Skyrme, *History of the Justices of the Peace*, ii, 20.

[69] Eastwood, *Governing Rural England*, 72.

[70] There is a summary in Skyrme, *History of the Justices of the Peace*, ii, 55–7. Many counties built new accommodation: C. W. Chalklin, *English Counties and Public Buildings, 1650–1830* (1998), 133–48, but see C. Graham, *Ordering Law* (Aldershot, 2003), 132 n.59.

[71] Moir, *Justices of the Peace*, 109; Eastwood, *Governing Rural England*, table 8.1, 197. According to V. A. C. Gatrell, 'The Decline of Theft and Violence in Victorian and Edwardian England', in Gatrell, C. Lenman and G. Parker (eds), *Crime and the Law: The Social History of Crime in Western Europe Since 1500* (1980), 238–371, committals in England and Wales rose sevenfold between 1805 and 1842.

[72] Eastwood, *Governing Rural England*, 46–7.   [73] Ibid., 45–6.

running of prisons consumed time and money,[74] and though statutory provision of lunatic asylums was permissive only, it became a practical necessity in populous counties.[75] Oversight of repair and maintenance of highways and bridges naturally became more onerous with increasing traffic and commerce,[76] and above all there was the poor law. Not only were quarter sessions busy with appeals from parish officers and with an endless stream of settlement cases[77] but justices at sessions were drawn inexorably into devising policies for the whole county; the widely imitated 'Speenhamland' scheme of wage supplements was controversial and costly.[78] In other ways too this 'rural House of Lords'[79] acted as a legislative body, attempting, not always effectually, to suppress or regulate fairs, begging, beer houses, and other features of rural life magistrates considered undesirable.[80]

Although assaults on their pleasures and pastimes made the justices unpopular with the poor, it was the cost of local government which imperilled the continuation of the system. The county rate and the poor rate rose alarmingly,[81] and as a result, besides radicals who condemned government by justices for its unrepresentative and class-based character and centralizing utilitarians who belittled it for inefficiency and lack of uniformity,[82] its critics included conservatives who cared for neither of these things but were indignant at the sheer expense.[83] Yet despite the temperate criticisms of several inquiries into county rates[84] and Joseph Hume's bills to establish county finance boards,[85] county quarter sessions survived the threatening decade of Whig reforms with their powers and duties largely intact, save one great exception: the revolution in poor relief practically ended the role of quarter sessions.[86]

---

[74] Gaols Act 1823 (4 Geo. IV c. 64). Above, pp. 459–60.

[75] Above, pp. 460–1. County Asylums Acts 1808 (48 Geo. III c. 96); 1826 (9 Geo. IV c. 40); Skyrme, *History of the Justices of the Peace*, ii, 196–7.

[76] Eastwood, *Governing Rural England*, 33–4.

[77] Skyrme, *History of the Justices of the Peace*, ii, 76. They filled an entire volume of later editions of the Rev. Richard Burn's *Justice of the Peace and Parish Officer*, the justices' bible from 1755 until superseded by Samuel Stone's *Justices' Manual* and G. C. Oke's *Magisterialist's Formulary*.

[78] See XIII, Pt 2, Ch. II. Much of Eastwood, *Governing Rural England*, deals with this subject.

[79] Moir, *Justices of the Peace*, Ch. 6. The Webbs called it an 'inchoate provincial legislature'.

[80] B. Osborne, *Justices of the Peace 1361–1848* (Shaftesbury, 1960), 210–12; Skyrme, *History of the Justices of the Peace*, ii, 59–62.

[81] County expenditure in Cumberland grew from £1600 in 1792 to £13,000 in 1830; in the West Riding between 1786 and 1826 it rose from £7279 to £47,787; in Warwickshire from 1782 to 1837 from £1803 to £20,393: Moir, *Justices of the Peace*, 115–16.

[82] Eastwood, *Governing Rural England*, 48.   [83] Webb and Webb, *Parish and County*, 595–6.

[84] Commons select committees (*PP* 1825 (461), vi and *PP* 1834 (532), xiv); a Lords' select committee (*PP* 1834 (206), xiv) and a royal commission (*PP* 1836 (58), xxvii).

[85] Eastwood, *Governing Rural England*, 74.

[86] According to John Cleave (Hertfordshire Clerk of the Peace) settlement cases had almost disappeared by 1850: *SC on Fees in Courts of Law and Equity Second Report*, *PP* 1850 (711), xiii, qq. 3712–13.

In several other areas, prisons and asylums are instances where central supervision and regulation made inroads into their virtual autonomy.[87] However, the loss of independence in these areas can be overstated, and how much remained is as notable as how much was lost.[88] The county was not superseded as the basis for local government by the poor law union districts and when counties were offered the opportunity for a police force in 1839 it was on the quarter sessions that the decision rested.[89] Even when counties were obliged to have a police force in 1856 quarter sessions shared operational responsibility in an often cosy but occasionally uneasy relationship with the chief constable.[90]

There were important new or enhanced responsibilities in other areas, such as arranging assessments for county rates and a steady stream of appeals from the outcomes.[91] When controls on liquor licensing were reimposed it was a standing committee of quarter sessions which had to confirm new licences.[92] As a residual local authority it was the recipient of a great miscellany of duties, from handling outbreaks of foot and mouth disease in cattle to appointing inspectors of weights and measures and making rules to govern the use of bicycles and traction engines on the highway.[93]

What had greatly changed was that quarter sessions and the county had ceased to be the basic elements of local government for rural England (and England was still predominantly rural), becoming just one of a bewildering range of authorities, old and new; some with a single function, others with several; some elected, others nominated; and with their boundaries overlapping and confusing.[94] The place of quarter sessions in this patchwork was threatened by its exclusive,

---

[87] Above, pp. 459–61. Skyrme, *History of the Justices of the Peace*, ii, 186–96. Further Acts of 1865 and 1877 practically ended the justices' involvement in lunacy.

[88] In contrast to the Webbs, who entitled a section on the 1830s 'the stripping of the oligarchy' (*Parish and County*, 602–5) and Lewis (['they] yielded one field of activity after another to the surveillance of the government departments, and derived a growing proportion of their revenue from the Treasury', *County Government Since 1835*, 231–2), Moir (*Justices of the Peace*, 130–43), emphasizes continuity, and Mill, Chadwick, and other Benthamites were frustrated at the persistence of magisterial government.

[89] This represented a signal defeat for Chadwick, who had hoped to make the report of the rural police commission a vehicle for a Benthamite scheme for local courts which would supersede the magistrates: A. Brundage, 'Ministers, Magistrates, and Reformers: The Genesis of the Rural Constabulary Act of 1839' (1986) 5 *Parl. Hist.* 55–64.

[90] See XIII, Pt 1, pp. 36–40.

[91] County Rate Act (15 & 16 Vict. c. 81). Appeals from poor rate assessment committees also came to quarter sessions under the Union Assessment Committee Act 1862 (c. 103). Skyrme, *History of Justices of the Peace*, ii, 209–10; F. W. Maitland, *Justice and Police* (1885), 86.

[92] Skyrme, *History of the Justices of the Peace*, ii, 202.

[93] Maitland, *Justice and Police*, 86–8.

[94] See the table compiled by N. Chester and reproduced in K. T. Hoppen, *The Mid-Victorian Generation* (Oxford, 1998), 107.

undemocratic character, which would gradually come to override considerations of economy and efficiency.

The position in the boroughs was quite different.[95] In some the quarter sessions had become the most powerful element in town government, while in places like High Wycombe it was little more than decorative.[96] Either way, the Municipal Corporations Commissioners saw no place for it in the reformed scheme of town government, and with a few exceptions of a 'quasi-judicial' character, notably licensing, borough quarter sessions were thereafter confined to criminal jurisdiction.[97] More than 50 years later the same fate befell the county justices, though they too retained a role in liquor licensing, along with a miscellany of duties in relation to highways, prisons, and lunatics and a not inconsiderable appellate jurisdiction in bastardy orders, rating appeals, poor law matters, and others.[98]

The criminal business of quarter sessions had consisted chiefly of petty larcenies and misdemeanours, since it was understood that capital offences and those likely to involve a difficult question of law should be reserved for the Assizes.[99] That still enabled the justices to prescribe brutal corporal punishments and transportation, the latter so convenient a means of removing troublesome petty criminals and saving expenditure on the rates, that some benches were tempted to use it rather freely.[100] When crime underwent a big surge from the 1790s[101] quarter sessions trials did not at first rise in proportion, because the proliferation of crimes made capital by statute took many out of their agreed limits, while an increasing number were being dealt with by the justices 'out of session'.[102] However, beginning with Peel's programme of criminal law reform, capital offences were

---

[95] Most of the more than 200 boroughs had the right to hold quarter sessions, but the powers of the sessions varied widely: 'the intricacy of all this, and the difficulty of spelling it out from the Acts of Parliament and other authorities relating to the matter, is a good instance of some of the causes which make our law obscure and repulsive': J. F. Stephen, *A History of the Criminal Law of England*, 3 vols (1883), i, 121. By 1885 they had been reduced to 105: Moir, *Justices of the Peace*, 168–9; Maitland, *Justice and Police*, 95.

[96] Moir, *Justices of the Peace*, 171–2.   [97] *Ibid.*, 179.

[98] *Halsbury's Laws of England*, ix (1909), 'Courts', paras 172–3. In London the quinquennial rating assessment generated a great number of appeals: F. W. Ashley, *My Sixty Years in the Law* (1936), 70–1.

[99] Stephen, *History of the Criminal Law of England*, i, 115, citing Chitty (1826). The removal of the graver offences made the 'quorum' provision in the commission of the peace, aimed at ensuring some legal expertise on the bench, a meaningless ritual which was eventually discarded: J. H. Baker, 'Criminal Courts and Procedure at Common Law 1550–1800', in J. S. Cockburn (ed.), *Crime in England 1550–1800* (1977), 15–48.

[100] Skyrme, *History of Justices of the Peace*, ii, 77–8.

[101] D. J. Bentley, *English Criminal Justice in the Nineteenth Century* (1998), 16–17.

[102] Poaching was one instance: P. B. Munsche, *Gentlemen and Poachers* (Cambridge, 1981), 84. Even so, 57% of jury trials in the first decade of the nineteenth century were at quarter sessions: D. Hay, 'Dread of the Crown Office: The English Magistracy and the King's Bench', in N. Landau (ed.), *Law, Crime and English Society 1660–1830* (Cambridge, 2002), 19–45, at 20.

greatly reduced and when in 1842 a formal statutory limitation was placed on quarter sessions' capacity to try the most serious offences it may in practice have slightly enlarged rather than reduced its operations.[103]

Nevertheless, from the 1840s the relentless enlargement of petty sessions' jurisdiction, coupled with the beginnings of a reduction in crime levels,[104] ensured that quarter sessions functioned as much as an appeal court as one of original jurisdiction, larceny still making up 70–80 per cent of the latter.[105] From the 1870s there were persistent suggestions that more of the serious offences should be tried at sessions instead of Assize, but the only major devolution was simple burglary in 1896.[106] Most judges were steadfastly opposed to such moves and had a plausible objection in the uncomfortable fact that most quarter sessions chairmen were laymen whose ability to conduct major criminal trials was questionable.[107] Nevertheless, by 1900 about three-quarters of jury trials were held at quarter sessions (twice as many at county sessions as in the boroughs).[108] Even so, in some rural counties the encroachments of petty sessions and relatively low levels of acquisitive crime robbed the quarter sessions of much of their business.[109]

Organization

As Eastwood remarks, the quarter sessions was an institution which proved capable of remarkable flexibility in adapting itself to changing circumstances.[110] Its essential peculiarity as an agency of government remained, duties being enforced by a quasi-criminal procedure initiated by a presentment, but some participants in the process, such as the hundred jury, had already faded into history and others, such as the grand jury and the high constable, were fast losing their importance.[111] Presentments now emanated mostly from the justices themselves and the

---

[103] Quarter Sessions Act 1842 (5 & 6 Vict. c. 38). For criminal business generally see XIII. Pt 1, pp. 115–121.

[104] Gatrell, 'Decline of Theft and Violence', 240–1 and table III; Bentley, *English Criminal Justice in the Nineteenth Century*,16.

[105] Skyrme, *History of the Justices of the Peace*, ii, 175.

[106] Burglary Act (c. 57); Alexander, *Administration of Justice in Criminal Matters*, 74. It was passed with little debate though L.E.H. Pickersgill objected that quarter sessions tended to severer sentencing: *PD* 1896 (s4) 44: 458–9. Bramwell had tried to pass a bill for this and forgery in 1882: (1881–2) 26 *Sol. J.* 488. On later initiatives see R. Abel-Smith and R. Stevens, *Lawyers and the Courts* (1967), 89.

[107] Simple burglaries were the utmost they would concede in 1878.

[108] Alexander, *Administration of Justice in Criminal Matters*, 75–6. They included bigamy, perjury, forgery, and sexual offences under the Criminal Law Amendment Act 1885.

[109] [J. A. Foote], *Pie-Powder* (1911), 64–7.   [110] Eastwood, *Governing Rural* England', 74.

[111] Webb and Webb, *Parish and County*, 446–79; Eastwood, *Governing Rural England*', 85–8. Many of the presentment obligations of high and petty constables were abolished by the Presentments by Constables Act 1827 (7 & 8 Geo. IV c. 38).

administrative side of quarter sessions was becoming less of a public and more of
a bureaucratic affair.

From 1819 sessions were explicitly allowed to operate as two courts where the
business was likely to exceed three days.[112] Criminal business, which had to be
held in public, was usually taken first and magistrates often dealt with the rest
in private session, sometimes over dinner.[113] The private sessions were probably
more for convenience than concealment, but it became more difficult to defend
the exclusion of press and public and by the mid-1830s more than half of the
counties had ceased trying, the others coming into line soon afterwards.[114]

As business grew, counties sought to improve the ways in which it was handled.
Delegating the examination of a bill or a set of accounts to one or more justices
with local knowledge or a special interest was superseded by formal committees,
and by 1835 most had a committee for prisons and one for finance.[115] New permanent officials, the treasurer and the surveyor, made their appearance,[116] and in
many counties a small inner group of regular attenders became established: this
was 'the efficient secret of the Quarter Sessions…orchestrated by an energetic
and authoritative chairman and serviced by an efficient clerk of the peace'.[117]

The key figures in determining how quarter sessions conducted its affairs were
the chairman and the clerk of the peace. The former was practically unrecog-
nized by statute until the twentieth century, and even passing references in the
Poor Prisoners' Defence Act 1903 and the Criminal Appeals Act 1907 at most only
implied the existence of a permanent chairman.[118] Yet by the 1820s many counties
elected such a chairman, though Devon at least maintained the older custom of
choosing afresh for every session. Others, like Surrey, had a different chairman
for each place where the sessions were held, and Surrey was also among those
with different chairmen for administrative and criminal business,[119] the latter
having become so burdensome that in 1832 the county made an unsuccessful

[112] Quarter Sessions Act 1819 (59 Geo. III c. 28). The custom was already widespread. Wiltshire
instituted a second court in 1821 (Lewis, 'County Government after 1835', 233), whilst in
Northamptonshire one court heard appeals while the other tried cases: Shorthouse, 'Justices in
Northamptonshire', 243.

[113] Webb and Webb, *Parish and County*, 437–9; Eastwood, *Governing Rural England*, 70–2.

[114] Eastwood, *Governing Rural England*, 71.

[115] Webb and Webb, *Parish and County*, 526–32; Eastwood, *Governing Rural England*, 72–3.
Wiltshire had half-a-dozen permanent committees, Shropshire four: Lewis, 'County Government
Since 1835', 233; Baugh, 'County Government 1834–1889', 144.

[116] Webb and Webb, *Parish and County*, 502–25.

[117] Eastwood, *Governing Rural England*, 55.

[118] 'The Powers and Duties of a Chairman of Quarter Sessions' (1910) 74 *JP* 110–11.

[119] Webb and Webb, *Parish and County*, 433–7; Eastwood, *Governing Rural England*, 55–61. In
1842 Gloucestershire elected one chairman of the 'Appellate and Judicial Court' and another for
'Financial and all General County Business': Skyrme, *History of the Justices of the Peace*, ii, 46.

attempt to emulate Salford in having a salaried chairman.[120] Middlesex was even more hard pressed and in 1844 was granted a salaried, legally qualified, assistant judge to preside over trials[121] but this was unique. There was a tendency to choose a prominent social figure and counties were encouraged to invite judges of various sorts as the role became more judicial and less administrative.[122] A long-serving and hard-working chairman like Sir Christopher Willoughby in Oxfordshire could do much to invigorate and reshape local government, but probably more typical of the nineteenth century was his successor W. H. Ashurst (1822–46), who favoured a more collective style of leadership and led the way into an era of 'cabinet-style government'.[123]

Until 1835 there was a variety of arrangements in the boroughs. In some a Recorder (not always legally qualified) presided over trials; in others the justices chose a temporary chairman and in others still the mayor and alderman held court.[124] The Municipal Corporations Act changed all that, imposing a uniform arrangement whereby the Recorder (now always a salaried barrister) became the sole judge; lay justices might sit with him and be consulted at his discretion, but responsibility was his alone.[125] In the counties the chairman was much less absolute, at least in theory. He was merely *primus inter pares*, 'only the mouthpiece of the majority of justices present', and might be overruled even if he (and the clerk) alone possessed and applied professional legal learning.[126] In practice such happenings were rare and probably became rarer with the increasing complexity of the criminal trial.[127]

This, and in particular the increasing tendency of prisoners to be legally represented,[128] no doubt exposed the shortcomings of many a chairman, though

---

[120] Webb and Webb, *Parish and County*, 436–7.

[121] Criminal Justice (Middlesex) Act 1844 (7 & 8 Vict. c. 71), s 8. The county sessions were to be held twice a month. In the metropolitan government reorganization of 1888 the judge was transferred to the new County of London sessions: Bentley, *English Criminal Justice in the Nineteenth Century*, 58. The new county also acquired parts of other neighbouring counties, including Surrey, and the London sessions were held at two locations; those for north London (much the busier) at Clerkenwell and those for south London at Newington Causeway.

[122] Skyrme, *History of Justices of the Peace*, ii, 46. In the 1920s some Surrey justices still felt that a peer or big landowner was desirable: C. Whiteley, *Brief Life* (1942), 264.

[123] Eastwood, *Governing Rural England*, 56.

[124] Bentley, *English Criminal Justice in the Nineteenth Century*, 57.

[125] Ibid., 69–70; Alexander, *Administration of Justice in Criminal Matters*, 79–80.

[126] 'Powers and Duties of a Chairman of Quarter Sessions', 110. This applied even to the assistant judge of Middlesex quarter sessions: *R v. Justices of Middlesex* (1877–8) 2 QBD, 516. Sometimes the judge (Sir Peter Edlin) overbore opposition (Ashley, *My Sixty Years in the Law*, 69–70), but now and then he was forced to yield: E. D. Purcell, *Forty Years at the Criminal Bar* (1916), 189–90.

[127] In 1900 only 15 of 65 chairmen possessed a legal qualification: J. De Grey, 'Is it Expedient to Have Paid Chairmen of Quarter Sessions?' (1900–01) 26 (s5) *LM & R* 385–95.

[128] XIII, Pt 1, pp. 71–83.

harshness in sentencing attracted more criticism.[129] Published recollections are mostly of the metropolitan area courts, which are hardly representative.[130] Sir William Hardman's 'brutal and ferocious' sentencing was widely condemned[131] and similar criticisms were levelled at Sir Peter Edlin and several of his deputies across the river at Clerkenwell Green.[132]

Administrative and clerical support for county quarter sessions was supplied principally by the clerk of the peace.[133] He was appointed by the *custos rotulorum* and held office during good behaviour, though between 1864 and 1893 he might be dismissed by the quarter sessions for misconduct outside his office.[134] The Webbs painted an unflattering picture of the clerks. Most were proteges of the *custos* and usually employed a deputy to do the work. Both positions were coveted by solicitors, and tended to become attached to particular firms.[135] The clerk or his deputy was often careless in his primary task of record-keeping and was concerned chiefly with extorting fees, which were practically unregulated until 1817.[136] The justices might be indifferent to exactions from suitors but as the county rate increased they became less complaisant about attempts to charge the county for the clerk's services, sometimes resulting in recurrent friction and leading to a more systematic scrutiny of accounts.[137]

---

[129] e.g. Sir C. Biron, *Without Prejudice* (1936), 93. This is not borne out by the statistical evidence: See XIII, Pt 1, pp. 124–7.

[130] Exceptions are [Foote], *Pie-Powder*, 47–75 and Sir R. Bosanquet, *The Oxford Circuit* (1951). W. J. Disturnal was emphatic against further extensions because of the varying capacity of chairmen: *RC on Delays in the KB Division Evidence II: PP* 1913 [Cd. 6762], xxx, q.925.

[131] Ashley, *My Sixty Years in the Law*, 72, echoed in other reminiscences. Hardman was a barrister and was annoyed when prominent counsel came down to 'bully' the magistrates: *The Hardman Papers* (1930), 21–2. He was chairman of the Surrey sessions 1856–90 and also Recorder of Kingston-upon-Thames from 1875. Contemporaries found it hard to reconcile the savage judge with the man of letters shown in *A Mid-Victorian Pepys: The Letters and Correspondence of Sir William Hardman*, ed. S. M. Ellis (1923, and 2nd series 1925).

[132] See e.g. Purcell, *Forty Years at the Criminal Bar*, 172–99, 315–26; Ashley, *My Sixty Years in the Law*, 68–72. See also B. C. Robinson, *Bench and Bar* (2nd edn, 1889), 258–63 on an earlier deputy, Joseph Payne.

[133] There is a list of clerks and an account of the evolution of the office in Sir E. Stephens, *The Clerks of the Counties, 1360–1960* (1961).

[134] Skyrme, *History of the Justices of the Peace*, ii, 182. The Clerks of the Peace Removal Act 1864 (c. 65) seems to have been the offspring of Lord Romsey: *PD* 1864 (s3) 173: 708. Repealed by the Statute Law Revision (No. 2) Act 1893 (c. 54), it remained applicable to clerks in office before the Local Government Act 1888. The tenure was confirmed in *Lord Leconfield* v. *Thornley* [1926] AC 10.

[135] Webb and Webb, *Parish and County*, 502–5.

[136] Justices of the Peace Fees Act 1817 (57 Geo. III c. 91). In 1844 Sir James Graham introduced a bill (not proceeded with) to substitute salaries for fees. One MP (B. E. Scott) attacked the 'gross system of extortion' and another (Gally Knight) said magistrates sometimes felt constrained to let offenders off because they had already been mulcted so heavily in fees: *PD* 1844 (s3) 76: 1940–4.

[137] Webb and Webb, *Parish and County*, 505–7.

More recent scholarship substantially modifies this unflattering view, at least for the first half of the nineteenth century. Deputies were not so common,[138] clerks were mostly solicitors,[139] and if some clerks held several county offices, this gave them a tighter grip on the overall administration, which was necessary for the 'chief executive officer' they had in many cases become.[140] There were more records to be kept, more returns to be made, and the clerk's duties look so formidable that it is not surprising that some became full-time officials.[141]

The move from fees to salaries was very gradual. An early initiative in the West Riding of Yorkshire was abandoned after doubts about its legality, but it was introduced in Hertfordshire and elsewhere on the strength of a recommendation of the County Rate Committee in 1834, receiving a belated statutory sanction in 1851.[142] Even then vested interests were so well protected that Sir Richard Wyatt, the clerk of the peace for Surrey, kept his fees until his death in 1904.[143]

Wyatt was one of many who enjoyed a long tenure, though few could match H. P. Markham's 58 years (1846–1904) in Northamptonshire.[144] The combination of long experience in office, sometimes in several posts, practical irremovability, and close acquaintance with criminal procedure made some clerks arrogant and high-handed, a tendency strengthened when they were made secretaries to the advisory committees on the appointment of justices.[145] However, their position was drastically altered by the Local Government Act 1888. The power of appointment was transferred to a standing joint committee of the county council and quarter sessions, with the clerk's salary fixed by the latter, and he was now to act also as secretary to the new council.[146] This made the county clerk's position closer

---

[138] See the list in Stephens, *Clerks of the Counties.*

[139] H. C. Johnson, 'The Origin and Office of Clerk of the Peace', in Stephens, *Clerks of the Counties*, 29–47, notes dynasties such as that of Fooks in Dorset (1825–1925) and Hodgson in Cumberland (1809–1942).

[140] 'The clerk of the peace, who at the beginning of this period [in 1660] was primarily a country lawyer, and might serve by deputy, had by the end gone far in metamorphosis into a county bureaucrat': Ward, 'County Government 1660–1835', 174.

[141] Eastwood, *Governing Rural England* , 61–6; Skyrme, *History of the Justices of the Peace*, ii, 182–3.

[142] Eastwood, *Governing Rural England*, 66–7; Skyrme, *History of the Justices of the Peace*, ii, 182–3. The concomitant increase in their fees (in Northants from £225 to £700 in the 1830s and 1840s: Shorthouse, *Justices in Northamptonshire*, 249) made whole time work feasible for some. When the Wiltshire clerk was first salaried, in 1864, it was at £1050: Lewis, 'County Government Since 1835', 233.

[143] Webb and Webb, *Parish and County*, 507 n.3. Wyatt was in charge of the south London sessions after the re-organization of 1888, but did none of the duties there. His north London counterpart Sir Richard Nicholson, with a salary of £3000 per annum, acted wholly by deputy: Purcell, *Forty Years at the Criminal Bar*, 323–5.

[144] Skyrme, *History of the Justices of the Peace*, ii, 238.

[145] *Ibid.*, 182–4, 238–40. As the Lord Chancellor's secretary for commissions from 1948–77, Sir Thomas Skyrme had personal and anecdotal experience of many clerks.

[146] *Ibid.*, 238–40.

to his borough counterpart, who usually doubled as town clerk. The Municipal Corporations Act 1835 vested the appointment and remuneration of the clerk of the peace in the corporation, and while it did not require the two posts to be held by the same person, for a time at least that remained usual. The chief duties of the borough clerk of the peace were arranging criminal trials: drawing indictments, preparing warrants and orders, and recording judgments.[147]

3. JUSTICES OUT OF QUARTER SESSIONS

Petty Sessions

The sittings of the justices at general sessions formed only a small part of their activities. The commission empowered them to act in many circumstances either alone or in pairs and to the single justice, often at home, came 'a succession of cases of every imaginable description'.[148] Moreover, the justice was not supposed to be merely a passive recipient of complaints but actively to seek out neglects of public duties and criminal behaviour.[149] However, in the eighteenth and early nineteenth centuries Parliament reposed confidence increasingly in what lawyers called 'the double justice'; pairs of justices were given responsibility for enforcing weights and measures legislation and (with unhappy results) power to sanction the stopping up or diversion of footpaths.[150] Quarter sessions too began to delegate to them more 'county business', such as that relating to bridges and prisons.

The justices out of sessions were not a court of record and their work was essentially informal. Though writers of manuals urged diligent record-keeping as good practice (and as some security if a justice were haled into the King's Bench), it was often sketchy and unsystematic.[151] The statutes which extended the powers and duties of the county justices seldom restricted their jurisdiction to any defined part of their own county, so a complainant might seek out a justice believed to be favourable and contradictory orders might be issued in ignorance by different justices.[152]

However, during the eighteenth century the haphazard practices of the justices out of sessions had been reduced to some regularity in most counties.[153] Alongside or between special sessions regular, publicly notified meetings of several justices

---

[147] Bentley, *English Criminal Justice in the Nineteenth Century*, 83.

[148] Webb and Webb, *Parish and County*, 387. There is a useful summary of their activities in Skyrme, *History of the Justices of the Peace*, ii, 62–5.

[149] Webb and Webb, *Parish and County*, 391–2; Eastwood, *Governing Rural England*, 83–4.

[150] Webb and Webb, *Parish and County*, 392–6, 418–19, 599–602. The self-interested exercise of the power over footpaths was a leading grievance of critics of the magistracy in the 1820s.

[151] *Ibid.*, 388–90; Skyrme, *History of the Justices of the Peace*, ii, 66.

[152] Webb and Webb, *Parish and County*, 392–6.

[153] *Ibid.*, 400–12; Eastwood, *Governing Rural England*, 88–92.

for a particular division were held, their frequency depending on the volume of business and the conscientiousness of the justices. In Middlesex, where pressure of business first led to this innovation, some districts were in practically daily session, while in other counties weekly or fortnightly meetings were the rule.[154] Most had also imitated quarter sessions by choosing a regular chairman.[155] There was nothing to prevent any county justice from attending one of these 'petty sessions', but custom confined it to the justices of that division.[156] Not all justices welcomed the growth of formality and collective activity, and many continued in the old ways; indeed, petty sessions nowhere displaced the magistrate at home, dispensing justice from his parlour.[157]

Parliament, however, evinced a clear preference for the new practice. One of Peel's reforming measures in 1828 permitted quarter sessions to revise the petty sessional divisions every ten years and allowed them to create additional divisions, and an 1836 Act encouraged the alignment of the divisions with poor law unions as far as county boundaries would allow.[158] The development of petty sessions has been called 'the most significant innovation in English county government within the early modern period'.[159] It practically eclipsed venerable offices such as the high constable in the oversight of parish administration and steadily accumulated a massive body of summary jurisdiction. In many places the justices coped with business like quarter sessions, by separating criminal work from their innumerable 'powers of a local and social character'[160] often doing the latter in private.[161]

Yet all this was bestowed upon an institution scarcely mentioned in statute. Petty sessions were still aptly described by the County Rates Commission 1836 'rather as a voluntary meeting of magistrates than a court specifically recognized by law. It has neither a regular establishment of officers, nor any formal or authentic memorial of its proceedings.'[162]

A badly needed overhaul of summary jurisdiction and out-of-sessions business was undertaken by the Attorney-General Sir John Jervis. Jervis's legislation fell well short of the full consolidation of magistrates' law he intended,[163] and his policy of shifting further criminal business onto an amateur, untrained

---

[154] Webb and Webb, *Parish and County*, 406–8.

[155] Skyrme, *History of the Justices of the Peace*, ii, 66.

[156] Bentley, *English Criminal Justice in the Nineteenth Century*, 21.

[157] Eastwood, *Governing Rural England*, 89.

[158] *Ibid.*, 92. The statutes are the Divisions of Counties Act 1828 (9 Geo. IV c. 43) and the Poor Law Amendment Act 1836 (6 & 7 Will. IV c. 12).

[159] *Ibid.*, 88.

[160] G. C. Oke, 'Magisterial Procedure' (1862) *TNAPSS* 146–57, summarized at 146–7.

[161] Webb and Webb, *Parish and County*, 408.

[162] Quoted in Eastwood, *Governing Rural England*, 89.

[163] Oke, 'Magisterial Procedure'; 'Justices of the Peace Procedure Bill' (1864) 17 (s3) *LM & LR* 280–8.

and questionably impartial magistracy did not meet with universal approba-
tion.[164] Nevertheless the collection of four statutes—the Summary Jurisdiction
Act, Indictable Offences Act, and Protection of Justices Act 1848, and the Petty
Sessions Act 1849, put in place a much needed framework.[165]

The interface of petty sessions and courts of summary jurisdiction was still
complicated. A court of summary jurisdiction was held before justices in petty
sessions or a stipendiary magistrate. A petty sessions court which exercised that
jurisdiction sat on a publicly announced day in a designated petty sessions court-
house. Two justices sitting in an 'occasional court house' might still hear and
determine cases but their sentencing powers were more limited, while a single
justice sitting at a petty sessions house retained a lesser criminal jurisdiction; he
was then a court of summary jurisdiction but not a petty sessions court.[166]

Petty sessions continued to handle an enormous range of not strictly or technically criminal matters, though in some cases—without any obvious logic—their
activities were not those of a court.[167] Beyond the confines of petty sessions justices still had a range of other powers and duties, such as backing and issuing
warrants and in keeping the peace, but by 1914 most of their duties were performed in court.[168] Government responsibility for the petty sessions lay with the
Home Secretary, and this included vetting the appointment of justices' clerks.[169]

Summary Jurisdiction and Committals

Blackstone was perturbed at the statutory inroads made upon the hallowed right
to trial by jury by extending summary trial by magistrates.[170] He would have

---

[164] e.g. 'E.B.A.', 'The Bill Against Trial By Jury' (1849) 11 (s2) *LM* 155–60. Jervis admitted that 'there
might be difference of opinion in the House as to the expediency of entrusting to the unpaid magistracy the large powers they now possessed': *PD* 1848 (s3) 96: 4.

[165] 11 & 12 Vict. cc. 42, 43, 44; 12 & 13 Vict. c.18. Jervis's Acts are appraised in D. Freestone and
J. Richardson, 'The Making of English Criminal Law (7) Sir John Jervis and his Acts' [1980] *Crim.
Law Rev.* 5–16.

[166] Maitland, *Justice and Police*, 89–90. Oke reckoned there were 790 petty sessions divisions
in the counties, 175 in cities and boroughs and 15 in the metropolis. Each had approximately ten
magistrates: 'Magisterial Procedure', 148. By 1914 there were about 20 to each division: Alexander,
Administration of Justice in Criminal Matters, 12.

[167] Their functions were 'increasingly illogical' (Abel-Smith and Stevens, *Lawyers and the Courts*,
91, and see also 98). Oke calculated in 1862 that one-fifth of the public Acts of the previous 20 years
related in some way to magistrates' duties ('Magisterial Procedure', 146). There is an exhaustive list
in *Halsbury's Laws of England*, ix, sub. 'Courts', 74–9.

[168] Maitland, *Justice and Police*, 91–3.

[169] The division of responsibility between Home Office and Lord Chancellor's Office was later seen
as unsatisfactory: Sir C. Schuster, memo. to Lord Chancellor Simon, 1943, NA PRO LCO 2/3630.

[170] D. Hay, 'Legislation, Magistrates and Judges', in D. Lemmings (ed.), *The British and their Laws
in the Eighteenth Century* (Woodbridge, 2005), 59–79, while documenting the vast predominance

been even more alarmed at subsequent developments, and he would not have been alone, for though Bentham was in favour there were both Tories and Whigs who deprecated at least some aspects of this tendency. The Tory C. D. Brereton inveighed against its informalities and unconstitutionality[171] while Brougham devoted a part of his marathon speech on law reform to attacking magistrates' justice.[172] There were certainly gross defects in both theory and practice. Few of the statutes prescribed a procedure to be followed and few allowed an appeal, leaving only the remote supervision of the King's Bench as a remedy for injustice, which occurred on a large scale.[173] In London there was some degree of regularity and professionalism in the conduct of sessions, but in the country summary justice was sometimes downright perfunctory.[174] One or two justices, at home or at an inn, untrained in the law and with only the assistance of a clerk of limited learning and a copy of Burn or some other manual, would often go astray through ignorance, in some cases compounded by prejudice. Poor men were at the mercy of the magistrate, while even the better off might find themselves denied counsel and tried in private, away from the publicity of the newspaper press.[175] Borough justices, as in Sheffield, often had a worse reputation than their county counterparts and since the justices took responsibility for keeping public order, their police function in suppressing strikes and demonstrations sat uneasily with their judicial role.[176]

Suspicions about the biases of magistrates were often well-founded. Landed gentry might be disinterested enough in most matters but scarcely when it came to the game laws or the stopping of footpaths.[177] The reluctance of lord-lieutenants to put manufacturers on the bench might be down to snobbery but the consequences when they did were often as predicted: an unmistakable pattern of anti-workman decisions and a conviction on the part of the men that only at

of summary trial (perhaps 83% of Staffordshire trials in the eighteenth century), cautions that Blackstone's complaint underestimates its importance in earlier centuries.

[171] Eastwood, *Governing Rural England*, 84.

[172] *PD* 1828 (s2) 18: 161–2, still being reproduced in support of attacks on justices 30 years later: 'Justice and Justices' (1859–60) 8 (s3) *LM & LR* 280–300.

[173] D. Hay, 'Dread of the Crown Office: The English Magistracy and the King's Bench', in N. Landau (ed.), *Law, Crime and English Society* (Cambridge, 2002), 19–45, concludes that the threat of such action was not very great.

[174] Bentley, *English Criminal Justice in the Nineteenth Century*, 22–3.

[175] *Ibid.*

[176] Philips, 'Black Country Magistracy'.

[177] Munsche, *Gentlemen and Poachers*, Ch. 4, gives a less severe verdict on their work under the Game Laws and Skyrme, *History of the Justices of the Peace*, ii, 7, also seeks to soften the accepted picture; see KJMS. However, T. Sweeney, *The Extension and Practice of Summary Jurisdiction in England, 1790–1860* (PhD thesis, Cambridge University, 1975), 382–99 is more critical.

appellate level could they expect justice.[178] There was also concern among MPs at the sentencing proclivities of some benches in other areas.[179]

Given this unflattering reputation it may seem surprising that the 1840s saw the beginnings of an enormous increase in the summary trial of offences. This was an indirect consequence of a major change in the deployment of the criminal law. A strategy based upon a highly selective use of prosecutions carrying the threat of punishments which were either literally lethal or at least so severe as to deter others (or so it was hoped) was gradually replaced by a 'policed' society in which a wider range of errant behaviour was criminalized and the emphasis placed on implacable prosecution and milder, reformative, punishments.[180] Prosecutors were encouraged by the more liberal award of expenses under Acts of 1818 and 1826, and this contributed to a steep rise in committals to quarter sessions and Assizes.[181] Since Assize judges had little appetite for a diet of trivial offences nor quarter sessions for the financial burdens this imposed, they cast around for alternatives for the trial of petty criminals.

Stipendiary magistrates were thought likely to become case-hardened and cynical; would be irremovable however unsatisfactory they proved; and would create patronage for government or borough corporations. New local courts or the revival of old ones would meet opposition on grounds of expense. Above all, the country gentlemen who still had a powerful voice in Parliament were sure to resist the erosion of the social control they were able to exercise through the magistracy.[182]

Even so, devolution to the great unpaid at petty sessions was a contentious solution.[183] It was not favoured by Peel, though his Vagrancy Act 1824 was an important precedent,[184] and successive attempts at further devolution, some urged by quarter sessions themselves, were rebuffed in Parliament.[185] The Times probably represented the prevailing opinion in 1840 when it pronounced that 'summary conviction is too apt to be conviction without law or justice, without

[178] Swift, *English Urban Magistracy*; C. Frank, 'The Defeat of the 1844 Master and Servants Bill' in D. Hay and P. Craven (eds), *Masters, Servants and Magistrates in Britain and the Empire, 1652–1955* (2004), 402–21.

[179] See e.g. the debate on the Shrewsbury magistrates in *PD* 1844 (s3) 75: 283–95, with Hume's breakdown of sentences. A general criticism of the lay justices is 'E.B.A', 'Bill Against Trial by Jury'.

[180] This is of course the subject of extensive debate and controversy: see XIII, Pt 1, Ch. V.

[181] Sweeney, *Extension and Practice of Summary Jurisdiction*, 125–6; D. Philips, '"A New Engine of Power and Authority"; The Institutionalization of Law Enforcement in England', in Gatrell et al., *Crime and the Law* 155–89, 179–80.

[182] O. MacDonagh, *Early Victorian Government 1830–1870* (1977), 104–6.

[183] For similar developments in Ireland see D. McCabe, 'Open Court: Law and the Expansion of Magisterial Jurisdiction at Petty Sessions in Nineteenth century Ireland', in N. M. Dawson (ed.), *Reflections on Law and History* (Dublin, 2006), 126–62.

[184] MacDonagh, *Early Victorian Government*, 119–26; 3 Geo. IV c. 40, replaced by 5 Geo. IV c. 83.

[185] McDonagh, *Early Victorian Government*, 127–51, the fullest account of these developments.

legal evidence or dispassionate enquiry'.[186] Nevertheless, the attractions were very strong, not least that it was notoriously much more difficult to secure a conviction for an indictable offence, with its procedural and evidential constraints[187] and magistrates, particularly the police magistrates of London, found ways of extending summary jurisdiction by local Acts or by stretching the law to its limits and beyond.[188]

If more work was to be devolved to petty sessions, they must be fitted to receive it. One step had been taken in 1836, when defence lawyers might no longer be barred,[189] but Jervis's Acts of 1848–9 were the principal instruments. The Summary Jurisdiction Act 1848 in particular provided a code of procedure and ensured that the court would be open to the public; as with county courts, the presence of the newspaper reporter went far to curb the grosser abuses of local tyrants.[190] Some courthouses remained unsuitable for many years, but governments would not wait upon improvements before further enlarging the summary jurisdiction.[191] The Juvenile Offenders Act 1847 (10 & 11 Vict. c. 82) had already begun the 'momentous transformation of petty sessions'[192] through a series of measures which encouraged first juveniles and then adults to waive their right to trial by jury across a range of indictable offences;[193] a speedier trial and restrictions on the maximum length of sentences were the principal inducements, and gradually the width of appeal provisions was also expanded, though the cost of appeals did more than the quality of summary justice to ensure that this facility did not overload quarter sessions.[194] The Summary Jurisdiction Act 1879 (c. 49), which also

---

[186] 10 August, quoted *ibid.*, 156.

[187] Sweeney, *Extension and Practice of Summary Jurisdiction*, 81–5.

[188] *Ibid.*, 167, 407–10.

[189] Bentley, *English Criminal Justice in the Nineteenth Century*, 23.

[190] Though reporting also made public the stigma of an appearance in the 'police court': Hay, 'England 1562–1875, the Law and its Uses', 107.

[191] Bentley, *English Criminal Justice in the Nineteenth Century*, 23–4; Skyrme, *History of the Justices of the Peace*, ii, 176–9; Abel-Smith and Stevens, *Lawyers and the Courts*, 31–2. There was particular concern at sessions being held in public houses; 358 out of 724 according to Sir G. R. Pechell, who sought to outlaw it. The only substantial reported debate on the second reading of any of Jervis's bills was on the Petty Sessions Bill 1849, with peers demanding changes to meet their fears of extravagant court building projects: *PD* 1849 (s3) 107: 156–7, 1364–7. New courts were often housed in town halls or with police stations: Graham, *Ordering Law*, 174–98.

[192] Hay, 'England 1562–1875, the Law and its Uses', 107. The Law Amendment Society claimed that it was based partly on one of its reports, but that had not been confined to juveniles: 'History of the Law Amendment Society... V: The Criminal Law' (1854) 20 *LR* 291–304 at 297–9.

[193] Beginning with the Criminal Justice Act 1855 (18 & 19 Vict. c. 126); Alexander, *Administration of Justice in Criminal Matters*, 44–51. The category of 'young persons' (14 to 16 years old) was introduced in 1908.

[194] Bentley, *English Criminal Justice in the Nineteenth Century*, 24–5. Magistrates were said to use the 1855 Act in a way not intended, giving lenient sentences to hardened offenders in order to save the county money: W. M. Tartt, 'On Summary Convictions under the Criminal Justice Act of 1855'

introduced the 'converse innovation' of offering an accused under 16 charged with a summary offence which carried the possibility of at least three months' imprisonment the right to elect for trial by jury,[195] was particularly important in enlarging the scope of summary jurisdiction and by 1900 not only were 98 per cent of all offences tried summarily, but over 80 per cent of indictable ones.[196]

Inevitably the quality of magistrates' justice was variable, yet there was little pressure to impose a training requirement upon them or substitute stipendiaries, even though they now dealt with all cases (other than homicides) where the accused were children or young persons. Some kept themselves informed through *The Justice of the Peace*,[197] or followed Alexander's advice to buy a copy of the consolidated Home Office circulars, which were issued both to explain new Acts and to correct misunderstandings.[198] Most probably left such things to their clerks, but for all their failings the lay justices in petty sessions were firmly entrenched in the criminal justice system, a position cemented by the Criminal Justice Act 1914.[199]

Another responsibility for justices, acting alone or, by custom rather than law, in pairs,[200] was to receive informations, summonses or warrants alleging the commission of an indictable offence and to establish by taking depositions of prosecution witnesses, whether they disclosed 'a strong or probable presumption' of guilt, which would justify committing the accused for trial at Assizes or quarter sessions.[201] What had once been an examination designed to elicit evidence of guilt had become a procedure more akin to a preliminary trial, albeit the justices did not comprise a court when sitting for this purpose.[202] The Indictable Offences Act 1848 placed the preliminary hearing on a long-lasting footing, and although it conferred no right to legal representation, it came to be standard practice to permit it.[203]

(1859) *TNAPSS* 481–5. Sweeney (*Extension and Practice of Summary Jurisdiction*, 14) regards the 1855 Act as intended largely to safeguard jury trial through its voluntarist stance, but that was not the view of all contemporaries, see e.g. 'E.B.A.', 'Bill Against Trial by Jury'.

[195]   42 & 43 Vict. c. 49 and 'Summary Jurisdiction of Magistrates' *TNAPSS* 1878, 247–62; Alexander, *Administration of Justice in Criminal Matters*, 51.

[196]   Alexander, *Administration of Justice in Criminal Matters*, 202–3. The number of trials rose by 11% in the first year after the 1879 Act: Gatrell, 'Decline of Theft and Violence', 303.

[197]   From 1837; Skyrme, *History of the Justices of the Peace*, ii, 211.

[198]   *Administration of Justice in Criminal Matters*, 70.

[199]   *Ibid.*, 71–4. Section 15 substantially raised the money limits of its jurisdiction over property offences; there is a commentary in (1914) 78 *JP* 531, 542.

[200]   Alexander, *Administration of Justice in Criminal Matters*, 26.

[201]   *Ibid.*, 25–6.

[202]   *Ibid.*, 26.

[203]   If the justices resolved upon a committal they had then to consider granting bail.

Special Sessions

Special sessions were defined in the early nineteenth century as 'a sitting convened by reasonable notice to the other justices of the Division'.[204] They had evolved out of divisional meetings and were called for a variety of purposes, but the dominant one was the regulation of liquor sales through licensing of premises. An Act of 1753 allocated this function to special sessions which became known as 'brewster sessions'.[205] The practically unfettered discretion exercised by the justices in granting and renewing licences came under severe criticism both for corruption—especially in Middlesex—and arbitrariness. The growth of free trade sentiment and a desire to wean the lower classes off cheap spirits also contributed to the relaxation of controls on beer houses in the Beer Act 1830.[206]

Though a few half-hearted measures were passed to moderate the undesirable consequences of the repeal, it was not until 1869 that the policy was reversed.[207] Special sessions regained most of their powers, but from 1872 new licences had to be confirmed by a standing licensing committee of quarter sessions. There was a general licensing meeting in February, with transfer sessions four to eight times a year, and the bench often contained justices who were otherwise inactive.[208] A combination of clashing economic interests and powerful moral and religious sentiment made for an undignified and sometimes riotous atmosphere; even appeals to quarter sessions were described as resembling a public meeting, with a good deal of canvassing and whipping up of sympathizers.[209] Though the sessions were not a court,[210] lawyers made a good thing of licensing[211] and in some places, particularly in London, it remained a most unsatisfactory affair until after the Second World War.[212]

---

[204] Bayley J., in *R.v. Justices of Worcestershire* (1818) 2 B & Ald., 228, 233; Webb and Webb, *Parish and County*, 396.

[205] The subject is covered exhaustively by S. and B. Webb, *The History of Liquor Licensing in England* (1903), and see above, pp. 462–3.

[206] Skyrme, *History of the Justices of the Peace*, ii, 111–16. The Act is 11 Geo. IV and 1 Will. IV. c. 64. As Albany Fonblanque pithily wrote, 'to stop the jobbing of the magistrates in licensing was Lord B[rougham]'s object': *England under Seven Administrations*, 3 vols (1837), iii, 47.

[207] Beerhouses etc. Act 1869 (c. 27); Skyrme, *History of Justices of the Peace*, ii, 204–5.

[208] *Ibid.*, 252–4.

[209] Whiteley, *Brief Life*, 21–5; M Williams, *Leaves of a Life*, 2 vols (1890), i, 206. Middlesex sessions for spirit licences had remained corrupt: W. S. Ballantine, *Some Experiences of a Barrister's Life* (6th edn, 1883), 32.

[210] Emphasized by Lord Halsbury in *Boulter* v. *Kent Justices* [1897] AC 556 but hardly grasped by many benches: Skyrme, *History of the Justices of the Peace*, ii, 253–4.

[211] Ashley, *My Sixty Years in the Law*, 29, 101; Williams, *Leaves of a Life*, i, 206.

[212] P. Polden, *A Guide to the Records of the Lord Chancellor's Department* (1988), 139–40. Liverpool was another city where licensing was notably contentious: J. Campbell, *F. E. Smith, First Earl of Birkenhead* (1983), 95–6.

The Clerk to the Justices

Most justices needed a clerk, sometimes simply for clerical duties, but increasingly for legal advice.[213] It was his clerk who restrained the ineffable Mr Nupkins
in his dealings with the Pickwickians, just as Squire Western's had tried to keep
the squire out of the King's Bench. The men employed by justices as their personal
clerks are elusive figures,[214] but they were becoming more visible as groups of justices meeting at petty sessions found it more efficient to leave their clerks at home
and employ collectively a local attorney. It then became the practice in many
districts to refer those seeking to do business at the justice's home to the office
of that same attorney, and those justices ceased to employ a personal clerk.[215] The
personal clerk survived in remoter areas, where the pickings at sessions were too
meagre to tempt a respectable attorney, and there were part-time clerks with no
legal qualifications ('the farmer, the steward, the school-master, the surveyor of
weights and measures, the grocer'[216]) were still employed. At the other extreme,
justices in Bradford were so busy that they could afford an attorney as their personal clerk besides having a clerk to the sessions.[217]

The amount of business was crucial because with very few exceptions clerks
depended upon fees. Indeed it became one of the commonest complaints against
them that they indulged in a 'shameless heaping up of fees'[218] and that even at
quarter sessions, where they were supposedly governed by a table drawn up in
1753, they were in practice uncontrolled.[219]

Another complaint, made by justices as well as laymen, was that some justices and sessions were ruled by their clerks, on whose often inadequate legal
knowledge they habitually relied. Reliance sometimes extended to the decision
whether to commit a prisoner for trial, and it was suspected that some clerks were
influenced by the rewards they could gain from committals in the many places
where they were habitually employed to conduct the prosecution.[220] A group of
Birmingham attorneys was believed to make a large income from this practice,
and although other clerks furiously denied the imputation, it may well have been a
factor in the suspiciously low success rate of prosecutions in Hertfordshire.[221] The

---

[213] Webb and Webb, *Parish and County*, 347–9, 412–16.

[214] Moir, *Justices of the Peace*, 91.   [215] Webb and Webb, *Parish and County*, 413–15.

[216] K. C. Clarke, 'The Nineteenth Century Justices' Clerk and his Critics' (1968) 132 *JP* 713–15,
728–30 at 729–30.

[217] *Ibid.*, 729.   [218] Webb and Webb, *Parish and County*, 416.   [219] *Ibid.*, 416–17.

[220] Bentley, *English Criminal Justice in the Nineteenth Century*, 26; Clarke, 'Nineteenth Century
Justices' Clerk and his Critics', 715–16, 728. Law societies protested at this practice, e.g. (1891) 10 *LN* 5.

[221] Clarke, 'Nineteenth Century Justices' Clerk and his Critics', 715–16; [C. Austin] 'The
Administration of Provincial Justice' (1825) 4 *Westminster Rev.* 315–36.

Municipal Corporations Act removed this temptation from borough clerks,[222] but the county rate committee even contemplated transforming the clerks—salaried rather than dependent upon fees—into regular public prosecutors.[223] That course did not appeal to the Criminal Law Commissioners, but attempts to outlaw the clerks' role in prosecutions were unsuccessful and it persisted despite frequent expressions of judicial disapproval.[224] In some divisions there was a much more questionable practice: clerks, either for the petty sessions or belonging to individual justices, represented parties before their own bench, although in licensing cases this was expressly prohibited.[225]

From 1877 all petty sessions were legally required to appoint a clerk, either whole or part time. Chosen by the justices of the division or the borough, and holding office at their pleasure,[226] he was to be salaried (a previous enactment on salaries in 1851 had been permissive) and appropriately qualified either by having served seven years as a clerk to a stipendiary, police, or metropolitan magistrate, or by being a lawyer.[227] There was, however, a 'striking anomaly',[228] for whereas any solicitor was eligible, barristers needed to be of at least 14 years' standing; the bar's lack of concern suggests a belief that few barristers would be attracted to the post. In the busier petty sessional divisions the duties prescribed for the clerk were such as to oblige him to recruit assistants, but they were his own employees and paid from his own salary.[229]

---

[222] 5 & 6 Will. IV c. 76.

[223] Clarke, 'Nineteenth Century Justices' Clerk and his Critics', 728. The proposal was in a bill of 1845: *PD* 1845 (s3) 78: 759–70.

[224] Bentley, *English Criminal Justice in the Nineteenth Century*, 26; Clarke, Nineteenth Century Justices' Clerk and his Critics', 728; (1913) 77 *JP* 370. Oke defended the practice: 'Magisterial Procedure', 155.

[225] Clarke, 'Nineteenth Century Justices' Clerk and his Critics', 728; Alexander, *Administration of Justice in Criminal Matters*, 15–16.

[226] The appointment being purely ministerial, it was immune from challenge by *certiorari*, and the clerk could be dismissed summarily: R. Burrows, 'The Justices' Clerk' (1946) 62 *LQR* 157–66 at 164.

[227] Justices' Clerks Act 1877 (c. 43); Skyrme, *History of the Justices of the Peace*, ii, 185; Criminal Justice Administration Act 1851 (13 & 14 Vict. c. 100), s. 9. Clerks to the metropolitan stipendiary magistrates came under the direct control of the Home Office through an Act of 1839.

[228] Alexander, *Administration of Justice in Criminal Matters*, 15.

[229] *Ibid.*, 16; Skyrme, *History of the Justices of the Peace*, ii, 185. Most clerks were part-time, since their net income was small—under £100 in 345 divisions as late as 1937: S. French, 'The Evolution of the Justices' Clerk' [1961] *Crim. Law Rev.* 688–97 at 697.

XIV
Coroners and their Courts

1. INTRODUCTION

In the nineteenth century the coroner's inquest came much more often into the public eye, and was the site for a range of conflicts over its purpose and effectiveness. These led to regular proposals for radical changes, sometimes extending to its complete abolition.[1]

Radical reformers extolled the Scottish system, in which the leading role was taken by the procurator–fiscal, and this 'secret system', which appealed to some doctors, had no real place for the coroner.[2] Ideas were floated for a body of 'public certifiers' who would scrutinize doctors' death certificates and pass only the suspicious cases on to the coroner,[3] or for 'medical examiners' who would carry out the preliminary investigation, replacing the view of the body by the coroner and his jurymen.[4] Traditionalists like Joshua Toulmin-Smith and Edward Herford vigorously championed the antiquity and democratic nature of the inquest, but they seemed to be fighting a losing battle.[5]

The 1870s was a crucial decade, with a series of inquiries and bills against a backdrop of sensational inquests which threw the failings of the institution into high relief.[6] Ominously, the Judicature Commissioners in 1873 were only prepared to recommend that 'the system of coroners' inquests may for the present be

---

[1] Between them P. J. Fisher, *The Politics of Sudden Death: The Office and Role of Coroner in England and Wales, 1726–1888* (PhD thesis, Leicester University, 2007) and D. Prichard, *The Office of Coroner 1860–1926: Resistance, Reluctance and Reform* (PhD thesis, Greenwich University, 2001) provide a full history. J. D. J. Havard, *The Detection of Secret Homicide* (1960) needs to be read with I. A. Burney, *Bodies of Evidence: Medicine and the Politics of the English Inquest* (Baltimore, 2000). O. Anderson, *Suicide in Victorian and Edwardian England* (Oxford, 1987), Ch. 1 is an excellent summary and the Brodrick Report, *PP* 1971–2 [Cmnd. 4810], xxi, has a useful historical introduction.

[2] Prichard, *Office of Coroner*, 122–4.

[3] Burney, *Bodies of Evidence*, 56–7, 168–70; Prichard, *Office of Coroner*, 290.

[4] Prichard, *Office of Coroner*, 181, 201, 244.

[5] *Ibid.*, 64–73; G. H. H. Glasgow, *The Role of Lancashire Coroners, c.1836–1888* (M Phil thesis, Manchester University, 2002), 134–92.

[6] Prichard, *Office of Coroner*, 74–121.

allowed to remain',[7] and a Commons select committee in 1879 sent for only two witnesses, both to expound the workings of the Scottish system.[8]

And yet the coroner and the inquest survived substantially intact, albeit with important changes. Despite Herschell's urgings, the 1887 consolidation Act was not a prelude to substantive reform and it perpetuated common law words and phrases which had proved notoriously difficult to interpret. The Home Office and the Local Government Board (succeeded by the Ministry of Health) showed little disposition to co-operate, and when the former set up a departmental committee in 1908 its recommendations were mired in politics and professional rivalries until the war provided a perfect excuse for continuing inaction.[9] By then the *Law Times* felt that inquests had lost much of their importance, relapsing into a backwater of the legal system.[10]

2. THE OFFICE OF CORONER

Types and Distribution

Apart from those exotic rarities the King's coroner, the coroner of the royal household,[11] and the Admiralty coroner,[12] and those High Court judges who were coroners *ex officio*,[13] coroners were of three sorts. The Municipal Corporations Act 1835 (section 62) obliged each borough with its own quarter sessions to appoint a coroner. Most counties had from two to a dozen coroners, each based in a district,[14] but when county justices created similar petty sessional divisions they seldom matched them to the coroners' divisions.[15] A more serious source of confusion was the existence of 'islands in the jurisdiction[16] of county coroners under coroners

---

[7] *Fifth Report 1874, PP* 1874 [C. 1090], xxiv, xviii.

[8] *PP* 1878–9 (279), ix; Prichard, *Office of Coroner*, 142–6.

[9] Prichard, *Office of Coroner*, 254–64

[10] (1909–10) 128 *LT* 485.

[11] *Halsbury's Laws of England*, viii (1909), 229–31. Halsbury rejected a proposal to abolish the Queen's coroner in 1892: Prichard, *Office of Coroner*, 176. The coroner of the royal household came unexpectedly into the public eye in 2007 through the inquest into the death of Diana, Princess of Wales.

[12] *Halsbury's Laws of England*, viii 231–4. '[R]ather a mystery at present', *DC on Coroners, Evidence I, PP* 1909 [Cd. 4782], xv, J. B. Little, q. 156.

[13] Judicature Act 1873, c. 25, s 12. Previously limited to the judges of the King's Bench. The Lord Chief Justice was chief coroner of England, an almost purely honorific title.

[14] S. and B. Webb, *A History of English Local Government, I, The Parish and the County* (rev. edn, 1963), 292. Shropshire had four, adding a fifth in 1850 (*VCH Shropshire* (1982), iii, 133–4, 163–4), whereas Wiltshire had only two, both in the north of the county (*VCH Wiltshire* (1957), v, 233–4).

[15] D. Eastwood, *Governing Rural England* (Oxford, 1994), 69 n.113.

[16] *DC on Coroners, Second Report and Evidence, PP* 1910 [Cd. 5039], xxi, 5.

appointed by the Duchy of Lancaster, Oxford University, and other franchisees,[17] the latter having sometimes to fight off attempts by their county rivals to encroach upon their territory.[18] Even when there was no conflict, the untidiness of over-lapping jurisdictions was confusing and inconvenient; Huntingdon was so fully covered by franchises that it had no county coroner at all, while neighbouring Norfolk was pockmarked with them, some covering a tiny area.[19]

The distribution of coroners bore no relation to population. Coroners numbered well over 300,[20] yet eight coroners performed 27 per cent of all inquests in England in 1860, 21 per cent in 1912.[21] A select committee of 1879 boldly proposed to substitute a much smaller number who would double as rural stipendiary magistrates,[22] but the changes actually made were much less drastic. The county divisions were put on a statutory footing in 1844, with a procedure for changes in the districts,[23] while under the Local Government Act 1888 boroughs with under 10,000 inhabitants lost their coroner.[24] The franchises remained intact, though criticized by an inquiry of 1910 as 'inconvenient and anomalous'[25] and only vanished under the long delayed overhaul of coroners' law in 1926.[26]

Qualifications

The only formal qualification for the office of county coroner was that he must 'hold land in fee sufficient in the county whereof he may answer to all manner of people'.[27] This was incorporated in the consolidation Act of 1887 notwithstanding

---

[17] *Ibid.*, 4–6. The oddest was the famous Tutbury horn: G. H. H. Glasgow, 'The Election of County Coroners' (1999) 20 *JLH* 75–108 at 76. There were also peculiar arrangements for the Cinque Ports and Cosham manor: *DC on Coroners, Second Report and Evidence 1910*, 4–5.

[18] The Duchy of Lancaster had to obtain a court order upholding its exclusive jurisdiction within the Honor of Pontefract: *Jewison* v. *Dyson* (1842) 9 M. & W. 540; R. Somerville, *A History of the Duchy of Lancasterii* (1970), 269–70.

[19] Fisher, *Politics of Sudden Death*, 64–91; *DC on Coroners Second Report and Evidence 1910*, 4 and qq. 6706–77 (H. O. Chislett).

[20] 360 in 1909, 56 of whom were franchise coroners: Havard, *Detection of Secret Homicide*, 204.

[21] Anderson, *Suicide in Victorian and Edwardian England*, 35. In 1858, 91 out of 324 held fewer than ten inquests in the year: Burney, *Bodies of Evidence*, 174 n.5.

[22] Prichard, *Office of Coroner*, 129, 146.

[23] Coroners Act 1844 (7 & 8 Vict. c. 92), esp. ss 2, 6. A county coroner was elected for the whole county but unless in emergencies would only sit in his own district (ss 19–20).

[24] Section 38(2)(a).

[25] *DC on Coroners, Second Report and Evidence 1910*, 4; Coroners (Amendment) Act 1926 (c. 59), s 4.

[26] However, see C. Schuster to A. Maxwell (Home Office), 3 March 1936, 'some of the very worst things...have been done by full-time coroners': NA PRO LCO 2/1245.

[27] Coroners Act 1887 (c. 41), s 12. One candidate qualified himself by purchasing a plot in Kensal Green cemetery: *DC on Coroners Evidence I, PP* 1909 [Cd. 4782], J. B. Little, q. 60.

its obscurity and complete practical inutility, the more glaring since a borough coroner had only to be 'a fit person' and there was no qualification at all for most franchise coroners.[28]

The lack of any need for a professional qualification occasioned criticism. Most eighteenth-century coroners were attorneys[29] and Blackstone had bewailed the social decline of the office.[30] However, improved possibilities of remuneration attracted professional men, while the rising social status of solicitors and doctors improved the reputation of the coronership. There was strenuous rivalry between these two professions, each claiming that its own qualifications were peculiarly apt for the post.[31]

Thomas Wakley[32] initiated a vigorous campaign for medical coroners.[33] Wakley was successful up to a point. When he died in 1862 there were 59 doctor-coroners and it had become accepted that the coroner should be either medically or legally qualified.[34] Nevertheless, the lawyers (particularly the solicitors) more than held their own. From a peak of 14 per cent in counties and 20 per cent in boroughs in the 1880s the proportion of doctor-coroners gently declined.[35] Though the 1879 Select Committee's recommendation that only lawyers should be coroners was not implemented, the best the doctors could hope for was that any requisite professional qualification should preserve their position, as the Chalmers Committee accepted.[36]

---

[28] Municipal Corporations Act 1835 (5 & 6 Will. IV c. 76), s 62; Municipal Corporations Act 1882, c. 50, s 171. Some franchisees were themselves the coroner, though they acted by deputy: Glasgow, *Role of Lancashire Coroners*, 10.

[29] *Ibid.*, 93.

[30] Eastwood, *Governing Rural England*, 68.

[31] Glasgow, 'Election of County Coroners', 88–92.

[32] S. Squire Sprigge, *The Life and Times of Thomas Wakley* (1897), but see also J. Hostettler, *Thomas Wakley—an Enemy of Injustice* (Chichester, 1993) and E. Sherrington, *Thomas Wakley and Reform* (D. Phil. thesis, Oxford, 1974). Wakley may have been the first 'medically qualified' coroner (Havard, *Detection of Secret Homicide*, 49) but there were surgeons and apothecaries as coroners before him: Fisher: *Politics of Sudden Death*, 92–100.

[33] The first time the question was canvassed may have been for the City of London coronership in 1829: T. R. Forbes, 'Crowner's Quest' (1978) 68 *Transactions of the American Philosophical Society*, 1–52, at 9. See also the Stroud East election of 1831: G. H. H. Glasgow, 'The Election of Gloucestershire Coroners 1800–1888, Part One' (1999) 13 *Gloucestershire History*, 20–6, 22–4.

[34] B. English, *Victorian Values: The Life and Times of Dr. Edwin Lankester* (c. 1990), 137. The best known Victorian coroner outside London was the cricketer Edward Mills Grace (Gloucestershire Lower Division 1875–1911), often styled 'the coroner': Glasgow, 'The Election of Gloucestershire Coroners, Part Two' (2000) 14 *Gloucestershire History*, 17–21, 18–19.

[35] Anderson, *Suicide in Victorian and Edwardian England*, 16.

[36] *SC on Coroners, Report 1879; DC on Coroners, Second Report and Evidence 1910*, 6. The London County Council was in a position to require a dual qualification: G. H. H. Glasgow, 'Three Liverpool Doctors and their Coronial Ambitions' (2005) 154 *Transactions of the Historic Society of Lancashire and Cheshire*, 63–91, 84.

Appointment

County coroners were elected by the freeholders.[37] Contested elections, relatively
unusual in the eighteenth century, were becoming more frequent,[38] sometimes as
a way to promote particular causes or, as in the northern Staffordshire election in
1826, 'a contest between two political parties who wanted to try their strength'.[39]
By the 1840s contests occurred more often than not,[40] and since the constituency
was often very large, contests could be expensive and irregularities extensive.[41]
The Queen's Bench occasionally set aside enough votes to make an election void,[42]
but in *Re Diplock* it adopted a very unambitious role in scrutinizing the sheriff's
actions.[43] In law the poll was restricted to ten days,[44] but subsequent reductions
first to two and then to one day cut the expenses of polling, making it unlikely
that the 6869 votes recorded over eight days in Gloucestershire in 1831 would be
repeated;[45] even so, Lancashire contests attracted more than 2000.[46] Inevitably
there was corruption, and the cost to candidates could be alarming, perhaps
£10,000 to £12,000.[47] The most famous contests, those involving Thomas Wakley
and Edwin Lankester in Middlesex, were especially costly: Wakley was £7000 out
of pocket after losing the 1830 east Middlesex election and Lankester's success in
1862 cost £3000 and permanently crippled him financially.[48] Experienced election agents were called into play and solicitors' experience in electoral business
gave them a big advantage over their medical rivals.[49]

Wakely liked to call the coroner 'the people's judge' because of his broad electoral basis, but by 1869 many shared the Home Secretary's view that besides being

[37] Fisher, *Politics of Sudden Death*, 24–63.

[38] Glasgow, 'Election of County Coroners', 77–8; Glasgow, *Role of Lancashire Coroners*, 83–133.

[39] Sir G. Strickland bart., MP.

[40] Glasgow, *Role of Lancashire Coroners*, 154. Nationally 42% of contests went to the poll between
1820 and 1844: Fisher, *Politics of Sudden Death*, 38–56.

[41] Glasgow, 'Election of County Coroners', 80–2. Claims to vote might be based on fishing rights
and other proprietary interests and even graveyard plots: Glasgow, *Role of Lancashire Coroners*, 94.

[42] e.g. *In re the Coronership of Hemel Hempstead* (1852) 5 De M. & G. 228; Glasgow 'Election of
County Coroners', 83.

[43] (1868–9) 4 QB 549. Mellor J. admitted that the freeholder's oath required by statute in 1818 was
a very flimsy safeguard.

[44] Glasgow, 'Election of County Coroners', 98.

[45] Coroners Act 1844, s 10, Coroners Act 1860 (23 & 24 Vict. c. 116), s 2; Glasgow, , 82; Glasgow,
'Election of Gloucestershire Coroners, Part One', 23.

[46] Glasgow, *Role of Lancashire Coroners*, 155. Several bills in the 1830s had aimed at reducing the
electorate and cutting the 'ruinous expense' (*PD* 1834 (s3) 21: 557, J. Cripps) of elections, but none had
passed: *ibid.*, 193.

[47] Glasgow, 'Election of County Coroners', 89. See also Glasgow, *Role of Lancashire Coroners*, 155.

[48] English, *Victorian Values*, 139.

[49] See e.g. the election of Brighouse for West Derby Hundred in 1884: Glasgow, *Role of Lancashire
Coroners*, 109–14.

'cumbrous and expensive', election was 'unsuited to the character of the office'.[50] Disagreements over patronage and lack of urgency delayed the change so long that it eventually came as part of the reform of county government in 1888.[51] With little debate and certainly without any popular protest the coroner was henceforth to be appointed by an elected county council.[52]

This change aligned the position with the boroughs, where the coroner was already chosen by the corporation.[53] To judge from Birmingham and the Lancashire boroughs the process was largely political, though local law societies in Liverpool and Manchester were powerful enough to ensure that a solicitor would be chosen.[54]

Tenure

Most coroners were appointed or elected for life, but some borough coroners were chosen for only a year and were vulnerable to changes in the political complexion of the borough; though after criticism of the ruthless purge by the Birmingham radicals in 1839, it became rare for coroners to be displaced.[55]

Some felt it an oddity that the Lord Chancellor, rather than the Lord Chief Justice, had acquired the power to remove a coroner who misconducted himself in office or had become incapable of performing its duties,[56] and both Eldon and his successors were vague in explaining its origin.[57] A statute of 1751 enabled the King's Bench to remove one convicted of 'extortion or wilful neglect of his duty or misdemeanour in his office',[58] and the Coroners Act 1860 placed the Lord Chancellor's powers of removal over county coroners for 'inability or misbehaviour' on a statutory footing.[59] These two provisions, with minor verbal changes, were infelicitously juxtaposed in the consolidating Act of 1887.[60]

---

[50] H. A. Bruce, *PD* 1869 (s3) 195: 792–3; Glasgow, 'Election of County Coroners', 99.

[51] Glasgow, 'Election of County Coroners', 99; Prichard, *Office of Coroner*, 128–55. A range of suggestions was offered in a debate of 1860: *PD* 1860 (s3) 159: 2110–17.

[52] Local Government Act 1888, s. 5. A bill of the Lord Chancellor's had proposed to give him these appointments but after Herschell's objections it was replaced with this provision: Prichard, *Office of Coroner*, 156–67. The last election, for north-east Middlesex, was held in June 1888.

[53] Glasgow, 'Election of County Coroners', 76–7.

[54] D. Fraser, *Power and Authority in the Victorian City* (Oxford, 1979), 88; Glasgow, *Role of Lancashire Coroner*, 15–132.

[55] Fraser, *Power and Authority in the Victorian City*, 88.

[56] *DC on Coroners Evidence I*, J. B. Little, q. 84.

[57] *Ex p. Parnell* (1820) 1 Jac. & W. 451, and cf. Lord Campbell in *Re Ward* (1861) 3 De G. F & J. 700.

[58] 25 Geo. II c. 29. This was not considered to displace the common law power: J. Jervis, *A Treatise on the Office and Duties of Coroners* (1829), 68–71. Jervis's work superseded the older one by T. Umfreville, *Lex Coronatoria* (2nd edn, by J. B. Grindon, Bristol, 1822) and became the standard authority.

[59] Section 6. The same formula was used for county court judges.

[60] Section 8.

The Lord Chancellor's role was a delicate one. He had to act judicially upon evidence and must not prejudge the issue, yet it was to his office (sometimes via the Home Office) that complaints came. He could take no disciplinary action unless someone was prepared to lodge a complaint, which rendered it 'peculiarly difficult for him to deal with any complaint where it appears that the complaint, if investigated or substantiated, would or might lead to the removal of the coroner from office'.[61] Where no one was prepared to make the formal complaint which would warrant judicial proceedings, the most the Chancellor could do was to invite the coroner's comments and, if appropriate, rebuke him.[62] 'Misbehaviour' in this office was very difficult to define. It was straightforward enough to dismiss a coroner who was mentally or physically disabled, or who was bankrupt or fled abroad,[63] but *R v. Hull* showed the difficulty arising from complaints that the coroner was not holding inquests when he should,[64] or indeed was holding them unnecessarily.[65] Where an undesirable practice had gained some currency a Home Office circular might be issued, but these had no authority. With little incentive to pleasing the authorities and very little to fear from displeasing them,[66] coroners were essentially independent.[67]

Remuneration

On one view the middle of the nineteenth century witnessed a 'vicious campaign of obstructing the medico-legal investigation of sudden deaths' by justices at quarter sessions, 'carried on in the face of incontrovertible evidence that they were facilitating and inviting the concealment of murder'.[68] The justices received encouragement from superior court judgments which supported their narrow construction of the duty to hold an inquest and made it nearly impossible to challenge magistrates' decisions on the propriety of coroners' expenses.[69]

---

[61] Sir C. Schuster, memorandum of 16 May 1935, LCO 2/1444, 4.

[62] *Ibid.* The memorandum lists all cases in the office files from 1892. The correspondence between the Lord Chancellor (Cairns) and the coroner in the case of Sir Charles Lyell's inquest was laid before Parliament (*PP* 1875 (298), lxi): Prichard, *Office of Coroner*, 92–100.

[63] See the cases in LCO 2/1444 and *Halsbury's Laws of England*, viii, 251–5.

[64] (1882) 9 QBD 689.   [65] See below.

[66] J. B. Edge became a county court judge, but he was one of the few barrister-coroners: Glasgow, *Role of Lancashire Coroners*, 63.

[67] The absence of pension arrangements led coroners to cling to the job, and they were reputed to be a long-lived breed; J. C. Malcolm of Leeds was almost 90 when he retired in 1919, having presided over some 25,000 inquests: S. M. Barnard, *Viewing the Lifeless Corpse: Coroners and Inquests in Victorian Leeds* (Leeds, 2001), 7. See D. Zuck, 'Mr. Troutbeck as the Surgeon's Friend: the Coroner and the Doctors—an Edwardian Comedy', (1995) 39 *Medical History* 259–87 at 260 n.6, for the notoriously incompetent 86-year-old William Carter.

[68] Havard, *Detection of Secret Homicide*, 38; 51.

[69] *Ibid.*, 38–66.

The expense of inquests lay at the root of these disputes. Many quarter sessions gave a higher priority to limiting the rate burden than to uncovering secret homicides and avoidable deaths in public institutions, while most justices felt the way coroners were remunerated offered a direct incentive to hold unnecessary inquests. A statute of 1751 entitled the coroner to a fee of 20s per inquest 'duly held', plus a travelling allowance of 9s a mile, payments needing to be authorized by quarter sessions.[70] Towards 1800 the justices began increasingly to question the amounts claimed, encouraged by several unsuccessful challenges to disallowances.[71] Behind these disputes was a rapid rise in inquests. Even in rural Wiltshire they doubled in the second half of the eighteenth century, while a single Oxfordshire coroner covered 325 miles for 160 inquests between 1829 and 1832.[72] It is hardly surprising that increasing coroners' expenses inclined justices towards a narrow view of coroners' duties.[73]

Subsequent legislation increased the incentive to vigilant economy. When the poor law commissioners ceased to pay incidental inquest expenses from the parish poor rate hasty legislation charged the county rate with all the expenses, including an enhanced payment of 6s 8d to the coroner;[74] Wakley also procured a specific witness allowance for medical evidence.[75] Faced with a sudden rise in inquests (Middlesex up 43 per cent in a few years, Bristol from 91 in 1836 to 221 in 1840[76]), probably linked to the introduction of registration of deaths in 1836, justices in Middlesex led the way in going beyond disallowing individual cases to passing resolutions detailing what expenses would be met.[77] Challenges met with mixed success, and did little to restrain the quarter sessions.[78]

---

[70] Coroners Act 1751, which also gave them an extra 13s 4d for homicides. Applied to borough coroners with minor variations by the Municipal Corporations Act 1835, s. 62.

[71] In R v. Kent Justices (1809) 11 East Rep. 229, Ellenborough CJ held that the justices' discretion in deciding whether an inquest was 'duly held' was, in the absence of evidence of bias, absolute. In R v. Oxfordshire Justices (1818) 2 B. & Ald. 203 the King's Bench restricted the mileage allowance to the journey to the inquest, with no payment for the return. See also Eastwood, Governing Rural England, 69 and Havard, Detection of Secret Homicide, 42–3.

[72] Eastwood, Governing Rural England, 68–9.

[73] Fisher, Politics of Sudden Death, 149–64. They may have drawn support from the view of a select committee in 1819 that '[i]n this country no atrocious crimes remain secret', quoted in Havard, Detection of Secret Homicide, 42.

[74] Coroners' Inquests (Expenses) Act 1836 (6 & 7 Will. IV c. 89), amended by 7 Will. IV c. 68.

[75] Sprigge, Thomas Wakley, 283–90.

[76] Havard, Detection of Secret Homicide, 48.

[77] Ibid., 55–8. In 1851 Middlesex quarter sessions circulated a copy of their resolutions to each county and most adopted them more or less entirely.

[78] Denman LCJ in R v. Justices of Caermarthenshire (1847) 10 Q.B. 796, was notably unsympathetic to the coroner, but in R v. Justices of Gloucestershire (1857) 7 E. & B. 805, the court agreed that the additional 6s 8d was payable even if the inquest was 'not duly held'. One decision favourable

Justices were often unjust in stigmatizing coroners as engaging in 'a species of petty tyranny'[79] and wrong to suspect them of self-interest in ordering unnecessary inquests. A parliamentary inquiry vindicated Wakley from the aspersions of the Middlesex bench[80] and a hapless coroner might find himself in trouble if he went too far to please his paymasters.[81] But not all coroners were disinterested. Ellenborough had insisted that they sometimes exceeded their powers and in Wiltshire there had been '[i]ncreasingly successful peculation [which] may well have been connived at by the justices of the peace'.[82]

Even so, the justices were felt by both Sir James Graham and the Lord Chief Justice to have become too restrictive[83] and *The Times* attacked the Middlesex and Staffordshire resolutions for their tendency to protect the workhouse and the prison.[84] With popular consciousness apprehensive of poisonings it was hardly reassuring that inquests had fallen steeply in Staffordshire, home to that celebrated poisoner William Palmer, and a sharp fall in inquests persuaded the Home Secretary to set up a royal commission.[85]

The Coroners' Society had been agitating for salaries to replace fees[86] and the same remedy commended itself to the Commission.[87] The new Home Secretary, Sir George Cornewall Lewis, had an old-fashioned preference for fees as providing an incentive to zeal and vigour but was overborne by a select committee and in 1860 county coroners became salaried, though at their own wish borough and franchise coroners were excluded from the Act.[88]

---

to coroners (*R v. Devon Justices* (7 *LT* (o.s.)) 228) was not fully reported: Fisher, *Politics of Sudden Death*, 168–9.

[79] P. B. Purnell, chairman of Gloucestershire sessions in 1857: Glasgow, 'Election of Gloucestershire Coroners, Part One', 22.

[80] *PP* 1840 (549), xiv, but the committee took a middle course and did not censure the justices.

[81] *R v. Hellier (otherwise Axford)*, Wells Assizes 1850, discussed in W. Baker, *A Practical Compendium of Recent Statutes, Cases and Decisions Affecting the Office of Coroner* (1851), 30–1. Havard (*Detection of Secret Homicide*, 57) wrongly identifies the judge as Coleridge LCJ; it was Sir J. T. Coleridge.

[82] *R v. Justices of Kent* (1809) 11 East 229, 231; R. F. Hunnisett, 'The Importance of Eighteenth Century Coroners' Bills', in *Law, Litigants and the Legal Profession*, ed. E. W. Ives and A. H. Manchester (1983), 126–39 at 134. Harrison of Cumberland was convicted of extortion by threatening to hold an inquest: *R v. Justices of Anglesea* (1799) 7 East P.C. 382. One enterprising coroner successfully claimed his expenses for an inquest on a mummy in transit but another was denied them for an inquest held on a skeleton unearthed in a long barrow: *SC on Coroners Evidence I*, J. B. Little, q. 115.

[83] Prichard, *Office of Coroner*, 29

[84] Leader of 29 January 1851 reproduced in Baker, *Office of Coroner*, 669–72.

[85] Havard, *Detection of Secret Homicide*, 57. Baker claimed there was a statistical relation between the number of inquests in a county and the incidence of poisonings: Prichard, *Office of Coroner*, 29.

[86] Glasgow, *Role of Lancashire Coroners*, 39; Havard, *Detection of Secret Homicide*, 62. Bills of 1850 and 1851 led to a select committee which made no report: Prichard, *Office of Coroner*, 43–8.

[87] *RC on the Expense of Coroners' Inquests*, *PP* 1859 sess. 2 (2575), xiii.

[88] Prichard, *Office of Coroner*, 48–51, *SC on the Office of Coroner*, *PP* 1860 (193), xxii.

Since the salaries were based on the number of inquests held over the past five years and were eligible for review every five years, there was still reason for the justices to scrutinize inquests.[89] One Lancashire coroner clashed repeatedly with quarter sessions, especially when he held 14 inquests in four days on deaths from a single colliery explosion[90] and Lancashire was one of several which took a narrow view of the 1860 Act.[91] Elsewhere justices delayed paying expenses, but though Wakley and Lankester were accused of maximizing inquests in pursuit of higher salaries, the change seems gradually to have muted antagonisms.[92] Naturally variations in salary were extreme. Wakley had £1800 and his successor Lankester eventually £1770.[93] Big cities, such as Liverpool and Birmingham, also paid four-figure sums,[94] and their coroners were whole timers, but in rural counties part-timers remained the rule; the four Oxfordshire coroners, for instance, made between £70 and £85 in 1870.[95]

Assistance

Coroners had to pay for their own assistance. County coroners frequently used deputies (usually their clerk) but in the Lees inquest case Best J. declared that since Ferrand's clerk, who had opened the inquest, had not been formally appointed deputy he could not conclude it.[96] Power to appoint a deputy was conferred upon borough coroners in 1836 and extended to county coroners in 1843.[97] In 1887 (counties) and 1892 (boroughs) a deputy was made compulsory,[98] to act in the coroner's indisposition or 'absence for any lawful or reasonable cause', a phrase which was often stretched to allow two inquests to be held simultaneously.[99]

[89] Coroners Act 1860, s. 43. The calculation (s. 3) was odd and illogical: Glasgow, *Role of Lancashire Coroners*, 47–8.

[90] C. E. Driffield: *ibid.*, 70–80.   [91] *Ibid.*, 46–87. The East Riding of Yorkshire was another.

[92] English, *Victorian Values*, 151–3.   [93] *Ibid.*, 141–2.

[94] Glasgow, 'Election of County Coroners', 79; *DC on Coroners Second Report and Evidence 1910*, evidence of T. E. Sampson, I. Bradley.

[95] Glasgow, 'Election of County Coroners', 79. In 1936 there were only 13 full-timers, and 81 coroners were earning less than £100 per annum: *DC on Coroners, PP* 1935–6 (5070), viii, 4.

[96] G. H. H. Glasgow, 'The John Lees inquest of 1819 and the Peterloo Massacre' (1998) 148 *Transactions of the Historic Society of Lancashire and Cheshire*, 95–118 at 103–4; *R v. Ferrand* (1819) 3 B. & Ald. 260, 660. Jervis (*Treatise on Coroners*, 54) asserted that there was no right to appoint a deputy.

[97] Administration of Justice (Boroughs) Act 1836 (6 & 7 Will. IV c. 105), s 6, Coroners Act 1843 (6 & 7 Vict. c. 83), s 1.

[98] He had to be approved by the Lord Chancellor in the counties and the mayor in the boroughs (see *PD* 1892 (s4) 5: 1781, 1866). Coroners Act 1887, s 13(1); Coroners Act 1892 (c. 92), s 1(1). The deputy was to be 'a fit person'. These provisions did not apply to franchise coroners, some of whom claimed a prescriptive right to appoint a deputy where the charter did not expressly confer it: *Halsbury's Laws of England*, viii, 237.

[99] Coroners Act 1892, s 1(3).

No allowance was given for clerical assistance[100] and most solicitor-coroners used their own clerks. Doctors were therefore at a disadvantage, as Lankester found to his cost.[101] Outdoor assistance, arranging the inquest for example, presented more difficulties. These tasks had usually fallen on the parish constable, who continued to perform the function in many places even after the establishment of a local police force because of its poor relations with the coroner.[102] Where it was feasible most coroners did make use of the police,[103] but some coroners preferred to use former policemen instead.[104]

3. INQUESTS

The Scope of the Duty

The extent of the coroner's duty to hold an inquest became a matter of persistent controversy. Grounded in what was eventually exposed as a fictitious statute[105] and deriving largely from the authoritative but historically unreliable Sir Matthew Hale, the duty had been narrowed to cases involving a reasonable suspicion that the deceased had met a violent or unnatural end: a sudden death from unexplained causes was insufficient.[106]

This narrow view appealed to the justices as guardians of the county rate but frustrated the more ambitious coroners;[107] men like Wakley who saw the potential of his office for preventing abuses in institutions for the poor, insane, and criminous;[108] 'sanitarians' like Baker and Lankester who envisaged it as part of the detective and preventive force against the spread of infectious and contagious

---

[100] Recommended by the *DC on Coroners Second Report and Evidence 1910*, 6.

[101] English, *Victorian Values*, 141. [102] Havard, *Detection of Secret Homicide*, 57–8, 141–3.

[103] e.g. in Birmingham: *DC on Coroners Evidence I*, Bradley, q. 3550.

[104] Havard, *Detection of Secret Homicide*, 141–3.

[105] *Officium Coronatoris*, attributed as 4 Edw. I statute 2 and exposed in F. M. Pollock and F. W. Maitland, *A History of English Law Before the Time of Edward I* (1895, re-issue 1968), ii, 641. It was regarded as declaring the common law.

[106] *R v. Great Western Railway* (1842) 3 Q.B. 333. Havard, *Detection of Secret Homicide*, 11–42 provides a detailed, though slanted, account, and see R. F. Hunnisett, *The Medieval Coroner, 1194–1487* (Cambridge, 1961).

[107] Compare the 'absolutist' view of Manchester's Edward Herford with the more selective approach of Rochdale's John Molesworth: Glasgow, *Role of Lancashire Coroners*, 157–64.

[108] Havard, *Detection of Secret Homicide*, 31–4; J. Hostettler, 'Thomas Wakley—An Enemy of Injustice' (1984) 5 *JLH* 60–76 at 67–72. In 1839 Wakley issued instructions that all workhouse deaths should be reported to him: J. Sim and T. Ward, 'The Magistrate of the Poor? Coroners and Deaths in Custody in Nineteenth Century England', in M. Clark and C. Crawford (eds), *Legal Medicine in History* (Cambridge, 1994), 249. Inquests on prison deaths were mandatory, and Henry 'Orator' Hunt, imprisoned in Ilchester gaol after 'Peterloo' drew public attention to the conduct of prison inquests: *ibid.*, 31–4.

diseases;[109] those alarmed at an apparent epidemic of poisoning and other surreptitious killings of unwanted infants;[110] and those, like Dr William Farr, anxious to improve the quality of official statistics.[111] With mass migration and industrialization having dislocated the traditional means of assisting accident victims,[112] made more numerous through machinery, inquests were a forum in which liability could be brought home to employers and undertakers.[113]

In 1860 a select committee, concerned at the fall in inquests, recommended a wider definition in words much quoted by coroners: 'it [is] desirable that an inquest should be held in every case of violent and unnatural death, and also that an inquest should be held in cases of sudden death where the cause of death is unknown, and also where, though the death is apparently natural, reasonable suspicion of criminality exists'.[114] but it was 1887 before it was given statutory effect: inquests should now be held:

(1) where the deceased was reasonably suspected of having met a violent or unnatural end;
(2) where the death was sudden and the cause unknown;
(3) where it took place in a prison or 'in such place or in such circumstances as to require an inquest in pursuance of any Act'.[115]

From around 1890 the proportion of inquests to total deaths rose from between 5 and 5½ per cent to between 6 and 7 per cent, suggesting that the Act had some effect.[116] The London County Council still fretted over inconsistent approaches among its coroners and some insisted on an inquest whenever no death certificate was available, but the Chalmers Committee did not recommend any further change.[117]

---

[109] 'Here then is a field open to the most immensurable extent for inquiry by the coroner', Baker, *Office of Coroner*, 7, and see also v–viii; English, *Victorian Values*, 143, Prichard, *Office of Coroner*, 53–64. Lankester issued annual reports of his work.

[110] Havard, *Detection of Secret Homicide*, 51–5. According to one MP, '[o]ne could scarcely take up a newspaper without seeing a case of suspected or proved murder by poison': *PD* 1860 (s3) 159: 2112 (J. M. Cobbett). Actual poisonings seem to have been much fewer: I. Burney, 'A Poisoning of No Substance: The Trials of Medico-Legal Proof in Mid-Victorian England' (1999) 38 *JBS* 59–92, at 69 n.32, and see K. Watson, *Poisoned Lives, English Poisoners and their Victims* (2004).

[111] Statistical superintendent at the General Register Office: Burney, *Bodies of Evidence*, 60–70.

[112] See A. W. B. Simpson's discussion of *Priestley* v. *Fowler*, 'A Case of First Impression', in *Leading Cases in the Common Law* (Oxford, 1995), 100–34.

[113] E. Cawthon, 'Thomas Wakley and the Medical Coronership—Occupational Death and the Judicial Process' (1986) 30 *Medical History* 191–202; T. Sutton, *The Deodand* (1997) 18 *JLH* 44–55 at 46–53.

[114] *SC on Coroners Report 1860*, iii; Prichard, *Office of Coroner*, 49.

[115] Coroners Act 1887, s. 3(1).   [116] *Evidence I*, App. 2, 610.

[117] *Evidence I*, R. H. Wellington, qq. 4997–9, J. B. Little, qq. 227 *et seq.*; recommendations of 1895, Prichard, *Office of Coroner*, 180–2. There is an interesting selection of inquest cases in Barnard, *Viewing the Breathless Corpse*.

Notification

The common law duty of individuals and communities to notify the coroner of sudden deaths had practically ceased to be enforceable, leaving the eighteenth-century coroner reliant on reports from parish officers, who still had a financial incentive, and the general public.[118] By degrees the state interested itself in a range of fatal situations, and statutes imposed a reporting duty for, inter alia, deaths in asylums, factories, prisons and reformatories, retreats, and 'baby farms'.[119] Two innovations in the late 1830s created the potential for a comprehensive arrangement for notification. However, no attempt was made to integrate the registration of deaths (1836) with inquests. The Act imposed no duty on the doctor providing a death certificate to notify the coroner of potential inquests; that was left to local deputy registrars, and even if they were punctilious, there were gaps in the system which led to deaths going uncertificated.[120] The select committee on death certification in 1893 was scathing about the deficiencies of this, as most aspects of certification and registration.[121]

Doctors were not always co-operative either. They often sought to shield their patients' families from an inquest in cases of suicide or other embarrassing deaths and, as criticism of the coroner in Sir Charles Lyell's case showed, respectable opinion mostly sided with the doctor.[122] The Coroners' Society unavailingly claimed there was an enforceable common law duty on a medical practitioner in attendance on the deceased to notify the coroner[123] and relations between doctors and coroners worsened when some coroners, responding to public concern, began insisting on holding inquests on all deaths under anaesthetic.[124] Then in 1908 the wayward Troutbeck broke an unwritten understanding by starting to hold inquests on deaths during or after surgical operations, provoking a furious response from the surgeons.[125]

The second event was the creation of local police forces. However, the police were not under the coroner's authority and in some places his attempts to require reports on all sudden deaths to him were countermanded by the local authority, as

---

[118] Anderson, *Suicide in Victorian and Edwardian England*, 19.

[119] *Ibid.*, 18. There is a full list in *Halsbury's Laws of England*, viii, 241–7.

[120] Havard, *Detection of Secret Homicide*, 67–76, 97–8.

[121] *PP* 1893–4 (373), (402), xi; Burney, *Bodies of Evidence*, 67–70.

[122] Prichard, *Office of Coroner*, 92–9.

[123] Havard, *Detection of Secret Homicide*, 85–6. They cited *R* v. *Clerk* (1702) 1 Salk. 377 as authority. The fifth and sixth editions of *Jervis on Coroners* agreed, but *Halsbury's Laws of England*, viii, 240 (1909) differed.

[124] Burney, *Bodies of Evidence*, 137–64. The terms of reference of the Chalmers Committee required a special report on this subject.

[125] Prichard, *Office of Coroner*, 22–7; Zuck, 'Mr. Troutbeck as the Surgeon's Friend', 280–6.

happened to Wakley and to Herford.[126] Even when left to their own discretion the police often reported only violent deaths, and as they became increasingly a detective force rather than a purely preventive one, they naturally tended to conduct a preliminary investigation, however cursory, rather than leaving this to the coroner.

Though there was no prospect of judges reviving the broad common law duty to notify the coroner of sudden deaths, they were obliged to create a new offence of obstructing a coroner in the course of his duties. This transpired because Stephen J.'s ruling that cremation was lawful[127] opened the way for murderers, particularly by poison, to destroy the evidence of their crime.[128]

Post-Mortems

The advance of pathology made the post-mortem examination an increasingly valuable tool in determining cause of death, but it did not fit comfortably into the ideology and practice of inquests. A prior autopsy which produced findings that removed the suspicion of foul play or misadventure made an inquest otiose, yet the common law required that if the coroner ordered an autopsy he must then hold an inquest.[129] This sometimes posed a dilemma, since families objected to the publicity and upset attendant upon an inquest, and would blame the coroner if it proved unnecessary.[130] Though still opposed by some coroners who feared being pressurized not to hold an inquest,[131] the view that the coroner should be able to hold a post-mortem without proceeding to inquest gained ground, but despite a recommendation in the Chalmers Report the obligatory yoking together of post-mortem and inquest persisted until 1926.[132]

Whether to order a post-mortem was a matter for the coroner,[133] and some, particularly medical coroners, enthused about its virtues. Lankester said that a verdict of 'found dead' was never acceptable; where there was doubt a post-mortem should be held and 'when he ordered a post-mortem examination to

---

[126] Havard, *Detection of Secret Homicide*, 57–8; Glasgow, *Role of Lancashire Coroners*, 146–8.

[127] *Re Price* (1884) 12 QBD 247. For background see S. White, 'A Burial ahead of its Time?': The Crookenden Burial Case and the Sanctioning of Cremation in England and Wales', in T. G. Watkin (ed.), *The Trial of Dic Penderyn and other Essays* (Cardiff, 2003), 151–79.

[128] *R v. Stephenson* (1884) 13 QBD 331; Havard, *Detection of Secret Homicide*, 80–4.

[129] Isaac Bradley of Birmingham told the Chalmers Committee that half his inquests were unnecessary: *Evidence I*, q. 3578.

[130] Wealthier families sometimes offered to have a private autopsy, which might obviate the necessity for an inquest: *ibid.*, J. B. Little, q. 250.

[131] Compare *DC on Coroners Evidence I*, R. Wellington (q. 5019) with G. P. Wyatt (q. 996) and F. J. Waldo (q. 1911).

[132] *Second Report and Evidence 1910*, 10.

[133] Coroners Expenses Act 1836, s 2. A majority of the jury might also call for a post-mortem but this was very unusual.

be made it was to be a thorough and not a partial one; all the organs were to be tested, as poison had frequently been found where there was no suspicion of anything of the kind'.[134] The sanitarians were naturally keen[135] and post-mortems were probably most frequent where they could be carried out free of charge by local hospital doctors.[136] This made possible the controversial practice of John Troutbeck, who resorted to a post-mortem in 99.2 per cent of his cases.[137]

Troutbeck stirred up professional hostility by making use of a single expert pathologist (and worse, a foreigner) to perform his autopsies.[138] Specialization had became more common and pathology achieved recognition as a distinct discipline,[139] but the 1836 Act did not require any special expertise in the doctor and many practitioners lacked experience.[140] Many actively disliked this duty, so that, while the number of autopsies steadily increased,[141] the results fell well short of Lankester's ideal. Outside major towns coroners often had little choice but to use the deceased's doctor, with obvious drawbacks, and though the specialists pointed to unsatisfactory results in sensational cases such as Harriet Staunton's, their opponents argued against placing undue reliance on clinical teleology divorced from familiarity with the case history.[142]

Some coroners felt their control of the inquest threatened by the sort of evidence produced by a post-mortem, which posed the question whether the view of the body continued to serve any useful purpose. It continued to be mandatory[143] but was unpopular with some jurymen[144] and was often very perfunctory.[145] Traditionalists defended its symbolic role in the 'open' inquest,[146] but even within

---

[134] English, *Victorian Values*, 144.   [135] Prichard, *Office of Coroner*, 59–60.

[136] Anderson, *Suicide in Victorian and Edwardian England*, 27.

[137] *Ibid.*; Prichard, *Office of Coroner*, 206–31. See above.

[138] Prichard, *Office of Coroner*, 211–14.

[139] Burney, *Bodies of Evidence*, 107–35. The Pathological Society of London was founded in 1846.

[140] They were liable to a fine if they refused: Coroners Expenses Act 1836, s. 6.

[141] According to Forbes, 'Crowner's Quest', table 15, in the 1820s the City and Southwark coroner held post-mortems in about 20% of his inquests. Between 1835–8 and 1865–6 the proportion in Westminster rose from 17% to 49% and in the LCC's jurisdiction there was a steady rise from 48% in 1894 to 62% in 1918: Burney, *Bodies of Evidence*, Ch. 2 n.25. The incidence in rural counties was probably much lower.

[142] Burney, *Bodies of Evidence*, 107–35.

[143] Re-enacted in the Coroners Act 1887, s 4(1), though by then the requirement for the jury to be sworn in the presence of the body had been held unnecessary.

[144] *DC on Coroners Second Report and Evidence*, E. A. Gibson, q. 8326, S. F. Butcher q. 10,637; *Evidence I*, I. Bradley q. 3901; Burney, *Bodies of Evidence*, 93.

[145] Burney, *Bodies of Evidence*, 96. In the Lyell case the jury barely glimpsed the body: Prichard, *Office of Coroner*, 92–100.

[146] Burney, *Bodies of Evidence*, 99, also noting that in 1898 it was defended by the Lord Chancellor's Office. Other defenders included Herford (Glasgow, *Role of Lancashire Coroners*, 178) and G. V. Benson (*DC on Coroners Second Report and Evidence*, qq. 6394–9).

the Coroners' Society the balance of opinion came to consider it unnecessary for the jury and many felt it should be discretionary even for the coroner.[147]

In other ways too the increasing resort to post-mortems threatened to change the nature of the inquest. Since it was difficult to perform one in a private home or in the public house where the inquest was to be held, pressure grew to provide special facilities, which did not always please the deceased's family and diminished the impact of the inquest as a public act.[148] Furthermore, though doctors were encouraged to make their findings intelligible, even non-medical coroners struggled to summarize post-mortem findings to the jury,[149] while its daunting technicality and imperviousness to lay questioning seemed to give it a peculiar authority. In poisoning cases the regular resort to a handful of experts gave them a particular, and rather dangerous, authority. Thomas Stevenson, called in 24 such cases, became the Home Office's official analyst and the fame of Sir Bernard Spilsbury spread through reports of sensational murder trials. At least at trial barristers could probe their testimony, but it must have become ever harder to dispute their findings at an inquest.[150]

The Conduct of the Inquest

The coroner's court was a peculiar one, 'a court of law, but it cannot be fitted into any classification of courts...a fact-finding body, incapable of trying any issue civil or criminal'.[151] This distinctiveness extended to the venue, which was usually a public house.[152] Traditionalists like Toulmin-Smith defended this custom,[153] with petty sessions and the new county courts mostly held in town halls and courthouses it seemed anomalous and undesirable.[154] Nevertheless change was very slow. The London County Council led the way, but Lancashire inquests of the 1890s were almost invariably in public houses, and even after the Licensing Act 1902 had restricted it to places where there was no alternative, it remained common in rural districts.[155]

---

[147] Burney, *Bodies of Evidence*, 211 n.65. The 1926 Act made the view discretionary and according to Watson, *Poisoned Lives*, 162, no jury afterwards viewed the body.

[148] *Ibid.*, 104–6; *DC on Coroners Evidence I*, G. P. Wyatt, q. 984.

[149] Burney, *Bodies of Evidence*, 118–20.

[150] Watson, *Poisoned Lives*, 166–73, especially table 5 on 167. The first to acquire a national reputation was Alfred Swayne Taylor, called in 31 cases.

[151] R. M. Jackson, *The Machinery of Justice in England* (Cambridge, 1940), 97. Regrettably, as the Wright Committee observed, these peculiarities extended to a failure to preserve records (*Report*, 3).

[152] 'The coroner frequents more public houses than any man alive': Dickens' description of an inquest in *Bleak House*, 196–200 is accurate. More than 80% of Middlesex inquests in the early nineteenth century were held there: Burney, *Bodies of Evidence*, 81 n.3.

[153] In a riposte to a critical article by Dickens in *Household Words*: Burney, *Bodies of Evidence*, 83.

[154] *Ibid.*, 84, citing in particular a parliamentary criticism of the Bravo inquest.

[155] *Ibid.*, 81.

This undignified venue contributed to an 'image problem' which led coroners to debate whether they should wear robes.[156] Nevertheless, the coroner was the judge of a court of record, immune from suit in respect of words or actions within his jurisdiction and in the exercise of it.[157] His court was subject to the supervisory jurisdiction of the King's Bench and anyone affected by the outcome might traverse the inquisition,[158] usually by way of *certiorari*, to have it amended or quashed.[159] The superior courts had the common law power to amend defects of form, but not substance,[160] and might adopt a highly technical approach; the use of paper rather than parchment sufficed to quash the verdict in one case,[161] as did the omission of the word 'instantly' in another.[162] It quashed one verdict on the grounds that the facts did not support the jury's conclusion[163] but not another where the evidence did not do so,[164] and in that same case (one where the judges were highly critical of coroners' inquests), it refused to confirm that a misdirection was sufficient ground either. However, in the Bravo case, Carter's refusal to admit relevant evidence did provide a ground for quashing the verdict.[165] How far coroners were influenced by the possibility of review remains unexplored.[166]

No rules provided a framework encouraging uniformity, no knowledgeable clerk gave law to an unqualified coroner and no regular bar constrained his autonomy.[167] Despite formal disclaimers of responsibility, the Home Office would usually provide guidance on difficult points if requested, but these opinions had no authority and do not seem to have been made available in collected form.[168] The Coroners' Society might have emulated the Association of County Court

---

[156] *Ibid.*, 102–3.

[157] *Garnett* v. *Ferrand* (1827) 6 B. & C. 611. In *Thomas* v. *Churton* (1862) 2 B. & S. 475, it was held (though Cockburn CJ had doubts) that this privilege extended to words spoken falsely and maliciously in addressing the jury.

[158] *Halsbury's Laws of England*, viii, 273–9.

[159] *Ibid.*, 283–8. Anyone charged with a criminal offence in an inquisition might seek amendment: Coroners Act 1887, s. 20.

[160] See e.g. *R* v. *Evett* (1827) 6 B. & C. 247.　　　[161] *R* v. *Whalley* (1849) 19 LJ QB 14.

[162] *R* v. *Brownlow* (1839) 11 Ad. & El. 119 (the court was probably anxious to find a way of avoiding the award of a large deodand). Cawthon, 'Thomas Wakley and the Medical Coronership', 196. However, in *R* v. *Ingham* (1864) 5 B. & S. 257, both Cockburn CJ and Blackburn J. took the view that the Coroners Act 1843 (s 2) which sought to avoid inquisitions being quashed for technical defects, should be given a purposive construction.

[163] *R* v. *Culley* (1833) 5 B. & Ald 230.　　　[164] *R* v. *Ingham* (1864) 5 B. & S. 257.

[165] *R* v. *Carter* (1876) 45 LJ (QB) 711.

[166] The Chalmers Committee was told that only three inquest verdicts had been set aside in the previous seven years: *Second Report and Evidence 1910*, 4.

[167] Counsel could not claim audience as of right (*Jervis on Coroners*, 239), though in practice it was unusual not to hear them and in some instances, as at the Lees inquest, they dominated the proceedings: Glasgow, 'John Lees Inquest and Peterloo Massacre', 106–8.

[168] Prichard, *Office of Coroner*, 234.

Registrars in compiling guidance, but although it originally aspired to 'promote regularity and uniformity', it was never fully representative, tended towards conservatism and seems seldom to have been consulted by its members.[169] The Lord Chancellor used his power to remove a coroner only in extreme cases, so a maverick like Troutbeck could safely take a completely different line from his London colleagues on controversial points.[170] The Chalmers Committee recommended the establishment of a rule committee but when a rule-making power was given in 1926, results were initially disappointing.[171]

The most contentious exercise of the coroner's discretion was whether to call medical evidence and, if so, what and whose,[172] and the 'open court'. Radicals and reactionaries alike were insistent that if this was indeed a 'people's court' and the coroner 'eminently the magistrate of the poor',[173] it must be open to the public and its proceedings freely reported.[174] However, the coroner's power to exclude some or all of the public was affirmed[175] and a bill to change that was lost through differences between Lords and Commons.[176] It had earlier been ruled in R v. Fleet that the publication of evidence which might prejudice a trial jury could be prevented,[177] and Mr Justice Park added further emphatic warnings in 1823, though the Whitcombe scandal indicated that suppression of reporting sometimes had undesirable consequences.[178] Newspapers took little notice and the judges gradually softened their attitude.[179] In general coroners did not attempt to ban reporting even where, as in Palmer's case, it would make it difficult to secure an unprejudiced trial jury.[180] In fact it was not in inquests of great public

---

[169] Ibid., 31, 120, 125, 342. It was founded in 1846, succeeding a committee of 1843. Isaac Bradley told the Chalmers Committee in 1909 that about two-thirds were members (Evidence 1, q. 2523), a considerable increase on the 154 of 1893 (Anderson, Suicide in Victorian and Edwardian England, 17). There was also a Northern Counties Coroners Association: Glasgow, Role of Lancashire Coroners, 162.

[170] For vain attempts to persuade him to tackle Troutbeck, see Zuck, 'Mr. Troutbeck as the Surgeon's Friend', 270–7, and see Prichard, Office of Coroner, 336–8.

[171] Second Report and Evidence 1910, 11; DC on Coroners Report 1936, 51.

[172] The BMA was incensed at some coroners' reluctance to seek medical evidence: Zuck, 'Mr. Troutbeck as the Surgeon's Friend', 262.

[173] The Times, 29 January 1851, quoted in Baker, Office of Coroner, 669.

[174] According to James Harmer at the Lees inquest, 'if all the people of England could be so compressed, they are entitled to be present': Glasgow, 'Lees Inquest and Peterloo Massacre', 105.

[175] Garnett v. Ferrand (1827) 6 B. & C. 610. The first edition of Jervis's treatise describes it as 'the subject of much controversy' (212).

[176] PD 1834 (s3) 21: 558; 25: 1048–52, 1251. For an earlier attempt see Burney, Bodies of Evidence, 33–7.

[177] (1818) 1 B. & Ald. 379; Jervis on Coroners, 242.

[178] D. J. Bentley, English Criminal Justice in the Nineteenth Century (1998), 45–6, citing especially R v. Pallett, The Times, 13, 15 December 1823.

[179] Ibid., 47–9.

[180] Burney, Poisoning of no Substance, 66–7. Palmer's was the first trial to be moved to another locality.

importance that the coroner sought to keep proceedings private,[181] so much as sensational deaths among the well-to-do. Troutbeck's action in the Duke of Bedford's case was characteristically bold[182] and it had become common enough for the National Union of Journalists to make representations to the Chalmers Committee in favour of a right to report. Unfortunately for them, their representative was obliged to admit that the only inquests they wanted to report were precisely those which the Committee felt ought not to be reported.[183]

The Jury

The coroner's jury differed from the common jury in several respects and despite strong criticism its peculiarities remained untouched. One distinctive feature was that any number from 12 to 23 might be summoned, though it was uncommon to call up more than 15.[184] Beyond needing to be male householders in the district these 'good and lawful men' needed no qualifications,[185] but one Birmingham coroner excluded only common labourers, while his Liverpool counterpart used the town directories to ensure a more socially select jury.[186] In London, however, the socially select often bought their way out of jury service.[187] In the country districts it is unlikely that the coroner's officer could afford to be choosy, speed being of the essence.[188]

Another peculiarity was that the verdict need not be unanimous; a valid inquisition needed only the agreement of 12 jurors, even if the jury was larger.[189] The Chalmers Committee was prepared to require only 12 jurors in all cases and still

---

[181] *DC on Coroners Evidence 1*, J. B. Little, q. 514. The Lord Chancellor had confirmed their right to do so in 1887: Zuck, 'Mr. Troutbeck as the Surgeon's Friend', 264 n.26.

[182] Prichard, *Office of Coroner*, 114–16. The family, with the coroner's connivance, almost succeeded in publicly passing off the suicide as an accidental death.

[183] *DC on Coroners Second Report and Evidence 1910*, 21 and J. T. Smith, qq. 10,412–599. See also Prichard, *Office of Coroner*, 118. In *Weldon* v. *Meignard* (1889) 87 LT 356 a judge refused to interfere with the publication of inquest evidence even with comments, though he deprecated it.

[184] *Halsbury's Laws of England*, viii, 259; Coroners Act 1887, s. 3. However, in the controversial Cully inquest there were 17. The coroner decided upon the number: Fisher, *Politics of Sudden Death*, 120.

[185] They were subject to the same disqualifications and exemptions as a petty jury: *Re Dutton* [1892] 1 QB 486. The question of calling up women seems not to have arisen, though Bradley of Birmingham said that he did not (*DC on Coroners Evidence 1*, q. 3888).

[186] *Ibid.*, and *Second Report and Evidence 1910*, q. 9030.

[187] As Dickens felt he was expected to do: Cawthon, 'Thomas Wakley and the Medical Coronership', 194–5.

[188] Burney, *Bodies of Evidence*, 4; Anderson, *Suicide in Victorian and Edwardian England*, 27–8; G. G. Alexander, *The Administration of Justice in Criminal Matters in England and Wales* (Cambridge, rev. edn, 1919), 99.

[189] Coroners Act 1887, s 3(5).

to allow a three-quarters majority verdict, but even in the 1920s this found no favour.[190]

Throughout the period critics, including some coroners,[191] wanted to abolish or curtail the jury, disliking its freedom from control.[192] In his first edition John Jervis noted that it was doubtful how far a coroner could impose his view of the law on his jury. His only resort in the case of a divided jury or a verdict he felt perverse was to send them off to the Assizes to be lectured by a judge, and that did not always work.[193] Respectable opinion was shocked by the verdict of justifiable homicide of the policeman Cully;[194] businessmen feared 'the upstart ideas of juries on accident compensation'[195] and the revival of the deodand in deaths from accidents on steamships and railways;[196] later on, institutional doctors were offended by unfavourable verdicts on the deaths of paupers and prisoners.[197] Against that, there was widespread approval for juries' stubborn refusal to return verdicts of *felo de se*, which still carried unpleasant consequences, on suicides.[198] Those who would medicalize the inquest made great play with the most egregious verdicts that emerged from inquests, though Wakley—a defender of juries—attributed these more to the inadequacy of the lawyer-coroner than to the deficiencies of the jurors.[199]

The jury survived all attacks, even though coroners themselves became divided over its merits.[200] Perhaps reluctantly, and with an eye to political realities, the

---

[190] *Second Report and Evidence, 1910,* 14. A majority of the Coroners' Society felt seven should be sufficient to form a jury: S. F. Butcher, q. 10,619.

[191] Prichard, *Office of Coroner,* 37.

[192] The jury, sometimes encouraged by the coroner, could also append a rider to the verdict apportioning praise or blame and suggesting reforms: Burney, *Bodies of Evidence,* 5.

[193] e.g. the Gosport jury on the accident to the 'Mistletoe', sunk in a collision with the royal yacht, had Bramwell expound the law to them but remained hopelessly divided: Prichard, *Office of Coroner,* 100–5.

[194] Burney, *Bodies of Evidence,* 37.

[195] Cawthon, 'Thomas Wakley and the Medical Coronership', 193.

[196] Sutton, 'The Deodand', 44–55.

[197] Sim and Ward, 'Magistrate of the Poor?', 262. Yet some murder verdicts (especially infanticides) may have been evaded through fear that the parish would be burdened with the expenses of a prosecution: Fisher, *Politics of Sudden Death,* 234–5.

[198] Anderson, *Suicide in Victorian and Edwardian England,* 219–30. One of Forbes's studies found only 16 suicides against 925 'suicide while lunatic' ('Crowner's Quest', 13, table 2) and in 1909 Wellington said he had known only two *felo de se* verdicts in 12 years and 600 suicides (*DC on Coroners Evidence I,* q. 5578). Jervis had urged that 'unsound mind' verdicts 'ought not to be carried to that length to which coroners' juries are too apt to carry it' (*Jervis on Coroners,* 112).

[199] e.g. those cited by William Ogle of the registration office: 'Died from stone in the kidney which stone he swallowed when laying on a gravel path in a state of drunkenness' and 'Child, three months old, found dead, but no evidence whether born alive': quoted in Burney, *Bodies of Evidence,* 68. As late as 1880 a Somerset jury brought in a verdict of 'visitation of God': Fisher, *Politics of Sudden Death,* 198.

[200] *DC on Coroners Evidence I,* I. Bradley (q. 3861); *Second Report and Evidence 1910,* S. F. Butcher (q. 10,619).

Chalmers Committee was only prepared to suggest majority verdicts and a power for the coroner to apply to a judge in chambers to set aside a perverse verdict.[201]

Committals

The most controversial power exercised by a coroner's court was to commit a person suspected of homicide for trial at the Assizes.[202] Coroners' committals had existed long before magistrates were given similar powers and the two co-existed on uneasy terms.[203] Jealous magistrates usually insisted on making their own investigation even when there was already a coroner's committal and the duplication could be embarrassing when each committed the prisoner to a different Assize town,[204] or where the justices (sometimes wrongly) discharged the committal. Wakley thwarted the Middlesex justices by making committals direct to Newgate but this was one of the complaints brought against him.[205]

Coroners had certain advantages over justices in getting at the truth, but these were the result of omitting safeguards for the suspect which were imposed upon magistrates.[206] The strict common law rules of evidence were not observed;[207] witnesses could be obliged to testify to their own peril[208] and until 1887 the accused was not entitled to copies of the depositions.[209] These features, and the notorious difficulty coroners found in drawing up a judge-proof inquisition, influenced the Criminal Law Commissioners to propose the abolition of coroners' committals in 1849, but many saw the coroner's court as a safeguard against misdeeds by public officers and in public institutions; they approved the notorious 'justifiable homicide' finding in Cully's case, Wakley's exposure of army flogging in the 1840s, and several investigations of workhouse deaths.[210] Nevertheless, judges came to

---

[201] *Second Report and Evidence 1910*, 14.

[202] The Middlesex Justices Special Committee of 1851 reported that barely 1% of inquests had this outcome: Sim and Ward, 'Magistrate of the Poor', 254, and see Forbes, 'Crowner's Quest', 13, table 2.

[203] Prichard, *Office of Coroner*, 37.

[204] *DC on Coroners Second Report and Evidence 1910*, 17. Remedied in 1926 by enabling the coroner to suspend his inquest until the magistrates' proceedings were completed.

[205] Havard, *Detection of Secret Homicide*, 171–2.   [206] *Ibid.*, 176–7.

[207] Judges seem gradually to have introduced restrictions; see e.g. *R v. Rigg* (1866) 4 F. & F. 1085 (*Halsbury's Laws of England*, viii, 291). Curiously, the DPP deplored the suggestion of the Wright Committee that coroners should conform to the rules of evidence: note in LCO 2/1245.

[208] In *Wakley v. Cooke* (1849) 4 Exch. 511 it was held that the coroner should warn anyone whose testimony went to incriminate himself that he need not do so, but the coroner should not refuse to receive such testimony.

[209] Coroners Act 1887, s 18(5).

[210] Fifth Report, *PP* 1849 (1100), xxi; draft bill, 11; Havard, *Detection of Secret Homicide*, 173–4. The inquest into the death of Corporal White at Hounslow Barracks in 1846 contributed to the ending of flogging in the army. Wakley gained favourable publicity from the inquest on an elderly pauper, Thomas Austin, who fell into a vat of boiling water at Hendon workhouse, especially for his much

regard the inquisition, unsupported by a justices' committal, as insufficient[211] and in 1864 Mr Justice Blackburn subscribed to the widespread sentiment that coroners' committals should be ended.[212] There was no consensus in official circles on how to deal with the overlapping jurisdiction, for within a year of a select committee urging that the inquest be empowered to commit directly for trial, by-passing both justices and the grand jury, Stephen's draft criminal code required their verdict to be submitted to the petty sessions.[213] There matters remained until the headline 'virtual trials' in the 1920s revived the controversy.[214]

4. OTHER DUTIES

Most of the coroner's other duties had either been abolished or become obsolete and only three survived the consolidating Act of 1887.[215] These were: certain duties in relation to outlawry (itself obsolescent); substituting for the sheriff in certain cases; and inquests on treasure trove.[216] The City of London coroner acquired an additional duty, to hold inquests on serious fires even if there were no loss of life.[217] An attempt to assert that power at common law had failed in 1860[218] and although the Chalmers Committee recommended that it be made general, that was never done.[219]

quoted retort to the protest of a workhouse official that the body had not been identified as Austin's: 'Pray sir, how many paupers have you boiled?': Burney, *Bodies of Evidence*, 42–50.

[211] Glasgow, *Role of Lancashire Coroners*, 186. In Manchester the police refused to produce suspected persons from custody to give evidence at inquests and the Home Secretary refused to interfere: *ibid.*, 143.

[212] *R v. Ingham* (1864) 5 B. & S. 257 at 277.

[213] Havard, *Detection of Secret Homicide*, 175. The criminal code proposal was foreshadowed in the Judicature Commissioners *Fifth Report 1874*, xviii, and was also in a Criminal Law Procedure Bill of 1894 which was not enacted.

[214] Prichard, *Office of Coroner*, 301–11; Schuster's memorandum, LCO 2/1244, 27.

[215] Holdsworth, *HEL*, i, 86–7.

[216] *Halsbury's Laws of England*, vol. 8, 237–8, 248–50; *DC on Coroners Evidence I*, William Brown (Assistant King's Proctor), q. 727.

[217] City of London Fire Inquests Act 1888 (c. xxxviii); *Halsbury's Laws of England*, viii, 296–7.

[218] *R v. Herford* (1860) 3 E. & E. 115; Glasgow, *Role of Lancashire Coroners*, 174–6. The Home Secretary had refused to extend it in 1860: Prichard, *Office of Coroner*, 125.

[219] *Second Report and Evidence 1910*, 8–9, and see *Evidence I*, F. J. Waldo, qq. 1819–2105.

Part Four

THE LEGAL PROFESSIONS

I

The Judiciary

1. THE JUDGES OF THE SUPERIOR COURTS

Note on Sources

Around 20 of the superior court judges of this period have written autobiographies or memoirs or, more commonly, been the subject of biographies.[1] Predictably, their value to the historian is enormously variable and few are of recent date;[2] compared with politicians, even the most renowned judges (unless they were Lord Chancellors) do not attract biographers.[3] However, almost all (Alexander CB is one notable exception) have an entry in the *Oxford Dictionary of National Biography*, and in some cases these have been considerably revised from the original *Dictionary of National Biography* entry; compare, for example, C. W. J. Allen's entry on Sir Fitzroy Kelly.[4] The best known also feature in the *Biographical Dictionary of the Common Law*.[5]

Collective judicial biographies are nothing new. Among the earliest, and best known, are John, Lord Campbell's sequences of *Lives of the Lord Chancellors*[6] (the volumes which are famously said to have added a new terror to death) and *Lives of the Lord Chief Justices*.[7] The former, which ended with Lyndhurst, has been continued in very different, and infinitely more reliable, fashion first by J. B. Atlay[8] and then by R. F. V. Heuston,[9] but the later Chief Justices (after Tenterden) are

---

[1] When completed, the London School of Economics project on legal biographies will provide full information. There may also be some autobiographies which have never been published besides that of Lord Lindley. On judicial biography generally, see P. Girard, 'Judging Lives: Judicial Biography from Hale to Holmes (2003) 7 *AJLH* 87–106.

[2] The subjects of the most recent, Geoffrey Lewis, *Lord Atkin* (1983) and Anthony Lethin, *The Last Political Law Lord: Lord Sumner* (1859–1934) (Cambridge, 2008), barely come within this period.

[3] There is none e.g. for Blackburn, Parke, or Willes, nor (on the Chancery side) for Grant.

[4] *ODNB* 31: 110.

[5] Edited by A. W. B. Simpson (1984).

[6] 8 vols (1845–69). For its complex publishing history see G. F. Holborn, *Sources of Biographical Information on Past Lawyers* (1999), which is the best guide to the literature on judges generally.

[7] 3 vols (1849–57).

[8] *The Victorian Chancellors*, 2 vols (1908).

[9] *Lives of the Lord Chancellors*, 1885–1940 (Oxford, 1964) and *1940–1970* (Oxford, 1987).

covered only briefly in A. Mockler's *Lions under the Throne* (1983). Campbell's compilations are not the only ones that require great caution in their use. James Grant's *The Bench and Bar*, 2 vols (1837–8) is tempting in its wide coverage and pungent style but is not to be trusted without corroboration.[10] Unfortunately, for the first half of the nineteenth century corroboration is hard to come by except in the often rather brief and not always very informative pages of Edward Foss's *The Judges of England*, 9 vols (1848–64), though that much reviled reporter Espinasse dealt interestingly with a few of his higher-achieving contemporaries[11] and a few of the most famous are in W. C. Townsend's *Lives of Twelve Eminent Judges*, 2 vols (1846) or W. H. Bennet's *Select Biographical Sketches* (1867). Obituaries, particularly in the *Law Magazine*, can be informative and not uncritical, but it is only after c.1870 that those in *The Times* regularly attained the amplitude later generations came to expect.

Posterity is better served for the later Victorian judges, not only through the much more numerous memoirs and autobiographies of members of the bar, but also in two much used collections, written by W. D. I. Foulkes[12] and Edward Manson,[13] respectively. There is also an interestingly idiosyncratic selection by 'E' (Edward Bowen Rowlands) in the *Strand Magazine* for 1896.[14] The fullest and most scholarly, however, is Van Veeden Vechter's survey in the volumes of *Select Essay in Anglo-American Legal History*.[15] After two post-First World War collections, Lord Birkenhead's *Fourteen English Judges* (1926) and Evelyn Graham's *Fifty Years of Famous Judges* (1930), the fashion for such publications waned, though Sir William Holdsworth maintained his practice of providing succint appraisals of the leading judges of the period.[16]

Some of these sources provide valuable material on their subject's judicial style and manner, but disappointingly few—Waddams' book on Lushington[17] and Bourguignon's on Stowell[18] are notable exceptions—offer a worthwhile analysis of the intellectual and ideological underpinnings of their judgments. In a few cases modern academic writings fill the gap; the *American Journal of Legal History*

---

[10] See the review by Abraham Hayward in (1838) 19 *LM* 88–103.

[11] 'My Contemporaries' (1832) 6 *Fraser's Mag.* 220–30, 314–24, 417–28; vol. 7, 44–53, 178–90, 555–64.

[12] *A Generation of Judges, by their Reporter* (1886)

[13] *Builders of our Law in the Reign of Queen Victoria* (1895, 2nd edn, 1904).

[14] 'Her Majesty's Judges' (1896), 456–65, 551–58, 689–95. For some more eccentric appraisals see e.g. E. Burnaby, *Memories of Famous Trials* (1907).

[15] Edited by a Committee of American Law Schools, 3 vols (Boston, USA, 1907), i, 730–836.

[16] *HEL* vols xv, 395–510; xvi (1965), 5–170, edited by A. L. Goodhart and H. G. Hanbury.

[17] *Law, Politics and the Church of England* (Cambridge, 1992).

[18] *Sir William Scott, Lord Stowell* (Cambridge, 1987).

issue 'For a Bramwell Revival' is one such,[19] as is Burns' article on Cottenham,[20] but they are strikingly few, and it is now 50 years since C. H. S. Fifoot's Hamlyn lectures on *Judge and Jurist in the Reign of Victoria*.[21]

There are also disappointingly few studies of the operation of particular courts, especially the common law courts sitting in banc. A notable exception is Robert Stevens' thorough examination of the jurisprudence of the House of Lords after the reconstruction of 1876, albeit couched in a rather constricting intellectual framework.[22] We know very little, for instance, of the interaction of the judges in Pollock's Exchequer, or the Queen's Bench under Cockburn; yet even so able a judge as Bowen had few opportunities to make his mark in the Court of Appeal, where the custom had developed very early to confine the junior judges to short judgments.[23]

On the larger stage, the gaps are even more notable. While the changing attitude to precedent has been explored in some detail, there have been few if any attempts to elaborate on Stephen Hedley's stimulating essay of more than a decade ago on such fundamental matters as the length of judgments; the resort to civil and other common law jurisdiction authorities; the role of textbooks and of extra-judicial authorities, religious, economic, sociological.[24] Here, surely, is a fruitful field of study.

Appointment: Eligibility

Judges were appointed from members of the English bar, or for the civilian courts, from the advocates of Doctors' Commons. After the Judicature Act 1875 a person appointed to the High Court had to be of 10 years' standing, and those appointed directly to the Court of Appeal and House of Lords, the Master of the Rolls and heads of divisions, of 15 years. Only once did these requirements threaten inconvenience, when Sir Edward Carson was offered to be President of the PDA in 1905 when not qualified; fortunately he declined.[25] Curiously, there is no formal legal qualification for Lord Chancellor, but as Canning found when

---

[19] (1994) 38.

[20] F. B. Burns, 'Lord Cottenham and the Court of Chancery' (2003) 24 *JLH* 187–214.

[21] (1959). Sir R. E. Megarry, 'The Vice-Chancellors' (1982) 98 *LQR*, 370–405, provides brief accounts of its subjects.

[22] *Law and Politics: The House of Lords as a Judicial Body 1800–1976* (1979).

[23] V. V. Veeder, 'The Judicial Career of the Late Lord Bowen' (1896–7) 10 *Harvard Law Rev.* 351–71.

[24] '"Words, Words, Words": Making Sense of Legal Judgments', in C. Stebbings (ed.), *Law Reporting in England* (1995), 169–86.

[25] E. Marjoribanks, *The Life of Lord Carson*, 2 vols (1932), i, 324.

he wished to make Plunket Master of the Rolls, the English bar would assert its monopoly: Englishmen might go as judges to Ireland but there would be no reciprocity.[26] Scotsmen and Irishmen were eligible to become additional members of the Judicial Committee, as Sir Joseph Napier did in 1868, and as 'persons who have held high judicial office' for two years they might, and did, become lords of appeal in ordinary after 1875.[27]

Since judges had to take the oath of allegiance, it was only with the repeal of the Test Act in 1828 that Roman Catholics and the most scrupulous dissenters became eligible. The first Roman Catholic, William Shee, was appointed in 1863 (followed by Mathew and Day), the first non-Christianized Jew, Sir George Jessel, in 1873.[28]

Well before 1914 it became a solecism to apply for a High Court judgeship, though someone who had turned down an offer might let it be known that he was open to a renewal;[29] however, since governments preferred refusals not to become public knowledge it is difficult to know how common they were. Of the ten whom Duman names between 1800 and 1875, nine later held high judicial office, and most who refused a puisne judgeship successfully aspired to higher things.[30] Once the Lord Chancellor acquired a permanent secretary who kept himself informed about the disposition of likely candidates, there were probably fewer rebuffs, and only a very few are known to have maintained their refusal; they include Sir Edward Clarke and Lord James because of political ambitions, and Harry Poland.[31]

RESPONSIBILITY FOR THE SELECTION OF JUDGES

Constitutionally the Crown was advised on the appointment of the Lord Chancellor, chief justices, and the Master of the Rolls by the Prime Minister and on the Chief Baron and all common law puisnes and barons by the Lord Chancellor. The Archbishop of Canterbury advised on the dean of Arches and the

---

[26] Atlay, *Victorian Chancellors*, ii, 25n. Following the Act of Union, Lord Redesdale, Lord Manners, Sir Anthony Hart, Sir Edward Sugden, and Sir John Campbell all served as Lord Chancellors of Ireland, but there no further instances.

[27] Above, pp. 538–40.

[28] Roman Catholic barristers, such as Charles Butler, had mostly gravitated towards conveyancing.

[29] C. Schuster to E. Shortt, 15 September 1917, NA PRO LCO 2/2226; H. Hawkins to Lord Cairns, 19 April 1875, Cairns Mss NA PRO 30/51/10.

[30] Hon. Mrs M. S. Hardcastle (ed.), *The Life of Lord Campbell*, 2 vols (2nd edn, 1881), i, 429; D. Duman, *The Judicial Bench in England, 1725–1875* (1982), 83 n.21. A later example is Herschell: Heuston, *Lives of the Lord Chancellors*, 24, 35, 93.

[31] E. Clarke, *The Story of My Life* (1918), 241 (though Clarke still cherished the notion that he might later become a judge, see 406); [G. R.] Lord Askwith, *Lord James of Hereford* (1930), 105, 113; Sir C. Biron, *Without Prejudice* (1936), 103.

judge of the Prerogative Court of Canterbury , and there was some uncertainty over the judge of Admiralty.[32] New positions of Vice-Chancellor of England and later the additional vice-chancellors fell within the Lord Chancellor's sphere, but the lords justices of Appeal in Chancery and the Probate judge in 1857 came under the Prime Minister. The Judicature Acts preserved a broadly similar division; the Prime Minister chose the Lord Chief Justice and President of the PDA, the lord justices of appeal and lords of appeal in ordinary, leaving the Lord Chancellor the puisne judges and the Master of the Rolls.

In practice the position was much less clear cut. Judicial appointments were part of the political process, and in the early nineteenth century the monarch could still exert personal influence in three areas: (1) over the choice of a Lord Chancellor;[33] (2) by vetoing personal enemies, as George IV did Thomas Denman; and (3) by advancing his favourites beyond their deserts, like Vaughan (the 'judge by prescription'), or more quickly than they merited, like Leach.[34] Royal influence, however, virtually ceased after 1830.

In practice, the appointment even of puisne judges was a government matter and one which in Salisbury's time was brought before the cabinet.[35] The Prime Minister and chief whip would expect to be consulted and at each end of the century Eldon and Halsbury accepted that party claims might suggest men they would not have chosen. Eldon did not conceal his low opinion of William Garrow and was seriously embarrassed at having to pass over Richard Richards as Vice-Chancellor for Liverpool's choice, the Attorney-General, Sir Thomas Plumer.[36] Halsbury willingly delayed filling his very first vacancy until election outcomes were clear and then chose an undistinguished lawyer, but prominent Tory campaigner, William Grantham.[37] Not all Lord Chancellors were so compliant, nor all Prime Ministers so exigent. Brougham predictably claimed the Chancellor had sole responsibility; Chelmsford refused to appoint a Tory at Disraeli's behest; Westbury told Palmerston he wanted to de-politicize puisne judgeships, and Gladstone claimed always to have let his Chancellors have the

[32] Duman, *Judicial Bench*, 78–9.

[33] Eldon was the last to claim a 'special relationship' with the sovereign, which conveniently justified him in deserting Addington's administration in 1804.

[34] Duman, *Judicial Bench*, 74, 82. Vaughan was so called because his father was the King's physician.

[35] Heuston, *Lord Chancellors*, 57.

[36] Campbell, *Lord Chancellors*, vii, 678; *ODNB*, 44: 609; 46: 788.

[37] Heuston, *Lord Chancellors*, 41. Even Salisbury described Grantham as 'no lawyer': to Duke of Richmond, 29 June 1885, quoted in H. J. Hanham, *The Nineteenth Century Constitution* (Cambridge, 1969), 416.

final say.[38] Personalities and political exigencies evidently affected the exercise of patronage; indeed other members of the government intervened at times, as Lord John Russell did in the 1830s.[39]

Conversely, Lord Chancellors had influence over the higher appointments. They were the best source of information for Prime Ministers who (Asquith excepted) had no personal knowledge of the bar, and after 1875 were responsible for the proper running of the courts.

Rather less clear is the role of the chiefs of the courts, and later the heads of the divisions of the Supreme Court. Lord Coleridge, who could draw upon family knowledge going back to Eldon's day, asserted it was almost a convention for the chief to be consulted about a vacancy in his court, although he claimed only something akin to the role of a Bagehotian sovereign. He deprecated Halsbury's break with the tradition[40] and there is evidence for the practice from earlier decades. Though it is unlikely that such wilful Chancellors as Brougham and Campbell acknowledged any obligation to consult, even Campbell approved Eldon's habit of consulting Ellenborough.[41] Until the creation of the Lord Chancellor's Office in 1885, no permanent official systematically influenced the process, but with the widening divide between common law and equity practitioners a Lord Chancellor's personal knowledge of the 'other' branch might be rather inadequate and Muir McKenzie was rumoured at the bar to have a hand in the distribution of the loaves and fishes. He left few traces of his handiwork, and only in Schuster's time can the officials' part in judicial appointments be glimpsed.[42]

AGE AT APPOINTMENT

Duman noticed a marked rise in the ages of judges at appointment, from 44 in the mid-eighteenth century to 56 in the third quarter of the nineteenth.[43] In fact the mean age peaked in the last of his cohorts and after the Judicature Acts

[38] Brougham airily claimed it as a 'good, long-established practice of a Chancellor making judges without any communication to any of his colleagues': H. P. Brougham, *Life and Times of Henry, Lord Brougham*, 3 vols (1868), iii, 86; Atlay, *Victorian Chancellors*, ii, 121; T. A. Nash, *The Life of Richard, Lord Westbury*, 2 vols (1888), ii, 69; Gladstone to Selborne, 2 November 1872, Lambeth Palace Library, Selborne Mss., vol. 1865, f. 166.

[39] Russell to Melbourne, 10 January 1836, R. Russell (ed.), *The Early Correspondence of Lord John Russell*, 2 vols (1913), ii, 69.

[40] Coleridge to Halsbury, 5 July 1892, in Heuston, *Lord Chancellors*, 47. Lyndhurst consulted Patteson J. over the choice of a judge (J. T. Coleridge) in 1834: Atlay, *Victorian Chancellors*, i, 114.

[41] Campbell, *Lord Chief Justices*, iii, 289. But Eldon objected to Ellenborough advising the Regent on his own successor: A. L. Lincoln and R. L. McEwen (eds), *Lord Eldon's Anecdote Book* (1960), 12.

[42] R. Stevens, *The Independence of the Judiciary* (Oxford, 1992), 40–1.

[43] *Judicial Bench*. Duman studied judges in six cohorts between 1727 and 1875. I have added two further cohorts for comparative purposes.

stabilized at around 51, the bottom of the range (50 to 55) which witnesses before a royal commission in 1913 advocated. Duman offered three suggestions (not mutually exclusive) to account for the rise. First, with judicial salaries after 1825 remaining relatively constant, rising incomes may have made leading barristers delay their readiness to quit the bar, though since Edwardian high-flyers were making more money than ever, that may have become a less important factor. Conversely, a more crowded bar may have meant that even the best men could not rise so quickly, though the end of special pleaders and equity draftsmen practising under the bar contributed to the trend whereby fewer judges had less than 20 years behind them. After Alfred Thesiger (14) only Barnes (16) and Evans (18, and a former solicitor) had less than 20 and some had been much longer in the profession, Pearson and Jelf each for 37 years.[44] The third possibility is that the path was blocked because men stayed on the bench longer, and there is some limited evidence to support this view.[45]

Another noticeable change is the rarity of the very young judge. It became almost unheard to reach the bench before the age of 40, as Patteson had in 1830. Alderson, 43, was made at the same time, and though these were additional judgeships, the advantages of younger judges had been urged in the debates on salaries in 1825 and this may have influenced appointments, for J. T. Coleridge (44) followed soon afterwards and common law judges tended towards (comparative) youth for some time; of 12 puisnes made between 1835 and 1854 only Crowder, Wightman, and Coltman were over 55.[46]

Thereafter, however, even this degree of precocity was unusual. In Duman's next cohort only Willes at 41 and J. P. Wilde at 43 were under 45 (though the under-50s were Cairns, Bramwell, Jessel, Blackburn, and Hannen—about as distinguished a group as could be found). After the Judicature Acts Alfred Thesiger's appointment at 39 (and direct to the Court of Appeal at that) was truly remarkable, and of the rest only Bowen and Barnes (each 44) and Atkin (45) were under 46. By 1917 Schuster was describing Hawke (48) as very young; the definition of youthfulness had advanced well into middle age.[47]

Really elderly new judges also became a rarity. Of the five men over 70 who were made judges, both Sugden and Campbell had already been Lord Chancellors of Ireland, Dodson was a stop-gap pending the abolition of his court and Bacon

[44] Duman, *Judicial Bench*, 72.

[45] Ibid. RC on Delays in the King's Bench Division, Evidence, *PP* 1913 [Cd. 6762], xxx, qq. 122, 1124, 1302.

[46] *PD* 1825 (s2) 13: 801, 1280. For convenience, the term puisne is used also of the Exchequer barons.

[47] Memorandum of 1917, LCO 2/601. Schuster may have wanted to delay Hawke's appointment for other reasons.

was already the bankruptcy judge, made a vice-chancellor to save public money. That leaves only the very odd choice of Anthony Hart (70), to be Vice-Chancellor in 1827. Sexagenarians continued to be chosen, though most were political lawyers like J. F. Pollock, Thomas Wilde, Page Wood, and Frederick Thesiger. Fitzroy Kelly (69), was a bad choice for Chief Baron at so advanced an age and when Henry Manisty was chosen at 67 in 1876 it transpired that the Lord Chancellor (Cairns) and the Chief Justice (Cockburn) each felt the other would think him too old.[48] He proved indeed to be the last one over 65 and after Fletcher Moulton (60) in 1906 the Liberals ceased to choose sexagenarians. There was no public explanation but since a 60-year-old would be eligible for full pension at 75, it helped meet criticism of elderly judges without imposing a retirement age.[49]

SOCIAL BACKGROUND

An examination of the occupational or social status of judges' fathers requires considerable caution.[50] Paternal occupations are frequently omitted or may have changed over time; thus Sir Charles Russell's father, a brewer, leased the business and settled down as a rentier.[51] Some occupations embrace a wide spectrum of wealth and status; there is, for instance, an enormous gulf between John Campbell, a poor son of the manse, and George Mellish, son of the Dean of Hereford. And parental occupation may seriously mislead. John Rolt and Thomas Pemberton-Leigh for instance, sons of a merchant and a barrister respectively, experienced poverty in childhood, while Charles Darling, son of a land agent, became wealthy by collateral inheritance.[52]

With these caveats, and using Duman's categories for convenience (but combining merchants and businessmen), at the start of the period judges were no longer drawn chiefly, or even largely, from major landed families. A few were baronets' sons or came from 'county' families, but none were sons of peers (other than judicial peers).

Increasingly, they were recruited from the professions and from the business community[53] and this remained true down to 1914, with the proportion hailing from the professions alone increasing from around a half to some 60 per cent.

---

[48] Cockburn to Cairns, 30 September 1876, Cairns Mss, PRO 30/51/10. The *Law Magazine and Law Review* said that he was passed over in 1873 (1873 2(ns), 176).

[49] Memorandum of 1917, LCO 2/601.

[50] Duman, *Judicial Bench*, 51–5. Other studies include J. A. G. Griffith, *The Politics of the Judiciary* (1977), 17–35; H. Cecil, *The English Judge* (1970), 26–31; and H. Perkin, *The Rise of Professional Society* (1990 edn), 88.

[51] R. B. O'Brien, *The Life of Lord Russell of Killowen* (1901, edn of 1903), 29.

[52] Sir J. Rolt, *Memoirs* (1939), 33–47; E. L. Pemberton (ed.), *Lord Kingsdown's Recollections of his Life* (1868), 1–10; D. Walker Smith, *A Life of Lord Darling* (1938), 29.

[53] *Judicial Bench*, 54.

Among the professions the law was the largest provider, followed by the clergy. While several of the best known judges (Parke, Bramwell, Jessel, Isaacs, Hamilton) came from a business background they never formed more than a quarter or so of the bench, which as a whole lacked business experience. Another of Duman's conclusions demolishes a cherished myth of the bar: the bench was indeed open to the impoverished middle class, but the lower class was excluded; the barbers' sons, Abbott and Sugden, were exceptions rather than examples, and not one judge of the nineteenth century had a working-class background.[54]

Where they were heterogeneous, however, was in their place of origin. They included a dozen Scots and nine Irishmen (either by birth or parentage), and at least seven from Wales. The Scots, remarkably, supplied four Lord Chancellors (Brougham, Campbell, Reid, Haldane) as well as Blackburn; Ireland contributed three of the greatest judges in Cairns, Macnaghten and Willes (some would give Russell a high place too); Sir William James was probably the most distinguished Welshman. If Cairns had adopted Coleridge's suggestion the bench would also have been adorned by that exotic character Judah Benjamin.[55]

EDUCATION

The boyhood of most of these judges preceded the rise of the modern public school. Pre-Victorian education even within the best known schools was narrow and often unsatisfactory; the 'bundle of virtues without a single redeeming vice' who became Lord Hatherley was expelled from Winchester for rioting[56] while that keen intellect J. F. Pollock quitted St. Paul's in disgust.[57] Some who missed out on a classical education regretted it[58] and the proportion who had one was rising. In the last cohort some 60 per cent were public school educated, many at the 'Clarendon schools'.[59] As a provider of judges Eton stood alone, with 24 , some 12 per cent of the total, and no other school comes close. Even so, the judiciary was not so public school dominated as other bastions of the establishment; the court, the cabinet and the Foreign Office.

Civilians apart, few judges read law at university, but almost three-quarters of them attended a university and a few, such as Herschell and Day, also studied

[54] *Ibid.*, and see below on county court judges.

[55] [Foulkes], *Generation of Judges*, 190.

[56] W. R. W. Stephens, *A Memoir of Sir William Page Wood, Baron Hatherley*, 2 vols (1883), i, 106–12. The characteristically wounding description is Lord Westbury's.

[57] Lord Hanworth, *Lord Chief Baron Pollock* (1929), 8.

[58] e.g. Campbell, Kelly, and even Barnes, despite his sojourn at Cambridge: Hardcastle, *Life of Lord Campbell*, i, 22; J. E. G. de Montmorency, *John Gorell Barnes, First Lord Gorell, a Memoir* (1920), 11; Manson, *Builders of Our Law in the Reign of Queen Victoria* (1904 edn), 302–10.

[59] There is no generally agreed definition of a public school. I have followed J. R. de S. Honey, *Tom Brown's Universe* (1977).

abroad.[60] However, perhaps reflecting the broadening of the judiciary's social composition, the proportion actually fell to not much more than half among those appointed in the third quarter of the nineteenth century, and considerably less among the common law puisnes. Many future judges distinguished themselves at university—Littledale, Maule, and Bickersteth were all senior wranglers for example—but as Maule, J. F. Pollock, and Bowen found, a great 'varsity reputation was not an unmixed blessing at the bar.[61]

In the first half of the nineteenth century Cambridge reversed Oxford's superiority as a provider of judges and for a time Trinity College acquired a quite remarkable record, supplying 14 of 33 judges appointed between 1835 and 1854; the college history suggests that its mathematical bent provided an analytical rigour which proved valuable to men who had to grapple with legal doctrine.[62]

If mathematics was valuable, it nevertheless lost its vogue and classicists came to dominate the bench. After 1895 all but a handful of new judges were university educated, and though a dozen post-Judicature Act judges were London graduates, it was the Oxbridge experience which was becoming increasingly characteristic of the bench. It brought future judges into early contact with other members of the ruling elite, removed the provincial accents of ambitious men like F. E. Smith and, if followed by a legal practice which did not embrace the ruder realities of economic and social existence, was prone to leave men like Ford North and Charles Bowen rather at sea with common juries and the experience of everyday life.[63]

PROFESSIONAL STANDING

There were no formal staging posts on the route to the bench. Becoming a bencher of an inn, even when it was not purely through seniority, was at best an indicator of existing status, and in the nineteenth century it became almost a perquisite of any new Crown counsel. [64] The serjeants no longer provided even junior judges on a regular basis and the rank no longer indicated either leadership in the profession or favour with the government.[65]

---

[60] At Bonn and Freiburg respectively.

[61] 'Sketch of the Life and Character of Mr. Justice Maule' (1896–7) 22 *LM* (s5), 3–6; Ellenborough and Cockburn (Pollock CB in another account) made clear their disappointment with Pollock and Bowen respectively: J. Grant, *The Bench and the Bar*, 2 vols (1838), ii, 56–62; H. S. Cunningham, *Lord Bowen, a Biographical Sketch* (1897), 114–15.

[62] Duman, *Judicial Bench*, 41–4; W. W. Rouse Ball, *Trinity College, Cambridge* (1906), 84.

[63] Manson, *Builders of our Law*, 259; Lord Birkenhead, *F.E.* (1959 edn), 45; P. Polden, 'Mingling the Waters' (2002) 61 *CLJ* 575–611 at 609–10. According to (1899–1900) 44 *Sol. J.* 441, the Court of Appeal was 'almost a Cambridge monopoly'.

[64] D. Lemmings, *Professors of the Law* (Oxford, 2000), 250–8, and see below, pp. 1078–79.

[65] See below, pp. 1055–58.

Crown counsel rank counted for more, but a more liberal approach gradually devalued the currency, which no longer created any expectation of a judgeship. Still, after the appointment of three stuff gownsmen as judges in 1830, that became a rarity,[66] hence the controversy when Campbell made Colin Blackburn a judge of the Queen's Bench in 1859. Critics pointed to at least a dozen eligible QCs, implicitly insisting that save for the government's law officers, judges should be drawn from the most successful members of the practising bar. There had been no similar outcry when Willes was appointed a few years earlier, but Willes had earned special consideration by drafting the Common Law Procedure Acts. Blackburn had neither great professional reputation nor public service to warrant his jumping the queue.[67] Of course, critics were quickly disarmed by Blackburn's remarkable quality as a judge. Even so, it remained exceptional for stuff gownsmen to become judges unless (like Hall, Wickens, J. C. Mathew, and Parker) they had refused silk.[68]

The government had a range of positions to bestow upon favoured barristers, but very few proved a reliable predictor of promotion and the elected recordership of London, which had once been, was no longer.[69] Before its abolition in 1830 the Chief Justiceship of Chester, the 'Welsh cheese' in the ministerial rat-trap, was a way station successively for Best, Copley, and Leach,[70] and later on it was said that selection to go as Commissioner of Assize was a pretty strong indication. However, an examination of these commissioners shows that Bompas and Rose-Innes only became county court judges, while J. P. Murphy, Alderson Foote and John Forbes never made the bench at all; nor did W. English Harrison, although he went on three different circuits.[71]

Any successful Crown counsel had some claim to be considered for a judgeship; indeed it is said that Henry Hawkins' great earnings and public fame virtually compelled his selection, and the reaction of his fellow judges confirms that unpopularity with the bench was not a disqualification.[72] The parliamentary bar was so specialized as to weaken their claims,[73] and the Old Bailey bar had such

---

[66] Apart from junior Treasury counsel, see below, pp. 977–8.

[67] Blackburn is said to have assumed he was being offered a county court judgeship: Sir W. F. Pollock, *Personal Reminiscences*, 2 vols (1887), ii, 81. For contemporary criticism see e.g. (1859) 7 (s3) *LM & LR* 450–9. For criticism of Coltman's appointment see Grant, *Bench and Bar*, (1837), i, 314.

[68] Foulkes, *Generation of Judges*, 60–70; Lord Selborne, *Memorials, Part Two, Personal and Political*, 2 vols (1898), i, 113; *ODNB* 37: 288; 42: 735.

[69] R. J. Blackham, *Sir Ernest Wild KC* (1935), 224.

[70] W. R. Williams, The *History of the Great Sessions in Wales, 1547–1830* (Brecknock, 1899), 28–55.

[71] *ODNB*, 10: 876; A. B. Schofield, *A Dictionary of Legal Biography, 1845–1945* (Chichester, 1998).

[72] (1898–99) 43 *Sol. J.* 137; Sir R. Bosanquet, *The Oxford Circuit* (1951), 37.

[73] Schuster's memorandum to Lord Finlay, 1917, LCO 2/601; J. H. Balfour Browne, *Forty Years at the Bar* (1916), 252.

a poor reputation that none of its regulars was chosen until Harry Poland, who twice refused. Horace Avory's appointment in 1910 was taken as a sign that it had become respectable and R.D. Muir might also have been made a judge had he been willing to give up being junior Treasury counsel and take silk.[74] As the provincial bars grew in reputation men were taken from their ranks, beginning with W. Rann Kennedy in 1891, soon followed by Bigham and Pickford.[75]

There were, however, good men who never received an offer. The collective memory of the bar held a list of the unlucky ones, though Sir Henry Dickens was unusual in openly acknowledging his acute disappointment when Haldane did not fulfil the expectations Loreburn had held out. The unfortunate case of Arthur Cohen was also well known. Persuaded to help out his party by declining Selborne's offer in 1881, he was repeatedly overlooked for no apparent reason. Nor could the profession understand why F. A. Inderwick, the Admiralty leader, was ignored, though some said he was too much a Liberal for Halsbury's taste. In some cases there were explanations not for public consumption, as with M. D. Hill, who had disclosed confidential government information.[76]

It was always acknowledged that successful advocates did not necessarily make good judges. Edward Marshall Hall, the most famous of his day, was never seriously in the running, not just because of his clashes with judges but because his whole personality seemed 'unjudicial'.[77] Strong and ostentatious religious beliefs do not seem to have been a disadvantage, though they were said to have held back Robert Lush. Indeed, while the Woolsack was occupied in succession by three men noted for their religious zeal (Cairns, Hatherley, and Selborne) piety may have been a positive commendation. It was insinuated that Cairns' prayerful levees attracted some opportunist aspirants, though probably mostly for junior posts, and Alfred Wills was said to have won Selborne's favour by his impeccable morals.[78]

A doubtful personal reputation could certainly count against a man. No one expressed much surprise that unstable 'characters' like William Ballantine and Charles Wilkins remained mere serjeants, and there were others with

[74] Biron, *Without Prejudice*, 106; E. Abinger, *Forty Years at the Bar* (1930), 243; F. W. Ashley, *My Sixty Years in the Law* (1936), 29; S. T. Felstead and Lady Muir, *Sir R.M. Muir* (1927), 2.

[75] Welcomed in (1891–2) 36 *Sol. J.* 859.

[76] Sir H. Dickens, *The Recollections of Sir Henry Dickens KC* (1934), 233; L. Cohen, *Arthur Cohen* (1919), 72–4; Biron, *Without Prejudice*, 44; E. Bowen Rowlands, *In the Light of the Law* (1931), 118; W. S. Ballantine, *Some Experiences of a Barrister's Life* (6th edn, 1883), 272.

[77] Schuster's memorandum of 1917, LCO 2/601.

[78] W. G. Thorpe, *Middle Temple Table Talk* (1884), 365; G. Alexander, *The Temple of the Nineties* (1938), 228; Atlay, *Victorian Chancellors*, ii, 323–4. In his *Memorials* (i, 379), Selborne listed several 'sincere christian judges', and W. G. Phillimore's very ostentatious religiosity did not prevent his appointment.

eccentricities thought too extreme for the bench. Sir Charles Wetherell is probably the most notable, though Peel was prepared to make him Vice-Chancellor,[79] and the best known instance in later times was W. O. Danckwerts ('Danky'), whose explosive rudeness and insensitivity more than offset his immense ability. J. G. Witt is mentioned as another too astringent for official taste and the tone of his memoirs suggests that J. H. Balfour Browne, despite his great earnings, may have been a third.[80]

POLITICS

Judicial appointments had been politicized and assimilated to the system of 'Old Corruption' which governed Hanoverian Britain. Though purely professional achievement might lead to the bench (if not offset by the unfashionable political ideas or connections), it would seldom open up one of the great judicial offices. These had become the preserve of MPs who had served the government capably (most often as law officers) and might be depended upon to protect its interests on the bench. If their performance in Parliament or government disappointed, they would still be in line for a puisne judgeship, competing with loyal and influential MPs, with the pure professionals and with personal favourites of the Lord Chancellor or the King. And prospects might be dramatically changed by a realignment of parties.[81]

Judicial appointments might serve at least three political ends. First, a ministry would want at least the key positions to be held by men who shared its views and values; those who had made their name as defenders in state trials had to prove that their advocacy could be equally impassioned for the prosecution.[82] Secondly, they attracted rising lawyers whose allegiance might be determined or at least influenced by prospects of preferment, and might detach opposition supporters, men who would 'rat' if their prospects seemed otherwise blighted.[83] Thirdly, they

[79] (1847) *LM* (s2) 280–7; Peel to Eldon, January 1835, Lord Mahon and E. Cardwell, *Memoirs of Sir Robert Peel*, 2 vols (1857), ii, 55.

[80] Alexander, *Temple of the Nineties*, 148; F. Pearson, *Memories of a KC's Clerk* (1935), 72–5; G. C. Whiteley, *Brief Life* (1942), 12; A. J. Ashton, *As I Went on My Way* (1924), 184. In an earlier generation John Adolphus was similarly tempestuous: E. Henderson, *Recollections of the Public Career and Private Life of the late John Adolphus* (1871), 292.

[81] Lemmings, *Professors of the Law*, 271–92 and 'The Independence of the Judiciary in 18th Century England', in P. Birks (ed.), *The Life of the Law* (1993), 125–50.

[82] Among those excluded from the bench for political principles were G. Lee (Campbell, *Lord Chief Justices*, ii, 104) and G. Wilson (J. and W. Romilly, *Memoirs of the Life of Sir Samuel Romilly*, 3 vols (1840), i, 434n).

[83] Baron Gurney is perhaps the last example: Ballantine, *Some Experiences of a Barrister's Life*, 173–5; Hardcastle, *Life of Lord Campbell*, i, 221; (1845) 2 (s2) *LM* 274–9.

were rewards for men who had fought costly elections or given solid and active support in the House.

The first of these considerations became much less important from the 1820s onwards, with the end of the treason trials and more sparing prosecutions for political libels. Victoria's ministries were seldom engaged in contests where the judges' political views were likely to be important, until a series of controversial trade union cases with inescapable political dimensions arose. Several leading judges notoriously held views which were unsympathetic to the Liberal political programme. W. S. Robson, the Liberal Attorney-General newly installed as a law lord, pointed out that the 'resolute bias of many of the Judges—there and elsewhere... will probably operate more than ever in cases that touch on labour, educational, constitutional and, for the future I might perhaps add, revenue questions'. Robson urged the need for more Liberals in the House of Lords.[84]

The prospect of judicial office attracted one or two 'rats',[85] but old party allegiances weakened after Liverpool's resignation in 1827, enabling Scarlett to join Canning's administration with the consent of the Whig leaders.[86] Thereafter there was no single party ascendancy to pose an acute dilemma to ambitious lawyers and some probably chose the party most likely to procure their advancement; others, such as A. L. Smith, were decidedly half-hearted in their politics. [87]

The third motive remained in full force. Eldon appointed some personal friends (e.g. Alexander) but only a minority of puisnes were MPs or active supporters of government; the likes of Littledale 'whose politics were those of a special pleader',[88] Burrough, Richardson, and Hullock were more typical.[89] After the 1832 Reform Act there were more practising barristers in the Commons and the new judges included a fair number of MPs.[90] Political opponents were no longer proscribed, indeed Lyndhurst was criticized by Tory newspapers for choosing the Liberal William Erle, but such even-handedness remained uncommon. Law reformers regretted the intrusion of a political element but it seems to have been accepted as a fact of public life.[91] However, though appointments such as

[84] Robson to Asquith, n.d., Heuston, *Lord Chancellors*, 151.

[85] For instance, Charles Warren KC, Attorney-General to the Prince of Wales, succeeded Copley as Chief Justice of Chester in 1820 within a few months of becoming an MP: (1829) 2 *LM* 710–12.

[86] *ODNB* 49: 188.

[87] *ODNB* 51: 41.

[88] Quoted in *ODNB* 34: 23.

[89] J. A. Park was made a judge at the behest of the Home Secretary (Lord Sidmouth), who was pleased with his handling of government prosecutions: Campbell, *Lord Chief Justices*, iii, 283.

[90] According to H. Laski, 'The Technique of Judicial Appointment', in *Studies in Law and Politics* (1932), 163–80, of 139 judges in the period 1832–1906, 80 sat in the House of Commons, another 11 had been parliamentary candidates, and 63 of the 80 were appointed by their own party.

[91] Atlay, *Victorian Chancellors*, i, 146; (1844) 1 (s2) *LM* 229; (1852) 16 (s3) *LM & LR* 92. The exchange between Peel and Henry Goulburn in 1835 (Sir C. S. Parker, *Sir Robert Peel*, 2 vols (1899, ii, 272–3) is instructive.

Hannen's, a radical Liberal chosen by a Conservative Chancellor, and Holker's, a Conservative former law officer made a lord justice by the Liberals, still caused surprise, the bipartisan co-operation of Cairns and Selborne over a long period gave the impression that political influences were a diminishing force.[92]

Then came Lord Halsbury. The myth that Halsbury cynically practised nepotism and 'political' appointments on a large scale has been modified by Heuston's careful study,[93] but the myth is itself revealing in suggesting that after the Third Reform Act public expectations were changing. In a culture of selection by merit, the choice of senior public servants on party grounds was felt to be anomalous. Some felt that after the Judicature Acts only the best men would do for the bench;[94] indeed, since the senior bar and the judges were themselves prone to lament that there were barely enough top-class men to fill the bench, it seemed hardly justifiable to appoint second raters. Halsbury went wrong not in being influenced by party considerations but in choosing from outside the range of men the profession regarded as qualified.

Of course, as Heuston points out, Salisbury as Prime Minister was insistent that party claims must have their weight, but he wrote to Halsbury in 1897 that 'the judicial salad requires both legal oil and political vinegar', and though the Chancellor was noted for skilfully disarming criticism about a bad job by following with an unexceptionable one (and selecting a political opponent on occasion), the worst choices seem to have been Halsbury's own.[95]

For most of the legal community it was acceptable to prefer on party grounds one man over another equally qualified, as with Anthony Cleasby over W. R. Grove.[96] However, Gainsford Bruce was a barely acceptable choice in any case, but leaving the vacancy unfilled for a month to have his safe seat free for any minister defeated at the general election made his selection more discreditable.[97]

Heuston successfully vindicates Halsbury on some of his criticised appointments, such as Sutton and Kekewich. Also, it was not unreasonable to widen the field of choice by taking Edward Ridley from among the Official Referees, though Halsbury's rooted antipathy to county court expansion led him to ignore that

---

[92] *Pump Court*, October 1883, 8; (1884–5); 29 *Sol. J.* 410 ('it might be said that by those on both sides who dispose of appointments politics have for many years been disregarded'); (1885–6) 30 *Sol. J.* 87. Some judges in this period were certainly seen as 'political appointments' however: W. G. Thorpe, *The Still Life of the Middle Temple* (1892), 317–20 (Bovill and Huddleston); *The Times*, 27 May 1892 (Butt).

[93] Heuston, *Lord Chancellors*, 36–66.

[94] (1881–2) 26 *Sol. J.* 487.

[95] Heuston, *Lord Chancellors*, 37, 52, 57; Bosanquet, *Oxford Circuit*, 33.

[96] Duman, *Judicial Bench*, 80.

[97] Heuston, *Lord Chancellors*, 46–7.

more promising source, and Ridley turned out far worse than anyone might have expected.[98]

Even so, three appointments were simply unjustifiable: J. C.Lawrance, Charles Darling, and William Grantham. Lawrance and Grantham were QCs but none had a good reputation as a lawyer. It might be argued that there was still a place in the QBD for men unfitted for higher courts but able to deliver commonsense justice, especially on Assize and in criminal cases, and this Grantham and Lawrence did. But many others with solid reputations could done have that as well or better and to prefer men not unfairly described in Darling's case as ' a party hack'; was to breach the tacit understanding about the limits of political influence.[99]

They were almost the last of their kind. Loreburn disliked anything that smacked of patronage but it was only when Asquith and Haldane, with their close political relationship, were in charge that it was agreed that the junior posts would be filled without reference to party needs or claims.[100]

THE LAW OFFICERS

The history of the most senior judges is somewhat different, for here the freedom of the government came to be constrained by the claims of its own law officers, which have been painstakingly analysed by J. Llewellyn Edwards.[101] These claims originated with that 'indefatigable seeker after office' Francis Bacon, who mendaciously claimed that 'the places of rest after the extreme painful places wherein we [the law officers] serve have used to be either the Lord Chancellor's place, or the Mastership of the Rolls, or the places of Chief Justices'.[102] The most persuasive, and most frequently advanced claim, was the Attorney-General's to the 'cushion' of the Common Pleas. John Scott successfully insisted upon it in 1799 and politicians and profession acknowledged that it would have fallen (rather fortuitously) to Frederick Thesiger in 1845 had Tindal CJ died a few days earlier; as it was, Thomas Wilde became the fortunate recipient, seemingly as of right.[103] The claim was admitted by Lord John Russell in 1850, and though his Attorney-General,

[98] *Ibid.*, 33, 49–51. For Sutton see below, p. 977.

[99] *Ibid.*, 41–2, 45, 54–6.

[100] *Ibid.*, 219. Horridge was one of the last judges who would not have been shortlisted by the bar: G. Rentoul, *This Is My Case* ([1944]), 61. Yet in 1920 a barrister claimed that no opposition MP would be offered a judgeship: R. Primrose in A. M. Kales, 'The English Judicature Acts' (1920–1) 4 *Journal of the American Juridical Society*, 133–47 at 145.

[101] J. Ll. Edwards, *The Law Officers of the Crown* (1964), 309–34.

[102] *Ibid.*, 311.

[103] *Ibid.*, 320–3; Atlay, *Victorian Chancellors*, ii, 101–2; Sir J. Hollams, *Jottings of an Old Solicitor* (1906), 130–1.

Sir John Jervis, disclaimed any absolute entitlement, he agreed that it was always allowed in practice.[104]

Other claims for the Attorney-General were tenuous. Campbell's brazen claim to the Rolls in 1834 was robustly rejected by Brougham and Melbourne and the 'venerable tradition' of a right to the Woolsack urged by Isaacs in 1912 had even less substance.[105] Edwards does not discuss the claim to be Chief Baron, suggested for Garrow in 1817,[106] and his discussion of the Chief Justice of the King's Bench is brief and inconclusive.

However, in focusing strictly on rights rather than practice Edwards' analysis is apt to mislead. The fact is that before the Judicature Acts at different times and on different advice Prime Ministers and Lord Chancellors gave varying degrees of acknowledgement to such pretensions. More important is that in practice all administrations felt obliged to make suitable provision for their law officers when they had had enough, and that if it was not possible to do so immediately their claim would be met when a suitable post became vacant.[107] The nature of the provision would naturally vary with what was available, with the length and quality of services rendered and with rival claims. As a result, it was very seldom that a vacancy among the great offices occurred that was not subject to such claims and sometimes, particularly in the 1830s and 1890s, they created serious difficulties.

Attorney-Generals were very successful in obtaining the great offices. Between 1801 and 1880 only Abbott breaks the sequence of Chief Justices of the King's Bench who were former Attorney-Generals, and then only because Sir Samuel Shepherd was ineligible through deafness. Others became chiefs of the Common Pleas or Exchequer, or Master of the Rolls, and when they did not fill the vacancies there was always a compelling political or personal reason. A few law officers went straight to the Woolsack.[108] Of the remaining Attorney-Generals, Sir William Follett died in office and Sir John Karslake became blind. Garrow was made an Exchequer baron, a position Atherton and Horne (the latter unwisely) declined; Cairns and Rolt became lord justices of appeal in Chancery and Sir Robert

---

[104] *SC on Official Salaries, PP* 1850 (611), xv, qq. 1347, 1789.

[105] Edwards, *Law Officers*, 325–6, 312–19. However, Pemberton-Leigh wrote that if he had agreed to become Solicitor-General in 1841 it would have led to the Woolsack: *Recollections of Kingsdown*, 102.

[106] H. W. Woolrych, *Lives of Eminent Serjeants at Law*, 2 vols (1869), ii, 843. In 1844 it was said in *The Times* that Pollock became Chief Baron ahead of Parke by right of this claim; the bar felt Parke was hard done by: Manson, *Builders of our Law*, 34–40.

[107] Thus Eldon urged Peel to ensure both law officers felt they would obtain one of the great law offices: Campbell, *Lord Chancellors*, vii, 51.

[108] Sir J. C. Sainty, *The Judges of England 1272–1990* (1993); Hardcastle, *Life of Lord Campbell*, i, 441; Nash, *Life of Lord Westbury*, i, 279.

Collier, under extraordinary circumstances, a judge of the Privy Council.[109] Only Wetherell received no firm offer of judicial preferment and he was at least considered. Among the Solicitor-Generals, Rolfe accepted an Exchequer barony but rose to the Woolsack and Dundas and Stuart-Wortley suffered from ill-health and withdrew from strenuous public offices;[110] Sir W. P. Wood became a vice-chancellor and eventually Lord Chancellor.

Gladstone clearly felt a continuation of this uncertain situation was undesirable and took the opportunity afforded by the Judicature Act 1873 to secure a cabinet resolution that 'all claims of either or both Law Officers to a succession as of right to any particular judicial office (claims which were never adequately established) have naturally dropped; so that their promotion would henceforth rest on qualification and service only, not on the possession of the post of Law Officer'.[111] This was presumably approved by his law officers, Coleridge and Sir Henry James, though James persistently disclaimed all judicial ambitions.

In practice the resolution made little difference. Indeed in 1897, when Lord Salisbury found himself in acute difficulties over a successor to the Master of the Rolls, he declared that 'there is no clearer statute in that unwritten law [of our party system] than the rule that party claims should always weigh very heavily in the disposal of the highest legal appointments'.[112] His problem was one law officer, Sir Edward Clarke, whom neither Salisbury nor Halsbury thought fit for the Rolls, and another, the Attorney-General, Sir Richard Webster, who did not want it. If Webster were persuaded to take it, Clarke must succeed him as Attorney-General, giving him 'a claim to higher vacancies which could not be passed over'. Though Clarke, happily unaware of these unflattering views, fortunately decided to remain in politics, the episode illustrated how an unlucky choice of law officer might have serious ongoing consequences.[113]

The Rolls was subsequently removed from the political equation, save in 1900 when a reluctant Webster accepted it at the second time of asking. However, all Lord Chief Justices came straight from Attorney-General save Russell, who had briefly been a law lord. The other Attorney-Generals (James apart) achieved various high positions—lord justices of appeal, law lord and, in Finlay's case, Lord Chancellor, he having turned down offers to be President of the PDA and, probably, to be a law lord.[114] The only exception is Walton, who died in office. Several

---

[109] P. A. Howell, *The Judicial Committee of the Privy Council 1833–1876* (Cambridge, 1979), 151–3; Nash, *Life of Lord Westbury*, ii, 67.

[110] *ODNB* 60: 368; 17: 273.

[111] Edwards, *Law Officers*, 323.

[112] Heuston, *Lord Chancellors*, 52.

[113] *Ibid.*

[114] *Ibid.*, 325–6.

Solicitor-Generals held high judicial office and Sir William Harcourt, whose ambition was to be Lord Chief Justice, became Home Secretary. Clarke rejected preferment, Sir Edward Carson rejected the Presidency of the PDA, the much loved Frank Lockwood died in office, and J. E. Gorst, rather mysteriously, seems to have become a victim of the split in the Tory ranks.[115] Brett is a rare instance of a law officer who took a puisne judgeship. His ambitions were always judicial rather than political and, seeing that the direct route to the higher posts was blocked, he gambled successfully on ascending via the bench. That it was his own choice did not prevent his seeking a peerage in recognition of his 'sacrifice'.[116]

In the result therefore, whatever their expectations, both law officers, but especially the Attorney-General, more often than not emerged with one of the great legal prizes—if they wanted one. A consequence was that the government's choice was sometimes undesirably restricted and unsuitable and second rate men filled crucial posts: Coleridge and Alverstone as Lord Chief Justice, Best and Bovill at the Common Pleas, Scarlett and (on account of his age) Kelly at the Exchequer, and Plumer and Romilly at the Rolls. This was the price governments paid to have the men they wanted as law officers, and it was sometimes a heavy one.

During the nineteenth century the Attorney-General himself acquired, in that haphazard way characteristic of the unwritten constitution, a piece of judicial patronage, for his 'devil' (the junior counsel to the Treasury), gradually gained a prescriptive right to a common law judgeship. To Collier in 1819 it was only a a possibility and as late as 1886 Foulkes was still only expecting it to become customary—indeed a few years earlier the *Solicitors Journal* had remarked that 'if the rule is to become inflexible... it is to be hoped that some care will be used in the choice of a successor to this office'.[117] It did become inflexible. Halsbury felt obliged to make Henry Sutton a judge in 1905 and doubts about his suitability were soon confirmed.[118] By then it seems also to have extended to his counterpart on the equity side[119] and it did ensure that men such as Willes and Bowen, rather scholarly for the rough and tumble of the practising bar, were able to reach the

---

[115] A. G. Gardiner, *The Life of Sir William Harcourt*, 2 vols (1923), i, 189–90 and compare Pollock, *Reminiscences*, ii, 165. J. T. Rees, *Reserved Judgment* (1949), 203; Marjoribanks, *Carson*, i, 324. Gorst was offered Solicitor-General but conditional on his taking the first vacancy as a puisne judge: A. Hunter, *A Life of Sir John Eldon Gorst, Disraeli's Awkward Disciple* (2001), 184–5.

[116] To Cairns, 9 August 1876, Cairns Mss, PRO 30/51/10. He became Baron Esher in 1885, possibly a consolation prize after Giffard was preferred as Lord Chancellor.

[117] [J. P. Collier], *Criticisms on the Bar* (1819), 94–6; Foulkes, *Generation of Judges*, 31; (1882–3) 27 *Sol. J.* 335.

[118] Heuston, *Lord Chancellors*, 62–3. Sutton retired after only five years.

[119] Stirling (1886), Joyce (1900), Parker (1906), Sargent (1913). On Parker's appointment Loreburn wrote to Campbell-Bannerman that he held 'a post which traditionally leads to the bench': Heuston, *Lord Chancellors*, 147.

bench without breaching the conventions; but like the law officers' 'right', a bad choice, like Webster's of Sutton, would result in an inadequate judge.

In Office: Length of Service

Judges of the superior courts held office during good behaviour, with no reference in their patent to incapacity.[120] In effect, therefore, they were judges for life, though in practice they could not remain if they became wholly incapable of performing their duties. No judicial scandals brought this tenure into question,[121] and if a few judges had a dissipated private life it was kept under wraps; though the adulterous indulgences of Cockburn and Westbury were well known, they stayed out of the divorce court and avoided public scandal.[122] None went bankrupt (though Kelly had to remain on the bench too long partly in order to recoup heavy financial losses) and though it was embarrassing that Coleridge was successfully sued by members of his own family and that Fletcher Moulton lost an action for breach of trust, neither was considered a ground for resignation.[123]

In 1799 the judges had become pensionable after 15 years' service or in the case of permanent incapacity, a great improvement, since pensions theretofore had been granted at the discretion of the government of the day and might be a means of influencing a judge.[124] In 1825, as part of the overhaul of judicial remuneration, pensions were raised to £3500, with the Chief Justice of the Common Pleas, Chief Baron, Master of the Rolls and Vice-Chancellor on £3750 and the Chief Justice of the King's Bench on £4000. These were raised considerably from the original suggestions as an encouragement to judges to quit before their faculties deteriorated,[125] and Duman suggests it did indeed have this effect, retirements rising from 35 per cent in the eighteenth century to 61 per cent. However, excluding Lord Chancellors (who usually went out with the ministry), almost half of the judges appointed between 1815 and 1875 died in office; only in the twentieth century did this become uncommon.[126]

---

[120] Specimen patents are in Sainty, *Judges of England*, App.

[121] S. Shetreet, *Judges on Trial* (Amsterdam, 1976), 143–4 outlines the 1830 case of the Irish judge Sir Jonah Barrington. Grantham came quite close for scandalously partisan handling of an election case: *ibid.*, 148–9, 175–6.

[122] *ODNB* 12: 328; Thorpe, *Still Life of the Middle Temple*, 297; Lord Birkenhead, *Fourteen English Judges* (1926), 255–77.

[123] Foulkes, *Generation of Judges*, 38–53; Bosanquet, *Oxford Circuit*, 31; Heuston, *Lord Chancellors*, 147.

[124] Sainty, *Judges of England*, 5, 21, 44, 91, 145; Lemmings, *Professors of the Law*, 273; Duman, *Judicial Bench*, 121–6.

[125] Judicial Salaries Act 1825 (6 Geo. IV c. 84), s. 4. *PD* 1825 (s2) 13: 611–43, 801–24.

[126] Duman, *Judicial Bench*, 125.

Not surprisingly, some judges expired, or retired through ill-health, within a very short period. All were middle aged or elderly men and some (e.g. Rolt and Robson) were already worn down by practice or government service.[127] Eight of those appointed between 1850 and 1875 served less than five years, as did six of the later ones, including Sir Henry Mather Jackson, the most evanescent of them all, who died before he could even take his seat. A few retired before their time, Richardson after just five years and Robert Romer, said to have tired of Vaughan Williams' tedious prolixity in the Court of Appeal.[128]

The median length of service rose slightly, from 13 years before 1875 to 16 years afterwards. At all times, and especially towards the end of the period, most judges were very experienced. Twenty-three pre-1875 judges and 18 post-1875 judges passed 20 years on the bench and they included many of the most distinguished or well known: Blackburn (28), Hannen (25), Brett (29), Lindley (30), J. F. Pollock (22), Bramwell (24), Parke (27), Cockburn (24), and J. D. Coleridge (20) in the earlier group; Atkin (31), Macnaghten (26), Sumner (20), and Scrutton (24) in the later.[129] The durability and reluctance to retire of so many mid-Victorian judges may be of some significance in the development of the common law. Lord Chancellors fall into a separate category, for their term of office was often intermittent and their judicial service prolonged by sitting in the House of Lords. After the everlasting Eldon (25 years as Chancellor), Cranworth (26 years in various posts), Lyndhurst (19), Hatherley (19), and Halsbury (17 years as Chancellor, more than 30 between his first and last judgments), each had a long innings.

Retirement became a sensitive matter once the judiciary fell out of step with other public servants. Though politicians frequently stayed on the public stage to an advanced age, even Prime Ministers were becoming younger and civil servants were, in general, made to retire at 65.[130] Attempts to impose a similar rule on court staff were stoutly resisted by the judges, no doubt in part because of the fear that it would be their turn next.

Despite occasional earlier suggestions, as late as 1895 a demand in the *Saturday Review* for judges to retire at 65 was called a 'strange proposal' by the *Solicitors Journal*.[131] The *Review* was characteristically outspoken in naming Esher, Hawkins, Day, and Pollock as immediate candidates for the rest home and mentioning,

[127] Rolt, *Memoirs*, 125; G. W. Keeton, *A Liberal Attorney-General* (1949), 210. Dampier was one who was unable to sustain the demands of his practice (*PD* 1825 (s2) 13: 633–7), while Bowen overworked for the Tichborne trials: Cunningham, *Lord Bowen*, 41–2.

[128] Bosanquet, *Oxford Circuit*, 74.

[129] Figures for Parke and Bramwell exclude service in the House of Lords.

[130] E. W. Cohen, *The Growth of the British Civil Service, 1780–1939* (1941, repr. of 1965), 59–65. The first two permanent secretaries in the LCO, however, did not retire until 75.

[131] (1894–5) 39 *Sol. J.* 844; (1895) 40 *Sol. J.* 2. See also Manisty's obituary in *The Times*, 1 February 1890.

without naming, a younger judge who was said to be senile. The question would not go away, and in 1913 a royal commission came out for retirement at 72 with a power for the Lord Chancellor to postpone it in individual cases.[132]

The recommendation was not implemented but undoubtedly had an effect on the age at which judges were normally chosen.[133] Opponents advanced three arguments. First, that judges mature on the bench and are at their best between 65 and 80 (or 75 at any rate), so a uniform retiring age would deprive the country of some of its best judges; they were fortunate in being able to instance Halsbury, a miracle of physical and intellectual vigour, though of course no longer a trial judge, where alertness was especially required. Such assertions are difficult to test. Sir Walter Phillimore argued that judges did not need 'elan and go' like other public servants, but omitted to mention that other, younger public servants, did not claim to need short hours and long vacations to recuperate.

The second argument was that potential judges might be discouraged if they had only a limited period on the bench, especially with the real value of salaries falling, but that was an argument for more generous pensions. The third argument was that a retiring age was in practice unnecessary because when the public interest required a judge's departure he either resigned unprompted or (rarely) was tactfully persuaded. Alverstone mentioned an instance in which he (rather than the Lord Chancellor) had induced the retirement of a judge who, although mentally alert, looked 'decrepit' and so presented an unacceptable image to a public which could not distinguish 'between apparent decrepitude and inability'. He maintained, however, that there had been only three cases within his knowledge where the public might say a judge was 'not up to it', and in the two which occurred while he was Lord Chief Justice he had persuaded the judge to retire.[134] Furthermore, as the opponents of compulsory retirement pointed out, an age limit would not have helped in the most notorious case of judicial incapacity, that of J. F. Stephen, who was barely into his sixties when the sensational trial of Florence Maybrick exposed his failings to the full glare of publicity. Stephen's resignation was procured by a 'wonderfully tactful' intervention from Halsbury, but only after parliamentary questions and a press campaign.[135] However, rather than furnishing an argument against compulsory retirement ages, Stephen's case exposed the want of any explicit incapacity ground for dismissal. Such a clause had been urged by Gladstone during discussions on Selborne's Judicature Bill but was not included.[136]

---

[132] *RC on Delays in the King's Bench Division, Second Report,* PP 1914 [Cd. 7177], xxxvii, para. 64.

[133] See above. Retirement was finally introduced in 1959. Lord Denning MR, appointed in 1945, at length retired in 1982.

[134] *RC on the KBD, Evidence,* qq. 122–4.

[135] L. Stephen, *The Life of J.F. Stephen* (1895), 477–8; Heuston, *Lord Chancellors,* 46.

[136] Gladstone to Selborne, 27 January 1873, Selborne Mss vol. 1867, f. 198.

There were, however, several more mundane cases where peer pressure was either not applied or did not work very well. In 1825 Baron Wood's state had become pitiful, 'he having at length lost one eye and the use of both ears'.[137] Later on Cottenham, Kelly, Blackburn, Esher, and Grantham all remained on the bench too long.[138] Some timed retirement to suit their own political associates; Pollock CB clung on until the Tories came in in 1866 for example. Others sought to keep out an unwanted successor (as Denman LCJ sought vainly to do with Campbell in 1850) or to secure the promotion of a friend, as Erle wanted to do for Roundell Palmer.[139] Some clung on for a full pension, as Coleridge did in the 1890s. Bayley simply enjoyed being a judge, while Wightman's wife did not want him at home.[140] There is no knowing how often a Chancellor or the chief of a court brought pressure on a lingering colleague. It happened with Honyman, but that was because Huddleston, who wanted the place for himself, planted questions in the House about his fitness. On the other hand it seems that Rigby for one was not asked to go when Halsbury believed he should.[141]

Elderly men were prone to deafness, real life counterparts to Dickens' Mr Justice Stareleigh. Bacon and Maule, Patteson and John Williams were all afflicted,[142] but the most often mentioned is Ventris Field, whose deafness contributed to his notorious ill-temper. Field did not recognize any need to retire and was extremely rude to Baron Pollock, who was given the unwelcome task of suggesting that he should.[143] The other common condition was sleepiness, which perhaps became harder to resist in the quieter courtrooms of the Strand than in the hubbub of Westminster Hall. For at least one important trial Coleridge LCJ had to have his wife beside him to keep him awake,[144] but the most notorious offender was Lewis Cave, whose post-prandial torpor became so blatant that he

---

[137] *PD* 1825 (s2) 13: 625–7, 802. According to Campbell, in 1813 half the judges were 'superannuated' (Hardcastle, *Life of Lord Campbell*, i, 288). It remained a problem, for in 1891 *The Times* fired a general broadside at sleeping judges: (1891–2) 36 *Sol. J.* 194.

[138] Atlay, *Victorian Chancellors*, ii, 410–12; Foulkes, *Generation of Judges*, 38–53; J. G. Witt, *A Life in the Law* (1906), 109; E. Graham, *Fifty Years of Famous Judges* (1930) 163; A. F. Engelbach, *Anecdotes of Bench and Bar* (1913), 101, 134.

[139] Witt, *Life in the Law*, 17; Sir J. Arnould, *A Memoir of Thomas, First Lord Denman*, 2 vols (1873), ii, 288–9; Campbell, *Lord Chancellors* (1869), viii, 549–50; Erle to Palmer, 27 November 1866, Selborne Mss, vol. 1862, f. 233.

[140] Coleridge to Roupell, 29 August 1893, E. H. Coleridge, *The Life and Correspondence of John Duke, Lord Coleridge*, 2 vols (1904), ii, 380; Engelbach, *Anecdotes*, 161.

[141] Coleridge to Cairns, 2 February 1875, Cairns Mss PRO 30/51/10; Heuston, *Lord Chancellors*, 60; KCL Library, *Lord Lindley's Autobiography*, 129.

[142] Bosanquet, *Oxford Circuit*, 68; B. C. Robinson, *Bench and Bar* (2nd edn, 1889), 121.

[143] Abinger, *Forty Years at the Bar*, 101; Bosanquet, *Oxford Circuit*, 28–9, 37.

[144] S. Mayer, *Reminiscences of a KC, Theatrical and Legal* (1924), 124; Bosanquet, *Oxford Circuit*, 30; Witt, *Life in the Law*, 111. Leach had also been sleepy in later years: (1834) 12 *LM* 427–34.

was carefully kept off jury trials.[145] The bar could regard such human weaknesses with amusement or at worst resignation, though few were perhaps so cynical as Lord Westbury who, when Erle protested his unfitness for duty on the Judicial Committee because he was old, deaf and stupid, retorted, 'Why, Chelmsford and I are old, Napier is very deaf and Colville is stupid, but we four make an excellent tribunal'.[146] As well as slowing down trials, these men helped create an image of judges as old, deaf, and dozy.

So the prospect of a pension, uncoupled from an explicit requirement of retirement through infirmity or age, was a mixed blessing. It kept a few admirable judges on the bench for longer and avoided controversies over the definition of judicial incapacity. On the other hand it encouraged a tendency for judges who were ailing like Butt, or simply worn out, like Neville, to stay too long.[147] A further drawback was that it hindered advance planning. The occurrence of vacancies could not be predicted and therefore when a ministry wanted to accommodate its law officers or other prominent lawyers it was tempted to offer inducements, perhaps coupled with hints of parliamentary questions about fitness, to create a vacancy. The most blatant case of this sort occurred in 1830, when Wellington's administration needed a place for the Solicitor-General, Sir Nicholas Tindal. They sounded out the Chief Baron (Alexander), the Master of the Rolls (Leach) and the Chief Justice of the Common Pleas (Best), eventually closing with Best, who extracted a peerage and a pension for disability based on a rather exaggerated diagnosis of the severity of his gout.[148]

PROMOTIONS

Making the great law offices berths for politicians and law officers severely reduced the likelihood that a man who accepted a puisne judgeship would win promotion. Some politicians approved of this since it would dissuade judges from currying favour with the government of the day and in the debates on judges' salaries in 1825 some claimed to detect a regular practice of promotions, which Brougham hysterically denounced as 'a system so foul, that [it] mocked all public decency'.[149] In fact there was no policy, merely a series of accidents, and it was rather curious of Whig lawyers to argue a preference for taking the highest judges straight from ministerial positions. Still, promotion did not look like a promising route and law

[145] Bowen Rowlands, *In the Light of the Law*, 96; E. A. Parry, *What the Judge Saw* (1912), 134–6; E. A. Bell, *Those Meddlesome Attorneys* (1939), 70.
[146] Nash, *Life of Lord Westbury*, ii, 174.
[147] (1891–2) 36 *Sol. J.* 515; *The Times*, 15 October 1918.
[148] (1845) 2 (s2) *LM* 308–16.
[149] *PD* 1825 (s2) 13: 811.

officers and ambitious KCs were seldom willing to take a puisne post without a clear expectation such as had been given to Gibbs and Richards.

It was different in Chancery because the creation of a Vice-Chancellor in 1813 created a distinct hierarchy. The first holder, Sir Thomas Plumer, was promoted to the Rolls in 1817 despite a poor reputation, perhaps to facilitate the appointment of the Regent's protege John Leach. Leach in turn become Master of the Rolls, though not on the next vacancy, and his own successor Sir Anthony Hart was sent to Ireland as Lord Chancellor. Sir Lancelot Shadwell, the next Vice-Chancellor, was not seriously considered for the Rolls in the highly charged political circumstances surrounding the next vacancy, in 1836,[150] but the creation of two more vice-chancellors in 1841 and then the two lord justices of appeal in Chancery in 1852 lengthened the ladder.

With Chancery leaders practising exclusively in one judge's court, it was difficult to overlook the claims of vice-chancellors to promotion, and in fact six of the 14 became lord justices of appeal in Chancery, as Sir James Parker would surely have done had he lived. Of the other lord justices, Cairns and Rolt were law officers, but outstanding equity lawyers too; Sir George Mellish was a deliberate common law appointment and that of C. J. Selwyn was coolly received at the bar.[151] Nevertheless, even on a Chancery vacancy it was Gladstone's view that they should first see if anyone who had held a great law office wanted it (he called this 'the Lyndhurst principle') before considering a promotion.[152]

The Judicature Acts brought a hierarchy to all three divisions of the High Court.[153] Lords of appeal in ordinary and lord justices of appeal might either be direct appointments or promotions, and it quickly became apparent that promotion would be more common. Initially several judges were elevated to the Court of Appeal, while Blackburn alone went straight to the Lords from the Queen's Bench. Thereafter only Macnaghten (1887), Russell (1894), and Robson (1910) went to the Lords direct from the English bar, with a further five direct to the Court of Appeal.

As against these direct appointments, there were 31 promotions from the High Court, so the prospects of promotion were distinctly good. Of 20 Chancery judges 12 went up (Pearson and Byrne died too soon to be considered) and prospects of advancement were even more favourable in the cinderella division, the PDA, where three out of four junior judges ended as President.

---

[150] He was offered the Lord Chancellorship of Ireland by Peel in 1834: Mahon and Cardwell, *Memoir of Peel*, ii, 55.

[151] Polden, 'Mingling the Waters', 594–5; (1869) 4 *LJ* 439.

[152] Gladstone to Earl Granville, 16 December 1868, in Nash, *Life of Lord Westbury*, ii, 185.

[153] For arguments on the desirability of a distinct class of judges of appeal, see Polden, 'Mingling the Waters', 594.

Because the Queen's Bench was bigger the chances were less good, but even so, 16 out of 45 were promoted and Bigham was rather surprisingly made President of the PDA. Only five lord justices ever reached the Lords, along with Parker, raised direct from the Chancery Division and Hannen, the President of the PDA.

It was no longer suggested that the prospect of promotion had sinister implications and it might have facilitated the appointment to the High Court of gifted men who were temperamentally unsuited for the role of a trial judge, but there is no evidence for this. There was no fast track to the Court of Appeal, but it was not Buggins' turn either.[154]

TRANSFERS BETWEEN COURTS

In theory, the common law courts had roughly equal standing and a judge was not expected (and could not be required) to move between them.[155] However, by the end of the 1820s the disparity in reputation between the overburdened King's Bench and the others was such that the Common Law Commissioners recommended some excellent appointments to the latter to restore suitors' confidence.[156] This implicitly admitted what the *Law Magazine* asserted, that great care had been taken in the selection of King's Bench judges but much less with Common Pleas, while the Exchequer was 'not infrequently a resting place for age and infirmity, or a reward for political subserviency'.[157] Eldon did not consider either Burrough or Garrow up to King's Bench standard and the Exchequer had to receive Vaughan, and Copley's favourite, William Bolland.

Accordingly, the government soon manouevred to strengthen the Exchequer. It was given Bayley in 1830, who presumably wanted an easier life in his old age, and Alderson and Patteson were appointed to the Common Pleas and King's Bench respectively on their undertaking to remove if required. In 1834 Alderson did go into the Exchequer, along with the highly regarded James Parke from King's Bench, Vaughan moving to the Common Pleas.[158] Not all commentators approved of this game of 'Puss in the Corner', feeling that different capacities of judges should not be openly signalled, but it did help.[159] There is a handful of later transfers,[160] but only in the making of the Judicature Acts was another significant attempt made to re-balance the courts, and this time the chiefs, particularly

---

[154] The most rapid promotions were Cozens-Hardy (within three years), Hamilton (four) and Bankes (five).

[155] Lemmings, *Professors of the Law*, 286; Foss, *Judges of England*, , viii, 325.

[156] *RC on the Common Law, First Report*, PP 1829 (46), ix, 23.

[157] 'The Constitution and Practice of the English Courts of Law' (1828–9) 1 *LM* 185–219 at 211.

[158] (1829–30) 3 *LM* 292; (1831) 5 *LM* 252; (1834) 11 *LM* 544.

[159] (1834) 12 *LM* 263.

[160] Erle from Common Pleas to King's Bench in 1846, then to Common Pleas as Chief Justice in 1859; Maule from Exchequer to Common Pleas in 1839; Rolfe from Exchequer to Chancery as

Coleridge, seem to have been the prime movers. High Court judges, unlike their predecessors, might be moved between divisions without their consent, but in fact after the transfer of Ford North to the Chancery Division in 1883 following his unsuccessful placing in the QBD by Selborne, there were no further simple translations of this sort.[161]

SALARIES

Until 1825 the incomes of the judges were made up of a salary, augmented by the income from certain suitors' fees and, in the case of the great offices, by the exploitation of patronage. In 1809 salaries stood thus: puisne judges, the Master of the Rolls and the Chief Baron £4000 (but made up to £5000 in 1813); the Chief Justice of the Common Pleas £3500; the Chief Justice of the King's Bench £4000; the Lord Chancellor £5000.[162] The Chancellor and the chiefs in particular actually had incomes far greater than this, and when Liverpool's ministry finally tackled the thorny question of fees and patronage in 1825, the proposed salaries had to reflect that. Puisnes were now to have £6000; the Master of the Rolls and Chief Baron £7000; the Chief Justice of the Common Pleas £8000; and the Chief Justice of the King's Bench £10,000. The Vice-Chancellor's salary of £5000 would be raised to £6000. In Parliament argument centred on the Chief Justice of the King's Bench's salary, and the desirable differential between his salary and those of the Chief Justice of the Common Pleas and his own puisnes, and on objections that the puisnes were being treated too generously.[163]

The government agreed to reduce the puisnes to £5500, which still put them among the highest salaried individuals in the country and well ahead of all but the very top earners at the bar.[164] Few other public officials, including cabinet ministers, could match these earnings, especially when supported by generous pensions,[165] and they soon came under fire. From November 1828 new puisnes were required to agree to accept only £5000.[166] Soon afterwards, when Denman became Chief Justice of the King's Bench, he put his earlier declaration that the

---

a lord justice, 1850. The Probate judges, Cresswell and J. P. Wilde, came from Common Pleas and Exchequer respectively.

[161] Polden, 'Mingling the Waters', 591–2, 609–10.

[162] Judges' Salaries Act 1809 (49 Geo. III c. 127); Duman, *Judicial Bench*, 111–16.

[163] *Ibid.*; PD 1825 (s2) 13: 801–24. The Master of the Rolls' salary had not been raised in 1813 as Sir William Grant disclaimed the need (col. 616).

[164] It was said that getting good judges was difficult: C. Cottu, *On the Administration of Criminal Justice in England* (1822), 139, instancing Richardson's reluctance.

[165] Duman, *Judicial Bench*, 113, table 9.

[166] Judges' Salaries Act 1832 (2 & 3 Will. IV c. 116), s. 1 made the reduction effective for appointments since 16 November 1828. Those judges had taken office on those terms.

judges were overpaid into practice by voluntarily taking only £8000.[167] Finally, in 1832, the Lord Chancellor was dealt with. Eldon had been making around £15,000 and his successors were now put on £10,000 with a £4000 addition as deputy speaker of the House of the Lords.[168] Further attacks on judicial salaries in the 1830s had no effect,[169] but the two extra vice-chancellors were paid only £5000 as against the Vice-Chancellor of England's £6000, which was also what the lord justices of appeals in Chancery received in 1852.[170] With Denman's retirement his successor Campbell was more or less compelled to accept the 'voluntary' reduction, but insisted that it be made statutory. Jervis, on becoming Chief Justice of the Common Pleas in the same year, had accepted the post at a reduced salary of £7000 and both reductions were made permanent.[171]

After a period of calm there was another battle at the time of the Judicature Acts. Gladstone had always considered the puisne judges overpaid in comparison with the higher civil service, but he could not persuade his cabinet to support a reduction to £4000, though he did manage to reduce the pensions.[172]

In the event, the lords of appeal in ordinary were to have £6000, with both puisnes and lord justices left on £5000 despite Cairns' urgent advocacy on behalf of the latter.[173] The Master of the Rolls was on £6000, the Lord Chief Justice (after the abolition of the other chiefs) £8000 and the President of the PDA £5000. The lack of adverse comment in the legal press and the seeming absence of any lobbying by the Lord Chancellor for an increase suggest that these salaries were regarded as sufficient to attract and retain suitable candidates for the bench. However, they had begun to seem less attractive by 1914 as bar earnings for the brightest stars climbed to unheard of heights and tax began to take its toll.[174]

The Judge in Court

There is a wealth of anecdotal and biographical information on nineteenth-century judges, but it must be used with care. Some sources are untrustworthy—Campbell's

---

[167] Arnould, *First Lord Denman*, 420–1.

[168] For the controversies about Eldon's income see R. A. Melikan, *John Scott, Lord Eldon* (Cambridge, 1999), 315–17.

[169] The *Law Magazine* ((1838) 11 *LM* 544) suggested that Hume's proposal to reduce the puisnes to £3500 reduced the attractions of the bench.

[170] Administration of Justice Act 1841 (5 Vict. c. 5) ss. 35, 37; Court of Chancery and Privy Council Act 1852 (14 & 15 Vict. c. 83), s. 19.

[171] Hardcastle, *Life of Lord Campbell*, ii, 295; Sainty, *Judges of England*, 44.

[172] H. C. G. Matthew (ed.), *The Gladstone Diaries* (1982), viii, 277.

[173] Cairns to Selborne, 18 April 1873, Selborne Mss, vol. 1865, f. 266; *PD* 1881 (s3) 258: 629.

[174] KBD judges, however, received liberal circuit allowances: *Lindley's Autobiography*, 80; Stevens, *Independence of the Judiciary*, 50–2.

Lives and Grant's *Bar and Bench* are familiar examples—and many biographies are uncritical. Since most of the writing has been done by members of the bar, the bar's perspective on a judge is what usually emerges so that a judge who was habitually unpleasant to counsel seldom gets a good press. And of course views are sometimes divergent. Lord Alverstone is a case in point. Few would hold his judgments in high regard, but while Dickens and Abinger regarded him as a good trial judge, Cancellor said he seemed bored in criminal trials; to Whiteley he was pleasant, but Morris called him 'a pig'.[175] Where the judge has featured in only one or two memoirs they may of course be wayward or untypical. [176]

Judges were prominent public characters, whose utterances were frequently in the newspapers. The unabashed exhibition of individual personality traits on the bench was regarded as normal and the bar generally accommodated itself to the foibles of the bench except when pressed to extremes. They all knew how Cockburn had to string out commercial cases overnight to allow him to look up the law and how he ensured that the most sensational cases came before him;[177] how Willes sought for a chance to display his prodigious legal learning from the Year Books downwards and how Darling was desperate to produce a not always spontaneous witticism; how the aged Kelly was obsessed with dates and Westbury and Esher loved to pounce on solecisms in the classical languages.[178] They knew that some judges were inclined to affirm (Lyndhurst) and others to reverse (Cottenham);[179] that some were plaintiffs' judges, others defendants'.[180] Gradually this unabashed individualism become less pronounced, perhaps because the judges collectively became less confident about their role. 'Characters' were still appointed to the bench—men like Scrutton, McCardie, and Swift—but they were no longer typical; even Avory, the best known of the judges of the 1920s, was self-effacing and remote.[181]

---

[175] Dickens, *Recollections*, 165–6; Abinger, *Forty Years at the Bar*, 44–5; H. L. Cancellor, *The Life of a London Beak* (1930), 233; Whiteley, *Brief Life*, 9–11; Sir H. Morris, *Back View* (1960), 126.

[176] Sir Henry Keating is an example: *ODNB* 31: 977 (S. Hedley).

[177] Hollams, *Jottings of an Old Solicitor*, 138; C. Yarnall (ed.), *Fifty Years of Friendship* (1911), 194. Coleridge's disclaimer of any similar attempts on his part (to E. Yarnall, 12 March 1881) would have amused some of his colleagues.

[178] Foulkes, *Generation of Judges*, 38–53, 60–70; Nash, *Life of Lord Westbury*, i, 89–90; Abinger, *Forty Years at the Bar*, 111–12.

[179] Campbell, *Lord Chancellors*, viii, 135.

[180] C. W. Crocker, *Far From Humdrum: A Lawyer's Life* (1967), 72; B. Lailey, *Jottings From a Fee Book* (Portsmouth, 1932), 130.

[181] It seems likely that the venting of party political opinions extra-judicially had come to be deplored since the days of Kelly CB, who made openly Conservative speeches: 'QC', 'The Vacant Chiefships' (1880–1) 6 (s4) *LM & R* 174–90 at 171. This remains to be explored, though see Stevens, *Independence of the Judiciary*.

It is also significant that while the oral tradition of the bar celebrated the more exuberant characters, the judge who was most often mentioned as epitomizing the judicial ideal was the imperturbable Sir William Grant MR.[182] The nearest later equivalent was perhaps Sir James Hannen, though Hannen made most of his reputation in the divorce court, where an especially decorous atmosphere was expected.[183]

Grant and Hannen are elusive personalities, almost devoid of minor eccentricities when on the bench, and after all not all foibles were harmless. Russell's intolerance of facial hair on counsel, and Bacon's of moustaches may not have impaired their possessors' chance of a fair hearing,[184] but other manifestations of dominion over 'my court' did put justice at risk.[185] Thus counsel and witnesses might find themselves chilled in the courts of Parke or Huddleston, or stifled in those of Wills or Hawkins. Hawkins and Parke were also notorious for protracting sittings beyond the point where anyone but themselves could concentrate.[186]

In Hawkins' case both traits were manifestations of a generally domineering attitude and though he pressed it to extremes, some claimed that there had been a deterioration in judicial manners since the days of courtly judges like Graham and Dallas,[187] and the impression may be more significant than the reality. Although Eldon's disarming urbanity set the tone for Chancery, Leach was so unpleasant that he was formally remonstrated with by leaders on behalf of the bar.[188] Conversely, while even the combative Jack Campbell found 'the four ruffians of the King's Bench' headed by Ellenborough daunting, and 'Vinegar' Gibbs deserved his nickname,[189] in the 1830s and 1840s Denman in the Queen's Bench and Lyndhurst in Chancery were models of polished courtesy.

It may be, however, that a clutch of 'strong' judges in the mid-century made an impression beyond their numbers. Certainly Alderson, James, Bramwell, Blackburn, Cottenham, and Jessel fell into that category, and their vigorous, masculine style was perpetuated after the Judicature Acts by men like Brett and

---

[182] Romilly, *Memoir of Romilly*, iii, 324; *Lord Kingsdown's Recollections*, 35–9.

[183] Manson, *Builders of our Law*, 332–43.

[184] T. E. Crispe, *Reminiscences of a KC* (2nd edn, 1909), 100; A. Underhill, *Change and Decay* (1938), 121.

[185] In the case of Kekewich J. this proprietorial attitude manifested itself in the form of local 'rules': P. Polden, 'Nineteenth Century Judicial Reputations', paper to the 19th British Legal History Conference, Exeter, 2009.

[186] Ballantine, *Some Experiences*, 106; 'Circuit Tramp' [J. A. Foote], *Pie-Powder* (1911), 127.

[187] Collier, *Criticisms on the Bar*, 47–8; *ODNB* 14: 599.

[188] *Lord Kingsdown's Reminiscences*, 29 (a m/s note in the London Library copy says it was Heald alone). Some years earlier the Yorkshire barrister Topping had performed a similar service with Gibbs: Hardcastle, *Life of Lord Campbell*, i, 218.

[189] Hardcastle, *Life of Lord Campbell*, i, 329; Townsend, *The Lives of Twelve Eminent Judges*, ii, 290–1.

Stephen.[190] At worst, however, it degenerated into sheer unpleasantness through the likes of Ridley, Hawkins, Kay, and Field.[191] Some carried it into the new century. Scrutton had to be bearded by the bar like Leach before him, but R. A. Wright was described as the last of the breed and when A. L. Smith took over Esher's division of the Court of Appeal there was a markedly less combative atmosphere there.[192] In general judges do seem to have become milder and less dictatorial in the new century; perhaps, like Page Wood earlier, they did not wish to inflict on juniors the treatment they had received themselves.[193]

Among the virtues possessed by Grant and Hannen was that they did not noticeably allow personal views to come into play. Of course, as Scrutton acknowledged in the 1920s all judges have such views, sometimes with a political dimension;[194] it was said, for example, that the early motorists found the judiciary generally hostile.[195] But some judges were well known for particular prejudices; Field was reckoned to be biased against railway companies, Gorell Barnes to favour wives in divorce cases, Robert Phillimore could not restrain his high church sympathies in ecclesiastical cases, W. G. Phillimore, Wills, and Day were thought to be quite unbalanced when sexual offences were being tried before them, and J. C. Lawrance always favoured the Revenue.[196] It was notoriously difficult to persuade Esher's Court of Appeal to question a jury verdict and Halsbury was equally reluctant—an especially serious hurdle at appellate level.[197]

Then again, there were judges who, unlike Cairns, could not be said to have 'heard well'.[198] Few things upset the bar more than a judge who frequently interrupted them in their speeches, and Lord Coleridge suggested that it had contributed to the decay in true forensic eloquence.[199] It is unlikely, as was alleged, that such interruptions were rare in Grant's day, for though it may have been unusual for puisnes sitting in banc to intervene, Ellenborough and Gibbs certainly had no compunction about doing so.[200] The impression is, however, that it became

---

[190] Graham, *Fifty Years of Famous Judges*, 89–107; Lailey, *Jottings*, 27.

[191] Bosanquet, *Oxford Circuit*, 41–2, 69–70; A. Smith, *Lord Goddard* (1959), 24–5; Alexander, *Temple of the Nineties*, 100; Mayer, *Reminiscences*, 133; Crispe, *Reminiscences of a KC*, 412.

[192] Bosanquet, *Oxford Circuit*, 39.

[193] Rentoul, *This Is My Case*, 60; Stephens, *Life of Lord Hatherley*, ii, 59.

[194] 'The Work of the Commercial Court' [1920] 1 *CLJ* 6–20 at 8.

[195] Crocker, *Far From Humdrum*, 72.

[196] Crispe, *Reminiscences of a KC*, 95; de Montmorency, *Lord Gorell*, 73; Graham, *Fifty Years of Famous Judges*, 201–8; Bowen Rowlands, *In the Light of the Law*, 100; *The Times*, 6 December 1912.

[197] Lailey, *Jottings*, 80; Graham, *Fifty Years of Famous Judges*, 105.

[198] Manson, *Builders of Our Law*, 203–14.

[199] Lord Alverstone, *Recollections of Bar and Bench*, 285.

[200] Woolrych, *Lives of Eminent Serjeants*, ii, 695.

commoner. Leach brought it into Chancery [201] and several common law judges were notorious for it, especially in the Exchequer. It was not confined to poor judges like Bovill, for among those named are Mellish and Blackburn, though Cairns coldly and decisively checked the latter when he attempted it in the Lords.[202] It may have been in part a response to lengthier speeches from counsel, for Langdale MR, who sought to emulate Grant's perfect stillness, was criticized for allowing cases to be drawn out and complained of the interminable ramblings of counsel.[203] However, that was certainly not the motive of the most extreme example, Sir George Jessel. Jessel developed a style which substituted a rapid fire dialogue with counsel for their conventional, and often ponderous speeches and such was the force of his personality that he was able to impose it without protest, though it could only work well in a court like the Rolls where the same few leaders appeared in case after case and were familiar with it. Even then it worked notably less well when Chitty attempted it.[204]

Once it had become widespread, the habit of interruption proved difficult to eradicate even for Halsbury in the Lords.[205] At least some of those who routinely hindered attempts to put forth an argument also failed to emulate Grant in another respect—they made up their mind early on and were hard to sway from their first opinion. Among the alleged culprits were Ellenborough, Erle, Robert Lush, Martin, Jelf, and William James.[206] Others angered counsel by ostentatious inattention. Eldon had been discreet in writing his letters on the bench but Brougham's more open impoliteness led to a famous row with Sugden.[207] It is revealing of the disregard for appearances that some judges had that men like Day and Bailhache could manifest open boredom in the sort of cases they disliked.[208]

Much worse, however, were judges who either favoured a particular counsel or the reverse. Twice at least this led to angry scenes in the courtroom; Adolphus, from the rough and tumble Old Bailey, gave voice to what King's

---

[201] *Lord Kingsdown's Reminiscences*, 30. It did not depart with Leach: Rolt, *Memoirs*, 88. Knight-Bruce was particularly notorious: J. C. Fox, *A Handbook of English Law Reports* (1913), 89.

[202] Hollams, *Jottings of an Old Solicitor*, 144; Witt, *Life in the Law*, 108; Foulkes, *Generation of Judges*, 109–11.

[203] T. D. Hardy, *Memoirs of the Rt Hon. Henry, Lord Langdale*, 2 vols (1852), ii, 57; (1851) 14(s2) *LM* 283. It was said at the bar that Samuel Romilly's speeches had seldom exceeded 15 minutes: G. Harris, *Autobiography* (1888), 99.

[204] Lord Bryce, *Studies in Contemporary Biography* (1903), 173–6.

[205] See above, p. 543.

[206] Townsend, *Lives of Eminent Judges*, ii, 90; Robinson, *Bench and Bar*, 195; Ballantine, *Some Experiences*, 222; Foulkes, *Generation of Judges*, 104; E. F. Spence, *Bar and Buskin* (1930), 333.

[207] Atlay, *Victorian Chancellors*, ii, 299.

[208] *ODNB* 15: 590; T. Humphreys, *Criminal Days* (1946), 127.

Bench practitioners all believed, that Abbott was too much under the influence of Scarlett,[209] while 20 years later, and perhaps with less cause, Frederick Thesiger accused Chief Baron Pollock of being biased in favour of his son-in-law Samuel Martin.[210] Gibbs and Jervis were also said to favour particular counsel, and it is unsurprising to read that Hawkins mistreated A. J. Cock.[211] However, it was most likely to occur in Chancery and in the civilian courts, sometimes due not so much to favouritism as inability to resist superior intellectual power. Shadwell was notoriously under the sway of a succession of domineering leaders, beginning with Sugden and climaxing with Bethell, who scarcely bothered to conceal a state of affairs which, Selborne wrote 'would be inconceivable to those who did not witness it'.[212] At the Rolls it was said that Langdale more or less adopted Pemberton Leigh's arguments and that the latter practically wrote the judgments,[213] but even more unsatisfactory was Malins' court; not only could he be readily provoked into a scene but he was openly bullied by Glasse.[214] Knight Bruce, who suffered from contending against favoured rivals at the Rolls, then had the misfortune as a vice-chancellor to incur the animosity first of Lord Chancellor Cottenham, who delighted in reversing his decrees, and then of Westbury, who would not even sit with him on appeals.[215]

Such internal animosities were, for the most part, kept behind the curtain, but it was notorious that Eldon and Leach were mutually hostile; that Westbury and Maule both hated Campbell; that Jessel disliked Selborne; and Cockburn disliked Willes. Brett and Jessel were openly at odds; practically the whole common law bench could not abide Hawkins and Fletcher Moulton's appeal court was perpetually riven by animosities.[216]

---

[209] Townsend, *Lives of Eminent Judges*, ii, 63.

[210] Hollams, *Jottings of an Old Solicitor*, 134.

[211] Townsend, *Lives of Eminent Judges*, ii, 297; Hollams, *Jottings of an Old Solicitor*, 135–6; Abinger, *Forty Years at the Bar*, 40.

[212] *Memorials, Part One, Family and Personal, 1866–75*, 2 vols (1896), i, 374.

[213] Rolt, *Memoirs*, 82. Ashton (*As I Went On My Way*, 99) says Davey wrote them for the indolent Wickens.

[214] Foulkes, *Generation of Judges*, 147–56; Witt, *Life in the Law*, 100.

[215] Rolt, *Memoirs*, 91.

[216] *Lord Kingsdown's Recollections*, 30–1; Birkenhead, *Fourteen English Judges*, 270; Graham, *Fifty Years of Famous Judges*, 100; Hollams, *Jottings of an Old Solicitor*, 152; Ballantine, *Some Experiences*, 141; Rentoul, *This Is My Case*, 61; E. Bowen Rowlands, *In Court and Out of Court* (1925), 54. A growing trend for judges to criticize each other was noted in (1880–1) 25 *Sol. J.* 292 and deplored by Sir Edward Clarke in 1890 (9 *LN* 2).

2. COUNTY COURT JUDGES

Appointment: Numbers, Qualifications, and Selection

The County Courts Act 1846 authorized the appointment of 'as many fit persons as are needed', and the government promptly made 60 new judges.[217] This unprecedented harvest of patronage was in fact drastically reduced by Cottenham's decision to employ as many of the judges of the liquidated local courts as were appointable, and barely one-third were selected from outside this pool. Experience suggested to many that the number of judges was excessive and their distribution misaligned with need, but despite strong recommendations by successive inquiries in the 1870s for a major reduction and redistribution, only modest changes were made and in 1914 there were still 55 judges.[218]

Despite vigorous lobbying by attorneys, the new judgeships were confined to barristers of seven years' standing, a less stringent qualification than the 10 years recommended by the Common Law Commissioners. [219]

The power to appoint judges was vested in the Lord Chancellor, but both temporary and permanent exceptions were inserted into the Act. The temporary ones were, first, that the judges of four local courts, the county clerk of Middlesex, and the steward of the manor of Sheffield were translated to the new courts, and secondly, that the lords of eight manors were allowed to fill the next vacancy in the county court which superseded their manorial court; the last of these judges, Thomas Ellison, sitting in Sheffield on the Duke of Norfolk's nomination, died in 1896.[220] The permanent exception gave the Chancellor of the Duchy the patronage of districts exclusively within the Duchy of Lancaster. One of his early choices, William Ramshay in Liverpool, turned out disastrously and there was some criticism of later appointments, but although local men tended to be favoured, the appointments generally seem no worse than the Lord Chancellors'.[221]

PATRONAGE AND POLITICS

Tradition has it that Cottenham packed the bench with good Whigs, and there are certainly obvious examples in David Leahy, a prominent journalist, and

---

[217] P. Polden, *A History of the County Court 1846–1971* (Cambridge, 1999), 38.

[218] *RC on the Judicature, Second Report*, PP 1872 [C. 631], xx, 14; *SC on Civil Service Expenditure, Second Report*, PP 1873 (248), vii at vii; *RC on the Legal Departments, Second Report*, PP 1875 [C. 1107], xxiv, 97.

[219] County Courts Act 1846, s. 10; Polden, *History of the County Court*, 241–2. The seven years might include time spent as a special pleader.

[220] Sections 10–12.

[221] Polden, *History of the County Court*, 241. For Ramshay see below, p. 1002.

W. M. Praed, son of a Whig politician.[222] Party loyalties continued to count. Joseph Pollock, for instance, was described as an O'Connellite and Liberal, but he was also a well-regarded judge of the Salford hundred court and criticism centred rather on appointments like T. F. Falconer, a man with no real practice who had just cadged a colonial secretaryship which he renounced upon procuring a judgeship, no doubt through the same agency, his brother in law J. A. Roebuck.[223]

The only known instances of actual nepotism belong to Halsbury, who chose his brother-in-law Robert Woodfall and another of his wife's relations, Robert Melville. Woodfall was well qualified but Melville was a flagrant job; Halsbury also put his brother J. W. Giffard onto the County Court Rule Committee at the first opportunity.[224]

There were too many Falconers, Bayleys, and Caillards,[225] men 'utterly unknown to the public, scarcely known even by name to the Profession'.[226] With the exceptions of St. Leonards' two appointees, all Lord Chancellors from Cottenham down to Halsbury chose some men on grounds which the legal press either could not understand or, if they did, condemned. Some critics were jealously defending the interests of the practising bar, but others lamented choices which would undermine the case for widening county court jurisdiction and also regretted the retention of the former judges of courts of requests, though as a group they seem no more prone to error or misbehaviour than others.[227] The attacks became more frequent and outspoken from about 1870 onwards, culminating in an exasperated leader in the *Solicitors Journal*:

having come to the conclusion that of late the preponderance of appointments of county court judges is so greatly on the side of those which, like the present, it is impossible to approve, we think it best to give up the attempt to estimate the merits of such appointments, and to reserve any comments until they come to be made in accordance with some standard which the profession can recognise or at least understand.[228]

One of the most controversial appointments, which Hatherley realized would arouse protest, was Edmond Beales in 1870. A radical MP, he had been deprived of a revising barristership by the Conservatives for his part in the Hyde Park

---

[222] *Ibid.*, 39–40; Atlay, *Victorian Chancellors*, i, 410.

[223] Polden, *History of the County Court*, 246; (1852) 16 (s2) *LM* 129; (1858) 31 *LT* 146.

[224] Polden, *History of the County Court*, 247, 274.

[225] *Ibid.*, 65; (1850) 3 *CCC* 17. Bayley, son of a superior court judge, was on the bench from 1849 to 1893.

[226] (1855) n.s. 1 *Jur.* 75, describing Christopher Temple.

[227] T. W. Snagge, *The Evolution of the County Court* (1904), 12.

[228] (1878–9) 23 *Sol. J.* 293. Compare (1891–2) 92 *LT* 382: '[i]t is impossible to gauge the influences brought to bear upon the Prime Minister and the Lord Chancellor, but it must be something prodigious to secure the appointments which have been made during the past twelve months'.

rally-turned-riot in 1866 and the judgeship was openly intended as a rather generous recompense. It was not only Conservatives who regarded this as particularly irresponsible, for it occurred while the Judicature Commissioners were wrestling with the problem of the extent of local jurisdiction.[229]

Nor was Beales an isolated case. Hatherley, who notoriously did not seek advice on judicial appointments, had already incurred criticism by choosing Gordon Whitbread, his own private secretary, and among his 'peculiar' appointments that of J. F. Collier caused astonishment since he had only a modest western circuit practice. Homersham Cox and J. T. Abdy, while acknowledged to raise the intellectual tone of the bench, were deprecated as not 'practical men'.[230]

Hatherley's successors continued on occasion to oblige Prime Ministers (as Halsbury did with A. G. Marten) and cabinet colleagues (as Cairns did with Horatio Lloyd).[231] They rewarded men for public service (T. J. Bradshaw and R. A. Fisher, successive secretaries to the Judicature Commission) or for serving them (W. L. Selfe, whose appointment provoked a parliamentary question), or to economize on pensions (Vernon Lushington, James Stephen).[232] Not all of these turned out badly, nor for that matter were all those praised by the press a success (Crompton Hutton is an example[233]) but they perpetuated the image of the county court bench as not being the repository of sagacity and proven ability as measured by the profession's own, narrow, test. Its reputation was also damaged by stories, whether true or not, like Cairns' selection of one judge when his secretary misunderstood Sir John Karslake's unflattering verdict on the man.[234]

As with the High Court, the new century saw a change. Loreburn's choices were admitted by an unenthusiastic critic to be 'in the main…middle aged men with a good circuit, local or commercial court practice, and not mere party hacks',[235] and though party political considerations were not eliminated from the selection process, a solid practice background had become almost a prerequisite.[236] Balfour Browne might refer contemptuously to the county court bench as a 'respectable shelf', but at least the shelf had become respectable.[237]

---

[229] (1870–2) 22 *CCC* 227; (1872) 7 *LJ* 127; D. Duman, *The English and Colonial Bars in the Nineteenth Century* (1983), 97.

[230] (1872–3) 17 *Sol. J.* 102; (1871–2) 16 *Sol. J.* 115; (1870–2) 22 *CCC* 131.

[231] Polden, *History of the County Court*, 246.

[232] *Ibid.*, 218; (1881–2) 28 *CCC* 449; (1877) 12 *LJ* 593; (1871) 6 *LJ* 795.

[233] (1873) 8 *LJ* 2; Parry, *What the Judge Saw*, 143–6; P. Polden, 'Judicial Independence and Executive Responsibilities, Part Two' (1996) 25 *Anglo-Am. Law Rev.* 133–62, 147–8.

[234] Engelbach, *Anecdotes*, 238.

[235] (1911–12) 56 *Sol. J.* 590.

[236] One likely exception is J. Shiress Will, a former Liberal MP who had not recovered his once big parliamentary practice: *ODNB* 59: 8.

[237] Browne, *Forty Years at the Bar*, 168.

Politics of a different kind were intruded into appointments to the Welsh districts. The influence of the Welsh language lobby within the Liberal party enabled them to extort a promise that certain districts would become the preserve of Welsh-speaking judges. This created a rather pernicious closed shop, for so few Welsh speakers had even halfway respectable practices that some men well below the general standard obtained judgeships; nevertheless it became too firmly entrenched to be challenged.[238]

AGE AT APPOINTMENT

In 1878 Henry Nicol testified that he felt that as their duties placed a premium rather on the vigour of (comparative) youth than the accumulated wisdom of age, these judges should usually be appointed at under 45, and certainly by 50. This view, endorsed by Haldane in 1913, had much to commend it, for their extensive travelling in most districts, year-round work, and anything but tranquil working conditions imposed strains that were more physical than intellectual.[239]

As it happened the original cadre of judges was, on the whole, a youthful one. J. W. Wing was just 34 and at least seven others were in their 30s, while probably only four were over 60, including two of the more distinguished of Cottenham's 'free' choices, James Manning and J. H. Koe.[240] As overcrowding at the bar made rapid progress harder, young judges became rarer, but not unknown; Joseph Pollock and D. Brynmor Jones were 33 and Edward Parry, probably the youngest of all, only 31, though he was chosen by the Chancellor of the Duchy.[241] Though doubts were voiced as to the wisdom of pitching the 37-year-old McKenzie Chalmers straight into the busy Birmingham court, the youthful judges were generally welcomed unless, like Caillard, there were other objections.[242]

Men in their 60s were harder to justify, though some were excellent in all other respects, like the 65-year-old C. E. Petersdorff and William Willis (62).[243] Halsbury chose some even older men, and what made William Paterson a suitable choice at 71 probably only Halsbury knew. Impervious to criticism of another such, James Mackonochie, he promptly appointed a former circuit colleague, Aeneas McIntyre, good in his day, but at 68 two years older than Mackonochie.[244]

---

[238] (1891) 26 LJ 712; (1885–6) 30 CCC 123; (1893–4) 34 CCC 187.

[239] Polden, *History of the County Court*, 247.

[240] Heath and Manning are in the *ODNB*; for the others see F. R. Boase, *Modern English Biography*, 6 vols (Truro, 1892–1921).

[241] Jones is in the *Dictionary of Welsh Biography* (Oxford, 1959), Pollock in *Modern English Biography*, Parry in *ODNB* 42: 881.

[242] (1884) 29 CCC 477. For Chalmers see *ODNB* 10: 876.

[243] *ODNB* 43: 879; 59: 395.

[244] (1889) 32 CCC 27; (1889) 24 LJ 1.

There was further criticism of Mansel Jones (66) in 1902, but perhaps the failure to raise salaries was making it more difficult to attract men in their prime. Those in their late 50s and early 60s were by now often the best available: thus the four made in 1914 were all between 58 and 63. Better record keeping then perpetuated this trend, for once a man made the shortlist his name would crop up on every vacancy, whereas earlier Lord Chancellors would consider only those who had written to them, except for rare instances where they chose someone who had not applied.[245]

STANDING AND EXPERIENCE

The regular criticism of appointments of men without an extensive practice is difficult to test and 'years since call' is an unreliable indicator. It was certainly said that of Halsbury's first 21 judges, no more than six 'ever enjoyed anything like a large practice at the Bar, with three or four of the others being experienced deputies and the rest practically unknown'.[246] This, even if accurate, may not be representative, and certainly quite a lot of the judges had some prior judicial experience. Taking as an example the 30 men with initials starting with 'B', nine had been recorders, one a judge of a court of requests, another judge of the Salford hundred court, two commissioners in bankruptcy, one a deputy Chairman of Quarter Sessions, at least two deputy county court judges, and one a Commissioner of Assize. In all, one-half of the sample had been on the bench in some capacity, not counting those 14 who were already, or subsequently became, JPs.

A particular issue arose with deputies. Several judges employed a deputy on a regular basis and it was inevitable for an expectation to arise that, if supported by the outgoing judge and local solicitors, the deputy would have a claim to the vacancy. To counter this Westbury laid down a rule that no deputy would be appointed to a vacancy in 'his' district and this was applied strictly even when local pressure was exerted.[247]

Attitudes differed over the suitability of members of the Chancery bar. With county courts dispensing no equity until 1867 and not much thereafter, such men would be unable to use their particular expertise. More seriously, the atmosphere of Chancery was far removed from most county courts and the two judges

---

[245] (1902) 37 *LJ* 511. Martineau was one who claimed not to have sought the post: *SC on the County Courts Bill*, PP 1878 (267), xi, q. 1956. For the permanent officials' role between the wars see P. Polden, ' "Oiling the Machinery": The Lord Chancellor's Office and the County Court Bench, 1927–44' (1998) 19 *JLH* 224–44.

[246] (1892) 27 *LJ* 491.

[247] Polden, *History of the County Court*, 249–50. However, by making William Nichols, registrar of the bankruptcy court in Manchester, a judge, Westbury was able to put Nichols' deputy George Harris into that position: Harris, *Autobiography*, 297–8.

who recoiled from what they found and returned rapidly to the bar were both Chancery men—C. C. Barber in 1874 and G. B. Hughes in 1885.[248] Yet if these judgeships were regarded as spoils of the profession, Lincoln's Inn would not take kindly to being excluded, and might expect support at least from those Lord Chancellors who were themselves equity lawyers, and who would have personal knowledge of their candidates. The junior Chancery bar apparently felt excluded until Westbury chose R. G. Welford in 1865 despite his being mostly a conveyancer with little court experience.[249] Westbury and his immediate successors made sure Chancery had its share and some felt indeed that they were too numerous, but by 1898 the Chancery bar was again complaining of neglect, though there is little to suggest that they were right.[250]

Local bars also began to furnish candidates, mostly to the Duchy districts (like Millis Coventry in 1886 and C. L. Shand in 1889) but sometimes elsewhere, such as Alfred Young, a very prominent and successful Birmingham leader (1898) and F. J. Greenwell of the Newcastle bar (1895).[251]

Throughout the period most vacancies were filled from the outer bar. The original judges included a handful of serjeants and QCs, but only gradually, as the rising number of QCs meant that most could no longer aspire to anything higher, did the proportion became significant.[252] Some fell into that embarrassing class of failed silks; W. H. G. Bagshawe, for instance, failed to adapt to Jessel's unique style in the Rolls court, while Samuel Prentice had been among the silks outraged by Blackburn's promotion.[253] Three of 23 QCs made in 1851 ended up on the county court bench; four of 17 made in 1861; two of the 18 of 1872. But the process was not uniform; the bench acquired just one apiece of the smaller cohorts of 1881 and 1891 and none at all from that of 1901.

BACKGROUND AND EDUCATION

As might be expected, the profile of these judges is broadly the same as that of superior court judges. There are, however, a few differences. First, the decline in the number from a landed background was more delayed; perhaps barristers of gentry background still sought appointments in their own locality.[254] Secondly,

---

[248] Hughes was Halsbury's first, and generally approved, appointment. It was perhaps a mistake to send them to Hull and Bradford respectively.

[249] (1864–5) 9 *Sol. J.* 259.

[250] (1867–8) 44 *LT* 436, 487; (1898) 33 *LJ* 352.

[251] (1886) 21 *LJ* 190; (1889) 32 *CCC* 103, (1900–01) 45 *Sol. J.* 85; (1895) 30 *LJ* 211.

[252] (1897–8) 36 *CCC* 87 noted 13 silks among the last 29 appointments, but felt the number was declining.

[253] (1893) 28 *LJ* 882; *The Times*, 6 November 1901.

[254] This is suggested by the presence of several judges in the several editions of E. O. Walford, *County Families* and *Burke's Landed Gentry*.

the proportion from a business background was distinctly lower—among the last cohort fewer than 10 per cent. The professions were overwhelmingly dominant, and while the church, army, and medicine provided a substantial input through-out, from the 1870s onwards recruitment from within the legal profession itself became very marked. Among 53 appointees between 1893 and 1914 with known father's occupations are eight solicitors' sons and 16 sons of barristers (including nine sons of judges of various sorts)—not far short of half the total.

Among the names are those of famous legal dynasties—Mellor, Vaughan Williams, Russell, and Stephen—and county courts had begun to produce some of their own: father and son Haringtons, Beresfords, Wheelers, and Atkinsons sat on the bench. Once again, even at this less exalted level, no one is to be found of truly humble birth. [255]

As with the superior court judges, a public school and university education became increasingly common. Around two-thirds of the original judges had been to university, rising to three-quarters among later appointments, and some three-quarters of those attended Oxford or Cambridge,[256] though 20 per cent of judges in the last cohort had been to London. On an impressionistic view, their academic records are, on the whole, somewhat less distinguished than their superior court counterparts, but they can show their share of wranglers, prizewinners, and fellows, plus distinguished academic lawyers in Andrew Amos, Thomas Starkie, J. T. Abdy, and J. A. Russell.[257]

In Office: Salaries

The County Courts Act 1846 empowered the Treasury to pay salaries of up to £1200 but, still pained by the experience with Brougham's ill-fated Court of Review, they deferred setting the figure until the fee yield had become clear. A very modest £1000 was the outcome and even when it was raised to £1200 in 1850 only 18 of the judges were gainers by the move from a fee-based income.

Aware that the extension of county court jurisdiction by an Act of 1852 which also raised the maximum salary to £1500 would generate demands for a pay rise, the Treasury proposed salaries differentiated by workload, keeping the total outlay within the fee income. Unable to persuade the County Courts Commission to do the dirty work of devising the formula, they had to concoct one themselves, under which just 18 judges were to receive either £1500 or £1350. It was naturally unpopular and was scrapped when the conferral of equity jurisdiction provided a suitable

---

[255] Polden, *History of the County Court*, 265–6.
[256] Trinity College, Cambridge far outstripped other colleges.
[257] Polden, *History of the County Court*, 269–70. Heath and Starkie were senior wranglers.

pretext. From 1867 all the judges were on £1500 and there they stayed for the next 70 years. Their judges' council made regular representations and a select committee of 1878 recommended £2000, but with no substantial increase in jurisdiction, no problem in recruiting, and persistent claims that some judges were underworked, there was little prospect of the claim succeeding. Early in the twentieth century officials toyed with reviving differential salaries but wisely let it drop.[258]

In addition to their salary the judges received travelling allowances, in some cases quite substantial—in 1870/1 T. H. Ingham claimed £450, W. Gurdon and F. T. Dinsdale over £400.[259] Some judges, quite legitimately, preferred to live outside their district and only rarely did the Lord Chancellor seek a personal undertaking about local residence. Nevertheless in 1872 the Treasury, 'with a distrustful meanness that would be resented by a third-rate commercial traveller',[260] sought to reduce expenses by calculating them on the presumption of residence in the central town of the district. Unwise insistence upon applying this to existing judges provoked a barrage of protest and lobbying which forced an undignified retreat.[261]

In the early years judges could augment their income by undertaking arbitrations and holding recorderships. When Thomas Terrell defied first a judicial rebuke and then a Lord Chancellor's circular, arbitrations had to be prohibited by statute and in time the weight of disapproval from the bar, which felt judges holding onto recorderships was greedy and unfair, was reinforced by Lord Chancellors, starting with Herschell, and by the Home Office which appointed recorders, and that practice gradually ceased.[262] By contrast, unpaid judicial duties as JP or Chairman of Quarter Sessions were positively encouraged. According to Sir Richard Harington, Selborne had supported a bill of his drafting to make the judges *ex officio* Commissioners of Assize, but it foundered because it included a provision for additional remuneration.[263] Selborne did, however, secure for them a defined place in the order of precedence and the right to style themselves 'judge' and be addressed as 'your honour'.[264]

LIFESTYLE AND WORKLOAD

For those on the rural circuits at least, it was 'very much the life of a bagman',[265] with all the travelling of the assize circuits and none of the fellowship and cer-

---

[258] *Ibid.*, 251.
[259] *Return of Expenses*, PP 1872 (246), l.
[260] (1873) 8 *LJ* 174.
[261] Polden, *History of the County Court*, 253–4.
[262] *Ibid.*, 257.
[263] *Ibid.*
[264] *Ibid.*, 255–6.
[265] *RC on the Judicature, Second Report 1872*, Serjeant Pulling, q. 7145.

emony. It was, of course, otherwise in the metropolitan courts and a few others which were more or less confined to one city, but even those judges shared their colleagues' isolation, never sitting in banc and seldom even sharing a building with a colleague. Even where there was a local bar a judge had to be wary of too enthusiastic a fraternization, which might be disapproved by local solicitors.[266] The work frequently lacked variety and intellectual stimulation, and even in 1914 it consisted mostly of the rapid disposal of one debt case after another, few of them with any real defence. It could be colourful enough in the east end of London and in the big cities, but it could be a hard life too. Courtrooms were often dreadful, and could even be lethal, and the workload could be heavy. London judges like Emden and Bacon ploughed grimly through their list, forgoing luncheon intervals or sitting late, and often in an atmosphere far removed from the orderly calm of the High Court.[267]

Yet there were obviously attractions since so many men, some of very high calibre, sought the posts and very few abandoned them unless sick or worn out. In a favoured locality a man could have a comfortable lifestyle as a country gentleman mingling with good society, like John Worlledge and William Gurdon in Suffolk and Cecil Beresford in the west country.[268] Others were attached to their native district and deeply involved in its affairs, like F. J. Greenwell, a judge in Durham for 35 years, whose 'interests…were bound up in his family house and in the welfare of the mining and agricultural people of Durham and Northumberland, among whom he had lived his life, and for whom he had an unbounded admiration and sympathy'.[269] Such prolonged and close engagement with a community was an aspect of localized justice that had its critics, suspicious of conflicts of interest and an unhealthy degree of intimacy with local solicitors and barristers, but it was an undoubted attraction.

Again, the degree of independence and even autocracy had its charms for some. So long as they kept their behaviour within bounds, these 'judicial Selkirks' were largely immune from challenge and could apply their own interpretations of law and practice (especially in the all-important area of committals), arrange their own sittings, choose their own registrar.[270]

And for some the workload was not very burdensome. This was in part an inevitable consequence of the basis on which the initial division had been made, but some judges undoubtedly exploited their discretion to give themselves a quiet

[266] H. Cecil, *Tipping the Scales* (1964), 231–5.
[267] *Ibid.*, 98, 316–18.
[268] *Ibid.*, 273–4. For these judges see *Modern English Biography* and *The Times*, 15 February 1911.
[269] C. Muir, *Justice in a Depressed Area* (1936), 106.
[270] P. Polden, ' "Judicial Selkirks": The County Court Judges and the Press, 1847–1880', in C. W. Brooks and M. J. Lobban (eds), *Communities and Courts in Britain, 1150–1900* (1997), 245–62.

life. The striking discrepancies gave ammunition to critics like Henry Fowler. Even their average sittings, 135 days a year in 1873, compared unfavourably with the superior courts' 200, and the range was unacceptably high—in 1864 it went from 74 to 174. Somewhat later the people of Nottingham compared their judge's record unfavourably with his neighbour in Derby and Bolton complained that Crompton Hutton managed only 85 days a year.[271] Even allowing for the days of travelling—Falconer claimed to have done 3635 miles in 11 months[272]—it was certainly the impression in the LCO, in the county courts department of the Treasury, and within the profession that some judges had an easy time of it.

PROMOTION AND TRANSFER

No county court judge was promoted until Edward Acton in 1919. Enthusiasts for county courts were deeply frustrated by this, especially since there was no formal bar and at least twice they seemed on the verge of a breakthrough. J. Pitt Taylor, author of an influential minority report for the County Courts Commission and an authority on the law of evidence, had expectations from Cranworth which were defeated by a change of ministry and nearly 40 years on the same thing happened to McKenzie Chalmers, who was openly said to have been sent as Commissioner of Assize in anticipation of promotion by Herschell.[273] There were always men of High Court standard, such as William Barber, William Elmsley, and Howland Roberts, but they tended to be rather elderly when their claims were considered, and that, along with the needs of party politics and the certainty of antagonizing the bar, all tended against promotions.[274]

A judge was appointed to a district but could be moved at any time whether he wished it or not. This executive power might have been a useful tool to reward a compliant judge or punish a recalcitrant one, but the practice was different. A well-regarded judge who wished to move would usually be accommodated if possible,[275] but some districts were more desirable than others, so possibilities were limited. An informal hierarchy of courts evolved, so that H. J. Stonor's move from Surrey to Southwark in 1877 was described in the legal press as a promotion; eventually Westminster came to be generally acknowledged to be the 'blue riband' court and Birmingham was also held in high regard. [276]

---

[271] Polden, *History of the County Court*, 87–8, 110, 270–1.
[272] *Ibid.*, 254.
[273] Polden, 'Judicial Independence and Executive Responsibilities, Part Two', 140–2.
[274] (1888–9) 33 *Sol. J.* 737; (1861–2) 6 *Sol. J.* 446; C. Schuster to Lord Stamfordham, 17 June 1920, LCO 2/2539.
[275] Polden, 'Oiling the Machinery', 231–8.
[276] P. Polden, 'Judicial Independence and Executive Responsibilities, Part One' (1996) 25 *Anglo-Am. Law Rev.* 1–38 at 8.

It soon became accepted that there would be no routine rotation of judges and by the 1870s it was tacitly understood that judges would not be moved against their will without a compelling reason. T. H. Jordan was therefore able to decline both Manchester and Birmingham whereas Homersham Cox was moved in 1883 because he had criticized his Welsh constituents for perjury. Moving Cecil Beresford in 1893 to install a Welsh speaker gave rise to justifiable criticism and probably strengthened the view of the Lord Chancellor's Office that such actions should be exceptional.[277] They already knew that where a judge could call upon strong local support it might not even be practicable. The most ambitious reconfiguration, involving the Manchester district, had to be modified to meet J. A. Russell's objections, and something similar occurred in 1912 when it was proposed to move Judge Sturges.[278] So by and large a judge could remain in his district until he died, resigned or—in extreme cases—was dismissed.

DISMISSAL AND RETIREMENT

One of the features that emphasized the inferiority of the county court judges was that they might be dismissed by the Lord Chancellor for 'inability or misbehaviour'.[279] This appeared to give him ample power to deal with wayward or incompetent judges, but such a drastic weapon was not to be lightly invoked given the sensitivity surrounding judicial tenure and the likelihood that the judges of the Queen's Bench would give the power a restrictive interpretation. They did so when a clerk (registrar) was dismissed by his judge and the court had held that his acute and undignified financial embarrassments (falling short of actual bankruptcy) amounted neither to inability nor to misbehaviour.[280]

Soon afterwards the behaviour of Judge William Ramshay in Liverpool made his dismissal unavoidable. Ramshay's conduct, culminating in his fining and imprisoning for contempt a newspaper editor whose robust criticisms offended him, was sufficiently gross to leave no doubt that dismissal was warranted and Lord Chief Justice Campbell was helpfully robust in making short shrift of Ramshay's attempt to enmesh the procedure in technicalities.[281] No other dismissal was made public but at least three other judges were forced to resign. T. E. P. Lefroy's behaviour was rather like Ramshay's in a less dramatic form; he had a running feud with an attorney and several local newspapers which eventually led

---

[277] *Ibid.*

[278] *Ibid.*, 9–10.

[279] County Courts Act 1846, s. 18.

[280] *R* v. *Owen* (1850) 15 Q.B. 476; Polden, *History of the County Court*, 289. The clerk/registrar later lost his security of tenure and became subject to the power of the Lord Chancellor rather than the judge.

[281] *Ex p. Ramshay* (1852) 18 Q.B. 174; Polden, 'Judicial Selkirks', 255–7.

to a deputation to the Lord Chancellor and Lefroy's resignation. Robert Vaughan Williams compounded an assault on a cabman (for which he was fined at the Assizes) by committing the unfortunate man for contempt; he was allowed to retire on a pension but clearly his position had become untenable. In the 1890s P. M. Leonard was forced to resign after some murky financial dealings which had led to a very severe rebuke from the Court of Appeal.[282]

These cases marked the outer limits of acceptable conduct, but short of that judges could engage in conduct which was eccentric, despotic, or capricious without necessarily coming to grief. In the 1850s T. H. Marshall in Leeds was judged to have fallen short of conduct warranting dismissal though he was successfully sued for defamation and remained disputatious despite a warning. Several petitions against Crompton Hutton in the 1870s were also found to merit only a rebuke, though Hutton did resign soon afterwards, and for some years the antics of J. W. Smith, a learned Chancery lawyer cast adrift in the backwaters of the Welsh Marches, enlivened the pages of the law press.[283]

Perhaps such excesses were inevitable in the absence of the restraints—juries, counsel, and colleagues—which checked such tendencies in some of the superior judges. Occasional put-downs by barristers[284] were less effective than determined and tenacious resistance from attorneys and the vigilance of the local press, which bought down Ramshay and Lefroy.

As in the High Court, however, there seems to have been a gradual improvement around the turn of the century, despite the 'offensive facetiousness' of W. S. Owen and the ill-manners of Arthur Emden. However, S. A. Hill Kelly, appointed in 1910, carried the tradition of unpleasant judges into the inter-war period.[285]

Retirement pensions as of right were proposed in a bill of 1852 but the clause was taken out and a similar recommendation by a select committee of 1878 was ignored.[286] There was a power to give a judge a gratuity of up to £1000 per annum if it was agreed that he should resign through ill-health and Muir McKenzie presented this as 'a most extraordinarily good bargain',[287] but it had serious disadvantages. First, elderly judges remained on the bench too long. Some may have been coaxed off the bench by Nicol and it looks as though Abdy and Bayley were either shamed or persuaded into retiring following some uninhibited press

---

[282] *Ibid.*, 256–9; Polden, *History of the County Court*, 262.

[283] Polden, 'Judicial Selkirks', 248–53, 255, 259.

[284] See e.g. J. Campbell, *F.E. Smith* (1983), 112–13.

[285] (1897–8) 104 *LT* 595–6; (1903–4) 116 *LT* 289; Polden, *History of the County Court*, 136.

[286] Polden, *History of the County Court*, 253.

[287] *Public Accounts Committee 1914*, PP 1914–16 (249), iv, q. 1278.

criticism, but there were obvious limits to what could be achieved;[288] after all the Queen's Bench could hardly hold that Trafford's deafness amounted to inability without casting invidious reflections on some of their own comrades.[289]

Even some of the best judges, men like Daniel and Stonor, outstayed their welcome and in 1870 20 of the originals were still on the bench, the last of them, Ingham, remaining until 1891.[290] Furthermore, unlike their counterparts in the higher courts, they could prolong their tenure by employing deputies, as G. L. Russell did for two years before he quit.[291] This may have resulted in a higher proportion dying in office: almost equal numbers died and retired among those appointed in the early 1870s. It was not such an imbalance as to justify sarcastic exaggerations in the press,[292] but it harmed the image of the judge, especially if, like Bayley, he employed a deputy almost as decrepit as himself.[293]

3. STIPENDIARY MAGISTRATES

London: Numbers and Organization

The creation of a paid magistracy in London was the result of the complete incapacity of the traditional institutions of police and unpaid justices to cope with crime and disorder in the great metropolis.[294] The Middlesex Justices Act 1792 provided for seven state financed 'public offices', each staffed by three magistrates paid £400 per annum and each with a small complement of constables.[295] In 1800 a separate Act added the Thames Police Office, with a much larger body of constables, to combat the endemic depredations on the river,[296] and including the older Bow Street office there were nine public offices and 27 paid magistrates.[297]

---

[288] (1892–3) 6 *LG* 161, 177.

[289] (1863–4) 39 *LT* 430. His loss of hearing probably contributed to his death: run down by a horse and cart.

[290] (1883) 29 *CCC* 3; (1905) 40 *LJ* 433. In 1887 Ingham gave a rather embarrassing interview to the *Pall Mall Gazette*: (1886–7) 31 *Sol. J.* 565.

[291] See also Polden, 'Judicial Independence and Executive Responsibilities, Part One', 20–1.

[292] e.g. (1895–6) 100 *LT* 209.

[293] The deputy, Scott, was 88: Crispe, *Reminiscences of a KC*, 115–16.

[294] A. Babington, *A House in Bow Street* (1969); D. Philips, '"A New Engine of Power and Authority": The Institutionalization of Law-Enforcement in England, 1780–1830', in V. A. C. Gatrell et al., *Crime and the Law: The Social History of Crime in Western Europe since 1500* (1980), 155–89 at 164–70.

[295] 32 Geo. III c. 53.

[296] S. French, 'The Early History of Stipendiary Magistrates' [1961] *Crim. Law Rev.* 663–8; [1965] 213–21, 281–91; [1967] 224–30, 269–77, 321–6, [1965] 285.

[297] Though in *PD* 1825 (s2) 12: 1129 Peel says there are 30 magistrates.

The stipendiary magistrates were intended to be principally judicial officers,[298] but since the offices were modelled on Bow Street, whose 'runners' had attracted widespread publicity, and the Thames Police Office was established chiefly as a crime prevention/detection institution, the public expectation was that the 'police offices' would perform similar functions and their magistrates were seen as 'chief constables primarily and only judges incidentally'.[299]

When Peel established a metropolitan police force in 1829 he disingenuously presented it as merely an extension of these arrangements, but though the New Police operated alongside the Bow Street patrols (not always harmoniously) and Thames Police Office, the Police Offices lost authority over their constabulary.[300] Successive chief magistrates, Sir Richard Birnie and Sir Frederick Roe, argued vainly to retain the magistrates' powers to investigate crime as well as adjudicate[301] and the Metropolitan Police Courts Act 1839, following enquiries into both the New Police and the Police Offices, put the latter, now officially styled Police Courts, on a new footing. Magistrates would be barristers of seven years' standing, paid £1200 per annum, and each court would have a defined and distinct area, which might be altered by order in council. Courts might be located anywhere within the metropolitan police district, though the number of magistrates was not to exceed 27.[302]

Since the police district extended 15 miles from Charing Cross, it might have been expected—and some certainly feared—that the police courts would be enlarged and extended alongside the expanding metropolis, but it was not so.[303] New courts were set up at Greenwich and Woolwich, served jointly by a pair of magistrates, and the Whitechapel court was moved to Lambeth, but Home Office inquiries reported against the need for other extensions,[304] and the new arrangement got under way with just 23 magistrates, two to each court, with the exception of Bow Street, which kept its three.

Two new courts, at Dalston (rapidly renamed the North London) and the Western, in Hammersmith, opened in the 1880s, single-magistrate courts on Treasury insistence, and magistrates' pleas for the full statutory number were met only by moving some of the Surrey suburbs into the jurisdiction of the Surrey

---

[298] Select Committee, 1812, quoted in French, 'Early History', 287.
[299] H. T. Waddy, *The Police Court and its Work* (1925), 2.
[300] Babington, *House in Bow Street*, 214–16; Philips, 'New Engine', 179–86.
[301] Babington, *House in Bow Street*, 218, 233–4; French, 'Early History', 287.
[302] 3 & 4 Vict. c. 61.
[303] See e.g. G. Palmer, *PD* 1839 (s3) 49: 912.
[304] French, 'Early History', 225; Sir W. T. C. Skyrme, *History of the Justices of the Peace*, 3 vols (Chichester, 1991), ii, 149–50.

justices.[305] This was one of the few areas of the judicial establishment where the Treasury enjoyed real success in enforcing economy, for not until 1928 was the magistracy raised to its full statutory complement. Bow Street apart, the 12 courts were paired into 'Unions' in a western and a northern group, each with 11 magistrates to accommodate holidays. Magistrates were based at one court but in substituting for absent colleagues they got to experience the others as well.[306]

QUALIFICATIONS AND SELECTION

The 1792 Act imposed no legal qualification and most of the original batch had none.[307] Some of the early magistrates were not without distinction, however. 'Glasgow trader' was Peel's unfair description of that noted writer on police matters Patrick Colquhoun, while Henry Pye was poet laureate, albeit an undistinguished one[308] and John Harriott of the Thames Police Office, having been 'midshipman, naval officer, soldier, administrator, judge advocate of the north circars in Madras, farmer, wine merchant, land speculator, acting chaplain, duellist, underwriter, and inventor' was a vigorous and efficient, if exasperatingly insubordinate and wilful, foe to the river pirates.[309] But they also included 'an illiterate and ignorant journeyman carpenter'[310] and the claims of others to responsible public positions are not apparent. Their unsuitability quickly became apparent and from 1812 Lord Sidmouth appointed only barristers of three years' standing, spurning the country magistrates who were the biggest class of applicants.[311] In 1825 Peel stated that only four were not barristers and select committees in the 1830s agreed this practice had 'had a very beneficial influence on the general character of the Police Establishment'; one committee wanted their attainments and reputation to fall 'not...far short of those of Commissioners of bankrupt or Judges in our Colonial Courts'—a rather modest aspiration.[312]

However, their practice was, in some cases, said to be anything but extensive: 'of all the barristers on the bench, not three ever had twenty briefs'.[313] Nor, of course, did qualifications guarantee the right character. Allan Laing—the Mr Fang of

[305] PRO HO 45/9668/A46382I; A. C. Plowden, *Grain or Chaff?* (1903), 288–90; Skyrme, *Justices of the Peace*, ii, 150.

[306] M. Williams, *Later Leaves* (1891), 20.

[307] *PD* 1825 (s2) 12: 1218 (Peel).

[308] See Vol. XIII, pp. 25–7; F. Milton, *In Some Authority* (1959), 34.

[309] Waddy, *Police Court*, 209.

[310] Milton, *In Some Authority*, 34, describing Nicholas Bond, a former Bow Street Runner.

[311] *PD* 1825 (s2) 12: 1129. Thus 'an old sea captain', Richbell, was replaced in 1822 by a barrister, William Broderip: Ballantine, *Some Experiences*, 51.

[312] *PD* 1825 (s2) 12: 1129; Select Committee on the Police Offices, 1838, quoted in French, *Early History*, 289.

[313] Milton, *In Some Authority*, 38, quoting *The Times* of 1828.

Dickens's *Oliver Twist*, sacked in 1838 after a complaint to the Home Office—was, according to Ballantine 'a thoroughly honourable gentleman, a good lawyer, and accomplished scholar'.[314] In 1839 a qualification of seven years from call (which might include up to three years as a special pleader) was imposed, with Thomas Wakley a lone voice in decrying the fetish for barristers.[315] No voice was raised to claim that attorneys should be eligible, perhaps because very few respectable firms handled London criminal cases.

SALARIES AND TENURE

Salaries were raised to £600 in 1821 and £800 in 1825, when Peel explained (somewhat unflatteringly to the incumbents) that he did not want to be reduced to taking 'the refuse of the bar'.[316] In 1839 Russell proposed £1200, with £1400 for the chief magistrate. Some felt that was excessive, and though it was narrowly carried (57–49), the chief magistrate's addition was lost.[317] There it stayed for almost a century, since Lord Chancellors would not support Home Secretaries in seeking a raise for the metropolitan stipendiary magistrates (MSMs) without maintaining the differential between their salaries and county court judges' £1500.[318] The chief magistrate had been generously treated in the way of allowances until the formation of the New Police, after which he had £400 more than the others, raised by a further £300 per annum at some point before 1855.[319]

Like other justices , the salaried magistrates held at pleasure and could, as the chief magistrate Sir Richard Baker found in 1821, and Laing later, be dismissed without ceremony.[320] The explicit intention of the Whig ministry in 1839 was to purge the police offices, 'to get rid of all the weak, worn out, imbecile old fixtures in Worship Street and Queen's Square. Yes, all the Whites and Gregorys and Nortons were to be swept away and in their stead we were to get young barristers of seven years' standing, distinguished for great learning and legal talent.'[321] The bill was not explicit about tenure and Charles Law argued unsuccessfully for the same good behaviour term as the superior court judges.[322] Brougham and

---

[314] *Some Experiences*, 53; P. Collins, *Dickens and Crime* (1962), 180–1.

[315] *PD* 1839 (s3) 49: 910; 47: 1301.

[316] *PD* 1825 (s2) 12: 1129–30.

[317] *PD* 1839 (s3) 47: 1292–1302; 49: 911–14.

[318] P. Polden, 'Safety First: The Appointment of Metropolitan Stipendiary Magistrates, 1950–61' (1996) 27 *Cambrian Law Rev.* 57–74 at 59.

[319] Babington, *House in Bow Street*, 201; *PD* 1839 (s3) 49: 911; HO memorandum on police magistrates, 1934, LCO 2/5726.

[320] Baker was made the scapegoat for the riots attending Queen Caroline's funeral procession: Babington, *House in Bow Street*, 207–9.

[321] *PD* 1839 (s3) 50: 446–7 (Thomas Duncombe).

[322] *PD* 1839 (s3) 49: 535. Law was Recorder of London.

Lyndhurst leagued in mischief to remove the clause which allowed superannuation[323] and Duncombe lamented 'that Ministers will not be able to supersede the existing magistrates…the result will be that these old, worn out, incompetent magistrates will get their £1,200 a year instead of the £800 which they now have and they will continue fixtures on the bench as long as they can either write, see or eat'.[324]

This did not happen, for the Superannuation Act of 1834 could be used to effect retirements. It was agreed, however, that the magistrates could not be dismissed without compensation save for wrongdoing or utter incompetence.[325] The Home Office took the view, on a rather strained construction of sections 1–3, that the stipendiaries still held at pleasure and it was never put to the test because the threat always sufficed.[326]

PROMOTION AND TRANSFER

There was no regular prospect of promotion for a MSM, though Clive (1847), Sir Richard Harington (1872), and Cluer (1911) successfully applied for the county court bench. But unlike the county court judges, the MSMs did have a chief, albeit one in a rather equivocal position. The Home Office regarded him as only *primus inter pares*, but besides his extra allowance he had an automatic knighthood, an invitation to the Lord Mayor's banquet and (a whimsical oddity), the obligation to hold a court at the Royal Ascot meeting.[327] He was the Home Office adviser on all matters concerning summary jurisdiction; he chaired the statutory quarterly meetings of MSMs, and transmitted their views to the Home Office, and the Home Secretary usually acted upon his recommendations when transfers of magistrates between courts were in question, which gave him considerable sway over his fellow magistrates.[328] Some were happy to remain in the same court for many years, as did Traill at Greenwich (1846–68); Bros at Camberwell (1888–1921), and Denman (1899–1922), Newton (1871–96), and Mead (1907–33) all at Great Marlborough Street. But few desired to remain long in the less salubrious districts such as Wandsworth and Old Street and most moved several times; thus Plowden went from Wandsworth to Marylebone via Lavender Hill and

[323] Voted down at the report stage by 43–30: *ibid.*, 50: 180–93, 217.

[324] *Ibid.*, 446–7.

[325] *Ibid.*, 447 (Chancellor of the Exchequer), 185–6 (Lord Chancellor).

[326] Memorandum, 1934, LCO 2/5726. In 1911 Winston Churchill contemplated dismissing one, probably Cecil Chapman, for his indiscreet support for the suffragettes: C. Chapman, *The Poor Man's Court of Justice* (1924), 214–21.

[327] Memorandum of 1934, LCO 2/5726; Biron, *Without Prejudice*, 295–9. Roe was made a baronet; James Read and Thomas Hall refused knighthoods.

[328] Memorandum of 1934, LCO 2/5726; Biron, *Without Prejudice*, 301–4; Metropolitan Police Courts Act 1839, s. 15.

Hammersmith; Chapman from Clerkenwell to Lambeth/Southwark to Tower Bridge to Westminster.[329] Magistrates laid claim to a vacancy by length of service but Bow Street and Marlborough Street were special cases where the Home Secretary determined how vacancies should be filled; the latter attracted sensational cases, which might generate bad publicity if handled maladroitly.[330] Within each two-man court there was a senior and a junior magistrate and Biron's tone suggests that the senior was very much in charge, something else which might lead the junior to seek a move.[331]

CONDITIONS OF SERVICE AND RETIREMENT

The Police Courts were open six days a week, with a magistrate required to be in attendance from 10 am to 5 pm and at other times at need or the Home Secretary's insistence.[332] The Home Office view in the 1930s was that a magistrate's working year should comprise around 184 days, with most of his statutory six weeks' holiday having to be taken during a vacation period in the summer.[333] Deputies might be appointed but seldom were because the deputy's remuneration came out of the magistrate's salary, so they all preferred to cover for absences.[334]

Being a MSM was a full-time post and there was no possibility of remaining in practice. The Home Office insisted that recorderships be given up, and though it did allow men like De Grey and Tennyson D'Eyncourt to remain as chairmen of quarter sessions, from the 1880s magistrates were barred from taking on any new ones.[335] With no provision for superannuation some men remained on the bench into old age; Frederick Mead, for example, sat at Marlborough Street until 1933, when he was 86.[336] However, from 1895 onwards the Home Secretary obliged all appointees to undertake to retire at 70, though with Treasury consent they might remain until 72.[337] The lack of superannuation was a long-standing grievance and

[329] Waddy, *Police Court*, 196–207; Williams, *Later Leaves*, 241, 284; Plowden, *Grain or Chaff?*, 200–2, 212; Cancellor, *Life of a London Beak*, 119 ; Chapman, *Poor Man's Court*, 20, 33–64, 114.

[330] Memorandum of 1934, LCO 2/5726; J. B. Sandbach, *This Old Wig* ([1950]), 67–74. However, Ballantine's father believed he was denied the chance to move to a better court because he had annoyed the Home Office: *Some Experiences*, 236.

[331] Biron, *Without Prejudice*, 251.

[332] Memorandum of 1934, LCO 2/5726; Home Office memorandum to Royal Commission on Justices of the Peace, 1947–8, 69. The 1792 Act had required the Police Offices to be open from 10 am to 8 pm, Mondays to Saturdays.

[333] Memorandum of 1934, LCO 2/5726.

[334] *Ibid.*; Plowden, *Grain or Chaff?*, 208–11.

[335] Memorandum of 1934, LCO 2/5726.

[336] C. Mullins, *Fifteen Years Hard Labour* (1948), 38. Mead had opted out of a post-war superannuation scheme.

[337] Memorandum of 1934, LCO 2/5726. Chapman and C. K. Francis were mistakenly allowed to claim extensions: Chapman, *Poor Man's Court*, 224–5.

Plowden had others, less serious; that they had no title to use other than JP; they had no distinctive dress and forfeited the chance to become benchers of their inn. In his view they were 'neither fish, nor fowl nor good red herring'. There is no sign in the other autobiographies, however, that these drawbacks were much resented.[338]

A PROFILE OF METROPOLITAN STIPENDIARIES

As foreshadowed in the debates on the 1839 bill, it was followed by a purge. Roe, the chief magistrate, inherited a fortune and resigned his post, while almost half of the rest left within the next three years;[339] among them were White and Gregorie, named by Duncombe, but not Norton, who remained at Lambeth until 1867.[340] Ten new men were appointed between 1839 and 1842, with a new chief magistrate in Thomas Hall from Liverpool.

Home Secretaries later took to consulting the Lord Chancellor and the Attorney-General on these appointments, though he did not always follow their advice,[341] but when this began is not clear.[342] No doubt, as with other judicial posts, party political considerations came into play on occasion, but there is only one MP among the MSMs and the posts were probably not coveted enough to be rewards for party services.[343]

Davis claims that most of them were 'either socially or professionally prominent and in some cases both', but this is perhaps an exaggeration for two of her five examples were chief magistrates and all are from the *Dictionary of National Biography*, which included few other MSMs.[344] There were certainly landed gentry (Tennyson–D'Eyncourts, father and son, Graham–Campbell) and even peers (Harington, de Grey, de Rutzen), but they seem to have been few.[345] There are fewer from an army or medical background than among other judges, the usual high proportion from the clergy among the earlier appointments, and a substantial number from the law. They also include a warehouseman and a tinplate

---

[338] Chapman, *Poor Man's Court*, 2; Plowden, *Grain or Chaff?*, 199.

[339] Ballantine, *Some Experiences*, 52–3.

[340] See above, p. 1007. George Norton had sued the Prime Minister, Lord Melbourne, for adultery with Norton's wife Caroline: Milton, *In Some Authority*, 36–7. Ballantine thought him capable: *Some Experiences*, 258.

[341] Polden, 'Safety First', 58–9.

[342] Schuster felt there had been some really bad appointments: to C. Chapman, 2 May 1924, LCO 2/955.

[343] A. E. H. Hutton, appointed 1906. One ferocious radical was appointed in 1846, Edward Yardley: Plowden, *Grain or Chaff?*, 293–5 and see Harris, *Autobiography*, 208.

[344] J. Davis, 'A Poor Man's System of Justice: The London Police Courts in the Second Half of the Nineteenth Century' (1984) 27 *Hist. J.* 309–35 at 311.

[345] The standard reference works contain a total of 87 men appointed between 1839 and 1914.

worker,[346] but Behlmer is probably correct to class them as 'typical products of the upper bourgeoisie'.[347] Like other judges, from the 1860s onwards most were public school men who had been to Oxford or Cambridge.[348]

Were they the 'young barristers distinguished by great learning and legal talent' that Duncombe had sarcastically described in 1839?[349] They were certainly young. Of 29 direct appointments between 1839 and 1864, at least six were under 40 and most of the rest under 50. Thereafter the under–40s became fewer, but 19 of 22 appointed between 1890 and 1914 were under 50, and all were under 55. The contrast with county court judges is striking, for just four MSMs were over 55, and only two of them over 60. [350]

They had less practising experience as a group than the other judges, but only 11 were fewer than 15 years since call and over half more than 20 years. Whether they practised successfully is another matter. They included no serjeants and only two Crown counsel, one of whom, Montagu Williams, had reluctantly quitted the bar on medical grounds.[351] Unless Home Secretaries passed over KCs in favour of younger men, these posts were not considered attractive even to those for whom silk had proved a wrong move.

It may be, however, that the successful applicants came disproportionately from the criminal bar, where it was not customary for even successful practitioners to take silk. Judges were seldom taken from the criminal bar, even for the county court bench[352] and Biron was said to regard these posts as peculiarly the preserve of the criminal bar. The names of the MSMs do not often feature in memoirs and it may be that many were men who were finding the going pretty hard.[353]

Few, however, were unknowns, most having held some post connected with the administration of the criminal law. Ten were provincial stipendiaries, which suggests that the Home Office welcomed men with appropriate experience. Of the rest about half had been recorders, though mostly of the smaller and less prestigious towns. Others were chairmen of quarter sessions, Treasury or Mint counsel etc. Most, however, had evidently made a judgement in their 30s or 40s that they would not go very far in the profession, whereas a good many county court judges had gone further and got tired or begun to lose their practice. For

[346] Chester Jones (1907) and Arthur Hopkins (1890).

[347] G. Behlmer, 'Summary Jurisdiction and Working Class Marriage in England, 1870–1940' (1994) 12 L & HR 229–75 at 237.

[348] Cambridge 38, Oxford 21, others 10.

[349] PD 1839 (s3) 49: 446–7.

[350] The elderly pair were John Hosack (1877, at 67/8) and T. W. Saunders (1878, at 64).

[351] The other QC was Richard Lane (QC 1890, MSM 1893). One serjeant (Thomas Cranley) was among the 1792 appointments.

[352] Biron, Without Prejudice, 233–4.

[353] Sandbach, This Old Wig, 119.

many years their number included survivors of the pre-1839 regime. At least one, Broughton, was fortunate to survive the purge, since he was chronically idle, but others, such as Broderip, seem to have been competent enough.[354]

The Provinces

A Tory journalist warned in 1830: '[l]et the system of stipendiary magistrates be carried to perfection, and the case will stand thus. The blue army, almost unlimited in numbers and powers, will be the servile instruments of the Executive; it will continually increase its encroachments on popular rights and the liberty of the subject.' [355] His fears of a national network of stipendiaries proved unfounded, but since some were already in existence the threat was not fanciful.

The unpaid magistracy had been found wanting outside London too, in rapidly growing industrial towns where few gentlemen lived. There were no 'trading justices', indeed there were few justices at all, for lord lieutenants were frequently reluctant to appoint factory owners and merchants.[356] In Manchester the hundred of Salford obtained an Act (1805) enabling the justices of the division to levy a rate for a salaried barrister as Chairman of Quarter Sessions at £400 per annum;[357] presumably he also undertook the everyday duties of a justice. Before long the desperate shortage of justices in Manchester itself prompted a further measure in 1813, providing a stipendiary magistrate for the two adjoining divisions of Manchester and Salford, appointed by the Home Secretary on the advice of the Chancellor of the Duchy; a barrister of at least four years' standing, he would receive £1,000 per annum, the lion's share paid by Manchester.[358]

At the end of the 1830s Manchester, now a corporation, secured its own stipendiary despite the protests of the satellite towns, adding insult to injury by securing the services of the existing magistrate, Daniel Maude.[359] In 1878 Salford and the Manchester Division separated, so that there were eventually three stipendiaries in the conurbation.

Other towns followed Manchester's lead. Some made use of local Acts, usually promoted for wider purposes,[360] but the Municipal Corporations Act 1835 empowered corporations wanting a salaried police magistrate or magistrates to

---

[354] Plowden, *Grain or Chaff?*, 291; Ballantine, *Some Experiences*, 51.

[355] Quoted in Philips, 'New Engine', 155.

[356] *PD* 1813, 26: 100–1 (Romilly). Bathurst defended the exclusion of manufacturers because so much of the work involved labour disputes.

[357] 45 Geo. III c. lix; French, 'Early History', 227–8.

[358] 53 Geo. III c. 72; French, 'Early History', 228–9.

[359] A. Redford with I. S. Russell, *A History of Local Government in Manchester*, 3 vols (1939), ii, 36–7; HO 45/677.

[360] Examples are Merthyr Tydfil, Pontypridd, and Chatham and Sheerness.

pass a bye law on which the Home Secretary might act. In 1863 that power was extended to places of 25,000 inhabitants within the scope of the Public Health, Local Government and Local Improvements Acts, though the by-law required a two-thirds majority of the Local Board. [361]

These various statutory provisions created a confusing situation; qualifications, tenure, salary, and even titles were quite different.[362] The 1863 Act, never used, required a barrister of five years, as did the 1835 Municipal Corporations Act, but when the 1835 Act was replaced in 1882 the qualification was raised to seven years in line with county court judges and MSMs.[363] The Manchester District Act stipulated four years, the Staffordshire Potteries Act 1839 six years, so there was no uniformity.

Disparities also arose with tenure. The Municipal Corporations Act made it during pleasure, which in the Home Office view also applied whenever a statute was silent.[364] As for salaries, the Municipal Corporations Act prescribed that the by-law would set a maximum, at or below which the Home Secretary would set the figure, and he seems invariably to have used the maximum to get the best man possible. Salaries varied widely, ranging in 1884 from Liverpool's munificent £1750 to Swansea's very modest £750 (Worcester had originally paid only £300), and until 1882 they could be altered only by terminating the appointment and going through the whole procedure again.[365]

The distribution of stipendiaries was extremely patchy. Only 25 places ever had one in this period and Leeds and Manchester City alone ever had more than one.[366] Neither the chronology nor the location quite matches expectations. Worcester was the first to follow Manchester, with more likely candidates like Leeds (1869) and Sheffield (1874) relative latecomers. There are the expected concentrations in the north-west (Manchester's three, Liverpool, Birkenhead); in Yorkshire (Leeds, Bradford, and Sheffield; Hull, and Grimsby may also be included); in the north-east (Newcastle, Middlesborough, South Shields); and in the west midlands (Birmingham, Wolverhampton, Worcester, the Potteries) and south Wales (Cardiff, Swansea, Merthyr Tydfil, Pontypridd). There are also oddities: Brighton, Chatham/Sheerness—a big dockyard area, but then one might have expected Portsmouth or Plymouth too—and West and East Ham.

---

[361] 5 & 6 Will. IV c. 76, s. 99; Stipendiary Magistrates Act 1863 c. 97.

[362] HO 45/54141.

[363] Municipal Corporations Act 1882, s. 161; RC on Justices of the Peace, PP 1947–8 (Cmd. 7463), xii, App. G, Home Office memorandum, 69.

[364] HO 45/9463/75249; except for Wolverhampton.

[365] e.g. Leeds, HO 45/946/A13301.

[366] They are listed in The Law List from 1878, and in PP 1873 (192), liv.

A major limiting factor is likely to have been local hostility to a further charge on the rates coupled with resistance from the local bench and their clerks. Graham's suggestion for paid chairmen of quarter sessions was vetoed by Peel even during the social unrest of 1842 because of the sensibilities of the country gentlemen[367] and the Home Office did not press the case though it was generally favourably disposed, making it clear that Brighton's claim to its own quarter sessions would be materially advanced by an associated bid for a stipendiary.[368] Grimsby's bid was welcomed because 'Grimsby has long been notorious for their lax enforcement of the Factory Acts',[369] but applications were refused from Barrow-in-Furness in 1868 and Accrington the following year, the latter perhaps because it wanted to pay only £200 per annum and to allow the magistrate to continue his bar practice, something to which both the Attorney-General and Lord Chancellor were opposed; evidently the Home Office officials were not keen either.[370] More predictably, an earlier attempt by Warrington to persuade the Treasury to fund a paid Chairman of Quarter Sessions was rebuffed.[371]

The most interesting case is West Ham. London's voracious eastward expansion had sent its population soaring and in 1878 the Local Board petitioned for a stipendiary. However, the petition was trenchantly opposed by the Chairman of Quarter Sessions, by the local MP, and the Ilford bench. Delegations left officials unconvinced that it met the requirements of the statute.[372] It 'originated in miserable pique' minuted Lushington and another wrote that it was intended 'to gratify the vanity of a few local big-wigs'.[373] The officials had no difficulty convincing R. A. Cross that it should be declined. If there was unmet need at all there should be an extension of the metropolitan police area (which the Treasury would not allow, as they well knew), but a change of government brought in Sir William Harcourt, who rejected their advice on the ground that 'why shouldn't they have one if they want, even if he is superfluous?' [374]

Not all towns which obtained a stipendiary kept one. Whenever a vacancy occurred they must petition for it to be filled, and a surprising number felt theirs was no longer needed. Five lapsed before the the First World War; South Shields

---

[367] C. S. Parker, *The Life and Letters of Sir James Graham*, 2 vols (1907), i, 438.
[368] HO 45/54141.
[369] HO 45/18361, note on file.
[370] HO 45/088266.
[371] HO 45/1820.
[372] HO 45/9562/73097.
[373] *Ibid.*, minutes of 1 October 1880 and May 1878.
[374] *Ibid.*, minutes of 1 October 1880.

lasted only five years and, surprisingly, Newcastle hardly longer—indeed they may have persuaded their magistrate to apply for a Manchester vacancy.[375]

Formally the town had no say in the selection process, though it was accepted that they might ask for someone with a particular expertise, as Cardiff did in 1897.[376] However, in 1851 Liverpool put forward J. S. Mansfield and assured the Home Office that both previous incumbents had been chosen on their recommendation. They got their way again, for although Sir George Grey saved face by insisting on his rights, he admitted that the better qualified candidate, J. K. Blair, had withdrawn, not wishing to be appointed against the desires of the council.[377] Birmingham too were able to secure their preferred candidate when the post was first created in 1856.[378]

This local involvement probably explains one noticeable difference between the backgrounds and careers of the provincial stipendiaries and their metropolitan counterparts:[379] they frequently had local connections. For instance, not a single non-Welshman was appointed to a Welsh town; many of those in the Manchester area were linked to the town by family or education: Tassell (Chatham) was the son of a local solicitor; Marshall at Leeds was from a minor judicial dynasty; and Sidebottom was already the judge of the Worcester court of Pleas. A stipendiary had no obvious career path though three became county court judges—two in Wales, and A. S. Hogg in a court in the Duchy. A more frequent promotion was to MSM. At least 13 made this move, some very quickly, others much later—Maude and Tassell after 22 years in Manchester and Chatham. Only one moved between provincial towns: C. E. Ellison from Newcastle to Manchester in 1860.[380]

The stipendiaries had several grievances, which Kynnersley rehearsed to the Home Office on their behalf in 1880.[381] Their salaries were lower than the MSMs', and whereas the MSMs, working in pairs or threes, could arrange cover in the event of sickness by transfers, their provincial counterparts had to pay for deputies out of their salaries if they were given sick leave.[382] The most serious was the lack

---

[375] Birkenhead, 1866–93; Brighton, 1855–1902; Newcastle, 1854–60; South Shields, 1875–81; Worcester, 1836–81.

[376] HO 45/9756/A61229.

[377] HO 45/3639. Blair was judge of the Salford hundred court and became a county court judge in Liverpool.

[378] C. Gill, A History of Birmingham (Oxford, 1952), i, 438.

[379] Based on details (sometimes incomplete) of 68, including one paid chairman of quarter sessions. There is no convenient list and some of the earliest are not included here.

[380] Cuthbert Ellison was appointed at 36 in 1854. He left Manchester in 1860 and ended at Lambeth from 1870 to 1883.

[381] Letter to Harcourt, 10 December 1880, HO 45/9603/A281.

[382] This was the Home Office interpretation of the Stipendiary Magistrates Act 1869 c. 34: RC on Justices of the Peace Report 1948, App. G.

of any possibility of superannuation. When Headlam grew old, his Manchester employers managed to arrange that a second man, Brierley, should be appointed, with Headlam's salary reduced. Brierley was evidently given to understand that when Headlam died or became incapable, he would succeed to the post.[383] Since this was not usually practicable, stipendiaries clung on to office when clearly past their best. The Home Office was disposed to support a private members' bill in 1886 and 1887,[384] but it was opposed by the 'Local Taxationists' and seemingly by the Treasury, perhaps because it would make the stipendiaries unique among local government officials and lead to emulative demands.[385] At all events, the initiative stalled and despite regular approaches by the stipendiaries it remained unfinished business until the Justices of the Peace Act 1949.[386]

[383] HO 45/10049/A62841.
[384] HO 45/9603/A281, esp. G. Lushington to H. C. E. Childers, 20 February 1886.
[385] *Ibid.*; minute by 'T.O.' on draft bill sent to R. A. Cross by T. S. Raffles, 21 January 1886.
[386] For discussions see LCO 2/4599.

II

Barristers

1. NUMBERS AND COMPOSITION

Numbers

Those who have studied its composition in the eighteenth and nineteenth centuries have experienced considerable difficulty in distinguishing the bar in the broader sense, those who were entitled to call themselves barrister-at-law, from the practising bar, who sought to make their living as barristers. The distinction was important to the bar. In the 1890s, for example, controversy arose when some reformers wished to reconstitute the Bar Committee so as to represent the interests of the practising bar rather than a broader constituency. The size of the bigger group can be estimated quite closely, but the size of the practising bar is uncertain.[1]

Around 40 men a year were called to the bar in the eighteenth century, about one-quarter of those admitted to the inns, but even among those called were many who did not intend to practise, including heirs to estates who wanted to pick up a smattering of legal knowledge to assist them in their role as landowner, magistrate, and perhaps MP. Others set out to practise but were deflected either by acquired wealth, an attractive office or a more palatable occupation.[2]

The number of regular practitioners barely exceeded 300,[3] but the profession was growing and growth continued unabated until the accession of Victoria. Admissions, averaging 1571 in the first decade of the century, reached 3105 in the third, when the proportion who were called approached one in two. From the 1860s that settled at two-thirds, so the expansion was driven by an influx of men with at least a provisional intention of practising rather than gentlemen rounding off their general education.[4]

---

[1] For the eighteenth century see D. Lemmings, *Gentlemen and Barristers* (Oxford, 1990) and *Professors of the Law* (Oxford, 2000). For the nineteenth, D. Duman, *The English and Colonial Bars in the Nineteenth Century* (1983).

[2] Lemmings, *Professors of the Law*, 66–70.

[3] *Ibid.*, 73.

[4] Duman, *English and Colonial Bars*, 24–9.

Contemporaries were in no doubt that such an expansion threatened traditional ways and far outstripped the business available. The 1840s were full of
warnings about the dire state of the bar, threatened by eager and often neces-
sitous newcomers and by the creation of county courts and recent procedural
reforms in the superior courts.[5] In the short term, perhaps partly because the
warnings did deter some, the incoming tide receded. Admissions and calls fell
dramatically before a more gentle rise resumed after 1860. In the last quarter of
the century numbers were surprisingly constant, and then came another great
spurt, with 503 men called in 1913.[6]

Contemporaries often overestimated the number actually in practice. *The Law
List* was apt to mislead and after 1840 it did not distinguish practitioners from
others.[7] Estimates of the former were necessarily vague. In 1850 the Attorney-
General could only tell an inquiry that they were between 100 and 1000,[8] and
the best scholarly estimate has parameters of 450 to 1010 for 1835 and 660 to 1450
in 1885. Since this does not include anyone over 65, which was not the end of all
careers, it is a slight underestimate, but it can be assumed that the practising bar
more than doubled over the course of the nineteenth century.[9]

Duman is probably right to stress that most of the fluctuations in size were
the result of exogenous factors, in particular economic change and population
growth, although the prolonged slump in admissions from 1837 to 1857 requires
further explanation. There were fluctuations in the main pool—young men from
about 18 to 25 educated at a public school and/or university—from whom the
inns drew students, and apparently an excess of educated men in parts of Europe
in the 1820s and 1830s. English population growth outstripped the capacity of
suitable occupations until the rise of newer professions such as architect, surveyor, engineer, and accountant relieved pressure on the more traditional ones.[10]
The popularity of the traditional alternatives also varied. Prospects in the armed
forces after the Napoleonic Wars were bleak indeed and when the church roused
itself from Augustan lethargy, its appeal to the less ardent university men may
have diminished. Towards the end of the century the competition for government and professional posts became ever more intense as the output of the multiplying public schools increased.[11]

[5] R. J. C. Cocks, *Foundations of the Modern Bar* (1983), 55–9.
[6] R. Abel, *The Legal Profession in England and Wales* (Oxford, 1988), 65–7, tables 1.10, 1.13. One
journal reckoned that as a proportion of the population the bar had increased thus: 1785 1:28,555; 1826
1:16,666; 1841 1:7200; 1861 1:5000; 1892 1:3400. No sources were given: (1892) 11 *LN* 68.
[7] Duman, *English and Colonial Bars*, 7.
[8] *SC on Official Salaries*, PP 1850 (611), xv, q. 1699.
[9] Duman, *English and Colonial Bars*, table 1.3.
[10] *Ibid.*, 3–4.
[11] D. Cannadine, *The Decline and Fall of the British Aristocracy* (rev. edn, 1996), 236–9.

There is also the matter of public image, so central a preoccupation of the bar. Writers addressing would-be students never failed to stress the arduous nature of the calling and the long odds against success, yet E. D. Purcell was inspired rather than deterred by Edward Cox's presentation[12] and even the 'brutal realism' of Rouse Ball was not wholly discouraging; the earlier editions of his work assured readers that 'given health, time, industry, and perseverance, everyone of ordinary abilities may reasonably rely on securing a competency'.[13] Some fathers, like W. V. Ball's, saw the bar as the avenue to many jobs in the public service and barrister friends sometimes encouraged men they thought could succeed, as F. A. Philbrick did Barnard Lailey.[14] However, the bar had a bad press for much of the century, especially in the immensely influential *Times* and the widely read *Punch*, and J. G. Witt's parents were probably not alone in having a horror of the whole legal establishment.[15] Yet accusations of cupidity and exploitation were as likely to attract men by the prospect of big earnings as to repel them, and the publicity which surrounded leading counsel in celebrated murder trials, from Palmer to Crippen, and in a few sensational civil actions, especially the Tichborne case, cast a glamour over the whole profession. The bar could be a route into politics, as it was for Robson and Asquith,[16] and for those undecided about a career, like Frederic Harrison, or hoping to make a living from their pen, like Crabb Robinson, it was a convenient base.[17] Not least of its attractions was that entry was easy: J. W. S. Armstrong, for instance, went to the bar after failing the Foreign Office examination.[18]

The loose-knit structure of the bar made any institutional response to overcrowding difficult. Sometimes individually, occasionally in concert, the inns did put in place some fresh obstacles. Disqualifying occupations, mostly those connected with the law or 'trade', were expanded and in 1829 the Inner Temple examined candidates in classics and 'general subjects of a liberal education'. Other inns did not follow suit and rather than lose students the Inner quietly dropped it in the 1840s.[19] Later examinations were not used to restrict entry. Not only would

---

[12] E. D. Purcell, *Forty Years at the Criminal Bar* (1916), 24. For Cox's publications see Cocks, *Foundations of the Modern Bar*, 72–3.

[13] Cocks, *Foundations of the Modern Bar*, 184; W. R. Ball, *The Student's Guide to the Bar* (1884 edn), 11.

[14] Sir W. Ball, *Lincoln's Inn* (1947), 82; H. Slesser, *Judgement Reserved* (1941), 15; B. Lailey, *Jottings From a Fee-Book* (Portsmouth, 1932), 14.

[15] J. G. Witt, *A Life in the Law* (1906), 1–2.

[16] J. A. Spender and C. Asquith, *The Life of Herbert Henry, Lord Asquith*, 2 vols (1932), i, 38; G. W. Keeton, *A Liberal Attorney-General* (1949), 9.

[17] F. Harrison, *Autobiographic Memoirs*, 2 vols (1911), i, 149–50; *The Diary, Reminiscences and Correspondence of Henry Crabb Robinson*, ed. T. Sadler, 2 vols (3rd edn, 1872), i, 141.

[18] H. B. Thomson, *The Choice of a Profession* (1857), 96; J. W. S. Armstrong, *Yesterday* (1955), 62.

[19] See below, p. 1022.

such a policy have been contrary to the bar's own conception of itself, but it would have been impossible to reach agreement on suitable criteria.

Composition

According to Duman, 8.7 per cent of the 1835 bar were Irish, 4.1 per cent Scottish, and 1.6 per cent Welsh, totalling one-seventh of the whole. In 1885 they comprised 7.9, 5.9, and 2.9 per cent respectively, making up one-sixth.[20] Some were sensitive about their nationality. John Campbell felt that J. A. Park discredited his countrymen by his 'extreme obsequiousness',[21] while the Irish were noted in the early nineteenth century for a distinctively flamboyant style of advocacy. Digby Seymour claimed in the mid-century that he was the victim of anti-Irish prejudice on the northern circuit,[22] though it did not hold back Russell and Carson; Tim Healy, however, was one who failed to get business in England.[23]

After the disappearance of students from the American colonies there was no substantial colonial presence at the English bar until the 1860s, though there were a few West Indians, among them Anthony Hart.[24] This changed with an influx of Indians, and others from the east, particularly to the Middle Temple, which began to assume a very cosmopolitan air. Their abstemiousness from alcohol made them desirable dinner companions to the more thirsty English students[25] and Frederic Harrison was greatly impressed with their academic prowess, claiming that in one year the best three were 'a Japanese, a Madras Mussulman, and a Hindoo'.[26] They did, however, meet disapproval when many of the Indians, most famously M. T. Gandhi, openly supported Indian nationalism.[27] Most returned home to practise, though Dube overcame the additional difficulties his race created to carve out a good practice in the Privy Council. 'Old King Cole' from the Gold Coast was another who tried his hand in England.[28]

---

[20] *English and Colonial Bars*, 9–15. The first practising Jew to be called was Francis Goldsmid, by Lincoln's in 1832. By the 1880s they made up between 1 and 3% of practitioners and included such luminaries as Jessel, Arthur Cohen, Isaacs, and Benjamin: J. Cooper, *Pride versus Prejudice* (Oxford 2003), 93–111.

[21] Hon. Mrs M. S. Hardcastle, *The Life of John, Lord Campbell*, 2 vols (1861), i, 219.

[22] (1829–30) 3 *LM* 303–40; 'William Digby Seymour, QC, MP' (1862) 13 (s3) *LM & LR* 158–85 at 162.

[23] G. Alexander, *The Temple of the Nineties* (1938), 134, attributed Healy's failure partly to the political antipathy of the big London solicitors.

[24] According to J. R. Lewis, *The Victorian Bar* (1982), 60, West Indians began to be admitted more frequently from the mid-century, but he does not distinguish their colour.

[25] Duman, *English and Colonial Bars*, 130–2 ; E. Bowen Rowlands, *In the Light of the Law* (1931), 62.

[26] *Autobiographic Memoirs*, i, 330. Their diligent use of the libraries made them the butt of jokes: Alexander, *Temple of the Nineties*, 66.

[27] (1908–9) 53 *Sol. J.* 558.

[28] Duman, *English and Colonial Bars*, 132; Sir R. Bosanquet, *The Oxford Circuit* (1951), 9; H. S. Theobald, *Remembrance of Things Past* (Oxford, 1935), 60.

The incentive offered in 1762 to university graduates of call after three years rather than five led to something of an 'aristocratic resurgence' at Lincoln's Inn[29] but the longer term trend for the sons of men from the older professions—church, army, law—to dominate, soon resumed, leading Byerly Thomson to insist that the bar was 'more than ever a profession of the middle class'.[30] Though men from landed backgrounds (generously interpreted) still made up over 40 per cent of those at the bar in 1835, 50 years later, and in a much larger profession, they had fallen to a third, and formed only one-quarter of the practising bar. Moreover, they were now more often younger than elder sons and came mostly from the less prosperous gentry. If the somewhat hazy categories of Inner Temple admissions can be relied upon, then even under the very broad description of 'gentleman', they had almost disappeared by the Edwardian era.[31]

In their place came sons of businessmen and, in greater numbers, of professional men. The law was not a caste, but from the 1830s one-quarter of students had a father in the law and given the advantage this gave them, it is hardly surprising that they figure more strongly among the successful than in the bar at large.[32] Fears arose that the higher branch was being swamped by sons and relations of the lower,[33] but in fact connections of barristers always outnumbered those of solicitors. For much of the century the clergy continued to provide as many entrants as all the other (non-legal) professions put together but there was a marked decline by the end.[34]

What remained constant was the near absence of the lower orders of society, not only labourers and industrial workers, but even artisans and small shopkeepers. Much was made of the fact that men of humble origins like Sir Edward Clarke could rise to the top of the profession, but Clarkes were few, and that may have owed more to the intimidating image of the barrister as a gentleman than to the barriers the inns erected to preserve a measure of social exclusivity, for being essentially financial they were as likely to deter sons of poor clergy and half-pay officers as tradesmen.[35] Young men of slender means would endure hardship and use great initiative to pursue their chosen career and it is noteworthy that

---

[29] P. Lucas, 'A Collective Biography of the Students and Barristers of Lincoln's Inn, 1680–1804: A Study in the "Aristocratic Resurgence" of the Eighteenth Century' (1974) 46 *JMH* 227–61, at 229; W. C. Richardson, *A History of the Inns of Court* (Baton Rouge, USA, 1975), 313–14.

[30] Thomson, *The Choice of a Profession*, 93.

[31] *English and Colonial Bars*, 16–19. Cannadine, *Decline and Fall*, explores the change from the aristocracy's perspective.

[32] Duman, *English and Colonial Bars*, 111.

[33] e.g. A. Polson, *Law and Lawyers*, 2 vols (1840), i, 146; 'Bar Etiquette' (1857) 3 (s3) *LM & LR* 236–59 at 255; Sir C. Biron, *Without Prejudice* (1936), 89.

[34] Abel, *Legal Profession*, table 1.21.

[35] Duman, *English and Colonial Bars*, 21–2.

Lincoln's Inn could not sustain its ban on journalism, which kept the wolf from many a door.[36]

2. PREPARATION FOR THE BAR

Education

A Georgian barrister was as likely to have been educated at home as at school,[37] but this changed as more public schools opened to provide an education geared to university entrance. Judges, and probably the bar in general, came increasingly from public schools but the proportion from the old elite schools fell.[38] Nevertheless, it was still a help to be an old Etonian or Wykehamist, since the disposal of minor offices so useful to a young barrister was often vested in someone from the old school.

A bigger and more significant change was the dramatic rise in the number of 'varsity men'.[39] In Victoria's reign it became very much the done thing to go to university, and for an aspiring barrister this was perfectly compatible with qualifying for the bar. It was not uncommon to enrol at an inn while still an undergraduate and not unknown to do it the other way around.

The bar became a predominantly graduate profession, graduates rising from 58 per cent to 70 per cent between 1835 and 1885, though with curiously large variations between the inns; Inner Temple and Lincoln's reached very high levels while Grays was only 33 per cent in 1913 and the Middle Temple fell sharply, from 61 per cent in 1890 to just 24 per cent in 1910.[40] The big Oxford and Cambridge colleges continued to dominate the bar and especially the judiciary.[41] Trinity College, Dublin provided a steady stream of Irishmen and as the century went on London University began to make an impact, perhaps a socially distinctive one. Graduates in law remained a small (and by and large undistinguished) minority.[42]

The predominance of university men at the bar had a considerable effect. It gave plausibility to the bar's claim to be a gentlemanly and cultivated profession without the bar having to impose its own qualifications. In particular, it helped

---

[36] See below, p. 1034.

[37] Lemmings, *Gentlemen and Barristers*, 113–15.

[38] See above, p. 967 and Duman, *English and Colonial Bars*, 22–3.

[39] Lemmings, *Professors of the Law*, 120; Lucas, 'Collective Biography of Lincoln's Inn', table A 10; Duman, *English and Colonial Bars*, table 1.9.

[40] Abel, *Legal Profession*, tables 1.13, 1.14. The influx of overseas students may partly explain the Middle Temple figure.

[41] Duman, *English and Colonial Bars*, 24.   [42] Ibid., 23.

maintain the social gap between the bar and the solicitors which was essential to the bar's collective self-esteem, and perhaps to preserve social cohesion as the profession expanded, by providing a common culture, albeit at the expense of the non-university minority.

At an individual level the value of a university education is more difficult to evaluate,[43] but it furnished contacts which might be crucial in the difficult early years; for instance, F. E. Smith as Chancellor was reckoned to favour members of his old college (Wadham).[44] A university career garlanded with distinctions certainly generated some momentum, and the insistence with which contemporary publications record them suggests they were viewed as important indicators of potential forensic prowess. And for some of the most distinguished students there was a tangible advantage in the shape of a university fellowship bringing in several hundred pounds a year with a minimum of duties.[45]

Pupillage

Pupillage emerged in the 1770s from the custom of apprenticing bar students to London solicitors and attorneys, desired by anxious fathers as much as a safeguard against the temptations of loose living as a training for the law.[46] This intensely practical and intellectually barren form of education still had its advocates well into the next century, and in 1840 Archer Polson offered a detailed appraisal of its merits. Admitting the advantages of acquiring miscellaneous, but often superficial knowledge, steady application to dull labour, tact and readiness, he felt the training incompatible with the ideal of a liberal profession.[47] Most evidently agreed, for the practice had long been in decline by then, but it did not wholly die out. In the 1880s Lailey, Richard Webster, and William Ball each spent a few months in a City solicitor's firm, but they were probably unusual.[48]

Though Blackstone had denounced its narrow and superficial character, what displaced it was often no more enlarged, if perhaps more 'scientific'.[49] The 'fetish for pupillage with a special pleader'[50] led to William Tidd having among his many

[43] Thomson, *Choice of a Profession*, 101, regarded it as doubtful.

[44] J. Campbell, *F.E. Smith* (1983), 48, 279.

[45] D. Duman, *The Judicial Bench in England, 1727–1875: The Re-Shaping of a Professional Elite* (1982), 59.

[46] Lemmings, *Professors of the Law*, 132–5.

[47] *Law and Lawyers*, i, 29–30.

[48] Ball, *Student's Guide*, 49; Lailey, *Jottings From a Fee-Book*, 14; Lord Alverstone, *Recollections of Bar and Bench* (1914), 4; Ball, *Lincoln's Inn*, 30–1.

[49] Lemmings, *Professors of the Law*, 134.

[50] *Ibid.*, 125. Sir John Bayley was a transitional figure, following a year in an attorney's office with two years with a special pleader.

pupils Copley, Campbell, Pepys, and Denman.[51] A generation of judges and leading common lawyers was thereby initiated into the mysteries of the pleader's art,
with serious consequences for the development of the common law. It also came
to be accepted that the budding barrister should attach himself to a conveyancer
and an equity draftsman, and by the time Edward Cox produced his prescription
for *The Advocate* (1852) he was in good company in suggesting the training period
should last between 18 months and three years.[52] Cox insisted that the novice at
common law or Chancery should start in a conveyancer's chambers, the former
moving on to a special pleader, the latter to an equity draftsman and both finish-
ing up with a busy junior 'General Practitioner'.[53] This last stage, however, was
the least common.

Because pupillage was not obligatory it is practically impossible to know how
many men followed Cox's prescription, let alone with what effect. Jeaffreson was
probably wrong in claiming in the 1860s that the full three years was normal,[54]
if only because the established rate of 100 guineas a year (50 for six months)
was beyond many.[55] Campbell was one who could not afford this and believed
that a year or two would be enough. Ball suggested two or three years[56] and to
judge from memoirs, relatively few undertook the full course Cox prescribed.
Frederick Thesiger was probably unusual in going from the conveyancer Walker
to the special pleader Sykes via an equity draftsman (Heald) and, a common law
junior (Holroyd),[57] for Palmer described as 'usual' his year apiece with Walters
for conveyancing and Booth (equity draftsman) and most mention only two
names, some just one.[58] Patrick Hastings was one of those who could not afford
to be a pupil at all.[59]

The choice of a pupil master was important since his formal obligations were
narrowly defined.[60] A fortunate student like A. J. Ashton had contacts at the bar

[51] *ODNB*, 54: 763.

[52] At 201–8.

[53] *Ibid.*

[54] J. C. Jeaffreson, *A Book About Lawyers*, 2 vols (1867). According to E. C. Whitehurst, 'Successful
Lawyers' (1877) 52 (n.s.) *Westminster Rev.*, 157–88, 'every page…is disfigured by inaccuracies' (176).
Lindley's four-and-a-half years was exceptional, but included an interval in Bonn: KCL Mss,
Autobiography (1918), 25–7.

[55] Hardcastle, *Life of Lord Campbell*, i, 134. Special pleaders set their own rate: J. H. Slater, *A Guide
to the Legal Profession* (1884), 381.

[56] *Student's Guide*, 41.

[57] J. B. Atlay, *The Victorian Chancellors*, 2 vols (1908), ii, 82 ('longer and more varied than most').

[58] Lord Selborne, *Memorials, Part One, Family and Personal, 1766–1895*, 2 vols (1896), i, 200.

[59] Sir P. Hastings, *The Autobiography of Sir Patrick Hastings* (1948), 72.

[60] See below, pp. 1176–7. See also J. A. Shearwood, *A Guide for Candidates of the Professions of
Barrister and Solicitor* (2nd edn, 1887), 50.

to make sure he was well served,[61] but for others it was a lottery. B. J. Robinson contrived to spend 300 guineas and three years with Nichols, who did only insolvency, while E. F. Spence was doubly unfortunate; first he went to Bousfield, but found his patent specialization unpalatable and then to Gill, who practised largely in the Mayor's Court with its antiquated and peculiar procedure.[62]

Many were advised to find a busy junior with a general practice, but too busy a man would have no time for his pupils.[63] Bowen fell into this class, and Bowen Rowlands named four less famous leading juniors who were similarly situated.[64] Day and Lindley, on the other hand, were reckoned very conscientious pupil masters, and Harrison, though he loathed conveyancing, found Joshua Williams eager to initiate him into its mysteries.[65] Alverstone was so proud of his record that he listed his pupils in full in his autobiography.[66]

Special pleaders with a chamber practice had more time to spend on their pupils than advocates but like Tidd and later G. B. Allen, were tempted to take on too many.[67] Chamber counsel were the same, with Tom Chitty perhaps the worst, taking up to 20 even when well past his prime. Generally more than half-a-dozen pupils was unusual and Campbell and Lindley restricted themselves to two at a time.[68]

Special Pleaders, Equity Draftsmen, and Conveyancers

Special pleaders and equity draftsmen had been admitted to an inn but had chosen to defer their call, usually because they felt uncertain of being able to make a living at the bar without having first built up a reputation and clientele among the lower branch.[69] They were allowed to charge half the minimum fee (half a guinea), could form partnerships, accept instructions directly from a lay client, and sue for fees.[70] The best known special pleader of the 1820s was William Tidd, whose writings were extolled by Uriah Heep in *David Copperfield*. Unlike his celebrated predecessor George Wood, Tidd remained a special pleader throughout

---

[61] *As I Went On My Way* (1924), 88.

[62] Robinson, *Bench and Bar* (2nd edn, 1889), 27–9; Spence, *Bar and Buskin* (1930), 119.

[63] Slater, *Guide to the Legal Profession*, 382.

[64] A. G. C. Liddell, *Notes from the Life of an Ordinary Mortal* (1911), 132–3; E. Bowen Rowlands, *In Court and Out of Court* (1925), 49–50.

[65] [A. F. Day] , *John C.F.S. Day, his Forbears and Himself* (1910), 171–8; Sir F. M. Pollock, *For My Grandson* (1935), 161; Harrison, *Autobiographic Memoirs*, i, 149.

[66] *Recollections*, App.

[67] Hardcastle, *Life of Lord Campbell*, i, 147; Theobald, *Remembrance of Things Past*, 71–2.

[68] Sir H. F. Dickens, *The Recollections of Sir Henry Dickens, KC* (1934), 136; Hardcastle, *Life of Lord Campbell*, i, 344; Lindley, *Autobiography*, 52.

[69] Lemmings, *Professors of the Law*, 34. But see below, p. 1055, for serjeants practising as special pleaders.

[70] *Poucher* v. *Norman* (1825) 3 B. & C. 744; 'Doctor in Jure Civil', *The Legal Profession* (1873), 219.

his career and had so many pupils that he was said to be making between £2000 and £3000 a year.[71] The reputation of special pleaders was enhanced by the fact that at one time all four judges of the King's Bench had come from their ranks, and in the 1840s they were numerous enough to have their own club.[72]

They needed an annual certificate costing £12,[73] which gave the inns a discretionary power disapproved by the Common Law Commissioners: '[t]o subject Special Pleaders...to a regulation so arbitrary, is to expose to inconvenience and disadvantage, a body of persons whose prosperity is of great importance to the Profession, and to the science of the Law itself'.[74]

Not everyone shared the Commissioners' fondness for special pleaders. They were able to undercut the bar, and study with them led to contracted minds:[75] 'enlarged notions of law and justice are smothered in laborious and absurd technicalities'.[76] It certainly turned out lawyers who were impressively proficient in the 'science' of pleadings—James Parke is the most celebrated example—and since many became judges it is not surprising that the virtues and vices of special pleading became so embedded in English jurisprudence; in the Regency Collier could allege, with spurious precision, that one-fifth of cases were decided purely on technical grounds.[77]

For some of the best known, a spell as a special pleader was usually a short one, though Gibbs (nearly 12 years) and Abbott (earning £1000) were notably cautious.[78] How many were never called, and how much they earned, remains unknown. The day of the special pleader was short and his eclipse was sudden. The Common Law Procedure Acts 1852 and 1854 demolished the elaborate artifice of special pleading erected by the New Pleading Rules and removed his raison d'être. Thereafter, any member of the junior bar ought to be competent to draw all the usual pleadings, and solicitors would expect them to do so. Training with a special pleader therefore became rapidly obsolete and the profession withered. The decline was precipitous—from 74 in 1850 to just 19 in 1860.[79] A few lingered

[71] Hardcastle, *Life of Lord Campbell*, i, 147.

[72] *Ibid.*, i, 138; (1845) 3 (s2) *LM* 161.

[73] Stamp Act 1804 (44 Geo. III c. 98).

[74] *Sixth Report*, PP 1834 (263), xxvi, 9.

[75] Hardcastle, *Life of Lord Campbell*, i, 138; Cox, *The Advocate*, 297–8; *RC on the Inns of Court*, PP 1854–5 [1998], xviii, qq. 1441–57 (A. Pulling).

[76] 'Amicus Curiae' [J. P. Collier], *Criticisms on the Bar* (1819), 5.

[77] *Ibid.* No doubt Lord Abinger exaggerated when he said that 'he never knew a civil case decided from beginning to end upon the merits': 'The Progress of English Jurisprudence' (1857) 12 ns *Westminster Rev.*, 511–32.

[78] W. C. Townsend, *The Lives of Twelve Eminent Judges*, 2 vols (1846), i, 243–4; John, Lord Campbell, *The Lives of the Chief Justices of England* (1857), iii, 271–2.

[79] Abel, *Legal Profession*, table 4.2. The inns had become reluctant to grant certificates (Ball, *Student's Guide*, 19), but oddly both Ball and Shearwood still recommended study under a special pleader.

into the new century but Dodgson (who died in 1884) was probably the last one of any note.[80] Well into the 1870s judges trained in this school were still on the bench, but it is unsurprising that Byles would not stay a day after his pension became due under a regime which had made pleadings even more loose, nor that Lush, so good in chambers, was lost in the new Court of Appeal.[81]

Much less is known about the conveyancers and equity draftsmen, many of whom combined both roles. The conveyancers became even more numerous than the special pleaders, but with them too the numbers in the *Law List* are erratic, falling from 96 in 1820 to just 20 in 1835 and fluctuating thereafter until a steady decline set in after the 1880s. The sharp fall in the 1820s is explicable. The possibility of practising without the restraints either of the bar or the solicitors' profession had attracted dubious characters who had no intention of being called and promptly set themselves up as conveyancers under the bar.[82] Under pressure from the other branch the inns began to require undertakings from all practitioners under the bar that they would not practise until they were qualified to be called.[83] In 1830 Lincoln's Inn expelled one man who was a land agent and auctioneer turned conveyancer, and the more careful scrutiny of applicants for certificates cured the evil.[84] Equity draftsmen went into decline with the simplifications in equity procedure which parallelled those at common law, though some barristers practised under this designation.

Chambers

Two major changes took place in the nineteenth century: chambers gradually ceased to be a place of residence as well as of work and came to be shared for that purpose. Fashionable lawyers (especially married ones) moved inexorably westwards, following Ellenborough from Bloomsbury to St. James's Square.[85] As suburban buses and then trains made commuting cheaper and quicker the less eminent fled to the suburbs. Thackeray evidently considered it quite normal for Pendennis to be living in chambers with Warrington, but by 1870 few men with any practice were living in their chambers.[86]

[80] (1883–4) 28 *Sol. J.* 769.
[81] [W. D. I. Foulkes], *A Generation of Judges, by their Reporter* (1886), 21–9, 71–82.
[82] Complaint of Randle Lewis, 1816, *Lincoln's Inn Black Books* (1902), iv, 139.
[83] *Ibid.*, 167 (11 November 1824), 179 (28 April 1830).
[84] (1829) 2 *LM* 705, 706; *Lincoln's Inn Black Books* iv, 179, 194.
[85] Lewis, *Victorian Bar*, 30–1; Sir W. F. Pollock, *Personal Reminiscences of Sir Frederick Pollock, second baronet*, 2 vols (1887), 3–4.
[86] *The History of Pendennis* (1850), Ch. 28; Thomson, *Choice of a Profession*, 100; 'The Inns of Court' (1869) 25 (s3) *LM & LR* 73–90.

Shared professional quarters have been traced no further back than 1839 and initially seem to have been confined to doubling up by young barrister friends to save costs.[87] Strahan, writing in 1919, suggested that sets arose from congregations based on school affiliation to provide mutual support, but another development contributing to the creation of 'sets' in the modern sense, with a head and a group of clerks, is illustrated by the case of Gorell Barnes, who made himself so useful to J. C. Mathew as his devil that the latter kept him on after pupillage.[88] Sets were certainly in vogue by the First World War; Salter's chambers were a western circuit set which emptied at Assize time, and in Liverpool F. E. Smith brought in Harold Jager and other juniors to share his chambers.[89]

The move to shared chambers made for significant changes in working practices.[90] In single chambers the novice had to adopt a very passive role. The unpleasantness of that situation was often described, though it also gave rise to a folklore of comforting stories, some of them true, of the miraculous deliverance that did come to the man who waited.[91] The solitary barrister in his own chambers was the individual idealized by the bar, an independent man making his own way in the world. But the position of a young man joining a set with an established hierarchy is very different. Besides inculcating the bar's values, the arrangement reinforces the authority of the bar establishment, tending to repress rebellious traits and promote conformity. Without guaranteeing work, it also ensures that a man who is accepted into chambers will, through the agency of the clerks, obtain at least a few briefs with which to demonstrate his abilities. As the trend to sets grew, the man who sat in chambers like patience on a monument, smiling at grief, became more unusual. And in time finding a tenancy would become one of the biggest obstacles to a career at the bar.[92]

Local Bars

Towards the end of the nineteenth century a further possibility opened up. There had long been individuals who, either from an attachment to their locality or because they had failed to get a foothold in London, confined themselves to one

---

[87] Duman, *English and Colonial Bars*, 58–60. This was still common in 1902: 'The Bar' (1902) *Cornhill Mag.*, n.s. 13, 474.

[88] Duman, *English and Colonial Bars*, 83–4; Ball, *Lincoln's Inn*, 99; J. E. G. de Montmorency, *John Gorell Barnes, Lord Gorell* (1920), 50.

[89] A. Smith, *Lord Goddard: My Years with the Lord Chief Justice* (1959), 16; H. Jager, *Brief Life* (Liverpool, 1934), 104.

[90] J. A. Strahan, *The Bench and Bar of England* (1919), 207–8; Cocks, *Foundations of the Modern Bar*, 9–10.

[91] See below, pp. 1039–40.

[92] Abel, *Legal Profession*, 56–60.

part of the provinces, but nowhere outside London was there enough business for more than two or three to carve out a full-time practice. Many counties could show one or two men like the younger Balguy, scion of an old Derbyshire house, who went the midland circuit, but would never go to London unless on circuit business, though he nominally had chambers there. 'The perfect English gentleman', Balguy collected local offices and was ambitious of nothing more.[93] Such men were too few and scattered to represent any sort of threat to the 'great central bar of England'.

With the creation of the new county courts and changes to the Assizes, the conditions for the development of local bars of modest size but distinct character gradually came into being.[94] Manchester, Liverpool, Leeds, and Birmingham all became Assize towns and district registries and the first two had specially lengthened Assize sittings. Several big cities had an active local court which besides being a venue for litigation above the county court money limits, offered the possibility of a local judgeship. All of them had a Recorder, and most had a stipendiary magistrate too. In 1880 Birmingham, Leeds, Bristol, and Newcastle had about a dozen barristers with local business addresses and Manchester and Liverpool each had over fifty.[95] By 1900 these two were approaching 100, while growth in the other regional centres remained much more modest.[96]

Local bars, if still unwelcome in some quarters, became a fact of life and had their share of talent. John Holker was perhaps the first to demonstrate in London that carefully nurtured artless bluntness which went down so well with northern juries, and even eminent circuiteers lacking a local connexion found that solicitors preferred locals familiar with the peculiarities of northern juries and business practices.[97]

The strength, and indeed legitimacy, of the Manchester bar was openly acknowledged in Herschell's choice of W. R. Kennedy for the bench in 1893 and by the abandonment of the rule that a KC must have chambers in London.[98] Manchester and Liverpool by then boasted sets of chambers on the London model and a wide range of barristers from the commercial silks that were their greatest strength to criminal defenders of the rough and breezy type like Charles McKeand.[99]

---

[93] R.Walton, *Random Recollections of the Midland Circuit* (1869), 24–5.

[94] See the forebodings in Cox, *Advocate*, vii.

[95] As early as 1850 Charles Le Blanc told the Select Committee on Official Salaries that there were reputed to be good local bars at Liverpool and Manchester (*Report 1850*, q. 1592).

[96] Ball, *Student's Guide*, 11; Abel, *Legal Profession*, table 1.26 (commencing 1894). By 1914 Bradford had also reached double figures.

[97] E. A. Parry, *My Own Way* (1932), 178–80; [Foulkes] *Generation of Judges*, 119–27.

[98] R. Jackson, *The Chief* (1959), 37, 55; E. S. Fay, *The Life of Mr. Justice Swift* (1939), 6. A. J. Ashton was the last KC appointed from the northern circuit who had not also belonged to a local bar: Ashton, *As I Went On My Way*, 216.

[99] E. A. Parry, *What the Judge Saw* (1912), 153–62.

The other provincial bars remained smaller. Birmingham had some good advocates but only H. A. McCardie was in the star class and the quality of the Leeds, Newcastle, and Bristol ones was rather moderate.[100] As a proportion of the practising bar they were still small in aggregate, but no longer insignificant.

Choice of Circuit

Most men had to choose between practising in the courts of common law or in Chancery, though the choice did not have to be immediate and while the equity side of the Exchequer lasted it was possible to practise on both sides of that court. After the opening of Divorce, Probate, and Admiralty courts to the common lawyers in the mid-century it was also possible to specialize from the outset in those areas, but few did so. There were, however, those who made the Old Bailey and the Surrey and Middlesex sessions their home, not venturing even onto the home circuit.

The Chancery bar was disengaging from the circuits. Charles Wetherell was the last of the big names to go, though J. L. Knight-Bruce went the South Wales for a few years until it interfered with his growing Chancery business. By the late 1820s, at all events, the habit was gone.[101] Edward Cox put great emphasis on the importance of choosing the right circuit. He felt the most obvious criterion, a local connection, could easily be overrated, but conceded that it was a significant advantage and for most men it was probably the decisive consideration.[102] Family connections were the most obvious, though some fathers forbade their sons to accompany them.[103] For those who had no usable connection it was more difficult. A. C. Plowden resolved on the Oxford because it took him to the Welsh marches where at least his name would have associations but for Scarlett, coming from the West Indies, it was more or less a random choice.[104] Cost could enter the equation, persuading Campbell to take the home and Copley the midland; later on Edward Clarke, who could ill-afford the £150 for the western, went the home instead.[105] For those who did not expect to get much business and were either too poor or too much in earnest to care for the social side of circuit life, compactness

[100] G. Pollock, *Mr. Justice McCardie* (1934), 10; F. E. Weatherly, *Piano and Gown* (1926), 217–21.

[101] J. and W. Romilly, *Memoirs of the Life of Sir Samuel Romilly*, 3 vols (1840), i, 72; Atlay, *Victorian Chancellors*, i, 386; A. C. Bruce, 'The Late Lord Justice of Appeal Sir J. L. Knight-Bruce' (1866–7) 22 (s3) *LM & LR* 278–94; C. Cottu, *On the Administration of Criminal Justice in England...* (1822), 42.

[102] *The Advocate*, 262–9.

[103] M. Williams, *Leaves from a Life*, 2 vols (1890), 57–8; C. Jay, *The Law* (1868), 13.

[104] A. C. Plowden, *Grain Or Chaff?* (1903), 94–5; P. C. Scarlett, *A Memoir of the R.H. James, First Lord Abinger* (1877), 48.

[105] Hardcastle, *Life of Lord Campbell*, i, 195; Atlay, *Victorian Chancellors*, i, 12; Clarke, *Story of My Life* , 77.

was a factor which made the midland more attractive than the northern, while from the 1850s the home allowed of a sort of commuting by railway. But men were various; Campbell moved to a circuit where the bar was weaker whereas Brett was one of the few who actually took the northern because the bar was strongest.[106] Towards the end of the period there were leading men who never went circuit; for the likes of T. E. Scrutton and F. D. Mackinnon it presumably seemed a waste of time.[107]

Clerks

A barrister had to employ a clerk but impecunious newcomers like Campbell had to settle for recruiting a nine-year-old boy and training him up. *Pendennis* indicates that such juveniles were still the norm in the 1840s[108] but with the coming of compulsory education these 'wonders of precocity' were usually between 12 and 14.[109] They were still seen as needing no more than a board school education,[110] for unlike articled clerks they were not expected to look for advancement beyond a clerkship and only a handful went to the bar.[111] So for all that KCs' clerks had to dress in silk hat and striped trousers they were for the most part cockneyfied.

If the clerk was satisfactory and the barrister successful the relationship might be a long term one, though few hero-worshipped a master as Bowker did Marshall Hall,[112] nor were many on such familiar terms with their master as Mingay's.[113] Clerk frequently followed their master if he became a judge, though for financial reasons they usually hoped such a move would be long delayed, and the reluctance of several judges to abandon long-serving clerks to an unpensioned existence precipitated the 'Colliery explosion' in 1871.[114]

---

[106] Hardcastle, *Life of Lord Campbell*, i, 242–3; E. Manson, *Builders of our Law in the Reign of Queen Victoria* (2nd edn, 1904), 392.

[107] Sir F. MacKinnon, *On Circuit* (1940), 4.

[108] Hardcastle , *Life of Lord Campbell*, i, 192; Thackeray, *History of Pendennis*, Ch. 28.

[109] M. Williams, *Later Leaves* (1891), 28; F. W. Ashley, *My Sixty Years in the Law* (1936), 18; A. E. Bowker, *A Lifetime in the Law* (1961), 16; T. E. Crispe, *Memories of a KC* (2nd edn, 1909), 201. Roundell Palmer was unusual in recruiting his clerks from the family servants: *Memorials, Family and Personal, Part One*, i, 245.

[110] Though some noted up cases and Leslie Scott used his devil: Alexander, *Temple of the Nineties*, 241; Jager, *Brief Life*, 56–7.

[111] F. Pearson, *Memories of a KC's Clerk*, 4; Bowker, *Lifetime in the Law*, 17. In the nineteenth century the inns would not call them: G. Shaw-Lefevre, 'Discipline of the Law' (1862) 13 (s3) *LM & LR* 1–33 at 7.

[112] J. Flood, *Barristers' Clerks, the Law's Middlemen* (Manchester, 1983), 101–11; Bowker, *Lifetime in the Law*, 9.

[113] [J. Espinasse], 'My Contemporaries' (1832) 6 *Fraser's Mag.* 426.

[114] See above, p. 561.

It was the financial aspect of the clerks' duties that led to repeated criticism. Bowker's romantic view that most successful barristers were not motivated primarily by the pursuit of money was made possible by what Hawkins' biographer described as the rapacity of barristers' clerks.[115] Once the practice of having a separate fee for the clerk endorsed on briefs was accepted by taxing masters and rapidly hardened into one of the bar's immutable traditions, it became necessary for a scale to be adopted in 1834 to curb their demands.[116] It failed to do so, leading to indignant protests by the Law Society in 1850 at attempts to extort extra fees and a further controversy in the 1880s, when solicitors seemed at one point ready to refuse to pay a separate fee at all.[117] By Lord Alverstone's day the clerks had succeeded in claiming 2½ per cent on the brief and 2s/6d or 5s for a conference,[118] but by then the move to sets was making important changes in the position of the clerk. Barristers had begun to share clerks when they began to share chambers,[119] but once a set became established it was ruled by a senior clerk, who took his percentage of the earnings of every member of the set, with each barrister having a junior clerk of his own.[120] As chambers increased in size, the earnings of a few clerks reached four figures, but as there were seldom more than three or four members in a set,[121] most got between £300 and £400 and Edward Spence reckoned that when he was making a little over £4000 his clerk got £170 (4 or 5 per cent).[122]

In this situation the senior clerk came to wield real power over the junior bar. Even the career of the head of chambers could be shaped by the levels at which his fees were set. Carson's clerk took care to ensure that he demanded as much as Isaacs, and this sort of thing, conducted by sharp, streetwise men with a keen eye on the market, was one factor in the inflation of counsel's fees before the First World War.[123] The clerk could also advance or retard the progress of a junior's career in such a way that the hapless sufferer might not immediately be aware of it; thus Newman, Salter's clerk, was felt by Smith to care little for Goddard and the other juniors.[124]

---

[115] *Lifetime in the Law*, 29–30; R. Harris (ed.), *The Reminiscences of Sir Henry Hawkins, Baron Brampton* (1904), 112.

[116] R. Abel-Smith and R. Stevens, *Lawyers and the Courts* (1967), 56 n.4.

[117] *Ibid.*, 230–1.

[118] Lord Alverstone, *Recollections of Bar and Bench*, 279–80.

[119] e.g. Pollock, *Personal Reminiscences*, i, 191.

[120] Bowker, *Lifetime in the Law*, 16; Williams, *Later Leaves*, 28–30; Ashley, *My Sixty Years in the Law*, 40.

[121] E. A. Bell, *Those Meddlesome Attorneys* (1939), 75.

[122] Smith, *Lord Goddard*, 23; Spence, *Bar and Buskin*, 165.

[123] E. Marjoribanks, *The Life of Lord Carson*, 2 vols (1932), i, 235–6. For complaints about clerks' rapacity see W. Durran, *The Lawyer, Our Old-Man-of-the-Sea* (1913), 527.

[124] Smith, *Lord Goddard*, 21.

For the junior clerks there was no expectation of promotion within chambers, where hours were long and working practices usually very conservative, with typewriters and telephones making only slow progress.[125] Young clerks had to be alert for vacancies in other chambers or in new sets. Thus Bowker entered Houghton's chambers in 1904, moved to Macaskie's as a junior then became senior clerk to Hans Hamilton and when Hamilton became a county court judge, moved to head a Birmingham set. He eventually achieved his long held desire to serve Marshall Hall, who passed over his own junior to take him.[126]

3. GETTING STARTED

Outlay

A university educated bar student in the mid-nineteenth century might expect to spend c.£400 per annum and, with board and lodging, perhaps another £600 per annum.[127] Being called, however, did not mean an immediate income. In *The Advocate* (1852) Edward Cox entered fully into the question of how much a man needed to live on at the bar until—hopefully—he acquired a worthwhile practice. Cox put chambers at £30, a laundress at £12, a clerk at £15, and books (limited to the 'regular reports') at £10. With various sundries he costed chambers etc. expenses at £77. To this he added five attendances at sessions (£40), a restricted attendance on circuit (£55), and the expenses necessary to keep up a gentlemanly appearance (£100); in all he would need to find at least £272 per annum.[128]

Other estimates naturally varied. In 1835 Samuel Warren felt one could manage on £150 (but revised it to £250–£300 following sharp criticism), whereas Lord Abinger CB probably put it too high at £400. Others put it at £250 (1857), £300 (1881), and £200 (1909).[129]

This sum would very likely have to be found for a good few years, for it usually took upwards of five years to show a profit.[130] It was cheaper to practise at a local bar and there were economies in sharing clerks, chambers, and reports.[131] Even so, without parental support, it was a precarious existence: a man must, as Eldon put it, 'live like a hermit and work like a horse'.[132] Some successful men in every

---

[125] G. Alexander, *After Court Hours* (1950), 8.
[126] *Lifetime in the Law*, 11–21.
[127] Duman, *Judicial Bench*, 47–9, 55–7.
[128] *The Advocate*, 27–42. Cottu, *Administration of Justice*, had put it at £600–£700 per annum.
[129] Polson, *Law and Lawyers*, i, 150; Thomson, *Choice of a Profession*, 99–100; Ball, *Student's Guide*, 58–60; Crispe, *Memories of a KC*, 98–102.
[130] *The Advocate*, 39–40; Ball, *Student's Guide*, 60.
[131] Sir H. Morris, *Back View* (1960), 117.
[132] Quoted in Sir T. Martin, *A Life of Lord Lyndhurst* (1884), 220.

generation—like Pemberton-Leigh, Brett, and Hastings—maintained that poverty was the best stimulus to success,[133] but the general advice was that a man should not venture to practise if he were poor.

Journalism

The bar knew all this perfectly well, but the character of the profession was held incompatible with supplementing their fees by other employment, and the need to be in chambers or in court when that elusive brief arrived precluded regular work.[134] Nevertheless in 1842 one barrister was found to be keeping a public house and another was in the confectionery trade.[135] Just one occupation was excepted from the general censure and became the staple of the briefless barrister—journalism, and its more respectable cousin, literature.

Jeaffreson (1867) probably exaggerated in claiming that 'three out of every five journalists attached to our chief London newspapers are Inns-of-Court men'[136] but they were certainly numerous and, by then, respectable. This had not always been so. When men like Spankie, Campbell, and James Stephen wrote for the newspapers in the first decade of the century they courted the disapproval of the more traditional members of the bar, for journalism was a dubious occupation.[137] But Lincoln's Inn had to withdraw a ban on those who had 'written for hire in the newspapers'[138] and the coming of the *Edinburgh* and other weighty reviews provided opportunities for more elevated writings of which the bar took full advantage. J. T. Coleridge was briefly editor of the *Quarterly* before he became a judge; Brougham poured forth his unstoppable learning in the *Edinburgh*, and when the *Saturday Review* started up in 1855 its recruits included J. F. Stephen, Henry Maine, Vernon Harcourt, and G. S. Venables; in 1865 Stephen and Maine migrated to the new *Pall Mall Gazette*, whose team also included the young Frederic Harrison.[139] Not all serial publications were so elevated in tone; Bracebridge Hemyng of the Middle Temple gave the world the vivid adventures of Jack Harkaway.[140] In fiction, Pendennis was as swiftly inveigled into the literary world as his creator had been, and Thackeray was one of many (John Buchan and Alfred Harmsworth

[133] *The Recollections of Lord Kingsdown*, ed. E. L. Pemberton (1868), 11; E. Graham, *Fifty Years of Famous Judges* (1930), 89–90; Hastings, *Autobiography*, 57.

[134] For an explicit assertion that the expense ensured a necessary union between property and education see (1843) 1 *LT* 42 (quoted in Cocks, *Foundations of the Modern Bar*, 70).

[135] Lewis, *Victorian Bar*, 42–3.

[136] Jeaffreson, *A Book About Lawyers*, i, 45.

[137] Polson, *Law and Lawyers*, i, 147.

[138] *Ibid.*, 147–8; *Lincoln's Inn Black Books*, iv, 117.

[139] *ODNB*, 12: 570; K. J. M. Smith, *James Fitzjames Stephen* (Cambridge, 1988), 38–40.

[140] E. S. Turner, *Boys Will Be Boys* (Penguin edn, 1976), 81–95.

were others) who were seduced from the bar.[141] For most, however, it was a temporary expedient and from the 1840s there were also at least three weekly legal newspapers as well as one or two scholarly periodicals.

Some, however, sought to use their position as a way of puffing their own career. In 'The Modern Way to Get On at the Bar' one writer boasted that 'the way which I choose, to get on is by paragraph puffs in the News...'. This practice, which often took the form of mutual boosting, was generally condemned but hard to eradicate.[142]

The importance of publicity to a young barrister's career was illustrated by the seriousness with which circuit messes took up complaints against *The Times* in the 1840s when it became inexplicably selective in naming the counsel appearing in cases on the Oxford circuit.[143] It was a foolish dispute, for the newspaper relied on court cases to fill its pages and it benefitted the bar to have reporting, even at a 'human interest' level, done by its members.[144] At least the Attorney-General confirmed that it was acceptable for barristers to write for the press, though the limits of acceptability were tested in 1908, when the Bar Council was divided on the practice of offering legal advice through a newspaper column.[145]

Books

In the first half of the nineteenth century a dictum appeared in various forms about the ways to get started at the bar. One version listed four: 'huggery', a miracle, quarter sessions, and writing a law book.[146]

In 1808 the young Thomas Denman told his father that he thought the market for law books was now saturated.[147] He was quite wrong, and if it became harder to find fresh subjects, or to rearrange existing ones, some writers still succeeded in establishing titles which passed through many editions; *Chitty on Contracts* is an obvious example. The less fastidious could improve their chances with fulsome dedications to leading judges and lawyers; much later Patrick Hastings unabashedly used this means to ingratiate himself with C. F. Gill.[148]

---

[141] *Pendennis*, Ch. 31, 'In which the printer's devil comes to the Inn'; Alexander, *Temple of the Nineties*, 57; E. Abinger, *Forty Years at the Bar* (1930), 16.

[142] Quoted, inter alia, in Polson, *Law and Lawyers*, ii, 119–21; Lewis, *Victorian Bar*, 39.

[143] The dispute can be followed in the legal press, e.g. (1845) 2 (s2) *LM* 421; 'The Newspapers and the Bar' (1845) 3 (s2) *LM* 165–87; (1846) 4 (s2) *LM* 218, 368; (1845) 9 *Jur.* 261.

[144] (1845/6) 3 *LR* 27–43. For law reporting, see below, Ch. V.

[145] Lewis, *Victorian Bar*, 45; (1907–8) 52 *Sol. J.* 484.

[146] Other versions include politics, on which see below, pp. 1057–8.

[147] Denman to his father, 26 July 1808; Sir J. Arnould, *A Memoir of Thomas, First Lord Denman*, 2 vols (1873), i, 169.

[148] [Collier], *Criticisms on the Bar*, 8; Hastings, *Autobiography*, 87.

The dominance of the junior bar in the book market is unsurprising. Absent a substantial body academic lawyers they alone had the time, the knowledge, and the access to a library which were needed to produce a book. Few were so precocious as Edward Sugden, who at 21 boldly aimed his *Vendors and Purchasers* at landowners, and few succeeded so well either.[149] An outpouring of statutes supplied plentiful opportunities and many offerings were mere scissors and paste jobs, but on new or under-explored subjects even they could have a decent sale: Sandbach and Cassels were self-depreciatory of theirs on Motoring Law and Hire Purchase respectively, but they served their purpose.[150] Success did not always go to the deserving. William Charley's book on the Judicature Acts was said to have been mostly the work of one Hughes, who died in a railway accident, yet it helped to gain Charley the post of Common Serjeant, while W. M. Best wrote 'perhaps the most scientific legal work of the present century', yet his practice never prospered.[151] Best's was one of the relatively few books that went into successive editions, thereby creating further opportunities once the original author was dead or too busy to revise it.[152] Thus William Barber gave Haldane Dart's *Vendors and Purchasers* to edit, while H. S. Theobald was even luckier: the publisher Stevens asked Farwell to write on wills and being too busy he suggested Theobald instead.[153]

The coming of law examinations made openings for a new sort of book, the student text, and Arthur Underhill seized the chance to write the first one on torts, to his considerable profit.[154] As the profession grew so did the number of books published; in 1853 the *Law Times* listed just 16 new books, but 83 in 1913, most by barristers. Some considered that authorship had become so commonplace that only a weighty treatise would bring a barrister to notice, but that might brand the writer as too theoretical.[155] Most preferred to attempt something modest which might bring in a few hundred pounds even if it did nothing for their reputation.

Quarter Sessions

The recommendation that fledgling barristers should ensure they went to quarter sessions was well grounded.[156] Because of the interaction of Assizes and quarter

---

[149] Atlay, *Victorian Chancellors*, ii, 3–4.

[150] J. B. Sandbach, *This Old Wig* [n.d.], 44–5; I. Adamson, *A Man of Quality: A Biography of Mr. Justice Cassels* (1964), 37.

[151] Purcell, *Forty Years at the Bar*, 230; (1869/70) 28 (s3) *LM & LR* 381.

[152] Vaughan Hawkins was eccentric in letting his expire rather than see it revised by another hand.

[153] D. Sommer, *Haldane of Cloan* (1960), 51; Theobald, *Remembrance of Things Past*, 79.

[154] A. Underhill, *Change and Decay* (1935), 74–5.

[155] R. J. Blackham, *Sir Ernest Wild KC* (1935), 38.

[156] Romilly, *Memoirs*, i, 92–4; Lemmings, *Professors of the Law*, 154–5.

sessions a man could choose only one county quarter sessions, but as many boroughs as he could fit in, though the key to getting any business was to attend each of them regularly.[157]

The intrusion of hungry barristers created ructions in places where the local attorneys had hitherto had the field to themselves, but the intruders' success was predictable given the judges' partiality for their own profession. In *R v. Justices of Denbighshire*[158] the Queen's Bench upheld a local bench in granting exclusive audience even where barristers had never established a foothold. A 'rule of four' (exclusive audience wherever the bar could muster at least four men) became fixed and by degrees the barristers' domain was extended to all but the least profitable sessions.[159]

Unfortunately for beginners the quarter sessions became less profitable once the new Poor Law drastically reduced the number of settlement cases. There was still abundant licensing business in the bigger boroughs but elsewhere it was mostly crime.[160] In Lancashire, where new industrial towns kept acquiring sessions of their own, the prospects were still good, but at Warwick George Harris had found just three rivals and no briefs which afforded the chance to impress the solicitors.[161] Furthermore, the junior bar suffered in places where the magistrates undertook prosecutions themselves and refused to fund counsel for prisoners, denying inexperienced counsel invaluable experience.[162]

Though a novice could embarrass himself even at sessions,[163] even less able practitioners like Liddell could handle most cases and Plowden found that if one persevered some briefs would eventually be forthcoming.[164] Still, local men often took all the best business, especially at the county sessions. Devon for instance had men like Sam Carter, a 'picturesque old savage' and Henry Clark, whose intimacy with the magistrates' clerks got him all the prosecutions.[165] Later on, as the

---

[157] *The Advocate*, 275–6.

[158] (1846) 15 LJ QB 335, discarding the dictum of Parke B. in *Collier* v. *Hicks* (1831) 2 B. & Ald. 663. Denman LCJ had thought they should enjoy pre-audience rather than exclusive audience: W. R. Dickenson, *Guide to the Quarter Sessions* (6th edn, by T. N. Talfourd, 1845), 152–3.

[159] (1907–8) 52 *Sol. J.* 166, 174, noted the last appearance of a solicitor at the Ripon Liberty quarter sessions.

[160] Polson, *Law and Lawyers*, i, 158; Thomson, *Choice of a Profession*, 123; 'Circuit Tramp' [J. A. Foote], *Pie-Powder* (1911), 49–54.

[161] Parry, *What the Judge Saw*, 95–6; G. Harris, *The Autobiography of George Harris* (1888), 113.

[162] See above, pp 932–3.

[163] Plowden, *Grain or Chaff?*, 142–3, tells of one who made a determined effort to introduce the prisoner's previous convictions.

[164] Ibid.; Liddell, *Notes From the Life of an Ordinary Mortal*, 137–42.

[165] [Foote], *Pie-Powder*, 49–54.

petty sessions acquired enlarged jurisdiction, the 20 or 30 barristers at quarter sessions might find fewer than a dozen prisoners.[166]

'Devilling'

Pre-Victorian prescriptions for getting started at the bar did not mention devilling, and although the term itself was familiar, it was usually applied only to the junior Treasury counsel who assisted the law officers. That was an official position with guaranteed remuneration and good prospects, whereas the essence of devilling as it came to be widely practised was informality. It was an arrangement between the brief holder and the 'devil' which might well be unknown to the client and the solicitor and whose terms, particularly whether there would be any payment, were a matter only for the two of them—and were usually dictated by the brief holder.[167]

It is precisely this informality which makes the incidence, terms and etiquette of devilling elusive. It seems to have grown with the explosion of KCs in the 1830s and with the concentration of lucrative business in leaders (including busy juniors) who routinely held more briefs than they could manage. The organization of Chancery, and the practice of splitting the fee, may have made it less prevalent there (though see the cases of Davey and Haldane, below) but among the big practitioners at common law and also in the criminal courts it became commonplace.[168]

The means through which devilling was obtained varied. An enterprising clerk such as Webster's might sniff out an opportunity; a pupil master like Haldane's might recommend him, and F. E. Smith used his own pupils.[169] Sometimes it arose from a man being in the right place and receiving a brief to hold or being asked to take a note. As noted above, Gorell Barnes won a place in Mathew's chambers and succeeded to most of his business when Mathew became a judge. Something similar befel Haldane after his introduction to Horace Davey, and at the criminal bar R. D. Muir devilled so successfully for Forrest Fulton that he assumed the latter's practice.[170] That was rare, however, and all three men were paid for their work, whereas gratuitous devilling was commoner, though this

---

[166] Ibid.; 'Sir Frank Lockwood—Some Notes by a Friend at the Common Law Bar' (1897–8) 23 (s4) LM & R 92–9.

[167] Alexander, After Court Hours, 29–36.

[168] 'Prospects in the Professions: The Solicitors' (1902) 13 (n. 5) Cornhill Mag., 635–50.

[169] Alverstone, Recollections of Bar and Bench, 8; Sommer, Haldane of Cloan, 53; Campbell, F.E. Smith, 58.

[170] Duman, English and Colonial Bars, 83–4; Sommer, Haldane of Cloan, 53; S. T. Felstead and Lady Muir, Sir Richard Muir (1927), 148.

may not originally have been the case.[171] No wonder some disliked the practice, regarding it as demeaning, but for the most part it was accepted as a fact of professional life.[172]

The role of the devil also varied. For the most part he was a 'research assistant',[173] reading and summarizing the brief, finding the cases, and checking the evidence. At the criminal bar, however, it seems that an overburdened Old Bailey leader would sometimes simply offload the brief onto his devil, giving him conduct of the trial.[174]

'Miracles'

The inclusion of the miracle in the prescription is an eloquent acknowledgment that while success at the bar had to be earned, the opportunity to earn it could not be guaranteed. As Crispe wrote: '[t]he day after your call you go to the empty desk, and, unless you have influence, you may so go for days, weeks, months and even years'.[175] Stories of the sudden, unexpected opportunity to make one's name by a single brilliant performance continued to emerge, albeit with warnings that it was not the usual route to success. More encouraging to the briefless were the tales of a first brief obtained by chance, as happened to Cairns[176] and to Buckley, who was briefed on the erroneous assumption that he was the son of a taxing master.[177] J. A. Rentoul was equally lucky in that a solicitor's clerk was impressed with his speech at a political rally.[178] But writers stressed that, while the deserving could not command an opportunity, these miracles happened only to the patient and diligent. 'Be always *en evidence*', wrote Henry Dickens,[179] and writer after writer urged an early and regular attendance at chambers followed by a day in court, where the opportunity might arise to take a note, which might lead a generous leader like Marshall Hall to mention your name to the judge, or to hold briefs.[180] These stories served a useful purpose. While accepting the role of luck (even Bethell said he was fortunate to have a name near the beginning of

---

[171] Alexander, *After Court Hours*, 29–36; Cocks, *Foundations of the Modern Bar*, 20.

[172] See the rebuttal of Plowden's criticism in Crispe, *Memories of a KC*, 210.

[173] Lemmings, *Professors of the Law*, 256, describing the Treasury devil.

[174] Biron, *Without Prejudice*, 101. Purcell, *Forty Years at the Criminal Bar*, 25, 28, noted that they were given all the hopeless cases.

[175] Crispe, *Memories of a KC*, 210–11.

[176] Atlay, *Victorian Chancellors*, ii, 294.

[177] Ball, *Lincoln's Inn*, 90–1.

[178] J. A. Rentoul, *Stray Thoughts and Memories* (1921), 112.

[179] Dickens, *Recollections*, 130.

[180] As happened to Morris: *Back View*, 114. A typical moral tale is given in Crispe, *Memories of a KC*, 211.

the alphabet[181]), they linked success to deserts, thereby squaring a particularly troublesome circle, and offered hope to the briefless.

'Huggery'

Huggery may be defined as 'to caress or court, especially in order to get favour or patronage'.[182] It was quite desirable to follow Crispe's suggestion and cultivate a wide and promiscuous acquaintance at the bar,[183] but any attempt to ingratiate oneself with an attorney or solicitor was deprecated. The circuits had rigid rules to make it difficult and offenders were sure to be visited with the full range of informal sanctions, as the hapless Dan Giles found when he turned up at York with a hatful of briefs obtained through recommendations from London solicitors of his acquaintance.[184] However, sanctions were not always effective and in London, and later in the cities with a local bar, it was practically impossible to police any but the most flagrant breaches. With an unpleasant twist of gratuitous snobbery, huggery was sometimes coupled with the sneering suggestion that one way forward was to marry a solicitor's ugly daughter, though this may have been heard less often once Halsbury (who had married a solicitor's daughter and was no oil painting himself) became Lord Chancellor.

The inclusion of huggery in the prescriptions for success indicates a rueful acceptance that for some beginners there was little alternative. Since solicitors had been given the role of gatekeeper to clients a newcomer's best chance of persuading them to employ him was through direct contacts or a connection with one or more of their major clients. It was all very well for an exceptional man like John Simon to insisted that it was not necessary,[185] and for Underhill and Parry to argue that it was not helpful for a young man to have demanding briefs bestowed upon him by well meaning friends; besides creating jealously in the circuit mess they risked a poor performance leading to loss of confidence by the tiro and the solicitor alike.[186] And certainly professional connections were no guarantee of success. Freshfields briefed Roundell Palmer as a favour to his uncle, and Haldane impressed a partner he met socially with his knowledge of wine; in each case further briefs followed, whereas Freshfields also briefed Dolly Liddell, but only once.[187]

---

[181] T. A. Nash, *The Life of Richard, Lord Westbury*, 2 vols (1888), ii, 62.

[182] *Shorter Oxford English Dictionary*.

[183] *Memories of a KC*, 208, 210–11.

[184] 'Recollections of a Deceased Welch Judge' (1845–6) 3 *LR* 1–14 at 3.

[185] Lord Simon, *In Retrospect* (1952), 47.

[186] Underhill, *Change and Decay*, 68–70; Parry, *What the Judge Saw*, 88.

[187] Selborne, *Memorials Part One, Family and Personal*, i, 246–7; Sommer, *Haldane of Cloan*, 51–2; Liddell, *Notes From the Life of an Ordinary Mortal*, 210.

Still, the desirability of a professional connection was a truth almost universally acknowledged, even if it led only [*sic*] to 'colonial attorney and solicitor generalships and appointments of a similar character'.[188] That is why the inns erected and defended barriers against solicitors wishing to transfer to the bar and maintained them for as long they could and why there were exaggerated estimates of the number and impact of solicitors' sons coming to the bar.[189] Relations of the lower branch were indeed disproportionately represented among the superior court judges,[190] and the careers of Palmer and Webster show that an early link with big business could be equally valuable.[191] In the provinces Robert Gifford rose so quickly because he was backed by Exeter's business community and Gerald Dodson's father's year as Norwich mayor ensured him some complimentary briefs from the local attorneys.[192] According to Bickersteth, there was also a period when the leading agency firms had strong northern connections and favoured barristers from the region.[193]

Sons of judges and famous leaders could trade on their name to get their start. Serjeant Parry's popularity certainly helped his son, as the names of Romilly, Erskine, and Law helped their less talented sons, and Witt retails the bar's bitter jest about the priorities at the beargarden: '[a]ny judge's son with a summons?'[194] The playing field was anything but level and a few openly objected that the rules against huggery only helped the already advantaged and the unscrupulous.[195] J. D. Coleridge shrank from seeking to muscle in on what he and his father both called 'the favour business' on the western circuit, which went overwhelmingly to the well connected,[196] but others could not afford to be so fastidious.

'Soup' and 'Dockers'

There were two substantial gaps in the wall erected between the barrister and the client, both in criminal proceedings. On the prosecution side there was 'soup', the name given to the system under which prosecution briefs at sessions were

[188] Polson, *Law and Lawyers*, i, 145.

[189] See below, pp. 1167–9.

[190] Duman, *English and Colonial Bars*, 91–3. But Hawkins denied that his family firm helped him at all: [E. Bowen Rowlands], *The Life in the Law of Sir Henry Hawkins* (1907), 12–13.

[191] Selborne, *Memorials Part One, Family and Personal*, i, 246–7; Alverstone, *Recollections of Bar and Bench*, 244. The less talented William Bovill profited from a connection with a big East End manufacturing concern and the patents it needed: (1873) 2 (n.s.) *LM & R* 1131.

[192] Hardcastle, *Life of Lord Campbell*, i, 294; G. Dodson, *Consider Your Verdict* (1967), 30–1.

[193] T. D. Hardy, *Memoirs of the R.H. Henry, Lord Langdale*, 2 vols (1852), i, 240.

[194] Witt, *Lifetime in the Law*, 38.

[195] Townsend, *Fourteen Eminent Judges*, ii, 244–5.

[196] E. H. Coleridge, *The Life and Correspondence of John Duke, Lord Coleridge*, 2 vols (1904), i, 181, 195.

prepared by a person employed by the county or borough and distributed by him among all counsel attending the sessions, usually in order of seniority.[197] The amounts were small—at the Old Bailey they ranged from one to three guineas depending on the number of witnesses—but worth having for the experience and the chance of publicity. Even Gorell Barnes could be found in the queue at Liverpool, and in Manchester, where the number of briefs was considerable, Edward Parry found them a very useful addition to his income.[198] Until the creation of a bar mess in 1891, soup was seen at its worst at the Old Bailey, where some elderly or incompetent practitioners, like the eccentric Langford, were wholly dependent upon it.[199] There was a waiting list to get on the rota and quarrels broke out over whose turn it was. Moreover, since the judges left the distribution to their clerks there was the suspicion of favouritism and touting for business.[200] The bar mess disgraced itself by blackballing an Indian barrister, who needed the Attorney-General's intervention to get him his soup ration.[201]

The equivalent to soup on the defence side was the 'in person' procedure, supplemented by the dock brief or 'docker'. A prisoner might, if he could find a guinea, plus a half crown for the barrister's clerk, choose counsel without the intervention of an attorney.[202] The benefit to a young counsel could far outweigh the modest fee; for example, the murder defence Gerald Dodson got in Norwich in 1903 won him priceless publicity.[203] Once again the Old Bailey was the centre of abuses. Regulars who established a reputation for giving their guineasworth, men like Purcell and Thorne Cole, made very worthwhile sums,[204] but the warders used to recommend favoured individuals and barristers' clerks indulged in touting for trade, at least one barrister being suspended for irregularities of this sort.[205]

Soon after 1900 Sir Richard Muir, as head of the Old Bailey bar mess, effectively put an end to the 'in person' and a new system for aiding impecunious defendants was introduced. This seems to have been subject to a similar abuse, with distribution frequently ending up in the hands of the head warder.[206] Apart

---

[197] 'Soup System—Prosecution by Magistrates' (1841) 26 *LM* 103–19.

[198] De Montmorency, *Lord Gorell*, 58; Parry, *What the Judge Saw*, 88.

[199] Williams, *Later Leaves*, 30. Bosanquet, *Oxford Circuit*, 64–5 describes similar men at the Staffordshire sessions.

[200] Morris, *Back View*, 118; T. Humphreys, *Criminal Days* (1946), 73–4.

[201] Humphreys, *Criminal Days*, 73–4; Dickens, *Recollections*, 161–2.

[202] Described in Williams, *Leaves of a Life*, i, 160 and Jay, *The Law*, 128–9. On occasion the money had to be 'earned' outside the court while the barrister waited.

[203] Dodson, *Consider Your Verdict*, 30.

[204] Ashley, *My Sixty Years in the Law*, 80–1.

[205] Felstead and Muir, *Sir Richard Muir*, 156–7.

[206] *Ibid.*

from those who intended to make a career in the criminal law, most new barristers abandoned the quest for soup and dockers as soon as they felt able, though Sandbach needed a hint from the Clerk of Assize that it was time he did so: presumably it did no good to a man's reputation.[207]

4. LIFE AT THE BAR

Earnings

Though there is little statistical information about barristers' incomes, it is clear from figures for the very end of the period and from the unanimous opinion of contemporaries throughout that the range of incomes far exceeded that in most other professions; in 1913/14 the top 10 per cent of barristers averaged £1820, the bottom quartile £155.[208] Since the latter hardly represented a living wage for anyone with pretensions to middle-class life, it may be assumed that it includes many who were just starting out and others who were not treating the profession as their sole or main source of income.

Some 60 years earlier Thomson, considering only the 500 or so men he felt made a living at the bar, reckoned a junior as likely to make between £500 and £1200 with a maximum of £2000.[209] It is unlikely that the late Georgian bar was as prosperous as that, though a few juniors like Scarlett and Abbott may have had unprecedented earnings.[210] Conveyancers and equity chambers counsel were said never to approach these levels.[211]

Most data concerns outstandingly successful men and suggests that their upward drift continued until the 1830s and resumed in the 1850s after a pause, but these trends are unlikely to hold good for the practising bar as a whole.[212] However, from 30 or so sources it is possible to extrapolate a tentative series of pathways. A few very able men began to make money almost immediately; Bethell and Clarke made 100 guineas in their first year and William Follett's meteoric rise from 300

---

[207] Sandbach, *This Old Wig*, 41.

[208] G. Routh, *Occupation and Pay in Great Britain, 1906–60* (Cambridge, 1965), 62–3; Duman, *English and Colonial Bars*, 143–53.

[209] *Choice of a Profession*, 95–7. But Jeaffreson reckoned that plenty of juniors made only £300–£400 per annum: *Book About Lawyers*, i, 269–71.

[210] Lemmings, *Professors of the Law*, 189–202. *The Gentleman's Magazine*, vol. 78 (1808), 408 claimed 50 out of some 600 men made above £1200; the rest made £300 plus, with 60 not covering their expenses.

[211] Pemberton-Leigh, quoted in 'The Masters' Offices' (1841) 25 *LM* 97–113 at 108–9; *SC on Official Salaries 1850*, q. 1621.

[212] Duman, *Judicial Bench*, 105–11. On a cautionary note, Bowen Rowlands claimed that barristers tended to exaggerate their earnings: [Bowen Rowlands], *Life in the Law of Sir Henry Hawkins*, 25.

guineas in his first year to 3000 in his fourth was regarded as unexampled, though later on Gordon Hewart bettered everyone with £1000.[213] More common was a slow start followed by a sudden acceleration at some point between three and seven years from call. This happened with Lindley, Haldane and Palmer, Russell and Barnes, and on a more modest scale with Dodson and Curtis Bennett.[214] The third path is a relatively smooth growth such as that experienced by Henry James and J. D. Coleridge.[215] How high a junior's earnings rose depended, inter alia, on whether and when he took silk. A few juniors who declined silk might be earning more than most leaders, in H. A. McCardie's case an unprecedented £20,000.[216]

Little is known about the make up of earnings, but E. F. Spence offers one useful breakdown: for two years between half and 60 per cent of his earnings came from interlocutories and cases for opinion as opposed to briefs for trial.[217] Whether this is typical there is no knowing at present.

Public Offices

In 1818 Crabb Robinson remarked on the number of offices reserved for a 'barrister of five years standing…while it is notorious that many such barristers are ill-qualified for any office'.[218] The bar did remarkably well in securing so many opportunities for its members and it was small wonder that purists like Denman grumbled that it was coming to be seen as a staging post to public offices.[219] Samuel Warren was criticized for degrading the noble spirit of the bar by pointing out the number and value of such posts, but William Ball's father was probably not the only one who was impressed with the possibilities they offered.[220]

Many positions were full-time appointments which meant abandoning the bar irrevocably, though a few colonial judges returned home to practise. However, there were also part-time positions offering modest rewards but raising the profile of the holder. For example, the only judicial post that eminent jurist (but unsuccessful

---

[213] Nash, *Lord Westbury*, i, 52; Clarke, *Story of My Life*, 87; 'Sir William Follett' (1845) 2 *LR* 436–50 at 450; Jackson, *The Chief*, 50.

[214] Sommer, *Haldane of Cloan*, 51; Selborne, *Memorials, Part One, Family and Personal*, i, 246–7; R. B. O'Brien, *The Life of Lord Russell of Killowen* (1901), 83; de Montmorency, *Lord Gorell*, 59–60; Dodson, *Consider Your Verdict*, 30–5; R. Wild and D. Curtis-Bennett, *'Curtis': The Life of Sir Henry Curtis-Bennett* (1937), 27–9.

[215] R. Askwith, *Lord James of Hereford* (1930), 16; Coleridge, *Life and Correspondence of Lord Coleridge*, i, passim.

[216] Pollock, *Mr. Justice McCardie*, 19.

[217] *Bar and Buskin*, 146–7.

[218] *Diary etc.*, i, 322.

[219] To J. T. Coleridge, 1847, Arnould, *Lord Denman*, ii, 228.

[220] 'Warren's *Law Studies*' (1845–6) 3 *LR* 67–84 at 68–72. Cf. Thomson, *Choice of a Profession*, 95; Ball, *Lincoln's Inn*, 81. Lists are in e.g. Durran, *The Lawyer*, and 'Prospects in the Professions', 480–1.

barrister) F. M. Pollock ever filled was the near-sinecure Admiralty judge of the Cinque Ports.[221] It was usually the well connected who got such pickings: Adolphus Liddell, of an aristocratic family and brother of a permanent secretary, was secretary to three royal commissions, an examiner to the Supreme Court, a revising barrister, counsel to the mint at Durham and an examiner for the inns of court.[222]

The three most common part-time employments were as recorders, bankruptcy commissioners, and revising barristers. Until the Municipal Corporations Act 1835 the boroughs appointed their own recorders, and still exerted influence after the Home Secretary acquired the patronage.[223] Where there was much criminal business they usually wanted a big name, preferably with local connections, but a sleepy hollow like Much Wenlock provided Plowden with barely 10 days' work in 10 years. The salary was proportionately low, but it served to distinguish him from the ruck.[224]

Until Brougham's reforms of the bankruptcy courts there were also more than 70 part-time commissioners appointed by the Lord Chancellor. At £300 per annum these posts were worth having, though they demanded quite a lot of time, and were used by Eldon to reward political services and oblige friends. Even after 1831 there were still commissioners in the provinces.[225]

Revising barristers were created by the 1832 Reform Act to determine election petitions and might have been expressly made as outdoor relief for the junior bar. Even when a qualification was imposed it was a mere three years from call, and since the Attorney-General had told the Commons that these positions were ideal for barristers without work it is hardly surprising to find the judges (the senior judge on each circuit had the patronage) accused of putting the interests of the profession, especially their own connections, before that of the public.[226] Charges of nepotism may not be fully substantiated, but the 1871 list includes a Channell, a Vaughan Williams, a Coleridge, and a Lushington among the 56 names, 16 with less than seven years' standing. Furthermore, at least one Lord Chief Justice, who nominated to London, ensured that the Chancery bar got its fair share even though its practitioners were ill-suited to handle the business.[227] Faced with the number of hungry mouths at the circuit mess the more fastidious

---

[221] M. De Wolfe (ed.), *The Holmes-Pollock Letters*, 2 vols (2nd edn, Cambridge, Mass., 1961), i, 214.

[222] Liddell, *Notes From the Life of an Ordinary Mortal*, 223.

[223] Duman, *English and Colonial Bars*, 97–8. Some early appointments were heavily politicized: R. and F. Davenport-Hill, *A Memoir of Matthew Davenport-Hill, Recorder of Birmingham* (1878), 148.

[224] *Grain or Chaff?*, 174–5. Ellis Hume-Williams described Bury St. Edmunds as practically a sinecure at £40 per annum: *The World, The House and The Bar* (1930), 41, and see Bosanquet, *Oxford Circuit*, 83–8.

[225] Duman, *English and Colonial Bars*, 97–8; Jay, *The Law*, 9–12.

[226] Duman, *English and Colonial Bars*, 97. By 1885 there were no fewer than 123.

[227] *Ibid.*; (1888/9) 33 *Sol. J.* 681.

judges would have agreed with what Denman wrote in 1847: 'I heartily wish the judges were deprived of all patronage of this kind. Towards the end of the Assizes the looks of expectation and disappointment are harrowing.'[228] That shows how much these casual titbits meant to the strugglers.[229]

Another useful position was deputy county court judge. Though creating no expectation of succeeding to the judge's place, it offered the chance to acquire judicial experience and make a name. Indeed some judges had regular deputies and until the 1880s controls on suitability were weak and judges often chose the needy rather than the capable.[230] Prosecuting counsel for the mint and, especially, the post office were also sought after posts, existing for each circuit as well as for the Central Criminal Court. W. F. Pollock, counsel for the mint on the northern circuit in 1841, and Chartres Biron, a post office prosecutor at a later date, found they yielded a good crop of cases.[231]

Besides positions at home, call to the bar made a man eligible for most judicial posts in the colonies. He might emigrate, set up as a barrister in the colony of choice and come in time to a judgeship;[232] one unfortunate example is John Cook, an undistinguished Old Bailey practitioner who emigrated to Trinidad, became a judge, and was sacked for drunkenness.[233] The alternative was to apply direct for a judicial post. Indian judgeships were by far the best paid, and after 1861 the chief justiceships were reserved for barristers, as were at least one-third of the seats on the High Court benches. Nevertheless, it was usually difficult to find men of suitable calibre; the Indian bench was seen throughout the period as a refuge for comparative failures.[234]

As the nineteenth century progressed, the 'white' settler colonies offered a more attractive environment but the professional prospects of an English barrister without connections diminished, for with the establishment of self-government judicial posts tended increasingly to be given to prominent local lawyers.[235] In Crown colonies the Colonial Secretary appointed judges. He was besieged by applicants, many with political connections, and lacked any knowledge of most of them. Some choices were strongly criticized, especially around the middle of the century. Modest salaries, unhealthy climates, and low prestige deterred most

---

[228] Arnould, *Lord Denman*, ii, 228.

[229] Hawkins had 60 or 70 applications for a single one: (1885) 33 *Sol. J.* 639.

[230] P. Polden, 'Judicial Independence and Executive Responsibilities, Part One' (1996) 25 *Anglo-Am. Law Rev.* 1–38 at 20–1.

[231] Pollock, *Personal Reminiscences*, i, 171; Biron, *Without Prejudice*, 222.

[232] Duman, *English and Colonial Bars*, 122. [Foote], *Pie-Powder*, 30–1 gives some names.

[233] Purcell, *Forty Years at the Criminal Bar*, 35–6; P. Polden, 'Doctor in Trouble: *Gorrie* v. *Anderson* and the Extension of Judicial Immunity From Suit' (2001) 22 *JLH* 37–68 at 43–7.

[234] Duman, *English and Colonial Bars*, 130–7.

[235] 'Prospects in the Professions', 41.

successful men and in the more desirable colonies there were plenty of local candidates with pretensions. However, more than half of the colonial chief justices in the last third of the century were taken from the English bar and by then it was probably easier to find men in good practice.[236]

Specialization[237]

Some writers noted an increasing trend towards specialization towards the end of the nineteenth century,[238] and certainly the Judicature Acts had done nothing to fuse the common law and equity bars; only a few—Giffard, Moulton, and Buckmaster among them—bestrode that divide.[239] Distinctive bars had also emerged out of the destruction of Doctors' Commons, both in Admiralty and (rather larger and very self-protective) in divorce. There was a semi-distinct patent bar and a wholly separate parliamentary bar.

Within the generous width of the common law bar, which was much the largest, there had long been specialists and new specialisms arose, such as the motoring cases which gave Curtis Bennett such a good living and in an earlier generation the railway cases from which Webster had profited.[240] West, the Manchester Recorder, was one of several who had been regularly in settlement cases and first Day and later Darling had been fashionable silks in breach of promise cases.[241]

The Common Law Bar

The career trajectories and life experiences of the common law bar were so diverse as almost to defy generalizations. It is possible to outline a pattern for the successful (essentially those who became KCs or reached the judicial bench), but they are necessarily untypical and there are too few individual studies of the

---

[236] Duman, *English and Colonial Bars*, 121–30.

[237] For the bar at the Central Criminal Court, see above, 641–2, 969–70.

[238] Biron, *Without Prejudice*, 90, Ashton, *As I Went On My Way*, 172.

[239] A. Wilson Fox, *The Earl of Halsbury* (1929), 46; H. F. Moulton, *The Life of Lord Moulton* (1932), 37; Alexander, *Temple of the Nineties*, 117.

[240] Wild and Curtis-Bennett, *Curtis*, 29; Lord Alverstone, *Recollections of Bar and Bench*, 34–46. Lopes gained a reputation for 'nervous shock' cases (G. Pitt-Lewis, 'Obituary: The R.H. Lord Lopes' (1898–9) 25 (s5) *LM* 311–37), while Lindley's performance in *Lumley* v. *Gye* made him the favourite counsel of the theatrical community: *Autobiography*, 60.

[241] Parry, *My Own Way*, 146; Day, *Sir John Day*, 94–6; D. Walker-Smith, *A Life of Lord Darling* (1938), 78.

rank and file, men like Thomas Blofield, to make more than a very sketchy out-line possible.[242]

With the recovery of business, especially in the King's Bench, in the early nine-teenth century the outlook for the bar was more promising, though Campbell's *Life* gives a graphic picture of how competitive and overcrowded it felt even then.[243] The noble oratory of Erskine was held up as the ideal[244] but the reality was that most trials were very short[245] and most of the successful men, even Scarlett and J. F. Pollock, were not orators but skilful conversational persuaders of juries or expert marshallers of fact and law.[246] Sir James Mackintosh, renowned for his oratory, was nonetheless considered a poor advocate.[247] At a less elevated level bluster and browbeating were the order of the day.[248] Much of the work of the junior bar was in motions of course and minor interlocutory matters, which had enjoyed a steady growth, perhaps as a means of nurturing what business there was during the prolonged slump in litigation.[249]

The reforms of the 1830s, while they preserved and extended the intricacies of special pleading, attempted to reduce this sort of work and the bar was made more uneasy at the threat of local courts removing business from Westminster Hall and the Assizes. The materialization of this threat in 1846 was especially demoralizing as it coincided with a great expansion of the bar, and this combina-tion of increased numbers pressing upon diminished opportunities put the bar under great strain. Its ideology was essentially individualistic but competition had been restrained and softened by its geographical compactness and the col-legiate influences of inns and circuit messes.[250]

At an ideological level the bar was now threatened with a crisis of identity posed by the new intellectual climate in which traditional justifications for the bar's role and practices were no longer readily accepted and on a practical level by the way in which the self-imposed code of etiquette seemed almost wilfully to

---

[242] Duman, *English and Colonial Bars*, 105–13; R. Cocks, 'Dignity and Emoluments' (1978) 8 *Kingston Law Rev.* 37–48.

[243] Vol. i, 60–276.

[244] B. W. Kelly, *Famous Advocates and their Speeches* (1921). The bar erected a statue to him by subscription: Jay, *The Law*, 156.

[245] According to Hardy, *Lord Langdale*, ii, 52, few trials at common law went into a second day.

[246] See Collier's critical account, *Criticisms on the Bar*, and Polson, 'Advocates and Advocacy', in *Law and Lawyers*, i, 162–221.

[247] 'Recollections of Sir James Mackintosh' (1832) 8 *LM* 160–73 at 170.

[248] [Collier], *Criticisms on the Bar*, 109–21; J. Grant, *The Bench and the Bar*, 2 vols (1837), ii, 201 *et seq.*

[249] 'The Bar' (1844) 31 *LM* 1–26 at 25–6.

[250] Cocks, *Foundations of the Modern Bar*, 34–82. M. Burrage, *The Revolution and the Making of the Contemporary Legal Profession* (Oxford, 2006), Ch. 10 argues rather unpersuasively that the threat was not especially serious.

deny juniors the chances they needed. But neither attempts to protect their interests by blatant trade union practices such as a complete two-counsel rule nor the attempt of the C. R. Kennedy-led rebels to destroy the concordat between barristers and solicitors by restoring the right of direct client access was successful.[251]

In the 1850s, after further reforms to the practice and procedure of the superior courts had altered the role of counsel, Thomson described the usual tasks of a common law junior as examining witnesses, raising objections, and in smaller cases addressing the jury.[252] Increasingly in the more substantial cases he would be acting in support of a QC and although some silks, such as Day and Huddleston, were singled out for criticism for their relentless hoovering up of even small briefs,[253] the proliferation of silks and the establishment of the two-counsel rule did ensure work for juniors. Furthermore, according to Webster, there was a profitable period when commercial clients seemed disposed to be relatively eager to fight for their rights, leading to an expansion of business.[254] At a less glamorous level, barristers also began to appear more frequently in the despised county courts.[255] These developments presumably went some way to make good the lost functions.

A second crisis appeared to have arrived in the late 1860s. Again there was received to be a great influx of young men, while the collapse of Overend Gurney marked a sharp downturn in commercial litigation. Indeed businessmen began to press hard for tribunals of commerce which would severely limit the role of lawyers,[256] while the Judicature Commission posed a serious threat to dismantle the 'great central bar of England' and create a network of regional justice in its place.

Fortunately for the bar, the threatening clouds quickly passed away; indeed the Judicature Acts created something of a bonanza for them in the shape of endless opportunities for applications in chambers which exhausted Tom Chitty and practically overwhelmed J. C. Mathew.[257] Following belated attempts to curb this feast in 1883, Lord Halsbury proved more indulgent than Selborne or Cairns and the creeping expansion of profitable interlocutory business and the lengthening of trials soon resumed. At the trial stage, Hollams claimed that the role of the junior had become less important, that they had formerly argued special

[251] Some of the less scrupulous, like R. M. Kerr, quietly resorted to undercutting the minimum fee of one guinea: G. Pitt-Lewis, *Commissioner Kerr, an Individuality* (1903), 48.

[252] Thomson, *Choice of a Profession*, 119–20.

[253] Clarke, *Story of My Life*, 79–86.

[254] Lord Alverstone, *Reminiscences of Bar and Bench*, 20–1.

[255] Polden, *History of the County Court*, 67.

[256] Cocks, *Foundations of the Modern Bar*, 20, and see above pp. 773–6.

[257] Alexander, *After Court Hours*, 9–13; de Montmorency, *Lord Gorell*, 50–4.

verdicts and pleaded demurrers, whereas they had become very much subordinate to the leader.[258] There were fewer juries too, which hastened the demise of the more florid style of eloquence; Digby Seymour was said to have been one of the last of the breed outside the Old Bailey.[259] By the end of the century it was even suggested that there was a prejudice against eloquent speakers as being unlikely to be good lawyers.[260]

Over the century observers claimed to have seen a gradual improvement in manners at the bar.[261] There was no shortage of snobbery[262] and anti-semitism,[263] and juniors still suffered arrogant or condescending treatment at the hands of some of their seniors, but the days when Bethell had provoked Neate to assault him in court and the bar had sent Adolphus and Andrews to Coventry for fighting with umbrellas were long over.[264] Danckwerts was celebrated for his rudeness to everyone but he was the exception; more often it was cooperation that was remarked rather than conflict. This extended to witnesses, who were no longer browbeaten unmercifully.[265]

The bar was still overcrowded but the earnings of the more successful juniors were borne aloft on the two-thirds rule as the leaders' fees soared. Circuit business may have fallen off but the King's Bench was unable to cope, not so much with the volume of cases as with their greater elaboration. For the juniors who did succeed the pickings were good.[266]

The Chancery Bar

Lord Eldon had seen the regular Chancery bar expand from 12–15 when he started out to 50–60 by the 1820s. It included a dozen or so KCs, two sets of new creations in the 1810s having broken a log-jam in the court and created opportunities for the leading juniors like Pemberton-Leigh.[267] Business grew steadily despite all the bad publicity and new courts were created or expanded.[268]

---

[258] Sir J. Hollams, *Jottings of an Old Solicitor* (1906), 128–9.

[259] [Foote], *Pie-Powder*, 82–3.

[260] 'E' [Bowen Rowlands], 'Her Majesty's Judges' (1896) 11 *Strand Mag.* 551.

[261] e.g. Witt, *Life in the Law*, 42–4.

[262] See e.g. Serjeant Parry's crushing retort to the supercilious barrister who sneered at Jessel's dropped aitches: Manson, *Builders of our Law*, 226.

[263] See e.g. Jay, *The Law*, 23–4; Abinger, *Forty Years at the Bar*, 8.

[264] Ashton, *As I Went on My Way*, 25; Jay, *The Law*, 289.

[265] Pearson, *Memories of a KC's Clerk*, 155; Strahan, *Bench and Bar*, 73–6.

[266] Alexander, *Temple of the Nineties*, 148, describes some of them.

[267] Campbell, *Lives of the Lord Chancellors* (1847), vii, 51; (1838) 20 *LM* 350; Pemberton, *Lord Kingsdown's Reminiscences*, 15.

[268] See above, Pt 3, Ch. IV.

The Chancery bar became increasingly introverted. They no longer went circuit and the most successful had to abandon practice in other courts.[269] There were men who seldom or never appeared in court, conveyancers like Charles Butler, Lewis Duval, and Richard Preston, increasingly a bar within a bar; for as Edward Sugden found, it was becoming ever more difficult to combine a thriving chamber practice with advocacy.[270]

Sugden and others gained Chancery leaders an unenviable reputation for snappishness and discourtesy to juniors which Bethell carried to extremes.[271] At times in the 1830s and 1840s there were also acrimonious scenes between leaders or with a judge. The leaders had sensibly met criticism that they dodged from court to court and were unable effectively to manage their loads by confining their practice to one of the courts, a process formalized in 1854 but practically universal for at least a decade before.[272] In the vice-chancellors' courts presided over by Shadwell and Malins in particular a single counsel might be utterly dominant, presenting regular opponents with an unenviable task.[273]

The luxuriant nature of Chancery proceedings made plenty of work through the endless motions of course and petitions and as recommended by the Chancery Commission in 1826, each counsel was limited to two motions at a time.[274] The role of the junior was different from his common law counterpart, for in Chancery he followed the leader(s)and summed up the evidence; he also drew the pleadings.[275] Observers were struck by the prolixity and repetitiousness of the arguments, which impatient judges like Langdale and Romilly were unable to curb.[276] Palmer, who began his career at that time, later remarked that at no time had the two bars seemed so widely separated. If Chancery men seldom achieved the public celebrity of their counterparts in Westminster Hall, he reckoned that they made more money, and if they aspired to the bench they were less at the mercy of politics and the Lord Chancellor's whims.[277]

---

[269] Hardy, Lord Langdale, i, 370; W. R. W. Stephens, A Memoir of the R.H. William Page Wood, Baron Hatherley, 2 vols (1883), i, 73.

[270] Atlay, Victorian Chancellors, ii, 5–6. For the conveyancers see Anderson, Lawyers and the Making of English Land Law, 6.

[271] Atlay, Victorian Chancellors, ii, 19; Nash, Lord Westbury, i, 74–7.

[272] SC on Official Salaries 1850, Sugden, q. 2147; Sir J. Rolt, The Memoirs of Sir John Rolt (1939), 115.

[273] See above, p. 991.

[274] Report 1826, proposition 139.

[275] J. R. V. Marchant, The Barrister at Law (1905), 108; Selborne, Memorials Part One, Family and Personal, i, 21.

[276] Hardy, Lord Langdale, ii, 57. Eldon had indulged them: Campbell, Lives of the Lord Chancellors, vii, 621–3.

[277] Selborne, Memorials, Family and Personal, i, 371. Thomson agreed: Choice of a Profession, 124.

The procedural reforms of the 1850s were felt to have harmed the junior bar,[278] just as conveyancing reforms later eroded the position of the conveyancers, but there was enough profitable work for specialists, even recondite ones like Charles Elton;[279] indeed the leading conveyancers like Joshua Williams had now an opening as counsel to the court. They also had their own club, and jocularly styled themselves, 'the forty thieves'.[280] Talk of fusion and the encroachments of the common law courts made possible by new statutory powers alarmed the Chancery bar and they were sufficiently cohesive to make a collective representation to ensure their interests were not disregarded in the discussions on the Judicature Bill.[281]

Although the Chancery division enjoyed a burst of popularity with suitors, it did not last and an investigating committee at Lincoln's Inn in 1891 was gloomy about future prospects.[282] The gloom proved ill-founded, however. Though the circuits repelled attempts by the Chancery juniors to sidestep the rules on special retainers, common law interlopers seldom came into Chancery and judges like Kekewich and Joyce made their dislike of them clear.[283] Its popularity may have been affected by the relative fewness of judicial posts[284] but Lord Chancellors, especially those from an equity background, had always done their best to ensure Chancery men their share of spoils as county court judges and revising barristers,[285] not always with happy results since they remained relatively unfamiliar with juries and unskilled in the art of examination. It was still a comparatively small world and a very distinctive one. One common law barrister sketched his Chancery rivals thus: 'as a rule Chancery counsel are denoted by a straggling beard, baggy trousers and a stutter'; he asserted that their jokes were vulgar and that they were combative and assertive; they were an uninteresting race, who often belonged to musical societies and some of them fished. In all 'they are a thing apart from the Common Law Bar, a society within themselves'.[286] This was no doubt a caricature which the Chancery bar would have rejected with some asperity, but there clearly was a difference, as Edward Parry affirmed in less coarse terms.[287]

---

[278] As Pemberton-Leigh had predicted: *SC on Official Salaries 1850*, q. 2188.

[279] Ashton, *As I Went On My Way*, 88.

[280] Underhill, *Change and Decay*, 102–3; J. S. Vaizey, *The Institute* (?1907).

[281] P. Polden, 'Mingling the Waters: Personalities, Politics and the Making of the SCJ' (2002) 61 *CLJ* 575–611 at 576–82.

[282] See below, p. 1086.

[283] Bosanquet, *Oxford Circuit*, 70; Ball, *Lincoln's Inn*, 208.

[284] Strahan, *Bench and Bar*, 251.

[285] See above, pp. 996–7, 1045–6.

[286] [Bowen Rowlands], 'Her Majesty's Judges', 551 *et seq.*

[287] Parry, *What the Judge Saw*, 150–1. See also Alexander, *Temple of the Nineties*, 184–95 and 'Lounger in the Courts', *Pen and Ink Sketches in Chancery* (c. 1872).

The Parliamentary Bar

Parliamentary business, the semi-judicialized stages in private bill procedure, was lucrative, though the leading practitioners in the 1820s—Warren and Harrison,—were not highly regarded.[288] A drawback to the parliamentary bar for ambitious lawyers was that convention forbade MPs to participate, so in terms of a legal/political career it was a dead end.[289] Nevertheless, it became immensely profitable in the 'the age of equipment',[290] for which the private or local Act was the principal vehicle. Above all, the 1840s was the decade of railway mania. With huge sums at stake and bitter in-fighting between competing promoters *inter se*, and with landowners, parliamentary agents and their clients needed the best men. It was a highly specialized practice and the specialists could name their price.[291]

The response was embarrassing to the profession. Men grabbed all the briefs that came their way without any reasonable expectation that they would be able to attend the hearing; they raised their fees beyond anything seen before, and imposed a restrictive practice which even the bar could not bring itself to defend—a minimum fee which effectively prevented outsiders from breaking into the magic circle, or the 'golden gallery' as it became known.[292] They plundered the railway promoters and there was no limit to their exactions set by the courts.

At the head of these buccaneers was John Austin's more worldly brother Charles, whose career ridiculed the noble ideals of the bar. In 1834 he refused to become Solicitor-General and scorned any aspirations to the bench. Instead he piled up sums not seen again until the next century—40,000 guineas in a single year at the height of the mania, or so it was rumoured. At 49 he retired exhausted to an estate in Suffolk to live the life of a gentleman, and a wag chalked upon his deserted chambers 'Gone to California'.[293] His successor as leader of this now distinct bar, Scott Hope, could not match this treasure, but his income still surpassed his more celebrated and probably abler peers in Westminster Hall and Lincoln's Inn.[294] Inevitably there was public criticism, and the defences would have been more persuasive had the parliamentary bar not sought to erect a wall around itself.

[288] [Collier], *Criticisms on the Bar*, 282–6.

[289] Stephens, *Baron Hatherley*, i, 62–5.

[290] Walter Eliot, quoted in Lord MacMillan, *A Man of Law's Tale* (1952), 72.

[291] R. W. Kostal, *Law and English Railway Capitalism 1825–1875* (Oxford, 1994), 116–23.

[292] Ibid.; Alverstone, *Recollections of Bar and Bench*, 47; Strahan, *Bench and Bar*, 254, and see *SC on Private Bill Legislation*, PP 1863 (385), viii.

[293] Kostal, *Law and English Railway Capitalism*, 123–4. For a sympathetic portrait see L. A. Tollemache, 'Charles Austin' (1875) 17 *Fortnightly Rev.* 321–38.

[294] Kostal, *Law and English Railway Capitalism*, 124.

The golden age passed but there were still rich pickings to be had. Balfour
Browne, the waspish Scot who wrote the best account, left a handsome fortune
and despite his assertion that it was no longer profitable[295] the failure of the referees' court and attempts at reducing costs in the 1860s and 1870s ensured that
a good living was still to be made.[296] Geographically separated, mostly in chambers near the Houses of Parliament, they were unfamiliar even to some of the
bar and unusual in regularly accommodating members of the Scottish and Irish
bars.[297] The parliamentary bar was disparaged in some quarters, for the technique of advocacy necessarily differed markedly from the courts and the rules of
evidence were not adhered to,[298] but it had able practitioners and pungent characters–the acrid Grimthorpe, the elephantine Sam Pope, and the poet and poseur
E. H. Pember among them.[299] It was always small and its leaders never abandoned
their addiction to multiple briefs, justified in some measure by the exigencies of
the parliamentary timetable.[300] With the decline of private bills its palmy days
were ending by 1914, and it was slowly metamorphosing into its sort of successor,
the planning bar.[301]

5. THE INNER BAR

The Serjeants

The serjeants-at-law occupied a peculiar position. Though drawn from the ranks
of barristers they left the bar upon joining the order of the coif, quitting their
inn and usually joining Serjeants Inn.[302] They possessed some of the attributes
of officers of the court—a life tenure and the right to sue by attachment of privilege—but not others—no Crown emoluments, no assigned place in court; they
probably held, through the terms of their writ, 'not only a degree but an estate'
and there was uncertainty about their precedence.[303]

---

[295] J. H. Balfour Browne, *Forty Years at the Bar* (1916), 149–54; MacMillan, *Man of Law's Tale*, 72.
[296] e.g. by Edward Chandos Leigh, later counsel to the Speaker: *Bar, Bat and Bit* (1913), 146–9.
[297] Browne, *Forty Years at the Bar*, 12–16; Alexander, *Temple of the Nineties*, 106–18; MacMillan,
Man of Law's Tale, 51–76.
[298] 'The easiest and most lucrative branch of the profession', according to J. B. Atlay, quoted in
MacMillan, *Man of Law's Tale* at 53, and see MacMillan's defence at 57–60. J. W. S. Armstrong found
it too boring to stay with: *Yesterday*, 62.
[299] Browne, *Forty Years at the Bar*, 50–71.
[300] Kostal, *Law and English Railway Capitalism*, 119.
[301] MacMillan, *Man of Law's Tale*, 72.
[302] J. H. Baker, *The Serjeants at Law* (Selden Society, supp. series, 1984), vii, 128, instancing Sir
R. Collier, Lord Monkswell, as one who did not.
[303] *Ibid.*, 45–9, quoting Sir John Fortescue, *De Laudibus...*

Serjeants enjoyed two valuable monopolies. From their ranks alone were drawn the judges of the courts of common law and in the court of Common Pleas they enjoyed an exclusive right to audience. But their monopoly of judicial posts was effectively abolished by the simple expedient of making any designated judge a serjeant immediately before his appointment, and the monopoly of audience was less covetable in a court which had lost most of its business.[304]

Just as the King's Counsel formed a 'bar within a bar', so did the 'King's Serjeants', a rank valued not for the £40 per annum salary but for conferring precedence in all courts not only over other serjeants senior in call but over King's Counsel too.[305] The most senior pair, the King's Ancient Serjeants, even had precedence over the law officers of the Crown.[306]

It was costly to become a serjeant—£350 from 1817[307]—and it was becoming doubtful whether the investment represented value for money. One major blight on the serjeants was the remorseless rise of their upstart competitors the King's Counsel. Although they were being made in greater numbers than serjeants, the criteria were more stringent, for anyone with a decent practice (and some whose practice was in decline) might take the coif for the asking.[308] Their reasons varied. Unlike a KC, a serjeant might practise at sessions without a licence to plead against the Crown;[309] he had priority over juniors on circuit, and might take out a licence as a special pleader, as was not uncommon.[310] The quality of the serjeants was generally disparaged and some evidently shared this estimation of their own talents and prospects, since they took lesser judicial and government positions at home (Sellon became a police magistrate, Palmer a commissioner for the relief of insolvent debtors[311]) or overseas (Rosset and Russell were chief justices of Bengal).[312]

King's Serjeants were more eminent, being made only when it was necessary to keep up the number of leaders in the Common Pleas.[313] The order received a much needed boost to its prestige when W. D. Best and J. S. Copley were made judges,[314] but while Copley would do his best to defend the serjeants' interests, Shepherd's refusal to resign as King's Ancient Serjeant when made Solicitor-General in 1813 obliged the government to give both law officers precedence over the King's Ancient Serjeants.[315]

---

[304] Ibid., 113–14.   [305] Ibid., 59–60.   [306] Ibid., 60–1.   [307] Ibid., 106.

[308] J. P. Collier wrote in 1819 that applications for serjeant were being scrutinized like those for KC, but he had rapidly to retract: Criticisms on the Bar, 235, 240.

[309] Chandos Leigh, Bar, Bat and Bit, 106.

[310] Baker, Serjeants at Law, 117.

[311] Ibid.   [312] Ibid.   [313] Ibid., 116.

[314] Best became Chief Justice of the Common Pleas in 1824, Copley was successively Master of the Rolls (1827), Lord Chancellor, and Chief Baron.

[315] Baker, Serjeants at Law, 115.

The future of the serjeants looked bleak when Brougham attacked their monopoly in 1828 and Peel referred it to the Common Law Commissioners,[316] but things took an unexpected turn for the better when Lyndhurst became Lord Chancellor and applied to two Tory serjeants an expedient already common with the bar, the grant of a patent of precedence. This avoided giving unwarranted precedence (such as a King's Serjeant had) while protecting the holder from being overtaken by new KCs.[317] Moreover, the Common Law Commissioners proved unexpectedly tender to the serjeants, recommending that the Common Pleas monopoly should be preserved. They were impressed by the Exchequer and Chancery solution to the problem of 'double booked' counsel then beginning to beset the King's Bench, whereby KCs confined themselves wholly or largely to a single court, and felt that a similar result was obtained by the serjeants' monopoly. They did, however, recommend that a counsel who had been engaged at *nisi prius* should be allowed to move for a new trial, obviating the need to employ a serjeant just for that purpose.[318]

This was an outcome more satisfactory to the serjeants than law reformers.[319] As Lord Chancellor, Brougham was determined to open up the Common Pleas, encouraging suitors to relieve pressure on the King's Bench, and in 1834 he resorted to bold steps. A warrant under the sign manual ordered Tindal CJ to admit all barristers to plead in his court. Unusually, on what amounted to a deprivation of property rights there was to be no financial compensation, but in exchange all serjeants who did not already have precedence over KCs were given precedence in all courts next after the most junior of the existing KCs.[320]

The move neither produced the hoped-for increase in business nor persuaded the solicitors who did resort to Common Pleas to make extensive use of the bar rather than the serjeants.[321] A challenge was puzzlingly slow in coming, and followed the death of William IV, which created uncertainty as to the precedence conferred by the warrant. It was orchestrated by the five senior serjeants who had not gained from the new arrangement[322] and who presumably hoped that the Whig ministry would not make room in its programme for a bill and that Lyndhurst would prevent the Tories from doing so.

The *Serjeants' Case* succeeded in turning the clock back. The verdict was a triumph for James Manning's exhaustive historical researches, and for Thomas

[316] *Ibid.*, 118.

[317] In Spankie's case it was probably a consolation prize for being passed over for the bench: *ODNB*, 51: 745.

[318] *First Report 1829*, 24–5.

[319] e.g. (1829) 2 *LM* 151–60.

[320] Baker, *Serjeants at Law*, 118.

[321] *Ibid.*, 119.

[322] Wilde, Taddy, Bompas, Spankie, and Atcherley.

Wilde, whose narrow-minded tenacity was perfectly suited to argue a case of this sort.[323] Tindal, who evidently approved of the verdict, gave it effect at the start of the session 1839–40 and five new serjeants, mostly of better calibre than of late, were soon coifed.[324] With Lyndhurst back on the Woolsack in 1841 everything was snug. The success, however, was illusory. Apart from the vulnerability of the monopoly to objections on 'free trade' grounds, the Common Pleas remained unattractive to suitors, and when the government fell the Whigs passed a brief measure to open it to all barristers. There was no real debate nor any suggestion that there should be compensation to the serjeants.[325]

The last inglorious phase of the serjeants lasted another 30 years.[326] Few took chambers in their expensively refurbished hall, which one of them termed 'the grave of the serjeants'.[327] New serjeants were still created, among them celebrated advocates in Parry, Ballantine, and Hayes and legal writers E. W. Cox and Charles Petersdorff. But in the 1860s they suspected that the order was being allowed to die out by a deliberate policy of attrition.[328] Chief Justice Erle, who was responsible for recommending new serjeants to the Lord Chancellor, had become so angry at his nominations being ignored that he was refusing to make any more.[329] The three serjeants created in 1868 were rumoured to be the last, and so it proved.[330] A clause in the Judicature Bill of 1873 proposing that it should no longer be necessary for a judge to be a serjeant was passed without debate[331] and though the Disraeli government would not admit to having decided to call no more serjeants, it could accomplish the same end by denying them any patent of precedence. A grudging exception was made for B. C. Robinson, but he was told his would be the last,[332] and from 25 non-judicial serjeants in 1868 the number slowly dwindled.

Once it had become clear that the order was doomed, the surviving members of Serjeants' Inn determined to dispose of their inn. Failing to entice any of the legal institutions to acquire it for public purposes, they sold it by auction to Serjeant

[323] Reported in J. Manning, *Serviens ad Legem* (1840). Wilde must have been motivated by attachment to the order, as he had a great practice.

[324] They included future judges W. F. Channell and William Shee, and Manning, who became a county court judge in 1847.

[325] Barristers and Serjeants-at-Law Act 1846 (9 & 10 Vict. c. 54).

[326] Campbell disparaged the serjeants of 1850 as a 'very degenerate race': Hardcastle, *Life of Lord Campbell*, ii, 277. W. S. Ballantine's rebuttal in *Some Experiences of a Barrister's Life* (6th edn, 1883), 142–3 is rather tepid.

[327] Jay, *The Law*, 167.

[328] 'Member of the Temple', *An Inquiry…* (1858).

[329] Robinson, *Bench and Bar*, 330.

[330] Baker, *Serjeants at Law*, 125.

[331] Judicature Act 1873, s. 88.

[332] Robinson, *Bench and Bar*, 257.

Edward Cox for some £57,000, disposed of the contents and shared the proceeds, to the indignation of elements of the public and legal press, who unconvincingly argued that the money should be dedicated to educational purposes.[333]

The last practising serjeant was the rather undistinguished Frederick Lowten Spinks, who died in 1899.[334] The best known of the last generation, Ballantine, had gone in 1887; Alexander Pulling, its historian and record keeper, in 1890;[335] Robinson, probably the last to achieve any reputation, in 1895. The order was not formally extinguished until Nathaniel Lindley, the last judicial serjeant, expired in 1921, and by then even the buildings of the inn had been demolished.

Crown Counsel

In 1820 there were 33 KCs living, but not all were in practice and so few were available that it was said that for major state trials the Crown had taken to calling up most of the better ones and that in the Shelley case the defendant had sought to retain them all.[336] While Eldon was Lord Chancellor there was no danger of the currency becoming debased. Even apart from the political considerations which he allowed to reduce the field of choice, he was miserly in adding to their number and made none between Sugden in 1821 and Pepys in 1826. His immediate successors compensated with unprecedented generosity (16 were made in 1834 alone), and by the early 1840s concerns were being voiced and the problem of the 'failed' silk began to emerge.[337] In fact with the great expansion of the bar the proportion of silks to juniors in practice fell if anything, and was probably not then above 3 per cent, but if Robinson's claim that by 1867 there were c.300 compared with 63 in 1837 looks exaggerated it reflects contemporary feeling.[338]

The growth in numbers proceeded in fits and starts, with substantial batches (28 in 1866) interspersing other years with none at all. Towards the end of the century their proportion of the practising bar had risen to one in six and in 1912 there were 236 alive, though this includes judges and those no longer active.[339] In a very few cases at the end of the reigns of George IV and William IV patents, which expired with the sovereign, were not renewed and three were revoked after

---

[333] Baker, *Serjeants at Law*, 126–9; Robinson, *Bench and Bar*, 308–11. Most of the judges gave their share to charity: Lindley, *Autobiography*, 82–3.

[334] Ashley, *My Sixty Years In The Law*, 13.

[335] Pulling's *Order of the Coif* (1884) was the fullest history of the order until Baker's definitive study.

[336] Polson, *Law and Lawyers*, i, 157.

[337] J. C. Sainty, *A History of English Law Officers, King's Counsel and Holders of Patents of Precedence* (Selden Society supp. vols, vii, 1987); (1842) 27 *LM* 244.

[338] *Bench and Bar*, 296.

[339] Abel, *Legal Profession*, table 1.24; Duman, *English and Colonial Bars*, 98–100.

disbarment (Edwin James, Edward Kenealy, and J. T. Woodroffe), but otherwise a patent was for life.[340]

For the most part the rank was given only to practising members of the English bar, though 18 distinguished Scottish advocates were appointed between 1868 and the creation of a separate roll for Scotland in 1896.[341] By then there were occasional creations of a more or less honorary nature, against the views of the permanent secretary to the Lord Chancellor, Kenneth Muir McKenzie, who was himself a reluctant beneficiary.[342]

Both the process and the criteria by which appointments were made remain opaque. Politics played some part throughout, but with very few exceptions (Rowland Blennerhasset seems to be one) men without a substantial practice were not elevated.[343] Eldon had quite unabashedly denied silk to men whose claims were unimpeachable but whose politics were unpalatable. Even Scarlett was kept waiting until 1816, while Brougham and Denman did not get patents of precedence until he had left the Woolsack.[344] It took Ellenborough's intervention to secure a patent for Giffin Wilson, a Whig but hardly an active political opponent.[345]

As Pemberton-Leigh observed, this costive approach sometimes meant men received the rank too late to profit by it[346] but it was important to create openings for rising juniors and as Brougham's case demonstrated, penalizing a political opponent had knock-on effects which might disadvantage even political allies. On the northern circuit it had left only Serjeant Cross, whom litigants did not regard highly, to contest with Scarlett as a leader while those senior in call to Brougham could not take briefs as his junior, leaving them high and dry.[347]

There was to be no continuation of this proscription. MPs and men whom the governing party wanted in Parliament always had better prospects of being made silks and because of the greater feasibility of combining professional and political career as a KC politicians were more anxious to take silk than some prosperous juniors.[348] MPs were also much more likely to receive the promotion from their

---

[340] Sainty, *History of English Law Officers*, 84.

[341] Ibid., 86.

[342] See NA PRO LCO 2/405.

[343] Lemmings, *Professors of the Law*, 264–71; Duman, *English and Colonial Bars*, 177–9.

[344] Scarlett, *Memoir of Lord Abinger*, 85–6; R. A. Melikan, *John Scott, Lord Eldon* (Cambridge, 1999), 203–4.

[345] Romilly, *Memoirs*, iii, 51.

[346] *Lord Kingsdown's Recollections*, 15–16.

[347] Lord Brougham, *The Life and Times of Henry, Lord Brougham*, 3 vols (1871), ii, 459–60.

[348] Duman, *English and Colonial Bars*, 178–9.

own party than another, but no one of real eminence is known to have been passed over other than Judah Benjamin, whose case was a peculiar one.[349]

Very little is known about the selection process. In general men were expected to apply rather than await an invitation, but Jervis and Follett were exceptions, though the latter in fact refused from 'professional prudence'.[350] However, unlike what has been claimed for the inter-war period, applications were not routinely granted to MP/barristers, and among those rejected on their first application were Haldane, Jessel, Russell, and Palmer.[351]

According to the *Solicitors' Journal* in 1910 Lord Chancellors took up one of two positions.[352] One was simply to assess the personal qualifications of each applicant (presumably age, reputation, earnings), the other to consider what openings there were at the bar. Loreburn evidently held the latter view and was censured for his slowness in making decisions, which cost known candidates briefs which impending promotion would oblige them to relinquish, and provoked McCardie into withdrawing his application.[353] It is not clear what Chancellors were really looking for, since the refusals which are known were mostly on the ground that the candidate lacked sufficient experience and should wait another year or two.[354] The minimum period had lengthened to nine years from call[355] but Herschell's attempt to apply it to Edward Carson, who was already an Irish QC, could not be sustained.[356] Age did not matter much, for Haldane was made at 33 (supposed to be the youngest for 50 years, though Webster boasted that his had been the shortest interval from call).[357] Under Eldon the average wait had risen to well over 20 years but in the nineteenth century some 20 per cent, and those the most successful in terms of career progression, were made within 15 years of call, usually in their late 30s or early 40s; a further 40 per cent were aged between 42 and 46.[358]

[349] *Ibid.*, 177–8; Witt, *Lifetime in the Law*, 159–60. Benjamin was given a patent of precedence in 1872.

[350] Grant, *The Bench and the Bar*, ii, 133–40; (1845) 2 *LR* 436–50, at 439. J. D. Coleridge spoke of wanting it to 'come of itself': A. Harwood, *Circuit Ghosts, a Western Circuit Miscellany* (Winchester, 1980), 91.

[351] Sommer, *Haldane of Cloan*, 75; O'Brien, *Life of Lord Russell*, 88–9; Selborne, *Memorials Part One, Family and Personal*, ii, 21–2; A. L. Goodhart, *Five Jewish Lawyers of the Common Law* (1949), 16–23.

[352] (1909–10) 54 *Sol. J.* 867.

[353] Blackham, *Sir Ernest Wild*, 91–2; Pollock, *Mr. Justice McCardie*, 25.

[354] For criticism see E. S. Roscoe, 'The Position and Prospects of the Legal Profession' (1885) 1 *LQR* 314–23 at 317 and E. Webster, 'On Promotion at the English Bar', *Papers Read Before the Juridical Society* (1861), ii, 475–95.

[355] Campbell, *Lives of the Lord Chief Justices*, iii, 112. Richard Webster put it at 12 years.

[356] Marjoribanks, *Lord Carson*, i, 75.

[357] Sommer, *Haldane of Cloan*, 82; Alverstone, *Recollections of Bar and Bench*, 80.

[358] Duman, *English and Colonial Bars*, table 3.3.

So in his mid-40s a successful junior could expect to be earning enough to be eligible for silk, but the decision to seek it was a notoriously difficult one and J. T. Coleridge and Gordon Hewart (not a man usually short of self-confidence) were among those who hesitated.[359] Bray advised that no one should contemplate silk unless he had made at least £4000 for three years running, and even then the risks were considerable.[360] It was by convention irreversible and if the attorneys and solicitors did not feel a man had the right qualities for a leader his plight was a serious one.[361] Some were rescued by the offer of a judgeship in the county court, the colonies, or occasionally, like Arthur Kekewich, the High Court.[362] Others, however, sank into obscurity and poverty; William Lee was a brilliant Chancery lawyer but hopeless in court; J. O. Griffits was an ideal junior but no good as a leader; and both J. B. Mathews, a Worcester solicitor turned successful circuit barrister, and that erudite writer and law reformer George Spence committed suicide.[363] Not surprisingly there were some, like Richards in the King's Bench and Bullen on the western circuit, who preferred not to take the chance.[364] Others, like Chartres Biron's father, regretted having waited too long.[365]

There were particular problems in Chancery. Once two leaders became well established in one of the courts they were almost impossible to shift except by a Jessel or a Cairns, and a new KC must await a promotion before he could expect much business. H. S. Theobald, who was warned by Muir McKenzie what lay in store, got virtually no business until sickness laid both leaders low and was well advised to take a judicial post.[366] However, the rewards were commensurate with the risks, and because silks could offload much of the burden of a case onto the junior, some found it less onerous than the relentless work of a successful junior. In the 1850s Thomson estimated that most QCs made only £3000 per annum, but a few years earlier there were five men earning over £11,000, three more between £8000 and £11,000 and 15 or 16 between £5000 and £8000.[367] There had always been one or two men whose earnings were spectacular. Scarlett at common law

---

[359] *Ibid.*, 98; Jackson, *The Chief*, 55.

[360] Morris, *Back View*, 180. Lindley was told that a new silk's income was likely to drop by one-third: *Autobiography*, 62.

[361] Nash, *Life of Lord Westbury* (1888) noted that 'stranded' QCs were much on the increase: i, 68.

[362] Atlay, *Victorian Chancellors*, ii, 56–7; (1907–8) 52 *Sol. J.* 72.

[363] Rolt, *Memoirs*, 122–3; Plowden, *Grain or Chaff?*, 128; Alexander, *Temple of the Nineties*, 57; (1851) 14 (s2) *LM* 130.

[364] Grant, *The Bench and the Bar*, ii, 110–15; (1898–9) 43 *Sol. J.* 2.

[365] Biron, *Without Prejudice*, 100.

[366] Theobald, *Remembrance of Things Past*, 89–90.

[367] *Choice of a Profession*, 97; *SC on Official Salaries 1850*, qq. 1699 *et seq.* (Sir John Jervis). *The Jurist* ((1845), 9, 81) claimed men were lured to the bar by the fame and fortune of a handful such as Follett, who were making £16,000 to £20,000 a year.

and Sugden in equity were regarded as prodigious in their day; Thomas Wilde's 4000 guinea brief in *Atwood* v. *Small* was a pinnacle for a single case and the 1000 guinea brief was still rare enough to be mentioned specially.[368] But even discounting the enormous sums that Charles Austin, Horatio Lloyd, and company had extracted in railway cases and that Henry Hawkins had made out of compensation claims, the top men like Bethell and Jessel pushed the earnings ceiling well above £20,000.[369] Russell was notably bold in demanding huge fees and stoked the fire for Isaacs, Carson, and F. E. Smith. Carson's clerk set his fees by what Isaacs was charging and the results were spectacular: in *Isaacs* v. *Chesterton* the fees were: Carson 1000 guineas; Smith 670; Muir 420; Wild 350; Swift 250; and Purcell 200.[370]

Of course these were exceptional, but clients seemed prepared to pay almost unlimited sums to secure their services and their fees dragged the rest upwards.[371] There were still men like Lewis Thomas, McCall, and Kemp prepared to scurry from court to court for fairly modest fees—the standard fee for a common jury case was said to be 10–15 guineas (15–20 for a special jury)–but the First World War would change all that.[372]

[368] Duman, *Judicial Bench*, 104–11; Atlay, *Victorian Chancellors*, i, 427. Sir Charles Wetherell was said to have had 7000g to oppose the Municipal Corporations Bill (Polson, *Law and Lawyers*, i, 153).

[369] See above, p. 1053, and Harris, *Hawkins*, 207; Duman, *Judicial Bench*, table 8.

[370] O'Brien, *Life of Lord Russell*, 115; G. Rentoul, *This Is My Case* (1944), 49; Blackham, *Sir Ernest Wild*, 94–6.

[371] *The Times* said that Hawkins' example had lifted fees generally and that KCs might price themselves out of the market: (1907–8) 52 *Sol. J.* 3.

[372] Bowker, *Lifetime in the Law*, 47–8; Smith, *Lord Goddard*, 27–8; Alexander, *Temple of the Nineties*, 146. Ordinary leaders made between £5000 and £6000 a year: 'Prospects in the Professions', 480.

III

The Institutions and Governance of the Bar

1. THE LAW OFFICERS

Introduction

Although Canning still included the judge-advocate general among the law officers in 1826,[1] the term was more usually confined to the Attorney-General, Solicitor-General and king's advocate. The division was essentially hierarchical. Each gave his opinions on important questions of law and Mansfield's judgment of 1770 in *R* v. *Wilkes*[2] ruled that except where expressly reserved, the Attorney-General's prerogative and statutory functions were exercisable also by the Solicitor-General.

How much influence the Solicitor-General had obviously depended upon the law officers' personalities and aptitudes. Thus while Campbell reduced Attorney-General Horne to a cypher and Palmer eclipsed Atherton,[3] others formed partnerships of equals, like James and Herschell,[4] and some Solicitor-Generals were quite overshadowed. It was recognized that the Solicitor-General had a strong claim to the senior post, but it fell short of an entitlement, so that Bovill had to accept that Rolt would leapfrog him once Cairns (also from the equity bar) ceased to be Attorney-General.[5]

---

[1] J. Ll. Edwards, *The Law Officers of the Crown* (1964), 47. This is the standard work on the law officers, supplemented by the author's *The Attorney-General and the Public Interest* (1984). For a list of holders see Sir J. C. Sainty, *A History of English Law Officers, King's Counsel and Holders of Patents of Precedence* (Selden Society, suppl. vol. vii, 1987).

[2] 4 Burr. 2527, in the Lords in Wilm. 322. Discussed in Edwards, *Law Officers of the Crown*, 123–6.

[3] J. B. Atlay, *The Victorian Chancellors*, 2 vols (1908), ii, 155; Edwards, *Law Officers of the Crown*, 130.

[4] R. F. V. Heuston, *Lives of the Lord Chancellors 1885–1940* (Oxford, 1964), 93–8.

[5] Lord Selborne, *Memorials Part Two, Personal and Political*, 2 vols (1898), i, 43.

The third law officer, the king's advocate, was always a leading civilian, and often also held a civilian judgeship.[6] The Foreign Office made regular use of his expertise in the civil law, questions of international law being sometimes sent to him alone, or, if they were more important, sent to him before the other law officers.[7] However, the circulation arrangements were dangerously informal, and their inadequacy was demonstrated with calamitous effect in the *Alabama* fiasco in 1862.[8] After that episode papers invariably went first to the Attorney-General and last to the queen's advocate. In 1872, when Sir Travers Twiss resigned,[9] the office was abolished[10] and Dr (later Sir James Parker) Deane was appointed legal advisor to the Foreign Office. The arrangement was not a success. Deane interpreted the terms of his employment narrowly and the Foreign Office continued to send almost everything to the law officers as well as Deane.[11] Another result of the change was that the law officers were landed with formal court appearances on behalf of the queen's proctor, for which they received no fees.[12] Later the Foreign Office acquired a legal assistant under secretary, but opinions on international law continued to make up much of the law officers' most challenging business.[13]

The Attorney-General as Head of the Bar

As noted earlier, in 1814 the Attorney-General was accorded precedence over all others at the English bar, and in 1834 the House of Lords affirmed that he had precedence over the Lord Advocate even in Scottish appeals. In this capacity it was generally allowed that he might speak authoritatively on behalf of the bar, though Giffard rebuffed Coleridge's attempt to exert this authority in the courtroom.[14] On the rare occasions where it was felt desirable to call the bar together to discuss a matter of major importance to the profession, such as Daniel's proposals for law reporting,[15] it was the Attorney-General who issued the call, and it also

---

[6] Holders were Sir John Robinson (1809–28); Sir Herbert Jenner (1828–34); Sir John Dodson (1834–52); Sir John Harding (1852–68); Sir Robert Phillimore (1862–7) and Sir Travers Twiss (1867–72).

[7] The fullest account of these developments is by Lord McNair, *International Law Opinions* (1956), iii, App. Edwards, *Law Officers of the Crown*, 131–40, draws extensively on this work.

[8] Edwards, *Law Officers of the Crown*, 135–6.

[9] For the sensational circumstances see M. Taggart, 'Alexander Chaffers and the Genesis of the Vexatious Actions Act 1896' (2004) 63 *CLJ* 565–84.

[10] To the regret of Sir John Karslake: *DC on the Legal Business of Government, First Report, PP* 1877 (199), xxvii, qq. 622–3.

[11] *DC on Government Legal Business First Report*, particularly Deane's evidence: qq. 479–566.

[12] *Ibid.*, Baggallay qq. 153–61.

[13] Following the example of the Colonial Office: Edwards, *Law Officers of the Crown*, 139–40.

[14] *Ibid.*, 276–82.

[15] See below, pp. 1216–18.

fell to him to pronounce upon matters of bar etiquette. After the creation of the Bar Council this role usually devolved upon them, although it was not formally yielded up. The Attorney-General's position as head of the bar and defender of its privileges sometimes sat uneasily with another function, that of presenting bills emanating from the Lord Chancellor's Office in the Commons. Certainly Muir McKenzie felt that the lack of a junior minister in the lower house was a signifi-cant handicap.[16]

CHOICE IN SELECTION

The choice of a law officer was limited by several considerations. He should be an eminent counsel[17] with suitable political opinions, and if not already an MP, he must be prepared to enter the House.[18] Before the first Reform Act these require-ments seldom created difficulties. The usual avenue to the highest judicial posts lay through serving the government, and ambitious Georgian lawyers took care that their politics would not disqualify them or were prepared to turn their coat at need.[19] Later on, in an era when 'every child that is born into the world alive is either a little Liberal or else a little Conservative', the choice was more restricted, particularly for the Whigs in the mid-1830s,[20] though there were always lawyers who wore their politics lightly and could be recruited by either party as soon as they rose to prominence in the profession.

It was also desirable that one law officer should be from the common law bar and the other from equity,[21] but this was not a binding convention.[22] However, it was necessary to have someone capable of examining witnesses and addressing a jury.[23] The choice had a long-term importance because, besides giving a claim

[16] P. Polden, *A Guide to the Records of the Lord Chancellor's Department* (1988), 21.

[17] The bar was said to have disapproved when Rolfe was made Solicitor-General in 1834, and the *Law Magazine and Review* ('The Law Officers and the Crown' (1873) n.s. 2, 1124–8) complained that Harcourt was not really a 'practising barrister'.

[18] Campbell was out of Parliament for three months after being defeated at Dudley. Pemberton-Leigh refused in 1834, not wanting to be in Parliament.

[19] An example is Copley, whose radical past was regularly brought up against him by opponents: Lee, *Lyndhurst, the Flexible Tory* (Colorado, 1994), 35–46. It is not clear that men who did refuse, Lens and Leach in 1813 for example, did so on party principle: H. W.Woolrych, *The Lives of Eminent Serjeants at Law*, 2 vols (1869), ii, 744–5. Perhaps, like Brougham later, they had higher ambitions.

[20] Before Rolfe's appointment, they had been obliged to resort to C. C. Pepys, who had not yet acquired a big reputation.

[21] See E. L. Pemberton, *The Recollections of Lord Kingsdown* (1868), 40–2, though the reason he gives for Gifford's appointment, that someone was needed to defend Eldon in the Commons, was a temporary one.

[22] (1875–6) 20 *Sol. J.* 1.

[23] Lord Selborne, *Memorials, Personal and Political*, i, 43; *DC on the Legal Business of Government First Report*, Sir W. Hart-Dyke, q. 370. Not that common lawyers were always knowledgeable

to judicial perferment,[24] the seniority acquired by the Attorney- General over the Solicitor-General, and his claim to re-appointment if a ministry came back in, could hardly be overlooked. No doubt, for instance, Palmerston would have much preferred to promote Palmer over the head of the inadequate Atherton, but did not,[25] and choosing Gorst in 1885 stored up trouble for the Conservatives when they later had to juggle his claims with those of Webster and Clarke.[26] Moreover, Webster's selection ahead of Clarke (over Clarke's protests) put him permanently ahead in their claims to office.[27]

GOVERNMENT AND PARLIAMENT

Law officers, even those most favoured by the Prime Minister, were not expected to have a seat in the cabinet, but in 1912 Asquith's need to mollify Rufus Isaacs for preferring Haldane as Lord Chancellor brought about a short-lived change, several of Isaacs' successors being similarly favoured.[28] Membership of the Privy Council, however, a consolation prize first offered to Sir J. D. Coleridge for being denied cabinet rank, was conferred upon most of his successors and some Solicitor-Generals.[29]

The law officers were expected to take a leading part in parliamentary business relating to the law and the courts, even though the Lord Chancellor (if anyone) was the minister with responsibility for law reform.[30] This could be awkward when their relations with the Chancellor were bad, as most notoriously between Cranworth and Bethell in the 1850s. If Coleridge's experience is typical, the Attorney-General was not always consulted in advance on law bills,[31] and neither was he always the best person to forward them; as head of the bar, the Attorney-General was unlikely

---

in key areas: Robson and Evans were said to be hopeless in revenue cases: E. A. Bell, *Those Meddlesome Attorneys* (1939), 94.

[24] See above, pp. 974–8. A law officer like Garrow or Gorst, who was considered barely suitable even for a puisne judgeship was a considerable embarrassment.

[25] T. A. Nash, *The Life of Richard, Lord Westbury*, 2 vols (1888), ii, 8. One of Westbury's typically spiteful jokes was that this would be impossible since Atherton had no head.

[26] A. Hunter, *A Life of Sir John Eldon Gorst, Disraeli's Awkward Disciple* (2001), 179–84; D. Walker-Smith and E. Clarke, *A Life of Sir Edward Clarke* (1939), 158–63.

[27] Walker-Smith and Clarke, *Life of Sir Edward Clarke*, 58–63, 191–2. The account in Webster's autobiography (*Recollections of Bar and Bench*, 1914) is very bland.

[28] Edwards, *Law Officers of the Crown*, 165–77; G. P. Judd, *Lord Reading* (1982), 82–5.

[29] Edwards, *Law Officers of the Crown*, 158–65. Coleridge became CJCP before he could be made a member, and his successor as Attorney-General, Sir Henry James, declined it, though he accepted it when it was again offered in 1885. Simon, in 1915, was the first Solicitor-General to be a privy councillor.

[30] Coleridge argued that he should be in the cabinet in order to ensure that such measures were given due attention: Edwards, *Law Officers of the Crown*, 158–9.

[31] *Ibid.*, 148.

to be enthusiastic about legislation such as Loreburn's County Court Bills which the bar vociferously opposed.

Canning expressed disappointment that the Admiralty advocate and king's advocate were no longer in the Commons, but the law officers' usefulness in debate varied enormously according to their ability and commitment.[32] Edward Law had been one of the most dependable speakers in Addington's administration, which was unusually weak in debate, and a century later Isaacs and Simon, both with serious political ambitions, were equally prominent; indeed all the law officers of the Liberal ministries worked hard on its heavy programme of social legislation.[33] In earlier times some had played a major role in seeing through particular bills, as Bethell did with the Succession Duty Bill and Page Wood with the Ecclesiastical Titles Bill.[34] Others, such as Cockburn, ostentatiously held aloof from non-legal matters[35] and some, however effective in court, had such limited parliamentary skills that whips and ministers would not call on them unless it was unavoidable; Rolfe, for example, was quite hopeless and Pollock and Jessel disappointing.[36]

In general, however, the governmental and parliamentary duties of the law officers were encroaching remorselessly on their private practice. Jervis voiced concerns about this in 1850[37] and though Jessel questioned Baggallay's claim that they were paid for attending at cabinet, he acknowledged that attendances on ministers now formed a major part of their duties.[38] So did sittings of the

---

[32] *Ibid.*, 47. Parke told the Committee on Official Salaries in 1850 that the priority was to get a good lawyer rather than a good speaker (q. 1897). See, however, the enigmatic (and none too tactful) remark of Jessel in 1875: '[i]n former days the Crown was able to select its law officers freely, and then it was quite certain to have for at least one of its law officers a good lawyer and a good advocate; but that is not so now. The Crown may be compelled to take two gentlemen, neither of whom have held the first position as advocates; they may be selected for other reasons ...' (*DC on the Legal Business of Government First Report*, q. 617).

[33] G. W. Keeton, *A Liberal Attorney-General* (1949), 142–61.

[34] Edwards, *Law Officers of the Crown*, 48; W. R. W. Stephens, *A Memoir of the R. H. William Page Wood, Baron Hatherley*, 2 vols (1883), ii, 86.

[35] Edwards, *Law Officers of the Crown*, 48 n.76. Cockburn may be one of those Sir William Harcourt had in mind when he wrote to Dilke: 'I don't see why I am not to be a politician because I am a law officer. Law Officers used to be politicians some years ago till the men of later days degraded the office': 21 November 1873, A. G. Gardiner, *The Life of Sir William Harcourt*, 2 vols (1923), i, 259. Harcourt and Sir Henry James successfully argued that they should attend the shadow cabinets of 1874–80 rather than merely being summoned when required: R. Askwith, *Lord James of Hereford* (1930), 71.

[36] Edwards, *Law Officers of the Crown*, 48; J. Grant, *The Bench and the Bar*, 2 vols (1838), ii, 56–62; J. Bryce, *Studies in Contemporary Biography* (1903), 170–83. Even the much loved Frank Lockwood became rather diffident in the Commons: A. Birrell, *Sir Frank Lockwood* (1898), 184–5.

[37] *SC on Official Salaries 1850*, q. 1794.

[38] *DC on Government Legal Business First Report*, q. 233.

Commons, where pressure from MPs was beginning to be felt by 1872.[39] The strain on the Attorney-General in particular led Sir Henry James to contend that the position had become impossible, and besides Cairns' breakdown after only a few months, it was thought to have contributed to the early deaths of Karslake and Holker.[40] Among their burdens was the annual Finance Act,[41] and as legislative programmes grew more ambitious and the legislation more complex it became harder for the law officers to set limits upon their participation.

These growing demands on their time highlighted the inherent ambiguities in the law officers' position. MPs might regard them as servants of the Crown like other ministers, but they preferred to see themselves as ordinary barristers with a retainer from the Crown to provide a range of legal services. This conception emphasized their independence and standing within a profession in which salaried barristers were an inferior rarity, but though it received some superficial endorsement from the withdrawal in 1831 of the £40 salary which law officers and KCs had received,[42] the conception gradually lost plausibility as their public duties expanded. Some, such as parliamentary engagements, were regarded as incidental to membership of the house, and therefore unremunerated; but in the case of opinions given to ministers, payment seems to have turned on the mode and channel through which the request came, which was plainly unsatisfactory.[43] The fees for contentious business where a brief was delivered were conventionally set well below the market rate,[44] but each law officer had a token 'complimentary' brief for each Crown prosecution irrespective of whether he was being asked to conduct it in person,[45] and a large income—£2500 a year in 1850 and rising— accrued from the scrutiny of patents, which most left to a competent clerk.[46]

The overall result (not unfamiliar in the courts and their offices) was that they were underpaid for important work and overpaid for purely formal business. For a long time it hardly mattered to the law officers themselves, for though Scott had greatly overstated the loss of income he suffered, and though others down to Jervis also experienced a fall, it was not steep enough for anyone (except perhaps

[39] Edwards, *Law Officers of the Crown*, 49–50; *PD* 1872 (s3) 212: 47–77.

[40] Edwards, *Law Officers of the Crown*, 64–5.

[41] *Ibid.*, 47. Coleridge noted that this had not been expected in his time: E. H. Coleridge, *The Life and Correspondence of John Duke, First Lord Coleridge*, 2 vols (1904), ii, 78.

[42] Campbell disapproved: Hon. Mrs M. S. Hardcastle, *The Life of John, Lord Campbell*, 2 vols (1861 edn), ii, 144.

[43] *SC on Official Salaries 1850*, Jervis, qq. 1799–1800; Edwards, *Law Officers of the Crown*, 76–7.

[44] *SC on Official Salaries 1850*, Jervis, q. 1729.

[45] *DC on the Legal Business of Government First Report*, Karslake q. 571.

[46] *Ibid.*, Harcourt, qq. 448–52, though cf. Karslake, qq. 586–95; Edwards, *Law Officers of the Crown*, 77–8.

Charles Austin) to refuse the place on that account.[47] Furthermore, few of those who were not translated to the bench if they wished remained law officers long enough for their practice to suffer irreparably.[48] The principle that public servants should be paid purely and fully for the actual services they rendered only slowly became established, and although the Select Committee on Official Salaries in 1850, finding that (exclusive of what their private practice produced), the law officers' bemusing arrangements yielded an excessive income, recommended that they be salaried instead, no action was taken.[49]

However, by the 1870s the law officers were feeling the strain. Some MPs were aggrieved that these junior ministers were not more readily available to justify their actions and those of the government, while the law officers themselves were having an increasing struggle to conduct their private practice and attend to the multifarious business of government; whereas Bethell had felt it prudent to limit his private practice, Holker gave up his altogether.[50] The Treasury viewed with disapproval the rising sums paid for their services and precipitated a change: Under the new arrangement the Attorney-General would have £7000 per annum and the Solicitor-General £6000 to cover all non-contentious business, with fees continuing to be paid for contentious business, but now on 'the ordinary professional scale'. There would no longer be complimentary briefs.[51] This scheme, embodied in a Treasury minute in December 1871, was inadequately explained in the Law Officers' Fees Act 1872 (c.70), which merely added that all other fees should henceforth be accounted for to the Treasury.

A combination of incompetence and concealment at the Treasury, and culpable lack of clarity in the definition of 'non-contentious' business, produced a row with the Attorney-General which obliged the government hastily to convene a committee under Jessel MR (a former Solicitor-General).[52] Even Baggallay, who favoured the old system, acknowledged that there could be no going back,[53] and the committee's narrow remit precluded a thorough review of the antediluvian

---

[47] *Ibid.*, 71–80.

[48] The average length was 22 months: *ibid.*, 114. It was apparently a matter of professional etiquette that a law officer might not return to his circuit (Jervis, *SC on Official Salaries 1850*, q. 1793) but the only one known to have experienced financial embarrassment was Sir William Horne .

[49] *Report 1850*, 7; Edwards, *Law Officers of the Crown*, 75–8.

[50] Nash, *Life of Lord Westbury*, ii, 129, 189; [W. D. I. Foulkes], *A Generation of Judges, by their Reporter* (1886), 129–37.

[51] *DC on the Legal Business of Government First Report*, App. B, reprinted in Edwards, *Law Officers of the Crown*, 80.

[52] The other members were Sir T. D. Archibald (a judge in the QBD), H. T. Holland (Colonial Office), R. R. W. Lingen (Treasury) and H. L. Pemberton (Official Solicitor). This unedifying episode is thoroughly explained in Edwards, *Law Officers of the Crown*, 80–9.

[53] *First Report*, q. 90.

way the law officers were obliged to do their business, though it did publicize it.[54] Greater precision in the distinction between non-contentious and contentious business (several departments had been encouraged by the Treasury to adopt a construction very unfavourable to the law officers[55]) was the only outcome directly affecting the law officers,[56] though the committee then proceeded to suggest the incorporation of standing counsel employed by sundry government departments into the office of Treasury counsel.[57]

The new system lasted less than 20 years. There had been strong criticism of the law officers combining private practice with public duties when Coleridge, upon becoming Solicitor-General in 1871, promptly undertook the prosecution of the Tichborne claimant, whom he had relentlessly cross-examined in the civil action a few months before.[58] Far more damage was done by Webster's representing *The Times* in Parnell's action and at the subsequent inquiry ordered by the government to which he belonged.[59] That insensitive action bolstered Gladstone's insistence that his law officers must abandon private practice, though he was either strangely ill-informed or deliberately misleading in telling them that their Conservative predecessors had also been severely restricted. He also substituted an inclusive salary (£10,000 and £9000 respectively) for the mixture of salaries and fees.[60] The Conservatives, Webster and Clarke, denied that they had been so restricted and, on the party's return to office in 1895, were supported by Halsbury in seeking a return to the old ways. Given the difficulty of finding adequate substitutes, they might have overcome cabinet opposition, but Webster, perhaps conscious that his past actions had made him vulnerable, ratted on his colleague, salving his conscience by securing the concession that fees would again become the basis for conducting contentious business. Clarke stood out on principle, but it was not one with which laymen sympathized, nor was it really compatible with the amount of assorted public business which now fell to the law officers.[61]

Private practice was gone for good, but the fees system was attacked again by Lloyd George in 1901, drawing ammunition from published figures showing incomes temporarily swollen by several big international arbitrations. However, that, and subsequent attacks, were repulsed, and the same structure continued

---

[54] Harcourt could not be restrained from forcefully airing the wider issues: qq. 443–78.

[55] *Ibid.*, Sir A. Stephenson (Treasury Solicitor), q. 36; Edwards, *Law Officers of the Crown*, 87–8.

[56] *First Report*, 3.

[57] *Second and Third Reports*, PP 1877 (199), xxii.

[58] Edwards, *Law Officers of the Crown*, 93–4.

[59] *Ibid.*, 94–8. The bar rallied to the defence of its head: Alverstone, *Recollections of Bar and Bench*, 142–56.

[60] Edwards, *Law Officers of the Crown*, 94–8.

[61] *Ibid.*, 98–105. Walker-Smith and Clarke, *Life of Sir Edward Clarke*, 239–42.

until the 1940s.[62] Men like Isaacs, Simon, and Smith could not hope to match the remarkable incomes they could make at the bar, and their incredulous and indignant clerks had to learn to accept briefs marked with what they thought contemptibly low sums,[63] but these were men with political ambitions who had been able to amass big sums much more quickly than most of their predecessors, so governments were still able to attract the biggest names at the bar.

ORGANIZATION

Whereas the Lord Chancellor had a collection of officers who could be employed on official business[64] the law officers had only their own personal clerks, who might well be entirely ignorant of the ways of government.[65] For professional assistance it had become the invariable custom for the Attorney-General to employ a devil[66] and there seems also to have been a clerk with knowledge of the patent business upon whom they could call.[67] Karslake reckoned that these services, and the payment to his own clerk on account of government business, cost him close to £1000 per annum.[68] The lack of any permanent location for a 'Law Officers' Department' does not seem to have been a concern in the first half of the nineteenth century, when (if Campbell is typical) law officers seem not to have troubled even to have a copy of the opinions they delivered,[69] but by Harcourt's time the 'archives of the Solicitor-General', comprising a coachload of assorted and unsorted opinions and papers, were passed unceremoniously from the chambers of one incumbent to the next.[70] More alarming was the practice of merely bundling up Foreign Office documents, sometimes highly secret ones, and sending them between law officers by a clerk on the railway.[71] With law officers dependent upon the department bespeaking the opinion to supply them with earlier relevant materials, and the department expecting the law officers to have a copy of anything emanating from their predecessors, it was a discreditable and inefficient way of doing business.[72]

---

[62] Edwards, *Law Officers of the Crown*, 105–8.

[63] Judd, *Lord Reading*, 69. The yardstick was the fee charged by ordinary QCs.

[64] See above, p. 785.

[65] See e.g. *DC on the Legal Business of Government First Report*, Harcourt, q. 447.

[66] See above, p. 1038. It was already established in the Regency: [J. P. Collier], *Criticisms on the Bar* (1819), 94–7.

[67] *DC on the Legal Business of Government First Report*, q. 447 (Harcourt).

[68] *Ibid.*, q. 568.

[69] Sir Samuel Shepherd was reputed to go obligingly around the ministries to answer questions, but Sir James Scarlett put a stop to that: Hardcastle, *Life of Lord Campbell*, ii, 94, 119n.

[70] *DC on the Legal Business of Government First Report*, q. 454.

[71] *Ibid.*, q. 459.   [72] *Ibid.*, qq. 453–4.

Harcourt's disclosure did not, as he had hoped, lead immediately to the establishment of a permanent secretariat, even after Selborne had argued that the law officers needed at least a secretary capable of ensuring that all relevant bills in the Commons were drawn to their attention.[73] Finally in 1893 they were given a small office in the RCJ, consisting of two clerks (raised to three just before the War) along with law officers' own clerks.[74] There was no equivalent to the Lord Chancellor's permanent secretary, and Simon was surprised at the old-fashioned way opinions were still prepared.[75]

OPINIONS

It had long been one of the law officers' chief duties to provide a minister upon request with an opinion on a question of law. Some requests arrived in a formal shape which attracted a fee, but others were contained in a letter and were treated more informally; curiously, there was no convention to distinguish which approach was appropriate.[76] As the law officers noted with suspicion, formal requests increased following the Minute of 1871 under which they need not be paid for individually, and Holland of the Colonial Office admitted that they now had less doubt about making them.[77] Baggallay reckoned there were then 600 a year, rising sharply when war conditions increased the demand for opinions on international law.[78] The law officers' main complaint, however, was the lack of discrimination rather than the number; in Harcourt's view 'an enormous mass of business was sent from the Foreign Office which had no possible relation to law at all, and might just as well have been sent to anybody else as to the law officers'.[79] The Foreign Office may have become more selective once it acquired its own in-house lawyer; at all events the number of formal opinions, 187 in 1893, remained fairly constant down to the First World War, though this may conceal a growing reliance on informal requests.[80]

Different views were expressed on whether these opinions were confidential. When Palmerston wished to quote from an opinion on the Belfast riots in 1865 the speaker ruled that it would not breach the rules of the House, and although in

---

[73] Draft letter to Treasury, 23 July 1886, NA PRO LCO 1/61.

[74] Edwards, *Law Officers of the Crown*, 144–6. The third clerk was required because the assumption that the personal clerks would undertake a goodly share of the public work proved unfounded.

[75] Lord Simon, *In Retrospect* (1972), 59.

[76] *SC on Official Salaries 1850*, Jervis, qq. 1729 et seq.

[77] *DC on the Legal Business of Government First Report*, Baggallay, q. 163 (who said many of them would previously have been sent to the junior counsel), 169 (many now came from the Local Government Board and Colonial Office), 175; Holland at 165.

[78] *Ibid.*, Baggallay, q. 164, Karslake, q. 621.

[79] *Ibid.*, q. 460, and cf. Karslake's example at q. 570.

[80] Edwards, *Law Officers of the Crown*, 151–2.

1901 Balfour made a very uncompromising pronouncement in favour of complete confidentiality, Isaacs provided the Commons with a full account of his opinion on the Archer-Shee case in 1911 and the question remained unsettled.[81]

The law officers were sometimes involved in the drafting of bills. Though Coleridge complained that he was sometimes unaware of the contents even of law reform bills until he had to commend them to the House,[82] it seems that in general they expected that once the draftsman had furnished a bill they would settle it with the minister and others who would be responsible for its passage. However, Baggallay jibbed at being expected to draft clauses himself, something Jessel thought was a novelty, although in the 1850s the struggle to get through the stages of controversial bills such as those on probate and divorce had required frequent recourse to extempore drafting under harassing circumstances.[83] It may be, however, that the involvement of the Parliamentary Counsel Office reduced such demands.[84]

IN COURT

In 1872 the Chancellor of the Exchequer claimed that advising on and conducting government prosecutions was the law officers' most important duty, but his view was out of date.[85] Most criminal proceedings instigated by government departments were for routine breaches of revenue law and were conducted on behalf of the Customs & Excise, Board of Trade, Post Office, and Mint. It had been customary to send a complimentary brief to the Attorney-General with a modest fee, in the expectation that he would usually return his opinion (often rather perfunctory) to the department, which would then hire junior counsel to conduct the case.[86] The move to salaries for non-contentious business in 1871 seems to have confused matters, with the Post Office in particular now treating the brief as a request for an opinion, which attracted no separate fee even where it led to a prosecution. Baggallay protested, insisting on his right to decide for himself whether to conduct the case, and on this being classed as contentious business.[87]

The law officers' position was safeguarded in most of the proposals to create public prosecutors, including the bill which finally succeeded in 1879.[88] Though

---

[81] *Ibid.*, 256–60.

[82] *Ibid*, 148–9.

[83] *DC on the Legal Business of Government First Report*, qq. 239–40.

[84] Webster, however, observed that more drafting, especially of amendments, was put upon them: Alverstone, *Recollections of Bar and Bench*, 138.

[85] *PD* 1872 (s3) 212: 55–6 (Robert Lowe).

[86] *DC on the Legal Business of Government First Report*, Baggallay, qq. 207–12, Karslake, qq. 570–1.

[87] *Ibid.*

[88] Edwards, *Law Officers of the Crown*, 340–66.

the Attorney-General lost out to the Home Secretary in the right to appoint the Director of Public Prosecutions, and was to exercise only a 'superintendence',[89] he kept intact his patronage, that is, the right to nominate the counsel whom the Director was to employ, not only at the Old Bailey[90] but elsewhere, defeating the Treasury Solicitor's bid for a formal advisory role.[91]

A more serious issue arose in those important cases where the Attorney-General as a member of the government was involved in the decision whether to bring a prosecution. Sir John Scott had insisted that he exercised an independent discretion, but when Denman advanced this view of the constitutional position to William IV he concluded with words suggesting that the government might nevertheless issue an express direction to him.[92] There are certainly later instances when the Home Secretary or the cabinet resolved on a prosecution before consulting the law officers, and Herschell was justified in demurring to Halsbury's reiteration of their absolute independence in 1896, although there was a distinction between the decision that a prosecution would be desirable and the advice of the law officers on whether the likelihood of success would warrant it.[93] Balfour also adopted the absolutist position in 1903, but this neither reflected the past nor would hold good for the near future.[94]

The law officers' very prolific use of informations for criminal libel (particularly by Vicary Gibbs) to suppress radical publications during the long war with France had been politically controversial, and although Copley desisted from using them,[95] Tenterden's complaisant acceptance of informations from both common informers ('Crown Office informations') and the law officers held out a strong temptation. However, dismayed by the failure to convict Cobbett in 1831, Denman, despite pressure from the King, gave them up,[96] and although

---

[89] *Ibid.*, 361–3, Prosecution of Offences Act 1879 (c. 22), s 2.

[90] In 1875 Stephenson told the Committee on Government Legal Business that Poland and Beasley were overworked (*First Report*, q. 634) and Webster doubled their number on Poland's retirement. He insisted on restricting these appointments to juniors: Alverstone, *Recollections of Bar and Bench*, 184

[91] Edwards, *Law Officers of the Crown*, 390–3. Stephenson's evidence to the SC on Public Prosecutions, PP 1888 (239), lxxx,

[92] Edwards, *Law Officers of the Crown*, 179–84. The memorandum is in Sir J. Arnould, *A Memoir of Thomas, First Lord Denman*, 2 vols (1873), i, 368–72. Denman was discussing *ex officio* informations, but his argument would not seem to be confined to those.

[93] Sir Edward Troup, permanent under-secretary at the Home Office, drew this distinction. The cases in question concerned Johann Most (1881), Taggart (1889), and Ben Tillett (1893): Edwards, *Law Officers of the Crown*, 185–6.

[94] *Ibid*, 188–91.

[95] W. C. Townsend, *The Lives of Twelve Eminent Judges*, 2 vols (1846), i, 239–98, 255–66; Lee, *Lyndhurst*, 205–6; Edwards, *Law Officers of the Crown*, 265, citing Coleridge LCJ in *R v. Labouchere* (1884) 12 QBD 320.

[96] Edwards, *Law Officers of the Crown*, 181; Arnould, *Life of Lord Denman*, i, 331–6, 368–73.

some of his successors (e.g. A. L. Smith[97]) regretted that they were not more readily used in appropriate cases, they became a rarity.[98]

The most objectionable thing about *ex officio* informations was that they sent the accused straight to trial, by-passing the normal safeguards of committal and grand jury,[99] and the Attorney-General's other privileges in litigation also came under scrutiny as the accused's position was gradually improved. He kept the right to insist on a trial at bar in cases where he claimed that the Crown had an interest in the outcome (though that claim might itself be disputed[100]), and if he waived a trial at bar his right to choose the venue was expressly enacted in the Crown Suits Act 1865.[101] However, his claim to be entitled to the last opportunity to address the jury in a criminal trial proved more difficult to sustain. It was upheld by Mansfield, at any rate for state trials,[102] and following the Prisoners Counsel Act 1836 the judges agreed it should apply to all prosecuting counsel in public prosecutions for felonies.[103] However, it was much criticized[104] and in 1884 it was confined to the law officers acting in person.[105]

Besides his role in the decision to bring prosecutions there were cases in which the Attorney-General exercised control over their continuation.[106] The broadest was the long-standing prerogative power to discontinue a prosecution on indictment by entering a *nolle prosequi*, whether the prosecution had been initiated by a private individual or by the Crown (Denman thereby extricated himself from embarrassment after the jury would not convict Cobbett of a criminal libel in 1831).[107] It was exercisable at any stage before the entry of the verdict (even after the jury's verdict, as in *R v. Johnson*[108]) but until the authoritative review in *R v. Allen*,[109] it remained unclear whether it only terminated proceedings on the

---

[97] *Ex p. Tomlinson* [1899] 1 QB 909, 914.

[98] Edwards, *Law Officers of the Crown*, 266–7. The unusual circumstances of a gross libel on the King, alleging a secret marriage, presumably justified its use in *R v. Mylius*, *The Times*, 2 February 1911.

[99] Holdsworth, *HEL*, ix, 242–4. Cockburn CJ had said they should be confined to 'cases of public importance' (*R v. Lord Winchilsea*, unreported 1865, in *R v. Labouchere*).

[100] Edwards, *Law Officers of the Crown*, 269–70. *Paddock v. Forrester* (1840) 1 Man. & G. 583; *Dixon v. Farrer* (1886) 18 QBD 43.

[101] Crown Suits Act 1865 (c. 104), s 46; Edwards, *Law Officers of the Crown*, 270.

[102] *R v. Horne* (1777) 2 Cowp. 672.

[103] Edwards, *Law Officers of the Crown*, 273.

[104] In *Lord Advocate v. Douglas* (1842) 9 Cl. & F. 173, the House of Lords declined to recognize it.

[105] Edwards, *Law Officers of the Crown*, 274.

[106] Unless expressly authorized by the Attorney-General, his fiat could not be exercised by other Crown prosecutors, not even by the Solicitor-General: *R v. Dunn* (1843) 1 Car. & K. 730.

[107] Edwards, *Law Officers of the Crown*, 226–37. Curiously, the power did not extend to summary prosecutions: 'Nolle Prosequi' [1958] *Crim. Law Rev.* 573–82 at 581.

[108] (1725) 1 Stra. 644.

[109] (1862) 1 B. & S. 850.

particular indictment or also barred future proceedings for the same offence. In *Allen* the court not only ruled that the Attorney-General's practice of consulting the prosecutor or his counsel beforehand, though desirable, was not a requisite, but held that the proceedings thus halted could not be revived.[110] The *nolle prosequi* appears to have been used chiefly for two reasons: 'to dispose of technically imperfect proceedings instituted by the Crown; and to put a stop to oppressive, but technically impeccable, proceedings issued by private prosecutors'.[111] Once the DPP was empowered to take over a private prosecution and, if he chose, discontinue it, the latter became unnecessary, and with the simplifications of the Indictments Act 1915 so did the former, rendering the *nolle prosequi* obsolescent until the 1950s.[112]

The Attorney-General also controlled appeals to the House of Lords from criminal convictions by writ of error.[113] A dictum of Mansfield's suggested that his consent ought not to be withheld 'if there be probable cause',[114] but in *Ex p Newton*[115] an attempt to obtain a *mandamus* against his refusal was not only unsuccessful, but led Campbell CJ to doubt the authenticity as well as the correctness of the dictum.[116] According to J. F. Stephen, 'the criminal law is for the most part now so well settled and understood that it is a matter of little practical importance',[117] but the rarity of successful applications probably also owed something to the deficiencies of the writ of error as a corrective mechanism. At any rate, during the passage of the Court of Criminal Appeals Act 1907 the writ of error was abolished and section 1(6) provided instead that an appeal would lie on a certificate of the Attorney-General that 'the decision of the Court of Criminal Appeal involves a point of law of exceptional public importance, and that it is desirable in the public interest that a further appeal should be brought'.[118] This provision placed the Attorney-General in a rather unsatisfactory position, and while the statutory terms looked very restrictive (and were intended to be), it was

---

[110] This was a case of a private prosecution, unlike *R* v. *Ridpath* (1712) 10 Mod. 152 where the Attorney-General was allowed to bring a fresh indictment. Cockburn CJ said that to allow proceedings to be resurrected would be 'fraught with great inconvenience' (at 854), but Blackburn J. would not commit himself on the validity of a fresh prosecution (855).

[111] 'Nolle Prosequi', 577.

[112] *Ibid.*, 577–80.

[113] Edwards, *Law Officers of the Crown*, 246–54; 'Appeals to the House of Lords' [1957] *Crim. Law Rev.* 566–76.

[114] *R* v. *Wilkes* (1770) 4 Burr. 2527, 2551.

[115] (1855) 4 E. & B. 869.

[116] At 871. This would appear to be a case of the biter bit. Mansfield was well known for disputing the accuracy of reporters in inconvenient cases and here Campbell questions Burrow, usually regarded as one of the more careful ones.

[117] *History of the Criminal Law*, quoted in 'Appeals to the House of Lords', 568 n.9.

[118] Edwards, *Law Officers of the Crown*, 248–9.

predictable that in capital cases there might be considerable newspaper and parliamentary pressure, as was soon demonstrated with Steinie Morrison and Roger
Casement.[119]

The Attorney-General's third restraint on proceedings was a new development, commencing with the Roman Catholic Relief Act 1829.[120] This and cer
tain later statutes provided that no prosecution might be brought without his
consent.[121] The justifications were usually either (as in the Roman Catholic Relief
Act) that it was likely to attract many malicious or vexatious private prosecutions
or, as with the Official Secrets Act 1911, that the offence was essentially against
the state rather than an individual. Before the Criminal Law Commission in
1854 Campbell CJ and the Attorney-General (Cockburn) differed fundamentally on whether this restraint should be adopted more widely, and though the
Commission produced a rather startling proposal that it should be necessary 'in
cases where the defendant has not previously been taken before a magistrate'[122]
no general rule was made. It spread piecemeal, and with no discernible rationale,
but did not become seriously problematic until these clauses proliferated in wartime emergency legislation.[123]

Quite distinct from these roles was the Attorney-General's position as the
guardian of the public interest.[124] Originally exercised (either directly or through
a relator action) chiefly in relation to alleged misuse of charitable funds, it was
expanded by degrees to other wrongs which were not particular enough to give
any individual interest or reason to bring an action or which for various reasons might otherwise escape challenge. Beginning with public nuisances, these
situations extended to a wide range of *ultra vires* actions by public bodies.[125] As
Lord Halsbury made clear in *LCC v. Attorney-General*,[126] his discretion fell outside the courts' control, though he could not claim an injunction as of right.[127]
Lastly, it was the Attorney-General who was made defendant in actions against
the Crown. RSC 1883 Ord. 25, r 5 enabled declaratory judgments to be obtained in
this way with a view to creating a strong moral obligation in lieu of an injunction,

---

[119] *Ibid.*, 251–2.

[120] 10 Geo. IV c. 7.

[121] In some the Solicitor-General was specified, alone or as an alternative, but there was no general provision to this effect until 1944.

[122] *PP* 1856 (206), vii, 355–7, quoted in Edwards, *Law Officers of the Crown*, 240.

[123] Edwards, *Law Officers of the Crown*, 237–41.

[124] See generally *ibid.*, 286–95 and S. A. de Smith, *Judicial Review of Administrative Action* (1959),
323–72.

[125] See above, Pt 2, Chs II, IV.

[126] [1902] AC 165.

[127] *AG v. Birmingham, Tam and Lee District Drainage Board* [1910] 1 Ch. 48.

but only after *Dyson* v. *Attorney-General*[128] where the rules were given a broad enough interpretation to encourage this course of action.[129]

2. THE INNS OF COURT AND CHANCERY

The Benchers

Each inn of court was governed by its benchers, a self-perpetuating body of unrestricted size who added to their number as and when they chose. The normal qualifications remained age, wealth, and personal convenience rather than professional competence or success,[130] and benchers became a byword for elderly men, remote from the concerns of juniors and students and more interested in their dinners than anything else.[131] Though the composition of the benches did change significantly it was fortuitous rather than a response to the discontent of juniors. It had become the practice to elect new KCs almost automatically and this created two unforeseen difficulties: that the size of the bench would become unwieldy, and that either any discrimination must be abandoned or its exercise must be defensible, lest it create an invidious position for the rejected silk.[132]

The latter surfaced first and in the most embarrassing fashion. In 1845 the Tory Abraham Hayward, outspoken former editor of the *Law Magazine*, was blackballed by the Whig J. A. Roebuck in retaliation for an old slight. Hayward took his case to the judges, who correctly decided that he had no 'inchoate right' capable of being infringed but deplored the Inner Temple's practice; the response, to substitute a requirement of four black balls for one, was scarcely the improvement the judges had in mind.[133]

QCs continued to be chosen (only a few refused[134]) except in a handful of cases, such as Edwin James, where the inn judged them unsuitable, and the benches therefore grew ever larger and ever more remote from the junior bar, since no attempt was made to balance this influx by the addition of younger men. By 1877

---

[128] [1911] KB 410, [1912] 1 Ch. 159.

[129] De Smith, *Judicial Review of Administrative Action*, 370–2.

[130] D. Lemmings, *Professors of the Law* (Oxford, 2000), 257. Holdsworth's account of the government of the inns by the benchers (*HEL*) is a rather complacent one. M. Burrage, *The Revolution and Making of the Contemporary Legal Profession* (Oxford, 2006), also takes a more favourable view than the one presented here.

[131] C. Lamb, 'Essays of Elia: Old Benchers of the Middle Temple', in *Prose Works of Charles Lamb*, (1838), 188–207.

[132] The process has not been elucidated: see Holdsworth, *HEL*, xii, 19–26.

[133] 'The Ballot for Benchers' (1846) 4 (s2) *LM* 46–53; (1848) 8 *LR* 152–7.

[134] *Lincoln's Inn Black Books*, iv, vii.

they numbered between 50 and 70, except at Grays (just 21).[135] This trend had not perturbed the Inns of Court Commission in the 1850s and when a challenge came it was the result of the bad publicity over the handling of the disciplinary cases of James and Seymour.[136]

Sir George Bowyer, an equity draftsman and conveyancer, and two non-practising barristers presented a bill in 1862 which coupled reforms of the disciplinary jurisdiction with proposals to have a slender majority of benchers elected. Though the contrary arguments, that elections were undignified affairs in which men of refinement would shrink from standing and even voting and that because the Crown (via the QCs) in effect controlled the benches all was well, were unconvincing there was little support for this part of Bowyer's bill and he let it drop.[137] Roundell Palmer's mild attempt at democratization in the 1870s was equally unsuccessful. His Inns of Court Bill of 1874 would have reduced the number of benchers (50 for Lincoln's, 40 for each of the Temples, 20 for Grays) by allowing alternate vacancies to remain unfilled and the others to be filled alternately by a QC and a practising barrister of at least five years' standing. Some minor changes were made. The inns had to confront the situation brought about by the Judicature Acts and the dissolution in 1877 of Serjeants Inn. The judges returned to their own inns and except at Lincoln's Inn (which was accustomed to having judges as benchers) were accorded a sort of honorary status on the benches.[138] Lincoln's also limited benchers to 70 in 1875 and later made rather faint-hearted moves towards getting juniors onto the bench, but even there, the government of the inns remained essentially oligarchical, and reflective observers wondered at the apathy of the members.[139] Despite the attempts of a few brave souls at the Middle Temple in the 1890s to demand more democratic selection of benchers and the publication of accounts, the finances of the inns, audited only in the most perfunctory and amateurish manner, remained shrouded in secrecy.[140]

---

[135] D. Duman, *The English and Colonial Bars in the Nineteenth century* (1983), table 2.1 (the figure for Lincoln's Inn is from 1874). The Inner Temple alone refused to accept admissions *ad eundem* from the other inns, which had apparently been a popular move among new silks.

[136] See below, pp. 1082–3.

[137] Duman, *English and Colonial Bars*, 56–8; *PD* 1862 (s3) 167: 1030–73.

[138] *Lincoln's Inn Black Books*, v (1914–45) ed. Sir R. Roxburgh (1968), lxii.

[139] G. Alexander, *The Temple of the Nineties* (1938), 245–7.

[140] R. Abel-Smith and R. Stevens, *Lawyers and the Courts* (1967), 217; W. G. Thorpe, *Middle Temple Table Talk* (1894), 365–70. The refusal of the inns to publish their accounts had been the subject of earlier criticisms, e.g. 'Inns of Court—Finance in the Temple' (1860) 9 (s3) *LM & LR* 21–35.

Admission and Call

The inns had acquired the right both to lay down general requirements governing entrance to the profession and to exclude either from admission or call any individual whom they felt undesirable.[141] Spasmodic attempts to harmonize their rules had produced a substantial, though not complete, uniformity; thus, while none of the inns would call a person 'in trade', Grays and the Inner Temple would not even admit him.[142] Moreover, for some 20 years from 1829 the Inner Temple was unique in also imposing an entrance examination, while candidates at Lincoln's Inn had still to be approved by the 'Bar Table' (those barristers who happened to be dining in hall when he was proposed for admission); this veto could be overridden by the benchers, who took a more generous view in cases such as an inspector of taxes and the editor of *The Satirist*.[143] The principal safeguard against undesirable entrants was a certificate signed by a bencher or two barristers that the applicant was 'a gentleman of character and respectability'. Though the Commissioners objected that it might work hardship on those without connections it does not seem to have been too rigorous in practice.[144]

The power to refuse admission or call, being exercised without reference to any published criteria, was certainly liable to criticism. Its origin was 'involved in considerable obscurity'[145] and was supposed to have been devolved by the judges, who retained the power to police its exercise, though which judges and whether as visitors or otherwise remained obscure. The King's Bench, which had consistently declined to intervene in disputes between the benchers and members of the inns,[146] abdicated all responsibility when Thomas Wooler, whom Lincoln's Inn had not only refused to admit but even to supply reasons for their refusal, sought a *mandamus*.[147] Littledale J . held that 'those are voluntary societies, not submitting to any government. They may in their discretion admit or not, as they please; and the Court…has no power to compel them to admit any individual.'[148]

Littledale distinguished this situation from a refusal to call, where an appeal did lie to the judges, on the doubtful ground that the candidate once admitted

---

[141] No inn would admit a man rejected by another: P. Brady Leigh, *The Law Student's Guide* (1827), 33.

[142] *RC on the Inns of Court, PP* 1854–5 [1998], xviii, 6–7; W. C. Richardson, *A History of the Inns of Court* (Baton Rouge, USA, 1975), 34–6; Holdsworth, *HEL*, xii, 22–7.

[143] *Lincoln's Inn Black Books*, iv, 113, 119–20, 128.

[144] *Report 1855*, 6.

[145] *Ibid.*, 5.

[146] Richardson, *Inns of Court*, 33–9.

[147] It was common knowledge that his production of the *Black Dwarf* made him unacceptable: *Lincoln's Inn Black Books*, iv, 168–9; *R v. Benchers of Lincoln's Inn* (1825) 4 B. & C. 855.

[148] *Ibid.*, at 860–1.

acquired 'an inchoate right to be called',[149] but this was not a distinction that commended itself to the Commissioners and in 1837 the inns had agreed to extend
the same right of appeal to admissions.[150] In fact no further refusals attracted
any public attention until those of Miss Day and Christobel Pankhurst in the
Edwardian era, and those refusals were upheld on the grounds of their sex rather
than personal characteristics.[151]

However, in the 1830s the benchers of the Inner Temple were courting trouble
by refusing to call D. W. Harvey, a former attorney with a dubious record, despite
admitting him 11 terms before.[152] Harvey's appeal did not persuade the judges to
overturn the benchers' refusal but he was elected MP for Colchester in 1832 and
returned to the charge. Though his attempts to have the inns compelled to frame
fairer regulations failed, the Common Law Commissioners were instructed to
investigate.[153] Meanwhile Harvey obtained a rehearing, but the benchers remained
obdurate even in the face of a critical select committee report.[154]

The Commissioners deplored the lack of any regulations governing the conduct of appeals and rejected Littledale's position: 'the ordinary immunities of
a voluntary society ought not to be allowed to any body of persons claiming to
be the medium of admission into one of the learned professions. If the body is
to enjoy this privilege, it is not longer a private association, but one in which the
public has a deep interest, and the proceedings of which, if not adapted to the
pruposes of general utility, ought to be made so by the interposition of law.'[155]

While pronouncing the inns' general rules unexceptionable, they recommended that any new rules should require the sanction of the judges; refusals of
admission and call should be subject to an appeal and the veto of the Lincoln's
Inn bar table should be abolished.[156] As we have seen, the inns did extend the
right of appeal and Lincoln's did abandon the bar table's veto. As usual, the inns
escaped regulation by taking the minimum action required to deflect criticism.

Discipline

Like any voluntary society the inns had the power to expel members. In keeping
with its general attitude, the King's Bench, through Lord Ellenborough CJ, had

[149] *Ibid.*
[150] *RC on the Common Law, 6th Report, PP* 1834 (263), xxvi, 7–10; Holdsworth, *HEL*, xii, 27–8.
[151] M. J. Mossman, *The First Women Lawyers* (Oxford, 2006), 113–15.
[152] *RC on the Common Law, 6th Report,* App.; 'Case of D. W. Harvey' (1833) 10 *LM* 94–146; (1834)
12 *LM* 373–427.
[153] *PD* 1832 (s3) 13: 648–714.
[154] *RC on the Common Law, 6th Report,* 93.
[155] *Ibid.,* 8.
[156] *Ibid.,* 9.

firmly refused to involve itself in disputes over non-payment of dues.[157] More difficult were allegations that a barrister had contravened the ethical norms of the profession since, as critics were pointing out with increasing frequency, the inns had taken no steps to inform the profession what those norms were. Cockburn CJ quite aptly likened their general tenor to the military's catch-all 'conduct unbecoming',[158] but the lack of definition meant that sanctions were restricted to the most blatant violations of the unwritten code.[159]

The range of sanctions was limited, with nothing between 'screening' a censure (perhaps coupled with a ban on dining in hall) and permanent disbarment, so seldom used that a good deal of uncertainty surrounded the procedure.[160] Though this could lead to complaints of unfairness and inconsistency, action was sometimes unavoidable.[161] James Townshend Saward, barrister, master forger and high-class receiver known to the London underworld as 'Jem the Penman', lived his double life so long and so notoriously that his downfall in 1857 was a humiliating episode for the high-minded profession.[162] Such delinquencies seemed to reflect a growing disregard among barristers for the etiquette of the profession, and the weaknesses of the disciplinary process as well as the moral shortcomings of individuals were scandalously exposed in several cases around 1860.

The most sensational involved Edwin James. James epitomized a new type of barrister. A flashy, sometimes effective advocate but a shallow lawyer, he had long been suspected of gaining publicity by unscrupulous use of the press and was rumoured to have been made Recorder of Rye for hushing up the part played by Sir John Jervis in a corrupt by-election. Fashionable, high living and free spending, James was tipped as a coming law officer but was so questionable a character that the Inner Temple had not made him a bencher when he took silk.[163]

In the end rumours of scoundrelly conduct in two law cases, of immense debts, and of leeching the young son of a peer compelled the benchers to take action,

---

[157]   *Rosslyn v. Jodrell* (1815) 4 Camp. 303; Richardson, *Inns of Court*, 33–4.

[158]   G. Shaw Lefevre, 'The Discipline of the Bar' (1863) 15 (s3) *LM & LR* 1–42 at 9–10. 'Screening' (posting of a defaulter's name in hall) for non-payment of dues was said to have been resorted to more systematically at the Middle Temple in the 1880s than before: W. G. Thorpe, *The Still Life of the Middle Temple* (1892), 335.

[159]   Wesley Pue has argued that the inns used their disciplinary powers in a more purposeful way than is suggested here, in order to reinforce conservative professional and political norms by exemplary action against notoriously radical barristers: 'Lawyers and Political Liberalism in Eighteenth and Nineteenth Century England', in *Lawyers and the Rise of Western Political Liberalism*, ed. T. C. Halliday and L. Karpik (Oxford, 1997), 167–205, esp. 199–205.

[160]   W. W. Pue, 'Rebels at the Bar, English Barristers and the County Courts in the 1850s' (1987) 16 *Anglo-Am. Law Rev.* 308–52 at 347–51.

[161]   J. R. Lewis, *The Victorian Bar* (1982), 42.

[162]   *Ibid.*, 91–3.

[163]   *Ibid.*, 93–5.

but because, as was customary, details of the disbarment were not published, James was able to restart his career in the United States, presenting himself as the aggrieved victim of a prejudiced establishment.[164] Meanwhile the Middle Temple was grappling with the less straightforward case of W. Digby Seymour, another who had not been offered a seat on his inn's bench when given silk, this time on account of some questionable business dealings, which had also led to expulsion from the northern circuit mess. He escaped with a censure, but not before benchers had lost their dignity by engaging in a farcical struggle with a witness for possession of a document, leading to charges of assault.[165] Seymour refused to accept the verdict, raised it in the Commons,[166] and pointed to numerous deficiencies in the process against him—in particular that the succession of after-dinner hearings had been attended by different benchers each time.[167]

To correct these manifest deficiencies, Bowyer and Sir John Romilly brought forward schemes[168] and though neither came to fruition the inns were sufficiently alarmed at the threat to their autonomy to hold their own discussions about establishing some body to deal with questions of practice.[169] As noted elsewhere, they yielded to Cairns's Bar Education and Discipline Bill which would have created a council of 30 members, including six Crown nominees, but when it was dropped the reform of the disciplinary process lapsed. The Judicature Act 1873 did substitute the Lord Chancellor and a single judge of the KBD for the common law judges as a domestic tribunal[170] and in the last of the century's scandals, the disbarment by Grays of Kenealy in 1876, it was confirmed that the accused had the right to be given reasons for an adverse decision.[171] However, the only joint body to be set up was a 20-man committee established in 1894 to report on general issues of discipline.[172]

Chambers and Libraries

Not all London barristers were located in the inns. Some conveyancing counsel such as Swanston and the eccentric Charles Trevelyan had spilled out of Lincoln's

---

[164] Ibid.; 'Disbarment of Edwin James' (1860) 9 (s3) LM & LR 263–86.

[165] Lewis, Victorian Bar, 26.

[166] He also sued the Law Magazine and was awarded nominal damages: 'Report of the Trial of the Cause of Seymour v. Butterworth for Libel with Remarks' (1862–3) 14 (s3) LM & LR 181–338.

[167] Ibid.; Shaw Lefevre, 'Discipline of the Bar', 12.

[168] PD 1862 (s3) 167: 1030–40; Lincoln's Inn Black Books, v, lxvi.

[169] Duman, English and Colonial Bars, 57, 62–5.

[170] Section 12.

[171] Manisty v. Kenealy (unreported 1876).

[172] Lincoln's Inn Black Books, v, 298–9.

Inn into Chancery Lane, but only the very best could afford to take that risk.[173] All the inns had gone over to yearly tenancies, lettings for life were gradually extinguished and the practice of designating some eligible sets as 'benchers' chambers' was phased out after criticism from the Commissioners in 1855.[174]

There were other changes besides. With the exception of underpopulated Gray's, the inns sought to confine lettings to their own members. They ceased to be family residences and being exclusively the haunt of bachelors, the Temple at night became notorious for loose women (dollymops) and prostitutes.[175] That changed with the evolution of chambers into places purely of business. Young and impecunious men who still needed residential chambers were pushed upwards into the less spacious, less client-friendly chambers on the upper floors.[176] The rising number of bar students was accommodated by carving small, inconvenient rooms out of former bedrooms and closets but the inns did also build new chambers. Inner undertook a joint venture with Middle when the Thames embankment gave them extra space towards the river, resulting in some rather grand chambers by E. M. Barry.[177] None of the inns seems actually to have run short of space, and despite complaints about exorbitant rents[178] and some mismanagement, they did show sensitivity to the laws of supply and demand. Inner cut rents by 7½ per cent in the early 1850s during the slump at the common law bar and the Lincoln's Inn investigation in the 1890s recommended lower rents to attract the uncommitted student who gravitated to the Temple partly through cheapness.[179]

What did not change until the end of the century was the tradition that chambers would be shabby, drab and dim—it was hackneyed enough to feature in verses in *Punch*.[180] Only the new breed of super-rich Edwardian counsel seems to have begun smartening them up, Fletcher Moulton using trophies from his patent cases, and Joseph Walton with pictures.[181]

All the inns had libraries which possessed rare and valuable items, but they were not well adapted to student use in the content of their collection, their buildings or

---

[173] *Ibid.*, v, 277; R. and F. Davenport Hill, *A Memoir of Matthew Davenport Hill, Recorder of Birmingham* (1878), 97; A. J. Ashton, *As I Went on My Way* (1924), 89–103.

[174] *Report 1855*, 7; Thorpe, *Middle Temple Table Talk*, 367–8; Holdsworth, *HEL*, xii, 37.

[175] Thorpe, *Middle Temple Table Talk*, 296–7; J. C. Jeaffreson, *A Book About Lawyers*, 2 vols (1867), i, 163–4; Lewis, *Victorian Bar*, 56–8.

[176] G. B. Hurst, *Lincoln's Inn Essays* (1949), 66.

[177] G. Noel, *A Portrait of the Inner Temple* (2002), 55–63; G. Godwin, *The Middle Temple* (1954), 108–13. They also spent heavily on restoring the Temple church.

[178] e.g. 'The Inns of Court Commission' (1854) 21 (s2) *LM* 49–50; Jeffreason, *Book About Lawyers*, i, 164.

[179] *RC on the Inns of Court 1855*, W. Whateley, q. 220; *Lincoln's Inn Black Books*, v, 280–1.

[180] Quoted in H. H. L. Bellot, *The Inner and Middle Temple* (1902), 81. Among many descriptions see Alexander, *Temple of the Nineties*, 91 and C. P. Hawkes, *Chambers in the Temple* (1930), 3.

[181] A. W. Myers, 'KCs and their Chambers' (1903) 25 *Strand Mag.* 135–42.

their opening hours.[182] In all cases, however, the buildings were either replaced and/ or enlarged.[183] They were not always generous with their spending, however, and it was said that the meanness of the Middle Temple librarian over textbooks led the British Museum to complain of too many law students resorting to its collection.[184] To their credit, however, all the inns contributed in proportion to their members to the expense of the bar library in the Royal Courts of Justice in 1884.[185]

The Four Inns

> Inner for the rich man, Middle for the poor, Lincoln's for the gentleman,
> Gray's for the boor.

When quoting the old rhyme in 1919, J. A. Strahan was careful to disclaim its continuing applicability to Gray's.[186] Nevertheless, for almost all of the period under consideration, Gray's was unfashionable and in a decline which at one stage threatened to become terminal. From an entry comparable with Middle Temple in the 1820s there was a rapid and inexplicable falling off to only 15 admissions in 1850, and not a single student was called in 1873.[187]

Gray's was less convenient for the courts, particularly while the London streets were in the condition described in *Bleak House*, and with the legal world so compact even a short distance could be isolating. However, that does not explain the earlier fluctuations nor the precipitate decline in mid-century and it meant that it was cheaper to rent chambers.[188] This attracted a considerable Irish contingent, and since for the most part they came to fulfil the two-year qualification period before returning home, cheapness was a serious consideration.[189] The Irish contributed to a convivial atmosphere but hibernian numbers and boisterousness were thought to have put off home students.[190] Gray's was unlike the other inns in not becoming exclusively a barristers' haunt and had a motley character as

---

[182] Hurst, *Lincoln's Inn Essays*, 69; 'Inns of Court' (1848) 8 *LR* 152–7.

[183] *Lincoln's Inn Black Books*, v, at xxxvi, xxxix, xlii, lxx–lxxi;. C. E. A. Bedwell, *A Brief History of Middle Temple* (1909), 95–9; Bellot, *Inner and Middle Temple*, 107–50, 290–3; W. R. Douthwaite, *Gray's Inn, its History and Associations* (1886), 171–82.

[184] Sir F. D. MacKinnon, *Inner Temple Papers* (1948), 101; Thorpe, *Still Life*, 348.

[185] *Lincoln's Inn Black Books*, v, lxxx.

[186] *Bench and Bar* (1919), 194.

[187] R. Abel, *Legal Profession in England and Wales* (Oxford, 1988), table 1.10; F. Cowper, *A Prospect of Gray's Inn* (1951), 114–15.

[188] W. R. Ball, *The Student's Guide to the Bar* (1878, 1884 edn), 14–15.

[189] H. B. Thomson, *The Choice of a Profession* (1857), 116.

[190] Thorpe, *Still Life*, 331; A. Polson, *Law and Lawyers*, 2 vols (1840), i, 121; Cowper, *Prospect of Gray's Inn*, 126.

'that straggling caravanserai for the reception of moneylenders, Bohemians, and eccentric gentlemen'.[191]

The critical state of its affairs in the 1870s finally prompted the benchers to action, and though scholarships and a new library[192] were offset by a rising overdraft and a peculating steward, rescue efforts led by Lewis Coward and Miles Mattinson and the urgings of F. E. Smith revived admissions dramatically from 29 in 1893 to 113 in 1910. Though still the smallest of the inns Gray's was no longer the poor relation.[193]

Lincoln's began the nineteenth century as the premier inn both for the 'gentleman' and for the ambitious practitioner.[194] In 1842 it mustered 42 per cent of barristers named in the *Law List* and had been busily buying back chambers, renovating old buildings and erecting new ones; £88,000 went on its new hall and library, opened in 1845.[195] Uniquely it still maintained the form of exercises for pupils but they had become a ritual farce and were abolished in 1856.[196]

From the 1850s Lincoln's went into a worrying decline. In part this was a direct result of its ever-closer links with the court of Chancery and the equity bar and its advocacy of concentrating the courts of equity within the precincts of the inn.[197] This made it almost necessary for leading equity counsel to reside in there, which drove up rents and put off newcomers whose aspirations lay at common law.[198] Top floors remained largely residential, it being felt that solicitors would not willingly climb so high[199] and by the time rents of the cheaper sets were reduced to competitive levels a rapid loss of popularity had already set in.[200]

By 1863 the inn's share of the bar had fallen abruptly to 13 per cent and the removal of the courts of equity to the Strand in 1883 and the difficulties of the junior equity bar hit hard. A committee set up by the benchers in 1890 was decidedly pessimistic about the prospects of the equity bar and the inn but the pessimism was misplaced.[201] Chancery rallied and with the general expansion of the bar Lincoln's returned to favour, though numbers did not match the Temple. More sedate than the Temple, it was closer to the big solicitors in the Fields outside the

[191] Jeaffreson, *Book About Lawyers*, i, 175.

[192] Cowper, *Prospect of Gray's Inn*, 114–16; Douthwaite, *Gray's Inn*, 179–80.

[193] Cowper, *Prospect of Gray's Inn*, 163; Lord Birkenhead, *F.E.: The Life of F.E. Smith, First Earl of Birkenhead*, 2 vols (1933, 1959 edn), i, 70; Abel, *Legal Profession*, table 1.12.

[194] Lemmings, *Professors of the Law*, 64–6.

[195] *Lincoln's Inn Black Books*, iv, 185–96; RC on the Inns of Court 1855, M. Dolye, q. 101.

[196] Richardson, *Inns of Court*, 319–21.

[197] See above, p. 782.

[198] *Lincoln's Inn Black Books*, v, 277.

[199] *Ibid.*, v, xxxiii–xxxv; Hurst, *Lincoln's Inn Essays*, 66.

[200] *Lincoln's Inn Black Books*, v, 281.

[201] *Ibid.*, v, xx–xxi, 276–81.

gate, and when the Land Registry and the Public Trustee were located there, it reinforced the 'property' character of the inn.

'Inner for the rich man' was only true if the rich man could be equated with the 'varsity man', for its reputation was certainly as the preferred inn for the public school and Oxbridge product.[202] Besides its shortlived entrance examination, it made laudable but unsuccessful attempts in the 1830s and 1840s to revive learning through the creation of lectureships.[203] Profiting from the fire started by the inattentive William Maule to improve some wretched old sets, equipped with a new hall and library, and offering the reduced rents in the 1850s, the Inner boomed. In 1878 it admitted more than 200, a figure unmatched until Middle Temple in 1910[204] and its 400 sets were all needed, since for the rest of the period it regularly admitted more than 150 a year, around 30 per cent of the total.

Among the inns the Middle Temple was the most cosmopolitan, the most democratic in its dining arrangements (being alone in not ordering the tables by seniority) and perhaps the most sociable.[205] If not 'for the poor' it was certainly the favourite among those who came late to the bar and later among graduates of London University.[206] From the 1880s onwards, however, it was most clearly distinguished from the other inns by the influx of students from the empire, in particular from the east. By 1914, when three-fifths of the intake were from overseas, it had become the biggest inn.[207] More generous scholarships were part of the attraction, but cheapness was probably a bigger one, though the most sought after chambers, those new ones towards the river, were expensive.[208]

The Inns of Chancery

Each of the inns of Chancery, reduced to eight in number by Coke's time, was loosely affiliated to an inn of court which exercised 'a certain supervisory jurisdiction over it'.[209] However, having first become the haunt of attorneys rather than barristers, they subsequently lost any real connection with the legal profession.[210]

---

[202] J. A. Shearwood, *A Guide for Candidates for the Professions of Barrister and Solicitor* (2nd edn, 1887), 1; Ball, *Student's Guide*, 17; Alexander, *Temple of the Nineties*, 78. Its examination had brought in more university men: *RC on the Inns of Court 1855*, Whateley, q. 329.

[203] *RC on the Inns of Court Report 1855*, G. Bryant, qq. 1670 et seq.

[204] Abel, *Legal Profession*, table 1.12

[205] Thorpe, *Still Life*, 331.

[206] Shearwood, *Guide*, 1–2; Ball, *Student's Guide*, 17.

[207] Abel, *Legal Profession*, table 1.12.

[208] Shearwood, *Guide*, 12–13; Godwin, *Middle Temple*, 108–9.

[209] Richardson, *Inns of Court*, 5.

[210] *Ibid.*, 5–7.

Their mostly ancient buildings occupied prime sites along Holborn and Chancery Lane and were all sold as the area was redeveloped.

Since the Inns of Court Commission had dismissively concluded that they held no property on charitable trusts, nor possessed any income which might be devoted to public purposes,[211] there seemed no reason to obstruct this process and the sale of Lyon's Inn in 1863 aroused little interest,[212] but controversy generated by the sale of Serjeants' Inn in 1877 and lively debates about legal education made the sale of Clement's Inn in 1884 less straightforward. The Law Society failed in its allegation that the inn was subject to charitable trusts, but some of the members who benefited by the windfall prudently made a large donation for the purpose of legal education.[213] Threats of a further challenge were made when the Prudential bought Staple and Furnival's Inns but seemingly did not materialize and an attempt to intervene in the sale of Barnard's in 1892 was unsuccessful.[214]

Nevertheless, when the last two, Cliffords and New Inn were disposed of, the latter as a compulsory purchase by the LCC for road widening, claims were made. The New Inn case was settled on terms which extracted £55,000 for the provision of legal education.[215] The other case was fought out and in *Smith* v. *Kerr* the bulk of its proceeds of £100,000 was held charitable; both sums went to swell the war chest of the proposed 'general school of law'.[216] The halls of Barnard's Inn and (more prominently) Staple Inn survive, but the inns themselves are dead and gone.

3. THE BAR COMMITTEE AND BAR COUNCIL

Many members of the junior bar, especially on the common law side, were aggrieved that during the threatening reformist ferment of the 1870s their interests were not adequately defended. The Attorney-General was in an equivocal position and the numerous barristers in Parliament were mostly eminent and successful men, remote from the concerns of the rank-and-file. The latter looked enviously at the solicitors' institutions, which were more vigorous in defence of their members than the gerontocracy of the inns.[217]

In 1883 this exasperation translated into purposeful activity. A new set of rules of court threatened drastically to reduce the openings for juniors and came hard

---

[211] *RC on the Inns of Court 1855*, 5.
[212] Richardson, *Inns of Court*, 7.
[213] Abel-Smith and Stevens, *Lawyers and the Courts*, 174–5.
[214] *Ibid*, 175; Richardson, *Inns of Court*, 7.
[215] *Ibid*.
[216] *Ibid*. Smith v. Kerr (1900) 2 Ch. 511, [1902] 1 Ch. 774. See below, pp. 1191, 1197.
[217] Abel-Smith and Stevens, *Lawyers and the Courts*, 214–15.

on the heels of legislation tending to diminish counsel's conveyancing role.[218] More than 1000 attended a bar meeting and a Bar Committee was formed 'to collect and express the opinion[s] of the members of the Bar on matters affecting the profession and to take such action thereon as may be deemed expedient'. A telling indication of the truculent mood of the juniors was the composition of the Committee, with equal numbers drawn from the QCs, the men of 10 years' standing and the more junior.[219]

The Committee failed in its immediate object, a review of the new rules, despite a forceful challenge by its chairman, Sir Hardinge Giffard, in the Commons.[220] However, the bar benefited from Giffard becoming Lord Chancellor in 1885. Selborne had agreed that the Bar Committee should be given an opportunity to make representations before new rules became effective, but Halsbury gave them the right to be consulted at the drafting stage. Their comments were usually conservative, as in their desire to revert to closing the Westminster courts during the circuits.[221] The Committee also sought a role in the internal regulation of the profession in such matters as the two-counsel rule and retainers,[222] but as it became clear that it had no real authority and external threats receded, early enthusiasm waned, attendance at annual meetings dropped, and despite the efforts of its energetic secretary S. H. S. Lofthouse, subscribers diminished.[223]

The apathy was dispelled in 1894, partly through the energetic efforts F. O. Crump, editor of *The Law Times*. His views were not generally accepted, not least because he sought to have the Committee operate explicitly in the interests of the 'working part' of the profession,[224] but they seem to have stirred the bar from its slumbers. Another very large meeting transformed the Bar Committee into a Bar Council with a wider remit, though one which still fell well short of Crump's grandiose ideas.[225]

The Bar Council was accepted as the counterpart of the Law Society and officially recognized in the Rule Committee Act 1909, which gave it two representatives (in practice a KC and a junior) on the Committee.[226] Moreover, it always provided a

---

[218] See above, pp. 765–6.

[219] Abel-Smith and Stevens, *Lawyers and the Courts*, 214–15.

[220] *PD* 1883 (s3) 283: 145–87.

[221] Abel-Smith and Stevens, *Lawyers and the Courts*, 216. For an example of their input see (1892–3) 37 *Sol. J.* 127.

[222] Abel-Smith and Stevens, *Lawyers and the Courts*, 217; (1889–90) 34 *Sol. J.* 423; (1890–1) 35 *Sol. J.* 209.

[223] Abel-Smith and Stevens, *Lawyers and the Courts*, 216–17; R. J. C. Cocks, *Foundations of the Modern Bar* (1883), 215–16.

[224] Cocks, *Foundations of the Modern Bar*, 217–19.

[225] The Council was the product of a committee chaired by Sir Henry James: (1893–4) 38 *Sol. J.* 603.

[226] S. Rosenbaum, 'Studies in English Civil Procedure II: The Rule-Making Authority' (1915) 63 *University of Pennsylvania Law Rev.* 151–82, 165 n.50. The Lord Chancellor had previously exercised the power given to him in 1894 to appoint a barrister to the committee.

nominee for royal commissions and departmental committees and to judge from the reports of the annual bar meeting it gave general satisfaction in that role.

The relationship of the Council with the circuits and the inns was more delicate. Gradually circuit messes acquiesced in the Council making rules of etiquette binding on their members[227] but it had been folly for the bar meeting to demand an annual subsidy of £1000 from the inns to fund a permanent secretariat while seeking to take over their disciplinary function. After some testy negotiations, the Council had to be satisfied with £600 a year and was forced to leave the inns' powers essentially intact.[228] In fact the new body soon found itself able to cohabit quite comfortably with the old. It was convenient for the inns to have another body pronounce upon difficult questions of etiquette, while the Council's existence masked their scarcely challengeable powers over admissions and calls. [229]

4. CIRCUITS AND BAR MESSES

Circuit life had an importance in the life of the bar which transcended the Assizes as a source of briefs.[230] On circuit barristers were most nearly able to live up to the elevated conception of their calling which they affected and, in their own eyes at least, made them more than a mere profession. On circuit they partook of the majesty of the law in its solemn progress round the counties and circuit etiquette emphasized that this was a company of gentlemen. The ban on travelling by public conveyance (and later the insistence on first-class rail travel); insistence on staying in lodgings rather than hotels, and communal dining, besides creating a *cordon sanitaire* preventing contamination by attorneys, were ways of maintaining social difference.[231]

Circuit life was also designed to emphasize the collective aspect of the bar and to soften the harsh individualism that underlay the competition for business. Men who went without any expectation of briefs were particularly welcomed and the customs of the mess—temporary inversions of status, mock courts, and fines—helped the unsuccessful to sublimate their envy of the successful.[232] Not

---

[227] A. Harwood, *Circuit Ghosts, a Western Circuit Miscellany* (Winchester, 1980), 111; Cocks, *Foundations of the Modern Bar,* 219.

[228] Abel-Smith and Stevens, *Lawyers and the Courts,* 218–19.

[229] The raising of the inns' grant to the £1000 originally sought in 1909 is an indication that demarcation disputes had been settled. On the eve of the war there was talk of establishing a bar association along the lines of the American Bar Association, but seemingly it came to nothing: (1914) 33 *LN* 162.

[230] The best scholarly account is Cocks, *Foundations of the Modern Bar.*

[231] e.g. E. Cox, *The Advocate* (1852), 272–3; [J. A. Foote], *Pie-Powder* (1911), 44.

[232] A good account of the bar mess in operation is in A. Ward, *Stuff and Silk* (Ramsey, ?1948).

everyone enjoyed the atmosphere of bachelor jollity; Campbell soon grew tired of it, Disraeli disparaged it in fiction as 'a cold and mercantile adventure', and the patrician intellectual Robert Cecil found the 'childish ceremony' an ordeal. [233]

Each circuit had its own character. They had their own songs and stories and a hard core of veteran circuiteers who were the custodians of circuit traditions, men like Thomas Blofield on the Norfolk.[234] Some of these customs were assembled into collections, yet the best account of circuit life, Alderson Foote's *Pie-Powder* (1911), is suffused with melancholy and is really an elegy for a passing world.[235] And many were marked by a common theme: circuit life was not what it was.[236]

In fact it is striking how much of circuit life survived well into the twentieth century. The nineteenth had opened with six English circuits and closed with six. The northern had been divided, the home and Norfolk amalgamated in the south-eastern, but of the others only the midland had undergone substantial alterations. Circuit membership had risen remarkably from 316 in 1820 to 1994 in 1900.[237] Whole sets of chambers like Salter's still emptied for the circuits and most of the ritual of the circuit mess was still intact.[238]

Yet the *laudatores tempori acti* were right. Making all allowances for their nostalgia, circuits were less attractive than before. On the south-eastern and the northern it became impossible to know all one's fellow circuiteers and at least from the 1850s some men were no longer going the whole circuit, something which Coleridge found especially saddening.[239] Successful men forsook the smaller towns, making it a farce in some places on the midland, as Atlay (a circuit enthusiast) lamented.[240] A small core kept up the old tradition but the railway, and at the very end of the period the motorcar, made it easy for men to drop in and out of the circuit and the rules had to bend to accommodate realities;[241] the sale of the western circuit's van in 1893 marked an epoch.[242] The circuits furthest from London found it easier to keep up a semblance of the old life, but it was no longer the same anywhere.

[233] Hardcastle, *Life of Lord Campbell*, i, 224; J. A. Lovat-Fraser, 'Disraeli and the Law' (1913–14) 49 (s5) *LM & R* 427–32; K. Rose, *The Later Cecils* (1975), 135; Cocks, *Foundations of the Modern Bar*, 171–2.

[234] Lewis, *Victorian Bar*, 10–11; Cocks, *Foundations of the Modern Bar*, 166–73.

[235] Foote is described in B. Coleridge, *This For Remembrance* (1925), 48. Even J. T. Coleridge's *My Recollections of the Circuit* (Exeter, 1859) strikes this note.

[236] Cocks, *Foundations of the Modern Bar*, 169–73.

[237] Duman, *English and Colonial Bars*, table 2.2.

[238] A. Smith, *Lord Goddard* (1959), 16.

[239] Cox, *The Advocate*, 270–5; Coleridge, *My Recollections of the Circuit*.

[240] [Foote], *Pie-Powder*, 3–11; Cocks, *Foundations of the Modern Bar*, 165.

[241] Ward, *Stuff and Silk*, 60, dates the motor car's appearance from c.1910.

[242] Harwood, *Circuit Ghosts*, 106.

'Social' circuiteers, the gentlemen barristers, were seen no more; Joseph Sharpe, a yeoman bachelor, was the last on the northern.[243] Assize balls disappeared, judges ceased to give dinners to local worthies and to their friends among the bar.[244] 'Grand Nights' remained, but much of their splendour had departed, and the hard-drinking culture which had been a feature of some circuits in their heyday also vanished.[245] Many blamed the railway, but other causes were intrinsic to the legal system. County courts and the extended jurisdiction of quarter sessions took away business and continuous sittings of the High Court in London (helped by the creation of district registries) offered litigants an alternative to waiting on the next Assize, as well as forcing barristers to choose whether to go circuit or remain in town.[246] Local bars created formidable competition for business just where it was heaviest and the wonder is perhaps that so many men continued to go circuit.[247]

The shrinking attendance at circuit dinners had its effect on the role of the bar mess as an arbiter of conduct. This echoed the way the inns sought to be private clubs exercising public functions and had been controversial enough when the Norfolk acted against Kelly and O'Malley in the 1830s and the home against Ellis-Davis in the 1870s,[248] but it could not be pretended that the deliberations of a handful of men (and often juniors at that) without access to precedents on their own, or practice on other circuits, represented the feeling of the circuit.[249] Some circuits resorted to delegating duties to their wine committee, since that necessarily met regularly for their primary purpose, and at least on the Norfolk and western, these acquired disciplinary functions—indeed Foote felt that the chairman had become something of a tyrant.[250]

With the formation of the Bar Council the role of the circuit messes in developing and defining etiquette became much diminished and a greater uniformity prevailed, so it was no longer necessary for the newcomer to ask the circuit leader what its rules were.[251] The mess could now concentrate on its social side.[252]

---

[243] J. B. Sandbach, *This Old Wig* [n.d.], 52.

[244] Lewis, *Victorian Bar*, 12–13; Sir F. D. Mackinnon, *On Circuit* (1940), 37.

[245] [Espinasse], 'My Contemporaries', (1832) 6 *Fraser's Mag.* 322.

[246] Foote believed the introduction of judgment by default (RSC Ord. 14) contributed: 'Pie-Powder', 6–7.

[247] The author of *The Legal Profession* (27–30), and 'Two Idle Apprentices', *Sketches of the Bar and the Press* (1872), 43–61, noted this trend, and see 'E' [Bowen Rowlands], 'Leaders of the Bar', (1896) 12 *Strand Mag.* 559–71.

[248] Cocks, *Foundations of the Modern Bar*, 15–17, 147–8.

[249] The western, for example, did not record any decisions until the 1920s: Harwood, *Circuit Ghosts*, 70.

[250] Cocks, *Foundations of the Modern Bar*, 151–2; [Foote], *Pie-Powder*, 38–40.

[251] *The Advocate*, 278. Some of the Oxford circuit's rules are in App. I to G. Williams, *Death of a Circuit* (2006).

[252] e.g. cricket matches; several are recorded in *MCC Scores and Biographies*.

Each circuit had its own distinctive character and rules. The western always prided itself on being rather special and thanks to the writings of the Coleridges (three generations went the circuit and attained the bench) and Foote is probably the best known. It included many west countrymen and was perhaps at its zenith in the 1830s and 1840s when Cockburn, Crowder, and Follett competed for the lead, but remained strong for most of the century.[253] Renowned for the discursiveness of its practitioners, even some leaders such as Crowder, which drove Assize judges to distraction,[254] it was barely affected by the changes of the 1870s and the Bristol bar was not strong enough to be much of a threat.[255] Traditions were upheld by Foote, E. U. Bullen, and 'Tommy' Bucknill, but though the numbers had risen to 200 from just 58 in 1820 the calibre declined, perhaps because it did not produce much commercial work.[256]

The chronicler of the Oxford circuit, Sir R. Bosanquet, tells the same tale of departing glories as Foote. The van was gone; men who could not get briefs gave up more quickly; the seniors were highly selective in their choice of towns, and for a time the nominal and invisible leader was Lewis Edmunds of the patent bar.[257] Perhaps the most of conservative of circuits, it preserved the old ways longer than most and much of the social life remained intact, the fortunate being entertained at Stavely Hill's country house.[258] It was weak in the 1820s, the leader, Dauncey being little regarded even in the Exchequer, not the strongest of courts.[259] His successor John Jervis was much more formidable, though it was not from men of the world like Jervis that the circuit gained its reputation for refinement,[260] but rather from Oxonians who liked the opportunity to keep in touch with their old college. Even so, it grew more slowly than most until near the end of the century, when it mustered 239.[261] Business failed to keep pace, hence perhaps its reputation for slow speech and a capacity for drawing out proceedings.[262] Even crime was not

[253] Coleridge, *Life and Correspondence of J.D. Coleridge*, i, 177–8, ii, 195; Sir E. Clarke, *The Story of My Life* (1918), 76–7; Harwood, *Circuit Ghosts*, 86–8.

[254] B. C. Robinson, *Bench and Bar* (1889 edn), 129–30, 140; Harwood, *Circuit Ghosts*, 76.

[255] Harwood, *Circuit Ghosts*, 222–3.

[256] H. L. Cancellor, *The Life of a London Beak* (1930), 235–46; E. Manson, *Builders of our Law in the Reign of Queen Victoria* (1895, 2nd edn, 1904), 355–67; Duman, *English and Colonial Bars*, table 2.2

[257] *The Oxford Circuit* (1951).

[258] A. C. Plowden, *Grain or Chaff?* (1903), 137. Jay (*The Law*, (1868) 324) believed it was one of the least strict on etiquette.

[259] Hardcastle, *Life of Lord Campbell*, i, 247–51; [Collier], *Criticisms on the Bar*, 135–48.

[260] Plowden, *Grain or Chaff?*, 140.

[261] Duman, *English and Colonial Bars*, table 2.2.

[262] Plowden, *Grain or Chaff?*, 121; Bosanquet, *Oxford Circuit*, 'E' [Bowen Rowlands], *Leaders of the Bar*, 560.

abundant except in the savage parts of Staffordshire and the Forest of Dean, and circuiteers found the Birmingham local bar a formidable competitor.[263]

Short and compact, except between 1864 and 1876, when York and Leeds were added to relieve the northern, the midland was favoured by juniors.[264] In 1884 Birmingham at last became an Assize town, inconveniently tacked onto the end of the circuit apparently to preserve the holidays of the Clerks of Assize.[265] Lord Birkenhead disparaged it as 'provincial in sympathy and prejudiced in influence', and it never seems to have been really fashionable.[266] M. D. Hill and Thomas Denman in the 1820s chose it for cheapness and small numbers[267] and it remained small (just 63 in 1860) until a spectacular rise with the addition of big cities, when numbers tripled in 20 years.[268] Ballantine found it highly convivial and it certainly had its share of 'characters' like the Clarkes, father and son, who were among the leaders in the 1820s and 1830s.[269] The local Birmingham bar contributed its share of oddities—apparently it 'ran to freaks', men like Pye, successively an anglican and roman catholic clergyman, and the tempestuous Pym Yeatman.[270] It was in Birmingham too that Charles Rann Kennedy and his 'rebels at the bar' had attempted to defy the convention against direct access to clients.[271]

The Norfolk was something of a backwater. Just 19 strong in 1800, it mustered barely 50 in 1860, and in 1876 its independent existence came to an abrupt end with its merger with the home to form the south-eastern.[272] A cosy, self-contained world in Crabb Robinson's time[273] it was riven by two linked controversies which shattered the old order in the 1830s and produced the peculiar feature of a 'mess club' performing the functions of the bar mess which was dissolved. One of the protagonists, O'Malley, later became circuit leader and with another Irishman, D. D. Keane, imparted such a 'combustible' air to it that the young J. G. Witt rapidly moved to the home.[274] Elderly judges put up with that atmosphere in exchange for light business, and the Norfolk remained the quietest of circuits until its abrupt demise. Most of the Assize towns in the home counties were transferred to the

[263] Plowden, *Grain or Chaff?*, 95; Bosanquet, *Oxford Circuit*, 21.

[264] Walton, *Random Recollections*; Ward, *Stuff and Silk*.

[265] Ward, *Stuff and Silk*, 21, 207; Walton, *Random Recollections, Second Series* (1873), 162–4.

[266] Lord Birkenhead, *Fourteen English Judges* (1926), 305.

[267] R. and F. Davenport-Hill, *Memoir of M.D. Hill*, 47; Arnould, *Lord Denman*, i, 58.

[268] Duman, *English and Colonial Bars*, table 2.2.

[269] W. S. Ballantine, *Some Experiences of a Barrister's Life* (6th edn, 1883), 105; Walton, *Random Recollections*, 18–23.

[270] Bosanquet, *Oxford Circuit*, 65; Polden, 'Doctor in Trouble', 37–40.

[271] See below, pp. 1098–9.

[272] Duman, *English and Colonial Bars*, table 2.2.

[273] Crabb Robinson, *Diaries etc.*, *passim*. It was also the scene of Matthew Arnold's flirtation with the bar: H. C. Merivale, *Bar, Stage and Platform*, 2 vols (1902), 278 *et seq.*

[274] Cocks, *Foundations of the Modern Bar*, 15–18; Witt, *Lifetime in the Law*, 42–3.

midland and the truncated Norfolk was swamped by the much greater numbers from the home, despite the gallant efforts of Thomas Blofeld, which did succeed in preserving some of its traditions.[275]

The home circuit had the regular social apparatus of bar mess, Grand Nights, balls etc., but due to the proximity of some centres to London there was never quite the same sense of an expedition; after all, the impecunious could and did walk from London to some of these towns.[276] It rapidly outgrew all but the northern, doubling in size to 141 by 1840 and again to 285 by 1860,[277] but many regulars were chiefly criminal practitioners and even in Campbell's time few went down into Sussex.[278] The commuting element on the home naturally became much stronger with the coming of the railway and John Day's anachronistic attempt to preserve the tradition of riding the circuit horseback seemed particularly forlorn. It was harder for such a circuit to agree and enforce rules of conduct and the home was curiously vague on many important rules. Despite its size fewer than half were regular circuiteers and it scarcely mustered enough for a decent circuit dinner.[279]

The home was a sitting target for reformers and was the sacrificial victim to the Judicature Commission. However, the Commissioners might differ on the future shape of provincial justice they could agree that Surrey business should be done in London, and without Surrey there was no rationale for the home circuit.[280] Its shotgun marriage with the Norfolk created the south-eastern, a pale shadow of the home and made up largely of Londoners without roots in the counties.[281] It was among the first where judges' dinners were discontinued and pomp and circumstance faded out. [282]

The northern also faced major surgery in the 1870s, but with less depressing consequences. It had always been dauntingly long and arduous, so much so that the winter Assize did not venture into its furthest recesses.[283] The expansion of its industrial towns demanded first a third Assize and then a fourth and altogether it posed the most severe tests for the viability of the circuit system. Apparently tiny

[275] Cocks, *Foundations of the Modern Bar*, 165–7.
[276] Robinson, *Bench and Bar*, 33–6.
[277] Duman, *English and Colonial Bars*, table 2.2.
[278] Hardcastle, *Life of Lord Campbell*, i, 209.
[279] Cocks, *Foundations of the Modern Bar*, 149, 165–7; R. Harris (ed.), *Reminiscences of Sir Henry Hawkins, Baron Brampton* (1904), 72.
[280] See above, pp. 776–80.
[281] Alverstone, *Recollections of Bar and Bench*, 7; Witt, *Lifetime in the Law*, 87–8. According to Parry, the abolition of local venue resulted in most of the better men deserting the circuit for London: *My Own Way* (1912), 145.
[282] J. S. Rentoul, *Stray Thoughts and Memories* (1921), 69; Cocks, *Foundations of the Modern Bar*, 156; 'E' [Bowen-Rowlands], 'Leaders of the Bar', 566.
[283] J. S. Cockburn, 'The Northern Circuit' (1968) 3 *Northern History* 118–30.

in the 1780s, it soon became rivalled only by the home in size and in the 1820s hosted the epic battles of Scarlett, Brougham, and Pollock.[284] It was therefore unfortunate, if understandable, that most of the senior judges tried to avoid it, Campbell being one who swore never to go again.[285]

In the mid-century it was rivalled by the western for the quality of the bar, though not the importance of its business, but it soon recovered preeminence.[286] Its Grand Nights and subscription dinners were splendid,[287] but if it was sociable it was also tough and hugely competitive, with solicitors and clients expecting a no-frills, robust style.[288]

The division of the circuit in 1876 was a logical step, mooted more than 30 years before, but it caused considerable friction.[289] The north-western towns won the right to the old name (by the toss of a coin according to one account) and the 'new' northern remained the stronger. Men of the quality of Herschell, Russell, and Gully had to fight to get a start, and no wonder the very 'Oxford' manner of A. V. Dicey was a failure.[290] Holker's plain, artless style had some successful imitators on both northern and north-eastern but so strong were the local bars on the former, that circuiteers could be dismissed as 'of no account'.[291]

5. THE ETIQUETTE OF THE BAR

Introduction

The etiquette of the bar prescribed a code of conduct for barristers in their dealings with clients, attorneys, and each other.[292] In the mid-nineteenth century it was pronounced 'somewhat vague and difficult to define precisely. So much uncertainty prevails in matters of detail, that the highest authorities differ on points

---

[284] Lemmings, *Professors of the Law*, 263; Duman, *English and Colonial Bars*, table 2.2. T. H. Ford, *Henry Brougham and his World* (Chichester, 1995), offers a detailed, if rather partisan, account.

[285] MacKinnon, *On Circuit*, 14; Hardcastle, *Life of Lord Campbell*, ii, 310.

[286] Jeaffreson, *Book about Lawyers*, ii, 273.

[287] Sir W. F. Pollock, *Personal Reminiscences of Sir Frederick Pollock, second Baronet*, 2 vols (1887) i, 216.

[288] [Foulkes], *Generation of Judges*, 54–9.

[289] (1841) 25 *LM*, 472; A. G. C. Liddell, *Notes from the Life of an Ordinary Mortal* (1911), 146–7. Biographical details of members of the northern circuit are given in D. Lynch, *The Northern Circuit Directory 1876–2004* (Liverpool, 2005).

[290] Heuston, *Lives of the Lord Chancellors*, 87; R. A. Cosgrove, *The Rule of Law: Albert Venn Dicey, Victorian Jurist* (Chapel Hill, USA, 1980), 29.

[291] 'E', [Bowen Rowlands] 'Leaders of the Bar', 561.

[292] C. R. Kennedy claimed that he was 'obliged to use the French word; England has no name for such an absurdity': quoted in Pue, *Rebels at the Bar*, 340 n.163.

of constant recurrence…',[293] and not surprisingly, with 'laws…so uncertain and indefinite…it is almost impossible that any one should be punished for their breach'.[294] These blurred outlines had some advantages, for changes could be brought about informally and individual and local breaches could be quietly ignored. However, over the century many of the elements constituting the etiquette of the bar were made more precise and formal.

Though they have been grouped into categories,[295] these categories overlap considerably. Nevertheless, '[t]aken together, these rules represented a starkly anti-commercial ideology of legal practice'.[296] These guidelines attempted to reconcile the bar's desire to preserve a gentlemanly code of behaviour with the necessary accommodation to a highly and openly competitive profession. The ideal was one in which merit would prevail over connection, influence etc. without men resorting to the 'deliberately business-like practice of law, actively seeking out clients, advertising their services, offering to do legal work at fees that were competitive with those charged by attorneys, taking steps to cut down on business overheads, and generally working to stimulate the market, increase income and decrease expenses'.[297] However, the rules also aimed to limit the triumph of pure merit, for example by protecting a circuit against outsiders and prescribing minimum fees.

To outsiders this looked uncommonly like the approach taken by trade unions, and in 1867 a 'Journeyman Engineer' complained in the press that that was what the bar was. The more thoughtful responses revealed just how uncertain and ambiguous the bar was about its rules. Dicey endorsed the defence that they served the public, rather than a sectional interest but was uneasy with some of the rules.[298] Most barristers preferred not to engage in discussion of this sort. The bar remained a strikingly anti-intellectual profession with a great addiction to 'common sense' and viewed the more academic journals in which theoretical issues might be pursued with a disdain which sometimes concealed unease.[299]

The Prohibition on Direct Access to Clients

It had become established that a layman contemplating, or facing, an action in the superior courts should not be permitted to approach counsel save through

[293] Shaw-Lefevre, 'Etiquette of the Bar', 237.
[294] 'Legal Etiquette' (1867) *Fortnightly Review*, 179, quoted in Pue, *Rebels at the Bar*, 317 n.292.
[295] Duman, English and Colonial Bars, 41.
[296] Pue, 'Rebels at the Bar', 318–19.
[297] *Ibid.*, 319.
[298] Cocks, *Foundations of the Modern Bar*, 127–9.
[299] *Ibid.*, 188–9. For a sympathetic account, arguing that these practices conduced to 'the division of legal labor…structured by notions of honor' and were beneficial to society, see Burrage, *Revolution and Making of Contemporary Legal Profession*, 478–82.

an attorney or solicitor,[300] but there was no such firm convention in criminal proceedings, nor was it settled practice for non-contentious business such as conveyancing. The leaders who set the tone for the bar were content with this self-denying ordinance, which reinforced the functional and social separation between the 'higher' and 'lower' branches. The solicitors naturally supported this particular practice and their organizations were vigilant to see that it was observed.[301] Even so, as Brougham's well-publicized defiance of the attorneys of the northern circuit in the 1820s demonstrated, it was not yet sufficiently entrenched to be enforced through a circuit mess.[302]

Direct access became an explosive issue in the late 1840s, when the prohibition was embodied in the County Courts Act 1846.[303] Here the bar did not have exclusive audience, and with an unprecedented number of young barristers desperately short of work the ban on direct access seemed to many of them unfair and unnecessary.[304] In county courts they were expected to compete as advocates with solicitors, yet were heavily handicapped by the etiquette of their own profession, which seemed to serve the interests only of the already successful and the well connected.[305] In 1852 a petition against the rule was signed by 130 juniors, testifying to the existence of a militant minority.[306]

These 'rebels' had powerful backing. They could count on the support of the uniquely influential *Times* and the Law Amendment Society since they were pleading for the very 'free trade' in legal services which the bar's etiquette seemed usually intent on restricting. If a client were free to approach a barrister direct there would be a saving of costs and a freedom of choice.[307] Fortuitously, the enforceability of the prohibition came before the courts in 1850 and in *Doe d. Bennett* v. *Hales and Davis*[308] the Queen's Bench in banc overturned Patteson J.'s refusal to hear directly instructed counsel. 'The etiquette of the bar is one thing; a practice which is to bind the world is another', said Campbell CJ,[309] unable to ground the practice in enacted law or immemorial usage. Nevertheless he was insistent that 'a confusion of the characters of attorney and counsel would be

---

[300] Lemmings, *Professors of the Law*, 25–9. The convention that client's communications with counsel should be routed through the solicitor gradually gained acceptance; see e.g. the correspondence of William Hoar in 1814: JHB MS 414, see (2008) 29 *JLH* 151.

[301] *Ibid.*, 28.

[302] Lord Campbell, *The Lives of the Lord Chancellors*, 8 vols (1869), viii, 369–70.

[303] County Courts Act 1846, s 91.

[304] Pue, 'Rebels at the Bar', 303–15.

[305] *Ibid.*, 306–10. By charging three guineas for a chambers appointment they were said to have yielded up much of this business to solicitors: (1838) 2 *Jur.* 833.

[306] Pue, 'Rebels at the Bar', 331–2.

[307] *Ibid.*, 329–30.

[308] (1850) 15 QB 170.

[309] At 174–5.

mischievous'[310] and anxiously hoped that the bar would not abuse their freedom. Soon afterwards the junior bar obtained a signal success in its county court campaign. It could not obtain what the leaders would have preferred, exclusive audience in actions above £20, but gained both direct access and a ban on their most dangerous competitors, the 'attorney-advocates' who took advocacy instructions from other solicitors.[311]

The rule of etiquette itself now appeared to be without formal sanction and at odds with a statute. Yet the rule was maintained, indeed it became progressively more entrenched. This was not achieved through the circuit messes and the inns, which proved impotent against the most outspoken and defiant of the 'rebels at the bar', C. R. Kennedy.[312] Nevertheless, Kennedy's Mutual Law Association soon folded and the other known individuals and groups who attempted to practise without the mediation of solicitors were few and undistinguished.[313] The threat to the fundamental demarcation between the professions came to nothing and by degrees even the conveyancers yielded to it.

The Honorarium

A barrister's services were not governed by a contract either with the client or with the solicitor who acted as their intermediary. Coke and Blackstone had provided dignified analogies with the Roman *patroni* who acted disinterestedly and without the expectation of reward, but gratifying as that comparison was, the reality was that English barristers seldom acted for nothing. The justifications which seem most plausible nowadays, policy considerations which underpin the barrister's immunity from suit, did not figure largely in nineteenth-century discussions. ˙

At the outset the practice seemed unproblematic. It was said in 1819[314] that a barrister wanting to ensure that he was paid should, as was said to be standard practice in the upper reaches of the profession, insist that payment accompanied the brief. Whatever the quality of the service counsel provided, the client would usually receive the document he wanted or have his case presented by the barrister he had chosen. Discontent surfaced in Chancery in the 1820s, when

---

[310] At 176.
[311] County Courts Act 1852, s 10. Pue, 'Rebels at the Bar', 326–34. The Lord Chancellor (Truro) emphasized that the repeal of the statutory prohibition on direct access would not make any change in practice which would go against the views of the profession. Lord Campbell feelingly agreed: *PD* 1852 (s3) 119: 491.
[312] Pue, 'Rebels at the Bar', 336–43. It was, however, affirmed by the Norfolk Circuit Bar Club in 1872: R. Cocks, 'The Bar at Assizes' (1976) 6 *Kingston Law Rev.* 36–52 at 46.
[313] Pue, 'Rebels at the Bar', 343–7.
[314] *Hunt* v. *Morris* (1819) 1 Chitt. 544.

leading counsel (the choice was not very wide) flitting from court to court began to miss engagements more frequently.[315] This was largely abated by leaders confining themselves to a single court, encouraged by Langdale MR's refusal to stand cases over in the complaisant way of his predecessors.[316] Unfortunately by then the habit had spread to the common law courts, especially the busy King's Bench, and a small clutch of leaders, notably Fitzroy Kelly and William Follett, attracted criticism for greedily accepting briefs without any likelihood of being able to attend to all of them, leaving the client to make do with the junior or find another leader at short notice.[317] The emergence of the two-counsel rule may well be linked to this phenomenon, which was worsened by the opening up of the Common Pleas. There was talk of replicating the Chancery practice at common law[318] but it was never really feasible. Successful leaders faced a genuine problem, for turning away business risked losing a client and a barrister's prime was often short: the temptation to take the brief and hope for the best was irresistible for some,[319] giving rise to a probably apocryphal story (told of Hardinge Giffard among others) of a fashionable silk found strolling in the park instead of being in court and disarmingly explaining that he would thereby avoid favouring one among the several clients he had undertaken to represent.[320]

The standard defence to accusations of greed and unscrupulousness, and one with a kernel of truth, was to blame the public's insistence on having the most fashionable counsel of the day, so that the solution lay with solicitors and their clients. It was also argued, less compellingly, that a great leader was often retained simply to deny his services to the other side.[321] Neither justified the practice that caused most indignation—that men like Kelly would not return the fee even if they could not appear; bar etiquette, so punctilious on other points of conduct, was silent on this one. It seemed that counsel managed to avoid both legal and moral responsibility; as *Punch* put it:

> The barristers of England, how with *sang-froid* sublime,
> They undertake to advocate two cases at one time,
> And when they find it is a thing impossible to do,
> They throw the client overboard and take the fee for two.

[315] Holdsworth, *HEL*, xii, 73.

[316] See above p. 658 and T. D. Hardy, *Memoirs of the R.H. Henry, Lord Langdale*, 2 vols (1852), ii, 53.

[317] See e.g. (1845) 2 *LR* 436–53; Sir J. Rolt, *The Memoirs of Sir John Rolt* (1939), 141; review of W. D. Lewis, *Horae Juridicae*, in (1845) 9 *Jur.* 98.

[318] (1838) 2 *Jur.* 505.

[319] 'Recollections of a Deceased Welch Judge' (1845/6) 3 *LR* 293–305.

[320] E. Bowen-Rowlands, *In Court and Out of Court* (1925), 44.

[321] Hawkins' biographer blamed his clerk for over-booking him: Harris, *Reminiscences of Hawkins*, 112.

The debate over double booking grew more strident in the 1850s,[322] and the barrister's financial relations with his client came inopportunely into the spotlight in the great Swinfen will case.[323] This showed leading members of the bar in a most unflattering light and the redoubtable Prudence Swinfen established that her counsel (Sir Frederick Thesiger) had no right to conclude a compromise without his client's consent.[324] She then defeated C. R. Kennedy's unwise attempt to recover his £20,000 fees by either enforcing an express engagement or indirectly via a mortgage over property in the suit.[325]

Kennedy v. *Broun* was one authoritative precedent the bar did not care to cite. Erle CJ relied on a host of precedents, and 'the tradition and understanding of the profession both as known to memory and as expressed in former times', but his principled justification was flimsy:

[i]f the law allowed the advocate to make a contract of hiring and service, it may be that his mind would be lowered, and that his performance would be guided by the words of his contract rather than by principle of duty.[326]

Despite the commendable willingness of some leaders, Roundell Palmer and Arthur Cohen among them, to return brief and fee promptly if they could not appear, it was not general practice.[327] C. M. Norwood launched a frontal assault on the honorarium, first by amendment to the Judicature Bill 1875 and then in the next session through a separate bill, but encountered what the *Law Times* predicted: 'the Bar possesses a gigantic influence in the country—an influence sufficient to defy all interference with its habits and customs'.[328] Barristers queued up to argue their own case, most not focusing on the practical problems that a contractual relationship would create (after all, solicitors acted as advocates in county courts on that basis) but on altogether more lofty grounds.[329] Presumably lay MPs as well as barristers accepted the interesting proposition that 'the interests of the profession and the public are identical in this matter',[330] for the bill was beaten by 237 to 130.

---

[322] Abel-Smith and Stevens, *Lawyers and the Courts*, 231–2.

[323] H. Clayton, *The Great Swinfen Case* (1980).

[324] *Ibid.*, 150–63; *Swinfen* v. *Lord Chelmsford* (1860) 5 Hurl. & Norm. 890.

[325] *Kennedy* v. *Broun* (1863) 32 LJ CP 137; 'On the Right of Counsel to Recover his Fees' (1870) 29 (s3) *LM & LR* 295–323.

[326] 5 Hurl. & Norm. 921, 924.

[327] Selborne, *Memorials Part Two: Personal and Political*, ii, App. (Horace Davey, 444–5); L. Cohen, *Arthur Cohen* (1919), 88.

[328] Quoted in Duman, *English and Colonial Bars*, 62.

[329] PD 1875 (s3) 226: 625–34; 1876, 229: 307–49.

[330] Sir H. M. Jackson at cols 322–3.

Neither the public nor a good many solicitors accepted this convenient coincidence, and leading firms and major clients were sometimes outraged by a leader's cavalier treatment.[331] Perhaps prompted by another bill in 1886, the Attorney-General indicated that fees should be returned when counsel could not appear in court—something of a revolution in practice, for which Haldane claimed an immediate and unexpected effect; leaders raised their fees sharply, suggesting how lucrative the former practice had been.[332] The client could still not be sure that the counsel of his choice would actually be in court, but it suggested a more responsible attitude among counsel. Carson and Marshall Hall were two who set a fine example, but solicitors still played safe by briefing the busiest as an insurance against being blamed if the case was lost.[333]

As C. R. Kennedy's experience had shown, the drawback of immunity from contractual liability was that unless they were paid in advance they could not be sure of recovering the fee. Erle was probably out of touch in asserting that advance payment was still the usual practice,[334] and by the end of the period it may have become the exception rather than the rule; Rentoul said that at least one big City solicitor's firm settled its accounts yearly.[335]

Unscrupulous solicitors had always taken advantage of young barristers anxious to get business and most learned the hard way not to count on the fee until it was actually in their clerk's hands.[336] Newcomers were in no position to demand advance payment like the great leaders and the serious nature of the problem is well illustrated by Edward Spence, a former solicitor and no greenhorn; of his first 89 guineas only 60 were paid; of the next 248 only 141, of the next 823 only 470. Even in his second decade 1377 guineas out of 10,223 were bad debts.[337] No doubt recovery rates were even lower in those Temple chambers which, contrary to bar etiquette, operated on a 'no win, no fee' basis.[338]

---

[331] D. Sommer, *Haldane of Cloan* (1960), 59–60; Liddell, *Notes From the Life of an Ordinary Mortal*, 143–4.

[332] Abel-Smith and Stevens, *Lawyers and the Courts*, 233. Raising fees may also have been a way of limiting the demand upon their services without actually refusing briefs. Giffard demanded 10,000 guineas to represent the Tichborne claimant at his criminal trial against his inclinations: Heuston, *Lives of the Lord Chancellors*, 14. In 1904 the Bar Council resolved that counsel should accept any brief in an area in which he professed to practise and where an appropriate fee was offered.

[333] E. Marjoribanks, *Lord Carson*, 2 vols (1932) i, 177; E. A. Bell, *Those Meddlesome Attorneys* (1939), 154.

[334] *Kennedy v. Broun*, 144. Bethell had complained about the difficulty in getting paid in 1834 (Nash, *Lord Westbury*, i, 60) and see (1842) 28 *LM* 206.

[335] *This Is My Case*, 63–4. Payment accompanying the brief was by then confined to criminal matters: H. H. L. Bellot, 'Counsel's Fees' (1908–9) 34(ss) *LM & R*, 394–407.

[336] See e.g. Hardcastle, *Life of Lord Campbell*, i, 266.

[337] *Bar and Buskin*, 143–8.

[338] *Ibid.*, 148; Ball, *Lincoln's Inn*, 160.

It is not surprising that juniors demanded action. A Norfolk circuit suggestion that defaulters be blackballed was scotched by the recollection that an Attorney-General 40 years before had ruled that it would be improper, and neither the inns nor the Bar Committee were keen to act, wary of encouraging further attacks on the honorarium. Recourse was also had to the Law Society, but it was only after the bar had curbed the most blatant of the abuses on its side—the cavalier attitude to briefs—that it would crack down on its own defaulters.[339]

The Two-Counsel Rule

Complaints had been made of the proliferation of counsel back in the 1690s, when the judges declined to countenance any limit on numbers, and it was again remarked upon in the 1730s.[340] In Chancery Eldon's expansive notion of what circumstances justified several counsel led even the cautious reformers on the Chancery Commission to recommended that it should normally be limited to two for any party, but that proposition sank without trace.[341] Nor was the extravagance confined to courts of equity. Thanks to the liberality of taxing masters, suitors on the northern circuit had frequently made use of several counsel; one writer instanced a case of ejectment with six on one side and five on the other.[342]

Soon KCs began invariably to demand the assistance of a junior, but when a custom hardened into an etiquette is uncertain. It was found on the Norfolk circuit in 1828,[343] but in 1851 the Attorney-General refused to endorse the Chester circuit mess's attempt to impose it. When the Bar Committee described it in 1890 as a generally recognized practice, it was making rather than declaring etiquette, at least in non-jury cases, but from that date it was firmly in place for all High Court actions, though not in the county courts.[344]

Solicitors were not antagonistic to a practice which ensured at least the presence of a junior while a double-booked leader was elsewhere, but they and their larger corporate clients became increasingly dissatisfied with the 'long-established practice' of fixing the junior's fee at two-thirds or three-fifths of his leader's. While this was obviously convenient for the bar, it produced an iniquitous result where leaders' fees were at a level which gave the junior a fee he could never

---

[339] Abel-Smith and Stevens, *Lawyers and the Courts*, 233. Even in 1909 T. E. Crispe still regarded it as unsettled whether brief fees needed to be returned on non-appearance: *Memories of a KC*, 279–81.

[340] Lemmings, *Professors of the Law*, 19, 188.

[341] *PP* 1826 (143), xv, proposition 139.

[342] 'Mr. Justice Patteson' (1852) 16 (s2) *LM* 90–104 at 91–2.

[343] Duman, *English and Colonial Bars*, 44–5.

[344] Abel-Smith and Stevens, *Lawyers and the Courts*, 223.

command on his own merits. Yet despite remonstrances, in 1900 the Bar Council made it a professional offence for a junior to accept a lower rate except in 'special circumstances'. The definition of these and the argument that the rule discouraged resort to the courts left a 'vexed question' between the Law Society and the Bar Council.[345]

Retainers

The old style of general retainer used by great men like the Duke of Chandos was gone by the end of the Regency.[346] What remained was the arrangement whereby institutions like the universities, the Bank of England, and the East India Company had one or more standing counsel regularly entrusted with their briefs.[347] There was a token fee of five guineas,[348] but the position was coveted as a mark of distinction and a reliable source of income; thus Serjeant Spankie, who had lost much of his general practice, had an EIC retainer which was enough to keep him afloat in lean times.[349] For more successful men like J. B. Bosanquet, for the Bank, Charles Abbott, with his clutch of cathedral retainers and Bethell, for Oxford University, retainers were a mark of reputation as well as a source of profit.[350] Though there were various problems in applying the rules about retainers in particular situations[351] and the *Solicitors' Journal* later denounced them 'an excrescence',[352] they remained popular with regular litigants as helping to secure the services of their favoured counsel. Guidelines were eventually agreed by the Bar Committee and the Law Society in 1892, but disputed points still arose; in particular, the obligations of a barrister offered a brief for a client who had given a colleague a general retainer was a frequent source of questions.[353]

The origins and spread of the special retainer, that is, the rule of etiquette that counsel offered a brief on a circuit or at a quarter sessions to which he does not belong must insist on an additional, standardized fee, are obscure, though like the restrictions on counsel changing circuits, it was intended to protect the entitlement of circuiteers to the business of their circuit.

[345] *Ibid.*, 223–5.

[346] Lemmings, *Professors of the Law*, 41–2.

[347] For their evolution see D. Lemmings, *Gentlemen and Barristers* (Oxford, 1990), 173–4.

[348] J. R. V. Marchant, *The Barrister at Law* (1905), 127–33.

[349] *ODNB*, 51: 745.

[350] [Collier], *Criticisms on the Bar*, 235; Lord Campbell, *Lives of the Lord Chief Justices of England* (1857), iii, 276; Nash, *Lord Westbury*, i, 74–5.

[351] 'The Practice Relating to Retainers' (1830) 4 *LM* 417–32.

[352] (1886–7) 31 *Sol. J.* 408; (1875–6) 20 *Sol. J.* 470–1.

[353] Marchant, *Barrister at Law*, 127–33.

The prohibition on changing circuits was still subject to variations between circuits and probably within circuits in the mid-nineteenth century,[354] but it was rapidly hardening as competition for business became fiercer; thus in 1876 the Norfolk adopted the practice the home had been following for 20 years in imposing a blanket four-year rule,[355] not an easy rule to justify in an age awash with free trade doctrines.[356] It was argued that demonstrably competent counsel on a circuit had a legitimate expectation that as juniors became leaders, leaders judges, and men died or dropped out, an increasing share of its business would accrue to them and that only thus could the gentlemanly character of the profession be sustained; otherwise 'the moment that a man having business should retire from the circuit, there would be a general scramble for the vacant place; men would rush in from all quarters, and you, who had been labouring and patiently waiting your turn through long years, would find yourself, as it were, thrust out of your inheritance by a stranger…all the existing brotherhood of the Circuit Bar would be broken up and the competition of opposition tradesmen take the place of the honourable and generous rivalry that now merely stimulates the energies of the mind without provoking personal hatreds'.[357] Another writer put it rather more sceptically: '[a]s every cock pheasant has his walk, so every QC expects to have undisturbed enjoyment of his brace of counties'.[358] Circuit leaders with little town practice, like Dauncey on the Oxford and Andrews on the Norfolk, were the beneficiaries of this protected status.

The coming of the railway made it feasible to hire a famous QC or rising junior for a single case, particularly on those circuits close to London.[359] Even on the western, Alexander Cockburn was repeatedly fined by his own circuit mess for breaking off to fulfil engagements elsewhere, and on that circuit it was a *quid pro quo* for allowing men to go special at all that they must be available on their own circuit at a reasonable fee.[360] Since it was not politically feasible to curb such marauders directly, the best the circuits could do was to discourage them by imposing a tax, something perhaps only the bar could have got away with.[361] Indeed in 1862 a meeting of circuit representatives led to the adoption of an agreed scale. At the top end—300 guineas for a QC—it reflected existing

---

[354] Cox, *The Advocate*, 272–3; Duman, *English and Colonial Bars*, 47; Jay, *The Law*, 324.

[355] Cocks, 'Bar at Assizes', 45–6.

[356] Cox, *The Advocate*, 262–4, 280–4.

[357] *Ibid.*, 280.

[358] Shaw-Lefevre, 'Etiquette of the Bar', 238.

[359] Though Jeaffreson (*Book About Lawyers*, i, 298) claimed that Erskine had had a dozen such briefs a year in the pre-railway era.

[360] Harwood, *Circuit Ghosts*, 83, 94.

[361] For a rare attack on the principle see J. A. Lovat-Fraser, 'The Bar and the Circuits' (1894) 9 *LQR* 261–3.

practice,[362] but at 100 guineas for a junior as leader and 50 guineas for other juniors it was calculated to make a client think long and hard about the value of a 'star' counsel. In 1870s the home, in its death throes, sought its abolition but found little support, apart from some members of the northern.[363] However, the bar felt vulnerable with the honorarium under threat so the impost was lowered to 100 guineas for a QC and 50 for a junior. It remained at that level even when the fees of leading counsel soared in the 1900s, suggesting that it was no longer serving its original purpose, if indeed it ever had. It is doubtful whether it either sustained circuit life or benefited the public.

The Law Society objected in vain when the same practice was imposed on quarter sessions. Since KCs by convention did not appear and the pickings were usually small, the levy was proportionately modest, varying from five to 15 guineas until the Bar Council set a standard minimum of 10 guineas in 1898.[364] At the same time the Bar Council endorsed the extension to quarter sessions of another custom which the circuits had smuggled in at some earlier stage, that the intruding counsel had to be 'assisted' by a member of the circuit bar or sessions mess.[365] The bar was not a trade union but sometimes acted very like one.

Something like the special retainer also found its way into Chancery, though stern moralists like Bickersteth disapproved.[366] Once a leader located himself in a particular court, he had to be paid a 'special fee' (50 guineas in Rolt's case) for appearing in another.[367] This was to enable leading counsel to set limits on the demands made upon them rather than to protect less popular brethren from their predations. Bethell was among the first, but many after him also 'went special' in the sense of demanding a special fee to appear in any court.[368] From equity the practice seems to have spread to common law, Webster claiming to have been the first, in 1883.[369] This form of special retainer was not open to the objections of the circuit rule, being merely a means for an individual to set a price on his services.

---

[362] As Jervis had told the SC on Official Salaries: *Report 1850*, q. 1730.

[363] Duman, *English and Colonial Bars*, 47; Cocks, *Bar at Assizes*, 45. For the resolution and the response of the western circuit see Harwood, *Circuit Ghosts*, 106–7.

[364] Abel-Smith and Stevens, *Lawyers and the Courts*, 221.There was no upper limit and some sessions messes were going as high as 30 guineas. On the western they were fixed at 25 guineas for county and 15 guineas for borough sessions: Harwood, *Circuit Ghosts*, 106–7

[365] *Ibid*. These were known as 'kite briefs'. In 1866 Holker, a leading junior, was unaware of the custom: to T. Baker, 10 April 1866, JHB MS 487, see (2008) 29 *JLH* 157.

[366] Hardy, *Lord Langdale*, i, 470.

[367] Rolt, *Memoirs*, 15.

[368] Nash, *Lord Westbury*, i, 470; Bosanquet, *Oxford Circuit*, 67; R. B. (Lord) Haldane, *An Autobiography* (1929), 49.

[369] Alverstone, *Recollections of Bar and Bench*, 112–13.

Refreshers

Though Campbell refers to it in the 1840s, the practice of requiring a refresher for the second and subsequent days of a trial seems to have become widespread only in the third quarter of the nineteenth century and at one time only in the Common Pleas were they allowed on taxation.[370] Themselves a product of lengthening trials and shorter court hours, they in turn probably contributed to spin trials out longer. The justification for refreshers was that it was difficult for a barrister's clerk to estimate at the brief delivery stage how long a trial would last and that it was in the client's interests as well as counsel's that rather than increasing the fee to allow for the trial lasting longer than expected, it should be supplemented by an amount which reflected the time actually spent in court.[371] This did not stop some clerks from trying to claim a refresher even for days when counsel was not actually in court.[372]

The argument for refreshers seems to have prevailed with at least some of the taxing masters at common law and with Malins VC in Chancery,[373] but it did not impress the Law Society, which first tried in vain to suppress refreshers altogether and then to confine them (in the absence of a clear agreement in advance) to what would be allowed on taxation,[374] though that was itself uncertain.[375] It came to be agreed that the working day for this purpose meant only five hours, and the normal allowance would be eight to 10 guineas a day.[376] However, leading counsel routinely asked for much more; in *Isaacs* v. *Chesterton* the refreshers ranged from 100 guineas a day for Carson down to 40 for Purcell, while in *Wyler* v. *Lewis*, which lasted 33 days in the KBD and 18 in the Court of Appeal, Carson and Isaacs each had 250 guineas a day.[377]

---

[370] Hardcastle, *Life of Lord Campbell*, ii, 134; (1880–1) 25 *Sol. J.* 292. According to Ashley (*My Sixty Years in the Law*, 22) they were still uncommon when Hardinge Giffard started out.

[371] Abel-Smith and Stevens, *Lawyers and the Courts*, 213.

[372] *Ibid.*, 230.

[373] *Ibid.*, 213.

[374] (1880–1) 25 *Sol. J.* 292, 320, 338; (1883–4) 28 *Sol. J.* 167.

[375] (1886) 33 Ch D 52; (1891–2) 36 *Sol. J.* 147–9; (1892–3) 37 *Sol. J.* 228.

[376] Abel-Smith and Stevens, *Lawyers and the Courts*, 213; Marchant, *Barrister at Law*, 141–5.

[377] R. J. Blackham, *Sir Ernest Wild* (1935), 95; G. Rentoul, *This Is My Case* (1944), 49.

IV

Solicitors[1]

1. INTRODUCTION: THE QUEST FOR RESPECTABILITY

Attorneys and solicitors had a deep concern, sometimes almost amounting to an obsession, with establishing a 'respectable' or 'liberal' profession. Their route to respectability involved a long, uphill struggle to displace the unflattering image of the pettifogger which literature insistently perpetuated and to which certain judges and barristers lent their imprimatur. It was made harder by the persistence, particularly in London, of practitioners (not all of them enrolled) who fully merited the bad reputation that critics fastened on the whole profession.[2] Progress was made, however. It was easier to achieve respectability, if not gentility, in the counties, where those who forsook litigation for conveyancing or became a factotum to landowners usually insinuated themselves at least into the lower levels of polite society. In big towns there was a great divide between the socially accepted elite, and the mass of more lowly attorneys. Still, the irresistible comparison with the bar remained dispiriting. There were barristers shabby in conduct and costume, but their existence never detracted from the standing of the profession: to be a barrister was to be a gentleman. By contrast, if an attorney were a gentleman—some unquestionably were—it was not by virtue of his profession but rather despite it.[3]

[1] Until 1873 attorneys (sometimes 'attornies') appeared in common law courts, solicitors in courts of equity, though many practised in both. For convenience I have referred to them all as attorneys before this period commences and solicitors thereafter except where the context requires them to be distinguished. Their equivalents in the civilian courts were the proctors, for whom see above, pp. 698–701.

[2] R. Robson, *The Attorney in Eighteenth Century England* (Cambridge, 1959), 134–54; P. J. Corfield, *Power and the Professions* (1995, 2000 edn), 47–52, 76–85; H. Kirk, *Portrait of a Profession* (1976), 203–8. For a wider perspective see D. Sugarman and W. W. Pue, 'Towards a Cultural History of Lawyers' in their *Lawyers and Vampires: A Cultural History of the Legal Professions* (Oxford, 2003), 1–25.

[3] Robson, *Attorney in Eighteenth Century England*, 144–6.

This was what gave point to the favourite jibe of their detractors, that an attorney was a gentleman [only] by Act of Parliament.[4]

The dogged pursuit of respectability brought successes. In 1852 Charles Dickens introduced readers *of Bleak House* to Mr Tulkinghorn, respectability incarnate, and Mr Vholes: 'Mr Vholes is a very respectable man. He has not a large business, but he is a very respectable man. He is allowed by the greater attorneys who have made large fortunes, or are making them, to be a most respectable man....'[5] However, in calling Vholes an attorney Dickens was consciously choosing a term which was going out of favour and one which, since Vholes was acting in Chancery, was inapt.

Most of the profession had long preferred the term solicitor, which had not acquired the seemingly irremovable stigma attached to attorney. The move was ridiculed by a versifier in 1815:

> And thus the most opprobrious fame
> Attends upon the attorney's name.
> Nay, the professors seem ashamed
> To have their legal title named;
> Unless my observation errs
> They're all become solicitors.[6]

Though conservatives like Samuel Warren deplored the abandonment of the venerable name, it received its *quietus* under the Judicature Act 1873, which made the members of the lower branch solicitors of the Supreme Court.[7]

Of course it took much more than a change of name to rescue the image of the profession and the Law Society and its provincial counterparts adopted several means. One was to improve the social quality of new entrants by offering shorter articles to graduates in 1821, imposing a preliminary examination in 1861 and reducing exemptions to 'ten year men'.[8]

It was also necessary to remove or marginalize the sort of practitioners whose activities brought the profession into disrepute. The Manchester Law Society had as its original aim 'putting down one or two practitioners of the very lowest

---

[4] P. Birks, *Gentlemen of the Law* (1960), 136–7. When Dickens makes this the boast of the unscrupulous Sampson Brass, he is clearly ridiculing the solicitors' pretensions: *The Old Curiosity Shop*, Ch. 60.

[5] *Bleak House*, Ch. 39. The authorial irony does not detract from the point.

[6] Birks, *Gentlemen of the Law*, 144.

[7] Judicature Act 1873 c. 66, s. 87; E. B. V. Christian, *A Short History of Solicitors*, (1896), 223–5; Kirk, *Portrait of a Profession*, 213–14.

[8] D. Sugarman, 'Bourgeois Collectivism, Professional Power and the Boundaries of the State. The Private and Public Life of the Law Society, 1825 to 1914' (1996) 3 *International Journal of the Legal Profession* 81–134, at 91; *SC on Legal Education*, PP 1846 (686), x, App. 3 (Manchester LS) and pp. 1198–9.

class',[9] spent hundreds of pounds in its early years in prosecuting them and only took its dirty linen indoors to wash in private when it felt it no longer needed to demonstrate its determination in public.[10] Once respectability was successfully claimed the local practitioners in Birmingham and elsewhere could 'define out' their 'black sheep' and disown them.[11]

Thirdly, it was necessary to create a professional etiquette to put down practices which laymen regarded as discreditable and/or which savoured too much of trade. Touting by clerks fell into the former class;[12] advertising into the latter, and while neither could be altogether prevented, both could be put beyond the professional pale and Christian (1896) felt (optimistically) that the latter had been effectively stamped out.[13] As with the bar, etiquette often embraced anti-competitive behaviour and Christian lamented that it had not been possible to prevent 'the higgling of the market', and to enforce a strict adherence to scale charges.[14]

There were, however, limits to what professional institutions could accomplish, and the position of solicitors would in the end depend upon the exertions of individuals in demonstrating their upright, gentlemanly qualities and insisting on fitting treatment by others.[15] Sometimes this meant standing up to judges. Fortunately the most severe and prejudiced critics on the bench—Kenyon, Thurlow, Tenterden, and Gibbs (who had called attorneys 'the growling jackals and predatory pilot fish of the law'[16]) had no successors in their exalted places, but Abinger CB passed a casual aspersion on the lower branch and several others allowed barristers undue latitude in disparaging solicitor witnesses.[17] Since plenty of lesser judges were also prone to assume the worst of solicitors, it was important, as well as courageous, for Fairfield to stand his ground against Master Stratford and that county court bullies such as Lefroy should not go unchallenged.[18]

---

[9] *SC on Legal Education 1846*, evidence of T. Taylor, q. 949.

[10] *Ibid.*, q. 887; V. Parrott, *A Route to Respectability: Solicitors and their Changing Image, 1830–1910*, Salford University Occasional Papers in Politics, 26 (1991).

[11] A. S. Rowley, *Professions, Class and Society: Solicitors in Nineteenth Century Birmingham* (PhD, Aston, 1988), 354–63.

[12] P. H. Williams, *A Gentleman's Calling* (Liverpool, 1980), 263; D. Sugarman, 'Simple Images and Complex Realities: English Lawyers and the Relation to Business and Politics 1750–1950' (1993) 11 *Law & Hist. Rev.* 257–302 at 269.

[13] *Short History of Solicitors*, 234–5; Birks, *Gentlemen of the Law*, 246–7. Ironically, in Blackpool one practice much condemned was advertising money to lend, which had done so much to advance the profession in the eighteenth century: D. Cameron, *Solicitors in Blackpool* (Blackpool, 1995), 80–3, 90. Indirect advertising continued: (1893) 12 *LN* 36.

[14] *Short History of Solicitors*, 234.

[15] G. Stephen, *Adventures of an Attorney in Search of a Practice* (1839, 2nd edn, 1840), 235–7.

[16] Quoted in *The Bristol Law Society, the First Two Hundred Years* (Bristol, 1970), 20.

[17] Stephen, *Adventures of an Attorney*, 241–9.

[18] *Ibid.*, 235–7; P. Polden, 'Judicial Selkirks: The County Court Judges and the Press, 1847–1880', in C. W. Brooks and M. J. Lobban (eds), *Communities and Courts, 1150–1900* (1997), 257–60.

Social relations with the bar were a matter of acute sensitivity. Stephen's assertion that 'there was not much intercourse' between the professions needs the caveat that their own etiquette made some barristers preternaturally wary of anything that might savour of 'huggery'.[19] In the 1880s, C. F. Follett's complaint was revealingly different: he felt gracious after-dinner assurances of perfect equality between the professions by leading barristers were just a 'convivial compliment', neither meant nor felt.[20]

Such protestations were not always insincere however, and Lord Selborne may be believed when he wrote that to treat solicitors as a separate, inferior, caste was 'simply absurd'.[21] It was the struggling barrister who was keenest to claim a distinction which, if it existed at all, could not pretend to that 'visible superiority' Stephen had so vehemently denied.[22] Solicitors sought to assert their place in the hierarchy of professions. Striving to elevate themselves onto the same social plane as the bar, the church, and the army, they acknowledged doctors as equals but claimed a superiority over the 'confessedly inferior' latecomers to professionalism, the architects, auctioneers, land valuers, estate agents, and civil engineers, and later tried to keep the upstart accountants in their place too.[23]

A measure of solicitors' success is that they gradually became less frequent targets for cheap invective by politicians. Brougham, who never seemed able to forgive his treatment at the hands of the attorneys on the northern circuit, was a notable offender[24] and in 1854 Pleydell Bouverie (a barrister) asserted, apparently seriously, that 'the two great evils of the country were taxes and attornies'.[25] Such sneers grew rarer and even in fiction (where given the Victorians' appetite for tales featuring inheritance and lawsuits they featured prominently) solicitors were less often found as villains.[26]

As Sir George Stephen and others emphasized, all depended upon character. A 'good' education was supposed to produce a good character, but even where it did not, the outward appearance could at least be preserved. William Duignan's father was a drunkard at home, but maintained his practice as a respectable Birmingham solicitor,[27] and he was not the only whited sepulchre in the profession.[28] An appearance of gentility helped attract the better sort of client and that

---

[19] Birks, *Gentlemen of the Law*, 231.
[20] *Ibid.*, 238.   [21] *Ibid.*, 171.
[22] Stephen, *Adventures of an Attorney*, i–xxxix.
[23] 'Grievances of Solicitors and Attorneys' (1838) 20 *LM* 114–24 at 117; D. Sugarman, 'Who Colonized Whom? Historical Reflections on the Interaction Between Law, Lawyers and Accountants in England', in Y. Delazay and D. Sugarman (eds), *Professional Competition and Professional Power: Lawyers and the Social Construction of Markets* (1995), 226–37 at 234–5.
[24] 'Grievances of Solicitors and Attorneys', 119.
[25] Kirk, *Portrait of a Profession*, 210.
[26] *Ibid.*, 213
[27] Rowley, *Professions, Class and Society*, 88.
[28] Examples from Liverpool are in Williams, *Gentleman's Calling*, 162–70.

in turn reinforced the respectability of the solicitor; for as Trollope wrote: '[i]s it not remarkable that the common repute which we all give to attorneys in general is exactly the opposite to that which every man gives to his own attorney?'[29]

The cumulative effect of each prosperous family having its own 'respectable' family solicitor gradually destroyed Trollope's paradox. By 1900 solicitors were no longer commonly found under 'trades' in street directories, nor did they prudently style themselves 'gentleman' rather than acknowledging their profession.[30] Criticisms of the law hardly diminished, but unlike Bentham's day, its defects were no longer routinely laid at the door of the lower branch.[31] It did not achieve that happy equation of practitioner with gentleman the bar commanded, and within the profession there were still big divisions; indeed, one consequence of the respectability of most solicitors was that disreputable clients would be driven to seek the other sort, and when the profession was overstocked there was seldom any difficulty finding such a one.[32] At the start of this period a substantial body of attorneys belonged to what has been called an 'uneasy class poised precariously just within the bourgeoisie'.[33] Most consolidated their position in respectable society, but a minority slipped into an unlabelled quasi-class along with other men whose professions were respectable but whose own practice was not. They were the men the law societies were anxious to disown or blacklist if they could not drive them from the district.[34]

The defalcation scandals of around 1900 cost solicitors some of the improved reputation they had so painstakingly built up,[35] but a fortuitous opportunity to repair the damage was at hand. Unlike barristers, solicitors who volunteered for service in the First World War were not automatically given a commission; nevertheless of 26 members of the Nottingham Law Society who gave their lives in the conflict, 23 died as officers. Solicitors had demonstrated that they could die as gentlemen.[36]

---

[29] Quoted in Kirk, *Portrait of a Profession*, 211.

[30] *Ibid.*, 211; Corfield, *Power and the Professions*, 53.

[31] Robson, *Attorney in Eighteenth Century England*, 143, but compare Christian, *Short History of Solicitors*, 234.

[32] 'Grievances of Solicitors and Attorneys', 114.

[33] Rowley, *Professions, Class and Society*, 78.

[34] *Ibid.*, 354–64.

[35] See below, pp. 1161–5.

[36] R. J. T. Smith, *A Short History of the Nottingham Law Society 1875–1975* (?Nottingham, 1975). Offer computes mortality among those solicitors who served at 17.1% (A. Offer, *Property and Politics* (1981), 64), but does not note differences in rank.

2. THE SOCIOGRAPHY OF THE SOLICITORS' PROFESSION

The Size of the Profession

In the view of most laymen in Georgian England there were too many attorneys and they included many pettifoggers, unscrupulous fomenters of discord, and promoters of lawsuits. Reputable practitioners attributed most of the disreputable practices to men who practised as attorneys without being properly qualified and it was Yorkshire attorneys whose petition for action had triggered the Attorneys and Solicitors Act 1729.[37]

A return produced in connection with the legislation showed more than 4600 attorneys and solicitors on the rolls of the superior courts.[38] This was felt excessive and the Act limited each attorney to two articled clerks at one time. It prescribed a five-year apprenticeship and an examination before a judge as a condition for enrolment, airily restricting the total number to that which 'by the ancient custom and usage of such court hath heretofore been allowed'.[39] Though the Act failed to curb numbers, it gave the Society of Gentlemen Practisers and local law societies a weapon against unlicensed practitioners, but an unknown number of these—'hedge lawyers' and failed businessmen—continued to make a living.[40]

The real constriction upon the size of the profession was the cost of entry, not only the premium paid for articles but the expense of living unwaged for those five years, especially as it became less common for apprentices to live in with their master. Pitt's taxes upon articles and admissions, and on the annual practising certificate, were further discouragements, yet the first 30 years of the nineteenth century witnessed rapid growth.[41] Between 400 and 600 sets of articles were being registered and practising certificates climbed from the 5000s to the 9000s, an annualized rate (3 per cent) remarkable even for a period of fast population growth. From the mid-1830s it slowed notably and entrants actually declined by 14 per cent in the 1850s. A period of equilibrium followed until the

[37] Robson, *Attorney in Eighteenth Century England*, 7–12, 134–44; Kirk, *Portrait of a Profession*, 202–4; Corfield, *Power and the Professions*, 74–80.

[38] Corfield, *Power and the Professions*, 78–9 and table 4.1. As each court maintained a separate roll the total enrolment of 10,000 plus counted many twice.

[39] Solicitors and Attornies Act 1729 (2 Geo. II c. 23), ss. 5–8, 15. Initially for 10 years, it was twice renewed and made permanent in 1757.

[40] Kirk, *Portrait of a Profession*, 72–3; Birks, *Gentlemen of the Law*, 172–3; Corfield, *Power and the Professions*, 77–8; P. Aylett, *The Distribution and Functions of Attorneys in the Eighteenth Century, with Special Reference to North-West England* (M. Phil., Manchester, 1984), 188.

[41] Robson, *Attorney in Eighteenth Century England*, 14–15; Birks, *Gentlemen of the Law*, 140–1. In 1820 the duty on articles was £80 (£120 in London), on admission £25 and the certificate £8 (£12 in London). For the position in Wales, see above, p. 633.

1870s, causing a fall in the ratio of solicitors to population.[42] In Birmingham it fell from 1:1690 in 1831 to 1:1790 in 1871, and Birmingham also shows the subsequent resumption of expansion, especially in the 1880s, to 1:1450 in 1901.[43] Nationally, practising certificates issued were in the 16,000s from 1900 but a decline in articles registered, from a peak of 900+ a year in the 1880s and above 600 almost every year to 1903, suggests that the profession was becoming less attractive; by 1913 they had slipped below 500, the lowest for half a century.[44]

In 1911 more than 11,000 practising certificates were issued against around 10,000 in the mid-nineteenth century, but it must be noted that the increasing number of qualified men working as managing clerks did not usually take out a certificate and that there was still an unknown number of unqualified practitioners. These were quite numerous to judge from the persistent complaints, but a more effective sanction in the Solicitors Act 1874 and determined action by local law societies probably reduced their number.[45]

The 'lower branch' was much bigger than the practising part of the 'higher', though the latter grew bigger in proportion: in 1841 there were five solicitors to each barrister; by 1911 there were four. In the 1841 census solicitors were outnumbered by clergy and doctors/surgeons but were much more numerous than other professions. By 1911 many of them had closed the gap appreciably and solicitors were not numerically pre-eminent.[46]

There is no simple explanation for the fluctuations in solicitor numbers. Internal factors contributed, the Edwardian contraction for instance resulting partly from a species of 'birth control', as a market response to the impact of a property slump.[47] But the experience of one profession cannot be treated in isolation from a consideration of opportunities elsewhere. Thus, while Robert Maugham attributed the slowdown in the 1840s to changes in the common law and bankruptcy rules, Sir George Stephen pointed to poor prospects in the armed forces having underlain the rapid expansion after Waterloo.[48]

Variations were partly the result of the Law Society's own professional examinations. Both the final (1836) and the preliminary and intermediate (1861) were at times manipulated to control numbers entering the profession. However, many

---

[42] R. Abel, *The Legal Profession in England and Wales* (1988), 164–5, tables 2.14, 15; Birks, *Gentlemen of the Law*, 140–1.

[43] Rowley, *Professions, Class and Society*, 69.

[44] Abel, *Legal Profession*, tables 2.14, 2.15; Offer, *Property and Politics*, 63; J. S. Anderson, *Lawyers and the Making of English Land Law* (Oxford, 1992), 224–5.

[45] Solicitors Act 1874 c. 68, s. 12, replacing 23 & 24 Vict. c. 12.

[46] W. J. Reader, *Professional Men* (1966), App. 1; H. Perkin, *The Rise of Professional Society* (1989, edn of 1990), 80.

[47] Offer, *Property and Politics*, 60–6.

[48] *SC on Legal Education 1846*, qq. 2115, 1971.

who failed first time persevered until they scraped through. Too much time and money had been invested, at any rate by the intermediate and final candidates, for many to abandon the profession after one reverse, and there were many family-based firms with a family member like J. E. Underhill of Preston's W. Banks & Co struggling to qualify, so standards could not be raised too high.[49]

Age, Race, and Social Class

The profession's age profile changed substantially over the nineteenth century, the proportion of young men falling steadily from a high point produced by the expansion of the early decades; under-35s comprised 31.5 per cent in 1851, only 26.5 per cent in 1911. Curiously, the trajectory for elderly men (55 plus) was different, peaking at 25.2 per cent in 1871, falling to 17 per cent but rising again to 21.8 per cent in 1911, which may reflect a tendency for successful practitioners to retire earlier in the most prosperous period. Throughout the period, however, the typical solicitor was a middle-aged man.[50]

He was also an Englishman.[51] Non-British citizens were not admitted and there are no complaints to suggest an influx of Scots or Irish. In 1854 the Law Society promoted a bill giving reciprocal rights to English and Irish solicitors, but its Irish counterpart, sensing that despite its disarmingly equitable appearance it would benefit London firms most, ensured its failure.[52] Despite its 'United Kingdom' title, the Law Society made no attempt to recruit Scots, and without mutual recognition of qualifications, the cost of qualifying in England probably deterred most Scots and Irish.[53] Unlike the bar it did not provide access to colonial posts, so there was no parallel to the bar's mass of colonial students. A few brave souls did set up in practice, but probably found the going hard.[54]

Unlike barristers, aspiring solicitors did not need to disclose their father's occupation, so we are less well informed about their background. It was once generally assumed that their struggle for respectability was accompanied and assisted by a gradual elevation in the social origins of new recruits, but this may be an oversimplification. Miles suggested that an influx of men of a higher class provided the impetus for that struggle, and though his method probably exaggerates the

---

[49] Cameron, *Solicitors in Blackpool*, 22.

[50] Abel, *Legal Profession*, 169–70 and table 4.5.

[51] It has been calculated that slightly less than 1% of London solicitors in 1883 were jewish, but only a handful elsewhere. Several are profiled in J. Cooper, *Pride versus Prejudice: Jewish Doctors and Lawyers in England 1890–1990* (Portland, Oregon, 2003), 151–63.

[52] E. G. Hall and D. Hogan (eds), *The Law Society of Ireland* (Dublin, 2002), 51.

[53] Corfield, *Power and the Professions*, 84.

[54] Few more so than George Edalji, the Parsee who was wrongly convicted of cattle-maiming and is the subject of J. Barnes, *Arthur and George* (2005).

profession's gentility, it may already have been more of a 'haven for the privileged' and less of a ladder for upwardly mobile men of humble birth than was once thought.[55]

As with the bar, the landed gentry's proportional decline as a social group was mirrored in their contribution to the profession, and it may be that the big intake in the first third of the nineteenth century included a high proportion of men from a lower class, including those 'low people', shopkeepers and mechanics, whom Stephen identified as a substantial sub-group in the 1840s.[56] However, lack of statistical evidence has allowed Stephen's breakdown of recruits undue prominence.[57] Stephen's omitted solicitors' sons, who would be expected to feature prominently; in a study of Birmingham solicitors they number 10 out of 28 in 1851 and 30 out of 78 in 1900,[58] and even if that over-represents family continuity it suggest that they formed the biggest single contributor to the profession.[59] By 1900 and probably long before, the second biggest was other professions, whose tendency to cross-fertilize each other was well known.[60] Among the others few were from the lower strata. It is not difficult to find examples of men climbing to eminence within the profession from humble birth (or more rarely, like David Lloyd George, to wider fame via the profession), but they were exceptional and unlike the bar, solicitors preferred to boast of their respectable origins rather than how accessible their profession was. Both exaggerated, but the difference is revealing.

In 1914 the profession was still exclusively, but precariously, male. Women had been refused permission to sit the examinations and a father had been denied the right to article his daughter.[61] A debate at the 1912 annual provincial meeting

---

[55] M. Miles, 'A Haven for the Privileged: Recruitment to the Profession of Attorney in England, 1709–52' (1986) 11 *Social History* 197–210; Corfield, *Power and the Professions*, 228. Compare Robson, *Attorney in Eighteenth Century England*, 57.

[56] *Adventures of an Attorney*, 202.

[57] *SC on Legal Education 1846*, q. 1963, quoted, inter alia, in Christian, *Short History*, 188–90. His three categories were (1) tradesmen, shopkeepers and merchants wanting a solicitor in the family for business reasons; (2) 'gentlemen of moderate means' with several sons; (3) men 'from a much lower stock', copying clerks who become articled.

[58] Rowley, *Professions, Class and Society*, 69 and table 8.1. Aylett, *Distribution and Functions of Attorneys*, using an admittedly crude method, counted more than a quarter as sons in the eighteenth century.

[59] Of William Roscoe's children, grandchildren and great-grandchildren, eight either became or married barristers, 16 solicitors: Williams, *Gentleman's Calling*, 227 n.2.

[60] 'The professions absorb aspirants from all classes, but return few or none to their source', *Saturday Review*, quoted in Reader, *Professional Men*, 120. In the Birmingham samples professional parents (including solicitors) outnumbered all others: Rowley, *Professions, Class and Society*, table 8.1.

[61] Kirk, *Portrait of a Profession*, 10; (1891) 10 *LN* 103. Women received law degrees from London University from 1888 , and from 1875 to around 1900 Eliza Orme and a succession of partners ran a conveyancing and patent office in Chancery Lane: M. J. Mossman, *The First Women Lawyers* (Oxford, 2006), 113–54, esp. 130–7.

confirmed that most solicitors were opposed to women in their ranks, but with several professions, especially medicine, having already yielded and in a climate of militant suffragism, a legal challenge was inevitable. It came in 1914, and with the authorities on either side of the flimsiest, the Court of Appeal preferred the status quo.[62] The relief of conservatives was to prove short-lived.[63]

Education

'Public school education, far more than university education, became the hallmark of the later Victorian professional man',[64] and at the Law Society's annual provincial meeting in 1881 a speaker asserted that 'our profession is now largely recruited from the public schools'.[65] Since the Committee on Legal Education in the 1840s was so impressed with the deficiencies in the general education of aspiring solicitors that it suggested an entrance examination to ensure a basic grounding in 'the so-called commercial education..., Latin, Geography, History, and the elements of Arithmetic and Ethics, and one or more modern languages', this suggests a remarkable transformation. It is likely, however, that the Committee was unduly disparaging and the speaker too sanguine.[66]

Since the lesser gentry were still providing a substantial proportion of entrants in the first half of the century there must have been plenty of public school men in its ranks. The best family firms were already public school educated; G. B. Gregory followed his father to Eton; Edward Boodle's sons went to Charterhouse and Harrow; sons of J. W. Freshfield and William Vizard were at Charterhouse and Eton respectively. In some towns a reinvigorated local school supplied a suitable education more cheaply and conveniently. Birmingham had King Edward VI Grammar School,[67] Manchester its grammar school, and York, St. Peter's, while nonconformists and evangelicals who shunned the public schools had academies of their own, such as Warrington. For most of the less affluent middle class, however, educating sons was a problem until the opening of new public schools whose education mimicked the older foundations' emphasis on character

---

[62] *Bebb* v. *The Law Society* [1914] 1 Ch. 286; Kirk, *Portrait of a Profession*, 110–11.

[63] Women became eligible for admission under the Sex Disqualification Act 1919 and Miss Carrie Morrison was the first admitted, in 1922.

[64] Reader, *Professional Men*, 115.

[65] Quoted in Kirk, *Portrait of a Profession*, 57.

[66] Also below, pp. 1181–83. They relied heavily on the evidence of Sir George Stephen, celebrated for his anonymous *Adventures of an Attorney in Search of a Practice* (1839) but opinionated and eccentric (Christian, *Short History*, 243–8), and also heard from an articled clerk, E. T. Payne (especially qq. 2656–7).

[67] Rowley, *Professions, Class and Society*, table 6.1.

and gentlemanliness while making limited concessions to 'usefulness'.[68] They proved popular with solicitors, Thomas Paine sending his sons to Rugby, Henry E. Norton his to Marlborough. Because only the more prosperous firms, which formed the core Law Society membership, could afford this, members were likely to gain a false impression of its prevalence. In fact many solicitors still had to rely on obscure private schools and even board schools, whose products needed crammers to help them through the preliminary examination.

Beyond school the legal professions remained distinct. University education was the norm for barristers but the preserve of a minority of solicitors.[69] The cost aside, many fathers felt it an extravagance for a son destined for the lower branch, especially as it postponed his entry into practice and therefore his financial independence.[70] Some fathers who were themselves solicitors felt with William Gray's that 'there is a dryness and a mechanical labour about the Attorney's desk which would be insupportable and irksome to a young man from a University'.[71] Such sentiments might be self-serving but the unreformed universities were a poor preparation for drudgery.

Nevertheless graduate numbers rose and 16 per cent of new articled clerks in 1881 were said, probably with some exaggeration, to be Oxbridge men.[72] Though a few of the best-known solicitors, Sir Albert Rollit (University College) and Sir George Lewis (King's College) for example, were London graduates, the older universities still dominated and their products gradually infiltrated the best firms. The brilliant Dudley Baxter joined Norton Rose from Trinity (Cambridge); R. S. Taylor IV (Charterhouse and Trinity) joined Taylor and Humbert (1893); Booth's of Leeds had W. H. Wade (Cambridge, 1894), and by 1913, when Henry Wansborough's son joined the family firm from Oxford, graduates were commonplace at Coward Chance.[73] Indeed, for some, the college connection served to win them clients. Few were so fortunate as John Withers, who perseveringly, and ultimately successfully, lobbied to become the London solicitor for King's College, Cambridge, which provided a steady flow of work over several decades.[74]

---

[68] J. Roach, *Public Examinations in England, 1850–1900* (Cambridge, 1971), 35–55.

[69] Abel, *Legal Profession*, 143.

[70] The concession of three-year articles for graduates in 1821 probably made little difference.

[71] W. Cobb, *A History of Gray's of York* (York, 1989) App. C (November 1821). See also *SC on Legal Education 1846*, evidence of Robert Maugham, esp. qq. 2170–1.

[72] Kirk, *Portrait of a Profession*, 57–8. Abel, *Legal Profession*, table 2.3.

[73] A. St. George, *A History of Norton Rose* (Cambridge, 1995), 62; D. Drummond, *Taylor and Humbert, 1782–1982* (1982), 36; *Booth & Co, 1775–1975* (n.d.), 14–15; *The First Hundred Years: A History of Wansboroughs 1882–1982* (Bristol, n.d.); J. Slinn, *Clifford Chance—its Origins and Development* (1993), 36.

[74] S. J. Cretney, 'Sir John Withers MP: The Solicitor in Private Practice and Public Life in England between the Wars' (2007) *CLJ* 200–27.

Geographical Distribution

Unlike barristers, most solicitors practised outside London, where about one-third were probably based throughout this period. Though legal services had become more concentrated during the eighteenth century and attorneys were found in fewer places, their number had fallen in proportion to the population and their distribution did not echo population shifts.[75]

There is no similar study for the nineteenth century, but on the one hand there were very large increases in solicitor numbers in parts of the midlands and north, notably in Liverpool and Birmingham,[76] and on the other village attorneys such as Benjamin Smith of Horbling and John Howarth of Rippondon became a rare breed; in Kent in 1802 Penshurst, Newington and Staplehurst each had its attorney, but only the last still had one in 1914.[77]

There were few complaints that solicitors were hard to find, as firms were quick to set up branches where they scented business opportunities. Wansboroughs, based in the market towns of Devizes and Melksham, tried the water at Weston-super-Mare in 1898; Blackpool was colonized from the 'legal honeypot' of Preston, which boasted 50 solicitors in 1820, and Alfred Tolhurst sent a son across the estuary from Gravesend to Southend.[78] With county courts in almost 500 locations even the smallest town could support a lawyer, and apart from the restrictive covenants which prevented former articled clerks from starting up a rival business, practices found no effective way of keeping out newcomers. Scale charges operated by local law societies may have some effect but the experience in Blackpool suggests they were not very effective; making a decent living, however, was much more difficult, at least in a venerable city like Canterbury with an entrenched core of long-established firms.[79]

---

[75] P. J. Aylett, 'A Profession in the Marketplace: The Distribution of Attorneys' (1987) 5 *L & HR*, 1–30 at 3–13; Offer, *Property and Politics*, 11.

[76] Kirk, *Portrait of a Profession*, 109.

[77] A. J. Schmidt, *A Country Attorney in Late Eighteenth Century England, Benjamin Smith of Horbling* (1990) 8 *L & HR* 237–71; Miles, ' "Eminent Practitioners", the New Visage of Country Attorneys', in D. Sugarman and G. R. Rubin, *Law, Economy and Society* (Abingdon, 1984), 470–503 at 470–9; Aylett, *Distribution and Functions of Attorneys*, App. 2.

[78] *History of Wansboroughs*; Cameron, *Solicitors in Blackpool*, 25–7; Law Society Library t/s, *The Martin Tolhurst Partnership, a Short History* (Gravesend, 1986), 10.

[79] Cameron, *Solicitors in Blackpool*; M. Dockray, 'Guineas by Gaslight', in Dockray et al., *City University Centenary Essays in Law* (1996), 27–46 at 34.

3. SOLICITORS IN PRACTICE

The Size and Shape of Practices

Solicitors' firms remained for the most part a cottage industry and the characteristic figure throughout was the sole practitioner, who in 1780 formed 90 per cent of provincial firms and more than 75 per cent of those in London.[80] The proportion slowly decreased but in 1843 Lincoln still had only two partnerships in its 16 firms, Canterbury in 1898 just three out of 11 and as late as 1925 two-thirds of Birmingham solicitors practised alone.[81] This sits oddly with claims that the Victorian solicitor needed to be more knowledgeable than his Georgian predecessor,[82] but several factors made sole practice easier than before. Greater dependence upon office-based work, especially conveyancing, coupled with the penny post and better transport, meant less time spent in court and on the road, and fellow practitioners could be consulted on an unfamiliar matter. Brougham said that London solicitors knew less because they so readily referred matters to counsel and named several from big northern towns as the best he had encountered.[83]

Many became or remained alone by choice. William Gray thought partnerships undesirable and John Taylor took a partner only when unable to find a good managing clerk.[84] For others a partner was a necessity if they were to practise at all. There were usually more men qualifying than openings and the cost of setting up alone, estimated at £200, restricted that option to those with family money or who, like W. H. Barber, had saved enough.[85] Each town had one or two like Stephen's Mr Sharp, who rented a cheap room with minimal furniture, acquired an office boy as clerk and hoped to live off debt-collecting, casual county court work, and the odd conveyance.[86] They were prone to undercutting, sent

---

[80] In some places outside London solicitors also practised as proctors of the ecclesiastical courts; see above, pp. 700–1.

[81] Abel, *Legal Profession*, tables 2.20, 2.21; Corfield, *Power and the Professions*, table 4.2; J. Davies and P. Race, *Andrew & Co., Lincoln Solicitors* (?1983), 3; Dockray, 'Guineas by Gaslight', 34. Even among London commercial solicitors the sole practitioner was not a rarity; see the profile of C. M. Barker (Law Society president 1905) in (1906) 25 *LN* 209.

[82] Stephen, *Adventures of an Attorney*, xxvii; Birks, *Gentlemen of the Law*, 176; Kirk, *Portrait of a Profession*, 52.

[83] J. Clegg (ed.), *The Autobiography of a Lancashire Lawyer* (1883), 356; *SC on Legal Education 1846*, q. 3778. Samuel Warren in *Moral, Social and Professional Duties of Attornies and Solicitors* (1848), at 163 cautioned against excessive reliance upon counsel.

[84] Cobb, *History of Gray's*, 169; Clegg, *Autobiography of a Lancashire Lawyer*, 62–3. Stephen (*SC on Legal Education 1846*, q. 2017) said country solicitors usually started out on their own immediately, often at just 21.

[85] Miles, 'Haven for the Privileged', 204–10. For Barber see below, p. 1160n.

[86] *Adventures of an Attorney*, 1–2.

their clerks touting for business and generally undermined the profession's worthy efforts to improve its image. Most men had to leave the town where they were articled because of the common restrictive covenant protecting the principal from having clients poached[87] and if a man lacked useful contacts his choice of town might be quite arbitrary; a casual remark on a stagecoach took W. B. Young to Hastings; Harry Cartnell chose Preston because his wife liked the name; Frank Sinclair picked out a midlands town at random.[88] Others, like Edward Spence and E. W. Field, were able to pool resources with a similarly circumstanced friend or, like Clifford Turner, found a partner with money but little energy.[89]

Georgian partnerships were generally two-man affairs, most often familial and most commonly father and son. This changed little.[90] In 1808 only one London firm (Winter and Kaye) had four partners, and by 1910 just four in a sample of 50 had that many, with one other having eight.[91] Outside London few exceeded three. Some City and West End firms had a more complicated structure: N. H. Smith took on a tax specialist and an administrator; Slaughter and May had assistant solicitors; Norton Rose principals, subsidiaries, and salaried partners.[92] The statutory maximum of 20 partners set in 1862 was never approached.[93]

An obvious reason for this was that few firms made very large profits and hiring employees made better sense. Moreover partnerships were inherently risky.[94] If one partner misused the firms' money in unsuccessful speculations like Robert Baxter, or embezzled it like Charles Kaye at Freshfields or Jacob Mould at Taylors, the other was fully liable for crippling debts.[95] Even without such dramas, disharmony or divergent ambitions led to many partnerships being dissolved before their term. Family members were safer, even if less able; hence reluctant sons like George Harris and Michael Letts were corralled into the business,[96] though

---

[87] Alfred Tolhurst paid his former principal to release him: *Martin Tolhurst Partnership*, 9.

[88] C. Langdon, *Square Toes and Formal* (Hastings, 2003), 19; Cameron, *Solicitors in Blackpool*, 69–70; F. Sinclair, *Reminiscences of a Lawyer* (1861), 79.

[89] E. F. Spence, *Bar and Buskin* (1930), 72; T. Sadler, *Edwin Wilkins Field, a Memorial Sketch* (1872), 15; J. Scott, *Legibus* (1980), 30–2.

[90] Aylett, *Distribution and Functions of Attorneys*, 54–81; Corfield, *Power and the Professions*, 82.

[91] Abel, *Legal Profession*, tables 2.20, 2.21; J. Slinn, *A History of Freshfields* (1980), 32.

[92] T. Phillips, *A History of Herbert Smith* (2007), 40–1; L. Dennett, *Slaughter and May, a Century in the City* (1989), 131; St. George, *History of Norton Rose*, 136. Salaried partners were not unknown elsewhere; e.g.. W. H. Goodwin in Hastings, on £700 per annum: Langdon, *Square Toes and Formal*, 50.

[93] M. Burrage, *Revolution and the Making of the Contemporary Legal Profession* (Oxford, 2006), 522, suggests solicitors' firms were aping the bar in this respect, but that seems improbable.

[94] S. Warren, *The Moral, Social and Professional Duties of Attorneys and Solicitors* (1848), 227–31; 'The Organization of a Solicitor's Practice' (1884–5) 29 *Sol. J.* 180.

[95] St. George, *Norton Rose*, 138–9; Slinn, *History of Freshfields*, 72–4; Drummond, *Taylor and Humbert*, 12–14.

[96] G. Harris, *The Autobiography of George Harris* (1888), 41; M. Letts, *The Old House* (?1942), 48.

some insisted on independence, like Thomas Wilde and at least one of the prolific
Badger family in Rotherham.[97] If there was no son, a nephew or son-in-law might
be pressed into service, W. M. Guichard resorting in succession to two sons-in-
law.[98] Firms' names are deceptive, for it gradually became commoner to retain
the founder's name when ownership changed, but published histories suggest
the family firm remained the norm. Greater continuity came about with more
investment in premises and office equipment and a bigger base of regular clients
as firms depended less upon litigation and more on conveyancing, probate, and
corporate business. This enlarged the value of goodwill, raising the price of purchasing a practice and making takeovers and mergers more frequent.[99]

In the Letts firm in the 1820s even the girls were called in to help bundle letters
etc and when Michael Letts reluctantly joined in the 1880s the three partner-
brothers were assisted by another brother (not a partner) and two clerks who
were nephews; only an elderly writ-server was not a blood relative.[100] That degree
of concentration was exceptional, but even in the leading firms partnerships were
often reserved for family unless circumstances necessitated otherwise. A succession of able men learned their trade at Freshfields without that opportunity,
while not until 1897 did Boodles, with one son too young and the other not capable, look outside. Even the progressive Norton Rose still had 'Norton shares' and
'Rose shares' and theirs was one of several cases where this inwardness had bad
consequences, since third and fourth generations seldom inherited the ability
and drive of the founders.[101] Some were more open, like Ashurst, Morris Crisp,
and Linklater and Paines, while in Birmingham, whereas Beales was decidedly
family oriented, Wragges was very willing to provide openings for Walter Barrow
and T. W. Horton, men with excellent business connections.[102]

Articled Clerks

The apprenticeship for attorneys had been fixed at five years in 1729, though
reductions to three years were offered to graduates in 1821[103] and '10-year men'

---

[97] A. G. Salmon, *A History of Wilde Sapte 1785–1985* (Trowbridge, 1985), 20; J. H. Cockburn,
Rotherham Lawyers During 350 Years (Rotherham, 1932), 40–3. John Withers started out in partnership with his father, but moved into one with his brother: Cretney, 'Sir John Withers', 203.

[98] Cockburn, *Rotherham Lawyers During 350 Years*, 61. London may have been different; of six
Cornhill partnerships in 1887 only one was a pure family affair: Dockray, 'Guineas by Gaslight', 32.

[99] Aylett, *Distribution and Functions of Attorneys*, 54–81. Goodwill became saleable after a decision in 1803 and was usually valued at three years' profits: Kirk, *Portrait of a Profession*, 117.

[100] Letts, *The Old House*, 42–7.

[101] Slinn, *History of Freshfields*, 133; V. Belcher, *Boodle, Hatfield & Co* (1985), 112–21; St. George,
History of Norton Rose, 167.

[102] Rowley, *Professions, Class and Society*, 343–5.

[103] 1 & 2 Geo. IV c. 48. A 'curious blunder' had to be rectified in the next session: Christian, *Short
History*, 180 n.1.

in 1860.[104] As country practitioners left off going to London to conduct litigation and concentrated on conveyancing it became common for their articled clerks to complete or follow their term with a year in a London practice, often their firm's agents.[105] London articled clerks sometimes spent their last year with a licensed conveyancer or conveyancing barrister, though this was becoming less common.[106]

The apprentice had customarily entered articles at 16, though many started earlier. He became a member of his principal's household (which usually doubled as his office) and the board and lodging he received offset the premium required of all but partners' sons.[107] By the 1820s market forces and changing customs were working in the employer's favour, enabling him to demand more and provide less. Openings did not keep pace with would-be entrants, and with a solicitor limited to two articled clerks at any time and some taking none but their own sons, it was a seller's market.[108] Moreover, it became easier to recruit literate clerks for copying work, so that articled clerks in their early years were less useful.[109]

Accordingly, the cost of becoming a solicitor increased. As well as the duty on articles, the aspirant had to find a 'liberal premium': £200 was given as the norm in mid-century but the better London firms wanted up to £500[110] and as he now had to find food and lodging besides, the overall cost of qualifying was £700 to £1000.[111] A few able and deserving office clerks were given their articles, leading to complaints in the 1840s that unscrupulous firms poached from their rivals by this lure, but they were the exception.[112]

It was a commonplace that the life of an articled clerk, especially in his first years, was one of drudgery. Office hours were long, working conditions often bad,

---

[104] See below, p. 1198.

[105] Birks, *Gentlemen of the Law*, 167. This added £150 or more to the cost of qualifying: 'Grievances of Solicitors and Attorneys' (1838) 20 *LM* 114–24 at 117, but clerks like Clement Francis had social reasons also in mind: C. Jackson, *A Cambridge Bicentenary* (Bungay, 1990), 78–80.

[106] *SC on Legal Education 1846*; Maugham at q. 2165, who estimated 10% did so.

[107] Birks, *Gentlemen of the Law*, 163–4; Robson, *Attorney in Eighteenth Century England*, 59–63. The minimum age for admission was 21.

[108] e.g. [W. E. Beasley], *The Early History of an Old Leicester Firm of Solicitors, 1767–1865* (Leicester, 1930), 14.

[109] *SC on Legal Education 1846*, Stephen at qq. 2024–5; 'The Education of Attorneys' (1873) 2 (n.s.) *LM & R* 47–62 at 61–2; Birks, *Gentlemen of the Law*, 163–5.

[110] Abel, *Legal Profession*, 149. In 1820 one Leicester attorney managed to extract 600 guineas: Beasley, *Early History of an Old Leicester Firm*, 24–7. By 1902 300 guineas was more usual: 'Prospects in the Professions: The Solicitors' (1902) 13 (n.s.) *Cornhill Mag.* 635–50 at 639.

[111] Offer, *Property and Politics*, 13–14. In (1829) 2 *LM* 705, it was costed 'on the liberal plan' at £1000. However, H. B. Thomson, *The Choice of a Profession* (1857) said a few were being paid in articles.

[112] Q. Dodd, *The Practice* (Wrexham, 2003), 98. Uriah Heep, in Dickens' *David Copperfield*, was so favoured, though hardly deserving, as was W. H. Barber in Tonbridge.

and the work monotonous and repetitive.[113] Though some toiled hard, others were underemployed. Busy principals tended to consign them to a managing clerk ('an illiterate man of middle age and considerable self-importance'[114]), who might well be jealous of them and begrudge them interesting work and practical education.[115] Near the end of articles the clerk might, like Thomas Loughborough, be given a degree of responsibility, and his life become more interesting,[116] but some could not endure to wait. One of the Farrars quit the family firm in disgust and T. C. Turner scraped enough money together to transfer his articles to a better firm.[117] Though it was notorious that service in articles often fell below an acceptable standard, there was no real possibility of imposing one.

With no formal training, the articled clerk was advised to prepare himself by private study and there were books advising him how to go about it. The early ones were mostly over-ambitious and unrealistic, so most probably muddled their way through on what they could find in the office.[118] Lectures provided by the Law Society from 1833 were felt too academic and anyway were open only to those whose principal was a member; later ventures in Manchester and Birmingham were also unsuccessful.[119] An attempt to organize on a national basis to promote their cause was conceived on too grandiose lines to attract the support of leading solicitors and other key figures,[120] and though student debating societies flourished at times (they held a national congress in 1872), clerks were too scattered and divided to push their interests effectively.[121] The most they achieved was the belated implementation of the Legal Education Committee's recommendation for leave to prepare for their examinations.[122]

Clerks

The attorney had always had his clerk, Sancho Panza to his Don Quixote, though some managed without one for a long time.[123] When E. W. Field became articled

---

[113] e.g. Christian, *Short History of Solicitors*, 224.

[114] 'Education of Attorneys', 59.

[115] *Ibid.*, 60–2; *SC on Legal Education 1846*, qq. 991 (Taylor), 2546 (Payne); Birks, *Gentlemen of the Law*, 176.

[116] Birks, *Gentlemen of the Law*, 228–9.

[117] [C. Jessel], *Farrer & Co.: A Firm of First-Rate Connection* (?2001), 3; Scott, *Legibus*, 27.

[118] e.g. 'A Course of Study for Articled Clerks' (1829) 2 *LM* 83–102; 'Articled Clerks' (1854) 20 *LR* 323–41; Kirk, *Portrait of a Profession*, 51.

[119] Kirk, *Portrait of a Profession*, 60.

[120] *SC on Legal Education*, 1846, App. viii.

[121] Kirk, *Portrait of a Profession*, 60. Their meetings were regularly reported in the professional weeklies.

[122] *Ibid.*

[123] Birks, *Gentlemen of the Law*, 199–205.

to the reputable London firm of Taylor Roscoe in 1821 he found only one clerk, but that was becoming unusual.[124] By 1832 it was reckoned that most such firms had at least four, with 7000 clerks to 3000 solicitors in London and 9000 to 4000 in the provinces. Census figures point to a rise overall from 16,000 in 1851, via 24,500 in 1881 to 34,000 in 1911, when the ratio of clerks to solicitors was estimated at 2½ to 1.[125] Among the bigger firms the normal range was between 5 and 9 to 1, but could go much higher—20 to 1 at Norton Rose in the 1860s. Indeed that firm had caused a sensation at the height of the railway boom by housing almost 300 clerks in temporary offices for a massive copying operation, but none of the firms with published histories comes near that on a regular basis; Norton Rose had 70 or so in the 1860s, Gregory Rowcliffe 56 in 1889, while Coward Chance needed six office boys and had to open a second office.[126]

Some firms developed an elaborate departmental structure but the threefold division into common law, conveyancing, and copying clerks seen at Ellison Nares in 1800 remained the commonest.[127] The outdoor clerks had the most varied and hectic life and were mostly of the sharp, combative type who jostled for chambers appointments at the 'beargarden', battled tenaciously over costs, and negotiated fees with equally abrasive barristers' clerks.[128] They had a reputation for boisterous joviality and a fondness for drink,[129] especially if they imbibed the 'unhealthy moral atmosphere' of the SCJ Central Office.[130] Conveyancing clerks were altogether more sedate, spending their lives hunting down and adapting precedents, assembling abstracts of title and suchlike.[131] Copying clerks were the least well paid and were seldom found in smaller offices.[132] In London and big towns formal documents were mostly sent to law writers and in a small place like

[124] *Ibid.*, 217.

[125] Kirk, *Portrait of a Profession*, 114–15; Offer, *Property and Politics*, 20. According to Abel, *Legal Profession*, 203, the ratio of clerks to solicitors changed from 0.86 in 1850 to 2.09 in 1900, but the former seems too low.

[126] St. George, *Norton Rose*, 38, 81; J. Slinn, *A History of Vizards 1797–1997* (1997), 41; Dennett, *Slaughter and May*, 130; P. Davis, *Number One: A History of the Firm of Gregory Rowcliffe & Co 1784–1984* (1984), 41–2; Slinn, *History of Clifford Chance*, 68.

[127] Robson, *Attorney in Eighteenth Century England*, 127; Birks, *Gentlemen of the Law*, 232. For a layman's view see Dickens, *Pickwick Papers*, Ch. 31.

[128] Birks, *Gentlemen of the Law*, 232; Stephen, *Adventures of an Attorney*, 153–7.

[129] Spence, *Bar and Buskin*, 39–40; Scott, *Legibus*, 26. Some disreputable firms employed struckoff solicitors: G. Pitt-Lewis, *Commissioner Kerr* (1903), 132.

[130] 'Organization of a Solicitor's Office' (1884–5) 29 Sol. J. 79.

[131] Birks, *Gentlemen of the Law*, 232. For a very old-fashioned one see W. Hine, *Confessions of an Un-common Attorney* (1946), 16.

[132] Birks, *Gentlemen of the Law*, 232.

Great Yarmouth when a mass of urgent copying came in everyone from the principal downwards went to work.[133]

The law writers were a distinct sub-profession, operating mostly through law stationers. There were three grades: an elite properly qualified through a five to seven-year apprenticeship; the 'trade', who for various reasons were no longer in regular work; and the 'wallers', unqualified men who had somehow picked up the know-how. By the time they featured in Booths', *Life and Labours of the People in London* law writers were an endangered species.[134]

There can be no typical firm, but Preston's W. Banks & Co illustrates the structure of a prosperous provincial practice of the 1880s. William Banks was assisted by his brother and a cousin and employed a conveyancing clerk, a shorthand writer, a bookkeeper/ledger clerk, a cashier, a general clerk, and several junior clerks.[135] In big firms with distinct departments the heads could earn considerable salaries; Norton Rose paid Edmund Harvey £400 as chief clerk of accounts, though he still embezzled £17,000.[136]

Most clerks had a much harder life. A few were so well entrenched that they worked what hours they pleased, though outdoor clerks needed careful watching or they would lounge around the courts when their mission was done.[137] In the 1820s standard office hours were 8 am to 9 pm, though many London practices were quite idle during outside term. However, in 1837 the Law Society persuaded the courts to close their offices earlier and 6 pm gradually became the norm for solicitors' clerks, though unpaid overtime could always be exacted. One after another, solicitors in provincial towns shut up shop at Saturday lunchtime, but only when the judges were persuaded to discontinue Saturday afternoon sittings in 1876 were metropolitan firms able to follow suit.[138]

If solicitors' clerks were working shorter hours, in other ways they were probably becoming worse off than other clerks. Solicitors had long been reckoned among the meanest employers, although comparisons with government, banks, and insurance companies were not wholly fair as they mostly demanded better educated employees than the boys whom solicitors took on at 12 or 13.[139] They usually started at 5s a week and once shorthand had become the vogue often

---

[133] Slinn, *Linklaters and Paines*, 18.
[134] 2nd series (1903), iv, 75–7 (G. H. Duckworth). In *Bleak House* the law stationer Snagsby employs 'Nemo' (Captain Hawden) on a casual basis.
[135] Cameron, *Solicitors in Blackpool*, 18–21.
[136] St. George, *History of Norton Rose*, 137–8.
[137] Birks, *Gentlemen of the Law*, 230–2; C. W. Crocker, *Far From Humdrum* (1967), 20–1; 'Organization of a Solicitor's Practice', 79.
[138] Kirk, *Portrait of a Profession*, 119–20; Birks, *Gentlemen of the Law*, 231.
[139] Williams, *Gentleman's Calling*, 282; Birks, *Gentlemen of the Law*, 233.

could not progress beyond about 15s without it.[140] Big firms were not necessarily the most generous payers. In 1874 one Liverpool employer paid 21 of his staff less than £100 per annum and another 26 no more than £200. Freshfields paid many clerks just £60–70, though by taking home copying and various other shifts they could raise earnings to £100. Linklater & Paine, at between £2 10s and £4 a week, were less tight, but on this clerks had to dress respectably and save for their old age.[141] Since no pensions were provided, many firms had a few decrepit veterans (at least one clocked up 80 years), and their presence reinforced the conservatism of most office management.[142] The situation of a clerk who was dismissed was desperate: no reputable firm would hire him and he must become a process server or worse.[143]

By 1900 solicitors' clerks, like many others in the black-coated army, were feeling aggrieved and anxious, their livelihoods under threat from a conjunction of circumstances.[144] The staple work of copying was being superseded by printed court documents and by the arrival of copying machines which, though messy and unreliable, proved unstoppable.[145] So did the typewriter, and with that came the woman typist. While in 1882 the suggestion that they be employed in solicitors' offices could be scorned, within 20 years it was becoming a reality. The less conservative firms recognized their one great advantage—cheapness (they were generally paid only £50–60 per annum)—and though women clerks were still few, their number was growing.[146]

The more senior clerks had another problem besides. A large pool of qualified solicitors was competing with them for the position of managing clerk which was the summit of their ambition, reducing opportunities and also depressing salaries.[147] There had been a United Law Clerks Society for the London area since 1832 but it was chiefly a benefit society. Now local associations were formed, some mounting a hopeless campaign to counter the trend towards a more gentlemanly, better educated profession by demanding an easier route to qualification for

[140] Offer, *Property and Politics*, 20. When Harry Edwards mastered shorthand his pay rose immediately from 7s to 15s a week: Langdon, *Square Toes and Formal*, 51.

[141] Kirk, *Portrait of a Profession*, 120; Slinn, *History of Freshfields*, 119–21; J. Slinn, *Linklaters and Paines, the First One Hundred and Fifty Years* (1987), 92–3.

[142] Birks, *Gentlemen of the Law*, 232–3; Hine, *Confessions of an Un-common Attorney*, 17; Offer, *Property and Politics*, 58.

[143] C. Jay, *The Law* (1868), 58.

[144] G. Anderson, *Victorian Clerks* (Manchester, 1976), 52–73.

[145] Offer, *Property and Politics*, 58; Letts, *The Old House*, 54–5.

[146] 'Solicitor of the Supreme Court', *The Modern Lawyer's Office* (1902), 9; Kirk, *Portrait of a Profession*, 121–2; (1879–80) 24 *Sol. J.* 884; (1881–2) 26 *Sol. J.* 160.

[147] Judges' chambers appointments were a particular focus for rivalry: see e.g. correspondence in (1890) 10 *LN* 140.

clerks. In reality, however, effective trade union action was impossible in such a fragmented occupation.[148]

Managing Clerks

The important role played by the managing clerk was a distinctive feature of the English legal profession. There was no formal definition,[149] but he was the man who (advertisements insisted) must be able to work without supervision and he bridged the divide between admitted and unadmitted. It was common, indeed perhaps usual in London, for the newly qualified to start in this way, though it is not known what proportion of managing clerks were admitted men.[150]

This practice reflected the shortage of opportunities. It was seldom less than three years before a former articled clerk would be offered a partnership, and then usually only in return for a substantial capital contribution. There were a few assistant solicitors and salaried partners in private practice,[151] but few openings in the civil service or the business world. Railway companies began to revive the practice of hiring an in-house solicitor with James Blenkinsop in 1862, but it only became common enough to rate discussion in Law Society circles in 1909.[152]

If some newly admitted solicitors became managing clerks through necessity, for others it was because they shunned the responsibilities and risks of striking out alone or in order to gain further experience. Considerable numbers came to the big City firms for the latter purpose (Gregory Rowcliffe had eight of them in 1899[153]) but it was not confined to London; Tilney Barton for example worked successively in Cirencester, Malvern, and Truro.[154]

[148] Kirk, *Portrait of a Profession*, 120–1; Offer, *Property and Politics*, 58–60.

[149] *PD* 1860 (s3) 157: 1905–15 (Attorneys and Solicitors Bill).

[150] Miles, 'Haven for the Privileged', 204–10; Birks, *Gentlemen of the Law*, 233. The *Legal Observer* (quoted by Kirk, *Portrait of a Profession*, 114) was probably on the high side in suggesting that 40% of qualified solicitors did not take out a practising certificate.

[151] A. T. Keene became an assistant solicitor on qualification in 1853 and again in a different town after his own practice failed: Dodd, *The Practice*, 44–53. As late as 1903 a county court judge called salaried partners 'new–fangled': (1903) 22 *LN* 336–7.

[152] R. W. Kostal, *Law and English Railway Capitalism 1825–1875* (Oxford, 1994, edn of 1997), 373; (1908–9) 53 *Sol. J.* 666; (1909–10) 54 *Sol. J.* 676. One eminent banker was reported as saying that 'he could not well have a trained solicitor on the premises without antagonizing the legal profession' (Slinn, *Clifford Chance*, 53), but by 1899 in-house solicitors had spread to insurance firms and breweries and arguments that such employment contravened s.6 of the Solicitors Act 1843 were rejected in *Galloway* v. *Corporation of London* (1867) 4 LR Eq. 90, and *Henderson* v. *Merthyr Tydfil UDC* [1900] 1 QB 434; (1909) 28 *LN* 16–19.

[153] Davis, *Number One*, 41–2; Slinn, *Clifford Chance*, 34–5.

[154] T. Barton, *The Life of a Country Lawyer in Peace and Wartime* (Oxford, 1937), 15–27.

Pay was generally low and as the profession expanded their bargaining position weakened. £150 had always been a common starting figure, though some accepted less (W. H. Armitage became an assistant solicitor in Halifax on just £75)[155] and the register opened by the Law Society in 1902 offered plenty of men willing to take a salary well below the minimum for a middle-class existence. They must have had private means or a parental subsidy, and it is no wonder unadmitted clerks were bitter when employers gave them preference.[156] Of course, a good managing clerk could expect substantial pay rises. Edward Spence's went up from £150 to £250 before he left for the bar, Thomas Paines's from £200 to £400 before he was offered a partnership.[157] Bourchier Hawkes got his partnership at Coward Chance by handling Cecil Rhodes's affairs so capably that he was indispensable,[158] and if no partnership was to be had there might be a new branch office opening; Wansborough's paid its Devizes manager £150 plus a 10 per cent commission on the introduction of new business.[159] Managing clerks were prominent in the United Law Clerks Society but eventually formed their own Solicitors' Managing Clerks Association in 1892. It proved equally unsuccessful in improving the conditions of its members however.[160]

Premises

The Law Institution's prospectus (1823) struck an anachronistic note in promising 'an exchange to be open to attorneys, solicitors, proctors and such principal officers at all hours of the day but some particular time to be fixed for the general time of assembling; to be furnished with desks or enclosed tables running on each side of the room for the whole length of it, affording similar accommodation to those in Lloyd's Coffee-House'.[161] In fact the days when attorneys 'in the evening were accustomed to frequent the coffee-house in the neighbourhood for the purposes of business'[162] were gone, and with them the peripatetic attorney with his business papers in a green bag, apt to be mysteriously elusive whenever documents

---

[155] Offer, *Property and Politics*, 13; Kirk, *Portrait of a Profession*, 120; *Booth & Co*, 23. Edwin James, however, claimed that many in the City were on £300–400 per annum: *PD* 1860 (s3) 157: 1910.

[156] Offer, *Property and Politics*, 141–5; *Organization of a Solicitors' Office*, 64. Abbott's argument that resort to managing clerks arose from manpower shortages seems misconceived: A. Abbott, *The System of the Professions* (Chicago, 1988), 251–2.

[157] Spence, *Bar and Buskin*, 74–5; Slinn, *Linklater and Paines*, 16–27.

[158] Slinn, *Clifford Chance*, 33–4.

[159] *History of Wansboroughs*. Such commissions were common: Kirk, *Portrait of a Profession*, 120.

[160] Kirk, *Portrait of a Profession*, 121.

[161] *Ibid.*, 26.

[162] Christian, *Short History of Solicitors*, 179.

were to be served on him.[163] Whether their chambers were in the inns of court (mostly in Gray's) or the inns of Chancery (especially Cliffords), or whether settled elsewhere, attorneys had acquired fixed business abodes.

It was still common for traders and professionals to live above the shop, sometimes (as for John Taylor when he set up in Bolton) from financial necessity, but it was declining.[164] Thomas Tyrell and the Wilde family were unusual among City solicitors in the 1840s to be living at their offices and the Letts family became distinctly eccentric in continuing to cram themselves into the upper floors of their Holborn house until the end of the century.[165]

Whether doubling as home or not, the office, even a high-class practice such as Vizards, was likely to be shabby, dingy, incommodious, and unwelcoming. Trollope's much quoted remark that 'there is, I think, no sadder place in the world than the waiting room attached to an attorney's chambers in London', was echoed in other fiction, in memoirs, and magazines.[166] Most solicitors affected at least a show of disorder and discomfort, perhaps to avoid the impression that they were profiting unduly from their clients.[167]

The habit was, of course, not universal. A few firms, like Paris Smith and Randall, were fortunate to have acquired imposing premises, and others had new ones built. Aristocratic Frere Cholmeley employed Lewis Vulliamy for theirs in Lincoln's Inn Fields and on a more modest scale Tolhursts made themselves unique among Gravesend firms with a brand new office in 1906.[168] George Lewis refurbished his to impress clients with its opulence and confidentiality, and for a very different clientele Sir Frank Crisp of Ashurst Morris Crisp equipped himself with a huge office, suitable for directors' meetings, and an imposing library.[169] In due course commercial firms in the great cities moved into more spacious and showy buildings, acquiring necessary space and emphasizing that they belonged as much in the business community as in the legal. Ashurst Morris Crisp for instance moved into grand premises in Throgmorton Avenue, while newcomers Slaughter and May mortgaged themselves heavily for a new office in Austin Friars.[170]

[163] Kirk, *Portrait of a Profession*, 117.

[164] Clegg, *Autobiography of a Lancashire Lawyer*, 75.

[165] Slinn, *Linklater and Paines*, 23; Salmon, *History of Wilde Sapte*, 121; Letts, *The Old House*.

[166] E. B. V. Christian, *Leaves of the Lower Branch* (1909), 85–6; 'Organization of a Solicitor's Practice', 21; Birks, *Gentlemen of the Law*, 246; E. A. Bell, *Those Meddlesome Attorneys* (1939), 190.

[167] Crocker, *Far From Humdrum*, 20. An 1884 inventory of furniture from a Liverpool firm is in Williams, *Gentleman's Calling*, 194.

[168] N. Kemish, *Lansdowne House* (Totton, 1998), 8–14; P. Frere et al., *Frere Cholmeley, 1950–1980* (1981), 9–10; *Martin Tolhurst Partnership*, 11.

[169] J. Juxon, *Lewis and Lewis* (1983), 176–7; Bell, *Those Meddlesome Attorneys*, 188. The author of *The Organization of a Solicitor's Practice* was scathing about solicitors' meanness in the matter of libraries.

[170] Dennett, *Slaughter and May*, 74.

In office equipment and working methods most solicitors were known for an 'intense conservatism'.[171] In 1879 Ashurst Morris Crisp were among the first to install a telephone, but even the big firms (Coward Chance, 1899; Gregory Rowcliffe, 1903; Linklater and Paines, 1907) were surprisingly slow to follow.[172] It was 1914 before Andrew's, one of Lincoln's biggest firms, had one and some senior partners, like Banks in Preston resisted still.[173] It was the same with typewriters. Entrepreneurial newcomers Kenneth Brown Baker had them early while stately Coward Chance still had only one in 1912.[174] Even electric lighting was for long too radical for Freshfields.[175] The adoption of new methods for filing, storage, and accounts was equally slow. Solicitors were far more anxious to impress clients with respectability and trustworthiness than innovation and efficiency.[176]

4. WORK

The Georgian Transformation

During the eighteenth century attorneys were transformed from men whose chief livelihood was lawsuits into men who undertook a much wider range of business and made themselves indispensable to the propertied classes.[177] Country attorneys in particular mostly sought to avoid litigation work and when they did undertake it, employed firms like Farrers as agents, sharing the profits.[178] They looked instead to perform the services landowners needed; they drew wills and settlements; were stewards to manorial courts; chased rents and arranged repairs; audited accounts; and collected debts.[179] Where landowners developed urban

[171] 'Solicitor', *Modern Lawyer's Office*, 1.

[172] Dennett, *Slaughter and May*, 26; Slinn, *Clifford Chance*, 68; Slinn, *Linklaters and Paines*, 93; Davis, *Number One*, 43. But see Dockray, *Guineas by Gaslight*, 28 n.5.

[173] Davies and Race, *Andrew & Co*, 14; Cameron, *Solicitors in Blackpool*, 22; Letts, *The Old House*, 53.

[174] B. J. Moughton, *Two Years Short of Two Hundred: Turner Kenneth Brown* (Law Society Library t/s, 2001), 15; Slinn, *Clifford Chance*, 67.

[175] Slinn, *History of Freshfields*, 137.

[176] 'Solicitor', *Modern Lawyer's Office*.

[177] Robson, *Attorney in Eighteenth Century England*, 68–154; Miles, 'Eminent Practitioners'; Aylett, *Distribution and Functions of Attorneys*, and 'Attorneys and Clients in Eighteenth Century Cheshire: A Study in Relationships, 1740–1785' (1986–7), 69 *Bulletin of the John Rylands Library*, 326–58; Birks, *Gentlemen of the Law*, 181–205.

[178] C. W. Brooks, 'Interpersonal Conflict and Social Tension: Civil Litigation in England, 1640–1830', *Lawyers, Litigation and English Society Since 1450* (1998), 27–63 at 46; Jessel, *Farrer & Co*, 1–2; Anderson, *Lawyers and the Making of English Land Law*, 23. The northern agents even had their own club.

[179] See above, also Schmidt, 'Country Attorney' and C. D. Webster, 'Robert Parker, Attorney' (1966) *Transactions of the Halifax Antiquarian Society*, 53–82.

property attorneys acted as middlemen between owner and builders.[180] Nor were they content to be just the servants of the landed classes. They were eager and active participants in enclosures, canals and turnpikes, insinuated themselves into local government and some, like J. S. Carsdale of Leicester, profited from the innumerable disputes over pauper settlements.[181]

Above all, they moved into conveyancing and allied work such as preparing auction particulars, and their extensive involvement in property transfers afforded them the opportunity to play a pivotal part in commercial and industrial development. They were the conduit between capital seeking a home and enterprises needing finance. Attorneys brought the parties together and drew the mortgages which secured the investment,[182] and when country banks started to supersede them in this role attorneys like William Alcock in Skipton were among the first to join those ventures.[183] In all these ways the attorney became an ubiquitous figure in small town and country society, far removed from the pettyfogger who still characterized most literary representations.

Litigation

Litigation in the superior courts, particularly in the King's Bench and Chancery, was reviving by the 1820s.[184] Provincial litigation was mostly channelled though a small number of London agency firms of great respectability for whom litigation was a major source of profit and business.[185] Although they were complicit in the defects of the courts, their reputation was unimpeachable, but there were others active in this field who undoubtedly justified the popular belief that the profession actively encouraged lawsuits for its own profit,[186] men like John Smith in

---

[180] V. Belcher, 'A London Attorney of the Eighteenth Century: Robert Andrews' (1986) 12 *London Journal* 40–50 and Belcher, *Boodle, Hatfield and Co.*

[181] Beasley, *Early History of an Old Leicester Firm*, 13; B. Keith-Lucas, *The Unreformed System of Local Government* (1980), 61–3.

[182] M. Miles, 'The Money Market in the Early Industrial Revolution' (1981) 23 *Business History* 351–74; B. L. Anderson, 'The Early Capital Market in Lancashire', in *Capital Formation and the Industrial Revolution*, ed. F. Crouzet (1972), 223–57.

[183] A. S. Rowley, *A History of Charlesworth, Wood and Brown, Solicitors* (1732–1982), Law Society Library t/s, n.d.

[184] See above, pp. 619, 652.

[185] The biggest was Gregory Rowcliffe: Davis, *Number One*, 15–16.

[186] To the Law Society representatives giving evidence to the Judicature Commission, Master Erle pointed out that he had to deal with 'a class of solicitors having business very different from that which you gentlemen are conversant with', who abused the facility of judgment by default: *Second Report, Evidence, PP* 1872 (C. 631–I) xx, q. 6179.

Birmingham and Roger Whitehead in Liverpool.[187] Every big town had its share of Smiths and Whiteheads, whose clerks touted for business around the courts, and a few exploited the possibilities of an old local court, as John Williams did with the Wirral Hundred Court;[188] a strong argument against proposals to expand local justice was that they would give more opportunities to such men. Even the courts of requests, which had originally discouraged legal representation, were being opened up to lawyers, often of the most dubious sort.[189]

The agency firms had a vested interest in keeping Westminster Hall as the focus for suits and were instrumental in defeating Brougham's local courts bill in 1833,[190] but they were not alone in being dismayed when the county courts were introduced in 1846. So were those who practised on their own account in the superior courts[191] and the many solicitors who got their livelihood from collecting debts or buying them up wholesale at a discount and pursuing the debtors themselves; this was how the respectable Cambridge firm of Gunning and Francis got started in 1839 but many were less reputable.[192] For them the establishment of a cheap, accessible forum for creditors seemed a disaster, for although solicitors had audience in the new courts, costs were set so low as to make it uneconomic.

In fact the volume of business, the extension of the money limits, and the enactment of a less miserly scale of costs soon altered the picture. Figures for Liverpool in the 1850s showed more than 1500 cases where one or both parties was represented, overwhelmingly by a solicitor rather than a barrister, and an indication of their importance to the profession is that in 1850 the Sheffield law society imposed a scale on its members and forbade undercutting.[193] The merits of county courts divided the profession. The Law Society, on which the agency firms were strongly represented, was itself so split that it sent several witnesses to the Romilly Commission to offer different views, while those who represented it before the Judicature Commission confessed to having no mandate.[194] Given their background, however, it is not surprising that they opposed further extensions of

[187] Stephen, *Adventures of an Attorney*, 205–10; 'Reform of the Legal Profession' (1887–8) 13 (s4) *LM & R* 191–200; Rowley, *Professions, Class and Society*, 106–7; Williams, *Gentleman's Calling*, 165–70.

[188] Williams, *Gentleman's Calling*, 162–3, and see Jay, *The Law*, 92, on the attorneys of the Palace Court.

[189] See above, p. 853.

[190] P. Polden, A *History of the County Court, 1846–1971* (Cambridge, 1999), 20, 25. They later joined with the bar in attacking the proposal to give them equitable jurisdiction: (1864) 40 *LT* 223.

[191] e.g. Thomas Angell: see his evidence to Judicature Commission (*Second Report 1872*, qq. 1982–2205).

[192] Jackson, *Cambridge Bicentenary*, 75; Stephen, *Adventures of an Attorney*, 209, Jay, *The Law*, 257–9.

[193] Polden, *History of the County Court*, 36, 43–4, 54–6, 171.

[194] *RC on County Courts, PP* 1854–5 [1914], xviii, evidence of J. Maynard, q. 2; *RC on the Judicature, Second Report 1872*, evidence of E. W. Williamson, q. 6107.

jurisdiction. In 1878 E. F. Burton, the president, maintained that 'a man of position cannot go into the county court' and 'when gentlemen are summoned to the county courts their solicitors cannot go with them'.[195] Some leading firms in the great cities aspired to reproduce the metropolitan position regionally, making themselves agents for the regional branches of the High Court which they demanded.[196]

In London and other big cities only a minority of solicitors regularly undertook county court business; indeed many shunned litigation altogether, like A. L. Howarth in Bolton, who 'had a horror of litigation and avoided as much as he could the bringing of actions and squabbling suits at law'.[197] Litigation at Gray and Dodsworth of York was so infrequent that cases were long remembered and George Wyman in Peterborough in the whole of a long life never tried to muster a court practice.[198] Though it was said that 150 Birmingham solicitors had appeared in the county court at one time or another, just three firms did the great bulk of the work, while it was estimated in 1878 that only one-fifth of Nottingham solicitors appeared in the county court.[199]

From the first some realized that a decent living could be made out of the county courts by acting as an 'attorney-advocate', conducting all the scattered cases of local solicitors for whom a day in the court would be a waste. This practice was outlawed in 1852 but while it was not a dead letter as Hollams (who never went there) claimed, the prohibition was enforced only sporadically and was readily evaded.[200] A class of advocates developed whose 'loud shop-boy manner' the *Law Times* deplored but who were often at least as effective as junior barristers,[201] men like T. W. Garrold in Shrewsbury, blessed with 'great energy, unbounded confidence in his own power, and plenty of impudence', who upset the staid local practitioners as well as Judge Smith.[202] County courts might not be places for gentlemen, but for the most part they were not the haunt of the doubtful characters who still plagued the surviving local courts.[203]

---

[195] *SC on County Courts (No. 2) Bill*, 1878, PP 1878 (267) xi, qq. 4221–2.

[196] Polden, *History of the County Court*, 82.

[197] Clegg, *Autobiography of a Lancashire Lawyer*, 354.

[198] Cobb, *Grays of York*, 55; R. Hill, *A History of Wyman Abbott* (?Peterborough, 1996), 12.

[199] Rowley, *Professions, Class and Society*, 136–8; *SC on County Courts (No. 2) Bill 1878*, evidence of R. Mellors, q. 5232.

[200] Polden, *History of the County Court*, 44–5; Sir J. Hollams. *Jottings of a Old Solicitor* (1906), 222–3.

[201] Kirk, *Portrait of a Profession*, 157; *RC on the Judicature, Second Report 1872*, R. G. Welford, q. 4718. Seemingly, even successful advocacy only gradually became completely reputable: Rowley, *Professions, Class and Society*, 139.

[202] W. J. Humfreys, *Memories of Old Hereford* (n.d.), 20; Polden, 'Judicial Selkirks', 245–62 at 249–50.

[203] Parrott, *Route to Respectability*, 5–8.

The county court advocates had often to fight for their business, however, and a much more serious set of rivals than the bar were 'agents', and 'accountants', essentially debt collectors. Among them were disreputable individuals claiming to be lawyers and others who used the names of broken down solicitors,[204] but many firms acted for bulk creditors such as mail order firms for whom the county court was just the last stage in the pursuit of a debtor.[205] Provincial solicitors were regularly frustrated by a seeming lack of vigour in the Law Society in defending this contested turf and local societies devoted considerable effort to ousting them. Success depended essentially on the attitude of the local judge and was generally greater in rural areas, since judges in large industrial towns often depended on the agents to help them get through the mass of judgment summonses.[206]

In the superior courts simplifications of procedure in the mid-century hit practitioners' profits hard and the loss of business to the county courts was a major setback for them.[207] There were, of course, specialist areas which were confined to the superior courts and firms could market their expertise in those; thus Lewis & Lewis were noted for libel; Farrers made a corner in Privy Council appeals, and Kenneth Brown Baker became well known defending motorists.[208] In addition, urbanization and industrialization brought in more contractual disputes and more torts arising out of damage to persons and properties. In the wake of railway accidents came 'ambulance chasers', who were later to be found pursuing motor accidents with the same vigour.[209]

The overall level of litigation in the High Court remained at a relatively low figure but it became more profitable. Interlocutory proceedings expanded, the volume of correspondence produced in commercial cases expanded and court hours shortened, so cases stretched out longer and costs rose.[210] All told, although few firms drew their sustenance primarily from litigation, there were many for whom it was still a valuable source of business and income.

One area still shunned by most respectable firms was crime. Stephen wrote that 'business of that class [theft] I could not undertake myself'[211] and the decline of private prosecutions made it less likely that the leading firms would be approached in a criminal matter. From the early nineteenth century criminal

---

[204] *Ibid.*

[205] M. C. Finn, *The Character of Credit* (Cambridge, 2003, edn of 2007), 99, 255–7.

[206] Polden, *History of the County Court*, 45–6; Rowley, *Professions, Class and Society*, 276–97; Cameron, *Solicitors in Blackpool*.

[207] Birks, *Gentlemen of the Law*, 223.

[208] Juxon, *Lewis and Lewis*, 78–9; Jessel, *Farrer & Co*, 25; Moughton, *Two Years Short of Two Hundred*, 9–11.

[209] Kostal, *Law and English Railway Capitalism*, 378–80; Crocker, *Far From Humdrum*, 73–5.

[210] See above, Part 3, Chs VI and IX.

[211] *Adventures of an Attorney*, 384.

prosecutions at the Old Bailey were almost monopolized by a handful of criminal practices,[212] while outside London it was difficult to get any funds even to organize a murder defence, as Taylor found in Bolton.[213] Solicitors did criminal work at the sessions however: in 1848 they were given the right to appear at petty sessions and in 1905 were enabled to do licensing work at most quarter sessions,[214] useful for a new practitioner. Bosanquet felt the quality and integrity of regular criminal advocates improved greatly over time. When he started out on circuit in the 1890s many were still 'rough and untrustworthy', though each county had its local Marshall Hall, men such as Evans of Breconshire and Prothero of Monmouthshire.[215]

Conveyancing

By the mid-nineteenth century conveyancing had become the basis of most practices, particularly outside London,[216] and by that time an assertion that it was the least remunerative work was not credible.[217] Unfortunately it is not possible before the 1890s to establish how profitable it was, nor even then what proportion of the profession's income it yielded, but dependence upon it was growing, and dangerously so, for many practices.[218]

The danger did not come from other professions. In the first part of the nineteenth century, solicitors extended their role in the preliminary stages of land transfer, whether by auction or private treaty, and although auctioneers recovered, and estate agents succeeded in establishing their own distinctive role in the land market,[219] after the demise of the certificated conveyancers solicitors had no serious rivals in the work of the conveyancer proper.[220] This was not due to the punitive sanctions protecting the statutory monopoly, which were clumsy and ineffectual, but to the obstructions a solicitor could deploy against an unqualified person acting for the other side and perhaps also because solicitors were pricing

---

[212] See above, p. 643. Freshfields were an exception, since they handled Bank of England prosecutions.

[213] Clegg, *Autobiography of a Lancashire Lawyer*, 84–5.

[214] Kirk, *Portrait of a Profession*, 160–1.

[215] Sir R. Bosanquet, *The Oxford Circuit* (1951), 101.

[216] Like the 'steady conveyancing practice' in Kirkby Lonsdale described by A. Pearson, *Doings of a Country Solicitor* (Kendal, 1947), 42, and Cruttwells of Frome, where Tilney Barton was articled: *Life of a Country Lawyer*, 6.

[217] Birks, *Gentlemen of the Law*, 227, 279; Kirk, *Portrait of a Profession*, 137–8.

[218] According to (1857) 28 *LT* 209 three-quarters of the business of provincial firms came from this source, but that was just guesswork.

[219] See Vol XII, pp. 95–6, 107–8. Offer, *Property and Politics*, 98–101. For auctions see e.g. Rowley, *Professions, Class and Society*, 287–90.

[220] For the bar's abandonment of its claim to receive direct instructions in conveyancing matters see Kirk, *Portrait of a Profession*, 135–7.

their services competitively, though they did their best to discourage price competition among themselves.[221]

How much solicitors actually did charge before the remuneration order of 1883
is not very clear. Notionally at least, charges were calculated in the same outdated
manner as those for litigation, by allowances for each attendance and each folio
of documents, providing a perverse incentive to long-winded conveyances and
unnecessary interviews. However, the taxations which were supposed to protect
against overcharging were comparatively infrequent and scale charges were produced by local law societies from the 1830s onwards, suggesting that the allow-
able elements in the bill may simply have been manipulated to produce what was
considered a reasonable charge. If that was the case, it will have done nothing to
endear either practitioners or the land transfer system to clients confronted with
such a concoction.[222]

Although the alternative of simple lump sum agreements was allowed from
1870 (subject to approval by a taxing master) it never became popular. Local scales
were widely used, since a national one could not be agreed. Finally in 1883 a statutory (maximum) scale was imposed. Local societies continued to use their own,
however, and tried to prevent undercutting; not always successfully, for develop-
ers and building societies could offer tempting inducements to impoverished or
raw practitioners. Still, competition was, at best, muted.[223]

The danger of relying on conveyancing became apparent when title registration, rather than deeds registration, came onto the political agenda in the 1850s.
Its practical effects were very limited before the Great War but the Edwardian
period did coincide with a downturn in the property cycle which seriously eroded
solicitor incomes from land transfer.[224]

Business and Commerce

A conventional narrative presents the role of solicitors in business as a gradual
decline from a time when 'inside the eighteenth century attorney, half-a-dozen
professional men—accountant, company secretary, and others, were struggling
to get out'.[225] In this story it was the accountant whose escape was seen as crucial.[226] There was no distinct accountancy profession until the 1870s and the

---

[221] *Ibid.*, 134.

[222] Anderson, *Lawyers and the Making of English Land Law*, 50–7.

[223] Anderson, *Lawyers and the Making of English Land Law*, 153–8; Offer, *Property and Politics*, 39–40; Cameron, *Solicitors in Blackpool*, 42–5, 57, 60, 66, 83–4.

[224] Offer, *Property and Politics*, 49–68.

[225] Reader, *Professional Men*, 27.

[226] Sugarman, 'Who Colonized Whom?', 227.

Institute of Chartered Accountants came only in 1880. However, accountants had been steadily evolving into a respectable profession at least from 1831, when they were named among those who might be 'official assignees' under the Bankruptcy Act (from which solicitors were rather curiously excluded), encouraged by subsequent legislation, first for railways and then for joint stock companies generally, which imposed an annual audit. This provided an essential opening for men like W. W. Deloitte, who became accountant for the GWR in 1849, and accountants acquired influence over clients because they claimed expertise not only in company finance but also in taxation. Solicitors are said to have been ousted from this pivotal and lucrative advisory role largely because of their own reluctance to educate themselves and engage with business in concerns where advice was required. In fact the story is a more complicated one.[227]

For instance, the early history of railways presents a very different picture. Since attorneys were deeply involved in canals and turnpikes, it is no surprise to find them equally eager to participate in railways and they did so enthusiastically, both as legal advisers and as promoters and backers. The extent and nature of their involvement has been viewed as profoundly bad for the infant industry, with the employment of solicitors on the conventional basis, a 'ruinous system', only cured when the companies, beginning with the LNWR in the 1860s, created in-house legal departments.[228]

In Kostal's view, solicitors ruthlessly and shamelessly exploited their indispensable knowledge and expertise by 'fee gouging'—inflating bills by unnecessary (and sometimes fictitious) charges for attendances and documents. This went largely unchecked because the directors were inexperienced, irresponsible, and complicit in various proportions and conscious of their dependence on lawyers to get enterprises up and running. Taxations of bills frequently demonstrated how exorbitant the charges were, yet until the 1850s they were seldom sought, and thereafter it was only the big companies who used them regularly. There is substance to these criticisms. Bills were sometimes huge, Robert Baxter's to the GNR for 1844–6 totalling a whopping £179,739. Some were certainly inflated, and many solicitors felt that this type of client, evidently careless with shareholders' money and seemingly going to be immensely profitable, could be charged at a much higher rate than a private individual. But bills included not only disbursements but often the fees of counsel, and it was not the fault of solicitors that the bills covered innumerable pages and comprised huge numbers of small items.

---

[227] Reader, *Professional Men*, 161; Sugarman, 'Simple Images and Complex Realities', 225–6. For a recent summary of the conventional story see Burrage, *The Revolution and the Making of the Contemporary Legal Profession*, 485–96.

[228] Kostal, *Law and English Railway Capitalism*, 322–57.

That was precisely the system they wanted changed and it made it difficult for a man like Baxter to place an open market value on his services or to negotiate a sensible reward in advance.[229]

Very few firms profited as much as Baxter, Norton Rose, which maintained 23 railway accounts even after the crash of 1846, or Henry Nelson in Leeds, the GNR agent in Yorkshire and the midlands from 1876 to 1895, whose offices often worked through the night.[230] But more small provincial firms had some railway business than might be supposed, since the landowners who funded or promoted a railway often insisted on their own solicitor acting for the company; Kelly and Keene in Mold were one firm which did well on a modest scale.[231] The big companies generally employed several firms in different locations—six in the case of the LNWR—so many firms shared in the railway business, at least before the very gradual trend towards taking the business in-house.

Kostal makes other charges against solicitors. He gives substantial credence to allegations that in the proliferation of sham railway companies before the crash of 1845, the 'most fecund source' was the 'scampish attorney…too idle for steady business, and too dissolute to preserve it if they had it'.[232] Many solicitors were certainly active participants in company promotion—Baxter Norton Rose was a product of the founders' financial support for rival schemes—and some of these schemes proved to be unsound; thus, John Duncan, solicitor to the Eastern Counties Railway, became involved in an acrimonious dispute over excessive billing and was also behind the Southampton, Petersfield, and London Direct Railway which collapsed in circumstances that suggested it had been always highly speculative.[233] Moreover their enthusiasm for promotions grew as the bubble expanded; of 75 schemes registered in May 1845, 31 had at least one-quarter of lawyers (mostly solicitors) among their principal promoters.[234] It was freely alleged in the railway press that many of these promotions were fraudulent bubble companies with lawyers exploiting their professional knowledge to become the most able and prolific joint-stock swindlers.[235] The evidence for such sweeping and serious accusations is inconclusive. It is unsurprising that solicitors should have entered so enthusiastically into the railway boom and if their commercial judgement was sometimes unsound that is equally unsurprising. Only one seems to have been convicted of fraud, however, and it is not known how many walked

[229] *Ibid.*, 334–49.
[230] St. George, *Norton Rose*, 81; *Booth & Co*, 9–10.
[231] Kostal, *Law and English Railway Capitalism*, 354; Dodd, *The Practice*, 84.
[232] Kostal, *Law and English Railway Capitalism*, 41.
[233] *Ibid.*, 42, 341–3; St. George, *Norton Rose*, 36–7.
[234] Kostal, *Law and English Railway Capitalism*, 45–6.
[235] *Ibid.*, 46.

away from the crash with their pockets lined.²³⁶ If the railway crash left a question mark about the profession's probity it also provided a confirmation of its entrepreneurial leanings.

Less controversial were banking and insurance, both of which offered profitable opportunities after the remodelling legislation of 1825.²³⁷ Farrers were keen on life insurance but benefited most from acting for Coutts Bank. At one time they had a 'Coutts partner' who visited the bank daily, and were also involved in setting up the Irish Bank and the National Provincial Bank for Thomas Joplin; subsequently they went in for advising on overseas banking development.²³⁸ Coward Chance had the Commercial Union and other insurers on their books and were heavily involved in the world of discount houses and merchant banking. Under Hollams' sway they persuaded the Institute of Bankers and the Association of Chambers of Commerce to fund Chalmers' Bills of Exchange Bill in 1882 and they had major banking clients overseas (such as the Bank of Persia) as well as in England.²³⁹ As with railways, there were some who sailed close to the wind. Thomas Tyrell helped to found the Bank of London in 1855 but committed such questionable acts when it ran into difficulties that his partner Paine was relieved when Tyrell retired.²⁴⁰

The enactment of the Companies Acts 1856–62 widened horizons, encouraging a boom in incorporation which also attracted business from abroad.²⁴¹ Solicitors had been condemned for their role in the stock market bubble of 1835–6, though some of them were dupes rather than fraudsters.²⁴² There were both sorts in the profession in the 1860s, but it was the enterprising and generally honest City men who were the biggest and most enduring successes. 'Practitioners were the architects of company law. They authored the basic textbooks and, most important, those collections of precedents that were used, re-used, and reworked in the everyday world of corporate practice.'²⁴³ Their activities went far beyond the mechanics of company formation, as a few examples will show.

Ashurst Morris Crisp benefited hugely from the connection with the great grocer James Morrison. John Morris, senior partner from 1862, had immense flair for commercial work, especially liquidations. He made his name in the salvage operation following the Overend Gurney collapse, helped draft the Companies

---

²³⁶ *Ibid.*, 42–8.
²³⁷ W. R. Cornish and G. de N. Clark, *Law and Society in England, 1750–1950* (1989), 250–4.
²³⁸ Jessel, *Farrer & Co*, 17–20.
²³⁹ Slinn, *Clifford Chance*, 36–62.
²⁴⁰ Slinn, *Linklater and Paines*, 60.
²⁴¹ Sugarman, 'Simple Images and Complex Realities', 274–6.
²⁴² Stephen, *Adventures of an Attorney*, 171–4.
²⁴³ Sugarman, 'Simple Images and Complex Realities', 275.

Act of 1870 and amassed a client base of over 300 companies at home and abroad, including Cuthbert Boulter's National Telephone Company.[244] According to Charles Norton, his firm and AMC were involved in practically every major company share issue between 1870 and 1914, so many that Sir Frank Crisp had a printing press on the premises to speed the issue of flotation documents.[245]

An offshoot of AMC was Slaughter & May, one of whose founding partners, William Slaughter, not only exploited family connections in the City but became intimately involved in building up Julius Drew's Home and Colonial Stores, though the biggest client was the international financier Emile Erlange & Co.[246] The firm's ingenuity in devising share dealing arrangements occasionally crossed the very blurred line into illegal share manipulation.[247]

Coward Chance was one of the first firms in the field and represented some of the biggest undertakings in the heyday of imperial exploitation, notably the Imperial Tobacco Company and Cecil Rhodes's British South Africa Company. The latter embroiled them in some rather murky business when they had to organize the defence in the trial of participants in the Jameson Raid.[248]

In Dudley Baxter, Norton Rose had one of the first real tax experts and in Philip Rose a man born for commercial law. Rose led them into lucrative foreign loan business, assisted from 1869 by Henry T. Norton, one of the new breed of commercial lawyers. They entered boldly on all the financial novelties of the age, instigated the corps of foreign bondholders to safeguard their interests, pioneered investment trusts in 1868, and branched out from railways into allied industries such as submarine cables.[249]

The story of Clifford Turner, founded only in 1900, shows that it was relatively easy for an ambitious and enterprising firm to break into the magic circle. Through Turner's partner Hopton they acquired a good deal of work in bus company formation and subsequent amalgamations, hitching themselves to the coat tails of the transport entrepreneur A. H. Stanley.[250]

When necessary these City firms could act collectively in defence of the regime which they served. They formed an exclusive 'City Law Club'[251] and ensured, through publications, discreet lobbying and appearance as select committee witnesses that the views of the City were heard; for example, 17 of them

[244] Dennett, *Slaughter and May*, 20–30.
[245] Sir C. Norton, *A Man of Many Parts* (1972), 17; Bell, *Those Meddlesome Attorneys*, 188.
[246] Dennett, *Slaughter and May*, 30–7.
[247] *Ibid.*, 99–105. For example the *Steam Loop* case [1892] 2 QB 724.
[248] Slinn, *Clifford Chance*, 58–62. Acquiring two of the 'randlords' as clients added greatly to the prosperity of Herbert Smith: Phillips, *Herbert Smith*, 33–6.
[249] St. George, *Norton Rose*, 84–111.
[250] Scott, *Legibus*, 47–9.
[251] Slinn, *Linklaters and Paines*, 68.

banded together to oppose the Joint Stock Companies Bill of 1888 which sought to improve shareholder protection.[252]

While the biggest firms were in London, there were emergent specialists in other major cities. Botterell and Roche was at the centre of a complex structure of partnerships and firms operating in London and the shipbuilding centres of the north-east, and in Wilson Roche they had the country's leading expert on shipping law. Roche inspired the formation of the British Ship Owners Association and the British Shipping Federation, from which they had a regular retainer, and frequently advised the Board of Trade. Between 1900 and 1920 the firm had at least 37 cases in the Court of Appeal on shipping matters alone.[253]

Liverpool too had commercial lawyers of excellent repute (notably W. G. Bateson and A. F. Warr) and in Birmingham John Moore-Bayley and R. H. Milward developed a speciality in corporate law, while Arthur Ryland established a national name for his role in trade mark reform.[254] Men of such stature were not confined to the big cities. Rotherham could boast Frederick Parker Rhodes, a man of high repute in the coalmining industry, active in railway development, in great demand as an expert witness, sometime president of the Sheffield Law Society and member of the Law Society's council.[255] Cornwall too had a very active commercial lawyer in Gerald Nalder, and F. W. Snell in Tonbridge specialized in company law and had Marconi and Daimler among his clients.[256]

Both in the City and elsewhere, there was clearly no shortage of interest in and commitment to, business enterprise, nor was this seen as incompatible with the notion of gentility which solicitors so much valued; after all Philip Rose was a confidant of Disraeli and a major figure in the Conservative party and John Hollams, known as 'the judgemaker', was one of the most prominent men in law reform; both, like Thomas Paine, were knighted.[257] And yet despite all this activity, there is substance in the contention that solicitors had begun to lose their place as advisers to business.

They were not passive in the face of what one writer called 'our invaders'.[258] Indeed the legal journals published regular complaints about the inactivity of the Law Society and sometimes the apathy of the profession, complaints which were

[252] Slinn, *Clifford Chance*, 32; Sugarman, 'Simple Images and Complex Realities', 275.
[253] St. George, *Norton Rose*, 153–4.
[254] Rowley, *Professions, Class and Society*, 119–20; Williams, *Gentleman's Calling*, 202.
[255] Cockburn, *Rotherham Lawyers During 350 Years*, 53–6.
[256] J. Pollock, *A Very Cornish Practice* (Truro, 2004), 89; M. Blatcher, *The First Four Hundred Years* (1970), 19–20.
[257] St. George, *Norton Rose*, 44–62; Slinn, *Clifford Chance*, 19–29 ; Slinn, *Linklaters and Paines*, 60–75.
[258] J. S. Salaman, quoted in Sugarman, 'Who Colonized Whom?', 231.

periodically echoed at annual meetings.[259] In 1874 the Law Society responded by sponsoring an unsuccessful bill aimed at both accountants and estate agents, extending the ban on preparing instruments for reward to cover bankruptcy documents and estate contracts.[260] Accountants had an unfair advantage in not needing a practising certificate and their lower income expectations probably enabled them to undercut solicitors' charges for some work. Nevertheless, solicitors acquired a deserved reputation for being ignorant and slovenly in bookkeeping and accounts,[261] examined in an antiquated system of trust accounts which was 'as unintelligible to the ordinary business man as it is to the most ignorant person'.[262] No wonder the accountants gloated. Furthermore, solicitors' examinations were based exclusively on private client work and disdained company law and taxation, which meant that only those articled in firms which practised extensively in those areas were likely to acquire a working knowledge of them.[263] In many places it must have become known to businessmen and professionals that it was vain to look to a solicitor for intelligent advice on financial matters. Solicitors' complaints to the Law Society arising from encroachments on their function in advising laymen formed a much smaller proportion of the total than in the United States, suggesting it was not something they conceived as central to their practice.[264]

From that standpoint it was no doubt perfectly sensible of the profession to seek to draw agreed boundaries by discussion. In Liverpool, for example, the newly founded Society of Liverpool Accountants immediately met the Liverpool Law Society to establish the demarcation of work under the Bankruptcy Act[265] and though no such agreement was struck nationally, the likelihood is that at least informal agreements were common; after all, although in competition for some work, each profession was in a position to send business to the other. Co-operation rather than conflict was probably the norm among the better class of practitioners who belonged to professional associations.[266]

---

[259] See e.g. 'The Rights and Wrongs of Solicitors' (1908) 27 LN 113–15, 339–40; (1909) 28 LN 161–9, 334–6; Offer, Property and Politics, 98–101.

[260] R. Abel-Smith and R. Stevens, Lawyers and the Courts (1967), 58–9.

[261] Sugarman, 'Who Colonized Whom?', 232. R. Brooke of Liverpool suggested to the Common Law Commissioners that by auditing landowners' accounts, lawyers might be 'unconsciously lowering the Profession' (Third Report, PP 1831 (92), x, App., 101).

[262] Sugarman, 'Who Colonized Whom?', 232 and see below, p. 1199.

[263] Ibid., 233.

[264] Abbott, The System of the Professions, 256–71.

[265] Williams, Gentleman's Calling, 328.

[266] Sugarman, 'Who Colonized Whom?', 229–30.

Insolvency[267]

Business failure was also a profitable source of work for solicitors.[268] Though the commissioners in bankruptcy were barristers, all commissions made use of solicitors and there were complaints of 'the total want of control by them [the commissioners] over the expenditure of the Solicitor to the Commission...'.[269] Brougham's reforms of 1831 came before the profession was organized to protect its interests, otherwise, for all Brougham's prejudice against solicitors, they would probably not have been omitted from the qualifying occupations for official assignees.[270] By the time further reforms were in contemplation the solicitors made sure their voice was heard. In 1843 local law societies petitioned alone and in conjunction with local business interests in favour of changes; a year later solicitors concerned with the collection of small debts were among the groups who secured the reversal of Brougham's misconceived measure abolishing imprisonment for debts under £20, and in 1861 the Law Society was able to rebuff the Attorney-General's desire to curtail the rights of audience in bankruptcy courts gained in 1849.[271]

The business was clearly worth protecting, for in the 1840s solicitors' fees were said to take around 10 per cent from an estate[272] and when a creditor-managed system of administration was substituted in 1869 the editor of the *County Courts Chronicle* suspected a plot by traders and accountants whereby the latter would grab the winding up business and milk it—'their charges are double those of the solicitor...'.[273] Predictions of abuses were amply fulfilled, but the 'whitewashing' of private liquidations frequently involved excessive payments to a compliant solicitor as well as an accountant,[274] justifying the cynical definition of bankruptcy as 'that state of things which exists when, a man being unable to pay his debts, his solicitor and an accountant divide all his property between them'.[275] Solicitors supported the return to 'officialism' in a better controlled form in the Bankruptcy Act 1883, though they had later to contend with the expansionist tendencies of Board of Trade officials.

The same recourse to supervision by the Board of Trade occurred in the winding up of the companies following similar complaints of exorbitant professional

---

[267] See Vol. XII, Pt 3, Ch. IV.

[268] Several jewish bankruptcy specialists are described in Cooper, *Pride versus Prejudice*, 152–3.

[269] V. M. Lester, *Victorian Insolvency* (Oxford, 1995), 37, quoting an official of the master's office in 1825.

[270] Sugarman, 'Who Colonized Whom?', 227.

[271] Lester, *Victorian Insolvency*, 63–4, 116, 145.

[272] *Ibid.*, 85.   [273] *Ibid.*, 156–7.

[274] *Ibid.*, 179; Sugarman, 'Who Colonized Whom?', 230.

[275] W. R. Cornish and G. de N. Clark, *Law and Society in England, 1750–1950* (1989), 236.

charges.[276] The Law Society mounted an ineffectual attack on the intrusion of the state into this field[277] and there was probably some substance in what Tilney Barton, who was appointed a part-time official assignee in bankruptcy in 1905, alleged—that its own full-time salaried officials were favoured.[278] For the larger firms which handled the bulk of company liquidations, however, there was still profit to be had from a failing client.

The Family Solicitor

Just as the solicitor's role in commerce was gradually narrowed by the rise of other professions, so his part in the management of landed estates tended to shrink. Big estates began to employ the new breed of land agent, though the process was gradual.[279] The Earl of Berkeley, for example, continued to employ Boodle, Hatfield for his Gloucestershire estates; it was not until 1885 that Wilde Sapte's dealings with the Portman estate were limited to strictly law business, and country landowners continued to provide the backbone of Grays' practice in York for much of the nineteenth century.[280] Estates in Chancery could be profitable too, since solicitors, besides their professional work, might be made receivers, though few were so profitable for so long as the Thellusson estates, which earned Benbow's firm an average of £2500 per annum for half a century.[281]

Even if solicitors were deprived of their function in estate management, they still profited from employment by landowners. Most big landowners used a local man for everyday matters and a specialist London firm for more complicated or important ones.[282] Among the leading London firms were Frere Cholmeley, Farrers, who handled the Duke of Wellington's estates, Gregory Rowcliffe, solicitors to the royal family and a firm which rather discouraged prospective

---

[276] C. Stebbings, '"Officialism": Law, Bureaucracy and Ideology in late Victorian England', in *Law and History* (*Current Legal Issues* 6 (Oxford 2003)), ed. A. Lewis and M. Lobban, 317–42.

[277] *Ibid.*

[278] Barton, *Life of a Country Lawyer*, 235–41. Barton reckoned his earnings from this source averaged £360 per annum.

[279] F. M. L. Thompson, *English Landed Society in the Nineteenth Century* (1963, edn of 1971), 151–83.

[280] Belcher, *Boodle and Hatfield*, 77–82; Salmon, *History of Wilde Sapte*, 255–6; Cobb, *Grays of York*, 27–9, and see V. Parrott, 'Nineteenth Century Manchester Solicitors: Provincial Leadership and Professionalization', *Salford Occasional Papers* 27 (n.d.), 1–2. Kingsford Wightwick in Canterbury in 1898 acted for three major estates, the dean and chapter, two Cambridge colleges and several of the biggest local business: Dockray, 'Guineas by Gaslight', 37 n.48.

[281] P. Polden, *Peter Thellusson's Will of 1797 and its Consequences on Chancery Law* (Lewiston, USA, 2002), 398. Peter Thellusson's outraged sons ensured that Townley Ward, who had drawn up the notorious will, were never employed by the family again.

[282] B. English and J. Saville, *Strict Settlement, a Guide for Historians* (Hull, 1983), 45.

commercial clients, and Boodles.[283] Boodles had only around 100 clients in the early nineteenth century, rising only to 140 in mid-century, but they were mostly valuable ones, and John Boodle at one time got £500 per annum for handling the Earl of Essex's affairs without even being his full-time agent.[284] The firm's biggest work, however, came for the Grosvenors and Comptons, both of whom were developing their properties in London. Such activities were highly profitable for the solicitors, especially if the leasehold system favoured by both families was used, since that generated continuing business. The Boodle–Grosvenor connection went back to the early eighteenth century and remained intact into the twentieth, though the Compton one ended acrimoniously.[285]

Much of the land in England was in settlement in the nineteenth century, but a large quantity of personalty was settled too and that encouraged the evolution of the family solicitor for the prosperous bourgeoisie as well as the gentry. A barrister, William Johnston, noted the 'very curious' position of such men, the 'Father Confessors' who alone understood the family trusts and whose 'exquisite discretion' ensured their confidentiality.[286] At the very same time Dickens was creating his archetype of such men, the sinister Mr Tulkinghorn. As the century wore on solicitors were increasingly chosen (and more readily offered themselves) as trustees rather than mere advisers. In 1854 John Taylor was disconcerted at being nominated a trustee by an occasional client, with a legacy of £100 as an inducement and a 'special provision authorizing me to charge for work to be done as a solicitor'.[287] Such an appointment was still unusual and rather problematic since the courts, with a grudging and narrow exception in the so-called 'rule in *Cradock v. Piper*' insisted that trusteeship was not an office of profit and construed charging clauses as narrowly as they could.[288] However, as trusteeship became more onerous so it became commoner to resort to solicitors, and before an inquiry in 1895 one claimed to be in 47 trusts, another between 20 and 30.[289] No wonder that the 'officialism' which created a Public Trustee in 1906 was contested by law societies on more than grounds of principle alone.

The role of solicitor to a family trust, whether or not combined with trusteeship, was extremely valuable. It cemented the solicitor's position as 'family solicitor' and unless he frustrated the family in its designs it virtually ensured that he

---

[283] Frere, *Frere Cholmeley*, 12; Jessel, *Farrer & Co*, 1, 13–15; Davis, *Number One*, 16; Belcher, *Boodle, Hatfield & Co.*

[284] Belcher, *Boodle, Hatfield & Co.*, 86, 96.

[285] *Ibid.*, 107–19.

[286] *England As It Is*, 2 vols (1851), 171. See also, Vol, XII, pp. 268–94.

[287] *Autobiography of a Lancashire Lawyer*, 267.

[288] (1850) 1 Mac. & G. 664; C. Stebbings, 'The Rule in *Cradock v. Piper*' (1998) 19 *JLH* 189–202.

[289] C. Stebbings, *The Private Trustee in Victorian England* (Cambridge, 2002), 34–42; *SC on Trusts Administration*, PP 1895 (403), xiii, qq. 939 (W. M. Walters), 1019 (J. Hunter)

would handle its legal business on a continuing basis. It was also an indicator of his social standing, for no one would be chosen to fill that role who was not considered a gentleman.[290]

Public Offices

One of the most persistently voiced grievances of solicitors was the bar's near-monopoly of legal and judicial offices, whether secured by formal reservation or practice.[291] Only a few (chief clerks and taxing masters in Chancery and county court registrars) were reserved to solicitors, and there were understandable complaints when the Croydon registrar was called to the bar without forfeiting his place.[292] Barristers were not the only competitors; district probate registrars were often taken from the clerks in Somerset House for example,[293] but barristers were the most favoured, especially when new posts such as those in the Land Registry and Public Trustee Office were created.[294]

The sense of grievance swelled as solicitors gained in social standing. The first outburst came when solicitors, who had been made eligible to be judges of small debts courts under an 1845 Act, were denied similar chances in the County Courts Act 1846 despite strenuous lobbying. Just two, qualified as being already judges of small debts courts, were appointed, and one of those later went to the bar, leaving James Stansfeld the only solicitor on the bench.[295] Although registrars gradually acquired judicial duties, the Judicature Commissions's recommendation that they be eligible for judgeships was ignored.[296]

However, the real disappointment was the disposition of administrative posts such as solicitors to government departments, Clerks of Assize, and commissioners in bankruptcy. The bar's stranglehold on these was not complete. A vociferous critic, C. F. Follett, became solicitor to the Customs and Excise in succession to a barrister and Hollams was offered both a chief clerkship in Chancery and solicitor to the Admiralty, but the perception was that the good things were mostly kept for the bar.[297] That complaints extended to the unpaid position of justice of

[290] Old-fashioned firms of this type clustered in Grays Inn, Bedford Row, and Lincoln's Inn Fields: Bell, *Those Meddlesome Attorneys*, 190.

[291] Kirk, *Portrait of a Profession*, 181–3. A contemporary example is 'Doctor in Jure Civil', *The Legal Profession* (1873), 274–7.

[292] (1890) 25 *LJ* 367.

[293] In 1914 only 10 of 40 were solicitors: see above, pp. 738–40.

[294] Anderson, *Lawyers and the Making of English Land Law*, 129–30.

[295] Polden, *History of the County Court*, 35–6.

[296] *Ibid.*, 276–80.

[297] Kirk, *Portrait of a Profession*, 182–3; Hollams, *Jottings of an Old Solicitor*, 242.

the peace suggest that professional pride was as much at stake as money. This disqualification was partly removed in 1871, though their continued exclusion from districts where they practised was resented as a slur on solicitors' integrity. On this point, however, they made no headway.[298]

In their own locality, however, solicitors often accumulated public or semi-public positions which were financially rewarding, socially desirable or both. This trend was well developed in the eighteenth century[299] and it is written of one Leeds practice in the 1820s that 'it is hard to imagine which further appointments the firm could have acquired'.[300] Some were near sinecures, but others, such as the clerk of the Liverpool vestry held by M. D. Lowndes, demanded a lot of time.[301]

Local government changes from the 1830s did not oust the solicitors from their places, in particular the key post of town clerk, which enabled William Statham to exert an influence on Liverpool affairs for 38 years.[302] Likewise in the counties, largely unaffected by those changes, the clerkship of the peace remained highly desirable; in Cambridgeshire it brought Christopher Pemberton £450 in the 1840s and he later added the receivership of taxes yielding another £500.[303] The clerk of the peace was one of many offices which became almost hereditary, for the *custos rotulorum* often chose his own solicitor; the under-sheriff in York, which the Gray family held in succession was another.[304] Even where a firm rather than a family monopolized an office the element of succession, especially in small towns, could be notable. Charlesworths provided three successive county court registrars for Bradford, while two partners and a managing clerk followed each other as chairman of the Skipton board of health; it also provided coroners for 137 years.[305] In Mold, Kelly & Keane so monopolized local offices as to create a real danger of conflicts of interest.[306] Individuals also collected positions, though few so assiduously as Charles Deacon in Southampton, as coroner, commissioner of bankrupts, clerk to the waterworks commission, town clerk, clerk to the board of health, registrar of the court of record, secretary to the cemetery

---

[298] See e.g. debates on the Solicitors Bill 1860, *PD* 1860 (s3) 157: 1905–15; 159: 515–19. A Birmingham solicitor, Arthur Ryland, may have influenced Selborne in his later relaxation of the rule: Rowley, *Professions, Class and Society*, 310–16.

[299] Robson, *Attorney in Eighteenth Century England*, 68–83.

[300] *Booth & Co*, 5.

[301] Williams, *Gentleman's Calling*, 214.

[302] *Ibid.*, 221–2.

[303] Jackson, *Cambridge Bicentenary*, 23–8.

[304] Cobb, *History of Gray's*, 16.

[305] Rowley, *History of Charlesworth, Wood and Brown*.

[306] Dodd, *The Practice*, 98–120.

company, commissioner of deeds for married women and for insolvent debtors' recognizances.[307]

However, monopoly was not invariable. Ten of Lincoln's 16 firms parcelled out 16 city clerkships, commissionerships etc and in Canterbury seven of 11 practices made at least £100 per annum from public offices.[308] Solicitors were sometimes in competition with others (such as doctors for coronerships) but more than held their own. In Birmingham, for example, between 1838 and 1914 they furnished all four clerks of the peace, all six town clerks, six out of seven magistrates' clerks and two out of four coroners, and in addition had the lion's share of other important positions, such as secretaryships to municipal charities.[309] True, some posts were lost in the course of local government reforms,[310] but others replaced them, at least until the major changes of 1888–94, which did reduce opportunities. This deep imbrication in local government was both a contributor to, and a consequence of, rising respectability and needs fuller examination.

Incomes

In comparison with other professions, including barristers, solicitors were doing rather well financially when the Great War came.[311] True, the top decile of barristers considerably outstripped their solicitor counterparts, but at lower levels solicitors were doing better than other professions. The top 10 per cent of solicitors earned at least £1410 per annum, and the top 25 per cent at least £790. The median figure was £390, but there was an uncomfortable residue, 25 per cent of the profession earning £185 or less.[312] Income tax did not yet take a big slice out of most solicitors' incomes and the cost of living was still much lower than it had been a century before.[313] It is difficult to reconcile this picture with Offer's view of a profession in a critical condition, but he is right to emphasize that many young solicitors were in financial straits; for the majority of the profession, however, times were not hard.[314]

---

[307] Kemish, *Lansdowne House*, 20–1.

[308] Davies and Race, *Andrew & Co.*, 3; Dockray, 'Guineas by Gaslight', 34–5.

[309] Rowley, *Professions, Class and Society*, 159–68 and App. 2.

[310] e.g. with the absorption of turnpike trusts by highways boards: Birks, *Gentlemen of the Law*, 213.

[311] Abel, *Legal Profession*, 15. This is also the conclusion of Dockray, 'Guineas by Gaslight', drawing on Inland Revenue figures for Cornhill (1887) and Canterbury (1898) solicitors.

[312] G. Routh, *Occupation and Pay in Great Britain, 1900–1960* (1965), table 29, 62, reproduced with variations in Kirk, *Portrait of a Profession*, 95.

[313] Kirk, *Portrait of a Profession*, 89–90. Using 1900 as a base (100) Kirk notes that the equivalent in 1820 would have been 172 and in 1914, 113.

[314] *Ibid.*, 89–92; Offer, *Property and Politics*, 15–19, 49–67; cf. Anderson, *Lawyers and the Making of English Land Law*, 221–6. The cost of keeping up appearances was rising: Perkin, *Rise of Professional Society*, 94.

For most of the nineteenth century there are only scattered figures for individual firms and the guesses of contemporaries, the former not necessarily representative and the latter often coloured by the author's aim. Thus Wade's *Extraordinary Black Book* in 1832 had a few London men making between £10,000 and £11,000 per annum and many more on between £3000 and 4000, which almost certainly overestimates the latter group.[315] James Anderton, who wanted to show that solicitors were rather badly off, maintained that fewer than 200 in the whole country made even £300 through common law practice, while Robert Maugham wrote that profits of £600 were uncommon and £1000 decidedly rare.[316] It is not difficult to find big earners: the three Freshfields partners shared £10,000 to £20,000 each between 1816 and 1821, while Disraeli claimed the five in his firm were dividing £15,000 and Gregory Rowcliffe had profits of £11,000 in 1835; yet even these men fell short of Wade's figures.[317]

Within the profession the talk in the 1830s and 1840s was often of declining profits as a result of changes in the courts,[318] but even if the pessimism was justified, it affected mostly London firms, whose continuing dependence upon litigation set them apart from most country solicitors. Yet W. H. Barber, starting from scratch in 1839, had 150 clients by 1844 and with a gross income of £3000 was dividing £2000 profits with his partner.[319] Moreover many established practitioners had at least one post which supplemented their income.[320] For example, William Young in Hastings took £337 as his share of the firm's profits in 1845 but had a further £20–30 as a notary and was shortly to become registrar of the county court; Kelly and Keane in Mold in 1862 reckoned on £900 per annum but both held an assortment of local positions.[321] Thomson reckoned that even a City or fashionable West End solicitor must work very hard to make £2000, and £1500 was generally felt to be a decent income for them.[322] Boodles certainly did little better than that, but the leading City firms were beginning to: Linklaters were reckoning on £9500 in the 1870s, rising to £13,500 in the 1880s.[323]

Solicitors continued to plead poverty and one Law Society president stretched credulity too far in 1880 by claiming that he never knew one who could keep a

---

[315] Quoted in Kirk, 88. The author, John Wade, was a radical with no love for lawyers.

[316] Birks, *Gentlemen of the Law*, 208.

[317] Slinn, *History of Freshfields*, 37; Kirk, *Portrait of a Profession*, 89; Davis, *Number One*, 15.

[318] Kirk, *Portrait of a Profession*, 87–8.

[319] *SC on the Petition of William Henry Barber, PP* 1857–8 (397), xx, R. Peckham qq. 1252–3.

[320] Above, pp. 1147–9, and see Dockray, 'Guineas by Gaslight', 33–5.

[321] Langdon, *Square Toes and Formal*, 20; Dodd, *The Practice*, 57–8.

[322] *The Choice of a Profession*, 134 ('with great anxiety and responsibility'); Kirk, *Portrait of a Profession*, 90. A future Lord Chancellor said that a solicitor should be satisfied with £500 since he should only to take on work he could do personally: [E. S. P. Haynes], *Concerning Solicitors* (1920), 31.

[323] Belcher, *Boodle, Hatfield & Co*, 101; Slinn, *Linklaters and Paines*, 41.

carriage out of his professional earnings.[324] True, large fortunes came largely from investment and speculation, but it was decidedly embarrassing for the pessimists when the *Daily Telegraph* in 1895 unearthed no fewer than 40 recent cases of very substantial fortunes (averaging £117,000) left by solicitors.[325] They were not all in London either: when Frederick Andrew of Lincoln died in 1916 he left £123,396.[326] Unfortunately there are few indications of the ratio of profits to income, though Freshfields' profits were some 60 per cent of total income (less disbursements) in the early nineteenth century and Slaughter & May's about 50 per cent of income in the early twentieth.[327]

In London a new firm, like Clifford Turner, could establish a good financial position quite quickly, profits rising from £900 in 1901 to £7000 in 1913,[328] but it had probably become harder. Firms everywhere benefited (though bigger firms benefited most) from the glut of well-qualified clerks and solicitors, which enabled salaries to be kept down. Average earnings among these men seem to have hovered somewhere between £200 and £300, leaving a good many solicitors on the margins of gentility and very vulnerable to a crisis in their affairs.[329] There was an extremely wide spread of earnings among firms. Partners in well-established practices, some with several branches, with a wide range of business and access to local positions, were making four-figure sums. Outside London newcomers, even well-connected ones, could only build up slowly to these levels, while some survived only through supplementary sources of income and others struggled to stay afloat.[330]

5. SOLICITORS IN POLITICS AND SOCIETY

Before 1832 few attorneys had been MPs, but they played an important part in political life as the agents who oiled the wheels of the unreformed electoral system, and if their near monopoly of election management only enhanced their reputation for corruption, such practices were generally accepted as a normal feature of public life.[331]

---

[324] Kirk, *Portrait of a Profession*, 88, and see Dockray, 'Guineas by Gaslight', 30.

[325] Kirk, *Portrait of a Profession*, 89. A further selection is in (1908) 27 *LN* 196, 228. John Morris left £370,405 in 1905 (Dennett, *Slaughter and May*, 88). Hollams was an exception; he left £601,587 in 1910 and claimed never to have speculated: *Jottings of an Old Solicitor*, 239–40.

[326] Davies and Race, *Andrew & Co*, 15 and App. 1, 38.

[327] Slinn, *History of Freshfields*, 35; Dennett, *Slaughter and May*, 133–4.

[328] Scott, *Legibus*, 34, 47.

[329] Kirk, *Portrait of a Profession*, 90–1; Offer, *Property and Politics*, 15–18, 60–2; Abel, *Legal Profession*, table 2.37.

[330] Dockray, 'Guineas by Gaslight', 45–9.

[331] Robson, *Attorney in Eighteenth Century England*, 96–103; Kirk, *Portrait of a Profession*, 189–91.

The 1832 Reform Act made the business more difficult, troublesome and expensive, but the *Law Times* confidently asserted that 'management of elections throughout the country is practically committed to solicitors'[332] and for some 20 years first Sir Philip Rose and then another member of his firm, Markham Spofforth, had charge of the central organization of the Conservative party.[333] It was often not the 'low attorney' who ran elections, but reputable solicitors, sometimes on an hereditary basis, though the less scrupulous party agents were said to provoke contests to increase their gains and these activities sat uncomfortably with the profession's concern for its public image. Even so, it was not until 1878 that a Law Society president appealed to members not to engage in this 'dirty work'.[334] By then a 'war on electoral corruption' had begun which gradually eliminated disreputable practices and the political parties increasingly employed full-time agents to manage election business; nevertheless, a good many solicitors still held that position in 1914.[335] More solicitors were in Parliament by then, though numbers, peaking at 34 in 1906, never matched the excessive representation of the bar. Only a handful achieved high office, for the trajectory of a successful professional career did not fit well with politics.[336] Henry Fowler was the first cabinet minister, and the most notable, David Lloyd George, was no friend to his profession.[337]

Though the role of solicitors in Parliament and government was modest, at a local level their influence was pervasive because of their near monopoly of the key positions of clerk of the peace and town clerk.[338] The magistrates and the parish vestry stood in the foreground, but 'in the background of that picture there must be seen the grey figure of the attorney, always at the elbow of the mayor or chairman unostentatiously advising and guiding'.[339] Poor Law unions, boards of health, and school boards all needed their secretary or clerk; and usually he was a solicitor.[340]

---

[332] Quoted in Kirk, *Portrait of a Profession*, 191.

[333] St. George, *History of Norton Rose*, 44–62. Rose was made county court treasurer for Buckinghamshire, Spofforth a Chancery taxing master.

[334] Kirk, *Portrait of a Profession*, 192–3. A contested election was reckoned to be worth £400 in fees, and even unpaid help might later be rewarded: J. R. Vincent, *The Formation of the Liberal Party* (1966, 1972 edn), 80.

[335] G. Orr, 'Suppressing Vote-Buying: The "War" on Electoral Bribery from 1868' (2006) 27 *JLH* 289–314.

[336] Kirk, *Portrait of a Profession*, 189.

[337] Fowler was a reluctant solicitor: E. Fowler, *The Life of Henry Hartley Fowler, First Lord Wolverhampton* (1912), 79.

[338] Keith-Lucas, *Unreformed System of Local Government*, 152–4, and see above, pp. 922–4.

[339] *Ibid.*, 154.

[340] Rowley, *Professions, Class and Society*, 155–6, 338–40.

In most counties it paid to be a Tory, as three-quarters of solicitors were reck-oned to be,[341] but in the bigger boroughs, politics was often volatile and even minor posts were strenuously contested along party lines. The Whig ascendancy in the boroughs following the Municipal Corporations Act 1835 displaced many a Tory solicitor who had been comfortably entrenched under the old oligarchy[342] and men like C. G. Beale in Birmingham, who followed Joseph Chamberlain, profited from loyalty to the new rulers.[343] In small country towns some solici-tors had already acquired a prominent position, like John Hawkins, the 'king of Hitchin'[344] and gradually they asserted themselves in larger communities. They became councillors, often influential ones through their legal expertise, and sometimes mayor;[345] indeed, the mayoralty had such symbolic value that the *Solicitors' Journal* at one time listed all solicitors who attained it.[346] Some law societies fostered the notion that active engagement in public affairs was a civic duty, a consequence of being a gentleman-professional, and many believed it.[347] Birmingham is an instance. Its first solicitor-councillor was Hawkes in 1846, who became mayor in 1852. Only two other solicitors became mayors before 1877 but solicitors then filled the position for 12 of the following 40 years, Beale on three occasions.[348] Men like Beale and Arthur Ryland gave so much time to the city's increasingly complicated affairs that sometimes, like the Rollits in Hull, they had to enlarge their firms to cover their frequent absences from the office;[349] promi-nence in civic affairs demonstrated prosperity as well as respectability and pro-bity. Further local government reforms, in 1888 and 1894, involving the creation of county councils, urban and rural district councils and a further tranche of county boroughs, afforded fresh opportunities. They also produced the London County Council, where one of the Simmons twins was among several solicitors who rapidly pushed themselves forward.[350]

---

[341] Birks, *Gentlemen of the Law*, 210. In Bristol the 13 solicitor-councillors between 1835 and 1851 comprised 10 Conservatives and three Liberals; from then to 1898 only 10 of 31 were Liberals: J. Lyes, 'A Strong Smell of Brimstone': *The Solicitors and Attorneys of Bristol 1740–1840* (Bristol, 1999), 28. For a rare example of a radical solicitor who acted regularly for chartists and trade unions see R. Challinor, *W.P. Roberts and the Struggle for Workers' Rights* (1990).

[342] e.g. James Nelson in Leeds: *Booth & Co*, 5.

[343] Rowley, *Professions, Class and Society*, 150–7.

[344] *Hawkins Russell Jones* (Law Society library t/s, n.d.).

[345] Examples are William Andrew in Lincoln and Harry Cartmell in Preston: Davies and Race, *Andrew & Co*, 7; Cameron, *Solicitors in Blackpool*, 69–70.

[346] Kirk, *Portrait of a Profession*, 197.

[347] Williams, *Gentleman's Calling*, 234; Rowley, *Professions, Class and Society*, 194–7.

[348] Rowley, *Professions, Class and Society*, 186–200.

[349] T. H. Farrell, *Rollit, Farrell and Bladon, 1841–1991* (Hull, 1991), 14.

[350] T. Henry, *Partnership: The Story of Simmons and Simmons* (Cambridge, 1996), 18–19.

Politics was only one way of insinuating oneself into a local elite. Another, often connected with party politics, was religion. In Birmingham the Beales, Rylandses, and Martineaus were part of a unitarian ruling group, while F. W. Martin in Gravesend benefited from being both secretary to the Liberal party and a prominent figure in the congregational church.[351] Every cathedral town had a firm whose practice was based upon ecclesiastical work[352] and it is likely that both roman catholics and protestant nonconformists favoured lawyers of their own creed.[353]

Other organizations, like the volunteers, brought together the cream of local society: William Scriven in Hastings, H. R. Wanborough in Bristol, and George Robinson in Skipton are examples of solicitors active in that movement.[354] Robinson was also a master of foxhounds and many others were prominent in founding and sustaining sporting clubs.[355] Cricket was a particular favourite since an approved style and a familiarity with its etiquette was usually associated with a public school or university education and it afforded opportunities to encounter wealthy wandering clubs and social counterparts from neighbouring towns; the keenness of Blackpool's law society to arrange an annual fixture against the medical practitioners is a clear indication that they regarded the two occupations as social equals.[356] Towards the end of the period golf became fashionable, welcomed not least as affording ample business opportunities.

A whole array of cultural, intellectual, and charitable societies had came into being in Georgian England which depended very largely upon the professions for their existence.[357] T. H. Gem was 'the founder of club life in Birmingham'; three solicitors were among the founder-members of the Kingston Debating Society; Taylor in Bolton was an earnest member of the Delta Society, and Charles Elmhirst was honorary secretary of the York Philosophical Society.[358] In London a select few even entered high society, sometimes steered by their wives as George Lewis and H. T. Norton were.[359] An uncharted influence was the freemasons;

---

[351] Rowley, *Professions, Class and Society*; *Martin Tolhurst Partnership*, 2.

[352] e.g. Hudsons of York, Cobb, *History of Grays of York*, 53–4.

[353] e.g. R. B. O'Brien, *The Life of Lord Russell of Killowen* (1901), 69.

[354] Langdon, *Square Toes and Formal*, 10; *Wansboroughs*; Rowley, *History of Charlesworth, Wood and Brown*.

[355] Rowley, *Professions, Class and Society*, 209–27.

[356] Cameron, *Solicitors in Blackpool*, 61.

[357] J. Brewer, *The Pleasures of the Imagination* (New York, 1997), esp. 39–50, 507–12.

[358] Rowley, *Professions, Class and Society*, 211; G. W. Fox, *Some Memories* (1931), 29; Clegg, *Autobiography of a Lancashire Lawyer*, 123; Cobb, *History of Grays of York*, 81.

[359] Juxon, *Lewis and Lewis*, 115–16; St. George, *History of Norton Rose*, 174–5.

Frank Sinclair was given immediate help by a fellow mason when he set up in a strange town and J. T. Last was a very active mason in Bradford.[360]

However shabby their offices, most solicitors felt it necessary to adopt a demonstrably gentlemanly lifestyle.[361] Even if it was no longer a general belief that the largest house in town would belong to an attorney, it was still important to have the right address and some were very ostentatious, like Henry Allcock who built himself a big new house outside Skipton and took out a coat of arms.[362] In the big cities solicitors joined the flight to the grander suburbs[363] and the most prosperous bought or leased a country house; Kentwell Hall for Henry Norton, Dene Park for Hollams, Standen for the Beales, and another Sussex place for G. B. Gregory.[364] Inevitably some, like William Wynne near Mold and Arthur Underhill's father not too far away, overreached themselves[365] and in the aftermath of the defalcation scandals there were claims that many failures were caused by solicitors trying to rise out of their class and 'hobnob with aristocrats, county people and plutocrats'.[366] Most solicitors had settled for something much more modest, but the social imperative of a gentlemanly lifestyle was no doubt a factor in some of the bankruptcies which so embarrassed the profession.

6. PROFESSIONAL ORGANIZATION

The Formation of the Incorporated Law Society

In August 1823 solicitors were invited to subscribe to a new professional body, a Law Institution, but though the invitation was extended to country solicitors, its real target was those in and around London.[367] There were already two law societies, but the promoters envisaged it as complementing rather than competing with them. Several of the moving spirits behind the Law Institution, such as Bryan Holme, J. W. Freshfield, and George Frere were also prominent in the venerable Society of Gentlemen Practisers (SGP) ('the law society'), though its

---

[360] Sinclair, *Reminiscences of a Lawyer*, 86; D. White, *Last Suddards* (1981), 3. There were many in Birmingham: Rowley, *Professions, Class and Society*, 222.

[361] Dockray, 'Guineas by Gaslight', 36.

[362] Rowley, *History of Charlesworth, Wood and Brown*.

[363] Rowley, *Professions, Class and Society*, 329–30.

[364] St. George, *History of Norton Rose*, 174–5; Slinn, *Clifford Chance*, 32; Davis, *Number One*, 21.

[365] Dodd, *The Practice*, 26–7; A. Underhill, *Change and Decay* (1938), 18–19.

[366] Quoted in M. Lunney, 'The Law Society and the Defalcations Scandals of 1900', (1996) 17 *JLH* 244–69 at 253.

[367] The original title was the London Law Institution, but the reference to London was dropped before the subscribers met in 1825: Sugarman, 'Bourgeois Collectivism', 91.

prolocutor/secretary held aloof for the time.[368] The aims of the new body were quite different from the SGP, formed in 1739 chiefly to raise and defend the standing of the profession. It had some notable achievements, especially the famous defeat of the scriveners, and had recently been instrumental in securing an increase in solicitors' court costs.[369] Nevertheless, it was declining into a predominantly social and convivial club, content with a small membership drawn from the major City firms.[370] It made little effort to promote legal education and was so slothful as guardian of the profession against unqualified practitioners that Jonathan Brundrett founded the Metropolitan Law Society in 1819 to perform that function.[371]

The Law Institution promised subscribers more tangible benefits, in particular a building in the heart of legal London which would contain a library and reading room, a registry of properties for sale and money to be lent, an agency for employment, a club room, and offices, facilities in which the SGP had never shown much interest.[372] It took two years to collect enough subscriptions but once the Law Institution was launched it opened negotiations with the Society for an amalgamation. They were never formally concluded but the old law society slipped quietly out of existence soon after 1832.[373]

The prospectus noted that 'numerous institutions for promoting literature and science amongst all ranks and conditions of society' had sprung up. In emulating those the profession would align itself not only with the inns (which were improving their own libraries) but with learned societies engaged in the disinterested pursuit of knowledge. If law was a science, the Law Institution would provide practitioners with a laboratory.[374]

And very soon it did. In 1832 Vulliamy's imposing neo-classical facade on Chancery Lane reinforced the message that the profession aspired to something more elevated than mere trade. If they remained cast out of the inns, at least the solicitors had laid down in columns of stone and a hall of marble a visible

---

[368] Kirk, *Portrait of a Profession*, 22–6; Birks, *Gentlemen of the Law*, 155–9. Several were also members of the 'Verulam Club'.

[369] Birks, *Gentlemen of the Law*, 144–53; Robson, *Attorney in Eighteenth Century England*, 20–34.

[370] Birks, *Gentlemen of the Law*, 153. It was not quite dormant however: Sugarman, 'Bourgeois Collectivism', n.47.

[371] Birks, *Gentlemen of the Law*, 153–4. Brundrett became involved in the formation of the Law Institution.

[372] *Ibid.*, 155–6; Sugarman, 'Bourgeois Collectivism', 90. For the ambitious proposals of John Day in the 1790s see Robson, *Attorney in Eighteenth Century England*, 31–4.

[373] Birks, *Gentlemen of the Law*, 158–60, Kirk, *Portrait of a Profession*, 28–30.

[374] Birks, *Gentlemen of the Law*, 155. Sugarman, 'Bourgeois Collectivism', 89–91, cites the Royal College of Surgeons, the Royal College of Physicians, and the Royal Institution as examples.

presence in the heart of the legal quarter.[375] They had a spacious and impressive library, 1000 volumes by 1832, 32,500 by 1891.[376] The hall was gradually embellished with portraits of the worthies of the profession, including those who had left it for the bar and become judges, thereby creating a sense of history and continuity. Among those commemorated is Bryan Holme, often regarded as the progenitor of the Society,[377] but not the other leading figure in the early history, Robert Maugham, whose long tenure as secretary gave him considerable influence.[378] Maugham and his successor E. W. Williamson, who served until 1908,[379] provided a crucial element of stability and continuity and the very fact that the Society, unlike its predecessor, had a permanent staff and an office through which it could communicate with members and issue publications, including the *Law Society's Gazette* from 1902, was important.[380]

Membership and Government

The prospectus of the Law Institution assured potential subscribers that it would be composed 'only of the most respectable and leading men in the Profession (it being intended carefully to exclude all disreputable characters)'. It was hoped that this scrutiny would itself operate as an inducement to high ethical standards.[381] As a joint stock company with shares costing £25 each, it was deliberately designed to keep out low attorneys and draw members from the profession's elite,[382] for at that price only a wealthy country solicitor would join a club he would seldom use, ensuring that the new body would be predominantly metropolitan and wholly respectable.

The joint stock character was preserved when it received a royal charter in 1831, and the title Law Institution was soon altered to the Incorporated Law Society, the demise of the SGP having ended any risk of confusion.[383] The title

---

[375] Kirk, *Portrait of a Profession*, 31–2; Sugarman, 'Bourgeois Collectivism', 91.

[376] Kirk, *Portrait of a Profession*, 33–4.

[377] 'The founder of the profession as we know it today' (*ibid.*, 27). The portrait is reproduced in Birks, *Gentlemen of the Law*, facing 160. It has a faint resemblance to Mr Pickwick.

[378] Kirk, *Portrait of a Profession*, 27; Sugarman, 'Bourgeois Collectivism', n.63. He remained secretary (on £400 per annum) until his death in 1862. He owned and edited *The Legal Observer* from 1830 and wrote the first major work on the law relating to solicitors.

[379] Williamson's *Recollections of Some Past Presidents of the Law Society* (1905) is disappointingly anodyne.

[380] Sugarman, 'Bourgeois Collectivism' n.38 points out that the SGP probably did have a base in its secretary's office, but the Law Society's secretariat was at the centre of its operations.

[381] Birks, *Gentlemen of the Law*, 156; Kirk, *Portrait of a Profession*, 26.

[382] Sugarman, 'Bourgeois Collectivism', 90.

[383] Via the cumbersome 'Society of Attorneys, Solicitors, Proctors and others not being Barristers practising in the Courts of Law and Equity in the United Kingdom'. The official title was not changed to the Law Society until 1903 but for convenience, it is here called the Law Society throughout.

was now appropriate but the constitution was seriously flawed: 'its structure was that of a social club; its legal form that of a commercial venture'.[384] The unacceptable feature was the inheritance of shares by non-solicitors, so a new charter was sought, and obtained in 1845 after stubborn resistance from a small minority.[385] This constitution, in the form of a subscription society much like other professional organizations, thenceforth remained unchanged in essentials.

In the new dispensation the chairman and vice-chairman were renamed president and vice-president and the managing committee became a council of 20 to 30 members, with 10 places up for election every year. In practice the everyday work was done by a small minority of senior men in City firms who could spare the time for what could be a very demanding task.[386] Many were men of weight and influence, possessing useful connections with politicians, businessmen, and judges, but it was easy for them to become 'a closed oligarchy with a penchant for complacent self-congratulation'.[387] Not surprisingly they were mostly elderly and in the 1890s it was forcefully pointed out that these characteristics put them out of touch with the concerns of most of the membership, especially the increasing number of country solicitors.[388]

In fact the Law Society faced serious problems in acting as a representative body. Until the 1890s, most solicitors were not members, indeed more than half were thought to belong to no law society at all. The founders had never envisaged that membership would be universal even in London and did not make it an inviting proposition for men of modest means. Apart from the cost, the grand surroundings—'its two porters dressed in livery-crimson waist-coats, gold-banded hats, black breeches fastened below knee and brown coats [which] contributed to the aura of power, authority and independence'[389]—were rather intimidating. However, in 1843 the Society acquired responsibility for keeping the roll of solicitors and actively promoting the interests of the profession. It then sought to enlarge the membership, though with modest success.[390] In 1870 fewer

[384] Anderson, *Lawyers and the Making of English Land Law*, 24.

[385] *Ibid.*; Kirk, *Portrait of Profession*, 42.

[386] Sugarman, 'Bourgeois Collectivism', 95. Kirk, *Portrait of a Profession*, 43, quotes the *Law Times* 1879 to the effect that of 60 members no more than 30 were active.

[387] Anderson, *Lawyers and the Making of English Land Law*, 24. It was almost impossible for anyone to get onto the Council who was not on the approved list made up by the outgoing council. Sir George Lewis stood in 1899 just to demonstrate this: (1900) 18 *LN* 257.

[388] Kirk, *Portrait of a Profession*, 42–6. In 1900 14 members were over 69 (Lunney, 'Law Society and Defalcations', n.120). A motion to bar the re-election of anyone over 70 was defeated.

[389] Sugarman, 'Bourgeois Collectivism', 91.

[390] Membership rose from 292 in 1825 to 1382 in 1845 (*ibid.*, 92) and became more affordable when the annual fee was cut from £15 to £5 (*ibid.*, 41). The 1845 figure still represented fewer than 10% of those with practising certificates.

than 10 per cent of country solicitors were members, and only in the 1890s did they become even a bare majority of the Society.[391] In dealing with the government and the bar, the inability to claim to speak for the whole profession was a handicap, especially when the Society sought powers over all solicitors, and it is not surprising that by 1900 the bolder souls in Chancery Lane were making noises about compulsory membership.[392]

One reason why some men would not join was the feeling, often outspokenly expressed, that the Law Society was run by and for the big London firms.[393] The Council often seemed indifferent to the encroachment of agents and accountants; opposed decentralization of the courts which many in the provinces wanted; and was lukewarm on the importance of local offices if title registration had to come. This was especially exasperating when contrasted with its vigorous, albeit unavailing, challenge to the law stationers' threat to the probate monopoly in London and lent plausibility to attacks which were sometimes unfair.

In an attempt to encourage country solicitors, when the charter was renewed in 1872 provision was made for up to 10 'extraordinary' members on a council of 60. They were usually presidents of local law societies, the bigger ones taking care to ensure they were included. Yet the council refused to seek an increase in country representation when the Metropolitan and Provincial Law Association (MPLA) was absorbed shortly afterwards[394] and some provincial law societies remained dissatisfied with the arrangements.[395] A handful of country solicitors, beginning with C. T. Saunders of Birmingham in 1884, became president and the country representation was enlarged in 1903,[396] but the council remained a basically metropolitan body.

One outcome of the absorption of the MPLA was the annual provincial meeting, which provided opportunities for public criticism. There and at the AGM regular dissidents, often with a particular bee in their bonnet and a wearisome pertinacity, kept the ruling group on its toes. A. H. Hastie regularly attacked them over the lack of rigour in controlling entry, Charles Ford vented his grievance about the position of the Law Club and J. S. Rubinstein kept up a running fire over title registration.[397] Unlike the gerontocracies which ran the inns, the Law Society's council was regularly attacked for its decisions and on occasion

[391] *Ibid.*, 37–40.

[392] *Ibid.*, 41–2.

[393] *Ibid.*, 37–41; Anderson, *Lawyers and the Making of English Land Law*, 30, 126–8; Sugarman, 'Bourgeois Collectivism', 102–4.

[394] Anderson, *Lawyers and the Making of English Land Law*, 127.

[395] e.g. Bristol: *Bristol Law Society, the First Two Hundred Years*, 34.

[396] Kirk, *Portrait of a Profession*, 40.

[397] Sugarman, 'Bourgeois Collectivism', 109; Kirk, *Portrait of a Profession*, 34–5; Anderson, *Lawyers and the Making of English Land Law*, 204–5.

it was defeated, as over its opposition to a committee to investigate frauds in 1906.[398]

Conduct and Discipline

Attorneys and solicitors were officers of the courts in which they were enrolled and it was for the judges to ensure that they alone practised before them and that no one was entered upon the roll without being properly qualified. Persistent complaints suggest that they were not very vigilant and they were even less successful in preventing practitioners from resorting to disreputable conduct. Only when misconduct came to light during the course of court proceedings or when someone made a complaint did the court take action.[399]

Moreover although some judges—Abbott near the beginning of the nineteenth century and Kay near the end are notorious examples—were only too willing to believe the worst of the lower branch, the courts' definition of what constituted malpractice justifying striking off the roll or a suspension from practice was much narrower than the standards set by the profession. Neither advertising nor touting came within it,[400] and although Lord Mansfield's dictum that any serious criminal offence disqualified a solicitor from practice was still confidently stated in the first edition of *Cordery on Solicitors* (1878), within 20 years it had been severely qualified.[401]

Plainly the profession needed to promulgate and enforce its own code of conduct, one which would demonstrate its gentlemanly status. In 1825 Robert Maugham gathered together the scattered provisions and decisions on solicitor's rights and duties in a compact volume,[402] but it was probably more through the legal weeklies and the operations of local law societies that they were disseminated. The more active local societies made determined, though not always successful, attempts to enforce both law and etiquette, and in some places a public spirited individual took on the task. In Bristol local solicitors presented Charles H. Walker with a piece of plate in recognition of his efforts to get rid of miscreants who had committed fraud

---

[398] Kirk, *Portrait of a Profession*, 101.

[399] Robson, *Attorney in Eighteenth Century England*, 12–13.

[400] Sugarman, 'Bourgeois Collectivism', 106–7.

[401] *Ex p Brounsall* (1778) 2 Cowp. 829; *Re a Solicitor* (1889); *Re Ware, a Solicitor* (1893) 2 QB 439, discussed in Kirk, *Portrait of a Profession*, 76–7; A. Cordery, *The Law Relating to Solicitors* (1878), 139. Many both within and without the profession were disturbed by the Law Society's stubborn opposition to the restoration of the practising certificate of W. H. Barber, pardoned after a wrongful conviction for forgery, when he returned from the prison colony on Norfolk Island.

[402] *A Treatise Upon Solicitors*. As Kirk points out (76 n.45), Cordery, which later established itself as the standard work, was rather weak on etiquette and conduct. The author was a barrister.

or perjury.[403] The unqualified and their abettors became somewhat easier to drive out once the Law Society had gained custody of the roll, but they and the disreputable could not be eradicated. The Law Society had started out boldly on that course but the formation of the Metropolitan and Provincial Legal Association in 1844 devoted to that end indicates its lack of success, albeit the new body soon collapsed for want of funds.[404] In every city there was a handful of rogues and a larger number whom failure tempted into misconduct; the better class of practitioners disowned them but could not remove the taint they brought to solicitors generally.[405]

In the 1850s another phenomenon began to receive very unwelcome publicity. Solicitors had always had custody of clients' money and occasionally and inevitably one had defaulted. Now this seemed to happen more frequently and with larger amounts; worse, the culprits often came from the outwardly respectable element. Hall's big fraud was followed by the even worse case of Hughes, who fled to Australia leaving debts of £160,000 and was given 10 years' penal servitude.[406] Such cases triggered off denunciations of the profession in *The Times* and elsewhere, and even when the culprit was negligent rather than fraudulent, that consoled neither his clients nor those who feared for their own money.[407]

In 1861 solicitors were brought within the scope of the bankruptcy jurisdiction and a disquieting number passed through the procedure. It was asserted that between 1861 and 1877 no fewer than 942 went bankrupt, 130 of them more than once, with one brazen individual managing to do so 12 times. The inference was inescapable: whatever their protestations of probity, solicitors could not be trusted to manage their own money, and their clients' money was too often mixed with it and lost in the bankruptcy. And bankruptcy did not prevent a solicitor from resuming practice after his discharge; it even emerged in 1902 that the Law Society could not refuse to renew the certificate of an undischarged bankrupt.[408]

Various solutions were suggested. Sir Henry Peek, who campaigned in Parliament on this issue through the 1870s, favoured a mark in the *Law List* indicating bankruptcy, but this and similar 'blacklisting' notions were felt only to make

---

[403] Lyes, *Strong Smell of Brimstone*, 17–18. Evidently a reformed character, for he had served six months for assault in 1803.

[404] Kirk, *Portrait of a Profession*, 76–7; Birks, *Gentlemen of the Law*, 152–3; *SC on Legal Education 1846*, Sir G. Stephen, q. 1976.

[405] Embarrassingly, some of the worst were in and around Chancery Lane and were exposed in *Tit-Bits*: (1894) 13 *LN* 130.

[406] (1857–8) 2 *Sol. J.* 274; (1859–60) 4 *Sol. J.* 154–7.

[407] Kirk, *Portrait of a Profession*, 96–7.

[408] Ibid., 100, citing *Re a Solicitor* [1902] 1 KB 128. In Canterbury Sankey, bankrupted and then struck off for misusing clients' money, could be found working for the man who had bought his practice, ostensibly as a clerk but in reality seemingly as a profit sharer: Dockray, 'Guineas by Gaslight', 40.

it easier for dishonest clients to find suitable collaborators.[409] Others declared that solicitors should stick strictly to their law business and eschew speculation in building schemes, mines, and other risky ventures.[410] However, this was impracticable: one of the attractions of the profession was the opportunities for 'safe speculations'[411] and many of the best-known City men made handsome fortunes in this way.[412] Even if it were in the public interest to keep men of enterprise and drive from employing those qualities, such a prohibition could scarcely have been enforced.

The root of the problem was the mixture of client funds with the office account. Georgian attorneys had seen themselves as bankers, fully entitled to use client money and take the interest it generated, and that outlook persisted except where the contract with the client contained a specific direction to the contrary, something few clients required, and even fewer solicitors suggested.[413] But solicitors' bookkeeping was proverbially slovenly.[414] An examination in bookkeeping and trust accounts was introduced in 1862, but dropped in 1877.[415] Of five methods commonly used by solicitors, three did not involve the creation of separate bank accounts and two of those did not adequately distinguish between the ownership of monies in the account.[416]

This situation gave the Law Society ammunition for its claim to extend its authority to non-members. In 1874 it won the right to be heard in striking-off applications, but its 1887 bill enabling it to empower it to investigate and determine such complaints with a right of appeal to the court went well beyond what was acceptable to the House of Commons. Instead investigation was delegated to a committee chosen by the Master of the Rolls from the council of the Society, the court retaining the decision-making power. In recognition that this was essentially a public function, the Society was given a subvention from the Treasury in 1897, which marked a significant stage in its progress to semi-official status.[417]

Not all solicitors were enthusiastic that the Society had become 'more a prosecuting Society than ever'.[418] The publicity given to the less costly proce-

---

[409] Kirk, *Portrait of a Profession*, 77, 99–100.

[410] *Ibid.*, 98 and cf. (1884–5) 29 *Sol. J.* 322, 337 (Brett MR in *Ex p Salaman* [1884–5] 14 QBD 936); (1891–2) 36 *Sol. J.* 101 (CA in *Re Keays* (1891)).

[411] Thomson, *Choice of a Profession*, 134–5.

[412] Kirk, *Portrait of a Profession*, 89.

[413] Birks, *Gentlemen of the Law*, 245–6.

[414] W. F. Hoyle was one whose unmethodical habits with money, coupled with heavy investment in tin mines, led him into difficulties: Cockburn, *Rotherham Lawyers During 350 Years*, 50.

[415] Birks, *Gentlemen of the Law*, 245–6; Sugarman, 'Who Colonized Whom?', 230–1.

[416] E. T. Turner, *The Organization of a Solicitor's Office* (1886), 48–55. It originally appeared as a series of articles in (1884–35) 29 *Sol. J.*

[417] Kirk, *Portrait of a Profession*, 78–9; Lunney, 'Law Society and Defalcation Scandals', 245–6.

[418] Kirk, *Portrait of Profession*, 79, quoting the *Solicitors Journal*.

dure helped bring about a rise in the number of complaints, even if many were dismissed without calling for an answer.[419] Solicitors confronted by a complaint were unhappy that their own professional body, so far from defending them, was, in effect, acting as prosecutor, the first signs of a tension inherent in its dual role which would become acute in the twentieth century.[420]

Still the defalcations continued. It might be true, as the Law Society argued in 1895, that they claimed only a tiny proportion of the trust funds administered by the profession, but in absolute terms they were very large[421] and a few years later collapsing share prices in the Boer War found out many an outwardly respectable firm.[422] In many towns a leading solicitor was disgraced. In Hastings W. B. Young died leaving a deficiency of £28,000, having been insolvent for at least seven years; in Cambridge William Peed was only the best known of several; in Birmingham it was Milward & Co, one of the biggest practices; their fall was spectacular with the junior partner imprisoned.[423] But it was London cases which made the biggest stir. One of the old-fashioned, straitlaced firms in Bedford Row turned out to have lost client funds through building speculations; Cartmell, Harrison, and Ingram of Lincoln's Inn Fields went under to the tune of £200,000 and Keighley, Arnold, and Sismey, seemingly never solvent, topped even that with £300,000.[424] Worst of all Benjamin Lake, former president of the Law Society and chairman of its disciplinary committee, defaulted for £170,000.[425] Newspapers regaled the public with further shocking cases, the grant in aid came under fire and the Law Society was subjected to intense criticism from within and without the profession.[426] Some was misguided, assuming that the disciplinary committee could itself take action against defaulters, but there were also damaging suggestions (not without some foundation) that the establishment shielded some of the bigger miscreants while treating the smaller fry with scant sympathy.[427] It was certainly

---

[419] Christian, *Short History of Solicitors*, 232.

[420] Kirk, *Portrait of a Profession*, 79.

[421] *SC on Trusts Administration Report 1895*, evidence of W. M. Walters, J. Hunter. A. H. Hastie had complained strenuously that the Council was too lenient in dealing with financial laxity: Sugarman, 'Bourgeois Collectivism', 98.

[422] Birks, *Gentlemen of the Law*, 271–2. But others lost in colliery speculations or at the tables in Monte Carlo: (1896) 15 *LN* 280–2.

[423] Langdon, *Square Toes and Formal*, 22; Jackson, *Cambridge Bicentenary*, 192–6; Rowley, *Professions, Class and Society*, 282.

[424] Bell, *Those Meddlesome Attorneys*, 190; Kirk, *Portrait of a Profession*, 98; Lunney, 'Law Society and Defalcations Scandals', 264 n.13.

[425] Anderson, *Lawyers and the Making of English Land Law*, 207–8.

[426] Lunney, 'Law Society and Defalcation Scandals', 246–50.

[427] *Ibid.*, 253–7.

no longer possible to maintain the old defence that these 'black sheep' were fringe practitioners of doubtful repute.[428]

The Society responded by setting up a special committee, only to have its best-known member, Sir George Lewis, resign when the committee rejected his suggestion that the Law Society should itself prosecute defaulters.[429] However, the momentum of public opinion enabled the Society to overcome the parliamentary obstructions which usually beset its attempts at reform. The Larceny Act 1901 at last made misappropriation of clients' money an offence and in 1906 the Solicitors Act enabled the Society to refuse renewal of a certificate to a bankrupt.[430] Lake became the essential scapegoat, humiliated in court by Sir Edward Carson and given 12 years' imprisonment.[431]

The real source of the trouble, however, remained the lack of security for client funds, and the committee had declared impracticable any indemnity fund. A further committee, set up against the council's opposition, made nine recommendations but three were decisively voted down at the AGM. These were controversial because they provided for checks that the other recommendations were being observed. Particularly objectionable to many solicitors was requiring an accountant to examine the books: it would be costly; it would not be a real safeguard against deliberate fraud; and it would be a 'degrading obligation', a humiliating submission to audit by a newer and inferior profession.[432] Even the six accepted recommendations were not implemented until many years later, despite the threat posed by the new Public Trustee and trust corporations and a further blow to the profession's reputation for financial competence with the failure of the Law Guarantee Trust in which several judges as well as practitioners had participated.[433] It was therefore wise of solicitors not to complain when the House of Lords held a firm vicariously liable for the frauds of a managing clerk.[434] Meanwhile the Society's own attempts to enlarge its disciplinary powers through bills giving it some of the powers refused in 1888 and enabling it to

---

[428] Rowley, *Professions, Class and Society*, 354–65.

[429] Lunney, 'Law Society and Defalcation Scandals', 251–3.

[430] Kirk, *Portrait of a Profession*, 100–1; Abel-Smith and Stevens, *Lawyers and the Courts*, 188–9.

[431] Lunney, 'Law Society and Defalcations Scandals', 260–2. Conveniently, he also served as a scapegoat for what some provincial societies considered the Law Society's sell-out over title registration: Anderson, *Lawyers and the Making of English Land Law*, 207–9.

[432] Kirk, *Portrait of a Profession*, 101–3.

[433] W. Durran, *The Lawyer, Our Old-Man-of-the-Sea* (1913), 23–5, 465. Harley Granville Barker's successful play *The Voysey Inheritance* also made uncomfortable viewing.

[434] *Lloyd* v. *Grace Smith* [1912] AC 716; M. Lunney, 'Insurance and the Liability of the Legal Profession' (1995) 16 *JLH* 94–106.

punish professional misconduct stalled in Parliament and those changes had to wait until 1919.[435]

Law Reform

From an early stage the Law Society began to interest itself in proposed law reforms. It was soon making good use of the handful of solicitor-MPs, co-opting them onto a parliamentary committee through which it began subjecting all law reform bills to thorough scrutiny.[436]

The Society denied that it was taking this trouble purely in the interests of solicitors and less convincingly denied any wish to meddle in wider matters of public policy. It sought rather to present itself as an expert witness commenting on proposals in its special areas, though they extended well beyond the range which governing bodies of other professions such as medicine might claim to pronounce upon.[437] When this role was explicitly included in the charter of 1845, it reflected a position the Society had already acquired; at Langdale's invitation it had, for example, been closely involved in the Solicitors Act 1843.[438] Its informed contributions helped to fill a vacuum at government level, where the Lord Chancellor had no permanent professional staff and the drafting of statutes was the subject of increasingly vociferous criticism.[439] Of course, the Law Society could not plausibly claim to be disinterested in proposals which had implications for solicitors, notably in the reform of the courts, in insolvency and the law of property; nevertheless, it could lay a claim to participate in the law-making process through the expertise and experience it could command. In recognition of this, it became established that the Society should be invited to give evidence to inquiries on such matters.

The attitude of the society might be summarily described as individualist and incrementalist. It tended to favour limited state intervention in cases of proven necessity and cautious piecemeal reform rather than sweeping plans of codification and reconstruction; hence in 1852 the more adventurous spirits of the Law Amendment Society attacked it sharply as an enemy to true law reform.[440] Its own members expected it actively to promote their interests and from their standpoint its record over its first 50 years was mixed. In the endless struggles with

---

[435] Kirk, *Portrait of a Profession*, 79, 103; Abel-Smith and Stevens, *Lawyers and the Courts*, 189.
[436] Sugarman, 'Bourgeois Collectivism', 93–4.
[437] *Ibid.*   [438] *Ibid.*, 96–7.
[439] Ibid., 97, 99; Anderson, *Lawyers and the Making of English Land Law*, 18, 27–8.
[440] 'The Condition and Policy of the Profession' (1852) 15 *LR* 1–48; Sugarman, 'Bourgeois Collectivism', 104–5.

the bar over audience and appointments it generally failed.[441] The fight to repeal the annual certificate duty was effectively ended by a shrewd tactical concession by Gladstone.[442] In the battle for a more sensible and generous method of calculating remuneration it made little progress until the 1880s.[443] Against that, it had unobtrusive successes in protecting solicitors from reforms which threatened their prosperity. Courts of requests were abolished and tribunals of commerce seen off; direct access to clients by the bar came to nothing; the law itself remained too daunting for many people to use without an intermediary; and if the Judicature Acts did not deliver all the solicitors wanted, they produced more work at the interlocutory stages.[444] The knighting of the president, Thomas Paine, at the opening of the new courts in 1882 was a fitting recognition of the major part played by the Law Society in bringing the courts to its own back door.[445]

However, from the 1880s tensions between the Society and successive governments mounted. The major cause was what the Society condemned as 'officialism', defined by Sugarman as 'the tendency of government departments to undertake or interfere in work previously assumed by individuals and their professional advisers under the supervision of the ordinary courts of the land'.[446] The depth and persistence of the Society's concern led to its publishing pamphlets in 1892 and 1893 and setting up of a special committee in 1905.[447] The reach of the state was extending into areas traditionally belonging to the private sector, and in particular to solicitors, who as they forcefully pointed out, paid a substantial tax for their privileges. Bankruptcy and winding up, trusts and conveyancing were the areas chiefly affected, and the threat of state intrusion exposed the contradictions inherent in the Society's role in law reform.[448] It sought to be what the *The Times* described as the 'best organized and most intelligent trade union', out to defend its members' interests,[449] and also a 'think-tank' offering an expert input into the process of law reform. The tension became acute at times, for the council's instincts were to cooperate with governments, seeking to ameliorate damaging legislation rather than to oppose it outright as many of its members expected.

[441] Kirk, *Portrait of a Profession*, 181–3.
[442] Kirk, *Portrait of a Profession*, 131–4.
[443] Birks, *Gentlemen of the Law*, 220–6; Christian, *Short History of Solicitors*, 193–202.
[444] See above, Pt 3, Chs VI, IX.
[445] Kirk, *Portrait of a Profession*, 155–6.
[446] 'Bourgeois Collectivism', 12.
[447] *Ibid.*; Stebbings, 'Officialism', 20.
[448] The best general account is Stebbings, 'Officialism'. The particular subjects are treated elsewhere in these volumes.
[449] Sugarman, 'Bourgeois Collectivism', 113–15.

The worst buffeting for the council came in the long and bitter struggle against title registration.[450] A similar mixture of self-interest and ideology permeated its opposition to a public trustee (though here there was no immediate threat of compulsion); to the extended role of Board of Trade officials in liquidations and the powers of the Inland Revenue under the Finance Act 1909.[451] These questions poisoned relations with both Halsbury and Loreburn and it was not until there was a new Law Society secretary (E. R. Cook from 1914) and a new permanent secretary (Claud Schuster, 1915) at the LCO to bring fresh minds to bear that fruitful cooperation became possible. Meanwhile, though the backwoodsmen grumbled that the Society was compromised by its management's closeness to the state and by the acceptance of a Treasury subsidy for its disciplinary functions, its special position was reinforced by a place on both rule committees.[452]

Amalgamation of the Professions and Interchange Between Them

Talk of amalgamation or 'fusion' between the two branches of the profession in the 1840s was itself a sign of how much the gulf in social standing had been narrowed. That ardent law reformer E. W. Field was an early advocate, drawing upon the experience of American states for its supposed benefits.[453] Thereafter it made fitful appearances on the law reform agenda; supported by *The Times*; debated by the Law Amendment Society, and treated as a serious proposition by the Inns of Court Commission in the 1850s; revived by a speech of Sir James Hannen in 1867 and debated at the Law Society's 1874 APM; to be found in *The Economist* and again in *The Times* and twice before the Society's APM in the 1880s.[454]

There was never a chance that it would be adopted. With a few exceptions (notably Sir Edward Clarke[455]) the bar would have none of it and Hannen was a lone voice on the bench. It had some appeal for young and ambitious solicitors who chafed at the bar's monopoly of public offices and the limits on solicitors' advocacy rights, and might have been acceptable to big firms which could then provide a full range of legal services.[456] However, there were few advantages to smaller firms and older men and the 1888 APM resolved that there was 'no sufficient reason for seriously entertaining any scheme having for its object the

---

[450] See Vol. XII, pp. 202–32.

[451] (1908–9) 53 *Sol. J.* 700.

[452] See above, pp. 789–91.

[453] Sadler, *Edwin Wilkins Field*, 25.

[454] Kirk, *Portrait of a Profession*, 175–6; Abel-Smith and Stevens, *Lawyers and the Courts*, 227–30. Walter Bagehot also came out in favour: 'Bad Lawyers or Good?', *Literary Studies*, (1870), iii, 251–79.

[455] Sir E. Clarke, *The Story of My Life* (1918), 271.

[456] Christian, *Short History of Solicitors*, 210–15.

amalgamation of the two branches of the profession'.[457] The principal argument in its favour was a supposed saving of costs, and the defenders of the status quo usually sidestepped that with mere assertions that the existing system worked perfectly well.[458] The shrewder opponents realized that owed its appeal to solicitors largely to grievances—access to offices, transfer between the professions—which could be ameliorated without anything so drastic.[459] In the absence of strong external pressure, nothing needed to be done and nothing was done.

Nothing better illustrates the raw sensitivities on both sides than the comparatively trivial matter of the terms on which men might move between them. Until Victorian times it was a rather one-sided exchange, for so few barristers wished to become attorneys that no special provisions seem to have been canvassed.[460] The bar, however, had developed a distaste for men from the 'lower branch' seeking to join its ranks and in the 1820s all the inns insisted that a solicitor must have discontinued his practice for two years before he was even admitted as a student, a rule they affirmed and strengthened in 1844.[461] This was intended as a deterrent, driven, it was said, by the disconcerting success of Thomas Wilde, a former City solicitor, though the ostensible ground was that a solicitor might command the patronage of his former clients and so obtain an unfair advantage.[462] The junior bar lamented the influx of solicitors' sons to the bar, but since the benchers seldom responded to their concerns, social snobbery was probably at least as strong a motive as concern at unfair practices.

Indignation among its members eventually forced the Law Society to act, and when an initial remonstrance in 1875 was dismissed they resorted to a mixture of carrot and stick. The carrot was a generous relaxation of their own rules (which as the bar's defenders pointed out had been given a very inflexible interpretation by the Queen's Bench),[463] allowing a barrister qualified for five years to be admitted to the roll immediately on passing the final examination. The stick was tactical action in Parliament and pressure on the Lord Chancellor which quickly forced a partial capitulation, followed in 1888 by virtually complete reciprocity.[464] Twenty years later the Bar Council attempted to resile from that, but was unwilling to

---

[457] Kirk, *Portrait of a Profession*, 176.

[458] A typically robust defence is in 'The English Bar and the English Courts' (1875) 138 *Quart. Rev.* 139–77.

[459] See e.g. 'The Amalgamation of the Two Branches of the Legal Profession' (1868–9) 26 (s3) *LM & LR* 285–315, with lengthy extracts from a pro-fusion paper by W. A. Jevons.

[460] Abel, *Legal Profession*, 163.

[461] Kirk, *Portrait of a Profession*, 179.

[462] 'Doctor-in-Jure Civil', *The Legal Profession*, 137.

[463] *Ibid.*, 144.

[464] Kirk, *Portrait of a Profession*, 179–80.

accept the concessions on county court audience that the Law Society demanded in exchange.[465]

Numbers moving in either direction were never large. As might be expected from the different size of the professions, more went to the bar than came from it, and they included several who became judges.[466] In the other direction there were those like J. H. Layton KC, who inherited a family practice, and some who were attracted to the big City firms; Freshfields paid Peter Williams a remarkable £1000 per annum as an articled clerk in 1865 and looked to W. H. Leese in 1903 when the firm could find no suitable member to be senior partner.[467] Since the number probably never exceeded 30 a year Barnard Lailey was probably atypical in having two of his pupils become solicitors.[468]

Local Law Societies

Several local law societies were in existence by the end of the eighteenth century and though some seem to have petered out, there were 17 in 1835.[469] In their published aims 'the very language they use is remarkable in its similarity',[470] and that continued to be true, for some new ones borrowed from others, especially from Manchester.[471] The Halifax (1884), is quite typical: 'Upholding the character and status of the profession; promotion of honourable professional practice; repression of professional improprieties; the settlement of points of practice and the decision of questions of professional usage and courtesy'.[472] Some explicitly included the provision of assistance to members and their families who had fallen on hard times, and whether they did so or not, it was often practised.[473] The Berks., Bucks. and Oxon. (1889) was probably unusual in having among its objects 'to make and administer regulations providing for minimum fees to be charged in respect of professional services'[474] but many practised that as well.

---

[465] Abel-Smith and Stevens, *Lawyers and the Courts*, 234–6.

[466] Abel, *Legal Profession*, 62, 163–4; Kirk, *Portrait of a Profession*, 181.

[467] Williams, *Gentleman's Calling*, 220; Slinn, *History of Freshfields*, 118, 139.

[468] B. Lailey, *Jottings From a Fee Book* (Portsmouth, 1932), 75.

[469] Robson, *Attorney in Eighteenth Century England*, 35–51, describes several.

[470] *Ibid.*, 51.

[471] *SC on Legal Education 1846*, T. Taylor q. 845. Its rules are in App. 3.

[472] *Halifax Incorporated Law Society, an Account of the First Hundred Years* [1984], 5.

[473] e.g. Glos. & Wilts.: H. H. Scott, *Notes on the History of the Gloucestershire and Wiltshire ILS During One Hundred Years, 1817–1917* (Gloucester, n.d.), 5.

[474] E. H. Duce, *The Berks., Bucks. and Oxfordshire Law Society, A Centenary History* (Oxford, ?1989), 13.

Like the Law Society, several owed their existence in part or wholly to the desire for a law library; this was true of Bristol (1819), Birmingham (1818), and Leicester (1861).[475] Unable to afford its own, Glos. & Wilts. supported one in Gloucester.[476]

The concerns and activities of the societies varied considerably. Yorkshire made strenuous efforts against licensed conveyancers;[477] Birmingham was particularly vigilant over the quality of men admitted to the roll; Nottingham and Sunderland were strenuously opposed to the admission of women to the profession.[478] On the wider stage, even some of the smaller ones were vigilant to defend their interests from unpalatable legislation; Glos. & Wilts. had William Vizard report on bills and Kent petitioned against proposals for deeds registration in 1831.[479]

By the mid-1830s the Law Society was keen to encourage the formation of more local societies, but their spread was surprisingly slow.[480] There were no more than 35 in 1873[481] and some were little more than social clubs; some even folded up, like the Cambridge Society, founded by just nine men in 1830 and dissolved in 1866.[482] Those in big cities, however, were much more purposeful—indeed Birmingham gave up its annual dinner in 1864[483]—and had an impressive membership; Liverpool's stood at 409 in 1906, Birmingham's at 364, and many others were between 100 and 200: Sheffield 172, Nottingham 155 (in 1914), Leicester 123 (in 1901) are examples. Rural and county ones were mostly smaller; Norfolk and Norwich had 76 in 1906, Cambridge and District 48. A few were very small indeed; the Isle of Wight was formed in 1903 by 18 of the island's 48 practitioners and struggled to stay in existence in its early years.[484]

The biggest acted in concert with other professional and business organizations to promote local rather than sectional interests.[485] They became convinced that the Law Society should not present itself as the voice of the profession and in March 1844 the Yorkshire Law Society proposed an association which would

[475] Robson, *Attorney in Eighteenth Century England*, 38; G. M. Butts, *A Short History of the Birmingham Law Society, 1818–1968*, 16–20; C. D. Geach, *A History of the Leicester Law Society*, 7.

[476] Scott, *History of the Glos. & Wilts. ILS*, 13.

[477] Robson, *Attorney in Eighteenth Century England*, 40.

[478] Rowley, *Professions, Class and Society*, 101–4; Smith, *Short History of the Nottingham LS*, 12; *Sunderland Law Society Sesquicentenary 1824–1974*.

[479] Scott, *History of the Glos. & Wilts. LS*, 9–10; W. Mowll, *History of the Kent Law Society* [1948], 5.

[480] Kirk, *Portrait of a Profession*, 37–8, quoting the annual report of 1836. The chronology at the end of Christian, *Short History of Solicitors*, gives the dates of their foundation.

[481] Kirk, *Portrait of a Profession*, 39. Sixteen counties and 81 large towns were reported to have no law society.

[482] *Ibid.*, 37; Jackson, *Cambridge Bicentenary*, 136–40.

[483] Butts, *Short History of the Birmingham LS*, 14.

[484] J. A. Matthews, *A History of the Isle of Wight Law Society* [1975], 6–8.

[485] Sugarman, 'Bourgeois Collectivism', 128.

'resist the various attempts to centralise the business of the Profession in the metropolis', to which the Law Society seemed at least indifferent.[486] The outcome was the Provincial Law Societies Association, formed in 1845 by 15 societies 'chiefly to promote the interests and watch over all legislative and other interference with the just rights of the profession; to assist in obtaining all useful and practical amendments of the law; and to adopt measures for preserving the respectability of the profession'.[487] In 1847, wishing to present itself as a national body and finding the Law Society resistant to amalgamation, it became the Metropolitan and Provincial Law Association, seeking in this way 'to construct a more decentralised and less hierarchical form of professional organization, while ensuring that the profession as a whole could act in a united fashion'.[488]

The emphasis on law reform was significant, and helped propel the Law Society into a similar stance, but the main aim was clearly defensive, indicating the anxiety of provincial solicitors at the encroachments of a voracious and expanding bar and the detested agents and accountants. With both the M&PLA and the Law Society (plus some individual societies) having standing committees on bills, there would be no lack of vigilance, and the voice of provincial solicitors would still be heard loud and clear.[489]

Unfortunately for both bodies, their attempts to recruit country members were not very successful. The Law Society could survive comfortably enough as an essentially metropolitan body but the M&PLA, lacking a headquarters and secretariat, soon began to falter, despite talented men like Field and William Shaen, a tireless propagandist.[490] The issues on which the Law Society and country practitioners differed also began to divide the management of the M&PLA along regional lines, leading to uncertainty about its true role. At one time 'virtually the Law Society of the North',[491] its membership remained small and in the end, after 'fraught negotiations',[492] it was absorbed by the Law Society in 1874. In its place the big northern societies created the Associated Provincial Law Societies, which met when concerted action was needed. It had at first to fight for official recognition but its pivotal role in the solicitors' resistance to the unacceptable

---

[486] *Ibid.*, 103.

[487] Anderson, *Lawyers and the Making of English Land Law*, 26.

[488] Sugarman, 'Bourgeois Collectivism', 103.

[489] Anderson, *Lawyers and the Making of English Land Law*, 26–32 gives the best account of this body.

[490] Sadler, *Edwin Wilkins Field*; 'The Late E.W. Field' (1872) 1 (n.s.) *LM & R* 35–50; R. J. Shaen (ed.), *William Shaen, A Brief Sketch* (1912).

[491] Anderson, *Lawyers and the Making of English Land Law*, 125.

[492] Sugarman, 'Bourgeois Collectivism', 103. The account in Kirk, *Portrait of a Profession*, 39 is very bland.

parts of Cairns' Land Transfer Bill showed its worth and it remained a powerful counterweight to the voice of London.[493]

Local societies continued to spread slowly. Though atypical in fairly obvious ways, and still largely served by offshoots of Preston firms, the business of the Blackpool and Fylde Law Society (1892) is probably similar to most smaller societies.[494] A major concern was to establish and enforce a local conveyancing scale, though in Leicester agreement had proved impossible and Halifax had to abandon one in 1901 because of lack of uniformity.[495] Local conditions of sale were less contentious and widely adopted but also had to be defended.[496] In Blackpool and elsewhere the local society sought to ensure that newcomers were properly qualified and that unqualified men did not do solicitors' business. Even the Isle of Wight managed to defeat an accountant who sought to handle land sales except for the actual conveyance,[497] and like Blackpool, it also tried to curb advertising.[498] On occasion, as over the Licensing Act 1904, the Blackpool society acted in concert with other Lancashire law societies. and there was regular cooperation among the Yorkshire societies.[499]

Cooperation was not easy for societies, however, since their views often differed. Thus Liverpool for a period was unusual in supporting compulsory title registration; Birmingham and Leicester were at one stage keen on fusion with the bar; Leeds (and Yorkshire generally) was more hostile to the Law Society cutting a deal over title registration than others.[500] Societies therefore continued to act independently, though few were so zealous as Liverpool, which besides gaining a notable triumph over the Law Society over conveyancing scales in 1883, regularly sent its views to the rule committees. It was therefore appropriate that when a second solicitor representative was added to the Supreme Court Rule Committee the Law Society chose one from Liverpool, the long-serving C. H. Morton.[501]

---

[493] Anderson, *Lawyers and the Making of English Land Law*, 127–8. In 1894, 49 of 63 law societies were members: (1894–5) 39 *Sol. J.* 293.

[494] Cameron, *Solicitors in Blackpool*. Some published histories are listed in G. F. Holborn, *Sources of Biographical Information on Past Lawyers* (1999), 142–3.

[495] Anderson, *Lawyers and the Making of English Land Law*, 55–6, 122, 153–7; Geach, *History of the Leicester LS*, 10; *Halifax LS*, 11. Kent established 'a uniform rule of charges in conveyancing' as far back as the 1780s: Mowll, *History of the Kent LS*, 4.

[496] D. Martin, *The Hertfordshire Law Society, 1883–1983*; D. H. G. Salt, *A Short History of the Shropshire Law Society, 1876–1976*, 2.

[497] Matthews, *History of the Isle of Wight LS*, 9–10.

[498] *Ibid.*, 9; Cameron, *Solicitors in Blackpool*, 47.

[499] Cameron, *Solicitors in Blackpool*, 77 (and see 94).

[500] Rowley, *Professions, Class and Society*, 250–3; Geach, *History of the Leicester LS*, 13; Anderson, *Lawyers and the Making of English Land Law*, 181, 202, 213.

[501] Anderson, *Lawyers and the Making of English Land Law*, 24–5, 157; NA PRO LCO 2/251.

In 1914 there were 56 societies in the *Law List*, and by then new ones usually came when a town had enough solicitors to merit seceding from the county, as with Hastings in 1920 and Eastbourne in 1924.[502]

7. Notaries Public

Notaries survived as an independent profession because the attempt by the solicitors to absorb them in the aftermath of the Judicature Acts was thwarted by the opposition of the City (including some City solicitors), the Church, and a former Lord Chancellor, Cairns. The Law Society's Bill, started in 1881[503] and defeated in 1884,[504] was the latest and most ambitious of a series of assaults upon the Scriveners' Company monopoly, previous efforts having succeeded in breaking in upon it in the provinces to a limited extent.

The notary performed a number of functions, but those in connection with shipping and foreign trade gradually dwindled, so that the authentication of legal documents for countries which would not recognize the signature of a commissioner for oaths as sufficient became the most important.[505] As revised by an Act of 1801, a notary (admitted to practise by the court of Faculties of the Archbishop of Canterbury[506]) needed to be articled for seven years to a notary or a member of the Scriveners Company practising as a notary.[507] Even in the bigger outports there was insufficient work to provide a notary with a living and in 1833 the notaries fought off a bill which would have allowed solicitors to act as notaries outside the City and its environs, but only by conceding that a 'district notary' might be appointed, his practice limited to a 20-mile radius, where the Master of the Faculties was satisfied by a local memorial that there was a shortage.[508] Further pressure led to a wider concession in 1843 which created a third category,

---

[502] C. M. F. Langdon, *The Hastings and District Law Society* (1978); J. V. C. Claremont, *A History of the Eastbourne Law Society* (Eastbourne, 1948), 45.

[503] (1881) 71 *LT* 286.

[504] *PD* 1884 (s3) 287: 139–45.

[505] Richard Brooke's *Treatise on the Office and Practice of a Notary of England* appeared in 1839 and became the standard work, the 5th edn coming out in 1913. For the notary's functions see the 10th edn (1988) by N. P. Ready, 18–24.

[506] Coke called this 'a court, although it holdeth no plea of controversie': quoted in *Brooke's Notary*, which describes this peculiar institution at 30–5. By the Welsh Church Act 1914 (c. 91), s. 37, appointments in Wales were transferred to the Lord Chancellor.

[507] Public Notaries Act 1801 (41 Geo. III c. 79). This and subsequent Acts did not apply to ecclesiastical notaries, appointed by the Master of the Faculties under an Act of 1533. They were normally registrars of an ecclesiastical court or their deputies: *Brooke's Notary*, 49–50.

[508] Public Notaries Act 1833 (3 & 4 Will. IV c. 70); C. W. Brooks, R. H. Helmholz, and P. G. Stein, *Notaries Public in England Since the Reformation* (1991), 125–6; *Brooke's Notary*, 41–7.

unlimited in area outside the scriveners' three-mile monopoly,[509] but needing to have served five-year articles (as opposed to the seven years for scriveners), which might be 'double articles', i.e. under a man practising as both solicitor and notary.[510]

Even in London notaries were never numerous. In the debates on the 1884 bill it was claimed there were only 33 scrivener-notaries in London, and 48 in all,[511] and the major ports had only a handful of general notaries.[512] District notaries, essentially solicitors, however, numbered several hundred.[513] They remained immune from examinations,[514] and though so few, organized themselves into distinct London and provincial societies,[515] neither of which acquired any control over the process of admission or discipline, which remained anomalously within the Church.[516]

[509] Distance was measured from the Royal Exchange: see the map in *Brooke's Notary*, 539–41.

[510] 'Double articles' had been a doubtful question for some years, since *R* v. *Scriveners Company* (1830) 10 B. & C. 511; Brooks et al., *Notaries Public Since the Reformation*, 124.

[511] *Ibid.*, 129. They included several jews: Cooper, *Pride and Prejudice*, 151.

[512] *Graham* v. *Smart* (1863) 9 Jur. (N.S.), 387; *Brooke's Notary*, 42.

[513] H. C. Gutteridge, ' The Origins and Development of Notaries Public in England', in P. H. Winfield and A. D. McNair (eds), *Cambridge Legal Essays* (Cambridge, 1926), 123–37.

[514] They did, however, have to furnish a certificate of good character: *Brooke's Notary*, 488.

[515] Brooks et al., *Notaries Public Since the Reformation*, 135.

[516] What was believed to be the first removal of a notary from the roll for misconduct under the inherent jurisdiction of the court of the Faculties took place in 1906: *Re Champion* [1906] P. 86. For this and other cases see *Brooke's Notary*, 33–5.

V

The Education of Lawyers

1. 1820–60*

The State of Legal Education

In 1820, no formal legal education was available for men who wished to be barristers. Instead, it was left to the market to determine whether those who wished to practise were competent to do so.[1] Before an aspiring advocate could practise, he had to be admitted to an inn of court, and be called to the bar. There were no educational qualifications for admission to an inn; but those who wished to be admitted had to submit a statement showing their respectability, signed by two people, and pay a £100 deposit.[2] Being voluntary societies, the inns had complete discretion both in respect to admissions and calls.[3] The benchers' aims appear to have been to ensure that all barristers were respectable, even if they were not learned. To obtain a call, a candidate had only to have been a member of his inn for five years—or three, if he was a university graduate—and to have 'kept' 12 terms, 'which means being present at the time that grace is said [at dinner], for a minute or two, a certain number of days in each term during those three years'.[4]

Legal education had once been vibrant at the 'third university of England', as the inns were once known. However, teaching at the inns had fallen into decline by the early eighteenth century,[5] and only the formal vestiges of their earlier functions remained. These included the appointment of Readers who gave no

---

* This Section by Michael Lobban.

[1] Many of those who were called to the bar had no intention of earning their living as practising barristers, but either aimed to 'qualify themselves for the duties of the legislature or magistracy' or simply wanted 'to gratify their vanity by the hope of being sometimes spoken of as "*the learned gentleman*"', S. Warren, *A Popular and Practical Introduction to Law Studies* (1835), 61–2.

[2] *The Records of the Honourable Society of Lincoln's Inn Black Books* (1902) iv, 74, 100. From 1829 the Inner Temple examined each candidate 'as to his classical attainments, but not at all regarding his legal attainments', *Select Committee on Legal Education*, PP 1846 (686), x, 1 q. 38; it went little 'beyond the mere ordinary knowledge of a schoolboy in classics', q. 137 (T. Starkie).

[3] See the cases of T. J. Wooler and D. W. Harvey, discussed above, pp. 101–2.

[4] SC on Legal *Education* (1846), q. 3774 (Lord Brougham).

[5] D. Lemmings, *Professors of the Law: Barristers and English Legal Culture in the Eighteenth Century* (Oxford, 2000), 113–31.

readings, and the requirement that students perform perfunctory exercises prior to their call.[6] Occasional courses of lectures were still given at the inns, but this was on the initiative of private individuals, such as Joseph Chitty, who gave a course of lectures at Lincoln's Inn on commercial law in 1810.[7]

Legal education at the ancient universities at this time was also moribund. Although the Regius chairs in Roman civil law in both ancient universities dated from the reign of Henry VIII, the subject was weak at both establishments. In Oxford (where J. G. Phillimore held the chair), no lectures were given. Cambridge's J. W. Geldart did lecture, and reinstated examinations, but did not attract many students, and left nothing in the way of a scholarly legacy. Degrees in civil law were taken by men who required them for a college fellowship, or who wished to practise in Doctors' Commons; but aspiring common lawyers did not see any benefit in them.[8] Both universities had also established chairs in English law in the eighteenth century, but these were no stronger than their civil law counterparts. Oxford's Vinerian chair was a sinecure by 1820. When appointed in 1823 to the Downing chair in Cambridge, Thomas Starkie began to give lectures; but he also gave up after two years.[9] Oxbridge had little to offer the aspiring lawyer in 1820.

Instead of a formal education in law, whether at the inns or at a university, students were expected to learn in the office of a practitioner. By 1820, those intending to practise normally paid an annual fee of 100 guineas to become the pupil of a special pleader, equity draftsman or conveyancer. Though reformers called for fixed hours of instruction from the pupil master, those who took in pupils were under no obligation to teach them.[10] Instead, it was left to the pupil to copy out precedents, and learn the law from observing the business of the chamber and

---

[6] *Select Committee on Legal Education*, q. 3774, 275 (Lord Brougham). By mid-century, this system had declined: *RC on the Inns of Court and Inns of Chancery*, PP 1854–55 [1998], xviii, 345 at q. 399 (W. Whateley).

[7] J. Chitty, Prospectus of a Course of Lectures on the Commercial Law, to be delivered immediately after the Michaelmas Term 1810 (1810). In 1824, Chitty published a four-volume Treatise on the Laws of Commerce and Manufactures, and the Contracts relating thereto. See also C. W. Brooks and M. Lobban, 'Apprenticeship or Academy? The Idea of a Law University, 1830–1860', in J. A. Bush and A. Wijffels (eds), *Learning the Law: Teaching and the Transmission of Law in England 1150–1900* (1997), 353–82 at 358 and J. H. Baker, *Legal Education in London, 1250–1850* (Selden Society, 2007), 25–6. Lectures had also been given at this inn in the 1790s by Michael Nolan and James Mackintosh.

[8] For the civilians see above, pp. 696–8.

[9] *SC on Legal Education*, q. 11. His tenure lasted until he was succeeded by Andrew Amos in 1849.

[10] Brougham felt the pupil master should spend five hours every evening reading with the pupil: (1850) 15 *LT* 35.

attending court.[11] By the 1820s, the system was frequently criticized by those who wanted a more scientific form of legal education. Nonetheless, the practical training it offered continued to be strongly defended by the profession. In his advice book to the law student, Samuel Warren therefore insisted that he could not learn the law simply by reading books, or hearing lectures, but could only learn by observing the material which came into his office 'under the superintendence of a competent teacher: one whose tact and experience will keep business and systematic reading ancillary to each other; who will chalk out a proper line of study, and illustrate it by actual practice'.[12] C. H. Whitehurst, treasurer of the Middle Temple, said that intending practitioners got the 'only instruction which is valuable to them' in a pleader or draftsman's office.[13]

If many students were left to fend for themselves in the office, some were taught by masters who took the education of their pupils seriously. Chitty, who had more than 20 pupils, gave them lectures, which formed the basis of the many treatises he published.[14] Andrew Amos also gave private classes at his chambers in the 1820s, attracting 'a very large number' thanks to the 'rather more philosophical view of the subject of law' which he offered.[15] Amos's teaching was by a form of seminar, in which he directed students on their readings, and discussed them. Students also formed their own debating societies and mooting clubs.[16] Like many others, his students formed a club, and he 'used to go and talk afterwards to them upon the faults in their reasonings or declamations'.[17]

Students were also advised to pursue their own course of reading, tailored to explain legal points they encountered while in chambers or attending court, and to attend their own law debating clubs.[18] Students had long suffered from a lack of systematic literature. Early nineteenth-century law students were still expected to learn property law from *Coke upon Littleton*; and as late as 1846, James Stewart pointed out that 'the best book that you can put in the hands of the student at the pleader's chambers' on many points of common law was Williams's edition

---

[11] See the criticisms of S. C. Denison, in *RC on the University and Colleges of Oxford*, PP 1852 [1482], xxii, 1 at 197.

[12] Warren, *Popular and Practical Introduction*, 34.

[13] *RC on the Inns of Court*, q. 528.

[14] Brooks and Lobban, 'Apprenticeship or Academy', 358. In the preface to his *Treatise on the Laws of Commerce and Manufactures, and the Contracts relating thereto* (4 vols, 1824) Chitty thanked two of his 'industrious pupils' for their assistance: i: xvi.

[15] *SC on Legal Education*, q. 1265 (A. Amos).

[16] For legal clubs, see (1836–7) 13 *Leg. Ob.* 118, 128.

[17] *SC on Legal Education*, q. 1269 (A. Amos). Chitty's pupils also started their own Forensic Society, which was open to pupils from other chambers.

[18] (1844–5) 1 *LR* 154 advised the student to spend half the day in court merely listening and taking notes, and the other half reading up for themselves what they had heard. The *Law Times* (1848) 11: 260 advised the young barrister to delay his call, and instead spend five years reading.

of Saunders' Reports, where the student had to find key points in two sets of notes on seventeenth century cases.[19] However, things were improving, for by 1820 there was a wider range of legal literature available to the student, given the growth of printed legal treatises often written by young practitioners and pupil masters.[20] The growth of a legal periodical press from the late 1820s, republishing lectures and offering the reader treatises on various aspects of the law in weekly instalments, also provided a means of acquiring legal knowledge.

In contrast to barristers, there were some formal educational requirements for those wishing to become attorneys. Under the 1729 Attorneys Act, those wishing to enrol as attorneys had to provide written articles to prove they had served a clerkship. The Act also confirmed the duty of the common law judges to examine the competence of the candidates.[21] Articles of clerkship were much like other kinds of articles of apprenticeship, with the master undertaking to train and maintain the young man. However, there was no control over the education offered in the attorney's office, and the examination given to articled clerks was largely perfunctory.[22] Much therefore depended on how busy the attorney's office was, and how much time he devoted to his clerk. Clerks learned the law by copying documents, as well as reading manuals on practice.[23] In practice, the kind of learning experienced by the young clerk was hence not very different in nature from that experienced by the would-be barrister. Indeed, many eighteenth-century parents, who wished their sons to be barristers, placed them first in the office of an attorney, a practice which persisted into the nineteenth century.[24]

Initiatives in Legal Education

By the 1820s, members of the 'lower' branch, who were keen to assert the respectable nature of their profession, were increasingly concerned to reform the education of attorneys. From the 1790s, the reform of their education was linked to the creation of a body which would regulate both admission to the profession and the

---

[19] SC on Legal Education, q. 3667.

[20] See A. W. B. Simpson, 'The Rise and Fall of the Legal Treatise: Legal Principles and the Forms of Legal Literature', in his Legal Theory and Legal History: Essays on the Common Law (1987), 273–320 and M. Lobban, 'The English Treatise and English Law in the Eighteenth Century', in S. Dauchy, J. Monballyu, and A. Wijffels (eds), Auctoritates (Iuris Scripta Historica vol. XIII, Brussels, 1997), 69–88.

[21] C. W. Brooks, 'Apprenticeship and Legal Training in England, 1700–1850', in his Lawyers, Litigation and English Society Since 1750 (1998), 149–78 at 155.

[22] See the criticisms of J. Day, Thoughts on the Necessity and Utility of the Examination directed by Several Acts of Parliament (1795).

[23] Brooks, 'Apprenticeship and Legal Training', 159–60; R. Robson, The Attorney in Eighteenth Century England (1959), 155–8.

[24] Lemmings, Professors, 133–4; Brooks and Lobban, 'Apprenticehip or Academy', 355–6.

conduct of solicitors and attorneys.[25] Education was therefore high on the agenda of the Law Society formed in 1825, and incorporated in 1831. In 1833, it began to provide lectures in its hall. The lectures were given by barristers, and attracted audiences of approximately 200 articled clerks, as well as attorneys.[26] Lectures were given on common law, conveyancing, equity, bankruptcy, and criminal law.[27] In 1836, the Law Society took control of the examination of attorneys, when new rules laid down by the judges specified that admission to practice would require candidates to pass a written examination taken in the Hall of the society.[28] Members of the council of the Law Society were the examiners, appointed annually by the judges.

Though the examination was compulsory for all aspiring attorneys, the Law Society's library was only open to its members and their clerks. The 1830s and 1840s accordingly saw clerks in the provinces to devise ways to assist each other in learning. Encouraged by periodicals aimed at attorneys, which republished the lectures given at the Law Society, clerks in the 1840s corresponded with each other on moot points, and set up their own debating clubs. Law students societies were set up in a number of provincial towns. There were also calls for local law societies to set up courses of lectures, acted on by some, as in Manchester.[29]

By 1833, a number of initiatives had also been taken to provide lectures for those wishing to become barristers, as well as aspirant attorneys. Private lectures continued to be given, such as those at Lyon's Inn hall in 1828 by Charles Petersdorff and in 1829 by J. B. Byles.[30] More significant were the lectures offered by London University, founded in 1826. Two professors were appointed, who began to give lectures in 1829. Amos was appointed to the chair of English law, and lectured to audiences of between 50 and 150, his popularity increased by the practical approach he took. The other lecturer, John Austin, whose approach was more dryly philosophical, was less successful in the size of his audience, though the lectures he gave would form the core of the most influential of nineteenth-century English works on jurisprudence. This institution intended to create more chairs and initiate a German-style legal education. At King's

[25] D. Sugarman, 'Bourgeois Collectivism, Professional Power and the Boundaries of the State. The Private and Public Life of the Law Society, 1825 to 1914' (1996) 3 *International Journal of the Legal Profession* 81–135 at 89–90.

[26] *SC on Legal Education*, q. 2097 (R. Maugham).

[27] Among the regular lecturers at this institution was J. W. Smith, whose lectures were later published as textbooks. Students were also occasionally addressed by experts such as Basil Montagu.

[28] Brooks and Lobban, 'Apprenticeship or Academy', 362.

[29] Brooks and Lobban, 'Apprenticeship or Academy', 364–5; W. W. Pue, 'Guild Training vs. Professional Legal Education: The Committee on Legal Education and the Law Department of Queen's College, Birmingham in the 1850s' (1989) 33 *AJLH* 241–87 at 251.

[30] Petersdorff's lectures were aimed at clerks and pupils: Baker, *Legal Education*, 36.

College, a combined chair of jurisprudence and English law was set up, with
J. J. Park appointed in 1831. In the event, by 1834, enrolment was falling, and the
chairs vacated by Austin and Amos (after their resignations) and Park (after his
death) soon declined into sinecures.[31] Amos later claimed that it was the success
of his lectures which encouraged others to emulate his efforts. The university's
initiative certainly fuelled the Law Society's interest in lectures,[32] and in 1833 the
Inner Temple provided a venue for courses of lectures by Thomas Starkie and
John Austin. But as yet, the demand for classroom teaching in London was not
sufficiently high to sustain the academic education for barristers which Amos
had in mind. Aspiring barristers had little appetite for abstract learning in the
lecture hall, which gave no professional advantages, and the Inner Temple's initiative itself soon stalled.

The spur for renewed attempts to revive legal education in England in the
1840s came from Ireland. In 1839 the Dublin Law Institute was set up, to provide
legal education for both branches of the profession. It obtained the financial support of the benchers of King's Inn, and five professors were appointed.[33] However,
by 1842, the institute ran into financial problems after the benchers withdrew
their backing. Despite stalling, this Irish initiative attracted much publicity in
England, notably after Thomas Wyse MP presented a petition to Parliament from
Tristram Kennedy, the founder of the Dublin Law Institute, calling for improvements in legal education. At the same time, English legal periodicals such as the
Law Times and *Legal Observer* gave strong support for the growing movement to
reform legal education, regularly printing articles critical of the legal education
currently offered.[34]

By this time, there was a growing interest among reformers in encouraging
the study of Roman law and legal history, as a way of introducing students to
a wider set of principles.[35] As Lord Brougham pointed out, even those students
who were in the busiest pleaders' offices 'acquire a practical and mechanical
rather than a systematic knowledge of law'.[36] Brougham and his acolytes in the

---

[31] See R. Cocks, *Foundations of the Modern Bar* (1983), 41–4. On Austin and Amos, see Baker,
Legal Education, 28–31 and W. E. Rumble, 'Austin in the Classroom: Why Were his Courses on
Jurisprudence Unpopular?' (1996) 17 *JLH* 17–39.

[32] Brooks and Lobban, 'Apprenticeship or Academy', 361.

[33] See C. Kenny, *Tristram Kennedy and the Revival of Irish Legal Training 1835–1885* (Dublin,
1996).

[34] Cocks, *Foundations*, 70–6. They also republished lectures given by the holders of chairs in
London: Baker, *Legal Education*, 32.

[35] M. Graziadei, 'Changing Images of the Law in XIX Century English Legal Thought (the continental impulse)', in M. Reimann (ed.), *The Reception of Continental Ideas in the Common Law World,
1820–1920* (Berlin, 1997), 115–64.

[36] [H. Brougham], 'Legal Education' (1844) 1 *LR* 144–57 at 148. See also 'Science and the Study of
Jurisprudence' (1844) 1 *LR* 1–25.

Law Amendment Society now began to argue for the establishment of a legal university in London, based on the inns of court, which would be open to all those in practice or preparing for it, whether as barristers, attorneys, advocates, or proctors.[37] They also turned their attention to persuading their own inns to offer a more systematic legal education. As early as 1843, Richard Bethell encouraged the Middle Temple to look into offering lectures, and instituting compulsory examinations. By the start of 1846, this inn had set up a committee which recommended appointing a lecturers in jurisprudence and civil law, by which they meant 'modern Roman law'. Bethell had specifically favoured such a chair 'because it is most desirable that young men coming from the universities should enter upon the study of the law, in a philosophical manner, as the highest branch of Ethical science'.[38] The committee agreed, and declared that these subjects would 'furnish the best means of preparatory legal culture, and the formation of an enlarged and comprehensive legal mind'.[39] It proposed instituting a voluntary examination, and to allow only those who had attended at least one of the courses of lectures to be called to the bar. It also expressed the hope that the other inns would offer lectures;[40] and in the following July, committees from the four inns agreed to set up four more lectureships, and to refuse a call to anyone who failed to attend at least two courses.[41]

The Select Committee on Legal Education and its Results

At the same time that the inns were seeking to revive the provision of lectures, in philosophical as well as practical subjects, a select committee was appointed, on the initiative of Wyse, to consider improvements in legal education both in England and Ireland. Witnesses before the committee argued for an academic education for lawyers which would help cultivate a more sophisticated and learned legal culture in England. Reformers pointed to the unscientific nature of English legal literature, when compared with the treatises written by continental jurists such as Savigny or Americans such as Joseph Story. Nonetheless, there were clear obstacles in the path to reform. To begin with, in 1846, the reform movement had yet to revive the curriculum at the ancient universities. At the same time, in the decade before procedural reforms paved the way for the demise

[37] [H. Brougham], 'Legal Education— Law University' (1844) 1 LR 345–52.
[38] Brougham MSS, University College, London, MS 2493 (Bethell to Brougham, 20 January 1846).
[39] Ibid.
[40] (1845–6) 31 Leg. Ob. 264; The Times, 24 January 1846, col. 7b.
[41] Lincoln's Inn Black Books, v, 9.

of the forms of action, lawyers remained convinced that the primary place to learn the law remained the practitioner's chamber.

When the Committee reported in August, it favoured reform, stating that 'no Legal Education, worthy of the name, is at this moment to be had', in England or Ireland. It was critical of the fact that the education of young barristers was left too much to 'the individual intelligence and exertion of the pupil'. Although 'well calculated to communicate minute practical knowledge of forms and technicalities', study in the office of a pleader or draftsman, 'cannot be considered as a substitute for that systematic and comprehensive information, and philosophic spirit, which are the highest qualities of the Lawyer'. Similarly, the education of the young solicitor 'though useful in training to the mechanical drudgery of the profession, is not sufficient for [its] higher and more important duties'.[42] The Committee was critical of the examination taken by members of the lower branch, feeling that it was too focused on technicalities and too little on general principles. It was also critical of the fact that the universities did not offer a course for the general student who did not wish to proceed to practise, but who might be 'called on to act as Magistrate, Legislator, Administrator, with insufficient knowledge, crude ideas, and false views'.[43]

The Committee therefore recommended an overhaul of legal education. It felt that university undergraduates should receive some education in the history and progress of law as well as jurisprudence; and that 'greater advantages should be attached to the Law degrees', with some careers being limited to those who had received the degree of doctor of law.[44] Since the lawyer could not learn his craft in the academy alone, those who wished to become barristers would proceed to a second stage of their education at a 'professional Law College' centred on the inns, with entry after 'an examination by way of Matriculation'. Lectures would be given at each inn, which would appoint the professors and set examinations. The Committee did not lay much stress on chamber teaching, though it did suggest that some lectures might be given which could be combined with attendance in a pleader's or draftsman's office. Significantly, it did not suggest that attorneys be educated with barristers. In its view, the lectures the inns 'would scarcely be appropriate and special enough for his wants', and there would be opposition from the bar to such a joint education. Though clerks might be allowed to attend some lectures at the inns, it was felt appropriate for the Law Society to offer lectures suitable to the profession. Under its proposals, attorneys would still be trained through apprenticeships. Prior to his admission to an apprenticeship,

---

[42] *SC on Legal Education*, lvi; Pue, 'Guild Training vs. Professional Legal Education', 254–55.
[43] *SC on Legal Education*, lvii.
[44] *Ibid.*, lviii.

the young man should be examined to show he had acquired a 'sound general education'.[45] The 'lower branch', which had been the driving force behind much of the movement to revive legal education in the 1830s, was hence to be excluded from proposals for an academic legal education.

The report of the Select Committee was not acted on by Parliament. Nonetheless, the inns did continue with the initiative begun by Bethell. Lecturers were appointed by each inn in 1847,[46] though attendance at their lectures was voluntary. No system of examinations was instituted, though at Gray's Inn, W. D. Lewis did set voluntary examinations for honours.[47] Many reformers felt that the inns should be doing more. In 1848, the four lecturers expressed their view to the benchers that attendance at the lectures be made part of the qualification for a barrister, and that a voluntary honours examination should obtain the public sanction of the inns. The Law Amendment Society was also critical of the efforts of the inns, and continued to urge the establishment of a law school, with students being offered a general series of lectures, as well as being given classes by barristers, pleaders, and conveyancers in their chambers.[48] In 1851, Bethell once more persuaded his inn to set up a committee to consider his proposal for a united scheme of legal education at the inns; and as a result of this, a joint committee of the four inns was set up which reported in February 1852. It proposed setting up a Council of Legal Education composed of benchers from each inn, which would supervise the legal education of would-be barristers. Five Readers were appointed, one by each inn, and one jointly, to teach Constitutional Law and Legal History.[49] Henceforth, a call to the bar was to be conditional on attending the lectures of two of the Readers for a full year, or passing a public examination. Awards would be given to those who had distinguished themselves in the examination. However, to the disappointment of many reformers, there was to be no compulsory examination.

If the creation of the Council of Legal Education was a significant breakthrough, the legal education it instituted remained a long way from perfect. Henry Maine, who was appointed Reader in jurisprudence and common law, bemoaned the lack of system in this education. As he pointed out in 1854, there

[45] *Ibid.*, liii, lx.

[46] George Long was appointed at the Middle Temple; the Inner Temple appointed Robert Hall to teach common law; Gray's Inn appointed W. D. Lewis to lecture on real property; and Lincoln's Inn appointed George Spence to teach equity.

[47] RC on the Inns of Court, 149–51.

[48] [Report of the] Special Committee [of the Law Amendment Society] on the Establishment of a Law School (1850) 12 *LR* 106–15. The society also felt that junior members of the bar could act as tutors: see (1855–6) 23 *LR* 44–52.

[49] *RC on the Inns of Court*, qq. 1394, 1402 (W. D. Lewis). Only 13 out of the 60 who attended Lewis's lectures took the examination.

were no rules prescribing the order in which students were to take up the different subjects. 'They look upon these new arrangements as so many onerous conditions imposed on the Call to the Bar', he said, 'they give themselves the minimum of time for satisfying them, and thus, when they do come into contact with the system, they are too late to avail themselves of its full advantages'.[50] Though the Readers offered private classes, they did not attract large numbers of students, whose time was taken in chambers.

In 1854, a royal commission was appointed to inquire into the educational arrangements made by the inns of court. There had been criticism for some time that the inns were wealthy institutions which had lost sight of their original function as educators. Instead of being taught, students were said merely to be subsidizing the benchers' fine dining.[51] The Commissioners accordingly investigated the revenues of the inns, to see if the money could be better spent on education; and found that there was 'every disposition' on the part of the benchers to render their funds available for the education of the students. There was no pot of unused gold which could be given over to legal education. But on the educational side, the inns were found wanting. The Commissioners pointed out that the traditional argument of lawyers, that a poor barrister would simply get no clients, was inappropriate in an age when many public offices were restricted to members of the bar: 'the community is surely entitled to require some guarantee—first, for the personal character, and next for the professional qualifications of the individuals called to the bar'.[52] The English system of educating lawyers compared woefully with that of continental Europe. They were especially troubled by the absence of any examination prior to the call. The Commissioners proposed uniting the inns into a university which would conduct examinations and confer degrees. Those who did not have a prior university degree would be required to take an admission examination.[53] In 1856, the Council of Legal Education agreed that a compulsory examination should be instituted, but this proposal was rejected by the benchers.[54] Three years later, a committee appointed by the four inns once more recommended a compulsory examination. However, in light of disagreement among the benchers of the different inns, the proposal was not implemented.[55]

---

[50] *RC on the Inns of Court*, q. 1107. On Maine's experiences as a teacher here, see R. Cocks, 'Who Attended the Lectures of Sir Henry Maine: And Does It Matter?', in J. A. Bush and A. Wijffels (eds), *Learning the Law: Teaching and the Transmission of Law in England 1150–1900* (1999), 383–96.

[51] 'Legal Education' (1847) 6 *LR* 225–42 at 229; see also Cocks, *Foundations*, 97.

[52] *RC on the Inns of Court*, 14.

[53] *Ibid.*, 5–6, 16–17.

[54] *Lincoln's Inn Black Books*, v, 61.

[55] *Ibid.*, 79–83.

Reform of legal education was deferred once more, thanks to the conservatism of the benchers.

Mid-century attempts to revive university law teaching also faltered. In 1850, a school of jurisprudence and history was set up in Oxford, while in 1854 Cambridge set up a new board of studies in law, offering an LLB degree with honours.[56] In an age of university reform, there were some signs that a reformed law degree might become part of the education of the gentleman and a foundation for those wishing to enter practice. However, since the bar continued to regard what happened at the universities as unrelated to their activities, and since a law degree from a university was not a prerequisite for admission to the inns, these degrees were not taken up with any enthusiasm. As one periodical put it, 'nine out of ten students who intend to become lawyers have the good sense to postpone the study of law until they have graduated'.[57] The experience of London University was not much better. Amos was succeeded in his chair at University College by a number of minor figures, while Austin's chair was only intermittently filled, generally by one of the few University College men who had excelled in the law examinations.[58] Only a small handful graduated in law each year from the college.[59] At King's College, Park's chair was filled until 1849, after which the college appointed a committee to investigate why the law course was such a failure.[60] King's also set up a chair in International Law in 1848, but this chair also fell into decline, after its holder, Travers Twiss, moved to Oxford.[61] There were also efforts after 1846 to create a scholarly form of professional legal education at Queen's College, Birmingham. But by the late 1850s, the education offered here was aimed more at the practical needs of the articled clerk, and by the mid-1860s, the college's law department had disappeared.[62]

---

[56] F. H. Lawson, *The Oxford Law School, 1850–1965* (Oxford, 1968), 20–1; D. A. Winstanley, *Early Victorian Cambridge* (Cambridge, 1940), 279–80, and *Later Victorian Cambridge* (Cambridge, 1947), 206.

[57] Cocks, *Foundations*, 114.

[58] These men included C. J. Hargreaves and C. J. Foster, who held the chair from 1850 to 1858.

[59] According to reports to the college's AGMs, between 1858 and 1868, less than four graduated on average each year. For the state of law teaching at the college in the mid-nineteenth century, see J. H. Baker, 'University College and Legal Education 1826–1976' (1977) 30 *Current Legal Problems* 1–13 at 6.

[60] Park was succeeded by J. W. Spurrier, Richard Preston, and Edward Bullock, whose tenure ended in 1849. In 1851 G. K. Rickards was appointed, rapidly succeeded by James Stephen. F. C. J. Hearnshaw, *The Centenary History of King's College, London, 1828–1928* (1929).

[61] King's also offered courses for students intending to go to India: see P. Mitchell, 'Law and India at King's College, London,' in A. D. E. Lewis, P. Brand, and P. Mitchell *Law in the City: Proceedings of the Seventeenth British Legal History Conference, London, 2005* (Dublin, 2007), 262–82.

[62] Pue, 'Guild Training vs. Professional Legal Education', 264–83.

2. 1860–1914

Introduction

For 60 years after the Inns of Court Commission there was an ongoing debate about the professional education of lawyers, punctuated by proposals to give it a more 'scientific' basis.[63] Scarcely anyone disputed the need for an apprenticeship of several years acquiring the practical skills of the trade, though some ardent advocates of chambers education for barristers ignored the inconvenient fact that it was not actually prescribed for them: indeed Bethell had been moved to call for a written examination on learning that a head of chambers was prepared to certify the fitness of a pupil he had met only once—at the Derby.[64] The disputes were over whether in addition to this, the apprentice should be taught law 'on scientific principles'. Only thus, it was argued, could English law be developed as a science and catch up with continental countries and the United States.[65] The publication of Austin's lectures and Maine's *Ancient Law* put broad jurisprudential and historical perspectives firmly back on the agenda[66] and the revival of law teaching at the universities, however limited in scope and popularity, produced a select body of eminent scholars.[67]

Not everyone agreed that English law did or could (unless codified) possess a scientific character, feeling that the student could only follow Tennyson's Leolin in

> Mastering the lawless science of our law,
> That codeless myriad of precedent,
> That wilderness of single instances,
> Through which a few, by wit or fortune led,
> May beat a pathway out to wealth and fame.[68]

No lectures could guide through that labyrinth nor examination test proficiency. It was, however, becoming a less tenable position as a new generation of textbooks

---

[63] The best account is R. Abel-Smith and R. Stevens, *Lawyers and the Courts* (1967), 63–76, 165–80.

[64] A. S. Strahan, *The Bench and the Bar in England* (1919), 121–2.

[65] See below, p. 1188 and C. W. Brooks and M. Lobban, *Idea of a Law University*.

[66] Cocks, *Foundations of the Modern Bar*, 106–13.

[67] Lawson, *Oxford Law School*, 33–60; Abel-Smith and Stevens, *Lawyers and the Courts*, 165–8.

[68] Quoted in W. B. Odgers, 'The Work of a School of Law' (1903) 19 *LQR* 55–70 at 65. Cf. *RC on the Proposed Gresham University, Evidence, PP* 1894 [C. 7425], xxiv, James Bryce (q. 16,844.): 'at present, such is the unsystematic character of the form of our English laws that a man rolls himself about in a heap of cases in the hope that some may stick to him'.

reduced even the jungles of criminal law and torts to a semblance of principled coherence.[69]

Questions of what students should learn, however, remained inextricably mixed with severely practical ones. Where should this teaching take place? Should it remain within the walls of the inns and the Law Society, or should part or all of it be given at the universities or at some new institution? And if the latter, what measure of control should the professional bodies have over the syllabus, teaching and examination? If only 'theoretical' subjects were suitable for a university, which were the 'theoretical' ones and which the 'practical'? Was that a real distinction or was the difference merely in how they were taught?[70] And was the same education appropriate for solicitors and barristers?: should the educational apartheid be perpetuated? And what provision ought to be made for the amateur, the 'pheasant shooter' who wanted a smattering of law to assist him as a JP or MP and to gratify himself with the title of barrister at law?[71]

Given the complexity of the subject and the number and strength of the vested interests engaged, it is not surprising that there was no clear resolution. In terms of structural changes the reformers were on the whole unsuccessful. Barristers and solicitors continued to be educated separately; their education continued to be controlled by their professional bodies even when it was in reality undertaken by crammers; the universities' role remained peripheral and the dominant ethos both at the bar and among solicitors was still essentially a practical and pragmatic one.[72] Yet there were changes. The inns had to accept compulsory examinations; university law studies entitled law graduates to exemptions, albeit small and grudging ones; perhaps the syllabuses even of 'practical' subjects became rather more systematic and 'scientific'. But few leading scholars would have shared Holdsworth's view that English legal education could hardly have been improved.[73]

---

[69] Compare *RC on Gresham University Evidence*, C. E. Pollock (q. 21,392) with Sir Charles Bowen (q. 24,392). See also Cocks, *Foundations of the Modern Bar*, 116–18.

[70] In evidence to the Gresham University Commission, W. R. Anson, holding the latter view, admitted he was in the minority (qq. 20,483, 20,603), but Dicey seems to have agreed with him (q. 17,159).

[71] *RC on Gresham University, Evidence*, Sir C. E. Pollock at q. 21,383. Abel-Smith and Stevens, *Lawyers and the Courts*, 75 mistakenly apply this to solicitors rather than country gentlemen. There was also concern to ensure that colonial administrators knew some law.

[72] Typical perhaps was the insistence of the *Law Times* that what was wanted was 'less Oxford professor and more practitioner in our education' (quoted in (1896) 15 *LN* 6).

[73] *The Holmes–Laski Letters*, ed. M. de W. Howe (Oxford, 1953), 1390. This remark was made in 1932, but there had been few changes of significance since Holdsworth's similarly sanguine views in *HEL*, xv, 232–48.

A 'General School of Law'

The most ambitious of the schemes to reconstruct legal education was Roundell Palmer's, and the vehicle was the Legal Education Association, formed by a small group of provincial solicitors who aspired to create a common initial stage of education for both legal professions.[74] Their organization was in place by 1867, but only assumed centre stage in 1870, when Palmer outlined its programme and progress.[75]

Palmer claimed a formidable range of supporters. Several judges lent their countenance[76] and he produced a petition signed by 18 QCs and more than 400 barristers.[77] Though the Law Society council was unfavourable, the membership forced it into line with the welcoming stance of the MPLA and sundry local law societies,[78] and while the senate of London University demurred to the proposed award of degrees, Oxford and Cambridge were in favour.[79] Palmer had even persuaded the benchers of the Inner Temple and Gray's to endorse the principle[80] although his plans were calculated 'to effect a complete revolution in the study of jurisprudence in England'.[81] Unlike earlier proposals, Palmer's 'National School or University of Law' would not be confined to the bar but would open its doors to would-be solicitors and those with no professional aspirations. It would deliver a legal education upon a 'broad and liberal' plan to match what was offered in Germany and other continental nations.[82] It would not only provide the teaching but would set and administer compulsory examinations which would be the only route into either legal profession. It would be governed by a senate drawn from all the main constituencies, and while it would eventually be financed by the fees

---

[74] Abel-Smith and Stevens, *Lawyers and the Courts*, 72. It was given impetus by a paper delivered by a 'brilliant and imaginative' Liverpool solicitor, W. A. Jevons: Cocks, *Foundations of the Modern Bar*, 113.

[75] 'The Legal Education Association' (1870–1) 30 (s3) *LM & LR* 126–40. 'The Meeting in Middle Temple Hall' (1871–2) 52 *LT* 76, updated the position.

[76] At the meeting of 1871 he was flanked by Sir John Wickens VC and Sir Edward Ryan of the JCPC.

[77] George Jessel claimed many were either not practising or held teaching posts: *PD* 1871 (s3) 208: 239.

[78] Abel-Smith and Stevens, *Lawyers and the Courts*, 72. The patrician element in the ILS remained opposed, see e.g. G. B. Gregory, *PD* 1872 (s3) 209: 1248.

[79] 'The Meeting in Middle Temple Hall', 76. Maine, Bryce, Digby, Bernard, and Abdy were all supporters. For the composition of its council see *RC on Gresham University, Evidence*, J. W. Longbourne, q. 16,976.

[80] *Ibid.* The inns were perhaps alarmed at the strength and persistence of criticism from several quarters: Cocks, *Foundations of the Modern Bar*, 120–1.

[81] 'Legal Education Association', 126.

[82] For an explicit reference to Germany see Lord Selborne, *Memorials Part Two: Personal and Political*, 2 vols (1898), i, 49.

of the students, the inns would be asked for some initial funding.[83] True, Palmer had to admit that a committee of the inns ('by a small majority') had reported against it,[84] but a scheme so strongly supported and so much in keeping with developments in other professions seemed to have every chance of success.

And yet nothing came of it. Despite the backing of Lord Chancellor Hatherley, the Liberal government declined to support it[85] and in 1872 resolutions were defeated in the Commons in a debate so monopolized by lawyers as to indicate apathy among laymen.[86] When Palmer became Lord Chancellor he was too preoccupied with the Judicature Bill to renew the attempt and when under the Conservative government he did introduce bills they failed to progress. Lacking government backing and with barrister supporters defecting, Selborne eventually abandoned the project.[87]

He ruefully attributed his failure to three causes.[88] In ascending order of importance they were; first, the hostility of London University and its law teaching colleges to this 'monster establishment', which threatened to eclipse their puny efforts;[89] secondly, the 'suspicious conservatism of the inns of court', whose benchers were indisposed to transfer any powers even to a body solely comprising their own members, much less to any outsiders;[90] the third, (a particular manifestation of the second), was a rooted objection to any combined education with solicitors. The justification was that most articled clerks would be several years younger than bar students and would not be 'varsity men'. This gulf

[83] *PD* 1871 (s3) 207: 1491–1500. The speech in 1872 (209: 1221–38) elaborated on some points but was still criticized for vagueness. The General School of Law Bill in 1874 met some of these criticisms.

[84] 'Meeting in Middle Temple Hall', 76.

[85] Gladstone's speech on Palmer's resolutions of 1872 was a temporizing one: *PD* 1872 (s3) 209: 1289–93.

[86] Sir George Denman, *ibid.*, 175. This led Gathorne Hardy to claim to speak against the resolution 'as a country gentleman' (176), but he was also a bencher of the Inner Temple. Palmer claimed the first set of resolutions were introduced only 'to break ground' and were not intended to be pressed to a vote ('Meeting in Middle Temple Hall', 77). Those of 1872 were lost by 116 to 103.

[87] *PD* 1874 (s3) 220: 1457–70; 1875 (s3) 224: 4–17; 1876 (s3) 228: 1892–4; 1877 (s3) 233: 104–5. The LEA was wound up and its remaining funds given to the Law Society: A. M. Carr-Saunders and H. Wilson, *The Professions* (1933), 50.

[88] *Memorials, Personal and Political*, i, 50. Solicitors became less enthusiastic about the project once the Law Society had gained control of their examinations in 1877: *RC on Gresham University, Evidence*, R. R. Pennington, q. 15,862.

[89] Sir F. Goldsmid, *PD* 1872 (s3) 209: 1262; J. H. Baker, *University College and Legal Education*, 6; W. L. Twining, 'Laws', in *The University of London and the World of Learning*, ed. F. M. L. Thompson (1990), 81–114 at 95–6.

[90] In public Selborne professed that the inns were 'of all the institutions in the world, the most completely open and accessible to reform' ('Meeting in Middle Temple Hall', 79). For a good instance of the attitude of the more reactionary benchers see J. Locke, *PD* 1872 (s3) 209: 1249–54. He felt that any sort of academic education with examinations would produce men who were clever rather than lively, and fatuously declared, 'Cicero was not examined before he pleaded'.

in education would make it impossible to teach them together. There were also fears that the clerks would 'swamp' the bar students by sheer numbers, and of course social snobbery underlay some of the objections.[91] A common education was also suspected of being a stalking horse for fusion of the professions, and though Selborne repeatedly and vehemently repudiated that aim, opponents did not scruple to play upon such fears.[92]

All this was true, but a fourth, crucial factor was the attitude of Lord Cairns, since only the bipartisan collaboration between the two Lord Chancellors had made the Judicature Acts possible. Selborne had thought Cairns 'favourable to the principle, though cautious in pressing it',[93] but it transpired that his views were far less ambitious. Cairns wanted the 'school of law' to be purely an examining body overseeing education provided by others, arguing that as a teaching institution it would either fail to get started through lack of funds or, if successful, would annihilate others, particularly the inns.[94] Moreover, while Selborne wanted to turn the inns into corporations, democratize them, and unite them under a single governing body, Cairns was content with something along the lines of the Oxbridge reforms, concerned only to ensure that neither individually nor collectively could they renege on their educational obligations and that the machinery for disciplining errant barristers was satisfactory.[95] In pursuit of this limited aim he made concession after concession,[96] at length extracting their reluctant consent to a bill creating a council composed only of barristers and a handful of crown appointees, but even that bill was mysteriously abandoned.[97] Against all expectations, the inns had fought off the threat to their autonomy as well as the indignity of being yoked to the inferior branch in teaching and examinations.

There was, however, a price to be paid. For 20 years there had been a stand-off within the inns between the advocates of compulsory examinations and their

---

[91] See e.g. Jessel (*PD* 1871 (s3) 208: 247–8) and Gathorne Hardy (1872 (s3) 209: 1279–80).

[92] Holdsworth's view was that Selborne did not appreciate how intimately bound up the two aims were, but his arguments are hardly convincing: *HEL*, xv, 246.

[93] *Memorials Personal and Political*, i, 50.

[94] *PD* 1874 (s3) 220: 1466–9.

[95] Cairns had persuaded Selborne to divide his measures into two separate bills, but after supporting his Inns of Court Bill (*PD* 1875 (s3) 224: 1891–4) he announced in the next session that the inns were preparing a bill of their own: *PD* 1876 (s3) 228: 1893.

[96] The negotiations can be followed in *Lincoln's Inn Black Books*, v, 200, 202, 208 and *PD* 1877 (s3) 233: 1250–62.

[97] Bar Education and Discipline Bill, *PD* 1877 (s3) 236: 787; Abel-Smith and Stevens, *Lawyers and the Courts*, 75; 'The Present Education of Solicitors' (1877) 52 n.s. *Westminster Rev.*, 101–26. Cairns disingenuously justified abandoning his earlier insistence that there should be a single authority regulating education for both branches by claiming that it was inappropriate for solicitors to be involved with questions of bar discipline: *PD* 1877 (s3) 233: 1253–4.

opponents. The latter included not only notorious reactionaries but luminaries such as Coleridge, who thought any attempt to teach English law by lectures was delusory, and Jessel, and they suffered a 'death-bed conversion' only when faced with the greater evil of the school of law.[98] The inns could now plead that their new system should be given a chance to prove itself and that, more than anything, probably saved them.[99] The examinations proved no barrier to the determined student, especially once the coaches and crammers got busy, nor did the Council of Legal Education emulate the Law Society in manipulating examinations to control numbers.[100] But there was one notable change. Except at Gray's, the proportion of calls to admissions rose significantly, while admissions fell.[101] The amateur element so cherished by the traditionalists was in decline and this was part of a more elusive change in the bar's own self-image and sense of distinctiveness. For all its boasted singularities it now looked more like other professions, and in the face of emphatic declarations by both Selborne and Cairns it was no longer possible to maintain the pretence that the inns were purely private societies, immune from state interference in the performance of their public functions.[102] That much at least the LEA had achieved.

Later efforts to revive the idea of a general school of law fared no better. It was vigorously urged by Lord Chief Justice Russell in the mid-1890s but he made no headway.[103] One of the most forthright opponents was Lord Halsbury, who did as much as anyone to defeat a more promising initiative promoted by the Attorney-General, Sir Robert Finlay, with the support of the Law Society and occasioned by the windfall of funds from the dissolution of the last two inns of Chancery.[104] Although a joint committee of the inns and the Law Society agreed on a plan for a charter, it needed only one inn to object for the proposal to fail and even if the probably spurious legal challenge to the use of Grays' Inn funds for the purpose could be seen off, the Inner Temple, where Halsbury was highly influential and staunchly opposed any 'system of which we know nothing' displacing one

---

[98] Sir G. O. Morgan (*PD* 1872 (s3) 209: 1240). Since the recommendation for compulsory examinations was in the committee report which rejected the LEA proposals the link was transparent and was admitted by Jessel: *Lincoln's Inn Black Books* v, 167–8; *PD*. 1872 (s3) 209: 1284.

[99] Petition of, and letter to Cairns, 19 January1874, *Lincoln's Inn Black Books*, v, 188. The new scheme was said to have been kept secret all through the long vacation: 'The New Scheme of Education for the Bar' (1872–3) 54 *LT* 33.

[100] R. Abel, *The Legal Profession in England and Wales* (1988), 42.

[101] W. C. Richardson, *A History of the Inns of Court* (Baton Rouge, 1975), 346.

[102] Selborne was more emphatic than Cairns, see e.g. *PD* 1877 (s3) 233: 104–5.

[103] R. B. O'Brien, *The Life of Lord Russell of Killowen* (1903 edn), 275–8; Cocks, *Foundations of the Modern Bar*, 191–4. The support of the *Law Times* was of doubtful value, since its editor, F. O. Crump, was engaged in a controversial attack on the Bar Committee: *ibid.*, 216–19.

[104] Abel-Smith and Stevens, *Lawyers and the Courts*, 174–6, and see Inns of Chancery above, pp. 1087–8.

responsible for a legal system which was 'the admiration of the world', could not be won over.[105]

Although this was an example of 'conservatism triumphant',[106] it should not be assumed that the general school of law was the best way to raise the intellectual tone of the education of English lawyers through the study of principles of jurisprudence, history, and comparative law. It is not necessary to adopt Holdsworth's rather complacent preference for adapting existing institutions[107] to share Cairns's doubts whether such a body would finance itself through student fees, since it had the extremely demanding task of providing what students wanted in order to pass their professional examinations either at a more attractive rate or on more appealing terms than its commercial or academic rivals, while also persuading enough men to subscribe to classes in the less practical subjects. C. R. Kennedy had failed ignominiously to achieve that at Queen's College, Birmingham in the 1850s[108] and though a London school would have a large pool of potential students (and teachers) to draw upon, the competitors were formidable, and most articled clerks (and many aspiring barristers) were understandably hard-headed and instrumental in seeking only the knowledge they felt professionally useful.

London University

Other initiatives emerged as by-products of a protracted series of wrangles over the future of London University and in particular of proposals for a 'university of the professors', an institution catering for full-time college-based students rather than what London University essentially was, an examining body for external degrees.[109] While law was a peripheral subject at the old universities it was considered essential to the success of this proposal, but the enfeebled state of law teaching at University College and King's College made the creation of a credible law faculty highly doubtful without the active participation of the Law Society and, more particularly, the inns.[110] Neither was attracted by the first proposal, the 'Albert Charter', floated in 1884 by an 'Association for Promoting a Teaching University for London',[111] but the better supported plan for a 'Gresham University' a few years later was given cautious acceptance in principle by the

---

[105] *Ibid.*, 175–6.

[106] *Ibid.*, 165, the title of their chapter.

[107] *HEL*, xv, 244–7.

[108] Pue, 'Guild Training versus Professional Education'. Kennedy's failure was, however, due in part to his notoriety and the professional views which made him unpopular with solicitors.

[109] Twining, 'Laws'.

[110] *RC on the Gresham University, Evidence*, Sir G. Young, q. 10,880, M. H. Crackanthorpe, q. 12,918. The Commission agreed: *Report*, PP 1893–4 [C. 7259], xxxi, p.xvii.

[111] Abel-Smith and Stevens, *Lawyers and the Courts*, 172.

Law Society. The inns, however, disdained even to enter into discussions.[112] In the event the idea of a new university was discarded in favour of a comprehensive review of the operations and structures of the existing one. Legal witnesses left the Commission in no doubt how difficult it was to persuade the inns to act co-operatively in anything[113] and how jealously they would defend their monopoly of bar education, entry, and discipline. Even so, most witnesses felt that under pressure of public opinion, backed if necessary by the threat of coercion, the inns might be induced to accept the degree or certificate of the university as a test of the 'theoretical knowledge' in the 'more general branches of law' required for the bar, provided that they were given a 'leading position' on the body which designed syllabuses and set examinations.[114]

They were wrong. For once the inns did speak with one voice, and rejected out of hand the proposals made to them in those terms. And they did so with impunity, for the Commissioners' threat that 'other steps' might be necessary to secure their co-operation carried no real menace while Halsbury was on the Woolsack and the bar so strongly represented in Parliament.[115]

A further attempt to link the professional schools and London University came in 1910 in the course of yet another attempt to rationalize the university's tangled constitution.[116] This Commission was chaired by Haldane and the parts dealing with law studies clearly bear the imprint of his thinking.[117] Haldane did not even waste time taking evidence from the inns,[118] and his questioning of Law Society witnesses was mostly directed at persuading them to explore the possibility of establishing an 'organic connection' which would infuse something of the 'university spirit' into their students.[119] He had little success, and there was equally strong resistance to the universities' attempts to secure exemptions from

---

[112] *Ibid.; RC on the Gresham University, Evidence*, Crackanthorpe, q. 12,950.

[113] e.g. Lord Coleridge CJ, q. 22,114, Sir Horace Davey, q. 18,212.

[114] Quotations are from the *RC on the Gresham University Report 1894*, xxviii. Among the witnesses who broadly shared this view were Sir John Rigby (Solicitor-General), Sir Richard Webster, Montagu Crackanthorpe QC, and Sir William Rann Kennedy. However, Frederick Pollock was 'not at all sanguine about the actions of the Inns of Court' (q. 16,206).

[115] *Report of Commissioners Appointed under the University of London Act 1898, PP* 1900 [Cd. 83], lxvi, para. 3; Abel-Smith and Stevens, *Lawyers and the Courts*, 173–4.

[116] Abel-Smith and Stevens, *Lawyers and the Courts*, 178–80.

[117] *RC on London University, First Report and Evidence, PP* 1910 (Cd. 5166), xxiii; *Third Report*, App., *PP* 1911 (Cd. 5911), xx; *Final Report and Evidence, PP* 1913 (Cd. 6717, 6718), xl. Haldane had been closely involved in an earlier attempt to reorganize the university; his account is in *Richard Burdon Haldane: An Autobiography* (1929), 124–7.

[118] The Commission used the evidence in the *RC on the Gresham University: Final Report 1913*, para. 332 and questioned Sir H. H. Cozens-Hardy MR.

[119] *Appendix to Final Report 1913*, qq. 15,836–16,050, esp. qq. 15,939 *et seq*. The Law Society's witnesses included Edward Jenks and Sir Albert Rollit.

professional examinations for subjects in which their syllabuses and questions were essentially similar.[120]

The report did break new ground[121] by departing from the insistence of Selborne and his followers that the way to escape the obsessive focus on 'practical training' was to integrate the philosophical and the practical in one course of study. Rather it espoused functional specialization, accepting Barrington's view that 'it is not the business of the university to turn out practising barristers or solicitors'.[122] University law study would ideally be postgraduate, taught outside the hours articled clerks and pupils would be spending in chambers. But though the report invited the inns to 'carefully consider' reviewing their approach to bar training, it must be doubted whether the chairman held much hope that they would.[123]

As for law at London University, since it was inadequately manned and funded to form a faculty, it was recommended that it be concentrated on one site, preferably King's College.[124] For the near future at least, most students would still be taking the external degree;[125] all teaching would take place in the evening, and the professional bodies would still exercise a sway over the syllabus and teaching through their powerful representation on senate.[126]

---

[120] The Law Society exempted holders of law degrees from the intermediate examination (other than accounts and book-keeping), while the bar gave exemption only for Roman Law. Both Oxford and Cambridge (through Professors Geldart and Kenny respectively) were anxious to widen this, as was Cecil Barrington for London. For Law Society resistance see *Appendix to Final Report, 1913*, qq. 15,856–76.

[121] Or rather, it reverted to the ideas of the 1846 Commission: Twining, 'Laws', 84.

[122] *Appendix to Third Report, 1911*, q. 6304; *Final Report, 1913*, paras 333–7; Abel-Smith and Stevens, *Lawyers and the Courts*, 179–80.

[123] *Final Report, 1913*, para. 336. Haldane had told Barrington, 'you are very sanguine about the power of the Government of this country' when the latter was suggesting that the inns might be compelled to make changes (*Appendix to Third Report*, q. 6308, and see qq. 6309–11).

[124] 349*Final Report, 1913*, para. 330. Since 1908 UC, King's, and the LSE had pooled their teaching for the Ll.B. Birkbeck's courses were too short to be acceptable: *Appendix to Third Report, 1911*, G. Armitage-Smith, qq. 9841–53; G. W. Keeton, 'University College, London, and the Law' (1939) 51 *JR* 118–33.

[125] The internal degree had been in existence only a few years and of 50 students taking Ll.B. finals in 1909 all but six were external candidates. UC had mustered just nine graduates in the previous 14 years (Baker, *University College and Legal Education*, 8). The Law Society favoured the external degree: *Appendix to Final Report, 1913*, q. 15,836.

[126] *First Report 1910, Evidence*, Cozens-Hardy, q. 1110; *Appendix to Third Report, 1911*, Barrington at q. 6333. Though the professional bodies had been given this representation largely in the hope of persuading them to become part of the university, they had no hesitation in making use of it. For example they vetoed a proposed course in the Constitutional Laws of the British Empire as unfair to external students because of the want of a suitable textbook.

Professional Education for Barristers

The Council for Legal Education set up by the inns in 1852 to create a uniform system for the legal education of students before admission to the bar hardly lived up to its high-sounding title.[127] Comprising two men from each inn, serving for two years, it was for a long time either supine or ineffectual. The Inns of Court Commission highlighted glaring weaknesses in the teaching the Council administered, and it had not been allowed to implement its crucial recommendation for compulsory examinations.[128] Its want of authority made the inns vulnerable to Cairns's demands for structural reform[129] and only heavy criticism in the late 1880s roused it from lethargy. Two influential and enterprising members, Nathaniel Lindley and J. C. Mathew, led the way, and although the Middle Temple vetoed a modest proposal for a few outsiders on the council, Lindley secured its enlargement to 20 members, with a high-powered board of studies in support, and an expansion of the range of teaching,[130] though even after the addition of a director of studies as a sort of 'dean of the faculty' in 1905,[131] it still had no authority to impose major changes.

In 1872 the inns had agreed to institute a preliminary examination akin to the Law Society's.[132] Being limited to non-matriculates, relatively few had to sit it and the high failure rate at first attempt suggests that some had not taken it seriously,[133] since it was later described as 'absurdly simple';[134] indeed by 1910 it was said to have become farcical, and the CLE successfully pressed for its replacement by prescriptive external qualifications.[135]

The revised scheme of 1873 for teaching law to bar students looked good on paper. The new lecturers would, it was hoped, be younger and would also undertake small group teaching.[136] Appointed for only three years, they would have the incentive of an attendance-related payment, while scholarships for proficiency

---

[127] Abel-Smith and Stevens, *Lawyers and the Courts*, 65–6.
[128] *Lincoln's Inn Black Books*, v, 59–60; Richardson, *Inns of Court*, 337–8.
[129] Richardson, *Inns of Court*, 347.
[130] Abel-Smith and Stevens, *Lawyers and the Courts*, 171.
[131] H. D. Hazeltine, 'The Present State of Legal Education in England' (1910) 26 *LQR* 17–39 at 20. W. Blake Odgers was 'a great favourite among the students' according to T. E. Crispe, *Reminiscences of a KC* (2nd edn, 1909), 206.
[132] Abel-Smith and Stevens, *Lawyers and the Courts*, 68. R. Abel (*The Legal Profession in England and Wales* (1988), 41) seems to be mistaken in dating it from 1888. The subjects were English language, Latin, and English History.
[133] Abel, *Legal Profession*, 41.
[134] J. A. Shearwood, *A Guide for Candidates for the Professions of Barrister and Solicitor* (2nd edn, 1887), 30.
[135] (1910) 29 *LN* 118; *Lincoln's Inn Black Books*, v, 79–82, 377–8.
[136] A. Edgar, 'The New Scheme of Education for the Bar' (1873) 2 (n.s.) *LM & LR* 62–7 expected it to be 'the sheet-anchor of the new scheme' (64).

(albeit only in Roman Law and Jurisprudence) would give a similar incentive to students.[137] As Cairns had wished,[138] the examinations were not too demanding, and though the failure rate was initially considerable—attributed by one commentator to university men arrogantly attempting to pass without serious study—it soon fell.[139]

Having secured the goal of a compulsory examination, the CLE lapsed into a complacency from which it was only aroused in 1889, when a committee of Lincoln's Inn issued a damning report.[140] Since 1873 'the system of Education has gradually been undergoing alteration for the worse, until it has been brought into a condition which is deplorable, and we feel bound to add is unworthy of the Inns of Court'.[141] Three well-paid lecturers delivered the bare minimum of lectures, and while one of the pair who shared the fourth lectureship discoursed amply on Roman Law, the other had to cover Public and Private International Law, Constitutional Law, Legal History, and Jurisprudence in the same allotted 18 hours.[142] None supplemented their lectures with smaller classes,[143] and most made no attempt to relate their course to the examinations.[144] Not surprisingly, most students, though contributing six guineas towards their cost, deserted them, attendances falling by between 6 and 8 per cent.[145] Instead they resorted to the crammers, who 'impart for a small fee, as nearly as may be, the exact amount of information which is required for a pass, and neither more nor less'.[146]

Fortuitously, the proposals for a 'Gresham charter' revived anxieties about outside intervention and although the reformers on the Council did not get all they wanted, they did secure major changes in the educational structure. The examination was divided into two parts. The first, taken at any time after admission, comprised Roman Law, Constitutional Law, and Legal History; Criminal Law and Procedure; and Real Property and Conveyancing.[147] Part Two, taken

---

[137] *Ibid.*, 66.

[138] *PD* 1876–7 (s3) 62: 444.

[139] Abel, *Legal Profession*, table 1.1; W.W. Rouse Ball, *A Student's Guide to the Bar* (3rd edn, 1884), 26–8, and cf. the 1st edn of 1879 quoted in Cocks, *Foundations of the Modern Bar*, 181–2. There was a noticeable rise in the pass rate of both Roman Law and Constitutional Law and Legal History in 1888.

[140] *RC on the Gresham University, Evidence*, M. H. Crackanthorpe, q. 12,866.

[141] *Lincoln's Inn Black Books*, v, 262–5.

[142] *Ibid.*

[143] This was encouraged, but not required: *ibid.*, 262.

[144] It was probably a mistake on the CLE's part to choose respected but elderly QCs such as A. S. Eddis and C. C. Barber: Strahan, *Bench and Bar of England*, 126–9.

[145] *Lincoln's Inn Black Books*, v, 263–4.

[146] *Ibid.*, 265.

[147] As an alternative to the last, Hindu and Mohammedan Law or Roman-Dutch Law might be taken. The former had been discontinued in 1874 (*Lincoln's Inn Black Books*, v, 186) but was revived

only after at least six terms had been kept, comprised papers in Common Law, Equity, Evidence, and Civil Procedure, and a general paper drawn from all these subjects.

The *Law Times* asserted that the inclusion of teachers among the examiners would make the examinations a farce,[148] but in fact the failure rate was well above the former level, stabilizing at around 30 per cent from 1908 until a sharp rise to over 40 per cent in 1913.[149] This is curious, for the questions were essentially tests of memory.[150] Contemporaries regarded bar examinations as easier than the Law Society's finals[151] and Oxford and Cambridge professors insisted that they were not on par with their own—hence their indignation that, with the grudging exception of Roman Law, the inns would not exempt candidates from subjects passed at university.[152]

The basis of the teaching was still lectures,[153] and by 1914 the lecturers (all part-time) included some very gifted men and others with great experience.[154] Attendance was not compulsory, but most men found it prudent because it was known that the examinations would be based upon the lectures.[155] Nevertheless, it was still possible to succeed by a burst of intensive private study, with or without a coach.[156]

in 1892 (*ibid.*, 290). Money from the dissolution of the inns of Chancery (see above) was used to provide teaching in these subjects (*RC on London University, Evidence*, Sir H. H. Cozens-Hardy, q. 1011) and the CLE classes in the latter proved fatal to the subject at UC: *ibid.*, T. G. Foster at qq. 1808–17.

[148] (1893–4) 96 *LT* 383.

[149] Abel, *Legal Profession*, table 1.1.

[150] Abel-Smith and Stevens, *Lawyers and the Courts*, 171. The *viva voce* element became very perfunctory and was dropped sometime before 1910: *RC on the Gresham University Evidence*, Crackanthorpe, q. 12,910; Hazeltine, 'Present State of Legal Education in England', 26.

[151] Gibson and Weldon, who prepared candidates for both, described the Law Society finals as 'the hardest law examination in England, probably in the world' (1889) 8 *LN* 131.

[152] *RC on the Gresham University, Evidence*, T. E. Holland (esp. q. 18,375); *RC on London University, Evidence*, W. M. Geldart, C. S. Kenny and C. Barrington. The big influx of overseas students, many of them from India, may have depressed pass rates (Strahan, *Bench and Bar of England*, 226–7; Abel, *Legal Profession*, 43–4), but Frederic Harrison, who was an examiner, claimed they were remarkably good at examinations (*Autobiographic Memoirs*, 2 vols (1911), i, 329–31) and Chan Toon, from Burma, carried off all the prizes in 1888.

[153] Hazeltine, *Present State of Legal Education in England*, 31; Strahan, *Bench and Bar in England*, 133.

[154] Strahan, *Bench and Bar in England*, 129; B. Lailey, *Jottings From a Fee Book* (Portsmouth, 1932), 17. The Haldane Commission criticised the CLE for having lecturers teach more than one subject (*Final Report 1913*, para. 335).

[155] E. Jenks, 'Possibilities in Legal Education' (1907) 23 *LQR* 266–81 at 273; *Lincoln's Inn Black Books*, v, 290; Hazeltine, *Present State of Legal Education in England*, 27, a practice deplored by F. M. Pollock at 29 n.1.

[156] As Patrick Hastings did: *Autobiography of Sir Patrick Hastings* (1948), 57–8.

Professional Education for Solicitors

A preliminary examination was introduced by the Solicitors Act 1860 following pressure from the MPLA.[157] It sought to ensure that candidates had a sound general education, initially testing them in Latin, French, English, History, Geography, and Arithmetic.[158] For those who complacently believed that the educational (and with it, the social) standard of the profession had reached a gratifyingly respectable level, the early results came as a rude shock.[159] Moreover, the failure rate would probably have been higher but for Chief Baron Kelly's indiscriminate granting of exemptions in 'special circumstances'.[160] So impervious was he to complaints that the Law Society resorted to legislation shortly before his resignation, though in the event the judges readily yielded control over exemptions to the Society and after that the backdoor to qualification was seldom opened.[161]

Before long, however, and despite a noticeable increase in the failure rate, there were demands for a higher standard.[162] The difficulty with that, however, was that statute granted entry through alternative qualifications, some of which, particularly the Oxford and Cambridge locals, were reckoned unduly easy.[163] Eventually the Law Society, having satisfied itself that this was so,[164] began the process of securing the repeal of the least demanding exemptions, something not accomplished until 1922.[165]

At the same time as the preliminary, an intermediate examination was introduced, whose only real purpose seems to have been to ensure that articled clerks acquired some substantive legal knowledge during their term. From 1895 university law degrees afforded exemption[166] and until 1901 it could not be taken until the halfway stage in articles, thereafter after one year. It was a rather sterile affair.

---

[157] Solicitors Act 1860 (23 & 24 Vict. c. 127), s. 8; (1857–8) 2 *Sol. J.* 977.

[158] Abel, *Legal Profession*, 157–8. By 1892 any two from a list of languages might be chosen, and algebra substituted for one paper: *RC on the Gresham University, Evidence*, Pennington, q. 15,719.

[159] Abel, *Legal Profession*, table 2.10, showing a pass rate of 72% for the first year. It then rose into the mid-80s, but fell back to the 70s from 1867. M. Birks, *Gentlemen of the Law* (1960), 238.

[160] Between 1877 and 1879 Kelly granted 217 applications, the other three chiefs 35.

[161] A bill was lost with the dissolution of 1880 and Kelly resigned soon afterwards: (1880) 69 *LT* 49, 180. Abel, *Legal Profession*, 158.

[162] H. Kirk, *Portrait of a Profession* (1976), 58. Jenks said they hoped to raise it to the level of the London matriculation: *RC on London University Evidence*, q. 15,842.

[163] Solicitors Act 1860, ss 5, 9. Gibson and Weldon were emphatic about this (see e.g. (1893) 12 *LN* 22, and many annual reviews of examination results thereafter).

[164] Abel, *Legal Profession*, 158–60. Figures produced for the Law Society showed that pass rates for the locals were lower than for the Law Society examinations (*ibid.*, table 2.11), but it does not follow that the preliminary was made progressively more difficult in this period as Abel suggests (160), since he admits the quality of candidates may have decreased.

[165] (1911) 30 *LN* 226.

[166] Abel, *Legal Profession*, 144.

Candidates had to answer 30 questions based entirely on Stephen's *Commentaries*, which was ideal material for the crammers,[167] and until the 1880s pass rates were very high. However, it became measurably stiffer, helped by the enlargement of the syllabus in 1904,[168] and with a further infusion of rigour in 1908 pass rates dropped into the low 60s.[169] In addition, there was an examination in accounts and book-keeping, but this was dropped in 1871 and not reinstated until 1906 (presumably as part of the Law Society's measures against solicitor defalcations). Unsurprisingly, it too had a high failure rate.[170]

The syllabus for the final examination changed little and important new areas such as company law and revenue law found no place. Four papers spread over two days and comprising 60 questions in all covered property and conveyancing; equity; common law; and an unsatisfactory miscellany of criminal justice, probate, divorce, Admiralty, and ecclesiastical law.[171] Once the Law Society had won control of the syllabus and the examinations in 1877 there was no room for 'theoretical' subjects and the questions continued to be of a severely practical kind.[172] A candidate did not need to pass each subject,[173] but his task evidently became harder, for the pass rate dropped back into the 70s during the 1880s, then into the 60s from 1900, remaining obstinately within that decile despite the best efforts of crammers and Law Society teachers alike.[174]

The Law Society faced a particular difficulty in meeting the needs of articled clerks both in London and the provinces. One president later claimed that 'in my time it was considered to be a reflection upon a man if he got assistance to pass his final examinations',[175] but even though the examination was eminently passable, by 1860 there were many candidates with little faith in the Society's lectures. 'Crammers' came forward to meet the need[176] and while the establishment might deplore this 'baneful system',[177] it posed a dilemma for the Society. On the

---

[167] (1893) 12 *LN* 22–7.

[168] Book 4 was added to books 1–3 and 5. Since the number of questions was unchanged this presumably forced candidates to widen their coverage.

[169] Abel, *Legal Profession*, table 2.10 and p.159.

[170] *Ibid.*, and see above, p. 1143.

[171] In 1891 the breakdown was: 15 on conveyancing and property; 15 on equity; 11 on common law; 4 on bankruptcy; 6 on criminal law and magistrates; 3 on probate, 3 on divorce, 2 on Admiralty and 1 on ecclesiastical law.

[172] Abel-Smith and Stevens, *Lawyers and the Courts*, 169.

[173] *RC on the Gresham University, Evidence*, Pennington, q. 15,726.

[174] Abel, *Legal Profession*, 157–63. There was also an optional Honours examination; trends in the pass rate were similar to those in the final examination (*ibid.*, table 2.10).

[175] *RC on the Gresham University, Evidence*, Pennington, q. 15,736.

[176] Abel, *Legal Profession*, 157; Kirk, *Portrait of a Profession*, 60–1.

[177] J. M. Clabon, Law Society president, (1880–1) 69 *LT* 392. Clabon had been a leading figure in the LEA and the Clabon prize was subsequently awarded out of the funds from its dissolution.

one hand it was unwilling to quit the teaching field—especially while pocketing £10,000 a year in examination fees—but on the other 'subsidized teaching'[178] could not compete effectively with the narrowly focused utilitarian service provided by the crammers.[179]

At length, and to the incredulity of observers, the Society conceded defeat, abandoned its lectures, and offered instead a correspondence course with limited tutorial assistance.[180] It was forced into an undignified retreat by a protest from articled clerks and reinstated lectures,[181] but it was not until it created a 'College of Law' in 1903, that it offered the sort of preparation the examinees wanted. Under the direction of Edward Jenks the College appointed suitable teachers and its well-populated classrooms were a marked contrast to earlier lectures.[182] However, with the examination becoming more demanding the crammers were not ousted, for they were able to concentrate on the revision stage while the College classes spanned the clerks' final year.[183] Clerks who attended the College and the best crammers received a sound grounding, but there was no longer any serious attempt to provide a broader legal education; for that they must attend College classes which prepared men for the London University LL.B.[184]

---

[178] So described in 'The Law Society and Articled Clerks' (1892) 11 *LN* 78–81, by Albert Gibson and Arthur Weldon, Chancery Lane solicitors who in 1876 founded the most successful and enduring of the crammers (a term they indignantly repudiated). Their journal, *Law Notes*, provides a valuable perspective on professional and legal developments, since these bodies were never invited to give evidence to inquiries and their teachers were pointedly excluded from the Society of Public Teachers of Law when it was founded in 1908. Gibson and Weldon survived until 1962, when it merged with the College of Law: R. H. Kersley, *Gibson's 1876–1962: A Chapter in Legal Education* (1973).

[179] It was claimed in 1883 that 7/8ths of candidates had attended no Law Society lectures(Kirk, *Portrait of a Profession*, 60); understandable if, as one examiner acknowledged, the lecturers made no attempt to relate their teaching to the examination: *RC on the Gresham University, Evidence*, E. H. Busk, qq. 768–9. The crammers were always fearful lest the Society allowed its lecturers to set the examination, thereby giving students an incentive to prefer its lectures: see e.g. 'The New Lectures' (1892) 11 *LN* 339–44.

[180] *RC on the Gresham University, Evidence*, Pennington, qq. 15,733–40. For criticism see Cozens-Hardy, *ibid.*, q. 22,933, Crackanthorpe, q. 12,924–5 and Longbourne, q. 16,989.

[181] Abel-Smith and Stevens, *Lawyers and the Courts*, 170. Correspondence courses continued and the writer learned his law through those in the 1970s. His colleagues and fellow authors claim always to have suspected as much.

[182] *RC on London University, Evidence*, Law Society witnesses (Jenks included), at q. 15,836; Kirk, *Portrait of a Profession*, 61. Jenks had experience both as professor of law at Liverpool and as a crammer: *RC on the Gresham University Evidence*, q. 24,427.

[183] 'Legal Education' (1903) 22 *LN* 314. According to A. Offer, *Property and Politics, 1870–1914* (1981), 14) some men spent up to £500 on crammers and coaches, but a writer in *The Cornhill Magazine* ('The Solicitors', 13 (n.s.) (1902), 635–50, at 641) reckoned on £25 for finals). There was a noticeable lessening of antagonism towards crammers, see e.g. B. G. Lake's presidential speech to the APM 1898 (1898) 17 *LN* 322.

[184] Hazeltine, *Present State of Legal Education in England*, 25. Jenks himself quirkishly took the Ll.B. in his 49th year and got a first: *ODNB* 29: 991.

The problem for provincial clerks, particularly those who did not spend their final year in London, was getting any useful tuition at all. From the outset some large local law societies, such as Manchester, arranged lectures, but these often had the same defects (from the students' viewpoint) as the London ones.[185] In Liverpool, for example, Bryce and Dicey failed to attract an audience,[186] nor did those hired by the Birmingham Law Society at the urging of the articled clerks.[187]

Once it controlled examinations and collected fees, it became impossible for the Law Society wholly to ignore the needs of the provinces, but it was not feasible to establish a nationwide network of classes.[188] Instead, a series of local arrangements emerged, with varying amounts of financial support from London.[189] The Society's favoured option was boards of studies along the lines pioneered in Yorkshire,[190] but in many places grants had to be given to a local society. The Society had to accept that much of the teaching would be provided by the new universities and university colleges, though it much preferred arrangements which gave the profession influence, if not control, rather than having to trust the dons as at Manchester.[191] By 1910 more than £10,000 per annum was being distributed and more than 400 students were enrolled[192] and with further university expansion envisaged, a Law Society president could even contemplate making attendance at classes a requirement for the examination.[193]

3. LEGAL PERIODICALS

Introduction

It seems probable that legal periodicals played a significant part in imparting law, and more particularly, lawyers' values, to the profession, and yet it has recently

---

[185] 'G.S', 'The Education of Attorneys' (1873) 2 (n.s.) *LM & R* 47–62.

[186] P. H. Williams, *A Gentleman's Calling* (Liverpool, 1980), 270.

[187] George Johnson's lectures, though apparently successful, were discontinued in the mid-1860s (Pue, 'Guild Training vs. Professional Education', 284). The Birmingham Law Society was a strong supporter of the LEA and included among its objects the encouragement of the study of law by articled clerks, but classes were not begun until 1882: A. S. Rowley, *Professions, Class and Society: Solicitors in Nineteenth Century Birmingham* (Ph.D. thesis, Aston University, 1988), 228–72.

[188] Even the congress of law students' societies in 1903 agreed: *Legal Education*, 43–6.

[189] *RC on London University, Evidence*, Law Society, q. 15,836.

[190] The Yorkshire and Liverpool boards were set up in the 1890s, followed shortly by Birmingham: Abel-Smith and Stevens, *Lawyers and the Courts*, 177; Rowley, *Professions, Class and Society*, 264–6.

[191] Abel-Smith, *Lawyers and the Courts*, 178–9.

[192] *Ibid.*, 177; *RC on London University Evidence*, Law Society, q. 15,836.

[193] Abel-Smith and Stevens, *Lawyers and the Courts*, 177. This came about in 1922.

been remarked that 'English legal historians have paid curiously little attention
to the legal periodical'.[194] Curious indeed, since while until the late 1820s they
were few and ephemeral, thereafter they were begun with increasing frequency,
reaching a peak in the 1840s when no fewer than 12 new ones were launched.[195]
The failure rate continued to be very high, but *The Law Magazine*, or *Quarterly
Journal of Jurisprudence* (1828) was the first of at least 10 which survived for more
than a decade.[196] The legal periodical became woven into the fabric of Victorian
legal culture, but while some scholars, beginning with Abel-Smith and Stevens
in the 1960s, have mined this rich source with productive results, its very volume,
particularly in the weeklies, remains a deterrent.[197]

Of course, the growth of legal periodicals was not an isolated phenomenon.
Beginning almost with the new century, serial publications of general interest,
from the high culture quarterly reviews which began with the *Edinburgh* and the
Quarterly to less sophisticated and 'highbrow' serials, along with proceedings of
learned societies and commercial magazines aimed at particular professions and
trades proliferated. The phenomenon was fuelled on the demand side by rising
numbers of literate men and women with enough money to buy or (better from
the publishers' viewpoint) subscribe, and on the supply side by advances in printing technology and business organization, improvements in postal services and
transport and relief from taxes on advertisements and paper and from stamp
duty. Nevertheless, despite the advances in communications, periodical publishing remained an almost exclusively metropolitan business.[198]

---

[194] D. Ibbetson, 'Legal Periodicals in England 1820–1870' (2006) 28 *Common Law and European
Legal History*, 175–94 at 175. The only previous general survey was R. A. Cosgrove, 'Victorian Legal
Periodicals' (1975) 8 *Victorian Periodicals Newsletter* 21–3. Neither H. Kay Jones, *Butterworths*
(1980), nor *Then and Now 1799–1974* (Sweet & Maxwell, 1974) pays much attention to the periodicals.
S. Vogenauer, '"to take up the ground hitherto unoccupied in periodical literature"—Die ersten
juristichen Fachzeitscrhriften Englands im 19. Jahrundert', in M. Stolleis and T. Simon, *Juristiche
Zeitschriften in Europa* (Frankfurt am Main, 2006), 533–64, reviews the development of legal literature more generally, and contains graphical information on the founding of the journals and their
average duration (546–7). In the same volume, see R. Zimmerman, 'Juristiche Zeitschriften und
Rechskultuir in Schottland', 565–96.

[195] Ibbetson, 'Legal Periodicals', 175–6

[196] The attrition rate means that the same title could be resurrected. For example, besides *The
Jurist*, the *Law Gazette* (see below) had a precursor of 1847 devoted exclusively to bankruptcy and
case reports, and substantially identical to a contemporary, *The Law Chronicle*, which was also the
title of a periodical for law students (1854–6). *The Legal Examiner* (1831) had a namesake of 1862.

[197] *Lawyers and the Courts* (1967), and see also J. S. Anderson, *Lawyers and the Making of English
Land Law, 1830–1940* (Oxford, 1992). To illustrate their formidable bulk, the 1907 volume of the *Law
Journal* (42) has 814 pages, the *Law Times* vol. 123 (May to October 1907), 560 excluding advertising
pages, the *Solicitors' Journal* (51, November 1906 to June 1907), 838.

[198] Ibbetson, 'Legal Periodicals', 176–9. For a comparative assessment of their significance, see
Vogenauer, 'Periodical Literature', 556–64.

The legal periodicals of the period have been conveniently classified as three distinct types, albeit with inevitable overlaps: the discursive, 'with lengthy essays and commonly a transparent political voice'; the informational, 'designed to disseminate useful information to the legal profession generally or to some specific branch of it'; and the pedagogic, aimed at law students.[199]

The Discursive Journals

It is probably no coincidence that two quarterlies of the first sort were launched in the late 1820s, for besides the more general context, developments within the law itself—the intellectual stimulus of Bentham's writings and the political impact of controversies over the courts, particularly Chancery, brought together in Brougham's famous law reform speech—seemed to make the times particularly propitious. The earlier, *The Jurist*, claimed to 'embrace the science of jurisprudence in its widest extent' but with a distinctly Benthamite stance. Under the aegis of Joseph Parkes and Sutton Sharpe it offered a scholarly mix of articles on the laws of European countries; printed James Humphrey's lectures and commented at length on those of John Austin and J. J. Park; it also treated extensively of the current issues in law reform.[200] 'Its style was that of the heavyweight quarterly, its content was intellectually robust, and its political stance was unmistakable.'[201] Unfortunately for its prospects, however, such a combination was too far removed from the immediate concerns of most lawyers (a more professionally oriented journal dismissed it as offering 'speculative opinions, forming a mere bundle of essays'[202]) and yet too narrowly 'legal' to find a general readership. *The Jurist* lasted only five years.

Its rival, *The Law Magazine*, despite its sub-title, struck a better balance for a lawyer audience. Its first editor, Abraham Hayward, had strong scholarly credentials and a pungent style of his own.[203] He shrewdly leavened the more scholarly and speculative pieces with features of a less elevated character, drawing on the bar to rework their counsel's opinions into articles, offering a 'necrology' and a

---

[199] *Ibid.*, following Cosgrove, 'Victorian Legal Periodicals'. They add law reports as a further category. See also Vogenauer, 'Periodical Literature', 548–55.

[200] Ibbetson, 'Legal Periodicals', 179–82. There were at least two subsequent journals with the same name, see below.

[201] *Ibid.*, 182.

[202] Quoted in *ibid.*, 182.

[203] Initially articled to a Somerset solicitor, then of the Inner Temple (special pleader, called 1832). Co-editor of the first few issues with W. F. Cornish. The recent study by A. Chessell (*The Life and Times of Abraham Hayward, Q.C., Victorian Essayist* (2008)), as the title suggests, treats only briefly of his editorship and identifies only one of his contributions.

selection of biographies of famous lawyers of the recent past, a selection of legal gossip ('Notes of the Quarter') and a substantial digest of recent case law.

Although the mixture of the loftily theoretical and the sometimes narrow and pedestrian makes some issues read oddly, *The Law Magazine* succeeded where *The Jurist* went under.[204] It survived the advent of a serious rival in *The Law Review* ('a Quarterly Journal of British and Foreign Jurisprudence') which emerged in 1844 and which, though smaller, covered much of the same ground. The *Law Review* became the mouthpiece of the Law Amendment Society, but while this focus on law reform gave it a greater coherence than its rival, it also limited its appeal among a largely conservative profession.[205] It 'gradually languished' and in 1856 was absorbed by the older journal, although its name survived and enough of the reformist stance to enable the retitled *Law Magazine and [Law] Review* to boast that 'it has been the principal advocate in the Press of such well-considered Law Reform as has commended itself to the great bulk of the profession...at times it has been almost the only advocate'.[206] It would be 30 years before the *Law Magazine* had another serious competitor, justifying the view 'that there was a market for the intelligent Law review is undoubted; but it was also a seemingly inelastic one'.[207] It was probably a precariously small one too, to judge from the fact that in 1873 the *Law Magazine* converted to monthly issues in an attempt to offer more coverage of matters of current interest. It continued to hold itself out as the promoter of law reform and promised to continue popular features such as legal biographies. Noting the publication of similar journals in other UK and common law jurisdictions, it also offered 'such topics of interest to the profession as affect Scotland, Ireland and our Colonies', along with coverage of the United States and European countries.[208]

The new format was seemingly a failure, for within a few years the journal reverted to quarterly publication. In this form it survived for the rest of its existence without substantial changes, though with its contributors no longer anonymous[209] and its editors' names disclosed.[210] Alongside notes of recent cases, regular features included a review of the annual judicial statistics and notes on international law cases. There was a strong representation of international and

---

[204] Ibbetson, 'Legal Periodicals', 182–4.

[205] *Ibid.*, 184.

[206] (1872) 1 (n.s.) *LM & R* 1. Hayward left the editorship—and active practice—in 1844 after being blackballed when proposed for the bench of his inn as a new QC: Chessell, *Life and Times of Abraham Hayward*, 88–106.

[207] Ibbetson, 'Legal Periodicals', 184.

[208] (1872) 1 (n.s.) *LM & R* 1–5.

[209] *Ibid.*, 5. In earlier volumes some are initialled and a few contributors can be identified with some confidence, e.g. 'JGP[hillimore]' and 'JP[itt]T[aylor]'.

[210] They included T. P. Taswell-Langmead and Sir G. Sherston Baker.

foreign law, legal history and education and current controversies. Thus among the 29 articles in the volume for 1900–1 were ones on Australia, Malaya, India, and France, as well as three on international or comparative law. Just nine were on substantive English law, and the only one of those which was really arcane was on Seamen's Advance Notes.[211] The last peacetime volume contained a similar mixture, though the number was reduced to 24. That reduction is one of several pointers to its declining fortunes, along with the absence of illustrious names among its contributors and a high turnover of publishers, the last of whom, Jordans, put an end to its long existence in 1915.[212]

One probable cause of its demise was competition from the *Law Quarterly Review*, which began in 1885.[213] Although Frederick Pollock, its editor until 1919, took pleasure in retorting to critics of its academic content ('very scientific, no doubt, but atrociously dull' is one example[214]) that it was edited and published in the heart of legal London, it originated at All Souls and the moving spirits, along with Pollock, were the Oxonians Sir William Markby, Sir William Anson, and Sir T. E. Holland.[215] Moreover, Pollock himself rightly claimed that it did something to pave the way for the *Harvard Law Review* (1887). Unlike the *Harvard*, however, the *Law Quarterly Review* did not inspire a flood of imitators, and it was not until 1921 that the *Cambridge Law Journal* became the next of the kind.[216] Its solitary splendour may have assisted Pollock in obtaining the pick of contributors, at least after the first few years when he leaned heavily on friends, albeit distinguished ones such as the founders, Dicey, Lindley, and Vinogradoff.[217]

These and others (Elphinstone, Maitland, Buckland, and T. C. Williams among them) made regular appearances,[218] but Pollock confessed that in early volumes he had succumbed to occasionally 'publishing barely passable articles out of compassion for writers who have evidently been at great pains'.[219]

The range of articles was very extensive, though not more so than the *LM & R*. Legal history and public international law were very well served and readers accustomed to the much narrower spread around the time of its centenary will

---

[211] Series 5, vol. 26.

[212] Series 5, vol. 39.

[213] Other quarterlies started in this period did not thrive. For the most idiosyncratic, the *Judicial Quarterly Review* of 1896, see P. Polden, 'Doctor in Trouble' (2001) 22 *JLH* 37–68.

[214] *Law Times* 1893, quoted in N. Duxbury, *Frederick Pollock and the English Juristic Tradition* (Oxford, 2004), 312.

[215] *Ibid.*, 309–11.

[216] Pollock, 'Our Jubilee' (1935) 51 *LQR* 5–10. Harvard was quickly emulated, inter alia, by Yale (1891), Columbia (1901), Michigan (1902), and California (1912).

[217] Dicey had complained about the state of legal periodicals a few years earlier: Cosgrove, 'Victorian Legal Periodicals', 22.

[218] Duxbury, *Frederick Pollock* , 314–15.

[219] Pollock, 'Our Jubilee', 9.

be surprised at the frequent inclusion of pieces on law reform and legal education. Pollock often contributed himself, though not perhaps his best work, but his most important contributions were the case notes which he modestly described as 'a mere rudiment of what they have become'.[220] Other journals had case notes but none so erudite; nor did others so frequently use them to urge the appeal courts to adopt a more expansive exercise of their functions in order to clarify an area of law, tidy up loose ends etc.[221] Another valuable inclusion was the more systematic reviewing of major legal books.

Informational Journals

The successful launch of Edward Cox's *Law Times* in 1843 and the survival in the face of that competition of *The Legal Observer* and *The Jurist* demonstrated that the market for weeklies aimed principally at solicitors could accommodate three titles, and the failure of others showed that it was three titles only. *The Legal Observer* was the oldest of these, founded by Robert Maugham in 1830. Since Maugham was also the secretary of the ILS it is hardly surprising that the *Legal Observer* became 'the mouthpiece of the council'[222] nor, for all that Maugham used it to urge provincial solicitors to join the Society, that the *Legal Observer* promoted the interests of the metropolitan elite. As such, it favoured a 'cautious incrementalism'[223] in law reform, opposing the devolution of business to local courts while advocating the abolition of the church courts to bring extra business to London solicitors.

The *Jurist* started up in 1838. Less well known, nowadays at any rate, than its rivals, it emphasized its case reporting service, but promised also information 'in a popular form' on conveyancing, pleading, practice, and evidence, while 'sometimes evils complained of, and the remedies suggested for their reform, will be considered'. Bankruptcies and other prosaic but necessary information, would also feature.[224] Before long the reports were hived off into a separate volume and for most subscribers they may have been the main attraction of the subscription.

The *Law Times* was one of the many publishing ventures of a remarkable man, Edward William Cox, 'barrister journalist scientist thinker entrepreneur and,

---

[220] *Ibid.*, 5; Duxbury, *Frederick Pollock*, 313–16. The content at the time of its silver jubilee was still akin to the early volumes.

[221] Duxbury, *Frederick Pollock*, 316–22.

[222] Anderson, *Lawyers and the Making of English Land Law*, 15.

[223] *Ibid.*, 15–20 at 18. See also Kirk, *Portrait of a Profession*, 26–7.

[224] Issue 1, p. 1. The first volume included short articles on bankruptcy, wills, attorney and client, and easements.

in general, alert man of affairs'.[225] Cox had promised that his magazine would be
'a purely practical one, and that it will not contain essays on abstract or specu
lative subjects; the publication we want is one which will teach us law and protect the interests of the profession'.[226] In fact he found that his readers were even
more narrowly focused than he had imagined and speedily dropped practically
all extraneous matter to produce a weekly which offered brief case notes, short
articles on aspects of English law and practice, current news, and coverage of
financial and property matters of direct relevance to his target audience.[227] And
that audience was mainly 'the disgruntled rural attorney';[228] early on, subscribers
numbered 1313 country solicitors against 191 London solicitors and just 43 barristers.[229] Nevertheless, he did not neglect to defend the interests of the junior
bar at a time when its prospects seemed lean. Cox's own journalism was trenchant, offering 'pithy brevity rather than intelligent discussion',[230] and he was
forthright and pugnacious in presenting his editorial view, not least on his particular interest, legal education. This style evidently went down well, as did the
larger, newspaper-style format, for he got the subscribers above 2000, enough to
attract advertisements in sufficient quantity to turn a profit, a rarity among legal
periodicals since 'the economics of production were loaded against publishing
success'.[231]

Until 1854 the *Law Times* and *Legal Observer* enjoyed a 'cosy relationship',[232]
but that was destroyed when plans were announced to relaunch the latter as *The
Solicitors Journal* in open rivalry to the *Law Times* and to do so, moreover, in what
Cox regarded as the cowardly guise of a limited company, the Law Newspaper
Company Ltd.[233] The *Law Times* was accused—not without justification—of
favouring the bar and the provincial solicitors over their London counterparts
and the new magazine aspired to emphasize the common interests which united,
rather than the differences which divided, the profession.[234] An incensed Cox
claimed that the MPLA, from which this scheme originated, had been infiltrated
by London agency firms (he targeted particularly W. S. Cookson) and that they

---

[225] Cocks, *Foundations of the Modern Bar*, 64 and Ch. 3 generally, also *ODNB* 13: 841. See also
Anderson, *Lawyers and the Making of English Land Law*, 98–103, and Ibbetson, 'Legal Periodicals',
184–8.

[226] (1843) 1 *LT* 3.

[227] Ibbetson, 'Legal Periodicals', 186.

[228] Cocks, *Foundations of the Modern Bar*, 65.

[229] Kirk, *Portrait of a Profession*, 59; Ibbetson, 'Legal Periodicals', 187–8.

[230] Ibbetson, 'Legal Periodicals', 188.

[231] *Ibid.*, 187.

[232] Anderson, *Lawyers and the Making of English Land Law*, 98.

[233] *Ibid.* It was the first periodical published by a limited company: 'To Present Ourselves…'
(1957) 101 *Sol. J.* 15–34.

[234] Anderson, *Lawyers and the Making of English Land Law*, 99.

would use the new weekly as a stalking horse to press the currently controversial proposals for title registration.[235] Whatever the truth of Cox's claim, it resulted in bitter exchanges in the respective journals and drove him to improve his own, and its associated reports. Whether though heightened competition or its own weaknesses, it was not many years before the Law Newspaper Company foundered. That was a triumph for Cox, but a heavily qualified one, for under new management *The Solicitors Journal* held its own and the rivalry between the owners ceased to be expressed through the editorial columns.[236]

In any case, before long they had a new rival to confront. In 1866 *The Jurist* disappeared, only to be replaced by *The Law Journal*, which rather modestly described itself as 'a weekly publication of Notes of Cases and Legal News'.[237] It was perhaps an attempt to enhance the appeal of the long-running Law Journal Reports in the face of the threat from the newly founded Incorporated Council for Law Reporting,[238] and evidently found a readership, as for almost a century these three publications would share the market for weekly legal papers, and despite differences in form, their coverage was in many respects similar.[239] As earlier, others made unsuccessful attempts to establish themselves.[240] Perhaps the most promising was the *Law Gazette* (1890). It aspired 'to represent the profession as a whole... and to combine the two essential points of cheapness and excellence'. It would offer 'carefully written articles on important legal questions from the pens of leading members of both branches and would include a 'law students gazette', all within 12 pages.[241] Retailing at one penny, it certainly achieved one essential, and the early numbers included some interesting material, but it lasted less than four years. Attempts to attract a bar readership with monthly issues by *The Law* (1874–5) and *Pump Court* (1883–6) were also doomed to failure.

---

[235] *Ibid.* The *Sol. J.*, however, claimed to 'owe... the seeds of its existence to two great provincial towns' (Birmingham and Liverpool), and its directors included A. Ryland from the former and M. D. Lowndes and A. Lace from the latter. Other well-known members included T. H. Bower, J. M. Clabon, E. W. Field, and F. Janson: 'To Present Ourselves'. The identity of the first editor is unknown.

[236] Anderson, *Lawyers and the Making of English Land Law*, 102–3. The *Solicitors Journal* had combined with the *Weekly Reporter* (1852).

[237] (1866) 1 *LJ* 1.

[238] The *Law Journal* is the least well known of these three. When it was amalgamated with the *Law Times* in 1965 to form *The New Law Journal* it was claimed to have been founded in 1822. This is rather tenuous, but suggests that it was an offshoot of the reports which began in that year.

[239] Though differences in indexing and presentation impede comparisons. To judge from the fact that the *Sol. J.* kept its subscription at 26s a month from 1870 to 1917, they do not seem to have engaged in price competition.

[240] They included *The Law Reporter* (1879), which seems to have mustered a single issue, and the sprightly, but very short-lived *The Lawyer* (1900).

[241] (1890) 1 *Law Gazette* 6.

Alongside the journals which aimed at the profession generally were others with a more particular focus. The most successful of these, in duration at any rate, is *The Justice of the Peace*, founded in 1837 and is surviving still.[242] It was neither the first nor the last journal to be aimed at this particular readership,[243] but its mixture of brief case notes, practical information about court sittings etc, and short, severely practical articles on magistrates' law and practice was evidently judicious. The *County Courts Chronicle* (1847–1920) owed much of its success to the economies of production contrived by its proprietor Cox. For the *County Courts Chronicle* was essentially an offshoot of the *Law Times*, incorporating much of the latter's copy in a similar format, supplemented by additional notes of county court cases and brief articles and notices of matters pertinent to their officers and practitioners. Attempts to create a readership out of practitioners in a particular field, as opposed to forum, were almost wholly unsuccessful; Cox's *Joint Stock Companies Law Journal* failed and *The Property Lawyer* of 1826 had been almost a century ahead of its market.[244] 1915 may not have seemed a very propitious year to revive such a project, but *The Conveyancer and Property Lawyer* endured and later prospered, a testimony to the unique importance of conveyancing to solicitors.

In a category of its own is *The Law Society's Gazette and Register*. This was not sold, but distributed to the Society's members from 1903, and as the title suggests, it was a means of publishing the information in the Society's registers of posts, partnerships, property, and so forth, supplemented with notices, reports from the Society's committees, brief obituaries of members, and notes of cases affecting solicitors.

Pedagogical Journals

The pedagogical journals, which began to spring up as soon as the solicitors's final examination was introduced in 1836 were, as has been written, 'uniformly dismal' in their want of scholarly or critical content, but then they were the printed equivalent of the crammers who ruthlessly discarded all unnecessary matter in carrying out their aim of propelling students through examinations.[245] Few of these publishing ventures were very long-lasting, and those with a slightly more ambitious agenda, like the *Jurist* of 1888, whose objects included 'to help forward as much as possible legal education throughout this country' and 'to discuss the desirability of all law students being required to have some sort of a University

---

[242] Ibbetson, 'Legal Periodicals', 188–9.
[243] e.g. *The Recorder* (1816) and Cox's *The Magistrate* (1848–53).
[244] Ibbetson, 'Legal Periodicals', 184, 188
[245] Ibbetson, 'Legal Periodicals', 189–90. Given their low salaries, *The Law Clerk* (1909) was an optimistic venture.

education', probably fared even less well.[246] To this list of failures there is one notable exception. From 1883 the most successful of the crammers, Gibson and Weldon, later the College of Law, provided their students with *Law Notes*, which continued in essentially the same format for more than a century. While necessarily containing, like the others of its kind, the usual examination-related content, its brief editorials (and occasional articles) not only throw useful sidelights on educational issues, but sometimes offered sharp criticisms of the law and its workings.

Influence

Circulation figures for these periodicals are rare, and their influence on the profession and the law even less clear. Some long-lasting editors[247] ensured a continuity of outlook over long periods and on enduring areas of contention—title registration and county courts for instance—there were marked divergences.[248] However, it is likely that editorials were intended at least as much to reflect and endorse the views of readers as to shape them. The *Legal Observer*'s denunciation of county courts as 'a ruinous piece of experimental quackery' no doubt resonated approvingly with its readers,[249] as did the persistent complaints about 'officialism' in the *Solicitors' Journal* and *Law Journal*.[250] Cox's attack on title registration in the late 1850s undoubtedly weakened the MPLA by encouraging defections, and by selective reporting and persistent editorializing professional opinion could be nudged in the desired direction, but it is not easy to find campaigns that achieved clear results. Certainly Cox's successor at the *Law Times*, F. O. Crump, was unsuccessful in his vigorous campaign to convert the Bar Committee into a body which explicitly represented the interests of the practising bar rather than the bar in its wider sense.[251]

The quarterlies, especially the *Law Quarterly Review*, had other aims. As noted above, case notes, and of course longer articles, might be a means of influencing the outcome of a case in progress at the next level or affecting the outcome of future ones. However, even the basic (and now less laborious) task of counting

---

[246] (1888) 1 *Jurist*, ii.

[247] Cox at the *Law Times* from 1843 to 1879; W. M. Fawcett (a conveyancer) at the *Sol. J.* from 1872 to 1912; he was followed by J. M. Lightwood, who subsequently migrated to the *Law Journal*.

[248] On title registration see Anderson, *Lawyers and the Making of English Land Law*. On county courts see e.g. their responses to the Gorell Report: (1908–9) 53 *Sol. J.* 442; (1909) 43 *LJ* 227; (1909) 127 *Law Times*, 235, 257.

[249] (1847) 34 *Leg.Ob.* 557.

[250] 'To Present Ourselves'. examples in the *Law Journal* include J. W. Reid, 'The Public Trustee Act 1906 and the March of Officialism' (1907) 42 *LJ*.

[251] Cocks, *Foundations of the Modern Bar*, 191–2, 217–19 and above, p. 1089.

the references to journals in reported judgments has still to be done, and at present it appears that when the *Law Quarterly Review* made its appearance judges' willingness to incorporate academic writings in their judgments was declining.[252] True, Pollock's campaign against the outcome of *Derry* v. *Peek*[253] may have contributed to the partial undoing of its mischief,[254] but criticism in this form might also be counter-productive.[255] On present evidence the direct influence of the *Law Quarterly Review* and *LM & R* in this period looks to have been small, though individual judges of a scholarly bent, such as Lindley and Haldane, no doubt found them instructive.

As this suggests, the influence of the journals, particularly the weeklies, is more subtle and indirect. For example, they brought the defects, and sometimes the virtues too, of local courts before the profession and in so doing helped to subject their judges to the values and doctrines of the higher courts.[256] They disseminated opinions on professional ethics and practices. They subjected the profession's own organizations to a critical scrutiny. They alerted readers to professionally threatening legislative initiatives. And by their narrowly national focus and general indifference (sometimes downright contempt) to jurisprudence and developments elsewhere, they contributed to the insularity which characterized English law.[257]

4. LAW REPORTS[258]

The System of Private Law Reporting

Besides their periodicals and textbooks, lawyers—at least the more intellectually or professionally ambitious—naturally read the law reports.

---

[252] S. Hedley, 'Words, Words, Words: Making Sense of Legal Judgments', in C. Stebbings (ed.), *Law Reporting in Britain* (1995), 169–86.

[253] (1889) 14 App Cas 337, HL.

[254] Duxbury, *Frederick Pollock*, 316–18.

[255] *Ibid.*, 318–19.

[256] See e.g. P. Polden, 'Judicial Selkirks, The County Court Judges and the Press, 1847–80', in C. W. Brooks and M. J. Lobban (eds), *Communities and Courts in Britain, 1150–1900* (1997), 247–62.

[257] Ibbetson, 'Legal Periodicals', 192–4.

[258] Two contemporary publications are the chief sources for most subsequent accounts: W. S. T. Daniel, *The History of the Law Reports* (1884) and J. W. Wallace, *The Reporters* (Boston, USA, 1855; the 4th edn, 1882, is the one in general use). Daniel consulted Wallace during his campaign for reform. The fullest modern account is Holdsworth's: *HEL*, xii, 102–62; xiii, 404–44, and xiv, 249–75. Shorter accounts are V. V. Veeder, 'English Law Reporting', in Committee of American Law Schools (ed.), *Select Essays in Anglo-American Law*, 3 vols (Boston, Mass. 1907, reprint 1968), ii, 123–54; J. P. Dawson, *The Oracles of the Law* (Ann Arbor, Michigan, 1967, reprint of 1978), 64–99; and J. C. Fox, *A Handbook of English Law Reports* (1913).

By the 1820s recognized reporters were regularly covering all the superior courts. Since 1812 the House of Lords had permitted the reasoning behind its decisions to be reported, and was unique in appointing official reporters to do so.[259] No longer were the Common Pleas and Exchequer reported only intermittently, so devaluing their authority.[260] The courts of equity, including the newly established Vice-Chancellor's court, were fully reported and so were the civilian courts.[261] *Nisi prius* reports had been begun by Peake in 1790 and though not always welcomed by judges, were by this time taken for granted,[262] and even the Bail court had its reporter. Most reporters followed the format pioneered by Burrow's King's Bench reports, which first appeared in 1765, and his successors Douglas and Cowper, which established the now familiar layout and sequence of headnote, statement of facts, arguments of counsel, and judgment.[263] Both the style and the quality of the reports was variable. Some differences reflected the nature of the proceedings; thus *nisi prius* reports tended to be terser than those of hearings in banc.[264] However, reporters in the same court acquired better or worse reputations: Campbell's *nisi prius* reports, for example, were generally preferred to those of Espinasse.[265] But although some reporters were very mediocre,[266] the general standard was much improved,[267] a far cry from the 'scambling reports' denounced by Chief Justice Holt at the beginning of the eighteenth century.[268]

The reliability of reports was particularly improved through the emergence of the so-called 'authorized reporters'. Though its origins remain something of a mystery,[269] the practice was well established in most of the superior courts of common law and equity, though not at *nisi prius*, while Doctors' Commons was such a small world that it would have been superfluous. There were two of these

[259] Holdsworth, *HEL*, xii, 104.

[260] J. C. Oldham, 'Underreported and Underrated: The Court of Common Pleas in the Eighteenth Century', in *Law as Culture, Culture as Law: Essays in Honor of Philip Reid*, ed. H. Hartog and W. E. Nelson (2000), 119–46.

[261] See the lists in Wallace, *The Reporters*, in Holdsworth, *HEL*, xiii, 428–34, and in *Halsbury's Laws of England*, viii (1909).

[262] J.C.Oldham, *Law-Making at Nisi Prius* (2004) 25 *JLH* 221–47.

[263] Veeder, 'English Law Reporting', 143–6; Holdsworth, *HEL*, xii, 110–12; Dawson, *Oracles of the Law*, 77.

[264] Holdsworth, *HEL*, xiii, 425.

[265] P. Luther, 'Campbell, Espinasse and the Sailors: Text and Context in Common Law' (1999) 19 *JLH* 526–51.

[266] For instance, Blackburn was critical of Lewin: Holdsworth, *HEL*, xiii, 430 n.2. C. P. Cooper's reports were eccentric and defective: *ibid.*, and see 'H', 'The Brougham and Cooper Reports' (1836) 15 *LM* 146–9.

[267] Holdsworth, *HEL*, xiii, 425.

[268] Quoted, inter alia, in Veeder, 'English Law Reporting', 125, and see R. E. Megarry, *A Miscellany-at-Law* (1955), 288–303.

[269] Dawson, *Oracles of the Law*, 80.

reporters in most courts, and each checked the other's work.[270] Their great advantage was that the judges granted them access to court documents and some would correct the reporter's version of their judgments.[271] The privilege was a valuable one and their substantial earnings attracted rising young lawyers; they included Maule, Alderson, and Cresswell in the 1820s and 1830s and Blackburn, Turner, and Crompton later.[272] The judges seem to have blessed the succession of a new reporter and there is no known case of an authorized reporter being deprived of his position.[273]

For the judges, more reliable reports of their judgments came at a price. No longer could they so readily put aside the inconvenient dictum of a colleague (much less one of their own) by blaming an error in the report, as Mansfield had been wont to do even with Burrow.[274] Nor were they so ready to scold counsel for the citation of certain older reports, as Kenyon had done when Park referred to Keble.[275] There were still 'unseemly discussions between bench and bar' over the reliability of reports,[276] and Maule's characteristically caustic dismissal of Espinasse became the stuff the bar's oral tradition, but few of Espinasse's successors suffered similar posthumous indignities.[277]

The judges' insistence that an authorized report should be cited in preference to others perhaps contributed to some of their less praiseworthy features. Slowness in appearing became a major complaint: the last volume of De Gex, Macnaghten, and Gordon, published in 1864, stretched back to 1857 and that of Ellis and Ellis to 1860.[278] The reports were often prolix and unfocused too, with the inclusion of the pleadings and counsel's argument features some felt unnecessary.[279] This helped make them unaffordable to most tiros. Sir J. F. Pollock reckoned it cost £30 a year to possess oneself of a complete set each year and with few chambers

---

[270] Holdsworth, *HEL*, xiii, 426–34, and see W. M. Best's description in Daniel, *History of the Law Reports*, 165.

[271] *Ibid.*

[272] *Ibid.*, 428–43, where the most notable reporters are described.

[273] *Ibid.*, 425–6.

[274] Wallace, *The Reporters*, 30–3.

[275] F. Pollock, 'English Law Reporting' (1903) 19 *LQR* 451–60, with updated version in his *Essays in the Law* (1922), 242–57 at 243.

[276] *The Times*, 2 December 1863, quoted in Daniel, *History of the Law Reports*, 77.

[277] Luther, 'Campbell, Espinasse and the Sailors', 531.

[278] Daniel to Sir R. Palmer, 29 October 1864, in Daniel, *History of the Law Reports*, 192, and cf. T. Webster at 217. Not a new problem: vol. 19 of Vesey's reports, for 1815, appeared in 1822: Fox, *Handbook of English Law Reports*, 39.

[279] In the sample analysed in 'The System of Law Reports' (1848) 9 (s2) *LM* 1–25 at 22, the arguments occupied more than a third of the text.

having more than one or two members and most solicitors working alone or in very small partnerships that was a daunting figure.[280]

In keeping with the prevailing economic dogma, some felt the cure lay in the wholesome discipline of competition. Accordingly, Denman CJ deprived the authorized reporters of the privilege of exclusive citation in the King's Bench in 1832 and the other common law courts followed suit.[281] Rival sets of nominate reports duly appeared,[282] but few established themselves as serious competitors to the authorized reporter, and some were decidedly inferior.[283] More dangerous competitors were the reports launched by the weekly law newspapers. The earliest, the *Law Journal*, carefully disclaimed any intention to compete with the authorized reports in fullness, claiming instead to furnish the profession with timely notice of pertinent cases and reporting them fully enough for use in argument in the absence of an authorized report.[284] The series succeeded well enough for it to be emulated by the *Legal Observer* (1830), the *Jurist* (1838) the *Law Times* (1843) and the *Weekly Reporter* (1852) as well as more ephemeral publications. Their style was generally different from the nominate reports, tending towards a summary of the judgment within a short explanation of the grounds for decision,[285] but over time they reduced the sale of the authorized reports from thousands to hundreds.[286] Some series of nominate reports were discontinued by the publishers[287] and in 1853 their association minuted in alarm that 'unless some radical change takes place with regard to publishing the Reports, they will all be annihilated'.[288]

---

[280] Sir N. Lindley, 'The History of the Law Reports' (1885) 1 *LQR* 137–49 at 138. According to 'JPT', 'Modern Common Law Reports' (1842) 27 *LM* 320–42 at 334, a set of Law Journal Reports cost £3 4s as opposed to £10 2s for the authorized reports of the common law courts.

[281] Holdsworth, *HEL*, xiv, 248, though at 249 he states that a few judges refused to accept unauthorized reports.

[282] According to an LAS report, '[i]t has long been considered a practicable scheme for any barrister and publisher who unite together with a view to notoriety or profit, to add to the existing list of Law Reports. It may be that such reports may be rarely referred to, that they may be inaccurate, that they may be of little or no authority, they nevertheless remain': 'The Reporting System' (1847–8) 7 *LR* 223–46 at 238.

[283] Holdsworth, *HEL*, xiii, 426, and see the generally unfavourable verdicts in 'Modern Common Law Reports'.

[284] Holdsworth, *HEL*, xiii, 427. The *Law Journal Reports* adopted a new style and monthly publication in 1830 and were more highly regarded than the others.

[285] Ibbetson, 'Legal Periodicals', 192–4.

[286] Daniel, *History of the Law Reports*, 39–48. Some estimates of circulations by J. W. Giffard are at 126. The *New Reports* appeared in 1862 and some Chancery reporters were prompted to reduce prices and accelerate publication but apparently without success: *ibid.*, 43.

[287] Bail Reports in 1851, Exchequer Reports in 1855: M. W. Maxwell, 'The Development of Law Publishing', in *Then and Now 1799–1974* (1974), 121–36 at 125.

[288] February 1853. The Associated Law Booksellers was a cartel comprising most of the leading publishers. They scotched a scheme floated by one of the reporters to publish reports independently of them: *ibid.*, 125–6.

However, competition also brought problems for judges and lawyers alike. Discrepancies between reports was one, but worse was the proliferation of reported cases. Selecting cases worth reporting had always required nice judgement but commercial imperatives drove the publishers of non-authorized reports to enhance the attractions of their volumes by encouraging their reporters to adopt lax criteria.[289] Acceptance (however reluctant) that any case vouched for by a barrister might be brought before the court marked the abandonment of any hope of confining citations,[290] and the economy of relying on a single set of reports was offset by insecurity. On circuit and in the county courts, this explosion of reports became a problem for judges as well as counsel, and Campbell sighed for the time when a good-sized bookcase could hold all the law reports worth consulting.[291] No longer was the chief criticism of the common law system that the law might not be known because it was not properly reported; rather, it was reported so extensively and indiscriminately that its guiding principles were submerged in a welter of fact-dependent, incoherent precedents, denounced by Westbury as 'a great chaos of judicial legislation'.[292] It was compounded by 'too facile adoption of anything as authority, however contrary it may be to common sense and legal principle, provided only it be or purported to be, a judicial determination'.[293] The situation was, as Nathaniel Lindley later observed, becoming intolerable.[294]

The Incorporated Council for Law Reporting

The remedy, however, was less easy to find. Reformist opinion was divided between those who favoured some form of official reporting and those who saw it as a matter for the profession to resolve. Among the former some argued that the judges or the registrar, aided by shorthand-writers, should undertake this function.[295] Even in Chancery it was unlikely to find favour with the judges and in common law

---

[289] Holdsworth, *HEL*, xiv, 250; 'Law Reports and Law Reporting' (1864–5) 18 (s3) *LM & LR* 270–300 at 287–9.

[290] Daniel, *History of the Law Reports*, 248–9. Westbury's unchallenged assertion to that effect in Parliament in 1863 (*PD* (s3) 171: 778) is usually regarded as authoritative.

[291] S. Rogers, 'The Study of Law Reports' (1897) 13 *LQR* 250–69 at 252.

[292] *PD* 1863 (s3) 171: 778.

[293] (1843) 7 *Jur.* 437.

[294] Lindley, 'History of the Law Reports', 137. However, despite this 'indiscriminate reporting' important cases still escaped the reporters' attention: see the undignified subterfuge resorted to in the case of the ship *Alexandria*: Daniel, *History of the Law Reports*, 87.

[295] e.g. John Pearson and Joshua Williams (Daniel, *History of the Law Reports*, 111, 124). On the Judicature Commission Sir William Erle objected to the suggestion that a shorthand writer should always be in attendance in court because such reports were 'so painfully accurate': J. Hollams, *Jottings of an Old Solicitor* (1906), 220. For their later adoption in criminal cases, see above, p. 807.

courts, where *The Times* claimed 99 per cent of judgments were still unwritten, it was quite unrealistic.[296] It was more plausible to argue for the appointment of reporters paid out of public funds, as did a LAS committee in 1853,[297] whose advocacy of an official board of superintendence was in keeping with the *zeitgeist* and pleased those who urged that the state had a duty to make judge-proclaimed law available to the public like statutes.[298] Moreover, since it was widely believed that medieval law reports—the Year Books in particular—had been official products, this represented a return to an older, and better, tradition.[299] Unfortunately for them, governments were not persuaded, and no Chancellor, law officer or leading politician showed any willingness to implement the report.[300] Furthermore, the most radical reformers, set upon codification, regarded such changes as either unimportant or even damaging to the bigger project.

Two groups favoured improvements to the existing private system.[301] One had ideological objections to either government or judges being able to restrict freedom to report what the judge actually said rather than his more polished second thoughts and to determine which cases were reported at all.[302] Others were simply pragmatic, preferring to attempt something the professions could bring about, though evidently with no aid from the inns of court.[303]

The initiative was seized by a barrister of reformist inclinations and energetic personality, W. T. S. Daniel.[304] Daniel spurned officialism, maintaining that the bar should assume responsibility for improving the condition of law reporting by establishing a superintending body and a coherent system.[305] He gained

---

[296] Daniel, *History of the Law Reports*, 77.

[297] 'Law Reporting' (1853) 18 *LR* 313–23; also in Daniel, *History of the Law Reports*, 15–21.

[298] e.g. Montague Smith, Gordon and Vernon Lushington, *The Jurist, The Law Magazine*: Daniel, *History of the Law Reports*, 21, 117, 149.

[299] See e.g. the 'historical review' in 'Law Reports and Law Reporting'.

[300] A LAS deputation in 1863 got no encouragement from Lord Westbury. Lord Cranworth refused the equity reporters' request to subsidize publication out of the suitors' fund. William Ewart gave notice of a motion for a select committee in 1855 but did not pursue it: Daniel, *History of the Law Reports*, 21, 26, 45.

[301] They included the short-lived and obscure Verulam Society, in which E. W. Cox, who founded the *Law Times* in the same year, was a leading light: *ibid.*, 3.

[302] e.g. George Denman, *ibid.*, 211. Others, like G. W. Hemming, disliked the extension of government patronage: *ibid.*, 105.

[303] This had been the tenor of an earlier LAS report of 1849, following an investigation prompted by Serjeant Pulling, who personally favoured official reporting: 'The Reporting System'; Daniel, *History of the Law Reports*, 4–14, 80–90.

[304] Described by Hemming as being of 'fervid and rhetorical temper' (*ibid.*, 220) and later a county court judge: *ODNB* 15: 80.

[305] First suggested in his paper privately circulated to the bar (18 May 1863) and printed in *The Jurist*; elaborated upon in *A Letter to Sir Roundell Palmer... On The Present System of Law Reporting* (12 September 1863). Both are in his *History of the Law Reports*.

considerable support from the Chancery bar and several vice chancellors, and although Lord Chancellor Westbury, busy on more ambitious schemes, declined to lend his countenance[306] Daniel secured the crucial support of Sir Roundell Palmer, the Solicitor-General. When Palmer became Attorney-General soon afterwards he agreed to call a meeting of the bar after sending Daniel off to procure a respectable show of support from the common law side, and in December 1863 a well-attended meeting agreed to refer his proposals to a committee.[307]

The committee circulated the profession and sought information on reporting arrangements in other countries,[308] but in a lengthy series of meetings the committee found it hard to reach agreement on several key issues. Only the chairman's casting vote defeated a motion to ask that all judgments be written ('so far as practicable'), and another, to grant the new reports ('the bar reports' as Daniel had proposed calling them) exclusive citation, was lost by a single vote.[309] A compromise which helped smooth the way was that instead of Daniel's 'host of reporting luminaries',[310] the authorized reporters were to be given preference.

The basis of Daniel's scheme remained intact, however. A new series of law reports would be published under the aegis of a body comprising representatives of the inns and the Law Society and funded by subscription. The governing council would employ reporters in all the superior courts under the supervision of editors[311] and to undermine the appeal of the rival series (an attempt to buy up the *Law Journal* had failed[312]), the reports would be supplemented by a weekly series giving the most important cases in an abbreviated form.[313]

The committee's report was debated at a further meeting in November 1864.[314] Given the celebrated individualism of the bar, it is perhaps surprising that only

[306] Daniel, *History of the Law Reports*, 26.

[307] *Ibid.*, 28–80. The attendance was estimated at 700.

[308] *Ibid.*, which prints a few of the responses. The sub-committee report on foreign practice (148–9) seems not to have been much used.

[309] *Ibid.*, 139, 142. The chairman was Sir R. P. Amphlett MP, a future High Court judge.

[310] Sir G. O. Morgan at 211.

[311] One Queen's Bench reporter, W. M. Best, could not stomach this ('a more direct attack on the independence of the Reporter it is hard to imagine': *ibid.*, at 205) and refused to participate.

[312] *The Law Journal Reports* were supposed to be the most profitable series: 'Present System of Law Reporting', 93.

[313] Daniel, *History of the Law Reports*, 145. The importance of such a series had been emphasized in the consultation: see e.g. E. E. Kay at 108–11.

[314] A meeting in September was adjourned as not having allowed enough time for consideration. It may have been convened prematurely to meet the wishes of Lord Westbury, who had urged haste 'as his own action in the House of Lords on the subject… was stopped by their proceedings' (*ibid.*, 197). His suggestion that reports should be reviewed annually by a 'Department of Justice' which would declare which cases ought to be regarded as worthwhile contributions to the law found few supporters: *PD* 1863 (s3), 171: 791.

one objection received enough support to throw doubt on the scheme's progress, and that was Hemming's resolution for more details of the financial data used by Daniel, who had mounted 'his chariot of Reform and [was] driv[ing], like Jehu or Pickford, furiously over us'.[315] It now needed only the approval of the inns and the Law Society to assemble the Council of Law Reporting. At first Gray's and Serjeant's Inn refused to take part, but the latter soon ceased to exist and Gray's quickly reconsidered.[316] As finally constituted, the Council comprised the three law officers, two solicitors and 10 barristers. Most of the former authorized reporters agreed terms and formed the backbone of the new team.[317]

The *Law Reports* began publication in January 1866 and were unquestionably a commercial success, signalled in 1885 by the decision to reduce the subscription from 5 guineas to 4.[318] For this modest outlay the subscriber received not only the reports but the *Weekly Notes* and a set of statutes, plus a *Digest* at intervals. But while no one seriously advocated a return to the old arrangements, lax editorial control meant the reports were not free from the faults which had beset their predecessors.[319] True, with the assistance of the judges in revising their decisions there were few complaints of inaccuracy, but it was almost inevitable that the reports should be accused of omitting important decisions (particularly in conveyancing[320]), while including those of no value, particularly turning merely on the construction of a private document or the exercise of a judicial discretion.[321] Important cases were slow to appear (the profession had to wait seven months

[315] At 222: it was lost by 111 to 126. Because the law publishers boycotted the scheme, Daniel had made arrangements with William Clowes.

[316] Serjeants' Inn stayed aloof because most of its members were judges, who felt it inappropriate to become involved. In May 1867 it nominated two members and one of them, Alexander Pulling, remained on the Council after the inn's dissolution. Gray's was allotted only one member, presumably because of its decayed condition. It was subsequently offered two, and nominated them in January 1867.

[317] One of those who refused, E. T. Hurlstone in the Exchequer, changed his mind too late once he found the financial position secure: Daniel, *History of the Law Reports*, 293–4. The last of the authorized reporters was M. R. Beavan who had 'taken his own independent course' with the backing of the Master of the Rolls, Sir John Romilly. His reports were much criticized, and his acceptance of the post of examiner in 1866 ended the awkward situation of a parallel series of Rolls reports: Daniel, *History of the Law Reports*, 300; Fox, *Handbook of English Reports*, 59.

[318] Holdsworth, *HEL*, xiv, 254; Lindley, 'History of the Law Reports', 138. Subscribers to the full series reached 5400: notes of second meeting of the Simonds Committee, NA PRO LCO 2/1152.

[319] Apparently the same latitude was practised in the other reports: F. Evans, 'Law Reporting: A Reporter's View' (1904) 20 *LQR* 88–93 at 92.

[320] (1893–4) 38 *Sol. J.* 302. See also (1888) 4 *LQR*, 115; (1894) 10 *LQR* 12.

[321] Lindley, 'History of the Law Reports', 144: J. Mews, 'The Present System of Law Reporting' (1893) 9 *LQR* 179–87. As the compiler of the standard *Digest of English Case Law* (1st edn 1884), Mews was well qualified to appraise the reports, but is likely to have had a prejudice in favour of a highly selective policy.

for *Walsh* v. *Lonsdale*[322]); headnotes were sometimes unsatisfactory and reports long-winded, often through the inclusion of interruptions from the bench during argument.[323] The most frequent criticisms were to be found in the *Law Quarterly Review*, whose editor, Frederick Pollock, printed critical articles and conducted a 'long and desultory campaign of footnotes'.[324] Pollock was particularly severe on the headnotes,[325] but his criticism extended to the whole undertaking, which he felt had lapsed into slovenly and dilatory ways.[326]

The Council evidently felt the force of these criticisms and in 1894 invited the poacher to turn gamekeeper with the new position of general editor. Pollock accepted and with minimal interference from the Council effectively ran the enterprise for the next 40 years.[327] Unexpectedly for such a famously reticent personality he seems to have presided over a genuinely co-operative organization, though it perhaps fell short of the perfect teamwork suggested by his own comparison with a college rowing crew.[328] He worked tirelessly to eliminate usages which he considered slovenly or illiterate (from judges as well as reporters) and to prune the reports of verbosity and redundant elements.[329] However, he was probably justified in claiming to give the reporters a pretty free hand, trusting to their judgement where he was doubtful whether a case merited inclusion. It was only near the end of his editorship that critics complained of the omission of significant cases, in some instances attributed to Pollock's disapproval of the decision.[330]

Pollock himself stated that 'utility to the profession is the only test',[331] and his judgement, and that of his reporters, seems generally to have coincided with those of the rival series.[332] A few cases which were not picked out of the *Weekly Notes*

---

[322] (1882) 21 Ch D 9; (1882–3) 27 *Sol. J.* 494. See also Lindley, 'History of the Law Reports', 145–6; (1890) 6 *LQR*, 332; (1890–1) 35 *Sol. J.* 325.

[323] Mews, 'Present System of Law Reporting', 179–87. Hemming, who had used great freedom in recasting and condensing the notoriously rambling judgments of Sir William Page-Wood, explained the difficulties involved: 'The Law Reports' (1885) 1 *LQR* 288–97 at 291, and see Jessel MR in *Re Mowlem* (1874) 43 LJ Ch 354.

[324] F. Pollock, *For My Grandson* (London, 1933), 187.

[325] Duxbury, *Frederick Pollock*, 295–6.

[326] Pollock, *For My Grandson*, 187. The first volume of the *LQR* included a defence by one of the *Law Reports* editors (Hemming), to a critical article by Lindley : 'The Law Reports', 288–97.

[327] Duxbury, *Frederick Pollock*, 294–8. The metaphor was Pollock's own.

[328] *Ibid.*, 297–300, quoting from Pollock's own account in *English Law Reporting*.

[329] Duxbury, *Frederick Pollock*, 302–4. Judges' corrections were almost always accepted (300), but Sylvan Mayer wrote of one instance where a reporter stoutly adhered to his own version: *Memories of a KC, Legal and Theatrical* (1924), 138–40.

[330] Duxbury, *Frederick Pollock*, 304–7.

[331] *English Law Reporting*, 249.

[332] Perhaps because the reporters by this stage shared their views on whether a case was worth reporting: Evans, 'Law Reporting', 92.

clearly should have been[333] and no doubt the other series were somewhat more expansive, though perhaps less than might have been expected.[334] Complaints were more likely to be of too many cases reported than too few.[335]

Though he disliked the multiplication of reports, Pollock did not revive the claim that the *Law Reports* should have the privilege of exclusive citation, though most judges insisted that its reports be preferred.[336] Both he and Lindley praised the unique arrangement, which was 'thoroughly English in its constitution and working'[337] but while Pollock seems genuinely to have been content with it, Lindley felt the continuation of other reports was 'the one great defect in the present system' and that it 'must be regarded as transitional and incomplete'.[338] The *Law Reports* failed to eliminate their rivals. The *LTR*, the *WR*, and *LJR* continued, the last being held in the highest esteem and being the only one to which judges would sometimes lend their assistance.[339] They competed successfully on price and, especially, on speed.[340] In addition there were several specialist series.[341] Some, such as *Aspinall's Maritime Cases* and *Cox's Criminal Cases*, predated the *Law Reports*, but new ones sprang up, particularly in areas of burgeoning litigation. Among them were *Knight's Local Government Reports*, *Reports of*

[333] e.g. *Re Cavendish–Browne's STs* [1916] WN 341 which featured regularly in textbook discussions on incompletely constituted trusts. In 1884 the *Times Law Reports* were started up, competing with *Weekly Notes* and *The Weekly Reporter* (the latter responded to the competition by improving its reports). They were popular with country solicitors: evidence of C. Clayton and T. Cunliffe to the Simonds Committee, PRO LCO 2/ 1152.

[334] Examples of cases not in the *Law Reports* are in C. Mullins, *In Quest of Justice* (1930) 51–4. A very cursory examination of the reports in the *Law Reports*, *LTR*, and *LJR* for 1913–14 suggests that almost all the *LR* cases were to be found in the others, plus a further 10% or so. Coverage in the *LJR* and *LTR* was very similar, and the *LR* may have been least generous in their coverage of shipping cases. Thirty years earlier the impression is that the differential between the *LR* coverage and that of the others was somewhat bigger; this is supported by lists of cases reported only in the *LTR* and taken from the indexes to the latest editions of *Chitty on Contracts* and *Jarman on Wills* given in evidence to the Simonds Committee (LCO 2/1153). The former declined from 32 of the 1870s to eight of the 1920s, the latter from 98 of the 1880s to 15 of the 1920s. A. L. Goodhart reckoned around 600 civil cases (750 all told) were being reported each year.

[335] This was certainly Pollock's view of the *Law Reports* in 1885: see his note to Lindley, 'History of the Law Reports', 138.

[336] Holdsworth, *HEL*, xv, 256; Duxbury, *Frederick Pollock*, 299.

[337] Lindley, 'History of the Law Reports', 142; Pollock, *English Law Reporting* 244.

[338] Lindley, 'History of the Law Reports', 141, 142.

[339] Dawson, *Oracles of the Law*, 83; Duxbury, *Sir Frederick Pollock*, 301; Rogers, 'Study of Law Reports', 261. The *Weekly Reporter* was absorbed by the *Solicitors Journal* in 1906: P. H. Winfield, *The Chief Sources of English Legal History* (Cambridge, Mass., 1925, reprint, New York, 1972), 193.

[340] Pollock claimed that most cases reached the *Law Reports* about two months after the judgment was handed down: *English Law Reporting*, 255.

[341] The *Justice of the Peace Reports* was the only one considered important: *DC on Law Reporting Report* (1940).

Commercial Cases, Patent, Design and Trademark Cases, and *Criminal Appeals Reports.*[342]

The proliferation of reports tended to perpetuate the old evil of reporting cases whose importance was at best limited. It was encouraged by the practice of excessive and rather undiscriminating citation which sprang partly from the defects in barristers' legal education, and though judges frequently complained (Esher said that in one case 'every case upon the subject that industry could find and ingenuity could torture was brought before the court'[343]), it was to no effect. Indeed, some fostered it in their desire to guard themselves from criticism in appeal courts and by embracing the doctrine of *stare decisis* in its most developed form. And while in theory reporters only reported what they personally heard in court, only Pollock's well-paid men could make a decent living from that; their less fortunate brethren had to cover several courts, relying on the shorthand writers for transcripts and sharing notes.[344]

One ambitious but ultimately unsuccessful attempt to set some bounds to the relentless accumulation of case law was the *Revised Reports,* begun in 1891 under Pollock's editorship. They aimed to 'republish the old reports of our Superior Courts of Common Law and Equity which are modern enough to be still of frequent utility, reducing them to a manageable bulk and cost by the omission of obsolete and unimportant matter'.[345] The *Revised Reports* performed a valuable function, but a few years later publication began of the *English Reports,* a monumental compilation which simply made more accessible most of the old reports.[346] In 1896 Pollock had estimated the total of English reports at some 1800 volumes,[347] and they were swelled by something over 20 a year. What made matters more arduous for the practitioner or scholar was the tendency of the leading

---

[342] There were said to be 18 series of reports in all by 1938, costing £45 13s 6d a year: Goodhart to Maugham LC, 26 November 1938, LCO 2/1151. From 1911 the *Law Reports Digest* included cases reported only in some of these specialist series and in the three general series mentioned above: Winfield, *Chief Sources of English Legal History,* 198. The last of the nominate reports, Best and Smith in the Queen's Bench, ended in 1870 and neither the *Jurist* nor the *New Reports* survived for long: 'Law Reports and Law Reporting', 298.

[343] Rogers, 'Study of Law Reports', 258.

[344] Evidence of C. G. Moran and T. R. Fitzwalter Butler to the Simonds Committee, LCO 2/1152. The evidence relates to the 1930s but the practices they describe were not new, see 'L', The Bar Scheme for the Amendment of the Present System of Law Reporting' (1865) 19 (s3) *LM & LR* 85–104 at 98–103.

[345] Prospectus, quoted in A. E. Randall, 'The Revised Reports' (1913) 28 *LQR* 276–82 at 276; Winfield, *Chief Sources of English Legal History,* 195–6. Publication was completed in 1920. Wallace had proposed something along these lines (*The Reporters,* 40–55) and it formed part of Westbury's plans, who reckoned they could be reduced to about a tenth of their then bulk: *PD* 1863 (s3) 171: 785.

[346] Winfield, *Chief Sources of English Legal History,* 196–7, noting that 'the exact scope of the work is difficult to ascertain'. Some reporters found in the *Revised Reports* are not included.

[347] Rogers, 'Study of Law Reports', 253

treatises to add new cases in successive editions without removing the older ones, whether from lack of time or confidence on the part of successive editors.[348] And as experience with the Workmen's Compensation Acts highlighted, the growing output of statutes led to a proliferation of reported cases which offered an interpretation of some statutory word or phrase, often in the hope that any authority would be better than none and would create some prospect of judicial consistency. The hope was often a forlorn one and the relentless accumulation of law reports posed an unresolved problem. The problem would become more acute with the arrival of Butterworths' *All England Law Reports* in 1936, whose cheapness and speedy production was thought to pose so serious a threat to the *Law Reports* themselves that it led to the setting up of the Simonds Committee.[349]

[348] Randall, 'Revised Reports', 277.
[349] P. Clinch, 'The Establishment v. Butterworths' (1990) 19 *Anglo-Am. Law Rev.* 209–38.

FURTHER READING

Part One: English Law in an Industrializing Society

Sources of Law

Allen, C. K., 'Case Law: an Unwarrantable Intervention' (1935) *51 LQR* 333–46.

Atiyah, P. S., *The Rise and Fall of Freedom of Contract* (Oxford, 1979).

Bryson, W. H. and Danchy S., (eds) *Ratio Decidendi: Guiding Principles of Judicial Decisions* (Berlin, 2006).

Duxbury, N., *The Nature and Authority of Precedent* (Cambridge, 2008).

Evans, J., 'Precedent in the Nineteenth Century' in L. Goldstein (ed.) *Precedent in Law* (Oxford, 1987) 35–72.

Ferguson, R. B., 'The Adjudication of Commercial Disputes and the Legal System in Modern England' (1980) *Brit.J.L.& Soc.* 141–57.

Goutal, J.-L., 'Characteristics of Judicial Style in France, Britain and the USA' (1973) 24 *Am. J. Comp. Law* 364–71.

Goodhart, A. L., 'Precedent in English and Continental Law' (1935) 50 *LQR* 40–65, 196–200.

Hedley, S. W., '"Superior Knowledge or Revelation": An Approach to Modern Legal History' (1989) 20 *Anglo-Am. LQR* 179–200.

Hedley, S. W., 'Words, Words, Words: Making Sense of Legal Judgments, 1875–1940' in C. Stebbings (ed.) *Law Reporting in England* (1995) 169–86.

Holdsworth, Sir W.S., 'Case Law' (1934) *50 LQR* 180–95.

Lawson, F. H., 'Comparative Judicial Style' (1977) *25 Am. J. Comp. Law* 314–71.

Lobban, M. J. W., 'Custom, Common Law Reasoning and the Law of Nations in the Nineteenth Century' in A. Perreau-Saussine and J.B. Murphy (eds) *The Nature of Customary Law* (Cambridge, 2007) 256–78.

Lobban, M. J. W., 'Custom, Nature and Authority: the Roots of English Positivism' in D. Lemmings (ed.) *The British and their Laws in the Eighteenth Century* (Woodbridge, 2005) 27–58.

Manchester, A. H., 'Simplifying the Sources of the Law: An Essay in Law Reform' (1973) 2 *Anglo-Am. Law Rev.* 395–415.

Murphy, J. D. and Rueter, R., *Stare Decisis in Commonwealth Appellate Courts* (Toronto, 1981).

Pugsley, D., 'London Tramways (1893)' [1996] *JLH* 172–83.

Simpson, A. W. B., 'The Rise and Fall of the Legal Treatise' (1981) 48 *U. Chicago LR* 632–79.

Stevens, R. B., *Law and Politics: The House of Lords as a Judicial Body 1800–1976* (Chapel Hill, 1979).

Theories of Law and Government

Burrow, J. W., *Evolution and Society: A Study in Victorian Social Theory* (Cambridge, 1966).

Capaldi, N., *John Stuart Mill: A Biography* (Cambridge, 2004).

Cashdollar, C. D., *The Transformation of Theology, 1830–1890: Positivism and Positivist Thought in Britain and America* (Princeton, 1989).

Claeys, G., *Citizens and Saints: Politics and Anti-Politics in Early British Socialism* (Cambridge, 1989).

Clarke, P. F., *Liberals and Social Democrats* (Cambridge, 1978).

Cocks, R. C. J., *Sir Henry Maine: A Study in Victorian Jurisprudence* (Cambridge, 1988).

Colaiaco, J. A., *James Fitzjames Stephen and the Crisis of Victorian Thought* (London, 1983).

Collini, S., *Liberalism and Sociology: L.T. Hobhouse and Political Argument in England, 1880–1914* (Cambridge, 1979).

Collini, S., *Public Moralists: Political Thought and Intellectual Life in Britain, 1850–1930* (Oxford, 1991).

Crimmins, J. E., *Secular Utilitarianism: Social Science and the Critique of Religion in the Thought of Jeremy Bentham* (Oxford, 1990).

den Otter, S. M., *British Idealism and Social Explanation: A Study in Late Victorian Thought* (Oxford, 1996).

Diamond (ed.), A., *The Victorian Achievement of Sir Henry Maine: a Centennial Reappraisal* (Cambridge, 1991).

Dinwiddy J. R., 'Adjudication under Bentham's Pannomion' (1989) 1 *Utilitas* 283–9.

Dinwiddy, J. R. *Bentham* (Oxford, 1989).

Dixon, T., *The Invention of Altruism: Making Moral Meanings in Victorian Britain* (Oxford, 2008).

Duxbury, N., *Frederick Pollock and the English Juristic Tradition* (Oxford, 2004).

Edwards, P., *The Statesman's Science: History, Nature and Law in the Political Thought of Samuel Taylor Coleridge* (New York, 2004).

Evans, R., *The Fabrication of Virtue: English Prison Architecture, 1750–1840* (Cambridge, 1982).

Feaver, G., *From Status to Contract: A Biography of Sir Henry Maine 1822–1888* (London, 1969).

Foucault, M., *Discipline and Punish: The Birth of the Prison* (1985).

Freeden, M., *The New Liberalism: an Ideology of Social Reform* (Oxford, 1986).

Finer, S. E., 'The Transmission of Benthamite Ideas, 1820–59' in G. Sutherland (ed), *Studies in the Growth of Nineteenth-Century Government* (1972), 11–32.

Goldman, L., *Science, Reform and Politics in Victorian Britain: The Social Science Association, 1857–1886* (Cambridge, 2002).

Halévy, E., *The Growth of Philosophic Radicalism*, trans. M. Morris (1972).

Hamburger, L. and J., *Troubled Lives: John and Sarah Austin* (Toronto, 1985).

Hamburger, J., *Intellectuals in Politics: John Stuart Mill and the Philosophic Radicals* (New Haven, 1965).

Harvie, C., *The Lights of Liberalism: University Liberals and the Challenge of Democracy, 1860–86* (1976).

Hart, H. L. A., *Essays on Bentham: Jurisprudence and Political Theory* (Oxford, 1982).

Himmelfarb, G., *Victorian Minds* (1968).

Himmelfarb, G., *Poverty and Compassion: the Moral Imagination of the Late Victorians* (New York, 1991).

Hoppen, K. T., *The Mid-Victorian Generation, 1846–1886* (Oxford, 1998).

Hume, L. J., 'Jeremy Bentham and the Nineteenth-Century Revolution in Government,' (1967) 10 *Hist. J.* 361–75.

Hume, L. J., *Bentham and Bureaucracy* (Cambridge, 1981).

Ignatieff, M., *A Just Measure of Pain: the Penitentiary in the Industrial Revolution, 1750–1850* (1989).

Lieberman, D., *The Province of Legislation Determined: Legal Theory in Eighteenth Century Britain* (Cambridge, 1989).

Lobban, M. J. W., *The Common Law and English Jurisprudence, 1760–1850* (Oxford, 1989).

Lobban, M. J. W., *A History of the Philosophy of Law in the Common Law World, 1600–1900*, vol. 8 of E. Pattaro (ed.), *Treatise of Legal Philosophy and General Jurisprudence* (Dordrecht, 2007).

Lobban, M. J. W., 'Was there a nineteenth-century "English School of Jurisprudence"' (1995) 16 *JLH* 34–62.

Lyons, D., *Rights, Welfare and Mill's Moral Theory* (Oxford, 1994).

McDonagh, O. R., 'The Nineteenth-Century Revolution in Government: a Reappraisal', (1958) 1 *Hist. J.* 52–67.

Morison, W. L., 'Some Myths about Positivism' (1958) 8 *Yale LJ* 212–33.

Morison, W. L., *John Austin* (London, 1982).

O'Brien, N.,. '"Something Older than law itself": Sir Henry Maine, Niebuhr and "the Path not Chosen"' (2005) 26 *JLH* 229–51.

Nicholson, P. P., *The Political Philosophy of the British Idealists: Selected Studies* (Cambridge, 1990).

Parker, C., *The English Idea of History from Coleridge to Collingwood* (Aldershot, 2000).

Parris, H., 'The Nineteenth-Century Revolution in Government: a Reappraisal Reappraised' (1960) 3 *Hist. J.* 17–37.

Postema, G. J., *Bentham and the Common Law Tradition* (Oxford, 1986).

Rosen, F., *Classical Utilitarianism from Hume to Mill* (2003).

Ryan, A.,*The Philosophy of John Stuart Mill*, 2nd edn (Basingstoke, 1987).

Rumble, W. E., *The Thought of John Austin: Jurisprudence, Colonial Reform and the British Constitution* (1985).

Rumble, W. E., *Doing Austin Justice: The Reception of Austin's Philosophy of Law in Nineteenth-Century England* (2005).

Schneewind, J. B., *Sidgwick's Ethics and Victorian Moral Philosophy* (Oxford, 1977).

Schofield, P., 'Jeremy Bentham, the Principle of Utility, and Legal Positivism' (2003) 56 *CLP* 1–40.

Schofield, P., *Utility and Democracy: the Political Thought of Jeremy Bentham* (Oxford, 2006).

Schultz, B., *Henry Sidgwick: Eye of the Universe* (Cambridge, 2004).

Semple, J., *Bentham's Prison: A Study of the Panopticon Penitentiary* (Oxford, 1993).

Skorupski , J., *John Stuart Mill* (1989).

Skorupski, J. (ed.), *The Cambridge Companion to Mill* (Cambridge, 1998).

Smith, K. J. M., *James Fitzjames Stephen: Portrait of a Victorian Rationalist* (Cambridge, 1988).

Stedman Jones, G., *Languages of Class: Studies in English Working Class History, 1832–1982* (Cambridge, 1983).

Taylor, M. W., *Men versus the State: Herbert Spencer and Late Victorian Individualism* (Oxford, 1992).

Thomas, W., *The Philosophic Radicals: Nine Studies in Theory and Practice, 1817–1841* (Oxford, 1979).

Vincent, A. and Plant, R., *Philosophy, Politics and Citizenship: The Life and Thought of the British Idealists* (Oxford, 1984).

Vincent, A. (ed.), *The Philosophy of T. H. Green* (Aldershot, 1986).

Wright, T. R., *The Religion of Humanity: the Impact of Comtean Positivism on Victorian Britain* (Cambridge, 1986).

Yeo, R., *Defining Science: William Whewell, Natural Knowledge and Public Debate in Early Victorian Britain* (Cambridge, 1993).

Law and Religion

Bebbington, D., *The Nonconformist Conscience* (1982).

Bebbington, D., *Evangelicalism in Modern Britain: A History from the 1730s to the 1980s* (1989).

Bradley, I., *The Call to Seriousness: The Evangelical Impact on Victorians* (1976).

Bristow, E., *Vice and Vigilance* (Dublin, 1977).

Chadwick, O., *The Secularization of the European Mind in the Nineteenth Century* (Cambridge, 1975).

Follett, R. *Evangelicalism, Penal Theory and the Politics of Criminal Law Reform 1808–1830*, (2001).

Hole, R., *Pulpits, Politics and Public Order in England 1760–1832* (Cambridge, 1989).

Machin, G., *Politics and the Churches in Great Britain 1869 to 1921* (Oxford, 1987).

Norman, E., *Church and Society in England 1770–1970* (Oxford, 1976).

Norman, E., *The Victorian Christian Socialists*, (Cambridge, 1987).

Parry, J., *Democracy and Religion, Gladstone and the Liberal Party 1867–1875* (Cambridge, 1986).

Paul, E., *Moral Revolution and Economic Science* (Westport, 1979).

Roberts, M., *Making English Morals: Voluntary Association and Moral Reform in England 1787–1886* (Cambridge, 2004).

Virgin, P., *The Church in an Age of Negligence: Ecclesiastical Structure and Problems of Church Reform 1700–1840* (Cambridge, 1989).

Law and Political Economy

Clark, J. C., *English Society 1660–1832, Religion, Ideology and Politics during the Ancien Regime* (Cambridge, 2000).

Collini, S., Winch, D. and Burrow, J., *That Noble Science of Politics* (Cambridge, 1983).

Collini, S., *Liberalism and Sociology: L. T. Hobhouse and Political Argument in 1880–1914* (Cambridge, 1979).

Cranston, R., *Legal Foundations of the Welfare State* (London, 1985).

Curthoys, M., *Governments, Labour and the Law in Mid-Victorian Britain* (Oxford, 2004).

Daunton, M., *Progress and Poverty, An Economic and Social History of Britain 1700–1850* (Oxford, 1995).

Daunton, M., *Trusting Leviathan, The Politics of Taxation in Britain, 1799–1914* (Cambridge, 2001).

Daunton, M., *Wealth and Welfare; An Economic and Social History of Britain 1851–1951* (Oxford, 2007).

Finn, M., *The Character of Credit: Personal Debt in English Culture, 1740–1914* (Cambridge, 2003).

Gordon, B., *Economic Doctrine and Tory Liberalism 1824–1830* (1979).

Hamlin, C., *Public Health and Social Justice in the Age of Chadwick 1800–1854* (Cambridge, 1998).

Harris, R., *Industrializing English Law: Entrepreneurship and Business Organisation 1720–1844* (Cambridge, 2000).

Hilton, B., *The Age of Atonement* (Oxford, 1988).

Hilton, B., *Corn, Cash, Commerce: The Economic Policies of the Tory Governments 1815–1830* (Oxford, 1977).

Hilton, B., *A Mad, Bad, and Dangerous People? England 1783–1846* (Oxford, 2006).

Howe, A., *Free Trade and Liberal England 1846–1946* (Oxford, 1997).

Kostal, R., *Law and English Railway Capitalism 1825–1875* (Oxford, 1994).

O'Brien, P., *Power without Profit: The State and the Economy 1688–1815* (1991).

Schmiechen, J., *Sweated Industries and Sweated Labour* (1984).

Searle, G. R., *Morality and the Market in Victorian Britain* (Oxford, 1998).

Steinfeld, R., *Coercion, Contract and Free Labor in the Nineteenth Century* (Cambridge, 2001).

Waterman, A., *Revolution, Economics and Religion: Christian Political Economy 1798–1833* (Cambridge, 1991).

Winch, D. and O'Brien, P. (eds), *The Political Economy of British Historical Experience 1688–1914* (Oxford, 2002).

Law in the British Empire

Buck, A., McLaren, J. and Wright, N. E., *Land and Freedom: Law, Property and the British Diaspora* (Aldershot, 2002).

Buck, A., McLaren, J. and Wright, N. E., *Despotic Dominion: Property Rights in British Settler Societies* (Vancouver, 2005).

Castles, A. C., *Introduction to Australian Legal History* (Melbourne, 1971).

Duman, D., *The English and Colonial Bars in the Nineteenth Century* (1983).

Howell, P. A., *The Judicial Committee of the Privy Council, 1838–1876* (Cambridge, 1976).

Karsten, P., *Heart versus Head: Judge-made Law in Nineteenth-Century America* (Chapel Hill, 1997).

Karsten, P., *Between Law and Custom: 'High' and 'Low' Legal Cultures in the Lands of the British Diaspora—the United States, Canada, Australia and New Zealand* (Cambridge, 2002).

Keeton, G. W. (author and editor), *The British Commonwealth: The Development of its Laws and Constitutions* (14 vols, 1952–68).

Keith, A. B., *The British Commonwealth of Nations: Its Territories and Laws* (1940).

Kercher, B., *An Unruly Child: A History of Law in Australia* (Sydney, 1995).

McHugh, P., *Aboriginal Societies and the Common Law: A History of Sovereignty, Status and Self-Determination* (Oxford, 2004).

McPherson, B. H., *The Reception of British Law Abroad.* (Brisbane, 2007).

Pitts, J., *A Turn to Empire: The Rise of Imperial Liberalism in Britain and France* (Princeton, 2007).

Roberts-Wray, K., *Commonwealth and Colonial Law* (1966).

Stokes, E., *The English Utilitarians and India* (Oxford, 1979).

Swinfen, D. B., *Imperial Appeal: The Debate on the Appeal to the Privy Council, 1833–1986* (Manchester, 1987).

Tompson, R. S., *Islands of Law: A Legal History of the British Isles* (New York, 2000).

International Law

Bell, D. S. A. (ed.), *Victorian Visions of Global Order* (Cambridge, 2007).

Cassesse, A., *International Law* (Oxford, 2001).

Craven, M. C. R., *The Decolonization of International Law: State Succession and the Law of Treaties* (Oxford, 2007).

Craven, M. C. R., Fitzmaurice M. and Vogiatzu, M. (eds), *Time, History and International Law* (Leiden, 2007).

Crawford, J. R., 'Public International Law in the Twentieth Century', in R. Zimmermann and J. Beatson, *Jurists Uprooted* (Oxford, 2004) 681–707.

Grewe, W., *Epochs of International Law* (Baden, 1983; trans. Byers, Berlin, 2000).

Higgins, Dame R., 'Time and the Law: International Perspectives on an Old Problem' (1997) 46 *ICLQ* 501–20.

Janis, M. W., *The American Tradition in International Law: Great Expectations, 1789–1914* (Oxford, 2004).

Johnson, D. H. N., 'The English Tradition in International Law' (1962) 11 *ICLQ* 416–45.

Koskenniemi, M., *The Gentle Civilizer of Nations: The Rise and Fall of International Law 1870–1960* (Cambridge, 2002).

Lauterpacht, Sir H. and Jennings, Sir R., 'International Law and Colonial Questions, 1870–1914', in E.A. Benions *et al* (eds) *Cambridge History of the British Empire*, iii (Cambridge, 1959) 667–710.

Lobban, M., 'English Approaches to International Law' in Craven M. C. R., Fitzmaurice, M. and Vogiatzu, M. (eds), *Time, History and International Law* (Leiden, 2007) 65–90.

Macalister-Smith P. and Schwietke, J., 'Bibliography of the Textbooks and Comprehensive Treatises on Positive International Law of the 19th Century' (1999) 1 *J. Hist. Int. L.* 136–212.

Neff, S. C., *War and the Law of Nations* (Cambridge, 2003).

Neff, S. C., 'A Short History of International Law' in M.D. Evans (ed.) *International Law* (Oxford, 2nd edn 2006) Ch. 2.

Simpson, G. H., *Great Powers and Outlaw States: Unequal States in the International Legal Order* (Cambridge, 2004).

Sylvest, C., 'International Law in Nineteenth Century Britain' (2004) 75 *BYIL* 1–69.

Sylvest, C., 'The Foundations of Victorian International Law', in Bell D. S. H. (ed.), *Victorian Visions of Global Order* (Cambridge, 2007), Ch. III.

Wilson, R. R., *International Law and Contemporary Commonwealth Issues* (Durham NC, 1971).

Private International Law

Lipstein, K., 'One Hundred Years of the Hague Conferences on Private International Law (1993) 42 *ICLQ* 553–653.

Lorenzen, K. G., 'Story's Commentaries on the Conflict of Laws – One Hundred Years After' (1934) *Harvard LR* 15–30.

Mills, A., 'The Private History of International Law' (2006) 55 *ICLQ* 1–50.

Mills, A., *The Confluence of Public and Private International Law: Justice, Pluralism and Subsidiarity in the International Constitutional Ordering of Private Law* (Cambridge, 2009).

Nadelmann, K. H., 'Joseph Story's Contribution to American Conflicts Law' (1961) 5 *AJLH* 230–53.

North P. M., 'Private International Law in the Twentieth Century', in R. Zimmermann and J. Beatson, *Jurists Uprooted* (Oxford, 2004) 483–515.

Sack, A., 'Conflict of Laws in the History of English Law' in M. Culp (ed.), *Select Readings on the Conflict of Laws* (St Paul, 1956).

Part Two Public Law

General

Le May, G. H. L., *The Victorian Constitution* (1979).

Parliament

Clifford, F., *A History of Private Bill Legislation* (1885).

Eastwood, D., 'Men, Morals and the Machinery of Social Legislation, 1790–1840' (1994) 13 *Parliamentary History* 190–205.

Fraser, P., 'The Growth of Ministerial Control in the Nineteenth-century House of Commons' (1960) 75 *EHR* 444–63.

Hawkins, A., '"Parliamentary Government" and Victorian Political Parties c. 1830-c. 1880' (1989) 104 *EHR* 638–69.

Redlich, J., *The Procedure of the House of Commons* (1908).

Rush, M., *The Role of the Member of Parliament Since 1868* (Oxford, 2001).

Rydz, D. L., *The Parliamentary Agents* (1979).

Williams, O. C., *The Historical Development of Private Bill Procedure and Standing Orders in the House of Commons* (1948).

Central Government

Aylmer, G. E., 'From Office-holding to Civil Service: the Genesis of Modern Bureaucracy', (1980) 30 *TRHS* (5th ser.), 91–108.

Bartrip J. and Burman, S. B., *The Wounded Soldiers of Industry* (Oxford, 1983).

Brewer, J., 'Servants of the Public—Servants of the Crown', in J. Brewer and E. Hellmuth, *Rethinking Leviathan* (Oxford, 1999).

Chester, N., *The English Administrative System 1780–1870* (Oxford, 1981).

Finer, S. E., *The Life and Times of Sir Edwin Chadwick* (1952).

Hamlin, C., *Public Health and Social Justice in the Age of Chadwick* (Cambridge, 1998).

MacDonagh, O., A *Pattern of Government Growth, 1800–1860: The Passenger Acts and their Enforcement* (1961).

Mitchell, J. D. B., 'The Causes and Effects of the Absence of a System of Public Law in the United Kingdom' [1965] *Public Law* 95–118.

Parris, H., *Constitutional Bureaucracy* (1969).

Parris, H., *Government and the Railways in Nineteenth Century Britain* (1965).

Pellew, J., *The Home Office 1848–1914* (1982).

Thomas, M. W., *The Early Factory Legislation* (Westport Conn., 1948).

Willson, F. M. G., 'Ministries and Boards: Some Aspects of Administrative Development since 1842', (1955) 33 *Public Administration* 43–58.

Wright, M., *Treasury Control of the Civil Service 1854–1874* (Oxford, 1969).

The Army

G. R. Rubin, 'The Legal Education of British Army Officers 1860–1923', (1994) 15 *JLH* 223–51.

G. R. Rubin, 'Parliament, Prerogative and Military Law' (1997) 18 *JLH* 45–84.

Strachan, H. *The Politics of the British Army* (Oxford, 1997).

Sweetman, J. *War and Administration: The Significance of the Crimean War for the British Army* (Edinburgh 1984).

Church and State

Best, G. F. A., *Temporal Pillars: Queen Anne's Bounty, the Ecclesiastical Commissioners and the Church of England* (Cambridge, 1964).

. Howell, P. A., *The Judicial Committee of the Privy Council 1833–1876* (Cambridge 1979).

Machin, G. I. T., *Politics and the Churches in Great Britain 1832 to 1868* (Oxford 1977).

Machin, G. I. T., *Politics and the Churches in Great Britain 1869 to 1921* (Oxford 1987).

Waddams, S.M., *Law, Politics and the Church of England* (Cambridge, 1992).

Local Government

Eastwood, D., *Governing Rural England* (Oxford, 1994).

Davis, J., *Reforming London* (Oxford, 1988).

Innes, J., 'Local Acts of a National Parliament', in D. Dean and C. Jones (eds), *Parliament and Locality, 1660–1939* (Edinburgh, 1998).

Innes J. and Rogers, N., 'Politics and Government 1700–1840', in P. Clark, (ed), *Cambridge Urban History*, ii (Cambridge, 2000) 529–74.

Lambert, R., 'Central and Local Relations in Mid-Victorian England: the Local Government Act Office, 1858–71' (1962) 6 *Victorian Studies* 121–50.

Owen, D., *The Government of Victorian London 1855–1889* (Cambridge, Mass., 1982).

Philips, D., 'The Black Country Magistracy 1835–1860' (1976) 3 *Midland History* 161–90.

Prest, J., *Liberty and Locality* (Oxford, 1990).

Judicial Review

Arthurs, H. W., *'Without the Law'* (Toronto, 1985).

Rubinstein, A., *Jurisdiction and Illegality* (Oxford, 1965).

Stebbings, C., *Legal Foundations of Tribunals in the Nineteenth Century* (Cambridge, 2006).

Part Three: The Courts

General Introduction

Holdsworth, Sir W. S., *A History of English Law* (16 vols, 1903–1966).

The Judicial Side of the House of Lords and Privy Council

Atiyah, P. S., *The Rise and Fall of Freedom of Contract* (Oxford, 1979).

Atlay, J. B., *The Victorian Chancellors* (2 vols, 1908).

Blom-Cooper, L., Dickson B. and Drewry G. (eds), *The Judicial House of Lords* (Oxford, 2009).

Howell, P. A., *The Judicial Committee of the Privy Council 1833–1876* (Cambridge, 1979).

Lowry, Lord, 'The Irish Lords of Appeal in Ordinary', in D.S. Greer and N.M. Dawson (eds), *Mysteries and Solutions in Irish Legal History* (Dublin, 2001).

Marsh, P. T., *The Victorian Church in Decline* (1969).

Paterson, A. A., 'Scottish Lords of Appeal, 1876–1988', [1988] *JR* 235–54.

Rodes, R. E., *Law and Modernization in the Church of England* (Notre Dame, Indiana, 1991).

Stevens, R. B., *Law and Politics: The House of Lords as a Judicial Body* (Chapel Hill, NC, 1979).

Stevens, R. B., *The Independence of the Judiciary* (Oxford, 1993).

Swinfen D. B., 'Henry Brougham and the Judicial Committee of the Privy Council' (1974) 90 *LQR* 396–411.

Swinfen, D. B., *Imperial Appeal* (Manchester, 1987).

Waddams, S. M., *Law, Politics and the Church of England: The Career of Stephen Lushington 1782–1873* (Cambridge, 1992).

The Superior Courts of Common Law, 1820–1875

Allen, C. J. W. *The Law of Evidence in Victorian England* (Cambridge, 1997).

Bauman, L. J., 'Evolution of the Summary Judgment Procedure', (1955–6) 31 *Indiana LJ* 329–56.

Bentley, D. J., *English Criminal Justice in the Nineteenth Century* (Hambledon, 1998).

Bodansky, J. N., 'The Abolition of Party-Witness Disqualification' (1981–2) 70 *Kentucky LR* 91–130.

Brooks, C. W., 'Interpersonal Conflict and Social Tension: Civil Litigation in England 1640–1830, in his *Lawyers, Litigation and English Society since 1450* (1998).

Crifo, C., 'The "Creation" of the Default Judgment in Nineteenth Century English Procedural Reforms', in A. Lewis *et al.*, *Law in the City* (Dublin, 2007).

Francis, C.W., 'Practice, Strategy and Institution: Debt Collection in the English Common Law Courts, 1740–1840' (1986) 80 *North-Western University LR* 808–954.

Gallanis, T. P., 'The Rise of Modern Evidence Law' (1999) 84 *Iowa LR* 499–559.

Hanly, C., 'The Decline of Civil Jury Trial in Nineteenth Century England' (2005) 26 *JLH* 253–78.

Holdsworth, W. S., 'The New Pleading Rules of the Hilary Term 1834' (1921 1 *CLJ* 261–78.

Kercher, B. 'The Transformation of Imprisonment for Debt in England, 1828–1838' (1984) 2 *Australian Journal of Law and Society* 60–109.

Lobban, M. J. W. *The Common Law and English Jurisprudence 1760–1850* (Oxford, 1991).

Lobban, M. J. W. 'The Strange Life of the English Civil Jury, 1837–1914', in J.W. Cairns and G. McLeod (eds), *The Dearest Birth Right of the People of England* (Oxford, 2002).

May, A. N. *The Bar and the Old Bailey* (Chapel Hill, NC, 2003).

Oldham, J. C., 'Special Juries in England: Nineteenth Century Usage and Reform' (1987) 8 *JLH* 148–62.

Schneider, W. E., '"Perjurious Albion": Perjury Prosecutions and the Victorian Trial', in A. D. E. Lewis and M. J. W. Lobban (eds), *Law and History* (Oxford, 2003).

Watkin, T. G. *The Legal History of Wales* (Cardiff, 2007).

Yeazell, S. C., 'Default and Modern Process', in W.M. Gordon and T.D. Fergus (eds), *Law in the Making* (1991).

The Court of Chancery, 1820–1875

Burns, F. B., 'Lord Cottenham and the Court of Chancery' (2003) 24 *JLH* 187–214.

Heward, E., *Masters in Ordinary* (Chichester, 1990).

Horwitz, H., 'Chancery's Younger Sister: the Court of Exchequer and its Equity Jurisdiction, 1689–1841' (1999) 72 *Historical Research* 160–82.

Horwitz H. and Polden, P., 'Continuity or Change in the Court of Chancery in the Seventeenth and Eighteenth Centuries?' (1996) 35 *JBS* 24–57.

Lobban, M. J. W., 'Preparing for Fusion: Reforming the Nineteenth Century Court of Chancery' (2004) 22 *LHR* 389–427, 566–99.

Megarry, Sir R. E., 'The Vice-Chancellors' (1982) 98 *LQR* 370–405.

Melikan, R. A., *John Scott, Lord Eldon: the Duty of Loyalty* (Cambridge, 1999).

The Civilian Courts and the Probate, Divorce and Admiralty Division

Bartrip, P. W. J., 'An Historical Account of the Evolution of the Registrars' Jurisdiction in Matrimonial Causes', in W.B. Baker *et al.*, *The Matrimonial Jurisdiction of Registrars* (1977).

Bourguignon, H. J., *Sir William Scott, Lord Stowell* (Cambridge, 1987).

Cretney, S.M., *Family Law in the Twentieth Century* (Oxford, 2003).

Horstman, A., *Victorian Divorce* (1985).

Hutton, B. G.,'"The Ecclesiastical Courts are the Sebastopol of the Tribunes. Will they ever be taken?"' [2002] *Cambrian LR* 93–100.

Hutton, B. G., *The Reform of the Testamentary Jurisdiction of the Ecclesiastical Courts, 1830–1857* (Ph.D. thesis, Brunel University, 2003).

Marsh, *The Victorian Church in Decline* (1969).

Outhwaite, R. B., *The Rise and Fall of the English Ecclesiastical Courts 1500–1860* (Cambridge, 2006).

Rodes, R. E., *Law and Modernization in the Church of England* (Notre Dame, Indiana, 1991).

Roscoe, E. S., *Studies in the History of Admiralty and Prize Courts* (1932).

Savage, G. L., 'The Divorce Court and the Queen's/King's Proctor: Legal Patriarchy and the Sanctity of Marriage in England, 1861–1937' (1989) *Historical Papers, Quebec*, 210–27.

Squibb, G. D., *Doctors' Commons* (1977).

Stone, L., *The Road to Divorce, England 1530–1857* (1990).

Thompson, G. H. M., *Admiralty Registrars* (ed. K.C.M. McGuffie, Belfast, 1958).

Waddams, S. M., *Law, Politics and the Church of England* (Cambridge, 1992).

Waddams, S. M., 'The English Matrimonial Courts on the Eve of Reform' (2000) 21 *JLH* 59–82.

Wiswall, F. L., *The Development of Admiralty Jurisdiction and Practice Since 1800* (Cambridge, 1970).

The Judicature Acts

Arthurs, H. W., *'Without the Law': Administrative Justice and Legal Pluralism in Nineteenth Century England* (Toronto, 1985).

Getzler, J. 'Patterns of Fusion', in P. Birks (ed.), *The Classification of Obligations* (Oxford, 1997), 157–92.

Graham, C., *Ordering Law* (Aldershot, 2003).

Jacob, Sir J. I. H., 'The Judicature Acts 1873–1875: Vision and Reality' in his *The Reform of Civil Procedural Law and Other Essays in Civil Procedure* (1982) 301–22.

Lobban, M. J. W 'Preparing for Fusion' Reforming the Nineteenth Century Court of Chancery' (2004) 22 *LHR*, 389–427, 566–99.

Polden, P., '"Mingling the Waters": Personalities, Politics and the Making of the Supreme Court of Judicature', (2002) 61 *CLJ* 575–611.

Rosenbaum, S., 'Studies in English Civil Procedure, II: The Rule-Making Authority', (1915) 63 *U. of Pennsylvania LR* 151–82.

The Government and Organization of the Supreme Court of Judicature

Heuston, R. F. V., *Lives of the Lord Chancellors, 1885–1940* (Oxford, 1964).

Polden, P., *A Guide to the Records of the Lord Chancellor's Department* (1988).

Stevens, R. B., *Law and Politics: The House of Lords as a Judiciary Body* (Chapel Hill, NC, 1979).

Stevens, R. B., *The Independence of the Judiciary* (Oxford, 1993).

Woodhouse, D., *The Office of Lord Chancellor* (Oxford, 2001).

The Courts of Appeal

Bentley D. J. (ed.), *Select Cases from the Notebooks of the Twelve Judges* (London, 1997).

Davies, S. D., 'The Court of Criminal Appeal: the First Forty Years' (1951) 1(ns) *JSPTL* 425–41.

Pattenden, R., *English Criminal Appeals: Appeals against Conviction and Sentence in England and Wales* (Oxford, 1996).

Polden, P., '"Mingling the Waters": Polities Personalities, polics and the Making of the Supreme Court of Judicature (2002) 61 CLJ, 575–611.

The King's (Queen's) Bench Division

Abel-Smith, B. and Stevens, R.B., *Lawyers and the Courts* (1967).

Brooks, C. W., 'Litigation and Society in England, 1200–1996, in his *Lawyers, Litigation and Society Since 1450* (Cambridge, 1998), 63–128.

Hedley, S. '"Words, Words, Words": Making Sense of Legal Judgments', C. Stebbings (ed.), *Law Reporting in England* (1995) 169–86.

Jackson, R. M., *The Machinery of Justice in England* (Cambridge, 1940).

Lobban, M. J. W. 'The Strange Life of the English Civil 1837–1914'. in J. W. Cairns and G. McLeod (eds), *The Dearest Birth Right of the People of England* (Oxford, 2002).

Polden, P., *A History of the County Court, 1846–1971* (Cambridge, 1999).

Stevens, R. B., *The Independence of the Judiciary* (above).

Taggart, M. J., 'Alexander Chaffers and the Genesis of the Vexatious Litigants Acts 1896' [2004] *CLJ* 565–84.

The Chancery Division

Ball, R. E., 'The Chancery Masters' (1961) 77 *LQR* 331–57.

Local Courts

H. W. Arthurs, ' "Without the Law": Courts of Local and Special Jurisdiction in Nineteenth Century England'(1984) 5 *JLH* 130–49.

Brooks, C. W., 'Interpersonal Conflict and Social Tension: 'Civil Litigation in England 1640–1830', in his *Lawyers, Litigation and English Society since 1450* (1998).

Cross, A. L., 'Old English Local Courts and the Movement for their Reform' (1942) 30 *Michigan LR* 369–85.

Finn, M. C., *The Character of Credit* (Cambridge, 2003).

Lobban, M. J. W., 'Henry Brougham and Law Reform' (2000) 115 *EHR* 1184–1215.

Mathew, T., 'The Mayor's Court, the Sheriffs' Courts and the Palace Court'(1919) 31 *JR* 134–51.

Webb, S. and B., *English Local Government: The Manor and the Borough* (2 vols, 1908).

Winder, W. H. D., 'The Courts of Requests' (1936) 52 *LQR* 369–94.

The County Courts

Abel-Smith, B. and Stevens, R. B., 1967 *Lawyers and the Courts* (above).

P. W. J. Bartrip, 'County Court and Superior Court Registrars, 1825–1875: the Making of a Judicial Official', in D. Sugarman and G.R. Rubin, *Law, Economy and Society in England 1750–1950* (Abingdon, 1984) 349–79.

Bartrip, P. W. B., *Workmen's Compensation in Twentieth Century Britain* (Aldershot, 1987).

Johnson, P., *Small Debts and Economic Distress in England and Wales, 1857–1913* (1993) 46 *Econ. Hist. Rev.* 67–87.

Johnson, P., 'Class Law in Victorian England' (1993) 141 *P & P* 147–69.

Polden, P., 'Judicial Independence and Executive Responsibilities' (1996) 25 *Anglo-Am. Law Rev.* 1–38, 133–62.

Polden, P., *History of the County Court, 1846–1971* (Cambridge, 1999).

Rosenbaum, S., 'Rule Making in the County Courts' (1915) 31 *LQR* 304–13.

Rubin, G. R., 'The County Courts and the Tally Trade, 1846–1914' and 'Law, Poverty and Imprisonment for Debt, 1869–1914', in Sugarman and G. R. Rubin, *Law, Economy and Society in England 1750–1950* (Abingdon, 1984).

Justices of the Peace and their Courts

Alexander, G. C., *The Administration of Justice in Criminal Matters in England* (Cambridge, 1915).

Baugh, G. C., 'County Government 1834–1889', *VCH Shropshire*, iii (1982), 135–66.

Bentley, D., *English Criminal Justice in the Nineteenth Century* (Hambledon, 1998).

Eastwood, D., *Governing Rural England* (Oxford, 1994).

Eastwood, D., *Government and Community in the English Provinces, 1700–1870* (Basingstoke, 1997).

Foster, D., 'Class and County Government in Early Nineteenth Century Lancashire'(1974) 9 *Northern History* 48–61.

French, S., 'The Evolution of the Justices' Clerk' [1961] *Crim LR* 688–97.

Lewis, R. A., 'County Government since 1835' and Ward, W.R., 'County Government 1660–1835', *VCH Wiltshire*, v (1957), 231–95, 170–94.

Moir, E., *The Justice of the Peace* (1969).

Olney, R. J., *Rural Society and County Government in Nineteenth Century Lincolnshire* (Lincoln, 1979).

Philips, D., 'The Black Country Magistracy 1835–1860: a Changing Elite and the Exercise of its Power' (1976) 3 *Midland History* 161–90.

Pue, W. W., 'The Criminal Twilight Zone: Pre-trial Procedures in the 1840s' (1983) 21 *Alberta LR* 331–63.

Skyrme, Sir W. T .C., *A History of the Justices of the Peace* (2 vols, Chichester, 1991).

Stephens, Sir E., *The Clerks of the Counties* (1960).

Sweeney, T., *The Extension and Practice of Summary Jurisdiction in England, 1790–1860* (Ph.D. thesis, Cambridge University, 1975).

Swift, R., 'The English Urban Magistracy and the Administration of Justice during the early Nineteenth Century: Wolverhampton 1815–1860' (1992) 17 *Midland History*, 75–92.

Webb, S. and B., *English Local Government: The Parish and the County* (1906).

Zangerl, C. H. E., 'The Social Composition of the County Magistracy in England and Wales, 1831–1887' (1971) 11 *JBS* 113–25.

Coroners' Courts

Burney, I. A., *Bodies of Evidence: Medicine and the Politics of the English Inquest* (Baltimore, 2000).

Burney, I. A., 'A Poisoning of no Substance: The Trials of Medico-Legal Proof in Mid-Victorian England' (1999) 38 *JBS* 59–92.

P. J. Fisher, *The Politics of Sudden Death: The Office and Role of Coroner in England and Wales, 1726–1888* (Ph.D. thesis, Leicester University, 2007).

Glasgow, G. H. H., *The Role of Lancashire Coroners, c.1836–1888* (M. Phil. thesis, Manchester University, 2002).

Glasgow, G. H. H.,'The John Lees Inquest of 1819 and the Peterloo Massacre' (1998) 148 *Transactions of the Historic Society of Lancashire and Cheshire* 95–118.

Glasgow, G. H. H., 'The Election of County Coroners' (1999) 20 *JLH*, 75–108.

Havard, J. D. J., *The Detection of Secret Homicide* (1960).

Prichard, D., *The Office of Coroner 1860–1926* (Ph.D. thesis., Greenwich University, 2001).

Sim J. and Ward, T., 'The Magistrate of the Poor? Coroners and Deaths in Custody in Nineteenth Century England', in M. Clark and C. Crawford (eds), *Legal Medicine in History* (Cambridge, 1994).

Zuck, D., 'Mr. Troutbeck as the Surgeon's Friend: The Coroner and the Doctors- -an Edwardian Comedy' (1995) 39 *Medical History* 259–87.

Part Four: The Legal Professions and their Education

The Judiciary

Atlay, J. B., *The Victorian Chancellors* (2 vols, 1908).

Davis, J., 'A Poor Man's System of Justice: the London Police Courts in the Second Half of the Nineteenth Century', (1984) 27 *Hist. J.* 309–35.

Duman, D., *The Judicial Bench in England, 1727–1875* (1982).

Fifoot, C. H. S., *Judge and Jurist in the Age of Queen Victoria* (1959).

French, S., 'The Early Stipendiary Magistrates', [1961] *Crim. LR*, 663–8; [1965] 213–21, 281–91; [1967] 224–30, 269–77, 321–6.

Hedley, S. W. 'Words, Words, Words: Making Sense of Legal Judgments 1875–1940' in C. Stebbings (ed.), *Law Reporting in England* (1995) 169–86.

Heuston, R. F. V, *The Lives of the Lord Chancellors, 1885–1964* (Oxford, 1964).

Lemmings, D., 'The Independence of the Judiciary in Eighteenth Century England', in P. Birks (ed.), *The Life of the Law* (1993).

Manson, E., *Builders of our Law in the Reign of Queen Victoria* (2nd edn, 1904).

Polden, P., *A History of the County Court, 1846–1971* (Cambridge, 1999).

Polden, P., 'Judicial Independence and Executive Responsibilities' (1996) 25 *Anglo-Am. LR* 1–38, 133–62.

Polden, P., 'Judicial Selkirks: The County Court Judges and the Press, 1847–1880', in C. W. Brooks and M.J.W Lobban (eds), *Communities and Courts in Britain, 1150–1900* (1997).

Simpson A. W. B. (ed.), *A Biographical Dictionary of the Common Law* (1984).

Stevens, R. B., *Law and Politics: The House of Lords as a Judicial Body 1800–1976* (Chapel Hill, 1979).

Stevens, R. B., *The Independence of the Judiciary: The View from the Lord Chancellor's Office* (Oxford, 1993).

Vechter, V. V., 'Bench and Bar', Committee of American Law Schools (eds), *Select Essays in Anglo-American Legal History,* vol. i (1907), 730–836.

Barristers

Abel, R., *The Legal Profession in England and Wales* (Oxford, 1988).

Abel-Smith, B. and Stevens R. B., *Lawyers and the Courts, 1750–1965* (1967).

Baker, J. H., *The Serjeants at Law* (Selden Society Supplementary Series, v, (1984).

Bosanquet, R., *The Oxford Circuit* (1951).

Burrage, M., *The Revolution and the Making of the Contemporary Legal Profession* (Oxford, 2006).

Cocks, R. J. C., *Foundations of the Modern Bar* (1983).

Duman, D., *The English and Colonial Bars in the Nineteenth Century* (1983).

Edwards, J. Ll., *The Law Officers of the Crown* (1964).

Flood, J., *Barristers' Clerks, the Law's Middlemen* (Manchester, 1983).

Harwood, A., *Circuit Ghosts* (Tiverton, 1980).

D. Lemmings, *Professors of the Law* (Oxford, 2000).

Lewis, J. R., *The Victorian Bar* (1982).

Pue, W. W, 'Lawyers and Political Liberalism in Eighteenth and Nineteenth Century England', in T.C. Halliday and L. Karpik (eds), *Lawyers and the Rise of Modern Political Liberalism* (Oxford, 1997).

Pue, W. W., 'Rebels at the Bar: English Barristers and the County Courts in the 1850s' (1987) 16 *Anglo-Am. Law Rev.* 308–52.

Richardson, W. C., *A History of the Inns of Court* (Baton Rouge, 1975).

Sainty, J. C., *A History of English Law Officers, King's Counsel and Holders of Patents of Precedence* (Selden Society Supplementary Series, viii, 1987).

Solicitors

Abel, R., *The Legal Profession in England and Wales* (Oxford, 1988).

Abel-Smith, B. and Stevens, R. B., *Lawyers and the Courts 1750–1965* (1967).

Anderson, J. S., *Lawyers and the Making of English Land Law 1832–1940* (Oxford, 1992).

Aylett, P., *The Distribution and Function of Attorneys in the Eighteenth Century, with Special Reference to North-West England* (M. Phil., Manchester University, 1984).

Bell, E. A., *Those Meddlesome Attorneys* (1939) .

Brooks, C. W., 'Interpersonal Conflict and Social Tension: Civil Litigation in England 1640–1830', in his *Lawyers, Litigation and English Society since 1450* (1998).

Brooks, C. W., Helmholz R. H. and Stein, P. G., *Notaries Public in England Since the Reformation* (1991).

Birks, M., *Gentlemen of the Law* (1960).

Burrage, M., *The Revolution and the Making of the Contemporary Legal Profession* (Oxford, 2008).

Cameron, D., *Solicitors in Blackpool* (Blackpool, 1995).

Christian, E. B. V., *A Short History of Solicitors* (1896).

Dockray, M., 'Guineas by Gaslight', in Dockray *et al.*, *City University Centenary Essays in Law* (1996), 27–46.

Kirk, H., *Portrait of a Profession* (1976).

Lunney, M., 'The Law Society and the Defalcation Scandals of 1900' (1996), 17 *JLH*, 244–69.

Miles, M., '"Eminent Practitioners": the New Visage of Country Attorneys', in D. Sugarman and G. R. Rubin, *Law, Economy and Society (in England 1750–1950)*, (Abingdon, 1984) 470–503.

Mossman, M. J., *The First Women Lawyers* (Oxford, 2006).

Offer, A., *Property and Politics, 1870–1914* (1981).

Robson, R., *The Attorney in Eighteenth Century England* (Cambridge, 1959).

Rowley, A. S., *Professions, Class and Society: Solicitors in Nineteenth Century Birmingham* (Ph.D, Aston University, 1988).

Stebbings, C., '"Officialism": Law, Bureaucracy and Ideology in late Victorian England', in A. D. E. Lewis and M. J. Lobban (eds), *Law and History* (Oxford, 2003).

Sugarman, D., 'Bourgeois Collectivism, Professional Power and the State. The Private and Public Life of the Law Society, 1825–1914' (1996) 3 *IJLP* 81–134.

Sugarman, D., 'Simple Images and Complex Realities: English Lawyers and their Relation to Business and Politics 1750–1950', (1993) 11 *LHR*, 257–302.

Williams, P. H., *A Gentleman's Calling* (Liverpool, 1980).

Legal Education and Law Reporting

Abel-Smith, B. and Steven R. B., *1750–1967 Lawyers and the Courts* (1967).

Baker, J. H., *Legal Education in London, 1250–1850* (Selden Society, 2007).

Baker, J. H., 'University College, London and Legal Education 1826–1976' (1977) 30 *CLP*, 1–13.

Brooks C. W. and Lobban, M. J. W., 'Apprenticeship or Academy? The Idea of a Law University, 1830–1860', in J.A. Bush and A. Wijffels (eds), *Learning the Law: Teaching and the Transmission of Law in England 1150–1900* (1997).

Dawson, J. P., *The Oracles of the Law* (Ann Arbor, Michigan, 1967).

Duxbury, N., *Frederick Pollock and the English Juristic Tradition* (Oxford, 2004).

Ibbetson, D., 'Legal Periodicals in England, 1820–1870' (2006), 28 *Common Law and European Legal History*, 175–94.

Kersley, R. H., *Gibson's 1876–1962, a Chapter in Legal Education* (1973).

Lawson, F. H., *The Oxford Law School, 1850–1965* (Oxford, 1968).

Pollock, F., 'English Law Reporting', in his *Essays in the Law* (1922), 242–57.

Pue, W. W., 'Guild Training vs. Professional Education: the Committee on Legal Education and the Law Department of Queen's College, Birmingham in the 1850s'(1989) 33 *Anglo-Am. Law Rev.* 241–87.

INDEX OF NAMES

This index relates mainly to persons who were active in the period 1820–1914. Double surnames are given under the first of the names. Peers with titles differing from their family name are given under the family name, with a cross-reference from the title.

* indicates a person who served as a superior court judge in Britain and/of as a judicial member of the House of Lords. The same indication is given to persons of equivalent status in other jurisdictions.

** indicates a person who served as a County Court judge.

*** indicates a person who served as a Stipendiary Magistrate or Recorder, or in other judicial office not mentioned above.

† indicates a firm of solicitors or a legal family.

INDEX OF SUBJECTS

This index is for the contents of Vol XI only. The reader may also consult the full index for Volumes XI–XIII, to be found in Volume XIII.